THE OXFORD COMPANION TO
AMERICAN LITERATURE

THE OXFORD

COMPANION TO

American Literature

SIXTH EDITION

JAMES D. HART

with revisions and additions by
Phillip W. Leininger

New York   Oxford
OXFORD UNIVERSITY PRESS
1995

Oxford University Press

Oxford New York
Athens Auckland Bangkok Bombay
Calcutta Cape Town Dar es Salaam Delhi
Florence Hong Kong Istanbul Karachi
Kuala Lumpur Madras Madrid Melbourne
Mexico City Nairobi Paris Singapore
Taipei Tokyo Toronto

and associated companies in
Berlin Ibadan

Published by Oxford University Press, Inc.
198 Madison Avenue, New York, New York 10016

Oxford is a registered trademark of Oxford University Press

Library of Congress Cataloging-in-Publication Data
Hart, James David, 1911–90
The Oxford companion to American literature / James D. Hart ;
with revisions and additions by Phillip W. Leininger. — 6th ed.
p. cm. Includes index.
ISBN 0-19-506548-4
1. American literature—Dictionaries. 2. American literature—Bio-bibliography.
3. Authors, American—Biography—Dictionaries.
I. Leininger, Phillip, 1928– . II. Title.
PS21.H3 1995
810.9'0003—dc20 94-45727

5 7 9 8 6 4
Printed in the United States of America
on acid-free paper

For Carol and Peter
and for Patti

PREFACE TO THE FIFTH EDITION

Designed to serve as a useful companion for students and general readers, this volume provides ready references, first of all, to the authors and writings, past and present, popular and polite, that are included in the area of American literature. In addition, the references extend to the written word in America outside conventional literary criteria but relevant to them. The volume treats major nonliterary aspects of the American mind and the American scene as these are reflected in and influenced by American literature. The scope of the work also embraces far more than belles lettres, yet, while it attempts to be as comprehensive as might be desirable for a reader concerned with the literature of this land, it excludes some forms of publication, such as cookbooks and comic books. It is a companion to reading rather than to literature alone, but literature is its focus.

In alphabetic arrangement, the work includes short biographies and brief bibliographies of American authors, with information regarding their style and subjects. Next most common as a category are separate entries printing over 1,100 full summaries of important American novels, stories, essays, poems (with verse forms noted), plays, biographies and autobiographies, tracts, narratives, and histories, all of them long enough to provide a good sense of the original works, and many of them containing succinct but salient quotations. Other subjects that receive substantial treatment include definitions and historical outlines of literary schools and movements, literary awards (in many instances with lists of winners and their works), literary societies, scholarly organizations, magazines, newspapers, anthologies, cooperative publications, book collectors, printers, colleges and universities and their alumni in the world of letters, and a wide variety of other matters related to writing in America. Literary terms that are sufficiently defined in dictionaries are not cited unless they have a distinctive history in the United States or warrant definition by American examples. Thus there are no entries on the conventional terms of prosody, but existentialism, free verse, impressionism, polyphonic prose, and stream of consciousness are all treated, and there are full entries on such subjects as the ballad, local color, romanticism, and the tall tale.

As indicated even by a glance at the column of Literary History in the Chronological Index that concludes this book, much of the writing that is discussed in these pages may not be distinguished as literature, but it is all important for a comprehensive review of expression in America. The written word does not exist in a vacuum, and the author of this book has therefore constantly kept in mind the idea that the fullest understanding of major works in literature, let alone lesser pieces of writing, depends upon an informed knowledge of the social and cultural atmosphere of their place and time. This view has led to the inclusion of entries on some social, economic, aesthetic, scientific, military, political, and religious subjects that have affected the actions and thoughts, and hence the writings, in the lands now forming the United States, from the time of their discovery to the present day. However, to keep the book within compass, some entries on peripheral subjects that appeared in earlier editions have been removed to make room for the addition of more authors, mainly those of recent years, and their writings.

The work continues to include some biographies of persons who are not authors but who have been important in the nation's social history and culture, brief articles on religious sects, Indian tribes, wars, law and documents, educational institutions, important cities and regions, popular songs, and other subjects that may seem outside the purview of literature but whose relationships with it are genuine and significant. Entries will be found on subjects that range alphabetically from Abolitionist to the Zuñi Indians, the former entry, for example, including references to authors as various as Samuel Sewall, Franklin, Crèvecœur, Richard Hildreth, Harriet Beecher Stowe, Hinton Helper, Lowell, and Whittier, and the latter including a reference to an author as current as Edmund Wilson.

Just as American materials that lie on the periphery of literature are treated, so some foreign materials that are relevant to this country's writings are also represented. In a few instances these include significant explorers and colonial historians of neighboring lands, but the writers of Canada, treated in earlier editions, are now deleted because they have their own *Companion.* Foreign authors are thanked with more specific acknowledgment of their contributions. In that edition I also noted that "Frederic R. Gunsky, my typist and secretary during most of the time, has come to know the work as intimately as I, typing and retyping the various articles. He has gone far beyond the limits of the work required of him, from research and the compilation of materials to excellent suggestions concerning the general plan." Later editions profited from the help of several student assistants, chief among them being Gordon O. Taylor for the fourth edition and Michael Griffith for this one.

When the work was first begun in 1936, my sister Ellen H. Barnsten rendered invaluable assistance to me. For the fourth edition I am happy to say that I again received help within the family, that time from my daughter Carol H. Field. I was always aided too by suggestions from my son Peter and from my brother-in-law, Joseph M. Bransten. But most of all I think back with happy memories to my wife Ruth. Over the years of our marriage she always provided interest and support to my concern with a work that has lasted so long as to have grown from the composition of a book into a part, almost a way, of life.

Berkeley, California   J.D.H.
March 1983

NOTE TO THE SIXTH EDITION

This Sixth Edition of *The Oxford Companion to American Literature* has again been entirely reset, for there are 181 full new entries, and several hundred more which have significant revisions, in addition to the requisite updating throughout. In preparing the Sixth Edition, I have used all or part of the 77 new entries James Hart had finished at the time of his death in 1990, but have revised and made them current, and I have added 104 new entries of my own, seeking the dynamic balance between past and contemporary literature that James Hart always sought to maintain. To make room for new material and for other considerations I have omitted Presidents of the U.S. except for the founding fathers of the Enlightenment and of the early Republic, and those few thereafter who were age-shapers or who left a significant literary legacy. Colleges have been omitted, except for two: Harvard, as the first and pattern for the rest, and Black Mountain, a brief and brilliant creation of poets. Readers will notice, however, that many of the colleges, with founding dates, and all of the Presidents, appear in the Chronological Index, which contains a new twelve years' worth of literary and social notes since the last edition.

I wish to thank the kind people at the Lucy Scribner Library, Skidmore College, and Claudia Hayes, Reference Librarian at Saratoga Springs Public Library, who was an angel. The new material is of course my responsibility entirely.

Saratoga Springs, N.Y.   P.W.L.
April 1995

THE OXFORD COMPANION TO
AMERICAN LITERATURE

NOTE

CHARACTERS and REAL PERSONS are entered under their surnames, the former in ordinary bold type, the latter in capitals (e.g. Natty Bumppo under **Bumppo**, NATTY, and Henry James under **JAMES,** HENRY), unless the surname is little known, or the two names are generally considered an indissoluble whole (e.g. **John Henry** and **Little Eva**). For the sake of convenience, a few famous characters are also entered under their Christian names.

AUTHORS and other persons are entered under their proper names rather than their pseudonyms (e.g. **CLEMENS,** SAMUEL, rather than Mark Twain, and **Cody,** WILLIAM, rather than Buffalo Bill). In all cases the pseudonym is entered with a cross reference to the proper name. Upon rare occasions, when the real name is forgotten or little known, the entry is under the pseudonym (e.g., **TRAVEN,** B. rather than **TORSVAN,** BERICK TRAVEN).

FULL NAMES are given; those parts not ordinarily used are enclosed in brackets (e.g. **CATHER,** WILLA [SIBERT], and **MENCKEN,** H[ENRY] L[OUIS]). Variant spellings and originals of altered names are enclosed in parentheses (e.g. **FAULKNER** (or FALKNER) and **O'SHEEL** (SHIELDS)).

When more than one member of a family is mentioned, the entry is under the name that is most celebrated (e.g. **WINSLOW,** EDWARD, followed in a separate paragraph by JOSIAH WINSLOW). When several members of a family are equally famous, separate entries are made (e.g., the James family).

A TITLE consisting of a Christian name and a surname is entered under the Christian name (e.g. *Tom Sawyer*). The TITLE OF A BOOK OR PAMPHLET is italicized; at the head of an article it is given in bold italics (e.g. ***Mosses from an Old Manse***). The title of a work not separately issued, i.e. printed in a periodical or as part of a book, is enclosed in quotation marks (e.g. "Young Goodman Brown"); at the head of an article it is given in bold italic type.

All publication DATES, except as otherwise indicated, are American. Plays are dated in reference to first production rather than publication, although both dates are given for plays which are separately summarized. All dates are based on the New Style Calendar.

The symbol ♦ is used to indicate a cross-reference.

A

ABBEY, EDWARD (1927–89), born and lived in the Allegheny Mountains of Pennsylvania, went to the University of New Mexico for A.B. and graduate study. He began his career as a novelist, but achieved wide recognition with the essays in *Desert Solitaire* (1968), which treats life in an open desert park from April to October and is based on Abbey's park ranger experience. His feeling for wilderness led to work on his childhood land in *Appalachian Wilderness* (1970) and to related nonfiction: *Skyrock: The Canyon Country of Southeast Utah* (1971) and *Cactus Country* (1973). *The Journey Home* and *Down the River* (1982) collect personal wilderness experiences. Later fiction includes *Black Sun* (1971), about human love involving a hermit-like park ranger; *The Monkey Wrench Gang* (1975), opposing industry's invading wild land; *The Fool's Progress* (1988); and *Hayduke Lives* (1989). Later essays appear in *Beyond the Wall* (1984) and *One Life at a Time, Please* (1987).

ABBOTT, ELEANOR HALLOWELL (1872–1958), granddaughter of Jacob Abbott and an author of children's books too, of which the best known is *Molly Make-Believe* (1912).

ABBOTT, GEORGE (1887–1995), born in western New York, graduated from the University of Rochester, and after a time as an actor had a long and very successful career as a director and a dramatist, always as a co-author. Among the plays and musicals on which he collaborated are *The Fall Guy* (1925), *Broadway* (1926), *Coquette* (1927), *Three Men on a Horse* (1935), *Pal Joey* (1940), *A Tree Grows in Brooklyn* (1951), and *Fiorello!* (1959, Pulitzer Prize). *Mister Abbott* (1963) is his autobiography. At age 92 he published his first novel, *Tryout* (1979), about a young actor. At 101 he directed his own new work, *Frankenstein*.

ABBOTT, JACOB (1803–79). Massachusetts educator and Congregational clergyman, whose first book, *The Young Christian* (1832), was followed by some 200 similar works. The best known are the 28 volumes of the Rollo series (1835ff.), which are instructive stories for children in the genre of *Sandford and Merton*. Many of Abbott's books were written in collaboration with his brother John S.C. Abbott (1805–77).

ABBOTT, LYMAN (1835–1922), son of Jacob Abbott, was the successor of Henry Ward Beecher both in the pulpit of his Plymouth Church (Congregational) in Brooklyn and as editor of *The Outlook* (originally *The Christian Union*). He was a leader of the modern rational outlook upon religion, opposing ultra-refined theological controversy and championing scientific views such as the reconciliation of the Darwinian theory with Christianity. His books include *Christianity and Social Problems* (1896), *The Theology of an Evolutionist* (1897), *Henry Ward Beecher* (1903), *Reminiscences* (1915), and *What Christianity Means to Me* (1921).

Abe Lincoln in Illinois, play by Robert Sherwood,♦ produced in 1938 and awarded a Pulitzer Prize. It was published in 1939 with an extensive commentary by the author on its "Substance" and composition.

The 12 scenes of the play carry the hero from his young manhood as an unsuccessful storekeeper at New Salem, through the years of his marriage and legal career, to his election to the presidency and departure for Washington.

Abie's Irish Rose, comedy by Anne Nichols, produced in 1922. Its sentimental plot is concerned with the love of a Jewish youth and an Irish girl in New York's Lower East Side. The play is credited with being one of the most popular ever produced in the U.S., having had a New York run of 2327 performances.

ABISH, WALTER (1931–), born in Austria, reared in China, took U.S. citizenship in 1960, and taught for ten years at Columbia University. Abish was a MacArthur Prize fellow ("the genius award"), and his fiction is experimental: for example, *Alphabetical Africa* (1974), a novel wherein every word of the first chapter begins with the letter A; the second with A or B; the third with A, B, or C. At Z the process reverses: the final chapter has words again beginning with A. Another novel, *How German Is It* (1980), received the PEN Faulkner Award (1981). Not as formally mannered as his previous novel, it concerns an American of German parentage and his return to a small German town to investigate his father's wartime death, and to answer his own question, how German am I? Abish has a volume of poetry, *Duel Site* (1970), and collections of short stories in *Minds Meet* (1975) and *In the Future Perfect* (1977). Later fiction includes *99: The New Meaning* (1990) and *Eclipse Fever* (1993). Set in Mexico at the time of a total eclipse, with a Mexican writer as one protagonist and an American teen-age girl as another (the two never meet), the latter novel is a meditation on the cultural and societal malaise of Mexico and other third world countries.

Abolitionist, name applied to one who aimed at or advocated the abolition of slavery. The term may be found at least as early as 1790, during the period when Thomas Clarkson, William Wilberforce, and the younger Pitt attacked the slave trade. In 1807 the British Parliament abolished slave traffic between England and her possessions, and in 1808 the traffic was abolished in the U.S. Despite universal outlawry, the slave trade continued illegally. During the 1830s, the territorial expansion of the U.S. made slavery and its abolition a vital issue, but though the North had freed its slaves it was still economically dependent on the cotton industry of the South, to which slavery was indispensable. Out of this conflict emerged three schools of Abolitionist thought: radical Abolitionism under W.L. Garrison♦; the philosophical attacks of Channing and Wayland; and Free-Soilism under Lincoln. Two events in 1831 accelerated the Abolitionist movement and the hostility to it: the South was alarmed by the defeat, by only one vote, of a bill in the Virginia Senate providing for the colonization of free blacks and encouraging private emancipation; and the first issue of *The Liberator.*♦ The New England Anti-Slavery Society was organized by Garrison and others in 1831, and in 1833 the American Anti-Slavery Society was established at Philadelphia by this and other local societies. The American Anti-Slavery Society, including such members as Wendell Phillips, Whittier, Edmund Quincy, Arthur Tappan, James G. Birney, and Amos Phelps, was not dissolved until 1870, although a schism occurred in 1840 and most of the membership resigned to join other groups. In 1859 John Brown♦ and his followers captured the armory at Harpers Ferry, intending to establish a base from which to free slaves by armed intervention. From then until the firing upon Fort Sumter, the Abolitionist drive and the opposition to it became increasingly powerful, being among the principal causes of the Civil War and influencing the Emancipation Proclamation and the 14th Amendment. The earliest antislavery prose is to be found in such works as Sewall's *The Selling of Joseph,* Franklin's "On the Slave Trade," and the ninth of Crèvecœur's *Letters from an American Farmer.* Hildreth's *The Slave* (1836) is credited with being the first antislavery novel, but of the reams of literature—sermons, tracts, treatises, periodicals, poems, plays, and novels—for this cause, the most popular and influential were Harriet Beecher Stowe's *Uncle Tom's Cabin* (1852) and H.R. Helper's *The Impending Crisis of the South* (1857). Other prominent antislavery authors were Lowell, Whittier, Benjamin Lundy, John Rankin, Samuel Crothers, T.D. Weld, Horace Mann, and Frederick Douglass.

Abraham Lincoln Walks at Midnight, poem in iambic pentameter quatrains, by Vachel Lindsay,♦ published in *The Congo and Other Poems* (1914). The poet describes his vision of the "mourning figure" of Lincoln, which paces the streets of Springfield on the eve of World War I, "sleepless" because of "the bitterness, the folly, and the pain" that are abroad in the world.

Absalom, Absalom!, novel by Faulkner,♦ published in 1936.

The story of Thomas Sutpen and the intricate patterns of other lives involved with his are narrated mainly through Quentin Compson, the grandson of Sutpen's befriender, General Compson. Born to a poor-white family in the West Virginia mountains in 1807, Sutpen runs away at 14 and makes his way to Haiti. There he later marries Eulalia Bon, a planter's daughter, and they have a son, Charles. Discovering his wife's partial black ancestry, Sutpen leaves her and the child, and two years later (1833) appears in Yoknapatawpha County, Mississippi, with a band of wild Haitian blacks. He obtains 100 acres of land questionably from the Chickasaw Indians, creates a plantation, and builds a large house on "Sutpen's Hundred." As a further part of his grand design to achieve aristocracy, Sutpen marries Ellen Coldfield, of a respectable family, and they have children, Henry and Judith. Years later, at the University of Mississippi, Henry meets and admires Charles Bon, Sutpen's Haitian son, who has grown to manhood in New Orleans. When Bon comes home with Henry for Christmas, he falls in love with Judith, but Sutpen forbids their marriage. To Henry he reveals that he is Bon's father (but conceals the black background), and Henry reacts by renouncing his birthright and leaving with Bon, and upon the outbreak of the Civil War, the two go off to fight. During the war Ellen dies but the men survive. Although Bon will not repudiate his octoroon mistress and their son, he still wants to wed Judith, being willing to leave only if Sutpen will acknowledge him as "Bon, my son." Learning of Bon's Negro blood, Henry murders him to prevent the marriage, and then disappears himself. Intent on begetting an heir and founding a dynasty, Sutpen gets engaged to his sister-in-law Rosa Coldfield, who leaves him when he suggests that they try to have a son before marrying. Attempting "to replace that progeny the hopes of which he had himself destroyed," Sutpen has relations with the granddaughter of Wash Jones, a poor-white squatter on Sutpen's Hundred. When he casts off Milly Jones and the child because it is a girl, Wash kills Sutpen with a scythe. Bon's son by his mistress, Charles Etienne De Saint-Valery Bon, is brought to the plantation by Clytemnestra (Clytie), another daughter of Sutpen by one of his slaves. Charles Etienne in turn marries a full-blood black woman and fathers an idiot son, Jim Bond. After Judith and Charles Etienne die of yellow fever, only Sutpen's black heirs, Clytie and Jim Bond, remain on the decaying plantation. In 1910, shortly before her death, Rosa, aided by Quentin, finds Henry, now aged and wasted, returned and hidden in the house, and when Rosa sends for an ambulance, Clytie, thinking it a police car come to arrest Henry for the old murder, sets fire to the house, violently ending the "doom" of Sutpen's own destructive career on a "land primed for fatality and already cursed with it."

Acadia, early Canadian province corresponding to present Nova Scotia, though of greater area, was claimed by the English but mainly settled by the French. When the Acadians refused to take an oath of allegiance to the British, during the last French and Indian War, several thousand of them were deported (1755) to British provinces farther south. Many families were accidentally separated, although most of the French sought refuge in Quebec and Louisiana. Longfellow's *Evangeline*♦ is the most famous account of these events. In Louisiana the Acadian exiles and their descendants are called "Cajuns," and have been described by Kate Chopin and other local-color writers.

Accent (1940–60), eclectic "quarterly of new literature" published at the University of Illinois but not an official university organ. Contributors included Katherine Anne Porter, Kay Boyle, Kenneth Burke, Thomas Mann, Wallace Stevens, R.P. Blackmur, Irwin Shaw, and J.C. Ransom. A selection appeared in *Accent Anthology* (1946).

Acres of Diamonds, see *Conwell, Russell.*

Across the Plains, autobiographical narrative by R. L. Stevenson,♦ was published in an abridged version in *Longman's Magazine* (1883) and in book form in 1892. A sequel to *The Amateur Emigrant,*♦ it is an account of Stevenson's journey by railroad (1879) from New York to San Francisco.

Actress of Padua, The, romantic tragedy by R.P. Smith,♦ produced in 1836, which survives only in his narrative version published the same year.

ADAIR, JAMES (*c.*1709–*c.*1783), Irish-born trader with the Indians in the South, came to America about 1735. His book *The History of the American Indians* (1775) is valuable as an account of the customs and languages of the Chickasaw and other tries, despite its thesis that Indians are descended from the ancient Israelites.

ADAMIC, LOUIS (1899–1951), wrote of his early life in the U.S. in *Laughing in the Jungle* (1932), and of his homeland, Yugoslavia, in *The Native's Return* (1934). His other books include

Dynamite: The Story of Class Violence in America (1931, revised 1934); two novels, *Grandsons: A Story of American Lives* (1935) and *Cradle of Life: The Story of One Man's Beginnings* (1936); *The House in Antigua* (1937), the history of a colonial house in Guatemala; *Two-Way Passage* (1941), proposing that European-Americans be returned to their homelands to educate Europeans in democracy, a scheme that led to Adamic's conference with Roosevelt and Churchill, described in *Dinner at the White House* (1946); *What's Your Name?* (1942); *My Native Land* (1943); and *A Nation of Nations* (1945), stressing the role of non-Anglo-Saxons in U.S. history. Adamic was the first editor of *Common Ground*♦ (1940–42).

ADAMS, ABIGAIL [SMITH], (1744–1818), wife of John Adams, from whom she had to be separated for long periods during the Revolution, occasioning her frequent, loving, lively, and outspoken letters. She also engaged in much correspondence with other family members. Her charming letters were published by her grandson Charles Francis Adams as *Letters of Mrs. Adams* . . . (2 vols., 1840) and *Familiar Letters of John Adams and His Wife* (1876). Better edited texts appear in the Adams Papers.♦

ADAMS, ALICE (1926–), Virginia-born author, educated at Radcliffe, long resident in San Francisco, whose novels include *Careless Love* (1966), *Families and Survivors* (1974), *Listening to Billie* (1978), *Rich Rewards* (1980), *Superior Women* (1984), sensitive studies of women—young to middle-aged—and their relations to family, friends, husbands, and lovers, and *Second Chances* (1988), a novel about a group of longtime friends having important relationships in older age. She is also known for stories, collected in *Beautiful Girl* (1979), *You Can't Keep a Good Woman Down* (1981), *To See You Again* (1982), *Return Trips* (1986), and *After You've Gone* (1989).

ADAMS, ANDY (1859–1935), born in Indiana, moved to Texas to become a cowboy, and during the mining boom went to Colorado, where he later wrote his stories of the cattle kingdom. He is one of the few authors of cowboy stories who are considered to have achieved high literary merit. Among his books are *The Log of a Cowboy* (1903), a novel of the cattle drive north from Texas; *The Outlet* (1905), treating a similar subject, and the sharp methods of the railway companies, contractors, and congressional lobbyists concerned with the drive; *Cattle Brands* (1906), short stories of frontier life in the 1880s; and *Reed Anthony, Cowman: An Autobiography* (1907), a novel about a Confederate army veteran who becomes a cattle rancher in Texas.

ADAMS, BROOKS (1848–1927), historian, whose works include *The Emancipation of Massachusetts* (1887), an iconoclastic study of the religious and political bondage of the colonists; *Law of Civilization and Decay* (1895); and *Theory of Social Revolutions* (1913). He wrote a lengthy history of the intellectual tradition of his family as a preface to the "Letter to American Teachers of History" by his brother Henry Adams,♦ and published both under the title *The Degradation of the Democratic Dogma* (1919). He was a grandson of John Quincy Adams and a son of Charles Francis Adams.

ADAMS, CHARLES FOLLEN (1842–1918), author of comic verse, is best known for his sentimental "Leedle Yawcob Strauss" (1876), in Pennsylvania Dutch. His verses were collected in *Yawcob Strauss and Other Poems* (1910).

ADAMS, CHARLES FRANCIS (1807–86), son of John Quincy Adams, entered politics as a "conscience" Whig, founded the *Boston Whig,* and in 1848 ran for the vice-presidency as a Free-Soil candidate. He later entered Congress as a Republican, and in 1861 was appointed minister to England, where he served during the Civil War. His diplomacy prevented England from continuing to furnish ironclad vessels to the Confederacy, and he was an arbitrator of the Alabama Claims. He edited the *Works of John Adams* (1850–56), the letters of Abigail Adams, and the *Memoirs of John Quincy Adams* (12 vols., 1874–77). Henry, Brooks, and Charles Francis Adams, Jr., were his sons.

ADAMS, CHARLES FRANCIS, JR. (1835–1915), a son of Charles Francis Adams, was active in civic affairs, and president of the Union Pacific Railroad (1884–90). His writings indicate the wide scope of his interests: *Chapters of Erie and Other Essays* (1871), written with his brother Henry; *Railroads: Their Origin and Problems* (1878); a biography of Richard Henry Dana (1890); *Three Episodes of Massachusetts History* (1892); and *Studies: Military and Diplomatic* (1911). He also wrote a biography of his father (1900), edited Morton's *New English Canaan* (1883), and wrote his interesting *Autobiography* (1916).

ADAMS, FRANKLIN P[IERCE] (1881–1960), columnist, radio performer, and humorist, began his journalistic career in Chicago (1903). He worked on various New York papers and was best known for his column, "The Conning Tower," which featured satirical verse and a personal diary in the manner of Pepys. Among his books are *Tobogganing on Parnassus* (1911), *Christopher Columbus* (1931), and other collections of verse, from which *The Melancholy Lute* (1936) is a selection; and *The Diary of Our Own Samuel Pepys* (2 vols., 1935), edited from his newspaper column, *Nods and Becks* (1944) collects newspaper pieces and poems. He usually signed his work with his initials.

ADAMS, HANNAH (1755–1831), is generally considered the first professional woman author of America. Her popular works included *Alphabetical Compendium of the Various Sects . . . from the Beginning of the Christian Era to the Present Day* (1784), *A Summary History of New England* (1799), *The Truth and Excellence of the Christian Religion Exhibited* (1804), and *The History of the Jews* (1812).

ADAMS, HENRY [BROOKS] (1838–1918), grandson of John Quincy Adams and son of Charles Francis Adams, claims in his autobiography that his conventional education was defective, despite the best Boston and Quincy background, Harvard, German postgraduate training, and his position as secretary during his father's ministry to England at the time of the Civil War. His first writing, an article on Captain John Smith published in 1867, was followed by other contributions to periodicals, including a review of Lyell's *Principles of Geology* (1868), clearly showing his belief in the importance of the evolutionary theory in human history and Adams's own divorce from the absolute standards of his ancestors. Returning from England to Washington, D.C. (1868), he continued to write carefully considered articles, and, completely out of sympathy with Reconstruction politics, abandoned former ideas of a political career to teach history at Harvard (1870–77), for most of this period also editing *The North American Review.* He next went to Washington to write history and to seek the companionship of such men as Secretary of State Evarts, John Hay, and Clarence King, for he said ironically, "So far as [I] had a function in life, it was as stable-companion to statesmen." There he wrote *Democracy*♦ (1880), an anonymous novel on Washington politics, and *Esther*♦ (1884), a pseudonymous novel of New York society. In 1872 he married Marian Hooper, whose suicide in 1885 tragically affected his life. Although he never mentions her in his writings, she probably served as a model for the heroine in *Esther.* Adams commissioned his friend Saint-Gaudens to design for her grave in Washington a symbolic statue, which he called "The Peace of God." When he could no longer endure life at Washington, he made a long trip through the Orient, from which he returned to complete his *History of the United States During the Administrations of Thomas Jefferson and James Madison* (9 vols., 1889–91), portraying politics and diplomacy in the early republic. He traveled widely during the following years, and among the literary results was the *Memoirs of Marau Taaroa, Last Queen of Tahiti* (1893, revised 1901). He "drifted back to Washington with a new sense of history" after a summer in Normandy (1895) and a visit to the Paris Exposition (1900), where he saw the huge dynamo that in his autobiography he was to take as a symbol of mechanistic power and energy in the multiplicity of the 20th century as contrasted to the force of the Virgin, "the ideal of human perfection," representing the unity of the 13th century, which he treated in *Mont-Saint-Michel and Chartres*♦ (1904). This scholarly descriptive work, interpretively studying a unified world, was Adams's first attempt to measure the life and thought of an era in terms of Force. In 1910 he published "A Letter to American Teachers of History," reprinted in *The Degradation of the Democratic Dogma* (1919) by his brother Brooks Adams.♦ This work sets forth Henry Adams's dynamic theory of history. The second law of thermodynamics supposes a universal tendency to dissipate mechanical energy and thus vitiates the idea of human history as evolving toward a state of perfection. On the contrary, according to Adams, human thought is a substance passing from one phase to another through critical points determined by attraction, acceleration, and volume (equivalent to pressure, temperature, and volume in mechanical physics), and he points out that history must be studied in the light of these principles. The complementary work to *Mont-Saint-Michel* is a study of 20th-century multiplicity, *The Education of Henry Adams*♦ (1907). The skepticism and cynicism in the account of his self-termed failures pass beyond autobiography to a study of the garment of education draped on the "manikin" Henry Adams, a figure used to measure motion, proportion, and human conditions. In later chapters the use of his dynamic theory of history is made explicit. Other books include *Chapters of Erie and Other Essays* (1871), written with his brother Charles Francis Adams, Jr.; *The Life of Albert Gallatin* (1879); *John Randolph* (1882); and *The Life of George Cabot Lodge* (1911). His letters have been printed in various collections, and those of his wife were published in 1936.

ADAMS, JAMES TRUSLOW (1878–1949), New York historian, educated at Brooklyn Polytechnic Institute and Yale, was in business in New York for 13 years before he devoted full time to historical writing. He won a Pulitzer Prize for *The Founding of New England* (1921), the first of a trilogy completed in *Revolutionary New England* (1923) and *New England in the Republic* (1926), reinterpreting the ideals and achievements of the Puritans and their descendants. Other books include *Provincial Society, 1690–1763* (1927); *The Epic of America* (1931); *The March of Democracy* (2 vols., 1932–33); *The American: The Making of a New Man* (1943); *Frontiers of American Culture* (1944), on adult education; and *Big Business in a Democracy* (1945). He wrote two works on the Adams family of Massachusetts, although he is not related to them: *The Adams Family* (1930) and *Henry Adams* (1933). He was general editor of the *Dictionary of American History*♦ (1940) and its companion works, *Atlas of American History* (1943) and *Album of American History* (6 vols., 1944–61). *Building the British Empire* (1938) and *Empire on the Seven Seas* (1940) reflect his interest in English history.

ADAMS, JOHN (1704–40), clergyman, scholar, and writer of verse. His *Poems on Several Occasions: Original and Translated* (1745) consists of Biblical paraphrases, translations from Horace, and devotional pieces.

ADAMS, JOHN (1735–1826), 2nd President of the U.S. (1797–1801), was born in Braintree (now Quincy), Mass., graduated from Harvard (1755), was admitted to the bar (1758), and soon entered public life. He opposed the Stamp Act and the Boston Port Act, was a delegate to the first Continental Congress, where he aided in drafting a petition to the king and a declaration of rights, and returned to the second Congress, in which he proposed Washington for military commander, hoping to draw Virginia into greater support of Revolutionary policies. He worked for independence, but disliked Paine's plan of government suggested in *Common Sense,* and set forth his own ideas in *Thoughts on Government* (1776), one of his several energetic publications on current questions, which also included letters to Daniel Leonard.♦ He helped draft the Declaration of Independence and, according to Jefferson, was "the pillar of its support on the floor of Congress," where he also served on many important committees. From 1777 to 1779 he was a commissioner to France, and in the latter year also consulted the French government concerning peace negotiations with England, although he failed to achieve anything because he alienated their foreign minister. His negotiations with the Dutch to secure a treaty and loan were ultimately successful. In 1782–83 he accompanied Jay and Franklin to England, where they negotiated the treaty of peace, and in 1785 he was appointed envoy to the Court of St. James's. During his residence in England, Adams wrote a three-volume *Defence of the Constitutions of Government of the United States of America against the Attack of Mr. Turgot* (1787). Upon his return (1788) he was elected the first Vice-President of the U.S., and, although his office was mainly a matter of routine, he worked without party alignment on the side of the Federalists. His *Discourses on Davila* (1791), drawing a moral for the U.S. from the history of France, alienated Hamilton, who thought the work tended to weaken the government, while Jefferson considered it as leaning toward hereditary monarchy and aristocracy. After another term as Vice-President, Adams was elected to the presidency in 1796, despite the opposition of Hamilton. Jefferson was antagonistic to Adams's administration, and Hamilton, with a strong influence in the cabinet, particularly opposed Adams's conciliatory policy toward France, by which war was averted. Hamilton's animus, as displayed in his *Letter Concerning the Public Conduct and Character of John Adams* (1800), played into the hands of the Jeffersonians, and after he failed of reelection Adams retired to private life in Quincy. His *Works* were collected in ten volumes

(1850–56), and many separate volumes of his correspondence have been issued, of which the most important are the letters addressed to his wife Abigail and the communications with Jefferson. His diary, autobiography, and family correspondence have been published as part of the Adams Papers. ◆

ADAMS, JOHN QUINCY (1767–1848), 6th President of the U.S. (1825–29), son of John and Abigail Adams, was born in Braintree (now Quincy), Mass., and received his early training by accompanying his father on diplomatic missions to France and Holland. He graduated from Harvard (1787), after which he was admitted to the bar (1790) and entered politics and political discussion. His answer to Paine's *Rights of Man,* signed "Publicola" (1791), and similar essays, led Washington to appoint him minister to the Netherlands (1794). In 1797 his father appointed him minister to Berlin, and he remained abroad until 1801. Literary results of this residence were his translation of Wieland's poetic romance *Oberon* (first published 1940) and his *Letters on Silesia* (1804). In 1803 Adams was elected to the Senate, where his want of allegiance to Federalist tradition caused his resignation (1808). He had already been appointed Professor of Rhetoric and Belles-Lettres at Harvard, and his college lectures were published (1810). In 1809 he was appointed minister to Russia, and six years later minister to England, to remain until Monroe invited him (1817) to be secretary of state. In this capacity he postponed the Oregon boundary question by treaty with England, secured Florida from Spain, and recognized the rebelling Spanish colonies. The principles underlying his policies were drafted by him in the Monroe Doctrine as it was enunciated by Monroe in 1823. After four years of independent policies as President, he was elected to Congress (1831) without any definite party support, and continued to serve until his death 17 years later. He was considered to be without peer as a parliamentary debater, and worked hard to oppose the extension of slavery and consequently the admission of Texas and the Mexican War. All his actions were characterized by an independence of party. His *Memoirs* (12 vols., 1874–77) cover half a century, and are valuable both as political commentary and as a study in American letters; they have been described by Allan Nevins in his edition (1928) as written "with malice towards all." His independent mind is indicated by the diversity of his other writings, which include the minor *Poems of Religion and Society* (1848), which he himself treasured, and the celebrated *Report on Weights and Measures* (1821), in which the subject is examined with the exactness of mathematical science, the sagacity of statesmanship, and the wisdom of philosophy.

ADAMS, JOHN TURVILL (1805–82), New England novelist, whose books include *The Lost Hunter* (1856), laid in 19th-century Connecticut; and *The White Chief Among the Red Men; or, Knight of the Golden Melice* (1859), a tale dealing with Sir Christopher Gardiner and the Pequot War.

ADAMS, LÉONIE [FULLER] (1899–1988), New York poet, whose books, *Those Not Elect* (1925), *High Falcon* (1929), *This Measure* (1933), and *Poems* (1954), have been described as works of a modern metaphysical poet because of their sensitivity, austere intensity, and emphasis on intellect. She taught English at New York University, Bennington College, and Columbia University. In 1969 and the '70s she received several major awards and grants for her poetic achievements.

ADAMS, SAMUEL (1722–1803), born in Boston, graduated from Harvard (1740), studied law, was unsuccessful in business and after 1764 turned to the serious use of his talent for political agitation. He was a leader in directing popular hatred against the conservatives, and strongly opposed the Sugar Act of 1764, the Stamp Act, and the Townshend acts. From 1765 to 1774 he was a member of the lower house of the Massachusetts general court, serving after 1766 as recording clerk, in which capacity he showed great skill as a polemical writer, drafting many important Revolutionary documents. As early as 1765 his writings pointed the way toward the Declaration of Independence, and at times, when revolutionary feeling was waning, he fanned the embers with bitter contributions to periodicals. He helped organize the Sons of Liberty, aided in the formation of the nonimportation association of 1768, and emphasized the revolutionary doctrines of the "rights of man," "the laws of nature," and American independence of Parliament. Inflamed by Lord North's Tea Act, he was the guiding spirit of the Boston Tea Party. As a member of the intercolonial congress, which he had proposed, and as a delegate to the Continental Congress, he worked for colonial union and against any compromise with England. After the signing of the Declaration of Independence his career waned, for he was essentially a revolutionary agitator and not a constructive statesman. His later career included membership in the Massachusetts Constitutional Convention (1779–80) and the lieutenant-governorship (1789–93) and governorship of Massachusetts (1794–97). His various writings were collected (4 vols., 1904–8).

ADAMS, SAMUEL HOPKINS (1871–1958), journalist and author, from 1900 to 1916 was associated with *McClure's, Collier's,* and the New York *Tribune,* for which he wrote muckraking articles. His books include *The Great American Fraud* (1906), on patent nostrums; *Success* (1921), a novel about modern journalism; *Revelry* (1926), a fictional account of the Harding administration, of which he also wrote a history, *Incredible Era* (1939); *The*

Godlike Daniel (1930), a biography of Webster; *The Harvey Girls* (1942), a novel about the Fred Harvey restaurants; *Canal Town* (1944), a novel set in Palmyra, N.Y., in 1820; *A. Woollcott: His Life and His World* (1945); *Grandfather Stories* (1955), reminiscent tales told him by his grandfather, born in the 18th century; and *Tenderloin* (1959), a novel about New York's fast nightlife of the 1880s and 1890s.

ADAMS, WILLIAM TAYLOR (1822–97), Boston author and schoolteacher, who adopted the pseudonym Oliver Optic (*c.*1850) and began to write juvenile books and magazine tales, comparable in manner and popularity to the works of Horatio Alger. In 1865 he quit teaching to give all his time to authorship and to the editing of such magazines as *Oliver Optic's Magazine for Boys and Girls* (1867–75). He wrote more than 1000 short stories, and more than 115 novels, most of the latter in series, which included The Boat Club Series (1854), Woodville Series (1861–67), Army and Navy Series (1865–94), Starry Flag Series (1867–69), Onward and Upward Series (1870), Yacht Club Series (1872–1900), and Great Western Series (1875–82). His heroes, like Alger's, were rather priggish, but Adams's were more concerned with patriotism and adventure than with rising in the business world.

Adams Papers, archives of the Adams family, housed in the Massachusetts Historical Society, originally made available to scholars in a microfilm collection. A letterpress edition being prepared under the editorship of Lyman Henry Butterfield draws also upon public and private collections for its selective but scholarly gathering of documents. Series I contains the diaries of the Adams family statesmen, 1755–1880; Series II deals with the family correspondence, 1761–1889; and Series III prints general correspondence and other papers of the statesmen.

ADDAMS, JANE (1860–1935), reformer and sociologist, founded the Chicago social settlement, Hull-House, in 1889. Among her books are *Democracy and Social Ethics* (1902), *A New Conscience and an Ancient Evil* (1912), *Twenty Years at Hull-House* (1910), *Peace and Bread in Time of War* (1922), and *The Second Twenty Years at Hull-House* (1930).

Adding Machine, The, expressionistic play by Elmer Rice, ♦ produced and published in 1923.

ADE, GEORGE (1866–1944), Indiana author, whose books are noted for their racy use of vernacular and sympathetic portrayal of country characters. His *Fables in Slang* (1899) is often credited with being one of the most acute literary examples of the language of the common American. The satire and speech of this book appear also in *People You Know* (1903) and *Hand-Made*

Fables (1920). Ade was also known as a playwright, being the author of several musical comedies, notably *The Sultan of Sulu* (1902), and such plays as *The College Widow* (1904) and *Just Out of College* (1905), farcical satires on student life.

ADLER, MORTIMER J[EROME] (1902–), after receiving his Ph.D. at Columbia, became a professor of the philosophy of law at the University of Chicago (1930–52) during Hutchins's administration. His writings of this period include his statement of adherence to the views of St. Thomas Aquinas, *What Man Has Made of Man* (1938), *St. Thomas and the Gentiles* (1938), *Problems for Thomists* (1940), and *A Dialectic of Morals* (1941). With Hutchins he edited *Great Books of the Western World* (54 vols., 1952), drawn from 76 authors from Homer to Freud, and for it created a monumental index called the *Synopticon.* Popularizations of his views about contemporary inability to read or think precisely appeared in his *How To Read a Book* (1940) and *How To Think About War and Peace* (1944). His ideas have been promulgated not only through "Great Books courses" but through his own Institute for Philosophical Research, out of which has come his *The Idea of Freedom* (1958) and *Great Ideas from the Great Books* (1961). His other activities have included chairing the Board of Editors, *Encyclopaedia Britannica,* and his other books include *The Time of Our Lives: The Ethics of Common Sense* (1970), *Philosopher at Large: An Intellectual Autobiography* (1977), *Aristotle for Everybody* (1978), and *Reforming Education: The Opening of the American Mind* (1978).

ADLER, RENATA (1938–), after graduation from Bryn Mawr and further education at Harvard, the Sorbonne, and Yale law school, wrote social and political essays for *The New Yorker* and literary criticism collected in *Toward a Radical Middle* (1970). Her film reviews for *The New York Times* were collected in *A Year in the Dark* (1970). *Speedboat* (1976) is a brilliant episodic novel about the education and experiences of a young woman journalist, and *Pitch Dark* (1983) is a similarly constructed novel about a woman journalist breaking off her long-standing affair with a married man. *Reckless Disregard* (1986) is a study of legal issues involved in two suits and trials concerning libel accusations: that of General Westmoreland vs. CBS on reporting concerning him during the war in Vietnam and that of Israel's former defense minister, General Sharon, vs. *Time* about Palestinians being killed in Lebanese refugee camps.

Adulateur, The, satirical play by Mercy Otis Warren, ♦ published in 1773.

Adventists, see *Millerites.*

Adventures of Augie March, The, see *Augie March, The Adventures of.*

Adventures of a Young Man, novel by Dos Passos,♦ the first volume (1939) of a trilogy, preceding *Number One*♦ (1943) and *The Grand Design* (1949).

Adventues of Captain Bonneville, The, (1837), narrative by Washington Irving from the papers of Captain Benjamin Louis Eulalie de Bonneville (1796–1878). Bonneville, a West Pointer, led expeditions through the western slopes of the Rockies in 1832–35. Irving, at work on his novel *Astoria,* met Bonneville at the home of John Jacob Astor, bought the explorer's papers and maps, and then shaped his story as a kind of sequel to *Astoria.*

Advertisements for the Unexperienced Planters of New England . . . , work by Captain John Smith.♦

Advice to the Privileged Orders, work by Joel Barlow.♦

Afloat and Ashore, romance by Cooper♦ (1844). *Miles Wallingford*♦ is a sequel.

Miles and Grace Wallingford, orphaned children of a Revolutionary naval officer, are raised on their Hudson River estate by the Rev. Mr. Hardinge, with his children Rupert and Lucy. Miles and Lucy have already fallen in love when the two boys run away to New York, accompanied by the black slave Neb. They sign on the *John,* a ship bound for the Indies, which is commanded by Captain Robbins, a friend of Miles's father. Miles and Neb become favorites of the mate, Mr. Marble. In the Strait of Sunda the *John* escapes capture by Malay pirates, but is afterward wrecked off Madagascar. The survivors reach the isle of Bourbon and ship home on the *Tigris,* but Robbins dies during the voyage. Rupert and Miles reach New York in time to deny reports of their death, and Rupert enters a lawyer's office. Miles ships under Mr. Marble as third mate of the *Crisis,* enlisting Neb as a seaman. After various adventures, they reach England and sail for the Pacific. They engage in trade on the South American coast, have their ship stolen by the crew of a wrecked French privateer, rebuild the privateer, retake the *Crisis,* and sail for China. When he returns to America after this voyage, Miles becomes master of his own ship, the *Dawn.*

After the Fall, two-act play by Arthur Miller,♦ produced and published in 1964.

According to the stage directions, the "action takes place in the mind, thought, and memory" of Quentin, a man aged about 50, as persons with whom he has been involved "appear and disappear instantaneously." These include his first wife, Louise, who berates him for failing to appreciate her as a person in her own right; a onetime friend and fellow Communist, now an informer to a congressional investigating committee; and another friend, also a former Communist, whom Quentin determines to defend but is happy not to have to when the friend commits suicide. The second act deals with the character Maggie, a onetime switchboard operator, then an enormously popular singer, Quentin's second wife, who sinks from guileless sexual love to neuroticism and pettiness destructive of him and finally of her, as she commits suicide. At the end Quentin seeks salvation through Holga, who has stood out against Hitler in Germany and who now appears destined to be Quentin's third wife.

Agapida, FRAY ANTONIO, fictitious Spanish priest through whom Irving expresses the attitude of "monkish zealots" in *Chronicle of the Conquest of Granada.*♦

AGAR, HERBERT [SEBASTIAN] (1897–1980), historian and critic, whose books include *The Garment of Praise* (1929), a study of English poetry, written in collaboration with his wife, Eleanor Carroll Chilton; *The People's Choice* (1933, Pulitzer Prize), a study of American Presidents; *Land of the Free* (1935), a survey of American culture; *The Pursuit of Happiness* (1938), a history of the Democratic party; and *Who Owns America?* (1936), a compilation edited with Allen Tate. As the editor of the Louisville *Courier-Journal* (1940–42) and the author of *Beyond German Victory* (1940) he helped arouse public opinion before the U.S. entered World War II. Other books include: *A Time for Greatness* (1942), appraising American culture and indicating a role for the U.S. in the world crisis; *The Price of Union* (1950), on the U.S. political system; *A Declaration of Faith* (1952), calling for a revival of natural law; *Price of Power* (1957), on U.S. foreign relations; *The Saving Remnant* (1960), on charitable work to save persecuted Jews abroad; *The Perils of Democracy* (1966); and *The Darkest Hour* (1973), about Britain at war, 1940–41.

AGASSIZ, [JEAN] LOUIS [RODOLPHE] (1807–73), Swiss-born scientist and educator. In 1831 he went to Paris, became associated with the Jardin des Plantes, and assisted in and continued the work of his friends Cuvier and Humboldt. During the following years he was professor of natural history at Neuchâtel, wrote on *The Fishes of Brazil,* the *History of the Fresh Water Fishes of Central Europe,* and on similar subjects, and made the pioneer classification of fossil fishes, as well as the first treatment of the laws of glacial movement and deposit. When Agassiz came to the U.S. in 1846, it is said that "American Natural history . . . found its leader." Exerting the characteristic vigor of his stimulating personality, he lectured to enormous audiences throughout the East, and beginning in 1848 was professor of natural history in the Lawrence Scientific School at Harvard, at the same time beginning the collections that became the Harvard Museum of Comparative Zoology. Continuing at Harvard until his death, he was also associated at various times with the Charleston Medical College, Cornell University, and the Smithsonian Institution, as well as collaborating in the work of the Coast Survey, and leading many explorations, including the Thayer Expedition to Brazil (1865–66). His influence as a teacher was great, especially in his urging of direct observation and experiment, his attacks on memorization and the study of "dead" classics, and his encouragement of graduate work. His most distinguished writing during his American period appears in the *Contributions to the Natural History of the United States* (4 vols., 1857–62), which includes the "Essay on Classification," summing up his views on paleontology and geology, following the theories of Cuvier, and opposing Darwinian natural selection.

ELIZABETH CARY AGASSIZ (1822–1907), his wife, was a founder and president (1894–1903) of Radcliffe College. She wrote a biography of her husband (2 vols., 1885).

Age of Anxiety, The, long poem by Auden.♦

Age of Fable, The, see *Bulfinch, Thomas.*

Age of Innocence, The, novel by Edith Wharton.♦ published in 1920. It received a Pulitzer Prize, and in 1928 was dramatized by Margaret Ayer Barnes.

In the highest circle of New York social life during the 1870s, Newland Archer, a young lawyer, is the fiancé of May Welland. Before their engagement is announced, he meets May's cousin Ellen Olenska, the wife of a dissolute Polish count, from whom she is separated although she does not divorce him because of the conventional taboo. The taboo extends so far that she is nearly ostracized by her former friends, and only the efforts of Archer and his mother save her position. She wins the toleration of her grandmother, Mrs. Manson Mingott, but even then she is distrusted. Archer's taste and intelligence distinguish him in this dogmatic society, and he discovers in Ellen the companion spirit he has sought but not found in May, who is the product of her strict, formal environment. The two fall in love, but it is too late for Archer to withdraw from his engagement. He marries May but is dissatisfied with their convention-bound relationship. Ellen moves to Washington, then returns to care for her grandmother, and her relation with Archer is rekindled. When May reveals to Ellen that she is pregnant, the situation becomes intolerable for the Countess, who goes to live in Paris. Archer is never sure how much his wife knows until after her death, many years later, when he visits Paris with his son Dallas. Ellen invites them to visit her, but at the last moment Archer sends Dallas alone, feeling that, though they are now free to marry, he prefers his ideal vision of Ellen to the reality.

Age of Reason, The, deistic work by Thomas Paine,♦ published in two parts (Paris, 1794–95). Between the writing of the first and second parts, Paine spent 11 months in prison because of his activities in the French Revolution.

Part I affirms the existence of God and offers proofs from the arguments of design and first cause. The knowledge of God has been obscured, according to the author, by the calumnies of the Bible and all national institutions of churches, which are no more than "human inventions set up to terrify and enslave mankind, and monopolize power and profit." Man's moral duty should be to observe the real and ever-existing word of God in the creation, and to strive to imitate this beneficence. Part II is mainly an attack on the Bible, pointing out the cruelty of Moses, the folly of Solomon, the exaggerations of the prophets, the improbability of Jesus' miraculous birth, and the general inconsistency that renders the Bible fallible.

AGEE, JAMES (1909–55), Tennessee-born author, after graduation from Harvard (1932) began his literary career with *Permit Me Voyage* (1934), a work issued in the Yale Series of Younger Poets. He served on the staffs of *Fortune* and *Time,* and for the former wrote a study of Alabama sharecroppers during the Depression, which when found inappropriate for *Fortune* was issued with photographs by Walker Evans as *Let Us Now Praise Famous Men*♦ (1941). *The Morning Watch* (1951), a novella sensitively depicting a day in the life of a 12-year-old boy in a Tennessee school, was a prelude to his major work of fiction, *A Death in the Family*♦ (1957), a partly autobiographical and poetic story of a happy, secure Tennessee family whose good life is shattered by the father's death in an auto accident. His motion picture reviews for *The Nation, Time,* and other journals were posthumously collected as *Agee on Film* (1958). *Agee on Film: II* (1960) contains five of his own screenplays, including Stephen Crane's *The Bride Comes to Yellow Sky* and *The Blue Hotel. A Death in the Family* was dramatized as *All the Way Home* (1960) by Tad Mosel and won a Pulitzer Prize. Agee's letters to his old schoolteacher and friendly mentor from his sixteenth year to his death were published as *Letters to Father Flye* (1962). *Selected Journalism* (1985) gathers unreprinted articles.

Ages, The, poem by Bryant,♦ presented as the Phi Beta Kappa poem at the Harvard Commencement (1821) and published the same year. In 35 Spenserian stanzas, the work recounts the historic achievements of man, and affirms the benevolence of God and the principle of human progress.

Aggawam, see *Simple Cobler of Aggawam.*

Agrarians, name applied to certain Southern writers, including J.C. Ransom, J.G. Fletcher,

R.P. Warren, Allen Tate, and Donald Davidson, who had championed an agrarian economy for the South and the more general movement known as Regionalism. ◆

Ah Sin, character in *Plain Language from Truthful James,* ◆ also the title character in a play by Harte and Twain, produced in 1877, printed in 1961.

Ah, Wilderness!, play by Eugene O'Neill. ◆

Ahab, CAPTAIN, character in *Moby-Dick.* ◆

AIKEN, CONRAD [POTTER] (1889–1973), was born in Georgia but reared in Massachusetts, from which his parents' families had come, and educated at Harvard (A.B., 1911), so that a strong sense of a New England heritage is evident in his writing. In his maturity he lived for many years in England but returned to make his home in Massachusetts. His early poetry is marked by subtle musical rhythms and is concerned with the problem of personal identity, what it is that constitutes one's own consciousness, how to achieve self-knowledge, and how to transcend the self so as to understand the world at large. The volumes that collect this early poetry include *Earth Triumphant* (1914); *Turns and Movies* (1916); *The Jig of Forslin: A Symphony* (1916); *Nocturne of Remembered Spring* (1917); *The Charnel Rose, Senlin: A Biography, and Other Poems* (1918); *The House of Dust: A Symphony* (1920); *Punch: The Immortal Liar* (1921); *Priapus and the Pool* (1922); and *The Pilgrimage of Festus* (1923). A more metaphysical expression is developed in *John Deth* (1930), *The Coming Forth by Day of Osiris Jones* (1931), *Preludes for Memnon* (1931), *Landscape West of Eden* (1934), and *Time in the Rock* (1936), philosophic poems dealing with consciousness and time. *And in the Human Heart* (1940) is a sequence of 43 sonnets extending the concern with consciousness to the intensity of love. *Brownstone Eclogues* (1942) picks up the setting and subject of *The House of Dust:* the city and the quest of the individual for identification with its good and evil. *The Soldier* (1944) traces the common soldier through history in treating the wars of armies and the wars of the spirit. In *The Kid* (1947) Aiken uses the figure of William Blackstone, an individualistic and very early New England settler, as a symbol for the American character which is developed in the guise of such diverse later figures as Thoreau, Johnny Appleseed, and Whitman. Later poetry showing great musical quality and setting forth his essentially existentialist position appears in *Skylight One* (1949), *A Letter from Li Po* (1955), *Sheepfold Hill* (1958), and *The Morning Song of Lord Zero* (1963). He published *Selected Poems* (1929, Pulitzer Prize), *Collected Poems* (1953), and another *Selected Poems* (1961). He is also known for his critical writing in *Scepticisms* (1919), commenting on contemporary poets, his introduction to an edition of Emily Dickinson's poems (1924),

which had much to do with establishing her reputation, and *A Reviewer's ABC* (1958). In 1927 appeared his first novel, a fantasy entitled *Blue Voyage,* which treats some of his poetic themes as it tells in stream-of-consciousness prose of a dramatist's voyage to England, supposedly for reasons of his career and his love for a girl, but actually in his quest for self-knowledge. Later novels are *Great Circle* (1933), another tale of a voyage and of the quest to discover oneself; *King Coffin* (1935), the story of a neurotic criminal; *A Heart for the Gods of Mexico* (1939), about a dying woman's last love as it takes her from Boston to Mexico; and *Conversation; or, Pilgrims' Progress* (1940), dealing with crises in a man's life as husband, father, and artist. His stories have appeared in *Bring! Bring!* (1925), *Costumes by Eros* (1928), and *Among the Lost People* (1934), the last-named including "Mr. Arcularis," dramatized by the author and published as a play in 1957, about a sad old man who is dying, as he lived, alone, and who imagines himself on a recuperative sea voyage while he is actually outward bound toward death on an operating table. *Ushant* (1952), subtitled "an essay," is a psychological autobiography, reissued (1971) with the names of actual people replacing the original pseudonyms. *Selected Letters* was published in 1978.

AIKEN, GEORGE L. (1830–76), actor, and author of many plays, who dramatized Harriet Beecher Stowe's *Uncle Tom's Cabin* and acted in its first performance at Troy, N.Y. (Sept. 27, 1852), where it ran for 100 nights.

AIMARD, GUSTAVE, pseudonym of Oliver Gloux (1818–83), who sailed to the U.S. from his native France as a boy midshipman, and lived for ten years in Arkansas and other regions of the Old Southwest, where he was supposedly adopted by an Indian tribe. His life as hunter, trapper, squatter, warrior, and miner furnished the material for his many romances, which caused him to be called the Dumas of the Indians. He later revisited America to gather further material for his fiction. He wrote more than 25 novels, and among those which have been translated are *Loyal Heart; or, The Trappers of Arkansas* (1858), *The Pirates of the Prairies* (1858), *The Tiger Slayer* (1860), *Lynch Law* (1860), *The Gold Seekers* (1861), *The Freebooters* (1861), *The Indian Chief* (1861), *The Prairie Flower* (1861), and *The Last of the Incas* (1862).

AINSLIE, HEW (1792–1878), Scottish poet whose first work, *A Pilgrimage to the Land of Burns* (1822), a narrative interspersed with songs and ballads, was published just before he came to the U.S. (1822). There he was for a time a member of the New Harmony colony, and later published a further collection of dialect poems, *Scottish Songs, Ballads, and Poems* (1855).

Air-Conditioned Nightmare, The, travel account by Henry Miller, ◆ published in 1945. Views of the U.S. based on the author's travels (1941–42), the year after returning from his long expatriation, the work dwells, generally negatively, not only on the natural scene but on the national spirit. *Remember To Remember* (1947) is a sequel.

Airways, Inc., play by Dos Passos,♦ published 1928, produced 1929.

The Turner family, resident in a suburban town during the 1920s, is nominally headed by Dad, an unsuccessful inventor, but he is overshadowed by his son Elmer, a celebrated aviator and aircraft designer. But Elmer is soon corrupted by his sudden fame and wealth, so that the family, including two inconsequential brothers, is held together by their sister Martha, in love with a radical labor organizer, Walter Goldberg. Disasters soon dog the family: Dad commits suicide; Elmer is injured in a plane crash; the brothers are unemployed because of a local depression occasioned by the strike called by Walter's union; Walter is framed on a false charge of murder and electrocuted, as penniless and desolate Martha is left to care for the crippled Elmer.

AITKEN, ROBERT (1734–1802), Scottish-born printer and publisher, settled in America (1771). His most famous publishing venture was the Aitken Bible (New Testament, 1777; complete edition, 1782), the first complete English-language Bible printed in America. Prior to the Revolution the English held a monopoly on the Bible by prohibiting its publication outside the mother country. Aitken also published the *Pennsylvania Magazine.* ♦

AKERS, ELIZABETH [CHASE] (1832–1911), literary editor of the Portland (Me.) *Daily Advertiser.* Her verse, popular at the time but now mainly forgotten, included the poem "Rock Me To Sleep," which contains the famous lines:

> Backward, turn backward, O Time, in your
> flight.
> Make me a child again just for tonight.

The poem was first printed in the *Saturday Evening Post* (June 9, 1860) under the pseudonym Florence Percy, and has since been set to music by more than 30 composers. Because of the pseudonym the authorship was disputed, but Mrs. Akers successfully defended her claim. The poem was later reprinted in her collections *Poems* (1866) and *The Sunset Song and Other Verses* (1902).

AKINS, ZOË (1886–1958), born in Missouri, began writing for *The Mirror* of W.M. Reedy, and came to New York to write plays for the Washington Square Players, achieving her first professional success with *Déclassée* (1919), a play showing the social decline of an English lady. This was followed by *Daddy's Gone A-Hunting* (1921), the story of a man who forsakes his wife to pursue his dream of becoming a great painter. Several less successful plays were produced during

the next ten years, among them *The Varying Shore* (1921), tracing in reverse chronology the career of a woman from her death as a gambler and demi-mondaine to her unhappy shy girlhood, and *The Texas Nightingale* (1922), revived as *Greatness* (1923), the story of an opera singer. Miss Akins returned to her full power with *The Greeks Had a Word for It* (1930), a satirical comedy of three unscrupulous girls whose only loyalty is to one another. In 1935 she won the Pulitzer Prize with *The Old Maid,* ♦ adapted from a novelette by Edith Wharton. *O, Evening Star* (1936) is the story of an aging actress whose burlesquing of serious drama in a motion picture reestablishes her career. *Forever Young* (1941), her first novel, deals with a Midwestern girls' school in the early 1900s.

Al Aaraaf, allegorical poem by Poe,♦ published in *Al Aaraaf, Tamerlane, and Minor Poems* (1829) and revised in later printings. With the sonnet "To Science"♦ as a "prologue," the poem is arranged in two parts, composed of octosyllabic groups, heroic couplets, and songs of two- and three-stress lines.

Al Aaraaf in Mohammedan mythology is a sort of limbo, but in the present allegory it is the brilliant star, briefly observed by Tycho Brahe, which the poet imagines to be the birthplace of the "Idea of Beauty." To this haven of ideal loveliness is carried the earth-born youth Angelo, but his worship is removed from the realm of the ideal by his passion for the maiden Ianthe. Because of their passion they do not hear the summons sent them by the presiding spirit Nesace, through her agent Ligeia, and they fall to perdition:

> . . . for Heaven to them no hope imparts
> Who hear not for the beating of their hearts.

ALBEE, EDWARD [FRANKLIN] (1928–), after a troubled youth came in his early thirties to the beginning of his career as playwright. He quickly became a leading figure of the new drama of the absurd that mingles the realistic with fantasy to present a savagely satirical attack on spiritual sterility, blandness, conformity, and hypocrisy, and to summon up with deep feeling the tragedy of alienation. His first play, *The Zoo Story* (Berlin, 1959; New York, 1960), a one-act drama, presents a young homosexual who, hating both the world he can't live in and the one he does inhabit, manages to trick an ordinary, middle-aged, and innocent stranger whom he encounters in New York's Central Park into killing him. Another short play, *The Death of Bessie Smith* (Berlin, 1960; New York, 1961), treats the agony of the black blues singer's death after an auto accident as the counterpointed background for a horrid fight involving a nurse, an intern, and an orderly in the all-white hospital to which she is brought. *The Sandbox* (1960) symbolically treats family relationships as Mommy and Daddy, tired of Grandma, an unusually vital person, leave her on a beach to be picked up by a young man representative of Death. *The American Dream*♦ (1961), another play in one scene, again presents a grotesque comedy about a middle-class Mommy and Daddy who tortured their adopted son to death because he seemed unlikely to grow up into the clean-cut "American Dream" type of young man. *Who's Afraid of Virginia Woolf?*♦ (1962), Albee's first three-act play, presents an all-night drinking bout of a middle-aged professor and his wife, joined by a vacuous instructor and his silly wife, in which through horrid verbal torturing of one another they eventually achieve catharsis by exorcising their fixation about a nonexistent son, which the older couple had created to sustain themselves, an illustration of what Albee has called the need to "try to claw our way into compassion." *Tiny Alice* (1965) is a more obscure and symbolic drama that presents the richest woman in the world corrupting a Catholic lay brother, whom she seduces, marries, and arranges to have murdered. In 1963 he dramatized Carson McCullers's *The Ballad of the Sad Café.* ♦ His other adaptations are: James Purdy's *Malcolm* (1965), Giles Cooper's *Everything in the Garden* (1967), and Nabokov's *Lolita* (1981). *A Delicate Balance*♦ (1966; Pulitzer Prize, 1967) depicts a family unhappily questing for love and purpose without success. In 1968 Albee produced *Box* and *Quotations from Chairman Mao Tse-Tung,* the former presenting a huge box on stage while the sole voice is an offstage monologue, and the latter presenting four characters who speak banal lines from Mao and the sentimental poet Will Carleton, the two linked dramas suggesting the lack of significant values in human relations. *All Over* (1971) treats the attitudes toward life of the diverse hangers-on who gather at the deathbed of a so-called great man. *Seascape* (1975) is a two-act play abstractly presenting a seemingly average man and wife who on a deserted beach encounter a humanoid couple in an earlier stage of evolutionary development and through conversation gain insights into curiosities of human behavior and beliefs. *The Lady from Dubuque* (1979) presents three fiercely captious couples to whom the Lady from Dubuque (Death) will come. *Counting the Ways* (1977) and *Listening* (1977) are short plays in which respectively two and three characters discuss their relationships. Similarly, *Finding the Sun* (1982) and *Walking* (1984) are one-act plays with some short scenes. *The Man Who Had Three Arms* (1983) is a full-length three-person rendition of a man called Himself who has a brief period of great prominence. *Three Tall Women* (1994, Pulitzer Prize) is a poetic play about three generations of women and their coming to terms with their pasts.

ALCOTT, [Amos] Bronson (1799–1888), born in Connecticut, had little formal education, and early attempted to support himself as a peddler in the Southern states and as a schoolteacher in New England and Pennsylvania (1823–33). His educational ideas, continued in his Temple School at Boston (1834–39) and later in his work as school superintendent at Concord and elsewhere, were characterized by an attempt to create the harmonious development of the physical, intellectual, aesthetic, and moral natures, with stress placed on imagination. To achieve this end, he favored a conversational method of instruction, attempted to beautify the school surroundings and to give study and instruction the aspect of recreation, and introduced such innovations as gymnastics, organized play, and the honor system. His philosophy, mediating between the extreme idealistic and materialistic positions, was summed up in the term Personalism. Alcott was an extreme Transcendentalist,♦ yet he was opposed to its doctrine of individualism and believed that all seemingly separate minds are linked by a common relation to a central Mind; that is, as he said, "all souls have a Personal identity with God and abide in Him." His philosophy, his theory of infant education founded "on the great principle that every infant is already in possession of the faculties and apparatus required for his instruction," his later emphasis on birth or heredity as more important than education and environment in determining character, and his social conscience were all bound up with his own integrated and benevolent personality. In 1835 Alcott's assistant at the Temple School, Elizabeth Peabody, edited his *Record of a School, Exemplifying the General Principles of Spiritual Culture;* this was followed by two volumes of his *Conversations with Children on the Gospels* (1836–37). These books, setting forth his theory and practice of education, won Alcott the support of such friends as Channing, Emerson, and J.F. Clarke, but lost him many pupils, whose parents considered his ideas dangerous and improper, so that the school was finally abandoned. In 1840 he moved with his wife and children to Concord, where he attempted to live by farming an acre of land, but this also failed. He then went to England (May– Oct. 1842), where an Alcott House had been founded to experiment with his educational ideas, and met Carlyle, who found the voluble American tiresome, but described him as being "like a venerable Don Quixote, whom nobody can laugh at without loving." In the U.S. again, in the company of a group of mystics, Alcott made plans for a cooperative community, which resulted in the ill-fated experiment at Fruitlands. ♦ This transcendental, communal, vegetarian organization persisted for only seven months, and in January 1845 the family returned to Concord. There and elsewhere, Alcott continued to lecture and to hold informal "conversations" to disseminate his ideas, meanwhile being supported mainly by the labors of his wife and his daughter Louisa May Alcott.♦ Not until 1868 did they become financially independent, when Louisa published *Little Women,* based on the family life during her childhood. In 1859 Alcott became superintendent of Concord schools, where he introduced the teaching of singing, dancing, reading aloud, and such novel subjects as physiology. This work and his endeavors in higher education that culminated in the Concord School of Philosophy (1879–88), a profound influence on U.S. education through his disciple W.T. Harris and others, embodied not only his philosophic ideas but also his genius for conversation and his personal influence. His serene unworldliness, his idealism in the midst of a material world, and his preoccupation with his own ideas and innumerable reforms made his practical relations with his family and friends difficult, although he considered the Family a golden mean between the hermit's cell and the phalanstery, and his home life was beautiful and generally happy. Carlyle had looked upon him indulgently as a man "bent on saving the world by a return to acorns and the golden age"; but Emerson said, "As pure intellect I have never seen his equal"; and Thoreau agreed that he was "the sanest man I ever knew." As an apostle of Transcendentalism, his medium was "conversation," in which he informally developed his ideas and personality. In this spontaneous art, Alcott exhibited the most lucid and brilliant aspects of his thought, but, as it inevitably died with him, his reputation waned when he could be approached only through the colder medium of his writings. Among his early books on education were *Observations on the Principles and Methods of Infant Instruction* (1830) and *The Doctrine and Discipline of Human Culture* (1836). Later writings include the mystical "Orphic Sayings," ♦ published in *The Dial* (1840–41); *Tablets* ♦ (1868); *Ralph Waldo Emerson* (1865, 1882), a laudatory estimate of Emerson's character and genius in both prose and verse; *Concord Days* (1872), a work based on his journals; and *Table Talk* (1877). *New Connecticut* (1887) is a poetical autobiography of his youth, and *Sonnets and Canzonets* (1882) is a volume written in memory of his wife. A selection from his *Journals* was published in 1938 and from his *Letters* in 1969.

ALCOTT, LOUISA MAY (1832–88), a daughter of Bronson Alcott, was born in Pennsylvania, spent most of her early years in Boston and Concord, and was educated by her father, receiving instruction and guidance also from such friends as Thoreau, Emerson, and Theodore Parker. She worked at various tasks to help support her family, and at the age of 16 wrote a book, *Flower Fables* (1854). Her ambition for a time was to be an actress, and she wrote several unproduced melodramas, as well as poems and short stories, some of which were published in the *Atlantic Monthly*. She was a nurse in a Union hospital during the Civil War until her health failed: her letters of this period were published as *Hospital Sketches* (1863). She issued her first novel, *Moods,*

in 1865, and toured Europe as a lady's companion the same year. Between 1863 and 1869 she published anonymous and pseudonymous Gothic romances and thrilling tales, like "Pauline's Passion and Punishment," in popular journals. These were discovered and collected by Madeleine B. Stern in *Behind a Mask* (1975) and *Plots and Counterplots* (1976), which also included, among other anonymously issued fiction, *A Modern Mephistopheles* (1877), a Faustian work much affected by Goethe, first reissued posthumously with her name (1889) and then by Stern in 1987. In 1867 she became editor of a juvenile magazine, *Merry's Museum*. *Little Women* ♦ (1868–69), her charming and immensely popular story for children, presents a cheerful account of her own early life in New England; in it she portrays herself as Jo, and her sisters May, Elizabeth, and Anna respectively as Amy, Beth, and Meg. This work brought the financial security she had been trying to achieve for her family, and she continued to write in the same vein in *An Old-Fashioned Girl* (1870). *Little Men* (1871), and *Work* (1873), a more feminist text. She revisited Europe (1870–71), returning to Boston to continue her participation in such reform movements as temperance and woman suffrage and her writing of moralistic fiction for children. Her later works include *Eight Cousins* (1875); *Rose in Bloom* (1876); *Silver Pitchers and Independence* (1876), containing "Transcendental Wild Oats," about her father's experiments at Fruitlands; *Under the Lilacs* (1878); *Jack and Jill* (1880); *Aunt Jo's Scrap-Bag* (6 vols., 1872–82); *Proverb Stories* (1882); *Spinning-Wheel Stories* (1884); *Lulu's Library* (3 vols., 1886–89); *Jo's Boys* (1886); and *A Garland for Girls* (1888). Recent publications of her writing include *Selected Letters* (1987) and *Journals* (1989). In late 1994 plans were announced for publication of a newly found manuscript of a romantic novel with the title *A Long Fatal Love Chase*.

ALDEN, ISABELLA [MACDONALD] (1841–1930), New York author of children's books, including some 75 in the series issued under her pseudonym, Pansy. She edited the magazine for children, *Pansy* (1873–96).

ALDEN, JOHN (c.1599–1687), a *Mayflower* Pilgrim who held various important colonial positions, was a friend of Miles Standish, with whom he founded Duxbury. He married Priscilla Mullens (or Molines) c.1621, but Longfellow's *The Courtship of Miles Standish* ♦ is based on a legend that arose in the 19th century. He also figures in novels by Jane G. Austin. ♦

Aldine, The (1868–79), journal of art and typography, was founded as the house organ of a New York firm of printers. It soon became a magazine for general circulation, under the editorship of R.H. Stoddard (1871–75). After his retirement, the magazine abandoned general literature and drifted into bimonthly publication. It was consistently praised for its fine engravings and typography.

ALDRICH, BESS STREETER (1881–1954), Iowa novelist, later a resident of Nebraska, whose works include *A Lantern in Her Hand* (1928), the story of a pioneer woman in Nebraska; *A White Bird Flying* (1931), a sequel dealing with the children of the pioneers; *Spring Came On Forever* (1935); *The Man Who Caught the Weather* (1936), a collection of short stories; *Song of Years* (1939), a story of pioneer life in Iowa; and *The Lieutenant's Lady* (1942), a novel of an army wife on the Indian frontier in the 19th century.

ALDRICH, THOMAS BAILEY (1836–1907), born in Portsmouth, N.H., lived in New Orleans, New York, and in his birthplace during his childhood. Portsmouth is the scene of his semiautobiographical novel, *The Story of a Bad Boy*◆ (1870). He had planned to enter Harvard, but when his father died in 1852 he took a business position instead, and soon began to write poetry for magazines. After the publication of his first collection, *The Bells* (1855), he held various posts on N. P. Willis's *Evening Mirror* and *Home Journal,* became a correspondent for the *Tribune* at the outbreak of the Civil War, and was managing editor (1862–65) of the *Illustrated News.* In 1865 began his permanent residence in Boston, the mecca of his ambition and home of the New England group of authors who were the objects of his lifelong veneration. He was editor of *Every Saturday* (1866–74), during which period he published *The Story of a Bad Boy,* such gracefully turned short stories as "Marjorie Daw" (1873), and the refined, delicately finished, but shallow verses, printed mainly in the *Atlantic Monthly,* which he collected in *Pampinea* (1861) and *Cloth of Gold* (1874). Later collections of poetry included *Flower and Thorn* (1877); *Friar Jerome's Beautiful Book* (1881); *Mercedes and Later Lyrics* (1884), whose title piece, dramatized by the author, was produced in 1894; *Wyndham Towers* (1890); and *Judith and Holofernes* (1896), whose dramatic version, retitled *Judith of Bethulia,* was later produced (1904). His novels, written during the same years, were also marked by technical skill and charm, though they lack depth of understanding. They include *Prudence Palfrey* (1874), a romantic tale set in a small New England town; *The Queen of Sheba* (1877), a fantastic story of a young man's meeting with a girl who thinks she is the Queen of Sheba, their second meeting years later after she has recovered her sanity, and their falling in love; and *The Stillwater Tragedy* (1880), a detective mystery, partly concerned with an employer's triumph in quelling a strike. His best-known short stories appeared in *Marjorie Daw and Other People* (1873), *Two Bites at a Cherry, with Other Tales* (1894), and later volumes. Aldrich's editorship of the *Atlantic Monthly* (1881–

90) was noted for his conservative policy and his adherence to "Boston-plated" traditions, which also appear in his collected essays, *From Ponkapog to Pesth* (1883), *An Old Town by the Sea* (1893), and *Ponkapog Papers* (1903).

ALFRED, WILLIAM (1922–), New York City–born author and educator, after graduation from Brooklyn College and previous service in the army went to Harvard on a GI scholarship, remaining there as a faculty member for more than 35 years after receiving an M.A. and a Ph.D. His first play, *Agamemnon* (1954), is an adaptation of Aeschylus' drama in verse, with a modern setting and situation. *Hogan's Goat* (1966), also a verse play, is a lively treatment of Irish-American life and politics in Brooklyn during the 1890s and was adapted by Alfred as a musical, *Cry for Us All* (1970). *The Curse of an Aching Heart* (1982) is a play also located in Brooklyn but during the 1940s.

ALGER, HORATIO, JR. (1832–99), was born in Massachusetts of an old Puritan family. He graduated from Harvard and its Divinity School, wrote books for boys, traveled abroad, and served in the Civil War before becoming a Unitarian minister. He was ousted (1866) for immoral relations with his choirboys and moved to New York to continue his literary career. While associated with the Newsboys' Lodging House as chaplain and philanthropist, he wrote about 130 popular books for boys, almost all fiction and all based on the concept that a struggle against poverty and temptation inevitably leads a boy to wealth and fame. His most famous hero was in the Ragged Dick series (1867 ff.); the Luck and Pluck (1869 ff.) and Tattered Tom (1871) series were next most popular. He also wrote lives of self-made statesmen. Over 20,000,000 copies of the novels are said to have been printed. Herbert R. Mayes's once accepted biography (1927) contains many fabrications.

Algerine Captive, The; or, The Life and Adventures of Dr. Updike Underhill, novel by Royall Tyler,◆ published in 1797.

Dr. Underhill, in this fictitious autobiography, first tells of the stupidity of contemporary New England college education, and then, while studying medicine, illustrates the quackery of the profession, in both New England and the South. After describing slavery as he sees it in the Southern states and on a slave ship, he narrates his own difficulties when he is abandoned in Africa. His picaresque adventures provide an ironic commentary on American life when, during a seven-year absence from the U.S., he is captured by the Algerines, is sold into slavery, and just escapes becoming a Mohammedan.

Algic Researches, treatise on Indian life, by H.R. Schoolcraft.◆

Algonquin (or ALGONKIN) **Indians,** name applied to nomadic hunting tribes in Quebec and Ontario, and later to the entire Algonquian linguistic family to which they belong. Located originally near Ottawa, the Algonquian tribe was driven northward by 17th-century wars with the Iroquois and British, whom they, as allies of the French, opposed. They had the characteristic attributes of a Plains tribe. ♦ The linguistic family, whose primitive culture preceded those of the Mound Builders and Iroquois, included the Arapaho, Blackfoot, and Cheyenne of the northern Plains; the Ojibway, Cree, Shawnee, Delaware, Mohegan, Narragansett, and Pequot of the eastern U.S.; and tribes as far south as the Powhatan. Longfellow uses Algonquian legends in his poem on the Mohawk hero Hiawatha.

Algonquin Round Table, informal meeting place in the dining room of the Algonquin Hotel (New York City), mainly from the 1920s through the 1940s, of a lively, witty group, whose participants included Franklin P. Adams, Robert Benchley, Heywood Broun, Marc Connelly, Russel Crouse, George S. Kaufman, Dorothy Parker, Robert E. Sherwood, Frank Sullivan, and Alexander Woollcott.

ALGREN, NELSON (1909–81), born in Detroit and reared in Chicago slums, grew up in poverty and insecurity in a Jewish family, with the name William Algren Abraham. His literary career as a writer of realistic novels of social protest began with *Somebody in Boots* (1935), about a poor-white Texas boy's vagabondage and criminality during the Depression, and was continued in *Never Come Morning* (1942), about a Polish hoodlum in Chicago who dreams of a better life as a prizefighter. *The Man with the Golden Arm♦* (1949) depicts the life of Frankie Machine (the Americanized version of his Polish name, Majcinek), a stud-poker dealer in a Chicago gambling club who becomes a dope addict and commits suicide, and places him in a panorama of the corrupt and violent lives of Chicago's underdogs who, like Frankie, are frustrated by their slum environment. *A Walk on the Wild Side* (1956) presents a somewhat similar underworld in New Orleans during the Depression, emphasizing the erotic and bohemian. The stories of *The Neon Wilderness* (1947) are less violent treatments of lower-class life. *Who Lost an American?* (1963) collects sketches of a lighter sort about life in New York and Chicago and on his travels abroad. *Conversations* (1964) issues tape-recorded recollections, *Notes from a Sea Diary* (1965) collects stories and a commentary on Hemingway, and *The Last Carousel* (1973) gathers short prose and poetry. His romance with Simone de Beauvoir is treated in her autobiography, *Force of Circumstance,* and to a degree in her novel *The Mandarins.*

Alhambra, The, 41 sketches by Irving, ♦ published in 1832 and revised and enlarged in 1852, the result of the author's residence (1829) in the ancient Moorish palace at Granada in Spain. His purpose was "to depict its half Spanish, half Oriental character; . . . to revive the traces of grace and beauty fast fading from its walls; to record the regal and chivalrous traditions . . . and the whimsical and superstitious legends of the motley race now burrowing among its ruins." Tales of medieval Moorish Spain are interspersed with architectural and other descriptions, and anecdotes of the author's experiences among the native residents.

Alias Jimmy Valentine, see *Porter, W. S.*

Alice Adams, novel by Booth Tarkington, ♦ published in 1921 and awarded a Pulitzer Prize.

Alice, a pretty girl, anxious to escape her Midwestern lower-middle-class life, dreams of the stage or a rich marriage. Her father, Virgil Adams, nagged by his wife, leaves his lifelong job at Lamb's drug company, to open a glue factory with the formula he invented for Mr. Lamb. Alice, forsaken by local beaux because of her family's pushing ways, falls in love with a wealthy newcomer, Arthur Russell. To snare him she fabricates a web of small lies about herself and her family, which turns him against her when he sees the truth at a pathetic family dinner party. As their affair ends, her brother Walter absconds with the drug firm's money, and Virgil's new business is ruined by competition from Mr. Lamb, who nevertheless aids Virgil when he has a paralytic stroke. He recovers, his wife opens a boardinghouse to support him, and Alice, sadly wiser, becomes a typist.

Alice of Old Vincennes, novel by Maurice Thompson, ♦ published in 1900.

Alice Tarleton, the child of an old colonial family, is abducted and reared on the frontier by Gaspard Roussilon, a French trader with the Indians, at Vincennes in the Wabash country of Indiana. At the outbreak of the Revolution, she aids the campaign of George Rogers Clark, and the story is mainly concerned with his capture of Vincennes for the patriots (1779). Alice's love affair with aristocratic Lieutenant Beverley, one of Clark's officers, turns out happily when her real parentage is disclosed.

Alison's House, play by Susan Glaspell, ♦ produced and published in 1930, and awarded a Pulitzer Prize. Alison Stanhope is considered to represent Emily Dickinson.

All God's Chillun Got Wings, play by Eugene O'Neill, ♦ produced and published in 1924.

All in a Bustle; or, The New House, farce by William Milns, written for the opening of the Park

Theatre, New York (1798). It deals with the difficulties of the stage manager and his actors and actresses, some of whom represented themselves in the production. The play is important as a source of information on early American theaters.

All the King's Men, novel by Robert Penn Warren, ♦ published in 1946, winner of a Pulitzer Prize. The protagonist is said to be based on Huey Long.

Willie Stark, a self-educated Southern backcountry man, infatuated with power and dreams of public service, is elected governor of his state. Vital, unscrupulous, and demagogic, he attracts into his employ Jack Burden, a newspaperman and "student of history" in search of truth; Sadie Burke, an intense and intrepid secretary, who becomes his mistress; and Tiny Duffy, a fat yesman. Willie sends Jack to Burden's Landing, his childhood home, to find something with which to blackmail Judge Irwin, a dignified, honorable, old family friend and former attorney general, who reneged on a promise to the Boss. In his "excursion into the past," Jack renews old friendships with Adam Stanton, an idealististic surgeon, and his sister Anne, the unmarried patrician who was his first love. Through Jack they become involved with the Boss, who fascinates and repels them and fulfills an incompleteness in their characters: Anne eventually replaces Sadie as his mistress and Adam becomes director of the hospital Willie built as an altruistic act. Jack gets evidence that Irwin took a bribe, but the Judge won't submit to Willie and commits suicide. From his grief-stricken mother Jack learns that Irwin was his father. Adam, after receiving news of Anne's affair by an anonymous telephone call instigated by Sadie, gets into the Capitol and, in shooting Willie, is himself killed. Jack returns to Burden's Landing, marries Anne, and comes to realize that Willie was corrupted by success and destroyed by a conflict between the will to power and the desire to perform good works. At last able to understand his own past and aware of the infinite consequences of a single act and the common guilt of men, Jack prepares to "go into the convulsion of the world . . . and the awful responsibility of Time."

ALLEN, ETHAN (1738–89), hero of the Revolutionary War, was earlier a leader of the Green Mountain Boys♦ in their opposition to the rule of New York state in the New Hampshire Grants. His irregular militia served under him in the Revolution, and, with a force of Connecticut soldiers under Benedict Arnold, captured Ticonderoga (May 10, 1775). According to his own unverified account, Allen called upon the British to surrender "in the name of the great Jehovah and the Continental Congress." In an expedition against Montreal, he was captured and imprisoned by the British (Sept. 1775–May 1778), an experience described in his blunt, egotistical,

and amusing *Narrative of Colonel Ethan Allen's Captivity* (1779). The deistic book, *Reason the Only Oracle of Man* (1784), is sometimes called "Ethan Allen's Bible," but scholars have contended that most of it was written by the freethinker Dr. Thomas Young (1732–77), to whose posthumously obtained manuscript Allen gave no credit. Allen appears as a character in Thompson's *The Green Mountain Boys* and in Melville's *Israel Potter.*

ALLEN, FREDERICK LEWIS (1890–1954), born in Boston and educated at Harvard, served on the staffs of the *Atlantic Monthly* (1914–16), *The Century* (1916–1917), and *Harper's* (1923–53, as editor after 1941). His major books are informal histories of the U.S.: *Only Yesterday* (1931), about the 1920s; *Since Yesterday* (1940), about the 1930s; *The Lords of Creation* (1935), about financial and corporate expansion since the 1890s; and *The Big Change* (1952), about the first half of the 20th century. He also wrote the text for two anthologies of photographs, *The American Procession* (1933) and *Metropolis* (1934).

ALLEN, [WILLIAM] HERVEY (1889–1949), born in Pittsburgh, graduated from the University of Pittsburgh and served in World War I, as he described in his autobiographical novel *Toward the Flame* (1926). He taught English at Charleston, S.C., where with DuBose Heyward he wrote the poems *Carolina Chansons* (1922). He is best known as a novelist and for his carefully documented biography of Poe, *Israfel* (1926). *Anthony Adverse* (1933), a lengthy picaresque romance of the Napoleonic era, sold a half-million copies during its first two years. *Action at Aquila* (1938) is a novel of the Civil War, and *It Was Like This* (1940) contains two World War I stories. *The City in the Dawn* (1950) collects three novels, *The Forest and the Fort* (1943), *Bedford Village* (1944), and *Toward the Morning* (1948), about Salathiel Albine, an 18th-century frontiersman and soldier reared by Indians in the colony of New York.

ALLEN, JAMES LANE (1849–1925), was born and reared in Kentucky, where he taught school until 1880, and then turned to writing critical and descriptive articles and short stories. *The Blue-Grass Region of Kentucky* (1892) is a collection of sketches contributed to *Harper's Magazine* during the '80s, while *Flute and Violin* (1891) contains romantic short stories of Kentucky local color, demonstrating his craftsmanship and polished style, and his interest in the interdependence of man and nature. This theme dominates his best-known novels, *A Kentucky Cardinal* (1894), its sequel *Aftermath* (1896), and *The Choir Invisible* (1897). Allen's numerous later writings include *A Summer in Arcady* (1896) and *The Reign of Law* (1900), realistic novels of simple farm folk; *The Mettle of the Pasture* (1903), a tragic tale of the aristocrats of a Southern town; *The Last Christmas*

Tree (1914), a prose poem describing the ultimate glacial conquest of the earth; *The Bride of the Mistletoe* (1909) and *The Doctor's Christmas Eve* (1910), novels concerned with the conflicts that arise from the desire of middle age for youthful passion; *The Sword of Youth* (1915), a novelette of the Civil War; *The Alabaster Box* (1923), a tale of ingratitude; and *The Landmark* (1925), collected short stories.

ALLEN, PAUL (1775–1826), born in Rhode Island, graduated from Brown University (1793) and lived in Philadelphia, where he was well known as a magazine contributor. His works include *Original Poems, Serious and Entertaining* (1801); *Noah* (1821), a narrative poem largely revised by John Neal, who was almost entirely the author of Allen's *History of the American Revolution* (2 vols., 1819); and, with Nicholas Biddle, the official *History of the Expedition of Captains Lewis and Clark* (1814).

ALLEN, PAULA GUNN (1939–   ), born in New Mexico of Laguna Pueblo, Sioux, and Lebanese Jewish forebears, was educated at the University of New Mexico. In both poetry, for which she is best known, and the novel, she portrays Native Americans under the pressures of Anglo culture, and their struggles in or against cultural assimilation. Her poems are printed in *Shadow Country* (1982) and *Skins and Bones: Poems 1979–87* (1988). *The Woman Who Owned the Shadows: The Autobiography of Ephanie Atencio* (1983) is a novel. She edited *Spider Woman's Granddaughters: Traditional Tales and Contemporary Writing by Native American Women* (1989). She is chair of Native American Studies at San Francisco State University.

ALLEN, WILLIAM (1784–1868), New England clergyman, educator, and historian. During his six years as assistant librarian and regent of Harvard, he compiled the first edition of his *American Biographical and Historical Dictionary* (1809). He was president of Bowdoin College (1819–31, 1833–38), but was unpopular because of his inflexible disposition and rigid insistence on church discipline.

ALLEN, WOODY (ALLEN STEWART KONIGSBERG) (1935–   ), New York-born actor, film director and producer, and author, began his career as a writer for television comedy and as a nightclub entertainer. Since 1964 he has been a very popular motion-picture actor whose persona is that of a wistful, wry, self-deprecating figure. In addition to films he has written comic plays, *Don't Drink the Water* (1966), *Play It Again, Sam* (1969), and *The Floating Lightbulb* (1981). Brief humorous sketches, mostly from *The New Yorker,* have been collected in *Getting Even* (1971), *Without Feathers* (1975), and *Side Effects* (1980). Among the recent comedy-dramas he has written for the screen are *Crimes and Misdemeanors*

(1989), *Husbands and Wives* (1992), and *Bullets Over Broadway* (1994).

ALLIBONE, S[AMUEL] AUSTIN (1816–89), author of the important reference work *A Critical Dictionary of English Literature and British and American Authors* (3 vols., 1858–71) and compiler of volumes of prose and verse quotations. After 1879 he was the librarian of the Lenox Library established in New York City by James Lenox.◆

ALLSTON, JOSEPH BLYTH (1833–1904), South Carolina poet, whose best-known work, "Stack Arms," was written while he was a prisoner at Fort Delaware during the Civil War.

ALLSTON, WASHINGTON (1779–1843), painter, teacher of S.F.B. Morse, was himself a student of Benjamin West, with whom he shared the doctrine that painting should tell a story and appeal to the spectator by virtue of its sentiment. Long a resident in England and on the Continent, Allston was an intimate of Coleridge, Wordsworth, Southey, and other prominent literary men. He was a brother-in-law of the elder R. H. Dana, and like him was a rather studied and affected poet, as exemplified in his work *The Sylphs of the Seasons* (1813). His other books include the Gothic romance *Monaldi* (1841) and his *Lectures on Art, and Poems,* posthumously collected (1850) by R.H. Dana, Jr.

Almanac in America followed much the same development as in England, where it began as a calendar with the addition of some astronomical data. The first American work of this nature, *An Almanack for New England for the Year 1639,* was compiled by William Pierce (or Peirce) and printed by Stephen Daye, and, with the exception of a broadside, was the first work printed in the British colonies. Until the close of the 17th century, this press, associated with Harvard, continued to issue annual almanacs, and together with other presses caused Boston to become a center of almanac-making. The first humorous almanac was compiled in 1687 by John Tulley, of Saybrook, Conn. Subsequently all American almanacs, like their English counterparts, contained not only calendars but compendiums of popular science, notices of remarkable events and dates, problems, proverbs, jests, and practical information of various kinds, illuminated by illustrations. Among important early almanacs were the *Astronomical Diary and Almanack* issued from Dedham, Mass., by Nathaniel Ames and his son, 1725–75; *The Rhode Island Almanac,* issued 1728–58 by James Franklin; *Poor Richard's Almanack*◆; and *The Farmer's Almanack.*◆ The Crockett almanacs◆ were a popular 19th-century series, noted for their tall tales of frontier heroes. Many religious sects and reform organizations issued almanacs, which have also been used by advertisers of medicines and other products. Several modern almanacs and books of facts are issued annually in large paperback editions.

ALSOP, GEORGE (1638–?), emigrated from England to America (1658), of which he wrote in *A Character of the Province of Mary-Land* (1666) to encourage emigration. This jocular mixture of prose and verse describes the country, the Indians, and the arrangements for conveying poor people to America.

ALSOP, RICHARD (1761–1815), one of the Connecticut Wits, ♦ frequently collaborated with other members of the group in such light verse as *The Echo* ♦ and *The Political Greenhouse.* ♦ His serious poetry, including *American Poems* (1793) and *The Charms of Fancy* (1856), is conventional, imitative, and bookish.

ALTGELD, JOHN PETER (1847–1902), born at Nassau, Germany, was brought as a child to Ohio, where he received little formal education. He moved to Chicago in 1875, and in 1886 was elected to the Superior Court of Cook County. In *Our Penal Machinery and Its Victims* (1884) he set forth his belief that American judicial systems were weighted against the poor, and after he was elected governor of Illinois (1892) he pardoned three anarchist leaders convicted of fostering the Haymarket Riot. ♦ During the Pullman strike, he protested against Cleveland's sending U.S. troops into Chicago without his permission. He was defeated for reelection in 1896 because of his alleged radical sympathies. He is the subject of Vachel Lindsay's poem "The Eagle That Is Forgotten" ♦ and Howard Fast's novel *The American* (1946).

Amateur Emigrant, *The,* autobiographical narrative by R.L. Stevenson, ♦ written in San Francisco in 1879. It is an account of his voyage as a second-class passenger across the Atlantic "from the Clyde to Sandy Hook." Later revised, it was published with its sequel, *Across the Plains,* ♦ in the Edinburgh Edition of the author's works (1894).

Ambassadors, *The,* novel by Henry James, ♦ published in 1903.

Lambert Strether, an intelligent, conscientious American editor, is sent by his wealthy fiancée, Mrs. Newsome, a rigorously conventional Massachusetts widow, to Paris to bring home her son Chad, who has spent several years in Europe and is now required to take charge of the family's business interests. She has been unable to learn why Chad chooses to remain abroad, and when Strether arrives he discovers the young man much changed by his Old World environment and his relations with the charming, cultured Countess de Vionnet, who later appears to be Chad's mistress. Gradually Strether comes to realize the fascinations and satisfactions that life offers in Paris but not in Woollett, Mass., and he virtually gives

up his mission. Then a new group of ambassadors is sent after him, including Chad's aggressively proper sister Mrs. Pocock; her husband, Jim; and Jim's appealing but inexperienced young sister Mamie, who has been expected to marry Chad. Their arguments are supplemented by those of Strether's American friend Waymarsh, and the situation becomes comic, for none of these people can comprehend the education that has reformed Chad and Strether. Chad's determination to remain in Paris is unmoved, but Strether's conscience is reawakened, and he is persuaded to return to America, even though this will end his attachment to the quiet, kindly Maria Gostrey, an expatriate who has been a sympathetic spectator of his cultural adventure and the comedy of contrasted manners it has involved.

Ambitious Guest, *The,* allegorical tale by Hawthorne, ♦ published in *The Token* (1835) and in *Twice-Told Tales* (1837).

A solitary youth stops for the night at a lonely cottage in the Notch of the White Mountains in New Hampshire. He tells of his hopes of fame and fortune, and each member of his host's family is moved to divulge his intimate desires. The head of the house would like "to be called Squire, and sent to General Court for a term or two"; the youngest child would like to go at once on an excursion to "take a drink out of the basin of the Flume"; his older sister hardly conceals her growing interest in the young stranger; and even the grandmother speaks of her wish to look well in her coffin. While they talk, a great landslide begins, which buries the whole company.

America, name first applied to the present continent of South America (1507) in a map by the German geographer Martin Waldseemüller (*fl.* 1470–1513), who coined the title in honor of the navigator Amerigo Vespucci. He applied it to the whole New World in his *Cosmographiae Introductio* (1507), a work intended to be an introduction to a new edition of Ptolemy. Mercator used "America" to indicate both North and South America (1538), but for more than two centuries the lands in the western hemisphere were known in Spain and Portugal as the "Indies," "West Indies," or "New World."

"America," patriotic hymn written by Samuel Francis Smith, ♦ was first sung at a Boston Fourth of July meeting (1831) and published in *The Choir* (1832), a collection edited by Lowell Mason. The tune is the British "God Save the King," often erroneously attributed to Henry Carey (1690?–1743), but actually a traditional air whose earliest known version is by John Bull (1563–1628). Smith's hymn is frequently known as "My country, 'tis of thee," its opening line.

"America the Beautiful," patriotic hymn by Katherine Lee Bates, ♦ written in 1893 and published in *The Congregationalist* (July 4, 1895). A revision was published in 1904, and in the author's *America the Beautiful and Other Poems* (1911). Of the 60 tunes composed for it by various musicians, those most frequently used are by W.C. Macfarlane and S.A. Ward.

American, *The,* novel by Henry James, ♦ published in 1877 and dramatized by the author in 1891.

Christopher Newman, a wealthy American on a visit to Paris, meets Claire de Cintré, a widow of noble birth, half French and half English. On his first call at her home, Newman is turned away by her ungracious brother Marquis Urbain de Bellegarde, but later he meets others of the family, Urbain's wife, the charming younger brother Count Valentin, the shrewd, proud old Marquise, and her maid, the sympathetic Englishwoman Mrs. Bread. The American becomes a close friend of Valentin, who encourages his courtship of Mme de Cintré, but the others tolerate him only because of his wealth. Finally his proposal is accepted, the engagement is formally announced, and the Marquis reluctantly introduces Newman to his aristocratic friends. Meanwhile the American comes to know Mlle Noémie Nioche, a copyist of paintings, whose meek, shabby-genteel father is Newman's French teacher. Newman benevolently orders a number of Noémie's paintings in order to provide her a dowry, and introduces her to Valentin. Although the young man realizes she is mercenary and unscrupulous, he continues to see her, and she is the cause of a duel in which he is fatally wounded. Before learning of this, Newman receives word that Mme de Cintré, influenced by her mother and brother, has broken their engagement. Summoned to Valentin's deathbed, he hears the young man's disgust with his family, and is told that Mrs. Bread knows a guilty secret about them that Newman may use to further his own ends. After Valentin's funeral, Mme de Cintré announces that she intends to become a nun. Through Mrs. Bread, Newman discovers that the Marquise killed her husband, and he threatens to expose the evidence, but Urbain and his mother still refuse to allow the marriage. At first Newman determines to fulfill his revenge, but in a revulsion of feeling he destroys the evidence of the murder.

American Academy of Arts and Letters, organization that amalgamated (1976) the American Institute of Arts and Letters (founded 1898), modeled on the French Academy, with 250 members divided into sections in Art, Literature, and Music, and the American Academy of Arts and Letters (founded 1904), an honorary circle of 50 members within the Institute. Both were chartered by acts of Congress. The Academy's purpose is to promote American literature, art, and music by honoring prominent persons in

these fields, presenting public addresses, bringing representatives of foreign academies to the U.S., and organizing conferences, publications, collections, and awards. Authors among the original Academy members included Henry Adams, Aldrich, Burroughs, Clemens, Hay, Howells, J.C. Harris, Henry James, C.E. Norton, and Stedman.

American Academy of Arts and Sciences, scholarly society of about 3300 elected Fellows, founded in 1780, and representing all areas of learning. It holds frequent meetings at which papers are delivered, makes some grants, publishes *Daedalus,* ♦ and since 1956 has annually presented its Emerson-Thoreau Medal for distinguished achievement in literature. Its headquarters have always been in or near Boston.

American Antiquarian Society was founded by Isaiah Thomas at Worcester, Mass. (1812). Its collections of Americana extend to 1876 and the holdings prior to 1821 are preeminent. A private institution, it has some 550 elected members.

American Anti-Slavery Society, see *Abolitionist.*

American Apollo, see *Massachusetts Historical Society.*

American Book Awards, see *National Book Awards.*

American Caravan (1927–36), yearbook founded by Paul Rosenfeld, Alfred Kreymborg, Lewis Mumford, and Van Wyck Brooks, was edited by the first three as "an affirmation of the health of the young American literature, and an earnest of a guild for the co-operative publication of its works." It underwent some changes of title, but the purpose remained the same despite lapses in publication. Contributors included Hemingway, Dos Passos, O'Neill, and Gertrude Stein.

American Chronicles of the Times, see *First Book of the American Chronicles of the Times.*

American Claimant, *The,* story by S.L. Clemens, ♦ written under his pseudonym Mark Twain and published in 1892. It is based on the play *Colonel Sellers,* written by Clemens with Howells (1883) and produced unsuccessfully (1886). The character of Sellers first appeared in *The Gilded Age.* ♦

Viscount Berkeley is an earnest young man who desires a just trial of the rights of American claimants to his father's earldom, and he goes to America to investigate the matter, as well as to see the democratic institutions he admires. The current claimant is Colonel Mulberry Sellers, in his old age still "the same old scheming, generous, goodhearted . . . failure he always was," and still on the trail of easy wealth. By a number of complicated coincidences, Berkeley, believed to have died in a hotel fire, disguises himself to seek work and test the institutions of Western democracy. Although disappointed in both quests until he is employed as a painter of chromos, he discovers Sellers, with whose beautiful and sensible daughter Sally he falls in love. Berkeley summons his father, who comes to America, is won over by Sally, and consents to a marriage. The families plan to return to England together, but as the ship is about to leave the colonel is missed. He has gone off on a scheme to control the sunspots, leaving a message that asks the others to watch for a vast sunspot which will mean: "Mulberry Sellers throws us a kiss across the universe."

American Commonwealth, *The,* political and social survey by James Bryce, ◆ published in two volumes in 1888, and supplemented and revised in 1910. This study of "the nation of the future," as Bryce considered the U.S., is presented in six sections: (1) the Constitution, the organization of the federal government, and its interrelations with the state governments; (2) the state and local governments; (3) the party system; (4) the nature of public opinion and its influence on policies and issues; (5) illustrations of previous arguments, with a discussion of the "strength and weakness of democratic government" in the U.S.; and (6) social, intellectual, and spiritual forces as they affect the course of life of the nation and its citizens. The work reasserted faith in democracy and the paradox that in general the wisdom of the mass is greater than that of the select few, although noting the following faults in American society: a lack of intellectual distinction, the apathy of the cultured and the leisure class, incompetence in legislation and administration, and laxity in the management of public business.

American Democrat, *The, or Hints on the Social and Civic Relations of the United States of America,* critical work by Cooper, ◆ published in 1838.

Returning from Europe in 1835, the author was struck by "a disposition in the majority to carry out the opinions of the system to extremes, and a disposition in the minority to abandon all to the current of the day," and he writes in order to express "the voice of simple, honest and . . . fearless truth" on the peculiarities of the American system in theory and practice. Following an introduction and general chapters on government and republican theories, he discusses government in the U.S., especially with regard to the doctrine of state rights. The 43 brief chapters that follow are concerned with "Distinctive American Principles," "Equality," "Liberty," "Advantages of a Democracy," "Disadvantages of a Democracy," "Prejudice," "The Private Duties of Station," "Language," "Demagogues," "The Press," "Property," and similar subjects, all discussed from the point of view of a conservative thinker who is convinced of the value of an aristocratic system.

American Dream, *An,* novel by Norman Mailer, ◆ published in 1965.

Stephen Richards Rojack, a former congressman from New York, friend of Jack Kennedy, World War II hero, and television star, a "personality . . . built upon a void," is torn between an urge to suicide and a desire to see Deborah Kelly, the society heiress wife from whom he has long been separated, although she remains "the armature of [his] ego." His nighttime visit to Deborah leads to a quarrel; he strangles her, and after making love to her maid he throws Deborah's body out of her apartment window, telling the police who take him into custody that she committed suicide. Her father, Oswald Kelly, arranges Rojack's release and he continues his dark night of adventure, including an attack upon Shago Martin, a black jazz singer patronized by Deborah, a brief romantic interlude with Cherry, an appealing blonde nightclub entertainer, and an encounter with Deborah's father, who attempts to push him off a skyscraper parapet. Returning to Cherry's apartment and finding her murdered by a friend of Shago Martin, Rojack leaves New York for Las Vegas, where he fantasizes an affectionate telephone conversation with Cherry.

American Dream, *The,* one-act play by Edward Albee, ◆ produced in 1961.

In a serio-comic vein of absurdity, two middle-class Americans, Mommy and Daddy, are presented as ignoring Grandma because she is old, and as having tortured and dismembered their adopted son because he was clearly not going to grow up to be a clean-cut young man who typified the American Dream. After his death they send for another adopted son. This one satisfies Mommy because he is handsome and athletic, even though it is also obvious that he lacks intelligence and sensitivity.

American Farmer, see *Letters from an American Farmer.*

American Folk-Lore Society, founded in 1888, through its quarterly *Journal of American Folk-Lore* and other publications, and the investigations of its branch groups, has made valuable contributions to the study of the lore of American Indians and blacks, as well as of the folk ballads and tales of the modern U.S.

American Geographical Society, founded 1852 in New York City, through the activities of its members and publication of a *Bulletin* (later called the *Geographical Review*) has encouraged exploration and disseminated geographical information. The library, the largest private collection on its subject in the western hemisphere, has been housed at the University of Wisconsin, Milwaukee, since 1978.

American Guide Series, see *Federal Writers' Project.*

American Heritage, magazine established in 1949 by the American Association for State and Local History but expanded as a commercial enterprise, beginning with Vol. VI, No. 1 (Dec. 1954), into a hardbound journal of American history addressed to a large public and featuring many colorful pictures. It was edited by Bruce Catton (1954–59) and is now co-sponsored by the Society of American Historians.

American Historical Association, THE, founded at Saratoga, N.Y., in 1884 and incorporated (1889) with a main office in Washington, D.C. It has aided in the classification of official documents, and promoted, organized, and published research in neglected subjects of American history. Its organ, the *American Historical Review* (1895–), special reports, annual bibliographies, and a cooperative *Guide to Historical Literature* (1931) are among its many important publications.

American Language, *The,* study by H.L. Mencken,♦ published originally in 1919, in revised editions in 1921 and 1923, and corrected, enlarged, and rewritten for its fourth edition, 1936, with supplementary volumes in 1945 and 1948. This "inquiry into the development of English in the United States" was begun in articles in the Baltimore *Evening Sun* as early as 1910 to investigate the differences between American and English, but by 1936 Mencken was convinced that the influence of American had become so strong that in "some not too remote tomorrow" the language of Englishmen will be "a kind of dialect of American, just as the language spoken by the American was once a dialect of English." In his investigation Mencken first treats his subject chronologically, then takes up specific elements, such as pronunciation, spelling, grammar, and slang. He also deals with proper names and with non-English dialects in the U.S.

American Literature (1929–), journal of literary history, criticism, and bibliography, published quarterly by the Duke University Press with the cooperation of the American Literature Group of the Modern Language Association.

American Magazine, *The* (Jan.–March 1741), first magazine published in the British colonies in America. Edited by John Webbe, it was published from Philadelphia by Andrew Bradford after Webbe became dissatisfied with Franklin's terms for publication. Only three issues of this "monthly view of the political state" were published, but because the first appeared three days before Franklin's *The General Magazine,* it is distinguished as the first publication of its kind. It contained proceedings of the colonial assemblies, essays on moral, scientific, political, and historical subjects, and brief reprints from *The London Magazine.*

A second *American Magazine* (Dec. 1787–Nov. 1788) was a monthly edited by Noah Webster from New York. Besides the usual periodical features, it had articles on education and subjects of interest to women. It included contributions from the Connecticut Wits♦ and was strongly Federalist.

A third publication with this title was founded as *Frank Leslie's Popular Monthly,*♦ assuming its later name in 1906, when it was purchased by a group of muckraking authors, including Ida Tarbell, Steffens, R.S. Baker, F.P. Dunne, and W.A. White. To make money, they tempered their muckraking with an emphasis on the homely affairs of average people, and in time this became the primary interest, when the original publishers gave up the magazine. It once had a circulation of more than 2,000,000, and was devoted to optimistic stories of people who reached success in spite of handicaps, and similar fiction aimed at average American families. It was discontinued in 1956.

American Magazine and Monthly Chronicle, *The* (1757–58), political magazine founded at Philadelphia by William Bradford, with William Smith as editor. It published contributions by Francis Hopkinson and Thomas Godfrey, and attacked the French and the Quakers, championed the development of an American nation, and sided with the proprietors against Franklin in the quarrel over the question whether the Penns should pay taxes on their Pennsylvania grants. The magazine's contributors formed a literary group known as the Society of Gentlemen.

American Men of Letters Series, 22 volumes of critical biographies also "illustrating the social, political and moral influences" upon the writers, issued from 1881 to 1904 under the editorship of Charles Dudley Warner. He wrote the first volume, *Washington Irving* (1881). Other authors and subjects included Holmes, *Emerson;* Lounsbury, *Cooper;* Higginson, *Margaret Fuller Ossoli.* It was similar but unrelated to the earlier English Men of Letters Series that also included American authors, e.g. James on Hawthorne and Higginson on Whittier. A second but unrelated series with the same title as Warner's and intended to employ modern techniques and critical attitudes was issued in 11 volumes (1948–51) under the editorship of Krutch, Margaret Marshall, Trilling, and Mark Van Doren. Authors and subjects included M. Van Doren, *Hawthorne;* Krutch, *Thoreau;* Matthiessen, *Dreiser;* Perry Miller, *Edwards;* Newton Arvin, *Melville;* and John Berryman, *Stephen Crane.*

American Mercury (1719–46), see *American Weekly Mercury.*

American Mercury, *The* (1924–80), monthly magazine founded by H.L. Mencken♦ and George

Jean Nathan♦ as a successor to their *Smart Set,* "to attempt a realistic presentation of the whole gaudy, gorgeous American scene," with all phases of American culture and institutions treated in a spirit of boisterous skepticism. The subject matter included not only lusty critical commentaries, but also short stories, poems, plays, and reviews of the arts, in keeping with the full-blooded editorial policy. After the first year Nathan ceased to be co-editor, and in 1930 he silently disappeared from the magazine. The many noted contributors included Dreiser, O'Neill, Sherwood Anderson, Cabell, Hergesheimer, Sandburg, Van Vechten, Sinclair Lewis, and Edgar Lee Masters. Among several celebrated departments, "Americana" was devoted to clippings from newspapers, ironically reflecting the alleged stupidity of the American mass mind. In 1934 Mencken left the magazine, but his decade and the next were memorialized in *The American Mercury Reader* (1944). In 1946 it absorbed *Common Sense,*♦ but it underwent more drastic changes of ownership and views until in 1952 it became a right-wing journal with no relation to the original magazine except for name. In 1968 it began publication in Orange County, Cal., but ceased publication in 1980.

American Minerva (1793–1905), founded at New York by Noah Webster, its editor to 1803, as a daily Federalist journal to combat French influences. The editor and Hamilton both wrote series of letters defending Jay's Treaty. In 1797 the name was changed to the *Commercial Advertiser,* and later editors included R.C. Sands, Thurlow Weed, Parke Godwin, and William L. Stone. In 1905 the paper was combined with the *New York Globe* to become the *Globe and Commercial Advertiser,* which in turn was bought by the New York *Sun* in 1923.

American Monthly Magazine (1829–31), literary journal published from Boston by N.P. Willis,♦ whose other contributors included J.L. Motley, Richard Hildreth, Lydia H. Sigourney, and Park Benjamin. Its levity and worldliness caused it to be a failure in Boston, and it was absorbed by the *New-York Mirror.*♦

American Monthly Magazine, The (1833–38), literary periodical edited by H.W. Herbert (1833–35), during which time its contributors included Paulding, Verplanck, and James Hall. In 1835 it absorbed *The New-England Magazine,*♦ after which it was edited by Park Benjamin and C.F. Hoffman, and included Poe among its contributors. During its last year, an attempt was made to invigorate the magazine by introducing such political contributors as Horace Greeley and Henry Clay.

American Museum, The (1787–92), monthly magazine published and edited at Philadelphia by Mathew Carey.♦ At first it contained mainly re-printed materials, although original contributions came from Francis Hopkinson,♦ Franklin,♦ Benjamin Rush,♦ and the Connecticut Wits.♦ In 1790 the subtitle *Universal Magazine* was added, and the policy was altered to include more belles lettres and original writing.

American Notes for General Circulation, travel account by Dickens,♦ published in 1842. Dickens visited the U.S. (Jan.–May 1842) in a tour that took him from Boston and New York to Canada and as far west as St. Louis. His book is almost wholly descriptive, and does not attempt to analyze institutions. He wrote in a complimentary fashion about much of America, but antagonized many readers by criticizing the penal system, the lack of copyright and hence the pirating of English works, and the entire system of slavery and its adherents.

American party, see *Know-Nothing movement.*

American Philosophical Society, first scientific society in America, founded at Philadelphia (1743) by Franklin, its first president. His successors were Rittenhouse and Jefferson. The Society issues *Transactions, Proceedings* (since 1838) and *Memoirs* (since 1900) and makes research grants. It has some 600 elected members.

American Prefaces (1935–43), little magazine sponsored by the University of Iowa. Although interested in regionalism, its contributors included T.S. Eliot, J.G. Fletcher, Muriel Rukeyser, Robert Frost, Paul Engle, C. Day-Lewis, Wallace Stegner, and Eudora Welty.

American Quarterly (1949–   ), scholarly journal of American civilization studies. Founded at the University of Minnesota, it moved (1951) to the University of Pennsylvania. In 1988 the American Studies Association arranged for publication by the Johns Hopkins University Press.

American Register, see *Literary Magazine.*

American Renaissance, seminal critical study by F. O. Matthiessen,♦ published in 1941, analyzing Emerson, Thoreau, Hawthorne, Melville, and Whitman in their concern with the relation of the individual to society, conceptions of good and evil, attitudes toward nature, relations to their times, predecessors and successors, relation to other arts, symbolism, and language.

American Review (1845–50), see *American Whig Review.*

American Review, The (1933–37), socio-economic magazine, founded by Seward Collins, after the suspension of *The Bookman,* to analyze contemporary life and letters from a traditionalist basis. It was devoted to such movements as Agrarianism, New Humanism, and Neo-Scholasticism.

American Revolution, see *Revolutionary War.*

American Scene, The, descriptive and interpretive work by Henry James,♦ published in 1907. The author toured the U.S. (1904) after an absence of "nearly a quarter of a century," and writes from a point of view that he claims to be almost as fresh as that of an "inquiring stranger" and as acute as that of an "initiated native." He describes his dramatic adventure in rediscovering an America occupied by "a society reaching out into the apparent void for the amenities, the consummations, after having earnestly gathered in so many of the preparations and necessities." The chapters of sensitive and cultivated appreciation include discussions of New England, New York, and Newport; the foreign aspects of New York City; "social notes" on upper-class life; and places associated with such authors as Hawthorne, Emerson, Thoreau, and Irving. The general impression is in keeping with his attitude as an expatriate:

> You touch the great lonely land—as one feels it still to be—only to plant upon it some ugliness about which, never dreaming of the grace of apology or contrition, you then proceed to brag. . . . You convert the large and noble sanities that I see around me . . . one after the other to crudities, to invalidities, hideous and unashamed. . . .

American Scholar, The, address by Emerson♦ delivered before the Phi Beta Kappa Society of Harvard (Aug. 31, 1837), published separately in 1837, and reprinted in *Nature, Addresses, and Lectures* (1849). Called "our intellectual Declaration of Independence" by Holmes, the work was immediately influential and remains important as an idealistic appeal for the active leadership of American society by native thinkers, developed through contact with the best products of former cultures and through free intercourse with nature and their fellow men.

The author announces that "Events, actions arise, that must be sung, that will sing themselves." The original unit, man, has been "minutely subdivided and peddled out," however, and "in this distribution of functions, the scholar is the delegated intellect . . . he is *Man Thinking.*" The scholar, following "the ancient precept 'Know thyself,' and the modern precept, 'Study Nature,'" must interpret the distinctive new culture, for "Each age must write its own books." Yet he must act, as well as think and write. His duties are all implied in the term "self-trust"; knowing himself and his function, he must be self-reliant and free of bondage to the "popular cry." Society's purpose is to produce perfect individuals, and the scholar's idealistic mission is both to embody this perfection in himself and to make use of his divine inspiration for the highest good of his fellows.

American Scholar, The (1932–   ), quarterly journal published by the United Chapters of Phi Beta Kappa and aimed at embodying and furthering the purposes and implications of Emerson's address from which its title is derived. In addition to articles and book reviews it occasionally publishes poetry. Hiram Hayden remained editor until his death in December 1973.

American Spectator, The (1932–37), monthly literary journal published in newspaper format, was founded by G.J. Nathan, Ernest Boyd, Cabell, Dreiser, O'Neill, and Sherwood Anderson, and constituted a spiritual offspring of *The American Mercury.* In a flip, satirical manner, it published stimulating articles concerned with "life, in general, and some of the specific problems of our time, in particular." Clarity, vigor, and humor were announced as the three indispensable qualifications of contributions. Although the magazine had a brilliant list of contributors and was financially successful, it was abandoned by its editors "because they were bored." It was then purchased (1935) by an anonymous group, but, lacking its former lively iconoclasm, was forced to become a bimonthly (1936).

American Tragedy, An, novel by Dreiser,♦ published in 1925 and dramatized by Patrick Kearney in 1926. The plot is based on an actual New York murder case.

Clyde Griffiths, son of street evangelists in Kansas City, desires to escape his family's drab life and to win wealth and social position. Becoming a bellboy in a hotel, he plunges into the worldly society of his fellow employees, but this life ends as the result of an automobile accident for which he is legally culpable. Providentially he meets his wealthy relative Samuel Griffiths, who is attracted by the youth's engaging manner and employs him in his collar factory in New York state. Here Clyde enters into a liaison with Roberta Alden, a working girl, and almost simultaneously falls in love with Sondra Finchley, who seems to him to represent the dazzling "four hundred" of the small town. Roberta discloses that she is pregnant and demands that Clyde provide for her. In a frenzy he plans to murder her, and takes her to a deserted lake resort. They row out on the lake, where, though Clyde lacks the courage to complete his plan, the boat is overturned, possibly by accident. He swims away leaving Roberta to drown. After a lengthy trial, he is condemned to death.

American Weekly Mercury, The (1719–46), Philadelphia newspaper founded by Andrew Bradford. Much of its material was copied from English journals. Franklin contributed six of the "Busy-Body Papers" to the *Mercury* in 1729.

American Whig Review (1845–52), political magazine founded to champion Clay's presidential campaign, was continued as a political and literary review. Poe contributed "The Raven," "Some Words with a Mummy," "The Facts in the Case of M. Valdemar," and "Ulalume." Other contributors included Lowell, Webster, Everett, Calhoun, and Greeley, and the magazine was a vigorous advocate of American literature. From 1845 to 1850 it was known as *The American Review*. The decisive defeat of the Whigs caused its suspension.

Americanization of Edward Bok, The, autobiographical narrative by E.W. Bok,♦ published in 1920 and awarded a Pulitzer Prize. It describes his arrival in the U.S., his rise to influential editorial positions, and his acquaintance with leading public figures.

America's Lost Plays, 20-volume series (1940–65), under the initial editorship of Barrett H. Clark, collecting from manuscripts and other sources obscure plays by some 18th- and 19th-century dramatists popular in their day.

AMES, FISHER (1758–1808), son of Nathaniel Ames, after graduation from Harvard was admitted to the bar (1781). His political essays in Boston newspapers and a powerful speech in the Massachusetts convention that ratified the Constitution made him the leading orator and pamphleteer of New England Federalism. Distrusting all signs of "French liberalism," he lustily argued that "the essence, and almost the quintessence, of good government is to protect property and its rights. . . . The major business of government becomes, therefore, the problem of keeping in due subjection to law and order the dangerous mass of the poor and vicious." From 1789 to 1797, as a Federalist member of Congress, he helped to force Hamilton's financial measures through the House. After he retired, his essays and correspondence with Federalist leaders maintained his reputation as a party sage. His *Works* were collected in 1809, and an enlarged edition was published in 1854.

AMES, NATHANIEL (1708–64), compiler of an annual *Astronomical Diary and Almanack* (1725–64), which attained a circulation of 60,000 copies and was among the works that served as models for *Poor Richard's Almanack*. His work was continued by his son, Nathaniel Ames, Jr., until 1775. The material in their almanacs has been edited as *The Essays, Humor, and Poems of Nathaniel Ames* (1891).

Amish, see *Mennonites.*

AMMONS, A[RCHIE] R[ANDOLPH] (1926–), North Carolina-born poet, after graduation from Wake Forest College and study at the University of California, Berkeley, where he was encour-

aged by Josephine Miles, wrote poetry while working in a glass factory before publishing his first small book, *Ommateum, with Doxology* (1955), whose title refers to the vision that insects have with compound eye structure. A move to teaching creative writing as a professor at Cornell (1964–) preceded his next book, nearly a decade later, *Expressions of Sea Level* (1964). With it began his career as a major poet. Writing in his own voice, he also relates clearly to the American transcendental tradition, recalling Emerson's concern with the relations of the One and the Many, Thoreau's isolation and concentration on nature, and Whitman's democratic sensibility and use of lengthy monologue. While waiting for the publication of his second volume, Ammons wrote a personal poetic journal, *Tape for the Turn of the Year* (1965), whose brevity in line and length in form were the result of his typing it, without revision, on a roll of adding machine paper. His collection of lyrics was quickly followed by another, *Corsons Inlet* (1965), in one of whose poems he wrote of "eddies of meaning . . . running like a stream through the geography of my work . . . but Overall is beyond me." In these works and those that followed, including *Northfield Poems* (1966), *Uplands* (1970), *Briefings* (1971), *Collected Poems* (1971, National Book Award), *Sphere: The Form of a Motion* (1974), *Diversifications* (1975), *The Snow Poems* (1977), *Highgate Road* (1977), *A Coast of Trees* (1981), *Worldly Hopes* (1982), *Lake Effect Country* (1983), and *Sumerian Vistas* (1987), he confirmed his position as a leading American writer of his time (he won a Bollingen Prize, 1973–74), whose poems are marked by a tension between specific observations and philosophic abstractions framed in an ecological context, often expressed in meditations inspired by solitary walks along a shoreline. *Garbage* (1993, National Book Award), is a single poem of 2200 lines in 18 sections, composed, like *Tape for the Turn of the Year,* on adding machine tape. It is a meditation on trash, which we and all other life forms finally are.

Anabaptists, religious sects that contend that infant baptism is unauthorized by Scripture, and that the sacrament may be administered only to believers. They were among the most radical during the Reformation and were widely persecuted because of their agitation for social and economic reforms. Although scattered in different sects, they possess certain fundamental beliefs in common, including the necessity of direct contact with God without the mediation of human agencies, absolute pacifism, and a refusal to obey the state whenever its demands conflict with conscience. During the first quarter of the 16th century, the belief spread through the Germanic peoples of Europe, particularly attracting the common people. Some communal experiments were tried, in which law, private property, and marriage were outlawed. Many Anabaptists moved to South Dakota from Russia in 1874 because of persecution.

Analectic Magazine, The, see *Literary Gazette.*

Anarchiad, The, 12 papers in mock-heroic verse, jointly composed by the Connecticut Wits, ♦ published anonymously in *The New Haven Gazette* and *The Connecticut Magazine* (1786–87), and reprinted with notes and appendices in 1861 as *The Anarchiad: A New England Poem.* Probably conceived by David Humphreys, the work is considered to have been written mainly by Lemuel Hopkins, supplemented by Joel Barlow, Timothy Dwight, John Trumbull, and Humphreys. It follows the plan of *The Rolliad,* an English satire of Tory politics, and the authors, representatives of the Connecticut aristocracy, were intent on counteracting the popular appeal of agrarian economics and democratic liberalism, converting the faltering alliance between states into a national unity, and establishing commercial security through a financial policy based on sound mercy.

ANAYA, RUDOLFO (1937–   ), born of Mexican-American parents in Pastura, N.M., took a degree at the University of New Mexico and has taught at Albuquerque public schools as well as at his alma mater. His first novel, *Bless Me, Ultima* (1972), established him in the first rank of Chicano writers, even though he writes in English rather than in Spanish. He uses magic realism in *Bless Me, Ultima* to create, in the person of a folk healer, a new identity out of Spanish, Indian, and Anglo elements. *Heart of Aztlan* (1976), *Tortuga* (1979), and *Lord of the Dawn* (1987) all focus on racial identities. *Alburquerque* (1992)—the title gives the original Spanish spelling—is both adventure and political satire, wherein a ruthless real-estate developer seeks to turn the city into a desert Venice by diverting the Rio Grande into new channels.

Ancestral Footstep, The, romance by Hawthorne. ♦

ANDERSON, MAXWELL (1888–1959), born in Pennsylvania, was reared in North Dakota, from whose state university he graduated in 1911. He received his M.A. from Stanford (1914), taught school in California and North Dakota, and entered a career of journalism, which brought him to New York and continued until 1924. His first play was *White Desert* (1923), a tragedy of repressed lives in North Dakota, and his second, written with Laurence Stallings, was the immensely successful war play, *What Price Glory?* (1924). With Stallings he also wrote *First Flight* (1925), about an episode in the youth of Andrew Jackson, and *The Buccaneer* (1925), about the pirate Sir Henry Morgan. These were collected in *Three American Plays* (1926). Anderson published

his only book of poems as *You Who Have Dreams* (1925). *Outside Looking In* (1925) was a dramatization of Jim Tully's *Beggars of Life,* and *Saturday's Children* (1927) a comedy of modern marital relations. His next play, written with Harold Hickerson, was *Gods of the Lightning* (1928), dealing with the Sacco-Vanzetti case, and he turned to blank-verse drama with *Elizabeth the Queen* (1930), concerned with Elizabeth's love for the Earl of Essex. *Night Over Taos* (1932), also in verse, dramatizes the end of the feudal era in New Mexico in 1847. *Both Your Houses* (1933, Pulitzer Prize) is a prose satire of political corruption in Congress. With *Mary of Scotland* (1933), the author returned to verse and to English and Scottish history, but *Valley Forge* (1934) has a distinctly American theme, as do many of his later plays, which include *Winterset* ♦ (1935), a verse tragedy suggested by the Sacco-Vanzetti case; *The Wingless Victory* (1936), an adaptation of the Medea theme, set in Salem in 1800; *The Masque of Kings* (1936), a verse play concerning the Mayerling affair; *High Tor* (1937), a satirical fantasy on the encroachments of industrialism on personal liberty; *The Star Wagon* (1937), a prose fantasy about an inventor who controls time; and *Knickerbocker Holiday* (1938), a musical comedy (with music by Kurt Weill) satirizing the New Deal through a story of Stuyvesant's New Netherland. Later verse plays include *Key Largo* (1939), about an idealistic American in the Spanish Loyalist army; *Journey to Jerusalem* (1940), about the young Jesus; and *The Eve of St. Mark* (1942), about an American farm boy killed in World War II. Two other plays concerned with this war are *Candle in the Wind* (1941) and *Storm Operation* (1944), the latter about U.S. soldiers in North Africa. After a lesser play, *Truckline Café* (1946), he wrote three historical dramas: *Joan of Lorraine* (1947), interpreting Joan of Arc as a mystic through a drama about a production of a play concerning different conceptions of her; *Anne of the Thousand Days* (1948), about Anne Boleyn and Henry VIII; and *Barefoot in Athens* (1951), about Socrates. *Lost in the Stars* (1948) was a dramatization of Alan Paton's *Cry, the Beloved Country* for a musical production, and *The Bad Seed* (1955) was a dramatization of the last novel by William March, ♦ concerning an evil child. *Eleven Verse Plays* (1940) collects some of his dramas. His radio plays include *The Feast of Ortolans* (1938), set in France in 1789. Essays are printed in *The Essence of Tragedy* (1938) and *Off Broadway* (1940).

ANDERSON, ROBERT W[OODRUFF] (1917–   ), New York City-born playwright, after receiving his A.B. and M.A. from Harvard and navy service in World War II taught playwriting and began writing his own dramas, including *All Summer Long* (1953); *Tea and Sympathy* (1953), about an unhappy preparatory school boy accused of homosexuality; *Silent Night, Lonely Night* (1959), about the effect of Christmas Eve on a man and woman who meet then by chance; *The Days Between* (1965), produced in small theaters throughout the nation by the American Playwrights' Theatre; *You Know I Can't Hear You When the Water's Running* (1967), four one-act plays; *I Never Sang for My Father* (1968), about a man's struggles with his domineering father; *Solitaire / Double Solitaire* (1971); and *Free and Clear* (1983), about family friction involving two midcareer-age brothers. He has written two novels: *After* (1973), about a man trying to find himself after the death of his beloved wife, and *Getting Up and Going Home* (1978).

ANDERSON, SHERWOOD (1876–1941), born in Ohio, at the age of 14 began his restless career, drifting from job to job and serving in the Spanish-American War. For a time he settled in his native state, was married, and became the manager of a paint factory; but he suddenly walked out of the factory, left his family, and made his way to Chicago. There, while writing advertising copy, he met such authors as Carl Sandburg and Floyd Dell, who encouraged him to publish his first book, *Windy McPherson's Son* (1916), a novel dealing with a boy's life in a drab Iowa town, his rise to success as a manufacturer, and his renunciation of this life to "find truth." This was followed by another novel, *Marching Men* (1917), set in the Pennsylvania coal region and showing the failure of a mystical movement to organize the workers in order to free them from oppressive routine. He also published a book of poems, *Mid-American Chants* (1918), but it was not until 1919, when *Winesburg, Ohio*♦ appeared, that he first attracted wide attention. These stories of small-town people voice the philosophy of life expressed in all his later works. Adopting a naturalistic interpretation of American life, he believed that the primal forces of human behavior are instinctive and not to be denied, as he supposed they are, by the standardization of a machine age. His characters are puzzled, groping, baffled, and possess no vision of order or channel for directing their energies against the frustrations of contemporary existence. Primarily through sex, which he endowed with a mystical significance, Anderson conceived man as having an opportunity to escape from the confinement of this regulated life. Similarly, he placed stress on the mystical identification of man with the primal forces of nature. In *Poor White*♦ (1920), a novel of the Midwest, "the town was really the hero of the book. . . . What happened to the town was, I thought, more important than what happened to the people of the town." What happens is that the machine comes to the town, destroying whatever beauty and significance it once possessed. The same themes and attitude of mind are evinced in subsequent books: *The Triumph of the Egg* (1921), stories and poems depicting frustration and maladjustment in typical American backgrounds; *Horses and Men* (1923),

stories mainly about horse racing; and *Many Marriages* (1923), a novel about a businessman's attempt to escape routine. In *Dark Laughter*♦ (1925), a novel contrasting the laughter and song of unrepressed blacks with the spiritual sterility of the whites, he reached artistic maturity both in his style—simple, direct, consciously naïve, and admittedly indebted to Gertrude Stein—and in his mastery of form. *Tar: A Midwest Childhood* (1926) is a fictional treatment of his own life, which he had begun to describe in *A Story Teller's Story* (1924). After issuing two volumes of sketches, *The Modern Writer* (1925) and *Sherwood Anderson's Notebook* (1926), and a volume of poetry, *A New Testament* (1927), he retired to a small Virginia town to edit two newspapers, one Republican and the other Democratic. His next book, *Hello Towns!* (1929), is a narrative of visits to small towns, and *Nearer the Grass Roots* (1929) sets forth his reasons for retirement, to be "in close and constant touch with every phase of life in an American community every day of the year." *Perhaps Women* (1931) is a critical work, placing hope for salvation from the sterility of mechanized life in the leadership of women. *Beyond Desire* (1932), his first novel in seven years, shows a shift of scene to the industrialized South, but is still concerned with the problem of modern frustrations. A book of stories, *Death in the Woods* (1933), and a survey of the U.S. during the Depression, *Puzzled America* (1935), were followed by another novel, *Kit Brandon* (1936), showing the author's characters still trapped in a situation with which they cannot cope. *Home Town* (1940) is a collection of essays. *Memoirs* (1942) and *Letters* (1953) were posthumously issued, as was *Letters to Bab* (1985), correspondence with his mistress, and *Love Letters to Eleanor . . .* (1989), communications with his fourth wife (1929–41).

Andersonville, novel by MacKinlay Kantor,♦ published in 1955, was awarded a Pulitzer Prize.

Set in the Civil War at the Confederate prison in Georgia whose name is the title of the book, it treats the dreadful conditions of confinement that led to the death of some 12,000 Union soldiers, for which the commander, Captain Henry Wirz, was in 1865 charged with murder and hanged.

André, blank-verse tragedy by William Dunlap,♦ produced and published in 1798. The author's revision was produced in 1803 as *The Glory of Columbia* (published 1817).

ANDRÉ, JOHN (1751–80), came to America (1774) as a lieutenant in the Royal Fusiliers, and during the Revolutionary War was promoted to the rank of major. In 1780 he carried on secret negotiations with Benedict Arnold, when that American officer attempted to betray West Point. André was tried as a spy at Washington's headquarters, and was hanged for this offense despite official British protests and popular sympathy aroused by his engaging personality. He is the subject of plays named for him by William Dunlap, Clyde Fitch, and Philip Freneau, and figures often in fiction, e.g. P.L. Ford's *Janice Meredith.*

ANDREWS, JANE (1833–87), schoolteacher of Newburyport, Mass., whose popular books for children included *The Seven Little Sisters Who Live on the Round Ball That Floats in the Air* (1861) and *The Stories Mother Nature Told Her Children* (1889).

ANDREWS, STEPHEN PEARL (1812–86), reformer interested in various radical movements, including the manumission of slaves by purchase. His religious and economic free-thinking led him to develop, in his book *The Science of Society* (1851), a semi-anarchistic social scheme which he called Pantarchy. His other books include *Cost the Limit of Price* (1851) and *Basic Outline of Universology* (1872). He helped Victoria Woodhull♦ and her sister to found *Woodhull and Claflin's Weekly* (1870–76). He was also a brilliant linguist, knew 32 languages, created a universal language he called Alwato, and wrote several books of instruction in shorthand.

Androboros, the first American play to be printed (1714), was written by Robert Hunter, governor of New York (1710–19), and has been reprinted from its rare first edition in the *Bulletin of the New York Public Library* (March 1964). A political satire, it was never produced, and the publication bears the fictitious imprint, Moronopolis ("fools' town"). It is an attack on the colonial administrator and military leader Francis Nicholson, who is given the name Androboros ("man eater"). The plot deals with Androboros's proposed attack on the Mulomachians (the French), and the senate's resolution that he has behaved courageously in the attack, which he has not yet made. When the keeper (the author, Hunter) asks why they pass the resolution before the expedition, he is told that it is because there will be less reason after the encounter.

ANDROS, SIR EDMUND (1637–1714), was the Duke of York's appointed governor of New York (1674), and later the governor of the consolidated northern colonies when James II concentrated British power against France in the New World (1686). He was an autocratic governor of this Dominion of New England until a Boston uprising led by Cotton Mather and probably instigated by Increase Mather precipitated reforms. Under William and Mary the colonies returned to their former charter governments. He was governor of Virginia (1692–97) until recalled because of charges by James Blair.♦ His New England period figures frequently in fiction.

Anecdote of the Jar, poem by Wallace Stevens,♦ published in *Harmonium.*♦ In three four-line

stanzas the speaker tells of placing a jar on a Tennessee hillside, illustrative of the way a work of art brings order to a slovenly wilderness.

ANGELOU, MAYA (1928–   ), St. Louis-born author, singer, dancer, playwright, and stage and screen actress, long resident in California, has achieved most success with her frank and warm-hearted autobiographical accounts of her life as a young black woman in America and her residence abroad in Egypt and Ghana, titled *I Know Why the Caged Bird Sings* (1970), *Gather Together in My Name* (1974), *Singin' and Swingin' and Gettin' Merry Like Christmas* (1976), *The Heart of a Woman* (1981), and *All God's Children Need Traveling Shoes* (1986). She has also written six collections of poems, *Just Give Me a Cool Drink of Water 'fore I Diie* (1971), *Oh Pray My Wings Are Gonna Fit Me Well* (1975), *And Still I Rise* (1978), *Shaker, Why Don't You Sing* (1983), *Now Sheba Sings the Song* (1987), and *Shall Not Be Moved* (1990). *Wouldn't Take Nothing for My Journey Now* (1993) is a memoir concerned with spirituality, sensuality, and healing.

ANGHIERA, PIETRO MARTIRE, see *Martyr, Peter.*

Anglican Church, see *Protestant Episcopal Church.*

Anglomaniacs, The, novel by Constance Cary Harrison.♦

Animal Kingdom, The, play by Philip Barry,♦ produced and published in 1932.

   Tom Collier, a wealthy young man, after years of happiness with his mistress Daisy Sage, a painter, breaks with her and resumes his former social position. He marries Cecilia Henry, who, though outwardly a good wife, actually fails to understand and sympathize with his views of the world. Eventually he discovers that it is his wife, not his former mistress, who lives in the wrong world for him, and he returns to Daisy.

Anna Christie, play by Eugene O'Neill,♦ produced in 1921 and published in 1922, when it received a Pulitzer Prize. It is a revision of his unsuccessful play *Chris Christopherson* (1920).

   Chris Christopherson, Swedish-American captain of the coal barge *Simeon Winthrop,* awaits the arrival of his daughter Anna in the saloon of Johnny-the-Priest on the New York waterfront. Several years before, he sent her to relatives on a Midwestern farm, away from the baneful influence of "dat ole davil sea," and he pictures her as an innocent country girl; but when she enters it is obvious to all except Chris that Anna is a coarse, hardened woman of the underworld. She confesses to her father's mistress, Marthy, that she was seduced by a cousin when she was 16, lived as a prostitute in St. Louis, was ill in a prison hospital, and has acquired a deep-seated hatred of men.

Father and daughter leave New York on a voyage of the barge, and the sea that Chris hates proves to be the means of Anna's regeneration, until the *Winthrop* picks up a boatload of shipwrecked sailors, one of whom is the rough Irishman Mat Burke. In love with Anna, Mat wants to marry her, but when she discloses her history, both he and Chris go off separately to get drunk, and sign for a voyage on the same ship. But Mat's love is stronger than his sense of Anna's shame, and both men go back to Anna, who promises to make a home for them when they return.

Annabel Lee, lyrical ballad by Poe,♦ posthumously published in the New York *Tribune* (Oct. 9, 1849). In six stanzas of alternate four- and three-stress lines, the poem has been called "the culmination of Poe's lyric style" in his recurrent theme of the loss of a beautiful and loved woman.

Annandale, GEORGE, see *Book of Annandale.*

Annie Kilburn, novel by Howells,♦ published in 1889.

The heroine, having lived in Italy for 11 years, after her father's death returns to her girlhood home, Hatboro', Mass. Aged 31, and refusing to be an old maid member of the local social set, she plunges into a career of indiscriminate philanthropy. Influenced by her aristocratic acquaintances, she plans an amateur theatrical production to raise funds for a Social Union to improve the conditions of the factory workers. Mr. Peck, the young Unitarian minister, points out the superficial and unjust effect the Union may have. Inspired by his arguments and by her new friend Dr. Morrell, Annie interests herself in other charities, sending several sick children to the seashore. When one of the little girls dies, Annie is heartbroken, finding that she cannot meet the bereaved family even on the ground of a common grief. Mr. Peck, nearly discharged for his liberal views, is retained because of popular agitation in his favor, and during the bitter controversy his motherless daughter Idella lives with "Aunt Annie," whom she comes to love. When the minister is killed in a railroad accident, Annie adopts Idella, and plans to carry on the Social Union enterprise, which everyone else has dropped. Finally she marries her adviser and friend in these activities, Dr. Morrell.

Annual, see *Gift Book.*

Another Country, novel by James Baldwin,♦ published in 1962.

Rufus Scott, a young, unemployed black jazz musician, deeply embittered by the sense that he and his people have few opportunities, hates the whites and yet is intrigued by them. His relations with his white mistress Leona turn sour, he refuses to see his friends, the aspiring white novelists Vivaldo Moore and Richard Silenski, or Richard's wife Cass, and he even neglects his idolizing young sister Ida. After nightmare wanderings through New York City, Scott commits suicide by jumping off the George Washington Bridge. Ida and Vivaldo, drawn together by grief, become lovers but their relations too are plagued by the fear, hatred, and contempt one race feels for the other. They are complicated also because Ida continues to brood about her brother and believes Vivaldo could neither understand nor appreciate him enough. But most of all they are tortured because of their involvements with Rufus's friends. Vivaldo, like Rufus, has a brief sexual relationship with an actor, Eric Jones, who for a time is also the lover of Cass, while Ida is temporarily the mistress of Steve Ellis, the white man who manages her career as singer. The relations of all are violent and brutal as they try to find the nature of their own identities through associations with other people.

Anthology Club, Boston literary society (*c.*1804–11), devoted to raising the standards of American literature. Its members included William Tudor and George Ticknor, who, with such contributing members as Daniel Webster, Allston, Bryant, and Joseph Story, wrote for the Club's *Monthly Anthology and Boston Review* (1803–11), predecessor of *The North American Review.* This journal of poetry, fiction, and criticism was liberal in theological matters, conservative in politics, and severe in literary reviews. Selections from it were edited by Lewis P. Simpson as *The Federalist Literary Mind* (1962). Although the members displayed a scholarly interest in Americana, their distrust of democratic "vulgarity" and fight against provincialism brought them into conflict with Noah Webster and caused them to be generally condemned as pro-English. Their reading room was the foundation of the Boston Athenaeum.♦

ANTHONY, SUSAN B[ROWNELL] (1820–1906), was a leader in the movement for woman suffrage and an ardent lecturer on abolition and temperance. Her test (1872) of the 14th Amendment as allowing women the vote led to a famous trial. With others she wrote a *History of Woman Suffrage* (4 vols., 1881–87, 1900). She is the heroine of Gertrude Stein's opera *The Mother of Us All* (1949).

Anthony Adverse, romance by Hervey Allen.♦

ANTIN, MARY (MARY ANTIN GRABAU) (1881–1949), born in Russian Poland, was brought to Boston (1894), where she attended public school and began to write poems which were published in local papers. While still a child, she wrote in Yiddish *From Plotzk to Boston,* an impressionistic description of life inside the Jewish Pale in Poland and the emigration of her family, which she translated into English for publication in 1899. She married a Columbia professor, and attended college at Columbia and Barnard (1901–4), but left before receiving a degree to become a settlement worker at Hale House in Boston. In 1912 she extended her early book to make *The Promised Land,* a full account of the customs and hardships of European Jews, as contrasted with the enlightenment and free opportunity they found in the U.S. A later work is *They Who Knock at Our Gates* (1914).

Antinomianism, any theory that holds that moral law as such, or the Old Testament legal system specifically, is not binding upon Christians. In America the Antinomian controversy was precipitated by Anne Hutchinson,♦ who was supported, in her protest against the legal system of the Massachusetts Puritans, by her brother-in-law John Wheelwright, Governor Vane, and other Bostonians. She was opposed by John Winthrop and by the people and clergy of the rural districts. The theological dispute became a political one, and, in 1637, when Winthrop was elected governor, Vane returned to England, and the Hutchinsons were banished to Rhode Island. Although the extreme emphasis upon the belief that Christians, saved by the sacrifice of Jesus and justified by their faith, have no obligation to regard moral law, often tends toward fanaticism, the New England Antinomians seem to compare favorably with their neighbors both in practical morality and in devotion.

Anti-Rent War, conflict of the agrarian feudal system with industrial democracy, centered in the Van Rensselaer land-holdings along the Hudson River. After the death (1839) of Stephen Van Rensselaer, his tenants sought to purchase the reservations in their leases and thus to terminate their tenure. When they were refused, Anti-Rent Associations were organized, and popular indignation led to disorders throughout north-central New York state. In the Constitutional Convention of 1846, the Anti-Renters managed to insert a clause abolishing feudal tenures and prohibiting the leasing of agricultural lands for more than 12 years. The movement was in force until 1854. Cooper's Littlepage Manuscripts♦ form a trilogy on the Anti-Rent War.

ANTONINUS, BROTHER, see *Everson, William.*

Apache Indians, group of tribes or bands related to the Navajo, characteristically unsettled, predatory, and ferocious. Ranging the southern Plains and the Southwest, they were known to the Spaniards as early as 1540, and their guerrilla warfare terrorized these regions until the surrender of Geronimo♦ (1886). Arizona, popularly called the Apache State, includes the present reservations of the tribe.

APES, WILLIAM (1798–?), Indian of mixed Pequot and white parentage, who fought for the Americans in the War of 1812, became a Methodist preacher (1829), and successfully championed the rights of the Cape Cod Indians. He later disappeared, and the date of his death is unknown. His writings include *A Son of the Forest* (1829), *The Experiences of Five Christian Indians* (1833), and *Eulogy on King Philip of the Pequot Tribe* (1836).

Apostle to the Indians, see *Eliot, John.*

APPEL, BENJAMIN (1907–79), New York author, graduated from Lafayette College (1929), whose novels include a trilogy, *Brain Guy* (1934), *The Powerhouse* (1939), and *The Dark Stain* (1943), about a college graduate who enters New York crime, labor rackets, and a fascist group; *Runaround* (1937), about political corruption; *But Not Yet Slain* (1947), about tensions in post-New Deal Washington; *Fortress in the Rice* (1951), set in the war-torn Philippines, which he knew as assistant to the U.S. High Commissioner; *Life and Death of a Tough Guy* (1955); *The Raw Edge* (1958); and *A Big Man, A Fast Man* (1961), about a tough labor leader. *Hell's Kitchen* (1952) and *Dock Wallopers* (1953) collect stories, and *Mixed Vintage* (1929) collects poems. *With Many Voices* (1963) presents impressions of Europe and its peoples' views of the U.S. Later works of nonfiction include *Man and Magic* (1967), a historical consideration of conjuring; *Age of Dictators* (1968); and *The Fantastic Mirror* (1970), about science fiction.

Apple-Tree Table, *The, and Other Sketches,* ten prose pieces by Melville,♦ collected in 1922. Originally published in *Harper's Magazine* and *Putnam's* (1850–56), the sketches range from the critical "Hawthorne and His Mosses" to the title story, an allegory of the appearance of two beautiful living insects in the dead wood of an ancient piece of furniture.

APPLESEED, JOHNNY, see *Chapman, John.*

APPLETON, THOMAS GOLD (1812–84), brother-in-law of Longfellow and son of Nathan Appleton, a rich cotton manufacturer, was a Boston virtuoso and great conversationalist. His thin talents are seen in his formal poetry, appropriately entitled *Faded Leaves* (1872), in pleasant little essays such as *A Sheaf of Papers* (1875), and in travel accounts like *A Nile Journal* (1876).

Appleton's Journal (1869–81), weekly magazine that published, in addition to fiction, articles of current interest on science, politics, foreign events, and the arts. O.B. Bunce, who became editor in 1872, originated a series of pictures by prominent artists to accompany texts by such authors as T.B. Thorpe and J.E. Cooke. The magazine became a monthly in 1876, but its character continued with little change. The writers included Constance F. Woolson, Julian Hawthorne, Bryant, Rebecca Davis., G.C. Eggleston, R.H. Stoddard, Burroughs, and Brander Matthews. During its last three years the *Journal* declined and was made up mainly of reprints from foreign magazines.

April Hopes, novel by Howells,♦ published in 1888.

The brief engagement of Dan Mavering and Alice Pasmer is broken when Alice fancies that her fiancé is secretly wooing another girl. Their differences are adjusted, but Alice's jealousy is again aroused, and the engagement once more broken. After a brief reconciliation, she leaves him to go abroad with her mother because of a disagreement about plans for their future. They are finally united when Dan promises always to be frank in their life together.

Arbella, flagship of the small fleet that arrived at Salem, Mass. (June 12, 1630), carrying some 600–700 persons from England to found a Puritan colony. Unlike the Pilgrims, who arrived on the *Mayflower* in 1620, these founders of the Massachusetts Bay Colony desired to reform the Established Church, not to separate from it. John Winthrop left a record of the *Arbella's* voyage in his *Journal.*

archy and mehitabel, humorous verses by Don Marquis♦ collected (1927) from his columns in the New York *Sun* and later from the New York *Tribune.* They present the adventures of archy, a literary cockroach, who writes free verse because he cannot manipulate a typewriter shift key, and of his friend mehitabel, a cat, whose motto is "toujours gai," as they consider and comment on contemporary U.S. life. First gathered in *archy and mehitabel;* there were several sequels.

Arcturus, see *Boston Miscellany.*

Arena, The, monthly journal edited in Boston (1889–1909) by Benjamin O. Flower. Devoted to social and economic reform and to realism in the arts, its contributors included Hamlin Garland.

ARENDT, HANNAH (1906–75), German-born scholar, emigrated to the U.S. (1941), where she held several major academic posts and published influential works of political theory, including *Origins of Totalitarianism* (1951) and *The Human Condition* (1958). Her correspondence with Mary McCarthy was published in 1994.

Arikara Indians, Plains tribe♦ devoted to bison hunting and maize agriculture, are considered a branch of the Pawnee. During the 19th century the Arikara lived in villages on the Missouri River in North Dakota, where, as early as 1700,

French traders had established relations with them. Warfare with aggressive tribes and the ravages of smallpox nearly exterminated some of their villages, and they became allies of the Mandan and Hidatsa. In 1804, when Lewis and Clark visited them, they were disposed to be friendly toward the U.S., but later they became hostile. Their conflicts with the Americans were concluded by a treaty (1825) in which they acknowledged the supremacy of the U.S. government and agreed to trade only with American citizens. They are frequently spoken of, from the name of their reservation, as the Fort Barthold Indians. They appear in Neihardt's *Song of Hugh Glass* and *Song of the Indian Wars.*

"Arkansas Traveler, THE," folk tune traditionally played on the fiddle, which originated in the backwoods entertainments of the Old Southwest. It is accompanied by humorous dialogue concerned with the arrival of a traveler at a rural tavern and his reception by the fiddling proprietor.

Armies of the Night, The, book by Norman Mailer,♦ published in 1968. The work is divided into two parts in keeping with its concern with the nature of its genre. The first, titled "History as a Novel," records Mailer's reactions as he recounts his participation in an anti-Vietnam march on the Pentagon in October 1967; the second, "The Novel as History," treats in more generalized fashion the sociopolitical background of the march.

Arminianism, doctrine developed by the followers of Jacobus Arminius (1560–1609), a Dutch theologian and critic of Calvinism. These followers, frequently called Remonstrants, differed from orthodox Calvinists on the following points: (1) predestination is conditional rather than absolute; (2) atonement is universal; (3) regeneration requires the Holy Spirit; (4) divine grace is needed for human effort, but it does not act irresistibly in man; (5) believers can resist sin but may fall from grace. These liberal ideas were inclined toward a belief in the freedom of man's will. The Remonstrants later became an independent church, and among those who shared their views were the Methodists, against whose doctrines Jonathan Edwards was led to write his *Freedom of the Will,* defending the orthodox Calvinist view.

Armory Show, name given to the International Exhibition of painting and sculpture (1913) held at the Armory of the 69th Regiment in New York City. It was organized by the Association of American Painters and Sculptors, of which Arthur Davies was president, and was largely aided by the progressive group known as "The Eight." It introduced Fauvism, Cubism, Futurism, and Expressionism to the American public, and provided a great stimulus for American painting and sculpture, and art criticism.

ARNOLD, BENEDICT (1741–1801), Revolutionary War general who, with Ethan Allen, captured Fort Ticonderoga (1775) and marched through the Maine woods in an attempt to seize Quebec. As commander of Philadelphia in 1778 he got in trouble with civil authorities and was sentenced to court-martial. At this time he began to make treasonable reports to Clinton, the British general. In 1780 he accepted the command of West Point, and plotted to deliver the garrison to André. When the plot failed because of André's capture, Arnold fled to the British army, later leading devastating raids against Virginia and his native Connecticut. The latter part of his life was spent in England and New Brunswick. He appears as a character in Brackenridge's play *The Death of General Montgomery,* dealing with the Quebec campaign, and in such plays on the affair of André as those by William Dunlap, Samuel Woodworth, W.W. Lord, and Clyde Fitch; and also in D.P. Thompson's novel *The Green Mountain Boys,* and F.J. Stimson's novel *My Story,* ostensibly an autobiography, and Harold Sinclair's *Westward the Tide.* Source materials concerning his expedition to Quebec were edited by Kenneth Roberts as *March to Quebec* (1938) and employed in the same author's novel *Arundel* (1930).

ARNOLD, GEORGE (1834–65), poet and humorist, was a member of the bohemian group that gathered at Pfaff's Cellar in New York. His writing, published under many pseudonyms, consisted largely of burlesques in verse and prose. Under the name McArone, he wrote a series of sketches for *Vanity Fair,* ♦ including the popular "Life and Adventures of Jeff Davis." After his death, Arnold's poems were collected and edited by William Winter in *Drift: A Sea-Shore Idyl and Other Poems* (1866) and *Poems, Grave and Gay* (1867), the two volumes being combined in the 1870 edition.

ARNOLD, MATTHEW (1822–88), English poet, critic, and educator, visited the U.S. in 1883 and again in 1886, at which times he delivered the lectures collected in *Discourses in America*♦ (1885) and gathered the impressions on which he based his essays in *Civilization in the United States*♦ (1888).

ARNOW, HARRIETTE (1908–86), Kentucky author of novels set in her Cumberland Mountains region, and of *The Dollmaker* (1954), contrasting the values of her native area with those she experienced in Detroit during World War II.

ARRINGTON, ALFRED W. (1810–67), lawyer, spent much of his life on the frontier. Under the pseudonym Charles Summerfield, he wrote *The Desperadoes of the Southwest* (1847), vividly portraying the operation of lynch law, and *The Rangers and Regulators of the Tanaha* (1856), a novel of the Southwest in transition.

Arrow and the Song, The, poem by Longfellow,♦ published in *The Belfry of Bruges and Other Poems* (1845). In three quatrains of four-stress iambic lines, the poet likens his art to the shooting of arrows into the air. As he finds an arrow embedded in an oak, long after losing it, so it is with his song, which ". . . from beginning to end, I found again in the heart of a friend."

Arrowsmith, novel by Sinclair Lewis,♦ published in 1925 and awarded a Pulitzer Prize, which Lewis declined.

Martin Arrowsmith attends the University of Winnemac, in a Midwestern state, where he is influenced by Max Gottlieb, a sincere though sardonic bacteriologist. At college he marries Leora Tozer, a nursing student. They settle in Wheatsylvania, N.D., but his medical practice there is so small that he is forced to accept a post in the health department of Nautilus, Iowa. Disillusioned by the charlatanry of his superior, Dr. Almus Pickerbaugh, Martin leaves this post to enter a fashionable Chicago clinic. After further disappointment, he joins Gottlieb at the McGurk Institute in New York, hoping to find in altruistic research the relief he desires from publicity-seeking and money-grabbing commercial medicine. Martin is now tolerably happy, disturbed only by the patronizing visits of Capitola McGurk, wife of the founder, and by the demand that he turn out results to make newspaper copy. His actual discovery of an "X Principle," an organism that preys on bacteria, is not publicized until a Frenchman has announced a similar discovery. When an epidemic breaks out on the West Indian island of St. Hubert, Gottlieb urges Martin to seize this opportunity to test the efficacy of his "bacteriophage." With Leora and Gustaf Sondelius, a titanic Swedish scientist, he goes to the stricken settlement. Leora and Sondelius die of the plague, after which Martin, instead of maintaining rigid scientific controls, administers the serum indiscriminately, thus destroying the results of his experiment. He returns to New York to marry a rich widow, whose social life interferes with his work. Finally, with Terry Wickett, an uncouth but conscientious chemist, he leaves the McGurk Institute and his wife, establishing himself on a Vermont farm to manufacture serum and pursue his research.

Arsenal at Springfield, The, poem by Longfellow,♦ published in *The Belfry of Bruges and Other Poems* (1845). In quatrains of alternately rhymed pentameter lines, this "peace poem" was inspired by a visit to the U.S. arsenal at Springfield, Mass., and likens the stored cannon to the pipes of a huge organ which will play "awful symphonies . . . when the death-angel touches those swift keys!" After recounting the horrors of war, the poet prophesies a time when Christ's message of peace will be heard, and "the blasts of War's great organ" no longer sound.

Art of Courting, *The,* didactic novel by Ebenezer Bradford. ♦

Artemus Ward, pseudonym of Charles Farrar Browne. ♦

ARTHUR, TIMOTHY SHAY (1809–85), author of nearly 100 moral tales and tracts, including *Temperance Tales* (1843), *Agnes; or, The Possessed. A Revelation of Mesmerism* (1848), and *The Debtor's Daughter; or, Life and Its Changes* (1850). His novel *Ten Nights in a Barroom and What I Saw There* ♦ (1854) was dramatized with great success by William W. Pratt in 1858. Arthur was also the editor of several magazines devoted to the cause of temperance.

Arthur Mervyn; *or, Memoirs of the Year 1793,* romance by C.B. Brown, ♦ published in two parts (1799–1800).

This complicated tale of romance, intrigue, and terror, set in Philadelphia, has for its main theme the career of Mervyn, a lad of 18, stricken with yellow fever during an epidemic, who is cured and befriended by a Dr. Stevens. The latter's friend Wortley accuses the youth of being an accomplice of the embezzler Thomas Welbeck. To clear himself, Mervyn tells how he was driven from his father's farm by a malicious stepmother, and came to Philadelphia, where he was employed as an amanuensis by Welbeck, whose career had included theft, forgery, seduction, and murder. Appropriating an Italian manuscript that Welbeck had stolen, Mervyn settled on the farm of a Mr. Hadwin, soon falling in love with his daughter Eliza. In the manuscript he found $20,000 in bills. Later, in Philadelphia on an errand, he found the city in the grip of the plague, and fell into the hands of Welbeck, who, in trying to regain the money, caused Mervyn to burn it. It was after this that he was found by Dr. Stevens. Satisfied by his account, the doctor cares for the youth and begins to train him in medicine. Mervyn visits the Hadwins, and discovers all dead of the plague except Eliza, whom he places in safety. Returning to the city, he finds Welbeck dying in prison. The repentant criminal asks Mervyn's aid in redressing his misdeeds, leading to the youth's receiving a large reward that makes him independent. During his education he is friendly with the young widow Mrs. Fielding, and, finding that his affection for Eliza is only "brotherly," he concludes by marrying Mrs. Fielding.

Artist of the Beautiful, *The,* allegorical tale by Hawthorne, ♦ published in the *Democratic Review* (1844) and in *Mosses from an Old Manse* (1846).

Owen Warland, a youthful watchmaker, obsessed with a desire to create something ideally beautiful, loves Annie Hovenden, daughter of his former master. She is unsympathetic toward his aspirations and his delicate nature, and Peter Hovenden and the blacksmith, Robert Danforth, both rough and unimaginative, oppress Owen and destroy his inspiration. Annie marries Danforth, and for a time Owen forsakes his dreams for grosser practical activities, but then devotes himself to creating a mechanical butterfly, fragile, lovely, and endowed with living qualities. When he exhibits his work to Annie and her family, Danforth and Hovenden seem to oppress the insect as they do its creator, while Annie prefers to admire her child. The child, who resembles his grandfather, rudely crushes the butterfly, but Owen looks on calmly; "he had caught a far other butterfly than this."

As I Lay Dying, stream-of-consciousness novel by Faulkner, ♦ published in 1930.

Addie Bundren lies dying, and her children prepare to fulfill her desire to be buried in her native Jefferson (Miss.), far from the crude backcountry surroundings of her married life. Cash, one of her sons, makes her coffin, and when she is dead the family unites to carry out the one wish of hers it has ever respected. Another son, Vardaman, still a child, in shock confuses the excitement of catching a big fish and of his mother's death so that he says "my mother is a fish," just as, remembering how he was stifled in a shut corn crib, he bores holes through the coffin so that she can breathe. Led by their mean, simple-minded, whining father, Anse, the family sets off in a mule-drawn wagon. Floods have washed out a bridge, and while fording a river they lose their team. Jewel, Addie's illegitimate son, also nearly loses his beloved horse as it too is plunged in the river, and as Cash is dragged out, he breaks his leg. But although the horse is saved from the river, it is lost to Jewel when Anse trades it for a new team. During the gruesome ten-day trek, although the body begins to decay, Cash rests on the coffin, his leg in a homemade cast that permanently cripples him. One night Darl, the most imaginative and intense of the sons, sets fire to a barn where the coffin is lying so as to cremate his mother and end the horrid pilgrimage, and Jewel, helping to rescue the animals, is badly burned. Arrived in Jefferson, Darl is seized by the authorities and sent to the insane asylum, and Cash is taken to a doctor. Dewey Dell, their sister, buys a "cure" for her pregnancy, paying the drug clerk by giving herself to him. Having fulfilled his duty to Addie, Anse "borrows" money from Dewey Dell, buys a set of false teeth, and, "kind of hangdog and proud, too," returns with a strange woman, saying, "Meet Mrs. Bundren."

ASBURY, FRANCIS (1745–1816), was sent to America in 1771 by John Wesley, founded there the system of circuit-riding, and became the first bishop of the Methodist Episcopal Church to be consecrated in America (1784). His journal, which gives a vivid picture of contemporary frontier society and religion, was published in 1852 and reissued with letters in three volumes (1958).

ASCH, NATHAN (1902–64), son of Sholem Asch, whose novels include *The Office* (1925), *Love in Chartres* (1927), and *Pay Day* (1930). *The Valley* (1935) collects stories, and *The Road* (1937) contains observations on a journey through the U.S.

ASCH, SHOLEM (name also spelled SHALOM or SHOLOM) (1880–1957), Polish-born novelist, came to the U.S. in 1914 and later lived in New York City and in London. His books are written in Yiddish or German, and among those which have been translated into English are *Uncle Moses, Chaim Lederer's Return,* and *Judge Not,* republished as *Three Novels* (1938); *The Mother* (1930, new translation 1937), the story of a Polish family in New York City; *Three Cities* (1933), a realistic trilogy of 20th-century Jewish life in Russia and Poland; *Salvation* (1934), a novel of Polish Jews of the 19th century; *The War Goes On* (1936), a plea for tolerance and humanity set in a story of Jews in postwar Germany; *East River* (1946), a novel of Jewish life in New York at the opening of this century; *A Passage in the Night* (1953), about a Jewish businessman discovering faith on approaching death; and a trilogy: *The Nazarene* (1939), presenting Jesus as the last and greatest Jewish prophet; *The Apostle* (1943), about St. Paul; and *Mary* (1949), about the Virgin. *The Prophet* (1955) is a novel about Isaiah. His many Yiddish plays include *Mottke the Vagabond* (1917), new translation, and *Mottke the Thief* (1935). *What I Believe* (1941) is a testament of faith.

Ash-Wednesday, poem by T.S. Eliot,♦ was published in 1930 as a profession of his faith in the Church of England and represented a statement of the faith which he had called for at the end of *The Waste Land.* By employing certain portions of Dante's *Divine Comedy* and a sermon of Lancelot Andrewes in the frame of reference within which this poem of doubt and faith is constructed, Eliot manages to objectify the emotions he desires to evoke, concerning the security, the emotional satisfaction, and the profound truth that he can find only by accepting the traditions of the Church.

ASHBERY, JOHN [LAWRENCE] (1927–   ), poet born in Rochester, N.Y., after an A.B. from Harvard and graduate study of French literature at Columbia and New York University became an art and literary critic in France. His first poems, *Turandot* (1953) and *Some Trees* (1956), the latter in the Yale Series of Younger Poets, appeared before his expatriation. The later works

have been influenced by French surrealism and relate to the abstractions of New York action painters, including Jackson Pollock and Robert Motherwell. They are melodious, dreamlike, and ever-shifting meditations that do not order the exterior world but in solipsistic fashion present the poet's personal associations and sensory responses to it. Opposed to conventional logic, realism, and the idea of a usable past, the poetry cannot be explicated in a traditional way. Ashbery's evocative images and musicality make fragments sensually beautiful, but the entirety of a work is opaque, lacking sequential development in syntax or theme. His collections include *The Poems* (1960); *The Tennis Court Oath* (1962); *Rivers and Mountains* (1966); *Selected Poems* (1967); *Three Madrigals* (1968); *Sunrise in Suburbia* (1968); *77, Fragment* (1969); *The Double Dream of Spring* (1970); *Three Poems* (1972); *Self-Portrait in a Convex Mirror* (1975, National Book Award, National Book Critics Circle Award, Pulitzer Prize); *Houseboat Days* (1977); *As We Know* (1979); *Shadow Train* (1981); *A Wave* (1984); *April Galleons* (1987); *Flow Chart* (1991), a 216-page poem displaying Ashbery making the stuff of his poetry from the midst of the daily minutiae of television watching, telephone calls, and other common interruptions; and *Hotel Lautréamont* (1993), a meditative series of lyrics. He has also published a novel (written with James Schuyler♦), *A Nest of Ninnies* (1969), a parody of modern U.S. life as seen through the experiences of two vacuous suburban families; and has written two one-act plays, *The Heroes* (1952), a light-hearted presentation of classical mythology in modern times, and *The Philosopher* (1962), a travesty of conventional detective story drama, and a three-act play, *The Compromise* (1956). As a frequent analyst of art, he was one of two critics to write a book on Fairfield Porter (1982).

ASHLEY, WILLIAM HENRY (c.1778–1838), Virginia-born fur trader, became lieutenant governor of Missouri (1820) and sent expeditions up the Missouri River to the Yellowstone (1822–23), employing such "mountain men" as Jedediah Smith, Fitzpatrick, Bridger, and Beckwourth. He was in Congress from 1831 to 1837. H.C. Dale's *The Ashley-Smith Explorations* (1918) is an account of his expeditions during the 1820s.

ASIMOV, ISAAC (1920–92), born in Russia, brought to New York City at age three, was graduated from Columbia University at 19 and after military service returned there to receive a Ph.D. in 1948. He was on the faculty of Boston University's School of Medicine for ten years, but his life was devoted to his career of prodigious authorship, which began with his sale of a science fiction story at age 18 to *Amazing Stories,* though it did not lead to book publication until the appearance of his novel *Pebble in the Sky* (1950), when he was 30. Since then he turned out book after book in diverse genres on a wide variety of subjects, many of them properly titled *Asimov's Guide to* . . . . He is well known for his science fiction stories and novels, particularly for his Foundation series: *Foundation* (1951), *Foundation and Empire* (1952), *Second Foundation* (1953), *Foundation's Edge* (1982), and *Foundation and Earth* (1986). His other works include nonfictional studies for adults and for teenagers on numerous scientific and technological subjects, essays on many topics, histories, Biblical studies, humor, and mysteries and fantasies for children and adults. He published numerous works every year, reaching his hundredth in 1969 and his *Opus 200* in 1979. At the time of his death, he had published 470 titles. His autobiography, *In Memory Yet Green,* telling of his life to age 34, appeared in 1979, and was continued in *In Joy Still Felt* (1980).

Aspern Papers, *The,* novelette by Henry James, ♦ published in 1888.

An American editor with an enthusiasm for the works of Jeffrey Aspern, a romantic poet of the early 19th century, goes to Venice to acquire the letters that Aspern wrote to his mistress, a Miss Bordereau, whom he called "Juliana." Under an assumed name he rents a suite in the ancient palace where she lives in poverty and seclusion with her niece, Miss Tina. He finds that the old lady is shrewd and haughty and accepts him as a lodger only to put aside money for the future of Miss Tina, a timid, unattractive spinster much in awe of her aunt. During his residence with them, the editor wins the friendship of Miss Tina, to whom he reveals his mission. Miss Bordereau falls ill and he attempts to rifle her desk, but she surprises him and frightens him off before suffering a relapse. Leaving Venice for a fortnight, he returns to find the old lady dead. Miss Tina welcomes him expectantly, and he realizes that she is in love with him. She says that she could give him the papers only if he were "a relative," and, alarmed at this proposal, he leaves. At their next interview he learns that she has destroyed the letters. Her suffering has matured and ennobled her, and she dismisses him with tact and restraint.

Assignation, *The,* story by Poe, ♦ published as "The Visionary" in *Godey's Lady's Book* (1834) and under its present title in *Tales of the Grotesque and Arabesque* (1840). It contains the poem "To One in Paradise."

Assiniboin Indians, northern Plains tribe, many of whom migrated in the 17th century from Dakota to Lake Winnipeg, and later to the upper Saskatchewan and Assiniboin rivers. Their southern branch was almost constantly at war with the Dakota Indians, until it was gathered on a Montana reservation. The Assiniboin figure in Neihardt's *Song of Three Friends.*

Assistant, *The,* novel by Bernard Malamud, ♦ published in 1957.

Morris Bober, a 60-year-old Jewish owner of a small grocery store in Brooklyn, hoping to sell out before competition, theft, and illness overwhelm him, is instead wounded by robbers. Good fortune comes his way when Frank Alpine, a stranger caught up in the robbery, assists Bober as he recuperates. Alpine is also a threat to Bober and his wife Ida because he falls in love with their daughter Helen but is unsuitable for her since he is not Jewish. When he pilfers from the cash register he is fired, but after Bober's death he returns to work and hopes to win Helen by converting to her faith.

ASTON, ANTHONY (*fl.* 1703–30), the first known professional actor in America. Apparently in 1703, he arrived in Charleston, "full of Shame, Poverty, Nakedness, and Hunger: I turned *Player* and *Poet* and wrote one Play on the Subject of the Country." That play is lost, but a negligible work, *The Fool's Opera; or, The Taste of the Age* (*c.* 1730), survives, and to it is prefixed the autobiographical sketch from which the above is quoted. This parody of *The Beggar's Opera* is the only extant work by this strolling English player.

ASTOR, JOHN JACOB (1763–1848), German-born merchant, emigrated to the U.S. in 1784. He arrived in New York practically penniless, but two years later had his own fur store there. The growth of his fur business was phenomenal, owing to his skill in bargaining and personal supervision of frontier posts. He had acquired a considerable fortune by 1800, when his ships called at London and Canton, and by 1817 his American Fur Company (founded 1808) enjoyed a virtual monopoly, with trading posts dotting the plains and mountains as far as Astoria ♦ on the Columbia River. His profits were invested in New York City real estate, which, together with his profiteering in government bonds during the War of 1812, made him the wealthiest man in the U.S. He retired from the fur trade (1834), and with his son William (1792–1875) occupied the rest of his life in managing the Astor holdings in New York, which later made William known as the city's "landlord." Part of the family fortune was contributed to found the Astor Library, later joined with the New York Public Library.

Astor Place riot, the result of a controversy between Edwin Forrest and the English actor William Charles Macready. Both actors were appearing in New York in 1849, and both had ardent followers, the elite favoring Macready, the rank and file, Forrest. To the latter the controversy was a struggle between democracy and Anglomania. On the evening of May 10, a mob led by E.Z.C. Judson, ♦ and possibly abetted by Forrest, invaded the Astor Place Opera House, where Macready was appearing in *Macbeth,* and in the ensuing fracas, which almost wrecked the structure, 22 persons were killed and at least 36 wounded. For helping direct the attack, Judson was sentenced to a year in the penitentiary.

Astoria, now a town near the mouth of the Columbia River in northwest Oregon, was founded as Fort Clatsop (1805) by the Lewis and Clark expedition. In 1811 John Jacob Astor♦ founded a fur trading post at the site, but during the War of 1812 the Astor interests were sold to the British. Astoria was restored to the U.S. in accordance with the Treaty of Ghent (1818). Irving's *Astoria* (1836, revised 1849) is a history of Astor's fur trade in the Northwest. The region also appears in fiction, e.g. Archie Binns's *You Rolling River.*

Asylum, The; or, Alonzo and Melissa, Gothic romance by Isaac Mitchell,♦ published in 1811. An almost verbatim plagiarism appeared the same year under the title *Alonzo and Melissa; or, The Unfeeling Father,* credited to Daniel Jackson.

Melissa decides to marry Alonzo rather than Beauman, his rival, but her father, finding Alonzo to be penniless, parts the lovers and confines Melissa in a haunted ruined castle. She escapes to Charleston, whence comes the notice of her sudden death. In despair, Alonzo joins the navy, and is captured by the British during the Revolution, finally reaching home by way of France, where he is aided by Franklin. He goes to Charleston to weep at Melissa's grave, and in that city, keeping a tryst with a mysterious lady, discovers her to be Melissa. The mysterious actions in the castle are explained by the discovery that the ghosts are the device of a group of smugglers in the service of the British. Alonzo regains the family estate of which he had long been deprived, and the novel ends: "And now, reader of sensibility, indulge the pleasing sensations of thy bosom—for Alonzo and Melissa are MARRIED."

Atala, romantic tale by Chateaubriand,♦ published in France (1801) and translated into English by Caleb Bingham (1802). Originally intended to be an episode in *Les Natchez,* ♦ it was later incorporated in *Le Génie du christianisme* (1802).

To René, a young Frenchman self-exiled in the American wilderness, Chactas, an old Natchez Indian, tells how he was reared among whites by Lopez, a kindly Spaniard, then captured by the enemy Muscogulges and how he escaped with Atala, the virgin bride of their chief and the daughter of Lopez. Although she returned Chactas's love, she was faithful to her vow of virginity and killed herself. Chactas and René are killed during a French massacre of the Indians.

ATHERTON, GERTRUDE [FRANKLIN] (1857–1948), California author, whose many novels include a series depicting life in her native state from Spanish times to the present, in such volumes as *Before the Gringo Came* (1894), revised as *The Splendid Idle Forties*♦ (1902); *The Californians* (1898, revised 1935); *Rezánov* (1906); *The Sisters-in-Law* (1921); and *The Horn of Life* (1942). She also wrote a fictional biography of Alexander Hamilton, *The Conqueror*♦ (1902), and several society novels which include *Julia France and Her Times*♦ (1912) and the sensational *Black Oxen*♦ (1923). Other works are essays, short stories, a history of California, *Golden Gate Country* (1945) in the American Folkways series, and several novels on classical themes. *Adventures of a Novelist* (1932) is her autobiography.

ATKINSON, [JUSTIN] BROOKS (1894–1984), drama critic (1925–60) and critic at large for *The New York Times,* except during World War II when he was a war and news correspondent, winning a Pulitzer Prize for journalism about China. His books include *Henry Thoreau: The Cosmic Yankee* (1927); *East of the Hudson* (1931), sketches of bucolic life; *Once Around the Sun* (1951), essays; *Tuesdays and Fridays* (1963) and *Brief Chronicles* (1966), from his columns in *The New York Times*; and *Sean O'Casey* (1982).

Atlantic Magazine, see *New York Review and Athenaeum Magazine.*

Atlantic Monthly (1857–), magazine of literature, art, and politics, was founded at Boston by leading New England literary figures. It was named by Holmes, who contributed his *Autocrat of the Breakfast-Table,* and the editor for the first four years was Lowell, who wrote for the magazine himself and also obtained contributions from Emerson, Longfellow, Motley, Whittier, Harriet Beecher Stowe, and other prominent authors. Although the editors denied that it was meant to be an organ of Bostonian or New England opinion, the *Atlantic* was generally accused of Brahminism and failure to recognize writers outside of its region. In politics they contended that it was "the organ of no party or clique," but it was considered to be strongly antislavery. It was, however, relatively uninterested in current affairs until purchased by the publishers Ticknor and Fields (1859), and edited by J.T. Fields (1861–71). During the Civil War there were articles on contemporary matters by Sumner, Carl Schurz, and others prominent in politics, and the *Atlantic* published such stirring verses as "The Battle Hymn of the Republic," "Barbara Frietchie," and the second series of *The Biglow Papers,* as well as *The Man Without a Country.* Under the editorship of Howells (1871–81) the magazine was less concerned with politics and, without ceasing to be representative of New England, drew its authors from farther afield. Nevertheless, the greatest success of his editorship was the publication of Aldrich's "Marjorie Daw." He added new departments, including book reviews, and sections on science, music, and education. Under Aldrich's editorship (1881–90), the Brahmin standards were returned to; contributors included Fiske, Henry James, Parkman, Mary N. Murfree, Sarah Orne Jewett, and Woodberry. H.E. Scudder's editorship (1890–98) emphasized social subjects in articles like those of Theodore Roosevelt on civil service; and his assistant W.H. Page, who succeeded him (1898–99), brought the magazine even more into the national scene. Under Page and Bliss Perry (1899–1909) contributors included J. J. Chapman, Woodrow Wilson, Riis, Booker T. Washington, Cleveland, and W.A. White. The later *Atlantic* preserves its heritage as an intelligent literary journal with a keen interest in contemporary affairs. *Jubilee* (1957) is an anthology from its first 100 years collected by its editor (1938–66), Edward Weeks.

Atlantic Souvenir, *The* (1826–32), annual gift book, whose authors included Bryant, Cooper, Halleck, Irving, Paulding.

Attaché, *The; or Sam Slick in England,* two series of humorous sketches (1843–44) by T.C. Haliburton, continuing the Yankee adventures in *The Clockmaker.* ♦

ATTAWAY, WILLIAM (1911–86), Mississippi-born black author, reared in Chicago, graduated from the University of Illinois, and held various jobs before writing his two novels, *Let Me Breathe Thunder* (1939), about two tough young white hoboes, and *Blood on the Forge* (1941), about Southern black farmworkers trying to compete in Pennsylvania steel-mill jobs. His only other book, *Hear America Singing* (1967), is for children.

AUCHINCLOSS, LOUIS [STANTON] (1917–), graduate of Yale with a law degree from the University of Virginia, is a New York lawyer whose polished fiction about high society began with several volumes issued under the pseudonym Andrew Lee. His very large authorship of novels includes *The Indifferent Children* (1947), about a dilettante during World War II; *Sybil* (1952), portraying an Edith Wharton kind of heroine; *A Law for the Lion* (1953); *The Romantic Egoists* (1954), stories told by one character; *The Great World and Timothy Colt* (1956), about a disillusioned New York lawyer; *Venus in Sparta* (1958) and *Pursuit of the Prodigal* (1959), portraying different kinds of rich, upper-class New Yorkers who leave their wives and move out of their usual world; *The House of Five Talents* (1960), tracing one of his kind of family from 1873 to 1948; *Portrait in Brownstone* (1962), about a New York society woman; *The Rector of Justin* (1964), a study of the founding headmaster of an Episcopalian boys' school in New England; *The Embezzler* (1966), about a socialite who misappropriates some bonds; *A World of Profit* (1968), presenting a young Jewish entrepreneur of New York and the WASP family whose estates he buys; *A Writer's*

Capital (1974), characterizing a lawyer who comes to write satires of the elite; *The Dark Lady* (1977), presenting a social climber in New York; *Watchfires* (1982), treating three generations of an elite New York family; *The Book Class* (1984), dealing with several generations of stylish New York ladies and their studies of literature; *Honorable Man* (1985), a biography of a fictive wealthy and intelligent man; *Diary of a Yuppie* (1986), characterizing a contemporary striver in business and law; *The Golden Calves* (1987), a satire on obtaining financial aid for an art museum; and *The Lady of Situations* (1990), about a woman whose family has lost money in the Depression and her struggles to regain social standing. Stories with similar themes have appeared in several volumes, beginning with *The Injustice Collectors* (1950) and continuing with *Skinny Island* (1987), tales of Manhattan, and *Three Lives* (1993), three novellas about complicated characters facing difficult choices. He has also written books on Henry James (1961 and 1975), Shakespeare (1969), Edith Wharton (1971), Richelieu (1973), and the Vanderbilts (1989); *False Dawn* (1984), on women in the 18th century; *Love Without Wings* (1991), which examines the concept of friendship in literature and politics; and *The Style's the Man: Reflections on Proust, Fitzgerald, Wharton, Vidal, and Others* (1994). *Life, Law and Letters* (1979) collects essays and sketches.

AUDEN, W[YSTAN] H[UGH] (1907–73), British-born poet, educated at Oxford. During the Depression of the 1930s he and other English authors—Spender, Isherwood, and C. Day-Lewis, among them—were deeply affected by Marxism, an interest that Auden called "more psychological than political." His works of that period include *Poems* (1930) and *The Orators* (1932), prose and poetry, bitter and witty, on the impending collapse of British middle-class ways and a coming revolution. During this decade he also experimented with lively plays using verse and the vernacular in the vein of Brecht; and after his own *The Dance of Death* (1933), a verse play, he collaborated with Christopher Isherwood on *The Dog Beneath the Skin* (1936), a fanciful prose and verse play satirizing the middle class; *The Ascent of F6* (1936); and *On the Frontier* (1938), all with incidental music by Benjamin Britten. His experiences as a traveler during the Spanish Civil War are reflected in the poem *Spain* (1937); other travels gave rise to *Letters from Iceland* (1937), verse and prose in collaboration with Louis MacNeice, expressing a holiday mood in temporarily escaping Europe; and *Journey to a War* (1939), a sad survey of the contemporary situation, issuing out of a voyage to China, with Isherwood's prose balancing Auden's verse. This decade and this period of ideas ended in 1939 with Auden's coming to live in the U.S., confirmed by his naturalization as a citizen in 1946. Although he tried an American theme in *Paul Bunyan,* a choral operetta written with Benjamin Britten and produced in 1941, his shift in this period was more in views and attitudes than in nationalism. New collections of poetry were *Another Time* (1940) and *The Double Man* (1941), a title showing he was cleft in his intense search for a belief or logic, while the English title, *New Year Letter*, comes from the longest poem in a collection including prose too. Having moved away from the Marxism of the 1930s, he came in the 1940s to the heritage of his Anglo-Catholic faith and to a Christian existential view. Books included *For the Time Being* (1945), a Christmas oratorio confronting the present day with a religious view and containing "The Sea and the Mirror," a commentary on *The Tempest* concerned with the relations of art and society; and *The Age of Anxiety: A Baroque Eclogue* (1948, Pulitzer Prize), an ironic idyl, set in a cheap New York bar, on man's isolated condition, intensified in an era without tradition or belief. In 1950 he issued his *Collected Shorter Poems, 1930–44,* and later lyrics were gathered in *Nones* (1951), a volume which opened themes that were developed in *The Shield of Achilles* (1955), *Homage to Clio* (1960), and *About the House* (1965), which in their contrast of human qualities and natural forces, and the treatment of the relation of nature to history, displayed great technical skill. In 1968 and 1970 he reassessed respectively the shorter and the longer poems he wished to preserve and issued new editions of them. These volumes were followed by poetry in *City Without Walls* (1969); *Epistle to a Godson* (1972); *Academic Graffiti* (1972), 61 clerihews about famous people; *Thank You, Fog* (1974), his last lyrics; and *Collected Poems* (1976), a final selection, often with revisions. His later prose included *The Enchafèd Flood: The Romantic Iconography of the Sea* (1951), lectures on the Romantics' attitudes toward man, God, and nature; an edition of *The Living Thoughts of Kierkegaard* (1952); *Making, Knowing and Judging* (1956), his inaugural lecture as Professor of Poetry at Oxford (1956–61); and *The Dyer's Hand* (1962), a major work collecting lectures, essays, musings, and aphorisms. His final prose works appeared in *Secondary Worlds* (1968), lectures on poetry, history, and music; *A Certain World* (1970), extracts with comments from Auden's reading; and *Forewords and Afterwords* (1973), a collection of minor commentary. In 1972 Auden returned to England to live out his last years at Oxford.

AUDUBON, John James (1785–1851), born in Haiti, was educated in France, where Rousseau's and Buffon's works led to nature study. After training by David, the French artist, he lived in 1804 on his father's estate near Philadelphia. In the next years he traveled and tried business, portrait painting, drawing instruction, decorating porcelain, taxidermy, and depicting the birds of Kentucky and neighboring wild areas, leading to his *The Birds of America*♦ (1827–

38). His narrative gifts and knowledge of the frontier are better seen in the extracts published as *Delineations of American Scenery and Character* (1926) and *Audubon's America* (1940). With the American naturalist John Bachman he worked on *Viviparous Quadrupeds of North America,* completed by his two sons (2 vols., plates, 1842–45; 3 vols., text, 1846–54). He painted many portraits but his fame rests on his bird paintings, whose scientific accuracy may be challenged but whose fresh vitality is unquestioned. His *Journal* was published in 1929 and his *Letters* in 1930.

Augie March, The Adventures of, novel by Saul Bellow,♦ published in 1953.

Augie March, a young Chicago Jew, leaves his charity-supported mother, tyrannical grandmother, and mentally retarded brother George, and with his opportunistic older brother Simon ventures into the world to make a living. He manages to graduate from high school but learns about life and himself through diverse jobs and experiences. He first works as a "man at arms" for the crippled William Einhorn, a learned but inept and dishonest businessman who instills in him a love of books; then he becomes a salesman in an elegant saddle shop, leaving when Mrs. Renling, the owner's wife, tries to refine and adopt him. He takes part in a robbery, tries to smuggle immigrants over the Canadian border, steals and sells expensive books, and is briefly a union organizer. Unlike Simon, Augie remains emotionally involved with his family, is deeply upset when his mother and George are institutionalized, and grieves when Grandma Lausch dies. Unwilling to emulate Simon, who married Charlotte Magnus for her money, he leaves his job with Simon and stops courting Charlotte's cousin Lucy, persisting in searching for his own fate in his own way. His love affair with Thea Fenchel, on their iguana hunt in Mexico, convinces him that independence and love are irreconcilable but, sometime later, back in the U.S., he marries Stella, an actress he aided in Mexico. Considering the shambles of Simon's marriage and reflecting on his own unachieved desires for a stable life, Augie recognizes that "everyone got bitterness in his chosen thing," but retains his optimism, humor, and amazement at man's "refusal to lead a disappointed life."

Aunt Polly, character in *Tom Sawyer*♦ and its sequels.

Aurora (1794–1822, 1834–35), Philadelphia anti-Federalist newspaper, supplanted the *General Advertiser* (1790–94). B.F. Bache's editorship was strongly pro-French and anti-Washington and the office was wrecked (1797) by veterans of Washington's army. After Bache's death (1798) William Duane continued the Jeffersonian policy to 1822, when publication was suspended. It was revived in 1834. The Alien and Sedition acts were partly aimed at the *Aurora*.

Aurora Community, see *Bethel.*

AUSLANDER, JOSEPH (1897–1965), poet, author of *Sunrise Trumpets* (1924), *Cyclops' Eye* (1926), *Letters to Women* (1929), *Hell in Harness* (1929), *Riders at the Gate* (1938), and *The Unconquerables* (1943), marked by romantic rhetoric. With his wife, Audrey Wurdemann, he wrote a novel, *My Uncle Jan* (1948), and *The Islanders* (1951), poems.

AUSTER, PAUL (1947–   ), born in Newark, N.J., and educated at Columbia University, worked in relative obscurity until the publication of his "New York Trilogy"—*City of Glass* (1985), *Ghosts* (1986), and *The Locked Room* (1987), all postmodern detective novels. *The Locked Room* is the least abstract and most accessible of the trio. Auster's vision of humanity is dark, seen best perhaps in *In the Country of Last Things* (1988). Here New York City and surroundings have become a dystopia, a horrible place where shills lure people to human abattoirs, where the New York Public Library, deserted, cold, and dark, provides shelter for a couple who meet there by chance and fall in love. Circumstances defeat them—even the weather has gone crazy, with snow in July, a hint of nuclear winter. *Moon Palace* (1989) has its protagonist driving from New York to the Far West to unearth an inheritance whose location has only been roughly described to him. *Leviathan* (1992) chronicles Peter Aaron's attempt to tell the truth (ultimately, for the FBI) about his best friend Benjamin Sachs, who lately blew himself to bits constructing a bomb. Aaron also seeks to discover his friend's true identity. It is the story of a deep friendship within which are elements of betrayal. Both friends are writers; Aaron is interrupted in his writing by an FBI agent who has solved the mystery of Sachs's identity. Aaron then hands over his manuscript, which we have been reading, to the agent. In *Mr. Vertigo* (1994) Walter Rawley tells mostly his boyhood story as he remembers it in old age. The story begins in 1924. Walter, like Huck Finn, is from Missouri and speaks a modern version of Huck's dialect. He is a similar free spirit, having not a mean father but a bad uncle. He is taken off the uncle's hands by Mr. Yehudi, a sort of Zen showman, who promises to teach Walt to fly. This is accomplished in three years in an arduous 33-step series of trials, including live burial. Walt learns to levitate and becomes famous as Walt the Wonder Boy. As the result of an ugly accident, he develops terrible headaches after each levitation and has to give up this gift. His mean Uncle Slim waylays him and Mr. Yehudi, stealing all their money. Mr. Yehudi, suffering from cancer, kills himself. Walt then hunts down and kills the uncle by making him drink strychnine. Walt goes through many other picaresque adventures before washing up in Wichita. The novel is redolent of the spirit of the times. At the end, Walt believes we all have it in us to fly—you let your *self* evaporate, and then you lift off. "Like so." *The Invention of Solitude* (1982) is a memoir of his dead father, seeking to rescue him "from vanishing completely." *Disappearances: Selected Poems* appeared in 1989. *The Art of Hunger* (1991) collects essays.

AUSTIN, JANE GOODWIN (1831–94), Massachusetts author of books for children, whose works include *A Nameless Nobleman* (1881), a romance dealing with a courtier of Louis XIV who comes to America, and the Pilgrim Books, including *Standish of Standish* (1889) and *Betty Alden* (1891).

AUSTIN, MARY [HUNTER] (1868–1934), born in Illinois, moved to California at the age of 18, and lived for many years on the desert, engaged in the study of Indian life. She was a member of the artist colony at Carmel, and later moved to Santa Fe, N.M., to teach and continue her study of the Indians. Her first book, *The Land of Little Rain*♦ (1903), is a sympathetic description of the beauties of Western desert life. After *The Basket Woman* (1904), a book of short stories, she wrote her first novel, *Isidro*♦ (1905), a romance of California in the days of the Franciscan missions and Mexican rule. *The Flock* (1906) is a factual but poetically conceived narrative of shepherd life. *Santa Lucia: A Common Story* (1908), her first writing concerned with contemporary city life, tells of the marriages of three women and their different adjustments to typical marital problems. *Lost Borders* (1909) is a collection of stories, while *A Woman of Genius* (1912) is a novel about a woman who attempts to escape from her restricted life through a stage career. This book has, according to the author, "the social ideal of Taylorville, Ohianna, for the villain." *The Green Bough* (1913) tells the story of Jesus' progress from the passion to the ascension, and *The Lovely Lady* (1913) is an idyl concerned with a boy's dreams, his disillusion, and his ultimate triumph. *The Ford* (1917), a realistic novel of social injustice and reform, is set in central California. After *The Trail Book* (1918), stories for children dealing with primitive life, and *Outland* (1919), a mystical romance exalting the primitive values, she wrote *No. 26 Jayne Street* (1920), a novel concerned with contemporary radical activities in New York City. The subjects of her other works are divided between life in the West and the position of the individual in an increasingly standardized machine culture. These include *California, the Land of the Sun* (1914); *Love and the Soul Maker* (1914), a discussion of modern problems of love, marriage, and divorce; *The Young Woman Citizen* (1918), a handbook of politics for newly enfranchised women voters; *The American Rhythm* (1923), studies of American Indian songs, and original poems expressing the same spirit and movement; *Everyman's Genius* (1925), a "personal research into the nature and processes of genius"; *A Small*

Town Man (1925), a revision of *The Man Jesus* (1915), presenting the author's concept of Christ as a human being and great mystical genius; and *Children Sing in the Far West* (1928), Indian songs and original poems, written with the "help" of the children in her classes, and preserving their youthful approach. Mrs. Austin left a record of her sympathetic understanding of the West, her mystical attitude, and her personal rebellion for the freedom of the individual in her distinguished autobiography, *Earth Horizon* (1932). She was also the author of three plays, of which the best known is *The Arrow Maker* (1911), a drama of Indian life dealing with a medicine woman's unhappiness in her sanctified position and her revenge when a young chief rejects her love to marry another woman. A collection of the author's letters appeared in 1979.

AUSTIN, WILLIAM (1778–1841), graduated from Harvard (1798) and wrote of the restraints of college life in his precocious Rousseauistic *Strictures on Harvard University.* While training in London for his later successful career as a Boston lawyer and legislator, he wrote the popular *Letters from London* (1804), which shows British lawyers and statesmen as they appeared to a New England Republican. Of his five uncollected tales, the most famous is "Peter Rugg, the Missing Man" (1824). This tells of a Bostonian who set out to drive to the city in a blinding storm, and continued to seek it for 50 years, during which his galloping jet horse with its white feet became a common sight, always heralding an approaching storm. This fable passed into New England folklore and has been used by Louise Imogen Guiney and Amy Lowell. It seems to foreshadow Hawthorne and may have influenced him, for he uses the figure of Peter Rugg in "A Virtuoso's Collection."

Authors' Club, New York literary society, founded in 1882 by Brander Matthews, Edward Eggleston, E.C. Stedman, R.W. Gilder, and others.

Authors League of America, founded in 1912 to protect copyright material. Its categories of membership have changed over the years, and in 1964 its structure added to the League an Authors Guild and a Dramatists Guild. Matters of concern to members in both Guilds (e.g. copyright, freedom of expression) remain the League's province, but matters in which their interests differ (e.g. contract terms, subsidiary rights) are the province of the respective Guilds.

Autobiography of Alice B. Toklas, The, personal narrative by Gertrude Stein. ♦

Autobiography of an Ex-Colored Man, The, novel by James Weldon Johnson. ♦

Autocrat of the Breakfast-Table, The, by Holmes, ♦ was published in 1858, although the germ of the idea may be seen in two papers published (1831–32) in *The New England Magazine* and never reprinted. These rambling Addisonian essays describe imaginary table talk at a Boston boarding house, and include a number of the author's poems: "The Deacon's Masterpiece," ♦ "The Chambered Nautilus," ♦ "Contentment," "The Living Temple," and others. The conversation comprehends many topics and expresses Holmes's urbane philosophy and his concept of the New England character in an easy, genial, witty style. Among those who participate are the Autocrat; the Schoolmistress, to whom he becomes engaged; the Landlady and her Daughter; the Old Gentlemen Opposite; the Divinity Student; and the Poor Relation. The success of the *Autocrat* led the author to write three other series: *The Professor at the Breakfast-Table* (1860), *The Poet at the Breakfast-Table* (1872), and *Over the Teacups* (1891).

Avon's Harvest, blank-verse narrative by E.A. Robinson, ♦ the title poem of a volume published in 1921.

Awake and Sing!, play by Clifford Odets, ♦ produced and published in 1935.

The Bergers, a poor Jewish family living in the Bronx, struggle for life "amidst petty conditions." Myron, the father, is a sententious failure; Bessie, his wife and the imperious leader of the household, is obsessed with the need for bourgeois respectability. Jacob, Bessie's father, is a "sentimental idealist with no power to turn ideal to action," and he encourages the rebellion of his grandson Ralph against their environment. Ralph's sister Hennie, a stenographer, is deserted by her lover after she becomes pregnant, and hurriedly marries her immigrant suitor Sam Feinschreiber, who believes it is his child she bears. She is still sought by her first lover, proud and passionate Moe Axelrod, a one-legged war veteran whose bitter view of the world is in direct contrast with that of Bessie's brother, Uncle Morty, the Bergers' rich relative. Ralph falls in love with the orphan girl Blanche, to the intense displeasure of his practical mother. His unhappiness and that of the others cause Jacob to commit suicide in order that Ralph may have his insurance. During this crisis, Hennie abandons Sam and her baby to elope with Moe. Ralph, realizing the significance of his grandfather's teachings and the selfishness of his love for Blanche, gives the money to the family and resolves to devote himself to radical agitation for an improved order of society.

Awakening, The, novella by Kate Chopin, ♦ published in 1899.

Edna Pontellier, still in her 20s, is vaguely discontented in her marriage to Léonce Pontellier, a 40-year-old stockbroker of New Orleans, whose main interests are business and bourgeois respectability. While at a vacation resort at Grand Isle, only joined on weekends by her husband, she begins to awaken from the submissiveness he expects of her as she discovers the freer, romantic society of Creoles and also becomes enamored of young Robert Lebrun. After he leaves suddenly for Mexico her life is empty when she returns to the city. She grows more estranged from her husband, turning frenetically to friends from Grand Isle. Upon Robert's return, they admit their love for one another, but when he says "Good-by—because I love you," she goes to the resort, deserted in off season, and naked swims suicidally far out from the shore, buoyed by "the touch of the sea . . . sensuous, enfolding the body in its soft, close embrace."

Awakening, THE GREAT, see *Great Awakening.*

Awkward Age, The, novel by Henry James,♦ published in 1899.

The story is concerned with the "awkward age" in the life of Nanda Brookenham, during the period just following her emergence from childhood segregation to the brilliant atmosphere of her mother's London salon. The girl and her mother are both in love with Vanderbank, a young government official, although Nanda is also fond of Mitchett, who wishes to marry her. Mrs. Brookenham's friend, the Duchess, wants Mitchett to marry her fragile, innocent niece Aggie, and the two older women wage a diplomatic battle over the match, using as weapons Mrs. Brookenham's relations with Vanderbank and the Duchess's liaison with Lord Petherton. Nanda, having learned of the world through such friends as the unhappily married Tishy Grendon, has a mind of her own during these maneuvers. Mr. Longdon, just reentering London society after 30 years' seclusion, sees in Nanda a resemblance to her grandmother, whom he once loved, and, interesting himself in her affairs, is converted to her modern point of view. He realizes that, though she wants Vanderbank, the young man is not anxious to marry her because of her sophistication and frank display of affection. He thereupon gives her a large dowry as bait, but

even then the ambitious Vanderbank fails to propose. Mitchett, finally discouraged, marries Aggie, and Mrs. Brookenham overplays her hand by demanding Nanda's return from a visit at Longdon's home. This alienates Vanderbank, and Nanda establishes herself in a separate suite at home. Longdon confers with Mitchett, who has found his marriage unsatisfactory, and they agree that they are Nanda's only remaining friends. They decide, and Nanda later agrees, that the best solution of the problem is for her to live permanently at Longdon's country place, since he is the one who has attained a truly modern point of view and can meet her on her own terms.

Axe-Helve, The, blank-verse dramatic narrative by Robert Frost,♦ published in *New Hampshire* (1923).

The poet, chopping wood, is interrupted by a neighboring farmer, the Frenchman Baptiste, who objects to his using an inferior machine-made axe-helve. He promises him a good hickory helve of his own cutting, and that evening the poet visits Baptiste's home, meeting his sociable wife, who speaks no English. He talks with the earnest workman, who proves to be a conscientious laborer who knows "how to make a short job long for love of it," and insists that his children shall not attend school, asserting the superiority of his own proud independence and appreciation of such essential things as the materials of a properly durable axe-helve.

Axel's Castle, critical essays on symbolism by Edmund Wilson,♦ published in 1931 with the subtitle "A Study in the Imaginative Literature of 1870 to 1930." The authors treated are Yeats, Valéry, Eliot, Proust, Joyce, Gertrude Stein, Rimbaud, and Villiers de l'Isle-Adam. The poetic prose drama *Axel* by the last-named author gives the work its title, for it treats a character, Count Axel, and has a setting that suggests the subjective and symbolic quality of the literature with which Wilson deals.

Azarian, tale by Harriet Spofford.♦

B

Babbitt, novel by Sinclair Lewis, ♦ published in 1922.

George Folansbee Babbitt, an enterprising, moral, stereotyped, and prosperous real-estate broker of the typical Midwestern city of Zenith, has been trained to believe in the virtues of home life, the Republican party, and middle-class conventions. Suddenly tiring of his life, he takes a vacation with Paul Riesling, an artist who has been forced into the role of a businessman. His return to Zenith is at first difficult, but he shortly discovers pleasure in campaigning for a friend for mayor, in several profitable real-estate deals, in the vice-presidency of the Boosters' Club, and in speeches before prominent local gatherings. During his wife's absence, he again tries to find an outlet from Zenith standards. After an unsuccessful and lonely trip to Maine, he enters into a liaison with Mrs. Tanis Judique, an attractive widow who fails to be the "fairy child" of his dreams when he sees her in clear light in relation to her group of nondescript would-be bohemians, "The Bunch." He next turns to liberalism, when impressed by Seneca Doane, a socialist lawyer. For this added heresy he is ostracized by all right-minded citizens. He is not again able to return to Zenith's outlook until his wife Myra is suddenly taken ill, and he once more feels a spiritual union with her and a sympathy with his city's point of view.

BABBITT, IRVING (1865–1933), born in Ohio, graduated from Harvard (1889), and after study abroad became a professor of Romance languages at Williams (1893–94) and of French at Harvard (1894–1933). He was an outstanding scholar and as a leader of the New Humanism was a trenchant critic of romanticism and its arch-apostle, Rousseau. Among the books in which he set forth his humanist doctrines are *Literature and the American College* (1908), a plea for the humanities; *The New Laokoön* (1910), on the romantic confusion in the arts; *Rousseau and Romanticism* (1919); *Democracy and Leadership* (1924), a philosophy of modern civilization; and *On Being Creative* (1932), a discussion of classic theories of imitation and romantic concepts of spontaneity. *Spanish Character* (1940), a posthumous collection of essays, contains a bibliography and index to his works.

BACHE, BENJAMIN FRANKLIN (1769–98), grandson of Franklin, at the age of 21 founded the Philadelphia *General Advertiser* (later the *Aurora* ♦) and in its columns bitterly attacked Washington, Adams, and Federalist policies.

BACHELLER, IRVING [ADDISON] (1859–1950), author of popular romances, which include *Eben Holden* (1900), a novel concerned with a homely hired man; *D'ri and I* (1901), a novel of the War of 1812; *Silas Strong* (1906); *A Man for the Ages* (1919), a story of Lincoln; *A Candle in the Wilderness* (1930), laid in early New England; and *The Winds of God* (1941), a boy's experiences in Vermont and upper New York. *Opinions of a Cheerful Yankee* (1926), *Coming Up the Road* (1928), and *From Stores of Memory* (1938) are memoirs.

Back Bay, reclaimed western addition of the city of Boston, on the south bank of the Charles River. Since the mid-19th century, it has been a fashionable residential district. *The Rise of Silas Lapham* is one of the many novels set in the Back Bay.

BACKUS, ISAAC (1724–1806), Baptist preacher of Connecticut, who led his church in its struggle for freedom of worship. His *History of New England, with Particular Reference to the Denomination of Christians Called Baptists* (3 vols., 1777–96) is a monument of early historical scholarship, despite its bias and turgidity. The work is partially based on materials gathered by John Callender.

Backward Glance o'er Travel'd Roads, A, Whitman's prose epilogue to *Leaves of Grass,* ♦ which served as a preface to *November Boughs* (1888), and appeared in the collected volume in 1889 for the first time.

Leaves of Grass, according to the essay, is intended "to articulate . . . uncompromisingly my own physical, emotional, moral, intellectual, and aesthetic Personality, in the midst of, and tallying, the momentous spirit and facts of . . . current America—and to exploit that Personality, identified with place and date, in a far more candid and comprehensive sense than any hitherto poem or book." Whitman abandons conventional themes, ornaments, euphemism, and rhyme so as "to conform with and build on the concrete realities of the universe furnish'd by science," and to root himself "in the emotional and imaginative action of the modern times." His purpose is to write "poems of realities and science and of the democratic average and basic equality," but he points out his literary influences, which might have come to naught had not the Civil War given a final reason for "an authochthonic and passionate song."

BACON, DELIA SALTER (1811–59), was among the first to propound the theory that Shakespeare's plays were written by a group headed by Bacon and including Raleigh and Spenser, and that a great system of thought was concealed in them by ciphers. Emerson and Carlyle encouraged her for a time, and Hawthorne, who describes her in *Our Old Home,* wrote a preface for her *Philosophy of the Plays of Shakspere Unfolded* (1857). She also wrote such fiction as *Tales of the Puritans* (1831) and *The Bride of Fort Edward* (1839), a closet drama on the Revolution. She was violently insane during her last two years.

BACON, LEONARD (1887–1954), poet, whose collection of lyrics, *Sunderland Capture* (1940), was awarded a Pulitzer Prize. *Day of Fire* (1943) is a book of wartime lyrics. His earlier volumes, often satirical, include *Ulug Beg* (1923), *Ph.D.'s* (1925), *The Legend of Quincibald* (1928), *Rhyme and Punishment* (1936), and *Bullinger Bound* (1938). He was professor of English (1910–23) at the University of California. *Semi-Centennial* (1939) is an autobiography.

BACON, NATHANIEL, see *Bacon's Rebellion.*

BACON, PEGGY [MARGARET FRANCES] (1895–1987), artist and poet whose satires and caricatures appear in *Off with Their Heads* (1934), *Cat-Calls* (1935), and *Starting from Scratch* (1945). *The Inward Eye* (1952) is a mystery novel.

Bacon's Rebellion was led by Nathaniel Bacon (1647–76), a Virginia planter who caused the people to take up arms (1676), ostensibly against the Indians, but actually to curb the dictatorial policy of Sir William Berkeley.♦ Berkeley made some concessions but did not keep faith with the insurgents, and the rebellion ended for want of a leader at Bacon's sudden death by fever. An epitaph is in the Burwell Papers,♦ and Bacon figures in W.A. Caruthers's *The Cavaliers of Virginia,* Mary Johnston's *Prisoners of Hope,* and other romances, and in a poem by Ebenezer Cook.

BAGBY, GEORGE WILLIAM (1828–83), Virginia journalist, lecturer, and author of humorous local-color sketches. He edited the *Southern Literary Messenger* (1860–64), but is best remembered for his sketches of antebellum Virginia, with their sentimental picture of a past era, enlivened by a realistic homely humor. "The Old Virginia Gentleman" (1877) and "Jud Browning's Account of Rubenstein's Playing" are among his best sketches. T.N. Page published a selected edition (1910).

BAILEY, JAMES MONTGOMERY (1841–94), Civil War journalist known as the "Danbury News Man," since his humorous articles appeared in his newspaper published at Danbury, Conn. He is often considered the father of the humorous newspaper column, and his witty comments on current events were collected in several popular books.

BAILYN, BERNARD (1922–), born in Connecticut, after an A.B. from Williams College and higher degrees from Harvard has been on its faculty since 1953 and has held distinguished appointments in more recent years. His numerous books in his field of history include *New England Merchants in the 17th Century* (1955); *The Ideological Origins of the American Revolution* (1967), awarded a Pulitzer Prize; and *Voyagers to the West: A Passage in the Peopling of America on the Eve of the Revolution* (1986), also awarded a Pulitzer Prize.

BAKER, BENJAMIN A. (1818–90), New York playwright whose melodrama *A Glance at New York* (1848) created a new theatrical genre by its realistic portrayal of Mose, the volunteer fireman and type of the Bowery boy. He wrote several similar plays.

BAKER, DOROTHY (1907–68), Montana-born novelist, attended Whittier College, and graduated from the University of California, Los Angeles. Her novels are *Young Man with a Horn* (1938), inspired by the music of Bix Beiderbecke; *Trio* (1943), dramatized (1944) with her husband Howard Baker, novelist and poet; *Our Gifted Son* (1948); and *Cassandra at the Wedding* (1962), a psychological study of two sisters and their family.

BAKER, GEORGE PIERCE (1866–1935), was instrumental in encouraging and inspiring many little theaters, stage designers, directors, and dramatists. His 47 Workshop at Harvard (1905–25) served as a laboratory for the staging of plays by such students as Edward Sheldon, Eugene O'Neill, Philip Barry, John Dos Passos, S.N. Behrman, Sidney Howard, and Thomas Wolfe. After 1925 he continued his work at Yale. Baker is the prototype of Professor Hatcher in Wolfe's *Of Time and the River.*

BAKER, LEONARD [STANLEY] (1931–84), Pittsburgh-born journalist and author of biographical and historical studies including *The Johnson Eclipse* (1966), *Roosevelt and Pearl Harbor* (1970), *John Marshall: A Life in Law* (1974), *Days of Sorrow and Pain: Leo Baeck and the Berlin Jews* (1978, Pulitzer Prize), and *Brandeis and Frankfurter: A Dual Biography* (1984).

BAKER, RAY STANNARD (1870–1946), a leading contributor to *McClure's Magazine* during its muckraking period, became an intimate of President Wilson and was director of the press at the Versailles Conference. His books include *Woodrow Wilson and World Settlement* (3 vols., 1922); with W.E. Dodd, an edition of the President's public papers (6 vols., 1925–26); and *Woodrow Wilson: Life and Letters* (8 vols., 1927–39), the last two volumes of which were awarded a Pulitzer Prize. Under the pseudonym David Grayson, he wrote seven volumes of familiar essays, the best known being *Adventures in Contentment* (1907). *Native American* (1941) and *American Chronicle* (1945) are his autobiography to the time of Wilson's death.

BAKER, RUSSELL [WAYNE] (1925–   ), born in countryside Virginia, after graduation from Johns Hopkins (1947) became a journalistic writer, moving on in 1962 to a position as an amusing editorial columnist for *The New York Times*. His witty and observant columns on government and all aspects of U.S. life have been gathered in numerous books including *American in Washington* (1961), *No Cause for Panic* (1964), *All Things Considered* (1965), *Our Next President* (1968), and *Poor Russell's Almanac* (1972). *Growing Up* (1982), an autobiography of youthful years, was awarded a Pulitzer Prize for biography, a grant previously made to him in the more general field of distinguished commentary. *The Good Times* (1989), again autobiographical, describes a more mature period.

BAKER, WILLIAM MUMFORD (1825–83), Presbyterian minister in Texas, Ohio, and Massachusetts, who was best known for his novel *Inside: A Chronicle of Secession* (1866), published under the pseudonym George F. Harrington and actually an autobiographical account of his life in the South during the Civil War. His other books include *The New Timothy* (1870), *Carter Quarterman* (1876), *The Virginians in Texas* (1878), *A Year Worth Living* (1878), and *His Majesty: Myself* (1880).

Balance, The, and New York Journal, see *Hudson Balance.*

BALDWIN, FAITH (1893–1978), popular author of more than 75 books, mainly romantic and light fiction for women, some inspirational poems, and a few books for children. Her first novel, *Mavis of Green Hill* (1921), was followed by many others, including *Office Wife* (1930), *White Collar Girl* (1933), *Men Are Such Fools!* (1936), *Temporary Address: Reno* (1941), *He Married a Doctor* (1943), and *The Lonely Man* (1964). *Testament of Trust* (1960) is an autobiography.

BALDWIN, JAMES (1924–87), born in Harlem, where for a short time in his youth he followed his father's footsteps as a preacher, and, as he says, "the rhetoric of the storefront church" has been among the influences on his prose. He left home at the age of 17 and subsequent travels included long expatriation in France. His first novel, *Go Tell It on the Mountain*♦ (1953), about a day in the lives of various members of a Harlem church and, through flashbacks, about their forebears, was immediately hailed as a major treatment of black life in the U.S. and helped to establish Baldwin as the leading black novelist since Richard Wright. His second novel, *Giovanni's Room* (1956), was set in his new residence of Paris and concerned a

man torn between homosexual love and love of a woman. His third novel, *Another Country*♦ (1962), is a lengthy tale of complex human relations between races and sexes. His next novel, *Tell Me How Long the Train's Been Gone* (1968), about a black actor recalling his youth in Harlem and his dramatic career, is by implication an assessment of the situation of American blacks. *If Beale Street Could Talk* (1974) is a novel about a pregnant young woman's struggle to free her falsely imprisoned fiancé. *Just Above My Head* (1979), Baldwin's sixth novel, retrospectively treats the life of a Harlem gospel singer as he and his family search for their identities and for salvation. Baldwin's nonfiction includes *Notes of a Native Son* (1955), containing personal essays, reminiscences of Harlem life, his harsh view of Richard Wright, and consideration of the situation of Northern black intellectuals; *Nobody Knows My Name*♦ (1961), intense personal essays on race relations, the relation of the artist to society, and his views of other authors; *The Fire Next Time* (1963), two "letters" vigorously describing the state of the black in the U.S. through his own youthful experiences and his encounter with the Black Muslim movement; *No Name in the Street* (1972), autobiographical fragments and an assessment of race relations in the U.S.; and *The Devil Finds Work* (1976), an essay about blacks and American films. He also wrote plays, including *Blues for Mister Charley* (1964), about the antagonism between the Negro and the white man (generically called "Mr. Charley"), which depicts a black boy who has become a successful singer in New York but also a drug addict and who, upon returning to his Southern home to start life anew, is murdered by a white man; *The Amen Corner* (1964) is concerned with a woman evangelist torn between religious fanaticism and love of her footloose, jazz-playing husband. *Going To Meet the Man* (1965) is a collection of short stories.

BALDWIN, JOSEPH GLOVER (1815–64), jurist of the Old Southwest, lived in Alabama and Mississippi during the 1830s and '40s, when speculation was rampant, politics turbulent, and law undefined. Later he settled in California, but his earlier surroundings are described in *The Flush Times of Alabama and Mississippi*♦ (1853), a volume of sketches composed at leisure moments. He also wrote *Party Leaders* (1855), serious studies of Jefferson, Hamilton, Jackson, Clay, and Randolph.

BALESTIER, [CHARLES] WOLCOTT (1861–91), author of several novels and short stories, is best known for his collaboration with his brother-in-law Kipling on *The Naulahka* (1892), a novel about a California speculator in India, to which Balestier contributed the American chapters. A brief residence in Colorado (1885) led to his writing *Benefits Forgot* (1892), a novel of the Rocky Mountain mining camps.

Ballad, narrative poem of communal origin, transmitted by a process of oral tradition among people usually free from literary influences. Folk ballads frequently deal with common people, are presented with simplicity, have little description, and depend mainly on dialogue and incremental repetition, i.e. structural repetitions of a preceding stanza with some variation to advance the story. Metrically, the ballad is usually composed of long seven-stress lines, conventionally printed as two lines of four and three stresses each, rhyming *abcb*. Among the classifications of American folk ballads are those dealing with occupations ("Casey Jones" of the railroad workers, "Git Along, Little Dogies" of the cowboys, and "The Jam on Gerry's Rock" of the lumberjacks), with regions ("The Roving Gambler" of the Kentucky and Tennessee mountains, "The Buffalo Skinners" of the Western plains, and the "The Erie Canal Ballad"), with wars ("Yankee Doodle" of the Revolution, and "The Battle of Shiloh Hill" of the Civil War), with racial groups ("John Henry" of the blacks), and with desperadoes ("Sam Bass" and "Billy the Kid"). Many of the ballads are of English origin, some of these surviving almost intact in the Southern mountains. Variations of the most popular ballads constitute cycles or groups, for example, those concerned with Jesse James,♦ Frankie and Johnny,♦ John Henry,♦ Casey Jones,♦ and Yankee Doodle.♦ The many collections of American folk ballads include Louise Pound's *American Ballads and Songs* (1922), Sandburg's *The American Songbag* (1927), Lomax's *American Ballads and Folk Songs* (1934), and Hudson's *Folksongs of Mississippi* (1936). Among literary adaptations of the ballad form are Longfellow's "Wreck of the Hesperus," Hay's *Pike County Ballads,* Whittier's "Skipper Ireson's Ride," Harte's "Plain Language from Truthful James," and Lindsay's "The Chinese Nightingale."

Ballad of the Sad Café, *The,* novella by Carson McCullers,♦ title piece of a book published in 1951. It was dramatized by Edward Albee in 1963.

In a small Georgia town the hardest working and best business person is Miss Amelia Evans, at 30 a tall, strong woman, able to outfight any man, and the owner of a store and a still that produces the best whiskey in the area. She had been married, for ten days only, to Marvin Macy, the town's toughest criminal, who doted on her. When she refused to sleep with him and threw him out of her house he went on a rampage of crime that led to his imprisonment. While he was in prison Miss Amelia was attracted by a distant relative, Cousin Lymon Willis, a dwarfish hunchback, whom she befriended and under whose spell she opened her store at night as the town's café. But after Marvin Macy is released and returns to the town, Cousin Lymon becomes fascinated by him, and it is clear that Miss Amelia will have to fight physically with her onetime husband for

leadership and for Lymon too. Soon a wrestling match does occur. Amelia is about to win when Lymon jumps on her back and she is downed in defeat. Marvin and Lymon vandalize the store, destroy the still, and leave town, also leaving Miss Amelia a physically and psychologically broken woman, huddling in her closed café.

Balloon Hoax, *The,* story by Poe,♦ published in the New York *Sun* (April 13, 1844) in the guise of an actual article of news. According to the author, the "*jeu d'esprit . . .* subserved the purpose of creating indigestible aliment for the *quidnuncs* during the few hours intervening between a couple of the Charleston mails." It is an account of a fictitious crossing of the Atlantic in 75 hours (April 6–9) by eight men in "Mr. Monck Mason's Flying Machine . . . the Steering Balloon 'Victoria.'" The balloon, inflated with coal gas, is supposed to have started from a place in north Wales, headed out over the ocean, and then been caught in a powerful gale that lasted two days, driving the craft at great speed until it was landed on Sullivan's Island, S.C.

BALLOU, ADIN (1803–90), founder of the Hopedale Community,♦ was originally a believer in Universalism, but withdrew to expound the doctrine of Restorationism, that all men will be ultimately restored to happiness in the future life. He published a magazine, the *Independent Messenger* (1831–39), and wrote such books as *Practical Christian Socialism* (1854) and *Primitive Christianity and Its Corruptions* (1870).

BALLOU, HOSEA (1771–1852), Boston clergyman, was the foremost exponent of Universalism. His works include *Notes on the Parables* (1804), *A Treatise on Atonement* (1805), and *A Series of Letters in Defense of Divine Revelation* (1816), a correspondence with Abner Kneeland. In addition to editing collections, he composed almost 200 hymns. He was remotely related to Adin Ballou.

BALLOU, MATURIN MURRAY (1820–95), son of Hosea Ballou, was a Boston publisher, editor, and author noted for his production of popular literature for the masses. His journals included *Flag of Our Union, Gleason's Pictorial Drawing Room Companion, Ballou's Dollar Monthly,* and the *Boston Globe.* He was the first American editor to demand a set form of construction and type of plot, and as such was the forerunner of the dime-novel publishers. In addition to many volumes of sensational fiction, most of them issued under the pseudonym Lieutenant Murray, he wrote several travel books.

Baltimore, largest city in Maryland, situated on the Patapsco River near Chesapeake Bay. The present city, founded in 1729, soon became an important shipping point for agricultural products, and later served as a port for privateers and clipper ships. The Continental Congress met for a time in Baltimore (1776), and Fort McHenry is famous for its role in the composition of "The Star-Spangled Banner." A great fire partially destroyed the city (1904), which since its reconstruction has been a leading industrial center. Educational institutions include Johns Hopkins University, Peabody Institute, and the University of Baltimore. Among Baltimore authors have been Lanier, Tabb, Lizette W. Reese, F.H. Smith, H.L. Mencken, Karl Shapiro, and D.L. Coburn.

BALTIMORE, LORD, see *Calvert, George.*

Baltimore *Sun* (1837–   ), nonpartisan penny daily, which, during the Mexican War, attracted wide attention by publishing news of the capture of Veracruz before the War Department issued the information. Its allegiance, like that of Maryland, was divided during the Civil War, since the paper favored the South but opposed secession. It was active at the end of the century in fighting the local Democratic machine. In 1910 began the publication of a separate edition, *The Evening Sun,* and during 1918–19 an overseas edition was issued for troops in France. H.L. Mencken was on the staff of the *Sun* (1906–16, 1918–41). Between 1931 and 1949 the paper or staff members won eight Pulitzer Prizes. The paper was bought by the Times Mirror Company of Los Angeles and is being technologically advanced through computerization.

BAMBARA, TONI CADE (1939–   ), in addition to dealing with civil rights and teaching African-American studies in American universities, is known for her books *Gorilla, My Love* (1970) and *The Sea Birds Are Still Alive* (1977), short stories about black people in both the North and the South. Her first novel, *The Salt Eaters* (1980), features two black women of Georgia.

BANCROFT, GEORGE (1800–1891), Massachusetts statesman and scholar, while holding various government posts obtained material for his monumental *History of the United States* (1834–76). As secretary of navy under Polk, he was instrumental in establishing Annapolis as the U.S. Naval Academy, and as secretary of war *pro tem* (May 1845) he sent General Taylor across the Texas border, precipitating war with Mexico. His standing order to Sloat to occupy California ports in case of war led to the early occupation of that territory. Bancroft was minister to Great Britain (1846–49) and minister to Germany (1867–74). His ten-volume *History* was revised in 1876 to six volumes. A final revision (6 vols., 1883–85) includes the *History of the Formation of the Constitution* (1882). Although the work is now outmoded, it is still important as an example of the aggressive yet spiritual nationalism of Ameri-

ca's mid-19th century. Some of Bancroft's many orations and essays are collected in *Literary and Historical Miscellanies* (1855).

BANCROFT, HUBERT HOWE (1832–1918), born in Ohio, came to California (1852) to be a miner and bookseller. In San Francisco he later founded the West's leading bookstore and publishing firm. In 1859 he began to collect a great library of regional source materials, now known as The Bancroft Library. ♦ On this collection he based his history of the *Native Races* (5 vols., 1874–75), *History of the Pacific States* (34 vols., 1882–90), *Chronicles of the Builders* (7 vols., 1891–92), and other works which establish him as the first great historian of the West Coast. Although all the books bear Bancroft's name alone, he depended upon assistants whose work included the preparation of drafts, some of which he altered only slightly in making the final texts. His books for general readers include *California Pastoral* (1888) and *California Inter Pocula* (1888), respectively on the Spanish and gold-rush eras, and the autobiographical works *Literary Industries* (1890) and *Retrospection, Political and Personal* (1910).

Bancroft Library, THE, formed by Hubert Howe Bancroft, ♦ sold by him to the University of California, Berkeley (1905), which continues to concentrate on his collecting fields: the western part of North America, emphasizing California, and Mexico and Central America. In 1969 it became the major library of rare materials of all sorts on the campus, including the manuscripts and other papers of Mark Twain, the basis of a major publishing program.

Band of Angels, novel by R. P. Warren, ♦ published in 1955.

Amantha Starr tells the story of her life, beginning in the 1850s as the pampered daughter of a Kentucky plantation owner educated in Ohio until upon her father's death she learns that her mother was a slave. To defray her father's debts, as a 16-year-old girl she is sold to Hamish Bond, an old man in New Orleans, who first makes her his mistress, then frees her. During the Civil War, when Union troops occupy New Orleans, Amantha meets and is married to Captain Tobias Sears, a proper New Englander who commands black soldiers, the most heroic of whom is Lieutenant Oliver Cromwell Jones, once known as Rau-Ru on Hamish's plantation. After the war, while separated from Sears, Amantha takes up with Rau-Ru/Jones, who causes the hanging of Hamish. Reunited, Amantha and Tobias in their middle age during the 1880s drift to Missouri and Kansas, living uneasily as he pursues his career as an idealistic lawyer opposed to the Gilded Age standards. Finally both achieve security with some money but, more important, through an understanding of their own identities.

BANDELIER, ADOLPH FRANCIS ALPHONSE (1840–1914), pioneer American archaeologist, was born in Switzerland and brought to the U.S. in 1848. He published many works concerned with his research among the remains of ancient man in Mexico, New Mexico, Peru, and Bolivia, and these are important sources for modern investigators. He is more widely known for his popular books, *The Delight Makers* (1890), a story of the prehistoric Pueblo Indians of New Mexico and their betrayal to the Navajo by their ruling class, the Delight Makers; and *The Gilded Man* (1893), concerned with the El Dorado legend.

BANGS, JOHN KENDRICK (1862–1922), lecturer, editor of *Puck* (1904–5) and other humorous magazines, whose writings were of great variety. He is best known for collections of extravagantly farcical tales, *Tiddledywink Tales* (1891), *The Idiot* (1895), *Mr. Bonaparte of Corsica* (1895), and *A Houseboat on the Styx* (1896). In the last he gathers together such diverse characters as Shakespeare, Delilah, Lucrezia Borgia, and Artemus Ward and lets his mind play freely with the absurd situations that ensue. It is illustrated by Peter Newell, of whom he wrote a biographical sketch. *The Pursuit of the Houseboat* (1897) is a sequel. With F. D. Sherman he wrote *New Waggings of Old Tales* (1888).

BANKS, RUSSELL (1940–), born in Newton, Mass., educated at Colgate and at the University of North Carolina, is a novelist who first had a career as publisher and editor of Lillabulero Press 1966–1975. He published a novel and a book of short stories before achieving national recognition with *Continental Drift* (1986). This novel moves between two protagonists: Bob Dubois, a New Hampshire oil-burner repairman who, restless and dissatisfied with his life, moves his family to Florida where he tries to manage his brother's liquor store; and Vanise Dorsinville, a Haitian woman with an infant son who becomes a boat person to emigrate to the U.S. The stories interlock and drift to a fatal intersection. *Affliction* (1989), set in working-class New Hampshire, is about friendship, rivalry, and murder. In *The Sweet Hereafter* (1991), again set in New Hampshire, a woman schoolbus driver is ostracized by the entire community after a bad accident for which she is blamed. *Trailerpark* (1981) and *Success Stories* (1986) are short fiction.

BANNEKER, BENJAMIN (1731–1806), freeborn black of Maryland, whose calculations of astronomical tables were published annually (1791–97) in his *Almanack and Ephemeris*. He served on a commission to survey and design the District of Columbia, being probably the first black to hold a civilian post in the federal government.

BANNING, MARGARET CULKIN (1891–1982), Minnesota author, graduate of Vassar College (1912), whose novels concerning contemporary problems of love, marriage, and parenthood include *This Marrying* (1920), *Country Club People* (1923), *The Women of the Family* (1926), *Mixed Marriage* (1930), *Too Young To Marry* (1938), *Clever Sister* (1947), *The Dowry* (1955), *Echo Answers* (1959), *The Vine and the Olive* (1964), *Mesabi* (1969), *Lifeboat Number Two* (1971), *The Splendid Torments* (1976), and *Such Interesting People* (1979). Other books include *Women for Defense* (1942), appraising the role of women in both world wars, and *Letters from England, Summer 1942* (1943).

BANNISTER, NATHANIEL HARRINGTON (1813–47), prolific Southern dramatist whose works are mostly historical melodramas. His most successful play was *Putnam* (1844), about the Revolutionary War. *England's Iron Days* (1837) is typical of his other work, being set in a period "when Normans and Saxons were at odds with each other and certainly with history," as Arthur Hobson Quinn said.

Baptists, followers of the religious doctrine that baptism should be administered only to believers. The modern Baptist movement originated in England (1608), but soon divided into two groups: the General Baptists, who hold to the Arminian belief that Christ's atonement is not limited to the elect; and the Particular Baptists, who follow Calvinistic doctrine in contending that atonement is individual. The first Baptists in America, of the Particular belief, established a church in Rhode Island (1639) under the leadership of Roger Williams, although Williams soon withdrew. The next group, in the same colony, was led by John Clarke and Anne Hutchinson. Because of their opposition to child baptism, the Baptists were persecuted in New England, although they flourished in Pennsylvania and throughout the South. The strict Calvinistic belief of the Particular Baptists in the South has led to their being called Hard Shell Baptists. There have been various schisms, occasioned by such events as the Great Awakening and the Civil War, but the Baptists have grown in number, so that in 1990 there were over 28,000,000 members in 12 different churches. The Baptists are distinguished for founding such educational institutions as Colgate and Brown, and for such missionary work as that of Adoniram Judson.

BARAKA, IMAMU AMIRI, see *Jones, LeRoi.*

Barbara Frietchie, poem by Whittier♦ in four-stress couplets, published in *In War Time and Other Poems* (1864). It relates a supposedly historic incident of Stonewall Jackson's entry into Frederick, Md. The 90-year-old heroine raises the Stars and Stripes:

> Shoot if you must, this old gray head,
> But spare your country's flag, she said.

Her courage impresses the general, who orders his troops to march on. Barbara Frietchie is the subject of a play (1899) by Clyde Fitch,♦ who makes her a youthful heroine. The name is also spelled Fritchie.

Barbary Wars, see *Tripolitan War.*

Barefoot Boy, The, poem in tetrameter couplets by Whittier,♦ collected in *The Panorama* (1856). It recounts the adventures of rural boyhood, with a nostalgic sense of their innocent sensuous enjoyments.

BARKER, JAMES NELSON (1784–1858), Philadelphia dramatist, five of whose ten plays survive in print. His contemporary prominence was due to his concern with American subjects. *Tears and Smiles* (1807) is a comedy of manners, evidently suggested by *The Contrast*♦; *The Indian Princess; or, La Belle Sauvage*♦ (1808) deals with Pocahontas; and *Superstition*♦ (1824), considered his best play, deals with the regicide Goffe in early New England. His adaptations included one of Scott's *Marmion* (1812), and *How to Try a Lover*♦ (1817), a stage version of a French picaresque novel.

BARLOW, JOEL (1754–1812), one of the Connecticut Wits,♦ graduated from Yale (1778), taught school, managed a business, preached, entered military service, was admitted to the bar (1786), contributed to *The Anarchiad,*♦ and wrote a new version of the Psalms, all of which occupations were incidental to his lifelong ambition to write the great American epic. This work, *The Vision of Columbus* (1787), was finally revised as *The Columbiad*♦ (1807), which he considered his masterpiece. He went to Europe (1788) and during 17 years of residence abroad changed from a conservative Connecticut Puritan to a cosmopolitan Democrat. As a reward for *A Letter to the National Convention of France* (1792) he was made a French citizen. Inspired by his friend Paine, he next wrote his *Advice to the Privileged Orders* (1792), in which he sets forth the thesis that the state is the responsible agent of all society rather than of any one class, and that its duty is to safeguard the social heritage as a common asset held in trust for future generations. It was during this residence in France that Barlow wrote his charming little poem *Hasty Pudding*♦ (1796), for which he is best remembered. In 1795 he was appointed consul to Algiers, where he effected important treaties. Upon his return to the U.S. (1805) he published a *Prospectus of a National Institution to be Established in the United States* for research and instruction in the arts and sciences. He lived the quiet life of a scholar for six years, and in 1811 was appointed minister to France. He died near Cracow, Poland, on his way to meet Napoleon, with whom he hoped to consummate a treaty.

BARNARD, GEORGE GREY (1863–1938), Chicago sculptor, studied in France, where he achieved fame for his *Two Natures* (1894), an allegory of dual personality. Among his works are the colossal *Hewer* in Cairo, Ill.; the two large groups of nude figures symbolizing *The Burden of Life* and *Brotherly Love and Work,* which flank the entrance of the Pennsylvania state capitol; the gaunt, homespun *Lincoln* in Cincinnati; and an unfinished memorial arch to World War I soldiers. Although he had a tendency to moralize in stone, this did not destroy the courage and vigor with which he endowed his work. His collection of medieval sculpture and architectural material was purchased by John D. Rockefeller, Jr. (1925) and presented to the Metropolitan Museum of Art. It forms the nucleus of The Cloisters, a museum of medieval art at New York.

BARNES, CHARLOTTE MARY SANFORD (1818–63), author of romantic melodramas, including *The Forest Princess* (1848), concerned with the adventures of Pocahontas in America and England, and *Octavia Bragaldi* (1837, published 1848), a blank-verse setting of the Kentucky Tragedy.♦ In the latter, events are transferred to 15th-century Milan, where Ann Cook becomes Octavia, Beauchamp becomes Bragaldi, and Sharp becomes Castelli.

BARNES, DJUNA (1892–1982), New York-born author long resident in Europe. Her first major work was *A Book* (1923) of short plays, stories, and poems, introspective analyses of people whose temperamental sympathies lie with the simple lives of animals. It was reissued with three new stories as *A Night Among the Horses* (1929), and the stories were somewhat refashioned as *Spillway* in her *Selected Works* (1962). *Ryder* (1928) is a satirical novel in the stream-of-consciousness style, concerned with a man's relations with his mother, his wife, and his mistresses. *Nightwood* (1936), a novel of the relationships of five psychopathic people, has been described by T.S. Eliot as having "a quality of horror and doom very nearly related to that of Elizabethan tragedy." *The Antiphon* (1958) is a blank-verse play. Other publications are *The Book of Repulsive Women* (1948), poems and drawings created in 1915, and *Vagaries Malicieux* (1975), two essays based on life in Paris of the 1920s but described as stories. *Smoke and Other Early Stories* (1982) collects juvenilia. *Interviews* (1985) gathers her journalistic talks with and drawings of persons as various as Joyce and Jack Dempsey. *New York* (1989) collects from newspapers her impressions between 1913 and 1919 of Coney Island and other local areas.

BARNES, HARRY ELMER (1889–1968), historian, historiographer, and sociologist, associated at various times with Columbia, The New School for Social Research, and Smith College. His books include *The Social History of the Western World* (1921), *The New History and the Social Studies* (1925), *The Genesis of the World War* (1926),

The Twilight of Christianity (1929), *The History of Sociological Thought* (1936), *Society in Transition* (1939), *Social Institutions in an Era of World Upheaval* (1942), *Historical Sociology* (1947), and *Perpetual War for Perpetual Peace* (1953).

BARNES, MARGARET AYER (1886–1967), novelist and playwright, whose fiction includes *Years of Grace* (1930, Pulitzer Prize), the story of a Chicago matron of the era of respectability who lives on into the jazz age; *Wisdom's Gate* (1938), a sequel; *Within This Present* (1933), about a Chicago family from the Civil War to the present; and *Edna, His Wife* (1935), dramatized by Cornelia Otis Skinner. Plays include an adaptation of *The Age of Innocence* (1928), and *Jenny* (1929) and *Dishonored Lady* (1930), both with Edward Sheldon. She is a sister of Janet Ayer Fairbank.

BARNUM, P[HINEAS] T[AYLOR] (1810–91), Connecticut-born impresario, began his career (1835) by exhibiting an aged black woman fraudulently claimed to have been George Washington's childhood nurse. His career as a New York City showman he continued in his American Museum (founded 1842), which combined sideshows, stage entertainment, and exhibition of curios. It attracted crowds by extravagant publicity and advertising, in which he originated methods that became characteristic of American show business. His international reputation began with his first European tour (1844) with his dwarf, "General Tom Thumb," and was extended when he brought to the U.S. foreign stars, such as the "Swedish nightingale" Jenny Lind, whose tour he managed in 1850–52. In 1871 he organized his circus, advertised as "the greatest show on earth," which dominated that type of entertainment, especially after his merger (1881) with his chief competitor, James A. Bailey. Barnum's books include his *Life* (1855, frequently revised) and *The Humbugs of the World* (1865).

BARR, AMELIA EDITH [HUDDLESTON] (1831–1919), English-born novelist, came to the U.S. with her husband in 1853, lived in Texas after the period of the Lone Star Republic, and went to New York in 1868 to write for the newspapers of Henry Ward Beecher and begin her career as an author of popular historical fiction. Among her numerous novels are *Romance and Reality* (1872), *Jan Vedder's Wife* (1885), *The Bow of Orange Ribbon* (1886), *Remember the Alamo* (1888), *The Belle of Bowling Green* (1904), and *The Paper Cap* (1918). *All the Days of My Life* (1913) is an autobiography.

BARR, STRINGFELLOW (1897–1982), born in Virginia, graduated from the University of Virginia, and after further study as a Rhodes Scholar became a professor of history there (1924–37). He was president of St. John's College (1937–46) and a professor of humanities at Newark College,

Rutgers (1955–64). His books include *Mazzini: Portrait of an Exile* (1935); *Pilgrimage of Western Man* (1949); *Let's Join the Human Race* (1950), extended as *Citizens of the World* (1952), proposing an international program of aid to underprivileged countries; *Purely Academic* (1958), a novel about university administration and faculty; *The Will of Zeus* (1961), on Greek culture from prehistoric times to Alexander's death; and *Voices That Endured* (1971), on great books of Western civilization.

Barren Ground, novel by Ellen Glasgow,◆ published in 1925.

Dorinda Oakley, daughter of a land-poor farmer in Virginia, at 20 goes to work in Nathan Pedlar's store. She falls in love with Jason Greylock, weak-willed son of the village doctor, and forgets her purpose of helping her father to rebuild the farm, but the day before their planned wedding Jason is forced to marry a former fiancée. Bitterly disillusioned, Dorinda seeks work in New York, where she is injured in a street accident. She is attended by Dr. Faraday, who later employs her as a nurse for his children. A young doctor proposes to her, but she refuses him, determined to "find something else in life." At her father's death, Dorinda returns to the family farm, which is impoverished and overgrown with broomsedge. Having studied scientific agriculture, she introduces progressive methods, gradually returning the "barren ground" to fertility and creating a prosperous dairy farm. Her mother becomes an invalid, and her brother Rufus is lazy and selfish, so that Dorinda must carry on unaided. After her mother's death she marries Nathan Pedlar, to provide a home for his children, and after he dies she shelters Jason, now penniless and ill from excessive drinking. He soon dies, and to the suggestion that she might marry again, Dorinda replies with an ironic smile, "Oh, I've finished with all that . . . I am thankful to have finished with all that."

Barriers Burned Away, novel by E.P. Roe,◆ published in 1872. This popular moral tale is concerned with the love of a poor but well-educated young man, Dennis Fleet, for his employer's daughter Christine Ludolph, which she does not return until his heroism and rescue of her in the disastrous Chicago fire convert her indifference to piety and affection.

BARRY, PHILIP (1896–1949), born in Rochester, N.Y., graduated from Yale (1919), and studied in the 47 Workshop of G.P. Baker at Harvard, where he wrote *You and I* (1923), in which a father, trying to guide his son into an artistic career, reveals his own thwarted ambition. Following *The Youngest* (1924), a satirical play concerning the revolt of a youngest son from the bourgeois standards of his family, and *In a Garden* (1925), a sophisticated comedy, he wrote *White*

Wings♦ (1926), an ironic fantasy. His next play, *John* (1927), based on the life of John the Baptist, was unsuccessful, but *Paris Bound* (1927) was a popular comedy concerned with contemporary moral standards. After collaborating with Elmer Rice in writing a fanciful mystery play, *Cock Robin* (1928), Barry returned to his earlier theme of a child's revolt against the standards of her parents in *Holiday*♦ (1928). *Hotel Universe* (1930) was a mystical play, and he further showed his interest in psychological investigation in *Tomorrow and Tomorrow* (1931) and in *The Animal Kingdom*♦ (1932), plays concerned with modern marital relations. After two unsuccessful plays, *The Joyous Season* (1934) and *Bright Star* (1935), and *Spring Dance* (1936), an adaptation, he wrote *Here Come the Clowns* (1938), also published as a novel, *War in Heaven* (1938), in which an "illusionist's" hypnotic powers reveal the inner tragedies of a group of vaudeville actors. *The Philadelphia Story* (1939) is a drawing-room comedy about a young heiress and an author; *Liberty Jones* (1941) is an allegory of the threats to democracy in the modern world; *Without Love* (1942) is a comedy of platonic marriage; and *Second Threshold* (1951) is a play left in manuscript and revised by Robert Sherwood.

BARRYMORE, family of American actors, which has included Maurice (1847–1905); his wife, Georgiana Drew (1856–93), a daughter of John Drew; their children, Lionel (1878–1954), John (1882–1942), and Ethel (1879–1959). Kaufman and Ferber's *The Royal Family* satirizes the Barrymores.

BARTH, JOHN [SIMMONS] (1930–   ), Maryland-born novelist, educated at Johns Hopkins, whose fiction set on the Eastern Shore of his native state includes *The Floating Opera* (1956), the experiences of a man recalled on the day in 1937 when he debates suicide, and *The End of the Road* (1958), another existential and nihilistic view of experience set in a travestied conventional love triangle. Although placed in the same setting, his third novel, *The Sot-Weed Factor*♦ (1960), is more fantastic and funnier in its lusty parody of an 18th-century picaresque tale re-creating the life and times of Ebenezer Cooke. This was followed by *Giles Goat-Boy*♦ (1966), another lengthy, complex, and comic novel full of ingenious parody in its satirical allegory of the modern world conceived in terms of a university campus. *Lost in the Funhouse* (1968) consists of 14 pieces of fiction related in part by their concern with what happens when a writer writes (he makes himself a persona) and a reader reads. *Chimera* (1972) is also a volume of short fiction, retelling in elaborate style tales of Scheherazade, Perseus, and Bellerophon dealing with social and psychological problems of modern life, also introducing the author Barth along the way. The last-named work won a National Book Award. Barth returned to the long novel in *Letters* (1979),

an unusual development of epistolary fiction, in which seven more or less parallel narratives are revealed through correspondence written by seven characters from his earlier fiction, including the author himself as just another imaginary figure, the intricate story comprising an inquiry into the patterns into which the characters have been previously set and the degree of freedom they may possess. *Sabbatical: A Romance* (1982) tells of the adventures and ideas occasioned by a long cruise of a college professor and her husband, an aspiring novelist. *The Friday Book* (1984) collects essays and other nonfiction. *The Tidewater Tales* (1987) is a lengthy novel about a novelist who claims he cannot write a projected novel as he and his wife sail full of friction around Chesapeake Bay. *The Last Voyage of Somebody the Sailor* (1991) probes the connections between memory and reality in a postmodern style of narration.

BARTHELME, DONALD (1931–89), author of stories collected in *Come Back, Dr. Caligari* (1964), *Unspeakable Practices, Unnatural Acts* (1968), *City Life* (1970), *Sadness* (1972), *Guilty Pleasures* (1974), *Amateurs* (1976), *Great Days* (1979), and *Overnight to Many Distant Cities* (1984), all possessed of a fantastic humor marked by a straightforward presentation of absurdly grotesque, illogical, and meaningless matters as if to indicate that their world, and therefore our own, is wholly irrational. The same attitudes and parodic style mark his novels, *Snow White* (1967), an oblique, incongruous version of the fairy tale in episodic form, and *The Dead Father* (1975), telling of 19 children hauling their father, both a living man and a gigantic carcass, across a city to his death. *Paradise* (1986) is a fantasy as a novel, considered somewhat lesser. *Forty Stories* (1987) nicely complements his *Sixty Stories* (1981). *The King* (1990) is a fanciful history of King Arthur at his Round Table transposed to 1940s England and Nazi bombings.

Bartleby the Scrivener: A Story of Wall Street, symbolic tale by Melville♦ published anonymously in *Putnam's Magazine* (1853) and reprinted in *The Piazza Tales* (1856). One view is that it reflects Melville's futility at the neglect of his novels ("Dead Letters") and his uncertainty about how to relate to society.

A Wall Street lawyer hires Bartleby, a curious, wraith-like figure, as a copyist. Bartleby refuses to mingle with the other employees, and, when asked to do anything besides copying documents, invariably says, "I would prefer not to." Some inner dignity or pathos in him prevents his being discharged, even when he ceases to work and uses the office for living quarters. The lawyer moves to another building, and the new tenant has Bartleby arrested. Visited in prison by the lawyer, he is silent and refuses favors. Soon he dies, and the lawyer hears a rumor that Bartleby was formerly a clerk in the Dead Letter Office, whose strange atmosphere affected his attitude toward life to the end.

BARTLETT, JOHN (1820–1905), owner of the University Book Store at Cambridge, a meeting place for Harvard professors and students. "Ask John Bartlett" was the customary saying when anyone sought a book or quotation. His reference book *Familiar Quotations* was first published in 1855.

BARTRAM, JOHN (1699–1777), pioneer American botanist, established the Philadelphia gardens described, along with a sketch of their creator, in Crèvecoeur's *Letters from an American Farmer.* Before and after his appointment as Botanist to the King, Bartram made several journeys, described in his journals, of which the best known is *Observations on the Inhabitants, Climate, Soil, . . . Made by Mr. John Bartram in his travels from Pensilvania to . . . Lake Ontario* (1751).

BARTRAM, WILLIAM (1739–1823), son of John Bartram, was also a botanist and accompanied his father on exploring trips. Although he was a good painter of flora and fauna, and did some important anthropological and ornithological investigation, his fame rests on his *Travels Through North and South Carolina, Georgia, East and West Florida, the Cherokee Country, the Extensive Territories of the Muscogulges, or Creek Confederacy, and the Country of the Chactaws* (1791), a travel book which Coleridge called a work of "high merit." In it the Quaker traveler reveals a philosophic vision of the idea of the "natural" man, and his rich descriptions influenced, among others, Chateaubriand, Coleridge, Wordsworth, and Lafcadio Hearn.

BARZUN, JACQUES (1907–   ), born in France, came to the U.S. (1919), received an A.B. and a Ph.D. from Columbia, where he taught history (1929–67) and was Dean of Faculties and Provost. His learned, gracefully written books include *The French Race* (1932); *Race: A Study in Modern Superstition* (1937); *Romanticism and the Modern Ego* (1943), a defense of romanticism and a view of man's potential nobility, revised and extended as *Classic, Romantic, and Modern* (1961); *Darwin, Marx, Wagner: Critique of a Heritage* (1941); *Teacher in America* (1945), essays on U.S. education; *Berlioz and the Romantic Century* (2 vols., 1950); *God's Country and Mine* (1954), essays; *Energies of Art: Studies of Authors, Classic and Modern* (1956); *Music in American Life* (1956); *The House of Intellect* (1959), an astringent analysis of democratic intellectual life, particularly American; *Science: The Glorious Entertainment* (1964), a humanist's view of the overestimation of science; *The American University* (1968); *The Use and Abuse of Art* (1974); *A Stroll With William James* (1983); *A Word or Two Before You Go—* (1986), essays on fine English usage; and *The Culture We Deserve* (1989).

BASSETT, JOHN SPENCER (1867–1928), founder of the *South Atlantic Quarterly* (1902) and professor of American history at Trinity College (1892–1906) and Smith College (1906–28). His works include *The Writings of Colonel William Byrd* (1901), *The Federalist System* (1906), *Life of Andrew Jackson* (1911), *The Middle Group of American Historians* (1917), and *The Southern Plantation Overseer As Revealed in His Letters* (1925).

BASSO, [JOSEPH] HAMILTON (1904–64), Louisiana-born novelist who was a chronicler of Southern society in moods that ranged from the satirical to the sunny, but that were generally temperate. His novels are *Relics and Angels* (1929); *Cinnamon Seed* (1934); *In Their Own Image* (1935); *Courthouse Square* (1936); *Days Before Lent* (1939); *Wine of the Country* (1941); *Sun in Capricorn* (1942), about a power-mad politician like Huey Long; *The Greenroom* (1949); *The View from Pompey's Head* (1954), about a Southerner, long resident in New York, called back by a legal case to his hometown, whose mores he rediscovers; *Light Infantry Ball* (1959), another view of the same town, this time during the disintegration caused by the Civil War; and *A Touch of the Dragon* (1964), a modern comedy of manners. *Beauregard* (1933) is a biography; *Mainstream* (1943) studies great Americans from Mather to F.D. Roosevelt; and *A Quota of Seaweed* (1960) contains travel sketches.

BATE, WALTER JACKSON (1918–   ), educated at Harvard, where he has been on the faculty of the Department of English since 1946. His books include *The Stylistic Development of Keats* (1945), *The Achievement of Samuel Johnson* (1955), and biographies *John Keats* (1963, Pulitzer Prize), *Coleridge* (1968), and *Samuel Johnson* (1977, Pulitzer Prize and National Book Award).

BATEMAN, SIDNEY FRANCES (1823–81), actress and playwright, whose plays include the social satire *Self♦* (1856), the romantic drama *Geraldine* (1859), and a dramatization of *Evangeline* (1860).

BATES, ARLO (1850–1918), born in Maine, graduated from Bowdoin (1876), was a Boston newspaper editor and later professor of English at the Massachusetts Institute of Technology (1893–1915). His novels include *Mr. Jacobs* (1883); *The Pagans* (1884); *A Wheel of Fire* (1885); *The Philistines* (1889), the story of a painter whose marriage into stultifying Boston society thwarts his art; and *The Puritans* (1898). With his wife, Harriet L. Vose, he wrote *Prince Vance* (1888), and she is the subject of *Sonnets in Shadow* (1887), one of his many books of poetry. He also wrote textbooks; a play, *A Mothers' Meeting* (1909); and stories, *The Intoxicated Ghost* (1908).

BATES, ERNEST SUTHERLAND (1879–1939), professor at the University of Oregon (1915–25) and literary editor of the *Dictionary of American Biography*. His books include *The Friend of Jesus* (1928); *This Land of Liberty* (1930); *Hearst, the Lord of San Simeon* (1936), written with Oliver Carlson; *The Bible Designed To Be Read as Living Literature* (1936); and *American Faith* (1940), interpreting U.S. religion, politics, and economics.

BATES, KATHERINE LEE (1859–1929), Massachusetts author, professor at Wellesley (1885–1925), whose writings include scholarly works, children's books, and poems, of which the most famous is "America the Beautiful"♦ (1893).

"Battle Hymn of the Republic, The," song popular among Union partisans in the Civil War, was written by Julia Ward Howe♦ at the suggestion of J.F. Clarke,♦ when both were visiting McClellan's troops in December 1861. The words, whose chief message Mrs. Howe described as "the sacredness of human liberty," were to be sung to the tune of "John Brown's Body," which is ascribed to William Steffe (*c.*1856). James T. Fields is said to have named the "Battle Hymn," and he was responsible for its publication in the *Atlantic Monthly* (Feb. 1862).

Battle of Bunkers-Hill, The, blank-verse tragedy by H.H. Brackenridge,♦ written in 1776 for production at Somerset Academy, Maryland, of which he was a master. It consists of two conversations, one between Revolutionary leaders and the other between British officers, whose theme is American courage.

Battle of the Kegs, The, Revolutionary War ballad by Francis Hopkinson,♦ was published in 1778, immediately after the Americans under David Bushnell had prepared certain "infernal machines" that were floated down the Delaware River in the form of kegs, intended to destroy British shipping at Philadelphia. The British opened a furious cannonade upon everything floating on the water. Hopkinson describes in rollicking verse the panic into which the British were thrown and their supposed belief that the kegs were filled with armed rebels.

Battle-Pieces and Aspects of the War, poems by Melville,♦ published in 1866. An appendix contains a prose supplement pleading for a humane and charitable Northern attitude toward Reconstruction.

BAUM, L[YMAN] FRANK (1856–1919), journalist, dramatist, and writer of juvenile tales, best known for his fantasies for children about the land of Oz,♦ of which the first was *The Wonderful Wizard of Oz* (1900), the story of a little girl, Dorothy, and her dog Toto whisked away on a cyclone from their drab Kansas home to a land of adventure and achievement inhabited by such creatures as a Cowardly Lion, a Tin Woodman,

an animate Scarecrow, a witch, and the Wizard himself. The success of this book and Baum's musical extravaganza adapted for the stage (1901) led to his 13 sequels, including *Ozma of Oz* (1907), *The Road to Oz* (1909), and *The Lost Princess of Oz* (1917), as well as many additions to the series by other authors after Baum's death. He himself wrote about 60 books, mostly for children, including 18 for girls, written under the pseudonym Edith Van Dyne.

Bay Psalm Book, name generally given to *The Whole Booke of Psalmes Faithfully Translated into English Metre,* the accepted hymnal of the Massachusetts Bay Colony. The translation was made by Richard Mather, John Eliot, and Thomas Weld, with the stated intention of sacrificing elegance to accuracy. It was published at Cambridge (1640) by Stephen Daye,♦ and except for a broadside and a brief almanac was the first work printed in the colonies. John Cotton wrote the Preface.

BAYLOR, FRANCES COURTENAY (1848–1920), Virginia author, whose *Juan and Juanita* (1888) deals with Mexican children captured by Comanches. *Behind the Blue Ridge* (1887), *Claudia Hyde* (1894), and *Miss Nina Barrow* (1897) are adult novels.

Bayou Folk, 23 stories and anecdotes of Louisiana local color by Kate Chopin,♦ published in 1894.

"A No-Account Creole" is the story of selfish, vain Placide Santien, whose faults are redeemed by his giving up his wealthy fiancée the day before their scheduled marriage, when he learns that she loves another man. "Désirée's Baby" tells of a Louisiana aristocrat who marries an orphan girl. Their son shows evidence of black ancestry, and Armand turns Désirée and the child out of his house. She disappears, and some weeks later he discovers an old letter of his mother, revealing that the Negro blood is in his own family. "La Belle Zoraïde" tells of a beautiful quadroon slave who goes mad because she is not allowed to marry the black father of her child. The child is taken from her, and she transfers her affection to a doll, which she refuses to give up even in return for her own infant.

BEACH, JOSEPH WARREN (1880–1957), professor of English at the University of Minnesota and literary critic, whose works include *The Comic Spirit in George Meredith* (1911), *The Method of Henry James* (1918; enlarged and revised, 1954), *The Technique of Thomas Hardy* (1922), *The Twentieth-Century Novel* (1932), *American Fiction 1920–1940* (1941), *A Romantic View of Poetry* (1944), *The Making of the Auden Canon* (1957), and *Obsessive Images: Symbolism in the Poetry of the 1930's and 1940's* (1960). *Beginning with Plato* (1944) and *Involuntary Witness* (1950) are books of poems.

BEACH, REX [ELLINGWOOD] (1877–1949), Michigan novelist, spent several years in the Klondike and wrote a number of novels concerned with the region, including *The Spoilers* (1906), based on a Nome gold-mining case; *The Silver Horde* (1909), a tale of the salmon fisheries; and *The Iron Trail* (1913). He later turned to other backgrounds, such as the Canal Zone, in *The Ne'er-do-well* (1911); New York City, in *The Auction Block* (1914); and Florida, in *Wild Pastures* (1935). *Personal Exposures* (1941) is an autobiography.

BEACH, SYLVIA (1887–1962), bookseller. An expatriate, she kept a bookshop at No. 12 Rue de l'Odéon, Paris, known as Shakespeare & Co. Beach was encouraging and generous to new writers of all nationalities throughout the 1920s. She wrote of this in *Shakespeare & Co.* (1959). She was the first publisher of Joyce's *Ulysses* (1922), using French typesetters.

Beacon Hill, elevation in Boston where a signal was placed (1635) to warn against possible Indian attacks. In 1795 the State House, designed by Bulfinch, was placed on the summit, and since then Beacon Hill has been a noted residential district. Beacon Street, one of the most fashionable streets in Boston, extends along the slope of the hill skirting the Common. James T. Fields and Francis Parkman are among those who lived on the Hill. Fiction treating it includes J.P. Marquand's *The Late George Apley,* Upton Sinclair's *Boston,* and Jean Stafford's *Boston Adventure.*

BEADLE, ERASTUS (1821–94), famous publisher of dime novels, began his career by issuing ten-cent song books and game manuals. *Malaeska, the Indian Wife of the White Hunter* (1860) by Ann S. Stephens was the first of his series advertised as "a dollar book for a dime." It is said to have sold 300,000 copies during its first year, and was followed by hundreds of similar works dealing with the desperate adventures of frontiersmen. Among Beadle's writers were "Bruin" Adams, W.F. Cody, Edward S. Ellis, Mayne Reid, and Fred Whittaker. After 1880, train robbers and detectives supplanted Indians and hunters, and the dime novel acquired the opprobrious reputation that has clung to it.

BEAGLE, PETER S[OYER] (1939–   ), novelist born in New York City, resident in northern California, whose works include *A Fine and Private Place* (1960), whose protagonist returns from his burial to join living people; *I See By My Outfit* (1965), about two young Beatniks motorscooting across the continent to California; and *The Last Unicorn* (1968), presenting a female unicorn transformed into a human and back again as symbolic of the wonder and beauty of love. He has also written *The California Feeling* (1969), a nonfictional travelogue, and *The Garden of Earthly*

Delights (1982), a study of the Flemish artist Hieronymous Bosch. In addition, he has written for films and television.

BEALS, CARLETON (1893–1981), graduated from the University of California (1916) and became a teacher in Mexico and a journalist. His social studies, ranging in date and subject from *Rome or Death: The Story of Fascism* (1923) to *The Incredible Incas* (1973), deal mostly with Latin America. He also wrote novels, biographies, and memoirs, *Glass Houses: Ten Years of Free-Lancing* (1938) and *Great Circle* (1940).

Bear, The, novelette by Faulkner,◆ published in *Go Down, Moses* in 1942. Early versions of parts of the work are "Lion" (*Harper's,* Dec. 1935) and "The Bear" (*Saturday Evening Post,* May 9, 1942), and an abbreviated form, without section 4 that treats of Isaac's dispossessing himself of his lands, appeared in *Big Woods* (1955).

One December day in the 1880s the 16-year-old Isaac McCaslin, heir of one of the good old families of Yoknapatawpha County, is taken to hunt the great bear Old Ben so that the boy may show his courage and be initiated into the ranks of men. Since the age of ten he has learned the woods and the ways of hunters on annual autumnal outings with other McCaslins, Major de Spain, General Compson, and men of Indian blood, like Boon Hogganbeck and Sam Fathers. When Ike was 13 Sam Fathers "had marked his face with the hot blood" of the first buck he had killed, and "in the next November he killed a bear." Now he faces more dangerous game, for Old Ben, who has killed dogs, a fawn, and a colt, is the prime subject of an annual quest by mature men. For this purpose Sam Fathers has trained a huge, almost wild dog, Lion, to hold the beast, but in their first encounter both the bear and the dog are killed. Boon too is ripped by the bear, but he survives to act on Sam's unspoken request, killing the exhausted man, who has lost his will to live. Five years later, when he is 21 and married, Ike makes clear the great meaningfulness of this experience as he tells his older cousin, McCaslin Edmonds, that he plans to give up the plantation he has inherited so as to free himself from the ownership of property, further cursed because it was dubiously acquired and was the site of his grandfather's incestuous relations with his slaves. Ike has come to love the wild beauty of nature, represented by Old Ben. This sacramental feeling he has learned from Sam, rather than from the land, which is only the object of human possession and is now typically despoiled by men.

BEARD, CHARLES A[USTIN] (1874–1948), historian and educator born in Indiana, after graduating from DePauw University (1898) attended Oxford, where he founded Ruskin College (1899) to train labor leaders. Returning to the U.S., he became professor of political science at Columbia

(1904–17). He wrote a number of textbooks on European history, such as *The Development of Modern Europe* (2 vols., 1907–8), with J.H. Robinson, ♦ but about 1909 discovered "that American history is more interesting." His most important early books on the U.S., reflecting his belief in economic determinism, are *An Economic Interpretation of the Constitution* (1913) and *Economic Origins of Jeffersonian Democracy* (1915). These volumes established him as a liberal historian, and profoundly affected the study of American history but alienated many traditionalists. Beard resigned from Columbia (1917) to protest the dismissal of pacifist professors, and the next year helped found The New School for Social Research. With his wife, Mary R. Beard, ♦ he wrote *The Rise of American Civilization* (2 vols., 1927), an analysis of U.S. institutions, emphasizing social and economic backgrounds; *America in Midpassage* (1939), a continuation; *The American Spirit* (1942), about the "idea of civilization" in the U.S.; and *A Basic History of the United States* (1944). Other works include *The Economic Basis of Politics* (1922, revised 1945); *The American Leviathan* (1930), a study of the machine age, written with William Beard; and *A Charter for the Social Sciences* (1932), a program of social planning for the U.S. Although Beard was once an adviser to Japan and Yugoslavia on governmental reforms, and was long known for activities to preserve civil liberties, he later held isolationist and conservative views expressed in *The Idea of National Interest* (1934) and *The Open Door at Home* (1934), both written with G.H.E. Smith as arguments for a continental economy. Other books illustrative of his later views include *The Old Deal and the New* (1940), also written with Smith; *Public Policy and the General Welfare* (1941); *The Republic* (1943); *American Foreign Policy in the Making: 1932–1940* (1946), and its sequel, *President Roosevelt and the Coming of the War* (1948).

BEARD, MARY R[ITTER] (1876–1958), is known for historical works written with her husband, Charles A. Beard, ♦ and for her work in the woman suffrage and labor movements. Her works include *A Short History of the American Labor Movement* (1920, revised 1925), *On Understanding Women* (1931), *America Through Women's Eyes* (1933), *Woman: Co-Maker of History* (1940), *Woman as a Force in History* (1946), and *The Making of Charles A. Beard* (1955).

Beare and Ye Club, Ye, first play performed in English in America, was composed by Cornelius Watkinson, Philip Howard, and William Darby, three citizens of Accomac County, Va., in 1665. When brought to trial for performing the play, they reproduced it for the court, which found them "not guilty of fault," and acquitted them of licentiousness. The play is otherwise unknown. The title is sometimes given as *Ye Bare and Ye Cubb.*

Beat movement, a bohemian rebellion against established society which came to prominence about 1956 and had its centers in San Francisco and New York. The term "Beat" expressed both exhaustion and beatification in that the writers, tired of conventional society, and disgusted by it, believed that thoroughgoing disaffiliation from all aspects of the manners and mores of what they saw as a corrupt, crass, commercial world would bring its own kind of blissful illumination, aided by drink and drugs. Writers of the movement expressed their views in their own "hip" vocabulary, combined with phrases from Buddhism, by which they were influenced, but there is a personal statement and power that goes beyond this jargon in the works of the leading literary figures, who include the poets Allen Ginsberg♦ and Gregory Corso♦ and their San Francisco publisher Lawrence Ferlinghetti♦ and the novelist Jack Kerouac. ♦ Older writers who related to the movement included Norman Mailer, ♦ Henry Miller, ♦ and Kenneth Rexroth. ♦ Close to them and yet removed in part from the Beat movement because of his greater violence is William Burroughs. ♦

BEATTIE, ANN (1947–), born in Washington, D.C. Her first novel, *Chilly Scenes of Winter* (1976), presents a man in his twenties lonely and yearning for love, a frustrated, bewildered figure of the 1960s; and her second, *Falling in Place* (1980), set in the late 1970s, treats the loveless marriage of an advertising executive aged 40; *Love Always* (1985) deals with a writer about love who is deserted by her lover; *Alex Katz* (1987) dramatizes a painter; and *Picturing Will* (1990) renders a special situation in depicting the life of 5-year-old Will, whose mother goes to work as a photographer when deserted by her now remarried husband (Will's father) and is having a romance with a new man. *Distortions* (1976), *Secrets and Surprises* (1978), *The Burning House* (1982), and *Where You'll Find Me* (1986) gather her stories.

Beauchamp family, characters in Faulkner's fiction, related to the McCaslin family, ♦ of whom the most prominent was Lucas, who figures in *Intruder in the Dust.* ♦

Beauchampe: or, The Kentucky Tragedy, novel by Simms, ♦ published in 1842 as a fictional account of the Kentucky Tragedy. ♦ In 1856 the first part was expanded into an independent novel, *Charlemont; or, The Pride of the Village.* In this part Warham Sharpe, a young attorney, assumes the name of Alfred Stevens and the guise of a theological student, to woo Margaret Cooper. After seducing her and failing to keep his promise of marriage, he departs; her illegitimate child dies, and she swears to kill the father.

The revised *Beauchampe,* the former second part, opens five years later, when Margaret, living in seclusion under the name Anna Cooke, accepts the proposal of a young lawyer, Beauchampe. She warns him that he "clasps a dishonoured hand," and requires him to kill her seducer. After their marriage, Beauchampe's friend Sharpe visits them. When he again attempts to seduce Margaret, Beauchampe discovers his identity, stabs him, and later is condemned to death. On the eve of the execution, he and his wife attempt suicide. Although she succeeds, he is hanged, proclaiming at the last, "Daughters of Kentucky! you, at least, will bless the name of Beauchampe!"

Beauties of Santa Cruz, The, poem by Freneau,♦ written in the West Indies in 1776 and printed in his *Poems* (1786). This piece, in iambic pentameter quatrains, extols the beauties of the tropics and describes the horrors of slavery, which blot the country's native charms.

Beaver, TONY, giant hero of tall tales told by lumberjacks of the Southern mountains, was "a sort of relative" of Paul Bunyan,♦ whose mythical exploits he equals. In the Cumberland Mountains, one of his camps was located "up Eel River"; another was "way up in the Smokies." His most famous associate was Big Henry, whose axe, when swung, came down "boo!" Tony Beaver was the author of many ingenious inventions, including that of peanut brittle, which he created when he stopped a flood by dumping into the stream the surplus crop of peanuts and molasses. His adventures are recorded by Margaret Montague in *Up Eel River* (1928).

Bech: A Book, novel by John Updike,♦ published in 1970. *Bech Is Back* (1982), a sequel, presents the author in his fifties breaking out of a writer's block to create a best seller but no happier or more personally fulfilled.

In seven episodes presented in the guise of lectures with a spurious bibliography, the work reveals the literary and personal life of Henry Bech, a distinguished Jewish author of New York. Revelatory incidents include Bech's travels in the 1960s as a kind of cultural ambassador in Russia and Eastern Europe, his visit as a lecturer to adulatory pupils at a girls' school, his diverse romantic affairs, his difficulties in writing as he ages, and his ultimate enshrinement as a major American author.

BECKER, CARL [LOTUS] (1873–1945), former professor of history at Cornell University, whose books include *Beginnings of the American People* (1915), *Eve of the Revolution* (1918), *The Declaration of Independence* (1922), *The Heavenly City of the Eighteenth Century Philosophers* (1932), *Everyman His Own Historian* (1935), *New Liberties for Old* (1941), *Modern Democracy* (1941), *Cornell University* (1943), *How New Will the Better World Be?* (1944), and *Freedom and Responsibility in the American Way of Life* (1945).

BECKWOURTH, JAMES P. (1798–*c.*1867), Virginia-born hunter and adventurer in the Rocky Mountains, California, and Missouri, began his career as a "mountain man" while still a boy, and in 1823 joined the expedition of Ashley which ascended the Missouri River. His daring exploits and his life among the Indians made him a famous hero of frontier tall tales. In 1856 T.D. Bonner wrote "from his own dictation" the colorful and bombastic book, based on facts but exaggerated and disproportionately heroic, which was published as *Life and Adventures of James P. Beckwourth, Mountaineer, Scout, and Pioneer and Chief of the Crow Nation of Indians*. It is probably the best account we have for the pre-1830 societies of the Crow, Cheyenne, and Comanche.

Becky Thatcher, character in *Tom Sawyer.*♦

BEDOTT, WIDOW, pseudonym of Frances M. Whitcher.♦

BEEBE, [CHARLES] WILLIAM (1877–1962), graduated from Columbia (1898), became curator of ornithology of the New York Zoological Society, and until his death was director of the Society's tropical research department. His numerous expeditions to various parts of the world have been recorded in a long series of popular books. Among these are *Beneath Tropic Seas* (1928), *Nonsuch: Land of Water* (1932), *Half Mile Down* (1934), describing his ichthyological investigations undersea in a bathysphere, and *Book of Bays* (1942), and the earlier *Two Bird-Lovers in Mexico* (1905), *The Log of the Sun* (1906), *Our Search for a Wilderness* (1910), *Jungle Peace* (1918), *Galapagos, World's End* (1924), *Jungle Days* (1925), *The Arcturus Adventure* (1926), and *Pheasant Jungles* (1927). Later works are *High Jungle* (1949) and *Unseen Life of New York* (1953).

BEECHER, CATHARINE E[STHER] (1800–1878), daughter of Lyman Beecher and sister of Henry Ward Beecher and Harriet Beecher Stowe. Her work as an educator and reformer included the founding of schools for young ladies at Hartford (1824) and Cincinnati, and main responsibility for the founding of women's colleges in Iowa, Illinois, and Wisconsin. Her writings include *An Essay on Slavery and Abolitionism* (1837); *The Evils Suffered by American Women and . . . Children* (1846); *Women Suffrage* (1871), on a movement she opposed; and *Educational Reminiscences and Suggestions* (1874).

BEECHER, HENRY WARD (1813–87), son of Lyman Beecher and brother of Catharine Beecher and Harriet Beecher Stowe, was a celebrated Congregational minister, moral crusader, and lecturer. At his Plymouth (Congregational) Church in Brooklyn, he became the outstanding pulpit orator of his day, being immensely popular for his sentimental and high-flown rhetoric in sermons on political, social, and religious subjects. He was an ardent champion of antislavery and during the Civil War delivered a popular series of lectures in England on behalf of the Union cause. His sermons were published in many volumes, and his other books include *Norwood; or, Village Life in New England* (1867), a sentimental novel; *The Life of Jesus, the Christ* (1871); *Yale Lectures on Preaching* (1872–74); and *Evolution and Religion* (1885). His reputation was seriously injured by the suit (1874) of Theodore Tilton, who accused Beecher of adultery with Mrs. Tilton. Although the jury disagreed, the scandal turned Beecher from a respected to a notorious figure for some years.

BEECHER, LYMAN (1775–1863), born in New Haven, after graduation from Yale (1797) became a Presbyterian minister on Long Island, at Litchfield, Conn., and at Boston, noted for his fiery and vigorous denunciation of liquor and his strongly anti-Catholic sermons. In 1832 he went to Cincinnati to become the first president of Lane Theological Seminary. There he was the defendant in a noted heresy trial, in which he was acquitted, although he resigned in 1850. His sermons and magazine articles were published in his *Works* (1852), and an *Autobiography* appeared in 1864–65. His children included Catharine Beecher, Henry Ward Beecher, and Harriet Beecher Stowe.

BEER, THOMAS (1889–1940), born in Iowa, graduated from Yale (1911), and devoted himself to writing following his service in World War I. In addition to three novels—*The Fair Rewards* (1922), a story of the New York stage, whose central figure is an impresario constantly divided between his artistic convictions and the commercial aspects of his work; *Sandoval* (1924), "a romance of bad manners" depicting New York in 1870; and *The Road to Heaven* (1928), a sophisticated romance praising the virtues of rural living —he wrote such humorous short stories as those collected in *Mrs. Egg and Other Barbarians* (1933). His biography of Stephen Crane (1923) did much to establish Crane's fame. *The Mauve Decade* (1926) is an interpretation of American life during the last part of the 19th century, and *Hanna* (1929) is a similar study centered on Mark Hanna. Both are written in an oblique and urbanely ironic style. *The Agreeable Finish* (1941) is a collection of short stories.

BEERS, ETHEL LYNN (1827–79), New York poet and author of fiction, was best known for her poem "All Quiet Along the Potomac," originally published as "The Picket-Guard" (*Harper's Weekly,* 1861), a sentimental account of the death of an unknown soldier during the Civil War. It was reprinted in *All Quiet Along the Potomac, and Other Poems* (1879).

Before Adam, novel by Jack London,♦ published in 1906.

The nameless narrator expounds a theory of the dissociation of personality to explain his strange dreams, which, he contends, are memories of a distant ancestor, Big Tooth, who roamed the forests during the mid-Pleistocene era. He describes in a somewhat sentimentalized fashion the life of Big Tooth and his mate Swift One, their fight with the Fire People, and the processes by which human beings defended themselves against beasts.

Beggar on Horseback, satirical play by George S. Kaufman♦ and Marc Connelly♦ with music by Deems Taylor. Produced and published in 1924, it was suggested by a German play, Paul Apel's *Hans Sonnenstössers Höllenfahrt.*

BEHRMAN, S[AMUEL] N[ATHANIEL] (1893–1973), graduated from Harvard (1916), where he studied in the 47 Workshop, did graduate work at Columbia under Brander Matthews and St. John Ervine, and contributed to newspapers and magazines, winning his first success as a playwright with a comedy of manners, *The Second Man* (1927). Later plays, mainly in the same genre, include *Serena Blandish* (1929), adapted from a novel published anonymously but attributed to Enid Bagnold, about a naïve Mayfair society girl; *Meteor* (1929); *Brief Moment* (1931), about marital difficulties of a young patrician and a nightclub singer; *Biography* (1932), about a portrait painter and the celebrities she attracts; *Rain from Heaven* (1934); *End of Summer* (1936); *Amphitryon 38* (1937), adapted from a French version of a Greek legend; *No Time for Comedy* (1939), about a playwright's attempt to do serious writing while tempted to continue with successful comedies; *The Talley Method* (1941), a surgeon's education in humanity; *The Pirate* (1942); *Jacobowsky and the Colonel* (1944), with Franz Werfel; *Dunnigan's Daughter* (1945); *Fanny* (1954), with Joshua Logan; *Lord Pengo* (1962); and *But for Whom Charlie* (1964). He also wrote motion-picture scripts; a life of the art dealer Duveen (1952); *The Worcester Account* (1954), stories about his youth which he dramatized as *The Cold Wind and the Warm* (1958); *Portrait of Max* (1960), an intimate memoir of Max Beerbohm; *The Suspended Drawing Room* (1965), presenting profiles; *The Burning Glass* (1968), a novel about a young playwright; and *People in a Diary* (1972), a memoir.

BEIN, ALBERT (1902–63), proletarian author, whose plays include *Little Ol' Boy* (1933); *Let Freedom Ring* (1935), adapted from Grace Lumpkin's novel *To Make My Bread*; and *Heavenly Express* (1940), based on firsthand knowledge of hobo life, depicting the afterlife imagined by railroad tramps. His novels are *Road Out of Hell* (1929), from which his first play was adapted; *Love in Chicago* (1929), written under the pseudonym Charles Walt; and *Youth in Hell* (1930), a semi-autobiographical novel about a reform school.

Being There, novel by Jerzy Kosinski,♦ published in 1971.

A man named Chance, adopted by the Old Man when a boy, remains illiterate and a complete innocent as an adult, having spent all his life tending a walled-off garden or watching television in his isolated room. When Chance is made homeless by the death of the Old Man he encounters a new protector, Mrs. Benjamin Rand, who, misunderstanding his name and occupation, calls him Chauncy Gardener. She takes him to the Rand mansion, where he meets the President of the U.S., who interprets Chance's comments on gardening as brilliant metaphors on finance. As a result Chance is catapulted to international prominence, which he accepts with calm detachment.

BELASCO, DAVID (1853–1931), born in San Francisco, where he first achieved recognition as actor, playwright, and producer, was intermittently associated with the New York stage during his youth, and after 1882 was constantly identified with it. He was famous not only for his plays, but also for his managership, discovery, and development of such actors as David Warfield and Mrs. Leslie Carter, his realistic stage settings, and his ability to obtain novel effects with newly invented electric lights. Many of his plays were written with collaborators: *Hearts of Oak* (1879), adapted from an English melodrama, with James A. Herne♦; *Lord Chumley* (1888), a domestic drama, with Henry C. De Mille; *The Girl I Left Behind Me* (1893), with Franklin Fyles; *The Return of Peter Grimm*♦ (1911), with Cecil B. DeMille; *Madame Butterfly*♦ (1900), *Adrea*♦ (1904), and *The Darling of the Gods* (1902), with John L. Long; and many other plays with these and other writers. Belasco's own plays include *The Heart of Maryland* (1895), a Civil War drama; *Zaza* (1898), adapted from the French; *DuBarry* (1901); and *The Girl of the Golden West*♦ (1905). Six of his plays were collected and edited by M.J. Moses (1928).

Belfry of Bruges, The, and Other Poems, volume of poems by Longfellow,♦ published in 1845, which contains such poems as "The Arsenal at Springfield,"♦ "The Bridge,"♦ and "The Arrow and the Song."♦ "The Belfry of Bruges," in rhymed couplets of eight-stress lines, recalling the ancient glories of the Belgian city, is prefaced by a "Carillon" in four-stress lines, describing the chimes as the poet heard them during a restless night.

BELITT, BEN (1911–), poet born in New York, after receiving an A.B. and M.A. from the University of Virginia became a professor of English at Bennington. His poems have been published in *The Five-Fold Mesh* (1938), *Wilderness*

Stair (1955), *The Enemy Joy* (1964), *Nowhere But Light* (1970), *The Double Witness* (1977), and *Possessions* (1986), gathering poetry since 1938. He wrote *Adam's Dream* (1977), about translation, and has translated poems of Rimbaud, Lorca, and Neruda.

BELKNAP, JEREMY (1744–98), Congregational clergyman and historian, was the author of a *History of New Hampshire* (3 vols., 1784, 1791, 1792), noted for its research, impartiality, and literary merit. His humorous allegory *The Foresters* (1792) narrates the founding and growth of British colonies in America, and his *American Biography* (2 vols., 1794–98) is the prototype of many later works. Belknap's nationalism, enthusiasm for research, and scholarship led him, with others, to found the Massachusetts Historical Society, the first organization of its kind in the U.S.

Bell for Adano, A, novel by John Hersey♦ (1944, Pulitzer Prize), dramatized (1944) by Paul Osborn.

Major Victor Joppolo, New Yorker of Italian descent, arrives during the invasion of the Sicilian town of Adano to serve as Allied Military Government officer. He and his sergeant Borth have a humane appreciation of the people and ignore the arbitrary orders of the arrogant General Marvin that mule carts may not enter the town. To inspirit the people he replaces the town's ancient bell, whose original the Fascists melted for munitions. Marvin, discovering the violation of his orders, transfers Joppolo elsewhere but not before the people can give him a party.

Bell Jar, The, novel by Sylvia Plath,♦ published (1963) under the pseudonym Victoria Lucas, and under her own name in 1966. The story is based on the author's own experiences.

Esther Greenwood, a 19-year-old Smith College student, during a summer internship working for a fashion magazine in New York undergoes a series of experiences that leave her unable to cope with competition, professional and personal, and cause her to attempt suicide. Assisted to a private institution by Philomena Guinea, the woman who had provided her college scholarship, she recovers, makes peace with a high-school boyfriend, is liberated by a sexual experience, and returns recovered to college.

BELLAMY, EDWARD (1850–98), born in Massachusetts, had a public school education, toured Europe in 1868, returned to study law, but, though admitted to the Massachusetts bar, never practiced. He entered journalism, edited the Springfield *Union,* and in 1880 founded the Springfield *Daily News.* He had already begun writing fiction, publishing *The Duke of Stockbridge* as a serial in 1879. This novel, completed after his death by a cousin and published in 1900, was a sort of proletarian romance dealing with Shays's Rebellion. Other novels included *Six to One: A Nantucket Idyl* (1878), the result of a voyage to Hawaii; and *Dr. Heidenhoff's Process* (1880) and *Miss Ludington's Sister* (1884), romances showing his interest in psychic phenomena. These were overshadowed by the immensely popular *Looking Backward: 2000–1887*♦ (1888), a Utopian romance predicting a new social and economic order, which led to the founding of a Nationalist party that advocated its principles. To aid this cause and further his social theories, he founded the *New Nation* (1891), lectured widely, and wrote *Equality* (1897), a sequel to *Looking Backward* but much more of a theoretical tract. Bellamy's only other writings were *The Blindman's World and Other Stories* (1898) and *The Religion of Solidarity* (a fragment, published 1940). His early death from tuberculosis ended a career of social reform in which he set forth a theory of state capitalism that has greatly affected U.S. economic thinking and the proletarian movement.

BELLAMY, JOSEPH (1719–90), associate of Jonathan Edwards in the Great Awakening,♦ and author of theological pamphlets, notably *True Religion Delineated* (1750).

Bellman, The (1906–19), literary review published at Minneapolis by William C. Edgar. Its urbane, conservative, dignified point of view led critics to consider it guilty of preciosity and Anglophilia. In addition to foreign authors, its contributors included C.M. Flandrau, Joyce Kilmer, Sara Teasdale, George Sterling, and Carl Van Vechten.

BELLOW, SAUL (1915–　), born in Canada of parents recently emigrated from Russia, was reared in Chicago and educated at the University of Chicago and at Northwestern (B.S., 1937). He has taught at Minnesota, Princeton, New York University, and elsewhere, but his career is that of a writer. His first two novels, presenting a Kafka-like atmosphere, are *Dangling Man*♦ (1944), a psychological study of a man waiting to be inducted into the army and living in limbo between civilian and military life, and *The Victim* (1947), about the agonizing, equivocal relations of Jew and Gentile. His next novel, *The Adventures of Augie March*♦ (1953), which won a National Book Award, is naturalistic in treating the picaresque adventures of a young Chicago Jew. *Seize the Day* (1956) includes a novella, stories, and a one-act play. *Henderson the Rain King*♦ (1959) opens with a realistic depiction of an intense middle-age Connecticut millionaire whose inner urge for fulfillment of self—"I want, I want"—drives him to primitive Africa, where in a symbolic tragi-comedy he encounters fantastic experiences. *Herzog*♦ (1964) is an intense revelation of the life and experiences of a middle-aged Jewish intellectual, presenting his involvements with two wives and other women, with his chil-

dren, with a friend who betrays him, and with his careers of teaching and writing. He is led through neurosis almost to suicide and emerges "pretty well satisfied to be, to be just as it is willed." *Mr. Sammler's Planet* (1969) is a fictive critique of modern society as seen by a survivor of a Nazi concentration camp resident in New York. *Humboldt's Gift*♦ (1975, Pulitzer Prize) depicts a crisis in the life of the narrator that is resolved by his friend, the poet Humboldt. Bellow did not publish another novel until *The Dean's December,*♦ issued seven years later, whose protagonist is in part an autobiographical figure, concerned with two opposing concepts of life and thought. *More Die of Heartbreak* (1987) treats in unnamed Chicago a distinguished professor of botany wed to a handsome wealthy woman who is sadly and humorously involved in a family feud and sexual confusion. The novel gives a sense of people, many ignorant and corrupt, in contemporary American society. This was followed by two paperback novellas: *Theft* (1988), with less plot than vintage ideas of the author; and *The Bellarosa Connection* (1989), treating Jews of European heritage, uneasy but successful in the U.S. *It All Adds Up* (1994) prints essays and memoirs, most previously published in periodicals, dating back in some instances 30 years. *Mosby's Memoirs* (1968) collects stories, *The Last Analysis* (1964) is a comic play, and *To Jerusalem and Back* (1976) deals with his visit to Israel. In 1976 he was awarded a Nobel Prize.

Bells, The, poem by Poe,♦ published in 1849. The four irregular stanzas, of varied meter, depict onomatopoetically, by means of reiterated alliteration, assonance, and phonetic imitation, four ways in which the sounds of bells influence moods: the merry tinkle of sleigh bells; the mellow, golden notes of wedding bells; the terrible shriek of alarm bells; and the solemn, melancholy roll of funeral bells. Poe's first version of this *tour de force* of "tintinnabulation" consisted of only 18 lines, suggested by his friend Mrs. M.L. Shew, but in its complete form the poem contains 113 lines. Its origin has been traced to a passage in Chateaubriand's *Le Génie du christianisme.*

BEMELMANS, LUDWIG (1898–1962), born in the Austrian Tyrol, came to New York in 1914, worked at various hotels, and became a restaurant proprietor. His adventures in this field form one of the principal subjects of his whimsical and witty books, illustrated with his drawings and watercolors. *My War with the United States* (1937), a humorous description of his service with the American army during World War I, was his first book for adults. Besides books for children, his stories appear in *Life Class* (1938), *At Your Service* (1941), *Hotel Splendide* (1941), *I Love You, I Love You, I Love You* (1942), and *Hotel Bemelmans* (1946). His novels include *Now I Lay Me Down To Sleep* (1943), about the travels of an Ecuadorian general; *Dirty Eddie* (1947), a farcical satire on Hollywood; and *The Eye of God* (1949), about an innkeeper in the Tyrolean Alps. Travel accounts include *The Donkey Inside* (1941), *The Best of Times* (1948), *Father, Dear Father* (1953), and *On Board Noah's Ark* (1962).

Ben Bolt, popular ballad by T.D. English,◆ first published in the *New-York Mirror* (1843), often set to music suiting its sentimentality, and revived by its introduction into Du Maurier's *Trilby* (1894), whose heroine sings the ballad beginning, "Don't you remember sweet Alice, Ben Bolt?"

Ben Jonson Entertains a Man from Stratford, blank-verse dramatic monologue by E.A. Robinson,◆ published in *The Man Against the Sky* (1916).
   This witty, jovial, and incisive characterization of Shakespeare is presented in the words of his fellow poet, supposed to be drinking in a London tavern with a Stratford visitor. Describing him as "this mad, careful, proud, indifferent Shakespeare," Jonson says that he is an incomparable genius, but solitary and passion-consumed, "empowered out of nature" by lacking "faith, innocence, illusion, Whatever 'tis that keeps us out o' Bedlam," and saved perhaps only by his thrift and ambition and "that House in Stratford."

Benbow family, characters in Faulkner's fiction, figure prominently in *Sartoris*◆ and *Sanctuary.*◆ In the former novel, Horace ("Horry") Benbow and his sister Narcissa ("Narcy") Benbow are introduced as members of an old but less extensive and less important family than the Sartoris clan, to which they are related. Horace comes home to Jefferson in 1919 from World War I, a lawyer by training and a lonely man, seeking tranquillity in art and poetry. Partly to escape his possessive sister he drifts into an affair with the coarse Belle Mitchell, whom he marries when she gets a divorce. Narcissa marries young Bayard Sartoris, also recently returned from the war and himself disoriented, but her resentment of his indrawn desperation and her exasperation at the recklessness of Sartoris men becomes an expression of deep-seated resentment of men generally. Bayard abandons her and on the day of his death in a plane crash in 1920 she gives birth to a son, naming him Benbow Sartoris, as if to fend off the destructiveness she associates with the Sartoris family name. In *Sanctuary* Horace becomes aware of Belle's shallow nature, leaves her, and gets enmeshed with bootleggers, idealistically defending one against a false murder charge. The widowed Narcissa, concerned for her social position, wants Horace to return to Belle, and contrives to thwart his handling of the case so that he loses it. The Benbows disappear from direct involvement in Faulkner's work after *Sanctuary,* although they are mentioned in *Absalom, Absalom!* and *The Unvanquished.*

BENCHLEY, ROBERT [CHARLES] (1889–1945), drama critic, humorist, and actor, after graduating from Harvard (1912) wrote for New York newspapers and magazines, and was theater critic of *Life* (1920–29) and *The New Yorker* (1929–40). His sketches of the tribulations of the average man are collected in *Of All Things* (1921), *Love Conquers All* (1922), *Pluck and Luck* (1925), *The Early Worm* (1927), *20,000 Leagues Under the Sea; or, David Copperfield* (1928), *The Treasurer's Report* (1930), *No Poems* (1932), *From Bed to Worse* (1934), *My Ten Years in a Quandary* (1936), *After 1903—What?* (1938), *Inside Benchley* (1942), and *Benchley Beside Himself* (1943). He also played in motion pictures and on the radio.
   His son NATHANIEL BENCHLEY (1915–81), also a humorist, was the author of light novels, films and plays, and lives of his father and of his friend Humphrey Bogart (1975).

BENCHLEY, PETER [BRADFORD] (1940–   ), son of Nathaniel, has written a travel account; two sensational underwater adventure novels, *Jaws* (1974) and *The Deep* (1976), the former made by him into a screenplay that was tremendously popular, melodramatic adventure tales; *The Island* (1976); and *Rummies* (1989), about an alcoholic, as well as many television shows.

BENEFIELD, [JOHN] BARRY (1877–1956?), novelist, whose works include *The Chicken-Wagon Family* (1925), *A Little Clown Lost* (1928), *Valiant Is the Word for Carrie* (1935), *April Was When It Began* (1939), and *Eddie and the Archangel Mike* (1943), all distinguished by whimsical fantasy. *Short Turns* (1926) is a volume of stories.

BENÉT, STEPHEN VINCENT (1889–1943), brother of W.R. Benét, was born in Pennsylvania, and graduated from Yale (1919). As an undergraduate he wrote two books of poetry, *Five Men and Pompey* (1915), dramatic monologues, and *Young Adventure* (1918); shortly after graduation he wrote his first novel, *The Beginning of Wisdom* (1921), a college story in the vein of F. Scott Fitzgerald. The poems in *Heavens and Earth* (1920), *King David* (1923), *The Ballad of William Sycamore* (1923), and *Tiger Joy* (1925) show a growing maturity, and the *Ballad* particularly indicates his interest in the American scene. He reached his full power with *John Brown's Body*◆ (1928, Pulitzer Prize), a long narrative poem of the Civil War. His *Ballads and Poems, 1915–30* were collected in 1931. *Nightmare at Noon* (1940) is a poem warning the U.S. to meet the fascist challenge. *Western Star* (1943, Pulitzer Prize), a section of a projected epic poem on the westward migration, depicts the settling of Jamestown and Plymouth. *America* (1944) is a short U.S. history written for distribution abroad by the Office of War Information. In addition to such novels as *Young People's Pride* (1922), *Jean Huguenot* (1923), and *Spanish Bayonet* (1926), he wrote librettos for two one-act folk operas. *The Headless Horseman* (1937) and *The Devil and Daniel Webster*♦ (1939), with music by Douglas Moore. Collections are *Tales Before Midnight* (1939), stories; *Selected Works* (1942); and *Selected Letters* (1960).

BENÉT, WILLIAM ROSE (1886–1950), New York poet and critic, whose exuberant, romantic verse, ranging from Oriental fantasy to cowboy balladry, has been published in *Merchants from Cathay* (1913), *The Falconer of God* (1914), *The Great White Wall* (1916), *The Burglar of the Zodiac* (1918), *Moons of Grandeur* (1920), *Man Possessed* (1927), *Day of Deliverance* (1944), and other volumes. *Rip Tide* (1932) and *The Dust Which Is God* (1941, Pulitzer Prize) are verse novels, the latter autobiographical. Among his anthologies is the *Oxford Anthology of American Literature* (1938), edited in collaboration with N.H. Pearson. He was wed to Elinor Wylie,♦ whose works he collected, and was a brother of S.V. Benét.

BENEZET, ANTHONY (1713–84), French-born Huguenot, converted to the Quaker faith, emigrated to America (1731), where he was a schoolteacher, first of boys, then girls, and later blacks. He wrote *A Caution to Great Britain and Her Colonies* (1766) on slavery to carry on the work of his friend Woolman♦; *An Historical Account of Guinea* (1771), on the slave trade; *The Mighty Destroyer Displayed* (1774), on alcoholism; a *Short Account of the People Called Quakers* (1780); and *Some Observations . . . on the Indian Natives of This Continent* (1784).

Ben-Hur: *A Tale of the Christ,* novel by Lew Wallace,♦ published in 1880 and dramatized by William Young in 1899.

Against the background of the life of Jesus is told the story of Judah Ben-Hur, a Jewish patrician youth wrongly accused by his former friend Messala of attempting to kill the Roman governor of Judea. He is sent to the galleys for life, and his mother and sister are imprisoned. Escaping, Ben-Hur returns as a Roman officer and enters the chariot race in which Messala has wagered heavily on himself. Messala hopes to ruin Ben-Hur, but instead is seriously injured during the race. His cruelties are discovered, and he is slain by his wife Isas. Ben-Hur rescues his mother and sister, now lepers, and all become Christians after the disease is cured through the intervention of Jesus.

Benito Cereno, story by Melville,♦ published in *The Piazza Tales* (1856). Its source is a chapter in Amasa Delano's *Voyages and Travels* (1817). Robert Lowell adapted Melville's story in a one-act verse play of the same title in *The Old Glory* (1965).

In 1799 Captain Delano puts in for water at an uninhabited island off Chile, where he encoun-

ters a Spanish merchantman in ruinous condition, commanded by Benito Cereno, a sensitive young Spaniard now gravely ill and enabled to pursue his duties only with the solicitous care of his black servant Babo. Cereno tells the American that he sailed from Buenos Aires for Lima, with a crew of 50 and a cargo including 300 Negroes owned by Alexandro Aranda. Off Cape Horn, he says, many of the crew were lost in a storm, and disease destroyed most of the other whites and blacks. Delano offers aid, but is uneasy at the insubordination of the slaves and the careless seamanship and seeming ingratitude of Cereno. He is about to return to his ship when Cereno jumps into his boat, precipitating an attack by the Negroes from which they barely escape. Cereno explains that the blacks had mutinied, led by Babo, and wanted to be carried to Africa. Delano seizes the slave ship, and takes it with his own to Lima, where Babo is executed. Cereno enters a monastery, but soon dies.

BENJAMIN, PARK (1809–64), editor and publisher, is best known for his *New World* (1839–45), a literary journal that reprinted British works without remunerating their authors. Among the American contributions was Longfellow's "The Wreck of the Hesperus." Benjamin was notorious for his sensational journalistic devices and vituperation, and was among those successfully sued for libel by Cooper. His verse was prominent in early anthologies but has never been collected.

BENNETT, EMERSON (1822–1905), wrote melodramatic fiction of intrigue and adventure set for the most part on the frontier. He was the author of more than 50 novels and several hundred short stories. His *Prairie Flower* (1849) and its sequel *Leni-Leoti* (1849) had a sale of 100,000 copies each. He also wrote novels concerned with *The League of the Miami* (1845) and *Mike Fink* (1848).

BENNETT, JAMES GORDON, see *New York Herald.*

BENNETT, JOHN (1865–1956), born in Ohio and resident in Charleston, S.C., is best known for his boys' book *Master Skylark* (1897), a historical novel "of Shakespere's time."

BENSON, SALLY (SARA MAHALA REDWAY SMITH BENSON) (1900–1972), New York writer, best known for short stories including *People Are Fascinating* (1936); *Emily* (1938); *Junior Miss* (1941), dramatized by Jerome Chodorov and Joseph Fields (1944); *Meet Me in St. Louis* (1942); and *Women and Children First* (1943).

BENTON, THOMAS HART (1782–1858), Democratic senator from Missouri (1820–50), was an ardent supporter of Andrew Jackson and like him opposed the Bank of the United States and advocated legislation favoring frontier interests. He was a leader in obtaining federal support for Western explorations, including the expeditions of his son-in-law Frémont. Benton edited a 16-volume *Abridgement of the Debates of Congress from 1789 to 1856. Thirty Years' View* (1854–56) is an autobiography.

BENTON, THOMAS HART (1889–1975), grandnephew of the Missouri senator of the same name, had a deep sense of relation to the traditions of that state, where he was born and which he depicted in paintings and murals, such as those in the Truman Library. He wrote two autobiographies, *An Artist in America* (1937) and *An American in Art* (1969), and illustrated an edition of *Grapes of Wrath.*

Bent's Fort, trading post on the Arkansas River near Rocky Ford, Colo., was founded (*c.*1829) by frontiersmen Charles and William Bent. A new fort was built (1853) downstream and leased (1859) to the government for a military post. Its appearance and life during the 1840s figure in many travel accounts, such as Parkman's *The Oregon Trail,* Ruxton's *Life in the Far West,* and Garrard's *Wah-to'-yah.*

BERCOVICI, KONRAD (1882–1961), in 1916 came to the U.S. from Rumania and wrote *Crimes of Charity* (1917), inspired by his work for a New York charity. His stories include *Dust of New York* (1919), about the Jewish Lower East Side and other foreign quarters, and depictions of European gypsy life in *Ghitza* (1921), *Murdo* (1923), *Iliana* (1924), *Singing Winds* (1926), and *Peasants* (1928). His novels include *The Marriage Guest* (1925), *The Volga Boatman* (1926), and *The Exodus* (1947), on Moses. Other works include *Costa's Daughter* (1923), a play; *Alexander* (1928), a romantic biography; *On New Shores* (1925); *Story of the Gypsies* (1928); and *The Incredible Balkans* (1932). *It's the Gypsy in Me* (1941) is his autobiography.

Berenice, tale by Poe, ♦ published in the *Southern Literary Messenger* (1835) and reprinted in *Tales of the Grotesque and Arabesque* (1840).

Egaeus, gloomy and unhealthy, grows up with his cousin Berenice, who is "agile . . . overflowing with energy" until she contracts a form of epilepsy that causes frequent trances. The youth's mind becomes diseased, and although he never loved Berenice while she was normal, he now madly proposes marriage. As the wedding approaches, he sees her as she is, pale and shrunken, but her white teeth fascinate him, and he feels insanely certain that to possess them would cure his own malady. When she is stricken with epilepsy and entombed as dead, Egaeus, unconscious of what he does, draws her teeth. He returns to the library, and there a servant makes him aware

of what he has done, telling him that Berenice has not been dead but in a trance.

BERENSON, BERNARD (1865–1959), art historian, born in Lithuania, reared in Boston, educated at Harvard, resident after 1900 at his estate, I Tatti, outside Florence, where he and his wife, sister of Logan Pearsall Smith, lived with his great collection of paintings and books. Recognized as the leading connoisseur of Renaissance art, wrote a great number of books and monographs on the subject, including *Venetian Painters of the Renaissance* (1894), *Florentine Painters of the Renaissance* (1896), *Central Italian Painters of the Renaissance* (1897), *Study and Criticism of Italian Art* (1901, 1902, 1915), *Venetian Paintings in America* (1916), and *Sienese Paintings* (1918). More general works of criticism, written with great grace and knowledge, include *Aesthetics and History in the Visual Arts* (1948), *Seeing and Knowing* (1954), and *Essays in Appreciation* (1959). Other works of his urbane observations include *Sketch for a Self-Portrait* (1949), *Rumor and Reflection* (1952), and *The Passionate Sightseer* (1960).

BERGER, THOMAS [LOUIS] (1924–   ), Cincinnati-born author, long resident in New York, whose works include *Crazy in Berlin* (1958), the beginning of a comic saga about Carlo Reinhart, a happy GI in occupied Germany at the end of World War II, whose fantastic picaresque tale is continued in *Reinhart in Love* (1962), with the anti-hero back in his conformist Midwest home, and concluded in *Vital Parts* (1970), in which Reinhart's curiously old-fashioned style appeals to the salesman Bob Sweet, who wants to preserve him through cryonics. *Little Big Man* (1964) is a fanciful parody of the Old West myth presented through the life of the ancient frontiersman Jack Crabb, kidnapped by Indians from an emigrant wagon and eventually a participant in Custer's last stand. *Killing Time* (1967) presents through the tale of a mass murderer many questions about sanity and madness, crime and legality. *Regiment of Women* (1973) fictively treats the dominance of women in the 22nd-century U.S. *Sneaky People* (1975) comically depicts the diverse involvements and deceptions of a Midwestern family in the 1930s. *Who Is Teddy Villanova?* (1977) is a parody of the detective novel; *Arthur Rex* (1978) is a satiric and parodic retelling of Arthurian legendry; *Neighbors* (1980) is a fantastic account of violent relations, real and imagined, between neighboring families; *Reinhart's Women* (1981) deals again with his unheroic figure, now in his fifties. *The Feud* (1983) is a melodramatic view of life and sudden death in middle U.S. towns of the 1930s; *Nowhere* (1985), a witty spy story set in eastern Europe; *Being Invisible* (1987), a humorous tale of a man with the power to become invisible. *The Houseguest* (1988) is about the difficult experiences of an initially happy newly wed woman; *Changing the Past* (1990), about a book editor in his fifties offered an eventually very sorry chance to alter his life entirely; *Orrie's Story* (1990) replays *The Oresteia* set in the U.S. after World War II; and *Meeting Evil* (1992) throws a decent man and a scoundrel together on a day's crime spree and leads eventually to the paradox that innocence can consort with evil. *Robert Crews* (1994) is a contemporary version of *Robinson Crusoe*, in which the title character, a hopeless alcoholic and skill-less man, achieves redemption by surviving in the north woods after his fishing companions are killed in a plane crash into a lake, Robert alone escaping from the underwater wreckage. His Friday is a woman who has been shot by her faux-macho husband in the course of a camping trip. Friday and Robert redeem each other in the struggle to live in the wild, and come to love each other. They also find and overcome Friday's husband. The novel, in the same genre as Dickey's *Deliverance*, is equally compelling.

BERKELEY, GEORGE (1685–1753), Irish-born bishop of the Church of England, is famous as an idealistic philosopher. By 1723 he had conceived the project of founding a college in Bermuda and wrote a poem to favor the cause, with the prophetic opening line, "Westward the course of Empire takes its way." While waiting to obtain funds for this project, he came to America (1729) and settled at Rhode Island for nearly three years. There he formed a Literary and Philosophical Society, and wrote *Alciphron* (1732), a series of Platonic dialogues opposing deism and finding proof of God's existence in Berkeley's own theory of vision. William Byrd and others pointed out the defects of the Bermuda plan, which failed completely, although King's College (now Columbia) was largely based on Berkeley's model. Berkeley Divinity School at New Haven is named in his honor, as is the city of Berkeley, the site of the original University of California campus.

BERKELEY, SIR WILLIAM (1606–77), was appointed colonial governor of Virginia in 1642 and served until 1652, when he was unseated by parliamentary order. He served again from 1660 until his death. During the early years of his administration he made many improvements, but later he assumed such a dictatorial policy that a group of colonists under Nathaniel Bacon♦ rose in rebellion. After Bacon's death, Berkeley entered upon a program of executions and confiscations that supposedly led Charles II to remark, "The old fool has killed more people in that naked country than I have done for the murder of my father." Before coming to America he published *The Lost Lady* (1639), a tragi-comedy.

BERLIN, IRVING (1888–1989), Russian-born song composer, was brought to the U.S. (1893). He became an innovator of jazz, rising from Tin Pan Alley to fame with such pieces as "Alex-

ander's Ragtime Band" (1911) and "Everybody's Doin' It" (1911). Broadway shows for which he wrote songs include various editions of the Ziegfeld *Follies, Face the Music* (1931), *As Thousands Cheer* (1932), *Louisiana Purchase* (1940), *Annie Get Your Gun* (1946), and *Call Me Madam* (1950). In the army (1917–18) he wrote music for *Yip-Yip-Yaphank*, in which he starred; he wrote a second army show, *This Is the Army* (1942). In 1938 he wrote "God Bless America." Woollcott wrote his biography (1925) as did his daughter, Mary Ellin Barrett, in 1994.

BERNARD, WILLIAM BAYLE (1807–75), dramatist who helped popularize the stage type of the eccentric rural American. Among the 100 successful plays that he wrote were *The Dumb Belle* (1831); *The Kentuckian; or, A Trip to New York* (1833), a revision of Paulding's *Lion of the West; His Last Legs* (1839); and an early dramatization of *Rip Van Winkle* (1832). His *Retrospections of America* (1887) was edited by Brander Matthews.

BERNSTEIN, CHARLES (1950–   ), born in New York City and educated at Harvard, published the first of his large collection of poems, *Parsing* (1976), which initiated an emphasis on sound but not a unified meaning. Among his many later books are *Poetic Justice* (1979), *Sense of Responsibility* (1979), *Artifice of Absorption* (1988), and *The Sophist* (1988). His essays have been collected in *Content's Dream* (1985).

BERNSTEIN, LEONARD (1918–90), Massachusetts-born composer, conductor, and pianist, graduated from Harvard (1939), conducted the New York City Symphony (1945–48), was on the faculty of the Berkshire Music Center (1948–55) and Brandeis University (1951–56), and was the conductor of the New York Philharmonic (1958–69), along with making world tours and conducting other major orchestras. His works include pieces for piano, brass instruments, and clarinet; song cycles; two symphonies, *Jeremiah* (1942) and *The Age of Anxiety* (1949), the latter inspired by Auden's poem; a one-act opera (music and libretto), *Trouble in Tahiti* (1952); ballets; a film score; and the musical shows *On the Town* (1945), *Wonderful Town* (1953), *Candide* (1956, 1974), and *West Side Story* (1957). His books include *The Joy of Music* (1959); *The Infinite Variety of Music* (1966); *The Unanswered Question* (1976), lectures delivered at Harvard; and *Findings* (1982), collecting a wide variety of writings from the author's school days forward.

BERRIGAN, TED (EDMUND J.M. BERRIGAN, JR.) (1934–83), poet whose experimental works, very diverse in style but often parodic, include *A Lily for My Love* (1959), *The Sonnets* (1964), *In the Early Morning Rain* (1971), and *Red Wagon* (1976). *Galileo; or Finksville* (1964) is a play, and

Bean Spasms (1967) is a medley of poems and prose pieces written with Ron Padgett. Berrigan's poems, old and new, are collected in *So Going Around Cities* (1980).

BERRY, DON (1932–   ), Minnesota-born novelist, long resident in Oregon, the setting of *Trask* (1960), depicting Indian and white relations in the mid-19th century; *Moontrap* (1962), dealing with mountain men; and *To Build a Ship* (1963), the last volume of this loosely related trilogy. *A Majority of Scoundrels* (1961) is an informal history of the Rocky Mountain Fur Company.

BERRY, WENDELL (1934–   ), Kentucky-born author and professor at his alma mater, the state university. His poems, redolent of the region and its people, are collected in *The Broken Ground* (1964), *Openings* (1968), *Findings* (1969), *Farming: A Handbook* (1970), *The Country of Marriage* (1973), *Clearing* (1977), *Collected Poems* (1985), *Sabbaths* (1987), and *Traveling at Home* (1988). His novels, also set in his native state, are *Nathan Coulter* (1960), about a boy growing up in the tobacco-farming land; *A Place on Earth* (1967), about a Kentuckian at home whose only son is missing in action during World War II; and *The Memory of Old Jack* (1974), in which a 92-year-old farmer recalls the ways of life of his earlier days. He has also written essays collected in *The Long-Legged House* (1969), *The Unforeseen Wilderness* (1971), *A Continuous Harmony* (1972), *The Unsettling of America: Culture and Agriculture* (1977), and *What Are People For?* (1990). *The Hidden Wound* (1970) contains recollections of childhood and the effect of racism on him. *A Part* (1980) contains translations and poems. *The Wild Birds* (1986) collects six stories of the pastoral life of his state. *Sex, Economy, Freedom and Community* (1993) contains essays on the pursuit of self-liberation.

BERRYMAN, JOHN (1914–72), born in Oklahoma, educated in the U.S. and England, a professor of humanities at the University of Minnesota, wrote a study of *Stephen Crane* (1950) for the American Men of Letters Series, but is best known for his poetry. His early works are *Poems* (1942); *The Dispossessed* (1948); *Homage to Mistress Bradstreet* (1956), a biographical ode, richly allusive, moving and meaningful to the present day in its inquiry into the personal and spiritual life of the colonial poet Anne Bradstreet♦; and *His Thought Made Pockets and the Plane Buckt* (1958). In 1964 he published *77 Dream Songs* (Pulitzer Prize), the opening of a series of 18-line poems that reached to 385 in all, presenting his own persona of Henry, who lives through personal and social crises and survives. It is a work complex in themes, celebrating a kind of negative courage with ironic humor, and employing diction and syntax that are very American and often derive from the stereotyped minstrel-show Negro. The poem is completed in *His Toy, His Dream, His Rest* (1968) and *The Dream Songs* (1969). Prior to the collection of the entirety of this major work, *Berryman's Sonnets* (1967) published 115 Petrarchan sonnets telling of a summer love affair; *Short Poems* (1967) gathered lyrics, and *Love and Fame* (1970) brought together autobiographical poems showing Berryman returning to his parents' faith of Catholicism. Despite this turn to religion, Berryman took his own life. *Delusions, etc.* (1972) posthumously gathers late poems, and *Henry's Fate* (1977) prints unpublished parts of the *Dream Songs* and other fragments. *The Freedom of the Poet* (1976) collects stories and essays, and *Recovery* (1973) is an incomplete autobiographical novel about an intellectual man's addiction to alcohol. *We Dream of Honour* (1988) gathers his letters to his mother.

Best sellers, term for books that are remarkably popular, for a brief time or over a period of many years. Seldom of great literary significance, such works are often ephemeral and dependent upon temporary tastes and interests. Nevertheless, the best-selling book in the U.S., as in other Christian lands, has been the Bible. Publications of special sects, like the *Book of Mormon* and *Science and Health,* have also been widely circulated. Best sellers of colonial times included the *New England Primer* and *The Day of Doom,* followed later by political tracts like *Common Sense,* by chapbooks like Weems's life of Washington, and by almanacs. In the mid-19th century gift books had huge sales, as did dime novels,♦ and children's literature.♦ Widely read poems included *Hiawatha, Nothing To Wear,* and "Plain Language from Truthful James," and later poets with great followings included Ella Wheeler Wilcox, James Whitcomb Riley, Robert Service, and Edgar Guest. Texts that have been popular include Webster's *Spelling Book* and dictionary, Caleb Bingham's primers, McGuffey's *Eclectic Readers,* and cookbooks.

The novel has been the most popular literary genre in the U.S., and widely read works include *Charlotte Temple* (1794), *The Spy* (1821), *Uncle Tom's Cabin* (1852), *The Lamplighter* (1854), *St. Elmo* (1867), *The Gates Ajar* (1868), *Barriers Burned Away* (1872), *The Adventures of Tom Sawyer* (1876), *Ben-Hur* (1880), *Looking Backward* (1888), *In His Steps* (1896), *Hugh Wynne* (1897), *When Knighthood Was in Flower* (1898), *David Harum* (1898), *Richard Carvel* (1899), *The Call of the Wild* (1903), *The Little Shepherd of Kingdom Come* (1903), *The Clansman* (1905), *The Winning of Barbara Worth* (1911), *Riders of the Purple Sage* (1912), *Dere Mable!* (1918), *The Covered Wagon* (1922), *Gentlemen Prefer Blondes* (1925), *Anthony Adverse* (1933), *Gone with the Wind* (1936), *The Robe* (1942), *The Naked and the Dead* (1948), *From Here to Eternity* (1951), *The Caine Mutiny* (1951), *Lolita* (1958), *The Group* (1963), and *War and Remembrance* (1978). The first American novel to sell over 1,000,000 copies was *Uncle Tom's Cabin. In His Steps* has been the most popular work with a religious theme, and *Gone with the Wind* has been fastest selling.

Very popular types of fiction, although not always represented by single books, are detective stories,♦ novels of Western adventure by such authors as Harold Bell Wright, Zane Grey, Max Brand, and Louis L'Amour; science fiction, like that of Isaac Asimov and Ray Bradbury; and novels by women, ranging from the moral and sentimental, like those of Kathleen Norris and Frances Parkinson Keyes, to the toughly realistic and frankly sexual, like the works of Jacqueline Susann and Erica Jong and the in-between work of Danielle Steel. In recent years authors whose works almost consistently appear on best-seller lists have included O'Hara and Steinbeck, and Michener, Irving Stone, Uris, Vidal, and Wouk. Popularity on first publication in hardbound editions is usually repeated in paperback reprints, but some authors, like Erskine Caldwell, find their large public only in reprints, as do works of certain desirable genres, such as the lushly romantic pseudo-historic novels called Gothic romances. Selection by major book clubs usually assists bookstore sales and popularity of reprints. Popular plays may be considered in the category of best sellers, even if they do not always sell very well when put into print. The greatest stage successes in the U.S. have included *The Drunkard, A Trip to Chinatown, The Old Homestead, Our American Cousin, Under the Gaslight, East Lynne, Rip Van Winkle, Sherlock Holmes, The Squaw Man, Lightnin', Abie's Irish Rose, The Green Pastures, Tobacco Road, Life with Father, Oklahoma!, My Fair Lady, Hello, Dolly!, Pal Joey, Guys and Dolls, The Fantasticks,* and *A Chorus Line.*

Bethel Community, partriarchal agricultural colony (1844–80) of Germans and a few Pennsylvania Dutch, directed by Dr. William Keil, a Prussian immigrant, occupied about 4000 acres in Missouri. Loosely organized, it insisted on community of goods and labor, but encouraged marriage and maintained strict standards of family life. It was dissolved soon after the death of Keil. The Aurora Community in Oregon (1856–81) was a similar organization founded by Keil.

BEVERIDGE, ALBERT J[EREMIAH] (1862–1927), insurgent Republican senator from Indiana (1899–1911), was an organizer of the Progressive party. After its defeat in his state, he turned to historical writing, producing a *Life of John Marshall* (4 vols., 1916, 1919, Pulitzer Prize), which is also a history of the early U.S. Supreme Court. His incomplete *Life of Abraham Lincoln* (2 vols., 1928) is noted for its treatment of Lincoln's career to 1858.

BEVERLEY, ROBERT (*c.*1673–1722), Virginia planter and minor statesman, wrote *The History and Present State of Virginia* (1705, enlarged 1722) to replace the work of John Oldmixon and other English historians whom he regarded as superficial. His work falls into four parts: (1) history to 1706; (2) natural resources; (3) native Indians; and (4) present state of the country. He writes in a shrewd, lively manner, with humor playing both on the Southern planter and the foreign critic.

Beyond the Horizon, play by Eugene O'Neill,♦ produced and published in 1920, when it won a Pulitzer Prize.

Robert Mayo, of poetic nature, dislikes work on his father's farm, and plans to seek adventure as a seaman. His brother Andrew, better adapted to farm life, has been his rival for the love of Ruth Atkins, but when she reveals that she loves Robert, Andrew goes to sea instead. In the next three years Ruth's passion fades, and Robert fails as a farmer. Persecuted by the complaints of his wife and his mother, he is consoled only by his daughter and his books, while Ruth hopes that Andrew still loves her and will return. Andrew, home for a day, shows that travel has made him hard and commonplace, and he reveals to Ruth that his love for her soon passed. Disillusioned and poverty-stricken, the family passes another five years on the farm. Robert's daughter dies, his wife is apathetic, and Andrew returns only when Robert is dying of consumption. Escaping from his bed, he watches the sunrise from a hill: "It isn't the end. It's a free beginning . . . beyond the horizon!"

Bianca Visconti, blank-verse romantic tragedy by N. P. Willis,♦ produced in 1837 and published in 1839. The play, set in 15th-century Italy, concerns the Duke of Milan, Francesco Sforza, and his wife Bianca Visconti.

Bible in Colonial America, originally brought from England and Europe in various versions, was first partially translated and published in the English colonies with the issuance of the Bay Psalm Book♦ (1640). The first publication of the complete Bible was the translation of John Eliot♦ into the language of the Massachuset Indians (New Testament, 1661; Old Testament, 1663). The British monopolistically refused to let an English-language Bible be printed in the colonies and so none was issued until after the Revolution, when Robert Aitken♦ of Philadelphia printed the New Testament in 1777 and the complete Bible in 1782.

Biblical Repertory (1825–88), the most important Presbyterian periodical until 1878, when it was rechristened *The Princeton Review* and shifted its emphasis to compete with *The North American Review.* After suspending publication in 1884, it was revived as *The New Princeton Review* (1886), an eclectic literary magazine whose contributors included C.D. Warner, Lowell, Theodore Roosevelt, Wilson, C.E. Norton, and Stedman.

Bibliographical Society of America, founded in 1904 as a development of the Bibliographical

Society of Chicago (1899–1904), to promote bibliographical study with emphasis on American materials. It publishes quarterly *Papers* and scholarly books, including sponsorship of the *Bibliography of American Literature.* ♦

Bibliography of American Literature, compiled by Jacob Blanck and sponsored by the Bibliographical Society of America, provides a detailed physical description of all first editions (books, pamphlets, broadsides, etc.) by some 300 authors who lived between the Federal period and 1930, with emphasis on writers of belles lettres. The nine volumes were published between 1955 and 1991.

BIDDLE, Nicholas (1786–1844), Philadelphia financier and scholar, edited the *Port Folio* (1812), and, assisted by Paul Allen, compiled and edited the notes and journals of the Lewis and Clark expedition, published as the *History of the Expedition of Captains Lewis and Clark* (1814). The exigencies of the War of 1812 caused Biddle to abandon literary scholarship to serve in the state senate and aid in financing the war. In 1819 he became a director and then (1822–39) president of the Bank of the United States.

BIDWELL, John (1819–1900), arrived in California (1841) from Missouri, as described in his *Echoes of the Past* (1914) and *A Journey to California* (1842). He took a prominent part in the separation from Mexico and in later state politics.

BIERCE, Ambrose [Gwinett] (1842–1914?), born in Ohio, served in the Civil War and became a brilliant and bitter journalist in San Francisco. In England (1872–75) he was on the staff of *Fun,* contributed to *Tom Hood's Comic Annual,* edited two issues of *The Lantern* for the exiled Empress Eugenie, and published under the pseudonym Dod Grile three collections of his vitriolic sketches and witticisms, *The Fiend's Delight* (1873), *Nuggets and Dust Panned Out in California* (1873), and *Cobwebs from an Empty Skull* (1874). Returning to San Francisco, he wrote for Hearst's *Examiner,* and his wit and satire made him the literary dictator of the Pacific coast, strongly influencing many writers, including his friend George Sterling. Many of his works were potboilers, but in 1891 he issued *Tales of Soldiers and Civilians,* ♦ stories reminiscent of Poe's tales of horror and marked by an ingenious use of the surprise ending, a sardonic humor, and a realistic study of tense emotional states. This was followed by *The Monk and the Hangman's Daughter* (1892), a medieval romance translated with a collaborator from the German of Richard Voss, and *Black Beetles in Amber* (1892), witty satirical verses. Later poems are collected in *Shapes of Clay* (1903). *Can Such Things Be?* ♦ (1893) is a second volume of tales, also dealing with episodes of the Civil War and the California frontier, with the supernaturalism,

horror, and sardonic humor of the earlier volume. In 1897 Bierce went to Washington as correspondent for the Hearst newspapers, and there he collected *The Cynic's Word Book* (1906), retitled *The Devil's Dictionary* ♦ (1911), a volume of ironic definitions whose temper is elaborated in *Fantastic Fables* (1899), an Æsopian collection about contemporary economics and politics. *The Shadow on the Dial* (1909) is a series of disillusioned essays on contemporary civilization. For several years Bierce was occupied with editing his *Collected Works* (1909–12), 12 volumes of his better prose and verse, interlarded with journalism. Tired of American civilization, in 1913 he disappeared into war-torn Mexico, to seek "the good, kind darkness." Although weird stories have been told concerning his fate, it is probable that in Mexico he found the euthanasia he desired.

A brief book, *Write It Right* (1909), "a blacklist of literary faults," was not included in his *Works.* Posthumously collected books include *The Letters of Ambrose Bierce* (1922), *Ambrose Bierce's Civil War* (1956), and *The Enlarged Devil's Dictionary* (1967).

Big Bear of Arkansas, The, story by T.B. Thorpe, ♦ one of the most famous tall tales of the Southwest, tells of a hunter's adventures in attempting to shoot "an unhuntable bear," finally killed because he "died when his time come." It first appeared in the *Spirit of the Times* (1841), and was reprinted in *The Hive of the Bee Hunter* (1854) and in a collection bearing its title edited by W.T. Porter.

Big Money, The, novel by Dos Passos, ♦ published in 1936. It is the last of the trilogy *U.S.A.* (collected 1938), following *The 42nd Parallel* ♦ (1930) and *1919* ♦ (1932). Interspersed in the narrative are brief biographies of Frederick Taylor, Ford, Veblen, Isadora Duncan, the Wright brothers, Valentino, Frank Lloyd Wright, Hearst, and Samuel Insull.

The war hero Charley Anderson returns to New York to organize an airplane factory, intending to produce better planes and avoid the profit motive. Progressively disillusioned, he joins a large Detroit plane factory, marries the heiress Gladys Wheatley, takes to drink, gambles in the stock market, and is swindled by his associates. In Florida to recuperate, he has an affair with Margo Dowling, is divorced by Gladys, enters a fraudulent land deal, and is killed in an automobile accident.

Margo, after an unhappy childhood, goes to New York, hopes to have a stage career, is seduced by her stepfather, and elopes with a Cuban dancer. Deserted by her husband, she becomes a New York chorus girl, drifts to Miami, and after her affair with Charley uses the last of his money to go to Hollywood. There she marries a producer, has a brief success in motion pictures, and sinks into obscurity.

Mary French, daughter of a Colorado doctor, attends Vassar, works on a Pittsburgh paper, and is discharged for her sympathetic reporting of a steel strike. She lives for a time with the dishonest labor leader G.H. Barrow, but leaves him to do union work and aid her Communist lover Ben Compton. Disillusioned by Ben's arrest, the loss of another lover, and the outcome of the Sacco-Vanzetti case, she temporarily quits these activities, but later plunges again into labor work.

Richard Ellsworth Savage is alone able to cope with the era, accepting its standards and opportunistically serving the "public relations" firm of J.W. Moorehouse, whose successor he promises to become.

The final character is a "vag," hitchhiking across the continent, who thinks of the comfort of the passengers in a plane overhead, and of his youthful beliefs: "went to school, books said opportunity, ads promised speed, own your own home, shine bigger than your neighbor. . . ."

Big Sky, The, novel by A.B. Guthrie,♦ published in 1947. *Fair Land, Fair Land* (1982) is a sequel carrying Dick Summers to the age of 70 in a changed West.

Leaving his mean father for dead after a fight, Boone Caudill, a simple taciturn, impulsive boy of 17, quits Kentucky in 1830 in pursuit of freedom as a "natural man" in the virgin territory of the West. He goes up the Missouri River on a keelboat with Jim Deakins, a fun-loving, redheaded young man, Teal Eye, the beautiful daughter of a Piegan chief, and Dick Summers, an experienced mountain man. In succeeding years of wandering in the wilderness Boone becomes more like an Indian. Teal Eye is his squaw. Jim, called Red Hair by the Indians, also lives with the Piegans. When Teal Eye gives birth to a boy "with a touch of red in its hair," Boone kills his friend in a burst of fury, leaves Teal Eye, and gives up the way of life he loved.

Big Sur and the Oranges of Hieronymus Bosch, personal narrative by Henry Miller,♦ published in 1957. An anecdotal account, it tells of the author's life on the rugged and rather isolated California coastal area south of Carmel, where he lived for more than a decade after returning from his lengthy European expatriation. Alluding to the Flemish painter's depiction of fruit as symbolic of a garden of earthly delights, Miller finds the natural scene and his enjoyable neighbors make for a good life.

Big Table, quarterly little magazine (1959–60) founded to publish the contents of a suppressed issue of the *Chicago Review* of the University of Chicago. That and subsequent issues featured writing by Kerouac, Dahlberg, and William Burroughs.

BIGELOW, JOHN (1817–1911), associate editor and owner of the New York *Evening Post*♦ (1848–61), whose Free-Soil interests led to his campaign *Life* of Frémont (1856). As consul general at Paris (1861–65) and minister to France (1865–66), he helped swing sympathy away from the Confederacy. Foreign experiences led to his writing *Beaumarchais the Merchant* (1870), *France and Hereditary Monarchy* (1871), and *France and the Confederate Navy* (1888). His other works include an edition of Franklin's *Autobiography* (1868) from the manuscript he discovered in France; a ten-volume edition of Franklin's *Works* (1887–88); a *Life* (1895) and *Writings* (1885) of Tilden, with whom he was politically associated; and two Swedenborgian works, *Molinos the Quietist* (1882) and *The Mystery of Sleep* (1897). He wrote *Retrospections of an Active Life* (5 vols., 1909–13), and he is the subject of Margaret Clapp's *Forgotten First Citizen* (1947).

BIGGERS, EARL DERR (1884–1933), born in Ohio, educated at Harvard, became a journalist in Boston and later won fame as a popular novelist and playwright. He is best known for his *Seven Keys to Baldpate* (1913), a melodramatic story set in a lonely mountain inn, and a series of detective novels whose hero is the enigmatic Chinese sleuth Charlie Chan. Among these are *The Chinese Parrot* (1926), *Behind That Curtain* (1928), and *The Black Camel* (1929).

Biglow Papers, The, two series of satirical verses in Yankee dialect by Lowell,♦ the first written in opposition to the Mexican War and the second in support of the North during the Civil War. The first of the verses appeared in *The Boston Courier* (1846), and the first series was published in book form in 1848, while the second appeared in the *Atlantic Monthly* during the Civil War and was collected in 1867. Both are purportedly written by the young New England farmer Hosea Biglow, and edited with a complicated pseudo-critical apparatus by Homer Wilbur, "Pastor of the First Church in Jaalam."

Of the nine "letters" in the first series, three represent versified epistles from Hosea's friend Birdofredom Sawin, "Private in the Massachusetts Regiment," who swallows the propaganda of "manifest destiny" but comes to disappointment and disillusion. ("Nimepunce a day fer killin' folks comes kind o' low fer murder.") The remaining six are Hosea's satirical portrait of a recruiting sergeant; his satire of a hypocritical politician, "What Mr. Robinson Thinks"; his parody of an address by a State Street stump speaker; "The Debate in the Sennit," burlesquing a speech by Calhoun; the pusillanimous "Pious Editor's Creed"; and the declaration of principles by a supposed presidential candidate, which leaves him uncommitted, "frontin' South by North."

The second series, with a critical introduction over Lowell's signature, includes "The Courtin'," a humorous narrative in dialect verse, and 11 satirical "letters," including two from Birdofredom Sawin, now resident in the South and gulled by Confederate propaganda; "Mason and Slidell: A Yankee Idyll"; malicious burlesque speeches by Jefferson Davis and a hypocritical man of wealth, "Honourable Preserved Doe"; an appeal to sentiment, "Sunthin' in the Pastoral Line"; a demand that the Confederate "system" be crushed ("Conciliate? it jest means *be kicked*"); "Kettleopotomachia," macaronic Latin verses by Parson Wilbur; an idyllic depiction of the approaching peace; and a view of Reconstruction, "Mr. Hosea Biglow's Speech in March Meeting."

Bill Arp, pseudonym of Charles H. Smith.♦

Bill of Rights, the first ten amendments to the U.S. Constitution,♦ passed in 1791, were framed largely by Madison, Patrick Henry, and R.H. Lee. Their main guarantees are the freedom of worship, of speech, of press, of assembly, of petition for redress of grievances, and against being deprived of life, liberty, or property without "due process of law." An important source was the Virginia Declaration of Rights (1776), framed by George Mason.

BILLINGS, JOSH, pseudonym of H.W. Shaw.♦

BILLINGS, WILLIAM (1746–1800), Boston tanner, became a professional composer because he wished to reform the bare and tedious psalmody of the period. He published *The New-England Psalm-Singer* (1770), his own novel settings of religious poetry, and during the Revolution wrote patriotic hymns and anthems, including the belligerent "Chester" and paraphrases of the Psalms invoking God's grace exclusively for the rebels.

Billy Budd, novelette by Melville,♦ was written during the five years before his death and published in 1924. The much revised manuscript, left without definitive form, was reissued in a very careful edition in 1962. A dramatization was made by Louis O. Coxe and Robert H. Chapman as *Uniform of Flesh* (1949), revised as *Billy Budd* (1951).

Billy Budd is the typical Handsome Sailor of 18th-century balladry, and because of his innocence and beauty is hated by Claggart, a dark, demon-haunted petty officer. In his simplicity, Billy cannot understand why Claggart should hate him, why evil should desire to destroy good. Claggart concocts a fantastic story of mutiny, supposedly plotted by Billy, whom he accuses to the captain. Billy, unable to speak, in his only act of rebellion strikes Claggart a fatal blow. Captain Vere, who sympathizes with Billy and recognizes his essential innocence, is nevertheless force to condemn him, and though Billy is hanged he lives on as a legend among sailors.

Billy the Kid, sobriquet of William H. Bonney (1859–81), desperado of the Southwest, who was

a leader in the Lincoln County cattle war in New Mexico. His subsequent career of wholesale cattle stealing brought his score of murders to 21 before he was finally killed by a sheriff. The Kid is the subject of many stories and ballads, and he has been apotheosized in dime novels and serious fiction.

BINGHAM, CALEB (1757–1817), author of school texts, whose books *The American Preceptor* (1794) and *The Columbian Orator* (1797) were constant companions of the Bible and the Psalms in New England schools. He translated Chateaubriand's *Atala* (1802).

BINNS, ARCHIE (1899–1971), born and reared in Washington, after service on a lightship, on a freighter, and in the army graduated from Stanford University (1922) and began his literary career. His novels include *Lightship* (1934), based on his experiences but treating the coastal vessel as a microcosm; *The Laurels are Cut Down* (1937), about a boy's life in the Puget Sound region, his service with his brother in the army sent to Siberia, and his disillusionment; *The Land is Bright* (1939), concerning the Oregon Trail in the 1850s; *Mighty Mountain* (1940), about a sea voyage in the 1850s to Puget Sound; *Timber Beast* (1944), about the lumber industry and the I.W.W. conflict; *You Rolling River* (1947), set in the Columbia River country of the 1890s; and *The Headwaters* (1957), about pioneer life on an island near Vancouver. *Northwest Gateway: The Story of Seattle* (1941), *Roaring Land* (1942), and *Sea in the Forest* (1953) are historical and descriptive accounts. With Olive Kooken he wrote *Mrs. Fiske and the American Theatre* (1955).

Birches, blank-verse lyric by Robert Frost,♦ published in *Mountain Interval* (1916). The poet describes his boyhood pleasure in climbing birch trees, swinging from the tops until the supple trunks bent in a curve to the ground. He dreams of being again "a swinger of birches," and finds in this occupation a symbol for his desired surcease from "considerations," in which he might

go by climbing a birch tree . . .
Toward heaven, till the tree could bear no
    more,
But dipped its top and set me down again.
That would be good both going and coming
    back.

BIRD, ROBERT MONTGOMERY (1806–54), born in Delaware, studied at the University of Pennsylvania (M.D., 1827) and taught at the Pennsylvania Medical College (1841–43), but is famous as a novelist and dramatist. His early romantic tragedies and comedies of Philadelphia life such as *The City Looking Glass* (1828, published 1933) were followed by *Pelopidas,* an unproduced historical drama about the Theban revolt against Sparta, and *The Gladiator*♦ (1831), his most popular play. In 1832 his friend Forrest produced

Oralloossa,♦ a tragedy concerned with the assassination of Pizarro, which he followed with Bird's best play, *The Broker of Bogotá*♦ (1834). Bird revised *Metamora*♦ (1836) for Forrest, but then, discouraged by the actor's failure to keep financial agreements, broke with him and turned to writing fiction. In 1834 he published anonymously *Calavar; or, The Knight of the Conquest,* a tale of the Mexican conquistadors, which was later praised by Prescott. *The Infidel; or, The Fall of Mexico* (1835) is a sequel. *The Hawks of Hawk-Hollow*♦ (1835), a romance of the Revolution, deals with a prominent Pennsylvania family's decline because of disloyalty to the patriot cause. *Sheppard Lee* (1836) uses a psychological study of metempsychosis to satirize contemporary social conditions, and reflects Bird's Whig sympathies in regard to slavery. His finest novel, *Nick of the Woods; or, The Jibbenainosay*♦ (1837), was followed by *Peter Pilgrim; or, A Rambler's Recollections* (1838), a series of realistic travel sketches, and *The Adventures of Robin Day* (1839), a picaresque novel. Because of ill-health, he wrote no more books, but in 1847, after some years of retirement, became literary editor and part owner of the Philadelphia *North American,* which he helped to edit until his death.

Bird Woman, see *Sacagawea.*

Birds' Christmas Carol, The, story for children by Kate Douglas Wiggin.♦

Birds of America, The, collection of color prints of some 500 species of birds by Audubon,♦ issued serially in an elephant folio edition (London, 1827–38), as engraved by Robert Havell, Jr. The original drawings by Audubon have disappeared, and it is uncertain how much of the fine artistic quality is due to the work of Havell. The accompanying text, written with the more scholarly William MacGillivray, was issued as *Ornithological Biography* (5 vols., 1831–39). An octavo edition of *The Birds of America* (7 vols., 1840–44) was prepared by Audubon for American publication. The *Synopsis of the Birds of North America* (1839) is a methodical catalogue of the birds then known, and was also prepared with the assistance of MacGillivray. The drawings were said by Cuvier to be "the most magnificent monument yet raised by art to science," but their scientific basis has been questioned in some instances. Audubon's firsthand acquaintance with his subject and his impressionistic art give the work its high value and wide popularity.

Birds of Killingworth, The, one of the *Tales of a Wayside Inn.*♦

BIRKBECK, MORRIS (1764–1825), emigrated to Illinois from England (1817), and attracted attention to the prairie region by his *Notes on a Journey . . . to the Territory of Illinois* (1817) and his *Letters from Illinois* (1818). These books were much criticized by Cobbett,♦ who was in the pay of Eastern land speculators.

BIRNEY, JAMES GILLESPIE (1792–1857), early Southern antislavery leader, set forth his beliefs in a *Letter on the Political Obligations of Abolitionists* (1839), and was later nominated for the presidency by the Liberty party.♦ His *Letters* have been published (2 vols., 1938).

Birth of a Nation, The, motion picture written by Thomas Dixon♦ and filmed by D.W. Griffith♦ in 1915. This story of the South during and after the Civil War provided the screen with its first large spectacle.

Birthmark, The, allegorical tale by Hawthorne,♦ published in *Mosses from an Old Manse* (1846).

Aylmer, a scientist, marries Georgiana, a beautiful woman whose single physical flaw is a tiny crimson birthmark on her left cheek, resembling a hand. The mark repels Aylmer, who determines to use his scientific knowledge to remove it. Assisted by his rude, earthy servant, Aminadab, he unsuccessfully tries every known method, finally using a powerful potion which, although it causes the birthmark to fade, causes her death also. Aminadab laughs, and the author concludes:

> Thus ever does the gross fatality of earth exult in its invariable triumph over the immortal essence which, in this dim sphere of half-development, demands the completeness of a higher state.

BISHOP, ELIZABETH (1911–79), poet, born in Worcester, Mass., was raised in her formative years chiefly in Nova Scotia by relatives after her father died and her mother institutionalized when the child was five. At about the time of graduation from Vassar, Bishop met Marianne Moore, who became mentor and friend. Her first poems in book form appeared in the anthology *Trial Balances* (1935), with an introduction by Moore. From 1939 to 1973 Bishop lived in Key West, then in Brazil; in 1974 she settled in Boston, teaching at Harvard until her death. *Poems* (1955) collects *North and South* (1946) and *A Cold Spring* (1955). It contains some of her most famous poems, such as "The Fish," in which she catches and, after minutely described examination, releases a huge trout, whereat "Suddenly everything was rainbow, rainbow, rainbow." Her move to Brazil illuminates *Questions of Travel* (1965). Recognition of Bishop as a major poet became widespread only at her death. Her best work, a series of meditations, is her last, *Geography III* (1976). Her poems build intricate details toward resolution, reminiscent of the work of Marianne Moore. She marries common experience to the strangeness of dreams. There are two posthumous books: *The Complete Poems 1927–1979* (1983) and *The Collected Prose* (1984). A selection of her letters, *One Art,* edited by Robert Giroux, was published in 1994.

BISHOP, JOHN PEALE (1892–1944), West Virginia-born author, lived on Cape Cod, whose poems are collected in *Green Fruit* (1917); *The Undertaker's Garland* (1922), written with Edmund Wilson; *Now with His Love* (1933); and *Minute Particulars* (1936). *Many Thousands Gone* (1931) is a book of stories, and *Act of Darkness* (1935) is a novel. Bishop is said to be the prototype of Tom D'Invilliers in *This Side of Paradise.* His *Collected Essays* and his *Collected Poems* were published in 1948. His correspondence with Allen Tate was printed in 1981.

BISHOP, MORRIS [GILBERT] (1893–1973), educated at Cornell, where he served as a professor of Romance languages (1921–60), about which he wrote *A History of Cornell* (1962). Besides his scholarly works, *The Odyssey of Cabeza de Vaca* (1933), *Champlain* (1948) and *The Life and Adventures of La Rochefoucauld* (1951), he wrote many volumes of light verse, including *A Bowl of Bishop* (1954). *The Widening Stain* (1942) is a mystery story published under the name W. Bolingbroke Johnson.

BISHOP, THOMAS BRIGHAM (1835–1905), song composer of Portland, Me., whose works were popular during the Civil War and much used by minstrel shows. He was the author of "When Johnny Comes Marching Home" and "Shoo, fly! don't bodder me!" and has been credited with the words of "John Brown's Body."

Black April, novel by Julia Peterkin,♦ published in 1927.
   April, giant black foreman of a South Carolina cotton plantation and patriarchal leader of the local blacks, has many illegitimate children, one of whom is the boy Breeze, through whose experiences the story is told. Sherry, another illegitimate son, becomes his father's rival in leadership on the plantation and in having a son by a young girl, Joy, who had been one of April's loves. April contracts gangrene in his legs, which are amputated, and he is broken in spirit as well as in body, pathetically asking only to be buried "in a man-size box— . . . six feet fo'!"

Black Beetles in Amber, satirical verse by Ambrose Bierce.♦

Black Boy, autobiography of Richard Wright,♦ published in 1945.
   This story of the author's life to the age of 19, when he went north, incorporates an evocation of the South, rural and urban, as he moved from place to place, living mainly in Jackson, Miss., and Nashville, Tenn., with a succession of relatives after his father abandoned the family and his mother was incapacitated by paralyzing strokes.

In addition to summoning up a sense of the sights, sounds, smells, and ways of life in the South, Wright explores the genesis of an artist, an individual who rebels against the beliefs and mores of pietistic relatives and against schoolmasters and schoolmates, finally finding a larger world in his voracious reading of Mencken, Dreiser, Sinclair Lewis, and other authors. The book also vividly presents racial conflict in the South, with its physical, political, social, and spiritual violence against blacks.

Black Cat, The, story, by Poe,♦ published in 1843, collected in *Tales* (1845).
   A condemned murderer tells of his crime and its discovery. For years he cherished a pet black cat, Pluto, until intemperate drinking led him to destroy one of its eyes during a fit of malevolence. The cat recovered, but its master's perverse mood continued, and he tied it by the neck to a tree. The same night, his home was destroyed by fire, except for a newly plastered wall that bore the image of a cat with a noose about its neck. Now poverty-stricken and degenerate, the man was haunted by this image, but nevertheless brought home a stray one-eyed cat, which had a single white mark on its black breast, resembling a gallows. He came to hate the animal, and one day attempted to kill it with an axe; murdering his wife when she interfered, he placed her body in a cellar recess that he concealed with plaster. When police came to make a search, they found nothing until a ghastly scream from the walled recess caused them to open it and discover the cat seated upon the head of the corpse.

BLACK HAWK (1767–1838), chief of the Sauk and Fox Indians, who refused to move west of the Mississippi in accordance with a treaty of 1804. Instead he made war on the frontier settlements (1832) in what is known as the Black Hawk War. His *Autobiography* (1833) defends his interpretation of the treaty and his subsequent action, which resulted in his temporary imprisonment and the dispersal of his force.

Black Mountain College, experimental liberal arts institution, near Asheville, N.C., founded (1933) by dissident faculty and students of Rollins College (Florida) for innovative and improvisory learning. Although it foundered (1956), its teachers, including Josef Albers, and its journal, *The Black Mountain Review* (1954–57), had a great effect far beyond its campus. The major figure was Charles Olson,♦ for a time the chancellor, whose important students include Creeley, Duncan, Levertov, and John Wieners. Creeley edited the *Review,* concentrating on the college's poets but including also Ginsberg, Kerouac, and Zukofsky.

Black Oxen, novel by Gertrude Atherton,♦ published in 1923.

Black Riders, The, and Other Lines, volume of free verse by Stephen Crane,♦ published in 1895. Influenced by reading Emily Dickinson, Crane in these concise, intense unrhymed poems foreshadows the work of the Imagists. Elliptical renderings of his naturalistic philosophy, they show his bewildered bitterness of youth buffeted by the great impersonal forces of the world.

BLACKBEARD, name commonly given to the pirate Edward Teach (also Thatch or Thach, *d.*1718), whose audacious cruelty in the West Indies and along the coast of Virginia and the Carolinas is the subject of numerous legends. The mania of searching for his supposed treasure is ridiculed in *The Disappointment*♦ (1767).

BLACKBURN, PAUL (1926–71), Vermont-born poet, for a time resident in Spain, whose translations are *Proensa* (1953) from troubadours and *El Cid Campeador* (1966). His own poetry, influenced by William Carlos Williams, appeared in *The Dissolving Fabric* (1955), *Brooklyn-Manhattan Transit* (1960), *The Nets* (1961), *Sing-Song* (1967), *The Cities* (1967), and *In, On, or About the Premises* (1968). *The Journals* (1975) and *Omitted Journals* (1983) form a posthumous collection of poems and a chronicle of his last years. Other posthumously issued works include *Against the Silences* (1980), poems introduced by Robert Creeley, and *Collected Poems* (1985).

Blackfoot Indians, group of bison-hunting Algonquian tribes in Alberta and Montana, of which the Blackfoot proper are the most prominent. They once ranged from the Yellowstone River to the Rocky Mountains, and they figure in diaries of 19th-century plainsmen, being noted for their constant warfare with the Crow, and their unwavering hostility toward whites. In Irving's *Adventures of Captain Bonneville* and the *Life* of Beckwourth they appear as horse thieves and ruffians, but they are romantically depicted in the operas of Arthur Nevin, whose music is based on a study of native themes. G.B. Grinnell and J.W. Schultz have also written on the Blackfoot.

BLACKMUR, R[ICHARD] P[ALMER] (1904–65), poet and critic, although without formal education after high school, was not only a learned critic but served as a resident fellow (1940–48) and professor (1948–65) at Princeton. His books include *From Jordan's Delight* (1937) and *Second World* (1942), poems; *The Double Agent* (1935), *The Expense of Greatness* (1940), *Language as Gesture* (1952), *The Lion and the Honeycomb* (1955), essays on literature; *Form and Value in Modern Poetry* (1957); and *Eleven Essays in the European Novel* (1964). *Henry Adams* (1980) is a posthumous gathering of studies of the historian.

BLAIR, JAMES (1655–1743), Scottish-born clergyman, politician, and leader of the Church of

England in Virginia, was successful in withstanding the opposition of the governor, Andros, and managed to have him recalled (1697). He acted as governor of the colony (1740–41). He also founded the College of William and Mary (1693), of which he was president until his death, and with Henry Hartwell and Edward Chilton he wrote *The Present State of Virginia and the College* (1727). His sermons in Virginia, including 117 on the subject *Our Saviour's Divine Sermon on the Mount,* appeared in 5 volumes in London (1722).

BLAKE, HARRISON GRAY OTIS (1816?–98), disciple and acquaintance of Thoreau, from whose sister he inherited the unpublished notebooks which he edited, often inaccurately, as *Early Spring in Massachusetts* (1881), *Summer* (1884), *Winter* (1888), *Autumn* (1892), whose titles for a time gave Thoreau a specious reputation as a naturalist.

BLANCK, JACOB, see *Bibliography of American Literature.*

BLAND, JAMES A. (1854–1911), black composer born in New York state, was educated at Howard University, and toured the U.S. and England with a minstrel troupe. He wrote some 700 songs, of which the best known are "Carry Me Back to Old Virginny" (1875), "Oh, Dem Golden Slippers," and "In the Morning by the Bright Light, In the Evening by the Moonlight" (1880).

BLAND, RICHARD (1710–76), Virginia antiquary and author of *An Enquiry into the Rights of the British Colonies* (1766), which asserted that the colonies owed their existence to the Crown alone, and were hence under no obligation of allegiance to Parliament.

BLATCH, HARRIET STANTON (1856–1940), daughter of Elizabeth Cady Stanton, was, like her mother, a leader of the woman suffrage movement, both in the U.S. and in England, where she lived for 20 years. Her works include *Mobilizing Woman-Power* (1918), *A Woman's Point of View* (1920), a biography of her mother (1921), and her own memoirs, *Challenging Years* (1940).

BLAVATSKY, HELENA PETROVNA HAHN (1831–91), leader of the Theosophic movement, was born in Russia and lived in America (1874–78) after a wildly romantic and erratic career on the Continent, in the Near East, and in Egypt and India. After a period of spiritualism in America, Mme Blavatsky with the aid of Colonel Henry S. Olcott founded her Theosophical Society and published *Isis Unveiled* (1877), a plagiarized occult work denouncing the spiritualism she had formerly advocated. After leaving the U.S., she continued her theosophic preaching in India, which ended with exposés that drove her to Europe and England. Although afflicted with enough diseases to kill any ordinary person, she lived to see herself venerated as a martyr. The most important of her mystical writings is *The Secret Doctrine* (2 vols., 1888), an involved exposition of Theosophy.

BLECHMAN, BURT (1932?–   ), New York novelist and New York University Medical School faculty member, whose works include the fantastic and satirical treatment of Jewish family life *How Much?* (1962), adapted for the stage by Lillian Hellman as *My Father, My Mother and Me* (1963); *The War of Camp Omongo* (1963), satirizing the values of middle-class children at summer camp; *Stations* (1964), a metaphorical story of homosexuality; *The Octopus Papers* (1965), a satirical view of the New York art world and pseudo-bohemians; and *Maybe* (1967), treating the loneliness of a Park Avenue widow whose only solace is to spend money.

BLEECKER, ANN ELIZA (1752–83), born in New York City, after her marriage at the age of 17 lived in Poughkeepsie and later in a frontier village near Albany. Her epistolary novel, *The History of Maria Kittle* (1797), deals with the capture of an American woman by Indians during the French and Indian War. Her melancholy verse was collected in *The Posthumous Works of Ann Eliza Bleecker* (1793), to which was added *A Collection of Essays, Prose and Poetical* by her daughter Margaretta Faugères (1771–1801).

Blithedale Romance, *The,* romance by Hawthorne,♦ published in 1852. Blithedale was suggested by Brook Farm, and the character Zenobia by Margaret Fuller, while Miles Coverdale is a fictional self-portrait.

Coverdale visits Blithedale Farm, near Boston, a socialized community for the betterment of mankind. He meets Silas Forster, a farmer, and his wife; Zenobia, a passionate and queenly woman; Hollingsworth, a former blacksmith, who brings his sledgehammer method to bear upon the evils of society but lacks the spark of spiritual light; and Priscilla, a delicate girl said to be a city seamstress. Zenobia and Priscilla both fall in love with Hollingsworth, who, however, loves mankind in the aggregate too fiercely to be gentle to individuals. Returning to the city, Coverdale meets the people of the community in a different atmosphere. Zenobia is again a wealthy woman of fashion, and actually Priscilla's half-sister, although this remains unknown. Priscilla falls under the mysterious influence of the mesmerist Westervelt, from whom she is rescued by Hollingsworth, and upon their return to Blithedale Hollingsworth gives his love to Priscilla, although he has previously wooed Zenobia to get money for his philanthropic work. Unable to bear defeat, Zenobia drowns herself. Hollingsworth marries Priscilla, but his energy and peace of mind are lost, and Priscilla is now the sole prop of his

broken spirit. Coverdale remains skeptical concerning human progress.

BLITZSTEIN, MARC (1905–64), Philadelphia-born composer, whose works, experimental in form, include *The Cradle Will Rock* (1937), an "opera" depicting decadent capitalism, social injustice, and labor unity; *No for an Answer* (1941) and *Reuben, Reuben* (1951); an adaptation and translation of *The Threepenny Opera* (1952); and also ballet music, music for motion pictures, and symphonies.

Blix, novel by Frank Norris,♦ published in 1899. The story is partly autobiographical.

Condé (Condy) Rivers, a San Francisco journalist, is friendly with Travis (Blix) Bessemer, the daughter of a socially prominent family. They agree in disliking conventional society, frankly decide they are not in love, and become close comrades. While they explore the city together, Blix helps Condy to overcome a fondness for gambling and encourages his ambition to write books. When they realize that they have fallen in love, they are in despair at Blix's approaching departure for an Eastern school. Just in time to make their marriage possible comes news that Condy's novel has won him a position as editor of an Eastern magazine.

Blockade, *The,* unpublished play by General John Burgoyne,♦ was performed in Boston (1775) while the British army occupied the city. It ridicules the valor of the rebel soldiers and makes light of the situation in which the British found themselves. Shortly after their evacuation of the city, the play was answered (March 1776) by an anonymous farce, *The Blockheads,* at first erroneously attributed to Mercy Otis Warren. *The Blockheads* is a dialogue between British soldiers and Tory refugees from Boston, concerned with Howe's abortive attempt to storm Dorchester Heights.

BLODGETT, LEVI, see *Parker, Theodore.*

BLOOD, BENJAMIN PAUL (1822–1919), philosopher, mystic, and poet. His principal poetic works are *The Bride of the Iconoclast* (1954), "a long Shelleyesque poem in Spenserian stanzas," and *The Colonnades* (1868), a philosophic blank-verse epic. *The Philosophy of Justice* (1851) and *Optimism* (1860) are subtly conceived, very unorthodox interpretations of Christianity. Blood's reputation is chiefly based on his belief in pluralism, induced through the use of anaesthetics. This philosophic creed he describes in *The Anaesthetic Revelation and the Gist of Philosophy* (1874), whose publication led to an extended correspondence with William James. The final statement of Blood's pluralism is contained in his *Pluriverse* (1920).

BLOOMER, Amelia Jenks (1818–94), temperance and woman suffrage reformer, who published *The Lily* (1848–54), a periodical devoted to these causes. She adopted a reformed trouser dress for women, which was named "bloomers" in her honor. She is the subject of *Bloomer Girl* (1944), a musical comedy.

Bloudy Tenent of Persecution, The, tract by Roger Williams, ♦ written primarily as an attack on John Cotton, was published in London (1644). The treatise is in the form of a dialogue between two fugitive angelic characters, Truth and Peace, who, after a long separation, are still unable to find a home in the civilized world and meet in a dark refuge. Their conversation, on intellectual freedom in civil and ecclesiastical governments, is an argument for democratic liberty and tolerance, and attacks persecution for cause of conscience. The "bloudy and slaughterous conclusions" of Cotton and the other persecutors are answered, according to the author, in "spiritually white milk." Cotton's reply, *The Bloudy Tenent Washed and Made White in the Bloud of the Lamb* (1647), was answered by another tract on liberty of conscience, *The Bloudy Tenent Yet More Bloudy, by Mr. Cotton's Endeavour To Wash It White in the Bloud of the Lamb* (1652).

Blue and the Gray, The, popular names respectively for the armies of the North and South during the Civil War, referring to the color of their uniforms. A song of this title was composed in 1867 by F.M. Finch. Judson Kilpatrick and J.O. Moore were the authors of *The Blue and the Gray; or, War Is Hell,* a play revised and revived by Christopher Morley in 1929. A song of the same title was written by Paul Dresser. ♦

Blue Hotel, *The,* story by Stephen Crane in *The Monster and Other Stories.* ♦

Blue laws, term applied to colonial legislation, especially in New England, which restricted personal action in order to improve community morality. A collection of such laws was made by the Rev. Samuel Peters in his derogatory *General History of Connecticut* (London, 1781), and he was the first to popularize the term. His hatred of republicanism and nonconformity led him to make gross misrepresentations about the stringency of these laws, but his discredited statements have generally found their way into the popular mind. Such blue laws as the prohibition of sports and work on the Sabbath, and compulsory church attendance, disappeared generally following the Revolution, but there are still similar laws in many places, like those in some states prohibiting the sale of tobacco or liquor.

Blue Voyage, novel by Conrad Aiken. ♦

BLY, Nelly, pseudonym of Elizabeth C. Seaman. ♦

BLY, Robert [Elwood] (1926–   ), Minnesota-born poet, whose first volume, *Silence in the Snowy Fields* (1962), contains spare poems of the native farm scene in which he continues to live, direct but also marked by striking imagery. The poems in *The Light Around the Body* (1967) differ in that some are more mystical, others more political in his intense hatred of the Vietnam War. The work was selected for a National Book Award, and Bly gave the prize money to an antidraft organization. Later numerous poems, some prose poems, appear in many separate works, including: *Chrysanthemums* (1967), *Water Under the Earth* (1972), *Sleepers Joining Hands* (1973), *Point Reyes Poems* (1973), *Old Man Rubbing His Eyes* (1975), *This Body Is Made of Camphor and Gopherwood* (1977), *Counting Small Boned Bodies* (1979), *This Tree Will Be Here for a Thousand Years* (1979), *News of the Universe* (1980), *The Man in the Black Coat Turns* (1981), *At the Time of Peony Blossoming* (1983), *Loving a Woman in Two Worlds* (1985), *In the Month of May* (1985), *The Moon on a Fencepost* (1988), and *Out of the Rolling Ocean* (1988), a large but incomplete selection. He has translated some fiction of Selma Lagerlöf and of Knut Hamsun, as well as poetry from German, Spanish, and Swedish, including that of Trakl, Neruda, Rilke, and Lorca, who have influenced him. His periodical, originally *The Fifties,* which changes its title with each decade, has printed some of these authors, as well as Americans. *Leaping Poetry* (1975) is a critical work, as are *The Eight Stages of Translation* (1983) and an interpretation of Carl Jung's work, *A Little Book on the Human Shadow* (1988). *Iron John* (1990), an interpretation of a medieval tale of the quest, contains instructions on becoming a whole man, and was a bestseller. *The Darkness Around Us Is Deep* (1994) is a selection of poems chosen by William Stafford.

Bobbsey Twins, series of books for girls by Edward Stratemeyer. ♦

BODENHEIM, Maxwell (1893–1954), born in Mississippi, moved to Chicago and then to New York, where he published *Minna and Myself* (1918), a volume of poems using the sharply pictorial technique of Imagism. The highly mannered use of language and the author's posturing as an aesthetic misanthrope is also evident in such later verse as *Advice* (1920), *Introducing Irony* (1922), *Against This Age* (1923), *The Sardonic Arm* (1923), *Returning to Emotion* (1927), *The King of Spain and Other Poems* (1928), *Bringing Jazz* (1930), and *Lights in the Valley* (1942). Bodenheim's novels, including *Crazy Man* (1924), *Replenishing Jessica* (1925), *Sixty Seconds* (1929), and *Naked on Roller Skates* (1931), show a similar vivacious cynicism, iconoclasm, and jazz-age paganism. He wrote several plays, including *The Master-Poisoner* (1918), with Ben Hecht, ♦ who later attacked him in his fiction. Always a bohemian drifter and drinker, he spent his last years in squalor and was murdered.

Body of Liberties, first written laws of Massachusetts, based on common law and like the Bill of Rights. This code of 100 basic laws was drafted by Nathaniel Ward and adopted by the General Court (Dec. 1641). *The Book of General Laws and Libertyes* (1648) replaced it.

BOGAN, LOUISE (1897–1970), Maine-born poet, lived in New York, whose books include *Body of This Death* (1923), *Dark Summer* (1929), *The Sleeping Fury* (1937), *Poems and New Poems* (1941), *Collected Poems* (1954), and *The Blue Estuaries* (1968). Her volume of *Selected Criticism* (1955) was extended in *A Poet's Alphabet* (1970), a posthumous collection. *What the Woman Lived* (1973) prints her letters. Her spare, sensitive poetry, mostly in traditional forms, is marked by intensity of personal expression and incisive imagery.

BOJER, JOHAN (1872–1959), Norwegian novelist, visited the U.S. (1923) to gather material for his novel, *The Emigrants* ♦ (1925), concerned with the settling of the Middle West by Norwegian farmers.

BOK, EDWARD WILLIAM (1863–1930), born in Holland, came to the U.S. at the age of 7, and at 26 became editor of the *Ladies' Home Journal.* ♦ *The Americanization of Edward Bok* (1920, Pulitzer Prize) is the best known of his books.

BOKER, GEORGE HENRY (1823–90), Philadelphia playwright, showed his romantic leanings by the medieval Spanish setting of his first blank-verse tragedy, *Calaynos* (1849). He tried romantic comedy in *The Betrothal* (1850), social satire in *The World a Mask* (1851), and blank-verse comedy in *The Widow's Marriage* (1852, unproduced), but his forte was romantic tragedy. *Leonor de Guzman* (1853) demonstrated his power in this form, contrasting the character of Leonor, the mistress of Alfonso XII, with that of his wife, Queen Maria. Boker's greatest achievement was *Francesca da Rimini* (1855), a verse tragedy of high literary quality as well as good theater, based on the story of Paolo and Francesca. It was successfully revived (1885–86), and this encouraged the author to write two similar plays, *Nydia* and *Glaucus,* suggested by Bulwer-Lytton's *Last Days of Pompeii,* but these were never produced. Some narrative and shorter poems were issued in *Plays and Poems* (1856). *Nydia* and *Sonnets* were issued in 1929. He was minister to Turkey (1871–75) and to Russia (1875–79).

Bollingen Poetry Translation Prize, awarded (1961–68) by the foundation that awards the poetry prize. After 1963 both became biennial.

Bollingen Prize in Poetry, established (1948) by the Bollingen Foundation, financed by Paul Mellon and named by him for the Swiss home of the psychoanalyst Jung. The award $1000 to 1960, $2500 to 1964, $5000 thereafter) was given annually for the highest achievement in American poetry issued the preceding year, but became a biennial award after 1963. The first award (1949), to Pound's *Pisan Cantos,* recommended by the Fellows in American Letters of the Library of Congress, precipitated a controversy spearheaded by Robert Hillyer and led the Library to discontinue all prizes under its auspices. The Prize has since been administered by the Yale University Library and later winners are Wallace Stevens (1950), J.C. Ransom (1951), Marianne Moore (1952), MacLeish and W.C. Williams (1953), Auden (1954), Léonie Adams and Louise Bogan (1955), Aiken (1956), Tate (1957), Cummings (1958), Roethke (1959), Delmore Schwartz (1960), Yvor Winters (1961), J.H. Wheelock and R. Eberhart (1962), Frost (1963), Horace Gregory (1965), R.P. Warren (1967), Berryman and Karl Shapiro (1969), Richard Wilbur and Mona Van Duyn (1971), James Merrill (1973), A.R. Ammons (1975), David Ignatow (1977), W.S. Merwin (1979), Howard Nemerov and May Swenson (1981), Anthony Hecht and John Hollander (1983), John Ashbery and Fred Chappell (1985), Stanley Kunitz (1987), Edgar Bowers (1989), Laura Riding Jackson and Donald Justice (1991), Mark Strand (1993), and Kenneth Koch (1995).

Bonhomme Richard, see *Jones, J.P.*

Bonifacius, essay by Cotton Mather, ♦ published in 1710 with the subtitle *An Essay Upon the Good, That Is To Be Devised and Designed . . . ,* often reissued as *Essays To Do Good.* Franklin liked it because it anticipated his practical Yankee view of good deeds.

BONNER, SHERWOOD, pseudonym of Katherine MacDowell. ♦

Bonneville, see *The Adventures of Captain Bonneville.*

BONTEMPS, ARNA [WENDELL] (1902–73), Louisiana-born author, educated in California, received an M.A. from the University of Chicago, and was librarian of Fisk University. His novels about his black people include *God Sends Sunday* (1931), about a jockey, dramatized with Countee Cullen as *St. Louis Woman* (1946); *Black Thunder* (1936), about a slave revolt in Virginia in 1800; *Drums at Dusk* (1939), about the slave revolt and emancipation in Haiti; and many children's books, including *Sam Patch* (1951), written with Jack Conroy. His nonfiction includes another work written with Conroy, *They Seek a City* (1945); *The Story of the Negro* (1948); *Chariot in the Sky* (1951), about the Jubilee Singers of Fisk University; and *One Hundred Years of Negro Free-*

dom (1961). His correspondence with Langston Hughes was published in 1979.

Book clubs select books issued by regular publishers for release to their members, at retail prices or less, and with dividends of extra books. The first U.S. organization, the Book-of-the-Month Club, was founded in 1926 with 4750 subscribers, and in 1946 had nearly 1,000,000 members. In 20 years it distributed some 70,000,000 volumes, and set the pattern for most book clubs. Its board of judges selects a newly issued book (or a dual selection of two short books) for the members, who guarantee to accept four selections the first year. Members receive a dividend upon joining, another for every two books purchased, and a monthly literary review. Another large club, The Literary Guild (founded 1927), operates on the same principle, except that a single editor makes the selections. In 1946, at the height of the plan, there were some 25 clubs distributing 75,000,000 books annually, and grossing one-sixth of all U.S. book sales. Many clubs are specialized, devoted to particular categories, e.g. religion, nonfiction, history, the arts, "classics," limited editions, and detective stories. The effect of these organizations on literary taste has been much discussed. It is conceded that they have increased reading and brought new books to regions without bookstores, but it is often contended that they have put literature on a standardized, mail-order basis, have inculcated a mediocrity of taste, and have focused attention on their selections to the exclusion of equally good or better books.

Book of Annandale, The, blank-verse narrative by E.A. Robinson,♦ published in *Captain Craig* (1902).

After the funeral of his wife Miriam, George Annandale contemplates his altered life and wonders at his lack of emotion. He thinks mainly of the curious, inspired book that he wrote years before, and of the dead Miriam, mingling the two in a dream vision: the woman Damaris, in some mysterious place, considers the loss, long before, of her husband Argan, who on his deathbed made her promise never to remarry. She gave her word gladly, but now doubts the wisdom of denying love in life. As the irretrievable promise haunts her, she is like "one long imprisoned in a twilight cave," until she finds release through the red-bound book of Annandale, which teaches her "the triumph and the magic of the soul" and her obligation to love and suffer, thus vindicating "the truth of what she was."

Book of Common Prayer, A, novel by Joan Didion,♦ published in 1977.

Grace Strasser-Mendana, a 60-year-old American woman, formerly an anthropologist, is a longtime resident of the equatorial country Boca Grande, and widow of a member of its leading political family. She is fascinated by Charlotte Douglas, a 40-year-old Californian, who has turned up in Boca Grande, traveling aimlessly and alone. She recently suffered a nervous breakdown because Marin, the daughter she and her second husband Lloyd had hoped to raise as a teenager playing tennis at the local country club, instead fled underground when she was found to be a member of a radical group that had bombed a San Francisco office building and hijacked a plane. Charlotte has an affair with Grace's son Gerardo, who is planning a coup to seize the government. When the revolution breaks out Charlotte refuses to flee Boca Grande with Grace and Gerardo, and she is soon killed by a soldier for no reason.

Book of . . . Libertyes, see *Body of Liberties.*

Bookman, The (1895–1933), monthly magazine of literature and criticism. Modeled after the English *Bookman,* it gave special attention to American literature, although prominent English authors were frequent contributors. Until 1902 it was edited by H.T. Peck, with F.M. Colby among the associate editors, and received much adverse criticism. Its standards were conservative until the editorship of Burton Rascoe (1927–28), who published in it such fiction as Upton Sinclair's *Boston.* Upon the suspension of *The Bookman,* its last editor, Seward Collins, founded *The American Review.*♦

BOONE, DANIEL (1734–1820), born in Pennsylvania, moved to North Carolina, and from 1769 to 1771 made an extended exploration of Kentucky. As an agent of the Transylvania Company, he led a band of colonists along the Wilderness Road♦ through the Cumberland Gap to the site of Boonesborough, where a fort was erected in 1775. After the region was made a county of Virginia (1776), he held many local offices, and his activities in behalf of the settlement were interrupted only by a brief captivity (Feb.–June 1778) by Shawnees. When his improperly registered land tracts were lost by a series of ejectment suits, he moved to Point Pleasant (now West Virginia), and in 1798 or 1799 moved again to a tract granted him by the Spanish in the Femme Osage valley, Missouri. The legend of Boone as the discoverer of Kentucky and the greatest of frontiersmen was begun with the biography written by John Filson♦ and extended by Byron in the eighth canto of *Don Juan* (1823), as well as by many laudatory references in contemporary literature and tall tales. Audubon, who met Boone in Missouri, retold one of his adventures in the *Ornithological Biography.* He is a frequent figure in fiction, as in Churchill's *The Crossing,* Elizabeth Madox Roberts's *The Great Meadow,* and Caroline Gordon's *Green Centuries.*

BOORSTIN, DANIEL J. (1914–), Atlanta-born educator and author, after an A.B. from

Harvard, Rhodes scholarship, and law degree from Yale had a distinguished academic career teaching American history, mainly at the University of Chicago, before becoming Director, National Museum of History and Technology, Smithsonian Institution, and then Librarian of Congress (1975–87). His books include: *The Americans: The Colonial Experience* (1958); *The Americans: The National Experience* (1965); *The Americans: The Democratic Experience* (1973, Pulitzer Prize); *The Discoverers* (1983), the first part of a world history; *The Creators,* the second part, which appeared in 1992; and *Hidden History* (1989), 24 essays.

BOOTH, Edwin Thomas (1833–93), son of Junius Brutus Booth, was also a prominent tragedian, best known for his Shakespearean roles. He was the founder and first president of the Players Club. Otis Skinner edited his letters, with a biographical commentary, as *The Last Tragedian* (1939).

BOOTH, John Wilkes (1838–65), son of Junius Brutus Booth and brother of Edwin Booth, was also a noted actor. During a performance of *Our American Cousin* at Ford's Theatre in Washington (April 14, 1865), he shot President Lincoln, and while escaping shouted "*Sic semper tyrannis!* The South is avenged!" A fortnight later at Bowling Green, Va., after the barn in which he was hiding was set afire, he was shot while attempting to escape. He often figures in fiction about Lincoln, and novels specially directed toward him include David Stacton's *The Judges of the Secret Court.*

BOOTH, Junius Brutus (1796–1852), British actor, emigrated to the U.S. in 1821. Here, despite attacks of insanity, intemperance, and general irresponsibility, he played in theaters throughout the country, augmenting his reputation as a great tragedian. His sons were the actors Edwin Thomas Booth and John Wilkes Booth.

BOOTH, Philip (1925–), New Hampshire-born poet, graduated from Dartmouth, has taught at Bowdoin, Wellesley, and Syracuse (1961–). His first book, *Letter from a Distant Land* (1957), contains a blank-verse autobiographical address to Thoreau. Later works which show his deeply ingrained feeling for the New England coast and the tough, terse turn of mind of the region, along with a Yankee wit, are published in *The Islanders* (1961); *Weathers and Edges* (1966); *North by East* (1967); *Beyond Our Fears* (1968); *Margins* (1970); *Available Light* (1976); *Before Sleep* (1980); *Relations* (1986), poems selected from 1950 through 1985; and *Selves* (1989).

BOOTHE, Clare (Clare Boothe Luce) (1903–87), wrote the plays *The Women* (1936), satirizing wealthy women in the U.S.; *Kiss the Boys Goodbye* (1938), ridiculing Hollywood's star system; and *Margin for Error* (1940), a melodrama

about the murder of a Nazi consul. *Europe in the Spring* (1940) recounts travels in Allied countries and recommends an American crusade for world democracy. She was married to Henry Robinson Luce (1898–1967), the publisher of *Time,* served as U.S. representative from Connecticut (1943–47), and as U.S. ambassador to Italy (1953–56).

BORDEN, Lizzie (1860–1927), was accused of hacking to death her aged father and stepmother in Fall River, Mass. (Aug. 4, 1892). The trial of the spinster Lizzie was a national sensation. Since there was only circumstantial evidence, she was acquitted, but her supposed crime won her a place in American popular legend. In addition to ballads and contemporary literature, the case has been the subject of several novels; of some plays, including John Colton's *Nine Pine Street* (1933); a ballet, *Fall River Legend* (1948) by Agnes de Mille; a scholarly investigation by Edmund Pearson (1924) that found Lizzie guilty but was severely attacked by Edward D. Radin (1961), who suggested another culprit; and an opera (1965) by Jack Beeson.

Border Beagles, *A Tale of Mississippi,* romance by W.G. Simms,♦ published in 1840. One of his Border Romances, it is a sequel to *Richard Hurdis.*♦

Harry Vernon is commissioned by his friend Carter to find and aid the Wilsons, Wilson having been Carter's successful rival in love years before. He is also commissioned by the governor of Mississippi to find the outlaw Foster. Accompanied by Harry Horsey, a stagestruck yokel, Vernon encounters many difficulties engineered by Foster, but saves the Wilsons from a highwayman. He is arrested on the false charge of murdering Horsey, who has been detained in the camp of the outlaws, whom he imagined to be a group of strolling players. Upon Horsey's return Vernon is freed, and, with a posse of honest settlers, captures Foster and rescues the Wilsons' kidnapped daughter Virginia, with whom he falls in love.

Border Romances, series of novels by W.G. Simms♦ dealing with colonial and 19th-century life in the South. The romances are *Guy Rivers, The Yemassee, Richard Hurdis, Border Beagles, Beauchampe, Helen Halsey, Charlemont, The Cassique of Kiawah, Voltmeier,* and *The Cub of the Panther.*

BORGLUM, [John] Gutzon [de la Mothe] (1871–1941), sculptor and painter, trained in San Francisco, Paris, and London, was influenced by Rodin's impressionism to employ sketchy surface modeling, casual poses, and moving contours in his naturalistic treatment of figures. His sculpture, often pictorial rather than plastic, includes the *Sheridan Monument* in Washington, D.C., the *Lincoln Monument* in Newark, the head of Lincoln in the rotunda of the national capital, and the *Apostles* in New York's Cathedral of St. John the Divine. He is best known, however, for two colossal projects: the memorial to the leaders of the Confederate army, carved on the side of Stone Mountain, Ga.; and the vast portraits of Washington, Jefferson, Lincoln, and Theodore Roosevelt, carved on the side of Mount Rushmore, S.D.

Boss, The, play by Edward Sheldon,♦ produced in 1911 and first published (1917) in *Representative American Plays* edited by A.H. Quinn.

Boston, situated at the head of Massachusetts Bay, is the principal seaport of New England♦ and the capital of Massachusetts. The present city includes such previously outlying communities as East and South Boston, Brookline, Roxbury, Charlestown, and Dorchester. The region may have been known to the Norsemen, but it was first explored and mapped by John Smith (1614). Individual settlers came from the Plymouth Colony (1621), and under Winthrop's leadership the site was colonized by the Massachusetts Bay Company♦ (1630), which established fisheries, agriculture, and the lumber trade, so that the town throve as a maritime center. Since it was colonized by Puritans, its early rule was theocratic, and such nonconformists as Anne Hutchinson, Roger Williams, and the Quakers were not tolerated. The Calvinists fostered education, for a literate clergy and laity were needed to understand the Bible, and Boston Latin School was the first American public school (1635), followed by Roxbury Latin School (1645). In 1636 Harvard was founded at Cambridge♦ across the Charles River. The views of the Puritans were further disseminated by such divines and laymen as John Cotton, Edward Johnson, John Eliot, the Mathers, Benjamin Thompson, Thomas Prince, Mather Byles, and others. The hold of the church began to decline with the rising power of the merchant class, and the beginnings of the Yankee attitude of mind may be observed in the writings of the Hell-Fire Club and of such men as Samuel Sewall. The protests of the merchant class against the Stamp Act (1765) and the Townshend acts (1767) helped foster the Revolution, and the ensuing friction led such Bostonians as Samuel Adams, John Hancock, and James Otis to form the Sons of Liberty, who met at Faneuil Hall. Their actions precipitated the attack on Lieutenant-Governor Hutchinson (1765), the Boston Massacre (1770), and the Boston Tea Party (1773), which was answered by the Boston Port Bill (1774). The closing of the port, which meant commercial ruin, was influential in provoking the outbreak of the war, in whose opening action Paul Revere and Boston members of the Minute Men were prominent. The British laid siege to the town after the battle of Bunker Hill,♦ but upon Howe's evacuation (March 1776) Boston ceased to be a theater of war.

During the early years of the republic, the city was a stronghold of Federalism, and its commercial interests led it to oppose the Embargo Act (1807), which crippled maritime development. This led to talk of secession and to refusal to cooperate actively in the War of 1812. Although the subsequent era of clipper trade brought prosperity, the city became increasingly industrial, and as it outgrew former limitations its intellectual attitude became more spacious and liberal. Despite 17th-century changes within the church, such as the Half-Way Covenant, the mid-18th-century reforms of such divines as Jonathan Mayhew, and the founding of King's Chapel (1749), the first Episcopal church and later the first Unitarian church, the shift to Unitarianism was not effected until the beginning of the 19th century, under the leadership of such men as Channing and Parker. Similar expressions of liberalism included the humanitarian activities of Dorothea Dix, Samuel G. Howe, and the antislavery, temperance, and feminist movements, in which Bostonians were leaders. The Brook Farm community was situated in West Roxbury. The democratization of education was fostered by Alcott's Temple School, the work of Horace Mann, the establishment of Lowell Institute (1839), and the growth of the lyceum. The city's supremacy in literary activity was marked by the founding of *The North American Review,* the Anthology Club, the *Atlantic Monthly,* the Saturday Club, and such publishing firms as Ticknor and Fields. Boston literary figures at this peak of New England culture included Parkman, Prescott, Motley, Holmes, Ripley, Palfrey, the elder Henry James, Howells, Aldrich, Julia Ward Howe, and E.E. Hale; nearby, in Cambridge and Concord, lived Longfellow, Lowell, Hawthorne, Dana, T.W. Higginson, and the Transcendentalists.

After the Civil War the idealism of what Holmes had called the intellectual "Hub of the Universe" cooled somewhat, while State Street, the financial district, directed energy toward making Boston a greater center for the importing of cotton, wool, and leather for the state's textile mills and shoe factories, whose products were shipped throughout the world. This caused a great influx of Irish and Italian workers, and the character of the city was changed, although its financial and social hegemony was still Brahmin. Its intellectual energies were less creative, and were turned to exploiting a pride of heritage, as in the scholarly antiquarianism of such bodies as the Massachusetts Historical Society. Nevertheless the Harvard professors contributed to the maintenance of cultural activities, among them being John Fiske, Agassiz, C.E. Norton, William James, C.W. Eliot, Royce, Barrett Wendell, and Santayana. At the same time, the aristocratic homes on Beacon Hill, under the shadow of Bulfinch's State House, or along the newly reclaimed Back Bay continued in their serene fashion, despite the advent of such newcomers as Howells depicted in *The Rise of Silas Lapham.* That some of the old stock realized the breakdown of their traditions may be seen in Henry James's novels, and *The Education of Henry Adams.* The new forces made themselves felt, on the other hand, when the growing consciousness of organized labor caused the Boston police to strike for higher wages (1919), and when the social discord was crystallized in the Sacco-Vanzetti case. More recent Boston authors include Amy Lowell, T.S. Eliot, M.A. DeWolfe Howe, J.P. Marquand, Ben Ames Williams, Robert Lowell, David McCord, and Edwin O'Connor, in addition to the many scholarly writers associated with Harvard and other educational institutions, including Massachusetts Institute of Technology (1859), Boston University (1869), Simmons College (1902), and Brandeis University (1948). Other educational foundations are the Boston Athenaeum (1805), Boston Public Library (1852), Boston Museum of Fine Arts (1870), and Gardner Museum (1902). Leading religious institutions include the Episcopal Trinity Church and the Mother Church of Christian Science. The cultural development of Boston has also partly derived from the influence of the painters, Smibert, Copley, Stuart, Earle, S.F.B. Morse, Chester Harding, Whistler, Homer, Sargent, William Hunt, La Farge, and Edwin Abbey; the sculptors, Greenough, Saint-Gaudens, and French; the architects, McIntyre, Richardson, McKim, and Cram; and such early hymnodists as William Billings, succeeded by the 19th-century musicians, Lowell Mason, J.K. Paine, Chadwick, and MacDowell, and the Handel and Haydn Society (1815), *Dwight's Journal of Music* (1852), the New England Conservatory of Music (1867), and the Boston Symphony (1881), as well as the later composers, Arthur Foote, F.S. Converse, E.B. Hill, and Roger Sessions.

For Boston newspapers other than those prefixed by the name of the city, see *Massachusetts Centinel, Independent Chronicle, New England Courant, Massachusetts Mercury, New England Weekly Journal,* and *The Weekly Rehearsal.*

Boston, novel by Upton Sinclair,♦ published in 1928.

The story of Sacco and Vanzetti♦ is told through the experiences of Cornelia Thornwall, who, at age 60 after the death of her husband, an ex-governor and industrial magnate, runs away from wealth and respectability to obtain a six-dollar-a-week job in the Plymouth Cordage Factory. Her fellow boarder is Bartolomeo Vanzetti, and through him Cornelia becomes acquainted with Sacco and other anarchists, witnesses a factory strike, sees pickets clubbed by police, and, in time, the arrests and trials of Sacco and Vanzetti, who are doomed to execution because of the views of Boston's ruling class, despite the help she, her granddaughter Betty, and others extend to the two men.

Boston Athenaeum, association of Boston literary men, was founded in 1805 as an outgrowth of the Anthology Club♦ and patterned after the Liverpool Athenaeum in England. A corporation was organized (1807), and a library, a museum, and a laboratory were founded. Although the institution underwent trying times and was criticized as being limited to the wealthy, the library became valuable and in 1845 was provided with its own large building. The society has continued to influence Boston's literary life, and it is mentioned in such journals as Hawthorne's *American Notebooks.* It serves as the setting of Hawthorne's posthumous story "The Ghost of Doctor Harris."

Boston Daily Advertiser (1813–1929), the first successful daily newspaper in New England. In 1840 it absorbed both the *Massachusetts Centinel* and the *Massachusetts Mercury,* and by the mid-century it had become nationally prominent, although it was accused of subservience to the interests of the Boston upper class. In 1917 it was purchased by Hearst, who changed it considerably, and in 1921 it became an illustrated tabloid.

Boston Daily Evening Transcript (1830–1941), newspaper representative of the conservative New England tradition, was long considered to be a leader in reporting cultural activities in Boston and elsewhere in the nation. T.S. Eliot wrote a witty poem on the stultification of Boston life, making the *Transcript* its symbol.

Boston Evening Post (1735–75), successor of *The Weekly Rehearsal,* was edited by Thomas Fleet with much attention to local news, brief satirical comments being sometimes appended to news items. All sides were allowed to express themselves in controversies, a policy continued by the editor's sons after his death (1758). With the coming of the Revolution, this neutral course was disliked, and the last issue of the paper appeared five days after the battles at Lexington and Concord.

Boston Gazette, *The* (1719–41), second newspaper in America, printed by James Franklin, became the organ of the conservative element after Franklin left it (1721) to found his *New England Courant,* which attacked Increase Mather and others behind the *Gazette.* In 1741 it was merged with the *New England Weekly Journal.*♦

Another paper of the same title (1755–98) was the leading New England journal to advocate the cause of independence, and had Samuel Adams as a contributor. In it were published the *Hutchinson Letters* and the letters of John Adams, written under the pseudonym Novanglus and attacking Daniel Leonard, as well as other important Revolutionary documents.

Boston Miscellany of Literature and Fashion (1842–43), monthly magazine, was an outgrowth of *Arcturus* (1841–42), a critical magazine founded by E.A. Duyckinck and Cornelius Mathews.

Its contributors included Lowell, E.E. Hale, Hawthorne, Edward Everett, Poe, and N.P. Willis.

Boston News-Letter (1704–76), originally a handwritten account sent to New England colonial governors by John Campbell, the Boston postmaster. The first printed issue appeared in 1704. Local news was gathered from many sources, and foreign news was reprinted in chronological order from English papers, so that the *News-Letter* was sometimes a year behind time in foreign information. Bartholomew Green, the editor (1704–32), adopted a semi-religious editorial policy, continued (1733–62) by his son-in-law John Draper. Richard Draper, the editor (1762–74), changed the title to *The Boston Weekly News-Letter and New-England Chronicle* and later to *The Massachusetts Gazette and Boston News-Letter,* making the journal the mouthpiece of the governor and loyalists. When he purchased the *Boston Post-Boy,* he published the papers separately. In 1768–69 the *Gazette* was the official government organ, and the second half of the paper was alternately composed of the *Post-Boy* and the *News-Letter.* Draper edited the *News-Letter* alone from 1769 to 1774. His widow and others ran the paper until February 22, 1776, when it was the only paper published during the British occupation of Boston.

Boston Post-Boy, see *Boston News-Letter.*

Boston Public Library, founded in 1852, is housed in a building designed by McKim, Mead, and White, which contains mural paintings by Sargent, Abbey, and Chavannes. Among its famous collections are those of U.S. colonial and Revolutionary history, feminist writings, newspapers, and the Ticknor collections of Spanish and Portuguese literature.

Boston Quarterly Review, The (1838–42), was founded and edited by Orestes Brownson, ◆ whose quest for truth in many fields of thought it reflected. Subscribers saw the magazine change in religion from Presbyterianism to Universalism to Unitarianism. It was at one time associated with the Democratic party, at another with the short-lived Workingmen's party, and a kind of Christian Socialism consistently permeated its thought. Contributors included Brisbane, Bancroft, Ripley, Alcott, Margaret Fuller, and Elizabeth Peabody. In 1842 it merged with the New York *Democratic Review.* When the columns were closed to Brownson after a year, he founded *Brownson's Quarterly Review.* ◆

Boston Transcript, see *Boston Daily Evening Transcript.*

Bostonians, The, novel by Henry James, ◆ published in 1886. Miss Birdseye is believed to represent Elizabeth Peabody. ◆

Basil Ransom, a Mississippi lawyer, comes to Boston to seek his fortune, and becomes acquainted with his cousins, the flirtatious widow, Mrs. Luna, and her neurotic sister, Olive Chancellor. He is taken by Olive, a radical feminist, to a suffragette meeting, where he meets Miss Birdseye, an aged, altruistic worker for lost causes. They hear an address by beautiful young Verena Tarrant, whose gift of persuasion interests Olive as an instrument for her own use. Olive removes the girl to her own luxurious home, converts her to the feminist cause, and even urges her to vow that she will never marry. Fleeing the attentions of Mrs. Luna, Ransom attempts to win Verena to his belief that her proper sphere is a home and a drawing room, not a career as lecturer for a preposterous political movement, and there is open hostility between Ransom and the jealous Olive. Their struggle reaches a climax when Verena is about to begin her lectures, for she loses confidence, especially after the death of Miss Birdseye. Completely unnerved by Ransom's presence at her initial appearance, she consents to marry him, and Olive, who must announce her protégée's defection, is left desolate.

Both Your Houses, play by Maxwell Anderson, ◆ produced and published in 1933, and awarded the Pulitzer Prize.

BOTTA, CARLO GIUSEPPE GUGLIELMO (1766–1837), Italian historian and physician, was exiled to France because of his republicanism. His *History of the War of Independence of the United States of America* (1809, translated 1820) was popular in this country as a study of the worldwide significance of the Revolution. Until the publications of George Bancroft it was without equal in its field.

BOUCHER, JONATHAN (1738–1804), came to Virginia as a tutor (1759), returned to England (1762) to take orders in the Anglican Church, and the following year returned to Virginia. He became a rector at Annapolis (1770), where he was the first president of the Homony Club, a genteel literary and social organization. Because of his Tory views he fled to England in 1775. He published 13 of his American sermons (1797), with a preface, *A View of the Causes and Consequences of the American Revolution.* He maintained that monarchial government was a divine instrument functioning under God's sanction, and "unless we are good subjects, we cannot be good Christians. . . . To suffer grievances nobly is proper, to disobey the established government is simply to resist the ordinances of God."

BOUCICAULT, DION (1820–90), Irish-born dramatist and actor, achieved some success in London both with his own plays and with adaptations from French drama. In 1853 he came to the U.S., where he turned out musical interludes, melodramas, adaptations from the French, dramatizations of Dickens's novels, and *The Poor of New York,* a "superficial but graphic picture" of the panic of 1857. His melodramatic problem play about slavery, *The Octoroon; or, Life in Louisiana* (1859), adapted from Mayne Reid's *The Quadroon,* ◆ created a contemporary sensation. With *The Colleen Bawn* (1860), Boucicault began a long series of Irish comedy dramas which brought him his greatest fame, although his collaboration with Joseph Jefferson on *Rip Van Winkle* (1865) was unusually successful. With the exception of a decade in London (1862–72), and shorter journeys abroad, he continued his declining dramatic career in New York, where most of his 132 plays were produced.

BOUDINOT, ELIAS (1740–1821), New Jersey Revolutionary statesman, member of the Continental Congress, and president of it (1782–83), in which capacity he signed the proclamation for cessation of hostilities and the treaties of peace with Great Britain. He was the first president of the American Bible Society and wrote *The Age of Revelation* (1801) and other anti-Deist works.

ELIAS BOUDINOT (c. 1803–39), his Cherokee Indian protégé, edited the *Cherokee Phoenix* (1828–35), a bilingual Georgia weekly, and wrote *Poor Sarah; or, the Indian Woman* (1833), a novel in his native language.

Bound East for Cardiff, one-act play by Eugene O'Neill, ◆ produced and published in 1916.

In mid-Atlantic on the British tramp steamer *Glencairn,* the seaman Yank has been injured in a fall and lies moaning in his bunk. His friend, the Irishman Driscoll, and the other seamen encourage him with rough expressions of good will, but Yank realizes that he is dying. Since he fears to be alone, Driscoll remains with him, and they discuss old adventures and their mean life at sea. Yank considers that "this sailor life ain't much to cry about leavin'," and refuses to accept his friend's comfortable piety. Before the night fog lifts he dies, with a vision of "a pretty lady dressed in black."

BOURJAILY, VANCE [NYE] (1922–), Ohioborn writer, after service in World War II wrote *The End of My Life* (1947), a novel about a young man's collapse in the war, and *The Hound of Earth* (1954), about a scientist who runs away from his army job and his family after the bombing of Hiroshima. Bourjaily then became the editor of *discovery,* ◆ a distinguished departure in little magazines, and after its demise returned to fiction, writing *The Violated* (1958), a long novel of character analysis; *Confessions of a Spent Youth* (1960), about a young man's life and loves before, during, and after World War II; *The Man Who Knew Kennedy* (1967), treating the era of the President; *Brill Among the Ruins* (1970), depicting sociocultural turmoil of the 1960s as it affects a middle-aged man; *Now Playing at Canterbury* (1976), a

kind of *Canterbury Tales* set in the U.S. of the '60s and '70s; *A Game Men Play* (1980), a panoramic social history and adventure tale of the 20th century; and *The Great Fake Book* (1987), about a man learning of the life of his father through various means, including a pen-and-ink private memoir. *Old Soldier* (1990) is a fictional account of fishing in Maine. *The Unnatural Enemy* (1963) and *Country Matters* (1973) are nonfictional works about rural life.

BOURNE, RANDOLPH SILLIMAN (1886–1918), while a student at Columbia, from which he graduated in 1913, and during the remainder of his short life, established himself as a spokesman of his generation through his critical examination of American institutions, attacks on big-business civilization, and criticism of sentimental ideas in literature and elsewhere. His books, *Youth and Life* (1913), *The Gary Schools* (1916), and *Education and Living* (1917), show him to be a disciple of John Dewey although he felt pragmatism failed to direct a war-torn world. His pacifist articles were posthumously collected as *Untimely Papers* (1919), and his philosophical and critical views are summed up in *The History of a Literary Radical* (1920), edited by Van Wyck Brooks.

BOWDITCH, NATHANIEL (1773–1838), navigator and mathematician of Salem, Mass., who corrected Moore's *Practical Navigator* and after substantial revision issued it under his own name as *The New American Practical Navigator* (1802). More than 60 editions have since appeared, and this standard work is still referred to as *Bowditch's Navigator.*

BOWEN, CATHERINE [SHOBER] DRINKER (1897–1973), biographer and writer on musical subjects, whose books include *Beloved Friend* (1937), on Tchaikovsky; *Free Artist* (1939), on Anton and Nicholas Rubinstein; *Yankee from Olympus* (1944), on Justice Oliver Wendell Holmes and his family; *John Adams and the American Revolution* (1950); *The Lion and the Throne* (1956), a life of Sir Edward Coke; and *Francis Bacon: The Temper of a Man* (1963). *Adventures of a Biographer* (1960) are autobiographical essays.

BOWERS, EDGAR (1924–), after receiving a Ph.D. from Stanford became a professor of English at the University of California, Santa Barbara (1958), where he has remained. He is distinguished as a controlled, highly serious poet often employing well-established forms and always marked by serious thought. His poetry is published in *The Form of Loss* (1956); *The Astronomer* (1965); *Living Together* (1973), adding some new works to those from the two earlier books; *Witnesses* (1981); and *Thirteen Views of Santa Barbara* (1989), issued not long after he was awarded a Bollingen Prize.

Bowery, THE, street in New York City, situated in lower Manhattan, whose name derives from the fact that it once ran through Peter Stuyvesant's farm, or *bouwerie,* as it was called by the Dutch settlers. The 19th-century-stage type of the Bowery boy, representing the characteristic exuberant, impudent rascal of the district, in the plug hat, red shirt, and turned-up trousers of the volunteer fire department, was introduced in the play *A Glance at New York* (1848). The Bowery was long notorious for its dance halls, gambling houses, and other criminal resorts, which were fliply commented upon in a song ("The Bowery! I'll never go there any more!") by a bumpkin recounting his misadventures in Charles Hoyt's play *A Trip to Chinatown.* Fiction about the squalid slum life there includes Stephen Crane's *Maggie* and *George's Mother* and Edward W. Townsend's *Chimmie Fadden, . . . and Other Stories* (1895).

BOWLES, JANE (1917–73), New York-born author, resident abroad for long periods as a child with her family and as an adult after marriage (1938) to Paul Bowles.♦ She created a reputation among the avant-garde with *Two Serious Ladies* (1943), an experimental novel about two women, one rich and prosperous, the other sensuous and sinful, whose lives touch only twice. A play, *In the Summer House* (1954), and her stories, *Plain Pleasures* (1966), were issued together as her *Collected Works* (1966). *Feminine Wiles* (1976) collects stories and sketches, another play, and letters.

BOWLES, PAUL (1910–   ), born in New York, graduated from the University of Virginia, after studying with Aaron Copland and Virgil Thomson became a composer himself, writing scores for many ballets and motion pictures, as well as an opera, *The Wind Remains* (1943). He left the U.S. in the 1940s. His later career has been that of an author and his works have generally been set in Morocco, where he has long been expatriated. His novels including *The Sheltering Sky* (1949), *Let It Come Down* (1952), and *The Spider's House* (1955) often deal with Occidentals in the Arab world, having as themes isolation, lovelessness, and the loss of tradition; *Up Above the World* (1966) deals with a couple in Central America. He issued *A Little Stone* (1950), *Collected Stories* (1979), *A Delicate Episode* (1988), and *Unwelcome Words* (1989) as volumes of short stories. *The Thicket of Spring* (1972) and *Next to Nothing* (1981) collect poems. *Their Heads Are Green and Their Hands Are Blue* (1963) chronicles his journeys through Hindu, Muslim, Buddhist, and Central American lands. *A Life Full of Holes* (1964) is a novel by an illiterate house servant in Morocco, tape recorded and translated from an Arabic dialect by Bowles, one of his many translations. *Without Stopping* (1972) is his autobiography, and *Points in Time* (1982) is a brief book evoking the Morocco where he has long lived. *In*

Touch, the Letters of Paul Bowles, covering a lifetime of correspondence, was published in 1994.

BOWLES, SAMUEL (1826–78), son of Samuel Bowles (1797–1851), founder of *The Springfield Republican,*♦ a spearhead of liberal Republicans. Incisive letters on his travels were reprinted from his paper as *Across the Continent* (1865) and *The Switzerland of America* (1869).

BOYD, ERNEST (1887–1946), Irish-born critic and author, who as a member of the British consular service came to the U.S. in 1913 and returned in 1920 to make his home here. He became an important literary figure of the period, and in addition to many magazine contributions and translations, particularly from the French and German, wrote *Contemporary Drama of Ireland* (1917); *Appreciations and Depreciations* (1918), studies of Irish literature; *Ireland's Literary Renaissance* (1922); *Portraits: Real and Imaginary* (1924), sketches of contemporary authors in the U.S. and abroad; *H.L. Mencken* (1925); *Studies from Ten Literatures* (1925); *Guy de Maupassant* (1926), a biography to accompany his translation of Maupassant's complete works; *Literary Blasphemies* (1927); and *The Virtue of Vices* (1930).

BOYD, JAMES (1888–1944), born in Pennsylvania, was reared in North Carolina, graduated from Princeton (1910), studied at Cambridge, served in World War I, and returned to North Carolina to write. His two major novels, *Drums*♦ (1925) and *Marching On*♦ (1927), use his experience of war, but are set respectively in Revolutionary and Civil War times, in keeping with his theory that a writer needs "perspective of years." His other novels are *Roll River* (1935), set in his native Harrisburg; and *Long Hunt* (1930) and *Bitter Creek* (1939), about the frontier West. *Eighteen Poems* (1944) is a posthumous collection.

BOYD, THOMAS [ALEXANDER] (1898–1935), born in Ohio, later lived in Vermont, and is best known for his World War I novel, *Through the Wheat* (1923), and his realistically treated romance of Ohio before the Revolutionary War, *Shadow of the Long Knives* (1928). *Simon Girty, the White Savage* (1928), *Mad Anthony Wayne* (1929), *Light-Horse Harry Lee* (1931), and *Poor John Fitch* (1935) are biographies; *Points of Honor* (1925) is a collection of stories about World War I; and *In Time of Peace* (1935) is a sequel to his first war novel.

BOYESEN, HJALMAR HJORTH (1848–95), Norwegian-born author and educator, emigrated to the U.S. in 1869. As professor of German at Cornell and Columbia, he was considered stimulating rather than scholarly, although his *Goethe and Schiller* (1879) and *Essays on Scandinavian Literature* (1895) were sound treatments of their subjects. He wrote many works of fiction for adults and children and some poetry, but is best known for four novels, *Gunnar* (1874), a tale of Norwegian life, established his lifelong friendship with Howells, who influenced his later works. Turning against the romanticism of *Gunnar*, Boyesen denounced the subservience of writers to the standards of the young American girl, "the Iron Madonna who strangles in her fond embrace the American novelist." Influenced by Howells, Tolstoy, Turgenev, and Björnson, he wrote *The Mammon of Unrighteousness* (1891), a realistic urban study, contrasting two brothers, one a social idealist, the other a ruthless politician. *The Golden Calf* (1892) portrays the disintegration of a young man's ideals when he is tempted by wealth. *The Social Strugglers* (1893) is the best of these novels, although lighter and less incisive in its criticism and vague in its social implications.

BOYLE, KAY (1903–94), born in Minnesota, was long an expatriate in France, returning to the U.S. in 1941. Her impressionistic stories appeared in *Wedding Day* (1930), *First Lover* (1933), *The White Horses of Vienna* (1936), *The Crazy Hunter* (1940), *Thirty Stories* (1946), *The Smoking Mountain* (1951), *Nothing Ever Breaks Except the Heart* (1966), and *Fifty Stories* (1980). Her novels include *Plagued by the Nightingale* (1931), dealing with an American girl and her French husband, torn between the need to have a child so as to receive his legacy and the desire to avoid transmitting his hereditary disease; *Year Before Last* (1932), on a similar problem; *Gentlemen, I Address You Privately* (1933), about perverts; *My Next Bride* (1934), about American expatriates who must choose between love and money; *Death of a Man* (1936), concerning an American girl's renunciation of the love of a Nazi doctor; *Monday Night* (1938), psychological probing of character; *The Youngest Camel* (1939), an allegorical tale; *Primer for Combat* (1942), in diary form, about France during the Occupation; *Avalanche* (1943), a tale of espionage; *A Frenchman Must Die* (1946), story of a manhunt by an American member of the *maquis; His Human Majesty* (1949), about a foreign legion of ski troops training to attack the Nazis; *Seagull on the Step* (1955); *Generation Without Farewell* (1959), about Germans and Americans just after World War II; and *The Underground Woman* (1975), about a woman jailed for anti-Vietnam War protest and her concern for her daughter involved in a cult. Poems are published in *A Glad Day* (1938); *American Citizen* (1944), about her Austrian refugee husband who became a U.S. soldier; *Testament for My Students* (1970), works written in the 1920s and '30s; and the selections mistitled *Collected Poems* (1962). *The Long Walk at San Francisco State* (1970) prints essays on social and political issues. She expanded the autobiography of Robert McAlmon♦ as *Being Geniuses Together* (1968) by interspersing her own memoirs with his. Her *Words That Must Somehow Be Said* (1985) collects essays since 1927; *This Is*

Not a Letter (1985) gathers poems; and *Life Being the Best* (1988) collects stories.

BOYLE, T. CORAGHESSAN (1948–), born and raised in Peekskill, N.Y., educated at the University of Iowa (Ph.D. 1977), Professor of English at the University of Southern California. Boyle displayed his fine comic sense in his first novel, *Water Music,* which has Mungo Park teamed with a drunken con man on a voyage in 1805 down the Niger River, from which the historical Park did not return. He followed with *Budding Prospects: A Pastoral* (1984), wherein a disillusioned teacher finds his life's purpose while tending a crop of marijuana. *World's End* (1987) follows both 17th- and 20th-century characters from the Peekskill vicinity of the Hudson Highlands, and employs magic realism. *East Is East* (1990) follows a half-Japanese sailor who feels himself a *gaijin*, or foreigner, in Japan, and jumps ship at Georgia or South Carolina in an effort to find his American roots, but much of the story concerns the antics of writers at a MacDowell-like colony, one of whom shields the sailor in her cabin in order to write his story. In *The Road to Wellville* (1993) the scene is the Battle Creek Sanitarium in 1907, where Dr. Kellogg, the inventor of cornflakes, administers strict and sometimes weird dietary and spiritual as well as physical regimens for his clients. *The Descent of Man* (1979), *Greasy Lake* (1985), and *If the River Was Whiskey* (1989) print short stories—humorous, tragic, and bizarre. Another gathering of stories, *Without a Here,* appeared in 1994.

BOYNTON, PERCY H[OLMES] (1875–1946), professor of English literature at the University of Chicago (1902–41). His books include *Some Contemporary Americans* (1924) and *More Contemporary Americans* (1927), studies of authors; *The Rediscovery of the Frontier* (1931); *Literature and American Life* (1936); and *America in Contemporary Fiction* (1940).

Boy's Will, A, first book of poems, published in 1913 by Robert Frost,♦ the title derived from the refrain of Longfellow's "My Lost Youth."♦

BRACE, GERALD WARNER (1901–78), received his A.B. from Amherst and graduate degrees from Harvard, and taught at various New England colleges, chiefly Boston University (1939–68). His novels, all dealing with New England people and scenes, include *The Islands* (1936), set in Maine; *The Wayward Pilgrims* (1938), about a chance meeting in a Vermont depot; *Light on a Mountain* (1941); *The Garretson Chronicle* (1947), depicting changing ways in three generations of a Massachusetts family; *A Summer's Tale* (1949); *The Spire* (1952); *The World of Carrick's Cove* (1957); *Winter Solstice* (1960); *The Wind's Will* (1964); and *Between Wind and Water* (1966). *The Department* (1968) is a novel about a professor recalling 40 years in an English department. *The Age of the Novel* (1957) and *The Stuff of Fiction* (1969) are critical works. *Days That Were* (1976) presents memories of his youth.

Bracebridge Hall; or, The Humorists: A Medley, 49 tales and sketches by Irving,♦ published in 1822 under the pseudonym Geoffrey Crayon, Gent. Resembling its predecessor, *The Sketch Book,* the collection includes stories with English, French, and Spanish settings, but is chiefly remembered for "Dolph Heyliger" and its sequel, "The Storm-Ship," which recount the adventures of a New York lad who undertakes to discredit the legend of a haunted house, but encounters its ghost and recovers a fabulous buried treasure, as well as marrying an heiress. Americanized versions of the Flying Dutchman theme are presented in "The Storm-Ship," and other stories in the volume are also based on European folklore.

BRACKENRIDGE, HENRY MARIE (1786–1871), the son of Hugh Henry Brackenridge, was also a prominent jurist. He wrote of his *Voyage to South America* (1819), and in a pamphlet, *South America* (1817), advocated a policy similar to the later Monroe Doctrine. His *Views of Louisiana* (1814) and *Recollections of Persons and Places in the West* (1834) afford interesting historical information.

BRACKENRIDGE, HUGH HENRY (1748–1816), born in Scotland, was brought to a Pennsylvania farm at the age of five, and entered Princeton in 1768, where he became intimate with Freneau and Madison, and collaborated with the former on *The Rising Glory of America* (1772), an ardent poetical expression of national consciousness. He studied theology, and in 1774 received his M.A., writing *A Poem on Divine Revelation*. During the Revolutionary War he served as a chaplain, and wrote two patriotic plays for amateur production. Both of these, *The Battle of Bunkers-Hill♦* (1776) and *The Death of General Montgomery♦* (1777), are neoclassical dramas in rather stilted blank verse, and his more pungent contributions to the cause are included in his sermons, *Six Political Discourses* (1778), and in his work as editor of the patriotic *United States Magazine.* Repelled by strict dogma, he gave up the ministry to practice law, and in 1781 settled in the frontier village of Pittsburgh. Here he had an active political career and showed himself to be an aristocratic democrat, attempting to mediate between the federal government and the local insurrectionists during the Whiskey Rebellion, as described in his *Incidents of the Insurrection in the Western Parts of Pennsylvania* (1795). His satirical contributions to the local paper mirrored his political and social ideas, which are more completely treated in his novel *Modern Chivalry♦* (1792–1815). In 1799 he was appointed justice of the Pennsylvania Supreme Court, and after his removal to Carlisle (1801) made his chief contribution to legal literature in his *Law Miscellanies* (1814).

BRADBURY, RAY [DOUGLAS] (1920–   ), born in Illinois, long resident in Los Angeles, began to publish in pulp magazines, but after 1945 became known for serious stories. These include works of both fantasy and science fiction, now macabre, now humorous, collected in volumes including *Dark Carnival* (1947); *The Martian Chronicles* (1950), titled *The Silver Locusts* in England), about Mars a century hence; *The Illustrated Man* (1951); *The Golden Apples of the Sun* (1953), satirical sketches; *October Country* (1955); *A Meditation for Melancholy* (1959); *R Is for Rocket, S Is for Space* (1962); *The Machineries of Joy* (1964); *Twice Twenty-Two* (1966); *Any Friend of Nicholas Nickleby's Is a Friend of Mine* (1968); and *I Sing the Body Electric* (1969). His novels include *Fahrenheit 451* (1953), presenting a future totalitarian state in which super-television presents all that people are to think or know, and the ownership of books is cause for the state to burn both volumes and owners; *Dandelion Wine* (1957) and *Something Wicked This Way Comes* (1962), about boyhood experiences in the Midwest; *Death Is a Lonely Business* (1985), a semi-autobiographical tale of crime; *A Graveyard for Lunatics* (1990), science fiction set in 1954 Hollywood; and *Green Shadow, White Whale* (1992), an affectionate homage to Ireland and director John Huston. He has written many plays, including *The Meadow* (1947), *The Anthem Sprinters* (1962), *The Wonderful Ice Cream Suit* (1965), *The Halloween Tree* (1968), *Pillar of Fire* (1975); and film scripts, including *Moby Dick* (1954). His poems appear in *When Elephants Last in the Dooryard Bloomed* (1973), *Where Robot Men and Robot Women Run Round in Robot Towns* (1977), and *Complete Poems* (1982). *The Toynbee Convector* (1988) is the latest of many collections of short stories.

BRADFORD, EBENEZER (*fl.*1795), Massachusetts author of a didactic epistolary novel, *The Art of Courting* (1795).

BRADFORD, GAMALIEL (1863–1932), Massachusetts author, who at age 50 found his most successful medium when he published *Lee, the American* (1912). This book employed a method he described as "psychography," which aims to extract the essential, permanent, and vitally characteristic strands out of the continuous texture of a man's entire life. Applying this subjective, analytical technique, Bradford wrote a great many other sketches, published in such books as *Confederate Portraits* (1914); *Portraits of Women* (1916); *Union Portraits* (1916); *American Portraits* (1922); *Damaged Souls* (1923), perhaps his best-known book, dealing with such Americans as Aaron Burr, P.T. Barnum, John Randolph, and Thomas

Paine; *Wives* (1925); *As God Made Them* (1929); *Daughters of Eve* (1930); and *The Quick and the Dead* (1931). His autobiographical works include *A Naturalist of Souls* (1917), *Life and I* (1928), and his *Journal* (1933), edited by Van Wyck Brooks.

BRADFORD, John (1749–1830), pioneer printer of Kentucky, in 1787 first issued his *Kentucke Gazette,* the earliest newspaper in the territory, in which he published his "Notes of Kentucky" (1826–29), an important historical source. He printed the first pamphlet in the territory, the *Kentucke Almanac* (1788).

BRADFORD, Roark (1896–1948), author of stories about African Americans and their folklore, whose books include *Ol' Man Adam an' His Chillun* (1928), from which the play *The Green Pastures♦* (1930) was adapted; *This Side of Jordan* (1929); *Ol' King David an' the Philistine Boys* (1930); *John Henry* (1931), about the legendary hero, dramatized by the author in 1940; and *How Come Christmas* (1934), a one-act "modern morality" play.

BRADFORD, William (1590–1657), as a boy joined the Separatist group of William Brewster, with whom he emigrated to Amsterdam (1609) and then to Leyden. He came to America on the *Mayflower* (1620), and the following April was elected governor of Plymouth Colony, an office to which he was reelected every year from 1622 to 1656, with the exception of 1633, 1634, 1636, 1638, and 1644, when he was an assistant, having "by importunity gat off" from the position of leadership. Bradford's life was inseparably bound with the settlement, of which he was long the outstanding authority in all executive, judicial, and legislative matters. In 1627 Bradford and seven leading Pilgrims, with four London merchants, assumed the £1800 debt to the original merchant adventurers. Although these "Undertakers" held a monopoly of fishing and trading, the land and cattle were distributed equally among the "Old Comers." Bradford willingly aided all common enterprises, including the New England Confederation, but considered his colony as a compact community. About 1630 he began to write his *History of Plimmoth Plantation,♦* which he completed in 1651. A fragment of his letter-book (1624–30) as well as his letters to Winthrop have been published in the *Collections* of the Massachusetts Historical Society. Other works printed by this organization and the Colonial Society of Massachusetts include his *Dialogue between some young men born in New England and sundry ancient men that came out of Holland;* a long descriptive poem of 1654; *A Word to New Plymouth; A Word to New England;* and *Of Boston in New-England.* He is also considered to be the author of the first half of *Mourt's Relation,♦* which chronicles the events from September 6, 1620, to March 23, 1621.

BRADFORD, William (1663–1752), established the first press in Philadelphia and the first paper mill in the English colonies. In 1693 he became the official royal printer at New York, and among the 400 items from his press during the next half-century were the first American Book of Common Prayer; *Androboros,♦* the first American play to be printed; and the almanacs and pamphlets of Daniel Leeds. He published the first newspaper of the colony, the *New York Gazette* (1725–44).

BRADFORD, William (1722–91), grandson of Bradford the printer, vehemently opposed the Stamp Act in his *Pennsylvania Journal and Weekly Advertiser* (1743–97), the most successful competitor of Franklin's *Pennsylvania Gazette.* He also published *The American Magazine and Monthly Chronicle♦* (1757–58) and was the official printer for the first Continental Congress.

BRADSTREET, Anne [Dudley] (*c.*1612–72), daughter of Thomas Dudley, governor of the Massachusetts Bay Colony, was born in England, where at age 16 she married Simon Bradstreet. Two years later she left her comfortable English home to accompany her husband and father on the voyage of the *Arbella,* settling first at Ipswich and later in North Andover, Mass. In the intervals of arduous household tasks and the care of her eight children, she found time for her literary interests, and in 1650 the first edition of her poems was published in England as *The Tenth Muse Lately Sprung Up in America,* the manuscript having been taken without her knowledge to a London publisher by an admiring brother-in-law. A posthumous second edition, with her own additions and corrections, was issued at Boston (1678), and a scholarly edition with some additional material was published in 1867. Mrs. Bradstreet's literary influences were obvious and acknowledged, for she was enamored of Quarles, Joshua Sylvester's translation of Du Bartas's *Divine Semaine,* Spenser, and Sir Philip Sydney, although she reproaches the latter "miracle of wit" for his *Arcadia.* Cotton Mather in the *Magnalia♦* praised her highly, and Nathaniel Ward and others were equally lavish in the commendatory verses that prefaced her poetry. Her longer work consists of poetic discourses on the four elements, the four humors, the four ages of man, the four seasons, and "A Dialogue between Old England and New." The long, rhymed history, "The Four Monarchies," is based closely on Raleigh's *History of the World* and treats the Persian, Greek, and Assyrian kingdoms, and the Roman Commonwealth. Her current fame is based rather on the later and shorter poems, in which she looked into her heart or out upon a real New England world, and was less dependent on stock poetic conventions. These include "The Flesh and the Spirit"; "Contemplations," her nature poem on the transiency of man's life; "On the Burning of Her

House"; "To My Dear and Loving Husband," showing a moving use of the Donnean conceit; "On My Son's Return Out of England"; and "The Author to Her Book." In the prose "Meditations Divine and Morall," written for her son, she composed simple, pithy, and sincere aphorisms, and in her short spiritual autobiography, "Religious Experiences," she also employs a sweet and simple prose. A moving biographical poem, *Homage to Mistress Bradstreet* (1956), was written by John Berryman.

BRADSTREET, SIMON (1603–97), husband of Anne Bradstreet, held several important administrative positions in the colony, including the governorship (1679–86, 1689–92). He figures in Hawthorne's "Howe's Masquerade," "The Grey Champion," and *The Dolliver Romance.*

BRADY, CYRUS TOWNSEND (1861–1920), Episcopal clergyman, was the author of some 70 novels, mainly historical romances of the Revolution, the War of 1812, and the Civil War.

BRADY, MATHEW B. (*c.*1823–96), first important American photographer, became acquainted with the new art while studying painting in Paris with S.F.B. Morse, and won great success during the 1840s by his sincere photographic portraits published in a *Gallery of Illustrious Americans* (1850). His famous *National Photographic Collection of War Views* (1869), part of which was purchased by the government, is important as a complete factual record of Civil War battles and camp life, and possesses aesthetic merit because of its simple, literal objectivity.

Bragg, ARISTABULUS, character in *Home as Found.* ♦

Brahma, poem by Emerson, ♦ published in 1857 and reprinted in *May-Day and Other Poems* (1867). In alternately rhymed tetrameter quatrains, the poem reflects the author's interest in Hindu religious thought, in which Brahma personifies the universal creative force, embodying his concept of an eternal, all-inclusive divine power.

Brahmins, name humorously applied to upperclass New England society, derived from the name of the highest or priestly caste among the Hindus. In *Elsie Venner,* Holmes speaks of "the harmless, inoffensive, untitled aristocracy" of New England, and specifically of Boston, "which has grown to be a caste by the repetition of the same influences generation after generation," so that it has acquired a distinct organization and physiognomy.

BRAINARD, JOHN GARDINER CALKINS (1796–1828), Connecticut author, was an editor of the *Connecticut Mirror,* from which he reprinted his *Occasional Pieces of Poetry* (1825). His poems were respected in his time for their piety, sentimentality, and gently elegant descriptions of nature. He also wrote a historical romance, *Letters Found in the Ruins of Fort Bradford* (1824). His *Fugitive Tales* were published in 1830, and his literary remains in 1832, with a biographical sketch by Whittier.

BRAINERD, DAVID (1718–47), Calvinist missionary to the Indians in Connecticut, New York, and New Jersey. His mystical experiences, teachings, travels, and methods of work are described in his diary, which was partially published during his lifetime as *Mirabilia Dei Inter Indicos* (1746) and *Divine Grace Displayed* (1746). Jonathan Edwards, to whose daughter Brainerd was engaged, published the complete journal in *An Account of the Life of the Late Reverend Mr. David Brainerd* (1749).

BRAITHWAITE, WILLIAM STANLEY BEAUMONT (1878–1962), black author and editor, whose poetry, first published in *Lyrics of Life and Love* (1904) and *The House of Falling Leaves* (1908), was gathered in *Selected Poems* (1948). He also wrote *Frost on the Green Tree* (1928), stories; *The House Under Arcturus* (1941), an autobiography; and *The Bewitched Parsonage: The Story of the Brontës* (1950). He was also well known for his annual *Anthology of Magazine Verse and Year Book of American Poetry* (1913–29).

BRANAGAN, THOMAS (1774–1843), born in Ireland, at age 16 became a buyer of slaves in Africa but, overcome by religious scruples, gave up this business and after emigrating to Philadelphia (*c.*1798) wrote hortatory works in prose and verse. His books include *A Preliminary Essay, on the Oppression of the Exiled Sons of Africa* (1804) and two poems, *Avenia; or, A Tragical Poem on the Oppression of the Human Species* (1805) and *The Penitential Tyrant; or, Slave Trader Reformed* (1805).

BRANCH, ANNA HEMPSTEAD (1875–1937), New York poet, is noted for her metaphysical lyrics published in *The Heart of the Road* (1901), *The Shoes That Danced* (1906), *Rose of the Wind* (1910), *Sonnets from a Lock Box* (1929), *Last Poems* (1944), and other volumes. Her play, *Rose of the World,* was produced in 1908.

BRANCH, TAYLOR (1947–   ), reared in Georgia, returned there from graduate study at Princeton to register voters. This led him into journalism for *Harper's* and *Esquire.* He then moved on to write *Parting the Waters: America in the King Years, 1954–1963* (1988), a lengthy study of civil rights focusing on Martin Luther King, Jr. It was awarded a Pulitzer Prize in history.

BRAND, MAX, pseudonym of Frederick Faust (1892–1944) used for his prodigious output of adventure fiction, including cowboy novels like

Destry Rides Again (1930) and a series about Dr. Kildare.

BRANDEIS, LOUIS D[EMBITZ] (1856–1941), became known as the "people's attorney" when, early in his career, without pay he defended Boston citizens against local public utilities. His book *Other People's Money* (1914) greatly influenced Woodrow Wilson, who in 1916 appointed him to the U.S. Supreme Court. His miscellaneous papers, edited as *The Curse of Bigness* (1934), show him to have been continuously devoted to a social liberal point of view. After his retirement from the Supreme Court (1939), he concerned himself with aiding Jewish refugees. *On Zionism* (1942) collects addresses and statements. Brandeis University (founded 1948) was named for him.

BRANN, WILLIAM COWPER (1855–98), journalist and lecturer, notorious for his violent, often unconventional treatment of moral and social problems. As editor of the *Iconoclast* of Waco, Tex., he was involved in a quarrel with a local religious college, which resulted in his murder. Among his works are *Potiphar's Wife* (1897) and *Brann's Scrap-Book* (1898). A collection of his writings was published after his death as *Brann, the Iconoclast* (1898), and his *Works* appeared in 1919.

BRANT, JOSEPH (1742–1807), Mohawk Indian chief, educated at Eleazer Wheelock's school, was the principal leader of Indian troops for the British during the Revolutionary War, and for his work was cordially received in England. Although he did not participate in the Wyoming Valley Massacre in Pennsylvania, as is frequently stated, he was responsible for similar attacks. He translated parts of the Bible into his own tongue (1787). He is treated in a life by W.L. Stone♦ and in Hoffman's *Greyslaer.*♦

Brass Check, The, tract on contemporary journalism by Upton Sinclair,♦ published in 1920. The first half treats his experiences with the press, denouncing newspapers and news agencies as saboteurs of democracy, and proposed an unbiased national "truth-telling" weekly. The remainder of the book contains corroboration by eminent persons.

BRAUTIGAN, RICHARD (1935–84), San Francisco author, whose loosely conceived short "novels" composed of comic, whimsical, and surrealistic sketches of gently anarchic, unselfish, and Beat♦ ways of life include *A Confederate General from Big Sur* (1964), *Trout Fishing in America* (1967), *In Watermelon Sugar* (1968), *The Abortion: An Historical Romance* (1971), *Revenge of the Lawn* (1971), *The Hawkins Monster: A Gothic Western* (1974), *Willard and His Bowling Trophies: A Perverse Mystery* (1975), and *Sombrero Fallout: A Japanese Novel* (1976). *Dreaming of Babylon: A Private Eye Novel*

(1977), *The Tokyo-Montana Express* (1980), and *So the Wind Won't Blow It All Away* (1992) show sadness mingling with humor, as in his other novels. *The Pill Versus the Springfield Mine Disaster* (1968), *Rommel Drives on Deep into Egypt* (1970), *Loading Mercury with a Pitchfork* (1976), and *June 30th, June 30th* (1978) collect brief poems. He committed suicide by shooting himself.

Bravo, The, romance by Cooper,♦ was published in 1831 and dramatized by R.P. Smith in 1837.

In Venice of the Renaissance, Jacopo Frontoni, to win freedom for his unjustly imprisoned father, pretends to be a "bravo" or hired assassin for the Senate, but he actually works against it by aiding the Neapolitan Don Camillo Monforte to win the hand of Violetta Tiepolo, the senators' wealthy ward, whose fortune they want to retain by marriage to a Venetian. When unrest follows the lovers' escape and the death of Jacopo's friend Antonio, Jacopo is falsely accused of murder and is executed at the behest of the Senate.

Bread and Cheese Club, formed (c.1822) as an informal social club of New York City, growing out of impromptu meetings by Cooper's circle of friends. Cooper was always acknowledged as the leader, and the society included some 35 members, among them being Bryant, Dunlap, James Kent, Verplanck, R.S.A. Durand, Philip Hone, J.G. Percival, J.A. Hillhouse, Halleck, and S.F.B. Morse. It lasted until at least 1827, later dividing to become the Sketch Club and the Literary Club.

Bread-Winners, The, novel by John Hay,♦ published anonymously in 1884. *The Money-Makers*♦ (1885) was a "reply."

Breakfast at Tiffany's, short novel by Truman Capote,♦ published in 1958.

An unnamed narrator, a onetime resident in the 1940s of an old brownstone apartment building in the East 70s of New York City, reminisces about a glamorous fellow tenant, Holly Golightly, with "a face beyond childhood, yet this side of belonging to a woman," and not yet 19. Independent since age 14, fay, and very appealing, she has already had a life for herself, including refusal of a Hollywood film career. Her background is as unusual as her life in New York: as a teenage hillbilly she married an older veterinarian in Texas, but she later became an uninhibited playgirl of café society. By a series of misadventures she is arrested as a go-between of a drug-smuggling gang and therefore flees to Brazil, never to be seen again by the admiring friend who writes her story as she passes into modern legendary.

Breitmann, HANS, see *Leland, C.G.*

BREMER, FREDRIKA (1801–65), Swedish novelist, traveled extensively in the U.S. between 1849 and 1861 and wrote a book describing *The Homes of the New World* (1853). Her letters from the U.S. were published as *America of the Fifties* (1924).

Brer Rabbit, character in the Uncle Remus stories. ♦

BRERETON, JOHN, see *Brierton, John.*

BREWSTER, HENRY B. (1850–1908), European-born American author, reared in France and long resident in Italy, whose metaphysical writings include *The Theories of Anarchy and of Law* (1887); *The Prison* (1891), a fictive work presenting the responses of persons of various beliefs to a manuscript of a prisoner condemned to death; *The Statuette and the Background* (1895), a dialogue on art and reality; and *L'Âme Paienne* (1901), a philosophical prose-poem.

Brewster's Millions, comic fantasy by G.B. McCutcheon, ♦ dramatized by Winchell Smith.

Bricks Without Straw, novel by A.W. Tourgée, ♦ published in 1880. Intended to demonstrate the fallacy of freedom for Southern blacks without the "straw" of an adequate social and economic basis for free development, the story is concerned with Reconstruction days on the North Carolina tobacco plantations.

Mollie Ainslie, a Northern schoolteacher, comes to the black community of Red Wing, where the success of her work arouses the fury of the neighboring whites against presumptuous "niggers" and "nigger-teachers." While Mollie is absent at the plantation of Hesden Le Moyne, nursing his dying son and incidentally falling in love with Hesden, a band of "Ku Kluckers" falls upon the Red Wing settlement. They burn the schoolhouse and church, nearly kill the crippled preacher Eliab Hill, and drive out the black farmer Nimbus Desmit. Hesden's haughty mother causes a misunderstanding between her son and Mollie, who takes Nimbus's family to the North with her. Later Hesden, who nurses Eliab and helps him to reestablish the Red Wing school, discovers papers which show that Mollie is the rightful heir to his estate. Notified, she declines the inheritance and only visits the plantation at the insistence of Hesden and his repentant dying mother. Reconciled and married, they resume their dangerous work for the betterment of the blacks.

Bride Comes to Yellow Sky, The, story by Stephen Crane in *The Open Boat.* ♦

BRIDGE, HORATIO (1806–93), classmate and friend of Hawthorne at Bowdoin, was the author of *Personal Recollections of Nathaniel Hawthorne*

(1893). His *Journal of an African Cruiser* (1845), based on his manuscript notes as a naval officer, was frequently attributed to Hawthorne, its editor.

Bridge, The, poem by Longfellow, ♦ published in *The Belfry of Bruges and Other Poems* ♦ (1845). In quatrains of three-stress lines, the poem recalls Longfellow's frequent crossings of the bridge over the Charles River between Boston and Cambridge, when he would stop at night to meditate on the "care-encumbered" lives of himself and others who cross, and the constant reflection of the moon in the water,

> . . . the symbol of love in heaven,
> And its wavering image here.

Bridge, The, long poem by Hart Crane, ♦ published in 1930.

Opening with a proem, "To Brooklyn Bridge," in which the structure, both "harp and altar," is conceived as lending "a myth to God," the eight succeeding sections begin with "Ave Maria," in which Columbus dedicates himself to the new world, and "Powhatan's Daughter," envisioning Pocahontas as an earth goddess but also drawing upon the legend of Rip Van Winkle, the author's own boyhood experiences, the movement of Americans flowing like a river, a dance of life and death associated with an Indian chief, and the farewell of a pioneer mother to her son who is leaving Indiana to go to sea. "Cutty Sark," the third section, presents a kaleidoscopic view of life at sea, at the Panama Canal, and in the Bowery. It is followed by "Cape Hatteras," hovered over by the spirit of Whitman and guided by him as elements of America, such as the achievements of the Wright brothers, are evoked. "Three Songs," treating the power of woman as Venus and Virgin, precede "Quaker Hill," which summons up the sense of degradation in American culture, a theme intensified in "The Tunnel," in which Poe is the author's Virgil in a Hell conceived as a modern subway. The work concludes in its eighth section, "Atlantis," with an affirmative vision that returns to the symbolism of the opening view of Brooklyn Bridge "iridescently upborne Through the bright drench and fabric of our veins. . . ."

Bridge of San Luis Rey, The, novel by Thornton Wilder, ♦ published in 1927 and awarded a Pulitzer Prize.

In 1714 a bridge over a canyon near Lima, Peru, collapses, and five travelers are killed. Brother Juniper, a Franciscan, resolves to help place theology "among the exact sciences" by proving the catastrophe to be an act of divine providence. He collects the results of his six years of investigation in a great book, which is pronounced heretical. He and his book are burned at the stake, but a copy survives, and from it comes these stories of the five who fell with the bridge. . . . The Marquesa de Montemayor has devoted her life to her daughter Clara, a brilliant, selfish woman who goes to Spain after her marriage. The Marquesa's wonderful letters are now her only way of showing her affection, but through her companion, the child Pepita, the Marquesa discovers she has not had true love for Clara and decides to reform. Two days later she and Pepita die on the bridge. . . . The twins Manuel and Esteban, who feel an intense fraternal bond, become scribes and lead a solitary life together. The actress La Périchole employs Manuel to write her letters, but when an infatuation threatens to separate him from his brother, Manuel ends their connection. He dies soon afterward, and the despairing Esteban, prevented from suicide, signs for a voyage as seaman, but is killed on the bridge. . . . Through the teaching of the old rogue Uncle Pio, La Périchole is the most celebrated of actresses, and mistress of the viceroy, to whom she has borne three children. Socially ambitious, she leaves the stage, but her beauty is ravaged by smallpox, and heartbroken she retires to seclusion, devoid of interest except in her son Jaimé. Uncle Pio persuades her to let the boy go with him for a year to begin his education, but Pio and Jaimé die in the fall of the bridge.

BRIDGER, James (1804–81), Virginia-born fur trader, frontiersman, and guide in the Far West, was a member of the expeditions of Ashley (1822) and Jedediah Smith (1823), and is the first white man known to have visited the Great Salt Lake (1824 or 1825). He visited the Grand Canyon (1830), and his tall tales of that region and the Salt Lake are particularly famous. Though illiterate, he had an unrivaled knowledge of the West and the Indian tongues. He built Fort Bridger (1843) on the Oregon Trail, opened the route through Bridger's Pass (1856), helped to survey the Bozeman Trail, and guided the expedition of Bonneville. Like Beckwourth♦ and Fitzpatrick,♦ with whom he worked, he was the hero of many folk legends, such as the one on which Neihardt based *The Song of Hugh Glass.*

BRIERTON, John (*fl.*1572–1619), English rector, participated in Gosnold's expedition (1602) along the New England coast. His enthusiastic account was published as *A Briefe and True Relation of the Discouerie of the North Part of Virginia* (1602). His name was also spelled Brereton.

BRIGGS, Charles Frederick (1804–77), edited the *Broadway Journal,* of which Poe was then an assistant editor, and *Putnam's Magazine* and *The New York Times.* He later turned against Poe, in the latter's critical controversies with Longfellow and Lowell. *The Adventures of Harry Franco* (1839) and *Working a Passage* (1844) are novels based on Briggs's early life, the first dealing with a financial panic in New York, and the

second with his life as a sailor. *The Trippings of Tom Pepper* (2 vols., 1847–50) bears the subtitle, "The Results of Romancing. An Autobiography by Harry Franco."

BRIGGS, Le Baron Russell (1855–1934), professor of creative writing at Harvard, who numbered among his pupils John Dos Passos, Robert Hillyer, E.E. Cummings, Conrad Aiken, and Stuart P. Sherman. As Dean Briggs he became something of a legend as a sympathetic and helpful teacher who was also interested in fostering competitive athletics. Among his books on education are *School, College and Character* (1901), *Routine and Ideals* (1904), and *Men, Women, and Colleges* (1925).

BRINIG, Myron (1900–1991), novelist born in Minnesota, whose works include *Madonna Without Child* (1929), a psychological study of an old maid whose love for her employer's daughter leads her to kidnapping; *Singermann* (1929), of a Jewish immigrant family in Montana; its sequel, *This Man Is My Brother* (1932); *Wide Open Town* (1931) and *Sun Sets in the West* (1935), of Montana mining life, respectively at the turn of the century and during the '30s; *The Flutter of an Eyelid* (1933), satirizing Los Angeles; *Out of Life* (1935), a study of a man's lethargic mind awakened to sensitivity when told that his wife is to have a child; *The Sisters* (1937), the story of the daughters of a Montana druggist; *May Flavin* (1938); *Anne Minton's Life* (1939); *All of Their Lives* (1941); *The Family Way* (1942), satirizing New York suburbanites; *The Gambler Takes a Wife* (1943), set in Montana in the 1880s; *You and I* (1945), about two adopted children meeting again in maturity; *Footsteps on the Stair* (1950), about Irish and Jewish families in Montana; *The Street of the Three Friends* (1953); and *Looking Glass Heart* (1958), set at the opening of the 20th century and portraying a selfish woman.

BRINNIN, John Malcolm (1916–   ), born in Canada, educated at the University of Michigan, has been director of the Poetry Center (1949–56) of New York City's YMHA, and is a professor at Boston University. His poetry has been collected in *The Garden Is Political* (1942), *The Lincoln Lyrics* (1942), *No Arch, No Triumph* (1945), *The Sorrows of Cold Stone* (1951), and *Skin Diving in the Virgins* (1970). He has also written the studies *Dylan Thomas in America* (1955), *The Third Rose* (1959), about Gertrude Stein, and *Sextet: T.S. Eliot & Truman Capote & Others* (1981). Part of the last work is expanded in *Truman Capote: Dear Heart, Old Buddy* (1986).

BRINTON, Daniel Garrison (1837–99), Philadelphia physician and anthropologist, in 1886 became a professor at the University of Pennsylvania. Among his most important writings are *Notes on the Floridian Peninsula* (1859); *The American Race* (1891), a pioneer attempt to classify the Indian racial groups; and *Religions of Primitive Peoples* (1897). He edited the *Library of Aboriginal American Literature* (8 vols., 1882–90), and in *The Lenâpé and Their Legends* (1885) made a translation of the *Walam Olum.* ◆

BRISBANE, ALBERT (1809–90), after studying under Charles Fourier in Paris, returned to the U.S. (1834) to popularize Fourierism through his column in the New York *Tribune,* which was also influential in the formation of more than 40 socialized communities in America. The most famous of these was Brook Farm, and the most successful the North American Phalanx. Brisbane had little to do with the organizations themselves, but defended their general theory in his books, *Social Destiny of Man* (1840) and *General Introduction to Social Science* (1876).

BRISBANE, ARTHUR (1864–1936), son of Albert Brisbane, was a newspaperman associated after 1897 with the publications of W.R. Hearst. His sententious columns, "Today" and "This Week," won him millions of readers.

British Prison Ship, The, poem by Freneau ◆ in four cantos of heroic couplets was published in 1781. In a revision the poem was recast in three cantos. It describes the author's experiences when seized by the British during the Revolutionary War. The first canto tells of his capture; the second describes with bitter satire the horrors of the prison ship *Scorpion,* where the combination of foul air, rotten food and water, and bad treatment soon made him violently ill; and the third tells of his transfer to a so-called hospital ship, the *Hunter,* where the treatment was equally inhumane.

British Spy, see *Letters of the British Spy.*

Broadway, long a residential street, became the main business thoroughfare of New York City in the mid-19th century. It often figures in Whitman's poetry. Its most famous section is the theatrical district at 42nd Street (Times Square), known popularly as The Great White Way, a nickname derived from the title of a play by A.B. Paine (1901), referring to its brilliant lighting.

Broadway Journal (1845–46), literary paper of New York City, was founded (Jan. 4, 1845) with Poe as a contributor and one-third owner. By July he was half owner, and by October sole owner. In the *Journal* he carried on his war with Longfellow and the Transcendentalists, accusing the New England poet of plagiarism, and making the paper more notorious than respectable. In it he published for the first time "The Premature Burial," and reprinted many of his short stories and poems. The final issue (Jan. 2, 1846) was partly edited by T.D. English. ◆

BRODKEY, HAROLD (1930–), a native of Illinois, educated at Harvard, made his sizable reputation as a writer of short stories, many first appearing in *The New Yorker* magazine. His material is often Jewish family life in the small-town Midwest. He published three collections, *First Love and Other Sorrows* (1958), *Women and Angels* (1985), and *Stories in an Almost Classical Mode* (1988), before his novel *The Runaway Soul,* many years in the writing, appeared in 1991. Its center of consciousness is Wiley Silenowicz, the 14-year-old adopted son of S.L. Silenowicz and his wife Lila, of St. Louis. Wiley is tormented throughout by his sister, a natural child of the family. Much use is made of inverted time and of wandering dialogue with many words like "thing" and "stuff." It is a postmodern self-exploration as challenging as—though more centered than—Pynchon's.

Broken-Face Gargoyles, free-verse poem by Carl Sandburg, ◆ published in *Smoke and Steel* (1920). The poet apologizes for his imperfect artistry ("All I can give you is broken-face gargoyles"), explaining that the time has not yet come for the creation of masterpieces in his medium:

> Such a beautiful pail of fish, such a beautiful
> peck of apples, I cannot bring you now.

Broker of Bogotá, The, domestic tragedy by R.M. Bird, ◆ produced in 1834 and first published in Quinn's *Representative American Plays* (1917).

Baptista Febro is an honest moneylender in 18th-century Santa Fe de Bogotá, Colombia. He loves his eldest son, Ramon, despite the fact that he keeps low company. Ramon's friend Cabrero urges him to rob his father to obtain money to marry his beloved Juana. The robbery is perpetrated, and Cabrero causes it to appear that Febro has robbed himself of funds deposited with him. Ramon, brought in as a witness, refuses to speak and his father is condemned. After Juana forces her lover to confess his guilt, he is overcome by remorse and kills himself. When Febro learns of this, he dies.

Brom Bones, character in "The Legend of Sleepy Hollow." ◆

BROMFIELD, LOUIS (1896–1956), born in Ohio, served in World War I, became a New York journalist and foreign correspondent, and long made his home in France. His first novel, *The Green Bay Tree* (1924), opens a tetralogy, *Escape,* including *Possession* (1925), *Early Autumn* (1926, Pulitzer Prize), and *A Good Woman* (1927), about efforts of individuals to escape the domination of family and tradition in different eras of American life. His twelve other novels include *The Farm* (1933), about a century in the life of an Ohio family. Story collections include *Awake and Rehearse* (1929), and plays include *The House of*

Women (1927), dramatizing *The Green Bay Tree.* Bromfield's conservative social views are set forth in *A Few Brass Tacks* (1946). *From My Experience* (1955) treats the pleasures and miseries of his farming in Ohio and Brazil.

Brook Farm, cooperative community (1841–47) near West Roxbury, Mass., nine miles from Boston. Under George Ripley, the Transcendental Club established the community to apply its theories, forming a stock company under the name Brook Farm Institute of Agriculture and Education. Among those interested in it were Hawthorne, C.A. Dana, J.S. Dwight, G.P. Bradford, G.W. Curtis, Theodore Parker, Orestes Brownson, Margaret Fuller, Elizabeth Peabody, C.P. Cranch, Bronson Alcott, W.E. Channing, and Emerson. Of these, only Hawthorne, who wrote about it in *The Blithedale Romance,* and Dana and Dwight lived there. Among the objectives were the promotion of the great purposes of human culture and brotherly cooperation, in order to secure the highest benefits of physical, intellectual, and moral education. The life of the community was simple, all members sharing in the work and the educational and social advantages, and receiving similar pay. Occupations included the tilling of the farm, industrial employments, and school teaching. In 1843 it came under the influence of Albert Brisbane and soon turned into a Fourierist phalanx. As the U.S. center of Fourierism it issued *The Phalanx* (1843–45) and *The Harbinger*♦ (1845). When an incomplete central phalanstery was burned, enthusiasm waned and the group dissolved (Oct. 1847). The Fourierist period is described in the *Letters* of Marianne Dwight Orvis.

Brooklyn, borough of New York, on the southwestern part of Long Island, was an independent city until 1898. First settled by Dutch farmers during the early 17th century, Brooklyn had become an important city by the time of the Revolution, when it was occupied by the British following the battle of Long Island (1776). Whitman and H. W. Beecher are prominent figures in its cultural history. Now a great manufacturing center and place of residence, in its eastern section it includes Brownsville, formerly a Jewish immigrant neighborhood, warmly described by Alfred Kazin in *A Walker in the City.* Brooklyn was long noted for its U.S. navy yard. It is the site of the amusement park zone of Coney Island. The first ferry across the East River was begun in 1642, and Whitman's poem has immortalized the Brooklyn Ferry, but Brooklyn is now connected with Manhattan by tunnel, subway, and by the Williamsburg, Manhattan, and Brooklyn bridges. Brooklyn Bridge, the earliest, was designed by J.A. Roebling, who began the work in 1869, and was completed by his son, W.A. Roebling, in 1883. A suspension type, it carries motor and pedestrian traffic, has a span of 1595 feet, and at

the center is 133 feet above the water. Authors born in or associated with Brooklyn and who have often written about it include Hart Crane, Daniel Fuchs, Joseph Heller, David Ignatow, Norman Mailer, Bernard Malamud, Wallace Markfield, Norman Podhoretz, Hubert Selby, Gilbert Sorrentino, and Ronald Sukenick.

Brooklyn Eagle, The (1841–1955), daily newspaper, a Democratic party organ, edited (March 1846–Jan. 1848) by Walt Whitman, whose writings for it were collected in *The Gathering of the Forces* (2 vols., 1920). The paper was continuously published except for a brief period in 1861 when barred from the mails for its proslavery position.

BROOKS, CHARLES T[IMOTHY] (1813–83), Unitarian clergyman of Newport, R.I., mainly known for his translations from the German, including *William Tell* (1838) by Schiller, *Songs and Ballads* (1842) by various lyric poets, and *Faust* (1856), retaining Goethe's meters. He also wrote original occasional poetry.

BROOKS, CLEANTH, see *New Criticism.*

BROOKS, GWENDOLYN (1917–   ), poet reared in Chicago's slums, whose works include *A Street in Bronzeville* (1945), lyrics; *Annie Allen* (1949, Pulitzer Prize), a verse narrative about a black girl's life to maturity in World War II, treating her race's isolation as both spiritual and social; *The Bean Eaters* (1960), about contemporary black life in the U.S.; and *Selected Poems* (1963). Later volumes of poetry, more militant in tone but continuing to treat the lives and problems of blacks, include *In the Mecca* (1968), *Riot* (1969), *Family Pictures* (1970), *Aloneness* (1971), and *To Disembark* (1982). *Maud Martha* (1953), a novelette about a black woman's romance, is set in Chicago; *Bronzeville Boys and Girls* (1956) is a book for children; and *Report from Part One* (1972) collects autobiographical pieces. She was Poetry Consultant to the Library of Congress (1985–86), becoming the first African-American woman named to that post.

BROOKS, MARIA GOWEN (c.1794–1845), Massachusetts poet, whose first volume, *Judith, Esther, and Other Poems* (1820), was praised by Southey, who dubbed her "Maria of the West," a name she later used as a pseudonym, along with its translation, Maria del Occidente. She removed to Cuba, where she wrote tragic dramas and further poetry, including her epic *Zóphiël* (1833). She was also the author of a romance, *Idomen; or, The Vale of Yumuri* (1843).

BROOKS, NOAH (1830–1903), born in Maine, became a California journalist (1854–62), then a Washington correspondent, and after another period of newspaper editorship in San Francisco continued his journalistic career in New York and New Jersey, until he retired to California in 1892. His knowledge of the West furnished the background for his popular boys' book, *The Boy Emigrants* (1877). Other works include *Tales of the Maine Coast* (1894); works on Lincoln, whom he knew intimately; and various American historical studies.

BROOKS, PHILLIPS (1835–93), from the pulpit of Trinity Church in Boston, the stronghold of Episcopalianism, won an international reputation as a vigorous leader of his faith, being made a bishop in 1891. Although he published such books as *Lectures on Preaching* (1877), *The Influence of Jesus* (1879), and *Essays and Addresses* (1892), his best-loved contribution is his Christmas hymn "O Little Town of Bethlehem."

BROOKS, VAN WYCK (1886–1963), born in New Jersey of a wealthy, cultivated family, after graduation from Harvard (1904) entered upon his literary career. In biographies and criticism, beginning with *The Wine of the Puritans* (1909), he first developed the thesis that the Puritan tradition crushed American culture and placed an undue emphasis on material values, neglecting the aesthetic side of life. This theory is illustrated in *America's Coming-of-Age* (1915), *Letters and Leadership* (1918), *The Ordeal of Mark Twain* (1920), and *The Pilgrimage of Henry James* (1925). He strikingly altered this belief in his later books, which, in addition to a revision of the Mark Twain study, include the very appreciative analyses of American life, *Emerson and Others* (1927) and *Sketches in Criticism* (1932). His "history of the writer in America," titled *Makers and Finders,* includes *The Flowering of New England* (1936, Pulitzer Prize), on the period 1815–65; *New England: Indian Summer* (1940), continuing to 1915; *The World of Washington Irving* (1944), concerning 1800 to the 1840s outside New England; *The Times of Melville and Whitman* (1947); and *The Confident Years* (1952), about the era 1885–1915. All of these present a rich, impressionistic, and anecdotal view of the American literary scene with its writers, great and small, all treated knowingly and appreciatively. Although he did some teaching early at Stanford University (1911–13), edited magazines, edited works by many writers, including Randolph Bourne and Gamaliel Bradford, and translated many French books, his main work throughout his life was devoted to interpreting the literary and cultural life of the U.S. in numerous books which show a steadfast humanism, a Jeffersonian liberalism, and an appreciation of the American past. His views of literature and antipathy to many 20th-century movements appear in *On Literature Today* (1941), *Opinions of Oliver Allston* (1941), *The Writer in America* (1953), and *From a Writer's Notebook* (1958). His other works on the literary and cultural traditions of this country include *John Sloan* (1955), a biography of his friend, the artist; *Helen Keller: Sketch for*

a Portrait (1956); *American Writers and Artists in Italy, 1760–1915* (1958); *Howells: His Life and World* (1959); and *Fenollosa and His Circle* (1962). His own impressionistic reminiscences appeared in *Scenes and Portraits: Memories of Childhood and Youth* (1954); *Days of the Phoenix* (1957), about the 1920s; and *From the Shadow of the Mountain: My Post-Meridian Years* (1961), from 1931 to his birthday—all collected in *An Autobiography* (1965). His correspondence with Lewis Mumford was published in 1970.

Brother Jonathan, sobriquet applied to America and the American people, which has been largely supplanted by the name Uncle Sam. The most commonly accepted origin attributes the term to Washington, who supposedly relied on the advice of Jonathan Trumbull, and once in a moment of perplexity remarked, "We must consult Brother Jonathan." The legend is questionable, since no contemporary evidence exists, and the British used the term as early as the 17th century in alluding to the Roundheads or Puritans. In the U.S. it often refers to a Yankee, as in the novel of this title published in 1825 by John Neal. ♦

Brother to Dragons, narrative poem in dramatic form by Robert Penn Warren ♦ treating the subject of an axe-murder of a slave by nephews of Thomas Jefferson, published in 1953 and revised by the poet (1979).

BROUGHAM, JOHN (1810–80), Irish-born actor and playwright, was for many years a member of the company of W.E. Burton. Among his plays were the three burlesques, *Metamora; or, The Last of the Pollywoags* (1847), a parody of Stone's *Metamora; Po-ca-hon-tas! or, Ye Gentle Savage* (1855); and *Columbus* (1857). He dramatized Harriet Beecher Stowe's *Dred* (1856), and wrote other successful plays, including *Temptation, or the Irish Immigrant* (1849) and *The Mustard Ball; or, Love at the Academy* (1858).

BROUGHTON, JAMES [RICHARD] (1913–   ), native-born California poet, graduated from Stanford, whose early volumes, *The Playground* (1949), *Musical Chairs* (1950), and *An Almanac for Amorists* (1952), related to the local Beat movement. ♦ Later poems include *A Long Undressing* (1971), *Seeing the Light* (1977), *Graffiti for the Johns of Heaven* (1982), and *Hooplas: Odes for Odd Occasions* (1988). He has also produced experimental films and plays.

BROUN, HEYWOOD [CAMPBELL] (1888–1939), New York columnist and critic, was a consistent opponent of social injustice through his articles in the New York *Tribune* and *World, The Nation,* and *The New Republic.* His books include *The A.E.F.* (1918), describing his experiences as a correspondent with the American forces in France; *Pieces of*

Hate, and Other Enthusiasms (1922) and *Sitting on the World* (1924), selected from his newspaper columns; and *Anthony Comstock* (1927), a biography written with Margaret Leech. A *Collected Edition* of the best of Broun's work was issued in 1941.

BROWN, ALICE (1857–1948), New Hampshire author, is best known for her stories of New England local color, collected in such volumes as *Meadow-Grass* (1895), *Tiverton Tales* (1899), *Vanishing Points* (1913), and *Homespun and Gold* (1920). Her novels, mainly portraits of New England characters, although some exhibit her interest in the supernatural, include *Fools of Nature* (1887), *The Day of His Youth* (1897), *Margaret Warrener* (1901), *Rose MacLeod* (1908), *The Story of Thyrza* (1909), *The Prisoner* (1916), *Bromley Neighborhood* (1917), *The Wind Between the Worlds* (1920), *Old Crow* (1922), and *Dear Old Templeton* (1927). In addition to many one-act plays, she wrote *Children of Earth* (1915), a drama dealing with a New England spinster's thwarted desire for love. With Louise Imogen Guiney♦ she wrote a critical study of Stevenson (1895), and in 1921 she wrote Guiney's biography.

BROWN, CHARLES BROCKDEN (1771–1810), after a brief career as a lawyer in his native Philadelphia, moved to New York to become the first professional author of the U.S. Under the influence of William Godwin, he wrote *Alcuin: A Dialogue* (1798), a treatise on the rights of women. Further stimulated by Godwin's *Caleb Williams* and his own critical ideas of fiction, Brown in two frenetic years composed his four best novels, *Wieland♦* (1798), *Arthur Mervyn♦* (1799), *Ormond♦* (1799), and *Edgar Huntly♦* (1799), quickly followed by *Clara Howard* (1801), which was published in England as *Philip Stanley,* and *Jane Talbot* (1801). These Gothic romances were carefully documented in fact and pseudo-science, and influenced by the moral purpose of Godwin, the sentimentalism and psychology of Richardson, and above all the horrors of the school of Mrs. Radcliffe. After this brief burst of fiction, Brown entered business, although he also edited *The Monthly Magazine and American Register♦* and *The Literary Magazine and American Register♦* and did such hackwork as the *Memoirs of Carwin.♦* He held high critical standards concerning American literature, believed in using distinctively American materials and in writing novels whose ideas would stir thinkers while their plots would attract ordinary readers. Although Brown was appreciated by Keats, Shelley, and Scott, and even influenced his own master, Godwin, he failed to achieve his aims because of his haste, immaturity, stilted language, fascination by the pathological, and inability to master completely the Godwinian plot structure. Despite his failings, his Gothic romances transferred to an American setting have a dark emotional intensity that gives his work more than historical significance. William

Dunlap♦ wrote a biography of Brown (1815). A scholarly edition of his works began publication in 1977.

BROWN, HARRY [PETER McNAB, JR.] (1917–86), first wrote humorous sketches about a Brooklyn GI in Britain during World War II, published originally in *Yank* and collected in *Artie Greengroin, Pfc.* (1945). His other writing about the war is serious, including *A Walk in the Sun* (1944), a novelette about an American platoon on an Italian beachhead, and *A Sound of Hunting* (1946), a play about U.S. soldiers in Italy trying to rescue a missing comrade. Other fiction includes *The Stars in Their Courses* (1960), set in the Western U.S. of the 1870s but written as a parallel to the story of the *Iliad; The Wild Hunt* (1973); and *The Gathering* (1977). His poetry has been collected in *The End of a Decade* (1941), *The Poem of Bunker Hill* (1941), *The Violent* (1943), and *The Beast in His Hunger* (1949).

BROWN, JOHN (1800–1859), Abolitionist leader, in 1855 moved with his five sons from Ohio to Osawatomie, Kan., following the passage of the Kansas-Nebraska Bill. Believing himself to be the special instrument of God intended to destroy proslavery settlers, he deliberately murdered five of his Southern-minded neighbors, and this, and similar acts, together with his previous reputation as an operator of the Underground Railroad, made him nationally celebrated as "Brown of Osawatomie." In 1859 he and his followers moved to Harpers Ferry, Va., where, on the night of October 16, he and 21 others captured the U.S. armory, with the intention of establishing a base from which they might free slaves by armed intervention. A force of U.S. marines under R.E. Lee attacked the armory, killed ten of Brown's men, and wounded and captured Brown. With the insurrection quelled, Brown was hanged (Dec. 2, 1859). His sincerity and dignity when on trial led many liberals to treat him as a martyr, e.g. Thoreau's *The Last Days of John Brown.* He is also lauded in Benét's *John Brown's Body,♦* the title too of a Civil War song, in Whittier's "John Brown of Osawatomie," Stedman's "How Old Brown Took Harpers Ferry," and Leonard Ehrlich's novel *God's Angry Man* (1932).

BROWN, JOHN MASON (1900–69), New York drama critic, whose books include *The Modern Theatre in Revolt* (1929), *Upstage* (1930), *Letters from Greenroom Ghosts* (1934), *The Art of Playgoing* (1936), *Accustomed as I Am* (1942), *Seeing Things* (1946), *As They Appear* (1952), and *Dramatis Personae* (1963). *To All Hands* (1943) and *Many a Watchful Night* (1944) treat the Allied invasion of Europe in World War II, in which he served in the navy. His biographical works include *Through These Men* (1956), about contemporary figures, and *The Worlds of Robert E. Sherwood* (1956).

BROWN, NORMAN O[LIVER] (1913–), professor of classics and comparative literature at the University of California, Santa Cruz (1971–), best known for his *Life Against Death: The Psychoanalytic Meaning of History* (1959), a Freudian study of human nature written in an aphoristic style. His other works include *Love's Body* (1966), an extension of the ideas in his earlier book; and *Closing Time* (1973), relating Vico's ideas to *Finnegans Wake.*

BROWN, RITA MAE (1944–), born in Pennsylvania, educated at the New York School of Visual Arts. Her first novel, *Rubyfruit Jungle* (1973), celebrating the joys of lesbian sexuality, won her acclaim. Other novels on similar themes are *In Her Day* (1976), *Six of One* (1978), *Southern Discomfort* (1982), and *Sudden Death* (1983). Her poetry is collected in *The Hand That Cradles the Rock* (1971) and *Songs to a Handsome Woman* (1973). A collection of essays, *Plain Brown Wrapper,* appeared in 1976. *Venus Envy* (1993), a novelistic comedy of manners, is a polemical parable concerning a wealthy lesbian owner of a Virginia art gallery.

BROWN, STERLING A[LLAN] (1901–89), born in Washington, D.C., educated at Williams College and Harvard and long a professor at Howard University, is known for poetry celebrating black people through the use of folk themes and dialect. These were first published in *Southern Road* (1932) and in a belated collection, *The Last Ride of Wild Bill* (1975), and gathered in *Collected Poems* (1980). He also wrote books about black poetry, fiction, and drama.

BROWN, THEOPHILUS (1811–79?), "the literary tailor," whose shop in Worcester, Mass., was a literary rendezvous, was a friend of Thoreau and Emerson. Excerpts from his letters published in 1879 reflect the cultural life of his time.

BROWN, WILLIAM HILL (1765–93), author of "the first American novel," *The Power of Sympathy*♦ (1789), long attributed to Mrs. Sarah Morton.♦ Another novel by Brown, *Ira and Isabella; or, The Natural Children* (1807), uses a similar plot, with a happy ending. He also wrote verse fables, a comedy, and *West Point Preserved* (1797), a tragedy about André.♦

BROWN, WILLIAM WELLS (1816?–84), African-American leader, born in Kentucky, reared in St. Louis, where he worked for Lovejoy's press until he found freedom in Ohio, where he aided fugitive slaves. His works include an autobiographical *Narrative* (1847); *The Anti-Slavery Harp* (1848), poems; *My Three Years in Europe* (1852); *Clotelle; or, The President's Daughter* (London, 1853), said to be the first novel by a black; this tale of a mulatto born to Jefferson's housekeeper was issued in the U.S. without references to the President as *Clotelle: A Tale of the Southern States* (1864); *The Escape* (1858), a play; and *The Black Man: His Antecedents, His Genius, and His Achievements* (1863), expanded as *The Rising Son* (1874).

BROWNE, CHARLES FARRAR (1834–67), humorist born in Maine, is better known under his pseudonym Artemus Ward. In 1857 he began to contribute to the Cleveland *Plain Dealer* the series of "Artemus Ward's Sayings," a record of the imaginary adventures of an itinerant showman. He capitalized on the traits of backwoods and Down East characters, and attracted attention with comic misspellings. He often wrote on current events and jibed at insincerities and sentimentality. For a short time he was editor of *Vanity Fair.* He was at the height of his fame as a London lecturer and contributor to *Punch* when he died of tuberculosis. A selection from his books was made by A.J. Nock (1924).

BROWNE, J[OHN] ROSS (1821–75), born in Ireland, was brought to Kentucky when 11, and as a young man began his life of traveling, which furnished material for books. His first book, *Etchings of a Whaling Cruise* (1846), was influenced by Dana and in turn influenced *Moby-Dick.* His trip around the Horn to California, where he served as official reporter for the first Constitutional Convention (1849), and other Far Western experiences as a customs house inspector, special inspector of Indian affairs, and commissioner of mines furnished material for *Crusoe's Island . . . with Sketches of Adventures in California and Washoe* (1864) and *Adventures in Apache Country* (1869), which anticipate the attitude and materials of Mark Twain's *Roughing It.* His frontier humorist's view of Europe in *Yusef . . . a Crusade in the East* (1853), the first of several foreign travel books, preceded Twain's *Innocents Abroad.* Browne also wrote governmental reports and was U.S. minister to China.

BROWNELL, W[ILLIAM] C[RARY] (1851–1928), literary critic, who, in search for ethical and social standards as measures of value that he felt the frequently provincial U.S. lacked, recommended an understanding of past culture and an attitude similar to that of Matthew Arnold. He preceded the New Humanists but is identified with their movement. His learned essays, also distinguished by their fine style, include *French Traits, An Essay in Comparative Criticism* (1889), *French Art* (1892), *Victorian Prose Masters* (1901), *American Prose Masters* (1909), *Criticism* (1914), *Standards* (1917), *The Genius of Style* (1924), *Democratic Distinction in America* (1927), and *The Spirit of Society* (1927). An anthology of his writings was collected in 1933.

Brownists, name applied by their opponents to those who separated from the Church of England at the beginning of the 17th century. The name was derived from that of Robert Browne (c.1550–c.1633), who, as a Separatist pastor, felt that some of the rites and ceremonies of the Established Church were superstitious, and that its power should rest in the people. Browne later returned to the Church, and this relapse, with the extreme character of some of his views, made the name Brownist very objectionable to the Congregationalists to whom it was applied.

BROWNLOW, WILLIAM GANNAWAY (1805–77), Tennessee preacher and editor, known as "the Fighting Parson." His pro-Union sympathies, voiced in his newspaper, caused him to be imprisoned and later driven from the South. His *Sketches of the Rise, Progress, and Decline of Secession* (1862) had a huge Northern circulation. As governor of Tennessee (1865–69), he disfranchised Confederate veterans and attempted to break the Ku Klux Klan. He served as U.S. senator (1869–75).

BROWNSON, ORESTES AUGUSTUS (1803–76), New England clergyman and liberal thinker, originally a Presbyterian, became successively a Universalist, an independent, a Unitarian minister, and a Roman Catholic. He was an ardent advocate of various liberal and socialistic projects, supported the Workingmen's party, and was interested in Transcendentalism and Brook Farm. His ideas were set forth in the magazines he edited: *The Boston Quarterly Review,*♦ *Democratic Review,*♦ and *Brownson's Quarterly Review.*♦ Some of his books are *New Views of Christianity, Society and the Church* (1836); *Charles Elwood, or the Infidel Converted* (1840), a semi-autobiographical novel; *The Mediatorial Life of Jesus* (1842); and *The Convert* (1857), an account of his conversion to Catholicism, which created a contemporary sensation. *The Spirit-Rapper* (1854) is subtitled "An Autobiography" but is actually a romance concerning spiritualism, which the author attributed to Satanic influence. His works were collected in 20 volumes (1882–87).

Brownson's Quarterly Review (1844–75), founded by Orestes Brownson♦ when the columns of the *Democratic Review,* which he had helped to edit, were closed to him because of its subscribers' complaints. The magazine reflected Brownson's conversion to Catholicism, although it attacked what he called "radicalism and despotism" in the Church. In 1864 he turned to a chauvinistic interest in American civilization, and then, after a year, returned to Catholicism after the sincerity of his former standards had been questioned.

Brutus; or, The Fall of Tarquin, romantic blank-verse tragedy by John Howard Payne,♦ produced and published in London (1818) and New York (1819). Based on seven previous plays on the same subject, Payne's work on the whole is nevertheless original. With a careful historical background, it is mainly a characterization of the Roman patriot Brutus and his establishment of the republic.

BRYAN, WILLIAM JENNINGS (1860–1925), after representing Nebraska in Congress (1890–94) continued to advocate free silver as a Chautauqua speaker. The greatest statement of his silver policy was in his "Cross of Gold" speech at the 1896 Democratic national convention at Chicago, when he was nominated for the presidency, although only 36 years old. After a campaign based on the platform of free, unlimited coinage of silver as a cure for the ills of farmers and workers, he was defeated by McKinley, who advocated the gold standard and protective tariff. He lost to McKinley again in 1900. In 1901 he founded the *Commoner,* a magazine expounding his reform policies, and until 1912 he was a power in every Democratic convention, winning the name of "the great commoner." In 1908 he was again defeated for the presidency, this time by Taft. He served as Wilson's secretary of state, formulating arbitration treaties with foreign nations that were never tested because of World War I; in 1915 his pacifist sympathies caused him to resign. His militant defense of Fundamentalism reached its greatest prominence when he served as the Tennessee prosecutor in the trial of J.T. Scopes.♦ His *Memoirs* were published in 1925. He figures frequently in literature as a folk figure, e.g. Vachel Lindsay's "Bryan, Bryan, Bryan, Bryan" and Dos Passos's *U.S.A.* The Scopes trial was the subject of *Inherit the Wind* (1955), a play by J. Lawrence and R.E. Lee.

BRYANT, EDWIN (1805–69), Kentuckian who led an emigrant party from Missouri to California (1846), where he became *alcalde* of the San Francisco district. His description of the journey and the conquest of California was published as *What I Saw in California* (1848), frequently reprinted as *Rocky Mountain Adventures.*

BRYANT, WILLIAM CULLEN (1794–1878), born at Cummington, Mass., was educated at home, at the district schools, and at Williams College. After writing *The Embargo* (1808), at the age of 14, indignant satires against Jefferson's administration, he wrote "Thanatopsis"♦ and "To a Waterfowl,"♦ but left them unpublished while continuing a legal career that lasted to 1825. His fame as a poet dates from the printing of "Thanatopsis" (1817). In 1821 he read "The Ages"♦ at Harvard as a Phi Beta Kappa poem and published his first mature book of *Poems.* In 1824–25 he wrote some 20 or 30 poems for the *United States Literary Gazette,* including "A Forest Hymn,"♦ "Monument Mountain,"♦ "Rizpah," and "An Indian at the Burial Place of His Fathers," which established him as the leading poet of the U.S. Early in 1825 he became co-editor of the *New*

York Review and Athenæum Magazine♦ and then of the New York *Evening Post,*♦ whose full editorship he assumed in 1829 and held for almost 50 years. By 1840 he had become one of the leading Democratic editors, but his vigorous opposition to slavery brought him into the new Republican party. In 1832 he published a new collection of *Poems,* which included "The Death of the Flowers,"♦ "To the Fringed Gentian,"♦ "Mutation,"♦ and "The Song of Marion's Men."♦ Although new additions and other books continued to appear, this edition contains all of the essential Bryant. Throughout he shows certain ideas growing always out of a limited range of emotional responses, and reporting a few aspects of man and nature. He was a poet of nature, and his work is often compared with that of Wordsworth, who profoundly influenced him, but Bryant's God remained ever a Divine Being distinct from His creation. Nature is simply the visible token of God's transcendent beauty and awful power, and thus nature influences man for good. There is a pervading sense of the transiency of earthly things, but he thinks of the somber certainty of the grave, rather than the earlier Puritan obsession with the terrors of hell. Although Bryant's themes were few and his thought not profound, he possessed a simple dignity and an impeccable, restrained style. The Doric nobility and dignity of the poet fitted him well for his translation of the *Iliad* (1870) and the *Odyssey* (1871–72), blank-verse renditions plain in style and simple in movement. His other publications include *The Fountain* (1842), *The White-Footed Deer* (1844), *A Forest Hymn* (1860), *Thirty Poems* (1864), *Hymns* (1869), *The Little People of the Snow* (1873), *Among the Trees* (1874), and *The Flood of Years* (1878). His best prose is found in the discourses on Cooper, Irving, Halleck, and Verplanck, in his *Letters of a Traveller* (1850; 2nd series, 1859), and in the collected *Orations and Addresses* (1873).

BRYCE, James (1838–1922), English historian and diplomat, after a career as an Oxford professor, a member of Parliament, and in various political posts, became ambassador to the U.S. (1907–13). His great work *The American Commonwealth*♦ was published in 1888, after five visits to this country and wide reading on American history and institutions.

BUCK, Pearl [Sydenstricker] (1892–1973), born in West Virginia, reared in China, where her parents were missionaries. Educated at Randolph-Macon and Cornell, she returned to be a missionary and teacher at Chinese universities. Of her many novels about China the best known is *The Good Earth* (1931, Pulitzer Prize), the first of a trilogy, *The House of Earth,* including *Sons* (1932) and *A House Divided* (1935). She was prolific, producing a book every other year. Most notable later works include *The Spirit and the Flesh* (1936),

moving portraits of her mother and father; a translation from the classic Chinese of one of China's most famous novels, *Shui Hu Chuan* (The Water Margin) as *All Men Are Brothers* (2 vols., 1933, 1937); and *Imperial Woman* (1956), a fictionalized life of China's last empress. She also wrote stories, plays, essays, and children's books. She won the Nobel Prize for literature in 1938.

BUCKE, Richard Maurice (1837–1902), English-born friend of Whitman, reared in Canada, and practiced there and in the U.S. as a doctor specializing in psychiatric disturbances. His uncritically enthusiastic and mystical writings on Whitman include *Walt Whitman* (1883) and *Walt Whitman, Man and Poet* (1897). His concern with the poet's mysticism led him to write *Cosmic Consciousness* (1901). As a literary executor of Whitman he joined Horace Traubel♦ and Thomas B. Harned in editing *The Complete Writings* (1902) and collecting critical essays and statements by followers published in *In Re Walt Whitman* (1893).

BUCKINGHAM, James Silk (1786–1855), English journalist, founder of the *Athenæum,* and member of Parliament, toured the U.S. (1837–40), which he described favorably in *America: Historical, Statistic, and Descriptive* (9 vols., 1841–43).

BUCKLEY, William F[rank], Jr. (1925–   ), born in New York, after graduation from Yale became a leading spokesman for conservatism in politics, partly as editor of the *National Review* (1955–90) and the author of numerous books, including *Up from Liberalism* (1959) and *Right Reason* (1985). He has also been the author of many popular mystery and espionage novels, including *Saving the Queen* (1976), *Who's on First* (1980), and *The Story of Henri Tod* (1984). Books on personal experiences at sea and on land are *Airborne: A Sentimental Journey* (1984), *Atlantic High: A Celebration* (1983), *Racing Through Paradise: A Pacific Passage* (1987), and *Windfall: The End of the Affair* (1992). *Happy Days Were Here Again: Reflections of a Libertarian Journalist* (1993) collects 120 articles and addresses written between 1985 and 1993.

BUCKMINSTER, Joseph Stevens (1784–1812), Boston Unitarian clergyman, was a founder of the Anthology Club.♦ His library became the nucleus of the Boston Athenæum. He was the brother of Eliza Buckminster Lee.♦

Budd, Lanny, see *Sinclair, Upton.*

BUDD, Thomas (d. 1698), English-born Quaker, came to New Jersey (1678), about which he wrote *Good Order Established in Pennsylvania and New Jersey* (1685).

BUECHNER, [Carl] Frederick (1926–   ), novelist and clergyman, after graduation from

Princeton (1947) taught English at Lawrenceville School (1948–53) until ordained to the Presbyterian ministry (1958), after which he became a teacher of religion and school minister at Phillips Academy, Exeter, until 1967. His first novel, *A Long Day's Dying* (1949), is an elaborately contrived and strenuously symbolic work which deals with the tensions in the relations among a widow, her son, and her mother when she is discovered to have had sexual relations with the boy's young college instructor and, to save her reputation, accuses the teacher of a homosexual relationship with her son. The psychological analysis of the first novel, as well as its Jamesian mannerisms and baroque syntax, is also observable in *The Seasons' Difference* (1951), a novel about the responses of a group of children and adults to a vision seen by the youngsters' tutor. *The Return of Ansel Gibbs* (1958) is a story more plainly told of the private and public life of a liberal man appointed to a U.S. cabinet post. *The Final Beast* (1965) draws religious meaning from its tale of a minister whose attempt to aid a member of his congregation leads to a tragic misinterpretation of his actions. *The Entrance to Porlock* (1970) is a strangely symbolic novel, again in an elaborate style, of an octogenarian and his family as he becomes involved with a mystic and his strange charitable community. *Lion Country* (1971), *Open Heart* (1972), *Love Feast* (1974), and *Treasure Hunt* (1977) form a series of novels that creates a parable related to individual involvement in evangelical religion. *Brendan* (1987) is a tale of a 6th-century Irish adventurer, and *The Son of Laughter* (1993) retells the story of Jacob, son of Isaac and grandson of Abraham. *The Magnificent Defeat* (1966) prints sermons; *The Hungering Dark* (1969), *The Alphabet of Grace* (1970), and *Wishful Thinking* (1973) contain meditations and prayers; *The Faces of Jesus* (1974) studies artists' interpretations of Christ; *Telling the Truth* (1977) collects essays on the Gospels; and *A Room Called Remember* (1984) gathers sermons. *The Sacred Journey* (1982), *Now and Then* (1983), and *Whistling in the Dark* (1988) form a memoir animated by the author's religious convictions.

Buffalo Bill, see *Cody, W. F.*

Building of the Ship, The, ode in four-stress trochaic verse by Longfellow,♦ published in *The Seaside and the Fireside* (1849). A long narrative describes the construction and launching of a sailing ship. It concludes with the famous apostrophe to the Federal Union, beginning: "Thou, too, sail on, O Ship of State!"

BUKOWSKI, CHARLES (1920–94), born in Germany, son of a U.S. soldier and German woman, reared in the U.S., worked mainly as an unskilled laborer until, aged 35, he began to write poetry. His prolific output, published in many limited-edition booklets, begun with *Flower, Fist*

and Bestial Wail (1960), includes larger collections: *It Catches My Heart in Its Hands* (1963), *Burning in Water, Drowning in Flame* (1974), *Love Is a Dog from Hell* (1977), *Dangling in the Tournefortia* (1981), *War All the Time* (1985), *You Get So Alone at Times That It Just Make Sense* (1986), and *The Last Night of the Earth, Poems* (1992). In them his attitude is that of a tough, lowbrow outsider, egocentric and very masculine, whose personal interests and literary subjects are drink and sex and violence. He also wrote stories: *Erections, Ejaculations, Exhibitions and General Tales of Ordinary Madness* (1972), *Life and Death in the Charity Ward* (1973), and *South of No North* (1973). *Notes of a Dirty Old Man* (1969) is partly memoir and partly fiction, while other novels are *Post Office* (1971), *Factotum* (1975), *Women* (1978), and *Ham on Rye* (1982), about the seedy life of the quasi-autobiographical Henry Chinaski. Wholly autobiographical works include *Confessions of a Man Insane Enough To Live with Beasts* (1965) and *Shakespeare Never Did This* (1979). *Hollywood, a Novel* (1989) is an account of the author's dealings with the film colony. *Septuagenarian Stew* (1990) prints a mixture of poems and stories.

BULFINCH, CHARLES (1763–1844), known as the first professional architect in the U.S., did his best work in his native Boston. Influenced by the Adam style, his outstanding achievements, marked by a simple treatment of lightly proportioned classical orders, include the central part of the Boston State House (1795–98), University Hall at Harvard (1815), and the Massachusetts General Hospital (1820). Franklin Crescent (1793) in Boston was a curved row of homes with the type of exterior known as the Bulfinch front, following the example of the Adam brothers in Adelphi Terrace in London and significant as the first American attempt to create a unified exterior grouping. As architect of the national Capitol (1818–30), Bulfinch executed the west portico and its approach, and completed the work of Latrobe.♦

BULFINCH, THOMAS (1796–1867), son of Charles Bulfinch, was the author of *The Age of Fable* (1855), a popular treatment of classic myths and also Scandinavian, Celtic, and Oriental myths. Other works include *The Age of Chivalry* (1858) on Arthurian and Welsh legends, *Shakespeare Adapted for Reading Classes* (1865), and *Oregon and Eldorado* (1866), treating a sea expedition to the Pacific Northwest which his father helped to organize.

BULL, OLE (1810–80), Norwegian violinist, made the first of his five tours of the U.S. in 1843. He encouraged nationalism among U.S. composers, and himself created such works as *Grand March to the Memory of Washington, Niagara,* and *Solitude of the Prairie.* He figures as the musician in Longfellow's *Tales of a Wayside Inn.* In

1852 he established the short-lived Norwegian colony, Oleana, in Pennsylvania.

BULLINS, ED (1935–   ), born in Philadelphia, studied at San Francisco State College among several schools. In the mid-1960s he was cultural director for the Black Panthers, an activist group in Oakland. At the end of the decade he moved to New York, where he became a prolific playwright. *Five Plays* (1969) collects his early one-acters. Among his best-known plays are *A Son, Come Home* (1968), *The Electronic Nigger* (1968), and *Four Dynamite Plays* (1971). All express political anger. *The Hungered One* (1971) prints short stories. *The Reluctant Rapist* (1973) is a novel. Bullins was editor of *Black Theatre,* 1968–73.

Bulwark, *The,* novel by Dreiser,♦ posthumously published in 1946.

Bumppo, NATTY, see *Leather-Stocking Tales.*

BUNCE, OLIVER BELL (1828–90), New York writer and editor, best known for his plays, *Love in '76*♦ (1857); *The Morning of Life* (1848), a rural comedy; and *Marco Bozzaris* (1850), about the recent Greek revolt. *The Opinions and Disputations of Bachelor Bluff* (1881) is a collection of social essays, reprinted from *Appleton's Journal,* which he edited (1872–81).

Bundren, family name of the principal characters in Faulkner's novel *As I Lay Dying.*♦

Bunker Hill, in Boston, was the approximate site of the first severe engagement of the Revolutionary War (June 17, 1775). The British attacked the newly constructed American fort on Breed's Hill, but were twice routed by the American defenders, who capitulated on the third charge, being out of powder. Although the battle was a British victory, American morale was strengthened by the demonstration of their small force. The battle is a frequent subject in American literature, as in Brackenridge's play *The Battle of Bunkers-Hill,*♦ Cooper's novel *Lionel Lincoln,*♦ and J.W. De Forest's novel *A Lover's Revolt.* A memorial obelisk has been erected on the site, the cornerstone being laid by Lafayette in 1825 and the monument completed in 1843, a famous speech by Daniel Webster being delivered on each occasion.

BUNNER, H[ENRY] C[UYLER] (1855–96), edited *Puck*♦ (1878–96), to which he contributed much of the familiar verse which appeared in such books as *Airs from Arcady and Elsewhere* (1884), and which was collected in a single volume in 1896. *The Midge* (1886) is a novelette about a New York bachelor and his ward, and *The Story of a New York House* (1887) traces two New York families through three generations. Bunner's craftsmanship and urbanity are best seen in the stories collected in *"Short Sixes"* (1891), *Zadoc Pine* (1891), and *More "Short Sixes"* (1894). His light stories and sketches about New York foreshadowed the work of O. Henry, but in technique he was so like Maupassant that when he adapted some of the French master's work as *"Made in France"* (1893), he was able to insert an original story without detection. *In Partnership* (1879) contains stories written with Brander Matthews.

BUNTLINE, NED, pseudonym of E.Z.C. Judson.♦

Bunyan, PAUL, giant hero of many tales told by lumberjacks of the Great Lakes region and the Pacific Northwest. Originally, the stories may have described a French Canadian, "Bon Jean," but in their later form they are pure mythology. They tell of the exploits of the greatest of all boss loggers, which include such fantastic feats as the creation of the Grand Canyon and Puget Sound, and the invention of the double-bitted axe and of a gigantic hotcake griddle, greased by flunkies who skate on it with sides of bacon strapped to their feet. Bunyan's crews included the one that logged on the Big Onion River during the winter of the blue snow, when it was so cold that cuss words froze in the air, thawing out the next Fourth of July with a great din. Among his companions were Babe the blue ox, who measured 42 axe handles and a plug of Star tobacco between the eyes; Sourdough Slim, the cook; and Johnny Inkslinger, the clerk. A similar hero of the South is Tony Beaver.♦ Books by Esther Shephard, T.G. Alvord, R.L. Stokes, and James Stevens collect Bunyan tales. Frost wrote a poem, "Paul's Wife," Louis Untermeyer wrote a verse version of many tales in *the Wonderful Adventures of Paul Bunyan* (1945), and the choral operetta *Paul Bunyan* by Auden and Benjamin Britten was produced (1941) but never published, except for three songs in Auden's *Collected Poems.*

BURDETTE, ROBERT JONES (1844–1914), newspaper editor and humorist, whose popular writings for an Iowa paper caused him to be called "the Burlington Hawkeye Man." His lecture, "The Rise and Fall of the Moustache" (printed 1877), is said to have been delivered nearly 5000 times.

BURGESS, GELETT [FRANK] (1866–1951), Massachusetts-born author, identified with San Francisco, where he led a literary group, Les Jeunes, in editing *The Lark*♦ (1895–97), in which appeared his quatrain, "The Purple Cow," and his drawings of "goops."♦ His many books include light verse, stories, and drawings, such as *Goops and How To Be Them* (1900), *Are You a Bromide?* (1906), and a local-color novel of San Francisco, *The Heart Line* (1907).

BURGESS, THORNTON W[ALDO] (1874–1965), Massachusetts author of children's books whimsically depicting nature and animal life. These include *Old Mother West Wind* (1910), *The Burgess Bird Book for Children* (1919), and *The Burgess Sea Shore Book for Children* (1929).

BURGOYNE, JOHN (1722–92), English general, dramatist, and politician, was sent to Boston to reinforce Gage, arriving after the Battle of Lexington. Distressed at the army's inaction, he returned to England (Nov. 1775), but was sent to Canada the following spring. In 1777 he was made commander-in-chief of the northern army, and, although he mustered only half the men he expected, he reoccupied Crown Point and captured Fort Ticonderoga. On his advance to Albany, Arnold cut off his retreat, Schuyler blockaded his advance, and Clinton failed to meet him. He lost men through desertion and in the battle at Bemis Heights (Sept. 24, 1777), where Gates met him with an army three times greater than his own. He surrendered to Gates at Saratoga (Oct. 17, 1777). In Boston, Burgoyne wrote *The Blockade*♦ (1775). He figures in Shaw's play *The Devil's Disciple* and in Kenneth Roberts's novel *Rabble in Arms.*

BURK, JOHN DALY (*c.*1775–1808), Irish-born dramatist, came to America in 1796, and wrote a *History of Virginia* (1804–16). His *Bunker Hill, or the Death of General Warren* (1797) was a bombastic blank-verse drama, popular for its spectacular battle scene. *Female Patriotism, or the Death of Joan d'Arc* (1798) is a blank-verse tragedy, characterizing Joan as a simple human being, and is untouched by the inflated rhetoric of Burk's other plays.

BURKE, EDMUND (1729–97), British statesman. See *Conciliation with the American Colonies* and *Letter to the Sheriffs of Bristol.*

BURKE, FIELDING, see *Dargan, O.T.*

BURKE, KENNETH [DUVA] (1897–1993), literary and philosophical critic, whose books include *Counter-Statement* (1931); *Permanence and Change: An Anatomy of Purpose* (1935), a philosophic investigation of the evolution of ethical ideas; *Attitudes Toward History* (2 vols., 1937), a psychological interpretation of historical events and characters; *The Philosophy of Literary Form* (1941), *A Grammar of Motives* (1945), and *A Rhetoric of Motives* (1950), linguistic analyses interpreting human motives; *The Rhetoric of Religion* (1961), further "studies in logology"; *Perspectives by Incongruity* (1964); *Language as Symbolic Action* (1966) and *Dramatism and Development* (1972). *Towards a Better Life* (1932) contains fictive "epistles and declamations"; *The White Oxen* (1924) prints stories; and poems are gathered in *Book of Moments* (1955) and *Collected Poems* (1968). He was

awarded the National Medal for Literature♦ in 1980. *The Selected Correspondence of Kenneth Burke and Malcolm Cowley* was published in 1988.

Burlesque, popular stage entertainment that originated in mid-19th-century New York, deriving from the minstrel show, variety theater, and travesties. Often considered somewhat illicit, it became very popular, and from New York companies grew the Columbia and Mutual circuits ("wheels") throughout the country and the Weber and Fields Music Hall and Minsky's. It featured dialect and slapstick comedians who specialized in double entendre; travesties of popular drama and current events; scantily dressed chorus girls; and song-and-dance acts.

BURMAN, BEN LUCIEN (1895–1984), Kentucky-born journalist, graduated from Harvard (1920), whose novels about river adventures include *Mississippi* (1929), *Steamboat Round the Bend* (1933), *Blow for a Landing* (1938), and *The Four Lives of Mundy Tolliver* (1953). *The Street of the Laughing Camel* (1959) deals with a Texan's amusing adventures in Africa. *High Water at Catfish Bend* (1952), *Seven Stars for Catfish Bend* (1956), *The Owl Hoots Twice at Catfish Bend* (1961), and *The Strange Invasion of Catfish Bend* (1980) are animal fables. *Big River To Cross* (1940) and *Look Down That Winding River* (1973) are informal accounts of life on the Mississippi, and *It's a Big Continent* (1961) deals with his travels to remote U.S. sites.

BURNETT, FRANCES [ELIZA] HODGSON (1849–1924), born in England, came to the U.S. (1865) and won her first success with *That Lass o' Lowrie's* (1877), a novel of the Lancashire coal mines. This was followed by romantic stories and novels, many of them for children, of which the most famous is *Little Lord Fauntleroy*♦ (1886), later dramatized with great success. She wrote a play, *Esmeralda* (1881), with William Gillette, and such novels as *Sara Crewe* (1888); *Editha's Burglar* (1888), dramatized by Augustus Thomas; *The Shuttle* (1907); *A Fair Barbarian* (1881); *The Secret Garden* (1911); and *The White People* (1917), dealing with the supernatural. *The One I Knew the Best of All* (1893) is an autobiography.

BURNETT, W[ILLIAM] R[ILEY] (1899–1982), author of novels about gangsters, prizefighters, and professional sportsmen, including *Little Caesar* (1929), *Iron Man* (1930), *The Silver Eagle* (1931), *Dark Hazard* (1933), *High Sierra* (1940), *Nobody Lives Forever* (1943), *Tomorrow's Another Day* (1945), and *The Asphalt Jungle* (1949). *The Giant Swing* (1932) is about a jazz pianist; *Goodbye to the Past* (1934) tells of a man's life beginning with his death and going back to his youth in the West; *King Cole* (1936) is an exposé of American politics; *The Goodhues of Sinking Creek* (1934) and *The Dark Command* (1938) deal with the Civil

War; *Adobe Walls* (1953) is about the last Apache uprising; and *Mi Amigo* (1959) deals with Billy the Kid. ♦

BURNS, JOHN HORNE (1916–53), born in Massachusetts, educated at Andover and Harvard, served in the army during World War II, and as a teacher at a boys' school. Before his early death he wrote the novels *The Gallery* (1947), about the conquering American army in World War II; *Lucifer with a Book* (1949), a sensational view of a boys' boarding school; and *A Cry of Children* (1952).

BURR, AARON (1756–1836), was a distinguished officer in the Revolutionary War, after which he became a New York lawyer serving as the state attorney general (1789) and as U.S. senator (1791–97). Owing to his unprecedented organization of New York Democrats through the previously nonpolitical Tammany Society, he received an equal electoral vote with Jefferson in the presidential election of 1800. The House of Representatives, after many ballots, chose Jefferson as President and Burr as Vice-President. His candidacy for New York's governorship (1804) was defeated mainly by Hamilton, whose "despicable opinion" of Burr led to a duel in which Hamilton was killed. Burr's political career thus ended, he went to the Old Southwest and became involved in the dealings with James Wilkinson that led to his trial for treason. Acquitted but still thought suspect, he went to England and France, concocted many wild schemes, and did not return to New York and law practice until age 56. In 1833 he married Mme Jumel. He figures in fiction in *The Conqueror, The Minister's Wooing,* Eliza Dupuy's *The Conspirator,* J.H. Ingraham's *Burton,* E.L. Bynner's *Zachary Phips,* Rupert Hughes's *The Golden Ladder,* and Anya Seton's *My Theodosia,* among many other romances. Gore Vidal's *Burr* is a fictionized biography.

BURRITT, ELIHU (1810–79), was called "the learned blacksmith" because in New Britain, Conn., and Worcester, Mass., he forged metals and Greek verbs with equal ease. Influenced by William Ladd, he conducted a weekly paper, *The Christian Citizen* (1844–51), which became an important organ of pacifism, and he traveled through the U.S. and England to advocate this cause. Besides his *Lectures and Speeches* (1866), he wrote many essays and travel accounts, reminiscent of Cobbett. The erudition of this self-educated blacksmith is also indicated by his translation of Longfellow's poems into Sanskrit.

BURROUGHS, EDGAR RICE (1875–1950), author of popular and fantastic adventure stories about Tarzan, the son of a British nobleman, deserted in the African jungle in infancy and reared by apes. *Tarzan of the Apes* (1914) is the first in a lengthy series of tales about the boy, who grows up to wed and have a son, and a grandson in the many sequels. He also wrote many works of science fiction.

BURROUGHS, JOHN (1837–1921), through keen observation of his native Catskills and under the influence of Emerson and Thoreau, became the greatest writer of nature essays after his two Transcendentalist masters. Although all his writing is characterized by a distinctive charm and simplicity, his first works, such as *Wake-Robin* (1871) and *Birds and Poets* (1877), are the most poetic in manner. *Locusts and Wild Honey* (1879) and *Squirrels and Other Fur-Bearers* (1900) are products of a period of more scientific observation, which lasted until *c.*1908. During his final years Burroughs held the belief that the salvation of society depends upon "the great teachers and prophets, poets and mystics," rather than upon cold scientific reason, and he expressed this creed in such books as *The Breath of Life* (1915) and *Accepting the Universe* (1920). He was a friend of Whitman, and his early appreciation of the poet may be seen in *Notes on Walt Whitman as Poet and Person* (1867), a book written in part by the subject. *My Boyhood* (1922) is autobiographical; *The Heart of John Burroughs's Journals* appeared in 1928. A good selection of his writings is *A River View, Hudson Valley* essays edited by Edward Renehan, Jr., who also wrote a fine critical biography, *John Burroughs, an American Naturalist* (1992).

BURROUGHS, WILLIAM S[EWARD] (1914–), born in St. Louis, long expatriated in Paris and elsewhere, best known for his frank accounts of his life as a drug addict, begun under the pseudonym of William Lee in *Junkie* (1953) and continued in *Naked Lunch* (Paris, 1959; New York, 1962), a bitter, existential account of an addict's life and a surrealistic evocation of the subjective horrors involved. *Queer* (1985) is a novel written in 1953 that carries on some problems and views close to *Junkie.* Other works, showing a relation to the Beat movement, include *The Exterminator* (1960); *The Soft Machine* (Paris, 1961); *The Ticket That Exploded* (Paris, 1962); *Nova Express* (1964), fiction about interplanetary gangsters that satirizes modern life; *The Wild Boys* (1971), a fantasy about revolutionary homosexuals; *The Last Words of Dutch Schultz* (1975), fiction about a real gangster, whose deathbed talk is recorded; and *Port of Saints* (1980), a quasi-autobiographical novel. *Cities of the Red Night* (1981), a novel about a Utopian settlement; and *The Place of the Dead Roads* (1984), a kind of science fiction fantasy involving a 19th-century writer of wild-west stories, are parts of a trilogy, completed in *The Western Lands* (1987), drawing upon ancient Egypt. *The Adding Machine* (1986) gathers essays, and *Tornado Alley* (1989) prints short prose pieces. Another late collection, *Interzone* (1989), assembles mainly unpublished autobiographical work of the 1950s. *The Yage Letters* (1963) prints correspondence from Mexico with

Allen Ginsberg. *Letters 1945–59* was published in 1993. *The Job* (1971) records interviews setting out his philosophy, and *The Third Mind* (1978), written with Brion Gysin, deals with Burroughs's ways of writing fiction.

BURT, [MAXWELL] STRUTHERS (1882–1954), taught at Princeton, served in World War I, and later lived in Wyoming, North Carolina, and Pennsylvania. His novels include *The Interpreter's House* (1924), *The Delectable Mountains* (1927), and *Along These Streets* (1942); and his shorter fiction in such volumes as *John O'May, and Other Stories* (1918), *Chance Encounters* (1921), and *They Could Not Sleep* (1928). *The Diary of a Dude-Wrangler* (1924) is autobiographical; *Powder River: Let 'Er Buck* (1938), an account of a Wyoming river; and *Philadelphia, Holy Experiment* (1945), an account of the city's history.

BURTON, WILLIAM EVANS (1804–60), came to the U.S. from England in 1834, to continue his career as a comic actor. He founded *The Gentleman's Magazine*♦ (1837), but sold it after failing to agree with his editor, Poe. Meanwhile he wrote the sketches collected in *Waggeries and Vagaries* (1848), and opened Burton's Theatre in New York. He wrote two domestic farces, and edited *The Literary Souvenir* (1838–40) and an *American Cyclopædia of Wit and Humor* (1858).

Burwell Papers, manuscript account of Bacon's Rebellion,♦ apparently written by a contemporary of Bacon, was given its present name at the end of the Revolutionary War, when it was found among the papers of Captain Nathaniel Burwell. In 1812 Josiah Quincy sent what is evidently an 18th-century copy of the lost original manuscript to the Massachusetts Historical Society, which printed it in its *Collections* (1814) and again, more accurately, in 1866, under the title "The History of Bacon's and Ingram's Rebellion." The manuscript was then placed in the keeping of the Virginia Historical Society. Besides the prose account, the manuscript contains a stately epitaph for Bacon written by "his man," and the reply "Upon the death of G.B." These poems, long attributed to one "Cotton of Acquia Creek," are now considered, like the body of the manuscript, to be the work of John Cotton, a contemporary of Bacon, who lived near Williamsburg, or of his wife, Ann Cotton. The Burwell Papers are believed to be the chief source of the first part of *The Maryland Muse* by Ebenezer Cook.♦

Bury the Dead, play by Irwin Shaw,♦ produced and published in 1936.

BUSCH, FREDERICK (1941–   ), a professor of English at Colgate (1966–   ), is best known for his fiction. It includes the novels *I Wanted a Year Without Fall* (1971), about two young men who

flee to encounter unusual experiences together; *Manual Labor* (1974), about a young married couple disintegrated by the loss of their children; *Domestic Particulars* (1976), short views of a small city family; *The Mutual Friend* (1978), a fictive consideration of Charles Dickens; *Rounds* (1980), containing exotic views of parents and children; *Take This Man* (1982), flash views of nearly 40 years of a special family; *Invisible Mending* (1984), a tale of a Jewish family experience; *Sometimes I Live in the Country* (1986), dealing with the difficult life of a teen-age boy; *Harry and Catherine* (1990), about the romance of two middle-aged people; *Closing Arguments* (1991), about a Vietnam veteran, now a lawyer involved with a failing marriage and a murder trial; and *Long Way from Home* (1993), which tells of a woman on the verge of divorce who leaves husband and child to search for her birth mother. Busch has published volumes of short stories: *Breathing Trouble* (1974), *Hardwater Country* (1979), *Too Late American Boyhood Blues* (1984), *Absent Friends* (1989), and *The Children in the Woods* (1994), as well as a novella, *War Babies* (1989). He has also written a book on the author John Hawkes (1973) and a study of authorship, *When People Publish* (1986).

BUSHNELL, HORACE (1802–76), religious thinker, as pastor of the North Church (Congregational) of Hartford, Conn. (1833–59), propounded a gospel attacking the harshness of Calvinism, upholding the oneness of deity and the goodness of man, accepting intuition as a basis of theological knowledge, and emphasizing the New Testament. His books include *Christian Nurture* (1847); *God in Christ* (1849); *The Age of Homespun* (1851), depicting the rural New England of his youth; *Nature and the Supernatural* (1858), attacking Transcendentalism; and *The Vicarious Sacrifice* (1866). His writings were collected (1876–81), and *The Spirit in Man* was published in 1903.

Busy-Body Papers, 32 articles in the form of letters contributed to Bradford's *American Weekly Mercury* during 1729. Six of these (1–5, 8) are definitely ascribed to Franklin, and the others are supposed to be the work of his friends. The papers follow the Addisonian form in their homely comments on social, moral, and religious conduct, and other topics. The character Critico is evidently a satirical portrait of Franklin's rival, Samuel Keimer, and the entire series was begun as an attempt to win readers from Keimer's *Pennsylvania Gazette*.

BUTLER, ELLIS PARKER (1869–1937), humorist, of whose 32 books the best known is the sketch *Pigs Is Pigs* (1906).

BUTLER, JAMES (1755?–1842), English author resident in Pennsylvania, whose romantic novel *Fortune's Foot-ball; or, The Adventures of Mercutio*

(1797–98) deals with the Algerian slave trade, British impressment of sailors, and other melodramatic matters.

BUTLER, NICHOLAS MURRAY (1862–1947), became a professor of philosophy at Columbia (1885) and was thereafter constantly identified with the university, serving as president (1902–45). During his administration the institution's scope was enlarged and academic standards raised. He was also prominent in civic affairs and as a leader of the Republican party. His books include *The Meaning of Education* (1898), *True and False Democracy* (1907), *Education in the United States* (1910), *A World in Ferment* (1917), *The Faith of a Liberal* (1924), *The Path to Peace* (1930), and his autobiography, *Across the Busy Years* (2 vols., 1939–40).

BUTLER, OCTAVIA E[STELLE] (1947–   ), born in Pasadena and educated at Los Angeles colleges, writes science fiction from the unique vantage point of the only African-American woman in the field. Her main characters are oftener than not black women and her themes social, sexual, and racial interrelationships. Her best-known novella, "Bloodchild" (1985), features human males transported to another planet and used to procreate with the aliens. Other works are novels: *Patternmaster* (1976), about a society run by telepaths, with sequels in *Mind of My Mind* (1977), *Survivor* (1978), and *Wild Seed* (1980). Another series, the Xenogenesis trilogy, has aliens mating with the few survivors of a nuclear holocaust to repopulate earth with a better gene pool than heretofore. The books in the trilogy are *Dawn* (1987), *Adulthood Rites* (1988), and *Imago* (1989). Set in Southern California in the year 2024, *Parable of the Sower* (1993) is a gripping tale of survival and a poignant account of growing up sane in a disintegrating world, as seen through the eyes of its teen-age heroine.

BUTLER, WILLIAM ALLEN (1825–1902), lawyer, teacher, and leader in New York civic affairs, was noted for his biographies, novels, and society verse. His best-known work was the satirical poem *Nothing To Wear,* published anonymously in *Harper's Weekly* (1857) and reprinted that year in book form without Butler's authorization. It was so popular that several claimants to its authorship appeared, and it was imitated, parodied, and frequently reprinted in the U.S., England, and France. This satire of Flora M'Flimsy, a society lady who claimed she had nothing to wear to parties, captured the public imagination at a time when social climbers were making themselves strenuously felt. Among the books it inspired were *Nothing To Do: A Tilt at Our Best Society* (1857) by Horatio Alger, and *Nothing To Say: A Slight Slap at Mobocratic Snobbery, Which Has "Nothing To Do" with "Nothing To Wear"* (1857) by Mortimer Thomson.

By Blue Ontario's Shore, poem by Whitman,♦ first published in the 1856 edition of *Leaves of Grass* as "Poem of Many in One." Formed partly from the prose preface of 1855, it was reprinted in 1867 as "As I Sat Alone by Blue Ontario's Shore," and under its present title in 1881.

At the command of a Phantom, "Chant me the poem that comes from the soul of America," the poet sings of "These States . . . the amplest poem" and "the great Idea, the idea of perfect and free individuals . . . that is the mission of Poets." He calls for poets freed from past conventions, coteries, schools, and religions, celebrates himself "a man before all—myself, typical before all," and declares "These States—what are they except myself?" "Thrilled with the Power's pulsations and the charm of my theme," he announces, "Bards for my own land, only, I invoke."

By Love Possessed, novel by James Gould Cozzens,♦ published in 1957.

Between the time that an ornate French gilt clock inscribed "amor vincit omnia" strikes three o'clock one afternoon and its striking of four o'clock two days later, Arthur Winner, Jr., undergoes a series of crises and discoveries that force him to alter the view he takes of himself, the rational standards of his revered late father (in whose living room the clock is situated), and his world, centered on his well-to-do and well-born family's community. During these trying 49 hours, Winner, a conservative lawyer, now about 50, is called on to defend Ralph Detwiler, the orphan son of family friends and the brother of his devoted spinster secretary, Helen. Although Ralph is corrupt, he is innocent of the crime of rape for which he has been arrested, and the prosecutor Garrett Hughes, an assistant district attorney, and Jerome Brophy, the district attorney who wants to be a judge, eager to have Winner's support for a judgeship, tacitly offer to drop the case. Winner believes his decision to back Hughes is impartial, but he does not bring himself to tell Helen of his knowledge that all will be well, and when Ralph jumps bail and leaves the state, his worshiping sister thinks his career is ruined and commits suicide. Meanwhile Winner is involved with the Detwiler family in another way because his firm serves as trustees in reestablishing the credit of the local bank from which Ralph and Helen's father has improperly diverted funds. In the course of this activity he finds that his senior partner, Noah Tuttle, who is also his father-in-law, has himself misused bank funds, even though he is accounted a pillar of decency in the community. This shock to Winner's values is compounded by circumstances that cause him to recall his passionate adultery during the time before he had come to find satisfying love and companionship in his second marriage. Through these experiences and memories Winner is moved out of his complacency to recognize in himself and others various kinds of love and disruptive passions.

BYLES, MATHER (1707–88), grandson of Increase Mather, continued the family tradition of pulpit oratory and authorship. His Tory sympathies led to the dissolution of his church, and though he remained a Congregationalist he tended toward Episcopalianism. *Poems on Several Occasions* (1744) is a collection of his verse, which is of uneven quality, sometimes witty and urbane but more frequently imitative and dull. He wrote many theological works and a long poem, *The Conflagration* (1755), and was noted among his contemporaries for his repartee.

BYNNER, EDWIN LASSETTER (1842–93), Massachusetts lawyer and author, is best known for his novel *Agnes Surriage* (1886), a dialect romance set in Marblehead, Mass., during the 18th century. *The Chase of the Meteor* (1892) was a book of stories for children, and his other novels include *Penelope's Suitors* (1884); *The Begum's Daughter* (1890), concerned with Leisler's Revolt; and *Zachary Phips* (1892), dealing with Burr during the War of 1812.

BYNNER, [HAROLD] WITTER (1881–1968), graduated from Harvard (1902), of which he wrote in *An Ode to Harvard* (1907), revised as *Young Harvard* (1925). He developed a melodious lyric style in such books as the *Grenstone Poems* (1917) and *A Canticle of Pan* (1920), and his *Indian Earth* (1929) and translation with Dr. Kiang Kang-hu of Chinese poetry, *The Jade Mountain* (1929), show a change toward a simplicity similar to Imagism. He published *A Book of Plays* (1922), and under the pseudonym Emanuel Morgan contributed to the hoax *Spectra*♦ (1916). *Against the Cold* (1940), satirical poems; *Take Away the Darkness* (1947); and *A Book of Lyrics* (1956) are later collections. He also wrote *The Way of Life According to Laotzu* (1944) and *Journey with Genius* (1951), his recollections of D.H. Lawrence. Richard Wilbur edited Bynner's *Selected Poems* (1978).

BYRD, RICHARD EVELYN (1888–1957), descendant of William Byrd, is known as an aviator and polar explorer, whose most important expeditions included a flight over the North Pole (1926), another across the Atlantic (1927), a long exploration of the Antarctic in 1929 with a flight over the South Pole, and another Antarctic expedition (1934). His autobiographical books include *Skyward* (1928), *Little America* (1930), and *Alone* (1938).

BYRD, WILLIAM (1674–1744), Virginia planter, resided at Westover on the James River, and in 1737 had the city of Richmond laid out on his lands. His library of more than 4000 volumes was reputedly the largest in the English colonies, and his cultural interests resulted in his membership in the Royal Society. He was a colonial agent in England (1697–1705, 1715–26). His commission as a surveyor of the boundary line between North Carolina and Virginia is reported in his *History of the Dividing Line,* ♦ and other frontier expeditions are described in his *Journey to the Land of Eden* ♦ and *Progress to the Mines,* ♦ posthumously published journals found among his Westover Manuscripts. *The Secret Diary of William Byrd of Westover* (1941) and *Another Secret Diary* (1942) are later discovered accounts written in shorthand in the years 1709–12, 1739–41, as is *The London Diary* (1958) concerning part (1717–21) of his second residence in England. Written as an avocation of this urbane and witty gentleman, none of his accounts was intended for publication.

BYRNE, DONN (1889–1928), Irish-American author, baptized Bernard Byrne, was also in various periods known as Brian Oswald Donn Byrne, and Brian Donn-Byrne. Educated in Dublin, he returned to his native New York (1911), where he wrote romantic poems and stories tinged with Celtic mysticism. *The Foolish Matrons* (1920), character studies of four women, was followed by his first popular book, *Messer Marco Polo* (1921), the story of Marco Polo's journey to China and his love for the daughter of Kubla Khan, told with Gaelic wistfulness by a venerable Ulsterman. *The Wind Bloweth* (1922) tells of an Irish sailor's life, and *The Changeling* (1923) contains short stories of quaint places and people. In *Blind Raftery* (1924), a tale of an 18th-century itinerant Gaelic poet and his Spanish wife, Donn Byrne expresses his consistent attitude, that what the world accounts good is often but vulgar and selfish, for kindness, needed in this "apart, dark place," is unknown to the shallow, soulless people who have never died in life. His other books include *Hangman's House* (1926), a tender love story set in 19th-century Ireland; *Brother Saul* (1927), a fictional account of Saul of Tarsus; *Crusade* (1928), the story of an Irish crusader who loves a Saracen girl; *Destiny Bay* (1928), stories of a romantic Irish family; *Field of Honor* (1929, published in England as *Power of the Dog*), a novel of Napoleonic times; and several posthumous collections of short stories.

C

Cabala, The, novel by Thornton Wilder. ♦

Cabbages and Kings, novel by W.S. Porter. ♦

CABELL, JAMES BRANCH (1879–1958), born in Virginia, graduated from William and Mary (1898), and began his literary career with *The Eagle's Shadow* (1904), a romance of modern money-worship. With *The Line of Love* (1905), short stories set in medieval times, he began his sophisticated romanticizing of historical themes, continued in *Gallantry* (1907) and *Chivalry* (1909). *The Cords of Vanity* (1909) is a romance of contemporary Virginia, and later novels with similar settings include *The Rivet in Grandfather's Neck* (1915), satirizing the romantic idealism of the South, and *The Cream of the Jest* (1917). He is best known for his series of urbane, highly mannered, pseudo-erudite romances of Dom Manuel, set in the mythical medieval country of Poictesme. The first of these was *The Soul of Melicent* (1913; revised as *Domnei,* 1920); others are *Jurgen* ♦ (1919), which attracted much attention because of an attempt to suppress it as obscene; *Figures of Earth* (1921), depicting Manuel as a pessimistic individualist striving for an unattainable ideal; *The High Place* (1923); *The Silver Stallion* (1926), dealing with the legends that arise after the death of Manuel; *Something About Eve* (1927); *The White Robe* (1928); and *The Way of Ecben* (1929). He also published criticism, including *Beyond Life* (1919), *Joseph Hergesheimer* (1921), *Straws and Prayer-Books* (1924), *Some of Us* (1930), and *Preface to the Past* (1936), which set forth his theory that fiction should be allegorical in interpreting a dream of life, since realism presents facts out of their relation to the spirit of life. *The Certain Hour* (1916) and *The Music from Behind the Moon* (1926) collect short stories, while the author's love of the archaic and of elaborate rhythms is also revealed in his poetry, which includes *From the Hidden Way* (1916) and *Sonnets from Antan* (1929). According to *The Lineage of Lichfield* (1922), *Beyond Life* and *Straws and Prayer-Books* are prologue and epilogue to his Poictesme series, which he arranges in sequence of action as *Figures of Earth, The Silver Stallion, Domnei, The Music from Behind the Moon, Chivalry, Jurgen, The Line of Love, The High Place, Gallantry, Something About Eve, The Certain Hour, The Cords of Vanity, From the Hidden Way, The Jewel Merchants, The Rivet in Grandfather's Neck, The Eagle's Shadow,* and *The Cream of the Jest.* To an autobiographical work, *These Restless Heads* (1932); two series of letters, real and fictitious,

Special Delivery (1933) and *Ladies and Gentlemen* (1934); and a trilogy, *Smirt* (1934), *Smith* (1935), and *Smire* (1937), he signed his name as Branch Cabell. Following two novels, *The King Was in His Counting House* (1938) and *Hamlet Had an Uncle* (1940), witty romances in his established manner, Cabell again assumed his full name, and wrote *First Gentleman of America* (1942), about an Indian prince who became a Spanish grandee; *The St. Johns* (1943), a social history of the Florida river, written with A.J. Hanna; *There Were Two Pirates* (1946), a novelette; *Let Me Lie* (1947), essays on Virginia; and *Quiet, Please* (1952) and *As I Remember It* (1955), volumes of reminiscences. *Between Friends* (1962) collects letters.

CABET, ÉTIENNE (1788–1856), French Communist, whose Utopian romance *Voyage et Aventures de Lord William Carisdall en Icarie* (1840) won him many followers. With more than 500 of these Icarians, he came to the U.S. to establish socialized communities. The most important were at Cheltenham, Mo.; Cloverdale, Cal.; and Corning, Iowa.

CABEZA DE VACA, ALVAR NUÑEZ (*c.*1490–*c.*1557), sailed on the expedition led by Pánfilo de Narváez in 1528 to conquer and exploit Florida. Some 300 Spaniards crossed from the Atlantic to the Gulf coast—the first overland trek on future U.S. soil—but suffered from the wilderness itself and from attacks by fierce Apalachee Indians. They built boats to escape to Mexico, but a storm wrecked them near Galveston Island. Finally only four men of the original 300 remained alive: Cabeza de Vaca, Alonzo del Castillo, Andrés Dorantes, and the Moroccan slave Estevan. For eight years they wandered on the Gulf coast, and probably to New Mexico and Arizona, living on wild fruits and prickly-pear cactus. They were taken captive by several bands of Indians and survived, it appears, by practicing faith healing. Their horrendous journey was set down in *The Narrative of Alvar Nuñez Cabeza de Vaca* (1542)—the first North American captivity literature. A good account is by Morris Bishop in *The Odyssey of Cabeza de Vaca* (1933).

CABLE, GEORGE WASHINGTON (1844–1925), born in New Orleans, served in the Confederate army, studied engineering, and was a warehouse clerk before he turned to writing as a career. His early sketches were published in the New Orleans *Picayune,* and his stories of Louisiana local color appeared in *Scribner's* and *Appleton's* at intervals from 1873 to 1879. In the latter year he published a collection, *Old Creole Days,*♦ which was followed by a novel of 19th-century Louisiana, *The Grandissimes*♦ (1880). Other books include *Madame Delphine*♦ (1881), a novelette about a quadroon woman; *Dr. Sevier* (1885), a novel set in New Orleans before and during the Civil War; *Bonaventure* (1888), concerned with a Creole among the descendants of Acadian exiles; *John March, Southerner* (1894), a novel of the Reconstruction, concerned with an amiable old judge and his dealings with Northern intrigues in a small town; *Strong Hearts* (1899), a collection of stories; *The Cavalier* (1901), a story of the Civil War; and *Bylow Hill* (1902), concerned with the unhappy marriage of a New England clergyman and a Southern girl. Cable, who continued to write until 1918, was a leader of the local-color movement, and his stories depicting the charm of New Orleans society, though slight in narrative value, are distinguished by their style and an appreciation of the locality, although there were those who attacked his treatment of the Creoles, Adrien Rouquette♦ for one.

CAHAN, ABRAHAM (1860–1951), who came to the U.S. from Russia (1882), was long the editor of the *Jewish Daily Forward.* Besides works in Yiddish he wrote realistic fiction in English, including *Yekl, a Tale of the New York Ghetto* (1896), *The Imported Bridegroom and Other Stories* (1898), and *The Rise of David Levinsky* (1917), a novel of the good and bad in a Jew's Americanization in New York. He also wrote an autobiography (5 vols., 1916–36). His journalism (1897–1903) was collected and posthumously published in *Grandma Never Lived in America* (1988).

CAIN, JAMES M[ALLAHAN] (1892–1977), novelist and journalist, known for his novels of racketeers and others on the criminal fringe. His books include *The Postman Always Rings Twice* (1934); dramatized, 1936; made into a film, 1946, 1981; adapted as an opera, 1982; a tough story, written in a popularization of Hemingway's style, about the plotting of a voluptuous girl and her lover, a young drifter, to murder her husband; *Double Indemnity* (1936); *Serenade* (1937); *Mildred Pierce* (1941), which treats a mother's fierce love for a thankless daughter; *Love's Lovely Counterfeit* (1942); *Past All Dishonor* (1946), set in Nevada during the Civil War; *The Butterfly* (1947); *The Moth* (1948); *Galatea* (1953); *Mignon* (1962), set in New Orleans just after the Civil War; *Rainbow's End* (1975); and *The Institute* (1976). *The Baby in the Icebox* (1981) collects stories.

Caine Mutiny, *The,* novel by Herman Wouk,♦ published in 1951. Part of the plot was dramatized by the author as *The Caine Mutiny Court-Martial* (1954).

Entering the navy as a midshipman in December 1942, Willie Keith, a wealthy, spoiled Princeton graduate, in love with a spirited nightclub singer, May Wynn, grows to manhood through his experiences in the South Pacific on the minesweeper *Caine.* When Philip Queeg comes aboard the wretched, filthy ship as commander he soon incurs the men's enmity because of his obsessive meticulousness, demonic orders and punishments, extreme emotional instability, and monomaniacal ambition. Tom Keefer, a clever intellectual, convinces the uneducated but loyal and capable executive officer, Steve Maryk, that Queeg is a classic paranoid who is too sick to hold command. During a typhoon, with Willie, now officer of the deck, Maryk takes command. He is court-martialed but acquitted, thanks to his shrewd lawyer, Barney Greenwald, who reveals at a triumphal dinner that Keefer, the author of the mutiny, had lied in order to keep his own future secure. Returning to the *Caine,* Willie becomes executive officer under Keefer, who shows cowardice at a decisive moment and Willie saves the ship. Keefer is discharged, Willie becomes commanding officer on the *Caine's* final voyage, and, the war ended, he looks forward to marriage with May and preparation for a university teaching career.

Cajun, see *Acadia.*

Calamus, section of Whitman's *Leaves of Grass*♦ containing 45 poems first published in the 1860 edition. Its theme of the spiritual love of man for man complements that of "Children of Adam."♦

The calamus, a plant generally known as the sweet flag, serves as a threefold symbol. Its leaves symbolize mortality; its fascicles, which cling together for support, represent "adhesive" love or friendship; and its perennial pink-tinged aromatic root is symbolic of immortal life, from which bloom successive transient forms. This mystical group of poems, frequently considered a reflection of the author's homosexuality, was said by Whitman to have "Political significance" in celebrating the "beautiful and sane affection of man for man" which would "make the continent indissoluble" and weld the states into a "Living Union."

The title was used by Richard Maurice Bucke♦ for his edition (1897) of letters written between 1868 and 1880 by Whitman to his friend Peter Doyle, a Washington streetcar conductor.

Caldecott Medal, named for the English illustrator of children's books Randolph Caldecott (1846–84), the award is made annually (since 1938) by the American Library Association to the children's book published in the U.S. that is judged to be the most distinguished pictorially.

CALDWELL, ERSKINE [PRESTON] (1903–87), born in Georgia, after study at the University of Virginia published two novelettes in 1930, *The Bastard* and *Poor Fool,* but first won fame with *Tobacco Road*♦ (1932), dramatized by Jack Kirkland. Like his next novel, *God's Little Acre*♦ (1933), it showed a rich sense of folk humor, indignation at social inequities, and a lusty bawdiness. One or more of these elements is seen in later novels, including *Journeyman* (1935); *Trouble in July* (1940), about race hatred in the South; *Tragic Ground* (1944), about a Georgia farmer stranded in a war-boom town; *House in the Uplands* (1946); *The Sure Hand of God* (1947), about a small-town woman's search for a man for herself and a husband for her daughter; *This Very Earth* (1948); *A Place Called Estherville* (1949), about black-white relations in a small Southern town; *Episode in Palmetto* (1950), about a young schoolteacher in a similar town; *Gretta* (1955), a portrait of a nymphomaniac; *Claudelle Inglish* (1958); and *Jenny By Nature* (1961), set in a small-town boardinghouse in Georgia. Other novels include *All Night Long* (1942), about guerrilla fighting in Russia; *A Lamp for Nightfall* (1952), set in Maine; *Love and Money* (1954), satirically portraying a best-selling author; *Sometimes Island* (1968), about friendships and conflicts of whites and blacks on a fishing trip; *The Weather Shelter* (1969), set in a Tennessee town; and *Annette* (1973), a portrait of a kindergarten teacher. Caldwell is considered to be best in the writing of short stories, and his many collections include *American Earth* (1931), *We Are the Living* (1933), *Kneel to the Rising Sun* (1935), *Southways* (1938), *Jackpot* (1940), *The Courting of Susie Brown* (1952), *Gulf Coast Stories* (1956), and *When You Think of Me* (1959). His short stories and novels have been enormously popular in paperback reprints, but since the 1930s little critical attention has been given to Caldwell's constant succession of newly published fiction. Other works include *Some American People* (1935), vignettes of U.S. life; *Call It Experience* (1951), about the art of writing; *Around About America* (1964), light essays treating his travels through the U.S., a subject continued in *Afternoons in Mid-America* (1976); *In Search of Bisco* (1965), about his attempt to find a black man who was his boyhood chum; and *Deep South* (1968), an informal account of religion in his native region. *With All My Might* (1989) is a posthumously published autobiography.

CALDWELL, [JANET] TAYLOR (1900–1985), English-born novelist, reared in the U.S., began her career of writing very popular and dramatic novels, usually set in the past, with *Dynasty of Death* (1938), about wealthy families of munitions manufacturers, a saga continued in *The Eagles Gather* (1940) and *The Final Hour* (1944). Other novels include *The Earth Is The Lord's* (1941), about Genghis Khan; *Time No Longer* (1941), about Nazi Germany, and written under the pseudonym Max Reiner; *The Arm and the Darkness* (1943), set in 16th-century France; *This Side of Innocence* (1946), about rich and powerful New York families in the Gilded Age; *Dear and Glorious Physician* (1959); *A Prologue to Love* (1961); *A Pillar of Iron* (1965), a fictive life of Cicero; and *Answer as a Man* (1981), her thirty-sixth novel, about a rags-to-riches American at the beginning of the 20th century. *Dialogues with the Devil* (1967) comments on the modern world, revealing her conservative views and religious bent.

CALEF, ROBERT (1648–1719), Boston merchant, author of *More Wonders of the Invisible World* (London, 1700), a well-documented, bitterly satiric attack on those responsible for the Salem witchcraft trials (1692), particularly Cotton Mather, who replied in *Some Few Remarks upon a Scandalous Book* (1701). Increase Mather is said to have ordered Calef's book burned in the Harvard Yard.

California gold rush, see *Forty-niners.*

CALISHER, HORTENSE (1911–   ), born in New York City, graduated from Barnard, and is known for her stories that subtly interpret character, collected in *In the Absence of Angels* (1951), *Tale for the Mirror* (1962), and *Extreme Magic* (1964). *False Entry* (1961) is a novel about a character known only by his pseudonym Pierre Goodman and his involvement in an Alabama trial, testifying against racists in the murder of a black. *Textures of Life* (1963) is a novel about relationships between parents and adult children and their respective marriages. *Journal from Ellipsia* (1965) is comic science fiction, and *The Railway Police and The Last Trolly Ride* (1966) are two novellas. Other novels include *Queenie* (1971), *Eagle Eye* (1973), and *On Keeping Women* (1977), all depicting modern New Yorkers in family relationships, themes also in *The Bobby-Soxer* (1986) and *Age* (1987), as well as the stories in *Saratoga, Hot* (1985). *Herself* (1972) and *Kissing Cousins* (1988) are memoirs.

Call It Sleep (1934), novel by Henry Roth.♦ The book is largely the lyrical stream of consciousness of David Schearl as he lives from his sixth to his ninth year. The setting is the teeming, vibrant Jewish community on the Lower East Side of New York just before World War I. David competes with his father, a peasant immigrant from Austria who earns a catch-as-catch-can living, for the total affection of the mother. He provokes his father to violence, leaving the mother no other option but to embrace her son at the price of alienating her husband. The novel evokes the true terror of childhood, as well as being a kind of rhapsody on Jewish ethnic solidarity.

Call of the Wild, The, novel by Jack London,♦ published in 1903.

Buck, offspring of a St. Bernard and Scotch shepherd dog, lives on a California estate until he is stolen and shipped to the Klondike. There he is trained as a sledge dog, and wins the leadership of the team from Spitz. He gives his entire allegiance to his master, John Thornton, even breaking the ice and dragging a 1000-pound load on a sledge so that Thornton may win a wager. After Thornton is murdered by Indians, Buck responds to the call of the wild, and abandons human civilization to lead a wolf pack.

CALLAGHAN, MORLEY (1903–90), Canadian-born author, whose novels include *Strange Fugitive* (1928), the story of a bootlegger; *It's Never Over* (1930), tracing the effects of disgrace upon the family and friends of a murderer; *A Broken Journey* (1932); *Such Is My Beloved* (1934), in which a priest defies his parishioners by trying to reform prostitutes; *They Shall Inherit the Earth* (1935), a study of an average family during the Depression; *More Joy in Heaven* (1937), about a reformed prisoner who finds that the world will not let him pursue his ideals; *The Loved and the Lost* (1951); *The Many-Colored Coat* (1960), the story of a corporate power struggle, revised as *The Man with the Coat* (1988); *A Passion in Rome* (1961); *A Fine and Private Place* (1975); *A Time for Judas* (1984), an unusual conception of Jesus with Judas as a friend; and *Our Lady of the Snows* (1985), about a noble Canadian prostitute. *A Native Argosy* (1929), *Close to the Sun Again* (1977), and *Lost and Found* (1985) collect stories. *No Man's Meat* (1931) and *Now That April's Here* (1936) are novelettes. *That Summer in Paris* (1963) prints his "memories of tangled friendships with Hemingway, Fitzgerald, and some others" during the 1960s.

CALVERT, GEORGE HENRY (1803–89), descendant of the Baltimore family, was born in Maryland, educated at Harvard and Göttingen, and settled in 1840 at Newport, R.I. He was the author of closet dramas, such as *Arnold and André* (1864); several volumes of poetry in "a diluted Tennysonian vein"; an essay on manners, *The Gentleman* (1863); critical analyses of the countries through which he traveled; "biographic aesthetic" studies of English and European authors; a Fourierist *Introduction to Social Science* (1856); and other works. Poe's criticism in *A Chapter on Autography,* "Essentially a feeble and commonplace writer of poetry, although his prose compositions have a certain degree of merit," is still considered valid.

CALVERTON, V[ICTOR] F[RANCIS] (1900–1940), Marxist literary critic, set forth his concept of the sociological interpretation of literature in *The Newer Spirit* (1925) and practiced it in *The Liberation of American Literature* (1932). His other books include *Sex Expression in Literature* (1926); *For Revolution* (1932); *The Awakening of America* (1939), a history of early America in "terms of the ruled instead of the rulers"; and *Where Angels Dared to Tread* (1941), describing Utopian ventures in the U.S. He edited *The Modern Quarterly: A Journal of Radical Opinion.* His real name was George Goetz.

Calvinism, system of theological thought found in the doctrinal expressions of the Reformed and Presbyterian churches, which derives its name from John Calvin (1509–64), the French Protestant reformer. In Calvin's own day, the element of his teaching that involved him in most conflict was his interpretation of Holy Communion, which differs from that of Luther, but his followers have been mainly distinguished by their emphasis upon predestination. The distinctive characteristics of Calvinism were formulated at the Synod of Dort (1618–19), in opposition to the Five Articles (1610) of the Arminians,♦ and are known as the Five Points: (1) total depravity, man's natural inability to exercise free will, since through Adam's fall he has suffered hereditary corruption; (2) unconditional election, which manifests itself through God's wisdom to elect those to be saved, despite their inability to perform saving works; (3) prevenient and irresistible grace, that anticipatory grace made available only to the elect; (4) the perseverance of saints, those who are predetermined as elect inevitably persevering in the path of holiness; and (5) limited atonement, man's hereditary corruption being partially atoned for by Christ, and this atonement being provided the elect through the Holy Spirit, giving them the power to attempt to obey God's will as revealed through the Bible. These five dicta were embodied in the beliefs of those whose church polity was Presbyterian, Baptist, and Congregational, and in the beliefs of certain other groups. In New England both Puritans♦ and Pilgrims♦ agreed with Calvinism in their creation of a theocratic state, but the Covenant theology♦ became as important as the original Calvinist doctrine. New Englanders tended to study Calvin less than later formulators of Protestant opinion as William Perkins and William Ames. In addition to reading Augustine and other church fathers, they emphasized above all the Bible. Expressions of 17th-century Calvinist thought in New England may be found in such works as *The Wonder-Working Providence of Sions Saviour in New England,*♦ *The Simple Cobler of Aggawam,*♦ the *Magnalia Christi Americana,*♦ and *The Day of Doom.*♦ Later, Calvinism in the Congregational Church was considerably modified and softened by the Half-Way Covenant,♦ although under evangelical stress the earlier doctrines were temporarily revived in the Great Awakening.♦ The doctrinal framework has been less successful in withstanding the changes in intellectual climate than have the ethical teachings, which have affected both orthodox Calvinists and such diverse thinkers as Franklin and the Transcendentalist writers.

Cambridge (originally NEWE TOWNE), Mass., is situated on the bank of the Charles River opposite Boston. ♦ It was founded (1636) by members of the Massachusetts Bay Company, and renamed (1638) in honor of the English university town, following the establishment of Harvard College. It has always been an intellectual center, and was the home of the first printing press in the English colonies, established by Stephen Daye. Craigie House, a colonial mansion occupied by Washington (1775) and later the home of Longfellow (1837–82), is situated there. Since Harvard, Radcliffe, and the Massachusetts Institute of Technology are all located there, it is not only a great center of higher education but a major axis for research in all fields of knowledge.

Cambridge History of American Literature, The, published in four volumes (1917–21), is a survey "of the life of the American people as expressed in their writings rather than a history of *belles lettres* alone," from colonial times to the end of the 19th century. It provided for the first time an extensive bibliography for all periods and subjects. The editors were W.P. Trent, John Erskine, Stuart P. Sherman, and Carl Van Doren, and among the 64 contributors were J.S. Bassett, V.L. Parrington, P.E. More, Woodbridge Riley, A.H. Quinn, W.E. Leonard, H.C. Lodge, Brander Matthews, F.L. Pattee, Norman Foerster, M.J. Moses, and Mary Austin.

Cambridge Platform, basic statement of New England Congregationalism♦ until the adoption of the Saybrook Platform (1708) in Connecticut. The Cambridge Platform was drafted by Richard Mather, amended and adopted by a church synod at Cambridge (1648), and printed as *A Platform of Church-Discipline* (1649).

CAMPBELL, BARTLEY (1843–88), author of popular melodramas, moral and domestic dramas, and a blank-verse tragedy. His best play, *My Partner* (1879), shows the influence of Bret Harte in the treatment of California frontier life. *The White Slave* (1882) contains the line, "Rags are royal raiment, when worn for virtue's sake," planted for the melodramatic effect that Campbell liked. His plays are collected in *America's Lost Plays* (1941).

CAMPBELL, JOSEPH (1904–87), born in New York City, was six years old when his mythic and anthropological interests were awakened by a visit to Buffalo Bill's Wild West Show at Madison Square Garden. He graduated from Columbia College in 1925, and after another year to complete a Master's thesis on Arthurian Romance, won a traveling fellowship to Europe, where he spent the next several years, mostly in Munich

and Paris, studying medieval philology, Sanskrit, and mythology; he was drawn to the theories of Carl Jung, especially that of a "collective unconscious," a deep racial reservoir common to everyone, out of which rise the universal symbols of the world's mythologies. In 1934 Campbell began teaching comparative mythology at Sarah Lawrence College, continuing there for 38 years. Gleanings from his lectures resulted in his most influential work, *The Hero with a Thousand Faces* (1949), showing the universality of the quest motif. Other major books include *The Masks of God* (1959–68), a 4-volume study of world mythology; *The Mythic Image* (1974); and the first half of his projected multi-volume opus *The Historical Atlas of World Mythology* (1983, 1988), left unfinished at his death. Campbell's great fame came posthumously, when the Public Broadcasting System (PBS) aired *The Power of Myth,* hours of talks with journalist Bill Moyers, taped over a number of years. The series made millions of people familiar with Campbell's thesis that myths embody profound and enduring truths about human societies.

CAMPBELL, THOMAS (1777–1844), English poet, author of *Gertrude of Wyoming*♦ (1809). His poems were edited by Irving (1810).

Can Such Things Be?, 24 stories by Ambrose Bierce, ♦ published in 1893. Mainly concerned with episodes of the Civil War and the California frontier, they are marked by a psychological realism, sardonic humor, and clever use of surprise endings and effects of supernatural horror, exhibited in such titles as "The Realm of the Unreal," "Some Haunted Houses," "Bodies of the Dead," and "Mysterious Disappearances."

"My Favorite Murder" is a perversely humorous narrative which concludes: "Altogether, I cannot help thinking that in point of atrocity my murder of Uncle William has seldom been excelled." "The Famous Gilson Bequest," anticipating Clemens's "The Man That Corrupted Hadleyburg," tells of a hanged California horse-thief who leaves his wealth to the man who convicted him, maliciously stipulating that anyone who can prove that Gilson robbed him shall receive the property instead. This results in years of litigation, the wrecking of moral conscience in the community, and the premature aging and death of his victim. "One Kind of Officer," a Civil War story, tells of Captain Ransome's fire on his own troops, owing to the mistaken orders of a general who is killed in battle, leaving Ransome to be punished for his superior's error.

CANBY, HENRY SEIDEL (1878–1961), former Yale professor of literature and editor of *The Saturday Review of Literature.* His books of literary and social criticism include *Classic Americans* (1931), studies of authors; *Thoreau* (1939) and *Whitman* (1943), biographies; *The Brandywine*

(1941), an informal history of the river; and *American Memoir* (1947), including *The Age of Confidence* (1934), a survey of American life in the 1890s, and *Alma Mater: The Gothic Age of the American College* (1936). *Family History* (1945) deals with his ancestry; *Turn West, Turn East* (1951) is a study contrasting Mark Twain and Henry James.

Cane, work by Jean Toomer,♦ published in 1923, is a major work of the Harlem Renaissance. A brief book incorporating stories, poetry, and a play, the first third presents black people, mainly women, in the South in prose and verse sketches; the next group of tales deals with light-colored persons in the North, uncertain about themselves and their place in society; and the last third of the work contains one story, "Kabnis," about a black of that name from the North who goes to the South as a teacher, meets blacks of diverse views, and is frustrated in his search for a way of life.

CANE, MELVILLE H[ENRY] (1879–1980), New York lawyer, authority on copyright, and author of graceful poems, light verse, and memoirs of authors and the Manhattan of his youth. Collections of poems include *January Garden* (1926), *Behind Dark Spaces* (1930), *A Wider Arc* (1947), *Bullet-Hunting* (1960), and *Snow Toward Evening* (1974). *All and Sundry* (1968) is an "oblique autobiography."

CANFIELD [FISHER], DOROTHY (1879–1958), born in Kansas, resident in Vermont after 1907, where she wrote many novels. Among them are *The Squirrel-Cage* (1912), dealing with the married life of an average American couple; *The Bent Twig* (1915), the story of a Midwestern professor's family; *The Brimming Cup* (1921), about a woman torn between husband and family and her love for another man; *Her Son's Wife* (1926), concerning a mother's attempt to dominate her son's family; and *The Deepening Stream* (1930), tracing the growth of a woman's character. *Four Square* (1949) collects 17 of her stories.

Cannery Row, novel by John Steinbeck,♦ published in 1945.

On Cannery Row in Monterey, California, live Doc, the sympathetic, wise, lonely owner of the Western Biological Laboratory; Dora, the tough-minded but warm-hearted madam of a brothel, the Bear Flag Restaurant; Lee Chong, the shrewd, kind proprietor of a remarkably well-stocked grocery store; and Mack and his five happy-go-lucky friends, compounded of "Virtues and graces and laziness and zest." Since they like and admire Doc, these pleasant, philosophic bums engage in a great expedition to catch frogs for which Doc will pay and thus finance a surprise party they plan for him. Fortified by liquor got from Lee, they begin their party at Doc's laboratory, of which they accidentally make a

shambles and from which their innumerable frogs escape long before Doc arrives. Ashamed of the disaster, the men settle into gloom until months later, forgiven by Lee and Doc, and with Dora's aid, they plan a birthday party for Doc, who locks up his valuables for a party that has "all the best qualities of a riot and a night on the barricades."

CANNON, CHARLES JAMES (1800–1860), New York author, whose best play is *The Oath of Office* (1850), a tragedy of 15th-century Ireland. He wrote several volumes of poetry and a number of tales, among them *Mora Carmody; or, Woman's Influence* (1844) and *Ravellings from the Web of Life* (1855).

CANONCHET (or CONANCHET) (*d.*1676), Narragansett chief, signed a treaty with the English during the early part of King Philip's War, but later violated it, was captured by the English, and was executed by the Pequots and Mohicans. He figures in Hubbard's *Narrative of the Troubles with the Indians in New England,* and is the hero of Cooper's *The Wept of Wish-ton-Wish.*

Cantos, The, long, fluid body of poetry by Ezra Pound.♦ Begun with the publication of the first three segments in *Quia Pauper Amavi* (1919), the work occupied Pound for most of the rest of his life. Succeeding volumes adding to the work are *A Draft of XVI Cantos . . . for the Beginning of a Poem of Some Length* (1925), *A Draft of Cantos XVII to XXVII* (1928), *A Draft of XXX Cantos* (1933), *Eleven New Cantos, XXXI–XLI* (1934), *The Fifth Decad of Cantos* (1937), *Cantos LII–LXXI* (1940), *The Pisan Cantos* (1948)—a particularly unified segment of ten sections based on Pound's incarceration in an Italian prisoner-of-war camp, in which he views himself as a romantic hero whose sensibility will bring order to a world of chaos, *Section: Rock-Drill, 85–95 de los Cantares* (1956), *Thrones; 96–109 de los Cantares* (1959). The writing begun in 1915 was finally collected in *The Cantos of Ezra Pound* (1970), but the work was not brought to any conclusion and simply trails off with fragments of Cantos 110 to 117.

In kaleidoscopic manner, lacking any evident overall plan or continuing narrative, the cantos move with very free association over diverse aspects and eras of history, American, European, and Oriental, for all time is treated as contemporary. Similarly there is no distinction made in the use of diverse languages, and the English is often peppered with Greek, Latin, Provençal, Italian, and Chinese, according to the subject of the passages of frequently shifting topics. Not only are subject and language very varied, but the elliptical style ranges from laconic and esoteric juxtapositions to lengthy allusive associations. Among all this variety there are, however, relationships which apparently are meant to evaluate history by comparison, and to present a morality for the individual based on Confucian thought and one for society depending upon the ostensibly humanitarian use of state-controlled credit and money. The *Cantos* are filled with esoteric lore, recondite theories, personal allusions, and the author's own crotchets so that they are extremely difficult to follow in their entirety, no matter how evocative or effective limited passages or particular images may be, with the result that the whole body of work breaks into fragments that are often not only pedantic but confusing. Nevertheless, the work, particularly in its earlier sections, has had a tremendous impact on modern poetry.

CANTWELL, ROBERT [EMMETT] (1908–78), proletarian novelist, whose books include *Laugh and Lie Down* (1931), about life in a lumber-mill city of the Northwest, and *The Land of Plenty* (1934), dealing with a strike in a similar setting. He also wrote lives of Hawthorne (1948) and of the ornithologist Alexander Wilson (1961) and a historical study, *The Hidden Northwest* (1972).

Cape Cod, descriptive work by Thoreau,♦ posthumously published (1865) and edited by the younger W.E. Channing, after chapters had been printed in *Putnam's Magazine* (1855) and the *Atlantic Monthly* (1864). Describing the natural environment and people of "the bare and bended arm of Massachusetts," the account is based on the author's experiences during three short visits to Cape Cod (Oct. 1849, June 1850, July 1855) and includes ten essays on the history and character of the inhabitants, "The Highland Light," Nantucket, the sea, the beach, and other aspects of the Cape.

CAPOTE, TRUMAN (1924–84), New Orleans-born author whose novels are *Other Voices, Other Rooms*♦ (1948), about a homosexually inclined boy painfully groping toward maturity; and *The Grass Harp* (1951, dramatized 1952), about innocent people, old and young, escaping social restraint by living in a tree house. *Breakfast at Tiffany's*♦ (1958) is a novella about a light-hearted, amoral playgirl of New York, Holly Golightly. *Tree of Night* (1949) contains stories, and *Local Color* (1950) collects travel sketches. *House of Flowers* (1954) is a musical play set in a West Indies bordello. *The Muses Are Heard* (1956) is a witty account of his travels with the black cast of *Porgy and Bess* through Russia. *In Cold Blood*♦ (1966) examines a notorious multiple murder. *A Christmas Memory* (1966) and *The Thanksgiving Visitor* (1969) are tales; *The Dogs Bark* (1973) collects essays and other short pieces; and *Then It All Came Down* (1976) contains interviews and comments on current criminal justice. *Music for Chameleons* (1980) is another collection of pieces, a true murder tale, some recollections, and short stories. Toward the end of his life Capote published a slight memoir, *One Christmas* (1983),

about traveling to spend the Yule with his father. After his death came *Jug of Silver* (1986), a previously anthologized story for youngsters, and an unfinished novel, *Answered Prayers* (1986), serialized a decade earlier in *Esquire,* presenting a malicious view of high society.

CAPPS, BENJAMIN (1922–), Texan whose writing begins with *The Hanging at Comanche* (1962, paperback), about conflict between a sheriff and wealthy, powerful ranch owners of his area. This first novel was followed by others, including *Sam Chance* (1965) and *The Trail for Ogallala* (1965), presenting additional aspects of the lives of Texan ranchers. Succeeding novels continued in the same vein, although *A Woman of the People* (1966) deals with the capture of two white girls by Comanche Indians.

Captain Craig, blank-verse narrative by E.A. Robinson,♦ the title poem of a volume published in 1902.

Captain Craig, aged vagabond, poet, and amateur philosopher, spends his penurious last years in Tilbury Town, where he is protected by a group of young men who, alone among the townspeople, value his wit, courage, and eccentric manners. The captain is a whimsical transcendentalist, who believes that all human striving should be directed toward learning to "laugh with God." When one of the young men leaves Tilbury, the captain writes him erudite, self-revealing letters, interspersed with his own romantic sonnets and ballads. On the youth's return, the old man reads to his assembled friends a discursive poetic testament, bequeathing to them the swashbuckling philosophy and heroic humor that underlie his vision of the universe. A few days later he dies, ending his contradictory career with a last request for a brass band at his funeral.

Captains Courageous, novel by Kipling,♦ published in 1897.

Harvey Cheyne, a 15-year-old pampered son of a Los Angeles millionaire, is lost overboard from a transatlantic steamer and picked up by the Gloucester fishing schooner *We're Here.* The schooner is commanded by Disko Troop, a seasoned Bank fisherman of high integrity and strong will, who hires the lad at $10 a month to work as a second boy. At first unwillingly, but later with interest and determination, Harvey learns the arts of sailing and fishing. From a weak, selfish, arrogant child he becomes a strong, self-reliant youth, and after many adventures with the fishing fleet returns home to develop further his interest in sailing ships. He partly repays his debt to Disko Troop by helping the latter's son Dan to become an officer on one of the elder Cheyne's Pacific ships.

Captivity narrative, account of kidnapping by Indians of white persons, usually women, taken by long journeys into the wilderness. The tale of Mary Rowlandson♦ (1682), the earliest example, is representative of New England colonial texts concentrating on the Indians as sons of the Devil removing a daughter of Zion into Satan's lands, often considering it a judgment or test of the Lord. Later accounts, like that of John Williams♦ (1707), telling of the seizure of a man, represent an 18th-century shift to a political point of view in presenting the French allies of the Indians as evil in trying to convert a captive to Catholicism. The genre passed into fiction with Ann Bleecker♦ (1797). In the 19th century the popular account about Mary Jemison♦ (1824) sentimentalized a white woman's romantically happy adjustment to primitive life. Later narratives were like melodramatic penny dreadfuls, as in R.B. Stratton's *The Captivity of the Oatman Girls* (1857) dealing with Far Western Indians.

CAREY, MATHEW (1760–1839), born in Ireland, escaped to France when his pamphlet in defense of Irish Catholics was considered treasonable. After a year in Franklin's printing office at Passy, he returned to Ireland to edit the *Volunteer's Journal,* a paper in which he militated against English rule. His violent editorial policy led to his arrest and later escape to America (1784). He edited the conservative *Pennsylvania Herald, The American Museum,* ♦ and *The Columbian Magazine.* ♦ From his Philadelphia publishing house, he issued his various books, which include a vivid pamphlet on the yellow fever epidemic of 1793; *The Porcupiniad; A Hudibrastic Poem* (1796), one of his attacks on William Cobbett; *The Olive Branch* (1814), a plea for reconciliation after the War of 1812; and many addresses before the Philadelphia Society for the Promotion of National Industry. Next to Hamilton's works, these are the most distinguished American arguments of the time in favor of the protective system, and are forerunners of the work of his son Henry C. Carey. Among his many tracts and books, the *Miscellaneous Essays* (1830) is an outstanding example of his vigorous writing. He published a volume of *Autobiographical Sketches* (1829).

CARLETON, HENRY GUY (1856–1910), humorist, and author of farce comedies including *The Gilded Fool* (1892) and *The Butterflies* (1894). His broad humor is further exhibited in *The Thompson Street Poker Club* (1884).

CARLETON, WILL (1845–1912), author of the sentimental *Farm Ballads* (1873), containing his best-known poem, "Over the Hill to the Poor House." Other collections include *Farm Legends* (1875) and *City Ballads* (1885). Some of his verse was used by Edward Albee♦ to convey a sense of banality in *Quotations from Chairman Mao Tse-Tung* (1968).

CARMAN, [WILLIAM] BLISS (1861–1929), Canadian-born poet, after 1888 made his home in New York and Connecticut. He edited *The Chap-Book* and published his first notable poetry in *Low Tide on Grand Pré: A Book of Lyrics* (1893), whose youthful buoyancy and pagan love of nature won it immediate success. In collaboration with Richard Hovey♦ he wrote *Songs from Vagabondia* (1894), which, being marked by a carefree gypsy spirit, helped to initiate a revolt against the scholarly and anemic poetry of the time. The collaboration was continued in *More Songs from Vagabondia* (1896) and *Last Songs from Vagabondia* (1901). In his more than 20 subsequent volumes, Carman retained his spontaneity in simple lyrics, although he was occasionally so captivated by rhythm and symbolism that his work contains an undue use of verbal music and coloring. The range of his verse is beyond nationalism, although Canada claimed him as unofficial poet laureate. His later books include *Behind the Arras: A Book of the Unseen* (1895); *Ballads of Lost Haven: A Book of the Sea* (1897); *Sappho* (1904), an imaginative reconstruction of one hundred fragments from the Greek poet; *Pipes of Pan* (1906); *Echoes from Vagabondia* (1912); *The Rough Riders and Other Poems* (1909); *April Airs: A Book of New England Lyrics* (1916); and *Wild Garden* (1929). He also wrote essays on *The Friendship of Art* (1904), *The Making of Personality* (1908), and *The Kinship of Nature* (1913).

Carmel (or CARMEL-BY-THE-SEA), California town 100 miles south of San Francisco, derives its name from that given to the bay (1602) by Carmelite monks from Palestine, who accompanied the Spanish discoverer Vizcaino. In 1769 the neighboring town of Monterey was founded by Portolá, and its mission established by Serra. Monterey, as capital of the Mexican province of California, is described in *Two Years Before the Mast.* It was captured by Sloat (1846), and later became the capital of territorial California until the admission of the state (1850). It has been written about by Stevenson and Steinbeck, temporary residents. Carmel became an artists' colony (*c.*1904) when Mary Austin, Sterling, and others moved there; later residents have included Upton Sinclair, Sinclair Lewis, Steffens, and Jeffers. Henry Miller lived at nearby Big Sur.

CARMER, CARL [LAMSON] (1893–1976), author and editor whose writings concentrate on the regional history and folkways of his native upstate New York and of Alabama, at whose state university he was a professor of English (1921–27). His books include *Deep South* (1930), poetry; *Stars Fell on Alabama* (1934), Negro and white folklore; *Listen for a Lonesome Drum* (1936), New York state folklore; *The Hudson* (1939) and *The Susquehanna* (1955), histories of life along these rivers; *Genesee Fever* (1941), a novel of early upstate New York; *Dark Trees to the Wind* (1949), New York state history; and *The Farm Boy and the*

Angel (1970), on the beginnings of the Mormon church in New York.

CARNEGIE, ANDREW (1835–1919), Scottish-born industrialist, began work in a cotton factory after his family moved to Pennsylvania (1848). By 1873 he was engaged in the steel industry, in which he showed remarkable organizing ability and shrewd judgment, as in the selection of such lieutenants as Henry C. Frick. His career was climaxed (1901) when the U.S. Steel Corporation purchased his interests for $250,000,000. During his retirement he wrote an essay, *The Gospel of Wealth* (1889), setting forth the idea that rich men are trustees for the public benefit, which he put into practice in large endowments to educational institutions, including the Carnegie Institute at Pittsburgh (since 1967 Carnegie-Mellon University), the Carnegie Corporation of New York to promote general knowledge of the U.S., the Carnegie Endowment for International Peace, and in gifts for the erection of libraries throughout the U.S. His books include *Triumphant Democracy* (1886), *The Empire of Business* (1902), and an *Autobiography* (1920).

Carolina Playmakers, writing and producing group founded at the University of North Carolina (1918) by Frederick Henry Koch (1877–1944), who had founded the Dakota Playmakers in 1910. The North Carolina group, now called the Playmakers Repertory Company, in their own theater and during frequent tours through the Southern states has been influential in the little-theater movement as a leader in regional and folk drama. Plays by student writers, including Thomas Wolfe and Paul Green, have been published in a series of *Carolina Folk-Plays.*

Carpet-Bag, The (1851–53), humorous weekly magazine edited at Boston by B.P. Shillaber, who contributed many of his "Mrs. Partington" sketches. The edition of May 1, 1852, contained the first published writing of three prominent humorists: "The Dandy Frightening the Squatter," by the 16-year-old Clemens; an essay by the 17-year-old Artemus Ward; and drawings and text by G.H. Derby. Other contributors included J.T. Trowbridge, C.G. Halpine, Sylvanus Cobb, C.B. Lewis, Elizabeth Akers, and Louise Moulton.

CARROLL, GLADYS HASTY (1904–), born in New Hampshire, graduate of Bates College, long resident in Maine, and author of many regional novels including *As the Earth Turns* (1933), *A Few Foolish Ones* (1935), *Neighbor to the Sky* (1937), *Dunnybrook* (1943), *West of the Hill* (1949), *One White Star* (1954), *Come with Me Home* (1961), *Man on the Mountain* (1969), *Next of Kin* (1974), *The Sleeping Beauty* (1982), *If You Call This Cry a Song* (1983), *Asphalt Georgics* (1985), and *Tell Me Again How the White Heron Rises . . .*

(1989). *Head of the Line* (1942) collects stories. *Only Fifty Years Ago* (1962) and *Years Away from Home* (1972) contain reminiscences.

CARRUTH, HAYDEN (1921–), Connecticut-born poet whose works, employing traditional forms, include *The Crow and the Heart* (1959), *Nothing for Tigers* (1965), *For You* (1970), and *From Snow and Rock, for Chaos* (1973). *The Bloomingdale Papers* (1975) is an early long poem chronicling his experiences in a mental hospital. *Appendix A* (1963) is a novel, and *Working Papers* (1982) collects essays and reviews. *Sitting In* (1986), treats jazz alone. *Collected Shorter Poems 1946–1991* was published in 1992.

CARRYL, CHARLES EDWARD (1842–1920), New York financier, was an author of juvenile fantasies in the tradition of Lewis Carroll. These include *Davy and the Goblin* (1886) and *The Admiral's Caravan* (1892), which are interspersed with such verses as "The Plaint of the Camel" and "Robinson Crusoe's Story."

CARRYL, GUY WETMORE (1873–1904), son of Charles Edward Carryl, was also an author of light verse, published in such volumes as *Fables for the Frivolous* (1898), *Mother Goose for Grown-Ups* (1900), and *Grimm Tales Made Gay* (1903). *The Transgression of Andrew Vane* (1902) and *Zut and Other Parisians* (1903) are collections of short stories, and *The Lieutenant-Governor* (1903) is considered the best of his three novels.

CARSON, KIT (CHRISTOPHER) (1809–68), frontiersman and guide, was born in Kentucky, grew up on the Missouri frontier, and in 1826 went to New Mexico, making his home at Taos and becoming a guide on the Santa Fe Trail. He accompanied one of the first overland expeditions to California (1829–31), and took part in many trapping and trading trips, especially in the employ of Thomas Fitzpatrick. Famous as one of the ablest "mountain men," Carson in 1842 became the guide of Frémont's Western expeditions, and he was prominent in the taking of California during the Mexican War. He served as a U.S. agent in the Southwest (1853–60), and during the Civil War organized a regiment of New Mexico volunteers, leading them against various Indian forces and rising to the rank of brigadier-general. He was the subject of many frontier legends, and figures in Willa Cather's *Death Comes for the Archbishop,* ◆ Harvey Ferguson's *Wolf Song,* and several works by Stanley Vestal. *Kit Carson's Own Story of His Life* was published in 1926.

CARSON, RACHEL (1907–64), zoologist whose sensitive interpretations of scientific data made her books, *Under the Sea Wind* (1941), *The Sea Around Us* (1951), and *The Edge of the Sea* (1955), popular successes. *Silent Spring* (1963) was also widely read but for more sensational reasons since it describes the potentially dangerous effects of misused insecticides.

Carter, NICK, see *Nick Carter.*

CARTWRIGHT, PETER (1785–1872), Virginia-born Methodist preacher, an outstanding leader of frontier camp meetings, for some 50 years rode the circuits of Kentucky, Tennessee, Indiana, Ohio, and Illinois. He was an unsuccessful candidate for Congress against Abraham Lincoln (1846). He published three vivid autobiographical works: *Autobiography* (1857); *The Backwoods Preacher* (1858); and *Fifty Years as a Presiding Elder* (1871).

CARUTHERS, WILLIAM ALEXANDER (1802–46), Virginia novelist, whose works include *The Kentuckian in New York* (1834), an epistolary romance contrasting Northern and Southern character; *The Cavaliers of Virginia* (1834–35), a romance of Bacon's Rebellion; and *The Knights of the Horseshoe* (1845), a romance dealing with the career of Governor Spotswood.

CARVER, JONATHAN (1710–80), served in the French and Indian War, and was sent (1766–67) by Major Robert Rogers to explore the western Mississippi and Great Lakes region and to investigate the Indian tribes. His *Travels Through the Interior Part of North America* (London, 1778), a popular work which had more than 30 editions, is noted for its firsthand knowledge of Indian languages and customs and of the geography of the frontier.

CARVER, RAYMOND (1939–89), born in Clatskanie, Ore., married at 18, supported two children by working evenings while studying at Chico State College in California, where he was inspired by John Gardner's creative writing class. Carver spent a year at the University of Iowa's Writers' Workshop, then returned to California, where he worked as janitor, waiter, and gas station attendant to provide for his family while writing in his spare time. His first collection of short stories, *Will You Be Quiet, Please?* (1976), was nominated for a National Book Award. Another collection, *Furious Seasons,* followed in 1977. Solidly based on felt experience, his spare stories honor and articulate the lives of America's working class and poor, as well as sometimes those of the upwardly mobile. He completed four more collections—*What We Talk About When We Talk About Love* (1981); *Cathedral* (1984); *Fires* (1984), a gathering of poems, stories, and essays; and *Where I'm Calling From* (1988)—before he died of lung cancer.

Carwin, the Biloquist, see *Memoirs of Carwin.*

CARY, ALICE (1820–71), Ohio-born author whose quasi-autobiographical stories and sketches,

Clovernook; Or Recollections of Our Neighborhood in the West (1852), give a good sense of a woman's life on the frontier. A "Second Series" (1853) introduced the coming of cities and commerce. With her sister Phoebe (1824–71) she moved to New York, gained a reputation for their *Poems* (1849), and became the subject of Whittier's poem "The Singer."

Casamassima, PRINCESS, character in *Roderick Hudson*♦ and *The Princess Casamassima.* ♦

Casey at the Bat, mock-heroic poem by Ernest Lawrence Thayer, first published in the San Francisco *Examiner* (June 3, 1888). The poem, which soon became enormously popular and was a favorite piece in the repertory of DeWolf Hopper, tells of the dramatic defeat of the Mudville baseball team when its hero, the great Casey, struck out.

Casey Jones, railroad engineer hero of a popular ballad that tells of his fatal last trip in the cabin of a "big eight-wheeler," which was "eight hours late with the western mail." His attempt to arrive in "Frisco" on schedule results in a head-on collision with another train. As with most ballads, there are many variants of both music and verses, and no definite origin is known. It is claimed that the original engineer was John Luther Jones, killed in a wreck on the Chicago and New Orleans Limited (March 18, 1900). The song has been attributed at various times to three railroad workers, Wallace Saunders, Cornelius Steen, and "Wash" Sanders. It may have been revised from a ballad about a black fireman, Jimmie Jones, but certainly has its roots in the tradition that "there's many a man killed on the railroad, and laid in his lonesome grave," which also produced "The Wreck of the Six-Wheel Drive," "Ol' John Brown," and "Charley Snyder." A vaudeville version of "Casey Jones" was published in 1909 by T.L. Siebert and E. Newton. The hero's career has become a folk legend, and is the subject of a famous labor-union song and of Robert Ardrey's play *Casey Jones* (1938).

Cask of Amontillado, The, tale by Poe,♦ published in *Godey's Lady's Book* (1846).
   During the excitement of the carnival in an Italian city, Montresor determines to avenge "the thousand injuries" of Fortunato, a connoisseur of wines who has offended him. He finds Fortunato drunk, but eager to taste the choice Amontillado that Montresor claims to have stored in his underground vaults. Although he has a cough, made worse by the damp air and clinging nitre of the tunnels through which they go, he refuses to turn back when he hears that his rival, Luchresi, may be allowed to try the wine. At last they reach a crypt at the end of a passage, where Montresor shackles the stupefied Fortunato and proceeds to wall him up with stone and mortar. Fortunato

cries for help, but there is no one to hear, and Montresor completes his work, the last sound from his victim being a faint jingling of bells on his carnival motley.

Cassandra, poem in iambic tetrameter quatrains by E.A. Robinson,♦ published in *The Man Against the Sky* (1916). This prophetic satire of thoughtless American ideals denounces the modern trinity of "Dollar, Dove, and Eagle," and predicts their defeat by "the merciless old verities," asserting that "the power is yours, but not the sight":

> You have the ages for your guide,
> But not the wisdom to be led.

CASSILL, R[ONALD] V[ERLIN] (1919–   ), born in Iowa, educated at the University of Iowa, where he has taught creative writing. His novels include *Eagle on the Coin* (1950), treating personal and political involvements in a black's campaign for a small-town school board; *Clem Anderson* (1961), about the degradation and death of a promising young author; *The President* (1964), about a psychotic, power-seeking college president; *La Vie Passionée of Rodney Buckthorne* (1968), a comic work about academia and Greenwich Village culture; *Dr. Cobb's Game* (1970), a lively tale drawing on Britain's Profumo case of 1963 to treat sexual and social motivations; *The Goss Women* (1974), another story of sex and society; *Hoyt's Child* (1976); *Labors of Love* (1980), presenting a failing author who overcomes his writer's block and begins to analyze women when deserted by his wife and his mistress; *Flame* (1980), a fictive character study of a female motion-picture star; and *After Goliath* (1985), a tale set in the place and period of the Bible's King David. *The Father* (1965) and *Three Stories* (1982) assemble short stories. He has also issued popular paperback novels under his own name and that of Owen Aherne.

Castilian Days, travel book by John Hay,♦ published in 1871. It contains 17 essays on the civilization of Spain and its domination by the Church since medieval times, as well as vivid observations on the conventions, manners, character, and scenery of the country.

Casting Away of Mrs. Lecks and Mrs. Aleshine, The, humorous novel by Frank Stockton,♦ published in 1886. *The Dusantes* (1888) is a sequel.

Cat on a Hot Tin Roof, play by Tennessee Williams,♦ produced and published in 1955 and awarded a Pulitzer Prize.

On his sixty-fifth birthday, Big Daddy Pollitt, vulgar, fat, ruthless, and the richest cotton planter of the Mississippi Delta, is surrounded by his family: Brick, his favorite son, a withdrawn, alcoholic ex-football hero, and Brick's wife Maggie,

the passionate, vital "cat" who is unrelenting in her struggle to get what she wants; Gooper, the hypocritical, avaricious elder son whose wife Mae is about to produce their sixth "no-neck monster" child; and Big Mama, his loud, garrulous wife of 40 years. Maggie, determined to have marital relations with her remote husband and to produce the heir for the plantation, turns on Brick to tell him that she and his closest friend, Skipper, now dead, had slept together because each needed the warmth that Brick's "godlike" superiority and ideally pure relationship would not provide, and that in forcing Skipper to face the truth of his latent homosexuality she drove him to drink, drugs, and destruction. Soon after, Big Daddy makes Brick see that his alcoholism stems not from a noble disgust with the "mendacity" of the world, but from disgust with himself for refusing to help Skipper when the basic nature of their relationship became evident. Faced by his own truth, Brick retaliates by telling Big Daddy that he is dying of cancer. Aware that there is no will and anxious to inherit the rich plantation, Gooper and Mae tell Big Mama the truth about her husband's health and are surprised by her outraged revulsion toward the trusteeship they have had prepared. Wanting to make Big Daddy happy and determined not to be disinherited, Maggie announces that she and Brick are expecting a child, and later that evening, having locked away the liquor, she sets about attempting to make the lie come true, hoping both to rekindle Brick's desire and to save him from his cold detachment and death-in-life.

Catch-22, novel by Joseph Heller,♦ published in 1961.

On the Mediterranean island of Pianosa during the last months of World War II, Captain John Yossarian of the U.S. air force attempts to avoid further combat after having experienced grisly events and observing his fellow officers being ridiculous in their lust for promotion. Trying to be grounded as insane, he turns up naked at the ceremony in which General Dreedle is to award him a DFC. But fantastic bureaucratic rulings, extending to a Catch-22, prevent him from achieving his objective, and he deserts to seek a saner world in neutral Sweden. His commander, Captain Cathcart, drives his men to more and more combat, so that he may look impressive, and General Peckham makes them fly in formations that will make his aerial photos look good, while Lieutenant Milo Minderbinder ignores the whole matter of war and enemy forces as he goes about making a fortune and gaining power in black-market schemes.

Catcher in the Rye, The, novel by J.D. Salinger,♦ published in 1951.

Holden Caulfield, a lonely, compassionate, and quixotic 16-year-old boy, plagued by the "phoniness" of his moral environment, leaves

Pencey, the Pennsylvania preparatory school from which he has been expelled, for New York City. Having said goodbye to his conceited athletic roommate Stradlater and the "pimply, boring" Ackley, and fearful of confronting his parents, he checks into a depressing, cheap hotel. Unable to see or telephone his innocent, affectionate sister Phoebe, of whom he is very fond, he goes in desperation to nightclubs. Returning to the hotel, he accepts the elevator operator's offer of a prostitute, but depressed by and sorry for the girl, he retains his virginity, only to be confronted soon by the girl and her pimp, Maurice, who demands more money and fights with Holden. The next morning he meets Sally Hayes, an old girl friend, takes her ice skating, tells her that he is tired of the ubiquitous hypocrisy that he encounters, and asks her to run away with him to the New England countryside. Righteously angered by his impractical scheme, the pseudo-sophisticated Sally refuses, they fight, and Holden leaves her. After becoming drunk and making a nostalgic visit to Central Park, he sneaks home that evening to see Phoebe, who is distressed by his negativism and challenges him to name one thing he would like to be. Holden replies that he would like to be "the catcher in the rye." Mistaken in his recollection of Burns's poem, he says, "Anyway, I keep picturing all these little kids playing some game in this big field of rye and all. Thousands of little kids, and nobody's around—nobody big, I mean—except me. And I'm standing on the edge of some crazy cliff. What I have to do, I have to catch everybody if they start to go over the cliff—I mean if they're running and they don't look where they're going . . . ," a persistent image indicative of his desire to preserve innocence. Leaving his parents' apartment, he spends the night at the home of Mr. Antolini, his former English teacher, whose homosexual advances repel Holden and set him in flight. "Confused and frightened and even sickened by human behavior," he decides to see Phoebe once more before running away to the West, but suddenly filled with love for her and the world, he knows he cannot leave. After going home, Holden has a nervous breakdown, but recovers to tell in his own vivid vernacular of these two dramatic days and of the experiences and feelings that lie behind them, as he is filled with sympathy for everyone he has known, "even . . . that goddam Maurice."

CATESBY, MARK (c. 1679–1749), English naturalist, studied the flora and fauna of the Carolinas and other Southern regions (1710–19), which he described in *The Natural History of Carolina, Florida, and the Bahama Islands* (1731–43), illustrated with more than 200 of his own plates. He returned to America (1722), eventually settling in the South. His *Hortus Britanno-Americanus* (1763–67) is said to have encouraged the introduction of American trees and shrubs into Europe.

Cathedral, The, blank-verse poem by J.R. Lowell, ♦ published Christmas 1869. A revised edition (1877) includes the "Ode Recited at the Harvard Commemoration."

CATHER, WILLA [SIBERT] (1873–1947), born in Virginia, as a child moved with her family to Nebraska, where she was reared among the immigrants who are the subjects of many of her novels. After graduation from the University of Nebraska (1895), where her study of Latin may have influenced her graceful Virgilian style, and a period of journalism and high-school teaching, she published a book of poems, *April Twilights* (1903, enlarged 1923), and a book of short stories, *The Troll Garden* (1905). She was on the staff of *McClure's* (1906–12), leaving to devote herself to creative writing after the publication of her first novel, *Alexander's Bridge* (1912), the story of an engineer torn between love for his wife and the woman he had loved during his youth. With *O Pioneers!*♦ (1913) she turned to the Nebraska prairies to tell of the heroic and creative qualities of the passing frontier. *The Song of the Lark♦* (1915) is again a study of a woman's character; and *My Ántonia♦* (1918), episodic in construction like her other novels, tells of a Bohemian immigrant girl's life on the frontier, and the pioneer strength that preserves her through numerous adversities. *One of Ours* (1922), which won a Pulitzer Prize although it is not considered to rank with her best work, tells of a young man's escape from his oppressive life on a Midwestern farm to vitalizing experiences as a soldier in France during World War I. *A Lost Lady♦* (1923) differs from Miss Cather's previous studies of women in the Middle West in that the heroine's grace, charm, and cultivated taste place her above and apart from the new grasping generation that succeeds the era of pioneers. *The Professor's House♦* (1925) is partly the story of an idealistic scholar's adjustment to middle age, and partly that of his favorite student's discovery of an ancient cliff city in New Mexico, the description of which foreshadows the setting of *Death Comes for the Archbishop.* *My Mortal Enemy* (1926) is a short novel concerned with a selfish and strong-willed woman who brings about her own downfall. The author's idealism and love of the past reach a climax in *Death Comes for the Archbishop♦* (1927), her celebration of the spiritual pioneering of the Catholic Church in New Mexico. Catholicism is also at the core of *Shadows on the Rock♦* (1931), which deals with 17th-century Quebec. *Lucy Gayheart* (1935) is the story of a Midwestern girl who gives up an early love affair to study music, then abandons her career to become the mistress of an egotistical concert singer and meets an accidental death after he deserts her. *Sapphira and the Slave Girl♦* (1940) is a novel based on a story recalled from her Virginia childhood. *Obscure Destinies* (1932) contains three novelettes set in small communities of the Middle West, and

Youth and the Bright Medusa (1920) is a volume of stories dealing with the careers of artists. *Not Under Forty* (1936) is a collection of essays presenting the author's theory of fiction, and describing literary encounters with writers who influenced her, such as Sarah Orne Jewett.

CATHERWOOD, MARY [HARTWELL] (1847–1902), Ohio-born author of fiction, was a schoolteacher in Illinois and New York, and achieved literary success with *The Romance of Dollard* (1889), the first of a series of historical romances set in French Canada and the Middle West. Others of these are *The Story of Tonty* (1890), *The Lady of Fort St. John* (1891). *Old Kaskaskia* (1893), *The Spirit of an Illinois Town* (1897), *Spanish Peggy* (1899), and *Lazarre* (1901). She also wrote *Heroes of the Middle West: The French* (1898) and other books for children, and published collections of short stories.

Catholic World, see *Hecker, Isaac.*

Catholicism, see *Roman Catholic Church in America.*

CATLIN, GEORGE (1796–1872), self-taught painter of Indian life, lived in Pennsylvania until 1832, when he made an eight-year expedition to various Indian tribes from the Yellowstone River to Florida, resulting in the 300 engravings and descriptive text of *The Manners, Customs and Condition of the North American Indians* (2 vols., 1841). From 1852 to 1857 he traveled in Central and South America and explored the Far West, as recorded in *Last Rambles Amongst the Indians of the Rocky Mountains and the Andes* (1867) and *Life Among the Indians* (1867). He also aroused interest in Indian culture by bringing troupes of Indians to the East and Europe, before the period of the shows of Buffalo Bill and P.T. Barnum. His artistic work, though uneven in quality and primitive in style, possesses the charm, sincerity, and documentary value of authentic records of American Indian life.

CATO, pseudonym of Provost William Smith. ♦

Cat's Cradle, novel by Vonnegut, ♦ published in 1963.
Jonah, a journalist, goes to Ilium, N.Y., the manufacturing city where the late Felix Hoenikker lived, so as to write a book about that eccentric scientist and his invention of an atom bomb and of a crystal named *ice-nine* that will freeze anything aqueous with which it comes in contact. On a magazine assignment Jonah next goes to the Latin American island nation of San Lorenzo. There he learns of the black adventurer and ex-soldier Earl McCabe, who was the land's autocratic ruler until superseded by Papa Monzano, a dictator, who has been aided by Hoenikker's son Franklin. Jonah learns too of another

black ex-soldier, Lionel Boyd Johnson, who has become the people's spiritual leader by the creation of a religion called Bokononism and the preaching of "foma," useful lies. Papa Monzano kills himself with a bit of *ice-nine* that he got from Franklin Hoenikker, and when by accident his frozen body slides into the sea, all the surrounding water is congealed and all the San Lorenzans are killed, save Bokonon, Jonah, and a few others.

CATTON, BRUCE (1899–1978), born in Michigan, attended Oberlin College, became a journalist, and served in World War II. His trilogy of historical studies about the Army of the Potomac is *Mr. Lincoln's Army* (1951), *Glory Road* (1952), and *A Stillness at Appomattox* (1953, Pulitzer Prize). Later works related to the Civil War, his central subject, include: *U.S. Grant and the American Military Tradition* (1954) and its sequels, *Grant Moves South* (1960) and *Grant Takes Command* (1969); *This Hallowed Ground* (1956), on the Union side of the war; a Centennial History of the Civil War in three volumes: *The Coming Fury* (1961), *Terrible Swift Sword* (1963), and *Never Call Retreat* (1965); and *Two Roads to Sumter* (1963), biographies of Lincoln and Jefferson Davis written in collaboration with his son William. He also wrote a memoir of his youth, *Waiting for the Morning Train* (1972), and *Michigan: A Bicentennial History* (1976).

Caulfield, HOLDEN, hero of *The Catcher in the Rye.* ♦

Cavender's House, dramatic narrative in blank verse by E.A. Robinson, ♦ published in 1929.

Cawdor, narrative poem by Robinson Jeffers, ♦ the title piece of a volume published in 1928.
Using a powerful unrhymed five- and ten-stress line, the poet sets his story in the farming country of the California coast in 1909–10. After a fire destroys their farm, Fera Martial and her blind father go to live with their neighbor Cawdor. When Cawdor desires her for her beauty, Fera marries him, but she falls in love with Cawdor's young son Hood. The lad refuses her advances, and for revenge Fera tells her husband that his son has raped her. Infuriated, Cawdor quarrels with Hood and accidentally kills him. Later, after Fera tells Cawdor the truth, he blinds himself in a passion of guilt.

CAWEIN, MADISON [JULIUS] (1865–1914), prolific writer of poems dealing with his native Kentucky, its scenes and its people. Lacking the faculty of self-criticism, he published 36 volumes, in which his occasionally sensitive lyrics are buried under a welter of mediocre verse. *Lyrics and Idyls* (1890) and *Vale of Tempe* (1905) are representative of his work. A selection by Edmund

Gosse was published in England as *Kentucky Poems* (1902).

Cayuga Indians, see *Iroquois Indians.*

Celebrated Jumping Frog of Calaveras County, The, sketch by Clemens♦ written under his pseudonym Mark Twain, was published in the New York *Saturday Press* (1865) and reprinted as the title piece of a series of sketches that formed his first book (1867). Although his source was an old folk tale that had been in print in California as early as 1853, Clemens was catapulted into fame by his version, which tells of the jumping frog Dan'l Webster, pet of gambling Jim Smiley, which is defeated when a stranger fills its gullet with quail shot while Smiley's attention is distracted.

Celestial Railroad, The, allegorical tale by Hawthorne,♦ published in 1843 and collected in *Mosses from an Old Manse* (1846).

The narrator travels the way of Christian in *Pilgrim's Progress,* from the City of Destruction to the Celestial City. Instead of going afoot, he finds that modern achievement has made possible an easy, convenient Celestial Railroad, on which he rides in the company of affable, bluff Mr. Smooth-it-away, who scoffs at the difficult path of old-fashioned pilgrims. The ancient landmarks and institutions are all changed, and on arriving at the end of the line, the passengers expect to cross the river by steam ferryboat. But here Mr. Smooth-it-away deserts them, laughing and showing his identity by breathing smoke and flame. About to drown, the narrator suddenly awakens to "thank Heaven it was a Dream!"

Centaur, The, novel by Updike,♦ published in 1963.

During three winter days of 1944 George Caldwell, a 50-year-old high-school teacher of science in Olinger, Pa., and his teenage son Peter have experiences that, though realistically told, are parallel to classic myths. Olinger is Olympus; the senior Caldwell is Chiron, the centaur who was a teacher of heroes, famed for surrendering his immortality and accepting death to be released from the pain of a wound; and Peter is not only an uneasy adolescent troubled by a skin disease, infatuated by a sweet girl, Penny, and envious of boys who are better athletes or more appealing, but he is Prometheus in love with Penelope and envious of Daedalus. While Caldwell copes with his wife Cassie (Ceres), who is eager to develop their property into a farm, and with his father-in-law, Pop Kramer (Kronos), he moves restlessly through life as he encounters a veritable pantheon of deities: the garage mechanic Al Hummel (Hephaistos), who helps him when he is wounded, as does Doc Appleton (Apollo); the school principal Zimmerman (Zeus), a petty tyrant enjoying an affair with a

school-board member, Mrs. Herzog (Hera); and the lascivious physical education teacher, Vera (Venus), who is attracted to the local minister, the Rev. March (Ares).

Center for Editions of American Authors, organized by the Modern Language Association (1963) to promote textual and bibliographical study and to oversee the creation of approved texts for definitive editions of classic American authors, including Cooper, Stephen Crane, John Dewey, Emerson, Hawthorne, Howells, Irving, Melville, Simms, Thoreau, Mark Twain, and Whitman. Its publication program was later directly overseen by the National Endowment for the Humanities.

Century Association, New York men's club of writers and artists, was founded (1847) as an outgrowth of the Sketch Club, which in turn had split from the Bread and Cheese Club.♦ Early members included Bryant, Irving, F.S. Cozzens, George Bancroft, H.T. Tuckerman, and Verplanck. It has long since outgrown the membership of 100 from which its name derives, but even with greatly increased membership, the purposes and qualifications for membership today remain basically the same.

Century Illustrated Monthly Magazine, The, (1881–1930), continuation of *Scribner's Monthly,*♦ was independently published, and edited by R.W. Gilder (1881–1909). The early contents included a series of Civil War Papers by outstanding generals and the serialization of Nicolay and Hay's biography of Lincoln (1887–90). Among the novels serialized at this time were Howells's *A Modern Instance* and *The Rise of Silas Lapham,* James's *The Bostonians,* Hay's *The Breadwinners,* London's *The Sea-Wolf,* and Mitchell's *Hugh Wynne.* Of its short stories, the most popular was "The Lady or the Tiger?," by the associate editor Stockton, although Harris's Uncle Remus stories had a wide following. R.U. Johnson was editor (1909–13), when the magazine was known simply as *The Century.* It declined under later editors, and in 1929 became a quarterly. The following year it was merged with *The Forum.*♦

Chactas, character in *Atala,*♦ *René,*♦ and *Les Natchez.*♦

Chad Newsome, character in *The Ambassadors.*♦

Chainbearer, The, novel by Cooper,♦ published in 1845 as the second part of his Littlepage Manuscripts.♦

Mordaunt, son of Cornelius Littlepage and heir to his New York estates, is educated at Princeton, and in the last year of the Revolutionary War is an ensign in the company of the bluff

Dutch surveyor Andries Coejemans, called Chainbearer, who later goes to Ravensnest and Mooseridge, the Littlepage frontier estates, as chief surveyor. There Mordaunt joins him, and falls in love with his niece Dus Malbone. Mordaunt and the Indian guide Susquesus are captured while spying on Aaron Thousandacres, a surly squatter who has been plundering the timber at Ravensnest. Susquesus escapes to summon Chainbearer, who comes to parley with Thousandacres. The squatter demands that Dus marry his son, and when the indignant uncle refuses there is an altercation in which he is killed. Thousandacres is killed by a posse while resisting arrest, and members of the Littlepage family arrive in time to learn of the betrothal of Mordaunt and Dus.

CHALKLEY, THOMAS (1675–1741), sea captain, divided his time between trading and missionary voyages and preaching his Quaker gospel in England and the colonies. He appears in Whittier's *Snow-Bound* as the "gentlest of skippers, rare sea-saint." His simple *Journal* (1747), recounting both his adventures and his quiet religious life, was widely admired by Quakers.

CHALMERS, GEORGE (1742–1825), Scottish antiquary, historian, and lawyer, resided in Maryland (1763–75). His writing include the *Political Annals of the Present United Colonies* (1780), *An Introduction to the History of the Revolt of the Colonies* (1782), and *Opinions . . . Arising from American Independence* (1784). In the last, he opposes with legalistic thoroughness the constitutional position of the rebellious colonies. A continuation of his *Annals* was posthumously published by the New-York Historical Society.

Chambered Nautilus, The, poem by Holmes,♦ included in *The Autocrat of the Breakfast-Table* (1858) and in later collections of poems. It consists of five seven-line stanzas, in the pattern of three iambic pentameters, three trimeters, and a final alexandrine: a5a3b3b5b5c3c6.

A chambered nautilus is a mollusk that begins life in a small shell and builds larger ones as it grows. In the poem this symbolizes human endeavor, and the reader is exhorted to build a broader and more comprehensive life, growing with his age and experience.

CHAMBERLAIN, JOSHUA LAWRENCE (1828–1913), professor of rhetoric at Bowdoin College when he joined the 20th Maine Regiment as lieutenant colonel in 1862. He commanded the 20th at Gettysburg, anchoring the crucial far-left flank of the Union army during the fight for Little Round Top. When his troops ran out of ammunition and looked to him, he ordered and led a bayonet charge which routed the Alabama regiment in front of him. He was awarded the Congressional Medal of Honor, and rose to brigadier general by war's end. He was later governor of Maine and president of Bowdoin. He wrote a good account of the last campaigns of the Army of the Potomac in the East, *The Passing of the Armies* (1915). He figures centrally in Shaara's♦ novel *The Killer Angels.*

CHAMBERS, ROBERT W[ILLIAM] (1865–1933), New York novelist, began his career as a painter and illustrator, but soon turned to the more profitable production of gracefully written pseudo-historical romances. Besides short stories and two plays, he published a long series of popular novels, including *In the Quarter* (1894), *The Red Republic* (1895), *A King and a Few Dukes* (1896), *Lorraine* (1898), *Ashes of Empire* (1898), *Cardigan* (1901), *The Fighting Chance* (1906), *The Tracer of Lost Persons* (1906), *The Firing Line* (1908), *Police!!!* (1915), *The Restless Sex* (1918), *The Hi-Jackers* (1923), and *The Drums of Aulone* (1927).

Chan, CHARLIE, detective hero of a number of mystery novels by Earl Derr Biggers.♦

Chance Acquaintance, A, novel by Howells,♦ published in 1873.

Chancellorsville, Battle of, Confederate victory during the Civil War (May 2–4, 1863), in which Lee and Stonewall Jackson routed Hooker and the Army of the Potomac. Jackson was fatally wounded, being accidentally shot by his own men. Crane's *Red Badge of Courage* is partly based on accounts of this battle, which also figures prominently in John Esten Cooke's *Surry of Eagle's Nest,* Mary Johnston's *The Long Roll,* and Thomas Dixon's *The Southerner.*

CHANDLER, ELIZABETH MARGARET (1807–34), Quaker poet who contributed antislavery and descriptive verse, such as "The Captured Slave" and "The Sunset Hour," to Benjamin Lundy's journal *The Genius of Universal Emancipation.* Lundy published her *Essays, Philosophical and Moral* (1836) and her *Poetical Works* (1836).

CHANDLER, RAYMOND (1888–1959), born in Chicago, reared in England, moved to southern California (1912) but did not begin to write his famous mystery stories until he was in his forties. He soon became the prime figure of the school of hard-boiled detective fiction, also distinguished for his presentation of the seamy side of his Los Angeles setting. His tough sleuth, Philip Marlowe, became a cult figure. Chandler's major works are *The Big Sleep* (1939), *Farewell, My Lovely* (1940), *The Lady in the Lake* (1943), and *The Long Goodbye* (1954), all of which were made into very popular films. An incomplete manuscript involving his figure Marlowe was rewritten and brought to an end by Robert B. Parker for publication as *Poodle Springs* (1989).

CHANNING, EDWARD TYRRELL (1790–1856), brother of the elder William Ellery Channing, a founder and editor (1818–19) of *The North American Review.* As professor of rhetoric and oratory at Harvard (1826–50), according to T.W. Higginson he "probably trained as many conspicuous authors as all other American instructors put together"; his students included Emerson, Holmes, Thoreau, and R.H. Dana, Jr. His *Lectures Read to the Seniors in Harvard College* (1856) was published with a memoir by Dana.

CHANNING, WILLIAM ELLERY (1780–1842), born in Rhode Island, became pastor of a Boston Congregational church (1803). In his sermon at the ordination of Jared Sparks (1819), he clearly indicated his break with orthodox Calvinism, and from this date he was considered the "apostle" of Unitarianism♦ and the leading opponent of Calvinism. As a stimulating force in the intellectual life of Massachusetts, he did much to prepare the way for Transcendentalism and other advanced social and cultural movements. His idealism and opposition to dogmatism may be observed in such sermons as the *Baltimore Sermon* (1819); *The Moral Argument Against Calvinism* (1820), in which he denies that human nature is essentially depraved; and *Unitarian Christianity Most Favorable to Piety* (1826). In his *Remarks on American Literature* (1830), he asks for a literary Declaration of Independence. His pamphlets on pacifism, antislavery, temperance, public education, and labor conditions are included in his collected *Works* (6 vols., 1841–43).

CHANNING, WILLIAM ELLERY (1818–1901), nephew of the elder W.E. Channing, ran away from Harvard to devote his life to poetry. His first recognition came when Emerson wrote an article on his poetry for *The Dial.* In order to be near Emerson he moved to Concord with his wife Ellen, the sister of Margaret Fuller. There he became an intimate of Thoreau and wrote the first biography, *Thoreau, the Poet-Naturalist* (1873, enlarged 1902), as well as editing several posthumous volumes of his friend's writings. Channing's own first volume of *Poems* (1843) is said by James Russell Lowell in his *Fable for Critics* to plunder the "orchard" of its editor, Emerson. During succeeding years, Channing wrote his *Poems, Second Series* (1847), *The Woodman* (1849), *Near Home* (1858), *The Wanderer* (1871), *Eliot* (1885), and *John Brown and the Heroes of Harper's Ferry* (1886). Thoreau called Channing's style "sublimoslipshod," and other friends deplored his insistence upon printing his "native wood-notes wild," which his thoroughgoing Transcendentalism would not let him polish or revise.

CHANNING, WILLIAM HENRY (1810–84), nephew of the elder W.E. Channing, was a Christian socialist and member of the Transcendental Club. He served as pastor of the Unitarian church at Cincinnati (1838–39), and there edited *The Western Messenger.*♦ He spent a few months at Brook Farm, was interested in the North American Phalanx, and, becoming converted to Fourierism, headed the Boston Religious Union of Associationists (1847), which included George Ripley and Albert Brisbane. He also edited the socioreligious magazines *The Present*♦ (1843–44) and *The Spirit of the Age* (1849–50). With Emerson and J.F. Clarke he wrote the *Memoirs* (1852) of Margaret Fuller, and his other writings include a *Memoir of William Ellery Channing* (1848).

Chanting the Square Deific, poem by Whitman,♦ published in the *Sequel to Drum-Taps* (1865–66) and added to the 1867 edition of *Leaves of Grass.*

This expression of Whitman's religious thought is presented in four stanzas, each dealing with an aspect of the deity. The first side of the square deific is Jehovah, or the relentless, inexorable laws of nature. The second is Christ, the affectionate "consolator." The third is Satan, the spirit of individual freedom in opposition to the omnipotent. The fourth is the feminine Santa Spirita, the soul which mystically pervades all, giving direction and form to the divine energies.

Chap Book, The (1894–98), semi-monthly little magazine, was founded at Cambridge as a house organ of the publishers Stone and Kimball. Moved with the firm to Chicago after six months, it had already become a separate publication, printing works by Henry James, Hamlin Garland, Eugene Field, Bliss Carman, and Julian Hawthorne, in addition to contributions from such foreign authors as Wells, Beerbohm, Stevenson, Henley, and Yeats. In typography, illustrations, and literary content, the magazine was faintly suggestive of the English *fin de siècle* publications, and in its turn affected *The Lark*♦ and other American periodicals. It was increased in size (1897) and later lost much of its charm and naïveté.

Chapbooks, pamphlet editions of popular literature, widely distributed in the early U.S., especially during the first quarter of the 19th century. Like the English publications of the same type, they included such various materials as jokes, ballads, marvelous accounts, fables, Gothic tales, biographies of popular heroes, model letters, moral stories, and orations. Mason Weems♦ was an author and peddler of chapbooks, and among the prominent publishers was Isaiah Thomas. Chapbooks shared with almanacs and newspapers the most important place in the dissemination of popular literature in their time.

CHAPLIN, CHARLES [SPENCER] (1889–1977), English-born actor, after a career in vaudeville in England and the U.S. became a motion-picture comedian, known for his brilliant pantomime and creation of the wistful tramp character that he portrayed in many short films as well as full features, including *The Kid* (1921), *The Gold Rush* (1925), and *City Lights* (1931). Later films, also created and directed by him, include *The Great Dictator* (1940), a satire on Hitler and Mussolini, and *Monsieur Verdoux* (1947). His character is symbolically portrayed in Hart Crane's "Chaplinesque," in *White Buildings*. He wrote *My Autobiography* (1964) and was knighted (1975).

CHAPMAN, JOHN (1774–1847), Massachusetts-born orchardist, known as "Johnny Appleseed" because of the fruit trees he planted for frontier settlers in Pennsylvania, Ohio, Indiana, and Illinois. Many legends and tall tales were told of his remarkable woodcraft and his adventures in aiding pioneers. He is the subject of a ballad by W.H. Venable and of many poems by Vachel Lindsay, including "In Praise of Johnny Appleseed."◆

CHAPMAN, JOHN JAY (1862–1933), literary critic, translator, essayist, was a strong individualist in his eclectic criticism based on an "essentially aristocratic" and Emersonian appreciation of individualism. His books include *Emerson and Other Essays* (1898), *Learning and Other Essays* (1910), *William Lloyd Garrison* (1913, revised 1921), *Memories and Milestones* (1915), *Greek Genius and Other Essays* (1915), *Letters and Religion* (1924), and *New Horizons in American Life* (1932). He was the author of many plays, including *The Treason and Death of Benedict Arnold* (1910), "a play for a Greek theatre." His *Songs and Poems* were collected in 1919, and in 1937 M.A. DeWolfe Howe issued *John Jay Chapman and His Letters*.

CHAPMAN, MARIA WESTON (1806–85), was associated with Garrison as treasurer of the Massachusetts Anti-Slavery Society and as an editor of the *Liberator*. She wrote many abolitionist articles, and her *Life of Harriet Martineau* (1877) was the result of a long personal friendship. She sponsored the publication of *The Liberty Bell*◆ (1839–58).

CHAPPELL, FRED (1936–) was born in North Carolina at whose state university he has been a professor of English since 1964. Beginning with his first novel, *It Is Time, Lord* (1963), his fiction is set in his native region, as is *The Inkling* (1965), concerning psychological problems of a family; *Dagon* (1968), about a minister driven to madness and murder; *The Gaudy Place* (1973), about a chance encounter between a professor and a prostitute and her pimp; *I Am One of You Forever* (1985), about a North Carolina boy and the diverse people he meets; and *Brighten the Corner Where You Are* (1989), a comic view of the days of a high school teacher. Chappell is a noted poet whose books include *The World Between the Eyes* (1971), followed by a tetralogy: *River* (1975),

Bloodfire (1978), *Wind Mountain* (1979), and *Earthsleep* (1980) gathered in the volume *Midquest* (1981), revealing both serious intensity and humor associated with broad cultural, geographic, and temporal relations as well as those of his native region. *Source* (1985) was published in the year the poet was awarded a Bollingen Prize;◆ it was followed by *First and Last Words* (1989).

Character and Opinion in the United States, essays by Santayana,◆ published in 1920.

Written several years after the author left the U.S., these critical memoirs interpret the temper of the American people and their philosophic thought, in terms of the author's observations at Harvard and elsewhere. Besides reminiscences of the university and of his fellow professors, William James and Josiah Royce, there is a discussion of the conflict between materialism and idealism, and the moral background embodied in New England Calvinism and the conditions of the frontier, "the primitive physical emptiness" accompanied by a "moral emptiness." The American character is "cheerfully experimental," imaginative, optimistic, "successful in invention, conservative in reform, and quick in emergencies." Its attitude is that of a "moral materialism," marked by a "love of quantity," but inconclusive because "the American has never yet had to face the trials of Job." The typical American, though unprovided with opportunities to develop a sense of beauty, is "wonderfully alive," youthful, inquisitive, and enthusiastic, and promises much for the future.

Chardon Street Convention, three meetings (Nov. 1840; March 1841; Nov. 1841) held at Boston in the Chardon Street Chapel under the leadership of Edmund Quincy and Bronson Alcott, for the consideration of religious questions. The dominant spirit was one of radical idealism, those who attended wishing to cleave through orthodoxy and ritual to a practical application of Christianity in contemporary American life. The meetings were reported by Emerson in *The Dial*.

Charles the Second; or, The Merry Monarch, comedy by J.H. Payne,◆ adapted with the anonymous assistance of Irving from a French play. It was produced in London and New York (1824), and published the same year.

The Earl of Rochester, at the instigation of his beloved Lady Clara, attempts to reform Charles II, and takes the king in disguise to a sailors' tavern. There he leaves the monarch without money, to be threatened with arrest by the landlord, until he escapes by a window. Lady Clara wins the king's pardon for Rochester by pretending that she will otherwise expose Charles. Rochester and Lady Clara plan to marry, and the king resolves to mend his ways.

Charlotte Temple: *A Tale of Truth,* sentimental romance by Susanna Rowson,◆ published in England (1791) and in the U.S. (1794). Based on experiences of the author's family, it was "designed . . . for the perusal of the young and thoughtful of the fair sex." By 1933 it had gone through 161 editions in the U.S. A sequel, *Charlotte's Daughter* (1828), is usually published as *Lucy Temple*.

At 15 Charlotte is a pupil in Mme Du Pont's school for young ladies. An army officer, Montraville, aided by an unscrupulous teacher, Mlle La Rue, seduces the girl, who elopes with him from England to New York. There he deserts her to marry an heiress, Julia Franklin. Charlotte gives birth to a daughter, Lucy, but, abandoned even by the heartless Mlle La Rue, now married to Colonel Crayton, she dies in poverty. Her father later adopts Lucy, but refuses to punish the repentant Montraville. The latter in a duel kills his former friend Belcour, who had further misled Charlotte, and returns to the tender Julia.

CHASE, MARY COYLE (1907–81), Colorado playwright, whose fantastic comedy about an inebriate whose companion is a huge, imaginary rabbit, *Harvey* (1944), won a Pulitzer Prize. Other plays include *Now You've Done It* (1937), *The Next Half Hour* (1945), *Bernardine* (1952), *Mrs. McThing* (1952), *Mickey* (1969), and *Cocktails with Mimi* (1974). She also wrote books for children.

CHASE, MARY ELLEN (1887–1973), was born in Maine, from whose state university she graduated, and whose land, traditions, and people she celebrated in many of her books. In addition to her career as a professor of English, mainly at Smith (1926–55), she is known as a popular author. Her fiction includes *Mary Peters* (1934) and *Silas Crockett* (1935), novels about New England seafaring families; *Dawn in Lyonesse* (1938), a modern parallel of the Tristan and Isolde story; *Windswept* (1941); *The Plum Tree* (1949); *The Edge of Darkness* (1957), set in northern Maine; and *Lovely Ambition* (1960), set partly in Maine, partly in England. Other writings include *This England* (1936); *The Bible and the Common Reader* (1944); *Jonathan Fisher* (1948), biography of a Maine minister; *Abby Aldrich Rockefeller* (1950); *Life and Language in the Old Testament* (1955); and three autobiographical works: *A Goodly Heritage* (1932); *A Goodly Fellowship* (1939), and *The White Gate* (1954). She also wrote many children's books.

CHASTELLUX, FRANÇOIS JEAN, Marquis de (1734–88), French author and major general under Rochambeau in the Revolutionary War, is noted for his *Travels in North-America, in the Years 1780, 1781, and 1782 . . .* (2 vols., 1787).

CHATEAUBRIAND, FRANÇOIS RENÉ, Vicomte de (1768–1848), French romantic author, made one visit to the U.S. (July 10–Dec. 10, 1791), which included a trip from Baltimore to Niagara Falls and a brief residence with an Indian tribe. *Voyage en Amérique* (1827) describes the trip with many fictional embellishments. His works with American settings include *Atala,* ♦ *René,* ♦ and *Les Natchez.* ♦

CHAUNCY, CHARLES (1705–87), pastor of the First Church of Boston (1727–87), opposed Jonathan Edwards and the revivalists of the Great Awakening in his *Seasonable Thoughts on the State of Religion in New England* (1743) and other pamphlets. He also published *A Compleat View of Episcopacy* (1771), arguments against an Anglican hierarchy in the colonies, and in other sermons and pamphlets set forth reasons for a distinct break from the mother country. Late in life he proclaimed himself a Universalist in *Salvation for All Men* (1782) and *The Mystery Hid from Ages and Generations* (1784).

Chautauqua movement, an outgrowth of the lyceum movement, ♦ originated at Lake Chautauqua, N.Y., where annual Methodist Episcopal camp meetings had been held until they were reorganized (1874) as assemblies for religious study. The program was extended to include other branches of education, as well as musical and dramatic entertainments. The resulting Chautauqua Institution offered correspondence courses, published books, issued *The Chautauquan* (1880–1914), and held an annual summer school. Its success caused other communities throughout the U.S. to imitate the venture, and "chautauqua" became a generic name for programs given by troupes of lecturers and entertainers, operated in the manner of traveling theatrical companies, and performing in rural settlements.

CHAYEFSKY, PADDY (1923–1981), born in New York City, after graduation from City College and army service in World War II became a writer of television dramas and a producer of films and legitimate plays. His works include *Marty* (1953, TV; 1955, film), a direct, sympathetic treatment of the romance of a lonely Bronx butcher and a spinster schoolteacher. *The Bachelor Party* (1954, TV; 1957, film) and *The Catered Affair* (1955, TV; 1956, film) also blend reportorial realism about commonplace people with a sentimental attitude toward their problems. A dedication to Judaism is seen in *The Tenth Man* (1959), a play using the theme of the Dybbuk but set in the Bronx, and in *Gideon* (1961). Another stage play, *The Passion of Josef D.* (1964), is a morality with music, depicting Stalin, Trotsky, and Lenin during the Russian Revolution. Six of his works are collected in *Television Plays* (1955). Later works include *The Latent Heterosexual* (1968), a play; *Network* (1975), a film he wrote and produced; and *Altered States* (1978), a science fiction novel.

CHEETHAM, JAMES (1772–1810), English-born journalist, was part owner of the New York daily *The American Citizen,* which supported DeWitt Clinton. His vindictive *View of the Political Conduct of Aaron Burr* (1802) involved him in a bitter newspaper battle with Peter Irving and others. He was also the author of a scornful *Life of Thomas Paine* (1809).

CHEEVER, JOHN (1912–1982), Massachusetts author whose formal schooling ended and literary career began with expulsion from Thayer Academy, the subject of his first story, published in 1930. His many stories since then, frequently dealing satirically with affluent New Englanders living in suburbia, have often appeared in *The New Yorker* and have been collected in *The Way Some People Live* (1943), *The Housebreaker of Shady Hill* (1958), *Some People, Places and Things That Will Not Appear in My Next Novel* (1961), *The Brigadier and the Golf Widow* (1964), and *The World of Apples* (1973). *The Wapshot Chronicle*♦ (1957), an episodic novel about the comically raffish lives of a wealthy Massachusetts family during the first half of the 20th century, was given a National Book Award. Its sequel, *The Wapshot Scandal*♦ (1964), continues the tale of the family decline in their hometown, St. Botolph. His third novel, *Bullet Park* (1969), also depicting a suburban family, is a firmer-structured work, more satirical and more of a morality story. *Falconer*♦ (1977), a later novel, deals with an ex-professor's experiences as an inmate in Falconer Prison, and is a story of human redemption. *Oh What a Paradise It Seems* (1982) is a novella about an aging man who is rejuvenated by an unusual romance and who uses his new energies to save the landscape of the area where he lived as a boy. His *Uncollected Stories* were published in 1988, and his *Letters* appeared the same year.

CHENEY, JOHN VANCE (1848–1922), born in New York, moved to California (1876), where he became known for his conventional lyric poems collected in *Thistle-Drift* (1887), *Wood Blooms* (1888), and *Poems* (1905). He was a friend of Joaquin Miller, Edwin Markham, and John Muir. He was librarian of the San Francisco Public Library (1887–94) and of the Newberry Library (1894–1909). His essays appeared in *The Golden Guess* (1892) and *That Dome in Air* (1895).

Cherokee Indians, large tribe that formerly occupied the mountains of Georgia, Alabama, Tennessee, and Carolina. They aided the British against the French, as well as in the Revolutionary War, when they attacked frontier settlers. In 1827 they adopted a government modeled on that of the U.S., after which, although the U.S. Supreme Court upheld their autonomy, they were forcibly deported (1838–39) to Oklahoma. Disbanded (1906) they became U.S. citizens. The high state of their culture is represented in such individuals as Sequoyah,♦ who created their alphabet. Elias Boudinot, an educated Cherokee,

edited the *Cherokee Phoenix* (1828–35), the first newspaper for an Indian tribe, and wrote *Poor Sarah; or, The Indian Woman* (1833). The "Deathsong of a Cherokee Indian," sometimes attributed to Freneau, appears as a song in Tyler's play *The Contrast.* Cherokee Indians of the colonial period appear in the novels of Mary N. Murfree,♦ and those of later times in stories by W.G. Simms,♦ who gained first-hand knowledge by a sojourn among them. *The Cherokee Night* is a play by Lynn Riggs. John R. Ridge, an early California poet and journalist, was of Cherokee descent.

CHESNUT, MARY BOYKIN [MILLER] (1823–86), daughter of a U.S. senator from South Carolina and married to the scion of a great plantation owner of the state, also a senator, was a passionate believer in states' rights. During the Civil War she kept a lively, sharp-eyed diary of life in the Confederacy, also expressive of sympathy for black people. *A Diary from Dixie* (1905) was reissued in an enlarged, revised text by Ben Ames Williams. The complete text (1981) of some 400,000 words was edited by C. Vann Woodward as *Mary Chesnut's Civil War* (1982) and awarded a Pulitzer Prize, although some historians questioned its authenticity since Mrs. Chesnut rewrote the work substantially during Reconstruction. *The Private Mary Chesnut* (1984), edited by Woodward and Elisabeth Muhlenfeld, prints the diary in the original words.

CHESNUTT, CHARLES W[ADDELL] (1858–1932), black author, best known for *The Conjure Woman* (1899), a series of dialect stories about incidents of slavery, told by an old black gardener to his Northern employers. This was followed by a biography of Frederick Douglass (1899), and a second collection of stories, *The Wife of His Youth* (1899), dealing with a free black's conflicting loyalties to the wife he had married in slavery and to the more refined black woman whom he later meets. His less successful novels are *The House Behind the Cedars* (1900), concerned with a light-complexioned black woman who is undecided whether to enjoy comfort as a white man's mistress or the sincere love of a black man; *The Marrow of Tradition* (1901), about the struggles of black and white half-sisters; and *The Colonel's Dream* (1905), telling of an idealist's unsuccessful attempt to root race hatred out of a Southern town.

CHESTER, GEORGE RANDOLPH (1869–1924), Ohio-born journalist and popular author, best known for *Get-Rich-Quick Wallingford* (1908), stories about a likable and ingenious rascal of high finance who, with his partner "Blackie" Daw, makes a fortune and just manages to stay on the right side of the law. Chester wrote many sequels, and George M. Cohan♦ successfully dramatized the character and some of the incidents in 1910.

CHEVALIER, MICHEL, see *Society, Manners, and Politics in the United States.*

Cheyenne Indians, Plains tribe♦ of the Algonquian family, inhabited a region near the Black Hills and then migrated to the headwaters of the Platte River, where in 1830 they divided into northern and southern bands. Treaties with the southern group were constantly violated, and, after an indiscriminate massacre by U.S. troops, there began the bitter war which culminated in Custer's annihilation of a great number of the Cheyenne in 1868, and the revenge of others, who joined Sitting Bull in the Battle of Little Big Horn. The Cheyenne are the subject of a study by G.B. Grinnell and figure in the novels of Hamlin Garland, in Howard Fast's *The Last Frontier,* and in a fanciful form in *Little Big Man* by Thomas Berger.

Chicago, free-verse poem by Carl Sandburg,♦ published in 1914 and collected in his *Chicago Poems* (1916). This ode to the city, which the poet accept as "wicked . . . crooked . . . brutal," but acclaims as proud . . . flinging magnetic curses amid the toil . . . fierce," is a celebration of its

> Laughing the stormy, husky, brawling laughter of Youth, half-naked, sweating, proud to be Hog Butcher, Tool Maker, Stacker of Wheat, Player with Railroad and Freight Handler to the Nation.

Chicago Daily News (1875–1978) won wide circulation as the first local paper to print the news of Hayes's nomination (1876). Although it was sensational and frequently issued extras, it was also known for its literary contributions, which included the "Sharps and Flats" column (1883–95) of Eugene Field. It was owned by Frank Knox (1931–44), who made it a Republican organ. After his death it became politically independent again, and in 1961 Marshall Field, Jr., became publisher and editor.

Chicago Times (1854–1918), known before and during the Civil War as an exponent of Southern Democracy because it denounced Lincoln, was considered a strong Copperhead paper. After the war, when it established special correspondents in Europe, even those who disliked its opinions read it for its news coverage. The *Times* was sold (1891) to Carter Harrison, and he and his heirs made it a radical Democratic paper. In 1895 it became the *Times-Herald,* merging with the Chicago *Herald,* which had been founded in 1881. Among the contributors was F.P. Dunne, who wrote for it many of his "Mr. Dooley" papers. After various changes of ownership and name, it was sold to and incorporated with Hearst's *Examiner* in 1918.

Chicago Tribune (1847–   ) became prominent under the editorship of Joseph Medill (1855–99),

who made it an ardently Republican journal when he became a founder of the party. It continued in the control of his descendants, of whom the best known was Colonel Robert Rutherford McCormick (1880–1955), a militaristic isolationist, also opposed to labor unions. Under him and thereafter the paper became sensational in handling news.

Chickasaw Indians, warlike tribe that originally inhabited northern Mississippi. During the colonial period they sided with the English against the French, and they continued to be friendly with the whites, aiding the U.S. against the Creek in 1793. They migrated to Oklahoma in accordance with later treaties, and served in the Confederate army. Ikkemotubbe♦ and other Indian characters in Faulkner's Yoknapatawpha saga belong to the tribe.

CHILD, LYDIA MARIA (1802–80), Massachusetts Abolitionist, whose *Appeal in Favor of that Class of Americans Called Africans* (1833) won many to the antislavery cause, as did her widely circulated *Correspondence* (1860) with the governor of Virginia. Her fiction, humane and didactic rather than creative, includes *Hobomok* (1824), a romance set in Massachusetts during Endecott's governorship and glorifying the "noble savage"; *The Rebels; or, Boston Before the Revolution* (1825), concerned with the Stamp Tax agitation; and *Philothea* (1836), a romance of classical Greece. She was editor of the *National Anti-Slavery Standard* (1841–43), but she lives for most of us now in two lines from her "Thanksgiving Day" (1857):

> Over the river and through the wood
> To grandmother's house we go.

She was a sister of Convers Francis.

Children of Adam, section of Whitman's *Leaves of Grass,* ♦ first published in the 1860 edition as "Enfans d'Adam," and given its present title in 1867. It contains 16 poems, all concerned with physical love, identifying the sexual impulse with the spiritual force of the universe. Among the poems in the section are "I Sing the Body Electric,"♦ "Spontaneous Me,"♦ "Once I Pass'd Through a Populous City,"♦ and "Facing West from California's Shores."♦ "Calamus,"♦ a section concerned with the spiritual love of man for man, forms a complement.

Children's Hour, The, poem by Longfellow,♦ published in *Birds of Passage* (1860). Ten jocund quatrains describe the nightly descent upon the poet's study of his three "blue-eyed banditti" daughters, "grave Alice, and laughing Allegra, and Edith with golden hair."

Children's Hour, The, play by Lillian Hellman. ♦

Children's literature in America first consisted of aids to piety, seemingly addressed to miniature adults. The earliest examples include Cotton's *Milk for Babes, Drawn out of the Breasts of Both Testaments* (1646) and the perennial *New England Primer* (1683?). In the colonial era most books for children were imported from England or, like the popular *Songs from the Nursery* (1719), were republished by American printers such as Isaiah Thomas. Since the early 19th century, many adult books, particularly humorous fiction and adventure tales, have been adopted by children, some of the earliest including works on American subjects by Irving, Cooper, and Dana. The trend away from the religious to the generally moral and didactic as suited to a child began in mid-19th-century works by Hawthorne and in the Peter Parley tales. The more modern desire to entertain as well as instruct is also found in the novels by Jacob Abbott. Other works of his time include new versions and additions to Old World fairy tales, folklore, and stories of chivalry. Popular verse included C.C. Moore's "A Visit from St. Nicholas," Sarah Josepha Hale's "Mary Had a Little Lamb," and Longfellow's poems. Separate traditions of works for boys and girls grew up, but several generations of both sexes made best sellers of Harris's Uncle Remus stories, Howard Pyle's tales of pirates and medieval heroes, Seton-Thompson's animal books, Palmer Cox's Brownies, Bennett's *Master Skylark,* Baum's Oz books, Gelett Burgess's Goops, the novels of Frank Stockton, and Thornton Burgess's stories of animal characters.

Among the most popular books for girls have been Mary Mapes Dodge's *Hans Brinker,* Louisa May Alcott's *Little Women,* Isabella Alden's Pansy series, Frances Baylor's *Juan and Juanita,* Harriet Lothrop's *Five Little Peppers,* Frances Hodgson Burnett's *Little Lord Fauntleroy,* Alice Hegan Rice's *Mrs. Wiggs of the Cabbage Patch,* Kate Douglas Wiggin's *Rebecca of Sunnybrook Farm,* L.M. Montgomery's *Anne of Green Gables,* Laura Ingalls Wilder's *Little House on the Prairie,* the American Girl series, and the novels about Nancy Drew by Edward Stratemeyer and his syndicate. Boy readers, reputedly enamored of dime novels and adult stories of manly adventures, like those by Jack London, also probably read many of these works, just as girls frequently read such popular books for boys as D.P. Thompson's *The Green Mountain Boys,* Trowbridge's *Cudjo's Cave,* the stories of Mayne Reid, Aldrich's *The Story of a Bad Boy,* Noah Brooks's *The Boy Emigrants,* Eggleston's *The Hoosier Schoolboy,* the popular series of C.C. Coffin and Horatio Alger, Clemens's *The Adventures of Tom Sawyer* and *Adventures of Huckleberry Finn,* Tarkington's *Penrod,* and the various series concerned with the Rover Boys, Tom Swift, Frank Merriwell, and the Hardy Boys.

Works in these veins continue popular, but later vogues include the flashily illustrated and diverse subjects of so-called comic books; highly imaginative science fiction novels with fantastic heroes like Tarzan and some supermen; quieter fantasies; histories, biographies, and studies of adult subjects (including scientific concepts and frank treatments of social and sexual issues), generally well written and illustrated for young people. Among the most popular of the many picture books for very young children are *The Little Engine That Could* (1930), Dorothy Kunhardt's *Pat the Bunny* (1942), and Margaret Wise Brown's *Goodnight Moon* (1947). Popular authors who write just for children include Dr. Seuss (Theodore Geisel), Maurice Sendak (equally noted for his illustrations), Walter Farley, the creator of a series about a black stallion, Walter Dean Myers, and, notable for nonfiction, Patricia Lauber and Seymour Simon. Those who also write for adults include Asimov, Bemelmans, Pearl Buck, Ray Bradbury, Mary Ellen Chase, Marchette Chute, Howard Fast, Rachel Field, Esther Forbes, Will James, MacKinlay Kantor, Ursula K. Le Guin, Phyllis McGinley, Sandburg, Saroyan, Steinbeck, Thurber, Van Loon, and E.B. White. Each year since 1921 the book judged best receives the Newbery Medal, named for an 18th-century chapbook publisher, and since 1938 the work considered to have the best illustrations receives a Caldecott Medal. Since *The Children's Magazine* (1789) there have been many periodicals edited exclusively for children, including *The Youth's Companion* (1827–1929), *Parley's Magazine* (1833–41), *Merry's Museum for Boys and Girls* (1841–72), *St. Nicholas* (1873–1940), *American Boy* (1899–1941), *Boy's Life* (1911–), *Highlights for Children* (1946–), *Cricket* (1973–), and *Cobblestone* (1980–).

Chillingworth, ROGER, character in *The Scarlet Letter.*◆

Chinese Nightingale, The: *A Song in Chinese Tapestries,* poem by Vachel Lindsay.◆ the title piece of a book (1917).

During a night visit to his friend Chang, a Chinese laundryman of San Francisco, the poet dreams of a "gray small bird" perched on Chang's wrist, and "a Chinese lady of high degree" who stands "on the snowy table wide," singing to the laundryman of their idyllic love in China, ages before. Chang is too busy to reply, but the nightingale sings ("I remember, I remember That Spring came on forever . . . "), evoking a delicate picture of ancient China, strongly contrasted with the present surroundings of Chang and the musing poet.

Chingachgook, Indian chieftain also known as John Mohegan, character in Cooper's Leather-Stocking Tales.◆

Chinook language, jargon developed by traders with the Chinook Indians, a Pacific Coast tribe, includes English, Canadian French, and Indian words.

Chippewa Indians, see *Ojibway Indians.*

Chisholm Trail, from the Red River in eastern Texas to Southern Kansas, was named for a half-breed Cherokee trader and government agent, Jesse Chisholm. For more than 20 years following the Civil War, it furnished owners of Texas range cattle with an outlet to the Indian Territory and successive railheads of the westward-building railways. *The Old Chisholm Trail* is a famous cowboy ballad.

Chita: *A Memory of Last Island,* tale by Lafcadio Hearn,♦ published in 1889. A narrative of the destruction of "Last Island" in the Gulf of Mexico by a tidal wave (1856), it is essentially a series of vivid descriptions unified by its account of a lost child.

CHIVERS, THOMAS HOLLEY (1809–58), born in Georgia, early abandoned medicine for a career as author, publishing *The Path of Sorrow* (1832), poems about his unhappy first marriage; *Conrad and Eudora* (1834), a verse drama based on the Kentucky Tragedy♦; and *Nacoochee* (1837), which has a preface on the transcendental nature of poetry. He is principally known for his association with Poe (1840–49), although the two were never actually friends. Charges of plagiarism followed the publication of Chivers's *Eonchs of Ruby* (1851), to which he replied with counter charges, and critics believe that his previously published "Isadore" and other poems influenced the writing of "The Raven" and "Ulalume." The title poem of *The Lost Pleiad* (1845) and "To Allegra Florence in Heaven" are elegies for his daughter, and after the death of three other children Chivers became increasingly interested in various mystical movements, writing a prose work on the *Search After Truth; or, A New Revelation of the Psycho-Physiological Nature of Man* (1848). Several later volumes of poetry exhibit his sentimentality, lack of critical judgment, and finally his unbalanced mind.

Choctaw Indians, agricultural tribe of southern Mississippi, who served against the British in the French and Indian Wars and in the Revolution. They later aided the U.S. against the Creek, and after ceding their lands to the national government moved to Oklahoma. The Choctaw of Louisiana inspired affectionate tributes in the poetry of the brothers Adrien Rouquette♦ and François Rouquette.♦

Choir Invisible, *The,* romance by J.L. Allen,♦ published as *John Gray* (1893) and revised under its present title (1897).

CHOPIN, KATE [O'FLAHERTY] (1851–1904), St. Louis author, from her marriage to a Louisi-

ana Creole until his death (1882) lived in New Orleans and on a Louisiana cotton plantation. Returning to her native city, she began to write tales for children and the local-color stories for which she is noted. *At Fault* (1890) is an undistinguished novel of Creole life in the Cane River section of central Louisiana. Her importance in the local-color movement depends primarily, however, on her interpretations of Creole and Cajun life in her collections of short stories and anecdotes, *Bayou Folk*♦ (1894) and *A Night in Acadie* (1897). These carefully polished tales are delicately objective in treatment and marked by a poignant restraint of which perhaps the greatest example is "Désirée's Baby" in the former volume. Mrs. Chopin's last novel, *The Awakening* (1899), caused a storm of criticism that ended her literary career because readers of the time were shocked not only by the story of a Southern lady's revolt against her husband and love of a young man but by the frank sense of sexuality.

Chorus Line, *A,* musical play about the lives of diverse men and women trying out for a Broadway musical. Conceived, choreographed, and directed by Michael Bennett, with a book by James Kirkwood♦ and Nicholas Dante, music by Marvin Hamlisch, and lyrics by Edward Kleban, it was a great success when first produced in 1975 and won a Pulitzer Prize for drama. It enjoyed the longest run of a production on Broadway: 5,137 performances over a 15-year period.

Christadelphians, members of a lay movement, sometimes called Thomasites after their English-born founder John Thomas (1805–71), who repudiated the name Christian as associated with anti-Christian beliefs and attempted to revive the early apostolic faith. They expect a second coming of Jesus to establish a theocracy centered at Jerusalem. Adherents have shrunk from 15,000 in 1960 to 5000 in 1980.

Christian Disciple, *The* (1813–69), Boston monthly magazine, became a bimonthly in 1819. The title was retained until 1823, when it became *The Christian Examiner.* Successively edited by Noah Worcester, Henry Ware, Jr., J.G. Palfrey, William Ware, and E.E. Hale, this Unitarian organ was the leading religious review of its time. In 1857 it became more liberal, espousing the Transcendentalist movement, but after its removal to New York (1866) its theological views were conservative and its influence declined.

Christian Examiner, *The, see Christian Disciple.*

Christian Philosopher, *The,* essay by Cotton Mather,♦ published in 1721, is a summary of scientific knowledge and an early attempt to reconcile religion and science. Marked not only by scientific observation but a poetic religious feeling, it argues that the beauty and wonder of the world are proof of an all-powerful benevolent creator, and that scientific research is to be used as a source of understanding these qualities.

Christian Science, religion founded upon principles formulated by Mary Baker Eddy♦ from New Testament teachings, in her book *Science and Health with Key to the Scriptures*♦ (1875). According to this text, science is Christ's revelation of the Eternal Mind, the source of all being, and his message is that the power of Mind (Truth, God, Spirit) overcomes illusions of sin, sickness, and death. The followers of Christian Science attempt to end the illusory conflict of mind and body by unceasing prayer and "the understanding of Truth and Love," which will dispel the belief in disease or the supposition that any evil can emanate from God. The Church of Christ, Scientist, founded at Boston (1879), since 1892 has been known as the Mother Church. Other churches are self-governing and self-supporting, but all accept Mrs. Eddy's tenets. The churches do not have pastors, and services are conducted by two persons, one reading from the Scriptures, the other from *Science and Health.*

Christian Science Monitor, The (1908–), daily newspaper founded in Boston by Mary Baker Eddy, partly as a protest against yellow journalism. It has never been a proselytizing organ nor emphasized Church news, but it is issued by the Church's Publishing Society and adheres to the founder's policy of avoiding emphasis on crime, disaster, and sensations. It is known for cultural features and good national and international coverage.

Christian Union, The, see *Outlook.*

Christmas, Joe, character in Faulkner's novel *Light in August.*♦

Christopher Caustic, pseudonym of T.G. Fessenden.♦

Christus: A Mystery, dramatic poem by Longfellow,♦ published in 1872, for the first time brought together *The Divine Tragedy,*♦ *The Golden Legend,*♦ and *The New England Tragedies,*♦ which were placed in the order suggested in the author's notebook: "Christus, a dramatic poem, in three parts: Part First. The Times of Christ (Hope). Part Second. The Middle Ages (Faith). Part Third. The Present (Charity)." *The Divine Tragedy* is a reworking in dramatic form of Biblical themes in the structural sequence of a cycle of medieval miracle plays. *The Golden Legend* presents a dramatic miracle cycle of nine parts dealing with the lives of saints. *The New England Tragedies* dramatizes two episodes of colonial New England history. Since the final section, dealing with the fanaticism of decadent Puritanism, is not a happy choice of subject, the theme is sometimes considered confused and irresolute.

CHRISTY, Edwin P. (1815–62), actor and singer, whose minstrel show,♦ organized in the early 1840s as the Virginia Minstrels and later known as Christy's Minstrels, toured the U.S. and England, receiving popular acclaim and being widely imitated. Christy himself performed as interlocutor, and his singing of the minstrel songs of Stephen Foster, which were first published under Christy's name, was partly responsible for their early popularity.

CHURCH, Benjamin (1639–1718), officer in King Philip's War, who described his experiences in a book compiled by his son Thomas Church.♦

CHURCH, Benjamin (1734–76), Massachusetts author, while supposed to be working for the Whigs was suspected of writing Loyalist answers to his own political essays. Tried by a Revolutionary court-martial (1775), he was found guilty of "holding criminal correspondence with the enemy." Among his publications were *The Times* (1765), a verse satire on the Stamp Act, and *An Oration To Commemorate the Bloody Tragedy of the Fifth of March, 1770* (1773). He was the grandson of the elder Benjamin Church.

CHURCH, Thomas (1673–1748), was the son of Benjamin Church, a soldier in King Philip's War, from whose notes he wrote *Entertaining Passages Relating to Philip's War . . .* (1716), a frank, vivid, bluff narrative of the adventures of Indian warfare.

Church of England, see *Protestant Episcopal Church.*

Churches Quarrel Espoused, The, controversial work by John Wise,♦ was published in 1710 as an answer to the *Questions and Proposals* (1705) propounded by Increase and Cotton Mather in their project to substitute a central association of clergy for the system of lay-controlled independent churches. With earnest logic and annihilating invective, Wise shows the danger or folly of each proposal, which he opposes with the theory of democracy. Because its democratic theme transcends the specific issues, the book was republished (1772) and widely read prior to the Revolution and again before the Civil War.

CHURCHILL, Winston (1871–1947), born in St. Louis, graduated from Annapolis (1894), and during his career as author lived mainly in New Hampshire. *The Celebrity: An Episode* (1898) is an amusing social satire, but with *Richard Carvel*♦ (1899), a Revolutionary romance, he began his serious consideration of historic forces and ideals in the nation's background. *The Crisis*♦ (1901), set in St. Louis, deals with society and politics before and during the Civil War, while *The Crossing*♦ (1904), considered his finest work, is a romance concerned with the settling of

Kentucky and the part the frontier played in the Revolution. From this celebration of the romantic aspects of manifest destiny and the heroism of early Americans, Churchill turned to contemporary politics, although his methods continued to be those of the popular romancer; most of his character portraits were superficial and his handling of plot was arbitrary. *Coniston*♦ (1906), concerned with ethical conflicts in New England politics of the mid-19th century, has for its central figure Jethro Bass, Churchill's most striking character. *Mr. Crewe's Career*♦ (1908) tells of a railroad monopoly's attempt to dominate a state government, and *A Far Country* (1915) is a story of the conflict of private interests with public-spirited idealism in a Midwestern city. This interest also resulted in the author's participation in New Hampshire politics, and he became a member of the state legislature and a candidate for the governorship. His other novels include *A Modern Chronicle* (1910), concerned with the problem of divorce; *The Inside of the Cup* (1913), dealing with the need of religion to adapt itself to modern conditions; and *The Dwelling Place of Light* (1917), the story of a New England factory strike. *Dr. Jonathan* (1919) is a play set in a New England mill town, intended to show that World War I stimulated the extension of industrial democracy. Churchill's only subsequent writing is *The Uncharted Way* (1940), a profession of religious belief, combining faith in self-abnegating Christian love with an evolutionary hypothesis concerning an afterlife.

Chuzzlewit, MARTIN, see *Martin Chuzzlewit.*

CIARDI, JOHN (1916–85), born in Boston, educated at Bates and Tufts, taught English at Harvard and Rutgers, and was poetry editor (1956–72) of *The Saturday Review.* His own poetry, often marked by vernacular diction and homely wit, includes *Homeward to America* (1940); *Other Skies* (1947); *Live Another Day* (1949); *From Time to Time* (1951); *As If, Poems New and Selected* (1955); *I Marry You* (1958), love poems; *In Fact* (1963); and *Lives of X* (1971), about his youth. He also wrote verse, often humorous or nonsensical, for children. He translated Dante's *Inferno* (1954). *Dialogue with an Audience* (1963) and *Fast and Slow* (1975) are collections of essays.

Cibola, see *Zuñi Indians.*

Cimarron, novel by Edna Ferber.♦

Cincinnati, Society of the, fraternal organization formed by officers of the disbanding Continental army (1783). Washington and Hamilton were the first presidents. It was attacked as being an aristocratic military order, and Tammany societies were founded partly to oppose it. The society figures in contemporary literature, e.g. *Modern Chivalry.* Although it has declined in

importance, it continues to exist as an organization of descendants of the founders.

Circuit Rider, *The,* novel by Edward Eggleston.♦

Circus, traveling company of acrobats, clowns, and animals, who usually perform in tents. The modern circus originated in the English equestrian troupes of the late 18th century, and the first of these to visit the U.S. was the Rickett's Circus, which came to New York in 1795. The distinctive American type of traveling tent show had developed by 1850, when American troupes were already touring Europe. Famous clowns and impresarios have included John Robinson, Adam Forepaugh, the Sells brothers, Dan Rice, James A. Bailey, and the Ringling brothers, while P.T. Barnum's "greatest show on earth," the most spectacular development of circus showmanship, was founded in 1871 and combined with that of Bailey in 1881. Since the time of Dan Rice, who was the last of the great "talking clowns" to perform in tents of moderate size, the circus has been devoted to large-scale spectacles, pantomimic humor, equestrian and aerial acrobatics, menagerie and freak exhibitions, and such special features as Wild West shows patterned after that of Buffalo Bill. Nineteenth-century circuses appear often in literature, including the boys' stories *Toby Tyler* by J.O. Kaler and *Chad Hanna* by Walter Edmonds.

Cisco Kid, character in O. Henry's "The Caballero's Way" of *Heart of the West,* who was transmuted into an almost mythic figure, a romantic Latin cowboy and Robin Hood of the U.S. Southwest, through a series of films and television serials.

City in the Sea, *The,* poem by Poe.♦

Civil Disobedience, essay by Thoreau,♦ originally delivered as a lecture and first printed as "Resistance to Civil Government" in Elizabeth Peabody's *Aesthetic Papers* (1849).

Asserting that "That government is best which governs not at all" and that "Government is at best but an expedient," the author points to such injustices and abuses as the prosecution of the Mexican War, the treatment of native Indians, and the institution of slavery. To cooperate with government, even to the extent of paying taxes, he says, is to condone its crimes and participate in them, and an "honest man" must "withdraw from this co-partnership." Individual conscience, not law, is the moral arbiter; "under a government which imprisons any unjustly, the true place for a just man is also a prison." He cites his own refusal to pay a tithing or poll tax, in order "to refuse allegiance to the State, to withdraw and stand aloof from it effectually." He will participate only in those governmental activities that he approves:

any man more right than his neighbors constitutes a majority of one already. . . . There will never be a really free and enlightened State until the State comes to recognize the individual as a higher and independent power, from which all its own power and authority are derived. . . .

Civil War, the conflict (1861–65) between the Northern states which remained in the Union and the Southern states which seceded to form the Confederacy. The underlying causes became more pronounced after the Missouri Compromise (1820) in the hostility that developed from the two fundamentally different economic and social systems of the U.S. The South, with its large plantations, staple crops, and institution of slavery, inevitably came into conflict with the free industrial and commercial North. States'-rights doctrines and tariff questions further complicated these differences. Clay, Webster, Calhoun, and others attempted solutions, but after the Compromise of 1850 and the Kansas-Nebraska bill, each side became more radical. Following Lincoln's election, the Southern states feared a hostile majority in Congress, and resorted to secession. The Confederacy was organized, South Carolina seized Fort Sumter (April 12, 1861), and the war began. Northern forces, beginning an advance on Richmond, the Confederate capital, were defeated in the first Battle of Bull Run (July 1861), although the Southerners failed to follow up this victory, while the North established a fairly successful blockade of Southern ports. In 1862 each side continued without decisive gains, Grant's forces taking much ground in the West, although at Shiloh (April 1862) he suffered severe losses. New Orleans was captured (May 1862), and the Union army had some success in eastern Tennessee and Kentucky. McClellan launched the Peninsular Campaign to take Richmond, which ended in failure in the Seven Days' Battles (June–July, 1862) after Stonewall Jackson prevented McDowell from joining McClellan. Under Jackson and Lee, the Confederate forces were again victorious at Bull Run (Aug. 30, 1862). Lee was checked in his march northward at Antietam (Sept. 1862), but Burnside's Union army was stopped in its advance on Richmond at the Battle of Fredericksburg (Dec. 13, 1862). The Emancipation Proclamation was issued to take effect in January 1863, and the beginning of that year saw the death of Jackson at Chancellorsville (May 1863), where the new drive on Richmond was stopped. Lee then made a Northern campaign, which ended disastrously at Gettysburg (July 1863), the most decisive battle of the war. The South was split by Grant's capture of Vicksburg (July 4, 1863), Rosecrans's seizure of Tennessee, and Banks's victories in Louisiana, although in September the Confederates won the bloody battle of Chickamauga. In 1864 Grant became commander in chief of the Union forces, continuing in command despite tremendous losses in the

Battle of the Wilderness (May 1864). Sherman captured Atlanta (Sept. 3, 1864) and began his devastating march to the sea. Meanwhile the Southern cruiser *Alabama* was defeated by the *Kearsarge* and the Confederacy was obviously doomed at sea and on land. On April 9, 1865, Lee surrendered to Grant at Appomattox. A few days later Lincoln was assassinated, and the settlement of the effects of the war, the Reconstruction, fell into other hands.

A great many of the generals wrote memoirs, as did numberless plainer soldiers and other participants in the war. From the outbreak of hostilities the war began to generate a great variety of literature. In the beginning, poetry ranged from popular songs such as "The Battle Hymn of Republic" and "Tramp, Tramp, Tramp" of the Union and "Maryland, My Maryland" of the Confederacy to serious works like H.H. Brownell's *Lyrics of a Day* (1864) and *War Lyrics* (1866), Lowell's *Biglow Papers, Second Series* (1867), Melville's *Battle-Pieces* (1866), Whitman's *Drum-Taps* (1865), and Whittier's *In War Time* (1864) in the North, and Simms's *War Poetry of the South* (1866), gathering Hayne's "Vicksburg—A Ballad" and other such expressions of the Confederates.

Civilization in the United States: First and Last Impressions of America, four essays by Matthew Arnold,♦ published in 1888.

"General Grant: An Estimate," written after reading Grant's memoirs, is a lengthy biographical discussion of "a man of sterling good-sense as well as of the firmest resolution. . . ." "A Word about America" deals with Arnold's view of the U.S. before his visits: "America has, like us, industry and conduct, and, what we have not, equality; but . . . America has . . . a middle class of stunted religion, intellect, and manners, and American civilization suffers accordingly." "A Word More about America," written after his first visit, mainly appraises political and social institutions, which, he finds, fit the condition of the people "like an excellent suit of clothes." "Civilization in the United States" deals with weaknesses of American culture on the "human" side. Despite the "inflated, self-congratulatory sentiment of most Americans," their nation lacks what is "interesting" in civilization. "The great sources of the interesting are distinction (or the elevated) and beauty."

CLAFLIN, Tennessee, see *Woodhull, V.*

CLAMPITT, Amy (1920–94), poet. A native of New Providence, Iowa, a region at the center of some of her richest verse, Clampitt graduated from Grinnell College. She describes herself as one of a "late blooming family." In the later 1970s her poems began to be published in *The New Yorker,* and in 1983 appeared *The Kingfisher,* a work at once perceived as that of a mature and various talent. Clampitt writes about growing up in rural Iowa, about the Maine coast, about the life of Keats. Later collections are *What the Light Was Like* (1985), *Archaic Figure* (1987), *Westward* (1990), and *A Silence Opens* (1994).

Clansman, The, novel by Thomas Dixon, ♦ published in 1905 as the second volume of a trilogy including *The Leopard's Spots* (1902) and *The Traitor* (1907), melodramatic and extremist Southern depictions of the Reconstruction era, violently racist in their characterizations of blacks, and laudatory of the Ku Klux Klan as potential saviors of the old Confederate region. The book was very popular, as was Dixon's dramatization for touring companies (1905–6). The work was adapted by D.W. Griffith for his film *The Birth of a Nation* (1915).

CLAPP, HENRY (1814–75), New York journalist, as the leader of the group which gathered at Pfaff's Cellar♦ was called "the king of Bohemia." He founded and edited the *Saturday Press,* ♦ to whose staff he brought Aldrich, Fitz-James O'Brien, and William Winter. He championed *Leaves of Grass,* translated Fourier, and wrote books including *The Pioneer; or, Leaves from an Editor's Portfolio* (1846). Figaro was his pseudonym.

CLAPPE, LOUISE AMELIA KNAPP SMITH (1819–1906), came to California from her native Massachusetts with her husband in 1849, and, over the pseudonym Dame Shirley, wrote letters (1851–52), ostensibly to her sister, which give a witty, feminine view of the gold rush. They were issued in San Francisco's *Pioneer Magazine* (1854–55) and as a book, *The Shirley Letters,* in 1922.

CLARE, ADA, pseudonym of Jane McElheney (1836–74), whose notoriety as a beauty, and as the "queen of Bohemia" at Pfaff's Cellar, ♦ was responsible for the popularity of her passionate poetry and fiction in various New York periodicals. After the decline of the group at Pfaff's, she became an actress.

Clarel: A Poem and Pilgrimage in the Holy Land, poem in 150 cantos by Melville, ♦ published in two volumes in 1876. Using the setting he observed on a trip to Palestine (1857), Melville treats the problems of a modern culture not based on religion, and the resultant spiritual and psychological turmoil of its peoples. The narrative describes the experiences of a young American theological student, Clarel, who, while visiting Jerusalem, falls in love with Ruth, a Zionist, and recounts his travels with various pilgrims to the great sites of the region. His fellows include a man deformed in body and spirit who doubts his Roman Catholic faith, an Anglican clergyman with easy belief in the goodness of man and nature, a cynic who feels the emulation of Christ

leads but to destruction, an apostate Jew whose scientism is used to attack religion, and an American of great moral qualities and aesthetic sensitivity but without clear commitments. Despite lengthy philosophic conversations, Clarel is unable to resolve his religious uncertainties, and he returns on Ash Wednesday to the grief of finding Ruth dead.

Clari; or, The Maid of Milan, play by J.H. Payne, ♦ produced and published at London (1823), was adapted from a French ballet-pantomime. Clari, an Italian country girl, is seduced by a duke, with whom she lives until a longing for home gives her courage to break the tie. At the end, the duke penitently marries her. The play is famous for the heroine's nostalgic song, "Home, Sweet Home," which Payne wrote to music arranged from a Sicilian air by Sir Henry Rowley Bishop (1786–1855).

CLARK, CHARLES HEBER (1841–1915), Maryland-born journalist in Philadelphia, whose literary reputation rested mainly on his first book, *Out of the Hurly-Burly* (1874), farcical sketches of life in a suburban town. *Elbow-Room* (1876), subtitled "a novel without a plot," is in the same vein, but his later novel *The Quakeress* (1905), the short story collection *By the Bend in the River* (1914), and other works are more regular in form and depend on local color and character rather than humor. He used the pseudonym Max Adeler.

CLARK, ELEANOR (1913–   ), author of *Rome and a Villa* (1952) and *The Oysters of Locmariaquer* (1964), local-color studies summoning up the sense of the Italian capital and of Brittany respectively. Twenty years later she wrote about her trip through the Sahara, *Tamrart* (1984). She also wrote *Eyes, Etc.* (1977), about her loss of vision, and three novels: *The Bitter Box* (1946), *Baldur's Gate* (1971), and *Gloria Mundi* (1979). She was long married to Robert Penn Warren.

CLARK, GEORGE ROGERS (1752–1818), Virginia soldier, served under Lord Dunmore against the Ohio Indians, was a surveyor for the Ohio Company, and helped secure his colony's sovereignty over Kentucky and Ohio. During the Revolutionary War, he led a campaign that captured Kaskaskia and Vincennes (1778–79), establishing American control of the Old Northwest. His narrative of these events is contained in M.M. Quaife's *The Capture of Old Vincennes* (1927). He was the brother of the explorer William Clark and figures in many historical novels, including Bird's *Nick of the Woods,* ♦ D.P. Thompson's *The Rangers,* M. Thompson's *Alice of Old Vincennes,* ♦ Churchill's *The Crossing,* ♦ and Harold Sinclair's *Westward the Tide.*

CLARK, LEWIS GAYLORD (1808–73), edited *The Knickerbocker Magazine* (1834–61), the outstanding literary periodical of its time. He edited *The Knickerbocker Sketch-Book* (1845), which contained contributions by Irving, and wrote *Knick-Knacks from an Editor's Table* (1852), an urbane, quietly humorous work.

WILLIS GAYLORD CLARK (1808–41), his twin, was co-editor of *The Knickerbocker Magazine*. His humorous contributions were collected as *Literary Remains . . . Including the Ollipodiana* (1844). The *Letters* of the brothers was published in 1940.

CLARK, WALTER VAN TILBURG (1909–71), born in Maine, reared in Nevada, was a professor of English and the author of *The Ox-Bow Incident*♦ (1940), a psychological novel about a lynching in Nevada's cattle country; *The City of Trembling Leaves* (1945; in England *Tim Hazard*, 1951), about a Reno boy whose ambition is to be a composer; and *The Track of the Cat*♦ (1949), a symbolic tale of hunting a panther in the Sierra. *The Watchful Gods* (1950) collects stories.

CLARK, WILLIAM (1770–1838), served in the U.S. army during campaigns against the Indians, and was commissioned by Jefferson to be co-commander of the Lewis and Clark expedition (1803–6) (see *Lewis, Meriwether*). He later headed independent surveys, notably one of the Yellowstone River, and was governor of Missouri Territory (1813–21), serving the rest of his life as Superintendent of Indian Affairs. He was the brother of George Rogers Clark.

CLARKE, JAMES FREEMAN (1810–88), Massachusetts Unitarian and liberal leader, whose first church was at Louisville, Ky. There he edited *The Western Messenger* (1836–39). For the following 40 years he was a Unitarian pastor at Boston, where he wrote *The Christian Doctrine of Prayer* (1854), *Ten Great Religions* (1871–83), *Common Sense in Religion* (1874), *Essentials and Non-Essentials in Religion* (1878), and *Self-Culture* (1880). He collaborated with Emerson and W.H. Channing on a memoir of Margaret Fuller (1852). To his *Hymn Book for the Church of the Disciples* (1844, enlarged 1852), he contributed ten original works.

CLARKE, JOHN (1609–76), was on the side of Anne Hutchinson in the Boston Antinomian dispute (1637), and two years later helped to found Newport, R.I., where he served as physician and Baptist minister. His *Ill News from New England* (1652) attacked the intolerance of the Massachusetts leaders in their suppression of religious liberty, and supplemented the writings of his friend Roger Williams.

CLARKE, MCDONALD (1798–1842), "the mad poet" of Broadway, was befriended by Halleck, who made him the subject of his humorous poem "The Discarded." Clarke is remembered for the couplet, "Now twilight lets her curtain down And pins it with a star." One volume containing verse was *Elixir of Moonshine by the Mad Poet* (1822).

Clark's Field, novel by Robert Herrick,♦ published in 1914.

CLAVERS, MRS. MARY, pseudonym of Caroline Kirkland. ♦

Claypoole's American Daily Advertiser, see *Pennsylvania Packet.*

Clean, Well-Lighted Place, A, story by Hemingway, published in *Winner Take Nothing.* ♦

At a sidewalk table of a Spanish café an old, deaf man sits drinking brandy late at night as the two waiters discuss him, the older one with sympathy because he too is lonely, fearful, confident of nothing, and also in need of the security of a clean, well-lighted place.

CLEMENS, JEREMIAH (1814–65), Alabama novelist, whose historical fiction includes *Bernard Lile* (1856), a story of the Mexican War; *The Rivals* (1860), about Burr and Hamilton; and *Tobias Wilson* (1865), a story of the Civil War.

CLEMENS, SAMUEL LANGHORNE (1835–1910), born in Florida, Mo., was the son of a Virginian imbued with the frontier spirit and grandiose dreams of easy wealth, who had married in Kentucky and spent the rest of his life in a restless search for profits from land speculation. The family settled in Hannibal, Mo. (1839), where Samuel grew up under the influence of this attitude, and passed the adventurous boyhood and youth that he recalls in *Tom Sawyer* and *Huckleberry Finn*. After his father's death (1847), he left school to be apprenticed to a printer, and was soon writing for his brother Orion's newspaper. He was a journeyman printer in the East and Middle West (1853–54), and in 1856 planned to seek his fortune in South America, but gave up this idea to become a steamboat pilot on the Mississippi, a position that he considered the most important discipline of his life. When the Civil War began, the riverboats ceased operation, and, after a brief trial of soldiering with a group of Confederate volunteers, Clemens went to Nevada with his brother, who had been appointed secretary to the governor. In *Roughing It* he describes the trip west and his subsequent adventures as miner and journalist. After he joined the staff of the Virginia City *Territorial Enterprise* (1862), he adopted the pseudonym Mark Twain,♦ by which he was thereafter known, and began his career as a journalistic humorist in the frontier tradition. His articles of the time are collected in *Mark Twain of the* Enterprise (1957).

During this period he met Artemus Ward and

others who encouraged his work, collaborated with Bret Harte in San Francisco, and wrote "The Celebrated Jumping Frog" ♦ sketch (1865), which won him immediate recognition. He increased his popularity with letters and lectures about his trip to the Sandwich Islands, went east to lecture, published *The Celebrated Jumping Frog of Calaveras County and Other Sketches* (1867), and made the tour of the Mediterranean and the Holy Land that he describes in *The Innocents Abroad* ♦ (1869), a humorous narrative that assured his position as a leading author and shows his typical American irreverence for the classic and the antique. In 1870 Clemens married Olivia Langdon, with whom he settled in Hartford, Conn. The effect of this marriage upon his career has been responsible for two divergent interpretations of his work. Mrs. Clemens belonged to a genteel, conservative society, and it has been claimed (mainly by Van Wyck Brooks) that the puritanical and materialistic surroundings into which Clemens was thrust frustrated his potential creative force for fierce revolt and satire. Others (principally Bernard De Voto) posit the idea that Clemens began as a frontier humorist and storyteller, and that his later work shows the unthwarted development of these essential talents.

In *Roughing It* (1872) he continues the method of *The Innocents Abroad,* seasoning the realistic account of adventure with humorous exaggerations in his highly personal idiom. Next he collaborated with C.D. Warner in *The Gilded Age* ♦ (1873), a satirical novel of post-Civil War boom times that gave a name to the era. *A Tramp Abroad* ♦ (1880) is another travel narrative, this time of a walking trip through the Black Forest and the Alps. England during the reign of Edward VI is the scene of *The Prince and the Pauper* ♦ (1882), while *A Connecticut Yankee in King Arthur's Court* ♦ (1889) is a realistic-satirical fantasy of Arthurian England. During this period, however, Clemens was dealing with the background of his own early life in what are generally considered the most significant of his characteristically American works. In *The Adventures of Tom Sawyer* ♦ (1876) he presents a nostalgic tale of boyish adventure in a Mississippi town and the Valley; and in *Life on the Mississippi* ♦ (1883) and *Adventures of Huckleberry Finn* ♦ (1884) he celebrates the flowering of Mississippi Valley frontier civilization, in terms of its own pungent tall talk and picaresque adventure.

External events soon interfered with the even flow of Clemens's creative activity. During his residence in Hartford, he had been a partner in the publishing firm of Charles L. Webster and Company, which reaped a fortune through the sale of Grant's *Memoirs* and Clemens's own writings, but bad publishing ventures and the investment of $200,000 in an unperfected typesetting machine drove him into bankruptcy (1894). To discharge his debts he made a lecturing tour of the world, although he had come to dislike lec-

turing, and the record of this tour, *Following the Equator* ♦ (1897), has an undercurrent of bitterness not found in his earlier travel books. During this decade, although he wrote *The Tragedy of Pudd'nhead Wilson* ♦ (1894) and the *Personal Recollections of Joan of Arc* ♦ (1896), most of his work is uneven in quality, and *The American Claimant* ♦ (1892), *Tom Sawyer Abroad* ♦ (1894), and *Tom Sawyer, Detective* ♦ (1896) are feeble echoes of earlier work. In 1898 he finished paying off his debts, but his writings show that the strain of pessimism he formerly repressed was now dominating his mind. *The Man That Corrupted Hadleyburg* (1900), *What Is Man?* ♦ (1906), and *The Mysterious Stranger* ♦ (1916) demonstrate this attitude. He continued to travel widely, lectured and wrote articles on contemporary events and such controversial works as *Christian Science* (1907) and *Is Shakespeare Dead?* (1909), but his bitterness was deepened by the loss of his wife and two daughters. His pessimism was perhaps no more profound than the optimism of his own Colonel Sellers, but his feeling that it was too mordant for publication caused him to instruct that certain of his works be published posthumously.

Since 1906 he had been engaged in dictating his autobiography to his secretary, A.B. Paine, who later became the first Literary Editor of the Mark Twain Estate, and issued a collection of *Letters* (1917), the authorized biography (3 vols., 1912), and the *Autobiography* (1924). The second editor, Bernard De Voto, edited volumes of materials from the papers left by Clemens, including *Letters from the Earth* (1963). Drawing on the same sources, the third editor, Dixon Wecter, collected *The Love Letters of Mark Twain* (1949); and the fourth editor, Henry Nash Smith, edited with William M. Gibson, *Mark Twain–Howells Letters* (2 vols., 1960). A scholarly edition of his *Works* began publication by the University of California Press in 1972, which also began issuing (1967) a scholarly edition of his previously unpublished *Papers,* most of whose originals are in the University's Bancroft Library.

An important early estimate of his work is *My Mark Twain: Reminiscences and Criticisms* (1910), by his friend and adviser Howells. The prevalent critical attitude has come to consider Clemens's most distinctive work as summing up the tradition of Western humor and frontier realism. Beginning as a journalist, he assumed the method and point of view of popular literature in the U.S., maintaining the personal anecdotal style that he used also in his capacity of comic lecturer. In travel books, he digresses easily from factual narrative to humorous exaggeration and burlesque. The novels are episodic or autobiographical, and not formed by any larger structural concepts. He wrote in the authentic native idiom, exuberantly and irreverently, but underlying the humor was a vigorous desire for social justice and a pervasive equalitarian attitude. The romantic idealism of *Joan of Arc,* the bitter satire of feudal tyranny in *A Connecticut Yankee*, the appreciation of human values in *Huckleberry Finn*, and the sense of epic sweep in *Life on the Mississippi* establish Clemens's place in American letters as an artist of broad understanding and vital, although uneven and sometimes misdirected, achievement.

Clements Library (THE WILLIAM L. CLEMENTS LIBRARY OF AMERICANA), donated to the University of Michigan (1923), is a collection of rare books and manuscripts on early America and the Revolution. R.G. Adams was the director (1923–51). Carl Van Doren's *Secret History of the American Revolution* is based on the manuscript materials there.

CLIFFTON, WILLIAM (1772–99), Pennsylvania poet, whose conservative political views in favor of England and against free-thinking France appear in *The Group: or, An Elegant Representation* (1796), an attack on Gallatin and defense of Jay's Treaty. His poems were collected in 1800.

Clithero Edny, see *Edgar Huntly.*

Clock Without Hands, novel by Carson McCullers,♦ published in 1961.

Treating the disintegration of individual human lives and of the way of life in the Old South, the story occurs during the final 15 months of a small-town Georgia druggist, dying of leukemia. J.T. Malone's last days are linked with the life of Judge Clane, a former congressman, fat and fatuous in his hope of reviving the antebellum society, and yet sentimentally kind in his attachment to his grandson and to another orphan, a black named Sherman Pew. The tragic pasts of these two young men, themselves involved in ambivalent emotional relations, are intertwined because the white boy's late father, a lawyer, had unsuccessfully defended the black boy's father, unjustly accused of murdering the white husband of Old Pew's white mistress. As the clock of Malone's life ticks toward a stop, the town erupts into violence. Sherman is murdered by a bomb because he has moved into a white neighborhood, and the judge, making a frenzied attempt to be the South's spokesman in a radio statement about the Supreme Court 1954 decision to ban segregation in schools, can only mindlessly shout the Gettysburg Address into a microphone while Malone, listening on his deathbed, quietly slips out of life.

Clockmaker, The; or, The Sayings and Doings of Samuel Slick, of Slickville, humorous sketches by T.C. Haliburton,♦ published in three series (1837, 1838, 1840).

The hero, Sam Slick, is a Yankee peddler in Nova Scotia, whose wide acquaintance, shrewd sagacity, and dry humor win him success on his circuit among the Canadian farms. A thread of plot connects the sketches, in which the clockmaker encounters a "Squire," with whom he travels in Nova Scotia and Connecticut, but the principal interest is in the humorous folk-wisdom of the Yankee. Sam Slick is responsible for such sayings as "Now, Marm Pugwash is like the minister's apples, very temptin' fruit to look at but desperate sour"; "We can do without any article of luxury we have never had, but . . . it is not in human natur' to surrender it voluntarily"; "Time is like a woman and pigs; the more you want it to go, the more it won't."

COATES, ROBERT M[YRON] (1897–1973), after graduation from Yale (1919) became an expatriate in France, where he wrote *The Eater of Darkness* (1929), a surrealist novel. Returning to the U.S., he turned to the American background in *The Outlaw Years* (1930), a history of the Natchez Trace pirates. Later fiction includes *Yesterday's Burdens* (1933), about a "modern Everyman" in New York City; *Bitter Season* (1946), about New York during World War II; *Wisteria Cottage* (1948), concerning a man with a Messiah complex; and *Farther Shore* (1955), about the pathetic love affair of a Hungarian resident in New York. *All the Year Round* (1943) and *Hour After Westerly* (1957) collect stories. *The View from Here* (1960) is a work of reminiscences.

COATSWORTH, ELIZABETH [JANE] (1893–1986), New York poet, whose works include *Fox Footprints* (1923), employing Oriental themes in the manner of Imagism; *Atlas and Beyond* (1924) and *Compass Rose* (1929), verses about many lands; and *The Creaking Stair* (1949). Her most popular children's book is *The Cat Who Went to Heaven* (1930). *Here I Stay* (1938), a novel for adults, and *Country Neighborhood* (1944), sketches, are set in Maine. *Personal Geography* (1976) is subtitled "Almost an Autobiography."

COBB, IRVIN S[HREWSBURY] (1876–1944), born in Paducah, Ky., after newspaper work in his hometown became noted as a New York journalist and humorous columnist. He wrote serious fiction, but is best known for his many books of humor, including *"Speaking of Operations—"* (1916), based on his personal experiences; *To Be Taken Before Sailing* (1930); and *Incredible Truth* (1931). The most prominent character in his short stories of Kentucky local color is Judge Priest, a kindly, hospitable old Confederate veteran, given to the frequent drinking of mint juleps and to active sympathy for those in distress. He figures in *Old Judge Priest* (1915) and many later collections. Cobb wrote the screenplay for and acted in *Steamboat Round the Bend. Exit Laughing* (1941) is Cobb's autobiography.

COBB, JOSEPH B[ECKHAM] (1819–58), Mississippi author, whose works include *The Creole; or, Siege of New Orleans* (1850), a historical romance about Laffite's pirates; *Mississippi Scenes* (1851), a collection of sketches; and *Leisure Labors* (1858), literary essays and political discussions, in which he criticizes Longfellow, N.P. Willis, and others for their insipid style and want of indigenous subjects.

COBB, SYLVANUS, JR. (1823–87), New England novelist, said to have been the first to undertake the wholesale production of popular fiction. He is credited with the authorship of over 300 novelettes and 1000 short stories, whose morality and adventure were suited to contemporary public taste. His novels include *The King's Talisman* (1851), *The Patriot Cruiser* (1859), *Ben Hamed* (1864), and *The Gunmaker of Moscow* (1888).

COBBETT, WILLIAM (1763–1835), British journalist, served in the army in Nova Scotia and New Brunswick, and fled to the U.S. (1792) to escape litigation resulting from his unsubstantiated exposés of army frauds. In Philadelphia he opened a bookstore, published *Porcupine's Gazette* (1797–99), and with delightful effrontery got into one scrape after another, reflected in his vituperative Federalist pamphlets against Republican friends of France. These include *A Bone to Gnaw for the Democrats* (1795), *A Kick for a Bite* (1795), *The Scare-Crow* (1796), and a scurrilous *Life of Tom Paine* (1796). This era is described in good homespun prose in *The Life and Adventures of Peter Porcupine* (1796). For two years he was a farmer on Long Island, after a return stay in England. During this second sojourn, Cobbett wrote his *Grammar of the English Language* for working-class students, as well as the graphic journal *A Year's Residence in the United States* (1818–19). Information about his life in America is also recorded in the *Political Register* (English), which he edited (1802–35), *The American Gardener* (1821), and *Advice to Young Men* (1829). *Peter Porcupine in America* (1940), by M.E. Clark, is a biography of Cobbett.

COBURN, D[ONALD] L[EE] (1938–), born in East Baltimore, long resident in Dallas as an advertising writer, wrote his first play, *The Gin Game,* had it successfully produced in a small Los Angeles theater (1976) and then on Broadway (1977). It was awarded a Pulitzer Prize for drama (1978), and published (1979). The two-character, two-act play depicts a series of gin rummy games between a man and a woman living in a home for old people, whose contests (always won by her) reveal their characters, their loneliness, and their relationships of a geriatric sexual sort. Later but less significant plays include *Guy* (1983) and *Noble Adjustment* (1986).

COCHRANE, ELIZABETH, see *Seaman, Elizabeth.*

Cocktail Party, The, verse play by T.S. Eliot,♦ produced in 1949, published in 1950.

At his cocktail party, Edward Chamberlayne tries to conceal the fact that his wife Lavinia has left him, but he is found out by his mistress Celia; talented, lonely Peter Quilpe; and a mysterious stranger, the psychiatrist Sir Henry Harcourt-Reilly. Harcourt-Reilly arranges Lavinia's return and although Edward still finds her his "angel of destruction," Sir Henry makes him see that they are bound together by "the same isolation," as her former lover Quilpe has now fallen in love with Celia, and if Edward is incapable of giving love, Lavinia cannot be loved. Celia too feels alone, and craving "the intensity of loving in the spirit" refuses to be reconciled to the human condition accepted by the others and chooses to journey in quest of faith. Two years later at a cocktail party given by Edward and Lavinia for the same guests, they learn that Celia, having become a nurse in a heathen country, has been crucified and is now worshipped as a goddess. Harcourt-Reilly tells the Chamberlaynes they should not feel guilt since the saintly way was right for Celia and another way is for them, since "there are two worlds of life and death."

Code, The, blank-verse dramatic narrative by Robert Frost,♦ published in *North of Boston* (1914).

An experienced farmhand tells a "town-bred farmer" of the pride his fellows take in their competence, and the resulting code:

> The hand that knows his business won't be told
> To do work better or faster—those two things.

For illustration he describes an incident that took place when he worked for a certain Sanders, of Salem, a prodigious worker himself. They were engaged in unloading a wagon of hay, and Sanders made the mistake, while standing below to pile the load, of saying to the hand on the wagon, "Let her come!" Offended at this breach of the code, the hand dumped the entire load down on the helpless farmer, regardless of the danger of suffocating him. Sanders extricated himself, and showed that he recognized the justice of his employee's act:

> "Discharge me? No! He knew I did just right."

CODY, WILLIAM FREDERICK (1846–1917), known by his sobriquet Buffalo Bill, served as a frontier scout during the Civil War, and again from 1868 to 1872, as well as in the battles against the Sioux. In 1883 he started his famous "Wild West" show, the prototype of many later ones, and he had previously acted in Western melodramas. The dime novels of Ned Buntline and Prentiss Ingraham are partially responsible for his popular reputation. He acted for two years in Buntline's play *The Scouts of the Plains* (1873). His autobiography (1904) is unreliable.

Coeur d'Alene, novel by Mary H. Foote,♦ published in 1894.

COFFIN, CHARLES CARLETON (1823–96), New England newspaper correspondent, whose experiences during the Civil War provided information for both autobiographical accounts and such popular children's books as *The Boys of '61* (1881). *The Boys of '76* (1876), concerned with the Revolution, was his most popular work, and he covered much American history in his series, *Drum-Beat of the Nation* (1887–91).

COFFIN, ROBERT P[ETER] T[RISTRAM] (1892–1955), Maine author, graduated from Bowdoin (1915), was a Rhodes Scholar at Oxford, and became professor of English at Wells College (Aurora, N.Y.). His honest, hearty pastoral poetry of Maine life includes *Ballads of Square-Toed Americans* (1933), *Strange Holiness* (1935, Pulitzer Prize), an early volume of *Collected Poems* (1939), *There Will Be Bread and Love* (1942), *Primer for America* (1943), *Poems for a Son with Wings* (1945), and *Apples by Ocean* (1950). *Lost Paradise* (1934) is an autobiography, while *Captain Abby and Captain John* (1939) is biography based on diaries of a 19th-century Maine family who lived aboard a sailing ship. Other works include *Book of Crowns and Cottages* (1925), *An Attic Room* (1929), *Book of Uncles* (1942), *Mainstays of Maine* (1944), and *Maine Doings* (1950), essays; *Kennebec, Cradle of Americans* (1937); biographies of Laud (1930) and the dukes of Buckingham (1931); and *Portrait of an American* (1931). *New Poetry of New England: Frost and Robinson* (1938) and *The Substance That Is Poetry* (1942) are essays.

COGGLESHALL, WILLIAM TURNER (1824–67), born in Pennsylvania, was a noted Ohio journalist and publisher. His novels, including *Oakshaw* (1855), are only slightly above the level of popular works of the time, but his criticism is valuable. *The Protective Policy in Literature* (1859) is a plea for regionalism. *The Poets and Poetry of the West* (1860), an anthology with biographical sketches, was to offset neglect of the West in the anthologies by R.W. Griswold and E.A. and G.L. Duyckinck.

COHAN, GEORGE M[ICHAEL] (1878–1942), New York comic actor, composer of such popular songs as "Over There" of World War I, and author of plays that include *Forty-Five Minutes from Broadway* (1906), *The Talk of New York* (1907), and *The Song and Dance Man* (1923).

COHEN, OCTAVUS ROY (1891–1959), South Carolina-born writer and humorist, best known for his depiction of small-town Southern blacks in such volumes as *Florian Slappey Goes Abroad* (1928) and *Florian Slappey* (1938).

COLDEN, CADWALLADER (1688–1776), born in Scotland, came to America (1710), and after a long political career became lieutenant-governor of New York (1761–76). His *History of the Five Indian Nations* (1727) was the first careful and well-documented study of the Iroquois Confederacy. Among his many treatises on medicine, moral philosophy, and natural science is the *Plantae Coldenghamiae* (1749, 1751). He attracted much attention by his implied criticism of Newton in the *Explication of the First Causes of Action in Matter, and, of the Causes of Gravitation* (1745, frequently revised).

COLE, THOMAS (1801–48), English-born painter brought to Ohio (1819). With Asher Durand he became a founder of the Hudson River School of landscape art. Trips to Europe (1821–31, 1841) made him concerned with allegory in such canvases as *The Course of Empire* and *The Voyage of Life,* incorporating dramatic and poetic views of nature. He was also a poet, e.g. "The Spirits of the Wilderness" (1835–37), but got into print only parts of his poetry, travel sketches, and memoirs.

COLES, ROBERT (1929–), staff member and professor at Harvard (1963–), a distinguished psychiatrist, educator, and author, whose numerous books include: *Children of Crisis* (1967); *Migrants, Sharecroppers and Mountaineers* (1972); *Irony in the Mind's Life* (1974), essays on novels, including work by James Agee; *Eskimos, Chicanos and Indians* (1978); *Walker Percy: An American Search* (1978); *Flannery O'Connor's South* (1980); and *Children of Crisis* (1967 and 1977), awarded a Pulitzer Prize for Vols. II and III. *Rumors of Separate Worlds* (1989) is one of his volumes of poetry.

Coliseum, The, poem by Poe,♦ interpolated in his tragedy *Politian.*♦

Collier's (1888–1957), weekly magazine founded by Peter F. Collier to promote his installment plan for selling books. It soon became an illustrated literary and critical journal, and under the editorship of Norman Hapgood (1903–12) and Mark Sullivan (1914–17) was a leading liberal and muckraking publication. After the editorship of F.P. Dunne (1918–19), it was less concerned with influencing social opinion and more with furnishing light fiction and articles for the average reader. Although it participated in new crusades, e.g. against the 18th Amendment, it concentrated on fiction, cartoons, and popular articles on current events written by famous persons, together with discussions of Hollywood, Broadway, and athletic events. Under this policy, the circulation rose to more than 2,500,000, but in the 1950s it hit hard times (becoming a fortnightly in 1953) as newsstand sales dropped and advertising declined. In 1957 *Look* assumed its debts in exchange for its subscriptions.

COLMAN, BENJAMIN (1673–1747), minister of the Brattle Street Church in Boston (1699–1747) and prominent among liberal Congregationalists, was active in civil and religious affairs, and a minor leader in the Great Awakening. ♦ Most of his more than 90 books are sermons, and these include *God Deals with Us as Rational Creatures* (1723), *The Government and Improvement of Mirth* (1707), and *Discourses upon the Parable of the Ten Virgins,* as well as works concerned with his defense of inoculation. His poetry included *Elijah's Translation* (1707), a neoclassical work on the death of the Rev. Samuel Willard. He is the subject of a biography by Ebenezer Turell (1749), who married Colman's daughter, Jane Colman Turrell. ♦

COLON and **SPONDEE,** pseudonyms respectively of J. Dennie ♦ and R. Tyler ♦ in their journalistic collaboration.

Colonel Carter of Cartersville, novelette by F. Hopkinson Smith, ♦ published in 1891, was successfully dramatized by Augustus Thomas (1892). *Colonel Carter's Christmas* (1903) is a sequel.

Colonel Sellers, play by Clemens ♦ and Howells, ♦ featuring the hero of *The Gilded Age.* ♦ Unsuccessfully produced in 1886, it was the basis of Clemens's story *The American Claimant.* ♦

Colonel Surry, pseudonym of J.E. Cooke. ♦

COLTON, JOHN (1889–1946), New York dramatist, whose plays include *Nine Pine Street* (1933), written in collaboration with others, and based on the Borden murder case; *Rain* (1922), in collaboration with Clemence Randolph, based on Somerset Maugham's short story "Miss Thompson" and telling of the prostitute Sadie Thompson's arrival on a South Sea island, where she is frightened into confessing to the Rev. Mr. Davidson, but returns to a defiant cynicism after he reveals his lust for her; and *The Shanghai Gesture* (1926), a sensational play depicting a Chinese brothel and the vengeance of its keeper on the Englishman who betrayed her, by placing his two daughters in her establishment.

COLTON, WALTER (1797–1851), author of *Ship and Shore* (1835), the account of his cruise as naval chaplain, and *Deck and Port* (1850), about his voyage to California (1845) with Commodore Stockton. He remained in California, became *alcalde* of Monterey, and founded *The Californian,* the territory's first newspaper. His *Three Years in California* (1850) is an important historical source.

"Columbia, the Gem of the Ocean," patriotic song attributed to two English actors, Thomas à Becket and David T. Shaw, and said to have been written for a Philadelphia benefit (1843). It is sometimes asserted that Shaw wrote it for à Becket in England, under the title "Britannia, the Pride of the Ocean," and later adapted it for American performance.

Columbiad, The, epic poem in heroic couplets by Joel Barlow, ♦ was published in 1807 and is a revision of *The Vision of Columbus* (1787). It is a tedious and turgid work modeled on Milton and influenced by Shenstone and Timothy Dwight.

According to the preface, Barlow's purpose is "to inculcate the love of national liberty, and to discountenance the deleterious passion for violence and war; to show that on the basis of republican principle all good morals, as well as good government and hopes of permanent peace, must be founded." The poem is concerned with the vision revealed by a "radiant seraph" to Columbus, an old man dying in prison. Columbus sees the future glories of America, and a distant vision of a league of all nations, "assembled to establish the political harmony of mankind."

Columbian Centinel, The, see *Massachusetts Centinel.*

Columbian Lady's and Gentleman's Magazine (1844–49), monthly literary journal, was published at New York as a competitor of *Graham's Magazine.* Its contributors included Poe, Paulding, and C.F. Hoffman.

Columbian Magazine, The (1786–92), monthly periodical published at Philadelphia by a literary group that included Mathew Carey and Francis Hopkinson. Its format was the most attractive of all American magazines of its time, and it featured agricultural and mechanical subjects, with an unusual amount of fiction. In its pages were first printed Belknap's *The Foresters,* William Byrd's description of the Dismal Swamp, and C.B. Brown's "The Rhapsodist." In 1790 the magazine was altered, afterward appearing as *The Universal Asylum and Columbian Magazine,* with Benjamin Rush as the leading contributor.

COLUMBUS, CHRISTOPHER (*c.*1446–1506), whose name in Italian is Cristoforo Colombo, and in Spanish Cristóbal Colón, was probably born in Genoa, to whose authorities he is said to have first proposed his expedition of discovery. He is supposed to have been influenced toward exploration by his older brother Bartholomew, an expert chart maker, and by his marriage (1477) to the daughter of a Portuguese navigator. After repeated rebuffs at the Portuguese and Spanish courts, he received the aid of Ferdinand and Isabella of Spain, and set sail (Aug. 3, 1492) with three small ships, the *Santa Maria* under his own command, the *Niña* under Vicente Pinzón, and the *Pinta* under Martin Pinzón. He landed in the Bahamas (Oct. 12) at an island that he named San

Salvador, now generally identified with Watling Island. After discovering Cuba and Hispaniola (Haiti), he returned to Spain. For these discoveries he was made "admiral of the ocean" and governor-general of all new lands. On his second voyage (1493) his discoveries included the Leeward Islands, St. Christopher, and Puerto Rico. On the third expedition (1498), he discovered Trinidad and the mouth of the Orinoco. His poor administration caused his popularity to wane, and greater attention was given to Vespucci and other navigators. In 1502 he left Spain for a fourth time, in the hope of sailing past his discovered islands to Marco Polo's Cathay, for which he had constantly searched. This expedition suffered terrible hardships, and he was forced to abandon his plans and return to Spain, where he was discredited. As the founder of American history, he is the subject of many biographies, notably Irving's *Life and Voyages of Christopher Columbus* (3 vols., 1828) and Samuel Eliot Morison's *Admiral of the Ocean Sea* (1942). Inevitably he has been the subject of a great deal of creative writing, of which perhaps the best known is the declamatory poem "Columbus" by Joaquin Miller.

COLWIN, LAURIE E. (1944–92), novelist and short story writer. Born in Manhattan, she grew up on Long Island, in Chicago and Philadelphia, and attended Bard College and Columbia University. Her material was the mores of middle- and upper-class New Yorkers; her love stories usually had happy endings, both in and outside of marriage. Her novels are *Shine On, Bright and Dangerous Object* (1975), *Happy All the Time* (1978), *Family Happiness* (1982), *Goodbye Without Leaving* (1990), and the posthumously published *A Big Storm Knocked It Over* (1993), in which the idealization of friendship supplants that of happy family life. Her short story collections are *Passion and Affect* (1974), *The Lone Pilgrim* (1981), and *Another Marvelous Thing* (1986).

Come-outers, name applied to those 19th-century New Englanders who, believing that ministers and creeds were unnecessary, found the only source of divine truth in what God said directly to their hearts. Members of this vigorous mystic movement came originally from Cape Cod.

COMMAGER, HENRY STEELE (1902–), educated at the University of Chicago and in Denmark and England, has been a professor of history at New York University (1926–38), Columbia (1939–56), and Amherst (1956–72). His many books include *The Growth of the American Republic* (2 vols., 1930), with S.E. Morison; *Theodore Parker* (1936); *The American Mind* (1951); *The Empire of Reason* (1977); and *The Era of Reform* (1982).

Commemoration Ode, see *Ode Recited at . . . Harvard University.*

Commentaries on American Law, see *Kent, James.*

Commentary (1945–), monthly journal, superseding *Contemporary Jewish Record* (1938–45), "to promote Jewish cultural interests and creative achievement in America." It is nonparochial and nonsectarian in its social and political articles, criticism, poetry, and fiction. American contributors have included James Baldwin, Hofstadter, Kazin, Mailer, Malamud, Riesman, and Trilling. An anthology, *Commentary on the American Scene,* was published in 1953. When Norman Podhoretz♦ assumed editorship (1960), the magazine became increasingly conservative in its social and political views.

Commercial Advertiser, see *American Minerva.*

Common Ground (1940–49), quarterly magazine published by the Common Council for American Unity to further an appreciation of contributions to U.S. culture by many ethnic, religious, and national groups. Louis Adamic was the editor until 1942.

Common Sense, pamphlet by Thomas Paine,♦ published anonymously at Philadelphia (Jan. 10, 1776). At a time of rising passion against the British government, the work was the first unqualified argument for complete political independence, and helped turn colonial thought in the direction that, six months later, culminated in the Declaration of Independence. Over 100,000 copies were sold by the end of March, and it is generally considered the most important literary influence on the movement for independence.

The argument is presented in four parts entitled: "Of the Origin and Design of Government in General; with Concise Remarks on the English Constitution"; "Of Monarchy and Hereditary Succession"; "Thoughts on the Present State of American Affairs"; and "Of the Present Ability of America. . . ." The most cogent points of the closely reasoned discussion may be summarized in these extracts:

> Here then is the origin and rise of government; namely, a mode rendered necessary by the inability of moral virtue to govern the world; here too is the design and end of government, viz. freedom and security. . . . Of more worth is one honest man to society, and in the sight of God, than all the crowned ruffians that ever lived. . . . We have boasted the protection of Great Britain, without considering, that her motive was *interest* not *attachment*. . . . I challenge the warmest advocate for reconciliation to show a single advantage that this continent can reap by being connected with Great Britain. . . . Our corn will fetch its price in any market in Europe, and our imported goods must be paid for buy them where we will. . . . Everything that is right or reasonable pleads for separation. The blood of the slain, the weeping voice of Nature cries, 'TIS TIME TO PART. . . . The republican form of government is the best because it is founded on the most natural

principles. . . . 'Tis not in numbers but in unity that our great strength lies; yet our present numbers are sufficient to repel the force of all the world.

Common Sense (1932–46), monthly liberal review of political, economic, and social affairs, whose contributors included Dos Passos, MacLeish, Upton Sinclair, Norman Thomas, Louis Adamic, John Dewey, and Max Eastman. In 1946 it was absorbed by the *American Mercury.*

Commoner, magazine edited by Bryan.

Commonweal, [*The*] (1924–　), weekly review of current events, literature, and art, expressing the point of view of Catholic laymen, although admitting contributions from writers of other faiths.

Compensation, essay by Emerson,♦ published in *Essays, First Series* (1841); also, a poem by Emerson, published the same year.

　The idea of compensation is implicit in Emerson's thought, and involves his concept of the "Over-Soul"♦: "An inevitable dualism bisects nature, so that each thing is a half, and suggests another thing to make it whole." Although the malicious are apparently rewarded rather than punished, the view that justice will be meted out in an afterlife is erroneous, for it "is not postponed. . . . What we call retribution, is the universal necessity by which the whole appears wherever a part appears. . . . Every act rewards itself." The necessary conditions that life involves may not be avoided: "Our action is overmastered and characterised above our will by the law of nature. . . . Our strength grows out of our weakness." But the author does not counsel indifference. "Under all this running sea of circumstance . . . lies the aboriginal abyss of real Being." Wisdom and virtue involve no penalty, but are qualities of being; "in a virtuous action, I properly *am.*" The individual, trusting instinct, acts in accord with a divinely balanced justice, and "the changes which break up at short intervals the prosperity of men, are advertisements of a nature whose law is growth."

Compson family, characters in Faulkner's fiction, an old family centrally involved in Jefferson history from the town's earliest years, figures most prominently in *The Sound and the Fury*♦ and more briefly in *Absalom, Absalom!,*♦ *The Town,*♦ and *The Mansion.*♦ The family is traced back to Quentin MacLachan Compson, who comes to Carolina from Scotland in the 18th century and who, while his son Charles Stuart Compson is fighting with the British in Georgia in 1778, takes his infant grandson Jason Lycurgus Compson to Kentucky. In 1811 Jason Lycurgus goes to the Chickasaw Agency in Mississippi, where he wins money racing horses against Ikkemotubbe♦ and obtains a square mile of land

from the Chickasaw chief, on which he builds an estate, while the town of Jefferson begins to grow around it. Jason Lycurgus's son Quentin MacLachan II becomes governor of Mississippi, and *his* son Jason Lycurgus II becomes a Confederate general, later helping to build the railroad to Jefferson. His son Jason III (Jason Richmond, Sr.), a lawyer, becomes a recluse who spends his time drinking, reading the classics, and exercising his cynical wit in the years after he marries Caroline Bascomb and fathers four children: a daughter, Candace (Caddy), and three sons, Quentin III, Benjamin (Benjy), originally named Maury, and Jason IV, whose sad stories are the subject of *The Sound and the Fury.* The last generation of the Compson family is Caddy's illegitimate daughter Quentin, for Jason remains a bachelor, Quentin commits suicide, and the idiot Benjy is castrated and, according to *The Mansion,* dies in the fire he sets to the family house.

COMPTON, Frances Snow, pseudonym of Henry Adams.♦

COMSTOCK, Anthony (1844–1915), was head of a YMCA campaign against obscene literature, special agent for the Post Office Department, founder of the Society for Suppression of Vice, and a leader of Boston's Watch and Ward Society. He was the father of the so-called Comstock law (1873) to exclude vicious matter from the mails. In his various campaigns, he caused the arrest of more than 3000 persons and destroyed 50 tons of books, 28,400 pounds of stereotyped plates for printing objectionable books, and nearly 4,000,000 pictures. He wrote several books on immorality in art and literature. *Anthony Comstock: Roundsman of the Lord* (1927) is a biography by Heywood Broun and Margaret Leech.

Comstock Lode, silver deposit discovered by H.T.P. Comstock on the site of Virginia City, Nev. (1856). By 1863 the settlement had mushroomed to 40,000 inhabitants, and the mines were producing $20,000,000 to $30,000,000 annually. Large quantities of ore were milled throughout the 1870s. Clemens was present (1861–64) during its heyday and describes it in *Roughing It.*♦ While in Nevada he first used his pseudonym Mark Twain (1863) and he also helped to edit the local newspaper, *The Territorial Enterprise.* Some 50 of his articles and dispatches were reprinted for the first time in *Mark Twain of the* Enterprise (1957) and his letters to the *Enterprise* in 1855–56 were collected in *Mark Twain: San Francisco Correspondent* (1957). Other authors of the region and the time included William Wright, known by his pen name Dan De Quille♦ and for his *History of the Big Bonanza,* and Fred H. Hart.♦

CONANCHET, see *Canonchet.*

Concerning the End for Which God Created the World, see *Edwards, Jonathan.*

Conciliation with the American Colonies, *On,* speech by Burke, delivered before the British Parliament (March 1775). Intending to prevent the defection of the colonies, Burke submitted 13 resolutions affirming the principle of autonomy for them, based on four fundamental assumptions: happiness is the true end of government; political expediency is the means to that end; the criterion for judging the end is the wisdom of the past; and the end must be obtained through the medium of the British Constitution.

Concord, Mass., village 20 miles northwest of Boston, was settled in 1635. It was the scene of the colony's first provincial congress (1774–75) and as a military supply depot was the objective of the British expedition that fought the Battle of Lexington♦ and then proceeded to Concord (April 19, 1775), where it encountered 500 minutemen who had been warned by Paul Revere and Rufus Dawes. This event is commemorated by French's monument *The Minute Man,* and by Emerson's "Concord Hymn":

> . . . Here once the embattled farmers stood
> And fired the shot heard round the world.

During the mid-19th century, Concord was the home of the Transcendentalist movement, whose leaders included Emerson, Thoreau, Hawthorne, Alcott, and the younger W.E. Channing. The "Old Manse" was the home of Emerson and of Hawthorne, and "Orchard House" was Alcott's while he conducted his Concord School of Philosophy (1879–88).

Condensed Novels and Other Papers, first collection of writings by Bret Harte,♦ published in 1867. It included 15 travesties of the works of such popular writers as Cooper, Dickens, Dumas, and Hugo, as well as three legends of Spanish California in the manner of Washington Irving, and "A Night at Wingdam," a gold rush story. A poorer collection was issued under the same title as a second series in 1902.

Conduct of Life, *The,* essays by Emerson,♦ published in 1860, based on lectures delivered in 1851. The author's ethical ideas are developed in nine essays: "Fate," "Power," "Wealth," "Culture," "Behavior," "Worship," "Considerations by the Way," "Beauty," and "Illusions."

Confederacy, name commonly given to the Confederate States of America, those Southern states that, by the ordinance of secession, withdrew from the Union to set up their own government in 1861. These included Virginia, North and South Carolina, Georgia, Alabama, Tennessee, Louisiana, Arkansas, Mississippi, Florida, and Texas. Jefferson Davis was president of the Confederacy, which existed until the end of the Civil War. Of the relatively few works of belles lettres published in the Confederacy, many were by British authors, but native works included R.M. Johnston's *Georgia Sketches,* J.B. Jones's *Wild Western Scenes,* Margaret J. Preston's *Beechenbrook,* and N.B. Tucker's *The Partisan Leader.* Literature about the Confederacy ranges from personal memoirs such as the posthumously published *A Diary from Dixie* (1905) by Mary Boykin Chesnut♦ through historical studies and biographies of individual leaders, like Douglas Southall Freeman's *Lee* (4 vols., 1934–35) and *Lee's Lieutenants* (4 vols., 1946); to a great deal of fiction concentrating upon the Civil War, itself as various as John Esten Cooke's trilogy *Surry of Eagle's Nest* (1866), *Hilt to Hilt* (1869), and *Mohun* (1869), Margaret Mitchell's *Gone with the Wind* (1936), and Faulkner's *Unvanquished* (1938). Freeman's *The South to Posterity* (1939) is a bibliography and "history of Confederate history."

Confession; *or, The Blind Heart, a Domestic Story,* novel by Simms,♦ published in 1841.

Edgar Clifford, melancholy and suspicious, marries his cousin Julia, to whom he introduces William Edgerton, who shares her interest in art and falls in love with her. Believing that his wife is encouraging William, Edgar moves to Alabama, where he and Julia are happy until the arrival of William, who remains to be nursed through an illness. Edgar challenges his rival to a duel, poisons his wife, and after her death discovers her innocence. He threatens to commit suicide, but is dissuaded and decides to begin a new life in Texas.

Confessions of Nat Turner, *The,* novel by William Styron,♦ published in 1967 and awarded a Pulitzer Prize. It stirred much controversy, mainly from blacks, who considered the interpretation of Turner to be inaccurate.

Told in the first person, yet, in the author's view, "less an 'historical novel' in conventional terms than a meditation on history," the account of an actual person and event is based on the brief contemporary pamphlet of the same title presented to a trial court as evidence and published in Virginia a year after the revolt of fellow slaves led by Turner in 1831. Imagining much of Turner's youth and early manhood before the rebellion that he headed at the age of 31, Styron in frequently rhetorical and pseudo-Biblical style has Turner recall his religious faith and his power of preaching to other slaves. Embittered and frustrated by the evils of slavery, including the failure to obtain the freedom promised by his first master, Turner is portrayed as unable to find surcease in human relations, black or white, sexually or spiritually. Impelled by supernatural visions, the basically kind Turner becomes the leader of a small band of Southampton County slaves, who raise a violent insurrection in which many white men and women are killed but which is put down with great speed and brutality so that more than twice as many blacks die. Those captured and hanged include Turner.

Confidence-Man, *The: His Masquerade,* unfinished satirical novel by Melville,♦ published in 1857. This last novel printed during the author's life shows a pessimistic view best described by the title of a handbill that figures in the story: "Ode on the Intimations of Distrust in Man, Unwillingly Inferred from Repeated Repulses, in Disinterested Endeavors to Procure His Confidence."

A deaf-mute boards the Mississippi steamboat *Fidèle,* bound from St. Louis for New Orleans, and displays to the passengers a slate on which he writes: "Charity thinketh no evil; suffereth long, and is kind; endureth all things; believeth all things; and never faileth." This is regarded as a proof of lunacy, although the passengers consider the barber's "No Trust" sign as wise and well expressed. Optimistic, faith-seeking mankind then appears in a variety of other disguises, as the "Masquerade" continues, and distrust replaces confidence in the course of each episode.

Congo, *The (A Study of the Negro Race),* poem by Vachel Lindsay,♦ published in *The Congo and Other Poems* (1914). With a sensational use of varied syncopated rhythms, occasional rhymes, and frequent alliteration, the poet presents this "roaring, epic, ragtime tune" on the traits of blacks: "Their Basic Savagery," "Their Irrepressible High Spirits," and "The Hope of Their Religion."

Congregationalism, system of church government in which each congregation is autonomous and democratic. No hierarchy exists, since Christ is in principle the head of each church, and the various congregations are related as fellow participants in the common family of God. This form of church polity in America was inaugurated by the Pilgrim Fathers, who were Separatists,♦ and by the later stream of Puritan colonists.♦ It was virtually the established religion in New England (*c.*1631–1833), and its basic statement was the Cambridge Platform (1648).♦ Increasing liberalism during the 17th century caused the adoption of the Half-Way Covenant.♦ In 1705, the proposal that higher church assemblies be created, similar to those of the Presbyterians, failed to be accepted in Massachusetts, largely because of the opposition of John Wise,♦ but the Saybrook Platform (1708) in Connecticut tended toward Presbyterianism. The Great Awakening♦ (1734ff.) revitalized the religious life of New England for a time, but eventually led to the breakdown of Congregationalism and the rise of Unitarianism during the mid-19th century. Most of the New England Congregationalists who went west became Presbyterians. In 1871 a National Council was formed, although local churches still remain

independent. The influence of Congregationalism in American culture may be seen throughout art and literature and in many political institutions and social attitudes. Virtually all the New England authors have been conditioned by Congregationalism, which also led to the founding of Harvard, Yale, Williams, and Amherst.

Congressional Library, see *Library of Congress.*

Congressional Record (1874–   ), report of the proceedings of the Senate and House of Representatives. It was preceded by the *Annals of Congress* (1789–1824), the *Register of Debates* (1825–37), and the *Congressional Globe* (1834–73). The *Journals of the Continental Congress* were first collected in 34 volumes (1904–37).

Coniston, novel by Winston Churchill,♦ published in 1906.

CONKLING, GRACE HAZARD (1878–1958), professor of English at Smith, was known for her gentle nature poetry, published in such volumes as *Afternoons of April* (1915) and *Wilderness Songs* (1920).

HILDA CONKLING (1910–   ), her daughter, won a reputation as a prodigy for her *Poems by a Little Girl* (1920) and *Shoes of the Wind* (1922).

Connecticut Courant, see *Hartford Courant.*

Connecticut Wits, literary group of the late 18th century, centered at Hartford (known also as the Hartford Wits), whose origin is ascribed to the quickening interest in literature at Yale during this period, when most of the group were tutors or students there. They patterned themselves after the Augustan wits, but preserved the intellectual and spiritual conservatism of Connecticut. Aiming to modernize the rigidly scholastic curriculum of Yale, they also wished to supply poetry that would celebrate America's literary independence by extolling native history and society. Although they copied London modes, after the Revolution they clung to their orthodox Calvinism and Federalism, bitterly opposing deism and equalitarianism. Their collaborations included *The Anarchiad*♦ (1786–87), *The Echo*♦ (1791–1805), and *The Political Greenhouse*♦ (1799). Members included John Trumbull, Timothy Dwight, Joel Barlow, Lemuel Hopkins, David Humphreys, Richard Alsop, Theodore Dwight, E.H. Smith, and Dr. Mason F. Cogswell.

Connecticut Yankee in King Arthur's Court, *A* (1889), realistic-satirical fantasy of Arthurian England by Clemens♦ under his pseudonym Mark Twain.

An ingenious Yankee mechanic, knocked unconscious in a fight, awakens to find himself at Camelot in A.D. 528. Imprisoned by Sir Kay the

Seneschal and exhibited before the knights of the Round Table, he is condemned to death, but saves himself by posing as a magician like Merlin, correctly predicting an eclipse, and becoming minister to King Arthur. He increases his power by applying 19th-century knowledge of gunpowder, electricity, and industrial methods; but when he attempts to better the condition of the peasantry he meets opposition from the church, the knights, Merlin, and the sorceress Morgan le Fay. He accompanies the king in disguise on an expedition among the common people, and, when they are captured, they are rescued by the Yankee's trained troop of 500 knights on bicycles. His daughter Hello-Central becomes ill, and with his wife Alisande (Sandy) he takes her to France. Back in England, he finds his work undone, Arthur killed, the land in civil war. Gathering friends in a cave with modern armed defenses, he declares a republic, fights off an attack, but is wounded. Merlin, pretending to nurse him, puts him asleep until the 19th century.

CONNELL, EVAN S[HELBY], JR. (1924–   ), born in Kansas City, educated at Dartmouth and four universities, has long lived in California. *Mrs. Bridge* (1959) is a humorous, ironic, and sad series of sketches about a suburban society matron who lives a life of quiet desperation. *The Patriot* (1960), with a similar tone but a more conventional novelistic technique, treats the maturing of an idealistic boy in World War II naval air force service. His other novels include *The Diary of a Rapist* (1966), on sexual violence; *Mr. Bridge* (1969), a companion piece to his first book; *The Connoisseur* (1974), a sensitive study of a man's aesthetic development through appreciation of Mayan art; and *Double Honeymoon* (1976), about a romance of the protagonist of his previous novel. Stories are collected in *The Anatomy Lesson* (1957), *At the Crossroads* (1965), and *St. Augustine's Pigeon* (1980). *Notes from a Bottle Found on the Beach at Carmel* (1963) and *Points for a Compass Rose* (1973) are long philosophic poems. *A Long Desire* (1979) and *The White Lantern* (1980) are nonfictional treatments of great acts of exploration, anthropology, and archaeology; *Son of the Morning Star* (1984) is a study of and meditation on Custer's Last Stand, from Native American as well as white perspectives; and *The Alchymist's Journal* (1991) attempts to re-create the world view of the 16th-century European alchemists through fabricated journal entries of 7 practicing alchemists.

CONNELLY, MARC[US COOK] (1890–1980), Pennsylvania-born journalist and playwright, is best known for his play *The Green Pastures*♦ (1930, Pulitzer Prize), based on Roark Bradford's stories of the black's conception of Old Testament history. With George S. Kaufman he wrote plays including *Dulcy* (1921), satirizing a well-meaning, stupid woman who jeopardizes her husband's chances; *To the Ladies* (1922), about a brilliant woman who saves her husband from his stupidities; *Merton of the Movies* (1922), dramatizing H.L. Wilson's novel; and *Beggar on Horseback*♦ (1924), satirizing the repression of the artist by bourgeois society. Other works include *Helen of Troy* (1923), a musical comedy; and *The Farmer Takes a Wife* (1934), from a novel by Edmonds. ♦ *A Souvenir from Qam* (1965) is a novel satirizing spy stories. *Voices Offstage* (1968) is a memoir.

CONNOR, RALPH, see *Gordon, C.W.*

Conqueror, The, novel by Gertrude Atherton,♦ published in 1902, a "dramatized biography" of Alexander Hamilton.

Conqueror Worm, The, poem by Poe,♦ published in *The Raven and Other Poems* (1845) and later included in "Ligeia." It consists of five eight-line stanzas, rhymed *ababcbcb,* the meter being free though most frequently iambic and anapaestic. The final lines convey the subject:

> . . . the play is the tragedy, "Man,"
> And its hero, the Conqueror Worm.

Conquest of Canaan, The, epic poem in 11 books of conventional heroic couplets, by Timothy Dwight,♦ published in 1785. Written between 1771 and 1773, the work is claimed by the author to be "the first epic poem to have appeared in America." Shuttling with sonorous declamation between Canaan and Connecticut, it is an allegory in which Joshua's conquest of Canaan suggests the struggle under Washington. Although contemporary events and characters are frequently mentioned, the epic is intended "to represent such manners as are removed from peculiarities of any age or country."

Conquest of Granada, A Chronicle of the, history by Irving,♦ published in 1829 and revised in 1850. Praised by Prescott and others for its careful documentation, the work is the result of research in Spanish archives and in the library of Obadiah Rich, but is presented within a frame of humorous and romantic fiction, and purports to be based on a work by the fictitious "Fray Antonio Agapida," who is "intended as a personification of the monkish zealots" of its period (1478–92). Through this chronicler, Irving emphasizes the barbarity of the Christian conquerors, the prejudices and ignorance of the court, and the heroism of the Moorish leaders in their hopeless struggle to retain Granada.

Conquest of Mexico and *Conquest of Peru,* histories by W.H. Prescott.♦

Conquistador, narrative poem by Archibald MacLeish,♦ published in 1932 and awarded a Pulitzer Prize. An epic employing a free terza-rima form, the work is based mainly on the account by Bernal Díaz, but the poet says he "altered and transposed and invented incidents," and his account of the topography derives from his own experience.

CONRAD, ROBERT TAYLOR (1810–58), Philadelphia journalist and dramatist, author of such tragedies as *Conrad, King of Naples* (1832) and *Jack Cade♦* (1835). He chaired the prize committee (1843) which awarded $100 to Poe's "The Gold-Bug" as the best story sent to *Dollar Magazine.* He was mayor of Philadelphia (1854–56).

CONROY, FRANK (1936–   ), born in New York City, educated at Haverford College. In his first book, *Stop-Time* (1967), a memoir, Conroy achieved a kind of breakthrough art in describing the metamorphosis from childhood to adolescence. After this hugely successful debut, 18 years elapsed before Conroy's next book, *Midair* (1985), which prints short stories. He published a novel, *Body & Soul* (1993), dealing with the transformation of a child prodigy into a master pianist and composer.

CONROY, JACK (JOHN WESLEY) (1899–1980), Missouri-born editor of *The Anvil* (1933–37) and *The New Anvil* (1939–41), dedicated to the proletarian movement, as were his novels about laborers, *The Disinherited* (1933) and *A World To Win* (1935). With Arna Bontemps he wrote *They Seek a City* (1945), expanded as *Anyplace But Here* (1966), on migration of blacks. *Writers in Revolt* (1973) is an anthology from *The Anvil. The Jack Conroy Reader* (1980) is a collection of his writings.

Constitution of the United States, framed by the Federal Constitutional Convention♦ (1787) to create the system of federal government, which began to function in 1789, superseding the Articles of Confederation. Madison has been called "the father of the Constitution," since he was secretary and spokesman for the signers. *The Federalist♦* played an important role in securing the adoption of the Constitution, and remains the most important commentary on constitutional interpretation have always existed. Article I, section 8, after expressly enumerating the powers of Congress, supplements them by the grant "to make all laws which shall be necessary and proper for carrying into execution the foregoing powers and all other powers vested by this Constitution in the government of the United States or in any department or officer thereof." The loose construction of the document, allowing a liberal use of these implied powers, and consequently favoring a strong central government, was advocated by Hamilton and the Federalist party. Those anti-Federalists like Jefferson, who wished the state governments to retain power, believed in a strict or limited interpretation of the implied powers. Marshall's judicial interpretations, from the point of view of

loose construction, did much to establish the principle of elaborating and expanding federal regulation, and since his time the Supreme Court has enjoyed a great growth of power by declaring certain legislation unconstitutional. The struggle between strict and loose constructionists was most pronounced during the mid-19th-century conflict over states' rights.

The original seven articles of the Constitution are concerned respectively with the legislative, executive, and judicial branches of the government; the regulation of state and territorial governments; the method of amendment; the validity of previous debts and engagements; and the supreme authority of the Constitution, as well as the method of ratification. The first ten amendments are generally known as the Bill of Rights.♦

Constitutional Courant, The, (Sept. 21, 1765), newspaper issued by James Parker to attack the Stamp Act, appeared in a single issue published at three separate places. It contained three articles and reproduced the *Pennsylvania Gazette* cartoon that represented a snake, symbolizing the colonies, divided into eight parts, and bearing the motto "Join or Die."

Contrast, The, social comedy by Royall Tyler,♦ produced in 1787 and published in 1790.

Maria is affianced by her American father, Van Rough, to wealthy Billy Dimple, Anglomaniac disciple of Chesterfield. Dimple meanwhile flirts with the coquettes Letitia and Charlotte. The latter's brother, Colonel Manly, a serious-minded Revolutionary officer, loves Maria but honorably forswears her. Losing his fortune by gambling, Dimple decides to break with Maria and marry the wealthy Letitia. When Van Rough discovers Dimple's duplicity and the noble filial sentiment of his daughter, who really loves Manly, he favors the officer's suit. Finally Dimple is foiled by the disclosure that he is simultaneously courting both Letitia and Charlotte, and Manly and Maria are united. The subplot is concerned with Jonathan, Manly's servant, whose homespun shrewdness is contrasted with the wiliness of the popinjay Jessamy, servant of Dimple. Jessamy educates Jonathan in the ways of the world and teaches him to court the maid Jenny, hoping to turn her affections toward himself by the Yankee's annoying blunders. Jenny, learning of the scheme, rejects both of them.

CONWAY, MONCURE DANIEL (1832–1907), Virginia Unitarian clergyman and liberal leader, whose more than 70 books include biographies of Emerson, Carlyle, and Hawthorne; novels, studies of Oriental religions and demonology; and pamphlets which, like his *Autobiography* (1904), show his very individual mind and extreme changes of opinion. *Pine and Palm* (1887) is a novel about the North and South prior to the Civil War, as seen by Harvard friends from the two sections. Conway was editor of the Cincinnati *Dial*♦ (1860). He edited *The Writings of Thomas Paine* (1894–96), of whom he also wrote a biography (1892).

Conway Cabal, during the Revolutionary War, was an alleged plot to replace Washington by General Horatio Gates, in the command of the Continental army. There was a movement in favor of Gates, who had been victorious at Saratoga while Washington had been defeated at Brandywine and Germantown, and a misunderstanding involving a letter by General Thomas Conway temporarily caused accusations of treason against Gates, who was later cleared. The intrigue figures in the plot of Maxwell Anderson's *Valley Forge.*

CONWELL, RUSSELL HERMAN (1843–1925), Massachusetts-born Philadelphia Baptist minister, founded Temple University (1888) and was its first president. His book *Acres of Diamonds* (1888) was delivered thousands of times as a lecture, and set forth his gospel of the reconciliation of orthodox Christianity with the dominant capitalist spirit, stressing individual initiative and the Christian responsibility of the wealthy class to society.

COOK, EBENEZER (*fl.*1708), author of the satirical poem *The Sot-Weed Factor*♦ (1708), of whom nothing definite is known. According to the poem, he was an Englishman who visited Maryland, but he is now considered to have been an American. *Sotweed Redivivus* (1730), a serious verse treatise on the overproduction of tobacco, is probably by him, and elegies on Nicholas Lowe and William Lock bear Cook's name, with the title "Laureat," which may have been granted by Lord Baltimore. To Cook is also attributed "The History of Colonel Nathaniel Bacon's Rebellion," a burlesque poem in the collection *The Maryland Muse* (1731), thought to be based on the Burwell Papers. He was the inspiration for a modern novel, *The Sot-Weed Factor* (1960) by John Barth.

COOK, GEORGE CRAM (1873–1924), founder and leader of the Provincetown Players.♦ Despite the success of this theater, he felt his creative impulses to be frustrated, and turned to a new outlet by making a pilgrimage to Greece. There he was accepted as a seer, and was said to have been honored in legends and songs of the peasants. *The Road to the Temple* (1926) is a romantic biography of Cook by his third wife, Susan Glaspell, with whom he collaborated in writing the one-act plays *Suppressed Desires* (1914) and *Tickless Time* (1918). His own books include *Evolution and the Superman* (1906), *The Chasm* (1911), and *Battle-Hymn of the Workers* (1912).

COOKE, [ALFRED] ALISTAIR (1908–), British commentator on the U.S., after graduation

from Cambridge and a Commonwealth Fellowship at Yale and Harvard, began his career of writing on American affairs, notably for *The Manchester Guardian* (1948–72). He early took American citizenship and his books on American subjects include *Douglas Fairbanks* (1940); *A Generation on Trial* (1950), about the Alger Hiss case; *One Man's America* (1952); *Christmas Eve* (1952); *A Commencement Address* (1954); *Talk About America* (1968), selections from his BBC broadcasts; *Alistair Cooke's America* (1973), based on a television series; and *The Patient Has the Floor* (1986), a collection of speeches.

COOKE, JOHN ESTEN (1830–86), Virginia author, brother of Philip Pendleton Cooke. His reputation derives mainly from his romances of colonial Virginia, *Leather Stocking and Silk*♦ (1854), *The Virginia Comedians*♦ (1854), and *Henry St. John, Gentleman*♦ (1859). He served in the Confederate army throughout the Civil War, and in the intervals of campaigning wrote a *Life of Stonewall Jackson* (1863). The war also prompted his military biography of Lee (1871); two volumes of essays on military subjects; a series of romances, including *Surry of Eagle's Nest* (1866), *Hilt to Hilt* (1869), and *Mohun* (1869), in which the Civil War is seen through the eyes of Surry, a fictitious aide of Stonewall Jackson; and *Hammer and Rapier* (1871), a panoramic novel from Bull Run to Appomattox. *The Heir of Gaymount* (1870), a novel pleading for agrarianism as the salvation of the postbellum South, also has a basis in Cooke's war experiences, although its story of buried treasure and a cryptogram are reminiscent of Poe's "The Gold-Bug." Other romances, showing Cooke's indebtedness to Irving, certain English novelists, and most of all Cooper, include *Fairfax* (1868), a romantic account of Washington's youth; *Her Majesty the Queen* (1873), a story of the Cavaliers; *Canolles* (1877), a romance of Virginia during the Revolution; *Fanchette* (1883), a novel of contemporary Washington life; and *My Lady Pokahontas*♦ (1885). *Virginia* (1883) is a history of his native state, emphasizing the colonial era. All of Cooke's fiction exhibits an idealization of the past, sentimentality, and dependence upon literary conventions of the day; his principal aim, however, was to entertain, and in this he was eminently successful.

COOKE, PHILIP PENDLETON (1816–50), like his brother John Esten Cooke, was also an author, best known for his poem "Florence Vane," published in *Burton's Gentleman's Magazine* (1840), which was long a parlor favorite in the then popular sentimental vein. His only volume of poetry, *Froissart's Ballads* (1847), contains versified transcripts from the French chronicler. Cooke contributed several prose romances to the *Southern Literary Messenger,* but these have not been reprinted. He was a literary critic.

COOKE, Philip St. George (1809–95), uncle of John Esten Cooke and Philip P. Cooke, was a military leader in the West and in the Mexican War, and served on the Union side in the Civil War, although others of his family were prominent in the Confederate army. He became a major general (1865). His early experiences form the basis of *Scenes and Adventures in the Army* (1857) and *Conquest of New Mexico and California* (1878).

COOKE, Rose Terry (1827–92), Connecticut short-story writer and poet, whose best tales, collected in *Somebody's Neighbors* (1881), *Root-Bound* (1885), *The Sphinx's Children and Other People's* (1886), and *Huckleberries Gathered from New England Hills*♦ (1891), are homely incidents of New England rural life, told in a simple, spontaneous, humorous manner. In her 50 years of writing, one may trace the development of the short story in America, from unlocalized, leisurely, sentimental tales to simple histories of commonplace people set in real locales.

Cool Tombs, free-verse poem by Carl Sandburg,♦ written in 1915 and collected in *Cornhuskers* (1918). Meditating upon death's negation of human ambition and turmoil, the poet concludes:

> . . . tell me if the lovers are losers . . .
> tell me if any get more than the lovers
> . . . in the dust . . . in the cool tombs.

COOLBRITH, Ina [Donna] (1842–1928), was born in Illinois, brought by covered wagon to California as a child, and after 1865 lived in the San Francisco Bay region. She helped Bret Harte to edit the *Overland Monthly* and was associated with the literary group that included Clemens, C.W. Stoddard, and Joaquin Miller. Her simple lyric poems were collected in *A Perfect Day* (1881), *The Singer of the Sea* (1894), and *Songs from the Golden Gate* (1895). In 1915 she organized a World Congress of Authors for the Panama-Pacific Exposition in San Francisco and was named the state's first Poet Laureate by the legislature.

COONEY, Seamus, see *Reznikoff, Charles.*

COOPER, Frank, pseudonym of Simms.♦

COOPER, James Fenimore (1789–1851), was born at Burlington, N.J., the son of William Cooper,♦ who in 1790 removed his family to Otsego Hall, a manorial estate at Cooperstown on Otsego Lake, west of Albany, N.Y. Educated at the local school and in Albany, Cooper went to Yale, from which he was dismissed (1806). During the next five years he served at sea as a foremast hand, was a midshipman in the navy (1808–11), and left to marry and settle as a country gentleman at Mamaroneck. He moved to Cooperstown (1814), but in 1817 moved again to a farm at Scarsdale.

At 30 he was suddenly plunged into a literary career, when his wife challenged his claim that he could write a better book than the English novel he was reading to her. The result was *Precaution* (1820), a conventional novel of manners in genteel English society. His second book, *The Spy*♦ (1821), was an immediate success and established Cooper's typical attitude toward plot and characterization, being significant for its use of the American scene as the background of a romance. In *The Pioneers*♦ (1823) he began his series of Leather-Stocking Tales,♦ but in his rapid quest for unusual subjects he turned to the sea in *The Pilot*♦ (1823), intending to prove that a sailor could write a better novel than the landsman Scott had done in *The Pirate* (1822).

Established as a leading American author, he moved to New York City, where he founded the Bread and Cheese Club.♦ To further his position as the outstanding American novelist, he planned to write 13 national romances, one for each of the original states, but wrote only *Lionel Lincoln*♦ (1825), dealing with Revolutionary Boston. Encouraged by the success of *The Pioneers* and the growing interest in the clash between savagery and civilization on the frontier, he continued his history of the pioneer scout Natty Bumppo in *The Last of the Mohicans*♦ (1826) and *The Prairie*♦ (1827). While traveling abroad (1826–33), nominally as U.S. consul at Lyons, he published *The Red Rover*♦ (1827), *The Wept of Wish-ton-Wish*♦ (1829), and *The Water-Witch*♦ (1830), romances about America and life on American ships. In addition, he wrote *The Bravo*♦ (1831), *The Heidenmauer*♦ (1832), and *The Headsman*♦ (1833), a trilogy intended to dispel the glamor of feudalism and to show its decline before the rise of democratic liberalism. *A Letter . . . to General Lafayette* (1831) champions republics against monarchies, and *Notions of the Americans* (1828) is an answer to English critics of U.S. society and government.

Upon his return, Cooper in turn was repelled by the absence of what he considered to be public and private virtue, the abuses of democracy, and the failure to perceive the best elements of the life he had conjured up in his novels. *A Letter to His Countrymen* (1834), petulantly expressing his conservatism, was followed by his satire, *The Monikins*♦ (1835), and four volumes of *Gleanings in Europe* (1837–38), containing brilliant descriptions and pungent social criticism. *The American Democrat*♦ (1838), a full statement of his aristocratic social ideals, was followed by *Homeward Bound*♦ (1838) and *Home as Found*♦ (1838), fictional statements of these themes.

During the ensuing years, the press attacked his books and personal character, and he brought suits for libel against various Whig papers, arguing his own cases so successfully that he was regularly victorious. He returned to live at Cooperstown, where his favorite companion and amanuensis for the rest of his life was his daughter Susan,♦ whose books describe their home. Here he carried his war with the press over to a war with the people concerning property rights, in which, although he was consistently vindicated, he stood alone and unpopular.

Meanwhile he wrote a scholarly *History of the Navy* (1839), whose simplicity and gusto were overlooked in a controversy centering on his treatment of the Battle of Lake Erie. With the publication of *The Pathfinder*◆ (1840) and *The Deerslayer*◆ (1841) he completed the epical Leather-Stocking series, and in a burst of creative energy wrote 16 works of fiction, a great amount of controversial literature, and some scholarly and factual works. *Mercedes of Castile* (1840) deals with the first voyage of Columbus; *The Two Admirals* (1842) is a story of the British navy before the Revolutionary War; and *Wing-and-Wing*◆ (1842) is concerned with a French privateer in the Mediterranean. *Ned Myers* (1843) is the fictional biography of a former shipmate, and the *Lives of Distinguished American Naval Officers* (1846) supplements the *History of the Navy*. *Wyandotté* (1843) deals with the outbreak of the Revolution in New York; *Le Mouchoir* (1843), republished as the *Autobiography of a Pocket-Handkerchief*, is a short romance of New York society and class distinctions; *Afloat and Ashore*◆ (1844) and its sequel *Miles Wallingford*◆ (1844) seem to present a self-portrait of Cooper; *The Crater* (1848) is a Utopian social allegory; and *Jack Tier* (1848), *The Oak Openings*◆ (1848), and *The Sea Lions* (1848) are all swift-moving historical romances. Cooper's last novel, *The Ways of the Hour* (1850), concerned with the perversion of social justice, is a forerunner of the modern mystery novel. Another late work is an unpublished comedy, *Upside Down, or Philosophy in Petticoats,* produced in New York. Of the novels written after 1840, the most important are those in the trilogy known as the Littlepage Manuscripts◆: *Satanstoe*◆ (1845), *The Chainbearer*◆ (1845), and *The Redskins*◆ (1846), tracing the growing difficulties between propertied and propertyless classes in New York. A collection of *Letters and Journals* (6 vols., 1960–68) by James F. Beard gathers all known previously unpublished manuscripts.

Cooper's achievement, although uneven and the result of brilliant improvisation rather than a deeply considered artistry, was nevertheless sustained almost to the close of a hectic, crowded career. His worldwide fame attests his power of invention, for his novels have been popular principally for their variety of dramatic incidents, vivid depiction of romantic scenes and situations, and adventurous plots. But a more sophisticated view caused a revival of interest in the mid-20th century concentrating on Cooper's novels in their creation of tension between different kinds of society, between society and the individual, between the settlement and the wilderness, and between civil law and natural rights as these suggest issues of moral and mythic import.

COOPER, MYLES (1735–85), English-born Anglican clergyman, came to American (1762), where he was president of King's College (1763–75). His Loyalist writings include *The American Querist* (1774) and *A Friendly Address to All Reasonable Americans* (1774), which urged moderation on the part of the patriots, and became a favorite target for rebel replies. He fled to England (1775).

COOPER, PETER (1791–1883), New York inventor, financier, and philanthropist, designed and built the first steam locomotive, *Tom Thumb* (1830), rolled the first structural steel, and invented a cloth-shearing machine. He founded Cooper Union◆ and circulated millions of documents against the growing financial hierarchy of his time. In *Ideas for a Science of Good Government* (1883) he advocates a national monetary system based on legal tender, a protective tariff, and an effective civil service.

COOPER, SUSAN FENIMORE (1813–94), daughter of J.F. Cooper,◆ to whose works she added biographical prefaces. She was the author of *Rural Hours* (1850), journal jottings on nature and life at Cooperstown, and *William West Skiles: A Sketch of Missionary Life* (1890).

COOPER, THOMAS (1759–1839), born in England and educated at Oxford, emigrated to Pennsylvania (1794) because of disputes arising from his sympathy with the French Revolution. Allying himself with the Jeffersonian opponents of the Federalist administration, he wrote many pamphlets and a volume of *Political Essays* (1799). After a brief political career, he became a professor of chemistry and then president of South Carolina College (1820–33). An early advocate of nullification and champion of free trade, he wrote many controversial pamphlets, showing his hostility to tyranny, whether clerical, political, or legal, as well as scholarly works on law and science.

COOPER, WILLIAM (1754–1809), father of J.F. Cooper,◆ settled on the shores of Otsego Lake in central New York (1790) and founded the town which bears his name. At one time his land holdings aggregated more than 750,000 acres, and he prospered as a land agent. He adopted a policy of installment payments for his tenants, and kept his land free of the Anti-Rent Wars.◆ A staunch Federalist, he was a member of Congress (1795–97, 1799–1801), and often left his magnificent home to show his prowess as a wrestler in some neighboring shanty. He died as the result of a blow struck by a political opponent. His son's *Chronicles of Cooperstown* (1838) tells of his settlement, which he himself vigorously describes in *A Guide in the Wilderness* (1810).

Cooper Union (COOPER INSTITUTE), free, privately supported college founded at New York

City (1859) by Peter Cooper and specializing in art, architecture, engineering, and science. It was also famous for its free public lectures. Among the speeches delivered in its auditorium was Lincoln's first address in the East (Feb. 27, 1860) as a potential presidential candidate.

Cooperstown, New York state settlement 59 miles west of Albany, founded by William Cooper♦ and described by him in *A Guide in the Wilderness* (1810) and by his son James Fenimore Cooper in *Chronicles of Cooperstown* (1838). The younger Cooper used the environs of the town on Otsego Lake as prototype for the setting of some of his fiction, notably *The Deerslayer* and *The Pioneers.* The town is also famous as the home of Abner Doubleday, the originator of baseball, and has a National Baseball Museum and Hall of Fame. Cooperstown has been restored, as a 19th-century frontier town with museums specializing in the life of that era. It is the site of annual summer seminars on American culture and folk art offered by the New York State Historical Association.

COOVER, ROBERT [LOWELL] (1932–), Iowa-born author, winner of a Faulkner Award for the best first novel in 1965 with *The Origin of the Brunists,* which fuses realism, satire, and fantasy in telling of a mystic cult founded by the survivor of an accident in a coal mine. It was followed by another fanciful novel of multilevel character, *The Universal Baseball Association, Inc., J. Henry Waugh, Prop.* (1968), about a lonely accountant who fantasizes a rich, warm life in the imaginary baseball league he has invented and avidly follows. *The Public Burning* (1977) is an even more surrealistic and satirical novel in its depiction of the U.S. at the beginning of the Eisenhower administration as Vice-President Nixon and Uncle Sam go golfing together while Ethel and Julius Rosenberg are condemned to death for espionage. *A Political Fable* (1980) is a novella about politics, first issued in a journal in 1968, and *Spanking the Maid* (1982), another novella, satirically treats the use of sadism in fiction. After these came *Gerald's Party* (1986), a black-humor novel about human chaos, and *Whatever Happened to Gloomy Gus of the Chicago Bears?* (1987), a tale about an athlete successful during the Depression. *Pricksongs and Descants* (1969) contains short fictional pieces juxtaposing famous legends with his own inventive stories; and *A Night At the Movies, Or You Must Remember This* (1987) is a collection of short pieces linking film and fiction in imagery. Coover has also written plays, *A Theological Position* (1972) and *The Water Pourer* (1972), and a film, *On a Confrontation in Iowa City* (1969).

COPELAND, CHARLES TOWNSEND (1860–1952), born in Maine, after graduation from Harvard (1882) became a professor of English literature there (1893) and influenced many later authors, including Cowley, John Reed, Dos Passos, and Hillyer. His wit and his beautiful reading voice charmed generations of students. He edited an anthology, *The Copeland Reader* (1926), and other works. His biography, *Copey of Harvard* (1960), was written by a former student, J. Donald Adams, with recollections from other students.

COPLEY, JOHN SINGLETON (1738?–1815), Boston portrait painter, known for his attention to detail and uncompromising truth in depicting his sitters. He went to England (1774), and his Tory leanings kept him there for the rest of his life except for a year in Italy, where he studied the works of the old masters. In England he executed successful portraits and large historical canvases, showing a greater facility, grace, and technical skill than in the firmer and more honest New England portraits on which his reputation rests. His most dramatic (and familiar) painting is *Watson and the Shark.*

Copperheads, epithet applied during the Civil War to Northern sympathizers with the Confederacy, or to the Peace Democrats, who opposed the waging of the war. The name is derived from that of the deadly snake that gives no warning before it discharges its venom. In earlier times, the name was applied to Indians and to the Dutch colonists. The most prominent of the Peace Democrats was C.L. Vallandigham, Ohio politician who in 1864 became president of the Knights of the Golden Circle, a secret society of Copperheads, powerful in the Middle West until the end of that year. This organization, which had originated in the South during the 1850s, was also known as the Order of American Knights and the Sons of Liberty. Harold Frederic's *The Copperhead* (1893) is a story of a New York farmer who opposes Abolitionism, and Augustus Thomas's play *The Copperhead* (1918) deals with a southern Illinois farmer selected by Lincoln to serve as an espionage agent among the Copperheads.

COPWAY, GEORGE (1818–c.1863), Ojibway chief, became a Wesleyan missionary, and wrote several volumes of reminiscences and Indian history, including *Life, History, and Travels* (1847), *Traditional History of the Ojibway Nation* (1850), and a poem, *The Ojibway Conquest* (1850). His style is said by *The Dictionary of American Biography* to be "an amalgam of Washington Irving, St. Luke, and elements derived from Methodist exhorters."

Coquette, The, epistolary novel by Hannah Foster,♦ anonymously issued in 1797. The plot, based on fact, is told in 74 letters, mainly from the heroine to her friend Lucy Freeman.

When the death of her disliked fiancé frees Eliza Wharton for flirtation, she is wooed by

J. Boyer, a minister, but keeps him waiting because she is entranced by the libertine Major Sanford. Boyer gives her up and Sanford deserts her to wed an heiress. Still attracted, Eliza has an affair with Sanford. Consumptive and melancholy, the pregnant Eliza leaves home and friends, and she and her baby die in childbirth.

CORBIN, ALICE, see *Henderson, Alice.*

COREY, GILES (*d.*1692), Salem, Mass., resident, was pressed to death for witchcraft when his wife was hanged for the same crime. An account of this folk hero appears in Calef's *More Wonders of the Invisible World,* and he is the subject of the second of Longfellow's *New England Tragedies,* of Mary Wilkins Freeman's play *Giles Corey, Yeoman,* and of Arthur Miller's *The Crucible.*

CORLE, EDWIN (1906–56), New Jersey-born author of books on the Southwest that include the novels *Fig Tree John* (1935), about a 19th-century Apache's unhappy relations with whites; *People on the Earth* (1937), with a similar but less tragic theme; *Listen, Bright Angel* (1946); *Three Ways to Mecca* (1947), a pseudo-philosophic social satire; and *In Winter Light* (1949), set on a Navajo reservation. *Mojave* (1934) collects stories with desert settings; *Burro Alley* (1938) presents fictive incidents of night life in Santa Fe; and *Billy the Kid* (1953) is a fictionized life. His nonfiction includes *Desert Country* (1941) and *The Gila, River of the Southwest* (1951).

CORMAN, CID (SIDNEY CORMAN) (1924–   ), Boston-born writer, graduated from Tufts University (1945), was much influenced by Charles Olson, edited *Origin* (1951–71), to which many Black Mountain♦ authors contributed. His own spare poems, suggestive of the Orient, appeared in 49 slight collections from 1944 through 1975, including *Thanksgiving Eclogue* (1954) and *Livingdying* (1970). *Aegis* (1984) contains selected poems, 1970–80, extended in *And the Word* (1987). Long expatriated in Japan, he has also translated from the Japanese, including 50 haiku in *One Man's Moon* (1984). He has also written essays.

CORSO, GREGORY [NUNZIO] (1930–   ), poet of the Beat movement♦ from New York City and friend of Allen Ginsberg, has led a checkered life in several lands and spent three years in prison. His poems of protest, now intensely bitter, now amusingly irreverent, appear in *The Vestal Lady of Brattle* (1955), *Gasoline* (1958), *Bomb* (1958), *The Happy Birthday of Death* (1960), *Long Live Man* (1962), *Elegiac Feelings American* (1970), *There Is Yet Time To Run Back Through Life and Expiate All That's Been Sadly Done* (1965), *Herald of the Autochthonic Spirit* (1981), *Wings, Words, Windows* (1982), and *Mindfield* (1989). *This Hung-Up Age* (1955) is a play;

The American Express (1961) is a novel; and *Some of My Beginnings and What I Feel Right Now* (1982) is a brief autobiographical work.

CORWIN, NORMAN [LEWIS] (1910–   ), Boston-born radio dramatist, who has written for such nationwide broadcast series as "Words Without Music" and the "Columbia Workshop." He was long known for his bold and unusual adaptations of current topics and his creation of new microphone techniques, as exhibited in the scripts in *Thirteen by Corwin* (1942), *More by Corwin* (1944), and *On a Note of Triumph* (1945), hailing victory in Europe. Later works include *Untitled and Other Radio Dramas* (1947); *Dog in the Sky* (1952), a radio play; *The World of Carl Sandburg* (1961); *Overkill and Megalove* (1963); *Prayer for the 70s* (1969); *Holes in a Stained Glass Window* (1978); and *Trivializing America* (1983). He became a professor at the University of Southern California in 1981.

CORYELL, JOHN RUSSELL, see *Nick Carter.*

Cosmopolitan (1886–   ), monthly magazine founded at Rochester, N.Y., as a conservative journal for family reading. It was moved to New York City (1887), and under the editorship of John B. Walker (1889–1905), who had such assistants as Howells and A.S. Hardy, it entered into competition with *McClure's* and *Munsey's.* Among its contributors were Clemens, Henry James, Kipling, and Conan Doyle. Articles on popular education led to the founding of Cosmopolitan University (1897), a correspondence school. After 1900, *Cosmopolitan* entered the muckraking movement, and later turned to featuring popular fiction and noncontroversial articles on the drama and notable personalities, a policy continued after its purchase by Hearst (1925). Beginning in 1965 a new editor, Helen Gurley Brown, employed sensational text and pictures to appeal to women who are career-oriented and seeking personal freedom.

COSTAIN, THOMAS B[ERTRAM] (1885–1965), born in Canada, after a journalistic career there came to the U.S. (1920) and became an associate editor of *The Saturday Evening Post.* His popular historical romances include *For My Great Folly* (1942), about a 17th-century pirate; *Ride with Me* (1943), set during the Napoleonic Wars; *The Black Rose* (1945), about a 13th-century English nobleman in Kublai Khan's China; *The Moneyman* (1947), about Jacques Cœur, the 15th-century French financier; *High Towers* (1949), set in 18th-century Montreal and New Orleans; *The Silver Chalice* (1952), dealing with the legend of the Holy Grail; *The Tontine* (2 vols., 1955), depicting the relations of two early 19th-century English families to an insurance lottery; *Below the Salt* (1957), a story within a story, the former about King John's England; *The Darkness and the*

Dawn (1959), about the era of Attila; and *The Last Love* (1963), about Napoleon at St. Helena. His nonfiction *Pageant of England is in four volumes: The Conqueror* (1949), *The Magnificent Century* (1951), *The Three Edwards* (1958), and *The Last Plantagenets* (1962). *The White and the Gold* (1954) is a history of Canada from discovery to 1763, and *The Chord of Steel* (1960) tells of Alexander Graham Bell's years in Brantford, Ontario, the author's hometown.

COTTON, JOHN (1584–1652), as dean of Emmanuel College, Cambridge, became interested in Puritanism. He emigrated to the Massachusetts Bay Colony (1633) and became a religious leader. Once close to the views of Anne Hutchinson,♦ he joined those who adjudged her a heretic. He wrote many works on the church, and a catechism for children, *Milk for Babes, Drawn out of the Breasts of Both Testaments* (1646). *The Keyes of the Kingdom of Heaven* (1644) was the standard Congregational guide in New England until the publication of the Cambridge Platform (1648). *The Way of the Churches of Christ in New England* (1645) and *The Way of the Congregational Churches Cleared* (1648) tended to identify the New England church with the aristocratic aspects of Calvinism. Cotton also wrote a second volume of *A Survey of the Summe of Church-Discipline* (1648), continuing the work of Thomas Hooker.♦ His authocratic views on civil and religious government provoked Roger Williams to write *The Bloudy Tenent of Persecution*♦ (1644), which was answered by Cotton's *The Bloudy Tenent Washed and Made White in the Bloud of the Lamb* (1647). He wrote the preface to *The Bay Psalm Book.*♦ He was the father-in-law of Increase Mather.

Cotton Boll, *The,* ode by Henry Timrod,♦ published in his *Poems* (1873). Written during the Civil War, it embodies the author's observations on the "small sphere" of a single boll of cotton, which symbolizes the cotton fields of the South in their "soft white fibres,"

> That, with their gossamer bands,
> Unite, like love, the sea-divided lands.

Country of the Pointed Firs, *The,* local-color sketches by Sarah Orne Jewett,♦ published in 1896.

A woman who spends her summers in the isolated seaport town of Dunnet, Me., describes the region in these portraits and anecdotes. She lives as a boarder with kindly Mrs. Almira Todd, through whose gossip she comes to know the lives and idiosyncrasies of the people. On a visit to Green Island, she meets Mrs. Todd's charming old mother, Mrs. Blackett, and her shy brother William. Other acquaintances are aged Captain Littlepage, who tells a fantastic story of discovering Purgatory in the Arctic; Abby Martin, the "Queen's Twin," born in the same hour as Victoria; old Mrs. Fosdick, "the best hand in the

world to make a visit," who tells of her childhood on her father's ship; and the gentle shepherdess Esther Hight, who, though courted by William Blackett for 40 years, continues to live with her invalid mother. A visit from Mrs. Fosdick leads Mrs. Todd to tell of her cousin, "Poor Joanna," who became a hermit on Shell-heap Island when "crossed in love." Later events are the death of old Mrs. Hight and the happy marriage of William and Esther.

Couples, novel by John Updike,♦ published in 1968.

In Tarbox, Mass. (a town like Ipswich), during the 1960s the young married set of stylish suburbanites is composed of men and women trying to find their own identities, often through finding themselves in bed with somebody else's mate. Frank and Albert Appleby and Herbert and Marcia Smith exchange partners and thus become known as The Applesmiths, while Ben and Irene Saltz, silently smarting over the community's alleged anti-Semitism, become involved with the Constantines—Eddie, a swinging airline pilot, and Carol, the town's sharpest gossip—and thus become The Saltines. Piet Hanema, a redheaded, well-built contractor and restorer of old houses, is proud of his Dutch heritage but as free and easy as any of his WASP neighbors. Among the women with whom he becomes involved is the well-bred Foxy Whitman, wife of a Boston University scientist, who becomes pregnant by Piet. She gets an abortion from the dentist Freddy Thorne, though his price for the operation is a night with Piet's pretty wife Angela. In time the couples drift apart from their marriages, their liaisons, and the town. Among them, Piet and Foxy, each divorced, later get married and move to Lexington, where they come to be accepted as just another couple in that town. Updike has stated that he wrote the closet drama *Buchanan Dying* as a penance for *Couples.*

Courtin', *The,* dialect verse narrative by Lowell, in *The Biglow Papers.*♦

Courtship of Miles Standish, *The,* narrative poem in unrhymed English hexameters by Longfellow,♦ published in 1858. The central theme is apocryphal, although material is drawn from early New England histories and tradition.

Miles Standish, captain of the Plymouth Colony, calls upon his better-educated friend John Alden to woo the maid Priscilla for him. Alden, also in love with the girl, yields to the duty of friendship and blurts out Standish's message, at which Priscilla makes her famous arch inquiry, "Why don't you speak for yourself, John?" Infuriated by Alden's failure, which he attributes to a betrayal of trust, Standish leaves on an Indian campaign without bidding farewell to his friend. During his absence, Alden and Priscilla are constantly together, and, receiving news of his death, plan to marry. The news proves to be false, Standish returns to attend the wedding and beg forgiveness for his anger, and the three are reunited as friends.

COUSINS, NORMAN (1912–   ), editor of *The Saturday Review* (1940–77), in which he expressed his humanitarian concern with democratic ideals, international understanding, and world unity. His books include *The Democratic Chance* (1942); *Who Speaks for Man?* (1952); *The Last Defense in a Nuclear Age* (1960); *Present Tense* (1967), about *The Saturday Review* and his contributions to it; *The Celebration of Life* (1974), on immortality; *Anatomy of an Illness* (1979) about curing his own sickness; *Human Options* (1982), "an autobiographical notebook" on the need for world unity; *The Pathology of Power* (1987), opposing national independent power; and *The Biology of Hope* (1989), demonstrating, from Cousins's work at Stanford, where he joined the medical faculty, the dramatic effect of emotions on bodily resistance to disease.

Covenant Theology (or FEDERAL THEOLO-GY), elaboration of the doctrines of Calvinism,♦ which became as important in New England as the original teaching. Developed in the writings of the English Puritans William Perkins and William Ames, and in those of early New England ministers, the Covenant Theology held that God promised Adam and his posterity eternal life, in return for obedience to moral law. After Adam broke this covenant of works, a new one was made with Abraham, this one a covenant of grace, requiring of man an active faith and indicating that man must still have reason and the ability to struggle toward moral perfection. Although this doctrine does not deny that God rejects or elects souls according to His pleasure, it softens the Calvinist statement of predestination by substituting for the divine decree a juridical relationship between man and God. Punishment for sin is considered not an inherent pollution but a judicial sentence of expulsion. During the Great Awakening, Jonathan Edwards repudiated the Covenant Theology to return to orthodox Calvinism.

Coverdale, MILES, character in *The Blithedale Romance.*♦

Cowboy, name given during the Revolution to lawless marauders who pillaged neutral territory and were supposedly favorable to the English. Those who favored the rebels were known as Skinners. Both figure in fiction about the Revolutionary War, particularly Cooper's *The Spy.*♦ The term "cowboy" has since been applied, particularly in the West, to cattle herders, and there are distinctive cowboy ballads♦ and tall tales.♦ Popular romancing about the cowboy dates back to dime novels and other pulp fiction beginning

in the 1870s, preceding infrequent realistic reminiscences like *A Texas Cowboy* (1885) by Charles Siringo. Owen Wister's *The Virginian*♦ (1902) became the classic handling of the type, far surpassing in popularity the literary works of writers who had more experience of cowboy life, such as Andy Adams's *The Log of a Cowboy* (1903) and E.M. Rhodes's *Good Men and True* (1910). The mythology of the masculine and heroic cowboy has been continued in a large body of fiction from the time of Clarence E. Mulford (*Hopalong Cassidy,* 1910), Zane Grey (*Riders of the Purple Sage,* 1912), and Max Brand (*Destry Rides Again,* 1930) to modern paperback publications of Louis L'Amour. The works of these authors and others in their vein have been further popularized in numerous film versions by stars who have included William S. Hart, Tom Mix, Gene Autry, Roy Rogers, and John Wayne. Cowboys have also been the subject of television programs.

COWLEY, MALCOLM (1898–1989), born in Pennsylvania, served in World War I, graduated from Harvard (1920), and later became an expatriate in France. *Blue Juniata* (1929) prints semi-autobiographical poems tracing his mental and emotional development during this period, to his final facing of the American scene. *A Dry Season* (1942), further poems, is partly about the "lost generation." Prose works, concerned with social and intellectual forces in contemporary society, include *Exile's Return: A Narrative of Ideas* (1934; revised, 1951), partly autobiographical, analyzing the postwar generation; *The Literary Situation* (1954), about the sociology of contemporary American authorship; *Think Back on Us* (1967), collecting his writings during and on the 1930s; *A Many-Windowed House* (1970), *A Second Flowering* (1973), and *And I Worked at the Writer's Trade* (1978), essays on modern American literature; *The Dream of the Golden Mountains* (1980), a memoir of the '30s, while *The Flower and the Leaf* (1985) recalls American writing since 1941 with some comment on famous early figures. His introduction to *The Portable Faulkner* (1946) marked the creation of Faulkner's reputation as a great writer. Much later he published *Unshaken Friend* (1985), a tribute to Thomas Wolfe's editor, Maxwell Perkins♦; and his *Correspondence* (of 1915–81) with Kenneth Burke (1988). He edited *After the Genteel Tradition* (1937) and many works by major American writers. *The View from 80* (1981) contains reflections on the life of an octogenarian.

Cowperwood, FRANK, major character in Dreiser's novels *The Financier,*♦ *The Titan,*♦ and *The Stoic.*

COX, PALMER (1840–1924), author and illustrator of books for children, was born in Quebec and came to the U.S. in 1876. Beginning with *The Brownies: Their Book* (1887), he published a long series of verse and pictorial treatments of this race of good-natured elves.

COXE, Louis O[sborne] (1918–), born in New Hampshire, after graduation from Princeton (1940) and naval service taught English at Lawrenceville, Harvard, Minnesota, and Bowdoin (1955–83). His poetry has been collected in *The Sea Faring* (1947), *The Second Man* (1955), *The Wilderness* (1958), *The Last Hero* (1965), and *Nikal Seyn and Decoration Day* (1966), whose sense of tradition, lofty subjects, and disciplined craftsmanship may be reasons why he has called himself "the first neo-Victorian"; *Passage* (1979) collects poems since 1943, and *The North Well* (1985), new poems. *The Middle Passage* (1960) is a book-length blank-verse narrative poem on the depravity of the slave trade. With Princeton classmate Robert H. Chapman he wrote the dramatic adaptation of *Billy Budd* (1951), first produced in an earlier version as *Uniform of Flesh* (1949). He is also the author of a critical book, *Edwin Arlington Robinson* (1969), and *Enabling Acts* (1976), critical essays.

COZZENS, Frederick Swartwout (1818–69), under the pseudonym Richard Haywarde, contributed burlesques and humorous articles to *The Knickerbocker Magazine* and other periodicals. These were collected in *The Sparrowgrass Papers (1856), The Sayings of Dr. Bushwhacker and Other Learned Men* (1867), and *Sayings, Wise and Otherwise* (1880).

COZZENS, James Gould (1903–78), born in Chicago but reared on Staten Island and educated at Harvard (1922–24), where he wrote his first novel, *Confusion* (1924), the story of an aristocratic, rebellious French girl. Leaving college to become a tutor in Cuba, he wrote *Michael Scarlett* (1925), a historical romance, and gathered background for *Cock Pit* (1928), set on a Cuban sugar plantation, and *The Son of Perdition* (1929), about a despotic American company official in Cuba. His more mature work begins with the novelette *S.S. San Pedro* (1931), based on the mysterious sinking of the *Vestris,* followed by *The Last Adam* (1933), published in England as *A Cure of Flesh,* introducing a representative Cozzens figure and setting in the story of a crusty, heterodox doctor in a rigid Connecticut town. *Castaway* (1934) is an atypical fantasy, presenting, with seeming realism, New York after a disaster that leaves the sole surviving man wandering in a great department store. The most characteristic novels begin with *Men and Brethren* (1936), a study of a liberal clergyman; *Ask Me Tomorrow* (1940), about an American in Europe; and *The Just and The Unjust* (1942), about a murder trial, for they deal with mature professional men in a stratified society who are called upon to resolve a conflict between the ideal and the possible and who acquiesce in the way things are, without complete loss of

principle. This point of view and the tone of detached disenchantment appear most markedly in *Guard of Honor*♦ (1948, Pulitzer Prize), about the clash between human and military values at an air force base in World War II; and *By Love Possessed*♦ (1957), depicting a lawyer, one of the men of reason, and his involvements in love. Cozzens's last novel, *Morning, Noon, and Night* (1968), in presenting the recollections of one man in his sixties also gives a sense of upper-middle-class New England life in the 20th century. *Children and Others* (1964) collects stories, half of them about boys' views of their teachers, parents, and other adults.

Cracker, name applied to one of the class of poor-white inhabitants of the backwoods of Georgia and Florida, supposedly because their chief article of diet is cracked corn. The Georgia cracker has appeared frequently in fiction, from A.B. Longstreet and W.T. Thompson to Erskine Caldwell.

Cracker-barrel humor, originally associated with the native American wise saws involved in the swapping of gossip, information, and social and political views around the cracker barrel of New England general stores, but later extended to all shrewd, homespun, idiomatic Yankee wit, such as that of Jack Downing, Sam Slick, the characters in Lowell's *Biglow Papers,* the Widow Bedott, and Mrs. Partington, and further extended to all horse-sense folk humor of the U.S., regardless of region.

CRADDOCK, Charles Egbert, pseudonym of Mary N. Murfree.♦

CRAFTS, William (1787–1826), South Carolina lawyer and orator, wrote essays, poems, and drama criticism for the Charleston *Courier,* and *The Raciad and Other Occasional Poems* (1810) and *Sullivan's Island, The Raciad, and Other Poems* (1820).

Craig's Wife, play by George Kelly,♦ produced in 1925 and published in 1926, when it won a Pulitzer Prize.

Harriet Craig, interested only in her personal security, makes a career of her immaculate, luxurious home. She merely tolerates her husband Walter, but he remains romantically in love with her until his aunt and a niece reveal her selfishness. Walter decides on a divorce, and Harriet is left desolate with her possessions.

CRANCH, Christopher Pearse (1813–92), Unitarian minister and member of the Transcendentalist movement, contributed poems to *The Dial, The Western Messenger,* and other magazines, which were collected in 1844. A second volume was published as *The Bird and the Bell* (1875). Cranch translated the Æneid (1872), became known as a painter, and wrote and illustrated such children's books as *The Last of the Hugger-muggers* (1856) and its sequel *Kobboltozo* (1857).

CRANE, [Harold] Hart (1899–1932), Ohio-born poet, although he published only two books during his lifetime, is recognized as an outstanding poet of his era. *White Buildings* (1926), despite its lack of a single theme to synthesize the author's experience of the American scene, is distinguished by a sonorous rhetoric and concrete imagery, revealing by tangential suggestion an acute mystical perception. The promise of this early work is fulfilled in *The Bridge*♦ (1930), a long mystical poem concerned with the American background and the modern consciousness to which it gives rise. Crane finds in America a principle of unity and absolute faith, through the integration of such symbols as Columbus, Pocahontas, Rip Van Winkle, Poe, Whitman, the subway, and, above all, Brooklyn Bridge, an image of man's anonymous creative power unifying past and present. The lack of discipline in the poet's personal existence, and his belief that his creative ability had been dissipated, caused him to commit suicide by jumping from a ship that was bringing him home from a year's residence in Mexico. His *Collected Poems* (1933) incorporate previously unpublished West Indian sketches and other new poems. His *Letters* were published in 1952, and his correspondence with Yvor Winters was printed in 1978.

Crane, Ichabod, hero of "The Legend of Sleepy Hollow."♦

CRANE, Nathalia [Clara Ruth] (1913–   ), created a stir when at 11 she issued *The Janitor's Boy* (1924), containing not only light, facile rhymed poems unusual for a child, but even verses verging on the metaphysical. Her later books, *Lava Lane* (1925), *The Singing Crow* (1926), and *Venus Invisible* (1928) are increasingly serious; but her adult books, including *Swear by the Night* (1936) and *Death of Poetry* (1941), a dramatic poem, are considered less remarkable. She also published an account of the Children's Crusade, *The Sunken Garden* (1926), and a novel, *An Alien from Heaven* (1929).

CRANE, Stephen (1871–1900), born in New Jersey, spent most of his youth in upstate New York; he attended Lafayette College and Syracuse University, each for a year, before moving to New York City to become a struggling author and do intermittent reporting for the *Herald* and *Tribune.* His first book, *Maggie: A Girl of the Streets*♦ (1893), was too grim to find a regular publisher, and remained unsold even when Crane borrowed from his brother to issue it privately. Early in 1893, with no personal experience of war, deriving his knowledge primarily from reading Tolstoy and *Battles and Leaders of the*

Civil War, he wrote *The Red Badge of Courage*♦ (1895), his great realistic study of the mind of an inexperienced soldier trapped in the fury and turmoil of battle.

The success of this book led to the reissue of *Maggie,* and Crane's reputation was established. In quick succession appeared his book of free verse, influenced by Emily Dickinson, *The Black Riders*♦ (1895); *The Little Regiment*♦ (1896), naturalistic Civil War Stories, issued in England as *Pictures of War; George's Mother* (1896), the story of the dull lives of a young workingman and his mother in New York; and *The Third Violet* (1897), a conventional novelette about the romance of a young artist.

Because of his successful treatment of war in his masterpiece, Crane was thrust for most of his remaining life into the field of war reporting. After a period as a correspondent in the Southwest and in Mexico, he was sent with a filibustering expedition to Cuba at the end of 1896. The sinking of the ship and his subsequent 50-hour struggle with the waves furnished the theme of his best-known short story, "The Open Boat." Inexperience and illness made his trip to Greece, to report the Turkish war, almost futile. Following a short residence in England, he went to Cuba to report the Spanish-American War, and his journalistic sketches and stories of this period are collected in *Wounds in the Rain* (1900). His observation of the Greco-Turkish War resulted in *Active Service* (1899), a satirical novel about a war correspondent.

Upon his return to New York, Crane's health was already broken by the hardships he had endured, and, possibly owing to his early treatment of squalor in *Maggie* and rumors about the immorality of his common-law wife, a myth now arose to the effect that he was a drunk, a drug addict, and generally depraved. Disgusted by unpleasant notoriety, he returned to England, having meanwhile published two collections of short stories, *The Open Boat*♦ (1898) and *The Monster*♦ (1899), and a second volume of free verse, *War is Kind* (1899). *Whilomville Stories*♦ (1900) is a collection of tales concerned with typical childhood incidents in a small New York town. Crane's last work shows a decrease in power, for he was broken in health and soon died of tuberculosis in Germany, where he had gone to seek a cure. Posthumously published volumes include *Great Battles of the World* (1901), an uninspired historical study; *Last Words* (1902), a collection of his early tales and sketches; *The O'Ruddy* (1903), an unfinished romance, completed by Robert Barr; and *Men, Women, and Boats* (1921), a selection, including several stories never before published. His *Letters* were collected in 1960, and the University of Virginia issued a scholarly edition of his works (10 vols., 1969–75).

CRAPSEY, Adelaide (1878–1914), author of a slender volume, *Verse* (1915), written in the last year of her brief life. Of her fastidious poetry, the best-known pieces are her *cinquains,* a stark metrical form of her own invention, resembling the Japanese *haiku.* The *cinquain* is a precise five-line stanza, the lines having respectively two, four, six, eight, and two syllables. Her *Verse* was edited by Jean Webster,♦ whose fictional heroines are said to be patterned after the poet.

CRAWFORD, FRANCIS MARION (1854–1909), son of noted sculptor Thomas Crawford (1813–57), and nephew of Julia Ward Howe, was born in Italy. Educated in the U.S. and abroad, he began his career as an author of romantic novels of cosmopolitan life with *Mr. Isaacs, A Tale of Modern India* (1882), the story of a diamond merchant. This was followed by more than 40 novels dealing with the various countries in which the author resided. Among those set in Rome are *A Roman Singer* (1884), a story of artist life; *To Leeward* (1884), concerning the unhappy marriage of an English girl and an Italian *marchese; Marzio's Crucifix* (1887), about an Italian silversmith's struggle between love for his religious art and hatred of his brother, a priest; *Saracinesca* (1887), a story of love in Italian high society, and its sequels, *Sant' Ilario* (1889), *Don Orsino* (1892), and *Corleone* (1896); *Pietro Ghisleri* (1983), the love story of an Italian gentleman and an English girl; *Casa Braccio* (1895), about an Italian nun's elopement with a Scottish nobleman, and the unhappy life of their daughter; and *The White Sister* (1909), dealing with a nun torn between devotion to her vows and her passion for a former lover. The novels set in Germany include *Greifenstein* (1889), a story of German university life; *A Cigarette-Maker's Romance* (1890), about an impoverished Russian count and his love for a Polish girl who works with him in a tobacco shop; and *Dr. Claudius* (1883), the story of a Swedish doctor in Germany. Crawford's seven novels set in the U.S. include *An American Politician* (1884), concerned with political corruption and reform during the Gilded Age; *The Three Fates* (1892), about the love affairs of a young author; *Katherine Lauderdale* (1894), dealing with wealthy New York society, and its sequel, *The Ralstons* (1895). He also wrote such historical romances as *Zoroaster* (1885), set in Persia at the time of Cyrus; *Via Crucis* (1898), the story of an English nobleman in the Second Crusade; *In the Palace of the King* (1900), set in Philip II's Spain; *Marietta* (1901), the story of a 15th-century Venetian glass worker; and *Arethusa* (1907), about 14th-century Constantinople. In addition to his short stories of the supernatural, *Wandering Ghosts* (1911), he wrote several plays adapting his novels for the stage, as well as *Francesca da Rimini*♦ (1902), written for Sarah Bernhardt. In *The Novel—What It Is* (1893), and implicitly in his work, Crawford set forth his concept of fiction, which he said is to be devoted exclusively to entertainment, for which purpose he preferred the historical novel or romantic narrative of cosmopolitan life, and avoided moralizing or any photographic representation of life.

CRAWFORD, JOHN WALLACE (1847–1917), known as Captain Jack, was a frontier scout and Indian agent of the Black Hills, popular for lecturing and reciting his own verses. Among his published works are *The Poet Scout* (1879) and *The Broncho Book* (1908).

CRAYON, GEOFFREY, pseudonym of Irving.♦ *The Crayon Miscellany* is a series of three volumes published (1835) under this pseudonym. The books are *A Tour of the Prairies,*♦ *Legends of the Conquest of Spain,* and *Abbotsford and Newstead Abbey.*

CRAZY HORSE (*c.*1849–77), chief and military leader of the Sioux and Cheyenne Indians, aided Sitting Bull♦ in annihilating the forces of Custer in the Battle of the Little Big Horn (1876). He figures in Neihardt's *Song of the Indian Wars* and is the subject of a biography by Mari Sandoz.♦

Cream of the Jest, *The,* novel by Cabell,♦ published in 1917 and revised in 1920.

Creek Indians, confederacy of tribes, also called Muscogulges, were once located in Georgia and Alabama. Because the Spaniards mistreated them, they became allies of the English. Their rebellion (1814) was quelled by Andrew Jackson. Later the tribe moved to Oklahoma. J.R. Swanton has written a *History of the Creek Indians,* and they figure in the works of Chateaubriand, Irving, and Simms.

CREELEY, ROBERT [WHITE] (1926–), Massachusetts-born poet, graduated from Black Mountain College, where he became close to Charles Olson, whose *Selected Writings* he edited (1966), and where he was editor of *The Black Mountain Review*♦ (1954–57). He subsequently traveled widely and became a faculty member (1963) of the State University of New York at Buffalo. With *Le Fou* (1952) he began publication of numerous brief collections of poetry, selected in *For Love* (1962), marked by terse, laconic treatments of love, presented with great immediacy. Later volumes—*Words* (1967), *Pieces* (1969), *The Finger* (1970), *St. Martin's* (1971), *A Day Book* (1972), *Thirty Things* (1974), *Away* (1976), *Later* (1978), *Mirrors* (1983), *A Calendar* (1983), 12 poems, one for each month, among others—show him continuing a stripped-down style and diction in presenting the problems of understanding in dealing with personal feelings and relations, and he has been described as more existential and spontaneous. Still later volumes of poems include *Memories* (1984), *Memory Gardens* (1986), *The Company* (1988), and *Windows* (1990). He has also written stories, *The Gold Diggers* (1954, enlarged 1965); a quasi-autobiographical novel, *The Island* (1963), about a young American writer living on Majorca; and critical essays, *A Quick Graph* (1970) and *Was That a Real Poem* (1979). *The Collected Poems, 1945–75* appeared in 1983 and *The Collected Prose* in 1984. The so-called *Collected Essays* (1989) includes a good deal of fiction written since 1951.

Creole, name applied to American-born descendants of the French and Spanish settlers of Latin America. The term did not originally mean persons of mixed white and Negro blood, although this is one of its various connotations in popular usage. In Louisiana it is used to distinguish descendants of the original French settlers from the "Cajun" heirs of the exiles from Acadia. ♦ Creole life in Louisiana has been depicted by such local-color authors as Cable, Hearn, Grace King, and Kate Chopin, and been the subject of critical comment by a descendant, Adrien Rouquette.

CRÈVECŒUR, MICHEL-GUILLAUME JEAN DE (1735–1813), known as J. Hector St. John de Crèvecœur, was born in France, and emigrated to Canada during the last of the French and Indian Wars. He served under Montcalm, and later seems to have explored near the Great Lakes and the Ohio River. He landed at New York (1759), took out naturalization papers (1765), traveled extensively in Pennsylvania and New York, and settled with his American wife in Orange Country, N.Y. His travels are described in his later book, *Voyage dans la Haute Pensylvanie et dans l'état de New-York* (3 vols., 1801), translated as *Journey into Northern Pennsylvania and the State of New York* (1963). He spent idyllic years on his New York farm until the Revolution, when, as a Loyalist, he was forced to flee to New York and then to France (1780). During the quiet decade prior to the Revolution, he probably wrote most of the charming *Letters from an American Farmer*♦ (1782) on which his reputation rests. Other informative and vivid essays written during this period have been published in *Sketches of Eighteenth-Century America* (1925), which also includes a play, "Landscapes," six scenes showing the hypocrisy, inhumanity, cupidity, and abuse of power which underlay the Revolution. In 1783 Crèvecœur returned to America only to discover that his wife was dead, his home burned, and his children had disappeared, as a result of an Indian raid. Eventually he found his children, and settled in New York, where as French consul he attempted to cement the friendly relations of the two countries. He returned to France (1790), where he passed the rest of his life. Although he did not consider himself a man of letters, the French thought of him as a true "man of feeling," and when his *Lettres d'un cultivateur Américain* appeared in France (1783), it was adulterated with artificial sentimentality and redundant rhetoric.

For this and other reasons, Crèvecœur has often been considered merely a sentimental Rousseauistic romancer, but current criticism looks upon him as being a fresh and vigorous recorder of events and scenes in early American rural life.

Crisis, The, magazine edited by W.E.B. DuBois. ♦

Crisis, The, novel by Winston Churchill, ♦ published in 1901.
      This narrative of life and issues in the South, before and during the Civil War, centers at St. Louis, and among the characters are descendants of Richard Carvel. ♦ Stephen Brice comes from Boston to practice law in the office of Judge Whipple, who, though a Republican and Abolitionist, is a close friend of Colonel Carvel, a typical Southern Democrat. Stephen is attracted by Carvel's daughter Virginia, but she spurns him because of his Northern sympathies and becomes engaged to the romantic cavalier Clarence Colfax. Stephen is wounded in the Union cause, and later becomes an aide to Lincoln, while Colfax fights with the Confederates. In spite of the machinations of the Yankee carpetbagger Eliphalet Hooper, Virginia breaks with Colfax, who is captured as a spy, and she finally marries Stephen.

Crisis, The American, series of 13 regular and three specially issued pamphlets by Thomas Paine, ♦ published between Dec. 19, 1776, and April 19, 1783. The first pamphlet appeared at a time of gloom and uncertainty, when the Revolutionary army faced defeat because of its retreat across New Jersey and the imminent defection of some of the colonies, and Washington the day before had written ". . . if every nerve is not strained to the utmost to recruit the new army with all possible expedition, I think the game is pretty near up." Paine's direct, incisive style, and his stirring opening, "These are the times that try men's souls," created an immediate reaction in favor of the patriotic cause, and Washington had the pamphlet read before every regiment. The subsequent crossing of the Delaware and the victories at Trenton and Princeton were partly credited to its influence. Later issues continued to oppose defeatism and compromise, and were influential in maintaining morale and a unified spirit in the colonies.

CRISTOFER, MICHAEL (1945–), New Jersey-born actor and dramatist, whose plays include *The Mandala* (1967), *Rienzi* (1968), *Dorian* (1969), *Plot Counter Plot* (1971), *Americomedia* (1972), and *The Shadow Box* (1977, Pulitzer Prize), which presents three separate persons dying of cancer and the ways each meets the end of life. Other plays include *Ice* (1974), presenting two men and a woman living in an isolated Alaskan cabin; *Black Angel* (1976), about the later life of a World War II German officer responsible for the deaths of many French civilians; and *The Lady and the Clarinet* (1980), a comedy of a woman's recollections.

Critic, The (1881–1906), weekly literary magazine and review, published by Jeannette and Joseph Gilder. It is remembered as one of the first magazines to welcome Whitman's writing, and as the first to publish the Uncle Remus stories outside of the author's native town. Other contributors included J.L. Allen, Julia Ward Howe, Stedman, R.W. Gilder, E.E. Hale, and Aldrich.

Critical Fable, A, humorous critical verse on contemporary poets by Amy Lowell,♦ published anonymously in 1922. The idea, the eccentric rhythms, and the ludicrous rhymes are patterned after James Russell Lowell's *Fable for Critics*. An elder poet (presumably J.R. Lowell) and a contemporary poet (Amy Lowell) meet to discuss modern American poetry, displaying in their conversation some common sense, some humor, and some malice. Of the 21 authors mentioned, emphasis is given to Frost, Robinson, Sandburg, Lindsay, H.D., and Amy Lowell, while T.S. Eliot and Ezra Pound are classified as "odds and ends."

Croaker Papers, name given to a series of satirical poems on current topics by Drake♦ and Halleck.♦ The authorship of these popular verses was never acknowledged, and they were sent with elaborate secrecy to the New York *Evening Post* and *National Advertiser* between March and July 1819. Of the initial series of 35 poems, 14 are attributed to Drake (Croaker); 13 to Halleck (Croaker, Jr.); and eight to their collaboration (Croaker and Co.). The pseudonym was suggested by the name of a character in Goldsmith's *The Good-Natured Man*. The first (unauthorized) collection was published in 1819 and contained 24 selections; the first complete edition was published in 1860.

Croatan see *Roanoke Island*.

CROCKER, HANNAH MATHER (1752–1829), granddaughter of Cotton Mather, was an early Massachusetts advocate of women's rights. Her *Series of Letters on Free Masonry* (1815) deals with her educational attempts in connection with women's Masonic lodges. She also wrote *Observations on the Real Rights of Women.* (1818).

CROCKETT, DAVY (DAVID) (1786–1836), born in Tennessee, spent a shiftless youth until his political career began (*c.*1816) with his appointment as justice of the peace. He boasted that none of his decisions was ever reversed because of his dependence on "natural-born sense instead of law learning." After being twice elected to the state legislature, he accepted a humorous proposal that he run for Congress, and to his surprise was elected, serving from 1827 to 1831, and again

from 1833 to 1835. Because of his opposition to Jackson, the Whigs adopted him as a convenient tool through whom to draw the backwoods democracy to its standard. Davy was soon turned by skillful politicians into a frontier hero, whose picturesque eccentricities, backwoods humor, tall tales, shrewd native intelligence, and lusty pioneer spirit were all aggrandized. Whig journalists were soon at work and in short order turned out such books, attributed to Davy, as *Sketches and Eccentricities of Col. David Crockett* (1833), *An Account of Col. Crockett's Tour to the North and Down East* (1835), *The Life of Martin Van Buren* (1835), and *Col. Crockett's Exploits and Adventures in Texas* (1836). With the exception of the last, which is posthumous, he may have had a hand in all these works, and he gladly claimed the *Tour* and life of Van Buren. Swallowing the Whig bait, he enjoyed his sudden rise to fame and was glad to aid in propagating the myth, which, however, removed him from office, since his constituents would not tolerate his desertion of Democratic principles. Piqued, he left Tennessee to participate in the war for Texan independence, and a few months later died in the heroic defense of the Alamo, adding a final dramatic chapter to his career. *A Narrative of the Life of David Crockett, of the State of Tennessee* (1834) passes as his autobiography, although the claim has often been disputed. In any case the book has the robust manner attributed to Crockett, and contains fine examples of the farce and exaggeration of the tall tale.

Crockett almanacs, popular pamphlets issued irregularly by various publishers under the name of Davy Crockett or his "heirs." About 50 appeared between 1835 and 1856. In addition to the usual features of the almanacs, these publications, printed at Nashville, New York, Boston, Philadelphia, and other cities, contain tall tales based mainly on legends of oral tradition, concerned with Crockett, Mike Fink, Daniel Boone, and Kit Carson, as well as such mythical figures as the sea serpent of Cape Cod. The historical Crockett may have been involved in the original enterprise, and the almanacs, capitalizing on his spectacular death at the Alamo, contributed largely to his widespread popularity in contemporary folklore.

CROLY, HERBERT [DAVID] (1869–1930), son of Jane Croly, was a New York editor and social critic. He edited the *Architectural Record* (1900–1906), remaining on its staff until 1913, and publishing two books on American architecture. He was the founding editor (1914–30) of *The New Republic.* ♦ His other writings include *The Promise of American Life* (1909), a consideration of democratic principles in view of changing economic and social conditions; a biography of Mark Hanna (1912); *Progressive Democracy* (1914), a study of the evolution of democracy since the time of Hanna; and *Willard Straight* (1924), a biography of a friend who was a writer and adventurer in the Far East. Croly sometimes used the pseudonym William Herbert.

CROLY, JANE CUNNINGHAM (1829–1901), English-born journalist, came to New York in 1841, where she later married the author and editor David Goodman Croly (1829–89). Under the pseudonym Jenny June, she wrote feature articles for New York newspapers. Besides founding and presiding (1868–82) over Sorosis, the first professional women's club in the U.S., she helped found the Federation of Women's Clubs. She edited *Demorest's Illustrated Monthly* (1860–87), was part owner of *Godey's Lady's Book,* and was a professor at Rutgers. Her books include *For Better or Worse: A Book for Some Men and All Women* (1875) and *The History of the Women's Club Movement in America* (1898).

Cross of Gold Speech, see *Bryan, William Jennings.*

Crossing, The, historical romance by Winston Churchill,♦ published in 1904.

Until he is ten, David Ritchie lives with his puritanical Scottish father on the North Carolina frontier. His father joins the rebel army at the outbreak of the Revolution, and sends him to live with the Temple family at Charleston. Here David finds a friend in Nick Temple, a quick-tempered lad of his own age, but, when news comes of his father's death, he returns to the frontier as a farmhand. He is befriended by Polly Ann Ripley, who marries Tom McChesney, and he accompanies the couple to a Kentucky settlement. Soon Tom becomes a soldier under George Rogers Clark, and precocious David, though only 11, goes along as Clark's drummer and trusted aide. Historical figures portrayed in the ensuing scenes of the Wilderness campaign include John Sevier, Boone, and Simon Kenton. After capturing Kaskaskia, Cahokia, and Vincennes, Clark turns back, realizing his goal of Detroit to be impracticable. David returns to grow up on the McChesney farm, goes to Richmond to study law, and at 21 begins his practice in Kentucky, where he is joined by his boyhood friend, Nick, who discloses that they are cousins, and both grandsons of a Scottish earl. After helping to prosecute the treasonable activities of James Wilkinson, David goes with Nick to New Orleans where the Temples, former Loyalists, live in exile, and there he marries Hélène d'Ivryle-Tour, a French exile, with whom he returns to the Kentucky frontier.

Crossing Brooklyn Ferry, poem by Whitman,♦ published in the 1856 edition of *Leaves of Grass* as "Sun-Down Poem" and given its present title in 1860. Based on the author's reminiscences of life in Brooklyn and the trip across the East River to Manhattan, it is a rhapsody of the daily crowds and of the panorama of the city as seen from the river, in which he mystically identifies himself with everybody and everything: "great or small, you furnish your parts toward the soul."

CROTHERS, RACHEL (1878–1958), Illinois-born playwright and director, had her first New York success with *The Three of Us* (1906), a play set in a Nevada mining camp. *A Man's World*♦ (1909) was her first play concerned with contemporary morality and with the position of women in the modern world. Later plays concerning these subjects include *He and She*♦ (1911), *Ourselves* (1913), *Young Wisdom* (1914), *Nice People* (1920), *Everyday* (1921), *Mary the Third* (1923), *Expressing Willie* (1924), *A Lady's Virtue* (1925), *Let Us Be Gay* (1929), *As Husbands Go* (1931), *When Ladies Meet* (1932), and *Susan and God* (1938). She also wrote one-act plays and other full-length dramas, frequently sentimental in their treatment of character. She dramatized *Mother Carey's Chickens* (1917) in collaboration with Kate D. Wiggin.

CROTHERS, SAMUEL MCCHORD (1857–1927), Presbyterian minister, was later a Unitarian minister at Cambridge (1894–1927) and preached to Harvard University. His volumes of mellow essays in the manner of Lamb include *The Gentle Reader* (1903), *The Pardoner's Wallet* (1905), *By the Christmas Fire* (1908), *Among Friends* (1910), *Humanly Speaking* (1912), *The Pleasures of an Absentee Landlord* (1916), and *The Dame School of Experience* (1920). He also wrote a book on Emerson (1921).

CROUSE, RUSSEL (1893–1966), New York journalist, playwright, and producer, best known for his collaboration with Howard Lindsay (1889–1968) on *Life with Father* (1939), adapted from the book by Clarence Day♦; *State of the Union* (1945, Pulitzer Prize), a political satire of a presidential aspirant who resembles Wendell Willkie; *Life with Mother* (1948), another adaptation from Clarence Day; *The Great Sebastians* (1956), a melodramatic comedy; and *Tall Story* (1959), a comedy based on Howard Nemerov's novel *The Homecoming Game.* With others he wrote musical shows, including *Anything Goes* (1934), *Hooray for What* (1936), *Red, Hot, and Blue* (1936), and *Call Me Madam* (1950). He also wrote a study of the printmakers *Mr. Currier and Mr. Ives* (1930).

Crow Indians, Plains tribe of the Sioux family, which once ranged along the upper Yellowstone and Big Horn rivers of Wyoming and Montana. The Crow were nomadic hunters and warriors, conducted a constant warfare with the Blackfoot, and aided the U.S. army against the Sioux. They are described as predatory ruffians in *The Adventures of Captain Bonneville* and in Beckwourth's *Life,* but F.B. Linderman's *American* gives a more favorable view of them. James Welch's♦ *Fools*

Crow (1986) examines them from a Blackfoot perspective.

CRUMMELL, ALEXANDER (1819–98), black minister of the Episcopal Church in his native U.S., after education at Cambridge and long residence in Liberia. His works include *The Future of Africa* (1862) and *Africa and America* (1892).

Crying of Lot 49, novel by Thomas Pynchon,♦ published in 1966.

When Mrs. Oedipa Maas learns that the will of her onetime lover, a real estate mogul, Pierce Inverarity, has made her an executor of his estate, she leaves her husband Mucho to investigate Inverarity's property. The investigation leads to the discovery of what she takes to be a conspiratorial underground communications system dating from the 16th century. As she travels through California on her new quest she encounters the system's symbol, the Tristero, a muted post horn, in many odd places and meets such curious people as Professor Bortz, editor of a 17th-century drama that treats the Tristero. Finally she believes she will solve the enigma through a mysterious bidder eager to buy Inverarity's stamp collection, but the novel concludes as Oedipa awaits the crying out at the auction of the salient lot numbered 49.

Cudjo's Cave, antislavery novel by J.T. Trowbridge,♦ published in 1864.

In seceding Tennessee at the outbreak of the Civil War, Penn Hapgood is a young Quaker schoolmaster whose Abolitionist sympathies arouse the enmity of the Confederate slaveholders and their poor-white allies, who tar and feather him. He is aided by Carl, a friendly German boy, and the blind minister Mr. Villars, whose daughter Virginia he loves. When Villars is threatened by the people of the community, led by Augustus Bythewood, a wealthy planter, and Silas Ropes, a drunkard, Penn flees to a great cave in the backwoods, occupied by Cudjo, a deformed runaway slave, and another runaway, Pomp, a dignified "lion of a man." During the developing conflict, the cave becomes a place of refuge for Union sympathizers, including the Villars family, and it is besieged by Bythewood and his men. The planter offers to end the struggle if Virginia will accept his proposal of marriage, but she refuses. Her sister Salina is killed, and Cudjo and Ropes die while fighting each other, but Bythewood is captured and the Confederates are routed. Penn and Virginia, who plan to wed, escape with Villars and Pomp to Ohio.

CULLEN, COUNTEE (1903–46), black author, a major figure of the Harlem Renaissance♦ of the 1920s, was educated at New York University (A.B., 1925) and Harvard (M.A., 1926). While he was only in his twenties, his poetry won prizes in journals and was collected in *Color* (1925), *Copper*

Sun (1927), *The Ballad of the Brown Girl* (1927), and *The Black Christ* (1929). As the titles indicate, the themes were racial, but he was also criticized for being unduly influenced by the romanticism of Keats and for failing to use black rhythms and idioms. A later collection, *The Medea and Some Poems* (1935), opens with a translation of Euripides' tragedy. His other works include *One Way to Heaven* (1932), a novel about Harlem life; *Caroling Dusk* (1927), an anthology of verse by black writers; an adaptation of Arna Bontemps's novel *God Sends Sunday* as a musical play, *St. Louis Woman* (1946); and two books for children.

Culprit Fay, The, poem by J.R. Drake,♦ the title piece of his first collection (1835). The basic meter is iambic, but the metrical principle, based on Coleridge's *Christabel,* is that each line has four primary stresses, irrespective of the number of syllables. More than 600 lines in length, it was written in three days in August 1816, according to Drake's friend Halleck. Delicately imaginative, with a background of Hudson River scenery, the poem is concerned with the adventures of a fairy who loves a mortal maid. As punishment he is ordered to catch a drop of the water raised by a sturgeon's leap in the bright moonshine, and the last faint spark of a shooting star.

CUMMINGS, E[DWARD] E[STLIN] (1894–1962), born in Cambridge, Mass., after receiving his A.B. (1915) and M.A. (1916) from Harvard joined the service of the American volunteer Norton Harjes Ambulance Corps in France before the U.S. entered World War I, and in 1917 was confined for several months in a French concentration camp on an unfounded charge of treasonable correspondence. This experience provided the basis for his first book, *The Enormous Room*♦ (1922), a prose narrative of a poetic and personal perception. His first book of poetry, *Tulips and Chimneys* (1923), followed by *&* (1925), *XLI Poems* (1925), and *is 5* (1926, substantially augmented in a reprint of 1985), clearly established his individual voice and tone. The poems show his transcendental faith in a world where the self-reliant, joyful, loving individual is beautifully alive but in which mass man, or the man who lives by mind alone, without heart and soul, is dead. The true individual Cummings praised, often reverently and with freshness of spirit and idiom, but the "unman" was satirized as Cummings presented witty, bitter parodies of and attacks on the patriotic or cultural platitudes and shibboleths of the "unworld." This poetry is marked by experimental word coinages, shifting of grammar, blending of established stanzaic forms and free verse, flamboyant punning, typographic distortion, unusual punctuation, and idiosyncratic division of words, all of which became integral to the ideas and rhythms of his relatively brief lyrics. These he continued to write with subtlety of technique and sensitivity of feeling and to publish in *ViVa* (1931), *No Thanks* (1935), *I/20* (1936), *Collected Poems* (1938), *50 Poems* (1940), *I x I* (1944), *Χαῖρε* (1950), *Poems: 1923–1954* (1954), *95 Poems* (1958), and the post-humously collected *73 Poems* (1963). His other works are *him* (1927), an expressionist drama in verse and prose, with kaleidoscopic scenes dashing from comedy to tragedy; a book which bears no title (1930); *Eimi*♦ (1933), a travel diary utilizing the techniques of his poetry and violently attacking the regimentation of individuals in the U.S.S.R.; *Tom* (1935), a satirical ballet based on *Uncle Tom's Cabin; CIOPW* (1931), drawings and paintings showing his ability in charcoal, ink, oil, pencil, and watercolor; *Anthropos, The Future of Art* (1944); *Santa Claus* (1946), a morality play; and *i* (1953), "six nonlectures" delivered at Harvard.

CUMMINS, MARIA SUSANNA (1827–66), Massachusetts author, contributor to the *Atlantic Monthly,* wrote the popular moralistic romance *The Lamplighter* (1854), concerned with the life of a Boston orphan girl who is befriended by the lamplighter Trueman Flint, grows up under his protection, and is rewarded for her goodness and purity when she marries a childhood sweetheart. Later novels include *Mabel Vaughan* (1857), *El Fureidis* (1860), and *Haunted Hearts* (1864).

CUNNINGHAM, J[AMES] V[INCENT] (1911–85), poet of the school of Yvor Winters, received his A.B. and Ph.D. from Stanford, and taught at Brandeis beginning in 1953. His disciplined poetry, often abstract and epigrammatic, sometimes mordant, and marked by fine craftsmanship, is printed in six volumes beginning with *The Helmsman* (1942) and gathered in *Collected Poems and Epigrams* (1971). *Collected Essays* was issued in 1977.

Curfew Must Not Ring Tonight, ballad by Rose Hartwick Thorpe. ♦

CURRIER and **IVES,** lithographers and print publishers, famous in the second half of the 19th century for depicting aspects of American life ranging from sporting events to caricatures to sentimental and homely subjects. Nathaniel Currier, who founded the New York firm (1835), was associated with J. Merritt Ives (1850), and after 1857 their two names were signed to the prints. Widely circulated, crudely colored, and naïvely drawn, the prints are topically interesting but have little artistic value despite their rarity as collectors' items.

CURTIS, GEORGE TICKNOR (1812–94), Massachusetts lawyer, defended Dred Scott and wrote biographies of his acquaintances Daniel Webster and James Buchanan, as well as a *Constitutional History of the U.S. . . . to the Close of the Civil War* (1889–96). *John Charaxes* (1889) is a novel about the Civil War.

CURTIS, GEORGE WILLIAM (1824–92), Rhode Island-born writer, spent some time at Brook Farm, and later traveled in the Near East as correspondent for the New York *Tribune.* His amusing impressions of his travels were published as *Nile Notes of a Howadji* (1851) and *The Howadji in Syria* (1852). *Lotus-Eating* (1852) is a collection of letters written to the *Tribune* from various spas. *The Potiphar Papers*♦ (1853) and *Prue and I*♦ (1856) contain essays contributed to magazines, and *Trumps* (1861) is a novel of New York society and Washington politics. Curtis's oration, *The Duty of the American Scholar to Politics and the Times* (1856), marked his transition to serious thought on contemporary affairs, and he became a noted editor and lyceum lecturer in the struggles for antislavery, women's rights, civil service reform, and industrial harmony. He was an official of many reform organizations, being president of the National Civil Service Reform League from its founding (1881) to his death. He was editor of *Harper's Weekly* after 1863, and three of his books are collections of "Editor's Easy Chair" papers for *Harper's Magazine.*

CURWOOD, JAMES OLIVER (1878–1927), Michigan journalist and novelist, won immense popularity for his many stories of adventure in the North Woods, which he termed "God's Country." Following the conventions of Jack London's robust fiction of the elemental struggle for survival by men and beasts, these novels include *The Courage of Captain Plum* (1908), *The Grizzly King* (1916), *Nomads of the North* (1919), and *The Valley of Silent Men* (1920).

CUSHING, FRANK HAMILTON (1857–1900), ethnologist and archaeologist, in 1879 accompanied a scientific expedition to New Mexico and lived among the Zuñi Indians for several years. During his association with the Bureau of American Ethnology he made many explorations in the pueblo regions of the Southwest, locating the "Seven Cities of Cibola," and making other important discoveries. His writings include a translation of the Zuñi epic, published as *Myths of Creation* (1882) and *Outlines of Zuñi Creation Myths* (1896), as well as volumes on *Zuñi Fetiches* (1881), *The Arrow* (1895), *Primitive Motherhood* (1897), *Zuñi Folk Tales* (1901), and other subjects.

CUSTER, GEORGE ARMSTRONG (1839–76), youthful major general in the Civil War, distinguished himself at the battles of Gettysburg and Winchester and in the Shenandoah campaign. He led an expedition into the Black Hills (1874), beginning a long campaign against the Sioux, who, under the direction of Sitting Bull♦ and Crazy Horse,♦ annihilated Custer and his force in the Battle of Little Big Horn (1876). Custer's graphic account, *My Life on the Plains,* was published in 1874.

ELIZABETH BACON CUSTER (1842–1933), his

wife, wrote *Boots and Saddles* (1885), an account of their life in Dakota, and several other books on the frontier army.

CUSTIS, GEORGE WASHINGTON PARKE (1781–1857), grandson of Martha Washington, was a Virginia planter who wrote historical plays as an avocation, and as a so-called kindness to "poor rogues of actors." Some of his works are *The Indian Prophecy, a National Drama in Two Acts, Founded on . . . the Life of George Washington* (1827), *Pocahontas* (1830), *The Railroad* (1830),

North Point (1833), and *The Eighth of January* (1834). He also wrote *Recollections and Private Memoirs of Washington* (1859, greatly enlarged 1860).

Custom of the Country, **The,** (1913), novel by Edith Wharton. ♦

Cuticle, SURGEON, character in *White-Jacket.* ♦

Cynic's Word Book, original title of Bierce's *The Devil's Dictionary.* ♦

D

Daedalus, quarterly magazine, founded in 1955, published by the American Academy of Arts and Sciences. Each issue contains scholarly and critical articles on one topic, e.g. mass culture and mass media, excellence and leadership in a democracy, the American reading public, and perspectives on the novel.

DAHLBERG, EDWARD (1900–1977), born in Boston, the illegitimate son of the Junoesque owner of the Star Lady Barbershop of Kansas City, as he describes in his autobiography, *Because I Was Flesh* (1964). This work also tells of his years in a Jewish orphan asylum in Cleveland, his education at the University of California (1922–23) and at Columbia (B.S.). For some time after 1926 he was an expatriate in Europe. His novels include *Bottom Dogs* (England, 1929), about a boyhood like his own, giving a sense of the horror of orphanage, slum, and hobo experiences; *From Flushing to Calvary* (1932), depicting the sordid lives of slum dwellers in New York City; and *Those Who Perish* (1934), treating the effects of German Nazism upon American Jews. His prophetic, mystical literary criticism, in the vein of his friend D. H. Lawrence, is printed in *Do These Bones Live?* (1941), revised as *Sing O Barren* (1947) and *Can These Bones Live?* (1960). Other works include *Flea of Sodom* (1950), essays and parables indignantly attacking contemporary civilization; *The Sorrows of Priapus* (1957), on the dichotomy of mind and body in Hellenic, Hebraic, and pre-Columbian cultures; *Truth Is More Sacred* (1961), correspondence with Herbert Read about modern literature; *Cipango's Hinder Door* (1966), poems; *The Carnal Myth* (1968), subtitled "A Search into Classical Sensuality"; and *The Olive of Minerva* (1976), a comic novel about sex and cuckoldry. *Epitaphs of Our Times* (1967) collects his letters, and *Confessions* (1971) contains reminiscences.

Daisy Miller: *A Study,* novel by Henry James,♦ published in 1878 and dramatized by the author in 1883.

Frederick Winterbourne, an American expatriate visiting at Vevey, Switzerland, meets commonplace, newly rich Mrs. Miller, from Schenectady, N.Y., her mischievous small son Randolph, and her daughter Daisy, an "inscrutable combination of audacity and innocence." The Millers have no perception of the complex code that underlies behavior in European society, and Winterbourne is astonished at the girl's innocence and her mother's unconcern when Daisy accompanies him to the Castle of Chillon. Some months later he meets the family in Rome, where Daisy has aroused suspicion among the American colony by being seen constantly with Giovanelli, a third-rate Italian. Ostracized by former friends, who think her "intrigue" has gone too far, Daisy denies to Winterbourne that she is engaged to Giovanelli, with whom the American meets her one night in the Colosseum. When he comments on her indiscretion in exposing herself to the danger of "Roman fever," Giovanelli says, "but when was the Signorina ever prudent?" A few days later she falls ill with malaria, and a week afterward dies. At her funeral Giovanelli tells Winterbourne that Daisy was "the most beautiful young lady I ever saw, and the most amiable . . . and the most innocent." He says that he had hoped to marry her, but believes she would not have accepted him.

Dakota Indians, see *Sioux Indians.*

DALY, [JOHN] AUGUSTIN (1838–99), author or adapter of more than 90 plays, most of which were radically altered from the original French or German, and often given an American setting. His own best plays were *Horizon* (1871), a romantic drama of the West, and *Divorce* (1871), a problem play, but he was also the author of melodramas such as *Under the Gaslight* (1867), in which heroes were tied to logs about to be sawed in two, or bound to railroad tracks in the paths of onrushing trains. The most successful of his ventures as a producer were in the theater in New York City that bore his name, where he staged many of his own adaptations, several of the leading English comedies of manners, and superb productions of Shakespeare.

DALY, THOMAS AUGUSTINE (1871–1948), Philadelphia poet and journalist. He is best known for his humorous, sympathetic treatments of Irish and Italian immigrants, in such dialect verse as *Canzoni* (1906), *Carmina* (1909), *Madrigali* (1912), *McAroni Ballads* (1919), and *McAroni Medleys* (1931).

DAMIEN, FATHER (JOSEPH DAMIEN DE VEUSTER) (1840–89), Belgian missionary priest, went to Hawaii (1864), where he worked among the natives, and in 1873 went to the leper colony, where he ministered to the sick until he himself contracted leprosy, from which he died. His work was brought to public attention when Stevenson published a defense (1890) against a minister who had slandered Damien. C.W. Stoddard, who wrote about Damien in *The Lepers of Molokai* (1885), probably attracted Stevenson's attention to the subject.

Damnation of Theron Ware, The, novel by Harold Frederic,♦ published in 1896. Its title in England is *Illumination*.

Dan De Quille, see *De Quille*.

DANA, CHARLES ANDERSON (1819–97), born in New Hampshire, was associated as a young man with the Brook Farm community, but left this group to work on the New York *Tribune,* of which he was managing editor under Greeley (1849–62). Although he opposed militant labor, Dana's point of view was generally liberal, and he was a brilliant editorial and business manager. His chauvinistic policy at the outbreak of the Civil War led to his dismissal, after which he became a special investigator for the War Department, and assistant secretary of war (1864). He became part owner of the New York *Sun*♦ in 1867 and edited it with a personal and perverse social and political policy but achieved his aim of "condensation, clearness, point, and . . . the most luminous and lively manner." He edited the *American Cyclopædia* (1858–64) with George Ripley, and wrote his *Recollections of the Civil War* (1898).

DANA, RICHARD HENRY, SR. (1787–1879), Massachusetts poet and journalist, was a founder of *The North American Review.* When his romantic criticism alienated many of this magazine's subscribers, he began his own journal in New York, *The Idle Man* (1821–22), modeled upon Irving's *Salmagundi.* Because of Dana's perpetual procrastination, he was satirized by Lowell as being "so well aware of how things should be done, that his own works displease him before they're begun." His slight literary production was collected in the two-volume *Poems and Prose Writings* (1833, enlarged 1850), but his famous lectures on Shakespeare have never been printed, and he was overshadowed during his last 40 years by his son.

DANA, RICHARD HENRY, JR. (1815–82), son of R.H. Dana, Sr., was born at Cambridge, where he was reared according to conventional New England standards. He suffered serious eye trouble as a sophomore at Harvard, and to regain his health sailed for California as a common sailor (1834). On the Pacific coast he worked for more than a year gathering hides, after which he returned to Boston and completed his education at Harvard law school. In fulfillment of his vows "to redress the grievances and suffering of that class of beings with whom my lot had so long been cast," his first publication was an article in the *American Jurist* (1839) on "Cruelty to Seamen." In 1840,

the year of his admission to the bar, he published the famous account of his voyage, *Two Years Before the Mast,* ♦ which won immediate popularity, created many imitators and followers of its realistic approach, and permanently influenced the literature of the sea. His second book, *The Seaman's Friend* (1841, called in England *The Seaman's Manual*), was designed to show common sailors their legal rights and duties, and constitutes a reference book of sea terms, customs, and laws. Dana was active in Free-Soil politics, and provided legal assistance without charge to slaves captured under the Fugitive Slave Law, thereby antagonizing those of his own class in Boston whose cotton mills were dependent on the Southern plantations. During the Civil War he was U.S. attorney for the district of Massachusetts, and succeeded in convincing the U.S. Supreme Court, despite its Democratic leanings, that the Northern blockade was legal. Although he held several minor offices, he never attained the diplomatic heights of which he was ambitious. His edition of *Elements of International Law by Wheaton* (1866) made him the object of an invidious and protracted suit for plagiarism, and the slanders involved caused the Senate to refuse his appointment as minister to England (1876). Wearied by many abortive attempts to obtain public office, he declared bitterly, "My life has been a failure compared with what I might and ought to have done," and "My great success— my book—was a boy's work, done before I came to the Bar." He went to Europe (1878) to rest and to write further books, but died before completing any of his proposed writings on international law, which he hoped might establish his reputation in this field. One of his several later voyages is described in *To Cuba and Back* (1859), which lacks, however, the qualities for which his first book is admired. Some of his addresses were collected as *Speeches in Stirring Times* (1910).

Danbury News Man, see *Bailey, J.M.*

Dangling Man, novel by Saul Bellow,♦ published in 1944.

At 27, a Chicagoan named Joseph, a university graduate, an intellectual, five years married, leaves his job with a travel bureau, and under the pressure of waiting to be taken to war as a draftee feels himself alienated from society. In his diary between Dec. 15, 1942, and April 9, 1943, he objectively describes his quarrels with friends, in-laws, his wife Iva, by whom he is supported in their mean rooming house, and his brother Amos, a go-getting success, as he undergoes intense self-analysis dedicated only to the belief "I must know what I myself am." Talks with his alter ego, "Tu As Raison Aussi," finally convince him that man creates his own destiny and send him to volunteer in the army rather than continue to wait indefinitely to be inducted.

DANIELS, Jonathan [Worth] (1902–81), North Carolina newspaper editor, a spokesman for progressive ideas in the South, whose books include *A Southerner Discovers the South* (1938); *Tar Heels* (1941); *The Man of Independence* (1950), a life of Truman; *The End of Innocence* (1954), recollections of the political career of his father, Josephus Daniels♦; lives of John S. Mosby, Stonewall Jackson, and Robert E. Lee; *The Time Between the Wars* (1966), an intimate history of the Harding to F.D. Roosevelt era; *The Randolphs of Virginia* (1972); and *White House Witness, 1942–45* (1975), about his times as administrative assistant and press secretary to F.D. Roosevelt and in several posts under Truman.

DANIELS, Josephus (1862–1948), editor and publisher of the Raleigh, N.C., *News and Observer,* was Wilson's secretary of the navy and ambassador to Mexico (1933–42). Besides *The Navy and the Nation* (1919), *Our Navy at War* (1922), and *The Life of Woodrow Wilson* (1924), he wrote his memoirs: *Tar Heel Editor* (1939), *Editor in Politics* (1941), *The Wilson Era* (2 vols., 1944, 1946), and *Shirt-Sleeve Diplomat* (1947).

Danites in the Sierras, The (produced 1877, printed 1882), play by Joaquin Miller.♦

The Danites, a secret society of Mormons, attempt to take revenge upon a young girl for her supposed crimes. She disguises herself as a man, alone in a cabin in the Sierras, to elude their pursuit. There are many suspenseful interludes, and *Danites* was one of the most popular frontier dramas in the country, as well as a success in London when it was produced there in 1880.

DARE, Virginia, see *Roanoke Island.*

DARGAN, Olive Tilford (1869–1968), Kentucky-born author whose verse dramas include *Semiramis and Other Plays* (1904), *Lords and Lovers and Other Dramas* (1906), and *The Mortal Gods and Other Plays* (1912). Lyric poems appeared in *Path Flower and Other Verses* (1914); *The Cycle's Rim* (1916), a sonnet sequence; *Lute and Furrow* (1922); and a late collection, *Spotted Hawk* (1958). Her prose includes *Highland Annals* (1925), stories of Kentucky mountain life; and, under the name Fielding Burke, *Call Home the Heart* (1932), a proletarian but non-Marxist novel about North Carolina textile mill workers; *A Stone Came Rolling* (1935); and *Sons of the Stranger* (1947), about the labor organization of miners at the end of the 19th century. *Innocent Bigamy* (1962) collects late stories.

Daring Young Man on the Flying Trapeze, The, first book by William Saroyan,♦ issued in 1934. It collects 26 stories, all brief, and some only a page long, in the author's own idiosyncratic vein, written with great speed during a time when he claimed to have written a story a day for 30 days.

The title work presents a poor, jobless, aspiring young author in San Francisco as he makes his way through a day conceiving, among many other things, of a "flight with grace . . . to some sort of eternity."

Dark Laughter, novel by Sherwood Anderson,♦ published in 1925.

John Stockton, a Chicago reporter, drifts apart from his wife Bernice, and decides suddenly to leave his routine life. He travels in an open boat down the Illinois and Mississippi rivers, dreaming of the epic Mark Twain might now write, "of song killed, of laughter killed, of men herded into a new age of speed, of factories, of swift, fast-running trains," and his story is accompanied by a chorus of "dark laughter" and song by the unrepressed blacks, contrasted with the spiritual sterility of machine civilization. In his childhood home, Old Harbor, Ind., as Bruce Dudley, he becomes a factory hand, painting wheels with old Sponge Martin, an expert craftsman, happily married, and satisfied by his pattern of life. The shop's owner is Fred Grey, a World War I veteran who met his wife Aline in the bohemian quarter of Paris, where she was under the influence of postwar disillusion. Although she had little in common with this conventional businessman, she married him for love and stability. Bruce and Aline become lovers, and after the birth of their child they elope, leaving Fred bewildered by his wife's preference for an irresponsible laborer.

DARLEY, Felix Octavius Carr (1822–88), is best known for his pen-and-ink illustrations for books, which show both a technical facility and a sense of humor. Among the works he illustrated were *The Library of Humorous American Works* (29 vols., 1846–53), and books by Cooper, Irving, Parkman, Simms, and by English authors. His own books include *Scenes in Indian Life* (1843) and *Sketches Abroad with Pen and Pencil* (1869).

Darling of the Gods, The, tragedy by David Belasco♦ and John L. Long,♦ produced in 1902 and published in 1928.

Yo-San, daughter of the Prince of Tosan, not wishing to marry the man to whom she is betrothed, stipulates that he must capture the outlaw Prince Kara. Kara, who had once rescued her when she did not know who he was, now comes to the palace and is hidden by her. When they are discovered, she saves his life by revealing the hiding place of his followers, and he makes his way to them to die honorably among his samurai.

DARROW, Clarence Seward (1857–1938), Ohio-born lawyer, mainly associated with Chicago, was noted for his defense of labor organizations, acting as counsel for Debs in the case resulting from the Pullman strike; for William D. Haywood, accused of instigating the murder of the governor of Idaho; and for the McNamara brothers, accused of dynamiting the Los Angeles *Times* building. He was also known as a criminal lawyer in such cases as the trial of Loeb and Leopold (1924) and the Fortescue-Massie case in Honolulu. His agnosticism was strikingly revealed in the Scopes trial.♦ He wrote several books, including *A Persian Pearl* (1898), literary essays; *Farmington* (1904), a novel about his own youth; *An Eye for an Eye* (1905), a novel concerned with the fallacy of the Mosaic law; *Crime: Its Cause and Treatment* (1922); and *The Story of My Life* (1932). *Attorney for the Damned* (1957) collects 13 major speeches.

Daughter of the Middle Border, *A,* autobiographical narrative by Hamlin Garland,♦ published in 1921 as a continuation of *A Son of the Middle Border.*♦ This volume deals with his later life, especially his marriage. It won a Pulitzer Prize.

DAVENPORT, Guy [Mattison, Jr.] (1927–), born in South Carolina, received his B.A. from Duke and a B.Litt. from Oxford as a Rhodes Scholar. He has taught English at U.S. universities, including the University of Kentucky, since 1963. His publications include a translation of Sappho (1965), and studies of modern foreign writings and of part of Pound's *Cantos* (1983). His own creative writing includes *Tatlin!* (1974), *Da Vinci's Bicycle* (1979), *Eclogues* (1981), *Troise Caprices* (1982), and *Apples and Pears* (1984), short fiction featuring cultural life from ancient to modern times, including notable figures of the arts as well as personally conceived individuals, viewed in ways both esoteric and exotic. He has also written *The Geography of the Imagination* (1981), essays ranging from Homer to Louis Zukofsky, and *Every Force Evolves a Form* (1987), more general essays on a wide scope of authors.

DAVENPORT, John (1597–1670), born in England, graduated from Oxford (1625), and came to America in 1637 with Theophilus Eaton because his nonconformist views had caused him to leave England and Holland. In 1638 he founded the colony at New Haven, becoming its pastor and most prominent leader next to Eaton. He wrote many devotional works, and a defense of theocracy. *A Discourse About Civil Government in a New Plantation Whose Design is Religion* (1663), attributed on the title page to John Cotton. His *Letters* were published in 1937.

DAVENPORT, Marcia (1903–94), music critic and author, daughter of the singer Alma Gluck, wrote *Mozart* (1932); and the novels *Of Lena Geyer* (1936), about a musician; *The Valley of Decision* (1943), tracing a Pittsburgh family and its steel mills from 1873 to 1941; *East Side, West Side* (1947); *My Brother's Keeper* (1954), about two reclusive rich men; and *Constant Image* (1960). *Too Strong for Fantasy* (1967) is a memoir.

David Harum, *A Story of American Life,* novel by Edward Noyes Westcott,♦ posthumously published in 1898.

David is a country banker in the New England town Homeville, where he is noted as a crusty widower, an oracle of pithy humor, and a sly horse trader. Unlearned and commonsensical, he holds that "The's as much human nature in some folks as th' is in others, if not more," and contends that "A reasonable amount of fleas is good for a dog—they keep him f'm broodin' on bein' a dog." He proves his kindliness by aiding John Lenox, a young New Yorker who comes to Homeville as David's assistant at the bank. Lenox through a misunderstanding has broken his engagement with Mary Blake, but they meet again and marry, and live in Homeville, where they are understood to be David's heirs, and name their son for him.

DAVIDSON, Donald [Grady] (1893–1968). Tennessee author, professor at Vanderbilt University was one of the exponents of regionalism♦ who founded *The Fugitive*♦ and contributed to the group's symposia. His own books include *The Tall Men* (1927), a blank-verse poem; *The Attack on Leviathan* (1938), essays opposing centralization of political and economic power in the North; *Lee in the Mountains* (1938), short narrative poems on Southern heroes; *The Tennessee* (2 vols., 1946–48), a history of the river and valley; *Still Rebels, Still Yankees* (1957), essays; *Southern Writers in the Modern World* (1958); *The Long Street* (1961), poems written over a long period of time; and *The Spyglass* (1963), early essays. His collected *Poems* appeared in 1966 and his correspondence with Allen Tate in 1974.

DAVIDSON, Thomas (1840–1900), Scottish-born philosopher and scholar, after graduation from Aberdeen University and teaching in Scotland and England, moved to Canada (1866) and shortly thereafter to the U.S., where as a public-school teacher in St. Louis he fell under the influence of W.T. Harris. In 1875 he settled in Boston, though making annual trips abroad during which he absorbed the teachings of Rosimini and developed his philosophy of pluralistic idealism. In London he founded the Fellowship of the New Life (1883), a precursor of the Fabian Society, and later instituted a branch in New York and a summer school variously situated in New Jersey, Connecticut, and the Adirondacks. In association with the People's Institute and the Educational Alliance of New York he organized a "Bread-Winner's College" for Lower East Side workers. His writings include *The Philosophical System of Antonio Rosimini-Serbati* (1882), *Aristotle and Ancient Educational Ideals* (1892), *Education of the Greek People* (1894), and *Rousseau and Education According to Nature* (1898).

DAVIS, ANDREW JACKSON (1826–1910), known as the "Poughkeepsie Seer," after a shiftless childhood fell under the influence of a mesmerist, who found him to be an ideal subject. In 1845, with his own hypnotist and reporter, Davis began a series of lectures delivered ostensibly in states of trance. From the verbatim reports he compiled his *Principles of Nature, Her Divine Revelations, and A Voice to Mankind* (1847), a mixture of mysticism, philosophy, science, and occult history, which seems to have influenced Poe's *Eureka* and Chivers's *Search After Truth*. His transition from mesmerism to spiritualism is shown in *The Great Harmonia* (1850) and 26 subsequent works.

DAVIS, CHARLES AUGUSTUS (1795?–1868?), New York merchant and journalist, was the most popular imitator of Seba Smith, and employed his character "Jack Downing" for similar satire of Jackson's administration. *Letters Written During the President's Tour, "Down East," by Myself, Major Jack Downing, of Downingville* (1833) was a pirated work containing a few original letters by Smith, and others by Davis and other imitators, while Davis's own book of his newspaper contributions was *Letters of J. Downing, Major, Downingville Militia . . . to Mr. Dwight of the New York Daily Advertiser* (1834).

DAVIS, CLYDE BRION (1894–1962), born in Nebraska, served on various newspapers (1919–37) until he began to write novels, which include *The Anointed* (1937), the story of a sailor who considers himself divinely inspired, but, ironically, becomes a grocery clerk when caught in the web of marriage; *The Great American Novel* (1938), about a roving newspaperman who dreams vainly of the novel he means to write, unaware that his own life is the great American novel; *Nebraska Coast* (1939), about a typical, unheroic pioneer; *Follow the Leader* (1942), satirizing a war hero who becomes a businessman; *The Rebellion of Leo McGuire* (1944), about a reformed burglar; *The Stars Incline* (1946), a study of a newspaperman; *Jeremy Bell* (1947), set in a 19th-century lumber camp; *Temper the Wind* (1948), about a prizefighter; *Playtime Is Over* (1949), about an ex-soldier of fortune; *Thudbury* (1952); *The Newcomer* (1954); *Unholy Uproar* (1957); and *The Big Pink Kite* (1960). *The Arkansas* (1940) is a history of the river; *The Age of Indiscretion* (1950) contains reminiscences; and *Something for Nothing* (1956) studies gambling. *Shadow of a Tiger* (1963) is a quasi-autobiographical novel.

DAVIS, ELMER [HOLMES] (1890–1958), Indiana-born journalist, author, and news analyst, and director of the Office of War Information (1942–45). While with *The New York Times* (1914–24) he wrote its *History* (1921). His books include novels and stories; *Show Window* (1927) and *Not To Mention the War* (1940), essays; *But We Were Born Free* (1954), on civil liberties; and *Two Min-*

utes *Till Midnight* (1955), on nuclear weapons and peace.

DAVIS, H[AROLD] L[ENOIR] (1896–1960), Oregon author whose novels are *Honey in the Horn* (1935, Pulitzer Prize), about Oregon in the homesteading era; *Harp of a Thousand Strings* (1947), contrasting French and American ways of life; *Beulah Land* (1949), a picaresque tale of Indian and white frontier life; *Winds of Morning* (1952), set in the Columbia River area of the 1920s; and *Distant Music* (1957), about three generations of a pioneer Oregon family. *Team Bells Woke Me* (1953) is a collection of stories; *Kettle of Fire* (1959) contains essays and articles about the Pacific Northwest; and *Proud Riders* (1942) is poetry about people in the Far West.

DAVIS, JEFFERSON (1808–89), born in Kentucky, graduated from West Point (1828), and served in the army on the Northwestern frontier and during the Mexican War. He was U.S. senator from Mississippi (1847–51) and Pierce's secretary of war (1853–57), championing the Gadsden Purchase and expansion in the Southwest. Again in the Senate (1857–61) he resigned and became President of the Confederacy. His dictatorial policies were criticized, but they were the result of the war, not his personality. After Lee surrendered, without his approval, Davis was imprisoned for two years. Later he spent time in Canada and Europe and wrote *The Rise and Fall of the Confederacy* (2 vols., 1881) and *A Short History of the Confederate States of America* (1890).

DAVIS, JOHN (1775–1854), English sailor, whose writings based on his voyages to American include *Travels of Four Years and a Half in the United States* (1803) and a novel, *The Post Captain* (1805). His walking trip through 15 states provided background for three other novels: *The Farmer of New Jersey* (1800), *The Wanderings of William* (1801), and *Walter Kennedy* (1808). Another novel, *The First Settlers of Virginia* (1805), contains the first fictional treatment of Pocahontas.

DAVIS, OWEN (1874–1956), born in Maine, graduated from Harvard (1893), and, after failing with serious verse tragedy, turned to the writing of some hundreds of melodramas, of which the most famous was *Nellie, the Beautiful Cloak Model.* His later serious plays include *The Detour*♦ (1921) and *Icebound*♦ (1923, Pulitzer Prize), character studies; and adaptations of *The Great Gatsby* (1926), *The Good Earth* (1932), and *Ethan Frome* (1936). He wrote an autobiography, *I'd Like To Do It Again* (1931).

DAVIS, REBECCA [BLAINE] HARDING (1831–1910), lived most of her life in Philadelphia, the background of several of her books. She first came into prominence with her realistic story

"Life in the Iron Mills" (*Atlantic Monthly*, (1861). *Margaret Howth* (1862), a novel of life in a mill town, is somewhat marred by an undue stress on moral contrasts, but shows her purpose "to dig into this commonplace, this vulgar American life, and see what is in it." *Waiting for the Verdict* (1868) is a novel strongly in favor of blacks, and *John Andross* (1874), about the Whiskey Ring and Pennsylvania corporation lobbying, shows the effect of political corruption. Mrs. Davis was the author of several other novels, an autobiography, and many short stories, some of which are collected in *Silhouettes of American Life* (1892). Some of her later writing drifts into sentimentality and prevailing literary conventions, but she is adept at character portrayal.

DAVIS, RICHARD HARDING (1864–1916), son of Rebecca H. Davis, was born in Philadelphia, where in 1886 he began the journalistic career that was to make him the leading reporter of his time. His reporting and "specials" for the New York *Sun* (1889–90) and his short stories for *Scribner's* attracted wide attention. In 1890 he became managing editor of *Harper's Weekly*. The letters reporting his various journalistic tours of this period were collected in *The West from a Car Window* (1892), *The Rulers of the Mediterranean* (1894), *Our English Cousins* (1894), *About Paris* (1895), and *Three Gringos in Venezuela and Central America* (1896). As correspondent for New York and London papers, he reported the Spanish war in Cuba, the Greco-Turkish War, the Spanish-American War, the Boer War, the Russo-Japanese War, and World War I. From his observations came the following books: *Cuba in War Time* (1897), *A Year from a Reporter's Note-Book* (1898), *The Cuban and the Porto Rican Campaigns* (1898), *With Both Armies in South Africa* (1900), *Notes of a War Correspondent* (1910), *With the Allies* (1914), and *With the French in France and Salonika* (1916). As a correspondent, Davis was a vivid and picturesque writer, always dramatizing the facts of his stories. After the publication of *Gallegher and Other Stories*♦ (1891), he collected more than 80 other short stories in 11 volumes, all of which show adept craftsmanship but are journalistic, with more stress on effect and form than on substance. *Van Bibber and Others* (1892) contains anecdotes of New York life concerning Courtlandt Van Bibber, a rich young clubman who breaks laws with one hand while befriending the weak and poor with the other. The title story of *The Exiles* (1894) deals with moral contrasts in a colony of American outcasts at Tangier. *The Lion and the Unicorn* (1899), *Ranson's Folly*♦ (1902), and *The Scarlet Car* (1907) are among the other collections of tales. His vivid but superficial novels include such treatments of the international scene as *Soldiers of Fortune* (1897), *The King's Jackal* (1898), *Captain Macklin* (1902), *The Bar Sinister* (1903), *Vera the Medium* (1908), *The White Mice* (1909). From Davis's facile pen also came 25

plays, of which the most popular were *Ranson's Folly* (1904), *The Dictator*♦ (1904), and *Miss Civilization* (1906).

DAVIS, WILLIAM STEARNS (1877–1930), Massachusetts novelist and scholar, taught at the University of Minnesota (1909–27). Among his scholarly works are *Influence of Wealth in Imperial Rome* (1910), *A Short History of the Near East* (1922), *Life on a Medieval Barony* (1923), and *Life in Elizabethan Days* (1930). His romantic novels, based on historical study, include *A Friend of Cæsar* (1900); *God Wills It* (1902), about the First Crusade; *Falaise of the Blessed Voice* (1904), concerned with Louis IX; *Friar of Wittenberg* (1912); *Gilman of Redford* (1927), a story of the American Revolution; and *The Whirlwind* (1929), about the French Revolution.

DAVISON, PETER [HUBERT] (1928–   ), New York City-born poet and editor, graduated from Harvard, was a Fulbright Scholar at Cambridge University, and won the award of the Yale Series of Younger Poets with *The Breaking of the Day* (1964). Later collections include *The City and the Island* (1966), *Pretending To Be Asleep* (1970), *Dark Houses* (1971), *Walking the Boundaries* (1974), *A Voice in the Mountain* (1977), *Barn Fever* (1981), *Praying Wrong* (1984), and *The Great Ledge* (1989). *Half Remembered* (1973) is an autobiography.

DAWES, RUFUS (1803–59), Massachusetts author whose books include *Geraldine, Athenia of Damascus, and Miscellaneous Poems* (1839), the first work being a long poem in the manner of *Don Juan,* and the second a drama set during the Turks' 7th-century siege of Damascus; and *Nix's Mate* (1839), a historical romance set in late 17th-century Massachusetts.

DAWSON, WILLIAM (1704–52), English-born poet, graduated from Oxford (1725), and emigrated to America, where he became a professor at William and Mary and later (1743–52) its president. His *Poems on Several Occasions* (1736), which appeared anonymously as "By a Gentleman of Virginia," were mostly written in England and show the influence of Pope and a frequent use of anacreontics.

DAY, CLARENCE [SHEPARD] (1874–1935), essayist, best known for his autobiographical works, *God and My Father* (1932), *Life with Father* (1935), *Life with Mother* (1937), and *Father and I* (1940), in which, with affectionate humor, he characterizes his family's Victorian traditions and typical upper-class life in 19th-century New York. *Life with Father,* dramatized (1939) by Howard Lindsay and Russel Crouse, once held the record of having the longest continuous run of any American play. Day was also noted for his genial, witty considerations of such matters as *This Simian World* (1920), satirizing human traits by speculating on possible evolutions from other animal families, and *Scenes from the Mesozoic and Other Drawings* (1935). Other books include *The Crow's Nest* (1921), enlarged as *After All* (1936); *Thoughts Without Words* (1928); and *In the Green Mountain Country* (1934).

Day of Doom, The, theological poem in ballad meter by Michael Wigglesworth,♦ published in 1662. The subject is indicated by the subtitle, *A Poetical Description of the Great and Last Judgment.* Few stanzas approach the poetic, and the work is now interesting only as a historical document, but in its own day it was immensely popular in both America and England. It is estimated that a copy was sold for one in every 20 persons then in New England, or one in every 45 in the colonies. Other versified theology of the same nature is annexed to the work as preface and postscript, while "Vanity of Vanities" serves as a "Song of Emptiness To Fill Up the Empty Pages Following."

Day of the Locust, The, novel by Nathanael West,♦ published in 1939.

Tod Hackett, a recent Yale graduate in the 1930s, moves to Hollywood to make set and costume designs for a film studio while also pursuing his own painting. There he meets Faye Greener and her father, Harry, a down-and-out actor reduced to selling homemade silver polish door to door. One of his customers, Homer Simpson, a bland 40-year-old bookkeeper, becomes enamored of Faye and in a "business arrangement" offers her lodging in his cottage just to aid her. She in turn houses a cowboy from Arizona and a young Mexican in the garage, stages a drunken party at Homer's house, and goes to bed with Miguel, the Mexican. Disillusioned, Homer walks to the railroad station to return to Utah but on the way is attacked by a pesky boy and knocks him down. Then Homer is attacked by a swarming crowd of people who had gathered to see the arrival of stars at a premiere and out of boredom were seeking any excitement they might find. In a frenzied scene, reminiscent of Tod's surrealistic painting, *The Burning of Los Angeles,* the mob overwhelms Homer and Tod loses his own self-control.

DAYE, STEPHEN (*c.*1594–1668), came to Boston (1638) under contract to the man who brought the first printing press to the English colonies. The owner died during the voyage, and Daye set up the press at Cambridge. Although untrained in typography, he became the first printer of New England. His first piece of printing was a broadside, the *Oath of a Free-man*♦ (1639), and during the next decade he issued more than 20 other items, of which the most famous is the *Bay Psalm Book* (1640).

Days, blank-verse poem by Emerson,♦ published in the *Atlantic Monthly* (1857) and reprinted

in *May-Day and Other Pieces* (1867). When the Days come to offer gifts "to each . . . after his will," the poet hastily chooses only "a few herbs and apples," realizing too late the scorn of the departing Day.

Days Without End, play by Eugene O'Neill.♦

Deacon's Masterpiece, The; or, The Wonderful "One-Hoss Shay," poem by Holmes♦ in *The Autocrat of the Breakfast-Table,* was first published in the *Atlantic Monthly* (1858). In its rhymed four-stress couplets, anapests are frequently substituted for iambs, and a humorous effect is derived from the monotonous rhyme and absurd rhythm. A parable of the breakdown of Calvinism, the poem tells of a deacon who wanted a carriage that would never break down, so that he built all of its parts with equal strength. Exactly a century after the construction of this masterpiece, the whole work fell apart at once.

Dead End, play by Sidney Kingsley,♦ produced in 1935 and published in 1936.

At the "dead end" of a New York street, the scene includes squalid tenements, a wharf over the East River, and an exclusive apartment building, whose rear entrance is in use because of repairs at the front. The tenants, among whom are Jack Hilton and his mistress Kay, and Mr. Griswald and his son Philip, are affronted by the sight of the "kids," who swim in the filthy river and play and fight in the streets. The five kids, Tommy, Dippy, T.B., Angel, and Spit, are shown to have developed a vicious antisocial attitude, despite the interference of Tommy's sister Drina and of Gimpty, an unemployed crippled young architect, who has grown up in the neighborhood and draws futile plans for its abolition. Gimpty and Kay, in love, are unable to face a penniless marriage. "Baby Face" Martin, a gangster, returns to the street to visit his mother, and Gimpty wins a reward for betraying him to police, who kill Martin. Even this wealth does not assure his future, and Kay leaves to marry Hilton. Tommy is arrested for abusing Philip and attacking Mr. Griswald. Drina, fearing that her brother will be permanently "bad" after reform school, appeals to Gimpty, whom she loves, and he promises to use his "blood-money" for Tommy's defense.

Deadwood Dick, sobriquet of Richard W. Clarke (1845–1930), English-born frontiersman in South Dakota, noted as an Indian fighter and express guard for Black Hills gold shipments. A series of dime novels was written about his exploits, mainly by Edward L. Wheeler, although they were later attributed to Clarke.

Dean's December, The, novel by Saul Bellow,♦ published in 1982.

Albert Corde, dean of men at a Chicago college, accompanies his Rumanian-born wife Minna, an astronomer, to Bucharest to be with her dying mother. Communist authorities deny visiting rights as a means of punishing the old woman, a lapsed Communist, and the young one because she defected to the West. This example of the state's control of individuals is balanced by the anarchy that the Dean witnesses in his home city when a campus murder case leads him to write articles dealing with the violent ways of life to which black people are driven, both those on the streets and those in jails.

Dear Judas, narrative poem by Robinson Jeffers. ♦

Death Comes for the Archbishop, novel by Willa Cather, ♦ published in 1927.

Bishop Jean Latour and his vicar Father Joseph Vaillant together create pioneer missions and organize the new diocese of New Mexico. Youthful friends in France, they are lifelong comrades, united by a love of their native country, as well as by their common purpose, but their characters are sharply contrasted. Latour is an intellectual and a patrician, highly sensitive but tolerant and possessed of an indomitable resolution and courage, remaining solitary in the midst of his people's love and his friend's devotion. Vaillant is practical, humane, companionable, and vigorous. The two combine to triumph over the apathy of the Hopi and Navajo Indians, the opposition of corrupt Spanish priests, and adverse climatic and topographic conditions. They are assisted by Kit Carson and by such devoted Indians as the guide Jacinto. When Vaillant goes as a missionary bishop to Colorado, they are finally separated, but Latour dies soon after his friend, universally revered and respected, to lie in state in the great Santa Fe cathedral that he himself created.

Death in the Afternoon, discursive work by Hemingway, ♦ published in 1932. In it he describes the rearing and fighting of bulls in Spain, and depicts the bullfight as a kind of microcosmic tragedy, in which the death of the bull is inevitable but must be achieved by the observance of ritual, which gives the animal a maximum chance to destroy the matador. The discussion includes lengthy digressions, in the form of conversations between the author and an old lady, presenting his philosophy through the discussion of various aspects of life and death.

Death in the Family, A, quasi-autobiographical novel by James Agee, ♦ left incomplete at his death, pieced together by others and published in 1957. It received a Pulitzer Prize. A play by Tad Mosel, ♦ *All The Way Home,* was based on the novel. Produced in 1960, published in 1961, it also won a Pulitzer Prize.

The intimacies of the life of Jay Follet in Knoxville, Tenn., are interrupted when he has to visit his ailing father and they come to an end

when he is killed in an auto accident. His wife Mary, his four-year-old daughter Catherine, and especially his six-year-old son Rufus grapple with the meaning of death, of faith, and of maturity.

Death of a Salesman, play by Arthur Miller, ♦ produced and published in 1949, won a Pulitzer Prize.

Willy Loman, a bewildered, well-intentioned, unsuccessful traveling salesman aged 63, is pleased by the return home for a visit of his sons Biff and Happy, but they are upset by his peculiar behavior and hallucinatory conversations with figures of a happier past, and they worry about the effect on Linda, their compassionate mother, who loves her husband and recognizes that his actions stem from the disparity of his "massive dreams" and a disappointing reality. Wanting desperately to be successful and well liked, Willy had fallen victim to the false values of society and cannot cope with his failure or that of Biff, once a high-school football hero, now moody and jobless. Linda persuades Biff to try for a good job to make his father proud, but when, with Happy, he meets his father in the restaurant where they intend to treat him to a celebration dinner, Biff tells the truth about his ill-fated appointment and destroys Willy's hopes. In confusion Willy goes to the washroom and relives the awful time when Biff, desperately needing his help, traveled to Boston, where he discovered him with his mistress. Realizing his responsibility for Biff's aimlessness and disillusionment, Willy stumbles back to the table, only to find that the boys have deserted him for two chippies. Humiliated and stunned, he returns home, fights with Biff, and then is touched by Biff's tears of concern and love. In a final hallucinatory talk with his brother Ben, a successful self-made man, Willy decides on suicide to provide Biff with insurance money. At the funeral, which none of his business acquaintances attend, a friend points out "Willy was a salesman . . . a man . . . riding on a smile and a shoeshine. . . . Nobody dast blame this man. A salesman is got to dream, boy. It comes with the territory."

Death of General Montgomery, *The,* blank-verse tragedy by H.H. Brackenridge, ♦ written in 1777 for production at Somerset Academy, Maryland, of which he was a master. Intended primarily as an exercise in oratory, it deals with the ill-fated attack of General Montgomery on Quebec.

Death of the Flowers, *The,* threnody by Bryant ♦ on the death of his sister, published in 1825 and collected in his *Poems* (1832). In six-line stanzas of rhymed seven-stress lines, the poem expresses Bryant's restrained but profound grief, identifying the passing of the woman with the decay of summer's beauty in "The melancholy days . . . the saddest of the year."

Death of the Hired Man, *The,* blank-verse dramatic narrative by Robert Frost, ♦ published in *North of Boston* (1914).

Warren and Mary, a farmer and his wife, discuss the return of Silas, an aged farmhand who has worked for them often in the past, always wandering off when other employment offered itself, and coming "home" at times of difficulty. Warren wants to dismiss him, but Mary describes the poignant contrast between his former proud competence and his present broken health, loneliness, and pitiful eagerness to serve. She tells of his infirm mind, which she thinks a sign of approaching death, and her husband is moved to reconsider. When he enters the house to talk with Silas, he discovers the old man dead.

Death Ship, The, novel by B. Traven.♦

DE BOW, JAMES DUNWOODY BROWNSON (1820–67), born at Charleston, first won prominence as editor of the *Southern Quarterly Review,*♦ which he left to found his own monthly, *De Bow's Review* (1846–80), issued with differing titles from New Orleans, Columbia, Nashville, and Washington. Mainly written by the editor, the magazine was influential in molding Southern opinion in antebellum days, through its violently partisan championing of Calhoun, the protective tariff, and slavery. After the Civil War, it was sympathetic to the Reconstruction. De Bow's *Industrial Resources of the Southern and Western States* (3 vols., 1853) reprints important articles from the *Review.*

DEBS, EUGENE VICTOR (1855–1926), born in Indiana, became a railway worker (1871), and in 1880 became secretary-treasurer of the Brotherhood of Locomotive Firemen and editor of the organization's magazine. He organized the American Railway Union (1893), and as its first president was an outstanding advocate of industrial unionism. The strike against the Pullman Company (1894) brought him national prominence, and a six-month jail sentence for conspiracy to obstruct the mails. He emerged from jail a convert to socialism and became a founder of the Socialist Democratic party (1899). As the leading Socialist of the U.S. he was five times a candidate for the presidency (1900, 1904, 1908, 1912, 1920), polling 402,321 votes in 1904 and 901,062 in 1912. Meanwhile he helped edit the party paper *The Appeal to Reason,* was an organizer of the I.W.W., from which he later withdrew, and led pacifist protest of World War I. In 1918 he was sentenced to jail for ten years, as a violator of the Espionage Act, because he had assailed the administration's prosecution of persons charged with sedition. While still in the Atlanta penitentiary (1920), he polled 919,799 votes for the presidency. He was released (1921) by order of Harding but did not regain his citizenship, lost when he was imprisoned. In 1925–26 he edited the *American Appeal,* organ of the combined Socialist and La Follette forces. His *Speeches* were collected in 1929, and he wrote such books as *Liberty*

(1895), *Unionism and Socialism, a Plea for Both* (1904), *The American Movement* (1904), *Industrial Unionism* (1905), *The Growth of Socialism* (1910), *The Children of the Poor* (1911), and *Walls and Bars* (1927).

DE CASSERES, BENJAMIN (1873–1945), Philadelphia-born journalist, critic, essayist, and poet, resident in New York City. His iconoclastic works, frequently reminiscent of the *fin de siècle* style, include *The Shadow-Eater* (1915), poems; *Chameleon—Being the Book of My Selves* (1922); *James Gibbons Huneker* (1925); *Forty Immortals* (1925), essays; *The Superman in America* (1929); *Mencken and Shaw* (1930), critical studies; and *Fantasia Impromptu: The Adventures of an Intellectual Faun* (1937).

Declaration of Independence, formal proclamation of the 13 colonies, announcing their separation from Great Britain, was adopted July 4, 1776. In the second Continental Congress on June 7, Richard Henry Lee, a Virginia delegate, proposed a resolution of independence, and four days later Jefferson, Franklin, Adams, Roger Sherman, and Robert Livingston were appointed as a committee to draft the declaration. The actual writing was done by Jefferson, although corrections were made by Franklin, Adams, and the Congress at large. The document is based on the natural-rights theory of government, derived from Locke and 18th-century French philosophers, and proclaims that the function of government is to guarantee the inalienable rights with which men are endowed. These include "Life, Liberty, and the pursuit of Happiness." The declaration contended that, since George III had willfully violated these rights, revolution was justifiable and necessary. The document was signed (Aug. 2) by 56 colonial representatives.

Deephaven, local-color sketches by Sarah Orne Jewett,♦ published in 1877.
    Deephaven, described by Helen Denis, who accompanies her friend Kate Lancaster on a summer visit to the Maine seaport town, is isolated and poor because of the decline of its port since the early 1800s. Its peculiar distinction, deriving from its decayed grandeur and fading memories, makes the place seem "more like one of the lazy little English seaside towns. . . . It was not in the least American." The population mainly consists of poor fishermen and farmers, and retired sea captains and their families, except for such relics of aristocracy as old Miss Chauncey, the lonely, half-insane resident of East Parrish, whose mind dwells still in her distant youth. "The Captains" are usually to be found "sunning themselves like turtles on one of the wharves," exchanging anecdotes of seafaring days. Life moves in a slow rhythm of reminiscence, and perhaps the busiest of the townspeople are such shrewd, methodical housewives as Mrs. Kew, wife of the lighthouse

keeper, "peart" old Mrs. Bonny, and the Widow Jim, tenderly faithful to the memory of her brutal husband.

DEERING, NATHANIEL (1791–1881), Maine editor and dramatist, whose works include *Cara-basset* (1831), a tragedy; *Bozzaris* (1851), a romantic blank-verse drama on the Greek revolt; and *The Clairvoyants,* a comedy first published in 1934.

Deerslayer, The, romance by Cooper,♦ published in 1841. An anonymous dramatization was produced the same year. The romance is the first in plot sequence of the Leather-Stocking Tales. ♦

At Lake Otsego, during the 1740s, early in the French and Indian Wars, lives the trapper Thomas Hutter, with his daughters Judith and Hetty. The frontiersmen, giant Hurry Harry and Natty Bumppo, known as Deerslayer among the Delaware Indians, help Hutter to resist an Iroquois attack and return to his log fortress. There Deerslayer is joined by his friend, the Mohican chief Chingachgook, and they attempt to ransom Hutter and Hurry Harry, who have been captured. Feeble-minded Hetty slips away to the Iroquois camp, where she is unharmed because of the Indians' veneration for the demented, and before her return she sees her father and Harry, as well as Chingachgook's bride Hist, also a captive. The trapper and Harry are released, but Deerslayer, who helps his friend rescue Hist, is captured, and Hutter is later killed. Judith, who discovers that she and Hetty are not Hutter's children but are actually of noble birth, tells Deerslayer, when he is released on parole, that she loves him. She tries to prevent his return to the Iroquois, but he keeps his word, returns, and is about to be tortured. Judith appears, delaying the executioners until Chingachgook arrives with a troop of British soldiers. Hetty is killed, and Judith disappears. Although Deerslayer later learns that Judith married one of the titled British officers, he always treasures romantic memories of the affair.

DE FOREST, JOHN WILLIAM (1826–1906), Connecticut-born novelist, utilized his experiences as a Civil War captain to write the first realistic novel of that conflict, *Miss Ravenel's Conversion from Secession to Loyalty*♦ (1867), which gives a vivid picture of a soldier's feelings in battle, the sordid corruption and inefficiency during the war, and the subtleties of the feminine mind. *Kate Beaumont* (1872) is a realistic study of South Carolina life and manners, which De Forest had observed as a district commander of the Freedmen's Bureau. Further examples of his vigorous realism and study of character are *Honest John Vane* (1875) and *Playing the Mischief* (1875), political novels set in the corrupt Washington of Grant's administration. Other, lesser novels are "Witching Times" (serialized in *Putnam's Maga-*

zine (1856–57), not separately published), about the Salem witchcraft trials; *Seacliff or The Mystery of the Westervelts* (1859), concerning a domestic tragedy in Connecticut; *Overland* (1871), set in frontier New Mexico and California; *The Wetherel Affair* (1873), a mystery story; *Justine's Lovers* (1878); *Irene the Missionary* (1879), set in Syria, where he had traveled in the 1850s; *The Bloody Chasm* (1881), dealing with the post-Civil War era; and *A Lover's Revolt* (1898), a romance of the Revolution. De Forest also wrote a scholarly *History of the Indians of Connecticut . . .* (1851), *Oriental Acquaintance: or, Letters from Syria* (1856), *European Acquaintance: Being Sketches of People . . .* (1858), and *Poems* (1902). *A Volunteer's Adventures* (1946) and *A Union Officer in the Reconstruction* (1948) collect letters and articles written during and after the Civil War.

Deformed, The; or, Woman's Trial, verse drama by R.P. Smith,♦ produced and published in 1830. The play is indebted to Dekker's *The Honest Whore* and Dunlap's adaptation, *The Italian Father.*

Deism, trend of religious thought, characterized by belief in the existence of a God who rules natural phenomena by established laws, not by miracles, and in the rational nature of men, who are capable of understanding these laws and of guiding their lives by them. In America, deism evolved partly as a protest against Calvinism, partly as an attempt to reconcile religious belief with scientific thought. The former attitude appears in the writings of Charles Chauncey and Jonathan Mayhew, and the latter in Cotton Mather's *The Christian Philosopher*♦ (1721), which attempts to give proof of benevolent design in the universe. A more positive deism, advocating a belief in a natural universal religion and having a more utilitarian basis, appears in the writings of Franklin and the eclectic philosophy of Jefferson. The political liberalism of the Revolution was related to the attitude exhibited in such deistic works as Ethan Allen's *Reason the Only Oracle of Man,* and the books of Elihu Palmer (1764–1806), who attempted to establish a republican religion. The most extreme expression of deism is Paine's *The Age of Reason*♦ (1794–95). By about 1810 its force was arrested by the emotional reaction of revivalism. The emphasis on the perfectibility of man and of human institutions engendered by the Revolution gave way to renewed concern with the preparation for immortality. Deism thus declined as a movement, but its views continued to appear sporadically, in such authors as Abner Kneeland, the two Owens, Orestes Brownson, and Frances Wright, and it is a source of later rational and skeptical philosophic thought, as well as of the liberalism of Unitarianism, Universalism, and other movements.

DE JONG, DAVID CORNEL (1905–67), born in the Netherlands, came to the U.S. at 13, graduated from Calvin College, Michigan (1929), and did graduate work at Duke and Brown. His novels include *Belly Fulla Straw* (1935) and *Light Sons and Dark* (1940), about American farm life; *Old Haven* (1938) and *Day of the Trumpet* (1941), about Holland; *Benefit Street* (1942), set in a Providence boardinghouse; *Somewhat Angels* (1945), showing the impact of war on women; *The Desperate Children* (1949), a psychological study of two boys; and *Two Sofas in the Parlor* (1952), about a Dutch family in the U.S. during 1913. *With a Dutch Accent* (1944) is autobiography; *Across the Board* (1943), poems; and *Snow-on-the-Mountain* (1946) and *The Unfairness of Easter* (1959), stories.

DE KRUIF, PAUL (1890–1971), born in Michigan, taught bacteriology at the state university until he served in World War I. His popular books on scientific subjects include *Our Medicine Men* (1922); *Microbe Hunters* (1926), stories of pioneers in bacteriology; *Hunger Fighters* (1928), about men who have worked to increase the North American food supply; *Seven Iron Men* (1929); *Men Against Death* (1932), about modern "microbe hunters"; *Why Keep Them Alive?* (1936), recounting scientific improvements not in use because of lack of money; *The Fight for Life* (1938); *Health is Wealth* (1940); *Kaiser Wakes the Doctors* (1943); *The Male Hormone* (1945); and *A Man Against Insanity* (1957). *The Sweeping Wind* (1962) is an autobiography. He provided background material for Lewis's *Arrowsmith*♦ and Howard's *Yellow Jack.*♦

DELAND, MARGARET[TA WADE CAMPBELL] (1857–1945), novelist born in a Pennsylvania town that forms the background of many of her books and has been described as being "not so much a place as a number of people and a state of mind." Her first novel, *John Ward, Preacher* (1888), concerned a 19th-century Calvinist minister torn between his doctrines and his love for his wife, a liberal thinker. *Sidney* (1890) and *Philip and His Wife* (1894) were also character studies. Her greatest works in this vein are considered to be *The Awakening of Helena Richie* (1906) and its sequel *The Iron Woman* (1911), portraying the life of a selfish woman and her gradual realization of her own limitations. Later works include *The Rising Tide* (1916), dealing with the woman suffrage movement; *The Vehement Flame* (1922), the story of the love of a young boy and a mature woman; *The Kays* (1926), a study of a flinty New England woman; and *Captain Archer's Daughter* (1932), a historical novel of Maine, contrasting the old families, the summer visitors, and the newly rich. Her short stories, also primarily character studies, have been collected in several volumes, including *Old Chester Tales* (1898), *Dr. Lavendar's People* (1903), *R. J.'s Mother and Some Other People*

(1908), and *Around Old Chester* (1915). *New Friends in Old Chester* (1924) contains three novelettes. *If This Be I* (1935) and *Golden Yesterdays* (1941) are autobiographical.

DELANO, ALONZO (1802?–74), born in Albany, N.Y., emigrated to Illinois, but became famous because of his later overland trip to California and residence there. The narrative of his overland voyage in 1849, *Life on the Plains and Among the Diggings* (1854), is one of the most interesting accounts of the great migration and is supplemented by 36 letters to newspapers collected in *Alonzo Delano's California Correspondence* (1952). As a frontier humorist resident in the mines, Delano made a great local reputation with works that include *Pen-Knife Sketches, or Chips of the Old Block* (1853); *Old Block's Sketch Book* (1856); *A Live Woman in the Mines* (1857), a play; and *A Sojourn with Royalty* (1936).

DELANO, AMASA (1763–1823), Massachusetts sea captain. Melville's "Benito Cereno" is based on his autobiographical *Narrative of Voyages and Travels* (1817).

DELANY, MARTIN R[OBINSON] (1812–85), free-born black of the present West Virginia, who published a newspaper in Pittsburgh, assisted Frederick Douglass with his journal, attended Harvard Medical School for a year before issuing *The Condition, Elevation, Emigration, and Destiny of the Colored People of the United States* (1852), which argues for emigration of blacks to a state of their own creation. His novel *Blake: or The Huts of America*, partly serialized (1859) and fully (1861–62), was first issued as a book in 1870. It deals with a West Indian kidnapped into U.S. slavery who escapes to plot an insurrection in his homeland. Delany was the first black major in the U.S. army during the Civil War. *Principia of Ethnology* (1878) is a defense of blacks' intelligence and achievements.

Delaware Indians, confederacy of Algonquian tribes, were given their present name by colonists who found them in the Delaware River valley, but their own name is Leni-Lenape. Their early history and migration to North America are told in their tribal chronicle, the *Walam Olum.*♦ In 1682 they made their famous treaty with Penn, which they retained for 50 years. Defeated by the Iroquois (1720), they moved into Ohio, where they sided with the French in the French and Indian War, and against the Americans in the uprising of Pontiac and the Revolution. The whites attacked a peaceful Delaware settlement in 1782, causing the remainder of these Christian Indians to flee to Ontario. Others ceded their lands to the U.S. and moved to Oklahoma. The Delaware figure as noble, wise, and just in the Leather-Stocking Tales, and appear also in Freneau's "Prophecy of King Tammany," Brown's

Edgar Huntly, Paulding's *Koningsmarke,* Nicholas Hentz's *Tadeuskund,* and outside of literature, in studies by Rafinesque, E.G. Squier, and D.G. Brinton. They are mentioned in Irving's *Tour of the Prairies,* but the most comprehensive early account of them was in Schoolcraft's six-volume *History, Conditions, and Prospects of the Indian Tribes in the United States* (1851–57), used as a source by Thoreau and Longfellow. A fictional view of them in modern life occurs in *The Light in the Forest* (1953) by Conrad Richter.

DE LA WARR, THOMAS WEST, Baron (1577–1618), first colonial governor of Virginia (1610–18), encouraged further colonization by writing a *Relation . . . of the Colonie, Planted in Virginia* (1611). The state of Delaware was named for him.

DE LEON, DANIEL (1852–1914), born in Curaçao, graduated from Columbia University and became a leader of the Socialist Labor party, editing its journal, *The People.* After some of his party's members joined Debs to found the Socialist Democratic party (later Socialist party) in 1899, De Leon helped to organize the I.W.W. and later promoted a rival group to work for industrial unionism. His major pamphlet is *Socialist Reconstruction of Society* (1905) and he also translated most of Eugène Sue's series *The Mysteries of the People.*

Delicate Balance, A, play by Edward Albee,♦ produced and published in 1966 and awarded a Pulitzer Prize.

During an October weekend in their suburban home, Tobias and Agnes, a couple in their fifties, and Agnes's sister Claire, who lives with them, spend their time in quiet desperation, drinking heavily and talking about the local country club; and Agnes wonders if she might be losing her mind. They are unexpectedly visited by their friends, Harry and Edna, who have been frightened by some unexplained cause. Harry and Edna move into the house, much to the displeasure of Julia, Tobias, and Agnes's 36-year-old daughter, who has come home after breaking up with her fourth husband. Stormy scenes occur between the two couples until Harry and Edna depart and the old delicate balance of the home is restored, with Agnes once again discussing the possibility that she might go mad.

Delineator, The (1873–1937), New York monthly magazine of women's fashions, founded by Ebenezer Buttrick, in 1894 began printing articles and fiction of interest to women. Its success was so great that four foreign editions were published. Under the editorship of Dreiser (1907–10), it dealt with such problems as divorce and woman suffrage and began crusades for improved living conditions in homes and public institutions. Under Honoré Morrow's editorship (1914–19), it was violently anti-German and was concerned with postwar morality and radical activities. After 1926 it emphasized fashions and had more than 2,000,000 circulation before it merged with the *Pictorial Review.*

DELL, FLOYD (1887–1969), born in Illinois, after a career in Chicago journalism moved to New York (1913), and for the next ten years was a prominent radical, serving as an editor of *The Masses* and *The Liberator.* He wrote one-act plays, such as *The Angel Intrudes* (1918), and also wrote a study of child psychology, *Were You Ever a Child?* (1919). His first novel, *Moon-Calf♦* (1920), won acclaim as a representative document of the disillusioned post-war generation. This was followed by a sequel, *The Briary-Bush* (1921), and by *Janet March* (1923), *Runaway* (1925), and other novels concerned with the hopelessness of youth in a confused world, the spirit of the jazz age, and the revolt against convention typified by the residents of Greenwich Village. Dell's many later works include *Intellectual Vagabondage; An Apology for the Intelligentsia* (1926); *An Old Man's Folly* (1926), a novel about World War I pacifists; *The Outline of Marriage* (1926); *An Unmarried Father* (1927), humorous novel, dramatized by the author with Thomas Mitchell as *Little Accident* (1928); *Upton Sinclair* (1927); *Love in the Machine Age* (1930); and *Homecoming* (1933), autobiography.

DE LILLO, DON (1936–), novelist born in New York City and educated at Fordham. His works include *Americana* (1971), about a TV executive who outgrows his business; *End Zone* (1972), which brought him major critical attention, like other of his novels is an existential comedy, its theme football as metaphor for both anomie and atomic war, with down-home characters. *Great Jones Street* (1973) concerns the worlds of jazz and drugs; *Ratner's Star* (1976) is a grim, surreal novel, its protagonist a 14-year-old mathematical genius and Nobel laureate, Billy Twillig, whose mission is to decode the message of a star and to invent a mathematical language to answer it. After *Players* (1977), about rich New Yorkers caught in terrorism, *Running Dog* (1978), on spies and murder, and *The Names* (1982), about a corrupt American expatriate in Athens, De Lillo published *White Noise* (1985), by general consent his best book, with rich characters depicted in minimalist language. Jack Gladney is chairman of Hitler Studies (a department he pioneered) at a small college. He is secretly trying to learn German for a forthcoming conference he is sponsoring. A toxic gas spill threatens him and his family, causing them to flee. The plot and characters are at once real and weird. In *Libra* (1988) Oswald's shooting of President Kennedy becomes a national allegory. *Mao II* (1991) concerns CIA operatives in Greece.

DELMAR, VIÑA (1905–   ), New York City author, whose novels, *Bad Girl* (1928; dramatized, 1930) and *Kept Woman* (1929), and short stories, *Loose Ladies* (1929), were sensations of the day for their sleek, hard-boiled treatments of jazz-age girls. Later works include two fictional treatments of Confederate heroes, *Beloved* (1956), about Judah P. Benjamin, and *The Big Family* (1961), about John Slidell. *The Becker Scandal* (1968) is a memoir about an event of 1912 that touched their parents. *A Time for Titans* (1974) is a novel featuring Jefferson, Napoleon, and Toussaint L'Ouverture. In 1936 she created a screenplay, *The Awful Truth,* successfully filmed but unpublished.

DELORIA, VINE, JR. (1933–   ), polemicist. A Standing Rock Sioux born and raised on a South Dakota reservation, Deloria read law and theology, and beginning with *Custer Died for Your Sins* (1969) he seized the politically and culturally right moment to become for a time a leading spokesperson for Native Americans of whatever tribe, with an agenda advocating legal separatism. His other works are *We Talk, You Listen* (1970), *God Is Red* (1973), *Behind the Trail of Broken Treaties: An Indian Declaration of Independence* (1974), *Indians of the Pacific Northwest* (1977), and *The Metaphysics of Modern Existence* (1979).

Delphian Club, Baltimore literary association, founded in 1816, whose membership included John Neal, Francis Scott Key, and Samuel Woodworth. Its literary organ was *The Portico.* ♦

DEMBY, WILLIAM (1922–   ), Pennsylvania-born novelist, after education at West Virginia State College for Negroes and Fisk University was long an expatriate in Rome, writing for Italian films. His first novel, *Beetlecreek* (1950), depicts evil in the relations between blacks and whites in a West Virginia town. *The Catacombs* (1965) is a novel about a novelist in Rome named William Demby caught up in the immoralities and crises of the times. *Love Story Black* (1978) was followed by *Blueboy* (1980), a shorter novel.

DEMING, P[HILANDER] (1829–1915), New York author, whose realistic accounts of life in upper New York state were published as *Adirondack Stories* (1880), *Tompkins and Other Folks* (1885), and *The Story of a Pathfinder* (1907).

Democracy: An American Novel, by Henry Adams, ♦ was published anonymously in 1880. "Old Granite" is believed to represent President Hayes.

Madeleine Lee, a young New York widow, moves to Washington to investigate "the tremendous forces of government, and the machinery of society, at work. What she wanted was POWER." With her sister Sybil, she creates a salon, attends Senate debates, and entertains legislators and diplomats. Through her admirer John Carrington, a lawyer, she captures as her guest the political boss, Senator Ratcliffe of Illinois, whose party has just elected the new President, "Old Granite." The President-elect, an unsophisticated Indiana lawyer, is lost among the capital's intrigues, and, though he hates and distrusts Ratcliffe, is forced to place control of patronage in his hands, and to appoint him secretary of the treasury. During the months before the inauguration, Ratcliffe falls in love with Madeleine, who is first repelled by his coarse vanity, then fascinated by his self-command and position. Carrington, who undertakes with Sybil a secret campaign against the senator, is sent to Mexico on business, but through Sybil he reveals to Madeleine that Ratcliffe is guilty of selling his influence. Disillusioned, she now refuses his proposal, at which Ratcliffe calls her a heartless coquette and departs wrathfully. Having learned enough of the mechanism and instruments of power, Madeleine deserts Washington for a tour of Europe, and Sybil writes Carrington that he may yet hope to win her sister's hand.

Democratic Review, see *United States Magazine.*

Democratic Vistas, prose pamphlet by Whitman, ♦ published in 1871, incorporating earlier essays. It was reprinted in *Two Rivulets* (1876).

The main themes are the ideals of democracy and individualism, which the author does not consider to be incompatible, and he outlines a new cultural order for the U.S. He condemns the degradation of democracy and the growth of cankerous wealth during the post-Civil War period, prophesies a future greatness, and announces that there must be a declaration of cultural independence to achieve a truly national indigenous literature.

Demos and Dionysus, blank-verse dialogue by E.A. Robinson, ♦ published in *Dionysus in Doubt* ♦ (1925).

DENNIE, JOSEPH (1768–1812), born in Boston and educated at Harvard, after a brief legal career turned to writing. At Walpole, N.H., he became the leader of a group of conservative Federalist literati, and edited the *Farmer's Weekly Museum* ♦ (1796–98), for which he wrote the graceful "Lay Preacher" essays. Under the pseudonym Colon he collaborated with Royall Tyler, who adopted the name Spondee, in contributing satirical prose and poetry to various newspapers. His later life was spent in Philadelphia, where he founded the Tuesday Club ♦ and edited *The Port Folio* (1801–9), for which he wrote further Lay Preacher essays, and for which he obtained original manuscripts from Thomas Moore, Leigh Hunt, and Thomas Campbell. Forty of his earlier essays were published in book form (1796), and another selection in 1816, but Dennie's reputation as an "American Addison" was eclipsed by that of Irving. His *Letters* were published in 1936.

DENTON, DANIEL (*d.*1696), planter and public official of Jamaica, N.Y., was the author of *A Brief Description of New-York* (London, 1670), the first separate work in English relating to the province, intended "for the encouragement of many that have a desire to remove themselves" and "for the satisfaction of others that would make a trade thither."

DE QUILLE, DAN, pseudonym of William Wright (1829–98), Far Western humorist and historian. Born in Ohio, he went to California and Nevada as a prospector in 1857. Unsuccessful in mining, he drifted into newspaper writing and became city editor (1861) of *The Territorial Enterprise* of Virginia City, Nev. In this capacity he became a good friend of his fellow worker Mark Twain, who later encouraged De Quille to write his *History of the Big Bonanza* (1877). The work bears an introduction by Twain and is known as a repository of information and anecdote about the Comstock Lode.♦ After Virginia City dwindled to a ghost town and his paper could no longer be published, De Quille finally moved away. Posthumously several works were made into books, including *Snow Shoe Thompson* (1954), *Dan De Quille of the Big Bonanza* (1980), *Little Lucy's Papa: A Story of Silverland* (1987), and *Dives and Lazarus* (1988).

DERBY, GEORGE HORATIO (1823–61), Massachusetts-born army officer and author, was famous as a wit and practical joker, but his writing was done chiefly for his own amusement, appearing in various newspapers and magazines, especially during his residence in California (1849–56). His friends collected these scattered pieces in two volumes, the popular *Phoenixiana* (1855) and *Squibob Papers* (1865), named from his pseudonyms, John Phoenix and Squibob. Although he is usually classed as a "Western humorist," Derby was a well-educated gentleman with an innate love of fun, who wrote in a spirit of satire, irony, and burlesque. To some extent he carries on the tradition of urbane humor represented by Irving and *The Knickerbocker Magazine,* but his boisterous quality is in the new Western spirit. His burlesques of contemporary subjects are somewhat dated, but modern readers can appreciate such *jeux d'esprit* as "A New System of English Grammar" and "Musical Review Extraordinary."

DERLETH, AUGUST [WILLIAM] (1909–71), Wisconsin author, noted for his regional writings and prolific literary career. After graduation from the state university (1930) he averaged nearly three published books annually. His long series of novels about Sac Prairie (whose prototype is Sauk City) includes *Still Is the Summer Night* (1937), *Wind over Wisconsin* (1938), *Restless Is the River*

(1939), *Evening in Spring* (1941), *Sweet Genevieve* (1942), *Shadow of Night* (1943), and *The Shield of the Valiant* (1945). He also wrote other novels with Wisconsin settings, including *Bright Journey* (1940) and its sequels, *House on the Mound* (1958) and *The Hills Stand Watch* (1960); poems about the region, collected in *Hawk on the Wind* (1938), *Man Track Here* (1939), *Rind of Earth* (1942), *And You, Thoreau!* (1944), and other volumes; short story collections like *Sac Prairie People* (1948); as well as detective novels; science fiction; a biography of Zona Gale, *Still Small Voice* (1940); *The Wisconsin: River of a Thousand Isles* (1942); and *Place of Hawks* (1935), collecting novelettes on psychic problems.

Descent into the Maelström, A, story by Poe,♦ published in *Graham's Magazine* (1841) and reprinted in *Prose Tales* (1843).

A Norwegian sailor and his brother are trapped in their fishing boat when a hurricane draws it into the fearful Moskoe-ström, a whirlpool that periodically forms and subsides. Whirled about the inner verge of the gulf, they face death, and the elder brother becomes insane. The other sees that of the many objects in the grasp of the whirlpool, small cylindrical ones are least likely to be destroyed, and, lashing himself to a cask, he jumps into the sea. When the Moskoe-ström subsides, he floats to safety and is rescued by fellow fishermen. They do not recognize him or believe his story, for his hair has turned white and his expression is completely altered.

Descent to the Dead, see *Jeffers, R.*

Description of New England, A, autobiographical narrative by John Smith.♦

Deseret, name given to the present state of Utah at its founding by the Mormons. Derived from the *Book of Mormon,* the name means "the land of the working bee."

Desire Under the Elms, play by O'Neill,♦ produced and published in 1924.

Ephraim Cabot, in his elm-shaded New England farmhouse in 1850, is a decadent Puritan, harsh and miserly. He acquired the farm from his dead second wife, mother of his son Eben, who works it with his elder half-brothers, Simeon and Peter. Eben, who resembles his gentle mother, hates Ephraim for having mistreated her, and the other sons are kept from joining the gold rush to California only by their avaricious interest in inheriting the farm. When Ephraim, despite his 75 years, takes a third wife, Simeon and Peter sell their shares to Eben and leave for California. Ephraim's third wife is Abbie Putnam, a young widow, greedy and sensual, whose only purpose is to gain her husband's wealth, and she seduces Eben in order to have a child who will inherit it. Ephraim exults over the birth of his supposed son, and when he reveals that the new child will inherit the property, Eben repudiates Abbie's love, which is by now genuine. She kills the child and in a rage confesses her crimes. Eben informs the police, but, overcome by love for Abbie, admits a part in the murder, and is arrested with her.

DE SMET, Pierre Jean (1801–73), Belgian Jesuit missionary among the Indians of the Northwest, erected many missions and won the confidence of his people, to whom he made many journeys. After the white immigration of the mid-century made Indian relations difficult, he often acted as intermediary and arbitrator, and was chiefly responsible for the eventual peace between the Sioux and the Americans. His missionary work was supplemented by his books, *Letters and Sketches* (1843), *Oregon Missions and Travels* (1847), *Western Missions and Missionaries* (1859), and *New Indian Sketches* (1863).

De Spain, Major Cassius, character in the Yoknapatawpha saga of Faulkner. After service in the Confederate cavalry, he becomes the sheriff who, in *Absalom, Absalom!,* kills Wash Jones after Jones has murdered Thomas Sutpen. Some of Sutpen's land becomes his, and to it he annually invites hunting parties as described in "The Bear." In *The Hamlet* his barn is burned, presumably by Ab and Flem Snopes. His son Manfred, a West Point graduate and veteran of the Spanish-American War, becomes mayor of Jefferson and president of the Sartoris Bank. In *The Mansion,* when Will Varner discovers that Eula Varner Snopes, his daughter, is De Spain's mistress, Manfred has to sell his bank stock to Eula's husband Flem and to leave Jefferson.

Detective story, form of fiction whose main structural characteristic is a reversal of the sequence of events: the catastrophe, generally a murder, is typically presented first, followed by the introduction of suspected criminals and of a series of clues whose significance the reader is not supposed to grasp until the story is ended by a climax of explanation, in which the detective hero shows how the crime was committed, the motives for it, and finally the identity of the criminal. Poe's "The Murders in the Rue Morgue," ♦ "The Purloined Letter," ♦ and "The Mystery of Marie Rogêt" ♦ are considered the first modern detective stories. In them there appears the prototype of fictional detectives, C. Auguste Dupin, an intellectual amateur who demonstrates an astounding ability to solve crimes by analyzing clues unobserved or misinterpreted by the police and his simple friend, the narrator of the tale. Some dime novels featured detectives like Nick Carter, but the detective novel did not become widely popular until the work of such foreign authors as Gaboriau, Wilkie Collins, and Conan Doyle was published in the U.S. The first

full-length detective novels of the U.S. of importance were those of Anna Katharine Green, the most popular being *The Leavenworth Case* (1878). The vogue of detective fiction has become tremendous in the 20th century.

DE TOCQUEVILLE, see *Tocqueville.*

Detour, The, play by Owen Davis, ♦ produced in 1921 and published in 1922.

DEUTSCH, Babette (1895–1982), New York poet, noted for her sensitive intellectual verse, highly charged with emotion and concerned with social questions and attitudes. Her reputation was established by her early volumes, *Banners* (1919), *Honey Out of the Rock* (1925), and *Fire for the Night* (1930). *Epistle to Prometheus* (1931) is on the Promethean spirit throughout the ages; *One Part Love* (1939), a protest against the spiritual darkness of today; *Take Them, Stranger* (1944), poems of war; and *Animal, Vegetable, Mineral* (1954) and *Coming of Age* (1959), new and selected earlier poems and translations. *Collected Poems* was issued in 1969. Besides novels, *A Brittle Heaven* (1926), *In Such a Night* (1927), *Mask of Silenus* (1933), and *Rogue's Legacy* (1942), she wrote a biography of Whitman (1941) for children. Critical works include *Potable Gold: Some Notes on Poetry and This Age* (1929); *This Modern Poetry* (1935), revised as *Poetry in Our Time* (1954); and anthologies of Russian and German poetry.

Devil and Daniel Webster, The, one-act folk opera by Stephen Vincent Benét ♦ and Douglas Moore, produced in 1939. It is based on a short story by Benét, published in *Thirteen O'Clock* (1937). *Scratch* (1971) is a prose dramatization by MacLeish.

Jabez Stone, a New Hampshire farmer, sells his soul to the devil in return for ten years of prosperity. When the devil comes to his wedding to collect, Jabez appeals to a guest, Daniel Webster, to defend him before the devil's jury of American villains. Appealing to them as men, Webster's eloquence touches their memories of freedom and wins an acquittal.

Devil's Dictionary, The, by Ambrose Bierce, ♦ was first published as *The Cynic's Word Book* (1906) and retitled in 1911. Collected from newspaper contributions (1881–1906), and addressed to "enlightened souls who prefer dry wines to sweet, sense to sentiment, wit to humor, and clean English to slang," the volume contains witty, concise "definitions" reflecting Bierce's bold social criticism, pessimism, and skeptical philosophy. Characteristic entries are: "Mugwump, *n.* In politics one afflicted with self-respect and addicted to the vice of independence. A term of contempt"; "Edible, *adj.* Good to eat, and wholesome to digest, as a worm to a toad, a toad to a snake, a snake to a pig, a pig to a man, and a man to a worm."

DE VINNE, THEODORE LOW (1828–1914), advanced the art of printing in the U.S. by the high quality of workmanship at his New York press and by his writings, which include *The Invention of Printing* (1876), *Historic Printing Types* (1886), *The Practice of Typography* (1900–1904), and *Notable Printers of Italy During the Fifteenth Century* (1910).

DE VOTO, BERNARD [AUGUSTINE] (1897–1955), Utah-born professor of English at Northwestern University (1922–27) and Harvard (1929–36), later edited *The Saturday Review of Literature* (1936–38), and occupied the "Easy Chair" of *Harper's* (1935–55). As Literary Editor of the Mark Twain Estate he issued previously unpublished manuscripts as *Mark Twain in Eruption* (1940) and *Letters from the Earth* (1962). His own studies of the writer include *Mark Twain's America* (1932) and *Mark Twain at Work* (1942). His study of "the continental experience," a trilogy on the impact of the West on the American mind, is contained in *The Course of Empire* (1952), about discovery and exploration from the 16th century to the 19th; *Across the Wide Missouri* (1947, Pulitzer Prize), about the Rocky Mountain fur trade; and *The Year of Decision: 1846* (1943). Other studies of American ideas include *Forays and Rebuttals* (1936), *Minority Report* (1940), and *The Easy Chair* (1955), collections of forthright essays; and *The Literary Fallacy* (1944), criticizing American authors of the 1920s for holding aloof from vital experience. His novels include *The Crooked Mile* (1924), *The Chariot of Fire* (1926), *The House of Sun-Goes-Down* (1928), *We Accept with Pleasure* (1934), *Mountain Time* (1947), and lesser fiction under the name John August. A collection of *Letters* (1975) was edited by Wallace Stegner, who also wrote a biography (1974).

DE VRIES, PETER (1910–93), born in Chicago, long resident in Connecticut, for a time an editor of *Poetry,* later on the staff of *The New Yorker,* is known for his humorous, sophisticated novels, beginning with *But Who Wakes the Bugler?* (1940), often about suburban Connecticut life, as in *Tunnel of Love* (1954), adapted with Joseph Fields as a play (1957); *Comfort Me with Apples* (1956); *The Mackerel Plaza* (1958); *The Tents of Wickedness* (1959), indulging not only in his exuberant punning but travestying the styles of Faulkner, Hemingway, and Fitzgerald; *Through the Fields of Clover* (1961), about the reunion of a fantastic New England family; and *Reuben, Reuben* (1964), presenting outsiders' views of an ex-urbanite community. Regardless of setting, his lively comedies of manners, though farcical and peopled with fantastic characters, have some serious concern with matters of religion or morality. His fiction also includes *Let Me*

Count the Ways (1965), concerning a man converted to religion after paradoxically suffering a sudden sickness at Lourdes; *The Vale of Laughter* (1967), a sardonic comedy narrated by a stockbroker and his former philosophy professor; *The Cat's Pyjamas and Witch's Milk* (1968), two related novellas of pathos told comically; *Mrs. Wallop* (1970); *Into Your Tent I'll Creep* (1971), satirizing women's liberation in relation to marriage; *Forever Panting* (1975); *The Glory of the Hummingbird* (1974), about a small-town Indiana boy's success through a television quiz show; *I Hear America Swinging* (1976), treating the effect of the new sexual liberation on an Iowa farming community; *Madder Music* (1977), portraying an author who comes to think of himself as Groucho Marx; *Consenting Adults, or The Duchess Will Be Furious* (1980), a tale with a light, lively plot set again in Illinois; *Sauce for the Goose* (1981), fliply presenting the love affair of a feminist journalist; *Slouching Towards Kalamazoo* (1983), a comic story of an affair between a boy and his eighth-grade teacher; *The Prick of Noon* (1985), about a rich "sexucational" film-maker; and *Peckham's Marbles* (1986), treating a man both professor and creative writer booked into a treatment place for alcoholics. *The Handsome Heart* (1943) and *The Blood of the Lamb* (1962) are more sober novels. *No, But I Saw the Movie* (1952) and *Without a Stitch in Time* (1972) collect stories.

DEWEY, JOHN (1859–1952), Vermont-born philosopher and educator, graduated from the University of Vermont (1879) and Johns Hopkins (Ph.D., 1884). He taught at the universities of Minnesota, Michigan, Chicago, and after 1904 at Columbia. While director of the University of Chicago's School of Education he founded the Laboratory School to test new educational techniques. His influence on education and thought came also from his books, teaching, and leadership of many learned societies, connection with the Socialist party, and work as adviser to foreign governments. His most important writings on education, following his *Psychology* (1887), include *The School and Society* (1899), *The Child and the Curriculum* (1902), *Moral Principles in Education* (1909), *Interest and Effort in Education* (1913), *Experience and Education* (1938), and *The Public Schools and Spiritual Values* (1944). *Problems of Men* (1946) is a collection of his essays. In these works he emphasizes the changes in educational needs due to the industrial revolution, the democratic point of view, and the concept of man as a biological entity required to adjust himself to his environment and the complex structure of modern society. His scientific realism, the basis of this attitude, springs from pragmatism, of which Dewey was the leading exponent after the death of William James.

Shifting the emphasis of pragmatic thought from religion and the will to believe to practical problems of social reconstruction, Dewey called his philosophy "instrumentalism," and in it he holds that, since reality changes and grows, truth consists in the success with which ideas, hypotheses, and beliefs are framed for the achievement of set purposes. The only reality is experience, and knowledge is necessarily functional, not abstract or theoretical. The natural sciences have advanced through devotion to observation, experiment, and revision in light of experience; the great need is for social sciences to advance to a commensurate point, at which they may direct all knowledge to human ends, enabling intelligence to control the human and extra-human environment. These ideas have been developed in *Outlines of a Critical Theory of Ethics* (1891), *Studies in Logical Theory* (1903), *How We Think* (1909), *The Influence of Darwin on Philosophy* . . . (1910), *Essays in Experimental Logic* (1916), *Democracy and Education* (1916), *Reconstruction in Philosophy* (1920), *Human Nature and Conduct* (1922), *Experience and Nature* (1925), *The Quest for Certainty* (1929), *Individualism, Old and New* (1930), *Philosophy and Civilization* (1931), *Art as Experience* (1934), *A Common Faith* (1934), *Liberalism and Social Action* (1935), *Logic, the Theory of Inquiry* (1938), and *Freedom and Culture* (1939). A scholarly edition of his works began publication in 1967.

DEWEY, MELVIL (1851–1931), as librarian of Amherst College (1874–76) evolved his Dewey Decimal Classification system of cataloguing. He later founded the *Library Journal* (1876) and established the first school of librarianship at Columbia (1887).

DEXTER, TIMOTHY (1747–1806), eccentric merchant of Newburyport, Mass., who dubbed himself "Lord" Timothy Dexter. He gained his wealth by unusual, though shrewd, business transactions and spent part of it for a curious mansion in his native town. His book, *A Pickle for the Knowing Ones* (1802), is an amusing expression of his idiosyncrasies, famous for its lack of punctuation except in the second edition, which had a page of punctuation marks at the end so that readers could "pepper and solt it as they plese." J. P. Marquand wrote a biography of Dexter (1925, revised 1960).

Dharma Bums, The, novel by Jack Kerouac. ◆

Dial, The, (July 1840–April 1844), quarterly magazine of literature, philosophy, and religion, was the organ of the New England Transcendentalist movement, and grew out of the informal meetings of the Transcendental Club. ◆ Although Alcott, who gave the magazine its title, thought it insufficiently transcendental, it was considered obscure by the general public, and savagely attacked by the press. Margaret Fuller, the editor, was assisted by George Ripley, but she failed to give the magazine unity, admitting many

contradictory articles. Among the early contributions were Thoreau's "Friendship"; Emerson's "The Problem" and "Man the Reformer"; Alcott's "Orphic Sayings"; Miss Fuller's "Goethe"; Theodore Parker's "German Literature"; Elizabeth Peabody's "Christ's Idea of Society"; and writings by George Ripley, C.P. Cranch, and W.H. Channing. Emerson succeeded as editor (July 1842), and gave *The Dial* a more unified attitude, publishing extracts from Oriental religious writings entitled "Ethnic Scriptures," his own "Lectures on the Times," and further writings by W.H. Channing, Miss Fuller, Parker, Charles Lane, Jones Very, J.F. Clarke, Lowell, and C.A. Dana.

Dial, The (1860), monthly literary and philosophic magazine, the Western organ of Transcendentalism, was edited from Cincinnati by Moncure Conway. Patterned after the Boston Transcendentalist magazine, it printed similar material, although individual contributions were less distinguished. The authors included Emerson, Alcott, Howells, and O.B. Frothingham.

Dial, The (1880–1929), monthly journal of literary criticism, was founded at Chicago as a conservative review. In 1892 it became a fortnightly, continuing the original policy until 1918, when it was moved to New York. New contributing editors, including Conrad Aiken, H.E. Stearns, Randolph Bourne, and Van Wyck Brooks, made it a radical journal of opinion, publishing such previously taboo authors as Dewey, Veblen, Laski, Beard, and R.M. Lovett. Under Scofield Thayer, after 1920, *The Dial* became the most distinguished literary monthly in the U.S. to champion modern artistic movements. It drew contributors from many nations and had as associates Thomas Mann, T.S. Eliot, James Stephens, and Paul Morand. It printed virtually all the distinguished authors of the period, and was noted also for its fine reproductions of modern graphic art. Marianne Moore was editor after 1926.

Dialogues in Limbo, ten Platonic discourses by Santayana, ◆ published in 1926.

Diamond as Big as the Ritz, The, story by F. Scott Fitzgerald, ◆ published in *Tales of the Jazz Age* (1922).
    John T. Unger, a teenager from Hades, Miss., becomes a friend of Percy Washington at their Massachusetts preparatory school and goes to spend the summer holiday at the Washington mansion in the wilds of Montana. It is located on isolated land that conceals a diamond mine and a single gem one cubic mile in extent, discovered by Percy's grandfather and concealed from the world. The summer ends when the diamond mountain is located from planes by aviators who land to scale its great peak. With his father and mother Percy disappears into the mine but the

mountain disintegrates, burying them and the aviators, while John and Percy's two sisters contemplate the scene of the disaster.

Diamond Lens, The, story by Fitz-James O'Brien. ♦

Diary of a Public Man, The, see *Ward, Samuel.*

Diary of Anne Frank, The, play by Albert Hackett. ♦

DICKENS, CHARLES (1812–70), English novelist, whose first tour of the U.S. (Jan.–May 1842) is described in his *American Notes for General Circulation*♦ (1842), and furnished the background for portions of *Martin Chuzzlewit*♦ (1843–44). He visited the U.S. again (Nov. 1867–April 1868), when he presented a popular series of readings in Eastern cities.

DICKEY, JAMES [LAFAYETTE] (1923–), Georgia-born poet, on the faculty of the University of South Carolina (1969–). His first volumes of poetry, *Into the Stone* (1960), *Drowning with Others* (1962), *Helmets* (1964), and *Buckdancer's Choice* (1965, National Book Award), were the sources from which he selected his *Poems* (1967). The last of the four separate volumes contained "The Firebombing," disputed as a major poem but with divergent conceptions of Dickey's treatment of the destruction of a city by atomic bombing from the air. In the same year that he issued his next volume of poetry, *The Eye-Beaters, Blood, Victory, Madness, Buckhead and Mercy* (1970), he also published a novel, *Deliverance.* A thrilling adventure story about four Georgia businessmen going by canoe down a rugged river on a hunting trip and fighting for their lives against the wilderness and malevolent mountaineers, it became a best seller and he later adapted it for a film version; his next novel, *Alnilam,* did not appear until 1987, and it is a rather opaque tale about a blind father and his missing son. In 1993 Dickey published a short novel, *To the White Sea.* Set in the closing days of World War II, it concerns a grotesque, elemental tail gunner, Muldrow, who after bailing out of his hit B-29 over Tokyo, survives the firebombing of the city and undergoes a series of savage and murderous adventures as he makes his way to Hokkaido, using the skills he learned during his upbringing in remotest Alaska. The narration is spare and first-person. His poetry had reappeared in 1976 as *The Zodiac,* a lengthy work in 12 parts. Meanwhile he had published prose works: *The Suspect in Poetry* (1964), frank, often polemical reviews of contemporary poets, followed by the similar *Babel to Byzantium* (1968); *Self-Interviews* (1970), based on tape-recorded commentary on his poetry; and *Sorties* (1971), extracts from his journals and essays on poets. Dickey returned to poetry with a new collection, *The Strength of*

Fields (1979), whose title work was written for President Carter's inaugural, while other poems, like those written before, often deal with masculine adventure and violence. *The Early Motion: "Drowning with Others" and "Helmets"* (1980) and *The Central Motion* (1983) collect previously published poems. *Puella* (1982) is a long poem about a girl developing from a child to a woman, while *Bronwen, the Traw, and the Shape-Shifter* (1986) is a lengthy poem about a young girl's problems. *The Poet Turns on Himself* (1982) and *Night Hurling* (1983) collect essays and miscellaneous minor writing.

DICKINSON, EMILY [ELIZABETH] (1830–86), the daughter of Edward Dickinson, a prominent lawyer of Amherst, Mass., was educated at Amherst Academy and for one year at Mount Holyoke Female Seminary, under Mary Lyon. Her life was outwardly eventless, for she lived quietly at home and for the last 25 years secluded herself from all but the most intimate friends. Though never married, she cultivated intense intellectual companionships with several men in succession, whom she quaintly called her tutors. The first was Benjamin F. Newton, a law student in her father's office, who introduced her to stimulating books and urged her to take seriously her vocation as poet. Religious questionings prompted by his early death led her to appeal for guidance to the Rev. Charles Wadsworth of Philadelphia, whom she met in 1854. She soon came to regard him as her "dearest earthly friend," and for purposes of poetry created in his image the "lover" whom she was never to know except in imagination. From the time of Wadsworth's removal to San Francisco, in the spring of 1862, may be dated her withdrawal from village society and her increasing preoccupation with poetry. She initiated a literary correspondence with T.W. Higginson, whom she knew only through his papers in the *Atlantic Monthly,* and his kindly encouragement was a support to her through years of loneliness. Besides Higginson, the circle of friends to whom she occasionally showed a few of her poems included Samuel Bowles, Dr. J.G. Holland, and Helen Hunt Jackson. For the most part, however, she wrote in secret and guarded her poems even from her family.

Before her death, she had composed well over 1000 brief lyrics, her "letter to the world," records of the life about her, of tiny ecstasies set in motion by mutations of the seasons or by home and garden incidents, of candid insights into her own states of consciousness, and of speculations on the timeless mysteries of love and death. Her mind was charged with paradox, as though her vision, like the eyes of birds, was focused in opposite directions on the two worlds of material and immaterial values. She could express feelings of deepest poignancy in terms of wit. Like Emerson, her preference for the intrinsic and the essential led her often to a gnomic concision of phrase, but her artistry in the modulation of simple meters and the delicate management of imperfect rhymes was greater than his. Her daringly precise metaphors made her seem to Amy Lowell a precursor of the Imagist school.

Publication, in Emily Dickinson's unworldly view, formed no part of a poet's business. Only six of her poems, not counting an early verse valentine, were printed during her lifetime, and none with her consent. From the chaotic mass of manuscripts found after her death, some carefully revised, others carelessly jotted down on odd scraps of paper, six volumes have been selected: *Poems* (1890) and *Poems: Second Series* (1891), edited by Mabel L. Todd and T.W. Higginson; *Poems: Third Series* (1896), edited by Mrs. Todd; *The Single Hound*♦ (1914), edited by Emily's niece Martha Dickinson Bianchi; *Further Poems* (1929) and *Unpublished Poems* (1936), edited by Mrs. Bianchi and Alfred Leete Hampson. A collection was issued as *Poems: Centenary Edition* (1930). Posthumous publication kept the poems from being presented in any effective order. Trifling pieces and fragments were included with major lyrics and the text was often inaccurate, badly punctuated, or poorly displayed on the page. However, *Bolts of Melody* (1945), poems long suppressed because of a family feud, was carefully edited by Mabel L. Todd and Millicent Bingham, and a complete *The Poems of Emily Dickinson* was issued in a scholarly edition (3 vols., 1955) including variant readings by Thomas H. Johnson, who, in addition to this definitive work, edited the poet's *Letters* (3 vols., 1958). *The Manuscript Books of Emily Dickinson* (1982) reproduces in facsimile the manuscripts of the canon of 1147 poems in the fascicles into which the author gathered them.

Emily Dickinson is considered the prototype of Alison Stanhope in Susan Glaspell's *Alison's House* and the heroine of Helen Hunt Jackson's *Mercy Philbrick's Choice* (1876).

DICKINSON, JOHN (1732–1808), Philadelphia lawyer, led the conservative group in the Pennsylvania legislature during the debates on proprietary government. He wrote *Protest against the Appointment of Benjamin Franklin* (1764), and the Sugar Act and proposed Stamp Act caused him to write *The Late Regulations Respecting the British Colonies on the Continent of America . . .* (1765). When England continued to assert its rights of taxation, he began to publish in the *Pennsylvania Chronicle* his *Letters from a Farmer in Pennsylvania*♦ (1768), whose thesis is that England's acts were contrary to her own constitutional principles. These letters established him as the leading conservative opponent of English policy, for his methods differed from those of Patrick Henry and Samuel Adams. A member of both Continental Congresses, he wrote *Essay upon the Constitutional Power of Great Britain . . .* (1774), *A Dec-*

laration by the Representatives of the United Colonies (1775), and other addresses and petitions. Although he supported military measures and wrote "A Song for American Freedom" (the Liberty Song), he still hoped for reconciliation and voted against the Declaration of Independence. After the war, he represented Delaware in Congress and wrote two series of *Letters of Fabius* (1788, 1797) in favor of the Constitution.

Dictator, The, play by R.H. Davis,♦ produced in 1904 and published in 1906.

Dictionaries, see *Worcester, J.E.,* and *Webster, Noah.*

Dictionary of American Biography, biographies of outstanding Americans, published in 20 volumes (1928–36), and based on the plan of the English *Dictionary of National Biography.* Published under the auspices of the American Council of Learned Societies, and financed mainly by *The New York Times,* the work was under the supervision of an editorial staff headed (1928–31) by Allen Johnson, and after his death by Dumas Malone, who edited volumes viii–xx. The work, which includes no accounts of persons living at the time of publication, contains sketches of 13,633 persons by 2,243 contributors, and totals 11 million words. Eight supplementary volumes (1944–88) bring the total to 18,110 persons. *A Comprehensive Index* (1990) was issued as an aid to the entire work.

Dictionary of American English, based on historical principles, was compiled at the University of Chicago under the editorship of Sir William Craigie and James R. Hulbert. The project was begun in 1925, and the work is in 4 volumes (1938–44). It contains words, phrases, and usages originating in the U.S., invented words, and English importations whose meanings have become distinctively American.

Dictionary of American History, reference work written by some 1000 historians under the general editorship of James Truslow Adams, the managing editorship of R.V. Coleman, and an advisory council of 17 scholars. It was begun in 1936 with the compilation of a list of 6000 topics, and published in six volumes (1940). It was expanded to eight volumes (1976). Each of the brief articles deals with a separate aspect of American history, but there are many "covering" articles presenting broader subjects in orderly summary, and cross references indicate collateral information.

DIDION, JOAN (1934–   ), California author whose novels include *Run River* (1963), depicting deteriorating ways of life in her native Sacramento Valley; *Play It as It Lays*♦ (1970), presenting a woman caught in the social disintegration of southern California; and *A Book of Common Pray-*

er♦ (1977), treating the growing self-awareness and shattering life of a California woman in Central America. *Slouching Towards Bethlehem*♦ (1968) and *The White Album*♦ (1979) are nonfictional works on contemporary life, mainly related to California, her synecdoche for a deteriorating modern world. Other works are *Democracy* (1984), a novel; *Essays and Interviews* (1984); *Miami* (1987), a nonfictional examination of the Cuban immigrants; and *After Henry* (1992), essays about lives of people in New York, Washington, D.C., and Los Angeles. She and her husband, John Gregory Dunne,♦ also write film scripts.

DI DONATO, PIETRO (1911–92), came to prominence with publication of *Christ in Concrete* (1939), an autobiographical novel about an Italian immigrant family whose father is killed in a construction accident when his son is aged 12. *Three Circles of Light* (1960) continues the family story. *Immigrant Saint: The Life of Mother Cabrini* (1960) and *The Penitent* (1962) are biographies of 20th-century saints. *Naked Author* (1970) collects stories and excerpts from longer works.

Diedrich Knickerbocker, see *Knickerbocker.*

DIGGES, THOMAS ATWOOD (1742–1822), an intimate of Washington, Jefferson, Franklin, and Madison, while residing in Lisbon during the American Revolution was active in the patriot cause. To him has been attributed *Adventures of Alonso: Containing Some Striking Anecdotes of the Present Prime Minister of Portugal* (1775), a novel "by a native of Maryland, some years resident in Lisbon," which was published in England. If actually by Digges or another American, it is the first novel by an American, since it precedes *The Power of Sympathy* by 14 years. It is a romantic, picaresque story of a young Portuguese merchant, and includes passages on the evils of despotic government. Digges's *Letters* was published in 1982.

DILLARD, ANNIE (1945–   ), Pittsburgh-born essayist on ecological subjects, author of *Pilgrim at Tinker Creek* (1974, Pulitzer Prize), a sensitive view of the natural surroundings in which she lives. She has also written *Tickets for a Prayer Wheel* (1974), poetry; *Holy the Firm* (1977); and *Teaching a Stone To Talk* (1982), further essays on nature. Other works are *Living by Fiction* (1978), essays on contemporary fiction and writers; *The Writing Life,* more essays; and a novel, *The Living* (1992), about the frontier settlement experiences of people in the American Northwest in the last decades of the 19th century.

DILLON, GEORGE (1906–68), born in Florida and reared in Kentucky and the Middle West, while an undergraduate at the University of Chicago became an editor of *Poetry.* The poems in *Boy in the Wind* (1927), published the year of his graduation, have a soft musical quality. *The Flowering Stone* (1931), a more vigorous work, won a Pulitzer Prize (1932). His later works are translations, of Baudelaire's *Flowers of Evil* (1936) with Edna St. Vincent Millay, and of Racine's *Three Plays: Andromache, Britannicus, Phædra* (1961).

Dilsey, character in Faulkner's novel, *The Sound and the Fury.* ♦

Dime novel, popular name for cheap thrilling tales of history, romance, warfare, or any violent action, many of which were set in America during the Revolution, Civil War, or frontier period. They attained an immense popularity in the U.S. from the publication of *Malaeska: The Indian Wife of the White Hunter* in 1860 by Ann Sophia Stephens♦ to about 1895, at which time they began to be superseded by pulp magazines♦ and such series as those concerning Frank Merriwell, the Rover Boys, and Tom Swift. Many of the novels, whose major publisher was Beadle and Adams of New York, cost only five cents. Although the development of plot closely followed conventional moral patterns, stern critics mistakenly called dime novels immoral. They probably fostered a nationalistic attitude, emphasizing as they did the democratic vigor and individualism of the American people. Among the most famous authors were E.Z.C. Judson, Prentiss Ingraham, Edward L. Wheeler, who created "Deadwood Dick,"♦ and J.R. Coryell, who created "Nick Carter."

Dimmesdale, ARTHUR, character in *The Scarlet Letter.* ♦

Dinner at Eight, play by George S. Kaufman♦ and Edna Ferber.♦

Dinsmore, ELSIE, character in novels for children by Martha Finley.♦

Dionysus in Doubt, poems by E.A. Robinson,♦ published in 1925, including "Demos and Dionysus."

In the title poem, Robinson denounces modern tendencies toward collectivism, standardization, and equalitarianism. "Freedom," Dionysus vouchsafes in an imagined conversation with the poet, "becomes a prodigy for men to fear" when "herd-servitude" thoughtlessly exalts it. Democracy is "an unransomed kidnapped juvenile," and the sole hope for humanity is that it may hide "intelligence . . . much as a tree's unguessed immensities are hidden in a seed." The concept of social equality is a snare, for "Humbug is no less himself in his best dress," and men dream of a Utopia impossible on earth, in their "confused assumptions of a state Not yet prepared" for them.

Disappointment, The; or, The Force of Credulity, comic opera by Andrew Barton (presumably a pseudonym of Colonel Thomas Forrest), published in 1767. It was arranged for production a few days before *The Prince of Parthia,* the first professionally produced American play, but was withdrawn because of its personal satire. It is concerned with the contemporary mania of searching for the supposed treasures of the pirate Blackbeard and ridicules various Philadelphians involved in such undertakings. A song set to the tune of "Yankee Doodle" is included.

Disciples of Christ, see *Campbell, Alexander.*

Discourses in America, three lectures by Matthew Arnold,♦ delivered during a tour of the Eastern states in 1883 and published in 1885.

"Numbers; or, The Majority and the Remnant," a discussion of national traits, shows the danger of assuming that what is popular or widespread need be praiseworthy. The author indicates the fallacy of the American pride in size and numbers; "in a democratic community like this, with its newness, its magnitude, its strength, its life of business, its sheer freedom and equality, the danger is in the absence of the discipline of respect; in hardness and materialism, exaggeration and boastfulness; in a false smartness, a false audacity, a want of soul and delicacy." "Literature and Science" is an argument against the tendency in modern schools to supplant literary education by scientific studies. The essay on Emerson states that the American author is not a great poet, writer, or philosopher, but rather occupies a position like that of Marcus Aurelius, "the friend and aider of those who would live in the spirit." Emerson's "insight is admirable, his truth is precious"; but his most valuable quality is his "hopeful, serene, beautiful temper," which makes him, together with Franklin, "the most distinctly and honourably American of your writers."

discovery, literary magazine in paperback book format, whose six issues appeared between 1953 and 1955. Its editor was Vance Bourjaily,♦ who wrote an article, "No More Apologies" in the second issue, comparing the great older generation of American authors, including Faulkner and Hemingway, with some of his contemporaries, including his contributors, Nelson Algren, Kenneth Fearing, Herbert Gold, Norman Mailer, and William Styron.

Disko Troop, character in *Captains Courageous.* ♦

Dismal Swamp, on the coast of southeast Virginia and northeast North Carolina, was formerly extensive and almost impenetrable. William Byrd describes it in his *History of the Dividing Line.* It is the setting of Harriet Beecher Stowe's *Dred* and is frequently mentioned in literature as a refuge for the fugitive slave, e.g. Longfellow's "The Slave in the Dismal Swamp."

DISNEY, Walt[er Elias] (1901–66), creator of animated cartoons, produced the first of his Mickey Mouse series in 1928. Other works, noted for their fantastic humor and technical brilliance, include the Silly Symphony series and the full-length pictures *Snow White and the Seven Dwarfs* (1938), *Pinocchio* (1940), *Fantasia* (1940), and *The Reluctant Dragon* (1941). During World War II he made training and goodwill films, and later produced nature films of birds and animals in their natural habitats, as well as films for children and adults with live actors, including *Mary Poppins* (1964). In 1955 he created Disneyland, an innovative kind of amusement park with scaleddown settings that convey the many visitors into environments of fantasy, adventure, and sentiment. The original park near Los Angeles inspired another (1971), Walt Disney World, near Orlando, Fla.

Dividing Line, see *History of the Dividing Line.*

Divina Commedia, sequence of six Petrarchan sonnets by Longfellow,♦ written (1864–67) to precede and follow each of the three parts of his translation (1865–67) of Dante's *Divine Comedy.* In the first sonnet, the *Divine Comedy* is likened to a cathedral that the poet enters, from day to day, for prayer and sanctuary from the cares he leaves outside. This figure is continued in the succeeding sonnets, which are concerned with the variety of themes and emotional attitudes in "this medieval miracle of song," Dante's benignant religious influence on the reader, his love for Beatrice, and a comparison of the emotional effect of his work to that of the Catholic Mass. The sixth sonnet deals with Dante's place in history as "forerunner of the day that is to be."

Divine Tragedy, The, dramatic poem by Longfellow,♦ published in 1871 and later included in *Christus*♦ (1872).

Divinity School Address, name commonly given to the address delivered by Emerson♦ before the senior class of Divinity College, Harvard (July 15, 1838), published that year, and reprinted in *Nature, Addresses, and Lectures* (1849). The discourse provoked a strong reaction among the faculty, and Andrews Norton attacked it as irreverent and atheistic in *On the Latest Form of Infidelity* (1839). Received with enthusiasm by such men such as W.E. Channing and Theodore Parker, the address had no immediate effect on the church, but caused Emerson's virtual ostracism from strict Unitarian circles.

In "The American Scholar," the author appeals for a return to original intellectual experience; here he appeals for a return to original spiritual experience. Truth is attainable only through intuition, "it cannot be received at second hand." Since historical Christianity has fallen into errors, its influence is baneful. By emphasizing past revolution, it limits and discourages the direct exploration of Moral Nature, which alone communicates spiritual greatness and the divine spirit. The formal church is dry, false, and moribund; the "great and perpetual office of the preacher is not discharged." Young men entering the ministry must search their own hearts, preach their own message:

> speak the very truth, as your life and conscience teach it, and cheer the waiting, fainting hearts of men with new hope and new revelations.

DIX, DOROTHEA LYNDE (1802–87), Massachusetts teacher, pioneer in American prison reforms and the creation of almshouses and insane asylums. Her study of institutional conditions resulted in a *Memorial to the Legislature of Massachusetts* (1843). She was superintendent of women nurses during the Civil War.

DIX, DOROTHY, pseudonym of Elizabeth Meriwether Gilmer (1861–1951), author of a column of advice to the lovelorn, begun (1896) in the *New Orleans Picayune* and later syndicated and distilled in such books as *How To Win and Hold a Husband* (1939).

"Dixie," patriotic song probably composed by Dan Emmett♦ (1859), member of Dan Bryant's minstrel troupe. Its greatest popularity has been in the South, where it was sung by Confederate soldiers. Dixie signifies "de land ob cotton," but the origin of the name is uncertain. It is sometimes supposed to be a corruption of the name of Jeremiah Dixon, who with Charles Mason (1763–67) surveyed the boundary which later separated slave and free states.

DIXON, THOMAS (1864–1946), born in North Carolina, was a Baptist minister and lyceum lecturer before he became an author. His most sensational novels are the trilogy *The Leopard's Spots* (1902), *The Clansman♦* (1905), and *The Traitor* (1907), extremist Southern views of the Reconstruction era, vigorously antiblack and strongly supportive of the original Ku Klux Klan. Of his 20 novels, all are tracts for his social views, and many concerned with contemporary issues, opposing feminism, socialism, and pacifism, among other matters. After the success of D.W. Griffith's adaptation of *The Clansman* as *The Birth of a Nation* (1915), Dixon made five films at his own Los Angeles studio, all based on his novels.

DOBIE, CHARLES CALDWELL (1881–1943), San Francisco author who celebrated his native city in many stories and novels, including *San Francisco Tales* (1935), and in nonfiction, including *San Francisco: A Pageant* (1933).

DOBIE, J[AMES] FRANK (1888–1964), Texas educator and author, whose books on Southwestern history and folklore include *A Vaquero of*

the *Brush Country* (1929), based on the reminiscences of the cattleman John Young; *Coronado's Children* (1931), tales of lost mines and buried treasures; *On the Open Range* (1931); *Tongues of the Monte* (1935), about northern Mexico; *Tales of the Mustangs* (1936); *Apache Gold and Yaqui Silver* (1939); *The Longhorns* (1941); *Guide to Life and Literature of the Southwest* (1943); *The Voice of the Coyote* (1949); *Tales of Old-Time Texas* (1955); and *Cow People* (1964). He was a professor of English at the University of Texas (1933–47) and his experiences as a visiting professor at Cambridge during World War II are described in *A Texan in England* (1945).

Dr. Grimshawe's Secret, romance by Hawthorne,♦ posthumously edited from an unfinished manuscript by his son Julian and published in 1883.

In a New England town in the early 19th century lives Dr. Grimshawe, an eccentric recluse, and two orphans, Ned and Elsie. The children are involved in a secret related to an estate in England, whence the doctor originally came. This estate has lacked a direct heir since the reign of Charles I, when the incumbent disappeared, leaving a bloody footprint on the threshold. After their guardian's death, the children are separated, but meet again years later, in England. Ned, now Edward Redclyffe, is injured while investigating the estate and is befriended by Colcord, his boyhood tutor. Lord Braithwaite, the estate's present owner, invites Edward to live at the Hall, where he meets Elsie, who warns him of a presentiment of danger. He finds the hiding place of an incredibly old man who "haunts" the Hall, and recognizes him as the Sir Edward Redclyffe of the time of the bloody footprint. When the old man dies, Colcord produces a locket that proves Edward to be the heir.

Dr. Heidegger's Experiment, allegorical tale by Hawthorne,♦ published in *Twice-Told Tales* (1837).

The doctor, an aged physician and scientist, invites four of his venerable, eccentric acquaintances to take part in a test of some water from the Fountain of Youth. Medbourne, an impoverished former merchant, Gascoigne, a ruined politician, Colonel Killigrew, a gouty old wastrel, and the Widow Wycherly, a faded beauty, see the doctor restore a dried rose by applying the water, and are eager to try it. Dr. Heidegger declares he merely wishes to see the results, and does not drink, but serves his guests full glasses. They become increasingly younger until they reach gay and reckless youth, when the three men vie for the favors of the Widow. They accidentally upset the table, and spill the water. Then the doctor notices that his rose has faded again, and gradually his guests resume their aged appearances. He says that he has learned from the experiment not to desire the delirium of youth, but his friends resolve to make a pilgrimage to Florida in search of the Fountain.

DOCTOROW, E[DGAR] L[AWRENCE] (1931–), New York City-born novelist, graduate of Kenyon College, editor in publishing firms, and faculty member at Sarah Lawrence College (1971–78) and NYU (1982–). His first novel, *Welcome to Hard Times* (1960), depicted the devastation of a Dakota frontier town by an evil outsider. More than a decade later it was followed by *The Book of Daniel* (1971), the fictive biography of a boy recalling his parents, who, like their models, Ethel and Julius Rosenberg, were executed for providing secret information to an enemy nation. He won great popularity and a National Book Critics Circle Award with *Ragtime* (1975), a jazzily written view of early-20th-century America that fuses tales of fictional characters and such real people as Henry Ford, Scott Joplin, Emma Goldman, and J.P. Morgan. *Loon Lake* (1980) is a picaresque novel about a Midwestern American's experiences in the 1930s and post-World War II U.S. *Drinks Before Dinner* (1979) is a play marked more by the conversation and ideas of one character than by action. He returned to the novel with *World's Fair* (1985), a tale of a Bronx boy growing to some maturity, and *Billy Bathgate* (1989), about another Bronx boy of the 1930s but one who drifts into the world of gangsters. Other works include the nonfictional *Essays and Conversations* (1983); *Lives of the Poets* (1984), stories and a related novella; and *Jack London, Hemingway, and the Constitution: Selected Essays 1977–1992* (1993). *The Waterworks* (1994), narrated by a newspaper editor who is marginal to the plot action, evokes New York City as it was in 1871; the plot concerns several never fully unravelled mysteries.

DODDRIDGE, JOSEPH (1769–1826), frontier clergyman, author of *Notes on the Settlement and Indian Wars of the Western Parts of Virginia and Pennsylvania from 1763 to 1783* (1824). He also wrote an unproduced prose drama, *Logan* (1821), based on the story of the Mingo chief.

DODGE, MARY ABIGAIL (1833–96), Massachusetts author, edited with J.T. Trowbridge and Lucy Larcom *Our Young Folks* (1865–67). Her essays, some of which attack woman suffrage, include *Country Living and Country Thinking* (1862), *A New Atmosphere* (1865), *Woman's Wrongs: A Counter-Irritant* (1868), and *Our Common School System* (1880). She wrote a biography of her kinsman J.G. Blaine (1895), and her own reminiscences, *Gail Hamilton's Life in Letters* (1901). She wrote under the pseudonym Gail Hamilton.

DODGE, MARY [ELIZABETH] MAPES (1831–1905), New York City author and editor of juvenile fiction, is best known for her popular *Hans*

Brinker; or, The Silver Skates (1865), a story of youthful adventures in a Dutch setting. She became editor of the magazine *St. Nicholas* in 1873, and in this position was the most important influence of the time on children's literature. Her other writings include *Irvington Stories* (1864), *A Few Friends and How They Amused Themselves* (1869), *Rhymes and Jingles* (1874), *Donald and Dorothy* (1883), and *The Land of Pluck* (1894).

Dodsworth, novel by Sinclair Lewis,♦ published in 1929, was dramatized by Sidney Howard and the author (1934).

Samuel Dodsworth, automobile manufacturer of the Midwestern city of Zenith, retires to devote himself to cultural pursuits and a trip to Europe. During 23 years of married life, he has adored his frivolous, pampered wife Fran, but he is soon disillusioned after abandoning his absorption in business. On the transatlantic ship she assumes an air of worldliness and flirts with an Englishman, Major Clyde Lockert; in Paris she joins the extravagant set of Renée de Pénable and has an affair with Arnold Israel. Sam quickly tires of this life and returns alone to America, but, fearing that Fran may be harmed by Israel, he rejoins her in Europe. Fran breaks with her lover and visits Germany with Sam, where she falls in love with an impoverished aristocrat, Kurt von Obersdorf. She asks Sam for a divorce, and he spends lonely months touring southern Europe. He is happy again only after he meets Edith Cortright, an American widow, in whose mature tolerance he finds companionship. Through Edith he learns to appreciate European traditions and art, and she encourages his plans for a building enterprise in Zenith. They intend to marry, but when Kurt's mother forbids him to marry Fran, Sam is persuaded to return to America with his wife. During the voyage he finds Fran still childish and egotistical, and he cables Edith that he will return to her by the next ship.

Doesticks, What He Says, 36 sketches by Mortimer Thomson,♦ published under the pseudonym Doesticks in 1855. The foibles of New York society are described by the humorous and sometimes gently satiric gay blade, Doesticks, and his companions, Damphool and Bull Dogge. Subjects of the sketches include Barnum's Museum, boardinghouses, "modern witchcraft," patent medicine, politics, fire companies, theaters, churches, the Millerites, inebriation, and Kentucky blacks.

Dogood Papers, essays in the manner of the *Spectator,* contributed by Franklin♦ to *The New England Courant* (March–Oct. 1722). Published anonymously when the author was only 17, they were not ascribed to him until the publication of Parton's biography (1864). The 14 papers purport to have been written by Silence Dogood, widow of a parson, and their range of subjects is indicated by such titles as "Pride and Hoop Petticoats," "Freedom of Thought," "Drunkenness," and "Receipt for a New England Funeral Elegy."

DOLE, NATHAN HASKELL (1852–1935), Massachusetts author, editor, and translator of Tolstoy and Daudet. His original works include *Not Angels Quite* (1893), a novel concerned with the romantic misadventures of two ill-matched couples and their eventual change of partners and happy marriages; *The Hawthorn Tree and Other Poems* (1895), *Omar, the Tent-Maker* (1899), and *Six Italian Essays* (1907).

"Dollar, The Almighty," expression first used by Irving, in *Wolfert's Roost* (1855), where he speaks of the dollar as "that great object of our universal devotion throughout our land." Another phrase, "dollar diplomacy," indicating the management of international relations for the benefit of U.S. commercial interests, was first applied (1910) to the policies of Secretary of State Philander Knox.

Dolliver Romance, The, unfinished novel by Hawthorne,♦ posthumously published in the *Atlantic Monthly* (1864, 1871) and in book form in 1876. The author's last work, it was an attempt to develop the theme of the elixir of life also essayed in *Septimius Felton.*

In a New England town lives an aged apothecary, with the sole remaining member of his family, his great-granddaughter Pansie. One day he tries a cordial presented to him by a stranger seven years before, and when the potion rejuvenates him he takes further doses. Colonel Dabney, an impetuous, sensual old man, comes to demand the cordial, which he says is rightfully his. When he threatens the apothecary with a pistol, he is given the drink. Swallowing a large amount of it, he rises to his feet, shrieks, and falls dead. The apothecary sees that for a moment the colonel's face becomes that of a young man, but then it is aged and withered in death. An inquest pronounces the death to have occurred "by the visitation of God."

Domain of Arnheim, The, descriptive tale by Poe,♦ published in 1847. It incorporates "The Landscape Garden" (1842), and "Landor's Cottage"♦ is a "pendant."

A fabulously beautiful estate is created by Ellison, a millionaire enthusiast of landscape gardening. After spending years in searching for the perfect site, he chooses Arnheim, and carries out a huge plan for disposing the waterways, landscape, and vegetation so as to make it the ideal setting for the "semi-Gothic, semi-Saracenic" architecture of his elaborate home.

Domestic Manners of the Americans, descriptive work by Frances Trollope.♦

DONALD, DAVID HERBERT (1920–   ), born in Mississippi, has had an academic career at several institutions and written many books in his career as a historian. These include *Lincoln's Herndon* (1948); *Charles Sumner and the Coming of the Civil War* (1960), awarded a Pulitzer Prize for biography; *The Nation in Crisis, 1861–1877* (1969); and *Look Homeward: A Life of Thomas Wolfe* (1987), also awarded a Pulitzer Prize for biography.

Donatello, character in *The Marble Faun.*♦

DONLEAVY, J[AMES] P[ATRICK] (1926–   ), was born in Brooklyn and served in the U.S. navy, but went to Trinity College, Dublin, in his parents' native Ireland, and has since lived there and in England. *The Ginger Man* (Paris, 1955; U.S., 1958) is a lusty comic novel about a red-bearded ex-GI and the grubby life he and his wife lead in Ireland and in London. Donleavy dramatized the work, produced in England (1959) and New York (1963), and published in New York (1961), and wrote another play, *Fairy Tales of New York* (1961), reworked as a novel, *A Fairy Tale of New York* (1973), a satire on contemporary America. Other broadly comic novels include *A Singular Man* (1963), *The Saddest Summer of Samuel S.* (1966), and *The Beastly Beatitudes of Balthazar B.* (1968), all dramatized by the author; *The Onion Eaters* (1971), a more surrealistic tale; *The Destinies of Darcy Dancer, Gentleman* (1977), another picaresque story; *Schultz* (1979), a farce about an American impresario in England; *Leila* (1983), further adventures of Darcy Dancer; *Are You Listening Rabbi Löw* (1987); and *A Singular Man* (1989). Donleavy collected stories in *Meet My Maker, the Mad Molecule* (1964) and wrote a parody of etiquette books, *The Unexpurgated Code* (1975). He also wrote reminiscences in *J.P. Donleavy's Ireland* (1986).

DONN-BYRNE, see *Byrne, Donn.*

DONNELLY, IGNATIUS (1831–1901), born in Pennsylvania, moved to Minnesota (1857), where he became a lawyer, and was elected lieutenant-governor, congressman (1863–69), and state senator (1873–78). He was a leader of liberal third-party movements and of the agricultural and reform groups whose views he expounded in his weekly *Anti-Monopolist* (1874–79), and was the Populist candidate for President when he died. His novel *Cæsar's Column: A Story of the Twentieth Century* (1891) depicts a future that is technologically Utopian for the wealthy and oppressive for the poor. His other books include *Atlantis: The Antediluvian World* (1882), *Ragnarok: The Age of Fire and Gravel* (1883), *The American People's Money* (1895), and *The Great Cryptogram* (1888) and *The Cipher in the Plays and on the Tombstone* (1899), two studies attempting to prove Bacon's authorship of Shakespeare's plays.

Donner Party, wagon train of emigrants who set out across the plains for California (1846). Taking a new cutoff south of the Great Salt Lake, they suffered great hardships and were so delayed that they were blocked by early snows in the Sierra Nevada. They camped at what is now called Donner Lake, and during the winter about half their number died of starvation. Rescue parties from California brought out survivors in the spring, after some of them had resorted to cannibalism. The gruesome yet heroic nature of these adventures has led to their figuring in many novels and poems, e.g. the opening of Harte's *Gabriel Conroy,* and Vardis Fisher's *The Mothers.* The recognized historian of the subject is George R. Stewart.

Dooley, MR., character in a series of books by F.P. Dunne. ◆

DOOLITTLE, HILDA (1886–1961), known by her initials, was born in Pennsylvania, went to Europe in 1911, married English author Richard Aldington in 1913, and lived in England thereafter. An early member of the school of Imagism, she is frequently considered the outstanding poet consistently practicing its principles. *Sea Garden* (1916), her first collection, shows the classically chiseled, objective method for which she became famous, and *Hymen* (1921) indicates her interest in the Hellenic tradition. Her later volumes, *Heliodora and Other Poems* (1924) and *Hippolytus Temporizes* (1927), a drama in classic form, foreshadowed her translation of the *Ion of Euripides* (1937). Editions of her *Collected Poems* appeared in 1925 and 1940, but later verse includes the trilogy, *The Walls Do Not Fall* (1944), *Tribute to Angels* (1945), and *Flowering of the Rod* (1946), while *By Avon River* (1949) contains both poetry and prose about Shakespeare and Elizabethan literature, and *Helen in Egypt* (1961) is a posthumously issued long poem. Her prose fiction is published in *Palimpsest* (1926), *Hedylus* (1928), *The Hedgehog* (1936), and *Bid Me to Live* (1960), the last being a stream-of-consciousness novel of Bloomsbury life in 1917, an obvious *roman à clef.* *Tribute to Freud* (1956) is a prose work on the psychoanalyst, whose patient she was. Other late works include *End to Torment* (1958), a memoir of Pound. *Hermetic Definition* (1972), a personal statement cast in philosophic terms, and *HERmione* (1981), an autobiographical novel about a young woman torn between love for a man (obviously based on Pound) and for a woman, are posthumously issued works.

Dorchester Company of Adventurers, joint stock company which attempted to establish a permanent fishing and farming colony on Cape Ann (1623). The organizers, who included John White, were identified with the Puritan party, but had no intention of establishing a Puritan refuge. When their colony failed, the settlers came under the temporary rules of John Endecott, but were reorganized as the New England Company for a Plantation in Massachusetts Bay, which became the Massachusetts Bay Company. ◆

DORN, ED[WARD MERTON] (1929–), Illinois-born poet, studied at Black Mountain College under Charles Olson, about whose work he wrote a critical study, *What I See in the Maximus Poems* (1960). His own poetry, often loose and idiomatic, appears in many collections, including the one long epic of 1960s events, *Gunslinger,* whose four "Books" were gathered in 1975, in *Selected Poems* (1978) and *Captain Jack's Chaps, or Houston/MLA* (1983), as well as many other volumes. He began teaching at the University of Colorado in 1977.

DORSEY, GEORGE AMOS (1868–1931), anthropologist associated with the Field Museum at Chicago, taught at the University of Chicago and The New School for Social Research. His studies of the American Indians include *Traditions of the Arikara* (1904), *The Mythology of the Wichita* (1904), *Traditions of the Caddo* (1905), and *Pawnee Mythology* (1906). Among his later popular works are *Why We Behave Like Human Beings* (1925), *The Evolution of Charles Darwin* (1927), and *Man's Own Show: Civilization* (1931).

DOS PASSOS, JOHN [RODERIGO] (1896–1970), born in Chicago, was educated abroad and in the U.S. After graduation from Harvard (1916), he went to Spain, nominally to study architecture, but he soon entered World War I as a member of the French ambulance service, later joining the U.S. medical corps. Experiences of this period furnished the material for his first book, *One Man's Initiation—1917* (1920, reissued with a new preface as *First Encounter,* 1945), a novel about an ambulance driver. This was followed by *Three Soldiers* ◆ (1921), showing the effects of war on three types of character. After publishing a volume of poetry, *A Pushcart at the Curb* (1922), and *Rosinante to the Road Again* (1922), essays on the art and culture of Spain, he returned to fiction with *Streets of Night* (1923), which has been characterized as a typical "art novel" of the time, and deals with a sensitive boy's attempt to escape from the crass conventions of his world. With *Manhattan Transfer* ◆ (1925), a collective portrait in hundreds of fictional episodes of the sprawling, diversified life of New York City, Dos Passos reached maturity both in his outlook upon the world and in his stylistic technique. His next book, *Orient Express* (1927), a travel diary, also shows a broadening point of view and a greater interest in social problems, as do the works collected as *Three Plays*

(1934); *The Garbage Man*♦ (1926), produced as *The Moon Is a Gong* and dramatizing the distressed lives of a representative New York couple; *Airways, Inc.*♦ (1929), contrasting the atmosphere of big business with the oppressed lives of workers, and showing the background of a building trades strike; and *Fortune Heights* (1933), showing a real-estate development during boom times, and its ruin in the Depression.

In 1930 Dos Passos published *The 42nd Parallel,*♦ the first novel in his *U.S.A.* trilogy (collected 1938), which also includes *1919*♦ (1932) and *The Big Money*♦ (1936). These novels, which tell the story of the first three decades of the 20th century in the U.S., have as their protagonist the social background of the nation, and as their major theme the vitiation and degradation of character in a decaying civilization based on commercialism and exploitation. The trilogy employs several distinctive fictional devices. Its basis is a number of episodes from the lives of diverse characters, whose actions either converge or run parallel. The panoramic background is the "Newsreel," a selection from contemporary headlines, advertisements, popular songs, and newspaper articles, which suggest the general atmosphere at the time of each episode. Among the narrative episodes are also interspersed brief biographies of prominent Americans of the period, whose lives form a counterpart, often ironic, of the lesser figures of the fiction. A third device is "The Camera Eye," presenting the author's point of view toward the subject matter, through impressionistic stream-of-consciousness passages. The wide panorama of American life is interpreted as being marked by corruption, futility, frustration, and defeat.

This view of the contemporary world is also exhibited in a travel book of this period, *In All Countries* (1934), which deals with such subjects as the Sacco-Vanzetti case, communism in Russia, and Mexican agrarian socialism. Excerpts from this book and from his two previous travel books are combined with new material on the Spanish Civil War in *Journeys Between Wars* (1938). *Adventures of a Young Man* (1939), about Glenn Spotswood, a naïve, idealistic Communist, betrayed by the party when he does not follow its program, is the first of a trilogy continued in *Number One*♦ (1943), about Glenn's brother Tyler, who works for a demagogue like Huey Long, and *The Grand Design* (1949), about the boy's father, a disillusioned liberal in Washington during the New Deal and World War II. The trilogy was collected as *District of Columbia* (1952).

His later fiction includes *The Prospect Before Us* (1950), a novel in the form of lectures on the contemporary world as Dos Passos gloomily saw it; *Chosen Country* (1951), a panoramic view of the U.S. from the mid-19th century to the Depression; *Most Likely To Succeed* (1954), a novel satirizing bohemians and Communist followers between the wars; *The Great Days* (1958), a novel

about a former war correspondent's unhappy recollections; and *Midcentury* (1961), a novel about contemporary America in which the techniques of *U.S.A.* and its faith in individualism now celebrate free enterprise. Nonfiction of these years includes *The Ground We Stand On* (1941), biographies of men who influenced American liberty; *Men Who Made the Nation* (1957), on American leaders from the end of the Revolution to Hamilton's death; and *Prospects of a Golden Age* (1959), other selected biographical sketches. *State of the Nation* (1944) and *Tour of Duty* (1946) describe wartime travels, while *Brazil on the Move* (1963) treats travels abroad. *The Theme Is Freedom* (1956) and *Occasions and Protests* (1964) collect essays also representative of his later, conservative views, while *Mr. Wilson's War* (1963) treats U.S. history from 1901 to 1921 from a point of view different from the liberalism of *U.S.A.,* the trilogy that covered the same era. *The Best Times* (1966) is an informal memoir, and *The Fourteenth Chronicle* (1973) collects letters and diaries.

DOUGLAS, LLOYD C[ASSEL] (1877–1951), Lutheran clergyman and author, whose novels include *Magnificent Obsession* (1929), *Forgive Us Our Trespasses* (1932), *Precious Jeopardy* (1933), *Green Light* (1935), *White Banners* (1936), *Disputed Passage* (1939), and *Invitation To Live* (1940), preaching self-enrichment by serving others; and *The Robe* (1942) and *The Big Fisherman* (1949), historical novels of the New Testament.

DOUGLAS, STEPHEN ARNOLD (1813–61), Vermont-born Illinois lawyer, early became a prominent Democrat and state official. He was a congressman (1843–47), and thereafter served in the U.S. Senate. As chairman of the Committee on Territories, he drafted bills for the government of New Mexico and Utah expressing his doctrine of "popular sovereignty," which allowed territorial governments to decide all legislative policies, including those on slavery. He was largely responsible for the Kansas-Nebraska Bill, based on the same principle. He failed to win the Democratic presidential nomination in 1852 and 1856 when his attempts at compromise between Northern and Southern party factions were unsuccessful. In the 1858 campaign for U.S. senator he spoke in seven debates against Lincoln, maintaining his "popular sovereignty" thesis, while Lincoln upheld his declaration that "A house divided against itself cannot stand." Although Douglas won the election, his power in the Democratic party waned because he opposed intervention in behalf of territorial slaveholders. He was the Democratic presidential candidate in 1860, but Southern delegates bolted in favor of Breckinridge, and the resulting schism won the election for Lincoln. Douglas continued to work for compromise, but from the outbreak of the Civil War gave his support to Lincoln's policies. Because of his slight stature and great personal vigor, Douglas was popularly known as the Little Giant. He figures frequently in literature, as in Masters's *Children of the Market Place* and Sherwood's *Abe Lincoln in Illinois.*

DOUGLAS, WILLIAM O[RVILLE] (1898–1980), associate justice of the U.S. Supreme Court (1939–75), whose books include *Of Men and Mountains* (1950); *Strange Lands and Friendly People* (1951), about travels in the Middle East and India; *Beyond the High Himalayas* (1952); *North from Malaya* (1953); *We the Judges* (1955), on U.S. and Indian constitutional law; *Russian Journey* (1956); *The Right of the People* (1958), lectures on civil liberties; *My Wilderness: The Pacific West* (1960); *Mr. Lincoln and the Negroes* (1963); *A Wilderness Bill of Rights* (1965); *Towards a Global Federation* (1968); *Holocaust or Hemispheric Cooperation* (1970); and *Go East, Young Man* (1974), autobiography to the year of his appointment to the Supreme Court, followed by *The Court Years* (1980).

DOUGLASS, FREDERICK (1817–95), born into slavery in Maryland, escaped to Massachusetts (1838), where he was employed as a lecturer by antislavery societies. He published a *Narrative of the Life of Frederick Douglass* (1845, revised 1892). Fearing capture as a fugitive slave, he spent several years in England and Ireland, returning to purchase his freedom and establish the antislavery newspaper *North Star.* ◆ Since he favored political methods for freeing the slaves, he became a follower of J.G. Birney rather than of Garrison. He organized two regiments of blacks in Massachusetts during the Civil War, and continued to labor for his people during the Reconstruction, later serving as secretary of the Santo Domingo Commission (1871), marshal of the District of Columbia (1877–81), recorder of deeds for the District (1881–86), and minister to Haiti (1889–91). Although his first book is his most famous, he wrote two other autobiographies: *My Bondage and My Freedom* (1855) and *Life and Times of Frederick Douglass* (1881). He is also the subject of biographies by C.W. Chesnutt and Booker T. Washington.

DOUGLASS, WILLIAM (c.1691–1752), Scottish-born physician in Boston, opposed the theory of inoculation for smallpox and wrote *The Practical History of a New Epidemical Eruptive Military Fever* (1736), describing scarlet fever. *A Summary, Historical and Political . . . of the British Settlements in North-America* (2 vols., 1749–51) contains information on a variety of subjects, including medicine and botany, but is marred by historical inaccuracies. In *A Discourse Concerning the Currencies of the British Plantations in America . . .* (1739), he wrote a trenchant work on the principles of exchange. He was a member of the Hell-Fire Club. ◆

DOVE, RITA (1952–   ), born in Akron, Ohio, and educated at Miami University and the University of Iowa Writers' Workshop, soon began her career of publishing her poetry. The list begins with *Ten Poems* (1977), continues with *The Only Dark Spot in the Sky* (1980); *The Yellow House on the Corner* (1980); *Mandolin* (1982); *Museum* (1983); *Thomas and Beulah* (1986, Pulitzer Prize)—lyrics about her grandparents, two black people from the rural South emigrating to industrial Akron, and experiencing there some early 20th-century U.S. history, including the Depression; and *Grace Notes* (1989). *Fifth Sunday* (1985) collects prose stories, and *Through the Ivory Gate* (1992) is a novel. She was chosen Poet Laureate by the Librarian of Congress for the term 1993–94, the youngest poet to be so honored, and the first black woman.

Down East, popular name for Maine, or for other districts on the New England and Nova Scotia coast. The Down East character, with his shrewd Yankee wit, was well defined in the humor of American almanacs and newspapers prior to the creation of Seba Smith's Jack Downing (1830), who was followed by a great many similar characters, including Sam Slick, Hosea Biglow, Frances Miriam Whitcher's Widow Spriggins and Widow Bedott, and Shillaber's Mrs. Partington.

Down-Easters, *The,* novel by John Neal, ◆ published in 1833.
    Following a scene aboard a Long Island Sound steamship, in which a comic Yankee is introduced, the story becomes a Gothic romance. Two rivals, the argumentative Gage and Middleton, a young Byronic Southerner, fall in love with a widow, who elopes with Middleton and then dies. Middleton's own unhappy past is revealed, and he dies in the arms of his earlier betrayed "wife," who takes poison. The main plot is melodramatic and overfurnished, but the Yankee descriptions are realistic.

DOWNING, MAJOR JACK, pseudonym of Seba Smith. ◆

DRAKE, DANIEL (1785–1852), born in New Jersey, reared in Kentucky, became a physician, educator, and civic leader, mainly in Cincinnati. He founded the Ohio Medical College (1819) and was the founder and editor of the *Western Medical and Physical Journal.* His books include *Picture of Cincinnati in 1815* (1815), describing the region's natural and social history; *Practical Essays on Medical Education and the Medical Profession in the U.S.* (1832); *Systematic Treatise . . . on the Principal Diseases of the Interior Valley of North America* (2 vols., 1850–54); and *Pioneer Life in Kentucky* (1870). His antislavery letters in the *National Intelligencer* (1851) were republished as *Dr. Daniel Drake's Letters on Slavery* (1940).
    BENJAMIN DRAKE (1795–1841), his brother, was also a pioneer resident of Cincinnati. His

books, valuable as sources, include *Cincinnati in 1826* (1827), *Tales and Sketches from the Queen City* (1838), *The Life and Adventures of Black Hawk* (1838), and *Life of Tecumseh and His Brother* (1841).

DRAKE, JOSEPH RODMAN (1795–1820), born in New York City, studied medicine and, after a trip abroad, ran a drugstore for a year prior to his early death from consumption. His only writing published during his lifetime was the "Croaker Papers," ♦ satirical verses written with his friend Fitz-Greene Halleck. On his deathbed, Drake instructed his wife to destroy the manuscript of his "trifles in rhyme," but the work was preserved, and in 1835 a selection was published as *The Culprit Fay and Other Poems.* ♦ Of these, the best known are the title poem and "The American Flag," an effusively patriotic lyric first unfurled in the Croaker series. Drake was an early member of the Knickerbocker Group, whose pretensions to fame were riddled by Poe's devasting reviews in "The Literati," but he received a compensating tribute from Halleck, whose poem "On the Death of Joseph Rodman Drake" is considered to be one of the finest elegies in American literature. Drake's *Works* were collected in 1935.

Drake, TEMPLE, character in Faulkner's *Sanctuary*♦ and its sequel, *Requiem for a Nun.*

Dramatists' Guild, see *Authors League of America.*

DRAYTON, WILLIAM HENRY (1742–79), South Carolina jurist, educated at Oxford, who boldly attacked the policies of Parliament in his *Letter from Freeman of South Carolina,* consequently losing his judicial positions. As Chief Justice of South Carolina, he declared, two months before the Declaration of Independence, that the king had no authority in his colony. Drayton was the first important advocate of political autonomy for America. *Memoirs of the American Revolution* (1821) was edited from his papers by his son John.

Dream Within a Dream, A, poem by Poe.♦

Dred: *A Tale of the Great Dismal Swamp,* novel by Harriet Beecher Stowe,♦ published in 1856. It complements *Uncle Tom's Cabin* by showing the demoralizing influence of slavery on the whites. Dred is modeled on Nat Turner. There were three dramatizations of *Dred,* including one by Brougham.

Nina Gordon places the management of her deceased father's North Carolina estate in the hands of Harry, a mulatto half-brother. On her sudden death from cholera, her brother Tom comes into possession of the property and cruelly forces Harry to flee. Seeking refuge in the Swamp, Harry is protected by Dred, a black religious fa-

natic, who is killed when Tom comes to search for his half-brother. A subplot tells a parallel story of a worthless trader, John Cripps, whose cruelty drives his slave, Old Tiff, to take Cripps's children to the Swamp among other refugees. Through Edward Clayton, Nina's former fiancé, the fugitives are transported to Canada and safety.

DREISER, THEODORE [HERMAN ALBERT] (1871–1945), born at Terre Haute, Ind., of a poor and intensely religious family, who taught him to shun many human experiences as degrading or destructive. He early developed a yearning for wealth, society, and the kind of life which he later gave to his hero Cowperwood, an unscrupulous magnate of big business, who is the subject of an exhaustive character study in *The Financier*♦ (1912), *The Titan*♦ (1914), and *The Stoic* (1947).

After a period of newspaper reporting in St. Louis, Chicago, Pittsburgh, and New York, stimulated by reading Balzac, and released from his crass success-worship by studying Huxley, Tyndall, and Spencer, he came to see life as a strangely magnificent composite of warring energies, having no plan or purpose. His journalism and hackwork were temporarily interrupted by the writing of *Sister Carrie*♦ (1900), the story of a working girl and her life as the mistress of a man who descends the social scale as she rises to success as an actress. The publishers withheld the novel from circulation because they were disturbed by its amoral treatment of Carrie's life, and so Dreiser did not earn enough royalties or gain a wide enough reputation to allow him to retire from commercial activities, including the editing of pulp magazines and women's fashion journals, until the publication of *Jennie Gerhardt*♦ (1911), the story of a woman who sacrifices her own interests rather than jeopardize her lover's social and economic security by opposing his marriage.

In *The "Genius"*♦ (1915), the story of a gifted but weak artist, and *An American Tragedy*♦ (1925), the story of a youth of unstable character trapped by circumstances that lead to his execution for murder, Dreiser sets forth his naturalistic concept of American society. This view, developed in the four previous books, concludes that, since the chaotic nature of life precludes spiritual satisfactions, it is normal and right to take the most one can from the economic grab bag. Dreiser has been acclaimed for this sincere and profound consciousness of the tragedy of life as he saw it in America, despite the ugliness of his heavy style, and his structural incompetence, chaotic verbosity, and sometimes confused character drawing. Often bogged down by clumsy writing, his books nevertheless are endowed with power by sheer force and an honest massing of details. In *Dreiser Looks at Russia* (1928), *Tragic America* (1931), and *America Is Worth Saving* (1941), he expressed hopeful belief in socialism, as opposed to his former confused naturalism, while *The Bulwark*♦ (1946) emphasized the place of spiritual values in the life of the modern individual.

His many other writings include *Plays of the Natural and Supernatural* (1916); *The Hand of the Potter* (1918), a tragedy; *Free* (1918), *Chains* (1927), and *A Gallery of Women* (2 vols., 1929), short story collections; *Moods, Cadenced and Declaimed* (1926, enlarged 1928), a book of poetry; *Hey Rub-a-Dub-Dub* (1920), essays setting forth his philosophic views; *The Color of a Great City* (1923) and *My City* (1929), vignettes of New York; *Twelve Men* (1919), studies of actual persons, including one of his brother, Paul Dresser, whom he is said to have assisted in writing "On the Banks of the Wabash"; and the autobiographical works, *A Traveler at Forty* (1913), *A Hoosier Holiday* (1916), *A Book About Myself* (1922), which was republished as *Newspaper Days* (1931), and *Dawn* (1931). His *Letters* was published in 1959 (3 vols.), and his *American Diaries, 1902–1926* was printed in 1982.

DRESSER, PAUL (1857–1911), composer of "The Blue and the Gray" (1890), "On the Banks of the Wabash, Far Away," which was popular during the Spanish-American War period, and many other songs for Tin Pan Alley. His surname was originally spelled like that of his brother Theodore Dreiser, who is said to have collaborated in writing "On the Banks of the Wabash" (1899).

D'ri and I, novel by Irving Bacheller.♦

Drum-Taps, poems by Whitman,♦ published in 1865, containing descriptive scenes at the front and in Washington hospitals during the Civil War, as well as "Pioneers! O Pioneers!"♦ A small supplement, issued after Lincoln's assassination as *Sequel to Drum-Taps* (1865–66), contained "When Lilacs Last in the Door Yard Bloom'd,"♦ "O Captain! My Captain!,"♦ "Chanting the Square Deific,"♦ and other poems. Both volumes were incorporated in the 1867 edition of *Leaves of Grass.*

Drums, historical novel by James Boyd,♦ published in 1925.

Johnny Fraser, son of a former Scottish rebel who has married the daughter of an aristocratic colonial family, grows up on a pioneer North Carolina plantation. At home his close companion has been Sally Merrillee, daughter of a neighbor, but in Edenton, where he completes his education, he turns to Eve Tennant, daughter of a British officer. At the outbreak of the Revolutionary War, the Tennants are forced to flee, while Johnny is recalled to his home, where his father discourages his interest in the patriot cause, reminding him of the failure of the Scottish rebellion. He goes to London to work in the exporting business and renews his relationship with Eve, but she is forced to abandon him for a

wealthier match. Through an Edenton friend, Johnny becomes involved in the plans of John Paul Jones, takes part in the battle between the *Bonhomme Richard* and the *Serapis,* returns home wounded, and fights again in the troops of Daniel Morgan. At the close of the war, he is crippled but optimistic because of the patriot victory and his love for Sally, which she returns.

Drunkard, The; or, The Fallen Saved, popular melodrama by W.H. Smith, was produced in 1844 as a sentimental plea for temperance, but has often been revived in the 20th century for purposes of burlesque.

DRURY, ALLEN [STUART] (1918–   ), Texas-born journalist and novelist, after graduation from Stanford (1939) worked on California newspapers and as a Washington correspondent for *The New York Times* and *Reader's Digest* before writing his popular and sensational novel *Advise and Consent* (1959, Pulitzer Prize), about the political and personal machinations in the Senate upon the occasion of considering confirmation of a secretary of state. He has written many more novels, none approaching the success of the first.

DUANE, WILLIAM (1760–1835), journalist in the U.S., India, and England, was associated with B. F. Bache in the editorship of the Philadelphia *Aurora,* and after Bache's death was sole editor of this Jeffersonian paper (1798–1822, 1834–35). Arrested under the Sedition Law, he was acquitted with a *nolle prosequi* by Jefferson. He was the author of *The Mississippi Question* (1803), *A Military Dictionary* (1810), *An Epitome of the Arts and Sciences* (1811), and *A Visit to Colombia* (1826).

DU BOIS, W[ILLIAM] E[DWARD] B[URGHARDT] (1868–1963), after graduation from Fisk (1888) and a Ph.D. from Harvard (1895) became a professor of economics and history at Atlanta University (1897–1910) and a dynamic leader of social reform activities on behalf of his fellow blacks. He opposed the views of Booker T. Washington as too conservative and limited, organized young black intellectuals in a Niagara Movement, helped to found the National Association for the Advancement of Colored People (1909), which he later disavowed (1948) as too conservative, and was an editor of the magazine *Crisis* (1910–34). Meanwhile he wrote *The Souls of Black Folk*♦ (1903) and *Darkwater* (1920), essays, sketches, and verses about the life of blacks in the U.S. His significant historical and sociological studies dealing with black people in Africa and the U.S. and over a long period of time include *The Suppression of the African Slave Trade to the U.S.A.* (1896), his doctoral thesis; *The Philadelphia Negro* (1899); *John Brown* (1909); *The Negro* (1915); *The Gift of Black Folk* (1924); *Black Reconstruction* (1935); and *Color and Democracy: Colonies and Peace* (1945), a tract against imperialism and for the independence of small nations. *Dusk of Dawn* (1940) he described as "not so much my autobiography as the autobiography of a concept of race." He also wrote novels: *The Dark Princess* (1928), and *The Black Flame: A Trilogy,* which incorporates *The Ordeal of Mansart* (1957), *Mansart Builds a School* (1959), and *Worlds of Color* (1961). In 1958 he was awarded the Lenin International Peace Prize and in 1961 he joined the Communist party. The year before his death he moved to Ghana and became a citizen of that nation. His *Correspondence* was published in 3 volumes (1979).

DU CHAILLU, PAUL BELLONI (1835–1903), explorer and author, probably born in France and reared in Africa, came to the U.S. (*c.*1852), and received the backing of the Philadelphia Academy of Natural Sciences for his African explorations (1856–59), described in his *Explorations and Adventures in Equatorial Africa* (1861). Because of its seemingly fantastic tales, this work won him notoriety and ridicule rather than scientific fame. A second expedition (1863–65) resulted in his *Journey to Ashangoland* (1867), *Stories of the Gorilla Country* (1868), *Wild Life Under the Equator* (1869), *Lost in the Jungle* (1869), *My Apingi Kingdom* (1870), and *The Country of the Dwarfs* (1871). A trip to Sweden, Norway, and Lapland (1871) was the source of his *The Land of the Midnight Sun* (1881) and *The Viking Age* (1889). He died in Russia.

DUCHÉ, JACOB (1737–98), Philadelphia-born Anglican clergyman, preached to the Revolutionary soldiers (1775–76), his most famous sermon being "The Duty of Standing Fast in Our Spiritual and Temporal Liberties," delivered after the Battle of Bunker Hill. Military reverses affected his allegiance, and he later supplicated God in behalf of the Loyalists with equal zeal. *Discourses on Various Subjects* (1779) is a product of his clerical career in Philadelphia, and his *Observations* (1774), better known as *Caspipina's Letters,* contains descriptions of the American scene, supposedly written by a young Englishman to friends at home, which show an unswerving deference to the Church and aristocracy.

DUGAN, ALAN (1923–   ), achieved great success with his first volume of *Poems* (1961), issued in the Yale Series of Younger Poets, which won a Pulitzer Prize and a National Book Award. *Poems 2* (1963), *Poems 3* (1968), *Collected Poems* (1970), and *Poems 4* (1974) are also directly stated, dry, bleak views of life. Later poetic achievements appear in *Sequence* (1976) and *New and Collected Poems* (1983).

DUGANNE, AUGUSTINE JOSEPH HICKEY (1823–84), author of poetry, a tragedy, dime novels, and popular economic and political treatises. *A Sound Literature the Safeguard of Our Na-*

tional Institutions (1853) and *Art's True Mission in America* (1853) are chauvinistic works; *Parnassus in Pillory* (1851) is an imitation of Lowell's *Fable for Critics;* and *Camps and Prisons* (1865) is a vivid account of the author's experiences in the Civil War. His *Poetical Works* were collected in 1855.

Duke of Stockbridge, The, novel by Edward Bellamy. ♦

Dukesborough Tales, local-color sketches by R.M. Johnston, ♦ four of which were published under the pseudonym Philemon Perch as *Georgia Sketches* (1864), and republished with additions and the present title in 1871. Studies of Georgia provincial life before the coming of the railroad, they belong in the tradition of Longstreet's *Georgia Scenes* and are sympathetically humorous stories emphasizing character and native setting, with little attention to plot.

DULANY, DANIEL (1722–97), Maryland lawyer, author of *Considerations on the Propriety of Imposing Taxes in the British Colonies* (1765), opposing the Stamp Act on legal grounds. He lost his colonial popularity when, in a newspaper controversy with Charles Carroll (1773), he defended the exacting of fees by government officials.

Dulcy, play by Marc Connelly♦ and George S. Kaufman. ♦

DUMMER, JEREMIAH (*c.*1679–1739), colonial agent for Massachusetts and Connecticut, wrote a closely reasoned *Defence of the New England Charters* (1721) to answer the Parliamentary attacks of the time. He was instrumental in persuading Elihu Yale to contribute to the college then named for him.

DUNBAR, PAUL LAURENCE (1872–1906), born in Dayton, Ohio, of parents who had been slaves in Kentucky, and resident in that city most of his short life, early displaying his talents as a poet. Under the auspices of the Moravian Church but with his own funds he issued a booklet of his lyrics, *Oak and Ivy,* in 1893, followed by *Majors and Minors* (1895), both treating black themes with both pathos and humor. He supported himself by menial jobs, including one that Frederick Douglass arranged at the Haiti Building in the Columbian Exposition at Chicago, but when Howells gave the second collection of poems a long and enthusiastic review, Dunbar's reputation was established. The best of the earlier poetry and some new works were then printed by a major publisher as *Lyrics of Lowly Life* (1896) with a preface by Howells. He became a popular reader of his poetry on a lecture circuit in the U.S. and England and held a job at the Library of Congress until sickness forced him to leave. Meanwhile he wrote further poems using folk materials and situations of plantation life set forth in dialect and exhibiting the influence of Burns and James Whitcomb Riley, and even the sentimental views of white interpreters of the Old South. These appeared in *Lyrics of the Hearthside* (1899), *Lyrics of Love and Laughter* (1903), and *Lyrics of Sunshine and Shadow* (1905). He also wrote a one-act musical play, *Uncle Eph's Christmas* (1900), and four novels: *The Uncalled* (1896), *The Love of Landry* (1900), *The Fanatics* (1901), and *The Sport of the Gods* (1902), melodramatic stories, the first three about whites, respectively concerning an orphan, an American aristocrat roughing it in Colorado, and conflicts between Southerners and Unionists in the Civil War era, while the last novel treats a black family from the South caught up in crime in Harlem. *The Collected Poetry of Paul Laurence Dunbar* (1993) includes 60 poems not in the previous *Complete Poems,* 16 of which were found in manuscript.

DUNCAN, ISADORA (1878–1927), dancer born in San Francisco, developed her theories of interpretative dancing, based on classic forms and such modern aesthetic thought as that of Whitman, during her long residence in Europe. Her autobiography, *My Life* (1927), is noted for its frank revelations of an eventful career. A brief biography appears in Dos Passos's *The Big Money.* Her letters to Gordon Craig were edited by Francis Steegmuller as *"Your Isadora"* (1974), and diverse writings and talks were collected as *Isadora Speaks* (1981).

DUNCAN, ROBERT [EDWARD] (1919–88), poet associated with the San Francisco Bay area, studied at the University of California and taught at Black Mountain College.♦ Influenced by Pound and holding to the belief of Charles Olson in an "open field" of composition in which a poem not only treats a theme but picks up associations of the moment of composition, Duncan's writing tends to be rhapsodic and orphic. His ongoing "Passages" relate to Pound's *Cantos* and Olson's *Maximus* poems. Duncan's collections include *Heavenly City, Earthly City* (1947); *Medieval Scenes* (1950); *Letters* (1958), containing poetry and prose; *The Opening of the Field* (1960); *Roots and Branches* (1964); *The Years as Catches* (1966), his early poems; *Passages 22–27* (1966), and *Bending the Bow* (1968). *Faust Foutou* (1960) and *Medea at Kolchis* (1965) are plays. Later works include *A Paris Visit* (1985), poems; *Fictive Certainties* (1985), essays; and *Ground Work II: In the Dark* (1987), a longer collection of poetry.

Dunkers, Baptist sect, officially called the Church of the Brethren, organized its first congregation in Germany (1708). A group came to Germantown, Pa. (1719), but the next year a schism was caused by Conrad Beissel's ascetic teachings, his observance of the seventh day as sabbath, and certain Old Testament ideas about food, and he led a group to found the Ephrata Community in 1732, where they became known as Seventh-Day Baptists. The Dunkers, sometimes called Dunkards and Tunkers (dippers), derive their name from their method of baptism by triple immersion, once for each member of the Trinity. They preserve the primitive simplicity of the apostolic church, and enjoin plainness of dress, settlement of disputes without recourse to oaths or law, and opposition to tobacco, alcohol, and war.

DUNLAP, WILLIAM (1766–1839), born in New Jersey, began his versatile career at 16 as a professional portrait painter, among his early subjects being George and Martha Washington. He returned to New York after three years of study in London under Benjamin West, but had only a moderate success as a painter. Inspired by the success of Royall Tyler's *The Contrast,* he wrote *The Father; or, American Shandyism*♦ (1789), which was so successful that he continued to focus his attention on the drama. New plays from his pen appeared on the New York stage at least once a year, and these included *Darby's Return* (1789); *Fatal Deception* (1794), which was published as *Leicester*♦ (1807); *Fontainville Abbey* (1795); and an opera, *The Archers* (1796). In 1796 he purchased a share in New York's Old American Company, and two years later became the sole owner of this unprofitable theatrical enterprise. He translated many popular French and German dramas, and his version of Kotzebue's *The Stranger* (1798) began a tremendous vogue for this dramatist, of which Dunlap took advantage by translating more than a dozen of his plays. His adaptations were frequently based on Schiller and other German dramatists, and he also drew heavily on French playwrights.

Although these works were popular, and although during this period Dunlap produced some of his own best plays, such as *André*♦ (1798) and *The Italian Father*♦ (1799), his theater failed and he went into bankruptcy (1805). After a season as an itinerant miniaturist, five years as a theatrical manager, and an attempt to publish a magazine, *The Monthly Recorder* (1813), he returned to his career as a painter. Meanwhile he wrote a *Life of Charles Brockden Brown* (1815), poorly organized but the primary source of biographical information about the novelist. In 1821 Dunlap began a series of large show canvases much indebted to Benjamin West, and he helped found the National Academy of Design (1826), where for a time he served as professor of historical painting. His *History of the Rise and Progress of the Arts of Design in the United States* (2 vols., 1834) is an indispensable authority, much of its information being based on firsthand knowledge. *The History of the American Theatre* (1832), the first account of our stage, is important for furnishing personal information about actors as well as material about early theaters and plays. Dunlap also wrote a temperance novel, *Thirty Years Ago; or, The Memoirs of a Water Drinker* (1836); a dialogue *History of New York for Schools* (1837), dealing with events up to 1789; and a *History of the New Netherlands, Province of New York, and State of New York* (2 vols., 1839–40), a careful work about the period before the adoption of the Constitution. He was the first American to make a serious business of writing for the stage, and of the 65 plays listed in his bibliography, 30 are original. Several of them have been republished by the Dunlap Society.

DUNNE, FINLEY PETER (1867–1936), Chicago journalist, editor of *Collier's* (1918–19), is best known as the author of a series of books in which Mr. Dooley, an Irish saloon keeper, criticizes current events, leaders, and aspects of the social scene, with a rich brogue and shrewd native humor. *Mr. Dooley in Peace and in War* (1898) was the first of this series, which concluded with *Mr. Dooley on Making a Will* (1919).

DUNNE, JOHN GREGORY (1932–), Connecticut-born writer resident in southern California since 1964, author of *True Confessions* (1977), a tough police novel in the vein of Raymond Chandler, and *Dutch Shea, Jr.* (1982), a novel of a similar nature, to which the tough view of the current U.S., *The Red, White, and Blue* (1987), is also related in a vital way. His nonfictional works include *Delano* (1967), about the labor movement of Cesar Chavez; *The Studio* (1969), about the film industry; *Vegas* (1974), depicting Nevada's gambling city; *Quintana and Friends* (1978), essays and reviews; and *Harp* (1989), a vibrant work dealing with autobiographic recollections of his family and deep concern with their Irish background. He and his wife Joan Didion♦ also have written successful film scripts.

DUNTON, JOHN (1659–1733), English bookseller, came to Boston (March 1686) to collect a debt. He remained two or three months, making excursions into neighboring towns to sell books, which, he said, "were most of them practical, and well suited to the genius of New England." His *Life and Errors of John Dunton* (1705) gives a glimpse of this visit, and eight fictional *Letters from New England* have been published by the Prince Society (1867).

Dupin, C. AUGUSTE, hero of "The Murders in the Rue Morgue,"♦ "The Purloined Letter,"♦ and "The Mystery of Marie Rogêt,"♦ and prototype of the intellectual amateur who is often the main character in the detective story.♦

DU PONCEAU, PIERRE ÉTIENNE (PETER STEPHEN) (1760–1844), born in St. Martin, Île de Ré, France, came to America (1777) as secretary to Baron Steuben, and served in the Continental army until illness forced him to retire (1780). As a U.S. citizen he was admitted to the Pennsylvania bar. In addition to works on international law he wrote philological treatises that include *English Phonology* (1817) and *Grammatical System of Some of the Languages of the Indian Nations of North America* (1838), and an early plea for native expression, *A Discourse on the Necessity and Means of Making Our National Literature Independent . . .* (1834). He also wrote books on Pennsylvania history and on the Constitution. His autobiography was published in the *Pennsylvania Magazine of History* (1939–40).

DUPUY, ELIZA ANN (1814–81), Southern author, whose historical romances include *The Conspirator* (1850), based on the life of Aaron Burr, and *The Huguenot Exiles* (1856).

DURANT, WILL[IAM JAMES] (1885–1981), popularizer of the history of ideas, whose books include *The Story of Philosophy* (1926), *The Mansions of Philosophy* (1929), *Adventures in Genius* (1931), and *The Story of Civilization* in ten volumes: *Our Oriental Heritage* (1935), *The Life of Greece* (1939), *Caesar and Christ* (1944), *The Age of Faith* (1950), *The Renaissance* (1953), *The Reformation* (1957), *The Age of Reason Begins* (1961), *The Age of Louis XIV* (1963), *The Age of Voltaire* (1965), and *Rousseau and Revolution* (1967). The last four were written with his wife Ariel and the last volume won the Pulitzer Prize for nonfiction (1968). Later works include *The Lesson of History* (1968), and, with his wife, *Interpretations of Life* (1970) and *A Dual Autobiography* (1977).

Dutch Reformed Church, see *Reformed Church in America.*

Dutch West India Company, see *New Netherland.*

Dutchman's Fireside, The, novel by J.K. Paulding,♦ published in 1831.
   Catalina Vancour, daughter of a Dutch patroon living near Albany, is loved by her adopted cousin Sybert Vancour, a bashful youth, who, despairing of her love, leaves for a hunting trip. He meets Sir William Johnson, who befriends him and restores his self-confidence. On Sybert's return home, he is able to save Catalina from death at the hands of a degenerate Indian, whom he kills after a desperate struggle. Soon Catalina, although in love with Sybert, goes to New York and becomes the belle of the city. Following her there, the youth is overcome by shyness. At the outbreak of the French and Indian War, he becomes a scout for Johnson, in company with Timothy Weasel (Lewis Wetzel). Sybert is seriously wounded in an engagement. Catalina hears that he has been killed, and his sudden return causes consternation and joy. The story concludes with their marriage.

DUYCKINCK, EVERT AUGUSTUS (1816–78), with his brother George Long Duyckinck (1823–63) edited the New York *Literary World* (1847–53), the leading weekly literary review of the period. Prominent in literary society, they were acquainted with Irving, Cooper, Halleck, Bryant, and Melville, and were instrumental in the first publication of many writers. The brothers continued their collaboration in the *Cyclopaedia of American Literature* (1855, revised 1866), the most comprehensive scholarly work of its kind at that date. Although no longer a standard reference, it is still valuable for students. E.A. Duyckinck edited other periodicals and many books, and assembled a large and important library, now in the New York Public Library. With Cornelius Mathews, he founded and edited the literary journal *Arcturus.* ♦

DWIGGINS, W[ILLIAM] A[DDISON] (1880–1956), book designer and calligrapher, known for his striking type design and arrangement, in harmony with the subject matter of the text. His own writings include *Towards a Reform of the Paper Currency Particularly in Point of Its Design* (1932) and *Layout in Advertising* (1928, revised 1949).

DWIGHT, JOHN S[ULLIVAN] (1813–93), Boston music critic, helped found the influential Harvard Musical Association (1837). After a few years as a Unitarian minister, he became one of the first members of the Transcendental Club, and later taught music and Latin at Brook Farm. He contributed to *The Dial* and *The Harbinger*, making the latter a leader in U.S. music criticism, and founded and edited *Dwight's Journal of Music* (1852–81), as well as establishing a professorship of music at Harvard. Through his criticism, in the orthodox romantic tradition of the time, he had a profound influence on American musical taste.

DWIGHT, MARIANNE (1816–1901), sister of John Dwight, joined him at Brook Farm, and there in 1846 married John Orvis. Her *Letters from Brook Farm, 1844–1847* (1928) gives an interesting and sprightly account of daily life under the Fourierist regime.

DWIGHT, THEODORE (1764–1846), Massachusetts lawyer, grandson of Jonathan Edwards and brother of Timothy Dwight, is remembered as one of the Connecticut Wits, ♦ of whom he was probably the most vehemently Federalist member. Democracy was anathema to him, as appears in his speeches and in his *History of the Hartford Convention* (1833) and *The Character of Thomas Jefferson* (1839). He also wrote *Sketches of Scenery and Manners in the United States* (1829), *The Northern Traveller* (1825), and a *History of Connecticut* (1841). His crisp Federalist verse, in

The Echo and *The Political Greenhouse*, shows a mastery of Hudibrastic verse. From 1815 to 1817 he conducted the Albany *Daily Advertiser*, and thereafter edited the *New York Daily Advertiser*.

His son THEODORE DWIGHT (1796–1866) edited an independent journal, *Dwight's American Magazine* (1845–52), and wrote several books about his travels.

DWIGHT, TIMOTHY (1752–1817), born in Massachusetts, was a grandson of Jonathan Edwards and brother of Theodore Dwight. He showed precocious brilliance by entering Yale at the age of 13, and as a tutor there (1771–77) worked and studied so excessively that he precipitated a physical breakdown. To recuperate, he turned to an equally disproportionate amount of hiking and horseback trips, and his observations furnished much of the material for his later *Travels in New England and New York* (4 vols., 1821–22). His literary interests at Yale and his attempts with John Trumbull to introduce contemporary English literature into the curriculum may be considered the genesis of the Connecticut Wits. ♦ After a brief period as an army chaplain and in local politics, he became pastor (1783–95) of the Congregational church at Greenfield Hill, Conn. Preacher, author, community leader, and proprietor of a coeducational school, Dwight established himself as a leading Calvinist and stalwart Federalist. His literary reputation as a leader of the Wits was based mainly on his poems, *The Conquest of Canaan* ♦ (1785), *Greenfield Hill* ♦ (1794), and *The Triumph of Infidelity* ♦ (1788). His staunch belief in theocracy and Federalism appears in such works as *The True Means of Establishing Public Happiness* (1795), *The Nature, and Danger, of Infidel Philosophy* (1798), and *The Duty of Americans, at the Present Crisis* (1798). As guardian of public morality, he wrote and preached on many subjects, including even a sermon on the *Folly, Guilt, and Mischiefs of Dueling* (1805), following the duel between his cousin Burr and Hamilton. He was president of Yale (1795–1817), where, despite his narrow political, social, and religious views, he proved a great teacher and college leader. The beginnings of Yale's modern importance are attributed to his enlargement of the curriculum and employment of prominent scholars. His series of 173 sermons delivered at Yale, *Theology, Explained and Defended* (5 vols., 1818–19), is a complete exposition of his theological system. His *Travels* is his most famous prose work, a thorough record of scenery, history, social and religious conditions, and statistical information. The best known of his short poems is the patriotic song, "Columbia, Columbia, to glory arise."

Dynamo, play by Eugene O'Neill. ♦

E

Each and All, poem by Emerson,♦ published in 1839 and reprinted in his *Poems* (1847). In couplets of four-stress verse, it expresses his apprehension of the beauty of complete nature, "the perfect whole," despite passing disappointments and the realization that isolated facts may be ugly:

> All are needed by each one;
> Nothing is fair or good alone.

Eagle, The; or Dartmouth Centinel (1793–99), country newspaper of Hanover, N.H., which had a distinctly literary character. During its first two years, many of the contributions came from Joseph Dennie and Royall Tyler. After 1796 it became an unimportant local journal.

Eagle That Is Forgotten, The, poem in five-stress anapestic meter, by Vachel Lindsay,♦ published in *General William Booth Enters into Heaven and Other Poems* (1913). This elegy on the memory of J.P. Altgeld,♦ liberal governor of Illinois, celebrates him as a "brave-hearted . . . wise man" who "kindled the flame" and served "the mocked and the scorned and the wounded, the lame and the poor," concluding that "To live in mankind is far more than to live in a name."

EAMES, WILBERFORCE (1855–1937), bibliographer of the New York Public Library, editor of *Sabin's Dictionary,*♦ was a scholar of many interests, although he was primarily distinguished for his bibliographical knowledge of American history and literature.

EARLE, ALICE MORSE (1853–1911), Massachusetts scholar whose works include *The Sabbath in Puritan New England* (1891), *Customs and Fashions in Old New England* (1893), *Colonial Days in Old New York* (1897), *Child Life in Colonial Days* (1899), and *Two Centuries of Costume* (1903).

Early Autumn: A Story of a Lady, novel by Louis Bromfield,♦ published in 1926, won a Pulitzer Prize.

Earth Horizon, autobiography of Mary Austin.♦

East Lynne, sentimental melodramatic novel by the English author Mrs. Henry Wood, published in 1861. Its dramatic version was extremely popular on the American stage during the later part of the century for its sensational and lachrymose plot about crime and licentious behavior in English high society.

East of Eden, novel by John Steinbeck,♦ published in 1952.

In the late 1890s Adam Trask marries Cathy Ames, a beautiful but viciously evil former prostitute, and moves from his family farm in Connecticut to the Salinas Valley, California. There, aided by Sam Hamilton, a warm-hearted Irishman, he develops a large ranch, and Cathy gives birth to their twin sons. Hating her situation and her husband, Cathy shoots Adam when he tries to prevent her leaving, and under the name of Kate Albey joins a house in Salinas run by a madam whom she slowly poisons so as to get a place of her own to cater to men's darkest and most perverted desires. Adam, withdrawn and detached, has the help of kindly Sam and of his educated Chinese servant Lee in rearing his children, Caleb and Aron, whom he had considered naming Cain and Abel, particularly since Lee interpreted the Biblical story to show that although God exiled Cain to the land east of Eden, He said to him, "if thou doest well . . . thou mayest rule over sin." Hoping to jar Adam from his numbness by confronting him with reality, Sam reveals Cathy's whereabouts, and Adam, after calling on Kate, discovers her inhumanity and her belief in evil, and at last is no longer in love with her. The boys grow up, Aron as a naïve, openhearted, and religious young man innocently loving a girl named Abra, while Caleb has a stormy adolescence, torn between desires for innocence and for adventures in evil, conceived by him to be a heritage from his mother, whom he comes to know. The relationship of the boys recalls those that as a young man Adam had with his brother Charles. To hurt Adam, who dotes on Aron, Caleb takes his brother to meet their mother, and Aron is so shocked by the experience that he gives up Abra and enlists in the army during World War I. Kate commits suicide, bequeathing her wealth to Aron, whose own death in war leads to Adam's paralysis by a stroke. Caleb is guilt-ridden by the sequence of events he set in motion, but Adam on his deathbed recalls Lee's Biblical interpretation, and in forgiving Caleb he gives him the chance, like that given Cain, to make a moral choice and thus to create of his life what he will.

EASTBURN, JAMES WALLIS (1797–1819), born in England, was brought to New York (1803), graduated from Columbia (1816), and became a clergyman of the Protestant Episcopal Church in Virginia. He collaborated with R.C. Sands in writing *Yamoyden*♦ (1820), a romantic poem about King Philip's War, and was the author of several hymns.

EASTLAKE, WILLIAM (1917–), born and reared in New York City, after army service and residence in Paris moved to a New Mexico ranch. His novels include *Go in Beauty* (1956), about rivalry between brothers; *Bronc People* (1958), again a contrast of brothers, but these younger, also set in New Mexico; *Portrait of an Artist with Twenty-Six Horses* (1963), a story of fantasy and suspense involving a white man about to die and his Navajo friend; *Castle Keep* (1965), concerning American soldiers seizing a European castle in World War II; *The Bamboo Bed* (1969), about a love affair during the Vietnam War; *Dancers in the Scalp House* (1975), about Navajos and a lady friend fighting the building of a dam in New Mexico; and *The Long, Naked Descent into Boston* (1977), a comic treatment of the American Revolutionary War. *A Child's Garden of Verses for the Revolution* (1970) uses prose and poetry as commentary on contemporary issues. Eastlake also publishes many short stories, e.g. "Jack Armstrong in Tangier" (1984).

EASTMAN, CHARLES ALEXANDER (1858–1939), South Dakota physician and author, of mixed Sioux Indian and white parentage, graduated from Dartmouth (1887) and received his M.D. (1890) from Boston University. His works include *An Indian Boyhood* (1902), *Red Hunters and the Animal People* (1904), *Old Indian Days* (1907), *Wigwam Evenings* (1909), *The Soul of the Indian* (1911), *From the Deep Woods . . . ; Chapters in the Autobiography of an Indian* (1916), and *Indian Heroes and Great Chieftains* (1918).

EASTMAN, MARY H[ENDERSON] (1818–80), as a result of knowing Indians at the frontier posts where her husband, Colonel Seth Eastman, was stationed, wrote *Dacotah; or, Life and Legends of the Sioux Around Fort Snelling* (1849), *The Romance of Indian Life* (1852), and *Chicora, and Other Regions of the Conquerors and Conquered* (1854), books which he illustrated, as he did some works by Schoolcraft. As a native Virginian she wrote the novel *Aunt Phillis's Cabin; or, Southern Life as It Is* (1852), a popular reply to *Uncle Tom's Cabin.*

EASTMAN, MAX [FORRESTER] (1883–1969), social critic, whose writings are devoted to literary criticism, the relation of art to life, and problems of economic inequality. He is best known for his social criticism, although his first book, *Enjoyment of Poetry*♦ (1913), had a success unsurpassed by any of his later works. His own verse was collected in *Poems of Five Decades* (1954). He was a founder and editor of *The Masses* and *The Liberator.* Among his later books are *Marx, Lenin, and the Science of Revolution* (1926); *The Literary Mind: Its Place in an Age of Science* (1931); *Artists in Uniform* (1934); a translation of Trotsky's *History*

of the Russian Revolution (3 vols., 1932–33); *Enjoyment of Laughter* (1936); *Marxism: Is It Science?* (1940); *Stalin's Russia* (1940), showing his hostility to the orthodox Communist party line; and *Reflections on the Failure of Socialism* (1955). Reminiscent works are *Heroes I Have Known* (1942), sketches of people including Debs, Isadora Duncan, Clemens, Chaplin, Anatole France, Trotsky, Freud, and John Dewey; *Great Companions* (1959), essays on 12 friends, including Hemingway, Millay, and Santayana; and *Love and Revolution* (1965), an autobiography.

Eben Holden, a Tale of the North Country, novel by Irving Bacheller,♦ published in 1900.

EBERHART, RICHARD [GHORMLEY] (1904–), Minnesota-born poet, educated at Dartmouth and Cambridge, has taught there and at schools and colleges, and since 1956 has been a professor of English and poet in residence at Dartmouth. His poetry assumes a variety of forms, ranging from romantic description to allegory, and is marked by intensity, honesty, and precision of diction. It includes *A Bravery of Earth* (1930), partly about his world tour on a freight steamer; *Reading the Spirit* (1937); *Song and Idea* (1942); *Burr Oaks* (1947); *Brotherhood of Man* (1949); *An Herb Basket* (1950); *Undercliff* (1953); *Great Praises* (1957); *The Quarry* (1964); *Thirty One Sonnets* (1967), written in his youth; *Shifts of Being* (1968); *Fields of Grace* (1972); *Poems to Poets* (1976); and *Collected Poems* (1976). Since then he has collected poetry in *The Long Reach* (1984) and other volumes, including *Maine Poems* (1988) and *Florida Poems* (1989). *Collected Poems 1930–1986* was published in 1988. "The Visionary Farms" (1952) is one of his *Collected Verse Plays* (1962). He has also published *Selected Prose* (1978), and *Of Poetry and Poets* (1979). Among many honors he has received a Bollingen Prize, Pulitzer Prize, and National Book Award.

Echo, The, verse satire published in the *American Mercury* (1791–1805), collected in 1807, by Theodore Dwight, Richard Alsop, Lemuel Hopkins, E.H. Smith, and Mason Cogswell. These Connecticut Wits' attacks on anti-Federalism in press and politics run from travesty of journalistic rodomontade to satire of Jefferson.

Eclectic Magazine, The (1819–1907), literary journal published from New York, Philadelphia, and Boston. It began as *The Philadelphia Register and National Recorder,* a weekly reprint of American newspaper material, and became successively *The National Recorder* (1819–21); *The Saturday Magazine* (1821–22), republishing writings from British literary magazines; *The Museum of Foreign Literature and Science* (1822–42); and *The Eclectic Museum* (1843–44). All these magazines were edited and published by Eliakim Littell, but when it became *The Eclectic Magazine* (1844), a monthly reprint of foreign writings, he sold it to publish the rival *Living Age.*

EDDY, MARY BAKER (1821–1910), discoverer and founder of Christian Science,♦ was born in New Hampshire. She was married three times, although for a long time an invalid. In 1862 she became a patient of Phineas P. Quimby, a mental healer of Portland, Me., with whom she had contact until 1865 and in whom for a time she had much confidence. To the spiritual enlightenment she received with recovery from a serious injury (1866) she attributed her discovery of Christian Science. She began to work out her own metaphysical system, and her students and followers increased rapidly after the publication of *Science and Health with Key to the Scriptures*♦ (1875). The following year the Christian Science Association was formed, and in 1879 the various associations were merged in the Church of Christ, Scientist. She founded (1883) and for a time edited the *Journal of Christian Science,* which won more recruits to her Metaphysical College and church. Although she retired in 1889 to a secluded home at Concord, N.H., and made few appearances thereafter at the Mother Church in Boston, Mrs. Eddy never ceased to be the actual leader of the Christian Science movement and the chief author of its writings.

EDDY, SHERWOOD (1871–1963), YMCA leader in the Orient, the Near East, and Russia, whose books include *India Awakening* (1911); *The New World of Labor* (1923); *Religion and Social Justice* (1928); *The Challenge of Russia* (1930); *A Pilgrimage of Ideas* (1934) and *I Have Seen God Do It* (1940), autobiographical volumes; *The Kingdom of God and the American Dream* (1941), an account of American religious and secular ideals; *Maker of Men* (1941); *Man Discovers God* (1942); *I Have Seen God Work in China* (1945); *Pathfinders of the World Missionary Crusade* (1945); and *Eighty Adventurous Years* (1955), autobiography.

EDEL, [JOSEPH] LEON (1907–), born in Pittsburgh but educated at McGill University, Toronto (M.A., 1928), and the University of Paris (Litt.D., 1932), served as a journalist before entering an academic career in 1950 as a professor at New York University. He is particularly known for his scholarly work on Henry James, including various editions such as *The Complete Plays* (1949) and the *Complete Tales* (12 vols., 1963–65) and selected *Letters* (2 vols., 1974–75), but particularly for his authoritative *Life* (5 vols., 1953–72), which won a Pulitzer Prize and National Book Award for two of its volumes. A one-volume version was published in 1985. Edel's other works include a study of Joyce (1947), *The Modern Psychological Novel* (1955), *Literary Biography* (1957), *Bloomsburg, A House of Lions* (1979), *Stuff of Sleep and Dreams: Experiments in Literary Psychology* (1982), and, with E.K.

Brown, *Willa Cather* (1953). Works he has edited include the *Papers* (1972) of Edmund Wilson.

Edgar Huntly; *or, Memoirs of a Sleep-Walker,* epistolary romance by C.B. Brown,♦ published in 1799.

Edgar, in his letters to Mary Waldegrave, tells of startling occurrences in a Pennsylvania town, and his investigation of morose Clithero Edny, whom he has observed sleep-walking at the site of the recent murder of Mary's brother. Clithero confesses that he has escaped from Ireland, believing that he killed his benefactress, Mrs. Lorimer; then, his mind evidently unbalanced, he runs away to a nearby cave. One night, after Edgar has visited Clithero in his retreat, he finds himself lying in an underground pit, unable to account for his being there. He is soon involved in a number of adventures, barely escaping death in the pit, killing a panther that is about to leap on him, killing five Indians in a series of battles, and spending several days in the woods in a state of near collapse. When he finds shelter, he unexpectedly meets his former tutor, Sarsefield, who has returned to America after marrying Mrs. Lorimer. Sarsefield discovers that Edgar is a sleepwalker, and that he fell into the pit while unconsciously in search of Clithero. The latter is disclosed to be a maniac, and takes his own life after attempting to kill Mrs. Sarsefield. It is then found that Indians, not Clithero, caused the death of Mary's brother.

Edict by the King of Prussia, satire by Franklin,♦ published in the Philadelphia *Public Advertiser* (1773). It is written in the form of a royal proclamation, claiming that England belongs to Prussia because of its original settlement by Anglo-Saxons from that country. Having established English dependence upon Prussia, the king imposes a long list of political and legal restrictions upon the English people. In this fashion, Franklin satirizes the British attitude toward the American colonies.

EDMONDS, WALTER D[UMAUX] (1903–), New York author, graduated from Harvard (1926), and is best known for his historical novels about his native state. These include *Rome Haul* (1929), a story of the great days of the Erie Canal; *The Big Barn* (1930); *Erie Water* (1933); *Drums Along the Mohawk* (1936), a novel of the American Revolution and its effect on Mohawk Valley farmers; *Chad Hanna* (1940) and *Young Ames* (1942), about boys in the 1830s; *Tom Whipple* (1942), the story of a Yankee lad, retold from a work by Lydia M. Child; *In the Hands of the Senecas* (1947), about the frontier of 18th-century New York state; *The Wedding Journey* (1947), a novelette set on an Erie Canal boat in 1855; and *The Boyds of Black River* (1953), about upper New York state farmers in the 1900s. He has also written children's books; *Mostly Canallers* (1934), short stories; and *They Fought with What They Had* (1951), about the army air forces in the southwest Pacific, 1941–42. *Rome Haul* was dramatized by Marc Connelly and F.B. Elser as *The Farmer Takes a Wife* (1934).

Education of Henry Adams, *The,* autobiography of Henry Adams,♦ privately printed (1907) and posthumously published (1918). Subtitled "A Study of Twentieth-Century Multiplicity," the work complements *Mont-Saint-Michel and Chartres*♦ (1904), in which Adams interprets the 13th century in Europe as "the point of history when man held the highest idea of himself as a unit in a unified universe." In *The Education,* embodying his theory of the acceleration of historical force, he describes the modern world as a "multiverse," leading to a metaphysics and science of multiple aspects and reactions. Using himself "for purpose of model, to become a manikin on which the toilet of education is to be draped in order to show the fit or misfit of the clothes," he asserts that his formal education, at Harvard and elsewhere, failed to prepare him for the conflicts he had to meet. The narrative is incomplete, for it omits any mention of his marriage, or other events between 1871 and 1892, but there are vivid descriptions of his encounters with Harvard education, as both student and teacher; with diplomacy in England during the Civil War; with the theories of Darwin; and with other intellectual influences. The chapter "The Dynamo and the Virgin" expresses his view that the mechanical dynamo, symbol of electrical energy, corresponds to the central symbol of the Virgin that unified the thought of medieval Europe. The concluding chapters are a more explicit discussion of the dynamic theory of history and the law of acceleration.

Education of H*Y*M*A*N K*A*P*L*A*N, *The,* sketches by Leo Rosten.♦

EDWARDS, HARRY STILLWELL (1855–1938), Georgia journalist and author, whose books include a novel, *Sons and Fathers* (1896), and two popular stories about blacks, *Æneas Africanus* (1919) and *Æneas Africanus, Defendant* (1921).

EDWARDS, JONATHAN (1703–58), born in Connecticut, entered Yale before he was 13 and graduated in 1720. His interest in scientific observation was manifested at the age of 11 in an account "Of Insects," on phenomena related to the flying spider (*Andover Review,* Jan. 1890), and a group of acute comments on "The Soul," "The Rainbow," "Being," and "Colours." While at Yale he read Locke's *Essay Concerning Human Understanding* with more delight than a "greedy miser" finds in "some newly discovered treasure," and began to combine reflections on the mind with his observations of natural science. He made a precocious venture into Berkeleyan ideal-

ism, evidently without knowing Berkeley, and, in his "Notes on the Mind," decided: "That which truly is the substance of all Bodies, is the infinitely exact, and precise, and perfectly stable Idea, in God's mind, together with his stable Will, that the same shall gradually be communicated to us, and to other minds, according to certain fixed and exact established Methods and Laws."

After two additional years of theological study at Yale, and a year of tutoring there, he became (1726) the colleague of his grandfather Solomon Stoddard in the Congregational pastorate at Northampton, Mass. He had made a series of formal "Resolutions" for his spiritual progress, but it is in his "Personal Narrative" (written *c.*1740) that he rehearses his spiritual autobiography. Here one sees his intense absorption in the idea of God's infinite will throbbing through the universe. Edwards married Sarah Pierpont (1727), whom he had described four years earlier in a famous lyrical passage. Upon the death of his grandfather (1729), he became the sole pastor of the Northampton church. With stern discipline and exalted fervor he fought the growing Arminianism♦ and the weakening of Congregational churches through the Half-Way Covenant,♦ writing a *Treatise Concerning Religious Affections* (1746) and *A Vindication of the Gospel Doctrine of Justifying Faith* (1746). His discourse *God Glorified in . . . Man's Dependence upon Him* (1731) attacked those who relied for salvation solely on moral effort, and his sermon on *Divine and Supernatural Light* (1734) argued that saving grace came solely from the mind's supernatural illumination by the loveliness of divine holiness. There ensued a tremendous revival of religious fervor, the Great Awakening,♦ in which the community, lacking its pastor's iron will, gave way to a wave of emotionalism and morbid belief in God's absolute justification in condemnation. Edwards's sermons ranged from those on *Charity and Its Fruits* (1738) to the notorious *Sinners in the Hands of an Angry God*♦ (1741). Although he criticized the hysterical excitement that accompanied the Awakening, he defended it as a vitally important crisis in *A Faithful Narrative of the Surprising Work of God* (1737), *The Distinguishing Marks of a Work of the Spirit of God* (1741), *Some Thoughts Concerning the Present Revival of Religion in New England* (1742), and *An Humble Attempt To Promote Visible Union of God's People* (1747). He explained that the two activities of the mind—understanding and inclination or will—are indispensable for true religion. Man wills what he loves, and, instead of depending upon mere understanding of God and obedience to worldly morality, he shares directly in the divine light.

When Edwards applied this criterion to admission to the Lord's Supper, excluding those who wished to ally themselves to the church without supernatural conversion, his parishioners grew resentful, and this and other matters led to his dismissal (1750). After preaching his dignified *Farewell Sermon* (published 1751), he became a missionary to the Housatonic River Indians and pastor of a small congregation at Stockbridge. He had meanwhile published his apologia, *An Humble Inquiry into the Rules of the Word of God* (1749), and *An Account of the Life of the Late Reverend Mr. David Brainerd* (1749), an example of piety. In his next attack on Arminianism, Edwards reverted to the "Notes on the Mind," developing his ethical point of view in *A Careful and Strict Enquiry into the Modern Prevailing Notions of . . . Freedom of Will*♦ (1754), his greatest work, which became a primary Calvinistic document. In *The Great Christian Doctrine of Original Sin Defended* (1758), he argues that depravity is inevitable, since an identity of consciousness and a continuity of divine action make all men as one with Adam. "The Nature of True Virtue," in *Two Dissertations* (1765), upholds virtue as moral beauty, which, in the form of love, seeks the highest good of all being. Since God is the supreme object, truly disinterested love will be directed toward Him. The lower form of natural virtue rests on self-love, and those not enlightened by saving grace will only perceive and approve justice and benevolence, rather than the essential and primary beauty of virtue. In the second of the *Dissertations,* "Concerning the End for Which God Created the World" (written 1755), he returned to the mystic pantheism of his youth, declaring the world to be an emanation of God's infinite fullness, created to express His glory. Since He is the supreme excellence, He loves the world as He is infused into it. In this, Edwards's tendency to negate the personal, Hebraic concept of God and to view Him as an infinite being foreshadows Transcendentalism. After his work in Stockbridge, he became president of the college of New Jersey, an office he held from January 1758 until his death in March.

JONATHAN EDWARDS (1745–1801), his son, edited his works, propagated his doctrines, and continued his career as a pastor in New Haven, where he was dismissed (1795) because of a similar objection to the Half-Way Convenant.

Effingham, surname of characters in *Homeward Bound,*♦ *Home as Found,*♦ the Leather-Stocking Tales,♦ and other novels by Cooper; and in works by J.E. Cooke.

EGGLESTON, EDWARD (1837–1902), born in Indiana, received a strict Methodist rearing and was educated in country schools. Both influences are important in his later writing. He was successively a Bible agent, a circuit-riding Methodist minister, a pastor of small churches, and a writer and editor of Sunday school and juvenile magazines. By 1874 he had abandoned Methodism and founded a Church of Christian Endeavor in Brooklyn, N.Y. He was pastor of this "creedless" congregation until 1879, when he retired to devote himself to writing. He was already famous for his novels, particularly *The Hoosier Schoolmaster*♦ (1871), marked by a pious sentimentalism but distinguished for its realism in depicting the backwoods country of Indiana. Other fiction includes *The End of the World* (1872), an Indiana love story, whose background is concerned with the belief of the Millerites in an approaching day of doom; *The Mystery of Metropolisville* (1873), a melodramatic novel about a real-estate boom in Minnesota; *The Circuit Rider* (1874), about a Methodist preacher in Ohio during the early 19th century, distinguished for its realistic exposition of the lawlessness of frontier society; and *Roxy*♦ (1878), which is set in Indiana during the same period, and vividly contrasts pioneer and "poorwhite" types. Although he considered his fiction to be "a contribution to the history of civilization in America," he believed didactic historical works to be of greater value and wrote a series of juvenile biographies of such Indian figures as Tecumseh (1878), Pocahontas and Powhatan (1879), and Montezuma (1880), as well as several history texts. Later novels include *The Hoosier Schoolboy* (1883), a boys' story condemning conditions in rural schools; *The Graysons* (1888), a historical romance of Illinois, featuring Lincoln's successful defense of an accused murderer; and *The Faith Doctor* (1891), a satire on wealthy devotees of Christian Science. He also completed two volumes of a history of life in the U.S., which was posthumously published (1904).

EGGLESTON, GEORGE CARY (1839–1911), brother of Edward Eggleston, was born in Indiana, and at 16 began teaching in a backcountry district school, where his experiences furnished the material for his brother's *The Hoosier Schoolmaster* (1871). After serving with the Confederates in the Civil War, he practiced law briefly, then entered an editorial career on newspapers and magazines, with some free-lance writing. He was literary editor of Bryant's New York *Evening Post* and served for 11 years on the editorial staff of Pulitzer's *World.* Meanwhile he wrote a number of books for boys, the autobiographical *A Rebel's Recollections* (1874), some biography and history, and several novels, including *Juggernaut* (1891), written with Dorothy Marbourg, based on Indiana life; and *A Man of Honour* (1873), *Dorothy South* (1902), *The Master of Warlock* (1903), and *Evelyn Byrd* (1904), romantic tales of the South.

***Eighth of January,** The,* play by R.P. Smith,♦ produced and published in 1829. It contrasts the loyal American soldier Charles Bull with his father, John Bull, an Englishman who will fight against neither his native nor his adopted country, and centers on Jackson's victory at New Orleans (Jan. 8, 1815). It celebrates the success of popular government by Jackson's election (1828). G.W.P. Custis wrote a play with the same title (1834).

Eimi, travel narrative by E.E. Cummings♦ of his 36-day visit to the Soviet Union, published in 1933. This long prose work employs the techniques of his poetry and, like it, also celebrates the individual of the title (Greek, "I am"), and with wit and vigor attacks the regimentation of people in the U.S.S.R.

EISELEY, LOREN [COREY] (1907–77), professor of anthropology at the University of Pennsylvania, whose scholarly writings include *The Immense Journey* (1957), a history of life on the planet earth; *Darwin's Century* (1960); and *Francis Bacon and the Modern Dilemma* (1963), revised as *The Man Who Saw Through Mirrors* (1973). He also wrote *The Unexpected Universe* (1969), reflections on life; poetry including *Notes of an Alchemist* (1972) and *Another Kind of Autumn* (1977); and an autobiography, *All the Strange Hours* (1975).

El Dorado (Spanish, "The Gilded Man"), mythical land of great wealth sought by explorers including Pizarro, Raleigh, Cabeza de Vaca, and Coronado. The legend may derive from a custom of the Chibcha Indians of Colombia, who anointed their chief, rolled him in gold, and washed him in a lake into which they threw gold and jewels, but it was attributed to many tribes, including Zuñi. Bandelier's *The Gilded Man* (1893) deals with the legend. The name was associated with the California gold rush, e.g. works as different as Bayard Taylor's *Eldorado,* a travel account, and Poe's "Eldorado," a symbolic poem written in 1849 about a knight who learns that the true Eldorado is not of this earth but is a wealth beyond the mundane.

Eleonora, story by Poe,♦ in *The Gift* (1842). This brief romance tells of a youth reared with his cousin Eleonora in the beautiful Valley of the Many-Colored Grass. They fall in love, but she dies after he pledges never to wed "any daughter of Earth." Grieving, he goes to a strange city to serve at the gay court of the king, where he falls in love with and weds "the seraph Ermengarde." One night he hears a "familiar and sweet voice" absolve him of his vow "for reasons which shall be made known to thee in Heaven."

ELIOT, CHARLES W[ILLIAM] (1834–1926), president of Harvard (1869–1909), made the university the leading American institution of higher learning through his improvement of the graduate and professional schools, the distinguished scholars he attracted, the raising of undergraduate standards, and such reforms as the "elective system." After his resignation, he interested himself in civil service reform, peace organizations, and public affairs. He edited *The Harvard Classics* (1910), a 50-volume selection from world literature, popularly known as "Dr. Eliot's Five-Foot Shelf of Books," for self-education of persons without college training. His books include *The Religion of the Future* (1909) and *The Durable Satisfactions of Life* (1910).

ELIOT, JOHN (1604–90), English-born missionary, educated at Cambridge, came to Boston (1631), where, as the first to preach to the Indians in their native tongue, he obtained the sobriquet "Apostle to the Indians." In 1651 he established the first of his 14 villages of Praying Indians, numbering 1100 converts, but mainly destroyed in King Philip's War. By the pamphlets known as "Eliot's Indian Tracts" he aroused interest that led to the formation of the Society for the Propagation of the Gospel (1649). His translation of the Bible into the language of the Massachuset Indians (New Testament, 1661; Old Testament, 1663) was the first complete Bible printed in the English colonies. Other works include a *Catechism* in the Indian language (1654), *The Christian Commonwealth* (1659), *The Indian Primer* (1669), and a part of the *Bay Psalm Book♦* (1640). Cotton Mather wrote a biography of Eliot (1691); Eliot's correspondence with Richard Baxter was published in 1931.

ELIOT, T[HOMAS] S[TEARNS] (1888–1965), born in St. Louis, graduated from Harvard (1910) and studied at the Sorbonne and at Merton College, Oxford. For a year he was an instructor in philosophy at Harvard, and his first articles were on this subject. In 1914 he went to Europe, and he did not return to the U.S. until 1932, when he held a lectureship at Harvard. In the intervening years he did some schoolteaching in England, became a London bank clerk, wrote reviews and poems, assisted in editing a literary journal, and in 1923 became editor of the quarterly review *Criterion.* In 1927 he became a British subject because of his interest in the English church and state.

His first volume of criticism, *The Sacred Wood* (1920), emphasized the importance of tradition, both in creative writing and in criticism, and through further critical work he was partly responsible for a revival of interest in Donne and Dryden, in whom he found a fusion of thought and feeling that gave a unified sensibility to their poetry. *For Lancelot Andrewes♦* (1928) showed that in the Church of England he found the symbol and expression of meaningful form and discipline that he judged necessary to adequate fulfillment of his own life and service to letters. In *After Strange Gods* (1934), lectures delivered at the University of Virginia, he revealed his increasing preoccupation with tradition as it relates to the expression of moral problems in contemporary literature.

Not only was his poetry in harmony with his critical standards, but it also showed his understanding and skillful use of the works of earlier authors in the presentation of his ideas. His first volume of verse, *Prufrock and Other Observations* (1917), had a tone of flippant despair, but he employed the rhythms and technique of ironic contrast of some of the French Symbolists in "The Love Song of J. Alfred Prufrock"♦ and other poems. A second volume, *Poems* (1920), contained a brilliant series of quatrains, including "Sweeney Among the Nightingales," "Sweeney Erect," "The Hippopotamus," and "Mr. Eliot's Sunday Morning Service," in which he further indicated that he felt life to be ignoble, sordid, or stultifying, while it had once been otherwise, using the figure of Sweeney,♦ among others, to show this. In this volume he also displayed the inanition of modern life in "Gerontion,"♦ and he reached the fullness of his poetic expression during this period of despair in *The Waste Land*♦ (1922).

After "The Hollow Men" (1925), which indicated this trend, he issued *Ash-Wednesday*♦ (1930), and made clear his allegiance to the Church of England. In this context he wrote the dialogues and choruses of *The Rock* (1934), a pageant representing the past and present difficulties of the Church and its ultimate triumph, and *Murder in the Cathedral*♦ (1935), a latter-day morality play concerning the assassination of Thomas à Becket and affirming the value of the Church as a medium for social action. Later verse plays were *The Family Reunion*♦ (1939), a drama of sin and expiation; two symbolic comedies on faith and the quest for personal identity, *The Cocktail Party*♦ (1950) and *The Confidential Clerk* (1954); and *The Elder Statesman* (1958), about a distinguished old man who sees not only the nature of his youthful follies but his son's imitations of them. In 1943 he collected *Four Quartets,*♦ poetic considerations of time and place, memory and consciousness. In 1948 he was awarded a Nobel Prize.

His poetry illustrated also two critical formulas expressed in his prose. In *The Sacred Wood* he declared, "The only way of expressing emotion in the form of art is by finding an 'objective correlative'; in other words, a set of objects, a situation, a chain of events which shall be the formula of that particular emotion," and in "Tradition and the Individual Talent," an essay also from *The Sacred Woods,* he declared, "Poetry is not a turning loose of emotion, but an escape from emotion; it is not the expression of personality, but an escape from personality."

His other works include *Ezra Pound: His Metric and Poetry* (1917); *Ara Vos Prec* (1919); *Homage to John Dryden* (1924); *Shakespeare and the Stoicism of Seneca* (1927); *The Journey of the Magi* (1927); *A Song for Simeon* (1928); *Dante* (1929); *Animula* (1929); *Marina* (1930); *Triumphal March* (1931); *John Dryden, the Poet, the Dramatist, the Critic* (1932); *The Use of Poetry and the Use of Criticism* (1933), his Harvard lectures; *Old Possum's Book of Practical Cats*♦ (1939); *The Idea of a Christian Society* (1940); *Notes Toward a Definition of Culture* (1949); and *On Poetry and Poets* (1957). His *Poems Written in Early Youth* (1904–10) was privately issued in 1950 and for sale in 1967. The first volume of his *Letters* was published in 1988.

Eliza, character in *Uncle Tom's Cabin.*♦

ELKIN, STANLEY [LAWRENCE] (1930–   ), novelist whose fiction is marked by black humor, symbolism, rich prose, and a satiric view of contemporary American life. His novels are *Boswell* (1964), a comic depiction of a young man who attaches himself to prominent people, including the Queen of England; *A Bad Man* (1967), about a department store owner who ends up in prison; *The Dick Gibson Show* (1971), describing the adventures, sometimes surreal, of an early-day radio announcer; *The Franchiser* (1976), depicting an American businessman who creates chains of motels and restaurants; *The Living End* (1979), about the death of an ordinary man and how God judges him in the afterworld; *George Mills* (1982), about a man's 1000 years of reincarnations; *The Rabbi of Lud* (1987), a comic view of a rabbi often active as a sexton, and *The MacGuffin* (1991), a densely plotted novel about midlife anxiety, marital infidelity, and small-town conspiracies. *Criers and Kibitzers, Kibitzers and Criers* (1966) collects stories, and *Searches and Seizures* (1973) prints three novellas. *The Six-Year-Old Man* (1987) prints an unproduced screenplay written in 1966. In 1985 *Early Elkin* collected stories, a critique, and a memoir written in the 1950s. He has also created assemblages of his own writings in *Stanley Elkin's Greatest Hits* (1980), and *Stanley Elkin's The Magic Kingdom* (1986), a novel. Born in New York City, Elkin has been a professor at Washington University, St. Louis, since 1959.

ELLIOTT, GEORGE P[AUL] (1918–80), born in Indiana, reared in California, after receiving an A.B. and M.A. (1941) from the University of California taught English and creative writing at his alma mater, Cornell, Barnard, Iowa, and St. Mary's College (California). His novels include *Parktilden Village* (1958), set in a California apartment-house development; *David Knudsen* (1962), about the son of a nuclear physicist who develops radiation sickness; *In the World* (1965); and *Muriel* (1972), a portrait of a narrow, possessive woman. His stories are collected in *Among the Dangs* (1961) and *An Hour of Last Things* (1968). His poems are in *Fever and Chills* (1961) and *From the Berkeley Hills* (1969). *A Piece of Lettuce* (1964) and *Conversions* (1971) are essays on literature and society.

ELLIOTT, MAUD HOWE (1854–1948), daughter of S.G. and Julia Ward Howe, wrote several books on Italy, where she resided for a time, and such biographies as *Julia Ward Howe* (1915, Pulitzer Prize), written with her sister, Laura E. Richards, and *My Cousin, F. Marion Crawford* (1934).

ELLIOT, SARAH BARNWELL (1848–1928), born in Georgia, lived most of her life in Tennessee, of whose mountain people she wrote in her realistic novel *Jerry* (1891). Her other works include *The Felmeres* (1879), *A Simple Heart* (1887), *John Paget* (1893), *The Durket Sperret* (1898), and a biography of Houston (1900).

ELLIS, EDWARD S[YLVESTER] (1840–1916), born in Ohio, came to New York, where he became a leading author of dime novels. His *Seth Jones; or, The Captives of the Frontier* (1886) is said to have sold 450,000 copies within six months.

ELLISON, RALPH [WALDO] (1914–94), Oklahoma-born author, a student at Tuskegee Institute (1933–36), was a visiting professor of creative writing, black culture, and humanities at various major universities, but is best known for his naturalistic novel, *Invisible Man*♦ (1952), winner of a National Book Award, tracing the life of a young black man trying to find himself as an individual as well as in relation to his race and society. It remains a major novel. He also wrote *Shadow and Act* (1964), essays, and *Going to the Territory* (1986), a later collection. Ellison had completed a portion of a second novel which was destroyed in a fire. He started again from scratch and was about to finish it at his death.

ELLMANN, RICHARD (1918–87), born in Michigan, received his B.A. from Yale. After his graduate studies he became an outstanding literary scholar teaching at universities in the U.S. and England, noted both for lectures and for his biographical and critical studies of major modern authors, including *Yeats: The Man and the Masks* (1948), *The Identity of Yeats* (1951), *James Joyce* (1959), and *Oscar Wilde* (1988), awarded a Pulitzer Prize.

Elmer Gantry, see *Lewis, Sinclair.*

Elsie Dinsmore, see *Dinsmore, Elsie.*

Elsie Venner; A Romance of Destiny, novel by Holmes,♦ published in 1861, was previously serialized as *The Professor's Story*. The prototype of the heroine is said to be Margaret Fuller. The author's intention was "to test the doctrine of 'original sin' and human responsibility," and he spoke of the work as "a medicated novel," since it was an early instance of scientific analysis of character and of the concept of a pattern of heredity.

A professor of medicine tells the story of Elsie Venner, a New England girl whose snake-like nature is traced to the prenatal influence of a snakebite that her mother received. Elsie loves Bernard Langdon, one of the professor's students, but Bernard does not return her affection, though she saves his life when he is almost killed by a rattlesnake. Her peculiar quality, which sets her

apart from others and fascinates Helen Darley, a teacher in the academy where Bernard teaches temporarily, is lost during her illness following Bernard's rejection, but she dies as a result.

EMBURY, EMMA CATHERINE (1806–63), New York author, whose conventional feminine novels, including *Guido* (1828) and *Constance Latimer; or, The Blind Girl* (1838), were popular in her time. A selected volume of her popular poems was published in 1869, and *Selected Prose Writings* in 1893.

EMERSON, RALPH WALDO (1803–82), born in Boston, the son of a Unitarian minister who was a member of an old Puritan family. After his father's death, he was raised by his mother and an aunt, Mary Moody Emerson, a zealously pious woman who expressed her sardonically critical mind in a style her nephew admired and imitated. At Harvard in 1820 he began to keep the voluminous journals that he continued throughout his life, and that formed the basis of most of his essays and poems. After graduation (1821) he took over his brother's Boston school for young ladies, although with some misgivings, and when he moved to Canterbury with his family in 1823 he expressed his relief at returning to the natural beauties of the countryside in the poem "Goodbye."♦ He taught for two more years, then entered the Divinity School at Harvard, where ill health and doubts on dogma made him a desultory student. Although approved as a candidate for the Unitarian ministry (1826), he had to go to Georgia and Florida for the winter because of a pulmonary disease. He married in 1829, but his wife died in 1831. A year later came the great turning point in his life; he resigned his pastorate of the Second Church of Boston, where he had been an effective and popular preacher, because he could not conscientiously administer the Lord's Supper.

During a tour of Europe (1832–33), he met Carlyle, Wordsworth, and Coleridge, through whom he became intimately associated with the transcendental thought and its sources in German idealism. Other influences on Emerson's later thinking included his own Unitarian-Yankee background, his admiration for Plato and the neo-Platonists, his study of the sacred books of the East, the skepticism of Montaigne, the new republican tradition, the line of British philosophy that ran through Berkeley, Hume, and Locke, and the mystical metaphysics of Swedenborg. On his return to Boston he did some preaching, but turned more and more to lyceum lecturing, for which he drew materials from his journals. His addresses, presented in such series as "The Philosophy of History," "Human Culture," "Human Life," and "The Present Age," in turn furnished the basis for his later essays, which, without formal unity, are bound together by pithy, stimulating sentences that contain the quintessence of his philosophy. Among these are "Self-Reliance,"♦ "The Over-Soul,"♦ "Compensation"♦ "Spiritual Laws," "Love," and "Friendship."

In 1835 Emerson remarried and settled in Concord,♦ the home of his forefathers, which was thereafter the center of his own activity. Here he was intimate with Thoreau, Alcott, Jones Very, Margaret Fuller, Brownson, Hawthorne, and others who shared in the movement of Transcendentalism.♦ His first book, *Nature*♦ (1836), is the fundamental document of his philosophy, and expresses also his constant, deeply felt love for the natural scenes in which he passed so much of his time. His Transcendental ideas were next applied to cultural and national problems in his oration *The American Scholar*♦ (1837). A year later, in his "Divinity School Address,"♦ he attacked formal religion and championed intuitive spiritual experience. As a result, it was 30 years before he was again invited to speak at Harvard.

To promulgate his ideas further, in 1840 he joined with other Transcendentalists in publishing *The Dial,* and, though he did not sympathize with the communal experiments at Brook Farm and Fruitlands, he became interested in many contemporary reform movements and extended the sphere of his lecturing. Some of these lectures received their final form in the first series of *Essays* (1841), whose 12 pieces were "History," "Self-Reliance," "Compensation," "Spiritual Laws," "Love," "Friendship," "Prudence," "Heroism," "The Over-Soul," "Circles," "Intellect," and "Art." With the second series of *Essays,* which appeared three years later, these works established Emerson's reputation throughout the U.S. and abroad. In 1845 he delivered the series of lectures published as *Representative Men*♦ (1850). His first volume of *Poems* (1847), together with *May-Day and Other Pieces* (1867), included such poems as "Threnody,"♦ "Compensation,"♦ "Each and All,"♦ "The Rhodora,"♦ "The Sphinx,"♦ "Days,"♦ "The Humble-Bee,"♦ "Voluntaries,"♦ "Concord Hymn,"♦ "May-Day," ♦ and "Brahma."♦ His poetry is intellectual, gnomic, and metaphysical.

During 1847–48 he visited England and France, renewed the friendship with Carlyle that had been maintained in their notable correspondence, and made new friends among the most distinguished European thinkers and writers. *Selected Letters* (1987) consists of correspondence with his wife Lillian. His lectures on England the following season formed the basis of his book *English Traits*♦ (1856). A collection of *Addresses and Lectures* was published in 1849, and *The Conduct of Life*♦ (1860) and *Society and Solitude*♦ (1870) contain the materials of the lectures in his lyceum circuit, which took him as far west as the Mississippi. He contributed, with Channing and Clarke, to the *Memoirs* of Margaret Fuller (1852), and in 1855 helped found the Saturday Club.

During the 1850s, Emerson's journals exhibit his great interest in antislavery, and he was an active sympathizer with the Northern struggle in the Civil War, but by 1866 realized that his career was nearly at its end. In the poem "Terminus" he declared:

Fancy departs; no more invent;
Contract thy firmament
To compass of a tent.

Thereafter, although in 1870 he gave a series of lectures at Harvard, published as *Natural History of Intellect* (1893), and continued to lecture and write, issuing *Letters and Social Aims* (1876), his mental capacities showed a slow but sure decline. He made journeys to California (1871) and to Europe (1872), but gradually slipped into a serene senility in which his mind finally became a calm blank. His son Edward Waldo Emerson (1844–1930) edited his *Complete Works* (1903–4), along with the *Journals* (10 vols., 1909–14), and several collections of correspondence. A complete edition of previously unpublished *Letters* was edited by R.L. Rusk (6 vols., 1939). *Early Lectures* appeared in three volumes (1959–64). Publication of a complete edition of the *Journals* and *Notebooks* (16 vols.) was begun (1960–), as was a scholarly edition of *Collected Works* (1972–).

Emerson, whose thought is often considered the core of Transcendentalism, stood apart from much of the activity of the movement, and, though he summed up the major development of romanticism in America, his philosophy is rooted in the Puritan background and tempered by the many systems of thought that converged in him. He had no complete philosophical system, but with a style now vibrant, now flinty, preached the great doctrine of a higher individualism, the spiritual nature of reality, the importance of self-reliance, the obedience to instinct, the obligation of optimism and hope, and the existence of a unifying Over-Soul which explains the many diverse phenomena of life.

EMERY, GILBERT, pseudonym of Emery Bemsley Pottle (1875–1945), New York playwright, who graduated from Amherst, served in World War I, and in 1921 wrote his first and most successful play, *The Hero.*♦ His later plays include *Queed* (1921), a dramatization of the novel by H.S. Harrison; *Tarnish* (1923), concerned with the triumph of a girl's love over her hatred of her fiancé's weakness; *Episode* (1925), a domestic drama in which a man submits to his wife's indiscretions because he does not wish to disturb their placid social life; *Love-in-a-Mist* (1926), a comedy written in collaboration with Amélie Rives; and *Thank You, Doctor* (1928), a one-act melodramatic farce.

Emigrants, The, novel by Johan Bojer,♦ translated from the Norwegian (1925) by A. G. Jayne.

EMMETT, DANIEL DECATUR (1815–1904), songwriter and early minstrel, was probably the author of "Dixie."♦ Among his songs are "Old Dan Tucker," "The Road to Richmond," "Walk Along, John," and "Here We Are; or Cross Ober Jordan."

Emperor Jones, The, expressionist play by O'Neill,♦ produced in 1920 and published in 1921. An operatic version by Louis Gruenberg was produced in 1933.

The giant black Brutus Jones, former Pullman porter and ex-convict, becomes in two years the feared, autocratic "emperor" of a West Indian island. Exploiting the superstition of the primitive natives, claiming that only a silver bullet can kill him, he enriches himself at their expense, and brags to a cockney trader, Smithers, that when the inevitable rebellion comes he will escape to France, where he has sent a fortune. The uprising suddenly begins, but he is unable to locate his hidden supplies in the forest, where he loses his way. The incessant thumping of a tomtom undermines his courage, and a series of brief, symbolic scenes shows his mental return to earlier phases of his own and his race's history: his murder of another black, Jeff, in a gambling altercation; his escape from a prison chain gang; the slave auction block; the slave ship; the witch doctor and crocodile god in the Congo jungle. In each episode he fires a shot from his pistol, the last silver bullet being fired at the sacred crocodile. During this imaginative retrogression to a savage state, he circles through the forest; emerging where he had entered, he falls riddled by the silver bullets of the rebel tribesmen.

Emperor of Ice Cream, The, poem by Wallace Stevens,♦ published in *Harmonium.*♦ Presenting the body of a slatternly woman at her wake attended by a man who represents pleasure and by wenches who are apparently fellow prostitutes, the refrain declares that the only ruling power is the emperor of ice cream, or physical satisfaction, but it is evident that death is the real ruler and that with it all pretense or seeming must yield to actuality.

Encantadas, The, or Enchanted Isles, sketches by Melville,♦ published under the pseudonym Salvator R. Tarnmoor in *Putnam's Magazine* (1854) and reprinted in *The Piazza Tales* (1856). Seven of the ten sketches are descriptions of the uninhabited Galápagos Islands in the Pacific, "a group rather of extinct volcanoes than of isles; looking much as the world at large might, after a penal conflagration." The remaining three are narratives of people who lived temporarily in the islands. These include a Creole adventurer from Cuba, who acquires title to Charles's Isle, brutally rules his colonists, and is overthrown and banished by them; a half-breed woman who is stranded on Norfolk Isle while searching for tor-

toise oil, and finally rescued by an American ship; and the hermit of Hood's Isle, who enticed and then enslaved deserting sailors, until he in turn was imprisoned by their captains.

Encyclopaedia Britannica, The, founded in Edinburgh in 1768, has grown from the three-volume first edition to 32 volumes (1988). It was first popular in the U.S. in pirated versions, and its first American contributor was Edward Everett on George Washington. Purchased in 1901 by Horace Hooper, an American bookseller, it was for a time conducted under the sponsorship of the London *Times.* Sears, Roebuck, and Co. bought and brought it to Chicago (1920), and in 1943 its ownership passed to William Benton, affiliated with the University of Chicago, which he made the beneficiary of the publication's profits. In 1974 it was revised into a one-volume *Propaedia* (an outline of entries), ten volumes of *Micropaedia* (short entries), and 19 volumes of *Macropaedia* (long entries by authorities). Two volumes were added to the *Micropaedia* in 1988.

Encyclopaedia of the Social Sciences, The, edited by E.R.A. Seligman and Alvin Johnson, was published in 15 volumes (1930–35). It contained articles by outstanding scholars dealing with the primary materials of social study. In 1968 it was revised and expanded to 18 volumes as *International Encyclopedia of the Social Sciences.*

End for Which God Created the World, see *Edwards, Jonathan.*

ENDECOTT, JOHN (*c.*1589–1665), emigrated from England (1628), and was governor of the Massachusetts Bay Colony (1629–30) until the arrival of Winthrop. He held other important posts in the colony and was several times governor. Although an able administrator, he was stern and intolerant, and persecuted Quakers, followers of Thomas Morton, and others who differed in creed. In "Endicott and the Red Cross,"♦ Hawthorne tells the story of his tearing the sign of the cross from the British ensign because he considered it to smack of popery. Robert Lowell made a verse adaptation in "Endicott and the Red Cross" in *The Old Glory* (1965). The first of Longfellow's *New England Tragedies*♦ deals with his persecution of Quakers. Endicott is a variant spelling.

Endicott and the Red Cross, story by Hawthorne,♦ published in *Twice-Told Tales* (1837). It is a brief account of the rebellious gesture of the Puritan governor John Endecott, who, when Charles I decided to send an Anglican governor to England, tore the Red Cross from the British ensign, because he wished to demonstrate the dislike of the Massachusetts Bay colonists for "the idolatrous forms of English Episcopacy." A passage in the tale describes the punishment of an adulteress, later the theme of *The Scarlet Letter.*

ENGLE, PAUL [HAMILTON] (1908–91), Iowa poet and member of the faculty of the University of Iowa, whose *American Song* (1934) won acclaim as the heir of the tradition of *Leaves of Grass,* more because the poet aimed at Whitman's vitality and American quality than because he approached his achievement. While at Oxford as a Rhodes Scholar, Engle wrote in similar verse *Break the Heart's Anger* (1936), protesting against American materialism. In *Corn* (1939) his thought and technique became more controlled, and he was content to express aspects of the simple life of Iowa farmers, while *West of Midnight* (1941), celebrating the "light in American sky" while Europe was blacked out, contains poems in his early manner as well as brief, taut lyrics. *American Child* (1945) is a sonnet sequence about his daughter, enlarged (1956) upon the birth of another daughter; and other lyrics appeared in *The Word of Love* (1951), *Poems in Praise* (1959), *A Prairie Christmas* (1960), *A Woman Unashamed* (1965), and *Embraced* (1969). *Always the Land* (1941) is a novel about conflicts between two generations of Iowa farmers, and *Golden Child* (1962) is a prose tale of Christmas, originally a libretto for a television opera. Later works include *Embrace: Selected Love Poems* (1969) and *Images of China: Poems Written in China, April-June, 1980* (1981).

ENGLISH, THOMAS DUNN (1819–1902), ballad writer, whose most famous poem, "Ben Bolt,"♦ has been set to music 26 different times, once by the author himself. Popular during the Civil War, it was revived by its introduction into Du Maurier's *Trilby.* English wrote many poems and some 50 plays, including *The Mormons* (1858). He is ridiculed as "Thomas Dunn Brown" in Poe's "The Literati."♦

English Traits, lectures by Emerson,♦ delivered in 1848 and published in 1856. Although he sketches his visits to Coleridge, Wordsworth, and Carlyle, the author devotes most of his attention to a keen analysis of the English people and nation, which he strongly admired.

Enjoyment of Poetry, critical study by Max Eastman,♦ published in 1913 and revised in 1921.

Drawing his thesis from a distinction between poetic and practical attitudes, which he claims to be fundamental in human experience, the author states that his purpose is "to increase enjoyment." "That the poetic in every-day perception and conversation should be known for what it is, and not separated from the poetic in literature, is . . . essential to the full appreciation of either." Poetic and practical attitudes dominate different types of people, but prevail in the childhood of all. The artist and the scientist differ in this way, as is evident in the history of words, which are poetic when newly applied, but lose their connotative value through repetitive and exacting use. The poetic impulse is defined as the impulse to realize,

and rhythms, figures of speech, and other poetic techniques are shown to be valuable in attaining this end. Finally "the knowledge of poetry" is related "to the art of enjoying it" and to the supreme aim of life, "an enthusiastic welcome of the world as it is or as it may be. . . ."

Enormous Room, The, autobiographical narrative by E.E. Cummings,♦ published in 1922.

As members of an American ambulance corps in France during World War I, the author and a friend are erroneously suspected of treasonable correspondence, and imprisoned by the French (Aug. 1917–Jan. 1918) in a concentration camp at La Ferté Macé, 100 miles west of Paris. Their fellow prisoners include the hyper-refined Count Bragard, the belligerent Fighting Sheeney, the tragic gypsy Wanderer and his family, the inarticulate but expressive Zulu, the servile, clownish Surplice, and the childish giant Jean le Nègre. All suffer under the needlessly cruel stresses of captivity, inhumane treatment by the officials and *plantons* (jailers), and the extremely filthy surroundings. Nevertheless they maintain the idiosyncratic beauties and humors of individual character, which the author exalts as the highest human values. The narrative is set in the form of a pilgrimage, and the intended resemblance to Bunyan's *Pilgrim's Progress* appears in the presentation of the *Directeur* as the fiend Apollyon, and of certain remarkable prisoners as the Delectable Mountains.

ENSLIN, THEODORE [VERNON] (1925–   ), Pennsylvania-born poet, resident in Maine. Influenced by Olson, his first poems were published by Cid Corman,♦ and, like his, are often spare meditations. He has published a great number of slim collections since *The Work Proposed* (1958), including five parts of *Forms* (1970–74).

Epic of the Wheat, The, see *Norris, Frank.*

Episcopal Methodist Church, see *Methodism.*

Episcopalians, see *Protestant Episcopal Church.*

Equality, novel by E. Bellamy.♦

EQUIANO, OLAUDAH [GUSTAVAS VASSA] (1745?–1801?), taken from his West African homeland of Benin by slave traders at age 10, was renamed and belonged to several masters, including a Quaker from Philadelphia who oversaw his rudimentary education. In 1789 was published *The Interesting Narrative of Olaudah Equiano, or Gustavas Vassa, the African.* Now regarded as the first book of true note in the genre of slave narratives, Equiano's *Narrative* had gone through eight printings by 1794, with many to follow on both sides of the Atlantic. The *Narrative* is full of riveting detail told in a naturally gifted style; his opposition to slavery is implicit, to be sure, but he remained through all his travels and adventures a self-conscious African. His narrative is especially rare in its genre in recounting an African childhood.

Era of Good Feelings, see *Monroe, James.*

ERDRICH, LOUISE (1954–   ), of German and Chippewa descent, grew up in Wahpeton, North Dakota, in the Turtle Mountain Band of Chippewa. She graduated from Dartmouth College in 1976. In 1984 her collection of poems *Jacklight,* was published. *Love Medicine,* her first book of fiction, also published in 1984, won the National Book Critics Circle Award, and established her reputation. *Love Medicine* is a series of free-standing narratives told by various voices of two families, the Kashpaws and the Lamartines, living on a N.D. reservation between 1934 and 1984. The characters appear in one another's stories. Sadness, humor, and despair of a dispossessed people are well chronicled. The series of stories is continued in *The Beet Queen* (1986) and *Tracks* (1988). *The Bingo Palace* (1994) completes the tetralogy begun with *Love Medicine.* Lyman Lamartine now owns a bingo parlor, but another member of the Chippewa, Lipsha Morrissey, is the central character, come home from a factory job in Fargo in search of a meaningful life. Magic realism figures prominently in the pattern that finally links the characters and their land into a loving community.

Erie Canal, from Albany to Buffalo, connects the Hudson River with Lake Erie. Gouverneur Morris first conceived the idea (1777), and Washington approved a plan suggested in 1783, as a means of unifying the nation. Governor Clinton authorized a thorough survey (1791), and work was begun two years later, but progress was slow until De Witt Clinton made the canal an issue in the gubernatorial campaign of 1817. The canal was opened in 1825, after an expenditure of more than $7,000,000 to create its length of 352 miles. Largely responsible for the commerce of New York state, it also did much to unify the interest of seaboard communities and the western country. During a later enlargement of the channel, politics entered into the management, and a fraudulent "canal ring" was disclosed in the mid-19th century. Herbert Quick's novel *Vandemark's Folly* ♦ and other fiction by W.D. Edmonds and Samuel Hopkins Adams deal with the great days of the Erie Canal, before the growth of railroads. There is also the well-known "Erie Canal Ballad."

Essays To Do Good, see *Bonifacius.*

Established Church of England, see *Protestant Episcopal Church.*

Esther, novel by Henry Adams, ♦ published in 1884 under the pseudonym Frances Snow Compton. The character of the heroine is modeled on the author's wife, and that of Wharton on the sculptor Saint-Gaudens.

Esther Dudley, a young painter, is introduced to Stephen Hazard, preacher at St. John's in New York City, whom she at first dislikes because he is absorbed in religious work, while she shares the free-thinking of her invalid father. When Esther is commissioned to work on the decoration at St. John's, under the direction of the prominent artist Wharton, she uses as a model her friend Catherine Brooke. During the progress of the work, Wharton falls in love with Catherine, while Esther becomes friendly with Stephen, who is enthusiastic about her painting and visits her father. After the latter's death she becomes engaged to the clergyman but soon realizes that their views of life are incompatible. In spite of their love, attempts at reconciliation fail, and Stephen announces that he will not trouble her again until she stands in need of his and the church's consolations.

***Eternal Goodness,** The,* poem by Whittier. ♦

***Ethan Brand:** A Chapter from an Abortive Romance,* story by Hawthorne, ♦ published in *The Snow-Image* (1851).

Ethan Brand, formerly a lime-burner, has sought the Unpardonable Sin, and now returns to his New England home, announcing that he has found it in his own soul, in intellectual pride and in the separation of mind and heart. The townspeople do not understand him and consider him mad. He takes the place of his successor at the limekiln, and during the night lies down to perish in the furnace. When the other lime-burner returns in the morning, he finds the lime all burnt snow-white, and on its surface a human skeleton within whose ribs is a piece of marble in the shape of a heart.

Ethan Frome, novelette by Edith Wharton, ♦ published in 1911. It was dramatized by Owen and Donald Davis (1936).

This grim story is told by a middle-aged engineer, who pieces together the history of the inhabitants of a bleak Massachusetts farm. Zenobia (Zeena) is a whining slattern who hugs imaginary ailments to her barren breast, and spends upon quacks and patent medicines the scant substance her husband, Ethan Frome, manages to wring from the grudging earth. Her cousin Mattie Silver is left destitute and comes to live with them. The friendship of Ethan and Mattie arouses Zeena's jealousy, and after a year Mattie is ousted to make way for a strong hired girl. On their way to the railroad station, Ethan and Mattie realize that they cannot bear to part, and when they are coasting down their favorite snow slide he purposely steers their sled into a great elm. Instead of being killed, they are crippled for life, and spend the remainder of their unhappy days on the barren farm under Zeena's surveillance.

Ethnogenesis, ode by Timrod, ♦ written in 1861 during the meeting of the first Confederate Congress, and published in his *Poems* (1873). It enthusiastically hails the new nation, optimistically proclaiming its inevitable victory in the war, and celebrates the character of the Southern people and the perfection of soil and climate in the South.

Eureka: A Prose Poem, metaphysical work by Poe, ♦ published in 1848.

Based on the author's reading in Newton, Laplace, and others, the work accepts intuition, as well as induction and deduction, among legitimate paths to knowledge. Unity and diffusion are truths, because they are felt to be so, and "irradiation, by which alone these two truths are reconciled, is a consequent truth—I perceive it." The universe, composed of atoms radiated outward from a primary divine unity to an almost infinite variety, is conceived to be governed by the complementary laws of attraction and repulsion, in terms of which all phenomena are explicable. This is shown by mathematical proof, and by reference to the principles of heat, light, and electricity. This view of a harmoniously ordered, perfect universe is then extended in a discussion of literary criticism, especially applied to fiction. "In the construction of plot . . . we should aim at so arranging the incidents that we shall not be able to determine, of any one of them, whether it depends from any one other or upholds it." The view has also an ethical application: "God—the material *and* spiritual God—*now* exists solely in the diffused Matter and Spirit of the Universe," and the regathering of these elements will reconstitute "the *purely* Spiritual and individual God," so that the operations of "Divine Injustice" or "Inexorable Fate" may at last be understood. We "no longer rebel at a *Sorrow* which we ourselves have imposed upon ourselves," and "in this view alone the existence of Evil becomes intelligible . . . it becomes endurable."

Europeans, The: A Sketch, novel by Henry James, ♦ published in 1878.

Eugenia, Baroness Münster, an expatriated American, is the morganatic wife of a German prince, who is about to repudiate her in favor of a state marriage. With her artist brother Felix Young she goes to Boston to visit relatives whom she has never before seen, in hopes of making a wealthy marriage. Mr. Wentworth, their uncle, establishes Eugenia and Felix in a nearby house, and his children, Gertrude, Charlotte, and Clifford, soon become intimate with them. Felix, gay and debonaire, enriches himself by painting flattering portraits of the Bostonians, and is involved in a love affair with Gertrude. Mr. Acton, a friend of the Wentworths and himself somewhat a man of the world, is attracted to Eugenia, who also makes a near-conquest of Clifford, an awkward youth suspended from Harvard for drunkenness.

She overplays her hand with Acton, who realizes her deceitfulness and attempts to stay away from her. Clifford, too, is not to be snared, and becomes engaged to Acton's sister Lizzie. Gertrude weds Felix, after refusing the minister, Mr. Brand, who marries Charlotte. Eugenia returns to Europe, feeling that her fortune-hunting scheme is impractical in unsusceptible America.

Eutaw, novel by Simms, ♦ published in 1856 as a sequel to *The Forayers,* ♦ one of his Revolutionary Romances.

The British face defeat in their attempt to hold the Carolinas, and the Tory villain Inglehardt tortures his prisoners, Henry Travis and his father, to force their consent to his marriage with Henry's sister Bertha. The elder Travis slowly loses his mind under the strain. Inglehardt's desperate confederate, Hell-Fire Dick, is converted to religion by Henry. Colonel Sinclair, Tory planter, leaves home in an attempt to reach safety with his daughters Carrie and Lottie and joins the British troops, only to witness their defeat. At the home of the "Widow Avinger," really Mrs. Travis, the Sinclairs become friendly with Bertha, whose marriage to the colonel's son Willie they have formerly opposed. Bertha is kidnapped, however, by Hell-Fire Dick, who takes her to Inglehardt. After the indecisive Battle of Eutaw Springs, Willie is guided to the camp by a wandering, half-mad girl, Nelly Floyd, who is killed while seeking her brother. The elder Travis, insanely attempting to kill Inglehardt, is himself killed, but Willie rescues Bertha and they marry.

Eutaw Springs, Battle of, Revolutionary War action in South Carolina (Sept. 8, 1781), in which the Americans under Greene unsuccessfully attacked a British force. The British failed to secure their gains, fell back to Charleston, and gave the Americans a strategic victory. The battle is described in Simms's romance *Eutaw,* ♦ a play by William Ioor, and poems by Simms and Freneau.

Eva St. Clare (LITTLE EVA), character in *Uncle Tom's Cabin.* ♦

Evangeline, A Tale of Acadie, narrative poem in unrhymed English hexameters, by Longfellow, ♦ published in 1847. Material was drawn from works by T.C. Haliburton, Schoolcraft, and possibly Chateaubriand, while Goethe's *Hermann und Dorothea* was a strong influence on the verse and manner of treatment. The subject was known to Hawthorne, who suggested it to Longfellow. A dramatization was made in 1860 by Sidney Frances Bateman.

Evangeline, daughter of Benedict Bellefontaine, is about to be married to Gabriel Lajeunesse, son of Basil, the blacksmith of the Acadian village of Grand Pré, when, during the French and Indian War, the English exile the French residents to safer British colonies. The lovers are separated, and Gabriel and Basil make their way to Louisiana, while Evangeline continues to seek them. Finding Basil, she goes with him on further quests and alone to the Michigan woods. Years of fruitless wandering cause her to become prematurely old, and she settles in Philadelphia as a Sister of Mercy. There, during a pestilence, she recognizes a dying old man as her former lover. The shock of his death kills her, and, united at last, they are buried together in the Catholic cemetery.

EVANS, AUGUSTA JANE (1835–1909), Alabama author of sentimental, moralistic novels, which include *Inez: A Tale of the Alamo* (1855), *Beulah* (1859), *Macaria; or, Altars of Sacrifice* (1864), and the enormously popular *St. Elmo*♦ (1867).

EVANS, CHARLES (1850–1935), born in Boston, was a librarian at the Boston Athenaeum, the Public Library of Indianapolis, and the Enoch Pratt Free Library (Baltimore). His *American Bibliography* (12 vols., 1903–4) chronologically catalogues 35,854 titles of works printed in America (1639–1799). Volume 13 (1799–1800) was added by Clifford K. Shipton (1954), who with James E. Mooney compiled a short-title *Index* (2 vols., 1969).

EVANS, DONALD (1884–1921), born in Philadelphia, became a leading Greenwich Village aesthete who supported himself as a journalist and music critic and who was significant as a poet. His friends included Mabel Dodge and Carl Van Vechten, about each of whom he wrote a verse "Portrait." His urbane, elegant poetry, a reminiscence of the *fin de siècle* and an anticipation of Wallace Stevens,♦ appeared in *Discords* (1912), *Sonnets from the Patagonian* (1914), *Two Deaths in the Bronx* (1916), *Nine Poems from a Valetudinarium* (1916), and *Ironica* (1919). His brief career ended by suicide.

EVANS, GEORGE HENRY (1805–56), editor of the *Working Man's Advocate* and other newspapers devoted to the interests of labor. His *History of the . . . Working Men's Party* (1840) opposed Fourieristic ideas of association and based its theories on Paine's individualism and Jefferson's agrarianism. In his agitation for "free homesteads," Evans foreshadowed Henry George's "single tax."

EVANS, NATHANIEL (1742–67), born in Philadelphia, graduated from the University of Pennsylvania, and became a clergyman of the Church of England. He edited the works of his friend Godfrey (1765), and his own *Poems on Several Occasions, with Some Other Compositions* was posthumously published (1772).

Eve Effingham, English title of *Home as Found.* ♦

EVERETT, ALEXANDER HILL (1790–1847), Boston diplomat, essayist, editor, and educator whose diplomatic experience in Russia, Holland, and Spain (1809–29) furnished the basis of the books *Europe* (1822) and *America* (1827). As an editor of *The North American Review* he contributed translations from European and Oriental literatures that influenced the Transcendentalist movement, as well as the material collected in *Essays, Critical and Miscellaneous* (1845–46).

EVERETT, EDWARD (1794–1865), brother of Alexander Hill Everett, as a young man distinguished himself as a Unitarian minister, professor of Greek at Harvard (1819–26), and editor of *The North American Review* (1820–23), before entering upon his political career. After serving in Congress (1825–35), he became governor of Massachusetts (1836–39) and, despite much Northern opposition because of his careful conciliatory stand on slavery, he was appointed minister to England (1841–45). He was president of Harvard (1846–49), but returned to politics to complete Webster's term as secretary of state (1852–53) and was U.S. senator from Massachusetts (1853–54). Throughout his career he was criticized for his policies of compromise, but he was widely admired for his florid orations (including the lengthy speech that Lincoln followed with his brief Gettysburg Address), collected in four volumes (1836–68).

Evergreen Review (1957–73), literary magazine, a quarterly to 1959, thereafter a bimonthly. Edited by Barney Rossett of Grove Press (New York City), it published fiction, poetry, drama, criticism, interviews, and occasional photo portfolios, emphasizing the avant-garde and foreign authors. In the 1970s it gave much attention to liberal political commentary, civil liberties, and counterculture.

EVERSON, WILLIAM (1912–94), California poet whose career began in part influenced by the pantheism and long poetic line of Jeffers,♦ later celebrated in an elegy, *The Poet Is Dead* (1964), and a critical study, *Robinson Jeffers: Fragments of an Older Fury* (1968), as well as later editing and annotation of Jeffers's writings. Everson's early poems (1934–40) were collected in *Single Source* (1966). During World War II he was a conscientious objector and while at a camp in Waldport, Ore., issued his own *War Elegies* (1943) and *Waldport Poems* (1944), the printing a crude forerunner of his distinguished handpress printing of the late 1940s to '70s. Later poems, some of his own printing, include *The Residual Years* (1948), *A Privacy of Speech* (1949), *Triptych for the Living* (1951), *The Crooked Lines of God* (1959), and *The Hazards of Holiness* (1962), marked by rhapsodic, mystic, and erotic power as well as by regional imagery, and particularly by his religious exaltation that took him into the Catholic church.

From 1951 to 1971 he was a Dominican lay brother, writing under the name of Brother Antoninus further poems collected in *The Rose of Solitude* (1967), *The Last Crusade* (1969), and other volumes. In 1974 appeared *Man-Fate,* his swan song of religious life. Later works, written while he taught both poetry and printing at the University of California, Santa Cruz, include the long and powerful poem of human love *River-Root* (1976), with explicit erotic imagery, and *The Marks of Drought: Poems 1972–1979* (1980). *On Writing the Waterbirds* (1983) collects forewords and afterwords of all periods.

Every Saturday (1866–74), eclectic weekly magazine, edited at Boston by Aldrich.♦ Its literary contributions were mainly pirated from foreign authors, but it specialized in original pictorial material.

Everybody's (1899–1928), founded as a house organ of Wanamaker's department store, but became an independent magazine (1903). This was during the muckraking period, and *Everybody's* enthusiastically entered the movement, publishing T.W. Lawson's series on "Frenzied Finance" (1904–5) and articles by Upton Sinclair, Ben Lindsey, Lincoln Steffens, and others. After 1910 it turned to popular fiction, and soon became a widely circulated journal featuring stories and general articles. This policy was continued until it was absorbed by the journal *Romance.*

Excelsior, poem by Longfellow,♦ published in *Ballads and Other Poems* (1841). In four-stress iambic couplets, with the title as a refrain, the poem figuratively depicts the life of a man of genius, as he maintains his individualistic purpose, resisting temptations and ignoring warnings. Climbing the mountain of his career, he passes beyond the village and the monastery, repeating his idealistic motto, until he is found dead on the highest glacier. Even then a voice is heard from the sky, proclaiming the motto as a promise of immortality.

Excursions, essays by Thoreau,♦ posthumously collected in 1863, with a biographical preface by Emerson. The pieces had appeared in various magazines during Thoreau's lifetime, being expanded from journal notes on such subjects as "Natural History of Massachusetts," "A Walk to Wachusett," "The Succession of Forest Trees,"

"Walking," "Wild Apples," "May Days," and "Days and Nights in Concord."

Executioner's Song, The, fictive biography by Norman Mailer.♦

Exile's Return, a partly autobiographical narrative of the "lost generation" by Malcolm Cowley.♦

Existentialism, European philosophic movement with various schools or attitudes of different eras, including the Christian concepts of Kierkegaard and Maritain, but affecting American literature primarily in terms of an atheistic view shared with or influenced by Sartre and Camus. Holding that there are no accepted bases to explain the mysteries of human existence and that the individual must develop his being free of society, existentialism contends that solitariness makes the right condition for freedom of choice. However, it also brings anguish to the individual as he recognizes the futility of attempting to treat the paradoxes of a meaningless universe and an absurd world and to achieve self-mastery in an atmosphere of entire freedom. Such views and such a sense of metaphysical isolation in the consideration of the individual in the present moment are found in the fiction of Saul Bellow, Paul Bowles, Ralph Ellison, William Styron, and Richard Wright. Frequently using the monologue to show the protagonist's growing consciousness of the human condition, since thought rather than action is dominant in existential fiction, their novels deal with depersonalization, alienation from society and belief in divinity, and an individual search for identity.

Expressionism, aesthetic movement in which the artist expresses his inner experience through the free representation of objective facts. Since it emphasizes the creator's mood and attitude, the movement is a development of Impressionism,♦ from which it differs by being more concerned with individual intellectual conceptions, and less with the structure of exterior facts. Both movements belong to the later phase of romanticism. Expressionism originated in European painting, and was brought to the U.S. by painters. Although exemplified in literature by T.S. Eliot and other poets, it has been more influential in the theater, in the work of such stage designers as R.E. Jones and in the dramatic technique of such plays as *The Hairy Ape, The Emperor Jones, The Adding Machine,* and *Beggar on Horseback.*

F

Fable, A, novel by Faulkner,♦ published in 1954 and awarded a Pulitzer Prize.

Under the pacifist influence of a corporal and his 12 followers in 1918, a French regiment refuses to attack the Germans, who for the same reason do not counterattack. The commander, concerned with his military record, requests that the entire regiment be executed, but the supreme French general, who knows the corporal to be his natural son and who has come to believe in the inextricable mingling of human rapacity and idealism, heads the tribunal considering the case. Wise and not without compassion, yet utterly cynical, he sees war not only as a political and economic necessity but as "so long ingrained in man as to have become an honorable tenet of his behavior and the national altar for his love of bloodshed and glorious sacrifice." Having been warned of the pacifist plan by a betrayer among the corporal's 12 men, he collaborates with the German command to resume the war on the continued bases of national hatred and narrow idealism for the armies and people, and a disillusioned yet god-like way of life for the aristocracy of senior officers. Discovering this deception, a young British flyer commits suicide. A British runner is convinced by the corporal's example that soldiers can end war if they simply throw down their weapons and meet between the lines, and having persuaded a handful of men to follow him, he is horribly injured when artillery on both sides shell the peacemakers. Also killed in this barrage are a taciturn British sentry and a black lay preacher, whose remarkable adventure in America with a superb, stolen racehorse is a long interpolated tale. As the local populace turns against the corporal, fearing that the whole regiment will be shot because of him, a reenactment of the Passion of Christ develops and becomes ramified. Wed to a woman named Magda, and already betrayed, the corporal is denied by the betrayer as he conducts a "last supper" in prison, and then is taken by the old general to a hilltop fortress to be tempted with life at the expense of his exalted hope for man's repudiation of war and urged to abandon "that aberrant and futile dream" that "man . . . will prevail." Unrelenting, the corporal is shot along with two criminals and given surreptitious but decent burial. But the resumption of war, in the form of an explosion near the grave, "resurrects" him, and through a combination of chance and the greed of men assigned to get the body of an unknown soldier, he is entombed beneath the everlasting flame in Paris.

Fable for Critics, A, verse satire by Lowell,♦ published anonymously in 1848. Its eccentric "slap-dash" rhythm has been characterized as a "genial anapestic gait," and the rhymes are equally careless, but besides the humor there are shrewd critical estimates of such contemporary authors as Holmes ("His are just the fine hands, too, to weave you a lyric Full of fancy, fun, feeling, or spiced with satiric"); Emerson ("A Greek head on right Yankee shoulders"); Alcott (". . . I believe no man ever talked better; Each sentence hangs perfectly poised to the letter"); Longfellow ("Why, he'll live till men weary of Collins and Gray"); Bryant ("A smooth, silent iceberg, that never is ignified"); Margaret Fuller ("She always keeps asking if I don't observe a Particular likeness 'twixt her and Minerva"); Irving ("To a true poet-heart add the fun of Dick Steele, Throw in all of Addison, *minus* the chill"); Whittier ("A fervor of mind which knows no separation 'Twixt simple excitement and pure inspiration"); Poe (". . . with his raven, like Barnaby Rudge, Three-fifths of him genius, and two-fifths sheer fudge"); Hawthorne ("His strength is so tender, his wildness so meek . . . He's a John Bunyan Fouqué, a Puritan Tieck"); Cooper ("He has drawn you one character, though, that is new . . . He has done naught but copy it ill ever since"); and Lowell himself (". . . who's striving Parnassus to climb With a whole bale of *isms* tied together with rhyme . . ."). A disputed passage concerning two anonymous authors is considered to deal with Thoreau and W.E. Channing ("Fie, for shame, brother bard; with good fruit of your own, Can't you let Neighbor Emerson's orchards alone?"). The fable in which these comments are set deals with a gathering of the gods on Olympus, whereat a critic, worshipper of Apollo, attempts to satisfy the god's desire for a lily. The critic searches assiduously, passing the various authors in review, and at last produces a thistle. Apollo is disgusted, speaks of the happy period before the advent of critics, and the gods disperse. A similar plan is followed by Amy Lowell in her *Critical Fable.*

Fables for Our Time, and Famous Poems Illustrated, by James Thurber,♦ published in 1940.

Twenty-eight brief, wry, witty fables in the style of a modern Aesop, illustrated by the author, whose indicative titles include "The Fairly Intelligent Fly" and "The Rabbits Who Caused All the Trouble." The nine poems, so popular as to be platitudinous, like "Excelsior" and "Curfew Must Not Ring To-Night," are printed with illustrative embellishments by Thurber. In 1956 he published *Further Fables for Our Time.*

Fables in Slang, sketches by George Ade. ◆

Facing West from California's Shores, poem by Whitman, ◆ published in the "Children of Adam" section of *Leaves of Grass* (1860), and given its present title in the 1867 edition.

The poet, "a child, very old . . . long having wander'd," represents himself as symbolic of mankind looking backward "towards the house of eternity," the mystic Orient, from the vigorous utilitarian West, and questioning where he is to find fulfilled his search for the complete man. The poem thus foreshadows the theme of "Passage to India." ◆ Its being placed in the "Children of Adam" section indicates that Whitman believed the instinct of sex to be both the physical and the spiritual force of creative progress in man and nature.

Fair God, The; or, The Last of the Tzins, romance by Lew Wallace, ◆ was published in 1873, although it had been begun in 1843 under the influence of reading Prescott. Based on research and on the author's knowledge of Mexico, the romance is concerned with the invasion of the Aztec empire by Cortés and his defeat by the prince Guatamozin, who kills his weak uncle Montezuma in a vain attempt to save his country.

FAIRBANK, JANET AYER (1879–1951), Chicago novelist, sister of Margaret Ayer Barnes. Her novels are *The Cortlands of Washington Square* (1923); *The Smiths* (1925); *The Lion's Den* (1930); *The Bright Land* (1932), about a mid-19th century woman from her girlhood in New Hampshire to later life on the Illinois frontier; and *Rich Man, Poor Man* (1936), about the suffragist movement and reforms of the early Progressive party. *Idle Hands* (1927) is a collection of stories.

FAIRFIELD, SUMNER LINCOLN (1803–44), born in Massachusetts, lived an insecure life, by turns teacher, actor, magazine publisher (*North American Magazine,* 1832–38), was the author of some ten volumes of verse, including *The Siege of Constantinople* (1822); *The Cities of the Plain* (1827), on the destruction of Sodom and Gomorrah; and *The Last Night of Pompeii* (1832), which he accused Bulwer-Lytton of plagiarizing. Duyckinck considered that "his imagination was active but undisciplined, and led him to undertake comprehensive and powerful themes which required greater judgment than he had." His *Poems and Prose Writings* were collected in 1841 and his widow wrote a *Life* in 1874.

Falconer, novel by John Cheever, ◆ published in 1977.

Ezekiel Farragut, descended from a wealthy, aristocratic New England family that fell on hard times and has been reduced to operating a gas station on its Cape Cod estate, by the age of 48 has served overseas with the army in World War II, where he contracted a drug addiction, become a university professor, and married, though unhappily, a beautiful woman, Marcia, and is the father of a son, Peter. At that age he is also confined to Falconer State Prison in Connecticut for the murder of his older brother Eben, who had taunted him with being their parents' unwanted child. In prison he is cured of his drug addiction but becomes involved homosexually with another inmate, Jody, until his friend escapes. Some time later a cellmate dies. Farragut removes the body from its shroud, zips himself in its place, and upon being carried out of the prison faces his future with a fearless sense of freedom.

FALKNER, WILLIAM CLARK (1825–89), great-grandfather of William Faulkner and prototype of Colonel Sartoris, was a Mississippi army officer, lawyer, and railroad builder, and author of *The White Rose of Memphis* (1880), a popular melodramatic novel; *The Little Brick Church* (1882), a reply to *Uncle Tom's Cabin;* and *Rapid Ramblings in Europe* (1884).

Fall of British Tyranny, The; or, American Liberty Triumphant, unproduced tragi-comedy attributed to John or Joseph Leacock of Philadelphia, was published in 1776. It was the first American chronicle play, covering the period from the Battle of Lexington to the evacuation of Boston.

Lord Catspaw (Lord North) plots with Judas (Governor Hutchinson) to mislead the cabinet concerning the purpose and strength of the American colonists, while Lord Justice (Camden), Lord Patriot (Wilkes), Bold Irishman (Burke), and Lord Wisdom (Pitt) show themselves to be friends of the Americans. The scene is then shifted to America, with a similar argument between a Whig and a Tory. The Battle of Lexington and the progress of the Revolution in Virginia are described, and, after a scene in which Lord Boston (Gage), Elbow Room (Howe), and Mr. Caper (Burgoyne) upbraid each other for failure of the royal cause, there is a scene at the Cambridge camp of the patriots, with flattering portrayals of Washington, Charles Lee, and Putnam.

Fall of the House of Usher, The, story by Poe, ◆ published in 1839, and reprinted in *Tales of the Grotesque and Arabesque* (1840). It contains the poem "The Haunted Palace." ◆

A childhood companion of Roderick Usher, who has not seen him for many years, is summoned to the gloomy House of Usher to comfort his sick friend. The decayed mansion stands on the edge of a tarn, and is fungus-grown and dreary. Roderick and his twin Madeline are the only surviving members of the family, and both suffer serious physical and nervous maladies. Roderick entertains his friend with curious musical and poetic improvisations, indicating his morbid tastes by his choice of reading. Madeline, in a cataleptic trance, is thought to be dead, and her body is placed in the family vault. During a storm, Roderick is overcome by a severe nervous agitation, and his friend reads aloud from a medieval romance, whose horrifying episodes coincide with strange sounds from outside the room. Finally Madeline appears, enshrouded, and she and her brother fall dead together. The friend rushes from the house, and, as he looks back in the moonlight, sees the whole House of Usher split asunder and sink into the tarn.

Family Reunion, The, verse play by T.S. Eliot,♦ produced and published in 1939.

Harry, Lord Monchensey, returns to his English country home, after eight years abroad following the death at sea of his young wife. The occasion is the birthday of his mother, Amy, imperious matriarch of the family, which also includes her sisters, Ivy, Violet, and Agatha, the last being principal of a women's college; her brothers-in-law, Gerald and Charles Piper; and the penniless cousin Mary. Harry does not conceal his contempt for the others, and shows his neurotic, guilt-ridden condition by a blurted confession that he murdered his wife. He has returned in search of inner peace, but the avenging spirits (Eumenides) now become visible, even to Agatha and Mary, although not to the others. Anxious for her son's sanity, Amy summons Dr. Warburton, and the doctor warns Harry that any sudden emotion may kill his mother. Harry and Agatha have a talk, and he discovers the basis of their sympathy when she reveals that his father had loved her, not Amy, who had used him merely to have the children and home she desired. The father's frustrated desire to murder his wife seems to have been inherited by the son, whose sense of guilt is part of the fated atonement. Harry departs to complete his "pilgrimage of expiation," and the shock kills Amy, at which the family unity she has sustained is destroyed.

Fanny, satirical poem by F.G. Halleck.♦

Fanny Fern, see *Willis, Sara P.*

Fanshawe, romance by Hawthorne,♦ published anonymously in 1828. It was probably written during the author's college years, and the background resembles Bowdoin.

Ellen Langton comes to live with a friend of her father, Dr. Melmouth, orthodox minister and head of Harley College. Her principal suitors are Edward Walcott, a normal young gentlemen, and Fanshawe, a scholarly ascetic who now begins to lead a more worldly life, although he realizes that he can never have much in common with Ellen. The three are walking one day in the woods when an enemy of Ellen's father attempts to kidnap her. Fanshawe rescues her, and the kidnapper is killed in a fall from a precipice. Mr. Langton arrives, but Fanshawe refuses his offer of money. When Ellen offers to marry him, Fanshaw refuses because of their incompatibility. He goes away, devotes himself to his studies, and soon dies. A few years later, Ellen and Edward marry.

Fantastic Fables, stories by Bierce.♦

FANTE, JOHN (1909–83), novelist long resident in California, the setting of his fiction, including *Wait Until Spring, Bandini* (1938) and *Ask the Dust* (1939), novels of Italian-American workers; *Full of Life* (1952), a light tale of a man's adjustment to his wife's pregnancy; and *Bravo Burro* (1969). *Dago Red* (1940) prints stories of an Italian-American family in Fante's native Colorado and was retitled in the 1980s *The Wine of Youth.* His later career was that of a screenwriter but he became blind (1978) and his last authorship was dictated. Results include the novels *The Brotherhood of the Grape* (1977), *Dreams from Bunker Hill* (1982), and *West of Rome* (1986). Two novellas appeared in *The Road to Los Angeles* (1985), derived in part from a novel written in the 1930s.

Far North, see *North Woods.*

Far West, region bounded by the Rocky Mountains, the Pacific Ocean, and the Northwest♦ and Southwest♦ regions, includes California, Nevada, and Utah, and parts of Idaho, Montana, Wyoming, and Colorado. The region varies from the desert wastes of Nevada to the forested Sierra Nevada and fertile valleys of California, and there are rich areas devoted to cattle raising, mining, and agriculture. Industrial activities are associated with the principal cities, San Francisco♦ and Los Angeles.♦ The earliest explorers on the Pacific coast were Cabrillo and Drake, but the Spanish did not effect their occupation until Serra began founding the California missions (1769). The Mission Indians figure in such romances as *Ramona* and *Isidro,* and California life during the Spanish period, described from personal observation by Dana in *Two Years Before the Mast,* is also depicted in the histories of H.H. Bancroft and the novels of Gertrude Atherton and Stewart Edward White. During the Mexican War, the province was seized by the U.S., following the declaration of the Bear Flag Republic. The gold rush of the forty-niners♦ marks the initial development of Far Western resources. Besides such factual accounts as the journals of Captain Sutter and Dame Shirley, and Bayard Taylor's *Eldorado,* these events gave rise to the frontier school of authors, which included Bret Harte, Clemens, and Joaquin Miller. Later gold rushes took place at Virginia City and Pikes Peak, and silver and copper were also discovered, but the principal development of the Far West was now in cattle and sheep ranching on the plains and deserts, and irrigated agriculture in California and in Utah, where the Mormons♦ founded their colony in 1847. John Muir and Clarence King have dealt with the Sierra Nevada; Mary Hallock Foote's fiction tells of Idaho and Colorado life; Vardis Fisher and Bernard DeVoto have written of Utah and Idaho; Walter Van Tilburg Clark sets his novels in Nevada; and 20th-century California authors include Alice Adams, Gertrude Atherton, Mary Austin, Bierce, Brautigan, Gelett Burgess, Evan Connell, Joan Didion, William Everson, Ferlinghetti, Oakley Hall, Jeffers, London, Norris, Saroyan, Schulberg, Upton Sinclair, Gary Snyder, Wallace Stegner, Steinbeck, George Sterling, and George R. Stewart.

Farewell Address, issued by Washington♦ to the people of the U.S. on his retirement from the presidency, was first published in *Claypoole's American Daily Advertiser* (Sept. 17, 1796). This monument of American policy, probably written with the aid of Hamilton and Madison, explains Washington's course as President, emphasizes the need for a firm central government, warns against party strife, and inveighs against "entangling alliances" with foreign governments.

Farewell to Arms, A, novel by Hemingway,♦ published in 1929, and dramatized by Laurence Stallings (1930).

Frederic Henry, an American lieutenant in the Italian ambulance service during World War I, falls in love with an English nurse, Catherine Barkley. She returns his feeling, and when Henry, wounded during a bombardment, is sent to a hospital at Milan, Catherine comes to nurse him. They spend a happy summer together while he recuperates, and in the autumn Catherine confesses that she is pregnant, but will not marry him, fearing to be sent back to England. Henry returns to his post, finds his comrade Rinaldi depressed by the monotonous horrors of the war, and shares the suffering during the disastrous retreat from Caporetto. He deserts, learns that Catherine has been transferred to Stresa, and joins her there. Although he is in civilian clothes, he is suspected, and forced to flee with Catherine to Switzerland. They go to Lausanne for the birth of their child, but both mother and baby die, leaving Henry desolate and alone in a strange land.

FARLEY, HARRIET (1817–1907), factory worker of Lowell, Mass., who edited the *Lowell Offering* (1842–45), which became the *New England Offering* (1847–50), a periodical of the writings of the women mill hands. *Mind Amongst the Spindles* (1844) collects some of these. Her own articles and tales were published as *Shells from the Strand of the Sea of Genius* (1847) and *Happy Nights at Hazel Nook* (1852).

Farm Ballads, verses by Will Carleton. ♦

Farmer in Pennsylvania, see *Letters from a Farmer in Pennsylvania.*

Farmer's Almanack (1793–   ), Massachusetts almanac, founded by Robert Bailey Thomas (1766–1846), and still published with his name as editor. It has later been called *The Old Farmer's Almanac,* to distinguish it from its many imitators, and issued from New Hampshire. Its importance as a source of information on New England life and manners appears in G.L. Kittredge's *The Old Farmer and His Almanack* (1904).

Farmer's Weekly Museum (1793–1810), newspaper of Walpole, N.H., was founded by Isaiah Thomas. Among its contributions were essays by T.G. Fessenden, John Davis, and Joseph Dennie and Royall Tyler, who wrote under the pseudonyms Colon and Spondee. Dennie was editor (1796–98), and continued to be associated with the paper, for which he wrote his "Lay Preacher" essays.

FARQUHARSON, MARTHA, see *Finley.*

FARRELL, JAMES T[HOMAS] (1904–79), Chicago novelist in the naturalist tradition, studied at the University of Chicago, and held several jobs as clerk, salesman, and newspaper reporter. His experiences as a baseball enthusiast and pupil of Catholic schools on the city's South Side are the basis of *Young Lonigan♦* (1932). This naturalistic stream-of-consciousness study of an adolescent in a squalid urban environment shows Farrell's chief influences to be Dreiser, Joyce, and Proust, but also exhibits his interest in the common facts of U.S. life, and his indignation at social and economic inequalities. *Gas-House McGinty* (1933) depicts the activities of employees in a city express office, but *The Young Manhood of Studs Lonigan♦* (1934) follows the hero through his moral disintegration as the result of contact with the Chicago underworld, and *Judgment Day♦* (1935), completing the trilogy, tells of his defeat and death.

A new series of novels telling the story of Danny O'Neill, a sensitive youth with a background like Lonigan's, includes *A World I Never Made♦* (1936), *No Star Is Lost* (1938), *Father and Son* (1940), *My Days of Anger* (1943), and *The Face of Time* (1953). Other novels are *Tommy Gallagher's Crusade* (1939), about a boy who joins a priest's anti-Semitic campaign; *Ellen Rogers* (1941), about a selfish, middle-class girl; *Bernard Clare* (1946), about a frustrated New York author in the late 1920s, and its sequels, *The Road Between* (1949) and *Yet Other Waters* (1952); *This Man and This Woman* (1951), about the breakup of a long marriage. *The Silence of History* (1963) begins a tetralogy about Eddie Ryan, a University of Chicago student in 1926, who loses his faith in Catholicism and searches to find his own way, continued in *What Time Collects* (1964), about an unhappy marriage; *Lonely for the Future* (1966); and *When Time Was Born* (1967). Later novels include *Boarding House Blues* (1961); *New Year's Eve, 1929* (1967); *Childhood Is Not Forever* (1969); *Invisible Swords* (1971), depicting the relationship of a New York publisher and his wife upon discovering their child is retarded; *A Brand New Life* (1972); *The Dunne Family* (1976), about the lives and fates of a Chicago Irish family; and *The Death of Nora Ryan* (1978). His many stories, similar in attitude and subject to the longer fiction, are collected in *Calico Shoes* (1934), *Guillotine Party* (1935), *Can All This Grandeur Perish?* (1937), *$1,000 a Week* (1942), *To Whom It May Concern* (1944), *When Boyhood Dreams Come True* (1946), *The Life Adventurous* (1947), *An American Dream Girl* (1950), *French Girls Are Vicious* (1956), *A Dangerous Woman* (1957), *Side Street* (1961), *Sound of the City* (1962), and *Judith* (1974), portraits of aging people, presumably based on actual friends.

Farrell's literary credo is set forth in *A Note on Literary Criticism* (1936), describing his views as Marxist but not of the usual "crass and oversimplified" sort; *The League of Frightened Philistines* (1945), defending the social value of naturalistic realism; *Literature and Morality* (1947); and *Reflections at Fifty* (1954). Other writings include *My Baseball Diary* (1957), reflections on his love of the national pastime; *It Has Come To Pass* (1958), about a visit to Israel; *Collected Poems* (1965); and *On Irish Themes* (1982).

Fashion: or, Life in New York, comedy of manners by Anna Mowatt,♦ produced in 1845 and published in 1850.

Mrs. Tiffany, a newly rich society woman, and her daughter Seraphina set their caps for Count Jolimaitre, who is attracted by Seraphina's fortune. Tiffany, however, is forced to promise his daughter to Snobson, a confidential clerk who discovers his use of forgery. Jolimaitre is exposed as a fraudulent count and the lover of Mrs. Tiffany's maid. He and Seraphina plan to elope, but wait until they can obtain her jewels, which are held because of Tiffany's financial troubles. Finally Tiffany's friend Adam Trueman frees him from Snobson, and Seraphina from Jolimaitre.

FAST, HOWARD M[ELVIN] (1914–   ), New York author of historical fiction. Some of his works are set during the American Revolution, including *Two Valleys* (1933); *Conceived in Liberty* (1939), about a private at Valley Forge; *The Unvanquished* (1942), depicting Washington's development as a leader; *Citizen Tom Paine* (1943), a fictional biography, dramatized in 1986; *April Morning* (1961), a boy's view of the beginnings of battles; *The Crossing* (1971), about Washington's crossing of the Delaware; and *The Hessian* (1972), telling of an innocent drummer boy tried for an atrocity, a victim of war's passions. Other fiction includes *The Children* (1937), about New York

slums; *The Last Frontier* (1941), treating an Indian campaign of 1878–79; *Freedom Road* (1944), about a Southern black who becomes a congressman during Reconstruction; *The American* (1946), the story of Altgeld; *Clarkton* (1947), about a mill strike; *My Glorious Brothers* (1948), about Israel's ancient freedom; *Spartacus* (1952), treating the Roman slave revolt; *Moses, Prince of Egypt* (1958); *The Winston Affair* (1959), set in World War II; *Power* (1963), dealing with American labor during the days of a John L. Lewis-like figure; *Agrippa's Daughter* (1964); *Torquemada* (1966); a four-volume series set in San Francisco: *The Immigrants* (1977), *Second Generation* (1978), *The Establishment* (1979), and *The Legacy* (1981); *Max* (1982), about the making of a Hollywood movie mogul; *The Outsider* (1984), presenting the life of a rabbi in post-World War II U.S.; *The Immigrant's Daughter* (1985), a fifth and presumably final novel in his series on San Francisco; *The Dinner Party* (1986), about a senator's personal and political life in present-day Washington, D.C.; *The Pledge* (1988), treating a journalist trapped in the era of Senator Joseph McCarthy; and *The Confession of Joe Cullen* (1989), dealing with a man caught in the CIA during and after the Vietnam War. *The Naked God* (1957) is an account of his membership in the Communist party (1943–56), during which time he won a Stalin International Peace Prize (1953), wrote propagandistic works, and was ostracized in some quarters, though novels of this period (e.g. *Spartacus*) were filmed after he left the Party. Fast's other writings include children's books, short stories, plays, biographies, and, under the pseudonym E.V. Cunningham, detective and police novels, but his greatest success has been as a historical novelist. *Being Red* (1990) is a graceful memoir dealing with his years as an American Communist Party associate.

Fatal Deception, *The,* see *Leicester.*

Father, *The; or, American Shandyism,* comedy of manners by William Dunlap,♦ produced and published in 1789. It was revised (1806) as *The Father of an Only Child.*

Mr. Racket is a young merchant whose neglected wife consoles herself with the attentions of Captain Haller's servant, Ranter, who masquerades as a British officer. Ranter hopes to marry Mrs. Racket's sister, Caroline Felton, in order to possess her fortune. Colonel Duncan, guardian of Caroline and Mrs. Racket, appears to rescue the girls from Ranter. He assents to the betrothal of Caroline to Haller, who turns out to be Duncan's long-lost son. In addition to the main characters, there are two comedy parts: Cartridge, Colonel Duncan's servant; and the doctor, variously called Quiescent and Tattle.

Father Abbey's Will, see *Seccomb, John.*

Father Abraham's Speech, see *Poor Richard's Almanack.*

"Father, dear father," see *Work, H.C.*

Fathers, SAM, character in the Yoknapatawpha saga by Faulkner, is the son of the Chickasaw chief Ikkemotubbe♦ and a quadroon slave woman, and is himself a former slave. In "The Bear"♦ he appears not only as a great hunter and the best of woodsmen but as one who conceives of nature as a sacrament that the young man Isaac must be prepared to receive.

FAUGÈRES, MARGARETTA, see *Bleecker, Ann Eliza.*

FAULKNER (originally FALKNER), WILLIAM [HARRISON] (1897–1962), grew up in Oxford, Miss., the great-grandson of William C. Falkner♦ and a member of a family like that of the Sartoris clan in his novels centered on "Jefferson" in his mythical Yoknapatawpha County. ♦ After desultory education he joined the British Royal Air Force in Canada because he was too slight for U.S. requirements, but World War I ended before he was commissioned or saw service beyond training. Following the war he took some courses at the University of Mississippi and published *The Marble Faun* (1924), pastoral poems. Drifting to New Orleans, where he worked on a newspaper and also wrote the fiction collected in *New Orleans Sketches* (1958), he met Sherwood Anderson, who helped him publish *Soldiers' Pay*♦ (1926), his first novel, about the homecoming of a dying soldier, in the vein of the "lost generation." Following a brief stay in Europe (1925), he issued *Mosquitoes* (1927), a satirical novel set in New Orleans, later the site of his minor novel *Pylon* (1935), about aviators at a Mardi Gras.

With the publication of *Sartoris*♦ (1929) he found his own themes and setting, for it is the first novel in his long, loosely constructed Yoknapatawpha saga, whose themes include the decline of the Compson,♦ Sartoris,♦ Benbow,♦ and McCaslin♦ families, representatives of the Old South, and the rise of the unscrupulous Snopes♦ family, which displaces them. The life of the region is treated from the days of Indian possession, through the pre-Civil War era, down to modern times. The saga of macabre violence and antic comedy is written in a sensitive but often baroque style and depicts its region as a microcosm in which its subjects often achieve mythic proportions. *The Sound and the Fury*♦ (1929) introduces the significant but decadent Compson family in a remarkably structured story. *As I Lay Dying*♦ (1930) reveals the psychological relationships of a subnormal poor-white family on a pilgrimage to bury their mother. *Sanctuary*♦ (1931) is a sadistic horror story, ostensibly written to make money but carefully reworked before publication as a serious novel. *Light in August*♦

(1932), although also filled with horrors, is a more balanced contrast of positive and negative forces of life in its presentation of violent adventures involved in the relations between men and women, black and white. *Absalom, Absalom!*♦ (1936), set in early 19th-century Jefferson, shows the tragic downfall of the dynastic desires of the planter Colonel Sutpen. *The Unvanquished*♦ (1938) uses earlier short stories to create a novel about the Sartoris family in the Civil War. *The Wild Palms* (1939) shows the effects of a Mississippi flood on the lives of a hillbilly convict and a New Orleans doctor and his mistress. *The Hamlet*♦ (1940), the first volume of a trilogy, shows the rise to power of the depraved Snopes family. *Intruder in the Dust*♦ (1948) is a more compassionate tale of a black man on trial and the concomitant growing moral awareness of a white boy. *Requiem for a Nun* (1951), a sequel to *Sanctuary,* combines the forms of play and novel to treat the tortured redemption of Temple Drake. *A Fable*♦ (1954, Pulitzer Prize) is a lengthy parable of the Passion of Christ set in a framework of false armistice and actual mutiny in World War I. *The Town*♦ (1957) carries on the story of the white trash Flem Snopes and his coming to Jefferson, while *The Mansion*♦ (1960) concludes the Snopes story by treating the family in the first half of the 20th century. *The Reivers*♦ (1962, Pulitzer Prize), published just before the author's death, is an amusing fictive "reminiscence" of a boy's various misadventures in 1905. Many of the novels' characters, settings, and themes appear in stories collected in *These 13* (1931); *Idyll in the Desert* (1931); *Miss Zilphia Gant* (1932); *Dr. Martino* (1934); *Go Down, Moses* (1942), including the symbolic novelette "The Bear"♦; *Knight's Gambit* (1949); *Big Woods* (1955), hunting tales; and *Uncollected Stories* (1979). *Salmagundi* (1932) gathers early essays and poems, and *A Green Bough* (1933) collects poems. Other works include *Early Prose and Poetry* (1962), *Essays, Speeches and Public Letters* (1965) and *Flags in the Dust* (1973), the original uncut text of *Sartoris.*

During the 1930s he was off and on in Hollywood as a script writer, but his works for film are not accounted as being of much consequence. Critical views stated while teaching in Japan, at the University of Virginia, and at West Point appear in *Faulkner at Nagano* (1956), *Faulkner in the University* (1959), and *Faulkner at West Point* (1964). Lesser works include posthumously published juvenilia, *Marionettes: A Play in One Act* (1975) and *Mayday* (1976), while *The Wishing Tree* (1967) is a book for children. *Vision in the Spring* (1984) publishes 14 poems that he gathered in 1921. *Selected Letters* appeared in 1977. For his literary accomplishments Faulkner was awarded a Nobel Prize in 1950 and in acceptance made a brief but important statement about his belief "that man will not merely endure: he will prevail . . . because he has a soul, a spirit capable of compassion and sacrifice and endurance" and "the writer's duty is to write about these things."

FAUSET, JESSIE REDMON (1882–1961), born in New Jersey of a long-established family of free blacks, was probably the first black woman to become a member of Phi Beta Kappa upon her graduation from Cornell (1905). After graduate study at the University of Pennsylvania and the Sorbonne she became a high-school teacher of French and Latin and an editor of DuBois's *The Crisis,* which she opened to new young writers of the Harlem Renaissance. She herself wrote four novels: *There Is Confusion* (1924), a love story concerning an educated black woman who wants to be a concert singer and a black man whom she helps in his fight to become a doctor; *Plum Bun* (1929), presenting two sisters, one who passes for white while living in Greenwich Village, where she has an unhappy love affair with a white man, the other, admitting her race and living affirmatively in Harlem; *The Chinaberry Tree* (1931), another story about black women and the need for them to accept their heritage; and *Comedy: American Style* (1934), depicting an insecure, frustrated black woman.

FAWCETT, EDGAR (1847–1904), author of satirical novels and plays on New York society. Among them are the novel *Purple and Fine Linen* (1873) and such plays as *The False Friend* (1880), *Our First Families* (1880), and *Americans Abroad* (1881). *The Buntling Ball* (1884) is a verse play. He also wrote poetry typical of his era, such as *Songs of Doubt and Dream* (1891), and *Agnosticism and Other Essays* (1889).

FAY, THEODORE SEDGWICK (1807–98), editor of the *New-York Mirror* (1828–33), after 1837 held various diplomatic posts in England, Germany, and Switzerland. His early essays in the *Mirror* were collected in *Dreams and Reveries of a Quiet Man* (2 vols., 1832), and among his other books are *Norman Leslie: A Tale of the Present Times* (1835); *Sydney Clifton; or, Vicissitudes in Both Hemispheres* (1839), a Gothic romance in a modern setting; *The Countess Ida: A Tale of Berlin* (1840); *Hoboken* (1843), a moralistic romance; and *Ulric; or, The Voices* (1851), a romantic poem of the Reformation in Germany.

FEARING, KENNETH (1902–61), poet and novelist, born in Chicago, resident in New York after graduation from the University of Wisconsin. *Angel Arms* (1929), *Poems* (1935), *Dead Reckoning* (1938), *Afternoon of a Pawnbroker* (1943), and *Stranger at Coney Island* (1949) are verse satires of disintegrating, contemporary, middle-class life. His *New and Selected Poems* appeared in 1956. His novels include *The Hospital* (1939), about a moment in the big institution; *Clark Gifford's Body* (1942), a modern parallel of John Brown's raid; *The Big Clock* (1946), a fast-paced tale of murder and a manhunt; and *The Crozart Story* (1960).

Feathertop, story by Hawthorne, dramatized by MacKaye as *The Scarecrow.* ♦

Federal Orrery (1794–96), semi-weekly Federalist journal, founded at Boston by R.T. Paine. Joseph Dennie and Sarah Wentworth Morton were among those who contributed poetry, satire, and criticism, usually leveled at the anti-Federalists.

Federal Theatre Project, operated (1936–39) by the Works Progress Administration as a measure for the relief of unemployed actors and other workers in the theater. Directed by Hallie Flanagan, who had been active in the little-theater movement, the Project's activities were stimulated by little-theater developments. Production units were established throughout the U.S., employing as many as 13,000 workers at one time. Some 1200 plays, by both foreign and native authors, were produced, and the aim was to supplement commercial theaters with groups presenting legitimate drama at low prices, often to audiences that had grown unaccustomed to live theater. Perhaps the most important achievement was the development of an experimental form, "The Living Newspaper," created in New York City under the editorship of Arthur Arent. Among these plays, dramatizing contemporary social and political problems by the use of quotations from newspapers and public addresses, and employing new mechanical devices, were *Triple A Plowed Under* (1936), *Injunction Granted* (1936), *Power* (1937), and *". . . one-third of a nation . . ."* (1938). Other successful productions included T.S. Eliot's *Murder in the Cathedral,* Marlowe's *Dr. Faustus,* marionette plays for children, Sinclair Lewis's *It Can't Happen Here,* and black productions of such works as *Macbeth* and *The Mikado.* Two series of *Federal Theatre Plays* were published (1938), and *Arena* (1940) by Hallie Flanagan is a history of the Project.

Federal Theology, see *Covenant Theology.*

Federal Writers' Project, operated (1935–39) by the Works Progress Administration as a measure for the relief of unemployed writers, journalists, editors, and research workers. Directed by Henry G. Alsberg, the Project employed as many as 6600 workers at one time, in state and local branches throughout the U.S. Its main program was concerned with the compiling and editing of the American Guide Series, a "series of books which would give the Nation a detailed portrait of itself." The scope ranged from geographical and travel information to folklore, architecture, and other phases of cultural and ethnological history, and the plan included volumes not only for the then 48 states but also for cities, towns, and highway routes. Among the by-products were local histories, studies of racial groups, biographies, social histories, and nature studies. In 1941, by the Congressional Emergency Relief Appropriation Act, the project was transferred to state sponsorship.

Federalist, The, 85 essays in support of the Constitution,♦ signed by the pseudonym Publius, and written mainly by Hamilton,♦ assisted by Madison♦ and Jay.♦ First printed (1787–88) in the form of letters to the New York *Independent Journal, Packet,* and *Daily Advertiser,* they were collected and revised by Hamilton (2 vols., 1788). There are many critical editions, including those of P.L. Ford and H.C. Lodge. The latter summarizes the long controversy over the authorship by attributing 51 essays to Hamilton, 14 to Madison, 5 to Jay, 3 to Hamilton and Madison in collaboration, and 12 to either Hamilton or Madison.

At the time of writing, the purpose was principally to persuade New York voters to accept the Constitution, but the collected essays have come to be considered an authority on abstract principles of American government, and many Supreme Court decisions have been based in part on statements in *The Federalist.* The first paper, written by Hamilton, outlines the intention of numbers 1 to 51: "to discuss the following interesting particulars:—The utility of the UNION to your political prosperity—The insufficiency of the present Confederation to preserve that Union—The necessity of a government at least equally energetic with the one proposed, to the attainment of this object—The conformity of the proposed Constitution to the true principles of republican government—its analogy to your own State constitution—and lastly, The additional security which its adoption will afford, to the preservation of that species of government, to liberty, and to property." Specific subjects include "Dangers from Foreign Force and Influence" and "from Dissensions between the States"; "The Union as a Safeguard against Domestic Faction and Insurrection"; "Commercial Relations and a Navy"; "Revenue"; "Economy in Government"; "The Powers Necessary to the Common Defense"; "Militia"; "Power of Taxation"; and "Restrictions on the Authority of the Several States." Numbers 52 to 83 proceed to a detailed analysis of the governmental functions as defined by the Constitution, while the last two essays refute objections and summarize the general argument.

FEIBLEMAN, PETER S[TEINAM] (1930–), novelist born in New York City, reared in New Orleans, for seven years resident in Spain, whose novels include *A Place Without Twilight* (1958) and *The Daughters of Necessity* (1959), treating families in the South, respectively black and wealthy white; *The Columbus Tree* (1972), about Americans in Spain; and *Charlie Boy* (1980). *Tiger Tiger Burning Bright* (1963) is his dramatization of his first novel. *Strangers and Graves* (1966) collects four novellas. *Lilly* (1988) is his memoir of Lillian Hellman. ♦

FEIKEMA, FEIKE, see *Manfred, Frederick.*

Felix Carmen, pseudonym of F.D. Sherman. ♦

Female Quixotism: *Exhibited in the Romantic Opinions and Extravagant Adventures of Dorcasina Sheldon,* novel by Tabitha Tenney,♦ published in 1801. This satire of sentimental fiction is obviously indebted to Charlotte Lennox's *The Female Quixote* (1752).

Dorcas Sheldon, only daughter of a rich family, is addicted to the reading of sentimental novels, and determines to pattern her behavior on that of a typical heroine. Transforming her simple name into Dorcasina, she rejects a suitor because he fails to propose in approved fictional fashion. Accompanied by her maid Betty, a female Sancho Panza, she spends her time reading novels in a romantically situated arbor, and reaches the age of 34 without finding the romance she desires. After being nearly seduced, because an adventurer proposes to her in a sentimental manner, she is wooed by Philander, a student given to practical jokes, who imposes on her credulity. Finally despairing of finding a lover, she reads *Roderick Random,* and discovers that the hero, a serving-man, fell in love with his employer, at which she forces her hired man, John Brown, to do likewise. Her friends rescue her, and at last, completely disillusioned, Dorcas settles down to a quiet spinsterhood.

Feminism, reform movement aiming at the social, educational, and political equality of women with men, which arose during the late 18th century. The first great document of feminism was the *Vindication of the Rights of Woman* (1792), by the English author Mary Wollstonecraft. American women, including Abigail Adams and Mercy Otis Warren, were just as early in agitating that the Constitution specifically state the rights of women. Later prominent leaders in America included Emma Willard, who wrote a *Plan for Improving Female Education* (1819); Margaret Fuller, who wrote *Woman in the Nineteenth Century* (1845); and Harriet Farley, who edited the *Lowell Offering.* As an early result of feminist agitation, Oberlin College was the first institution of higher learning to grant degrees to women (1837). After the convention led by Elizabeth Stanton, Lucretia Mott, and others (1848), the movement became a predominantly political one for woman suffrage. With suffrage gained by the 19th Amendment (1920), further work for women's rights moved spasmodically and, on the whole, slowly. It finally became dynamic in the 1960s with the creation of the National Organization for Women (NOW) as a leader of the cause of feminism, thereafter called Women's Liberation. A major thrust was toward passage of an Equal Rights Amendment (ERA) to the Constitution, although it failed, but that was only part of a large movement for social changes rather than mere political action as women worked for full equality in every way, socially, legally, educationally, commercially, and sexually. Outstanding expositions of the so-called Women's Lib include *The Feminine Mystique* (1963) by Betty Friedan and *Sexual Politics* (1970) by Kate Millett, but there are many other champions of the cause and journals for it, like *Ms.*, founded in 1971 by Gloria Steinem and others. Aspects of the feminist dynamic have become more evident in diverse ways by women writers of very various sorts, ranging, for example, over the warm-hearted autobiographies of Maya Angelou, the sociopolitical essays and fiction of Renata Adler, the personal poetic statements of Anne Sexton, and the frank expressions of sexuality and individual independence of Erica Jong.

FENNO, JOHN, see *Gazette of the U.S.*

FENOLLOSA, ERNEST FRANCISCO (1853–1908), was an American pioneer in the study of Oriental literature and art. After 12 years of teaching in Japan, he returned to the U.S. to become a curator of the Boston Museum of Fine Arts. His writings include *East and West: The Discovery of America and Other Poems* (1893), *The Masters of Ukioye* (1896), and *Epochs of Chinese and Japanese Art* (2 vols., 1911). His literary executor, Ezra Pound, edited from his notes *Certain Noble Plays of Japan* (1916); *Noh; or, Accomplishments* (1916); *Cathay* (1915), Chinese poetry translated; and *The Chinese Written Character as a Medium for Poetry* (1936). Van Wyck Brooks wrote *Fenollosa and His Circle* (1962).

FERBER, EDNA (1887–1968), Michigan-born novelist and playwright, resided in New York City. After her first novel, *Dawn O'Hara* (1911), she wrote the short stories about the business woman Emma McChesney, collected in *Roast Beef, Medium* (1913), *Personality Plus* (1914), and *Emma McChesney and Co.* (1915). Besides other collections of stories, including *Mother Knows Best* (1927), she was the author of successful novels: *Fanny Herself* (1917); *The Girls* (1921), a study of three generations of women; *So Big* (1924, Pulitzer Prize), about Selina, a truck gardener, and her sacrifices for her son Dirk; *Show Boat* (1926), the romantic story of Magnolia Hawks, leading lady of her father's showboat troupe, who marries Gaylord Ravenal, a gambler, and after he deserts her becomes a successful singer; *Cimarron* (1930), about the 1889 land rush in Oklahoma and the region's later development; *American Beauty* (1931), about Polish immigrants in Connecticut; *Come and Get It* (1935), about the Wisconsin logging industry; *Saratoga Trunk* (1941), about a Creole adventuress and a cowboy gambler at a Saratoga (N.Y.) spa in the 1880s; *Great Son* (1945), about four generations of a Seattle family; *Giant* (1950), set in Texas; and *Ice Palace* (1958), set in modern Alaska but presenting its past too.

Show Boat was made into a musical play (Kern and Hammerstein, 1927); and with George S. Kaufman she wrote plays, including *Minick* (1924), based on one of her stories; *The Royal Family* (1927), lampooning the Barrymores; *Dinner at Eight* (1932); and *Stage Door* (1936). *A Peculiar Treasure* (1939) and *A Kind of Magic* (1963) are autobiographies.

FERGUSSON, HARVEY (1890–1971), New Mexico novelist, resident in California. *Followers of the Sun,* a trilogy about the Santa Fe Trail, includes *Blood of the Conquerors* (1921), showing the degeneration of the Spanish landowners; *Wolf Song* (1927), about the era of American settlement; and *In Those Days* (1929), about a Southwest pioneer living on to modern times. Other fiction includes *Capitol Hill* (1923), about Washington, D.C.; *Footloose McGarnigal* (1930), about a boy in the Santa Fe and Taos art colonies; *Grant of Kingdom* (1950), about a mountain man's Spanish land grant; and *The Conquest of Don Pedro* (1954), about a Jew's life in a New Mexico town after the Civil War. *Rio Grande* (1933) is an informal history of the Southwest, and *Home in the West* (1945) is autobiographical.

FERLINGHETTI, LAWRENCE (1920–), New York-born poet, painter, and publisher resident in San Francisco, with whose Beat movement♦ he is identified. He was the publisher of Ginsberg's♦ *Howl,* and his City Lights Bookshop continues as a center for many writers and artists. His own works include *Pictures of the Gone World* (1955); *A Coney Island of the Mind* (1958), a very popular work; *Starting from San Francisco* (1961); *After the Cries of the Birds* (1967); *The Secret Meaning of Things* (1969); *Tyrannus Nix* (1969); *Open Eye, Open Heart* (1973); *Who Are We Now?* (1976); and *Endless Life* (1981), colloquial poems, often topical in subject, and suited to public reading; *Her* (1960), a novel about an artist's search for the ideal in the guise of a woman; *Love in the Days of Rage* (1988), another novel, set in the student revolt of 1968 in Paris; *Unfair Arguments with Existence* (1962), experimental plays; and *Routines* (1963), proposals for happenings. With Nancy Peters he created *Literary San Francisco* (1980), a pictorial history.

FERN, FANNY, pseudonym of Sara P. Willis.♦

FERNALD, CHESTER BAILEY (1869–1938), born in Boston, lived in San Francisco (1889–93), where he obtained the material for his best-known books, *The Cat and the Cherub* (1896) and *Chinatown Stories* (1899), both collections of stories about the city's Chinese quarter. *Under the Jack-Staff* (1903) contains dramatic tales of life at sea, based on Fernald's travels in Alaska, Europe, and the Orient. After 1907 he lived in England, where he became known as a dramatist.

FERRIL, THOMAS HORNSBY (1896–1988), Colorado author and journalist, whose writings include *New and Selected Poems* (1952) and *And Perhaps Happiness* (1957), a verse play. *I Hate Thursday* (1946) contains prose sketches from his *Rocky Mountain Herald* and contributions to *Harper's*. He also published the non-journalistic *Poems in Words for Denver* (1966) and *Anvil of Roses* (1983).

FESSENDEN, THOMAS GREEN (1771–1837), New Hampshire author, whose varied career included law practice, invention, and the editing of newspapers in New York, Brattleboro, and Boston. His Hudibrastic satire *Terrible Tractoration* (1803) was aimed at English critics of Elisha Perkins's "metallic tractors," an invention for which Fessenden was the agent. His *Original Poems* (1804) include "The Country Lovers," which is thought to have suggested Lowell's "The Courtin'." *Democracy Unveiled* (1805) is a virulent attack on Jefferson and the Democrats. He used the pseudonym Christopher Caustic.

FICKE, ARTHUR DAVISON (1883–1945), Iowa-born poet, whose early romantic volumes included *From the Isles* (1907), *The Happy Princess* (1907), *The Earth Passion* (1908), *The Breaking of Bonds* (1910), *Sonnets of a Portrait Painter* (1914), *The Man on the Hilltop* (1915), and *An April Elegy* (1917). *Mr. Faust* (1913), later revised for stage production, presents Faustus as a modern New Yorker who enlists Satan's aid in hope of overcoming his disillusion, and finally attains a spiritual peace. Ficke's objection to modernism in poetry may be seen in the satirical hoax *Spectra*♦ (1916). His later poems showed him to be "homesick in modernity," and terrified by the natural beauty of the world, as in *Out of Silence and Other Poems* (1924), *Mountain Against Mountain* (1929), and *Tumultuous Shore* (1942). *Mrs. Morton of Mexico* (1939) is a novel.

FIEDLER, LESLIE A[ARON] (1917–   ), professor at State University of New York, Buffalo, whose lively and often very witty literary criticism appears in his works of "literary anthropology," *Love and Death in the American Novel* (1960); *Waiting for the End* (1964), on 20th-century American literature and culture; and *The Return of the Vanishing American* (1968), on the Western as genre; *The Stranger in Shakespeare* (1972); and *Collected Essays* (1971), often pursuing archetypal myths and making psychic explorations. *What Was Literature?* (1982) suggests that the popular products of mass society, literary and other, are more important than the high art of sophisticated culture. *The Inadvertent Epic* (1980) in five essays deals with the epic in relation to American literature, from *Uncle Tom's Cabin* to Haley's *Roots*. *Olf Stapledon, a Man Divided* (1983) studies the literary career of the noted British writer of science fiction. He has written stories, *The Last Jew*

in America (1966) and *Nude Croquet* (1969), and a novel, *The Messengers Will Come No More* (1974). *Being Busted* (1969) deals with his arrest for possession of marijuana, and *Freaks* (1978) surveys myths about and social responses to physical abnormality.

FIELD, EUGENE (1850–95), born in St. Louis, always considered himself a Westerner, and, in his writings for the Denver *Tribune* and his column "Sharps and Flats" in the Chicago *Daily News* (1883–95), showed his special province to be the journalization of literature. He filled his column with whimsical humor and with verse—often in real or imaginary dialects—that appealed to the popular taste in humor and sentiment. Among his best-known poems are the sentimental "Little Boy Blue" and the "Dutch Lullaby" ("Wynken, Blynken, and Nod"), both set to music by Reginald DeKoven and also by Ethelbert Nevin. His collections of newspaper contributions include *A Little Book of Western Verse* (1889), *A Little Book of Profitable Tales* (1889), *With Trumpet and Drum* (1892), *A Second Book of Verse* (1892), *The Holy Cross and Other Tales* (1893), *The Love Affairs of a Bibliomaniac* (1896), and *The House* (1896).

ROSWELL MARTIN FIELD (1851–1919), his brother, had a parallel career as journalist and music and dramatic critic. The two collaborated on a volume of paraphrases of Horace, *Echoes from the Sabine Farm* (1892).

FIELD, JOSEPH M. (1810–56), St. Louis actor, theatrical manager, and journalist, whose newspaper and magazine sketches were collected in *The Drama in Pokerville* (1847). Not one of his many plays was published, but he is remembered for such tales of frontier humor as "Mike Fink, the Last of the Boatmen."

FIELD, RACHEL [LYMAN] (1894–1942), Massachusetts author of such children's books as *The Cross-Stitch Heart and Other One-Act Plays* (1927) and *Hitty, Her First Hundred Years* (1929), and novels for adults, including *Time Out of Mind* (1935), *All This, and Heaven Too* (1938), and *And Now Tomorrow* (1942).

FIELD, STEPHEN J[OHNSON] (1816–99), New York lawyer, emigrated to California (1849), where he drafted codes of civil and criminal procedure and established the basis of Western mining law. He was chief justice of the state supreme court (1859–63), resigning to become a member of the U.S. Supreme Court, in which he served until 1897. His *Reminiscences of Early Days in California* was published in 1880.

FIELDS, JAMES T[HOMAS] (1817–81), partner of W.D. Ticknor♦ in a prominent Boston publishing firm bearing their names and in the ownership of the Old Corner Bookstore, was editor of the *Atlantic Monthly*♦ (1861–71). He wrote several volumes of poetry, including *A Few Verses for a Few Friends* (1858), which contains the lines, "'We are lost!' the captain shouted, As he staggered down the stairs." *Underbrush* (1877) is a collection of essays and sketches, and *Yesterdays with Authors* (1872) is one of his several reminiscences.

ANNIE ADAMS FIELDS (1834–1915), his wife, established a literary salon in their home, and also wrote poetry, a biography of her husband (1881), *Authors and Friends* (1896), and a diary from which M.A. DeW. Howe edited *Memories of a Hostess* (1922).

FIERSTEIN, HARVEY (1954–), playwright, author of *Torch Song Trilogy* (1981), a breakthrough serious drama about homosexuals, made into a movie (1988) with the playwright as lead. He adapted from the French *La Cage Aux Folles* (1983), a comic musical with homosexual characters. Other plays are *Safe Sex* (1987) and *Spook House* (1987).

"Fifty-four forty or fight," slogan of the Democrats during the election campaign of Polk (1844), expressing the view that U.S. rights extended over the entire Oregon territory to latitude 54° 40', a boundary which the British would not recognize. The slogan is the title of a book by Emerson Hough, which deals with the controversy.

FIGARO, pseudonym of Henry Clapp.♦

Figure in the Carpet, The, tale by Henry James,♦ collected in *Embarrassments* (1896).

Considered to be a self-revelation of the author, this is the narrative of an earnest young critic's study of the works of the brilliant novelist Hugh Vereker—his search for "the figure in the carpet," which Vereker tells him cryptically is the key to an appreciation of his books, although no one has yet understood it. The young man repeats this to his friend Corvick, an experienced critic, who dedicates himself to discovering the secret figure, and claims to have done so when he marries Gwendolyn Erme, who has been equally anxious to know the solution. Corvick is accidentally killed before writing his projected essay, and the young critic can urge from Gwendolyn only the assertion that her husband told her the secret. Later she marries another critic, Drayton Deane. After both Gwendolyn and Vereker have died, the young man meets Deane and implores him to divulge the secret. The astonished Deane knows nothing of it, and the disappointment of the young man is mitigated by the torment of the second husband, who thinks his wife may have considered him unworthy of sharing the sacred confidence.

FILSON, JOHN (c.1747–88), author of *The Discovery, Settlement, and Present State of Kentucke*

(1784), the first history of the state. The most famous passage in the book is "The Adventures of Col. Daniel Boon" (*sic*), probably based on the scout's dictation, which was primarily responsible for the beginning of Boone's legendary reputation. Filson also drew a *Map of Kentucke* in the same year.

Financier, The, novel by Dreiser,♦ published in 1912 and revised in 1927. The story and its sequel *The Titan*♦ are based on the career of C.T. Yerkes, a flamboyant financier of Philadelphia, Chicago, and London.

FINCH, FRANCIS MILES (1827–1907), born in Ithaca, N.Y., graduated from Yale (1849), became a prominent lawyer and judge, lecturer and dean and professor of law at Cornell's College of Law. His posthumously published writing, *The Blue and the Gray and Other Verses* (1909), was done as an avocation but is remembered today for the title piece, the poem "Nathan Hale," and some college songs.

FINEMAN, IRVING (1893–?), author of novels which include *This Pure Young Man* (1930), a story of adolescent development; *Lovers Must Learn* (1932), concerned with American expatriates in Paris; *Hear, Ye Sons* (1933), a story of life in Russian Poland in the 19th century; *Doctor Addams* (1939), about the contrast between the laboratory work of a research scientist and the disorder in his personal life; *Jacob* (1941), an autobiographical novel; *Ruth* (1949), a version of the Biblical story; and *Helen Herself* (1957), a modern novel. *Woman of Valor* (1961) is a biography of Henrietta Szold, the founder of Hadassah.

FINK, MIKE (1770?–1823?), keelboatman on the Ohio and Mississippi rivers, noted for tall tales of his exploits, which made him as fabulous as Paul Bunyan. Accounts of his adventures appeared as early as 1829, when tales derived from oral sources found their way into print. There are 11 versions of his death, and his daughter Sal is probably an entirely mythical creation. He figures in works by many writers, including Emerson Bennett, T.B. Thorpe, J.M. Field, and John Neihardt.

FINLEY, MARTHA FARQUHARSON (1828–1909), who wrote under the name Martha Farquharson, was the author of some 100 novels for children. Her character Elsie Dinsmore, who appeared in the 28 Elsie books (1867–1905), and similar figures in other pious tales were very popular.

First Book of the American Chronicles of the Times, The, anonymous burlesque, probably written by a Philadelphian, and published serially (1774–75). It is a satirical account, in the manner of the Scriptures, of American history leading up to the Revolution.

FISHER, DOROTHY CANFIELD, see *Canfield.*

FISHER, M[ARY] F[RANCES] K[ENNEDY] (1908–92), a Californian by birth and long-time residence, wrote about a far larger world of fine foods, also inhabited, beginning with *Serve It Forth* (1937) and continuing in *The Gastronomical Me* (1943); *A Considerable Town* (1978), about Marseilles; *Long Ago in France* (1991), concerning Dijon; and many other works based on fact and experience. Her final publications are *To Begin Again: Stories and Memoirs, 1908–1929* (1992) and *Stay Me, Oh Comfort Me: Journals and Stories, 1933–1941* (1993).

FISHER, VARDIS [ALVERO] (1895–1968), Idaho author, for a time taught English at the University of Utah (1925–28) and at New York University (1928–31), but is best known for his fiction concerned with his region, his own experiences, and man's civilization. After his early works, *Toilers of the Hills* (1928) and *Dark Bridwell* (1931), novels dealing with the repressive effects of frontier life, he wrote his tetralogy concerned with the life of Vridar Hunter, his not too subtly named alter ego. The first of these, *In Tragic Life* (1932), published in England as *I See No Sin* (1934), is the story of the boyhood and adolescence of the hypersensitive Vridar, who is terrified by the hardships of life on a Western farm, and by the Puritan rigidity of family standards. *Passions Spin the Plot* (1934) deals with his disillusion at failing to discover the meaning of life through attending college at Salt Lake City, and his marriage to the half-Indian girl Neloa. *We Are Betrayed* (1935) tells of his attempt to escape inner confusion by going to war, his return to college, and the conflicts between his Mormon background and the doctrines of Freud. In this state of mind, his mental cruelty drives Neloa to suicide. *No Villain Need Be* (1936) shows Vridar as a professor at a Mormon college and as a struggling author among New York bohemians, and his eventual discovery that there can be no peace for the individual until all men reach "a splended fellowship."

Fisher next wrote several independent novels: *April, A Fable of Love* (1937), about a girl's escape from the monotony of Idaho ranch life; *Forgive Us Our Virtues* (1938), the story of a psychology professor's discovery of the way lives are affected by sexual inhibitions; *Children of God* (1939), a historical novel of Joseph Smith, Brigham Young, and the Mormon movement; *City of Illusion* (1941), a story of the Comstock Lode; *The Mothers: An American Saga of Courage* (1943), about the Donner Party; *Pemmican* (1956), about the Hudson's Bay Company; *Tale of Valor* (1958), about the Lewis and Clark expedition; and *Mountain Man* (1965), about the Rocky Mountain fur trade.

The Testament of Man, a series of 12 novels on human development, includes *Darkness and the Deep* (1943), about primitive ape-men; *Golden Rooms* (1944), about Neanderthal man; *Intimations of Eve* (1946), about the period when men were hunters and women, tillers of the soil; *Adam and the Serpent* (1947), about the beginning of social institutions and a developing patriarchy; *The Divine Passion* (1948), about the era recorded in the Old Testament; *The Valley of Vision* (1951), about Solomon's times; *The Island of the Innocent* (1952), about Greek and Jew in the time of the Maccabees; *A Goat for Azazel* (1956), about the origins of Christianity; *Jesus Came Again* (1956), the life of a man named Joshua which parallels that of Jesus; *Peace Like a River* (1957), about the asceticism of early Christianity; *My Holy Satan* (1958), subtitled "a novel of Christian twilight," about medieval Christianity and the Inquisition; and *Orphans in Gethsemane* (1960).

Other works include a revision and extension at great length of the Vridar Hunter tetralogy; *Sonnets to an Imaginary Madonna* (1927); *The Neurotic Nightingale* (1935), essays; *God or Caesar? The Writing of Fiction for Beginners* (1953); *Love and Death* (1959), collected stories; *Suicide or Murder? The Strange Death of Governor Meriwether Lewis* (1962); and *Thomas Wolfe as I Knew Him* (1973).

FISKE, JOHN (1842–1901), Connecticut-born author, lecturer at Harvard, and professor of American history at Washington University (St. Louis). As a young man he was a follower of Comte and Herbert Spencer and, through such works as *The Outlines of Cosmic Philosophy* (1874), *Darwinism and Other Essays* (1879), and *The Destiny of Man Viewed in the Light of His Origin* (1884), became the chief popularizer of Victorian science and philosophy in the U.S. After 1879 he was principally known as a lecturer and author, but his importance was that of a popularizer, not of an original thinker. In *The Critical Period of American History, 1783–1789* (1888) and *The Beginnings of New England* (1889), he attempted to apply Comtean ideas of sociological evolution to American history. He helped edit *Appleton's Cyclopædia of American Biography* (1887–89), and his later works include *Civil Government in the United States* (1890), *The Mississippi Valley in the Civil War* (1900), *Essays: Historical and Literary* (1902), and *New France and New England* (1902). His *Letters* were published in 1940.

FISKE, NATHAN (1733–99), Massachusetts clergyman, was the author of *The Moral Monitor* (1801), a collection of essays following the plan of the *Spectator.* His *Historical Discourse* (1776) of his native town of Brookfield contains an account of the conflicts with the savages and the English.

FITCH, [WILLIAM] CLYDE (1865–1909), author of more than 30 popular plays, usually vehicles for specific stars. *Barbara Frietchie* (1899) was written for Julia Marlowe, *Nathan Hale* (1899) for Nat Goodwin, *Beau Brummell* (1890) for Richard

Mansfield, and *Her Great Match* (1905) for Maxine Elliott. Fitch was extremely versatile, writing farces, society dramas, historical plays, and problem plays, always with an understanding of what would be effective on the stage. Serious studies of the social, financial, and political aspects of New York City are contained in *The Climbers* (1901) and *The City* (1909). His popular farce, *Captain Jinks of the Horse Marines* (1901), was revised in 1925 as a musical comedy. *The Girl with the Green Eyes*♦ (1902), a psychological study of jealousy, is generally considered to be his most important work. His collected plays were edited by M.J. Moses (1915).

FITTS, DUDLEY (1903–68), instructor of English at Phillips Academy, Andover, was well known for colloquial metrical translations of Aristophanes' plays, *Lysistrata* (1954), *The Frogs* (1955), *The Birds* (1957), and *Ladies' Day* (1959), a version of *Thesmophoriazusae*. With Robert Fitzgerald he translated Euripides' *Alcestis* (1935) and Sophocles' *Oedipus* (1949), and he also wrote other translations as well as original poetry. He edited the Yale Series of Younger Poets (1960–68).

FITZGERALD, FRANCES (1940–), after graduation from Radcliffe and further study of Chinese and Vietnamese history and culture, became a foreign correspondent on those subjects. Her book *Fire in the Lake: The Vietnamese and the Americans in Vietnam* (1972) won a Pulitzer Prize and a National Book Award. She also wrote *America Revised* (1979) and *Cities on a Hill* (1986).

FITZGERALD, F[RANCIS] SCOTT [KEY] (1896–1940), born in St. Paul, Minn., where part of his youth was spent until he went to Princeton (1913). There he was a friend of Edmund Wilson♦ and John Peale Bishop♦ and was a leader in theatrical and literary activities until he left because of academic difficulties, and then, after a brief return, to enter the army (1917). While being trained in U.S. camps he wrote the initial draft of his first novel, *This Side of Paradise*♦ (1920), set at his alma mater and an expression of a new generation and its jazz age. His book having caught the flavor and interests of the changing era, his stories were in great demand by both the popular *Saturday Evening Post* and the critical *Scribner's* as he became a chronicler of the manners and moods of the time. From these journals came his next works, *Flappers and Philosophers* (1920) and *Tales of the Jazz Age* (1922), the latter including "The Diamond as Big as the Ritz."♦ In keeping with the tone of the stories, he himself became a character of the period, the handsome, witty, charming author married to a glamorous woman named Zelda, and both living life as though it were one great party. His lesser, second novel, *The Beautiful and Damned* (1922), was a minor work telling of a rich, aristocratic young

artist and his wife foundering in dissipation, suggesting something of the Fitzgeralds' own extravagant life. This was followed by his satirical play, *The Vegetable; or, From President to Postman* (1923), reissued (1976) with previously cut scenes. Then came *The Great Gatsby*♦ (1925), his finest novel, a sensitive and symbolic treatment of themes of contemporary life related with irony and pathos to the legendry of the "American dream." Although he continued to write stories, collected in *All the Sad Young Men* (1926) and later in *Taps at Reveille* (1935), and worked ahead on his most extensive novel, *Tender Is the Night*♦ (1934), his personal life suffered the tragedies of his wife's nervous breakdown and his own loss of security as he became sick and saw his critical esteem and public reception deteriorate, leading him to write the touching essays posthumously collected by Edmund Wilson in *The Crack-Up* (1945). His view of the psychological and spiritual malaise of modern life in *Tender Is the Night* he tried to clarify by a revision not published until after his death. He managed to pick up pieces of his life as a motion picture scenarist in Hollywood, about which he wrote his impressive final novel, *The Last Tycoon*♦ (1941), portraying a studio mogul and his industry, a work not completed because of the author's death by heart attack. *Afternoon of an Author* (1958) collects lesser stories and essays, and *The Pat Hobby Stories* (1962) are 17 tales, written just before his death, about a Hollywood hack writer down on his luck. A great resurgence of popularity led to several new collections of his magazine contributions, including *The Apprentice Fiction* (1969), *In His Own Time* (1971), *The Basil and Josephine Stories* (1976), and *The Price Was High* (1979). His correspondence, beyond that in *The Crack-Up*, appears in *Letters* (1963) and *As Ever, Scott Fitz-* (1972). His *Poems* were collected in 1981.

FITZGERALD, ROBERT STUART (1910–85), after graduation from Harvard became a writer for *Time* (1936–49) and a professor of creative writing, after 1965 at Harvard. In addition to his own poetry collected in *A Wreath for the Sea* (1943), *In the Rose of Time* (1956), and *Spring Shade* (1971), he translated the *Odyssey* (1961), for which he received a Bollingen Prize, the *Iliad* (1974), with Dudley Fitts, plays of Sophocles and Euripides, and, on his own, a translation of the *Aeneid* (1983). *Enlarging the Charge* (1984) collects literary criticism. In 1993 was published *The Third Kind of Knowledge: Memoirs and Selected Writings*, edited by P.L. Fitzgerald. It contains literary essays, recollections, and reminiscences.

FITZGERALD, ZELDA (1899–1948), wife of F. Scott Fitzgerald, whose turbulent life and marriage are reflected in his *Tender Is the Night* and her novel, *Save Me the Waltz* (1932), her version of their life together.

FITZHUGH, GEORGE (1806–81), Virginia lawyer and author, whose books, including *Sociology for the South; or, The Failure of Free Society* (1854) and *Cannibals All! or, Slaves Without Masters* (1857), are arguments for slavery and the plantation system, contending that laissez-faire capitalism and Northern industrialism had proved a failure.

FITZPATRICK, THOMAS (*c.*1799–1854), Irish-born frontiersman, was a member of Ashley's 1823 expedition, helped to establish the South Pass route, and guided emigrants to California and Oregon.

Five Little Peppers and How They Grew, book for children by Harriet Lothrop. ◆

Five Nations, see *Iroquois.*

Five-Foot Shelf, see *Eliot, C.W.*

Fixer, The, novel by Bernard Malamud, ◆ published in 1966, winner of a National Book Award and a Pulitzer Prize.

Yakov Bok, a middle-aged Jew, eking out a living as a handyman or "fixer" in Czarist Russia about 1910, after an unhappy marriage leaves his home province for Kiev. There he chances to rescue a man named Lebedev who was undergoing some kind of physical seizure. As a reward he is made an accountant at Lebedev's brickworks and has to live in an area closed to Jews. When a local Christian boy is found murdered in a grisly way, Yakov is arrested as a scapegoat by officials who want a reason to start a pogrom. After two years in prison, often in solitary confinement, he is finally brought to trial, innocent but aware that there is "no such thing as an unpolitical man, especially a Jew."

FLAGG, JAMES MONTGOMERY (1877–1960), painter and illustrator of fiction both for children in *St. Nicholas* and for adults, as well as a poster artist, whose best-known patriotic work, done for recruiting in World War I, depicted the finger-pointing Uncle Sam declaring, "I want you." Flagg's own books include *Yankee Girls Abroad* (1900), *City People* (1909), and an autobiography, *Roses and Buckshot* (1946).

Flammonde, poem in iambic pentameter couplets by E.A. Robinson, ◆ published in *The Man Against the Sky* (1916). It describes the mysterious elderly citizen of Tilbury Town, Flammonde, who, although outwardly a failure, is a constant source of sympathy for the town's troubled and needy.

FLANAGAN, THOMAS (1923–   ), born in Connecticut, for many years a professor specializing in Irish literature at the University of California, Berkeley. Currently at SUNY, Stony Brook.

Flanagan published a lengthy historical novel in 1979, *The Year of the French,* which won the National Book Award. It depicts characters in the failed Irish uprising—to have been coordinated with Napoleon's invasion—of 1798. His other novels are *The Tenants of Time* (1988), treating Irish history fictionally from the Fenian Rising in 1867 to the death of Parnell in 1891, and *The End of the Hunt* (1995), coming up through the Easter Rising to the 1920s.

FLANDRAU, CHARLES MACOMB (1871–1938), Minnesota author and journalist, a Harvard graduate, wrote many stories about undergraduate life, collected in three volumes, *Harvard Episodes* (1897), *The Diary of a Freshman* (1901), and *Sophomores Abroad* (1935). He also wrote two volumes of witty and perceptive essays, *Prejudices* (1911) and *Loquacities* (1931), and a notable book of sketches, *Viva Mexico!* (1908), based on the years he spent on his brother's coffee plantation.

FLANNER, JANET (1892–1978), Indianapolis-born foreign correspondent who, from its founding in 1925, contributed an occasional Letter from Paris to *The New Yorker.* Other writings include *The Cubical City* (1926), a novel; *An American in Paris* (1940), New Yorker "profiles"; and *Men and Monuments* (1957), about modern French artists, Malraux, and Goering's art collecting. Her *Paris Journal* (vol. I, 1965) won a National Book Award; volume II (1971) continued her account to date of publication. She used the pseudonym Genêt.

Flathead Indians, name applied to several Northwestern tribes that practiced occipital flattening on their children, and even to such other tribes as the Nez Percé. The Salish of western Montana, the only tribe now known by the name, actually never employed this practice. The Flatheads figure in the *Journals* of Lewis and Clark, *The Adventures of Captain Bonneville,* and James Hall's *The Wilderness and the War Path.*

FLAVIN, MARTIN [ARCHER] (1883–1967), California playwright and novelist, whose first Broadway play, *Children of the Moon* (1923), was followed by many others, the more successful including *The Criminal Code* (1929) and *Broken Dishes* (1929). His novels include *Mr. Littlejohn* (1940), a humorous account of a businessman who abandons conventional life for travel and adventure; *Corporal Cat* (1941), the story of a German parachute soldier who comes down by mistake in his own country, and is killed by the people; *Journey in the Dark* (1943, Pulitzer Prize), the story of Sam Braden, a small-town boy who attains wealth as a Chicago businessman but fails to achieve personal maturity; *The Enchanted* (1947), about children seeking a world away from adults; and *Cameron Hill* (1957), a fictional study of a murderer.

FLETCHER, JOHN GOULD (1886–1950), Arkansas author, was influenced by Southern traditions, although from 1908 to 1933 he lived mainly in Europe. In England he was a leader of the Imagists, whose poetic theory is exemplified in *Irradiations: Sands and Spray* (1915) and *Goblins and Pagodas* (1916), and he experimented with polyphonic prose. His later work, beginning with *Breakers and Granite* (1921) and including *Branches of Adam* (1926), *The Black Rock* (1928), *XXIV Elegies* (1935), *The Epic of Arkansas* (1936), *South Star* (1941), and *The Burning Mountain* (1946), shows a return to the American scene, a more mystical tone, and a tendency toward classic forms. After his return to Arkansas he became a leader of the Agrarians.♦ He won a Pulitzer Prize for his *Selected Poems* (1938). His prose works include *Paul Gauguin* (1921); *John Smith—Also Pocahontas* (1928); *The Two Frontiers* (1930), about Russia and the U.S.; *Arkansas* (1947), a social history; and his autobiography, *Life Is My Song* (1937).

FLINT, TIMOTHY (1780–1840), Massachusetts missionary, whose *Recollections of the Last Ten Years* (1826), an account of his preaching pilgrimages in the Mississippi Valley, shows a firsthand acquaintance with the scenes used in his later novels. *Francis Berrian; or, The Mexican Patriot* (1826) is a romantic story of a New England Puritan in the Mexican revolution of 1822. *George Mason, the Young Backwoodsman* (1829) is a historical romance, and *The Life and Adventures of Arthur Clenning* (1828) is a fantastic tale of castaways in the South Seas and their later life on the Illinois frontier. *The Shoshonee Valley* (1830) tells the story of a New England mariner and his Chinese wife, who abandon civilization to live among the Indians. Flint was a professed follower of Chateaubriand, but, although he generally romanticizes the background, some of his writing on the Far West has a claim to realism. He also published *The Western Monthly Review* (1827–30), a literary journal interpreting the West, was the editor and probably largely the author of the *Narrative* of Pattie,♦ and a popular *Memoir of Daniel Boone* (1833).

Floating Bear, little magazine published (1961–69) in 37 numbers from New York by Diane di Prima and LeRoi Jones, whose contributors included Burroughs, Creeley, Duncan, McClure, and Whalen. It served as a newsletter and rapid means of publication because its simple mimeographed format allowed for frequent issuance.

Flowering Judas, title story of a collection by Katherine Anne Porter,♦ issued with five others in 1930 and with still another four in 1935.
Laura, a 22-year-old American resident in Mexico, has an uneasy relationship with the revolutionary leader Braggioni, who courts her, and with the principles of the revolution that she vaguely assists. When Braggioni returns to his wife one evening, Laura falls asleep, dreaming of Eugenio, another revolutionary leader, who killed himself in prison with sleeping pills she had brought him. In the dream he asks her to eat the flowers of a Judas tree so as to travel with him to the land of death, but when he accuses her of being a murderer, she awakens herself, crying aloud "No," in negation of the nameless disaster that she has long feared.

Flowering of New England, *The*, literary history by Van Wyck Brooks.♦

Flush Times of Alabama and Mississippi, *The*, 26 sketches by J.G. Baldwin,♦ published in 1853, dealing with the bench and bar of the Old Southwest during the early years of settlement, and ranging from comic anecdotes to careful biographies of legal notables. The work is vivid both as satire and as a realistic picture of the period, due to the bluff humorous exaggeration with which Baldwin presents backwoods lawyers, spreadeagle orators, liars, crooked gamblers, boasters, and tellers of tall tales.

FLYNT, JOSIAH, pseudonym of Josiah Flint Willard.♦

FOLGER, PETER (1617–90), grandfather of Benjamin Franklin, was a pioneer of Nantucket. His *A Looking-Glass for the Times* (1676), in homespun quatrains of ballad meter, cried out for religious liberty, and asserted that the Indian wars were intended by God to punish the bigotry of Massachusetts.

Folger Shakespeare Memorial Library, Washington, D.C. (dedicated 1932), is the gift of Henry Clay Folger (1857–1930) and his wife and is administered by his alma mater, Amherst. It contains the greatest collection in the U.S. of Shakespeareana, including 79 copies of the First Folio, and a great collection dealing with English culture before 1800.

Folklore of the U.S., see *American Folk-Lore Society; Ballad; Beaver, Tony; "Big Bear of Arkansas"; Billy the Kid; Boone, Daniel; Bridger, James; Bunyan, Paul; Carson, Kit; Casey Jones; "Celebrated Jumping Frog of Calaveras County"; Crockett, Davy; Fink, Mike; Frankie and Johnny; Frontier; James, Jesse; John Henry; Pacing Mustang; Spiritual; Tall tale; Uncle Remus; "Yankee Doodle."*

Folkways, see *Sumner, W.G.*

FOLLEN, CHARLES (1796–1840), born in Germany, emigrated to the U.S. because of his republican sympathies, and became Harvard's first professor of German literature. He was a leader of Abolitionism and other liberal movements, some of his lectures on these subjects being included in his *Works* (1841–42), edited by his wife Eliza Lee Cabot Follen (1787–1860), also influential in Massachusetts liberal movements, and the author of *Hymns for Children* (1825) and *Poems* (1839).

Following the Equator, autobiographical narrative by Clemens,♦ published in 1897 under his pseudonym Mark Twain. Describing the Australian section of his lecture tour around the world (1895), he works up, in a rather pedestrian way, second-hand materials concerning the aborigines, early settlers, and local animals. Although there are witty interludes, vivid accounts such as the one of the Sepoy Mutiny, and satirical disquisitions on the Boer War and imperialistic morality, the book has little of the inspiration that distinguishes Clemens's other travel accounts. In India, he is oppressed by the overpopulation, superstition, plagues, famines, and disasters, and by the disillusioned society resigned to the constant repetition of barren and meaningless processes, which foreshadows the pessimism of the books he wrote in 1898.

FONT, PEDRO (*d*.1781), Franciscan missionary, accompanied Anza's expedition (1776) up the California coast to San Francisco Bay. His diary, giving a graphic account of the expedition, was translated in the *Publications of Pacific Coast History* (1913).

Fool's Errand, A, semi-autobiographical novel by Albion W. Tourgée,♦ published in 1879 with the signature, "By One of the Fools." It was dramatized by Steele MacKaye (produced, 1881; published, 1969).

The "Fool," Comfort Servosse, is a Union colonel during the Civil War, and afterward buys a plantation near Verdenton (Greensboro, N.C.), to which he brings his family. His actions as an influential Republican, and his sale of land to the blacks, whom he befriends, win him many enemies, including General Gurney, whose son Melville falls in love with Servosse's daughter Lily. He consistently fights both carpetbaggers and the Ku Klux Klan, and he advances a plan to abolish state boundaries in the South, so that it might be readmitted to the Union on a territorial basis. His life is endangered by an infuriated mob, but he is saved by a timely message from General Gurney, who thereby wins Lily's gratitude. When Melville proposes marriage, Servosse accepts for his daughter, but she refuses unless the general will agree. This makes the marriage impossible until years later, when Servosse is dying of a fever contracted during a trip to Central America, and Gurney, with the rest of the "Fool's" enemies, is reconciled with his sincere and honorable opponent.

FOOTE, MARY HALLOCK (1847–1938), New York-born novelist, married a civil engineer (1876), and spent her later life in Colorado, Idaho, and California. Her stories of Western life include *The Led-Horse Claim*♦ (1883), *The Chosen Valley* (1892), and *Cœur d'Alene*♦ (1894). Among her later works of fiction are *Edith Bonham* (1917) and *Ground-Swell* (1919). Her reminiscences were edited by Rodman Paul as *A Victorian Gentlewoman in the Far West* (1972). *Angle of Repose* (1971) by Wallace Stegner is partly based on her life.

FOOTE, SHELBY (1916–   ), Mississippi-born author whose novels include *Tournament* (1949), *Follow Me Down* (1950), and *Love in a Dry Season* (1951), a trilogy depicting changed ways of life on a cotton plantation from the Civil War to World War II. *Shiloh* (1952) is a fictive view of the battle as seen by a few Union and Confederate soldiers. *September September* (1978) is a novel about the kidnapping of a rich black boy by three whites from Memphis. *Jordan County* (1953) collects stories and novellas. He also wrote a play (1964) with the same title. *The Civil War* (3 vols., 1958, 1964, 1973) is a narrative history.

For Lancelot Andrewes, critical essays by T.S. Eliot,♦ published in 1928. The title essay is an examination of the style and thought of the 17th-century Anglican bishop, whom Eliot finds to be not only important in the history of the church, but also distinguished for his prose and his vital thought. Other subjects include Bramhall, Machiavelli, Bradley, Baudelaire, Middleton, and Crashaw. In "The Humanism of Irving Babbitt," Eliot questions the possibility of a long life or significance for the New Humanism, since it is presented as an alternative to religion. He demonstrates that Babbitt's faith in civilization must have as discipline a center of dogmatic moral reference, derived from religious authority.

For the Union Dead, collection of poems by Robert Lowell,♦ published in 1964.

The last of the 35 poems of the book is the title poem, first published with a different title in the paperback edition (1960) of *Life Studies.* In 17 unrhymed, meterless quatrains it treats with bitter irony an example of degradation in New England as symptomatic of modern life, presenting the Boston Common dug up for an underground garage so that its monument to the noble, idealistic Colonel Shaw and his black regiment in the Civil War has to be propped up by a plank while "giant finned cars nose forward . . . a savage servility slides by on grease." Other poems deal with the Puritan heritage, the threat of nuclear war, the corruption of modern society, and personal relations, of which the most intense is the double sonnet, "Night Sweat," presenting the poet's own emotional turmoil.

For Whom the Bell Tolls, novel by Hemingway,♦ published in 1940. The title is derived from a sermon by Donne: "No man is an *Iland,* intire of it selfe; every man is a peece of the *Continent . . .* And therefore never send to know for whom the *bell* tolls; It tolls for *thee.*"

Robert Jordan, an American, has entered the Loyalist army during the Spanish Civil War of the 1930s, and has been sent to join a guerrilla band in the mountains near Segovia to blow up a strategic bridge at the exact minute that will help a Loyalist advance. During the three days and nights that he spends in the guerrillas' cave, he awaits with a romantic opposition to heroism what he suspects will be his own destruction and that of his companions. He falls in love with Maria, daughter of a Republican mayor, who has seen her parents killed and was herself raped by Falangists. Her close-cropped hair is a symbol of her tortures; Jordan helps her to regain her desire to live. Their passionate love is abetted by the powerful woman Pilar, who dominates the group by her force of character, gusto, and love of the Republic. Her man Pablo is wily but lacks belief and hence courage. The others include foul-mouthed Agustín; pedantic, dignified Fernando; the gypsy Rafael; and the adoring Andrés. A sense of impending disaster develops, with smol-dering opposition within the group, a Falangist attack on the guerrilla leader El Sordo on a neighboring hill, acts of cowardice by Pablo, and a mission by Andrés to Loyalist headquarters to carry a note from Jordan saying the advance is likely to fail, with the messenger impeded by the Communists' bureaucracy and suspicion. The generals finally realize they should have cancelled the attack, but it is too late. Leaving the retreat, Jordan successfully blasts the bridge. In the attempt to flee he is wounded, and forces the others to leave him. He lies on the hillside almost delirious, restraining himself from suicide so that he may shoot the leader of the Fascists, and thinks, "I have fought for what I believed in for a year now. If we win here we will win everywhere. . . ."

Forayers, The; or, The Raid of the Dog Days, novel by Simms, ◆ published in 1855. Its sequel in the Revolutionary Romances is *Eutaw.* ◆

In Carolina during 1781, Willie Sinclair, a rebel officer, loves Bertha Travis, whose weak-willed father falls into the power of the Tory soldier Inglehardt. Willie's father is Colonel Sinclair, an ardent Tory, whose home is nevertheless raided by a band of Tory irregulars, led by rough, villainous Hell-Fire Dick. Willie arrives, drives off the raiders, then learns of a plan to attack the Travis plantation. He hides his men in ambush and drives off Inglehardt, but old Travis and his son Henry are captured, while Bertha and her mother are saved.

FORBES, ESTHER (1891–1967), Massachusetts author, known for the biography *Paul Revere and the World He Lived In* (1942, Pulitzer Prize) and her historical novels: *O, Genteel Lady* (1926),

about a lady who rebels against 19th-century Boston conventions; *A Mirror for Witches* (1928), set in 17th-century New England; *Paradise* (1937), about the era of King Philip's War; *The General's Lady* (1938), about the Revolution; *The Running of the Tide* (1948), about clipper ship days in Salem; and *Rainbow on the Road* (1954), about a 19th-century New England itinerant limner. *Johnny Tremaine* (1943), a juvenile, is set in the Revolution.

FORBES, JAMES (1871–1938), New York dramatist, whose early farces were succeeded by the more important social comedies, *The Famous Mrs. Fair* (1919) and *The Endless Chain* (1922), about 20th-century standards in New York City.

FORCE, PETER (1790–1868), born in New Jersey, after serving in the War of 1812 became a Washington printer, publishing the *National Journal* (1823–31), a Whig newspaper, and was drawn into politics, becoming mayor (1836–40). He is best remembered for his historical works, including *National Calendar and Annals of the United States* (1820–24, 1828–36), an annual compilation of historical and statistical information; *Tracts and Other Papers, Relating Principally to the Origin, Settlement, and Progress of Colonies in North America* (4 vols., 1836–46), reprinting scarce early pamphlets; and *American Archives* (9 vols., 1837–53), a supplementary collection of rare official and private manuscript material covering the period 1774–76. He planned to publish at least 36 volumes of the last work, covering the period from the 17th century to 1789, having received authorization from the State Department and Congress. When Secretary of State Marcy refused to sanction further publications, he was forced to quit and to sell his collection of 22,000 books and 40,000 pamphlets to the Library of Congress. One of his historical works first proved (1855) the spuriousness of the Mecklenburg Declaration.

FORCHE, CAROLYN [LOUISE] (1950–), born in Detroit of Slovak lineage, was recognized immediately with her first book of poetry, *Gathering of the Tribes* (1976), in which she ranges from meditations on her Michigan childhood and stories of her Slovak forebears to tales of American Indians of the Southwest. Her second book of poems, *The Country Between Us* (1982, Lamont Prize), reflects her work with Amnesty International in El Salvador. These verses embody cruelty and pain, including, in "The Colonel," a particularly vivid encounter in which the colonel of the title casually empties a bag of human ears before the poet, who imagines the ears hearing the colonel's voice.

FORD, JESSE HILL (1928–), Alabama-born author, graduated from Vanderbilt University, for some time was a resident of Tennessee, the region where his fiction is set. *Mountains of Gilead* (1962), *The Liberation of Lord Byron Jones* (1965), *The Feast of St. Barnabas* (1969), and *The Raider* (1975) are novels, the last about a pre-Civil War period marked by violence, part of it between blacks and whites. *The Conversion of Buster Drumwright* (1963) is a play later converted by him to a musical version, *Drumwright* (1982). Ford was co-author of a film version (1969) of his second novel. *Fishes, Birds and Sons of Men* (1967) collects stories.

FORD, PAUL LEICESTER (1865–1902), novelist, scholar, and bibliographer, at the age of 11 precociously began work in his father's library of Americana, which resulted in his many scholarly editions, making available historical materials long unknown. These include *The Writings of Thomas Jefferson* (10 vols., 1892–94), and *The True George Washington* (1896), a series of essays presenting the first President's human traits, but not detracting from his greatness. Ford's versatility and energy caused him also to become a novelist, and his best-known works of fiction, *The Honorable Peter Stirling*♦ (1894) and *Janice Meredith*♦ (1899), reflect his knowledge of American life and history. While at the height of his activities, he died tragically at the hands of his disinherited brother, Malcolm.

FORD, RICHARD (1944–   ), author of fiction, wide-ranging in region and treatment. His work includes the novels *A Piece of My Heart* (1976), set in his youthful home area of the Arkansas and Mississippi border; *The Ultimate Good Luck* (1981), about U.S. citizens in the drug business of Oaxaca; and *The Sportswriter* (1986), a tale of a man probing his life in the town of Princeton. *Wild Life* (1990) is a short novel chronicling the ruin of a Montana family seen through the eyes of a 16-year-old son. *Rock Springs* (1987) collects short stories, often set in Montana.

Ford, The, novel by Mary Austin,♦ published in 1917.

FORD, WORTHINGTON CHAUNCEY (1858–1941), a brother of P.L. Ford,♦ was long associated with the Library of Congress, the Boston Public Library, and the Massachusetts Historical Society. His editorial work includes *Winnowings in American History* (15 vols., 1890–91), in collaboration with his father and brother, and a complete edition of Washington's writings (12 vols., 1899), a two-volume *Letters of Henry Adams* (1930, 1938), and other important editions of works by the Adams family.

Ford Foundation, created (1936) by Henry Ford and his son Edsel, after their deaths became the world's largest philanthropic endowment, with assets of over $6 billion. The diverse programs it has supported are mostly in the fields of world law and peace, advancement of basic democratic principles, improvement of the world's economic conditions, strengthening of education, and scientific study of forces affecting humanity.

Foregone Conclusion, A, novel by Howells,♦ published in 1875.

Florida Vervain and her invalid mother, American expatriates in Venice, meet Henry Ferris, a young American painter. He recommends Don Ippolito, an Italian priest, as Florida's tutor. Ippolito confesses his agnosticism to the girl, and she, in a spirit of friendship, advises him to give up the sacerdotal life and go to America. Mistaking her interest for love, he confesses his feelings for her. Ferris, believing Florida to be in love with Ippolito, leaves Venice. Ippolito dies of a broken heart, and on his deathbed reveals the truth about his relations with Florida, but Ferris, unconvinced, roams Europe for years before he returns to America to marry Florida.

Forest Hymn, A, blank-verse poem by Bryant,♦ published in 1825, and reprinted as the title piece of a volume (1860).

Expressing a concept of nature akin to that of Wordsworth, Bryant proclaims, "The groves were God's first temples," where He raised shrines for beauty before the advent of human religion, and the flower still seems "an emanation of the indwelling Life" which pervades all things. The poet communes in the forest with "the perpetual work of thy creation, finished, yet renewed forever," and prays that men, in meditation there, may

. . . to the beautiful order of thy works
Learn to conform the order of our lives.

Forest Rose, The; or American Farmers, melodrama by Samuel Woodworth,♦ produced and published in 1825. It is distinguished for its comic Yankee, Jonathan, and it revived interest in this type.

FORESTER, pseudonym of T. Paine.♦

FORESTER, FANNY, pseudonym of Emily C. Judson.♦

FORESTER, FRANK, pseudonym of H.W. Herbert.♦

FORREST, EDWIN (1806–72), tragedian noted for Shakespearean roles and for performances in Bird's *Metamora, The Gladiator,* and *The Broker of Bogota.* Owing to his failure to reimburse Bird fully, the two friends quarreled, and Forrest's unfortunate jealousy was again exhibited in his treatment of his English rival, Macready, leading to the Astor Place riot♦ (1849). Forrest's fear of rivalry caused him to forbid the publication of plays written for him, so that they exist either in manuscript or in modern scholarly editions.

FORREST, LEON (1937–), Chicago-born and reared, has long taught African-American Studies at Northwestern University, and written novels often said to be particularly influenced by Faulkner. They are: *There Is a Tree More Ancient Than Egypt* (1973), about some illegitimate children of a one-time slave-owning family; *The Bloodworth Orphans* (1977); and *Two Wings To Veil My Face* (1984), about a black woman who first appeared in his earliest novel. He has also written *Re-Creation* (1978) and *Soldier Boy, Soldier* (1982), libretti for musicals.

FORREST, THOMAS, see *Disappointment, The.*

FORT, CHARLES [HOY] (1874–1932), journalist and author acclaimed by enthusiasts who organized The Fortean Society (1931) and founded its magazine *Doubt.* His books containing esoteric theories on psychic and other phenomena, *The Book of the Damned* (1919), *New Lands* (1923), *Lo!* (1931), and *Wild Talents* (1932), are based on library research and presumably agree with scientific facts; they deal, according to one reader, with "portents, the horrors and mysteries of Nature, disappearances, strange forms of demise."

Fort Barthold Indians, see *Arikara* and *Mandan.*

Fortune (1930–), magazine of business, finance, and industry, founded by the publishers of *Time.* It was a monthly noted for lengthy articles based on the work of a large research staff but written by associate editors, who have included Archibald MacLeish and John Chamberlain. Both technological and sociological in approach, it was more dignified in tone than *Time* or *Life,* even though serious subjects were mingled with considerations of such fringe matters as café society and debutante budgets. Its authors included James Agee, Alfred Kazin, Louis Kronenberger, and Dwight Macdonald. In 1978 it became a fortnightly, changed from its grand format, and grew more journalistic with shorter articles and an emphasis on timeliness and on regional and demographic issues for separate editions.

Forty-niners, emigrants to California in the gold rush of 1849, which followed the discovery of gold by James Marshall (Jan. 1848). By June 1848, the local rush to the gold fields was in full course, and President Polk's message to Congress (Dec. 5), incorporating news of the possibilities of great wealth, inaugurated the international excitement. Ships were diverted from their usual routes to carry gold seekers from European countries, China, Australia, and the South Seas. Many Mexicans came by overland routes, and it is believed that a total of nearly 100,000 persons had entered the territory by the end of 1849. The thousands of emigrants from the eastern U.S. used three principal routes: by ship around Cape Horn; a combination of sea and land travel, crossing Central America by the Panama or Nicaragua route; and in wagon trains across the Plains. The common goal was the Mother Lode region. ◆ Innumerable diaries, letters, and other writings of the period have been published, including those by Alonzo Delano, ◆ "Dame Shirley," ◆ and Bayard Taylor, ◆ and the forty-niners figure frequently in literature, the earliest major fictional interpretation being by Bret Harte.

42nd Parallel, The, novel by Dos Passos, ◆ published in 1930. It is the first of the trilogy *U.S.A.* (collected 1938), including *1919* ◆ (1932) and *The Big Money* ◆ (1936). Interspersed in the narrative are brief biographies of Debs, Burbank, Haywood, Bryan, Minor Keith, Carnegie, Edison, Steinmetz, and La Follette. (For critical discussion, see *Dos Passos.*)

Fainy ("Mac") McCreary, imbued with social idealism by his uncle Tim O'Hara, works for a book distributing company whose proprietor defrauds him. With a socialist friend he bums across the continent, works for an anarchist printer in San Francisco, edits an I.W.W. paper, marries, deserts his wife and children, and goes to Mexico with a revolutionist.

J. Ward Moorehouse, son of an Ohio station agent, becomes a shrewd, ruthless trader, marries and moves to Paris with Annabelle Strang, divorces her, and enters Pittsburgh journalism and advertising. He marries a steel heiress, Gertrude Stagle, and fosters a plan of "co-operation" between capital and labor at the outbreak of World War I.

Eleanor Stoddard and Eveline Hutchins become interior decorators in Chicago; Eleanor alone continues the business, decorates the Moorehouse home, and becomes intimate with the capitalist.

Janey Williams, left friendless when her brother Joe enlists in the navy, has an unhappy affair with Jerry Burnham, who becomes a war correspondent, and gets a job with G.H. Barrow, a dishonest labor leader, through whom she meets Moorehouse. Becoming the latter's secretary, she accompanies him to Mexico in a vain attempt to "buy" Mac; again in New York, she quarrels with her brother over U.S. participation in the war, which he denounces as the plot of munitions makers. She becomes intimate with Barrow, when Moorehouse concentrates his ardor on Eleanor. His wife is jealous until she feels her position assured when they go to Washington, where he aids in the impending entrance into the war.

Charley Anderson, a poor North Dakota boy, is attracted to socialism and the I.W.W., travels through the U.S., meets Ben Compton, brother of Janey's roommate Gladys, and learns of Moorehouse's big business propaganda. Disillusioned by the suppression of socialism, and craving action, he and his friend Doc Rogers join a French ambulance corps.

47 Workshop, see *Baker, George P.*

Forum, The (1886–1950), monthly magazine concerned with the discussion of contemporary problems. W. H. Page was its editor (1891–95), and the original policies were continued by most of his successors, although the magazine was a quarterly (1902–8), and published fiction as well as articles (1925–36). In 1923, H.G. Leach became editor, and his policies made *The Forum* also a magazine of controversy, actively debating national and international questions. In 1930 it absorbed *The Century,* and was called *Forum and Century* until it merged with *Current History* to become *Current History and Forum* (1940).

FOSDICK, CHARLES AUSTIN (1842–1915), known by his pseudonym Harry Castlemon, wrote some 58 novels for boys, many based on his own adventures or on experiences on gunboats during the Civil War. The works (1864–1904) were written in series: The Boy Trappers Series (hunting); The Sportsman's Club Series (sports); War, Afloat and Ashore Series (war); and Pony Express and Rocky Mountain Series (Western adventure).

FOSS, SAM WALTER (1858–1911), after education in his native New Hampshire and graduation from Brown University (1882), became owner, editor, and humorous columnist for the *Saturday Union* of Lynn, Mass., and then writer in Boston for other papers. His homespun, humorous poems, of which the best known is "The House by the Side of the Road," were collected in volumes including *Back Country Poems* (1892) and *Songs of the Average Man* (1907).

FOSTER, HANNAH WEBSTER (1759–1840), wife of a Massachusetts clergyman, was the author of *The Coquette*◆ (1797), a popular sentimental novel, and *The Boarding School; or, Lessons of a Preceptress to Her Pupils* (1798), a series of didactic lectures to young ladies.

FOSTER, STEPHEN COLLINS (1826–64), songwriter and composer, was born near Pittsburgh, Pa., and educated in local schools and at home. He early showed an interest in music, and although he received no formal training composed his first song, "Sadly to Mine Heart Appealing," when he was 13. In 1846 he went to Cincinnati, and while working as a bookkeeper wrote a number of songs, making a present of them to a local publisher, who issued them without Foster's name as *Songs of the Sable Harmonists* (1848). This collection, which included "Oh! Susannah,"◆ "Uncle Ned," and other popular pieces, was so successful that Foster gave up bookkeeping to

make a business of composing songs. The works of the following years included some 175 songs; among them "Old Folks at Home" ("Swanee River"), "Old Black Joe," "My Old Kentucky Home," "Nelly Was a Lady," "Camptown Races," "Nelly Bly," "Massa's in de Cold, Cold Ground," "Old Dog Tray," "Hard Times Come Again No More," "Jeanie with the Light Brown Hair," and "Come Where My Love Lies Dreaming." Some of these were sentimental ballads of the conventional kind, although distinguished for melodic content, but most of them were "Ethiopian songs" intended for performance by the popular black minstrel shows. In 1851 Foster made an agreement with E.P. Christy whereby his songs were to be first performed by Christy's Minstrels, and published with Christy's name as composer. The various editions of *Ethiopian Melodies,* in which many of Foster's songs appeared, bore the minstrel's name. Although these works capture the spirit of the black people so perfectly that they are often considered folk songs, Foster had never visited the South until he made a brief journey to New Orleans in 1852. His knowledge of the South and its people was derived mainly from minstrel shows and black camp meetings. His few instrumental compositions are seldom heard, but his songs have become popular classics, and he has been called "one of the greatest *melodists* we have ever produced." The tradition that he spent his life in dire poverty is untrue, for he was well paid for most of his early works, but an unhappy family life and an extreme sensitiveness led him to drink, and during the last years he was reduced to want, finally dying as the result of an accidental fall in his room in a Bowery lodging house.

Fountain, The, play by O'Neill,◆ produced in 1925 and published in 1926.

Fountainhead, The, novel by Ayn Rand,◆ published in 1943. It celebrates the achievements of an architect (presumably suggested by Frank Lloyd Wright) who is fiercely independent in pursuing his own ideas of design and who is therefore an example of the author's concept of Objectivism, which lauds individualism and "rational self-interest."

Four Hundred, THE, term applied to the leaders of fashionable society in the U.S. It is supposed to have referred to the exclusive group invited to an entertainment of Mrs. William Astor in New York City (1892), when Ward McAllister cut her list of guests to 400 because her ballroom would accommodate no more.

Four Million, The, 25 short stories by W.S. Porter,◆ published in 1906 under his pseudonym O. Henry. A preface explains the title: "Not very long ago some one invented the assertion that there were only 'Four Hundred' people in New York City who were really worth noticing. But a wiser man has arisen—the census taker—and his larger estimate of human interest has been preferred."

"The Gift of the Magi" is a tale of two New Yorkers who sell their most valued possessions to buy Christmas gifts for each other. Unknown to her husband, the wife sells her hair in order to purchase a chain for his watch, while he secretly sells the watch to buy her a pair of combs. "Of all who give and receive gifts, such as they are wisest. . . . They are the magi. . . ." "The Furnished Room" tells of a cheap boardinghouse room haunted by the "ghosts" of unfortunate residents. An attractive girl, penniless and despairing of her career as a singer, commits suicide in it. A week later her former sweetheart rents it. When he scents a trace of the mignonette she used to wear but can find no clue of her presence, he too commits suicide.

Four Quartets, cycle of poems by T.S. Eliot,♦ collected in 1943. These religious and philosophic meditations have a musical structure implied by their title, and are composed of four long lyrics titled by place names: "Burnt Norton," the site of an English country house; "East Coker," the English village that was the Eliot family's ancestral home; "The Dry Salvages," a group of rocks off Cape Ann, Massachusetts; and "Little Gidding," the British site of a 17th-century Anglican community. The dominant themes are time present, time past, time future, timelessness, identity, memory, consciousness, and place.

Four Saints in Three Acts, opera with libretto by Gertrude Stein♦ and music by Virgil Thomson.

Fourierism, communistic Utopian system for the reorganization of society, devised by Charles Fourier (1772–1837), French socialist author. He argued that the universe was so created that there is a harmonious connection between the organic and inorganic, between man and God, man and the world, and the world and the universe. Human passions are unchangeable, but, with due allowance for the variety of individual aptitudes and abilities, they may be brought to an equilibrium or harmony. For this purpose, Fourier wished to create phalansteries, social units of some 1600 persons, who would divide their labor according to their natural inclinations and abilities. Thereby the artificial restraints of ordinary civilized life would be destroyed, while a systematic agricultural society would be created in which all could live as one family, and yet retain many individual rights. Albert Brisbane, Horace Greeley, and Parke Godwin were the principal figures in developing Fourierism in the U.S. The best-known colony was the North American Phalanx.♦ Brook Farm♦ was for a time Fourierist, and a colony was founded in Texas by Fourier's chief disciple, Victor Considérant.♦ The movement had a temporary vogue among U.S. reform groups, but declined after the 1850s.

FOX, GEORGE, see *Quakers.*

FOX, JOHN [WILLIAM], JR. (1862–1919), born at Stony Point, Ky., spent part of his youth among the mountaineers of the Cumberlands, whose life is the main subject of his fiction. With the publication of *A Cumberland Vendetta* (1896), he began his series of novelettes about stereotyped pure mountain girls, savage villains, and the grimly beautiful mountains. Such works include "Hell fer Sartain" (1897), *The Kentuckians* (1898), and *A Mountain Europa* (1899). As a correspondent for *Harper's Weekly* during the Spanish-American War, Fox gained the material for *Crittenden* (1900), the story of a Southerner whose patriotism for the Union is aroused by a foreign war. Although still steeped in sentiment, his later novels, *The Little Shepherd of Kingdom Come*♦ (1903) and *The Trail of the Lonesome Pine*♦ (1908), brought him his greatest recognition. *Erskine Dale, Pioneer* (1920) is a romance of Kentucky and Virginia during the Revolution.

FOX, MARGARET (1836–93), with her sisters Katherine and Leah conducted a sensational series of spiritualistic séances in upstate New York, and, although they were later discredited, inaugurated the vogue of spiritualism in the U.S. Her affair with the Arctic explorer Kane was the subject of an anonymous book, *The Love-Life of Doctor Kane* (1856).

FOX, WILLIAM PRICE (1926–   ), Illinois-born author, reared in South Carolina, the setting for his stories collected in *Southern Fried* (1962) and *Southern Fried Plus Six* (1968) and his novel *Moonshine Light, Moonshine Bright* (1967), the salty tale of two teenaged boys involved in a variety of skulduggery. *Ruby Red* (1971), another novel, whose setting is extended to Nashville, presents the seamy life of girls trying to get into country-singer show business. Still another, *Dixiana Moon* (1981), is about the antic adventures of a young man in show business. *Dr. Golf* (1963) collects his humorous articles on golf, and *Chitlin Strut and Other Madrigals* assembles 13 of his stories.

Fox Indians, see *Sauk Indians.*

Francesca da Rimini, title of plays by G.H. Boker♦ and F.M. Crawford.♦

FRANCHÈRE, GABRIEL (1786–1863), Canadian fur trader, entered Astor's service in New York (1810) and assisted in the founding of Astoria, where he remained until 1814, as described in his *Relation d'un voyage á la côté du nord ouest de L'Amérique Septentrionale* (1820; revised in an English translation, 1854), a source of Irving's *Astoria.* He was later an Astor agent in Canada and established his own fur-trading company in New York.

FRANCIS, CONVERS (1795–1863), Unitarian minister at Watertown, Mass. (1813–36), professor at Harvard Divinity School (1842–63), and member of the Transcendental Club. He influenced the Transcendentalist movement mainly through his teaching of German idealistic philosophy. Lydia M. Child was his sister.

FRANCO, HARRY, see *Briggs, C.F.*

FRANK, WALDO [DAVID] (1889–1967), New Jersey-born novelist and critic, graduated from Yale (1911), spent some time abroad, and in 1916–17 was a founder and editor of *The Seven Arts.*♦ His novels, marked by mysticism, poetic style, and introspective analysis, include *The Unwelcome Man* (1917), the story of a sensitive, unloved child; *The Dark Mother* (1920); *Rahab* (1922), about a woman's descent to prostitution, while ever striving after God and truth; *City Block* (1922); *Holiday* (1923), about race problems in the South; *Chalk Face* (1924), a horror tale; *The Death and Birth of David Markand* (1934), about an American businessman who deserts his commonplace life to seek faith and understanding; *The Bridegroom Cometh* (1939), a Marxist novel about a woman's discovery of faith through her work for social reform; *Summer Never Ends* (1941); *Island in the Atlantic* (1946), about New York City from the Civil War to World War I; and *The Invaders* (1948), a parable of contemporary society. Besides an expressionistic play, *New Year's Eve* (1929), Frank, who called himself "a philosophical social revolutionary," wrote *Our America* (1919), on U.S. society; *Salvos* (1924), essays and social studies; *Virgin Spain* (1926, revised 1942), *South American Journey* (1943), and *Dawn in Russia* (1932), travel accounts; *The Re-Discovery of America* (1928), an analysis of the U.S., past and present; *America Hispaña* (1931), on South American history and ideals; *In the American Jungle* (1937), on industrial America; *Chart for Rough Water* (1940), setting forth a plan for an idealistic leadership by the Americas; *The Jew in Our Day* (1944); *Birth of a World* (1951), about Bolivar; *Bridgehead* (1957), impressionistic sketches of Israel; and *Cuba: Prophetic Island* (1961).

Frank Leslie's Popular Monthly (1876–1906), was founded by Frank Leslie.♦ Although it passed out of the hands of his family (1904), it was continued with similar policies as *Leslie's Monthly Magazine* until 1906, when it was sold and became *The American Magazine.*♦

FRANKFURTER, FELIX (1882–1965), born in Austria, was brought to the U.S. (1894), and after graduation from Harvard Law School (1906) became a professor there (1914–39). During World War I he held such offices as assistant to the secretary of war, assistant to the secretary of labor, and chairman of the War Labor Policies Board. An important liberal adviser to the administration of Franklin Roosevelt, he was appointed to the U.S. Supreme Court (1939) and served until

1962. His writings include *The Case of Sacco and Vanzetti* (1927); *The Business of the Supreme Court* (1928), in collaboration with J.M. Landis; *The Public and Its Government* (1930); and *Mr. Justice Holmes and the Supreme Court* (1938). His "occasional papers" (1913–38) were edited as *Law and Politics* (1939).

Frankie and Johnny, folk ballad of uncertain origin, first known in the mid-19th century and first printed in 1912. It is believed that the ballad describes the actual murder of a St. Louis black man (Johnny) by his mistress (Frankie). Early versions called the lovers Frankie and Albert, and there are some 300 variants of the music and verses. A play of this title was written in 1930 by John Huston.

FRANKLIN, BENJAMIN (1706–90), born in Boston, was a grandson of Peter Folger.♦ At the age of ten he began to work with his father, a tallow chandler and soap boiler, and from 12 to 17 was apprenticed to his half-brother James Franklin, to whose *New England Courant* he contributed his Dogood Papers♦ (1722). He had little formal education, but read widely, being particularly influenced by Locke, Shaftesbury, Xenophon, the *Spectator,* and some of Cotton Mather's works. After a quarrel with his brother (1723), he ran off to Philadelphia, where he entered the printing shop of Samuel Keimer. Under the patronage of Governor Keith, he was sent to England to buy equipment for his own press, but, failing to receive the necessary money, he worked in a London printing house. While abroad he wrote *A Dissertation on Liberty and Necessity, Pleasure and Pain* (1725) to refute Wollaston's *Religion of Nature Delineated,* which he had set in type.

He returned to Philadelphia (1726), and four years later had his own press, from which he issued *The Pennsylvania Gazette*♦ (1729–66), contributing such pieces as the letters of Anthony Afterwit and Alice Addertongue, and "A Witch Trial at Mount Holly." He also wrote, at this time, the Busy-Body Papers♦ and "Dialogues between Philocles and Horatio" (1730). He made a common-law union (1730) with Deborah Read, daughter of his first landlady, by whom he had two children. He was also the father of two illegitimate children. By frugality, industry, and native shrewdness he established a successful business. His popularity and prestige were enhanced by his *Poor Richard's Almanack*♦ (1733–58) and the Junto Club♦ (1727).

In his pragmatic way, he devised at 22 a "religion" for the attainment of useful virtues, holding firmly to the belief that the most acceptable service to God is doing good to men. When he had kept his shop so well that it kept him, he became a leader in philanthropic, scientific, and political affairs. He initiated projects for establishing city police, for paving, cleaning, and lighting the streets, and for the first circulating library. He also founded the American Philosophical Society, a city hospital, and an Academy for the Education of Youth, which was the forerunner of the University of Pennsylvania. For a time he published the second monthly magazine issued in America. *The General Magazine*♦ (1741), and some of his diverse interests are reflected in *A Proposal for Promoting Useful Knowledge* (1743), *Plain Truth, or Serious Consideration on the Present State of the City of Philadelphia* (1747), and *Proposals Relating to the Education of Youth in Pensilvania* (1749). He was interested in every sort of natural phenomenon, and made many scientific experiments, including his famous kite experiment to show the identity of lightning and electricity (reported in *Experiments and Observations on Electricity*, 1751–54). He had already invented the Franklin Stove (described in his *Account of the New Invented Pennsylvania Fire Place*, 1744), as well as a new kind of clock.

After holding minor public offices, he was made deputy postmaster-general for the colonies (1753–74), and was Pennsylvania's representative at the Albany Congress (1754), at which his "Plan of Union" was seriously considered. In 1757 he was sent to England to attempt to secure better governmental conditions for the colony, and he remained abroad, with brief interruptions, until 1775. There he was intimate with Burke, Hume, Adam Smith, Chatham, and other thinkers; received degrees from three British universities; continued his scientific interests; wrote a pamphlet that anticipated the Malthusian theory of population; and published *An Historical Review of the Constitution and Government of Pennsylvania* (1759) and an influential argument for the retention of Canada, *The Interest of Great Britain Considered with Regard to Her Colonies* (1760). He protested against the Stamp Act, and in his examination before the House of Commons (1766) increased his prestige by his lucid replies, which showed that the tax was contrary to custom.

When Georgia, New Jersey, and Massachusetts joined Pennsylvania in designating him as their agent, Franklin's position assumed virtually ambassadorial importance. Meanwhile he published his *Cool Thoughts on the Present Situation of Our Public Affairs* (1764) and a *Preface to the Speech of Joseph Galloway* (1764), asking for the replacement of the proprietary government of Pennsylvania by a royal charter. He demanded no colonial rights except those already possessed by all British subjects, and his admiration for England lessened in proportion to his increasing loyalty to the colonies. He strongly opposed the Townshend acts, and expressed his feeling in two satires, the "Edict by the King of Prussia"♦ (1773) and "Rules by Which a Great Empire May Be Reduced to a Small One"♦ (1773).

Because of his connection with the affair of the *Letters* of Thomas Hutchinson♦ (1772), he was dismissed from his postal position. Feeling that Lord North was driving the colonies into rebellion, he returned to America to serve in the Continental Congress, become postmaster-general, and aid in drafting the Declaration of Independence, after which he was sent to France to negotiate a treaty. Enthusiastically welcomed by the French as a witty and benign backwoods sage, a sort of Rousseauistic Socrates who was going to restore the Golden Age, he succeeded in securing a treaty of commerce and defensive alliance (Feb. 1778), after Burgoyne's surrender inspired confidence in America's prospects. In this year he was appointed plenipotentiary to the French court, obtained repeated loans from France, and negotiated commercial treaties with Sweden and Prussia. He also found time for scientific matters, for a frivolous correspondence with Mme Helvetius and Mme Brillon, and for amusing his friends by such urbane bagatelles from his private press at Passy as *The Ephemera* (1778), *The Morals of Chess* (1779), *The Whistle* (1779), and *The Dialogue Between Franklin and the Gout* (1780). He was a member of the commission that signed the Treaty of Paris (Sept. 1783), and in 1785 he returned home. After serving three years as president of the executive council of Pennsylvania, he became a member of the Federal Constitutional Convention, in which capacity he signed the Constitution, although he did not entirely approve of it. His last public act was the signature of a memorial to Congress for the abolition of slavery, and less than a month before his death he wrote an ironic letter "On the Slave Trade" to *The Federal Gazette*, as brilliant as the similar "Edict by the King of Prussia," which he had composed 17 years before.

His *Autobiography*, commenced in 1771, was never finished, and breaks off abruptly during the account of the year 1757, with a few random comments on the years 1757–59. It was published in England, France, and Germany before the American edition of 1818, but the complete work did not appear in English until 1867. This account is the epitome of Franklin's spirit. In it one sees him as a typical though great example of 18th-century enlightenment, a Yankee Puritan who could agree with Rousseau and Voltaire, and use the language of Defoe and Addison with a genial homely twang. His style, perfectly adapted to the ends to which he devoted it, is lucid, precise, and salty, revealing both his mental and moral temper. His mind was pragmatic, and though his greatest enthusiasm was reserved for science, he had a mellow tolerance for all types of thought. With candor and common sense, he relished the various turns in his life and took them easily, understanding and sharing the Gallic spirit while remaining pungently American. A definitive, scholarly edition of his *Papers* (1959–) under the editorship of Leonard W. Labaree (vols. 1–14) and William B. Willcox (vols. 15–) is planned in 40 volumes, 30 of which have now been published.

FRANKLIN, JAMES (1697–1735), Boston printer, issued *The Boston Gazette* ♦ from his press (1719–21), until the contract was taken from him to be given to another printer. He then founded *The New England Courant* ♦ (1721–26), a Yankee version of the *Spectator,* which, after his imprisonment for libelous remarks, appeared (1723–26) under the name of his half-brother and apprentice, Benjamin Franklin. In 1726 he moved to Rhode Island, taking with him the first press to be used in that colony, and printing on it *The Rhode Island Almanack* and the *Rhode Island Gazette* (1732–33). While associated with the *Courant,* he was the founder of the Hell-Fire Club. ♦ His son James Franklin, Jr., founded the *Newport Mercury.* ♦

FRANKLIN, WILLIAM (1730?–1813), son of Benjamin Franklin, grew up in Philadelphia, where he was comptroller of the general post office and clerk of the provincial assembly until 1757, when he went to England as his father's companion and secretary. He was royal governor of New Jersey (1763–76), but his Tory attitude led to his arrest and imprisonment during the Revolution, and after 1782 he lived in England. His father's *Autobiography* was written for his benefit. His son William Temple Franklin (1760–1823) was Benjamin Franklin's secretary in later years, and edited his works.

Franklin Evans, temperance tract by Whitman. ♦

Franny and Zooey, stories by J.D. Salinger. ♦

FREDERIC, HAROLD (1856–98), New York author, at 19 was a reporter on the *Utica Observer* and three years later became its editor. He was next editor of the *Albany Evening Journal* and London correspondent of *The New York Times.* His first novel, *Seth's Brother's Wife* (1887), is a realistic picture of New York farm life, local politics, and the less glamorous aspects of journalism. *The Lawton Girl* (1890) is the story of a girl who tries to live down a tarnished reputation in her native New York town. After a fantasy, *The Return of the O'Mahony* (1892), he wrote *The Copperhead* (1893), his first significant work, depicting the intolerant attacks upon Abner Beach, a New York farmer who opposes Abolitionism when this movement is sweeping the North during the Civil War. *The Damnation of Theron Ware* ♦ (1896), a realistic story of the fall of a Methodist minister, was his most popular work. He also wrote a historical novel, *In the Valley* (1890), dealing with the Revolution, and *Marsena and Other Stories* (1894), about the Civil War. *March Hares* (1896), *Gloria Mundi* (1898), and *The Market Place* (1899) are romantic stories based on his knowledge of English life. A scholarly edition of his *Major Works* began publication in 1978.

Free Enquirer, The, see *New Harmony.*

Free Religious Association, founded (1865) by liberal religious thinkers as a nonsectarian faith for people of intelligence, was a communion of various religions with no fetters of church, creed, or nation. Its supporters included O.B. Frothingham, R.D. Owen, T.W. Higginson, Alcott, and Emerson. *The Index* ♦ (1870–86) was an affiliated magazine.

Free verse (*vers libre*), poetry without a fixed metrical pattern, having a loosely organized rhythm. It is to be found in the work of some 19th-century American poets, e.g. Whitman and Stephen Crane, but it has been commonly employed only since World War I, its earlier users including the Imagists, Sandburg, Masters, Pound, and E.E. Cummings.

Freedom of Will, treatise by Jonathan Edwards, ♦ published in 1754. The full title is *A Careful and Strict Enquiry into the Modern Prevailing Notions, of that Freedom of Will which is supposed to be Essential to Moral Agency, Vertue and Vice, Reward and Punishment, Praise and Blame.* Written to uphold the doctrine of necessity against Arminianism, ♦ the work was frequently translated and reprinted, became a primary document in Calvinistic theology, and won Edwards eminence among American philosophers.

Defining the will as "that by which the mind chooses anything," and freedom or liberty as "the power, opportunity, or advantage, that any one has to do as he pleases, or conducting in any respect, according to his pleasure," the author bases his case for predestined necessity on the postulate that every event must have a cause. "That whatsoever begins to be which before was not, must have a Cause why it then begins to exist, seems to be the first dictate of the common and natural sense which God hath implanted in the minds of all mankind. . . ." Since volitions are events, they must have causes: "It is that motive, which, as it stands in the view of the mind, is the strongest, that determines the Will." Human motives impel us in the direction of what seems most agreeable, and this direction is determined entirely without independent activity on the part of the individual will. There is, then, no liberty of choice; liberty consists in the ability to act as one chooses. Having established this fundamental position, the author proceeds to refute the fallacies of "the Arminian notion of Liberty of Will," to answer possible objections, and to assert that his necessitarian position is the basis of Calvinistic doctrine.

FREEMAN, DOUGLAS SOUTHALL (1886–1953), editor of the Richmond *News Leader* (1915–53), professor of journalism at Columbia, and author of *R.E. Lee* (4 vols., 1934–35, Pulitzer Prize); *Lee's Lieutenants: A Study in Command* (3 vols., 1942–44); *The South to Posterity* (1939), lectures on the Confederacy; and *George Washington*

(6 vols., 1948–54; vol. 7, 1957, completed by two assistants, and all awarded a Pulitzer Prize).

FREEMAN, JOSEPH (1897–1965), Marxist critic, whose works include *The Soviet Worker* (1932); *Voices of October: Soviet Literature and Art* (1930); a critical introduction to *Proletarian Literature in the United States* (1935), an anthology; *An American Testament* (1936), an autobiography of his changing mind among "rebels and romantics"; and the novels, *Never Call Retreat* (1943), about a liberal Austrian refugee's frustrating background, and *The Long Pursuit* (1947), about a USO unit in Germany.

FREEMAN, MARY E[LEANOR] WILKINS (1852–1930), was born in Randolph, Mass., and spent most of her life there until her marriage in 1902, when she moved to New Jersey. The scenes she knew in eastern Massachusetts form the background for most of her tales of New England rural life. Her early work is a dispassionate observation of local character and constitutes an important contribution to the local-color school by its study of repressed people in a decaying social system, capturing their spirit through their dialect. Her first collections of tales, *A Humble Romance*♦ (1887) and *A New England Nun*♦ (1891), established her reputation and contain her finest work. The novels *Jane Field* (1893), *Pembroke* (1894), and *Jerome, a Poor Man*♦ (1897), show that her forte was not the novel but the short tale revealing a dominant characteristic. Mrs. Freeman was also the author of works in other forms, including *Giles Corey, Yeoman* (1893), a play about the Salem witchcraft trials; *The Heart's Highway* (1900), a historical novel; *The Portion of Labor* (1901), a social novel; and *The Wind in the Rose Bush* (1903), stories of the supernatural. *Edgewater People* (1918) is a collection of short stories of the type and nearly of the caliber of her early work. Her *Collected Letters* appeared in 1985.

Freeman, The (1920–24, 1930–31), weekly magazine of political and aesthetic criticism, edited with a liberal point of view, was founded by Van Wyck Brooks, A. J. Nock, and others. Financial failure caused its suspension, but it was revived as *The New Freeman* under the editorship of Suzanne La Follette.

Freemans Oath, see *Oath of a Free-man.*

FRÉMONT, JOHN CHARLES (1813–90), born in Georgia, as a lieutenant in the Topographical Corps, aided by his father-in-law, Senator Benton, was put in command of the governmental exploring expedition (1842) that scientifically reported and mapped the Oregon Trail through South Pass. The success of his *Report of the Exploring Expedition to the Rocky Mountains* (1843), written with his wife Jessie, led to command of an expedition (1843) to the Columbia which made a winter crossing of the Sierra to California, described in *Report of the Exploring Expedition to Oregon and North California* (1845), also sponsored by the Senate. On a third expedition, again accompanied by Kit Carson, this time to survey the central Rockies and the land to the Sierra, he crossed into California and led the Bear Flag revolt. Appointed governor of the newly won land by Commodore Stockton, he refused to recognize the authority of Kearny, sent to organize the local government, and was returned to Washington for a court-martial, in which he was found guilty of mutiny, but his sentence was remitted by President Polk and he was made a public hero. Resigned from the army, he led a disastrous expedition to survey routes for a transcontinental railway (1848–49), made a fortune in the gold rush, was elected U.S. senator from California (1850), led another private exploration for railroad interests (1853–54), and was the Republicans' first presidential candidate (1856). In his later, anticlimactic years he had a checkered Civil War career as a Union general, lost his wealth in railroad ventures, became territorial governor of Arizona (1878–93), and left incomplete his *Memoirs of My Life* (1887).

FRÉMONT, JESSIE BENTON (1824–1902), may have contributed to her husband's *Reports* beyond her work as amanuensis. Her own books include *The Story of the Guard* (1863), an autobiographical account of the Civil War; *A Year of American Travel* (1878), about California; and *Far West Sketches* (1890).

FRENCH, ALICE (1850–1934), born in Massachusetts, lived most of her life in Arkansas and Iowa, which provided the settings for her fiction written under the pseudonym Octave Thanet. A conventional figure in the local-color movement, she added nothing to its traditions except a certain interest in labor problems in the West. She is best known for her short stories, which are collected in such volumes as *Knitters in the Sun* (1887), *Stories of a Western Town* (1893), *The Missionary Sheriff* (1897), *The Captured Dream* (1899), and *Stories That End Well* (1911). Among her novels are *Expiation* (1890), *The Man of the Hour* (1905), and *A Step on the Stair* (1913).

FRENCH, MARILYN (1929–), New York City–born author, received a B.A. from Hofstra and a Ph.D. from Harvard, leading to her first book, *The Book as World—James Joyce's "Ulysses"* (1976). A later scholarly study is *Beyond Power* (1985), on the treatment of women for 2500 years. She has also written novels, *The Women's Room* (1977), a feminist view of a woman's life; *The Bleeding Heart* (1980), about an affair between two Americans in their forties, resident in England; *Her Mother's Daughter* (1987), about four generations of women in a family; and *Our Father* (1994), a novel about the lives of four half-sisters born of the same father, whose stroke is the occasion of their reunion. Scarcely having known each other before, they discover that their father had raped each as a young girl.

French and Indian Wars, name applied to the conflicts over Canada and the West involved in the territorial rivalry of France and Great Britain, and related to their larger imperial struggles abroad.

KING WILLIAM'S WAR (1689–97), roughly the American counterpart of the War of the Grand Alliance, had as its most important result the capture of Port Royal (Annapolis, Nova Scotia) by Sir William Phips and his Massachusetts troops, who failed in their campaign against Quebec. The Treaty of Ryswick (1697) restored all captured towns and districts.

During QUEEN ANNE'S WAR (1702–13), which corresponded to the War of the Spanish Succession, several New England towns were sacked, but, by the Peace of Utrecht (1713), Acadia,◆ Newfoundland, St. Kitts, and the Hudson's Bay territory were given to England.

KING GEORGE'S WAR (1744–48), part of the War of Jenkins' Ear and the War of the Austrian Succession, was signalized by Pepperell's capture of Louisburg, which was restored to France by the Treaty of Aix-la-Chapelle (1748).

Rivalry now centered about the Ohio Valley, which was captured by the British during the French and Indian War (1755–63), the American counterpart of the Seven Years' War. Washington defeated the French at Fort Necessity (Great Meadows, 1754), but was shortly forced to surrender, and Braddock was unsuccessful (1755) in his attempt to take the neighboring Fort Duquesne (Pittsburgh). In the ensuing battles, Sir William Johnson obtained the assistance of the Iroquois, Amherst captured Louisburg (1758) and Ticonderoga (1759), and Fort Duquesne was seized by the British (1758). Montcalm, the leading French general, had captured Fort Ontario (Oswego) and Fort William Henry (Lake George) in 1757, and was pitted against Wolfe in the battle for Quebec at the Plains of Abraham (1759). Both generals died in action, but the British gained Quebec and in 1760 took Montreal. In the Treaty of Paris (1763), France ceded her colonial empire in the St. Lawrence Valley, as well as all territory west to the Mississippi.

Parkman's are the best-known histories of the wars and Cooper wrote romances, including *The Last of the Mohicans* and *The Deerslayer*, concerning them. They also figure in later fiction, including Willa Cather's *Shadows on the Rock*.

FRENEAU, PHILIP [MORIN] (1752–1832), born in New York of Huguenot ancestry, was educated privately and at the College of New Jersey (Princeton). There he was a classmate of Madison and Brackenridge, and with the latter wrote the poem *The Rising Glory of America,*

which was read at the graduation exercises (1771) and published the following year. While at college he also wrote "The Power of Fancy" and other poems. After assisting Brackenridge in teaching in Maryland (1772), at the outbreak of the Revolution he wrote eight biting satirical poems, which included *General Gage's Soliloquy* (1775) and *General Gage's Confession* (1775). He discovered poetry to be a poor profession, however, and turned to a secretaryship in the home of a prominent planter on the island of Santa Cruz in the West Indies, where he wrote "The Beauties of Santa Cruz,"◆ "The Jamaica Funeral,"◆ and "The House of Night,"◆ romantic poems inspired by the lush tropical atmosphere. On his voyage home (June 1778) he was captured by the British, but was soon set free. After a short stay at home, he set out again for the West Indies (1780), only to be captured and, after a questionable trial, remanded to the British prison ship *Scorpion* in New York harbor. After a period of brutal treatment and starvation he was exchanged as a prisoner of war (July 1780). His experiences inspired the poem *The British Prison Ship*◆ (1781). During the next three years he was employed in the Philadelphia post office, and in his leisure poured forth a steady stream of satirical poetry that confirmed his title of "the poet of the American Revolution." In 1784 he sailed as master of a brig bound for Jamaica, and during the following six years led a life filled with dangers on the Atlantic and Caribbean. Meanwhile he wrote poems of life at sea, and published his first collection, *Poems* (1786), as well as a volume of *Miscellaneous Works* (1788). After his marriage in 1790 he abandoned the sea to become editor of the New York *Daily Advertiser,* and later, after an appointment by Jefferson as translating clerk of the State Department, on October 31, 1791, began the publication of his *National Gazette,* a sparkling Jeffersonian paper that particularly attacked Hamilton. During the two years of his editorship and his government appointment, Freneau was accused by Hamilton of being Jefferson's anti-Federalist mouthpiece, and even Washington called him "that rascal Freneau." He published *Poems Written Between the Years 1768 and 1794* (1795), and after a brief editorship of the *Jersey Chronicle* edited the New York *Time-Piece* (1797–99). On retiring to his plantation at Mount Pleasant, he issued a series of essays entitled *Letters on Various Interesting and Important Subjects* (1799). His last years were spent in New Jersey, although from 1803 to 1807 he was driven by poverty to serve again as a master of coastline freighters. In 1809, he published a two-volume edition of his collected poems, and in a final edition of 1815 included the patriotic and satirical poems prompted by the War of 1812. A scholarly edition of his poems was edited by F.L. Pattee (3 vols., 1902–7), and a selection of his prose, edited by H.H. Clark as *The Philosopher of the Forest,* appeared in 1939. *Last Poems* (1946) contains 50 poems, mainly on topics of the day, originally published in periodicals between 1815 and 1832. Among his best-known short poems of freedom are "Libera Nos, Domine," the ode "God Save the Rights of Man," "To the Memory of the Brave Americans," "On the Memorable Victory of John Paul Jones," and "To My Book," while among his noteworthy poems of romantic fancy are "The Indian Burying Ground,"♦ "The Wild Honey Suckle,"♦ "The Indian Student,"♦ "On a Honey Bee," "On Retirement," "To a Catydid," and "Advice to a Raven in Russia."

Frescoes for Mr. Rockefeller's City, poems in free verse by Archibald MacLeish,♦ published in 1933. In six "panels" for the walls of Rockefeller Center in New York City, from which the murals of Diego Rivera had been removed, the poet celebrates the American Land and its people, contrasting the vigorous laboring millions with the handful of capitalists ("It was all prices to them: they never looked at it: why should they look at the land").

"Landscape as a Nude" describes the American natural environment ("She has brown breasts and the mouth of no other country"). "Wildwest" tells of the defeat of the Indians before the drive of the railroad builders. "Burying Ground by the Ties" is the plaint of the immigrant laborers who built the tracks ("Not for this did we come out— to be lying here Nameless under the ties in the clay cuts"). "Oil Painting of the Artist as the Artist" satirizes expatriates and escapists. "Empire Builders" contrasts the manipulations of financiers with the constructive realities of the Lewis and Clark expedition. "Background with Revolutionaries," although satirizing doctrinaire radicals, expresses the poet's faith that the land and the people will be able to adjust social errors and correct abuses ("She's a tough land under the oaktrees mister: It may be she can change the word in the book . . .").

FRIEDAN, BETTY (1921–), born in Illinois, graduated from Smith College (1942), and has been a leader of feminist activities. Her major writing, *The Feminine Mystique* (1963), was followed by *It Changed My Life: Writings on the Women's Movement* (1976) and *The Second Stage* (1981), calling for a restructuring of institutions and therefore of power for women. *The Fountain of Age* (1993) is both a celebration of wisdom and acceptance in aging and a condemnation of American's treatment of the elderly, male and female.

FRIEDMAN, BRUCE JAY (1930–), New York City author, whose first novel, *Stern* (1962), presents a neurotic Jewish man with black humor, characteristic of later novels including *A Mother's Kisses* (1964), comically portraying a Jewish mother who not only chaperons her son Joseph at college but is an erotic figure in her

own right; *The Dick* (1970), dealing with a Jewish public relations man in police headquarters; and *About Harry Towns* (1974), portraying a middle-aged screenwriter. His other works include the plays *Scuba Duba* (1968), *Steambath* (1970), and *Foot in the Door* (1979); stories collected in *Far from the City of Class* (1963), *Black Angels* (1966), and *Let's Hear It for a Beautiful Guy* (1984), short fiction; a comic self-help manual, *The Lonely Guy's Book of Life* (1978); and *Tokyo Woes* (1985).

Friend of Peace, The, see *Worcester, Noah.*

Friendly Club, literary group of Hartford (c.1785–1807), whose members included John Trumbull, Timothy Dwight, Joel Barlow, Richard Alsop, and E.H. Smith, the Connecticut Wits♦ who contributed to *The Anarchiad*♦ and *The Echo*♦ (1785–1807).

Friendly Club of New York, organized some time after 1789 as an outgrowth of the Philological Society.♦ It was strongly patriotic and, aiming to further the literature of the new nation, sponsored *The Monthly Magazine and American Review.*♦ Members included James Kent, William Dunlap, C.B. Brown, E.H. Smith, and Richard Alsop.

Friends, RELIGIOUS SOCIETY OF, see *Quakers.*

Friendship Village, 20 sentimental stories in the local-color tradition, by Zona Gale,♦ published in 1908. The narrator is a woman who moves from a large city to a Midwest village, which she depicts as representative of "The little real home towns, their kindly, brooding companionship, their doors to an efficiency as intimate as that of fairy fingers."

"The Debut" describes the busy intrigue when Mrs. Ricker, who takes in washing, invites her patrons to a "coming out reception" for her daughter Emma Ella, 30 years old and engaged to be married. Mrs. Postmaster Sykes deliberately holds a reception the same evening; Emma Ella does not appear, having eloped; but all ends well when Mrs. Sykes brings her guests to join the other party. "The Grandma Ladies" is a Christmas story about Calliope Marsh, who cannot afford material gifts but entertains the "grandma ladies" of the Old Ladies Home, whom she gratifies by bringing a little child to join the celebration. "The Tea Party" tells of Mrs. Merriman, two years a widow, who will not appear at parties because she wishes to wear out her mourning costume before buying a new "best" dress. She solves her problem by appearing after a tea party has begun, and accepting refreshment apart from the other guests.

Fringed Gentian, see *To the Fringed Gentian.*

FRINGS, KETTI (1910–81), after writing two novels, *Hold Back the Dawn* (1940) and *God's Front Porch* (1944), and a play, *Mr. Sycamore* (1943), adapted Wolfe's *Look Homeward, Angel* (1957), for which she won a Pulitzer Prize for drama.

FROHMAN, CHARLES (1860–1915), New York theatrical manager, head of the theatrical trust of the 1890s, extended his operations to London after 1897 and created a system of exchange productions between the two cities, bringing to New York the works of Barrie, Galsworthy, Shaw, and Granville Barker.

FROHMAN, DANIEL (1851–1940), brother of Charles Frohman, was also famous as an impresario, and was the author of *Memories of a Manager* (1911), *Daniel Frohman Presents* (1935), and *Encore* (1937).

From Here to Eternity, novel by James Jones,♦ published in 1951.

Private Robert E. Lee Prewitt reports to a U.S. army base in Hawaii in 1941 and is subjected to psychological and physical harassment because, though known as a boxer in civilian life, he refuses to fight in the division championship since he had once accidentally blinded a friend in the ring. He breaks under "the treatment" and hits a noncom, for which he is sent to the stockade; there he experiences the brutality of Fatso Judson, the sergeant in charge, a sadist responsible for the death of his fellow prisoner Blues Berry, but from whom his friend Angelo had escaped by discharge after feigning madness. Prewitt kills Judson in a knife fight and runs off to hide with Lorene, a prostitute he loves. When the Japanese attack Pearl Harbor, Prewitt is killed by an M.P. as he tries to return to his company.

Front Page, The, play by Ben Hecht♦ and Charles MacArthur. ♦

FRONTENAC, LOUIS DE BUADE, Comte de (1620–98), French governor of New France (1672–82, 1689–98) whose attempts to obtain political independence for Canada were restrained by the home government. He was frequently in conflict with the sovereign council, the intendant or royal tax collector, and the Jesuits, and was recalled in 1682, only to be returned in 1689 to suppress uprisings of the Iroquois and to bring about their final submission (1696). He aided the explorations of Jolliet, Marquette, and La Salle, established military posts, repulsed the attack on Quebec by Sir William Phips, and made war on the New England coast. He is the subject of a work by Parkman, and figures in *Shadows on the Rock*. ♦

Frontier, in America the wilderness region marked by the farthest advance of white coloni-zation. The most popular conception of the significance of the frontier is derived from F.J. Turner,♦ although his theory has been attacked as "poetic," contradictory, and oversimplified. He contended that "the existence of an area of free land, its continuous recession, and the advance of American settlement westward, explain American development. . . ." This development is said to result from a return to primitive conditions on a continually advancing frontier, which is the meeting point of savagery and civilization. American democracy, according to Turner, came out of the American forest, whence it gained strength each time it touched a new frontier.

> . . . To the frontier the American intellect owes its striking characteristics. That coarseness and strength, combined with acuteness and acquisitiveness; that practical, inventive turn of mind, quick to find expedients; that masterful grasp of material things, lacking in the artistic but powerful to effect great ends; that restless, nervous energy; that dominant individualism, working for good and for evil, and withal that buoyancy and exuberance which comes with freedom—these are the traits of the frontier, or traits called out elsewhere because of the existence of the frontier.

The frontier has helped to shape some distinctive aspects of American literature, affecting the ballad,♦ the tall tale,♦ and the local-color movement.♦ It has less directly influenced American writing in so many ways as to defy concise summary. The physical frontier, which had a beginning at the Atlantic coast and moved westward until free land was exhausted (c.1890), during its progression may be said to have had some influence on virtually every American author, and especially formed the attitude and manner of such writers as Crèvecœur, William Byrd, Timothy Flint, Caroline Stansbury Kirkland, Irving, Cooper, Simms, Longstreet, Crockett, Edward Eggleston, Clemens, Harte, Joaquin Miller, Garland, Frank Norris, E.W. Howe, Rölvaag, Jack London, E.L. Masters, Sinclair Lewis, and Willa Cather. Successive frontiers likewise had their folk idols, among whom may be named Samuel Brady (Pennsylvania), Simon Kenton (Ohio), Lewis Wetzel (West Virginia), Davy Crockett (Tennessee and Texas), Sam Houston (Texas), Billy the Kid (New Mexico), Hugh Glass (Missouri), Kit Carson and Jim Bridger (the Great Plains), Wild Bill Hickok (Kansas), Daniel Boone (Kentucky), Mike Fink (the Mississippi River), and Paul Bunyan (the lumber frontier).

Frontier, The (1920–39), regional literary magazine, founded by Professor H.G. Merriam of Montana State University in connection with a class in creative writing. The first issue was called *The Montanan,* but its scope as a magazine of the Northwest brought about a change of title. Its contents included fiction, poetry, and criticism, as well as source materials relating to the early history of the Northwest. In 1933 the magazine merged with *The Midland* to become *Frontier and*

Midland. The *Midland* (1915–33), published from Iowa City, was also a regional magazine, and included among its "discoveries" MacKinlay Kantor, Paul Engle, and Phil Stong.

FROST, A[RTHUR] B[URDETT] (1851–1928), illustrator and cartoonist, noted for his subtly humorous pen-and-ink interpretations of such rural American types as the farmer, the plantation black, and the sportsman. He illustrated the Uncle Remus stories, fixing the images of their characters, and works by Mark Twain, Max Adeler, J.K. Bangs, and H.C. Bunner. Some of his drawings in narrative sequence he collected in *Stuff and Nonsense* (1884) and other volumes.

FROST, ROBERT [LEE] (1874–1963), member of a New England family, was born in San Francisco and taken at the age of ten to the New England farm country with which his poetry is identified. After a brief attendance at Dartmouth, where he disliked the academic attitude, he became a bobbin boy in a Massachusetts mill, and a short period at Harvard was followed by further work, making shoes, editing a country newspaper, teaching school, and finally farming. This background of craftsmanship and husbandry had its effect upon his poetry in more than the choice of subjects, for he demanded that his verse be as simple and honest as an axe or hoe. After a long period of farming, he moved to England (1912–15), where he published his first book of poems, *A Boy's Will* (1913), whose lyrics, including "Into My Own," "Revelation," "Mowing," and "Reluctance," are marked by an intense but restrained emotion and the characteristic flavor of New England life. He returned to the U.S. to settle on a New Hampshire farm, having achieved a reputation as an important American poet through the publication of *North of Boston* (1914), described by the author as "a book of people," and showing brilliant insight into New England character and the background that formed it. Among the poems in this volume are "Mending Wall,"♦ "The Death of the Hired Man,"♦ "The Code,"♦ "The Wood-Pile,"♦ "Home Burial,"♦ and "A Servant to Servants."♦ The same expressive idiom and brilliant observation appear in *Mountain Interval* (1916), containing such characteristic poems as "The Road Not Taken,"♦ "Birches,"♦ "Bond and Free,"♦ "A Time To Talk," "Snow," "Putting in the Seed," and "An Old Man's Winter Night."

The shrewd humor and Yankee understatement that distinguish such poems as "The Cow in Apple Time," "A Hundred Collars," and "Brown's Descent" are exhibited also in Frost's witty self-critical remarks, such as "I might be called a Synecdochist; for I prefer the synecdoche in poetry—that figure of speech in which we use a part for the whole." In both emotion and language he was restrained, and conveyed his messages by implication. Although his blank verse is colloquial, it is never loose, for it possesses the pithy, surcharged economy indigenous to the New Englander. His genre pieces, in the form of dramatic idylls or monologues, capture the vernacular of his neighbors north of Boston. Frost explained his realism by saying, "There are two types of realist—the one who offers a good deal of dirt with his potato to show that it is a real one; and the one who is satisfied with the potato brushed clean. . . . To me, the thing that art does for life is to clean it, to strip it to form." His next book, *New Hampshire* (1923, Pulitzer Prize), shows his ability to deal with genial, informal subjects, as in "The Star-Splitter,"♦ "Maple,"♦ "The Axe Helve,"♦ "New Hampshire,"♦ and "Paul's Wife," and to concentrate emotional impact into a few clean-stripped lines, as in "To Earthward,"♦ "Two Look at Two,"♦ "Stopping by Woods on a Snowy Evening,"♦ "Gathering Leaves," "Fire and Ice," and "Fragmentary Blue." In 1928 he issued a fifth new volume, *West-Running Brook,* with the same warm lyric quality that had characterized his first book. His *Collected Poems* (1930, Pulitzer Prize) assembled in one volume the work that has a lifelong continuity in its rhythms, its clear focusing on the individual, and its observation of the native New England background.

After collecting his poems, although he held positions as an affiliated teacher at Amherst, Harvard, and Michigan, he continued his literary career and in 1936 published *A Further Range* (Pulitzer Prize), whose lyrics, though more playful in blending fact and fantasy, have beneath their frivolity a deep seriousness. A new edition of *Collected Poems* (1939) was followed by *A Witness Tree* (1942, Pulitzer Prize); two blank-verse plays, *A Masque of Reason* (1945), about Job, and *A Masque of Mercy* (1947), in which Biblical characters in modern setting discuss ethics and man's relation to God; and *Steeple Bush* (1947) and *In the Clearing* (1962), later lyrics. The standard collected edition is *The Poetry of Robert Frost* (1969), edited by Edward C. Lathem. His correspondence appears in *Letters to Louis Untermeyer* (1963) and *Selected Letters* (1964), edited by Lawrance Thompson. Thompson published a controversial full biography—as official biographer—*Robert Frost* (3 vols., 1966–77), giving a harsh view of the poet. A less tendentious treatment is by William H. Pritchard, *Frost: A Literary Life Reconsidered* (1984).

FROTHINGHAM, OCTAVIUS BROOKS (1822–95), Unitarian minister, chief disciple of Theodore Parker, wrote a life of Parker (1874), *Transcendentalism in New England* (1876), and religious works.

Fruitlands, cooperative community led by Alcott♦ (June 1844–Jan. 1845) at Harvard, Mass. In his original plan for a "Concordium," Alcott proposed an institution in the country, where members would labor on the land and live a vegetarian life, basing their unity on religious love, with education and mutual labor leading to "the harmonic development of their physical, intellectual, and moral natures." The experiment died mainly because of the conflict between Alcott's love of family life and his admiration for the ideas of the English "Alcott House" of Charles Lane, who desired to submerge the individual in a communistic society. Louisa Alcott's *Transcendental Wild Oats* is a fictional account of Fruitlands.

FUCHS, DANIEL (1909–   ), New York City writer whose *Summer in Williamsburg* (1934), *Homage to Blenholt* (1936), and *Low Company* (1937) attracted little attention until republished as *Three Novels* (1961), when they were praised as a moving depiction of the humor and pathos of Lower East Side Jewish life. During his later years as a Hollywood script writer he published a fourth novel, *West of the Rockies* (1971), set in Hollywood, and collected stories and sketches in *The Apathetic Bookie Joint* (1979).

Fugitive, The (1922–25), bimonthly little magazine published at Nashville, Tenn. It contained poetry and criticism championing regionalism♦ and attacking "the highcaste Brahmins of the Old South." Most of the contributors were associated with Vanderbilt University, among them being Donald Davidson, Andrew Lytle, Merrill Moore, John Crow Ransome, Laura Riding, Allen Tate, and Robert Penn Warren. A collection from the magazine was issued as *Fugitive Anthology* (1928).

FULLER, CHARLES (1939–   ), Philadelphia-born playwright whose themes draw upon his experiences as a black and in the army (1959). His works include *Perfect Party* (1968); *Candidate* (1974); *In the Deepest Part of Sleep* (1974); *The Brownsville Raid* (1976), about black soldiers dishonorably discharged because of racial prejudice during the era of Theodore Roosevelt; *Zooman and the Sign* (1980), depicting a tough teenager in Philadelphia; and *A Soldier's Play* (1981, Pulitzer Prize), treating the trial of a black soldier for murder. A five-play series about black Americans in the second half of the 19th century has begun with *Sally, Prince, Jonquil* (1990), and *Burner's Frolic* (1990).

FULLER, HENRY BLAKE (1857–1929), Chicago novelist whose writing varied between the two genres of realistic depiction of the Middle West and fanciful portrayals of courtly Europe, which he knew through his travels. His first novel, published under the pseudonym Stanton Page, was *The Chevalier of Pensieri-Vani* (1890), an episodic work contrasting American and European cultures. *The Châtelaine of La Trinitée* (1892) is in the same cosmopolitan spirit. His most successful realistic work, *The Cliff-Dwellers♦* (1893), a high-

ly dramatic story of social and financial life in Chicago centered on the activities of office workers in a skyscraper, was followed by *With the Procession♦* (1895), a story of social strivings in Chicago. *The Last Refuge* (1900) is an idealistic and fanciful Sicilian romance, while *Under the Skylights* (1901) contains stories about Chicago artist life, one of which, "The Downfall of Abner Joyce," is a fictional treatment of Hamlin Garland. After *Waldo Trench and Others* (1908), stories set in Italy and contrasting American and continental standards, he returned to the Chicago scene in *On the Stairs* (1918), portraying two men who go up and down the stairs of economic and social life. *Bertram Cope's Year* (1919) deals with a University of Chicago instructor. *Gardens of This World* (1929), a continuation of his first book, and *Not on the Screen* (1930), a satire on motion pictures as well as a realistic account of Chicago, were both posthumously published, and show Fuller to have been still preoccupied with two contrasting types of fiction.

FULLER, [SARAH] MARGARET (1810–50), born at Cambridgeport, Mass., was educated by her father, read Ovid at the precocious age of eight, and as a young woman developed friendships with the Transcendentalists, who accepted her as their intellectual equal. From 1839 to 1844 she held a series of conversational classes at Elizabeth Peabody's home, and had a strong influence on the most cultivated circle of Boston society. In her discussions with this group originated the material of her book *Woman in the Nineteenth Century* (1845), the first mature consideration of feminism by an American touching every aspect of the subject, intellectual, economic, political, and sexual. She edited *The Dial♦* (1840–42) and in 1844 published her *Summer on the Lakes in 1843*, an optimistic view of Western life based on a visit to Chicago. During her two years in New York, on the staff of the *Tribune*, she established a wide reputation as a critic, and in the summer of 1846 she visited Europe, writing letters which appeared on the front page of the *Tribune*. She had intended to publish a book on the Roman revolution of 1848–49, but this was not completed. After *Papers on Literature and Art* (1846), her works were posthumously published. They are *At Home and Abroad* (1856) and *Life Without and Life Within* (1859). In Italy she was an ardent adherent of Mazzini, and married one of his followers, the Marquis Angelo Ossoli. The ship that brought them to the U.S. was wrecked in a storm off Fire Island, near New York. The body of her child was the only one recovered, and her manuscript on the Roman revolt was lost. Her *Memoirs* (1852) were written by Emerson, W.H. Channing, and J.F. Clarke. Because of her dynamic personality, she figures frequently in literature, being probably the prototype of Elsie Venner,♦ and of Zenobia in *The Blithedale Romance.♦* In Lowell's *Fable for Critics,* as Miranda,

She always keeps asking if I don't observe a
Particular likeness 'twixt her and Minerva.

Fundamentalism, conservative religious movement of various Protestant denominations during
the 20th century, embodying a protest against the
incursions of science into revelation. Its object is
to maintain traditional interpretations of the Bible and fundamental doctrines of Christian faith.
The five points of the doctrine whose literal acceptance is demanded are the Virgin birth, physical resurrection of Christ, inerrancy of the Scriptures, vicarious atonement, and the physical
second coming of Christ. The struggle against the
teaching of evolutionary theories, which are considered to threaten orthodoxy, became a national
issue in the Scopes trial in Tennessee (1925), in
which Clarence Darrow defended J.T. Scopes, a
public-school teacher who expounded evolution,
while William Jennings Bryan upheld the Fundamentalist point of view, winning the case for the
prosecution. The trial was the subject of the play
Inherit the Wind (1955) by Jerome Lawrence and
Robert E. Lee. Fundamentalist views have been
widely revived and extended during the 1980s
and 1990s by some ministers in their churches
and allied institutions and on their television programs, becoming a political force under the
rubric "The Moral Majority." As in the past, the
theory of evolution is challenged, as is the practice of abortion, while they fulminate against or
urge censorship of books, films, and the media
whose expression or values they disapprove.

FURNESS, HORACE HOWARD (1833–1912),
ranked as one of the most important Shakespeare
scholars of the U.S. because of the *New Variorum*
edition that he began in 1871, and which was
continued (1908–28) by his son and namesake
and later by others.

Furnished Room, The, short story in *The Four
Million.* ♦

FUSSELL, PAUL (1924–   ), southern California-
born professor of English literature at the University of Pennsylvania, has intellectual interests far
beyond his fine early books, *Poetic Meter and Poetic
Form* (1965) and *Samuel Johnson and the Life of
Writing* (1971). He has long been noted for his
social and intellectual history of modern English
and American life as represented in *The Great War
and Modern Memory* (1975, National Book
Award), on attitudes toward World War I; and
*Wartime: Understanding and Behavior in the Second
World War* (1989). He has also written *Abroad:
British Literary Traveling Between the Wars* (1980)
and *The Anti-Egotist: Kingsley Amis, Man of Letters*
(1994).

G

Gabriel Conroy, novel by Bret Harte. ◆

GADDIS, WILLIAM (1922–   ), born in New York City, after four years at Harvard and much foreign travel published *The Recognitions* (1955), a long, elaborate, experimental, satirical novel with settings as diverse as the author's travels, treating a Yankee artist whose original talent is overwhelmed by his career as a copyist of old masters. His second novel, *J R* (1975, National Book Award), is again a rich parodic treatment of hypocrisy and corruption. The eponymous hero, a sixth-grader, amasses a corporate empire, using the telephone and the mails in questionable legality. The novel nimbly satirizes both public education and standard business practices. His third novel, *Carpenter's Gothic* (1985), is a far shorter work, less experimental, though employing his trademark disconnective dialogue, and more accessible than the first two. Its themes are the helplessness engendered by dependent love and family disorder. *A Frolic of His Own* (1994, National Book Award) is an almost 600-page novel centering upon the complexities and bafflements of the law, with much technical legal detail. Written in his hallmark disconnected unpunctuated dialogue, the book is yet accessible. Its protagonist is Oscar Crease, a community-college teacher who sees himself as "the last civilized man." In trying to hotwire his own car, he has it run him over and injure him, whereupon he spends much effort and time figuring out whom to sue. The book is both harsh and funny.

GAGE, THOMAS (*c.*1596–1656), English priest, became a Roman Catholic missionary for Spain and traveled through Mexico, Guatemala, and other parts of Central America (1625–37). His book *The English-American: His Travail by Sea and Land* (1684) stimulated English exploration because of its account of the wealth and defenseless condition of Spanish possessions. After repatriating himself and becoming an Anglican chaplain, he accompanied the expedition that seized Jamaica, where he died.

Gail Hamilton, see *Dodge, Mary A.*

GAINES, ERNEST J. (1933–   ), Louisiana-born author, since age 13 resident in the San Francisco Bay area, has drawn on his background for stories of blacks in his native state. His novels include *Catherine Carmier* (1964); *Of Love and Dust* (1967); *The Autobiography of Miss Jane Pitman* (1971), a saga of black history in the South seen through the reminiscences of a 110-year-old woman; *In My Father's House* (1978); and *A Gathering of Old Men* (1983). *A Lesson Before Dying* (1993) has for narrator a black primary school teacher, Grant Wiggins, who tells the story of Jefferson, a condemned man in a Louisiana prison in 1948. *Bloodline* (1968) collects stories of children's views of adult life. Since 1983 he has taught at the University of Southwestern Louisiana.

Galaxy, The (1866–78), monthly literary magazine, published at New York and intended to counteract the supposed provincialism of the *Atlantic Monthly.* Clemens was one of its assistant editors, conducting a department of "Memoranda" (1870–71) devoted to humorous sketches. Other contributors included Henry James, J.W. De Forest, Rebecca H. Davis, H.H. Boyesen, Rose Terry Cooke, Whitman, Hayne, and E.C. Stedman. In addition to fiction, the magazine was distinguished for its literary criticism, historical and political articles, and scientific essays. Financially unsuccessful, it sold its subscription list to the *Atlantic Monthly.*

GALE, ZONA (1874–1938), Wisconsin author, known for her short stories in the local-color tradition, collected in such volumes as *Friendship Village* ◆ (1908), *Yellow Gentians and Blue* (1927), and *Bridal Pond* (1930). She won a Pulitzer Prize for her dramatization of her novel *Miss Lulu Bett* ◆ (1920), a study of a woman repressed by the bleak life of the Middle West. Other novels include *Birth* (1918), dramatized as *Mr. Pitt* (1924), the story of a similarly repressed man, whose simple honesty is scorned by the wife who deserts him and the son who is ashamed of his insignificance; *Faint Perfume* (1923), a character study of a poor relation; *Preface to a Life* (1926), dealing with the frustrated life of a businessman; *Borgia* (1929), the story of a morbid girl who thinks herself a modern Lucrezia Borgia; and *Papa La Fleur* (1933), the story of a country girl whose ideas of liberty for the younger generation hurt the feelings of both her father and her sweetheart. *The Secret Way* (1921) is a book of poems, *Magna* (1939) is a posthumously published novelette, and *Portage, Wisconsin* (1928) completes the autobiographical narrative begun in *When I Was a Little Girl* (1913). *Still Small Voice* (1940), a biography, was written by August Derleth.

GALLAGHER, WILLIAM DAVIS (1808–94), Ohio frontier editor, whose poetry, imitative in technique but original in its descriptions of nature, is among the region's best. It is contained chiefly in his *Erato* (3 vols., 1835–37) and *Miami Woods* (1881). He also edited a regional anthology, *Selections from the Poetical Literature of the West* (1841).

GALLATIN, ALBERT (1761–1849), born in Switzerland, emigrated to America at the age of 19 and became a frontier political leader, after 1797 being the recognized spokesman for the Republican minority, whose criticism of the Federalist management of the Treasury resulted in the Alien and Sedition acts, partially aimed at him. As Jefferson's secretary of the treasury, he severely curtailed army and navy appropriations, and materially reduced the public debt. He was later blamed for the inadequate preparation of the U.S. for the War of 1812, which he bitterly opposed. He was primarily responsible for the Treaty of Ghent, held the posts of minister to France and minister to England, and upon his retirement founded the bank that bears his name. He wrote *The Oregon Question* (1846), but considered his most important work to be the *Synopsis of the Indian Tribes . . . of North America* (1836), which led to his reputation as "the father of American ethnology." Henry Adams edited his *Writings* (3 vols., 1879) and wrote *The Life of Albert Gallatin* (1879).

Gallegher: A Newspaper Story, title story of a collection by R.H. Davis,♦ published in 1891.

GALLOWAY, JOSEPH (c.1731–1803), Loyalist writer and statesman of Philadelphia, attacked the policy of the English ministry toward the colonies, while opposing the extremism of radical colonists. In his *Plan of a Proposed Union Between Great Britain and the Colonies* (1774), he outlines a scheme for home rule that anticipated 19th-century British policies. *A Candid Examination of the Mutual Claims of Great Britain and the Colonies* (1775) proposes redress through a liberal constitutional union with England. His logic could not delay the current of more violent forces, and Galloway abandoned argument to serve in the British army, later becoming an efficient adviser to the Crown.

Game, The, novel by Jack London,♦ published in 1905.

Joe Fleming is asked by his fiancée Genevieve to give up his career as a prizefighter, since she is jealous of the attraction which "the game" exerts over her lover. To convey an idea of the fascination of the sport, Joe proposes that she watch him fight. She witnesses his bout with John Ponta, a brutal, bull-like pugilist. While Joe is hammering Ponta to the canvas, he slips and is simultaneously hit by his opponent. Hurled to the floor with a crushed skull, he dies in a few moments.

GANN, ERNEST K[ELLOGG] (1910–91), Nebraska-born author, whose works include the popular novel *The High and the Mighty* (1953), about the passengers of a disabled plane flying from Hawaii to San Francisco, and *Fate Is the Hunter* (1961), a memoir of his experiences as a flyer, including service as an airline pilot and during World War II in the Army Air Transport Command.

Gant, EUGENE, hero of *Look Homeward, Angel*♦ and *Of Time and the River.*♦

Garbage Man, The: A Parade with Shouting, play by John Dos Passos,♦ produced in 1925 as *The Moon Is a Gong,* and published under the present title in 1926. Experimental in form, the play is a poetic arraignment of oppressive forces in contemporary society.

GARCÉS, FRANCISCO TOMÁS HERMENEGILDO (1738–81), Spanish missionary and explorer, established missions on the Gila and Colorado rivers, and accompanied Anza to California (1774–75). He was killed by Indians. His diaries were published in Elliott Coues's *On the Trail of a Spanish Pioneer* (2 vols., 1900).

GARDINER, SIR CHRISTOPHER (*fl.*1630–32), arrived in Massachusetts (1630), bringing with him, according to Bradford, "a comly yonge woman, whom he caled his cousin, but it was suspected, she (after ye Italian maner) was his concubine." He was a mysterious figure, and was left undisturbed until it was discovered that he had deserted two wives, was a Papist, and was an agent of Ferdinando Gorges. Gardiner and his mistress, Mary Grove, were apprehended but released. For a time thereafter, he lived in Brunswick, Me., where his "known harlot" married one Thomas Purchase. In 1632 he turned up in Bristol, England, as the star witness before the Privy Council in Gorges's attempt to break the Massachusetts charter. He has figured in fiction and poetry, as in *The Tales of a Wayside Inn,* Motley's *Merry Mount,* and Maria Sedgwick's *Hope Leslie.*

GARDNER, ERLE STANLEY (1889–1970), California lawyer and writer of detective fiction whose central figure is the lawyer Perry Mason, who serves as sleuth. Earliest in his lengthy series were *The Case of the Velvet Claws* (1933) and *The Case of the Sulky Girl* (1933). In the 30 years following publication of these works, sales of his books in the U.S. totaled 135,740,861 copies.

GARDNER, ISABELLA [STEWART] (1915–81), Massachusetts-born poet, whose lively and loving lyrics written in diverse forms appear in *Birthdays from the Ocean* (1955), *The Looking Glass* (1961), and the collection *West of Childhood* (1965). Edith Sitwell said, "the poems arise from her personality," and the author herself said, "they are the poems of a poet who is woman first and poet second. . . . My poems celebrate and affirm life, but they are also elegiac. My central theme is the . . . failure of the I–Thou relationship." She was married to Allen Tate (1959–66) and was an associate editor of *Poetry* (1952–56).

GARDNER, JOHN [CHAMPLIN, JR.] (1933–82), after graduation from Washington University, St. Louis, and a Ph.D. from Iowa State University, became a professor of English at several universities and, beginning in the 1960s, a prolific and popular author. His novels include *The Resurrection* (1966), about a professor of philosophy who returns to his upstate New York childhood home when he is dying; *The Wreckage of Agathon* (1970), a metaphysical analysis of civilization through the dialogue of a dying Greek philosopher and his disciple; *Grendel* (1971), a *tour de force* in telling the story of *Beowulf* from the sympathetic viewpoint of the monster; *The Sunlight Dialogues* (1972), a multi-charactered philosophic and allegorical tale set in his birthplace, Batavia, N.Y.; *Nickel Mountain* (1973), a pastoral set in the Catskills characterizing a man through his relationships; *October Light* (1976, National Book Critics Circle Award), about the conflicts between an elderly brother and sister over political and philosophical issues; *Freddy's Book* (1980), a novel within a novel, ostensibly written by a monstrous 20th-century author, treating 16th-century Scandinavian history and related moral dilemmas; and *Mickelsson's Ghosts* (1982), about a philosophy professor caught up in emotional problems, personal and academic, and even in a violent Mormon mystery. Gardner also wrote *The King's Indian* (1974) and *The Art of Living* (1981), stories; *Dragon, Dragon* (1975), fairy tales for children; *A Child's Bestiary* (1977), in verse; and *In the Suicide Mountains* (1977), a fairy tale. *Jason and Medeia* (1973) is his epic poem of the classic story. His scholarly works include a biography of Chaucer (1977) and a study of his poetry (1977). His critical writings include *The Forms of Fiction* (1961) and *On Moral Fiction* (1978), a cantankerous consideration of modern American novels and their lack of moral content.

GARLAND, [HANNIBAL] HAMLIN (1860–1940), born in Wisconsin, after sharing the oppressive labor of farm life there and in Iowa and South Dakota went to Boston, where he came under the influence of Howells. Returning to the farmland of the Middle Border, he chose the hardships of the farmer for the subject of his stories, which are characterized by objective realism and ethical romanticism. They were collected in *Main-Travelled Roads♦* (1891), *Boy Life on the Prairie* (1899), and *Other Main-Travelled Roads* (1910), the last containing stories from two previous books, *Prairie Folks* (1893) and *Wayside Courtships* (1897). The writing of these stories, all of which were completed before 1890, led Garland to believe that something besides realistic fiction

was needed to ameliorate agricultural conditions. Accordingly, he wrote *Jason Edwards: An Average Man* (1892) as propaganda for the single tax theories of Henry George, and *A Spoil of Office* (1892), a novel that, in exposing political corruption, also campaigned for the Populist party. After *A Member of the Third House* (1892), a novel showing the legislative power of the railroads, he wrote *A Little Norsk* (1892), depicting the bleak life of a Dakota farm girl, and *Rose of Dutcher's Coolly♦* (1895), telling of a girl's revolt against this life. *Crumbling Idols* (1894), a book of essays, sets forth the author's theory of "veritism," combining realism for a democratic purpose with individualism, stemming from Whitman and flavored by local color. *The Captain of the Gray-Horse Troop* (1902) deals with the unjust treatment of the Indians by frontiersmen and cattlemen, and *Cavanagh, Forest Ranger* (1910) with the conflict between cattle ranchers and representatives of the government attempting to conserve natural resources. After the force of his youth had partially been spent, he wrote his comparatively mellow autobiography, *A Son of the Middle Border♦* (1917), continued in *A Daughter of the Middle Border♦* (1921, Pulitzer Prize), and the thinner, semi-fictional works, *Trail-Makers of the Middle Border* (1926) and *Back-Trailers from the Middle Border* (1928). Subsequent volumes, *Roadside Meetings* (1930), *Companions on the Trail* (1931), *My Friendly Contemporaries* (1932), and *Afternoon Neighbors* (1934), dwindled into the category of garrulous memoirs. His last books were concerned with psychic research.

GARRARD, LEWIS H. (1829–87), author of *Wah-tó-yah, and the Taos Trail* (1850), an account of his journey as a 17-year-old boy along the Santa Fe Trail to Taos. It is a valuable, well-written source of information about the mountain men.

GARRETT, GEORGE [PALMER, JR.] (1929–   ), born in Florida, educated at Princeton, to which he returned as a professor after teaching writing and criticism at Hollins College and the University of South Carolina. His first publication was poetry, continued in *The Sleeping Gypsy* (1958), *Abraham's Knife* (1961), *For a Bitter Season* (1967), *Welcome to the Medicine Show* (1978), and *Love's Shining Child* (1981). He is also known for his fiction, his stories being collected in *King of the Mountain* (1958), *In the Briar Patch* (1961), *Cold Ground Was My Bed Last Night* (1964), *A Wreath for Garibaldi* (1969), and *The Magic Striptease* (1973). His novels include *The Finished Man* (1959), about Florida politics; *Which Ones Are the Enemy?* (1961); *Do, Lord, Remember Me* (1965), concerning religious revival show people; *Death of the Fox* (1971), a fictional biography of Sir Walter Raleigh; *The Succession* (1984), about Queen Elizabeth and her successor, James I; and *Poison Pen* (1986), a humorous and often epistolary story. Modern biography and literary criticism occur in *James Jones* (1984). *Sir Slob and the Princess* (1962) is a play for children.

GARRIGUE, JEAN (1914–72), Indiana-born poet, educated at the University of Chicago, published her poetry in *The Ego and the Centaur* (1947), *The Monument Rose* (1953), *A Water Walk by Villa d'Este* (1959), *Country Without Maps* (1964), *New and Selected Poems* (1967), and *Studies for an Actress* (1973). The poems are marked by glittering imagery influenced by Wallace Stevens and by sensitivity to the natural scene and to art. She also wrote a novel, *The Animal Hotel* (1966).

GARRISON, WILLIAM LLOYD (1805–79), spearhead of New England Abolitionism,♦ was born in Newburyport, Mass. During 1829–30 he edited *The Genius of Universal Emancipation* with Benjamin Lundy at Baltimore, but after imprisonment for libel, he returned to his home to pursue policies that were too radical for Lundy. In 1831 he began to publish *The Liberator,*♦ which he continued for 34 years. An ascetic, moralist, pacifist, and noble agitator, Garrison constantly demanded immediate and complete emancipation of the slaves. Although the circulation of his paper was small, it drew wide attention because of the direct, forcible expression of its owner's passionate beliefs. He attacked the moderate elements who opposed him, disliked the actions of the Anti-Slavery Society, which he split asunder, and his own vituperation was equaled only by that of the slaveholders. He outdid the Southerners in advocating secession, since the Constitution, which permitted slavery, was to him a "Covenant with Death and an Agreement with Hell." After the Civil War, he retired from public activity. His books include *Thoughts on African Colonization* (1832), *Sonnets* (1843), and *Selections* (1852) from his speeches and writings. He was the subject of many works, including one of Whittier's finest poems.

GASS, WILLIAM H[OWARD] (1924–   ), graduated from Kenyon College, received a Ph.D. from Cornell, became a professor of philosophy while carrying on a literary career, and was appointed to Washington University (St. Louis) in 1980. His fiction includes a novel, *Omensetter's Luck* (1966), about a symbolically significant man who comes to settle in an Ohio River town; *In the Heart of the Heart of the Country* (1968), stories and novellas, also evoking small-town life in the Midwest; and *Willie Masters' Lonesome Wife* (1970), a lively novella about a stripteaser's recollections and activities, which is a commentary on art in general. His essays appear in *Fiction and the Figures of Life* (1970) and *The World Within the Word* (1978). *On Being Blue* (1976) is a brief, fanciful meditation on the significance, sexual and other, of the color blue. *Habitations of the Word* (1985) collects literary essays.

GATES, HORATIO (1727–1806), British soldier in the French and Indian War, returned to England (1765–72), where he retired from the army. Urged by Washington, he moved to a West Virginia plantation, and at the outbreak of the Revolution became a patriot officer. In 1776, promoted to major general, he began to hold important commands, and the following year led the campaign against Burgoyne, which ended with the victory at Saratoga. His popularity at this time led to the Conway Cabal,♦ a frustrated attempt to replace Washington by Gates as commander in chief. He continued in high commands until 1780, when, after the rout of his soldiers at Camden, he was replaced by Greene. A Congressional investigation of his actions was ordered, and he retired for two years. In 1782 the ordered inquiry was cancelled, and Gates served again at the close of the war. He figures often in historical fiction, e.g. Simms's *The Partisan* and *Eutaw,* Kennedy's *Horse-Shoe Robinson,* and Kenneth Roberts's *Rabble in Arms.*

Gates Ajar, The, novel by Elizabeth Ward,♦ published (1868) under her maiden name, Elizabeth Stuart Phelps.

A New England girl, Mary Cabot, is overcome by grief at the death of her brother Royal in the Civil War, and remains inconsolable until her aunt, Winifred Forceythe, comes to visit her, accompanied by her daughter Faith. Mary finds comfort in the little girl, and a great source of solace in the series of long conversations with her aunt, which she records in her journal. Slowly her aunt persuades her of the validity of a future life in which she will meet Royal, and presents convincingly her conception of Heaven.

GATH, pseudonym of George Alfred Townsend. ♦

Gatsby, JAY, see *Great Gatsby.*

GAYARRÉ, CHARLES ÉTIENNE ARTHUR (1805–95), New Orleans historian who, at the age of 30, was forced by ill health to resign his newly won seat in the U.S. Senate, and spent seven years in France, where he did much historical research. After returning to American politics, he retired in 1853 to become a leader of Louisiana literary circles, and wrote a monumental *History of Louisiana* (4 vols., 1851–66), which, though it began under the popular influence of Scott's romances, ended as a vivid and accurate narrative. He was also the author of a humorless satirical novel, *The School for Politics* (1845); a brilliant psychological study, *Philip II of Spain* (1866); *Fernando de Lemos* (1872), an autobiographical novel; and other fiction.

Gazette of the United States (1789–1847), weekly newspaper founded at New York by John Fenno (1751–98) as a Federalist journal, was moved to Philadelphia the following year, and became a daily in 1793. It was financed by Hamilton, who used it to attack Jefferson and the Jefferson-controlled *National Gazette*♦ of Freneau. After Fenno's death, his son became editor. In 1804 the title was changed to *United States Gazette*. The paper later merged with another Philadelphia paper to become the *North American and United States Gazette*.

GELBER, JACK (1932–　), Chicago-born author, whose first and most successful play, *The Connection* (1959), gives a sense of the lives of drug addicts by presenting their story as though it were real, with the heroin shots said to be real doses and the actors ostensibly drifters paid for their performances by the drugs received on stage. Later plays include *The Apple* (1961), a plotless series of confrontations among actors supposedly trying to devise a play; *Square in the Eye* (1966), a more conventional play about a man frustrated by family from his attempt to be a painter; and *The Cuban Thing* (1969), on Castro's revolution. Later plays include *Sleep* (1972), a treatment of scientists in a laboratory for sleep as a psychopathology of dreams; *Rehearsal* (1976), fully presented as *Jack Gelber's New Play: Rehearsal* (1976), concerning an ex-convict writing about a prison rebellion; and *Starters* (1980), treating an activist minister who is betrayed by young radicals. *Barbary Shore* (1973) is a stage adaptation of Norman Mailer's novel. Gelber himself wrote a novel, *On Ice* (1964), about life in the Beat generation.

GELLHORN, MARTHA (1908–　), foreign correspondent for *Collier's* (1937–45), whose war reports from the Spanish Civil War, Finland, China, Europe in World War II, and Java appear in *The Face of War* (1959). Her fiction includes *The Trouble I've Seen* (1936), about urban workers on relief during the Depression; *Two by Two* (1958), stories about marriage; *Pretty Tales for Tired People* (1965), stories; *The Lowest Trees Have Tops* (1969), a novel set in Mexico; and *The Weather in Africa* (1980). She was married to Hemingway (1940–45). *Travels with Myself and Another* (1979) is an autobiography.

General Advertiser, see *Aurora*.

General Magazine, *The* (Jan.–June 1741), subtitled a "Historical Chronicle for All the British Plantations in America," was edited and published by Franklin.♦ It was the first American magazine to be projected, but the second to be published, since John Webbe, the proposed editor, betrayed the publisher, and with Andrew Bradford issued *The American Magazine* three days earlier. During the six months of publication, attention was given mainly to the war with Spain, the French and Indian alliance, international trade, the Whitefield controversy, extracts from

the histories of Robert Beverley and Patrick Tailfer, and reprints of poetry. Franklin does not mention the enterprise in his *Autobiography*.

General Repository and Review, *The* (1812–13), Boston quarterly journal, affiliated with Harvard. Under the editorship of Andrews Norton, it championed Unitarianism.

General William Booth Enters into Heaven, title poem of a volume by Vachel Lindsay,♦ published in 1913. Intended to be sung to the music of the hymn "The Blood of the Lamb," its vigorous drumbeat rhythms describe the apotheosis of the Salvation Army founder, who enters the gates of Paradise at the head of a troop of criminals and slum dwellers:

> Christ came gently with a robe and crown
> For Booth the soldier, while the throng knelt down.

Generall Historie of Virginia, New England, and the Summer Isles, *The,* narrative by John Smith.♦

"Genius," *The,* novel by Dreiser,♦ published in 1915.

Handsome Eugene Witla, son of a middle-class family in an Illinois town, cherishes his bent toward drawing and writing, and is looked upon as a dreamer. He has the earliest of many amours at the age of 17, when he begins to work for the local newspaper. Then, ambitious and curious about the world, he goes to work in Chicago, spending his spare time in art study. Engaged to Angela Blue, a schoolteacher older than himself, he is employed in the art department of a Chicago paper, after which he goes to New York to achieve fame as an illustrator. Sincere but restless, he has affairs with several women, including Christina Channing, a concert singer, who ends their liaison because she considers her career more important. He marries Angela, who is unsuited to him, being prudent and conventional and incapable of understanding his tastes or his essential amorality. Eugene's paintings make him famous, but he suffers a nervous collapse, due to overwork and an intemperate sexual life. His savings gone and unable to paint even after a year's rest, he works for some time as a laborer. Then he rapidly climbs the ladder of business success to become managing director of a great publishing firm. Angela, jealous of his philanderings, attempts to win him back by becoming pregnant. He falls in love, however, with a society girl, Suzanne Dale, whose mother ends the affair by causing Eugene to lose his position. Angela dies at the birth of their daughter, and Eugene, belatedly penitent, devotes himself to the care of the child and to his true vocation of realistic painting.

Genteel Tradition at Bay, *The,* essay by Santayana,♦ published in 1931.

Gentle Art of Making Enemies, The, see *Whistler.*

Gentle Grafter, The, short stories by W.S. Porter. ♦

Gentle People, The: A Brooklyn Fable, comedy by Irwin Shaw, ♦ produced and published in 1939.

Jonah Goodman and Philip Anagnos, middle-aged, poverty-stricken New Yorkers, find their only pleasure in fishing from their rowboat below Coney Island's Steeplechase Pier. They have saved a small amount toward the purchase of a boat in which they hope to fish off the Florida coast. Jonah's wife, Florence, is an ill-tempered invalid, and his pretty daughter Stella is a stenographer, certain that she is "different," and dissatisfied with her commonplace suitor, Eli Lieber, a barker at Coney Island. Philip is the Greek chef in the restaurant of Angelina Esposito, who employs her enormous energy to persuade him to marry her, although he fears and dislikes her. The companions are hopeful of achieving their ambition, despite these hindrances, until a gangster, Harold Goff, forces them to pay for "protection" and tries to seduce Stella. Eli announces his intention of killing Goff, but Jonah and Philip dissuade him. They carry the gangster out to sea, take his money, drown him, and, escaping detection, are at last able to make their dream come true.

Gentleman from Indiana, The, novel by Tarkington. ♦

Gentleman's Magazine, The (1837–40), monthly Philadelphia periodical, founded by W.E. Burton, ♦ who later added his name to the title. Its contents were light and entertaining, with attention to art and literature, sports, the theater, and reprints and translations from English and foreign magazines, as well as tales of frontier adventure. Poe was the editor (July 1839–June 1840), and his contributions included "William Wilson," "The Fall of the House of Usher," and "The Journal of Julius Rodman." The different temperaments and editorial aims of Poe and Burton made their collaboration impossible, and Burton, tiring of the enterprise, sold it to George R. Graham, who merged it with *Atkinson's Casket* to create *Graham's Magazine.* ♦

Gentlemen Prefer Blondes, novel by Anita Loos. ♦

GEORGE, HENRY (1839–97), left his middle-class, devoutly Episcopalian Philadelphia home (1855) to sail as a foremast boy to Calcutta, where he was struck by the contrast between poverty and wealth. In 1857 the promise of work drew him to San Francisco, where he struggled against want intermittently for ten years, as printer, gold hunter, publisher, and free-lance editor and author, observing the rich new country come gradually under the control of a few land-hungry speculators. His first article in the *Overland Monthly* (Oct. 1868) anticipated his later thesis, contending that the railroads would bring riches to a few and poverty to many. His first separate publication, *Our Land and Land Policy* (1871), a pamphlet, urged that we "charge the expenses of government upon our land," thus stating the essence of the single-tax idea. During the depression and labor troubles of 1877 he began writing his great work, *Progress and Poverty* ♦ (1879), which attributes poverty to rent, and proposes a tax on land as the remedy for social ills. This doctrine, developed in six other books, numerous periodicals, and his own weekly, *The Standard* (1886–92), won national prominence for its author, as well as the support of labor in his two unsuccessful New York mayoralty campaigns. *The Irish Land Question* (1881) extends his basic tenets to the subject of Irish distress, which he saw at first hand for a year. *Social Problems* (1884) applies the principles of *Progress and Poverty* to various social maladjustments. *Protection or Free Trade* (1886) is a discussion of tariffs and free trade, stating George's belief that poverty would continue under either system, and that a single tax on land would furnish the only solution. *Science of Political Economy* (1897) is a general restatement of his principles. George lectured extensively in the U.S. and abroad, and in England influenced the circle of intellectuals who later founded the Fabian Society. In Germany and Austria his theories contributed to the introduction of increment taxes, while in the U.S. they have led to an increasing concern with problems of wealth distribution.

George's Mother, novelette by Stephen Crane. ♦

Georgia Scenes, Characters, Incidents, &c. in the First Half Century of the Republic, 18 humorous sketches by A.B. Longstreet, ♦ published in 1835. The author's aim "was to supply a chasm in history which has always been overlooked—the manners, customs, amusements, wit, dialect, as they appear in all grades of society to an eye and ear witness of them." The style is frequently Addisonian, but the best passages are derived from the oral anecdotes of the Old Southwest, distinguished by a genial humor, an eye for detail, and an ear for dialect, as well as a genuine, sympathetic realism. One of the sketches, "Georgia Theatrics," was used in Crockett's *Autobiography.*

German Reformed Church, see *Reformed Church in the U.S.*

GERNSBACK, HUGO, see *Science fiction.*

Gerontion, poem by T.S. Eliot, ♦ published in his *Poems* (1920), presents the fragmented thoughts of "an old man in a dry month," who without vital experience of faith is representative of the inanition of modern life and who, by means of images and allusions, yet shows his longing for spiritual rebirth and the expression of emotion.

GEROULD, GORDON HALL (1877–1953), husband of Katharine Fullerton Gerould, was a professor of English at Bryn Mawr and Princeton and, in addition to many scholarly works, was the author of the novels *Peter Sanders, Retired* (1917); *Youth in Harley* (1920), set in Vermont; and *A Midsummer Mystery* (1925).

GEROULD, KATHARINE FULLERTON (1879–1944), teacher of English at Bryn Mawr, and author of novels and short stories in the vein of Henry James and Edith Wharton. Her stories have been collected in such volumes as *Vain Oblations* (1914), *The Great Tradition* (1915), and *Valiant Dust* (1922). Among the novels are *A Change of Air* (1917); *Lost Valley* (1922), set in New England; *Conquistador* (1923), the story of a Scottish covenanter in Mexico during the time of Pancho Villa; and *The Light That Never Was* (1931).

GERSHWIN, GEORGE (1898–1937), born on the Lower East Side of New York City, began his musical career as a Tin Pan Alley composer, writing many popular jazz songs, and from the age of 20 composing musical comedies, among his greatest successes being *Lady, Be Good!* (1924), *Girl Crazy* (1930), and *Of Thee I Sing* (1931). Although he continued to write popular music, he became interested in serious composition, and after study under Rubin Goldmark began to produce works illustrating his belief in jazz "as an American folk-music" that "can be made the basis of serious symphonic works of lasting value." The *Rhapsody in Blue* for piano and orchestra was composed for Paul Whiteman's Concert of Jazz Music (1924), and the orchestral poem *An American in Paris* (1928) was commissioned by Damrosch. Other major works include the *Concerto in F* for piano (1925) and the *Second Rhapsody* (1931), utilizing in classic forms the rhythms previously identified with ephemeral dance music. Gershwin's most ambitious composition is the folk opera *Porgy and Bess* (1935), interpreting the Negro spirit in an adaptation of DuBose Heyward's *Porgy.* ◆

GERSHWIN, IRA (1896–1983), brother of George Gershwin, wrote lyrics for *Lady, Be Good!* (1924), *Girl Crazy* (1930), *Of Thee I Sing* (1931), and other musical comedies, as well as for *Porgy and Bess* (1935) and many films.

GERSTÄCKER, FRIEDRICH (1816–72), German adventurer and author, arrived in the U.S. in 1837, and spent several years wandering about the country in various capacities, writing about his adventures after his return to Germany. In 1849 he went to South America, California, the Sandwich Islands, and Australia; in 1860 to South America; and in 1867–68 to the U.S., Mexico,

Central America, and the West Indies. His books are reminiscent of those of Sealsfield, whose creative ability he lacked but whom he surpassed in popularity. Translations of his works include *The Wanderings and Fortunes of Some German Emigrants* (1848), *The Daughter of the Riccarees* (1851), *Narrative of a Journey Round the World* (1853), *The Regulators of Arkansas* (1857), and *The Young Gold-Digger* (1860).

Gertrude of Wyoming, narrative poem in Spenserian stanzas, by the English poet Thomas Campbell,◆ published in 1809.

Get-Rich-Quick Wallingford, stories by George R. Chester.◆

Gettysburg Address, delivered by Lincoln at the dedication of a national cemetery (Nov. 19, 1863) on the site of the Pennsylvania battlefield where there occurred (July 1–3, 1863) the action that is considered the turning point of the Civil War. Lincoln's speech of three brief paragraphs, following a two-hour address by the principal orator, Edward Everett, was considered unimportant at the time, but has come to be viewed as one of the noblest and most significant expressions of American democracy. Calling for "increased devotion to that cause" for which the Gettysburg dead "gave the last full measure of devotion," he stated that the aim of the Civil War was to make possible "a new birth of freedom . . . that government of the people, by the people, for the people, shall not perish from the earth."

Ghost of the Buffaloes, *The,* poem by Vachel Lindsay,◆ published in *The Chinese Nightingale and Other Poems* (1917). It describes the poet's dream-vision of the primitive Plains region before the coming of white civilization, and a mystic procession of Indians, eagles, and stampeding "royal old buffaloes," celebrated as the "far golden splendors" of a romantically superior world.

Giants in the Earth: *A Saga of the Prairie,* novel by Rölvaag,◆ published in Norway (1924–25) and in translation in the U.S. (1927). *Peter Victorious*◆ and *Their Fathers' God*◆ are sequels. The novel formed the basis for an opera (1951) by Douglas Moore.

In 1873 a small company of Norwegian farmers treks from Minnesota to settle in Dakota Territory. There are four families in this Spring Creek settlement: Per Hansa, his wife Beret, and their two sons and daughter; Hans Olsa, his wife Sörine, and their daughter; Syvert Tönseten and his wife Kjersti; and the brothers, Sam and Henry Solum. They erect rude sod huts and break the virgin surface of the prairie to plant their first crop; as years pass they make improvements, but their hold remains insecure, and the environment seems to seek ways of showing malevolence.

Winter blizzards terrify them, destroying cattle and crops, and for five years a plague of locusts despoils their grain, but they persist. Per is a daring, ambitious fellow, but his schemes are often thwarted by the fears and melancholy of his pious wife, who cannot feel at home in this wilderness. Hans Olsa, equally strong and purposeful, is steadier; while Tönseten is a craven braggart, although he conceives plans for a school and church, and persuades newcomers to join the community. Beret nearly dies at the birth of a third son, whom Per names Peder Victorious, and later she has periods of insanity, in which her fear of the evil powers of the land is accentuated. Per ages under the strain of violent labor and family difficulties, but Beret is cured when a visiting minister reassures her and consecrates Peder to a holy life. During a phenomenally hard winter, Hans Olsa is fatally stricken by pneumonia, and Beret, concerned over his spiritual welfare, asks Per to bring a minister. He sets out on this errand, but dies in a bitter snowstorm.

GIBBONS, JAMES SLOAN, see *We Are Coming, Father Abraham.*

GIBBS, JOSIAH WILLARD (1839–1903), professor of mathematical physics at Yale (1871–1903), is significant for his contributions to the science of thermodynamics. His *Scientific Papers* were collected in 1906, and his works were collected in 1928. Muriel Rukeyser published a prose study of him in 1942.

GIBBS, WOLCOTT (1902–58), drama critic for *The New Yorker* (1940–58) and occasional contributor to the magazine's "Talk of the Town." His pieces from the journal were collected as *Bed of Neuroses* (1937), *Season in the Sun* (1946), and *More in Sorrow* (1958). He also wrote a comic play, *Season in the Sun* (1950), about a journalist who leaves his job to write a novel.

GIBSON, CHARLES DANA (1867–1944), New York illustrator, obtained a great vogue during the 1890s for his so-called Gibson Girl drawings, glorifying American womanhood and reflecting the refined gaiety of fashionable society. He was a regular contributor to *Life,* which he edited for a time, and to *Collier's* and other magazines. The Gibson Girl was featured in his series *The Education of Mr. Pipp* (1899), which inspired a popular play of the same title (1905) by Augustus Thomas. He published several books of his drawings, and appealed to the period's romantic and sentimental tastes in his drawings for books by Richard Harding Davis and other popular authors.

GIBSON, WILLIAM (1914–), New York City-born dramatist, whose popular plays include *Two for the Seesaw* (1958), a comedy about the brief romance between a sweet girl from the Bronx and a Nebraska lawyer; *The Miracle Worker* (1960), about Helen Keller; and *Golda* (1977), about Golda Meir. Other works include *The Seesaw Log* (1959), about the production of his play with that title; *A Mass for the Dead* (1968), family memoirs; a musical adaptation of Odets's *Golden Boy* (1965); and poems.

Gideon Society, which places copies of the Bible in hotel rooms throughout the U.S. for the use of travelers, was founded in Wisconsin (1899).

Gift books, annual miscellanies widely distributed (*c.*1825–65), contained stories, essays, and poems, usually with a polite or moral tone, and were lavishly printed and adorned for use as Christmas or New Year gifts. Beginning with *The Atlantic Souvenir* (1825–32), the gift books contained some of the best art and literature of the period, when the popular monthly magazine was not yet fully developed. With the coming of the Civil War, some organizations employed the gift book as a medium of propaganda, e.g. *The Liberty Bell.*◆ *The Token*◆ was important for introducing many distinguished authors. Before the vogue spent itself, it was responsible for the publication of more than 1000 different volumes, ranging in format from muslin-bound 32mos at $37\frac{1}{2}$¢ to magnificent folios at $20.

***Gift of the Magi,** The,* short story in *The Four Million.*◆

GILBERT, SIR HUMPHREY (1539?–83), half-brother of Sir Walter Raleigh, and like him an explorer and colonizer. In 1583 he took possession of part of Newfoundland, but he was lost in a wreck on the return voyage. The Prince Society has published a narrative of this voyage by Edward Haies, *Sir Humphrey Gilberte and His Enterprise of Colonization in America* (1903). Later accounts include a poem by Longfellow.

***Gilded Age,** The: A Tale of To-day,* novel by Clemens◆ and C.D. Warner,◆ published in 1873 but dated 1874. It was dramatized by G.S. Densmore (1874), and Clemens revised the play the same year. The theme is that of unscrupulous individualism in a world of fantastic speculation and unstable values, and the title has become a popular name for the era depicted in the book, the boom times of post-Civil War years, when unbridled acquisitiveness dominated the national life.

"Squire" Si Hawkins moves, with his wife and family, from Tennessee to a primitive Missouri settlement, the current speculative project of his visionary friend, Colonel Beriah Sellers. During the journey, Hawkins adopts two unrelated orphans, Clay and Laura. Ten years pass, Sellers's optimism costs Hawkins several fortunes, and the children grow in constant expectation of great wealth. When the Squire dies, his family moves to Sellers's new promotion center, Hawkeye, where Laura is attracted by a philanderer, Colonel Selby, who abandons her after a mock-marriage. Harry Brierly, a New York engineer, collaborates with Sellers in a railroad land speculation scheme, which fails, bankrupting them. Brierly falls in love with Laura at this time, but Laura, hardened by her experience, considers him a mere tool for her advancement. Her beauty impresses Senator Dilworthy, who invites her and her foster brother to Washington, and there they and Sellers are involved in the intrigues and financial deals of the unscrupulous senator. When Selby reappears, Laura resumes her liaison with him, later murdering him when he attempts to desert her again. She is acquitted after a spectacular court trial, but dies of a heart attack when her career as a lecturer is a failure. A subplot is concerned with the love affair of Philip Sterling, a friend of Brierly, with Ruth Bolton, a Quaker girl, who takes up a medical career but finally marries him after he successfully exploits her father's coal-mining enterprise.

GILDER, RICHARD WATSON (1844–1909), was an assistant editor of *Scribner's Monthly* after 1870, and when it was succeeded by *The Century* (1881) remained as editor until his death. In this position he was a leader of New York artistic, civic, and social life. The best of his 16 volumes of poetry is *The New Day* (1875), a cycle of love sonnets. He characterized his verse as "insufficient but irrepressible," and called himself a "squire of poesy." He also wrote books on Lincoln (1909) and Cleveland (1910), and his *Letters* (1916) were edited by his daughter Rosamond, later a writer on theatrical subjects and editor of *Theatre Arts Monthly* (1945–48). His sister Jeannette (1849–1916) assisted him on *Scribner's,* wrote columns for various newspapers, of which "Chats about Books" was distinguished as probably the first American literary gossip column, and with another brother, Joseph B., wrote *Authors at Home* (1888).

Giles Goat-Boy; or, The Revised New Syllabus, novel by John Barth,♦ published in 1966.

In the metaphoric world called the University, control is held by a computer, WESAC, which is able to run itself and to tyrannize people, for it has the ability to subject them to a radiating and disintegrating force, that is, to EAT them, an acronym for its power of "Electroencephalic Amplification and Transaction." WESAC is so out of hand that one of its developers, Max Spielman, believes it can only be controlled through reprogramming by a Grand Tutor, a prophet, who will bring a "New Syllabus," that is, a new philosophy. For this role and this purpose he selects George Giles, whom he had raised among goats as a goat, though he was actually a human found as an infant in the tapelift of WESAC. In his under-

taking George has to contend with a troublemaker, Maurice Stoker, who alone fully understands the operation of WESAC, and with a minor poet, Harold Bray, who contends that he is a Grand Tutor. George enters the computer to destroy it, and learns to confound WESAC by answering its questions through paradoxes that paralyze the machine. When George emerges, authorities eager to put WESAC back into operation seize him and send him back to the animal site of his boyhood, for he is now the University's scapegoat.

GILLETTE, WILLIAM (1855–1937), made his debut as an actor in 1875, and as a dramatist in 1881 with *The Private Secretary,* based on a German drama, and *Esmeralda,* based on Frances Hodgson Burnett's novel. His 13 original plays include *Held by the Enemy* (1886) and *Secret Service* (1895), about the Civil War; *Too Much Johnson* (1894), a farce; and *Clarice* (1905). His most popular vehicle was *Sherlock Holmes* (1899), his own arrangement of Conan Doyle stories, in which he continued to act until within a few years of his death.

GILLISS, WALTER (1855–1925), New York printer, whose press, noted for the classical simplicity of its products, was considered at the turn of the century to be the most distinguished in the U.S. except for that of De Vinne.♦ Gilliss wrote his *Recollections of the Gilliss Press* (1926).

GILMAN, CAROLINE HOWARD (1794–1888), born and reared in Massachusetts, came to know and love the South when her husband Samuel (also a New Englander and author of the hymn "Fair Harvard") accepted a Unitarian pulpit there. Her first book, *Recollections of a Housekeeper* (1834), a light narrative of domesticity, looked back to her old home in the North, but with her sense of a dual allegiance she followed it with *Recollections of a Southern Matron* (1838), another domestic narrative. They illustrated her belief that a common faith in the homely morality of family life shared by women North and South was more important than the societal and political beliefs that divided the men of these increasingly antagonistic regions. A similar attitude informs her autobiographical *The Poetry of Travelling in the United States* (1838). Other lesser works include *Tales and Ballads* (1839), prose stories and verses, and *Verses of a Life Time* (1849), as well as books for children.

GILMAN, CHARLOTTE PERKINS (1860–1935), short story writer, novelist. Her father, Frederick Beecher Perkins, nephew of Henry Ward Beecher♦ and Harriet Beecher Stowe♦, deserted his family soon after Charlotte's birth in Hartford, Conn., and her childhood was difficult. In 1884 she married Charles Stetson. She wrote her best known work, "The Yellow Wallpaper" (1892), after being institutionalized as a consequence of post-natal depression. She divorced Stetson in 1887 and moved with her daughter to California. In the 1890s she lectured widely on women's rights. In *Women and Economics* (1898) she maintained that the dependence of women on men, economically, hinders the happiness of all. Other books, *Concerning Children* (1900), and *The Home* (1904), propose changes to liberate women for more productive lives. *Man Made World* (1911) and *His Religion and Hers* (1923) envision important roles for women in world affairs and church, leading to fewer wars. In 1900 she married her cousin George Houghton Gilman. It was a happy marriage. Late in her career, Gilman wrote novels, often utopian, including *Moving the Mountain* (1911), *Herland* (1915), and *With Her in Ourland* (1916), all touching on social evils and giving feminist remedies. In the same year as her death appeared *The Living of Charlotte Perkins Gilman, an Autobiography.* Her Diaries were published in 1994.

GILMAN, DANIEL COIT (1831–1908), founder of the Sheffield Scientific School at Yale, was professor of geography there (1855–72), president of the University of California (1872–75), and first president of Johns Hopkins (1876–1901). His stimulating personality, emphasis on creative research and freedom of thought and teaching, and the brilliant scholars he attracted, soon made Johns Hopkins an important American university and medical center. He resigned to accept the presidency of the Carnegie Institute, and remained active in other foundations and societies. His books include *University Problems* (1898) and *The Launching of a University* (1906).

GILMER, FRANCIS WALKER (1790–1826), born in Virginia, graduated from William and Mary, read law with his brother-in-law William Wirt. Although appointed professor of law at the University of Virginia, he died before serving. However, he had aided it previously as Jefferson's agent in England, collecting faculty and books. His own works include *Sketches of American Orators* (1816) and *Sketches, Essays and Translations* (1826).

GILPIN, WILLIAM (1813–94), editor, soldier, and politician, figured in Western history as a soldier in the Indian wars and the Mexican War, and as first territorial governor of Colorado. He wrote two visionary works: *The Central Gold Region* (1860), later published as *The Mission of the North American People* (1873), in which he pictured the Mississippi Valley as the future home of civilization; and *The Cosmopolitan Railway* (1890), proposing a railway to connect America with Asia by way of the Bering Strait.

GILROY, FRANK D[ANIEL] (1925–), Bronx-born playwright, educated at Dartmouth and the Yale Drama School, began his career with *Who'll Save the Plowboy?* (1962). His first Broadway production, *The Subject Was Roses* (1964), treating an Irish-American family of the Bronx, won a Pulitzer Prize. Later plays include *That Summer—That Fall* (1967), *The Only Game in Town* (1968), and *Present Tense* (1972), the last dramatized from his novel of the same title. He has published several other novels.

Ginger Man, The, novel by J.P. Donleavy, ♦ published in Paris in an unexpurgated edition (1955), in the U.S. in an expurgated edition (1958) and then complete (1965). The author dramatized it for London and Dublin production (1959) and U.S. publication (1961) and production (1963).

Sebastian Dangerfield, a redheaded American studying law at Trinity College, Dublin, after U.S. naval service in World War II, is living in poverty with his wife Marion and their baby because, contrary to his hopes, she receives no money from her wealthy father and because Sebastian squanders whatever cash he can get on liquor. While his friend Kenneth cannot lose his virginity, much as he tries to, Sebastian has constant affairs with women, sometimes, as with Miss Frost, their spinster roomer, to borrow funds, but mostly for fun. Marion leaves him but in time she lets him come to her, and he looks forward to temporary comfort from her and eventual inheritance from his father.

GINSBERG, ALLEN (1926–), New Jersey-born poet, after graduation from Columbia and work at odd jobs found his voice in San Francisco during the time of the Beat movement ♦ with the publication of *Howl and Other Poems* (1956), which became famous when its publisher, Lawrence Ferlinghetti, ♦ was tried and acquitted for issuing that allegedly obscene work. Its rhapsodic, passionate, Whitmanesque view of modern corruption brought Ginsberg a great reputation, enhanced by *Kaddish and Other Poems* (1961), whose title work was a moving, lyrical lament for his recently dead mother. He issued other, lesser collections with great rapidity, including *Empty Mirror* (1960), early poems; *Reality Sandwiches* (1963); written between 1953 and 1960; *Planet News* (1968), poems of the '60s; *T.V. Baby Poems* (1968); and *Ankor Wat* (1968). He also traveled widely, freely expressing his antiauthoritarian views as well as his new belief in Zen Buddhism, which made him the guru of a new generation, a cult figure for "drop-outs" of all ages who espoused the romantic, mystic, and pacifistic idea of "flower power," a phrase Ginsberg coined. A special sort of spokesman of the '60s, Ginsberg received formal honors in the next decade when *The Fall of America: Poems of These States* (1973) was granted a National Book Award. Other later collections include *The Gates of Wrath* (1973), rhymed poems written 1948–51; *Iron Horse* (1973); *First Blues* (1975); *Sad Dust Glories* (1975); *Mind Breaths* (1977); *Poems All Over the Place,*

Mostly 'Seventies (1978); *Plutonian Ode* (1981), poems dating back only to 1977; *Collected Poems 1947–1980* (1984); and *White Shroud* (1986), poems of 1980–85. His prose includes *The Yage Letters* (1963), correspondence with William Burroughs♦; *Indian Journals* (1970); *Allen Verbatim* (1974), lectures; *The Vision of the Great Rememberer* (1974), concerning his friendship with Neal Cassady and Jack Kerouac; *Journals* (1977), texts of the 1950s and '60s; *As Ever* (1977), correspondence with Cassady; *Composed on the Tongue* (1980), interviews; and *Straight Hearts' Delight* (1980), letters and love poems exchanged with Peter Orlovsky.

GIOVANNI, NIKKI (YOLANDE CORNELIA GIOVANNI, JR.) (1943–   ), born in Tennessee, educated at Fisk (B.A., 1967), is best known for her poetry, the early work often militantly black and socially conscious, the later, more personal and mellow. It has been published in *Black Feeling, Black Talk* (1968), *Black Judgement* (1968), *Re: Creation* (1970), *Poem of Angela Yvonne Davis* (1970), *My House* (1972), *The Women and the Men* (1975), and *Cotton Candy on a Rainy Day* (1978). Her poems for younger readers appear in *Spin a Soft Black Song* (1971) and *Ego Tripping* (1973). *Gemini* (1971) collects essays, many autobiographical and others socially revolutionary or literary criticism. *A Dialogue* (1972) transcribes a tape-recorded talk with James Baldwin on racial and literary subjects, and *A Poetic Equation* (1974) is a similar dialogue with Alice Walker. *Sacred Cows and Other Edibles* (1988) treats American racial prospects and related matters.

GIOVANNITTI, ARTURO (1884–1959), Italian-born poet, came to the U.S. (1902), where, disillusioned by his observation of exploited labor, he became a lecturer, pamphleteer, and labor organizer. His only book in English, *Arrows in the Gale* (1914), is an impassioned prose poem condemning the prison system, which he had come to know at first hand through his activity in strikes.

***Girl of the Golden West,** The,* play by Belasco,♦ produced in 1905 and published in 1925. It became the libretto of an Italian opera by Puccini (1910).

"The Girl," saloon keeper and schoolmistress in a Far Western mining community, falls in love with Dick Johnson, an outlaw who loves her too. Johnson, wounded, is tracked to her cabin by the sheriff, Jack Rance, who also loves the Girl but accepts her offer to decide by a game of poker whether he shall have her or, if he loses, discontinue his search for her lover. The sheriff is bested by her cheating, but Johnson is captured when he leaves the cabin. When the miners see how much she loves her outlaw, they free him, and Johnson and "The Girl" start eastward to a new life.

***Girl of the Limberlost,** A,* novel by Gene Stratton-Porter.♦

***Girl with the Green Eyes,** The,* play by Clyde Fitch,♦ produced in 1902 and published in 1905.

GIST, CHRISTOPHER (*c.*1706–59), frontiersman in the employ of the Ohio Company, was the first white man to explore southern Ohio and northeastern Kentucky, preceding Boone by 18 years. He accompanied Washington on a journey to warn the French out of the Ohio Valley (1753–54), and at this time saved Washington's life. He later guided the expedition of Braddock. His *Journals* were published in 1893.

Give Your Heart to the Hawks, free-verse narrative by Jeffers,♦ the title poem of a volume published in 1933.

At a drunken beach party near their California home, Lance Fraser discovers his brother Michael and his wife Fayne in an embrace, and kills his brother. No one else has seen the incident, and Fayne, independent of ordinary moral standards, persuades her husband to conceal his crime, making it appear an accident. ("Oh, give your heart to the hawks for a snack o' meat But not to men.") Conscience-stricken, Lance torments himself by sleeping in Michael's room, seducing Michael's fiancée, Mary Abbey, and making love to Fayne on Michael's grave. Mary confesses to Fayne that she is pregnant, goes to San Francisco for an abortion, and later commits suicide. Fayne, herself pregnant, tries desperately to keep Lance from surrendering to police, but he is morbidly obsessed, and confesses to his puritanical old father, who becomes insane. Fayne packs their belongings and persuades her husband to leave the farm with her. At their first camp, on a trail near the coast, he becomes insane, kills their horses with an axe, and leaps from a cliff to his death. Fayne buries him on the beach and returns, her courage and faith unwavering. ("I could not keep you, but your child in my body Will change the world.")

***Gladiator,** The,* blank-verse play by R.M. Bird,♦ written in 1831 for Edwin Forrest, who acted in it more than 1000 times. It was not published until 1919, because the actor feared it might be performed by another person.

GLASGOW, ELLEN [ANDERSON GHOLSON] (1874–1945), born in Richmond, Va., of an aristocratic Southern family, in 1897 published her first novel, *The Descendant. The Freeman, and Other Poems* (1902) is her only volume of verse. *The Voice of the People* (1900) was the first of a long series of novels recording the social and political background of her state from 1850 to the 1940s, and represented her revolt from the sentimental tradition of Southern fiction in depicting the genteel code of the Old South at bay before the new industrial revolution. This study, concerned with the rise of a farm boy to political prominence, and his death in a mob riot, was followed by such contrasts of life in the old and new social classes of the South as *The Battle-Ground* (1902), *The Deliverance* (1904), *The Wheel of Life* (1906), *The Ancient Law* (1908), *The Romance of a Plain Man* (1909), and *The Miller of Old Church* (1911). In *Virginia*♦ (1913) and *Life and Gabriella*♦ (1916) she wrote novels of Southern women victimized by a decaying code of chivalry. Three realistic studies of political and social conflicts followed: *The Builders* (1919); *One Man in His Time* (1922); and *Barren Ground*♦ (1925). At this time she declared that "what the South needs now is—blood and irony," and she proceeded to write three satirical novels of manners, *The Romantic Comedians*♦ (1926), *They Stooped to Folly*♦ (1929), and *The Sheltered Life*♦ (1932). In *Vein of Iron*♦ (1935) she returned to the study of rural life in Virginia. *In This Our Life* (1941, Pulitzer Prize) is a novel of an aristocratic Virginia family fallen into decadence. *The Shadowy Third* (1923) collects stories; her *Works* were collected in 1938. *A Certain Measure* (1943) collects essays prefatory to her novels. *The Woman Within* (1954) is her autobiography. Her *Letters* were collected in 1958; and an edition of her *Collected Stories* appeared in 1963.

GLASPELL, SUSAN (1882–1948), with her husband, George Cram Cook,♦ was a founder and leader of the Provincetown Players♦ and The Playwrights' Theatre, for which, sometimes in collaboration with him, she wrote such one-act plays as *Suppressed Desires* (1914), satirizing psychoanalysis; *Trifles* (1916), dealing with the death of a man and the arrest of his wife on suspicion of murder; *Close the Book* (1917); *A Woman's Honor* (1918); and *Tickless Time* (1918), satirizing romantic escapists from modern civilization. Her longer plays include *Bernice* (1919), which reveals the character of a dead woman through her effect upon her family and friends; *The Inheritors* (1921), concerned with a Midwestern college founded by liberal families whose third generations clash because one remains liberal but the other has become conservative; *The Verge* (1921), a psychological study of a neurotic woman driven to insanity; and *Alison's House*♦ (1930, Pulitzer Prize), dealing with the effect of a poet's life on her surviving family, and supposedly suggested by the life of Emily Dickinson. Her other works include *Lifted Masks* (1912), a book of short stories; *The Road to the Temple* (1926), a romantic biography of her husband; and novels which include *The Glory of the Conquered* (1909), the story of a scientist who goes blind and dies just as he is about to make a great discovery; *The Visioning* (1911), set at an army post; *Fidelity* (1915), about a girl who elopes with a married man; *Brook Evans* (1928), describing the lives of a mother and daughter; *The Fugitive's Return* (1929), dealing with an Iowa girl and her experiences on Cape Cod and in Greece; *Ambrose Holt and Family* (1931); *The Morning Is Near Us* (1940), about the homecoming of an American woman

traveler; *Norma Ashe* (1942), tracing the careers of a group of college students through 30 years; and *Judd Rankin's Daughter* (1945), about an American "grass roots" philosopher and his family.

GLASS, HUGH (*fl.* 1822–33), Far Western trapper, during an expedition to the mouth of the Yellowstone (1823) was attacked by a grizzly bear and left as dead by his companions, young James Bridger and a certain Fitzgerald. He regained his strength and made his way to Fort Kiowa. Upon encountering his former companions, he forgave Bridger because of his youth and Fitzgerald when he returned his rifle. He is believed to have been killed by the Blackfoot in 1833. His adventures were the basis of many legends, which have frequently been retold, as in Neihardt's poem *Song of Hugh Glass* (1915), and Frederick Manfred's novel *Lord Grizzly* (1954).

Glass Menagerie, The, play by Tennessee Williams,♦ produced in 1944 and published in 1945.

Laura Wingfield, who wears a leg brace because of a crippling childhood illness and is hypersensitive about it, lives with her mother Amanda and brother Tom in a St. Louis tenement. Her father has long since deserted them, though a dashing photo remains as a reminder of his charm. Amanda, a victim of illusions about her past as a Southern belle and about Laura's future, persists in preparing her daughter for hypothetical secretarial work and for nonexistent "gentlemen callers." She likewise wants Tom to get ahead in his warehouse job, which largely supports the family, but as a poetic dreamer his thoughts, like his father's, are often about escape from the family, as he turns to compulsive movie-going or plans for merchant-marine service. Amanda persuades Tom to invite a friend from the warehouse for dinner, and lets herself leap to romantic conclusions concerning a relationship between the visitor and Laura, even though the pathetically withdrawn girl is only at home in her private world, which centers on a collection of glass animal figurines. On the appointed evening Tom arrives with Jim O'Connor, who turns out to be a high-school acquaintance whom Laura admired and who has since been part of her dream life. Her shy, nervous confusion is eased by Jim's warmth and she shows him her favorite animal, a tiny unicorn, but when he later teaches her a few dance steps while trying to build up her self-confidence, they bump the table and the unicorn's horn is broken. She discounts the accident, saying that now the unicorn will "feel less—freakish," and Jim is moved to tell her that she herself is different from others "in a nice way," like "Blue Roses," his high-school nickname for her. He tells her that she is pretty and kisses her. He is sincere but casual and, suddenly embarrassed, explains that he cannot call again because he is engaged to another girl. Furious at Tom for bringing home an engaged man,

Amanda goads him beyond the breaking point, and he leaves home, haunted by the memory of his sister, who now retreats even further into herself.

Gleason's Pictorial Drawing-Room Companion (1851–59), Boston weekly magazine, modeled on the *London Illustrated News.* Contributors included Sylvanus Cobb, T.S. Arthur, A.J.H. Duganne, T.B. Read, Alger, and Lydia Huntley Sigourney. In 1854 it was sold to M.M. Ballou, who substituted his name for Gleason's in the title.

Glory of Columbia, *The,* see *André.*

Go Down, Moses, collection of seven stories by Faulkner,♦ published in 1942, which treat the McCaslin family,♦ white and black, from the time of Lucius, the founder at the opening of the 19th century, to the mid-20th century, all together representative of Southern history. Hunting and rituals of initiation are basic metaphors. The longest and most significant of the stories is "The Bear."♦

Go Tell It on the Mountain, novel by James Baldwin,♦ published in 1953.

On his fourteenth birthday in 1935, John Grimes faces the issue of religious conversion in the storefront Temple of the Fire Baptized while he wrestles with boyhood problems of sex and anger at his parents. His father, Gabriel, like other relatives and ancestors of young John, is revealed through flashbacks that illuminate John's own problems. Gabriel had had an affair with Esther, by whom he had his first son Royal, dead at age 18, and Gabriel atoned by wedding the sexless Deborah. Like Esther, Deborah died, and Gabriel then married Elizabeth. Before her marriage to Gabriel, Elizabeth had had an idyllic romance with Richard, by whom her illegitimate son John was born. After Richard's suicide following a beating by police, Elizabeth married Gabriel, who adopted her son John. Guilt, bitterness, a sense of doom, and spiritual strivings affect young John, as they have his family before him.

"Go west, young man," expression used in an editorial by Horace Greeley in the New York *Tribune,* and erroneously attributed to him. It was first used by John Babsone Lane Soule (1815–91) in an article in the Terre Haute *Express* (1851), and expressed the spirit of manifest destiny, exhorting young men to grow up with the country by taking advantage of opportunities in the unsettled West.

God Bless You, Mr. Rosewater; *or Pearls Before Swine,* novel by Vonnegut,♦ published in 1965.

In a free-form text the history of the Rosewater family is traced from two brothers of the Civil War era: Noah, who hired a substitute to fight while he made money manufacturing armaments, and George, blinded in battle and dispossessed by his brother. Noah's descendants include Senator Lister Ames Rosewater, creator of the Rosewater Foundation, managed by his son Eliot, who by accident during World War II had killed members of a volunteer fire department and ever thereafter gives Foundation funds to volunteer firefighters or down-and-outers in general. George's descendants include Fred, an insurance salesman who leads a middle-class life of desperation. The two branches of the family are united only by a lawsuit fomented by Norman Mushari, counsel for the Foundation, who attempts to prove Eliot insane so as to benefit himself and, incidentally, Fred too. The basic case is sidetracked when 57 separate paternity suits are brought against Eliot, who acknowledges all 57 children and arranges for each to become seriatim the president of the Rosewater Foundation.

Godey's Lady's Book (1830–98), monthly miscellany founded at Philadelphia by Louis Antoine Godey (1804–78). Sarah J. Hale, the editor from 1837 to 1877, exerted an important influence on fashions and manners, for the magazine was considered a criterion of taste. Among the articles and pictures of fashions were included stories and other contributions from Emerson, Longfellow, Holmes, Hawthorne, Harriet Beecher Stowe, Poe, W.G. Simms, and Paulding, although most of the writers were of a far lower caliber, conforming to the sentimental, moral, and didactic standards of the day. In 1892 the magazine was moved to New York, where as *Godey's Magazine* it published novelettes by Gertrude Atherton, Julian Hawthorne, H.H. Boyesen, and others. It was absorbed by Munsey's *Puritan.*

GODFREY, THOMAS (1736–63), Philadelphia poet, whose poems contributed to the *American Magazine* were imitative of the Cavalier poets. *The Court of Fancy* (1762), as he acknowledged, was strongly indebted to Chaucer and Pope. He is best known for his romantic tragedy, *The Prince of Parthia,*♦ which he wrote in 1759. *Juvenile Poems on Various Subjects. With the Prince of Parthia, a Tragedy* was a posthumous collection (1765).

GODKIN, EDWIN LAWRENCE (1831–1902), came to America from Ireland at the age of 25, and founded *The Nation*♦ (1865), a liberal weekly commenting on public affairs, literature, and the arts. He was a disciple of the Bentham-Mill-Grote school of philosophy, believing that the ultimate social object is the greatest happiness of the greatest number, attained through liberty, under reason and justice. He edited the New York *Evening Post*♦ (1883–1900), with which he had merged *The Nation* in 1881. His fearless independence, zeal, and wide knowledge made it an extremely influential newspaper. He was consistently liberal, believed wholeheartedly in democracy, sympathized with the Union during the Civil War, attacked the corruption of Grant's regime, led the Mugwump revolt against Blaine, supported Cleveland but attacked his jingoism, was an implacable foe of "free silver," advocated a moderate tariff, deplored territorial expansion, and consistently worked for civil service reform. Thirty years prior to the formulation of F.J. Turner's ideas on the frontier Godkin found that the democratic tide in the U.S. "owed most of its force and violence" to the influence of frontier life, which proved a dangerous leveling influence and caused the rise of the demagogue and spoilsman. His books include *Problems of Democracy* (1896) and *Unforeseen Tendencies of Democracy* (1898).

God's Little Acre, novel by Erskine Caldwell, ♦ published in 1933.

A Georgia "cracker," Ty Ty Walden, has devoted 15 years to digging for gold on his farm. Always a "religious man," he has set aside one acre whose income shall go to the church, but has had to shift "God's little acre" constantly, so as not to interfere with the digging. Ty Ty's sincere but adaptable morality appears also in the shiftless lives of his children: Buck, who is brutally jealous of his wife Griselda; Shaw, lazy at work but more diversified in his affections; promiscuous Darling Jill, who despises her timid fat suitor, Pluto Swint, a candidate for sheriff; and Rosamond, whose husband, Will Thompson, is a cotton weaver in a Carolina mill. Pluto drives Darling Jill to Scottsville, to bring the Thompsons back to dig, since the mill workers have long been on strike. Although Rosamond returns with her husband to the farm, she nearly kills him in the morning when she finds him sleeping with Darling Jill. Ty Ty, in need of funds, goes to Augusta to borrow money from his wealthy eldest son, Jim Leslie. Pluto, Darling Jill, and Griselda take Will and his wife back to Scottsville, where the mill owners have finally refused the union's demands. Will spectacularly fulfills his desire to possess Griselda, and next day dies a hero's death in a violent attempt to reopen the mill. Jim Leslie appears at the farm, mad with days of desire for Griselda. When he refuses to leave, Buck shoots him. Ty Ty, grief-stricken at this "blood on my land," allows Buck to commit suicide, and wonders "how soon Shaw would come back to help him dig."

Gods of the Lightning, play by Maxwell Anderson ♦ and Harold Hickerson.

God's Trombones, volume of poetry by James Weldon Johnson. ♦

GODWIN, PARKE (1816–1904), New Jersey-born journalist and reformer, graduated from Princeton (1834). He was a leading Fourierist, ♦ publishing *The Harbinger* ♦ from Brook Farm and

writing *Democracy, Constructive and Pacific* (1843) and *A Popular View of the Doctrines of Charles Fourier* (1844). Among his other books are *Vala* (1851), a fantastic tale; a partial translation of Goethe's *Autobiography* (1846–47); a biography of his father-in-law, Bryant (1883); and an edition of Bryant's works. Godwin was associated with the New York *Evening Post* ♦ (1836–81), during the last four years succeeding Bryant as editor. He also edited the *Commercial Advertiser.*

GOFFE, WILLIAM (c. 1605–79), English Puritan, signer of the death warrant of Charles I. During the Restoration he fled to America, where he lived mainly in seclusion at Hadley, Mass. He is said to have been instrumental in repelling an Indian attack during King Philip's War. He figures in Cooper's *The Wept of Wish-ton-Wish,* Barker's *Superstition,* Paulding's *The Puritan and His Daughter,* Hawthorne's "The Grey Champion," McHenry's *The Spectre of the Forest,* and Delia Bacon's *Tales of the Puritans,* as well as in Scott's *Peveril of the Peak.* A factual account of Goffe is contained in Ezra Stiles's *History of the Judges of Charles I* (1794). His father-in-law and fellow regicide, Edward Whalley, accompanied Goffe to America.

Gold, play by Eugene O'Neill. ♦

GOLD, HERBERT (1924–   ), born in Cleveland, after army service in World War II received an A.B. and M.A. from Columbia, and taught at Midwestern and California universities. He lived in France and Haiti and later moved to San Francisco. His novels are *Birth of a Hero* (1951), about a conventional, middle-aged man who learns to discover himself; *The Prospect Before Us* (1954); *The Man Who Was Not with It* (1956), a vivid tale, raffish and poetic in jargon and attitude, about a carnival barker who is a dope addict; *The Optimist* (1959), a portrait of a man bent on success and wanting to be wanted; *Therefore Be Bold* (1960), an amusing tale of Jewish adolescents in the Midwest; *Salt* (1963), depicting with wit and satire the massive metropolitan anonymity of New York City and the lives of three people, each telling one part of a romance in which all are involved; *Fathers* (1967), "a novel in the form of a memoir," dealing with Gold's father and his own experiences as a father; *The Great American Jackpot* (1969), a wry view of contemporary U.S. seen by a black college professor and a white student; *Swiftie the Magician* (1974), depicting a writer-producer-director in the 1960s; *Waiting for Cordelia* (1977), a comic view of prostitution; *He / She* (1980), presenting an unusual marriage; *Family* (1981), a saga of an immigrant Jewish family in the U.S.; *True Love* (1982); *Mister White Eyes* (1984), his 15th novel, about a U.S. journalist often abroad; and *Dreaming* (1988). Story collections include *Love and Like* (1960), *The Magic Will* (1971), *Stories of Misbegotten Love* (1985), *Lovers* *and Cohorts* (1986), and *Travels in San Francisco* (1990). Essays are printed in *The Age of Happy Problems* (1962), and both essays and stories in *A Walk on the West Side* (1981), about California. *My Last Two Thousand Years* (1972) is an autobiography of himself as a Jew.

GOLD, MICHAEL, pseudonym of Irwin Granich (1893–1967), born and reared on New York's Lower East Side. His experience of the slums and as a worker led him to become a Communist. He was an editor of *The Liberator.* His writings include *120 Million* (1929), sketches of American workers; *Jews Without Money* (1930), a semi-autobiographical work; *Change the World* (1937), articles from the *Daily Worker* and the *New Masses; The Hollow Men* (1941), critical articles on literature; and *Life of John Brown* (1960), the subject also of a play, *Battle Hymn* (1936), written with Michael Blankfort. He also wrote several plays of his own, some unpublished.

Gold-Bug, The, tale by Poe,♦ published as a prize story in the Philadelphia *Dollar Magazine* (1843) and reprinted in *Tales* (1845). The cryptograph on which the story depends is a development of the interest that prompted Poe's essay "Cryptography" (*Graham's Magazine,* 1841).

William Legrand, an impoverished Southern gentleman, lives in seclusion on Sullivan's Island, South Carolina, his only companion being the black servant Jupiter. One day, when they capture a rare golden scarab beetle, marked with a sort of death's-head, they come upon a curious piece of parchment, which when heated proves to contain a secret cipher and a drawing of a death's-head. Legrand ingeniously decodes the cipher, which directs them to the buried treasure of Captain Kidd. With the aid of a friend and the superstitious Jupiter, both of whom he deliberately mystifies, Legrand locates an indicated tree, in which a skull is nailed, and, by dropping the beetle through an eye of the skull, they are able to establish a line on the position of the cache. Besides several skeletons, they exhume a fortune in old coins and jewels, with which Legrand reestablishes himself in society.

Gold rush, see *Forty-niners* and *Klondike gold rush.*

Golden Book of Springfield, The, Utopian narrative by Vachel Lindsay.♦

Golden Bowl, The, novel by Henry James,♦ published in 1904.

Charlotte Stant, a daring, intelligent, but penniless American, has a brief affair in Rome with Prince Amerigo, an impoverished Italian aristocrat. They recognize that life together without money would be fatal to their love, and Charlotte returns to America. The Prince then falls in love with Maggie Verver, who, with her wealthy father, Adam, represents the best qualities of American culture: enthusiasm, moral fineness, the ability to assimilate new values, and a refreshing innocence and delicacy of outlook. Charlotte, a close friend of Maggie, returns to London, and, while shopping one day with the Prince, considers as a possible gift for Maggie a certain gilded crystal bowl, perfect except for an invisible flaw. She is persuaded not to buy it, but the bowl becomes a symbol of the Prince's character and the various flawed relationships in the narrative. Maggie, after her marriage, realizes that she has ended the happy relationship with her father, who, when he finds her worried about him, marries Charlotte. In England Maggie is happy with her reunited father, husband, and friend, as well as in the care of her son, but gradually she becomes aware of the renewed liaison of Charlotte and her husband. But when by chance she buys the golden bowl as a birthday present for her father, Maggie learns something from the shopkeeper that makes her suspect the Prince's infidelity. However, her friend Fanny Assingham declares that her theory is as cracked as the bowl, which she dramatically dashes to the floor. Maggie therefore proceeds cautiously, concealing her suspicions, and quietly works to restore the proper grouping of the couples. The Prince senses that she knows the truth, and is touched by her generosity and delicacy. Adam too realizes that she has learned that his wife and son-in-law are lovers; with the same tact and self-sacrifice that she has exhibited, he takes Charlotte to America, never to return. The Prince understands that, by losing his mistress, he has gained a new depth of character and a wife whose value he has only begun to appreciate. The process of "conversion," which began with the smashing of the golden bowl, is thus completed.

Golden Era, The (1852–93), newspaper and literary journal of San Francisco, during its heyday published writings by Bret Harte, Mark Twain, C.W. Stoddard, Prentice Mulford, Fitz Hugh Ludlow, Alonzo Delano, Ada Clare, Joaquin Miller, Adah Menken, and R.H. Newell. After the 1860s, the paper dwindled in significance.

Golden Legend, The, dramatic poem by Longfellow,♦ published in 1851 and incorporated in *Christus*♦ (1872). It is based on *Der arme Heinrich,* by Hartmann von der Aue, 12th-century German minnesinger.

GOLDMAN, EMMA (1869–1940), Russian-born exponent of anarchism,♦ came to the U.S. (1886) and soon began to write and lecture in behalf of various reform movements, including feminism and birth control. Her anarchist speeches, and the magazine *Mother Earth,* which she founded in 1906, attracted wide attention. She was twice jailed, once for advocating pacifism during World War I. In 1919 she and an associate, Alexander Berkman, were deported to Russia, but their dislike for the Bolshevist regime and their criticism of it led to their leaving the country. Miss Goldman's autobiography, *Living My Life* (1931), was published from her home in France, and her other works include *Anarchism and Other Essays* (revised edition, 1911), *The Social Significance of the Modern Drama* (1914), and *My Disillusionment in Russia* (1925).

Gone with the Wind, novel by Margaret Mitchell,♦ published in 1936 and awarded a Pulitzer Prize. A tremendously popular and frequently revived film was created (1939) from a script written by Sidney Howard.

Set in Georgia during the Civil War and Reconstruction, this long romantic tale centers on the adventures of Scarlett, a high-spirited willful girl, daughter of Gerald O'Hara, an Irish immigrant who has become owner of Tara, a large plantation. Sixteen years old at the outbreak of the war, and in love with their neighbor Ashley Wilkes, she learns that Ashley plans to marry his cousin, the gentle Melanie Hamilton. Out of spite, Scarlett marries Melanie's brother Charles, youthful suitor of Honey Wilkes, Ashley's sister. Charles soon dies in the war, and Scarlett, living in Atlanta with her aunt "Pittypat," is plunged into poverty by the city's fall to the Northern invaders. In the struggle to survive after the war, Scarlett must carry the load of supporting her own family and also Ashley's, for her mother has died, her father has lost his mind, and Ashley, an idealistic aristocrat, is unable to adjust himself to the harsh realities of the new South. Scarlett is determined to keep Tara and to win financial security at any cost. She works in the fields, does other menial tasks, and, to get money for taxes, marries Frank Kennedy, her sister's fiancé. With Frank's money and her own unscrupulous determination, she establishes a lumber business in Atlanta, and forces Ashley to become manager of one of her mills. Frank is killed in avenging an insult to her, and Scarlett, now 27, marries the war profiteer Rhett Butler, who attracts her by qualities similar to her own. Her selfishness and continuing infatuation for Ashley destroy Rhett's love, however, and he deserts her. When Melanie dies, and Ashley rejects Scarlett's sympathy, she realizes too late that Rhett is the one man she has ever really loved.

Good Earth, *The,* novel by Pearl Buck,♦ published in 1931, awarded a Pulitzer Prize, and dramatized by Owen and Donald Davis (1932). With *Sons* (1932) and *A House Divided* (1935), it forms a trilogy, *The House of Earth.*

Wang Lung, a Chinese peasant, rises to become a rich landowner and founder of a powerful family, but throughout his life he is dominated by a reverence for the soil. His marriage to O-lan, formerly a kitchen slave in the House of Hwang, intensifies this feeling, for her starved youth has impressed upon her the lessons of careful husbandry and the security that comes only from possession of land. Slowly but surely, during strenuous years of hardship, famine, flood, disease, and ceaseless labor, Wang Lung and patient, homely O-lan accumulate their acres, many of them bought from the declining House of Hwang. Three sons and two daughters are born to them, and they live more luxuriously. Wang Lung takes as second wife the attractive former prostitute Lotus, but O-lan patiently manages the household until her death. Their sons grow to manhood, the two eldest superintending their father's affairs, while the youngest becomes a revolutionary leader. All three divorce their lives from the soil, however, and although they plan to maintain their power as a family, they do not possess the vigor and intensity that has given significance to the life of Wang Lung.

Good Gray Poet, sobriquet of Whitman, first applied to him by W.D. O'Connor.♦

Good Morning, America, poem in free verse by Sandburg,♦ delivered as a Phi Beta Kappa poem at Harvard, is the title piece of a volume (1928). This Whitmanesque panorama of American life and ideals, distinguished by an apt use of vernacular phrases and folk sayings, sly humor, and skepticism of fashionable values, nevertheless exhibits a profound faith that the obstinate, misguided will of the people will triumph over the errors and abuses of modern mechanical civilization.

Good News from New England, see *Winslow, Edward.*

Good News from Virginia, sermon by Alexander Whitaker.♦

Good Speed to Virginia, see *Gray, Robert.*

Good-bye, poem by Emerson,♦ written in 1823 and published in *The Western Messenger* (1839). In couplets of four-stress lines, it is an early expression of the theme of *Nature.*♦ The poet rejects the traditional institutions of the "proud world," in favor of "going home" to the untrammeled solitude of nature, where "man in the bush with God may meet."

Good-Bye, My Fancy, poems and prose by Whitman,♦ published in 1891. The verse is reprinted in the final edition of *Leaves of Grass*♦ and the prose in the *Complete Writings* (1902).

GOODMAN, PAUL (1911–72), New York psychoanalyst and author, whose writings include *Communitas* (1947), with his brother Percival, on city planning; *Growing Up Absurd* (1960), an intense personal and sociological attack on the "eclectic, sensational, . . . phony" U.S. culture and its baneful effect on youth; *The Community of*

Scholars (1962) and *Compulsory Mis-Education* (1964), which criticize contemporary U.S. education; *New Reformation* (1970), advice to young dissidents; *Like a Conquered Province: The Moral Ambiguity of America* (1967); several volumes of poetry, gathered in *Collected Poems* (1974); plays, including *Faustina* (1949) and *The Young Disciple* (1955); novels, including *The Grand Piano* (1949), *The Dead of Spring* (1950), and *Making Do* (1963), experimental in form but setting forth the same nonconformist views of his nonfiction; and literary criticism in *The Structure of Literature* (1954). He had a great following among youth in the 1960s, and his writings continued to be collected posthumously through the 1970s.

GOODRICH, SAMUEL GRISWOLD (1793–1860), Boston publisher, founder of the annual gift book *The Token*♦ (1827–42). Under his pseudonym, Peter Parley, were published more than 100 moralistic books for juvenile instruction, beginning with *The Tales of Peter Parley About America* (1827). Sugarcoated with fiction, they were significant for their break away from religious didacticism. Goodrich was also the author of poetry, prose sketches, and volumes of advice to parents. His *Recollections of a Lifetime* (2 vols., 1856) tells of the many authors he knew, including Hawthorne and Epes Sargent, who were among those he employed to write children's books under his pseudonym.

GOOKIN, DANIEL (1612–87), born in England or Ireland, at the age of 18 was living on his father's Virginia plantation, and there later became a burgess, captain, and large landholder. An ardent Puritan, he emigrated to Massachusetts (1644), where for 35 years he was reelected as deputy to the General Court, and among other officers was appointed major general of the colony's forces (1681). He was interested in the welfare of the Indians, and was "chosen to be ruler over the praying Indians," protecting them during King Philip's War. *Historical Collections of the Indians in New England* (1792) and *An Historical Account of the Doings and Sufferings of the Christian Indians* (1836) are attempts at scientific history, marked by a humanitarianism toward the Indians.

Goops, characters in pictures and text created by Gelett Burgess♦ for his journal, *The Lark,* as boneless, quasi-human figures divided by their creator into two types: sulphites, independent thinkers, and bromides, platitudinous bores. In *Goops and How To Be Them* (1900), the first of a long series of amusing books intended to teach manners to youngsters, Burgess reincarnated the term but not the types, now presented as naughty, balloon-headed children.

GORDON, CAROLINE (1895–1981), Southern author, whose novels include *Penhally* (1931), about four generations of a Kentucky family; *Al-*

eck Maury, Sportsman* (1934), about a Southerner who is both scholar and sportsman; *None Shall Look Back* (1937), about a Kentucky family during the Civil War; *The Garden of Adonis* (1937), concerning Southern social and economic conflicts; *Green Centuries* (1941), about 18th-century Southern frontier life; *The Women on the Porch* (1944), a psychological analysis of a woman's life; *The Strange Children* (1951); *The Malefactors* (1956), a sensitive study of an aging, frustrated poet; and *The Glory of Hera* (1972), a particularly mythic tale. Her stories are collected in *The Forest of the South* (1945), *Old Red* (1963), and *Collected Stories* (1981). With Allen Tate, she wrote a textbook, *The House of Fiction* (1950), whose point of view animated her *How To Read a Novel* (1957). Some of her early letters were published in 1984. She and Allen Tate♦ were married (1924–59).

GORDON, WILLIAM (1728–1807), born in England, came to Massachusetts (1770) out of sympathy for the American cause. To collect materials for a contemporary history he hobnobbed with leading figures, but his book was too outspoken to be published in England or America. It was entirely recast before being printed in London as *The History of the Rise, Progress, and Establishment of the Independence of the United States of America* (1788). Probably some 100 of the most offensive pages were stricken from the manuscript, and plagiarized sections from Dodsley's *Annual Register* and the work of David Ramsay substituted for them.

GORDONE, CHARLES (1926–), Cleveland-born actor, director, producer, and playwright whose plays include *No Place to Be Somebody* (1969, Pulitzer Prize), a dark comedy about blacks in a rundown Greenwich Village saloon, whose owner is determined to be free of the local white Mafia; *The Last Chord* (1976), a melodrama with a related plot; and *Gordone Is Muthah* (1970), almost a one-man show.

GOREY, EDWARD [ST. JOHN] (1925–), after graduation from Harvard began publishing his numerous hand-lettered books, whose brief cryptic narratives and morbidly comic pen-and-ink illustrations are marked by a fey Gothic humor that has created a cult for works bearing such titles as *The Unstrung Harp* (1953), *The Hapless Child* (1961), *The Broken Spoke* (1976), *The Doubtful Guest* (1978), and *The Raging Tide* (1987). *Amphigorey* (1972) is a collection of 15 of his small books.

GORGES, SIR FERDINANDO (c.1566–1647), English soldier, was one of the organizers of the Virginia Company of Plymouth (1606), employed John Smith to head successive unsuccessful settlements in Maine, and himself directed commercial voyages to New England. He obtained a revised charter for a Council for New

England (1620), which set the boundaries of "New England" between 40° and 48° N. latitude, and wrote *The Briefe Narration of the Original Undertakings of the Advancement of Plantations into Parts of America* (1647) in a vain attempt to win financial support for the enterprise. His schemes for an aristocratic Anglican settlement failed because of the surprising success of the grants to the Pilgrims (1620) and to the Massachusetts Bay Colony (1628). Negotiations to make all New England a royal province, under the governorship of Gorges, were never completed because of the growing power of the Puritans in England. He received instead the title to the province of Maine (1639), but could not acquire the finances needed for extensive colonization.

FERDINANDO GORGES (1630–1718), his grandson, author of *America Painted to the Life* (1658–59), sold to Massachusetts his inherited title to Maine (1677). His account of Massachusetts is indebted to Johnson's *Wonder-Working Providence*.

GORMAN, HERBERT S[HERMAN] (1893–1954), New York author and journalist, whose books include the biographies *A Victorian American: Henry Wadsworth Longfellow* (1926); *Hawthorne: A Study in Solitude* (1927); *The Incredible Marquis* (1929), the story of Dumas *père*; *Scottish Queen* (1932), the life of Mary of Scotland; and *James Joyce* (1940). His historical novels include *Jonathan Bishop* (1933), about the end of Napoleon III's empire; *The Mountain and the Plain* (1936), about the French Revolution; *Brave General* (1942), about the French military hero Georges Boulanger; *The Wine of San Lorenzo* (1945), about the Mexican War; and *The Cry of Dolores* (1948), about the Mexican Revolution of 1810.

GORTON, SAMUEL (*c.*1592–1677), came to Boston from England (1637), but was soon banished because of his Antinomian beliefs. He followed Roger Williams to Providence, but seceded from his group to found Shawomet, R.I. (1643). Imprisoned in 1644 as an enemy of "civil authority among the people of God," he spent four years in exile in England, returning (1648) to live peaceably at Shawomet, which he renamed Warwick in honor of his protector. Gorton contended that Christ was the only proper object of worship, denied the Trinity, claimed that each man should be his own priest, wished to abolish all outward ordinances, taught a conditional immortality dependent upon individual character, claimed that by union with Christ one partook of God's perfection, and denied the existence of heaven and hell. Among his pamphlets setting forth these theories were *Simplicities Defense against Seven-Headed Policie* (1646), a reply to Edward Winslow's *Hypocrisie Unmasked* (1646); *Saltmarsh Returned from the Dead* (1655); and *An Antidote Against the Common Plague of the World*

(1657). His followers, the Gortonites, persisted as a distinct group for nearly a century.

Gospel of Wealth, *The,* essay by Andrew Carnegie. ◆

Gotham, sobriquet of New York City, derived from the jocular reputation of the "wise men" of Gotham, England, noted for their foolish actions. The name was first so used in Irving's *Salmagundi* (1807–8).

Gothic romance, variety of fiction widely popular in 18th-century England, whence it spread to the U.S. and throughout Europe, especially influencing German literature. The vogue of medievalism, sensationalism, and supernatural horrors was developed by Walpole's *Castle of Otranto* (1764), set in a background of romantic "Gothic" architecture; Beckford's *Vathek* (1786); M.G. Lewis's *The Monk* (1795); *The Mysteries of Udolpho* (1795) and other romances of horror by Ann Radcliffe; and later by Godwin and Mary Wollstonecraft Shelley. In the U.S., Charles Brockden Brown ◆ was the leading author of Gothic romances, and *The Asylum* ◆ is a typical example of the genre, which strongly influenced such writers about the mysterious and the supernatural as Poe ◆ and Hawthorne, ◆ although Poe's statement, "the terror of which I write is not of Germany, but of the soul," is applicable to both of them. In the 1970s and '80s the term was applied to a very different kind of fiction, generally published in paperback editions, addressed to women, broadly but simply plotted stories of sensual relations between a hero and heroine, often also period pieces set in distant and ostensibly romantic periods or places.

GOUDY, FREDERIC W[ILLIAM] (1865–1947), type designer and printer, founded his Village Press (1903) in Illinois, and three years later moved it to New York, where until its destruction by fire (1939) it was famous for expressing the character of the text in its design and printing of books. Goudy designed some 100 new type faces. His writings include *The Alphabet* (1918), *Elements of Lettering* (1921), *The Capitals from the Trajan Column at Rome* (1936), *Typologia* (1940), and a new edition of *The Alphabet, and Elements of Lettering* (1942).

GOUGH, JOHN BARTHOLOMEW (1817–86), English-born bookbinder in New York, was rescued from alcoholism by a temperance pledge and, beginning in 1842, devoted himself entirely to lecturing in the cause of temperance. He wrote an *Autobiography* (1845, revised 1869) and *Platform Echoes* (1885). Honoré Morrow's *Tiger! Tiger!* (1930) is a fictional biography of Gough.

GOULD, EDWARD SHERMAN (1805–85), New York author of a novel, a comedy, sketches, and a good deal of hackwork. His lectures, *American Criticism of American Literature* (1836), decried native letters and praised the British.

GOYEN, [CHARLES] WILLIAM (1915–83), Texas-born author, educated at Rice, after service in the navy taught writing at the University of Houston and elsewhere. His works include *The House of Breath* (1950), a lyric novel about a boy's life in a Texas town; *In a Farther Country* (1955), a fanciful romance about a Spanish-American woman who in her mean New York room receives real and fancied visitors whose troubled lives she purges of conflict; *Ghost and Flesh* (1952), stories with a Texas setting; *The Faces of Blood Kindred* (1960), a novella and stories; *The Fair Sister* (1963), expanding an earlier story about a black woman evangelist and the world of store-front churches; *Come the Restorer* (1974), a comic fantasy partly set in Texas. *A Book of Jesus* (1973) is a nonfictional work; and *Arcadio* (1984), the tale of a hermaphrodite who is a wandering outcast. He also wrote plays: *The House of Breath* (1956), *The Diamond Rattler* (1960), *Christy* (1964), and *The House of Breath Black/White* (1971). *Had I a Hundred Mouths* (1985) collects early and late stories.

GRADY, HENRY WOODFIN (1850–89), Georgia journalist and orator who, as editor of the *Atlanta Constitution* (1879–89) and as a speaker was an important influence in the rebuilding of the South by pointing the way to economic and racial readjustments. His famous oration "The New South" was delivered before the New England Club in New York City, in December 1886, and published in *The New South and Other Addresses* (1904) and in his *Complete Orations and Speeches* (1910).

Graham's Magazine (1826–58), monthly literary journal founded at Philadelphia as *Atkinson's Casket,* was an unimpressive miscellany until 1839, when it was purchased by George Rex Graham (1813–94). After he merged it with *Burton's Gentleman's Magazine*♦ (1840), it became one of the best periodicals in the country. Poe was literary editor of *Graham's Magazine* (1841–42), and increased its circulation from 5000 to 37,000. Among his contributions were such acute criticism as his review of the *Twice-Told Tales;* stories including "The Murders in the Rue Morgue," "A Descent into the Maelström," and "The Masque of the Red Death"; and poems including "To Helen." R.W. Griswold supplanted Poe (1842–43), and later editors included Bayard Taylor and C.G. Leland. The success of the magazine demonstrated the feasibility of paying liberally for contributions, so that it had such contributors as Lowell, N.P. Willis, Bryant, Cooper, Longfellow, C.F. Hoffman, Paulding, and Simms. It was also noted for its colored fashion plates and the engravings of John Sartain.

Grandfather's Chair, stories for children by Hawthorne.♦

Grandissimes, *The: A Story of Creole Life,* novel by G.W. Cable,♦ published in 1880.

During the early 19th century there is a feud between the Grandissimes and the De Grapions, aristocratic Louisiana families. One of its results has been the death in a duel of Nancanou De Grapion, and his beautiful widow, Aurora, is the last of the family to survive. She lives with her daughter Clotilde in impoverished seclusion in New Orleans. Joseph Frowenfeld, a young apothecary, through his friend old Dr. Keene and his whimsical Creole clerk Raoul Innerarity, becomes acquainted with both Honoré Grandissime, banker and head of his family, and the De Grapions, who nurse him during an illness. The apothecary falls in love with Clotilde, and Honoré loves Aurora, but various intrigues and their social positions keep them apart. Finally, haughty old Agricola Fusilier, who killed Nancanou, antagonizes Honoré's quadroon half-brother, who stabs him. At the old man's deathbed, Honoré's sister effects a reconciliation of the families, and the two couples are enabled to marry.

Grangerford family, characters in *Huckleberry Finn.*♦

GRANT, ANNE MCVICKAR (1755–1838), Scottish author, as a young girl lived for some years near Albany, N.Y., where her father, a captain in the British army, was stationed. Of her life at this time she left a record in the anonymous *Memoirs of an American Lady* (1808), an interesting source of information on contemporary manners.

GRANT, ROBERT (1852–1940), Boston jurist and author, graduated from Harvard (1873), and won his first literary success with *An Average Man* (1883), a study of two young New York lawyers, one of whom is willing to pursue a simple, honest career, while the other attempts by every means to gain money and fame. His other novels include *Face to Face* (1886), contrasting American and English standards; *Unleavened Bread*♦ (1900), about a woman whose desire for prestige and dominance outweighs all moral considerations; *The Undercurrent* (1904) and *The Orchid* (1905), studies of divorce in wealthy society; *The Chippendales* (1909), about a conservative Boston family, and the thinning out of its original fine qualities; *The High Priestess* (1915), dealing with a woman's attempt to have a career; *The Bishop's Granddaughter* (1925), satirizing American divorce laws; and *The Dark Horse* (1931), concerned with Boston politics and society. In addition to a volume of poetry and several collections of essays, Grant wrote an autobiography, *Fourscore* (1934). His public and judicial activities included service with President Lowell of Harvard and President Stratton of MIT on a committee to review evidence used to convict Sacco and Vanzetti, ♦ finding the trial and conviction to be fair.

GRANT, ULYSSES S[IMPSON] (1822–85), 18th President of the U.S. (1869–77), was reared on an Ohio farm, attended West Point, served in the Mexican War, and then retired to enter business. Early in the Civil War he was made a major general, following a successful campaign in western Kentucky. In July 1863, by a joint land and river campaign, he captured Vicksburg and Port Hudson, splitting the Confederacy in two, and after his successful Tennessee campaigns Lincoln made him commander in chief of the Union forces. Grant himself led the Army of the Potomac against Lee in the Wilderness campaign, the siege of Petersburg, and the subsequent strategy that led to Lee's surrender at Appomattox. His personal popularity, and his stand with the radical Republicans against President Johnson, caused his presidential nomination, and after his election he authorized punitive Reconstruction policies in the South, keeping alive sectional hatred. His cabinet appointments were misguided, and he was duped by disreputable financiers and politicians, so that serious scandals involved some of the highest in his administration. Nevertheless he was reelected. Upon retirement, Grant invested his funds in a private banking house in which his son Buck was a partner. The other partner, Ferdinand Ward, absconded with the firm's assets in 1884, causing Grant to seek financial recovery by writing his *Personal Memoirs* (2 vols., 1885–86), cited by Edmund Wilson ♦ as the best autobiography written by an American and without question ranking high among the world's historical military accounts—direct in style and unassuming in manner. Biographies of Grant include those by Hamlin Garland and W.E. Woodward. Matthew Arnold wrote a critical appraisal in his *Civilization in the United States* ♦; studies of his military career include works by Bruce Catton.

Grapes of Wrath, *The,* novel by Steinbeck, ♦ published in 1939 and awarded a Pulitzer Prize. The narrative chapters alternate with panoramic essays that show the social significance of the migrant labor problem.

The Joads, expropriated Oklahoma farmers from the Dust Bowl region, set out in a dilapidated automobile for California, which they believe is a land of plenty. The family includes Grampa, a lusty old man who was never "house broke"; Granma, weary and fanatically religious; lonely Uncle John; Pa, who has tacitly surrendered the rule of the family to his wife; Ma, brave, strong, and patient, who dreams and plans for the others; dull-witted Noah; Tom, just released from a jail term for killing a man in a fight; Al, a cocky youth who admires Tom's calm strength; Rose of Sharon, absorbed in love for her weak husband Connie and her unborn child;

and the children, Ruthie and Winfield. The caravan also includes Casy, an ex-preacher and rustic socialist. During the hard journey, Grampa and Granma die and Noah deserts, but the Joads drive on ("It don't take no nerve to do somepin when there ain't nothin' else you can do."). In California they are hounded by sheriffs and labor contractors, Casy is jailed, and Connie runs away. Haunted by starvation, they spend some time in a government camp, but leave reluctantly to pick fruit at a blacklisted orchard. Tom meets Casy, who is leading the strikers, and during an attack by vigilantes Casy is killed, and Tom in turn kills his murderer. The Joads escape, and, while hiding Tom, work at picking cotton. Exhausted and fearful, Ma finally sends Tom away, and he plans to continue Casy's work as a labor organizer. During a storm, Rose of Sharon gives birth to a stillborn child. Jobless, the Joads face starvation, but Ma cries, "We ain' gonna die out. People is goin' on—changin' a little, maybe, but goin' right on."

Grass Harp, *The,* novel by Truman Capote. ♦

GRATTAN, THOMAS COLLEY (1792–1864), British consul at Boston (1839–46), whose book, *Civilized America* (2 vols., 1859), which he calls "a record of events, a gallery of portraits, and a miscellany of opinions," is an important contemporary record combining contempt for U.S. social standards with praise for the country's independence, order, and energy.

GRAU, SHIRLEY ANN (1929–), New Orleans novelist whose works include *The Hard Blue Sky* (1958), presenting the life of an isolated Louisiana island community; *The House on Coliseum Street* (1961), set in her native city and treating the sad, loveless experience of a young girl there; *The Keepers of the House* (1964, Pulitzer Prize), portraying personal and political problems of a Southern family with a background of miscegenation; *The Condor Passes* (1971), chronicling three generations of a Louisiana family and its corrupt patriarch; and *Evidence of Love* (1974), about the tortured relations between father, son, and daughter-in-law. *The Black Prince* (1955), *The Wind Shifting West* (1973), and *Nine Women* (1986) collect stories.

Graustark, romance by G.B. McCutcheon. ♦

Gravity's Rainbow, novel by Thomas Pynchon, ♦ published in 1973.

Lieutenant Tyrone Slothrop, toward the end of World War II, is stationed in London as part of the intelligence unit ACHTUNG (Allied Clearing House, Technical Units) to monitor V-2 rocket attacks. He is also under surveillance by the PISCES (Psychological Intelligence Schemes for Expediting Surrender) section of the Firm, a mysterious shadow government within the military, since Teddy Bloat and Pirate Prentice of the Firm have discovered that the sites of Slothrop's numerous romantic liaisons in London correspond exactly to the locations subsequently hit by rockets. Ned Pointsman of PISCES is convinced that the relationship is associated with the experiments with Imipolex G that were inflicted upon Slothrop as a child by a German scientist, Laszlo Jamf, once at Harvard, now a developer of the V-2. Slothrop himself, always victimized by others, quests for the meaning of such matters, naïvely believing there is a way to understand events, past and present. Therefore he determines to learn about Jamf, and while engaged in an ever-shifting but phantasmagorically related search Slothrop is caught up in great power struggles that, among other affairs, involve a mysterious Captain Blicero (the Nazi officer Weissman) and some Herero tribesmen from Africa who have been trained as German rocket technicians. Slothrop also encounters Major Marvey of U.S. Army Ordnance, a black marketeer named Schnorp, some hashish runners, the director of a pornographic horror film, and diverse other strange men and women. They all appear to be involved somehow in a great conspiratorial cartel. As Oberst Enzian, a leader of the Herero command, says, the "War was never political at all, the politics was all theatre, all just to keep the people distracted . . . secretly, it was being dictated instead by the needs of technology." The rocket takes on metaphoric and mythic significance, answering "to a number of different shapes in the dreams of those who touch it—in combat, in tunnel, on paper" for "each Rocket will know its intended and hunt him . . . shining and pointed in the sky at his back . . . rushing in, rushing closer . . ." like a rainbow arched downward, as if by a force of gravity that is dragging mankind to death.

GRAY, ASA (1810–88), Harvard professor and leading botanist of his time in the U.S., and also famous as the foremost American advocate and supporter of Darwin, in such books as *Darwiniana* (1876).

GRAY, ROBERT (*fl.* 1609), author of *Good Speed to Virginia* (1609), a tract in the form of a sermon, published in London to promote colonization in Virginia. This was the third printed work relating to the colony, and its chief argument for immigration was that of the overpopulation of Great Britain.

GRAYDON, ALEXANDER (1752–1818), captain of a volunteer battalion during the Revolutionary War, wrote a volume of *Memoirs* (1811), valuable as a historical source.

GRAYSON, DAVID, pseudonym of R.S. Baker.♦

GRAYSON, WILLIAM J[OHN] (1788–1863), South Carolina author, lawyer, and politician,

represented his state in Congress (1833–37). An ardent champion of slavery, he is remembered for his long didactic poem *The Hireling and the Slave* (1854), contrasting the idyllic life of a black slave with the harsh existence of a Northern wage-slave. He also wrote *Letter to Governor Seabrook* (1850), against secession; *Letters of Curtius* (1851), defending slavery as a social scheme in which "labor and capital are associated on a large scale and their interests combined"; and *The Country* (1858), a neoclassical poem praising rural life. A later edition of *The Hireling and the Slave* (1856) includes "Chicora," a romantic verse treatment of an Indian legend.

Graysons, *The,* novel by Eggleston. ♦

Great Awakening, THE, series of religious revivals, which began (*c.*1734) with the evangelicalism of Jonathan Edwards. ♦ Revivalism was soon spread by such leaders as Theodore Frelinghuysen of the New Jersey Dutch Reformed Church; Gilbert Tennent, a New Jersey Presbyterian; and such lesser men as Benjamin Colman, Joseph Bellamy, George Whitefield, and James Davenport. Although the movement centered in New England, it extended throughout the colonies (*c.*1740–50). After the emotional fervor had spent its force in New England, a controversy developed between the New Lights of western Massachusetts, who held to the theology of Edwards, and the Old Lights of Boston, who were led by Charles Chauncy, and developed a liberalism that culminated in Unitarianism. A similar division in the Presbyterian Church split into a New Side and an Old Side, the former led by William and Gilbert Tennent, being instrumental in the founding of Princeton University. The original frenzied revival occasioned renewed missionary work among the Indians, in which Eleazar Wheelock was active, and which led to the founding of Dartmouth College.

Great Divide, *The,* play by William Vaughn Moody. ♦

Great Emancipator, THE, sobriquet of Lincoln.♦

Great Gatsby, *The,* novel by F. Scott Fitzgerald, ♦ published in 1925. It was dramatized by Owen Davis (1926).

Nick Carraway, a young Midwesterner who sells bonds in New York, lives at West Egg, Long Island, which is separated from the city by an ashdump, whose distinctive feature is an oculist's faded billboard with a pair of great staring eyes behind yellow spectacles, symbolic of an obscenely futile world. Nick's neighbor is mysterious Jay Gatsby, whose mansion and fabulous entertainments are financed by bootlegging and other criminal activities. As a poor army lieutenant, Gatsby had fallen in love with Nick's beautiful cousin Daisy, who later married Tom Buchanan, an unintelligent, brutal man of wealth. Through Nick, he manages to meet Daisy again, impresses her by his extravagant devotion, and makes her his mistress. Her husband takes as his mistress Myrtle Wilson, sensual wife of a garageman. When her husband becomes jealous and imprisons her in her room, Myrtle escapes, runs out on the highway, and is accidentally hit by Daisy, who drives on. Gatsby tries to protect Daisy, and Tom, to whom she has become reconciled, brings his hatred of her lover to a climax by telling Myrtle's husband that it was Gatsby who killed her. Wilson shoots Gatsby and then himself. At the end Nick broods over the setting whose

> big shore places were closed now . . . until gradually I became aware of the old island here that flowered once for Dutch sailors' eyes—a fresh, green breast of the new world. . . . I thought of Gatsby's wonder when he first picked out the green light at the end of Daisy's dock. . . . his dream must have seemed so close that he could hardly fail to grasp it. He did not know that it was already behind him, somewhere back in that vast obscurity beyond the city, where the dark fields of the republic rolled on under the night.

Great God Brown, The, play by Eugene O'Neill,♦ produced and published in 1926. The concept of multiple personality is expressed in the changeable masks worn by the characters, removed only when they are alone or in the presence of sympathetic persons.

Great Meadow, The, novel by Elizabeth M. Roberts,♦ published in 1930.

Great Stone Face, The, allegorical tale by Hawthorne,♦ published in *The Snow-Image and Other Twice-Told Tales* (1851). "Old Stony Phiz" is said to represent Webster.

In a mountain valley dominated by a towering rock formation that resembles a noble, majestic face lives the boy Ernest, who learns from his mother the legend that some day a great man bearing the features of the Face will visit the community. He eagerly awaits the coming of this man, but, though he grows to old age and sees Mr. Gathergold the banker, Old Blood-and-Thunder the general, and Old Stony Phiz the statesman, all reputed to resemble the Face, his expectations are disappointed. He has meanwhile lived an honest, helpful life, communing with the spirit of the landmark, and has come to be honored and revered. A poet visits him, in whom again Ernest hopes to see the features of the image but fails. At an outdoor meeting where Ernest preaches, the poet sees that it is Ernest himself who resembles the Stone Face. The simple, venerable old man, unconscious of this, continues to await his hero.

Greek Revival, neoclassical movement in architecture and the arts, occurred in Europe and the U.S. during the late 18th and early 19th centuries, and was directly influenced by archaeological excavations in Greece, and at Pompeii and Herculaneum. Although Jefferson's design for the Virginia state capitol (1785) had the plan of a Roman temple, the revival was really Greek, and had as its most influential architects Latrobe, Mills, Strickland, and T.U. Walter. The Capitol and most other federal and state buildings were created under the influence of this style, which later shared supremacy (*c.*1850–60) with that of the Gothic Revival.

GREELEY, HORACE (1811–72), born in New Hampshire, worked at journalistic and printing jobs until he was 23, when he founded the *New Yorker,* a critical weekly which he continued until 1841. He also edited Whig campaign papers, and, encouraged by Seward and Thurlow Weed, founded the *New-York Tribune,*♦ which he edited for 30 years. His chief assistant (1849–62) was Charles A. Dana.♦ The great influence of the paper was due to Greeley's trenchant editorials, which attacked monopolies and advocated labor organization, a protective tariff, temperance, and a homestead law, supporting the latter with the famous phrase "Go West, Young Man!"♦ He also championed Fourierism, helped found the North American Phalanx, and opposed all aids to slavery, particularly the Mexican War, the Compromise of 1850, and the Kansas-Nebraska Bill. He exerted his influence in behalf of Lincoln's election, and after the Civil War favored giving blacks the right to vote. In 1872 he was the presidential candidate of the Liberal Republican and Democratic parties, but was defeated. This disappointment and the death of his wife caused him to become insane, and he soon died. His books include *The American Conflict* (2 vols., 1864–66), a history of Abolitionism and the Civil War, and *Recollections of a Busy Life* (1868), and he himself appears not only in histories but occasionally in fiction too, e.g. Irving Bacheller's *Eben Holden.*

GREEN, ANNA KATHARINE (1846–1935), author of *The Leavenworth Case* (1878), which, though not the first detective story or the greatest, established the formula and the popularity of this new literary form in the U.S. She wrote many other detective novels.

GREEN, ANNE (1899–   ), Georgia-born author, like her brother Julien (originally Julian) Green has lived most of her life in France, which is the background of her novels. These include *The Selbys* (1930), *Reader, I Married Him* (1931), *Marietta* (1932), *Fools Rush In* (1934), *That Fellow Perceval* (1935), *16 Rue Cortambert* (1937), and *Just Before Dawn* (1943), mostly light, satirical stories of expatriates from the Southern states. *A Marriage of Convenience* (1933) is a humorous treatment of changing French standards; *Paris* (1938) is a character study of a French business woman;

The Silent Duchess (1939) is set in 18th-century France; *The Delamer Curse* (1940) tells of the exorcising of a curse laid on a Franco-American family; *The Lady in the Mask* (1942) is a historical novel of Renaissance Milan; and *The Old Lady* (1947) brings a French woman to the U.S. She has also published fiction in French, e.g. *Le Goret* (1954), stories, and *La Porte des Songes* (1969), a novel, that has not been translated or issued in the U.S. *With Much Love* (1948) recalls her childhood in France.

GREEN, Julien [ORIGINALLY Julian] (1900–   ), brother of Anne Green, ♦ was born in Paris of American parents and has lived most of his life in France. His first book, *Le Voyageur sur la terre* (1927), a novelette translated as *The Pilgrim on the Earth* (1929), concerns an American college student who dies after being driven insane by hallucinations. Later novels, also written in French, are equally somber psychological studies of individuals, superficially commonplace but actually the prey of deep tortured passions. These include *Mont-Cinère* (1926), translated as *Avarice House* (1927); *Adrienne Mésurat* (1927), translated as *The Closed Garden* (1928); *Léviathan* (1929), translated as *The Dark Journey* (1929); and, in a recent listing from a prolific career as novelist, *Moira* (1951); and some untranslated texts, including *L'Autre* (1983), about a woman's romantic experiences, and *Les Pays lointains* (1987). *Personal Record* (1939) is his journal (1928–39), and other works in English translation include the fiction *Christine and Other Stories* (1930), *The Strange River* (1932), *The Dreamer* (1934), *Midnight* (1936), *Then Shall the Dust Return* (1941), *If I Were You* (1949), *The Transgressor* (1957), about a girl's unhappy love for a homosexual, and *Each in His Darkness* (1961). *Memories of Happy Days* (1942) and *To Leave Before Dawn* (1967) are memoirs and, like his *Diary 1928–1957* (1964), were translated by his sister. Still further autobiographical texts are in *Terre lointaine* (1966); *Memories of Evil Days* (1976); *Ce qu'il faut d'amour a l'homme* (1978), about his conversion to Catholicism; *Paris* (1983); and *Villes* (1985), concerning various travels. He has also written many journals published in French. *God's Fool* (1985) is an appreciative study of St. Francis of Assisi.

GREEN, Paul [Eliot] (1894–1981), North Carolina playwright, professor at the state university, began his career with the Carolina Playmakers ♦ and was the author of many one-act plays about blacks. Collections have been issued as *The Lord's Will and Other Carolina Plays* (1925), *Lonesome Road* (1926), and *In the Valley* (1928). Perhaps the best known of his one-act plays is *Hymn to the Rising Sun* (1936), an indictment of prison-camp conditions. *In Abraham's Bosom* ♦ (1927, Pulitzer Prize) is a long play about the lives of blacks, based on his earlier play (1924) of this title and *Your Fiery Furnace* (1932). Other full-length

plays include *The Field God* (1927), about repressed, deeply religious poor whites; *Tread the Green Grass* (1929), a folk play; *Roll, Sweet Chariot* (1934), presenting the tragic spirit and philosophy of black people; *The House of Connelly* (1931), concerned with the decadence of Southern planters; *Johnny Johnson* (1937), a musical play written with Kurt Weill; *The Lost Colony* (1937), produced annually on Roanoke Island, a historical pageant of the early settlement there; *Native Son* (1941), a stage adaptation with Richard Wright of the latter's novel; and *The Highland Call* (1941), a historical play of life in the Carolinas using folk music; and other so-called symphonic dramas, including *The Common Glory* (1947), *Faith of Our Fathers* (1950), *The Confederacy* (1958), and *The Stephen Foster Story* (1959). *Out of the South* (1939) is a collection of 15 previously published plays; *Wide Fields* (1928), *Salvation on a String* (1946), *Home to My Valley* (1969), and *Land of Nod* (1976) collect stories. *This Body the Earth* (1935) is a novel about the tragic lives of sharecroppers. *The Hawthorn Tree* (1943), *Drama and the Weather* (1958), and *Plough and Furrow* (1963) gather essays.

Green Bay Tree, *The,* novel by Bromfield, ♦ published in 1924 and dramatized (1927) as *The House of Women.*

Green Grow the Lilacs, folk comedy by Lynn Riggs, ♦ produced and published in 1931. It is intended "to recapture in a kind of nostalgic glow . . . the great range of mood which characterized the old folk songs and ballads." An adaptation, *Oklahoma!* (1943), by Richard Rodgers and Oscar Hammerstein II, is a musical play that won an outstanding success and was awarded a special Pulitzer Prize.

The scene is a farm community in Indian Territory (Oklahoma) in 1900, and among the characters are Aunt Eller Murphy; her orphaned niece Laurey Williams: Jeeter Fry, their hired man, whose passion and vindictiveness Laurey fears; and the handsome cowboy, Curly McClain, who loves Laurey. All of them attend a "play-party" at the home of Old Man Peck, and there Curly and Laurey announce their engagement, arousing the rage of Jeeter, who vows revenge. On their wedding night they are victims of a traditional "shivaree," during which Jeeter attacks Curly and is accidentally killed. Curly is arrested, but, on the eve of the court hearing that is expected to exonerate him, breaks jail to visit his bride. When a posse arrives to recapture him, Aunt Eller persuades the friendly deputies to allow Curly to spend the night with Laurey.

Green Mountain Boys, irregular militia led by Ethan Allen, ♦ originally organized to defend the New Hampshire Grants of Vermont against the interference of New York land-jobbers. Later the Vermonters were prominent in the Revolution as captors of Fort Ticonderoga. D.P. Thompson's romance and works by Rowland Robinson celebrate their deeds. Vermont is popularly called the Green Mountain state.

Green Mountain Boys, The, romance by D.P. Thompson,♦ published in 1839.

Colonel Reed buys a Vermont tract from a group of New York land-jobbers, evicts the settlers who have occupied it under the New Hampshire Grants, establishes a log fort, and returns to Canada. To defend the rights of the former settlers, Captain Warrington and his band of local patriots capture the fort and its occupants, who include Reed's daughter Jessie. Selden, Warrington's friend, who takes Jessie to a friend's home, falls in love with her. Meanwhile Warrington goes to his estate on Lake Champlain, opposite Crown Point, and finds his old friends, Captain Hendee and his daughter Alma, who are ignorant of his ownership, having purchased the land from the New Yorkers. Darrow and Sherwood, New York agents, capture Warrington, but when Ethan Allen, disguised as "Smith," comes with news of the Battle of Lexington, he and Warrington escape, planning to organize the Green Mountain Boys♦ to fight the British. Sherwood, now a Loyalist spy, attempts to malign Warrington's character, in order to further his own suit with Alma, but is unsuccessful. Allen, after Warrington reconciles his differences with Benedict Arnold, leads the Green Mountain Boys in capturing Crown Point and Hubbardton. Darrow, fatally wounded, confesses his duplicity and Sherwood's and reveals that Selden is Hendee's long-lost son. Selden and Jessie are married, as are Warrington and Alma.

Green Pastures, The, play by Marc Connelly,♦ produced and published in 1930, and awarded a Pulitzer Prize, is based on Roark Bradford's *Ol' Man Adam an' His Chillun* (1928).

Mr. Deshee, a black preacher in Louisiana, gives a Bible lesson to his country Sunday school class, and the action of the play dramatizes his narratives, presenting black people's anthropomorphic conception of God and Heaven, and representing Old Testament history in terms of Southern black life.

GREENBERG, SAMUEL BERNARD (1893–1917), born in Vienna, brought to New York's Lower East Side (1900), reared in poverty and sickness, during his years in hospitals wrote lyric poems whose manuscripts were shown by a mutual friend to Hart Crane in 1923. Crane was greatly influenced by the poetry, which also had its impact upon other writers when a selection of 22 lyrics was published in 1939. A larger selection, *Poems,* appeared in 1947 with a brief, personal, and touching prose "Autobiography."

GREENE, ASA (1789–*c.*1837), Massachusetts physician and journalist, wrote several sportive

novels with a humor varying from the genial to the burlesque. *Travels in America by George Fibbleton* (1833) is a reply to Mrs. Trollope's *Domestic Manners of the Americans* (1832) and a satire on the *Observations . . . in the United States* (1833) of the Rev. Isaac Fiddler. *The Life and Adventures of Dr. Dodimus Duckworth* (1833) is mock-heroic biography of a New Englander; *The Perils of Pearl Street* (1834) presents a humorous story against a realistic background of New York business and high finance; and *A Yankee Among the Nullifiers* (1833) is a fictional autobiography with a truthful depiction of what the author saw during a visit to South Carolina.

GREENE, SARAH PRATT, see *McLean, Sarah.*

Greenfield Hill, discursive poem by Timothy Dwight,♦ published in 1794. Mainly in heroic couplets, although there are some Spenserian stanzas, octosyllabics, and blank-verse passages, the work is obviously modeled on Denham's *Cooper's Hill,* and also consciously imitates Goldsmith, Thomson, Beattie, Gay, and Pope. It was intended to answer European critics who asserted that America afforded no poetic settings.

Subjects of the poem's seven parts include "Prospect of the Country between Greenfield Hill and the Sound" and a contrast of its people with those of other nations; a description of the flourishing village and the felicity of its inhabitants; such historical events as the successful war against the Pequots and the burning of Fairfield; the moral advice of a clergyman and a wise farmer; and finally a "Vision, or Prospect of the Future Happiness of America."

GREENOUGH, HORATIO (1805–52), Boston-born sculptor, set the vogue for study in Italy. In his life there (1828–51) he was influenced toward classical forms and sentimental attitudes. His huge, half-nude statue of Washington as an Olympian god was the first monumental marble by an American. It was too heavy for its place under the Capitol dome, and it was scorned by the public. His reputation as a sculptor is now slight but he is praised for his functional concept of art, set forth in *Aesthetics in Washington* (1851) and other writings.

Greenwich Village, district of New York City, situated in lower Manhattan, during the colonial period was a separate village and later became an exclusive residential district. Paine wrote *The Crisis* in Greenwich Village, and Poe later lived there, but it was not until the end of the 19th century that it became famous for its bohemianism as an artistic and literary colony. Among those who lived in the Village, and among those who contributed to its long succession of little magazines, including *The Little Review, The Masses, The Seven Arts,* the *Bohemian,* the *Pagan,* the *Quill,* and the *Playboy,* were E.E. Cummings,

Floyd Dell, Mabel Dodge, Max Eastman, Donald Evans, Emma Goldman, Edna St. Vincent Millay, Eugene O'Neill, and Carl Van Vechten. The Greenwich Village Theatre was an outgrowth of the Provincetown Players.♦ Authors and artists have continued among the area's residents, including Edward Albee and Gregory Corso, and among its recent playhouses has been the Caffe Cino, where plays of Lanford Wilson♦ were produced. The Village has a lively nightlife, including jazz clubs, and is a great tourist attraction. Students from nearby New York University and other young people live there, but in large part Village residents are now professional people and business executives with some successful writers and artists.

GREENWOOD, GRACE, pseudonym of Sara Jane Lippincott.♦

GREGG, JOSIAH (1806–50), trader of the Santa Fe Trail, was the author of the *Commerce of the Prairies* (2 vols., 1844), an important contemporary account of frontier history. His *Diary and Letters* was published in two volumes (1941, 1944).

GREGORY, HORACE [VICTOR] (1898–1982), born in Milwaukee and educated at the University of Wisconsin, began his poetic career with *Chelsea Rooming House* (1930), which illustrates the reaction of a romantic nature swept from the surroundings of home and the academic world into the tough, vital life of Manhattan. Later collections of poetry include *No Retreat* (1933) and *Chorus for Survival* (1935), exhibiting his belief that life is bitter and destructive but must be challenged by the will to survive, and *Medusa in Gramercy Park* (1961). His *Collected Poems* (1964) was followed by a final volume of poetry, *Another Look* (1976). Other works include translations of Catullus (1931) and Ovid (1964); *Pilgrim of the Apocalypse* (1933), a critical study of D.H. Lawrence; *The Shield of Achilles* (1944), essays on poetry and art; a portrait of *Amy Lowell* (1958); *The World of James McNeill Whistler* (1959); and *Dorothy Richardson* (1967). *The Dying Gladiators* (1961) collects essays. *The House on Jefferson Street* (1971) is a memoir. With his wife Marya Zaturenska he wrote a *History of American Poetry, 1900–1940* (1946). He taught at Sarah Lawrence College (1934–60) and received the Bollingen Prize (1964).

GREY, ZANE (1872–1939), writer of Western novels, the 20th-century heir of the dime novel, whose more than 60 books sold over 13,000,000 copies during his life. His stories, chiefly dealing with cowboy life, are melodramatic and lack characterization, presenting life as a struggle between ruthless villains and self-reliant, brawny heroes who are loyal to their friends and the fictional ethics of the frontier and chivalrous toward

their naïve heroines. Grey's most popular novel was *Riders of the Purple Sage* (1912), but all his fiction was widely read and many of his works have been adapted for motion pictures. His many books on deep-sea and fresh-water game fishing describe his own experiences.

Grey Champion, The, historical sketch by Hawthorne,♦ published in *Twice-Told Tales* (1837). It is concerned with the appearance of the regicide Goffe♦ in Boston, at a time when rebellion threatened the colony. In his intimidation of Andros, Goffe is presented as "the grey champion" of the spirit of independence and colonial rights.

Greyslaer, romance by C.F. Hoffman,♦ published in 1840 and anonymously dramatized the same year. Its sources include the life of Brant♦ and the Kentucky Tragedy.♦

In the Mohawk Valley at the outbreak of the Revolution, Max Greyslaer, a young lawyer, is jailed for patriot agitation. Aided by Whig friends, he escapes to the home of his guardian, Mr. de Roos, which is then attacked by Joseph Brant and his Loyalist Mohawks. De Roos and his daughter Tyntie are killed, while another daughter, Alida, is captured with Greyslaer, who loves her. She reveals that she was forced into a secret marriage, years before, with the ruffian Bradshawe. Even when the marriage is discovered to have been illegal, and she and Greyslaer make their escape, she refuses to marry him until her reputation is cleared. He serves in the patriot army, in which Alida's brother Derrick is killed, leaving in her care a half-breed child who is then rumored to be her son. Heartbroken over this scandal, she breaks off with Greyslaer, who goes to Albany to seek vengeance on Bradshawe, the cause of their troubles. They fight, and Bradshawe, who disappears, is thought to have been killed. Greyslaer is tried for murder, and only saved by the evidence of the hunter Balt, who testifies that he himself killed Bradshawe. When a document is discovered proving the boy to be Derrick's son, Alida and Greyslaer are married.

GRIERSON, FRANCIS, pseudonym of Benjamin Henry Jesse Francis Shepard (1848–1927), who was brought from England as an infant and raised in a log cabin in Illinois and elsewhere in the Midwest. Self-educated as a musician, he made his way to Paris (1869) to become a sensational success as a singer and pianist, later touring Europe and the U.S. Given a house in San Diego by admirers, he lived there (1886–88) but returned to Europe to begin a literary career under a pseudonym. His books include *La Révolte idéaliste* (1889), oracular and sententious essays, in part translated as *Modern Mysticism* (1899); *The Celtic Temperament* (1901), displaying apocalyptic theories; *The Valley of Shadows: Recollections of the Lincoln Country, 1858–63* (1909), a clear and sensitive view of Midwest pioneers, possessing also a mystic sense of impending great events; *Parisian Portraits* (1910); *La Vie et les hommes* (1911), aphorisms; *The Humour of the Underman* (1911) and *Abraham Lincoln, The Practical Mystic* (1918), both complementing his major book on Lincoln's land; *Illusions and Realities of the War* (1918); and *Psycho-Phone Messages* (1921), spirit utterances of great Americans written during Grierson's last, poverty-stricken days in Los Angeles.

GRIFFITH, D[AVID LEWELYN] W[ARK] (1875–1948), motion-picture producer and director, who as a pioneer in the medium introduced such devices as the close-up and fade-out. His picture *The Birth of a Nation*♦ (1915), based on Thomas Dixon's *The Clansman,* was the first large screen spectacle in the genre. His other productions include *Intolerance* (1916), *Hearts of the World* (1918), *Broken Blossoms* (1919), and *Orphans of the Storm* (1921).

Griffiths, CLYDE, character in *An American Tragedy.*♦

GRIMKÉ, SARAH MOORE (1792–1873) and ANGELINA EMILY (1805–79), daughters of a wealthy South Carolina planter, converted to the Quaker faith and its opposition to the slavery of blacks. Moving to Philadelphia in their twenties, they never returned to the South, but their writings for the American Anti-Slavery Society were addressed in part to readers in their ancestral region. These included *An Appeal to the Christian Women of the South* (1836) and *Appeal to the Women of the Nominally Free States* (1837) by Angelina and *Epistle to the Clergy of the Southern States* (1836) by Sarah. Their pamphleteering and public lecturing next led them into the field of women's rights, a cause for which Sarah wrote *Letters on the Equality of the Sexes and the Condition of Woman* (1838). Sarah married the antislavery orator Theodore Dwight Weld,♦ moving with him to New Jersey and then to Massachusetts. The two compiled *American Slavery as It Is: Testimony of a Thousand Witnesses* (1839), used by Harriet Beecher Stowe as a source for *Uncle Tom's Cabin.*

Grimm, PETER, see *Return of Peter Grimm.*

GRINNELL, GEORGE BIRD (1849–1938), naturalist and ethnologist, accompanied Custer to Dakota, visited Yellowstone Park (1875), was an explorer in Alaska (1899), and made many expeditions in the western U.S. He edited *Forest and Stream* (1876–1911), was prominent in the conservation movement, and wrote books which include *Pawnee Hero Stories* (1889), *The Story of the Indian* (1895), *The Fighting Cheyennes* (1915), and *The Cheyenne Indians* (2 vols., 1923).

GRISWOLD, RUFUS WILMOT (1815–57), born in Vermont, was a prominent Philadelphia and New York journalist, editing *Graham's Magazine*♦ (1842–43) and *The International Monthly Magazine* (1850–52). As the literary executor of Poe, he wrote a biography, which was partly malicious and partly false, and in his edition (1850) of the poet's works published some letters in which he made interpolations favorable to himself. His compilations, *The Poets and Poetry of America* (1842), *The Prose Writers of America* (1847), and *The Female Poets of America* (1849), although often faulty in critical judgment, remain valuable for the student. His other works include a social history, *The Republican Court, or American Society in the Days of Washington* (1855).

Grolier Club, New York City organization founded (1884) for the study and promotion "of the arts pertaining to the production of books." It has published many books and catalogues of its exhibitions, including *One Hundred Influential American Books Printed Before 1900* (1947).

Group, The, satirical play by Mercy Otis Warren,♦ published in 1775, the day before the Battle of Lexington. It deals with the king's abrogation of the Massachusetts charter and his appointment of a Tory upper house.

Lord Chief Justice Hazelrod (Peter Oliver), Judge Meagre (Foster Hutchinson, brother of the governor), Brigadier Hateall (Timothy Ruggles), Sir Sparrow Spendall (William Pepperell), and Beau Trumps (Daniel Leonard) belong to the group that supports the royal prerogative and desires to take freedom away from the populace. They discuss their points of view at length, and the only real drama occurs when they import Sylla (General Gage) to put their ideas into action, although he is shown as torn between his duty as a soldier and his realization of the justice of the popular cause.

Group Theatre, New York organization, conducted (1931–41) by a group of insurgents from the Theatre Guild♦ under the leadership of Harold Clurman, Lee Strasberg, and Cheryl Crawford. Their first professional production, after a series of performances as a little theater, was Paul Green's *The House of Connelly* (1931), sponsored by the Theatre Guild and financed by O'Neill, Maxwell Anderson, and others. During its career, the group produced all the plays of Odets, formerly an actor with the company. Its many other productions included *Night Over Taos, Men in White, Bury the Dead,* and *The Gentle People.* Clurman described its history in *The Fervent Years* (1945).

GRUND, FRANCIS JOSEPH (1798–1863), emigrated to Boston from his native Austria about 1827 and began writing school texts before publishing *The Americans in Their Moral, Social and Political Relations* (1837), a work far more laudatory than his *Aristocracy in America* (2 vols., 1839), ostensibly by a German nobleman. As an American he wrote campaign biographies of several presidential candidates to appeal to German-speaking voters, and was rewarded by consular posts. He published and edited a Philadelphia journal, *Age* (1842–63).

Guard of Honor, novel by James Gould Cozzens,♦ published in 1948 and awarded a Pulitzer Prize.

Landing at his Florida air force base, the plane of Major General Ira N. ("Bus") Beal, a boyish hero of "simple-minded integrity," is almost hit by a B-26 piloted by black 2d Lieutenant Stanley Willis, who is angrily thrashed by Beal's friend and pilot, the brave but arrogant Lieutenant Colonel Benny Carricker. The same day, Al James, a black journalist writing an article about the base, discovers that it illegally practices segregation and that there is a mystery about Willis's hospitalization and the arrest of some black officers who had protested against discrimination. The problem is intensified when Lieutenant Edsell, a "sorehead," brings Willis's father to the base, expecting to stir up further inquiry into, and the abolition of, discrimination. Unable to control himself or the situation, General Beal escapes on a solo flight, and matters have to be handled by Colonel Norman Ross, the judicious older man on whom he is usually dependent, and General "Jo-Jo" Nichols, a candid, mature officer who has learned to live without illusions. The original problems are just being settled when new ones occur upon Beal's return, for, at maneuvers honoring his forty-first birthday, seven parachutists miss their target and drown in a lake. The dreadful weekend is further saddened by the suicide of Bus's friend, Colonel Woodman, when he is passed over for advancement, but it finally ends with Beal back in command and Ross reflecting that since good and bad are inextricably bound together in the human condition, one can expect no more than that "a man must stand up and do the best he can with what there is."

Guardian Angel, The, novel by Holmes,♦ published in 1868.

Myrtle Hazard, an orphan, is reared by her spinster aunt, Miss Silence Withers, whose brother Malachi leaves Myrtle a fortune, contingent upon a certain lawsuit. When the girl is 15 she rebels against her tyrannous aunt and runs away disguised as a boy. Endangered in her boat by a precipitous waterfall, she is rescued by Clement Lindsay, a talented young artist, and brought home by Master Byles Gridley, her "guardian angel." The shock leaves her in a nervous condition, which is taken advantage of by Miss Silence and others who try to convert Myrtle to Calvinism. Later she becomes conscious of her fascinating beauty, when she is courted by the poetaster Gifted Hopkins, the ambitious lawyer Murray Bradshaw, and Clement, who is, however, engaged to Susan Posey. She refuses a proposal from Bradshaw, who enlists in the Civil War and is killed. Susan falls in love with Gifted Hopkins and breaks her engagement to Clement. Through Gridley's aid, Myrtle receives her inheritance and marries Clement, who has become a colonel in the war.

GUARE, JOHN (1938–), playwright. A graduate of the Yale Drama School, Guare has written two plays that gained him national recognition, both produced in Off-Broadway theaters. These are *The House of Blue Leaves,* about a piano player who longs for the return to sanity of his wife "Bananas" (best play 1971, New York Drama Critics Circle), and *Six Degrees of Separation* (1990), about a young black man who cons his way into a wealthy white couple's graces by claiming to be the son of the film actor Sidney Poitier. Both plays are set in Guare's native New York City, as are several other of his works.

GUESS, GEORGE, see *Sequoyah.*

GUEST, EDGAR A[LBERT] (1881–1959), English-born newspaper poet, whose daily poem in the *Detroit Free Press* was widely syndicated and extremely popular with the people he called "folks" for its homely, saccharine morality. His verse has been collected in such books as *A Heap o' Livin'* (1916), *Just Folks* (1917), and *Life's Highway* (1933).

Guggenheim Fellowships, given annually for creative work in the arts, or research in any branch of knowledge, by the John Simon Guggenheim Memorial Foundation, founded in 1925 by Senator and Mrs. Simon Guggenheim. In the 1980s the number of annual awards ranged from 292 in 1983 to 198 in 1989. They allow winners funds for travel and research to carry on scholarly and creative projects.

GUINEY, LOUISE IMOGEN (1861–1920), born in Boston, began writing poetry and essays as a young woman. Throughout her later years, partly spent in England, she showed a steadfast admiration for Tennyson, Hazlitt, and the Cavalier poets, and a deeply ingrained devotion to the Catholic tradition. Her poems were collected in *Songs at the Start* (1884), *A Roadside Harp* (1893), *England and Yesterday* (1898), *The Martyrs' Idyl* (1899), and *Happy Ending* (1909, enlarged 1927). *A Little English Gallery* (1894) contains literary portraits, and *Patrins* (1897, 1901) is a collection of familiar essays. Alice Brown, with whom she wrote a study of Stevenson (1895), wrote her biography (1921), and her *Letters* have been published (2 vols., 1926).

GUITERMAN, ARTHUR (1871–1943), New York poet and journalist, best known for his humorous verse and ballads dealing with American history and legends. His books include *The*

Laughing Muse (1915), *The Mirthful Lyre* (1918), *Chips of Jade* (1920), *The Light Guitar* (1923), *A Poet's Proverbs* (1924), *I Sing the Pioneer* (1926), *Wildwood Fables* (1927), *Song and Laughter* (1929), *Death and General Putnam* (1935), and *Brave Laughter* (1943). He also wrote librettos for both light and grand operas, including Damrosch's *The Man Without a Country* (1937).

Gullah, linguistically corrupt dialect of blacks of the South Carolina and Georgia coast, and northeast Florida. It employs an African intonation and many West African words. Examples may be found in the novels of Julia Peterkin.

Gunmaker of Moscow, The, popular novel by Sylvanus Cobb, Jr.♦

GUNTER, ARCHIBALD CLAVERING (1847–1907), English-born author, lived in California (1853–79), where he attended the state university and won his first success with the play *Found the True Vein* (1872), featuring local characters similar to those Bret Harte was beginning to popularize. After a career in the West as chemist and civil engineer, he went to New York to write his best-known work, *Mr. Barnes of New York* (1887), a novel which is said to have had a sale of more than a million copies. He also wrote a play, *Prince Karl* (1886), and 39 novels in all, including *Miss Nobody of Nowhere* (1890) and *A Princess of Paris* (1894).

GUNTHER, JOHN (1901–70), graduated from the University of Chicago and became a foreign correspondent widely known for lively socio-political surveys: *Inside Europe* (1936), *Inside Asia* (1939, revised 1942), *Inside Latin America* (1941), *Inside U.S.A.* (1947), *Inside Africa* (1955), *Inside Russia Today* (1957), and *Twelve Cities* (1969). *D Day* (1944) is a wartime diary; *Behind the Curtain* (1949) deals with Russian and Middle European politics; *Roosevelt in Retrospect* (1950) is about F.D.R. *Death Be Not Proud* (1949) is a memorial to his son, and he published *A Fragment of Autobiography* (1962), as well as several novels, including *The Lost City* (1964), about prewar Vienna.

GURNEY, A[LBERT] R[AMSDELL, JR.] (1930–   ), graduated from Williams College, after graduate study at Yale became a teacher of literature at MIT (1960–87) until he left to devote himself fully to his already distinguished career of writing for the theater. His canon includes at least 17 plays, beginning with *Golden Fleece* (1969). They are known for a limited number of characters, frequently set in his hometown of Buffalo's elegant upper-class society, with some sophisticated humor as in *The Dining Room* (1981) and *The Cocktail Hour* (1987), among his most popular works. In *Later Life* (1993), a sad comedy, a middle-aged banker is trapped in Bostonian aristocratic gentility and feels out of place in a demo-cratic society. This man, Austin, meets an old almost-lover, Ruth, at a cocktail party, and the play is about the reunion.

GUTHRIE, A[LFRED] B[ERTRAM], JR. (1901–91), born in Indiana, reared in Montana, from whose state university he graduated (1923), lived in Kentucky, where he was a journalist (1926–47) before he began writing fiction. His novels are *The Big Sky♦* (1947), about a mountain man from Kentucky, who traps beaver and lives with the Indians in the West during the 1830s and 1840s; *The Way West* (1949, Pulitzer Prize), about an overland caravan from Missouri to Oregon in 1846; *These Thousand Hills* (1956), set in Montana in the later 19th century; *Arfive* (1971), about a new high-school principal's struggles in the Montana town of Arfive around the turn of the century; *Wild Pitch* (1973), *The Genuine Article* (1977), and *No Second Wind* (1980), light mysteries set in a modern cattle town; *The Last Valley* (1975), presenting life in Arfive around the time of World War II; *Fair Land, Fair Land* (1982), a sequel to *The Big Sky,* carrying one of its characters to the age of 70 in a changed West; and *Playing Catch-Up* (1985), another detective story, set in a Montana town. *The Big It* (1960) collects stories. *The Blue Hen's Chick* (1965) is an autobiography. The screenplay of *Shane* by Jack Schaefer was written for filming in 1953.

GUTHRIE, WOODY [WOODROW WILSON] (1912–67), song writer and folksinger. As a young man during the Great Depression, Guthrie, born in Oklahoma, rode freight trains with other hard-up itinerant crop workers; using guitar and harmonica, he composed songs about the unraveling of the American dream ("Pastures of Plenty") as well as songs of celebration and of mourning ("The Good Reuben James," "Plane Wreck at Los Gatos"), union songs ("Union Maid"), songs of adversity ("So Long, It's Been Good to Know Ya," "Hard Travelin'"), even religion ("This Train Is Bound for Glory"), and his best-known, "This Land Is Your Land," which has from time to time been proposed as a new national anthem. Guthrie was paralyzed and speechless from the effects of Huntington's chorea when his songs peaked commercially in the 1960s. His autobiography is *Bound for Glory* (1943, revised edition, 1968). A collection of his poetry and prose pieces, *Born to Win,* was published in 1965.

Guy Rivers, first of the Border Romances by Simms,♦ published in 1834. It deals with the outlawry in northern Georgia during the gold rush of the 1820s.

Ralph Colleton, who loves his cousin Edith, is driven from their home by his uncle, because he is penniless. On the road, he is wounded by a highwayman but he is aided by the backwoodsman Mark Forrester and nursed by Lucy Munro, whose father Wat is a member of the outlaw band led by Guy Rivers, Ralph's assailant. Rivers is really Edward Creighton, a brilliant lawyer turned desperado because of his failure to win social and political advancement and because of his rejection by Edith. Ralph participates in a battle between the outlaws and the state militia, and further incurs the enmity of Rivers, who had originally been jealous of Edith's love for him. In an attempt to kill Ralph, Rivers and Munro mistakenly kill Forrester. They engineer Ralph's arrest for the crime, and nearly gain a conviction. Munro, at the behest of his daughter, confesses before dying as a result of a scrape with the sheriff. Ralph is cleared; Rivers, captured, commits suicide; and Edith, having obtained her father's consent, weds Ralph, taking the orphaned Lucy into their home.

H

H.D., pseudonym of Hilda Doolittle.♦

H.H., pseudonym of Helen Hunt Jackson.♦

HABBERTON, JOHN (1842–1921), New York journalist whose novel *Helen's Babies* (1876) won tremendous popularity for its humorous account of a bachelor uncle's supervision of two mischief-loving boys during their parents' vacation, and their successful encouragement of his love affair. Later less successful works included a novel, a play, and children's fiction.

HAGEDORN, HERMANN (1882–1964), New York author, known both for his works about his friend Theodore Roosevelt, including a *Life* (1918), *Roosevelt in the Bad Lands* (1921), a selection of his speeches, *The Americanism of Theodore Roosevelt* (1923), and *The Bugle That Woke America: The Saga of Theodore Roosevelt's Last Battle for His Country* (1940), and for his poetry, ranging from *Poems and Ballads* (1912) to *The Bomb That Fell on America* (1946), treating the implications of the Hiroshima bombing for Americans, and such novels as *The Rough Riders* (1927). Other works include a biography of Edwin Arlington Robinson (1938) and *The Hyphenated Family* (1960), a saga of his own family of German-Americans, appreciative of both cultures.

"Hail Columbia," patriotic song by Joseph Hopkinson,♦ to the tune originally written for "The President's March," attributed to Philip Phile (variously spelled) or Johannes Roth. It was introduced by the actor Gilbert Fox (1798) when war with France was thought inevitable, since it appealed for a unified national spirit. It was published in *Porcupine's Gazette* (April 20, 1798).

HAINES, JOHN MEAD (1924–), born in Norfolk, Va., and trained in art schools, homesteaded 90 miles east of Fairbanks, Alaska, for over 20 years. He is best known as a poet: *Winter News* (1966), *The Stone Harp* (1971), *Cicada* (1977), and *News from the Glacier: Selected Poems 1960–1980* (1982). His poems and his collections of essay/memoirs are strikingly visual. The latter are *Living Off the Country: Essays on Poetry and Place* (1981) and *The Stars, the Snow, the Fire: Twenty-Five Years in the Northern Wilderness* (1989).

Hairy Ape, The, expressionist play by O'Neill,♦ produced and published in 1922. It is symbolic of the perversion of human strength by technological progress.

In the cramped forecastle of a transatlantic liner, Yank—brutal, stupid, and profane—is the recognized leader of the stokers, who are the ultimate products of a society subservient to machines. When Mildred Douglas, daughter of the ship's owner, makes a slumming visit to the stokehole, she is shocked by the lurid atmosphere, and faints at encountering Yank's unashamed brutality. Although he is completely adapted to this environment, he now discovers that there is a world in which he does not belong, and "the Hairy Ape," as his friend Paddy calls him, becomes sullen and morose, beginning to think of his position. In New York on Easter Sunday, he swaggers in dirty dungarees up Fifth Avenue, trying in vain to insult the aristocratic strollers, who politely ignore him. Arrested, he is sent to Blackwell's Island, where the prisoners, misunderstanding his rebellion, advise him to join the I.W.W. Rejected by the labor organization, he goes to the zoo to see the ape, the only creature with whom he can now feel kinship. When he liberates it, to help him wreak destruction, the beast crushes him to death.

HAKLUYT, RICHARD (1552?–1616), British geographer and compiler of narratives of exploration. Among his valuable publications dealing with America, preserving original accounts that would otherwise have been lost, are *Divers Voyages Touching the Discoverie of America* (1582); *A Notable Historie Containing Foure Voyages Made by Certayne French Captaynes into Florida* (1587), including the narrative of Laudonnière; *Virginia Richly Valued* (1609), including the account of De Soto's discoveries; and his greatest work, *The Principall Navigations, Voyages, Traffiques, and Discoveries of the English Nation* (1589: 3 vols., enlarged, 1598–1600). The work of Hakluyt was continued by Samuel Purchas,♦ who collected his unpublished papers in *Hakluytus Posthumus* (4 vols., 1625).

HALBERSTAM, DAVID (1934–), New York City-born and Harvard-educated (1955) author of a great many books, mostly journalistic, but beginning with two novels: *The Noblest Roman* (1961), about a bootlegger who is the king of a Southern county; and *One Very Hot Day* (1968), treating two companies of foot soldiers, one American, the other Vietnamese. His great nonfictional work includes: *The Making of a Quagmire*

(1965), the author's personal narrative of working during the war in South Vietnam, a major subject for his newspaper reporting that won him a Pulitzer Prize the year before; *The Unfinished Odyssey of Robert Kennedy* (1969); *Ho* (1971), on Ho Chi Minh as Communist party and Vietnam leader; *The Best and the Brightest* (1972), a study of the workings and decisions of top U.S. political leadership; *The Powers That Be* (1979), an inquiry into the workings of major U.S. media; *The Breaks of the Game* (1981), about a professional basketball team; *The Amateurs* (1985), on an Olympic rowing team; *The Reckoning* (1986), about economic and social effects upon U.S. and Japanese automobile makers; *Summer of '49* (1989), about the race for the American League pennant; and *The Fifties* (1993), in which Halberstam revisits "America's last great age of optimism."

HALE, EDWARD EVERETT (1822–1909), nephew of Edward Everett and great-nephew of Nathan Hale, was a Boston Unitarian clergyman, philanthropist, and popular author. He wrote prolifically on many subjects, but is principally remembered for his tale *The Man Without a Country♦* (1865). His other books include *If, Yes, and Perhaps* (1868), miscellaneous tales ranging from the patriotism of the reprinted "Man Without a Country" and the whimsy of "A Piece of Possible History" to the satirical fantasy of "My Double and How He Undid Me"; *Sybaris and Other Homes* (1869), a Utopian satire of American society; *Ten Times One Is Ten* (1871), a novelette concerned with the ethical influence of a dead man's ghost on his friends; *In His Name* (1874), concerned with the 12th-century Waldenses; *Philip Nolan's Friends* (1877), a romantic account of the real Nolan; *The Fortunes of Rachel* (1884), dealing with an orphaned English girl and her social career in the U.S.; *East and West* (1892), a story of frontier Ohio; and two autobiographical works, *A New England Boyhood* (1893) and *Memories of a Hundred Years* (1902). *Franklin in France* (2 vols., 1887–88) was the most important of his scholarly works.

HALE, LUCRETIA PEABODY (1820–1900), sister of Edward Everett Hale, was educated at Elizabeth Peabody's school and, like other members of her large family and of her coterie in Boston, she became interested in social work, feminism, and education. Although she began writing fiction for the *Atlantic* in 1858 and collaborated with her brother Edward on a novel, *Struggle for Life* (1861), and with him and others on another novel, *Six of One by Half a Dozen of the Other* (1872), it was not until she collected *The Peterkin Papers* (1880) that she established a wide reputation. This sprightly satire on the culture of Boston bent on self-improvement in which the ingenuousness of other characters is always offset by the commonsensical Lady from Philadelphia was contin-

ued in later sketches, *The Last of the Peterkins* (1886). In addition to her literary activities, Miss Hale was one of the first two women members of the Boston School Committee, in which capacity she fostered kindergartens and vacation schools.

HALE, NANCY (1908–88), Boston-born granddaughter of Edward Everett Hale, resident in Virginia since marriage (1942) to bibliographer Fredson Bowers. Her novels include *The Young Die Good* (1932), about sophisticated New York society; *Never Any More* (1934), treating antagonisms of three girls whose mothers are friends; *The Prodigal Women* (1942), about the adolescence of two sisters from the South and their New England friend; *Dear Beast* (1959), about a Vermont girl's life in Virginia with her Southern husband; and *Secrets* (1971), fictive reminiscences of a New England woman, akin to her earlier *A New England Girlhood* (1958). *The Life in the Studio* (1969) is a real memoir of her youth with her parents, both painters. Stories, often treating emotional situations of women, appear in *The Earliest Dreams* (1936), *Heaven and Hardpan Farm* (1957), *The Pattern of Perfection* (1960), and other volumes, and she also wrote fiction for children. Her biography of the painter Mary Cassatt was published in 1975.

HALE, NATHAN (1755–76), born in Connecticut, graduated from Yale (1773), became a captain in the Revolutionary War, and volunteered to serve as a spy among the British forces on Long Island. Apprehended and sentenced to be executed, before he was hanged he uttered the famous words, "I only regret that I have but one life to lose for my country." He was the subject of a popular song of the period, and later of a play by Clyde Fitch.

HALE, SARAH JOSEPHA [BUELL] (1788–1879), is celebrated as the author of "Mary Had a Little Lamb,"♦ published in *Poems for Our Children* (1830). In addition to her work in behalf of child welfare, feminine education, and other humanitarian movements, she edited the Boston *Ladies' Magazine* (1828–37), *Godey's Lady's Book♦* (1837–77), and various compilations, and wrote many works typical of Victorian feminine productions, including plays, further volumes of poetry, the antislavery *Northwood: A Tale of New England* (1827) and other novels, *Sketches of American Character* (1829) and other short stories, and *Woman's Record* (1854), a history of distinguished women.

HALEY, ALEX [PALMER] (1921–92), born in Ithaca, N.Y., after service with the coast guard (1939–59), in which he was a journalist, became the aid or ghost writer of *The Autobiography of Malcolm X* (1965), of which a film scenario was later created by James Baldwin. ♦ Then, intrigued by a desire to discover his own black heritage, through research involving oral traditions in Gambia, he traced his family back seven generations to an African, Kunta Kinte, enslaved and brought to Annapolis in 1767. Of these facts, and many fictive improvisations, he created the family chronicle *Roots* (1976), awarded a special Pulitzer Prize (1977). In 1988 he had published a book for young people, *A Different Kind of Christmas,* about a young North Carolinian of 1855 becoming converted to antislavery activities.

Half-Way Covenant, doctrinal revision of New England Congregationalism,♦ drafted by Richard Mather and approved by a church synod (1662). First-generation Congregationalists were admitted to full membership in the church only after a personal experience of conversion, but their children shared in the privileges of full membership except for the Lord's Supper. The Half-Way Covenant proposed to extend this same status of baptism to the children of second-generation members, even though the latter may have confessed no experience of conversion to bring them into full communion.

HALL, BASIL (1788–1844), British naval officer and traveler, whose three-volume *Travels in North America* (1829) aroused much protest in the U.S. because of its Tory view of the crude democratic society. *The Aristocratic Journey* (1931) is a collection of the letters which his wife, Margaret H. Hall, wrote during this trip.

HALL, BAYNARD RUSH (1798–1863), Presbyterian clergyman and teacher of classics in Indiana, the site of *The New Purchase: or, Seven and a Half Years in the Far West* (1843), his quasi-fictive depiction of frontier life issued under the name Robert Carlton. *Frank Freeman's Barber Shop* (1852) is a novel about a black barber.

HALL, DONALD [ANDREW] (1928–), Connecticut-born poet, educated at Harvard and Oxford, where his "Exiles" won the Newdigate Prize (1952). He was a professor at Michigan (1957–77). His early poetry in *Exiles and Marriages* (1955) was marked by traditional meters and rhythms and formalism as well as ironic wit. *The Dark Houses* (1958), poems about suburban and small-town life, is freer and more emotional. This change is further developed in later works, which are more subjective and rich in sensuous imagery: *The Alligator Bride* (1969), new poems and revised earlier ones; *A Roof of Tiger Lilies* (1964); *The Yellow Room* (1971), about a romance; *The Town of Hill* (1975), a small collection; *A Blue Wing Tilts at the Edge of the Sea* (1975); *Kicking the Leaves* (1978); *The Toy Bone* (1979); *The Happy Man* (1986); and *The One Day* (1988), a long poem of a man and woman exploring middle age. He has collaborated in two prose works about baseball, *Playing Around* (1974) and *Dock Ellis in the Country of Baseball* (1976), as well

as writing *Fathers Playing Catch with Sons* (1985), essays on sports, mostly baseball. He has also written essays on many diverse subjects in *To Keep Moving* (1980); *Seasons at Eagle Pond* (1987), about seasonal change at his New Hampshire home; and *Poetry and Ambition* (1988). *String Too Short To Be Saved* (1961) recalls in prose his youthful summers on a New Hampshire farm, and *Remembering Poets* (1978) contains reminiscences and assessments of Dylan Thomas, Frost, Eliot, and Pound. In addition he has written critical studies of the sculptor Henry Moore (1966) and the poet Marianne Moore (1970), has been the author of stories in *The Ideal Bakery,* and created a play, *The Bone Ring* (1987), as well as writing several tales for children (1959–85). *Goatfoot Milktongue Twinbird* (1978) collects interviews, essays, and notes on poetry, as does *The Weather for Poetry* (1982). *Old and New Poems* (1990) gathers old favorites. In 1993 appeared *The Museum of Clear Ideas,* the long title poem a set of imitations from Horace, but others on a favorite subject, baseball. *Life Work,* also published in 1993, is an autobiography shaped by the author's confrontation with imminent mortality after an operation for cancer of the liver. Hall edited the *Oxford Book of American Literary Anecdotes* (1981).

HALL, G[RANVILLE] STANLEY (1844–1924), Massachusetts-born professor of psychology at Antioch and Johns Hopkins (1881–88), where John Dewey was his student; and president of Clark University (1888–1920). He founded and edited the *American Journal of Psychology* (1887–1921). His books include *The Contents of Children's Minds on Entering School* (1894), which influenced the U.S. movement toward child study; *Adolescence* (1904); *Jesus the Christ, in the Light of Psychology* (1917); *Morale: The Supreme Standard of Life and Conduct* (1920); *Recreations of a Psychologist* (1920); and *Life and Confessions of a Psychologist* (1923), an autobiography.

HALL, JAMES (1793–1868), circuit judge, banker, and editor in frontier Illinois, edited the *Illinois Gazette* (1820–22) and the *Illinois Intelligencer* (1829–32) and founded the *Illinois Monthly Magazine*♦ (1830), the first literary periodical west of Ohio. He is chiefly remembered for his record of pioneer life and legends. His many books include the romantic *Letters from the West* (1828); *Legends of the West* (1832), containing "The Seventh Son," a realistic sketch; *Sketches of History, Life, and Manners in the West* (1834); and a *History of the Indian Tribes* (3 vols., 1836–44), written with T.L. McKenney.

HALL, JAMES NORMAN (1887–1951), co-author with Charles B. Nordhoff♦ of novels set in the South Pacific. His own works include narratives of his World War I experiences; essays; *The Friends* (1934), a poem about Robinson's poetry; and novels, including *Lost Island* (1944), about the effect of war on a small Pacific island, and *The Far Lands* (1950).

HALL, OAKLEY (1920–), California novelist, whose works include *Corpus of Joe Bailey* (1953) and its sequel, *Report from Beau Harbor* (1971), wry depictions of generational and ideological conflicts in California families; *Warlock* (1958), set in a Southwest frontier mining town during the 1880s; *The Downhill Racers* (1963), about skiing enthusiasts; *The Adelita* (1975), concerning an American's involvement in the Mexican Revolution; *The Bad Lands* (1978), portraying conflicts between cattlemen and farmers in South Dakota during the 1880s; *Lullaby* (1982), the story of dreadful events in the life of a family in Hawaii, perhaps attributable to an ancient curse; *The Children of the Sun* (1983), treating the voyage of Cabeza de Vaca♦; *The Coming of the Kid* (1985), dwelling on long-established regional myths; and *Apaches* (1986), about the war in New Mexico against Apaches in the 1880s. Hall has also written *The Art and Craft of Novel Writing* (1988), and he ventured out to write the libretto for the operatic version (1976) of Wallace Stegner's *Angle of Repose.*

HALLECK, FITZ-GREENE (1790–1867), born in Connecticut, was a leading member of the Knickerbocker Group♦ and co-author with J. R. Drake of the "Croaker Papers"♦ (1819), which catapulted him to fame. In the same year he published his long poem *Fanny,* a satire of New York society, imitating Byron's *Beppo* and *Don Juan,* which was so popular that he added 50 stanzas to it two years later. He visited Europe (1822) and there wrote the poem "Alnwick Castle," in which he attempted to combine the sentimental romance of Scott with Byron's sophisticated satire. Three years later he published "Marco Bozzaris," a stirring poem about the heroic fighter against the Turks in the Greek struggle for freedom, which again exhibits his debt to Byron. After the publication of *Alnwick Castle, with Other Poems* (1827), Halleck did little writing, but his collected *Works* appeared in 1847. Among his best-known short poems are "Connecticut," "Burns," "The Field of the Grounded Arms," "Red Jacket," and "On the Death of Joseph Rodman Drake."

HALPER, ALBERT (1904–84), Chicago-born proletarian novelist, whose *Union Square* (1933), about economic pressures on workingmen, artists, and agitators, tended to satirize radicalism toward which his later books are sympathetic. *On the Shore* (1934) contains semi-autobiographical sketches of Chicago. *The Foundry* (1934) deals with workers in a Chicago electrotype foundry during the year preceding the 1929 stock market crash, and *The Chute* (1937) deals with workers in a mail-order house. *Sons of the Fathers* (1940) depicts the strain of America's entrance into World War I upon a Jewish immigrant who hoped his sons would never know war; *Only an Inch from Glory* (1943) deals with the frustrations of four New Yorkers; and *The Golden Watch* (1953) tells of a boy growing up in Chicago before World War I. *Little People* (1942) contains stories about Chicago clothing-store employees. Later novels include *Atlantic Avenue* (1956), about physical and emotional violence in Brooklyn and along New York's waterfront, and *The Fourth Horseman of Miami Beach* (1966), about lonely, middle-aged men. *Good-Bye, Union Square* (1970) is a memoir.

HALPINE, CHARLES GRAHAM (1829–68), born in Ireland, came to the U.S. (1851), and became a brigadier general in the Union army. He was best known for his humorous description of Civil War events in *The Life and Adventures . . . of Private Miles O'Reilly* (1864).

HAMILTON, ALEXANDER (1755–1804), was born in the Leeward Islands, the illegitimate son of a Scottish merchant. A letter he wrote to the local newspaper describing a West Indian hurricane won popular attention and led to his aunt's sending him to be educated at Elizabethtown, N.J., and at King's College. Unsettled political conditions interrupted his education, and although he was only 17, he published two anonymous pamphlets, *A Full Vindication of the Measures of Congress* (1774) and *The Farmer Refuted* (1775), answering the arguments of Samuel Seabury and brilliantly defending the patriot position and justifying the appeal to arms. During the Revolutionary War he served as captain, lieutenant colonel, and aide-de-camp to Washington. After the victory he was appointed receiver-general of continental taxes, was elected to the Continental Congress (1782–83), practiced law in New York, and served as a delegate to the Annapolis Convention (1786).

As a member of the Federal Constitutional Convention he considered its accomplishments in many ways unsatisfactory, but as an advocate of strong centralized government he worked for the ratification of the Constitution, especially as the principal author of *The Federalist*♦ (1787–88). As the first secretary of the treasury (1789–95), he presented a series of influential reports. These included: (1) issued January 14, 1790, proposing that the national government take over state debts incurred in aid of the Revolution, and that both national and state debts be refunded at par; (2) issued December 13, 1790, advising that an excise tax be levied to provide revenue for the government; (3) issued the next day, recommending the establishment of a bank of the U.S., modeled on the national bank of England; and (4) issued December 5, 1791, a *Report on Manufactures,* advocating a protective tariff for military self-sufficiency and the preservation of the home market. In the last, he pointed out that, as long as the U.S. remained an exclusively agricultural country, it would depend upon uncertain foreign markets for the sale of its goods. He therefore urged the encouragement of manufacturing to provide a reliable market, and the protection of infant industries by import duties or bounties. These measures tended to strengthen the federal government at the expense of states, and to ally it with monied interests, a policy known as the Hamiltonian system, as opposed to the agrarian system of Jefferson and his followers.

Resigning from the cabinet, Hamilton declined the office of Chief Justice of the Supreme Court, and returned instead to law practice. In 1798, when war threatened with France, he became a general, second in command to Washington. After peaceful settlement of the dispute, he was a bitter critic of Adams. In New York politics, he was twice instrumental in defeating the political aspirations of Aaron Burr, and in 1800 he supported his old political enemy Jefferson against Burr for President. Embittered by these attacks, Burr challenged him to a duel, as a result of which Hamilton died.

Among the many novels in which he appears are Gertrude Atherton's *The Conqueror,* Jeremiah Clemen's *The Rivals,* Howard Fast's *The Unvanquished,* and P. L. Ford's *Janice Meredith.* Hamilton's *Papers* were published in 26 volumes (1961–79).

HAMILTON, Dr. Alexander (1715–56), Scottish-born physician, practiced in Maryland after 1738. He was a founder of the Tuesday Club of Annapolis♦ and is best known for his *Itinerarium* (1744), a diary of his journey through the Middle Colonies and as far as Boston, which provides an excellent account of contemporary society and manners.

HAMILTON, Gail, see *Dodge, Mary A.*

Hamlet, The, novel by Faulkner,♦ published in 1931, the first of a trilogy including *The Town*♦ and *The Mansion.*♦

In the 1890s, Will Varner, the mild-mannered economic power of Frenchman's Bend, Yoknapatawpha County, Mississippi, rents some land to Ab Snopes, whose grotesque, ruthlessly greedy son Flem is installed by the 30-year-old Varner heir Jody as a clerk in the Varner store to dissuade Ab from burning the barn, his usual way with landlords. Instead, Flem takes over Varner positions, property, and power as his relatives, including the shrewd, weasly I.O., the idiot Ike, and the primitive Mink, begin to dominate or demoralize the town, to the horror of the compassionate and rational V. K. Ratcliff, a backcountry trader. When Varner's daughter Eula, a mindless, sensual female, becomes pregnant, she is married off to Flem in return for cash and the deed to the crumbling pre-Civil War mansion, Frenchman's Place. A different passion overwhelms Ike, who falls in love with a cow belonging to the morose farmer Jack Houston, and their daily relationship is made another subject of profit as Lump Snopes sells secret viewing places of the encounters. Another heifer causes different troubles between Houston and a Snopes when Mink's rudimentary sense of justice is outraged because he is charged for letting his stock graze on the farmer's land, and in retaliation he kills Houston and hides his body. Lump's demands for the $50 carried by Houston almost lead to another murder, but Mink is imprisoned for life and comes to realize that Flem, absent in Texas, will not aid him. Flem returns from his trip with a herd of savagely wild horses, which he auctions to the townspeople. He then mulcts them of even more money by inducing them to buy Frenchman's Place as a site of hidden treasure, but it is actually only the place where Flem has buried, and publicly dug up, a little bit of gold. Henry Armstid not only breaks a leg capturing a wild pony, but is maddened by fruitless digging for riches, thus representing the whole community as it is bilked and corrupted by the Snopeses.

Hamlet of A. MacLeish, The, blank-verse poem by MacLeish,♦ published in 1928.

Reinterpreting *Hamlet* as spiritual questioning and pessimism in the modern world, the poet sees the dead king as the consciousness of evil urging revenge; Claudius as "the jay jeer of the sun in the ear of our pain"; Gertrude as the mother force reproducing pain and evil; Ophelia as temptation; and Hamlet as the poet himself, melancholy and despairing. Science and philosophy lead nowhere, man has lost significance by divorcing himself from the earth and tradition, and even death has become "a gesture away from us," and artistic expression a "hoarse grief . . . shouted at the narrow stars." He accepts the challenge of Laertes, resigning himself to "the staged encounter and the game-pit rules" of life, in which he hopes to "Cancel this bloody feud, revoke All tears, all pain. . . ."

Hamlin, Jack, character in *Gabriel Conroy* and short stories by Bret Harte.♦

HAMMERSTEIN, Oscar (1847–1919), New York impresario and builder of theaters, the Harlem Opera House (1888), and the Manhattan Opera House (1892, rebuilt 1906). His productions of new operas, including works by Debussy and Strauss, made him a rival of the Metropolitan Opera Company, which bought his interests (1910) on the condition that he stop producing opera in the U.S. His biography was written (1956) by Vincent Sheean.

HAMMERSTEIN, Oscar II (1895–1960), grandson of Oscar Hammerstein, was the author of librettos and lyrics for musical plays, written with such composers as Gershwin, Kern, and Richard Rodgers. His works include *Rose-Marie*

(1924), *Sunny* (1924), *The Desert Song* (1926), *Show Boat* (1927), *Oklahoma!*♦ (1943), *Carmen Jones* (1943), *Carousel* (1945), *South Pacific* (1949, Pulitzer Prize), *The King and I* (1951), *Flower Drum Song* (1958), and *The Sound of Music* (1959).

HAMMETT, [SAMUEL] DASHIELL (1894–1961), born in Maryland, went to San Francisco as a Pinkerton detective and soon drew upon the city's atmosphere and his own business for the novels he began to write. Cool, tough, and hardboiled in attitude, his works employ Hemingway's mood and spare, realistic dialogue in the genre of the detective story. He took murder out of the settings of polite society and put it into a corrupt urban environment where, as his follower, Raymond Chandler, said, he gave it "back to the people that commit it for reasons, not just to provide a corpse." Hammett's major works including *Red Harvest* (1929) and *The Maltese Falcon* (1930), also introduced a new kind of sleuth, the cynical, tough Sam Spade. These works, along with *The Thin Man* (1932), became very popular films, and Hammett himself moved to southern California to write scripts. When he refused to testify about so-called un-American activities in Hollywood he was sent to prison. His friend Lillian Hellman wrote about his stand and his era in *Scoundrel Time* (1976).

HAMMETT, SAMUEL ADAMS (1816–65), Southwestern frontier humorist, who embroidered his adventures with typical frontier anecdotes, dialect, and tall tales and published them as *A Stray Yankee in Texas* (1853), *The Wonderful Adventures of Captain Priest* (1855), and *Piney Woods Tavern, or Sam Slick in Texas* (1858). He used the pseudonym Philip Paxton.

HAMMON, JUPITER (*c.*1720–*c.*1800), black slave on Long Island, whose first poem, *An Evening Thought* (1760), antedated by several years the work of Phillis Wheatley, the more famous black poet to whom he addressed his second poem (1778). Of more importance than his religious verses is *An Address to the Negroes of the State of New York* (1787), urging fellow slaves to be patient, and asking masters to manumit the children.

HAMMOND, JOHN (*fl.*1635–56), English colonist, came to Virginia in 1635, and after 19 years moved to Maryland, where he remained for two years. Upon returning to England he published *Leah and Rachel; or, The Two Fruitfull Sisters, Virginia and Maryland* (1656), a racy, vigorous pamphlet contrasting living conditions in England and the colonies, and pleading for the amelioration of the status of poor Englishmen by their removal to America.

HANDY, W[ILLIAM] C[HRISTOPHER] (1873–1958), Alabama-born black composer of jazz and St. Louis song publisher. He became famous as the composer of "Memphis Blues" (1912), which won him the title of "father of the blues." The best known of his later compositions is "St. Louis Blues" (1914), included in *Blues: An Anthology* (1926), which he edited. *Father of the Blues* (1941) is his autobiography, and *Unsung Americans Sung* (1944), edited by him, is a collection of song tributes to outstanding blacks and articles on black culture and history.

HANSBERRY, LORRAINE (1930–65), Chicago-born dramatist, became the first black woman to have a play produced on Broadway with *A Raisin in the Sun* (1959), an easy-going comedy of a family of black Chicagoans who plan to move into a white neighborhood, illustrative of Langston Hughes's poem: "What happens to a dream deferred, Does it dry up like a raisin in the sun?" She followed this success with *The Sign in Sidney's Brustein's Window* (1964), depicting Jews and other whites as well as blacks in Greenwich Village. After her early death her husband assembled from her plays, letters, diaries, and other writings a dramatic presentation, *To Be Young, Gifted and Black* (1969). For *The Movement* (1964) she wrote wry captions for photographs of blacks in their struggle for equality. *Raisin* (1973) was a musical adaptation of her first play by others.

HAPGOOD, HUTCHINS (1869–1944), born in Chicago, graduated from Harvard (1892), and was a journalist in Chicago and New York. His realistic narratives include *The Autobiography of a Thief* (1903), *The Spirit of Labor* (1907), *An Anarchist Woman* (1909), and *Types from City Streets* (1910). *Enemies* (1916) is a novel written with his wife, and *The Story of a Lover* (1919) is a semi-autobiographical novel. *A Victorian in the Modern World* (1939) is an autobiography, telling of his relations with Chicago left-wing groups and his postwar association with Greenwich Village and Provincetown.

HAPGOOD, NORMAN (1868–1937), brother of Hutchins Hapgood, was editor of *Collier's* (1903–12) during its muckraking period, and later edited *Harper's Weekly* (1913–16) and *Hearst's International* (1923–25). His books include *Literary Statesmen* (1897), biographies of Washington, Lincoln, and Webster; *The Stage in America* (1901); *Industry and Progress* (1911); and his autobiography, *The Changing Years* (1930).

Hapless Orphan, *The; or, Innocent Victim of Revenge,* anonymous novel by "an American Lady," published in 1793. It is a typically sentimental didactic romance concerned with Caroline Francis, a Philadelphia girl who attracts the fiancé of Eliza and is the object of Eliza's remorseless revenge after the young man's suicide. After innumerable machinations, Caroline is killed, and her corpse is barely saved from the dissecting room through the aid of another suitor, Mr. Helen.

HARBEN, WILLIAM NATHANIEL (1858–1919), born in Georgia, later lived in New York and abroad, becoming known for his popular short stories and novels concerned with life in northern Georgia. His novels include *The Woman Who Trusted* (1901), *Abner Daniel* (1902), *The Georgians* (1904), *Ann Boyd* (1906), and *Mam' Linda* (1907).

Harbinger, The (1845–49), weekly Fourierist newspaper, edited by George Ripley, was dedicated to "the examination and discussion of the great questions in social science, politics, literature, and the arts, which command the attention of all believers in the progress and elevation of humanity." Until 1847 it was the official organ of Brook Farm, and it attained a circulation of approximately 1000. It was later edited from New York by Ripley and Parke Godwin for the American Union of Associationists. Among the contributors were Lowell, Whittier, C.A. Dana, Greeley, the younger W.E. Channing, and J.S. Dwight, whose critical articles made the paper one of the leading musical journals of the U.S.

Harbor, The, novel by Ernest Poole,◆ published in 1915.

HARDWICK, ELIZABETH (1916–), Kentucky-born author of novels, including *The Ghostly Lover* (1945), presenting a Kentucky family as seen by a young girl member; *The Simple Truth* (1955), a character study related to the trial of a college student accused of murdering his sweetheart; and *Sleepless Nights* (1979), a "meditation" on a woman's life. *A View of My Own* (1962) prints essays on literature and society, mostly from the *Partisan Review,* and *Seduction and Betrayal* (1974) collects essays on women writers. A co-founder of *The New York Review of Books,* she was married (1949–72) to Robert Lowell.

HARDY, ARTHUR SHERBURNE (1847–1930), born in Massachusetts, was known as a professor of civil engineering and mathematics before the success of his fiction. He later served as U.S. minister to Persia, Greece, Rumania, Serbia, and Spain. Besides mathematical texts and a book of verse, he was the author of several popular novels: *But Yet a Woman* (1883), a stylized tale of contemporary France; *The Wind of Destiny* (1886), a romantic story set in Europe and the U.S., and its sequel, *His Daughter First* (1903); *Passe Rose* (1889), a romance of the time of Charlemagne; and *Helen* (1916), a novel of international society, set in France. *Diane and Her Friends* (1914) is a collection of stories.

HARE, ROBERT (1781–1858), professor of chemistry at the University of Pennsylvania, was the author of *Brief View of the Policies and Resources of the United States* (1810); *Standish the Puritan* (1850), a romance of the Revolutionary War; and *Experimental Investigation of the Spirit Manifestations . . .* (1855).

HARIOT, THOMAS (1560–1621), English mathematician and geographer, accompanied Grenville on his second expedition to Virginia (1586). The two-year sojourn resulted in his *Briefe and True Report of the New-Found Land of Virginia* (1588), which was accompanied in the 1590 edition by the imaginative drawings of a fellow colonist, John White, and was republished by Hakluyt. Raleigh was indebted to Hariot in *The History of the World* for points of chronology and geography. The name is also spelled Harriot and Harriott. Muriel Rukeyser◆ wrote *The Traces of Thomas Hariot* (1971), a study.

HARJO, JOY (1951–), born in Tulsa, Okla., of Creek and Cherokee-French heritage, draws on her experience of contemporary problems of Native Americans, and on their history and mythology in her poems. Her books of poetry are *The Last Song* (1975), *What Moon Drove Me to This?* (1980), *She Had Some Horses* (1983), and *In Mad Love and War* (1990).

HARLAN, LOUIS R[UDOLPH] (1922–), historian born in Mississippi, attended Emory University and became a professor at the University of Maryland (1966). His biography, *Booker T. Washington* (vol. I, 1972), was awarded a Pulitzer Prize for its second volume (1983). He has also been the editor of Washington's papers in 13 volumes (1972–85).

HARLAND, HENRY (1861–1905), born in New York City and educated at its City College (1877–80), liked to pose as Russian-born, European-schooled, and a Harvard student. Under the name Sidney Luska he wrote some sensational novels dealing with the lives of immigrant Jews, including *As It Was Written: A Jewish Musician's Story* (1885), *Mrs. Peixada* (1886), *The Yoke of the Thorah* (1887), and *My Uncle Florimond* (1888). In 1889 he moved to Paris, cultivating new themes and using his own name for the collection of stories and four novels that he published within two years, respectively *A Latin-Quarter Courtship* (1889), *Grandison Mather* (1889), *Two Women or One* (1890), *Two Voices* (1890), and *Mea Culpa* (1891). He took up residence in London in 1890 and became one of the leading expatriate aesthetes, and the original editor of *The Yellow Book* (1894–97), a very influential *fin de siècle* literary and artistic journal. During this later period he wrote a number of courtly and decorative tales, collected in *Mademoiselle Miss* (1893), *Grey Roses* (1895), and *Comedies and Errors* (1898), as well as the extremely popular *The Cardinal's Snuff-Box* (1900), concerned with the love of an English novelist and an Italian duchess, which comes to a happy fulfillment through the mediation of his uncle, the cardinal. *My Friend Prospero* (1904) is a similar romance about a young English nobleman and an Austrian princess.

HARLAND, Marion, pseudonym of Mary Terhune. ♦

Harlem, section of upper Manhattan, whose central area had 100,000 blacks in 1990. It was originally an independent village of Dutch settlers who named it for Haarlem, and was later a residential section for whites until it became predominantly black (*c.*1914–18). The section figured in literature as early as J. W. Johnson's *The Autobiography of an Ex-Colored Man* (1912), and was widely exploited in the fiction and poetry of the 1920s, the era of the so-called Harlem Renaissance. Leading authors of the period included Countee Cullen, Jessie Redmon Fauset, Langston Hughes, James Weldon Johnson, Claude McKay, Wallace Thurman, and Jean Toomer, and a major commentator on the blacks' situation was W.E.B. Du Bois. Writings by whites about the era include Van Vechten's *Nigger Heaven,* O'Neill's *All God's Chillun Got Wings,* and Bodenheim's *Naked on Roller Skates.* Later black authors associated with Harlem include James Baldwin, Ralph Ellison, Zora Neale Hurston, and LeRoi Jones.

Harmonium, first volume of poetry by Wallace Stevens, ♦ published in 1923, when he was almost 44, although some of the poems were printed in journals as early as 1915. The 74 poems include "Sunday Morning," ♦ "The Emperor of Ice Cream," ♦ "Thirteen Ways of Looking at a Blackbird," ♦ "Anecdote of the Jar," ♦ "Le Monocle de Mon Oncle," "The Comedian as the Letter C," and "Peter Quince at the Clavier." In 1931 the work was reissued with three poems (none of the above) omitted and 14 added.

Harmony Society, an outgrowth of a German pietist sect founded at Württemberg by George Rapp. After persecution abroad, and the establishment of several temporary colonies, Rapp and 600 adherents settled in Pennsylvania (1804), naming their settlement Harmony. The society moved to Indiana (1815–25) but returned to settle at Economy, Pa., near Pittsburgh. In 1831 "Count Maximilian De Leon," an adventurer who undermined their religious beliefs, split the Harmonists in two, and escaped with the funds of his minority party. The majority, who continued successfully under the original leadership, are popularly known as the Rappists. Part of their religious system embraced communism, and another distinguishing feature was the doctrine of celibacy. The latter in 1807 led them to dissolve marriage ties and prohibit further marriages, and finally caused their extinction, although there were still four members in 1903. (See *New Harmony.*)

Harp-Weaver, The, poems by Edna St. Vincent Millay. ♦

HARPER, Frances Ellen Watkins (1825–1911), only child of free black parents, gave her time and energy to the people of her race: *Poems on Miscellaneous Subjects* (1854), geared to antislavery ideas; *The Martyr of Alabama* (1894), praising a black boy who had been lynched; *Iola Leroy, or Shadows Uplifted* (1892), a novel about a seized and enslaved black girl, and an active program of public speaking.

Harper's Bazar (1867–), weekly women's magazine, was published to complement *Harper's Weekly.* In 1901 it became a monthly, and in 1913 was purchased by Hearst, who made it more modern and sophisticated. Since 1929 the title has been spelled *Bazaar.*

Harpers Ferry, see *Brown, John.*

Harper's Monthly Magazine (1850–), founded at New York by Harper and Brothers, with Henry J. Raymond as editor during the first six years. This eclectic literary periodical at first drew widely on British authors, including Dickens, Thackeray, Charles Lever, Trollope, Wilkie Collins, and Hardy, but under the editorship (1869–1919) of Henry M. Alden it printed an increasing amount of American material, including contributions by such diverse authors as Melville, De Forest, Nordhoff, Elizabeth S. Phelps, Henry James, C.D. Warner, Howells, Garland, E.E. Hale, Sarah Orne Jewett, Brander Matthews, and Owen Wister. Among the popular serials were Du Maurier's *Trilby* (1894) and Clemens's *Joan of Arc* (1895–96); featured illustrations were by such artists as E.A. Abbey, A.B. Frost, Howard Pyle, and Winslow Homer. A separate English edition published abroad was edited by Andrew Lang. After 1900, the American publication devoted more space to contemporary politics and social problems, with articles by public figures including Wilson, Theodore Roosevelt, and H.C. Lodge, and following World War I its policy became more notably liberal. The best-known department was long the now-canceled "Editor's Easy Chair," whose occupants have included D.G. Mitchell (1851–53), G. W. Curtis (1853–92), Howells (1901–21), E.S. Martin (1921–35), and Bernard De Voto (1935–55). From 1900 to 1925 the title was *Harper's New Monthly Magazine;* since then it has been simply *Harper's Magazine,* with only the first word featured. Purchased in the early 1960s by the *Minneapolis Tribune,* the magazine lost circulation and nearly went out of business, but was acquired by the MacArthur Foundation and has enjoyed success as a nonprofit institution.

Harper's Weekly (1857–1916), illustrated political and literary journal. Although it always published serials, including works by Dickens, Wilkie Collins, Elizabeth Gaskell, and Bulwer-Lytton, it was best known for its engravings and woodcuts, which constitute a pictorial history of the times. In 1862 Thomas Nast joined the staff, and made the magazine notable for its war pictures and political cartoons. His bitter caricatures of the corrupt Tweed Ring did much to shape public opinion, as did his cartoons, which created the accepted symbols of the Tammany tiger, the Republican elephant, and the Democratic donkey. The magazine was later noted for its photographs and wash drawings, and the writings of such contributors as Kipling, Conan Doyle, Henry James, Howells, H.B. Fuller, R.H. Davis, and Hamlin Garland. Among the editors were G.W. Curtis (1863–92), Carl Schurz (1892–94), and J.K. Bangs (1898–1901). It was absorbed by *The Independent.* ◆

HARRIGAN, EDWARD (1845–1911), author of popular songs, variety sketches, and 39 plays, in all of which he acted the leading parts. His song "The Mulligan Guard" (1873) was the seed of many farce-comedies containing popular lyrics, the most famous being the cycle begun with *The Mulligan Guard Picnic* (1878). These satires on the amateur military organizations that flourished in society and politics after the Civil War depict a typical stage Irishman and German, the latter acted by Harrigan's partner, Tony Hart.

HARRIOT, THOMAS, see *Hariot.*

HARRIS, BENJAMIN (*fl.*1673–1716), English bookseller and publisher, lived in Boston (1686–95), where he issued *Publick Occurrences Both Foreign and Domestick,* ◆ the first newspaper printed in America. It was immediately suppressed, but Harris published writings by such authors as Cotton and Increase Mather, and his own compilation, *The New England Primer.* ◆

HARRIS, CHARLES K., see *Tin Pan Alley.*

HARRIS, FRANK (1856–1931), born in Ireland, came to the U.S. (1870), where he worked at jobs ranging from boot-blacking to cow punching, the latter occupation being described in *My Reminiscences as a Cowboy* (1930). After attending the University of Kansas, he became an American citizen and was admitted to the state bar (1875). He drifted to Europe for further education, and in England became editor of various magazines and an intimate of such men as Beerbohm, Wilde, and Shaw. He attained a literary reputation for books of short stories such as *Elder Conklin* (1894) and *Montes the Matador* (1900), his novel *The Bomb* (1908), dealing with the Haymarket Riot, and his play *Mr. and Mrs. Daventry* (1900), which critics have contended was mainly written by Wilde. Of this London period, Wilde said, "Frank Harris has been received in all the great houses—*once.*" He returned to the U.S., where he edited *Pearson's Magazine,* but his pro-German views during World War I caused him to retire to Nice. Meanwhile he had won noto-

riety through his biography *Oscar Wilde: His Life and Confessions* (2 vols., 1916), which has been called maliciously inaccurate; his five volumes of *Contemporary Portraits* (1915–27), impressionistic and frequently scandalous sketches of acquaintances; and his very frank *My Life and Loves* (3 vols., 1923–27). His other works include *The Man Shakespeare* (1909) and *The Women of Shakespeare* (1911), psychological studies; *Great Days* (1914) and *Love in Youth* (1916), novels; *Unpath'd Waters* (1913), *The Veils of Isis* (1915), *A Mad Love* (1920), and *Undream'd of Shores* (1924), short-story collections; *Shakespeare and His Love* (1910) and *Joan la Ramée* (1926), plays; and *Bernard Shaw* (1931), a biography of which Frank Scully later claimed the authorship.

HARRIS, GEORGE WASHINGTON (1814–69), Tennessee River steamboat captain, later became a political writer and contributed humorous sketches to local newspapers and *The Spirit of the Times.* He is best known for his *Sut Lovingood. Yarns* ◆ (1867), a collection of the tall tales and humor of the Old Southwest.

HARRIS, JOEL CHANDLER (1848–1908), born and reared in a small town in Georgia, worked on newspapers in Macon, New Orleans, and Savannah before joining the staff of the *Atlanta Constitution,* with which he was associated from 1876 until the founding of his own *Uncle Remus's Magazine* (1907). His first Uncle Remus story appeared in the *Constitution* in 1879, and the first collection in book form, *Uncle Remus: His Songs and His Sayings* ◆ (1881), was followed by *Nights with Uncle Remus* (1883), *Uncle Remus and His Friends* (1892), *Mr. Rabbit at Home* (1895), *The Tar-Baby and Other Rhymes of Uncle Remus* (1904), *Uncle Remus and Br'er Rabbit* (1906), and other collections, all more exclusively addressed to children than was the first. These works were among the first, and remain the greatest, in the school of black folk literature. Uncle Remus is both typical and strongly individual, and his tales, based on native legends, are told with a simple humor and authentic dialect that is in perfect harmony with the thing said and the way of saying it. The rich plantation background and the elaborate dialogue of the animals are also remarkably fine. *Mingo and Other Sketches in Black and White* ◆ (1884) was the first of a number of volumes in which Harris portrayed Georgia aristocrats, poor whites, and ex-slaves with fidelity, understanding, and humor. These include two novels, *Sister Jane: Her Friends and Acquaintances* (1896) and *Gabriel Tolliver: A Story of Reconstruction* (1902), and such volumes of short stories as *Free Joe and Other Georgian Sketches* (1887), *Tales of the Home Folks in Peace and War* (1898), and *The Making of a Statesman* (1902), all of which contribute to Harris's eminence among authors of local-color fiction.

HARRIS, MARK (1922–), New York-born author, received his Ph.D. in American Studies from the University of Minnesota and has taught at San Francisco State College (1954–68) and elsewhere. His novels are *Trumpet to the World* (1946), about a young black in the army married to a white girl; *The Southpaw* (1953), the first of four works "by" and about a big-league baseball player Henry W. Wiggen, which include *Bang the Drum Slowly* (1956), telling of a catcher dying of Hodgkin's disease and of the loyal affection of his teammates, *A Ticket for a Seamstitch* (1957), further revelations of a young pitcher for the New York Mammoths, and *It Looked Like for Ever* (1979), about Henry's being dropped by the Mammoths; *Something About a Soldier* (1957), the story of an idealistic young draftee; *Wake Up, Stupid* (1959), a humorous epistolary novel revealing a month in the life of a professor who is also a novelist; *The Goy* (1970), a portrait of a Gentile professor's relations with Jewish colleagues; *Killing Everybody* (1973); and *Lying in Bed* (1984), another epistolary novel involving the man in *Wake Up, Stupid*. *Speed* (1990) is a later novel. Works drawing directly on his own life include *Mark the Glove Boy, or The Last Days of Richard Nixon* (1964), related to Nixon's campaign for the California governorship; *Twentyone Twice* (1966), a journal of his forty-second year; and *Best Father Ever Invented* (1976). *City of Discontent* (1952) is an interpretation of Vachel Lindsay and his region. *Friedman and Son* (1962) is a play about the unhappy relationship between Solomon Friedman and his 45-year-old son Abraham, known to the world under the non-Jewish name A.B. Ferguson. *Short Work of It* (1980) collects articles written between 1946 and 1978. *Saul Bellow, Drumlin Woodchuck* (1980) is a very autobiographical biography of Bellow.

HARRIS, THOMAS LAKE (1823–1906), English-born poet and religionist, began his career in 1845 as a minister of Universalism,♦ was converted to spiritualism by Andrew Davis, and later established communities of believers in the Brotherhood of the New Life, which aimed at the creation of a new social system through the spiritual regeneration of mankind. He wrote mystic poetry, which he claimed to dictate while in a state of trance.

HARRIS, WILLIAM TORREY (1835–1909), philosopher and educator, founded the St. Louis school of Idealism, which initiated the systematic study of German thought in the U.S. Influenced by Alcott and Theodore Parker, he became the foremost exponent of Hegel in the U.S. upon publishing *Hegel's Logic* (1890), although he had already used Hegelian interpretation in *The Spiritual Sense of Dante's Divina Commedia* (1889). His academic career, beginning as a St. Louis schoolteacher (1857) and ending as U.S. Commissioner of Education (1889–1906), was marked by his application of Hegel's principles to educational problems. He founded *The Journal of Speculative Philosophy* (1867–93), which published the early writings of Dewey, James, and Royce, and with Alcott he established the Concord School of Philosophy (1880). The extensive bibliography of his writings includes *Introduction to the Study of Philosophy* (1889) and *Psychologic Foundations of Education* (1898). He contributed to P.B. Sanborn's study of their friend Emerson (1885).

HARRISON, CONSTANCE CARY (1843–1920), born in Virginia, later lived in New York and England, and became known for her essays, stories, and novels depicting American social life during the latter part of the 19th century. *The Anglomaniacs* (1890), published anonymously, won wide attention for its comic portrayal of American social climbers in Europe. Her other fiction includes *Belhaven Tales* (1892), *Sweet Bells Out of Tune* (1893), *A Son of the Old Dominion* (1897), *Good Americans* (1898), and *Latter-Day Sweethearts* (1906). She published her autobiography as *Recollections Grave and Gay* (1911).

HARRISON, HENRY SYDNOR (1880–1930), born in Tennessee, graduated from Columbia, and served on the staff of the Richmond *Times-Dispatch* (1900–1910). His later life was devoted mainly to fiction, the best of his seven novels being *Queed* (1911) and *V.V.'s Eyes* (1913). The first, dramatized by Gilbert Emery (1921), is a complacently realistic story of American city life, concerned with a young "revolutionary sociologist" whose conviction of his mission in life is broken by contact with actuality when he becomes a newspaper reporter. *V.V.'s Eyes,* about an enthusiastic young doctor, V. Vivian, who attempts to reform the selfish daughter of a factory owner, includes pleas for improved factory conditions, child-labor legislation, and women's rights.

HARRISON, JIM (1937–), part native American, Harrison was born in rural northern Michigan, where he still lives on a farm. He reached national critical attention and readership with *Legends of the Fall* (1979), three novellas on the theme of violent vengeance. His fiction includes *Wolf: A False Memoir* (1971); *A Good Day To Die* (1973); *Warlock* (1981); *Sundog* (1984); and *The Woman Lit by Fireflies* (1990), which prints three novellas, the title tale a haunting one of a woman suddenly deserting her insufferably mundane husband at a highway rest stop, spending a night in a cornfield; it is imagined from her viewpoint only. *Julip* (1994) is a collection of dark novellas built on the myths of maleness. Harrison's poetry is collected in *Plain Song* (1965), *Locations* (1968), *Outlyer* (1969), *Letters to Yesenin* (1973), *Returning to Earth* (1977), and *Selected and New Poems* (1982).

HARRISSE, HENRY (1829–1910), French bibliographer of American history, resident in the U.S. (1847–66). His works include *Bibliotheca Americana Vetustissima* (1866), a bibliography of 300 books referring to America between 1493 and 1551, and *Additions* (1872); *Notes on Columbus* (1866) with S.L.M. Barlow; *Notes . . . de la Nouvelle-France* (1872); *Découverte de l'Amérique du Nord* (1892), concerning the Cabots; and *John Cabot, the Discoverer of North America* (1896).

HART, FRANCES NOYES (1890–1943), author of fiction, including such detective novels as *The Bellamy Trial* (1927), *Hide in the Dark* (1929), and *The Crooked Lane* (1934). She pioneered several techniques of fictional legal proceedings and scientific research in the detective novel.

HART, FRED H. (*fl.*1873–78), Nevada frontier journalist and humorist, author of *The Sazerac Lying Club* (1878), a collection of character sketches and local narratives in the vein of the tall tale.

HART, JOHN S[EELY] (1810–77), professor at Princeton who taught what is thought to be the first college course on American literature (1872) and wrote *A Manual of American Literature for Schools and Colleges* (1872).

HART, JOSEPH C. (1798–1855), New York lawyer and journalist, lived for a time in Nantucket, and wrote *Miriam Coffin; or, The Whale-Fishermen* (1834), the first American novel on whaling, written to obtain congressional support for the industry, of which it gives a vivid picture. *The Romance of Yachting* (1848) is a farrago of travel and literary essays, including one of the earliest analyses of Shakespeare's plays intended to prove Bacon's authorship. Hart was later U.S. consul in the Canary Islands, where he died.

HART, MOSS (1904–61), New York playwright, was best known for his collaborations with George S. Kaufman,♦ which include *Once in a Lifetime* (1930), *You Can't Take It with You*♦ (1936, Pulitzer Prize), *I'd Rather Be Right* (1937), *The Man Who Came to Dinner* (1939), and *George Washington Slept Here* (1940). He also wrote the librettos for the Irving Berlin revues *Face the Music* (1932) and *As Thousands Cheer* (1933), and the musical comedy *Lady in the Dark* (1941), with songs by Kurt Weill and Ira Gershwin. *Winged Victory* (1943), a play about the air force, was performed by soldiers. *Act One* (1959) is his autobiography.

HARTE, [FRANCIS] BRET[T] (1836–1902), born in Albany, N.Y., went to California (1854), where he engaged in various occupations, including a brief attempt at mining in the Mother Lode. In 1860 he settled in San Francisco, where he became a printer and journalist, and through his contributions to the *Golden Era* and the *Californian* became a prominent literary figure, whose successes included tales about Spanish California in the vein of Washington Irving and a novelette, "M'liss,"♦ about a young girl's adventures in the gold-rush mining country. *Outcroppings* (1865), an anthology of local verse; *The Lost Galleon* (1867), a collection of his poems; and *Condensed Novels and Other Papers*♦ (1867), distinguished for its satirical parodies of famous authors, were his first books. The following year Harte became editor of the newly founded *Overland Monthly,* in which he published his local-color stories, mainly concerned with moral contrasts, including "The Luck of Roaring Camp,"♦ "The Outcasts of Poker Flat,"♦ "Tennessee's Partner,"♦ "Miggles," and "Brown of Calaveras." His famous comic ballad, "Plain Language from Truthful James"♦ (1870), often called "The Heathen Chinee," also appeared at this time, and, with the collection of *The Luck of Roaring Camp and Other Sketches* (1870), he was swept into popular favor throughout the U.S. He immediately made a triumphal trip east, where he received a contract from the *Atlantic Monthly* for $10,000 for 12 contributions. He fulfilled the contract with mediocre writing, and his short-lived popularity came to an end. During subsequent years, Harte collected his magazine contributions in *Mrs. Skagg's Husbands* (1873), *Tales of the Argonauts* (1875), *An Heiress of Red Dog and Other Sketches* (1878), *A Sappho of Green Springs and Other Stories* (1891), and *Colonel Starbottle's Client and Some Other People* (1892). He also wrote two short novels, *Gabriel Conroy* (1876) and *Jeff Briggs's Love Story* (1880), and two plays, *Two Men of Sandy Bar* (1876) and *Ah Sin*♦ (1877), the latter adapted with Clemens, as well as many other works, but none of these approached the success of his earliest writings. He became U.S. consul at Crefeld, Rhenish Prussia (1878), and at Glasgow (1880–85). He lived the remainder of his life in London, where editors accepted his stories more readily than did the American magazines. During his last years he was little better than a hack writer, turning out imitations of the California stories that had won him fame.

Hartford Courant (1764–   ), weekly newspaper published at Hartford. As the *Connecticut Courant,* it was a patriotic journal during the Revolution, and it later supported the Federalist party. Becoming a daily, it continued to be the leading news organ of its state, renamed the *Hartford Daily Courant* (1837) and the *Hartford Courant* (1887), and it claims to be the oldest continuously published newspaper in the U.S.

Hartford Wits, see *Connecticut Wits.*

HARTMANN, [CARL] SADAKICHI (1869?–1944), born in Japan of a Japanese mother and German father, by whom he was sent (1882) to the U.S., where he was naturalized (1894) and where he was said to have been championed by the aged Whitman, of whom he wrote *Conversations with Walt Whitman* (1895). His other writings include *Christ* (1893), a verse drama; *Buddha* (1897), *Confucius* (1923), and *Moses* (1934), prose plays; *A History of American Art* (1902); and *Drifting Flowers of the Sea* (1906), poems. He was identified with bohemian circles of Greenwich Village and later of Hollywood, the latter phase being described in Gene Fowler's *Minutes of the Last Meeting* (1954).

Harvard Classics, *The,* see *Eliot, C.W.*

Harvard University, first North American institution of higher learning, founded (1636) at Newe Towne (Cambridge) under a grant of the Massachusetts Bay Colony. Three years later, the college was named for John Harvard (1607–38), a colonist who bequeathed half his estate (£780) and his library of more than 400 volumes to the new institution. In its early years, the college was closely allied with church and state, but in the mid-19th century this alliance was completely severed, the clergy no longer being formally represented on the board of overseers, which is elected by the alumni rather than the legislature. Harvard Divinity School (founded 1819) was originally a stronghold of Unitarianism, but has later been a nonsectarian graduate school of theology. Other prominent schools are those of medicine (founded 1782), law (founded 1817), Lawrence Scientific School (1847–1907, now the school of engineering), and business administration (founded 1908). Among the notable institutions within the university are the Agassiz museum of comparative zoology, Peabody museum of archaeology, Fogg art museum, Arnold arboretum, and Widener Memorial Library, the largest university library in the U.S. Famous presidents of Harvard include Increase Mather (1685–1701); Josiah Quincy♦ (1829–45); Edward Everett (1846–49); Jared Sparks (1849–53); C.W. Eliot♦ (1869–1909), under whom Harvard took its place as a leading university of the U.S.; A.L. Lowell♦ (1909–33), who introduced the tutorial system and house plan and made other reforms and innovations; and James B. Conant (1933–53). Radcliffe College♦ for women, once an affiliate, is wholly integrated into the university. Throughout its history, Harvard has played an important role in American cultural life, and its faculty and alumni have included many outstanding men. Among the literary figures on the faculty have been Holmes, Lowell, C.E. Norton, George Bancroft, John Fiske, Parkman, Longfellow, Henry Adams, Santayana, Whitehead, William James, Bliss Perry, Irving Babbitt, G.P. Baker, G.L. Kittredge, Robert Hillyer, MacLeish, William Alfred, and Bernard Bailyn. Graduates noted for their writings include Michael Wigglesworth (1651), Increase Mather (1656),

Benjamin Tompson (1662), Samuel Sewall (1671), Cotton Mather (1678), Thomas Prince (1707), Mather Byles (1725), Royall Tyler (1776), Prescott (1814), Edward Everett (1811), Jared Sparks (1815), George Bancroft (1817), Emerson (1821), Holmes (1829), Motley (1831), Theodore Parker (1836), Jones Very (1836), Thoreau (1837), R.H. Dana, Jr. (1837), Lowell (1838), Parkman (1844), C.E. Norton (1846), Henry Adams (1858), John Fiske (1863), William James (M.D., 1869), Wister (1882), Santayana (1886), Herrick (1890), Van Wyck Brooks (1907), S.E. Morison (1908), T.S. Eliot (1909), Conrad Aiken (1911), Benchley (1912), Cummings (1915), Marquand (1915), Dos Passos (1916), Behrman (1916), W.D. Edmonds (1926), Agee (1932), Boorstin (1934), R.W. Anderson (1939), Nemerov (1941), Mailer (1943), K. Koch (1948), John Hawkes (1949), Donald Hall (1951), and Updike (1954).

Harvey, play by Mary C. Chase.♦

HARVEY, WILLIAM HOPE (1851–1936), known as "Coin" Harvey, the pseudonym he used in the magazine and books he published from his Chicago home to disseminate views on bimetallism. Among his works on free coinage of silver, which for a time had great influence, are *Coin's Financial School* (1894), *A Tale of Two Nations* (1894), *Coin's Financial School Up to Date* (1895), *Coin on Money, Trusts, and Imperialism* (1899), *The Remedy* (1915), and *Common Sense, or the Clot on the Brain of the Body Politic* (1920).

Hashimura Togo, character in humorous books by Wallace Irwin.♦

HASLAM, GERALD (1937–), California author dealing mainly with the Central Valley area where he was resident while completing an M.A. at San Francisco State studying themes and language of the region. His writing has mainly been short stories, e.g. *Okies* (1975) and *Snapshots: Glimpses of the Other California* (1985). He has also written a novel of the region, *Masks* (1976), and works of nonfiction that include *The Language of the Oil Field* (1972).

HASS, ROBERT (1941–), San Francisco-born poet resident in Berkeley, where in 1989 he became a professor of the University of California. He has written verse sympathetic to people in *Field Guide* (1973), *Praise* (1979), and *Human Wishes* (1989). He has also published *Twentieth Century Pleasures* (1984), subtitled "prose on poetry." He has edited some of the shorter poems by Jeffers♦ and translated poems by Milosz.♦ He succeeded Rita Dove♦ as Poet Laureate in 1995.

HASTINGS, THOMAS (1784–1872), born in Connecticut and reared in upstate New York, moved to New York City (1832), where he conducted church choirs, composed music and words for hymns, and compiled several hymn books. His first collection, *Spiritual Songs for Social Worship* (1931–32), was edited with Lowell Mason, and most of his original works were collected in *Devotional Hymns and Religious Poems* (1850), which includes his music for Toplady's "Rock of Ages."

Hasty Pudding, The, mock-epic in three cantos of heroic couplets, composed in 1793 by Joel Barlow,♦ published in 1796. While in France, the poet one evening, in a Savoyard inn, encountered a steaming dish of boiled Indian meal (hasty pudding). It reminded him of Connecticut and caused him to write his merry epic on this native dish, ranking "simplicity of diet among the virtues."

Haunted Palace, The, poem by Poe,♦ published in the *Baltimore Museum* (1839), and as one of the hero's "rhymed verbal improvisations" in "The Fall of the House of Usher." The six stanzas (rhymed *ababcdcd*) depict in allegory the progress of insanity within the phantom-haunted "palace" of a decaying mind.

HAVIGHURST, WALTER [EDWIN] (1901–94), Wisconsin-born professor at Miami University, Ohio, graduated from the University of Denver. His works include *Upper Mississippi: A Wilderness Saga* (1937, revised 1944); *Long Ships Passing* (1942), about Great Lakes shipping; *Voices on the River* (1964), a history of the Mississippi; *Alexander Spotswood* (1967), biography of a colonial Virginia governor; *River to the West* (1970), on the Ohio River; and *Ohio* (1977), on the state. His novels include *Pier 17* (1935), about a West Coast dock strike; *The Quiet Shore* (1937), set near Lake Erie; *The Winds of Spring* (1940), about pioneer Wisconsin; *No Homeward Course* (1941), about a German sea raider; and *The Signature of Time* (1949), about generations of a Lake Erie family.

HAWKES, JOHN [CLENDENNIN BURNE, JR.] (1925–), Connecticut-born novelist, a graduate of Harvard, has taught English at Brown University (1958–). His fiction includes *The Cannibal* (1949), two related stories presenting almost surrealistically the horrors of devastation in postwar Germany; *The Beetle Leg* (1951), a novel about a construction worker buried alive during the building of a dam and the psychological effect of his death upon friends and co-workers; *The Goose on the Grave* (1954) and *The Owl* (1954), two short novels set in Italy; *The Lime Twig* (1961), about the psychopathic effects on a man of life during and after the London blitz; *Second Skin* (1964), about an aging former navy officer who sheds his old life of violence, horror, and sadness to live a new one that is joyous and sensuous; *The Blood Oranges* (1971), about a contempt-

ible American couple in Greece who destroy a friendly visiting couple; *Death, Sleep and the Traveler* (1974), a man's phantasmagoric view of events that involve himself, his wife, and his friend who is her lover; *Travesty* (1976), a Frenchman's monologue that serves as a suicide note while he prepares to kill his daughter, a friend, and himself; *The Passion Artist* (1979), presenting a middle-aged widower's fantastic encounters in a European city; *Virginie* (1982), about a girl who has experienced two previous lives in France, both marked by bizarre sexual experiences; *Adventures in the Alaskan Skin Trade* (1985), a tale of a boy encountering hunting and sex in an excursion to Alaska, of which *Innocence in Extremis* (1985), a segment less than 100 pages long, was separately issued; and *Whistlejacket* (1988), about a gifted photographer fascinated by a major subject, a great show horse. *The Innocent Party* (1966) collects four short plays, and *Lunar Landscapes* (1969) collects stories and novellas. The plots of Hawkes's fiction are often oblique, set in a nightmare or a dream kind of world, told in an intricate, highly personal style that frequently verges on the abstract, and marked by a macabre humor.

Hawkeye, see *Leather-Stocking Tales.*

Hawks of Hawk-Hollow, The. *A Tradition of Pennsylvania,* romance by R. M. Bird,♦ published in 1835, and anonymously dramatized in 1841.

At the Delaware Water Gap in Pennsylvania, in 1780, there is a feud between the Gilbert and Falconer families. Years before, Colonel Richard Falconer seduced Jessie Gilbert, and her brothers, a wild group known as the Hawks, vowed revenge but fled during the Revolution. Herman Hunter, an artist, now comes to the valley, where he falls in love with Catherine Loring, daughter of the colonel's steward, after he rescues her from drowning, being in turn saved by a dark stranger. Herman's rival is Henry Falconer, the colonel's nephew. When Catherine prepares to marry Henry, the dark stranger, revealing himself to be Oran Gilbert, helps Herman to surprise the wedding party, killing Henry and kidnapping Catherine. Herman is captured and jailed, Oran fails to carry out his plan to seize the jail, and Elsie, an old crone, reveals to the colonel that Herman is actually Hyland, his son by Jessie Gilbert. The colonel has Hyland released, confesses that he had secretly married Jessie, and dies. Oran commits suicide, and Hyland and Catherine marry.

HAWTHORNE, JULIAN (1846–1934), son of Nathaniel Hawthorne, was educated in the U.S. and abroad, and spent part of his early life in England. Beginning with the publication of *Bressant* (1873), a melodramatic novel, he became a popular author, and his best-known fiction includes *Garth* (1877), a novel concerned with an

Indian curse on a New England family dwelling in Jamaica; *Archibald Malmaison* (1884), a story of split personality; and *A Fool of Nature* (1896). In addition to such books on his family as *Nathaniel Hawthorne and His Wife* (1884) and *Hawthorne and His Circle* (1903), his autobiographical works include *Shapes That Pass* (1928) and *The Memoirs of Julian Hawthorne* (1938).

HAWTHORNE, NATHANIEL (1804–64), was born at Salem, Mass., of a prominent Puritan family, which had spelled the name Hathorne and included a judge at the Salem witchcraft trials, who figures as the accursed founder of *The House of the Seven Gables*. Nathaniel's father, a sea captain, died of yellow fever in Dutch Guiana in 1808, leaving his widow to mourn him during a long life of eccentric seclusion, and this influenced her son's somber and solitary attitude. During his childhood, he read extensively in the poets and romancers, and spent an impressionable year at a remote Maine lake, after which he attended Bowdoin College, graduating in 1825. Returning to Salem, he began to write historical sketches and allegorical tales, dealing with moral conflicts in colonial New England.

In 1828 he published anonymously, at his own expense, an immature novel, *Fanshawe,*♦ whose hero resembles the author at this period. The work went practically unnoticed, but interested S.G. Goodrich, who then published many of Hawthorne's stories in *The Token.*♦ These were reprinted in *Twice-Told Tales*♦ (1837, enlarged 1842) and included "The Maypole of Merrymount,"♦ "Endicott and the Red Cross,"♦ "The Minister's Black Veil,"♦ "Mr. Higginbotham's Catastrophe,"♦ "Dr. Heidegger's Experiment,"♦ "The Gray Champion,"♦ "The Ambitious Guest,"♦ and the "Legends of the Province House," containing "Lady Eleanore's Mantle"♦ and "Howe's Masquerade."♦ These tales, which the author said had "the pale tint of flowers that blossomed in too retired a shade," deal with the themes of guilt and secrecy, and intellectual and moral pride, and show Hawthorne's constant preoccupation with the effects of Puritanism in New England. In imaginative, allegorical fashion, he depicts the dramatic results of a Puritanism that was at the roots of the culture he knew, recognizing its decadence in his own time.

In 1836 he emerged from his seclusion at Salem to begin a career of hack writing and editing. For Goodrich he edited the monthly *American Magazine of Useful and Entertaining Knowledge* (1836), and later compiled the popular *Peter Parley's Universal History* (1837), as well as writing such books for children as *Grandfather's Chair* (1841), *Famous Old People* (1841), *Liberty Tree* (1841), and *Biographical Stories for Children* (1842). Meanwhile he had also been employed in the Boston Custom House (1839–41), and now spent six or seven months at Brook Farm, where his sensitiveness and solitary habits, as well as his lack of enthusiasm for communal living, unfitted him for fruitful participation. He married Sophia Peabody, an ardent follower of the Concord school, but even this marriage, although it was a happy turning point in his life, did not bring Hawthorne to share the optimistic philosophy of Transcendentalism. Settling in Concord at the Old Manse, he continued his analysis of the Puritan mind in the tales that were collected in *Mosses from an Old Manse*♦ (1846), including "Young Goodman Brown,"♦ "The Celestial Railroad,"♦ "Rappaccini's Daughter,"♦ "The Artist of the Beautiful,"♦ "The Birthmark,"♦ and "Roger Malvin's Burial."♦

As Surveyor of the Port of Salem (1846–49), he wrote little, but satirically observed his associates, as he described in the introduction to *The Scarlet Letter*♦ (1850). This novel, written after Hawthorne's dismissal from his post owing to a change of administrations, proved to be his greatest work, and indeed summed up in classic terms the Puritan dilemma that had so long occupied his imagination. Other books of this period include *The House of the Seven Gables*♦ (1851), another great romance, concerned with the decadence of Puritanism; *The Blithedale Romance*♦ (1852), in which he turned to the contemporary scene and his Brook Farm experiences; *The Snow-Image and Other Twice-Told Tales*♦ (1851), containing "The Snow-Image,"♦ "The Great Stone Face,"♦ and "Ethan Brand"♦; and *A Wonder Book*♦ (1852) and *Tanglewood Tales*♦ (1853), stories for children.

During these years, he lived for a time in the Berkshires, where he was friendly with his admirer, Melville. After he wrote a campaign biography of his college friend Franklin Pierce (1852) he was rewarded with the consulship at Liverpool. His departure for Europe (1853) marks another turning point in his life. The ensuing years abroad were filled with sightseeing and keeping a journal, and, although his new cultural acquirements had little influence on his writing, they throw significant light on his character of mind. After his consular term (1853–57), he spent two years in Italy, returning to settle again in Concord (1860). *Our Old Home*♦ (1863), shrewd essays on his observations in England, and *The Marble Faun*♦ (1860), a romance set in Italy, were results of his European residence.

His last years, during which he continued to contribute to the *Atlantic Monthly,* were marked by declining creative powers. His attempts to write a romance based on the themes of an elixir of life and an American claimant to an English estate resulted only in four posthumous fragments: *Septimius Felton*♦ (1872); *The Dolliver Romance*♦ (1876); *Dr. Grimshawe's Secret*♦ (1883); and *The Ancestral Footstep* (1883). Other posthumous publications include *Passages from the American Notebooks* (1868), *Passages from the English Notebooks* (1870), and *Passages from the French and Italian Notebooks* (1871), all edited by his wife. The *English Notebooks* were newly edited from original manuscripts (1942) by Randall Stewart.

Hawthorne has long been recognized as a classic interpreter of the spiritual history of New England, and in many of his short works, as well as in *The Scarlet Letter* and *The House of the Seven Gables,* he wrote masterpieces of romantic fiction. Like Poe, but with an emphasis on moral significance, he was a leader in the development of the short story as a distinctive American genre. The philosophic attitude implicit in his writing is generally pessimistic, growing out of the Puritan background, although his use of the supernatural has an aesthetic rather than a religious foundation, for he presented New England's early Puritanism and its decay in terms of romantic fiction. Emphasis on allegory and symbolism causes his characters to be recalled as the embodiment of psychological traits or moral concepts more than as living figures.

HAY, JOHN [MILTON] (1838–1905), Indiana-born statesman and author, as a law student at Springfield met Lincoln, whose assistant secretary he became. With John Nicolay, another secretary, who also served the President until his assassination, he gathered material for *Abraham Lincoln: A History* (10 vols., 1890). After holding minor posts in foreign legations, he entered journalism, and wrote *Castilian Days*♦ (1871) and *Pike County Ballads*♦ (1871), dialect poems about the Illinois frontier. Reentering the government as assistant secretary of state under Hayes, he moved in the circle which included Henry Adams, H. C. Lodge, and Clarence King, and wrote an anonymous novel, *The Bread-Winners*♦ (1884). He was McKinley's ambassador to Great Britain (1897–98), and secretary of state under McKinley and Theodore Roosevelt (1898–1905). He was responsible for the Open Door policy in China and the Hay-Pauncefote Treaty (1901), which gave the U.S. control of the Panama Canal and supremacy in the Caribbean.

HAYDEN, ROBERT (1913–80), born in Detroit, educated at the University of Michigan, was a professor of English at Fisk and his alma mater. His first volume of poems, *Heart-Shape in the Dust* (1940), shows him as a spokesman for his fellow blacks, but though he continued to use racial subjects, e.g. "The Ballad of Nat Turner," his fine craftsmanship and broader view of human experience rise to a more universal level in the poems of later volumes: *Figure of Time* (1955), *A Ballad of Remembrance* (1962), *Selected Poems* (1966), *Words in the Mourning Time* (1970), and *American Journal* (1978).

HAYES, ALFRED (1911–85), English-born author and scenarist, reared in New York City. His novels, written after army service in Italy, are *All Thy Conquests* (1946), about differences between American troops and Roman citizens; *Shadow of Heaven* (1947), about an aging labor organizer; *The Girl on Via Flaminia* (1949), about a bittersweet affair between a lonely American soldier and a respectable Italian girl, adapted as a play by Hayes (1954); *In Love* (1953); *The End of Me* (1968), about the strained relations among family members; and *The Stockbroker, the Bitter Young Man, and the Beautiful Girl* (1973), an ironic novella. *The Big Time* (1944), *Welcome to the Castle* (1950), and *Just Before the Divorce* (1968) collect poems. *The Temptation of Don Volpi* (1960) contains three novellas.

HAYNE, PAUL HAMILTON (1830–86), South Carolina author, called "the last literary cavalier," was known before the Civil War for his nature poetry, published in *Poems* (1855), *Sonnets and Other Poems* (1857), and *Avolio* (1860). He was a leading member of the Russell's Bookstore Group♦ and edited *Russell's Magazine* (1857–60). During the war he was too ill to serve in the army, and lived in poverty after his home was destroyed, but won fame for his martial lyrics. His fragile, charming poetry finds its best expression during the postwar period in his *Legends and Lyrics* (1872). He edited the poems of his friend Timrod and for this volume (1873) wrote a pathetic and penetrating introductory essay. He also wrote a life of H. S. Legaré (1878). His own *Collected Poems* was published in 1882.

HAZARD, EBENEZER (1744–1817), Pennsylvania antiquarian and postmaster-general (1782–89), whose *Historical Collections, State Papers, and Other Authentic Documents* (2 vols., 1792–94) influenced the work of his friend Jeremy Belknap and constituted a significant early attempt to preserve American source materials.

HAZARD, THOMAS ROBINSON (1797–1886), Rhode Island agriculturist generally called "Shepherd Tom" because of his sheep-raising. This and his textile manufacturing were so successful that at 43 he retired from business, moved to an estate near Newport, and devoted the remainder of his life to spiritualism, to a variety of reforms that included better asylums for the poor and insane, abolition of capital punishment, antislavery, pacifism, and feminism, and to antiquarianism. His writings include *Recollections of Olden Times* (1879) and *The Jonny-Cake Letters* (1882). This collection, enlarged as *The Jonny-Cake Papers of "Shepherd Tom"* (1915), recounts Yankee folklore of Rhode Island in a whimsical fashion.

Hazard of New Fortunes, *A,* novel by Howells, ♦ published in 1890. Basil March also figures in *Their Wedding Journey* (1871), *An Open-Eyed Conspiracy* (1897), and *Their Silver Wedding Journey* (1899).

Basil March becomes editor of a magazine promoted by slangy, affable little Fulkerson and financed by Dryfoos, a farmer who has become a millionaire through the discovery of natural gas on his farm and who backs the magazine in order to give practical business experience to his son Conrad. March engages on his staff a German socialist, Lindau, whose point of view antagonizes Dryfoos. The capitalist orders March to discharge Lindau, but March refuses, and Fulkerson sides with him. During a strike of streetcar employees, Conrad is killed and Lindau is fatally injured while trying to pacify the strikers. Prostrated by the death of his son, Dryfoos magnanimously provides for Lindau's funeral, and sells the magazine to Fulkerson and March.

HAZZARD, Shirley (1931–   ), Australian-born author, in foreign service and later the United Nations, settled in New York City. Her books, in addition to *Defeat of an Ideal* (1973), condemning the U.N., and *Countenance of Truth* (1990), concerning the U.N. and the Kurt Waldheim case, include *The Evening of the Holiday* (1966), a novella about an unhappy romance, set in Italy; *People in Glass Houses* (1967), subtitled "Portraits from Organization Life," witty views of fictional bureaucrats; *The Bay of Noon* (1970), a novel about romantic entanglements in Italy; *The Transit of Venus* (1980), a novel treating the complex emotional relationships experienced by two expatriate Australian sisters; and a volume of stories, *Cliffs of Fall* (1963), collected from *The New Yorker*. She was married to Francis Steegmuller.

He and She, play by Rachel Crothers,♦ produced in 1911 as *The Herfords* and under its present title in 1920. It was published in 1921.

Tom and Ann Herford, both sculptors, are happily married until she wins a prize for which they both competed, and it becomes obvious that she is more interested in her career than in her home. While they are arguing, their young daughter Millicent arrives and announces that she has run away from boarding school to marry a chauffeur. Ann, realizing her responsibilities, prepares to take Millicent to Europe, and resigns her commission in favor of Tom.

Headless Horseman, see *Legend of Sleepy Hollow*.

Headsman, The; or, The Abbaye des Vignerons, romance by Cooper,♦ published in 1833.

During the early 18th century, Balthazar, headsman or executioner of Berne, conceals the identity of his supposed son Sigismund so that the youth may not be forced to continue the family's hereditary profession. Sigismund loves Adelheid, daughter of Baron Melchior de Willading, but, when questioned concerning his birth, he reveals his secret. Adelheid continues to love him, and it is later disclosed, when Balthazar is unjustly accused of murder, that Sigismund is actually the son of the Doge of Genoa, having been stolen as a child.

HEARN, Lafcadio (1850–1904), born in the Ionian Islands, of Irish-Greek parentage, was educated in France and England, and emigrated to the U.S. in 1869. Handicapped by poverty, semi-blindness, a morbid inferiority complex, and a scandal resulting from his relations with a mulatto woman, he had an unsuccessful career as a journalist in Cincinnati, and then lived for a time in New Orleans, where he wrote "Fantastics," a series of weird newspaper sketches. His first book, *One of Cleopatra's Nights* (1882), stories translated from Gautier, was followed by *Stray Leaves from Strange Literature* (1884), reconstructing fantastically beautiful stories from the exotic literature which fascinated him; *Gombo Zhêbes* (1885), a collection of Negro-French proverbs; and *Some Chinese Ghosts* (1887), beautifully polished Oriental legends. After a visit to Grand Isle, he wrote *Chita: A Memory of Last Island*♦ (1889). *Two Years in the French West Indies* (1890) contains sketches based on his residence in Martinique (1887–89), from which he also drew material for his novel *Youma*♦ (1890). During a brief residence in New York, he wrote *Karma,* a weak novel, and did some hackwork that enabled him to go to Japan (1890). There he spent the rest of his life, marrying the daughter of a Samurai family, and becoming a Japanese citizen under the name Koizumi Yakumo. As a schoolteacher in the small town of Matsue he observed the feudal customs described in his *Glimpses of Unfamiliar Japan* (1894). For almost ten years he occupied the chair of English literature at the Imperial University of Tokyo, and his lectures were posthumously published from verbatim transcripts made by his students. During this period he wrote 12 books on the life, customs, flora, and fauna of his adopted country. His stories of Japan were frequently set in the form of essays, and among the volumes in which he best catches the mood of the place and the people, or in which he most successfully treats the supernatural, are *Out of the East* (1895), *Kokoro* (1896), *In Ghostly Japan* (1899), *Shadowings* (1900), *A Japanese Miscellany* (1901), *Kottō* (1902), *Kwaidan* (1904), and *The Romance of the Milky Way* (1905). *Japan: An Attempt at Interpretation* (1904) was the summation of his sympathetic and acute observations on the mind and the soul of the people among whom he had chosen to live.

HEARST, William Randolph (1863–1951), son of George Hearst (1820–91), California mine operator and U.S. senator, was born in San Francisco, and assumed charge of his father's San Francisco *Examiner* in 1887. Beginning with this paper and the New York *Morning Journal,* he built up a powerful chain of newspapers throughout the U.S. and eventually became ruler of a domain, with headquarters on his San Simeon estate, that has included such properties as motion-picture and radio companies, some 30 newspapers with a circulation of many millions, and a number of popular magazines, including *Harper's Bazaar, Hearst's International-Cosmopolitan, Good Housekeeping,* and *Town and Country.* He served as a congressman from New York (1903–7), and was an unsuccessful candidate for mayor and governor on the Democratic ticket. He lived his life in a flamboyant style, and his newspapers reflected his views. They were often attacked as "yellow journalism" because of his sensational handling of news, including strident advocacy of war with Spain (1897–98) and later with Mexico, an extreme nationalism, and vigorous opposition to radical movements.

***Heart Is a Lonely Hunter,** The,* novel by Carson McCullers,♦ published in 1940.

In a small Georgia town, an intelligent and sympathetic deaf-mute, John Singer, is lonely and saddened when his only friend, another mute, Spiros Antonapoulos, is committed to an institution. He takes a room in the Kelly family home and eats his meals at Biff Brannon's café, but lives only for visits to Antonapoulos, the one person with whom he can communicate. Biff, a warm-hearted, magnanimous, impotent man, and Jake Blount, an intense, alcoholic wanderer, obsessed by a desire to convert others to Marxism, both feel that Singer somehow has a superhuman understanding that brings calm. They visit Singer in his room to tell him their innermost feelings, as do Mick Kelly, a sensitive adolescent tomboy with an intense spiritual hunger, and Dr. Benedict Copeland, an intellectual black man passionately devoted to the improvement of his people's lot. Singer becomes an important and mysterious figure in the town, as "everyone described the mute as he wished him to be," although he himself feels isolated. Each of his admirers meets tragedy: Dr. Copeland is jailed and savagely beaten by the sheriff when he protests the cruel mistreatment of his imprisoned son; Blount's "do nothing theories" and inability to cope meaningfully with life are shown up by the embittered Copeland; and Mick and Biff suffer when her brother accidentally fractures the skull of his niece. Soon after, Singer discovers that Antonapoulos is dead and, considering himself an exile without hope, he commits suicide. Confused and deeply saddened, each of Singer's four admirers feels the loss of peace and understanding he seemed to offer. Mick, having had her first sexual experience, leaves school to help support her parents, and feels cheated of her dreams, of an "inner room" of music and hopes. Blount, hunted by the police as an agitator, leaves the city, again a wanderer. The sick Dr. Copeland grieves for the only white man who had been his friend. Biff, now completely alone, suspended between the past and the future, between "radiance and darkness," tries to compose himself to face the unknown.

***Heart of the West,** short stories by W. S. Porter.♦

***Hearth and Home** (1868–75), weekly journal of agricultural information and literature for the rural home. The editors included D.G. Mitchell, Harriet Beecher Stowe, Mary Mapes Dodge, the two Egglestons, and Frank Stockton. In time the magazine became almost completely a literary miscellany, and, in addition to the serialization of *The Hoosier Schoolmaster* and other writings of its editors, printed contributions from E.E. Hale, Rebecca Davis, E.P. Roe, and Louisa May Alcott.

***Hearts of Oak,** play by David Belasco♦ and James A. Herne.♦

HEATH, JAMES EWELL (1792–1862), Virginia author and public official, whose books included *Edge-Hill* (1828), a romance of plantation life, and a comedy, *Whigs and Democrats* (1839).

***Heathen Chinee,** The,* see *Plain Language from Truthful James.*

HEAT-MOON, WILLIAM LEAST [TROGDON, WILLIAM] (1939–   ), memoirist. Trogdon graduated from the University of Missouri and taught English at Stephens College before in 1978 undertaking an odyssey in an RV around the country on secondary roads. He took extensive notes, counterpointing meditations on a struggling marriage. Out of this experience he made *Blue Highways* (1982), a bestselling book akin to Steinbeck's *Travels with Charley,* though darker in tone. After an interval of silence, Trogdon published *PrairyErth (A Deep Map)* (1991), a close inspection of rural Chase County, Kansas, including geologic history, people, flora, and fauna in affectionate and exhaustive detail.

***Heaven's My Destination,** novel by Thornton Wilder.♦

HECHT, ANTHONY [EVAN] (1923–   ), New York-born poet, whose infrequent volumes are carefully crafted, formal in manner but moving in their treatment of personal and philosophic subject matter. *A Summoning of Stones* (1954) was in part reprinted with new poems in *The Hard Hours* (1967, Pulitzer Prize). Other collections include *The Seven Deadly Sins* (1958), *A Bestiary* (1960), *Millions of Strange Shadows* (1977), *The Venetian Vespers* (1979), and *The Transparent Man* (1989). *Collected Earlier Poems* was also published in 1989. His skill in metrics and his wit are seen in *Jiggery-Pokery: A Compendium of Double Dactyls* (1967), written and edited with John Hollander. He also translated Aeschylus' *Seven Against Thebes* (1973) with Helen Bacon. *Obbligati* (1986) collects ten of his essays on poets from Shakespeare to his own contemporaries. In 1981 he was awarded a Bollingen Prize.

HECHT, BEN (1894–1964), born in New York, reared in Wisconsin, after refusing to go to college became in turn an acrobat, a violinist, and a newspaper reporter. As a bohemian member of the literary group that flourished in Chicago just after World War I, he became known as an ironical, cynical, ultra-romantic writer, who was variously dubbed an "intellectual mountebank" and "Pagliacci of the Fire Escape." He drew attention to himself in various ways, such as having a well-publicized literary feud with his friend Maxwell Bodenheim, with whom he wrote *The Master Poisoner* (1918) and other plays; publishing the *Chicago Literary Times* (1923–24), a gaudy iconoclastic little magazine; and vociferously espousing the cause of art-for-art's-sake. His attitude of mind was well revealed in his novels *Erik Dorn*♦ (1921) and *Gargoyles* (1922). *1001 Afternoons in Chicago* (1922), *Tales of Chicago Streets* (1924), and *1001 Afternoons in New York* (1941) are romantic stories of city life. *Fantazius Mallare* (1922), a book with a decadent erotic theme, was followed by several other novels: *The Florentine Dagger* (1923); *Humpty Dumpty* (1924); *The Kingdom of Evil* (1924); *Count Bruga* (1926) and *A Jew in Love* (1930), both about Maxwell Bodenheim; and *The Sensualists* (1959); and by collections of short stories: *Broken Necks* (1924), *The Champion from Far Away* (1931), and *A Book of Miracles* (1939). *Collected Stories* was published in 1945. *A Guide for the Bedevilled* (1944) is a study of anti-Semitism, and *Perfidy* (1961) is an angry attack on ostensible compromises in the creation of Israel. In 1928 was produced his play *The Front Page,* written in collaboration with Charles MacArthur,♦ a tough, swift-moving portrayal of newspaper life. His other plays include *20th Century* (1932); *The Great Magoo* (1933), written with Gene Fowler; *To Quito and Back* (1937); and *Ladies and Gentlemen* (1939), written with MacArthur, with whom he also wrote motion-picture scripts. *A Child of the Century* (1954) is his autobiography; *Gaily, Gaily* (1963) recalls rowdy, pre-World War I Chicago; and *Letters from Bohemia* (1964) contains recollections of and letters from Sherwood Anderson, Bodenheim, Mencken, and other friends.

HECKER, ISAAC THOMAS (1819–88), born in New York, early came under the influence of Orestes Brownson, visited Brook Farm and Fruitlands, and was intimate with the Transcendentalists. He entered the Roman Catholic Church (1844) and was expelled from the Redemptorist order 13 years later, but was permitted by the pope to found the Paulist Fathers, of which he was the superior until his death. *The Catholic World,* an eclectic monthly magazine that he founded (1865) and edited until his death, is still in existence, having become a bimonthly and changing its name to *New Catholic World* in 1971.

HECKEWELDER, JOHN GOTTLIEB ERNESTUS (1743–1823), was brought from England to America at the age of 11. He became a Moravian missionary to the Indians on the Susquehanna and aided in their removal to Ohio and Canada. His wide knowledge of the Indians is recorded in his *Account of the History, Manners, and Customs of the Indian Nations Who Once Inhabited Pennsylvania* (1819) and *A Narrative of the Mission of the United Brethren Among the Delaware and Mohegan Indians* (1820). Cooper drew strongly on these works, and was criticized for following the missionary's partiality for the Delaware, hatred of the Iroquois, and generally romantic interpretation.

HEDGE, FREDERIC HENRY (1805–90), Unitarian clergyman in Massachusetts, Maine, and Rhode Island, professor in Harvard Divinity School, is noted for helping to bring Emerson and other Transcendentalists the knowledge of German idealistic philosophy that he had acquired abroad. The Transcendental Club♦ was sometimes called the Hedge Club. His many books include *Prose Writers of Germany* (1848), *Hymns for the Church of Christ* (1853), *Ways of the Spirit and Other Essays* (1877), *Atheism in Philosophy* (1884), *Hours with German Classics* (1886), *Martin Luther and Other Essays* (1888), and many sermons, orations, and translations, some of the latter included in *Specimens of Foreign Standard Literature* (14 vols., 1838–42), edited with George Ripley.

HEGAN, ALICE, see *Rice, Alice.*

HEGGEN, THOMAS [ORLO] (1919–49), on the basis of naval service in the Pacific during World War II and a knowledge of the interests of a mass audience gained through his prior career with *Reader's Digest,* wrote the very popular novel *Mister Roberts* (1946), about the dull day-to-day life aboard a cargo ship, its stupid captain, and its decent cargo officer. It was also successfully adapted as a play.

Heidenmauer, The; or, The Benedictines, romance by Cooper,♦ published in 1832.

In 16th-century Bavaria the Benedictines of the abbey of Limburg strive to maintain their temporal power in the town of Dürkheim, which they finally lose to the feudal lord Count Emich of Leiningen-Hartenburg. This theme, showing a society emerging from domination by Catholicism and superstition to secular rule and critical Protestantism, is amplified by a subplot dealing with the love and marriage of the count's forester, Berchtold Hintermayer, with Meta Frey, daughter of a leading citizen of Dürkheim. The title refers to a ruined fortress near the town, home of the hermit Baron Odo von Ritterstein, once the fiancé of Meta's mother.

HEINLEIN, ROBERT A[NSON] (1907–88), graduated from Annapolis, served in the navy (1929–34), and did graduate work in physics at the University of California, Los Angeles, before beginning his career as a writer of science fiction whose first book was published in 1947. He became a master of the field in technique and output, producing 64 books, of which over 45 were best-sellers. His books were translated into 29 languages. His very popular and influential works deal mostly with the future, outer space, and eugenic breeding of humans but are also often tinged with mysticism and marked by sociopolitical views variously called rightist or anarchistic. His Future History, composed of relatively short fictive sketches, includes *The Man Who Sold the Moon* (1950), *The Green Hills of Earth* (1951), *Revolt in 2100* (1953), *Methuselah's Children* (1958), and *Orphans of the Sky* (1963). Of his numerous longer novels the most popular is *Stranger in a Strange Land* (1961), whose hero is a human born of space travelers from earth and raised by Martians. He is brought to the totalitarian post-World War III world that is in many ways depicted as a satire of the U.S. in the 1960s, marked by repressiveness in sexual morality and religion. The plot, which tells how the heroic stranger creates a Utopian society in which people preserve their individuality but share a brotherhood of community, made Heinlein and his novel cult objects for young people dedicated to a counterculture. Heinlein continued to publish prolifically other novels, including *The Moon Is a Harsh Mistress* (1967), *Time Enough for Love* (1973), *The Number of the Beast* (1980), and *Friday* (1982); works of nonfiction; many books for children; stories for magazines not collected into volumes; and film and television scripts.

HELD, JOHN, JR. (1889–1958), illustrator known for his woodcuts and drawings imitating this technique, which burlesqued the style and subject matter of the 1890s. Both as author and as artist, in such books as *Grim Youth* (1930) and *The Flesh Is Weak* (1931), he was considered a leading interpreter of the younger generation of the jazz age.

Helen's Babies, novel by John Habberton. ♦

Helicon Home Colony, communal experiment founded at Englewood, N.J. (1906), by Upton Sinclair♦ and some 40 associates, mostly young married writers. The mothers cooperated in the care of their children, and the household workers, one of whom was Sinclair Lewis, were treated as equals by the residents. Distinguished visitors included John Dewey, William James, and Emma Goldman. The project suffered much vilification in the press and was abandoned (1907) when the main building was destroyed by fire.

Hell-Bent fer Heaven, play by Hatcher Hughes, ♦ produced and published in 1924, and won a Pulitzer Prize.

HELLER, JOSEPH (1923–), New York author who served in the air force in World War II.

Later he received an A.B. from New York University, an M.A. from Columbia, studied at Oxford, and taught briefly before writing *Catch-22* ♦ (1961). This grotesquely comic tale of a madcap bombardier's resistance to his fanatic commander's ambition for promotion at the expense of his American squadron on a Mediterranean island satirizes military illogicality and glorification. It became enormously popular, particularly among younger readers during the Vietnam era, and its title became a catch phrase. Heller's next novel, *Something Happened* (1974), is a dark view of the life of a business executive, disgusted with what he does and is. *Good as Gold* (1979) is a long novel more in the comic vein of his first in its farcical treatment of Jewish family life and of the Washington political scene. *God Knows* (1984) is a lively first-person novel of the Biblical David. *Picture This* (1988) is a novel treating Rembrandt's painting of Aristotle contemplating the bust of Homer that contrasts two eras. In 1994 appeared *Closing Time,* a sequel to *Catch-22,* with Yossarian, twice divorced, living alone in Manhattan with the knowledge that this time he can in no way outwit death. The novel's main character, however, is one Sammy Singer, whose life affirms marriage as the best of all possible worlds. He collaborated with Speed Vogel on *No Laughing Matter* (1986), a serious treatment, though sometimes humorous, of Heller's sudden paralytic sickness. Much earlier he wrote two plays, *We Bombed in New Haven* (1968) and *Clevinger's Trial* (1974).

Hell-Fire Club, popular name of the Couranteers (1721–24), a Boston literary coterie, including Benjamin Franklin and William Douglass, which frequented the office of James Franklin, and contributed to his *New England Courant.* It received its name from the Mathers, who accused it of resembling the notorious London organizations of that name. Actually, it brought the spirit of the coffeehouses to Boston, and opposed reactionary tendencies.

HELLMAN, LILLIAN (1905–84), New York dramatist whose plays include *The Children's Hour* (1934), a tragedy of a malicious child accusing the owners of her boarding school of lesbianism; *Days To Come* (1936), about a strike; *The Little Foxes* (1939), about a reactionary Southern family's struggle to retain wealth and power despite internal feuds and the encroachments of modern society; *Watch on the Rhine* (1941), about an anti-Nazi in the U.S., with his American wife, who is forced to murder to fight against Hitlerism; *The Searching Wind* (1944), about the family of a former U.S. ambassador in wartime Washington and prewar Europe; *Another Part of the Forest* (1946); *The Autumn Garden* (1951), about middle-aged people trying to recapture a sense of youth; and *Toys in the Attic* (1960), set in New Orleans and treating the theme of miscegenation. *My Mother, My Father and Me* (1963) is an adaptation of the novel *How Much?* by Burt Blechman. She collaborated with Richard Wilbur on the comic opera *Candide* (1957), based on Voltaire's work. Her memoirs appeared as *An Unfinished Woman* (1969), emphasizing her personal experiences rather than her literary career; *Pentimento* (1973), about interesting persons she knew; *Scoundrel Time* (1976), an account of her experiences and those of friends during the McCarthy era's hunt for "un-American activities," all brought together as *Three* (1979); and *Maybe* (1980).

HELPER, HINTON ROWAN (1829–1909), North Carolina author, spent three years in California during the gold rush, and wrote his impressions in *Land of Gold: Reality Versus Fiction* (1855). He then became interested in the problem of slavery, and wrote *The Impending Crisis of the South: How To Meet It* (1857), discussing the question from an economic point of view and advocating free labor, although only in the interest of the whites, since he despised blacks. Unpopular in the South, this antislavery argument was widely distributed by Republicans and Abolitionists and won Helper the post of U.S. consul at Buenos Aires. After his return (1866), he wrote three passionate books denouncing the very existence of colored races, the first of these being *Nojoque: A Question for a Continent* (1867), a furious satire demanding the extinction of blacks and prophesying a happy "golden age" to be inaugurated by "the total absence of all the swarthy and inferior races of men." He devoted most of the rest of his life to an unsuccessful project that is described in *The Three Americas Railway* (1881).

HELPRIN, MARK (1947–), novelist. A native of Ossining, N.Y., after graduation from Harvard, Helprin served in the Israeli army. His fiction has been called "moral fantasy." *Ellis Island and Other Stories* (1981) mixes realism with fantasy, as do the stories in *A Dove of the East* (1975). *Winter's Tale* (1983) established his reputation. Combining history, myth, and fable, it is a visionary epic of New York City trying to free itself from crime and poverty. *A Soldier of the Great War* (1992) tells of the fantastic adventures—in flashback—of an Italian officer on the Austria-Italy front in World War I. It is a mainly lyrical, sometimes harrowing story told by a narrator, now an old man, to a boy as they trudge from the outskirts of Rome to a small village in the mountains.

HEMINGWAY, ERNEST [MILLER] (1899–1961), born in Illinois, while attending school made frequent hunting and fishing expeditions in northern Michigan, which helped condition his later primitivistic attitude. After working as a Kansas City reporter, he joined a volunteer ambulance unit in France, then transferred to the Italian infantry until the close of World War I, after which he reported battles in the Near East

for the Toronto *Star,* and settled in Paris as a member of the expatriate group.

Influenced by Ezra Pound and particularly by Gertrude Stein, whose style strongly affected him, he published *Three Stories & Ten Poems* (Paris, 1923) and *In Our Time*♦ (U.S., 1925). These early stories already exhibited the attitude of mind and technique for which he later became famous. As the leading spokesman for the "lost generation" he expressed the feelings of a war-wounded people disillusioned by the loss of faith and hope, and so thoroughly defeated by the collapse of former values that, their atrophied nerves not permitting them to attack their betrayers, they could turn only to a stoic acceptance of primal emotions. The stories are mainly concerned with "tough" people, either intelligent men and women who have dropped into an exhausted cynicism, or such primitives as frontiersmen, Indians, and professional athletes, whose essential courage and honesty are implicitly contrasted with the brutality of civilized society. Emotion is held at arm's length; only the bare happenings are recorded, and emphasis is obtained by understatement and spare dialogue.

After Hemingway returned to New York and wrote the lesser satirical novel *The Torrents of Spring* (1926), he carried the style and attitude of his short stories into the novel *The Sun Also Rises*♦ (1926), which tells of the moral collapse of a group of expatriated Americans and Englishmen, broken by the war, who turn toward escape through all possible violent diversions. Success in fictional craftsmanship and in portraying the mind of an era was again achieved in *A Farewell to Arms*♦ (1929), the poignant love story of an English nurse and an American ambulance lieutenant during the war. Besides further distinguished collections of short stories, *Men Without Women*♦ (1927) and *Winner Take Nothing*♦ (1933), he wrote only two lesser books during the next few years, although his work continued to exercise a great influence on the literature of the period. *Death in the Afternoon*♦ (1932), a book on bullfighting, and *Green Hills of Africa* (1935), an account of big-game hunting with digressions on literary matters, show a further cultivation of the primitive and brutal levels, contrasted with the hollow culture that had cheated his generation.

In *To Have and Have Not*♦ (1937), Hemingway for the first time showed an interest in a possible solution of social problems through collective action. This attitude continued in newspaper articles from Spain about its civil war, whose espionage was the subject of his realistic play, *The Fifth Column,* adapted for the stage (1940) by Benjamin Glazer, and printed in *The Fifth Column and the First Forty-Nine Stories* (1938), in which appeared two of his finest stories, "The Short Happy Life of Francis Macomber"♦ and "The Snows of Kilimanjaro."♦ *For Whom the Bell Tolls*♦ (1940), his longest novel, on an incident in the Spanish Civil War, has universality in its thesis that the loss of liberty in one place means a loss everywhere. He edited an anthology, *Men at War* (1942), but issued no new novel until *Across the River and into the Trees* (1950), which was considered to show that Hemingway had become bitter and defeatist like his tale's protagonist, an aging colonel. With *The Old Man and the Sea*♦ (1952), a parable of man against nature in a poignant novelette, he recaptured his critical acclaim, recognized in a Nobel Prize (1954).

In his last years he published nothing, and he had been seriously ill for some time before his death as a suicide by gunshot. However, several posthumous works followed, most notably *A Moveable Feast*♦ (1964), sketches of his life and acquaintances in Paris, 1921–1926, and *Islands in the Stream* (1970), a novel in three parts about a painter's unhappy marriage, his affection for his sons, their deaths, his bravery in war, his pleasure in deep-sea fishing, and his loneliness. Another novel, written in the 1940s, edited and published in 1986, *The Garden of Eden,* begins with the honeymoon of an enticing young couple, David and Catherine Bourne, he a good writer, she an heiress, who break up over serious sexual differences. Later compilations include *The Wild Years* (1962), his journalism for the Toronto *Star; By-Lines* (1967), selected journalism of four decades; *The Nick Adams Stories* (1972), eight of them previously unpublished; and three collections of verse, the last and most inclusive being *88 Poems* (1979). *Selected Letters* was issued in 1981.

HENDERSON, ALICE CORBIN (1881–1949), was an editor of *Poetry* (1912–16), and published her first book of poems, *The Spinning Woman of the Sky* (1912). She moved to New Mexico (1916), whose folklore she employed in her poems, *Red Earth* (1920) and *The Sun Turns West* (1933). Her other books include *Adam's Dream and Two Other Miracle Plays for Children* (1907); *The Turquoise Trail* (1928), an anthology of New Mexico poetry; and *Brothers of Light* (1937), an account of the Penitentes.

Henderson the Rain King, novel by Saul Bellow,♦ published in 1959.

Gene Henderson, an intense, vital millionaire, leaves his Connecticut home for Africa in quest of wisdom, and to satisfy his inner voice's cry, "I want, I want." With Romilayu, a loyal guide, he visits the Arnewi, a humane, cattle-loving people suffering from drought. He makes friends with the king Itelo and his aunts, Mtalba and Queen Willatale, serene, wise women, tries to aid them by cleansing the polluted water supply, but accidentally destroys it, and leaves, disgraced and saddened. Traveling to the island of the Wariri, he finds drought again and he wagers the king, Dahfu, there will be no rain, but overwhelmed by a tremendous "wish to *do* something . . . to work the right stitch into the design of destiny

before it was too late," he persuades Dahfu to let him try to move an immense idol, the statue of the goddess of clouds. He succeeds, a deluge follows, and although he is made Sungo, the rain king, he is also delivered into the power of the ruler to whom he lost the bet. From Dahfu he learns the fate of Wariri kings: when one weakens, he is killed and his spirit becomes a lion cub that the king's successor must catch within two years. Dahfu, still in his period of trial, has yet to capture Gmilo, the lion spirit of his father, but his uncle Horko, the Queen Mother, and Bunam, the high priest, force him to his obligation, and in his attempt he is clawed to death. As Sungo, Henderson succeeds Dahfu, into whose tomb he is placed near the cub that symbolizes the late king's spirit. Sure that Horko and Bunam effected Dahfu's death, Henderson and Romilayu escape, taking the cub. His inner voice at last quieted, and with an understanding of himself, Henderson and the cub, named Dahfu, take off for his home, after a life "discontinuous with civilization."

HENDERICK, BURTON J[ESSE] (1870–1949), journalist and historian, whose books include *The Victory at Sea* (1920), written with Admiral William S. Sims, *The Life and Letters of Walter Hines Page* (1922), and *The Training of an American: The Earlier Life and Letters of Walter Hines Page* (1928), all three winning Pulitzer Prizes; *Bulwark of the Republic: A Biography of the Constitution* (1937); *Statesmen of the Lost Cause* (1939); and *Lincoln's War Cabinet* (1946).

HENLEY, BETH (1952–   ), Mississippi-born playwright, attended Southern Methodist University, had her first full-length play, *Crimes of the Heart,* performed (1979) in Louisville, where it won a major local prize, and then, after an off-Broadway production, won a Pulitzer Prize (1980). With Gothic humor it presents the antics of three eccentric sisters in a small Mississippi town. *The Miss Firecracker Contest* (1980), produced in her new home in southern California, concerns other bizarre characters and situations in a small Mississippi town. *Am I Blue,* a one-act play produced in 1982, was written seven years before *Crimes of the Heart,* which was in turn rewritten as *The Wake of Jamey Foster* (1982). These were followed by *The Debutante Ball* (1985), related to a lurid social event and a family background in Mississippi, and *The Lucky Spot* (1986), about a Louisiana gambler, his post-prison wife, and an orphan daughter.

HENNEPIN, LOUIS (1640–1710?), Belgian-born Franciscan friar, came to Canada (1675), and became chaplain of the exploring expedition of La Salle, who detailed him to accompany Aco on the first exploration of the upper Mississippi Valley. Captured in Minnesota by the Sioux, they were rescued by Duluth. After returning to France, Hennepin published a *Déscription de la*

Louisiane (1683, translated 1880), *Nouvelle Décou-verte* (1697, translated 1698), and *Nouveau Voyage* (1698), interesting and important accounts in which, however, he exaggerates his own part in the expedition, which was actually led by Aco. His assertion that they reached the mouth of the Mississippi is unfounded, and his description of the lower river is plagiarized from Membré, a friar who traveled with La Salle.

HENRY, JOSEPH (1797–1878), New York physicist whose electromagnetic experiments and discoveries, independent of and evidently slightly prior to those of Faraday, were the foundation of the development of the telegraph, telephone, radio, and electric motor. He was a professor at the College of New Jersey (1832–46), and director of the Smithsonian Institution (1846–78), which published his *Scientific Writings* (1886).

HENRY, O., pseudonym of W. S. Porter.◆

HENRY, PATRICK (1736–99), Virginia statesman, during the years leading up to the Revolution was a member of the colonial House of Burgesses and of the Continental Congress. His revolutionary speeches were marked by force and sincerity, as in his famous phrases, "Tarquin and Cæsar each had his Brutus, Charles the First his Cromwell, and George the Third may profit by their example. . . . If this be treason, make the most of it!" (speech on the Stamp Act, May 29, 1765, in the Virginia legislature); and "I know not what course others may take, but as for me, give me liberty or give me death!" (speech in the Virginia Convention, March 23, 1775). Outlawed by Lord Dunmore, Henry succeeded him as governor of Virginia (1776–79), when he supported Washington and sent George Rogers Clark on his Northwestern expedition. Although originally a radical, he broke with his friend Jefferson and became a conservative member of the Federalist party. He declined membership in the Constitutional Convention and the U.S. Senate, as well as Washington's offers to appoint him secretary of state and chief justice of the Supreme Court. He was mainly responsible for the drafting of the Bill of Rights. He figures frequently in fiction, e.g. J.E. Cooke's *The Virginia Comedians* and John Erskine's *Give Me Liberty.* William Wirt's adulatory *Life* (1817) did much to ensure his fame for posterity.

Henry Esmond, Esquire, The History of, romance by Thackeray,◆ published in 1852. *The Virginians*◆ is a sequel.

Henry St. John, Gentleman, romance by J.E. Cooke,◆ published in 1859 as a sequel to *The Virginia Comedians.*◆ It was reissued under the title *Bonnybel Vane* (1883).

Set in the Shenandoah Valley at the outbreak of the Revolutionary War, the narrative tells of the hero's love for Bonnybel Vane. Contrasting the Whig and Tory classes, the author shows the changing sentiments of the landholders under the stress of historical events.

HENSON, JOSIAH (1789–1883), black slave who escaped from Maryland to Canada and became a Methodist preacher. He dictated *The Life of Josiah Henson* (1849), to which Harriet Beecher Stowe wrote an introduction. Regarded as a prototype of Uncle Tom, he figures in her *Key to Uncle Tom's Cabin.*

HENTZ, CAROLINE LEE (1800–1856), a New Englander (Massachusetts) who moved south, was a bestselling author of sentimental, domestic novels. She also wrote novels depicting slavery in a happy light, the most popular being *The Planter's Northern Bride* (1854). Another of her commercial successes was *Ernest Linwood* (1856), about the anguish of a young woman married to a pathologically jealous man. Her tales of Southern life include *Linda* (1850), and she also produced collections of tales and tragedies like *De Lara; or, The Moorish Bride* (1831) and *Werdenberg; or, the Forest League* (1832).

HENTZ, NICHOLAS MARCELLUS (1797–1856), French-born novelist, whose best-known work, *Tadeuskund, the Last King of the Lenape* (1825), is a melodramatic tale of the Delaware Indians in the manner of Cooper. He conducted several schools in the South with his wife, Caroline Lee Whiting Hentz.◆

HERBERT, HENRY WILLIAM (1807–58), English-born author and editor, came to New York (1831), where he taught school and edited *The American Monthly Magazine* (1833–35). Besides translating classical literature, he wrote a well-known series of historical romances, including *The Brothers: A Tale of the Fronde* (1835), and, under the pseudonym Frank Forester, wrote sporting manuals and such novels as *My Shooting Box* (1846), *The Deerstalkers* (1849), and *The Quorndon Hounds; or, A Virginian at Melton Mowbray* (1852).

HERBERT, VICTOR (1859–1924), New York composer, cellist, and conductor, was born in Ireland and had a career in Germany before he came to New York (1886) to be first cellist of the Metropolitan Opera. He later wrote two grand operas, the Indian *Natoma* (1911) and *Madeleine* (1914), but his fame is based on his gay and tuneful operettas, which number nearly 40. The most popular American works in this genre, they include *The Fortune Teller* (1898), *Babes in Toyland* (1903), *Mlle. Modiste* (1905), *The Red Mill* (1906), *Naughty Marietta* (1910), and *Eileen* (1917). Some of the songs from these operettas continue to be popular, among them "Ah, Sweet Mystery of Life" and "Gypsy Love Song."

HERBST, JOSEPHINE [FREY] (1892–1969), Iowa-born proletarian author, graduated from the University of California (1918). Her major fiction is a trilogy about an American family, the Trexlers: *Pity Is Not Enough* (1933) tells of a son who loses health, wealth, and faith during the Gilded Age; *The Executioner Waits* (1934) shows the family during the years 1918 to 1929, typifying the era's social conflicts and personal frustrations; and *Rope of Gold* (1939) follows the younger Trexlers through the economic chaos of the 1930s. Other novels include *Nothing Is Sacred* (1928), *Money for Love* (1929), *Satan's Sergeants* (1941), and *Somewhere the Tempest Fell* (1947). *The Unknown Americas* (1939) is a social study of Latin America; *New Green World* (1954) depicts John Bartram and other early American naturalists. *The Starched Blue Sky of Spain* (1991) contains, in the title memoir, an account of her time as a journalist based in Madrid during the Spanish Civil War, and of her friendship with Hemingway, Dos Passos, and others. In the same book she tells of an Iowa childhood in Sioux City and of youthful friendship with Katherine Anne Porter, Ford Madox Ford, and Allen Tate, among others, during Greenwich Village days in New York.

HERFORD, OLIVER (1863–1935), English-born humorist, reared in Boston and educated at Antioch College, in his twenties began to contribute to popular journals, by the turn of the century began to publish his long series of books of prose and verse, many illustrated by his pen-and-ink caricatures. In both media he was an accomplished craftsman possessed of a pleasant wit. His volumes include *The Bashful Earthquake* (1898), *A Child's Primer of Natural History* (1899), *A Little Book of Bores* (1906), *Confessions of a Caricaturist* (1917), *Excuse It, Please* (1929), and *The Deb's Dictionary* (1931). He also wrote plays.

HERGESHEIMER, JOSEPH (1880–1954), born in Philadelphia, began his career as a novelist with *The Lay Anthony* (1914), an idealistic romance, followed by *Mountain Blood* (1915), contrasting the newly rich with the old Virginians of Highland stock. *The Three Black Pennys*♦ (1917) is a portrait of the rise and decline of a family, with a background of the Pennsylvania iron industry. *Gold and Iron* (1918) contains three novelettes, each a character study of a powerful person whose aggression wins him what he desires. In *Java Head*♦ (1919), Hergesheimer turned to historic New England, writing an atmospheric novel concerned with the tragic results of miscegenation, while *Linda Condon*♦ (1919), a romantic character study, marked the end of this period of conscientious work and artistic sincerity. His earlier writing had not always been on the highest level, but now his novels tended to move progressively further toward the artistic shallows of cheap popular fiction. They follow two main lines: that of highly decorated, weak portraits of a futile society, as in *Cytherea* (1922) and *The Party Dress* (1930); and that of romances depending on picturesque settings for their vigor, as in *The Bright Shawl* (1922), set in the West Indies and recalling an incident in Cuba during the Spanish-American War, *Balisand* (1924), dealing with post-Revolutionary Virginia, *Tampico* (1926), a romance set in Mexico, *The Limestone Tree* (1931), concerned with Kentucky pioneers and their descendants, and *The Foolscap Rose* (1934), describing the rise to power of a Pennsylvania family. *The Happy End* (1919) is a book of short stories, of which the best known is "Tol'able David."♦ Hergesheimer also wrote *San Cristóbal de la Habaña* (1920), sketches of the Cuban city; *Quiet Cities* (1928), stories set in the past of nine American cities; *Sheridan* (1931), a biography; *Swords and Roses* (1929), essays on the Civil War; *From an Old House* (1925), an autobiographical narrative; and other fiction, travel accounts, and biography.

HERLIHY, JAMES LEO (1927–   ), Detroit-born author, educated at Black Mountain College, has written novels including *All Fall Down* (1960), depicting the disintegration of a middle-class American family; *Midnight Cowboy* (1965), presenting an ingenuous cowboy who goes to New York City, where he participates in its seamy nightlife and lovingly takes up with a crippled pickpocket; and *The Season of the Witch* (1971), about a young girl who runs away from home and also finds refuge among New York's drifters. He has written plays, including *Blue Denim* (1958), *Crazy October* (1958), and *Stop, You're Killing Me* (1968), and stories collected in *The Sleep of Baby Filbertson* (1959) and *A Story That Ends with a Scream* (1967).

HERNDON, WILLIAM HENRY (1818–91), Kentucky-born lawyer, the junior partner of Lincoln's law firm after 1844 and formally associated with the firm until Lincoln's death. His antislavery views are supposed to have influenced Lincoln, whose political career Herndon is also said to have encouraged. With Jesse W. Weik he wrote *Herndon's Lincoln: The True Story of a Great Life* (3 vols., 1889), noted for new material on Lincoln's early life.

HERNE, JAMES A. (1839–1901), New York actor and playwright, first came into prominence during his association with Belasco in San Francisco. His plays, first published in a collected edition in 1928, include *Margaret Fleming* (1890), a somber, realistic story of marital infidelity; *Shore Acres*♦ (1892), a realistic depiction of New England life; *The Reverend Griffith Davenport*♦ (1899), a Civil War play; and *Sag Harbor*♦ (1899), a reworking of *Hearts of Oak* (1879), originally written with Belasco, a final example of his mastery of homely realism and his break with the old tradition.

Hero, The, play by Gilbert Emery,♦ produced in 1921 and published in Quinn's *Contemporary American Plays* (1923).

HERR, MICHAEL (1940–   ), memoirist, novelist. Herr was a correspondent in Vietnam for *Esquire* magazine. In 1977 he published *Dispatches,* a spare and moving personal narrative considered one of the best accounts of combat by Americans in that war. Herr wrote the narration for the film *Apocalypse Now* and *Walter Winchell: A Novel* (1990), a fictional biography of the journalist famed in the 1930s and '40s, emphasizing his Jewishness and told in form of a screenplay.

HERRICK, ROBERT (1868–1938), born at Cambridge, graduated from Harvard (1890) and served in the English department at the University of Chicago (1893–1923). His first published work, "The Man Who Wins" (1897), is the story of a scientist upon whom family and financial pressures are so great as to exert a kind of deterministic influence, even though he is convinced of man's freedom of will. This novelette was followed by novels that showed his continued concern with contrasts of personal and professional demands but that emphasized individual freedom and moral responsibility opposing a corrupt, materialistic society. Among these are *The Gospel of Freedom* (1898), *The Web of Life* (1900), and *The Real World* (1901). The novels that followed, still primarily concerned with the conflict between the desire for material success and the maintenance of personal integrity, and with the place of women in this society, include some of his most notable writing: *The Common Lot* (1904), in which a young Chicago architect succumbs to the temptation of get-rich-quick methods, building a flimsy tenement that burns and destroys its tenants, but who is saved from moral disintegration by the faith of his wife; *The Memoirs of an American Citizen* (1905), the story of an unscrupulous industrialist; *The Master of the Inn* (1908), a novelette showing the effects of modern city life on physical and mental health; and *Together* (1908), an analysis of modern marriage. *A Life for a Life* (1910) is a novel of mysticism and muckraking about the fight against a power trust, but in *The Healer* (1911), *His Great Adventure* (1913), and *One Woman's Life* (1913), Herrick returned to his preoccupation with problems of personal relations in a hostile, complex world. *Clark's Field* (1914) is about the conflicts over the control and use of a valuable city lot; *Homely Lilla* (1923) and *Waste* (1924) are pessimistic studies of character; *Chimes* (1926) is a satirical novel about the big-business methods of a university; *The End of Desire* (1932) is about the belated love affair of two professional people; and *Sometime* (1933), a satir-

ical Utopian narrative. In these and in his several collections of short stories, Herrick frequently reveals the workings of industrialism, graft, and the disorders of modern civilization, but he rises above muckraking through his capacious, humane, and critical attitude. He treats literary structure much as he does social structure, denying and rejecting it, yet fails to create an adequate substitute, so that his books generally lack unity.

HERSEY, JOHN [RICHARD] (1914–93), born in Tianjin, China, of American missionary parents, was educated in China, the U.S. (Yale, 1936), and England. He was Sinclair Lewis's secretary (1937), became a correspondent for *Time,* and wrote books about events in World War II: *Men on Bataan* (1942), *Into the Valley* (1943), and *Hiroshima* (1946). His novels, also using a documentary technique, include *A Bell for Adano*♦ (1944, Pulitzer Prize), about the early days of Allied rule in a Sicilian village; *The Wall* (1950; dramatized, 1961, by Millard Lampell), about the ill-fated uprising in Warsaw's ghetto against the Nazis; *The Marmot Drive* (1953), a symbolic tale of depraved New Englanders ridding a valley of woodchucks; *A Single Pebble* (1956), contrasting Occidental and Oriental ways of life in a story about an American engineer in China; *The War Lover* (1959), an antiwar appeal in the tale of a U.S. pilot in World War II who becomes enamored of his experiences; *The Child Buyer* (1960), a satirical parable about modern education, which tells of a governmental buyer of brilliant children later used as thinking machines, dramatized by Paul Shyre (1964); *White Lotus* (1965), a parable of race relations, treating a mythical Oriental land in which white people are enslaved; *Too Far To Walk* (1966), a tract-like tale of New England college students self-indulgently seeking experience; *Under the Eye of the Storm* (1967), a symbolic tale of two couples aboard the boat *Harmony* as a hurricane sweeps them to sea; *The Conspiracy* (1972), an epistolary telling of the Pisonian uprising against Nero; *My Petition for More Space* (1974), the attempt of a man to gain better living conditions in a future overpopulated and overregulated U.S.; *The Walnut Door* (1977), treating two young people caught in the failure of their idealism; and *The Call* (1985), about an innocent young American boy who becomes a missionary in China. *Fling* (1990) collects 11 short stories. *Here To Stay* (1963) collects *Hiroshima* and eight other "studies in human tenacity." Later nonfiction includes *The Algiers Motel Incident* (1968), about an episode in the Detroit racial riots of 1967; *Letter to the Alumni* (1970), a discussion of dissidence and other problems of students at Yale, where he was affiliated with the faculty; *The President* (1975), an account of a week spent with Gerald Ford, revised, with a profile of Truman, as *Aspects of the Presidency* (1980); and *Blues* (1987), treating angling for bluefish off Cape Cod. *Life Sketches* (1989) collects some brief published pieces. *Key West Tales* (1994) prints 15 short stories completed shortly before the author's death.

Herzog, novel by Saul Bellow,♦ published in 1964.

Moses Herzog, a professor of history in New York City, undergoes a crisis when his wife Madeline divorces him. To find surcease he goes to Martha's Vineyard and occupies himself composing letters in his mind and on paper, addressed to friends and public figures, living and dead, on issues that plague him. Told that Madeline and her lover, Valentine Gersbach, once Herzog's best friend, are neglecting his daughter June, he rushes to Chicago to get custody of the girl and even plans to murder his former wife and one-time friend. Serio-comic misadventures frustrate his plans, and he goes back to Massachusetts "pretty well satisfied to be, to be just as it is willed . . ." with "no messages for anyone."

Hester Prynne, see *Scarlet Letter.*

HEWAT, ALEXANDER (*c.*1745–1829), Scottish-born Presbyterian clergyman, emigrated to South Carolina (1763), where he remained as a Loyalist until the outbreak of the Revolutionary War. He wrote *An Historical Account of the Rise and Progress of the Colonies of South Carolina and Georgia* (2 vols., 1779), interspersing social and natural history with a political narrative. David Ramsay, who declared that Hewat's Tory bias rendered untrustworthy the account of the Revolutionary background, used the rest of the history as a source of his own work.

HEWITT, JAMES (1770–1827), born in England, came to New York in 1792, where he became a conductor, instrumentalist, and composer, after 1812 continuing these activities in Boston. His compositions include sentimental songs; piano sonatas; program pieces for orchestra; and operas, of which *Tammany or the Indian Chief* (1794), with a libretto by Anne Julia Hatton, was one of the earliest U.S. operas.

Heyliger, DOLPH, see *Bracebridge Hall.*

HEYWARD, DuBOSE (1885–1940), South Carolina author, began his career with *Carolina Chansons* (1922), poems written with Hervey Allen, followed by his own poems in *Skylines and Horizons* (1924). He is best known for his novel about blacks in Charleston, *Porgy*♦ (1925), whose dramatic version, written with his wife Dorothy, won a Pulitzer Prize and was made into an opera by George Gershwin, as *Porgy and Bess* (1935). *Mamba's Daughters* (1929), another novel about the life of blacks, was also dramatized by the author and his wife (1939). His other works include the poems in *Jasbo Brown* (1931), and the novels *Peter Ashley* (1932), about South Carolina before the Civil War, and *Star Spangled Virgin* (1939),

dealing with the effects of the New Deal program on the population of the Virgin Islands.

HIAWATHA (*fl.c.*1570), Indian statesman and legislator, probably born a Mohawk, was one of the medicine men responsible for organizing the Iroquois confederacy. Schoolcraft and others recorded legends about him. Longfellow used his name only, not his personality or deeds.

Hiawatha, The Song of, narrative poem by Longfellow♦ in unrhymed trochaic tetrameter, published in 1855. Its novel and facile meter has led to many parodies and imitations. The meter derives from the Finnish epic *Kalevala,* which the poem resembles in spirit as well as in several striking passages. Among its sources of information are the works of Schoolcraft, Heckewelder, and Catlin. It is the subject of a series of Currier and Ives prints and has been set to music.

Hiawatha is reared by his grandmother, Nokomis, daughter of the Moon, among the Ojibway on the southern shore of Lake Superior. He learns the language of the birds and animals, secures magic mittens that will crush rocks and magic moccasins that enable him to take mile-long strides, and he seeks vengeance on his father, Mudjekeewis, the West Wind, for a wrong committed against his mother, Wenonah. The fight ends in a reconciliation, and Hiawatha returns as the defender and civilizer of his people. Later he defeats Mondamin, the Corn Spirit, from whose buried body springs the maize, after which he builds a birchbark canoe, has a contest with Nahma, the sturgeon, who swallows both canoe and warrior, and destroys Pearl-Feather, sender of disease and death. The youth then marries Minnehaha, lovely daughter of an arrow-maker of the once hostile Dakotah. The wedding feast and Song of the Evening Star inaugurate an idyllic time of peace and culture, over which Hiawatha rules until the death of his friends, Chibiabos the musician and Kwasind the strong man. Although he kills Pau-Puk-Keewis, who had insulted him, famine and fever visit the people and claim Minnehaha. Golden swarms of bees appear as forerunners of the whites, whose coming Hiawatha prophesied. Telling his people to heed a missionary offering a new religion, he departs for the Isles of the Blest in Keewaydin to rule the kingdom of the Northwest Wind.

HICKOK, WILD BILL, sobriquet of James Butler Hickok (1837–76), Illinois-born scout, stagecoach driver, and frontier marshal in Kansas. He had many encounters with desperadoes, and his name is famous in frontier tales. He toured the East with Buffalo Bill (1872–73), and was murdered at Deadwood, S.D.

HICKS, ELIAS (1748–1830), Quaker preacher whose liberal opposition to evangelical doctrines led to a separation (1827) of the Quakers♦ into

Hicksites and Orthodox Quakers. His doctrines, closely approaching Unitarian views, seemed to undervalue the Scriptures in emphasizing the "Inward Light." His *Journal* was published in 1832; *The Quaker* (4 vols., 1827–28) contains his sermons. The Hicksites founded Swarthmore College.

HICKS, GRANVILLE (1901–82), born in New Hampshire, graduated from Harvard (1923), wrote *Eight Ways of Looking at Christianity* (1926), and taught at Smith College and Rensselaer Polytechnic Institute. A leading Communist critic and editor of *The New Masses,* he wrote a Marxist interpretation of American literature since the Civil War, *The Great Tradition* (1933). With John Stuart he wrote a biography of John Reed (1936), he was appointed a Fellow in U.S. History at Harvard (1938), and with Ella Winter he edited the *Letters of Lincoln Steffens* (1938). In an autobiographical work, *I Like America* (1938), he explained his position as a Communist critic of the contemporary scene. *Figures of Transition* (1939), published the year he resigned from the Communist party, is a Marxist study of British literature at the end of the 19th century. His novels are *The First To Awaken* (1940), written with Richard M. Bennett, about a New Hampshire man, anesthetized in 1940, who wakes a century later to find revolutionary social and industrial improvements; *Only One Storm* (1942), about a New Englander who weathers a storm of intellectual doubt; and *Behold Trouble* (1944), about a wartime conscientious objector. *Small Town* (1946) is nonfiction, and *Where We Came Out* (1954) describes the appeal of, and disillusionment with, communism. He wrote essays titled *Literary Horizons* (1970) and collected his articles from *The New Masses* (1974). *Part of the Truth* (1965) is his autobiography.

HIGGINS, GEORGE V. (1939–   ), novelist. As a former assistant district attorney, Higgins brings a special focus to his novels about the criminal justice system. *The Friends of Eddie Coyle* (1971) remains his strongest book in a prolific output. In it, Higgins makes the criminal underside of Boston live in the character of Coyle, a born loser. Written entirely in riveting dialogue, this novel is a compelling study of motive. Some of Higgins's other works are *Digger's Game* (1973), *Cogan's Trade* (1974), *The Patriot Game* (1982), and *Trust* (1990).

HIGGINSON, FRANCIS (1586–1630), English nonconformist clergyman, emigrated to Salem (1629), where he was elected pastor, but died from the hardships of the winter. Part of his journal was published in England as *New-Englands Plantation* (1630), and the complete journal in the *Life* (1891) by T. W. Higginson.

HIGGINSON, THOMAS WENTWORTH (1823–1911), born at Cambridge, graduated from Har-

vard (1841) and Harvard Divinity School, and became a Unitarian minister. During the Civil War, he was colonel of the first regiment of black soldiers, and his war experiences are described in *Army Life in a Black Regiment* (1870). After being wounded, he retired to Newport, later returning to Cambridge to devote himself to writing, teaching, and social reform, being particularly interested in equal rights for blacks and in the woman suffrage movement. His books include *Malbone* (1869), a novel; sketches, including *Oldport Days* (1873) and *Old Cambridge* (1899); the lives of Whittier (1902) and Longfellow (1902) for the Men of Letters series; biographies of Margaret Fuller (1884) and of his ancestor, Francis Higginson (1891); and an autobiographical account, *Cheerful Yesterdays* (1898), valuable for its information about his contemporaries. Higginson was the first to encourage Emily Dickinson, although he tended to "correct" her poems. He edited two volumes of her verse with Mabel L. Todd (1890–91).

HIGHSMITH, PATRICIA (1921–95), author of very popular mystery novels and comparable short stories produced nearly annually since her first novel of mystery and intrigue, *Strangers on a Train* (1950).

HIJUELOS, OSCAR (1952–   ), born in New York City of Cuban parents, graduated from the City College of New York and became a writer. His second novel, *The Mambo Kings Play Songs of Love* (1989), treats two Castillo brothers who come from Havana to stardom in New York during a period of popularity of mambo music. It won a Pulitzer Prize.

HILDRETH, RICHARD (1807–65), Massachusetts historian, author, and jurist, whose most famous work is a *History of the United States* (6 vols., 1849–52), which discusses the subject, with a Federalist bias, down to 1821. In reply to those who objected to the lack of philosophy in his works, he wrote a *Theory of Politics* (1853), setting forth an economic interpretation of history based on the ideas of Robert Owen. His novel *The Slave; or, Memoirs of Archy Moore* (1836), republished under the titles *the White Slave* and *Archy Moore,* enjoyed great popularity and is said to have been the first antislavery novel. It is a romantic recital of the adventures of an octoroon slave who escapes from a Virginia plantation and eventually becomes the commander of a British privateer in the War of 1812.

HILL, GEORGE HANDEL (1809–49), comedian popularly known as Yankee Hill, because of his acting of Yankee parts in such plays as Woodworth's *The Forest Rose* and J. S. Jones's *The People's Lawyer.* As his fame increased, he acted not only in his native Boston, but throughout the East and abroad. To capitalize on his popularity a publisher concocted *Hill's Yankee Story Teller's Own Book* (1836), and an editor created *Life and Recollections of Yankee Hill* (1850).

HILL, JOE (1879–1915), balladeer, labor organizer. The folksong "I dreamed I saw Joe Hill last night/Alive as you or me" celebrates this Swedish immigrant's martyrdom. As a member of the Industrial Workers of the World—the Wobblies—from 1910 until his death, he composed songs for the movement, including "The Preacher and the Slave," with the jeering line "You'll get pie in the sky when you die." He was, labor legend has it, framed for a grocery store robbery and murder, and was in part executed by firing squad in Utah. His guilt or innocence, like the later case of Sacco and Vanzetti, has been a subject of debate. His final words to his colleague Big Bill Haywood, another labor martyr, "Don't waste any time in mourning. Organize!," have enshrined him in the American labor movement.

HILLHOUSE, JAMES ABRAHAM (1789–1841), Connecticut poetaster, author of romantic verse dramas; *Percy's Masque* (1819), *Hadad* (1825), and *Demetria* (1839).

HILLYER, ROBERT [SILLIMAN] (1895–1961), New Jersey-born poet, graduated from Harvard (1917), served in World War I, and returned to Harvard, where he was a professor (1919–45). His poetry, in the academic tradition of romanticism, is included in *Sonnets and Other Lyrics* (1917), *The Five Books of Youth* (1920), *Alchemy: A Symphonic Poem* (1920), *The Hills Give Promise* (1923), *The Halt in the Garden* (1925), *The Happy Episode* (1927), *The Seventh Hill* (1928), *The Gates of the Compass* (1930), *A Letter to Robert Frost and Others* (1937), *In Time of Mistrust* (1939), *Pattern of a Day* (1940), *Collected Verse* (1933, Pulitzer Prize), *Poems for Music* (1947), *The Death of Captain Nemo* (1949), *The Relic* (1957), and *Collected Poems* (1961). *Riverhead* (1932) and *My Heart for Hostage* (1942) are novels; and *Some Roots of English Poetry* (1933), *First Principles of Verse* (1938), and *In Pursuit of Poetry* (1960) are critical works.

him, play by E.E. Cummings.♦

HIMES, CHESTER [BOMAR] (1909–84), Missouri-born novelist about the life of fellow blacks in the U.S., attended Ohio State University but began his literary career while in Ohio State Penitentiary (1929–36) for armed robbery. His first novel, *If He Hollers Let Him Go* (1945), depicts with fury the prejudice met by a black worker in California defense plants, an experience he suffered. It was followed by *Lonely Crusade* (1947), about a black laborer meeting discrimination in unions and the Communist party; *Cast the First Stone* (1952), a naturalistic novel about blacks and whites in prison; and *Third Generation* (1954), a saga of a black family from slavery

to the mid-20th century. The year of the last publication he became an expatriate in Europe, and his next novel, *The Primitive* (1955), is quasi-autobiographical in its story of a black author and his white mistress. In France he published Harlem murder tales featuring black detectives, including *For Love of Imabelle* (1957), reissued as *A Rage in Harlem* (1965), *The Crazy Kill* (1959), *The Real Cool Killers* (1959), *All Shot Up* (1960), *The Big Gold Dream* (1960), *Cotton Comes to Harlem* (1965), *The Heat's On* (1966), and *Blind Man with a Pistol* (1969), reissued as *Hot Day, Hot Night* (1971). *Run Man Run* (1966) is a related thriller, and *Pinktoes* (Paris, 1961; U.S., 1965) is a slight novel about erotic relations of blacks and whites. He also published *Black on Black* (1973), a collection of shorter works, and a two-volume autobiography, *The Quality of Hurt* (1972) and *My Life as Absurdity* (1976).

HINDUS, MAURICE [GERSCHON] (1891–1969), Russian-born author, came to the U.S. (1905), graduated from Colgate (1915), and often revisited Russia, of which his studies include *Russian Peasant and Revolution* (1920), *Broken Earth* (1926), *Humanity Uprooted* (1929), *Red Bread* (1931), *The Great Offensive* (1933), *Russia and Japan* (1942), *Mother Russia* (1943), *The Cossacks* (1945), and *House Without a Roof* (1961). *Moscow Skies* (1936), *Sons and Fathers* (1940), *To Sing with the Angels* (1941), and *Magda* (1951) are novels. *Green Worlds* (1938) is an account of his youth.

HINOJOSA [-SMITH], ROLANDO (1929–   ), born in the Lower Rio Grande Valley, prefers to write in Spanish. He has translated some of his books and written others in English. He is best known for his "Klail City Death Trip" series (1972–82) of six novels, all written in Spanish and all set on the Texas-Mexican border; they constitute a personal portrait of the Chicano Southwest in the last 75 years. Long a professor of English at the University of Texas at Austin, Hinojosa also wrote a detective thriller, *Partners in Crime* (1985).

Hireling and the Slave, *The,* poem by W.J. Grayson.♦

HIRST, HENRY BECK (1817–74), eccentric Philadelphia poet, was a friend of Poe until he parodied "The Haunted Palace." He later claimed to be the author of "The Raven." His poems include *The Coming of the Mammoth* (1845), *Endymion* (1848), and *The Penance of Roland* (1849).

His Family, novel by Ernest Poole,♦ published in 1917 and awarded a Pulitzer Prize.

Hist, character in *The Deerslayer.*♦

History of New York, *A, From the Beginning of the World to the End of the Dutch Dynasty,* by Diedrich

Knickerbocker, burlesque history by Irving,♦ published in 1809 and revised in 1812, 1819, and 1848. It satirizes the methods of contemporary historians, the heroic style of epic poetry, and men and events during the Dutch administration as well as during its own period. Although Irving follows the history of New Netherland as then known, his satirical intention causes him to alter or disregard faets, as when, in the figure of William the Testy (William Kieft), he draws a Federalist caricature of Jefferson. According to the preface, the fictitious chronicler was "a small brisk looking old gentleman . . . a very inquisitive body . . . although a little queer in his ways."

Book I contains a cosmogony and description of the world, parodying contemporary histories, and a burlesque account of the discovery and peopling of America. Book II chronicles the voyage of Hudson, early Dutch colonization, and the founding of New Amsterdam, and gives traditional portraits of Dutch colonial types. Book III describes the "golden reign" of the stolid governor Wouter Van Twiller, who was "exactly five feet six inches in height, and six feet five inches in circumference," and whose head was "a perfect sphere"; the profound deliberations of his burgomasters over their pipes; conditions in early New Amsterdam; the hostility of the neighboring Yankees of Connecticut; and the establishment of Fort Goed Hoop. Book IV tells of the governorship of William the Testy, so learned that he was "good for nothing"; his pugnacity; his war "by proclamation" with the Yankees; his many laws, partisan quarrels, and border disputes. Books V, VI, and VII chronicle the reign of Peter Stuyvesant (Peter the Headstrong): his political reforms and military adventures in Delaware; and his unsuccessful defense of New Amsterdam against the conquering British force.

History of Plimmoth Plantation, see *Plimmoth Plantation, History of.*

History of the Dividing Line, journal of William Byrd♦ during 1728, found among his Westover Manuscripts and first published in 1841. These offhand daily jottings about Byrd's survey of the Virginia-North Carolina border begin with a sparkling sketch of Virginia history, and proceed to caustic comments upon the residents of North Carolina. This vivacious account and its various digressions show Byrd to be a witty, observant, and graceful writer. A variant, *The Secret History of the Line,* was published in 1929.

HITCHCOCK, ENOS (1744–1803), born in Massachusetts, graduated from Harvard (1767) and became a chaplain in the Revolutionary army and minister in Rhode Island. His didactic moral novel, the *Memoirs of the Bloomsgrove Family* (1790), is credited with being the second American novel, since it followed *The Power of Sympathy* by a year. He also wrote a *Treatise on Education*

(1790) and *The Farmer's Friend: or, The History of Mr. Charles Worthy* (1793), an edifying story of the worldly success of a moral New Englander.

Hive of the Bee Hunter, The, sketches by T.B. Thorpe.♦

HOAGLAND, EDWARD (1932–), New York City-born author, graduated from Harvard. His novels include *Cat Man* (1956), about circus life; *The Circle Home* (1960), dealing with prizefighters; and *The Peacock's Tail* (1965), set in a city's slums. Other works include a book about travel in British Columbia, *Notes from the Century Before* (1969), and *The Courage of Turtles* (1971). *Walking the Dead Diamond River* (1972), *Red Wolves and Black Bears* (1976), *The Tugman's Passage* (1982), and *Balancing Acts* (1992), are essays on rural and urban life, ecology, and animals, with subjects indicated by titles, as is true also of *African Calliope: A Journey to the Sudan* (1979). More imaginative is his novel *Seven Rivers West* (1986), about a Bostonian on the prairies and in the Rockies in 1887, although more atmospheric than plot-organized. *City Tales* (1986) are four stories set in New York City.

HOBAN, RUSSELL (1925–), Pennsylvania-born writer of moral fantasy and of children's books. Hoban has written over 50 books for children. Of particular note are *The Mouse and His Child* (1967) and *The Lion of Boaz-Jachin and Jachin-Boaz* (1973), both successful with adults as well as children. Hoban emigrated to England in 1969. His best-known adult books include *Turtle Diary* (1975), about two lonely people who meet in an English aquarium and conspire to set free a sea turtle. *Riddley Walker* (1980) is a fantasy narrated by a cockney Huck Finn. Civilization has been destroyed and mankind is living in Hobbesian savagery. The English language itself has degenerated to a weird dialect as spoken by the narrator. *Pilgermann* (1983) is a fantastic account of the First Crusade.

HOCKING, WILLIAM ERNEST (1873–1966), professor of philosophy at Harvard (1914–43) and elsewhere, whose books on religion and philosophy include *The Meaning of God in Human Experience* (1912), *Human Nature and Its Remaking* (1918), *Man and the State* (1926), *The Self, Its Body and Freedom* (1928), *The Spirit of World Politics* (1932), *Living Religions and a World Faith* (1939), *What Man Can Make of Man* (1942), *Science and the Idea of God* (1944), and *Experiment in Education* (1954).

HODGE, FREDERICK WEBB (1864–1956), anthropologist and author, served in the Southwest with the U.S. Geological Survey (1884–86) and later expeditions, and joined the Bureau of Ethnology in 1889, becoming its head (1910–18). He edited the *Handbook of American Indians North of*

Mexico (2 vols., 1907–10) and *The American Anthropologist* (1899–1910, 1912–14), and was the author of many important works on the background of the Southwest.

HOE, RICHARD MARCH (1812–86), as the head of the press-manufacturing business founded by his father, in 1846 invented the Hoe rotary press, which, by fastening type to a central cylinder around which impression cylinders revolved, greatly speeded the process of printing. He also invented a folder to fold newspapers as they come from the press.

ROBERT HOE (1839–1909), his son, also an inventor of printing processes, was the founder of the Grolier Club, and formed one of the finest rare book collections in the U.S.

HOFFMAN, CHARLES FENNO (1806–84), New York author and editor, whose career included editorial positions on the *American Monthly Magazine, Knickerbocker Magazine,* the *New-York Mirror,* and other periodicals. Before he became insane (1849), he was well known for his writings, which included *A Winter in the West* (1835), describing his horseback trip through sparsely settled Michigan and Illinois; *Wild Scenes in the Forest and Prairie* (1839); the novel *Greyslaer*♦ (1840), based on the Kentucky Tragedy and successfully dramatized; and the lilting lyrics and other popular poems collected in *The Vigil of Faith* (1842), *The Echo* (1844), and *Love's Calendar* (1847).

HOFFMAN, DANIEL [GERARD] (1923–), New York City-born author, educated at Columbia, is a professor at the University of Pennsylvania. His first book of poetry, *An Armada of Thirty Whales* (1954), was selected for the Yale Series of Younger Poets. Later volumes include *A Little Geste* (1960); *Striking the Stones* (1968); *Brotherly Love* (1980), a long poem celebrating the city of Philadelphia; and a volume of selected poems, *Hang-Gliding from Helicon* (1988). He has also written critical works on Stephen Crane (1957), Poe (1972), and Faulkner (1989).

HOFSTADTER, DOUGLAS R. (1945–), California-reared professor of computer science at the University of Indiana and then Michigan is the author of *Gödel, Escher, Bach* (1979, Pulitzer Prize), tracing intellectual relations among the mathematician, artist, and composer; *Metamagical Themes* (1985), essays mainly from *Scientific American;* and *The Mind's I* (1981).

HOFSTADTER, RICHARD (1916–70), received his Ph.D. from Columbia (1942) and was a member of its history department beginning in 1946. His influential books include *Social Darwinism in American Thought* (1944), *The American Political Tradition* (1948), *The Development and Scope of Higher Education in the U.S.* (1952), *The Age of*

Reform: From Bryan to F.D.R. (1955, Pulitzer Prize), *The Development of Academic Freedom in the U.S.* (1955), and *Anti-Intellectualism in American Life* (1963, Pulitzer Prize).

HOGAN, LINDA (1947–), a Chickasaw poet. Collections of her verse include *Calling Myself Home* (1979), *Daughters, I Love You* (1981), *Eclipse* (1983), and *Seeing Through the Sun* (1985). That *Horse* (1985) and *The Big Woman* (1987) collect stories.

HOLBROOK, JOSIAH (1788–1854), educational reformer, was born in Connecticut, graduated from Yale (1810), and founded an industrial school (1819) whose curriculum included manual training, farming, and scientific subjects. When this failed, he established an Agricultural Seminary (1824–25) and in 1826 founded the first American lyceum,♦ at Millbury, Mass. He remained the leader of the lyceum movement, for which, beginning in 1830, he published a series of *Scientific Tracts Designed for Instruction and Entertainment . . . ,* and edited a weekly newspaper, the *Family Lyceum* (1832).

HOLBROOK, STEWART H[ALL] (1893–1964), journalist and popular historian, born in Vermont and long resident in Oregon, whose books include *Holy Old Mackinaw: A Natural History of the American Lumberjack* (1938), *Burning an Empire: America's Great Forest Fires* (1943), *Lost Men of American History* (1946), and *The Columbia* (1956).

Holgrave, character in *The House of the Seven Gables.*♦

Holiday, play by Philip Barry,♦ produced in 1928 and published in 1929.

Johnny Case, a young lawyer, and Julia Seton, a New York heiress, meet during a winter holiday and return to announce their engagement. Johnny has not realized Julia's wealth and social position, and he is disconcerted by her father's cool reception and also by his realization that she shares her father's conventional beliefs and interests. He finds himself much more sympathetic to Julia's sister Linda, a more dynamic person, particularly when Julia, like her father, opposes his desire to forgo the earning of money by taking a holiday for a few years. After Julia breaks with Johnny, he and Linda elope to Europe.

HOLLAND, EDWIN CLIFFORD (*c.*1794–1824), Charleston poet, whose *Odes, Naval Songs, and Other Occasional Poems* (1813) are considered to mark the beginning of romantic poetry in South Carolina. He dramatized Byron's *Corsair* (1818).

HOLLAND, JOSIAH GILBERT (1819–81), Massachusetts author, was long associated with Samuel Bowles as an editor of the *Springfield Republican,* and became the first editor of *Scribner's*

Monthly♦ (1870–81). His many books were popular in their day, being well suited to the homely taste for sentimental didacticism. His novels include *The Bay-Path* (1857), dealing with the religious background of 17th-century Connecticut; *Miss Gilbert's Career* (1860), set in contemporary Connecticut; *Arthur Bonnicastle* (1873), a semiautobiographical novel of a New England boy's life at Yale and in New York; *Sevenoaks* (1875), the story of an unscrupulous financier; and *Nicholas Minturn* (1877), about a wealthy and idealistic young social reformer. Besides many poems, including *Bitter-Sweet* (1858) and *Kathrina, Her Life and Mine in a Poem* (1867), Holland wrote histories and such works as *Letters to Young People* (1858), using the pseudonym Timothy Titcomb.

HOLLANDER, JOHN (1929–   ), New York City-born poet, received his A.B. from Columbia and Ph.D. from Indiana University and since 1959 has been a member of Yale's faculty, except 1966–77, when he was at Hunter College. *A Crackling of Thorns* (1958), sophisticated poems, was selected by Auden for the Yale Younger Poets Award, and Auden has been an influence on him, along with the metaphysicals and the tradition of English song represented by Campion and Jonson. Hollander is himself an accomplished musician and wrote the scholarly study *The Untuning of the Sky: Ideas of Music in English Poetry, 1500–1700* (1961). These two earliest books were followed by *Movie-Going* (1962) and *Visions from the Ramble* (1965), poems whose inspirations came from his native city's Broadway and Central Park. His next book, *Types of Shape* (1968), further displayed his virtuosity through its shaped poems reminiscent of Quarles and Herbert. *The Night Mirror* (1971), *Town and Country Matters: Erotica and Satirica* (1972), and *The Head of the Bed* (1973) are further collections showing his remarkable variety, ranging from the philosophic to the sprightly, as well as his command of accented syllabic versification, which in *Tales Told of the Father* (1975) became purely syllabic. *Reflections on Espionage* (1976) contains his witty poetic commentary on contemporary poets and his own concepts of poetry. *Spectral Emanations* (1978) contains selected poems; *Jiggery-Pokery* (1967) is a collection of double-dactylic poems created with Anthony Hecht♦; and *Powers of Thirteen* (1983), the poet's 13th collection, contains 169 (13 × 13) poems of 13 lines, each containing 13 syllables. Other volumes of poetry include *In Time and Place* (1986), also including prose work, and *Harp Lake* (1988), including physical and psychic relations to Israel. *Various Owls* (1963) contains nonsense poems for children, and *The Quest of the Gole* (1966) is a mock-epic written for young people. Other works include a masque, *An Entertainment for Elizabeth* (1972), and critical works: *Images of Voice* (1969); *The Figure of Echo* (1981); *Rhyme's Reason* (1981), a guide to English verse forms, illustrated by Hollander's own witty ex-

amples; and *Melodious Guile: Fictive Pattern in Poetic Language* (1988). He was awarded a Bollingen Prize in 1983.

HOLLEY, MARIETTA (1836–1926), popular humorist whose pseudonym, "Josiah Allen's Wife," was a household word for many years because of her great literary output, which began with *My Opinions and Betsy Bobbet's* (1873) and ended with *Josiah Allen on the Woman Question* (1914). The humorous but sane homely philosophizing of Josiah's wife, Samantha, was often used as propaganda for temperance and woman suffrage.

Hollingsworth, character in *The Blithedale Romance.* ♦

HOLLISTER, GIDEON HIRAM (1817–81), Connecticut lawyer, was the author of *Mount Hope* (1851), a romance about King Philip; *Kinley Hollow* (1882), a novel about 19th-century Puritanism; *Thomas à Becket* (1866), a poetic drama produced by Edwin Booth; and a history of his state (1855).

Hollow Men, The, poem by T.S. Eliot.♦

Hollywood, district of Los Angeles, situated eight miles northeast of the city's downtown and long famous as the center of motion-picture♦ production for the world. Because of this association the area became synonymous with the flamboyance and glamour attached to the industry and its stars. Besides inspiring a great quantity of romantic fiction as well as serious sociological studies, the place has been the subject of much satirical treatment, e.g. Kaufman's plays, *Once in a Lifetime* and *Stage Door,* and such novels as H.L. Wilson's *Merton of the Movies,* Van Vechten's *Spider Boy,* Fitzgerald's *The Last Tycoon,* Elmer Rice's *A Voyage to Purilia,* John O'Hara's *Hope of Heaven,* Nathanael West's *The Day of the Locust,* Schulberg's *What Makes Sammy Run?,* and Bemelmans's *Dirty Eddy.* Among the dramatists and novelists who have spent time in Hollywood writing for films are Maxwell Anderson, Ray Bradbury, Bromfield, Joan Didion, Dreiser, John Gregory Dunne, Faulkner, F. Scott Fitzgerald, Daniel Fuchs, Ben Hecht, Sidney Howard, George S. Kaufman, Jeremy Larner, Charles MacArthur, Thomas McGuane, David Mamet, Odets, Dorothy Parker, S.J. Perelman, Robert Sherwood, Phil Stong, and Nathanael West. In the post-World War II era of vigorous anticommunism a group labeled the Hollywood Ten (including the writers Alvah Bessie, Ring Lardner, Jr., John Howard Lawson, Albert Maltz, and Dalton Trumbo) were indicted for refusing to testify before the Congressional Committee on Un-American Activities and as a result were blacklisted by film studios for a long time.

HOLM, SAXE, pseudonym of Helen Hunt Jackson. ◆

HOLMES, ABIEL (1763–1837), father of O.W. Holmes, was a Congregational clergyman at Cambridge (1792–1829), and wrote *The Annals of America,* a chronological compilation of facts from 1492 to 1826. He also wrote a *Life* (1798) of his father-in-law, Ezra Stiles.

HOLMES, JOHN CLELLON (1926–88), born in Massachusetts, after navy service in World War II and studies at Columbia and the New School for Social Research, began to publish poetry in magazines and later in *The Bowling Green Poems* (1977), *Death Drag* (1979), *Dire Coasts* (1988), and *Night Music* (1989). He is best known for his novels, *Go* (1952), about Beat intellectual drifters in New York City; *The Horn* (1958), about the sad latter days of a black saxophonist; and *Get Home Free* (1964), about the misalliance of a bohemian couple. *Nothing More To Declare* (1967) is an autobiographical backward look at Beat writers. He also wrote *Gone in October* (1985), memoirs of Kerouac; *Representative Men* (1988), biographical essays; *Displaced Person* (1987), telling of his own wide travels; and *Passionate Opinions* (1988), general cultural essays. He used his middle name and surname to sign his early works.

HOLMES, MARY JANE [HAWES] (1825–1907), popular post-Civil War novelist of Massachusetts, whose 39 sentimental, moral, and stereotyped novels sold more than 2,000,000 copies. Her best-known work was *Lena Rivers* (1856).

HOLMES, OLIVER WENDELL (1809–94), son of Abiel Holmes, was born at Cambridge, reared in the traditions of the Brahmin class, and graduated from Harvard in the class of 1829, which he helped to make famous by his long series of reunion poems. His first verse to bring him popularity was "Old Ironsides" ◆ (1830). While studying medicine at Harvard and in Boston, he published in *The New-England Magazine* (1831–32) two papers entitled "The Autocrat of the Breakfast-Table," which were precursors of his later famous work. After two years of study in Paris hospitals, he received his M.D. from Harvard (1836), and his collection of witty occasional *Poems* (1836) was his last literary contribution for some time, since he turned to his chosen profession, holding the post of Professor of Anatomy at Dartmouth (1838–40) and publishing two important medical works, *Homeopathy and Its Kindred Delusions* (1842) and *The Contagiousness of Puerperal Fever* (1843). From 1847 until his retirement in 1882, he was Parkman Professor of Anatomy and Physiology at Harvard, and for the first six years also served as dean of the Harvard Medical School.

His stimulating qualities as a lecturer soon brought him before the public in the lyceums. As a witty, urbane conversationalist, he reigned supreme in Boston society and club life and became the unofficial poet laureate of all important gatherings in the intellectual "hub of the Universe." As a reformer he was simply a scientific rationalist opposing the Calvinistic dogmas by which he had been reared. He was probably the most militant Unitarian among Boston laymen, and he attacked the religion of his fathers consistently in prose and poetry, notably in "The Deacon's Masterpiece" ◆ (1858) and the more vituperative "The Moral Bully," which satirizes a preacher's hypocritical virtues.

When the *Atlantic Monthly* was founded (1857), Holmes not only named it but also, as a leading contributor, was influenced to become primarily a man of letters. He contributed *The Autocrat of the Breakfast-Table* ◆ (1858), which he followed with *The Professor at the Breakfast-Table* (1860), *The Poet at the Breakfast-Table* (1872), and *Over the Teacups* (1891), all reflections of the original. Selections from his endless flow of poetry peppered these volumes, notably "The Chambered Nautilus" ◆ and "The Deacon's Masterpiece" ◆ in the first volume. He also turned to fiction, and in *Elsie Venner* ◆ (1861) wrote the best of his three "medicated novels." All exhibit his theological and biological views and are studies of abnormal psychology, but *The Guardian Angel* ◆ (1867) and *A Mortal Antipathy* ◆ (1885) show diminishing ability. He reprinted from the *Atlantic* two collections of essays, *Soundings from the Atlantic* (1864) and *Pages from an Old Volume of Life* (1883), wrote biographies of Motley (1879) and Emerson (1885), and collected a volume of *Medical Essays* (1883). His addresses, lectures, and minor essays would constitute a large collection.

Besides the several enlarged editions of his *Poems,* his verse was issued in many volumes, including *Songs in Many Keys* (1826), *Songs of Many Seasons* (1875), *The Iron Gate* (1880), and *Before the Curfew* (1888). Although most of his poems were written for specific occasions, some have transcended their occasional nature. Among the best known are "The Ballad of the Oysterman" (1830), a parody of romantic balladry; "The Last Leaf" ◆ (1831), on an aged survivor of the Boston Tea Party; "My Aunt" (1831), on the "sad, ungathered rose" of his ancestral tree; "The Boys," written for the thirtieth reunion of his Harvard class; "Bill and Joe" (1851), another reunion poem; "A Sunday Hymn" (1860), which begins "Lord of all being! throned afar"; "Contentment," a humorous poem on "simple pleasures," from the *Autocrat;* "The Living Temple," also from the *Autocrat,* a hymn on man's "wondrous frame"; "Brother Jonathan's Lament for Sister Caroline" (1861), a patriotic poem on the secession of South Carolina; and "Dorothy Q." (1871), a sentimentally humorous piece on a family portrait.

HOLMES, Oliver Wendell, Jr. (1841–1935), son and namesake of the well-known writer and professor of medicine, was himself professor of law at Harvard, chief justice of the Massachusetts supreme court (1899–1902), and associate justice of the U.S. Supreme Court (1902–32). His writings include *The Common Law* (1881), *Speeches* (1891, 1913), and *Collected Legal Papers* (1920), all exhibiting his distinction of mind and liberal views. Felix Frankfurter wrote *Mr. Justice Holmes and the Constitution* (1927). *Touched with Fire* (1946) collects his Civil War diary and letters. His correspondence with Sir Frederick Pollock was published in 1941, and his letters to and from Harold J. Laski, in 1953. He is the subject of more popular treatment in Catherine Drinker Bowen's biography, *Yankee from Olympus* (1944), and Emmet Lavery's play *The Magnificent Yankee* (1946).

HOLMES, William Henry (1846–1933), artist and geologist with the U.S. Geological Survey (1874–89), wrote important descriptive works on Yellowstone Park, the Grand Canyon, and the Southwest. As a leading anthropologist, he headed the National Museum, the Bureau of Ethnology, and the National Gallery of Art. His books include a *Handbook of Aboriginal American Antiquities* (1919).

Home as Found, novel by Cooper,♦ published in 1838 as a sequel to *Homeward Bound.♦* In it, Cooper satirizes his neighbors at Cooperstown, and, as a result of the controversies and libel suits that followed, he was himself satirized in an anonymous novel, *The Effinghams; or, Home as I Found It* (1842).

After their return from Europe, the Effinghams open their house in New York City, where they participate in many social affairs, during whose course their young relative Grace Van Cortlandt is wooed by Sir George Templemore. After Grace and Sir George go to England to be married, the Effinghams go to their estate at Templeton, a small upstate community, where they are joined by Paul Powis, John Effingham's newly found son, who is the suitor of his cousin Eve. Mlle Viefville, Eve's vivacious maid, marries Aristabulus Bragg, the village lawyer and an inveterate "booster," while other Templeton citizens are depicted as hypocritical demagogues or foolish democrats. Paul gives up his life of travel and adventure to marry Eve, and the Effinghams settle down to their duties as landowners and civic leaders.

Home Burial, dramatic dialogue in blank verse by Robert Frost,♦ published in *North of Boston* (1914).

The incompatibility of a New England farm couple is revealed in the tragic conflict between them following the death of their only child. The husband has buried the child in the nearby family plot, and the wife becomes obsessed by his seemingly unfeeling attitude. Oppressed by loneliness, she comes to hate him and now feels that the transitoriness of his grief is a further proof that "the world's evil." She is determined that she "must go—somewhere out of this house," but her husband declares obstinately, "I'll follow and bring you back by force. I *will!*—"

Home Journal, The (1846–1901), weekly magazine, founded by N.P. Willis and G.P. Morris as an outgrowth of the *New-York Mirror.♦* It was devoted to society news, gossip, light essays, and verse. Willis remained editor until 1867, and his policies were continued until 1901, when, as *Town and Country,* it became a more elegant society journal. Purchased by Hearst in 1925, *Town and Country* is still published.

"Home, Sweet Home," song in *Clari.♦*

Homeward Bound; or, The Chase, novel by Cooper,♦ published in 1838. *Home as Found♦* is a sequel.

Edward and John Effingham, New York landowners, with Edward's daughter Eve, have spent several years in Europe, and now sail for home on the American packet *Montauk,* commanded by Captain Truck. Their fellow passengers include the vulgar American, Steadfast Dodge; foppish Sir George Templemore; Mr. Sharp, a handsome young English aristocrat; and Mr. Blunt, an American adventurer, who falls in love with Eve. The *Montauk* encounters many hazards during the voyage: a port officer attempts to arrest a steerage passenger and is ordered off the ship; it is chased by the English war sloop *Foam;* in order to escape, Captain Truck heads for the Bay of Biscay and is caught in a storm; anchored for repairs on the African coast, it is attacked by Arab raiders, who are beaten off. Finally crossing the ocean, the packet arrives off Sandy Hook, only to find the waiting *Foam,* whose captain recognizes Mr. Sharp as the real Templemore and explains that his mission has been to arrest the imposter, a fleeing defaulter. Mr. Blunt reveals that he is actually Paul Powis, and it is learned that John Effingham is his long-lost father.

Homos, Mr., character in *A Traveler from Altruria♦* and *Through the Eye of the Needle.♦*

HONE, Philip (1780–1851), New York businessman, Whig political leader, and member of social and literary circles. His diary, of which selections have been published (1889, 1927), gives a comprehensive description of New York life during the second quarter of the 19th century.

Honey in the Horn, novel by H.L. Davis.♦

Honorable Peter Stirling, The, novel by P.L. Ford♦ published in 1894. Although the author denied it, the hero is considered to represent Grover Cleveland.

Peter Stirling, a "practical idealist," rises from a plain New England background and Harvard education to a leading position in New York society, law, and politics. He loves Helen Pierce, daughter of a banker, but is unselfishly reconciled to her marriage with his best friend, Watts d'Alloi. When d'Alloi fathers an illegitimate child, Stirling accepts the responsibility to spare Helen the knowledge of her husband's infidelity. In an environment of corrupt municipal and state politics, Stirling moves with unprejudiced fairness and honesty, seeking always the public interest. He is a candidate for governor, but when his sincere conservatism threatens to lose votes during a great strike, he maintains his position, saying "Votes be damned!" When he is wounded in a bombing while leading his regiment of militia against the strikers, he is cared for by Helen and d'Alloi's daughter Leonore, whom he later marries.

HOOKER, [WILLIAM] BRIAN (1880–1946), author of the poetic librettos for two operas by Horatio Parker, *Mona* (1912), concerned with early Britain under Roman rule, and *Fairyland* (1915), a romantic fantasy set in 13th-century Europe. *The White Bird* (1924) is an opera dealing with 19th-century New York. He translated *Cyrano de Bergerac* in 1923 for the successful production by Walter Hampden, and with W.H. Post adapted *The Squaw Man*◆ as the libretto of the musical play *White Eagle* (1927).

HOOKER, THOMAS (1586–1647), Englishborn Congregationalist, was forced to flee to Holland because he exhibited Puritan leanings in his religious lectures at Cambridge. After preaching in Amsterdam, Delft, and Rotterdam, he emigrated with John Cotton and Samuel Stone to Massachusetts (1633). He was pastor at Newe Towne (Cambridge) for three years, and then, because of his democratic views, took his entire congregation of some 100 families to found the Connecticut Colony. His liberal spirit shaped the character of the new community, in which authority was held with the free consent of the people. Because his ideas were so opposed to those of Winthrop and other Massachusetts leaders, it was not until 1643 that Hooker was able to persuade them to join with his colony in a New England confederation. His views were embodied in the "Fundamental Orders" (1639), which served as Connecticut's constitution, and his many published sermons reveal his dramatic oratorical power. In *A Survey of the Summe of Church Discipline* (1648), he defended New England Congregationalism and postulated the principle of divine absolutism, making temporal absolutism unnecessary. The sovereign will of God, he held, was represented by no ecclesiastical hierarchy, but was communicated directly to the individual

believer. The people, walking together in the fellowship of faith, communicate power by voluntary subjection to the governing pastor. A second volume of this work was written by John Cotton.◆

HOOPER, JOHNSON JONES (1815–62), born in North Carolina, later settled in Alabama, where he was a lawyer and newspaper editor. His tales of a backwoods gambler, *Some Adventures of Captain Simon Suggs, Late of the Tallapoosa Volunteers* (1845), present a vivid picture of flush times on the frontier of the Old Southwest. Similar sketches were collected in *The Widow Rugby's Husband, A Night at the Ugly Man's, and Other Tales of Alabama* (1851), and in 1858 he published *Dog and Gun, A Few Loose Chapters on Shooting.*

Hoosier, name applied to the residents of Indiana. Its origin is uncertain. One theory attributes it to one Aaron Short, who, after winning a prizefight, shouted "Hurrah for the Hoosier!," meaning perhaps "the Husher," a term applied to a champion fighter who could hush all comers. The first-known literary use is in John Finley's poem "The Hoosier Nest" (1830), and in course of time all Indiana authors have come to be called Hoosier authors. The most prominent among them are Edward Eggleston, who wrote *The Hoosier Schoolmaster* and *The Circuit Rider;* his brother George, who wrote *A Man of Honor* and *Juggernaut;* Lew Wallace; Maurice Thompson, author of *Hoosier Mosaics* but best known for *Alice of Old Vincennes;* James Whitcomb Riley, called the "Hoosier poet"; George Ade; Booth Tarkington, who wrote *The Gentleman from Indiana* and *The Magnificent Ambersons;* Theodore Dreiser, who described his native state in *A Hoosier Holiday;* Meredith Nicholson, who wrote *A Hoosier Chronicle* and other novels as well as studies of Indiana life; and Ross Lockridge, whose *Raintree County* poignantly evokes the period 1840–85.

Hoosier Schoolboy, *The,* novel by Edward Eggleston.◆

Hoosier Schoolmaster, *The,* novel by Edward Eggleston,◆ published in 1871. It is based on experiences of his brother George.

Ralph Hartsook, a schoolteacher in backwoods Indiana, loves Hannah Thompson, a hired girl whose brother, Jack Means, wants to marry his sister Mirandy to Ralph. The young man is persecuted by the settlers when a false accusation of theft is lodged against him, and his pupils attempt to drive him out. In the ensuing trial Ralph is acquitted, and he marries Hannah when she is found to be of age and therefore illegally "bound" to the Meanses.

Hopalong Cassidy, character in fiction by Clarence Mulford.◆

Hopedale Community was founded at Milford, Mass. (1842), by Adin Ballou and other

Universalists, who professed a kind of Christian socialism, advocated women's rights, and opposed intemperance, war, and slavery. Because of internal dissension and financial difficulties, the association disbanded in 1856.

Hopi Indians (also called MOQUI or MOKI), agricultural tribe inhabiting a group of pueblos on the mesas of northeastern Arizona. First known to the Spaniards in 1540 through Coronado's expedition, they were made vassals by Juan de Oñate in 1598. Missionary work among them was carried on precariously from 1629 to 1700, when their hostility compelled its abandonment. After the Pueblo Revolt of 1680, their villages were built on mesas for defense against the Spaniards. The Hopi are noted for their mythology and ceremonial dances, including the biennial snake dance. They figure in Willa Cather's *Death Comes for the Archbishop* and in Edna Dean Proctor's *Song of an Ancient People*.

HOPKINS, LEMUEL (1750–1801), Connecticut physician and poet, member of the Connecticut Wits,♦ a Yale graduate and resident of Hartford. A staunch Federalist and Calvinist, he contributed to *The Anarchiad,*♦ *The Echo,*♦ and *The Political Greenhouse.*♦ His separate works include *The Guillotina, or a Democratic Dirge* (1796); and "Epitaph on a Patient Killed by a Cancer Quack"; an arraignment of Deism, "Verses on General Allen"; and "The Hypocrite's Hope," a satire on irreligious persons.

HOPKINS, MARK (1802–87), Massachusetts physician, Congregationalist minister, and teacher, was president of Williams College (1836–72). Although President Garfield said, "Give me a log hut, with only a simple bench, Mark Hopkins on one end and I on the other, and you may have all the buildings, apparatus, and libraries without him," he was unimportant as theologian or philosopher. His books include *Lectures on the Evidences of Christianity* (1846), *The Law of Love and Love as a Law* (1869), and *Teachings and Counsels* (1884). He was president of the American Board of Commissioners for Foreign Missions (1857–87).

HOPKINS, PAULINE (1859–1930), born in Portland, Maine, and educated in Boston public schools, began writing early and became the most productive African-American woman writer of the pre-World War I era. She worked in the genres of novel, biography, short story, history, and the essay—all work of quality. Her best-known work—and the only fiction she published in book, as opposed to magazine serial, form—is *Contending Forces: A Romance Illustrative of Negro Life North and South* (1900). She wrote the book "to do all that I can in an humble way to raise the stigma of degradation from my race." Her intended audience was white, even though her

portrayal of most of the whites in the novel is negative. The book is a powerful sentimental romance, with its main theme female virtue besieged. She achieved little recognition in her time and was ignored by other black writers during the Harlem Renaissance in the 1920s. She was working as a stenographer at MIT when she died. Both *Contending Forces* and *The Magazine Novels of Pauline Hopkins* are reprinted in the Schomburg Library of Nineteenth-Century Black Women Writers (1988).

HOPKINS, SAMUEL (1721–1803), Congregational minister in Massachusetts, Rhode Island, and his native Connecticut, was the leading disciple of Jonathan Edwards,♦ on whose philosophy he based his own "Hopkinsianism." His *System of Doctrines Contained in Divine Revelation . . .* (1793) and other writings were more influential than his dull, logical preaching.

HOPKINS, STEPHEN (1707–85), governor of Rhode Island and signer of the Declaration of Independence, contributed to the Revolutionary cause an important pamphlet, *The Rights of Colonies Examined* (1765), that studied problems of parliamentary authority and justified the colonial attitude toward England's policy. To counteract it, Martin Howard♦ wrote *A Letter from a Gentleman in Halifax to His Friend in Rhode Island* (1765).

HOPKINSON, FRANCIS (1737–91), born in Philadelphia, was the first student to enroll in the Academy of Philadelphia, and the first to receive a diploma from the College of Philadelphia. After studying law, and serving as collector of customs at Salem, N.J. (1763), he sailed for England to seek political preferment. He was unsuccessful, but on returning to the law rose rapidly, and was appointed to the New Jersey governor's council (1774) and elected to the Continental Congress (1776).

He was a distinguished harpsichordist and leader of Philadelphia musical society, and revised and composed music for Thomson and Mallet's *Alfred, a Masque,* presented at the College of Philadelphia (1757). He published a collection of psalm tunes and a number of songs, and his later claim to "being the first Native of the United States who has produced a Musical Composition" is generally considered justified. His literary ability was exhibited in the many poems that he wrote in this early period, including "The Treaty" (1761), an Indian poem; "Exercises" for his college (1761, 1762); "Science" (1762), prophesying a great future for the college; and "Dirtilla" (1772), a humorous work. To the *Pennsylvania Magazine* he also contributed a series of Addisonian essays, on subjects ranging from "A New Plan for Education" to the state of bachelorhood. In 1774 he began his career as a political satirist with *A Pretty Story,*♦ and two years later he attacked the "Letters of Cato" in *A Prophecy,* which allegorically reviewed the contention with the mother country.

Meanwhile he was a signer of the Declaration of Independence, chairman of the Continental Navy Board (1776–78), treasurer of loans (1778–81), and judge of admiralty for Pennsylvania (1779–89). In *Letter Written by a Foreigner on the Character of the English Nation* (1777), he satirized the peculiarities of the English. This was followed by *A Political Catechism* (1777); a stirring "Camp Ballad"; and his *Answer to General Burgoyne's Proclamation* (1777), burlesquing the general's manifesto. He further satirized the English in "The Battle of the Kegs" ♦ (1778), the most popular of his writings, and "Date Obolum Bellisario" (1778), a poetical allegory in which wretched England, driven to beggary, tells of the grief caused her by her worthless son George. Hopkinson also satirized his fellow countrymen who sympathized with England, in "The Birds, the Beasts, and the Bat," a Hudibrastic fable on men who turn their allegiance according to the state of the military weather; *Two Letters* (1776), supposedly written by a Tory, acknowledged the unscrupulous lies which the Americans were then attributing to the Loyalists; and *Letter to Joseph Galloway* (1778) accused the prominent Loyalist of treachery to country and friends. Among other *jeux d'esprit* was his publication of a mock advertisement of the King's Printer, Rivington, who it proclaimed was retiring after the surrender of Cornwallis, and auctioning off his stock of abusive books and maps.

During the war, Hopkinson also employed his several talents in writing *The Temple of Minerva* (1781), a "dramatic allegorical cantata," "consisting of an overture, arias, ensembles, and choruses in praise of the American alliance with France"; in designing seals for various departments of the new government, a number of coins and issues of paper money, and the American flag, known as the Stars and Stripes. ♦ After the war, he was a federal judge in Pennsylvania, supported the Federalists in various writings, and published many literary essays, including "Modern Learning Exemplified" (1784), satirizing educational fads, and "A Plan for the Improvement of the Art of Paper War" (1786), ridiculing newspaper quarrels. *Seven Songs, for the Harpsichord or Forte-Piano* (1788), actually containing eight pieces, was the first book of music published by an American. *The Miscellaneous Essays and Occasional Writings* was issued in 1792.

HOPKINSON, JOSEPH (1770–1842), son of Francis Hopkinson, was a noted lawyer and jurist, served in Congress (1814–19), and was a member of the Tuesday Club of Philadelphia, president of the Academy of Fine Arts, and author of "Hail Columbia" ♦ (1798).

HOPWOOD, AVERY (1882–1928), Ohio-born playwright, graduated from Michigan (1905). Af-

ter writing his first play, *Clothes* (1906), with Channing Pollock, he had a long career of successful melodramas, farces, adaptations, and collaborations, including *The Gold Diggers* (1919); *The Bat* (1920), with Mary Roberts Rinehart; and *Getting Gertie's Garter* (1921), with Wilson Collison. Since 1930–31 his alma mater has sponsored an annual creative-writing contest in his name and an annual Hopwood Lecture by a major literary critic.

HORGAN, PAUL (1903–95), born in Buffalo, N.Y., reared there and in New Mexico. His novels include *The Fault of Angels* (1933), about professional musicians; *The Habit of Empire* (1939), about 16th-century New Mexico; *A Distant Trumpet* (1960), set on an Arizona army post of the 1880s; and *Things as They Are* (1964), beginning a trilogy about the life and early death of a rich young man in Philadelphia and New Mexico, continued in *Everything To Live For* (1968) and *The Thin Mountain Air* (1977). *Figures in a Landscape* (1940) and *The Peach Stone* (1967) collect stories, the former with essays. *Great River* (1954), a history of the Rio Grande, earned him a Pulitzer Prize, as did *Lamy of Santa Fe* (1975), a study of a pioneer bishop. Lincoln figures in *Yours, A. Lincoln* (1942), a play; *Citizen of New Salem* (1961), an essay; and *Songs After Lincoln* (1965), poetic tributes. Historical studies include *Centuries of Santa Fe* (1956) and *Conquistadors in North American History* (1963). *Tracings, a Book of Partial Portraits* (1993) gives affectionate sketches of the famous artists in many fields Horgan knew.

Horizon, play by Augustin Daly, ♦ produced in 1871 and printed in 1885.

Alleyn Van Dorp, a West Point graduate on his first command, combines army duties in the Far West with a search for the long-lost husband and daughter of his foster mother. In the Indian country he finds a vigilance committee ejecting the drunkard Wolf and his daughter Med, loved by the gambler Loder and the Indian chief Wannemucka. Alleyn falls in love with Med, discovers that she and her sick father are the two he seeks, and twice rescues her from Wannemucka's Indians. Loder kills Wannemucka but, realizing that Med deserves a better life than he can give her, departs, leaving her to Alleyn.

Horse-Shoe Robinson: *A Tale of the Tory Ascendancy,* novel by J.P. Kennedy, ♦ published in 1835. It was dramatized by Clifton W. Tayleure (1856).

In Virginia and the Carolinas, during the closing years of the Revolutionary War, Mildred Lindsay, daughter of a Tory who wants her to marry the British spy Tyrrel, loves the patriot Arthur Butler and is herself an ardent rebel. She secretly marries Butler, who is captured, leaving her to be squired through various difficulties by the frontier hero Horse-Shoe Robinson, a resourceful blacksmith. Tyrrel is eventually hanged as a traitor, and Mildred and Butler are reunited.

HORTON, GEORGE MOSES (1798?–1880?), enslaved black on a farm near Chapel Hill, N.C., where he was befriended by university students for whom he used his natural gifts as a poet in writing love poems they passed off as their own. He published three volumes of verse, concluding with *Naked Genius* (1865).

HOSMER, WILLIAM H[OWE] C[UYLER] (1814–77), lawyer of upstate New York known for his poetry, including *Yonnondio, or Warriors of the Genesee* (1844), a sympathetic treatment of the 17th-century Seneca Indians, and *Poetical Works* (2 vols., 1854), containing further "Indian Traditions and Songs" and nature poetry.

"Hot Time in the Old Town To-Night, A," song composed for a minstrel show (1886) by Theodore Metz, with words added by Joseph Hayden (1896). It was a popular marching song of the Spanish-American War, and later the campaign song of Theodore Roosevelt.

Hotel Universe, play by Philip Barry,♦ produced and published in 1930.

HOUGH, EMERSON (1857–1923), born in Iowa, graduated from the state university (1880) and began to practice law at Whiteoaks, N.M., "half cow town and half mining camp." There he began to write magazine sketches on the local outdoor life and sports, and he soon abandoned the law for work on Midwestern newspapers and the magazine *Forest and Stream.* He wrote many articles concerned with Yellowstone National Park, and was influential in the movement for the preservation of wild life in this and other regions. His first book, *The Singing Mouse Stories* (1895), was followed by his most popular early work, *The Story of the Cowboy* (1897). Besides a series of stories for boys, The Young Alaskans, he wrote *The Story of the Outlaw* (1907), *The Passing of the Frontier* (1918), and many popular historical romances set in the West. Among these are *The Mississippi Bubble* (1902), *The Law of the Land* (1904), *54–40 or Fight!* (1909), *The Sagebrusher* (1919), *The Covered Wagon* (1922), *North of 36* (1923), and *Mother of Gold* (1924).

Hound and Horn (1927–34), little magazine, founded as a "Harvard Miscellany" by Lincoln Kirstein and Varian Fry. The title came from Ezra Pound's "The White Stag": "'Tis the white stag Fame we're hunting, bid the world's hounds come to horn." R.P. Blackmur and Bernard Bandler II became editors (1929), and the following year the magazine moved to New York, losing its association with Harvard. Kirstein became the sole editor, and the quarterly vacillated there-

after among humanism, Southern regionalism, Marxism, and the neoclassicism of its Western editor, Yvor Winters. In its attempt to publish the best avant-garde authors, *Hound and Horn* printed works by Katherine Anne Porter, Kenneth Burke, Allen Tate, Ezra Pound, Gertrude Stein, T.S. Eliot, and many others, whose reputations it helped to establish. *The "Hound and Horn" Letters* (1982) collects correspondence of editors and contributors.

HOUSE, EDWARD MANDELL (1858–1938), Texas-born statesman, was instrumental in nominating Wilson for the presidency (1912), afterward becoming the chief executive's intimate adviser and "other self." He interviewed diplomats and rulers in attempts to avert war (1914–15); was a special representative at the Inter-Allied Conference of premiers and foreign ministers for coordination of war activities (1917); represented the U.S. on the Supreme War Council; gathered and prepared data for the Peace Conference; helped draft the Treaty of Versailles; was on the commission that drafted the Covenant of the League of Nations; and was a member of the Commission on Mandates (1919). He wrote *Philip Dru, Administrator: A Story of Tomorrow, 1920–1935* (1912), an anonymous novel whose proposed governmental reforms helped cement his friendship with Wilson. *The Intimate Papers of Colonel House* (4 vols., 1926–28) form a valuable source of information on American relations during World War I.

House by the Side of the Road, The, poem by Sam Walter Foss.♦

House of Earth, The, trilogy by Pearl Buck, which includes *The Good Earth.*♦

House of Mirth, The, novel by Edith Wharton,♦ published in 1905.

Although she has beauty and charm and is related to prominent New York families, Lily Bart is unmarried at 29. Ambitious for wealth and position, she makes a career of her search for a husband, and among her suitors are Simon Rosedale, a vulgar rich Jew, and Lawrence Selden, a lawyer who is the one love of her life but lacks the wealth she requires. Gambling at a house party, she loses a large sum to Gus Trenor, who undertakes to invest her small capital, gaining power over her by advancing money from his own pocket, although she does not realize this until later. His demand that she satisfy his passion by way of repayment frightens Lily, but she manages to escape and promises to return the money. She goes on a yachting trip to the Mediterranean in a party headed by George Dorset, whose wife Bertha conceals a meeting with her lover by accusing Lily of being George's mistress. The ensuing scandal ends Lily's career in fashionable society, and after the death of her aunt, Mrs.

Peniston, she becomes a milliner. Following a last interview in which she reveals her love to Selden, she returns, ill and overwrought, to her boardinghouse room, where she takes an overdose of sedative, which kills her. Selden arrives, intending to ask her to marry him. Her lifeless body has already been discovered, and when he searches her effects he finds that she has put aside her aunt's entire bequest to repay her debt to Trenor.

House of Night, The, poem by Freneau,♦ published in 1779 and enlarged in his *Poems* (1786). It was suggested by the Scriptural aphorism, "the last enemy that shall be conquered is Death."

Death, in his solitary palace at midnight, is represented as being on his deathbed. After composing his epitaph, which indicates that even Death has vanity, he makes a bargain with an avaricious undertaker, a reflection upon the inhumanity of man who will not perform a charitable act without certain reward. After the passing and funeral of Death, the poem concludes with reflections on the impropriety of too great attachment to the present life, and incentives to virtue that may conduct one to a better existence.

House of the Seven Gables, The, romance by Hawthorne,♦ published in 1851. It is based on the tradition of a curse pronounced on the author's family when his great-grandfather was a judge in the Salem witchcraft trials.

In Salem stands the ancestral home of the Pyncheons, cursed by Wizard Maule when the first Colonel Pyncheon despoiled him of his wealth. In the mid-19th century, the house is owned by hypocritical Judge Jaffrey Pyncheon, whose studied benevolence makes him an honored citizen. He does not live in the dilapidated mansion, whose occupants are his poor cousin Hepzibah, reduced to operating a cent-shop; a country relative, Phoebe; a single lodger, the young daguerreotypist Holgrave, who falls in love with Phoebe; and Hepzibah's brother Clifford, ill and feeble-minded, just released from prison after a term of 30 years for the supposed murder of a rich uncle. Jaffrey, who had obtained Clifford's arrest, now harasses him in an attempt to find the missing deeds to their rich uncle's property, and threatens to have Clifford confined in an insane asylum. Hepzibah attempts to aid her brother and circumvent the judge, but the latter's sudden death frees them and makes them his heirs. Holgrave reveals that he is actually the last of the Maules, and that the judge, like the rich uncle, died by the curse on the house. Revealing the location of the missing deeds, he marries Phoebe, leaving the House of the Seven Gables, freed of its curse, to Hepzibah and Clifford.

HOUSTON, JAMES D. (1933–), born in San Francisco and since 1969 a teacher of creative writing at the University of California, Santa Cruz, is known for his novels: *Between Battles* (1968), about mock military action to prepare for the real; *Gig* (1969), treating the ways and work of a jazz pianist; *A Native Son of the Golden West* (1971), depicting a playboy Californian in Hawaii; *Continental Drift* (1978), about the very uneasy life of a newspaperman in Houston's region; and *Love Life* (1986). Besides other fiction he and his wife wrote *Farewell to Manzanar* (1974), about Japanese-Americans mistreated during World War II, and he himself wrote *Californians* (1982).

HOVEY, RICHARD (1864–1900), born in Illinois, early began to write poetry and published his first small volume at the age of 16. After graduating from Dartmouth (1885), he was successively an art student, theological student, journalist, actor, and lecturer. He was in England and France (1891–92), and, influenced by the French Symbolists, translated eight of Maeterlinck's plays. His own poetic vitality found an outlet in the exuberant *Songs from Vagabondia* (1894), written in collaboration with Bliss Carman. In this and the later volumes written with Carman, *More Songs from Vagabondia* (1896) and *Last Songs from Vagabondia* (1901), he reveled in the idea of the open road and happily proclaimed the joys of youthful living and companionship. The outbreak of the Spanish-American War swept him into an excited chauvinism, and in such poems as "Unmanifest Destiny" and "The Word of the Lord from Havana" he nationalized the Deity and deified the nation. With these poems, which appeared in *Along the Trail* (1898), was published his longer poem, "Spring," whose popular interlude, "A Stein Song," has the refrain,

> For it's always fair weather
> When good fellows get together . . .

During these years, Hovey was also writing an ambitious cycle of poetic dramas based on the *Morte d'Arthur,* with love as a central theme and the thesis that the social system has not yet evolved sufficiently to become "a medium in which all lives can move at all times in all respects in freedom." He projected three trilogies, each consisting of a masque, a tragedy, and a drama, but in the posthumous collection of fragments *The Holy Graal* (1907) are only the first trilogy and the masque of the second. During the last two years of his life, he lectured at Barnard College. *To the End of the Trail* (1908) is a posthumous collection of poems.

How Beautiful with Shoes, play by W.D. Steele♦ and Anthony Brown, produced in 1935. It is based on a short story by Steele.

How To Try a Lover, comedy by J.N. Barker,♦ published in 1817 and probably unproduced. Founded on a French picaresque novel, it is set in 13th-century Catalonia and deals with the efforts of young Carlos to win the fair Eugenia, over the supposed disapproval of their two fathers, who concoct a scheme to bring them together through apparent difficulties, on the assumption that their love will be stronger if opposed. The play ends with a Court of Love, at which Eugenia presides and gives the fathers a bad time in revenge for their deception, until she finally awards her hand to Carlos.

How To Write Short Stories (with Samples), book by Ring Lardner,♦ published in 1924, with a humorous, mock-critical preface and ten stories to "illustrate in a half-hearted way what I am trying to get at." These tales of baseball players, boxers, songwriters, and other American types constitute a sardonically humorous use of the vernacular to expose native foibles and vices.

"The Facts" tells of an idyllic love affair, which proceeds smoothly until the hero, with his best friend, spends a drunken Christmas Eve in buying precisely the wrong gifts for his fiancée's entire family. "Some Like Them Cold," an account of a casual meeting of a songwriter and a stenographer, and their tentatively affectionate letters, exposes them as selfish and mercenary. "Alibi Ike" is the story of a competent baseball player who continually makes trouble for himself by seeking unnecessary excuses for his every action. "The Golden Honeymoon" describes the dull, commonplace, and quarrelsome lives of a superficially amiable old couple. "Champion" presents the cruel, mean, and unprincipled side of a prizefighter's life, which "would never have passed the sporting editor" of a newspaper. "A Caddy's Diary" reveals the hypocrisy and lack of sportsmanship of his patrons. "A Frame-Up" describes the deception of a champion boxer by his manager, who takes advantage of the youth's innocence to further his own ends.

HOWADJI, THE, pseudonym of G.W. Curtis.♦

HOWARD, BLANCHE WILLIS (1847–98), novelist born in Maine, lived after 1875 in Germany, marrying there and becoming the Baroness von Teuffel. She wrote many exotic romances, of which the most popular was *Guenn: A Wave on the Breton Coast* (1883), the story of an egocentric American artist who causes the suicide of a Breton peasant girl when he fails to return her love.

HOWARD, BRONSON [CROCKER] (1842–1908), Michigan-born dramatist, came to New York in 1865, where he became a pioneer in the drama of contemporary manners with his farce *Saratoga*♦ (1870) and of social criticism in *Young Mrs. Winthrop*♦ (1882). *Old Love Letters* (1878) was a popular one-act social comedy. *Baron Rudolph* (1881) and *The Henrietta* (1887) were satires on American business. *One of Our Girls* (1885) was a social comedy contrasting French and American standards, a theme further elaborated in *Aristocracy* (1892), contrasting a *nouveau*

riche Californian, an old established New Yorker, and a European patrician. *Shenandoah*♦ (1888), a Civil War drama, was his greatest and most popular work. Although Howard did much to improve the American drama, he was bound by both convention and his own desire to achieve effects at the expense of realism.

HOWARD, MARTIN (*d.*1781), Loyalist pamphleteer, wrote *A Letter from a Gentleman at Halifax to His Friend in Rhode Island* (1765), in reply to a publication by Stephen Hopkins.♦ To answer angry retorts, he wrote *A Defense of the Letter from a Gentleman at Halifax to His Friend in Rhode Island* (1765), distinguished for its urbanity, satire, and clear legal reasoning. He fled to England during the Revolution.

HOWARD, RICHARD [JOSEPH] (1929–), Ohio-born poet, after a B.A. and M.A. from Columbia and study at the Sorbonne published his first collections, *Quantities* (1962) and *The Damages* (1967), followed by the Pulitzer Prize-winning *Untitled Subjects* (1969), written in syllabic verse and presenting 15 dramatic monologues of 19th-century writers, artists, and composers. *Findings* (1971) and *Fellow Feelings* (1976) present further dramatic monologues, while *Two-Part Inventions* (1974) consists of six fictitious dialogues, such as one between Oscar Wilde and Whitman in the latter's home. *Misgivings* (1979) contains commentaries of Sarah Bernhardt, Victor Hugo, and other subjects on their portraits by the French photographer Nadar, while *Lining Up* (1984) contains further dramatic monologues and dialogues of the same genre. *Alone with America* (1969) is a prose work on 41 contemporary U.S. poets, and *Preferences* (1974) is his edition with commentary on works chosen by 51 contemporary American poets from their own writings and from favorite works of the past. Howard has also translated (1982) Baudelaire's *Les Fleurs du mal*. *No Traveller* (1986) is a later gathering of his own poems.

HOWARD, SIDNEY [COE] (1891–1939), California-born playwright, graduated from the state university (1915), studied at Harvard in the 47 Workshop of G.P. Baker, served in World War I, and returned to become a magazine editor. His first major play, *Swords* (1921), a romantic blank-verse tragedy set in medieval times, was followed by adaptations from foreign dramas, including *S.S. Tenacity* (1922), *Casanova* (1923), and *Sancho Panza* (1923), and an original play, *Bewitched* (1924), written with Edward Sheldon. Although he continued to make adaptations, his reputation as an original dramatist was established with *They Knew What They Wanted*♦ (1924, Pulitzer Prize), which was followed by *Lucky Sam McCarver*♦ (1925), *Ned McCobb's Daughter*♦ (1926), and *The Silver Cord*♦ (1926). With Charles MacArthur, he wrote *Salvation* (1928), a play about a woman revivalist. A further series of adaptations included *Olympia* (1928); *Marseilles* (1930); and *The Late Christopher Bean* (1932), which transfers a French play to a New England setting and shows the triumph of a hired girl in recognizing the greatness of a struggling artist, who marries her when he becomes successful. Howard's next play was *Alien Corn* (1933), the story of a music teacher in a small college, who forsakes her dream of becoming a concert pianist because of her love for the married college president, and, when their affair ends, stifles her feelings and continues her teaching. Later plays include *Dodsworth*♦ (1934), in collaboration with Sinclair Lewis; *Yellow Jack*♦ (1934); *Paths of Glory* (1935), a dramatization of a war novel by Humphrey Cobb; and *The Ghost of Yankee Doodle* (1937), the story of a liberal's fight against war propaganda.

HOWE, E[DGAR] W[ATSON] (1853–1937), born in Indiana, reared in Missouri and Nebraska, was editor and proprietor of the *Daily Globe* of Atchison, Kan. (1877–1911), and later of *E.W. Howe's Monthly* (1911–37), which was noted for his aphoristic editorials. His most famous novel, *The Story of a Country Town* (1883), is a powerful, melodramatic tale of the narrow life of a Midwestern community, which was privately printed after being rejected by numerous publishers, but has come to be recognized as a significant pioneering work of naturalistic fiction and, in spite of the stilted dialogue and the author's pessimism, has been widely read and frequently republished. Howe's other works include *The Confession of John Whitlock* (1891); *Country Town Savings* (1911); *Ventures in Common Sense* (1919); *Plain People* (1929), his autobiography; and *The Indignations of E.W. Howe* (1933). He was known as "the Sage of Potato Hill."

HOWE, IRVING (1920–93), professor at Hunter College (1963–86) and literary and social critic. His books include *Sherwood Anderson: A Critical Biography* (1951); *William Faulkner: A Critical Study* (1952, revised 1962); *Politics and the Novel: A World More Attractive* (1963); *Steady Work* (1966), essays on the politics of democratic radicalism; *Thomas Hardy* (1967); *The Decline of the New* (1969), a study of the decline of modernism in literature; *The Critical Point* (1973), literary essays; *World of Our Fathers* (1976, National Book Award), about the experiences of East European Jews in the U.S.; *Leon Trotsky* (1978); and *Celebrations and Attacks* (1979), a collection of occasional writings. *A Margin of Hope* (1982) is subtitled "An Intellectual Biography." It was followed by *Socialism and America* (1985) and *The American Newness: Culture and Politics in the Age of Emerson* (1986).

HOWE, JULIA WARD (1819–1910), poet and lecturer on social reform, was particularly interested in Abolitionism and woman suffrage. With her husband, Samuel G. Howe, she edited the Boston *Commonwealth,* an antislavery paper, and among her books are *Sex and Education* (1874), *Modern Society* (1881), and a life of *Margaret Fuller* (1883). She is famous as the author of "The Battle Hymn of the Republic"♦ (1862). She was the sister of Sam Ward♦ and the mother of Laura E. Richards and Maud Howe Elliott. Her collected poems include *Passion Flowers* (1854) and *Later Lyrics* (1866).

HOWE, M[ARK] A[NTONY] DeWOLFE (1864–1960), New England editor, poet, and scholarly antiquary. His numerous books on the New England background include *Boston, the Place and the People* (1903); *Life and Letters of George Bancroft* (1908); *Boston Common: Scenes from Four Centuries* (1910); *Letters of Charles Eliot Norton* (1913), edited with Sara Norton; *The Atlantic Monthly and Its Makers* (1919); *Memories of a Hostess* (1922), based on the journals of Mrs. J.T. Fields; *Barrett Wendell and His Letters* (1924, Pulitzer Prize); *Classic Shades* (1928); *James Ford Rhodes* (1929), a biography; and *Holmes of the Breakfast-Table* (1939). *A Venture in Remembrance* (1941) is his autobiography.

HOWE, SAMUEL GRIDLEY (1801–76), Boston philanthropist and champion of oppressed peoples, organized the Massachusetts School for the Blind (Perkins Institution), and aided the deaf and feeble-minded. With his wife, Julia Ward Howe, he founded the Boston *Commonwealth,* an antislavery paper. Late in life he aided the Cretans in their struggle for independence from Turkey, just as his earliest philanthropic act had been to aid the suffering Greeks in their revolt against the Turks. His principal book was *An Historical Sketch of the Greek Revolution* (1828). He was the father of Laura E. Richards and Maud Howe Elliott.

HOWE, WILLIAM, 5th Viscount (1729–1814), commander in chief of the British army in the American Revolution. After taking part in the Battle of Bunker Hill, he held Boston until the spring of 1776 but subsequent failure was travestied in the anonymous play *The Blockheads,* a patriot reply to Burgoyne's *The Blockade.*♦ A fictional incident of this period is the subject of Hawthorne's "Howe's Masquerade."♦ He subsequently captured Long Island and New York, defeated Washington at White Plains, Brandywine, and Germantown, and settled at Philadelphia during the winter when the Americans were rallying their forces at Valley Forge. Later military failures led to his resignation (1778). He appears often in literature about the period, e.g. Maxwell Anderson's *Valley Forge.*

HOWELLS, WILLIAM DEAN (1837–1920), born in Ohio, began at the age of nine to set type in his father's printing office. As he tells in *My*

Year in a Log Cabin (1893) and "The Country Printer" in *Impressions and Experiences* (1896), his formal education was very slight and he had to school himself in the pressroom and from his father's bookcase. The family life in Hamilton, one of several Ohio towns to which they migrated, is revealed in the autobiographical *A Boy's Town* (1890). After many moves, the family settled in Columbus, where from 1856 to 1861 Howells wrote for the *Ohio State Journal,* and with J.J. Piatt♦ published the *Poems of Two Friends* (1860). Meanwhile he was passionately studying languages and reading what literature he could obtain, activities which in later life he described in such volumes as *My Literary Passions* (1895), *Literary Friends and Acquaintance* (1900), *Years of My Youth* (1916), and others.

In 1860 he wrote a campaign biography of Lincoln, which won him the consulate at Venice. During his four years there he found time to write a pleasant observation of *Venetian Life* (1866) and *Italian Journeys* (1867), and his study of the language and literature later bore fruit in *Modern Italian Poets* (1887). Returning to America (1865), he was associated briefly with *The Nation,* and then accepted the subeditorship of the *Atlantic Monthly,* ♦ a post he held for five years, until he became editor in chief (1871–81). During these years, he lived in and near Boston, and, although he retained the democratic equalitarianism of the Ohio frontier, he also became an adopted son of Brahmin culture.

His first novel, *Their Wedding Journey*♦ (1872), grew naturally out of his travel sketches, as did *A Chance Acquaintance*♦ (1873) and *A Foregone Conclusion* (1875), the latter depicting an Italian background. *The Lady of the Aroostook*♦ (1879) and *A Fearful Responsibility* (1881) both contrast American and Venetian characters and deal with conflicts between love and social rank. Other works of this first period were "Private Theatricals" (*Atlantic,* 1875–76; in book form as *Mrs. Farrell,* 1921); *The Undiscovered Country* (1880), a study of the sordidness of spiritualism and the true spirituality of the Shakers; and *Dr. Breen's Practice* (1881), which deals with the incompetence of a society woman as a physician.

In 1881 Howells forsook the *Atlantic* and began serializing his stories in the *Century Magazine.* At the same time, he departed from his earlier comedies of manners and studies of contrasting types to begin a series of realistic character studies, particularly of characters grappling with ethical problems. The first of these, *A Modern Instance*♦ (1882), was followed by *A Woman's Reason* (1883), which in its study of feminine nature and Boston social values lacked the breadth of its predecessor and of the masterpiece on Boston and the self-made man that followed it, *The Rise of Silas Lapham*♦ (1885). *Indian Summer*♦ (1886), the subtle portrait of a middle-aged widow and her problem of romance, is considered second only to the portrait of Silas Lapham. *The Minis-*

ter's Charge (1887) presents the theme that one cannot disclaim complicity with lives that surround one, while *April Hopes*♦ (1888) shows a return to the comedy of manners, although it includes a tragic presentation of young love.

In *Annie Kilburn*♦ (1889), Howells deals with the contrasts among the "summer people," the substantial inhabitants, and the laboring class of a New England town, and his consideration of false charity as against true justice shows an indictment of the existing economic system. This novel marked the change that now came to Howells's life. He moved to New York as a member of the editorial staff of *Harper's,* where he ranged more widely than he had under the Boston influence, and became interested in the larger problems of industrialism. A New York street railway strike, the conviction of the anarchists of the Haymarket Riot, the influence of Tolstoy, and the reading of such social reformers as Henry George, all caused him to turn toward socialism and to adapt his realistic fiction to the problems of the machine age. This transition is reflected in his first novel about New York, *A Hazard of New Fortunes*♦ (1890), followed by *The Quality of Mercy* (1892), a study of the ramifications of a crime for which the economic order is primarily responsible. These were followed by *An Imperative Duty* (1893), a slight treatment of the problem of miscegenation; *The World of Chance* (1893), a record of New York literary life; and *The Coast of Bohemia* (1893), dealing with a young woman art student.

In *A Traveler from Altruria*♦ (1894) and again in its sequel *Through the Eye of the Needle*♦ (1907), he returned to his study of social and economic problems, through the medium of a Utopia. Several minor novels followed, which revert to earlier themes: *An Open-Eyed Conspiracy* (1897) and *Their Silver Wedding Journey* (1899) reintroduced the Marches from his first novel; *Ragged Lady* (1899) is a story of American rusticity and European sophistication; *The Landlord at Lion's Head*♦ (1897), with its portrait of Jeff Durgin, is one of the author's great works of character study; and *The Son of Royal Langbrith* (1904) is a dramatic handling of a moral problem. In his last novel, *The Leatherwood God* (1916), he deals with the Ohio frontier of his youth, which is also the scene of *New Leaf Mills* (1913), the chronicle of a year of his childhood.

Throughout his life, Howells wrote short stories, of which two volumes are concerned with the supernatural, but all are less important than his novels. He was also the author of 31 dramas, ranging from farce to blank-verse tragedy, of 11 travel books, of several autobiographical works, and of a few volumes of verse. A scholarly *Selected Edition* of his writings (32 vols.) began publication in 1968, and *Selected Letters* was projected in four volumes.

During his later life, Howells was frequently considered the preeminent American man of letters, and he received many honors both in the U.S. and abroad, as well as the offer of many academic posts. In addition to advising his friend Clemens, he used his important position to aid and encourage such authors as Boyesen, Garland, Stephen Crane, Frank Norris, and Robert Herrick, who were following the trail he had blazed. Both in his articles in the "Easy Chair" of *Harper's Monthly* and in such volumes as *Criticism and Fiction* (1891), *My Literary Passions* (1895), and *Literature and Life* (1902), he was an important critical force. His own literary credo was summed up in *Criticism and Fiction,* in which he championed realism and its truthful delineation of the motives, the impulses, and the principles that shape the lives of actual men and women. The sources of this realism he ascribes not only to science but to democracy, since the realist "feels in every nerve the equality of things and the unity of men." To this concept he also attached certain dicta of his age: that art must serve morality, that it should teach rather than amuse, and that truthfulness to American life would inevitably picture the smiling aspects of experience.

HOWES, BARBARA (1914–   ), New York-born poet, reared near Boston, educated at Bennington, where she was influenced by Genevieve Taggard, is married to the poet William Jay Smith. ♦ Her own lyrics, often quite formal, appear in *The Undersea Farmer* (1948), *In the Cold Country* (1954), *Light and Dark* (1959), *Looking Up at Leaves* (1966), *The Blue Garden* (1972), *A Private Signal* (1977), and *Moving* (1983). *The Road Commissioner* (1983) collects short stories.

Howe's Masquerade, story by Hawthorne, ♦ published in *Twice-Told Tales* (1842).

At the Boston tavern, the Old Province House, once headquarters of the royal governors, the proprietor tells a visitor this legend: When Governor Howe gave an entertainment, the night before the patriots' victory in the siege of Boston, the guests were costumed as figures of history and fiction, with comic individuals in rags representing Washington and his generals. Late in the evening, a funeral march was heard, and a solemn procession of ancient figures passed through the ballroom. Colonel Joliffe, an aged patriot detained during the siege, was present with his granddaughter, and identified the apparitions as early Puritan governors, "summoned to form the funeral procession of royal authority in New England." According to legend, the procession reappears on each anniversary of the occasion.

Howl, poem by Allen Ginsberg, ♦ issued as the title work of a booklet (1956) for which Lawrence Ferlinghetti ♦ was tried and acquitted of publishing and selling obscene work. In long Whitmanesque lines, opening with "I saw the best minds of my generation destroyed by madness, starving hysterical naked," part 1 presents these figures living and dying intensely in a modern hell which, in the briefer part 2, is denounced as the destructive product of Moloch's materialism, mechanization, and conformism. The concluding part 3 is a lyrical address of empathy from the poet to a friend confined in a madhouse as the victim of this society.

HOWTH, MARGARET, pseudonym of Rebecca H. Davis. ♦

HOYT, CHARLES HALE (1860–1900), popular dramatist whose farcical plays, depending on amusing situations, caricatured characters, and satire, included *A Texas Steer* (1890, published 1925), a satire on politics, and *A Trip to Chinatown* (produced 1891, unpublished), which incorporated a song by a bumpkin about his comic misadventures in the Bowery. ♦

"Hub of the Universe," phrase applied to Boston, derived from a statement by Holmes in *The Autocrat of the Breakfast-Table:* "Boston State-house is the hub of the solar system."

HUBBARD, ELBERT (1856–1915), born in Illinois, after a career as a salesman and the writing of several poor novels, turned self-conscious bohemian. Finding the Hubbard cupboard rather bare, he sought intellectual nutriment in the theories of the English craftsman William Morris, whose ideas on decoration, printing, and medieval design he followed, generally with more enthusiasm than success. As a result, Hubbard's Roycroft Press at East Aurora (near Buffalo, N.Y.), produced a shoddy imitation of Morris's Kelmscott Press. From this ostentatiously simple artist colony, he also edited an inspirational magazine, the *Philistine* (1895–1915), whose platitudinously "arty" content was mainly written by himself. A similar magazine, *The Fra* (1908–17), whose title derived from the sobriquet he conferred upon himself, never attained the enormous popularity of the earlier publication. Among his numerous writings is the series of 170 Little Journeys ♦ to the homes of great men. His best-known work is the narrative essay *A Message to Garcia* ♦ (1899), a typical, timely, Hubbard-inspirational account of an incident in the Spanish-American War, which appealed to industrial magnates so poignantly that they distributed countless copies to promote greater efficiency among their employees. Hubbard died in the sinking of the *Lusitania.*

HUBBARD, FRANK MCKINNEY (1868–1930), Indiana humorist, as "Kin" Hubbard was widely known for his syndicated columns and caricatures, originally published in the *Indianapolis News* (1892–1930). These were concerned with the "Sayings" of his shrewd, humorous character,

Abe Martin, whose dialect quips were collected in an annual series of books.

HUBBARD, WILLIAM (*c.*1621–1704), born in England, graduated from Harvard in the first class (1642) and became active in colonial affairs, entering the ministry at Ipswich (1656). *A General History of New England from the Discovery to MDCLXXX* depended greatly upon Morton's *Memorial* and Winthrop's *Journal,* just as later historians, such as Prince and Cotton Mather, in turn depended upon Hubbard's manuscript, first printed in 1815. In his *Narrative of the Troubles with the Indians in New-England* (1677), he quivered with fury in telling of the Indians, "the treacherous villains" and "dross of mankind." Although the narrative lacks artistic unity and digresses into many details, it has a tremendous zest, and was very popular. Another of his works is the sermon *The Happiness of a People in the Wisdome of their Rulers* (1676).

Huckleberries Gathered from New England Hills, 11 local-color stories by Rose Terry Cooke,♦ published in 1891.

"Grit" is the story of obstinate old Reuben Fyler, who, because of a family quarrel with the Potters, refuses to let his daughter marry Tom Potter. When the girl manifests her "Fyler grit" and elopes, his anger is overcome by his admiration, and he astonishes the town by approving the match. "Odd Miss Todd" is a character study of Miny (Hermione) Todd, who, after the death of her eccentric father, at the age of 30 cultivates a taste for friendship and becomes noted for her charity, especially after her brief love affair with a fortune-seeking minister she has befriended who abandons her to marry another. "Hopson's Choice" tells of the romance of Hopson Bunnell and his cousin Prudence. Their love hits a snag when Prudence mistakes *p* for *b* in an overheard reference to "Hopson's Choice," but a friend corrects the misunderstanding, and all ends well. "A Town Mouse and a Country Mouse" is the story of the Hart sisters, Amanda and Melinda, who are separated when the latter marries a farmer and the former becomes a maid-of-all-work in town. After many years, they visit each other, and Melinda finds the noisy town unendurable, while Amanda dislikes the lonely farm, so that they continue to live apart.

Huckleberry Finn, Adventures of, novel by Clemens,♦ written under his pseudonym Mark Twain. A sequel to *Tom Sawyer,*♦ it was begun in 1876 and published in 1884, omitting the chapter included in *Life on the Mississippi.* Although it carries on the picaresque story of the characters in *Tom Sawyer,* the sequel is a more accomplished and a more serious work of art as well as a keener realistic portrayal of regional character and frontier experience on the Mississippi.

Narrated by Huck, the sequel begins with its unschooled hero under the motherly protection of the Widow Douglas and her sister, Miss Watson. When his blackguard father appears to demand the boy's fortune, Huck tricks him by transferring the money to Judge Thatcher, but his father kidnaps him and imprisons him in a lonely cabin. During one of the old man's drunken spells, Huck escapes to Jackson's Island, where he meets Miss Watson's runaway slave, Jim. They start down the river on a raft, but, after several adventures, the raft is hit by a steamboat and the two are separated. Huck swims ashore, and is sheltered by the Grangerford family, whose feud with the Shepherdsons causes bloodshed. The boy discovers Jim, and they set out again on the raft, giving refuge to the "Duke of Bridgewater," itinerant printer and fraud, and the "Dauphin," "Louis XVII of France," actor, evangelist, and temperance faker. At stopping places, the "King" lectures as a reformed pirate, and they present, as "Kean" and "Garrick," dramatic performances culminating in the fraudulent exhibition of the "Royal Nonesuch." Huck witnesses the murder of a harmless drunkard by an Arkansas aristocrat, whose contempt discourages a mob of would-be lynchers. The rogues learn of the death of Peter Wilks and claim legacies as his brothers. Huck interferes in behalf of the three daughters, and the scheme is foiled by the arrival of the real brothers. Then he discovers that the "King" has sold Jim to Mrs. Phelps, Tom Sawyer's Aunt Sally, and at the Phelps farm he impersonates Tom in an attempt to rescue Jim. When Tom arrives, he masquerades as his brother Sid, and concocts a fantastic scheme to free Jim. In the "mixed-up and splendid rescue," Tom is accidentally shot, and the slave is recaptured. While Tom is recuperating, he reveals that Miss Watson has died, setting Jim free in her will, and that the rescue was necessary only because he "wanted the *adventure* of it." It is also disclosed that Huck's fortune is safe, since his father is dead, but he concludes: "I reckon I got to light out for the territory ahead of the rest, because Aunt Sally she's going to adopt me and sivilize me, and I can't stand it. I been there before."

Hudson Balance (1801–9), Federalist newspaper of Hudson, N.Y. Its editor, Harry Croswell, was unsuccessfully defended by Hamilton in a libel suit caused by the paper's attacks on Jefferson. Hamilton's remarks on Burr led to their fatal duel. The paper moved to Albany (1809) and continued its policies as *The Balance and New York Journal.*

Hudson Review, The (1948–   ), quarterly literary journal, published in New York. Contributors include William Arrowsmith, Saul Bellow, Blackmur, Kenneth Burke, Eliot, Herbert Gold, Richmond Lattimore, W.S. Merwin, Marianne Moore, Pound, Schorer, W.D. Snodgrass, Tate, Eudora Welty, and Yvor Winters. Frederick Morgan♦ was a founder and editor.

Hudson River school, group of American painters who, rebelling against the classical 18th-century tradition of aristocratic portraiture, turned to romantic depictions of the American landscape. This transition in interest and taste coincides with the rising nationalism that followed the War of 1812, and had as its literary parallel the novels of Cooper and the poetry of Bryant. The leaders of the school, Thomas Cole (1802–48), Asher Durand (1796–1886), and Thomas Doughty (1793–1856), were followed by the more sentimental or more literal Frederick Church (1826–1900), Albert Bierstadt,♦ John F. Kensett (1818–72), Thomas Moran (1837–1926), and others, whose subjects were now often not Hudson River scenery but the national parks of the Far West.

Hugh Selwyn Mauberley, poem by Ezra Pound,♦ published in 1920.

The poem begins with an ironic "ode" on Pound's poetic career as seen by his critics at the end of his London period, and continues through 12 parts of the opening section, which presents with complex allusions and varied rhythms the "tawdry cheapness" and degradation of culture in modern civilization, stigmatized as corrupt, commercial, mechanical, and lacking in cultural distinctions. The sources of degradation and sterility are traced from the aesthetics of the Pre-Raphaelites and the *fin de siècle* writers, and the effects are related to five characters variously symbolic of the times. After an "Envoi" that acts as summation, the themes of the first section are ironically employed in the second section to reveal Mauberley, a passive aesthetic poet, as distinct from Pound, an active creative force, for in this second section Mauberley, the lover of beauty, only drifts through life without a vital understanding of relations to past or present, and leaves as legacy but one poem, "Medallion," a precise, pedantic, passionless imagistic work.

Hugh Wynne, Free Quaker, romance by S.W. Mitchell,♦ published in 1897.

HUGHES, [James] Langston (1902–67), Missouri-born major figure of the Harlem Renaissance,♦ had a nomadic life in the U.S. and Europe until he began his prolific literary career with *The Weary Blues* (1926), poems on black themes in jazz rhythms and idiom, whose success made possible his college career at Lincoln University, Pa. (A.B., 1929). His subsequent publications were in diverse media, but he is most widely known for his poetry issued in more than ten books and pamphlets, including *Fine Clothes to the Jew* (1927), *Dear Lovely Death* (1931), *The Negro Mother* (1931), *The Dream Keeper* (1932), *A New Song* (1938), *Shakespeare in Harlem* (1941), *Fields of Wonder* (1947), *One-Way Ticket* (1949), *Montage of a Dream Deferred* (1951), and *Ask Your Mama* (1961). His concern with his race, mainly in an

urban setting, is evident in these works, as is his social consciousness, evident also in the topical *Scottsboro Limited* (1932), four poems and a one-act play on the Scottsboro Case.♦ He also wrote two novels, *Not Without Laughter* (1930) and *Tambourines to Glory* (1958), and collections of stories including *The Ways of White Folks* (1934) and *Something in Common* (1963), but his major prose writings are those concerned with his character Jesse B. Semple, satirical sketches of a shrewd but supposedly ignorant Harlem resident who, under his nickname Simple,♦ appears in five volumes. For the stage Hughes wrote several plays, including *Mulatto* (1936), revised as a musical drama, *The Barrier* (1950); a musical version of *Tambourines to Glory* (1963); and *Simply Heavenly* (1963), also a musical play, based on his stories about Simple. He wrote two autobiographical volumes, *The Big Sea* (1940), about his youth and his life in the 1920s, and *I Wonder as I Wander* (1956), carrying his experiences to 1938. Other writings include *Fight for Freedom* (1962), about the NAACP, while his correspondence with Arna Bontemps, with whom he also collaborated on the musical *Tambourines to Glory,* was published in 1979.

HUGHES, Rupert (1872–1956), Missouri-born author, long resident in California, is best known for *George Washington* (3 vols., 1926–30), treating the President as a great man but stripping him of myths. Hughes's many popular novels include *What Will People Say?* (1914); *Souls for Sale* (1922); *No One Man* (1931); *The Man Without a Home* (1935), about John Howard Payne; and *The Giant Wakes* (1950), about Gompers. He also wrote *American Composers* (1900), plays, songs, motion pictures, a world history, and *City of Angels* (1941), about Los Angeles.

HUGO, Richard [Franklin] (1923–82), Seattle-born poet and the director of creative writing at the University of Montana (1964–82). His poetry concentrates on bleak views of derelict towns in his native Northwest, yet in his first book, *A Run of Jacks* (1961), he apostrophizes the region's fish and in his third, *Good Luck in Cracked Italian* (1969), he recalls the Italy he knew in the air corps during wartime. Other books include *Death of the Kapowsin Tavern* (1965); *The Lady in Kicking Horse Reservoir* (1973); *What Thou Lovest Well, Remains American* (1975); *31 Letters and 13 Dreams* (1977), which is partly epistles addressed to other contemporary poets; *Selected Poems* (1979); *White Center* (1980); and *The Right Madness on Skye* (1980). *The Triggering Town* (1979) prints lectures and essays on poetry. He also wrote under his own name a detective story, *Death and the Good Life* (1981).

Huguenots, French Protestants, whose church was Calvinistic in doctrine and Presbyterian in government. They were bitterly persecuted until the Edict of Nantes granted them freedom of worship (1598). Upon its revocation (1685), many of them fled to America. Some had previously made settlements in Florida and South Carolina, and many of the settlers of New Amsterdam were Huguenots. They became an important element in the society of Virginia and South Carolina, and also settled in Rhode Island, Connecticut, New York, Delaware, Maryland, and Pennsylvania. The only surviving church is in Charlestown.

HULME, THOMAS, see *Cobbett, William.*

Humanism, THE NEW, philosophical and critical movement that flourished in the U.S. during the 1920s, under the leadership of Irving Babbitt♦ and P.E. More.♦ It stresses human elements of experience as distinguished from supernatural or animal elements, assuming that the essential quality of human experience is ethical, that there is a dualism of man and nature, and that man's will is free. The New Humanists desire a discriminating, harmonious cultivation of every part of human nature, based upon a universal scale of values rather than the temporary codes of any particular society. They transcend the scientific method, finding their ultimate ethical principle in restraint, recognizing freedom as the "liberation from outer constraints and subjection to inner law." They turn to the Hellenic doctrine of reason, and away from romanticism; although they draw upon Christianity, Oriental philosophy, and certain modern thinkers and tend to make intellect rather than formal theology the universal test. T.S. Eliot♦ and Norman Foerster♦ are among the important followers of this school, although Eliot criticized some of its basic concepts. S.P. Sherman♦ was an early popular spokesman for its philosophy, but later adopted different standards. *Humanism and America* (1930), a symposium by its proponents, was answered by the symposium *The Critique of Humanism* (1930), and also by Santayana's *The Genteel Tradition at Bay*♦ (1931).

Humble-Bee, *The,* poem by Emerson,♦ published in 1839 and reprinted in *Poems* (1847). In six stanzas of irregular four-stress couplets, the verses celebrate the wisdom and virtues of the "yellow-breeched philosopher," who mocks at care, "sipping only what is sweet," and taking account of only what is cheerful and excellent.

Humble Romance, *A, and Other Stories,* collection of 28 tales by Mary Wilkins Freeman,♦ published in 1887. Studies of the New England environment and its typical characters, they show the influence of the local-color movement and are representative of Victorian morality and sentimentality.

"A Humble Romance" is the story of Jake Russell, an itinerant tin peddler, who un-

knowingly commits bigamy after his first wife elopes with another man. She returns to blackmail Jake, but his second wife remains faithful, carrying on his business until he is able to rejoin her. "Old Lady Pingree" tells of a kindly old spinster whose charity during her bare, poverty-stricken life is rewarded by the granting of her pathetic last wish to be buried "respectably" in the family plot. "Cinnamon Roses" is a tale of the frustrated romance of a New England villager and the spinster who mistakenly believes he is courting her more attractive sister, and the correction of their misunderstanding in later life. "An Independent Thinker" tells of Esther Gay, who nearly alienates her granddaughter's fiancé and his family by her seeming irreligion, but ingeniously manages to regain their friendship while still clinging to her beloved "principles." "The Bar Light-House," set on the stormy New England coast, is concerned with a lighthouse keeper's paralytic wife and her religious conversion owing to a succession of apparently miraculous circumstances.

Humboldt's Gift, novel by Saul Bellow,♦ published in 1975 and awarded a Pulitzer Prize.

The saga of Charlie Citrine begins with him as a bright, bookish, ambitious young man from the Midwest intent on literary success, coming, by way of Chicago, to Greenwich Village. There he becomes the friend and disciple of the visionary poet Von Humboldt Fleisher, obviously modeled on Delmore Schwartz. In time the vexatious Humboldt dies alone, poor and mad, but he continues to affect the life of the middle-aged Charlie, who recapitulates some of the dead poet's folly while also striving for his wisdom. Worldly success comes to Citrine with the winning of two Pulitzer Prizes, respectively for a play and a biography, and an honorary award from the French government. But financial problems plague him and bring a variety of serio-comic difficulties in personal relations with his greedy divorced wife and his voluptuous girlfriend. Most troublesome of all is Ronald (Rinaldo) Cantabile, a minor hoodlum to whom Charlie owes money and whose wife, oddly enough, is writing a dissertation on Fleisher, about whom she seeks information as she pursues Citrine through Chicago and even across the Atlantic. From these difficulties Citrine is saved by money from the tremendously popular film whose fantastic script, written many years ago by Humboldt and Charlie, is a comedy of sorts about cannibalism, a recurrent metaphor in Bellow's novel.

HUMES, H[AROLD] L[OUIS] (1926–   ), New York–born novelist, educated at Massachusetts Institute of Technology and Harvard, a founder of the *Paris Review,*♦ whose novels are *Underground City* (1958), a story of personal conflicts of an American and others involved with the Resistance movement and politics in France during the 1940s, and *Men Die* (1959), treating the relationships of black and white survivors of an explosion of a naval ammunition dump.

HUMPHREY, WILLIAM (1924–   ), born in the east Texas area of the Red River, the setting of most of his fiction. His novels are *Home from the Hill* (1958), about a family whose men are hunters and live and die by the bloody code of their region; *The Ordways* (1965), a larger family chronicle of four generations from Tennessee to Texas; *Proud Flesh* (1973), portraying the matriarch of a cotton-raising family; *Hostages to Fortune* (1984), depicting the relentless tragic relations with family and friends of a middle-aged author; and *No Resting Place* (1989). *The Last Husband* (1953) and *A Time and a Place* (1968) collect stories. *The Spawning Run* (1971) and *My Moby Dick* (1978) are accounts of Humphrey's fishing for sport, and *Farther Off from Heaven* (1977) is a memoir of his youth.

HUMPHREYS, DAVID (1752–1818), born in Connecticut, graduated from Yale (1771), and during the Revolutionary War became a lieutenant colonel and aide-de-camp to Washington. His stirring patriotism appears in *A Poem Addressed to the Armies of the United States* (1780), and his military knowledge in *An Essay on the Life of the Honorable Major-General Israel Putnam* (1788). After the peace, he spent two years abroad as secretary to the Commission for Negotiating Treaties of Commerce, and then returned to Mount Vernon for a year with his "Dear General." At the threat of war between Spain and England (1790), he was appointed a secret agent abroad, and, appointed sole commissioner in Algerine affairs (1793), spent three more years in Spain as minister plenipotentiary. Returning to the U.S. (1802), he interested himself in the production of wool from the Spanish merino sheep, wrote a dissertation on the subject, and imported some of the sheep, establishing a successful woolen mill. A typical 18th-century squire, having directed his pen to *A Poem on the Happiness of America* (1780) and *The Glory of America; or, Peace Triumphant over War* (1783), he now addressed "to the Citizens of the United States" a didactic *Poem on the Industry of the United States of America* (1783). Here he expressed his faith in the nation's glorious future, with a social and economic conservatism characteristic of a Yankee industrialist and staunch Federalist. Associated with the Connecticut Wits,♦ he wrote poetry that is pompous and lacking in imagination, although he contributed a few light bagatelles and participated in the satire, *The Anarchiad*♦ (1786–87). He was also the author of a romantic drama, *The Widow of Malabar* (1790), and a comedy, *The Yankey in England*♦ (1814).

HUMPHRIES, [GEORGE] ROLFE (1894–1969), graduated from Amherst (1915), to which

he returned as a lecturer in English (1957) after a long career of teaching Latin in high school. He wrote poetry published in several volumes and gathered in *Collected Poems* (1965), and verse translations, including Lorca's *The Poet in New York* (1940), *The Aeneid* (1951), and Ovid's *Metamorphoses* (1955). Late poems appear in *Coat on a Stick* (1969).

HUNEKER, JAMES GIBBONS (1857–1921), after studying piano in Paris, where he was affected by the romanticism of contemporary painters, writers, and musicians, became a music critic in Philadelphia and New York. From 1900 to 1917 he wrote for the New York *Sun* on matters concerned with art, literature, drama, and music, and his wit, lush phrasing, and connoisseur's gusto made his criticism stand far above that of other journalists of the time. His best-known early books include *Mezzotints in Modern Music* (1899), essays on Brahms, Chopin, Liszt, and others; *Chopin: The Man and His Music* (1900), a biographical sketch and critical analysis generally considered his best work; and *Melomaniacs* (1902), satirical sketches. From this exclusive concern with music he turned to wider interests in such books as *Iconoclasts, a Book of Dramatists* (1905); *Egoists: A Book of Supermen* (1909); *Promenades of an Impressionist* (1910); *Ivory Apes and Peacocks* (1915); *New Cosmopolis* (1915), a study of New York City; *Unicorns* (1917); and *Variations* (1921). *Old Fogy* (1913) and *Steeplejack* (1920) are autobiographical works that exhibit the variety of interests, facility of criticism, and vivacity of thought that won Huneker the personal and artistic allegiance of such men as Mencken and Nathan. His sonorous style and love for the voluptuous and colorful are also exhibited in his novel, *Painted Veils*♦ (1920), concerned with New York artists.

HUNT, HELEN, see *Jackson, Helen Hunt.*

HUNT, ISAAC (*c.*1742–1809), born in Barbados, graduated from the Academy of Philadelphia (University of Pennsylvania) in 1763, served as a tutor, and then became a pamphleteer. *A Letter from a Gentleman in Transilvania* (1764) attacked the Pennsylvania proprietors, and Hunt lampooned the college authorities in a series of satires, beginning with *A Humble Attempt at Scurrility* (1765), nevertheless receiving a master's degree (1771). *The Political Family* (1775) championed a continued union with Great Britain, and as a Loyalist he was forced to escape to England, where he barely managed to live by preaching and tutoring. His last political pamphlet was written against Thomas Paine (1791). He was the father of Leigh Hunt.

HUNT, WILLIAM GIBBES (1791–1833), graduated from Harvard (1810), and moved to Lexington, Ky., where he established *The Western*

Review and Miscellaneous Magazine♦ (1819–21), an important journal of Western culture.

HUNTER, DARD (1883–1966), Ohio paper-maker and typographer, whose *The Etching of Figures* (1915) and *The Etching of Contemporary Life* (1917) are said to be the first books in the history of printing ever produced entirely by one man. His other works include *The Art of Bookmaking* (1915), *Primitive Papermaking* (1927), *Papermaking Through Eighteen Centuries* (1929), *Papermaking: The History and Technique of an Ancient Craft* (1943), and *My Life with Paper* (1958).

"Hunters of Kentucky, THE," song by Samuel Woodworth.♦

Huntington Library, properly titled the Henry E. Huntington Library and Art Gallery, is situated at San Marino, Cal., near Pasadena, on the estate of its founder, a railroad financier, who between 1910 and his death in 1927 accumulated vast collections of books, including the Beverly Chew, Robert Hoe, and Bridgewater libraries, and a fine collection of English paintings, particularly from the 18th century. These collections, valued at $30,000,000 upon Huntington's death, have been operated as a public trust with a large endowment. From its incunabula, book and manuscript collections of English and American literature, Americana, and Spanish-American history have come many important scholarly studies. The library's publications are an outgrowth of its research program.

HUNTLEY, LYDIA, see *Sigourney.*

Huron Indians (properly, WANDOT or WYAN-DOT), confederacy of nomadic Iroquoian tribes, which originally inhabited Ontario, where Champlain visited them (1603). They were bitter enemies of the Iroquois proper, who virtually destroyed them (1648–49). Some survivors fled to Quebec and descendants of others settled in Michigan and Ohio. They fought against the U.S. in the Revolution and the War of 1812, but later moved to Oklahoma. In the Leather-Stocking Tales♦ the Hurons are depicted as treacherous and cruel, and they figure also in *Satanstoe.*♦

Hurry Harry, character in *The Deerslayer.*♦

HURST, FANNIE (1889–1968), born in Ohio, graduated from Washington University (1909), taught school for a time, and moved to New York to begin her literary career. Her first four books were volumes of short stories, *Just Around the Corner* (1914), *Every Soul Hath Its Song* (1916), *Gaslight Sonatas* (1918), and *Humoresque* (1919). The last contains eight stories of New York City's Jews; the title work, concerning a prodigy on the violin, was dramatized by the author in

1923. Later collections include *The Vertical City* (1922), *Song of Life* (1927), *Procession* (1929), and *We Are Ten* (1937). Her novels, reflecting her interests in the stage, music, and the role of women, are *Star-Dust* (1921); *Lummox* (1923), about a Scandinavian servant girl; *Mannequin* (1926); *A President Is Born* (1928); *Five and Ten* (1929); *Back Street* (1931); *Imitation of Life* (1933); *Anitra's Dance* (1934); *Great Laughter* (1936), about a matriarch's rule; *Lonely Parade* (1942), about career women in New York; *Hallelujah* (1944), about a small-town girl's sacrifices; *The Hands of Veronica* (1947); *Anywoman* (1950); *Family!* (1960); and *God Must Be Sad* (1961). *Anatomy of Me* (1958) is autobiographical.

HURSTON, ZORA NEALE (1901?–60), born in Florida, after graduation from Barnard continued her study of anthropology, as evidenced in *Tell My Horse* (1938), about her research into folk-ways of Haiti and the West Indies; and *Mules and Men* (1935), stories of voodoo among blacks of the South. Her novels include *Jonah's Gourd Vine* (1934), about a black preacher's loves, and *Their Eyes Were Watching God* (1937), her masterpiece. It celebrates the self-liberation of Janie, a girl who dreams of a life redolent and symbolic of pear-tree blossoms. She goes through two marriages with domineering men. Janie publicly humiliates and leaves the first husband and suffers the second one for years until she meets her true love, Tea-cake, a gambler and migrant crop-picker, with whom she gladly works in the fields of Florida but kills in self-defense when he is mad with rabies. At her trial, the black community of men try to convict her of murder, but a white doctor and sheriff who were witness to Teacake's sick-ness testify for her and she is acquitted. The novel brilliantly explores the themes of male oppression and female autonomy. It has become a key feminist text. *Moses: Man of the Mountain* (1939) is a black folk interpretation of Biblical Jews, and *Seraph on the Suwanee* (1948) describes the marrying and civilizing of a Florida cracker woman. *Dust Tracks on a Road* (1942) is her autobiography. She taught at North Carolina College for Negroes. An anthology of her writings was edited by Alice Walker (1979), and *Spunk* (1985) collects stories.

HUTCHINS, ROBERT MAYNARD (1899–1977), graduated from Yale (1921) and was successively secretary of the university, professor in the law school (1927), and dean of the law school (1928). As president of the University of Chicago (1929–45) and its chancellor (1945–51), he reorganized the administration and abolished compulsory courses and the conventional grading system. In *The Higher Learning in America* (1936), *No Friendly Voice* (1936), *Speaking of Education* (1940), *Education for Freedom* (1943), and *Morals, Religion, and Higher Education* (1950) he stated his theory that education devoted to "the accumulation of observed facts" of science is anti-intellectual. He advocated the study of basic texts in the history of ideas, and concentration on basic abstractions, through "rational analysis which is logically prior to the empirical observations involved."

HUTCHINSON, ANNE (1591–1643), emigrated from England to Massachusetts (1634), where her vigorous intellect soon led her to hold informal weekly meetings of women, in which she discussed the sermons of the previous Sunday and advocated a "covenant of grace" based on the individual's direct intuition of God's grace, as opposed to the orthodox belief in a "covenant of works" based on obedience to the statutes of church and state. She was called an Antinomian, ♦ was said to be "traducing the ministers and their ministry," and, although Governor Vane, her brother-in-law John Wheelwright, and others supported her views, a synod of churches excommunicated her, and Governor Winthrop banished her from the colony. She and her family went to Rhode Island (1638), then to New York (1642), where Indians massacred all but one of them.

HUTCHINSON, THOMAS (1711–80), member of a prominent Boston family, enjoyed a brilliant political career. At one time he was simultaneously member of the council, judge of probate, chief justice, and lieutenant governor. He was the last royal governor of Massachusetts Bay Colony (1771–74). Although he was the most influential man in the colony, his "hard money" policy and decided Tory leanings made him unpopular with the Adams family and others. His strict enforcement of the Stamp Act and the fact that a family member was a stamp distributor led to the burning of his mansion in 1765. He was also hated because the *Hutchinson Letters,* said to have been sent to a former secretary of British Foreign Secretary Grenville, urged drastic measures to curb "what are called English Liberties" in the colonies. Franklin came upon the letters and sent them to a friend with instructions to keep them private, but they were published (1772) and the resulting scandal led to Franklin's removal from the post of deputy postmaster-general. Hutchinson's hatred of the liberal colonists increased, and it was his strenuous Tory policy that led to the Boston Tea Party, after which he left for England. His *History of the Colony of Massachusetts Bay, from its First Settlement in 1628 to the year 1750* (2 vols., 1764, 1767) was based on a wide study of manuscript sources, but he was better equipped for minute than for general analysis, and lacked creative imagination with which to reconstruct the past. A third volume, bringing the history down to 1774, was published (1828), and he was the author of several pamphlets dealing with colonial history. A continuation of the *History* was made by George Minot. ♦ Hutchinson is satirized in Mercy Otis Warren's *The Adulateur.*

HUTTON, LAURENCE (1843–1904), New York drama critic, wrote some 50 chatty, impressionistic books, mainly on the theater and his literary pilgrimages abroad, e.g. *Curiosities of the American Stage* (1891) and *Literary Landmarks of Florence* (1897). He edited the *American Actor Series* (5 vols., 1881–82).

HWANG, DAVID HENRY (1957–), playwright. The son of immigrants, Hwang won acclaim and an Obie Award for *FOB* (1981), about "fresh off the boat" Chinese immigrants and their tactics for survival. *Family Devotions* (1983) is written on a similar theme. *The Dance and the Railroad* (1982) concerns an 1867 strike by Chinese laborers building a railroad. *M. Butterfly* (1988) won the Tony Award as best play of that year.

Hyacinth Robinson, hero of *The Princess Casamassima.* ♦

Hyman Kaplan, character in fiction by Leo C. Rosten. ♦

Hymn to the Night, poem by Longfellow, ♦ published in *Voices of the Night* (1839). In quatrains of alternate five- and three-stress lines, the poem hails the soothing night with a verse from the *Iliad,* "Welcome! Thrice prayed for!" and celebrates the peace-bringing "fountain . . . the calm majestic presence of the Night."

Hymns have been collected by all American Protestant sects and sung in their church services. The scruples of the Puritans forbade original hymns, and they created only new versions of the Psalms. Although the 16th-century English versions of Henry Ainsworth, John Hopkins, and Thomas Sternhold were probably brought over on the *Mayflower,* the first American collection was the *Bay Psalm Book* ♦ (1640). Cotton Mather, in his *Psalterium Americanum* (1718), made another translation, as did Thomas Prince (1758), while Thomas Walter ♦ gave further impetus to psalmody through his discourse on "singing by note" (1721), and William Billings ♦ introduced other reforms in his musical settings (1770). During the late 18th century, Congregationalists began to admit hymns as well as psalms, and, besides the amended versions of Isaac Watts's *Psalms and Hymns* by Joel Barlow (1785) and Timothy Dwight (1800), original religious songs were written by Mather Byles. Later Congregational hymnodists included J.G.C. Brainard and Ray Palmer, and H.W. Beecher's *Plymouth Collection* (1855) was an important Congregational compilation. The Presbyterians, like the Congregationalists, long used versions of Watts, the first of their original hymnodists being Samson Occom. During the 19th century, hymnody was stimulated by Thomas Hastings ♦ and by Lowell Mason, ♦ whose settings included those for "From

Greenland's Icy Mountains" and "Nearer, My God, to Thee." Mason's collection, *The Choir* (1832), included S.F. Smith's "America," and other prominent Baptist hymnodists were Adoniram Judson and Lydia Huntley Sigourney. Members of the Protestant Episcopal church known for their hymns include Francis Scott Key, Sarah Josepha Hale, J.W. Eastburn, and Harriet Beecher Stowe. Other hymnodists of the time included Hosea Ballou, Alice and Phoebe Cary, Lucy Larcom, and Whittier. The Unitarians contributed more to American hymnody than any other sect, their authors including J.Q. Adams, Bryant, J.F. Clarke, Emerson, E.E. Hale, Holmes, Higginson, Longfellow, John Pierpont, and Jones Very. The evangelists Moody and Sankey made hymns more popular in the mid-19th century.

Hyperion, romance by Longfellow, ♦ published in 1839. The thin thread of story connects philosophical discourses, romantic legends, literary criticism, and translations of German poetry. The romantic creation is in the mood of Jean Paul Richter, but the events correspond with those of the author's second visit to Europe, from the death of his first wife to his friendship with Frances Appleton, whom he later married.

I

I Have a Rendezvous with Death, poem by Alan Seeger. ♦

I Sing the Body Electric, poem by Whitman, ♦ untitled in the 1855 edition of *Leaves of Grass,* later called "Poem of the Body" as a section of "Children of Adam," and given its present title in 1867. It celebrates the anatomy and the form of men, women, and children, declaring, "These are not the parts and poems of the Body only, but of the Soul, O I say now these are the soul!"

I.W.W., abbreviation for Industrial Workers of the World—the Wobblies. Figures such as Bill Haywood and Joe Hill ♦ of the Wobblies appear in many novels, including Dos Passos's *42nd Parallel,* Winston Churchill's *The Dwelling Place of Light,* and Josephine Herbst's *The Executioner.*

Icarian Colonies, see *Cabet, Étienne.*

Icebound, play by Owen Davis, ♦ produced and published in 1923, was awarded a Pulitzer Prize.

Members of the tight-lipped, "ice-bound" Jordan family, in Veazie, Me., await the death of old Mrs. Jordan, whom none of them loves. She has a secret fondness for her youngest son Ben, the "black sheep," and he is summoned by Jane Crosby, a poor cousin and household servant, who is in love with him. Jane's influence over Mrs. Jordan is disliked by the older son, Henry, his mean wife Emma, and vain step-daughter Nettie, and by the widowed daughter Sadie and her children, Ella and Orin. They plan to dismiss Jane on acquiring the estate. Mrs. Jordan dies before Ben arrives, risking arrest on a charge of arson that is dropped in time. The lawyer, Judge Bradford, discloses that Jane inherits the bulk of the estate, and she keeps Ben out of jail by paying bail for him, making him stay to help on the farm until his trial in the spring. He distrusts her, resents working for her, and is attracted by Nettie, who, like the others, becomes dependent upon Jane's generosity. But after Ben has proved to be a hard worker and honest, Jane transfers his mother's entire estate to him, in keeping with Mrs. Jordan's desire. The rest of the family, reversing their former attitude, now flatter him and try to become his friends. When Bradford reveals to Ben that Jane loves him, and shows him a letter from his mother, Ben breaks the "ice" of his Jordan character, confesses his love for his mother, and asks Jane to marry him.

Iceman Cometh, *The,* play by Eugene O'Neill, ♦ produced and published in 1946.

Harry Hope's run-down New York saloon and rooming house harbors a group of alcoholics, among them Hope himself, a former Tammany man; Willie Oban, a Harvard Law School graduate; "Jimmy Tomorrow," a onetime newspaper correspondent; and Larry Slade and Don Parritt, former anarchists. All are guilt-ridden by their ruined lives and all cling to "pipe dreams" about their condition and the future. They eagerly await a visit from Hickey, a cheerful salesman they consider one of them, though he is outwardly more successful. Upon his arrival to give his annual party, however, the pattern changes because Hickey's traditional joke about his wife and the iceman is not forthcoming, and he threatens the men's pipe dreams with talk of bringing to others the peace he claims to have found through having given up drink and discarded all illusions. Larry sees that Hickey's view that one should "sink down to the bottom of the sea" is poisonous, for "the lie of the pipe dream is what gives life" to people like themselves. In their deprivation they turn to hard, humorless cynicism, Hickey most of all in confessing he killed his wife out of hatred, not to give her peace; Parritt admits he betrayed his mother and anarchism out of hatred. Both in effect commit suicide: Hickey by summoning the police, Parritt by leaping from the fire escape. The idea that Hickey is insane slowly develops as a new pipe dream, allowing the others to resume their old relationships, banter, and illusions, and only Larry, who perceives Hickey as the "Iceman of Death," remains truly and despairingly aware of reality.

Ichabod, poem by Whittier, ♦ published in 1850. In quatrains of alternate four- and two-stress lines, the work, whose Hebrew title means "inglorious," expresses the disappointment of the antislavery factions when Webster supported the compromise of 1850 in his "Seventh of March Speech." In "The Lost Occasion" (1880), Whittier, praising Webster's "nobler self," condones his "sad concessions" in this episode.

Ichabod Crane, hero of *The Legend of Sleepy Hollow.* ♦

Idiot's Delight, play by Robert Sherwood, ♦ produced and published in 1936, was awarded a Pulitzer Prize.

[313]

At a resort hotel in the Italian Alps, "in any imminent year," several foreign travelers are detained because the nearby frontiers have been closed. Among them are Harry Van, an American vaudeville promoter, and his troupe known as "Les Blondes"; the Cherrys, a honeymooning English couple; Dr. Waldersee, a German scientist who is working on a cancer cure; Quillery, a radical French pacifist; and Achille Weber, a munitions manufacturer, and his Russian mistress Irene. Harry recognizes the exotic Irene as a vaudeville performer with whom he once had a casual love affair in Omaha, although she denies this and maintains an affected pose. The outbreak of a world war is announced, and Quillery, learning that planes from a local base have bombed Paris, delivers a violent patriotic outburst and is arrested and shot. Irene tells Weber "the truth" concerning his responsibility for death and destruction; this he cannot forgive, and the following day he refuses to endorse her questionable passport. Waldersee abandons research to join the "obscene maniacs" at home, Cherry goes to join the army, and even Dumptsy, the gentle little waiter, appears in uniform. Only Irene cannot cross the frontier, but, when she confesses to Harry that she did know him, "slightly, in Omaha," he suddenly decides to remain with her, and they are trapped when the hotel is destroyed during an air raid.

If, Yes, and Perhaps, tales by E.E. Hale. ♦

IGNATOW, DAVID (1914–   ), Brooklyn-born poet of immigrant parents, whose hard struggles in youth and through the Depression are the stuff from which he has made his poetry, briefly told in Brooklynese speech. This has appeared in *Poems* (1948), *The Gentle Weight Lifter* (1955), *Say Pardon* (1962), *Figures of the Human* (1964), *Earth Hard* (1968), *Rescue the Dead* (1968), *Poems, 1934–69* (1970), *Facing the Tree* (1975), *Tread the Dark* (1978), *Whisper to the Earth* (1981), *Leaving the Door Open* (1984), and *New and Collected Poems: 1970–1985* (1987). His *Notebooks* (1973) treats both his personal life and his aims as poet.

Ik Marvel, pseudonym of D.G. Mitchell. ♦

Ikkemotubbe, Chickasaw chief in Faulkner's fiction, variously presented as the son or nephew, but always the heir, of Issetibbeha, and himself the sire of Sam Fathers. He sells the Yoknapatawpha land that becomes Sutpen's Hundred and the McCaslin family property. He is mentioned in *The Sound and the Fury, Requiem for a Nun,* "The Bear," and other works, and in the early story "Red Leaves," where his family relationships are inconsistent with those in other accounts.

I'll Take My Stand, anthology published in 1930 by 12 Southerners to set forth their concept of regionalism♦ as members of the Agrarians. ♦ The contributors to the symposium, actually called a manifesto, included Donald Davidson, John Gould Fletcher, John Crowe Ransom, Allen Tate, R.P. Warren, and Stark Young, most of them former contributors to *The Fugitive.* ♦

Illinois Monthly Magazine, The (1830–37), edited and mainly written by James Hall,♦ was the first literary periodical west of Ohio. In 1832, when Hall moved to Cincinnati, he changed the title to *The Western Monthly Magazine* and continued it as a dignified literary journal and local review. His editorship ended in 1836.

Illustrious Providences, see *Remarkable Providences.*

Imagism, poetic movement of England and the United States, flourished from 1909 to 1917. Its credo, expressed in *Some Imagist Poets* (1915), included the use of the language of common speech, precision, the creation of new rhythms, absolute freedom in choice of subject matter, the evocation of images in hard, clear poetry, and concentration. Originating in the aesthetic philosophy of T.E. Hulme, the movement soon attracted Ezra Pound, who became the leader of a small group opposed to the romantic conception of poetry and inspired by Greek and Roman classics and by Chinese, Japanese, and modern French poets. In the U.S., the group was represented in *Poetry: A Magazine of Verse* by Pound, H.D., John Gould Fletcher, and Amy Lowell, and by such English poets as F.S. Flint, Richard Aldington, and D.H. Lawrence. Pound collected some of their work in *Des Imagistes: An Anthology* (1914), after which his interest began to wane; Amy Lowell then assumed active leadership, advocating that the group subscribe to a fixed program and hold together for at least three years. Under her guidance were published several anthologies, all entitled *Some Imagist Poets.*

IMLAY, GILBERT (*c.*1754–1828), Revolutionary War captain, adventurer, and author of *A Topographical Description of the Western Territory of North America* (1792) and *The Emigrants* (3 vols., 1793), a sentimental romance of the frontier near Pittsburgh, which, in addition to its adventurous quality, champions such social reforms as divorce and the rights of women. During his later life in Europe he lived for a time with Mary Wollstonecraft.

Imp of the Perverse, The, story by Poe,♦ published in *Graham's Magazine* (1845). A condemned murderer explains his confession, which followed years of safe concealment, in terms of a perverse impulse, and states that perversity is an unrecognized major motive for men's actions.

Impending Crisis, The, tract by H.R. Helper. ♦

Impressionism, aesthetic movement in which the artist attempts to present the impressions an object makes upon him, rather than a realistic version of the object itself. Impressionists are thus more concerned with moods or sensations than with the observation of details. The name derives from the French school of painting of the late 19th century, whose exponents included Degas, Monet, Manet, Renoir, and Pissarro, and which was brought to the U.S. by such painters as J.A. Weir, Maurice Prendergast, and Childe Hassam, who were similarly concerned with transitory effects of light and with capturing a momentary luminous atmosphere. Their theories were taken up by writers, especially Baudelaire and other followers of Poe, and Symbolists such as Mallarmé, who attempted to capture the fleeting impressions of a moment, or held that the personal attitudes and moods of an author were more important than any objective depiction of character, setting, and action. In music, the leading impressionist is Debussy, whose American followers include such composers as Griffes and Loeffler. Impressionistic art was most influential at the end of the 19th century and during the early decades of the 20th, when its leading proponents in American criticism included Huneker, Vance Thompson, and G.J. Nathan. In poetry the movement is exemplified in such authors as Pound, Sandburg, Amy Lowell, Conrad Aiken, Marianne Moore, and Wallace Stevens, who were influenced by a mingling of trends, including Imagism.♦ Impressionists in prose include such diverse writers as Van Vechten, Huneker, Gertrude Stein, E.E. Cummings, and Thomas Beer. Expressionism♦ is both an extension and a negation of this point of view.

In Abraham's Bosom, play by Paul Green,♦ produced in 1926 and published in 1927, when it won a Pulitzer Prize. It includes the earlier one-act plays *Your Fiery Furnace* (1923) and *In Abraham's Bosom* (1924).

Abraham McCranie is the son of a black woman by her white master, Colonel McCranie, a North Carolina plantation owner. Raised by his aunt, Muh Mack, who has a typical pessimistic view of her race's status, Abraham is moved to passionate rebellion. His education is meager and his experience limited, but he dreams of wider opportunities for blacks and attempts to found a school. Opposed by both whites and blacks, he is driven from place to place after the death of his well-meaning father leaves him at the mercy of his cruel white half-brother, Lonnie. His marriage with Goldie McAllister is unfortunate, and he is disappointed in his son Douglas. Following years of wandering, Abraham returns to the plantation, intending to open a school. His plans are accidentally disclosed by Douglas, just released from prison, and Abraham is beaten and injured by a party of masked white men. Lonnie tells him his farm crop is to be seized, and Abraham, infu-

riated, kills him, but is shot by a mob as he shouts a defiant prophecy of freedom for his race.

In Cold Blood, work by Truman Capote,♦ published in 1966. Described by its author as a "non-fiction novel," it tells of the murder of a well-to-do farmer of Holcomb, Kan., his wife, and two children, by two ex-convicts in the process of committing a robbery of their home in 1959. The aftermath of the criminals' escape to Mexico, capture, trial, appeals to the Supreme Court, and hanging in April 1965 is followed, in a fashion that opens larger social issues.

In Dubious Battle, novel by Steinbeck,♦ published in 1936.

Jim Nolan, a young man whose "whole family has been ruined by this system," joins the Communist party in San Francisco. He meets Mac, who "knows more about field work than anybody in the state," Dick, a "bedroom radical," and Joy, an agitator who has been "smacked over the head too much." When Mac is ordered to Torgas Valley, where a strike of fruit pickers is expected, Jim accompanies him to be trained. At Torgas they meet Al Anderson, a "sympathizer," and go to the camp of the fruit tramps, where Mac wins the gratitude of the leader, London, by assisting at the birth of his daughter's child. When the strike begins, Mac advises London concerning methods and finds a camping place for the 1000 strikers on the farm of Anderson's father. Mac summons Dick, who provides supplies, and Dr. Burton, a "fellow traveler," to take charge of sanitation. The orchardists unsuccessfully attempt to bribe and intimidate London and his fellow chairman Dakin, but the morale of the strikers is maintained. Strikebreakers arrive from the city, and Joy, who has accompanied them, is killed by a vigilante's bullet. This is the first of the misfortunes, which Mac impersonally turns to use, including the stoppage of food supplies, the shooting of Jim and other pickets, newspaper attacks, unrest and espionage, and the destruction by vigilantes of Anderson's crop. Burton and Dick disappear, Al is injured, Dakin is arrested, and the strikers are driven off the farm and warned of an armed attack. After being wounded, Jim grows in assurance and practically assumes leadership until he is led out of camp by a ruse and brutally murdered. In desperation, Mac places his friend's corpse on a platform and harangues the men: "'Comrades! This guy didn't want nothing for himself—'"

In His Steps, novel by C.M. Sheldon. ♦

In Ole Virginia, six local-color stories by T.N. Page,♦ published in 1887.

"Marse Chan," told in dialect by a black ex-slave, is a romance of the Civil War, concerned with a pair of aristocratic lovers separated by the political rivalry of their parents. The young man dies a hero in battle, and the girl dies of grief. "'Unc' Edinburg's Drowndin','" also in dialect, is a similar tale of lovers parted by a family quarrel, which ends, however, with their reconciliation. "Ole 'Stracted" tells of a slave who becomes "distracted" when his wife and children are taken from him to be sold. Freed at the close of the war, he is obsessed by his desire to earn their freedom, and, after many years, having saved the exact amount, finds his son only to die in his arms. "'No Haid Pawn'" (No Head Pond) is a sensational tale of ghosts and horrors set on a mysterious deserted plantation in the swamps. "Polly" is the story of a hotheaded Virginia colonel, his love for his niece, whom he rears from infancy, his anger at her secret marriage, and their reconciliation at a Christmas feast.

In Our Time, 15 short stories by Hemingway♦ with vignettes serving as interchapters, published in the U.S. in 1925. *In Our Time* (Paris, 1924) contains only the vignettes. Most stories treat life in the Middle West, but the interpolated sketches describe war in Europe and bullfights.

"Indian Camp," "The Doctor and the Doctor's Wife," "The Three Day Blow," and others tell of the boyhood experiences of Nick, the author's counterpart, who grew up in the Great Lakes region, learning the bitter as well as the beautiful facts of existence through the work of his father, a physician, and through his association with Indian guides and their families. Such stories as "Mr. and Mrs. Elliot," "Out of Season," and "Cross Country Snow" are brief, poignant tales of American expatriates in Europe and their complex loves and friendships. "My Old Man" is the story of a boy's loyalty to his father, an American jockey forced to work in Europe because of unsportsmanlike conduct at home, and of the boy's disillusion following his father's death. The author's enthusiasm for sport and the American wilderness is shown in "Big Two-Hearted River," an account of a trout-fishing expedition.

In Praise of Johnny Appleseed, free-verse poem by Vachel Lindsay,♦ published in his *Collected Poems* (1923). It celebrates the pioneering career of his favorite hero, John Chapman,♦ whom he considers a symbol of the restless, creative American spirit. The work is in three parts: "Over the Appalachian Barricade," "The Indians Worship Him, But He Hurries On," and "Johnny Appleseed's Old Age."

In the American Grain, essays by William Carlos Williams,♦ published in 1925.

In 20 impressionistic essays on significant persons of the western hemisphere, chronologically from Eric the Red to Lincoln, and including Cotton Mather, Franklin, and Poe among writers, Williams treats the ways in which these men viewed new worlds, often employing their own words so as to convey their ways of vision and

expression. The emphasis on discovery, the idealistic conception of liberty and freedom, and the opposition to Puritanism as a doctrine of denial mark the book as a precursor of elements of *Paterson, White Mule,* and other later writings by Williams.

In the Cage, novelette by Henry James,♦ published in 1898.

A telegraph clerk in a London department store despises her complacent suitor, Mr. Mudge. Curious about the lives of her wealthy patrons, she is particularly fascinated by the liaison of Lady Bradeen and young Captain Everard, details of which are revealed through their frequent telegrams. Although she "hates" the frivolous rich, she comes to have a tender interest in the affairs of Everard, and the two recognize a certain mutual understanding. When her friend Mrs. Jordan asks her to become a business partner, the girl postpones accepting either this offer or Mr. Mudge's proposal. She helps Everard to avoid a scandal by producing a copy of an intercepted telegram, and her brief association with him ends when Lord Bradeen dies and the lovers are able to marry. Mrs. Jordan's offer is withdrawn, and the girl quickly settles her problems by accepting Mr. Mudge.

In the Midst of Life, see *Tales of Soldiers and Civilians.*

In the Tennessee Mountains, eight local-color stories by Mary N. Murfree,♦ published in 1884 under her pseudonym Charles Egbert Craddock.

"Drifting Down Lost Creek" is the pathetic story of Cynthia Ware, a mountain girl whose lover is wrongfully convicted on a murder charge and sent to the penitentiary. She gathers evidence in his favor and a year later succeeds in having him pardoned, but, ignorant of her aid and fascinated by the outside world, he does not return. She never marries, and sees him only once again, ten years later, when he pays a brief visit to his birthplace, having become a successful machinist and married, although unhappily. "A-Playin' of Old Sledge at the Settlemint" is concerned with the evil results of an epidemic of gambling in a mountain village. "The Star in the Valley" is a poetic narrative of a girl too fine for her crude mountain environment, who seeks vainly to end the murderous family feuds and meets an early death, unappreciated save by an occasional visitor. "Electioneerin' on Big Injun Mounting" tells of an attorney general, born in a backwoods settlement, who nearly loses the vote of his native region for reelection because he is thought to have taken on "airs." The sentiment is changed by his act of generosity in refusing to prosecute a man who sought his life.

Independent, *The* (1848–1928), New York weekly periodical, was at first a religious journal affiliated with the Congregationalists. H.W. Beecher was the editor (1861–63), and when he was succeeded by his assistant, Theodore Tilton (1863–70), the latter made it a secular periodical interested in such reforms as woman suffrage, and drew contributions from Whittier, Lowell, Greeley, Harriet Beecher Stowe, and Garrison. Under later editors, it became an interdenominational religious and literary organ, with contributions from Bryant, Longfellow, Holmes, Harte, Aldrich, J.W. Riley, Helen Hunt Jackson, and Hovey. It became active in political discussion, and, after absorbing *Harper's Weekly* (1916), printed many pictures of the European war. After several changes of ownership and policy, it was merged with *The Outlook.*

Independent Chronicle (1776–1819), published at Boston as a Whig newspaper favoring the Revolutionary cause. Early contributors included William Gordon, John Hancock, and Samuel Adams. After the war, it continued to oppose the Tories, favored France, denounced the Alien and Sedition laws, and advocated the War of 1812. It was merged with the *Boston Patriot.*

Independent Journal, see *New York Independent Journal.*

Index, *The* (1870–86), liberal socioreligious weekly journal, advocating religious emancipation, was affiliated with the Free Religious Association.♦ Contributors included C.P. Cranch, the elder Henry James, Elizabeth Peabody, Moncure Conway, T.W. Higginson, O.B. Frothingham, and L.M. Child.

Indian Bible, see *Eliot, John.*

Indian Burying Ground, *The,* poem by Freneau,♦ published in his *Miscellaneous Works* (1788). In ten iambic tetrameter quatrains, it portrays sympathetically the spirit of the nomadic Indian hunters, who were traditionally buried in a sitting posture and with images of the objects they knew in life. Freneau's treatment of the immortal "children of the forest" appealed strongly to Scott and Thomas Campbell, who echoed his images in their poetry.

Indian Princess, *The; or, La Belle Sauvage,* play by J.N. Barker,♦ produced and published in 1808. The first Indian play by an American to be performed and the first to use the story of Pocahontas, the play with its accompanying songs was called "an operatic melodrame." Based on Smith's *General History of Virginia,* it bathes its subject in a romantic atmosphere, and the characters are conventional types.

Indian Student, *The,* poem by Freneau,♦ published in his *Miscellaneous Works* (1788). A short piece in iambic tetrameter quatrains, it tells of

Shalum, taken from his tribe on the Susquehanna to be educated at Harvard, but who left civilization to die amidst his native woods.

Indian Summer, novel by Howells,♦ published in 1886.

Theodore Colville, a middle-aged Indiana publisher, goes to Florence for a vacation and there meets his boyhood acquaintance Evalina Bowen, now a middle-aged widow, and her young friend Imogene Graham. Imogene's sympathy is aroused when she learns that Colville had been disappointed in love, and her pity leads to their engagement. She then falls in love with a young clergyman, Mr. Morton. When she finally recognizes her true feelings, she breaks the disparate bond with Colville, who marries Mrs. Bowen.

Infidel, *The,* novel by R.M. Bird.♦

INGE, WILLIAM (1913–73), Kansas-born dramatist, whose plays about seemingly ordinary Midwestern people include *Farther Off from Heaven* (1947); *Come Back, Little Sheba* (1950), about a drunkard's dreadful marriage; *Picnic* (1953, Pulitzer Prize), about a simple young girl and boy who entertain fatuous and frustrating dreams of glamorous lives; *Bus Stop* (1955), depicting a diverse group of snowbound people who represent the varied and fluid society of the U.S.; *The Dark at the Top of the Stairs* (1957), a symbolic treatment of loneliness in a family; *A Loss of Roses* (1959), about the Oedipal relation of a 21-year-old son and his widowed mother; *Natural Affection* (1963); and *Where's Daddy?* (1966), a comedy about the quest of a young couple to find values. *Good Luck, Miss Wyckoff* (1970) is a novel about a small-town Kansas schoolteacher involved with a black college football player, and *My Son Is a Splendid Driver* (1971) is a novel about a Kansas boy in the 1930s.

INGERSOLL, CHARLES JARED (1782–1862), Philadelphia lawyer, member of Congress (1813–15, 1840–49), and author. Although his works are varied, and include *Edwy and Elgiva* (1801), and *Julian* (1831), dramas, two histories of the War of 1812, books of poetry, and works on political economy, he is best known for *Inchiquin, the Jesuit's Letters . . .* (1810), an anonymous set of essays purportedly by a Jesuit traveler in America who appreciates the native scene and thus indirectly attacks the criticisms of contemporary English travelers. The scathing criticism of this book in the *Quarterly Review* (English) precipitated such defenses as Timothy Dwight's *Remarks on the Review of Inchiquin's Letters* (1815) and Paulding's *The United States and England* (1815).

INGERSOLL, ROBERT GREEN (1833–99), practiced law in Illinois and entered Democratic politics before the Civil War, in which he served as a colonel of cavalry and turned to the Republican party. In 1876 he nominated Blaine for the presidency with the famous epithet, "the plumed knight." He himself was known as "the great agnostic," because of his long campaign in behalf of free-thinking, including celebrated antireligious lectures on "Superstition," "The Gods," "Some Mistakes of Moses," and similar subjects, criticizing theology and the Bible from a rationalist point of view. His lectures, which had an important influence on American thought during the late 19th century, were published in several collections, and his complete *Works* appeared in 12 volumes (1900).

INGRAHAM, JOSEPH HOLT (1809–60), born in Maine, became popular as a historical romancer with such thrilling tales as *Lafitte: The Pirate of the Gulf* (1836); *Burton; or, The Sieges* (1838), an infamous portrait of Burr; and *Leisler; or, The Rebel and the King's Man* (1846). As an Episcopal clergyman in the South, Ingraham later wrote epistolary religious romances, including *The Prince of the House of David* (1855), concerned with the life of Christ; *The Pillar of Fire* (1859), the story of Moses; and *The Throne of David* (1860), telling of the land of Canaan to the time of Absalom's revolt.

INGRAHAM, PRENTISS (1843–1904), son of Joseph Holt Ingraham, after service in the Civil War and as a soldier of fortune in Mexico, Austria, Crete, and Cuba became a popular writer like his father. *The Masked Spy* (1872) was the first of more than 600 dime novels he wrote under his own name and many pseudonyms, perhaps 200 of the novels about his friend Buffalo Bill. He also wrote several popular plays.

Injun Joe, character in *Tom Sawyer.* ♦

Innocents Abroad, *The; or, The New Pilgrim's Progress,* travel narrative by Clemens, ♦ published in 1869 under his pseudonym Mark Twain. It is based on letters written during 1867 to the San Francisco *Alta California* and the *New-York Tribune* and *Herald,* describing the tour of the steamship *Quaker City* to Europe, Egypt, and the Holy Land. In this autobiographical account, Clemens has an opportunity to ridicule foreign sights and manners from the point of view of the American democrat, who scorns the sophisticated, revels in his own national peculiarities and advantages, and is contemptuously amused by anything with which he is unacquainted. Characteristic passages are concerned with the comical difficulties of "innocent" tourists, their adventures among deceptive guides, inefficient hotels, and misunderstood customs; a comparison of Lake Como with Lake Tahoe, to the general advantage of the latter; a burlesque account of the ascent of Vesuvius; experiences of various Turkish "frauds"; an awestruck meeting with the Russian royal

family; and a naïvely sentimental description of Biblical scenes in Palestine.

International Episode, *An,* novelette by Henry James, ♦ published in 1879.

Lord Lambeth and his friend Percy Beaumont come to America for a visit and at Newport they meet Mrs. Westgate and her sister Bessie Alden. The latter fascinates Lord Lambeth, being bold, intelligent, and typically American, and he is on the verge of falling in love with her when he is suddenly recalled to England. Later the situation is reversed, when Bessie and Mrs. Westgate visit London. The older woman discourages her sister from notifying Lord Lambeth of their arrival, but they meet accidentally, and Lambeth, increasingly charmed by Bessie's independence and frankness, is about to propose to her. His mother and sister, alarmed, call on the Americans and make plain their disapproval of the match. Bessie keeps her own counsel, but, when Lambeth proposes, she surprises everyone by refusing him.

International Monthly Magazine of Literature, Art, and Science, *The* (1850–52), was edited by R.W. Griswold, for the first six weeks as a weekly, and thereafter as a monthly competitor of *Harper's,* with which it was finally merged. Contributors included Bulwer-Lytton, Thackeray, Dickens, R.H. Stoddard, Bayard Taylor, Hawthorne, and Simms.

Intruder in the Dust, novel by William Faulkner, ♦ published in 1948.

Lucas Beauchamp, an aging black farmer whose grandparents were the white Carothers McCaslin ♦ and a slave woman, is arrested for the murder of Vinson Gowrie, one of a clan of hillsmen known for administering their own violent law. Hope Hampton, Yoknapatawpha County sheriff, brings Lucas to the Jefferson jail, where a crowd expects the Gowries to lynch him. Charles ("Chick") Mallison, County Attorney Gavin Stevens's 16-year-old nephew, goes to see Lucas, recalling the old man's kindness in caring for him some years earlier when he fell into an icy creek. Lucas asks Gavin to defend him but will tell only Charles that an examination of Vinson's body will prove that his gun was not the murder weapon. Charles persuades Aleck Sander, his black companion, and Eunice Habersham, a 70-year-old spinster, to help him dig up the grave, in which they find Jake Montgomery's body rather than Vinson's. Crawford Gowrie had actually shot his brother Vinson in such a way as to implicate Lucas when Lucas threatened to reveal that he was stealing lumber from Vinson. Crawford then murdered Jake and put him in Vinson's grave because Jake also knew of Crawford's crime and had disinterred Vinson for proof of the shooting through ballistic evidence. When Vinson's body is found Crawford is arrested and commits suicide in jail. Lucas is exonerated and the proud, dignified, and courageous black man, who will accept no white man's charity, pays Gavin his fee of two dollars, painstakingly counted out in pennies, as the last act in the events have made him "now tyrant over the whole county's white conscience."

Invisible Man, novel by Ralph Ellison,♦ published in 1952.

The nameless black narrator living in an underground "hole" in New York City, brilliantly lighted by electricity he taps from Monopolated Light and Power, is invisible because people with whom he comes in contact "see only my surroundings, themselves, or figments of their imagination." Such vision is illustrated by his reminiscences of the Kafkaesque pilgrimage he has made from his beginnings in the South. As a bright high-school student he is invited by his town's most important men to deliver an oration to them on the virtues of humility. Before he is allowed to speak he must watch ribald entertainment and is forced to join other "niggers" in a blindfold fistfight. When he finally delivers his speech he mistakenly speaks of "social equality" instead of "social responsibility" and has to apologize abjectly so as to retain his prize of a scholarship to a college for blacks. At the college he finds the head to be a tyrannical hypocrite in his treatment of the students and fawningly humble to the white community. Expelled from the college, he goes to New York and soon falls in with the ruthless Brother Jack, leader of the Communist Brotherhood, more concerned with party politics and an authoritarian platform than with true aid to blacks. He is equally disillusioned by Ras the Exhorter, a West Indian rabble-rousing street leader, basically a self-promoter, and the Rev. B.P. Rinehart, "spiritual technologist" and preacher and a petty criminal as well. His experiences are climaxed by a surrealistic view of a Harlem race riot and its arson and looting. From this he retreats to his hideaway hole, reflecting upon the dehumanization visited not only on blacks but on all modern men.

Invitation to a Beheading, novel by Nabokov,♦ published in Russia in 1938 and in the U.S. in 1959.

Cincinnatus C. is in prison awaiting execution for his crime of "gnostical turpitude" or "opacity" since his soul has been impenetrable and not open to other people. There he recalls his past life, including marriage to Marthe, a nymphomaniac mother of two deformed children, and his own teaching of crippled children in a kindergarten. He also spends time thinking of ways to escape or talking with the prison director, Rodrig Ivanovich, and M'sieur Pierre, ostensibly another prisoner but actually his executioner. In time he learns to avoid his confusion of dreams of the past with present reality and discovers how to surround his soul with a structure of words that

permits him to communicate with others. Nevertheless he is led to his execution, but as one part of him puts his head on the block, another part leaves to join the onlooking crowd of people who are "beings akin to him."

IOOR, WILLIAM (*fl.*1780–1830), South Carolina dramatist, whose plays included *Independence, or Which Do You Like Best, the Peer or the Farmer?* (produced 1805), a social comedy adapted from an English novel, praising America's unsophisticated virtues, and *The Battle of Eutaw Springs* (published 1807, produced 1813).

Iron Heel, The, novel by Jack London,♦ published in 1908.

Purportedly written in 1932, this "Everhard Manuscript" tells of events said to take place between 1912 and 1918, when, by a process of evolutionary development, the great capitalistic monopolies of the U.S. band together in a fascistic organization, the Iron Heel, which seizes control of the country. Stamping out all democratic forms and free institutions, the Iron Heel creates a caste system with a plutocratic aristocracy at the top, supported by secret police, a military oligarchy, and a few powerful subsidized unions that aid in suppressing the majority of organized labor. Originally motivated by fear of the growing revolutionary Socialist party, the Iron Heel succeeds in driving the equalitarian movement underground, but there it continued to militate against the "Oligarchs" and their barbarous tyranny. One of the Socialist leaders is Ernest Everhard, a Californian, whose wife Avis, converted by him to the cause, tells their story in this manuscript. For 20 years they maintain their secret, partially terrorist, organization, which averts war with Germany by a general strike in collaboration with German Socialist unions, instigates armed revolts, and in general advocates the use of force against force. The manuscript breaks off, following Everhard's execution, but footnotes written 700 years later inform the reader that the Iron Heel retained power for 300 years, was overthrown, and was succeeded by a golden age of collectivism.

Ironweed, novel (1983) by William Kennedy.♦

Francis Phelan, once a major league pitcher in the Grover Cleveland Alexander era, now an alcoholic bum, returns to his native Albany, N.Y., in the 1930s. Francis continually sees accusing ghosts of figures from his past. He attempts small amends to his long since deserted wife and hostile grown daughter, and struggles merely to stay alive with his present consort Helen, another alcoholic. He bears up. Kennedy creates his own hymn to the human condition at its ugliest and grittiest. Rejected by 17 publishers as "not commercial," the novel was immediately hailed on publication as a masterpiece, became a bestseller, and received the 1983 National Book Award and the Pulitzer Prize.

Iroquois Indians, confederacy of war-like but highly cultured tribes in western New York (united *c.*1570), which consisted originally of Five Nations: Seneca, Cayuga, Onondaga, Oneida, and Mohawk. Among the chiefs who supposedly effected this league was the Mohawk immortalized as Hiawatha by Longfellow. The trade relations of the Iroquois with the Dutch led to their obtaining firearms, with which they became great conquerors of other tribes in the mid-17th century. During the French and Indian Wars they were allies of the British, and in the American Revolution most of the chiefs supported the Loyalists. The Tuscarora Indians joined the confederacy (1715), which became the Six Nations. Besides *Hiawatha* and the Leather-Stocking Tales, the Iroquois figure in such works as Alfred B. Street's *Frontenac, or the Atotarho of the Iroquois* (1849), a metrical romance based on Frontenac's expedition of 1696 against the confederacy. Cadwallader Colden's *History of the Five Indian Nations* (1727) was the first careful study of the subject. Among later works, L.H. Morgan's *League of the Ho-dé-no-sau-nee, or Iroquois* (1851) superseded Schoolcraft's *Notes on the Iroquois* (1847). Edmund Wilson's *Apologies to the Iroquois* (1960) tells of the modern situation of the confederacy.

IRVING, JOHN [WINSLOW] (1942–　), New Hampshire-born author, whose first serio-comic novels, *Setting Free the Bears* (1968), a tale of two young men's adventures motorcycling through Austria; *The Water-Method Man* (1972), about an Iowa graduate student's fantastic misadventures; and *The 158-Pound Marriage* (1974), presenting two couples who engage in mate-swapping, were followed by the enormously popular *The World According to Garp*♦ (1978), a fanciful story of a wonderfully talented novelist whose life and works are rich and various, but who is murdered at 33 by a disgruntled reader; *The Hotel New Hampshire* (1981), portraying an exotic family; *The Cider House Rules* (1985), about the attitudes and perils attending the question of abortion; and *A Prayer for Owen Meaney* (1989), about a gnomelike figure, Meaney, who has the gift of prophecy and a deep belief that he is God's instrument. Almost totally obsessed with the nature of faith, the narrator, a friend of Meaney's, tells his tale against the background of America's war in Vietnam. *A Son of the Circus* (1994) is the tale of a Hindu film star, an American missionary, twins separated at birth, a dwarf chauffeur, and a serial killer, on a collision course in India.

IRVING, JOHN TREAT (1812–1906), nephew of Washington Irving, whose urbane interest in the frontier he reflects in his *Indian Sketches* (1835) and in *The Hawk Chief: A Tale of the Indian Country* (1837), also titled *The Hunters of the Prairie*. *The Van Gelder Papers* (1887) are Dutch sketches under similar influence. As John Quod he wrote *The Quod Correspondence* (1842), also titled *The Attorney*, a novel about legal affairs.

IRVING, PETER (1771–1838), older brother of Washington Irving, helped him in planning *Salmagundi*, the *History of New York*, and the *Tales of a Traveller*. His own writing is unimportant, although he was for a time a political journalist and member of literary society, and wrote such works as *Giovanni Sbogarro* (1820), a historical romance set in Venice. He edited the New York *Morning Chronicle* and *The Corrector*, to which his brother contributed.

IRVING, PIERRE MUNRO (1803–76), lawyer and author, graduated from Columbia (1821) and during his subsequent travels became the confidant of his uncle, Washington Irving, whom he visited in Spain (1827). *Astoria* (1836) was a result of their collaboration, and, during his uncle's residence at Sunnyside (1846–59), Pierre was his agent and secretary and recorded their conversations. He was his uncle's literary executor, wrote the first biography, *The Life and Letters of Washington Irving* (4 vols., 1862–64), and edited *Spanish Papers and Other Miscellanies* (1866).

IRVING, WASHINGTON (1783–1859), was born in New York City, the youngest of 11 children of a wealthy merchant who had sided with the rebels in the Revolution. Precocious and impressionable, the boy was early influenced by the literary interests of his brothers William and Peter, but in 1798 concluded his education at private schools and entered a law office. His legal studies soon lost their appeal, although he continued in various offices until 1804, varying his occupation by a frontier journey (1803) through upper New York state and into Canada, and by writing for the *Morning Chronicle* and *The Corrector*, newspapers edited by his brother Peter. For the *Chronicle* (1802–3) he wrote the "Letters of Jonathan Oldstyle, Gent.," a series of youthful satires on New York society, which won him recognition. To restore his failing health and to further his education, he traveled in Europe (1804–6), where he collected material later used in stories and essays.

Although he was admitted to the bar upon his return, he lost interest in the law and turned seriously to literature. *Salmagundi; or, The Whim-Whams and Opinions of Launcelot Langstaff, Esq., and Others*♦ (1807–8) is a series of satirical miscellanies concerned with New York society. The leading essays were written by Irving, his brothers, and William Irving's brother-in-law, J.K. Paulding, all members of the group known as the "Nine Worthies" or "Lads of Kilkenny" of "Cockloft Hall." Federalist in politics, conservative in social attitude, and humorous in intention, these early essays represent the position and manner to which Irving was to cling throughout his career. He was now famous as author, wit, and man of society, and, to further his reputation, turned to the creation of the comic Dutch-American scholar Diedrich Knickerbocker, on whose burlesque *History of New York*♦ he was occupied until 1809. This work, called "the first great book of comic literature written by an American," although ostensibly concerned with the history of the Dutch occupation was also a Federalist critique of Jeffersonian democracy and a whimsical satire on pedantry and literary classics.

Before its completion, Irving suffered a tragic loss in the death of his fiancée, Matilda Hoffman. According to sentimental biographers, who disregard later love affairs, he remained a bachelor to be faithful to her memory. Certainly he was profoundly affected at the time. In spite of the success of the *History,* he deserted creative literature during the next six years, when he was occupied in business with his brothers, in collecting the poems of Thomas Campbell (1810), in editing the *Analectic Magazine* (1813–14), a popular miscellany of reprints from foreign periodicals, and in social and political activities in New York, Philadelphia, and Washington. Toward the end of the War of 1812, he served as an aide-de-camp to the governor, and in 1815 he planned a cruise to the Mediterranean with Decatur; but, when this became impossible, he sailed alone for Liverpool, to take charge of the family business there.

During the next two years, he tried desperately to maintain the failing business, but in 1818 it went into bankruptcy, and he was forced to write for a living. He had already been impressed by the beauties of the English countryside as interpreted by the romantic poets, and, encouraged by Scott, now returned to writing his most successful work, *The Sketch Book*♦ (1819–20), containing familiar essays on English life, and Americanized versions of European folk tales in "Rip Van Winkle" ♦ and "The Legend of Sleepy Hollow."♦ As Geoffrey Crayon, the pseudonym by which the book was signed, Irving was now a celebrity, lionized in English and French society, and the intimate of such men as Scott, Byron, and Moore. In Paris (1820) he wrote plays with J.H. Payne,♦ a collaboration to which he occasionally returned for several years. *Bracebridge Hall*♦ (1822) is another book of romantic sketches, less important than *The Sketch Book,* but equally well received.

Continuing his search for fictional materials, Irving now traveled in Germany (1822–23), spending the winter at Dresden, where he fell in love with an English girl, Emily Foster, who seems to have refused his proposal of marriage. After a year in Paris, he returned to England and published *Tales of a Traveller*♦ (1824), so adversely criticized that Irving was nearly discouraged from further literary activity. After two unproductive years in France, during which he is supposed to have vied with Payne for the affections of Mary Wollstonecraft Shelley, he became a diplomatic attaché in Spain (1826–29), living for a time in Madrid at the home of bibliographer Obadiah Rich, and engaged in research for his scholarly but popular *History of the Life and Voyages of Christopher Columbus* (1828), based principally on the work of the Spanish scholar Navarrete. This was followed by *A Chronicle of the Conquest of Granada*♦ (1829), and a "Spanish Sketch Book," *The Alhambra*♦ (1832), recounting Spanish legends and describing the famous monument.

Irving was secretary of the U.S. legation in London (1829–32), and then returned to New York, after an absence of 17 years, to be welcomed enthusiastically as the first American author to achieve international fame. Again seeking picturesque literary backgrounds, he made an adventurous trip to the Western frontier. This was described in *A Tour on the Prairies,* ♦ published as a part of *The Crayon Miscellany*♦ (3 vols., 1835). The tour also resulted in *Astoria* (1836), an account of the fur-trading empire of John Jacob Astor, written with Pierre Irving♦; and *The Adventures of Captain Bonneville, U.S.A.* ♦ (1837). Irving's *Western Journals* were published in 1944.

After a few years at his home, Sunnyside,♦ during which he declined the nomination for mayor of New York City and the secretaryship of the navy offered him by Van Buren, as well as giving up a plan to write a *Conquest of Mexico* in favor of Prescott, Irving returned to his favorite place of exile, becoming minister to Spain (1842–45). His position was made difficult by the Spanish insurrection (1843), and after his resignation two years later he spent a year in London on a diplomatic mission concerning the Oregon Question. Again at Sunnyside, he passed the remaining 13 years of his life in the company of his beloved nieces and innumerable friends, acknowledged as the leading American author, in spite of his waning powers, as evidenced in *Oliver Goldsmith* (1840), a biography of one of his literary masters; *A Book of the Hudson* (1849) and *Wolfert's Roost*♦ (1855), collections of sketches; *Mahomet and His Successors* (2 vols., 1849–50), conventional biographies; and the monumental *Life of Washington* (5 vols., 1855–59), planned as early as 1825, but completed in the last year of his life, just before his health finally failed. Bare of the graces of his early writing, this triumph of scholarship crowned an erratic career that seldom retained its literary focus for more than a few years at a time, but which served in many ways to consolidate the culture of the U.S. and Europe. Unlike his contemporary, Cooper, Irving saw the European past in an aura of romance, and, except for the gentle satire of his early works, consistently avoided coming to grips with modern democratic life. His graceful, humorous, stylistically careful writing is in the tradition of Addison, Steele, and Goldsmith. In subject and method he sought the traditional and the picturesque. A scholarly edition of his *Complete Works* began publication in 1969.

IRVING, WILLIAM (1766–1821), father of Pierre Munro Irving and eldest brother of Washington Irving, contributed light satirical verse to *Salmagundi*♦ (1807–8). He was a moving spirit, with his brothers and brother-in-law, J.K. Paulding, in the informal literary group known as the "Nine Worthies" or "Lads of Kilkenny" of "Cockloft Hall."

IRWIN, WALLACE [ADMAH] (1875–1959), born in Oneida, N.Y., attended Stanford (1896–99), and began his literary career as a San Francisco journalist. At this time he wrote humorous poems including *The Love Sonnets of a Hoodlum* (1902), *The Rubáiyát of Omar Khayyám, Jr.* (1902), *Nautical Lays of Landsman* (1904), and *Random Rhymes and Odd Numbers* (1906). While continuing his journalistic career in New York, he became widely popular for his Hashimura Togo letters, ostensibly written by a Japanese, commenting on politics and society, published in *Letters of a Japanese Schoolboy* (1909), *Mr. Togo, Maid of All Work* (1913), and *More Letters of a Japanese Schoolboy* (1923). Besides stories, he later wrote novels, including *Seed of the Sun* (1921), about the strife of Japanese and white farmers in California, and *The Days of Her Life* (1931), with a background of California history.

IRWIN, WILL[IAM HENRY] (1873–1948), brother of Wallace Irwin, was born in New York, reared in the West, graduated from Stanford (1899), and became a New York journalist. Among his works are such books as *Old Chinatown* (1908); *A Reporter in Armageddon* (1918), on his experiences as a World War I correspondent; *The Next War: An Appeal to Commonsense* (1921); *Christ or Mars?* (1923); *How Red Is America?* (1927); and *Propaganda and the News; or, What Makes You Think So?* (1936). He collaborated on two plays, *The Thirteenth Chair* (1916), with Bayard Veiller, and *Lute Song* (1930), with Sidney Howard.

Isaac and Archibald, blank-verse narrative by E.A. Robinson,♦ published in *Captain Craig* (1902).

The narrator tells how, as a small boy, he was taken by the old farmer Isaac to visit his lifelong friend Archibald. During the journey, Isaac confided his uneasiness about Archibald's failing health and competence, and also his mellow philosophy of life, based on honest emotion and sympathy. They arrive at Archibald's comfortable farm, to find its owner hearty and amiable. When Isaac walks out to inspect his friend's acres, Archibald confesses doubts of Isaac's health, and makes a like confession of simple faith in "the light, my boy,—the light behind the stars. . . . Live to see clearly, and the light will come." The narrator reflects on this day, which has passed with his friends "to the silence of the loved and well-forgotten," and concludes reverently, "They were old men, and I may laugh at them because I knew them."

Isabel Archer, heroine of *The Portrait of a Lady.* ♦

ISHERWOOD, CHRISTOPHER (1904–86), English-born author, studied at Cambridge, collaborated with Auden♦ on three satirical prose and verse plays, *The Dog Beneath the Skin* (1936), *The Ascent of F6* (1936), and *On the Frontier* (1938), and with him also wrote about their voyage to China in *Journey to a War* (1939). He had already published his first novel in 1928 and had lived in Berlin for four years, the city which was the setting of his novel *The Last of Mr. Norris* (1935), and the sketches *Goodbye to Berlin* (1939), the latter involving a fictive character bearing the author's name, and therefore retitled *I Am a Camera* when dramatized (1951) by John Van Druten. Isherwood came to the U.S. (1939), settled near Los Angeles, and was naturalized in 1946. His fiction written in the U.S. includes *Prater Violet* (1945), a symbolic novelette involving the story of an Austrian motion-picture director who produces a film about Vienna in London; *The World in the Evening* (1954); *Down There on a Visit* (1962), the frank, autobiographical story of the quest for selfhood by a character called by the author's name; *A Single Man* (1964), about a day in the sad, lonely life of a middle-aged homosexual professor in a California university after the death of the man he loved; and *A Meeting by the River* (1967), a philosophical tale of brothers with different values who meet in India, one to become a Hindu monk, the other to find a site to film a motion picture. Three very personal books are *Kathleen and Frank* (1972), an account of his parents and their influence on him; *Christopher and His Kind* (1976), about his own life and male lovers from 1929 to 1939; and *My Guru and His Disciple* (1980), about both worldly and spiritual experiences. *October* (1981) is a diary of how he and his beloved friend spent October 1979. *The Condor and the Cows* (1949) deals with a trip to South America. *Exhumations* (1966) collects stories, verse, and articles. *People One Ought To Know* (1981) contains poems written for children when he was only 21.

Ishmael, character in *Moby-Dick.* ♦

Isidro, romance by Mary Austin,♦ published in 1905.

During the Mexican rule of California, Don Isidro Escobar sets out for Monterey to fulfill his parents' vow that he shall serve the Church. He views this vocation with simple faith, although he is not prevented from having such adventures on the way as returning a flock of sheep to the shepherds of its murdered owner, leading to his being suspected of the crime; meeting the crafty trapper Peter Lebecque, whose shy ward, El Zarzo ("the Briar"), becomes Isidro's companion; and saving the life of the renegade Indian Mascado. At Monterey he places himself in the hands of Padre

Saavedra, who plans to train him as his successor. El Zarzo, actually the disguised Jacinta, long-lost daughter of the local Comandante, has fallen in love with Isidro, and remains to be near him. The innocent Isidro is imprisoned for murder, and, before Saavedra obtains his release, Jacinta is kidnapped by Mascado, who takes her to a mountain retreat. Awed by the girl's defiance, he does not harm her, and Isidro comes to the rescue. They return to the mission, where they are married to protect her name from scandal, but do not consummate the marriage because of Isidro's priestly vow. He is captured by Mascado and taken to a camp of renegade Indians, while Jacinta goes to her father's home. The Comandante leads a force against the renegades, and Jacinta, learning of her husband's plight, goes to him. Mascado's men withstand the siege until the Comandante routs them by setting a forest fire. Isidro and Jacinta are saved, and, on their return to Monterey, he renounces his intention of becoming a priest. Their marriage is celebrated by the community, and the Comandante takes them to Mexico to live.

Islandia, Utopian novel by Austin T. Wright. ◆

Israel Potter: His Fifty Years of Exile, romance by Melville, ◆ published in 1855. It is largely based on an anonymous *Life and Remarkable Adventures of Israel Potter* (1824).

Israel Potter, a New England boy, after youthful experiences as a farmer, surveyor, and peddler becomes a sailor on whaling ships. He joins the Revolutionary army in time to participate in the Battle of Bunker Hill, but is captured by the British and taken to England. There he escapes, goes to London as a laborer, is befriended by rebel agents, and joins them in secret activities. Traveling between London and Paris, he meets Horne Tooke, Franklin, and John Paul Jones, and, becoming a friend of the last, takes part in naval affairs, including the battle between the *Bonhomme Richard* and the *Serapis.* In England again,

Israel is associated with Ethan Allen, flees to London in fear of apprehension, and becomes a workman again, marrying and living in alternate want and moderate plenty. Finally, 45 years after his departure, he returns to America, infirm and impoverished, to seek a pension. He is refused, dictates his memoirs, and dies in poverty.

Israfel, poem by Poe, ◆ published in *Poems* (1831) and several times revised in later editions. It is prefaced by an altered quotation from the Koran: "And the angel Israfel, whose heart-strings are a lute, and who has the sweetest voice of all God's creatures." In eight stanzas of great metrical variety, ranging from four- to two-stress lines, the poem contrasts the ideal dwelling place of the angel with the poet's own "world of sweets and sours," and concludes that if they were to change places

> He might not sing so wildly well
>   A mortal melody,
> While a bolder note than this might swell
>   From my lyre within the sky.

It Can't Happen Here, novel by Sinclair Lewis, ◆ published in 1935. It was dramatized by the author and John C. Moffitt (1936) for simultaneous presentation by all units of the Federal Theatre.

Italian Father, The, play by William Dunlap, ◆ produced in 1799, and published in 1810. Based on Dekker's *The Honest Whore, Part II,* the play deals with Michael Brazzo, who, disguised as a servingman, watches over his daughter Astrabel after he casts her off for having become the mistress of the worthless Beraldo. Beraldo's friend Hippolito converts Astrabel to a chaste life, but later, at the request of Brazzo, tries to undo his work in order to test her fidelity.

Ivory Tower, The, unfinished novel by Henry James. ◆

J

J.B., poetic drama by Archibald MacLeish♦ treating the theme of Job's trials in a modern setting and idiom.

J R, novel by William Gaddis.♦

J.S. of Dale, see *Stimson, F. J.*

Jack Cade, the Captain of the Commons, romantic tragedy in blank verse by R. T. Conrad,♦ produced in 1835. It was rewritten as *Aylmere; or, The Bondman of Kent* for Edwin Forrest (1852) and was published in both versions. The story is concerned with the Kentish rebellion of 1450, interpreted from a social and economic point of view, and takes liberties with history in the depiction of Jack Cade, or Aylmere, and his friends and enemies.

Jack Downing, pseudonym of Seba Smith.♦

Jack Tier, novel by Cooper.♦

JACKSON, ANDREW (1767–1845), 7th President of the U.S. (1829–37), was born in the backwoods country of South Carolina, and at the age of 13 participated in Revolutionary War battles. He was admitted to the bar in North Carolina (1787), in a western district that is now a part of Tennessee. He helped draft the constitution of Tennessee (1796), and served in Congress as a representative (1796–97) and a senator (1797–98), later becoming a judge of the state supreme court and major general of the state militia. He took the side of Burr in the latter's trial for treason (1807), and retired to private life on his plantation until 1812.

The following year he led the militia in the defeat of the Creek Indians at Talladega and at Horseshoe Bend in 1814, and then became a major general in the U.S. army, capturing Florida and commanding the defense of New Orleans against the British. His spectacular victory in the Battle of New Orleans, although fought after the peace was signed, made him the hero of the War of 1812, and for it he was celebrated in literature in his own time, such as Samuel Woodworth's ballad "The Hunters of Kentucky" (1826) and two plays bearing the same title, *The Eighth of January,* respectively by Richard Penn Smith (1829) and G.W.P. Custis (1834).

In 1818 Jackson again entered the military service, exceeding his orders in quelling the Seminole Indian rebellion, so that the U.S. became involved in serious troubles with Great Britain and Spain. He was nevertheless appointed military governor of Florida (1821), a post which he soon resigned. Considered the leading representative of the frontier spirit, Jackson was again elected to the U.S. Senate (1823–25), and in 1824 was a candidate for the presidency. His opponents were J.Q. Adams, W.H. Crawford, and Henry Clay; though Jackson received the largest number of electoral votes, there was no majority, and a congressional poll gave the election to Adams.

In 1828, however, Jackson was swept into power by a popular vote based on his personal influence, expansionist policies, and advocacy of a protective tariff. He opposed Calhoun's doctrines of states' rights and nullification, but also opposed the centralization of power represented by the Bank of the United States. His stand pleased the backwoods people who suspected banks as privileged institutions, and, despite a dictatorial attitude and his spoils system, he was reelected by a large majority (1832). His destruction of the Bank and his policy of distributing government funds among state banks helped cause the financial panic of 1837, which he left to his successor, Van Buren. This and other aspects of his policies alienated former supporters, who formed the Whig party, which was victorious in 1840. He spent his last years at his Tennessee home, The Hermitage. Besides being the subject of many histories, e.g. Arthur Schlesinger, Jr.'s *The Age of Jackson,* he often figures in fiction, Winston Churchill's *The Crossing* and Meredith Nicholson's *The Cavalier of Tennessee* being among the romances in which he plays a part. An episode in his youth was dramatized by Maxwell Anderson and Laurence Stallings as *First Flight.*

JACKSON, CHARLES [REGINALD] (1903–68), author of *The Lost Weekend* (1944), a psychological novel of five days in an alcoholic's life; *The Fall of Valor* (1946), about a man with homosexual tendencies; *The Outer Edges* (1948), about the effects of a horrid newspaper story on readers; and *Earthly Creatures* (1953), stories.

JACKSON, DANIEL, see *Mitchell, Isaac.*

JACKSON, HELEN [MARIA] HUNT (1830–85), was born at Amherst, Mass., and in 1863 began to write poetry for publication, which was collected in *Verses by H.H.* (1870) and *Sonnets and Lyrics* (1886). Later she wrote a travel book, children's books, many magazine contributions, and several novels. *A Century of Dishonor* (1881) is a historical account of governmental injustice in the treatment of the Indians, and her indictment was stated even more strongly in the romance *Ramona*♦ (1884), inspired by her work in a government investigation of the Mission Indians. Her novel *Mercy Philbrick's Choice* (1876) is said to be a fictional study of her friend Emily Dickinson. Many of her early writings were published under the pseudonym Saxe Holm.

JACKSON, SHIRLEY [HARDIE] (1916–65), California-born author, educated at Syracuse University, lived in Vermont, where her husband, Stanley Edgar Hyman (1919–70), a literary critic, taught at Bennington College. Her novels include *The Road Through the Wall* (1948), *Hangsaman* (1951), and *The Bird's Nest* (1954), all depicting adolescents in disturbed states of mind. Other novels are *The Sundial* (1958), about people who believe the end of the world is near; *The Haunting of Hill House* (1959), concerning occult experiences; *We Have Always Lived in the Castle* (1962), presenting a woman writer who poisons her family; and *Come Along with Me* (1968), a posthumously published fragment. *The Lottery* ♦ (1949) collects stories of weird or psychopathic subjects placed in direct, realistic settings. *Life Among the Savages* (1953) and *Raising Demons* (1957) are amusing accounts of her life with her children. *The Witchcraft of Salem Village* (1956); *The Bad Children* (1959), a play; and *Nine Magic Wishes* (1963) are works for children.

JACOBS, HARRIET A. (1813–97), memoirist. Born in slavery in North Carolina, Jacobs wrote a narrative of her life under the pseudonym Linda Brent. It was published in 1861 as *Incidents in the Life of a Slave Girl: Written by Herself*. But the excellent account remained obscure until a new edition in 1987 found a receptive African-American and feminist audience. The narrative details the sexual exploitation that was the nightmare of all slave women. To escape the lechery of a white master she became the lover of another white man and bore him two children. He promised her emancipation, but reneged and threatened her life. She hid for seven years in a small space in her grandmother's house, able to see but not speak to her children. She and the children escaped to the North in 1842, but for years after lived in fear of being returned.

Jamaica Funeral, The, poem by Freneau,♦ written during his residence in the West Indies (1776) and published in his *Poems* (1786). This bitter satire on the sensual, hypocritical clergy of the colonial church tells how a "hectoring priest" beat a man at the funeral for objecting to his dunning the mourners for parish dues, and then without conscience glutted himself at the funeral feast.

JAMES, ALICE (1848–92), sister of Henry James, Jr., and William James, reared, like her four brothers, to find her own values without neighborhood, school, or church affiliations, from the age of 16 suffered recurrent psychosomatic sicknesses that were capped by a severe depression during the last 14 years of her life. Bedridden in her later years, in 1889 she began a work variously printed as her *Journal* (1894, 1934) and, complete, as her *Diary* (1964), marked by perceptive observation and psychological understanding.

JAMES, HENRY, SR. (1811–82), father of Henry James, Jr., William James, and Alice James, was a lecturer and writer on religious, social, and literary topics. Born of a wealthy and rigidly orthodox family of Albany, N.Y., he revolted against Calvinism and felt that the social order was unjust. An accident that happened to him as a schoolboy resulted in the amputation of a leg, and drove him further upon his mental resources. After his graduation from Union College (1830), he entered Princeton Theological Seminary (1835), but withdrew after two years, finding himself out of sympathy with orthodox theology. On a visit to England (1837) he became influenced by Robert Sandeman, a Scottish opponent of Calvinism, one of whose books he edited (1838). During the 1840s and '50s, James lived in New York, and traveled abroad frequently, until in 1864 he settled in Boston. In the 1840s he was introduced to the doctrines of Swedenborg, and underwent a kind of religious conversion. Although he never literally embraced these doctrines, they affected his whole later thought and gave him a strongly mystical bias. He was a friend of Emerson and Carlyle, and frequently lectured on them. After 1847 he was an intimate of Parke Godwin, C.A. Dana, Albert Brisbane, and George Ripley and found his social philosophy in the doctrines of Fourierism.♦ Most of his writings were devoted to expressing his religious doctrine, "the immanence of God in the unity of mankind." Among his books are *Christianity the Logic of Creation* (1857), *Substance and Shadow; or Morality and Religion in Their Relation to Life* (1863), *The Secret of Swedenborg, Being an Elucidation of . . . Divine Natural Humanity* (1869), and *Society the Redeemed Form of Man, and the Earnest of God's Omnipotence in Human Nature* (1879). He figures in his son Henry's books *A Small Boy and Others* and *Notes of a Son and Brother.*

JAMES, HENRY, JR. (1843–1916), son of Henry James, Sr., was born in New York City, and, with his brothers William, Garth (1845–83), and Robertson (1846–1910), received a remarkably cosmopolitan, eclectic education. The father, desiring his sons to be citizens of the world, believed that they should avoid forming definite habits of living or of intellect, until prepared to make wise choices of their own. Accordingly,

Henry was privately educated by tutors until 1855, when the family went to Europe for a three-year stay. He also lived for a time in Newport (1858, 1860–62) before he entered Harvard Law School (1862). After 1866, although he lived mostly in Europe, his American home was at Cambridge. His conception of himself as a detached spectator of life was maturing, as was his idea that the American scene was hostile toward creative talent and offered no adequate subject matter.

For the time being, however, he divided his interest between European and American materials. During the late 1860s, encouraged by Howells, C.E. Norton, and others, he wrote critical articles and reviews, exhibiting admiration for the technique of George Eliot, and also produced short stories, frequently showing the influence of Hawthorne, one of his masters; a realistic novelette, "Watch and Ward" (*Atlantic Monthly,* 1871; in book form, 1878), concerned with a guardian who loves and marries his ward; and a farce, "Pyramus and Thisbe" (1869). His first important fiction was "A Passionate Pilgrim" ♦ (1871), in which he deals with the first of his great themes, the reactions of an eager American "pilgrim" when confronted with the fascinations of the complex European world of art and affairs.

The author himself during this period was often a pilgrim to the transatlantic world, which he came to regard as his spiritual fatherland, moving there permanently in 1875. During a year in Paris he associated with such masters of his art as Turgenev and Flaubert, but after 1876 he made his home mainly in London, with which much of his writing is concerned. His first novel, following *A Passionate Pilgrim and Other Tales* (1875) and *Transatlantic Sketches* (1875), mainly treating his views of England and Italy, was *Roderick Hudson* ♦ (1876), concerned with the failure of an American sculptor in Rome, resulting from a lack of inner discipline. Other novels and tales of this early London period, when James's course of life was still for him a matter of doubt and self-questioning, include *The American* ♦ (1877), contrasting French and American standards of conduct; *The Europeans* ♦ (1878), reversing the situation by bringing Europeans into a New England background; *Daisy Miller* ♦ (1879), whose wide popularity is probably owing to its portrayal of a charming, ingenuous American girl; *An International Episode* ♦ (1879), a novelette showing the reactions of Englishmen to the American scene and of an American heiress to aristocratic Britain; *The Madonna of the Future and Other Tales* (1879); and *Confidence* (1880), a romantic, melodramatic novelette about a group of expatriated Americans.

In *Washington Square* ♦ (1881), James again revealed American character, this time in its native environment, but after *The Bostonians* ♦ (1886), a satirical novel of New England reformers and philanthropists, he devoted himself to British and continental themes. *The Portrait of a Lady* ♦

(1881), the first of his mature masterpieces, is a triumph of his method of psychological realism, analyzing the relations of a young American woman with a group of Europeans and expatriated Americans, who objectify her conscientious moral attitude, her sensitive appreciation, and her endurance under suffering. In nearly all of James's fiction, the environment is one of affluence and leisure, in which the preoccupations are with manners and the appreciation of character and the arts, including that of conversation. He treats this society with an infinite refinement of particulars, and in a prose style considered to be unapproached in English for subtlety of phrase and rhythm.

Following *The Portrait of a Lady,* James temporarily turned from the writing of novels. He collected his fiction (14 vols., 1883), and published several new works: a dramatization of *Daisy Miller* (1883); *The Siege of London* ♦ (1883), short stories; *Portraits of Places* (1883), a travel book; *Tales of Three Cities* (1884); *A Little Tour in France* (1885); and *Stories Revived* (3 vols., 1885), reprinting earlier tales.

He returned to the novel with *The Princess Casamassima* ♦ (1886), a melodramatic story of revolutionaries and lower-class life in London, told, as all of James's later fictions are, through the observations and reactions of one character, who usually remains outside the events. This was followed by *The Reverberator* (1888), a novelette concerned with American travelers on the Continent; *The Aspern Papers* ♦ (1888), a novelette which tells of the attempt of a critic to gain a celebrated poet's letters; *A London Life* (1889), short stories; *The Tragic Muse* ♦ (1890), a novel dealing with the lives of artists in English society; *The Lesson of the Master* (1892), short stories; *The Real Thing and Other Tales* (1893); *The Private Life* (1893) and *The Wheel of Time* (1893), collections of tales. At this time he also wrote four comedies, collected in *Theatricals* (2 vols., 1894–95), but none of them was successful in the theater, owing perhaps to his essentially cerebral attitude toward life, his extreme refinement of motive and situation, and his unlifelike dialogue and inability to create dramatic simplifications.

His next series of fictional works includes *Terminations* (1895) and *Embarrassments* (1896), books of stories, the latter containing "The Figure in the Carpet" ♦; *The Other House* (1896), an unsuccessful melodramatic novel; *The Spoils of Poynton* ♦ (1897), a tragic novel of mean passions magnified by the excellence of their object, a household of precious objects of art; *What Maisie Knew* ♦ (1897), a novel told through the medium of a little girl's mind; *In the Cage* ♦ (1898), in which a telegraph clerk observes her aristocratic patrons; *The Two Magics* (1898), containing the fine tale of the supernatural "The Turn of the Screw" ♦; *The Awkward Age* ♦ (1899), portraying a British society girl between adolescence and marriage; *The Soft Side* (1900), a collection of tales; *The Sacred Fount*♦ (1901), a novelette that seems to satirize the typical "detached observer" of James's novels; *The Wings of the Dove*♦ (1902), another of his masterpieces in subtle character portrayal; *The Better Sort* (1903), short stories; *The Ambassadors*♦ (1903), a novel that shows the author's genius for formal structure, as well as his discernment of the values of Old World culture; and *The Golden Bowl*♦ (1904), his last completed novel, which also exhibits him at the height of his artistry.

With the addition of two volumes of stories, *The Altar of the Dead* (1909) and *The Finer Grain* (1910), and two unfinished novels, *The Ivory Tower* (1917) and *The Sense of the Past* (1917), this completed his prolific output of fiction. He edited a second collection of his novels and tales (1907–9), which included the valuable critical prefaces, and other writings of his last decade include *William Wetmore Story and His Friends* (2 vols., 1903); *English Hours* (1905), essays; *The Question of Our Speech, and The Lesson of Balzac* (1905), two lectures delivered in the U.S.; *The American Scene*♦ (1907), a descriptive work written after a long journey through the U.S.; *Views and Reviews* (1908), essays; and the autobiographical books, *A Small Boy and Others*♦ (1913), *Notes of a Son and Brother*♦ (1914), and *The Middle Years* (1917). He also returned to playwriting, but of three plays only *The High Bid* was produced (1908).

These last years were troubled ones, saddened by deaths, including that of his brother William, and at the outbreak of World War I he was particularly agitated. To show allegiance to the Allied cause, he became a British subject in 1915. Always strongly conscious of the formal and theoretical phases of his work, he kept *Notebooks* (published 1948) and wrote criticism of his own practice and that of other masters of fiction. Even his *Letters* (3 vols., 1974, 1975, 1980), edited by Leon Edel, display his creative and critical turn of mind. His formal critical writings, sufficient in themselves to establish an author's reputation, were published in *French Poets and Novelists* (1878); *Hawthorne* (1879); *Partial Portraits* (1888), including the essay "The Art of Fiction"; *Picture and Text* (1893); *Essays in London and Elsewhere* (1893); *Notes on Novelists* (1914); *Within the Rim and Other Essays* (1918); and *Notes and Reviews* (1921). Thus he fulfilled his cosmopolitan destiny, detached even from the art that absorbed him, for his self-judgments are as subtle and well formed as is the substance of his fiction.

His artistry was conscious at every point, but his intellectual perceptivity in later life seemed to make him a rarefied observer, apparently largely out of touch with many of the more commonplace realities of his times. His eminence in the realm of his choice, however, is unquestioned, as is his influence in the history of the novel, in which he was a pioneer of psychological realism and formal architectonics, and the master of a rich, highly complex prose style and an extremely sensitive apprehension of values of character.

JAMES, JESSE [WOODSON] (1847–82), born and reared on a Missouri farm, joined the Quantrill gang during the Civil War, and afterward, with his brother Frank (1843–1915), led what became the most notorious band of robbers in U.S. history. Their field of operations included several Midwestern states, and they executed daring and melodramatic robberies of banks and railroad trains throughout the 1870s, causing many deaths. Public sentiment was strongly in favor of the brothers, Jesse especially having become a hero during his lifetime, but a large reward was offered for their capture dead or alive, and Jesse, who was in hiding under the alias Thomas Howard, was killed by one of his accomplices, Robert Ford. Frank, never convicted, gave up his life of crime to become a respectable farmer. As a sort of American Robin Hood, Jesse is the hero of a popular ballad, dime novels, and folk tales, as well as the play *Missouri Legend* (1938), and the musical pantomime *The Saga of Jesse James,* by Douglas Moore.

JAMES, MARQUIS (1891–1955), author of *The Raven: A Biography of Sam Houston* (1929, Pulitzer Prize), *Andrew Jackson: The Border Captain* (1933), *Andrew Jackson: Portrait of a President* (1937), *Alfred I. du Pont* (1941), and *Biography of a Business* (1942) and *Metropolitan Life* (1947), histories of insurance companies. *The Cherokee Strip* (1945) is an account of his Oklahoma boyhood.

JAMES, WILL[IAM RODERICK] (1892–1942), cowboy author and illustrator, whose tales of the West include *Cowboys, North and South* (1942), *The Drifting Cowboy* (1925), *Smoky* (1926), *Cow Country* (1927), *Sand* (1929), *Sun-Up* (1931), *Horses I've Known* (1940), and *The American Cowboy* (1942). *Lone Cowboy: My Life Story* (1930) is his autobiography, fictively embellished.

JAMES, WILLIAM (1842–1910), son of Henry James, Sr., was born in New York City, and spent his boyhood, with his brother Henry and two other brothers, in private study in Europe and at Newport. In 1860–61 he tested one of his apparent aptitudes by studying painting under W. M. Hunt at Newport, but abandoned this career to study at Lawrence Scientific School, Harvard (1861–64), and then at Harvard Medical School, which he left to accompany Agassiz on an expedition to collect zoological specimens in Brazil (1865–66). After another year in the Medical School, and a year abroad, he received his M.D. (1869). Physical weakness and a nervous condition that prevented his entering practice or laboratory research caused a period of pessimistic self-doubt, which ended in 1870, partly owing to his reading of Renouvier, whose psychological theories convinced him of the possibility of moral freedom. His long career of teaching at Harvard began in 1872, when he became an instructor in physiology. This work led him into problems of psychology and philosophy, and he soon became interested in the hypotheses of Darwin and Spencer, in 1879 commencing a course on "The Philosophy of Evolution." He had already transferred his instruction to the department of philosophy, and in 1876 had inaugurated a pioneering laboratory of psychology.

From the year of his marriage (1878) until 1890, James's chief occupation outside of his teaching was the writing of The Principles of Psychology (1890; abridged as a school text, 1892). This "positivistic" treatise, carefully documenting contemporary psychological knowledge and embodying its author's discoveries and hypotheses, remains a classic text, although somewhat superseded by later investigations, which it helped to inspire. Among the chapters previously published in periodicals is "What Is an Emotion?" (Mind, 1884), first stating the so-called James-Lange theory, which suggests that emotions do not cause behavior, but are, rather, collateral results of the same bodily reactions.

James's many trips to Europe and close association with leading continental psychologists and philosophers influenced his entry into the wider realm of philosophic problems. During the '80s and '90s, he was also active in the Society for Psychical Research, increasing the prestige of this organization and reinforcing his own impartial speculative attitude. Other activities demonstrating his altruistic idealism and championing of truth regardless of its source included opposing legislative discrimination against Christian Scientists and Spiritualists, campaigning against the Spanish-American War and other imperialist policies of the U.S., advocacy of temperance though not of prohibition, and criticism of the Dreyfus case. At the same time he was publishing many lectures and articles on philosophic subjects, and in 1897 issued The Will To Believe, ◆ a collection of essays defining his position as a "radical empiricist" and asserting the right to accept metaphysical hypotheses on grounds beyond the possibility of experimental proof. A lecture tour in 1896, made to spread these and similar ideas among influential audiences, resulted in the publication of Talks to Teachers on Psychology; and to Students on Some of Life's Ideals (1899), while another phase of his interest in human values appears in Human Immortality: Two Supposed Objections to the Doctrine (1898), defending the possibility of life after death.

James's international reputation was further strengthened by his appointment as Gifford Lecturer on Natural Religion at the University of Edinburgh (1901–2). There he delivered the two series of lectures printed in The Varieties of Religious Experience ◆ (1902), in which he considers religion as an area of psychological facts and treats it, in his brilliant expositional style, from the points of view of science and common sense. He indicates the practical values of religious belief in terms of action and of happiness, and concludes with a statement of his personal dualistic belief.

As early as 1898, while lecturing at the University of California, James had used the term and concept of "pragmatism," adopted from C.S. Peirce, ◆ to express his philosophic attitude. During the intervening years, he continued to develop this concept of the mind and its relation to action, and in Pragmatism ◆ (1907) he defined and amplified this eminently modern philosophic position, according to which an idea has meaning only in relation to its consequences in the world of feeling and action. This pragmatism, differing from that of Peirce, immediately won followers, including John Dewey, but also precipitated attacks, which were answered by James in The Meaning of Truth ◆ (1909). He had retired from Harvard (1907), but during his last years continued to write and to lecture, and was honored as the foremost American philosopher of his time.

His late and posthumous publications include "The Energies of Men" (1907) and "The Moral Equivalent of War" (1910), expressing his abhorrence of warfare and proposing a substitute, the conscription of youth for projects of manual labor in order to secure discipline and liberate the martial impulses; A Pluralistic Universe (1909), defining his metaphysical tenets, in a series of lectures delivered at Oxford in 1908; Some Problems of Philosophy. A Beginning of an Introduction to Philosophy (1911), edited by H.M. Kallen; Memories and Studies (1911), edited by his brother Henry; Essays in Radical Empiricism (1912), edited by R.B. Perry; The Letters of William James (2 vols., 1920), edited by his son Henry; and Collected Essays and Reviews (1920), edited by Perry. A scholarly edition of his Works was published (7 vols., 1975–78). Selected Letters (1961) was edited by Elizabeth Hardwick. A sketchy biography is contained in his brother's A Small Boy and Others and Notes of a Son and Brother, and Santayana's Character and Opinion in the United States includes a study of James and his philosophy.

Jamestown, capital of Virginia (1607–98), situated on what is now an island but was formerly a peninsula in the James River, about 40 miles above Norfolk. The first permanent English settlement within the boundaries of the present U.S., Jamestown was founded (May 13, 1607) on what may once have been the site of a Spanish colony by some hundred colonists under the command of Sir Christopher Newport. During the winters of 1608 and 1609, the colony was threatened with extinction by disease, starvation, and Indian attacks, and it was preserved only by the leadership of such men as John Smith. ◆ Fear of Spanish attack was also almost constant. Newport, Sir Thomas Gates, and Sir George Somers reached Jamestown with 150 colonists (1610), but found conditions so deplorable that they were about to give up the settlement. Lord De la Warr arrived unexpectedly at this juncture, bringing more colonists and supplies, and hope was renewed. In 1611, 650 additional colonists were brought. The rapid expansion of tobacco cultivation soon made the community self-supporting. An outstanding example of the acceptance of the whites by the Indians is the marriage of Pocahontas♦ to John Rolfe. America's first legislative assembly was held at Jamestown (1619), and slavery was introduced on this continent that year. Never prosperous, the town had several severe fires, one deliberately set by insurgents in Bacon's Rebellion (1676). Abandoned after Williamsburg became the capital (1699), its ruined buildings were partly restored (*c.*1900). Contemporary treatments of early Jamestown include those by Captain John Smith, Richard Rich, and George Sandys, and later historical novels include John Davis, *The First Settlers of Virginia* (1806), J.E. Cooke, *My Lady Pokahontas* (1885), and Mary Johnston, *To Have and To Hold* (1900).

Janice Meredith, novel by P.L. Ford,♦ published in 1899.

Coquettish Janice and her family are involved in the major events of the Revolutionary War. Patriotic Colonel John Brereton finally wins her, after the capricious heroine has captivated many soldiers of both armies. Washington, Hamilton, and others are vividly sketched, and the general atmosphere seems more real than the hero and heroine.

JANVIER, THOMAS ALLIBONE (1849–1913), born in Philadelphia, traveled widely in Mexico and France, which formed the backgrounds for his fiction, including *Color Studies* (1885), sketches of life in Mexico and in Greenwich Village during the 1880s; *The Aztec Treasure-House* (1890), a story of an archaeologist's adventures in Mexico; *Stories of Old New Spain* (1891); *The Uncle of an Angel* (1891) and *The Passing of Thomas* (1901), collections of stories satirizing Philadelphia conservatism through the eyes of a young girl; *From the South of France* (1912), stories of modern Provence; and *At the Casa Napoléon* (1914), stories of residents in a small New York hotel.

JARRELL, RANDALL (1914–65), Tennessee-born author, graduated from Vanderbilt (1935), and taught at various colleges. From poems published in *Blood for a Stranger* (1942), *Little Friend, Little Friend* (1945), *Losses* (1948), and *The Seven-League Crutches* (1951) he chose his *Selected Poems* (1955). Later poetry and translations appear in *The Woman at the Washington Zoo* (1960, National Book Award) and in *The Lost World* (1965). His other works include *Poetry and the Age* (1953), critical essays; *A Sad Heart at the Supermarket* (1962), essays on literature, the arts, and mass culture; and three posthumous volumes: *The Third Book of Criticism* (1969), *The Complete Poems*

(1969), and his translation of *Part One of Goethe's Faust* (1973). *Jerome* (1971) prints his worksheets for an incomplete poem. *Kipling, Auden & Co.* (1980) gathers uncollected essays and reviews. He also wrote a satirical novel about faculty at a progressive college for women, *Pictures from an Institution* (1954), and four books for children. In 1985 an autobiographical and literary selection of his letters was published, and his so-called *Complete Poems* was issued in 1990.

JARVES, JAMES JACKSON (1818–88), born in Boston, during his wide travels became editor of the *Polynesian* (1840–48), the first Hawaiian newspaper. His books include *Scenes and Scenery in the Sandwich Islands* (1843), *Parisian Sights* (1852), *Italian Sights* (1856), and several works of art criticism, mainly dealing with Italian painting, of which he formed a great collection, in part now owned by Yale University.

Java Head, novel by Hergesheimer,♦ published in 1919.

JAY, JOHN (1745–1829), New York lawyer, statesman, and jurist, was educated at King's College, and, admitted to the bar (1768), practiced in partnership with Robert Livingston. A conservative aristocrat, allied with the commercial class, he opposed separation from England until the Declaration of Independence, but thereafter was a leading supporter of the Revolutionary cause. As a member of the two Continental Congresses, he was the author of the celebrated *Address to the People of Great Britain* (1774) and of appeals to Canada, Jamaica, and Ireland to join in the rebellion (1775). He helped to draw up the New York state constitution, and served as chief justice of the state, and later as governor (1795–1801). His federal appointments included minister to Spain (1780–82); peace commissioner to England (1782); secretary of foreign affairs (1784–89); and first chief justice of the U.S. Supreme Court (1789–95). His five essays in *The Federalist*♦ (1787–88), numbers 2, 3, 4, 5, and 64, deal with the Constitution in relation to foreign affairs, and are marked by a lucid style and reasoning power. He is also noted for the so-called Jay's Treaty with England, concluded in 1794, which provided for the British evacuation of northwestern posts, allowed Loyalists full protection in becoming American citizens, permitted unrestricted navigation of the Mississippi, and authorized trade between the U.S. and Canada and equal privileges for vessels of both nations in Great Britain and the East Indies, while restricting American trade in the West Indies. Considered unduly favorable to British interests, the treaty aroused indignant protests in the U.S. but was finally ratified.

Jazz Age, epithet applied, often invidiously, to the era of the 1920s in the U.S., whose frenetic youth of the postwar period were conceived as more juvenile and hedonistic than the contemporary "lost generation" of expatriates. F. Scott Fitzgerald's *Tales of the Jazz Age* (1922) was a classic representation of the period, as was Percy Marks's *The Plastic Age* (1924). The manners of the times were also depicted in the caricatures of John Held. Treatments of jazz music, as distinct from the jazz-age ethos, occur in many works, including Vachel Lindsay's poem *The Daniel Jazz* (1920) and Dorothy Baker's novel *Young Man with a Horn* (1938).

JEFFERS, [JOHN] ROBINSON (1887–1962), born in Pittsburgh, traveled widely on the Continent until his family settled in California when he was 16. After graduation from Occidental College (California) and desultory graduate study of medicine and other subjects in the U.S. and abroad, he settled with his wife in the town of Carmel, ♦ whose surrounding country is the setting of his poetry. After two undistinguished volumes, *Flagons and Apples* (1912) and *Californians* (1916), containing his first California narratives and descriptive pieces, he published *Tamar and Other Poems* ♦ (1924), including two long works: the title narrative, adapting the Biblical legend to modern experience in a California scene, and "The Tower Beyond Tragedy ♦" his own version of the legend of Orestes and Electra, in which Orestes finds salvation from the madness of self-centered humanity by "falling in love outward" with his nonhuman surroundings. Other characteristic poems in the volume include the lyric "Night" ♦; "'Boats in a Fog" and "Granite and Cypress," expressing Jeffers's love of the spare enduring beauty of the rocky coast on which he made his home; "Shine, Perishing Republic," advising his sons to "be in nothing so moderate as in love of man . . . When the cities lie at the monster's feet there are left the mountains"; "The Coast-Range Christ," a tragically ironic narrative of California mountain people at Christmas; and the apostrophe "To the Stone-Cutters," comparing the poet's work to that of the stone-cutter, both being conscious of ultimate futility, "Yet stones have stood for a thousand years, and pained thoughts found The honey peace in old poems." These were reprinted with additions, the following year, in *Roan Stallion, Tamar, and Other Poems,* the new title piece ♦ being an allegorical legend of pantheism.

In *The Women at Point Sur* ♦ (1927), through the mad preacher Barclay, the poet again sets forth his conception of the need "to uncenter the human mind from itself," while yet indicating the dangerous aspects of action in accordance with such a philosophic attitude. "Cawdor" ♦ in *Cawdor, and Other Poems* (1928), is a bitterly tragic narrative, in which Jeffers considers "human affairs . . . looking eastward against the earth, reclaiming a little dignity from that association. . . ." Also included in this volume is "Hurt

Hawks," expressing the poet's concept of "the wild God of the world . . . intemperate and savage . . . beautiful and wild . . . ," whom the "communal people" have never known, or have forgotten. In 1929 he published *Dear Judas, and Other Poems,* whose title piece retells the story of the betrayal of Christ, describing Judas's motive as one of love. "The Loving Shepherdess," in the same collection, is a parable of self-sacrifice in its story of a girl who, knowing herself doomed to die, wanders over the countryside, devotedly caring for the dwindling flock of her dead father. *Descent to the Dead* (1931), written in England and Ireland, is a volume of elegies in the manner and often in the mood of their Greek models, forming a concise expression of Jeffers's poetic themes, the desire for an end of life, the breaking of the human mold, and the escape to nonhuman nature. In *Thurso's Landing, and Other Poems* (1932), the title narrative ♦ describes the fatally violent struggle of a California farmer and his rival for his wife's love. *Give Your Heart to the Hawks, and Other Poems* (1933) is a collection whose title narrative ♦ deals with the poet's frequent subject of a man who violates a human code, in this case by murdering his brother, and then finds himself alone in a world, beyond humanity, which is inhabited only by the fierce hawks of freedom and soaring flight. The title narrative of *Solstice, and Other Poems* (1935) is a retelling of the Medea legend, while "At the Birth of an Age," in the same volume, is a drama set in the time of Attila. In *Such Counsels You Gave to Me, and Other Poems* (1937), the title narrative ♦ is a modern tragedy based on the old Scottish ballad "Edward, Edward." The *Selected Poetry of Robinson Jeffers* was issued in 1938.

Later books include *Be Angry at the Sun* (1941); *Hungerfield and Other Poems* (1945), including a version of Euripides' *Hippolytus; Medea* (1946), including a free adaptation of Euripides' drama to fit the modern theater; *The Double Axe* (1948); and a posthumous collection, *The Beginning and the End* (1963). "*What Odd Expedients*" (1981) prints uncollected and unpublished poems. *Rock and Hawk,* a selection of shorter poems, was published in 1987, and other, very incidental writings have also been printed posthumously. In addition, his *Collected Poetry* is being issued in a multi-volume edition.

Jeffers's plots have a realistic setting of the granite cliffs, surf-beaten shore, and towering redwoods of California, yet Jeffers never obscured the symbolism in his use of this background. Accepting a scientific view of the universe, in which man appears to be of but trivial importance, he made the core of his thought the renunciation of humanity and the reliance upon nature. Thus the melodramatic subjects of his narratives have an allegorical significance, and the frequent use of the incest theme symbolizes man regarding man exclusively and leading himself to destruction. From this stemmed his intense re-

vulsion from society, expressed in such statements as "Cut humanity out of my being, that is
the wound that festers." He looked forward to
the time when man would be driven from the
universe, and the grass and the cliff would

> . . . enjoy wonderful vengeance and suck
> The arteries and walk in triumph on the faces.

In this profound contempt for "the animals
Christ was rumored to have died for," and belief
that solace will come to the earth only when,
freed from humanity, it has attained a "white and
most clean, colorless quietness," he found war or
any other negative force to be good, in that it
cleansed civilization and led back to "the primal
and the latter silences."

Jefferson, capital of Yoknapatawpha County,♦
the fictional setting in northern Mississippi of a
substantial part of the saga of novels and stories by
Faulkner, modeled on his hometown, Oxford,
Miss.

JEFFERSON, JOSEPH (1829–1905), Philadelphia-born actor, was prominent on the American
stage for 71 years. Noted for his comic roles, he is
primarily identified with the play *Rip Van Winkle,* adapted with Boucicault in 1865, in which he
continued to act for the remainder of his career.
He wrote an *Autobiography* (1890).

JEFFERSON, THOMAS (1743–1826), 3rd President of the U.S. (1801–9), was a member of a
prominent Virginia family, studied at William
and Mary, and practiced law (1767–74). After he
entered the House of Burgesses (1769), he was
almost constantly in the political service of Virginia and of the nation until his retirement from
the presidency. At the outset he identified himself
with the aggressive anti-British group, and he
made an important contribution to the Revolutionary cause in *A Summary View of the Rights of
British America* (1774), a brilliant exposition contending that Parliament had no authority in the
colonies, whose only bond with England was allegiance to the same king.

As a member of the Continental Congress
(1775–76), he was almost wholly responsible for
the spirit and phrasing of the Declaration of Independence,♦ his great monument in literature and
political theory. In the Virginia House of Burgesses (1776–79) and as governor (1779–81) he
attempted to translate the ideals of this document
into reality, by advocating laws which would
make impossible the maintenance of a landed aristocracy or an established church. His revision of
the state laws and constitution embodied liberal
policies, not all of which could be made effective,
concerning education, religious freedom, economic equality, antislavery, and other humanitarian reforms.

When the British invaded Virginia, he virtually resigned his governorship, intending to retire from public life, and used his leisure to write

his *Notes on the State of Virginia.*♦ Again in the
Continental Congress (1783), he headed the
committee that debated the peace treaty, suggested the plan of the present monetary system,
and prepared a report (March 1784) that formulated the plan of government of western territories later embodied in the Ordinance of 1787.

After traveling in Europe and serving as minister to France (1784–89), he returned to the U.S.
to become the first secretary of state (1789–93).
His antagonism toward the attitude and policies
of Hamilton, then secretary of the treasury, had
already arisen in their differences over the new
Constitution, which Jefferson opposed until the
adoption of the Bill of Rights. Jefferson, as a
thoroughgoing republican, feared that Hamilton's program would lead in the direction of
monarchy. He championed states' rights, individual liberties, and the ascendancy of the agrarian
faction—all in opposition to the Hamiltonian
attitude—and objected to the Bank of the
United States, the protective tariff, and other
measures that would ally the federal government
with the monied interests. To further his views,
which made him the leader of the anti-Federalist
Democratic Republican party♦ then in process
of formation, he backed Freneau's *Federal Gazette,* which attacked the Hamiltonian *Gazette of
the United States.*

He retired from office (1793–96), but in 1796
was the Democratic Republican candidate for the
presidency, and, running second to Adams, became Vice-President (1797–1801). His most important contribution during this period was his
drafting of the Kentucky Resolutions (1798),
complementing Madison's Virginia Resolutions
in reply to the Federalist Alien and Sedition acts.
In 1800 Jefferson and Burr, both Democratic Republican candidates, received equal electoral
votes for the presidency. In the congressional
election to determine which should be chief executive, Hamilton placed his influence on the
side of Jefferson, who was elected. During his
two terms, he authorized the Louisiana Purchase,
commissioned the expedition of Lewis and
Clark, dispatched the naval force of Decatur
against the Tripolitans, prosecuted Burr for his
unwarranted and bellicose expedition into the
Spanish Southwest, and was responsible for the
Nonimportation Act and the Embargo Act in
retaliation for foreign interference with American
trade. These last acts impoverished sections of the
country that had previously supported him and
revivified partisan opposition in New England,
but his party remained in power long after his
retirement, his immediate successors being Madison and Monroe, both his friends and protégés,
whom he continued to advise.

After he left the presidency he was primarily
interested in the University of Virginia, which he
founded and planned as a modern, broad, and
liberal institution of higher education. His designs for his home, Monticello, and for the Vir-

ginia state capitol and part of Washington, D.C., stimulated the classical revival in U.S. architecture. Besides his importance in politics and political history, he influenced American culture by his scholarship in sciences and languages, and as a connoisseur and patron of the arts. The variety of his interests and attainments is indicated by his nonpolitical writings, which include *An Essay Towards Facilitating Instruction in the Anglo-Saxon and Modern Dialects of the English Language,* prepared for the University of Virginia and printed by it in 1851, and *The Life and Morals of Jesus of Nazareth,* his personal polyglot compilation of the Gospels, published in facsimile in 1904. He composed his own epitaph: "Here was buried Thomas Jefferson, Author of the Declaration of American Independence, of the Statute of Virginia for Religious Freedom, and Father of the University of Virginia," summing up his lifelong quest of liberty, political, religious, and intellectual. His papers are being published in a projected 60-volume edition (1950–   ), of which the first 20 were edited by Julian P. Boyd (1903–80).

JEMISON, MARY (1743–1833), "the White Woman of the Genesee," was captured by Indians from her western Pennsylvania home at the age of 15, and, developing a deep affection for them, married into the Delaware tribe and remained with them for the rest of her life. James E. Seaver's *A Narrative of the Life of Mrs. Mary Jemison* (1824), although a late example of the accounts of Indian captivities, is one of the most popular.

Jennie Gerhardt, novel by Dreiser,♦ published in 1911.

As a poor young girl in Columbus, Ohio, Jennie Gerhardt has an affair with Senator Brander, who dies before he can marry her. With their child Vesta she moves to Cleveland and there, attracted by the kindliness and domineering personality of Lester Kane, son of a rich manufacturer, becomes his mistress, although she insists he leave her when she learns that the elder Kane's will provides that Lester receive only a small legacy as long as he remains with Jennie. Lester does leave Jennie to marry Letty Gerald, a woman of his own social class and interests, but installs Jennie in a modest home where she lives with two adopted children after Vesta dies. When Lester falls ill during his wife's absence, he summons Jennie and confesses that she has been his only true love, and she nurses him until he dies.

Jerome, A Poor Man, novel by Mary Wilkins Freeman,♦ published in 1897.

Jerome Edwards, a New England boy, is left by his father's mysterious disappearance to provide for his mother and his sister Elmira. During the difficulties of his youth, he preserves pride and independence, refusing aid, and is intent on paying his own way. He falls in love with a childhood friend, Lucina Merritt, and Elmira loves

Lawrence Prescott, son of a wealthy doctor who is virtually dictator of the district, but marriage seems impossible for both of them. Disaster follows disaster; the mill on which Jerome has founded his hopes is destroyed by a flood, but he continues his labors. He receives a large inheritance, but gives it away in order to keep a promise. Finally Dr. Prescott permits his son to marry Elmira, and Jerome submerges his pride, proposing to Lucina although she has a fortune and he has nothing, only to find that her inheritance has actually been left to her as a dowry, so that his arduous career is at last rewarded.

Jerry of the Islands, novel by Jack London,♦ published in 1917.

Jerry, an Irish setter pup, idolizes his master, Van Horn, who operates a ship to obtain indentured labor from the Solomon Islands. When Van Horn is killed by cannibals, Jerry is taken by the native chief and trained to act as a sentinel. He escapes to the jungle, and ends his quest for a white master when he is found by a California couple who are yachting in the South Seas. Following further adventures, they take Jerry back to the Pacific coast with them.

Jessel, MISS, character in "The Turn of the Screw."♦

Jesuits, name given to members of the Society of Jesus, a religious order of the Roman Catholic Church, founded by Ignatius Loyola (1534). Originally conceived as a band of spiritual soldiers to convert the Moslems, the order has been distinguished for its missionary work and scholarship. The Jesuits were powerful in the Spanish, French, and Portuguese possessions in the Americas, and were associated with the Calverts in founding Maryland. Among the notable French leaders were Marquette and Jogues, among the Spanish was Kino, and the Belgians included De Smet. The *Jesuit Relations,* translated by R.G. Thwaites (73 vols., 1896–1901), includes reports and narratives of the missionaries in New France. Among the learned institutions that they founded in the present U.S. are Georgetown University (1789) and Fordham (1841). A famous historical account is Parkman's *The Jesuits in North America in the Seventeenth Century.*

Jethro Bass, character in *Coniston.*♦

Jeunes, LES, see *Lark, The.*

JEWETT, SARAH ORNE (1849–1909), was born and reared in South Berwick, Me., near York, which resembles "Deephaven." She was early stimulated by Harriet Beecher Stowe's sympathetic depiction of her state's local color, and determined to follow her in recording the life of the dwindling farms and deserted, shipless harbors. Her keen perception led to the *Atlantic*

Monthly's accepting a story when she was 19. In 1873 it also printed "The Shore House," beginning the series gathered as *Deephaven*♦ (1877), which established her reputation, although she far exceeded it in her later writing. Her great friendship with Annie Fields brought her frequently to Boston, but she always returned to her native town to write her books. The most characteristic of these include *A Country Doctor* (1884), a novel about a New England girl who refuses marriage so as to become a doctor; *A Marsh Island* (1885), a novel depicting the love of a rich painter and the daughter of a New England farmer; *A White Heron* (1886), a collection of stories whose title piece deals with the conflict in the heart of a little girl between her adoration of a young ornithologist and her desire to protect the white heron for which he is searching; and further collections, *The King of Folly Island* (1888), *A Native of Winby* (1893), and *The Life of Nancy* (1895). Her masterpiece is *The Country of the Pointed Firs*♦ (1896), a series of closely knit sketches of a Maine seaport town during the era of its decay from the grandeur of West Indian trading days. Her precise, charmingly subdued vignettes of the gently perishing glory of the Maine countryside and ports have won her a place among the most important writers of the local-color school, and she was a significant influence on the writing of Willa Cather, as the latter tells in *Not Under Forty*. In 1901 Miss Jewett turned to historical romance in *The Tory Lover,* concerned with a young American officer during the Revolution and his conflicting duty to his king and to his native land. Her poems were collected in *Verses* (1916), and she also wrote three books for children.

Jim Bludso, poem in *Pike County Ballads.*♦

Joad, family name of the principal characters in *The Grapes of Wrath.*♦

Joan of Arc, Personal Recollections of, fictional biography by Clemens,♦ published in 1896. To conceal his authorship, so that the book might be received without bias, Clemens invented "The Sieur Louis de Conte," Joan's supposed "page and secretary," whose work is "freely translated by Jean François Alden." The biography follows the known facts in the life of the 15th-century French heroine but amplifies them with several fictional characters and interprets such documents as those relating to the ecclesiastical trial at Rouen in the light of Clemens's lifelong idealistic reverence for "the noble child, the most innocent, the most lovely, the most adorable the ages have produced." Her traits have been said to resemble those of women in the author's family. Other figures, like the comically boastful Paladin and laughing Noël Rainguesson, are related to characters in his earlier fiction. In general, the mood is that of serious, although romanticized, history, but there are characteristic Clemens

touches in the use of European folklore, humor, and American tall talk.

John Barleycorn, memoir by Jack London. ♦

John Brent, novel by Theodore Winthrop,♦ posthumously published in 1862.

Richard Wade, leaving for the East, trades his unsuccessful California mine for Don Fulano, a proud "unmanageable" black stallion, which in his hands becomes docile. The "Indianesque Saxon" John Brent, his friend and a veteran Western adventurer, accompanies him, and on their way across the plains they are joined by Murker and Larrap, two rascals who call themselves Smith and Robinson. In Utah they encounter a company of Mormons, headed by the unscrupulous Sizzum, who has in his power the impoverished Englishman Hugh Clitheroe and his daughter Ellen. Murker and Larrap kidnap Ellen and are followed in a melodramatic chase on horseback by Wade and Brent. The latter, losing his horse, continues with Wade on Don Fulano, and when Brent is shot in an encounter with the abductors, the horse tramples Murker to death. Brent recovers, and the rescued Ellen, although in love with Wade, returns to England with her father. Wade and Brent seek the Clitheroes in London, and the lovers are finally united.

"John Brown's Body," popular Civil War song, commemorating Brown's raid on Harpers Ferry. The origin of the tune is uncertain, although there is evidence that it was a Sunday-school hymn composed by a South Carolina musician, William Steffe, as early as 1856, which became popular in the North with various sets of words. The "John Brown" verses have been attributed to Charles S. Hall, H.H. Brownell, and anonymous Union soldiers, but Thomas B. Bishop♦ is most often credited with their authorship. "The Battle Hymn of the Republic"♦ was written for the same tune.

John Brown's Body, verse narrative of the Civil War by Stephen V. Benét,♦ published in 1928 and awarded a Pulitzer Prize.

A prelude, "The Slaver," sketches the background of intersectional antagonism with its account of an early slave ship, its harsh, pious master, Captain Ball, and the experiences of a conscience-stricken mate. Then, with vivid impressionistic characterizations and rapid changes of scene, the poem tells of Brown's raid on Harpers Ferry, and his execution; of the opening of the war, with episodes concerning Lincoln, Davis, Lee, Jackson, Grant, and other figures; and of the personal lives, now interrupted, of the fictional protagonists: Jack Ellyat, New England law student who joins the Union army; Clay Wingate, aristocratic Georgian who enlists in the Black Horse Troop, and his beautiful fiancée, Sally Dupré; Luke Breckinridge, ignorant mountaineer, who is not sure who the Yankees are, except that "they ain't Injuns neither"; Spade, renegade black; Jack Diefer, burly Pennsylvania farmer; Melora, a mountain girl with whom Ellyat has an idyllic interlude before his incarceration in a Southern prison; and others. The course of events until 1865 are thus described and interpreted, with a final passage concerned with the war's termination of the Southern dream of a patriarchal aristocratic nation, and the inauguration instead of an America of equalitarianism and industrial mechanization.

John Henry, hero of a cycle of Negro ballads♦ and tall tales,♦ a "natchal man," born in the "Black River country, where the sun don't never shine," who is sometimes a steel driver in the building of the "Yaller Dog" or "Yaller Ball" railroad line for "Mister Billie Bob Russell," sometimes a roustabout on riverboats. Other figures in the ballads and tales include John Hardy, the gambler; innumerable rivals of John Henry, all named Sam; and the women, Poor Selma, Julie Ann, and Ruby. John Henry's chief exploit is his competition with a steam drill in driving steel, in which he drives faster than the machine, but dies, "with his hammer in his hand," as a result of the exertion. In some versions, the contest is with a steam winch in loading cotton on a riverboat. The legend seems to have originated *c.*1870, when an actual John Henry of such a contest may have existed. The ballads about John Hardy may have arisen from the same source, but their hero differs from John Henry in that he comes to a bad end, murdering a man and dying on the gallows. Roark Bradford's *John Henry* (1931) combines and reconciles the various tales, while Guy B. Johnson's *John Henry: Tracking Down a Negro Legend* (1931) is a collection of variants of the ballads.

John Marr and Other Sailors, poem by Melville,♦ published in 1888. Besides the vigorous title piece, the collection includes such sea pieces as "Bridegroom Dick," "Tom Deadlight," and "Jack Roy." *John Marr and Other Poems* (1922) is a selection from all of Melville's poetic works.

John Phoenix, pseudonym of G.H. Derby.♦

Johnny Appleseed, sobriquet of John Chapman.♦

JOHNSON, CHARLES [RICHARD] (1948–), African-American novelist, cartoonist, television script writer, born in Evanston, Ill. Johnson is a professor at the University of Washington, Seattle. His novel *Faith and the Good Thing* (1974) concerns the adventures of Faith Cross, a Southern black girl going to Chicago in quest of life's "Good Thing." Another novel, *Oxherding Tale* (1982), explores the coming of age of Andrew Hawkins, a slave conceived of a black father and white mother in the pre–Civil War South. One of Andrew's achievements is eluding a bounty hunter with telepathic powers called Soulcatcher. *The Sorcerer's Apprentice* (1986) collects short stories.

JOHNSON, DIANE [LAIN] (1934–), born in Illinois, long resident in California, where she earned a Ph.D. from the University of California, Los Angeles, and taught at the University of California, Davis. Her novels include *Fair Game* (1965), a comic portrayal of four men variously involved with the same woman; *Loving Hands at Home* (1968), a farcical treatment of a Mormon family; *Burning* (1971), an apocalyptic view of lives in Los Angeles; *The Shadow Knows* (1972), portraying the terrifying experiences of a victimized woman; *Lying Low* (1978), depicting a young woman hiding out as a fugitive in a small California town; and *Persian Nights* (1987), about the social and emotional life of a young American woman in Persia on its eve of revolution. *Lesser Lives* (1972) is a biography of the daughter of Thomas Love Peacock, who was the wife of George Meredith, and she also wrote *Dashiell Hammett: A Life* (1983). *Terrorists and Novelists* (1982) collects book reviews.

JOHNSON, DOROTHY [MARIE] (1905–), reared in Montana but moved to Washington and Wisconsin, both background for her early book of stories, *Beulah Bunny Tells All* (1942) and the succeeding *The Hanging Tree* (1957). She also wrote several books of nonfiction and of stories for young readers, all based on the Western region she knew. *All the Buffalo Returning* (1979) is a novel presenting a sympathetic view of Native Americans.

JOHNSON, EDWARD (1598–1672), colonial Massachusetts chronicler and captain of militia, came to Boston in 1630 to trade with the Indians, and after a short stay sailed for England to bring his family, with whom he returned in 1636. He was a founder of Woburn (1640), and until his death was active in the affairs of that town. As a devout and stalwart Puritan, in 1650 he commenced writing *A History of New-England,* better known by its running title, *The Wonder-Working Providence of Sions Saviour in New-England*♦ (1654). In this anonymously published work, intended to suppress the calumniations of English critics and celebrate the Puritan religious commonwealth in America, Johnson writes with vigor both of homely facts and of great events, and rhapsodizes with an epic view of the founding of New England as a spiritual crusade by soldiers of Christ at war with unbelievers and the wilderness.

JOHNSON, JAMES WELDON (1871–1938), black educator, civil rights leader, and author, was born in Jacksonville, Fla., educated at Atlanta University, and became the first African American to be admitted to the Florida bar (1897) before moving to New York City and a wider area of activities. With his brother John Rosamond Johnson (1873–1954) he created a song-and-dance act for which they composed such songs as "Under the Bamboo Tree" (popularized by Lillian Russell and later drawn upon by T.S. Eliot in *Sweeney Agonistes*), as well as the so-called black anthem, "Lift Every Voice and Sing," and contributed to the musical comedy *The Shoo Fly Regiment* (1907). In New York he also became active in Republican party politics, leading to appointments as U.S. consul in Nicaragua and Venezuela. He next became the field, later the executive, secretary (1916–30) of the NAACP, increasing its membership enormously (from three to 131 branches in the South), investigating and publicizing the brutal U.S. occupation of Haiti, and fought valiantly against lynching. During the period of these diverse careers he became a leader of the Harlem Renaissance,♦ distinguished for both his prose and his poetry. *The Autobiography of an Ex-Colored Man* (1912) is a novel about a light black man who passes as a white and thereby is able to see further into the injustices suffered by his people in the U.S. Other prose writings include *Black Manhattan* (1930), a historical study of New York City; *Negro Americans, What Now?* (1934), his lectures at Fisk University; and *Along This Way* (1933), his autobiography. His poetry appears in *Fifty Years and Other Poems* (1917); *God's Trombones: Seven Negro Sermons in Verse* (1927); *Saint Peter Relates an Incident of the Resurrection Day* (1930), a satire on racial prejudice; and *Selected Poems* (1935). He also edited *The Book of American Negro Poetry* (1922, enlarged 1931) and, with his brother, two collections (1925, 1926) of black spirituals.

JOHNSON, JOSEPHINE [WINSLOW] (1910–), Missouri author, whose works include *Now in November* (1934, Pulitzer Prize), a realistic novel of drudgery on a Midwestern farm; *Winter Orchard* (1935), a collection of short stories; *Jordanstown* (1937), the story of a young Midwesterner who during the Depression edits a newspaper in a vain attempt to help the oppressed; *Year's End* (1937), a volume of poetry; *Wildwood* (1946), a novel of a frustrated young girl's upbringing in the home of relatives; *The Dark Traveler* (1963), about the rehabilitation of a schizophrenic young man; and *The Sorcerer's Son* (1965), stories. *The Inland Island* (1969), observations about nature, is also a critical view of contemporary America. *Seven Houses* (1973) is a memoir.

JOHNSON, MERLE [DEVORE] (1874–1935), a cartoonist on the staff of *Puck,* later compiled bibliographies of Mark Twain (1910) and Cabell (1921), *American First Editions* (1929), and *High Spots of American Literature* (1929). *You Know These Lines* (1934) is a list of books containing famous verse quotations.

JOHNSON, OLIVER (1809–89), a founder of the New England Anti-Slavery Society (1832), was associated with Garrison in the editorship of *The Liberator.*♦ As a reformer and journalist, he was a contributor to many humanitarian movements.

JOHNSON, OWEN [MCMAHON] (1878–1952), son of R.U. Johnson,♦ wrote popular novels about boys, including *The Varmint* (1910), set in a preparatory school; *Stover at Yale* (1911); and *The Tennessee Shad* (1911).

JOHNSON, ROBERT UNDERWOOD (1853–1937), was associated with the *Century Magazine* from 1873 and succeeded R.W. Gilder as editor (1909). His many occasional poems in the romantic tradition of the Gilded Age, including *Saint-Gaudens, an Ode* (1910), won him a reputation as the unofficial poet laureate of the U.S. and were collected in *Poems of Fifty Years* (1931). After 1919 he served as director of the Hall of Fame, and he was ambassador to Italy (1920–21). His memoirs were published as *Remembered Yesterdays* (1923).

JOHNSON, SAMUEL (1696–1772), was a Congregationalist minister until 1712, when he joined the Church of England, becoming its acknowledged leader in New England. He was the first president of King's College (1754–63) and, as a friend and disciple of the English philosopher Berkeley, became the leading American exponent of Berkeley's idealism, which he made palatable by his pleasing style, while rendering Calvin ridiculous by satirical paraphrase. His principal book, *Ethices Elementa* (1746), was enlarged as *Elementa Philosophica,* published by Franklin in 1752.

JOHNSON, SAMUEL (1709–84), English lexicographer and author, in 1775 was employed by the ministers in power to write a tract, *Taxation No Tyranny,* in answer to the resolutions and addresses of the Continental Congress. In it he ridicules the attempt of the Americans to resist the will of the mother country, asserts the supreme power of the home government to require contributions for the purposes of maintaining public safety or prosperity, and contends that in Parliament all British subjects possess a "virtual representation."

JOHNSON, SIR WILLIAM (1715–74), colonial superintendent of Indian affairs north of the Ohio, aided the English during King George's War (1744–48) by securing Iroquois loyalty. He helped to formulate the Indian policy of the Albany Congress, and, until the arrival of Gage, was in charge of the defense of the northern frontier, where he repulsed the French. He is the subject of a biography by W.I. Stone and his son, and figures in fiction in Paulding's *The Dutchman's*

Fireside, Hoffman's *Greyslaer,* Robert Chambers's *Cardigan,* Kenneth Roberts's *Northwest Passage,* and Margaret Widdemer's *Red Cloak Flying.*

JOHNSTON, ANNIE FELLOWS (1863–1931), author of children's stories, best known for the series beginning with *The Little Colonel* (1895). *In the Desert of Waiting* (1905) is based on a legend of an Arizona mountain.

JOHNSTON, MARY (1870–1936), Virginia author of 22 popular romances, the best known of which is *To Have and To Hold*♦ (1900), telling of a young English noblewoman who leaves her country to avoid marriage with a man she hates, and weds an unbelievably heroic Virginian. Fifteen of her stories deal with various periods of Virginia history, and *The Long Roll*♦ (1911) and its sequel, *Cease Firing* (1912), are romantic tales of the Civil War, constructed with minute attention to historical facts. Her books are idealistic, sometimes verging on the mystical, and are peopled by stilted or artificial figures, despite her ability to re-create atmosphere.

JOHNSTON, RICHARD MALCOLM (1822–98), Georgia jurist, educator, and author, wrote humorous local-color stories for the *Spirit of the Times* and similar publications, which he gathered in *Georgia Sketches* (1864), a work indebted even in its title to Longstreet's *Georgia Scenes.* Republished as the *Dukesborough Tales*♦ (1871) under the pseudonym Philemon Perch, the sketches are vivid studies of Georgia life in the best humorous tradition of the Old Southwest. In several editions between 1864 and the early 1890s, the revived sketches evolved from the coarse and direct Longstreet type to a more subdued and precise pattern. Among his other books are *Old Mark Langston, a Tale of Duke's Creek* (1884), a rambling, sketchy novel set in a rural Georgia town; *Mr. Absalom Billingslea and Other Georgia Folk* (1888); *Mr. Billy Downs and His Likes* (1892), six stories; *Widow Guthrie* (1890), a serious novel of life in a small Georgia community; *Old Times in Middle Georgia* (1897); *Pearce Amerson's Will* (1898), a melodramatic novelette; and an *Autobiography* (1900).

JOLAS, EUGENE, see *transition.*

Jonathan, character in *The Contrast.*♦

Jonathan, BROTHER, see *Brother Jonathan.*

Jonathan Oldstyle, pseudonym of Washington Irving.♦

Jones, CASEY, see *Casey Jones.*

JONES, GAYL (1949–   ), born in Lexington, Ky., educated at Connecticut College and Brown University, and currently a professor of

English at the University of Michigan. An African-American, Jones achieved fame with her first novel, *Corregidora* (1975), which traces the effects of slave heritage and sexual abuse upon a late 20th-century black woman. Her second novel, *Eva's Man* (1976), explores again even greater brutality; for example, the heroine is imprisoned for dentally castrating a man. *White Rat* (1977) prints short stories. Jones's poetry includes *Song for Anninho* (1981), *The Hermit Woman* (1983), and *Xarque and Other Poems* (1985). She has published a play, *Chile Woman* (1974).

JONES, HOWARD MUMFORD (1892–1980), professor of comparative literature at the University of Texas (1919–25), of English at North Carolina (1925–30), Michigan (1930–36), and Harvard (1936–60), and of humanities at Harvard (1960–62), author of more than 20 books, including poetry and plays. Among his best-known works are *America and French Culture, 1750–1848* (1927); *The Life of Moses Coit Tyler* (1933); *The Harp That Once* (1937), a life of Tom Moore; *The Theory of American Literature* (1948); *One Great Society: Humane Learning in the United States* (1959); *O Strange New World* (1964, Pulitzer Prize), a study of the formative years of American culture from the 15th to the 19th century; and *Revolution and Romanticism* (1974).

JONES, HUGH (c.1670–1760), Virginia minister, professor of mathematics at William and Mary, and historian, whose *An Accidence to the English Tongue* (1724) was the first English grammar written in America. His historical monograph *The Present State of Virginia* (1724) has been regarded as the best contemporary account of the social, economic, and ecclesiastical life of the colony.

JONES, JAMES (1921–77), Illinois-born author, served in the Pacific with the army (1939–44), his experiences furnishing background for *From Here to Eternity*♦ (1951), a naturalistic novel about army life in Hawaii on the eve of the Pearl Harbor attack. His later fiction includes *Some Came Running* (1957), a long, panoramic novel set in a Midwestern town between World War II and the Korean War; *The Pistol* (1959), a novella about an army private who accidentally obtains a pistol that comes to be his symbol of safety in war; *The Thin Red Line* (1962), a novel about a U.S. infantry company on Guadalcanal in 1942–43, a sequel to his first novel; *Go to the Widow-Maker* (1967), presenting a successful playwright's quest for manhood through his experiences in learning to skin-dive; *The Merry Month of May* (1971), depicting crises, personal and political, of an American family in Paris during the riots of May 1968; *A Touch of Danger* (1973), a detective tale set on a Greek island; and *Whistle* (1978), the final volume of Jones's World War II trilogy, depicting the difficulties four wounded soldiers have in adjusting to civilian life. *The Ice-Cream Headache* (1968) collects stories and a novella, and *Viet Journal* (1974) describes his trip to Vietnam in 1973. His collected letters were gathered under the title *To Reach Eternity* (1989).

JONES, JAMES ATHEARN (1791–1854), Massachusetts-born author and editor, whose books include *Tales of an Indian Camp* (3 vols., 1829), 56 romantic legends based on the folklore of Eastern and Plains Indians; an early volume of poems, of which the most popular was "The Lay of a Mountain Spirit"; *The Refugee* (1825), a fantastic romance of the Revolutionary War; and another novel, *Haverhill; or, Memoirs of an Officer in the Army of Wolfe* (1831).

JONES, JOHN BEAUCHAMP (1810–66), frontier novelist, was born in Baltimore and reared in the Kentucky and Missouri border country. His pioneer boyhood is reflected in the narrative *Wild Western Scenes* (1841), in which Daniel Boone is described. Other novels include *The Western Merchant* (1849), *Freaks of Fortune; or, The History of Ned Lorn* (1854), and *The War Path* (1858). In the interests of the South, he founded *The Southern Monitor* at Philadelphia (1858). His *A Rebel War Clerk's Diary at the Confederate Capital* (1866) gives a good picture of conditions within the Confederacy.

JONES, JOHN PAUL (1747–92), Scottish-born naval adventurer, served in the West Indian slave trade before he entered the Revolutionary navy (1755). He was highly successful in destroying British ships, harassing the Nova Scotia fisheries, and capturing a British transport. Franklin procured for him an old French vessel, renamed the *Bonhomme Richard,* with which, accompanied by a small fleet, he fought the most important naval engagement of the war (Sept. 23, 1779), which resulted in the capture of the British warship *Serapis.* "I have not yet begun to fight" is said to have been Jones's reply to the question of Captain Pearson of the British ship, "Have you struck?" The *Bonhomme Richard* sank within a few hours after Jones transferred his crew to the *Serapis.* In 1788 he entered the Russian naval service, but resigned the following year to reside in Paris. A dashing figure, he and his exploits appear in a poem by Freneau and several historical romances, notably Cooper's *The Pilot,* Melville's *Israel Potter,* Sarah Orne Jewett's *The Tory Lover,* Winston Churchill's *Richard Carvel,* and James Boyd's *Drums.*

JONES, JOSEPH STEVENS (1809–77), Boston actor, author of more than 150 melodramas, farces, and comedies. *The People's Lawyer* (1839) and *The Silver Spoon* (1852) are distinguished for their characterizations of the shrewd rural Yankee. The former play was also known as *Solon Shingle,* from its hero's name. Jones's other popular plays include *The Liberty Tree* (1832), *The Carpenter of Rouen* (1840), and *Paul Revere and the Sons of Liberty* (1875).

JONES, LEROI (1934–), New Jersey-born militant black author, reared in a middle-class environment, attended Rutgers and Howard University (B.A., 1954), served in the Strategic Air Command (1954–57), and studied philosophy and German literature respectively at Columbia and The New School for Social Research before becoming a revolutionary spokesman for his people. He turned his back on Greenwich Village, on the personal and romantic expression that marked his first poetry, *Preface to a Twenty Volume Suicide Note* (1961), divorced his white wife, took the name Imamu Amiri Baraka (1965) as part of his commitment to Afro-Americanism, and founded a black community center, Spirit House, in Newark. An intense black nationalist, he lashes out at whites in his violent one-act plays, *Dutchman, The Slave,* and *The Toilet* (1964). His bitterness and frustration are also evident in his episodic novel *The System of Dante's Hell* (1965), equating Newark slums and the Inferno. Anguish, violent response, and lyrical appreciation of the black spirit mark succeeding volumes of poetry: *The Dead Lecturer* (1964), *Black Magic . . .* (1969), *In Our Terribleness* (1971), *AM/TRAK* (1979), *Spring Song* (1979), *Reggae or Not* (1981), and *Thoughts for You* (1984). Further plays include *A Recent Killing* (1964), about an aviator intent upon becoming a poet, and the one-act *Four Black Revolutionary Plays* (1969). His stories, some of them clearly autobiographical, are collected in *Tales* (1967). His nonfiction includes *Blues People* (1963), on jazz as an expression of the black people in white America; *Black Music* (1967); *Black Art* (1967); and *Black Magic* (1969). Essays are collected in *Home* (1966), powerful social statements for a black nation; *Raise Race Rays Raze* (1971), written in black idiom; and *Daggers and Javelins* (1971). He has also published *A Black Value System* (1969); *Spirit Reach* (1972); *African Revolution* (1973); and, with his wife Amina Baraka, *The Music* (1987), related to his earlier *Blues People* and *Black Music. The Autobiography of LeRoi Jones* appeared in 1984. Since 1983 he has been on the African-American Studies faculty of SUNY at Stony Brook.

JONG, ERICA [MANN] (1942–), born in New York City, graduated from Barnard College (1963). Her books include *Fear of Flying* (1973), about an intense, neurotic New York woman in her thirties enjoying a lively sexual experience for two weeks with an existentialist Englishman; *How To Save Your Own Life* (1977), a sequel in which the woman's first novel becomes a best seller and she prepares to write another while enjoying sexual encounters with a man and a woman; *Fanny* (1980), a picaresque novel in a pseudo-18th-century style, written from the point of view of a woman; *Parachutes and Kisses* (1984), about later experiences of the heroine of *Fear of Flying; Serenissima* (1987), concerning an American movie actress in Venice who is mesmerized as the daughter of Shylock and the friend of Shakespeare; *Any Woman's Blues,* about a woman addicted to sex; and *Fear of Fifty* (1994), which details the sexual and other adventures of a woman in her fifties. *Witches* (1981) investigates the whole concept of the witch. Her poems appear in *Fruits and Vegetables* (1971), *Half-Lives* (1973), *Loveroot* (1975), *At the Edge of the Body* (1979), and *Ordinary Miracles* (1983).

JONSON, ROBERT (*fl.* 1609–12), author of *Nova Britannia: offeringe most excellent Fruites by Planting in Virginia* (London, 1609), a tract intended to promote colonization and investment in the Virginia colony. A second part, *The New Life of Virginia* (1612), is attributed to him.

JORDAN, DAVID STARR (1851–1931), first president and chancellor of Stanford University (1891–1916), which he helped make into a major American university. Besides his scientific works on fishes, he was the author of *The Human Harvest* (1907), *War's Aftermath* (1914), and other pacifist works, as well as an autobiography, *The Days of a Man* (2 vols., 1922).

JORDAN, JUNE (1936–   ), born in Harlem, is a poet, novelist, essayist, and writer of children's books. Best known as a poet, she expresses black consciousness and the effects of everyday racism, but withal in faith and ultimate optimism. Her poems are *Some Changes* (1971), *New Days: Poems of Exile and Return* (1973), *Things That I Do in the Dark: Selected Poetry* (1977), *Passion: New Poems 1977–1980* (1980), and *Living Room: New Poems 1980–1984* (1985). Essays, articles, and lectures are printed in *Civil Wars* (1981) and *On Call: New Political Essays 1981–1985* (1985).

JOSEPHSON, MATTHEW (1899–1978), New York author, known for a time as a member of the postwar expatriate group and an editor of *Secession* (1922–24), achieved prominence upon publishing the study *Zola and His Time* (1928). His *Portrait of the Artist as American* (1930) presents such Americans as Henry James, Whistler, and Bierce to support the thesis of Van Wyck Brooks that industrial America frustrates artistic creation. Later works include *Rousseau* (1931); *The Robber Barons* (1934), a study of the rise to power of 19th-century American industrialists; *The Politicos* (1938), a companion volume dealing with the political background of this era; *The President Makers* (1940), concerned with political maneuvers from the time of McKinley to that of Wilson; *Empire of the Air* (1944), an account of the growth of an airline; *Stendhal* (1946), *Sidney Hillman* (1952), and *Edison* (1959), biographies; *Union House, Union Bar* (1957), a history of the hotel,

restaurant, and bartenders' union; and *Among the Surrealists* (1962) and *Infidel in the Temple* (1967), memoirs. With his wife he wrote a life of Al Smith (1969).

Josiah Allen's Wife, pseudonym of Marietta Holley. ◆

JOSSELYN, JOHN (*fl.* 1638–75), English scientific writer, visited Boston and Maine (1638–39), where his brother was the representative of Gorges. His second visit (1663–71) was occupied by scientific observation and resulted in *New-England's Rarities Discovered* (1672) and *An Account of Two Voyages to New-England* (1674). Although there is some scientific value in his botanical observations, he makes many credulous statements concerning mermen, and Indians who talk "in perfect hexameter verse." With this lore he combines information for colonists, local history, and animadversions on the Puritans, whom he disliked, possibly because the Bay Colony's expansion threatened his brother's affairs.

Journal of Julius Rodman, The, fictional travel narrative by Poe, ◆ published anonymously in *Burton's Gentleman's Magazine* (1840). It purports to be an account of "the first passage across the Rocky Mountains of North America ever achieved by civilized man," as accomplished in 1792 by an English emigrant, Julius Rodman, with several companions, and described in a diary discovered by his heirs. The character of Rodman and the dates are fictitious, but the adventures and descriptions are based on fact, being largely paraphrased from Irving's *Astoria* and the accounts of Lewis and Clark and Sir Alexander Mackenzie.

Journey to the Land of Eden, A, journal written by William Byrd◆ during 1733, was found among his Westover Manuscripts, from which it was published in 1841. An account of his trip "to the land of Eden," his tract of land near the River Dan in North Carolina, the journal contains urbane and witty observations by a patrician Virginian concerning the boorish backcountry people and the Indians.

JUDAH, SAMUEL B[ENJAMIN] H[ELBERT] (1804–76), youthful author of *The Mountain Torrent* (1820) and *The Rose of Arragon* (1823), melodramas produced in his native New York; *Odofriede* (1822), a dramatic poem; *A Tale of Lexington* (1823), a three-act comedy; *Gotham and the Gothamites* (1823), a verse satire attacking identifiable contemporaries; and *The Buccaneers* (1827), a romance issued under the pseudonym Terentius Phlogobombos. The rest of his long life was devoted to the law.

JUDD, SYLVESTER (1813–53), Unitarian minister, graduate of Yale (1836) and Harvard Divinity

School (1840), during his second year at the graduate school published *A Young Man's Account of His Conversion from Calvinism.* As a pastor at Augusta, Me. (1840–53), he advocated several idealistic reforms, including a "birthright church" in which all individuals would by birth automatically become members. He was a pacifist, opposed capital punishment, and believed in temperance and antislavery. His religious and social ideas are exhibited in his two novels, *Margaret*♦ (1845) and *Richard Edney and the Governor's Family* (1850), and in his didactic metaphysical epic *Philo, an Evangeliad* (1850). His novels are distinguished both for their realistic depiction of the Down East region and for their idealistic quality, reminiscent of Hawthorne and Melville.

Judge (1881–1939), comic weekly founded by a group of authors and artists who seceded from *Puck.* The new magazine imitated its prototype closely, but failed of success until 1884, when a group of Republicans, recognizing the power wielded by the Democratic *Puck,* turned *Judge* into a satirical organ for political purposes. The Republican connection was dissolved in 1910, but the circulation was then so large that the magazine survived on its own power as a comic weekly. It was particularly successful during this and the next decade, but during the Depression of the '30s was forced to become a monthly (1932), losing its leadership in its field to *The New Yorker.* In 1936 it purchased "the humorous tradition and features of *Life.*"

Judgment Day, novel by James T. Farrell,♦ published in 1935 as the concluding part of his naturalistic trilogy concerned with the Chicago youth Studs Lonigan.♦

At 27, Studs contemplates the failure and unhappiness of his family and friends. Worried and suffering because of his weak heart, he fears loneliness, yet almost against his will is involved in an affair with Catherine Banahan, whom he asks to marry him. Events rapidly conspire to defeat him: he loses his savings on an unwise investment in stocks; is unable to buy insurance because of his heart ailment, which has been aggravated by unwholesome living; cannot persuade Catherine to have an abortion when she becomes pregnant; is unemployed during the business depression; and dies, after a brief illness, at the age of 29.

Judgment Day, play by Elmer Rice.♦

JUDSON, ADONIRAM (1788–1850), Massachusetts-born Baptist missionary in Burma, endured extreme hardships in founding his mission, including 17 months' imprisonment during the war with the British. He translated the Bible into Burmese and was the author of an English-Burmese dictionary. He is the subject of several romantic biographies, and of Honoré Morrow's novel *The Splendor of God* (1929).

EMILY [CHUBBUCK] JUDSON (1817–54), his third wife, returned from Burma to New York, where she wrote several popular moralistic works, including *Alderbrook* (1847), rural sketches and poems, and *Allen Lucas, the Self-Made Man* (1847), a novel. She used the pseudonym Fanny Forester.

JUDSON, EDWARD ZANE CARROLL (1823–86), known by his pseudonym Ned Buntline, was an adventurer, trapper, and soldier in the Far West, a founder of the Know-Nothing party,♦ leader of the Astor Place riot,♦ accused murderer, editor, and author, whose boisterous life reads like one of his own dime novels. In 1869 he met W.F. Cody, and, endowing him with the name Buffalo Bill, made him the hero of a series of dime novels, as well as the leading figure in his play *The Scouts of the Plains* (1873), in which Cody himself took the leading part. Judson was the author of more than 400 dime novels, a genre of which he was a creator.

Julia France and Her Times, novel by Gertrude Atherton,♦ published in 1912.

Julius Rodman, see *Journal of Julius Rodman.*

Jumping Frog, see *Celebrated Jumping Frog.*

June Moon, play by Ring Lardner♦ and George S. Kaufman.♦

Jungle, The, novel by Upton Sinclair,♦ published in 1906. This exposé of the Chicago meat-packing industry prompted the investigation by Roosevelt and the federal government that culminated in the pure-food legislation of 1906.

Jurgis Rudkus, a Slav immigrant, marries frail Ona Lukoszaite and seeks security and happiness as a workman in the Chicago stockyards. Foremen abuse him, real-estate sharks filch his meager savings, and at every turn he is beset by misfortunes arising from the poverty, brutality, and disease that are the conditions of his employment. At the birth of a second child, amid direst want, Ona dies. Jurgis's morale temporarily disintegrates and he becomes successively a tramp, common thief, highwayman, and pawn of a corrupt politician. Then, having thought his way through this morass of chicanery and brutality, and despairing of the individual's capacity to face modern society alone, he arrives at a belief in socialism.

Junto Club (THE JUNTO), social and debating society, founded by Franklin at Philadelphia (1727), with a membership restricted to 12 of his friends, all workingmen. The club was first known as the Leather Aprons and in plan of organization was similar to the neighborhood benefit societies founded at Boston by Cotton Mather, but the thought was directed along deistic and utilitarian lines. It existed approximately 40 years, during which time it was an important cultural influence, and affiliated clubs were organized. In 1731 it formed a subscription library, which was the first American public library. It was also the forerunner of the American Philosophical Society. ♦

Jurgen: A Comedy of Justice, romance by Cabell, ♦ published in 1919.

In mythical, medieval Poictesme, Jurgen is a middle-aged poetical pawnbroker, married to Dame Lisa, "a high-spirited woman, with no especial gift for silence." By special dispensation of the Devil, Lisa vanishes, and Jurgen unwillingly seeks her, forced by conscience and local gossip. By the Centaur Nessus, whose magic shirt he is given to wear, he is carried to "the garden between dawn and sunrise," and here encounters Dorothy la Désirée, the sweetheart of his youth, who does not recognize him. Continuing his search, he meets the earth goddess, Mother Sereda, and, when she promises him any gift in her power, he chooses a Wednesday of his youth to live over again. In this state, Dorothy loves him, but he discovers that his desire is a lost illusion. In various disguises, followed by his note-taking shadow, he pursues his skeptical pilgrimage among mythical and fictional figures, and has erotic adventures with Guenevere, Dame Anaïtis (The Lady of the Lake), Merlin, Queen Helen, a hamadryad, and others, visiting the legendary lands of Cocaigne, Pseudopolis, and Leukê. He lives in Hell, where he marries a vampire, and then, as Pope John XX, visits the Heaven of his grandmother, where he ascends the throne of God. At last he finds Koshchei, "who made things as they are." Offered various great beauties, Jurgen declines each of them and, after Koshchei dubiously returns Lisa to him, husband and wife take up again their prosaic but comfortable life.

JUSSERAND, JEAN JULES (1855–1932), French ambassador to the U.S. (1902–15), who in addition to being known as a diplomat was recognized as an author and scholar. His works include *English Wayfaring Life in the Middle Ages* (1889); and *With Americans of Past and Present Days,* awarded the first Pulitzer Prize in the area of history (1917).

"Just Before the Battle, Mother," song by G.F. Root. ♦

JUSTICE, DONALD [RODNEY] (1925–), Florida-born poet, professor at various institutions, including University of Florida beginning in 1982, has published gentle, well-controlled poems in *The Summer Anniversaries* (1960), *Night Light* (1967), *Departures* (1973), *Selected Poems* (1979, Pulitzer Prize), *Tremayne* (1984), and *The Sunset Maker* (1987), which combines poems, two stories, and a memoir of youth. He also edited the poems of Weldon Kees (1960) and wrote the libretto for an opera, *The Death of Lincoln* (1988). *Platonic Scripts* (1984) contains essays.

Juvenile literature, see *Children's literature.*

K

KAEL, PAULINE (1919–   ), California-born film critic for *The New Yorker* who retired in 1991. Her reviews are collected in *I Lost It at the Movies* (1965), *Kiss Kiss Bang Bang* (1968), *Going Steady* (1970), *Deeper into Movies* (1973; National Book Award, 1974), *Reeling* (1976), *When the Lights Go Down* (1980), *5001 Nights at the Movies* (1982), *Taking It All In* (1984), *State of the Art* (1985), *Hooked* (1989), *Movie Love, Complete Reviews 1988–1991* (1992); and *For Keeps,* a vast selection of movie reviews from 1961–91 (1994).

KAH-GE-GA-GAH-BOWH, CHIEF [GEORGE COPWAY] (1818–63), writer. An Ojibway chief born in Canada and educated in Illinois, Copway became a highly respected writer and a friend of Longfellow's. His works include *The Life, Letters, and Speeches of Chief Kah-ge-ga-gah-bowh* (1850); *The Ojibway Conquest, a Tale of the Northwest* (1850), an epic-length poem; and *Running Sketches of Men and Places in Europe* (1851).

KALER, JAMES OTIS (1848–1912), Maine author of stories for boys, of which the best known was *Toby Tyler; or, Ten Weeks with a Circus* (1881). He wrote under the pseudonym James Otis. His other tales include *At the Siege of Quebec* (1897), *With Perry on Lake Erie* (1899), and *The Minute Boys of the Wyoming Valley* (1900).

KALLEN, H[ORACE] M[EYER] (1882–1974), German-born professor at The New School for Social Research, translated and edited the works of philosophers, including William James and Benjamin Paul Blood, and wrote many books exhibiting liberal and idealistic social interests. These include *Creative Intelligence* (1917), written with John Dewey and others; *The Structure of Lasting Peace* (1918); *Zionism and World Politics* (1921); *Culture and Democracy in the United States* (1924); *Frontiers of Hope* (1929); *Individualism: An American Way of Life* (1933); *A Free Society* (1934); *The Decline and Rise of the Consumer: A Philosophy of Consumer Cooperation* (1936); *Art and Freedom* (2 vols., 1943), on the interrelation of philosophy, psychology, history, and the arts; *The Liberal Spirit* (1948); *Democracy's True Religion* (1951); *Cultural Pluralism and the American Idea* (1956); and *The Book of Job as a Greek Tragedy* (1959).

KALM, PETER (1716–79), Swedish scientist and traveler, a pupil of Linnaeus, was sent to America (1748–51) by the Swedish Academy of Sciences. He visited Pennsylvania, New York, New Jersey, and southern Canada, was the guest of such prominent men as Franklin, and, although chiefly concerned with botanical studies, was a shrewd observer of people and institutions. He wrote an account of his journey, published in Sweden (3 vols., 1753–61) and translated as *Travels into North America . . .* (1770–71). The manuscript of his fourth volume was destroyed by fire, but notes for it were discovered and published in 1929. A complete American edition was edited by Adolph B. Benson as *The America of 1750: Peter Kalm's Travels in North America* (2 vols., 1937).

KANE, ELISHA KENT (1820–57), naval surgeon and Arctic explorer, wrote of his first voyage to the Arctic in the popular narrative *The U.S. Grinnell Expedition in Search of Sir John Franklin* (1853), abridged and reprinted as *Adrift in the Arctic Ice Pack* (1915). Kane made a second expedition with the *Grinnell,* reaching 80° 10′ N., a "farthest North" record. The rigor of this journey caused his death after the publication of *Arctic Explorations* (2 vols., 1856). A scurrilous anonymous publication, *The Love-Life of Doctor Kane* (1866), tells of his romance with the spiritualist Margaret Fox.

KANIN, GARSON (1912–   ), New York-born actor, producer, director of plays and motion pictures, whose own stage plays include *Born Yesterday* (1946), a farce about wartime Washington; and *Smile of the World* (1949), about a brilliant young lawyer who becomes a pompous, reactionary Supreme Court justice. He has also written novels: *Do Re Mi* (1955), *Blow Up a Storm* (1959), *A Thousand Summers* (1973), *A Hell of an Actor* (1977), *Moviola* (1979), *Smash* (1980), and *Cordelia?* (1982), all in some ways bearing on the theater world; *Hollywood* (1974); memoirs of people he has known, such as *Together Again* (1978); and his own brief and grudging memoir, *It Takes a Long Time To Become Young* (1978).

KANTOR, MACKINLAY (1904–77), Iowa-born author, best known for his novels, which include *Long Remember* (1934), about the Battle of Gettysburg; *The Voice of Bugle Ann* (1935), about a foxhound whose master shoots the man suspected of killing her; *Arouse and Beware* (1936), about Yankees escaping from a Confederate prison; *The Romance of Rosy Ridge* (1937), a love story of post–Civil War Missouri; *The Noise of Their Wings* (1938), about plans to reintroduce passenger pigeons to the U.S.; *Cuba Libre* (1940), about an idealistic Cuban revolutionist; *Gentle Annie* (1942), set in early 20th-century Oklahoma; *Happy Land* (1942), the life of a boy killed in World War II; *Wicked Water* (1949), about early cattle wars; *Signal Thirty-Two* (1950), about a New York City policeman; *Andersonville*♦ (1955), dealing with the horrid life in a Confederate prison during the Civil War; *Spirit Lake* (1961), about an Indian massacre of white settlers in 19th-century Iowa; *Beauty Beast* (1968), about a Gulf Coast widow's involvement with one of her slaves; and *Valley Forge* (1975), a historical novel. *Turkey in the Straw* (1935) is a book of "American ballads and primitive verse"; stories are collected in *Author's Choice* (1944) and *Storyteller* (1967). *Missouri Bittersweet* (1969) treats the state, and *Hamilton County* (1970) deals with the ten U.S. counties of that name. *But Look, the Morn* (1947) is a memoir of Kantor's youth, and *The Day I Met a Lion* (1968) collects reminiscent pieces.

KAPLAN, JUSTIN (1925–), literary historian, born in New York City, graduated from Harvard at 19, long resident in Cambridge, Mass., is the author of *Mr. Clemens and Mark Twain* (1966, Pulitzer Prize, National Book Award), *Lincoln Steffens, A Biography* (1974), and *Walt Whitman* (1980).

KARNOW, STANLEY (1925–), after graduation from Harvard became a journalist-foreign correspondent and the author of several books in that vein. His *In Our Image: America's Empire in the Philippines* (1989) was awarded a Pulitzer Prize for History.

Katharine Walton, a Revolutionary Romance by Simms,♦ published in 1851, is a sequel to *The Partisan.*♦

Shortly after the Battle of Camden (1780), Katharine's father, Colonel Walton, is rescued from his captivity in the British garrison at Dorchester by her fiancé, Robert Singleton. Colonel Balfour, commandant at Charleston, to avoid responsibility for the loss of a prisoner, accuses Major Proctor, guard of the garrison, of treason. Walton's estates are confiscated and at Balfour's order Katharine is taken to Charleston. Singleton, disguising himself as Captain Furness, a Loyalist, becomes a friend of Proctor, revealing Balfour's treachery to him. Meanwhile Walton is again captured, and Balfour tells Katharine that if she does not marry him her father will be hanged. Proctor, having killed Balfour's henchman Vaughan, joins Singleton's rebels, among whom is the comic Captain Porgy. Before they can rescue the Waltons, Katharine agrees to marry Balfour, whose order to reprieve her father is intercepted by Balfour's former sweetheart. Since Walton is hanged, Katharine is freed from her promise to wed Balfour.

KAUFMAN, GEORGE S[IMON] (1889–1961), New York journalist, playwright, and director,

wrote popular plays and musical comedies in collaboration with many authors. Among these were Marc Connelly,♦ with whom he wrote such plays as *Dulcy* (1921), *To the Ladies* (1922), *Merton of the Movies* (1922), and *Beggar on Horseback*♦ (1924); Ring Lardner,♦ with whom he wrote *June Moon* (1929); Edna Ferber,♦ with whom he wrote *Minick* (1924), *The Royal Family* (1927), *Dinner at Eight* (1932), *Stage Door* (1936), and *The Land Is Bright* (1941); Morrie Ryskind and George Gershwin, with whom he wrote such musical comedies as *Of Thee I Sing*♦ (1931, Pulitzer Prize) and *Let 'Em Eat Cake* (1933), satirizing revolutionaries; Katherine Dayton, with whom he wrote *First Lady* (1935), a comedy of Washington political and social life; and Moss Hart,♦ with whom he wrote *Once in a Lifetime* (1930), a satire of Hollywood; *Merrily We Roll Along* (1934), a play in reverse chronology, tracing the hero from his failure in middle age back to his youthful promise; *I'd Rather Be Right* (1937), a travesty of the F.D. Roosevelt administration; *You Can't Take It with You*♦ (1936, Pulitzer Prize); *The American Way* (1939), a patriotic panorama of recent history; *The Man Who Came to Dinner* (1939), a farce about an author like Alexander Woollcott; and *George Washington Slept Here* (1940). With J.P. Marquand he wrote an adaptation of *The Late George Apley* (1944); and with Howard Teichmann, *The Solid Gold Cadillac* (1953).

Kavanagh, novel by Longfellow,♦ published in 1849.

A young Roman Catholic, Kavanagh, is converted to Protestantism and becomes the popular pastor of a New England village church. Alice Archer is enamored of his brilliance, but he marries her less timid friend Cecilia Vaughan, and after they leave for Italy, Alice languishes and dies. Meanwhile, the young schoolmaster Churchill, seemingly adjusted to the humdrum village life, broods in his search for the sublime subject suited to a romance he longs to write.

KAZAN, ELIA (1909–), Turkish-born theatrical and motion-picture director, graduated from Williams College (1930), and after study at Yale became an actor with the Group Theatre.♦ Plays he has directed include *The Skin of Our Teeth, A Streetcar Named Desire, Death of a Salesman, Cat on a Hot Tin Roof,* and *J.B.;* motion pictures he directed include *On the Waterfront* and *East of Eden.* He has written novels: *America, America* (1962), somewhat in the form of a screenplay (and made into a film, which he directed, 1963), about a Greek youth escaping poverty and persecution in Turkey by coming to the U.S. at the opening of the 20th century; *The Arrangement* (1967); *The Assassins* (1972); *The Understudy* (1974); and *Acts of Love* (1978); and his own first play, *The Chain* (1983), partly about the making of a classic drama. His autobiography, titled *Elia Kazan,* appeared in 1988.

KAZIN, ALFRED (1915–   ), literary critic, best known for his critical works, *On Native Grounds*♦ (1942), a study of American prose literature after Howells; *The Inmost Leaf* (1955), essays on European and American literature; *Contemporaries* (1962), essays on American authors, past and present; and *Bright Book of Life* (1973), treating American fiction from Hemingway to Mailer; and his moving autobiographical writings, *A Walker in the City* (1951), a lyrical treatment of his youth in Brownsville, then a Jewish immigrant section of Brooklyn; *Starting Out in the Thirties* (1965), reminiscences of his young manhood; and *New York Jew* (1978), considering his life into the 1970s. *An American Procession* (1984) is on U.S. authors from 1830 to 1930, and *A Writer's America* (1989) concerns landscape in literature. *Our New York* (1990), heavily illustrated, combines memoirs and social history.

KECKLEY, ELIZABETH (1827–1907), modiste and memoirist. After an early life as a slave, including bearing a child by her master, she earned her own and her son's emancipation in 1855 for $1200 by making dresses. In Washington she established herself as a custom dressmaker and had as clients Mrs. Jefferson Davis, Mrs. Stephen Douglas, and, for four years, Mary Todd Lincoln. From this experience she wrote a historically important memoir used by all Lincoln biographers: *Behind the Scenes; or Thirty Years a Slave and Four Years in the White House* (1868). Mary Todd Lincoln confided to Elizabeth Keckley her extravagances that must be kept from Mr. Lincoln, and many other family matters before and after Lincoln's death. Though her own son was killed in the war, Mrs. Keckley keeps herself in the background, and gives the foreground to the famous whom she knew. She wrote to Frederick Douglass and others asking support for a plan of lecture series that would raise money for Lincoln's impoverished widow. These did not come off, but Congress finally appropriated $22,000 for Mrs. Lincoln's relief. Intimate correspondence between the dressmaker and the President's widow continued for several years, and the letters are included in the memoir.

KEELER, RALPH OLMSTEAD (1840–73), Ohioborn journalist, whose *Vagabond Adventures* (1870) describes his life in a minstrel show, as a Heidelberg student, tramping through Europe, and as a San Francisco columnist. He also wrote feature articles for Eastern journals, became a proofreader on the *Atlantic* through Howells's aid, and wrote a novel set in California, *Gloverson and His Silent Partners* (1869).

KEENAN, HENRY FRANCIS (1850–1928), author of the anonymously published novel *The Money-Makers*♦ (1885), intended as a reply to Hay's *The Bread-Winners.* It shows the selfish, unprincipled actions of capitalists, which lead to the conditions attacked in Hay's anti-union novel.

KEES, WELDON (1914–55), poet. Born in Nebraska, Kees lived most of his brief life in New York City and in San Francisco. He worked for *Time* magazine and was a painter, jazz pianist, and composer. His early collections of poetry are *The Last Man* (1943), *The Fall of the Magicians* (1947), and *Poems 1947–1954,* all formalist in structure and tone. His reputation has grown steadily since the publication of *Collected Poems* (1960, revised 1975), edited by Donald Justice. A final posthumous work, *Fall Quarter* (1990), a satiric novel of academia, was edited by James Reidel Kees.

KEIMER, SAMUEL (1688–1739), English-born printer, author of *A Brand Pluck'd from the Burning* (1718) and *A Search after Religion* (1718), dealing with his connections with various religious sects. In 1722 he came to Philadelphia, where he later employed Franklin in his printshop. After the latter left him to start a newspaper, Keimer founded the weekly *Universal Instructor in All Arts and Sciences, and Pennsylvania Gazette* (Dec. 1728–Sept. 1729), but was overwhelmed by the competition of Franklin and Andrew Bradford. He sold the paper to Franklin, and after Franklin's day one of its later publishers founded *The Saturday Evening Post.* Reduced to bankruptcy, Keimer went to Barbados, where he founded the first newspaper in the Caribbean. He is remembered mainly because of the lively account of him in Franklin's autobiography. It also tells of Franklin's setting into type Keimer's *Elegy on the Much Lamented Death of . . . Aquila Rose* (1723).

KEITH, GEORGE (*c.*1638–1716), Scottish clergyman, came to America (1684) and became headmaster of the William Penn Charter School (1689). At first he agreed with the Quakers, but his differences with them on such points as the Inner Light, and his contentious manner, caused him to be denounced by Penn (1692). Keith returned the attack in *The Deism of William Penn and His Brethren* (1699), and formed a strong separatist party of Christian Quakers (Keithians). His *Exhortation and Caution to Friends* (1693) is said to be the first antislavery statement printed in the colonies. In 1700 he joined the Anglican Church, into which he took his followers, traveling widely throughout the colonies in 1702–4. Of this later period he left a record in *A Journal of Travels from New-Hampshire to Caratuck* (1706).

KELLAND, CLARENCE BUDINGTON (1881–1964), popular novelist whose works included *Mark Tidd* (1913), the first of a series of novels for boys, of the genre of *Tom Sawyer;* novels for adults, most of them dealing with current fads and manners, such as *Conflict* (1920), *Rhoda Fair*

(1925), *Hard Money* (1930), *The Great Crooner* (1933), *Arizona* (1939), and *Dangerous Angel* (1953); and detective fiction. His stories about a shrewd Yankee who pretends ingenuousness first appeared in *Scattergood Baines* (1921).

KELLER, HELEN [ADAMS] (1880–1968), author and lecturer, who, though blind and deaf from the age of two, graduated with honors from Radcliffe (1904) and became a prominent worker for social reforms. Her books include *The Story of My Life* (1902), *The World I Live In* (1908), *Out of the Dark* (1913), *My Religion* (1927), *Midstream: My Later Life* (1929), and *Let Us Have Faith* (1940). Van Wyck Brooks wrote *Helen Keller: Sketch for a Portrait* (1956).

KELLEY, EDITH SUMMERS (1884–1956), Canadian-born author, was secretary of Upton Sinclair at his Helicon Home Colony, ♦ later migrated to Kentucky, where she and her long-time friend, C. Frederick Kelley, were tenant farmers of tobacco, the subject of her novel *Weeds* (1923). Further wandering took them to San Diego, where she wrote her second sociological novel, *The Devil's Hand,* set in the Imperial Valley, and not published until 1974.

KELLEY, WILLIAM MELVIN (1937–), New York-born novelist, inspired to write by John Hawkes and Archibald MacLeish, his teachers at Harvard, has since become a leading African-American author. His first novel, *A Different Drummer* (1962), is a mythic tale of a black sharecropper who in destroying his farm and discarding his heritage inspires others to seek a better future. Later fiction includes *A Drop of Patience* (1965), about a blind black jazz musician who turns to his people's evangelical religion; *dem* (1967), a satirical and sometimes surrealistic story of a white Madison Avenue advertising executive as he searches for the father of the black baby to which his wife has given birth; and *Dunfords Travels Everywhere* (1970), contrasting a Harvard-educated black in France and a Harlem swindler. *Dancers on the Shore* (1964) collects stories.

KELLOGG, ELIJAH (1813–1901), Congregational clergyman of Maine, author of the famous declamatory piece, "Spartacus to the Gladiators," first published in the *School Reader* (1846) of Epes Sargent. His novel for children, *Good Old Times* (1867), a story of pioneer Maine, was followed by 28 other stories, mainly children's novels of Down East folk.

KELLY, GEORGE [EDWARD] (1887–1974), actor, director, and playwright. He wrote many one-act plays, and his longer works include *The Torch-Bearers* (1922, revised 1938), a satire on the little-theater movement; *The Show-Off* (1924), a comedy dealing with a successful braggart; *Craig's Wife♦* (1925, Pulitzer Prize), a character study of

a domineering woman who turns her family against her; and *Daisy Mayme* (1926). Later plays include *Behold the Bridegroom* (1927), *Maggie the Magnificent* (1929), *Philip Goes Forth* (1931), *Reflected Glory* (1936), and *The Fatal Weakness* (1946).

KELLY, JONATHAN FALCONBRIDGE (1817?–55), journalist and humorist, under the pseudonyms Falconbridge and Cerro Gordo, contributed to many periodicals. A collection of his work appeared as *The Humors of Falconbridge* (1856). He also wrote a biography of Dan Marble (1851).

KEMBLE, E[DWARD] W[INDSOR] (1861–1933), illustrator and cartoonist, best known for his light but sympathetic interpretations of blacks and mischievous boys, as in his drawings for the first edition of *Huckleberry Finn*.

KEMBLE, FRANCES ANNE (FANNY KEMBLE) (1809–95), member of a famous English stage family, had a successful career as an actress in London, and came to America (1832), acting for two years before retiring to marry Pierce Butler, owner of a Georgia plantation. Her *Journal of Frances Anne Butler* (2 vols., 1835) is a record of her theatrical tour, freely criticizing many American customs. Her *Journal of a Residence on a Georgian Plantation,* written during the winter of 1838–39, was not published until 1863, when it was meant to influence British opinion against the South, whose slavery she detested. In 1846 she left her husband, returned to the London stage, wrote *A Year of Consolation* (1847), and a year later became involved in a notorious divorce suit. Afterward, in the U.S., she gave public readings of Shakespeare and wrote plays, volumes of poetry, criticism, and autobiography, and *Far Away and Long Ago* (1889), a rambling novel of the Berkshires, where she made her home. Owen Wister was her grandson.

KEMP, HARRY (HIBBARD KEMP) (1883–1960), born in Ohio, has been called "the tramp poet" because of his vagabond career. His early poetry in *The Cry of Youth* (1914) and *The Passing God* (1919), quiet neoclassical verse, was completely out of keeping with his personality as revealed in *Chanteys and Ballads* (1920). *Tramping on Life* (1922) is a lusty autobiographical narrative, and *More Miles* (1926) is a novel based on his life. Besides volumes of translations and a later book of verse, *The Sea and the Dunes* (1926), Kemp published such varied volumes as *Boccaccio's Untold Tale and Other One-Act Plays* (1924); *The Bronze Treasury* (1927), "an Anthology of Eighty-one Obscure English Poets"; *Don Juan's Note-Book* (1929); and *Mabel Tarner, an American Primitive* (1936).

KENDALL, GEORGE WILKINS (1809–67), with Francis A. Lumsden, founded the *New Orleans Picayune*♦ (1837). After an adventurous expedition to Mexico (1841), he wrote the *Narrative of the Texan Sante Fe Expedition* (2 vols., 1844) and served in the Mexican War. He and his partner became, through the *Picayune,* the originators of the art of war correspondence, and he graphically described the conflict in *The War Between the United States and Mexico* (1851).

KENNAN, GEORGE (1845–1924), wrote of his experiences as a young man surveying a route to extend the Western Union telegraph system in his *Tent Life in Siberia* (1870), and thus became known as a writer and traveler, leading to his being sent to investigate Russian prisons, of which he wrote in *Siberia and the Exile System* (2 vols., 1891). Later works include *Campaigning in Cuba* (1899), *Folk-Tales of Napoleon* (1902), *The Tragedy of Pelée* (1902), about the Martinique volcanic eruption, and *E.H. Harriman: A Biography* (2 vols., 1922).

KENNAN, GEORGE F[ROST] (1904–   ), nephew of George Kennan, after graduation from Princeton (1925) began a diplomatic career which later included ambassadorships to the Soviet Union and to Yugoslavia. His books include *American Diplomacy 1900–1950* (1951); *Realities of American Foreign Policy* (1954); *Russia Leaves the War* (1956, Pulitzer Prize) and *Decision to Intervene* (1958), both comprising *Soviet-American Relations 1917–1920;* and *Russia and the West Under Lenin and Stalin* (1961). His *Memoirs* (1967) won him another Pulitzer Prize and a National Book Award. Its sense of significant detail and of controlled emotion along with sharp insight is later found in *Sketches from a Life* (1989). Other significant books include *The Cloud of Danger: Current Realities of American Foreign Policy* (1977), *The Decline of Bismarck's European Order* (1979), and *The Nuclear Delusion: Soviet-American Relations . . .* (1982).

KENNEDY, ADRIENNE (1931–   ), playwright of African-American heritage whose works exhibit the conflict between her inheritances— black father, light mother—especially in *Funnyhouse of a Negro* (1962), in which the main character, Sarah, discovers strands of herself in Queen Victoria and in a colored Jesus, but the play ends with Sarah hanging herself. She wrote expressionistic and surreal plays in the 1960s, more realistic ones in the 1970s, but came back to her earlier mode in 1976 with *A Movie Star Has To Star in Black and White.*

KENNEDY, CHARLES RANN (1871–1950), English dramatist, long resident in the U.S., whose plays, all concerned with ethical problems, include *The Servant in the House* (1908), a study of human relationships, applying the teachings of

Jesus to modern life; *The Winterfeast* (1908), set in 11th-century Iceland, dealing with the effects of love and friendship turned to hate; *The Terrible Meek* (1912), a plea for pacifism; *The Necessary Evil* (1913); *The Idol-Breaker* (1914); and *The Salutation* (1925).

KENNEDY, JOHN PENDLETON (1795–1870), born in Baltimore, graduated from Baltimore College (1812) and began to practice law. Disliking this profession, he soon entered politics, educational affairs, and literature. *The Red Book* (1818–19) was a publication in the manner of Irving's *Salmagundi*. *Swallow Barn*♦ (1832), a series of Virginia sketches, appeared under the pseudonym Mark Littleton, and in 1835 he issued a novel, *Horse-Shoe Robinson.*♦ A second novel, *Rob of the Bowl*♦ (1838), was less successful. His literary associations at this time included contacts with most of the leading U.S. authors, and he was a patron of Poe, awarding first prize in a short story contest to "MS. Found in a Bottle." In 1838 Kennedy's political career began with his election to Congress as a Whig. He was reelected (1840, 1842), and wrote a satire of Jacksonian democracy, *Quodlibet: Containing Some Annals Thereof . . . by Solomon Second-Thoughts, Schoolmaster* (1840). After the death of President Harrison, Kennedy wrote *A Defense of the Whigs* (1843), attacking Tyler's political defection. His last important literary work was a two-volume biography of William Wirt (1849). In 1852 he became Fillmore's secretary of the navy and urged the expedition to Japan under Commodore Perry, as well as the second Arctic voyage of Kane. Kennedy met Thackeray during the English author's visit to the U.S. (1855–56) and furnished him information later used in *The Virginians*. He supported the Union cause during the Civil War, about which he wrote *Mr. Ambrose's Letters on the Rebellion* (1865). Posthumous publications include *Political and Official Papers* (1872), *Occasional Addresses* (1872), and *At Home and Abroad* (1872).

KENNEDY, WILLIAM (1928–   ), a native of Albany, New York, Kennedy has stayed home for all his material. Albany is the setting for all his books, the most celebrated being *Ironweed*♦ (1983, National Book Award and Pulitzer Prize). In sharply evocative realistic prose it tells of the return to Albany in the 1930s of a onetime major league pitcher, Francis Phelan, now an alcoholic bum, and his episodes in and out of reality. *Legs* (1975) is a novelistic treatment of the gangster Jack "Legs" Diamond. *Billy Phelan's Greatest Game* (1978) is again about familiar characters in Depression Albany. *Quinn's Book* (1988) is an Albany novel set in the Civil War period. Another novel, *Very Old Bones* (1992), digs into the author's own past and family history. Three essay and journalism collections are *The Ink Truck* (1969), *O Albany!* (1983), and *Riding the Yellow Trolley Car: Selected Nonfiction* (1993).

KENT, JAMES (1763–1847), known as "the American Blackstone," was a New York jurist, legal commentator, and professor of law at Columbia (1794–97, 1824–26). As chief justice of the state supreme court (1804–14) and chancellor of the New York Court of Chancery (1814–23), he began the practice of delivering his opinions in writing, and some of them have been widely influential in later cases. He modified English chancery practice to conform to American constitutions, and became the virtual creator of equity jurisdiction in the U.S. His reputation depends both upon his judicial decisions and upon his *Commentaries on American Law* (4 vols., 1826–30), whose six parts deal respectively with (1) international law, (2) the Constitution and government of the U.S. from a Federalist point of view, (3) state laws, (4) rights of persons, (5) personal property, and (6) real property.

KENT, ROCKWELL (1882–1971), New York author and artist, whose books, illustrated by himself, are accounts of sea voyages and residences in the Arctic and South America. They include *Wilderness* (1920), concerning his experiences in Alaska; *Voyaging Southward from the Strait of Magellan* (1924), about his journey to Tierra del Fuego; *N by E* (1930) and *Salamina* (1935), dealing with his life in Greenland; and *This Is My Own* (1940) and *It's Me, O Lord* (1955), autobiography. In addition to illustrations for many books, he is known for his work as a painter, primarily of landscapes distinguished for a use of simple masses of color, and as a pen-and-ink artist and lithographer who uses a striking, stark line in a highly stylized manner.

KENTON, SIMON (1755–1836), Kentucky and Ohio frontiersman, Indian fighter, and scout under Boone, served in Clark's expedition to Kaskaskia and Vincennes. Although captured at Detroit by the British, he escaped (1779), served in attacks on the Indians in Kentucky, was a major under Wayne (1793–94), and finally served with the Kentucky volunteers in the War of 1812. He was famous in frontier legends, and figures in Thompson's *Alice of Old Vincennes* and Churchill's *The Crossing.*

Kentucky Cardinal, *A,* novelette by J.L. Allen,♦ published in 1894. *Aftermath* (1896) is a sequel.

Kentucky Tragedy, celebrated crime known also as the Beauchamp case. Ann Cook, after having been seduced by Colonel Solomon P. Sharp, solicitor-general of Kentucky, married an attorney, Jeroboam O. Beauchamp (1824), making him swear to kill Sharp. Several times challenged, Sharp refused to fight, and Beauchamp's murder plans were equally unsuccessful. Finally Beauchamp, in disguise, stabbed Sharp to death (Nov. 5, 1825). He pleaded not guilty after his arrest, but was convicted after a long trial marked by corruption on both sides. Beauchamp was refused a pardon by the governor, and the night before the execution, Ann joined him in his cell, where both took laudanum. When this did not kill them, they stabbed themselves. Ann died, but Beauchamp was hanged. The affair has been written about in Beauchamp's *Confession* (1826), containing poems by Ann, in plays by Chivers♦ and Charlotte Barnes,♦ R.P. Warren's *World Enough and Time,* and Poe's *Politian,♦* Hoffman's *Greyslaer,♦* and Simms's *Beauchampe.♦*

Kenyon Review (1939–70, 1979–), quarterly journal edited to 1959 by J.C. Ransom from Kenyon College, Ohio. It included many former contributors to *The Southern Review,♦* carrying on its program of close textual scrutiny of modern poetry, and the printing of essays on aesthetics along with important new fiction and poetry. Robie Macauley was editor (1959–67), shifting emphasis to essays on contemporary culture. In 1970 the journal ceased publication, but it was revived in 1979, again addressing itself to literature but not of any one school. Ransom and Macauley edited anthologies of its publications, respectively of criticism (1951) and fiction (1966).

KEROUAC, JACK (1922–69), Massachusetts-born writer who attended Columbia University (1940–42) and roamed about and took odd jobs before he became associated with the Beat movement.♦ His fiction, very loose in style and structure, includes *The Town and the City* (1950), tracing the Martin family from 1910 in Lowell, Mass., through the war years and the dispersal of the eight children; *On the Road♦* (1957), a quasi-autobiographical tale of Beat people ranging around America seeking experience and fulfillment; *The Dharma Bums* (1958), a similar novel but with more emphasis on the discovery of truth or "dharma" through Zen Buddhism; *The Subterraneans* (1958), about a love affair between a Beat writer and a black girl; *Doctor Sax* (1959), an early novel fictively re-creating the author's youth; *Maggie Cassidy* (1959), about the adolescent Jack Duluoz searching for love and identity; *Tristessa* (1960), portraying the morphine addiction of a Mexico City prostitute; *Big Sur* (1962), a sequel to *On the Road,* about the crack-up and withdrawal to the Carmel area of a leader of the Beat movement; *Visions of Gerard* (1963), about the great grief of a French-Canadian family of Lowell, Mass., when its religious young son dies; *Desolation Angels* (1965), treating the Beat generation just prior to the time of *On the Road;* and *Vanity of Duluoz* (1968), again drawing on his youth in a tale of "moral death and resurrection." *Pic* (1971), a posthumously published novel, tells of a black jazz musician making his way from the South to Harlem. *Mexico City Blues* (1959) collects poems, *Lonesome Traveler* (1960) gathers travel sketches, *Book of Dreams* (1960) recounts his dreams in stream-of-consciousness style, *Satori in Paris*

(1966) describes his French travels in quest of his ancestry and of illumination, or satori, and *Visions of Cody* (1960, in part; 1970, in full) gathers recollections, some about Neal Cassady, his traveling companion.

KERR, ORPHEUS C., see *Newell, R.H.*

KERR, WALTER [FRANCIS] (1913–), drama critic for the *New York Herald Tribune* (1951–66) and *The New York Times* (1966–83), won a Pulitzer Prize (1978) for his drama criticism. His own writing of plays includes *Murder in Reverse* (1935), adaptations of *Rip Van Winkle* (1937), *The Vicar of Wakefield* (1938), Molière's *The Miser* (1942), and *Sing Out, Sweet Land* (1944), an opera libretto that is a musical biography of America. His books include *How Not To Write a Play* (1955), *Criticism and Censorship* (1957), *Pieces of Eight* (1957), *The Theatre in Spite of Itself* (1963), *Tragedy and Comedy* (1967), *Thirty Plays Hath November* (1969), *God on the Gymnasium Floor* (1971), *The Silent Clowns* (1975), and *Journey to the Center of the Theater* (1979).
  JEAN [COLLINS] KERR (1923–), his wife, collaborated with him in adapting Werfel's *The Song of Bernadette* (1946) and on the musical comedy *Goldilocks* (1948). Her own humorous plays include *Mary, Mary* (1961), *Poor Richard* (1964), *Finishing Touches* (1973), and *Lunch Hour* (1980). *Please Don't Eat the Daisies* (1957), *The Snake Has All the Lines* (1960), and *How I Got To Be Perfect* (1978) are humorous autobiographies.

KESEY, KEN (1935–), born in Colorado, graduated from the University of Oregon, later studied at Stanford, and once worked as a ward attendant in a mental hospital which provided background for his comic macabre novel *One Flew Over the Cuckoo's Nest*♦ (1962), whose tone also animates his second novel, *Sometimes a Great Notion* (1964), about a feud between two brothers in an Oregon lumber town. *Kesey's Garage Sale* (1973) collects diverse writings, mainly autobiographical, while *Demon Box* (1986) collects essays, poems, and stories. His loose life-style during the '60s, touring around in a bus with his so-called Merry Pranksters, was the subject of an essay by Tom Wolfe♦ in his *Electric Kool-Aid Acid Test. The Further Inquiry* (1990) is Kesey's own account of the Merry Pranksters period.

KETTELL, SAMUEL (1800–1855), Massachusetts hack writer employed by S.G. Goodrich, edited *Specimens of American Poetry* (3 vols., 1829), an ardently patriotic collection of 189 writers, from Cotton Mather to Whittier, conceived as an answer to Sydney Smith's query, "Who reads an American book?"

KEY, FRANCIS SCOTT (1779–1843), author of "The Star-Spangled Banner"♦ (1814), was known in his own time as a Maryland lawyer, tempo-

rarily associated in practice with his brother-in-law, R.B. Taney, and for his other songs and devotional pieces, posthumously published in *Poems* (1857). He also wrote *The Power of Literature and Its Connection with Religion* (1834).

Key into the Language of America, A, by Roger Williams,♦ published at London (1643), is an early attempt to record the language of the Indians near Massachusetts and to describe the habits and customs of the Narragansett Indians.

KEYES, FRANCES PARKINSON (1885–1970), Virginia-born and -associated writer known for 50 conventional romantic historical novels, including *Dinner at Antoine's* (1948) and *I, the King* (1966), the latter treating Philip of 17th-century Spain.

KIDD, WILLIAM (c.1645–1701), British pirate known as Captain Kidd, made his home in New York City (c.1690ff.). In 1697 he was authorized by the governor to proceed as a privateer against pirates, but failure and disease caused a mutiny among his crew, and Kidd, to save himself, was forced to turn pirate. When he returned to his home, he expected to be pardoned, but instead was sent to London under guard and was hanged for piracy and murder. His estate was surprisingly small, and this led to tales of buried treasure, none of which has been proved true. Captain Kidd and his treasure figure in many stories, e.g. Poe's "The Gold-Bug" and Irving's *Tales of a Traveller.*

KIEFT, WILLEM (1597–1647), governor of New Netherland (1638–47), noted for his autocratic policies and for causing a long, bloody Indian war. Irving satirizes him as William the Testy in his *History of New York.*

Kilburn, ANNIE, see *Annie Kilburn.*

Killers, The, story in *Men Without Women.*♦

KILMER, [ALFRED] JOYCE (1886–1918), poet, journalist, and critic, whose best-known work is the title piece in *Trees and Other Poems* (1914). He died in the second Battle of the Marne, becoming a symbol of courageous poetic idealism destroyed by war. His other books of poetry are *Summer of Love* (1911) and *Main Street* (1917).
  ALINE KILMER (1888–1941), his widow, was known as a poet in her own right, having published *Candles That Burn* (1919), *Vigils* (1921), and other books.

KIMBALL, RICHARD BURLEIGH (1816–92), a New York lawyer mainly associated with Wall Street affairs (1840–54), until he went to Texas to become a banker and railroad financier. Among his many books are four novels valuable for their early fictional presentation of the American millionaire and the background of Wall Street:

Under-Currents of Wall-Street (1862), *Was He Successful?* (1864), *Henry Powers, Banker* (1868), and *To-day in New York* (1870).

KIMBROUGH, EMILY, see *Skinner, Cornelia Otis.*

KING, CHARLES (1844–1933), army officer in the Civil War, various Indian campaigns, and the Spanish-American War. Besides military accounts of frontier encounters, he wrote books for boys and such novels as *The Colonel's Daughter* (1883), *A War-Time Wooing* (1888), and *Under Fire* (1894).

KING, CLARENCE (1842–1901), born at Newport, graduated from Yale (1862), after which he made a horseback trip across the continent to work in the mines of the Comstock Lode and California. He was next engaged (1866–77) in a geological survey of the Cordilleran ranges from eastern Colorado to California, whose results were published in the cooperative *Report of the Geological Exploration of the Fortieth Parallel* (7 vols., 1870–80). This is said to have been the most thorough and the most exact government survey published to that date. After heading the U.S. Geological Survey (1878–81), he continued his own important writings on geological and geophysical problems. His most popular work was the series of sketches *Mountaineering in the Sierra Nevada*♦ (1872), scientifically accurate as well as charmingly descriptive of the region. His ability as an author is further seen in "The Helmet of Mambrino" (*Century,* May 1886), and in the discussions with his friends John Hay and Henry Adams, which are said to have been partly responsible for the novels *The Bread-Winners* and *Democracy.*

KING, GRACE ELIZABETH (1851–1932), New Orleans author, whose short stories and novels of that city were a late development of the local-color movement. Her books include *Monsieur Motte* (1888); *Tales of a Time and Place* (1892); *Balcony Stories* (1893); *The Pleasant Ways of St. Médard* (1916), a novel of Reconstruction days in New Orleans; and historical and biographical works concerning the region.

KING, MARTIN LUTHER, JR. (1929–68), Baptist pastor in Montgomery, Ala., as president of the Southern Christian Leadership Conference was a leading spokesman of American blacks for nonviolence in the civil rights movement. *Stride Toward Freedom* (1958) tells of the boycott he led against the Jim Crow buses of Montgomery, *Strength To Love* (1963) collects sermons, and *Why We Can't Wait* (1964) treats both the Birmingham demonstrations of 1963 and his larger views on civil rights. In 1964 he was awarded the Nobel Prize for Peace. He was assassinated while planning a peaceful march.

KING, THOMAS STARR (1824–64), born in New York, became a Boston Unitarian clergyman noted for his writings on natural beauties of the American landscape, including *The White Hills* (1860) and articles collected in *A Vacation Among the Sierras* (1962). During the last four years of his life, he was a Unitarian pastor in San Francisco and was influential in California's choice of the Union side in the Civil War.

King Coal, novel by Upton Sinclair,♦ published in 1917. It is based on "sworn testimony, taken under government supervision," during an investigation of the Colorado coal-mining industry following the strike of 1914–15.

King Cotton, term personifying the chief staple product of the South, indicating its financial and social supremacy. Although the pamphlet *Cotton Is King* was published in 1835 by David Christy, the term was popularized in a speech (1858) by Senator James Henry Hammond of South Carolina during his controversy with Seward.

King George's War, see *French and Indian Wars.*

King Jasper, blank-verse narrative by E.A. Robinson,♦ posthumously published in 1935. The symbolism is considered to refer to the destruction of the capitalistic social structure by vengeful acts of the disinherited, who also perish in the holocaust, leaving only the enduring creative principle of life itself.

The industrialist "King" Jasper, at the climax of a ruthless career, is apparently satisfied by his power, but actually is disturbed by the neurotic obsession of his wife Honoria, and by his knowledge that ". . . there are somewhere some hands at work That may destroy us if we live too long." The dignified, tradition-bound Honoria is troubled by the love of their son for Zoë, an orphan girl of exotic beauty and cryptic wisdom. Shocked by the fact that the couple is not legally married, and frightened by Zoë's "evil" power, Honoria refuses to recognize the girl, even when she joins the household. The elder Jasper finds Zoë's charm irresistible and takes her into his confidence, confessing his dream in which his dead friend Hebron, an inventor whose work he stole, appeared to haunt him and ride his shoulders like Sinbad's Old Man of the Sea. This dream is fulfilled when Hebron's son arrives to seek revenge, and destroys Jasper's kingdom. As the symbolic factory chimneys fall, Honoria quietly commits suicide. Jasper grimly awaits his doom, which comes when Hebron shoots him and his son, and seizes Zoë. Knowing in her mysterious way that she is destined to go on living, but "alone," Zoë kills Hebron, and escapes into the night.

King of Prussia, Edict by the, see *Edict by the King of Prussia.*

KING PHILIP (*d.*1676), name given by English settlers to Metacomet, chief of the Wampanoag Indians during New England's most important Indian war. The struggle, known as King Philip's War (1675–76), consisted of sudden raids on the border towns by the Wampanoag, the Nipmuck, and the Narragansett, the latter led by Canonchet. The Nipmuck, Abnaki, and some Praying Indians later joined the struggle. The massacre at Deerfield (autumn 1675) was a prominent attack. Philip was at first successful, but in 1676 his power began to decline, and the war ended when he was treacherously shot by another Indian. The result was the practical extermination of tribal life in southern New England. The character of Philip has been variously estimated by many historians. Increase Mather's *Brief History of the War with the Indians* (1676) and William Hubbard's *Narrative of the Troubles with the Indians* (1677) are examples of the immeasurable rage of the early historians. The only historian of the time who wrote of Philip temperately is Gookin in his *Historical Account . . . of the Christian Indians.* Benjamin Tompson wrote a versified account of the war, Mary Rowlandson told of her captivity, and Thomas Church collected *Entertaining Passages Relating to King Philip's War . . .* (1716). Later versions, in which sympathy lies with Philip's followers, include *Yamoyden* by Eastburn and Sands; Stone's play *Metamora;* Irving's essay in *The Sketch Book;* Cooper's *The Wept of Wish-ton-Wish;* D.P. Thompson's *The Doomed Chief;* and Esther Forbes's *Paradise.*

King William's War, see *French and Indian Wars.*

KING, STEPHEN (1947–), born in Maine and educated at its state university, early became and has long continued to be a very popular novelist of science fiction and horror stories, including *Carrie* (1973), *The Stand* (1978), *The Dead Zone* (1979), *Pet Sematary* (1983), and *The Dark Half* (1989). King is ultra prolific, publishing a book a year, nearly all bestsellers, the most recent of which are *Needful Things* (1991), *Gerald's Game* (1992), *Dolores Claiborne* (1993), and *Insomnia* (1994).

KINGSLEY, SIDNEY (1906–95), New York playwright and actor, whose plays include *Men in White♦* (1933), on the medical profession; *Dead End♦* (1935), about New York's slums; *Ten Million Ghosts* (1936), about munitions makers; *The World We Make* (1939), dramatizing Millen Brand's novel *The Outward Room,* about the cure of a psychopathic girl through sharing in the life of the poor; *The Patriots* (1943), written with his wife Madge Evans, about Jefferson and Hamilton's struggle over the future of the U.S.; *Detective Story* (1949); *Darkness at Noon* (1951), based on Arthur Koestler's novel; *Lunatics and Lovers* (1954), a farce; and *Night Life* (1962).

KINGSTON, MAXINE HONG (1940–), California-born author, graduated from University of California, Berkeley, long resident as a schoolteacher in Hawaii, wrote *The Woman Warrior* (1976), a partly fictional work about her girlhood as it was affected by the beliefs of her Chinese family, and *China Men* (1980), again blending family history and legendry in treating the lives of men in her family who left their Oriental culture to live and work in the U.S. *Tripmaster Monkey* (1989), far more a work of fiction, concentrates on an intense, rather strange young American of Chinese heritage who wants to be a dramatist.

KINNELL, GALWAY (1927–), born in Rhode Island, after receiving his A.B. from Princeton (1948) and an M.A. from the University of Rochester, has taught at various universities. Early poems, published in *First Poems, 1946–1954* (1970), *What a Kingdom It Was* (1960), and *Flower Herding on Mount Monadnock* (1964), are marked by vivid observation and religious and social consciousness presented in pure, though idiomatic, language. Later poems, often darker and more symbolic, appear in *Body Rags* (1966); *The Lackawanna Elegy* (1971); *The Book of Nightmares* (1971), a sequence of ten intense and personal poems; *The Avenue Bearing the Initial of Christ into the New World* (1974), whose title poem presents Whitman-like religious feelings about the ordinary people encountered on New York's Avenue C; *Mortal Acts, Mortal Words* (1980); *Angling, a Day* (1980); *Selected Poems* (1982), awarded a Pulitzer Prize; and *The Past* (1985) whose lyrics are quite often autobiographic. Kinnell has also translated poems by Yves Bonnefoy, Yvan Goll, and Villon and has written a taut novel, *Black Light* (1966), set in Iran, where he taught for a year. *Walking Down the Stairs* (1978) contains his views on poetry set forth in interviews. A recent collection is *When One Has Lived a Long Time Alone* (1990).

KIPLING, RUDYARD (1865–1936), British poet, novelist, and writer of short stories, came to the U.S. (1889) via California, resided for several years after 1892 at Brattleboro, Vt., with his brother-in-law Wolcott Balestier,♦ with whom he wrote *The Naulahka* (1892), but with whom he later quarreled. *Captains Courageous♦* (1897) is Kipling's own work concerned with the American scene.

KIRKLAND, CAROLINE STANSBURY (1801–64), granddaughter of Joseph Stansbury, was born in New York City. She married Samuel Kirkland, with him conducted a seminary at Geneva and then at Detroit, and became one of the first settlers of Pinckney, Mich. Her ideas of the West, formed by such works as Chateaubriand's *Atala,* were considerably altered when she went to live on the frontier, as indicated in *A New Home—*

Who'll Follow?♦ (1839), written under the pseudonym Mrs. Mary Clavers, and reissued (1874) as *Our New Home in the West*. Mrs. Kirkland's later works on the frontier, *Forest Life* (1842), a series of essays, and *Western Clearings* (1845), loosely woven stories, are more self-conscious and sentimental than her humorous first book. After her return to New York City (1843), her work became conventional, and she issued various stereotyped anthologies, travel letters, and didactic literary collections. She also edited *The Union Magazine*♦ during its first year (1847).

KIRKLAND, JOSEPH (1830–94), son of Caroline Stansbury Kirkland, also possessed the ability to describe the Middle West realistically. His novels are based primarily on his own experiences and observations, and are frankly and forcefully told, lacking the romanticism so common in their time. His chief work, *Zury: The Meanest Man in Spring County*♦ (1887), was followed by a sequel, *The McVeys* (1888), depicting the drab life of Anne McVey and her illegitimate children by Zury. *The Captain of Company K* (1891) is a realistic novel of the Civil War, based on Kirkland's own experiences.

KIRKWOOD, JAMES (1924–89), reared in the motion-picture and film areas of his parents, won a Pulitzer Prize as co-author of *A Chorus Line*♦ (1975).

KITTREDGE, GEORGE LYMAN (1860–1941), authority on Shakespeare and early English literature, professor at Harvard (1888–1936) whose teaching and writing had a profound influence on American scholarship. His works include *The Old Farmer and His Almanack* (1904), *Chaucer and His Poetry* (1915), *Shakspere* (1916), *A Study of Gawain and the Green Knight* (1916), and *Witchcraft in Old and New England* (1929).

KIZER, CAROLYN (1925–   ), born in Spokane, was a founder and editor of *Poetry Northwest* (1959–65). Her lyrics and translations from Pakistani and Chinese have appeared in *The Ungrateful Garden* (1960), *Knock Upon Silence* (1965), and *Midnight Was My Cry* (1971). After busy times at work in various colleges and universities, she published *Mermaids in the Basement: Poems for Women* (1984); *Yin: New Poems* (1984, Pulitzer Prize); *The Nearness of You* (1986); and *Carrying Over* (1988), translations ranging from Chinese to Yiddish.

KLEIN, CHARLES (1867–1915), popular dramatist, won success with such sentimental plays as *The Auctioneer* (1901) and *The Music Master* (1904), both produced by Belasco, with Warfield in the leading roles. His later works are cleverly constructed and depend upon timely subjects for their temporary effectiveness.

KNAPP, SAMUEL LORENZO (1783–1838), popular Massachusetts hack writer, whose *Bio-*

graphical Sketches (1821) contains personal essays ornate and somewhat effusive in style. He then went on to his *Lectures on American Literature* (1829), an early attempt to study a generally unrecognized subject, but, because he could not find enough material, Knapp padded his book with chapters on "The Naval Character of Our Country" and other rather remote literary material.

KNEELAND, ABNER (1774–1844), New England Universalist clergyman and free-thinker, whose doubts concerning the divine origin of the Scriptures appear in *A Series of Letters in Defense of Divine Revelation* (1816), a correspondence with Hosea Ballou, and in successive liberal religious magazines that he edited. In 1838 he was jailed for his unorthodox views, although defended by Channing, Ripley, Alcott, Garrison, and Emerson, as well as Theodore Parker, who said, "Abner was jugged for sixty days; but he will come out as beer from a bottle, all foaming, and will make others foam." In 1839 he made an unsuccessful attempt to found a colony in Iowa for his First Society of Free Enquirers.

KNICKERBOCKER, DIEDRICH, fictitious chronicler of Irving's humorous *History of New York*♦ (1809) and in shorter tales and sketches dealing with the Dutch background of the state. Owing to Irving, the name became synonymous with the Dutch in respect to New York. The real Knickerbocker family came to America *c.*1674 and lived chiefly in Albany County.

Knickerbocker Group, school of writers whose association was primarily geographical and due to similar literary tastes. The name was a tribute to Irving's *Knickerbocker's History of New York* (1809), and the members attempted to carry his Addisonian spirit into their superficially sophisticated work. Other than Irving, Bryant, and Paulding, the writers most generally identified with this group included Hoffman, Drake, Halleck, Verplanck, Sands, Willis, Lydia M. Child, and Epes Sargent. This New York City group was represented in *The Knickerbocker Magazine,*♦ but may be said to have waned after its founding. Most of the writers were pilloried in Poe's "The Literati."

Knickerbocker Holiday, musical play by Maxwell Anderson♦ and Kurt Weill.

Knickerbocker Magazine, *The* (1833–65), monthly literary magazine, published at New York, was edited by Lewis G. and Willis G. Clark (1834–61). The name was a tribute to Irving, who was a contributor during its heyday, as were Longfellow, Parkman, Paulding, Hoffman, Halleck, Willis, Hawthorne, Whittier, Holmes, Bird, and Bryant. C.G. Leland was editor (1861–62), writing most of the contents himself, although

Howells, Aldrich, and Fitz-James O'Brien also contributed. *The Knickerbocker Gallery* (1855) was an anthology selected from the magazine.

KNIGHT, Sarah Kemble (1666–1727), known as Madam Knight, was a Boston teacher, also employed in the recording of public documents. She is said to have been an early teacher of Benjamin Franklin. Entrusted with some family business, during the winter of 1704–5 she made an unaccompanied trip from Boston to New York City and back, which occupied five months. During the pauses of her horseback journey, she kept a journal, which records events in a most amusing fashion and comments entertainingly upon the rough roads, river crossings, intolerable inns, and the manners and speech of the inland rustics. The diary was first published by Theodore Dwight (1825), and has since been frequently reprinted, although the original manuscript is now lost.

Knight's Gambit, collection of closely related stories by Faulkner,♦ published in 1949, in which Gavin Stevens,♦ the county attorney of Yoknapatawpha, solves various crimes and sees that justice is done.

Knights of the Golden Circle, see *Copperheads.*

KNOWLES, John (1926–   ), West Virginia-born author, educated at Yale, whose novels include *A Separate Peace* (1960), reminiscences of the unhappy experiences of boys at a New England boarding school; *Morning in Antibes* (1962), depicting Americans on the French Riviera; *Indian Summer* (1966), presenting the uneasy relations of two men; *The Paragon* (1971), a portrait of a brilliant, iconoclastic college student during the Korean War; *Spreading Fires* (1974), a psychological thriller set in the south of France; *A Vein of Riches* (1979), about the waning fortunes of a West Virginia family made rich by coal mining; *Peace Breaks Out* (1980), a sequel to his first novel, treating malevolence that leads to murder at a boys' boarding school; *A Stolen Past* (1983), a reminiscent tale of college friendships; and *The Private Life of Axie Reed* (1986), revelations about the personal experiences of a 50-year-old youthful woman. *Phineas* (1968) collects stories, and *Double Vision* (1964) is a travel book.

Know-Nothing movement sponsored secret societies that flourished in the 1840s and '50s, whose purpose was to oppose the political influence of foreign-born groups, especially those who were Roman Catholics. Although not an actual party, the several organizations within the movement had considerable influence on local and state elections through the American Republican party and similar groupings, and in 1854 they abandoned secrecy to become the American party with Fillmore as their presidential candidate

(1856). Carleton Beals's *Brass-Knuckle Crusade* (1960) treats the movement.

KOBER, Arthur (1900–1974), was born in Poland and brought to New York as a child. He was the author of *Having Wonderful Time* (1937), a comedy of New York City office workers at a summer camp in the Catskills, and of another comedy written in collaboration, *Wish You Were Here* (1952); vernacular sketches of life in the Bronx, collected in *Thunder Over the Bronx* (1935), *My Dear Bella* (1941), *Bella, Bella, Kissed a Fella* (1951), and *Ooh, What You Said!* (1958); and *Pardon Me for Pointing* (1939) and *That Man Is Here Again* (1947), sketches of Hollywood. In addition to another play, *A Mighty Man Is He* (1959), he wrote many film scripts.

KOCH, Frederick Henry, see *Carolina Playmakers.*

KOCH, Kenneth [Jay] (1925–   ), Cincinnati-born author, educated at Harvard (A.B., 1948) and Columbia (Ph.D., 1959), has been on Columbia's faculty since 1959. He is associated with the so-called New York school of poetry of John Ashbery and Frank O'Hara, and his early *Poems* (1953) are marked by a surrealistic use of language. *Ko, or A Season on Earth* (1960) is a long comic poem of complex plots written in Byronic ottava rima. Later collections of poems, including *Thank You* (1962), *The Pleasures of Peace* (1969), and *The Art of Love* (1975), all marked by an exuberant wit, were followed by *The Duplications* (1977), another capricious Byronic epic, and *The Burning Mystery of Anna in 1951* (1979), combining poetry and prose. All of these books formed the source of *Selected Poems* (1985) and were followed by *On the Edge* (1986), two long poems. *Bertha and Other Plays* (1966) and *A Change of Hearts* (1973) collect his very short plays. *The Red Robins* is a fantasy that he dramatized (1980). His successful teaching of poetry to children is treated in *Wishes, Lies, and Dreams* (1970) and *Rose Where Did You Get That Red?* (1973). Similar teaching to sick, aged people in a nursing home is the subject of *I Never Told Anybody* (1977). He was awarded the 1995 Bollingen Prize.♦

KOMROFF, Manuel (1890–1974), born in New York, attended Yale, and became a journalist in New York and later in Russia during the revolution. Returning to New York, he published *The Grace of Lambs* (1925), short stories, followed by a novel, *Juggler's Kiss* (1927), and *Coronet* (2 vols., 1929), a romance tracing the decay of aristocracy from the 17th to the 20th century. *Two Thieves* (1931) is a novel about the men who were crucified with Jesus. Later novels include *A New York Tempest* (1932); *I, the Tiger* (1933); *Waterloo* (1936); *The March of the Hundred* (1939), an allegorical story of humanity in the 20 years after World War I; *The Magic Bow* (1940), about Paganini; *In the Years of Our Lord* (1942); *Feast of the Jesters* (1947), about the Congress of Vienna; *Echo of Evil* (1948), about a paroled murderess and her small-town relatives; and *Jade Star* (1951), about a Chinese girl at Kubla Khan's court. *All in Our Day* (1942) collects stories.

Koningsmarke, the Long Finne; *A Story of the New World,* romance by J.K. Paulding,♦ published in 1823, and later retitled *Koningsmarke; or, Old Times in the New World.*

This historical narrative of New Sweden is partly a burlesque of Scott's *The Pirate,* and also satirizes Cooper's Indian characters, the Swedes, and Paulding's contemporaries. Koningsmarke, a handsome young Finn, comes to the Swedish community of Elsingburgh on the Delaware, governed by Heer Peter Piper. Jailed for passing English coins, he is rescued when the jail catches fire. He has been badly injured and is nursed back to health by Christina, Heer Piper's daughter, with whom he falls in love. The town is betrayed by a black man into the hands of the Indians and several of the townspeople are captured, among them Christina and Koningsmarke, who are adopted into the tribe. Just as the Finn is in danger of execution for refusing a native marriage, they are rescued by the Quaker Shadrach Moneypenny, who ransoms them as the emissary of William Penn. Later, when the English seize the Swedish *holsings,* Koningsmarke is kidnapped, but Christina pleads for him and he is released by the governor of New York.

KOPIT, ARTHUR L. (1937–   ), born in New York and educated at Harvard (A.B., 1959), where he wrote and directed several plays, culminating with *Oh Dad, Poor Dad, Mama's Hung You in the Closet and I'm Feelin' So Sad* (1960). This work, published in 1960 and professionally produced in 1962, is subtitled "a pseudoclassical, tragifarce in a bastard French tradition," and presents in wildly farcical but moving style a fantastic treatment of the "silver cord" theme. *Indians* (1969) presents scenes from the lives of Buffalo Bill and Sitting Bull to denounce U.S. treatment of Indians. It was followed by *Wings* (1978), a portrait of a woman, produced on the air a year before the stage date; *Good Help Is Hard To Find* (1981), a one-act work; and *End of the World* (1984), dealing with the nuclear arms race. He wrote the book for a musical play, *Nine* (1982), and later gathered six of his short plays in *The Day the Whores Came Out To Play Tennis* (1985).

KOSINSKI, JERZY [NIKODEM] (1933–91), Polish-born, Russian-reared author, came to the U.S. (1957), where he was a graduate student at Columbia and began to write in English. His first novel, *The Painted Bird* (1965), presents a six-year-old Polish boy trapped during the German occupation, in which he suffers endless brutalities. It was followed by further spare fiction

treating other violent or perverse situations: *Steps* (1968) presents an anonymous narrator's account of diverse cruelties; *Being There*♦ (1971) is an ironic fable with a different tone in its tale of a gentle, illiterate gardener who achieves national leadership in the U.S. by chance; *The Devil Tree* (1973) is another fable, this one about a very rich young man seeking to find himself; *Cockpit* (1975) is like his other novels in avoiding a sequential plot as it tells of an ex-spy's violent acts of vengeance and quest for intimacy, mainly sexual; *Blind Date* (1977) is an amoral picaresque story, whose protagonist, an antihero, indulges in wild, perverse, and horrid activities; *Passion Play* (1979) depicts another picaresque figure, an impassioned horseman who is also an esoteric novelist; *Pinball* (1982) is about a seedy musician's quest to learn the true identity of a very popular rock star; and *The Hermit of 69th Street* (1988) is about the struggles of a creative writer. Kosinski also wrote two nonfictional books about people in the USSR, *The Future Is Ours, Comrade* (1960) and *No Third Path* (1962), under the name Joseph Novak.

KRAMER, LARRY (1935–   ), born in Connecticut and graduated from Yale, began his literary career with a film version of D.H. Lawrence's *Women in Love* (1969) but began his own authorship with the novel *Faggots* (1978) which "reflected homosexuality as I was living it," followed by the plays *The Normal Heart* (1985), about attacks upon homosexuals from society and from AIDS, and *Just Say No* (1988), a comic satire mainly on political figures. He also wrote *Holocaust* (1989), nonfiction dealing with AIDS.

KRAMM, JOSEPH (1908–   ), Philadelphia-born dramatist and actor, who wrote *The Shrike* (1952, Pulitzer Prize), a play about a man who attempts suicide to be free of a madly possessive wife. *Giants, Sons of Giants* (1962) is a later play, about an unhappy doctor.

KRAUSE, HERBERT (1905–76), born and partly raised in western Minnesota whose farm life is treated in his first novel, *Wind Without Rain* (1939), as is his critical concern with his Lutheran background. His next two novels are slightly farther west and very critical: *The Thresher* (1946), treating the difficult life of a young man enmeshed in large-scale wheat farming, and *The Oxcart Trail* (1954), further presenting frontier town life. *Neighbor Boy* (1939) is a collection of some of his poetry.

KREYMBORG, ALFRED (1883–1966), New York City poet and playwright, whose first collection, *Mushrooms* (1916), was an attempt to achieve direct simplicity in poetry. He next turned to poetic drama, writing *Plays for Poem-Mimes* (1918), *Plays for Merry Andrews* (1920), and *Puppet Plays* (1923), many of which were first presented by the Provincetown Players. ◆ *Less Lonely* (1923) shows the juxtaposition of personal themes and conventional verse forms. He continued to experiment with the sonnet form in *The Lost Sail* (1928), while *Manhattan Men* (1929) represents a midway point between his early experimentation and his later more conventional poetry published in *Prologue in Hell* (1930), *The Little World* (1932), and *No More War* (1950). His *Selected Poems* was published in 1945. *Our Singing Strength* (1929) is a history of American poetry, complemented by *Lyric America* (1930), an anthology. *Troubadour* (1925) is the autobiography of his youth on the Lower East Side and his later life in Greenwich Village and elsewhere, during part of which time he was a contributor to little magazines, including *Others* and *Broom*. His other books include the novels *Erna Vitek* (1914) and *I'm No Hero* (1933) and a book for children, *Funnybone Alley* (1927). He was active in the Federal Theatre and in radio drama, writing for the latter medium such plays as *The Planets* (1938), a modern pacifist allegory.

KRUTCH, JOSEPH WOOD (1893–1970), born in Tennessee, graduated from the state university (1915), and received his Ph.D. from Columbia (1923). He was long on the faculty of Columbia (1925–31, 1937–52) and on the editorial staff of *The Nation* (1924–52) mainly as a drama critic. His books include *Edgar Allan Poe: A Study in Genius* (1926), an analytical biography employing psychoanalysis; *The Modern Temper* (1929), a pessimistic analysis of contemporary life, by a "modern intellectual" who finds that science has destroyed his faith in a beneficent universe, and psychology his belief in his own nobility, so that he "finds only in the pursuit of knowledge that which makes life worth living"; *Five Masters: A Study in the Mutations of the Novel* (1930), an analysis of Boccaccio, Cervantes, Richardson, Stendhal, and Proust, to determine whether their greatness springs from the life of their times or from an essential universality; scholarly biographies, *Samuel Johnson* (1944) and *Thoreau* (1948); and *The Measure of Man* (1954), a return to the themes of *The Modern Temper*, with a humanistic plea for "Moral Discourse." After he moved to Arizona many of his books dealt with natural history, the Western scene, and a humanist's view of man and his environment, including *The Desert Year* (1952), *The Great Chain of Life* (1957), *Human Nature and the Human Condition* (1959), and *The Forgotten Peninsula; A Naturalist in Baja California* (1961). *More Lives Than One* (1962) recalls his varied experiences.

Ku Klux Klan, secret terrorist society widespread in the South during Reconstruction. It intended to keep freed blacks subservient, and used various methods of instilling fear, ranging from masks, flowing white robes, and horseback parades to raids by night, whippings, and tarring

and feathering. It figures in Thomas Dixon's *The Clansman,* Evelyn Scott's *A Calendar of Sin,* and Robert Lewis Taylor's *A Voyage to Matecumbe.* The more recent Ku Klux Klan movement has been nationwide, originating in Georgia (1915) but spreading, as an outgrowth of World War I emotionalism, to many Northern regions. Based on a program of white supremacy, native Americanism, fundamentalism, anti-Semitism, and anti-Catholicism, it had considerable political influence, especially in the early 1920s. The opposition of many Southerners to civil-rights legislation caused the Klan's revival in the 1960s, and it was joined by other extremist organizations that adopted some variation of its name.

KUMIN, MAXINE [WINOKUR] (1925–), born in Philadelphia, where her father was the city's major pawnbroker, was educated at Radcliffe (A.B., 1946; M.A., 1948). Her first novel, *Through Dooms of Love* (1965), titled with a line from Cummings, dealing with the conflict between a radical Radcliffe girl and her pawnbroker father, was followed by *The Passions of Uxport* (1968), with a setting like that of Updike's *Couples,* which presents stormy married life in a Boston suburb. *The Abduction* (1971) and *The Designated Heir* (1974), portrayals of different kinds of women, are later novels. Stories are collected in *Why Can't We Live Together Like Civilized Human Beings?* (1982). Her poetry is collected in *Halfway* (1961), *The Privilege* (1965), *The Nightmare Factory* (1970), *Up Country; Poems of New England* (1972, Pulitzer Prize), *House, Bridge, Fountain, Gate* (1975), *The Retrieval System* (1978), *Our Ground Time Here Will Be Brief* (1982), *Closing the Ring* (1984), *The Long Approach* (1985), *Nurture* (1989), and *Looking for Luck* (1993). She herself sees all her writing as "private experience giving rise to elegy and celebration." Her essays are collected in *To Make a Prairie* (1979) and *In Deep Country* (1987), and she has written many books for children, two with Anne Sexton.

KUNITZ, STANLEY J[ASSPON] (1905–), poet and editor of reference books, graduated from Harvard (1926), and has frequently been a teacher of poetry at colleges and literary workshops. His modern metaphysical poetry appears in *Intellectual Things* (1930); *Passport to the War* (1940); *Selected Poems* (1958, Pulitzer Prize), a third of them new; and *The Testing-Tree* (1971), marked, as he says, by "a more open style, based on natural speech rhythms." Later poetry appears in the small *The Wellfleet Whale* (1983) and *Next-to-Last Things: New Poems and Essays* (1985). He has also translated several contemporary Russian poets. *A Kind of Order, A Kind of Folly* (1975) prints essays and other prose. His reference works include *American Authors 1600–1900* (1938), with Howard Haycraft.

KYNE, PETER B[ERNARD] (1880–1957), California author whose popular books include *Cappy Ricks* (1916), a collection of short stories dealing with a shrewd though kindly retired sea captain and his adventures as owner of a coastwise navigation line and a lumber company. He published several other collections of Cappy Ricks stories. *The Go-Getter* (1922), the story of a canny businessman, was popular among the sort of men who served as prototypes for the leading character.

L

LACY, ERNEST (1863–1916), Philadelphia playwright whose blank-verse dramas include *Chatterton* (1894), produced by Julia Marlowe, *Rinaldo* (1895), and *The Ragged Earl* (1899). *The Bard of Mary Redcliffe,* an unproduced drama also concerned with Chatterton, was published with his poems and other romantic plays (1916).

LADD, JOSEPH BROWN (1764–86), Rhode Island physician, was the author of *The Poems of Arouet* (1786), which, though in the sentimental style of the Della-Cruscan school, are interesting as American predecessors of romantic poetry.

LADD, WILLIAM (1778–1841), New England author and lecturer on world peace, founded the American Peace Society (1828), edited the *Harbinger of Peace,* and wrote *An Essay on a Congress of Nations* (1840), proposing institutions whose essential features are to be found in the League of Nations, the World Court, and the Hague Conferences. His ideas were popularized by Elihu Burritt.

Ladies' Companion, The (1834–44), eclectic literary journal, was published monthly at New York as an imitation of *Godey's Lady's Book.*◆ Poe's "The Mystery of Marie Rogêt" appeared in it, and other contributors included Willis, Paulding, Longfellow, Simms, and Hoffman.

Ladies' Home Journal (1883–   ), monthly magazine founded by C.H.K. Curtis, was edited by his wife until 1889. It was popularized by its second editor, E.W. Bok (1889–1920), who not only obtained famous contributors, but also indulged in mild campaigns for social reform and aesthetic improvements in urban life. Later editors have continued his policies with such success that the circulation in 1994 was about 5,000,000.

Ladies' National Magazine, see *Peterson, C.J.*

Ladies' Repository, The (1841–80), Cincinnati monthly periodical of literature and religion, founded by the Methodists. After 1876 it was entitled the *National Repository.*

Lady Eleanore's Mantle, allegorical tale by Hawthorne,◆ published in 1838 and reprinted in *Twice-Told Tales* (1842).

Lady Eleanore Rochcliffe comes to live at the Boston Province House, in the family of her guardian, Colonel Shute. Her haughty beauty distracts Jervase Helwyse, whose love she scorns, and affects all who see her. The curious mantle she wears is said to have supernatural powers and to have some influence in the epidemic of smallpox that soon breaks out, striking first the aristocratic circle of Lady Eleanore, and then the common people she despises. At last she herself is stricken, and as she is dying confesses, "I wrapped myself in Pride as in a Mantle, and scorned the sympathies of nature; and therefore has nature made this wretched body the medium of a dreadful sympathy." Helwyse takes her mantle, which is burned by a mob, and the pestilence begins to subside.

Lady of the Aroostook, The, novel by Howells,◆ published in 1879.

Lydia Blood, a Massachusetts schoolteacher, sails for Venice on the *Aroostook.* She becomes the object of the attentions of Hicks, a drunken ne'er-do-well, and is saved from his advances by James Staniford, a member of Boston society. Staniford, gradually made aware of Lydia's native nobility that has been veiled by her provincialisms, falls in love with her and they are married in Venice.

Lady or the Tiger?, The, short story by Frank Stockton,◆ which was sensationally popular when it was published in *The Century* (Nov. 1882). It was reprinted in a collection (1884) and was the subject of an operetta (1888).

LA FARGE, CHRISTOPHER (1897–1956), author, painter, and architect. His verse novels are *Hoxie Sells His Acres* (1934), set in New England; *Each to the Other* (1939), about a young man trying to find his place in the modern world; and *Beauty for Ashes* (1953), about social responsibility and personal independence. *The Sudden Guest* (1946), a prose novel about a New England spinster's disregard for fellow citizens during a hurricane, is an oblique comment on U.S. international relations. *Mesa Verde* (1945) is a verse drama about the cliff dwellers. *The Wilsons* (1941) includes sketches of social climbers; other collections are *Poems and Portraits* (1941); *East by Southwest* (1944), stories and a poem about the war in the Pacific; and *All Sorts and Kinds* (1949), stories.

LA FARGE, JOHN (1835–1910), artist and author, was born in New York of French parentage. He went abroad (1856) to study painting with Couture and met the Pre-Raphaelites and other intellectual and artistic leaders of the time. In 1876 he executed the mural decorations for Trinity Church, Boston, and thereafter he devoted himself to mural painting and the design and manufacture of stained glass. While in Japan, Samoa, and the South Seas with Henry Adams he produced fine watercolors and paintings. His decorative, refined murals, in the tradition of the Italian masters, are in many churches and in the Minnesota state capitol. His books include *Considerations on Painting* (1895), *An Artist's Letters from Japan* (1897), *Great Masters* (1903), *The Higher Life in Art* (1908), and *Reminiscences of the South Seas* (1912). Christopher and Oliver La Farge are his grandsons.

LA FARGE, OLIVER [HAZARD PERRY] (1901–63), ethnologist and author, after graduation from Harvard (1924) conducted archaeological investigations in Arizona, Mexico, and Guatemala, and with Frans Blom wrote *Tribes and Temples* (2 vols., 1925, 1927). *Laughing Boy*◆ (1929, Pulitzer Prize) is a novel of life among the Navajo Indians, and his later novels include *Sparks Fly Upward* (1931), set in Central America; *Long Pennant* (1933), a story of 19th-century New England seamen; *The Enemy Gods* (1937), about Navajo inability to adapt to white civilization; and *The Copper Pot* (1942), about a New England painter in New Orleans. *All the Young Men* (1935) and *A Pause in the Desert* (1957) collect stories. *As Long as the Grass Shall Grow* (1940) surveys the history and conditions of American Indians, and other works of nonfiction include *Behind the Mountains* (1956), sketches of New Mexico village life in an earlier day, and *Santa Fe: The Autobiography of a Southwestern Town* (1959), collecting local newspaper comments with a commentary. *The Eagle in the Egg* (1949) deals with his wartime service as an officer of the air corps, and *Raw Material* (1945) contains reminiscences of his intellectual development.

LAFFITE (or LAFITTE), JEAN (c.1780–c.1825), French smuggler and pirate leader, with his brother Pierre operated off the coast of Louisiana. Their headquarters included the Barataria region near the mouth of the Mississippi, and the island site of the present Galveston, Tex. During the War of 1812, the Laffites refused British remuneration to engage in an attack on New Orleans, and turned over the documents containing the proposal to the U.S. An American naval force was at first sent against them, but later Jackson accepted the aid of Laffite in the Battle of New Orleans, giving him and his men a pardon in return for their services. Another force was sent against Laffite when he resumed operations in Texas, and he departed peaceably. His end is not definitely known, and his piratical adventures and rumors of buried treasure have made him a prominent figure in folk legends. He figures in much popular historical literature, including Joseph Holt Ingraham's *Lafitte*, Hervey Allen's *Anthony Adverse*, and O. and W. Shepard's *Holdfast Gaines*.

LAHONTAN, LOUIS-ARMAND, Baron de (1666–c.1713), French explorer, came to New France (1683) and made an unsuccessful expedition against the Iroquois. In 1687 he was sent with Duluth to Fort St. Joseph, near Detroit, a post which he capriciously abandoned the following year to make a journey of his own to the upper Mississippi. In favor with Frontenac and having distinguished himself in service, he was made lieutenant-governor of Newfoundland, which he erratically left (1693) to become an exile from French domains. His *Nouveaux Voyages,* published in Holland (1703), was translated into English with an added series of "Dialogues" with a supposed Huron chief, Adario. His book has important information on the Indians and the flora and fauna, but contains willfully misleading information on such subjects as the fictional River Long. His Dialogues, contrasting savage with civilized life, were a source of the writings of Chateaubriand and other believers in the noble savage.

LAMANTIA, PHILIP (1927–   ), San Francisco poet whose works are often surrealist and marked by a rapture, now religious, now inspired by drugs. His books include *Erotic Poems* (1946), *Ekstasis* (1959), *Destroyed Works* (1962), *Touch of the Marvelous* (1966), *The Blood of the Air* (1970), *Becoming Visible* (1981), and *Meadowland West* (1986), written during his life in Mexico, France, Morocco, and the Sierra Nevada mountains.

LAMAR, MIRABEAU BUONAPARTE (1798–1859), arrived in Texas from his native Georgia (1835) and distinguished himself at the Battle of San Jacinto. He successively held important positions in the Lone Star Republic, becoming its president (1838–41) between the two terms of Houston. He conducted his regime at Austin in a high-handed manner, and carried out his own ideas in opposition to Houston's desire for annexation by the U.S. His romantic strain may be observed in his Byronic *Verse Memorials* (1857). After serving in the Mexican War, he retired to his Richmond plantation, except for a year (1858–59) as minister to Nicaragua and Costa Rica.

Lambs, THE, private club founded in New York City (1874) as an American counterpart of a dining society for theater people. In its centennial year (1974) it went bankrupt and its clubhouse, designed by Stanford White, was auctioned. However, the organization continues in rented quarters.

L'AMOUR, LOUIS [DEARBORN] (1910?–88), North Dakota-born novelist, long resident in Los

Angeles, whose huge output of 200 novels and 14 books of stories, all on the Far West, sold 182,000,000 copies by 1987. He was awarded a Presidential Medal of Freedom (1984). His posthumously published *Education of a Wandering Man* (1989) reveals that his name was originally Louis LaMoore.

Lamplighter, The, novel by Maria Cummins.♦

Lancelot, blank-verse dramatic narrative by E.A. Robinson,♦ published in 1920. It belongs with *Merlin*♦ and *Tristram*♦ in the author's Arthurian trilogy.

On the eve of Lancelot's departure from Camelot on his pilgrimage, his liaison with Queen Guinevere has ended in suspicion and his own conscience-stricken resumption of his quest after "the Light." King Arthur, finally aware of his queen's infidelity, orders her burned at the stake. Lancelot and his friends rescue Guinevere, and the lovers flee to Joyous Gard, where they remain for six months, during the siege that Gawaine persuades Arthur to wage. At last Lancelot sees the futility of the slaughter, and on orders from Rome returns Guinevere to Camelot. Still in banishment, he journeys to France to participate in the war which destroys Arthur's rule. Later he returns to Camelot, attends the deathbed of the penitent Gawaine, and visits Guinevere's convent, but she refuses to go to France with him.

Land of Eden, see *Journey to the Land of Eden.*

Land of Little Rain, The, 14 sketches by Mary Austin,♦ published in 1903. Based on long personal observation, this familiar account of the land, the people, and the animals and plants is concerned with the California region "between the high Sierras south from Yosemite—east and south . . . beyond Death Valley and on illimitably into the Mojave Desert."

"The Pocket Hunter," "Shoshone Land," and "The Basket Maker" are quiet portraits of representative citizens in this region of high mountains and vast deserts: a gold miner who spends his life in an infrequently successful search for stray "pockets" of precious metal; an ancient Shoshone medicine man, homesick in exile among the Paiute; and a widowed Paiute woman who devotes herself to rearing her son and to weaving beautiful willow baskets "for the satisfaction of desire." "The Scavengers" is a study of the carrion creatures of the desert—vultures, buzzards, ravens, and coyotes—embodying the author's sense of the delicate economy of nature. "Jimville—A Bret Harte Town" is a genial depiction of a mountain town whose life contains all the themes of Harte's sentimental fiction.

Landlord at Lion's Head, The, novel by Howells,♦ published in 1898.

Westover, a Boston painter, while sketching in northern New England, boards at the home of Mrs. Durgin, whose wholesome and simple young son Jeff wins his admiration. When he returns several years later, he finds Mrs. Durgin running a summer hotel to put Jeff through Harvard. Jeff, detesting academic life, manages to get himself suspended and goes abroad. In Europe he meets Genevieve Vostrand, with whom he becomes infatuated. When Mrs. Vostrand forces her daughter to marry a worthless Italian count, Jeff courts Cynthia Whitwell, a childhood friend, who urges him to return to Harvard. After completing his studies, Jeff returns to Florence, where he again meets the Vostrands. Genevieve's Italian husband has died, and she and Jeff are married, as are Westover and Cynthia.

LANDON, MELVILLE DE LANCEY (1839–1910), New York journalist and humorous lecturer, who used the pseudonym Eli Perkins. He belongs to the school of Artemus Ward, whose complete works he edited (1879). His own numerous books include *The Franco-Prussian War in a Nutshell* (1871), *Eli Perkins at Large* (1875), and *Thirty Years of Wit . . .* (1891).

Landor's Cottage, descriptive story by Poe,♦ published in 1849 as a "pendant" to "The Domain of Arnheim."♦ It is a detailed depiction of the New York country estate of a Mr. Landor, a simple but exquisite creation of architecture and landscape gardening, and a less elaborate counterpart of the rich domain described in the earlier story.

LANE, SIR RALPH (c.1530–1603), English maritime adventurer and American colonist, governed the Roanoke Island colony (1585–86), of which he wrote a glowing report, published in Hakluyt's *The Principall Navigations.* . . .

LANGER, SUSANNE K. (1895–1985), philosopher and professor at Columbia, whose early works on philosophy, including *An Introduction to Symbolic Logic* (1937), were followed by widely influential works relating philosophy to aesthetics and significant form in art, including *Philosophy in a New Key* (1942), *Feeling and Form* (1953), *Problems of Art* (1957), *Reflections on Art* (1958), and *Mind* (two of three projected volumes, 1967, 1973), on mind and body and aesthetics.

LANGSTAFF, LANCELOT, pseudonym of J.K. Paulding.♦

LANIER, SIDNEY (1842–81), born in Macon, Ga., was educated at Oglethorpe University, where he early showed an inclination toward a musical career. Plans for further study were interrupted by his service in the Civil War and his four months' imprisonment at Point Lookout, Md. Seriously ill with consumption, and suffering from poverty, he said that in the eight years after his return in 1865 "pretty much the whole of life had been merely not dying." His novel *Tiger-Lilies* (1867), about his experiences in the Civil War, helped him to decide that he would not settle "down to be a third-rate struggling lawyer for the balance of my little life." Accordingly, he turned to the writing of poetry, published his *Poems* (1877), became a flutist in the Peabody Orchestra at Baltimore, and supplemented his small income by delivering lectures, which were posthumously published as *Shakspere and His Fore-runners* (2 vols., 1902). These talks brought him the position of lecturer in English literature at Johns Hopkins in 1879, and the work for his classes resulted in *The Science of English Verse* (1880) and *The English Novel* (1883). In his book on prosody he illuminates his own method by his thesis that the laws governing music and verse are identical, and that time, not accent, is the important element in verse rhythms. Lanier's complete *Poems* were collected in 1884 and are noted for the ballads and lyrics that embody his attempt to produce in verse the sound patterns of music. His arrangements of lines and rhythms were frequently strained as well as novel, in both the emphasis on pattern-making and the interest in metaphysical conceits, and the imagery is often vague as a result of the attention to musical quality. Nevertheless, the poet's theories were successfully practiced in some of his works, outstanding among which are "The Song of the Chattahoochee,"♦ "The Symphony,"♦ and "The Marshes of Glynn."♦ New editions of his *Poems* (1884) were issued with slight additions in 1891 and 1916. A full critical edition of his works was published in ten volumes (1945).

LANIGAN, George Thomas (1845–86), Canadian-born journalist and humorist, began his newspaper career in his native country but continued it in St. Louis, Chicago, New York, and Philadelphia. His verse *Fables by G. Washington Aesop* (1878) shows his wit and his facility, as does his improvisation occasioned by the headline "The Ahkoond of Swat Is Dead," entitled "Threnody for the Ahkoond of Swat" (1878) and containing the lines "The great Ahkoond of Swat Is not!"

LAPINE, James [Elliot] (1949–), long a successful playwright and director, whose works in the former capacity, but in association with Stephen Sondheim, are *Sunday in the Park with George* (1984), awarded a Pulitzer Prize for drama, and *Passion* (1994).

LARCOM, Lucy (1824–93), Massachusetts Abolitionist and author of simple poetry about nature and children, whose homely sincerity was pleasing to her generation. Her autobiographical *A New England Girlhood* (1889) gives a vivid picture of life in the Lowell mills and homes.

LARDNER, Ring[gold] [Wilmer] (1885–1933), born in Michigan, was known as a sports

writer and columnist in Chicago and New York before the great success of his short stories. His first collection, *You Know Me Al; A Busher's Letters* (1916), employs the racy idiom of the baseball diamond and describes the career of a novice on a professional team. Other books of this early period displaying the author's talent for the humorous use of the vernacular in portraying typical Americans include *Bib Ballads* (1915), a collection of verse; *Gullible's Travels* (1917), satirical stories; *Treat 'Em Rough* (1918); and *The Big Town* (1921), a humorous novel. The publication of *How To Write Short Stories*♦ (1924), a collection, first attracted critical attention to Lardner as a sardonic humorist exposing follies and vices through his characters' conversational speech. Though they seem to follow traditional methods of American humor, his stories are actually cynical and mordant treatments of the subjects. The boxers, baseball players, salesmen, stockbrokers, songwriters, barbers, actresses, stenographers, and other "average" characters whom he depicts are reduced by the author's implied bitterness to their essential commonplaceness, cruelty, viciousness, dullness, and stupidity. This pessimistic view, as well as his ability to reproduce the idioms and habits of mind of everyday people, continued to appear in Lardner's later collections of short stories: *What of It?* (1925), *The Love Nest*♦ (1926), *Round Up* (1929), and *First and Last* (1934). "The Love Nest" was dramatized by Robert Sherwood in 1927, and *June Moon* (1929), written by Lardner in collaboration with George S. Kaufman, is a comedy satirizing the songwriters of Tin Pan Alley. *The Story of a Wonder Man* (1927) is a satirical "autobiography." Some of his letters were published in 1979.

Lark, The (1895–97), little magazine published by Les Jeunes, a San Francisco group of literary aesthetes led by Gelett Burgess,♦ who contributed drawings of "Goops" and nonsense verses, including his "Purple Cow," first pastured there. Although influenced by *The Chap-Book* and English *fin de siècle* magazines, it had "no more serious intention than to be gay," and was stopped because Burgess "wanted it to die young and in its full freshness."

LARNER, Jeremy (1937–), author of the novels *Drive, He Said* (1964) and *The Answer* (1968), treating college students attempting to cope with an irrational society, in the latter book by resorting to drugs. He wrote the screenplay of his first novel and of *The Candidate.* His other works include edited, tape-recorded interviews with heroin users, *The Addict in the Street* (1965), and *Nobody Knows* (1970), reflections on the presidential campaign of Eugene McCarthy, for whom he was a speech writer.

LARPENTEUR, Charles (1807–72), born in France and reared on a Maryland farm, moved to

St. Louis (1828) and had a career as clerk, factor, trader, and sutler reported in *Forty Years a Fur Trader on the Upper Missouri* (2 vols., 1898), a prime source on the trade and the region.

LARSEN, NELLA (1891–1964), born in Chicago, daughter of a West Indies black man and a Danish mother, spent some time in Denmark as well as the U.S. She wrote a novel, *Quicksand* (1928), about a woman of parentage essentially identical to her own who marries an African-American evangelist and has to live with him in Alabama, where she experiences total alienation. It was followed by her only other novel, *Passing* (1929), about the tragic life and quick end of a black woman whose fair skin allows her to wed a white man and share his life for a time.

LA SALLE, RENÉ ROBERT CAVELIER, Sieur de (1643–87), French explorer and trader, whose expeditions in Canada were aided by Frontenac. He made exploring trips south of the Great Lakes during the 1670s, and returned to France to secure a trade monopoly in the valley of the Mississippi. In 1682 he descended the Mississippi and took possession of the region for France, naming it Louisiana. Given four ships and 200 colonists, he was made viceroy of North America to rule from Illinois to the Spanish borders. His fleet landed (1684) in Texas instead of at the mouth of the Mississippi, and, while La Salle was trying to find the river, his men mutinied and killed him. Narratives of his enterprise appear in I.J. Cox, *The Journeys of . . . La Salle* (2 vols., 1905). He is the subject of both colorful history by Parkman and popular fiction, including Mary Hartwell Catherwood's *The Story of Tonty*.

Last Frontier, *The,* historical novel by Howard Fast,♦ published in 1941, in which Captain Murray is the only purely fictional character.

In 1878, 300 Northern Cheyenne, resettled in an unhealthy Indian Territory, are virtual prisoners, many of them sick. When the local agent, unable to supply medicine or food, summons military aid to force them to give ten hostages for three of their number who escape, the entire band flees for its northern homeland, led by Dull Knife and Little Wolf, a philosophic old chief who understands that the white men "must do whatever they have to do," but that his people are doomed in their attempt to regain freedom and livelihood. Colonel Mizner at Fort Reno dispatches two cavalry troops commanded by indignant but disciplined Captain Murray, to capture the Indians. During the chase, more than 50 whites are killed as the Cheyenne battle with buffalo hunters, posses, and various army units. Through the fall and winter their flight takes them north through Kansas and Nebraska; Dull Knife leads part of the tribe into the Sand Hills, only to be captured, starved, and massacred. Little Wolf brings his group to the Powder River country, where, with the only understanding displayed by the government, they are allowed to remain. The epic of the Indians' struggle for freedom against the might of the U.S., intent on their slavery or extinction, is realized only by Captain Murray, who, sickened by what has happened, feels he must resign from service.

Last Leaf, *The,* poem by Oliver Wendell Holmes,♦ first published in *The Amateur* (1831) and reprinted in his *Poems* (1836), and, according to the poet, "suggested by the appearance in one of our streets of a venerable relic of the Revolution, said to be one of the party who threw the tea overboard in Boston Harbor." The subject is Major Thomas Melville, Herman Melville's grandfather, and the poet's smile leveled at him is not meant disrespectfully,

> But the old three-cornered hat,
> And the breeches, and all that,
> Are so queer!

Last of the Mohicans, *The,* romance by Cooper,♦ published in 1826, is the second of the Leather-Stocking Tales.♦

While the French and Indians besiege Fort William Henry on Lake George (1757), Cora and Alice Munro, daughters of the English commander, are on their way to join their father, accompanied by Major Duncan Heyward, Alice's fiancé, the singing teacher David Gamut, and the treacherous Indian Magua, who secretly serves the French. Magua's plan to betray the party to the Iroquois is foiled by the scout Hawkeye (Natty Bumppo) and his companions, old chief Chingachgook and his son Uncas, only survivors of the Mohican aristocracy. Escaping, Magua obtains Iroquois aid and returns to capture the girls. He promises them safety if Cora will become his squaw, but she refuses, and Hawkeye arrives to rescue them. Reaching the fort, they remain until Munro surrenders to Montcalm, who gives them a safe-conduct. When they leave they are set upon by Indians, and the sisters are captured. Hawkeye pursues them, finding Cora imprisoned in a Delaware camp and Alice in a Huron camp. Uncas is captured by the Hurons, and Heyward enters the camp in disguise, rescues Alice, and with Uncas escapes to the Delaware camp, where they are cordially received. Old chief Tamenund, learning Uncas's identity, hails him as his destined successor. Magua then claims Cora as his rightful property, and Uncas is unable to object, but, joined by the English, leads his tribe against the Hurons. When Magua attempts to desert, Uncas follows, and tries to rescue Cora. Uncas and Cora are killed, and Hawkeye shoots Magua, who falls from a precipice to his death. The others return to civilization, except for Hawkeye, who continues his frontier career.

Last Puritan, *The: A Memoir in the Form of a Novel,* by Santayana,♦ published in 1936.

Oliver Alden, in whom "puritanism worked itself out to its logical end," is the heir of a wealthy, effete New England family. His father, Peter, a drug addict, travels about the world on his yacht, vainly seeking a purpose in life to replace the dogmas of his puritanical brother Nathaniel, and of Harriet, his conventional, narrow-minded wife. Oliver grows up without understanding or love, reared by his mother and a sentimental German governess, Irma Schlote. A solemn, precocious child, he develops an athletic body, a passion for achieving the highest and best, and a keen intelligence, which soon begins to question the decadent society in which he lives. At 17 he accompanies his father on a cruise and finds a friend in Peter's paid companion, Jim Darnley, who is frankly animalistic and unscrupulous. Oliver attends Williams College, where he studies and plays football with equal zeal, since both are duties he must fulfill. After Peter's suicide, antagonized by Jim's parasitism, Oliver befriends Mario Van de Weyer, a cousin his father has helped to support. Educated on the Continent and at Eton, Mario is a cheerful hedonist, a dilettante of florid tastes, who sincerely appreciates Oliver's austere moral distinction but cannot admire his passionless approach to love with their cousin Edith. During a world tour following his graduation, Oliver stays with the Darnleys in England, falling in love with Jim's gentle sister Rose. Mario, who has joined the army at the outbreak of the World War, visits the Darnleys while on leave, and Rose falls in love with him, preferring his vitality to Oliver's ascetic intellectualism; but Mario does not realize this, and she is heartbroken. Oliver is meanwhile increasingly self-absorbed, obsessed by spiritual questionings that sap his strength and make him febrile and neurotic. Before entering the army, he asks Rose to marry him so that she may inherit his fortune, but she refuses. Willing his estate to the Darnleys, he leaves, dejected and hopeless, to be killed in France.

Last Tycoon, *The,* novel by F. Scott Fitzgerald, ♦ published in 1941. Left unrevised and incomplete at the author's death, it was edited for publication by Edmund Wilson. A large part of the novel's later plot was put together after his death from his notes.

Cecilia Brady, the daughter of a great motion-picture producer, reminisces about events that began five years earlier when she was an undergraduate at Bennington College, starting with a flight home to Hollywood on a plane whose other passengers include Wylie White, a script writer down on his luck, Manny Schwartz, once an influential film producer, and Monroe Stahr, another producer and a partner of Cecilia's father, Pat Brady. Cecilia becomes much attracted to Stahr, but he is caught up in an affair with an English woman. When the woman marries her fiancé, Stahr turns to Cecilia at the very time that

he has a falling out with her father and each of the partners conceives the idea of murdering the other. On the way to New York to establish an alibi, Stahr repents and decides to revoke his orders that will result in Brady's death, but his plane crashes before he can carry out his new plans, and Cecilia is deprived of both her father and the man she loves.

Late George Apley, *The,* novel by J.P. Marquand, ♦ published in 1937 and awarded a Pulitzer Prize. A dramatization by Marquand and George S. Kaufman ♦ was produced in 1944 and published in 1945.

Mr. Willing, contemporary and friend of the late George Apley, is requested by Apley's son John to describe his life in a book so that the conventional public eulogy may be amplified and humanized. The biography by Willing, based on family letters, adheres to the conventional attitudes it describes. It opens with Apley's birth in 1866 to a wealthy and socially prominent Boston family. His childhood is secure and serene, as he learns to move with the "right people" and to accept a family tradition of protective unity, as well as familial financial, charitable, and cultural responsibility. Apley displays a certain "erratic strain" of rebellion in school and at Harvard, but generally the "essential, undeviating discipline of background" prevails. He is taken into his father's club, works for a summer in the Apley textile mills, is admitted to the Law School, and emerges socially unscathed from an affection for a girl "from Central Square" by bowing to his father's opposition. He marries Catharine Bosworth, the girl of his family's choice, and becomes the father of John and Eleanor Apley. As they develop, his advice to and expectations of them increasingly resemble those of his father toward him. Personal inclinations are more and more subdued by a Puritan sense of duty, and even the desire to escape convention takes a conventional form as his retreat of Pequod Island becomes an exclusive resort. Apley's idealism leads him to attack civic corruption, but social prudence makes him accept a compromise when he is falsely implicated in a scandal. World War I and the Depression alter the tenor of American life and widen the gulf between Apley and his children, but he continues to find refuge in insularity as in a "safe . . . harbour."

LATHROP, George Parsons (1851–98), associate editor of the *Atlantic Monthly* (1875–77), wrote 15 books, ranging from travel accounts to society novels. Following his marriage to Rose Hawthorne, he wrote *A Study of Hawthorne* (1876), edited her father's works (1883), and in 1896 adapted *The Scarlet Letter* as a libretto for the opera by Damrosch. Lathrop and his wife became Roman Catholics, and after his death she became a nun under the name Mother Alphonsa.

Latter-Day Saints, see *Mormon.*

LATTIMORE, OWEN (1900–1989), brother of Richmond Lattimore, was a member of the Johns Hopkins faculty (1938–63) and of the University of Leeds in England (1963–70) but is also known for his government service. His writings on his travels, on geography and history, and on current events include *The Desert Road to Turkestan* (1929), *Manchuria, Cradle of Conflict* (1932), *Inner Asian Frontiers of China* (1940), *Solution in Asia* (1945), *The Situation in Asia* (1949), *Nationalism and Revolution in Mongolia* (1955), *Nomads and Commissars* (1962), and *History and Revolution in China* (1974). *Ordeal by Slander* (1950) describes the attack on him during the era of McCarthyism for his political views and his policy advice on China.

LATTIMORE, RICHMOND [ALEXANDER] (1906–84), brother of Owen Lattimore, after graduation from Dartmouth (1926) and a Rhodes scholarship did graduate work, and was a member of the Bryn Mawr faculty (1935–71). He is known for his translations, including *The Odes of Pindar* (1947), *The Iliad* (1951), *The Oresteia of Aeschylus* (1953), Aristophanes' *The Frogs* (1962), and Euripides' *Iphegenia* (1973), and for scholarly writings as well as his own poetry, including *The Stride of Time* (1966), *Poems from Three Decades* (1972), and *Continuing Conclusions* (1983).

LAUDONNIÈRE, RENÉ GOULAINÉ DE (*fl.*1562–82), French Huguenot navigator, with Jean Ribaut was sent to found an American colony, and settled the present Port Royal, S.C. After a revolt during the leaders' absence, another attempt was made at colonization on St. Johns River, Florida. Further dissension caused Laudonnière's purchase of a ship from Sir John Hawkins, to take his people home. When Ribaut arrived, shortly afterward, to bring supplies and an order for Laudonnière's return, the departure was forestalled by a fight with the Spanish, who massacred most of the colonists. Laudonnière managed to make his way to France, where he wrote *L'Histoire notable de la Floride* (1586), translated and published the following year in Hakluyt's *A Notable Historie.* Further information about the colony is found in a book by one of the colonists, Jacques Le Moyne, whose drawings of natives and animals are among the best of those made in early America, as well as in the account written by Ribaut.♦ A modern account is in Parkman's *Pioneers of France,* and he figures as a character in Kirk Munroe's *The Flamingo Feather.*

Laughing Boy, novel by Oliver La Farge,♦ was published in 1929 and won a Pulitzer Prize.

A young Navajo silversmith and horse trader, Laughing Boy, loves Slim Girl, who unlike him has been educated at an American school, and they elope despite the warning of his uncle, who hears from jealous Red Man that Slim Girl is a "bad woman." Far from Laughing Boy's people,

they live at the girl's cabin, where she weaves fine blankets and he makes silver jewelry, absorbed in their idyllic love and in saving money for the home of which they dream. During his horse-trading expeditions, Slim Girl continues to meet a white lover, whom she hates, but whose gifts will soon make possible a complete break with her unhappy past. Laughing Boy feels a gap between himself and Slim Girl, which even their love cannot bridge, but remains unaware of her infidelity until he surprises her with her lover, and shoots them both. Neither is fatally wounded, and Laughing Boy, matured by his disillusion, is reconciled with Slim Girl. They pack their possessions and begin a homeward trek, but during the journey Red Man shoots from ambush and kills Slim Girl. Purged of grief and vengefulness by his funeral vigil, Laughing Boy returns to the life of his tribe.

LAURENS, HENRY (1724–92), South Carolina planter and merchant, whose opposition to the Townshend acts caused him to publish *Some General Observations on American Custom House Officers and Courts of Vice-Admiralty* (1769). He was active in the Revolution, and served as president of the Continental Congress (Nov. 1777–Dec. 1778). On his way to Holland to negotiate a loan and treaty, he was captured by the British, and imprisoned for more than a year in the Tower of London, until exchanged for Cornwallis. The *Narrative* of his captivity was published with other papers in 1857.

LAURENTS, ARTHUR (1918–), born in New York and educated at Cornell, after army service began his career as playwright with *Home of the Brave* (1945), continued with *The Time of the Cuckoo* (1952) and several musical plays, including *West Side Story* (1957), an adaptation of *Romeo and Juliet* to a modern American socio-cultural view, and *Gypsy* (1959), as well as other dramas, including *Hallelulah, Baby* (1967). He has also written novels that include *The Way We Were* (1972) and *The Turning Point* (1977), as well as scenarios for films and radio plays, some of which he has directed.

Laus Deo!, poem by Whittier,♦ published in 1865. In six-line stanzas of predominantly four-stress lines, the work is the poet's joyous celebration of the passage of the 13th Amendment abolishing slavery, and was inspired by the "clang of bell and roar of gun" that announced the news (Dec. 18, 1865).

LA VÉRENDRYE, PIERRE GAULTIER DE VARENNES, Sieur de (1685–1749), French-Canadian explorer, after military service in America and Europe began in 1730 to explore western Canada, in return for a fur trade monopoly. With his sons and a nephew he built a fort on the site of Winnipeg (1738) and traveled overland to the upper Missouri. Two sons got as far west as the Black Hills (1742–43) and other expeditions went to the Saskatchewan and may have reached Wyoming. His *Journals and Letters* and his sons' were issued (1927).

LAWRENCE, D[AVID] H[ERBERT] (1885–1930), English novelist, poet, and critic, in 1915 began to consider U.S. sites for an ideal community, "Rananim." Interest in American culture led to his trenchant *Studies in Classic American Literature* (1923), essays on "The Spirit of Place" and eight authors from Franklin to Whitman. Early versions of the essays have been collected in *The Symbolic Meaning* (1962). In 1922 Lawrence and his wife Frieda moved to a ranch near Taos, N.M., and lived there until 1925, except for a long visit to Mexico. At Taos he finished *Kangaroo* (1923), wrote another novel, *The Plumed Serpent* (1926), the novelettes *St. Mawr* and *The Princess* (1925), "The Woman Who Rode Away" (1928) and other stories with American settings, and most of the essays in *Mornings in Mexico* (1927) and *Reflections on the Death of a Porcupine* (1934). Views of Lawrence in New Mexico are to be found in many memoirs, including *Lorenzo in Taos* (1932) by Mabel Dodge Luhan and *Journey with Genius* (1951) by Witter Bynner.

LAWRENCE, JOSEPHINE (1890–1978), New Jersey-born author of popular fiction, beginning in 1922 for children, but later for adults, mainly women, on various contemporary domestic and social issues. Her 33 novels include *If I Had Four Apples* (1935), *But You Are Young* (1940), *There Is Today* (1942), *Double Wedding Ring* (1946), *The Pleasant Morning Light* (1948), *My Heart Shall Not Fear* (1949), *Hearts Do Not Break* (1960), *Not a Cloud in the Sky* (1964), *Retreat with Honor* (1973), and *Under One Roof* (1975).

LAWSON, JAMES (1799–1880), Scottish-born businessman and author in New York, contributed verse and articles to magazines, and was a friend of Poe, Simms, and Paulding. His books, published anonymously, include *Ontwa, the Son of the Forest* (1822), a verse narrative of Indian warfare; *Tales and Sketches, by a Cosmopolite* (1830), sentimental stories with a Scottish background; *Poems* (1857); *Liddesdale* (1874), a blank-verse tragedy concerned with Indians; and *The Maiden's Oath* (1877), a domestic tragedy.

LAWSON, JOHN (*d.*1711), English explorer, came to the Carolinas (1700) and later traveled some 1000 miles through unexplored land in the Carolinas and Georgia. His minute records were issued as *A New Voyage to Carolina* (1709), reprinted as *The History of Carolina* (1714, 1718), mixing folklore and science. After seeing the book through the press in London, he returned to be surveyor-general of North Carolina and, with a Swiss adventurer, to found a colony of Palatines, but he was killed by Indians.

LAWSON, JOHN HOWARD (1895–1977), New York dramatist, whose first plays, *Roger Bloomer* (1923) and *Processional* (1925), are noteworthy examples of Expressionism. His later plays, which also show his interest in the proletarian movement, are *Loud Speaker* (1927), a farce about American politics; *The International* (1928), depicting a future world revolution of workers; *Success Story* (1932), a character study of a man who gains material power at the expense of his soul; *The Pure in Heart* (1934), concerned with the struggles of a small-town girl in New York, and her love for a convict; *Gentlewoman* (1934), a study of a rich woman who attempts an unsuccessful compromise between her love of wealth and her sympathy with the poor; and *Marching Song* (1937), concerned with a sit-down strike. Lawson's nonfiction writings include *Theory and Technique of Playwriting* (1936) and *Film in the Battle of Ideas* (1953). His motion-picture work led to *Film: The Creative Process* (1964). As one of the Hollywood Ten who refused to answer questions put by the Congressional Committee on Un-American Activities, he was jailed for a year, and thereafter forced to have his scripts issued under a pseudonym.

LAWSON, THOMAS W[ILLIAM] (1857–1925), multimillionaire Boston stockbroker, because of a grudge wrote muckraking articles on "Frenzied Finance" for *Everybody's* (1904–5) and other books on the subject, including *Friday, the Thirteenth* (1907), a novel. His clients turned on him and began the downfall that left him a poor man.

LAZARUS, EMMA (1849–87), New York poet, best known for her *Songs of a Semite* (1882), which includes the poetic drama "The Dance to Death," about 12th-century Thuringian Jews and constitutes an impassioned answer to the persecution of her race in Russia. She also wrote *Admetus and Other Poems* (1871); *Alide* (1874), a romance based on the life of Goethe; and *By the Waters of Babylon* (1887). She translated the *Poems and Ballads of Heine* (1881), and her collected *Poems* appeared in 1889. Miss Lazarus's love of the U.S. as a refuge for the oppressed is expressed in her sonnet to the Statue of Liberty, which was carved on the pedestal of the statue.

Lazarus Laughed, poetic drama by O'Neill,♦ produced in 1928 but published in 1927. This mystic affirmation of life employs masked choruses.

LEA, HENRY CHARLES (1825–1909), Philadelphia publisher and historian, whose first book, *Superstition and Force* (1866), a history of jurisprudence, led him into a lifetime study of the Catholic Church and its influence on medieval institutions, resulting in such books as *Studies in Church History* (1869), *A History of the Inquisition of the Middle Ages* (3 vols., 1888), *A History of the Inquisi-*

tion of Spain (4 vols., 1906–7), and *The Inquisition in the Spanish Dependencies* (1908). Besides other scholarly work, Lea engaged in many philanthropies, was active in politics, and aided such reforms as those in the civil service and copyright law.

LEA, HOMER (1876–1912), born in Colorado, educated in California, early decided on a military career even though he was a hunchback. In 1899 he went to China and took part in the relief of Peking during the Boxer Uprising. His strategy so impressed the Chinese that he became a general and a leader in the revolution under Sun Yat-sen. His writings include *The Valor of Ignorance* (1909), warning the U.S. against a coming Japanese attack, and *The Day of the Saxon* (1912), a comparable notice to the British of Oriental threats to the empire.

***Leather Stocking and Silk:** or, Hunter John Myers and His Times,* romance by J.E. Cooke,♦ published in 1854.

Set in Martinsburg (Williamsburg), Va., at the beginning of the 19th century, this comedy of manners has as protagonists the bourgeois and aristocratic classes of the region. Hunter John is a veteran frontiersman patterned after the middle-aged Natty Bumppo, but his Meadow Branch home is an outpost of Martinsburg society, rather than a backwoods establishment. His daughter Sally has the leading role in an amateur production of *Romeo and Juliet,* and the Romeo is young Max Cortlandt, who loves Nina Von Horn, and thus there begins the plot of romantic intrigue, involving William Lyttelton, an attorney, and Hans Huddleshingle, an unpopular aristocrat, both in love with Nina. Nina becomes engaged to Lyttelton, Huddleshingle is disgraced by his attempt to prevent the marriage, and Max is heartbroken and honorably disappears. Lyttelton dies, and five years later Nina, an accomplished woman of the world, weds Max, who has taken the name Dr. Thomas. At the same time, Sally Myers and Nina's cousin Barry, who have grown up together, are married. The narrative skips to the second generation, with old Hunter John happy among his children and grandchildren. Nina has died, Max is remarried, and his son weds Sally's daughter.

Leather-Stocking Tales, series of five novels by Cooper,♦ depicting the life of the early American frontier, and deriving its title from the nickname of the hero Natty Bumppo, so called because of his long deerskin leggings. The novels in order of composition are *The Pioneers* (1823), *The Last of the Mohicans* (1826), *The Prairie* (1827), *The Pathfinder* (1840), and *The Deerslayer* (1841). Their sequence in relation to plot is *Deerslayer,*♦ *Last of the Mohicans,*♦ *Pathfinder,*♦ *Pioneers,*♦ *Prairie.*♦ The hero is known by the following names: "Bumppo" or "Deerslayer" in *Deerslayer;* "Hawk-eye" in *Last of the Mohicans;* "Pathfinder" in *Pathfinder;* "Natty Bumppo" or "Leather-Stocking" in *Pioneers;* and "the trapper" in *Prairie.* His character remains strikingly consistent throughout the series, which treats his life and adventures from youth to old age and death. The perfect woodsman, who dislikes the restraints and destructiveness of settlements, he understands and loves the forest, and his moral qualities are as great as his understanding. Generous both to friends and to enemies, he possesses a simple, staunch morality, and a cool nerve and never-failing resourcefulness.

***Leavenworth Case,** The,* novel by Anna Katharine Green.♦

Leaves of Grass, poems by Whitman,♦ the first edition of which (1855) contained 12 poems, including those later entitled "Song of Myself,"♦ "I Sing the Body Electric,"♦ and "There Was a Child Went Forth."♦ The first edition was anonymous and had a preface, later omitted, in which the author declares that the ideal poet must be a complete lover of the universe, draw his materials from nature, as a seer reveal the cosmic plan which harmoniously unites past, present, and future, be commensurate with his nation, and in America serve as representative of the common people, differing from them only in his superior vision. He is to discover what is permanent in flux, explain its development, and be a realist in his art. His style is to be simple and natural, without such ornamentation as conventional rhyme or meter, since it must have an organic growth like that of a perfect animal or tree, in which each part is in proportion and harmonious with the whole.

The second edition (1856) contained 33 poems, including "Salut au Monde,"♦ "By Blue Ontario's Shore,"♦ "Crossing Brooklyn Ferry,"♦ "Spontaneous Me,"♦ and "Song of the Broad-Axe,"♦ as well as a fulsome reply to the author's "dear Friend and Master," Emerson, in acknowledgment of a laudatory letter which is reprinted.

The third edition (1860) was enlarged to 456 pages, containing 122 new poems, including "Starting from Paumanok"♦ and "Out of the Cradle Endlessly Rocking"♦ and two new sections, "Calamus"♦ and "Children of Adam."♦ The latter contains "Facing West from California's Shores"♦ and "Once I Pass'd Through a Populous City."♦

The fourth edition (1867) reprints, in the copies that came last from the press, those poems published as *Drum-Taps*♦ (1865) and *Sequel to Drum-Taps* (1865–66), including the poems on the death of Lincoln, "When Lilacs Last in the Door Yard Bloom'd"♦ and "O Captain! My Captain!"♦; the statement of religion, "Chanting the Square Deific"♦; and "Pioneers! O Pioneers!"♦ and "One's-Self I Sing."♦

The fifth edition (1871) was a reprint, with some copies having as annexes "After All Not To

Create Only," published separately as an ode for the American Institute; and "Passage to India." ◆

The sixth edition (1876), known as the Author's or Centennial Edition, was in two volumes, the first a reprint of the 1871 edition without the annexes, and the second entitled *Two Rivulets,* ◆ containing the annexes to the 1871 edition and other poems and prose. This edition contained a new preface, not later retained, expounding the plan and purpose of the poems.

The seventh edition (1881–82), containing 20 new poems and organizing all poems in groups that represent his final order, was first published in Boston, but, because of official protests against asserted indecency, was withdrawn and reissued by a Philadelphia publisher.

The eighth edition (1889), a special pocket edition, reprinted the poems of *November Boughs* (1888) as "Sands at Seventy," and, as epilogue, the prose preface of that book, "A Backward Glance o'er Travel'd Roads." ◆

The final edition under the author's supervision (1891–92) included "Old Age Echoes," as well as two annexes, "Good-Bye, My Fancy" (separately issued, 1891) and "A Backward Glance o'er Travel'd Roads."

The standard edition was prepared by the author's executors as part of his *Complete Writings* (10 vols., 1902).

LE CONTE, JOSEPH (1823–1901), studied at Harvard under Agassiz and was a professor of natural sciences at several Southern universities before becoming professor of geology, zoology, and botany at the University of California (1869–1901). His most important work was concerned with the origins of mountain systems, and he was an early supporter of the theories of Darwin and Lyell. His many publications include *Religion and Science* (1874), *Elements of Geology* (1878, frequently revised), *Evolution and Its Relation to Religious Thought* (1888), *Outlines of the Comparative Physiology and Morphology of Animals* (1900), an *Autobiography* (1903), and a journal of experiences in the Confederate army, *'Ware Sherman* (1937). Some of his theories influenced Frank Norris, a student in his classes.

Ledger, see *New York Ledger.*

Led-Horse Claim, The: A Romance of a Mining Camp, novel by Mary Hallock Foote, ◆ published in 1883.

Cecil Conrath, sister of the superintendent of the Shoshone mine in Colorado, meets Hilgard, superintendent of the rival Led-Horse mine, and they fall in love, although the affair is hindered by enmity between the personnel of the two enterprises. Conrath secretly pushes his shafts into the Led-Horse claim, and attempts to jump it, but Hilgard's men defend their property, and in a skirmish Conrath is supposedly killed. Although the shooting was justified, and it is not certain that Hilgard fired the fatal shot, Cecil refuses to marry him. He goes to New York, falls ill, and is saved from death only by Cecil's arrival to nurse him. Her family disapproves, but the two are married. Later her brother is found to have escaped, continued his criminal career, and not to have died until long afterward.

LEDYARD, JOHN (1751–89), abandoned his studies at Dartmouth to go to the Mediterranean, and subsequently accompanied Cook to the Sandwich Islands, where he made acute observations on the people and their society, publishing *A Journal of Captain Cook's Last Voyage to the Pacific Ocean* (1783). Prior to his return to America (1782), Ledyard was in the British navy and went to Cadiz. He next made his way on foot across Europe and Russia until he was seized in Irkutsk (eastern Siberia), where he was briefly imprisoned (1788) as a supposed spy. There he wrote an informal journal of recollections and anthropological information deduced from his travels. Returning to London, he began a trip to Africa, but died at Cairo.

LEE, ANN (1736–84), known as Mother Ann, was the leader of the sect called The United Society of Believers in Christ's Second Coming, commonly called Shakers because of its members' physical manifestations of spiritual influence during worship. She emigrated from her native England to America (1774) to preach against war, oaths, and sexual relations. Her New England tour (1781) aroused much antagonism because her followers accepted her as the second coming of Christ and because she claimed the gifts of discerning spirits and working miracles.

LEE, ARTHUR (1740–92), member of the famous Virginia family, was educated at Eton and Edinburgh (M.D., 1764), practiced medicine at Williamsburg, and went to London (1768) to study law and prepare for his diplomatic career. In the *Virginia Gazette* (1768), he published "The Monitor's Letters," which supplemented Dickinson's *Letters from a Farmer,* and he continued his literary contributions to the colonial cause in other letters and in *An Appeal to the Justice and Interests of the People of Great Britain* (1774) and *A Second Appeal* (1775). As a result of these pamphlets, he was appointed the London agent for Massachusetts (1770–75) and secret agent of the Continental Congress (1775). With Franklin and Silas Deane he was appointed (1776) to negotiate a treaty of alliance with France, and to solicit aid for the Revolution. Although they accomplished their ends, Lee and his colleagues were troubled by constant friction because his vivid imagination led him to accuse them of treason and fraud, when at worst they were guilty only of errors.

RICHARD HENRY LEE (1732–94), his brother, was also a distinguished Revolutionary patriot whose service in the House of Burgesses (1758–

75) included work with Patrick Henry and Jefferson for radical measures. In the Continental Congress he signed the Declaration of Independence. He opposed the Constitution mainly because it had no bill of rights. His views were set forth in two pamphlets printing "Letters of the Federal Farmer," respectively *Observations . . .* (1787) and *An Additional Number of Letters . . .* (1788), which were the chief literary opposition to *The Federalist.* After the ratification, he was elected a U.S. senator (1789–92), and was instrumental in the passage of the Bill of Rights, being himself the author of the 10th Amendment.

LEE, ELIZA BUCKMINSTER (*c.*1788–1864), New Hampshire author, whose works include *Sketches of a New England Village* (1838), *Delusion; or, The Witch of New England* (1840), *Naomi: or, Boston Two-Hundred Years Ago* (1848), and translations from Richter and other German authors to whom she had been introduced as a follower of Carlyle. Her *Memoirs* of her father, Joseph Buckminster, and her brother Joseph Stevens Buckminster♦ were published in 1849.

LEE, [NELLE] HARPER (1926–   ), Alabama author, educated at the state university, won a Pulitzer Prize with the publication of her first novel, *To Kill a Mockingbird* (1960). The plot turns on the sensational trial of a black man charged with raping a white woman, as seen through the eyes of the young daughter of the white defense lawyer.

LEE, HENRY (1756–1818), known as "Light-Horse Harry," was an officer in the Revolutionary War, whose cavalry and infantry, known as "Lee's Legion," won a notable victory at Paulus Hook near New York and was active in the Southern campaign. After the war, he was governor of Virginia (1792–95) and headed the army that quelled the Whiskey Rebellion in Pennsylvania. As a member of Congress, he wrote the *Resolutions* on the death of Washington (Dec. 26, 1799), containing the words, "first in war, first in peace, and first in the hearts of his countrymen." His *Memoirs of the War . . .* were published in 1812. He was the father of Robert E. Lee.

LEE, RICHARD HENRY, see *Lee, Arthur.*

LEE, ROBERT E[DWARD] (1807–70), son of Henry Lee, was born in Virginia, graduated from West Point (1829), and served as an army engineer and as an officer in the Mexican War. He was superintendent of West Point (1852–55), and commanded a cavalry regiment in Texas, although he spent much time at his Virginia home, Arlington, and commanded the troops that suppressed John Brown's raid on Harpers Ferry. Although he sympathized with the Union cause and hoped for a successful compromise, Lee was determined not to fight against his own state. He

was offered the field command of the Union army by Lincoln, but declined, resigned his post, and became commander of the Virginia troops in the Confederate army. He shortly became a general and military adviser to President Davis. He was successful in the Seven Days Battles which checked McClellan, and in the second Battle of Bull Run and the battles of Antietam, Fredericksburg, and Chancellorsville. His second attempt to invade the North was checked in the Battle of Gettysburg♦ (July 1863), following which he attempted to resign but was persuaded to continue in command. Thereafter he fought courageously in the battles of the Wilderness, Spottsylvania, and Cold Harbor. Appointed commander in chief of the Confederate forces in February 1865, he was forced to surrender at Appomattox. After the war he served as president of Washington College (Virginia), which was renamed Washington and Lee in his honor (1871). Lee has won universal admiration for his sincerity, chivalry, and courage. The best-known biography is that by D.S. Freeman (4 vols., 1934–35), but he figures in much literature, Northern as well as Southern, e.g. Masters's *Lee: A Dramatic Poem* (1926) and MacKinlay Kantor's novel *Long Remember* (1934); John Reuben Thompson's poem "Lee to the Rear" and Mary Johnston's novel *Cease Firing* (1912).

LEECH, MARGARET [KERNOCHAN] (1893–1974), New York author, graduate of Vassar (1915), whose books include *The Back of the Book* (1924) and *Tin Wedding* (1926), novels; *Roundsman of the Lord* (1927), a biography of Anthony Comstock written with Heywood Broun; *Reveille in Washington* (1941, Pulitzer Prize), a lively account of the capital during the Civil War; and *In the Days of McKinley* (1959, Pulitzer Prize).

LEEDS, TITAN (1699–1738), Philadelphia publisher of *The American Almanack,* mainly remembered as the victim of a hoax by Benjamin Franklin. In *Poor Richard's Almanack* (1733), Franklin predicted Leeds's death, "on Oct. 17, 1733, 3 hr. 29 m., P.M." Despite Leeds's denial, dated October 18, Franklin in his almanac declared "there is the strongest probability that my dear friend is no more. . . . Mr. Leeds was too well bred to use any man so indecently and so scurrilously" as Poor Richard had been in Leeds's protest. The amusing controversy, inspired by the "Bickerstaff" hoax of Swift (1708), continued until the actual death of Leeds.

DANIEL LEEDS (1652–1720), his father, had established the family reputation as almanac makers by his annual publications begun in 1687. Although originally a Quaker, he later wrote pamphlets accusing George Fox of forgeries and William Penn of concealing evidence of them.

LEFFLAND, ELLA (1931–   ), born and reared in the backwater area east of San Francisco Bay, the setting of some of her fiction, whose novels include *Mrs. Munck* (1970), the story of a woman in her forties meanly victimized by a double standard; *Love Out of Season* (1974), presenting a woman's experiences in San Francisco's frenetic Beat world of the 1960s; and *Rumors of Peace* (1979), depicting a girl of grammar-school age growing up during World War II. The author has long lived in San Francisco but over an eight-year period of work on *The Knight, Death and the Devil* (1990) she visited Germany three times and presented a life of Göring and the Hitler-steeped Germany of his era. The far earlier *Last Courtesies* (1980) collects stories.

LE GALLIENNE, Richard (1866–1947), English journalist, essayist, poet, and novelist, was originally associated with the *fin de siècle* aesthetes. His early verse and epigrammatic prose show the influence of Oscar Wilde. After settling in the U.S. (1903), he modified his early preciosity, although his work continued to indicate his allegiance to the English school of the 1890s. His books include *My Ladies' Sonnets* (1887) and *The Lonely Dancer* (1913), poems; *The Quest of the Golden Girl* (1896), a prose fantasy; *Orestes* (1910), a tragedy; *The Romantic Nineties* (1925), his literary reminiscences; and anthologies exhibiting the tastes of his own period.

Eva Le Gallienne (1899–1991), his daughter, was born in London, where she made her stage debut in 1915. She founded (1926), managed, directed, and acted at New York's Civic Repertory Theatre. *At 33* (1934) and *With a Quiet Heart* (1953) are memoirs.

LEGARÉ, Hugh Swinton (1797–1843), South Carolina lawyer and statesman, served as U.S. attorney general under Tyler, and as secretary of state *ad interim* (1843) upon the resignation of Webster. He was the great champion of Charleston literature, and his critical opinions had a profound effect upon the Southern cultural renaissance, which was partly expressed in his *Southern Review* (1828–32). His miscellaneous writings were collected in two volumes (1845–46).

Legend of Sleepy Hollow, The, short story by Irving,♦ possibly based on a German source. It was published in *The Sketch Book* (1820). An operetta, *The Headless Horseman* (1936), with music by Douglas Moore and libretto by Stephen Vincent Benét, is based on it.

Ichabod Crane, an assertive, ingenuous Yankee schoolmaster, lanky and angular in appearance, lives among the Dutch folk of Sleepy Hollow on the Hudson, in post-Revolutionary days. He loves Katrina Van Tassel, daughter of a rich farmer, and is the victim of many pranks by the friends of his chief rival for her affections, Brom Van Brunt or Brom Bones, a reckless horseman and neighborhood hero. At an autumn quilting party at Van Tassel's, the guests entertain themselves with stories of ghosts and witches, and Brom tells of the headless horseman said to haunt the region. Ichabod is discouraged in his suit for Katrina, and on his way home, late at night, riding a borrowed plow horse, is frightened by a headless apparition that rides after him and throws a round object at his head. Ichabod is never again seen in Sleepy Hollow, although the next morning the round object is discovered to be a pumpkin. Brom marries Katrina, and Ichabod's tale becomes a legend of the countryside.

Legends of the Province House, see *Twice-Told Tales.*

LEGGETT, William (1802?–39), was assistant editor and part owner of the New York *Evening Post* (1829–36) under Bryant, in which capacity he advocated Jacksonian principles and was an oracle of radical Democrats and Abolitionists. In 1836 he established *The Plaindealer,* in which he continued his trenchant editorial policy. *Leisure Hours at Sea* (1825) and *Journals of the Ocean* (1826) were volumes of poetry which grew out of his early life as a midshipman, and *Naval Stories* (1834) was a prose collection. His short stories concerned with the West were published as *Tales and Sketches. By a Country Schoolmaster* (1829), and his *Political Writings* were collected in two volumes (1840).

Legrand, William, character in "The Gold-Bug."♦

Legree, Simon, character in *Uncle Tom's Cabin.*♦

LE GUIN, Ursula K. (1929–), born in Berkeley, Calif., daughter of the distinguished anthropologist of the university, Alfred Louis Kroeber, graduated from Radcliffe, has lived in Portland. Since 1966 she has written science fiction for young people, including *A Wizard of Earthsea* (1968), *The Tombs of Atuan* (1971), and *The Farthest Shore* (1972), a trilogy shaped by Taoist philosophy in which the character of Ged in volume one is succeeded by a girl priestess in volume two and by Ged's apprentice Arren in the third volume; a tetron was completed with a fourth volume, *Tehanua* (1990). In addition to romantic novels, she has also published volumes of poetry, *Wild Angels* (1974) and *Hard Words* (1981); collections of essays, including *Dramas Must Explain Themselves* (1975) and *The Language of the Night* (1978); and short stories, *The Wind's Twelve Quarters* (1975), *Orsinian Tales* (1976), *Interfaces* (1980), and *The Compass Rose* (1982). She has also written novels of distinction: *The Dispossessed* (1975), contrasting imperfect utopias; *Tenth Millennium: The Beginning Place* (1979), depicting a young girl and boy terrified by passing events; and *Always Coming Home* (1986), about the impact of earlier days upon living persons.

Leicester, romantic tragedy by William Dunlap, ♦ produced in 1794 as *The Fatal Deception* and published under the present title (1807).

Matilda persuades her paramour, Henry Cecil, to murder his friend Leicester. Instead, he mistakenly stabs his own brother Dudley, who with his wife Edwina has sought refuge with him after slaying another brother. Edwina goes mad, accusing herself of the murder of her husband, while Matilda commits suicide and Henry kills himself with Leicester's sword. Leicester, pardoning his fellow sinners, departs.

LEISLER, JACOB (1640–91), German-born settler of New York, in 1689 led an anti-Catholic group to seize the government and name him lieutenant-governor. Although he acted as de facto governor, he was not recognized by the Crown, and a new governor and military commission were dispatched, whose conflict with Leisler almost brought about a civil war. After a trial for treason, he was hanged. For several decades, the colony's politics continued to be split between Leislerians and Anti-Leislerians. He figures in the historical plays, *Jacob Leisler* (1848) by Cornelius Mathews, and *Old New York, or Democracy in 1689* (1853) by Elizabeth Smith, as well as in Ingraham's romantic novel *Leisler; or, The Rebel and the King's Man* (1846), and E.L. Bynner's *The Begum's Daughter* (1890).

Leisure Class, Theory of the, see *Theory of the Leisure Class.*

LELAND, CHARLES GODFREY (1824–1903), Philadelphia author and editor, whose early teachers included Bronson Alcott, attended the College of New Jersey and universities in Heidelberg and Munich. His first book, *Meister Karl's Sketch-Book* (1855), was halfway between the Irving tradition and his own dialect humor, which asserted itself in "Hans Breitmann's Barty," published in *Graham's Magazine* (May 1857) during his brief editorship. He continued to write amusing dialect poems, which were finally gathered in *Hans Breitmann's Ballads* (1914). He edited *Vanity Fair* (1860–61), *The Knickerbocker Magazine* (1861), and a strong Union paper, *The Continental Monthly* (1862–63). His many activities included the study of gypsy lore and language, about which he wrote; Roman historical and literary scholarship; the study of Indian legends; mystic and occult knowledge; and the introduction of industrial education in public schools.

Leni-Lenape, see *Delaware Indians.*

Lennie Small, character in *Of Mice and Men.* ♦

LENNOX, CHARLOTTE RAMSAY (1720–1804), born in New York, was sent to England at the age of 15, and during her long life there won a literary reputation, mainly for her sentimental novels of manners. Her most successful work, *The Female Quixote; or, The Adventures of Arabella* (1752), however, burlesqued the lengthy French romances by telling of the adventures of a girl who molded her life on such works. She dramatized this as *Angelica; or, Quixote in Petticoats* (1758). *The Life of Harriot Stuart* (1750), *The History of Henrietta* (1758), *Sophia* (1762), and *Euphemia* (1790) resemble the romances she burlesqued in her satire, and the first and last are set partly in America. Her other books include *The Sister* (1769), a dramatization of *Henrietta; Old City Manners* (1775), a modernization of John Marston's *Eastward Hoe;* and *Shakespear Illustrated* (1753). She was a friend of Johnson, Richardson, Fielding, and Garrick.

Lenore, lyrical ballad by Poe, ♦ published as "A Paean" in *Poems* (1831) and considerably revised in later versions (1836, 1843). In four stanzas of seven-stress lines, preserving the fundamental ballad rhythm, it celebrates the death of the poet's beloved:

> Ah, broken is the golden bowl!—the spirit
> flown forever!
> Let the bell toll!—a saintly soul floats on the
> Stygian river.

LENOX, JAMES (1800–1880), heir to one of New York's greatest fortunes, spent much of his mature life in philanthropy, including the creation of the Lenox Library for his great collection of incunabula, Bibles, English literature, and for other sources of scholarship, including his own historical and bibliographical studies. Samuel Allibone was his librarian, and the library itself has become part of the New York Public Library. Henry Stevens, the bookseller, wrote *Recollections of Mr. James Lenox of New York and the Formation of His Library* (1886).

LEONARD, DANIEL (1740–1829), Loyalist writer, contributed to *The Massachusetts Gazette and Post-Boy* a series of articles, signed Massachusettsis, which in that critical period (Dec. 1774–April 1775) was said by John Adams to shine among the Tory writings "like the moon among the lesser stars." Adams replied to these letters under the pseudonym Novanglus in *The Boston Gazette.* During the Revolution, Leonard fled to Halifax and England, and was rewarded with the office of Chief Justice of Bermuda.

LEONARD, WILLIAM ELLERY (1876–1944), New Jersey-born professor of English for many years at the University of Wisconsin. In addition to scholarly works and translations of Lucretius and *Beowulf* he published a large body of poetry which, though often conventional in form and traditional in diction, is marked by a passionate intensity, and a revelation of personal situations seen psychologically. His first volume, *Sonnets and Poems* (1906), was followed by *The Vaunt of*

Man (1912); *The Lynching Bee* (1920), showing his concern with social injustice; *Two Lives* (1922); *Tutankhamen and After* (1924); *A Son of Earth* (1928), selected poems; *This Midland City* (1930); and *A Man Against Time, An Heroic Dream* (1945), a sonnet sequence. *Two Lives,* reprinted (1925) from its private edition, is a sonnet sequence frankly describing his romance with the young woman who became his wife and who killed herself. *Red Bird* (1923) is a drama of Wisconsin pioneering. He wrote his autobiography, *The Locomotive-God* (1927), in psychoanalytic terms, describing his "fear of spatial distance from a centre of safety."

LEONARD, ZENAS (1809–57), trapper and trader, whose *Narrative of the Adventures of Zenas Leonard* (1839) is a valuable source on the life of the trapper and on Walker's expedition to California (1833), of which he was a member. He later entered the Indian and Santa Fe trade.

LEOPOLD, ALDO (1887–1948), conservationist. Born in Iowa, Leopold began his professional career with the U.S. Forest Service. In 1933 he published a landmark conservation textbook, and the same year the University of Wisconsin created a chair of game management for him. He was a co-founder of the Wilderness Society in 1935. His articles in various periodicals were gathered and published posthumously as *A Sand County Almanac* (1949), an influential book with a theme of "land ethic" that has sold over a million copies. Leopold was posthumously awarded the John Burroughs Medal for his life's work in 1978. He died fighting a grass fire on a neighbor's farm shortly after becoming adviser on conservation to the U.N. *The Wisconsin State Journal* wrote, "His shadow has come to be the conscience of the monster ambition to make a great pinball machine of the world."

LERNER, ALAN JAY (1918–86), born in New York City, after graduation from Harvard (1940) met Frederick Loewe (1904–88), an Austrian-born composer, for whose music he wrote lyrics in their successful collaboration on musical comedies including *Brigadoon* (1947); *My Fair Lady* (1956), adapted from Shaw's *Pygmalion; Camelot* (1960), based on T.H. White's Arthurian tale *The Once and Future King;* and the motion picture *Gigi* (1958), based on the story by Colette. *The Street Where I Live* (1978) is a memoir. *The Musical Theatre* (1986) follows the London and New York musical stages from the 19th century.

LERNER, MAX (1902–92), Russian-born political scientist, teacher, and editor, graduate of Yale (1923), was an editor of *The Encyclopaedia of the Social Sciences,* and as a "neo-Marxian liberal" wrote essays on a variety of subjects. His books include *It Is Later Than You Think* (1938); *Ideas Are Weapons* (1939); *Ideas for the Ice Age* (1941);

The Mind and Faith of Justice Holmes (1943), selections from Holmes's writings; *Public Journal* (1945) and *Actions and Passions* (1949), editorials written for the New York paper *P.M.; America as a Civilization, Life and Thought in the United States Today* (1957); *The Unfinished Country* (1959), collecting his columns from the New York *Post; The Age of Overkill; A Preface to World Politics* (1963); *Values in Education* (1976); and *Ted and the Kennedy Legend* (1980).

Les Jeunes, see *Lark, The.*

LESLIE, ELIZA (1787–1858), Philadelphia author and editor, whose stories, juvenile tales, and books of advice were immensely popular in her time. *Amelia, or a Young Lady of Vicissitudes* (1848) was the only one approaching the dimensions of a novel, and her reputation was mainly based on magazine pieces, such as "Mrs. Washington Potts," which won a prize in *Godey's Lady's Book.* She published three series of *Pencil Sketches, or, Outlines of Character and Manners* (1833, 1835, 1837).

LESLIE, FRANK (1821–80), the assumed name of Henry Carter, English-born engraver and publisher of illustrated journals, emigrated to New York (1848), and there had a great success with such magazines as *Frank Leslie's Popular Monthly,* ◆ which he founded in 1876. This was partly due to his method of illustrating current events, dividing his drawings into blocks to be distributed among several engravers and afterward reassembled. In this way, his illustrations reached the public long before those of his competitors.

MIRIAM F. LESLIE (1836–1914), his widow, previously married to Ephraim Squier ◆ and subsequently to Oscar Wilde's brother Willie, carried on Leslie's business with great ingenuity and success, even legally adopting his name. She wrote many books, including the travel account *California: A Pleasure Trip from Gotham to the Golden Gate* (1877), and such feminist pleas as *A Social Mirage* (1899).

LE SUEUR, MERIDEL (1900–), journalist, novelist, poet. Child of a lawyer of the radical left, Le Sueur was born in Iowa and raised in Texas, Oklahoma, and Kansas. She quit high school and lived in a New York City socialist commune, where she met Emma Goldman. She was a factory worker and contributor to the *Daily Worker* and *The New Masses.* Her novel *The Girl* (1939) and *Salute to Spring and Other Stories* (1940) portray hardships of women in the Depression. *North Star Country* (1945) is based on her midwestern childhood experiences, and *Crusaders* (1955) is an account of, and tribute to, her parents. She was hounded during the McCarthy era of communist witchhunts in the early 1950s and published mainly journalism for the next 20 years. She tells of her struggles during this period in *Song for My Time: Stories of the Period of Repression* (1977). Other nonfiction works are *Conquistadors* (1973); *The Mound Builders* (1974); a book of poems, *Rites of Ancient Ripening* (1975); *Women on the Breadlines* (1977); and *I Hear Men Talking and Other Stories* (1984). *Ripening: Selected Work 1927–1980* was published in 1982.

Let Us Now Praise Famous Men, nonfictional work by James Agee♦ with photographs by Walker Evans, published in 1941. Commissioned (1936) by *Fortune* magazine, it was rejected because the collaborators could not treat their subject in a conventional journalistic fashion. Instead they converted and expanded their assignment on cotton tenantry in the U.S. to reveal the ways of life and the personalities of the members of three families in warm, personal terms. Almost 50 years later a sequel was created by Dale Maharidge♦ and Michael Williamson.

Letter to the Sheriffs of Bristol, by Edmund Burke, published in 1777. After the parliamentary defeat of a resolution for the revision of all acts which antagonized the American colonies, members of the British Whig party withdrew on all questions relating to America. This partial secession called forth Burke's letter, which elaborately defended his opposition to the government measures and reaffirmed the principles of his speeches *On American Taxation*♦ and *On Conciliation with the American Colonies.*♦

***Letters from a Farmer in Pennsylvania* to the Inhabitants of the British Colonies,** by John Dickinson,♦ published in the *Pennsylvania Chronicle* (1767–68) and reprinted as a pamphlet (1768). In these letters, Dickinson applied the political philosophy of Locke to the objections to British taxation. He contends that as the authority of government rests on a social compact and its object is the protection of the inalienable right of property, any attempt at external, arbitrary taxation is contrary to English principles and law. In a clear, sober style, he urges the colonists to attempt legal petition, then boycott, and finally, if peaceable methods fail, force of arms.

Letters from an American Farmer, 12 essays by Crèvecœur,♦ published in London in 1782 under the pseudonym J. Hector St. John. These charming and informative essays sketch the physical and social conditions of American rural life. The author fluctuates between the lover of nature and Rousseauistic idealist, and the realistic farmer writing of hard, unpleasant facts. As a theorist, he was ecstatic concerning America as an asylum for the oppressed and a melting pot for many races; as a farmer he described the frontier as it actually was, the difficulties of agriculture, and the warfare between different parts of animal nature. Half of the letters are concerned with the

education, employment, manners, and customs of Americans at Nantucket, Martha's Vineyard, Charleston, and elsewhere. The third answers the question "What is an American?" by stating that, as the product of the melting pot, he is a man who acts on new principles, and must therefore entertain new ideas. The eleventh letter describes a visit to John Bartram, and the last depicts the difficulties of a "frontier man," menaced on one side by savages, and on the other by the unsettled conditions of a Revolution in which he agrees with neither of the opposed groups.

Letters of Fabius, see *Dickinson, John.*

Letters of Jonathan Oldstyle, Gent., see *Irving, Washington.*

Letters of the British Spy, ten Addisonian essays by William Wirt,♦ published in 1803. Purportedly from an English traveler to a member of Parliament, they present a vivid picture of life in the contemporary Southern states of the U.S.

Letters of the Federal Farmer, see *Lee, Richard Henry.*

LEVERTOV, DENISE (1923–), born in England of a Welsh mother and a Russian-Jewish father who became an Anglican clergyman, was educated at home and came to the U.S. in 1948 after marriage to an American. Her earlier poems were published in *The Double Image* (1946), and since coming to this country she has issued *Here and Now* (1957), *Five Poems* (1958), *Overland to the Islands* (1958), *With Eyes at the Back of Our Heads* (1959), *The Jacob's Ladder* (1961), *O Taste and See* (1964), *The Sorrow Dance* (1967), *Relearning the Alphabet* (1970), *To Stay Alive* (1971), *Footprints* (1972), *The Freeing of the Dust* (1975), *Life in the Forest* (1978), *Pig Dreams* (1981), *Candles in Babylon* (1982), *Oblique Prayers* (1984), *Breathing the Water* (1987), and *A Door in the Hive* (1989), whose free verse presents compact and intensely immediate perceptions of people, things, and feelings, and is not only socially active but has become more spiritual. *The Poet in the World* (1973) collects essays on poetry, teaching, and the Vietnam War. Poetry on the last subject appeared in *Light Up the Cave* (1981).

LEVIN, IRA (1929–), born in New York City, after education at New York University and service in the army's Signal Corps began a literary career that includes novels in the vein of fantastic horror stories: *A Kiss Before Dying* (1953), about a girl murdered by her lover; *Rosemary's Baby* (1967), about a woman who gives birth to a satanic infant; *This Perfect Day* (1970), presenting a computerized anti-Utopian world; *The Stepford Wives* (1972), a fantasy about robot women; and *The Boys from Brazil* (1976), a thriller. His several plays include *No Time for Sergeants*

(1955), a comedy about army life, and *Deathtrap* (1978), a mystery-comedy.

LEVIN, MEYER (1905–81), Chicago author, graduated from the University of Chicago (1924) before becoming a journalist, which career formed the background of his first novel, *Reporter* (1929). His other novels are *Frankie and Johnny* (1930); *Yehuda* (1931), dealing with life on a Zionist farm commune in Palestine; *The New Bridge* (1933), about a family evicted from its tenement home; *The Old Bunch* (1937), a realistic story of the children of Russian-Jewish immigrants in Chicago from 1921 to 1934; *Citizens* (1940), an analysis of the Chicago Little Steel strike and Memorial Day battle of 1937 as seen by a doctor who figured in *The Old Bunch; My Father's House* (1947), about a boy's escape from Poland to Palestine; *Compulsion* (1956), a tense psychological tale based on the Loeb-Leopold case, of which he published his dramatized version (1958), which differed from the Broadway production; *Eva* (1959), about a Jewish girl's escape during World War II from Poland and a German concentration camp to Israel; and *The Fanatic* (1964), about an American-Jewish author's dramatization of philosophic fiction by a victim of the Nazis and the attacks upon the playwright by followers of the Communist line, which the play opposes. This novel reflects Levin's own problems related to his dramatization of *The Story of Anne Frank,* whose rejection he dealt with again in *The Obsession* (1973). Later novels include *The Stronghold* (1965), about post–World War II Germany; *Gore and Igor* (1968), presenting comic adventures of an American and a Russian in Israel during the Six Day War; *The Settlers* (1972), depicting a Russian immigrant family in Palestine, c. 1904–18; *The Harvest* (1978), a sequel; *The Spell of Time* (1974), a novella set in Jerusalem; and *The Architect* (1982), a novel based on the life of Frank Lloyd Wright. *The Search* (1950) is an autobiography.

LEVINE, PHILIP (1928–), Detroit-born poet, long resident in California as a professor at the state university campus, Fresno (1958–), whose volumes of verse, including *On the Edge* (1963), *Not This Pig* (1968), *5 Detroits* (1970), *Pili's Wall* (1971), *Red Dust* (1971), *They Feed, They Lion* (1972), *1933* (1974), *The Names of the Lost* (1976), *Seven Years from Somewhere* (1979), *Ashes* (1979), *One for the Rose* (1981), *Sweet Will* (1985), *A Walk with Tom Jefferson* (1988), *What Work Is* (1991), and Pulitzer Prize winner *Simple Truth* (1995), show an antipathy to the stylish wealthy class and a sympathy for the oppressed working class of the U.S. *Don't Ask* (1981) contains interviews with Levine. A collection of autobiographical essays, *The Bread of Time: Toward An Autobiography* (1994), has an account of his becoming a poet, especially as a student of John Berryman at the Iowa Writers' Workshop.

LEWIS, ALFRED HENRY (c.1858–1914), was born in Cleveland, Ohio, where he was a lawyer and city attorney until 1881, when he became a wandering cowboy in the Southwest. Returning to Kansas City, he entered journalism, and later went to Washington as a newspaper correspondent. During the last 17 years of his life he contributed fiction and articles to magazines, and for a time edited *The Verdict* (1898–1900), a Democratic paper. His fictional biographies are negligible, as are his novels of politics and the underworld, but he wrote important fiction concerning the Western frontier life he knew as a young man. His six volumes of Wolfville stories, published under the pseudonym Dan Quin, present an authentic picture of cowboy and mining life in the Southwest, in the form of discursive, humorous, drawling reminiscences by an "Old Cattleman." They include *Wolfville*♦ (1897), *Sandburrs* (1900), *Wolfville Days* (1902), *Wolfville Nights* (1902), *Wolfville Folks* (1908), and *Faro Nell and Her Friends* (1913).

LEWIS, CHARLES BERTRAND (1842–1924), Ohio humorist, whose sketches in the *Detroit Free Press* won him a contemporary reputation. Much of his writing was collected in books, typical examples being *Brother Gardener's Lime Kiln Club* (1882), a parody of a black society, and *Trials and Troubles of the Bowser Family* (1889), about the domestic tribulations of a middle-class family. He wrote under the pseudonym M. Quad.

LEWIS, JANET (1899–), born in Chicago and educated at the University of Chicago, has long been a resident of California. Like her husband, Yvor Winters, she is a poet, and her verse has been published in *The Indians in the Woods* (1922); *The Wheel in Midsummer* (1927); *The Earth-Bound* (1946), collecting earlier work; *The Ancient Ones* (1979); and *Poems Old and New, 1918–1978* (1981). Her fiction, marked by a pure, quiet style, includes *The Invasion* (1932), a novel about an upper Michigan family of Irish and Ojibway heritage; *The Wife of Martin Guerre* (1941), a novella dealing with a famous legal case of 16th-century France; *Against a Darkening Sky* (1943), a novel portraying the dignified character of a woman in a contemporary California setting; *The Trial of Sören Qvist* (1947), another fictive character study, set in 17th-century Denmark and treating the unjust execution of an innocent pastor for an alleged murder; *The Ghost of Monsieur Scarron* (1959), set in the France of Louis XIV; and *Good-Bye, Son* (1946), short stories. She has also written libretti that include an adaptation of *The Wife of Martin Guerre* (1956), an adaptation of *The Last of the Mohicans* (1976), and another adaptation, of Wilde's *The Birthday of the Infanta* (1977), as well as one of her own first novel, *The Invasion,* as *The Legend* (1987).

LEWIS, MERIWETHER (1774–1809), was reared in Virginia and Georgia, and first entered military service as a member of the militia that suppressed the Whiskey Rebellion. After 1795 he was stationed at various frontier posts and had an opportunity to learn the language and customs of the Indians. Upon the election of his friend and former neighbor Jefferson, Lewis received the post of private secretary to the President. Jefferson favored Lewis's project of exploring a land route to the Pacific, and Congress appropriated $2500 for this purpose. With his companion officer William Clark♦ he mustered his men in Illinois in the winter of 1803–4. The expedition followed the Missouri River to its source, made a long portage overland through the Rockies, and descended the Columbia River to the Pacific Ocean. Sacagawea, the Shoshone "Bird Woman," aided them as interpreter, guide, and peacemaker. After many difficulties, including encounters with hostile Indians, they returned overland to St. Louis (Sept. 1806). Lewis, although nominally co-commander, was the ultimate authority during the journey, and was rewarded for his success with the governorship of Louisiana Territory. He died mysteriously in central Tennessee while on his way to Washington, probably having been murdered, although Jefferson assumed that his death was a suicide. The subject is treated in Vardis Fisher's *Suicide or Murder?* The first report of the expedition appeared as a *Message from the President . . . Feb. 19, 1806*. The *History of the Expedition under the Command of Captains Lewis and Clark* was edited in 1814 by Nicholas Biddle and Paul Allen, from material left by Lewis and lent by Clark. The most complete account was edited by R.G. Thwaites as *Original Journals of the Lewis and Clark Expedition* (8 vols., 1904–5).

LEWIS, RICHARD (1699?–1733?), emigrated to Maryland (c.1725) and published a translation of Edward Holdsworth's *Muscipula* (1728), a popular 18th-century Latin satire on the Welsh. Through Governor Calvert he obtained a clerkship in the Assembly, and he seems to have been a schoolmaster at King Williams School (Annapolis). He wrote a "Description of Spring," a characteristic 18th-century descriptive poem dealing with American scenery, published anonymously in the English *Weekly Register* (Jan. 1, 1732). His "Carmen Saeculare" (1732) was addressed to Calvert on his becoming governor, and Lewis is also thought to be the author of "A Rapsody" (1732).

LEWIS, R[ICHARD] W[ARRINGTON] B[ALDWIN] (1917–), Chicago-born scholar of American literature, received his A.B. from Harvard and Ph.D. from Chicago, and taught at Yale for many years. His books include *The American Adam* (1955), an intellectual history and literary study of concern in 19th-century U.S. with the American as an Adam in a bright new land, and

the biography *Edith Wharton* (1975, Pulitzer Prize). Some interest in French and English literature in addition to American shows in his essays, *Trials of the Word* (1965). His biography, *The Jameses,* was published in 1991. He has been an editor of the letters of Edith Wharton (1988).

LEWIS, SARAH ANNA (1824–80), Baltimore poet, friend and benefactor of Poe, known as his "Estelle." Her romantic, sentimental works include *Records of the Heart* (1844), *Child of the Sea and Other Poems* (1848), and *Sappho* (1868), a poetic drama which was translated into Greek and produced in Athens.

LEWIS, [HARRY] SINCLAIR (1885–1951), born in Sauk Centre, Minn., graduated from Yale (1907), although he left college for a time to work at the Helicon Home Colony, Upton Sinclair's socialist experiment in New Jersey. After engaging in hack writing, travel in the U.S., and editorial positions in New York, he wrote several minor novels, including *Our Mr. Wrenn* (1914), *The Trail of the Hawk* (1915), and *The Innocents* (1917). *The Job* (1917), a realistic novel of life in New York, was his first distinguished work of fiction, and with the publication of *Main Street♦* (1920) he achieved wide recognition. This story, which contrasts cosmopolitan and Midwestern small-town culture, was followed by *Babbitt♦* (1922), a satirical portrayal of an "average" American businessman, and *Arrowsmith♦* (1925), on the career of a man of science. The latter was awarded a Pulitzer Prize in 1926, which Lewis declined. *Elmer Gantry* (1927) is a satirical novel concerned with religious shams and hypocrisy in the U.S., and *The Man Who Knew Coolidge* (1928) is a depiction of a mediocre businessman. These books, although inferior as fiction, are examples of the author's popular iconoclasm, influenced by the criticism of H.L. Mencken. *Dodsworth♦* (1929), generally ranked with his better novels, is a sympathetic portrayal of a retired manufacturer who seeks new interests in European travel.

In 1930 Lewis became the first American author to be awarded the Nobel Prize for distinction in world literature. His later books are *Ann Vickers* (1933), about a woman social reformer; *Work of Art* (1934), the story of a successful businessman; *It Can't Happen Here♦* (1935), concerned with a future fascist revolt in the U.S.; *Selected Short Stories* (1935); *The Prodigal Parents* (1938), on family relations; *Bethel Merriday* (1940), about a girl in a theatrical touring company; *Gideon Planish* (1943), an exposé of organized philanthropy; *Cass Timberlane* (1945), about the marital problems of a middle-aged Minnesota judge and his young wife; *Kingsblood Royal* (1947), on race prejudice as met with by a Midwestern banker who finds he has some black blood; *The God Seeker* (1949), about a New England missionary to Minnesota Indians; and *World So Wide* (1951), about the romances of a Coloradan in Italy with young American girls. *From Main Street to Stock-holm* (1952) collects letters, and *The Man from Main Street* (1953) collects essays and ephemera.

Lewis is an ingenious satirist of the American middle class, mimicking its speech and actions with what seems to be photographic realism but is actually more or less good-humored caricature. Critics have accused him of romanticism in over-stressing his effects, and often declared that he was himself proof that his charges against American culture were just. *It Can't Happen Here* shows his shift from large-scale social analysis to a more immediate political concern, with a bias seemingly in favor of middle-class liberalism. His plays include *Dodsworth* (1934), written with Sidney Howard; *Jayhawker* (1934), about Free-Soil battles in Kansas before the Civil War, written with Lloyd Lewis; and *It Can't Happen Here* (1936), with John C. Moffitt. Mark Schorer wrote a comprehensive biography, *Sinclair Lewis: An American Life* (1961).

Lewis and Clark expedition, see *Lewis, Meriwether.*

LEWISOHN, LUDWIG (1882–1955), novelist and critic, was born in Berlin and brought as a child to the U.S. Among his many writings, *Upstream* (1922) and *Mid-Channel* (1929) are autobiographical treatments of the problems of Jews in America. His novels include *The Broken Snare* (1908); *Don Juan* (1923); *Roman Summer* (1927); *The Case of Mr. Crump* (1926), his masterpiece, a harrowing story about the implacable refusal of a wife to consent to a divorce and the torments endured by the husband; *The Island Within* (1928); *Stephen Escott* (1930); *Trumpet of Jubilee* (1937); *For Ever Wilt Thou Love* (1939); *Renegade* (1942); *Breathe Upon These* (1944); *Anniversary* (1948); and *In a Summer Season* (1955). *Expression in America* (1932) studies the American spirit in literature, using Freudian analysis to attack the Puritan tradition. Besides many translations, his works include critical studies, among them *The Modern Drama* (1915), *The Drama and the Stage* (1922), *The Creative Life* (1924), and *Cities and Men* (1927), marked by idealistic individualism. Sociological studies of Jews, advocating Zionism, include *Israel* (1925), *The Answer: The Jew and the World* (1939), and *The American Jew* (1950). *Haven* (1940), written with his wife, presents matched diaries of a honeymoon.

Liberal Imagination, The, work by Lionel Trilling,♦ published in 1950, collects essays on literature and society in the intellectual tradition of liberalism in the U.S. Marked by the variety that is said to be representative of that tradition, the subjects include considerations of Freud and Literature, Art and Neurosis, Manners, Morals and the Novel, and studies of works by Sherwood Anderson, Henry James, Mark Twain, Kipling, Wordsworth, and F. Scott Fitzgerald.

Liberator, The, (1831–65), Abolitionist weekly, was founded at Boston by W.L. Garrison.♦ Its editorial policy was of a militant-pacifist type, denouncing slavery, calling for its immediate abolition and the enfranchisement of all American blacks, but having no specific program for attaining these ends. For years its editor proved the sincerity of the statement in the first issue: "I am in earnest—I will not equivocate—I will not excuse—I will not retreat a single inch—*and I will be heard.*" The paper inevitably attracted much opposition. Garrison was mobbed, his press destroyed, a law passed prohibiting its circulation to free blacks, a reward offered for the apprehension of anyone who circulated it in South Carolina, and a resolution passed in the Georgia senate offering a reward for the arrest of Garrison. In 1835 a South Carolina mob broke into the U.S. mails and burned copies of *The Liberator,* along with effigies of its editors. Garrison also aroused enmity by his espousal of liquor prohibition and pacifism. The paper printed the writings of the more intelligent free blacks as well as those of leading Abolitionists, but its circulation has been estimated as being about 1400 in 1837, and never more than 3000. The last issue of *The Liberator* was published upon the ratification of the 13th Amendment.

Liberator, The (1918–24), see *Masses, The.*

Liberty Bell, The (1839–58), gift book devoted to antislavery literature, was published from Boston under the sponsorship of Maria Chapman. The volumes appeared annually except in 1849, 1853, 1854, and 1856. Among the contributors were Emerson, Longfellow, Lowell, Parker, Wendell Phillips, Harriet Beecher Stowe, and Bayard Taylor. The foreign contributors, numbering nearly 75, included Elizabeth Browning, Harriet Martineau, and Tocqueville. Ignoring the economic issues involved, the volumes were confined to emotional appeals to popular morality.

Library of America, The, collection begun in 1982 of major writings by leading American authors (Literary Classics of the United States) in a series of well-made, readable volumes addressed to a general public rather than to scholars. In keeping with a proposal made in 1968 by Edmund Wilson, each volume contains several works by one author in authoritative texts, introduced by a brief essay and a basic chronology but with a minimum of annotation and editorial apparatus. Approximately 100 volumes are projected, some to contain the writing of more than one author and some to include works of literary significance by historians, philosophers, social and religious thinkers, travelers, explorers, and nature writers.

Library of Congress, U.S. national library at Washington, D.C., established by act of Congress

(1800), and housed until 1897 in the Capitol. The purchase (1815) of Jefferson's library of 6457 volumes formed the nucleus of the present collections. Other great early purchases included the manuscripts of Jefferson, Washington, Hamilton, and Madison, and the collection of Peter Force. The library is located in three large buildings near the Capitol, containing 64.6 acres of floor space. In 1990 it contained over 80,000,000 items, including more than 22,000,000 books and pamphlets, great collections of bound newspapers; pieces and volumes of music; maps and views; photographic negatives, prints, and slides; motion-picture reels; phonograph recordings; reels and strips of microfilm; and a vast assemblage of manuscript pieces, including the originals of the Declaration of Independence and the Constitution. After 1846 the copyright law required a copy of every book copyrighted in the U.S. to be deposited in the library, and since 1870 two copies have been required. Most U.S. libraries use its printed catalogue cards. Librarians include Herbert Putnam (1899–1939), Archibald MacLeish (1939–45), Luther Evans (1945–53), L. Quincy Mumford (1954–74), Daniel Boorstin (1975–87), James H. Billington (1987–).

Lie Down in Darkness, novel by William Styron,♦ published in 1951.

In Port Warwick, a ship-building city of tidewater Virginia, during the last days of World War II, Milton and Helen Loftis and their family meet to bury their daughter Peyton, who committed suicide in New York City. The parents have long been alienated, in part because Milton, an unsuccessful lawyer, has been dependent on Helen, a bitter woman, in whose family house they live, in part because of tensions created by the fact that their eldest daughter, Maudie, was a retarded cripple, dead in her twentieth year. Milton had an almost unpaternal affection for Peyton, long ago took to drink, and has long had a mistress, Dolly Bonner, who accompanies him to the funeral. Peyton was sent to the proper college, Sweet Briar, but, affected by her unhappy home life, left it to live in New York, to marry Harry Miller, a struggling artist, to separate from him, and to take lovers in a frustrated search to find her own way. Finally she threw herself from a skyscraper. Even her funeral does not go smoothly. The hearse breaks down and during the humid day the procession to the cemetery is interrupted by a traffic jam caused by a revival meeting of blacks. In it are servants of the Loftis family, ecstatic because of their redemption by Daddy Faith, in contrast to the hopeless despair of Milton and Helen Loftis.

LIEBER, FRANCIS (1800–1872), German-born political philosopher, emigrated to the U.S. (1827) after his liberalism led to difficulties in his native country. He originated and edited the *Encyclopaedia Americana* (13 vols., 1829–33). From 1835 to 1856 he was a professor of history and political economy at South Carolina College (University of South Carolina), and while there produced his most famous books. His *Manual of Political Ethics* (2 vols., 1838–39) discusses the moral obligations arising from the citizen's participation in government. *Legal and Political Hermeneutics* (1839) is an outgrowth of his first work, and *On Civil Liberty and Self-Government* (2 vols., 1853) is a further study of political science, discussing elements of freedom in their relation to law. In 1857 he was given an appointment to Columbia College, and from 1865 until his death taught at Columbia's law school. *A Code for the Government of Armies* (1863) was reissued by the War Department as *General Orders No. 100,* and became a standard international work on military law and the conduct of war.

LIEBLING, A[BBOTT] J[OSEPH] (1904–63), after study at Dartmouth, from which he was expelled for refusing to attend chapel, became a newspaperman and was with *The New Yorker* after 1935, writing its "Wayward Press" column and other articles. His books include *The Telephone Booth Indian* (1942), about raffish New York City characters; *The Road Back to Paris* (1944), about experiences as a war correspondent; *The Wayward Pressman* (1947), about early newspaper experiences; *Mink and Red Herring* (1949), New Yorker columns; *Chicago: Second City* (1952); *The Honest Rainmaker* (1953), about a racing columnist; *The Sweet Science: A Ringside View of Boxing* (1956); *The Jollity Building* (1962), combining tales from the two preceding books; *Normandy Revisited* (1958), on battle sites he had known; *The Earl of Louisiana* (1961), about Governor Earl Long; *Between Meals: An Appetite for Paris* (1962); *The Press* (1962); *Molly and Other War Experiences* (1964); and *Liebling at Home* (1982).

Life (1883–1936), magazine founded by J.A. Mitchell and E. S. Martin, young Harvard graduates, was intended to be a satirical weekly "of higher artistic and literary merit" than *Puck* and *Judge*. *Life* played the role of *arbiter elegantiarum,* and its early volumes represent the school of genteel humor. Among its artists were F.W. Attwood, E.W. Kemble, Palmer Cox, Peter Newell, Oliver Herford, and C.D. Gibson, who created his "Gibson Girl" for it; and such authors as J.K. Bangs, Agnes Repplier, and Brander Matthews wrote stories and articles. Besides being the outstanding humorous magazine of the U.S., *Life* was known for its reviews of books and the theater, and its editorial campaigns against vivisection, the Hearst newspapers, and other matters, as well as against Germany during World War I. After the war it was purchased by Gibson, who had Robert Sherwood edit it (1924–28), continuing the dual policy of humor and editorial crusades, now in behalf of its fresh-air camps for poor children and in opposition to the 18th

Amendment. Eventually, however, the magazine lost its subtlety and was eclipsed by *The New Yorker*. In 1933 it became a monthly, and in 1936 *Judge* bought its "humorous traditions and features."

Life (1936–72, 1978–   ), a weekly issued by the publishers of *Time*, ♦ who purchased the title of the humorous journal *Life* (1883–1936), presents news and feature articles mainly through photographs, with editorial standards akin to those of *Time*. The journal ceased publication in 1972, although a few "Special Report" issues appeared occasionally thereafter. In 1978 it was revived as a monthly with less emphasis on current news and more on personalities, although each January issue features "The Year in Pictures."

Life Amongst the Modocs, autobiographical narrative of adventures almost wholly fanciful by Joaquin Miller, ♦ published in 1873 but under various other titles in later editions.

Life and Gabriella: *The Story of a Woman's Courage*, novel by Ellen Glasgow, ♦ published in 1916.
   Gabriella Carr, raised in a Southern town, is a girl of unusual energy and resolution, with a "vein of iron" in her character that distinguishes her from the conventionally gentle, unassertive girls of her class. She marries George Fowler, an essentially selfish, complacent man, and they go to New York to live. His attraction for her is mainly physical, and when after a few years he deserts her for Florrie Spencer, she is soon reconciled to her condition, and turns her attention to raising her children and creating a business career for herself. As "Madame Dinard" she becomes head of a leading dressmaking establishment, and years later marries a Westerner, Ben O'Hara, whose bluff, sturdy nature makes him one of her own kind.

Life in the Far West, novel by George Frederick Ruxton, ♦ published in 1848. This tale of the ways of mountain men among whom the author lived for a time is noted for its use of the vernacular speech they affected and for its presentation of many realistic adventures in a romantic plot.

Life of Reason, The, study of the function of reason in common sense, society, religion, art, and science, by Santayana, ♦ published in five volumes (1905–6).

Life on the Mississippi, autobiographical narrative by Clemens, ♦ published under his pseudonym Mark Twain (1883). The book opens with a brief history of the Mississippi River since its discovery, and Chapters 4 to 22 deal with Clemens's life as a boy on the river. These chapters, originally published in the *Atlantic Monthly*, give a vivid account of his participation in the steam-

boat age, the science of steamboat piloting, and the life of the river as seen by the pilot. Chapter 3 also contains a lively passage written for *Huckleberry Finn* but never used in the novel. The second part of the book, written some seven years after the first, is an account of Clemens's return to the river as a traveler, 21 years after he had been a pilot. During his trip from St. Louis to New Orleans, he finds that the glamour of the river has been destroyed by railroad competition. Interspersed with his descriptions of the river, his accounts of meeting Cable and Joel Chandler Harris, and Horace Bixby, who first taught him piloting, are anecdotes of the past, and a vigorous attack on Scott's romanticism and its effect on Southern thought. The second part of the book lacks the unity of the first, has none of its verve and gusto, and is more descriptive and reminiscent.

Life on the Ocean Wave, A, poem by Epes Sargent. ♦

Life Studies, collection of poetry and prose by Robert Lowell, ♦ published in 1959.
   Divided into four parts, the volume opens with a section whose religious and social themes develop from Lowell's earlier works. Part Two contains prose recollections of family and youth, set forth in an ironically level tone. Part Three invokes four authors—Ford Madox Ford, Santayana, Delmore Schwartz, and Hart Crane— whose experiences and writings affect Lowell. Part Four, which gives the book its title, opens with recollections in poetic form of the author's family and his childhood, and concludes with four poems about Lowell's mature experiences of marriage, imprisonment for conscientious objection to service in World War II, and hospitalization for mental problems.

Life with Father, affectionately humorous memoir by Clarence Day, ♦ published in 1935 and dramatized by Lindsay and Crouse (1939).

Life Without Principle, essay by Thoreau, ♦ posthumously published in the *Atlantic Monthly* (1863).
   Modern American culture is criticized as being excessively preoccupied with acquisition, at the expense of an awareness of values. "The aim of the laborer should be, not to get his living . . . but to perform well a certain work. . . . An efficient and valuable man does what he can, whether the community pay him for it or not. . . ." Most men dwell thoughtlessly on the surface of existence, obsessed by the need for busyness, small gossip, and conformance to convention. They lack independence and self-expression, as appears in such phenomena as the gold rush to California: "The philosophy and poetry and reli-

gion of such a mankind are not worth the dust of a puffball."

All of us have desecrated ourselves:

the remedy will be by wariness and devotion to reconsecrate ourselves, and make once more a fane of the mind. . . . Even the facts of science may dust the mind by their dryness, unless they are . . . rendered fertile by the dews of fresh and living truth.

Ligeia, tale by Poe,♦ published in 1838 and reprinted in *Tales of the Grotesque and Arabesque* (1840). The poem "The Conqueror Worm"♦ was not included in the tale until 1845.

An aristocratic young man marries Ligeia, a woman of strange, dark beauty and great learning. They are deeply in love, and share an interest in the occult, until a wasting illness triumphs over Ligeia's passionate will to live, and she dies. In melancholy grief, her husband leaves his lonely home on the Rhine to purchase an English abbey, where he grows mentally deranged under the influence of opium. He marries fair-haired Lady Rowena Trevanion, although they are not in love, and Rowena soon dies in a strange manner. Her husband watches by the bier and sees signs of returning life in the body, but considers these to be hallucinations. At last she rises to her feet and loosens the cerements from her head so that masses of long black hair stream forth. When she opens her eyes, he realizes that the lost Ligeia's will to live has triumphed, for she has assumed what was formerly the body of Rowena.

Light, CHRISTINA, character in *Roderick Hudson*♦ and *The Princess Casamassima.* ♦

Light in August, novel by William Faulkner,♦ published in 1932.

Joe Christmas is the son of Milly Hines and a traveling circus man, who is murdered by Milly's father, Eupheus Hines, because Hines is fanatically convinced of the man's Negro blood. When Milly dies in childbirth, Hines leaves the infant on the steps of a white orphanage on Christmas night (the source of Joe's surname) and takes a job there to watch, with mingled hatred and religious fervor, the working out of God's will. When he is five, Joe innocently surprises Miss Atkins, the dietician, and an intern making love, and, convinced that Joe will tell on her, she informs the matron that he is a black. Accordingly he is sent away to be adopted by Simon McEachern, a puritanical farmer who believes only in hard work and austere religion. Stoically enduring McEachern's whippings, Joe does not rebel until he is 18 and has his first romantic experience, with a waitress, but when they are pursued by the suspicious McEachern, Joe strikes and perhaps kills him. The girl refuses to go away with him, and with her employers she leaves him robbed, beaten, and deeply embittered. Joe em-

barks on 15 years of compulsive wandering along the nightmare-like "empty street" of restless experience, sometimes passing for a white, sometimes living as a black among black people, hating both by turns and often flaunting his mixed blood. At 33 he takes work in the Jefferson planing mill, and lives in a cabin near the house of Joanna Burden, a reclusive white woman of New England descent who is liberal toward blacks, believing them "forever and ever a part of the white race's doom and curse for its sins." They become lovers, she giving way to a primitive passion, and he persisting in his bitter detachment. Joe drifts into bootlegging with a white man who calls himself Joe Brown but who is really named Lucas Burch and who has fled to Jefferson from Alabama to escape a country girl, Lena Grove, whom he has seduced. Busy with his new life, Joe neglects Joanna, who becomes intensely religious. Her efforts to convert him make him so enraged that he cuts her throat and sets her house afire. Although Joe is not detected, Brown is seen drunk in the blazing house, where the body is discovered, and has to hide. Meanwhile the pregnant Lena arrives in Jefferson to search for Lucas Burch, and because of the similarity of surnames, is led to meet Byron Bunch, another millworker and a choir leader. He not only realizes that the man called Brown is really Burch but he also falls in love with Lena. As her time is near, Bunch finds her a place to stay and creates in the disgraced minister Gail Hightower a compassionate interest in her situation. When Brown hears that $1000 is offered for the capture of Miss Burden's killer, he returns to accuse Joe, and when he himself is suspected, tells the sheriff that Joe is a black, thus convincing the sheriff of Joe's guilt. After Hightower delivers Lena's child, Byron contrives to have Brown confronted with her and the baby, and Brown gives up the reward to flee once more. Joe is caught, and Hines, his grandfather, who still thinks himself an avenging angel of the white race, comes to Jefferson to stir up a lynch mob, from which Joe escapes to take refuge in Hightower's house. There he is found by Percy Grimm, a racist who shoots and castrates him. The district attorney, Gavin Stevens, sends Joe's body to his grandmother, who has dazedly confused Lena's baby with the infant "Joey" of 36 years before, and Byron accompanies Lena, still serenely self-sufficient, as she travels on toward the "destiny" Hightower sees for her: "peopling in tranquil obedience to it the good earth."

Lightnin', play by Winchell Smith♦ and Frank Bacon.

Lilacs, poem by Amy Lowell. ♦

Lily Bart, heroine of *The House of Mirth.* ♦

LINCOLN, ABRAHAM (1809–65), 16th President of the U.S. (1861–65), was born in a log cabin in Kentucky, of a typically illiterate and shiftless frontier family. They soon migrated to another place in Kentucky, then to the Indiana woods, where the boy labored on the homestead, garnered a little learning in frontier schools, avoided church membership, and pursued his bent for reading in what books he could obtain. In 1830 the Lincolns moved to Illinois, where Abraham temporarily helped to build the new cabin, split fence rails, and otherwise assist in the tasks of homesteading. After navigating a flatboat to New Orleans, he returned to New Salem, Ill., where he spent six formative years (1831–37) working at odd jobs, studying, reading law, making a wide personal acquaintance, and serving as surveyor, postmaster, captain of volunteers in the Black Hawk War, and in the state legislature (1834–41). As a Clay Whig, he supported the Bank of the United States, opposed Jackson and Van Buren, and opposed the Abolitionists because he thought they tended to increase the evils of slavery. Meanwhile Lincoln courted Ann Rutledge, whose father kept the inn where he boarded. Her sudden death (1835), while Lincoln's suit was unsettled, has led to a great deal of sentimental conjecture. His peculiar courtship of and marriage to Mary Todd has also become part of the Lincoln legend.

He was a practicing attorney, beginning in 1836 at New Salem and then at Springfield, and served in Congress (1847–49), opposing the Mexican War as a Democratic-fomented campaign for the extension of slave territory, and consequently becoming unpopular in his home state. In his legal practice he now had as a partner William H. Herndon, whose papers afford an important source of information on the future President. Not only as a circuit-riding lawyer, but also in the higher courts, he was noted for his thoroughness, shrewdness, common sense, and ability to argue a case. He became a good stump speaker, known for his clear, pithy, and witty statements, brilliant by contrast with the trite verbosity then common.

After an unsuccessful campaign for the senatorship (1855), he became a Republican at the formation of the new party, and at the state convention (1856) was a leading figure because of his adroit and earnest dealing with the problem of slavery. As the Republican nominee for the U.S. Senate (1858), he delivered in the party convention his famous speech declaring, "A house divided against itself cannot stand." He challenged his opponent, Stephen Douglas,♦ to seven debates in which he showed the Democrat's inconsistency in favoring both popular sovereignty and the Dred Scott decision, and stressed a conservative attitude toward antislavery, thus winning many followers who disliked outright Abolitionism. Although Douglas won the election, Lincoln's fame was greatly enhanced. In his Cooper

Union speech (Feb. 27, 1860), as a potential presidential candidate, he spoke against slavery in the territories, and through his conservative and dignified attitude increased his power in the East. He was elected to the presidency in 1860 by a considerable electoral majority over Douglas and Breckinridge, although he lacked the popular vote.

Prior to his inauguration, the secession movement grew rapidly in the South. While Lincoln was still new in the executive functions, and his power was being threatened by members of his own cabinet, he vacillated and for some time failed to take a clear stand in relation to the firing on Fort Sumter. From the outbreak of the Civil War until the convening of Congress (July 1861), he treated the conflict as a huge insurrection to be met by executive measures, summoning the militia, proclaiming a blockade, expanding the army beyond the legal limit, directing governmental expenditures, suspending *habeas corpus,* and launching many military measures. During the progress of the war, he so extended his executive powers that he became a virtual dictator. Although faced with dissension in his cabinet and his own party, with radical Abolitionism on one side and defeatist cries for peace on the other, and despite maladjusted governmental and military functions, he managed to steer a middle course, favoring a war policy that was as little vengeful as possible. In military affairs there was confusion, ignorance, personal ambition, political pressure, lack of morale, and experimentation, which brought the pressure of military duties directly upon him. He nevertheless remained tolerant, selfless, and moderate. His search for a winning commander in chief led him to try in turn McClellan, Pope, Burnside, Hooker, Meade, and Grant.

The most famous of his executive acts was the Emancipation Proclamation (1862), which freed slaves in rebellious territory, while those in loyal or conquered states were to be freed by later legislation. As it was naturally ineffective in Confederate-controlled areas, the Proclamation was largely an announcement of Lincoln's aims and policies, and had a great moral effect. Foreign affairs and the threat of war with Great Britain were primarily handled by his secretary of state, Seward, although Lincoln aided in preserving a moderate policy. He made few public addresses, except for his inaugurals, the Gettysburg Address♦ (1863), and the speech on Reconstruction (April 1865). To express his attitude, he depended greatly upon letters addressed to individuals or delegations, intended for public consumption.

In 1864, during an atmosphere of national depression, war weariness, low financial credit, and sniping from defeatists, radicals, and other dissatisfied elements, Lincoln was nevertheless reelected over McClellan. His second inaugural address loftily declared, "With malice toward none; with charity for all, let us strive on to finish the work we are in . . . to do all which may achieve and cherish a just and lasting peace. . . ." He advocated a fair restoration of the Southern states to the Union, pardoning Confederates who would swear allegiance and promoting loyal governments in the Southern states, and, though he insisted on reunion and the abolition of slavery, he was generous concerning collateral issues. He was shot by John Wilkes Booth ♦ (April 14, 1865) and died the following morning. Stanton's comment, "Now he belongs to the ages," separates the real Lincoln, who encountered calumny, hatred, and misinterpretation of his plans, from the legendary Lincoln, who has been raised to the status of a symbol of American democracy and the Union.

The President's writing, in speeches and letters, is famous for its homespun dignity, lucidity of thought, trenchancy of expression, richness of idea, flexibility of style, adaptability to the audience, and peculiarly American flavor. He was close to the homely idiom of the common man, and his pungent provincialisms and native humor derive from his frontier education and account for his enthusiasm for such humorists as Artemus Ward. There are many collections of anecdotes attributed to him; his letters, speeches, and state papers have been frequently published; and his *Complete Writings* was edited by John Hay and J.G. Nicolay (2 vols., 1894, enlarged to 12 vols., 1905). But to this compilation have been added many others, such as *New Letters and Papers of Lincoln* (1930), edited by Paul Angle; *The Lincoln Papers* (2 vols., 1948), from family-owned documents given to the Library of Congress; and the *Collected Works* (9 vols., 1953), edited by Roy P. Basler.

Biographies began with lives written for presidential campaigns, including one by William Dean Howells in 1860 and one by Henry Jarvis Raymond in 1864. Later lives include *Herndon's Lincoln* (1889); Nicolay and Hay's *Abraham Lincoln: A History* (10 vols., 1890), based on the papers of his secretaries and some of the President's; Ida Tarbell's *Life* (2 vols., 1900), using a wide variety of sources; Lord Charnwood's *Abraham Lincoln* (1916), a British interpretation; Sandburg's six-volume study (1926, 1939); Beveridge's *Life* (2 vols., 1928), emphasizing the early career; Edgar Lee Master's *Lincoln, the Man* (1931), which attacks its subject as it praises Douglas; James G. Randall's scholarly account (4 vols., 1945–55); and compilations including an *Autobiography* (1926), drawn from various sources, and a day-by-day calendar.

Lincoln figures frequently in literature. Poems honoring him include Whitman's "O Captain! My Captain!" and "When Lilacs Last in the Dooryard Bloom'd," Lowell's "Commemoration Ode," Edwin Markham's "Lincoln," Robinson's "The Master," and Vachel Lindsay's "Abraham Lincoln Walks at Midnight." The historical fiction in which he figures is less distinguished although it is plentiful, including Edward

Eggleston's *The Graysons* (1888); Winston Churchill's *The Crisis* (1901); Upton Sinclair's *Manassas* (1904); Mary Raymond Shipman Andrews's *The Perfect Tribute* (1906); Irving Bacheller's *A Man for the Ages* (1919); Honoré Wilson Morrow's trilogy, *Forever Free* (1927), *With Malice Toward None* (1928), and *The Last Full Measure* (1930); and the more esteemed *Lincoln: A Novel* (1984) by Gore Vidal. The best known treatments in drama are John Drinkwater's *Abraham Lincoln* (1919) and Robert Sherwood's *Abe Lincoln in Illinois* (1938).

LINCOLN, JOSEPH C[ROSBY] (1870–1944), Massachusetts author, was born on Cape Cod, the setting of his many novels and short stories concerned with New England sea captains and Down East landsmen. His first book was *Cape Cod Ballads* (1902), but he was later known for his fiction, which includes *Cap'n Eri* (1904), *Mr. Pratt* (1906), *The Postmaster* (1912), *Galusha the Magnificent* (1921), *Rugged Water* (1924), *Bradshaws of Harness* (1943), and three novels written with his son Freeman Lincoln: *Blair's Attic* (1929), *The Ownley Inn* (1939), and *The New Hope* (1941).

LINCOLN, VICTORIA (1904–81), popular novelist whose best-known work, *February Hill* (1934), is set in her native Fall River, Mass., and was adapted for the stage by George Abbott as *Primrose Path* (1939). Other novels include *Out from Eden* (1951) and *Dangerous Innocence* (1958). *Grandmother and the Comet* (1944) collects stories. *A Private Disgrace* (1967) treats the case of Lizzie Borden ♦ of Fall River.

Linda Condon, novel by Hergesheimer, ♦ published in 1919.

LINDBERGH, ANNE MORROW (1906–), wife of Charles Lindbergh, has written *North to the Orient* (1935) and *Listen! the Wind* (1938), narratives of her flights with her husband (1933), exploring routes for commercial aviation. *The Wave of the Future* (1940), a "confession of faith," advocates U.S. domestic reforms in keeping with her husband's isolationist views of the time. *Steep Ascent* (1944) is an introspective novelette of a flight over the Alps by an American woman and her British flyer husband. *Gift from the Sea* (1955) contains musings on modern problems, particularly those of married women. *The Unicorn* (1956) collects her poems. *Dearly Beloved* (1962) is a novel that by means of flashbacks tells of the tangled lives of relatives and friends gathered at a wedding. *Earth Shine* (1969) prints two essays. *Bring Me a Unicorn* (1972), *Hour of Gold, Hour of Lead* (1973), *The Flower and the Nettle* (1976), *Locked Rooms and Open Doors* (1974), and *War Within and Without* (1980) contain diaries and letters.

LINDBERGH, CHARLES A[UGUSTUS] (1902–74), on May 20–21, 1927, flew his monoplane, *The Spirit of St. Louis,* in a nonstop flight of 3,610 miles from New York to Paris in 33½ hours. Lindbergh's accounts of this first solo flight across the Atlantic, which made him an international hero, are *"We"* (1927) and *The Spirit of St. Louis* (1953, Pulitzer Prize). His *Wartime Journals* was published in 1970. *Autobiography of Values* (1978) was edited from a lengthy manuscript.

LINDERMAN, FRANK BIRD (1869–1938), Montana author, whose books include *On a Passing Frontier* (1920), sketches; *Bunch-Grass and Blue-Joint* (1921), verse; several volumes of Indian lore; and fiction concerned with frontier and Indian life, including *Lige Mounts, Free Trapper* (1922), *American* (1930), *Red Mother* (1932), and *Beyond Law* (1933).

LINDSAY, HOWARD, see *Crouse, Russel.*

LINDSAY, [NICHOLAS] VACHEL (1879–1931), born in Springfield, Ill., attended Hiram College (1897–1900), studied art at Chicago and New York (1900–1905), and decided, after unsuccessful attempts to find employment, to be "a tramp and a beggar." Although he spent his winters in lecturing on art and temperance, much of the time during the following years was devoted to tramping tours of the U.S., on which he bartered verses for food and lodging. His poetic broadsides and leaflets included *The Tree of Laughing Bells* (1905) and *Rhymes To Be Traded for Bread* (1912). In 1912 he began to lecture on "The Gospel of Beauty" and in 1913 he published his first collection, *General William Booth Enters into Heaven and Other Poems,* whose title piece♦ displays the qualities of vivid imagery, vigorous rhythm, and dramatic conception for which Lindsay is best known. The volume also contains such conventional but equally sincere poems as "The Eagle That Is Forgotten."♦ With the publication of *The Congo and Other Poems* (1914), he was widely recognized as an exponent of the "new poetry," and came to be in great demand as a public reader of his own works. Still preaching the gospel of beauty, he tried to stimulate a popular taste for poetry through a method that he called "the higher vaudeville," in which his recitations were marked by a dramatic use of gesture and chant, emphasizing his strong rhythms and syncopation. This second volume includes "Abraham Lincoln Walks at Midnight,"♦ "The Congo,"♦ and "The Santa-Fé Trail,"♦ all characteristically vivid, imaginative "visions," in which the poet embodies his romantic faith in nature and a life close to the soil, and his fervent patriotism and love for democracy. *The Chinese Nightingale and Other Poems* (1917) marked the peak of his artistic achievement, its title poem♦ and "The Ghost of the Buffaloes"♦ having a subtle beauty of melody and image that he never surpassed, although "In

Praise of Johnny Appleseed,"♦ commemorating the deeds of his favorite pioneer hero, is one of his most significant pieces. Losing the faculty of self-criticism, he became more prolific but quickly declined in power, and his later poetry is of comparatively little value. Among his later collections are *The Daniel Jazz* (1920), *The Golden Whales of California* (1920), *Collected Poems* (1923, revised 1925), *The Candle in the Cabin* (1926), and *Johnny Appleseed* (1928). His prose works include *Adventures While Preaching the Gospel of Beauty* (1914); *A Handy Guide for Beggars* (1916); *The Golden Book of Springfield* (1920), a mystic Utopia based on his gospel of beauty; and *The Litany of Washington Street* (1929), a book of political essays. His biography (1935) was written by his friend Edgar Lee Masters, and Mark Harris's *City of Discontent* (1952) is an interpretation of his life and his region.

LINN, JOHN BLAIR (1777–1804), Pennsylvania poet and Presbyterian clergyman, whose writings include *The Poetical Wanderer* (1796), composed when he was a graduate student at Columbia; *The Death of Washington. A Poem* (1800), in the manner of Ossian; *The Powers of Genius* (1801), reminiscent of Shenstone and Akenside; and *Valerian* (1805), an unfinished narrative poem. His lost play, *Bourville Castle* (1797), was revised by William Dunlap and his brother-in-law, C.B. Brown.

***Lion of the West,** The,* comedy by J.K. Paulding,♦ produced in 1830 and revised (1831) as a melodrama by J.A. Stone, and again as *A Kentuckian's Trip to New York* (1833) by W.B. Bernard. The adaptations are known only by reputation, and Paulding's text was first published in 1954. The play was very popular because of its character Nimrod Wildfire (generally identified with Davy Crockett and W.P. Duval), a Kentucky backwoodsman who visits the East and confounds New Yorkers.

***Lionel Lincoln;** or, The Leaguer of Boston,* romance by Cooper,♦ published in 1825 and dramatized as *The Leaguer of Boston.*

Lionel Lincoln arrives at Boston (April 1775) as an officer with the British troops. On shipboard he has met an old man, "Ralph," who is actually his father, Sir Lionel, supposed to be in an English insane asylum. Another companion, whose true identity is unknown to either of them, is Job Pray, Lionel's half-wit stepbrother, who guides them to the house of his mother, Abigail. The latter is terrified at the sight of Sir Lionel. They go then to the home of Mrs. Lechmere, Lionel's aunt, with whose granddaughter, Cecil Dynever, Lionel falls in love. Job serves among the Minute Men at Lexington, and, although Lionel's father fails to convince his son of the justice of the rebel cause, Ralph saves his son's life during the battle. The young man vainly attempts to solve the mystery of their relationship, before he is called to serve at Bunker Hill. Seriously wounded, he is nursed to recovery by Cecil, and the two marry, encouraged by the strange insistence of Mrs. Lechmere, who soon dies. Finally Sir Lionel explains the various mysteries. Mrs. Lechmere, years before, had wished him to marry her daughter, but instead he had married her ward, Lionel's mother, whose death caused him to become temporarily insane. Somewhat earlier, he had assumed the character of "Ralph," during his liaison with Abigail. Mrs. Lechmere has insisted on the marriage of Cecil and Lionel in order to achieve her long cherished scheme of union between the families. The story ends with the sudden deaths of Sir Lionel, Abigail, and Job, the British evacuation of Boston, and the departure for England of Lionel and Cecil.

LIPPARD, George (1822–54), eccentric Philadelphia author, whose sensational novels are of two types: tales of the immorality of large cities, such as *New York: Its Upper Ten and Lower Million* (1853), and romantic historical fiction, such as *Blanche of Brandywine* (1846) and *Legends of Mexico* (1847). His popular plays deal with similar subjects. Lippard's most notorious work was *The Monks of Monk Hall* (1844), reprinted as *The Quaker City; or, The Monks of Monk Hall* (1844), pirated under variant titles, a melodramatic exposé of Philadelphia vice. In 1850 he founded the Brotherhood of the Union, whose purpose was to destroy social evils that produced poverty and crime. He befriended Poe, on whom his romantic, melodramatic fiction is said to have had some influence.

LIPPINCOTT, Sara Jane [Clarke] (1823–1904), popular mid-19th-century poet, newspaper woman, and essayist, whose best-known works are *Greenwood Leaves* (1850), a collection of sketches and letters, and *Haps and Mishaps of a Tour in Europe* (1854). She wrote under the pseudonym Grace Greenwood.

Lippincott's Magazine (1868–1916), Philadelphia literary monthly, was more national in scope than the *Atlantic,* but its contributions were of a similar high caliber. During the 1880s, the magazine was distinguished for the first printing in the U.S. of such English fiction as Wilde's *The Picture of Dorian Gray,* Kipling's *The Light That Failed,* and the first Sherlock Holmes stories. Contributors during its early decades included Frank Stockton, Henry James, Lanier, Simms, Constance F. Woolson, Rebecca H. Davis, and Rose Terry Cooke, and during the 1890s Edgar Saltus, Julian Hawthorne, Gertrude Atherton, P.L. Ford, J.L. Allen, Hearn, Wister, Crane, and Harte. In 1915 the magazine was moved to New York, where its title became *McBride's Magazine.* The following year it was merged with *Scribner's.*

LIPPMANN, Walter (1889–1974), born in New York, graduated from Harvard (1909, class

of 1910), and was associated with *The New Republic* at its inception. In 1917 he resigned to become an assistant to the secretary of war, and to aid in preparing data for the peace conference. After another period with *The New Republic* (1919–21), he became the leading editorial commentator for the New York *World,* then for the *Herald Tribune* (1931–62), the *Washington Post* (1963–67), and *Newsweek* (1963–70). His social philosophy was opposed to any planned society or collectivism, and he placed his faith in a liberalism regulated by the necessities of economic markets, justifying governmental interference only in cases of abuse. *A Preface to Morals* (1929) expounds his thesis that modern society requires realistic analysis and objective virtue for the attainment of individual freedom, rather than loyalty to persons or causes. His other books include *A Preface to Politics* (1913), *Drift and Mastery* (1914), *The Stakes of Diplomacy* (1915), *The Political Scene* (1919), *Public Opinion* (1922), *The Phantom Public* (1925), *The Method of Freedom* (1934), *The Good Society* (1937), *Some Notes on War and Peace* (1940), *U.S. Foreign Policy: Shield of the Republic* (1943), *U.S. War Aims* (1944), *The Cold War* (1947), *Isolation and Alliances* (1952), *The Public Philosophy* (1955), *The Communist World and Ours* (1959), and *The Coming Tests with Russia* (1961). He was awarded special Pulitzer Prize citations in 1958 and 1962.

Literary and Philosophical Society of Newport, debating club that owed its organization to the intellectual stimulus of Bishop Berkeley's visit. The Society existed from 1730 to 1747, and its members included Samuel Johnson and William Ellery.

Literary Classics of the United States, see *Library of America.*

Literary Digest (1890–1938), weekly magazine, founded as a repository of newspaper and magazine comments on current questions, prospered greatly under this policy, and during the 1920s reached a circulation of almost 2,000,000. During this decade it originated straw polls sampling public opinion on important issues, but its striking miscalculation of the probably outcome of the 1936 presidential election caused a loss of public confidence. The competition of such news magazines as *Time* made the old formula of juxtaposing contrary newspaper opinions seem antiquated, and attempts at modernization were made. Combination with the *Review of Reviews* as *The Digest* (1937) and *The Literary Digest* failed, and it was bought by *Time.*

Literary Gazette, The (1809–21), Philadelphia journal, was edited by Irving (1813–14) as *The Analectic Magazine,* and contained some of his writings. Under the editorship of Thomas Isaac Wharton, the journal by 1817 had lost its eclectic character, and it was later virtually a service magazine of the U.S. Navy. It dwindled to a weekly filled with book reviews.

Literary History of the United States, cooperative "redefinition of our literary past" from the vantage point of the mid-20th century, issued in three volumes (1948) under the editorship of Robert E. Spiller, Willard Thorp, Thomas H. Johnson, and Henry Seidel Canby, with Howard Mumford Jones, Dixon Wecter, and Stanley T. Williams as associates. The first two volumes were written by 55 scholars, including those above, and the third volume, a bibliography, is the work of Thomas Johnson, with a *Bibliography Supplement* (1959) by Richard M. Ludwig, followed by a *Supplement II* (1972). A later redefinition of our literary past is the one-volume *Columbia Literary History of the United States* (1988), Emory Elliott, general editor; Martha Banta, Terence Martin, David Minter, Marjorie Perloff, and Daniel Shea, associate editors. Its editors assign very different meanings to the terms "literary," "history," even "the United States." Its thrust is ethnic diversity, a downplaying of "canonicity." Many extra-literary matters—the Cold War, Vietnam, civil rights struggles, sexual politics—figure in the choosing of writers and works to be discussed.

Literary Magazine and American Register, The (1803–10), Philadelphia monthly, edited until 1807 by C.B. Brown. It printed both scientific and literary articles, and such contributions by Brown as "Memoirs of Carwin, the Biloquist." In 1807 it became *The American Register* and was a bulky semi-annual almanac containing little of literary value.

Literary World, The (1847–53), New York weekly journal of society, literature, and art, edited by the Duyckinck brothers and C.F. Hoffman. In addition to the editors' writings, Paulding, Simms, and others wrote sketches, reviews, portraits of manners, and literary gossip. Another magazine of this name was published at Boston (1870–1904).

Literati of New York City, The, critical review by Poe♦ of the Knickerbocker Group♦ and other New York authors, published in *Godey's Lady's Book* (1846). Among the 38 authors are Halleck (the third principal contemporary poet, "a somewhat better position than that to which on absolute grounds he is entitled"); C.P. Cranch ("unusual vivacity of fancy and dexterity of expression . . . one of the least intolerable of the school of Boston transcendentalists"); Caroline Stansbury Kirkland ("has a province of her own, and in that province has few equals"); Epes Sargent ("one of the most prominent members of a very extensive American family—the men of industry, talent, and tact"); E.A. Duyckinck ("the excessively tasteful"); Anna Mowatt ("She evinces more feel-

ing than ideality"); Lewis G. Clark ("he is noticeable for nothing in the world except for the markedness by which he is noticeable for nothing"); C.F. Hoffman ("a true idealist . . . one sensitively alive to beauty in every development"); Margaret Fuller ("tainted with the affectation of the transcendentalists, but brimful of the poetic sentiment"); and N.P. Willis ("As a poet he is not entitled to as high a rank as he may justly claim for his prose"). Poe's unfavorable comments on T.D. English, whom he satirizes as "Thomas Dunn Brown," provoked a scurrilous reply by English, to which Poe retaliated with a successful libel suit.

LITTELL, ELIAKIM (1797–1870), magazine editor and publisher, began his career in 1819 with the *Philadelphia Register and National Recorder,* which, with various changes of title, he edited until 1844. Then he sold it, as *The Eclectic Museum,♦* to found a rival publication, *The Living Age.♦*

LITTELL, WILLIAM (1768–1824), writer of numerous books on Kentucky law, who also wrote a collection of satirical essays on his contemporaries, *An Epistle from William, Surnamed Littell, to the People of the Realm of Kentucky* (1806), and *Festoons of Fancy: Consisting of Compositions Amatory, Sentimental, and Humorous in Verse and Prose* (1814).

Little Blue Books, paperback series of small nickel and dime booklets issued by Emanuel Haldeman-Julius from Girard, Kansas, mainly in the 1920s and '30s. The more than 2000 titles featured classic works of literature, socialist and free-thinking tracts, sex books, and some original works by Will Durant, E.W. Howe, Upton Sinclair, and others.

Little Breeches, poem by John Hay included in his *Pike County Ballads.♦*

Little Eva, a character in *Uncle Tom's Cabin.♦*

Little French Girl, The, novel by Anne Douglas Sedgwick,♦ published 1924.
Madame Vervier, a worldly Frenchwoman, sends her daughter Alix to England to make a good match. There Alix meets a girl, "Toppie," once engaged to Owen Bradley but since his death wooed by his brother Giles. Alix, learning that her mother was once Owen's mistress, tells this secret to Toppie so that she will be freed of faithfulness to his memory and thus willing to wed Giles. As a friendly act to Alix, Giles goes to tell Mme Vervier that her plan to wed Alix to a rich Englishman is opposed by the boy's family, but suddenly finds he loves her himself. Mme Vervier refuses to permit their marriage, but Alix, following the different standards she has learned in England, defies her mother and plans to wed Giles.

Little Giant, sobriquet of Stephen Douglas. ♦

Little Journeys, biographical sketches by Elbert Hubbard♦ telling of his sentimental journeys to the homes of the great, begun in January 1895 with a pamphlet on George Eliot, and continued for 170 monthly issues to 1909, and later collected in 14 volumes.

Little Lord Fauntleroy, novel by Frances H. Burnett, ♦ published in 1886 and dramatized by the author in 1888.

The son of an English earl alienates his arrogant old father by marrying an American, who after his death raises their son in New York, calling him Cedric Errol. The boy wears his hair in long curls, converses with grave volubility, and endears himself to everyone by his cheerfulness, generosity, and affection. His special friends are Mr. Hobbs the grocer and Dick the bootblack, whom he leaves regretfully when he goes to England as heir to Dorincourt, following the deaths of his uncles. As Lord Fauntleroy he is indulged by the gouty old earl, who, however, refuses to meet the boy's mother, giving her a house nearby, where the seven-year-old lord visits her daily. Fauntleroy enjoys his new wealth and wins his grandfather's devotion, persuading him to undertake charitable projects and improve his tenants' living conditions. When another American woman appears to claim the estate for her son, the earl is furious but helpless. Dick, in New York, recognizes the woman from a newspaper picture as the former wife of his brother Ben. With Mr. Hobbs the brothers go to England and discredit the woman's false claim. The earl is reconciled with Fauntleroy's mother, and the three live happily at Dorincourt.

Little magazine, name applied to an advance-guard literary journal, primarily concerned with the publication of writers or writing not likely to be acceptable to established journals of larger circulation. *The Yellow Book* (1894–97), founded by Henry Harland, and *The Savoy* (1896), both English magazines that revolted against Victorian rationalism, morality, and emphasis upon science, set the standards that others followed. Their art-for-art's sake credo was imitated by such American magazines as *The Bibelot* (1895–1915), a monthly reprint of prose and poetry from obscure works, edited by T.B. Mosher, and *The Chap Book*♦ (1894–98), issued from Chicago. *The Lark*♦ (1895–97), published at San Francisco, was a distant reflection of this school, but had gaiety as its only policy. The little magazine came into particular importance in the U.S. just before and after World War I, as a protest by those who believed artists were being enslaved and repressed by Mammon and Puritanism. *Poetry: A Magazine of Verse*♦ (1912–   ) is an eclectic publication, championing new poets of all nations and schools. *The Little Review*♦ (1914–29),

frequently considered the most significant American magazine of the type, had tremendous vitality and never settled into any one pattern. During the postwar period, some magazines, like *The Seven Arts*♦ (1916–17), were concerned with an objective scrutiny of American culture. Others, like *The Frontier*♦ (1920–39), *The Fugitive*♦ (1922–25), and *The Reviewer*♦ (1921–25), were regional in tendency; and still others, like *Secession*♦ (1922–24), *Broom* (1921–24), *transition*♦ (1927–50), and *This Quarter* (1925–32), were eclectic in character and were edited from abroad by expatriates. *The Dial*♦ (1917–29) was in a sense the heir of the previous experimentation, but maintained a more detached, urbane, and cosmopolitan tone. *Hound and Horn*♦ (1927–34), the outstanding little magazine edited by university students, held policies similar to those of other publications in the movement.

During the Depression after 1929, advance-guard writers turned their attention to social and economic reform, and for a time the significance of little magazines began to disappear. Some of their purposes were taken over by literary quarterlies issued from universities, but many new little magazines continued to appear, some with an international view, like *Paris Review*♦ or *Botteghe Oscure* (1949–60); some were issued as journals, like *Evergreen Review,* and some published as paperbacks, like *discovery*♦ and *New World Writing.* ♦

The publication of little magazines increased greatly beginning in the 1950s. In 1978 the editors of a book on the subject guessed that at least 1500 such journals were being published in the U.S. They are and have been of the most diverse sorts, championing a great range of aesthetic, critical, social, and cultural views. Some, like *The Floating Bear*♦ (1961–69), were essentially newsletters for rapid communication among authors of experimental literature; others, like *Big Table*♦ (1959–60), were founded to print what was unacceptable to more conventional publications; some, like *The Black Mountain Review*♦ (1954–59), were organs of a special school of literature; some, like Reed Whittemore's *Furioso* (1939–53), Cid Corman's *Origin* (1951–71), and Gilbert Sorrentino's *Neon* (1956–60), reflected the views of a major young writer; some, like *Salmagundi*♦ (1965–   ) and *Tri-Quarterly*♦ (1958–   ), are closely related to a university or college; and some, like *Yardbird Reader*♦ (1972–   ), are dedicated to the writings of ethnic minorities.

Over the hundred years or more that they have flourished, little magazines have printed a good deal of insignificant or bizarre work, but they have justified themselves by providing a medium for all kinds of aesthetic experimentation and innovative and unpopular beliefs. By initial circulation in these magazines the novelties, heresies, and unknown authors of one era have often become accepted and valued in a succeeding period.

Little Regiment, The, and Other Episodes of the American Civil War, six short stories by Stephen Crane,♦ published in 1896 and issued in England as *Pictures of War* (1916).

The title story tells of two brothers in the Union army, whose seeming antagonism conceals a deep affection. During a battle, one of them is believed killed, and the other shows signs of bitter grief. When his brother suddenly reappears, they greet each other with a curt "hello" and resume their pose of hostility. "Three Miraculous Soldiers" shows the reactions of an ignorant Southern girl, who is terrified when a Union detachment camps on her mother's farm. She helps three Confederate prisoners to escape, but breaks into hysterical tears over a sentry they have wounded. "A Mystery of Heroism" is concerned with the reckless feat of a private who crosses a field during a violent battle to fetch a pail of drinking water. When he returns, apparently by miracle, the water is accidentally spilled before any of it can be used. "The Veteran" tells of the heroism of an aged ex-soldier who sacrifices his life to save the animals in a burning barn.

Little Review, The (1914–29), monthly little magazine founded at Chicago by Margaret C. Anderson "as an organ of two interests, art and good talk about art." "Making no compromise with the public taste," the *Review* was best known for its serialization of Joyce's *Ulysses;* Ezra Pound was its foreign editor (1917–19). Such special issues were published as the one devoted to the works of Henry James (Aug. 1918), and in general the magazine tended toward favorable criticism of all extreme modern theories of art, although its aesthetic bias was temporarily interrupted (1916–17) when the editor became interested in social problems and the writings of Emma Goldman. This social concern was abandoned when Miss Anderson "found the tenets of anarchism to be simple and beautiful but quite uninteresting." For a short time, the magazine was published at San Francisco, and later at New York. With Miss Anderson's removal to Paris, it was published there as a quarterly (1924–29), mainly edited by Jane Heap, who had long been associated with it. The *Review* gave space to "23 new systems of art . . . representing 19 countries," and published works by such authors as T.S. Eliot, W.C. Williams, W.B. Yeats, Malcolm Cowley, Ford Madox Ford, Wallace Stevens, Amy Lowell, Ben Hecht, Sherwood Anderson, and Carl Sandburg. Miss Anderson has written of her editorship in *My Thirty Years' War* (1930).

Little Shepherd of Kingdom Come, The, novel by John Fox,♦ published in 1903 and dramatized by Eugene Walter (1916).

Chad Buford, a young shepherd, comes to the Cumberland Mountain settlement of Kingdom Come, where he is befriended by the Turner family, whose adopted daughter Melissa falls in love with him. Separated from the Turners during a trip, he is picked up by Major Buford, who becomes interested in his namesake and takes him to Lexington. There Chad falls in love with Margaret Dean, but, shunned by her because his antecedents are unknown, he returns to the mountains. When his parentage is established by kinship with the major, he becomes engaged to Margaret, but they are estranged when he enlists in the Union army at the outbreak of the Civil War. Melissa makes a hazardous trip to warn Chad that his life is in danger, and dies as a result of exposure. After the peace, he returns home a major, is forgiven, and marries Margaret.

Little theater, name applied to an organization whose dramatic productions are outside the scope of the commercial theater, because of either financial or conventional limitations. The little-theater movement originated in Paris with Antoine's Théâtre Libre (1887), which led to the establishment of Stanislavsky's Moscow Art Theater (1890), the Independent Theatre in England (1891), and the Irish Literary Theatre of the Abbey Players (1899). The movement did not reach the U.S., however, until the second decade of the present century, when the regular stage was diluted by melodrama and extravagant romance, and motion pictures were beginning to supplant road companies and small-town theaters. Although predominantly amateur, some little-theater groups employed professional talent. Their origins were various, some, like the Hull-House Players, springing from social settlements, and others, like Mrs. Gale's Toy Theatre, being dependent upon wealthy patrons. Among the important early organizations were Winthrop Ames's Little Theatre, in New York City; Maurice Browne's Little Theatre, in Chicago; the Washington Square Players♦ and Provincetown Players♦; and two which derived their stimulus from college drama, the 47 Workshop directed by G.P. Baker♦ at Harvard and later at Yale, and the Carolina Playmakers♦ established by F.H. Koch at Chapel Hill (1918). By 1918 there were some 50 little theaters in the U.S., and estimates of the number in 1924 have been as high as 2000. The most notable success has been the Theatre Guild,♦ founded in 1918 by former members of the Washington Square Players. Although it was distinctly a little-theater group when founded, the Guild's shrewdness in play selection, skill in production, and ability in financial management led in 1925 to the building of its own million-dollar theater, and thus took it beyond the usual scope of the movement. The little theaters have had a profound effect on the stage in the U.S. Besides raising the standards for commercial productions and supplying opportunities for such important talents as O'Neill, Paul Green, Philip Barry, Thornton Wilder, and R.E. Jones, they have caused the establishment of permanent little theaters and community theaters throughout the country. The zest for experiment and cooperation in production and the awakening of a community spirit are values that were also influential in the Federal Theatre Project♦ and in such professional ventures as the Group Theatre.♦ Experimental theater has continued to flourish in New York City, in the American Place Theater, which in the 1960s staged, among other works, Robert Lowell's *The Old Glory* (1964), and in off-Broadway and off-off-Broadway productions, and also in city after city in the U.S., e.g. in the Magic Theatre in San Francisco, which introduced the work of Sam Shepard. Innovative interpretations of classic dramas from Shakespeare to Ibsen are also often part of the repertoire of little theaters along with the basic productions of avant-garde plays by foreign and young American dramatists.

Little Women, novel by Louisa May Alcott,♦ published in 1868–69.

This favorite book for children, based on the author's own youthful experiences, describes the family life of the Marches in a small New England community. Mrs. March is busy, cheerful, and sympathetic; her husband is an improvident army chaplain in the Civil War; and there are four daughters, Meg, Jo, Beth, and Amy. Jo at 15 is ungainly, unconventional, and enterprising, with an ambition to be an author. Meg, a year older, is pretty and wishes to be a lady. Beth is a delicate child of 13 with a taste for music. Amy is a blonde beauty of 12. Their domestic adventures, their attempts to increase the family's small income, their friendship with the neighboring Laurence family, and their later love affairs are the interests of the narrative. Meg marries John Brooke, tutor of Laurie, Mr. Laurence's grandson. Laurie loves Jo, but when she does not respond he goes to Europe to forget her. There he meets and falls in love with Amy, whom he marries. Beth falls ill and dies. Jo becomes a writer of melodramatic fiction, and later marries Dr. Bhaer, a middle-aged professor.

Littlepage Manuscripts, trilogy of novels by Cooper♦ tracing the history of the Littlepage family through three generations in New York state, during the difficulties between the propertied and propertyless classes that ended in the Anti-Rent War.♦ The novels are *Satanstoe,*♦ *The Chainbearer,*♦ and *The Redskins.*♦

LITTLETON, MARK, pseudonym of J.P. Kennedy.♦

Living Age, *The* (1844–1941), eclectic magazine of fiction, poetry, and comment, founded by Eliakim Littel,♦ who edited it until his death (1870). Until 1925 it was a weekly, reprinting the cream of foreign periodicals, but after 1938 it was surreptitiously financed by the Japanese government as an organ for propaganda.

Living Temple, *The,* poem in *The Autocrat of the Breakfast-Table.*♦

LLOYD, HENRY DEMAREST (1847–1903), after practicing law and opposing Tammany in his native New York City moved to Chicago to serve as an editorial writer on the *Tribune* (1873–85) but turned his whole attention to independent fighting against monopolies and to muckraking. These ideas and his practical experience defending men convicted in the Haymarket Riot and Debs in the Pullman strike lay behind his *Wealth Against Commonwealth* (1894). Later works praised social and industrial reforms in England in *Labour Copartnership* (1898), in New Zealand in *A Country Without Strikes* (1900), and in Switzerland in *A Sovereign People* (1907).

Local color, term applied to fiction or verse which emphasizes its setting, being concerned with the character of a district or of an era, as marked by its customs, dialect, costumes, landscape, or other peculiarities that have escaped standardizing cultural influences. The earliest American writing reflects its locale, as all literature must, but the local-color movement came into particular prominence in the U.S. after the Civil War, perhaps as an attempt to recapture the glamour of a past era, or to portray the sections of the reunited county one to the other. Specifically, American influences upon those authors known as local-color writers may be found in Down East humor and in the frontier tradition of tall tales. Other influences include the writings of Irving, the English tradition of Scott, Maria Edgeworth, and Bulwer-Lytton, and the French romantic tradition of *couleur locale* represented by Hugo, Mérimée, and Bernardin de Saint-Pierre. According to Edward Eggleston, another influence was the national and racial bias of the historical works of Taine, which specifically impelled him to a closer observation of his own region. In local-color literature one finds the dual influence of romanticism and realism, since the author frequently looks away from ordinary life to distant lands, strange customs, or exotic scenes, but retains through minute detail a sense of fidelity and accuracy of description. Harte's "The Luck of Roaring Camp"♦ (1868) is usually considered the first local-color story. The most distinguished writing engendered by the movement was in the form of the short story, whose development was thus deeply affected. Besides Harte, the local-color school produced such prominent authors as Harriet Beecher Stowe, Sara Orne Jewett, Mary W. Freeman, Rose Terry Cooke, and R.E. Robinson in New England; T.N. Page in Virginia; J.C. Harris in Georgia; G.W. Cable and Kate Chopin in Louisiana; Mary N. Murfree and John Fox in Tennessee and Kentucky; John Hay in Illinois; Riley and the Egglestons in Indiana; Clemens in California and on the Mississippi; E.W. Howe, Garland, and Zona Gale in the

Middle West; and R.H. Davis, H.C. Bunner, Brander Matthews, and O. Henry in New York City. A broader concept of sectional differences lies behind regionalism. ♦

LOCKE, ALAIN [LE ROY] (1886–1954), seminal influence in starting the Harlem Renaissance through his ground-breaking anthology *The New Negro: An Interpretation* (1925). It focused critical attention on the work of hitherto ignored writers and was a source of inspiration to many other black writers. Locke, a Philadelphian with degrees from Harvard and Oxford, conceived the plan of his book after a six-month tour of the American South in 1911 which left him convinced that black people must tell their own stories to lift themselves. From this same experience came his 1916 social study, *Race Contacts and Inter-Racial Relations.* Among his other books are *Frederick Douglass: A Biography of Anti-Slavery* (1935) and *The Negro in Art: A Pictorial Record of the Negro Artist and of the Negro Theme in Art* (1940). Locke was chairman of the philosophy department at Howard University for 35 years.

LOCKE, DAVID ROSS (1833–88), born in New York state, became an itinerant printer and journalist mainly in Ohio, where he achieved fame during the Civil War as a humorist under the pseudonym Petroleum V. Nasby. The first Nasby letter appeared in the Findlay *Jeffersonian* (March 21, 1861), of which he was editor. "Petroleum Vesuvius Nasby, late pastor uv the Church uv the New Dispensation, Chaplain to his excellency the President, and p. m. at Confederate x roads, kentucky," was a dissolute, illiterate country preacher, who intended to support the South by his foolish arguments and "advenchers," but ironically made its cause appear ludicrously inept. In his caricature of this stupid and corrupt Copperhead, Locke followed the humorous style of Artemus Ward, using the devices popular among literary comedians of the time; ridiculous spellings, deformed grammar, monstrous logic, puns, malapropisms, incongruous juxtaposition of ideas, and anticlimax. In 1865 he became editor of the Toledo *Blade,* and later its owner, contributing to it his immensely popular letters until his death. Lincoln greatly admired Locke's humor, and even read the latest Nasby letters to his cabinet, as comic relief, before outlining the Emancipation Proclamation. *The Nasby Papers* (1864) was the first of several collections, and Locke also published a political novel, *The Demagogue* (1891), and other writings on politics, especially in favor of liquor prohibition.

LOCKE, RICHARD ADAMS see *Moon Hoax.*

LOCKRIDGE, ROSS [FRANKLIN, JR.] (1914–48), Indiana-born novelist, after graduation and an M.A. from the state university did further graduate work at Harvard and taught at Simmons.

His sole book, *Raintree County* (1948), told with great fullness and many flashbacks of a single day (July 4, 1892) in the life of a high-school principal in a mythical Indiana county. Its achievement in summoning up a region and a way of life brought great acclaim, in the midst of which Lockridge mysteriously committed suicide. A biography by his son Larry was published in 1995.

LOCKWOOD, RALPH INGERSOLL (1798–1858?), born in Connecticut, became a prominent New York lawyer prior to writing his two novels, *Rosine Laval* (1833), a story of contemporary life published under the pseudonym Mr. Smith, and *The Insurgents* (1835), a story of Shays's Rebellion, published anonymously. His later books were legal treatises.

LODGE, HENRY CABOT (1850–1924), member of a prominent Boston family, graduated from Harvard (1871), became an editor of *The North American Review* (1863–76), received his Ph.D. (1876) after study in political science under Henry Adams, and turned actively to public affairs. Elected to Congress (1886–93) and to the Senate (1893–1924), he was a leading conservative Republican, known for his defense of civil-service laws, championing of a high protective tariff, opposition to free silver, interest in a strong army and navy, and, during his last years, his successful opposition to U.S. participation in the League of Nations. His writings include *A Short History of the English Colonies in America* (1881), *Alexander Hamilton* (1882), *Daniel Webster* (1883), *George Washington* (2 vols., 1888), collections of essays and speeches, and the autobiographical *Early Memories* (1913).

GEORGE CABOT LODGE (1873–1909), his son, was a poet known for his sonnets and other works distinguished for an awareness of the realities of modern life. His books include *The Song of the Wave* (1898), *Poems* (1902), *Cain, a Drama* (1904), *The Great Adventure* (1905), *Herakles* (1908), and *The Soul's Inheritance* (1909).

Loeb Classical Library, series of Greek and Latin texts with English translations, published since 1912 as a project initiated by the New York banker and scholar James Loeb (1867–1933).

Log of a Cowboy, The, semi-autobiographical novel of "The Old Trail Days," by Andy Adams, ♦ published in 1903.

LOGAN, CORNELIUS AMBROSIUS (1806–53), Baltimore-born playwright and popular actor-manager, noted for his comic roles and especially for his creation of Yankee types. His extremely successful farces included *Yankee Land; or, The Foundling of the Apple Orchard* (1834), *The Wag of Maine* (1835), *The Vermont Wool Dealer* (1840), and *Chloroform; or, New York a Hundred Years Hence* (1849).

OLIVE LOGAN (1839–1909), his daughter, was known in the U.S. and abroad for her acting and lecturing, her novels and books about the theater, and her comedies, *Surf* (1870) and *Newport* (1879).

LOGAN, JAMES (1674–1751), Irish-born statesman and scholar, came to Philadelphia (1699) as Penn's secretary. He became the political leader of the wealthy and aristocratic interests, in a successful conflict with the democratic antiproprietary party. Also famous as a bibliophile, botanist, and natural scientist, he wrote on such varied subjects as the impregnation of seeds, lightning, and an improvement of the quadrant. He translated *Cato's Moral Distichs* (1735) and *M.T. Cicero's Cato Major* (1744), both published by Franklin.

LOGAN, JAMES (*c.*1725–80), chief of the Mingo Indians, whose English name, although sometimes given as John Logan, was probably taken in honor of the Pennsylvania statesman. After 1774, when his family was massacred by white settlers on the banks of the Ohio, he began a series of attacks on the colonists, and was a leader in Dunmore's War. Although defeated, he refused to make peace, delivering a speech in reply to treaty offers that is often cited as a great example of Indian eloquence, and that was printed in Jefferson's *Notes on the State of Virginia*. During the Revolution, Logan aided the British. Later he became dissipated and degraded, and was killed in a family dispute. He figures frequently in literature, as in Neal's *Logan, A Family History* (1822).

LOGAN, JOHN (1923–   ), Iowa-born poet, after graduation from Coe College and an M.A. from Iowa University has taught at Notre Dame and the State University of New York, Buffalo. His vigorous poetry, marked by vivid imagery and great variety of technique, often deals with religion. It has been issued in *Cycle for Mother Cabrini* (1955), *Ghosts of the Heart* (1960), *Spring of the Thief* (1963), *The Zig-Zag Walk* (1969), *The Anonymous Lover* (1973), *The Bridge of Change* (1981), *A Ballet for the Ear* (1983), and *The Collected Poems* (1989).

Lolita, novel by Nabokov,♦ published in Paris (1955) and in the U.S. (1958).

In the psychopathic ward of a prison while awaiting trial for murder, 37-year-old Humbert Humbert writes out his life story. Though once wed to a woman about his age, he has long been obsessed by a passion for nymphets: girls between the ages of nine and 14. Coming from Europe to the U.S. on business, he meets and marries the widowed Charlotte Haze only to be near her 12-year-old daughter Lolita. To achieve this he considers murdering Charlotte, but when she is killed by accident he takes Lolita on a cross-country junket, planning to seduce her, only to

be seduced by her, for she is no longer a virgin. Lolita escapes from his jealous protection, and he does not learn of her again until she is 17, married, and pregnant. Then she tells him that during her days with him she had loved Clare Quilty, a famous playwright. Even though their affair is long in the past, the infuriated Humbert Humbert murders Quilty and is jailed but dies of a heart attack before his trial.

LOMAX, JOHN A[VERY] (1872–1948), scholarly collector of American ballads and folk songs published in *Cowboy Songs and Other Frontier Ballads* (1910, revised 1916, 1927, and 1938). *Adventures of a Ballad Hunter* (1947) is an autobiographical account. With his son Alan (1915–   ), Lomax made several collections, including *American Ballads and Folk Songs* (1934), *Our Singing Country* (1941), and *Negro Folk Songs as Sung by Lead Belly* (1936), a volume transcribed from the improvisations of the black guitarist who was discovered in a Louisiana penitentiary. The independent work of the younger Lomax includes *The Folk Songs of North America* (1960).

LONDON, JACK (JOHN GRIFFITH LONDON) (1876–1916), born in San Francisco, is said to have been the illegitimate son of William Henry Chaney (1821–1903), an itinerant astrologer. Reared by a family without fixed occupation or residence, he lived along the Oakland waterfront described in *Martin Eden* and *John Barleycorn,* and attended school only until he finished grammar school at 14. As a boy he bought a sloop and with some cronies raided the oyster beds about the bay, as he later told in *The Cruise of the Dazzler* (1902) and *Tales of the Fish Patrol* (1905). He abandoned this lawless, reckless occupation in 1893, to join a sealing cruise which took him as far as Japan. After a tramping trip through the U.S. and Canada, and a period of education including a semester at the University of California (1896), he returned to the Oakland waterfront with an interest in sociology and the Socialist party, which appears in several of his later books. In 1897 he joined the gold rush to the Klondike, where he made an unsuccessful attempt at mining, came to know the men who were prototypes of his elemental, hard-living heroes, and continued to read Spencer, Darwin, and Karl Marx. Stricken with scurvy, he returned to Oakland the following year and began to write of his experiences.

His short stories of the Yukon were published in the *Overland Monthly* (1898) and the *Atlantic Monthly* (1899), and in 1900 his first collection, *The Son of the Wolf,* was issued, bringing him national fame for his Kiplingesque portrayal of the brutal, vigorous life of the Far North. He continued to write in this vein, producing an enormous output of stories and novels, and in 1902, with an established reputation, went to London, where he made a close study of slum conditions for his descriptive work *The People of the Abyss* (1903). The remainder of his short but full life was spent under the balmy influence of popularity and success. He reported the Russo-Japanese War for the Hearst papers, made lecture tours, went on sailing voyages to the Caribbean and the South Seas, was a correspondent for *Collier's* in Mexico, and lived on his great patriarchal estate in California. His popularity, journalistic training, and eagerness for money caused him to write too prolifically, but his energy and ability as a storyteller gave even his worst writing a great appeal.

Besides several collections of short stories, including *Love of Life* (1907); *Lost Face* (1910), in which was printed the popular "To Build a Fire"♦; *South Sea Tales* (1911); and *On the Makaloa Mat* (1919), giving a sense of rugged life close to nature, his longer fiction also showed a deep concern with physical energy, the cult of "red blood," and a breed of Nietzschean supermen engaged in violent struggles of various sorts. This includes many novels, the best known of which are *The Call of the Wild*♦ (1903), the story of a dog in the Far North, who escapes from civilization to lead a wolf pack; *The Sea-Wolf*♦ (1904), about the powerful, ruthless captain of a sealing ship; *The Game*♦ (1905), the story of a prizefighter; *Before Adam*♦ (1906), concerned with the life of prehistoric savages; *White Fang*♦ (1906) telling of a wild dog who is tamed; *Martin Eden*♦ (1909), a semi-autobiographical novel about a writer's struggles; *Burning Daylight* (1910), the story of Daylight, a man of tremendous energy who wrests a fortune from the Klondike, then idealistically renounces his hard-won wealth; *Smoke Bellew*♦ (1912), about a journalist's strenuous adventures in the Yukon; *John Barleycorn* (1913), an autobiographical memoir intended as propaganda for temperance; and *Jerry of the Islands*♦ (1917), the story of an Irish setter pup in the South Seas.

London also wrote socialistic treatises, such as *War of the Classes* (1905) and *The Human Drift* (1917), as well as novels concerned with socialists and class struggle, of which the most famous are *The Iron Heel*♦ (1908), prophesying a fascist revolution to be followed eventually by an equalitarian golden age, and *The Valley of the Moon*♦ (1913), in which the economic problem is solved by a return to the land.

In spite of his belief in collectivism as an inevitable next step in human evolution, London was most convincing in his depiction of individualistic struggle and primitive violence. The very titles of many of his books, e.g. *The Strength of the Strong* (1911) and *The Abysmal Brute* (1913), indicate his preoccupation with the concept of the brute which underlies the social behavior of men and animals. Buck, in *The Call of the Wild,* shows a retrogression, while *White Fang* and *Jerry of the Islands* depict the brute under control or in process of subjugation. Wolf Larsen is a combination

of civilized brain with primitive force. In *The Iron Heel,* one of the most impressive scenes shows the people of the abyss fighting with bestial, reckless fury against their oppressors. London worshipped Marx and Nietzsche impartially, grasping what he could of their diametrically opposed theories, and championing now one, now the other, both in his novels and in his own life. London's *Letters* from 1896 to 1916 were published in three volumes (1989).

LONG, HUEY P[IERCE] (1893–1935), Louisiana politician, admitted to the bar in 1915, served on state commissions and as a state attorney in public utility legislation until his election to the governorship (1928). In 1931 he became a U.S. senator, resigning his governorship to one of his henchmen and continuing to hold the political reins in his state. Although he improved the university, roads, and public buildings, he was frequently criticized for corrupt practices. His economic views were expressed in a "Share-the-Wealth Plan." The famous phrase, "Every man a king," which is the title of his autobiography (1933), was taken from Bryan's "Cross of Gold" speech. Long's book *My First Days in the White House* (1935), published after his assassination, shows clearly his political desires and programs and his demagogic attitude. He has been the subject of several novels, including R. P. Warren's *All the King's Men,* Dos Passos's *Number One,* and Hamilton Basso's *Sun in Capricorn.*

LONG, JOHN LUTHER (1851–1927), author of novels, plays, and librettos, who collaborated with Belasco in dramatizing his short story *Madame Butterfly*♦ (1898), later made into an opera by Puccini. Long collaborated with Belasco on two other plays, *The Darling of the Gods*♦ and *Adrea.*♦

Long Day's Journey into Night, semi-autobiographical play by Eugene O'Neill,♦ written in 1941, posthumously produced and published (1956).

Recently released from an institution as cured of her drug addiction, Mary Tyrone, a handsome, nervous woman, is, in August 1912, once again at her summer home with her husband James, an aging former matinee idol, and their sons, Jamie, at 33 a hard-drinking, cynical Broadway hanger-on, and Edmund, a sickly, morbid intellectual. Mary's appearance and detached conversations soon make clear that she is not cured, and as the men drink heavily to escape reality, she nostalgically revives past dreams of becoming a nun or a concert pianist, and seems an innocent girl again. But she also reveals her addiction began when her miserly husband chose a quack doctor who treated her with morphine after her sickness in giving birth to Edmund. Like his mother, Edmund wants to "be alone . . . in another world . . . where life can hide from itself." Like her too, he shows both love and hate for his family as he confronts his limited future as a consumptive, realizing that his father will send him to the cheapest state sanitarium, since he is expected to die. A similar ambivalence is exhibited by the debauched Jamie, who drunkenly tells Edmund how much he loves him and yet how much he hates him as responsible for their mother's addiction. As James curses the sad spectacle, Mary appears, trailing her wedding gown, utterly immersed in the happier past. Realizing that she is forever lost to them and that their fates are intimately bound with hers, they impassively contemplate their own destruction.

Long Ghost, DR., character in *Omoo.* ♦

Long Roll, *The,* novel by Mary Johnston, ♦ published in 1911. *Cease Firing* (1912) is a sequel.

General Warwick Cary of Greenwood and members of his family are among the Virginians prominent in the political activities of secession and the battles and intrigues of the Civil War. His son Edward is a Confederate volunteer, as are the suitors of his three daughters, Unity, Molly, and Judith. Judith prefers Richard Cleave to Maury Stafford. When the two leave to join the army, Stafford alters an order for Cleave's regiment from General Stonewall Jackson, so that Cleave is involved in difficulties that lead to a court-martial. Dismissed in disgrace, Cleave reenlists as an artillerist under the name Philip Deaderick and distinguishes himself in action. Stafford is captured, after being finally rejected by Judith. Jackson promises Cleave a new court of inquiry, but dies in battle the following day.

Long Tom Coffin, character in *The Pilot.* ♦

Long Valley, *The,* 13 short stories by Steinbeck, ♦ published in 1938. "The Red Pony" and "Saint Katy the Virgin" had previously appeared in separate editions.

Set in towns and on farms of the Salinas Valley in California, these realistic tales are mainly concerned with the relations of people with growing things, and dramatize the author's frequently mystical concept of animal and vegetable nature. "The Red Pony" presents three episodes in the boyhood of Jody Tiflin, a farm boy whose knowledge of life matures through his loss of a beloved red pony, his meeting with the mysterious *paisano* Gitano, and the death of a mare during the birth of her colt. "The Snake" tells of a woman's morbid obsession with the natural functions of a captive male rattlesnake. "The Leader of the People," which has the same characters as "The Red Pony," is concerned with the pathetic old age of Jody's pioneer grandfather. "Saint Katy the Virgin," in a different mood and style, is an ironic parable of medieval times, telling of the conversion and beatification of a brood sow.

Longdon, character in *The Awkward Age.* ♦

LONGFELLOW, HENRY WADSWORTH (1807–82), descendant of a colonial family, was born at Portland, Me., and educated in private schools and at Bowdoin, where he graduated (1825) as a classmate of Hawthorne. His first poem, about John Lovewell, ♦ was published in a Portland newspaper (1820). Soon after graduation, he was offered a professorship of modern languages at Bowdoin, on the condition that he prepare himself by studying abroad. Accordingly, he spent the years from 1826 to 1829 in France, Spain, Italy, and Germany. While professor and librarian at Bowdoin (1829–35), he contributed essays and sketches to many magazines, and his teaching was so successful that he was recommended by George Ticknor to be his successor in the Smith professorship of French and Spanish at Harvard. To improve his knowledge of languages, Longfellow went abroad in 1835. His wife, to whom he had been married in 1831, died at this time. In 1836 began his 18 years of teaching at Harvard, during which he became a significant figure in the literary and social life of Cambridge.

His first prose work, *Outre-Mer: A Pilgrimage Beyond the Sea* (1833–34), reminiscent of Irving's *Sketch Book,* was followed by *Hyperion* ♦ (1839), a semi-autobiographical romance, interspersed with prose and verse concerned with German romanticism, which had greatly impressed him. *Voices of the Night* (1839), his first book of poetry, contains "Hymn to the Night," ♦ "A Psalm of Life," ♦ and other poems foreshadowing his later work. *Ballads and Other Poems* (1841) contains such favorites as "The Village Blacksmith," ♦ "The Wreck of the Hesperus," ♦ "Excelsior," ♦ and "The Skeleton in Armor," and did more to establish his fame than *Poems on Slavery* (1842), an outgrowth of his antislavery interests.

In 1843 he married Frances Appleton, the prototype of the heroine of *Hyperion,* whom he met abroad. Her father, a wealthy cotton-mill proprietor, presented the couple with Craigie House as a wedding present. Longfellow's life now flowed on placidly in the congenial Cambridge society, which included his brother-in-law, T.G. Appleton. Besides the three daughters who figure in his poem "The Children's Hour," ♦ two sons were born of this second marriage.

Meanwhile his fame increased with the publication of *The Spanish Student* (1843), a poetic drama; *The Belfry of Bruges and Other Poems* ♦ (1845), including "The Arsenal at Springfield," ♦ "The Bridge," ♦ "The Arrow and the Song," ♦ and "The Belfry of Bruges"; *Evangeline* ♦ (1847), his narrative poem on the Acadians; *Kavanagh* ♦ (1849), a semi-autobiographical prose tale; *The Seaside and the Fireside* (1849), a volume of poems best known for "The Building of the Ship" ♦; *The Golden Legend* ♦ (1851), a dramatic poem on medieval Germany, later incorporated in *Christus;* and

Hiawatha♦ (1855), his celebrated "Indian Edda." In 1854 he resigned his professorship, which he said was "a great hand laid on all the strings of my lyre, stopping their vibration."

His popularity throughout the U.S. and Europe was so great that, on the publication of *The Courtship of Miles Standish*♦ (1858), more than 15,000 copies were sold during the first day in Boston and London. His happiness and the even course of his writing were sharply broken, however, when his wife was burned to death (1861). For a long time his grief stopped his creative work, and it was so persistent that it is implicit in "The Cross of Snow," written 18 years afterward. The *Tales of a Wayside Inn,*♦ including "Paul Revere's Ride",♦ began to appear in book form in 1863, but they were in large part completed before the death of his wife. For solace he turned to his translation of Dante's *Divine Comedy* (published 1865–67), done with the aid of Lowell and C.E. Norton, who met with him every week in the Dante Society that they formed. He added two lengthy pieces to *The Golden Legend,* which appeared in final form as *Christus*♦ (1872); added to the *Tales of a Wayside Inn;* and wrote many sonnets, including a sequence of six, "Divina Commedia,"♦ now considered to be among his most significant work.

During his remaining years, honors were heaped upon him and his home became a shrine for Americans and a point of visit for distinguished foreigners. During a tour of Europe (1868–69), he received degrees from Cambridge and Oxford, and was given a private audience by Queen Victoria. His last poems, including "Morituri Salutamus,"♦ were collected in *The Masque of Pandora* (1875), *Kéramos* (1878), *Ultima Thule* (1880), and *In the Harbor* (1882). After his death, he became the only American to be honored with a bust in the Poet's Corner of Westminster Abbey.

The gentleness, sweetness, and purity for which his poetry was popular during his lifetime were the very qualities that caused the reaction against it after his death. His writings belong to the milder aspects of the romantic movement, and he was strongly influenced by the German romantic lyrists. Throughout his work and his life, he was consistently high-minded but conventional, and untouched by the religious and social struggles that disturbed his contemporaries, with the exception of his interest in antislavery, for which his friendship with Sumner was partly responsible. He exercised a great influence in bringing European culture to the U.S., and likewise did much to popularize American folk themes abroad, where his work was immensely popular and widely translated. In his own time he was universally respected, except by a very few detractors, such as Poe in his article "Longfellow and Other Plagiarists." Even today Poe's criticism cannot be accepted, despite Longfellow's indebtedness to foreign models, e.g. *Hiawatha* to

the meter of the Finnish *Kalevala,* and "The Wreck of the Hesperus" to the ballad "Sir Patrick Spens." A later age, with different standards, has also accused him of undue didacticism and excessive symbolism, as in "A Psalm of Life," "Excelsior," "The Village Blacksmith," and "My Lost Youth."♦ The very simplicity that has made him a children's poet has lessened his mature audience, since, despite his great metrical skill, he is lacking in passion and high imagination, and is too decorous, benign, and sweet. More recent serious scholarly interest is indicated by the editing of his *Letters* (6 vols., 1966–82).

LONGFELLOW, SAMUEL (1819–92), brother of H. W. Longfellow, was a prominent Unitarian clergyman, and was active in the Transcendentalist movement. His writings include several books of hymns, a biography of his brother (2 vols., 1886), and *Thalatta: A Book for the Seaside* (1853), in collaboration with T.W. Higginson.

LONGSTREET, AUGUSTUS BALDWIN (1790–1870), Georgia jurist, educator, and author. He is best known for his *Georgia Scenes, Characters, and Incidents*♦ (1835), humorous realistic sketches of the life of the Old Southwest, which were forerunners of the work of such writers as J.G. Baldwin, G.W. Harris, J.J. Hooper, W.T. Thompson, and Clemens. He was a fervent advocate of nullification, establishing a newspaper and writing several pamphlets for this cause. He served successively as president of Emory College (1839–48), Centenary College (1849), the University of Mississippi (1849–56), and the University of South Carolina (1857–65). *Master William Mitten* (1864) is a semi-autobiographical novel of his youth in Georgia. Later stories and sketches in the vein of his first book were less successful.

Lonigan, STUDS, character whose life from a squalid adolescence on Chicago's South Side to his physical and moral disintegration and death in his late twenties is chronicled in the trilogy of novels, *Young Lonigan,*♦ *The Young Manhood of Studs Lonigan,*♦ and *Judgment Day,*♦ by James T. Farrell.

Look Homeward, Angel: *A Story of the Buried Life,* autobiographical novel by Thomas Wolfe♦ published in 1929. A dramatization (1957) by Ketti Frings♦ won a Pulitzer Prize. *Of Time and the River*♦ is a sequel to the novel.

Eugene Gant grows up in Altamont, Catawba (Asheville, N.C.), the youngest of six children of Oliver Gant, stonecutter and amateur orator, whose demonic passions both fascinate and terrify Eugene, and whose love of craftsmanship and rhetoric dominate the boy's character. Eliza, Oliver's crafty, miserly wife, has frequent quarrels with her husband, and leaves him, while Eugene is yet a child, to operate a boardinghouse. The other children include Steve, lazy, selfish, and corrupt; Daisy, shy and retiring; Helen, her father's favorite, "strung on the same wires"; Ben, quiet and intelligent, who becomes a newspaperman, and whose death is Eugene's most poignant loss; and Luke, exuberant and lovable. Eugene, the "baby" of the family, has a relatively solitary youth, delivering newspapers in the black quarter and becoming acquainted with the town's "characters." He reads and memorizes English classics, attending a private school where he receives a limited but more balanced education. At 16 he enters the state university, where he continues to feel lonely and "different," but by the time of his graduation makes important personal adjustments to the world, editing the literary magazine, having his first sexual encounters and youthful love affairs, and finally breaking with his family to make what he conceives to be a pilgrimage in search of "the lost lane-end into heaven, a stone, a leaf, an unfound door. . . ."

Looking Backward, 2000–1887, Utopian romance by Edward Bellamy,♦ published in 1888. Its immense popularity led to the founding of Bellamy clubs and a Nationalist party. *Equality* (1897), a sequel, is more a tract than a novel.

Conceived as a "fairy tale of social felicity," the book describes a future social and economic order through the narrative of Julian West, a young Bostonian, who enters a hypnotic sleep in 1887 and is revived 113 years later in the changed city. He falls in love with Edith Leete, a descendant of his former fiancée, and through her father, a physician, learns of the scientific and social developments that have taken place. In contrast with the squalor of the slums and the injustices and inequalities of the earlier time, he finds an America in which the business monopolies have evolved to become "The Great Trust," economic chaos having been replaced by a democratic form of state capitalism. Private enterprise has disappeared, each citizen is both an employee and a member of the state, and the collective organization of wealth and industry has eradicated crime, poverty, advertising, warfare, and many diseases. The cultural level of the people has consequently risen, and Dr. Leete ascribes these changes to the spread of social intelligence and social ethics among a good people formerly victimized by an evil system.

Loop, district of Chicago that forms the city's financial, shopping, theatrical, and hotel center. It received its name from the elevated railroad tracks (installed 1897) that "loop" the section. As the turbulent heart of the largest Midwestern city, the Loop has figured in the poetry of Sandburg, and in such fiction as Norris's *The Pit* and Fuller's *The Cliff-Dwellers.*

LOOS, ANITA (1893–1981), author of *Gentlemen Prefer Blondes* (1925), subtitled the "Illuminating Diary of a Professional Lady," a novel satirizing a pair of naïve, pert sirens of the jazz age. This was followed by a less successful sequel, *But Gentlemen Marry Brunettes* (1928). Later fiction includes *No Mother To Guide Her* (1961), a satire set in Hollywood. Other views of Hollywood are in her memoir *The Talmadge Girls* (1979), about two early-day film stars, and her autobiographical *This Brunette Prefers Work* (1956), *A Girl Like I* (1966), *Kiss Hollywood Goodby* (1974), and *Cast of Thousands* (1977). Her plays include a dramatization of her first book (1926); *Happy Birthday* (1947); *A Mouse Is Born* (1951); and *Gigi* (1952), based on Colette's novel; as well as motion pictures. *Twice Over Lightly* (1972) prints her memoirs and reactions to New York City and those of Helen Hayes.

LORD, WILLIAM WILBERFORCE (1819–1907), New York poet and Episcopal clergyman, was hailed as "the American Milton" on the appearance of his *Poems* (1845), although Poe, whose hostility he had incurred by a parody, wrote a scathing criticism, accusing Lord of plagiarism. Among his other works were *Christ in Hades* (1851), a religious epic, and *André* (1856), a blank-verse narrative. His *Complete Poetical Works* appeared in 1938. He was a chaplain in the Confederate army and for a time a minister in the South.

Lord Weary's Castle, collection of poems by Robert Lowell,♦ published in 1946.

Deriving its title from a folk ballad about Lord Weary's refusal to pay his stonemason Lambkin for building his castle, and Lambkin's murder of the lord's wife and child, the symbolic significance, as John Berryman pointed out in a review, is that the "castle is a house of ingratitude, failure of obligation, crime and punishment." These are among the themes of the volume's lyrics, some of which were revised from Lowell's previous book, *Land of Unlikeness,* some of them related to World War II and others to the author's New England heritage. Major works include "The Quaker Graveyard in Nantucket," an elegy for a cousin, alluding to Melville and Thoreau and treating man's equivocal relations to nature and the theological issues of innocence, corruption, sin, and redemption; "'Mr. Edwards and the Spider," drawing with antipathy upon Jonathan Edwards's *Sinners in the Hands of an Angry God;* and "Christmas Eve Under Hooker's Statue," relating the Civil War and World War II, and contrasting childhood innocence and adult materialistic belligerence.

LORDE, AUDRE (1934–92), poet. Born in New York City of West Indian parents, Lorde was educated at the National University of Mexico, Hunter College, and Columbia University. The main themes of her fiery verse are love, race, and being female, with a feminist agenda. Among her books of verse are *The New York Head Shop* *and Museum* (1974); *Coal* (1976); *The Black Unicorn* (1978), containing poems about Africa; and *Our Dead Behind Us* (1986). Her prose works include *The Cancer Journals* (1980), about her fight to overcome the disease; *Zami: A New Spelling of My Name* (1982), which she calls a "biomythography"; *Sister Outsider* (1984); and *Burst of Light* (1988). Her last work is *The Marvelous Arithmetics of Distance, Poems 1987–1992.*

LORIMER, GEORGE HORACE (1867–1937), as editor (1899–1936) of *The Saturday Evening Post* raised the magazine from a circulation of 1800 to 3,000,000 by both his business acumen and his sense of middle-class taste. He laid much stress on business as a subject in articles and in fiction, including Frank Norris's *The Pit*, George Randolph Chester's Get-Rich-Quick Wallingford series, and stories by Dreiser, Lewis, Booth Tarkington, and Peter B. Kyne. However, his range of interest was wider as indicated by publication of works by Stephen Crane, Jack London, Fitzgerald, and Marquand. He himself wrote the uplifting and hortatory *Letters from a Self-Made Merchant to His Son* (1902).

Lost Colony, The, see *Roanoke Island.*

Lost generation, name applied to the disillusioned intellectuals and aesthetes of the years following World War I, who rebelled against former ideals and values but could replace them only by despair or a cynical hedonism. The remark of Gertrude Stein, "You are all a lost generation," addressed to Hemingway, was used as a preface to the latter's novel *The Sun Also Rises,* which brilliantly describes an expatriate group typical of the "lost generation." Other expatriate American authors of the period to whom the term is generally applied include Malcolm Cowley, E.E. Cummings, F. Scott Fitzgerald, Archibald MacLeish, and Ezra Pound.

Lost Lady, A, novel by Willa Cather,♦ published in 1923.

Niel Herbert, a boy in the Midwestern town of Sweet Water, tells the story of Marian Forrester, who brings a knowledge of gracious living to the new country as the youthful wife of old Captain Forrester, retired railroad builder and aristocrat of the pioneer generation. Mrs. Forrester's beauty and charm set her apart from her crass, commonplace neighbors, as do her husband's rugged strength, integrity, and love of fine possessions. The captain is devoted to his wife, but her passionate nature causes her to become the secret mistress of his bachelor friend Frank Ellinger. When Forrester loses his fortune by assuming responsibility in the failure of his bank, he suffers a paralytic stroke. His wife nurses him carefully, but after his death she is left in financial straits. Ivy Peters, a pushy businessman of the new generation, acquires her beautiful home and

becomes her lover, to the bitter disillusion of Niel, who regards her as "a lost lady," although he never ceases to admire her. She goes West to her childhood home when Peters marries and occupies the Forrester mansion, and for Niel this symbolizes the end of the great era of the pioneers. Years afterward, he learns that she married a wealthy Englishman in South America, and until her death won admiration for her gracefulness, charm, and taste.

Lost Weekend, The, novel by Charles Jackson.♦

LOTHROP, HARRIET MULFORD STONE (1844–1924), author of books for children, wrote under the pseudonym Margaret Sidney. Her best-known work was *Five Little Peppers and How They Grew* (1881), which in 50 years sold more than 2,000,000 copies.

Lotos Club, New York City club of journalists, authors, actors, musicians, artists, and patrons of the arts, was founded in 1870 to offset the conservatism of the Century Association.♦ Its early members included Edwin Booth, Augustin Daly, John Hay, Bronson Howard, Brander Matthews, and Whitelaw Reid.

Lottery, The, title story of a collection by Shirley Jackson,♦ first issued in *The New Yorker* and published in the book in 1949.

On the morning of June 27 of a recent year, the 300 townspeople of an American village prepare for the annual lottery in a mood of excitement. The tradition of the lottery is so old that some of its ritual has been forgotten and some has been changed, and its basic purpose is entirely unremembered, but all residents are present to take part in it when the civic-minded Mr. Summers, having been sworn in, hands a piece of paper to the head of each household. When it is discovered that the Hutchison family has drawn the marked slip, each member of the family—Bill, Tessie, and the three children—is given another slip. Silence prevails as suspense hovers over the proceedings. After resignedly protesting the unfairness of the first drawing, Tessie finds that she holds the marked slip. Set in a cleared space, desperately afraid, she feels the first pebbles hitting her as the people, holding stones, push forward, "and then they were upon her."

LOUDON, SAMUEL (c.1727–1813), New York printer and publisher, in 1776 founded *The New York Packet and the American Advertiser,* a patriotic weekly newspaper. Although a staunch patriot, he became unpopular with the radical element when he issued *The Deceiver Unmasked; or, Loyalty and Interest United* (1776), an anonymous reply to Paine's *Common Sense.* While the British occupied New York, the *Packet* was suspended (Aug. 1776–Jan. 1777). It was then resumed irregularly in Fishkill, N.Y., until Loudon could return to the city. In 1787–88 the paper printed many of the *Federalist* essays. After 1792 it was known as the *Diary or Loudon's Register,* under which title it was continued by his son.

Louisville *Daily Journal* (1830–68), founded as an anti-Jackson newspaper by G.D. Prentice,♦ became noted for its editor's witty *bons mots* and stinging squibs, collected in *Prenticeana* (1860). During the Civil War the paper was loyal to the Union, and it is often credited with having prevented the secession of Kentucky. During Reconstruction, Prentice wavered between Republican and Democratic points of view, and in 1868 he retired, when the paper was merged with its rival, the Louisville *Courier.*

The Louisville *Courier-Journal* (1868–), the product of this merger, was edited by "Marse" Henry Watterson♦ and bore the stamp of his personality, typically Southern and symbolic of the Lost Cause. Despite this attitude, and his slow, picturesque, reminiscent style, his opinions were frequently opposed to those of his neighbors, and he advocated free trade, closer friendship with the North, and opposition to the Ku Klux Klan. The paper was sold in 1918, becoming a typical metropolitan daily, and Watterson resigned the following year. Herbert Agar was editor (1940–42). The paper won a Pulitzer Prize (1967) for Meritorious Public Service, and individual reporters won Pulitzer Prizes (1921, 1976, 1978, 1980) for their articles.

LOUNSBURY, THOMAS RAYNESFORD (1838–1915), professor of English literature at Yale, was the author of *A History of the English Language* (1879), a life of *James Fenimore Cooper* (1882), and *Shakespearean Wars* (3 vols., 1901–6).

LOVE, ALFRED HENRY (1830–1913), Quaker whose religious and social ideas made him an outstanding pacifist. His refusal to compromise during the Civil War led to the writing of *An Appeal in Vindication of Peace Principles* (1862) and the formation of the Universal Peace Society. Throughout his life he continued his vigorous though somewhat naïve attempts to prevent war, and for his spirited criticism of the Spanish-American War he was hanged in effigy.

Love in '76, play by Oliver B. Bunce,♦ produced and published in 1857.

Love Nest, *The, and Other Stories,* nine short stories by Lardner,♦ published in 1926. The title story was dramatized by Robert Sherwood (1927).

These accurate transcriptions of American speech reveal the self-deception and hypocrisies of typical Americans and express the author's sardonically humorous view of native character. "The Love Nest," telling of a motion-picture magnate's introduction of a reporter to his "hap-py wife and family," exposes the man's crude, selfish willfulness and the unhappiness of his frustrated, dipsomaniac wife. "Haircut," a barber's monologue while serving a customer, tells of the murder of an intolerable practical joker by a half-wit youth. "Rhythm" is the story of a cynical Tin Pan Alley composer, showing his egotism and meanness. "Who Dealt?," presenting the conversation of a stupid, frivolous woman during a bridge game, reveals the tragedy of her husband's previous love affair.

Love Song of J. Alfred Prufrock, The, poem by T.S. Eliot,♦ first published in *Poetry* (June 1915) and collected in *Prufrock and Other Observations* (1917). In the form of a dramatic monologue it presents with irony and pathos the musings of an aging young man, uncertain, uneasy, and unable to commit himself to the love he desires or to life at all, a figure representative of frustrations in modern life and of the aridity of a sterile upper-class culture.

LOVECRAFT, H[OWARD] P[HILLIPS] (1890–1937), author of science fiction for popular magazines, whose posthumously collected works include *The Outsider and Others* (1939) and *Beyond the Wall of Sleep* (1943). August Derleth published a critical biography (1945) of him.

LOVEJOY, ELIJAH PARISH (1802–37), born in Maine, became editor of the Abolitionist St. Louis *Observer* (1833), but was forced to move to Alton, Ill. (1836), when he was threatened with violence. The press on which he printed the Alton *Observer* was attacked four times, and he was killed in defending it.

OWEN LOVEJOY (1811–64), his brother, carried on the cause, became a leading Illinois Abolitionist, championed Lincoln, and served in Congress (1856–64).

LOVETT, ROBERT MORSS (1870–1956), professor of English at the University of Chicago, whose many books include *Richard Gresham* (1904) and *A Winged Victory* (1907), novels; *Cowards* (1914), a play; *Edith Wharton* (1925), a critical study; *A Preface to Fiction* (1930); two works on English literature in collaboration with William Vaughn Moody, whose poems he edited in 1930; and *All Our Years* (1948), autobiography. He edited *The Dial* (1919) and was long an associate editor of *The New Republic.*

LOVEWELL, JOHN (1691–1725), Massachusetts Indian fighter, was paid 2½ shillings a day and a bounty for scalps by the General Court. Decoyed by Pequawkets in Maine, he and some partners were killed, as told in "Lovewell's Fight" and other ballads; in Longfellow's first poem, "The Battle of Lovell's Pond"; and Parkman's *A Half-Century of Conflict.* Hawthorne's "Roger Malvin's Burial" tells of two survivors.

Lovingood, SUT, see *Sut Lovingood Yarns.*

LOWELL, ABBOTT LAWRENCE (1856–1943), brother of Amy Lowell, was a Boston lawyer and professor of political science at Harvard, of which he became president (1909–33). During his presidency the undergraduate curriculum was revised to include tutorial programs offered in residential houses like the colleges of Oxford and Cambridge. His books include *Essays on Government* (1889), *The Influence of Party upon Legislation* (1902), *Public Opinion and Popular Government* (1913), *Public Opinion in War and Peace* (1923), and *Conflicts of Principle* (1932).

LOWELL, AMY [LAWRENCE] (1874–1925), collateral descendant of James Russell Lowell, was born in Brookline, Mass. Her first book, *A Dome of Many-Coloured Glass* (1912), lacks the vivid individuality and technical experimentation that characterize the poetry in *Sword Blades and Poppy Seed* (1914), *Men, Women, and Ghosts* (1916), *Can Grande's Castle* (1918), *Pictures of the Floating World* (1919), and *Legends* (1921).

In 1913 Miss Lowell became identified with the movement of Imagism,♦ and after Ezra Pound abandoned the group she was its dominating force. Her technical experimentation includes not only the modes of the Imagists but also polyphonic prose,♦ a free-verse method of which she and John Gould Fletcher were the leading exponents. Although her work attracted wide attention, it has been criticized as dealing too exclusively with sensual images, particularly visual ones, and as neglecting emotional values. Her distinctive personality informs *A Critical Fable*♦ (1922), a witty *Who's Who* of contemporary poets patterned after *A Fable for Critics.* Her biographical study *John Keats* (1925) has been called an uncritical amassing of materials, although it is distinguished by the zest that marks all her work. Among the most noted of her poems are "Patterns," published in *Men, Women, and Ghosts,* a free-verse dramatic monologue on the clash between desire and convention within the mind of a woman of the 18th century, and "Lilacs," an Imagistic descriptive piece published in *What's O'Clock?* (1925), a volume for which she was posthumously awarded the Pulitzer Prize (1926).

Her other books of verse include *East Wind* (1926) and *Ballads for Sale* (1927), and she wrote two further critical studies, *Six French Poets* (1915) and *Tendencies in Modern American Poetry* (1917). Her correspondence with Florence Ayscough about translations from the Chinese (*Fir-Flower Tablets,* (1921) was published in 1946.

LOWELL, JAMES RUSSELL (1819–91), descendant of a distinguished colonial family, was born at Cambridge, and graduated from Harvard as class poet (1838; LL.B., 1840; M.A., 1841). Finding law not to his liking, he was generally confused about his place in life and went through a morose period from which he was rescued by his future wife, Maria White Lowell.♦ His early poetry, in *A Year's Life* (1841), shows a sharp difference from the *Poems* (1844) published the year of his marriage. Under the influence of his wife, an ardent Abolitionist and liberal, he temporarily submerged his native conservatism and was stimulated to forceful thinking and writing. His first journalistic venture was the short-lived *Pioneer*♦ (1843), but inspired by his wife he became a contributor to and editor of the *National Anti-Slavery Standard*♦ (1848–52) and contributed to the *Pennsylvania Freeman.*

The year 1848 marked his most important writing in his youth, for it included the publication of works that established him as a poet, critic, humorist, and political satirist: *Poems . . . Second Series,*♦ *A Fable for Critics,*♦ the first series of *The Biglow Papers,*♦ and *The Vision of Sir Launfal.*♦ His prose and poetry continued in these varied categories, and his great facility permitted him to become a competent, if not brilliant, author in all these fields. With the exception of these four books, published in his twenty-ninth year, most of his writing lacks vitality, is too hortatory, depends too much on verbal pranks, ingenious rhymes, and pleasant sounds, and represents the output of a man of taste who was a Bostonian and a Victorian.

His wife died in 1853, and it is significant that until the publication of *Fireside Travels* (1864), a volume of literary essays, he published no books. He entered the academic world in 1855, succeeding Longfellow as Smith Professor of French and Spanish at Harvard, in which capacity he continued his predecessor's task of directing Americans to the literature of Europe, past and present. After a European journey to perfect his linguistic knowledge, he occupied the post and was nominally professor until 1886, although his teaching career really ended in 1876. As a professor he published little poetry and turned to scholarly interests, emphasizing literary criticism and losing contact with the immediate world.

His criticism, contributed to periodicals and later assembled in book form, includes *Among My Books* (1870), *My Study Windows* (1871), a second series of *Among My Books* (1876), *Latest Literary Essays and Addresses* (1891), and *The Old English Dramatists* (1892). Lowell was the first editor of the *Atlantic Monthly*♦ (1857–61), in this position being a leader among the mid-19th-century authors who are said to have brought a renaissance to New England.

In 1864 he temporarily joined C.E. Norton as editor of *The North American Review,* and here also exerted a powerful influence on public taste and opinion. His *Political Essays* (1888) were gathered from his prose articles in these magazines, and in addition he contributed to the *Atlantic* his second series of *The Biglow Papers*♦ (1867), trenchantly criticizing England's part in the Civil War and stating the patriotic sentiments of Northerners. His feeling for the Union cause was also expressed in one of his most important poems, "Ode Recited at the Harvard Commemoration"♦ (1865), in honor of the Harvard men who died in the war. *The Cathedral*♦ (1869) is probably the best of his later poems.

As a staunch Republican, he was appointed a presidential elector in 1876; his firm stand for Hayes was rewarded by his appointment as minister to Spain (1877–80), and Garfield appointed him minister to England (1880–85). As a charming gentleman who had long since reverted to his natural conservatism, he was popularly received in European and English society and helped interpret American ideals to the Old World, both through personal contacts and through more formal addresses, such as *On Democracy* (1884). After the death of his second wife (1885) he gave up public life and returned to his Cambridge home, Elmwood. The works on which his reputation rests most securely were written before he was 30. Most of his books are periodical or lecture collections, and his writings, loosely connected, though brilliant in parts, have a diffused totality.

LOWELL, MARIA WHITE (1821–53), married J.R. Lowell♦ (1844), and was important in her own right as the author of poems, 20 of which were published in 1855, and a complete collection in 1907 and 1936. She stimulated her husband's interests in antislavery and the Transcendentalist movement. Her poetry, with a few exceptions, is considered cultivated but derivative, and her greatest work is the Abolitionist poem "Africa."

LOWELL, ROBERT [TRAILL SPENCE, JR.] (1917–77), grandson of the 19th-century poet and novelist of the same name and member of the prominent Boston family, was himself reared in Boston, as frankly described in *Life Studies,* and educated at Harvard and at Kenyon College. The year of his graduation (1940) was also marked by his marriage to his first wife, the writer Jean Stafford (he was later married—1949–72—to the novelist Elizabeth Hardwick), and his conversion to Catholicism. During World War II he was refused the status of a conscientious objector and was jailed. His poetry, first published in *Land of Unlikeness* (1944), is marked by themes of rebellion, depiction of corruption and chaos in the modern world, and quest for spiritual values in his adopted faith. A baroque intensity continues in his later poems collected in *Lord Weary's Castle*♦ (1946, Pulitzer Prize), *The Mills of the Kavanaughs* (1951), and *For the Union Dead*♦ (1964), as does his great technical skill, but his rich allegory shows a greater sense of acceptance in a more philosophical mood after he became an agnostic. *Life Studies*♦ (1959) includes frank prose and poetry about his family and himself. Lowell next wrote verse adaptations of foreign poems, collected in *Imitation* (1961), and made a free

translation of Racine's play as *Phaedria* (1961). Translations also appeared with original poems in *Near the Ocean* (1967). In 1965 he published *The Old Glory,* three one-act plays based on Melville's "Benito Cereno" and Hawthorne's "My Kinsman, Major Molyneux" and "Endicott and the Red Cross," and in 1969 he issued a prose *Prometheus Bound* derived from Aeschylus. *Notebooks, 1967–68* (1969) contains 274 sonnets on the contemporary scene and Lowell's personal situation in a time of upheaval, those dealing with his wife and daughter being reprinted in *For Lizzie and Harriet* (1973). *History* (1973) also draws upon the poems from his *Notebooks* and adds others that convey the poet's reflections on world events, past and present. *The Dolphins* (1973, Pulitzer Prize) is a cycle of sonnets about Lowell's life in England and New York, his third marriage, and the birth of a son. It was followed by a final collection of poems, *Day by Day* (1977). His *Collected Prose* was issued in 1987.

LOWELL, ROBERT TRAILL SPENCE (1816–91), elder brother of J.R. Lowell, graduated from Harvard (1833) and for some time was an Episcopal clergyman in Newfoundland, the basis for his novel *The New Priest in Conception Bay* (1858). *Anthony Brade, A Story of a School* (1874) derives from his experiences as headmaster of St. Mark's, and *A Story or Two from an Old Dutch Town* (1878) is set in Schenectady, where he taught at Union College. The best known of his *Poems* (1864) is "The Relief of Lucknow," about the Sepoy rebellion in Lahore (1857).

Lowell Institute, Boston adult educational institution, founded by John Lowell (1799–1836), as a center providing free lectures on all subjects by outstanding scholars. The lectures are also printed.

Lowell Offering, see *Farley, Harriet.*

Lower East Side, section of New York City bounded by the East River, the Bowery, and the fringe of the uptown area. It has long been known as a densely populated slum district of tenements housing poor, recent immigrants, whose foreign customs, such as shopping from sidewalk pushcart markets, were retained. For many years it was a ghetto for newly arrived Jews, but in more recent years other ethnic groups, including Puerto Ricans, have found their home in this district. Alfred E. Smith was reared in the district, as were Edward MacDowell and the more representative composers Irving Berlin and George Gershwin. Those who have written about the Lower East Side include Jacob Riis, Ernest Poole, Clifford Odets, Elmer Rice, Waldo Frank, Michael Gold, Alfred Kreymborg, Sholem Asch, Alfred Kazin, Bernard Malamud, and Henry Roth. Its life was painted by George Luks.

LOWES, JOHN LIVINGSTON (1867–1945), born in Indiana, was a professor of English at Swarthmore, Washington University, and after 1918 at Harvard. He lectured widely and edited many scholarly works, but is best known for his books, *Convention and Revolt in Poetry* (1919), tracing main currents in English poetry; *The Road to Xanadu* (1927), an exhaustive analysis of Coleridge's creative imagination; *Of Reading Books and Other Essays* (1929); and *The Art of Geoffrey Chaucer* (1931). He edited the *Selected Poems* of Amy Lowell (1928).

LOY, MINA (MINA GERTRUDE LOWY) (1882–1966), English-born poet whose contributions to little magazines of the 1920s are collected in *Lunar Baedecker* (1923). She was praised by T.S. Eliot, and called by Yvor Winters a master of free verse "so simplified, so denuded of secondary accent, as to be indistinguishable from prose." Her cool poems of the first volume and some additions were issued as *Lunar Baedeker & Time-Tables* (1958) and with further additions as *The Last Lunar Baedeker* (1982).

LUCE, CLARE BOOTHE, see *Boothe, Clare*.

Luck of Roaring Camp, The, story by Bret Harte,♦ published in the *Overland Monthly* (1868) and reprinted in *The Luck of Roaring Camp and Other Sketches* (1870). It is often called the first example of local-color fiction.

A child is born to Cherokee Sal, a prostitute in the California gold-mining settlement of Roaring Camp. The mother dies, and the child, christened Thomas Luck, is adopted by the hardened miners, whose spirit is changed to a beautiful though awkward sympathy. The following year, when the river rises, Roaring Camp is engulfed, and Kentuck, one of the miners, is drowned with The Luck in his arms.

Lucky Sam McCarver, play by Sidney Howard,♦ produced in 1925 and published in 1926.

LUDLOW, FITZ HUGH (1836–70), born in New York City, graduated from Union College, and the following year won notoriety for his book *The Hasheesh Eater* (1857), based on his own experiences as a drug addict. Among his periodical contributions was a series of descriptive sketches written during a tour of the West (1863) for the *Atlantic Monthly* and later collected as *The Heart of the Continent* (1870); an article on the effects of opium, "What Shall They Do To Be Saved?"; and the short stories collected in *Little Brother and Other Genre-Pictures* (1867).

LUHAN, MABEL DODGE (1879–1962), born at Buffalo, N.Y., severed her ties with her socially prominent family and became a leader of liberal intellectual and aesthetic movements. In Italy (1902–12) and in New York City (1912–18) she established salons to which were attracted such figures as Eleonora Duse, Gertrude Stein, Steffens, Isadora Duncan, John Reed, Walter Lippmann, Van Vechten, and Max Eastman. She moved to New Mexico (1918), and there in 1923 married her fourth husband, Antonio Luhan, a Taos Indian. Her life at Taos is described with painful detail in several books. *Lorenzo in Taos* (1932) is an account of her turbulent intimacy with D.H. Lawrence, while *Winter in Taos* (1935) is a narrative of the region's background. Her autobiography, *Intimate Memories,* comprises four volumes, *Background* (1933), *European Experiences* (1935), *Movers and Shakers* (1936), and *Edge of Taos Desert* (1937).

LUKAS, J. ANTHONY (1933–), New York City-born journalist, educated at Harvard and associated with it as a lecturer. His books include *Don't Shoot—We Are Your Children* (1971), *Nightmare: The Underside of the Nixon Years* (1976), and *Common Ground: A Turbulent Decade in the Lives of Three American Families* (1985), awarded a Pulitzer Prize for general nonfiction.

LUKENS, HENRY CLAY (1838–1900?), New York journalist, author of parodies, lampoons, and humorous verse, usually signed by his pseudonym Erratic Enrique. He wrote *Lean Nora* (1870), a parody of Burger's *Lenore; Jets and Flashes* (1883), a book of lampoons; and an article on "American Literary Comedians" (*Harper's Magazine,* (1890).

LUMMIS, CHARLES FLETCHER (1859–1928), spent most of his life in California, where he labored in many ways to create interest in the historical, archaeological, and ethnological backgrounds of the Southwest. His books include *The Land of Poco Tiempo* (1893), *The Spanish Pioneers* (1893), *Spanish Songs of Old California* (1923), *Mesa, Cañon, and Pueblo* (1925), and other works of fiction, history, and poetry. In 1894 he founded and edited the *Land of Sunshine,* a magazine of life and history in the Far West, later entitled *Out West.* Although more a popularizer than a scholar, as librarian of the Los Angeles Public Library he assembled an important collection of Southwest material. He also founded the Southwest Museum (Los Angeles) and the Landmarks Club.

LUMPKIN, GRACE (1903?–), proletarian novelist, author of *To Make My Bread* (1932), the story of a North Carolina mill strike, which was dramatized by Albert Bein as *Let Freedom Ring* (1936). Her other novels include *A Sign for Cain* (1935), dealing with Southern sharecroppers, *The Wedding* (1939), and *Full Circle* (1962).

LUNDY, BENJAMIN (1789–1839), Quaker Abolitionist, in Ohio established (1815) the Union Humane Society, and there began to publish *The*

Genius of Universal Emancipation (1821–35, 1838–39), a journal that appeared irregularly from the editor's various temporary residences in Tennessee, Maryland, and other states. Garrison was an associate editor during 1829, but, because his articles were too vitriolic, Lundy soon broke with him. From 1825 to 1835 Lundy also made journeys to Haiti, Canada, and Texas, searching for suitable places to colonize freed blacks. *The War in Texas* (1836) exposes the plot to wrest Texas from Mexico as a slaveholders' scheme. In 1836 he founded *The National Enquirer and Constitutional Advocate of Universal Liberty,* which in 1838 was taken over and edited for two years by Whittier. The latter changed its name to *The Pennsylvania Freeman,* and secured important contributions from Lowell. Lundy thereupon reestablished *The Genius,* issuing 12 further numbers before his death.

LURIE, ALISON (1926–   ), Chicago-born novelist, a member of the English department at Cornell, as is her husband. Her fiction, generally marked by quiet satire and dealing with the lives of academics and authors, includes *Love and Friendship* (1962), a witty view of a faculty wife's romancing out of marriage; *The Nowhere City* (1965), again about a scholar's wife, this one taken from Harvard to California with displeasure until she finds a pleasing man; *Imaginary Friends* (1967), a satiric tale of a woman, part of a pseudo-spiritual group, who comes to be the subject of academic consideration; *Real People* (1969), depicting a middle-aged writer of fiction experiencing an artists' colony visit; *The War Between the Tates* (1974), about the lively stress between the parents and their adolescent children, with an academic background; *Only Children* (1979), presenting the experiences and changing affections of two sets of parents and their young children weekending in the home farm of the head of the school attended by their girls; *Foreign Affairs* (1984), about two American professors (man and woman) of English on leave in London, getting involved with love affairs; and *The Truth About Lorin Jones* (1988), a comic view of supremely feminist potential as related to a museum worker and the study she makes of a woman artist. Lurie has also written *The Language of Clothes* (1981), a nonfictional study of the ways people dress; tales for children; and *Don't Tell the Grown-Ups* (1990), a study of children's literature. For *Foreign Affairs* she was awarded a Pulitzer Prize.

LUSKA, SIDNEY, pseudonym of Henry Harland. ♦

LUTHER, SETH (*fl.*1817–46), pioneer in American labor reform, who attacked child labor in the cotton mills of New England in his pamphlet *An Address to the Working-Men of New England* (1832). Other pamphlets were *An Address on*

the Right of Free Suffrage (1833) and *An Address on the Origin and Progress of Avarice* (1834). He was secretary of the General Trades Convention in Boston (1834), and helped to draw up the *Boston Circular* (1835), advocating the ten-hour day.

Lutherans, Protestants who adhere to the teachings of Martin Luther. The views of the Evangelical Church, which stem from his principles, are compared with those of the Reformed Church, based on Calvinistic doctrines. Luther emphasized the responsibility of the individual conscience to God alone, taught that the Scriptures are the only necessary guide to truth and that baptism is essential for regeneration, and permitted the retention of altars and vestments. A synodical form of church organization has developed, but the unity is one of doctrine rather than of organization, since each church makes its own decisions. The first Lutherans in America came to Manhattan from the Netherlands (1623). Another congregation was established in Delaware by Swedish settlers (1638). Others were attracted by the tolerance of the Quakers in Pennsylvania, but the creation of the first Lutheran synod and its independence from European affiliation resulted from the work of the German-born minister Heinrich Melchior Mühlenberg, who came to America in 1742. In 1990 there were almost eight and a half million Lutherans in the U.S.

Lyceums, popular societies for literary and scientific education. The first "American Lyceum" was founded at Millbury, Mass. (1826), by Josiah Holbrook, ♦ and under his leadership nearly 100 branches were established during the next two years, embodying his program of providing educational opportunities for adults, stimulating teacher-training and interest in schools, and founding museums and libraries. At first chiefly concerned with the cooperative study of natural history, the lyceums extended their curricula to include a wide range of subjects, and eight years after Holbrook began the work, approximately 3000 lyceums had been founded in towns and cities throughout the U.S., providing the most important stimulus to general education up to that time. In 1839 the American Lyceum Union held a national convention, and lesser organizations were already established in states and cities, of which the most notable was the Boston lyceum, with Daniel Webster as president. The movement flourished until the end of the century, interrupted only by the Civil War, and local programs of reading, debates, and classes were amplified by the addresses of professional lecturers. Among the popular and well-paid lyceum speakers were Emerson, whose essays were often first presented as lyceum lectures, Webster, Thoreau, Parker, Holmes, Hale, H.W. Beecher, Agassiz, Lowell, Curtis, C.A. Dana, Bayard Taylor, Clemens, Barnum, and Henry M. Stanley.

Reform movements were stimulated by such lecturers as Garrison, Greeley, Lucy Stone, and Elizabeth Stanton. With the rise of mercantile libraries and systems of public schools and higher education institutions, for which the lyceum movement had been largely responsible, local groups assumed the nature of forums that were supplied with lecturers from central booking offices, such as the American Literary Bureau of New York, and the Boston Lyceum Bureau of Redpath.◆ After 1890, Chautauqua◆ societies took the place of the original lyceums, which became centers of popular entertainment.

LYND, ROBERT S[TAUGHTON] (1892–1970), professor of sociology at Columbia, with his wife Helen Merrell Lynd (1896–1982) wrote *Middletown* (1929) and *Middletown in Transition* (1937), comprehensive sociological studies of a small American city (Muncie, Ind.), which she continued in *Update: Middletown Families: Fifty Years of Change and Continuity* (1982). *Middletown*, a television series based on the books, was produced in 1982 by Peter Davis, author of the novel *Hometown* (1982), set in a small Ohio town.

LYNES, [JOSEPH] RUSSELL [JR.] (1910–   ), graduated from Yale (1932), and was managing editor of *Harper's Magazine* (1947–67). His books include *Highbrow, Lowbrow, Middlebrow* (1949), a witty study of cultural levels; *Snobs* (1950), clever definitions; *Guests; or, How To Survive Hospitality* (1951); *The Tastemakers* (1954), an amusing interpretation of shapers of taste; *A Surfeit of Honey* (1957), on current U.S. manners and customs; *Cadwallader* (1959), a light fantasy about a cultivated rat resident at Columbia University; *The Domesticated Americans* (1963), a lively account of the American home of the 19th and 20th centuries; *The Art-Makers of Nineteenth-Century America*

(1970), putting art and architecture in its social setting; *Good Old Modern* (1973), on New York's Museum of Modern Art; and *The Lively Audience* (1985), a social history of the performing and visual arts in the U.S.

LYON, HARRIS MERTON (1883–1916), New Mexico-born author resident in New York City, where he was a journalist and critic. *Sardonics* (1908) contains 16 sketches and three poems; other realistic stories appeared in *Graphics* (1913), published by William Marion Reedy.◆

LYON, JAMES (1735–94), Presbyterian minister of Nova Scotia and Maine, as a psalmodist and writer of hymn tunes was one of the earliest American composers. Born in New Jersey, he graduated from Princeton (1759) and in 1761 published his *Urania, or A Choice Collection of Psalm-Tunes, Anthems, and Hymns*. During his pastorates in the northern colonies, he continued to compose religious music, which was published by later anthologists.

LYTLE, ANDREW NELSON (1902–   ), born in Tennessee, graduated from Vanderbilt, where he was part of the group active with *The Fugitive*.◆ He has taught history at Florida and the University of the South and edited *The Sewanee Review*. His books include *Bedford Forrest* (1931), a biography; *The Long Night* (1936) and *The Velvet Horn* (1957), novels set respectively just before and just after the Civil War; *At the Moon's Inn* (1941), a historical novel about De Soto; and *A Novel, A Novella, and Four Stories* (1958), reprinting *A Name for Evil* (1947), a ghost story about the restoration of a Southern mansion told with symbolic significance. *The Hero with the Private Parts* (1966) collects literary essays, and *A Wake for the Living* (1975) is his family chronicle.

M

Names beginning with "Mc" are placed as though beginning with "Mac."

M. Quad, pseudonym of C.B. Lewis.♦

McALMON, ROBERT (1896–1956), expatriate U.S. author, whose books, published mainly in France, made him a spokesman of the postwar nihilistic pessimists of the "lost generation." His poems in free verse were published in *Explorations* (1921), *The Portrait of a Generation* (1926), *North America, Continent of Conjecture* (1929), and *Not Alone Lost* (1937). *Village: As It Happened Through a Fifteen Year Period* (1924) is a group of impressionistic sketches showing the repressive effect of an American village on its youth, in the manner of Anderson's *Winesburg, Ohio. Being Geniuses Together* (1938) is his autobiography, extended (1968) by Kay Boyle,♦ who interspersed chapters of her own recollections. *McAlmon and the Lost Generation* (1962) is a self-portrait created by Robert E. Knoll from autobiographical fragments.

MacARTHUR, CHARLES (1895–1956), Pennsylvania-born playwright, as a journalist in Chicago was an intimate of its literary group. His plays include *Lulu Belle* (1926), written with his uncle Edward Sheldon♦; *Salvation* (1927), with Sidney Howard; and *The Front Page* (1928), *20th Century* (1932), and *Ladies and Gentlemen* (1939) with Ben Hecht, with whom he also wrote motion pictures. His wife, the actress Helen Hayes (1900–93), starred in Barrie's *What Every Woman Knows,* Housman's *Victoria Regina,* and Anderson's *Mary of Scotland. A Gift of Joy* (1965) is her autobiography.

MACAULEY, ROBIE [MAYHEW] (1919–), born in Michigan, graduated from Kenyon College (1941), to which he returned to become the editor of the *Kenyon Review* (1959–66). His writings include *The Disguises of Love* (1952), a novel about a psychology professor's extramarital affair and its impact upon him, his wife, and their son; *The End of Pity* (1957), stories; and *A Secret History of Time To Come* (1979), about human reversion to barbarism after a global war. He has also written *Technique in Fiction* (1964, revised 1987).

McCARTHY, CORMAC (1933–), novelist born in Rhode Island, educated in Tennessee, and since 1976 resident in El Paso. His fiction includes *The Orchard Keeper* (1965), concerning grim lives and a murder in the Great Smoky Mountains; *Outer Dark* (1968), another gothic tale in a Southern setting, treating the wanderings of a woman searching for the son she had by her brother; *Child of God* (1974), presenting grotesque characters of the Kentucky backwoods; *Suttree* (1979), about a dropout loner in the violent tenderloin district of Knoxville; *Blood Meridian, or The Evening Redness in the West* (1985), which starts in Nagodoches, Texas, in 1849 and follows a runaway boy as he joins a pirate army to fight in Mexico, and later hooks up with a band of bounty killers from Indians in wide-ranging pillaging and murder; and *All the Pretty Horses* (1992, National Book Award), which is the first volume of *The Border Trilogy.* It involves two boys, Cole and Rawlins, horse lovers both, and their dangerous adventures in mid-19th-century Mexico. *The Crossing* (1994), the second novel of the Border Trilogy, has its young protagonist Billy Parham dragging on horseback from New Mexico a trapped wolf which he means to release in the Sierra de la Madera mountains of Chihuahua, in the course of which journey he has many memorable encounters with men and beasts. *The Stonemason* (1994), a play, presents a multigenerational black family living in Louisville in the 1970s. The main character, Ben Telfair, has learned the art of freestone masonry from his 101-year-old grandfather, and the drama largely concerns Ben's love of his art and his refusal to adulterate or compromise it commercially.

McCARTHY, MARY [THERESE] (1912–89), born in Seattle, was orphaned as a child and reared by diverse relatives, as she recalled in *Memories of a Catholic Girlhood* (1957), a memoir continued in *How I Grew* (1987), dealing with her experience and intellectual development from age 13 to 21. After graduation from Vassar (1933) she became a drama critic of the *Partisan Review,* and her reviews and articles from 1937 to 1956 were collected in *Sights and Spectacles* (1956). She also taught English briefly at Bard and at Sarah Lawrence College. She was wed to and divorced from Edmund Wilson. She wrote *Venice Observed* (1956) and *The Stones of Florence* (1959), descriptive profiles of two cities she knows well, and published literary essays in *On the Contrary* (1961), *The Writing on the Wall* (1970), and *Ideas and the Novel* (1980), but is best known for social commentary and fiction. Her novels are *The Company She Keeps* (1942), a witty portrait of a bohemian, intellectual young woman; *The Oasis* (1949), a brief satirical tale of a Utopia created by some intellectuals on a New England mountain top; *The Groves of Academe* (1952), a satirical portrait of faculty life at a liberal college for women; *A Charmed Life* (1955), set in an artists' colony where life is more destructive than creative; *The Group* (1963), about the misadventures of eight Vassar alumnae of 1933 in the 30 years after their graduation: *Birds of America* (1971), treating strained relations between a mother and son because of their different generations and values; and *Cannibals and Missionaries* (1979), treating modern terrorism in an airplane hijacking. *Cast a Cold Eye* (1950) collects stories. *Vietnam* (1967), *Hanoi* (1968), and *Medina* (1972) are short books collected in *The Seventeenth Degree* (1974), about the U.S. war in Vietnam. *The Mask of State* (1974) contains portraits of persons involved in the Watergate scandal. *Occasional Prose* (1985) collects book reviews, essays, political reporting, and obituaries. *Intellectual Memoirs: New York 1936–1938* (1992) chronicles her 24th to 26th years and includes her liaison with Philip Rahv,♦ work on the *Partisan Review,♦* and Edmund Wilson's♦ pursuit of her, ending in marriage. The book deftly captures McCarthy in the swift process of becoming a critic and then, at Wilson's insistence, a novelist.

McCaslin family, characters in the fiction of Faulkner,♦ an old Jefferson (Mississippi) family figuring most prominently in the stories in *Go Down, Moses,* particularly "The Bear,"♦ in *Intruder in the Dust,♦* and in *The Reivers,♦* although frequently mentioned elsewhere. The McCaslin family perhaps embodies more clearly than any other single genealogy Faulkner's concern with the historical and moral implications of relations between the black and white races. A son of Lancaster McCaslin, Lucius Quintus Carothers ("old Carothers") McCaslin comes to Mississippi in 1813, buys land from the Chickasaw, and builds a plantation house near what is to become Jefferson. He legitimately fathers twin sons, Theophilus and Amodeus, and a daughter, Mary, but also takes a black mistress, his slave Eunice, and sires her daughter Tomasina (Tomey). This daughter dies while herself bearing him a son, Terrel (called Turl or Tomey's Turl), a relationship that leads Eunice to drown herself in despair upon learning of her daughter's incestuous pregnancy. In course of time Turl marries Tennie Beauchamp, a slave girl, and founds the black Beauchamp family. Theophilus (Uncle Buck) and Amodeus (Uncle Buddy), morally opposed to slavery, free the McCaslin blacks. Buck, long a confirmed bachelor, marries Sophonisba Beauchamp, sister of a neighboring plantation owner, and they have a child, Isaac (later Uncle Ike) McCaslin, who, born in 1867 and orphaned early (see *The Bear*), learns woodcraft and respect for nature from Sam Fathers, the Negro-Chickasaw bought long ago from Ikkemotubbe♦ by old Carothers. When he falls heir to the family estate, Isaac renounces the inheritance on grounds which he debates with McCaslin (Cass) Ed-

monds, the grandson of Mary McCaslin, who eventually inherits the lands. Having learned that old Carothers left legacies to his illegitimate grandchildren, Isaac tries to deliver the money to Tennie and Turl's surviving children, James Thucydides (Tennie's Jim), Sophonisba (Fonisba), and Lucas Beauchamp. Lucas wins in a showdown with Zachary (Zack) Edmonds, Cass's son and the new owner of the estate, over the return of Lucas's wife Mollie from the main house, where she has nursed Zack's son Carothers (Roth) Edmonds. Later Lucas again is victorious, this time against a false murder charge. Lucas remains on the place and is the oldest descendant of old Carothers when Roth inherits the lands. Roth has an illegitimate son by a girl who, unbeknownst to him, is a granddaughter of Tennie's Jim, thus echoing his great-great-great-grandfather's original incest. When she appears with the child, Roth asks Isaac, now an old man, to send her away, and Isaac, in anger and despair at McCaslin behavior, laments, "No wonder the ruined woods don't cry for retribution! The people who destroyed it [the land] will accomplish its revenge."

McCLURE, MICHAEL [THOMAS] (1932–), Kansas-born author, long resident in San Francisco and since 1962 a professor at Oakland's California College of Arts and Crafts. He has been associated with the regional Beat movement. His very numerous examples of personal and passionate poetry include *Passage* (1956), *Hymns to St. Geryon* (1959), *For Artaud* (1959), *Dark Brown* (1961), *Thirteen Mad Sonnets* (1965), *Star* (1970), *September Blackberries* (1974), *Jaguar Skies* (1975), and *Fragments of Perseus* (1983), as well as *Selected Poems* (1986). *Ghost Tantras* (1964) is verse meant for oral presentation, moving toward his dramas, of which the best known is *The Beard* (1967), an erotic conversation between the symbolized figures of Jean Harlow and Billy the Kid, while *Gorf* (1976) is another intense fantasy play, as is *Josephine: The Mouse Singer* (1980), a verse drama adapted from a story by Kafka. *Freewheelin Frank Secretary of the Angels* (1969) deals with Hell's Angels motorcyclists. *The Mad Club* (1970) contains two novellas dealing with young drug addicts, and *The Adept* (1971) is a novel about a cocaine dealer. *Meat Science* (1963, revised 1966) prints essays animated by poetry and biology, and later essays appear in *Scratching the Beat Surface* (1982).

McClure's Magazine (1893–1929), popular monthly, was published and edited by S[amuel] S[idney] McClure (1857–1949), Irish-born publisher who in 1884 established the first newspaper syndicate in the U.S. and went on from that success to found the magazine that bore his name. It was intended to present at a small price the work of the most famous contemporary English and American authors, as well as to report current scientific knowledge and world affairs. It became a leading vehicle in muckraking♦ (1901–12), producing lively articles on complex subjects, and was a spearhead of the reform movement, investigating every aspect of American life. Contributors included O. Henry, F.P. Dunne, Jack London, and W.A. White, and among the leading articles were "The History of the Standard Oil Company," by Ida Tarbell; "The Shame of Minneapolis," by Lincoln Steffens; and "The Right to Work," by R.S. Baker. Its period of significance passed with the waning of public enthusiasm for reform, and McClure's own success diminished. The work he called *My Autobiography* (1914) was written by Willa Cather.

McCONKEY, JAMES [RODNEY] (1921–), Ohio-born professor of English at Cornell (1956–) and author whose novels include *Crossroads* (1968), subtitled an "autobiographical novel" that in fragmented fictionized sketches presents moments of experience from boyhood on; *A Journey to Sahalin* (1971), treating violent racial conflict on a campus like Cornell, its title alluding to a Russian concentration camp once visited by Chekhov; and *The Tree House Confessions* (1979), about a 50-year-old man remembering his past while visiting the tree house he once built for his now dead son. *Court of Memory* (1983) contains two series of meditative memoirs, the first published as *Crossroads*.

McCORD, DAVID [THOMPSON WATSON] (1897–), graduated from Harvard (1921) and was long an editor of its *Alumni Bulletin*. The many volumes of his light verse include *Bay Window Ballads* (1935), *On Occasion* (1943), and *Selected Poems* (1957), while familiar essays include *Oddly Enough* (1926), *Stirabout* (1928), and *About Boston* (1948). *One at a Time* (1977) collects five volumes of poems for children.

McCOSH, JAMES (1811–94), Scottish-born philosopher and educator, came to the U.S. to become president of the College of New Jersey (1868–88). In Scotland and at Princeton, he set forth his philosophy of Intuitionism, opposed to the doctrines of Kant and J.S. Mill. He maintained that commonsense principles or intuitions have their beginnings in simple cognition, take on singular and concrete forms, and pass into higher judgments and beliefs, to become universal and necessary principles. His philosophy led him to become a theist, and at the same time to champion the doctrine of evolution as evidence of God's method of creation. His books include *The Intuitions of the Mind Inductively Investigated* (1860), *An Examination of Mr. J. S. Mill's Philosophy* (1866), *The Laws of Discursive Thought* (1870), *Christianity and Positivism* (1871), *The Scottish Philosophy* (1875), and *Realistic Philosophy Defended* (1887).

McCOY, HORACE (1897–1955), born in Tennessee, after service in World War I was for many years the sports editor of a Dallas newspaper but also spent time in Paris among expatriate U.S. writers, to whose little magazines he contributed. In 1931 he became a Hollywood screenwriter. His first novel, *They Shoot Horses, Don't They?* (1935), a first-person narrative of a man awaiting execution for the murder of his marathon dance partner, at her insistence, is a violent tale of sordid experience that won him a reputation, in France even more than in the U.S., as a serious writer in the vein of what was to be called existentialism. His other novels are *No Pockets in a Shroud* (1937), about crime and corruption in a seemingly decent American town; *I Should Have Stayed Home* (1938), about degradation in Hollywood; *Kiss Tomorrow Good-Bye* (1948), about a decent college graduate who seeks out a life of crime and brutality; and *Scalpel* (1952).

McCULLERS, CARSON [SMITH] (1917–67), was born in Georgia, where most of her works are set, although she was long resident in New York City. She immediately achieved great critical prominence with her first novel, *The Heart Is a Lonely Hunter♦* (1940), in which a deaf-mute in a Southern town loses his only friend, another mute, and turns to others who give him their confidence, such as a lonely, music-loving girl, a black doctor, and a young radical. It was appreciated for its compassionate treatment of individualism and its sensitive style, and also because it was considered a symbolic commentary on fascism. Her second novel, *Reflections in a Golden Eye* (1941), is a shorter work, a macabre story of experiences in an army camp in the South before World War II. *The Member of the Wedding♦* (1946) with great sensitivity presents the feelings of a 12-year-old girl on the occasion of her brother's impending wedding, and was successfully dramatized by the author in 1950. Her next work was also a play, *The Square Root of Wonderful* (1958), about the maturing of a woman twice married to and twice deserted by the same husband. Her next novel, *Clock Without Hands♦* (1961), set in a small Georgia town, treats the involvements of some whites and a black boy, thereby illuminating her common theme, the discovery of selfhood. *The Ballad of the Sad Café♦* (1951) collects stories and novels, the title work being dramatized by Edward Albee (1963), and *The Mortgaged Heart* (1971) collects early stories.

McCUTCHEON, GEORGE BARR (1866–1928), Indiana novelist, author of some 40 works of fiction within 28 years. His *Graustark* (1901) follows the style popularized by Anthony Hope's *Prisoner of Zenda* (1894) and deals with court intrigue in a fictional land, with high-flown romance between American heroes and titled heroines. This was followed by a series of romances dealing with the same mythical principality. His comic fantasy *Brewster's Millions* (1902) was equally popular and was successfully dramatized by Winchell Smith in 1906. He wrote one realistic novel of Midwestern life, *Mary Midthorne* (1911).

MACDONALD, DWIGHT (1906–82), after graduation from Yale and editorial posts on *Fortune* and *Partisan Review* founded his own journal, *Politics* (1944–49), as an organ of philosophical anarchism and pacifism. His later work on the staff of *The New Yorker* and as motion-picture critic for *Esquire* was more sociological than political. His books include *Henry Wallace: The Man and the Myth* (1948); *The Ford Foundation: The Man and the Millions* (1956); *Memoirs of a Revolutionist* (1957), essays in political criticism written over the previous 20 years; *Against the American Grain* (1963), sociocultural essays written from an astringent, minority point of view; *The Ghost of Conspiracy* (1965), a critique of the Warren Commission's report on President Kennedy's assassination; and *Discriminations* (1974), political and literary essays.

MacDONALD, JOHN D[ANN] (1916–86), popular writer of mystery novels under his own name and several pseudonyms, some of the works featuring his detective, Travis McGee. He also wrote several works of science fiction. In addition to 65 novels (1946–80) said to have sold 70,000,000 copies, he published 500 stories in magazines.

MACDONALD, ROSS, pseudonym of Kenneth Millar (1915–83), California-born novelist, reared in Canada. After graduation from the University of Western Ontario, naval service, and a Ph.D. from the University of Michigan, he published under his own name *The Dark Tunnel* (1944), a spy story set in Hitler's Germany. It was the beginning of a prolific career, best known for his hard-boiled detective novels set in southern California, featuring the private investigator Lew Archer and having as background generational differences in families. These works include *The Galton Case* (1959), *The Goodbye Look* (1964), *The Far Side of the Dollar* (1965), and *The Underground Man* (1971). *Self-Portrait* (1982) collects essays on ideas and experiences.

MacDOWELL, EDWARD ALEXANDER (1861–1908), New York-born composer, went abroad to study (1876) at Paris, Stuttgart, and Frankfurt, and taught piano at the Darmstadt Conservatory (1881–82). Before returning to the U.S. (1888), he composed his first and second piano concertos and other works for piano and orchestra. In Boston (1888–96), he taught, appeared as a concert pianist, and composed such piano works as the *Twelve Virtuoso Studies, Woodland Sketches,* the *Tragica* and *Eroica* sonatas, and many songs, tone poems, and the first and second (*Indian*) suites for orchestra. He headed Columbia's department of music (1896–1904), but after many difficulties resigned the post, and, exhausted and embittered, lost his reason after 1905. While at Columbia he produced his *Norse* and *Keltic* sonatas, the *Sea Pieces,* the *Fireside Tales,* and the *New England Idyls,* all for piano. MacDowell, like Grieg, was a leading composer of the late romantic tradition, but his nationalism, less marked than Grieg's, is found only in occasional use of Indian themes. He was often inspired by the countryside at his Peterboro, N.H., farm, where his widow, the pianist Marian Nevins MacDowell, established the MacDowell Colony for composers, artists, and writers. Authors who have stayed there include E.A. Robinson, Willa Cather, the Benéts, Thornton Wilder, and Hervey Allen.

MacDOWELL, KATHERINE SHERWOOD [BONNER] (1849–83), Mississippi local-color writer, whose sketches were collected in *Dialect Tales* (1883) and *Suwanee River Tales* (1884). *Like Unto Like* (1878) is a semi-autobiographical novel set in the era of the Civil War and Reconstruction. Her later stories of life in the Tennessee mountains and southern Illinois were more realistic. During the early 1870s she lived in Boston and served as Longfellow's amanuensis. She wrote under the pseudonym Sherwood Bonner.

McELROY, JOSEPH (1930–), born in Brooklyn, after an A.B. from Williams and Ph.D. from Columbia has been a professor of English at Queens College, CUNY (1964–). His writing is *A Smuggler's Bible* (1966), about adventures of a young antiquarian bookseller; *Hind's Kidnap* (1969), a man's inquiry into a seizure that he suffered as a boy; *Ancient History* (1971); *Lookout Cartridge* (1974), concerning a film maker caught in sinister situations; *Plus* (1977), about the relationship of a brain to an engineer dying of a radiation burn; *Ship Rock* (1980); *Women and Men* (1987), a lengthy treatment of the lives of a man and woman unconnected except that they live in the same apartment building; and *The Letter Left to Me* (1988), a short account of a 15-year-old boy who receives a letter from his father who has just committed suicide.

McFEE, WILLIAM [MORLEY PUNSHON] (1881–1966), born in London, was educated in England, and, following the family tradition, became a ship's engineer. His experiences furnished the material for *Letters from an Ocean Tramp* (1908, revised 1921). In 1911 he entered the American merchant marine and established his home in the U.S., although in World War I he served in the British navy. After the war he returned to the U.S. (1922), became an American citizen (1925), and settled at Westport, Conn. His first novel, *Aliens* (1914, revised 1918), set in New Jersey, is about British ships' officers and their families. *Casuals of the Sea* (1916) tells of a London family and its aimless struggles, while *Captain Macedoine's Daughter* (1920) is an adventure story with a

Mediterranean setting, showing McFee's indebtedness to Joseph Conrad. *Harbours of Memory* (1921) is a collection of sketches on experiences at sea and in foreign ports. Later books include *An Engineer's Note Book* (1921); *Studies in Patriotism* (1922); *Command* (1922), about a ship's officer who is a nonentity until war experiences bring him self-knowledge and authority; *Race* (1924), portraying middle-class London life in the late 19th century; *Swallowing the Anchor* (1925), autobiographical essays; *Sunlight in New Granada* (1925), about Colombia; *The Life of Sir Martin Frobisher* (1928); *Pilgrims of Adversity* (1928), an adventure novel set in Central and South America; *Sailors of Fortune* (1929), short stories set in the Mediterranean and Caribbean; *North of Suez* (1930), a romantic novel of the Near East; *The Harbourmaster* (1931), an exotic tale set in Salonika and South America; *No Castle in Spain* (1933), a romance contrasting modern American standards with the traditions of a South American aristocrat; *Reflections of Marsyas* (1933), a book of verse; *More Harbours of Memory* (1934), essays on travel and life at sea, including "A Six-Hour Shift," the title piece of an English collection (1920); *The Beachcomber* (1935), set in the West Indies; *Derelicts* (1938), a novel about an Englishman who escapes his frustrating home life to begin life anew in the tropics; *Watch Below* (1940), a study of tramp steamers, combining analysis and fiction; *Spenlove in Arcady* (1941), a novel about the love affair of a retired ship's engineer; *Ship to Shore* (1944), concerning the romance of a New York business woman and a middle-aged sea captain; and *Family Trouble* (1949), Spenlove's story about a friend's marital problems. *In the First Watch* (1946) is an account of McFee's early days on tramp steamers.

M'Fingal, mock epic by John Trumbull,♦ of which the first two cantos were published separately (1775–76) and the complete work in 1782. This burlesque, in four cantos of Hudibrastic couplets, satirizes the events of the year 1775 and deals humorously with the leading figures of the Revolution.

The first canto begins with a political discussion by Honorius (seemingly John Adams), which attacks the course of British government and the local defenders of its injurious colonial policy. This is interrupted by M'Fingal, a burly monarchist New England squire, who defends the Tory policies so ineptly that he ironically clinches every argument of Honorius. The argument between these two champions and their respective cohorts becomes more heated in the course of the second canto. In the third canto, their verbal argumentation is interrupted by the attempt of the Whigs to erect a liberty pole. When M'Fingal attempts to disperse the crowd, a general fracas ensues, and he is tarred and feathered and stuck to the pole. In the fourth canto, M'Fingal has sneaked to a secret Tory meeting, where he mournfully recites a vision of future events, and foretells the English defeat and the great rise of the American nation. In the midst of his recital, the mob discovers the meeting, and M'Fingal jumps out the window, to seek temporary safety.

McGINLEY, PHYLLIS (1905–78), Oregon-born author of light verse, educated at the universities of Utah and California, resident in New York. Her collections include *On the Contrary* (1934), *A Pocketful of Wry* (1940), *Stones from a Glass House* (1946), *A Short Walk from the Station* (1951), *The Love Letters of Phyllis McGinley* (1954), *Merry Christmas, Happy New Year* (1958), and *Times Three: Selected Verse from Three Decades* (1960, Pulitzer Prize). Other works include children's books; lyrics for the revue *Small Wonder* (1948); and *Province of the Heart* (1959) and *Sixpence in Her Shoe* (1964), light essays on suburban life.

MacGRATH, HAROLD (1871–1932), author of popular romances that include *The Man on the Box* (1904), *Half a Rogue* (1906), and *A Splendid Hazard* (1910). He wrote "Perils of Pauline," the silent movie serial.

McGUANE, THOMAS [FRANCIS III] (1939–   ), Michigan-born author whose novels include *The Sporting Club* (1969), a lively satiric comedy about wealthy sportsmen and their Michigan forest club; *The Bushwacked Piano* (1971), also marked by black humor in its tale of a young man rebelling against his Establishment background; *Ninety-Two in the Shade* (1973), a much darker story of fishermen guides in Florida; *Panama* (1979), a novelette about a rock musician on the way down; *Nobody's Angel* (1982), set in Montana's cattle-ranching country, where he has long lived; *Something To Be Desired* (1985), about a man who deserts his wife and son until he becomes the owner of a Montana health spa and with wealth retrieves them; *Keep the Change* (1989), about an artist living an oddly ecstatic life; and *Nothing But Blue Skies* (1992), a bitter novel about a real estate developer in Deadrock, Montana. *An Outside Chance* (1980) collects essays on McGuane's enthusiastic participation in sports; *To Skin a Cat* (1986) collects stories. He has also written many film scripts.

McGUFFEY, WILLIAM HOLMES (1800–1873), born in Pennsylvania, was educated in rural schools and was thought to be a prodigy because of his remarkable memorization. He graduated from Washington and Jefferson College (1826), taught school in Kentucky, and became professor of languages, philosophy, and philology at Miami University (Oxford, Ohio, 1826–36), president of Cincinnati College (1836–39) and Ohio University (1839–43), and professor at Woodward College, Cincinnati (1843–45), and the University of Virginia (1845–73). While at Miami, he began to compile his *Eclectic Readers,* six schoolbooks (1836–57) that combined literary lessons, obvious moral teachings, and carefully selected extracts from great English writers. Their estimated sales totaled 122,000,000 copies, and their constant use in mid-19th-century schools had a profound effect upon the moral and cultural shaping of the American mind.

McHENRY, JAMES (1785–1845), Irish-born poet and novelist, emigrated to Pennsylvania in 1817. His works include *The Pleasures of Friendship* (1822), miscellaneous verse; *Waltham* (1823), a poem dealing with the Revolution; *The Wilderness; or, Braddock's Times* (1823), a historical novel concerning Ulstermen during Braddock's campaign in Pennsylvania in the French and Indian War; *The Spectre of the Forest* (1823), a romance of 17th-century New England; and Irish historical fiction, a blank-verse drama on the Druids, and other miscellaneous literature.

McINERNEY, JAY (1955–), novelist. Born in Connecticut and educated at Williams College, McInerney went to New York City as a fact-checker for *The New Yorker* magazine. His first novel, *Bright Lights, Big City* (1984), about a young man's experience of existential furor in the city, won critical praise. A comic novel is *Ransom* (1985), set in Japan. *The Story of My Life* (1988) is another novel. *Brightness Falls* (1992) is a satiric novel about the excesses of city people in the 1980s.

McINTYRE, JOHN T[HOMAS] (1871–1951), Philadelphia author, studied the meaner aspects of the city in his realistic novel *The Ragged Edge* (1902) and then devoted himself to writing books for children. After 1923 he returned to fiction for adults, publishing in that year *Blowing Weather,* a romance of pirates, the sea, and the old port of Philadelphia. *Shot Towers* (1926) is a Dickensian depiction of city and country life in the 19th-century U.S.; *Stained Sails* (1928) is a romantic story about John Paul Jones; and *Drums in the Dawn* (1932) is a romance of the Revolutionary War. McIntyre's later realistic fiction about city life includes *Slag* (1927), a story of the New York slums and the criminals that flourish there; *Steps Going Down* (1936), which won an international novel prize for its melodramatic study of the Philadelphia underworld; *Ferment* (1937), a story of strikebreaking and labor racketeering in Philadelphia; and *Signing Off* (1938), contrasting the seamy side of the city's life with its more respectable aspects. *A Young Man's Fancy,* produced as a play in 1919 and revised as a novel in 1925, is a fantastic story of youthful romance.

McKAY, CLAUDE (1890–1948), black author, emigrated from his native Jamaica to the U.S. (1912). His books include *Songs of Jamaica* (1912) and *Harlem Shadows* (1922), poems; and the virile novels *Home to Harlem* (1928), the story of a black

soldier deserting from the army in France to return to America; *Banjo* (1929), set on the Marseilles waterfront, where McKay worked for a time; and *Banana Bottom* (1933), about a black girl in Jamaica, who is torn between racial traditions and the education she has received in England. *Gingertown* (1932) collects short stories. His novels have sometimes been criticized for emphasizing the primitive and voluptuous aspects of black life dwelt upon by Van Vechten. *A Long Way from Home* (1937) is his autobiography. *Harlem: Negro Metropolis* (1940) is a sociological study.

MacKAYE, PERCY [WALLACE] (1875–1956), son of Steele MacKaye, was born in New York City, and after graduation from Harvard (1897) and teaching school began to write poetry and plays. *The Canterbury Pilgrims* (1903) deals with an imaginary sentimental episode between Chaucer and the Prioress, and was made into a libretto for an opera by De Koven (1917). MacKaye wrote two other blank-verse plays, *Jeanne d'Arc* (1906) and *Sappho and Phaon* (1907). *The Scarecrow*♦ (1908) is a prose play based on a story by Hawthorne. His first play with a modern subject, *Mater* (1908), was a comedy of American politics, while *Anti-Matrimony* (1910) was a satire on the influence of continental playwrights upon naïve Americans, and *Tomorrow* (1913) was a problem play about eugenics. *Yankee Fantasies* (1912) is a series of one-act plays about New England life. *Rip Van Winkle* (1920) is a libretto for a De Koven opera, and *Washington, the Man Who Made Us* (1920) is a "ballad play." MacKaye was consistently interested in large pageants and communal productions of drama, producing the *Saint-Gaudens Masque-Prologue* (1905), followed by a spectacular pageant version of his *Canterbury Pilgrims* (1909), *Sanctuary, a Bird Masque* (1913), *Caliban, by the Yellow Sands* (1916), and *The Evergreen Tree* (1917), the last concerned with the celebration of Christmas. In 1921 he made the first of several visits to the Kentucky mountains, which resulted in *This Fine-Pretty World* (1923), a comedy based on native materials; *Tall Tales of the Kentucky Mountains* (1926); *Kentucky Mountain Fantasies* (1928), folk plays; *Gobbler of God* (1928), a narrative poem based on a mountain legend; and other writings. *The Mystery of Hamlet, King of Denmark; or, What We Will,* produced in 1949 and published in 1950, is a tetralogy of verse plays meant as a "prologue" to *Hamlet,* for they develop characters and plot to a point just before the beginning of Shakespeare's drama. *Poems and Plays* (2 vols., 1916) includes his poetry, and *My Lady Dear, Arise!* (1940) poems in memory of his wife. *Epoch* (2 vols., 1927) is a biography of his father.

MacKAYE, [JAMES MORRISON] STEELE (1842–94), New York actor and playwright, whose more than 20 plays, all sentimental melodramas, include *Hazel Kirke*♦ (1880), a domestic drama laid in England; a dramatization (1881) of Tourgée's *A Fool's Errand;* and *Paul Kauvar* (1887), a love story of the French Revolution. He also invented many stage devices, including an elevator stage and novel scenic and lighting effects. *Epoch* (2 vols., 1927), by his son Percy MacKaye, is his biography.

McKENNEY, RUTH (1911–72), author of *My Sister Eileen* (1938), humorous sketches about the youth of her sister, later married to Nathanael West. This work was dramatized (1941) and made into the musical comedy *Wonderful Town* (1953). Other works on her family include *The McKenneys Carry On* (1940) and *The Loud Red Patrick* (1947). *Industrial Valley* (1939) is nonfiction about labor strife in Akron, and *Jake Home* (1943), a novel sympathetically treating a Communist labor organizer, deals with the Sacco-Vanzetti case.

McKUEN, ROD (1933–), popular author of sentimental poems and songs, native and resident of California. His books include *Stanyan Street and Other Sorrows* (1966), *Listen to the Warm* (1967), *Come to Me in Silence* (1973), and *Looking for a Friend* (1980). *Finding My Father* (1976) is a prose account of his quest for his unknown father.

McLEAN, SARAH PRATT (1856–1935), New England author, best known for her stories and novels of Cape Cod village life. *Cape Cod Folks* (1881) is a local-color romance, based on real characters, and concerned with the life of a schoolteacher in a community of seafaring people. Her later books include *Towhead* (1883), *Last Chance Junction* (1889), *The Moral Imbeciles* (1898), *Vesty of the Basins* (1900), and *Winslow Plain* (1902). Several of her works were published under her married name, Sarah P. McLean Greene.

MacLEISH, ARCHIBALD (1892–1982), born in Illinois, graduated from Yale (1915), served in World War I, and received his LL.B. from Harvard (1919), after which he practiced law. His poetic career falls into three principal divisions. The first, signalized by his expatriation in Europe (1923–28) and in part the result of his reactions to the war, extends from *Tower of Ivory* (1917) to *The Hamlet of A. MacLeish*♦ (1928). These works, along with *The Happy Marriage* (1924), *The Pot of Earth*♦ (1925), *Streets in the Moon* (1926), and *Nobodaddy* (1926), a verse drama, show the influence of Ezra Pound and T.S. Eliot, and are subjective in content. MacLeish's work at this time was a voice of the hopeless individual in a chaotic postwar world.

Upon his return to the Depression-ridden U.S., he showed, from the publication of *New Found Land* (1930) to *Frescoes for Mr. Rockefeller's City*♦ (1933), a new attitude, in which his poetic influences were less obvious and his awareness of a national, social, and cultural heritage more sensitive and pronounced. *New Found Land* contains his poem "You, Andrew Marvell," addressing the 17th-century poet who heard "Time's wingèd chariot hurrying near," and, three centuries before MacLeish, discovered, in the words of the latter, that "the shadow of the night comes on . . ." to bury the struggling heart in final darkness. His main book of this period was *Conquistador*♦ (1932, Pulitzer Prize), an epic of the conquest of Mexico, in which Díaz tells of the battles to win territory named "for the kings that bear no scars" and "the bishops, rich-men, generals, cocks-at-arms." The end of the period was marked by the collection of *Poems, 1924–1933* (1933).

In *Panic*♦ (1935), a verse drama, he turned his attention to immediate social issues of the American scene, while in *Public Speech* (1936) he definitely announced his intention to take his part in collectivist social thought. This dual interest in drama and social ideas was extended in the radio plays in verse, *The Fall of the City* (1937), exposing totalitarian dictatorship as a hollow mockery of leadership, and *Air Raid* (1938), depicting the impersonal cruelty of modern warfare. He chose the medium of these works in accordance with his belief that "the imagination works better through the ear than through the eye." In *America Was Promises* (1939), he restated in poetry his theme of the need for action to save democracy, and *Colloquy for the States* (1943) is another poetic statement of patriotism.

Later poetry includes *Actfive* (1948); *Songs for Eve* (1954), lyrics; and *Collected Poems, 1917–1952* (1952, Pulitzer Prize). He returned to verse drama with *This Music Crept by Me Upon the Waters* (1953); *J.B.* (1958, Pulitzer Prize), treating Job's trials in a modern setting and idiom; *Herakles* (1967), relating aspects of the myth of Hercules to modern man; and *The Great American Fourth of July Parade* (1975), in which Adams and Jefferson comment on the U.S. of the 1970s. MacLeish brought together his poetry from 1917 onward in *New and Collected Poems* (1976). His prose includes *The Irresponsibles* (1940), an attack on American scholars and authors of the time for allegedly failing to take an active stand for democracy; *The American Cause* (1941), asserting the artist's usefulness in a democracy; *A Time To Speak* (1941) and *A Time To Act* (1943), addresses; *The American Story* (1944), radio sketches; and *Poetry and Opinion* (1950), *Poetry and Experience* (1960), *A Continuing Journey* (1968), and *Riders on the Earth* (1978), essays, addresses, memorials, and memoirs. *Scratch* (1971) is a prose dramatization of S.V. Benét's *The Devil and Daniel Webster.*♦ *His Letters 1907 to 1982* was published in 1983. His many important posts included Librarian of Congress (1939–44), Assistant Secretary of State (1944–45), and Boylston Professor at Harvard (1949–62).

McLELLAN, ISAAC (1806–99), graduated from Bowdoin, forsook a journalistic career to become a devoted sportsman and laureate of the subject in such works as *Poems of the Rod and Gun* (1886) and *Haunts of Wild Game* (1896), which versify "Elephant-Hunting in the Island of Ceylon" and "My Parker Gun" and similar topics dear to his heart.

McMURTRY, LARRY [JEFF] (1936–), novelist. After childhood and high school in Archer City, Texas, he attended North Texas State University and later Rice and Stanford. His first novel, *Horseman, Pass By* (1961), about the passing of old-time cattle ranching, set the theme and locale of his best work: a half-mythic West of values, freedom, and heroic friendship, not without drawbacks. *Horseman* was made into the movie *Hud* (1963). *Leaving Cheyenne* (1963) again explored conflicts between old ways and new. *The Last Picture Show* (1966), about a boy growing up in a small Texas town in the 1950s, also reached film, as did *Terms of Endearment* (1975), about a terminally ill woman and her eccentric mother. After *Somebody's Darling* (1978), *Cadillac Jack* (1982), and *The Desert Rose* (1983), McMurtry wrote *Lonesome Dove* (1985), a bestseller and winner of the Pulitzer Prize that later was the basis for a successful television miniseries. It chronicles the adventures of two former Texas Rangers and their sidekicks on a migratory cattle drive from Texas to Montana, with a villainous Indian, Blue Duck, as main adversary. In sweep and feeling it recalls *The Big Sky. Anything for Billy* (1988) has a Philadelphia dime novelist narrator hooked up with The Kid. *Buffalo Girls* (1990) features Bill Cody, Calamity Jane, and Sitting Bull dramatizing for urban audiences a West already gone. *The Evening Star* (1992) returns to the Houston and characters of *Terms of Endearment,* including the eccentric Aurora, who struggles to come to terms with aging. *Streets of Laredo* (1993) is a sequel to *Lonesome Dove,* set about 1890, with Captain Woodrow Call, the surviving former Texas Ranger, now an old man; he is chasing a Mexican train bandit. Some characters from the earlier work appear, others are new. The novel does not reach the level of its predecessor. McMurtry's nonfiction includes *In a Narrow Grave: Essays on Texas* (1971) and *Flim Flam: Essays on Hollywood* (1987).

McPHEE, JOHN [ANGUS] (1931–), graduate of Princeton, where he has been a professor of journalism, became a staff writer for *The New Yorker* in 1965. For its "Profiles" he has written on such diverse people as a professional basketball player from Princeton, the director of the Metropolitan Museum of Art, championship tennis stars, and a nuclear physicist, all reissued as books. His early books on natural history include *Oranges* (1967), on the botany, history, and industry of the fruit; *The Pine Barrens* (1968), about a wilderness area of New Jersey; *The Survival of the Bark Canoe* (1975); and the more substantial *Coming into the Country* (1977), about Alaska. *Basin and Range* (1981), *In Suspect Terrain* (1983), and *Rising from the Plains* (1986) resulted from his field trips with geologists. Other recent books include *Outcroppings* (1988), drawing on that series in part to deal with western U.S. geology and ecology. *In Suspect Terrain* and *Table of Contents* (1985), like others, were first printed in *The New Yorker.*

McPHERSON, JAMES ALAN (1943–), Georgia-born author, after graduation from a local college and degrees from Harvard Law School and Iowa's writing curriculum became a professor of literature at the University of California, Santa Cruz, the University of Virginia, and the University of Iowa and wrote stories, mostly set in the South, published in *Hue and Cry* (1969) and *Elbow Room* (1977), the latter collection a Pulitzer Prize winner, succeeded by *A World Unsuspected* (1987).

McPHERSON, JAMES M[UNRO], (1936–), born in North Dakota, received an A.B. from Minnesota's Gustavus Adolphus College and a Ph.D. from Johns Hopkins, has been professor of history at Princeton since 1962. His sizable bibliography includes *Struggle for Equality* (1962); *The Negro's Civil War* (1965); *The Abolitionist Legacy* (1975); *Battle Cry of Freedom* (1988), concerning the U.S. from the Mexican War through the Civil War, awarded a Pulitzer Prize; and *Abraham Lincoln and the Second American Revolution* (1991). He edited *The Atlas of the Civil War* (1994).

McTeague, novel by Frank Norris, ♦ published in 1899.

McTeague, a strong but stupid San Francisco dentist, marries Trina Sieppe, having met her through Marcus Schouler, her cousin and his friend. Trina wins $5000 in a lottery, and by careful saving, investment, and shrewd deception increases the sum. Schouler, who formerly hoped to marry Trina, feels he has been cheated of this fortune. In revenge he exposes McTeague's lack of either diploma or license, so that, forbidden to practice, he becomes mean and surly. Trina, grown miserly, refuses to let him use her money, and they sink into poverty. Greed, the motive underlying these events, also dominates the two figures of the subplot, Maria Macapa, a mad charwoman, and Zerkow, a Jewish junk dealer; fascinated by her obsession with a set of gold plate, he marries her, becomes insane, kills her, and commits suicide. Meanwhile McTeague has deserted Trina, stealing some of her savings. In an attempt to obtain the remainder, he murders her. Fleeing, he tries to cross Death Valley, where he is apprehended by Schouler. McTeague kills his captor, but before he dies the latter manages to handcuff their wrists together, so that McTeague is doomed to die of thirst, locked to the body of his enemy.

McWILLIAMS, CAREY (1905–80), California attorney and sociologist, whose books include *Ambrose Bierce* (1929), a biography; *Factories in the Field* (1939), a survey of migratory agricultural workers in California; *Ill Fares the Land* (1942), discussing changes in U.S. agriculture, especially the dislocation of workers; *Brothers Under the Skin* (1943), about nonwhite minorities in the U.S.; *Prejudice; Japanese-Americans: Symbols of Racial Intolerance* (1944); *A Mask for Privilege* (1948), about anti-Semitism in the U.S.; *North from Mexico* (1949), on Spanish-speaking people in the U.S.; *Witch Hunt* (1950), about civil rights; and *Southern California Country* (1946) and *California: The Great Exception* (1949), sociological analyses. *The Education of Carey McWilliams* (1979) is a memoir. He was editor of *The Nation* (1955–79).

Madame Butterfly, one-act tragedy by Belasco♦ and J.L. Long♦ (1900), adapted from a story by Long (1898). It was made into an opera by Puccini (1906).

Cho-Cho-San, a Japanese girl, has a liaison with Pinkerton, an American naval lieutenant, which she considers a marriage. For two years, with their infant son, she awaits his return. Then she finds he has married an American girl, and, realizing her status, kills herself.

Madame Delphine, novelette by G.W. Cable,♦ published in 1881.

Delphine Carraze, a New Orleans quadroon, lives in seclusion with her 17-year-old daughter Olive, whose white father left them his property when he died. The girl falls in love with Ursin Lemaitre, a white banker known as M. Vignevielle, who is associated with the pirate Lafitte. Through the aid of Père Jerome, the banker and Olive are engaged, but an investigation of his affairs forces him to hide with friends who prevent his "insane" marriage. Delphine, moved by maternal devotion, swears that Olive is really the daughter of a white woman. Even the heartbroken Olive is convinced, and the marriage is assured. Delphine confesses to Père Jerome and dies receiving absolution.

M'lle New York, see *Thompson, Vance.*

MADISON, DOLLY (DOLLEY PAYNE MADISON) (1768–1849), wife of James Madison, was famous as a leader of Washington society, acting as "first lady" during Jefferson's incumbency as well as her husband's. When the British burned the White House during their invasion of Washington (1814), she rescued many important state documents. Her *Memoirs and Letters* was published in 1886.

MADISON, JAMES (1751–1836), 4th President of the U.S. (1809–17), was born in Virginia, reared on his father's plantation, and educated at the College of New Jersey, from which he graduated (1771) as a classmate of Brackenridge and Freneau. He entered the Revolutionary struggle as a member of the local Committee of Safety, the Virginia Council of State (1778–79), and the Continental Congress (1780–83), where he favored increased power of the central government. Later, he practiced law and served in the Virginia House of Delegates, being the principal advocate of Jefferson's statute for religious liberty and other liberal measures. Madison was largely responsible for calling the Federal Constitutional Convention (1787), drew up the Virginia Plan, and won the name "Father of the Constitution" for his leadership of the Convention. Knowledge of its deliberations depends greatly on his *Journal of the Federal Convention* (3 vols., 1840). With Hamilton and Jay, he contributed many papers to *The Federalist*♦ (1787–88), and he was a leader in his state's ratifying convention, as well as the chief advocate of the Bill of Rights.♦ In Congress (1789–97) he supported the policies of Jefferson, with whom he wrote the Kentucky and Virginia Resolutions (1798), and under whom he served as secretary of state (1801–9). He was chosen by Jefferson to be his successor in the presidency. During his two terms in this office, he was strongly opposed to English military policy, because of the impressment of American seamen and interference with American trade during the Napoleonic Wars, as well as the supposed incitement of Indian hostilities on the frontier. His Federalist opponents dubbed the War of 1812, into which he plunged the country, "Mr. Madison's War," and blamed him for its inefficient prosecution. Not a single American aim was achieved, and, had it not been for the late victories at Baltimore, Plattsburg, Lake Erie, and New Orleans, he would have been extremely unpopular. Before his retirement, he inaugurated policies of internal improvement and a protective tariff. The most complete account of his administration is contained in Henry Adams's *History of the United States During the Administrations of Thomas Jefferson and James Madison* (9 vols., 1889–91). A definitive, scholarly edition of his *Papers* (1962–   ) is being published in 20 volumes.

Maggie: *A Girl of the Streets,* novel by Stephen Crane,♦ privately issued (1893) under the pseudonym Johnston Smith, but not regularly published until 1896.

In a slum district of New York City called Rum Alley, Maggie Johnson and her brother Jimmie are the maltreated and neglected children of a brutal workingman and his dipsomaniac wife. Maggie, attractive though ignorant and ill cared for, somehow preserves an inner core of innocence in her miserable, filthy environment. She finds work as a collar maker in a sweatshop, while Jimmie becomes a truck driver, typically hard-boiled and fight-loving. Their mother, now widowed, is constantly drunk and has acquired a lengthy police record. Maggie falls in love with

Jimmie's tough friend Pete, a bartender, who easily seduces her. For a brief time she lives with Pete, having been melodramatically disowned by her mother. Jimmie offers only the questionable assistance of administering a beating to his former friend. Pete abandons Maggie, who becomes a prostitute for a few months. Then, heartbroken and unable to succeed in this uneasy, exacting occupation, she commits suicide. Her mother makes a great display of grief, sends Jimmie to fetch home the body, and allows herself to be persuaded by her drinking companions to "forgive" her "bad, bad child."

Maggie Verver, heroine of *The Golden Bowl.* ◆

Magnalia Christi Americana, ecclesiastical history of New England by Cotton Mather, ◆ published at London in 1702. The work is in seven parts: (1) the settlement of New England; (2) lives of the governors; (3) biographies of 60 famous divines; (4) an account of Harvard College, with the lives of some famous graduates; (5) a history of the Congregational Church in New England; (6) a record of remarkable providences, i.e. events in which God directly revealed His power in the colonies; and (7) a history of various disturbances in the churches, with an appendix on remarkable occurrences in the wars with the Indians (1688–98). The *Magnalia* reprints many of the author's sermons, biographies, and historical narratives, insofar as they could be worked into a rather loose general scheme. The unity of the whole appears in Mather's intention to exalt godliness and celebrate the triumphs of Christ in the New World. It is valuable as a historical source, and the second and third parts indicate Mather's most significant writing to be in the form of biography. The feeling that he was writing a religious epic, buried by the scholarship and digression, is seen in the epic line of the introduction, "I write the wonders of the Christian religion, flying from the depravations of Europe, to the American strand. . . ."

Magnificent Ambersons, The, novel by Tarkington, ◆ published in 1918, won a Pulitzer Prize. It is the second part of the trilogy *Growth,* which also includes *The Turmoil* (1915) and *The Midlander* (1923).

Isabel is the daughter of old Major Amberson, who acquired his fortune during the Gilded Age and used it to win a dominating position for his family in a Midwestern town. She was in love with Eugene Morgan during her youth, but they separated owing to a misunderstanding, and Isabel married Wilbur Minafer, dull and sober, for whom she never cared. When her son George is nearly grown, Eugene, a widower, returns with his daughter Lucy to settle in the town and establish an automobile factory. Although Lucy is aware of George's arrogance and conceit, she falls in love with him, and Eugene and Isabel drift into

their old relation. After his father's death, George returns from an Eastern college, quarrels with Lucy because she objects to his idleness, and then, horrified at the prospect of his mother's remarriage, prevents it by exploiting her affection and fear of displeasing him. George and Isabel live abroad for a few years, until he brings her home to die of a heart ailment. The major's estate having been depleted, George goes to work in a chemical factory, unwilling to approach his former friends or Eugene, now wealthy, who occupies the social position the Ambersons once held. Having long since received the "comeuppance" his acquaintances desired for him, George is injured in an automobile accident, and at last Eugene, cherishing his love for Isabel, and Lucy, still faithful, are reconciled with him.

MAHAN, ALFRED THAYER (1840–1914), graduated from Annapolis (1859), served in the Civil War, later lectured on naval history and tactics at the Newport War College and was its president (1886–89). After retirement from the navy (1896), he was made a rear admiral. His lectures, *Influence of Sea Power Upon History, 1660–1783* (1890) and *The Influence of Sea Power Upon the French Revolution and Empire, 1793–1812* (2 vols., 1892), propounding new views of naval significance in political history, greatly influenced the policies of Germany, England, Japan, and the U.S. His many other books include lives of Nelson and Farragut, works on naval strategy, American naval histories, and a memoir, *From Sail to Steam* (1907).

Mahican Indians, Algonquian confederacy that originally occupied both banks of the upper Hudson River. Crowded by the white settlements, the Mahicans moved to Pennsylvania and thence with the Delawares to the Ohio region, where they were dispersed. The only Mahicans who have preserved the tribal identity are the Stockbridge Indians. In *The Last of the Mohicans* Cooper confuses Mahicans with Mohegans, ◆ with whom they were closely affiliated.

MAILER, NORMAN (1923–), born in New Jersey, reared in Brooklyn, began writing fiction before graduation from Harvard (1943). After serving with the army in the Pacific he wrote *The Naked and the Dead* ◆ (1948), a realistic and naturalistic novel of the fates of 13 men in an infantry platoon who survive the invasion of a Japanese-held island. Both a popular and a critical success, it was followed by two novels in which he turned from naturalistic to existential and allegorical views and which were far less well received: *Barbary Shore* (1951), a symbolic treatment of the conflict between leftist and rightist political forces in the U.S., and *The Deer Park* (1955, dramatized 1967), a bitter view of Hollywood as representative of the entire nation, seen through the stories of three men, a film director whose desire to create honest pictures is threatened by the rightist

House Committee on Un-American Activities, an air force veteran who can find no significant place in the postwar society, and a pimp who is both ambitious and philosophic in the style of a modern Faust. *The White Negro* (1957) is really part of the Beat Movement, calling upon contemporaries to resist media-driven culture. Mailer next published *Advertisements for Myself* (1959), in which he not only collected fiction but began his authorship of distinguished nonfictive works analyzing aspects of his times, in this one concentrating on himself as author in the postwar setting. Mailer returned to fiction with *An American Dream*♦ (1965), a lurid depiction of a disintegrating marriage and a corrupt society, and the coruscating and symbolic *Why Are We in Vietnam?* (1967), in which an obsessed disc jockey in Texas tells of an Alaskan bear hunt made in his youth with his father and a friend, whose quest to prove masculinity and relish the kill is a commentary on America's foray into Vietnam. The investigation of American character in that novel also animated his succeeding nonfiction: *The Armies of the Night*♦ (1968, Pulitzer Prize), treating his experiences and reflections during a pacifist march on the Pentagon (1967); *Miami and the Siege of Chicago* (1968), his view of the current Republican and Democratic presidential conventions; *Of a Fire on the Moon* (1970), analyzing the lunar landings; and *The Executioner's Song* (1979, Pulitzer Prize), a very lengthy so-called true life novel about Gary Gilmore, a convicted murderer, the first person to be executed (1977) in the U.S. for more than a decade. Other nonfictional works are *Cannibals and Christians* (1966), mainly essays; *The Prisoner of Sex* (1971), a reply to a proponent of women's liberation; *Marilyn* (1973), a speculative biography of the film star Marilyn Monroe; and *Of Women and Their Elegance* (1980), an "imaginary memoir" of Marilyn Monroe. *Ancient Evenings* (1983) is a massive novel set in Egypt during the years 1320–1121 BC, which has for a protagonist one Menenhetet, who in the course of the novel is reborn three times and rises from a peasant childhood to become an adviser to pharaohs; *Tough Guys Don't Dance* (1984) is a lively mystery novel; and *Harlot's Ghost* (1991), another lengthy novel, is about two generations of CIA operatives. In *Oswald's Tale: An American Mystery* (1995), Mailer returns to the true-life novel technique in an attempt to discover Lee Harvey Oswald's personality, examining especially his two years in Russia by using interviews with Russian friends and family and, most especially, KGB files containing transcripts from the Oswalds' bugged apartment in Minsk. No Russian, including the widow, Marina, believes Oswald capable of acting alone in assassinating JFK. Mailer collected his poems in *Death for the Ladies and Other Disasters* (1962) and his stories in *Short Fiction* (1967).

Main Street, novel by Sinclair Lewis,♦ published in 1920 and dramatized in 1921 by Harvey O'Higgins♦ and Harriet Ford.

Carol Milford, a girl of quick intelligence but no particular talent, after graduation from college meets and marries Will Kennicott, a sober, kindly, unimaginative physician of Gopher Prairie, Minn., who tells her that the town needs her abilities. She finds the village to be a smug, intolerant, unimaginatively standardized place, where the people will not accept her efforts to create more sightly homes, organize a dramatic association, and otherwise improve the village life. A few characters stand above the apathy and provinciality of the rest: Vida Sherwin, the repressed and acidulous schoolteacher; Guy Pollock, the learned lawyer who has been entrapped by the "village virus"; and Miles Bjornstam, a laughing, iconoclastic Swedish vagabond. Carol draws away from her husband, falls in love with Erik Valborg, a kindred spirit, and finally goes to Washington to make her own life. When Kennicott comes for her, two years later, she returns with him, for, though she feels no love, she respects him, and being incapable of creating her own life appears not unhappy to return to the familiar, petty Gopher Prairie.

Main-Travelled Roads, short stories by Hamlin Garland,♦ published in 1891. Late examples of the school of local color, these tales deal with farm life in the Middle West. The volume is unified by the author's conception of "The Main-Travelled Road in the West," which "may lead past a bend in the river where the water laughs eternally over its shallows. . . . Mainly it is long and wearyful. . . . Like the main-travelled road of life it is traversed by many classes of people, but the poor and the weary predominate."

Maine Woods, The, autobiographical narrative by Thoreau,♦ posthumously published (1864) as edited by the younger W.E. Channing. It contains three accounts of trips to Maine: "Ktaadn" (*Union Magazine,* 1848), describing an excursion to Mt. Ktaadn in 1846; "Chesuncook" (*Atlantic Monthly,* 1858), about a journey from Bangor to Chesuncook Lake in 1853, with an Indian guide, Joe Aitteon; and "The Allegash and East Branch," concerned with a voyage (1857) with "a relative" and the Indian guide Joe Polis, from Bangor to the St. John's lakes by way of Moosehead and Chesuncook, returning by the East Branch of the Penobscot. During this excursion, Thoreau made an extended study of Polis, "one of the aristocracy" of the Penobscot Indians, a silent, capable hunter and backwoodsman.

MAJOR, CHARLES (1856–1913), Indiana author, whose most popular work was the historical romance *When Knighthood Was in Flower* (1898), in which the master of the dance, Sir Edwin Caskoden, tells of the love of Queen Mary and Charles Brandon, with a romantic background of 16th-century England. *Dorothy Vernon of Haddon Hall* (1902) is another romance of this period. Both stories were successfully dramatized and, since their first vogue, have passed into the field of juvenile literature. Major wrote several other historical novels and attempted local-color fiction.

MAJOR, CHARLES (1936–), born in Atlanta, received degrees from SUNY at Albany and the Union for Experimenting Colleges and Universities, has taught English at the University of Colorado since 1977. His very full literary career began with *Love Poems of a Black Man* (1965), poetry continued in *Human Juices* (1966); *Swallow the Lake* (1970), about the difficult lives of black people in a city; *Private Line* (1971); *The Syncopated Cakewalk* (1974); and *Some Observations of a Stranger at Zuñi* (1988). Equally extensive is his body of fiction beginning with *All-Night Visitors* (1969), a rambling tale concerning the sexual and other experiences of a young black man; *No* (1973), about the maturing of a young black boy; *Reflex and Bone Structure* (1975), relating the murder of a black actress; *Emergency Exit* (1979), treating the falling apart of two black lovers; *My Amputations* (1986), about a black man trying to become an author; *Such Was the Season* (1987), comically displaying the lives of a black family in Atlanta; and *Painted Turtle* (1988), about a Native American folksinger. He has also collected stories in *Fun and Games* (1988) and published essays in *The Dark and Feeling: Black American Writers and Their Work* (1974).

MAKEMIE, FRANCIS (c.1658–1708), Presbyterian clergyman born in Ireland, emigrated to Maryland (1683) and eventually settled in Virginia. His missionary work and preaching throughout the colonies has sometimes caused him to be considered the founder of Presbyterianism in America. He was opposed in a controversy by George Keith, to whom he replied in *An Answer to George Keith's Libel* (1694), and also by the Church of England, to which he replied in *Truths in a True Light* (1699). While in England to obtain funds and workers for the Presbyterian cause, he published *A Plain and Friendly Persuasive to the Inhabitants of Virginia and Maryland for Promoting Towns and Cohabitation* (1705). In 1707 he was fined for preaching without a license in New York, and his pamphlet *A Narrative of a New and Unusual American Imprisonment* (1707) helped to do away with such intolerance.

Making of Americans, The, novel by Gertrude Stein,♦ written in 1906–8 and published in 1925. It deals with the wanderings and mental development of three generations of her own family, beginning as the history of a family's progress, but becoming the history of "everyone who ever was

or is or will be living." The simple language is marked by recurrent phrases and other devices to create the feeling of a prolonged present and a constant "beginning again and again."

Making of an American, The, autobiography of Jacob Riis.♦

MALAMUD, BERNARD (1914–86), born in Brooklyn of immigrant Russian parents, after graduation from the City College of New York and holding various odd jobs worked for an M.A. at Columbia while teaching night classes in a high school. His first novel, *The Natural* (1952), is a comic treatment of baseball in terms of a mythic view of the American hero. His second novel, *The Assistant*♦ (1957), is more realistic in its depiction of a pathetically unfortunate family of New York Jews and the assistant in their failing grocery store, but its treatment of the main character's search for the good life and his attempt to change himself is as much concerned with moral issues. His next novel, *A New Life* (1961), is both witty and satirical in its treatment of the life of a Jewish professor of English literature at an Oregon "cow college," but it too presents the theme of a man changing his life. Later novels include *The Fixer*♦ (1967, National Book Award, Pulitzer Prize), the story, based on a Russian case in 1913, of a Jew falsely accused of murder and the resultant attempt to break his spirit and that of all Jews in the country; *Pictures of Fidelman* (1969), about a middle-aged Bronx resident who goes to Italy to be an artist; *The Tenants* (1971), treating conflicts between a white and black writer, the sole residents of a Lower East Side tenement; *Dubin's Lives* (1979), about a famous author's marriage and love affair; and *God's Grace* (1982), a pseudo-Biblical fable about a man who is the sole human survivor of a nuclear war and begins a new civilization among apes. Malamud's stories, also often wryly treating unhappy experiences of Jews, are collected in *The Magic Barrel* (1958, National Book Award), *Idiots First* (1963), and *Rembrandt's Hat* (1973); 25 of them are reprinted in a selected *Stories* (1983). *The People* (1989) posthumously published an unfinished novel and uncollected but lesser stories. He taught English at Oregon State University (1949–61) and at Bennington College from 1961 until his death.

MALCOLM X (MALCOLM LITTLE) (1925–65), Omaha-born militant black leader, a preacher in the Black Muslim religion until ousted (1963) when he founded the Organization of Afro-American Unity, soon after which he was shot to death. *The Autobiography of Malcolm X* (1964) was told to Alex Haley.♦ It tells movingly of his self-education in prison (for thieving), his sense of self-worth buttressed by his conversion to Islam, and his taking a name of his own and not the heritage of a white man. A movie written and directed by Spike Lee (1992) maximized Malcolm's posthumous charisma as a black leader. *One Day, When I Was Lost* (1972) by James Baldwin is an unfilmed scenario of the *Autobiography*. Two volumes of his speeches have been published (1965, 1968).

Male Animal, *The,* play by James Thurber♦ and Elliott Nugent.

Mallison, CHARLES, JR., character, nicknamed Chick, in Faulkner's novels *Intruder in the Dust,*♦ *The Town,*♦ *The Mansion,*♦ and *Knight's Gambit,* each of which he partly narrates.

MALONE, DUMAS (1892–1986), professor of American history at Columbia (1945–59), an editor of the *Dictionary of American Biography* and editor in chief of its last 13 volumes. His books include *Saints in Action* (1939), lectures on American clergymen, educators, and reformers, and a six-volume biography of Jefferson (1948–81, Pulitzer Prize).

MALTZ, ALBERT (1908–85), dramatist, novelist, and scenarist, born in Brooklyn. After graduation from Columbia and study at the Yale Drama School he began writing plays: *Merry-Go-Round* (1932), about political corruption, and *Peace on Earth* (1933), an antiwar plea, both written with George Sklar; *Black Pit* (1935), about a coal miners' strike; and *Private Hicks* (1936), a one-act drama about the breaking of a strike. His novels are *The Underground Stream* (1940), about the struggle to unionize auto workers; *The Cross and the Arrow* (1944), about a German factory worker's aid to British bombers; *The Journey of Simon McKeever* (1949), a symbolic tale of an old man's quest for the good life; *A Long Day in a Short Life* (1957); and *A Tale of One January* (1966). *The Way Things Are* (1938) and *Afternoon in the Jungle* (1970) collect stories. *The Citizen Writer* (1950) collects essays. He was one of the so-called Hollywood Ten.♦

MAMET, DAVID [ALAN] (1947–), Chicago playwright whose works include *Sexual Perversity in Chicago* and *Duck Variations,* two one-act plays (produced 1974, published 1977), lively comedies respectively about two young men on the prowl for women and two loquacious old men who can't do much but talk. *American Buffalo* (1975, published 1977) is a two-act naturalistic play presenting some petty criminals. *Reunion* and *Dark Pony,* one-act productions (on stage respectively in 1976 and 1977 and in print in 1979), followed. *A Life in the Theater* (produced 1977, published 1978) is a work in the same category, a one-act play depicting a seasoned and a young actor on and off stage with symbolic overtones about different ways of life. It was followed by *Shoeshine* (1979), which was included with other Mamet works in the publication *Short Plays and*

Monologues (1981). *Edmond* (1982) is a play about a middle-class New Yorker who leaves wife and home to find his true nature by experiencing life in the city's corrupt and violent subculture. *Glengarry Glen Ross* (1984), presenting tough, crooked real estate salesmen, was given a Pulitzer Prize when simultaneously published. *Writing in Restaurants* (1986) is a book of essays, and *Some Freaks* (1989) is a volume of memoirs, as is *The Cabin, Reminiscence and Diversions* (1993). In 1981 he created the film script for the remake of Cain's *The Postman Always Rings Twice*. He wrote the screenplay for and directed the film *House of Games* (1987), about a woman among a nest of thieves and con artists. *The Woods* (1977) is a drama about a would-be romantic weekend. Then came the brilliant *Speed-the-Plow* (1988), excoriating Hollywood and its denizens, marked by crude and melodious dialogue. In 1992 *Oleanna* was produced successfully. A female student at a university wants help and clarification from her professor, and reacts to what she perceives as his self-satisfied attitude by denouncing him to the tenure committee as a sexist. He is denied tenure, his career ruined. The girl can be seen as rightly aggrieved or as a conniver working with her "group" in a kind of political cleansing. His first novel, *The Village* (1994), is a satire of an urbanite's efforts to take on small-town, old-fashioned values. Mamet is a poet of acidic dialogue, our most impressive theater voice since the early Albee.

Man Against the Sky, *The,* ode by E.A. Robinson,♦ with a basic pentameter line and varying meters and rhymes, the title piece of a volume published in 1916.

A figure seen on a hilltop, against the sunset sky, symbolizes mankind looming "before the chaos and the glare As if he were the last god going home Unto his last desire." Conjecturing as to the attitude of mind of this solitary figure, the poet reviews the various *raisons d'être* advanced by philosophy, mysticism, common sense, and emotion, but indicates his skeptical view that men "Must each await alone at his own height Another darkness or another light. . . ." Life seems a "blind atomic pilgrimage," to which we are led by "crass chance," yet we have hints of some deeper meaning. This he conceives as "an orient Word that will not be erased," vouchsafed in "incommunicable gleams Too permanent for dreams." Earthbound and narrow-visioned, men gain only "a little wisdom and much pain"; but if they are to continue living they must cling to hope, realizing that "Eternity records Too vast an answer for the time-born words We spell. . . ."

Man That Corrupted Hadleyburg, *The,* story by Clemens,♦ published under his pseudonym Mark Twain as the title piece of a collection of essays and fiction (1900).

Hadleyburg is proud of its distinction as "the

most honest and upright town in all the region round about." A stranger, offended in some way by its people, determines to ruin its reputation. He leaves a sack with bank cashier Edward Richards that he says contains a fortune in coins, and a note announcing that the money is to go to a townsman who once befriended him, and who can be identified by a remark he made, which is written on an enclosed paper. Nineteen of Hadleyburg's leading men then receive notes pretending to divulge the remark. Scruples dissolve under this temptation, and even the hitherto honest Richards begins to think he may have made the remark. At a town meeting, 18 of the citizens are exposed to ridicule, when the Rev. Mr. Burgess reads the notes setting forth their claims to the remark. Burgess has lost Richard's note, and the cashier becomes a hero. The victims pay an enormous sum to avoid having their names recorded on the lead slugs that prove to be the sole contents of the sack, and this amount is given to Richards as a reward for his supposed integrity. Conscience destroys the health of the old man and his wife, who in their dying delirium expose their guilt; thus "the town was stripped of the last rag of its ancient glory."

Man Who Died Twice, *The,* blank-verse narrative by E.A. Robinson, ♦ published in 1924.

Fernando Nash, a musician of great though unfulfilled genius, is impatient, indolent, and dissipated, allows his talent to atrophy, and drifts into a life of immorality and extravagance. After many years, penniless in a lonely garret, he reviews his frustrated career, and with sudden revulsion destroys the manuscripts of his two symphonies. Following a last debauch, he resigns himself to death by starvation but, as he lies on his couch, has a final experience of the creative force whose betrayal is his tragedy. With a feeling of spiritual peace he has never before known, he hears the "drums of death," which always formed the background of his creative imagination. The drums grow louder and more terrible, and his "Third Symphony" plays itself to his mind's ear in a "great golden choral fire." He weeps "blinding tears of praise and of exhaustion," gropes his way into the dark hall to call "for paper—not for food," and falls unconscious down the stairs. During his convalescence, he becomes resigned to life, finding in religion "far more than I have lost." He joins a group of street evangelists, to make "a joyful noise unto the Lord," which the narrator admits may be "earnest of thanksgiving, confusion, penance, or the picturesque," but cannot nullify his "fire of personality" and genius.

Man with the Blue Guitar, *The,* title poem of a collection by Wallace Stevens, ♦ published in 1937.

Divided into 33 parts, the poem, in four-stress unrhymed couplets, is constructed like variations played on a guitar. Suggested by Picasso's use of a guitar and the color blue, the poem is a statement by Stevens about the relations between reality (often symbolized by green), imagination (symbolized by blue), and understanding or interpretation through art. "Things as they are Are changed upon the blue guitar."

Man with the Golden Arm, *The,* novel by Nelson Algren, ♦ published in 1949.

Francis Majcinek, called Frankie Machine, comes back to Chicago's Polish community from World War II with a Purple Heart and a morphine habit. In the seedy setting of Division Street he is a dealer in a poker parlor, and is known as the "Man with the Golden Arm," because of both his rapid reflexes and his drug addiction. His wife Sophia, called Zosh, has been crippled in an auto accident caused by Frankie's drunken driving and spends her dreary days making him feel guilty. In Molly Novotny, a sweet 20-year-old part-time prostitute, Frankie finds love and solace, but he remains trapped in his marriage and morphine habit. He accidentally breaks the neck of his drug supplier, Nifty Louie Fomorowski, and next gets caught committing a robbery with his friend Solly Saltskin, variously called "The Punk" or "The Sparrow." After serving a brief prison term for the latter offense he returns to his old haunts and to Molly, but when about to be arrested for the killing, he hangs himself just before the police arrive.

Man with the Hoe, *The,* poem by Edwin Markham. ♦

Man Without a Country, *The,* story by E.E. Hale, ♦ published in the *Atlantic Monthly* (1863), reprinted in pamphlet form (1865), and collected in *If, Yes, and Perhaps* (1868). Written to inspire patriotism during the Civil War, it was suggested by the remark of Vallandigham, a former Ohio congressman, that he did not wish to live in a country that tolerated Lincoln's administration. Although entirely fictitious, the story has a realism reminiscent of Defoe. There was a real Philip Nolan, ♦ whose true history forms the basis of Hale's complementary novelette, *Philip Nolan's Friends* (1876). Arthur Guiterman adapted Hale's first story as a libretto for an opera by Damrosch (1937).

On trial with Aaron Burr for conspiracy, Philip Nolan cries out, "Damn the United States. I wish I may never hear of the United States again." The court-martial accordingly condemns him to a life at sea, where he will be denied any news of his country. His spirit is broken when one day he reads the lines from the *Lay of the Last Minstrel,*

> Breathes there a man with soul so dead
> Who never to himself hath said,
> "This is my own, my native land."

Thereafter he is a pathetic figure, desiring to aid the U.S. and showing great bravery in a sea battle during the War of 1812. After 57 years of exile, he dies happily, having learned of his country's increased greatness.

MANCHESTER, WILLIAM (1922–), biographer, historian. Manchester has published novels, but his reputation rests on his histories and biographies. Among these are *Disturber of the Peace: The Life of H.L. Mencken* (1951); *The Death of a President* (1967), on the assassination of JFK; *The Glory and the Dream: A Narrative History of America 1932–1972* (1968); and two of three projected volumes on the life of Winston Churchill, *The Last Lion: Visions of Glory 1874–1932* (1984) and *The Last Lion: Alone, 1932–1940* (1988). Some of his other works are *Controversy and Other Essays in Journalism* (1976); *Goodbye, Darkness* (1980), a memoir of his service as a Marine sergeant in the South Pacific island campaigns of World War II; and *A World Lit Only by Fire: The Medieval Mind* (1992).

Mandan Indians, northern Plains tribe affiliated with the Arikara, combined bison hunting with agricultural pursuits. La Vérendrye visited the Mandan in 1738, and every later expedition up the Missouri knew them. By 1776 smallpox and attacks by neighboring tribes had reduced them to a single village. In 1870 they settled with other tribes on the Fort Berthold reservation in North Dakota. The Mandan figure in the journals of Lewis and Clark and are the subject of a study and many paintings by George Catlin.

MANFRED, FREDERICK (FREDERICK FEIKEMA) (1912–), Iowa-born author of Frisian ancestry who also called himself Feike Feikema (1944–51). He began his career as a journalist but in his thirties became a prolific novelist of his native region, which he calls Siouxland, the area of the Minnesota and South Dakota border. His energetic and also poetic novels, often primitive in vision and rough in style, include *The Golden Bowl* (1944), about a conflict between two generations of Midwest farmers; *Boy Almighty* (1945), a semi-autobiographical tale of a writer's life as a patient in a Midwest tuberculosis sanitarium; *This Is the Year* (1947), portraying a willful Frisian farmer; *The Chokecherry Tree* (1948), depicting an aspiring boy in conflict with Midwest society; *The Primitive* (1949), *The Brother* (1950), and *The Giant* (1951), gathered in the trilogy *Wanderlust* (1962), about a farm boy who goes to New York; *Lord Grizzly* (1954), based on the life of the mountain man Hugh Glass; *Morning Red* (1956), treating journalism and politics in a small Minnesota town; *Riders of Judgment* (1957), about cattle wars in Wyoming during the 1890s; *Conquering Horse* (1959), presenting the adolescence of an Indian boy; *Scarlet Plume* (1964), about a white woman captured by the Sioux in 1862; *King of Spades* (1966), in part depicting the gold rush of the 1870s into the Black Hills of South Dakota;

Eden Prairie (1968), a frank tale of the lives of Midwest rural schoolteachers in the 1920s; *The Manly-Hearted Woman* (1976), about Indian experiences of life and death; *Milk of Wolves* (1976), portraying a stonecutter who becomes a sculptor; *Green Earth* (1977), about a Frisian family of tenant farmers in Iowa at the opening of the 20th century; and *Sons of Adam* (1980), presenting the dramatic experiences of two related young Midwest men. *Arrow of Love* (1961) and *Apples of Paradise* (1968) collect stories. *Winter Count* (1966) is a volume of poems. *The Wind Blows Free* (1980) is a memoir of hitchhiking from Iowa to the Rockies in the 1930s. *Prime Fathers* (1987) is a book of essays, some autobiographical, followed by *Selected Letters* (1989). *No Fun on Sunday* (1990) treats elements of playing serious baseball.

Manhattan Transfer, novel by Jon Dos Passos, ◆ published in 1925. It is marked by stylistic innovations, impressionistic descriptive effects, and a naturalistic attempt to depict the complex life of modern New York City. The careers of a dozen or more representative citizens are traced simultaneously, in a succession of brief dramatic episodes.

A country youth, Bud Korpenning, comes to the city to seek work, but after ten years of infrequent employment, and very close to starvation, commits suicide. Joe Harland, the "Wizard of Wall Street," loses fortune and power through excessive drinking and is reduced to common labor and beggary. Gus McNeil, a wealthy contractor, and Joe O'Keefe, a radical union organizer, exhibit the opposite ends of the scale in the building trades. Ellen Thatcher Oglethorpe, with various changes of name, rises from the lower middle class to become a featured actress, at the cost of integrity and happiness. Her first husband, John Oglethorpe, is a homosexual, whom she divorces. She endures the attentions of the impresario Harry Goldweiser, whom she despises. The one man she really loves, Stan Emery, takes to drink, marries another actress, and dies in an apartment-house fire. Ellen marries devoted Jimmy Herf, but even though they have a child and she quits the stage they cannot be happy and are soon divorced. Jimmy, a cousin of Joe Harland, has an unhappy, struggling career in journalism, which he leaves to begin life anew outside the city. These and such other characters as Congo Jake, the bootlegger, James Merivale, the banker and society man, George Baldwin, the unscrupulous lawyer and politician, and Cassandra Wilkins, the absurd aesthete, serve to illustrate the author's pessimistic view of the decadent city and to bind together his portrait of its teeming activity.

"Manifest Destiny," jingoistic phrase popular with mid-19th-century politicians, who believed that the U.S. should overspread the continent and annex such neighboring countries as Cuba. It was first used by John L. O'Sullivan, in the July

1845 issue of his *United States Magazine and Democratic Review.*

MANLY, WILLIAM LEWIS (1820–1903), in July 1849 set out along the Oregon Trail for the gold rush but upon reaching Fort Bridger thought he could float down the Green and Colorado rivers to California. With rough portages he did make his way to Arizona, then trekked via desert land to southern California (arriving March 1850) as later recounted in *Death Valley in '49* (1894, edited version 1927). Lesser sketches were collected in *The Jayhawkers' Oath* (1949).

MANN, HORACE (1796–1859), secretary of the Massachusetts state board of education (1837–48), raised the standards and improved the equipment of the free schools of the state. His influence was widespread, and he was instrumental in improving common school education throughout the U.S. In 1852 he founded and became the first president of Antioch College, a progressive institution. He was also identified with such liberal movements as the Free-Soil party, temperance agitation, and efforts to establish state insane asylums. His *Lectures on Education* was published in 1845.
     MARY TYLER PEABODY MANN (1806–87), his wife, a sister of Elizabeth Palmer Peabody, aided him in his educational and philanthropic work and published the self-effacing *Life and Works of Horace Mann* (3 vols., 1865–68).

Mannon, LAVINIA, character in *Mourning Becomes Electra.*♦

Man's Woman, *A,* novel by Frank Norris,♦ published in 1900.

Man's World, *A,* play by Rachel Crothers,♦ produced in 1909 and published in 1915.
     "Frank" Ware, a woman writer, rears the illegitimate son of a woman who died in childbirth at her Paris home. She becomes convinced that the morality that permits the father to escape responsibility is basically unfair. When she falls in love with Malcolm Gaskell, another suitor, Lione Brune, draws her attention to the resemblance Malcolm bears to the child. Questioning him, she discovers that he is the father and, in keeping with her moral attitude, refuses to marry him.

Mansion, *The,* novel by William Faulkner,♦ published in 1959, the third of a trilogy including *The Hamlet*♦ and *The Town.*♦
     In 1908 Mink Snopes, a poor sharecropper in Frenchman's Bend, Yoknapatawpha County, Mississippi, kills a rich neighbor in a dispute over a fee charged for pasturing his cow. Sent to prison, in part because his cousin Flem would not help him, Mink is determined to seek revenge. Meanwhile Flem has moved to Jefferson, become wealthy, and gained a respectable position as president of the Sartoris bank but, fearing Mink,

concocts a plot to have another relative, Montgomery Ward Snopes, aid Mink to escape from prison in such a way that he will be captured and receive an added sentence. The plot fails, but Mink is reconfirmed in his belief in Old Moster, a personification of vengeance who "jest punishes," as he himself lives for the time when he can kill Flem. Linda Snopes, the daughter of Flem's wife Eula by her lover, is also intent on vengeance against her stepfather since Flem had cheated her of her inheritance and driven her mother to suicide. Linda is aided by her lawyer, Gavin Stevens, who has had a long-standing fight with the rest of the Snopes family. Through Gavin's efforts Mink is pardoned after 38 years of imprisonment. As soon as he is free he goes to Flem's mansion and kills him. Linda helps Mink to escape, as does Gavin, but, utterly spent, Mink "jest lay down" to sleep and to die.

Manuductio ad Ministerium, by Cotton Mather,♦ published in 1726, is a simple set of directions for candidates for the ministry, and contains an important digression expounding Mather's concept of literary style.

MS. Found in a Bottle, story by Poe,♦ published in 1833 and reprinted in *Tales of the Grotesque and Arabesque* (1840).
     The narrator takes passage on a ship bound from Batavia to the Sunda Islands. During a terrible storm, the entire crew is swept overboard, except for this passenger and a Swedish sailor. The storm continues for several days, when suddenly a huge ship under full sail bears down on them, the narrator alone being saved by being hurled upon the rigging of the strange craft. This is the beginning of his long stay aboard the ship, whose aspect is unlike anything he has known, and whose ghostly sailors neither see nor speak to him. He writes a journal of his experiences, intending to seal it in a bottle and throw it into the sea "at the last moment." It concludes with a description of a fearful driving current and final whirlpool in which the ship is going down.

Many Marriages, novel by Sherwood Anderson.♦

Map of Virginia, *A,* narrative by John Smith.♦

Maple, narrative poem in blank verse by Robert Frost,♦ published in *New Hampshire* (1923).
     Although others commonly misunderstand it as "Mabel," Maple, the name of a New England girl, given her at birth by her dying mother, guides her life and endows her with a mysterious poetic quality. Her father is unable or unwilling to make clear the intended meaning, and Maple is able to find only partial clues, but the man she marries discerns her kinship with the spirit of the trees, and they share this secret as a motive of their love.

Mapple, FATHER, character in *Moby-Dick*◆ based on the Boston preacher E.T. Taylor.◆

MARBLE, DAN[FORTH] (1810–49), actor born in Connecticut, famous for his Yankee roles, of which the most popular was the title part in *Sam Patch* by E.H. Thompson. His circuit extended from Boston to New Orleans and from Savannah to St. Louis, while he was equally popular in New York, London, and Scotland. He is generally called Dan Marble, and sometimes received the nickname "Game Cock of the Wilderness" from the title of a play by the same name in which a Yankee goes to the frontier.

Marble Faun, *The,* romance by Hawthorne,◆ published in 1860. It was issued in England as *Transformation.*

Kenyon, an American sculptor, Hilda, a New England girl, and the mysterious Miriam are friends among the art students in Rome. They become acquainted with Donatello, Count of Monte Beni, a handsome Italian who resembles the Faun of Praxiteles, not only physically, but also in his mingling of human and animal qualities, his amoral attitude, and his simple enjoyment of the life of the senses. The dark, passionate Miriam is loved by Donatello, but she is haunted by an unrevealed sin and by the persecution of a mysterious man who dogs her footsteps after an accidental meeting in the Catacombs. Donatello is enraged by this man, and after an encouraging glance from Miriam flings him to his death from the Tarpeian Rock. Thereafter they are linked by their mutual guilt, which they keep secret. Donatello becomes brooding and conscience-stricken, and, though humanized by his suffering, is a broken spirit when he finally gives himself up to justice. Hilda, who saw the crime committed, is also involved in the sin until she forsakes Puritan tradition and pours out her secret at a church confessional. The unhappy Miriam disappears into the shadowy world from which she came, and Hilda and Kenyon are married.

March, BASIL, character in *A Hazard of New Fortunes*◆ and *Their Wedding Journey.*◆

MARCH, WILLIAM, pseudonym of William Edward March Campbell (1893–1954), Alabama author whose service in World War I inspired his related short stories, *Company K* (1933), in which each soldier of the unit succinctly tells his experiences to create a composite portrait. Besides other collections, *The Little Wife* (1935), *Some Like Them Short* (1939), and *Trial Balance* (1945), he wrote the novels *Come In at the Door* (1934); *The Tallons* (1936); *The Looking Glass* (1943), presenting tortured and psychological experiences of individuals, set in his native state; and *The Bad Seed* (1954), about an eight-year-old murderess, dramatized (1955) by Maxwell Anderson.

Marching On, historical novel by James Boyd,◆ published in 1927. The characters are descendents of those in his Revolutionary War novel *Drums.*

"Marching Through Georgia," popular Union marching song, composed in 1865 by H.C. Work,◆ and celebrating Sherman's famous march to the sea.

Marco Millions, drama by O'Neill,◆ published in 1927 and produced in 1928.

Mardi: And a Voyage Thither, allegorical romance by Melville,◆ published in 1849.

Taji, the hero, and his Norse companion Jarl desert from a whaling ship in southern Pacific waters and meet the brigantine *Parki,* abandoned except for the comic Polynesian husband and wife, Samoa and Annatoo. The four pass pleasant days aboard the *Parki,* until it sinks during a storm and Annatoo is drowned. Adrift in a whaleboat, Taji, Jarl, and Samoa meet a native priest and his ward, the mysterious white maiden Yillah, whom he is taking to be sacrificed. They rescue the maiden and reach Mardi, the realm of transcendental beauty, where Taji and Yillah spend a blissful period in love. When she suddenly vanishes, beauty and delight are also gone, and Taji searches for her through the islands of Mardi. He is accompanied by Media, king of Odo, Mohi (Braidbeard) the historian, Babbalanja the philosopher, and Yoomy the poet; as they travel, they discourse on many topics, and their search brings them to Dominora (Great Britain), Vivenza (the U.S.), and other lands, which are the subjects of Swiftian satire. They also visit Serenia, ruled by Alma (Christ), in whose doctrine of love Babbalanja finds the ultimate in earthly wisdom, but Taji, seeing the doctrine disregarded in practice, remains dissatisfied. At last they reach Flozella-a-Nina, where Queen Hautia has transformed Yillah into one of her dusky handmaidens. Hautia nearly overwhelms Taji by her sensual blandishments, but, leaving his companions, he sets sail alone, pursued by "three fixed spectres," to continue his search "over an endless sea."

Ma-re-Mount, see *Merry Mount.*

Margaret, novel by Sylvester Judd,◆ published in 1845 and revised in 1851. Subtitled "A Tale of the Real and Ideal," it combines a vivid description of the Down East region with a transcendental Fourierist fantasy.

Margaret, an orphan with a native sensitivity and intellectual interests, is reared by a backwoods Maine family. To the small town in which they live come Mr. Evelyn, a Transcendentalist, and Rose, a seduced woman. At a husking bee, a rustic lout pays unwelcome attentions to Margaret, and Rose induces Margaret's foster brother Chillion to kill him. Chillion is hanged for this crime. Margaret and Mr. Evelyn fall in love and marry, and together they transform the little town into an ideal community of prosperous, pious, philosophical Transcendentalists.

Margaret Fleming, play by James A. Herne. ♦

Marginalia, brief critical notes published by Poe♦ in various periodicals, including *Graham's Magazine* and the *Southern Literary Messenger,* during the 1840s. These were frequently excerpts from previously published reviews and articles, and dealt with such diverse subjects as "Defoe," "The Drama," "Antigone," "Plagiarism," "Rhetoric," "The Dash," and "Men of Genius."

Maria del Occidente, pseudonym of Maria Brooks. ♦

Marie Rogêt, see *Mystery of Marie Rogêt.*

MARION, FRANCIS (*c.*1732–95), South Carolina soldier, commander of militia in the Revolutionary War, who lacked sufficient men for regular organization and became famous for his guerrilla tactics. He was nicknamed "the Swamp Fox" because he retired to the swamps when confronted by superior forces. He became a brigadier general and fought under Greene in the Battle of Eutaw Springs. His reputation became almost legendary, and he figures in many of the Revolutionary Romances♦ of Simms. The latter also wrote his biography and the poem "The Swamp Fox," and Bryant wrote a "Song of Marion's Men."

Marjorie Daw, epistolary short story by Aldrich, ♦ the title piece of a collection published in 1873.

Mark Littleton, pseudonym of J. P. Kennedy. ♦

MARK TWAIN, pseudonym of Samuel L. Clemens. ♦ The name, a phrase meaning "two fathoms deep," was employed in making soundings on Mississippi riverboats. According to Clemens's questionable account in *Life on the Mississippi,* the name had been used previously by an older pilot, Isaiah Sellers (1803–64), to sign the pompous articles he contributed to the *New Orleans Picayune.* Clemens claims he burlesqued these in the New Orleans *True Delta* and that the parody so affected Sellers that he never published again. Therefore, Clemens declares, he adopted the name as a form of reparation. In that account he also paid tribute to Sellers as "the patriarch of the craft" of steamboat piloting. Clemens's first-known use of the name occurs in a contribution to the Virginia City *Territorial Enterprise* on February 3, 1863.

MARKFIELD, WALLACE (1926–), Brooklyn-born novelist whose books include *To an Early Grave* (1964), a wry, comic view of New York's Jewish intellectual life; *Teitlebaum's Window* (1970), a story of a boy growing up in Brooklyn during the 1930s; and *You Could Live It If They Let You* (1974), another treatment of New York Jewish experience. *Multiple Orgasms* (1977) collects stories.

MARKHAM, EDWIN [CHARLES] (1852–1940), Oregon-born poet, lived in California (1857–1901), where he became a schoolteacher. He won widespread popularity for the title poem of *The Man with the Hoe and Other Poems* (1899), inspired by Millet's painting. This blank-verse depiction of a brutalized farmer, "bowed by the weight of centuries . . . The emptiness of ages in his face," is a somewhat rhetorical protest against the degradation of exploited labor. *Lincoln and Other Poems* (1901), in the same vein, was also very popular. His many later volumes are generally mediocre, marked by a lofty and occasionally tumid melody. The character Presley in Norris's *The Octopus♦* is said to represent Markham.

MARKOE, PETER (*c.*1752–92), born in the Danish West Indies and educated at Oxford, probably came to America during the Revolutionary War. He wrote the unproduced play *The Patriot Chief* (1784), a romantic tragedy set in Lydia, indicating the dangers of aristocracy, and an unproduced opera, *The Reconciliation* (1790). He was also the author of *The Times* (1788), a satirical poem on prominent persons of Philadelphia, where he made his home. *The Algerine Spy in Pennsylvania* (1787), an epistolary novel, and *The Storm* (1788), a descriptive poem, have been attributed to him.

Marmion, play by J.N. Barker, ♦ adapted from the poem by Scott, produced in 1812 and published in 1816. Attributed to the British playwright Thomas Morton for fear that a work by an American would not be appreciated, it was soon immensely popular, partially owing to public sentiment during the War of 1812, since it places in the mouths of the Scots the resentment that Americans felt toward British arrogance.

MARQUAND, J[OHN] P[HILLIPS] (1893–1960), Massachusetts author, born in Wilmington, Del., whose literary career began with popular romances, including *The Unspeakable Gentleman* (1922), *The Black Cargo* (1925), *Warning Hill* (1930), and *Ming Yellow* (1935), and detective stories about Mr. Moto, a Japanese sleuth. His more serious comedies of manners, often observing the struggle between inherited conformity and personal desire, include *The Late George Apley♦* (1937, Pulitzer Prize), a supposed memoir of Boston Brahmin life; *Wickford Point* (1939), a similar satire of a New England family; *H. M. Pulham, Esquire* (1941), about a New Englander 25 years out of college; *So Little Time* (1943), about a play doctor who regrets an uncreative career; *B. F.'s Daughter* (1946), characterizing an industrialist's daughter who tries to dominate her husband; *Point of No Return* (1949), about a middle-aged banker, no longer able to turn from his path of materialism; *Melville Goodwin, USA* (1951), tracing the stultifying career of an army officer; *Sincerely, Willis Wayde* (1955), an ironic character study of an egocentric tycoon's rise to power; and *Women and Thomas Harrow* (1958), presenting a New Englander, once a successful dramatist, as he remembers his first wife and his happier past. *Lord Timothy Dexter* (1925) is the life of an 18th-century New England eccentric, and *Timothy Dexter Revisited* (1960) adds autobiographical information about Dexter's and Marquand's hometown, Newburyport. *Thirty Years* (1954) collects stories and articles, and *Life at Happy Knoll* (1957) assembles sketches in epistolary form about the problems of a country club.

MARQUETTE, JACQUES (1637–75), French Jesuit missionary and explorer, came to Canada in 1666. In 1673 with Jolliet he descended the Mississippi to the mouth of the Arkansas, establishing the existence of a waterway from the St. Lawrence to the Gulf of Mexico. In 1674 he set out to found a mission among the Illinois Indians, but he died during the journey. His journal of the voyage with Jolliet, published in 1681, has been translated in Thwaites's *The Jesuit Relations and Allied Documents* (1900), which also contains his journal of the later trip, first published in 1852.

MARQUIS, DON[ALD ROBERT PERRY] (1878–1937), Illinois-born journalist in Atlanta (1902–9) and New York (1909–22), became noted as a humorist through his columns, "The Sun Dial" in the New York *Sun* and "The Lantern" in the *New York Tribune*. His most famous works are *The Old Soak* (1921), which he dramatized successfully in 1922, "a kind of goldinged autobiography of what me and Old King Booze done before he went into the grave and took one of my feet with him"; and *archy and mehitabel*♦ (1927) and its sequels, which provided a medium for Marquis's opinions on contemporary life. His mordant satire, in the vein of Mark Twain, also appears in *Hermione and Her Little Group of Serious Thinkers* (1916); *Carter and Other People* (1921), including sketches of black characters and the ironic one-act play "Words and Thoughts"; *The Revolt of the Oyster* (1922), stories; *The Old Soak's History of the World* (1924); *The Almost Perfect State* (1927); *A Variety of People* (1929), stories; *Off the Arm* (1930), a novel set in Paris, Hollywood, and New York; *Chapters for the Orthodox* (1934), stories; and *Master of the Revels* (1934), a four-act comedy set in Tudor times. His books of humorous verse, besides those dealing with archy, include *Noah an' Jonah an' Cap'n John Smith* (1921), *Sonnets to a Red-Haired Lady (by a Gentleman with a Blue Beard) and Famous Love Affairs* (1922), and *Love Sonnets of a Cave Man*

(1928). Marquis was less successful with his serious works, which include the poems in *Dreams and Dust* (1915), *Poems and Portraits* (1922), and *The Awakening* (1924); the dramas *The Dark Hours* (1924, produced 1932), dealing with the last days of Jesus, and *Out of the Sea* (1927), a version of the Tristram and Isolde legend; and an unfinished autobiographical novel, *Sons of the Puritans* (1939).

MARRYAT, FREDERICK (1792–1848), British naval captain and popular novelist about life at sea, went to the U.S. and Canada (1837–39) to compare British and American governments. His tactless remarks and behavior led to attacks by the U.S. press in which he was accused of assaulting women, insulting Clay, and being a spy. At Detroit he was burned in effigy with hundreds of his books. His *Diary in America, with Remarks on Its Institutions* (1839) is sharp and often humorous reporting with many caustic comments. *Monsieur Violet* (1843), a melodramatic novel about California, plagiarizes the *Narrative* of G.W. Kendall.

Marse Henry, see *Watterson, Henry.*

MARSH, GEORGE PERKINS (1801–82), Vermont lawyer and scholar, because of his linguistic ability became minister to Turkey (1849–54) and minister to Italy (1860–82). He was the author of *A Compendious Grammar of the Old-Northern or Icelandic Language* (1838), *The Goths in New-England* (1843), *Lectures on the English Language* (1860), and *The Origin and History of the English Language* (1862), as well as collaborating on the *Oxford New English Dictionary.* His greatest work was *Man and Nature* (1864), revised as *The Earth as Modified by Human Action* (1874), in which he suggested methods by which man might restore the physical conditions of the organic and inorganic world that he had disturbed, and thereby improve wasted and exhausted regions. This book has been considered the fountainhead of the 20th-century conservation movement in the U.S. and elsewhere.

MARSH, JAMES (1794–1842), born in Vermont, graduated from Dartmouth (1817), and became a Congregational minister and professor of languages. He was president of the University of Vermont (1826–33). Opposed to both revivalism and stern Calvinism, he sought a religion that would "satisfy the heart as well as the head," and edited Coleridge's *Aids to Reflection* (1829), adopting its distinctions between reason and understanding. This work and his preliminary essay to it had a formative influence on the Transcendentalist movement.

Marsh Island, *A,* novel by Sarah Orne Jewett. ♦

MARSHALL, HUMPHREY (1722–1801), Pennsylvania botanist, whose book, *Arbustrum Ameri-*

canum: The American Grove (1785), is considered the first indigenous botanical essay published in America.

MARSHALL, PAULE (1929–   ), born in Brooklyn of Barbadian heritage, educated at Brooklyn and Hunter colleges. Her autobiographically grounded first novel, *Brown Girl, Brownstones* (1959), though a commercial failure on first publication, has become a classic in the female coming-of-age genre. *Praisesong for the Widow* (1983), her other widely read novel, concerns a financially comfortable middle-class widow in her sixties who has completely lost touch with her West Indian and African-American roots but determines to recover them during a luxury cruise through the West Indies in the course of which she has disturbing dreams. *Soul Clap Hands and Sing* (1961) prints short stories, as does *Reena and Other Stories* (1983).

Marshes of Glynn, The, poem by Lanier,♦ published anonymously in the anthology *A Masque of Poets* (1878). It is one of six projected "Hymns of the Marshes," of which the poet completed only three others, "Sunrise," "Individuality," and "Marsh-Song—At Sunset." In anapestic measure, it employs shifting accents, initial truncation, and from one to 17 syllables in a line, to achieve a musical cadence. The poem describes the sea marshes of Glynn County, Georgia, where the author is stimulated to a pagan ecstasy:

Oh, what is abroad in the marsh and the
     terminal sea?
Somehow my soul seems suddenly free
From the weighing of fate and the sad
     discussion of sin,
By the length and the breadth and the sweep of
     the marshes of Glynn.

MARTIN, VICTORIA, see *Woodhull.*

Martin Chuzzlewit, The Life and Adventures of, novel by Dickens,♦ published in 1844. It was partially an outgrowth of his American tour (1842).

Martin, the grandson of wealthy, misanthropic old Martin Chuzzlewit, is in love with Mary Graham, his grandfather's ward. When the old man refuses to allow him to marry Mary and has him dismissed from his position with his cousin, the architect Pecksniff, Martin sails to the U.S. to make his fortune, accompanied by Mark Tapley, his servant. He is defrauded in his work as an architect for the Eden Land Corporation (Cairo, Ill.), loses his money, and nearly dies of a fever. The example of his devoted, cheerful servant, also stricken, teaches him unselfishness. When he returns to England, his grandfather appreciates his newly revealed good qualities, becomes aware of the hypocritical Pecksniff's meanness and treachery, and gives his blessing to the wedding of young Martin and Mary.

Martin Eden, novel by Jack London,♦ published in 1909.

Like the author, the hero is a sailor and laborer whose endurance and intellectual curiosity lead him to educate himself so that he may share what he conceives to be the fine, high-thinking life of the wealthy bourgeoisie. He is inspired by Ruth Morse, a college-trained society girl, to him a symbol of what he considers are the values of her class. He becomes a writer, expressing the view of life to which his reading of Spencer has guided him, but only Russ Brissenden, a socialist poet (said to be based on George Sterling), understands the power and beauty of his work. His fiancée Ruth, like her family and class, "worshipping at the shrine of the established" and financially successful, deserts him, believing him a failure when magazines will not buy his writing, and is outraged by the notoriety attaching to a newspaper's false accusation that he is a socialist. When one of his books makes him wealthy and famous, she attempts to resume their engagement, but his love is killed by recognition that she really admires only his acclaim and financial success. This realization, the suicide of Brissenden, the loss of affiliation with his own class, and the contempt for the values of the class to which he has climbed rob him of his zest for living. He makes a voyage to the South Seas, and, his will to live destroyed, jumps from the ship and drowns.

Martin Faber, novel by Simms,♦ published in 1833 and revised as *Martin Faber, the Story of a Criminal* (1837).

Martin, a brilliant but evil young man, seduces Emily and deserts her to marry Constance Claiborne. When Emily threatens to expose him, he strangles her and hides her body in the cleft of a rock. He then accuses Constance of having an affair with his friend William Harding, who ingeniously reconstructs the murder and exposes it in a painting he hangs in the village gallery. Frightened, Martin goes with Harding to the scene of the crime, where he is held by the villagers while the rock is blasted and the body recovered. He attempts to stab Constance when she visits him in prison, but fails and is taken to be hanged.

MARTINEAU, HARRIET (1802–76), English author, wrote popularizations of social, philosophic, and economic subjects, as well as novels and stories for children. In 1834–36 she traveled from New England and New York to the Great Lakes and New Orleans. Returning to England, she published *Society in America* (1837), a study of American economic, political, and social institutions, and *Retrospect of Western Travel* (1838), sketches of her experiences. The latter was entertainingly written and had a popular success, but the former, although sympathizing in general with American principles, was antagonistic toward the South. A typical reply was Simms's *Slavery in America* (1838), which not only attacked Miss Martineau's ideas, but also vilified her character and made sport of her deafness. Although adversely criticized in *Blackwood's,* her book was well received in England and was among the most popular of her 52 volumes. Her *Autobiography* (1877) was edited by her friend Maria W. Chapman.

MARTYR, PETER (PIETRO MARTIRE ANGHIERA) (1455–1526), Italian chaplain, whose residence in Spain brought him acquaintance with Columbus, da Gama, Cortés, Magellan, and other discoverers. They furnished him with information, supplemented by official documents, for his letters on contemporary history and discovery. His *De Orbe Novo* (1516), known as the *Decades,* and his *Opus Epistolarium* (1530) give him claim to the title "the first historian of America."

MARVEL, IK, see *Mitchell, D.G.*

"Mary had a little lamb," first line of "Mary's Lamb," a poem by Sarah Josepha Hale,♦ first published in *The Juvenile Miscellany* (Sept. 1830) over her initials, and reprinted in *Poems for Our Children* (1830).

Mary of Scotland, blank-verse drama by Maxwell Anderson,♦ produced in 1933 and published in 1934.

Maryland Gazette, The, (1727–1839), first newspaper in Maryland, was founded and edited by William Parks, an Englishman resident at Annapolis until 1736. Among the literary contributions were an allegory, "The Plain Dealer," which took a conservative point of view regarding constitutional liberty, and a Defoe-like letter purporting to be by a South Carolina gentleman reporting a mutiny by mulattoes. The paper was revived by Jonas Green (1745–65), and then was suspended because of hostility toward the Stamp Act. In 1766 it was revived, and was continued by Green and his family until superseded by *St. Mary's Gazette.*

"Maryland, My Maryland," song by J.R. Randall.♦

MASON, BOBBIE ANN (1940–   ), short story writer, novelist. On publication of *Shiloh and Other Stories* in 1982, Mason was greeted as a major talent—a perfect voice for the rural shopping-mall frequenters and strivers after a meaningful and fully materialist life. Mason was born and raised near Mayfield, Ky., a region most of her characters are drawn from. At the University of Connecticut, she wrote a dissertation on Nabokov's novel *Ada,* later published as *Nabokov's Garden* (1974), followed by *The Girl Sleuth: A Feminist Guide to the Bobbsey Twins, Nancy Drew and Their Sisters* (1975). But she was, she says, "haunted by the people I went to high school with" and found her true voice writing

about them. Later novels were *In Country* (1985), about a young woman whose father died in Vietnam, and *Spence + Lila* (1988), which examines love strained by a woman's trials with breast cancer. *Feather Crowns* (1993) is set in Hopewell, Ky., in 1900, where Christie Wheeler gives birth to quintuplets; she and her husband become instant celebrities, but the fame is not an unmixed blessing, and the novel explores dealing with uncertainties. The stories in *Love Life* (1989) revisit the domain of *Shiloh.*

MASON, JOHN (*c.*1600–72), arrived in the Massachusetts Bay Colony (*c.*1630), where he became the military hero of the Pequot War and later commander in chief of the colony and holder of various offices. From memory he wrote a simple, honest, and blunt account of the war, originally published in Increase Mather's *A Relation of the Troubles Which Have Hapned in New-England . . .* (1677) and erroneously attributed to John Allyn. The work was edited by Thomas Prince as *A Brief History of the Pequot War* (1736).

Mason, PERRY, hero of many detective stories by Erle Stanley Gardner.♦

Masque of Kings, The, play by Maxwell Anderson.♦

Masque of the Red Death, The, story by Poe,♦ published in *Graham's Magazine* (1842).

In a land devastated by a horrible plague, the "Red Death," Prince Prospero determines to preserve himself and his friends, and removes to a secluded castle, where, with 1000 knights and ladies, he spends several months in extravagantly gay pursuits. At a masquerade in the imperial suite, when the courtiers appear in masks and fantastic costumes, a terrifying corpse-like figure joins them, garbed as the Red Death. Attempting to stab him, the Prince dies; when others seize the apparition, it is discovered to have no tangible body. They realize that this is the Red Death itself, and, as midnight strikes, they die: "and Darkness and Decay and the Red Death held illimitable dominion over all."

MASQUERIER, LEWIS (1802–?), Kentucky-born sociologist and pioneer in phonetic spelling, invented a new alphabet of 11 vowels and 22 consonants, published in *The Phonotypic Spelling and Reading Manual* (1867). Influenced by George Henry Evans, he developed a plan for an agrarian Utopia, in which the wage system and rents would be abolished, and his individualism eventually led him to anarchism. His various pamphlets were collected in *Sociology, or the Reconstruction of Society, Government, and Property* (1877) and *An Appendix to Sociology* (1884).

Massachuset Indians, tribe or tribes of Algonquian stock, inhabited the New England coast at the arrival of the white colonists, although their power was already on the decline. John Eliot♦ preached to them, and they joined the Praying Indians. ♦

MASSACHUSETTENSIS, see *Leonard, Daniel.*

Massachusetts Bay Company, English chartered company, was a Puritan♦ reorganization of the New England Company for a Plantation in Massachusetts Bay, in itself an outgrowth of the fishing and farming colony organized by the Dorchester Company of Adventurers. ♦ The Massachusetts Bay Company was organized for trading and settlement as a large colonial counterpart to Virginia, with a Puritan flavor. In 1628 it received a new patent, from George's Council for New England, with a grant of land between the Charles and Merrimac rivers, extending indefinitely westward. The royal charter (1629) confirming the patent was given entirely into the hands of the proposed settlers, who arrived on the *Arbella*♦ (1630) to settle at Salem and later at Boston. Self-government was conducted by a governor and General Court, although suffrage was extended only to church members. The Crown's objections to the colony's coining of money, suffrage restrictions, extension of authority over Maine and New Hampshire, refusal to comply with the Navigation Acts, and general independence led to the rescinding of the charter (1684), when the colony joined with that at Plymouth. ♦ The original settlers of the Bay Colony were Puritans, as distinguished from the Plymouth Separatists. The leading governors were John Endecott♦ and John Winthrop,♦ and the latter kept an important journal on the voyage and the founding. The Company's records have also been published.

Massachusetts Centinel and the Republican Journal (1784–1840), Boston newspaper distinguished for its impartial news coverage and literary contributions. J.Q. Adams attacked Paine and other sympathizers with the French in three series of essays (1791–93), under the pseudonyms Publicola, Marcellus, and Columbus. The paper was also famous for its effective use of cartoons, of which the most popular was the Gerrymander drawing. In 1790 the name was changed to *The Columbian Centinel,* and in 1840 to *Massachusetts Centinel and the Federalist Journal* when the paper was merged with the *Boston Daily Advertiser.* ♦

Massachusetts Gazette, see *Boston News-Letter.*

Massachusetts Historical Society, founded in 1791 by Jeremy Belknap and other historical scholars, whose gift of books and manuscripts became the nucleus of its present great collection. This, the first organization of its kind in the U.S., began to make available its Americana by publishing volumes of collections, augmented by a series of *Proceedings* and special publications. Among the many notable documents thus published for the first time are Bradford's *History of Plimmoth Plantation* and *The Diary and Letter Books of Samuel Sewall.* Its collections were first published in the *American Apollo* (1792–94), a Federalist weekly newspaper.

Massachusetts Magazine, The (1789–96), Boston monthly, published music and fiction, as well as articles on current events. Contributors included Sarah W. Morton, Joseph Dennie, and William Dunlap.

Massachusetts Mercury, The (1793–1840), Boston triweekly newspaper. Until 1797 it was called *The Mercury,* and after 1801 *The Mercury and New England Palladium.* Its conservatism was represented by such Federalist contributors as Fisher Ames. It was purchased by the *Boston Daily Advertiser.* ♦

Massachusetts Quarterly Review, The (1847–50), literary, philosophical, and humanitarian journal, edited from Boston by Emerson, Parker, and J.E. Cabot, and intended, according to Parker, to be "the *Dial* with a beard." Although its contributors included Lowell, Julia Ward Howe, the elder Henry James, and other prominent, militantly aggressive authors, T.W. Higginson considered it to be "the beard without the *Dial.*"

Massachusetts Spy (1770–1904), newspaper founded by Isaiah Thomas, ostensibly as a nonpartisan journal, but actually to serve the Revolutionary cause. In May 1775 it was moved from Boston to Worcester, and part of the time it was edited by others. In 1781 the title was changed to *Thomas's Massachusetts Spy, or the Worcester Gazette,* and from 1785 to 1788, to avoid the stamp tax on newspapers, it appeared as *The Worcester Magazine.* In addition to news, the paper published agricultural articles by Crèvecœur, and such complete works as Robertson's *History of America* and William Gordon's history of the Revolution. In 1814 it passed out of Thomas's hands. It became a daily (1845) concentrating on current news but cultivated an air of patrician traditionalism. Finally it lost circulation because it was considered to be old-fashioned.

Massachusetts to Virginia, poem by Whittier♦ read at the Essex County Convention (Jan. 2, 1843), called to protest the arrest of fugitive slaves. It was published that month in *The Liberator* and collected in *Voices of Freedom* (1846). In stirring seven-stress lines it addresses the Southern state, in the name of the aroused Massachusetts counties, recalling the common struggle for liberty in the Revolution, indicating the inconsistency of the slaveholders' position, and rejoicing in the vigorous democratic idealism of the Abolitionists.

"Massa's in de Cold, Cold Ground," song by Stephen Foster. ◆

MASSASOIT (*d.*1661), chief of the Wampanoag Indians, whose real name seems to have been Ousamequin or Wousamequin. As Indian ruler of all Massachusetts and Rhode Island, he made a treaty of peace with the Plymouth Colony (1621), which was not broken until the time of his son King Philip. ◆ He is mentioned in the writings of Winthrop, Williams, and Bradford.

Masses, The (1911–53), weekly journal of news and social criticism, founded at New York by Piet Vlag as "an outgrowth of the cooperative side of Socialist activity." Under the editorship of Thomas Seltzer, it pursued no consistent political policy, and stressed literature with a liberal bias, drawing largely upon European fiction by such authors as Sudermann and Bjorkman. In 1912 Max Eastman became editor, assisted by Floyd Dell, John Reed, and others, and the magazine followed a more consistently Socialist policy, until it was suppressed by the government (Dec. 1918). Three months later, the editors founded *The Liberator*, a weekly journal of social criticism with an increasingly radical point of view. In 1922 the staff voted to affiliate the magazine with the Communist party. Suspended in 1924, it was revived in 1926 as the *New Masses* and combined the political views of *The Liberator* and the aesthetics of *The Masses*. In 1948 it merged with another Marxist journal to become the monthly *Masses and Mainstream*.

Master of the Inn, The, novelette by Robert Herrick, ◆ published in 1908.

MASTERS, EDGAR LEE (1868?–1950), Kansasborn lawyer in Chicago (1891–1920), first entered literature as an avocation. His early works included *A Book of Verses* (1898) and *Maximilian* (1902), a blank-verse drama. He was suddenly catapulted into fame with the publication of *Spoon River Anthology* ◆ (1915), free-verse epitaphs revealing the secret lives of the persons buried in a Midwestern cemetery. Masters did not again achieve the directness and simplicity that characterize these poems, although he employed the same method in *The New Spoon River* (1924), a bitter commentary on the vicious urban standards of changing America. *Domesday Book* (1920) and its sequel, *The Fate of the Jury* (1929), are considered to be among the best of his later poetry, which also includes *Songs and Satires* (1916); *The Great Valley* (1916); *Toward the Gulf* (1918); *Starved Rock* (1919); the dramatic poems *Lee* (1926), *Jack Kelso* (1928), and *Godbey* (1931); *Lichee Nuts* (1930), statements of philosophy in the Chinese manner; *Invisible Landscapes* (1935); *Poems of People* (1936) and *The New World* (1937), panoramas of America and its outstanding figures; and *Illinois Poems* (1941). *The Sangamon* (1942) is

in the Rivers of America series. His other prose books include *Mitch Miller* (1920), *Skeeters Kirby* (1923), and *Mirage* (1924), novels based on his youth; *Children of the Market Place* (1922), a novel about Stephen Douglas; *The Tide of Time* (1937), another novel; *The Tale of Chicago* (1933), an iconoclastic history; and such biographical studies as *Lincoln, the Man* (1931), bitterly attacking its subject, *Vachel Lindsay* (1935), *Whitman* (1937), and *Mark Twain* (1938), the last presenting Clemens as a frustrated genius. *Across Spoon River* (1936) is an autobiography.

MATHER, COTTON (1663–1728), eldest son of Increase Mather, and grandson of Richard Mather and John Cotton, was so impressed by his heritage that he not only thought of himself as the destined leader of the Massachusetts church and state, but attempted to recapture the spirit of his forefathers in a time when such a spirit was no longer progressive. He entered Harvard at the age of 12, the youngest student ever admitted, and was justifiably considered a prig by his fellows. After some study of medicine, he prepared for the church, received an M.A. (1681), and assisted his father at the Second Church in Boston, where he was co-minister until 1723, and afterward minister. When his father went to England to plead for the restoration of the Massachusetts charter, Cotton conducted the church and worked at home for the same political ends, writing the manifesto against Andros *The Declaration of the Gentlemen, Merchants, and Inhabitants of Boston* (1689). He had now written some dozen works, given evidence of being a great preacher, and been made an overseer of Harvard.

When his father returned with the new charter and the new governor, Phips, Cotton wrote much to defend both, two of his works being *Political Fables* ◆ and *Pietas in Patriam* (1697), a life of Phips. The latter began the investigation known as the Salem witchcraft trials, ◆ in which Mather became fervently interested. Although he believed that the possessed persons should be treated by fasting and prayer, rather than executed, he affirmed the justice of the verdicts and made no public protest except in his semi-scientific writings. *Memorable Providences, Relating to Witchcrafts and Possessions* (1689) was an early study of a victim whom he took into his home. *The Wonders of the Invisible World* (1693) was a narrative of some of the Salem trials, containing theological observations on the operations of devils. This was answered by Robert Calef, a rationalist opponent of the Mather influence in church and state. Mather was himself as rational as Calef, as may be seen in his scientific interests and writings, recognized by his election to the Royal Society of England (1714), and in his statement of opposition to the methods of the witchcraft trials in his *Magnalia Christi Americana* ◆ (1702). Nevertheless, his aggressiveness in controversy, arrogant manner, and indication that he felt himself to be the political and religious leader of Massachusetts, all made him the butt of the critics of the Salem trials.

His inability to succeed his father as president of Harvard or to control Governor Joseph Dudley, and his general conservatism in a period of change, made him feel that many of his ambitions were frustrated, even though he remained a great power in the church. His irritable nerves were overtaxed by his indefatigable industry, and he was given to transports of religious feeling, which sometimes seemed self-conscious attempts to prove the existence of a saintly fire within him. On the other hand, he showed himself in harmony with the new age by championing smallpox inoculation, urging tolerance in the ministry in his *Manuductio ad Ministerium* (1726), and propounding ideas looking toward deism in his *Christian Philosopher*♦ (1721). Possessing a library of nearly 2000 volumes, he was probably more widely read than any other American of his time, and he knew seven languages well.

His writing was scholarly, sometimes pedantic, and exhibited a zeal which occasionally led him into specious reasoning. His more than 450 works include histories, biographies, essays, sermons, fables, verses, theological treatises, philosophy, science, medicine, and practical piety. He had a definite theory of style, believing that though a work should be replete with allusions and quotations, richness of content was more important than elegance of expression; and that the chief function of writing being instruction, the more information it conveyed the better its style. Among his important writings are *A Poem to the Memory of . . . Urian Oakes* (1682); *The Present State of New England* (1690); *Eleutheria: Or an Idea of the Reformation in England* (1698); *A Family Well-Ordered* (1699); *La Fe del Christiano* (1699), a work in Spanish; *Reasonable Religion* (1700); *Some Few Remarks upon a Scandalous Book . . . by One Robert Calef* (1701); *Le Vrai Patron des saines paroles* (1704), in French; *The Negro Christianized* (1706); *The Good Education of Children* (1708); *Bonifacius*♦ (1710), usually called *Essays To Do Good; Psalterium Americanum* (1718), a translation of the psalms; *Sentiments on the Small Pox Inoculated* (1721); *An Account . . . of Inoculating the Small-Pox* (1722); *The Angel of Bethesda* (1722), a medical manual; *Parentator* (1724), a biography of his father; *Ratio disciplinæ* (1726), on Congregational polity; and *Ratio disciplinæ* (1726), on Congregational polity; and *Biblia Americana,* an unpublished compilation of material illustrating and interpreting the Bible. His enormous *Diary* has been published in seven volumes by the Massachusetts Historical Society (1911–12).

MATHER, INCREASE (1639–1723), youngest son of Richard Mather, was reared in the strict Puritan tradition of his father's household, educated at Harvard (1656), and received an M.A. from Trinity College, Dublin (1658). He

preached in England at Congregational churches, until the Restoration and the return to Anglicanism forced him to quit England for his native land. He became teacher of the Second Church in Boston (1664), where he worked fervently until his death, and in 1674 was appointed a fellow of Harvard College. His intellectual activities outside of the church may be judged from his publication of some 25 books before 1683, his organization of a society to discuss scientific matters, and his central position in many types of Massachusetts activities. After having once refused the presidency of Harvard College, by placing his duty to his church before anything else, he was nevertheless appointed acting president in 1685, and the following year took complete charge with the title of Rector. During his presidency to 1701, he encouraged scientific study, while at the same time resisting all efforts to undermine the college's fundamental Congregationalism.

In 1688 he sailed for England, after having been appointed by the Congregational churches to bring a petition in the matter of the abrogated colonial charter. His interviews with James II came to naught when the king was deposed by the Revolution of 1688, but he continued to appeal to William III, and in 1690 was made an official representative of the colonial government. His work was successful, for Governor Andros was replaced by Sir William Phips, and a new charter gave the colonists some of the powers they demanded.

After his return his power waned, since many rebelled against his influence in church and state, were dissatisfied with the charter, and in time opposed the attitude of Phips and himself in the Salem witchcraft trials. ♦ The witchcraft excitement had begun before his return, but, though he avoided the matter for some time, he was accused by Calef and others of responsibility for Phips' actions. Actually, Mather's book *Cases of Conscience Concerning Evil Spirits* (1693) disapproved the emphasis the court put on "spectral evidence," and generally had the attitude that it was better for a guilty witch to escape than for an innocent man to die. His rational point of view may also be seen in his championship of the unpopular cause of inoculation during a smallpox epidemic.

Although he was by no means as bigoted as later popular opinion has claimed, he was firmly convinced of the rectitude of his own ideas, and supported them by his hot temper and tremendous power, in the belief that what he did was for the public good. He was the author of some 130 books, and contributed to more than 65 works by others. His style was simple, strong, and direct, although without brilliance. The works, which sweep the entire circuit of sacred and secular themes of the day, include *Life and Death of That Reverend Man of God, Mr. Richard Mather* (1670); *A Brief History of the War with the Indians* (1676); *A*

Relation of the Troubles Which Have Hapned in New-England by Reason of the Indians There (1677); *An Essay for the Recording of Illustrious Providences* (1684), generally known as *Remarkable Providences*♦; and many political tracts. *Parentator* (1724), his biography, was written by his son Cotton Mather.

MATHER, RICHARD (1596–1669), preached in England until 1633, when he was suspended from the ministry for his Puritanism. Stimulated by John Cotton and Thomas Hooker, he emigrated to Massachusetts Bay (1635) and the following year became teacher of the church in Dorchester, where he continued his ministry until his death. He was a prominent preacher and a leader in the development of the church polity. His anonymously published works included *Church-Government and Church-Covenant Discussed* (1643), the earliest complete exposition of the New England theory of the church, and *Apologie of the Churches in New-England for Church Covenant* (1643), arguing for a covenant of members as the basis of the Congregational Church. With John Eliot and Thomas Welde, Mather was an author of the *Bay Psalm Book*♦ (1640). His most important work was the original draft of *A Platform of Church-Discipline* (1649), the celebrated Cambridge Platform,♦ which was the basic statement of New England Congregationalism. He also drafted the original Half-Way Covenant.♦ He was the author of many other works and was the subject of biographies by his son Increase and his grandson Cotton, being famous as the founder of the "Mather Dynasty" in New England.

MATHER, SAMUEL (1706–85), son of Cotton Mather, was graduated from Harvard (1723) and the following year began preaching. He married a sister of Thomas Hutchinson, and in 1732 became pastor of the Second Church in Boston. Charges that are now uncertain caused him to be dismissed (1741), and more than 90 of his congregation withdrew with him to found a new church, which he ministered until his death. His writings include some 20 books, marked by erudition rather than intellectual strength or style. Among them were a *Life of the Very Reverend and Learned Cotton Mather* (1729), *Attempt To Shew That America Must Be Known to the Ancients* (1773), and the poem *The Sacred Minister* (1773). The last of the "Mather Dynasty," he appears to have been an unsuccessful preacher with little public influence. A contemporary said that "though a treasury of valuable historical anecdotes," he was "as weak a man as I ever knew."

MATHEWS, CORNELIUS (1817–89), New York editor, contributor to various magazines, dramatist, novelist, and poet. His first important writing was the romance *Behemoth: A Legend of the Mound-Builders* (1839) and a comic novel on New York politics. *The Career of Puffer Hopkins*

(1842), serialized in *Arcturus* (1841–42), a literary journal he founded with E.A. Duyckinck (1840). His verse was published in *Poems on Man in His Various Aspects Under the American Republic* (1843), and he was also the author of *Indian Fairy Book* (1856; reissued as *The Enchanted Moccasins,* 1877), a work based on information from H.R. Schoolcraft. His plays include *Witchcraft, or the Martyrs of Salem* (1846), an enormously successful blank-verse play, which was even translated into French; *Jacob Leisler* (1848), a historical drama based on the life of the early governor of New York; *The Politicians* (written in 1840 but unproduced), an indictment of New York politics; and *False Pretences; or, Both Sides of Good Society* (1855), a light social comedy on *parvenus.*

MATHEWS, HARRY (1930–), New York City-born author, long expatriated in France, whose esoteric, experimental works include short novels concerned with curiously convoluted quests. *The Conversions* (1962) presents a person who can inherit a huge fortune if able to answer three recondite riddles. *Tlooth* (1966), also told by an obscure narrator, is a kind of plotless story of a search for revenge. *The Sinking of the Odradek Stadium* (1975) is an odd epistolary account of a search for treasure. *Selected Declarations of Dependence* (1977) prints a novella and "Proverbs and Paraphrases." *Cigarettes* (1988), another odd novel, deals with complex relations among a small group of people of different generations in Saratoga Springs and New York City. *20 Lines a Day* (1988) is a work dealing with various and often odd personal issues. *The Ring* (1970), *The Planisphere* (1974), *Trial Impressions* (1977), and *Armenian Papers* (1987) collect his poems.

MATTHEWS, [JAMES] BRANDER (1852–1929), born in New Orleans, graduated from Columbia (1871) and two years later received an LL.B. After the loss of his family's wealth, he devoted himself to writing fiction and criticism and became prominent in literary and artistic circles in New York and London, being a founder of the Authors' Club, The Players, and other societies. In 1880–81 he wrote two books on the French stage, and with Laurence Hutton he edited *Actors and Actresses of Great Britain and the United States* (5 vols., 1886). Meanwhile, besides collaborating with H. C. Bunner♦ on a book of short stories, Matthews wrote a comedy, *Margery's Lovers* (1884), and collaborated on two other successful plays, *A Gold Mine* (1887), a comedy, and *On Probation* (1889), a farce, as well as writing several one-act plays. After lecturing at Columbia (1891–92), he became professor of literature there (1892–1900), and from 1900 to 1924 was professor of dramatic literature, being the first to hold such a position at any American university. His influence on playwrights, criticism, and public taste was great, through his many texts, compilations, and books of essays, including *The De-*

velopment of the Drama (1903), *Molière* (1910), *Shakspere as a Playwright* (1913), *A Book About the Theater* (1916), *Principles of Playmaking* (1919), and *Rip Van Winkle Goes to the Play* (1926). *These Many Years* (1917) is an autobiography, and he wrote several volumes of fiction about New York, including *Vignettes of Manhattan* (1894), *His Father's Son* (1895), *Outlines in Local Color* (1897), and *Vistas of New York* (1912). He lectured widely in the U.S. and abroad, was an original member and president (1913–14) of the National Institute of Arts and Letters, and has been called "perhaps the last of the gentlemanly school of critics and essayists" in America.

Matthias at the Door, blank-verse narrative by E.A. Robinson,♦ published in 1931.

Matthias at 50, wealthy and "wrapped in recti-tude," is unaware of the falsities in his life, and pities his neighbor Garth, not realizing that the latter, through bitter failure, is wiser than himself. Garth speaks strangely of death, and the next day commits suicide inside the curious door of a huge rock on Matthias's estate. "The rich web of his complacency" is abruptly destroyed when Mat-thias discovers that his wife Natalie married him as an expedient, and really loves his friend Tim-berlake, who, shaken by Garth's suicide, now disappears. The embittered Matthias takes to drink, and Natalie, to escape his violence, be-comes the rock's second suicide. A year later Timberlake returns, pitifully ill, and lonely Mat-thias welcomes his one remaining friend. He fears that Timberlake will seek an exit through "the door," but his friend reassures him, "I shall not go until my name is called." Feeling that Garth and Natalie are summoning him, Timberlake at-tempts to reach the rock, collapses, and a few days later dies. Weary of defeat and futile self-exploration, Matthias goes to the rock, but is halted by Garth's ghostly admonition, "You can-not die, Matthias, till you are born." He must live and suffer, he is told, before he can begin to know himself. Convinced and expectant, he re-turns to take his place ". . . in a new world That Timberlake and Garth and Natalie Had strangely lived and died to find for him."

MATTHIESSEN, F[RANCIS] O[TTO] (1902–50), graduated from Yale, was a Rhodes Scholar, and received a Ph.D. from Harvard before be-coming an instructor at Yale (1927–29) and pro-fessor at Harvard (1929–50). An influential teach-er, he was liberal in politics, deeply religious, and incisive in literary judgments. His books include *Sarah Orne Jewett* (1929); *The Achievement of T.S. Eliot* (1935, revised 1947); *American Renaissance*♦ (1941), analyzing "art and expression in the age of Emerson and Whitman"; *Henry James: The Major Phase* (1944); *The James Family* (1947); *The Note-books of Henry James* (1947), with Kenneth Mur-dock; *From the Heart of Europe* (1948); *The Oxford Book of American Verse* (1950); and *Theodore Dreiser* (1951).

MATTHIESSEN, PETER (1927–), began his literary career with three short novels, *Race Rock* (1954), *Partisans* (1955), and *Raditzer* (1960), fol-lowed at much later dates by a novel, *At Play in the Fields of the Lord* (1965), about missionaries and outsiders despoiling Indian tribal culture in the Amazon jungle; *Far Tortuga* (1975), another novel; and by *Midnight Turning Gray* (1984) and *On the River Styx* (1989), stories. His main career comes with *The Cloud Forest* (1961), recording his observations of primitive people and wild fauna in the wilderness of South America; *Under the Mountain Wall* (1963), dealing with his experi-ence of a savage tribe in New Guinea; *Oo-mingmark* (1967), concerning a expedition, of which he was a member, to a Bering Sea island, searching for a rare breed of musk ox; *Blue Merid-ian* (1971), about another expedition, this one for a great white shark; *The Tree Where Man Was Born* (1972), dealing with his trips to East Africa; *The Snow Leopard* (1978, National Book Award), telling of his trek to Tibet in quest of enlighten-ment; *Sand Rivers* (1981), about a safari in Tan-zania; and *Men's Lives* (1986), about a severe storm and its wreckage affecting the lives of fish-ermen and others on Long Island, New York. His travels through the U.S. to observe the spoli-ation of Indian lands resulted in *In the Spirit of Crazy Horse* (1983), on mistreatment of Native Americans, likewise *Indian Country* (1984). *Sal si Puedes* (1970) is a profile of Cesar Chavez, and *Nine-Headed Dragon River* (1986) treats his old-time pilgrimage to the Zen culture of the Hima-layas and to Japan. *Killing Mr. Watson* (1990) is an account, part fiction, part history, of the man said to have killed the outlaw Belle Starr.

Mauberley, see *Hugh Selwyn Mauberley.*

Maud Muller, poetic idyll in four-stress couplets by Whittier,♦ published in 1854 and collected in *The Panorama and Other Poems* (1856). It tells of the brief meeting of a wealthy judge with the rustic maiden Maud Muller, of their momentary thoughts of love, and of the memories of the incident that recur during their years of toil and disappointment.

MAULDIN, BILL (WILLIAM H. MAULDIN) (1921–), New Mexico-born cartoonist, fa-mous for his realistic, bitterly humorous drawings of front-line soldiers in World War II, printed with his complementary text on army life and war in *Up Front* (1945). After the war he ex-tended his subjects in *Back Home* (1946), wrote *A Sort of a Saga* (1949), about his youth, and treated from high school to his mid-twenties in *The Brass Ring* (1971). His career as a cartoonist has been for the Chicago *Sun Times* since 1962. He re-ceived two Pulitzer Prizes (1944, 1959) for car-tooning and has collected work in such books as *What's Got Your Back Up ?* (1961) and *Let's De-*

clare Ourselves Winners and Get the Hell Out (1985).

Mauve Decade, *The,* see *Beer, Thomas.*

MAVERICK, SAMUEL (*c.*1602–*c.*1676), came to Massachusetts about 1624, when he was evidently associated with Gorges, and engaged in commerce in the Bay Colony. He returned to England after the Restoration, and wrote *A Briefe Discription of New England and the Severall Townes Therein* (1660), probably in the interests of more rigid colonial supervision. He returned to Massachusetts as a royal commissioner (1664).

Maximus Poems, *The,* see *Olson, Charles.*

MAXWELL, WILLIAM (1908–   ), born in Illinois, graduated from the state university and, after an M.A. from Harvard, taught there briefly before trying his hand at a variety of jobs, including editorial work for *The New Yorker.* His novels include *Bright Center of Heaven* (1934); *They Came Like Swallows* (1937), about a woman of character and warmth who helps diverse people and leaves them to find themselves upon her death; *The Folded Leaf* (1945), quietly and tenderly treating the lives of two boys who are friends through school and college; *Time Will Darken It* (1948), about an impossibly idealistic man, set in Illinois in 1912; *The Château* (1961); *The Old Man at the Railroad Crossing* (1966); and *So Long, See You Tomorrow* (1979), about two 13-year-old boys whose friendship is abruptly ended after a murder in their Midwestern town. *Over by the River* (1977) collects stories. *Ancestors* (1971) is a history of the author's forebears and their religious views. *The Writer as Illusionist* (1955) studies fiction, and *The Outermost Dream* (1989) gathers some of his essays and book reviews, the latter mostly from *The New Yorker.*

MAY, SAMUEL JOSEPH (1797–1871), born in Boston, was Connecticut's first Unitarian clergyman, and was active in pacifist, Abolitionist, temperance, and feminist reform movements. He was involved in so many humanitarian movements that Alcott called him "the Lord's chore boy." His writings include *The Rights and Condition of Women* (1846), a widely circulated sermon; *A Brief Account of His Ministry* (1867); and *Some Recollections of Our Anti-Slavery Conflict* (1869).

May-Day, title piece of a volume of poems by Emerson,♦ published in 1867. It is a rhapsodic ode in praise of nature's beauties, in irregular tetrameter verse, alternately rhymed or in couplets. The poet conceives Spring, "Daughter of Heaven and Earth," to be languishing "with sudden passion" on May Day, following the snowbound winter. In a series of vivid images, he evokes the specific beauties of the season and their invigorating effect on all life. In accord with the philo-

sophic doctrines developed in *Nature,* he shows that as lovely Spring complements unlovely Winter, so nature contains a variety of elements, which must be seen in their complex interrelations in order that the whole may be understood.

Mayflower, ship that brought 102 Pilgrims♦ from England to Plymouth Colony.♦ After twice setting sail accompanied by the unseaworthy *Speedwell,* the voyagers abandoned this smaller ship, and left Plymouth, England (Sept. 16, 1620), arriving in the present Provincetown harbor (Nov. 21). A land party went to the present Plymouth (Dec. 21), followed five days later by the ship. The Mayflower Compact (drafted Nov. 11) was an agreement among the 41 adult males, binding them together in a civil body politic to enact, constitute, and frame laws, ordinances, acts, constitutions, and offices, with reference to the general good of the proposed colony. *Mourt's Relation*♦ contains a journal of the voyage and a record of the compact, as does the *History of Plimmoth Plantation*♦ by Bradford.

MAYHEW, EXPERIENCE (1673–1758), born at Martha's Vineyard, from the age of 20 until his death was employed by the Society for the Propagation of the Gospel in New England, as a preacher among the Indians. He translated into the Indian tongue a lecture by Cotton Mather, and his *Massachusee Psalter* (1709), an Indian version of the Psalms and the Gospel of St. John, is declared to be the greatest monument of the Massachuset language after the Indian Bible of Eliot. Mayhew's other writings include *Indian Converts* (1727), a defense of his work; *Grace Defended* (1744), a theological tract upholding a measure of free will against the Calvinist doctrine of total depravity; and *Observations on the Indian Language* (1884), a personal letter written in 1722. Other works remain in manuscript. He was a grandson of Thomas Mayhew.

MAYHEW, JONATHAN (1720–66), son of Experience Mayhew, was pastor of the West Church, Boston, from 1747 until his death. He preached a rational, practical Christianity based on the Scriptures rather than Calvin, and affirmed the doctrine of free will, rejecting the Trinitarian view and defending the right of private judgment. His advanced outlook led to many controversies, and among his replies is the caustic *Letter of Reproof to Mr. John Cleaveland* (1764). He was also a liberal in regard to civil rights; in his *Discourse Concerning Unlimited Submission and Non-Resistance to the Higher Powers* (1750), he defended popular disobedience when civil commands were contrary to divine ordinances. *The Snare Broken* (1766) was a sermon counseling observation of the Stamp Act laws, although defending the preservation of individual rights. Mayhew was a friend of the Adamses, James Otis, and other liberal leaders.

MAYHEW, THOMAS (*c.*1621–57), grandfather of Experience Mayhew, was owner and governor of Martha's Vineyard, where in 1643 he undertook missionary work among the Indians. This was three years prior to John Eliot's similar work on the mainland. With Eliot he wrote a number of Indian tracts, including *The Glorious Progress of the Gospel* (1649) and *Tears of Repentance* (1652).

MAYLEM, JOHN (1739–?), New England soldier, fought in the French and Indian War, about which he wrote two lusty poems, *The Conquest of Louisburg* (1758) and *Gallic Perfidy* (1758), the latter recounting his capture by the French and Indians under Montcalm. Appended to his name on the title pages is the designation, "Philo-Bellum." There is no record of him after 1762.

MAYO, FRANK (1839–96), actor and dramatist, began his career in California and became famous for his character parts, of which the greatest was the title role in *Davy Crockett* (1872), written by F.H. Murdoch but progressively revised by Mayo until it was as much his as Murdoch's. He performed it more than 2000 times during a successful English tour. He also dramatized and successfully produced Clemens's *Pudd'nhead Wilson* (1895).

MAYO, WILLIAM STARBUCK (1811–95), New York doctor whose voyage to Spain and northern Africa resulted in the novel *Kaloolah; or, Journeyings to the Djébel Kumri* (1849), a romance about the Yankee Jonathan Romer and his marriage to an African princess. The contrast between the U.S. and Africa gives rise to a Gulliverian satire. *The Berber* (1850) is a novel with a careful depiction of contemporary Moorish life, which was the result of firsthand observation. *Never Again* (1873) is a novel about a Yankee in wealthy New York society. *Romance Dust from the Historic Placer* (1851; republished as *Flood and Field*, 1855) collects short stories.

Maypole of Merrymount, The, allegorical tale by Hawthorne,♦ published in 1836 and collected in *Twice-Told Tales* (1837). It is based on historical accounts of the Anglican settlement at Merry Mount.♦

Among the revelers about the Maypole at Merrymount are a handsome youth and a beautiful maiden, who, at the height of the festivities, are married by a jolly Anglican priest. At this moment the proceedings are interrupted by a raid of Endecott and his Puritan followers. The latter are dissuaded from punishing the pair when each pleads for the other, and they join the Puritan colony, becoming sober and respectable citizens.

MEAD, MARGARET (1901–79), anthropologist, whose works include *Coming of Age in Samoa* (1928), *Growing Up in New Guinea* (1930), a treatment of the Manus tribe to whom she returned in

New Lives for Old (1956), and *Sex and Temperament in Three Primitive Societies* (1935), collected in *From the South Seas* (1939); *And Keep Your Powder Dry: An Anthropologist Looks at America* (1942); *Male and Female: A Study of the Sexes in a Changing World* (1949); *An Anthropologist at Work* (1959), a study of Ruth Benedict; *Anthropologists and What They Do* (1965); *A Rap on Race* (1971), an exchange with James Baldwin; and *Blackberry Winter: My Earlier Years* (1972).

Meaning of Truth, The, essays by William James,♦ published in 1909 as a sequel to *Pragmatism.*♦ In this reply to his critics, James reasserts and amplifies the basic principles of his concept of pragmatism: "The fundamental fact about our experience is that it is a process of change . . ."; "The true . . . is only the expedient in the way of our thinking, just as the right is only the expedient in the way of our behaving . . ."; "Truth *happens* to an idea. It *becomes* true, is *made* true to events"; "True ideas are those that we can assimilate, validate, corroborate, and verify. False ideas are those that we cannot." He discusses the theories of his fellow pragmatists, Schiller and Dewey, and points out certain weaknesses in their positions, but upholds his own concepts as essential to the doctrine of "radical empiricism" and contrary to untenable forms of idealism and absolutism.

MEDILL, JOSEPH (1823–99), born at St. John, New Brunswick, became one of the great journalists of his time and a founder of the Republican party, to which he may have given its name. In 1855 he bought an interest in the *Chicago Tribune,*♦ which he edited until his death and from 1874 controlled financially. The paper was ardently Republican, and championed Lincoln at an early date. He was elected mayor of Chicago in 1872.

MEEKER, NATHAN COOK (1817–79), first showed his interest in socialistic colonization by joining a Fourierist phalanx in Ohio, and during the 1850s he wrote a novel, *The Adventures of Captain Armstrong,* combining romance with social teachings. On the staff of the New York *Tribune* (1865), he wrote a series of articles on the Oneida Community, and from a newspaper appointment to investigate the Mormons grew his plan for an agricultural colony in the West. Supported by his editor, Horace Greeley, he launched the Union Colony (1870) at Greeley, on the Platte River north of Denver, as a cooperative organization in which private ownership of land and individual control of activity were permitted. During the eight years in which the colony flourished, he published a newspaper, the Greeley *Tribune.* He later became an Indian agent, but his attempt to reform his charges was unsuccessful, and he was killed by the Utes.

MEIKLEJOHN, Alexander (1872–1964), born in England, was brought to the U.S. as a child, and after graduation from Brown (1893) became a professor of philosophy there (1897–1912). He was president of Amherst College (1912–24). His progressive ideas of education were carried out when he headed the Experimental College at the University of Wisconsin (1926–38) and further practiced in the School for Social Studies, an adult education institution founded in San Francisco in 1933. His books include *The Liberal College* (1920), *Freedom and the College* (1923), *The Experimental College* (1932), *What Does America Mean?* (1935), *Education Between Two Worlds* (1942), *Free Speech and Its Relation to Self-Government* (1948), and *Education for a Free Society* (1957).

MELISH, John (1771–1822), born in Scotland, traveled extensively through the U.S., where he settled in 1809. His *Travels in the United States* (1812) was an attempt to promote emigration and was hailed by reviewers as a fair depiction of American life. The maps he drew for this work led him into cartography, and he next published *A Military and Topographical Atlas of the United States* (1813). His other works include statistical and geographical accounts of the U.S. and *Information and Advice to Emigrants to the United States* (1819).

MELLEN, Grenville (1799–1841), Maine author, whose books include *Sad Tales and Glad Tales* (1828), published under the pseudonym Reginald Reverie, showing the influence of Irving but foreshadowing the short story form as developed by Hawthorne and Poe. His verse, in *The Martyr's Triumph* (1833), was strongly influenced by Byron.

Mellichampe, a Legend of the Santee, Revolutionary Romance by Simms,♦ published in 1836.

Blonay, a hideous half-breed, hates the patriot Humphries for having accidentally killed his mother, and joins the Tory soldiers under Barsfield. Their machinations are opposed by Ernest Mellichampe, a young patriot whose father Barsfield had killed. Ernest is captured in a raid, and Barsfield plots to have him escape so that he may be killed and Barsfield thus be freed to continue wooing Janet Berkeley, Ernest's beloved, and to hold the Mellichampe plantation, Kaddipah, without fear of dispute. Blonay, remembering Janet's past kindness, tells her of the plot, but is himself imprisoned by Humphries in a hollow tree, until the remorseful Humphries releases him in time to save Ernest. In the unsuccessful attempt to carry out his plan, Barsfield is killed, as are Blonay and Ernest's companion, the scout Thumbscrew Witherspoon.

"Melting pot," phrase commonly used to signify the mixture and assimilation of different races that have immigrated to the U.S. An early suggestion of the phrase occurs in Crèvecœur's essay, "What Is an American?" It is used as the title of a play by Israel Zangwill, the 19th-century English author.

MELTZER, David (1937–), New York-born poet identified with the Beat movement♦ of San Francisco. His poems include *Ragas* (1959), *The Process* (1965), *The Dark Continent* (1967), *Tens* (1973), and *The Name* (1984). Additional writings include some anthologies with his own text on multicultural learning and legendry, an oral history with San Francisco poets (1971), experimental fiction marked by erotic themes, and *We All Have Something To Say to Each Other* (1962), which includes an essay on Kenneth Patchen and four poems.

MELVILLE, Herman (1819–91), was born in New York City, a descendant of English and Dutch colonial families in whom he took great pride. His father, a cultivated gentleman, underwent financial reverses, entered bankruptcy, and died when Herman was 12 years old. The boy's mother, left virtually destitute with seven other children, seems from the portrait of Mrs. Glendinning in *Pierre* to have been an imperious, unsympathetic woman. His schooling ended when he was 15, and, after clerking in a New York bank, working in his brother's fur and cap store, farming, and teaching, he shipped as a cabin boy to Liverpool (1839). This voyage, described in *Redburn,* was both romantic and harrowing, and ingrained in him a love for the sea. Upon his return, he again taught school in upstate New York, until he sailed on the whaler *Acushnet* for the South Seas (Jan. 1841). The 18-month voyage provided a factual basis for his later novel *Moby-Dick.* When he tired of whaling, he jumped ship at the Marquesas (July 1842) with a companion, Richard Tobias Greene, and lived for a month in the islands, as he later described in *Typee* and *Mardi.* He escaped from the savages who were holding him captive in the valley of Typee on an Australian trader, from which he deserted at Papeete (Sept. 1842). In Tahiti he worked for a time as a field laborer, studying the island life that he later depicted in *Omoo.* He left Tahiti on a whaler, and at Honolulu enlisted as an ordinary seaman on the frigate *United States* (Aug. 1843). His life aboard the man-of-war until his discharge at Boston (Oct. 1844) is the basis of *White-Jacket.* Having completed his education in what he later termed the only Harvard and Yale that were open to him, he returned home to begin fashioning novels from his experiences, and to enter literary society in New York and Boston.

His first five books, *Typee*♦ (1846), *Omoo*♦ (1847), *Mardi*♦ (1849), *Redburn*♦ (1849), and *White-Jacket*♦ (1850), won him fame and a wide following. He became a member of the literary circle of the Duyckinck brothers, who opened a new world of literature to him through their great libraries. In 1849 he made a trip to England to arrange for foreign publication, and visited Paris. The following year, with his wife, whom he had married in 1847, he moved to the Massachusetts farm that was his home for the next 13 years. Here he formed a friendship with his neighbor Hawthorne, who became his confidant after he outgrew the Duyckinck set of New York literati. His greatest work, *Moby-Dick♦* (1851), was dedicated to Hawthorne, and it is worth noting that the tortured novel *Pierre♦* (1852) was published at the same time as Hawthorne's *Blithedale Romance,* since both deal with idealists who are crushed in their attempts to pursue the ways of heaven upon earth.

Melville's popularity, which began to wane with the publication of *Moby-Dick,* was entirely lost through the confused metaphysics and iconoclasm of *Pierre,* for the public's preference was always for his early exotic romances. Opportunity for revaluation was lost when a fire at his publishers (1853) destroyed the plates of his books and most of the unsold copies. Hawthorne's removal to Concord deprived him of his last great stimulus, and from this time he drew farther within himself in his tireless search for a key to the universal mystery. *Israel Potter♦* (1855), the story of the Revolutionary soldier, was a weak historical romance, but it was followed by Melville's finest achievements in short fiction, *The Piazza Tales♦* (1856), which includes "Bartleby the Scrivener,"♦ "Benito Cereno,"♦ and "The Encantadas."♦ After *The Confidence Man♦* (1857), an abortive satire on the commercialism and selfishness of the age, he wrote no further prose except the novelette *Billy Budd,♦* completed just before his death.

Clarel♦ (1876), a long, involved poem concerned with his search for religious faith, grew out of a tour to the Holy Land (1857). His diary of the trip was published as *Journal Up the Straits* (1935). Melville's other verse includes *Battle-Pieces and Aspects of the War♦* (1866), *John Marr and Other Sailors♦* (1888), and *Timoleon* (1891), the last containing poems based on his travels in Greece and Italy. *Clarel, John Marr,* and *Timoleon* were privately financed and published in small editions. About 80 short uncollected poems were first printed in the collected edition of his works (1924).

Melville's great creative period having perished from public neglect and his own inanition, he attempted to eke out a living by lecturing. Failing to receive a desired consulship, after a trip to San Francisco (1860) on a clipper ship commanded by his brother, he moved to New York City (1863), and three years later received a mean appointment as an outdoor customs inspector, in which position he continued for 19 years. His last years were spent in complete obscurity, and his death passed virtually unnoticed. It was not until 1920 that he was rediscovered by literary scholars, and in subsequent years the previous neglect was atoned for by a general enthusiasm. An elaborate collected edition appeared (12 vols., 1922–23), including some work left in manuscript; individual works were frequently reprinted; and some magazine sketches were collected as *The Apple-Tree Table♦* (1922). Other books published for the first time included *Journal of a Visit to London and the Continent* (1948), *Journal of a Visit to Europe and the Levant* (1955), and *Letters* (1960), including all 271 then known.

A wealth of scholarly research on his life and writings has been made, and recent students have revaluated his long-obscure literary reputation. Publication of a scholarly edition of his *Writings* was begun in 1968 by the Newberry Library and Northwestern University Press, and by the 15th volume had reached the *Journals* (1989). He has come to be considered not only an outstanding writer of the sea and a great stylist who mastered both realistic narrative and a rich, rhythmical prose, but also a shrewd social critic and philosopher in his fiction.

Member of the Wedding, The, novel by Carson McCullers,♦ published in 1946 and dramatized by the novelist in 1950.

Frankie Adams, a lonely, sensitive, 12-year-old girl, lives in a small Southern town with her widowed father and Berenice Sadie Brown, the warm, understanding, thrice-married black cook. Except for play with Berenice and John Henry West, her bespectacled six-year-old cousin, Frankie is "a member of nothing" until her brother Jarvis and his fiancée, Janice, ask her to be a member of their wedding and she suffers the misapprehension that they will live as a happy threesome. On the day before the wedding, sure that it is her last at home, she makes a farewell tour of the town, meets a drunken soldier who invites her to a tryst, another of her many experiences with problems of love, chance, and selfhood, and she violently resists his advances. The wedding itself becomes another unhappy experience because of her unbudging refusal to get out of the honeymoon car as she hysterically cries "Take me, take me." Sadly determined to escape home and find experience, Frankie runs away, but is found at the café where she had met the soldier and is brought back to her house. Although John Henry dies of meningitis and Berenice leaves for her own new marriage, Frankie, now 13, manages to recover from her painful past in the new happiness of close friendship with a contemporary, Mary Littlejohn, with whom she imaginatively plans a trip around the world.

Memoirs of an American Lady, autobiography of Anne Grant.♦

Memoirs of Carwin, the Biloquist, unfinished story by C.B. Brown,♦ intended as a sequel to

Wieland.♦ Published serially in the author's *Literary Magazine* (1803–5), it appeared in book form in London (1822) and was reprinted with *Wieland* (1926).

Memoranda During the War, prose account by Whitman♦ of his Civil War experiences, published in 1875, and reprinted in *Specimen Days and Collect*♦ (1882).

Men in White, play by Sidney Kingsley,♦ produced and published in 1933, and awarded a Pulitzer Prize.

Men Without Women, 14 short stories by Hemingway,♦ published in 1927.

"The Undefeated" tells of the futile heroism of Manuel Garcia, a Spanish bullfighter just released from a hospital, who stubbornly refuses to retire, secures an ill-paid "nocturnal" engagement, and gives an adequate performance before an unappreciative audience, but is seriously injured and returned to the hospital. "The Killers" describes the tense atmosphere in a small-town lunchroom, when two Chicago gangsters enter to await Ole Andreson, whom they have been paid to murder. He fails to arrive, and they finally leave. Nick, the waiter, goes to Andreson's room, and finds the victim aware of his impending doom but paralyzed by fear and unwilling to attempt escape. "Fifty Grand" is the story of a champion prizefighter, Jack Brennan, and his bout with the contender Walcott. The middle-aged champion, worried by his responsibilities, cannot train properly, decides he is bound to lose, and bets $50,000 on his own defeat. He fights well for several rounds, until brutally fouled by his opponent. Insisting that this was an accident, he continues with difficulty, then suddenly ends the matter by an obvious foul on Walcott. "'It's funny how fast you can think when it means that much money,'" he says.

MENCKEN, H[ENRY] L[OUIS] (1880–1956), Baltimore journalist, critic, and essayist, began his career on local newspapers in 1899, becoming editor of the *Evening Herald* (1905–6), and thereafter serving on the staff of the *Evening Sun,* during 1916–17 as war correspondent in Germany. He became literary critic of *The Smart Set*♦ in 1908, and was co-editor of this lively periodical with George Jean Nathan (1914–23). His collaboration with Nathan continued during the early years of *The American Mercury,*♦ which they founded in 1924 and which Mencken edited until 1933. He is best known for the aggressive iconoclasm of his editorial policies in these magazines, especially during the decade following World War I, when he exhibited a savagely satirical reaction against the blunders and imperfections of democracy and the cultural gaucheries of the American scene. Although this attitude implied doubt of the ultimate effectiveness of American

institutions, he was equally vehement in his denunciation of European patronage of this country, and in his advocacy of an indigenous civilization. His critical views were widely influential, especially in his encouragement of such writers as Dreiser, Lewis, Cabell, and Sherwood Anderson, although he aroused much popular antagonism.

He published many books, of which the earliest were the Kiplingesque *Ventures into Verse* (1903) and two critical works, *George Bernard Shaw—His Plays* (1905) and *The Philosophy of Friedrich Nietzsche* (1908). Collaborations with Nathan include two plays, *The Artist* (1912) and *Heliogabalus* (1920); *The American Credo* (1920); and *Europe After 8:15* (1914), a travel book to which W. H. Wright also contributed. His most important work of scholarship is *The American Language*♦ (1919, revised 1921, 1923, 1936; supplementary volumes, 1945 and 1948), a discussion of the English language in the U.S., noting its significant American development. Besides the celebrated six series of *Prejudices*♦ (1919–27), he also wrote introductions and notes for editions of Ibsen, Nietzsche, and others; *A Book of Burlesques* (1916); *A Book of Prefaces* (1917); *In Defense of Women* (1918); *Notes on Democracy* (1926); *Treatise on the Gods* (1930); *Making a President* (1932); *Treatise on Right and Wrong* (1934); *Happy Days, 1880–1892* (1940), *Newspaper Days, 1899–1906* (1941), and *Heathen Days, 1890–1936* (1943), humorous autobiographical sketches; and *Minority Report* (1956), jottings drawn from his notebooks. He compiled *A New Dictionary of Quotations, on Historical Principles* (1942). His *Letters* (1961) prints some correspondence on literary matters only. His *Diary,* full and open, was finally published in 1989. An autobiography, *My Life as Author and Editor,* appeared in 1993, having been sealed for 35 years after his death.

Mending Wall, blank-verse poem by Robert Frost,♦ published in *North of Boston* (1914). Describing the time he and a neighboring farmer spent the day in replacing fallen stones on the wall which divides their land, the poet declares, "Something there is that doesn't love a wall." and expresses his philosophy of tolerance, generosity, and brotherhood in the contrast between his neighbor's dogmatic "Good fences make good neighbours" and his own more considered

> Before I built a wall I'd ask to know
> What I was walling in or walling out.

MENKEN, ADAH ISAACS (1835–68), born near New Orleans, began her dramatic career in that city (1857) and married a Cincinnati merchant, Alexander Isaac Menken. Her stage career took her to New York (1859), where she became a friend of Whitman, O'Brien, and others at the bohemian rendezvous Pfaff's Cellar. In 1861 she first played her famous title role in Byron's *Mazeppa,* noted for the scene in which, semi-nude, she was strapped to the back of a wild horse. Her acting in this and other parts made her a favorite, in San Francisco and Virginia City, of the literary group which included Clemens, Harte, and Artemus Ward, and in London of Dickens, Reade, Swinburne, Rossetti, and Burne-Jones, as well as in Paris, where her admirers included Gautier and Dumas *père*. She was meanwhile married three times after leaving Menken, once bigamously to the prizefighter Heenan, and once to Robert Henry Newell. Her adventures became so fabulous that she once declared, "I never lived with Houston; it was General Jackson and Methuselah, and other big men." Her poetry, like her life and acting, was rich, garish, and romantic. The rhythms, generally ascribed to the influence of Whitman, seemed to have sprung from the writings of the Hebrew prophets, and the subjects were always passionately autobiographical. Her poems were collected as *Infelicia* (1868).

Mennonites, members of a Protestant sect that originated in Friesland in the 16th century, deriving its name from the Dutch religious reformer Menno Simons (1492–1559). They accept the Bible as their sole rule of faith, wish to restore apostolic Christianity, administer baptism to adult believers only, are ardently pacifistic, and attempt to live apart from other groups. Suffering persecution in Europe, they emigrated to America, first settling in Pennsylvania (1683) and spreading throughout the South and Middle West. Their numbers have greatly increased, although they are divided into several branches. One of these is the Amish, followers of Jacob Amman, who separated from the orthodox body in the 17th century. In 1990 there were more than 200,000 Mennonites in various churches.

MEREDITH, WILLIAM [MORRIS] (1919–), poet born in New York City, after graduation from Princeton and service as a navy aviator taught for a time at Connecticut College. *Love Letter from an Impossible Land* (1944) was in the Yale Series of Younger Poets, and succeeding volumes—*Ships and Other Figures* (1948), *The Open Sea* (1958), *The Wreck of the Thresher* (1964)—use his naval background for themes and show the influence upon him both of Frost and of a metaphysical tradition. *Earth Walk* (1970) gathers these poems and in new verse reflects upon them. *Hazard, the Painter* (1975) presents poetic reflections upon a fictional painter's life and art; and *The Cheer* (1980) collects recent poems. *Partial Accounts* (1987) contains 93 poems from his earlier 7 books and 11 new ones; it won him a Pulitzer Prize. Meredith also translated Apollinaire's *Alcools* (1964).

MERGENTHALER, OTTMAR (1854–99), German-born inventor, came to the U.S. (1871) and perfected the linotype machine that bears his name (1885), which was first used to set type for a daily newspaper by the *New-York Tribune* (1886).

Merlin, blank-verse dramatic narrative by E.A. Robinson,♦ published in 1917. It belongs with *Lancelot*♦ and *Tristram*♦ in the author's Arthurian trilogy.

The wizard Merlin abandons worldly power to spend an idyllic decade with his mistress, Vivian, at Broceliande, in Brittany. At Camelot, meanwhile, Arthur is troubled by the schemes of his illegitimate son Modred, and by the infidelity of Guinevere with his trusted knight Lancelot. His rule is threatened by civil strife, and he summons Merlin to him, chiding him for having "gone down smiling to the smaller life," and asking him to correct the evils of the time. Merlin replies that he can prophesy but not control events, and that he can only advise Arthur to consider his kingdom his queen, since Guinevere is fated to love Lancelot, while England's future depends on Arthur. Still doubting and grieving, the king allows Merlin to return to Broceliande, but there the wizard and his mistress find their blissful preoccupation with each other vanished. He acknowledges that he has "seen too far" and "known too much," and they sadly part. Merlin returns to Camelot, "the stricken city" that he cannot save. With Dagonet, the fool who is so bitterly wise, he contemplates the ruin of the kingdom, and they find "a groping way Down through the gloom together."

MERRILL, JAMES [INGRAM] (1926–95), born in New York, after graduation from Amherst (1947) began his literary career with *First Poems* (1951), followed by further and increasingly philosophic poetry marked by an elegant and disciplined style in *The Country of a Thousand Years of Peace* (1959), *Water Street* (1962), *Nights and Days* (1966, National Book Award), *The Fire Screen* (1969), *Braving the Elements* (1972), *The Yellow Pages* (1974), and *Divine Comedies* (1976, Pulitzer Prize), including the long narrative "Book of Ephraim." That work, partly a Platonic symposium incorporating fictive and real characters (principally Auden), was continued and elaborated in his next two volumes of verse, *Mirabell* (1978) and *Scripts for the Pageant* (1980). *From the First Nine Poems* (1982) and *The Changing Light at Sandover* (1982) collect his poems. Merrill won a Bollingen Prize in 1973. His works of the 1980s were *Late Settings* (1985) and *The Inner Room* (1988), collections of poems, and *Recitative* (1986), a volume of diverse prose over a 40-year period. He also wrote prose plays, *The Immortal Husband* (1956) and *The Bait* (1960), and novels, *The Seraglio* (1957), about an aging, much-married businessman's involvements with women, and *The (Diblos) Notebook* (1965), about the attempts of a young American author to transform his experiences on a Greek island into a novel. *A Different Person Memoir* (1993) is an account of years abroad in his twenties; in it he tells how he found his poetic voice.

MERRILL, STUART FITZRANDOLPH (1863–1915), lived most of his life in France, whose language he used for all of his writing except *Pastels in Prose* (1890), short translations of French authors. *Les Gammes* (1887) and *Les Fastes* (1891) show the influence of Wilde, the Pre-Raphaelite school, and William Morris's socialism, and he sympathized with and influenced the Symbolist movement. His greatest work was *Une Voix dans la foule* (1909), a stirring poetic plea for the oppressed and wretched.

Merriwell, FRANK, character in the juvenile stories by W.G. Patten.♦

Merry Mount, settlement at Mount Wollaston (now Quincy), Mass., founded in 1625 by Captain Wollaston and Thomas Morton.♦ When the captain withdrew to Virginia with his indentured white servants, Morton took possession of the site, which was renamed Ma-re-Mount. There, according to Bradford, the Anglican settlers established a "schoole of athisme," whose members revived "the beastly practices of the madd Bachanalians." The frolicking of the colonists about a Maypole and their trading of weapons to the Indians caused Myles Standish to be sent to seize Morton, who was transferred to England under arrest (1628). Although the colony was dispersed, several "revelers" lingered on. Morton's *New English Canaan*♦ (1637) presents his version of events, while Bradford and John Winthrop represent the Puritan and Separatist views in their histories. Hawthorne's "The Maypole of Merrymount"♦ (1837) is an allegorical tale, and other literary treatments include Motley's romance *Merrymount* (1849), and the operatic ·version by Howard Hanson and R.L. Stokes, *Merry Mount* (1934).

MERTON, THOMAS (1915–69), religious writer, an American born in France, reared there, in England, and the U.S., while at Columbia University was converted to Roman Catholicism. In 1941 he became a Trappist at a Kentucky monastery and was later ordained as Father M. Louis. His books include *The Seven Storey Mountain* (1948), autobiography; *The Waters of Siloe* (1949), on the Trappists; *Seeds of Contemplation* (1949), on the spiritual life; *The Ascent to Truth* (1951), *The Sign of Jonas* (1953), *No Man Is an Island* (1955), *The Silent Life* (1957), *Silence in Heaven* (1957), *Thoughts in Solitude* (1958), *The New Man* (1962), *Life and Holiness* (1963), *Seeds of Destruction* (1964), *Conjectures of a Guilty Bystander* (1966), and *Mystics and Zen Masters* (1969), meditations and essays. His poetry includes *A Man in the Divided Sea* (1946), *Figures for an Apocalypse* (1947), and *Cables to the Ace* (1968). Other publications include a *Secular Journal* (1959) and his correspondence with Van Wyck Brooks (1970).

MERWIN, SAMUEL, see *Webster, Henry Kitchell.*

MERWIN, W[ILLIAM] S[TANLEY] (1927–   ), New York-born poet, after graduation from Princeton (1948) and further study of Romance languages began his career with *A Mask for Janus* (1952), issued in the Yale Series of Younger Poets. This collection has been followed by others, including *The Dancing Bears* (1954), *Green with Beasts* (1956), *The Drunk in the Furnace* (1960), *The Moving Target* (1963), *The Lice* (1967), *The Carrier of Ladders* (1970, Pulitzer Prize), *Writings to an Unfinished Accompaniment* (1973), and *The Compass Flower* (1977), in which his poetry has moved from the relatively formal and traditional early work to poems that are intense and existential. In 1979 he was awarded a Bollingen Prize for his poetry, continued in *Finding the Islands* (1982), *Opening the Hand* (1983), *The Rain in the Trees* (1987), *Selected Poems* (1987), and *Travels* (1993)—a series of portraits and dramatic monologues dealing with Rimbaud in Africa and various naturalists, including William Bartram,♦ and two Native American artists. The volumes *The Miner's Pale Children* (1970), *Houses and Travellers* (1977), *Unframed Originals* (1982), and *Regions of Memory* (1987) are gatherings of prose, including some stories, memories of friends and family, and critical commentary. Another prose work, *The Lost Upland: Stories of Southwest France* appeared in 1992. *Darkling Child* (1956), *Favor Island* (1957), and *The Gilded West* (1961) are plays, the first written with Dido Milroy. He has also made translations, including *Poem of the Cid* (1959), *The Satires of Perseus* (1961), and *The Song of Roland* (1963).

Message to Garcia, A, essay by Elbert Hubbard,♦ published in 1899. It recounts an incident in the Spanish-American War, when Lieutenant Andrew S. Rowan was sent by McKinley to meet General Calixto Garcia y Inigues, head of the Cuban insurgent forces, in order to ascertain what help was needed by Garcia against the Spanish. Because of the heroic aspects of Rowan's persistence during his difficult journey, and the inspirational moral drawn from it by Hubbard, the essay became tremendously popular. Its circulation to 1940 was estimated at 40,000,000 copies, many of which appeared in special editions issued by industrialists to promote efficiency among their employees. It also served as regulation equipment to soldiers on both sides in the Russo-Japanese War.

METACOMET, see *King Philip.*

Metamora, or the Last of the Wampanoags, romantic tragedy by J.A. Stone,♦ produced in 1829 and revised for Edwin Forrest by R.M. Bird (1836). It deals with the defeat of King Philip, depicted as a noble savage, at the hands of unscrupulous English colonists.

Metaphysical verse, term applied to writing like that of the 17th-century British poets Donne,

Crashaw, Cowley, Herbert, and Vaughan, which conveys a direct emotional apprehension of thought, employing a psychological analysis of love or religion, using the conceit to bring into eccentric and startling juxtaposition the contradictions of life, and usually placing more stress on subtlety of thought than on conventional form. American poets of this sort include Edward Taylor, Emerson, Jones Very, and Emily Dickinson. Many modern poets have been influenced by T.S. Eliot's interest in the 17th-century metaphysicals. They include Aiken, Louise Bogan, Cummings, Horace Gregory, Marianne Moore, MacLeish, Ransom, Wallace Stevens, Taggard, Tate, W.C. Williams, and Elinor Wylie.

Methodism, the doctrines, polity, and worship of those religious organizations developed from the evangelistic teaching of John Wesley (1702–91), his brother Charles, and George Whitefield.♦ As students at Oxford, they conducted meetings for religious exercises according to such precise rules that they were dubbed Methodists. They accepted the teachings of the Church of England, and, although influenced by the Moravians, intended no more than a revival of personal religion, emphasizing the immediacy of the Holy Spirit. Their zeal led the Anglican churches to be closed to them, but they carried on their evangelistic work in open-air meetings. No legal constitution was adopted until 1784, and it was not until 1791 that they broke from the Church of England to found the Wesleyan Methodist Church, known in America as the Methodist Episcopal Church. There have been many schisms on matters of government and, in America, also on issues raised by the Civil War. The Wesleys visited Georgia in 1735, and Whitefield made many visits, beginning in 1738–39, when he was a leader of the Great Awakening. The beginnings of the organized church are attributed to the preacher Philip Embury, who arrived in 1776. Francis Asbury was sent to America by Wesley in 1771, and became one of the church's first American bishops (1784). The three main branches of the church were united in 1938. In 1990 there were more than 13,000,000 Methodists in the U.S.

Mexican War, mainly precipitated by the annexation of Texas by the U.S. (Dec. 1845), but other contributing factors included the claims of U.S. citizens against Mexico, the desire to acquire California, and the ambition of imperialists for an increase in slaveholding territory. Hostilities began in April 1846, when the Mexicans resisted an advance at the disputed boundary of southern Texas by American troops under Zachary Taylor. War was declared the following month, when President Polk announced the U.S. territory had been invaded. Santa Anna, temporarily President of Mexico, led his country's forces, while various U.S. expeditions were led

by Sloat, Stockton, and Frémont in California; Kearny in New Mexico; Taylor, Wool, and Doniphan in northern Mexico; and Winfield Scott, the commander in chief, who captured Vera Cruz (March 1847) and led a long inland march to Mexico City, which capitulated after the Battle of Chapultepec (Sept. 1847). By the treaty of Guadalupe-Hidalgo (Feb. 2, 1848), Mexico ceded two-fifths of her territory to the U.S., receiving in return an indemnity of $15,000,000 and the cancellation of certain American claims.

So much writing has been related to the war that Justin H. Smith stated in his Pulitzer Prize-winning *The War with Mexico* (2 vols., 1919) that his work was based on 1200 books and pamphlets. Many Civil War generals began their careers in this war and wrote about it in their autobiographies, as Grant did in his *Personal Memoirs*. *The Diary of James K. Polk During His Presidency* (4 vols., 1910) also provides an intimate view from a war leader. The literature was various, ranging from the views of those who opposed the war as a means to extend slavery territory, such as Lowell's *Biglow Papers*♦ and Whittier's "The Angels of Buena Vista," to those who saw the war as a subject of patriotic romance, such as the poetry of Simms's *Lays of the Palmetto* (1848) and C.F. Hoffman's "Monterey," and the popular fiction that included Lippard's *Legends of Mexico* (1847) and Mayne Reid's *The Rifle Rangers; or, Adventures of an Officer in Southern Mexico* (1850).

MICHAELS, LEONARD (1933–), born in New York City, a professor of English at the University of California, Berkeley, is the author of collections of short stories, *Going Places* (1969) and *I Would Have Saved Them If I Could* (1975), and the novel *The Men's Club* (1981), about a rambunctious night out of a gathering of chauvinist males in California, that he recast as a film (1986). He also wrote a play, *City Boy* (1985) that was adapted from some of his stories.

MICHENER, JAMES A[LBERT] (1907–) New York-born novelist, after graduation from Swarthmore (1929), study at Colorado State College, teaching of social sciences, and work as a book editor, was led into literature by his naval experiences in World War II. His 18 related sketches, *Tales of the South Pacific* (1947, Pulitzer Prize), were adapted by Rodgers and Hammerstein as a musical comedy, *South Pacific* (1949). *The Fires of Spring* (1949) is a more conventional novel, concerning a boy's growth to maturity during the 1920s and the Depression. After *Return to Paradise* (1951), which dealt with the scene of his first work in a mingling of fact and fiction, and *The Voice of Asia* (1951), a study of the contemporary Orient, he wrote the novels *The Bridges at Toko-ri* (1953) and *Sayonara* (1954), using the Korean war as background, the latter emphasizing Japanese and American good relations through its love story. *Hawaii* (1959) is a panoramic novel of the fiftieth state's social history; *Caravans* (1963) is a novel about a romantic American girl in Afghanistan; *The Source* (1965) is a novel about the Holy Land, ancient and modern. *The Drifters* (1971), a contemporary tale, depicting six young people of various nations, all wandering the world in search of their diverse conception of the good life, was followed by further lengthy novels: *Centennial* (1974), presenting life in Colorado from prehistory through 200 years of life, Indian and white, concentrating on the last century: *Chesapeake* (1978), a chronicle of 400 years of life on Maryland's Eastern Shore, some of which was excerpted in *The Watermen* (1979); *The Covenant* (1980), a sweeping historical novel about South Africa from earliest days to the present; *Space* (1982), about U.S. astronauts involved in a flight to the dark side of the moon; *Poland* (1983), fiction about a nation's history; and *Texas* (1985), *Alaska* (1988), and *Caribbean* (1989), long novels that elicit the history and events of the titular place. Rather different are *Legacy* (1987), a short novel celebrating the Constitution of the U.S., and *Recessional* (1994), set in a Florida retirement community, about the challenges and rewards faced by older adults and their families. *The Eagle and the Raven* (1990) celebrates the friendship of Andrew Jackson and Sam Houston; recent nonfiction are *Pilgrimage: A Memoir of Poland and Rome* (1990) and *The World Is My Home: A Memoir* (1992).

The Floating World (1954) is a study of an art form continued in *Japanese Prints* (1959). *The Bridge at Andau* (1957) is a documentary account of the Hungarian revolt against the Communists in 1956. *Report of the County Chairman* (1961) treats his experiences as chairman of the Bucks County, Pennsylvania, Citizens for Kennedy; and other nonfictional writings include *Iberia* (1968), presenting experiences and reflections on Spanish travels; *Presidential Lottery: The Reckless Gamble in Our Electoral System* (1969); *The Quality of Life* (1970); *Kent State: What Happened and Why* (1971), treating the demonstration on the Ohio university campus that ended with the shooting of four students by the National Guard; and *Sports in America* (1976). With A. Grove Day he wrote *Rascals in Paradise* (1957), sketches of colorful characters in the Pacific.

Middle Border, the prairie region of Minnesota, Wisconsin, Nebraska, and the Dakotas, which was an important agricultural frontier (*c.* 1870–1900) when Scandinavian, Slavic, and Irish immigrants settled there to establish one of the great grain-raising areas of the U.S. Authors who have written of the region and its people during the frontier period include Garland, Rölvaag, Willa Cather, Bess Streeter Aldrich, and Frederick Manfred.

Middle Colonies, name applied to colonial New York, New Jersey, Pennsylvania, and sometimes Delaware, which now form the region known as the Atlantic states or Eastern states.

Middle of the Journey, The, novel by Lionel Trilling, ♦ published in 1947.

John Laskell, a middle-aged man recuperating from an almost fatal sickness, still feels close to death and attracted by it. He is assisted to life by an affair with Emily Caldwell but plunged into a new crisis when her drunken husband, Duck Caldwell, accidentally kills their young daughter. The event affects Laskell not only emotionally but intellectually as he finds his friends, Professor Croom and his wife, contending that not Duck but social forces are responsible for the tragedy, while another friend, Gifford Maxim, a doctrinaire Christian, argues that Duck, being responsible for his acts, is eternally damned unless saved by God's mercy. Faced by these opposing views, Laskell finally reaches his own view that man is not entirely governed by external forces nor entirely possessed of a free will.

Middle Years, The, title of a short story and of an autobiographical fragment, both by Henry James. ♦

Midland, The, see *Frontier* (magazine).

Midnight Ride of Paul Revere, The, see *Paul Revere's Ride.*

MIFFLIN, LLOYD (1846–1921), Pennsylvania poet who devoted himself chiefly to the sonnet form. Among his many volumes are *The Slopes of Helicon* (1898); *Echoes of Greek Idyls* (1899), versions of Bion, Moschus, and Bacchylides; *The Fields of Dawn* (1900); *The Fleeing Nymph* (1905); and *Flower and Thorn* (1909).

MILES, GEORGE HENRY (1824–71), Maryland author, whose plays included *Mohammed, the Arabian Prophet* (published 1850), a blank-verse romantic tragedy awarded a prize by Edwin Forrest, but produced by another actor (1851); *Hernando de Soto* (1852), romantic drama; and *Señor Valiente* (1859), a light comedy. His religious novels and *Christine* (1866), a collection of verse, are marked by his strong Catholicism.

MILES, JOSEPHINE (1911–85), after graduation from the University of California, Los Angeles, and graduate degrees in English from Berkeley, in 1940 joined the faculty of the latter campus. Her concise, disciplined, observant, and often witty poetry appeared in *Lines at Intersection* (1939), *Poems on Several Occasions* (1941), *Local Measures* (1946), *Prefabrications* (1955), *Poems 1930–1960* (1960), *Kinds of Affection* (1967), *Fields of Learning* (1968), *To All Appearances* (1974), and *Coming to Terms* (1979). She wrote scholarly studies of poetic diction in *The Vocabulary of Poetry* (1946), *The Continuity of English Poetic Language* (1951), *Eras* and Modes in English Poetry (1957), *Renaissance, Eighteenth Century and Modern Language in Poetry* (1960), and *Poetry and Change* (1974).

Miles Wallingford, romance by Cooper,♦ published in 1844 as a sequel to *Afloat and Ashore.*♦

Believing his childhood sweetheart, Lucy Hardinge, loves another man, Miles decides to remain a bachelor, makes a compact with a cousin to will their property to one another, and with his friends Marble and Neb, a black, sets sail in his ship, the *Dawn,* to Hamburg. Anxious to reach Hamburg to pay off a mortgage on his estate, he is harried when his ship is seized first by the British for carrying French goods, then by the French, and, after a second escape, is wrecked. Taken aboard a British warship, Miles is imprisoned and his friends pressed into service. Escaping to New York, Miles finds his cousin is dead and his estate seized by a distant relative, Daggett, who has Miles jailed for debt. Lucy, though plagued by the problem of her spendthrift brother Rupert, provides bail for Miles. Once freed, Miles dispossesses Daggett and weds Lucy.

MILLAY, EDNA ST. VINCENT (1892–1950), born in Maine, graduated from Vassar (1917) having already won fame with the publication of "Renascence"♦ (1912), the title poem of her first volume, *Renascence and Other Poems* (1917), which exhibited technical virtuosity, startling freshness, and a hunger for beauty. *A Few Figs from Thistles* (1920) showed that though the disillusion of the postwar years was crowding in upon her, she was attempting to maintain gaiety with a consciously cynical flippancy. With *Second April* (1921) she revealed a more mature emotional tone, which, like her use of Elizabethan words and tight metrical forms, marked her subsequent volumes. While living in Greenwich Village, she became associated with the Provincetown Players,♦ for whom she wrote *The Princess Marries the Page* (1918, published in 1932), *Aria da Capo* (1919, published 1921), and *Two Slatterns and a King* (1921), all one-act satirical fantasies. *The Lamp and the Bell* (1921), written for a Vassar commencement, is a five-act poetic drama. *The Ballad of the Harp-Weaver* (1923, Pulitzer Prize), later retitled *The Harp-Weaver and Other Poems,* is noted for poems showing a further deepening from her earlier arch attitude to a more disillusioned bitterness. Her mature technical ability, particularly in the sonnet, her lyric gift, and her directness were exhibited in further volumes: *The Buck in the Snow* (1928); *Fatal Interview* (1931), a sonnet cycle in the Elizabethan manner; *Wine from These Grapes* (1934); *Conversations at Midnight* (1937), a dramatic narrative showing her increasing interest in contemporary social problems; *Huntsman, What Quarry?* (1939); *Make Bright the Arrows* (1940), "poems for a world at war"; and *The Murder of Lidice* (1942), a ballad written for radio. Her *Collected Sonnets* appeared in 1941,

Collected Lyrics in 1943, and *Collected Poems* in 1956. Other works include *Distressing Dialogues* (1924), a volume of sophisticated prose sketches, written under the pseudonym Nancy Boyd; *The King's Henchman* (1927), the libretto of an opera by Deems Taylor, set in Saxon England; and a translation of Baudelaire's *Flowers of Evil* (1936) with George Dillon. *Mine the Harvest* (1954) posthumously collects 66 poems, and her *Letters* was published in 1952.

Millennial Church, see *Shakers.*

MILLER, ARTHUR (1915–), New York author, graduated from the University of Michigan (1938), where he began to write plays. His first, *Man Who Had All the Luck* (1944), treats an auto mechanic whose success in marriage and business is the result of work and care, and was followed by a nondramatic work of reportage, *Situation Normal* (1944), about military life at army bases, and *Focus* (1945), a novel about anti-Semitism. He returned to the drama with *All My Sons* (1947), about a manufacturer whose defective airplane parts cause the death of his son and other aviators in wartime. His most impressive play is *Death of a Salesman*♦ (1949, Pulitzer Prize), fusing realism and symbolism in reviewing the tragic life of a salesman victimized by his own false values and those of modern America. It was followed by *The Crucible* (1953), treating the Salem witch trials of 1692 as a parable for America during the era of McCarthyism, as the play probes into problems of individual conscience and guilt by association. *A View from the Bridge* (1955, Pulitzer Prize) presents two Italian longshoremen illegally in the U.S., and *A Memory of Two Mondays,* another short play included with it in production and publication, presents varied views of workers in a Manhattan warehouse. *The Misfits* (1961), a so-called cinema-novel, that is, fiction based on what the camera can see, is actually the script of a motion picture for his wife Marilyn Monroe, which deals with a beautiful woman in Nevada for a divorce who falls in with three men who herd old horses for slaughter and of her emotional relations with the men and feelings for the animals. *After the Fall* (1964) is a play in two long acts in which the quasi-autobiographical protagonist seeks self-knowledge, a sense of the meaning of his past and its meaning for his future as he reviews his marriages and other major experiences. *Incident at Vichy* (1965), a short play, concerns the treatment of diverse Frenchmen picked up by the Nazis in 1942. *The Price* (1968) is a play contrasting two brothers' views and ways of life as they meet after long separation to dispose of their parents' possessions. Later plays include *The American Clock* (1980), dealing with the Great Depression; *Elegy for a Lady* and *Some Kind of Love,* two one-act plays both presented in 1982; and *I Can't Remember Anything* and *Clara,* two more one-act plays that were produced together in 1987 as

Danger: Memory! In 1990 a screenplay, *Everybody Wins,* was published. *The Last Yankee* was produced in 1993, a 70-minute one-acter set in a state mental institution that may be a metaphor for the U.S.A. in decline on all fronts—physical, moral, intellectual. In *Broken Glass* (1994), Miller attempts to connect the troubled lives of a middle-aged Brooklyn Jewish couple and the wife's mysterious paralysis to the hysteria sweeping over Germany in 1938. *I Don't Need You Anymore* (1967) collects nine stories, including "The Misfits"; *The Creation of the World and Other Business* (1972) is a serio-comic treatment of the book of Genesis; *Theater Essays* (1978) includes interviews. With his wife Inge Morath, a photographer, he has created books of text and pictures: *In Russia* (1969), *In the Country* (1977), set in rural Connecticut, and *Chinese Encounters* (1979). *Salesman in Beijing* (1984) is an account of producing his play in China in 1983. He made an adaptation of Ibsen's *An Enemy of the People* (1951). In 1987 his full autobiography *Timebends,* was published.

MILLER, HENRY (1891–1980), New York-born author, lived in various parts of the U.S., as an expatriate in Europe (1930–40), and after 1942 in California. His books are essentially autobiographical, expressing with gusto his intense individualism, his love of freedom, his affection for natural responses, his hatred of all that blocks or blunts human impulses, and his enthusiastic search for intellectual and aesthetic adventure. Their energetic lyrical prose merges Rabelaisian dialogue and descriptions with sprawling statements of the author's own emotions, moods, and beliefs. Among his many works the best known is *Tropic of Cancer♦* (France, 1934; U.S., 1961), an intense personal narrative in fictive form of the emotional and intellectual life of an American expatriate in Paris, marked by its frank treatment of sexual relations and animated by a belief that "more obscene than anything is inertia." A similar autobiographical narrative is *Tropic of Capricorn♦* (France, 1939; U.S., 1962), treating the adolescence of the author in New York, and a related work is *Black Spring* (France, 1936; U.S., 1963), gathering autobiographical essays and sketches ranging from his Brooklyn boyhood to his Paris experiences. His other writings include *Aller Retour New York* (1935), a letter about a round-trip voyage during his expatriation; *Max and the White Phagocytes* (1938), on one of his unusual friends; *The Cosmological Eye* (1939), fiction and essays; *The Wisdom of the Heart* (1941), a similar collection; *The Colossus of Maroussi* (1941), an unconventional travel account on the spirit of Greece, emphasizing people, not sites, in a search for "a world of light"; *Sunday After the War* (1944), sketches; *The Air-Conditioned Nightmare♦* (1945) and its sequel, *Remember To Remember* (1947), on his responses to the American scene; *The Smile at the Foot of the Ladder* (1948), a tale;

The Books in My Life (1952), about the very varied reading that affected him; *Nights of Love and Laughter* (1955), stories; *The Time of the Assassins* (1956), a study of Rimbaud; *Big Sur and the Oranges of Hieronymus Bosch♦* (1957), treating his life in California; *To Paint Is To Love Again* (1960), containing reproductions of his art; *Stand Still Like a Hummingbird* (1962), essays; *Just Wild About Harry* (1963), a play; and *My Life and Times* (1971), tape-recorded interviews. *The Rosy Crucifixion,* composed of *Sexus* (1949), *Plexus* (1953), and *Nexus* (1960), is a memoir of his youth and life prior to expatriation in a form partly fictive, partly essay-like. *Genius and Lust* (1976) is an anthology of his writings selected by Norman Mailer, who wrote a lengthy introduction to it. Many volumes of Miller's correspondence have been printed, including *Hamlet* (2 vols., 1939, 1941), philosophic exchanges with Michael Fraenkel; and with Durrell (1963) and with Anaïs Nin (1965). *Letters to Emil* [Schnellock] (1990) document the years 1922 through 1934. Miller was also a major influence on the Beat movement. ♦

MILLER, JASON (1939–), Long Island-born actor and playwright whose plays include *Nobody Hears a Broken Drum* (1970), about Irish militants during the U.S. Civil War, and *That Championship Season* (1972), depicting the reunion of four middle-aged members of a championship basketball team and their adored coach, all basically corrupt men living by false values and fooling themselves, granted a Pulitzer Prize for drama, and made by him into a film (1982). He has also written *Three One-Act Plays* (1973) and several television dramas.

MILLER, JOAQUIN, pseudonym of Cincinnatus Hiner (or Heine) Miller (1841?–1913), at first a nickname, as his earliest writing was a defense of the Mexican bandit Joaquin Murietta. His early biography is cloaked in exaggeration; he was born in Liberty, Ind., supposedly went West in a covered wagon, lived in frontier Oregon and with the Indians in northern California, was at various times horse thief, Portland lawyer, pony-express messenger, newspaper editor, and Indian fighter, before turning to the poetry published as *Specimens,* (1868) and *Joaquin et al* (1869). He drifted to San Francisco to enter literary society, and to London, where his private printing of *Pacific Poems* (1870) and *Songs of the Sierras* (1871) brought him acclaim from the English, who were fascinated by the discovery of a "frontier poet." Hailed as "the Byron of Oregon," he dramatically attempted to live up to his title. He soon returned to America, where his energetic rhetorical poems continued to appear, although later his bombast, coupled with his imitativeness and metrical weakness, caused him to lose the acclaim he first received. *The Danites in the Sierras* (1877), a Mormon play, was the most popular of his dramas, and besides several novels he wrote the autobiographical *Life Amongst the Modocs* (1873) and *Memorie and Rime* (1884).

MILLER, PERRY [GILBERT EDDY] (1905–63), scholar of American literature, member of the Harvard faculty, best known for his writings on Puritanism and the intellectual history of New England. His books include *Orthodoxy in Massachusetts* (1933), *The New England Mind: The Seventeenth Century* (1939), *The New England Mind: From Colony to Province* (1953), *Jonathan Edwards* (1949), *Roger Williams* (1953), *The Raven and the Whale . . . the Era of Poe and Melville* (1956), and *Errand into the Wilderness* (1956) and *Nature's Nation* (1967), the latter two collecting essays. He also compiled several important anthologies, including *The Puritans* (1938) with T.H. Johnson.

Millerites, religious sect more properly called Second Adventists. These followers of the New York farmer William Miller (1782–1849) believed in the physical second advent of Christ in 1843. After the Day of Judgment failed to arrive that year, the date was set for October 23, 1844. Even after the second disappointment many followers remained faithful, continuing to anticipate a second coming. Another group, the Seventh-Day Adventists, holding to a similar belief, adopted Saturday as the sabbath. In 1990 this body had 700,000 members, and other Adventist sects some 31,000. Edward Eggleston's *The End of the World* and the works of Jane M. Parker♦ are among books dealing with Millerites.

MILLETT, KATE (KATHERINE MURRAY) (1934–   ), feminist activist, whose doctoral dissertation for Columbia University (1970) was published as *Sexual Politics* (1970), a study of the history and nature of the exploitation of women and the relationships between men and women. She followed this seminal book with two autobiographical works, *Flying* (1974), telling of her marriage to a Japanese sculptor and her love affairs with women, and *Sita* (1977), describing a mental breakdown and a lesbian romance. *The Basement* (1979) is an inquiry into an actual case of sadism: the torture and murder of a teenage girl by a woman who served her as a kind of foster mother. *Going to Iran* (1982) is a rather lengthy book about the short visit she made to the changed society of a foreign land. *The Loony-Bin Trip* (1990) relates her bout with mental illness.

MILLHAUSER, STEVEN (1943–   ), born in New York City, reared in Connecticut, graduated from Columbia (1965) and later studied and taught at Brown. His novels are *Edwin Mullhouse: The Life and Death of an American Writer, 1943–1954 by Jeffrey Cartwright* (1972), a comic Nabokovian biography in great depth of the 11-year life of a precocious novelist by his young chum; *Portrait of a Romantic* (1977), the memoir by a

29-year-old man of his juvenile, romantic high-school years that were spent with his realistic-minded doppelgänger; and *From the Realm of Morpheus* (1986), about a young man who penetrates the underground realm of the god of sleep and the kinds of stories he brings forth. *In the Penny Arcade* (1986) gathers short stories by the author, as does *The Barnum Museum* (1990). *Little Kingdoms* (1994) prints three novellas: "The Little Kingdom of J. Franklin Payne," about a newspaper cartoonist and movie animator of the 1920s; "The Princess, the Dwarf, and the Dungeon," about unfounded jealousy; and "Catalogue of the Exhibition: The Art of Edmund Moorash (1810–1846)," presenting the sinister career of a 19th-century American painter.

MILOSZ, CZESLAW (1911–   ), Lithuanian-born poet and man of letters, mainly reared and educated in Poland, in whose diplomatic corps he served (1945–50). He emigrated to the U.S. (1960) and joined the faculty of the University of California, Berkeley. He was naturalized in 1970. His books, written in Polish, in translation include *The Captive Mind* (1953), about the effect of communism on Polish writers; *Native Realm* (1968), an autobiography; *Selected Poems* (1972); *Bells in Winter* (1978), poems; *Visions from San Francisco Bay* (1982), essays; as well as novels and translations into Polish and English. He was awarded a Nobel Prize in 1980. *Collected Poems* was published in 1988.

Mingo, name applied by the Delaware Indians and their allies to the Iroquois♦ and cognate tribes, and more particularly, in colonial times, by the Americans to a detached band of Iroquois on the upper Ohio River in Pennsylvania. In the Leather-Stocking Tales, the name is always associated with cunning, treachery, and ferocity. Magua the Huron, in *The Last of the Mohicans,* is called a Mingo.

Mingo, and Other Sketches in Black and White, four local-color tales by Joel Chandler Harris,♦ published in 1884.

"Mingo: A Sketch of Life in Middle Georgia" is the story of the black servant Mingo, who remains faithful to his mistress even when she marries into a poor-white family. After her death, following the loss of her husband in the Civil War, Mingo remains to care for her child and manage the farm of her coarse but well-intentioned mother-in-law. "At Teague Poteet's" is a novelette about the Georgia backwoodsman, moonshiner, and Civil War draft evader Teague Poteet; his marriage to Puss Pringle; and their daughter Sis, who falls in love with Philip Woodward, agent sent to investigate the moonshiners. Woodward resigns his commission, allays suspicion by helping the mountaineers outwit federal officers, marries Sis, and takes her to the city, to the sorrow of her parents, who are however "proud that Sis was going to marry Somebody."

Minister's Black Veil, The, parable by Hawthorne,♦ published in *The Token* (1836) and in *Twice-Told Tales* (1837).

The Rev. Mr. Hooper, a New England Puritan minister, appears one Sunday with his face covered by a black veil. Refusing to explain his action to his terrified congregation, or to his fiancée, who leaves him, he goes through life concealing his face, saying only that the veil is a symbol of the curtain that hides every man's heart and makes him a stranger even to his friend, his lover, and his God.

Minister's Wooing, The, novel by Harriet Beecher Stowe,♦ published in 1859. It is set in Newport, a New England town, shortly after the Revolution. Aaron Burr is a minor character.

Mary Scudder has been taught by her widowed mother to follow the orthodoxy of their pastor, Dr. Hopkins. His cousin James Marvyn loves her, but, when she refuses him because he has no religious faith, he goes to sea and is reported to have died in a shipwreck. Mary becomes engaged to Dr. Hopkins, who is much older than she. Even when James writes that he has been converted by a miraculous escape from death, and then comes to resume his courtship, she announces that she will keep her promise to the minister. Miss Prissy Diamond, the friendly dressmaker, and Candace, the devout black servant, encourage James's suit, and when Dr. Hopkins learns their true feelings, he sacrifices his own happiness, making possible the marriage of the young couple.

Miniver Cheevy, poem in iambic tetrameter quatrains by E.A. Robinson,♦ published in *The Town Down the River* (1910).

This satirical portrait of Miniver, a worldly failure in Tilbury Town, shows him to be unaware of his personal inadequacies, consoling himself with a romantic melancholy that he carries to absurd lengths. "Born too late," he "sighed for what was not," dreaming of "medieval grace" and "the days of old." Thus his life consists of futile yearnings and frustration, to no end except that "Miniver coughed, and called it fate, And kept on drinking."

Minnehaha, character in *Hiawatha.*♦ The name is first mentioned in Mary Eastman's *Life and Legends of the Sioux* (1849), as the Indian name for a waterfall near Minneapolis.

MINOT, GEORGE RICHARDS (1758–1802), Massachusetts jurist, author of *The History of the Insurrection in Massachusetts in the Year 1786* (1788), a hostile account of Shays's Rebellion. He continued Hutchinson's *History of Massachusetts Bay* (2 vols., 1798, 1803), but his work was eclipsed

by the posthumous publication of Hutchinson's own continuation (1828).

Minstrel show, type of variety entertainment presenting white men in blackface performances of Negro songs, dances, and jokes, originated in the U.S. and was extremely popular here and in Europe during the 19th century. Thomas Dartmouth Rice (1808–60) has been called "the father of American minstrelsy" because of his blackface performance of the song "Jim Crow" (1830ff.) and his subsequent success in programs of pseudo-black songs and dances. Dan Emmett♦ was another early minstrel. The most famous troupe was organized by E.P. Christy♦ (1842). Stephen Foster wrote for Christy's Minstrels, publishing under Christy's name such popular minstrel songs as "Oh! Susanna!," "Uncle Ned," "Old Folks at Home," "Camptown Races," and "Massa's in de Cold, Cold Ground." Among the works of Dan Emmett were "Dixie"♦ and "Old Dan Tucker." By the middle of the century, the program of the minstrel show had become traditional. A row of performers was seated in a semicircle on the stage, with an interlocutor in the center, and two "end men" called "Mr. Tambo" and "Mr. Bones," who played the tambourine and bone castanets. These three maintained a running dialogue of jokes supposedly in the character and idiom of black people, while the whole company presented dances, songs, and farces, performing on banjos, fiddles, and percussion instruments, concluding in a grand finale, comically parading in review in a so-called walk around. Although probably intended in good humor, the minstrel show actually denigrated black culture in the vulgar white caricatures of ignorant, happy-go-lucky, shiftless people reveling in spirited dancing and sentimental singing.

Miriam, heroine of *The Marble Faun.*♦

Miss Leslie's Magazine (1843–46), periodical of literature and fashions for women, whose contributors included N.P. Willis, Lydia H. Sigourney, Park Benjamin, and Longfellow. The name was changed to *The Ladies' Magazine* (1844), and to *Arthur's Ladies' Magazine* (1845), before it was merged with *Godey's Lady's Book.*

Miss Lonelyhearts, short novel by Nathanael West,♦ published in 1933. A dramatization in two acts by Howard Teichmann was produced and published in 1959.

A nameless middle-aged man, the son of a Baptist minister, unable to find any other job, becomes the writer of a column of advice to the lovelorn for a New York newspaper, and is so troubled himself that he spends much of his time drinking. As Miss Lonelyhearts he is sought out by Fay Doyle, a woman married to a cripple, and ends up going to bed with her. Later he meets Fay's husband Peter, toward whom he feels a sympathetic sense of communion, but Peter, torn between reciprocal love and hatred, plans to shoot him with a gun that he has concealed in a package. Upon embracing Peter, Miss Lonelyhearts jostles the package and is accidentally shot to death.

Miss Lulu Bett, novel by Zona Gale, ♦ published in 1920. Her dramatization (1920) won a Pulitzer Prize.

Miss Ravenel's Conversion from Secession to Loyalty, novel by J.W. De Forest, ♦ published in 1867.

At the outbreak of the Civil War, Dr. Ravenel, a scholar who is loyal to the Union, leaves New Orleans for "New Boston" (New Haven, Conn.). With his daughter Lillie, whose sympathies lie with the aristocratic South, he grows concerned at the entrance into the girl's life of two suitors: Edward Colburne, an intelligent but modest New Boston lawyer; and Lieutenant-Colonel John Carter, a Virginia-born soldier in the Union army, whose dashing manners and aristocratic tendencies match her ideal of Southern manhood. Dr. Ravenel prefers Colburne, an Abolitionist like himself, and fears Carter's reputation for dissipation and lack of scruples. Meanwhile Lillie's conversion has begun, and she has a vital interest in the Northern success when Colburne and Carter participate in the capture of New Orleans. Soon the Ravenels return to their old home, and Carter gives up his life of drink and mistresses to court Lillie and intrigue for promotion. After their marriage, he remains faithful for a time, but during a trip to Washington has a secret affair with her carefree young aunt, Mrs. Larue. This ends with the birth of Lillie's son, but Dr. Ravenel, now engaged in the education of freed slaves, learns of Carter's infidelity and informs his daughter, who leaves her husband shortly before he dies as a hero in battle. At the close of the war, Lillie is converted to Abolitionism through her return to New Boston and her marriage to Colburne.

Mission Indians, general term applied to Indians of many tribes, chiefly the Yuma and Shoshone, who were Christianized and gathered into communities by the Spanish Franciscans in southern California (1776–1830s). They were driven out of the missions by the Mexicans, and were neglected by the Americans until after the Civil War, when, largely at the instigation of Helen Hunt Jackson, the government took steps to care for them. Since 1974 they have been located on 31 small reservations in southern California. Mary Austin's *Isidro* and Helen Hunt Jackson's *Ramona* are romantic depictions of the life of the Mission Indians.

Mississippi River, principal river of the U.S., drains the great central basin between the Appa-

lachian and Rocky Mountains. Having its source in northern Minnesota, and flowing through the center of the Prairie ♦ and Southern ♦ states, the river has for its chief tributaries the Missouri and Ohio rivers. Dominating the economic life of the South and Middle West until the Civil War and the coming of the railroads, the Mississippi was the focus of a distinctive type of American culture during the glamorous period of steamboats and showboats (1811–61), whose most celebrated literary interpreter has been Mark Twain, especially in *Huckleberry Finn* and *Life on the Mississippi,* although other popular treatments, respectively in poetry, the novel, and nonfiction, include John Hay's "Jim Bludso," Edna Ferber's *Show Boat,* and Ben Lucien Burman's *Big River To Cross.* Other writers include those associated with its principal cities, St. Louis ♦ and New Orleans. ♦ Its earlier history included discovery by De Soto, domination by the French following the explorations by Jolliet, Marquette, La Salle, and Iberville, control by Spain (1763–1800), settlement and exploitation of its valley by the U.S. after the Louisiana Purchase (1803), and the pre-steamboat period of keelboating whose typical folk hero was Mike Fink. ♦ By 1860 there were more than 1000 steamboats on the river, helping to tie the Middle West to the South. During the Civil War, the Northern attempts to gain control were finally successful through the siege of Vicksburg and the capture of New Orleans. The river is still of primary importance to U.S. agriculture and trade, as both a constructive and a destructive force; popular conceptions of its power have included the black's personification of "Ol' Man River" and the Indian's of the "Father of Waters."

Mr. Crewe's Career, novel by Winston Churchill, ♦ published in 1908.

Mr. Higginbotham's Catastrophe, story by Hawthorne, ♦ published in *The Token* (1834) and in *Twice-Told Tales* (1837).

Dominicus Pike, an itinerant tobacco peddler, is informed of the hanging of wealthy old Mr. Higginbotham of Kimballton. He spreads the rumor as he travels, only to have it denied by persons who have seen the old man since his supposed death. Hearing again of the hanging, and being contradicted by Higginbotham's niece, he goes to Kimballton and arrives just in time to save her uncle from actual murder. It is revealed that the murder was planned by three men, two of whom successively lost courage and fled, spreading the rumor. Dominicus is rewarded by becoming Higginbotham's heir, as well as marrying the niece.

Mr. Roberts, novel by Thomas Heggen. ♦

Mrs. Partington, character in the stories by B.P. Shillaber. ♦

Mrs. Wiggs of the Cabbage Patch, story by Alice Hegan Rice,♦ published in 1901 under her maiden name, Alice Caldwell Hegan.

Mrs. Nancy Wiggs, who lives in a ramshackle house in the "Cabbage Patch," a city tenement section along the railroad tracks, is a middle-aged widow with two sons, Jim and Billy, and three daughters, Asia, Australia, and Europena. They live amid hardships and dire poverty, but "the substance of her philosophy lay in keeping the dust off her rose-colored spectacles." When Jim dies, the family is aided by wealthy Lucy Olcott, and later by her former fiancé, Robert Redding. Through the intervention of these two, and by their own persistent endeavors, the Wiggses maintain life and optimism. They are able to repay their benefactors by causing their reconciliation, and when the people of the Cabbage Patch gather to celebrate Mrs. Wiggs's fiftieth birthday, Robert and Lucy come to announce their approaching marriage. The widow concludes, "Looks like ever' thing in the world comes right, if we jes' wait long enough!"

MITCHELL, Donald Grant (1822–1908), is commonly known as Ik Marvel, or Ike Marvel, a name that resulted from the misprinting of the pseudonym J.K. Marvel, which he adopted in 1846 for his contributions to the *Morning Courier and New York Enquirer.* Although he himself preferred his writings about model farming and rural pleasures, such as *My Farm of Edgewood* (1863) and *Rural Studies* (1867), his most popular works were the gently fanciful and subjective *Reveries of a Bachelor*♦ (1850) and *Dream Life* (1851), books on the borderline between fiction and the essay. His novel *Dr. Johns* (1866) is a delicate and leisurely story of New England village life in the early 19th century, concerned with the contrast between the rigid Calvinism of Connecticut and the external influence of Catholicism through two French women characters.

MITCHELL, Isaac (c.1759–1812), newspaper editor of Albany and Poughkeepsie, in his Poughkeepsie *Political Barometer* (1804) published serially the novel that appeared in book form as *The Asylum; or, Alonzo and Melissa*♦ (1811). An almost verbatim plagiarism of this Gothic romance appeared in the same year as *Alonzo and Melissa; or, The Unfeeling Father.* This was signed by Daniel Jackson (fl.1790–1811), a teacher at Plattsburg Academy, and achieved great popularity. Mitchell died before he could sue for damages, but posterity has awarded the novel to its rightful author.

MITCHELL, John (d.1768), British physician and botanist, resident in Virginia (c.1725–46), wrote on botany and zoology, and may have been the author of anonymous works on contemporary American history and American husbandry. His most important work was *Map of the*

British and French Dominions in North America (1755), the most reliable cartography of the period, frequently used during his lifetime and down to the present in boundary disputes.

MITCHELL, John Ames (1845–1918), New York novelist, editor, and artist whose writings and drawings were frequently contributed to the magazine *Life,*♦ which he founded in 1883 and guided until his death. His best-known novels were *Amos Judd* (1895) and *The Pines of Lory* (1901). The former concerns a young Indian rajah who is taken to Connecticut to save his life during a civil war, and, though reared as the New Englander Judd, shows the contrast between the shrewd, unimaginative Yankee type and the mystical Hindu character.

MITCHELL, Langdon [Elwyn] (1862–1935), son of S. Weir Mitchell, was born in Philadelphia, and began his career as a dramatist with *Sylvian* (1885), a romantic tragedy. His most important play is *The New York Idea* (1906), a problem drama exposing frivolous attitudes toward love and marriage. Mitchell also made stage adaptations of novels, including *Becky Sharp* (1899), from Thackeray's *Vanity Fair; The Adventures of François* (1900), from his father's novel; and *Major Pendennis* (1916), from Thackeray's *Pendennis.* *Understanding America* (1927) is a book of essays.

MITCHELL, Margaret (1900–1949), Georgia author and journalist, from 1926 to 1936 wrote her one book, *Gone with the Wind*♦ (1936, Pulitzer Prize). This long romantic novel of Georgia during the Civil War and Reconstruction, told entirely from the point of view of the middle class in the Old South, won an immediate and unprecedented popularity throughout the U.S. Said to be the fastest-selling novel in the history of American publishing, it had a sales record of 50,000 copies in one day and approximately 1,500,000 during its first year. By May 1941 the sales reached 3,368,000 in the hardbound editions in the English language, and of the 18 translations made in those first five years, the German was the most popular, selling 500,000 copies. The book's great initial popularity was further enhanced by a lavish motion-picture version first released in 1939.

MITCHELL, S[ilas] Weir (1829–1914), Philadelphia physician and author, prior to beginning his career in literature achieved fame for his investigations and writings on clinical medicine, toxicology, and the nervous system. His contributions to these medical subjects were treated in 119 specialized papers and various popular books. The trend of his literary career, marked by his ability in historical romances and in character portrayal, was clearly foreshadowed in his first tale, "The Case of George Dedlow" (*Atlantic Monthly,* July 1866), a story of the Civil War and its psychological effect on an injured army surgeon. Mitchell's first novels, *In War Time* (1885) and *Roland Blake* (1886), continue the use of this theme, the first by showing the psychology of cowardice in a New England doctor during the Civil War, and the second by depicting the accentuation of certain human characteristics during the stress of conflict, particularly the hero's confusion between good sense and romantic impulses, and the neurotic quality of a woman obsessed with a desire for power over others. His greatest historical novel, *Hugh Wynne, Free Quaker*◆ (1897), tells of a Quaker in the Revolutionary War. His other books include *Characteristics* (1892), a novel consisting primarily of character studies through the conversations of a group at whose center is Dr. Owen North; *Dr. North and His Friends* (1900), a sequel; *The Adventures of François* (1898), a picaresque novel of the French Revolution, whose hero, though refined in manner, is lacking in conscience; *Circumstance* (1901), the psychological study of an adventuress; *Constance Trescot* (1905), the analysis of a woman possessed of the one idea of seeking revenge for her husband's murder; *The Red City* (1907), a study of social contrasts in post-Revolutionary Philadelphia; *John Sherwood, Iron Master* (1911), the analysis of the split between the sympathetic and hard materialistic qualities of a businessman; and *Westways* (1913), a story of the Civil War seen through the eyes of two soldiers. Mitchell was also the author of several volumes of poetry, and short stories and novelettes. He was the father of Langdon Mitchell, who dramatized *The Adventures of François* in 1900.

M'liss, novelette by Bret Harte◆ which in its characterization of a willful young girl and her adventures in the mining country represented an early treatment of life in the gold rush. The earliest version appeared in the *Golden Era* (1860), from which it was expanded for serialization in the same journal (1863) and collection in *The Luck of Roaring Camp and Other Sketches* (1870).

Moby-Dick; or, *The Whale,* novel by Melville,◆ published in 1851. Within this realistic account of a whaling voyage is set a symbolic account of the conflict between man and his fate. Captain Ahab declares, "All visible objects are but as pasteboard masks," and Melville, holding this thesis, strikes through the surface of his adventurous narrative to formulate concepts of good and evil imbedded as allegory in its events.

The outcast youth Ishmael, feeling "a damp, drizzly November" in his soul, goes to New Bedford, planning to ship on a whaler. There he draws as a roommate Queequeg, a Polynesian prince, and the two become comrades. After Ishmael hears a symbolic sermon by Father Mapple, he and Queequeg go to Nantucket and sign on the *Pequod,* which sails on Christmas Day. The captain, Ahab, is a monomaniac whose one purpose is to capture the fierce, cunning white whale, Moby-Dick, which had torn away his leg during their last encounter. He keeps below deck for some time, but finally declares his purpose and posts a doubloon on the mast as a reward for the man who first sights the white whale. The characters of the sailors are revealed by their reactions. The chief mate, Starbuck, earnest, prudent, and fretful, dislikes it. Stubb, the second mate, is happy-go-lucky and takes perils as they come. Flask, the third mate, is incapable of deep thought and for him killing whales is simply an occupation. Others in the crew include Fedallah and his mysterious Asiatics; the American Indian harpooner, Tashtego; the African, Daggoo; and the black cabin boy, Pip. Through the plot of the voyage, which carries the *Pequod* nearly around the world, runs a comprehensive discussion of the nature of the whale, the history of science and art relating to the animal, and the facts of the whaling industry. Whales are captured during the pursuit, but circumstances seem to conspire against Ahab: storms, lightning, loss of the compass, the drowning of a man, and the insanity of Ahab's favorite, Pip. The white whale is finally sighted, and in the first day's chase he smashes a whaleboat. The second day, another boat is swamped, and the captain's ivory leg is snapped off. On the third day the whale is harpooned, but Ahab, fouled in the line, is pinioned to Moby-Dick, who bears down on the *Pequod.* The ship is sunk and, as the final spars settle in the water, one of the men nails to the mast a sky hawk that pecks at the flag he is placing as a signal. The ship, "like Satan, would not sink to hell till she had dragged a living part of heaven along with her, and helmeted herself with it." Ishmael, the only survivor, is rescued by another whaler, the *Rachel.*

Mocha Dick, fierce white whale, which, during the 1840s and '50s, is said to have had 19 harpoons put in him, caused the death of more than 30 men, stove three whaling ships and 14 boats, and sunk an Australian trader and a French merchantman. An account of him was published by J.N. Reynolds in *The Knickerbocker Magazine* (1839), 12 years before Melville's *Moby-Dick,* which may have been partly suggested by the article or the legends.

Modern Chivalry, satirical picaresque novel by H.H. Brackenridge.◆ The first two parts were published in 1792, the third and fourth in 1793 and 1797, a revision in 1805, and a final addition in 1815. The influence of Cervantes is obvious, as is in less degree that of Swift, Fielding, and Samuel Butler, but the work is distinguished as the first extended depiction of backwoods life in American fiction.

Captain John Farrago and his servant, Teague O'Regan, set out from the captain's farm in western Pennsylvania to ride through the country and observe the life and manners of the people.

Farrago is an intelligent democrat, part Jeffersonian and part independent, inclining to the ideas of Tom Paine. Teague is a red-headed, long-legged Irish immigrant, part fool and part knave, whose unbounded self-assurance arises from his ignorance. At each stage of their journey they meet some foolish group that admires Teague, and the captain must invent excuses to keep them from bestowing various honors on his servant. Each adventure is followed by a chapter of reflections upon the abuses of democracy. Teague is a universal success, meets the President, becomes an idol of politicians, beautiful ladies, and scientists, and is finally appointed collector of excise on whiskey, all of his predecessors in this office having been tarred and feathered. Teague receives the same treatment, and is captured as a strange animal by a philosophic society, which sends him to France. There the tar and feathers wear off, and his only article of clothing being in an imperfect state, he is mistaken for a sansculotte and borne off in triumph. In the later addition, the author describes a settlement founded by the captain and his friends, but the lack of the early comedy and satire expose his plainly didactic purpose of attempting to raise the standards of democracy.

Modern Instance, A, novel by Howells,♦ published in 1882.

Bartley Hubbard, a clever but unscrupulous Boston journalist, is married to Marcia Gaylord, from whom he becomes alienated because of his shady business practices and his philanderings. Marcia, though still in love with her husband, leaves him, and he sues for divorce. His action is defeated and the divorce granted to Marcia. Hubbard goes to Arizona, where he is killed by a man whose personal affairs he has discussed too frankly in his newspaper. Ben Halleck, who has constantly attended Marcia through her trials, debates with his friend Atherton whether he should forsake the ministry to marry her, but does not come to a decision.

Modern Language Association of America, a major scholarly and academic society, was founded in 1883. It is best known for an annual meeting at the Christmas season with a tremendous attendance and huge array of gatherings on specialized subjects and for its *Publications of the Modern Language Association.* Abbreviated as PMLA, it was founded in 1884 but changes in name, format, and contents have transformed stodginess into lively contemporary journals issued six times a year. To its numerous segments in 1921 the MLA added an American Literature Group. That division's journal, *American Literature,*♦ was first issued in 1929.

Modoc Indians, tribe of southwest Oregon and northern California. In 1864 the Modoc and the Klamath ceded their territory to the U.S., re-

moving to the Klamath reservation in Oregon. In 1870 a chief known as Captain Jack led a part of the tribe back to the California border, and in the subsequent Modoc War (1872–73) two peace commissioners were killed. After the Indians were overcome and their leaders hanged, the tribe was divided, part being sent to Oklahoma and the rest to the Klamath reservation. Joaquin Miller wrote a colorful but romantically imaginative account supposed to tell of his *Life Amongst the Modocs* (1873).

MOELLER, PHILIP (1880–1958), New York playwright, began his career with the Washington Square Players, for whom he wrote one-act plays such as *Helena's Husband* (1916), a satirical account of Helen's abduction by Paris. He was best known for *Madame Sand* (1917), a sophisticated biographical comedy, in which vein he also wrote *Molière* (1919) and *Sophie* (1919), the latter concerned with the opera singer Sophie Arnold in the time of Louis XV. Later plays include *Camel Through the Needle's Eye* (1929) and *Fata Morgana* (1931), adapted from the Hungarian in collaboration with J.L.A. Burrell. His early one-act dramas were published as *Five Somewhat Historical Plays* (1918). He was also well known as a stage director for the Theatre Guild.

Mohawk Indians, easternmost tribe of the Iroquois confederacy, located mainly along the Mohawk River, was noted for its ferocity and constant warfare. In the early 17th century, obtaining firearms from Dutch traders, the Mohawk conquered many neighboring tribes, including the Delaware. They were allied with the British in the French and Indian Wars and in the Revolution, after which most of them removed to Canada. The historical Hiawatha was probably a Mohawk, and Joseph Brant♦ was a Mohawk chief. Edmund Wilson's *Apologies to the Iroquois* (1960) treats the modern situation of the tribes in the confederacy.

Mohegan (or MONHEGAN) **Indians,** Algonquian tribe of Connecticut, united with the Pequot under Sassacus, and rebelled against him under the leadership of Uncas. They were allied with the English, and after the death of King Philip (1676) became the only important tribe south of Maine. They finally settled on a reservation near Norwich. Samson Occom♦ was a member of the tribe. In *The Last of the Mohicans,* Cooper confuses Mahicans♦ with Mohegans. The Mohegan figure in *Holdfast Gaines* by Odell Shepard and W.O. Shepard.

Mohican Indians, see *Mahican* and *Mohegan Indians.*

Moki Indians, see *Hopi Indians.*

MÖLLHAUSEN, HEINRICH BALDUIN (1825–1905), German traveler and author, in the U.S. on three trips, on which he respectively journeyed as far west as Fort Laramie (1849–53), trekked across the country from Fort Smith to Los Angeles (1853–54), and helped survey the Colorado River (1857–58). This life on the frontier was crystallized in some 30 romantic novels. His stirring depictions of Indian and pioneer life and adventure on the seas gave him a reputation as "the German Cooper." His *Diary of a Journey from the Mississippi to . . . the Pacific* (1858) is the only work translated into English, but his most famous novels are the trilogy of frontier life, *Der Halb Indianer* (1861), *Der Flüchtling* (1861), *Der Majordomo* (1863).

MOMADAY, N[AVARRE] SCOTT (1934–   ), Oklahoma-born author of Kiowa ancestry whose books include *House Made of Dawn* (1969, Pulitzer Prize), a novel about a young Indian man unable to be at home in either the white or his ancestral society; *The Way to Rainy Mountain* (1969), Kiowa legends told in relation to history and his own youth; *Angle of Geese* (1973) and *The Gourd Dancer* (1976), poems; *The Names* (1976), a memoir; and *The Ancient Child* (1989), about a young Indian who lives first in San Francisco, then in Paris with success as an artist. Momaday was a professor of English at Stanford (1972–81), from which he received a Ph.D. for his critique and edition of the poems of Frederick Goddard Tuckerman. He is currently teaching at the University of Arizona.

Money-Makers, *The*, novel by H.F. Keenan,♦ published anonymously in 1885 as a reply to Hay's *The Bread-Winners.*

Monikins, *The*, allegorical satire by Cooper,♦ published in 1835.
   Sir John Goldencalf meets Noah Poke, a Yankee sea captain, in Paris, where they become acquainted with four monkeys who have been traveling in Europe: Dr. Reasono, Lord Chatterino, Lady Chatterissa, and Mistress Vigilance Lynx. The knight and the captain, after being enlightened concerning the superior institutions of these "Monikins," accompany them to their homeland in the polar regions. Sir John visits the countries of Leaphigh (England), whose society is founded on a rigid system of castes and a false social hierarchy; Leapthrough (France), which he considers unprincipled, erratic, and selfish; and Leaplow (the U.S.), where the leveling tendency of democratic politics has destroyed virtue and distinction. Leaplow is governed according to a National Allegory (the Constitution), by a Great Sachem (President), Riddles (senators), a Legion (representatives), and Supreme Arbitrators (Supreme Court). The system operates by the institution of contrasting parties, "Perpendicular" and "Horizontal," sometimes supplemented by a third group, "Tangents." These parties are led by the Godlikes, who bow to the dominant commercial interests, allowing society to become "the great moral eclipse," in which "the great moral postulate of principle" is overshadowed by "the great immoral postulate known as interest," and public opinion is manipulated by scheming demagogues and a powerful press. When Sir John returns to England, he marries his patient fiancée, Anna Etherington, while Captain Poke returns to Connecticut.

MONK, MARIA (*c.*1817–50), author of *Awful Disclosures* (1836), an account of her supposed life as a nun in Montreal, filled with horror tales of misconduct in the Catholic convents. Since there was a strong anti-Catholic feeling at the time, Maria won as many converts as enemies. Investigating committees proved her tales to be false, but the slanderous controversies she had precipitated were still hot enough to ensure the popularity of her *Further Disclosures* (1837). After this period of notoriety, she faded from the limelight.

Monk and the Hangman's Daughter, *The*, romance by Ambrose Bierce.♦

MONROE, HARRIET (1860–1936), Chicago poet and editor, first attained notice with her *Columbian Ode* (1892, published 1893), written in celebration of the World's Columbian Exposition in her native city. Besides *Valeria and Other Poems* (1891), she published a biography of her brother-in-law, John Wellborn Root (1896), and a book of five verse plays, *The Passing Show* (1903). With the founding of *Poetry: A Magazine of Verse*♦ (1912), she became a leader in the championing of new poetry, and she edited this organ until her death, remaining better known for it than for her several subsequent volumes of minor poetry. Her other works include *Poets and Their Art* (1926, revised 1932), a book of essays, and *A Poet's Life* (1937), her autobiography. *The New Poetry* (1932), edited in collaboration with Alice Corbin Henderson, is an anthology of 20th-century verse. The Harriet Monroe Poetry Award established by her will is given, without competition, under the University of Chicago's direction, when sufficient income ($500) is available. Winners include Cummings, Robert Lowell, Marianne Moore, Wallace Stevens, and Yvor Winters.

MONROE, JAMES (1758–1831), 5th President of the U.S. (1817–25), was born in Virginia, left William and Mary College to become a soldier in the Revolutionary War, and afterward studied law under Jefferson, who remained his model and mentor in matters of policy. In the Virginia legislature (1782–83) and the Continental Congress (1783–86), he upheld Jeffersonian principles and favored a balance between federal and state powers. He opposed the adoption of the Constitution, as a member of the Virginia Convention (1788), fearing the central government would be too powerful. Elected to the U.S. Senate (1790–94), he was bitterly critical of Washington's administration and of Hamilton in particular. His ministry to France (1794–96) ended in recall because of his excessive sympathy with the French Revolution and his failure to follow Washington's instructions. He published his version of the controversy in *A View of the Conduct of the Executive, in the Foreign Affairs of the United States* (1797). Still popular in his own state, he was its governor (1799–1802) and in 1803 was appointed by Jefferson as an envoy to France and Spain. He participated in the negotiation of the Louisiana Purchase, and went to England in an attempt to settle various disputes between that country and the U.S. Again governor of Virginia (1811), he resigned to become Madison's secretary of state (1811–17). He was also secretary of war (1814–15) and was prominent in the events of the War of 1812 and the subsequent peace. Monroe was virtually unopposed in the presidential elections of 1816 and 1820, and the period of his administration, because of the apparent absence of partisan controversy, is known as the "era of good feelings." The principal events were the adoption of the Missouri Compromise, the Seminole War by which the U.S. acquired Florida, and the framing by Secretary of State J.Q. Adams of the U.S. foreign policy known as the Monroe Doctrine. *The Writings of James Monroe* have been published in seven volumes (1898–1903). Fragmentary reminiscences written in his old age were put together as an *Autobiography* in 1959.

Monsieur Beaucaire, romance by Tarkington. ♦

Monster, The, and Other Stories, seven tales by Stephen Crane,♦ published in 1899.

"The Monster," a novelette set in Whilomville, N.Y., is a bitterly ironic commentary on the cruelty and lack of sympathy of ordinary people for an act of humanity they do not understand. Henry Johnson, a black servant in the home of Dr. Trescott, rescues the physician's young son from a fire. He is terribly disfigured and loses his sanity, so that no home can be found for him in the town. Horrified by the "monster," the townspeople ostracize the doctor and his family because they harbor the man. It finally appears that Trescott has sacrificed his entire happiness for an ethical principle he formerly considered unquestionable. "The Blue Hotel" describes the events that lead to quarrels and a murder at a bar in a small Nebraska town. The victim, a stupid, paranoid Swede, who dies with his eyes fixed on the ironic and symbolic text on a cash register, "This registers the amount of your purchase," is partly responsible for his own death, and his murderer is hardly more responsible than others involved in a sequence of events, although he is sentenced to the penitentiary, because "ev-

ery sin is the result of a collaboration," and the one who gets the punishment is the one who happens to be at "the apex of a human movement." "His New Mittens" is concerned with the inner reactions of a small boy who runs away from home, and the remaining stories are studies of men in sensational situations or moments of intense excitement.

Mont-Saint-Michel and Chartres, critical work by Henry Adams,♦ privately printed in 1904, and published in 1913. It is subtitled "A Study of Thirteenth-Century Unity." This interpretation of the dominant attitude of mind from 1150 to 1250 precedes *The Education of Henry Adams*♦ in the author's plan to study historical forces by relating two points in time. He chose the 13th century as "the point of history when man held the highest idea of himself as a unit in a unified universe," in order to "measure motion down to his own time" in his autobiography, "a study of Twentieth-Century Multiplicity." In *Mont-Saint-Michel,* he shows philosophy, theology, and the arts to be informed by a spiritual unity, illogical but founded on simple faith and strength of energy. The 16 chapters discuss Norman architecture, giving way to Gothic "flinging its passion against the sky"; the subordinate arts of sculpture and glass; the *Chanson de Roland;* courts of love; the metaphysical system of Aquinas; and the religious mysticism of a period that found its highest symbol in the Virgin, apotheosis of the feminine ideal. Thus there is a unified attitude of mind in men's reaction to the universe, contrasting with the concept of a 20th-century "multiverse" which leads to a philosophy and science of multiple aspects and reactions.

Monthly Anthology, see *Anthology Club.*

Monthly Magazine and American Review, The (1799–1802), New York periodical edited by C.B. Brown. In 1801 it became a quarterly, entitled *The American Review and Literary Journal.* Primarily educational, it included scientific and literary subject matter, and among Brown's contributions was part of *Edgar Huntly.*

Monument Mountain, blank-verse poem by Bryant,♦ published in 1824 and collected in *Poems* (1832). Concerned with the name-legend of a mountain near Bryant's childhood home, the poem recounts the story of an Indian princess who loved her cousin. Because their union would have been considered incestuous, she threw herself from a precipice to her death.

MOODY, ANNE (1940–), memoirist of the civil rights movement. *Coming of Age in Mississippi* (1968) tells of her experiences growing up Southern and black and the confrontation of what Martin Luther King called "physical force with soul force."

MOODY, DWIGHT LYMAN (1837–99), Massachusetts evangelist, associated after 1870 with Ira David Sankey (1840–1908), organist and singer, with whom he carried on a great revivalist campaign in the U.S. and Great Britain. Their collections of gospel hymns were extremely popular. Moody established a chain of educational institutions based on his own plans. Their work is described in Sankey's *My Life and the Story of the Gospel Hymns* (1906).

MOODY, WILLIAM VAUGHN (1869–1910), Indiana playwright and poet, graduated from Harvard (1893) and taught English there (1894–95) and at the University of Chicago (1895–99, 1901–7). His first poetic play, *The Masque of Judgment* (1900), deals with the conflict between man and God and the rightful exercise of man's free will, which leads him to rebel. A second verse drama, *The Fire Bringer* (1904), stresses man's duty of rebellion in the story of Prometheus. These works were to have been brought to philosophic completion in a third play dealing with the reconciliation of God and man through the creation of woman. This part of the trilogy, *The Death of Eve* (1912), remained incomplete at Moody's death, and none of the works was ever produced. *The Great Divide* (1906), originally produced as *A Sabine Woman* (1906) and published (1909) under its second title, is a play concerned with the contrast between Ruth Jordan, a modern product of inherited Puritan traditions and inhibitions, and Stephen Ghent, a free individualist representative of the frontier West. This was followed by another prose play, *The Faith Healer* (1909), which was less successful because of its exalted idealism. It concerns Ulrich Michaelis, an occult healer whose power is lost when he gains the earthly love of Rhoda Williams, but regained when he purifies his love in a higher, unselfish realization that her anguish, like that of the whole world, needs healing. Moody's lyric *Poems* (1901) also recognizes that men's spirits are plagued and possessed by confused desires, but he voices a highly spiritual and idealistic belief in the greatness of their eventual destiny. His *Poems and Plays* were collected in two volumes (1912), and collections of his *Letters* have been published (1913, 1935).

Moon-Calf, semi-autobiographical novel by Floyd Dell,♦ published in 1920.

Felix Fay, the son of a poor family in a small Illinois town, hates the mean everyday world that surrounds him, and moons through life "in the day-dreams which books unfold before him." His adolescent education includes toying with atheism and socialism, the writing of romantic poetry, and being admired by older women with literary inclinations. He becomes a newspaper reporter and has an affair with a girl, Joyce, whom he considers to be a person with beliefs and standards like his own, until he loses his job and, going away to write a novel, leaves her free to marry a man who represents the philistine world he hates. Still a sensitive, idealistic youth frustrated by his surroundings, he goes to Chicago, hoping to find a world closer to his dreams.

The Briary-Bush (1921), a sequel, is concerned with Felix's career as a Chicago reporter and dramatic critic, and his life as a typical jazz-age rebel against convention, until he finally settles down to marriage and achieves literary success.

Moon Hoax, result of an article contributed to the New York *Sun* (Aug. 1835) by a reporter, Richard Adams Locke (1800–1871), who pretended to reveal a discovery by Sir John Herschel that men and animals existed on the moon. The revelations, supposedly reprinted from the actually defunct Edinburgh *Journal of Science,* were so clever as greatly to increase the *Sun's* circulation, cause a delegation from Yale to ask to see the original article, and produce pamphlet reprints in England and on the Continent. Poe, who was a friend of Locke and described him in *The Literati,* said that the hoax anticipated most of his "The Unparalleled Adventure of One Hans Pfaall"♦ and caused him to leave that tale unfinished, although he published it and later published his "Balloon Hoax"♦ in the *Sun* itself in 1844.

Moon of the Caribbees, The, one-act play by O'Neill,♦ produced and published in 1918.

The British tramp steamer *Glencairn* is anchored off a West Indian island, from which is heard a melancholy, crooning chant. On deck, the seamen await the arrival of Bella, the bumboat woman, who brings three girls and a boatload of fruit in which they smuggle bottles of rum. The Irishman Driscoll distributes the liquor, and an orgy of drinking and dancing begins. The prettiest of the girls, Pearl, leaves Yank to make advances to Smitty, a quiet Englishman burdened by memories of an unfortunate love affair that sent him to sea. When he does not respond, Pearl turns on him furiously and goes off with Yank. The party becomes riotous, ending with a fight in which a man is stabbed to death. The mate finally arrives to send the women ashore, and the men leave the deck, as the melancholy chant continues from the island.

MOORE, CLEMENT CLARKE (1779–1863), professor of Biblical learning and author of the poem popularly known as " 'Twas the Night Before Christmas," published anonymously in the *Troy Sentinel* (Dec. 23, 1823), widely copied, and reprinted in the author's *Poems* (1844). The poem's proper title is "A Visit from St. Nicholas."

MOORE, [HORATIO] FRANK[LIN] (1828–1904), New Hampshire-born scholar of American history, editor of such works as *Songs and Ballads of the American Revolution* (1856), *American Eloquence* (1857), and *Diary of the American Revolu-*

tion from Newspapers and Original Documents (2 vols., 1859–60).

MOORE, GEORGE HENRY (1823–92), brother of Frank Moore, was also a historical scholar, whose works include *Mr. Lee's Plan* (1860), a pamphlet on the treason of Charles Lee; . . . *Negroes in the . . . Army of the Revolution* (1862); and *John Dickinson* (1890).

MOORE, JOHN TROTWOOD (1858–1929), author of *Songs and Stories from Tennessee* (1897), local-color sketches and poems; *The Bishop of Cottontown* (1906), a novel concerned with the effects of industrialism on Southern life; *Uncle Wash, His Stories* (1910); *Tennessee, the Volunteer State* (4 vols., 1923); and *Hearts of Hickory* (1926), a romantic novel based on the early life of Jackson. His *Taylor-Trotwood Magazine* (1905–10), founded as *Trotwood's Monthly,* was a miscellany of local history and literature in Tennessee. Merrill Moore was his son.

MOORE, JULIA A. (1847–1920), better known as "The Sweet Singer of Michigan," upon publication of her first book, *The Sweet Singer of Michigan Salutes the Public* (1876), attracted wide attention because her writing was so bad that it seemed to possess almost a touch of genius. Her poems ranged from elegies on deaths caused by yellow fever and choking on roast beef to occasional verse on the Grand Rapids Cricket Club. Her unconsciously childish grammar, and rhymes that went from verse to worse, delighted Clemens, who declared that she had "the touch that makes an intentionally humorous episode pathetic and an intentionally pathetic one funny." Her first book, later retitled *The Sentimental Song Book,* was followed by *A Few Words to the Public with New and Original Poems by Julia A. Moore* (1878). She seems to have thought long before publishing her third book, *Sunshine and Shadow* (1915), a romance of the Revolution.

MOORE, MARIANNE [CRAIG] (1887–1972), born in St. Louis, graduated from Bryn Mawr (1909), and lived mainly in New York City, where she edited *The Dial*♦ (1925–29). She did not publish a book until she was in her mid-thirties, with the issuance of the neutrally titled *Poems* (1921), followed by the more aptly named *Observations* (1924). A long hiatus was followed by *Selected Poems* (1935), which T.S. Eliot in his Introduction declared to be "descriptive rather than lyrical or dramatic." She herself said in the early poem titled "Poetry" that despite "contempt for . . . all this fiddle . . . one discovers in it, after all, a place for the genuine," and the "genuine" she defined as "imaginary gardens with real toads in them." Succeeding collections of poetry appeared in *The Pangolin, and Other Verse* (1936), *What Are Years* (1941), *Nevertheless* (1944), *Collected Poems* (1951, Pulitzer Prize), *Like*

a *Bulwark* (1956), and *O To Be a Dragon* (1959). In keeping with her conception of the genuine in poetry, these were marked by piquant but precise observation serving as surprising metaphors that often alluded to exotic creatures (e.g. pangolin) based on her knowledge of biology and interest in zoos, as great and enthusiastic as that which she had for her hometown baseball team, the Brooklyn Dodgers. The poems were marked by a disciplined though unconventional use of metrics ("I tend to write in a patterned arrangement, with rhymes . . . to secure an effect of flowing continuity"), and an angular witty, cerebral, ironic attitude. Her so-called *Complete Poems* (1967) gathers all she wished to preserve. Her other works include *The Fables of La Fontaine* (1954), a verse translation; *Predilections* (1955), essays on favorite writers; and *Tell Me, Tell Me* (1966), poems and prose pieces.

MOORE, MERRILL (1903–57), son of J.T. Moore, was born in Tennessee, and began his poetic career as a member of the regionalist group that published *The Fugitive*♦ (1922–25). Although a practicing psychiatrist in Boston, Moore found time for a prodigious body of poetry, all using, with great fluency and flexibility, the sonnet form. His several collections of poems include *The Noise That Time Makes* (1929), *It Is a Good Deal Later Than You Think* (1934), *Six Sides to a Man* (1935), *M: One Thousand Autobiographical Sonnets* (1938), and *Clinical Sonnets* (1949).

Moqui Indians, see *Hopi Indians.*

MORAGA, CHERRIE (1952–), born in Whittier, Cal., of Anglo-Chicana parents and educated at San Francisco State, writes in many genres from a Chicana, feminist, and lesbian perspective. Her own works are *Loving in the War Years: Lo que nunca pasó por sus labios* (1983), poetry and essays; *Cuentos: Stories by Latinas* (1983); and *Giving Up the Ghost: Teatro in Two Acts* (1984), poetic monologues spoken in a mixture of Spanish and English by two women. But she is best known for editing, with Gloria Anzaldúa, *This Bridge Called My Back: Writings by Radical Women of Color* (1981), bilingual edition *Esta puente, mi espalda: Voces de mujeres tercermundistas en los Estados Unidos* (1988).

Moran of the Lady Letty, romance by Frank Norris,♦ published in 1898. It was issued in England as *Shanghaied* (1899).

Ross Wilbur, on his way to a San Francisco social affair, is shanghaied aboard the *Bertha Millner,* a fishing schooner commanded by brutal Captain Kitchell, with a Chinese crew. He grows hardened and alert during the voyage to the fishing grounds off Lower California. While seizing the derelict *Lady Letty* for salvage, Kitchell is drowned and Wilbur saves the *Lady Letty's* only survivor, Moran Sternerson, the captain's daughter, a rough, strong blonde who scorns femininity. She takes command of the schooner, but is coerced by the crew to Magdalena Bay, where they are joined by a beachcombing Chinese junk, and find a valuable piece of ambergris. During a fight in which they capture the crew of the junk, Wilbur and Moran become friends, and soon they fall in love. They bring the schooner to San Francisco, where Wilbur's friends are astonished by his strange companion. While he is ashore, one of the crew steals the ambergris and kills Moran. A storm drives the ship out through the Golden Gate, as Wilbur helplessly watches.

Moravian Church, evangelical Protestant communion that emphasizes Christian unity and personal service, retains a historical episcopacy, and accepts the Scriptures as the sole moral guide. It originated (1457) in Moravia and Bohemia, among the followers of the martyred John Huss, but met severe persecution. The renewed church dates from 1722, when Count Nicolaus Ludwig Zinzendorf (1700–1760) established a refuge in Saxony. The missionary movement began shortly afterward, and Zinzendorf came to America (1741–43), founded a colony at Bethlehem, Pa., and from this and other centers unsuccessfully tried to organize all German sects into the Church of God in Spirit. His biographer, Augustus Gottlieb Spangenberg (1704–92), was also a leader in America after 1735.

MORE, PAUL ELMER (1864–1937), born in St. Louis, graduated from Washington University (1887), and continued his studies there and at Harvard. He taught Sanskrit and the classics at Harvard and Bryn Mawr, but then became a critic in New York, editing *The Nation*♦ (1909–14), finally returning to scholarship as a lecturer at Princeton. His broad classical knowledge is shown in his *Shelburne Essays*♦ (14 vols., 1904–36), and in other critical works that include *Platonism* (1917), *The Religion of Plato* (1921), *Hellenistic Philosophies* (1923), *The Christ of the New Testament* (1924), *Christ the Word* (1927), *The Demon of the Absolute* (1928), and *The Catholic Faith* (1931). *Pages from an Oxford Diary* (1937) is an autobiographical work. More was associated with Irving Babbitt as a leader in the New Humanist movement.♦

More Wonders of the Invisible World, tract by Robert Calef.♦

Morella, story by Poe,♦ published in 1835 and reprinted in *Tales of the Grotesque and Arabesque* (1840).

Morella, a student of the German mystics, is a woman of extraordinary learning and mental power. Her husband is devoted to her, and acknowledges her intellectual superiority, but she realizes that he does not love her. When she declines in health, he is repelled by her melancholy beauty. She seems resigned, but at last tells him that she is dying and yet shall live, that "her whom in life thou didst abhor, in death thou shalt adore." She dies in childbirth, leaving a daughter who is loved by the lonely father, even though he recognizes her increasing resemblance to his dead wife. He neglects to name the child, but when she is 14 decides to have her baptized. At the font, a perverse impulse causes him to utter the name Morella, at which she falls dead, saying "I am here!" Distracted, the father bears her corpse to the tomb, where he finds no trace of the first Morella.

MORFORD, HENRY (1823–81), New York journalist and author, whose works include *The Rest of Don Juan* (1846), a Byronic poem; *Shoulder-Straps* (1863). *The Days of Shoddy* (1863), and *The Coward* (1864), novels describing corruption and incompetence in the Northern army and its contractors: *Red-Tape and Pigeon-Hole Generals as Seen from the Ranks* (1864), a narrative of his experiences in the Civil War; *The Bells of Shandon* (1867), a play written with John Brougham; *The Spur of Monmouth* (1876), a romance of the Revolution; and several popular guidebooks and travel accounts.

MORGAN, [GEORGE] FREDERICK (1922–   ), New York City-born poet, after graduation from Princeton became a founder and the editor of *The Hudson Review.*♦ His first volume, *A Book of Change* (1972), is frequently autobiographical in its quest for values, while *Poems of the Two Worlds* (1977) deals with body and spirit, the mundane and the ideal. Later works are *The Tarot of Cornelius Agrippa* (1978), a prose poem of legendry; *Death Mother* (1979) and *Northbook* (1982), collections of shorter poems; *The Fountain and Other Fables* (1985), allegories in prose; and *Poems: New and Selected* (1987).

MORGAN, SIR HENRY (c.1635–88), British buccaneer, came to the West Indies as a youth and later led his forces in raids on many Spanish towns, which he unmercifully plundered and outraged. In 1671 he captured Panama from its far more numerous Spanish defenders, for which he was rewarded by being knighted (1674) and made lieutenant-governor of Jamaica. Exquemelin, who served under Morgan, wrote of him in *The Bucaniers of America . . .* (1681); English translation, 1684). He figures often in literature, e.g. *The Buccaneer* by Maxwell Anderson and Laurence Stallings, and *Cup of Gold* by John Steinbeck.

MORGAN, JOHN (1735–89), Philadelphia physician and educator, graduated from the College of Philadelphia (1757), served in the French and Indian War, studied abroad, received his M.D. from the University of Edinburgh (1763), and returned in 1765 to found the University of

Pennsylvania's medical school, where he became a professor. He was medical director of the Revolutionary Army (1775–77). His writings include *A Discourse Upon the Institution of Medical Schools in America* (1765), one of *Four Dissertations on the Reciprocal Advantages of a Perpetual Union Between Great-Britain and Her American Colonies* (1766), and *A Recommendation of Inoculation . . .* (1776).

MORGAN, LEWIS HENRY (1818–81), called "the Father of American Anthropology," became interested in ethnology through his membership in a New York secret society, the Gordian Knot, later called The Grand Order of the Iroquois, superficially patterned after the Iroquois Confederacy. The casual desire to know more about Indian matters led Morgan into a serious investigation of the Iroquois, which in turn led to research concerning other tribes and eventually world anthropology. His *League of the Ho-dé-no-sau-nee, or Iroquois* (1851) is considered the first scientific account of an Indian tribe. His discovery that the kinship system of the Iroquois was similar to that of all American Indians was set forth in *Systems of Consanguinity and Affinity of the Human Family* (1871), an important work on primitive society in general. This led him to propound the doctrine of a common origin and psychic unity of all races, and a theory of social evolution in *Ancient Society; or Researches in the Lines of Human Progress* (1877). He wrote many pamphlets and articles on related matters of ethnology and made an important study of the minds of lower animals in *The American Beaver and His Works* (1868). A small selection from his unpublished diary was issued in 1938, and his *Indian Journals, 1859–1862* was published in 1958.

Morgan Library (properly, THE PIERPONT MORGAN LIBRARY), originally the private library of the elder J.P. Morgan, was given to the public by his son. It is housed in an art gallery constructed by McKim, Mead, and White (1905) and an adjoining library building (1920), adjacent to the old Morgan residence in New York City. In addition to an important collection of books and manuscripts, there are significant paintings, drawings, bookbindings, coins, and medals. Among the noteworthy categories in the collection are illuminated manuscripts, incunabula, early liturgical works, and manuscripts or first editions of English and American literature and history. Since its establishment as a public institution (1924), it has been open for research, lectures have been given by prominent scholars, and important exhibitions of its own and of borrowed materials have been arranged.

MORISON, SAMUEL ELIOT (1887–1976), professor of American history at Harvard and an editor of *The New England Quarterly.* His books include *Maritime History of Massachusetts* (1921); *The Oxford History of the United States, 1783–1917* (2 vols., 1927); *Builders of the Bay Colony* (1930); *The Founding of Harvard College* (1935); *Harvard College in the Seventeenth Century* (2 vols., 1936); *The Puritan Pronaos* (1936), a study of 17th-century New England intellectual life; *Portuguese Voyages to America in the Fifteenth Century* (1940); *Admiral of the Ocean Sea* (1942, Pulitzer Prize), a biography of Columbus; and with H.S. Commager, *The Growth of the American Republic* (2 vols., 1930, revised 1962). He was the navy's official historian in World War II, and wrote 14 volumes on its many engagements in his *History of U.S. Naval Operations* (1947–60). *The Two-Ocean War* (1963) is a short history of the subject. His study of *John Paul Jones* (1959) earned him another Pulitzer Prize. *One Boy's Boston* (1962) is a brief work recalling his youth. Even as he moved into and beyond his eighth decade he continued his publications with his *Oxford History of the American People* (1965), lives of Commodore Perry (1967), Harrison Gray Otis (1969), a new version of a study issued in 1913, and *Champlain* (1972); and a major work, *The European Discovery of America* (2 vols., 1971, 1974).

Morituri Salutamus, poem in heroic couplets by Longfellow,♦ written for the fiftieth anniversary of his class at Bowdoin, was collected in *The Masque of Pandora* (1875).

The title derives from the cry of the Roman gladiators, "O Cæsar, we who are about to die salute you!," and in the name of his now aged classmates the poet salutes the familiar scenes, the former teachers, and the young men who are taking the place of his generation, finally addressing his comrades themselves. In an elegiac mood, he recalls the joys and griefs of their long lives, then tells a story, adapted from the *Gesta Romanorum,* of the coming of death, and concludes by urging their continued activity and achievement, while life affords opportunity.

MORLEY, CHRISTOPHER [DARLINGTON] (1890–1957), New York author and journalist, was born in Pennsylvania, and educated at Haverford College and as a Rhodes Scholar at Oxford (1913). His more than 50 books are widely diverse in nature, and all mainly integrated by the author's personality. His interest in bookselling is indicated in his novels *Parnassus on Wheels* (1917), concerned with an itinerant bookseller, and *The Haunted Bookshop* (1919). Other novels include *Where the Blue Begins♦* (1922) and another fantasy, *Thunder on the Left* (1925); *The Swiss Family Manhattan* (1932); *Human Being* (1932); *The Trojan Horse* (1937), a modernized version of the story of Troilus and Cressida; *Kitty Foyle* (1939), a story of a lower-middle-class girl; *Thorofare* (1942), about an English boy who becomes an American citizen; and *The Man Who Made Friends with Himself* (1949), dealing with the conflict of reality and imagination in a serious fantasy. Morley's poetry, sentimental and derivative from the many dissimilar authors he liked, includes *The Rocking Horse* (1919), *Chimneysmoke* (1921), *Parson's Pleasure* (1923), and such books of humorous verse as *Mandarin in Manhattan* (1933), *The Middle Kingdom* (1944), and *Gentlemen's Relish* (1955). He wrote many books of essays and sketches, combining gossip and travel notes, which reflect his enthusiasms and crotchets: among them are *Shandygaff* (1918), *Tales from a Rolltop Desk* (1921), *John Mistletoe* (1931), *Hasta la Vista* (1935), *History of an Autumn* (1938), and *The Ironing Board* (1949). Besides one-act plays, he revised and revived melodramas for a Hoboken theater he helped manage (1928–30).

Mormon, name applied to the sect founded (1830) by Joseph Smith♦ and properly titled the Church of Jesus Christ of Latter-day Saints. The headquarters of the worldwide organization are in Salt Lake City, Utah, while the Reorganized Church, founded by the younger Joseph Smith,♦ has headquarters in Independence, Mo. The membership of the former in 1990 was well over 2,500,000; of the latter more than 200,000. Brigham Young,♦ who succeeded Smith as head of the church, led its great exodus 1100 miles westward to Salt Lake (1846–47). In addition to the King James version of the Bible, the church has as its primary documents the *Book of Mormon,* first published in 1830 after Smith had translated it from inscribed golden plates with the aid of a magical device called Urim and Thummim, and two other works, the *Doctrine and Covenants* (1835) and the *Pearl of Great Price* (1851), later revelations to Smith. The *Book* by the fifth-century prophet Mormon tells how the Israelites were led by Lehi to America, of their history to the 5th century A.D., of the future creation of a New Jerusalem in America, and prophesies the Second Coming, a millennium of peace, and an afterworld under Christ. One revelation to Smith (1843) sanctioned polygamy, but in 1890 this practice was prohibited by a church manifesto. The belief that members can have their ancestors baptized into the church has led to the creation of great genealogical libraries for needed research.

MORRELL, WILLIAM (*fl.* 1623–25), Anglican clergyman, came to Massachusetts (1623) as a member of the ill-fated colony of Gorges. After the colony's failure, he remained for a year at Plymouth, returning to England to publish his poem *Nova Anglia* or *New-England, or a Brief Enarration* (1625). This poem in Latin hexameters, with its author's translation into English heroic couplets, gives a description of the country and the Indians, ending in an appeal for Christian help.

MORRIS, GEORGE POPE (1802–64), New York journalist and poet, who occupied a minor position in the Knickerbocker Group. He became editor of the *New-York Mirror♦* (1824), and

won a temporary reputation for his drama *Brier Cliff* (1826) and his operetta *The Maid of Saxony* (1842), but is best known for his sentimental poems, which include the popular "Woodman, Spare That Tree!" (1830), reprinted in *The Deserted Bride and Other Poems* (1838). His best prose work was *The Little Frenchman and His Water Lots, with Other Sketches of the Times* (1839), the title piece telling of a shrewd New York realtor and a guileless foreigner.

MORRIS, GOUVERNEUR (1752–1816), graduated from King's College (1768) and, after a brief but brilliant law career, entered politics. As a member of the New York landed aristocracy, he was a conservative, but he supported the patriots in the Revolution. In the New York provincial congress he was a moderate and helped frame the state constitution. In the Continental Congress (1778–79) he drafted important documents and wrote *Observations on the American Revolution* (1779). Failing reelection, he moved to Philadelphia, resumed law practice, and wrote anonymous articles on finance that led to his appointment to assist Robert Morris as superintendent of finance (1781–85). In the Constitutional Convention he favored a strong centralized government controlled by the upper class, for he was frankly cynical about democracy. He was a business agent and later U.S. minister to France (1792–94), but was recalled at French request because he opposed their Revolution. In the Senate (1800–1803) he remained a staunch Federalist. His *Diary and Letters* (2 vols., 1888) and *Diary of the French Revolution* (2 vols., 1938) have been issued.

MORRIS, THOMAS (*fl.* 1741–67), English-born soldier, served in America in the French and Indian Wars (1758–67), leaving a record of his very dramatic activities in his *Miscellanies in Prose and Verse* (1791). *Quashy; or, The Coal-Black Maid* (1796) is a light narrative poem, and other poems are collected in *Songs Political and Convivial* (1802).

MORRIS, WRIGHT (1910–   ), Nebraska-born author, has set much of his fiction in the Midwest although he attended Pomona College and moved to California in 1961. His numerous finely crafted novels present acute observations of characters, often in an oblique fashion, as they make relations or undergo cleavages with other people. Sometimes these concentrate on one situation diversely affecting the different people involved in it. His novels are *My Uncle Dudley* (1942); *The Man Who Was There* (1945); *The World in the Attic* (1949); *Man and Boy* (1951), a brief but pungent view of a search for a meaningful life, just as another book, *The Works of Love* (1952), treats another basic theme of Morris's, the quest for significant loving relationships; *The Deep Sleep* (1953); *The Huge Season* (1954), a longer book than usual in its revelation of the ethos of the 1920s; *The Field of Vision* (1956, National Book Award), presenting recollections of significant experiences evoked in a group of Americans as they view a bullfight in Mexico; *Love Among the Cannibals* (1957); *Ceremony in Lone Tree* (1960), portraying family members isolated from one another as they assemble in a Nebraska ghost town to celebrate the ninetieth birthday of one of them; *What a Way To Go* (1962) and *Cause for Wonder* (1963), more broadly comic and with a different setting—Europe—than his other novels; *One Day* (1965), depicting the reactions of diverse Californians to the assassination of President Kennedy; *In Orbit* (1967), concerning the aimless rebellion of a high-school dropout of the time; *Fire Sermon* (1971) and its sequel, *A Life* (1973), further insights into generational relations; *Here Is Einbaum* (1973); *The Fork River Space Project* (1977); and *Plains Song: For Female Voices* (1980), about three generations of lonely Midwestern women. Stories are collected in *Real Losses, Imaginary Gains* (1976) and *Collected Stories 1948–86* (1986). He has created special memoirs: *Will's Boy* (1981) and *Solo: An American Dreamer in Europe* (1983), the first on his youth, the second on his young manhood, continued in *A Cloak of Light: Writing My Life* (1985). Morris is a distinguished as well as a sensitive and sharp-eyed photographer who has created books in which prose and pictures reinforce one another: *The Inhabitants* (1946), *The Home Place* (1948), *God's Country and My People* (1968), *Love Affair* (1972), about Venice, and *Photographs and Words* (1982). *The Territory Ahead* (1958) is a critical study of American literature and the native tradition, further investigated in books of essays: *A Bill of Rites, a Bill of Wrongs, a Bill of Goods* (1968), *About Fiction* (1975), and *Earthly Delights, Unearthly Adornments* (1978).

MORRISON, THEODORE (1901–88), long the director of composition classes at Harvard (1931–51), whose own works include *The Serpent in the Cloud* (1931), *The Devious Way* (1944), *The Dream of Alcestis* (1950), and other volumes of poetry, and *The Stones of the House* (1953), *To Make a World* (1957), and *The Whole Creation* (1962), novels of ideas exploring the university world.

MORRISON, TONI (1931–), Ohio-born novelist, originally named Chloe Anthony Wofford, a graduate of Howard University, writes about the problems of black women in the North, like herself. Her novels include *The Bluest Eye,* (1970), about a young black woman who moves from the old South with the belief that if only she had blue eyes she would be well accepted; *Sula* (1973); *Song of Solomon* (1977); *Tar Baby* (1981); and *Beloved* (1987), about a black woman after the Civil War recalling her need and thus her action of killing her baby, Beloved, but now pleasantly

greeted by a young woman of that name, aged about 20, some years after the war. It was awarded a Pulitzer Prize. *Jazz* (1992), set in Harlem of the 1920s, details the experiences, often bitter, of a couple, Joe and Violet. *Playing in the Dark: Whiteness and the Literary Imagination* (1992) collects the William E. Massey Sr. Lectures, at Harvard, in the History of American Civilization. Morrison won the Nobel Prize in 1993, the first African-American writer to be so honored.

MORROW, HONORÉ WILLSIE (1880–1940), born in Iowa, before making her home in New York lived for a time in Arizona. The West was the background of her early novels, mainly concerned with pleas for desert and forest reclamation and a return to the faith of the pioneers: *The Heart of the Desert* (1913), *Still Jim* (1915), *Lydia of the Pines* (1917), *The Forbidden Trail* (1919), *The Enchanted Canyon* (1921), *Judith of the Godless Valley* (1922), *The Exile of the Lariat* (1923), and *The Devonshers* (1924). From 1914 to 1919 she edited *The Delineator.* ◆ Her later books include *We Must March* (1925), dealing with Marcus Whitman and his wife, pioneers of the Northwest; *Forever Free* (1927), *With Malice Toward None* (1928), and *The Last Full Measure* (1930), a trilogy dealing with Lincoln; *The Father of Little Women* (1927), a study of Alcott; *Mary Todd Lincoln* (1928); *The Splendor of God* (1929), a novel concerned with Adoniram Judson; *Tiger! Tiger!* (1930), about John B. Gough, a temperance lecturer; *Black Daniel* (1931), the story of Daniel Webster; and *Demon Daughter* (1939), "the confession of a modern girl and her mother."

MORSE, JEDIDIAH (1761–1826), orthodox Congregational clergyman of Connecticut, founded *The Panoplist* (1805), a periodical to combat the growing Unitarianism. He was interested in missionary work among the Indians, his visits to various tribes resulting in the important *Report to the Secretary of War . . . on Indian Affairs* (1822). He was conservative in politics as in religion, and to oppose the influence of French republicanism founded a Federalist periodical, *The Mercury and New England Palladium* (1801). His *Geography Made Easy* (1784) was the first geography published in the U.S., and, along with his later works in this field, won him the title "father of American geography." With Elijah Parish he wrote *A Compendious History of New England* (1804), which brought accusations of plagiarism from Hannah Adams. He was also the author of *Annals of the American Revolution* (1824). He was the father of Samuel F.B. Morse.

MORSE, SAMUEL F.B. (1791–1872), inventor, artist, memoirist. Morse, born in Massachusetts, was educated at Yale and then studied painting in England. In the first part of his career he was a successful portrait artist, and founder in 1825 of the National Academy of Design. He then turned a new direction and spent 12 years perfecting his telegraph and devising the new code for it. He demonstrated the device to Congress in 1844. His letters and journals, edited by E.L. Morse, were published in 1914.

Mortal Antipathy, A, novel by Holmes,♦ published in 1885.

Maurice Kirkwood, son of a wealthy American family, is educated in Europe, and grows to manhood normal except in one respect. He suffers from "a mortal antipathy" to beautiful young women, the result of an experience during his infancy, when his young cousin Laura accidentally dropped him into a thornbush. The shock to his nervous system had a permanent effect and he has always associated young women with pain and terror. Once in Italy, however, a gypsy fortune-teller told him: "Fair lady cast a spell on thee—Fair lady's hand shall set thee free." As a young man he returns to America, where he lives in a small New England village as a recluse. During an attack of typhoid, he is tended by Dr. Butts, who learns his story. While he is still ill, Kirkwood's house is burned, and he is saved only by the strength and daring of Euthymia Tower, an athletic enthusiast and student at the local young ladies' school. Kirkwood's antipathy is cured by this new shock, after which he is able to associate beautiful womanhood with salvation. Euthymia helps nurse him to health, and they marry. Kirkwood anxiously watches for evidence of his phobia in their son, but his cousin Laura visits them and the child fearlessly cuddles in her arms.

MORTON, CHARLES (*c.* 1627–98), English Puritan clergyman and founder of a school for Nonconformists, whose pupils included the English author Daniel Defoe. Opposition to his school caused him to emigrate to Massachusetts in 1686, where after failing to achieve his desire of becoming president of Harvard he founded a school that might have become a rival college, had not Harvard authorities managed to end it, although they compensated by electing him fellow (1692) and vice-president (1697) of Harvard. He was an intellectual leader of the community, a prominent minister, and the author of textbooks on science and logic, and several volumes on religious subjects.

MORTON, GEORGE (1585–1624), converted to Puritanism by William Brewster, became closely associated with the leaders of the movement in England and Holland. When others went to America, he returned to England to become the chief agent of the Pilgrims. At this time he used the name Mourt, and *Mourt's Relation*♦ is the title generally given to *A Relation . . . of the . . . Plantation Setled at Plimoth . . .*♦ (1622). Morton came to New England in 1623, where his son Nathaniel Morton was later prominent.

MORTON, NATHANIEL (1613–86), emigrated to the Plymouth Colony (1623) with his father, George Morton, after whose death he lived with his uncle, William Bradford, whom he served as clerk and amanuensis. He became secretary of the colony and keeper of its records (1647–85), held a similar position in the Congregational Church, and was prominent in colonial affairs. His book *New Englands Memorial* (1669), a history of New England from its beginnings to the date of publication, was, he admitted, based on the journal of Edward Winslow and his uncle's papers; it was considered extremely important until 1855, when the lost manuscript of Bradford's *History of Plimmoth Plantation* was discovered, and it was found that Morton had transcribed large parts of it almost verbatim. Until that date, however, Morton's work had been the basis of histories by William Hubbard, Thomas Prince, and Cotton Mather. An extended version was written in 1680 and published in 1855, but again was drawn largely from Bradford's papers.

MORTON, SARAH WENTWORTH (1759–1846), Boston writer, long supposed to be the author of *The Power of Sympathy* (1789), which is now attributed to William Hill Brown.♦ This, the first novel written in America, dealt with a contemporary scandal of incest and suicide in the Morton family, and its anonymity gave rise to the mistaken theory of authorship. Under the pseudonym "Philenia, a Lady of Boston," Mrs. Morton wrote *Quâbi; or, The Virtues of Nature* (1790), an Indian tale in four cantos, celebrating the "noble savage"; *Beacon Hill: A Local Poem, Historic and Descriptive* (1797), an unfinished epic in heroic couplets, influenced by Milton and Gray; and "The African Chief," quoted in Whittier's *Snow-Bound.* Part of *Beacon Hill* appeared separately as *The Virtues of Society* (1799), telling of a wounded English major and his wife during the Revolution. In 1823, under her real name, appeared *My Mind and Its Thoughts,* fragments of prose and poetry.

MORTON, THOMAS (1590?–1647), British trader and adventurer, probably originally a lawyer, first visited New England in 1622 or 1624, and returned in 1625 as a member of the party of Captain Wollaston, to settle on the site of the present Quincy, Mass. When Wollaston left for Virginia at the end of the winter, Morton remained as head of the settlement, which he renamed Ma-re-Mount, whence it was called Merry Mount.♦ He was soon in the bad graces of the nearby Plymouth Colony, because he was an Anglican given to what the Pilgrims considered licentious practices, and because he hampered the Plymouth trading and violated the frontier code by trading gunpowder and liquor to the Indians for furs. In 1628 a band under Myles Standish attacked Morton's colony in a comic-opera skirmish, captured the leader, and sent him under arrest to England, on charges of trading arms to the Indians and harboring runaway servants. He returned in 1629, to find most of his colony scattered. In 1630 he was taken into custody, sentenced to have his goods confiscated, his house burned, and himself again returned to England. There he was released from jail through the aid of Gorges, who used him in an attempt to void the charter of the Massachusetts Bay Company. In 1637 his *New English Canaan*♦ was published. He returned to Massachusetts (1643), was ordered to leave, and went to Maine and Rhode Island. When he once again ventured into the colony, he was imprisoned for a year on slight pretext. Released, he made his way to Maine, where he died two years later. The Plymouth view of him and his group appears in Bradford's *History of Plimmoth Plantation* and in Winthrop's *Journal*.

MOSEL, TAD (GEORGE AULT MOSEL, JR.) (1922–), after graduation from Amherst (1947), study at the Yale Drama School, and an M.A. from Columbia began playwriting for television and in 1960 dramatized for the stage James Agee's *A Death in the Family*♦ under the title *All the Way Home*, a work for which he won a Pulitzer Prize. In a collaboration he wrote *Leading Lady* (1978), a life and study of the actress Katharine Cornell.

MOSES, MONTROSE J[ONAS] (1878–1934), editor and dramatic critic whose works include *The Literature of the South* (1909), *The American Dramatist* (1911), and an edition of the plays of Clyde Fitch (4 vols., 1915), whose biography he wrote (1924).

MOSHER, THOMAS BIRD (1852–1923), Maine publisher, whose Mosher Books, a series begun in 1891, were attractively printed, cheap editions of great works of literature little known in the U.S. *The Bibelot* (1895–1915) was a monthly reprint of prose and poetry from obscure but significant works, which both in selection and in printing was marked by his usual good taste.

MOSS, HOWARD (1922–87), New York City poet and poetry editor of *The New Yorker* (1948–87), whose graceful lyrics have been collected in *The Wound and the Weather* (1946), *The Toy Fair* (1954), *A Swimmer in the Air* (1957), *A Winter Come, A Summer Gone* (1960), *Finding Them Lost* (1965), *Second Nature* (1968), *Selected Poems* (1971, National Book Award), *Buried City* (1975), *A Swim Off the Rocks* (1976), *Notes from the Castle* (1979), and *New Selected Poems* (1985). He also wrote *The Magic Lantern of Marcel Proust* (1962); *Writing Against Time* (1969): *Instant Lives* (1974), brief biographical sketches of authors, written in parodies of their own styles; *Whatever Is Moving* (1981), essays and reviews; and *Minor Monuments: Selected Essays* (1986). *The Folding Green* (1958), *The Oedipus Mah-Jongg Scandal* (1968), and *The*

Palace at 4 A.M. (1972) are plays that have been produced.

Mosses from an Old Manse, tales and sketches written by Hawthorne♦ during his residence (1842–46) at the Old Manse in Concord. They were published in two volumes (1846), with an introductory essay, "The Old Manse," followed by 25 short stories and historical sketches. Among them are historical pieces, like "Roger Malvin's Burial"♦: satirical allegories, like "The Celestial Railroad"♦; and allegorical tales of the supernatural, like "Young Goodman Brown,"♦ "Rappaccini's Daughter,"♦ "The Birthmark,"♦ and "The Artist of the Beautiful."♦

Mother Carey's Chickens, story for children by Kate Wiggin.♦

Mother Goose, see *Songs for the Nursery.*

Mother Lode, name applied to the gold-mining region of northern and central California, specifically to a belt running northeast by southwest from Mariposa, near Yosemite, to Georgetown, a distance of *c.*120 miles. Gold was first mined there in 1848, but the great period began in 1849. In the first 25 years through 1874 production amounted to approximately $200,000,000. Literary associations of the region derive primarily from Bret Harte, who wrote a great number of stories about the gold rush days that preceded his own acquaintance with the area. Mark Twain also derived from the area the folk tale of "The Celebrated Jumping Frog of Calaveras County," and wrote about the region in *Roughing It*. Other writers about the Forty-niners and their followers include Alonzo Delano, "Dame Shirley," and Bayard Taylor.

Mother's Recompense, The, novel by Edith Wharton,♦ published in 1925.

Kate Clephane, after aimless, unattached years as an expatriate in Europe, returns to New York to live with her daughter Anne, whom she has not seen since deserting her husband and infant child long before. Kate has always been governed by her selfish impulses, and she is glad to be taken in charge by Anne's strong will. She finds New York society more tolerant than it had been in her youth, and since no one remembers the history of her indiscretions she is happy for a time. Among Anne's friends, however, is Chris Fenno, an artist and major in the World War. Although ten years younger than Kate, he has lived with her in Europe, and she regards him as the great love of her life. When Anne reveals that she and Chris are to be married, Kate makes him promise to give up Anne, whom he had not known was her daughter. In the ensuing conflict between mother and daughter, Anne finds that it was her mother who drove Chris away, and demands to know the reason. Kate cannot bring herself to confess that Chris has been her own lover, and Anne's superior will dominates. Chris and Anne are married, but Kate, who has announced she will marry Fred Landers, an old friend and Anne's guardian, cannot face this fate, and, once more acting on impulse, returns to the Riviera to forget her sorrows in this familiar Nirvana.

MOTLEY, JOHN LOTHROP (1814–77), descendant of an old and prominent Boston family, after graduation from Harvard (1831) studied for two years in Germany, toured the Continent, returned to Boston and married the sister of Park Benjamin, and began to study law, though primarily interested in literature. He wrote two novels, *Morton's Hope* (1839), a semi-autobiographical account of an American at a German university, and *Merry Mount* (1849), a romantic novel concerning the colony of Thomas Morton. After a year as secretary of legation at St. Petersburg and another in Massachusetts politics, he turned in 1847 to his lifelong work of a historical study of the Netherlands. The subject may have been chosen because he liked the analogy between the United Provinces and the United States, and because it gave him an opportunity to study the triumph of Protestantism in northern Europe and show how it brought freedom where previously there was despotism. He began his work in the U.S., then went to Germany and Holland for further material. The book appeared as *The Rise of the Dutch Republic* (3 vols., 1856) after ten years of preparation. In a picturesque, enthusiastic, and dramatic manner, he presented the political and religious history of the country, although he neglected economic and social matters. He arranged his whole canvas around the two subjects of Protestantism and absolutism, making William of Orange the Protestant hero and Philip II the dark-dyed autocratic, Catholic scoundrel. His continued research bore fruit in the *History of the United Netherlands* (4 vols., 1860, 1867), which deals with the period from William's death to the truce of 1609. The period from 1609 to the Thirty Years' War was treated in *The Life and Death of John of Barneveld* (2 vols., 1874). A fourth section dealing with the Thirty Years' War and bringing the history down to 1648 was planned but never completed. Although the series was unfinished, his books have a great sweep and a unified pattern, which possess as a core the study of the Protestant movement in developing civilization and liberty, which Motley thought had determined the course of European and American history for the modern ages. The long interval between the appearance of the first two volumes and the second two of the *History of the United Netherlands* was partly owing to his duties as minister to Austria (1861–67), in which he proved himself an able diplomat, but was recalled by President Johnson as the result of a political struggle. In 1869–70 he was minister to Great Britain, from which post he was recalled

because of disagreement concerning the Alabama claims.

MOTLEY, WILLARD (1912–65), author of naturalistic novels drawing upon his life in Chicago's slums but little upon his heritage as a black: *Knock on Any Door* (1947), about a boy growing from a juvenile delinquent to a murderer; *We Fished All Night* (1951); and *Let No Man Write My Epitaph* (1958), telling of the search for a decent life by the son of the protagonist of his first novel. *Let Noon Be Fair* (1966) depicts tourist trade corrupting a town in Mexico, the country in which Motley lived from 1951 on. His stories appear in *Soon, One Morning* (1963), and his *Diaries* was published in 1979.

Motley Assembly, The, see *Warren, Mercy Otis.*

Motor Boys, THE, series of books for boys by Edward Stratemeyer. ♦

MOTT, FRANK LUTHER (1886–1964), professor and later dean of the School of Journalism at Missouri (1925–51). His books include *Six Prophets out of the Middle West* (1917); *The Literature of Pioneer Life in Iowa* (1923); *A History of American Magazines* (3 vols., 1930–38, Pulitzer Prize; vol. IV, 1957; vol. V, 1968); *American Journalism* (1941); *Jefferson and the Press* (1943); *Golden Multitudes* (1947), on American best sellers; and *The News in America* (1952).

MOULTON, [ELLEN] LOUISE CHANDLER (1835–1908), Connecticut author of juvenile stories, travel books, short biographies, and such fiction as *Juno Clifford* (1855), a novel, and *This, That, and the Other* (1854), sketches. She was best known for her melancholy, subjective poetry, collected in *Poems and Sonnets* (1909).

Mountaineering in the Sierra Nevada, sketches of explorations and experiences in the California mountains, by Clarence King, ♦ published in 1872 and revised from the author's notes in 1902. King had been employed in the U.S. Geological Survey since 1863, and the book gives an accurate account of the geology and geography of the Sierra. Its chief importance, however, is based on its vivid narratives of mountain-climbing adventures in Yosemite Park and on Mount Tyndall, Mount Shasta, and Mount Whitney, and of meetings with picturesque and typical characters, such as the chapters on "The Newtys of Pike County," concerning a family of emigrants from Pike County; "Cut-Off Copples's," describing a frontier artist and his rustic romance; "The People," explaining the behavior of Californians by a theory of climatic influence; and "Kaweah's Run," an account of an escape from desperadoes.

Mountains of California, The, descriptive work of John Muir, ♦ published in 1894 and revised in

1911. Describing the geological history and the varieties of flora and fauna of the region, the study is the result of many summers spent by the author in both the Sierra Nevada and the Coast Range and, besides its scientific authority, presents an enthusiastic appreciation of the beauties of the California wilderness. The text, accompanied by Muir's own drawings, describes the glacial actions that created such landmarks as the Yosemite Valley, tells of the lakes, forests, and animals, including wild sheep and domesticated bees, and recounts anecdotes of the author's mountaineering adventures. Famous chapters deal with "The Water-Ouzel," "A Wind-Storm in the Forests," "Sierra Thunder-Storms," "The River Floods," and "The Douglas Squirrel."

Mourning Becomes Electra, dramatic trilogy by O'Neill,♦ produced and published in 1931. Based on the ancient Greek legend, its three parts are: (I) *Homecoming;* (II) *The Hunted;* (III) *The Haunted.*

I. At the close of the Civil War, Brigadier-General Ezra Mannon, descendant of a Puritan family, returns to his New England home, where he is awaited by his wife Christine and daughter Lavinia. During his absence and that of her adored soldier son Orin, Christine has had a liaison with the clipper captain Adam Brant, son of Ezra's brother and a family servant, who intended to avenge his mother's disgrace, but instead fell in love with the sensual Christine. Mother and daughter hate each other, for Lavinia is the victim of an inner conflict between her Mannon heritage and the elements of her nature inherited from Christine. Herself in love with Brant, she suspects her mother's relations with him and forces from him the truth. Peter Niles, a childhood friend, loves Lavinia, but she tells him that she hates love and will never marry. When Ezra comes home, it is revealed that he hates his son Orin for possessing Christine's love, which he himself never attained. Pretending to give him medicine, Christine poisons her husband from a box which Brant supplied her, and which Lavinia discovers.

II. Orin returns, to find his father dead and his mother distracted and changed. He resumes an old affair with Hazel, Peter's sister, but Lavinia persuades him to join her revenge plot. They follow Christine to a rendezvous on Brant's ship, and, after she leaves, Orin kills Brant. When Christine learns of this, she commits suicide.

III. Lavinia and Orin go on a long voyage that takes them to the South Sea islands. By the time they return, Orin, harried by guilt and remorse, has grown to resemble his father, while Lavinia, freed of the puritan repressions, has the beauty and amorality of her mother. She wants to marry Peter and now encourages Orin's affair with Hazel, but Orin, preoccupied with writing a confession, breaks with his fiancée, makes an incestuous proposal to Lavinia, and shoots himself. Lavinia

makes love to Peter, but he leaves her, repelled by her eagerness. She concludes, "Love isn't permitted to me. The dead are too strong!," and enters the shuttered house, to spend the rest of her life alone with the memory of the Mannon dead.

MOURNING DOVE (1888–1936), storyteller. Her Native American name was Hum-Ishu-Ma, and she is thought to be the first Native American novelist, publishing late in life *Cogewea the Half-Blood: A Depiction of the Great Montana Cattle Range* (1927). She also recorded Okanagan songs and stories.

Mourt's Relation, journal of the voyage of the *Mayflower,* record of its Compact, and description of the earliest days of Plymouth Colony. This anonymous document, published in England (1622) as *A Relation or Journall of the Beginning and Proceedings of the English Plantation Setled at Plimoth in New England,* has received its usual name from the signature "G. Mourt," attributed to George Morton,♦ who at that time used the name Mourt. It may be the work of Edward Winslow and William Bradford, with Morton merely acting as publisher, or a compilation by Morton of their narratives and information from other colonists. This first account of the Plymouth settlement is a vivid piece of prose, but the fact that it consists of extemporaneous jottings has caused it to be overshadowed by subsequent works.

Moveable Feast, A, memoir by Hemingway♦ of his life in Paris (1921–26), published in 1964. In brief sketches the work summons up the sense of what Paris meant to him as a writer beginning a career and to other expatriate Americans. It tells how Gertrude Stein came to employ the term "lost generation" and of his friendship and falling out with her, of Pound, Fitzgerald, and other associates.

MOWATT, ANNA CORA (1819–70), pursued a literary career in New York as a hack writer of widely varied material, until in 1845 her farcical social comedy *Fashion*♦ made her a respected author. This play was followed by a romantic prose and verse drama of the reign of Louis XV, *Armand, the Child of the People* (1847). In 1845 she went on the stage, and achieved great success, which she discussed in her *Autobiography of an Actress* (1854), and which furnished material for her romantic narratives of stage life, *Mimic Life* (1856) and *Twin Roses* (1857). After 1861, she lived abroad, where she wrote romantic novels and historical sketches. Her earlier novels of New York society include *The Fortune Hunter* (1844) and *Evelyn; or, A Heart Unmasked* (1845).

Muckraking movement received its name from Theodore Roosevelt (1906) in his attack upon allegedly biased and sweeping charges of corruption in politics and business. The term originally alluded to a character in *Pilgrim's Progress,* who was so intent upon raking up muck that he could not see a celestial crown held over him. The muckraking movement in the U.S. began in 1902 and in four years had spread throughout the nation. It reached another climax in 1911, but ended as a movement with America's entry into World War I. *The Arena,* a dignified journal of protest, was the precursor of many popular magazines that became the medium for the exposure of unscrupulous methods and motives in private business and in city, state, and national government. *Everybody's, McClure's, The Independent, Collier's,* and *Cosmopolitan* were the leading periodicals devoted to the movement, and among their principal authors were Ida Tarbell ("History of the Standard Oil Company"), Lincoln Steffens ("The Struggle for Self-Government"), T. W. Lawson ("Frenzied Finance"), R. S. Baker, S. S. McClure, Mark Sullivan, and Samuel Hopkins Adams. A few newspapers, particularly the New York *World* and Kansas City *Star,* aided materially in the campaign, and such books as Sinclair's *The Jungle* and the novels of D. G. Phillips carried the movement into fiction. An account of its development is given in the *Autobiography* of Steffens.

Mudjekeewis, character in *Hiawatha.* ◆

MUIR, JOHN (1838–1914), naturalist and explorer, was born in Scotland, brought to the U.S. (1849), and educated in chemistry, geology, and botany at the University of Wisconsin. Inspired to further study of these subjects, he made extended journeys throughout the U.S., often on foot. The journal of his trip (1867) from Indiana to the Gulf of Mexico was edited as *A Thousand-Mile Walk to the Gulf* (1916). In 1868 California became his home, and in the following years he studied the glacial formations of the West and the forests of the region, becoming a leader in the forest-conservation movement through his impassioned writings. His books include *The Story of My Boyhood and Youth* (1913); *The Mountains of California◆* (1894); *Our National Parks* (1901); *Stickeen* (1909), a sentimental short story about a dog; *My First Summer in the Sierra* (1911); *The Yosemite* (1912); *Travels in Alaska* (1915); and *Steep Trails* (1918).

MULFORD, CLARENCE E[DWARD] (1883–1956), author of popular romantic novels about the Western cowboy, ◆ which include *Bar-20* (1907), *Hopalong Cassidy* (1910), *Hopalong Cassidy Returns* (1924), and *Bar-20 Rides Again* (1926). They have been adapted for motion pictures and television programs.

MULFORD, PRENTICE (1834–91), California humorist and journalist, whose newspaper writings earned him a local reputation. *Prentice Mul-*

ford's Story (1889) is an account of his life up to 1872, when he left California, and *The Swamp Angel* (1888) is a description of his Thoreau-like retreat to the woods of New Jersey in the 1880s. His attitude of mind changed during this period, and he turned to writing theosophic essays.

MUMFORD, LEWIS (1895–1990), born in New York, after being educated at City College, Columbia University, and New York University, without receiving a degree, became a critic for magazines in London and New York. His first of more than 30 books was *The Story of Utopias* (1922), followed by *Sticks and Stones* (1924), which interpreted American life and thought in terms of its architecture. *The Golden Day* (1926) analyzed it in relation to its literature, particularly that of the romantic period. *Herman Melville* (1929) is a critical biography, primarily psychological. *The Brown Decades* (1931) is a study of the arts in the U.S. from the close of the Civil War to 1895, seeing that period's development in artistic fields as comparable with the earlier "Golden Day" in literature. In a series of four volumes, *Technics and Civilization* (1934), *The Culture of Cities* (1938), *The Condition of Man* (1944), and *The Conduct of Life* (1951), he analyzes the physical and social composition of cities in the Western world since the 10th century, and pleads for a reconstruction of the 20th-century "megalopolis" through regional planning and communal ownership of land. *Faith for Living* (1940) is a plea for moral regeneration based on renewal of family ties, relation to the soil, and discipline. *The South in Architecture* (1941) emphasizes the contributions of Jefferson and H.H. Richardson. *City Development: Studies in Disintegration and Renewal* (1945) collects essays; *Values for Survival* (1946) includes letters on politics and education written after World War II to German friends; *In the Name of Sanity* (1954) is a plea for decent actions to meet contemporary scientific and social issues. *The Transformations of Man* (1956) is an interpretive study of human history and of degradations of human values. Later works include *The City in History* (1961) and *The Highway and the City* (1963); *The Myth of the Machine* (2 vols., 1967, 1970), *The Urban Prospect* (1968), and *Interpretations and Forecasts* (1973), collections; and the autobiographical *Findings and Keepings* (1975), *My Works and Days* (1978), and *Sketches from Life* (1982).

MUNFORD, ROBERT (1730?–84), Virginia planter, member of the House of Burgesses, and major in the Revolution. His writings were published in the posthumous *A Collection of Plays and Poems* (1798) made by his son William Munford. In addition to his light poems and his translation of Ovid's *Metamorphoses* (Book One), the work contains his plays, *The Candidates,* probably written in 1770 and unproduced, a satire on country elections that introduces perhaps the first black in

American drama, and *The Patriots,* ♦ also unproduced but printed in 1776.

MUNFORD, WILLIAM (1775–1825), son of Robert Munford♦ and collector of his works, was himself the author of poems and compositions in *Prose on Several Occasions* (1798) and the first American translator of the *Iliad,* a work posthumously published in 1846.

MUNROE, KIRK (1850–1930), author of books for children. *The Flamingo Feather* (1887), inspired by a residence among the Seminole Indians of Florida, is concerned with 16th-century René de Veaux, a companion of Laudonnière, who became a member of an Indian tribe allied with the French. His other books deal with adventures in remote regions of the U.S. or with historical events ranging from Pontiac's Rebellion to the Spanish-American War.

Munsey's (1889–1929), New York weekly magazine founded by Frank A. Munsey as a popular journal "with pictures and art and Good Cheer and human interest throughout." In 1891 it became a monthly, patterned on *McClure's* and *Cosmopolitan.* Although it featured articles of popular interest, in addition to fiction, the magazine never entered into the muckraking movement with the fervor of its competitors. Its policy continued with little change until it was combined with the popular fiction magazine *All-Story.*

MÜNSTERBERG, HUGO (1863–1916), born in Danzig, was educated in Germany, where he was a professor of philosophy and psychology until he came to the U.S. to teach psychology at Harvard (1892–95, 1897–1916). There he distinguished himself in the fields of applied psychology and philosophy, and wrote such books as *The Principles of Art Education* (1905); *The Eternal Values* (1909), an idealistic view of philosophy, morality, and aesthetics; and *American Traits from the Point of View of a German* (1901).

MURAT, ACHILLE (1801–47), son of Joachim Murat, king of Naples (1808–15), and Caroline, a sister of Napoleon I, emigrated to the U.S. in 1823, where he settled in Florida and married an American woman. Although he spent a short while on the Continent, attempting to advance the Bonapartist cause, he lived most of the latter part of his life in the U.S. His works include *Lettres sur les États-Unis* (1830), a republican manifesto to Europe; *Esquisse morale et politique des États-Unis* (1832), a philosophic account of American society (English translations 1833, 1849); and *Exposition des principes du gouvernement républican, tel qu'il a été perfectionné en Amérique* (1833).

Murder in the Cathedral, verse drama by T.S. Eliot,♦ produced and published in 1935.

In A.D. 1170, Archbishop Thomas Becket returns to Canterbury from his seven-year exile in France. A women's chorus represents the helpless attitude of the common people toward the schism between church and state, while the ecclesiastical party is represented by Becket's priests, and the royal party by the officers of Henry II. The archbishop, having established relations with the Pope and the king of France, is determined to bring the argument to a crisis, even though he realizes that his life is at stake. Four Tempters show the inner conflict involved in his decision: his youthful love of pleasure, his later ambition for power, the demands of the feudal barons, and the desire for martyrdom. Rejecting all four, he is certain that he must give his life "to the Law of God above the Law of Man," and on Christmas morning delivers a sermon defending this position. Four days later the king's knights arrive, insolent and self-assured, to murder him by royal command, and he refuses to attempt escape. After they stab him to death, the knights address the audience with a pompous, foolish defense of their deed. They withdraw, leaving the stage to the priests, who thank God for having "given us another Saint in Canterbury," and the chorus, which supplicates divine mercy.

Murders in the Rue Morgue, The, story by Poe,♦ published in 1841 and collected in the *Prose Tales of Edgar A. Poe* (1843). It is his first tale of ratiocination and in it he is considered to have created the genre of the detective story.♦

The narrator lives in Paris with his friend C. Auguste Dupin, an eccentric genius of extraordinary analytic powers. They read an account of the murders of a Mme L'Espanaye and her daughter Camille in their fourth-story apartment in the Rue Morgue. The police are puzzled by the crime, for its brutal manner indicates that the murderer possessed superhuman strength and agility; his voice, overheard by neighbors, was grotesque and unintelligible; and they can discover no motive. Dupin undertakes to solve the mystery as an exercise in ratiocination. After examining the evidence and visiting the scene of the murders to find new clues, he deduces the fact that the criminal is an ape. An advertisement brings to Dupin's apartment a sailor who confesses that an orangutan, which he brought to Paris to sell, escaped and committed the murders. The police release a former suspect, and the ape is recaptured and sold to the Jardin des Plantes.

MURDOCH, FRANK HITCHCOCK (1843–72), actor and playwright, none of whose plays has been published. They include *The Keepers of Lighthouse Cliff,* which supposedly influenced Herne's *Shore Acres; Only a Jew* (1873), a sentimental comedy; *Davy Crockett* (1872), a melodramatic backwoods story, written for Frank Mayo♦ and substantially revised by him as he acted in it; and *Bohemia, or The Lottery of Art* (1872), an anonymous satire on dramatic critics.

MUREL, John A., see *Murrell.*

MURFREE, Mary Noailles (1850–1922), born in Murfreesboro, Tenn. spent most of her life in her native state, which she described in her local-color fiction published under the pseudonym Charles Egbert Craddock. She published dialect short stories of life in the Cumberland Mountains in *Lippincott's* and the *Atlantic Monthly,* during the 1870s, and in 1884 issued her first collection, *In the Tennessee Mountains,* ♦ but it was not until the following year that the editor of the *Atlantic* and the public discovered that the author was a frail, crippled spinster whose pseudonym was derived from the name of the hero in a very early story. The rhythmical prose and general atmosphere of her tales, and the poetic descriptions of landscape, are romantic, although the careful reproduction of the native dialect and faithful descriptions of specific details give them a realistic appearance. The first volume of stories was followed by more than ten others, including *The Mystery of Witch-Face Mountain* (1895), *The Young Mountaineers* (1897), and *The Frontiersmen* (1904). In addition, Miss Murfree wrote a series of Southern historical novels, which include *Where the Battle Was Fought* (1884) and *The Storm Centre* (1905), Civil War tales; *The Story of Old Fort Loudon* (1899); and *A Spectre of Power* (1903) and *The Amulet* (1906), on the colonial period in the old Southwest, and the life of the Cherokee. Other novels include *Down the Ravine* (1885) and *The Prophet of the Great Smoky Mountains* (1885).

MURIETA, Joaquin, see *Murrieta.*

MURRAY, John (1741–1815), founder of Universalism ♦ in America, was born in England, and reared as a Calvinist and Wesleyan. He joined the congregation of Whitefield, but was excommunicated by him when he openly accepted Universalism. Emigrating to America (1770), he became an itinerant preacher of this doctrine in New Jersey, New York, and New England, although he was not ordained. He established a congregation in Gloucester, Mass. (1774), the next year was appointed chaplain of the Rhode Island regiments by Washington, and became pastor of a Universalist society in Boston (1793–1809). His *Letters and Sketches of Sermons* was published in three volumes (1812–13), and his autobiographical *Records* in 1816.

Judith Sargent [Stevens] Murray (1751–1820), his wife, wrote a series of essays, two mediocre plays, and the short prose pieces and poems collected in *The Gleaner* (3 vols., 1798). She added concluding chapters to his *Records.* She used the pseudonym Constantia.

MURRAY, Lindley (1745–1826), a Quaker minister and grammarian, emigrated from his na-

tive Pennsylvania to England (1784), where he spent the rest of his life. Although the author of many religious tracts and a number of schoolbooks, he is best known for his *English Grammar* (1795, revised 1818), which until about 1850 monopolized this field in England and the U.S. His *Memoirs* was published in 1826.

MURRELL, John A. (*fl.*1804–44), bandit leader and folk hero of the Old Southwest, whose gang supposedly numbered some 1000 members. His highway robberies took place in eight states, and the spoils included money, horses, and black slaves. His specialty was stealing a slave from his owner, selling him to another, and repeating this process until the black became so well known that Murrell was forced to murder him. The bandit was captured in 1834 and imprisoned for ten years. Virgil A. Stewart, his captor, temporarily masqueraded as a member of the gang, and in this fashion obtained the information contained in *A History of the Detection, Conviction, Life, and Designs of John A. Murel* (1835). Murrell's gang figures in Simms's novels *Richard Hurdis* and *Border Beagles.*

MURRIETA, Joaquin (*c.*1832–53), California bandit leader, probably emigrated from Mexico during the gold rush, and because of some real or imagined grievance swore vengeance against the Americans, whom for two years he and his gang indiscriminately murdered, robbed, and terrorized. He, or an individual supposed to be him, was killed in 1853. The legendry that transformed him from a border ruffian to a Robin Hood and gave various men's exploits to him alone began with *Life and Adventures of Joaquin Murieta* (1854) by John R. Ridge. ♦ Joaquin Miller got his first name as a result of writing a similar defense in his youth.

Muscogulges, see *Creek Indians.*

Music Master, The, play by Charles Klein. ♦

Mustang, see *Pacing Mustang.*

Mutation, sonnet by Bryant, ♦ published in 1824 and collected in his *Poems* (1832).

The poet observes that painful experiences pass swiftly, releasing the "young limbs" of joy in "the welcome morning with its rays of peace." "Weep not that the world changes," he concludes, for an unchanging world would be intolerable.

Mutiny on the Bounty, first novel in the trilogy about the 18th-century mutiny against Captain Bligh written by James N. Hall ♦ and Charles B. Nordhoff. ♦

MUYBRIDGE, Eadweard (1830–1904), English-born photographer who, as a youth, changed his name from Edward James Muggeridge. He emigrated at an early age to the U.S., where, under the auspices of Leland Stanford in California, he began photographic investigations in the field of animal locomotion, which were forerunners of motion pictures. His first book, *The Horse in Motion* (1878), was followed by *Animal Locomotion* (11 vols., 1887), which reproduced 100,000 photographs, and *The Human Figure in Motion* (1901).

My Antonia, novel by Willa Cather,♦ published in 1918.

Jim Burden and Antonia Shimerda arrive as children in pioneer Black Hawk, Neb., he from Virginia and she with her family from Bohemia. With his companion, Jake Marpole, and the frontiersman and hired man Otto Fuchs, Jim lives on his grandparents' prosperous farm; but the Shimerdas are tricked into buying a squalid, undeveloped tract, where the impractical, music-loving father attempts to create a farm, aided by his vulgar, nagging wife, their grown son Ambrosch, the adolescent Antonia, her young sister Yulka, and the idiot boy Marek. Although the Burdens aid him with food and supplies, Shimerda in homesick despair commits suicide, and Jim's grandfather employs Ambrosch and Antonia, who later has to work in the fields. After the Burdens move to town, Antonia becomes a maid in the household of their neighbors. Despite her trying experiences with various employers, including amorous old Wick Cutter, she remains quiet, sincere, and industrious. Jim, after attending the state university and Harvard, learns of Antonia's elopement with Larry Donovan, a railway conductor who deserts her and her child. She then returns in disgrace to work on her brother's farm. Twenty years later when Jim visits Nebraska, he finds her a stalwart, middle-aged farm wife, married to mild, friendly Anton Cuzak. They have many children, and it is Antonia's strength that maintains the family, but she still possesses the laughter and inner core of pioneer integrity which always distinguished her. "She was a rich mine of life, like the founders of early races."

"My country, 'tis of thee," first words of the hymn "America."♦

My Heart and My Flesh, novel by Elizabeth M. Roberts,♦ published in 1927.

Theodosia, member of an aristocratic Kentucky family, is reared by her proud old grandfather, Anthony Bell, who encourages her ambition to be a violinist. She is downcast by her teacher's criticism, but far greater unhappiness comes when she discovers her father's dissolute past and that she is the half-sister of the mulattoes Americy and Lethe. When her grandfather's death leaves her destitute and she does not marry, Theodosia seeks out her black relatives to share their hatred of their white oppressors. After a

long sickness and sharing a kind of nightmare existence with an aged aunt whose only companions are a pack of hounds, Theodosia recovers to become a schoolteacher, returns to her music, finds peace in her bucolic locale, and comes to love a simple, straightforward farmer.

My Heart's in the Highlands, play by William Saroyan.♦

My Kinsman, Major Molineux, tale by Hawthorne,♦ first published in *The Token* (1832) and collected in *The Snow-Image.* Robert Lowell adapted it as a one-act verse play in *The Old Glory* (1965).

Set in Boston during a period when the colonists were opposing the royal government, the story tells of an 18-year-old country boy, Robin, who comes to town to make his fortune and to seek the aid of his important kinsman, one Major Molineux. He is rebuffed by everyone of whom he inquires, and spends an unhappy "evening of ambiguity and weariness" in his quest. Finally he discovers the Major being hauled through town, tarred and feathered, as all the citizenry laugh at him, and as the contagion seizes Robin his "shout was the loudest there."

My Lady Pokahontas: A True Relation of Virginia, romance by J.E. Cooke,♦ published in 1885.

My Life Is Like the Summer Rose, popular poem by Richard Henry Wilde,♦ set to music by Lanier.

My Lost Youth, poem by Longfellow,♦ published in 1855 and collected in *The Courtship of Miles Standish* (1858). In nine-line stanzas, whose meter is reminiscent of ballad measure, the lyric recalls the author's youth in Portland, Me. Each stanza ends with the refrain of a Lapland song: "A boy's will is the wind's will, And the thoughts of youth are long, long thoughts." The title of Frost's collection *A Boy's Will* is derived from this passage.

My Mortal Enemy, novel by Willa Cather.♦

My Old Man, story in *In Our Time.*♦

My Sister Eileen, humorous biography by Ruth McKenney.♦

MYERS, PETER HAMILTON (1812–78), New York lawyer and author whose historical novels include *The First of the Knickerbockers* (1848), *The Young Patroon* (1849), and *The King of the Hurons* (1850).

Mysterious Stranger, The, story by Clemens,♦ posthumously published in 1916. It was edited from various manuscripts by A.B. Paine. A new edition (1969) based on a final manuscript and titled *No. 44, The Mysterious Stranger,* shows that Paine had silently deleted about one-quarter of Mark Twain's text, created a new character (the Astrologer), altered the names of other characters, and conflated three manuscript drafts to create his own version.

The Paine version is set in the medieval Austrian village of Eseldorf, where a mysterious stranger visits young Theodor Fischer and his friends Nikolaus and Seppi. He is discovered to be Satan, and shows his power by building a miniature castle that he peoples with clay creatures, destroying them almost as soon as he brings them to life. He then exerts his power on the villagers, and, when Father Peter is falsely accused of theft by the Astrologer and Father Adolf, he confounds the evil and makes the innocent crazy, since he says earthly happiness is restricted to the mad. Other "kindness" includes the drowning of Nikolaus, who would otherwise live as a cripple. His total indifference to mankind and its conceptions of good and evil shocks the boys' natural moral sense, yet Satan shows that from this moral sense came wars, tortures, and inequalities. Finally he departs, and Theodor realizes that this was a dream, as false as morality, and as illogical as a God who tortured men yet commanded them to worship Him.

The version first published in 1969 is also set in Eseldorf. To it in 1490, not long after the invention of movable type, comes a likable young printer's devil, called only No. 44, who is actually possessed of satanic powers that allow him to master the craft of printing in a few hours. Single-handedly he speedily produces a Bible and magically summons up phantasmagoric people to print innumerable copies. He enjoys playing tricks on the town's magician and on the cruel, hypocritical Father Adolf, while he also travels back and forth in space and time between 19th-century U.S. and medieval Europe. The story of his activities, both diabolical and whimsical, is told by his 17-year-old friend August Feldner, a curious person with a split personality. August's

doppelgänger or "Dream-Self," named Emil Schwarz, has powers like those of No. 44 and is caught up in similar adventures and activities. The fanciful tale compounded of burlesque and satire concludes with the revelation of No. 44 to August that "Life itself is only a vision, a dream . . . ," the creation of "a God . . . who mouths morals . . . and has none himself . . . who could make good children as easily as bad, yet preferred to make bad ones."

Mystery of Marie Rogêt, The, detective story by Poe,♦ published in 1842–43 as a sequel to "The Murders in the Rue Morgue"♦ and reprinted in *Tales* (1845). The principal details are based on the actual New York murder case of Mary Cecilia Rogers.

Marie Rogêt, a Parisian beauty of uncertain reputation, leaves her mother's home, saying she intends to spend the day with an aunt, but is not seen again. Four days later, her corpse is recovered from the Seine. The Prefect of Police offers a reward to C. Auguste Dupin, scholarly amateur detective, for a solution to the puzzle. One of the girl's admirers, St. Eustache, is proved innocent after his suicide, and by a process of ratiocination Dupin shows that another, Beauvais, cannot be guilty. The newspapers have hinted that the corpse may not be that of Marie, but Dupin refutes this possibility. He sets aside other suggestions, also by logical proof, and decides that the murder must have been committed by a secret lover, who would have thrown the body into the river from a boat, and then cast the boat adrift after reaching shore. Dupin's proposal that the boat be found and examined for clues is followed by the successful solution of the mystery.

Mystery story, general term applied to fiction whose objective is the solution of an enigma, but that is as various as the Gothic romance,♦ which is a tale of horror, and the detective story,♦ which is based on ratiocination.

N

NABOKOV, VLADIMIR (1899–1977), born in Russia of a patrician family, educated at Trinity College, Cambridge, came to the U.S. (1940) and was naturalized in 1945. He was a professor of Russian literature at Cornell (1948–59) until his own literary success allowed him to retire. His ingenious, witty, stylized, and erudite novels include *Laughter in the Dark* (1938), published in England as *Camera Obscura* (1936), after the original Russian title, about the moral deterioration of a respectable Berliner; *The Real Life of Sebastian Knight* (1941), in which the narrator, a young Russian in Paris, discovers the true nature of his half-brother, an English novelist, by writing his biography; *Bend Sinister* (1947), about a politically uncommitted professor in a totalitarian state who tries to maintain personal integrity; *Pnin* (1957), amusing sketches about the experiences of an exiled Russian professor of entomology at an upstate New York college; *Lolita*♦ (Paris, 1955; U.S., 1958), a farcical and satirical novel of the passion of a middle-aged, sophisticated European émigré for a 12-year-old American "nymphet," and their wanderings across the U.S.; *Invitation to a Beheading*♦ (Russia, 1938; U.S., 1959), a Kafkaesque story of a man sentenced to die for some unknown expression of individuality and his resultant discovery that he has a real soul; *Pale Fire*♦ (1962), a satirical fantasy called a novel, which is a witty, ironic, and complex *tour de force* concerning a poem about an exiled Balkan king in a New England college town and the involved critical commentary on the poem by the king himself; *The Gift* (Russia, 1937; U.S., 1963), a pseudo-autobiography about Russian expatriates in Berlin after World War I; *The Defense* (Germany, 1930; U.S., 1964), about a young Russian master of chess who treats life as another game; *The Eye* (1965), about a Russian émigré living in Berlin; *Despair* (1966), about a man who contrives his own murder; *King, Queen, Knave* (1968), his second novel, originally published in Germany (1928), also the setting for the story of a young man's affair with his married aunt; *Ada or Ardor* (1969), a witty parody whose involved plot, set in a fanciful land, deals with a man's lifelong love for his sister Ada; *Mary* (1970), the author's first novel (Germany, 1926), about a young Czarist officer exiled in Berlin and his first love affair; *Glory* (1971), the fifth (Paris, 1932) of his nine novels written in Russian, a comic portrait of a Russian émigré's wanderings; *Transparent Things* (1972), a novella about a rootless American's marriage and murder of his wife; and *Look at the Harlequins!* (1974), a novel about an author who very much resembles Nabokov himself. His stories have been gathered in several collections; his light, witty verse appears in *Poems* (1959) and *Poems and Problems* (1971), the latter including also problems in chess, and *The Waltz Invention* (1966) is a play. *Conclusive Evidence* (1951), revised as *Speak, Memory* (1966), gathers autobiographical sketches of life in Imperial Russia. *Strong Opinions* (1973) prints replies to journalists' questions about himself, literature, and public issues. He wrote a study of *Nikolai Gogol* (1944) and made a translation with commentary of *Eugene Onegin* (4 vols., 1964, revised 1977). The correspondence of Edmund Wilson and Nabokov, much of it about his translation of Pushkin, appeared in 1979. Other posthumous publications include *Lectures on Literature* (1980) and *Lectures on Russian Literature* (1981).

Naked and the Dead, The, novel by Norman Mailer,♦ published in 1948.

An American division led by General Cummings invades the Japanese-held island of Anopopei, securing a position in spite of heavy losses. The varied members of Sergeant Croft's reconnaissance platoon are characterized through flashbacks and through their violent language and behavior under the stress of jungle warfare. Despite being undermanned, they withstand a Japanese counterattack, but shoot prisoners and hunt drunkenly among corpses for souvenirs. Personal conflict develops between Cummings, an intellectual who believes that "the morality of the future is a power morality," and Lieutenant Hearn, who is unwilling to fit into the general's "fear ladder," while Private Valsen opposes Croft's brutal implementation of Cumming's military philosophy. For a combination of personal and strategic reasons, the platoon is sent on a dangerous patrol across a mountain range, and returns, decimated by casualties, to find the Japanese destroyed and the island taken independently of their efforts.

Naked Lunch, novel by William Burroughs,♦ published in Paris (1959) and in New York (1962). Based upon the author's notes during a period of deep addiction to drugs, the book's first-person narrator, William Lee, is presented as a "recording instrument" of a surrealistic collage of nightmare fantasies purposefully without any sequential plot. Instead, the spokesman's psychic states, his alienation, and his fight against authority are depicted.

Narragansett Indians, Algonquian tribe, now extinct, which formerly occupied Rhode Island and Long Island. They were induced by Roger Williams, whose study of the tribe is contained in his *Key into the Language of America* (1643), to assist the colonists in the Pequot War. During King Philip's War they were suspected of treachery, and in an engagement of 1675, known as the "Swamp Fight," the tribe was virtually annihilated. The Narragansett figure in Cooper's *The Wept of Wish-ton-Wish.*

Narrative of Arthur Gordon Pym, of Nantucket, The, novelette by Poe,♦ published in 1838. Like "The Journal of Julius Rodman," it is an account of exploration and adventure, heightened by fictional additions, but based on fact. It is extensively paraphrased from Benjamin Morell's *Narrative of Four Voyages to the South Seas and Pacific* (1832) and a manual of seamanship, and owes its origin to a "Report of the Committee on Naval Affairs" (1836), concerning the expedition proposed by J.N. Reynolds, with whom Poe was acquainted. In the novelette, the fictitious Pym recounts his experiences as a passenger on the *Grampus,* which sailed from Nantucket for the South Seas in June 1827. Mutiny, shipwreck, and "horrible sufferings" are followed by a rescue and further sensational adventures in the Antarctic Ocean and on Pacific islands.

NASBY, PETROLEUM V., pseudonym of D.R. Locke.♦

NASH, OGDEN (1902–71), New York author of light verse, which ranges from acidulous satire and irrepressible good humor to the mildly mad. Nash says that he is indebted to "The Sweet Singer of Michigan,"♦ having humorously employed the mannerisms of her bad verse: hyperdithyrambic meters, pseudo-poetic inversions, gangling asymmetrical lines, extremely pat or elaborately inexact rhymes, parenthetical dissertations, and unexpected puns. His collections include *Free Wheeling* (1931), *Hard Lines* (1931), *Happy Days* (1933), *The Primrose Path* (1935), *The Bad Parents' Garden of Verse* (1936), *I'm a Stranger Here Myself* (1938), *The Face Is Familiar* (1940), *Many Long Years Ago* (1945), *Versus* (1949), *Family Reunion* (1950), *Parents Keep Out* (1951), *The Private Dining Room* (1953), *You Can't Get There from Here* (1957), and *Everyone But Thee and Me* (1962). As a lyricist he collaborated with Kurt Weill and S.J. Perelman on the musical comedy *One Touch of Venus* (1943). *Loving Letters* (1990) gathered his correspondence with family.

NAST, THOMAS (1840–1902), political caricaturist and illustrator, born in Germany, was brought to the U.S. (1846) and commenced his career as an illustrator at 15. After sketching events of Garibaldi's campaign in Italy for French, English, and American papers, he joined the staff of *Harper's Weekly* (1862) to draw Civil War cartoons that attacked Northern defeatists, leading Lincoln to call him "our best recruiting sergeant." He reached the height of his success in the 1870s, with his biting caricatures of the corrupt Tweed Ring. Although his greatest work was completed by 1886, he helped determine public opinion for almost a quarter of a century through his keen, forceful satire. He was the creator of the symbolic Tammany tiger, Republican elephant, and Democratic donkey, and popularized the use of Shakespearean scenes for political cartoons.

Natchez, Les, romance by Chateaubriand,♦ included in the manuscript containing *Atala* and *René,* written 1797–1800 but lost and not published until 1826.

A poetic novel, concerning an older and more despairing René, who, following the massacre of the French colony of the Natchez (1727), is adopted by the Indians and weds one of them. His wife Celuta is torn between love and duty when she thinks he has betrayed the tribe. When the true traitor, Ondouré, is discovered, the tale ends in a catastrophe of violence, suicide, and murder.

NATHAN, GEORGE JEAN (1882–1958), born in Indiana, after graduation from Cornell (1904) began his career as a drama critic in New York. In 1908 he became associated with *The Smart Set,*♦ of which he was co-editor (1914–23) with H.L. Mencken, with whom he then founded *The American Mercury*♦ (1924), serving as an editor until 1930 and establishing himself as one of the literary arbiters of the period. With Mencken and W.H. Wright he wrote *Europe After 8:15* (1914), and with Mencken he was the author of such works as *Heliogabalus* (1920), a satirical play, and *The American Credo* (1920), "a contribution toward the interpretation of the national mind," which travesties common beliefs and attitudes. While Mencken was considered the great satirical realist of the era, Nathan formed his counterpart as a philosophical snob, cynic, and sophisticate, who adopted a pose of detachment, following the attitude of his master, Huneker, in holding to standards of art for art's sake. In *The World in Falseface* (1923) he said, "What interests me in life is the surface of life: life's music and color, its charm and ease, its humor and its loveliness. The great problems of the world—social, political, economic, and theological—do not concern me in the slightest." His many books on the contemporary theater, mainly reprinting essays and reviews, include *The Eternal Mystery* (1913), *Mr. George Jean Nathan Presents* (1917), *The Popular Theatre* (1918), *The Theatre, the Drama, the Girls* (1921), *The Critic and the Drama* (1922), *Materia Critica* (1924), *Art of the Night* (1928), *The Morning After the First Night* (1938), and *Encyclopaedia of the Theatre* (1940). Important for their early championing of O'Neill and other talents, these works vary from scathing attacks on sentimentalities to boundless enthusiasms, for Nathan claimed to write "with a pestiferous catholicity of taste that embraces *Medea* and the Follies, Eleanora Duse and Florence Mills." His other books include *The Autobiography of an Attitude* (1925), epigrammatic self-revelations; *The New American Credo* (1927); *Testament of a Critic* (1931); *The Intimate Notebooks of George Jean Nathan* (1932), presenting views of friends; *The Avon Flows* (1937), a comedy adapting parts of *Romeo and Juliet, The Taming of the Shrew,* and *Othello* to present the lives of a Romeo and Juliet who do not commit suicide; *The Bachelor Life* (1941), an apologia; *The Entertainment of a Nation* (1942); *Beware of Parents* (1943), a bachelor's advice to children; and an annual *Theatre Book of the Year* (1943ff.).

NATHAN, ROBERT [GRUNTAL] (1894–1985), born in New York, was educated in the U.S. and abroad and was the author of many short novels, noted for their delicate prose and satirical fantasy. These include *Peter Kindred* (1919), the story of a boy's experiences in preparatory school and at Harvard; *Autumn* (1921), a pastoral tale whose chief figure is a Vermont schoolmaster and philosopher; *The Puppet Master* (1923), a fantasy concerned with the puppet maker Papa Jonas and his animated dolls; *Jonah* (1925, published in England as *Son of Amittai*), a witty reconstruction of the Biblical story; *The Fiddler in Barley* (1926), the story of a country musician; *The Woodcutter's House* (1927), a sentimental fable of a mountain girl; *The Bishop's Wife* (1928), about an angel who poses as an archdeacon and falls in love with the bishop's wife; *There Is Another Heaven* (1929), the story of a converted Jew in a Calvinist heaven; *One More Spring* (1933), a parable of Christian charity; *Road of Ages* (1935), about an imagined pilgrimage of Jewish exiles into the Gobi Desert; *Journey of Tapiola* (1938), travel adventures of a Yorkshire terrier, a canary, and an old gray rat; *Winter in April* (1938), a realistic story of everyday affection; *Portrait of Jennie* (1940), an idyll of a painter inspired by an elfin child; *They Went On Together* (1941), about wartime evacuees; *Tapiola's Brave Regiment* (1941); *The Sea-Gull Cry* (1942), about refugee children on Cape Cod; *But Gently Day* (1943), in which a dead soldier returns to his family's Civil War past; *Mr. Whittle and the Morning Star* (1947), about a professor's mystical view of the world's ending; *Long After Summer* (1948); *The River Journey* (1949); *The Innocent Eve* (1951); *The Train in the Meadow* (1953); *Sir Henry* (1955), a parable about an aging, moonstruck knight; *Rancho of the Little Loves* (1956) and *So Love Returns* (1958), gentle fantasies; *The Color of Evening* (1960); *A Star in the Wind* (1962); *The Devil with Love* (1963), a fantasy about an archdemon coming from Hell to the U.S. in quest of a human heart; *The Fair* (1964), a whimsical tale of the time of King Arthur; *The Mallot Diaries*

(1965), an ironic view of two anthropology professors living with a Stone Age-culture tribe; *Stonecliff* (1967), the fanciful tale of a young writer interviewing an old novelist; and *Mia* (1970) and *The Elixir* (1971), romances related to travels through time. *Youth Grows Old* (1922), *A Cedar Box* (1929), *A Winter Tide* (1940), *Darkening Meadows* (1945), *The Green Leaf* (1950), and *Evening Song* (1973) collect poems, and *A Morning in Iowa* (1944) is a narrative poem. *Jezebel's Husband & the Sleeping Beauty* (1953) and *Juliet in Mantua* (1966) are plays.

NATION, CARRY (1846–1911), temperance agitator, after an unhappy youth and irregular schooling during her family's journeying from Kentucky to Texas and Missouri married the intemperate Reverend Gloyd. A second marriage (1877) gave her the name Nation, and following a short period of school teaching she became absorbed in emotional religious activity, convinced that she was divinely appointed to destroy the institution of the saloon. She began her crusade at Medicine Lodge, Kan. (1899), and continued with a spectacular destruction of property in saloons. Her favorite weapon was the hatchet, and she referred to her exploits as "hatchetings" or "hatchetations." Her temperance lectures took her through the U.S. and Europe, and in 1904 she published *The Use and Need of the Life of Carry A. Nation.* Frequently jailed and ridiculed, she gladly suffered martyrdom. Carleton Beals's *Cyclone Carry* (1962) is a lively life.

Nation, The (1865–), New York weekly journal founded "to discuss current affairs . . . to maintain true democratic principles; to work for the equality of 'the laboring class of the South'; . . . the elevation of the Negro; to fix public attention on the importance of public education; . . . criticize books and works of art soundly and impartially." Its first editor (1865–81) was E.L. Godkin; early contributors included C.E. Norton, Howells, the three Jameses, D.C. Gilman, W.C. Brownell, Fiske, Parkman, C.F. Adams, Sumner, and F.W. Taussig. Among the causes for which the magazine worked were civil service and tariff reforms, proportional representation in the legislature, and the ousting of corrupt politicians such as the Tweed Ring. *The Nation* was also rigorous in its criticism of literature and the arts. It was sold to the New York *Evening Post* (1881), of which Godkin became the editor. Under W.P. Garrison (1881–1906), it continued its original policies, although as a subsidiary of the *Post* it lost its prestige. Garrison and later editors, including P.E. More (1909–14), drew on the same distinguished contributors, although adding many new literary figures. In 1918 O.G. Villard became editor and severed the connection with the *Post.* He continued the magazine's liberal stand, opposing the ratification of the Versailles Treaty, sympathetically interpreting the new Russian state, and making the journal a distinguished commentary on international affairs. The literary editors whose views influenced liberal letters included the Van Dorens, John Macy, Ludwig Lewisohn, and J.W. Krutch, and James Agee reviewed films during the 1940s. Villard retired in 1933, selling the magazine in 1935, but it continued its campaign for social justice, although for a time under the editorship of Freda Kirchwey (1933–55) this characteristic was thought to be diminished. Carey McWilliams, who had been associated with the magazine since 1945, was editor, 1955–79. Under him and since his time it continues to be a feisty left-wing commentator on the national and international scene, as well as a review of books and the arts by writers who include E.L. Doctorow, Studs Terkel, and Kurt Vonnegut.

National Anti-Slavery Standard (1840–72), published from New York by the American Anti-Slavery Society, advocated complete and immediate abolition, education for blacks, and perpetuation of the Union. Among its contributors were Eliza Lee Follen, Wendell Phillips, and Lowell. In 1848–49 Lowell was an active editor, and he was associated with the magazine until 1852. His contributions, posthumously collected in separate volumes, include *The Biglow Papers*. After 1870 the unstable magazine several times changed its title, periods of publication, and crusades, which included women's rights and temperance.

National Book Awards, founded (1950) by the American Book Publishers Council, American Booksellers Association, and Book Manufacturers Institute, and after 1976 sponsored by the National Book Committee for the year's most distinguished works in the areas of Arts and Letters, Children's Literature, Contemporary Affairs, Fiction, History and Biography, and Poetry. Discontinued in 1979, they were replaced by The American Book Awards of the Association of American Booksellers (1980–85) with numerous categories for hardcover and paperback works, but many authors made strong objection to the criteria of selection. Since 1985 again called the National Book Awards, sponsored by the National Book Foundation, the awards are made in the areas of Fiction, Nonfiction, and Poetry. The sponsoring organizations have also awarded an annual National Medal for Literature. ♦

National Book Critics Circle, organization of 300 professional critics and editors, founded (1974) to select the "most distinguished" volumes of fiction, general nonfiction, poetry, and criticism of the preceding year. Each member nominates three books in each category, and the board of directors, which may add selections of its own, votes to elect the winners.

National Era (1847–60), antislavery journal, edited from Washington, D.C., by Gamaliel Bai-

ley. In addition to Abolitionist news, it was known for its literary contributions, which included Hawthorne's "The Great Stone Face," most of Whittier's writings during its years of publication, and the serialization of *Uncle Tom's Cabin* (1851–52).

National Gazette (1791–93), newspaper of the Democratic Republican party, edited at Philadelphia by Freneau, and financed by Jefferson to oppose Fenno's Federalist *Gazette of the United States*. It ceased publication when Jefferson resigned from the secretaryship of state. A contributing cause of its demise was the Philadelphia yellow-fever epidemic.

National Institute of Arts and Letters, see *American Academy of Arts and Letters.*

National Intelligencer and Washington Advertiser (1800–1870), triweekly newspaper (daily after 1813), founded at Washington, D.C., by S.H. Smith, as a continuation of his Philadelphia *Independent Gazetteer,* which became the new paper's weekly edition. It was the recognized organ of the administrations of Jefferson, Madison, and Monroe, and until 1825 was the only printed record of the debates and proceedings of Congress. J.Q. Adams used another paper as his official organ, and during Jackson's presidency the *National Intelligencer* opposed the administration, being the outlet for many of the writings of Webster, Clay, and Calhoun. It was again the government organ during the administrations of Polk and Fillmore, but after this time no one paper was considered the dominant administration journal. Lincoln nevertheless used it when he replied to Greeley's "Prayer of Two Millions." The paper was suspended (1866–69). It was removed to New York (1870) and assumed a different complexion.

National Medal for Literature, annual award to honor the achievements of an American's literary career, established by the National Book Committee, a nonprofit educational society founded in 1954. The sponsors have been The National Institute of Arts and Letters (1975–77), The American Book Awards (1979–83), and the New York Public Library (1978, 1984–85). Medalists are Thornton Wilder (1965), Edmund Wilson (1966), Auden (1967), Marianne Moore (1968), Conrad Aiken (1969), R.P. Warren (1970), E.B. White (1971), Lewis Mumford (1972), Nabokov (1973), no awards (1974–75), Tate (1976), Robert Lowell (1977), MacLeish (1978), no award (1979), Eudora Welty (1980), Kenneth Burke (1981), John Cheever (1982), no award (1983), Mary McCarthy (1984), award discontinued (1985).

National Medal of Arts, founded by President Reagan (1985) and placed under the control of the National Endowment for the Arts. Each year the Medal is given to a number of persons in a variety of the arts. Awardees include: Ralph Ellison (1985), Eva Le Gallienne, Lewis Mumford, Eudora Welty (1986), Howard Nemerov, Robert Penn Warren (1987), Saul Bellow (1988), Czeslaw Milosz, John Updike (1989), George Abbott (1990), Stephen Sondheim (1992, refused), Stanley Kunitz, Arthur Miller, William Styron (1993), and Richard Wilbur (1994).

National Police Gazette, The (1845–1937), weekly magazine, was ostensibly intended to expose criminals, but obviously catered to morbid sensationalism, both in its fiction and in its lengthy accounts of current crimes. In course of time, its shocking pink cover was less devoted to criminal records than to exposing the feminine form. Theatrical gossip and sporting news were added features, and the magazine became known as "the barber shop Bible." Although it went bankrupt in 1932, it was revived as a monthly with the archaic format and a similar policy and limped along under changing ownership for five years.

Nationalist party, see *Bellamy, Edward.*

Native Son, novel by Richard Wright,♦ published in 1940. With Paul Green he dramatized it (1941), and also produced and acted in a film version (1951).

Bigger Thomas, a black boy, reared in the slum world of Chicago, is led by his environment into a life of crime. His patronizing reception by Communist associates of his employer's daughter, combined with other circumstances, throw him into a confused mental state in which he accidentally murders the girl. In the ensuing flight, pursued by a mob, he kills his own sweetheart before he is captured and condemned to death.

Natty Bumppo, see *Leather-Stocking Tales.*

Naturalism, critical term applied to the method of literary composition that aims at a detached, scientific objectivity in the treatment of natural man. It is thus more inclusive and less selective than realism,♦ and holds to the philosophy of determinism. It conceives of man as controlled by his instincts or his passions, or by his social and economic environment and circumstances. Since in this view man has no free will, the naturalistic writer does not attempt to make moral judgments, and as a determinist he tends toward pessimism. The movement is an outgrowth of 19th-century scientific thought, following in general the biological determinism of Darwin's theory, or the economic determinism of Marx. It stems from French literature, in which Zola emphasizes biological determinism, and Flaubert economic determinism. The Russian novelists also added

their influence to the trend. American leaders of the naturalistic movement are considered to include Crane, Norris, Herrick, London, and Frederic, and later such significant figures as Dreiser, Dos Passos, and Farrell.

Nature, essay by Emerson,♦ published anonymously in 1836 and reprinted in *Nature, Addresses, and Lectures* (1849). Based on his early lectures, this first book expresses the main principles of Transcendentalism. An introduction states that "Our age is retrospective," seeing God and nature at second hand through the ideas and experiences of previous generations, and asks, "Why should not we also enjoy an original relation to the universe?" The eight brief chapters discuss the "lover of nature," the rare, poetic person "whose inward and outer senses are still truly adjusted to each other"; the "uses" of nature; the idealist philosophy in relation to nature; evidences of spirit in the material universe; and the potential expansion of human souls and works that will result from a general return to direct, immediate contact with the natural environment. The four uses of nature are (1) "Commodity," or its utilitarian and sensuous contributions to the life of mankind; (2) "Beauty," or the delight in the perception of natural forms, of the high and noble spiritual elements essential to them, and of the intellectual truths inherent in them; (3) "Language," or the symbolic character of natural facts, which convey transcendental meanings to minds prepared for their reception; and (4) "Discipline," or the function of natural environment in educating "both the Understanding and the Reason." In expressing his belief in the mystical "unity of Nature—the unity, in variety,—which meets us everywhere," the author develops his concept of the "Over-Soul" or "Universal Mind." Nature is "to us, the present expositor of the divine mind," which is the spiritual essence everywhere present in, and represented by, material nature, and in which man himself shares.

Nauset Indians, Algonquian tribe formerly living on Cape Cod in Massachusetts. In 1622 they supplied the starving Plymouth colonists with corn and beans. Most of them became Christians, and they remained friendly to the colonists through King Philip's War. They were among those called Praying Indians.

Navajo (or NAVAHO) **Indians,** numerous shepherd tribe now living on a large reservation in the mountains of northern Arizona and New Mexico, and southern Utah. After a long-continued war with the Spanish and American settlers, they were finally subdued by Kit Carson (1863–64) and have since been peaceful and industrious agriculturists, known for the high state of their native culture. They figure in Bandelier's *The Delight Makers,* La Farge's *Laughing Boy,* Cather's *Death Comes for the Archbishop,* and William Eastlake's *Portrait of an Artist with Twenty-Six Horses.*

NEAL, DANIEL (1678–1743), English Nonconformist clergyman and historian, author of a *History of New England . . . to . . . 1700* (2 vols., 1720), which, though it drew strongly on Cotton Mather's work, was hostile to his family and their part in the witchcraft trials. Neal's *History of the Puritans* (4 vols., 1732–38) was also indebted to Mather for its information on the New England Puritans down to 1689.

NEAL, JOHN (1793–1876), was born in Portland, Me., of a Quaker family. He began his feverish literary career during his twenties, when he was studying law in Baltimore, by editing *The Portico* and doing some hackwork on Paul Allen's history of the Revolution. His own writing during this period included two narrative poems, "Battle of Niagara" and "Goldau, or, the Maniac Harper," published in 1818 under the pseudonym Jehu O'Cataract, and a blank-verse romantic tragedy, *Otho* (1819). His early novels include *Keep Cool* (1817), partly a tract against dueling; *Logan, A Family History* (2 vols., 1822), a romantic account of the Indian chief; *Errata; or, The Works of Will. Adams* (2 vols., 1823); *Seventy-Six* (2 vols., 1823), a Revolutionary Romance, considered his best work; and *Randolph* (1823), a romantic epistolary novel. The last, in addition to containing much criticism of English and American authors, had a lengthy attack on the Baltimore statesman William Pinkney, whose son Edward♦ challenged the author. Neal, who was much opposed to dueling, ignored the challenge. In the same year, he sailed for England, where *Blackwood's Magazine,* notoriously hostile to American writers, accepted some two dozen of his articles. The most notable of these form a series of five papers (Sept. 1824–Feb. 1825) on 135 American authors. Written without access to the books, the papers abound in errors of fact as well as of prejudice, but are significant as the first attempt at a history of American literature, and as such have been reprinted under Neal's title *American Writers* (1937). While abroad, he wrote and published *Brother Jonathan* (3 vols., 1825), a long romantic novel concerned with New England prior to the Revolution. In 1827 he returned to Portland, where he continued to contribute to periodicals, edited a literary journal, practiced law, and wrote four further novels, *Rachel Dyer* (1828), a study of the Salem witchcraft trials; *Authorship* (1830), a picaresque tale of a New Englander abroad; *The Down-Easters♦* (1833), a melodramatic story with realistic details about New England; and *True Womanhood* (1859). He also published *One Word More* (1854), a religious treatise; dime novels of Indian adventures; *Great Mysteries and Little Plagues* (1870), anecdotes and sayings of children; and *Portland Illustrated* (1874), describing the city. *Wandering Recollections of a Somewhat Busy Life* (1869) is a garrulous autobiography that, although not completely trustworthy, gives a fine understanding of the general character of this enthusiastic, flamboyant writer.

NEAL, JOSEPH CLAY (1807–47), Philadelphia journalist and humorist, whose first book, *Charcoal Sketches; or, Scenes in a Metropolis* (1838), satirized Philadelphia types, and was popular not only in this country but also in England, where it was reprinted in *The Pic Nic Papers* (1841) by Dickens, whose work it resembled. Other similar collections are *In Town and About* (1843); *Peter Ploddy and Other Oddities* (1844); *Charcoal Sketches; Second Series* (1848); *The Misfortunes of Peter Faber, and Other Sketches* (1856); and *Charcoal Sketches: Three Books Complete in One* (1865).

NEARING, SCOTT (1883–1983), economist, environmentalist. Removed from a tenured professorship at the University of Pennsylvania for his radical political and economic views in 1915, Nearing, a native of Pennsylvania, was also fired by the University of Toledo for his radical pacifist statements when the U.S. entered World War I. For a time a communist, he was expelled from the party as a deviationist from the Lenin line. Nearing and his wife Helen decided in 1932 they would live outside the money economy as much as possible. They bought cheap land in Vermont, built a stone house, and grew their vegetarian and fruit diet—without electricity. They found they could live comfortably by working mornings only and devoting afternoons to reading, writing, crafts, or music. They described their life in *Living the Good Life* (1954), which became one of the testamentary documents of the 1960s counterculture. The Nearings collaborated on *The Maple Sugar Book: Together with Remarks on Pioneering as a Way of Living in the Twentieth Century* (1950). Nearing's last book was *The Making of a Radical: A Political Autobiography* (1972).

Ned McCobb's Daughter, play by Sidney Howard,♦ produced and published in 1926.

Ned Meyers, biography of a former shipmate, cast as a novel by Cooper,♦ and published in 1843.

Neighbor Jackwood, antislavery novel by J.T. Trowbridge,♦ published in 1856 and revised in 1895. It was dramatized by the author (1857).

Camille ("Milly") Delisard, daughter of a French merchant and a nearly white slave, after her father's death is sold into slavery by his legitimate wife. Her mother dies of grief and maltreatment, and the girl passes through various distressing adventures until she is rescued by a Northerner, Robert Greenwich, who helps her to reach Vermont by way of the Underground Railroad. Befriended by Abimelech Jackwood, a benevolent Green Mountain man, she calls herself Charlotte Woods, and becomes a servant of the Dunbury family. When Hector Dunbury asks her to marry him, she reveals her history. At first repelled, he later returns to marry her. Greenwich, moved by an uncontrollable passion, now seeks to claim Camille as a fugitive slave. She is forced to hide, but Greenwich recovers his sense of moral values and rescues her from a slave hunt that he himself originated. Tormented by conscience, he commits suicide, after which Camille and Hector are brought together and their marriage is approved by his parents.

NEIHARDT, JOHN G[NEISENAU] (1881–1973), born in Illinois, after a varied career including teaching and farming lived among the Omaha Indians (1901–7), and from his study of this tribe came themes of his poetry and fiction. His five-part epic poem deals with the Plains Indians and their conquest during the westward movement of the white frontier, and is published as *The Song of Hugh Glass* (1915), concerned with the legendary episode of 1823, when the frontier trapper was injured, and abandoned at the approach of hostile Indians by his youthful companion, Jim Bridger; *The Song of Three Friends* (1919), telling of the Ashley-Henry expedition of 1822–23; *The Song of the Indian Wars* (1925), recounting the last great struggle for the bison herds of the Plains; *The Song of the Messiah* (1935), telling of the last phase of Indian resistance to the white invasion, when the Indians could only hope that a messianic prophet would arise to deliver them; and *The Song of Jed Smith* (1941). These five works were gathered as *A Cycle of the West* (1949). *Collected Poems* (1926) contains the rugged lyrics published in earlier volumes, and other books include *The River and I* (1910), an account of a boating trip on the Missouri River; *The Lonesome Trail* (1907) and *Indian Tales, and Others* (1926), short stories about Indians and frontier heroes; *Life's Lure* (1914), a novel of the Black Hills mining camps; *The Splendid Wayfaring* (1920), the story of Jedediah Smith; *Black Elk Speaks, Being the Life Story of a Holy Man of the Oglala Sioux* (1932), which transcribes dreams and reminiscences told to Neihardt, including the Custer fight as seen through a child's eyes; a play, *Two Mothers* (1921); a volume of essays, *Poetic Values* (1925); and *When the Tree Flowered* (1951) and *Eagle Voice* (1953), fictional accounts based on facts of Sioux life. *All Is But a Beginning* (1972) and *Patterns and Coincidences* (1978) are memoirs of his early years.

Nelly Bly, see *Seaman, E.C.*

NEMEROV, HOWARD (1920–   ), after graduation from Harvard and service as a pilot in World War II became a teacher of English at Bennington, Brandeis, and Washington University, St. Louis. His fiction includes *The Melodramatists* (1949), a satirical portrait of a Boston family's inabilities to find a meaningful way of life; *Federigo, or The Power of Love* (1954), a comedy; *The Homecoming Game* (1957), a satire about a professor failing a star football player, dramatized

by Howard Lindsay and Russel Crouse as *Tall Story* (1959); and *A Commodity of Dreams* (1959), stories. His well-wrought poetry has been collected in *Image and the Law* (1947), *Guide to the Ruins* (1950), *The Salt Garden* (1955), *Mirrors and Windows* (1958); *The Next Room of the Dream* (1964), including two verse plays with Biblical themes; *The Blue Swallows* (1967); *Gnomes & Occasions* (1973), epigrammatic works; *The Western Approaches* (1976); *Collected Poems* (1977), for which he won a Pulitzer Prize, a National Book Award, and in 1980 a Bollingen Prize; *Inside the Onion* (1984); and *War Stories* (1987). His essays appear in *Poetry and Fiction* (1963); *Journal of the Fictive Life* (1966), a psychological inquiry into the creative process; *Reflections on Poetry and Poetics* (1972); *Figures of Thought* (1978); *New and Selected Essays* (1985), introduced by Kenneth Burke; and *The Oak in the Acorn* (1987), lectures delivered at Brandeis University. He was awarded a National Medal of Arts (1987) and named the nation's Poet Laureate in 1988.

"Neutral Ground," term for Westchester County, N.Y., during the Revolution, because its residents' sympathies were divided and neither army occupied it for any length of time. It is the setting of Cooper's romance *The Spy*.

NEVINS, ALLAN (1890–1971), after a career in journalism became a professor of American history at Columbia (1931–58) and, upon retirement from teaching, was senior research associate at the Huntington Library. Prior to his academic career he had already made a reputation as a scholar with such books as *The Life of Robert Rogers* (1914), *The Evening Post—A Century of Journalism* (1922), *The Emergence of Modern America* (1927), and *Frémont: The West's Greatest Adventurer* (1928), revised as *Frémont: Pathmarker of the West* (1939). His later books include *Grover Cleveland* (1932, Pulitzer Prize); *Hamilton Fish* (1936, Pulitzer Prize); *John D. Rockefeller* (2 vols., 1940); *This Is England Today* (1941); *America, The Story of a Free People* (1942), with H.S. Commager; *The U.S. in a Chaotic World* (1948); *The New Deal and World Affairs* (1950); *Ordeal of the Union* (2 vols., 1947), on the U.S., 1847–57, and its sequel, *The Emergence of Lincoln* (2 vols., 1950); and, as sequel to these four volumes, another four-volume work under the collective title *The War for the Union*, of which the first were *The Improvised War* (1960) and *The War Becomes Revolution* (1961). With Frank E. Hill he wrote a lengthy work, *Ford* (3 vols., 1954, 1957, 1963), that, as the subtitle of Volume I says, deals with "the times, the man, the company." He also wrote *Herbert H. Lehman and His Era* (1963). *The Gateway to History* (1938) studies methods of historiography.

New Criticism, literary analysis identified mainly with concentration on elements of an isolated literary work (usually a poem) as they illuminate the whole. It concentrates on semantics, meter, imagery, metaphor, and symbol and deals with the work's tone, texture, and tensions to explicate a fused form and content in a piece of writing, rather than dealing with the relation of that piece to an age, a tradition, or an author's whole body of writing. Its views of psychology, of a disrupted moral order, and of organic unity derive from many earlier sources, but its immediate forebears include Pound, I.A. Richards, and T.S. Eliot. Diverse American critics associated with the beliefs and practices of New Criticism to some substantial degree include R.P. Blackmur; Cleanth Brooks; Kenneth Burke; J.C. Ransom, who wrote a book on the subject (1941); Allen Tate; R.P. Warren; and Yvor Winters. However, they differed very much from one another and most did not continue to practice these critical ways so stringently or exclusively as time went on, and the heyday of New Criticism did not outlast the 1950s. The term was also used by Spingarn♦ for his own criticism.

New Directions (1936–　), collection of experimental or new prose and poetry founded by James Laughlin IV as an annual, but since 1942 issued sporadically. Its interest in new ideas and forms is akin to that of the publishing house of the same name which issues it. Sections have been devoted to "New Directions in Design" in photography, architecture, and city planning, and issues often emphasize foreign authors. Contributors have included Kay Boyle, Kenneth Burke, Cummings, Dahlberg, Kerouac, Denise Levertov, Henry Miller, James Purdy, Rexroth, Sorrentino, Wallace Stevens, and W.C. Williams. A *New Directions Reader* (1964) printed works of 58 authors from the first 28 years.

New Eclectic (1868–75), Baltimore monthly magazine, an outgrowth of the *Richmond Eclectic* (1866–68), was noted for its contributions from R.M. Johnston, Simms, Lanier, Hayne, and Longstreet. In 1871 the title was changed to the *Southern Magazine,* and it became the organ of the Southern Historical Society.

New England, region including the present states of Maine, New Hampshire, Vermont, Massachusetts, Rhode Island, and Connecticut, was named by Captain John Smith in his map of 1616. The harsh climate, rocky soil, and paucity of natural products discouraged colonization, except by the Puritans who sought a new home in which to cultivate their faith, and there early developed a homogeneity emphasized by their intolerance of beliefs at variance from orthodox Calvinism. Accordingly, cooperative action was common in such matters as the public school system, civic rule by town meetings, the organization of the Congregational Church, and the New England Confederation. The resulting early New England mind may be traced through the writings of such divines as the Mathers and Jonathan Edwards, and of such laymen as Bradford, Winthrop, and Sewall. Economic considerations also produced a unity, shipbuilding and fishing being the most characteristic occupations, but the very barrenness of the soil, lack of a staple, and inaccessibility of markets forced the people to develop an ingenuity that flowered in the shrewd, thrifty, independent, and resourceful type known as the Yankee. ♦ Because of its great foreign commerce, which led to the rise of such ports as Boston♦ and Salem, the region was particularly affected by the British Navigation acts, and played an important part in shaping colonial ideas toward the Revolution, producing such leaders as Samuel and John Adams.

After the Revolution the commercial classes became increasingly powerful as the transition to industrialism advanced, calling forth a generally conservative temper that came to be buttressed by a pride of heritage. This attitude, evident in the writings of the Connecticut Wits, may be observed later in the policies of the Cotton Whigs, whose guiding lights were the textile mill owners closely affiliated with the Southern cotton planters. The Brahmin class♦ was therefore long averse to the antislavery movement, but others, with equal pride of heritage and thoughtful of the spirit of Yankee independence, identified themselves passionately with the humanitarian movements of the mid-19th century. Thus Garrison, Whittier, and others agitated for improved conditions of labor in both North and South. Liberalism manifested itself likewise in the growth of Unitarianism, under Channing and Parker, and in the philosophic and literary movement of Transcendentalism, whose school, flourishing at Concord,♦ included Emerson, Thoreau, Alcott, and Margaret Fuller. True to the cultural tradition that had led to the founding of Harvard as early as 1636, others also maintained the region's distinction as the center of American intellectual activity, and this renaissance of the pre-Civil War years has been termed by such critics as Van Wyck Brooks "the flowering of New England." Among the representative authors of the time may be mentioned Longfellow and Lowell, who show the scholarship and romantic influences of the Cambridge authors; Bryant and Whittier, the love of nature and social liberalism frequently to be observed in New England thought; Holmes, the genteel Brahmin attitude; Hawthorne, the interest in moral problems and in the Puritan past; and Harriet Beecher Stowe, the humanitarianism and later the preoccupation with local color.

The great days of commerce and clipper ships, romantically depicted in such later novels as Hergesheimer's *Java Head,* were now long past, and after the Civil War increasing consciousness of decadence and nostalgia for earlier glories led to a literary Indian summer, represented by such writers of local-color stories as Mary Wilkins Freeman and Sarah Orne Jewett, who were concerned with the decayed grandeur of deserted shipping ports and dwindling farms; T.B. Aldrich, who recalled the glamour of a New England boyhood; and Louisa May Alcott, who presented a cheerful view of Concord in an earlier day; while her contemporary, the recluse Emily Dickinson, distilled both Yankee wit and Transcendentalist mysticism in her gnomic verse. Immigration and a constant rise of *nouveaux riches* altered the character of both upper and lower classes in New England, and the transitional society was described by such novelists as Howells, in *The Rise of Silas Lapham* and other books, and Henry James, who contrasted the nature of New England manners, ranging from those in *The Bostonians* to those in *The Ambassadors,* with views of life elsewhere in the U.S., in England, and on the Continent.

The region has drawn increasingly on non-English immigrants for its labor, and the resulting social discord is best symbolized by the Sacco-Vanzetti case, described in Upton Sinclair's *Boston,* which shows the bases of such conflict in 20th-century New England. The earlier homogeneity of culture is thus lost, and the rise of other regions has tended to destroy the leadership of New England in the creative arts, although its schools, including Harvard, Yale, Dartmouth, Williams, Amherst, Smith, Andover, and Exeter, are still leaders in American education. Among more recent authors, Robinson, Frost, Coffin, and Robert Lowell reveal facets of the original New England spirit in their works, but others have been concerned with the decadence of the tradition, as in O'Neill's *Mourning Becomes Electra,* Santayana's *The Last Puritan,* Marquand's *The Late George Apley,* and Cheever's *The Wapshot Chronicle.*

New England Company, see *Massachusetts Bay Company.*

New England Courant, The (1721–26), third newspaper in Boston, was founded and edited by James Franklin.♦ A Yankee imitation of the *Spectator,* it gave Boston the best and most lively journalism it had yet encountered. Because of his flippant remarks about civil and ecclesiastical authorities, the editor was sentenced to jail for one month and forbidden by the court to print the *Courant* or any paper of a like nature. Beginning in February 1723, the paper was published under the name of his half-brother and apprentice Benjamin Franklin, who had already contributed to it his Dogood Papers♦ (1722). An account of the enterprise is contained in Benjamin Franklin's *Autobiography.* The Hell-Fire Club♦ was an organization of the contributors.

New-England Magazine, The (1831–35), is considered the most important magazine published in New England before the *Atlantic Monthly.*

Contributors included Longfellow, Holmes, Whittier, Everett, Noah Webster, J.G. Percival, and Hawthorne. In politics it favored Webster and Everett, opposed Van Buren. It was absorbed by the *American Monthly Magazine.*

New England Nun, A, and Other Stories, 24 tales by Mary Wilkins Freeman,♦ published in 1891. Realistic but frequently sentimental, they are influenced by the local-color movement.

"A New England Nun" tells of Louisa Ellis, whose fiancé spends 14 years in Australia gathering a fortune with which to marry her, but is rejected on his return because she does not wish to disturb the delicate domestic arrangements to which she has become accustomed. "A Gala Dress" is a humorous sketch, concerned with the adventures of a spying gossip and the two maiden sisters who can afford but one fine dress and are never seen together at the simple village entertainments. "Sister Liddy," set in an almshouse, tells of grotesque, crippled old Polly Moss, whose only pleasure is derived from describing to her fellow paupers a fictitious sister of marvelous beauty and attainments. "Christmas Jenny" is the story of an eccentric spinster's charity and humane love for the dumb child and the injured birds and beasts to whose care she devotes her life. "Life Everlastin'" tells of another humanitarian, Luella Norcross, who returns to the church after a lifetime of agnosticism because religion seems "the only way out of it" for a murderer whom she has befriended.

New-England Palladium, The, see *Massachusetts Mercury.*

New England Primer, The, Calvinist school book, compiled and published by Benjamin Harris,♦ probably in 1683 and certainly before 1690. In its frequent revisions, it is estimated to have sold more than 5,000,000 copies. Besides the letters of the alphabet, illustrated by crudely rhymed couplets and woodcuts, the book contained simple moral texts based on Old Testament history and wisdom, and the prayer "Now I lay me down to sleep."

New England Quarterly, The (1928–   ), scholarly literary and historical review of New England life and letters, founded by S.E. Morison, A.M. Schlesinger, and other prominent scholars.

New England Renaissance, term sometimes applied to the cultural awakening of the mid-19th century aroused by Unitarianism♦ and Transcendentalism.♦

New England Tragedies, The, long dramatic poem by Longfellow,♦ which was first published separately in 1868 and later incorporated as the final section of *Christus.♦* The poem is composed of two dramas, each with a prologue and five acts: I. *John Endicott;* and II. *Giles Corey of the Salem Farms.*

The first play concerns Governor Endicott's persecution of the Quakers in Boston in 1665. He condemns Wenlock Christison, a Quaker, to death, and his daughter Edith to lashing and banishment. The governor's son is renounced by his father when he aids Edith, and he unsuccessfully attempts to find her after she is banished. Under the king's orders, the Quakers are pardoned, and Endicott, broken by the loss of his son, dies shortly thereafter, as do several others of the cruel Puritans.

The second play concerns the witchcraft epidemic in Salem in 1692. Tituba, a villainous Indian woman, leads a sick girl, Mary Walcot, to accuse Goodwife Corey of bewitching her. Meanwhile, John Gloyd turns Giles Corey's cattle loose and claims their loss is caused by witchcraft. Goodwife Corey is then tried by Cotton Mather and Justice Hathorne for witchcraft and is convicted by the evidence of Mary Walcot and her own husband, from whom certain seemingly damaging facts are extracted. Giles is next tried and condemned by the evidence of Gloyd and Mary Walcot, but at the end of the farcical testimony, Cotton Mather, less bigoted than Hathorne, exclaims, "this poor man whom we have made a victim, Hereafter will be counted as a martyr."

New England Weekly Journal (1727–41), founded by Samuel Kneeland, was the fourth regularly published newspaper in Boston. In addition to news of current events, it printed essays, letters, and poems by Increase Mather, Thomas Prince, and Mather Byles, as well as a letter from Pope to Byles, on the subject of the latter's poetry. The paper was merged with *The Boston Gazette,* ♦ becoming *The Boston Gazette, or Weekly Journal.*

New Englands First Fruits, tract published in London (1643), dealing with the climate, products, and religion of New England and giving a description of Harvard College. It was evidently intended to serve as publicity literature and was edited and probably composed by Thomas Weld and Hugh Peter.

New Englands Memoriall, history by Nathaniel Morton. ♦

New Englands Prospect, descriptive book by William Wood, ♦ published in England (1634). This lively work, reminiscent of the full-blooded Elizabethan pamphleteers, is interspersed with the author's own verse. It is divided into two parts, the first a description of the country and its flora and fauna, the second an account of the Indian tribes, which the author says is "in a more light and facetious style . . . because their carriage and behavior afforded more matter of mirth and laughter, than gravity and wisdom."

New Englands Trials, autobiographical narrative by Captain John Smith. ♦

New England Canaan, descriptive work by Thomas Morton, ♦ subtitled *New Canaan, Containing an Abstract of New England,* published at Amsterdam (1637). The first part deals with the Indians, the second with the natural endowments of the country, and the third with the settlements there and the attack of the Plymouth colonists upon Morton's colony of Merry Mount. ♦ In a highly diverting style, Morton tells his side of the quarrel and satirizes the Pilgrims, particularly Myles Standish, the leader of the attack upon him, whom he calls Captain Shrimp.

New Hampshire, blank-verse poem by Robert Frost, ♦ published in 1923 as the title piece of a volume which won a Pulitzer Prize.

In this familiar monologue, the poet presents a witty defense of his manner of life and philosophic attitude. He describes New Hampshire as "one of the two best states in the Union. Vermont's the other," and as a compact community having "one each of everything as in a show-case." Answering the "glorious bards of Massachusetts" who "taunt the lofty land with little men," he names friends among the New Hampshire people he admires and would not change. "I choose to be a plain New Hampshire farmer," he says, in condemning extremists who demand that he take a radical attitude.

New Harmony, socialized community on the Wabash River in Indiana, founded by the Rappists ♦ (1814) as an outgrowth of their Harmony Society. ♦ Upon their failure, it was purchased by Robert Owen ♦ (1825) for use in applying his communal theories. Although some 1000 settlers arrived, most of them were impractical theorists. During the two years of its existence, New Harmony had seven different forms of government or constitutions. Dissensions and ten group secessions led to the final dissolution of the community (1828). *The New-Harmony Gazette* (1825–35), its weekly periodical, interpreted and recorded the progress of the colony. After the community disbanded, Robert Dale Owen, Frances Wright, and others broadened the scope of the magazine. It became a socialist and agnostic periodical, and in 1829 the title became *The Free Enquirer.*

New Home, A,—*Who'll Follow? or, Glimpses of Western Life,* sketches by Caroline Kirkland, ♦ published in 1839 under the pseudonym "Mrs. Mary Clavers, An Actual Settler." These realistic sketches of frontier Michigan during the 1830s describe the log houses, conditions in the towns, the land booms, and the backwoods social standards. Among the characters delineated are a silly romantic girl who marries a clerk, a young blood who embezzles the funds of a wildcat bank, squatters, English upper-class settlers, old-maid gossips, and rampant democrats. The book was reissued as *Our New Home in the West* (1874).

New Jerusalem, Church of the, see *Swedenborgianism.*

New Light, see *Great Awakening.*

New Masses, see *Masses.*

New Orleans, largest city in Louisiana and chief port of the Gulf states, is situated on the eastern bank of the Mississippi River,♦ 100 miles above its mouth. The site was known to survivors of De Soto's expedition, and to La Salle, Tonty, and Iberville, prior to the city's founding (1718) by the French governor Sieur de Bienville. Louisiana was ceded to Spain by the Treaty of Paris (1763), but reverted to France (1803) and in 1803 came into the possession of the U.S. by the Louisiana Purchase. The city's population was augmented by the real-estate scheme known as the Mississippi Bubble, and the opening of the West brought it new prosperity when it became capital of the state (1812). It is a city steeped in European culture, whose Latin character, enhanced by the semi-tropical climate, is evident in its Vieux Carré or French Quarter and its exotic ways of life with lively parties, opera, theater, and Mardi Gras celebrations drawing on a Creole and Cajun heritage. During the War of 1812, the Battle of New Orleans was the final engagement and a decisive American victory. The advent of steam navigation soon made New Orleans both the queen city of the Mississippi and a lawless river town, a center for showboats, gamblers, plantation owners, and slave and cotton traders. During the Civil War it was a strategic point in the Confederate defense until its surrender (1862), when it was placed under the harsh military governorship of Benjamin Butler. It suffered under the pressure of carpetbaggers and scalawags during Reconstruction, and, besides the civic strife, the diminishing of river trade caused a partial loss of the former commercial importance of the city. During the present century, when the population has increased to over a half-million, New Orleans was long under the virtual dictatorship of the political machine of Huey Long and his successors. The home of Tulane University (founded 1845), it is represented in the arts by its distinctive architecture, many of whose landmarks still survive; by the Creole and Cajun songs that influence the sentimental compositions of Gottschalk, and the black music that has had its effect on jazz; by the paintings of Audubon and Vanderlyn in the early 19th century; and by its literature. The early literature was predominantly French and, in the tradition of Chateaubriand, largely romantic. The flush period prior to the Civil War was depicted by Vincent Nolte and, in *Life on the Mississippi,* by Clemens. Newspapers have included the *Crescent,* for which Whitman worked briefly, and the *New Orleans Picayune.*♦ The city was one of the centers of the local-color movement, and its romantic past figured in the works of Cable, Hearn, Grace King, Kate Chopin, and Ruth Stuart. A more mystical but less sentimental view was expressed by the Rouquette brothers. After World War I, a more realistic attitude was inaugurated by the little magazine *Double Dealer,* whose contributors included Sherwood Anderson and Faulkner. Other modern authors who have used the city's background include Roark Bradford, Lyle Saxon, Tennessee Williams, Hamilton Basso, Truman Capote, and John Kennedy Toole.

New Orleans Picayune (1837–), founded by G.W. Kendall and F.A. Lumsden as an independent paper whose price per copy was a picayune, a Spanish coin current in the Southern states before the Civil War, worth 6¼¢. The newspaper was distinguished for its field reports of the Mexican War, on which the U.S. government relied in part for information. It has always been considered the leading New Orleans newspaper and its only break in publication was for two months during the Civil War, although during Reconstruction it was forced to issue its own currency in order to continue publication. In 1914 it was combined with the *Times-Democrat* to become the *New Orleans Times-Picayune.* In 1933 it acquired the *New Orleans States,* an evening journal, and merged it (1958) with another acquisition, the New Orleans *Item,* to create the *States-Item.* A further merger (1980) of all these combinations created an "all day" paper, *The Times-Picayune and the States-Item,* but under the recent ownership of Newhouse Newspapers it has become an "all-day" paper on weekdays and a morning paper on weekends.

New Republic, The (1914–), weekly journal of opinion and liberal views was founded by Willard D. Straight for editing by Herbert Croly.♦ Croly conceived the purpose of the magazine as being "less to inform or entertain its readers than to start little insurrections in the realm of their convictions." It supported American participation in World War I, and, though it originated the phrase "peace without victory," it broke with Wilson and opposed U.S. ratification of the Treaty of Versailles. It has been consistently distinguished as a liberal organ, and over the years editorial board members have included Walter Lippmann, Stark Young, Malcolm Cowley, Joyce Carol Oates, and Robert Pinsky.

New School for Social Research, THE, founded at New York City in 1919 by C.A. Beard, Herbert Croly, Alvin Johnson, J.H. Robinson, and others to provide adult education in the social sciences and other fields of learning in a spirit of free inquiry and with a faith in liberal democracy. The school began with fewer than 900 students, and its early professors included H.E. Barnes,

John Dewey, H.M. Kallen, Roscoe Pound, and Veblen. In 1930 it moved into a modern building designed by Joseph Urban and noted for both its functional architecture and its murals by Orozco and T.H. Benton, but it now has several New York locations as well as a School of Design and Art Institute in Los Angeles. In 1994 it enrolled 5500 students, most of them part-time. Over the years its teachers have included Carleton Beals, Franz Boas, Kay Boyle, John Chamberlain, Aaron Copland, Waldo Frank, Lewis Gannett, Robert Heilbroner, Alfred Kazin, J.W. Krutch, Lewis Mumford, Gorham Munson, E.R.A. Seligman, Mark Van Doren, and Stark Young. Beginning in 1933 and for some years it was particularly noted for its Graduate Faculty of Political and Social Science, drawn from scholars driven from their posts in totalitarian countries, which came to be known as the "University in Exile," although it was an integral division of the New School.

New Side, see *Great Awakening.*

New World Writing (1952–59), eclectic anthology of fiction, drama, essays, and poetry from all the world presenting in paperback book format and to a large public the kinds of writings usually restricted to little magazines or literary quarterlies. Contributors included not only such established authors as Auden, Farrell, Jeffers, Lorca, Schorer, and Dylan Thomas, but newer writers including Algren, James Baldwin, Ionesco, and Kerouac.

New York, City of, situated at the mouth of the Hudson River and formed of the five boroughs of Manhattan, Brooklyn, the Bronx, Richmond, and Queens, is the largest city of the U.S. The first white occupation occurred when Hudson established a trading post on Manhattan in 1609, and New Amsterdam was the capital of New Netherland long before Minuit's purchase of the island from the Indians (1626). The events of the Dutch occupation, until the British seized the colony in 1664, are widely known through Irving's burlesque *Knickerbocker's History of New York.*◆ Despite the rebellion led by Leisler,◆ New York grew rapidly during the century of English occupation, although it remained smaller and less important than Boston and Philadelphia. King's College (Columbia) was founded in 1754, and many of the city's theaters, newspapers, and educational institutions had already been established. It was a center of disaffection during the events that led up to the Revolution, and Washington made New York his headquarters after the British captured Boston. The Battle of Long Island was the city's chief event of the war, and as the national capital (1784–90) it was the scene of Washington's inauguration and Farewell Address.

It soon became the principal city of the U.S., having a population of 60,000 in 1800, over a half-million in 1850 (surpassing all European cit-ies except London and Paris), 3,347,202 in 1900, and 7,322,564 in 1990. The building of railroads, the opening of the Erie Canal (1825), and the importance of New York harbor contributed to the city's rise and to the increasing significance of Wall Street,◆ while Tammany Hall maintained political domination for more than a century. The growth in population has been the result of three streams of immigration: (1) from many foreign countries, which gave rise to such settlements as those on the Lower East Side◆; (2) from the Southern states to the black community of Harlem◆; and (3) the influx from all parts of the U.S. of persons with careers in business, finance, and the arts, in all of which New York City is considered to be the national capital. As the home of the United Nations it is also a cosmopolitan international capital.

The city's many educational institutions include Columbia, the College of the City of New York, Fordham, New York University, the New School for Social Research, and a great number of specialized ones. Other major cultural institutions include Lincoln Center for the Performing Arts with buildings devoted to opera, symphony, and theater, the Metropolitan Museum of Art, the Museum of Modern Art, the Guggenheim Museum, the Whitney Museum of American Art, the Museum of the City of New York, and the New York Public Library. The city's vitality in the arts and literature is not necessarily associated with such imposing institutions, for its distinction is often that created by individuals, who at one time made Greenwich Village◆ a locale where bohemians lived, or who made up the Algonquin Round Table,◆ a gathering of wits. Similarly, in recent times the little theater◆ of off-Broadway or off-off-Broadway has been more dynamic than that of the established stages.

During its long history the numerous literary movements, groups, and figures have been as diverse as the city itself. After the Dutch poet Steendam and such English colonial writers as Cadwallader Colden and the authors of *Androboros,* the significant authors include Freneau, Paine, Barlow, and Hamilton during the Revolution; such figures of the early 19th century as Dunlap, C.B. Brown, J.H. Payne, Irving, Paulding, the Knickerbocker Group,◆ Cooper, Bryant, Poe, Bayard Taylor, and the Duyckincks; Whitman and the bohemian group at Pfaff's Cellar◆; other 19th-century figures, including Parke Godwin, William Winter, Howells, Henry James, Melville, Stedman, and Brander Matthews; Stephen Crane, Riis, Saltus, D.G. Phillips, Steffens, O. Henry, H.C. Bunner, R.H. Davis, Huneker, Edith Wharton, and other pre-World War I authors; the Greenwich Village writers; and such modern figures as Mencken, Nathan, F. Scott Fitzgerald, Christopher Morley, Dorothy Parker, Kaufman, Dos Passos, Van Vechten, the Harlem◆ authors, Ernest Poole, James Oppenheim, Hart Crane, Odets, Irwin Shaw, F.P.

Adams, Maxwell Bodenheim, Michael Gold, Kreymborg, Konrad Bercovici, some of whom are also to be included in writers from Brooklyn♦ who interpreted Jewish culture. Other more recent New York authors include the so-called New York school,♦ Louis Auchincloss, Peter Beagle, Jane Bowles, E.L. Doctorow, Anthony Hecht, John Hollander, Frederick Morgan, Howard Moss, Jack Richardson, and Muriel Rukeyser. Tom Wolfe caught the spirit of the racial politics, financial maneuvering, and criminal justice system of the city in the 1980s in his novel *The Bonfire of the Vanities.*

New York American (1819–45), daily newspaper, early distinguished as a Whig and National Republican journal, which had great influence among the aristocratic circles of New York. Gulian C. Verplanck was a founder and assistant editor (1819–29) and Charles King was editor (1827–45), assisted for a time by C.F. Hoffman. The paper was absorbed by the *New York Courier and Enquirer,* a Whig paper, and King remained as an assistant editor with H.J. Raymond (1843–51). It is not to be confused with the Hearst newspaper of the same name.

New York *Evening Post* (1801–) was founded as a Federalist organ, and at first subordinated news to biased political discussion. Early literary contributions included the "Croaker Papers" of Drake and Halleck. Bryant joined the staff in 1826 and edited the paper (1829–78), which he made an organ of Jacksonian Democracy and later an advocate of the Free-Soil and Republican parties. John Bigelow♦ was an associate editor and owner (1848–61). After 1881 the *Evening Post* was published by the Villard family, and E.L. Godkin♦ and Carl Schurz♦ became its editors. Following Schurz's resignation, Godkin edited the paper and also *The Nation,* which was then virtually a weekly edition of the *Post.* It was noted for its crusades against jingoism and political corruption, and as a leader in the Mugwump movement. In 1918 O.G. Villard sold it and it came into the hands of the Curtis Publishing Company. J.D. Stern, who owned it (1934–39), changed the name to the New York *Post,* under which it was published (1939–76) by a new owner, Dorothy Schiff, who maintained its liberal editorial tradition. She sold it (1976) to the Australian publisher Rupert Murdoch. It has dropped "Evening" in its name, is "all day" Monday through Friday and morning alone on Saturday.

New York Gazette (1725–44), first newspaper in New York City, was a semi-official chronicle of current events, edited and published by William Bradford.

New-York Gazetteer, see *Rivington's New-York Gazetteer.*

New York Globe, see *American Minerva.*

New York *Herald* (1835–1966), founded by James Gordon Bennett (1795–1872) as a penny daily of dignified standards, which, when they failed to bring an income, were changed to those of yellow journalism. His sensational paper became proslavery and pro-Tammany until the Civil War, when popular feeling caused it to become strongly pro-Union. It was famous for its full news coverage, a policy further extended by the younger James Gordon Bennett (1841–1918) when he succeeded to the editorship (1872). He edited the paper primarily from his home in France, establishing European correspondents and making extensive use of cable communications. He also founded the Paris *Herald* (1887), which became the outstanding English-language paper on the Continent. In addition to excellent straight reporting, the younger Bennett's editorship won attention by the feature writing of such authors as Clemens and Richard Harding Davis, and by the organization of Stanley's expedition to Africa (1869–72) to find Livingstone. In the years prior to his death, Bennett's paper lost circulation; in 1920 it was purchased by Frank Munsey and merged with the New York *Sun,* but they were soon separated, and in 1924, the *Herald* was purchased by Ogden Reid, who merged it with the *New-York Tribune*♦ to create the New York *Herald Tribune,* a Republican daily noted both for its news coverage and for its many columnists, including Walter Lippmann, as well as for *Books,* a Sunday supplement of book reviews. It continued as a distinguished journal until, plagued by circulation problems and labor disputes, it ceased publication in April 1966, although a Sunday edition merged with the *Sun* and *World-Telegram* and continued to April 1967.

New York Idea, The, problem play by Langdon Mitchell,♦ produced in 1906 and published in 1908.

New York *Independent Journal, The,* or *General Advertiser* (1783–88), newspaper that published many of *The Federalist* papers (Oct. 1787–April 1788). In 1788 it became the *New York Daily Gazette.*

New York Ledger (1855–1903), outgrowth of the *Merchants' Ledger* (1847–55), was the most widely read weekly paper of its time, incorporating characteristics of both newspapers and magazines. "Fanny Fern," E.D.E.N. Southworth, Lydia H. Sigourney, and Sylvanus Cobb contributed regularly, attracting readers by their sensational and pathetic stories, while the more sophisticated readers were drawn by contributions from Everett, Bryant, Harriet Beecher Stowe, Halleck, Longfellow, and such English authors as Tennyson and Dickens. Robert Bonner, who purchased the *Ledger* in 1851, was noted as the Barnum of publishers because of his sensational advertising schemes. He retired in 1887 and in 1898 the paper became a monthly magazine.

New York Magazine, The (1790–97), monthly "Literary Repository," most of whose material was not original, but whose special contributors included C.B. Brown and Dunlap. The latter's "Theatrical Register" was first printed there.

New-York Mirror (1823–60), weekly newspaper devoted to literature, art, and society, founded by Samuel Woodworth and others. G.P. Morris became editor (1824) and in 1831 N.P. Willis became an associate editor, when the *Mirror* absorbed his *American Monthly Magazine.* Contributors included Cooper, Halleck, Whittier, Irving, T.D. English, John Neal, C.F. Hoffman, and Lydia H. Sigourney. In 1842 it became the *New Mirror,* and in 1844 the daily *Evening Mirror,* of which Poe was the literary critic (1844–45). Although Morris had retired, Willis still kept his connection, until he went abroad (1845). Upon his return the following year, he joined Morris's *National Press* to create *The Home Journal,* but the *Mirror* continued until 1860 under the management of their former partner, Hiram Fuller. The original *Mirror* is not to be confused with the 20th-century tabloid of that name, owned by Hearst.

New York Packet, see *Loudon, Samuel.*

New York *Post,* see *New York Evening Post.*

New York Public Library, consolidated (1895) from the collections of several previous libraries, including the Astor library founded by J.J. Astor, the scholarly Lenox Library founded by James Lenox, ♦ and the English and American literature collection of E.A. Duyckinck. Most of the city's independent libraries were consolidated with the main collection (1901–4). The Library had (1981) 83 publicly supported branches, but the Central Research Library, headquartered at Fifth Avenue and 42nd Street, receives two-thirds of its operating budget from private sources. Its holdings, including the Berg Collection of English and American Literature, contained, as of 1994, more than 6,000,000 books and more than 13,500,000 manuscripts.

New York Review and Athenaeum Magazine, The (1825–26), monthly literary journal which superseded *The Atlantic Magazine,* was edited by R.C. Sands, Bryant, and others. Among the contributors were Halleck, Longfellow, N.P. Willis, George Bancroft, and the elder R.H. Dana. Lack of an aggressive policy brought about its merger with *The United States Literary Gazette.* ♦

New York Review of Books, The (1963–   ), founded during a printers' strike against New York newspapers as a single-issue journal to dramatize the need for a new kind of book review as well as to fill the gap left by the suspension of the book-review sections of *The New York Times* and

the *Herald Tribune.* Its success led to regular biweekly publication, except for single issues in July and August, that feature lengthy, critical, and informed treatments of a few books, some poetry, and an occasional special article. It is much concerned with sociopolitical matters, national and international, from a liberal point of view. Reviewers include leading U.S. and English critics. Their texts are illustrated by sharp, witty caricatures of authors by the staff artist David Levine, by apposite pictures of animals in human guise from the works of the mid-19th-century French artist Grandeville, and by other exotic or satirical 19th-century illustrations. For the overseas edition, a *London Review of Books* was founded in 1979.

New York school, name applied to a group of poets including John Ashbery, Kenneth Koch, Frank O'Hara, and James Schuyler, ♦ whose writing, distinguished for visual detail, relates to New York's Abstract Expressionist painters of the 1950s. Several in the group have been art critics or museum curators, and they have collaborated with artists in their publications, as well as among themselves.

New York Sun (1833–1966), newspaper founded by Benjamin H. Day ♦ as a penny daily to feature human interest stories. Its news was local, with little emphasis on politics, although it leaned toward the Democratic party. It first attracted wide attention with its sensational Moon Hoax ♦ (1835). In 1838 Day sold the paper to Moses Y. Beach, who edited it until 1848, stressing news scoops. His sons controlled the *Sun* until 1860, tending to support the Democrats, although opposing secession and slavery. During 1860–62 the paper passed into other hands, becoming an organ of evangelical religion, but returned to the Beach family until 1868, when C.A. Dana ♦ became editor and manager. His sole rule was "Be interesting," and his forte was personal journalism. He early turned against Grant and was influential in attacking the corruption of the period. Upon his death (1897), his son became editor, to be succeeded (1903) by Edward P. Mitchell, who was associated with the paper for 50 years, editing it until 1920. Frank A. Munsey bought the *Sun* (1916) and merged it with the New York *Herald,* to become *The Sun and New York Herald,* but they were soon separated, and the *Sun* was made into an evening paper, which purchased the *New York Globe* (1923). It was merged with the *World-Telegram* (1950). Labor disputes led to its closing in April 1966, although a Sunday journal, the *World Journal Tribune,* lingered on to April 1967.

New York Times, The (1851–   ), daily newspaper founded by Henry J. Raymond ♦ as a conservative journal to be known for its accuracy, although reflecting the views of its Whig backers, Seward and Weed. After 1856 the paper was strongly Republican, but it continued its policy of conservative journalism under Raymond, who was editor until his death (1869). During the 1870s it became somewhat more sensational in its work for reforms and leadership of the attack on the Tweed Ring. Its original publisher, George Jones, died in 1891, and during the next five years the *Times* declined in standards and dropped to a circulation of 9000. In 1896 it was purchased by Adolph Ochs, who returned it to its original standards by adhering to the slogan, "All the News That's Fit to Print." Its careful reporting of World War I through a large corps of correspondents helped raise the circulation to nearly 370,000 (1918). Since the death of Ochs (1935), his family has maintained the *Times*'s reputation as the most eminent of American newspapers, and increased its daily circulation to 1,187,950 and its Sunday issue to 1,767,836 in 1994.

New-York Tribune (1841–1966), daily newspaper founded by Horace Greeley,♦ who edited it until his death (1872) and made it distinguished not only for his trenchant editorials, but also for the journalists he attracted to it. These included H.J. Raymond, who founded *The New York Times* in 1851; C.A. Dana, who was the managing editor from 1849 to 1862; George Ripley, who as literary critic (1849–80) wrote the first daily book reviews in the U.S.; and Whitelaw Reid, who succeeded Greeley as editor. Among Greeley's policies were opposition to monopolies and advocacy of labor organization, a protective tariff, and a homestead law. Although he began as a Whig, he became a Free-Soil leader, and was influential in the election of Lincoln. After the Civil War, he favored suffrage for blacks but opposed the punitive Reconstruction policy. During Reid's editorship (1872–1912), the *Tribune* remained the most distinguished and powerful Republican organ in the country. His policies were continued by his son Ogden Reid, who succeeded him as editor, although the paper lost circulation until in 1924 it purchased the New York *Herald,♦* becoming the *Herald Tribune.*

New-York Weekly Journal (1733–52), founded by J.P. Zenger♦ to oppose the official political views of the *New York Gazette.* Its repeated attacks on authorities caused Zenger to be imprisoned and to become the subject of the first trial for newspaper libel in the colonies. The paper was edited by his family while he was in prison (1735), and upon his acquittal, which is considered instrumental in establishing American freedom of press, he resumed editorship, which he continued until 1746. It was later edited by his son John to 1751.

New York *World* (1866–1931), founded as a penny daily religious newspaper. Since morality did not pay, it was forced to go through several mergers, and soon became worldly in fact as well as in name as the organ of the Albany Regency. In 1883 it was purchased by Joseph Pulitzer, who made it a flamboyant crusading paper and attracted an audience by espousing popular causes. In 1894 it inaugurated the multicolored comic strip "Hogan's Alley," whose hero's name, the Yellow Kid, is said to have been the original of the term "yellow journalism." The paper vied with the Hearst publications during the Spanish-American War in gaudy and unscrupulous sensationalism. Under the editorship of Pulitzer's son, its standards were raised, when it championed the Democratic party and became known for such columnists as Walter Lippmann, F.P. Adams, and Heywood Broun. In 1931 it was combined with the *New York Telegram* to become the *World-Telegram,* a member of the Scripps-Howard chain, which in turn absorbed the New York *Sun* to become the *New York World-Telegram and The Sun* (1950–66), continued to 1967 by merger with the *Herald-Tribune* and *Journal-American.*

New Yorker, The (1925–   ), weekly humorous magazine, founded and edited by Harold Ross (1892–1951), initially said to be for the "caviar sophisticates" and "not for the old lady in Dubuque." Though founded in the 1920s, it retains the special characteristics and quality that it originated: a crisp, satirical style, a warm-hearted concern with humane values, sophisticated amusement at human follies, and urbane attitudes, diversely evident in departments that include "Notes and Comments" and "Talk of the Town," both anonymous, the latter long written by E.B. White. Other distinctive features include "Profiles," sketches not only of persons, but of places and things, occasional "Annals of Crime," contributions from a "Reporter at Large," a frequent "Letter" from its foreign correspondents, and perceptive reviews of films, theater, music, art, and books, whose staff authors or frequent contributors have included Pauline Kael, Wolcott Gibbs, Brendan Gill, Edmund Wilson, and John Updike. Not infrequently it devotes a large part of an issue to a feature article concentrating on a significant social issue (John Hersey's "Hiroshima" occupied an entire issue in 1946), or extends it over several weeks. The body of the journal is composed of stories, poems, and comic drawings. The fiction frequently emphasizes a mood or dwells quietly on a slight but meaningful incident and is said to have an effect on the genre itself or to be "a typical *New Yorker* story," although there cannot be a type since authors have ranged from John O'Hara and S.J. Perelman (long steady contributors) to Donald Barthelme. The poets are just as diverse and have included Ogden Nash and John Ashbery. The drawings often are accompanied by one-line captions, a form the magazine is said to have popularized, but many are without text or jokes. Over the years the various artists have included Charles Addams, Alajalov, Peter Arno, Rea Irvin (whose first-issue cover appears annually on the anniversary of the founding, symbolically depicting a skeptical dandy, Eustace Tilley, and is also indicative of the journal's sense of continuity), Steig, Steinberg, and Thurber. Numerous anthologies have been collected from contributions, and accounts of the magazine by insiders include Thurber's *The Years with Ross* (1959) and Brendan Gill's *Here at The New Yorker* (1975). Since 1992, under new editorial management, the magazine has taken on a radically different tone.

Newbery Medal, see *Children's literature in America.*

Newberry Library, private institution in Chicago, founded (1887) with a bequest from Walter Loomis Newberry (1804–68), a local banker. A reference and research collection of rare books and manuscripts concentrating on the humanities, it emphasizes western Europe and America, being particularly famous for its holdings on bibliography, the Renaissance, music, English and American literature and history, Portugal and Brazil, the trans-Mississippi West, American Indians, and fine printing. The library conducts research and educational programs.

NEWELL, PETER (1862–1924), humorist, author, and illustrator, best known for his flat wash drawings and whimsical captions in such books as *Topsys and Turvys* (1893), *Peter Newell's Pictures and Rhymes* (1899), *The Hole Book* (1908), and *The Slant Book* (1910).

NEWELL, ROBERT HENRY (1836–1901), New York journalist and humorist, best known for his comic treatment of contemporary matters in newspapers, written under the pseudonym Orpheus C. Kerr. This name, a pun on the words "Office Seeker," was suggested by the great number of political aspirants at the time of Lincoln's inauguration and became a stock character for political lampooning. Newell's writings, significant for their comic interpretation of Civil War history, are in the vein of the crackerbox philosophy of Jack Downing, and are marked by mock-heroic jibing at solemnity, gross exaggeration or understatement, and purposeful misspelling. In addition to *The Orpheus C. Kerr Papers* (5 vols., 1862–71), under his own name Newell wrote sentimental verse; romantic fiction; *The Cloven Foot* (1870), a continuation of Dickens's unfinished *The Mystery of Edwin Drood;* and *There Was Once a Man* (1884), a novel attacking Darwinism. He married Adah Isaacs Menken.

Newes from Virginia, see *Rich, Richard.*

Newport Mercury (1758–   ), second newspaper in Rhode Island, was founded by James Franklin, Jr., nephew of Benjamin Franklin. After its founder's death (1762), the paper was successfully continued by others. Except for three years, when it was published in Massachusetts during the British occupation of Newport, it has continued to be published in Rhode Island. It ceased to be a daily in 1928, when through mergers it became the Newport *Mercury and Weekly News.*

NEWTON, A[LFRED] EDWARD (1863–1940), Philadelphia book collector, whose charming writings in a manner resembling that of the 18th-century essayists are primarily concerned with his avocation. These include *The Amenities of Book-Collecting and Kindred Affections* (1918), *A Magnificent Farce and Other Diversions of a Book-Collector* (1921), *The Greatest Book in the World and Other Papers* (1925), *This Book-Collecting Game* (1928), *A Tourist in Spite of Himself* (1930), *End Papers* (1933), and *Derby Day and Other Adventures* (1934). He also wrote two plays, *Doctor Johnson* (1923) and *Mr. Strahan's Dinner Party* (1930), and many brochures privately printed for his friends. His desire that the books, drawings, and manuscripts in his collection should "not be consigned to the cold tomb of a museum" led to the sale of his library in 1941.

Nez Percé Indians, Northwestern tribe whose name is derived from the custom of wearing nose pendants. First encountered by Lewis and Clark, they were praised in Irving's *Adventures of Captain Bonneville* for their high culture and longstanding friendliness with the whites. After a fraudulent treaty by which the Americans obtained their gold lands, an uprising occurred (1877), led by Chief Joseph.

NICHOLS, THOMAS LOW (1815–1901), journalist known for his reform and radical ideas, whose book *Forty Years of American Life: 1821–1861* (1864) furnishes one of the most interesting sources of information on everyday American life in its period. Among his other works are three novels on contemporary life in New York City, *Ellen Ramsay* (1843), *The Lady in Black* (1844), and *Raffle for a Wife* (1845). When he could not subscribe to the principles of a government prosecuting a Civil War, he left (1861) to spend the rest of his life expatriated in London.
   MARY SARGEANT NICHOLS (1810–84), his wife, was a well-known reformer and wrote an autobiographical novel, *Mary Lyndon; or, Revelations of a Life* (1855).

NICHOLSON, MEREDITH (1866–1947), Indiana novelist, who served as minister to Paraguay (1933–34), minister to Venezuela (1935–38), and to Nicaragua (1938–41). His books include *The Main Chance* (1903); *The House of a Thousand Candles* (1905), a mystery story; *The Port of Missing Men* (1907); *The Lords of High Decision* (1909); *Siege of the Seven Suitors* (1910); *A Hoosier Chronicle* (1912), a semi-autobiographical novel; *Hope of Happiness* (1923); and *The Cavalier of Tennessee*

(1928). In addition to short stories, essays, and poems, he also wrote *The Hoosiers* (1900), a study of Indiana authors, and *The Poet* (1914), a fictional biography of James Whitcomb Riley.

Nick Carter, name of the hero of many dime novels, also used by many of their authors. John Russell Coryell probably first used it in the 1880s, but more prolific writers produced most of the more than 1000 Nick Carter books.

Nick of the Woods; or, The Jibbenainosay, novel by R.M. Bird,♦ published in 1837. This popular novel opposing the idea of the Indian as a "noble savage" was dramatized by Louisa Medina (1838).

At the end of the Revolution Captain Roland Forrester travels through the Kentucky border wilderness with his beloved Edith, who is captured by Indians during one of their many raids and massacres. The only man who will not fight is the Quaker derisively called Bloody Nathan, an unctuous hypocrite who is really Nick of the Woods, the Jibbenainosay, or devil, feared by the Indians because he brutally kills them to avenge their murder of his family. When he finds Wenonga, a Shawnee chief, was the sole killer of his family, Nick, disguised as an Indian, slays him with a tomahawk and disappears, to haunt the forests no more. George Rogers Clark saves Roland and Edith from the stake.

NICOLAY, JOHN GEORGE (1832–1901), brought to the U.S. in 1838 from his native Germany, grew up in Illinois, where after a journalistic career during his twenties he was appointed Lincoln's private secretary in 1860. His lifelong friend John Hay held a similar position, and the two men, who revered Lincoln, enjoyed an unusual opportunity for intimate study of their hero. From 1875 to 1890 they collaborated on the great biography *Abraham Lincoln: A History* (10 vols., 1890). Nicolay's other works include *The Outbreak of Rebellion* (1881), *A Short Life of Abraham Lincoln* (1902), and the editorship with Hay of Lincoln's writings (12 vols., 1905).

NIEBUHR, REINHOLD (1892–1971), Missouri-born theologian, received his M.A. and B.D. from Yale Divinity School, was a pastor in Detroit's Bethel Evangelical Church (1915–28), where he was concerned with labor union issues before becoming a professor at Union Theological Seminary (1928–60). His neo-orthodox theology, treating the relevance of Christianity to modern man and society, holds that because of original sin man cannot reach Utopia through social reform or revolution, but that social dilemmas can be met in terms of the Christian beliefs and spiritual values contained in the Bible. His views are set forth in *Moral Man and Immoral Society* (1932), *Reflections on the End of an Era* (1934), *Beyond Tragedy* (1937), *Christianity and Power Politics* (1940), *The Nature and Destiny of Man* (2 vols.,

1941–43), *The Children of Light and the Children of Darkness* (1944), *Faith and History* (1949), *The Irony of American History* (1952), *The Self and the Dramas of History* (1955), *Pious and Secular America* (1958), and *Christianity and Power Politics* (1969).

Nigger, The, play by Edward Sheldon,♦ produced in 1909 and published in 1910.

Philip Morrow, a Southern patrician, becomes governor of his state through the aid of his cousin, Clifton Noyes, on a platform opposing new freedoms of blacks and favoring the commercial interests of Noyes. Turning against his cousin's plans, Morrow is threatened by him with the revelation, previously unknown to him, that he has some black ancestry. Nevertheless, urged by his fiancée, Georgiana, he signs the bill harming his cousin's business and prepares to address the citizens on his black heritage.

Nigger Heaven, novel by Carl Van Vechten,♦ published in 1926. It is noted for its depiction of the various strata of black society in Harlem.

Mary Love, a young librarian, meets Byron Kasson, a penniless writer. They fall in love, but are unhappy because his ambition meets constant obstacles, owing to the inferior position in society of their race. Mary refuses to marry the wealthy gambler Randolph Pettijohn, disliking his meanness and vulgarity. Lasca Sartoris, a celebrated, exotically fascinating actress, takes Byron's affections from Mary for a time, and his interest from his career, but then she tires of him and turns to Pettijohn. Byron thinks that to win Mary again he must prove that he hates Lasca. He goes to a nightclub intending to shoot both Lasca and Pettijohn. There another former lover of Lasca kills Pettijohn; Byron, maddened, fires into the dead body and police arrest him for the murder.

Night, lyric poem by Jeffers,♦ published in *Roan Stallion, Tamar, and Other Poems* (1925).

In stately free verse, the poet celebrates the beauty of the rhythmic return of night to the California coast. "Sun-lovers" worship a "father of lights and noises, wars, weeping and laughter . . . ," but nobler night, death, and darkness, "the primal and the latter silences," must prevail over life, "the flicker of men and moths and the wolf on the hill." This ultimate truth, which men dared not face before, has been unveiled by modern science and philosophy.

Night Before Christmas, poem by C.C. Moore.♦

Night Over Taos, verse drama by Maxwell Anderson,♦ produced and published in 1932. The play deals with the personal and political problems of the Montoya family in Taos, N.M., as this outpost of a crumbling empire is under attack by American soldiers and frontiersmen in 1847.

NILES, SAMUEL (1674–1762). Congregational clergyman of Rhode Island, was a prominent religious controversialist and historian. His works include *Tristitice Ecclesiarum* (1745), an account of the New England churches and an attack on Whitefield: "A Summary Historic Narrative of the Wars in New England with the French and Indians" (Collections of the Massachusetts Historical Society, 1837, 1861); and *A Brief and Plain Essay on God's Wonder-Working Providence . . . in the Reduction of Louisburg* (1745), a rhymed account.

Niles' Weekly Register (1811–49), journal published at Baltimore by Hezekiah Niles (1777–1839), an ardent economic nationalist. It was also titled *Niles' National Register* (1836–39). The paper's generally unbiased record of current events is of great value to the historiographer.

NIMS, J[OHN] F[REDERICK] (1913–   ), born in Michigan, educated at Notre Dame (A.B., 1937; Ph.D., 1945), where he taught English and creative writing (1939–61), a career continued at the University of Illinois, the University of Chicago, and the Chicago campus of the University of Illinois (1965–85). He has also been an editor of *Poetry.* His poems have been collected in *The Iron Pastoral* (1947), *A Fountain in Kentucky* (1950), *Knowledge of the Evening* (1960), *Of Flesh and Bone* (1967), and *The Kiss* (1982), 44 light verses on kissing. His translations are the *Poems of St. John of the Cross* (1959); sections of *The Poem Itself* (1960), a new mode of translation, edited by Stanley Burnshaw; and *Sappho to Valery* (1971). *A Local Habitation* (1985) prints his essays on poetry.

NIN, ANAÏS (1903–77), French-born author of Spanish-Cuban heritage, brought to the U.S. at the age of 11, lived here intermittently thereafter. Her first book, *D.H. Lawrence, An Unprofessional Study* (1932), was a critical work, but of her later books she has said: "I write as a poet in the framework of prose and appear to claim the rights of a novelist. . . . I intend the greater part of my writing to be received directly through the senses, as one apprehends painting and music." Her fiction includes *The House of Incest* (1936), a treatment of narcissism; *Winter of Artifice* (1939), a psychiatric investigation of the relations between a father and daughter; *Under a Glass Bell* (1944), stories: *This Hunger* (1945), interrelated stories about women who fear human society, and men in particular; *Ladders to Fire* (1946), stories of women who search for their identity; *The Four-Chambered Heart* (1950), a novel about a triangular love conflict; *A Spy in the House of Love* (1954), on a woman's self-questioning about her many transient loves; *Cities of the Interior* (1959), gathering works, including the three preceding ones, into a "continuous novel"; and *Collages* (1964), portraits of characters, real and fictive, in a "novel" set in Los Angeles. *Cities of the Interior* (1965) collects shorter fiction. *Realism and Reality* (1946), *On Writing* (1947), *The Novel of the Future* (1968),

A Woman Speaks (1975), and *In Favor of the Sensitive Man* (1976) are critical works. *Delta of Venus* (1968) reissues early pornographic work. Her full and frank *Diary* appeared in six volumes (1966–76), and *Linotte* (1978) is a diary kept between the ages of 11 and 17. Henry Miller's letters to her were published in 1965.

Nine Worthies, see *Irving, William.*

1919, novel by Dos Passos published in 1932. It is the second in the trilogy *U.S.A.* (collected 1938), including *The 42nd Parallel*♦ (1930) and *The Big Money*♦ (1936). Interspersed in the narrative are brief biographies of John Reed, Randolph Bourne, Theodore Roosevelt, Paxton Hibben, Wilson, J.P. Morgan, Joe Hill, Wesley Everest, and the Unknown Soldier. (For critical discussion, see *Dos Passos.*)

Joe Williams deserts from the navy, gets a forged seaman's certificate, and sails on tankers and freighters across the Atlantic, continuing his wanderings until the Armistice, although several times jailed and aboard torpedoed ships. Richard Ellsworth Savage, son of a genteelly poor New Jersey family, is aided by a politician, who sends him to Harvard. There he is an aesthete until, stirred by the war, he joins an ambulance corps in France and then, through the politician's influence, gets a commission in the U.S. Army. His eye ever on the main chance, he gets a post at the Peace Conference with the public relations office of J. Ward Moorehouse. Meanwhile he has an affair with Anne Trent, a confused Texas debutante who is on her way to do relief work in the Near East, but Dick refuses to marry her when she becomes pregnant, for fear of losing his chance to rise with Moorehouse. She gets hysterical, goes on a wild air flight, and is killed when the plane crashes. Eveline Hutchins, daughter of a wealthy Chicago minister, and her friend Eleanor Stoddard become interior decorators in New York City. Going to Paris with the Red Cross, Eveline has an affair with Jerry Burnham, an American correspondent, then with a young soldier, Paul Johnson, whom she inveigles into marriage. Eleanor resumes a former friendship with Moorehouse, but it does not develop because of his fickle attentions. Ben Compton, a bright young Brooklyn Jew, once a friend of Anne Trent, is active in a strike, becomes a Socialist, is an agitator at a Passaic mill strike, and is jailed. When released, he bums across the U.S., is beaten by police in Seattle because he is an I.W.W. radical, and is sent to prison for his pacifist agitation.

Nipmuck Indians, Massachusetts tribe allied with King Philip♦ in his war against the white colonists. Eliot's translation of the Bible was in the Nipmuck language.

NOAH, MORDECAI MANUEL (1785–1851), born in Philadelphia of a distinguished Portuguese-Jewish family, active in law, politics, and as a writer. His plays include *Paul and Alexis* (1812), a melodrama retitled *The Wandering Boys* (1821); *She Would Be a Soldier*♦ (1819); *The Siege of Tripoli* (1820), also produced as *Yuseff Caramalli* but unprinted; *Marion; or, The Hero of Lake George* (1821); and *The Grecian Captive* (1822). As consul to Tunis (1813–15) he won the release of Americans imprisoned by Algerian pirates. He wrote of his *Travels . . .* (1819) and collected *Gleanings . . .* (1845) from the six dailies he founded and edited.

Nobel Prizes, provided by the bequest of Alfred B. Nobel (1833–96), Swedish scientist, have been given annually since 1901 for the most significant contributions in the fields of chemistry, physics, medicine, and literature, and in the cause of peace. Awards are determined by committees at Stockholm and Oslo, and may be given to persons of any nationality. Each prize amounts to approximately $825,000 (1993). American-born recipients in literature are Sinclair Lewis (1930), O'Neill (1936), Pearl Buck (1938), T.S. Eliot (1948), Faulkner (1950), Hemingway (1954), Steinbeck (1962); Saul Bellow (1976), who, though born in Montreal, was raised in Chicago and calls himself "a Chicagoan out and out"; and Toni Morrison (1993). Recipients have also included two naturalized U.S. citizens who write in other languages: Isaac B. Singer (1978) and Czeslaw Milosz (1980).

Noble Savage (1960–62), magazine issued twice a year from New York in paperback book format, described by "Arias," an anonymous contributor to each issue, as having "no case to make for natural goodness," since "the man of nature is gone from this earth," but "we ourselves must pray to attach some nobility to our savagery." Saul Bellow was one of the three editors and contributing editors included Ralph Ellison, Herbert Gold, Arthur Miller, Wright Morris, and Harvey Swados, but other writers also contributed poetry, fiction, and essays, and each issue had an "Ancestors" section with texts by Samuel Butler, Lawrence, Pushkin, etc.

Nobody Knows My Name, personal essays by James Baldwin,♦ published in 1961, treating his ten-year expatriation in Europe, his return to Harlem, and his visit to the South during the period of school integration. Baldwin deals with black and white relations in the U.S. and Europe, with the relation of the artist to society, with Richard Wright, Faulkner, and Norman Mailer, and also with his views on the relationships of sexes.

NOCK, ALBERT JAY (1870–1945), iconoclastic author, by turns a minister, a muckraking journalist, a professor, and an independent commentator on social issues and ideas. His diverse writings appeared under his own name and

pseudonyms, independently and in various collaborations. His books include *How Diplomats Make War* (1915); *The Myth of a Guilty Nation* (1922); *Jefferson* (1926), a "study in conduct and character"; *The Theory of Education in the United States* (1932); *A Journal of These Days* (1934), a personal record, exhibiting the author's wit and irony as well as his prejudices; *Our Enemy, the State* (1935), expressing his extreme individualism; *Henry George: An Essay* (1939); *Meditations in Wall Street* (1940), aphorisms; and *Memoirs of a Superfluous Man* (1943), autobiography. He edited works of Artemus Ward (1924) and Rabelais (1931).

NOGUCHI, YONE (1875–1947), Japanese-born poet, came to the U.S. as a young man and became associated with Les Jeunes♦ of San Francisco and Joaquin Miller. Under their encouragement he wrote some odd, personal verse in seemingly uncertain English, *Seen and Unseen; or, Monologues of a Homeless Snail* (1897), which was praised by some for bohemian originality but was satirized by Norris in *The Octopus* and scorned by reviewers. *From the Eastern Sea* (1903) contains more conventional lyrics nostalgically recalling Japan from England, to which he moved. He returned home and was for a long time a professor at the University of Tokyo. Isamu Noguchi, the sculptor, is his son.

Nokomis, character in *Hiawatha.*♦

NOLAN, PHILIP (*c.*1771–1801), contraband horse trader along the Mexican border, who was killed in a skirmish resulting from his activities. His name was used for the leading figure in "The Man Without a Country," whose author, E.E. Hale, also wrote *The Real Philip Nolan* (1901), in which he explains that the historical Nolan is not the prototype of his character, although he was the subject of his other novel, *Philip Nolan's Friends* (1876).

NOLTE, VINCENT (1779–1853?), Italian-born merchant of German parentage, traveled widely, visited the U.S. several times, resided in New Orleans during the War of 1812, and was involved in various American ventures, including the United States Bank enterprise. His adventurous career, during which he encountered such figures as Napoleon, Victoria, Audubon, Jackson, Cooper, Delacroix, and Nicholas Biddle, is described in his *Fifty Years in Both Hemispheres, or Reminiscences of the Life of a Former Merchant* (translated from the German, 1854). He was also the author of works in German on finance and political economy, and is a principal character in *Anthony Adverse* by Hervey Allen.

NORDHOFF, CHARLES (1830–1901), Prussian-born journalist and author, whose earliest books are based on his youthful experiences as an American sailor. These are *Man-of-War Life* (1855), *The Merchant Vessel* (1855), *Whaling and Fishing* (1856), *Stories of the Island World* (1857), and a compilation of his first three books, *Nine Years a Sailor* (1857), edited by his grandson as *In Yankee Windjammers* (1940). He was an editor of the New York *Evening Post* (1861–71) and Washington correspondent of the New York *Herald* (1874–90). His newspaper assignments resulted in such books as *Secession Is Rebellion* (1860); *America for Free Working Men* (1865); *Communistic Societies in the United States* (1875), his most important contribution to social history; and *The Cotton States* (1876), an impartial political and economic investigation.

NORDHOFF, CHARLES BERNARD (1887–1947), grandson of Charles Nordhoff, served in World War I, where he met James N. Hall,♦ with whom he moved to Tahiti and wrote popular novels, including *Mutiny on the Bounty* (1932), *Men Against the Sea* (1934), and *Pitcairn's Island* (1934), a trilogy about the 18th-century mutiny against Captain Bligh; *The Hurricane* (1936), about contemporary Polynesian life; *Botany Bay* (1941); *Men Without Country* (1942); and *High Barbaree* (1945).

NORMAN, MARSHA (1947–), Kentucky-born dramatist whose first two-act play, *Getting Out* (1977, published as a book in 1979), is about a shattered woman emerging from prison and picking up her life. Two minor plays were produced by Actors Theatre in Louisville and a third by American Conservatory Theatre in San Francisco. She had far better staging of *'night, Mother* (1983, Pulitzer Prize), presenting a young woman about to commit suicide. After producing two more minor plays and then her novel, *The Fortune Teller* (1987), she wrote the book for a musical version of the classic children's novel *The Secret Garden* (1991). *Lunch with Lyn* (1994) is a one-act witty collage of lunchtime encounters between a fretful novelist and three friends.

NORRIS, CHARLES G[ILMAN] (1881–1945), brother of Frank Norris, author of novels dealing with such problems as modern education, women in business, hereditary and environmental influences, big business ethics, and birth control, which include *Salt* (1917), *Brass* (1921), *Bread* (1923), *Pig Iron* (1925), *Zelda Marsh* (1927), *Seed* (1930), *Bricks Without Straw* (1938), and *Flint* (1944).

KATHLEEN NORRIS (1880–1966), his wife, issued a steady flow of popular novels, beginning with *Mother* (1911), all characterized by a wholesome sentimental concern with domestic comedies and tragedies. *Family Gathering* (1959) is an informal autobiography.

NORRIS, FRANK (BENJAMIN FRANKLIN NORRIS) (1870–1902), was born in Chicago, but in 1884 moved to San Francisco with his parents.

After a year in a California preparatory school, he was sent to study art in Paris, where he spent his spare time writing medieval romances. While at the University of California (1890–94), he wrote short stories and sketches for student and local publications, as well as a romantic poem in three cantos, *Yvernelle, A Tale of Feudal France* (1892). Under the influence of Zola's fiction, he soon turned from his juvenile romanticism to naturalism and began a novel of lower- and middle-class life in San Francisco, which he later completed as *McTeague*♦ (1899). He next spent a year at Harvard, where he wrote more of *McTeague* and parts of *Vandover and the Brute* (1914).

In 1895–96 he was in South Africa, but failed in his project of writing travel sketches because of fighting between the English and Boers, which he reported for *Collier's* and the San Francisco *Chronicle*. He was ordered to leave the country, after being captured by the Boers, and returned to join the staff of *The Wave,* a San Francisco magazine, in which he serialized *Moran of the Lady Letty*♦ (1898). From his many contributions to this periodical also came the novelette *The Joyous Miracle* (1906) and two collections of short stories, *A Deal in Wheat* (1903) and *The Third Circle* (1909). These works exhibit his divided loyalty to the currently popular romantic realism of Kipling and the naturalistic attitude of Zola. The former influence caused him, like Stephen Crane, to go to Cuba (1898), where he reported the Santiago campaign of the Spanish-American War for *McClure's Magazine*. Upon his return (1899), he was employed by the publishing firm of Doubleday, Page, which that year issued *McTeague* and *Blix,*♦ a semi-autobiographical love story. *A Man's Woman*♦ (1900) is a romantic work in the vein of Jack London's novels.

About this time, moved by his growing concern with social and economic forces, Norris conceived the plan of his "Epic of the Wheat," a trilogy to consist of *The Octopus,* a novel dealing with the raising of wheat in California, and the struggle of the ranchers against the railroad; *The Pit,* a tale of speculation in the Chicago wheat exchange; and *The Wolf,* about the consumption of the wheat as bread in a famine-stricken European village. He visited a wheat ranch in California and wrote *The Octopus*♦ (1901), which is considered his finest work. Before his sudden death following an appendix operation, he had written *The Pit*♦ (1903), which became extremely popular. "The Wolf" was left unwritten.

The Responsibilities of the Novelist (1903), a collection of essays and articles, contains a statement of his artistic credo, in which he says that the novelist "of all men cannot think only of himself or for himself," but must rather sacrifice money, fashion, and popularity for the greater reward of realizing that he has told the truth. The best type of novel, according to Norris, "proves something, draws conclusions from a whole congeries of forces, social tendencies, race impulses, devotes itself not to a study of men but of man." In *McTeague* and *The Octopus,* despite their romantic elements and occasional extravagances, he is considered to have achieved his idealistic purpose and to have presented a vivid, authentic portrayal of contemporary life in California. Other posthumous publications include *Vandover and the Brute,* ♦ printed in 1914 from the uncorrected draft of his second novel; *Frank Norris of The Wave* (1931), a selection of his magazine fiction; and *Works* (10 vols., 1928), containing other previously uncollected articles and stories, with introductions by leading authors, including his brother Charles Norris. His *Letters* were first collected in 1956 and in a greatly enlarged edition in 1986.

North American Phalanx, most scientifically planned of all the American experiments in Fourierism, ♦ was founded at Red Bank, N.J. (1843), by Albert Brisbane, with the advice of Parke Godwin, W.H. Channing, Horace Greeley, and George Ripley. The colony maintained a three-story phalanstery, a gristmill, and a large orchard, and occupied a considerable area of fertile land. The members, mostly people of culture and refinement, ate their meals together, but each family had separate quarters and each member was allowed to work at the task which best suited him. Careful attention was paid to the education of children. When the mill burned (1854), the association was dissolved.

North American Review, The (1815–1939, 1963–), Boston magazine, founded as an outgrowth of *The Monthly Anthology,* was edited by William Tudor, with the assistance of E.T. Channing, R.H. Dana, Sr., and others, as a quarterly literary, critical, and historical review on the order of its English contemporaries, with the purpose of achieving a greater national scope than any previous American magazine. It was nevertheless scholarly and was closely affiliated with Harvard and Boston Unitarianism. Among its early contributions were Bryant's "Thanatopsis" (1817) and "To a Waterfowl" (1818). Edward Everett, Jared Sparks, and J.G. Palfrey, as later editors, continued the magazine's high standards, but were more inclined toward history than belles lettres. The *Review* later became a monthly and included among its editors C.E. Norton, Lowell, Henry Adams, and H.C. Lodge. Among its contributors were Emerson, Irving, Longfellow, Parkman, E.P. Whipple, Motley, Holmes, Howells, Boyesen, Whitman, Clemens, and Henry James. It moved to New York City (1878), where, separated from the Brahmin atmosphere, it plunged into a maelstrom of contemporaneity, becoming concerned with the latest political and social movements. At the turn of the century, it had a diverse list of authors, including Tolstoy, D'Annunzio, Maeterlinck, H.G. Wells, Alan Seeger, Bryan, James Bryce, Clemens, Howells, and Hen-

ry James. After World War I, circulation diminished greatly and the magazine became again a quarterly. It was revived as a quarterly in 1963, published by Cornell College of Iowa, now named the University of Northern Iowa.

North of Boston, poems by Robert Frost. ♦

North Star (1847–64), antislavery newspaper founded at Rochester, N.Y., by Frederick Douglass. ♦ A weekly journal, it was later called *Frederick Douglass's Paper* and was considered a noteworthy example of contemporary journalism, irrespective of its stand against slavery. It differed from *The Liberator* by favoring peaceful political methods.

North Woods, region of lakes and coniferous forests, including northern Minnesota, Wisconsin, and Michigan, and parts of southern Canada. Northwestern Canada, the region extending as far as the Klondike, is known as the Far North. The primitive lives of the few inhabitants of these regions in the 19th and early 20th century, chiefly miners, trappers, woodsmen, and Indians, have been treated, since Jack London, by many authors of popular adventure fiction, notably James Oliver Curwood, Rex Beach, and Stewart Edward White, and in the Nick Adams stories of Ernest Hemingway, while the ballads of Robert Service depict conventional heroes and scoundrels in the icy Far North from a similar point of view. Ernest Thompson Seton has written of the animals of the North Woods, as have other authors of fiction for children. In the late 19th century, the North Woods was the scene of an invasion by lumbermen, who deforested large areas. During this spectacular period, the lumberjacks developed a unique body of legends concerned with the fictional hero Paul Bunyan. ♦

Northwest, as distinguished from the old Northwest Territory, ♦ is the region including the states of Oregon, Washington, and western Montana and Idaho. Characterized on the Pacific coast by a humid, forested area, and east of the Cascade Mountains by a high arid tableland and great fertile valleys, the region has varied industries, the most prominent being salmon fishing, lumbering, agriculture, and cattle raising. Its central waterway, the Columbia River, was discovered and claimed for the U.S. in 1792, and the Lewis and Clark expedition, as well as the fur-trading activities of John Jacob Astor, further established U.S. interests in the Northwest, later the cause of the Oregon Question, which was not finally settled until 1846. Up to this time, the history of the territory had been that of the fur trade and of pioneer immigration by way of the Oregon Trail, ♦ whose most famous figures were Jedediah Smith and Marcus Whitman. ♦ After 1850 began the marked development of agriculture and industry, with later homesteading encouraged by the railroading accomplishments of Henry Villard and James J. Hill. Washington Irving described the fur trade in *Astoria*♦; Honoré Morrow's novel *We Must March* tells the story of Marcus Whitman; Emerson Hough's *54–40 or Fight!* and other books are concerned with the Oregon Question; Frank B. Linderman has written of frontier Montana; James Stevens and others have collected the Paul Bunyan stories of the Northwest lumber camps; Oregon in the early 1900s is described in H.L. Davis's *Honey in the Horn;* and modern life in the region is the subject of novels by Archie Binns and Robert Cantwell.

Northwest Passage, novel by Kenneth Roberts. ♦

Northwest Territory, the Old Northwest, as distinguished from the present Northwest, ♦ was formed by the Great Lakes region between the Ohio and Mississippi rivers, including the present states of Ohio, Indiana, Illinois, Michigan, Wisconsin, and a portion of Minnesota. It was first traversed by such French explorers as Duluth, La Salle, Jolliet, Cadillac, and Marquette, and was governed in conjunction with Louisiana and Canada. After the French influence became widespread, British interests represented by the Ohio Company began the conflict that led to Washington's expedition and the French and Indian Wars. After the British obtained Canada and the Old Northwest by the Treaty of Paris of 1763, the territory was involved in the uprising of Pontiac and the actions of Robert Rogers. During the Revolutionary War, it was conquered by George Rogers Clark, and by the Treaty of Paris of 1783 was given to the U.S. Several of the new states claimed the area, but it was finally placed under the control of the U.S. Congress and organized under the Ordinance of 1787. Subsequent unrest occurred due to Indian hostility, British agitation, and conflict of settlers. Even after the area was split into several different territories, the conflict with British influence had much to do with precipitating the War of 1812, and the problem of domination did not finally end until the Treaty of Ghent. Many authors of historical fiction have written of events in the history of the Territory; among their works are Kenneth Roberts's *Northwest Passage,* Winston Churchill's *The Crossing,* and Maurice Thompson's *Alice of Old Vincennes.*

NORTON, ANDREWS (1786–1853), Massachusetts Biblical scholar, associated with Harvard (1811–30). He founded and edited *The General Repository and Review* (1812–13), a Unitarian magazine, and his most important work, *The Evidences of the Genuineness of the Gospels* (3 vols., 1837, 1844), examined the New Testament in the light of information outside the Bible, being complemented by *Internal Evidences of the Genuineness of the Gospels* (1855). Other works written from his conservative Unitarian point of view include *On the Latest Form of Infidelity* (1839), a reply to Emerson's Divinity School Address and the publications of George Ripley, and *Tracts on Christianity* (1852). This was in turn answered by Theodore Parker.

NORTON, CHARLES ELIOT (1827–1908), son of Andrews Norton, is best known as professor of the history of fine art at Harvard (1873–98), although his broad range of scholarship, lofty and catholic taste, and great personal charm extended his influence far beyond the confines of the university. He was a frequent contributor to the *Atlantic Monthly,* co-editor of *The North American Review* (1864–68), a founder and co-editor of *The Nation* (1865), and the author of books as widely varied as a bibliography of Michelangelo and a biography of Kipling. In addition to his Italian scholarship, whose main fruit was a prose translation of the *Divine Comedy* (3 vols., 1891–92), his editorial activities extended from *The Poems of John Donne* (2 vols., 1895) to *The Early Letters of Thomas Carlyle* (2 vols., 1886). His friendships with distinguished artists and writers of his time, on both sides of the Atlantic, formed a powerful cultural influence in the U.S. His *Letters* (2 vols., 1913) are justly famous, and separate collections of his correspondence with particular individuals have been published.

NORTON, JOHN (1606–63), after receiving a B.A. (1624) and an M.A. (1627) from Cambridge and serving as a private chaplain in England emigrated to New England (1635) because of his Puritan sympathies. He immediately assumed an important place in the Massachusetts Bay Colony, becoming a "teacher" in the Ipswich church, a leading opponent of the Antinomians, a moving force in the drafting of the Cambridge Platform, and later pastor of the First Church of Boston and an overseer of Harvard. His scholarship and commanding manner gave him his prominence, which he lost in the later part of his life through his bigoted insistence on the persecution of the Quakers and his failure to aid the colony when sent as an agent to Charles II. His writings include *Responsio ad Guliel* (1648), a Latin treatise on New England church government; *A Discussion of that Great Point in Divinity, the Sufferings of Christ* (1653), an attack on the heresy of William Pynchon; *Abel Being Dead Yet Speaketh; or The Life and Death of . . . John Cotton* (1658), considered the first separately published biography of an American; and *The Heart of N-England Rent at the Blasphemies of the Present Generation* (1659), an attack on the Quakers.

Notes of a Native Son, a body of essays written between 1948 and 1955, the year of their book publication, that established James Baldwin's♦ reputation as a major essayist and spokesperson for African Americans. It is a three-part book. The first part, on African-American identity, contains "Everybody's Protest Novel" and "Many Thousands Gone," both critical of Richard Wright.♦ Part 2, containing the title essay, treats life in Harlem and Baldwin's life under his father. Part 3 is meditations by Baldwin as an expatriate in France and Switzerland.

Notes of a Son and Brother, autobiographical narrative by Henry James,♦ published in 1914. A sequel to *A Small Boy and Others,* ♦ this volume is concerned with the years from the late 1850s to 1870, and the central figures are again the author, his brother William, and the elder Henry James.

Notes on English Verse, see *Rationale of Verse.*

Notes on the Mind, see *Edwards, Jonathan.*

Notes on the State of Virginia, by Jefferson,♦ privately published at Paris in 1784 (dated 1782), is an unpretentious, patriotic compendium of statistical information on the geography, fauna and flora, and social and political life of the region. It was originally written (1781–82) in answer to questions from the Marquis de Barbé-Marbois, secretary of the French legation at Philadelphia. A French translation (1786) was followed by the first general edition, issued in London in 1787.

Notes Toward a Supreme Fiction, long poem by Wallace Stevens, ♦ published in 1942.

Composed of a prologue, 30 poems divided into three sections ("It Must Be Abstract," "It Must Change," "It Must Give Pleasure"), and an epilogue, each seven stanzas long, containing three verses in a metric form like iambic pentameter, the poem does not attempt to develop a sequential argument but is made up of meditations concerned with the nature of reality, man's perceptions, and poetic imagination. Reality is always changing; to treat reality requires imagination that may comprehend its variety. The poet in treating reality is concerned with providing a fiction that will please in the way that once a belief in a personal deity gave spiritual joy. In turn such fiction provides a faith by which man, a soldier in wartime, can live and die.

Nothing To Wear, see *Butler, W.A.*

NOTT, Henry Junius (1797–1837), South Carolina jurist and professor whose *Novelettes of a Traveller; or, Odds and Ends from the Knapsack of Thomas Singularity, Journeyman Printer* (2 vols., 1834) is a series of humorous sketches in a picaresque plan. Its realistic depiction of frontier life is a less brilliant but earlier example of the humor of the Southwest, as represented by Longstreet, Hooper, Baldwin, and others.

NOVANGLUS, pseudonym used by John Adams♦ in his attacks on Daniel Leonard.♦

November Boughs, collection of poems and prose by Whitman,♦ published in 1888. Its verse was

incorporated in *Leaves of Grass* as "Sands at Seventy," and its prose preface, "A Backward Glance o'er Travel'd Roads,"♦ became the epilogue of *Leaves of Grass* in 1889. The other prose later appeared in the *Complete Writings* (1902).

NOYES, John Humphrey (1811–86), born in Vermont, after graduation from Dartmouth (1830) studied theology at Andover and Yale. He lost his license to preach (1834) when he propounded his doctrine of perfectionism,♦ or complete freedom from sin. His colony of Bible Communists at Putney, Vt. (1836–46), a socioreligious community of perfectionists, came to an end when he fled from charges of adultery, which arose from the colony's system of complex marriages. He carried out his theories more successfully at the Oneida Community♦ (1848–79), but was again threatened with legal action, and removed to Canada, where he died. His views were expounded in *The Berean* (1847), and developed in *Bible Communism* (1848), *Male Continence* (1848), *Scientific Propagation* (c.1873), and *Home Talks* (1875). He also wrote *History of American Socialisms* (1870).

No. 44, The Mysterious Stranger, see *Mysterious Stranger.*

Number One, novel by Dos Passos,♦ published in 1943. It is the second volume in the trilogy that also includes *Adventures of a Young Man* and *The Grand Design.*

Tyler Spotswood is secretary and spokesman for Chuck Crawford, Southern politician and demagogic propagandist of a movement based on his slogan, "Every Man a Millionaire." As Crawford's ambition and greed carry him through unscrupulous oil deals and lower offices to the U.S. Senate, with the presidency frankly his goal, Tyler stifles his latent decency and his growing love for Crawford's wife. His health wrecked by excessive drinking and hard campaigning in behalf of Crawford, Tyler spends a long period recuperating. During his absence, federal attorneys, who set out to scotch Crawford's career, discover that Tyler and others are implicated in mishandling of funds. When Crawford abandons him to a probable prison sentence, although the misdeeds and their benefits were his own, Tyler's sick mind grasps the ultimate rascality and danger of the senator, but he refuses to escape punishment by betraying him.

NYE, Edgar Wilson (1850–96), better known as Bill Nye, was born in Maine, reared in the frontier country of Wisconsin, and removed to Wyoming Territory (1876), where he was admitted to the bar and edited the *Laramie Boomerang* (1881–84), a local newspaper. His humorous writings were frequently reprinted and won him international fame. In 1889 he moved east and continued to write in a similar vein for the New

York *World*. His writings were characterized by the loud and obvious humor typical of the period, and he employed such stylistic devices as misquotation, punning, malapropisms, and understatement, all juxtaposed in magnificently deformed sentences. Under his pseudonym, he published a series of very successful books, beginning with *Bill Nye and Boomerang* (1881). Some of these were compiled from his brief newspaper sketches, while others have a lengthy continuity of subject, as in the comic *History of the United States* (1894) and *History of England* (1896). After 1885 his reputation was increased by his humorous lectures, in which he frequently appeared with James Whitcomb Riley.

O

O Captain! My Captain!, poem by Whitman,♦ published in *Sequel to Drum-Taps* (1865–66) and in *Leaves of Grass* (1867). Although Whitman thought far less of this elegy on the death of Lincoln than he did of that entitled "When Lilacs Last in the Door Yard Bloom'd," it has attained great popularity because of its relatively regular stanzaic form, rhyme, rhythmic pattern, and refrain. It tells of a ship, representative of the Union, coming safely into port, with "the people all exulting," while the poet sadly walks the deck on which lies his Captain, "fallen cold and dead."

O. HENRY, pseudonym of W.S. Porter. ♦

O. Henry Awards, prizes granted annually to winners included in the anthologies *Prize Stories: The O. Henry Awards* (1919–) of works by American authors that appeared during the year in American periodicals. Winners have included Dorothy Parker, Faulkner, Saroyan, Eudora Welty, Flannery O'Connor, and Alice Adams.

O Pioneers!, novel by Willa Cather,♦ published in 1913.
    John Bergson, a strong-willed Swedish immigrant, struggles to build a farm on the Nebraska prairie, aided by his wife, their sons Lou and Oscar, and his favorite, the capable, intelligent daughter, Alexandra. At his death, Alexandra assumes responsibility for the farm and the family, since her mother lacks ingenuity or determination, and her older brothers are obstinate and plodding, while her brother Emil is a child of five. She possesses the heroic, creative quality of the passing frontier, and over a period of years her faith in the soil is rewarded by rich harvests. She is not satisfied by her increasing prosperity, however, for after the departure of Carl Linstrum, who seeks a career as an engraver, she lacks companionship in a society of weaker and meaner individuals. Emil is now a grown youth, sensitive and intelligent, for whom Alexandra has great hopes, but he has a secret affair with her friend Marie Shabata, and the two are killed by Marie's jealous husband Frank. Meanwhile Carl has visited the Bergsons on his way to the Klondike, and he and Alexandra find in each other the complementary qualities each needs. When he learns of Emil's death, Carl returns to marry Alexandra, and they plan to share the responsibilities and fulfillments of life on the farm.

Oak Openings, The; or, The Bee-Hunter, romance by Cooper,♦ published in 1848.

In Michigan, at the opening of the War of 1812, the bee-hunter Benjamin Boden, called *Le Bourdon* ("The Drone"), is joined at his "Honey Castle" (*Château au Miel*) by the drunken settler Gershom Waring, and the Indians Elksfoot and Pigeonswing. He learns that the British have captured the fort at Mackinaw, and that Pigeonswing is a U.S. army messenger, while Elksfoot is a British spy. On his way with Waring to the latter's home, Boden finds the corpse of Elksfoot, who has been scalped by Pigeonswing. At Waring's home, he meets the settler's wife and his attractive sister Margery, and wins their gratitude by destroying Waring's supply of liquor. Just before the arrival of a band of pro-British Potawatami, they abandon the cabin. After rescuing Pigeonswing, they are joined by Parson Amen and the American corporal Flint, both bound for Mackinaw in the company of a renegade Indian, Onoah, or Scalping Pete. At Boden's "Castle," they are surrounded by the Potawatami, with whom Pete pretends to parley while actually plotting the massacre of the whites. He is friendly to Boden, however, and urges him to marry Margery, so that the two may escape. They do marry, and afterward Amen and Flint are killed, but, with the aid of Pigeonswing and the repentant Pete, the other whites escape.

OAKES, URIAN (*c.*1631–81), Massachusetts poet and clergyman, born in England, graduated from Harvard (1649), returned to his native country to teach and preach, but settled in New England (1671) because of his staunch Puritan orthodoxy. His one published poem, an *Elegie* (1677) on Thomas Shepard, has been highly praised, as has the prose in his various published sermons. While pastor of the Church of Cambridge, he was also acting president of Harvard (1675–80), and he is accused of having allowed the near extinction of the college.

Oakhurst, JOHN, character in *The Outcasts of Poker Flat*♦ and other stories by Bret Harte. ♦

Oakley, DORINDA, character in *Barren Ground.* ♦

OATES, JOYCE CAROL (1938–), born in Lockport, N.Y., after graduation from Syracuse University and an M.A. from the University of Wisconsin became a professor of English, first at the University of Detroit, then the University of Windsor, Ontario, and since 1987 at Princeton, and a remarkably prolific author. Her novels are

With Shuddering Fall (1964); A Garden of Earthly
Delights (1967); Expensive People (1968); them
(1969, National Book Award); Wonderland
(1971); Do with Me What You Will (1973); The
Assassins (1975); The Childwold (1976); The Tri-
umph of the Spider Monkey (1978); Bellefleur (1980);
A Bloodsmoor Romance (1982); Last Days (1984);
Solstice (1985); Marya, a Life (1986); You Must
Remember This (1987); Raven's Wing (1987);
American Appetites (1989); Because It Is Bitter, and
Because It Is My Heart (1990); I Lock the Door Upon
Myself (1990); Black Water (1992), a novella about
a young woman who drowns in a car driven off a
bridge by a U.S. senator; Foxfire: Confessions of a
Girl Gang (1993), which features an outlaw band
of female warriors in a grim upstate New York
city, and their fierce loyalty to their leader and
founder; and What I Lived for (1994), her 23rd
novel, about a complex and troubled man. Her
fiction is peopled with realistically presented but
often demonic persons whose attempts to express
their own characters are frustrated by the grotesque and virulent culture of the U.S. (often
symbolized by Detroit) and thus lead them into
convulsive violence. The savage psychological
portrayals of these people caught up in their passions and also victims of forces beyond their control or comprehension are presented as those of
dwellers in a dark and destructive society. Her
numerous stories have been collected in By the
North Gate (1963), Upon the Sweeping Flood
(1966), The Wheel of Love (1970), Marriages and
Infidelities (1972), The Hungry Ghosts (1974), The
Goddess and Other Women (1974), Where Are You
Going, Where Have You Been? (1974), The Poi-
soned Kiss (1975), The Seduction (1975), Crossing
the Border (1976), Night-Side (1977), and Where Is
Here? Stories (1992). Haunted, Tales of the Grotesque (1994) prints new short stories. She has also
written poetry, collected in Women in Love
(1968), Anonymous Sins (1969), Love and Its De-
rangements (1970), Angel Fire (1973), Dreaming
America (1973), Women Whose Lives Are Food,
Men Whose Lives Are Money (1978), Invisible
Women: New and Selected Poems 1970–1982 (1982),
and The Time Traveler: Poems 1983–1989 (1990).
Her essays and critical writings are gathered in
The Edge of Impossibility (1971), The Hostile Sun
(1973), New Heaven, New Earth (1974), Contraries
(1981), The Profane Art: Essays and Reviews (1982),
On Boxing (1987), and (Woman) Writer: Occasions
and Opportunities (1988).

Oath of a Free-man, legal formulary of Massachusetts probably first drafted in 1631, revised
(1634) to include a statement of the freeman's
obligation, again revised (c.1648) as the Freemans
Oath, fitted to the status of one "now to be made
free" instead of one already an "Inhabitant, and
Freeman," and finally revised (1664) to include
an oath of allegiance to the Crown, lacking in the
previous forms. The 1634 version was probably
the one employed for Stephen Daye's broadside

(1639), the first piece of printing in what is now
the United States. No copy of Daye's printed
form exists, but its text is known through John
Child's pamphlet New Englands Jonas cast up at
London (1647).

Objectivist, school of poetry influenced by William Carlos Williams that came to prominence in
the 1930s. It sees poetry as process whose form
begins with the object dealt with and moves by
improvisation through verbal associations inspired by the initial object. Leading Objectivist
poets are George Oppen, Charles Reznikoff, and
Louis Zukofsky.

O'BRIEN, FITZ-JAMES (c.1828–62), Irish-born
journalist and author, came to the U.S. (c.1852),
where he was soon a conspicuous figure at Pfaff's
Cellar and other New York bohemian rendezvous. Although he had previously contributed
to Irish and English periodicals, his reputation is
based on his writings for American journals, especially his rococo short stories dealing with psychological subjects reminiscent of Poe. The most
notable of these, "The Diamond Lens" (Atlantic
Monthly, Jan. 1858), tells of the inventor of a
powerful microscope, who was enabled to see a
sylph-like human being enclosed in a drop of
water. After becoming obsessed by this fascinating creature, he went mad when she died. "The
Wondersmith" and "What Was It?" were similar
fantastic stories. O'Brien also wrote some plays
and many commonplace verses. His most notable
play was The Gentleman from Ireland (1854). He
died from a wound received in a Civil War battle. His Poems and Stories were collected by his
friend William Winter (1881).

O'BRIEN, FREDERICK (1869–1932), journalist
and globe-trotting vagabond, whose first book,
White Shadows in the South Seas (1919), an account of his life in the Marquesas, had a nationwide vogue with a public weary of wartime realities. He wrote two similar books, has been
credited with reviving interest in the works of
Melville, and inspired a host of imitations exploiting the glamour of the Pacific islands.

O'BRIEN, [WILLIAM] TIM[OTHY] (1946–   ),
novelist. Born in Minnesota, O'Brien was drafted
immediately after graduation from Macalester
College and sent to Vietnam, where he was
wounded near My Lai. That experience has been
the material of his novels, especially in three
thinly fictionalized books that rank high in 20th-
century American war literature. If I Die in a
Combat Zone, Box Me Up and Ship Me Home
(1973), his first book, is a series of linked sketches;
his second, Going After Cacciato (1978), employs
magic realism as it follows some breakaway
members of a platoon marching across Asia to
Paris (National Book Award, 1979); and The
Things They Carried (1990), again platoon experi-

ences, brings out the futility of getting at the truth of what actually happens, and why, in war. *In the Lake of the Woods* (1994) is a mystery in which the shadowy legacy of Vietnam stands as a symbol for the traumatic changes in society over the past few decades.

Obscure Destinies, novelettes by Willa Cather. ♦

O'CATARACT, JEHU, see *Neal, John.*

OCCOM, SAMSON (1723–92), Mohegan Indian of Connecticut, was converted to Christianity by Whitefield (1739) and educated by Eleazar Wheelock. He preached to the Montauk, Stockbridge, and other Indians, received Presbyterian orders (1759), and visited England (1766–67), where he preached to raise money for Dartmouth College. He edited a *Choice Collection of Hymns and Spiritual Songs* (1774), and several hymns are attributed to him.

Occurrence at Owl Creek Bridge, An, story by Bierce in *Tales of Soldiers and Civilians.* ♦

OCHS, ADOLPH S[IMON] (1858–1935), born in Cincinnati, reared in Tennessee, began his career as a newspaper publisher by purchasing the *Chattanooga Times* (1878). In 1896 he acquired *The New York Times*♦ and, by avoiding partisan or personal bias and sensationalism, raised it to a position generally considered the most eminent among U.S. papers. *An Honorable Titan* (1946) is a biography by Gerald Johnson.

O'CONNOR, EDWIN (1918–68), born in Rhode Island, after graduation from Notre Dame and service in the Coast Guard during World War II became a radio writer and producer. His books are *The Oracle* (1951), a caricature of a popular radio broadcaster; *The Last Hurrah* (1956), a lively portrayal of a big city boss, a demagogue and a rogue, but withal a warmly human Irish-American, presumably suggested by Boston's longtime mayor James M. Curley; *The Edge of Sadness* (1961, Pulitzer Prize), again set in a city modeled on Boston, portraying with sympathy the rector of a small Catholic parish, himself a reformed drunkard, and other vivid Irish-American characters; and *I Was Dancing* (1964), about an aging vaudeville performer's cunning fight to keep from being sent to a home for old people.

O'CONNOR, FLANNERY (1925–64), Georgia author, whose Gothic novels are *Wise Blood*♦ (1952), about a young religious fanatic who tries to establish a Church Without Christ in his Georgia mountain region; and *The Violent Bear It Away* (1960), a macabre tale set in the backwoods of Georgia and presenting the fanatical mission of a boy intent on baptizing a still younger boy. Her stories, set in the South and also grotesque, are

collected in *A Good Man Is Hard to Find* (1955, titled *The Artificial Nigger* in England), *Everything That Rises Must Converge* (1965), and *Complete Stories* (1971). Occasional prose was collected as *Mystery and Manners* (1969) and letters as *The Habit of Being* (1979). O'Connor represents a combination unique in modern American fiction: a writer deeply religious exploring the conflict between the sacred and the profane, and sometimes their merger, in a grittily regional setting. Her most memorable stories, "Good Country People," "A Good Man Is Hard to Find," and the title story in *Everything That Rises Must Converge,* are haunting, comic, and realistic depictions of the struggle of souls to know themselves, to escape evil, and to reach God. Most of her fiction is printed in a Library of America edition; she is the only author of her generation to be thus honored.

O'CONNOR, WILLIAM DOUGLAS (1832–89), journalist and minor government official, is best known for *The Good Gray Poet* (1866), a defense of his friend Whitman written upon the latter's dismissal from a governmental clerkship. The title of his book gave the poet his sobriquet. Whitman in turn wrote a preface for O'Connor's posthumous collection *Three Tales* (1892), containing "The Carpenter," and idealized Christlike depiction of the poet. O'Connor was also the author of an Abolitionist novel, *Harrington* (1860), and of two pamphlets that contended that Bacon was the author of Shakespeare's plays.

Octave Thanet, pseudonym of Alice French. ♦

Octopus, The: A Story of California, novel by Frank Norris, ♦ published in 1901 as the first part of his uncompleted trilogy, "The Epic of the Wheat."

The central theme in this realistic study of California farm life is the growing and harvesting of the wheat. Magnus Derrick operates the great Rancho de los Muertos, near Bonneville in the San Joaquin Valley, and is the leading spokesman for the farmers of the community. His son Harran helps him to manage their tenants and agricultural activities, while another son, Lyman, is a corporation lawyer in San Francisco. Among the neighboring farmers are Broderson, Osterman, and Annixter, all of whom are associated in a struggle to resist the encroachments of the Pacific and Southwestern Railroad, which dominates the state government and gradually extends its monopoly over other industries. The railroad is in complete control of Bonneville, for it subsidizes Genslinger, editor of the town paper, and, through S. Behrman, its unofficial agent, influences prices, interest rates, and all financial transactions. When Dyke, a veteran engineer, quits his position rather than accept a wage cut and becomes a farmer, he is ruined because of exorbitant freight rates, and in desperation robs a train, later ending up in prison. Presley, a poet from the East, stays for a time at Derrick's ranch and learns to sympathize with the cause of the oppressed farmers. He writes a poem about them that is widely popular, but finds it has no effect in the conflict of tremendous issues and resigns himself to being only an observer of the stirring events which follow. The farmers hold much of their land an option from the railroad, which raises the price enormously and puts up the land for public sale. Outraged by the broken promises and unfair tactics of Behrman and the corporation, the farmers form a protective league to protest and influence the state administration in their interests, electing Magnus Derrick their president. The league succeeds in placing Lyman on the state commission to fix rates, but he is bribed by the railroad and betrays his backers. When the railroad causes legal authorities to dispossess the farmers of their land, they revolt and in an armed clash many are killed, including Annixter, who has just married Hilma Tree. The railroad has now won complete domination, and the families of the insurgents are thrown into poverty and suffering. Magnus has been disgraced and ruined and is forced to enter the employment of Behrman, who is later accidentally smothereed to death while watching the loading on shipboard of his own dishonestly gained wheat. Presley, indignant over the outrages he has witnessed, visits Shelgrim, president of the railroad, but instead of the inhumane criminal he had expected finds Shelgrim sentimental and genial, convinced that his actions are dictated by circumstances and economic laws.

Octoroon, The, melodramatic play about slavery by Dion Boucicault,♦ produced in 1859. It was based on *The Quadroon*♦ by Mayne Reid.

Ode Recited at the Commemoration to the Living and Dead Soldiers of Harvard University, by Lowell,♦ privately printed in 1865 and published in *The Cathedral* (1877). It is in the irregular form of the Pindaric ode as adapted by Cowley.

Although song is "weak-winged," yet "feathered words" will recall the love for Truth that inspired the sons of Harvard to sacrifice their lives and make faith "whole with deed." Such sacrifice for an ideal gives the world of constant change "a high immunity from Night." Lincoln is symbolic of the courageous warrior against falsehood, and as long as men are loyal to an inspiring goal "outside of Self" they shall revere those who have died for its preservation. In gratitude, they shall give "that plain civic wreath," nobler than the feudal rewards of Europe, for it is no one man who is celebrated, but rather "the pith and marrow of a nation."

Ode Sung at the Occasion of Decorating the Graves of the Confederate Dead, delivered at Charleston (1867), was written by Timrod♦ and

published in his *Poems* (1873). In five quatrains of octosyllabic lines, this elegy on "martyrs of the fallen cause" declares that, though no marble column yet honors their defeated valor, the blossom of their fame is blown,

> And somewhere, waiting for its birth,
> The shaft is in the stone.

ODELL, GEORGE C[LINTON] D[ENSMORE] (1866–1949), professor of English (1895–1924) and of dramatic literature (1924–39) at Columbia, and author of *Shakespeare from Betterton to Irving* (1920) and *Annals of the New York Stage* (15 vols., 1927–49).

ODELL, JONATHAN (1737–1818), was born in New Jersey, and after graduation from the College of New Jersey (1759) became a surgeon in the British army. During a residence in England he was an Anglican minister. In his native colony, at the outbreak of the Revolution, he indicated his sympathies by writing "A Birthday Song" (1776) in honor of the king, attacking the patriots. He escaped to New York, and, remaining within the British lines until the end of the war, served as an army chaplain, as secretary to Sir Guy Carleton, and as a go-between in the treasonable negotiations of André and Benedict Arnold. He also aided the British by contributing essays and satirical poetry to *Rivington's New York Gazetteer.* Although less poetic than the other Loyalist writer, Joseph Stansbury, he was more virulent, and showed his ability at versified invective in such works as "Word of Congress" (1779), an attack on the Continental Congress, and "The American Times" (1780), published under the pseudonym Camillo Querno and generally attributed to him, which denounced the American leaders. His poetry was first collected in *The Loyal Verses of Joseph Stansbury and Doctor Jonathan Odell* (1860). After the war, he went temporarily to England, and he spent his later life in New Brunswick.

ODETS, CLIFFORD (1906–63), born in Philadelphia and reared in the Bronx, quit school at 15 to become an actor. After acting with the Theatre Guild, he became a founder of the Group Theatre (1931), and was catapulted to fame by its production of his one-act play *Waiting for Lefty*♦ (1935), dealing with a taxi strike. This success was followed by the production of *Awake and Sing*♦ (1935) and the one-act play *Till the Day I Die* (1935), about the struggle of the German Communists at the beginning of the Hitler regime. These plays brought Odets a reputation as the leading proletarian playwright at the time, although he was less concerned with the problems of the worker than with the "fraud" of middle-class civilization, deprived by its economic insecurity of its former status and becoming aware that most of its cherished ideals no longer correspond to realities. Further realistic plays written for the Group are *Paradise Lost* (1935); *Golden Boy* (1937; revised as a musical, 1964), about a young Italian-American violinist whose desire for wealth and fame leads him to become a pugilist, and who dies in an automobile crash, having attempted to find an escape in speed from the loss of his inner security; *Rocket to the Moon* (1938), portraying a Bronx dentist who attempts to find happiness in a belated love affair, but fails because his will has been vitiated by the meanness of his past life; *Night Music* (1940), the love story of a lower-middle-class couple in New York; and *Clash by Night* (1941), a love "triangle." Later plays, infrequent because of motion-picture work, are *The Big Knife* (1948), about an idealistic actor corrupted by money easily earned from motion pictures; *The Country Girl* (1950), about an alcoholic actor's marriage; and *The Flowering Peach* (1954), a retelling of the Noah tale.

ODIORNE, THOMAS (1769–1851), New Hampshire poet, graduate of Dartmouth (1791), who wrote *The Progress of Refinement* (1792), a long romantic poem displaying a philosophical interest in nature. Influenced poetically by James Thomson and Akenside, Odiorne was a precursor of the romantic movement in his use of the philosophy of Locke and David Hartley to show the mutual adjustment of man and nature, and the way in which man can attain an ideal ethical state.

Of Mice and Men, novelette by Steinbeck,♦ published in 1937 and dramatized by the author in 1937.

George Milton and Lennie Small, itinerant farm laborers, come to work on a Salinas Valley ranch in central California. Lennie has tremendous strength but a feeble intellect, and possesses a morbid desire to handle soft objects. George compensates for Lennie's deficiencies by exploiting his strength and cherishing their mutual dream of a small farm of their own. Curley, son of the boss, is an arrogant bully whose bride's promiscuity has already caused quarrels among the farmhands. When jealousy prompts him to pick a fight with Lennie, he emerges with a crushed hand, and his wife begins to admire the unwilling Lennie. She seeks a pretext to be alone with him, and one day in the hayloft tries to arouse his desire. He begins to stroke her hair, and, when she resists, he accidentally breaks her neck. He flees to the river, planning to escape. George and a friend discover the body, and George hurriedly follows, ahead of a mob led by the enraged Curley. Finding Lennie beside a secluded pool, George calms his fears with the frequently repeated description of the farm of their hopes, and shoots him in the head.

Of Thee I Sing, musical comedy, with music by George Gershwin♦ and text by George S. Kaufman,♦ Morrie Ryskind, and Ira Gershwin. Pro-

duced in 1931, it was published in 1932 and won a Pulitzer Prize.

Of Time and the River: A Legend of Man's Hunger in His Youth, semi-autobiographical novel by Thomas Wolfe,♦ published in 1935 as a sequel to *Look Homeward, Angel.*♦

Eugene Gant leaves his Southern home for graduate work at Harvard, where the scope of his immense romantic appetite for experience is broadened as he reads voraciously, studies playwriting in the class of Professor Hatcher, and cultivates eccentric acquaintances, including his absurdly erudite uncle, Bascom Pentland. After losing his first bewildered feeling of strangeness, he finds a valued friend in Hatcher's youthful assistant, Francis Starwick, a cultured, fastidious, and affected scholar. During these two years, Eugene tries to bend his creative talent to the exacting dramatic form, and achieves a limited success before he leaves for a brief visit at home, where his father dies after a long and terrible illness. He goes north again, this time to serve as a college instructor of English in New York City, which provides the setting for his tumultuous mystic vision of the modern "manswarm." Companions of this period include Abe Jones, an earnest Jewish student; Joel Pierce, who introduces Eugene to the luxurious life of the Hudson River social set, and whose sister is one of a number of girls who are the objects of Eugene's sudden passions; and bitter, disillusioned Robert Weaver and his mistress, Martha Upshaw. Careful saving makes possible a European tour, during which Eugene meets Starwick, now even more febrile and affected. With Ann and Elinor, two Boston girls, they spend several weeks as tourists in Paris and the provinces. Eugene falls in love with Ann, Elinor with Eugene, and Ann with Starwick, who responds to neither, giving himself up to dissipation during mysterious disappearances. Appalled and disgusted when he discovers that Starwick is a homosexual, Eugene leaves his friends, to tour Europe alone until he is forced by lack of funds to return to the U.S.

OGILVIE, JAMES (1775–1820), emigrated to Virginia (1794) from his native Scotland and made a great reputation for orations delivered at the school he founded and to a larger public. He wrote for *The Port Folio,* and his *Philosophical Essays* (1816) gave him a minor place among the philosophic realists. Always unstable and addicted to opium, he committed suicide when his claim to a Scottish earldom was denied.

OGLETHORPE, JAMES EDWARD (1696–1785), English general, in 1732 obtained a charter for the colony of Georgia as an asylum for the debtor class and persecuted Protestants of England. To raise revenue for his venture, he wrote *A New and Accurate Account of the Provinces of South-Carolina and Georgia* (1732). The following year he arrived in Georgia, and with 120 colonists under his governorship founded the city of Savannah. During the English war with Spain (1739–43), he successfully repulsed Spanish attacks, although failing in an attempted siege of St. Augustine. His policy of religious toleration attracted many diverse sects, but dissatisfaction with his colonial policy occasioned his permanent return to England (1743), where he resigned his post (1752). His administration was attacked in a book by Patrick Tailfer, ♦ *A True and Historical Narrative of the Colony of Georgia* (1741).

"Oh! Susannah," song by Stephen Foster, ♦ published in his *Songs of the Sable Harmonists* (1848). With new words it was popular among Forty-Niners and is identified with the westward migration.

O'HARA, FRANK (1926–66), poet and art critic whose poetry, published in *A City Winter* (1952), *Meditations in an Emergency* (1957), *Second Avenue* (1960), *Odes* (1960), *Lunch Poems* (1964), and *Selected Poems* (1973, National Book Award), is marked by an extremely autobiographical relation to his New York environment and an immediacy that John Ashbery compared to the painting of Jackson Pollock (about whom O'Hara wrote a book-length catalogue, 1959), for "Like Pollock, O'Hara demonstrates that the act of communication and the finished creation are the same." *Art Chronicles* (1975) collects his criticism; *Standing Still and Walking in New York* (1975) is a gathering of essays and notes, followed by *Early Writing* (1977).

O'HARA, JOHN [HENRY] (1905–70), after a journalistic career in his native Pennsylvania and in New York, began to write stories of acid observation on the country-club set, actors, and barroom figures, collected in *The Doctor's Son* (1935), *Files on Parade* (1939), *Pipe Night* (1945), and *Hellbox* (1947). His novels are *Appointment in Samarra* (1934), an ironic, toughly realistic treatment of the fast country-club set of a Pennsylvania city; *Butterfield 8* (1935), based on a New York murder, revealing the sordid and sensational lives of people on the fringe of café society and the underworld; *Hope of Heaven* (1938), about an unhappy love affair between a scenario writer and a bookshop clerk; *A Rage To Live* (1949), about the tormented life of a woman who could not be faithful to the husband she really loved; *The Farmers Hotel* (1951), a novelette about snowbound people involved in a violent tragedy; *Ten North Frederick* (1955), a character study of a leading Pennsylvania citizen's public and very private life; *A Family Party* (1956), a novella in the form of a speech at a testimonial dinner; *From the Terrace* (1958), following a man through his upperclass life during the first half of the 20th century, treating social as well as personal history; *Ourselves To Know* (1960), about a man who mur-

dered his wife undetected and his life thereafter; *The Big Laugh* (1962), set in Hollywood in the '20s and '30s; *Elizabeth Appleton* (1963), portraying the married life of a society girl and a professor; *The Lockwood Concern* (1965), depicting the dramatic, tangled lives of four generations of an upper-class Pennsylvania family; *The Instrument* (1967), about a Broadway playwright and his manipulation of people; *Lovey Childs* (1970), presenting a wealthy Philadelphia woman's romantic entanglements; and *The Ewings* (1972), treating a Cleveland lawyer's life as illustrative of the era of World War I. *Pal Joey* (1940) presents letters from a nightclub singer, dramatized by O'Hara and others as a musical comedy. *Five Plays* (1961) were all unproduced but one he had fictionized in 1951 as *The Farmers Hotel*. Stories are collected in *Sermons and Soda-Water* (1960), *Assembly* (1961) *The Cape Cod Lighter* (1962), *The Hat on the Bed* (1963), *The Horse Knows the Way* (1964), *And Other Stories* (1968), *The Time Element* (1972), and *Good Samaritan* (1974). *Sweet and Sour* (1954) collects columns on books and authors, and selected *Letters* was issued in 1978.

O'Hara, SCARLETT, character in *Gone with the Wind.* ♦

O'HARA, THEODORE (1820–67), Kentucky poet and journalist, whose varied career included legal practice, minor diplomatic positions, and service in the Mexican War and the Civil War. Although his poetry has not been collected, the rhetorical "The Old Pioneer" and "The Bivouac of the Deaf," honoring Kentuckians in the Mexican War, are anthology pieces.

O'HIGGINS, HARVEY [JERROLD] (1876–1929), Canadian-born author, whose popularizations of special subjects, written with authorities in their fields, include *The Beast* (1910), a study of the social environment of city-bred children; *Under the Prophet in Utah* (1911), an analysis of the Mormon church; and *The American Mind in Action* (1924), psychoanalyses of eminent Americans. His fiction includes *Some Distinguished Americans* (1922), a fictional use of the method employed in *The American Mind in Action; Julie Cane* (1924) and *Clara Barron* (1926), portraits of modern American women. He also wrote *Polygamy* (1914), a drama of Mormon marriage, and dramatized Sinclair Lewis's *Main Street* (1921).

Oil!, novel by Upton Sinclair, ♦ published in 1927.

Based on the oil scandals of the Harding administration, especially the Teapot Dome affair, the narrative tells of the struggles of "Bunny" Ross and his father, a good-natured independent oil operator, against the encroachments of monopoly. Involved in the detailed account of business transactions are the thinly disguised characters of senators, oil magnates, and other public figures. Bunny's experiences lead him to realize that the bribery of public officials, the oppression of workers, and international conflicts are inherent in the private ownership of the industry, and he turns for a solution to socialism.

Ojibway Indians (also OJIBWA or CHIPPEWA), Algonquian hunting tribe of the Great Lakes region. They sided with the French during the French and Indian Wars, and shared in Pontiac's Rebellion. Later most of them were won over to the British side in the War of 1812. One of their chiefs, George Copway,♦ has written about them, and they are the subject of an ethnological study by Schoolcraft. The Ojibway figure in *Hiawatha* as the tribe to which the hero belongs, and they appear in Cooper's *Oak Openings* and Janet Lewis's *The Invasion.*

OKADA, JOHN (1923–71), born in Seattle of Japanese-American parents, was an Air Force sergeant in World War II, then earned degrees from the University of Washington and Columbia University. He wrote a bitter play, *No-No Boy* (1957), about a Nisei who resisted the war draft, depicting the disastrous treatment of the time for Nisei. The play was critically dismissed. UCLA declined Okada's widow's offer of his manuscripts, and she burned them. Okada is now highly regarded and his play read in college courses in Asian-American literature.

Okies, name applied to refugees from Oklahoma, Texas, and other Dust Bowl states, who, because of the destruction of their farms by drought and dust storms, in the 1930s emigrated to seek employment elsewhere, mainly in California. Steinbeck's novel *The Grapes of Wrath*♦ is concerned with an Okie family.

Oklahoma!, see *Green Grow the Lilacs.*

Ol' Man Adam an' His Chillun, Negro folk versions of Old Testament stories, written by Roark Bradford♦ and published in 1928. The book suggested *The Green Pastures.*♦

"Old Black Joe," song by Stephen Foster.♦

Old Block, see *Delano, Alonzo.*

Old Corner Bookstore, established in 1828 in Boston on the corner of Washington and School streets, famous under the ownership of William D. Ticknor and James T. Fields as an adjunct of their publishing firm and as a gathering place of such literati as Emerson, Holmes, Hawthorne, Longfellow, Lowell, and Whittier, so that it was dubbed "Parnassus Corner."

Old Creole Days, seven short stories by G.W. Cable,♦ published in 1879. Later editions also include the novelette *Madame Delphine,*♦ and all

deal with the local color of 19th-century New Orleans.

"Café des Exilés" is a romantic tale of a smuggling plot of 1835, set in the café of kindly old M. D'Hemecourt. Major Galahad Shaughnessy, gallant leader of the conspirators, causes their failure by an excess of cunning, but wins the hand of D'Hemecourt's daughter Pauline. "Jean-ah Poquelin" tells of a former slave trader who suddenly goes into retirement in his suburban house. Because of the disappearance of his brother Jacques, the ruinous aspect of his grounds, and his fierce exclusion of trespassers, old Poquelin comes to have an evil reputation. When he dies, it is revealed that Jacques is a helpless and gruesome leper, whom Jean has personally concealed and cared for during these years. "'Tite Poulette" is the story of Kristian Koppig, a young Dutchman who falls in love with Poulette, daughter of his neighbor, Madame John. Kristian is injured while championing Poulette in a quarrel, and she nurses him to health. He proposes marriage, but she refuses, heartbroken, because Madame John has a strain of Negro blood. The romance concludes happily when the older woman reveals that she is only Poulette's foster mother, the girl's white parents having died during her infancy. "Madame Délicieuse" tells of the 15-year-long misunderstanding between General de Villivicencio, who clings to the outmoded Creole code of honor, and his gentle and retiring son Dr. Mossy, who champions science and common sense. Mossy will not marry his beautiful fiancée, Madame Délicieuse, because his father has disinherited him. Through a complicated intrigue, the young woman brings about their reconciliation.

Old Farmer's Almanac, The, see *Farmer's Almanack.*

"Old Folks at Home," song by Stephen Foster,♦ published in 1851 under the name E.P. Christy,♦ for whom it was written. It is also known as "Swanee River."

Old Homestead, The, play by Denman Thompson.♦

Old Ironsides, popular name of the 44-gun frigate *Constitution,* launched in 1797, which served in the Tripolitan War and the War of 1812. Under the command of Isaac Hull (1773–1843), the *Constitution* won the battle with the British vessel *Guerrière,* off Cape Race, Newfoundland (Aug. 19, 1812). The frigate was ordered to be dismantled (1830), but was saved when public sentiment was aroused by Holme's poem "Old Ironsides" (1830), and was rebuilt (1833).

Old Lights, see *Great Awakening.*

Old Maid, The, novelette by Edith Wharton,♦ published in 1924 as one of the series Old New York. Zoë Akins dramatized it (1935).

Delia Lovell and her cousin Charlotte both love Clem Spender, and Charlotte has an illegitimate daughter by him after Delia leaves to marry wealthy Jim Ralston. Ever-domineering and afraid of scandal, Delia takes the child Tina into her home as her own daughter, and maneuvers Charlotte into breaking her engagement to Joseph Ralston. Charlotte lives with them as the maiden aunt, stifling the truth through love of her child, even when Tina regards her as a quaint survival whose presence is rather a nuisance. The cousins quarrel violently the night before Tina's wedding, but when they are left alone Delia recognizes that she has done a "sacrilegious thing" in interfering with another "human being's right to love and suffer after his own fashion," and they settle down to a quiet understanding and old age.

Old Man and the Sea, The, novelette by Hemingway,♦ published in 1952.

This parable of man's struggle with the natural world, of his noble courage and endurance, tells of the Cuban fisherman Santiago, who for 84 luckless days has rowed his skiff into the Gulf Stream in quest of marlin. At first accompanied by the boy Manolin, with whom he talked of better days and about the great sport of baseball, he is now alone. Aged and solitary, he goes far out and hooks a great fish that tows his boat all afternoon and night and into the next day as he pits his skill and waning strength against it the way he once did as a wrestler called "El Campéon." As the second night turns to dawn he finally harpoons his catch, lashes it to his small boat, and makes his weary way home. As he sails slowly to port sharks attack his catch and he fights them as best he can with a knife lashed to the tiller gripped in raw hands. When he makes land his marlin is but a skeleton. Proud in defeat, Santiago furls his sail and staggers to his shack, to be found by the boy and other fishermen, who marvel at his catch, while the spent man sleeps and dreams of past experiences.

Old Manse, residence of the Emerson family, at Concord. Hawthorne lived there (1842–46) during the writing of his *Mosses from an Old Manse.*

"Old Oaken Bucket, THE," lyric by Samuel Woodworth.♦

Old Possum's Book of Practical Cats, by T.S. Eliot,♦ published in 1939. It collects 15 humorous poems in Edward Lear-like verse, originally written for children Eliot knew. The little volume begins with the significance of "The Naming of Cats" and continues through the presentation of such diverse felines as Growltiger, Mr. Mistoffelees, Gus: The Theatre Cat, Bustopher Jones: The Cat About Town, Cat Morgan, and Old Deuteronomy, "a cat who has lived many lives in succession. He was famous in proverb and famous in rhyme A long while before Queen

Victoria's accession." A very popular musical and dancing show titled *Cats* was adapted from Eliot's book and produced in London (1981) and New York (1982).

Old Side, see *Great Awakening.*

Old Soak, The, autobiographical work by Don Marquis.♦

Old Southwest, as distinguished from the present Southwest,♦ included the region between the Savannah River and the Mississippi,♦ which constituted the southwestern frontier from colonial times to the early 19th century. The pioneer settlers of this wilderness area, some of whom were called "crackers," created a distinctive folklore, which in turn gave rise to the frontier stories and sketches of T.B. Thorpe, Davy Crockett, G.W. Harris, Joseph Baldwin, J.M. Field, J.J. Hooper, Sol Smith, and A.B. Longstreet, and affected the writings of Mark Twain.

Old Swimmin'-Hole, The, and 'Leven More Poems, first book by James Whitcomb Riley,♦ published in 1883 under the pseudonym "Benj. F. Johnson, of Boone," but having the author's own name in brackets. The poems were originally written for *The Indianapolis Journal,* and include "When the Frost Is on the Punkin." These simple, sentimental poems in the homely Hoosier dialect established Riley's popularity.

OLDMIXON, JOHN (1673–1742), English poet, historian, and hack writer, whose *British Empire in America* (2 vols., 1708), although inaccurate, was advanced for its time, viewing the American colonies and the West Indies as a single community of interests in British imperialism.

OLDS, SHARON (1942–), San Francisco-born poet, educated at Stanford, with graduate study at Columbia, has taught at various places. She is best known for these volumes of poetry: *Satan Says* (1980), about the lives of women; *The Dead and the Living* (1984), a woman's view of her life and her family; *The Gold Cell* (1987), concerning a girl's social and erotic encounters; and *The Father* (1993), a daughter's vigil and grief for a father dying of cancer.

OLDSTYLE, JONATHAN, pseudonym of Irving.♦

OLDSTYLE, OLIVER, pseudonym of Paulding.♦

Oldtown Folks, novel by Harriet Beecher Stowe,♦ published in 1869 and dramatized by the author the same year.

Horace Holyoke, who has grown up in Oldtown, Mass., during the post-Revolutionary period, describes the town's typical institutions, its preoccupation with theological discussion, and its leading citizens, scholarly Parson Lothrop and his aristocratic, Episcopalian wife, known as "Lady" Lothrop. Henry and Tina Percival, foundling orphans, are taken into the family of "Old Crab" Smith and Miss Asphyxia Smith, whose harshness and miserliness cause the children to run away, although they are brought back by Horace's Uncle Fly and Sam Lawson, the humorous idler and oracle. Tina is adopted by Miss Mehitable Rossiter, daughter of the former clergyman, and Henry lives with Madam Lothrop. On her annual Easter trip to Boston, the children attend Church of England services and meet leaders of Boston society, including Ellery Davenport, an aristocratic Revolutionary officer who resembles Aaron Burr. After the orphans are discovered to be members of a wealthy British family, Henry attends the academy at Cloudland, and then goes to Harvard with Horace, who falls in love with Tina. The girl marries Davenport, but her happiness is short-lived, for Miss Rossiter's sister Emily appears to accuse Davenport of seducing her and being the father of her daughter. Tina adopts the child, and goes with her husband to Europe. Henry goes to England and becomes an Anglican clergyman. When the Davenports return to Massachusetts, Ellery becomes a political leader, and is killed in a duel. Two years later, Horace and Tina are married.

OLIVER, MARY (1935–   ), poet born in Cleveland, educated at Ohio State and Vassar, long a resident of Provincetown, Mass., while teaching at various places. Oliver celebrates our connection to all nature, both intuitive and actual, as evidenced by the titles of many of her poems. Her verse is subtly formal. Her works, all poems, are *No Voyage and Other Poems* (1963, enlarged 1965), *The River Styx, Ohio and Other Poems* (1972), *The Night Traveler* (1978), *Sleeping in the Forest* (1978), *Twelve Moons* (1979), *American Primitive* (1983, Pulitzer Prize), *Dream Work* (1986), *House of Light* (1990), and *New and Selected Poems* (1992, National Book Award). Oliver has also won the Shelley Memorial Award.

OLMSTED, FREDERICK LAW (1822–1903), landscape architect and conservationist, noted for his unbiased travel books, *A Journey in the Seaboard Slave States* (1856), *A Journey Through Texas* (1857), and *A Journey in the Back Country* (1860), which were condensed and reissued as *The Cotton Kingdom* (2 vols., 1861). He also wrote *Walks and Talks of an American Farmer in England* (1852). His greatest works in landscape architecture include Central Park and Riverside Park in New York City; the Boston park system; the Capitol grounds at Washington, D.C.; the 1893 World's Fair at Chicago; and the campuses of the University of California and Stanford University. Olmsted was instrumental in making public lands of Niagara Falls and Yosemite, and published works relating to public parks.

OLNEY, JESSE (1798–1872), Connecticut educator whose *Practical System of Modern Geography* (1828) was a standard American text of extensive influence during the 19th century. Its method was to familiarize the student with his own environment, and then progress to a knowledge of distant lands and geographical phenomena.

OLSEN, TILLIE (1913–   ), Nebraska-born author, worked as a domestic servant and raised her own four daughters before she found time to write, drawing upon her own experience. Four stories written in the 1950s were collected as *Tell Me a Riddle* (1962). *Yonnondio* (1974) is a novel about life in the 1930s. *Silences* (1978) prints essays and lectures delivered at colleges on writers who have been silenced because of their class or sex. She sympathetically introduced an edition of Rebecca Harding Davis's *Life in the Iron Mills* (1973), and she also edited, in *Mother to Daughter, Daughter to Mother* (1984), family relations set forth in poems, letters, short fiction, and diaries.

OLSON, CHARLES (1910–70), born in Massachusetts, educated at Harvard, first became known for *Call Me Ishmael* (1947), a rhapsodic study of Melville, including Shakespeare's influence on him, but subsequently became distinguished for his poetry and poetic theory. His ideas, set forth as instructor and Rector of Black Mountain College,♦ greatly influenced Creeley, Duncan, and Levertov, among other students there. His Projective Verse conceived of the poem as an "open field" through which energy moves from its source to the reader, the measure being based on the breath of the speaker-poet. Olson's shorter poems printed in *In Cold Hell, in Thicket* (1953) and *The Distances* (1960) are collected in *The Archaeologist of Morning* (1971). *The Maximus Poems* (1–10, 1953; 11–23, 1956; combined, 1960), *Maximus IV, V, VI* (1968), and *The Maximus Poem* (1975) form a long, organic work in which the persona of Maximus concentrates on the past and present of Olson's hometown, Gloucester. An enlarged and corrected edition appeared in 1983. Other works include *The Mayan Letters* (1953), written to Creeley from Mexico about anthropology and views of language; *A Bibliography on America for Ed Dorn* (1964), succinct commentary on the U.S.; *Human Universe* (1965), essays; *Letters for Origin* (1969), written to Cid Corman♦ about poetry and its publication; *Causal Mythology* (1969), on myth; *Poetry and Truth* (1971), lectures delivered at Beloit; and *The Fiery Hunt* (1978), verse plays. Creeley edited *Selected Writings* (1966).

OLSON, ELDER [JAMES] (1909–   ), Chicago-born poet and critic, professor at the University of Chicago, is known as a leader of its school of neo-Aristotelians, whose critical views were based on the *Poetics* of Aristotle. His poetry, cerebral and formal, appeared in *Thing of Sorrow*

(1934), *The Cock of Heaven* (1940), *The Scarecrow Christ* (1954), *Plays and Poems* (1958), *Collected Poems* (1963), *Olson's Penny Arcade* (1975), and *Last Poems* (1984). His critical works include *Tragedy and the Theory of Drama* (1961), *The Theory of Comedy* (1968), and *On Value Judgments in the Arts* (1976).

Omoo, a Narrative of Adventures in the South Seas, fictional account by Melville♦ of his experiences in the Society Islands (1842). It was published in 1847 as a sequel to *Typee.*♦

At Nukuheva the narrator is taken aboard the short-handed Australian trader *Julia* (actually the *Lucy Ann*). Despite his injured leg, he signs on as a seaman, being assured that he may leave the ship at the next port. He discovers that the ship is in poor condition, and that Captain Guy is ill and untrustworthy, but he admires the mate Jermin and finds a friend in jovial, well-traveled, well-read Dr. Long Ghost. At Papeetee, the consul Wilson orders the *Julia* to sea again, but the unruly crew disobeys, bringing the ship into harbor. Imprisoned for insubordination, the men oppose efforts to force them aboard and at last are deserted when the *Julia* sails with a new crew. They annoy the natives, whose scanty supplies they share, although the old guide "Captain Bob" is friendly. The narrator and the doctor leave Tahiti for Imeeo, where they work for two planters, the Yankee Zeke and the cockney Shorty. Soon tiring of farm labor, they desert the plantation to explore the islands and study the people. Then, leaving Long Ghost in Tahiti, the narrator ships on a whaler, *The Leviathan.*

On Native Grounds, literary study by Alfred Kazin,♦ published in 1942. Subtitled "An Interpretation of Modern American Prose Literature," the work covering the half century 1890–1940 conceives that "our modern literature in America is at bottom only the experience of our modern life in America" and that this study "is in part an effort at moral history, which is greater than literary history, and is needed to illuminate it."

On the Road, novel by Jack Kerouac,♦ published in 1957.

Sal Paradise (a self-portrait of Kerouac), a struggling author in his mid-twenties, tells of his meeting Dean Moriarty (based on Neal Cassady), a fast-living teenager just out of a New Mexico reform school, whose soul is "wrapped up in a fast car, a coast to reach, and a woman at the end of the road." During the next five years they travel coast to coast, either with each other or to each other. Five trips are described. In the first Sal travels to Denver in July 1947 to be with Dean, whom he finds to have left his recent wife Marylou for a woman named Camille. After ten days of wild parties, Sal goes to San Francisco, then Los Angeles, picking up jobs and women before returning to New York to work on his novel. A

year and a half later, Dean, back with Marylou, joins Sal in the East to drive to San Francisco. When Dean again deserts his wife for Camille, she and Sal have a brief affair before Sal returns alone to New York. In the spring of 1949 Sal goes to California to find Dean, still living with Camille, who expects her second child, and the two reunited friends leave her to drive to New York, where Dean finds another love, Inez, who bears him a child. Later, Sal, having sold his novel to a publisher, goes with Dean to Mexico, partly so that Dean may divorce Camille. But when Sal falls sick, Dean leaves him, returning to New York and Inez. After a time Sal, settled in New York, and Dean in San Francisco, again with Camille, plan further travels, when Dean goes east and remains there temporarily while Sal goes west again, this time alone.

Once I Pass'd Through a Populous City, poem by Whitman,♦ published in the "Children of Adam"♦ section of *Leaves of Grass* (1860). Although the poem in its original manuscript referred to a man, and Whitman denied that the poem was autobiographical, its declaration that "of all that city I remember only a woman" has led biographers to contend that it refers to a love affair in New Orleans in 1848 which substantially altered Whitman's character.

One Flew Over the Cuckoo's Nest, novel by Ken Kesey,♦ published in 1962. It was dramatized by Dale Wasserman (1974).

Chief Bromden, so named because he is of Indian descent but also because he is the chief sweeper in the psychopathic ward of an Oregon mental hospital, tells how he and the other inmates with whom he has shared confinement for ten years are buoyed by the arrival of Randle Patrick McMurphy. McMurphy, who has gotten himself transferred to the hospital from a prison, where he was serving time for statutory rape of a teenage girl, is a loud, laughing Irishman. He challenges the sadistic control of Head Nurse Ratched, who has browbeaten the frightened men into abject docility. Bit by bit he restores some self-esteem in the men and even stirs the long mute Chief to talk. For fomenting rebellion, and assaulting the Head Nurse, however, he is subjected to repeated shock treatment and a lobotomy that reduces him to blank passivity. As an act of mercy the Chief then smothers McMurphy and escapes into the outer world.

One Woman's Life, novel by Robert Herrick,♦ published in 1913.

One-Hoss Shay, see *Deacon's Masterpiece.*

Oneida Community, religious society established in central New York state by J.H. Noyes♦ (1848). The evolution of perfectionist doctrines, coupled with the reading of Fourierist publications, gradually led the group to communism. The original 40 members, grown to some 300, settled on a 900-acre farm, governed themselves democratically, and practiced a system of mutual criticism that took the place of trials and punishments, serving as a cure for both moral delinquencies and physical ailments. The community acquired a reputation for its excellent school system and its profitable manufactures, which included steel traps and silver-plated ware. Among the many books and periodicals published from Oneida and its affiliated communities, the most popular was the weekly *Oneida Circular* (1864–76). Despite the perfectionist doctrine of immediate and total cessation of sin, public opinion was aroused by the community's system of complex marriage, which combined polygamy and polyandry, attempting to propagate children scientifically by pairing the young of one sex with the aged of the other. This was abandoned in 1879, and Noyes soon removed to Canada. When the community was reorganized as a business corporation (1881), its property was valued at $600,000.

Oneida Indians, see *Iroquois Indians.*

O'NEILL, EUGENE [GLADSTONE] (1888–1953), born in New York City, as a child accompanied his father, James O'Neill (1847–1920), a popular romantic actor, on theatrical tours, and later attended a Catholic boarding school and a Connecticut preparatory school. He entered Princeton (1906), but remained there only a year. After secretarial work in New York, he went on a gold prospecting trip to Honduras (1909), but contracted malaria, and returned to the U.S. to be assistant manager of his father's company. Soon tiring of their mediocre vehicle, he shipped as a seaman for Buenos Aires. Employed for a time in Argentina, he then worked his way to South Africa and back on a cattle steamer, and after a period of beachcombing in Buenos Aires returned to New York. His last experience at sea followed, when he worked on ships between New York and Southampton. Next he tried acting during one of his father's tours, and reporting for a Connecticut newspaper, but suffered a physical breakdown and was sent to a sanatorium for six months. He had already written verses, and during this period of enforced rest and reflection turned to the drama as a medium for expressing the view of life he began to develop, based on his life at sea and among outcast and oppressed people in many places.

During the following winter (1913–14), he wrote his first play, *The Web,* seven other one-act plays, and two long plays. He gained further experience as a student in G.P. Baker's 47 Workshop (1914–15), and spent a winter in Greenwich Village. In 1916 he became associated with the Provincetown Players, who during the next three years produced many of his one-act plays, includ-

ing *Bound East for Cardiff*♦ (1916) and *The Moon of the Caribbees*♦ (1918). This period of practical experiment brought to a climax his years of apprentice work, and he began to win general recognition when three of his plays were printed in *The Smart Set.* With the New York production of *Beyond the Horizon*♦ (1920, Pulitzer Prize), O'Neill was acknowledged as the foremost creative American playwright.

Although he was associated with Robert Edmond Jones in managing the Greenwich Village Theatre (1923–27) and was a director of the Provincetown Players and a founder of the Theatre Guild, which produced his later plays, he became increasingly absorbed in writing, to the exclusion of other interests. He followed *Beyond the Horizon* with further naturalistic studies of tragic frustration set in modern American backgrounds: *Chris Christopherson* (1920), rewritten as *Anna Christie*♦ (1921, Pulitzer Prize); *Diff'rent* (1920); *Gold* (1921); *The Straw* (1921); and *The First Man* (1922). From the same period came his achievements in symbolic expressionism, *The Emperor Jones*♦ (1920) and *The Hairy Ape*♦ (1922); but he continued the naturalistic approach in *All God's Chillun Got Wings*♦ (1924), and *Desire Under the Elms*♦ (1924). In the same year he turned to the use of symbolic masks in a Provincetown production of Coleridge's *The Ancient Mariner,* which he adapted and directed.

The romantic and poetic elements of his nature, which had hitherto appeared in details of his plays, dominated *The Fountain*♦ (1925), an affirmation of life and spirit, and "the Eternal Becoming which is Beauty." His next play, *The Great God Brown*♦ (1926), fused symbolism, poetry, and the affirmation of a pagan idealism, in an ironic tragedy of modern materialism; and *Lazarus Laughed*♦ (1927) and *Marco Millions*♦ (1928) similarly attack the contemporary emphasis on acquisition and material standards, in terms of poetic emotion, exotic color, and satirical irony. Always an experimenter in forms, O'Neill attempted in *Strange Interlude*♦ (1928, Pulitzer Prize) to create a dramatic technique using the stream-of-consciousness method, in a nine-act tragedy of frustrated desires. This psychological analysis of motives was followed by a trilogy, *Mourning Becomes Electra*♦ (1931), adapting the Greek theme and preserving the dominant emotions of fear, horror, and a brooding sense of a malignant fate. O'Neill's deep interest in problems of religion in the modern world appears in two plays of this later period: *Dynamo* (1929), in which an electrical dynamo becomes a divine symbol, replacing the old God but destroying its worshippers; and *Days Without End* (1934), in which the hero is irresistibly attracted to Catholicism.

Ah, Wilderness! (1933) is a pleasant New England folk comedy, very different from O'Neill's usual concerns. *The Iceman Cometh*♦ (1946) is a tragedy, realistically set in a Bowery bar, symbolically portraying the loss of illusion and the coming of Death. *Long Day's Journey into Night*♦ (1956, Pulitzer Prize), an autobiographical tragedy written in 1940, and depicting a day in 1912 in the unhappy life of the Tyrone family, was the first of his posthumously produced and published plays. In 1958 came *Hughie,* a one-act character study. Of his projected eleven-play cycle, "A Tale of Possessors Self-Dispossessed," about the effect possessions had on an American family from the colonial era to the present day, two have been acted and issued: *A Touch of the Poet* (published 1957, produced 1958) and its immediate sequel, *More Stately Mansions* (1964).

O'Neill's works are deeply affected by his wide reading, especially in Greek tragedies, Ibsen, and Strindberg, but it is his own stage experience and his own insight into character that made them so distinguished and earned him a Nobel Prize (1936). His *Poems,* minor works, were collected in 1980, and *"As Ever, Gene"* (1980) assembled 130 letters to George Jean Nathan.

One's-Self I Sing, poem by Whitman, ♦ published as "Inscription" in *Leaves of Grass* (1867) and given its present title in 1871. According to Whitman's plan, the poem is printed first in his book. It celebrates the "simple, separate Person" as a physical, moral, intellectual, emotional, and aesthetic being, but declares that when he sings of himself, he uses the "word *En-masse*" to show that he represents the modern democratic man.

Only Yesterday, social history by F.L. Allen. ♦

Onondaga Indians, New York tribe that belonged to the Iroquois Confederacy. ♦ The Onondaga aided the British in the French and Indian Wars and in the Revolution. Most of them have since lived in Ontario, although some remain on a New York reservation. They figure in Cooper's *Wyandotté,* and in the Littlepage Manuscripts an Onondaga is one of the heroes.

Open Boat, The, and Other Tales of Adventure, eight short stories by Stephen Crane, ♦ published in 1898, mainly "after the Fact" of his own experiences as a reporter and war correspondent.

"The Open Boat" is a realistic account of the thoughts and emotions of four men who escape in a small dinghy from the wrecked steamer *Commodore* off the Florida coast. The captain, the cook, an oiler, and a newspaper correspondent, unable to land because of the dangerous surf, see the beach tantalizingly near, but are forced to spend the night on the sea. Next morning they employ their last strength to swim ashore, and all but the oiler survive. "Death and the Child," reminiscent of *The Red Badge of Courage,* has for its scene a battle of the Greco-Turkish War and is concerned with the psychological reactions of a Greek newspaperman in his first experience of warfare. At first he desires to fight with his coun-

trymen, but as he views the battle more intimately he is overcome by fear and panic, and flees to a nearby mountain, where his self-centered emotion is contrasted with the indifference of an abandoned peasant child. "Flanagan, and His Short Filibustering Adventure" narrates a melodramatic incident of arms smuggling in Cuba before the Spanish-American War. The remaining stories are sardonically realistic adventure tales in Mexico and the Far West. One is "The Bride Comes to Yellow Sky," about a newly married couple, the marshal of Yellow Sky, Tex., and his bride from San Antonio, who arrive on the train in his town at the moment that the local bad man goes on a drunken shooting spree. After a tense moment, the marshal is spared, not because the bad man was a "student of chivalry; it was merely that in the presence of this foreign condition he was a simple child of the earlier plains."

OPPEN, GEORGE (1908–84), poet reared and resident in California, a protégé of Ezra Pound and a leader of the Objectivist♦ school, whose terse poems appear in *Discrete Series* (1934). *The Materials* (1962), *This in Which* (1965), *Of Being Numerous* (1968, Pulitzer Prize), *Seascape* (1973), *Collected Poems* (1975), and *Primitive* (1978).

OPPENHEIM, JAMES (1882–1932), born in Minnesota, was reared in New York City, studied at Columbia (1901–3), and became a settlement worker on the Lower East Side, the background of his short stories in *Dr. Rast* (1909). The same year saw the publication of *Monday Morning,* his first book of verse. He wrote further stories, novels, and plays, expressing his radical social ideas, but it was not until *Songs for the New Age* (1914) that he clearly broke from his bourgeois background. These poems, containing both introspective analysis of the individual and social analysis of the times, showed an indebtedness to Whitman and the Old Testament of his own Semitic background. His social fervor and personal intensity were further illustrated in *War and Laughter* (1916), but his spirit was broken by the coming of World War I and the failure of his little magazine *The Seven Arts*♦ (1916–17), due to its pacifism. He turned to psychoanalysis, and *The Book of Self* (1917) is a poetic product of this period. His collected volume, *The Sea* (1924), includes *The Mystic Warrior* (1921), a free-verse autobiography; *Golden Bird* (1923), love lyrics; and the previous poems, all fused by new connecting verses.

Opposing Self, The, work by Lionel Trilling, ♦ published in 1955, collects nine discrete essays in criticism, mostly written as introductions to books from the previous 150 years and therefore said to be concerned with the idea of the self and its relation to modern culture. The works include *Little Dorrit, Anna Karenina, The Bostonians,* and *Mansfield Park,* to which are added considerations of Keats, Howells, Wordsworth, Orwell, and Flaubert.

OPTIC, OLIVER, pseudonym of W.T. Adams. ◆

Options, short stories by W.S. Porter. ◆

Oralloossa, Son of the Incas, romantic tragedy by R.M. Bird, ◆ produced by Edwin Forrest in 1832 and first published in 1919. Set in 16th-century Peru, it deals with Oralloossa, son of the Inca, or emperor, who has been killed by Pizarro. The prince in turn kills the conquistador, but, through the treachery of the Spaniards, is betrayed and killed by his own people.

O'Regan, TEAGUE, character in *Modern Chivalry.* ◆

Oregon Trail, emigrant route from Missouri to the "Oregon country" whose western part was first traveled by the expedition sent to Astoria ◆ (1811–12). It was not generally known until after Jedediah Smith used it (1824). Although Bonneville took wagons over part of the trail (1832), the first real emigrant train to use it was that of John Bidwell (1841). It was extensively used during the 1840s, and part of it was employed in the Mormon emigrations. Parkman's *The Oregon Trail* deals only with the eastern end of the route.

Oregon Trail, The, autobiographical narrative by Parkman, ◆ serialized in *The Knickerbocker Magazine* (1847) and issued in book form as *The California and Oregon Trail* (1849). The original title was resumed in later editions.

This account of the author's trip over the eastern part of the Oregon Trail, with his cousin, Quincy Adams Shaw (April–Aug. 1846), tells of their travels from St. Louis by steamboat and horseback to Fort Laramie, Wy., in company with guides and occasional other travelers. They encounter typical adventures in storms, buffalo hunts, and meetings with Indians, soldiers, sportsmen, and emigrants. At Fort Laramie, then a trading post, they find an encampment of Sioux and learn of a war party that is being sent against the Snake Indians. Attempting to join this party, they meet difficulties, and Parkman goes on alone with a guide, promising to rejoin Shaw later. After a dangerous mountain journey, he finds the Sioux band and lives with them for several weeks, sharing their food and shelter and taking part in buffalo hunts and ceremonials, although he sees no battles. Parkman was in ill health, and only managed by strenuous and painful activity to keep the respect of his untrustworthy hosts. After gaining much information and insight into Indian character, which influenced his writings and made this a classic description of Indian life, Parkman rejoined Shaw, and returned east.

O'REILLY, JOHN BOYLE (1844–90), Irish-born writer, came to the U.S. (1869) after escaping from an Australian prison, where he had been confined for Fenian activities. His novel *Moondyne* (1879) is concerned with Australian convict life, and his volumes of poetry include *Songs from Southern Seas* (1873) and *Songs, Legends, and Ballads* (1878). From 1870 to his death he edited the *Pilot,* a Catholic paper in Boston.

O'REILLY, MILES, pseudonym of C.G. Halpine. ◆

Ormond; or, The Secret Witness, romance by C.B. Brown, ◆ published in 1799.

Stephen Dudley, a Philadelphia merchant, is blinded and later bankrupted because of embezzlement by Thomas Craig, so that his daughter Constantia must work as a seamstress to support him. They live through a yellow-fever epidemic, but when out of work Constantia seeks aid from Osmond, a wealthy eccentric, who finds she belies his theory about the mental inferiority of women. He employs her as a seamstress for his mistress, Helena Cleves, who commits suicide when Ormond will not marry her. Helena leaves her wealth to the Dudleys, returning them to affluence and making possible an operation that restores Stephen's sight. Because he will not let Ormond marry Constantia, Stephen is murdered by Craig on Ormond's orders. In turn Ormond murders Craig, brings the body one night to Constantia, and then tries to rape her. After she stabs him to death, a friend establishes her innocence and takes her to live in England.

Orphan Angel, The, novel by Elinor Wylie. ◆

Orpheus C. Kerr, pseudonym of R.H. Newell. ◆

Orphic Sayings, 100 aphorisms expressing the mystical idealism of Bronson Alcott, ◆ printed in *The Dial,* ◆ July 1840, Jan. 1841, and as a book in 1939.

ORTIZ, SIMON (1941–), Acoma Pueblo poet and short story writer born in Albuquerque. Ortiz is known best for his poetry, beginning with the major collection *Going for the Rain* (1976). In it he recites the creation myth of the Acomas and ranges far to the present. *A Good Journey* (1977) features poems about the Acomas and their customs. *Fight Back: For the Sake of the People, for the Sake of the Land* (1980) is a collection of poetry and prose about Pueblos, Navajos, and Anglos in New Mexico's uranium mining country and how their destinies interlock. *From Sand Creek: Rising in This Heart Which Is Our America* (1981) collects poems set in a Colorado veteran's hospital; Ortiz draws parallels between the killing of 133 Native Americans, mostly women and children, at Sand Creek and the indiscriminate massacres of the Vietnam War. Two more poetry collections appeared in 1991: *Woven Stone* and

After and Before the Lightning, about the Great Plains. Stories are collected in *Howbah Indians* (1978) and *Fightin'* (1983).

ORVIS, MARIANNE DWIGHT, see *Dwight, Marianne.*

Osage Indians, war-like Plains tribe♦ related to the Sioux, were encountered (1673) on the Osage River in Missouri. Besides waging war on many tribes, they were allied with the French in the French and Indian Wars. Irving describes the Osage enthusiastically in *A Tour on the Prairies,* and their descendants, who have become wealthy through the discovery of oil on their Oklahoma lands, figure in Edna Ferber's *Cimarron.* John Joseph Matthews, an Osage, wrote *Wah'kon-tah: The Osage and the White Man's Road* (1932).

OSBORN, LAUGHTON (*c.*1809–78), New York litterateur, whose works include *Sixty Years of the Life of Jeremy Levis* (2 vols., 1831), a novel in the vein of *Tristram Shandy,* and *The Vision of Rubeta* (1838), a romantic story of some of New York history containing attacks on contemporary authors, particularly W.L. Stone and Wordsworth. He also wrote miscellaneous poems and unproduced dramas.

OSBOURNE, [SAMUEL] LLOYD (1868–1947), novelist and playwright, accompanied his stepfather, R.L. Stevenson, on the sojourn described in *The Silverado Squatters* and on travels to Europe and the South Seas. He collaborated with him on *The Wrong Box* (1889), *The Wrecker* (1892), and *The Ebb Tide* (1894), and later wrote fiction and plays of his own, as well as collaborating on dramas with his nephew, Austin Strong.♦

OSGOOD, FRANCES SARGENT [LOCKE] (1811–50), Massachusetts poet whose *The Casket of Fate* (1840) and *The Poetry of Flowers and Flowers of Poetry* (1841) are typical of the sentimental feminine verse of the Victorian era. After she moved to New York, she was a friend of Poe, who praised her work extravagantly in "The Literati."

O'SHEEL (SHIELDS), SHAEMAS (1886–1954), New York poet, whose verse is in the tradition of Yeats and the Irish renaissance. *Jealous of Dead Leaves* (1928) contains poems revised and selected from his two earlier books, *The Blossomy Bough* (1911) and *The Light Feet of Goats* (1915). His poem "They Went Forth to Battle, But They Always Fell" is widely known.

Osmond, GILBERT, character in *The Portrait of a Lady.*♦

OSSOLI, MARGARET, see *Fuller, Margaret.*

OSTENSO, MARTHA (1900–1963), Norwegian-born author, reared in Minnesota, South Dakota,

and Canada, whose first novel, *Wild Geese* (1925), is a realistic portrayal of an Icelandic community in Manitoba. Later novels, about family relations in the upper Midwest and Canada, include *The Dark Dawn* (1926), *The Mad Carews* (1927), *The Young May Moon* (1929), *The Waters Under the Earth* (1930), *There's Always Another Year* (1933), *The Stone Field* (1937), *The Mandrake Root* (1948), *O River, Remember!* (1943), *Milk Route* (1948), *The Sunset Tree* (1949), and *A Man Had Tall Sons* (1958).

Other Voices, Other Rooms, novel by Truman Capote,♦ published in 1948.

Joel Knox, an unloved 13-year-old boy, quests to find his real nature as he matures on a Louisiana plantation and its surroundings, where through reality and dream he loses his innocence and finds his homosexual identity.

OTIS, JAMES (1725–83), brother of Mercy Otis Warren, graduated from Harvard (1743) and became a prominent Boston lawyer, upholding the rights of the colonists as Englishmen in his opposition to the Sugar Act, Stamp Act, and Townshend acts. He was a prominent champion of free speech and an opponent of royal and Parliamentary prerogative, against which he invoked natural law in such pamphlets as *A Vindication of the House of Representatives . . .* (1762) and *The Rights of the British Colonies . . .* (1764), which laid the foundation for later Revolutionary writings. Although he did not champion revolution, he attacked the arguments of Soame Jenyns and Martin Howard, headed the Massachusetts Committee of Correspondence, and was active until 1769 in the colonial assembly. As the result of a political quarrel, he was physically attacked by an opponent and received injuries that put an end to his public career.

OTIS, JAMES, pseudonym of J.O. Kaler.♦

Ottawa Indians, tribe originally located on the Ottawa River in Canada, were first noted by Champlain (1615). They were allied with the French and Hurons, and consequently opposed the Iroquois. The latter forced them to flee to the Great Lakes region, and their later wanderings took them throughout the central U.S. Pontiac♦ was an Ottawa chieftain. The tribe figures in Rogers's *Ponteach* and in Doddridge's *Logan.*

Ouâbi, poem by Sarah Wentworth Morton.♦

Our American Cousin, comedy of Yankee life by the English dramatist Tom Taylor, first produced in 1858. It is remembered as the play that Lincoln was watching at Ford's Theatre in Washington (April 14, 1865) when he was assassinated by Booth.

Our New Home in the West, see *New Home, A,—Who'll Follow?*

Our Old Home, sketches by Hawthorne,♦ published in 1863, describing his observations and experiences during his residence in England.

Our Town, play by Thornton Wilder,♦ produced and published in 1938, when it won a Pulitzer Prize.

The intimate history of a typical American town, Grover's Corners, N.H., is sketched during the years 1901–13. On a bare, uncurtained stage, set with a few chairs and tables, the activities of the townspeople are enacted under the visible direction of the friendly Stage Manager, who addresses the audience, describing the characters and commenting on the action, in what the author calls a "hang-over from a novelist technique." Professor Willard and Editor Webb describe the scientific and social backgrounds, and other incidental figures are Joe Crowell, the newsboy; Howie Newsome, the milkman; Simon Stimson, a frustrated creative artist, the town organist and drunkard; Constable Warren; Mr. Morgan, the druggist; Mrs. Soames, the gossip; and Joe Stoddard, the undertaker. Interest is centered in the families of Editor Webb and Dr. Gibbs. The first act, "Daily Life," shows the common occupations of cooking, gardening, school, baseball, the church choir, and domestic concerns. The second act, "Love and Marriage," deals with the courtship and wedding of George Gibbs and Emily Webb. "Death," the third act, presents the funeral of Emily, who has died in childbirth. The buried dead become articulate, expressing the quiet and patience resulting from a view of the world outside of time, and their knowledge of "something way down deep that's eternal about every human being." Finally aware of the mysterious beauty and terror of life, they embody the author's aim "to present illustrations of harmony and of law . . . affirmations about mankind and his ends."

Out of the Cradle Endlessly Rocking, poem by Whitman,♦ published as "A Word Out of the Sea" in *Leaves of Grass* (1860) and given its present title in 1871.

At night, a boy steals out from his Long Island farm home to listen to the calls of a pair of mockingbirds by the sea. One night the female is gone, and her mate, from the nest to which she will never return, issues his plaintive call. The solitary singer becomes a symbol of the poet's daemon, and his mysterious aria is interpreted by the whispering current of the sea as "Death." The sea, symbol of the spiritual world, thus shows the boy that physical love is spiritualized through death for poetic creation, and the poet says, "my own songs awaked from that hour."

Outcasts of Poker Flat, *The,* story by Bret Harte,♦ published in 1869 and reprinted in *The Luck of Roaring Camp and Other Sketches* (1870). It is a leading example of local-color fiction.

This study of moral contrasts tells of the exile from Poker Flat, a California mining camp of 1850, of the gambler John Oakhurst, two prostitutes known as "the Duchess" and "Mother Shipton," and a drunken sluice-robber, "Uncle Billy." This group is joined by "The Innocent," Tom Simson, and the young girl Piney, who are eloping. When all are trapped by the snow, Mother Shipton starves to save her rations for Piney, Oakhurst gives the one chance of safety to Tom by killing himself, and the Duchess pillows her head on Piney's breast as the two die together.

Outland, TOM, character in *The Professor's House.*♦

Outlook, *The* (1893–1935), was an outgrowth of *The Christian Union* (1870–93), a "family magazine" edited by H.W. Beecher and Lyman Abbott, numbering among its contributors Louisa May Alcott, Harriet Beecher Stowe, Edward Eggleston, C.D. Warner, Whittier, Hayne, M.C. Tyler, Helen Hunt Jackson, Burroughs, and E.P. Roe. When the new name was adopted, the former policies were continued, but more emphasis was placed upon political commentary, and among the new contributors were Theodore Roosevelt, Riis, and Booker T. Washington. Roosevelt became an editor (1909) and contributed many of his writings. Another important contributor was H.W. Mabie, who was associated with *The Outlook* from 1879 to 1916. During the 1920s it began to decline, and in 1928 it was merged with *The Independent.* It became a monthly (1932) as *The New Outlook,* with Alfred E. Smith as editor for a year.

Outre-Mer, narrative by Longfellow.♦

Outsider, *The,* novel by Richard Wright,♦ published in 1953.

Cross Damon, a black man who works in the Chicago post office, is caught in a subway accident but escapes without serious injury, though because of a mistaken identity his death is announced. He decides to take advantage of this error to start life anew and thus free himself of his entanglements with women and debts. He goes to New York to live under an assumed name and before long becomes enmeshed in the Communist party. By it he is used as a murderer, until he is himself killed by a Party member.

Over the Hill to the Poor House, see *Carleton, Will.*

Over the Teacups, essays by Holmes.♦

"Over There," popular World War I song by George M. Cohan.♦

Overland Monthly (1868–75, 1883–1935), California regional magazine, published from San

Francisco, during its first two and a half years was edited by Bret Harte, who contributed "The Luck of Roaring Camp," "Plain Language from Truthful James," and other works that made both author and magazine famous. In its early years, the *Overland* published writings by such authors as C.W. Stoddard, Ina Coolbrith, E.R. Sill, and Prentice Mulford. It was less significant when revived, and rested so obviously on its former reputation that Bierce dubbed it "the warmed-Overland Monthly." For a time it attracted such authors as Gertrude Atherton, Jack London, Edwin Markham, J.G. Neilhardt, Frank Norris, and George Sterling, but it finally died of inanition.

Overland Trail, name given to various routes of Western migration but particularly to that which began at Independence, Mo., was for some distance identical with the Oregon Trail,♦ branched from it to follow the South Platte River to Fort Laramie, and continued thence to the Great Salt Lake and California. This route was first traversed by Jedediah Smith in 1826, was later used by trappers, traders, and such emigrants as the Donner Party, and was a principal route during the 1849 gold rush. George R. Stewart has dealt with the westernmost section in several of his works and has written the authoritative *The California Trail* (1963).

Over-Soul, *The,* essay by Emerson,♦ published in *Essays, First Series* (1841). The Over-Soul is "that great nature in which we rest . . . that Unity within which every man's particular being is contained and made one with all other." This Platonic concept, first stated in Emerson's early lectures and in such works as *Nature* and the "Divinity School Address," is here developed as a basic principle in the thought of Transcendentalism.

"We live in succession, in division, in parts, in particles. Meantime within man is the soul of the whole." Perceptible only through intuition and not to be communicated through words, this divine spirit is the source of all moral and intellectual growth, for "the heart, which abandons itself to the Supreme Mind, finds itself related to all its works and will travel a royal road to particular knowledge and powers." The revelations of truth received by various original thinkers and teachers proceed from "an influx of the Divine mind" into their minds. "The nature of these revelations is always the same: they are perceptions of the absolute law." What we call genius is simply the true insight derived from an influx of this "same Omniscience . . . into the intellect." This universal and benign omnipresence is neither "our god of tradition" nor "our god of rhetoric," but a God known to men only in moments of mystic enthusiasm, whose visitation leaves them altered, self-reliant, and purified of petty aims. The man who has received intimations of the "Highest Law" in this fashion "will weave no longer a

spotted life of shreds and patches, but he will live with a divine unity."

OWEN, ROBERT (1771–1858), "the father of English socialism," at an early age made a commercial success of his cotton mills at New Lanark, Scotland, and then, to ameliorate the conditions of his workers, instituted successful social experiments in economic, moral, and educational reform. In *A New View of Society* (1813), he set forth the principles of his educational philanthropy, contending that human character is formed by circumstances and that to create a good man one must surround him with the proper physical, moral, and social influences. This philosophy led Owen to propose the foundation of socialized agricultural communities of some 1200 persons. To test his theories he came to America (1824) and founded New Harmony.♦

ROBERT DALE OWEN (1801–77), his son, emigrated to the U.S. in 1825, and was active in the New Harmony community and with Frances Wright♦ in the Nashoba Community, as well as in other reform associations. He put his theories of public education into practice as a member of the Indiana legislature, and, while a Democratic member of Congress (1843–47), was instrumental in organizing the Smithsonian Institution. He was American chargé d'affaires and minister to Italy (1853–58), and there became interested in spiritualism, about which he wrote two books. Upon his return to the U.S., he wrote *The Policy of Emancipation* (1863), which supposedly influenced Lincoln's views. Other works include *Pocahontas* (1837), a historical drama; *Hints on Public Architecture* (1849); *The Future of the North-West* (1863); *The Wrong of Slavery* (1864); *Beyond the Breakers* (1870), a novel; and *Threading My Way* (1874), an autobiography of his youth.

Ox-Bow Incident, *The,* novel by Walter Van T. Clark,♦ published in 1940.

A trailhand, Art Croft, in 1885 tells the story of cattle rustlers who murdered a rancher and stole his stock near the Nevada mountain town of Bridger's Wells. A posse is formed to find and lynch the culprits, although the storekeeper Arthur Davies, the sanctimonious Reverend Osgood, and pompous Judge Tyler argue weakly for a fair trial. They are quickly overwhelmed by the old Confederate Major Willard Tetley, a prominent rancher, the tough stage driver Bill Winder, the town drunk Monty Smith, and others who ride out and in a small valley with an ox-bow-shaped river find the Mexican Juan Martinez, the senile Alva Hardwick, and a young rancher, Donald Martin, with cattle which they cannot prove they own. Despite Martin's convincing statement about his innocence, the three are hanged, Martin in a bungled way by Tetley's son Gerald, who is forced to the act by the Major. Upon returning to town the posse finds that the three men were innocent. Gerald hangs himself

in his father's barn, the elder Tetley kills himself
with his old cavalry sword, and Davies, filled
with self-pity as much as with remorse, takes up a
collection for Martin's widow and children.

Oz, mythical land that is the setting for 14 novels
for children by L. Frank Baum,♦ beginning with
The Wonderful Wizard of Oz (1900). This fanciful
region, traversed by a long yellow brick road, is
accidentally discovered by Dorothy, a little girl
from Kansas, when she and her dog Toto are
blown off to it by a cyclone. In this delightful
region of surprising adventures dwell such odd
characters as a good-hearted Cowardly Lion, a
friendly Tin Woodman, and an animate Scarecrow, all basically pleasant and joyful, presided
over by a kindly, eccentric Wizard. Although
there are threats from external forces, like the
Wicked Witch of the West, all turns out happily
in Oz.

Baum created a musical extravaganza for the
stage (1901), the first of many adaptations that
have included a Technicolor musical film featuring Judy Garland (1939) and a Broadway musical,
The Wiz (1975), with a black cast and using a
modern urban setting.

OZICK, CYNTHIA (1928–   ), Bronx-born fiction writer and literary critic. Her first novel,
Trust (1966), she herself describes as "Jamesian."
She began it after doing a master's thesis on James
at Ohio State. The involved plot has a female
narrator emotionally abandoned and financially
deprived by relatives, who becomes witness to
aftershocks of the Holocaust. Her first book of
stories, *The Pagan Rabbi and Other Stories* (1971),
is about immigrant intellectual Jews in America;
The Cannibal Galaxy (1983) is a short novel about
a Swedish book reviewer entranced by Judaism
and by the discovery of a manuscript of the Polish
author Bruno Schulz, a Holocaust victim; *The
Shawl* (1989) contains two novellas. American
Jews and the Holocaust experience feature in stories in *Levitation* (1982) and in the novellas in
Bloodshed (1976). Essays have been gathered in
Art and Ardor (1983), *Metaphor and Memory* (1987),
and *Metaphor and Myth* (1989).

P

Pacing Mustang, legendary wild stallion in the folk tales of the Western frontier, famed for his extraordinary beauty, size, strength, cunning, and untamable independence of spirit. He appears in *Moby-Dick* as "the White Steed of the Prairies," but his color varies in other versions, being black in "The Pacing Mustang" by Ernest Thompson Seton. Among the other works in which he appears are Irving's *A Tour on the Prairies,* Hough's *North of 36,* and Feikema's *Conquering Horse.*

PACK, ROBERT (1929–), poet born in New York City, after graduation from Dartmouth and an M.A. from Columbia has taught at Middlebury College. His controlled poems, whose themes range from the satiric to the comic, have appeared in *A Stranger's Privilege* (1959), *Guarded by Women* (1963), *Home from the Cemetery* (1969), *Nothing But Light* (1973), *Keeping Watch* (1976), *Waking to My Name* (1980), and *Faces in a Single Tree* (1984). He has also published *Affirming Limits* (1985), essays, and a critical book on Wallace Stevens (1958); edited anthologies of poetry; and published verse for children.

PAGE, THOMAS NELSON (1853–1922), Virginia author distinguished as a leader of the local-color movement. His first short story appeared in 1884, and in 1893 he forsook his legal career to become a professional writer. His first volume of stories, *In Ole Virginia♦* (1887), depicts romantic aspects of his region before and during the Civil War. Frequently employing Negro dialect, his stories are generally concerned sentimentally with the aristocratic Old South, as in such collections as *Elsket and Other Stories* (1891), *The Burial of the Guns* (1894), and *Bred in the Bone* (1904). Page's novels, dealing with the same background, include *On Newfound River* (1891), the story of a Virginia feud in the period before the Civil War; *The Old Gentleman of the Black Stock* (1897), a romantic tale of an old man who reunites a quarreling pair of young lovers; *Red Rock* (1898), telling of the oppressive military rule of the South during Reconstruction; *Gordon Keith* (1903), contrasting a well-born Southerner with a Northern *nouveau riche; John Marvel, Assistant* (1909), presenting a typical Southerner against the background of contemporary Chicago. His essays and social studies, linked to his fiction in theme and tone, include *The Old South* (1892), *Social Life in Old Virginia* (1897), and *The Old Dominion* (1908). He also wrote semi-historical works and eulogistic biographies, such as *Robert E. Lee, Man and Soldier*

(1911), and a volume of dialect verse, *Befo' de War* (1888). His literary career ended when he became U.S. ambassador to Italy (1913–19).

PAGE, WALTER HINES (1855–1918), born in North Carolina, began his journalistic career in 1880, reported on the South for the New York *World* (1881–83), edited the Raleigh *State Chronicle* (1883–85), *The Forum* (1890–95), the *Atlantic Monthly* (1896–99), and the *World's Work* (1900–1913). The prestige thus acquired caused his appointment as ambassador to Great Britain (1913–18), in which position he helped Anglo-American relations, sympathizing strongly with Great Britain even while the U.S. was attempting to maintain neutrality in World War I. His *Life and Letters* (3 vols., 1922–25, Pulitzer Prize) was the work of Burton J. Hendrick.

PAGLIA, CAMILLE (1947–), iconoclastic scholar and cultural critic, educated at Harpur College and at Yale, where Harold Bloom was her mentor, and for many years Professor of Humanities at the University of Arts in Philadelphia. She came to sudden national attention with her first book, long in the making and even longer in finding a publisher: *Sexual Personae: Art and Decadence from Nefertiti to Emily Dickinson* (1990). It was a stunning critical and popular success, a scholarly tour de force, and it established her as the leading critic of many articles in the feminist credo. Her writing is fresh and pyrotechnic, above all supremely confident in the attack and fearless of the response of the conventional scholarly establishment. She singles out as foolishly welcomed, baneful influences on American scholarship and teaching the writings of the post-existential French school of language philosophers, especially the work of Derrida, Lacan, and Foucault, as can be seen particularly in her second book, *Sex, Art, and American Culture* (1992), which had even more impact than the earlier one upon our ongoing cultural debate. *Vamps and Tramps: New Essays* (1994) is a compendium of her thoughts and media triumphs.

PAIN, PHILIP, author of *Daily Meditations* (1666). Nothing is known of his life except the information on the title page, that he "lately suffering shipwrack, was drowned." Since the work was published in Massachusetts, he may have been a New Englander, and the poems indicate that he was a very young man. They are concerned with the doubts, fears, and hopes of a devout man who is restive in his faith. The poetry has a deep personal note and is strongly influenced by the English metaphysical poets. If Pain was an American, as is supposed, his work is the earliest-known original verse printed in the American colonies.

PAINE, ALBERT BIGELOW (1861–1937), editor, dramatist, biographer, and author of several novels, is best known for his authorized three-volume biography of Mark Twain (1912) and for his editorship of Twain's letters (1917). The title of one of Paine's plays, *The Great White Way* (1901), gave a familiar nickname to New York City's theatrical district.

PAINE, ROBERT TREAT (1773–1811), was reared in the best society of Boston, but after his graduation from Harvard (1792) drifted from business into bohemianism, and through his writing and actions estranged himself from his conventional background. He edited the *Federal Orrery* (1794–96), a strongly Federalist journal that specialized in satire of Jacobin politics. His marriage to an actress, constant indebtedness, and vehement manner placed him beyond the pale of Boston society, but his satirical ability, facile versification, and general eccentricity caused him to be considered a genius. His poetry, including "The Invention of Letters" (1795) and "The Ruling Passion" (1796), was widely read. "Adams and Liberty"♦ (1798), his most famous work, was sung throughout the nation. Until 1801 he used his christened name, Thomas Paine, but that year he adopted the name of a dead brother, presumably because of his opposition to the ideas of the pamphleteer. His *Works* (1812) includes early neoclassical verse, later political satire, and patriotic prose.

PAINE, THOMAS (1737–1809), born in England, was the son of a corset maker, to whose trade he was apprenticed when his schooling ended at the age of 13. His unsettled life to 1774 included residence in various towns, two brief unhappy marriages, and such occupations as schoolteacher, tobacconist, grocer, and exciseman. He was twice dismissed from the last post, and was forced into bankruptcy after the publication of *The Case of the Officers of Excise* (1772), a plea to Parliament for higher wages. While lobbying for the excisemen, he met Franklin, who was impressed by his learning and interests and helped him to start anew in America.

Arriving at Philadelphia (1774), Paine contributed extensively to the *Pennsylvania Magazine* and achieved wide fame with the publication of *Common Sense*♦ (1776), which urged an immediate declaration of independence at a time when others were debating only matters of reform. Under the pseudonym Forester, in the *Pennsylvania Packet* (1776), he defended his theories against attacks by William Smith. While serving as a soldier in the Continental army, he continued his political journalism in *The American Crisis*♦ (Dec. 1776–April 1783), a series of 16 pamphlets in support of the Revolutionary War. He was rewarded by an appointment (1777–79) as secretary to the congressional committee on foreign affairs, but was forced to resign, after he charged corruption in the negotiations of Silas Deane with France and implied that the French, while still at peace with England, had aided the colonies. The plea for a strong federal union that he had made in *Common Sense* was reiterated in *Public Good* (1780), opposing Virginia's claims to western land.

After an appointment as clerk of the Pennsylvania Assembly and a trip to France (1781) for money and stores, he retired to the farm at New Rochelle that New York presented to him. *Dissertations on Government . . .* (1786), a blast against paper money inflation, was his only political work during this period, when he was engaged in perfecting his invention of an iron bridge. He went to France and England (1787), had his bridge constructed in the latter country, and traveled between Paris and London in the cause of a world revolution.

The Rights of Man♦ (1791–92), a defense of the French Revolution against the attacks of Edmund Burke, urged the English to create a republic. Having fled to France, he was not directly affected by his English trial for treason and sentence of banishment (1792). He was made a French citizen by the Assembly (1792) and was elected to the Convention, where he allied himself with the moderate republicans, who lost power during the Terror (1793). His citizenship was thereupon revoked, and, although he was outlawed by England, he was arrested by France as an enemy Englishman. In jail (Dec. 1793–Nov. 1794), he wrote *The Age of Reason*♦ (1794–95), his great deistic work.

At this time he considered himself the victim of a plot contrived by his conservative enemy, the American minister Gouverneur Morris, but it appears that Morris deliberately left him in jail because he was unnoticed there and might be sentenced to death if his case were reopened. Released at the request of Morris's successor, Monroe, Paine returned to the Convention (1795) after the passing of the Terror. Although he did not return to the U.S. until 1802, he played a vicarious part in American politics through his *Letter to George Washington* (1796), accusing the President and Morris of plotting against him, and, through Jefferson's championing of *The Rights of Man,* causing a bitter partisan dispute with J.Q. Adams, who attacked both Paine and Jefferson.

Paine's last years in the U.S. were marked by poverty, ill health, and ostracism. Malevolent persons of all parties, who feared his radical free-thinking, accused him of drunkenness, cowardice, adultery, and atheism. He was buried on his

New Rochelle farm when consecrated ground was refused, and in 1819 William Cobbett removed the remains to England, with the intention of erecting a monument to Paine. This was never accomplished, and after Cobbett's death the bones of Paine were lost.

Painted Veils, novel by Huneker,♦ published in 1920.

Set among the bohemian society of New York artists, critics, and dilettantes, this impressionistic narrative exhibits the author's love of the exotic and the voluptuous, his acceptance of the decorative aspects of Oriental mysticism, and his intimate knowledge of art and artists in his time. His aesthetic enthusiasms are shown by the incidental inclusion of such figures as Saltus, de Reszke, Lilli Lehmann, Huysmans, Gourmont, Mary Garden, and Seidl, and digressions concerning Wagner, the Symbolists, Ibsen, Henry James, Stendhal, Petronius, à Kempis, Flaubert, and others. The principal characters are fictional, and include Esther Brandés, later called "Easter" and finally "Istar," a beautiful and gifted Southern girl who wins a great success as a Wagnerian soprano, while maintaining her independence equally of men and of morals; Ulick Invern, a wealthy amateur and critic, who cherishes a hopeless passion for the singer, and, after frenetic years of sexual and alcoholic excess, artistic passions, and mysticism, dies in Paris; Mona Milton, a "maternal nymphomaniac," who is for a time Invern's mistress; her brother, a theological student deliberately debauched by Istar, who becomes a Catholic missionary in the Orient; Dora, a prostitute; Paul Godard, a music critic who "shares" Dora with Invern and becomes Istar's lover, but afterward marries Mona, to become a conventional *père de famille;* and Alfred Henderson, another critic, who observes the careers of this "queer crowd" with envious cynicism.

Pal Joey, 12 stories by John O'Hara♦ about a heel, published in 1940. They formed the basis for a hit musical the same year, with music by Richard Rodgers, lyrics by Lorenz Hart, and book by O'Hara.

Pale Fire, novel by Nabokov,♦ published in 1962.

An unfinished poem of 999 lines of heroic couplets, titled "Pale Fire," by John Shade is the subject of an inept but lengthy exegesis of 160 pages by Charles Kinbote. Although ostensibly a literary scholar, Kinbote admits he is actually Charles Xavier, last king of Zembla (1936–58), overthrown in a revolution. One of the revolutionary leaders, Gradus, has pursued the monarch to New Wye, Appalachia, in the U.S., where as Kinbote he is teaching at Wordsmith College. There Kinbote has made friends with the poet John Shade in the hope of persuading him to write an epic immortalizing Zembla and its last

monarch. However, Gradus accidentally kills Shade while trying to assassinate the ex-king. Charles makes off with the manuscript of the unfinished poem that he persuades himself is a cryptic version of the desired epic, and therefore in editing the work for publication he creates the very elaborate commentary that forms the body of the novel.

Pale Horse, Pale Rider, volume♦ of short stories by Katherine Anne Porter.♦

PALEY, GRACE (1922–   ), born in New York City, a member of the Sarah Lawrence faculty, has published *The Little Disturbances of Man* (1959), *Enormous Changes at the Last Minute* (1974); *Later the Same Day* (1985), short stories about people often tough and seeking; and *Leaning Forward* (1985), a collection of poems.

PALFREY, JOHN GORHAM (1796–1881), Unitarian clergyman of Boston, owned and edited *The North American Review*♦ (1835–43). In addition to books on religious subjects, he wrote a *History of New England* (5 vols., 1858–90), in its time considered impartial and revelatory because of its paralleling of colonial and English events. Later critics have found the work biased in favor of New England, particularly of Massachusetts.

Palladium, *The,* see *Massachusetts Mercury.*

PALMER, GEORGE HERBERT (1842–1933), professor of philosophy at Harvard (1873–1913), also known for his scholarly works on Greek and English literature. In addition to his *Autobiography of a Philosopher* (1930), he wrote a *Life* (1908) of his wife Alice Freeman Palmer (1855–1902), who was president of Wellesley College (1882–87).

PALMER, JOEL (1810–81), pioneer of the Pacific Northwest, who left his Indiana home (1845) for the voyage to Oregon described in his *Journal of Travels Over the Rocky Mountains* (1847), an account that became a guide for later emigrants.

PALMER, RAY (1808–87), born in Rhode Island, was reared in Boston and graduated from Yale (1830). He became a pastor of Congregational churches in Maine and New York, and is best remembered for his original hymns, published in *Hymns and Sacred Pieces* (1865), *Hymns of My Holy Hours* (1868), and other collections.

Panic, verse play by MacLeish,♦ produced and published in 1935. "A Note on the Verse" explains the intention to accommodate the verse to characteristic American speech rhythms by the use of lines of five accents but unlimited syllables, and, in the case of crowd effects, of similar lines of three accents.

PANSY, see *Alden, Isabella.*

Paris Bound, play by Philip Barry, ♦ produced in 1927 and published in 1929.

Paris Review, The (1953–   ), quarterly journal of poetry, fiction, art and literary criticism and commentary, edited from Paris and New York. It emphasizes the contemporary but its tastes are catholic as indicated by its contributors who have included Malcolm Cowley, Jack Kerouac, Philip Roth, W.D. Snodgrass, William Styron, and Joyce Carol Oates. It has featured a notable series of interviews with a variety of authors, including Eliot, Frost, Hemingway, Huxley, Voznesensky, and Joan Didion, some gathered in collections, beginning with *Writers at Work* (1958), that reached a sixth volume in 1984. One of the founders, William Styron, edited a collection of its *Best Short Stories* (1959) from the early years.

PARISH, ELIJAH (1762–1825), orthodox Congregational clergyman of Connecticut, whose sermons incidentally reveal his reactionary adherence to the Federalist party. With Jedidiah Morse, he wrote *A Compendious History of New England* (1804). In addition to his own works on modern and Biblical geography, he wrote a biography of Eleazar Wheelock with David McClure (1811).

PARKE, JOHN (1754–89), Delaware soldier in the Continental army, was known for his anonymous book *The Lyric Works of Horace . . . to Which Are Added, a Number of Original Poems . . .* (1786). His Horatian translations are adapted to American history by such substitutions as Washington for Augustus. The original verses are in the neoclassical manner, and include, in addition to some poems by other hands, his pastoral drama *Virginia* and a life of Horace.

PARKER, DOROTHY [ROTHSCHILD] (1893–1967), after a career as a dramatic and literary critic in her native New York City, during which she achieved an almost legendary reputation for her malicious and sardonic *bons mots,* published her first book of poetry, *Enough Rope* (1926). This and the two volumes which followed, *Sunset Gun* (1928) and *Death and Taxes* (1931), all collected in *Not So Deep as a Well* (1936), are works of light, satirical verse, characterized by brilliant concision, flippant cynicism, and caustic variations on certain dominant themes, such as frustrated love and cheated idealism in modern living. Her short stories and sketches, published in *Laments for the Living* (1930) and *After Such Pleasures* (1933), and collected in *Here Lies* (1939), possess the same wry quality and polished technique that are found in her poems. She was a newspaper correspondent in Spain during that country's civil war, and later wrote motion-picture scenarios in collaboration with her husband, Alan Campbell, and

with Arnaud d'Usseau wrote a two-act play, *Ladies of the Corridor* (1953), about the lonely lives of wealthy widows in a New York hotel.

PARKER, JAMES (c. 1714–70), New Jersey-born printer and journalist, after working with the younger William Bradford (1727–33) and with Franklin (1742–48) became public printer of New York (1743–60). In addition to his various printing businesses, he established several newspapers: the *New York Gazette, or the Weekly Post-Boy* (1743–73), the *Independent Reflector* (1752–53), the *Occasional Reverberator* (Sept.–Oct. 1753), *John Englishman* (April–July 1755), the *Instructor* (March–May 1755), the *Connecticut Gazette* (1755–68), and *The Constitutional Courant ♦* (1765).

PARKER, JANE MARSH (1836–1913), New York author, whose revolt from her father's fanatical belief in the Millerites ♦ may be seen in the semi-autobiographical *Barley Wood* (1860). *The Midnight Cry* (1886) is another novel based on the Millerites.

PARKER, SAMUEL (1779–1866), Congregational clergyman of Massachusetts, who in 1835 with Marcus Whitman ♦ went west to select sites for Indian missions. He continued to Oregon alone, while Whitman returned to organize a missionary party. His *Journal of an Exploring Tour Beyond the Rocky Mountains* (1838) is an account of this trip.

PARKER, THEODORE (1810–60), born at Lexington, Mass., early showed a precocious ability at scholarship, although poverty limited his schooling. From the age of 17 until he was 21, he taught at district schools, and then, after passing the Harvard entrance examination, being too poor to enroll, received special credit and graduated from the Divinity School (1836). He became a Unitarian clergyman in a Boston suburb (1837). Increasingly dependent upon the direct intuition of an Absolute Being, he turned away from the belief in miraculous revelation. In agreement with such liberal thinkers as Channing, Emerson, Alcott, Ripley, and Wendell Phillips, who were his friends, he developed his intuitive religious beliefs into a system, expressed in *The . . . Question Between Mr. Andrews Norton and His Alumni . . .* (1839), written under the pseudonym Levi Blodgett, and a sermon on "The Transient and Permanent in Christianity" (1841). Having become a Transcendentalist, he was ostracized by the orthodox Unitarian circles, and only enabled to deliver the lectures printed as *A Discourse of Matters Pertaining to Religion* (1842) when laymen invited him to Boston. After a trip to Europe (1843–44), he still found Boston churches closed to him. When he was finally installed as minister of a new Congregational Society of Boston, he devoted his pulpit not only to religious education but to the discussion of problems of war, slavery, temperance, women's rights, and other reforms, in the belief that social wrongs would be cured when men attained consciousness of the infinite perfection of God. Outside the church, he made passionate speeches against slavery, aided New England emigrants to Kansas in the struggle that followed the passage of the Kansas-Nebraska bill, abetted John Brown, was active in attempts to rescue fugitive slaves, and wrote such works as his *Letters . . . Touching the Matter of Slavery* (1848). His strenuous public life came to an end through exhaustion and illness (1859). In an attempt to regain his health, he went to Italy, where he died. His *Works* was published in 15 volumes (1907–13).

PARKER, THOMAS (1595–1677), English-born minister who emigrated to Massachusetts (1634), was an orthodox Calvinist, although in matters of ecclesiastical polity he favored Presbyterianism rather than Congregationalism, as may be seen in his *True Copy of a Letter written by Mr. T. Parker . . .* (1644). He conducted a preparatory school for Harvard students, among his pupils being Samuel Sewall, and also wrote *The Visions and Prophecies of Daniel expounded* (1646).

PARKMAN, FRANCIS (1823–93), member of a prominent Boston family, graduated from Harvard (1844), having already indicated his interest in frontier life through excursions to the northern woods to study Indian life. After a European trip (1843–44), he attended Harvard Law School (LL.B., 1846), although he never applied for admission to the bar. In 1846 he set out from St. Louis on a journey to Wyoming, with the dual purpose of studying Indian life and improving his frail health. He observed frontiersmen and Indians at first hand, and gained valuable information, but his strenuous exercise led to a complete breakdown rather than recovery. Incapable of writing, he dictated to his cousin and companion, Quincy A. Shaw, his account of the journey, which he entitled *The Oregon Trail♦* (1849).

Parkman continued to suffer from a complete exhaustion and derangement of his nervous system, a mental condition prohibiting concentration, and an extreme weakness of the eyes. Although he was frequently unable to compose more than six lines a day, had to hire others to read and write for him, and employed a special instrument enabling him to write without looking at his manuscript, he nevertheless began in 1848 his *History of the Conspiracy of Pontiac* (1851), the first of a long series of histories of the French and English struggle for colonial America. His only novel is the semi-autobiographical *Vassall Morton* (1856). A new nervous crisis caused him to seek cures in European travel (1858–59) and in an interest in horticulture, which resulted in *The Book of Roses* (1866) and his later appointment as Harvard professor of horticulture (1871).

By sheer will power, he forced himself to return to his historical project. The series concern-

ing the conflict for domination in the New World includes seven separate works: *Pioneers of France in the New World* (1865), concerned with the struggle between French Huguenots and Spanish Catholics for Florida, and the history of Champlain; *The Jesuits in North America in the Seventeenth Century* (1867), telling of the struggle to Christianize the Indians, and the Iroquois victory over the converted tribes (c. 1670); *La Salle and the Discovery of the Great West* (1869), originally published as *The Discovery of the Great West,* dealing with La Salle's attempts to colonize the Mississippi Valley; *The Old Regime in Canada* (1874), showing the French feudal dominion of Acadia, the problems of the missionaries, and the faults of autocratic rule; *Count Frontenac and New France Under Louis XIV* (1877), depicting Frontenac as the hero who alone attempted to maintain France's untenable position; *Montcalm and Wolfe* (1884), dealing with the Seven Years' War in America, and the dramatic conclusion of French influence with the defeat of Montcalm on the Plains of Abraham; and *A Half-Century of Conflict* (1892), concerned with border warfare and the siege of Louisburg in the years 1700–1741, between Frontenac's government and the final downfall of France's colonial empire. The series was written in historical sequence, except for the last two works, and the *History of the Conspiracy of Pontiac,* which describes events following those of *Montcalm and Wolfe.*

Parkman depicted history in terms of the two forces of progress and reaction, represented respectively by England and France. He saw the former as ordered democracy, the latter as dictated military despotism, but, placing his faith in neither, admitted in *The Old Regime* what was everywhere implicit: "My political faith lies between two vicious extremes, democracy and absolute authority. . . . I do not object to a good constitutional monarchy, but prefer a conservative republic. . . ." As he was a believer in a middle-of-the-road policy for government, likewise in his approach to history he combined Scott's romantic attitude with the scientific method of German scholarship, to create work both accurate as history and important as literature. His lost *Journals* were printed in 1948 and his *Letters* in 1960.

PARLEY, PETER, see *Goodrich, S.G.*

Parnassus on Wheels, novel by Christopher Morley.♦

PARRINGTON, VERNON L[OUIS] (1871–1929), scholar of American literature, professor at the University of Washington (1908–29), whose books include *The Connecticut Wits* (1926), *Sinclair Lewis, Our Own Diogenes* (1927), and *Main Currents in American Thought* (3 vols., 1927–30). The last work, of which the third volume was left incomplete, is a historical examination of American ideas and their primary expression in literature, written from the point of view of a Jeffersonian liberal. The first two volumes were awarded a Pulitzer Prize (1928) and the entire work influenced others to reevaluate American literature, following him in an economic interpretation of literary movements.

PARRISH, ANNE (1888–1957), author of *The Perennial Bachelor* (1925), a fictional study of a pampered, charming ne'er-do-well whose mother and sisters sacrifice themselves in order that he may enjoy a genteel life. Her other novels include *Semi-Attached* (1924), *Tomorrow Morning* (1926), *All Kneeling* (1928), *The Methodist Faun* (1929), *Loads of Love* (1932), *Sea Level* (1934), *Golden Wedding* (1936), *Poor Child* (1945), and *A Clouded Star* (1948).

PARSONS, THOMAS WILLIAM (1819–92), Massachusetts author, is best known for his translations of Dante, which began to appear in 1843 and were collected by C.E. Norton in *The Divine Comedy of Dante Alighieri* (1893), containing the entire *Inferno,* two-thirds of the *Purgatorio,* and fragments of the *Paradiso.* His original poems were collected in 1893. He is represented as "the Poet" in Longfellow's *Tales of a Wayside Inn.*

Partisan, The, first of the Revolutionary Romances by Simms,♦ published in 1835. Set in South Carolina, it covers the period between the capture of Charleston and the American defeat at Camden.

Robert Singleton, a young partisan (patriot) leader, comes in disguise to Dorchester, where he aids Davis, a young provincial, in his quarrel with the British officer Hastings over their love for Bella Humphries. Davis and Bella's brother Dick accordingly join Singleton's rebel band, as does Singleton's uncle, Colonel Walton, with whose daughter Katherine Singleton is in love. In his raids on the British, Singleton captures Captain Travis and his man Ned Blonay (Goggle), whose mother in revenge aids Hastings's attempt to seduce Bella. Meanwhile, Singleton is joined by Porgy, a gourmand and Falstaffian warrior, and Frampton, a mad bloodthirsty Whig whose plantation has been burned and whose wife has been murdered by the British. All of the partisans join the "Swamp Fox," Marion, and with him assist Gates and De Kalb. Gates stupidly misdirects the Battle of Camden, and the Americans are defeated. With a small band, Singleton rescues Colonel Walton just as he is about to be hanged, and the story ends with Mother Blonay's death, the reuniting of Bella and Davis, and Katherine's engagement to Singleton.

Partisan Leader, The, novel by N.B. Tucker,♦ published in 1836 under the pseudonym Edward William Sidney, with the fictitious publication date 1856. In order to excoriate the followers of Jackson, laud Calhoun, and promote the doctrine of secession, Tucker wrote this romantic fantasy as an account of events supposed to take place during 1849. Van Buren has become dictator of the U.S. and, in operating his great political machine for the benefit of himself and the North, has so exploited the South that South Carolina secedes and Virginia is on the point of joining in a confederacy that will trade freely with England and flourish unhampered as a great agrarian nation. The work was intended to sway the election of 1836 against Van Buren, but, because of its political philosophy, was reissued as propaganda during the Civil War.

Partisan Review (1934–), quarterly magazine, originally a partisan of the Communist party, but independent since 1938. Its fight for intellectual freedom has opposed regimentation, whether fascist or communist, but in later years it has been less concerned with specific social or political issues and more with sociocultural subjects and literary and art criticism. It is also noted for its fiction and poetry. Editors have included Philip Rahv (1934–69) and Delmore Schwartz (1943–55). Contributors have included Auden, Barzun, Bellow, I. Howe, Jarrell, Kazin, Levertov, Robert Lowell, Dwight Macdonald, MacLeish, Mailer, Oates, Roethke, Roth, Sontag, Sorrentino, Tate, Trilling, W.C. Williams, and Edmund Wilson. In earlier years the journal was a monthly for a time and long a bimonthly (until 1955). William Phillips, a founder, is the author of *A Partisan View* (1983), a memoir of literary life, coedited three anthologies drawn from the journal.

PARTON, JAMES (1822–91), born in England, was brought to New York (1827) and established his literary reputation with the publication of *The Life of Horace Greeley* (1855). His ability at realistic portrayal and the vivid ordering of comprehensive factual material made him a noteworthy biographer of his time. His other subjects were *Aaron Burr* (1857), *Andrew Jackson* (3 vols. 1859–60), *Benjamin Franklin* (2 vols., 1864), *John Jacob Astor* (1865), *Jefferson* (1874), and *Voltaire* (2 vols., 1881). In addition to these works, which remain excellent personal portraits, he wrote on contemporary political, social, and economic topics, and made collections of short biographies. His wife was Sara P. Willis.

PASQUIN, ANTHONY, pseudonym of John Williams.♦

Passage to India, poem by Whitman,♦ the title piece of a pamphlet (1871), was incorporated in *Leaves of Grass* (1876).

Ostensibly celebrating the completion of the Suez Canal and the transcontinental railroad (1869), and such other links as the Atlantic cable (1866), which would effect "the marriage of continents," the poem asserts that it is not only the "facts of modern science," but also the "myths and fables of eld . . . The deep diving bibles and legends," which will unify the world. The welding process must be carried on "not for trade or transportation only, But in God's name, and for thy sake, O soul." The long history of mankind, from Oriental antiquity to the present culture of the West, is now to be crowned in America, when "the Poet, worthy that name; The true Son of God shall come, singing his songs." The new nation shall combine the physical and intellectual vigor of the West with the spirituality and mystical wisdom of the East. The voyages of the former explorers symbolize the search for God, which is to be completed by the passage of the soul to "more than India," through the poet who will restore the divine trinity of God (the universal), Nature (the particular), and Man (the individual).

Passionate Pilgrim, A, story by Henry James,♦ published in 1871 and collected in *A Passionate Pilgrim and Other Tales* (1875).

Clement Searle, a middle-aged American widower, comes to England to prosecute his claim to a rich estate. Although a melancholy invalid, he is enthusiastic concerning his pilgrimage to the mother country, which has been his lifelong dream, and he shares his new experiences with the narrator, an impressionable American tourist. Penniless, and feeling the approach of death, Searle determines to enjoy to the full his last days. With the narrator, he visits the Searle estate, is received by its furiously conservative and selfish proprietor, and falls in love with his gentle sister. The brother drives his visitors away, and the shock further weakens Searle, who that night believes he sees a traditional family specter. With his companion, he goes to Oxford, still the "passionate pilgrim," but after a few days becomes weaker and dies. On his deathbed he asks for Miss Searle, who is summoned. She appears in mourning, since her brother has been accidentally killed, leaving her "free . . . with what use for freedom?"

PASTORIUS, FRANCIS DANIEL (1651–c.1720), German-born lawyer and author, came to Pennsylvania (1683) as the agent of Frankfurt Quakers to purchase the land on which he established Germantown. He held many public offices while studying seven languages and many fields of learning. His works include *Four Boasting Disputers of This World Briefly Rebuked* (1697), attacking George Keith's followers; *A New Primmer . . . of English* (c.1698); and a description of Pennsylvania in German (1700). The "Beehive," a store of the honey of his reading, contains original verse printed in a biography (1908).

PATCHEN, KENNETH (1911–72), born in Ohio and educated at the University of Wisconsin (1929–30), lived in New York and later in California. His poetry, marked by religious sym-

bols and intricate figures recalling the metaphysicals, is also free in structure and associations. Collections include *Before the Brave* (1936), *First Will and Testament* (1939), *The Teeth of the Lion* (1942), *Cloth of the Tempest* (1943), *An Astonished Eye Looks Out of the Air* (1945), *Sleepers Awake* (1946), *Selected Poems* (1946, enlarged 1958), *Red Wine & Yellow Hair* (1949), *To Say If You Love Someone* (1949), *Hurrah for Anything* (1957), *Because It Is* (1960), *But Even So* (1968), and *Collected Poems* (1969). He has written poems in cadenced prose, among them: *Panels for the Walls of Heaven* (1947) and *The Famous Boating Party* (1954). Many of his works are illustrated with his own abstract, expressionistic art, including *Because It Is* and *Hallelujah Anyway* (1966). His prose includes *The Journal of Albion Moonlight* (1941) a stream-of-consciousness account; *The Memoirs of a Shy Pornographer* (1945), a satirical novel; and *See You in the Morning* (1948), a love story about a dying man. His produced but unpublished plays were printed as *Patchen's Lost Plays* (1977).

Paterson, long poem by William Carlos Williams,♦ divided into five Books published in 1946, 1948, 1949, 1951, and 1958. Fragments of the incomplete Book Six were published posthumously (1963) as an appendix to the collection of the first five parts.

Written in the "variable foot" of Williams's free verse, the work incorporates prose passages from historical documents, newspaper accounts, geological surveys, literary texts, and personal letters ranging from one by an anonymous semi-literate black man to those by Edward Dahlberg, Alan Ginsberg, and Ezra Pound, all reinforcing the poem's themes.

The Author's Note declares: "a man in himself is a city, beginning, seeking, achieving and concluding his life in ways which the various aspects of a city may embody—if imaginatively conceived—any city, all the details of which may be made to voice his most intimate convictions."

Using the city of Paterson on the Passaic River near his hometown of Rutherford, N.J., as subject so as to bring forth the universal from a local setting ("there are no ideas but in things"), the poem presents local history and the natural scene (particularly the Falls and Garrett Mountain) as well as the consciousness of a gigantic, mythic man (Paterson) and of the author, poet and doctor. Book One ("The Delineaments of the Giants") mythologizes "the elemental character of the place": the city (a masculine force) the landscape (a feminine principle), and the vital, unifying river. Book Two ("Sunday in the Park"), concerned with "modern replicas," meditates on failures in communication through language, religion, economics, and sex, but suggests redemption through art, imagination, and memory. Book Three ("The Library") moves from the previous section's "confused uproar" of the Falls to find that "books will give rest sometimes," a sanctuary for "dead men's dreams," but the past represents only desolation, destruction, and death, and "I must find my meaning and lay it, white, beside the sliding water." Book Four ("The Run to the Sea") treats the polluted river below the Falls in terms of human corruption by modern civilization, while recognizing innovations in science, economics, and language, but finally the identity of the river is lost in the sea, although the individual man (Paterson) survives and strides inland to begin again. Book Five (untitled but dedicated to Toulouse-Lautrec) is like a separate work, an oblique commentary on the poem by an aged poet from a point of view more international and universal than local.

Pathfinder, The; or, The Inland Sea, romance by Cooper,♦ published in 1840 as the third in plot sequence of the Leather-Stocking Tales.♦

In 1759, Mabel Dunham is on her way to join her father at the British fort at Oswego, Lake Ontario, accompanied by her uncle, Charles Cap; Arrowhead, a Tuscarora Indian; his wife, Dew-in-June; Pathfinder, the scout aged about 40; the Mohican chief Chingachgook; and Jasper Western, a young sailor called Eau-douce by the French. Arrowhead and his wife disappear during skirmishes with the Iroquois, but the others reach Oswego. Then Dunham, Cap, Pathfinder, Mabel, and Lieutenant Muir, who wants to marry her, sail on Jasper's *Scud* to relieve a post in the Thousand Islands. Jasper's loyalty is suspected and he is returned to Oswego. While Dunham and his men are off destroying French supply boats, the rest are warned by Dew-in-June of an Iroquois attack to be led by Arrowhead. Cap and Muir are seized, Dunham is badly wounded, and Mabel, who defends the blockhouse, promises to wed Pathfinder if he protects her father. After Jasper and Chingachgook rout the Iroquois, Jasper is arrested by Muir as a traitor. Muir is proved the only guilty one and is killed by Arrowhead. Dunham dies, hoping Mabel and Pathfinder will marry, but Jasper has won Mabel's love.

PATRICK, JOHN, pseudonym of John Patrick Gogan (1905–), playwright, whose works include *The Hasty Heart* (1945), *The Story of Mary Surratt* (1947), *The Curious Savage* (1950), *Lo and Behold* (1951), and 20 other productions during the 1970s, as well as screenplays. His most famous play, *The Teahouse of the August Moon* (1953, Pulitzer Prize), an adaptation of Vern Sneider's novel, is a comic fantasy about American soldiers building a teahouse to please natives in Okinawa.

Patriotic Gore, Studies in the Literature of the American Civil War, by Edmund Wilson,♦ published in 1962.

Under a title derived from James Ryder Randall's "Maryland, My Maryland," the work in 16 essays ranges discursively over writings related to the war, including those of soldiers North and South (Grant and Sherman, Mosby and Lee), Confederate women diarists (Sarah Morgan and Mary Chesnut), statesmen North and South (Lincoln, Stephens), and writers of fiction North and South (Bierce and De Forest, Tourgée Cable and Page), among other subjects for reflection on literary expression associated with the war.

Patriots, The, play by Robert Munford,♦ published in 1776 and reprinted in his *Collection of Plays and Poems* (1798), but probably never produced. It represents the nonpartisan attitude at the beginning of the Revolutionary War. The soldiers are depicted as braggarts or cowards, and the rebel committee as ignorant and intolerant. Tackabout, a Tory masquerading as a rebel, causes Trueman and Meanwell, two nonpartisan pacifists, to be jailed, but when his duplicity is discovered, the moderates are released.

PATTEE, FRED LEWIS (1863–1950), professor at Pennsylvania State College (1894–1928), is said to have been the first incumbent of a chair of American literature. His works include *History of American Literature Since 1870* (1915), *The New American Literature, 1890–1930* (1930), and *The Feminine Fifties* (1940). *Penn State Yankee* (1953) is autobiography.

PATTEN, WILLIAM GILBERT (1866–1945), under the pseudonym Burt L. Standish wrote dime novels and several series of juvenile stories about college life and amateur sports. The best-known series deals with Frank Merriwell, a wholesome college athlete. The series began in 1896, included more than 200 novels, and sold over 25,000,000 copies. After a long interval *Mr. Frank Merriwell* (1941) appeared, presenting a mature hero facing contemporary problems, and Patten's autobiography was published as *Frank Merriwell's "Father"* (1964).

Patterns, poems by Amy Lowell.♦.

PATTIE, JAMES OHIO (1804–50?), Kentucky-born explorer and trapper, engaged in several lengthy and hazardous journeys, which took him to Santa Fe, Lower California, and Mexico (1824–30). His *Personal Narrative* (1831), describing these adventures, was edited and perhaps largely written by Timothy Flint.♦ Although the work mixes fiction and history, it is an important contribution to frontier literature. It was plagiarized in *The Hunters of Kentucky* (1847), which purported to tell the adventures of one B. Bilson. Except that he went to California (1849), little is known of Pattie's later life.

PAUL, ELLIOT [HAROLD] (1891–1958), Massachusetts-born author, served in World War I and became an expatriate while working as literary editor of American newspapers in Europe and later as founder and editor with Eugene Jolas of the little magazine *transition*. His novels include *Indelible* (1922), about two young musicians; *Impromptu* (1923), dealing with the warping of a young couple's lives by the World War and their community's intolerance; *Low Run Tide* (1929), about a declining New England fishing village, complemented by *Lava Rock* (1929), about a vigorous Western mining camp; *The Amazon* (1930); *The Governor of Massachusetts* (1930); and *Concert Pitch* (1938), about "lost generation" expatriates in the Parisian musical world. *The Life and Death of a Spanish Town* (1937) contrasts the idyllic life in the Balearic Islands with havoc wrought by the Spanish Civil War, and another narrative, *The Last Time I Saw Paris* (1942), intimately reveals the life of Parisians and expatriates. His autobiographical series, "Items on the Grand Account," includes *Linden on the Saugus Branch* (1947), *A Ghost Town on the Yellowstone* (1948), *My Old Kentucky Home* (1949), and *Desperate Scenery* (1954). He also wrote satirical mystery novels.

Paul Revere's Ride, narrative poem by Longfellow,♦ published in 1861 and included as the landlord's tale in his *Tales of a Wayside Inn*♦ (1863). In galloping anapestic tetrameter, this literary ballad tells of "the midnight ride of Paul Revere" from Charlestown to Lexington and Concord, to warn the inhabitants of the approach of British troops at the outbreak of the Revolution. Apparently based on Revere's account, the poem, which crystallized an American legend, is very inaccurate, since Revere never waited for signals from lanterns, and it was "a young Dr. Prescott" who carried the news to Concord, while Revere went to Lexington.

PAULDING, HIRAM (1797–1878), naval officer, distinguished himself in the Battle of Lake Champlain, the Tripolitan War, and the arrest of William Walker (1857), which delighted the Nicaraguans but caused Buchanan to relieve Paulding of his command. His *Journal of a Cruise of the United States Schooner* Dolphin (1831) tells of his pursuit of mutineers in the Pacific, and *Bolivar in His Camp* (1834) describes his 1500-mile horseback trip in the Andes (1824), carrying dispatches from Admiral Hull to Bolivar.

PAULDING, JAMES KIRKE (1778–1860), born in New York state, was reared at Tarrytown, where he became intimate with Washington Irving, whose brother William had married Paulding's sister. He was a member of their informal literary group, the "Nine Worthies of Cockloft Hall," and with them collaborated on *Salmagundi*♦ (1807–8), of which he published a second series alone (1819–20).

Stimulated by this venture and Irving's *History of New York*, Paulding wrote *The Diverting History of John Bull and Brother Jonathan* (1812), a comic account of the settlement, growth, and revolt of the American colonies. His flair for satire and opposition to the romanticism of Scott led him to write *The Lay of the Scottish Fiddle* (1813), while he defended his own conception of a hero as an oppressed individual who finds freedom on the frontier in the long poem *The Backwoodsman* (1818). His admiration for homespun American qualities and dislike of Tory England led him to answer British critics in a series of books employing both realistic descriptions of the U.S. and burlesques of the English.

The United States and England (1815) is a wholly serious work; *Letters from the South* (2 vols., 1817) is an agrarian, Jeffersonian defense of the South; and *A Sketch of Old England, by a New England Man* (2 vols., 1822) and *John Bull in America; or, the New Munchausen* (1825) are further contributions to this cause. These books, besides making him famous, brought him an appointment to the Board of Navy Commissioners (1815–23).

Having completed his work on the Anglo-American controversy, he wrote a series of realistic tales, some of which were published in *Tales of the Good Woman* (1829) and *The Book of St. Nicholas* (1836), which continue to show his dislike of the English, attacking their current literary styles, as represented in Byron and Scott. His novels also continue this realism and satire of false romanticism, in the treatment of historical subjects. *Koningsmarke, the Long Finne*♦ (1823) is concerned with the early Swedish settlement on the Delaware; *The Dutchman's Fireside*♦ (1831) deals with life in upper New York during the French and Indian War; *Westward Ho!* (1832) tells of a Virginia family pioneering in Kentucky; *The Old Continental; or, The Price of Liberty* (1846) is a realistic account of lower-class New Yorkers during the Revolution; and *The Puritan and His Daughter*♦ (1849) deals with 17th-century life in Virginia and New England, condemning the mutual intolerance of Puritans and Cavaliers. Other works include *The Merry Tales of the Three Wise Men of Gotham* (1826), satirical fiction; *The Lion of the West*♦ (1830), a comedy about a backwoodsman in New York; *A Life of Washington* (1835); *Slavery in the United States* (1836); and *The Bucktails; or, Americans in England* (1847), a satirical play.

Paulding's writings showed, despite his affiliation with the Knickerbocker Group,♦ that he was a consistent Jeffersonian in his social creed and that he attempted to deal with all phases of American life. His constant interest in naval affairs culminated in his appointment as Van Buren's secretary of the navy (1838–41), which capped his political career. After 1849 he retired to his estate at Hyde Park and ceased to write. His selected *Letters* was published in 1962.

Paumanok, Indian name of Long Island, N.Y., which is separated from Manhattan by the East River and runs almost parallel to the shore of Connecticut. The aboriginal name is frequently used in the works of Whitman, who was born on the island, notably in "Starting from Paumanok." ♦

Pau-Puk-Keewis, character in *Hiawatha.* ♦

Pawnee (or PANI) **Indians,** four bison-hunting Plains tribes, formerly living in Nebraska and Kansas, on the Platte and Republican rivers, whose descendants reside in Oklahoma. They had highly developed tribal and ceremonial systems and a rich mythology. Their folk tales were collected by Grinnell (1893) and a scholarly *Mythology* was published by G.A. Dorsey (1906). The Pawnee figure in Irving's *Tour on the Prairies,* Cooper's *The Prairie,* and Custis's *The Pawnee Chief.*

PAXTON, PHILIP, pseudonym of S.A. Hammett. ♦

PAYNE, JOHN HOWARD (1791–1852), born in New York City, showed a precocious interest in the drama, publishing the *Thespian Mirror* (1805–6), a theatrical review that attracted the attention of New York literary and theatrical figures, who encouraged him in the writing of *Julia; or, The Wanderer* (1806), a melodrama; the publication of another paper, *The Pastime* (1807–8); and his debut as an actor. After the production of *Lovers' Vows* (1809), adapted from Kotzebue, and further acting, a reaction set in against the tremendous acclaim that had greeted him as a prodigy. Friends then collected a fund to send him to England to reestablish his fame and fortune. Although received fairly well upon his arrival (1813), he was forced to turn to theatrical hackwork, from which he was rescued by Kean's successful production of his blank-verse tragedy *Brutus; or, The Fall of Tarquin* ♦ (1818). This triumph led him to produce his own melodramas but so unsuccessfully that he was sent to jail for debts. From Paris, whence he fled to escape duns, he sent plays to London for production, including *Clari; or, The Maid of Milan* ♦ (1823), set as an opera by Sir Henry Bishop and remembered for the heroine's song "Home, Sweet Home." Back in London he collaborated with Irving on *Charles the Second* ♦ (1824), *Richelieu* ♦ (1826), and five other plays. Returning to the U.S. (1832), he was honored as an eminent writer and rewarded with appointment as consul at Tunis (1842–45, 1851–52), where he died, in debt but working on great literary and dramatic plans.

PEABODY, ANDREW PRESTON (1811–93), Unitarian clergyman of Massachusetts, who graduated from Harvard at the precocious age of 15 and returned there from his pulpit in New Hampshire (1860) to become professor of Christian morals. He was extremely conservative in thought, and yet his importance at Harvard lay in his personal influence, rather than in the 190

works he wrote. He was editor of *The North American Review* (1853–63), to which he contributed some 1600 pages of text.

PEABODY, ELIZABETH PALMER (1804–94), sister-in-law of Hawthorne and Horace Mann, was like them interested in social reform and education. Her Boston home was the scene of the famous conversational classes of Margaret Fuller (1839–44), and her bookshop was a favorite meeting place of the Transcendental Club. She opened the first kindergarten (1860) in the U.S., and her association with Alcott in his Temple School is described in *Record of a School* (1835). *A Last Evening with Allston* (1886) contains further reminiscences of her life, and reprints some of her essays from *The Dial.* She is said to be the prototype of Miss Birdseye in James's *The Bostonians.* Her *Letters* was published in 1984.

PEABODY, JOSEPHINE PRESTON (1874–1922), born in New York, was educated at Radcliffe (1894–96), where under the influence of William Vaughn Moody, she turned from the light lyric poetry of *The Wayfarers* (1898) to poetic drama. Her plays include *Fortune and Men's Eyes* (1900), a one-act play about Shakespeare; *Marlowe* (1901), a five-act tragedy; *The Wings* (1905), a one-act play set in 8th-century Northumbria; *The Piper* (1910), a five-act drama that won the Stratford-on-Avon prize competition, using the Pied Piper theme to depict the struggle between Christianity and the power of the devil; *The Wolf of Gubbio* (1913), a drama about St. Francis, like its predecessor concerned with the conflict between love and greed; and *Portrait of Mrs. W.* (1922), a prose play dealing with the love of Mary Wollstonecraft and William Godwin. *The Singing of Leaves* (1903), *Pan, a Choric Idyl* (1904), and *Harvest Moon* (1916) are collections of lyrics. Her plays and poems were collected in 1927.

PEALE, REMBRANDT (1778–1860), son of the painter Charles Willson Peale (1741–1827), one of 11 children, all named for painters, and himself an artist of portraits and large allegorical canvases, wrote *Notes on Italy* (1831), based on a residence abroad, and *Portfolio of an Artist* (1837), which contained some of his poetry.

Pearl of Orr's Island, The, novel by Harriet Beecher Stowe, ♦ published in 1862.

On Orr's Island, a fishing community on the Maine coast, the orphan Mara Lincoln is reared by her grandparents, Zephaniah and Mary Pennel, who consider her a "pearl of great price." They also adopt a Spanish boy, Moses, who is washed ashore during a shipwreck. The children grow up together, and among the family friends are the stern spinster, Aunt Roxy Toothacre, and the whimsical retired sea captain who is the father of Mara's friend Sally Kittridge. Mara adores Moses, but he does not realize he loves her until his return from a voyage to China. Then he is jealous of the attentions paid her by "a Mr. Adams of Boston," and in retaliation woos Sally. Although a flirt, Sally is true to her friend and shows Moses that his real love is for Mara. After a brief period of happy understanding with Moses, Mara dies of tuberculosis. The young man returns to his life at sea, but after four years settles on Orr's Island and marries Sally.

PEARSON, EDMUND [LESTER] (1880–1937), New York librarian, bibliophile, and author of books and essays about murders and eccentricities of the past. His works include *Books in Black or Red* (1923), *Studies in Murder* (1924), *Queer Books* (1928), and *Dime Novels* (1929).

Pearson's Magazine (1899–1925), monthly magazine devoted to literature, politics, and the arts, was founded as a New York affiliate of the London periodical of this name, some part of whose contents it reprinted. From 1916 to 1923 it was edited by Frank Harris, with a policy of being "frankly opposed to the mad individualism we Americans name Liberty" and a "forum of sincere opinion for the Truth." Much of the material was written by the editor, and other contributors included Upton Sinclair, La Follette, Debs, and such foreign authors as Shaw and Maxim Gorki.

PEATTIE, DONALD CULROSS (1898–1964), graduated from Harvard (1922) and served with the Department of Agriculture. His books vary from scientific studies of botany to popular nature studies. The best known of the latter are *Singing in the Wilderness: A Salute to John James Audubon* (1935); *An Almanac for Moderns* (1935) and its "pendant," *A Book of Hours* (1937), records of a sensitive mind reacting to the wonders of nature; *Green Laurels: The Lives and Achievements of the Great Naturalists* (1936); *A Prairie Grove* (1938), tracing the history of an acre of American soil; *Flowering Earth* (1939); and *A Natural History of Trees* (1950). Other books include *Forward the Nation* (1942), on the Lewis and Clark expedition; *Journey into America* (1943), sketches of the National spirit; *Immortal Village* (1945), on the Provençal town of Vence, near which he lived in the 1920s; other books of travel; books for children; and four novels; *Up Country* (1928), with his wife Louise Redfield Peattie; *Port of Call* (1932); *Sons of the Martian* (1932); and *The Bright Lexicon* (1934). *The Road of a Naturalist* (1941) is his autobiography.

PECK, GEORGE WILBUR (1840–1916), Wisconsin journalist and humorist, wrote comic articles in Irish dialect on political events, which were published as *Adventures of One Terence McGrant* (1871). In 1874 he founded his own paper, *The Sun,* in which he published humorous

articles concerning the practical jokes played by a mischievous boy on his father. These were collected in *Peck's Bad Boy and His Pa* (1883) and several subsequent volumes. *How Private Geo. W. Peck Put Down the Rebellion* (1887) contains humorous sketches of his Civil War experiences. Peck's popular reputation swept him into politics as mayor of Milwaukee (1890–91) and governor of Wisconsin (1891–95).

PECK, HARRY THURSTON (1856–1914), professor of Latin at Columbia (1882–1910), was an author and editor of various scholarly works. He edited *The Bookman* (1895–1902) and wrote a biography of Prescott (1905) and a history from Cleveland to McKinley, *Twenty Years of the Republic* (1906). He was considered an outstanding critic until he was ostracized following a breach of promise suit (1910), which caused his collapse and suicide.

PECK, JOHN MASON (1789–1858), Baptist preacher of New York, after 1817 founded and administered missions and schools in Illinois, Indiana, and Missouri. He founded newspapers, and wrote a *Guide for Emigrants* (1831), *Life of Daniel Boone* (1847), and *Father Clark; or, The Pioneer Preacher* (1855), considered to be authoritative works on the West.

Peck's Bad Boy and His Pa, humorous sketches by George W. Peck.♦

Pecos Bill, giant folk hero of Southwestern tales, whose cowboy exploits resemble those of Paul Bunyan and Tony Beaver in the logging camps.

Peder Victorious, novel by Rölvaag,♦ published in Norway (1928) and in translation in the U.S. (1929), the second volume of a trilogy that includes *Giants in the Earth*♦ and *Their Fathers' God.*♦

PEGLER, WESTBROOK (1894–1969), journalist whose syndicated column, "Fair Enough" (1933–62), was a cynical, right-wing survey of contemporary events from which he collected pieces in books including *'T Aint Right* (1936), *The Dissenting Opinions of Mister Westbrook Pegler* (1938), and *George Spelvin, American* (1942). He won a 1941 Pulitzer Prize for columns exposing corruption in certain labor unions.

PEIRCE, CHARLES SANDERS (1839–1914), son of Benjamin Peirce (1809–80), Harvard professor of astronomy and mathematics, and eminent mathematician of his time, was himself a physicist, logician, and philosopher. A member of the U.S. Coast Survey, he made philosophy his avocation, and, except for rare academic appointments, pursued his work single-handed. He was a founder of the school of pragmatism, but, since his principles were more in accord with the separately developed idealism of Josiah Royce than with those popularized by his friend William James, he coined for his beliefs the term "pragmaticism," which he said was "ugly enough to be safe from kidnappers." He believed in the dependence of logic upon ethics, opposed a mechanical philosophy, defended the reality of absolute chance and the principle of continuity, and developed a theory of an evolutionary universe. His extreme precision, highly technical vocabulary, and lack of full explanation for those who were not on his philosophic plane made him a philosopher's philosopher rather than a teacher, and publishers were unwilling to print his works. From his mass of manuscript were collected *Chance, Love, and Logic* (1923) and a six-volume *Collected Papers* (1931–58).

PENHALLOW, SAMUEL (1665–1726), emigrated from England to New Hampshire (1686), where he became prominent in public affairs. He wrote a *History of the Wars of New-England with the Eastern Indians* (1726), a vivid, realistic account of Indian assaults, containing frequent parallels between the heroism of Indian fighters and the deeds of Greek and Roman warriors.

PENN, WILLIAM (1644–1718), English Quaker, in 1668 published a tract attacking the doctrine of the Trinity, *The Sandy Foundation Shaken,* for which he was imprisoned in the Tower of London, where he wrote *No Cross, No Crown* (1669), a defense of his faith, and another pamphlet in his own defense. After another term in prison for defying the Conventicle Act, he continued to work for his faith, through books and preaching, both in England and on the Continent. He established American colonies where Quakers ♦ might be free from persecution, and in 1681 secured the charter for Pennsylvania, named in honor of his father by Charles II. In America (1682–84), he personally organized the colony, framed its liberal government guaranteeing fundamental democratic liberties, and made equitable treaties with the Indians. After the accession of William and Mary (1688), he continued on friendly terms with James II, and being accused of treason temporarily lost his colony (1692–94). During this troublous time, he wrote his maxims of faith and life contained in *Some Fruits of Solitude* (1693), and *Essay Towards the Present and Future Peace of Europe* (1693), a plan for a general European confederation for arbitration of disputes. A similar idea was applied to a plan (1697) for the union of all the American colonies. After Pennsylvania was returned to him, he revisited it (1699) and revised its charter (1701) toward further democracy. In the same year, he left it for the last time, to oppose an English plan for annexation of all proprietary colonies to the Crown. He was temporarily imprisoned for debt when the colony's affairs were mismanaged by untrustworthy deputies; their administration was assumed by his wife

Hannah in 1712, when he lost his memory, and was continued by his sons after her death in 1727.

PENNELL, JOSEPH (1857–1926), born in Pennsylvania, first achieved fame as the illustrator of Cable's *The Creoles of Louisiana* (1884) and further established himself through his illustrations for Howells's *Tuscan Cities* (1885). In 1884 he married Elizabeth Robins (1855–1936), a niece of C.G. Leland. She had written the texts for some of his drawings, and together they produced *A Canterbury Pilgrimage* (1885). After taking up residence in England (1884–1918), they became intimate with such authors and artists as Henry James, Aubrey Beardsley, and Shaw. Under the influence of Whistler, Pennell turned first to etching and later to lithography, and (c. 1909–12) created the series "The Wonder of Work," which depicted such industrial subjects as the factories at Birmingham and Sheffield, and the construction of the Panama Canal. With his wife he wrote *The Life of James McNeill Whistler* (1908) and edited *The Whistler Journal* (1921). In 1929 Mrs. Pennell published her husband's *Life and Letters.*

PENNELL, JOSEPH STANLEY (1908–63), born in Kansas, after graduation from the state university and further study at Oxford, became a journalist and novelist. *The History of Rome Hanks* (1944) is a panoramic story of the Civil War. *The History of Nora Beckham* (1948), about small-town Kansas life at the end of the 19th century, involves some of the persons of the earlier novel. *Darksome House* (1959) collects poems.

Pennsylvania Chronicle (1767–73), Philadelphia newspaper founded to oppose the proprietary party in the colony. It attempted to be impartial, however, and is remembered for publishing John Dickinson's *Letters from a Farmer in Pennsylvania* ♦ (1767–68).

Pennsylvania Dutch, popular misnomer for the German-American people of Pennsylvania, or for their language, which was originally a High German idiom, but in modern times is a corrupt German and English dialect. The region was widely colonized by German immigrant groups, beginning in 1683 with the settlement of the Mennonites and others, who migrated for religious, political, and economic reasons, the greatest numbers coming during the 18th and 19th centuries. Owing to their persistent segregation in separate settlements, each with its own school and church, the Pennsylvania German communities retained their original language and customs until a recent date. They had many authors of religious and theological works in German, and their modern dialect appears in the humorous writings of C.G. Leland and C.F. Adams. Elsie Singmaster's novels are concerned with these people, as is Thames Williamson's *D Is for Dutch.*

Pennsylvania Farmer, pseudonym of John Dickinson. ◆

Pennsylvania Freeman, The, see *Lundy.*

Pennsylvania Gazette, The (1728–1815), was founded at Philadelphia by Samuel Keimer as *The Universal Instructor . . . and Pennsylvania Gazette,* when he heard that his rival, Franklin, was planning a similar paper. To snipe at Keimer, Franklin joined forces with *The American Weekly Mercury,* and so successfully drew attention from Keimer's paper that it was sold to Franklin (Oct. 2, 1729), who gave it the shorter title and continued to manage it until 1766. Besides making it a successful news organ, he created a number of imaginary characters with whom he engaged in dispute, wrote many essays on matters of contemporary interest, and introduced weather reports into American journalism. At the time of the Albany Congress (1754), he published and probably drew what appears to be the first American cartoon, a picture of a snake in eight parts, representing the principal colonies, with the caption "Join or die." The paper was continued with various changes of editorship by David Hall, Franklin's partner after 1748, and by Hall's descendants. During 1776 the *Gazette* carried the "Cato" letters of William Smith, attacking *Common Sense,* to which Paine replied in the *Pennsylvania Packet.*

Pennsylvania Journal, see *Bradford, William* (1722–91).

Pennsylvania Magazine (Jan. 1775–July 1776), published monthly by Robert Aitken. Thomas Paine was nominally the editor (Feb. 1775–May 1776) and contributed many articles. The magazine printed war reports, letters from Washington and other leaders, the text of the Declaration of Independence, scientific contributions by Benjamin Rush and others, and literary contributions by Francis Hopkinson, John Witherspoon, and William Smith.

Pennsylvania Packet or General Advertiser (1771–1839), Philadelphia newspaper, founded by John Dunlop. During 1776, Paine replied in its columns, under the signature Forester, to the attacks of William Smith in *The Pennsylvania Gazette.* Formerly a triweekly, in 1784 the paper became a daily. It passed into the hands of Dunlop's partners (1795) and was called *Claypoole's American Daily Advertiser.* It was this paper that first published Washington's "Farewell Address." In 1800 it was sold to Zachariah Poulson (1761–1844), who gave it his name, and in 1839 it was absorbed by the *Philadelphia North American,* which was published until 1925.

Penny, Howat, character in *The Three Black Pennys.* ◆

Penrod, novel by Tarkington, ◆ published in 1914. *Penrod and Sam* (1916) and *Penrod Jashber* (1929) are sequels.

This humorous narrative tells of the typical adventures of a 12-year-old American boy, Penrod Schofield, reared according to middle-class standards in a small Midwestern city. With his mongrel dog, Duke, and such intimates of his own age as Sam Williams and the black brothers Herman and Verman, Penrod is involved in characteristic frays and scrapes, and exhibits a healthy attitude toward the tyranny of parents and teachers, sometimes tolerating them but generally engaging in active warfare and subterfuge. He writes a fearsome dime novel about "Harold Ramorez, the Roadagent"; reluctantly enacts "the Child Sir Lancelot" in a school pageant; submits to dancing lessons, and falls under the spell of little Marjorie Jones; organizes a circus with Herman and Verman as principal performers; persecutes his sister's suitor, receiving a dollar by way of blackmail, then buying an incredible supply of sweets that makes him violently ill; is temporarily influenced by the bully Rupe Collins; becomes comically disfigured in the "Great Tar Fight"; and is consistently misunderstood by his elders until he meets his great-aunt, Mrs. Sarah Crim, who pronounces the realistic judgment, "'He's had to repeat the history of the race and go through all the stages from the primordial to barbarism. You don't expect boys to be civilized, do you?'"

People, Yes, The, free-verse poem by Sandburg, ◆ published in 1936.

The authentic American rhythms and idioms of the verse embody native legends, folk tales, proverbs, and slang, and employ the daily speech of the people to show their many-sided observations and experiences, their amusements and sufferings, and the values inherent in their lives. Capitalism's tyranny and social injustices are indicated, and a hope for revolution appears in many passages:

> On the horizon a cloud no larger than a man's
>   hand rolls
> larger and darker when masses of people begin
>   saying,
> "Any kind of death is better than this kind of
>   life."

In substance, the poem is an affirmation of faith in the enduring though blundering progress of the common American people toward justice and a free society:

> They will be tricked and sold and again sold
> And go back to the nourishing earth for
>   rootholds. . . .

Pequod, whaling ship which is the scene of *Moby-Dick.* ◆

Pequot Indians, Algonquian tribe originally united with the Mohegans, ◆ which moved south to the Connecticut Valley and there dominated neighboring tribes. The war-like spirit of the Pequot under Sassacus led to one of the most serious of the New England Indian wars (1637), after which members of the tribe were dispersed among other groups. The best account of the Pequot War is that of the English commander John Mason in his *Brief History of the Pequot War,* edited by Thomas Prince (1736). Another officer, John Underhill, described the war in his *News from America* (1638), as did the Rev. Philip Vincent in *A True Relation of the Late Battell Fought in New England* (1638). William Apes♦ was a Pequot.

PERCH, PHILEMON, see *Johnston, R.M.*

PERCIVAL, JAMES GATES (1795–1856), born in Connecticut, graduated from Yale (1815), studied for his M.D. at the University of Pennsylvania and Yale, had a brief career as a doctor, was a journalist in South Carolina, Connecticut, and New York, and taught chemistry at West Point. He chiefly fancied himself as a romantic poet, and for a time shared this conviction with others, enjoying a great vogue until the ascendancy of Bryant. Percival's *Poems* (1821) includes the long Spenserian "Prometheus," accounted by his compatriots the equal of *Childe Harold; Clio* (3 vols., 1822–27) consists of dream-haunted soliloquies; and *The Dream of a Day* (1843), with more prosaic subjects, is noted for its metrical experimentation. Although he was a man of unquestionable intellect, he was a lifelong eccentric and paranoiac, and for some time resided by his own choice in the New Haven State Hospital. He shuttled pathetically between various professions, but failed to attain greatness in any of them. Besides being an able linguist and philologist he served as state geologist of Connecticut (1835–42) and Wisconsin (1854–56), gathering much scientific information and formulating at least one important geological law.

PERCY, FLORENCE, pseudonym of Elizabeth Akers.♦

PERCY, GEORGE (1580–c.1632), English colonist in Virginia (1607–12), became deputy governor upon the recall of John Smith (1607–10), and again during the absence of Gates (1611–12). His first administration was known as "the starving time," when the 500 settlers dwindled to threescore, partly because of maladministration and dissension. His "Discourse of the Plantation of the Southern Colony in Virginia," an account of his voyage and the early settlement, was published by Purchas (1613). *A True Relation of the Proceedings . . . in Virginia . . . ,* defending his administration against the attack of a writer, presumably John Smith, was written in 1622, but was not printed in its entirety until 1922.

PERCY, WALKER (1916–90), Alabama-born author, after graduation from the University of North Carolina and an M.D. from Columbia gave up medicine because of his own ill health and began a literary career. His first novel, *The Moviegoer* (1961, National Book Award), deals with an alienated young stockbroker of New Orleans, addicted to the movies, who during Mardi Gras finally finds his own involvement in life through a compassionate relationship with a woman who has suffered a personal tragedy. *The Last Gentleman* (1966) presents another existential character, a courtly young Southerner resident in New York, where he suffers amnesia but finally returns to his own region in quest of himself. *Love in the Ruins* (1971) is a fanciful satire about Dr. Thomas More, a scientist and "bad Catholic" who attempts to redeem the mechanistic culture of the U.S. *Lancelot* (1977) is a more melodramatic and moralistic story about a New Orleans man's murder of his wife's lover. *The Second Coming* (1980) reintroduces the protagonist of *The Last Gentleman,* now a rich, lonely widower of 50, restored to hope by affection for a troubled young girl. *The Thanatos Syndrome* (1987) reintroduces Dr. More from *Love in the Ruins* upon his release from prison to discover his former patients suffering from physical and spiritual sickness. *The Message in the Bottle* (1975) contains essays on the philosophy of language, while *Lost in the Cosmos: The Last Self-Help Book* (1983) consists of both essays and other nonfiction. The orphaned author was reared by a cousin, William Alexander Percy (1885–1942), a Mississippi poet, whose *Lanterns on the Levee* (1941) is a lyrical autobiography of a Southern gentleman.

PERELMAN, S[IDNEY] J[OSEPH] (1904–79), born in Brooklyn, after education at Brown University became a writer for *Judge* and for 45 years was a contributor to *The New Yorker* of short humorous and satirical pieces, often in the form of brief, fantastic dramas which, with a surrealistic style and a Joycean use of words, lampoon the world of advertising, motion pictures, popular fiction, and other vacuities. His writings have been collected in many books, including *Dawn Ginsbergh's Revenge* (1929), *Parlor, Bedlam and Bath* (1930), *Strictly from Hunger* (1937), *Look Who's Talking* (1940), *The Dream Department* (1943), *Keep It Crisp* (1946), *Westward Ha!* (1948), *Listen to the Mocking Bird* (1949), *The Ill-Tempered Clavichord* (1953), *The Road to Miltown; or, Under the Spreading Atrophy* (1957), *The Rising Gorge* (1961), *Chicken Inspector No. 23* (1966), *Baby, It's Cold Inside* (1970), *Vinegar Puss* (1975), and *Eastward Ha!* (1977), a travel account. His comic plays include *One Touch of Venus* (1943) with Ogden Nash and *The Beauty Part* (1963). *The Last Laugh* (1981) posthumously collects an unfinished autobiography and comic sketches.

Perfectionism, radical religious doctrine, assuming the immediate and total cessation of sin, advanced by J.H. Noyes,♦ was the leading principle of his Oneida Community.♦ Perfectionism was a manifestation of the mid-19th-century enthusiasm for liberal social and religious beliefs that particularly affected New England, and was allied in temperament to the spirit that created Millerism, Shaker communities, Come-outers, and even Transcendentalism. Noyes's religious Utopianism held that a church on earth was rising to meet the approaching kingdom in heaven, and that the element of connection was direct communion with God, which leads to perfect holiness or complete salvation from sin.

PERKINS, ELI, see *Landon, M. DeL.*

PERKINS, FREDERIC BEECHER (1828–99), nephew of H.W. Beecher and brother-in-law of E.E. Hale, was a journalist and librarian in his native Connecticut, Massachusetts, and California. In addition to bibliographical works, he wrote a biography of Dickens (1870); *Scope; or, The Lost Library* (1874), a novel; and *Devil Puzzlers and Other Studies* (1877), short stories.

PERKINS, LUCY FITCH (1865–1937), author of such books for children as *The Dutch Twins* (1911), *The Japanese Twins* (1912), and *The French Twins* (1918), intended to create an understanding of foreign nations and their contributions to American culture.

PERKINS, MAX[WELL] EVARTS (1884–1947), book editor whose name became synonymous with what every aspiring young editor wanted to be: discoverer and nurturer of genius. Perkins's career was entirely with Charles Scribner's Sons, where he was editor for Lardner, Fitzgerald, Hemingway, Thomas Wolfe, and James Jones. All of these except Wolfe published exclusively with Scribner's. Perkins worked beyond the line of duty in helping Wolfe to cut and shape *Look Homeward, Angel,* by Wolfe's own testimony. Later Wolfe became sensitive to assertions that Perkins was helping too much, and took his last works to Harper, where another editor did the yeoman's work required for publication standards. Perkins's correspondence with his authors was published in 1950 as *Editor to Author.*

PERLEY, see *Poore, B.P.*

PERRY, BLISS (1860–1954), editor of the *Atlantic Monthly* (1899–1909), was a professor of English at Williams, Princeton, and finally Harvard (1907–30). He edited many works on English and American literature and was the author of several novels and informal essays; biographies of Whitman (1906), Whittier (1907), Carlyle (1915), and Emerson (1931); studies of *The American Mind* (1912) and *The American Spirit in Literature* (1918); and his autobiography, *And Gladly Teach* (1935).

PERRY, MATTHEW CALBRAITH (1794–1858), brother of Oliver Hazard Perry, was also a naval

officer and had a distinguished career before 1852, when he was commissioned by Fillmore to negotiate a treaty with Japan, a country then closed to all intercourse with the Occident. The following year he arrived at Yedo, impressed the Japanese by his armed strength, and delivered the President's request. After a trip to China, he returned to Yokohama (1854) to negotiate a treaty opening Japan to Western trade and providing for a U.S. consul in Japan. He wrote *Narrative of the Expedition of an American Squadron to the China Seas and Japan* (3 vols., 1856).

PERRY, OLIVER HAZARD (1785–1819), born in Rhode Island, entered the navy in 1799, and served in the Tripolitan War. At the outbreak of the War of 1812, he built and commanded a fleet of ten ships, headed by the *Lawrence,* and became a national hero following his defeat of the British on Lake Erie (Sept. 10, 1813). He figures in Irving Bacheller's *D'ri and I* and other historical fiction. M.C. Perry was his brother.

PERRY, RALPH BARTON (1876–1957), professor at Harvard, a follower of William James. His books include *The Moral Economy* (1909); *The New Realism* (1912); *The Present Conflict of Ideals* (1918); *The Thought and Character of William James* (2 vols., 1935, Pulitzer Prize); *Shall Not Perish from the Earth* (1940), an analysis of American democracy; *Puritanism and Democracy* (1944); *The Hope for Immortality* (1945); and *One World in the Making* (1945).

PERRY, THOMAS SERGEANT (1845–1928), born in Rhode Island, after graduation from Harvard (1866) went with William James to study in Germany, returning to become a tutor in French and German at Harvard (1868–72), member of *The North American Review* staff (1872–77), and a member of the department of English at Harvard (1877–82). In his critical writings for various magazines, including *The Nation* and the *Atlantic Monthly,* he showed his interest in realism and his knowledge of contemporary foreign literature, and through his brilliant conversations with his friends Howells and Henry James is said to have introduced them to Turgenev and influenced their theories on the novel. Perry was a great student of languages and in addition to translating from foreign literature he became acquainted with many foreign authors during his travels, and on one journey served as professor of English at the University of Keiogijiku in Japan (1898–1901). His writings include *The Life and Letters of Francis Lieber* (1882), *English Literature in the Eighteenth Century* (1883), *From Opitz to Lessing* (1885), *The Evolution of a Snob* (1887), *History of Greek Literature* (1890), and *John Fiske* (1906). Perry's *Letters* was edited by his friend E.A. Robinson in 1929.

PERSHING, JOHN J[OSEPH] (1860–1948), Missouri-born army officer, graduated from

West Point (1886) and served in Indian campaigns, in the Spanish-American War, in the Philippines, on the Mexican border against Villa, and as commander of the American Expeditionary Force in World War I. His book *My Experiences in the World War* (1931) won a Pulitzer Prize.

Personae, poems by Ezra Pound.◆

Personal Recollections of Joan of Arc, see *Joan of Arc.*

PETER (or PETERS), HUGH (1598–1660), English Puritan clergyman, was in Massachusetts (1636–41), where he succeeded Roger Williams as pastor of the Salem church, was prominent in colonial affairs, and helped found Harvard College. He returned to England as an agent of Massachusetts Bay Colony (1641), and there, with Thomas Weld, edited and probably wrote in part *New Englands First Fruits*◆ (1643). An important figure in Cromwell's revolution, he was later executed.

Peter Parley, pseudonym of S.G. Goodrich◆ and his staff.

Peter Porcupine, pseudonym of William Cobbett.◆

PETERKIN, JULIA [MOOD] (1880–1961), novelist of South Carolina, known for her sympathetic depiction of the Gullah◆ blacks, whom she understood through long association with them as the wife of a plantation manager. The poignant characterizations of the daily lives and folklore of these tragic, isolated laborers are presented in the novels *Black April*◆ (1927), *Scarlet Sister Mary*◆ (1928, Pulitzer Prize), and *Bright Skin* (1932); a collection of sketches, *Green Thursday* (1924); and a descriptive narrative accompanying a book of photographs, *Roll, Jordan, Roll* (1933).

Peterkin Papers, The, stories for children by Lucretia Hale.◆

PETERS, SAMUEL ANDREW (1735–1826), Connecticut Loyalist and Anglican clergyman, in 1781 published his derogatory *General History of Connecticut, by a Gentleman of the Province,* famous for its account of colonial blue laws. His strong hatred for the republicanism and nonconformity of his native land, whence he fled to England just before the Revolution, led him to make misrepresentations about the stringency of blue laws that have been innocently copied by later historians. In 1805 he returned to the U.S. and purchased land claims of Jonathan Carver, which Congress in 1826 disallowed. He also wrote *A History of the Reverend Hugh Peters* (1807), falsely claiming that Hugh Peters was his great-grand-uncle.

PETERSON, CHARLES JACOBS (1819–87), Philadelphia author, editor, and publisher, was associated with *Graham's Magazine* and *The Saturday Evening Post,* prior to founding the *Ladies' National Magazine* (1842), called *Peterson's Magazine* after 1848, an imitation of *Godey's Lady's Book,* which it surpassed in circulation. It was a highly popular women's magazine until it ended publication in 1898. In addition to such historical novels as *Grace Dudley; or, Arnold at Saratoga* (1849) and *Kate Aylesford, A Story of the Refugees* (1855). Peterson wrote *History of the United States Navy* (1852), and works on the heroes of the Revolution, the War of 1812, and the Mexican War.

Petrified Forest, The, play by Robert Sherwood,◆ produced in 1934 and published in 1935. Set in the Black Mesa Bar-B-Q, a gasoline station and lunch room in the Arizona desert, it melodramatically brings together representatives of a decadent civilization, in which Nature is "taking the world away from the intellectuals and giving it back to the apes."

PETRY, ANN (1911–), born in and still a resident of Old Saybrook, Conn., after graduation from the state university and work in the family drugstore published *The Street* (1946), a novel in the Richard Wright tradition, about blacks trapped in the ghetto life of Harlem. It was followed by *Country Place* (1947), a novel depicting class conflict in a setting like her hometown, and *The Narrows* (1953), which combines previous themes in its concern with black people like herself in a New England community but dramatically presents the romance of a talented black boy and a patrician white girl. Short stories are collected in *Miss Muriel* (1971), and books for children include *The Drugstore Cat* (1949), *Harriet Tubman* (1955), *Tituba of Salem Village* (1964), and *Legends of the Saints* (1970), hagiography for youngsters.

Pfaff's Cellar, bohemian rendezvous on Broadway above Bleecker Street in New York City, during the 1850s. The cellar is famous as the gathering place of Whitman, Fitz-James O'Brien, Bayard Taylor, William Winter, George Arnold, Adah Menken, Henry Clapp, Louis Gottschalk, and Ada Clare. It came to an end with the dispersion of its artistic clientele during the Civil War.

Phaenomena quaedam apocalyptica . . . , by Samuel Sewall,◆ published in 1697, bears the subtitle, "A Description of the New Heaven . . . to those who stand upon the New Earth." Sewall predicts that New England will be the final "rendezvous for Gog and Magog" and the true seat of the New Jerusalem. This work is the subject of Whittier's poem "The Prophecy of Samuel Sewall."

PHELPS, ELIZABETH [STUART] (1815–52), Massachusetts author of popular religious tales, which include *The Sunny Side; or, The Country Minister's Wife* (1851) and two semi-autobiographical novels, *A Peep at Number Five* (1852), the story of a clergyman's home, and *The Angel Over the Right Shoulder* (1852), the tale of a woman's difficulties in reconciling her domestic life with a genius for writing. These were published under the pseudonym H. Trusta. She was the mother of Elizabeth Stuart Phelps Ward, ♦ most of whose works were published under her maiden name.

PHELPS, WILLIAM LYON (1865–1943), professor of English literature at Yale (1892–1933), began his career as an academic scholar with such works as *The Beginnings of the English Romantic Movement* (1893) and *Browning: How To Know Him* (1915). He was best known as a popularizer of the humanities through his many lectures and his column "As I Like It" in *Scribner's,* endorsing innumerable new books and containing random commentaries on his many enthusiasms. In 1939 he published his *Autobiography with Letters.*

Phi Beta Kappa, honorary scholarship society, was founded at William and Mary (1776) as a secret social and literary club of undergraduates. It was the first college fraternity, and its name is said to derive from the initials of its Greek motto, translated as "Philosophy the guide of life." Chapters were soon established at other colleges, and secrecy was abandoned by 1831. Women have been admitted since 1875. Eligibility is restricted to the best students, usually selected in their senior year. Many famous poems have been first delivered as Phi Beta Kappa poems at college commencements, and it was before the Harvard chapter that Emerson delivered "The American Scholar" (1837). *The American Scholar*♦ is the quarterly of general circulation published by the society.

Philadelphia, largest city in Pennsylvania, 4th largest in the U.S., is situated on the Delaware River, 100 miles from the Atlantic. The site was occupied by an Indian settlement and a Swedish community before 1682, when William Penn founded the city as the proprietary capital of his Quaker colony, under its present Greek name ("brotherly love"). The next year, Pastorius brought German and Dutch settlers to establish Germantown in its environs. During this early period, the city was famous not only as a trading post but as a refuge for many diverse sects. In Franklin's time, Philadelphia saw the decline of the power of the Penn family and of Quaker dominance, as it became noted for its shipping industry and such figures as the wealthy merchant Stephen Girard. Democratic feeling arose during the pre-Revolutionary period, when the city assumed leadership through the writings and actions of such men as Franklin and John Dickinson, and the gathering of the two Continental

Congresses at Independence Hall, where the Declaration of Independence was adopted. Howe occupied the city following the rebels' defeats at Brandywine and Germantown, and held it through the incident known as the Battle of the Kegs, finally evacuating in the summer of 1778. After the Revolution the city was the capital of the U.S. (1790–1800), and the scene of the Constitutional Convention.

During the 19th century, Philadelphia became an important industrial center, and its character changed with the influx of Irish and German immigrants. It prospered during the Civil War from various war manufactures, and fortunes were acquired by such financiers as Jay Cooke, although the fighting came no closer to the city than the Battle of Gettysburg. Further expansion occurred during the Gilded Age, marked by labor strife, financial panics, and political corruption, and the ascendancy of such speculators as Yerkes. By the end of the century, the city had settled down as a leading metropolis, whose financial and social figures included C.H.K. Curtis, publisher of *The Saturday Evening Post,* the Drexel family, and John Wanamaker. The Philadelphia Centennial Exposition (1876), an industrial and educational exhibit celebrating the 100th anniversary of the Declaration of Independence, was the first great international exposition held in America.

Philadelphia has long been one of the centers of education in the U.S. As early as 1689 George Keith founded the present William Penn Charter School; the University of Pennsylvania was founded by Franklin and others in 1751; and other educational institutions include The Library Company (1731), American Philosophical Society (1744), Pennsylvania Academy of Fine Arts (1805), Franklin Institute (1824), La Salle College (1867), Temple University (1884), Drexel Institute (1891), Dropsie College (1907), and the nearby Haverford College (1833), Swarthmore College (1864), and Bryn Mawr College (1880).

Even before Franklin's time, the city was noted for its publishers, who included William Bradford, Andrew Bradford, and Samuel Keimer, while later publishers have included Claypool, Poulson, Duane, Godey, Graham, Lippincott, Curtis, and Bok. The city's literary history may be said to date from the tracts of Penn and Pastorius, but its fame as a literary center began in the time of Franklin. Authors associated with Philadelphia include James Logan, Jacob Duché, Woolman, Thomas Godfrey, Nathaniel Evans, Paine, Hopkinson, Seabury, John Bartram, Robert Proud, Joseph Galloway, Crèvecœur, Brackenridge, C.B. Brown, Joseph Dennie, Cobbett, Matthew Carey, Freneau, J.N. Barker, R.M. Bird, J.A. Stone, Sara J.B. Hale, George Lippard, T.D. English, T.S. Arthur, Poe, Whitman, Bayard Taylor, Rebecca Davis, Frank Stockton, S.W. Mitchell, T.B. Read, G.H. Boker, C.G. Leland, J.L. Long, R.H. Davis, Owen Wister, Agnes Repplier, Huneker, T.A. Daly, Langdon

Mitchell, A.E. Newton, J.T. McIntyre, Herge-sheimer, and Christopher Morley. Daniel Hoffman, a New Yorker, has written a major long poem about the city, *Brotherly Love* (1980).

(For Philadelphia newspapers other than those prefixed by the name of the city, see *American Weekly Mercury; Aurora; Gazette of the United States; National Gazette; Pennsylvania Chronicle; Pennsylvania Journal; Pennsylvania Packet;* and *Porcupine's Gazette.*)

Philadelphia North American, see *Pennsylvania Packet.*

Philadelphia Public Ledger (1836–1934, 1934–42), founded as the city's first penny paper by A.S. Abell, W.H. Swain, and A.H. Simmons. Abell left (1837) to found the Baltimore *Sun,* and Simmons soon died, so that Swain was its head, advocating independent voting and a free press, and fighting the Bank of the United States. Maintaining its price, despite rising paper costs during the Civil War, caused great losses, and the *Ledger* was sold to G.W. Childs (1864), who raised the price and made it distinguished for its carefully substantiated attacks on war profiteering, monopolies, and the debased currency, and for its stringent editorials on political and moral corruption. In 1913 the paper was purchased by C.H.K. Curtis. The *Philadelphia Inquirer* took over the journal (1934) and renamed it the *Evening Public Ledger.* Stanley Williams became its editor (1938) and Cary W. Bok its publisher (1939). It ceased publication in 1942.

Philadelphia Story, The, play by Philip Barry.◆

Philemon Perch, pseudonym of R.M. Johnston.◆

PHILENIA, pseudonym of Sara Wentworth Morton.◆

PHILIP, see *King Philip.*

Philistine, see *Hubbard, Elbert.*

PHILLIPS, David Graham (1867–1911), born in Indiana, began his journalistic career at Cincinnati (1887) and moved to New York (1890), where he worked on the *Sun* and *World.* In 1902 he began to write muckraking magazine articles and fiction concerned with contemporary social problems. During the few years of creative work that followed, he wrote 23 novels, a play, and a book of essays. The novels, which show his training as a reporter as well as his muckraking zeal against fraud and oppression, include *The Great God Success* (1901); *Golden Fleece* (1903), dealing with the American adventures of a fortune-hunting earl; *The Master-Rogue* (1903), the autobiography of a modern Croesus; *The Cost* (1904) and *The Deluge* (1905), both exposing

Wall Street manipulation; *The Plum Tree* (1905), about the operations of a political boss; *Light-Fingered Gentry* (1907), a fictional treatment of recent insurance scandals; *The Second Generation* (1907), contrasting the evils of inherited wealth with the virtues of the hard-working lower classes; and *The Fashionable Adventures of Joshua Craig* (1909), *The Conflict* (1911), and *George Helm* (1912), depicting respectively national, municipal, and state corruption. The remainder of his works deal with the contemporary interest in the "new woman." *Old Wives for New* (1908), *The Hungry Heart* (1909), and his play *The Worth of a Woman* (1908) are concerned with the changed standards of women in love and marriage. *The Husband's Story* (1910) and *The Price She Paid* (1912) are novels treating respectively feminine social ambitions and the independence of the new woman. Phillips's greatest novel, *Susan Lenox; Her Fall and Rise*◆ (1917), combines his previous themes in a muckraking exposé of Cincinnati slum life and New York political corruption, which serve as a background for the life of a country girl who reaches success through prostitution. The promise that Phillips showed in this work, published posthumously, was cut short when he was murdered by a lunatic.

PHILLIPS, Jayne Anne (1952–   ), born in West Virginia, educated at the state university there and later at the University of Iowa, is best known for *Black Tickets* (1979), short stories about the poor, murderers, people in despair, and people dying of cancer. Her best novel is *Machine Dreams* (1984), about the collapse of a family, told from each member's point of view. Her other works include the short story collections *How Mickey Made It* (1981) and *Fast Lanes* (1987).

PHILLIPS, Wendell (1811–84), born in Boston, after graduation from Harvard (1831) and admission to the bar became a prominent Boston Abolitionist and supporter of Garrison. He was an active lyceum lecturer for this and other causes, and was a contributor to *The Liberator* and *National Anti-Slavery Standard.* His *Speeches, Lectures, and Letters* were collected in 1863 and 1891.

Philo Vance, hero of detective novels by W.H. Wright.◆

Philological Society, New York organization (*fl.*1788–89), devoted to mutual improvement and the promotion of the American language. Its members included Noah Webster and William Dunlap. It was the forerunner of the Friendly Club of New York.

Philosophy of Composition, The, critical essay by Poe,◆ published in *Graham's Magazine* (1846). It purports to describe the author's usual procedure in composing poetry and is mainly devoted to an analysis of "The Raven" as an example of this procedure. Among the famous dicta announced in the essay are: "If any literary work is too long to be read at one sitting, we must be content to dispense with the immensely important effect derivable from unity of impression. . . . What we term a long poem is, in fact, merely a succession of brief ones"; "Beauty is the sole legitimate province of the poem"; "Beauty . . . in its supreme development, invariably excites the sensitive soul to tears. Melancholy is thus the most legitimate of all poetical tones"; "The death of a beautiful woman is, unquestionably, the most poetical topic in the world." Poe further discusses his principles of versification, use of a refrain, diction, and imagery, and the primary importance of the climax ("The Raven," stanza 16), which was written first so that every effect in the poem should lead in its direction.

PHIPS (or **PHIPPS**), SIR WILLIAM (1651–95), born in Maine, was knighted for his recovery of sunken West Indian treasure (reputedly worth £300,000), and was appointed provost marshal general at Boston (1687), in which position he led the colonial expedition against the French in the first French and Indian War. He aided Increase Mather to restore charter rule in Massachusetts, and, at Mather's behest, Phips was named governor under a new charter (1692). His administration was charged with neglect of military activities and other errors, for which he was summoned to answer in London, but he died before proceedings against him began. Cotton Mather's biography (1697) emphasizes the "self-made man," and its laudatory manner was attacked by Calef. Phips figures as "The King's Fisher" and "The Elephant" in Mather's *Political Fables.*

PHOENIX, JOHN, pseudonym of G.H. Derby. ♦

Piazza Tales, The, sketches by Melville, ♦ collected in 1856. They are "The Piazza," ♦ about the author's farmhouse, Arrowhead, in Pittsfield, Mass.; "Bartleby, the Scrivener" ♦; "The Encantadas" ♦; "Benito Cereno" ♦; "The Lightning-Rod Man"; and "The Bell-Tower."

Picayune, see *New Orleans Picayune.*

PICKERING, JOHN (1777–1846), Boston lawyer whose avocation was philology; he learned 20 languages, was the outstanding authority of his time on some languages of North American Indians, made the first study of Americanisms in his *Vocabulary . . . of Words and Phrases . . . Peculiar to the United States* (1816), and wrote a *Comprehensive Lexicon of the Greek Language* (1826).

Pictures of War, see *Little Regiment.*

PIERCY, MARGE (1936–   ), grew up poor and white in a black section of Detroit and was the first in her family to go to college (University of Michigan). Piercy early experienced class discrimination, racism, and the sufferings of women at the hands of men, all of which themes inform her nine books of poetry and ten novels. Her verse takes pleasure in the mundane—love and nature—as well as dramatizing the injustices of sexism. Her poetry includes *Breaking Camp* (1968), *Hard Loving* (1969), *To Be of Use* (1973), *Living in the Open* (1976), *The Twelve-Spoked Wheel Flashing* (1978), *The Moon Is Always Female* (1980), *Circles on the Water: Selected Poems* (1982), and *Stone, Paper, Knife* (1983). Among her fiction are *Going Down Fast* (1969), *Dance the Eagle to Sleep* (1971), *Small Changes* (1973), *Woman on the Edge of Time* (1976), *The High Cost of Living* (1978), *Vida* (1980), *Braided Lives* (1982), *Fly Away Home* (1984), *He, She and It* (1991), and *The Longings of Women* (1994).

PIERPONT, JOHN (1785–1866), born in Connecticut, graduated from Yale (1804) and practiced law at Newburyport, Mass., where he wrote *The Portrait* (1812), a Federalist poem extolling Washington and Hamilton and excoriating Jefferson. *Airs of Palestine* (1816), a poem in heroic couplets praising sacred music, written during a period of shopkeeping at Baltimore, put him in the front rank of American poets of the time. After graduation from Harvard Divinity School (1818), he became minister of the Hollis Street Church in Boston (1819), where his advocacy of antislavery, pacifism, and temperance irritated his congregation, who conducted a long campaign to oust him. He was accused of failing to confine himself to proper ecclesiastical subjects and of wasting his time in "the making of Books," which included poems based on a trip to the Holy Land (1835–36) and hymns and odes on religious, political, and liberal subjects, such as *The Anti-Slavery Poems of John Pierpont* (1843). After his resignation (1845), he was a pastor of other Unitarian churches, a Civil War chaplain, and a clerk in the U.S. Treasury Department. J.P. Morgan was his grandson.

Pierre; or, The Ambiguities, novel by Melville, ♦ published in 1852. It is considered to be semiautobiographical.

Pierre Glendinning, only son of an affluent and haughty widow, is engaged to Lucy Tartan, daughter of another prominent family in upstate New York. He accidentally meets Isabel, discovers that she is his illegitimate half-sister, and feels that it is his duty to protect her in opposition to his proud mother. To acknowledge Isabel as his sister would disgrace his father's memory, so Pierre pretends to marry her. They seek refuge in New York, and Pierre, poor and without friends, turns to writing a book that no publisher will issue. Lucy, still in love with Pierre, follows him to New York. Threatened by her brother and his own cousin, Pierre kills the latter. Both Lucy and

Mrs. Glendinning die of grief, and Pierre and Isabel, now in love with each other, commit suicide in his prison cell. In grappling with the ambiguities of good and evil, Pierre has followed the "chronometrical" standards of ideal Christian conduct, instead of the "horological" standards of contemporary society. He is accordingly undone by his ideals, and becomes "the fool of Truth, the fool of Virtue, the fool of Fate."

Pike, type character in American humor, a genus of Western immigrant during the pioneering period of the mid-19th century. The Pike characters were traditionally natives of Pike County, although this locality was variously assigned to Missouri, Arkansas, southern Illinois, northern Texas, or generally to the frontier area. A man from Pike County was usually depicted as an ignorant, suspicious backwoodsman, good-natured as the butt of frequent jokes, but savagely acquisitive. His exaggerated, droll speech was characterized by an expressive, imaginative dialect. In Bayard Taylor's *At Home and Abroad* (1860), he is described as:

> the Anglo Saxon relapsed into semi-barbarism. He is long, lathy, and sallow; he expectorates vehemently; he takes naturally to whisky; he has the "shakes" his life long at home, though he generally manages to get rid of them in California; he has little respect for the rights of others; he distrusts men in "store clothes," but venerates the memory of Andrew Jackson.

The Pike as a specific character was launched in the works of George Derby, but it was not until 1871 that he became generally known to the reading public, through Harte's *East and West Poems* and Hay's *Pike County Ballads.*

PIKE, ALBERT, (1809–91), born in Boston, went to the Southwestern frontier (1831), and two years later settled in Arkansas, where he became a prominent journalist and lawyer, and wrote of his frontier adventures in *Prose Sketches and Poems, Written in the Western Country* (1834). After serving in the Mexican War, he continued to practice law in various Southern cities, although during the Civil War he commanded Indian troops in the Confederate army, whose atrocities were bitterly criticized by other generals, provoking his *Letter to the President of the Confederate States* (1862) and causing his temporary arrest and flight to Canada. He was a leader of the Freemasons and published poetry, legal works, and books on Masonic dogma and ritual. Of his poems, published in *Nugae* (1854) and *Hymns to the Gods* (1872), the best known is "Dixie" (1861).

PIKE, MARY HAYDEN [GREEN] (1824–1908), Maine novelist, whose antislavery interests led her to write *Ida May* (1854), the story of a child sold into slavery, and *Caste* (1856), the story of a quadroon who is forbidden to marry a white

man. *Agnes* (1858) is a historical novel of the Revolution.

PIKE, ZEBULON MONTGOMERY (1779–1813), New Jersey-born army officer, was commissioned by James Wilkinson to seek the source of the Mississippi, and in 1805–7 explored the region westward from St. Louis to New Mexico, Colorado, and Louisiana Territory. At this time he sighted but did not climb the peak that bears his name. He entered Mexican territory, where he was arrested and forced to leave. In 1810 he published his *Account of Expeditions to the Sources of the Mississippi and Through the Western Parts of Louisiana.* He was a brigadier general in the War of 1812 and was killed in the assault on York (Toronto), Canada.

Pike County Ballads, dialect poems by John Hay,♦ published in 1871. They show an appreciation of the candor, crudeness, and self-reliance of frontiersmen in Pike County, Ill., during the 1860s, and include "Jim Bludso," the story of a Mississippi steamboat engineer who is burned to death while saving his passengers from a fire, and "Little Breeches," about the four-year-old son of a Pike man, who is miraculously rescued from a wagon accident.

Pilgrims, name applied to the persons who came to Massachusetts on the *Mayflower*♦ (1620), or by extension to all the early settlers of Plymouth Colony.♦ Unlike the Puritans, the Pilgrims were Separatists,♦ opposing the episcopal jurisdiction, rites, and discipline of the Church of England. They originated (*c.*1606) at Scrooby, England, whence they emigrated to Amsterdam (1608), and then to Leiden. Almost half of this group came to Plymouth on the *Mayflower.* These 41 believers, including William Bradford, William Brewster, and Edward Winslow, were called Saints; others, including Myles Standish, were called Strangers.

PILLSBURY, PARKER (1809–98), Massachusetts Abolitionist and woman suffrage leader, for a time edited the *National Anti-Slavery Standard.* His *Acts of the Anti-Slavery Apostles* (1883) is a history of the New England Abolitionist movement.

Pilot, The, romance by Cooper,♦ published in 1823. The unnamed hero is supposed to represent John Paul Jones.

During the Revolutionary War, the schooner *Ariel* and an unnamed frigate appear off the coast of England near the residence of Colonel Howard, an expatriated South Carolina Loyalist. Lieutenants Griffith and Barnstable love Howard's two nieces, but their romances are thwarted by conflicting political views. The officers return to their ships with the mysterious "Pilot," who takes charge of the frigate. The schooner puts to sea through a channel that the frigate cannot navigate, but, during a terrible storm, the Pilot guides his ship to safety through a difficult shoal passage. The mission of the Americans is to capture prominent Englishmen, in order to force a modification of British impressment, and they decide to raid the guarded Howard residence. In the attempt, the Pilot and others are captured, but make their escape despite the precautions of villainous Christopher Dillon, a suitor of one of the girls. Dillon warns the crew of a British cutter, which is, however, defeated in battle by the *Ariel.* Long Tom Coffin, a daring old salt, is sent with the captured Dillon to attempt an exchange, but attempts to escape, is recaptured and taken back to the ship, which is wrecked in a storm. Only Barnstable and a few others survive. The Pilot captures the Howards, and imprisons them on the cutter. In a fierce battle with British warships, the frigate escapes through the shoal waters. Colonel Howard has been wounded, but before he dies he surrenders to the inevitability of American victory in the war, and permits the marriage of his nieces with the officers. The Pilot goes to Holland, while his ship sails for America.

PINKERTON, ALLAN (1819–84), Scottish-born detective, became famous in Illinois for his exposure of a band of counterfeiters, and organized a private detective agency to protect the property of railroads and other corporations. He prevented an attempted assassination of Lincoln (1861), and became a leader of espionage during the Civil War, when he called himself Major E.J. Allen. This work led to the establishment of the Federal secret service. His agency, continued after his death by his sons, was notorious for its methods in suppressing labor disputes, especially in the Homestead strike (1892). It was subjected to a congressional investigation during industrial disputes over the recognition of unions (1937). Pinkerton was the author of *Criminal Reminiscences and Detective Sketches* (1879), *The Spy of the Rebellion* (1883), and *Thirty Years a Detective* (1884).

PINKNEY, EDWARD COOTE (1802–28), son of William Pinkney, a leading statesman and diplomat of his time, was born in London and reared partly there and partly in Baltimore. He edited *The Marylander* (1827–28), a paper which supported J.Q. Adams. When his father was attacked for his haughty manner in John Neal's *Randolph* (1823), the younger Pinkney challenged the novelist to a duel. Pinkney's few *Poems* (1825) were praised by Poe for their lyric gift but were often imitative of Byron and Tom Moore.

PINSKY, ROBERT (1940–), New Jersey-born poet, after graduation from Rutgers and a Ph.D. from Stanford became a professor of English at Wellesley, the University of California,

Berkeley (1980–89), and Boston University. His collections include *Sadness and Happiness* (1975), *An Explanation of America* (1979), *History of My Heart* (1984), and *The Want Bone* (1990). Critical works *Landor's Poetry* (1968), *The Situation of Poetry* (1977), and *Poetry and the World* (1988), gather Pinsky's book reviews. His critically acclaimed translation of *The Inferno of Dante* (1994) is rendered in *terza rima,* using slant rhyme and near-rhyme to avoid distortion of the original. It was published in a facing-page bilingual format.

Pioneer, *The* (1843), monthly literary magazine, founded by Lowell and Robert Carter, was published in only three issues, since it was a critical but not a financial success. It included among its contributions Poe's "The Tell-Tale Heart" and "Notes on English Verse," Hawthorne's "Hall of Fantasy" and "The Birthmark," and works by Jones Very, Lowell, J.S. Dwight, and Whittier.

Pioneers, *The; or, The Sources of the Susquehanna,* romance by Cooper, ♦ published in 1823. It is the fourth in plot sequence of the Leather-Stocking Tales. ♦

During the decade after the Revolutionary War, Judge Marmaduke Temple, a retired Quaker merchant, is the leading landowner of Otsego County on the New York frontier, having acquired the estate of the Loyalist father of his friend Edward Effingham. While hunting deer he accidentally shoots Oliver Edwards, young companion of Natty Bumppo (Leather-Stocking), a veteran frontiersman. The judge and his daughter Elizabeth befriend the young man, who becomes their overseer, although persisting in his mysterious association with Bumppo and old chief Chingachgook (John Mohegan), who is rumored to be his father. Elizabeth and her friend Louisa Grant, the rector's daughter, disdain the company of the supposed half-breed. After Bumppo is released from jail, following his arrest for shooting deer out of season, Elizabeth visits him and is trapped by a forest fire. She is saved by Edwards, but Chingachgook dies after his rescue by Bumppo. Elizabeth and Edwards now admit their love, and his identity is made known when a searching party discovers demented old Major Effingham, and it is revealed that Edwards is his grandson, that Bumppo had been an employee of his family, and that Chingachgook had adopted them into his tribe. The young couple is betrothed and given half of the judge's estate.

Pioneers! O Pioneers!, poem by Whitman, ♦ published in *Drum-Taps* (1865) and in the "annex" to *Leaves of Grass* (1867).

In 26 quatrains, each ending with the refrain that gives the poem its title, Whitman celebrates the frontier spirit with a paean of praise concerning the unique American qualities of optimism, self-reliance, equality, and revolt against the European past.

PIRSIG, ROBERT M[AYNARD] (1928–), philosopher, novelist. Pirsig taught English at Montana State before publishing *Zen and the Art of Motorcycle Maintenance* (1974), which recounts a cross-country trip of the narrator Phaedrus with his young son. Interspersed in the travel narrative are meditations on madness, Plato, and quality. The book built a cult following. After long silence Pirsig published *Lila: An Inquiry into Morals* (1991). The narrative concerns Phaedrus on a sailboat trip around America and his adventures with a woman picked up on the voyage. Phaedrus formulates a metaphysics of quality, with observations on sex, human rights, and, once again, madness.

Pit, The: A Story of Chicago, novel by Frank Norris,♦ posthumously published in 1903 as the second part of his "Epic of the Wheat."

Laura Dearborn comes to Chicago from Massachusetts to live with her Aunt Wess and her younger sister Page. She soon attracts three suitors: Sheldon Corthell, wealthy artist and dilettante; Landry Court, a young stockbroker who later marries Page; and Curtis Jadwin, a powerful, virile capitalist, who is lonely despite his wealth and position. She is won by Jadwin's honesty and simplicity, although she does not respond fully to his possessive affection. He succumbs to the lure of the Board of Trade and becomes a leading speculator, by a combination of boldness and luck gaining a "corner" in the wheat market. His preoccupation with business affairs causes him to neglect Laura, who drifts into an affair with Corthell, returned from a long absence in Europe. Natural laws defeat Jadwin's speculative coup, when his monopoly is broken by an unforeseen production of wheat in the West. His financial ruin is accompanied by a physical breakdown, and Laura, who has been about to elope with Corthell, nurses her husband to health, coming to realize the bond between them. Although they lose their mansion and rich possessions, they face a future of hard work and simple living in the West with renewed hope and enthusiasm.

Pit and the Pendulum, The, tale by Poe,♦ published in *The Gift* (1843).

A prisoner of the Spanish Inquisition at Toledo describes his horrible tortures. Sick from long suffering, he faints when the death sentence is pronounced; upon recovering consciousness, he finds himself on the stone floor of a dark dungeon. Exploring the cell, he is saved from plunging into a deep pit when he accidentally trips and falls. He sleeps, and awakes to discover that he is now strapped to a wooden framework, while a great pendulum swings slowly back and forth overhead, its end being a steel crescent sharpened

to a razor edge. The menacing blade gradually descends, and rats swarm about his highly seasoned food and over his body. As the pendulum reaches him, the rats gnaw his bonds, from which he frees himself to find the cells' metal walls are heated and are slowly closing in. Just as he gives way to an agony of terror, the city is captured by French soldiers, and the hand of General Lasalle stays him from tumbling into the pit.

Plain Language from Truthful James, comic ballad by Bret Harte,♦ published in the *Overland Monthly* (Sept. 1870). This narrative of a euchre game, in which Truthful James and his friend Bill Nye intend to cheat the Chinese gambler Ah Sin but are themselves deceived by the "ways that are dark" of their wily opponent, soon had a popular vogue throughout the country, was frequently quoted, and was pirated in broadside and pamphlet editions as *The Heathen Chinee.*

Plains Indians, general term applied to the many tribes that lived in the Plains and Prairie regions. Their more or less homogeneous culture was based economically on the hunting of bison, although some of the eastern tribes also grew maize. Principally nomadic, they used dogs and later horses for transportation, and were noted for their vigorous and constant warfare and for their mystical pursuit of visions and supernatural power. The popular conception of the heroic Indian brave—tall, muscular, and dignified, with braided hair, costume of skins, and feathered headdress, living in tepees and skilled in horsemanship—derives from contact with the Plains tribes. Among the most prominent of these were the Sioux,♦ Comanche,♦ Cheyenne,♦ Pawnee,♦ Blackfoot,♦ Osage,♦ and Mandan.♦ The Plains Indians figure in the writings of Cooper, Neihardt, Garland, Parkman, and Lewis and Clark, in Longfellow's *Hiawatha* and novels and nonfiction by Mari Sandoz, as well as in the more scientific descriptions by Schoolcraft, Catlin, Grinnell, Dorsey, and Wissler.

Plains region, country sloping gradually from the Rocky Mountains eastward to the Prairie region,♦ includes Nebraska, Kansas, Oklahoma, and Texas, as well as the eastern parts of Montana, Wyoming, Colorado, and New Mexico, and the western parts of North and South Dakota. The region is marked by broad, level river valleys and rolling plains, which were the habitat of great herds of bison and the Plains Indians♦ who hunted them. Later the plains were devoted to cattle raising, but during most of the 20th century they have been planted in wheat and other crops. This change, involving the removal of grass and consequent erosion of the topsoil, resulted in dust storms and drought, especially in the 1930s, and caused the region to be called the Dust Bowl. Oklahoma and Texas in particular were disastrously affected, causing a great migration of refugees, popularly and invidiously called "Okies," to other regions, notably California. Parkman's *Oregon Trail* is the most famous narrative of the Indians and white pioneers on the plains; Andy Adams has written of the cattle industry; the plays of Lynn Riggs deal with the transitional Indian Territory; Edna Ferber's *Cimarron* tells of the Oklahoma land rush and its aftermath; E.W. Howe and William Allen White, both Kansas editors, wrote stories of local life; Willa Cather describes the life of the region in many novels; Mari Sandoz treats Nebraska, past and present, in novels and nonfiction, as does Wright Morris, and Steinbeck's *Grapes of Wrath*♦ tells of the migrants from the Dust Bowl.

Platform of Church-Discipline, A, see *Cambridge Platform.*

PLATH, SYLVIA (1932–63), born in Massachusetts, attended Smith College on a scholarship endowed by Olive Higgins Prouty,♦ who later befriended her and appeared in her fiction. She suffered a nervous breakdown (1953) but returned to Smith to graduate (1955). These experiences formed the basis of her moving novel *The Bell Jar*♦ (1963), published under the pseudonym Victoria Lewis. A scholarship took her to England, where she married the British poet Ted Hughes. They lived briefly in the U.S., while she taught at Smith, but after returning to England and seemingly settling down with family and as an author, she suddenly took her life. Her intense, candid, and personal poems were published in the U.S. as *The Colossus* (1962), *Ariel* (1966), *Crossing the Water* (1971), and *Winter Trees* (1972). *Johnny Panic and the Bible of Dreams* (1977) collects various prose writings. *Letters Home* (1975) is a selection of correspondence. Her *Journals* was published in 1982. Her *Collected Poems* (1981) was awarded a Pulitzer Prize.

Play It as It Lays, novel by Joan Didion,♦ published in 1970.

Maria Wyeth, a 31-year-old former motion-picture actress, separated from her husband Carter, a film director, and the mother of Kate, a retarded, institutionalized child, reaches a degree of nihilism so intense that day after day she leaves her Beverly Hills house to drive aimlessly on the freeways of southern California. When she discovers that she is pregnant by Carter, who persuades her to have an abortion, her depression is deepened and she gives herself to meaningless, frenetic sex. She has a nervous breakdown, and in the institution to which she is sent for cure she dreams of a time when she and Kate can be together in a happy home; but she is determined that whatever happens she will not resort to suicide but live instead with the knowledge of "what nothing means and keep on playing."

Players, THE, New York City club for actors, writers, painters, sculptors, and musicians, was founded by Edwin Booth (1888), who was president until his death, and presented the organization with a building designed by Stanford White. Later presidents included Joseph Jefferson and John Drew. William Tecumseh Sherman was a member.

Playwrights' Company, theatrical production organization, founded in 1938 by Robert Sherwood, Maxwell Anderson, Elmer Rice, Sidney Howard, and S.N. Behrman, to produce their plays and those of others. In 1959, when Elmer Rice, the last of the founders, retired, the company was reorganized. Its greatest successes were *Abe Lincoln in Illinois* and *There Shall Be No Night,* by Sherwood.

Playwrights Theatre, see *Provincetown Players.*

Plimmoth Plantation, History of, was begun by William Bradford,♦ about ten years after the landing of the Pilgrims. Book I was completed within a year or two, Book II written between 1646 and 1650, and the list of *Mayflower* passengers added in 1651. The manuscript, probably not intended for publication, came at Bradford's death into the hands of his nephew, Nathaniel Morton, who drew on it heavily for *New Englands Memoriall,* and it was similarly used by a later owner, Thomas Prince, for his *Chronological History of New England,* as well as by Thomas Hutchinson as a source of his *History of the Colony of Massachusetts Bay.* During the Revolution the manuscript disappeared. Discovered in the library of the Bishop of London (1855), it was returned to the Commonwealth of Massachusetts. The entire work was first published in 1856, although Book I had been printed from the Plymouth church records (1841). In presenting his narrative, Bradford endeavors to go to "the very root and rise of the same," and the opening book sketches the origin of the Separatist movement, the flight from England to Holland, the settlement at Leiden, the plans for the settlement in New England, and the *Mayflower* voyage. The second book, which includes the major part of the history, is in the form of annals from 1620 to 1646, and describes every aspect of the life of the Pilgrims. Besides being a primary historical source, the work has artistic value because of its dignified, sonorous style, deriving from the Geneva Bible. The narrative is naturally grave, but it has vigorous qualities and an occasional strain of pithy sarcasm.

Pluralistic Universe, A, lectures by William James.♦

Plymouth Colony, settlement founded on the Massachusetts coast (1620) by the Pilgrims,♦ who arrived on the *Mayflower.* They obtained their charter from the Council for New England. John Carver was the first governor, and the May-

flower Compact remained the basis of government until 1691. This group was independent of
the Puritan colony of Massachusetts Bay until the
merger in 1684. William Bradford was the most
notably early governor of the Plymouth Colony.
Among the sources of the colony's early history
are *Mourt's Relation,* Bradford's *History of Plimmoth Plantation,* Winslow's *Good News from New
England,* and Winthrop's *Journal.*

Plymouth Company, see *Virginia Company.*

PM, New York City tabloid newspaper (1940–
48), was published daily except on Saturday and
Sunday, but a digest, *PM's Weekly,* was issued on
Saturday. The newspaper, stapled together and
bearing a cover consisting of a large picture and a
headline, was suggestive of a magazine. The news
was departmentalized, somewhat in the fashion
of a news magazine, and there was a liberal use of
photographs and specially drawn illustrations that
occupied about a third of the paper. No advertising was accepted, although there was a digest of
advertisements selected from the other major papers of the city; other unconventional features
included a listing of "good buys" in food and
suggested menus employing these products.
The paper was noted for its very liberal pro-
labor policies. The editor, Ralph Ingersoll, was
formerly the publisher of *Time.* It was owned
(1945–48) by Marshall Field. Contributors included Ben Hecht, Louis Kronenberger, Margaret Bourke-White, J.T. Winterich, Leane Zugsmith.

POCAHONTAS (*c.*1595–1617), daughter of
Indian chief Powhatan,♦ was really named
Matoaka. Her popular name means "sportive."
The fame of Pocahontas is largely based on the
story in Book III, Chapter 2, of John Smith's
Generall Historie (1624), which is considered
apocryphal. In 1608, according to Smith,♦ when
Powhatan was about "to beate out his brains,
Pocahontas the Kings dearest daughter, when no
intreaty could prevaile, got his head in her armes,
and laid her owne upon his to save him from
death." The story has been frequently studied by
historians and repeated in literature. The first
treatment in the latter form was John Davis's
novel *The First Settlers of Virginia* (1805), and later
examples include J.N. Barker's *The Indian
Princess,* G.W.P. Custis's *Pocahontas,* and Robert
Dale Owen's *Pocahontas,* all dramas; and Seba
Smith's metrical romance *Powhatan.* Hart Crane
treats Pocahontas as a mythic and symbolic figure
in *The Bridge,* as, in a manner closer to history,
does Louis Simpson in *At the End of the Open
Road.* In 1613 she was held as hostage for English prisoners, and in Jamestown became converted to Christianity and married John Rolfe.
She went to England with him (1616), and died
there. Their descendants include many prominent Virginia families. Her name has been spelled

Pokahontas, as in J.E. Cooke's novel *My Lady
Pokahontas.*

PODHORETZ, Norman (1930–),
Brooklyn-born literary critic, as a student at Co-
lumbia was influenced by Lionel Trilling, at Clare
College, Cambridge, by Leavis. His sociocultural
essays are collected in *Doings and Undoings: The
Fifties and After in American Writing* (1964). *Making
It* (1967) is a witty, self-deprecatory revelation of
the writer's successful efforts to succeed in New
York intellectual society. *Breaking Ranks* (1979) is
an equally candid memoir of recent political issues
and his turn toward the right. *Why We Were in
Vietnam* (1982) supports the purposes of the U.S.
intervention and attacks the New Left's views. He
became editor of *Commentary* in 1960 and moved
it to his neoconservative views. His literary views
stand out in the essays of *The Bloody Crossroads:
Where Literature and Politics Meet* (1986).

POE, Edgar Allan (1809–49), son of itinerant
actors, was born in Boston. His father died the
following year, and may have deserted his wife
before that time, for she continued to support
herself, taking the child with her from place to
place until her death at Richmond, Va. (1811),
when she left penniless Edgar and two other children: William Henry Leonard Poe (1808–31),
who became a poet and may have collaborated
with his brother; and Rosalie Poe (1810–74).
Edgar was taken into the home of a Richmond
merchant, John Allan. Although never legally
adopted, for a long while he used his foster father's name, employing it as a middle name after
1824. He went to England (1815–20) with the
Allans, and there attended school, as described in
the semi-autobiographical story "William Wilson."♦ After their return to Richmond, Mr. Allan, who had inherited a great fortune, was neither faithful to his wife nor sympathetic with his
stepson, whose favoring of Mrs. Allan caused him
to counter with remarks besmirching the character of Edgar and hinting at the possible ille-
gitimacy of Rosalie. The relationship was further
strained during Poe's attendance at the University of Virginia (1826), when Allan would give
him no money, and he resorted unsuccessfully to
gambling.

Allan insisted on Poe's preparation for a legal
career, and after a violent quarrel the youth went
to Boston, where he published *Tamerlane*♦
(1827), issued anonymously at his own expense,
which found no public. Under an assumed name
and an incorrect age, he entered the U.S. army
(1827) and was sent to Sullivan's Island, South
Carolina, the setting for his later stories "The
Gold-Bug"♦ and "The Balloon Hoax."♦ Mrs.
Allan's deathbed plea caused a cool reconciliation
with Allan, who aided Poe in obtaining an appointment to West Point and sent him a small
sum to live on meanwhile in Baltimore, where

he stayed with his brother and his aunt, Mrs. Maria Clemm, while arranging for the publication of *Al Aaraaf*♦ (1829), which contained the sonnet "To Science"♦ and "Tamerlane." Admitted to West Point (1830), he soon set about by gross neglect of duty to get himself dismissed (1831), since his reason for attendance, the desire to reinstate himself with Allan, had already been lost.

During a short stay in New York, he published *Poems by Edgar A. Poe* (1831), containing early versions of "Israfel,"♦ "To Helen,"♦ and "The City in the Sea," and then went to live with Mrs. Clemm in Baltimore (1831–35), where he began to publish stories in magazines. He first attracted attention with "MS. Found in a Bottle,"♦ which won a contest and brought him to the attention of J.P. Kennedy, who got him an editorial position on the *Southern Literary Messenger,* although he was discharged because of his drinking. At Baltimore he obtained a license (1835) to marry his cousin, Mrs. Clemm's daughter Virginia, aged 13, and may have married her before the public ceremony (1836). Reemployed by the *Messenger,* he moved with Mrs. Clemm and Virginia to Richmond, where, before he was finally discharged (1837), he had published the unfinished tragedy *Politian,*♦ 83 reviews, 6 poems, 4 essays, and 3 short stories, and greatly increased the magazine's circulation.

He moved his family to New York (1837–38), where he did hackwork and published *The Narrative of Arthur Gordon Pym,*♦ then going to Philadelphia, where as co-editor of *Burton's Gentleman's Magazine* (1839–40) he contributed "The Fall of the House of Usher,"♦ containing the previously published "Haunted Palace"♦; "William Wilson"♦; "The Journal of Julius Rodman"♦; "Morella"♦; and other works; and published *Tales of the Grotesque and Arabesque*♦ (1840), his first collection, which included "Berenice"♦; "Ligeia,"♦ containing "The Conqueror Worm"♦; "The Assignation"♦; "The Unparalleled Adventure of One Hans Pfaall"♦; and other stories. Leaving Burton, he made plans for his own magazine, which led to an acquaintance with T.H. Chivers,♦ whose similar poetry caused attacks and counterattacks of plagiarism after Poe's death. Poe was literary editor of *Graham's Magazine* (1841–42), to which he contributed "The Murders in the Rue Morgue,"♦ "A Descent into the Maelström,"♦ "The Masque of the Red Death,"♦ and other works, including some acute criticism which heightened his reputation. To the same magazine he later contributed "The Imp of the Perverse"♦ (1845) and "The Philosophy of Composition"♦ (1846). He came to know R.W. Griswold,♦ who followed him as editor and bitterly attacked him after his death.

In 1842–43 he published "The Mystery of Marie Rogêt"♦ in a New York magazine, and won a prize in a Philadelphia newspaper for "The Gold-Bug," but even this did not help him, since he had wasted opportunities for further publication in Philadelphia. In New York (1844), he wrote "The Raven,"♦ became associated with the *New-York Mirror,* and as literary critic (1844–45) conducted his war there with Longfellow, whom he accused of plagiarism. These attacks he continued after becoming proprietor of the *Broadway Journal*♦ (1845), where he also printed "The Pit and the Pendulum,"♦ "Eleonora,"♦ and "The Premature Burial," and reprinted "The Tell-Tale Heart"♦ and other works. His eighth book, *Tales* (1845), reprinted previous works selected by E.A. Duyckinck, and included "The Black Cat"♦ and "The Purloined Letter."♦ *The Raven and Other Poems* appeared the same year. Next associated with *Godey's Lady's Book,* Poe published "The Cask of Amontillado"♦ and his articles on "The Literati of New York City,"♦ whose harsh criticism of T.D. English prompted an answer, to which Poe replied with a successful libel suit.

Lacking regular employment, he with his wife and Mrs. Clemm nearly starved in their Fordham home, and Virginia died of tuberculosis during the winter. Although he published "Ulalume"♦ and "The Domain of Arnheim,"♦ and was at work on "The Bells"♦ and *Eureka,*♦ he was now more than ever in a thoroughly abnormal condition of body and mind, for which he attempted to find solace in the company of a Mrs. Shew, the poet Sarah Whitman, and the Mrs. Richmond addressed in "To Annie." Torn between the love of the latter two, he attempted suicide. His erratic mind, depressed in personal affairs, nevertheless showed extreme exaltation in the lecture *Eureka,* in which he attempted to establish an all-embracing theory of cosmogony. Upon his return to Richmond (1849), where he wrote "Annabel Lee,"♦ he made a vigorous attempt to end his addiction to liquor, and became engaged to Mrs. Shelton, a former neighbor of the Allans, with whom he had had an early affair. On his way North to bring Mrs. Clemm to the wedding, he stopped in Baltimore, where five days afterward he was discovered in a delirious condition near a saloon that had been used for a voting place. It has been supposed that he was captured in a drunken condition by a political gang, which used him for the then common practice of repeating votes. Four days later he died, and was buried in Baltimore beside his wife.

There have been strongly divergent evaluations of Poe's literary significance, from Emerson's dismissal of him as "the jingle man" and Lowell's "three-fifths genius and two-fifths sheer fudge" to Yeats's declaration, "always and for all lands a great lyric poet." The difference of opinion is at heart directed at his criticism, for the poetry consistently exemplifies the theories set forth in "The Philosophy of Composition,"♦ "The Rationale of Verse,"♦ and "The Poetic Principle,"♦ in which he indicated his conception of poetic unity to be one of mood or emotion, and especially emphasized the beauty of melancholy. This romantic attitude has led to the criticism that his poetry is no more than a sustained tone, entirely dominated by its atmosphere. His reputation is also grounded on his use of the short story, which he preferred to the novel on the same basis that he preferred the short poem to the long. The stories may be said to fall into two categories, those of horror, set in a crepuscular world, and those of ratiocination, which set the standard for the modern detective story and conform to the critical theories expounded in *Eureka*. Although Poe was strongly influenced by many authors—e.g. Tennyson in his poetry, Coleridge in his criticism, and C.B. Brown in his fiction—he himself proved a source of influence on such Americans as Bierce and Hart Crane, and such Englishmen as Rossetti, Swinburne, Dowson, and Stevenson, besides having a profound effect on the French Symbolists.

Poet at the Breakfast-Table, *The,* essays by Holmes,♦ published in 1872. It is a sequel to *The Autocrat of the Breakfast-Table.*♦

Poetic Principle, *The,* lecture by Poe,♦ delivered in various cities (1848–49) and posthumously published in *The Union Magazine* (1850). Partly an elocutionary vehicle, it contains short poems by Willis, Longfellow, Bryant, Shelley, Thomas Moore, Hood, Byron, and Tennyson.

Developing the theories already stated in "The Philosophy of Composition"♦ and other places, Poe declares that "a long poem does not exist. . . . A poem deserves its title only inasmuch as it excites, by elevating the soul. . . . That degree of excitement . . . cannot be sustained throughout a composition of any great length." This is true because of "that vital requisite in all works of Art, Unity," and the "absolute effect of even the best epic under the sun is a nullity." He proceeds to "the heresy of the Didactic": "there neither exists nor *can* exist any work more thoroughly dignified, more supremely noble than [the] poem which is a poem and nothing more—[the] poem written solely for the poem's sake." The proper mood for teaching a truth is completely opposed to the poetic mood. Poetry arises in the passionate reaching out "to apprehend the supernal Loveliness," to attain a vision, however brief, of the ideal beauty which is usually beyond our ken. "I would define, in brief, the Poetry of words as *The Rhythmical Creation of Beauty. Its sole arbiter is Taste.*" Love, "the purest and truest of all poetical themes," is the highest variety of beauty, and beauty is "the province of the poem. . . . The incitements of Passion, or the precepts of Duty, or even the lessons of Truth, may . . . be introduced . . . but the true artist will always contribute to tone them down in proper subjection to . . . Beauty."

Poet Laureate, salaried post authorized by the U.S. Senate in 1985 as an adjunct to the Consultant for Poetry in the Library of Congress. No ceremonial verse is required. Honorees include R.P. Warren (1986), Richard Wilbur (1987), Howard Nemerov (1988), Mark Strand (1990), Joseph Brodsky (1991), Mona Van Duyn (1992), and Rita Dove (1993).

Poetry: A Magazine of Verse (1912–   ), founded at Chicago by Harriet Monroe♦ and edited by her until 1936. Later editors have included Karl Shapiro and John Frederick Nims. Long the major journal exclusively devoted to poetry, and the precursor of many other little magazines, *Poetry* has had an extremely stimulating influence on American literature. Without confining itself to any school or type, it has published the work of such diverse authors as Sandburg, Amy Lowell, T.S. Eliot, Frost, H.D., Ezra Pound (for a time an editor), Vachel Lindsay, and Hart Crane, and in many cases first brought them to public attention.

Poictesme, mythical medieval country, the scene of *Jurgen* and other romances by Cabell.♦

POKAHONTAS, see *Pocahontas.*

Police Gazette, see *National Police Gazette.*

Politian: A Tragedy, unfinished blank-verse drama by Poe,♦ of which selected scenes were published in the *Southern Literary Messenger* (1835–36). The work remained in manuscript until 1923, when it appeared in its entirety in a scholarly edition arranged by T.O. Mabbott. "The Coliseum" (1833) was incorporated in the text by Poe. *Politian* is based on the Kentucky Tragedy,♦ but the scene is 16th-century Rome.

Castiglione, son of the Duke Di Broglio, seduces his father's orphan ward Lalage. When he becomes engaged to his cousin Alessandra, Lalage swears that she will be avenged. Politian, Earl of Leicester, comes to Rome from England, falls in love with Lalage, and accepts her demand that he kill Castiglione. Irresolute, he postpones the act and goes to the Coliseum to meditate. There he is joined by Lalage, who reminds him that Castiglione's marriage is about to take place, and Politian departs to fulfill his promise.

Political Fables, *The,* three tales by Cotton Mather,♦ circulated in manuscript (c.1692) and printed in *The Andros Tracts* (1868). They defend Sir William Phips♦ and the new Massachusetts charter, warning New Englanders to abstain from internal disputes when they are endangered from outside.

Political Greenhouse, *The,* Federalist verse satire on events in 1798 by Richard Alsop,♦ Lemuel Hopkins,♦ and Theodore Dwight,♦ reprinted in 1799 from the *Connecticut Courant.*

Political Litany, *A,* mock litany by Freneau,♦ published in 1775. Beginning with the traditional "Libera Nos, Domine," this slashing satire in anapestic couplets proceeds to pray for complete and final deliverance from association with the British.

Politician Outwitted, *The,* comedy attributed to Samuel Low, a federal official, was produced in 1788 and published in 1789. Obviously modeled on Royall Tyler's *The Contrast,* it presents its political opinions through Old Loveyet, who disinherits his son because of his adherence to the new Constitution, and Trueman, who staunchly upholds it. Old Loveyet is completely routed in love and politics, while his son Charles and Trueman emerge victorious.

POLLARD, [JOSEPH] PERCIVAL (1869–1911), born in Germany, was educated in England, and came to the U.S. (1885), where he won a great contemporary reputation as a critic, through his interpretation of European literature for the American public and his pungent attacks on sentimentality and puritanical morality in American literature. He influenced such writers as Bierce and Mencken, but collected little of his magazine writings and is now relatively obscure. *Their Day in Court* (1909) is the most important collection of his criticism. His plays, *Nocturno* (1906) and *The Ambitious Mrs. Alcott* (1907), were never published. He did much work without credit as an adapter for Richard Mansfield, whom he satirized in his novel *The Imitator* (1901).

POLLOCK, CHANNING (1880–1946), born in Washington, D.C., became a New York journalist and dramatic critic, and began his career as a playwright with an adaption of Norris's *The Pit* (1900). This was followed by a long series of farces, melodramas, and musical comedy librettos, but in 1922 he turned to the thesis drama with *The Fool,* about a modern minister who attempts to emulate the career of Christ. *The Enemy* (1925), another homiletic play, is a plea for pacifism, set in Austria at the beginning of World War I. *Mr. Moneypenny* (1928) is an allegory of a wage slave who sells his soul to the modern devil, Mr. Moneypenny, for wealth, but eventually returns to his original poverty and honesty. *The House Beautiful* (1931), another allegory, is about a clerk whose wife thinks him a modern Galahad. The critical disapproval of these plays led Pollock to retire from the theater. His later books include *The Adventures of a Happy Man* (1939), *Guide Posts in Chaos* (1942), and *Harvest of My Years* (1943), an autobiography.

Pollyanna, character in the juvenile novels of Eleanor Porter. ♦

Polyphonic prose, free-verse form that employs a succession of varied rhythms and all the devices of poetry, but is printed as prose and follows a mood rather than a strict metrical pattern. French in origin, it was frequently used by Amy Lowell and John Gould Fletcher.

Ponteach, *or, The Savages of America,* blank-verse play by Robert Rogers,♦ published in 1766. It was the first tragedy to be written about the Indians. Rogers had served in the expedition to crush Pontiac's Rebellion, but in the play he extols the noble Indian warrior and depicts the baseness of the English methods. The facts are still regarded as authentic, aside from the idealization of the chief, and Parkman used the play as a principal source of his *History of the Conspiracy of Pontiac.*

PONTIAC (*c.*1720–69), Ottawa Indian chief, considered a moving spirit in the struggle known as Pontiac's Rebellion or Pontiac's Conspiracy, although he was present only at the siege of Detroit. According to the Treaty of Paris (1763), the Ohio Valley and other Western areas were assigned to the Indians, but the uprising had already commenced. From spring until winter of that year, Pontiac laid siege to Fort Detroit, but his various schemes and attacks were unsuccessful. Great slaughter occurred elsewhere, outposts were destroyed, and the frontier settlements of Pennsylvania, Maryland, and Virginia were terrorized. The success of the English campaign in Pennsylvania led to a treaty of peace (1764), to which Pontiac finally acceded in July 1765. The English commanders included Amherst, Gage, and Sir William Johnson. Robert Rogers, who was also active in the struggle, wrote the popular drama *Ponteach♦* (1766), which was largely responsible for the reputation of the chief as a romantic hero, and he often figures in later historical fiction, e.g. John Richardson's *Wacousta* (1882) and Sir Gilbert Parker's *The Seats of the Mighty* (1896). Parkman's *History of the Conspiracy of Pontiac* (1851) is the most famous account.

POOLE, ERNEST (1880–1950), born in Chicago, graduated from Princeton (1902) and lived at University Settlement, New York City, while working for the abolition of child labor and other social reforms. He helped Upton Sinclair gather material for *The Jungle,* and then published his first novel, *The Voice of the Street* (1906), depicting New York's impoverished Lower East Side. New York was also a major setting for his major novel, *The Harbor♦* (1915). He also served as a war correspondent in Germany and France, going to Russia (1917) to view the October Revolution sympathetically and at first hand. *His Family♦* (1917, Pulitzer Prize) treats changing standards in U.S. life.

Making his home in New York, Poole continued his literary career with a long succession of novels and stories, including *His Second Wife* (1918), about a woman who married her widowed brother-in-law and wages a long struggle with the influence of her dead sister; *The Dark People* (1918) and *The Village* (1918), sketches of Russian peasant life; *Blind* (1920), a semi-autobiographical novel of tenement life in New York, the European war, and revolution in Russia; *Beggars' Gold* (1921), the story of a teacher who achieves his dream of visiting China; *Millions* (1922), an ironic tale of a family awaiting the death of a relative who, unknown to them, has lost his fortune; *Danger* (1923), concerned with a neurotic woman who wrecks the lives of her brother and sister-in-law; *The Avalanche* (1924), dealing with the conflict between a neurologist's ideals and his wife's desire for success; *The Hunter's Moon* (1925), telling of a boy's dream of a trip to the peaceful woods, away from his loveless home; *The Little Dark Man* (1925), Russian sketches; *With Eastern Eyes* (1926), describing a Russian scientist's reactions to American society; *Silent Storms* (1927), a novel dealing with the conflicting standards of an American financier and his young French wife; *The Car of Croesus* (1930), about Russian visitors in the U.S.; *The Destroyer* (1931), about a conflict between brothers; *Nurses on Horseback* (1932), an account of the frontier nursing service in the Kentucky mountains; *Great Winds* (1933), contrasting the complex life of a modern family with its New Hampshire background; *One of Us* (1934), describing changed New England life as seen by an old storekeeper; and *The Nancy Flyer* (1949), about a New Hampshire stagecoach builder.

Nonfiction includes *The Bridge* (1940), autobiography; *Giants Gone: Men Who Made Chicago* (1943); and *The Great White Hills of New Hampshire* (1946), about the state where he lived.

POOLE, William Frederick (1821–94), Massachusetts librarian, as an undergraduate at Yale in 1848 began his *Alphabetical Index to Subjects Treated in the . . . Periodicals . . . ,* the precursor of the present *Reader's Guide to Periodical Literature.* He compiled catalogues for the Boston Athenaeum, the public libraries of Cincinnati and Chicago, and the Newberry Library (Chicago), all of which he headed at different times. His writings include *The Battle of the Dictionaries* (1856), *The Popham Colony* (1866), and *Cotton Mather and Salem Witchcraft* (1869).

Poor Richard's Almanack, written and published by Franklin♦ at Philadelphia (1733–58), is the most famous of American almanacs, ♦ although it followed the pattern previously established in the colonies and in England. *Poor Richard's* undoubtedly derives from *Poor Robin's,* the English almanac which began publication in 1663, and the name Richard Saunders, with which Franklin signed his prefaces, is the same as that of the English editor of *Apollo Anglicanus.* Franklin likewise owed other debts to predecessors, particularly to his Pennsylvania contemporary, Titan Leeds, ♦ on whom he played a hoax that resembles Swift's humorous prognostication of the death of a rival almanac maker. To the almanac Franklin introduced characters on whom he draped his humor and homely wisdom, and the figures Richard and Bridget Saunders became popular in the contemporary American mind. Many of the shrewd maxims and proverbs that Franklin wrote and collected were brought together in *Father Abraham's Speech,* the harangue of a wise old man to the people attending an auction, and were published in the almanac of 1758. They were separately published under that title the following year, but many later reprints appeared with a title that was not Franklin's: *The Way to Wealth.* The title was not inappropriate for the gathering of apothegms included only those that inculcated virtue and frugality, and not the many other witty and cynical observations. The almanacs from 1748 on were called *Poor Richard Improved,* and probably did not contain any writing by Franklin, who sold the almanac (1758), although it continued to be published until 1796.

Poor White, novel by Sherwood Anderson, ♦ published in 1920.

POORE, Benjamin Perley (1820–87), journalist and author, known for his many popular biographies of people ranging from Louis Philippe to General Burnside, and for his reporting of Washington politics for the Boston *Journal* and other papers, under the signature Perley. He also wrote *Perley's Reminiscences of Sixty Years in the National Metropolis* (1886).

Popeye, a vicious, degenerate, and criminal character in Faulkner's novel *Sanctuary.* ♦

Populist party was formed in 1891 by a combination of farmer and labor reform groups, chiefly from the West. For more than a decade its importance was exceeded only by that of the Republican and Democratic parties, and in 1896 the Populist candidate, Bryan, captured the Democratic convention with his advocacy of free coinage of silver. Other Populist policies included demands for government ownership of railroads, the eight-hour day, pensions, a graduated income tax, increased paper money, and loans on nonperishable agricultural commodities. After Bryan's defeat, the party dwindled until its demise in 1904. Writers affected by Populist views included Hamlin Garland, whose *A Spoil of Office* (1892) particularly championed its politics.

Porcupine, *The,* play by E.A. Robinson. ♦

Porcupine's Gazette and Daily Advertiser (1797–99), Federalist, pro-British daily newspaper, published from Philadelphia by William Cobbett. ♦ His coarse partisanship led him into a controversy with the anti-Federalist *Aurora* and its editor, B.F.

Bache, as well as many others. The paper was discontinued when Benjamin Rush won a $5000 judgment for libel.

Porgy, character in *The Partisan,*♦ *Woodcraft,*♦ and other Revolutionary Romances of Simms.♦

Porgy, novel by DuBose Heyward,♦ published in 1925. The dramatization by the author and his wife Dorothy was awarded a Pulitzer Prize. Gershwin's *Porgy and Bess* (1935) is an opera based on the story.

In the black tenement section of the Charleston waterfront, known as Catfish Row, Porgy is a crippled beggar, celebrated for his luck with dice. He gambles regularly with the black men Robbins and Crown, until Crown kills Robbins in a quarrel and escapes to a thicket outside the town. Porgy denies knowledge of the crime, but old Peter, another denizen of the tenement, is imprisoned as a witness. Thus losing the friend who has helped him to move about, Porgy buys a goat cart, and continues to beg. Bess, formerly "Crown's Bess," becomes his mistress, and for a time they live happily together, until she returns to her addiction to narcotics and discovers Crown's hiding place. Porgy is forced to stab Crown, to protect Bess from his influence. He is not suspected of the murder, but is wanted as a witness, and is jailed when he tries to escape. After his release, he resumes his life in Catfish Row, but Bess, who has lost hope of his return, has left with a group of river workers for the cotton plantations.

Port Folio, The (1801–27), Philadelphia literary magazine founded by Joseph Dennie,♦ was published weekly during the first eight years, which constituted its most significant period. It followed Dennie's conservatism, which was both political and literary, decried the failure of American democracy and Webster's encouragement of an American idiom, and was typified by its editor's Addisonian "Lay Preacher" essays. Other contributors included the English poet Tom Moore, Joseph Hopkinson, Alexander Wilson, Nicholas Biddle, C.B. Brown, Royall Tyler, J.Q. Adams, Gouverneur Morris, T.G. Fessenden, and James Hall. The magazine became a monthly (1809) and later had a succession of editors. After 1816 it undertook to "vindicate the character of American literature and manners," and published much material about the West.

PORTER, COLE (1892–1964), wrote both music and lyrics of his works. Author of many "standards," Porter composed for Broadway musicals and for movies. Born to wealth in Peru, Ind., he went from Yale to Harvard Law, but switched to the School of Music and later studied at Schola Cantorum, Paris. His lyrics, nearly always highly sophisticated, can speak of sorrow ("Love for Sale"), or even "country" ("Don't Fence Me In"). Many of his intricately linked melodies and lyrics are haunting ("Night and Day," "Begin the Beguine"), but sometimes jubilant ("Blow, Gabriel, Blow," "You're the Top").

PORTER, DAVID (1780–1843), as a naval officer during the War of 1812 served in the Pacific, protecting American trade, capturing British whaling ships, and taking possession of the Marquesas islands, although the U.S. did not officially recognize this seizure. His account of his voyage, *A Journal of a Cruise Made to the Pacific Ocean, 1812–1814* (2 vols., 1815), contains a passage that suggested a sketch in Melville's *The Encantadas.* His later hostile acts against the friendly Spanish while he was suppressing piracy in the West Indies caused his suspension from the navy. With his son David Dixon Porter (1813–91) he went to Mexico and commanded its navy (1826–29), until his friend Jackson became President, and appointed him U.S. consul general to Algiers and later minister to Turkey. His letters to J.K. Paulding were published as *Constantinople and Its Environs* (2 vols., 1835). A *Memoir* of his life was published (1865) by his son, who rose to the rank of admiral, served in the Civil War, was superintendent of Annapolis, and wrote a naval history of the Civil War, his own memoirs, and two novels.

PORTER, ELEANOR HODGMAN (1868–1920), author of juvenile novels, best known for her character Pollyanna, the "glad girl." Her works include *Cross Currents* (1907), *Miss Billy* (1911), *Pollyanna* (1913), and *Pollyanna Grows Up* (1915).

PORTER, GENE STRATTON, see *Stratton-Porter.*

PORTER, KATHERINE ANNE (1890–1980), born in Texas of a family with a long Southern heritage, was educated in convent and private schools. She later traveled widely, and the settings for her fiction, in addition to her native state, include Mexico, where she lived for some time, and Germany, where she resided more briefly. France, where she lived during her first marriage, presumably did not affect her literary career, except that she translated an old *French Song-Book* (1933). Her early stories, published as *Flowering Judas*♦ (1930), immediately won her a critical reputation as a pure stylist who handled complex subjects with economy while penetrating the psychology of characters with great subtlety. *Hacienda* (1934) and *Noon Wine* (1937) are stories of intense emotions, the former being set in Mexico and concerned with the making of a film by the Soviet cinema director Eisenstein, the latter set on a Texas farm and dealing with a homicidal maniac. *Pale Horse, Pale Rider* (1939) incorporates *Noon Wine* with two other long stories, "Old Mortality" and the title piece, about a girl's love for a soldier who dies in an epidemic during

World War I. Stories were also gathered in *The Leaning Tower* (1944) and *Collected Stories* (1965). *The Days Before* (1952) collects personal essays, articles, and book reviews. In 1962 appeared the long awaited novel *Ship of Fools,* a moral allegory about the voyage of life and, according to the author, the way in which "evil is always done with the collusion of good," treated by means of presenting a variety of people—most of them Germans on the eve of Hitler's accession—as they travel on the *Vera,* a passenger freighter, from Mexico to Germany during 27 days of 1931. Her life work as a creator of stories was recognized by both a National Book Award and a Pulitzer Prize in 1966. In 1977 she published a brief memoir, *The Never-Ending Wrong,* about her protests during the Sacco-Vanzetti case. Her *Letters* (1990) appeared next.

PORTER, NOAH (1811–92), professor of moral philosophy and metaphysics at Yale (1846–71) and president of the college (1871–86). Although a staunch Calvinist and bitter opponent of Darwinism, he is considered a leader of modern thought because his book *The Human Intellect* (1868) was an important early work on psychology. His other books include *The Sciences of Nature Versus the Science of Man* (1871) and *Science and Humanity* (1872).

PORTER, WILLIAM SYDNEY (1862–1910), best known by his pseudonym O. Henry, was born in North Carolina, where after a brief schooling he worked in a drugstore. In 1882 he went to Texas to seek his fortune, and after trying his hand at various types of work, including a position as teller in an Austin bank (1891–94), founded a humorous weekly, *The Rolling Stone* (1894–95), and wrote for a Houston paper (1895–96) a daily column whose main staple was humorous anecdotes. In 1896 he was indicted for alleged embezzlement of funds at the bank for which he had worked. Since the bank was loosely run and his loss of a small sum was a case of technical mismanagement rather than crime, he might have been acquitted had he not fled to Honduras, from which he returned to Austin when his wife was on her deathbed. During his three-year imprisonment, he began to write short stories based on the life he knew in Texas, Honduras, and elsewhere, and it was the penitentiary ordeal that changed him from a newspaper columnist to a mature author.

After his release he went to New York (1902) to continue his literary career, and remained there for the rest of his life, making the city the scene of much of his fiction. As a contributor to magazines he became immensely popular, turning out stories at the rate of one a week. *Cabbages and Kings* (1904), his first book, is a series of stories of revolution and adventure in Latin America, integrated by a loose general plot and a single group of characters into the form of a novel. His

later collections of stories followed each other with great rapidity: *The Four Million* (1906), *Heart of the West* (1907), *The Trimmed Lamp* (1907), *The Gentle Grafter* (1908), *The Voice of the City* (1908), *Options* (1909), *Roads of Destiny* (1909), *Whirligigs* (1910), and *Strictly Business* (1910). He had written so prolifically that after his death posthumous collections continued to appear, including *Sixes and Sevens* (1911), *Rolling Stones* (1913), *Waifs and Strays* (1917), and *Postscripts* (1923). "A Retrieved Reformation," his story of a reformed burglar, was the basis of Paul Armstrong's popular play *Alias Jimmy Valentine* (1909).

Although his stories are set in many parts of the U.S., as well as in Central and South America, Porter is best known for his observations on the diverse lives of everyday New Yorkers, "the four million" neglected by other writers. He had a fine gift of humor and was adept at the ingenious depiction of ironic circumstances, in plots frequently dependent upon coincidence. A master in presenting vignettes of the whirligig of fortune, he saw life always in episodic form and was incapable of longer unified work or any philosophic generalization of his fatalistic outlook. His characters, plain, simple people, and his plots, depending often on the surprise ending, have little diversification, but he was skilled at ringing the changes on a few themes. "The Gift of the Magi" and "The Furnished Room," in *The Four Million,* ◆ are among the best known of the tales that illustrate his technique of ironic coincidence and the surprise ending. *O. Henry Encore* (1939) is a collection of stories and illustrations recovered from his early contributions to the Houston *Post.*

PORTER, WILLIAM T[ROTTER] (1809–58), born in Vermont, began his journalistic career there before moving to New York City, where in 1831 he established the *Spirit of the Times,* ◆ a racy chronicle primarily distinguished for its publication of tales of the Old Southwestern frontier. From it he collected material by such authors as T.B. Thorpe, G.W. Harris, J.J. Hooper, and W.T. Thompson in *The Big Bear of Arkansas* ◆ (1845) and *A Quarter Race in Kentucky* (1847).

Porter's Spirit of the Times, see *Spirit of the Times.*

Portico, The (1816–18), monthly literary magazine, published from Baltimore by the Delphian Club. ◆ It was chauvinistic in its admiration of the U.S. and sternly criticized foreign authors. John Neal was an editor, and J.P. Kennedy may have been an anonymous contributor.

PORTIS, CHARLES [MCCOLL] (1933–), novelist born in Arkansas, educated at the University of Arkansas, and a resident of Little Rock. After a hitch in the Marines and a career as reporter and London correspondent for the New York *Herald Tribune,* Portis published *Norwood* (1966), a novel about a Kerouac-like cross-country journey, with high humor in a Southern accent. But it was his next book, *True Grit* (1968), that established him as an original comic voice. It has as narrator a 14-year-old girl seeking vengeance against her father's killer. She chooses for her instrument one Rooster Cogburn, a Falstaffian marshal possessing "true grit." Both characters are memorable. *The Dog of the South* (1979) is a quest by the narrator to find the wife who took his car, her trail festooned by charges to his credit cards all the way to Mexico. *Gringos* (1991) features an expatriate American in Mexico and Guatemala and his picaresque adventures.

Portnoy's Complaint, novel by Philip Roth,♦ published in 1969.

Told as if to a psychiatrist, Dr. Spielvogel, the story is the autobiography of Alexander Portnoy of Newark, N.J., the bright but driven son of Sophie, a quintessential "Jewish mother" type, given to playing Mah-Jongg, worrying about warm clothes, fatty foods, money, and manners, and her passive husband Jack, a life insurance salesman. The price Portnoy pays for his mother's domination and his accomplishments at school is his compulsive masturbation, carried on in all ways and all places. As he matures, with achievements at Columbia Law School and as a lawyer for a congressional committee, he graduates also to more mature but equally compulsive sexual activity with a variety of Gentile girls, though with a final Oedipal irony, during a visit to Israel, he becomes impotent when attempting to have sex with the forceful Jewish women he meets there.

Portrait of a Lady, *The,* novel by Henry James,♦ published in 1881.

Mrs. Touchett, estranged wife of an expatriated American banker, brings to England her penniless niece, Isabel Archer, in her early twenties, intelligent and beautiful, who immediately attracts old Mr. Touchett, his invalid son Ralph, and their wealthy neighbor, Lord Warburton. The nobleman proposes marriage, but Isabel refuses him, and her courage and independence win the admiration of the Touchetts. Casper Goodwood, a sincere, persistent suitor, comes from America to renew his proposal, but Isabel tells him that her personal independence is her most valued possession and that she must have two years before giving him her answer. Ralph is also in love with her, but realizes that they cannot marry and arranges for her financial security by persuading his father to make her his heir. At the old man's death, Isabel becomes wealthy and goes to Florence with Mrs. Touchett. There Madame Merle, a gracious expatriate, introduces her to Gilbert Osmond, an American dilettante and widower. Incapable of perceiving that he desires her fortune, Isabel is won by Osmond's taste and intellectual detachment, despite the protests of Casper and her other friends. During the following years, she becomes aware of her husband's shallow aestheticism and lack of moral depth, but decides against a separation because of her pride, determination to fulfill her obligations, and sympathy for Pansy, Osmond's frail young daughter. Warburton, who still loves her, becomes a constant visitor and seeks to marry Pansy. Madame Merle is active in this new matchmaking, and she and Osmond urge Isabel to use her influence with Warburton, but Isabel withdraws when Pansy shows that she does not desire the marriage. This widens the breach between Isabel and her husband, who accuses her of an affair with Warburton. Summoned to England, where Ralph is dying, Isabel feels that she may never return to Italy, especially when she learns that Pansy's mother is Madame Merle. After comforting Ralph on his deathbed, she is joined by Casper, for whom she finally admits her affection. Conscience and her duty to Pansy dominate her desires, however, and she dismisses Casper and returns to her unhappy home.

PORY, John (1572–1635), English geographer and colonist, studied under Hakluyt and came to Virginia (1619) as secretary of state for the colony. While on a trading voyage, he was wrecked in the Azores and captured by Spaniards, but managed to return to England. His lively accounts of Virginia were published in Smith's *Generall Historie* and later scholarly collections.

POST, Emily (1873–1960), author of *Etiquette* (1922, frequently revised), a very popular and widely accepted guide to good behavior and social proprieties.

POST, Melville Davisson (1871–1930), popular author of mystery novels and detective stories, whose ability at plot structure in the latter form won him attention from serious literary critics. His books include *The Man of Last Resort* (1897); *Corrector of Destinies* (1909); *The Nameless Thing* (1912); and *Uncle Abner: Master of Mysteries* (1918), tales of the sleuthing of a colonial Virginia squire.

POSTL, Karl, see *Sealsfield, Charles.*

Postman Always Rings Twice, *The,* novel by James M. Cain.♦

Pot of Earth, *The,* free-verse narrative by MacLeish,♦ published in 1925.

Based on a primitive fertility legend in Frazer's *The Golden Bough,* concerning the gardens of Adonis, this bitter, sensuously wrought narrative is presented in three parts: "The Sowing of the Dead Corn," describing the mystery and terror of the heroine's sexual awakening; "The Shallow Grass," telling of her marriage and pregnancy; and "The Carrion Spring," in which her child is born dead, and she herself dies, ending a futile life, symbolic of the poet's pessimism.

Potawatami Indians, Algonquian tribe affiliated with the Ojibway and Ottawa. They aided the French in the French and Indian Wars, joined in Pontiac's Rebellion, and were on the side of the British during the Revolution and the War of 1812. They figure in Cooper's *Oak Openings.*

Potiphar Papers, The, seven satirical sketches of New York society by G.W. Curtis,♦ published in 1853. Portraying the hypocrisies and foibles of "our best society," the author considers this class to be composed of three types: first, the rich; second, those who belong to "the good old families"; and, third, "a swarm of youths who can dance dexterously, and who are invited for that purpose" to stupid, absurd parties. Beneath the surface of comedy there is an undercurrent of serious thought, for Curtis perceived dangerous tendencies in this society. The book is notable for its depiction of such characters as the socially ambitious Mrs. Potiphar, her philosophically resigned husband, and the tenderly sympathetic Reverend Cream Cheese.

POTTER, PAUL MEREDITH (1853–1921), English-born dramatist, after his early journalistic career in the U.S., won a reputation as a dramatizer of such romantic novels as Du Maurier's *Trilby* (1895), Ouida's *Under Two Flags* (1901), and Balzac's *The Honor of the Family* (1907). Potter's best-known original play was *The Ugly Duckling* (1890).

Poulson's American Daily Advertiser, see *Pennsylvania Packet.*

POUND, EZRA [WESTON LOOMIS] (1885–1972), Idaho-born poet and critic, reared in Pennsylvania, attended the University of Pennsylvania and Hamilton College, and taught briefly at Wabash College, until dismissed because of his impatience with academic ways, despite his scholarly ability. He went to Italy (1908), where his first book, *A Lume Spento* ["a dim light"] (1908), was published. He later lived in London (1908–20), in Paris (1920–24), and until the end of World War II at Rapallo, Italy.

In 1909 he published two volumes of verse, *Personae* and *Exultations* (poems from both reprinted as *Personae,* 1926), whose intensity and disciplined metrical experimentation attracted attention, as did his knowledge of medieval literature, Provençal singers, and troubadour ballads. *Provença* (1910), *Canzoni* (1911), and *Riposes* (1912) extended the paths he had marked for himself, but also indicated his tendency to allow esoteric lore to become an unduly important part of his poetry. This trend continues in his translation of *The Sonnets and Ballate of Guido Cavalcanti* (1912); *Cathay* (1915), translations from the Chinese, based on notes of Fenollosa; *Umbra* (1920); translations and selections from some of his earlier poems; and *Hugh Selwyn Mauberley♦* (1920).

He began to scatter his interests and became a leader of the Imagists,♦ and sponsored diverse authors in the anthologies and little magazines that he helped edit. He established the importance of such journals as *Poetry* and *The Little Review,* and wrote much about his successive enthusiasms, later generally acknowledged as significant. Those he championed include T.S. Eliot, James Joyce, Tagore, the musician George Antheil, and the sculptor Gaudier-Brzeska.

Lustra (1916), including earlier work, was followed by *Quia Pauper Amavi* (1919), containing the first three cantos of a lengthy work, with a flexible, conversation-like structure. His later poetry was almost entirely devoted to these *Cantos,♦* finally collected in 1970. They are so filled with esoteric lore and recondite theories that they often seem pedantic and confusing, yet they have had a tremendous influence on modern poetry, and works that are indebted to them include *The Waste Land, The Bridge,* and *Conquistador.*

Pound's prose includes *The Spirit of Romance* (1910); *Certain Noble Plays of Japan* (1916) and *Noh—or, Accomplishment* (1916), edited from the notes of Fenollosa, whose literary executor he was; *Gaudier-Brzeska* (1916), a biography; *Pavannes and Divisions* (1918); *Instigations* (1920); *Indiscretions* (1923); *Antheil and the Treatise on Harmony* (1924); *ABC of Economics* (1933); *ABC of Reading* (1934); *Make It New* (1934); *Jefferson and/or Mussolini* (1935); *Polite Essays* (1937); *Guide to Kulchur* (1938, revised 1952); *Money Pamphlets by Pound* (1950–52); *The Literary Essays* (1954), collected with an introduction by T.S. Eliot; *Pavannes and Divagations* (1958); and *Impact, Essays on Ignorance and the Decline of American Civilization* (1960), a compilation on politics, economics, and literature. His *Letters, 1907–41* was published in 1950. Later translations include *Confucius: The Unwobbling Pivot and the Great Digest* (1947); *Confucian Analects* (1951); *The Classic Anthology* (1954), Chinese poems; *Great Digest and the Unwobbling Pivot* (1954); and *The Women of Trachis* (1956), a version of Sophocles' play. Other late published books include *Patria Mia,* reflections on American culture, issued in *The New Age* in installments (1912) and as a book in 1950, and *Redondillas,* a poem of 114 lines issued in Australia in 1967 and in the U.S. in a 110-copy edition (1968).

Pound, who termed himself a "Jeffersonian Republican," professed to find "the heritage of Jefferson" in Mussolini's Italy, and prior to World War II espoused political views that included opposition to capitalism, the Jews, and the English, and support of the principle of censorship. During the war he broadcast Fascist propaganda over the Rome radio, and was afterward returned to the U.S. to face trial for treason. Adjudged to be of unsound mind, he was committed (1946–58) to a sanitarium instead of being tried. When the indictment was finally withdrawn he was released, and he returned to Italy.

POUND, ROSCOE (1870–1964), Nebraska-born jurist, dean of the Harvard Law School (1916–37), was later a "roving" professor at Harvard. His books include *The Spirit of the Common Law* (1921), *Introduction to the Philosophy of Law* (1922), *Law and Morals* (1924), and *Criminal Justice in America* (1930).

POWELL, JOHN WESLEY (1834–1902), reared in Illinois, after service in the Civil War, in which he rose to be a major but lost his right arm, he taught geology and led expeditions, the most notable being one which by boats explored, mapped, and obtained geologic data on the Green and Colorado rivers (1869). This and a second trip (1872) are reported in *Exploration of the Colorado River of the West and Its Tributaries* (1875), revised as *Canyons of the Colorado* (1895), a scientific but colorful book. After more geographic and geologic work, he entered the U.S. Geological and Geographical Survey (1875) and wrote a precise, sociologically realistic *Report on the Lands of the Arid Region of the U.S.* (1878). Under his administration (1881–94), the greatly expanded Survey issued many detailed maps and surveys clarifying Western topography, geology, irrigation, and ethnology. His scientific standards, concepts of government planning, and organization of bureaus helped shape U.S. reclamation and conservation policies. His "second opening of the west" is the subject of Wallace Stegner's *Beyond the Hundredth Meridian* (1954).

POWELL, THOMAS (1809–87), English-born hack writer, collaborated with Wordsworth, Leigh Hunt, and others in *The Poems of Geoffrey Chaucer Modernized* (1841), but came to the U.S. (1849) when accused of literary forgery that still causes some of his work to be attributed to Browning and Hunt. He became a bohemian habitué of Pfaff's Cellar and a journalist, and wrote *The Living Authors of America* (1850) and "Leaves from My Life" (1886).

Power of Sympathy, *The; or, The Triumph of Nature,* anonymously published in 1789, is called "the first American novel." Although now known to be by William Hill Brown,♦ it was long attributed to Sarah W. Morton♦ because it deals partly with events in her life.

An epistolary romance, the work fulfills the purpose announced in its preface, "To Expose the dangerous Consequences of Seduction" and to set forth "the Advantages of Female Education." The main plot deals with the threatened incestuous marriage of Harrington and Harriot, both children of the elder Harrington, the first by his legitimate marriage, the second by his mistress Maria. When the relationship is discovered, Harriot dies of shock and sadness and Harrington commits suicide. A subordinate incident deals with the suicide of Ophelia Shepherd after her seduction by her brother-in-law Martin. This parallels the suicide of Mrs. Morton's sister after her alleged seduction by Mr. Morton.

POWERS, J[AMES] F[ARL] (1917–), born and educated in Illinois, first achieved a reputation with his stories of the various lives of the Catholic clergy of the Midwest in *Prince of Darkness* (1947) and *The Presence of Grace* (1956). *Morte d'Urban* (1962), which won a National Book Award, is a novel about the life of Father Urban, a worldly but dedicated worker for his order in modern America. Later stories, many also about priests, and a short play appear in *Look How the Fish Live* (1975). Powers returned to the novel in *Wheat That Springeth Green* (1988), a work marked by a comic point of view in treating the experiences of a young priest concerned with the flesh and other temptations.

Powhatan Indians, confederacy of Algonquian tribes in Virginia and Maryland, were visited by some of the earliest explorers and are noted for their relations with the settlement at Jamestown (1607). Hostilities provoked by the exactions of the colonists ended when Pocahontas,♦ daughter of the chief known as Powhatan, married the English settler John Rolfe. After Powhatan's death (1618), a successor, Opechancanough, led a general uprising that resulted in the destruction of every white settlement except those around Jamestown. The ensuing war of extermination lasted 14 years (1622–36). Another serious uprising was led by the same chief in 1641. After his capture and execution, the confederacy was broken up and its tribes declined.

POWNALL, THOMAS (1722–1805), British statesman and colonial governor, came to America (1753) and was governor of Massachusetts (1757–59). After returning to England he wrote *The Administration of the Colonies* (1764), urging a centralized organization of all British possessions on a basis of commercial interests. Before, during, and after the Revolution he showed a desire for good relations with the colonies, again on a commercial basis.

Pragmatism: *A New Name for Some Old Ways of Thinking,* lectures by William James♦ delivered at the Lowell Institute and at Columbia (1906–7), and published in 1907. *The Meaning of Truth*♦ is a sequel.

Asserting the inadequacy of both rationalism and empiricism in "the present dilemma in philosophy," James proposes pragmatism as "a mediating system."

> A pragmatist . . . turns away from abstraction and insufficiency, from verbal solutions, from bad *a priori* reasons, from fixed principles, closed systems, and pretended absolutes and origins. He turns towards concreteness and adequacy, towards facts, towards action and towards power.

Pragmatism is not new; it is a more radical empiricism, which regards theories not as answers, but as instruments. The laws of science are useful only "to summarize old facts and to lead to new ones," and, more generally, "ideas (which themselves are but parts of our experiences) become true just in so far as they help us to get into satisfactory relation with other parts of our experience." A truth is anything that "proves itself to be good in the way of belief, and good, too, for definite, assignable reasons." Having established this distinction, James applies it to such metaphysical problems as those of substance, personal identity, materialism, design, and "free-will." He opposes the dogmatism of absolute monism and states his own pluralistic belief. Common sense is on the side of pragmatism, and is indeed its origin, for truth is "expedient thinking," having its text and context in human experience, which is its center and justification. Finally he discusses pragmatism in relation to religious questions, and contends that here too it mediates between extreme views, being conducive to useful possibilities, and, in the aptest sense, moral, for it is grounded in the present world of acts and facts.

Prairie, free-verse poem by Sandburg, ♦ published in *Cornhuskers* (1918). This warm appreciation of the fertility and beauty of the lands "between the sheds of the Rocky Mountains and the Appalachians," which were the poet's home, expresses an optimistic faith in the will and ability of the "cornhusker" and the "prairie girl," and concludes that though "yesterday is a wind gone down," there is "an ocean of to-morrows, a sky of to-morrows."

Prairie, The, romance by Cooper, ♦ published in 1827. It is the fifth in plot sequence of the Leather-Stocking Tales. ♦

Natty Bumppo, though nearly 90 in 1804, is still competent as a frontiersman and trapper on the Western plains, clinging to his faithful hound Hector and his rifle Killdeer. He encounters an emigrant train led by surly Ishmael Bush and his rascally brother-in-law Abiram White, in whose party are also the naturalist Dr. Obed Battins; a woman captive concealed in a covered wagon; her attendant, Ellen Wade; and the bee-hunter Paul Hover, who is in love with Ellen. The old trapper barely averts an Indian raid on the train, which he then guides to a safe camp. He is joined by a young soldier, Duncan Uncas Middleton, whom he is overjoyed to recognize as a descendant of an old friend, Duncan Heyward (see *Last of the Mohicans*). Middleton, on an army mission, is also seeking his betrothed, Doña Inez de Certavallos, who has been kidnapped for ransom. Discovering that she is Ishmael's captive, he rescues her with the aid of the trapper. With Paul and Ellen, they leave the emigrants, only to be captured by the Sioux. Escaping, they are endangered successively by a prairie fire and a buffalo stampede, but saved by the skill of Bumppo. Recaptured by the Sioux, they are rescued by a suc-

cessful Pawnee attack, but during the confusion Ishmael captures them. He accuses Bumppo of the murder of one of his men, but Abiram is found to be guilty. After his friends find safety with Middleton's soldiers, Bumppo finally yields to the weakness of his years, and dies quietly, surrounded by his Pawnee and white friends.

Prairie region, the level, unforested farming area, formerly grassland, that stretches westward from the Ohio River to the Plains region. ♦ The Prairie states include Ohio, Indiana, Illinois, and Iowa, as well as eastern North and South Dakota, northern Missouri, and southern Wisconsin, Minnesota, and Michigan, encompassing much of the Midwest. The Mississippi River ♦ flows through the center of the region, originally the Northwest Territory, ♦ whose culture has come to be considered distinctively American, with Abraham Lincoln as its typical hero. Since the pioneering period of the late 18th and early 19th century, described by James Fenimore Cooper and others, the Prairie states have become the nation's food-producing center, with a large, stable farming population, and with great cities like Chicago ♦ as points of distribution. Representative authors include Edward Eggleston, Booth Tarkington, James Whitcomb Riley, and other Hoosiers; Wisconsin writers such as Hamlin Garland, Zona Gale, and Glenway Wescott; O.E. Rölvaag, who wrote of Norwegian and Irish immigrants in the Dakotas; and many whose careers are in some way associated with the Chicago school, including Dreiser, Herrick, E.L. Masters, Sandburg, Lindsay, Sinclair Lewis, Sherwood Anderson, and Hemingway. The paintings of Grant Wood are expressive of the life of rural Iowa; Louis Sullivan and J.W. Root were the first of the Chicago school in architecture that has influenced urban construction by introducing the skyscraper; and Frank Lloyd Wright's "Prairie style" of domestic architecture was designed to be appropriate to the Midwestern landscape.

Prairie Schooner, *The* (1927–), literary quarterly associated with the University of Nebraska, founded and edited until 1956 by Lowry Charles Wimberly, who was succeeded by Karl Shapiro (1956–63), who made the magazine less regional and placed more emphasis on poetry.

Prayers of Steel, free-verse poem by Sandburg, ♦ published in *Cornhuskers* (1918). Symbolizing the attitude of the modern worker, the poet represents the unformed metal as supplicating.

> Lay me on an anvil, O God. Beat me and hammer me into a steel spike . . . Let me be the great nail holding a skyscraper through blue nights into white stars.

Praying Indians, name applied to the New England tribes, including the Nauset and Massachuset, which were early converted to Christianity. They remained friendly with the colonists during King Philip's War, and were led for a time by Daniel Gookin.♦ Among the missionaries to these Indians were John Eliot,♦ Thomas Mayhew,♦ and Experience Mayhew.♦

Precaution, novel by Cooper.♦

Preface to Morals, A, philosophic work by Walter Lippmann.♦

Prejudices, six series of critical essays by H.L. Mencken,♦ published in 1919, 1920, 1922, 1924, 1926, and 1927. A selected volume appeared in 1927.

These frankly biased, raucous effusions, on a wide variety of literary and cultural topics, won Mencken both devoted followers and indignant opponents during the 1920s. First published in *The Smart Set, The American Mercury,* the New York *Evening Mail,* and the Boston *Evening Star,* they exhibit their author's bold iconoclasm, vital prose, and crusading zeal against university education, equalitarianism, puritanical morality, sentimentalism, religion, the New Humanism, poetry, and business-class culture. Through these essays, he inspired and campaigned for critical American fiction, championing Dreiser, Cabell, and Sinclair Lewis, and pressed his enthusiasms for such writers as Clemens, Poe, Huneker, and Bierce, and for the music of the great German composers. Besides his mélange of classicism and journalistic audacity, he was noted for his ability at destructive criticism, typified in "The Sahara of the Bozart," attacking the sterility of Southern culture; "Bryan," ridiculing the statesman's provincialism and Fundamentalism; "Professor Veblen," decrying the obscure style and allegedly empty generalizations of the economist; and "The National Letters," asserting that American literature is on a mediocre level because of the absence of a cultural background and a civilized aristocracy.

PRENTICE, GEORGE DENNISON (1802–70), Connecticut-born editor of the *Louisville Daily Journal*♦ (1830–68), a prominent Kentucky paper, to which he contributed the caustic squibs and *bons mots* collected as *Prenticeana* (1860). His *Poems* were collected in 1876 and 1883.

Presbyterianism, system of church polity, occupying a middle position between episcopacy and congregationalism. Its organization is administered by representative courts, composed of clerical and lay presbyters of equal status, divided, according to their functions, into ministers and ruling elders. Such polity may be found throughout the history of the Christian church, but its modern movement is primarily attributed to the doctrine of Calvin. In its simple form of worship, the Bible is considered the sole rule of faith and conduct, the two sacraments being baptism and the Lord's Supper. Presbyterianism was first introduced in America by French Huguenot followers of Jean Ribaut, who settled in South Carolina (1562) and by followers of Laudonnière, who settled in Florida (1564). Groups of Presbyterians settled in most of the English colonies during the 17th century, many of them coming from Scotland. They flourished particularly in New England, whose churches have been described as representing "a Congregationalized Presbyterianism." The first organization of the various churches was accomplished by Francis Makemie in the late 17th century. During the Great Awakening, a split occurred between the evangelical New Side and the conservative Old Side, the former group, under the direction of the Tennents, being responsible for the founding of Princeton University. Presbyterians were particularly strong on the frontier, where under a Plan of Union with Congregationalists they frequently presided over mixed congregations. There have been various schisms, most of them temporary.

PRESCOTT, HARRIET, see *Spofford, Harriet.*

PRESCOTT, WILLIAM HICKLING (1796–1859), member of a prominent Massachusetts family, was born at Salem and educated at Harvard (A.B., 1814; M.A., 1817), where the course of his life was changed when, during boyish play, he was hit in the eye by a hard crust of bread. Although blinded in one eye and virtually incapable of using the other, he determined upon a literary career. He went to Europe (1815–17) to convalesce and get background for historical writing. His first works in his chosen field of Spanish history were articles and reviews, which, with other essays and a short "Life of Charles Brockden Brown," were collected in *Biographical and Critical Miscellanies* (1845). Three years of preparation preceded the writing of the first chapter of the *History of . . . Ferdinand and Isabella,* begun in 1829 and published in three volumes (1838). The reception of this accurate but picturesque history encouraged him to write his *History of the Conquest of Mexico* (3 vols., 1843), upon which he began research in 1839. This work, in an almost neglected field, has come to be considered his greatest triumph, not only because of its historical accuracy, but because of its epic sweep, which, following in the vein of Scott, arranged itself around the two heroic figures of Cortés and Montezuma to create a dramatic tragedy. The only criticism of the *Conquest of Mexico,* leveled also at Prescott's other writings, is that he was so concerned with the large panorama that he tended to neglect social and economic problems, and based his structure on documented romance rather than a philosophy of history. *History of the Conquest of Peru* (2 vols., 1847) is a shorter companion piece, utilizing the same method of a dramatic, large-scale canvas, with the figure of Pizarro as its center. It is considered to be less unified and less valuable, however, because of its less comprehensive survey of the background of civilization. After a trip abroad (1850), during which his English reputation was signalized by an Oxford degree and a reception by the queen, Prescott returned to write *History of the Reign of Philip the Second,* begun in 1849 and hastened by his realization that, with his failing sight, he might never cover the extensive materials. Planned to include four volumes, the work included only three by the time of his death (the first two in 1855, the last in 1858). His work on this book was interrupted by his preparation of an appendix to *The History of the Reign of the Emperor Charles the Fifth* (1857) by William Robertson, who, with Scott, was his master.

Present, *The* (Sept. 1843–April 1844), monthly periodical edited by W.H. Channing "to aid all movements which seem fitted to produce union and growth in Religion, Science and Society." Its brief life may be attributed to the excessive breadth, enthusiasm, and indefiniteness of its program of reform. Contributions included translations from French and German authors, some of Alcott's "Orphic Sayings," poems by C.P. Cranch and W.E. Channing, and writings by Margaret Fuller, Lowell, and C.A. Dana.

Present State of the New-English Affairs, *The,* broadside printed and published by Samuel Green of Boston (1689), "to prevent False Reports." It was concerned with the attitude of William III toward New England after the overthrow of the Andros government, as exhibited in an account of an interview between Increase Mather and the king, a letter on the same subject from Increase to his son Cotton, and an order by William to return Andros to England. Although frequently called the first American newspaper, it gives no evidence that another issue was intended.

Presidential Medal of Freedom, initially (1945–63) to honor government service, since 1963 has been given upon occasion to acknowledge contributions in the arts. Winners include Thornton Wilder and Edmund Wilson (1963); J. Frank Dobie, T.S. Eliot, Samuel Eliot Morison, Lewis Mumford, Sandburg, and Steinbeck (1964); Ralph Ellison (1969); Bruce Catton, Ariel and Will Durant, MacLeish, and Michener (1977); Rachel Carson (posthumous), R.P. Warren, Eudora Welty, Tennessee Williams (1980); Eric Hoffer, Clare Booth Luce, Dumas Malone (1983); and Louis L'Amour (1984).

PRESTON, MARGARET JUNKIN (1820–97), Pennsylvania-born poet of the Confederacy, whose works include *Beechenbrook: A Rhyme of the War* (1865), *Old Song and New* (1870), and *Cartoons* (1875). Her major prose work is *Silverwood: A Book of Memories* (1856). Her sister was the wife of "Stonewall" Jackson.

Pretty Story, *A,* pamphlet by Francis Hopkinson,♦ published under the pseudonym Peter Grievous. A satirical political allegory, tracing the events that led up to the first Continental Congress, it was issued at Philadelphia (Sept. 1774) during the assembling of the Congress.

An old Nobleman (George III), possessing a valuable farm (England), permits some of his children to settle on his new farm (America), with the provision that they must purchase from his shop all their merchandise (Navigation Acts), although they may make some of their own laws. The Nobleman's Wife (Parliament) lays taxes upon the New Farm, and sends lazy servants to spy upon it. Meanwhile the Steward (Ministry) debauches the old Nobleman's Wife, and, gaining power over her, orders the children to stamp all their plate with a certain mark, for which they are to pay a stipend (Stamp Act). He also orders the new settlers to pay a tax on Water-Gruel (tea tax), but one of them named Jack (Boston), driven to despair, demolishes a cargo of this gruel (Boston Tea Party). Vengeance follows when Jack's gate is padlocked (Boston Port bill), and an overseer (General Gage) is sent to hector him and his family. Finally Jack and the other families of the New Farm are so irritated that. . . . Here the story breaks off with a row of 13 stars.

PRICE, REYNOLDS (1933–), North Carolina-born author, graduated from Duke and has taught there, after a Rhodes scholarship to Oxford. His fiction, set in his native state, includes *A Long and Happy Life* (1962) and *A Generous Man* (1963), both concerning a small-town North Carolina family; *Love and Work* (1968), about a young teacher-novelist's problems with marriage and writing; and *The Surface of the Earth* (1975), presenting the saga of rural Virginia and North Carolina families during the first 40 years of the 20th century, continued in *The Source of Light* (1981), concentrating on a grandson studying at Oxford in the 1960s until called back to his ancestral home. Succeeding novels are *Kate Vaiden* (1986), telling of a woman's new relationship with a son deserted many years early and of other strange associations; *Good Hearts* (1988), treating the mid-life experiences of characters from the early *A Long and Happy Life;* and *The Tongues of Angels* (1990), about young men at a summer camp for boys. *Blue Calhoun* (1992) has as narrator a 65-year-old salesman in a music store in Raleigh, N.C. Blue's tale is told in a long letter to his granddaughter and ranges over the signal events of his life. *The Names and Faces of Heroes* (1963) and *Permanent Errors* (1970) print stories; *Collected Stories* appeared in 1993. *Things Themselves* (1972) and *A Common Room* (1972) collected personal and critical essays. *A Palpable God* (1978) is an essay on and translation of Biblical stories. *Vital Provisions* (1982) and *The Laws of Ice* (1986) are books of poetry. *Clear Pictures, First Loves, First Guides* (1984) is a memoir of Price's youth.

PRIESTLEY, JOSEPH (1733–1804), English physicist and educator, wrote *Essay on the First Principles of Government* (1768), which suggested the doctrine of "the greatest happiness of the greatest number" to Jeremy Bentham. His utilitarian and republican views were extended in pamphlets favoring the American colonies and the French Revolution. Popular hostility was aroused by his *Letters to . . . Edmund Burke* (1791), with the result that his house and scientific apparatus were destroyed, and he emigrated to Philadelphia (1794). There he continued his scientific experimentation and religious and political liberalism, expounded in such books as *Unitarianism Explained and Defended* (1796) and *A General History of the Christian Church* (1802). He was bitterly attacked by Cobbett in *Observations on Dr. Priestley's Emigration* (1794).

PRIME, BENJAMIN YOUNGS (1733–91), New York physician whose poems on the French and Indian Wars were published in *The Patriot Muse* (1764). During the Revolution he produced several popular political songs and the lengthy poetical review of the entire war *Columbia's Glory* (1791).

PRINCE, THOMAS (1687–1758), member of a prominent Massachusetts family, graduated from Harvard (1709), preached in England, and became pastor of the Old South Church in Boston. He was an orthodox Congregationalist, as appears in his many published sermons, writings on the Indian conversions of Experience Mayhew, and pamphlets on remarkable providences. His *Chronological History of New England in the Form of Annals* (1736) was carefully based on such sources as the manuscript *History of Plimmoth Plantation* by Bradford, and on the plan of recording events in the order of time with exactness and brevity. Because he conceived of New England's history as the apex of the preceding history of the world, his introductory chronology presents great events from Adam to the accession of James I, but even the body of his text does not get beyond the year 1633. His religious orthodoxy was disturbed when he fell under the sway of Whitefield's evangelicalism, which he describes enthusiastically in *The Christian History* (1744–45). In 1758 he made a metrical translation of *The Psalms, Hymns, & Spiritual Songs of the Old and New Testaments.* The enormous library in which he carried on his zealous scholarship was partly destroyed during the Revolutionary War.

Prince and the Pauper, *The,* novel by Clemens,♦ published in 1882 under his pseudonym Mark Twain. Designed to be a children's book, it shows an essentially adult point of view in its attack on the social evils of Tudor England.

Prince Edward (later Edward VI) discovers Tom Canty, a pauper boy, to be his exact twin in appearance. When they exchange clothes, the prince is by error driven from the court, and the pauper is forced to act the part of royalty. Edward finds Tom's family, is mistreated, and runs away with Sir Miles Hendon, a disinherited knight, who takes pity on him, thinking his assertions of royal birth a sign of madness. In their wanderings, the prince sees the cruelty of church and court toward the poor, and learns the sufferings of his people through such dramatic incidents as the burning of two women whose only crime is that of being Baptists. Tom meanwhile is also thought unbalanced because of his peculiar behavior; becoming accustomed to his situation, however, he attempts to act the part of the real prince. On the morning of his coronation, Edward gets to Westminster Abbey and proves his identity by revealing the hiding place of the Great Seal, which Tom did not recognize after having taken it to crack some nuts. During his brief reign, Edward tempers the harshness of the law with a sense of justice, learned during his contact with the common people.

Prince of Parthia, *The,* romantic blank-verse tragedy by Thomas Godfrey,♦ written in 1759 and published in 1765. If it was actually produced in 1767, it was the first play by an American to be produced professionally. Set at the beginning of the Christian era, it has a plot derived form Elizabethan dramatic conventions and is a patchwork of passages imitating the work of Shakespeare, Addison, Marlowe, Rowe, Dryden, Beaumont, and Ambrose Philips.

Princess Casamassima, *The,* novel by Henry James,♦ published in 1886. The Princess also appears in *Roderick Hudson.*♦

Hyacinth Robinson, an illegitimate orphan, is raised by the quiet spinster Miss Pynsent in lower-class London, where he is influenced by the anarchist musician Anastasius Vetch and the French Communist bookbinder M. Pupin, who teaches him his trade. The youth's sympathy for the downtrodden is further stimulated by the realistic revolutionary Paul Muniment, who leads him to pledge his life to the cause. He also meets the Princess Casmassima, who is separated from her wealthy Italian husband, and in her Hyacinth encounters for the first time a spirit like his own, combining an artistic and aristocratic temperament with a profound, restless sympathy for the oppressed. After Miss Pynsent's death, he uses her small legacy to travel in Europe, where he discovers values whose existence he has never suspected, and returns realizing that revolution cannot effect his personal salvation. He is determined, however, to devote himself to the cause, and is soon called upon by Muniment to assassinate a certain duke. The Princess, partly to save Hyacinth, partly to associate herself more closely with the revolutionaries, sets herself to fascinate Muniment, who nevertheless refuses to interfere. Hyacinth is in despair, believing that the two have abandoned him. Finally the Princess offers herself as a substitute in the assassination, and goes to inform Hyacinth. On arriving at his rooms, she finds that he has committed suicide.

Princeton Review, The, see *Biblical Repertory.*

Priscilla, heroine of *The Courtship of Miles Standish.* ♦ Another character of this name appears in *The Blithedale Romance.* ♦

Professor at the Breakfast-Table, The, essays by Holmes, ♦ published in 1860. It is a sequel to *The Autocrat of the Breakfast-Table.* ♦

Professor's House, The, novel by Willa Cather, ♦ published in 1925.

Godfrey St. Peter, professor at a Midwestern university, on reaching middle age completes his great work on the Spanish adventures in America. He is now well-to-do, but does not desire material comfort, and, when he and his pleasure-loving wife Lillian move to a beautiful new home, he keeps the homely old house whose garret study he has long shared as a workroom with the German seamstress Augusta. His daughters have grown away from him since their marriages. Rosamond to Louie Marsellus, a lavish, enterprising Jew, and Kathleen to Scott McGregor, a journalist who suppresses his artistic leanings to write "glad" pieces for a living. Marsellus is rich, having marketed a gas patent bequeathed to his wife by her former fiancé, Tom Outland, the professor's favorite student, who died in World War I. The story of Outland's exploration, with his companion Roddy Blake, of an ancient New Mexican cliff city, is recalled by the professor. Marsellus's patronizing attitude toward the dead Outland alienates the professor, but his generosity and love of beauty strike a sympathetic chord in Lillian, who tours Europe with him and Rosamond. During a lonely summer, the professor loses interest in life, and when gas from a faulty stove fills his study one night, he is about to let it suffocate him when he is saved by Augusta. This crisis, and his appreciation of the quiet patience of the old seamstress, reconcile him to continued existence, which he faces with a certain apathy but "at least . . . the ground under his feet."

Professor's Story, The, see *Elsie Venner.*

Progress and Poverty, economic treatise by Henry George, ♦ published in 1879.

Attempting to discover why individual poverty increases while the nation is becoming more prosperous, George indicates a solution in the fact that private property in land confines interest and wages to marginal gains, while landlords, who are nonproducers, reap the benefits of social advance. This follows from the nature of rent, which measures the difference between the yields per acre on the richest and on the leanest soil with a like outlay of capital. According to George, social forces are responsible for the differences in real value, hence the return on the more valuable land is an unearned increment. Land is necessary to labor, but since it belongs to private owners every increase in production only increases rent, which is the price that labor must pay for the opportunity to utilize its own power. This in turn affects capital, for capital is produced by labor, being in fact labor impressed upon matter. Therefore labor and capital should be freed of this incubus, so that the community-created value may be returned to the community. George advocates for this purpose a "Single Tax," amounting to the whole or almost the whole of economic rent. This would permit the abolition of all other taxation, leaving production unpenalized, and improve the conditions of both capital and labor.

Progress of Dulness, The, satirical poem in octosyllabic couplets by John Trumbull, ♦ published in three parts (1772–73).

The first part of this satire on contemporary education tells of the difficulties at college of Tom Brainless, who learns how to manage without studying and achieves a diploma that crowns him as learned. As a conservative, he is welcomed into the ministry, and becomes a pontifical fool. The second part deals with Dick Harebrain, a wealthy fop, who, though he learns nothing solid at college, manages to pick up cheap infidelity secondhand from Hume and Voltaire, and finally, running the course of coxcombery and dissipation, ends in jail, racked by disease. The third part recounts the adventures of Miss Harriet Simper, who, lacking any sensible education, becomes a coquette, modeling her life on romantic novels. After jilting her other admirers, she falls victim to Harebrain, and when discarded by that beau finally settles down to dullness by marrying Tom Brainless.

Progress to the Mines, A, journal written during 1732 by William Byrd, ♦ was found among his Westover Manuscripts, from which it was published in 1841. A brief account of his least arduous journey, it is told in the witty and observant manner of all his charming memoranda, and includes comments on London literary gossip and Gay's *The Beggar's Opera,* typical of this Virginian's influence by English authors of the time.

PROKOSCH, FREDERIC (1908–89), Wisconsin-born author, whose wide-ranging interests and extensive travels are suggested by the subjects and settings of his novels, which include *The Asiatics* (1935), about an American who travels across Asia; *The Seven Who Fled* (1937), concerned with demoralized Russian exiles, the torments of their flight, and their conclusion that the only victory is that of having lost with "dignity of heart . . .

and nobility of spirit"; *Night of the Poor* (1939), a tale of a boy's impressions as he drifts from Wisconsin to Texas; *The Skies of Europe* (1941), a panorama of Europe on the eve of World War II; *The Conspirators* (1943), a novel of spies and refugees in wartime Lisbon; *Age of Thunder* (1945), a tale in poetic prose about *maquisards; The Idols of the Cave* (1946), about postwar decadence; *Storm and Echo* (1948), about men's search for themselves as they travel in darkest Africa; *A Tale for Midnight* (1955), a fictional account of Beatrice Cenci; *A Ballad of Love* (1960); *The Seven Sisters* (1963); *The Dark Dancer* (1964), about the Indian prince who built the Taj Mahal; *The Wreck of the Cassandra* (1966), dealing with people shipwrecked on a desert isle; *The Missolonghi Manuscript* (1968), a fictive autobiography of Byron; and *America, My Wilderness* (1972), a foundling black's wanderings through and affection for America. Prokosch's poems, including *The Assassins* (1936), *The Carnival* (1938), and *Death at Sea* (1940), are romantic and individualistic. *Voices* (1983) prints vignettes of the literary famous friends and others that Prokosch knew.

Proletarian literature, name applied to the school of writing that contends that experience is primarily conditioned by the social, economic, and political environment and that the author is able to understand this environment by Marxist theory, which explains the dialectical relation of class cultures to the prevailing economic and social structure. During the Depression, when they flourished, proletarian writers contended that it was life itself, not the Communist party, that forced them to be interested in such phenomena as strikes, agricultural and industrial conditions, and persecution and oppression of racial minorities and the working class. In studying the history of American literature, proletarian critics found the progenitors of the movement in such men as Emerson, Thoreau, and Whitman, who were individualistic rebels against the oppressions of their day; Howells, H.B. Fuller, Markham, Garland, Norris, Herrick, and D.G. Phillips, who went a step farther in their concern with the collective good; Steffens and the other muckrakers, who attacked specific abuses; Jack London, Upton Sinclair, and John Reed, who subscribed definitely to socialistic theories; Dreiser, Lewis, and Sherwood Anderson, who helped to break taboos and brought literature closer to contemporary social problems. During the 1920s and '30s Dos Passos, Farrell, and Steinbeck were among the leading writers who sympathized with the broader concepts of proletarian literature, but they refused to be confined by what they viewed as dogmatic restrictions. During the Depression other authors who moved to the far left in their social views and were avowedly or apparently in major accord with the tenets of proletarian literature included the novelists Robert Cantwell, Jack Conroy, Waldo Frank, Albert Halper, Josephine

Herbst, and Grace Lumpkin; the dramatists John Howard Lawson, Clifford Odets, and Irwin Shaw; and the critics V.F. Calverton, Joseph Freeman, Michael Gold, and Granville Hicks. *The Masses* and its successor, the *New Masses,* were the leading proletarian journals, and the movement affected the theater through the Group Theatre and the Theatre Union. Events of the late 1930s, including the mass treason trials in the U.S.S.R. and the Nazi-Soviet pact, caused many leftist writers to become thoroughly disillusioned with Marxism and thus to turn away from proletarian literature, which dwindled away as a subject and a theory in the 1940s.

Protestant Episcopal Church, the U.S. institution of the Anglican Communion, directly descended from the established Church of England. The creeds are the Apostles' and the Nicene, and the standards of doctrine are the Thirty-Nine Articles and the Book of Common Prayer. Church of England services were first regularly held in America at Jamestown (1607), and the Church flourished in the Southern colonies, particularly in Virginia and Maryland. In New England the Puritans forbade Anglican services, and it was not until the revocation of the Massachusetts colonial charter (1686) that Church of England clergymen were appointed to this region, leading to the establishment three years later of King's Chapel, Boston. In the same year, Trinity Church was consecrated in New York City. The earliest educational institution founded by the Church was William and Mary (1693). King's College (Columbia University) was founded in 1754; and other Episcopalian-founded institutions include Kenyon College, Ohio; Trinity College, Connecticut; the University of the South, Tennessee; and Hobart College, New York. During the Revolution the Church was severely torn, many of its clergy being Loyalists who returned to England. The majority of the laity were patriots, however, and these included Washington and two-thirds of the signers of the Declaration of Independence. In 1784 Samuel Seabury was consecrated the first bishop of the Church in America, which began its separate existence as an American ecclesiastical body with its own episcopate in 1789.

PROUD, ROBERT (1728–1813), English-born schoolmaster of Philadelphia and collector of source materials for local history, which he employed in his *History of Pennsylvania* (2 vols., 1797–98), a heavily documented and authoritative work on the colony through 1742.

PROUTY, OLIVE HIGGINS (1882–1974), Massachusetts author of popular fiction for women. Her best-known novel, *Stella Dallas* (1922), about a poor, self-sacrificing New England woman, was later a successful radio and television serial. Mrs. Prouty endowed the scholarship at her alma mater Smith College held by Sylvia Plath, ♦ whom she also befriended personally, and she is the model for Philomena Guinea in Plath's novel *The Bell Jar.* ♦

Providence Journal, The (1820–), Rhode Island newspaper, has been a nonpartisan paper since its founding, and has more than once been called "the conscience of Rhode Island."

Providence Plantations, earliest settlement in Rhode Island, established at Providence (1636) by Roger Williams, ♦ who with five others had been exiled from the Massachusetts Bay Colony. He attracted other colonists of liberal beliefs, and a plantation covenant was adopted (1637) in which the civil and religious authorities were separated. Another unprecedented feature of Williams's administration was his purchase of the territory from the Narragansett Indians, through their leaders Canonicus and Miantonomo. William Coddington, ♦ Anne Hutchinson, ♦ and John Clark (1609–76), all Antinomians, meanwhile settled at Portsmouth (1638) and Newport (1639), and Samuel Gorton ♦ seceded from Williams's group to found Warwick (1643). After a struggle between Williams and Coddington for leadership, the four settlements were united (1647) under Williams's charter of 1644 for the Providence Plantations in the Narragansett Bay. The union split (1651) into two groups, the one including Providence and Warwick, the other Portsmouth and Newport, but it was reunited by Williams (1654), who obtained a new charter for Rhode Island and Providence Plantation (1663).

Province House, *Legends of the,* see *Twice-Told Tales.*

Provincetown Players, THE, little-theater group of authors, actors, and artists, first drawn together at Provincetown, Mass. (1915). Their association continued, with changes of place and personnel, until *c.*1929. The first plays were produced under the direction of George Cram Cook in a remodeled fishing smack, The Wharf Theatre. One-act plays continued to be produced at Greenwich Village, in The Playwright's Theatre, and later the expanded organization presented three-act plays in this and the Greenwich Village Theatre. By 1925 the Provincetown productions had included 93 new plays by 47 playwrights, greatly influencing the standards of American drama. Among these plays were all the works of Eugene O'Neill up to date, Edna St. Vincent Millay's *The Princess Marries the Page* and *Aria da Capo,* Susan Glaspell's *The Inheritors,* Sherwood Anderson's *The Triumph of the Egg,* and others by prominent authors. Later plays included Paul Green's *In Abraham's Bosom* and E.E. Cummings's *him* (1928). R.E. Jones, Lewis Beach, Floyd Dell, Edna Ferber, and Kenneth Macgowan were other authors and artists associated

with the group, which published *The Provincetown Plays* (6 vols., 1916–18).

Prue and I, sketches by G.W. Curtis, ♦ published in 1856. They describe the fanciful reveries of an old clerk who lives in New York but in imagination tours the world of romance with his beloved Prue.

Prufrock and Other Observations, a small collection of poems by T.S. Eliot, ♦ published in 1917, whose title piece is "The Love Song of J. Alfred Prufrock." ♦

Prynne, HESTER, heroine of *The Scarlet Letter.* ♦

Psalm of Life, A, poem by Longfellow, ♦ published in *Voices of the Night* (1839). In nine quatrains of alternately rhymed trochaic tetrameters, this popular didactic piece stresses the importance of a full and sincere activity in making the most of life's brief span, rather than succumbing to moods of vain regret or dejection.

Psalms, see *Hymns.*

Publick Occurrences Both Forreign and Domestick, colonial newspaper published at Boston by Benjamin Harris. ♦ It was intended to be a monthly stressing American rather than foreign news. Since it was not licensed, the paper was suppressed by the governor after one issue (Sept. 25, 1690), because it "contained reflections of a very high order" and "sundry doubtful and uncertain Reports." It is, however, considered the first American newspaper.

Publishers Weekly (1872–), trade journal of publishers addressed to those in the industry, especially booksellers, containing data on current books and publishing people and trends.

PUBLIUS, pseudonym of Hamilton, Madison, and Jay, in *The Federalist.* ♦

PUCCINI, GIACOMO (1858–1924), Italian composer, whose works include two operas adapted from American plays: *Madame Butterfly* ♦ (1906), by Belasco and J.L. Long, and Belasco's *The Girl of the Golden West* ♦ (1910).

Puck (1877–1918), weekly magazine of humor and satire, noted for its brilliantly colored cartoons and for its incisive, witty text, of which a great part was written by H.C. Bunner, the editor (1878–96). Besides the sketches satirizing contemporary society, *Puck* printed trenchant attacks on Tammany and other examples of political corruption. During the 1890s the satire was lighter and less concerned with politics, and this attitude was continued under the editorship of H.L. Wilson (1896–1902) and J.K. Bangs (1904–5). Later contributors included F.P. Adams, Arthur

Guiterman, G.J. Nathan, Huneker, and Ralph Barton. The paper was sold to Hearst (1917), who removed the sting and made the tone one of light persiflage.

Pudd'nhead Wilson, *The Tragedy of,* novel by Clemens, ♦ published in 1894 under the pseudonym Mark Twain. It was dramatized by Frank Mayo (1895).

On the Mississippi during the 1830s, at Dawson's Landing, Mo., lives Percy Driscoll, a prosperous slave owner. On the day his son Tom is born, his nearly white slave Roxy gives birth to a son, Chambers, whose father is a Virginia gentleman. Since Tom's mother dies when he is only a week old, he is raised by Roxy along with Chambers, whose twin he is in appearance. Roxy, fearful that her son may some day be sold down the river, changes the two children, and upon the death of Percy, his brother Judge Driscoll adopts Chambers, believing him to be Tom. The boy grows up a coward, a snob, and a gambler. Even though Roxy tells him that she is his mother, he sells her to pay his gambling debts. On escaping, she blackmails him. To obtain money he robs the judge and murders him with a knife stolen from Luigi, one of a pair of Italian twins with whom the judge once fought a duel. The evidence is against the twins, who are defended by David Wilson, an unsuccessful lawyer, whose "tragedy" consists in the ridicule that has resulted from his eccentric originality and iconoclasm; his humor and his interest in palmistry and fingerprints cause the people of Dawson's Landing to call him "Pudd'nhead." Wilson feels secure in his case for the twins, since the fingerprints on the knife are not those of the accused. One day he acquires the fingerprints of the spurious Tom, and with this evidence is able to vindicate his methods, and to win at last the admiration of his fellow townsmen, by saving the twins and convicting Chambers, who is sold down the river while the real Tom is restored to his rightful position.

Pueblo Indians, see *Hopi* and *Zuñi Indians.*

PULITZER, JOSEPH (1847–1911), Hungarian-born newspaper proprietor, came to the U.S. (1864), worked in St. Louis on the German Republican paper of Carl Schurz, and published his own paper there. He purchased the New York *World* ♦ (1883), which he made into a flamboyant symbol of yellow journalism, although it later turned to a more conservative policy, championing the Democratic party. He bequeathed funds to found the Pulitzer Prizes.

Pulitzer Prizes in Journalism and Letters, created as a result of Joseph Pulitzer's bequest of $2,000,000 to found the Columbia University School of Journalism, with the income from $500,000 of that sum to be devoted to annual prizes "for the encouragement of public service, public morals, American literature, and the advancement of education." Pulitzer's will established four categories of American literature: novel, play, U.S. history, and American biography. The will empowered an Advisory Board, which was retitled the Pulitzer Prize Board (1979), to alter these categories or to create new ones. Its annually appointed juries for each of the categories make their nominations to the Advisory Board, which may accept or reject them or even substitute its own choices. The Advisory Board (until 1950 associated with the School of Journalism) passes its nominations to the Board of Trustees of Columbia University (in 1975 the Trustees delegated their power to the University president), which can accept or reject nominations but cannot make substitutions. The Advisory Board has the power to withhold awards if nominees do not meet its unpublished criteria. Prizes for novels, plays, U.S. history, and American biography were established in 1917, but that year no works were judged acceptable in the first two categories. Prizes for poetry were first established for the year 1922, but Columbia University gave its approval to prizes granted in 1918 and 1919 by the Poetry Society of America. With the powers granted to it, the Advisory Board in 1947 redefined the award for novels to "fiction in book form" so that it might select for the award of 1948 a work comprising short stories. In 1962 it created a new category: general nonfiction. The dollar value of the prizes has varied over the years but is currently $3000.

Pulitzer Prize novels, since 1947,
"fiction in book form":

1917—No award
1918—Ernest Poole, *His Family*
1919—Booth Tarkington, *The Magnificent Ambersons*
1920—No award
1921—Edith Wharton, *The Age of Innocence*
1922—Booth Tarkington, *Alice Adams*
1923—Willa Cather, *One of Ours*
1924—Margaret Wilson, *The Able McLaughlins*
1925—Edna Ferber, *So Big*
1926—Sinclair Lewis, *Arrowsmith* (declined)
1927—Louis Bromfield, *Early Autumn*
1928—Thornton Wilder, *The Bridge of San Luis Rey*
1929—Julia Peterkin, *Scarlet Sister Mary*
1930—Oliver La Farge, *Laughing Boy*
1931—Margaret Ayer Barnes, *Years of Grace ·*
1932—Pearl Buck, *The Good Earth*
1933—T.S. Stribling, *The Store*
1934—Caroline Miller, *Lamb in His Bosom*
1935—Josephine Johnson, *Now in November*
1936—H.L. Davis, *Honey in the Horn*
1937—Margaret Mitchell, *Gone with the Wind*
1938—J.P. Marquand, *The Late George Apley*
1939—Marjorie K. Rawlings, *The Yearling*

1940—John Steinbeck, *The Grapes of Wrath*
1941—No award
1942—Ellen Glasgow, *In This Our Life*
1943—Upton Sinclair, *Dragon's Teeth*
1944—Martin Flavin, *Journey in the Dark*
1945—John Hersey, *A Bell for Adano*
1946—No award
1947—Robert Penn Warren, *All the King's Men*
1948—James A. Michener, *Tales of the South Pacific*
1949—James Gould Cozzens, *Guard of Honor*
1950—A.B. Guthrie, *The Way West*
1951—Conrad Richter, *The Town*
1952—Herman Wouk, *The Caine Mutiny*
1953—Ernest Hemingway, *The Old Man and the Sea*
1954—No award
1955—William Faulkner, *A Fable*
1956—MacKinlay Kantor, *Andersonville*
1957—No award
1958—James Agee, *A Death in the Family*
1959—Robert Lewis Taylor, *The Travels of Jamie McPheeters*
1960—Allen Drury, *Advise and Consent*
1961—Harper Lee, *To Kill a Mockingbird*
1962—Edwin O'Connor, *The Edge of Sadness*
1963—William Faulkner, *The Reivers*
1964—No award
1965—Shirley Ann Grau, *The Keepers of the House*
1966—Katherine Anne Porter, *Collected Stories*
1967—Bernard Malamud, *The Fixer*
1968—William Styron, *The Confessions of Nat Turner*
1969—N. Scott Momaday, *House Made of Dawn*
1970—Jean Stafford, *Collected Stories*
1971—No award
1972—Wallace Stegner, *Angels of Repose*
1973—Eudora Welty, *The Optimist's Daughter*
1974—No award
1975—Michael Shaara, *The Killer Angels*
1976—Saul Bellow, *Humboldt's Gift*
1977—No award
1978—James A. McPherson, *Elbow Room*
1979—John Cheever, *The Stories of John Cheever*
1980—Norman Mailer, *The Executioner's Song*
1981—John Kennedy Toole, *A Confederacy of Dunces*
1982—John Updike, *Rabbit Is Rich*
1983—Alice Walker, *The Color Purple*
1984—William Kennedy, *Ironweed*
1985—Alison Lurie, *Foreign Affairs*
1986—Larry McMurtry, *Lonesome Dove*
1987—Peter Taylor, *A Summons to Memphis*
1988—Toni Morrison, *Beloved*
1989—Anne Tyler, *Breathing Lessons*
1990—Oscar Hijuelos, *The Mambo Kings Play Songs of Love*
1991—John Updike, *Rabbit at Rest*
1992—Jane Smiley, *A Thousand Acres*
1993—Robert Olen Butler, *A Good Scent from a Strange Mountain*
1994—E. Annie Proulx, *The Shipping News*
1995—Carol Shields, *The Stone Diaries*

Pulitzer Prize plays:

1917—No award
1918—Jesse L. Williams, *Why Marry?*
1919—No award
1920—Eugene O'Neill, *Beyond the Horizon*
1921—Zona Gale, *Miss Lulu Bett*
1922—Eugene O'Neill, *Anna Christie*
1923—Owen Davis, *Icebound*
1924—Hatcher Hughes, *Hell-Bent for Heaven*
1925—Sidney Howard, *They Knew What They Wanted*
1926—George Kelly, *Craig's Wife*
1927—Paul Green, *In Abraham's Bosom*
1928—Eugene O'Neill, *Strange Interlude*
1929—Elmer Rice, *Street Scene*
1930—Marc Connelly, *The Green Pastures*
1931—Susan Glaspell, *Alison's House*
1932—George Kaufman and Morrie Ryskind, *Of Thee I Sing*
1933—Maxwell Anderson, *Both Your Houses*
1934—Sidney Kingsley, *Men in White*
1935—Zoë Akins, *The Old Maid*
1936—Robert Sherwood, *Idiot's Delight*
1937—George Kaufman, Moss Hart, and Ira Gershwin, *You Can't Take It with You*
1938—Thornton Wilder, *Our Town*
1939—Robert Sherwood, *Abe Lincoln in Illinois*
1940—William Saroyan, *The Time of Your Life* (declined)
1941—Robert Sherwood, *There Shall Be No Night*
1942—No award
1943—Thornton Wilder, *The Skin of Our Teeth*
1944—No award; special award for a musical play to Richard Rodgers and Oscar Hammerstein II for *Oklahoma!*
1945—Mary Chase, *Harvey*
1946—Russel Crouse and Howard Lindsay, *State of the Union*
1947—No award
1948—Tennessee Williams, *A Streetcar Named Desire*
1949—Arthur Miller, *Death of a Salesman*
1950—Richard Rodgers, Oscar Hammerstein II, and Joshua Logan, *South Pacific*
1951—No award
1952—Joseph Kramm, *The Shrike*
1953—William Inge, *Picnic*
1954—John Patrick, *The Teahouse of the August Moon*
1955—Tennessee Williams, *Cat on a Hot Tin Roof*
1956—Albert Hackett and Frances Goodrich, *The Diary of Anne Frank*
1957—Eugene O'Neill, *Long Day's Journey into Night*
1958—Ketti Frings, *Look Homeward, Angel*
1959—Archibald MacLeish, *J.B.*
1960—Jerome Weidman and George Abbott, *Fiorello!*
1961—Tad Mosel, *All the Way Home*
1962—Frank Loesser and Abe Burrows, *How To Succeed in Business Without Really Trying*
1963—No award

1964—No award
1965—Frank D. Gilroy, *The Subject Was Roses*
1966—No award
1967—Edward Albee, *A Delicate Balance*
1968—No award
1969—Howard Sackler, *The Great White Hope*
1970—Charles Gordone, *No Place To Be Somebody*
1971—Paul Zindel, *The Effect of Gamma Rays on Man-in-the-Moon Marigolds*
1973—Jason Miller, *The Championship Season*
1974—No award
1975—Edward Albee, *Seascape*
1976—Michael Bennett, James Kirkwood, Nicholas Dante, Marvin Hamlisch, and Edward Kieban, *A Chorus Line*
1977—Michael Cristofer, *The Shadow Box*
1978—Donald L. Coburn, *The Gin Game*
1979—Sam Shepard, *Buried Child*
1980—Lanford Wilson, *Talley's Folly*
1981—Beth Henley, *Crimes of the Heart*
1982—Charles Fuller, *A Soldier's Play*
1983—Marsha Norman, *'night, Mother*
1984—David Mamet, *Glengarry Glen Ross*
1985—Stephen Sondheim and James Lapine, *Sunday in the Park with George*
1986—No award
1987—August Wilson, *Fences*
1988—Alfred Uhry, *Driving Miss Daisy*
1989—Wendy Wasserstein, *The Heidi Chronicles*
1990—August Wilson, *The Piano Lesson*
1991—Neil Simon, *Lost in Yonkers*
1992—Robert Schenkan, *The Kentucky Cycle*
1993—Tony Kushner, *Angels in America*
1994—Edward Albee, *Three Tall Women*
1995—Horton Foote, *The Young Man From Atlanta*

Pulitzer prize poetry:

(Special prizes were awarded, from gifts provided by the Poetry Society, in 1918 to Sara Teasdale for *Love Songs,* and in 1919 to Margaret Widdemer for *Old Road to Paradise* and to Carl Sandburg for *Cornhuskers.*)

1922—Edwin Arlington Robinson, *Collected Poems*
1923—Edna St. Vincent Millay, *The Ballad of the Harp-Weaver; A Few Figs from Thistles; Eight Sonnets*
1924—Robert Frost, *New Hampshire*
1925—Edwin Arlington Robinson, *The Man Who Died Twice*
1926—Amy Lowell, *What's O'Clock?*
1927—Leonora Speyer, *Fiddler's Farewell*
1928—Edwin Arlington Robinson, *Tristram*
1929—Stephen Vincent Benét, *John Brown's Body*
1930—Conrad Aiken, *Selected Poems*
1931—Robert Frost, *Collected Poems*
1932—George Dillon, *The Flowering Stone*
1933—Archibald MacLeish, *Conquistador*
1934—Robert Hillyer, *Collected Verse*
1935—Audrey Wurdemann, *Bright Ambush*

1936—Robert Coffin, *Strange Holiness*
1937—Robert Frost, *A Further Range*
1938—Marya Zaturenska, *Cold Morning Sky*
1939—John Gould Fletcher, *Selected Poems*
1940—Mark Van Doren, *Collected Poems*
1941—Leonard Bacon, *Sunderland Capture*
1942—William Rose Benét, *The Dust Which Is God*
1943—Robert Frost, *A Witness Tree*
1944—Stephen Vincent Benét, *Western Star*
1945—Karl Shapiro, *V-Letter and Other Poems*
1946—No award
1947—Robert Lowell, *Lord Weary's Castle*
1948—W.H. Auden, *The Age of Anxiety*
1949—Peter Viereck, *Terror and Decorum*
1950—Gwendolyn Brooks, *Annie Adams*
1951—Carl Sandburg, *Complete Poems*
1952—Marianne Moore, *Collected Poems*
1953—Archibald MacLeish, *Collected Poems, 1917–1952*
1954—Theodore Roethke, *The Waking*
1955—Wallace Stevens, *Collected Poems*
1956—Elizabeth Bishop, *Poems—North & South*
1957—Richard Wilbur, *Things of This World*
1958—Robert Penn Warren, *Promises: Poems 1954–1956*
1959—Stanley Kunitz, *Selected Poems: 1918–1958*
1960—W.D. Snodgrass, *Heart's Needle*
1961—Phyllis McGinley, *Times Three: Selected Verse from Three Decades*
1962—Alan Dugan, *Poems*
1963—William Carlos Williams, *Pictures from Brueghel*
1964—Louis Simpson, *At the End of the Open Road*
1965—John Berryman, *77 Dream Songs*
1966—Richard Eberhart, *Selected Poems*
1967—Anne Sexton, *Live or Die*
1968—Anthony Hecht, *The Hard Hours*
1969—George Oppen, *Of Being Numerous*
1970—Richard Howard, *United Subjects*
1971—W.S. Merwin, *The Carrier of Ladders*
1972—James Wright, *Collected Poems*
1973—Maxine Kumin, *Up Country*
1974—No award
1975—Gary Snyder, *Turtle Island*
1976—John Ashbery, *Self Portrait in a Convex Mirror*
1977—James Merrill, *Divine Comedies*
1978—Howard Nemerov, *Collected Poems*
1979—Robert Penn Warren, *Now and Then*
1980—Donald Justice, *Selected Poems*
1981—James Schuyler, *The Morning of the Poem*
1982—Sylvia Plath, *The Collected Poems*
1983—Galway Kinnell, *Selected Poems*
1984—Mary Oliver, *American Primitive*
1985—Carolyn Kizer, *Yin*
1986—Henry Taylor, *The Flying Change*
1987—Rita Dove, *Thomas and Beulah*
1988—William Meredith, *Partial Accounts*
1989—Richard Wilbur, *New and Collected Poems*
1990—Charles Simic, *The World Doesn't End*
1991—Mona Van Duyn, *Near Changes*

1992—James Tate, *Selected Poems*
1993—Louise Glück, *The Wild Iris*
1994—Yousef Komunyakaa, *Neon Vernacular*
1995—Philip Levine, *Simple Truth*

Pulitzer Prize biographies:

1917—Laura E. Richards and Maude H. Elliott, assisted by Florence H. Hall, *Julia Ward Howe*
1918—William C. Bruce, *Benjamin Franklin, Self-Revealed*
1919—Henry Adams, *The Education of Henry Adams*
1920—Albert J. Beveridge, *Life of John Marshall*
1921—Edward Bok, *The Americanization of Edward Bok*
1922—Hamlin Garland, *A Daughter of the Middle Border*
1923—Burton J. Hendrick, *Life and Letters of Walter Hines Page*
1924—Michael Pupin, *From Immigrant to Inventor*
1925—M.A. DeW. Howe, *Barrett Wendell and His Letters*
1926—Harvey Cushing, *Life of Sir William Osler*
1927—Emory Holloway, *Whitman; An Interpretation in Narrative*
1928—C.E. Russell, *The American Orchestra and Theodore Thomas*
1929—Burton J. Hendrick, *The Training of an American: The Earlier Life and Letters of Walter Hines Page*
1930—Marquis James, *The Raven: A Biography of Sam Houston*
1931—Henry James, *Charles W. Eliot*
1932—Henry Pringle, *Theodore Roosevelt*
1933—Allan Nevins, *Grover Cleveland*
1934—Tyler Dennett, *John Hay*
1935—Douglas Freeman, *R.E. Lee*
1936—Ralph B. Perry, *The Thought and Character of William James*
1937—Allan Nevins, *Hamilton Fish: The Inner History of the Grant Administration*
1938—Odell Shepard, *Pedlar's Progress: The Life of Bronson Alcott;* and Marquis James, *Andrew Jackson*
1939—Carl Van Doren, *Benjamin Franklin*
1940—Ray Stannard Baker, *Woodrow Wilson* (vols. 7 and 8)
1941—Ola Elizabeth Winslow, *Jonathan Edwards*
1942—Forrest Wilson, *Crusader in Crinoline* (Harriet Beecher Stowe)
1943—Samuel Eliot Morison, *Christopher Columbus: Admiral of the Ocean Sea*
1944—Carleton Mabee, *The American Leonardo: The Life of Samuel F.B. Morse*
1945—Russel B. Nye, *George Bancroft: Brahmin Rebel*
1946—Linnie Marsh Wolfe, *Son of the Wilderness: The Life of John Muir*
1947—William Allen White, *Autobiography*
1948—Margaret Clapp, *Forgotten First Citizen: John Bigelow*

1949—Robert E. Sherwood, *Roosevelt and Hopkins*
1950—Samuel Flagg Bemis, *John Quincy Adams and the Foundations of American Foreign Policy*
1951—Margaret Louise Coit, *John C. Calhoun: American Portrait*
1952—Merlo J. Pusey, *Charles Evans Hughes*
1953—David J. Mays, *Edmund Pendleton, 1721–1803*
1954—Charles A. Lindbergh, *The Spirit of St. Louis*
1955—William S. White, *The Taft Story*
1956—Talbot Faulkner Hamlin, *Benjamin Henry Latrobe*
1957—John F. Kennedy, *Profiles in Courage*
1958—Douglas S. Freeman, *George Washington* (vols. 5 and 6); and John A. Carroll and Mary W. Ashworth, *George Washington* (vol. 7)
1959—Arthur Walworth, *Woodrow Wilson* (2 vols.)
1960—Samuel Eliot Morison, *John Paul Jones*
1961—David Donald, *Charles Sumner and the Coming of the Civil War*
1962—No award
1963—Leon Edel, *Henry James* (vols. 2 and 3)
1964—Walter Jackson Bate, *John Keats*
1965—Ernest Samuels, *Henry Adams* (3 vols.)
1966—Arthur M. Schlesinger, Jr., *A Thousand Days*
1967—Justin Kaplan, *Mr. Clemens and Mark Twain*
1968—George F. Kennan, *Memoirs (1925–1950)*
1969—B.L. Reid, *The Man from New York* (John Quinn)
1970—T. Harry Williams, *Huey Long*
1971—Lawrance Thompson, *Robert Frost*
1972—Joseph P. Lash, *Eleanor and Franklin*
1973—W.A. Swanberg, *Luce and His Empire*
1974—Louis Sheaffer, *O'Neill, Son and Artist*
1975—Robert A. Caro, *The Power Broker: Robert Moses*
1976—R.W.B. Lewis, *Edith Wharton*
1977—John E. Mack, *A Prince of Our Disorder, The Life of T.E. Lawrence*
1978—Walter Jackson Bate, *Samuel Johnson*
1979—Leonard Baker, *Days of Sorrow and Pain: Leo Baeck and the Berlin Jews*
1980—Edmund Morris, *The Rise of Theodore Roosevelt*
1981—Robert K. Massie, *Peter the Great*
1982—William S. McFeely, *Grant: A Biography*
1983—Russell Baker, *Growing Up*
1984—Louis R. Harlan, *Booker T. Washington*
1985—Kenneth Silverman, *The Life and Times of Cotton Mather*
1986—Elizabeth Frank, *Louise Bogan: A Portrait*
1987—David J. Garrow, *Bearing the Cross: Martin Luther King . . .*
1988—David Herbert Donald, *Look Homeward: A Life of Thomas Wolfe*
1989—Richard Ellmann, *Oscar Wilde*

1990—Sebastian de Grazia, *Machiavelli in Hell*
1991—Steven Naifeh and Gregory White Smith, *Jackson Pollock, an American Saga*
1992—Lewis B. Puller, Jr., *Fortunate Son*
1993—David McCullough, *Truman*
1994—David Levering Lewis, *W.E.B. DuBois: Biography of a Race, 1868–1919*
1995—Joan D. Hedrick, *Harriet Beecher Stowe: A Life*

Pulitzer Prize histories:

1917—J.J. Jusserand, *With Americans of Past and Present Days*
1918—James F. Rhodes, *A History of the Civil War*
1919—No award
1920—Justin H. Smith, *The War with Mexico*
1921—William S. Sims and Burton J. Hendrick, *The Victory at Sea*
1922—James Truslow Adams, *The Founding of New England*
1923—Charles Warren, *The Supreme Court in United States History*
1924—Charles H. McIlwain, *The American Revolution, A Constitutional Interpretation*
1925—Frederic L. Paxon, *A History of the American Frontier, 1763–1893*
1926—Edward Channing, *The War for Southern Independence*
1927—Samuel F. Bemis, *Pinckney's Treaty: A Study of America's Advantage from Europe's Distress*
1928—Vernon L. Parrington, *Main Currents in American Thought* (vols. 1 and 2)
1929—Fred Albert Shannon, *Organization and Administration of the Union Army, 1861–1865*
1930—Claude H. Van Tyne, *The War of Independence*
1931—Bernadotte E. Schmitt, *The Coming of the War: 1914*
1932—John J. Pershing, *My Experiences in the World War*
1933—Frederick J. Turner, *The Significance of Sections in American History*
1934—Herbert Agar, *The People's Choice*
1935—Charles McL. Andrews, *The Colonial Period of American History* (vol.1)
1936—Andrew C. McLaughlin, *Constitutional History of the United States*
1937—Van Wyck Brooks, *The Flowering of New England*
1938—Paul H. Buck, *The Road to Reunion*
1939—Frank L. Mott, *A History of American Magazines*
1940—Carl Sandburg, *Abraham Lincoln: The War Years* (4 vols.)
1941—Marcus Lee Hansen, *The Atlantic Migration*
1942—Margaret Leech, *Reveille in Washington*
1943—Esther Forbes, *Paul Revere and the World He Lived In*

1944—Merle Curti, *The Growth of American Thought*
1945—Stephen Bonsal, *Unfinished Business*
1946—Arthur M. Schlesinger, Jr., *The Age of Jackson*
1947—James Phinney Baxter, *Scientists Against Time*
1948—Bernard De Voto, *Across the Wide Missouri*
1949—Roy F. Nichols, *The Disruption of American Democracy*
1950—O.W. Larkin, *Art and Life in America*
1951—R. Carlyle Buley, *The Old Northwest, Pioneer Period, 1815–1840*
1952—Oscar Handlin, *The Uprooted*
1953—George Dangerfield, *The Era of Good Feelings*
1954—Bruce Catton, *A Stillness at Appomattox*
1955—Paul Horgan, *Great River: The Rio Grande in North American History*
1956—Richard Hofstadter, *The Age of Reform*
1957—George F. Kennan, *Russia Leaves the War*
1958—Bray Hammond, *Banks and Politics in America: From the Revolution to the Civil War*
1959—Leonard D. White, *The Republican Era: 1869–1901*
1960—Margaret Leech, *In the Days of McKinley;* special award to Garrett Mattingly for *The Armada*
1961—Herbert Feis, *Between War and Peace: The Potsdam Conference;* special award to the *American Heritage Picture History of the Civil War*
1962—Lawrence Gipson, *The Triumphant Empire: Thunder Clouds Gather in the West*
1963—Constance M. Green, *Washington, Village and Capital*
1964—Sumner Chilton Powell, *Puritan Village: The Formation of a New England Town*
1965—Irwin Unger, *The Greenback Era*
1966—Perry Miller, *The Life of the Mind in America*
1967—William H. Goetzmann, *Exploration and Empire*
1968—Bernard Bailyn, *The Ideological Origins of the American Revolution*
1969—Leonard W. Levy, *Origins of the Fifth Amendment*
1970—Dean Acheson, *Present at the Creation*
1971—James M. Burns, *Roosevelt, The Soldier of Freedom*
1972—Carl N. Degler, *Neither Black Nor White*
1973—Michael Kammen, *People of Paradox*
1974—Daniel J. Boorstin, *The Americans*
1975—Dumas Malone, *Jefferson and His Time*
1976—Paul Horgan, *Lamy of Santa Fe*
1977—David M. Potter, *The Impending Crisis*
1978—Alfred D. Chandler, Jr., *The Visible Hand*
1979—Don E. Fehrenbacher, *The Dred Scott Case*
1980—Leon F. Litwack, *Been in the Storm So Long*
1981—Lawrence A. Cremin, *American Education*
1982—C. Vann Woodward (ed.), *Mary Chesnut's Civil War*

1983—Rhys L. Isaac, *The Transformation of Virginia, 1740–1790*
1984—No award
1985—Thomas K. McGraw, *The Prophets of Regulation*
1986—Walter A. McDougall, *The Heavens and the Earth: A Political History of the Space Age*
1987—Bernard Bailyn, *Voyagers to the West: A Passage in the Peopling of America on the Eve of the Revolution*
1988—Robert V. Bruce, *The Launching of Modern American Science, 1846–1876*
1989—Taylor Branch, *Parting the Waters,* and James M. McPherson, *Battle Cry of Freedom*
1990—Stanley Karnow, *In Our Image: America's Empire in the Philippines*
1991—Laurel Ulrich, *A Midwife's Tale: The Life of Martha Ballard*
1992—Mark E. Neely, Jr., *The Fate of Liberty: Abraham Lincoln and Civil Liberties*
1993—Gordon S. Wood, *The Radicalism of the American Revolution*
1994—No award
1995—Doris Kearns Goodwin, *No Ordinary Time: Franklin and Eleanor Roosevelt: The Home Front in World War II*

Pulitzer Prize general nonfiction:

1962—Theodore H. White, *The Making of the President 1960*
1963—Barbara W. Tuchman, *The Guns of August*
1964—Richard Hofstadter, *Anti-Intellectualism in American Life*
1965—Howard Mumford Jones, *O Strange New World*
1966—Edwin Way Teale, *Wandering Through Winter*
1967—David Brion Davis, *The Problem of Slavery in Western Culture*
1968—Will and Ariel Durant, *Rousseau and Revolution*
1969—René Jules Dubos, *So Human an Animal;* and Norman Mailer, *The Armies of the Night*
1970—Eric H. Erikson, *Gandhi's Truth*
1971—John Toland, *The Rising Sun*
1972—Barbara W. Tuchman, *Stilwell and the American Experience in China*
1973—Frances Fitzgerald, *Fire in the Lake*
1974—Ernest Becker, *The Denial of Death*
1975—Annie Dillard, *The Pilgrim at Tinker Creek*
1976—Robert N. Butler, *Why Survive?*
1977—William H. Warner, *Beautiful Swimmers*
1978—Carl Sagan, *The Dragons of Eden*
1979—Edward O. Wilson, *On Human Nature*
1980—Douglas R. Hofstadter, *Gödel, Escher, Bach*
1981—Carl E. Schorske, *Fin-de-siècle Vienna*
1982—Tracy Kidder, *The Soul of a New Machine*
1983—Susan Sheehan, *Is There No Place on Earth for Me?*

1984—Paul Starr, *Social Transformation of American Medicine*
1985—Studs Terkel, *The Good War: An Oral History of World War II*
1986—Joseph Lelyveld, *Move Your Shadow: South Africa, Black and White,* and J. Anthony Lukas, *Common Ground: A Turbulent Decade in the Lives of Three American Families*
1987—David K. Shipler, *Arab and Jew: Wounded Spirits in a Promised Land*
1988—Richard Rhodes, *The Making of the Atomic Bomb*
1989—Neil Sheehan, *A Bright and Shining Lie*
1990—Dale Maharidge and Michael Williamson, *And Their Children After Them*
1991—Edward O. Wilson and Burt Holldobler, *The Ants*
1992—Daniel Yergin, *The Prize: The Epic Quest for Oil*
1993—Garry Wills, *Lincoln at Gettysburg*
1994—David Remnick, *For Lenin's Tomb*
1995—Jonathan Weiner, *The Beak of the Finch: A Story of Evolution in Our Time*

Pulp magazine, name applied to a periodical printed on coarse wood pulp paper and containing short stories, novelettes, and serials usually of violent and exotic adventure. This type of magazine carries on the tradition of the dime novel, combining melodrama and conventional romance based on innocent morality. Produced by hack writers, the fiction is based on a few accepted formulas, which have been described as "making all heroines very young girls, presenting the West purely as a cowboys' Valhalla, and bringing all criminals—except those of the Robin Hood type—to summary and violent justice." The pulp magazines generally specialize in a single variety of fiction, e.g. crime detection and the chase of criminals; "Western" adventure; "horror"; pseudo-erotic or saccharine "love"; and pseudo-scientific "amazing" stories. Always the basis of the tale is sensational situation rather than plot, and development of character is frowned upon, for, as a critic has termed it, pulp-magazine publishing is "the business of purveying predigested daydreams to people who cannot dream for themselves." Many journals of this sort have been superseded by series of paperback books devoted to analogous themes and subjects.

PURCHAS, SAMUEL (1575?–1626), English clergyman, whose best-known religious writing is *Purchas his Pilgrim. Microcosmus, or the histories of Man* (1619). He is famous for carrying on the work of Hakluyt, although his editions of contemporary travel narratives are considered inferior in style and scholarship to those of his predecessor. In 1613 he published his first collection, *Purchas his Pilgrimage; or, Relations of the World and the Religions observed in all Ages and places discovered, from the Creation unto this Present.* The final revision of this work (1626) constitutes a supplementary volume to his comprehensive extension of Hakluyt's collection, *Hakluytus Posthumus, or Purchas his Pilgrimes, contayning a History of the World in Sea Voyages and Lande Travells, by Englishmen and others* (4 vols., 1625). The first half of this enthusiastic work is devoted to travels in the Old World and the Far East, while the second half contains narratives of voyages to America.

PURDY, JAMES (1923–   ), Ohio-born author of *Malcolm* (1959), a bizarre, comic novel of the picaresque, presenting the strange experiences of a 15-year-old boy as in his search for his lost father he wanders through a world of depravity. It was dramatized (1965) by Albee. *The Nephew* (1960), his second novel, tells of the revelations following the death in war of the nephew of a doting spinster, a retired schoolteacher, in a small Midwest town, who decides to write a memorial booklet. She thereby learns more than she wants to about him and about life as she discovers he was a homosexual. *Cabot Wright Begins* (1964), a satirical novel on the American scene, presents a compulsive but mild-mannered rapist who is himself "raped" by editors and publishers wanting to create a best seller out of his experiences. *Eustace Chisholm and the Works* (1967) treats loving relations as well as destructive encounters between homosexuals. *I Am Elijah Thrush* (1972) presents a story of even more complex relations among men of different ages, backgrounds, and natures. *In a Shallow Grave* (1975) is about a hideously disfigured veteran trying to return to his childhood sweetheart, a different instance of alienation. *Sleepers in Moon-Crowned Valleys* is a trilogy composed of *Jeremy's Version* (1970), *The House of the Solitary Maggot* (1974), and *Mourners Below* (1981), about the strained, bizarre relations of a Midwest family. *Narrow Rooms* (1978) is a novel about homosexual passions, and *On Glory's Course* (1984) treats the lives and often odd loves of a town of Midwesterners in the 1930s. His next novel, *In the Hollow of His Hand* (1986), treats the generally unhappy adventures of the son of a Midwestern Indian and his illegal mother, a society lady. *Garments the Living Wear* (1989), a shorter tale, presents characters caught in the general corruption of New York City. *Out with the Stars* (1994) evokes scenes of the gay community in New York City in the last moments before AIDS and Stonewall, in terms half nostalgic, half satiric. *The Color of Darkness* (1957) collects stories and a novella, which Purdy and a collaborator adapted for the stage (1963). *Children Is All* (1962) also collects stories and two plays, and further plays appear in *A Day After the Fair* (1977) along with poems. *The Running Sun* (1971) and *Sunshine Is an Only Child* (1973) are volumes of poetry; *The Candles of Your Eyes* (1987) collects stories.

Puritan and His Daughter, *The,* novel by Paulding,♦ published in 1849.

Puritanism, attitude of a party within the Established Church of England, which, under Elizabeth I and the Stuarts, desired a more thoroughgoing reformation of the Church in the direction of continental Protestantism. At first the Puritans wished only to eliminate certain ceremonial vestments and rituals, and, having no doctrinal quarrel, they were not Separatists,♦ but definitely believed in a state church. As the conflict grew that led to the Revolution of 1640–60, there arose many political Puritans, whose main interest was in the establishment of parliamentary authority as opposed to the regal theory of divine right. The Puritan movement was at its height when it found an outlet in American colonization, and, though the Pilgrims♦ were Separatists, the later colonists were primarily Puritans who came from the English middle class. The Puritans' doctrine, as expressed in the Cambridge Platform (1646), had the theology of Calvinism♦ and the church polity of Congregationalism.♦ The word Puritan is used to refer either to this theology or to this polity. Later the word has been used to denote a strictness in morality that verges on intolerance, and refers to a supposed parallel with the moral severity of the early New England settlers.

Purloined Letter, *The,* detective story by Poe,♦ published in his *Tales* (1845).

The prefect of the Paris police visits C. Auguste Dupin, scholarly amateur detective, for advice on a baffling case concerning a cabinet minister who has gained power over, and consequently practiced blackmail upon, a royal lady from whom he has stolen a letter than she cannot have made public. After several months of elaborate search, the prefect concludes that the letter is not on the minister's person or premises. Dupin soon finds the letter, explaining later that the police seek only obscure hiding places such as would be avoided by the acute minister. Dupin, therefore, visited him openly, looked in the most obvious places, and found the letter, turned inside out and disguised in an exposed card rack. Diverting the minister the next day by means of an arranged street disturbance, he substituted a facsimile and took the purloined letter with him.

Purple Cow, *The,* see Burgess, Gelett.

PUTNAM, ISRAEL (1718–90), Massachusetts-born soldier, a major in the last French and Indian War, served in the expedition against Havana (1762), his journal of this and a later trip to West Florida being published in *The Two Putnams . . .* (1931). He commanded Connecticut troops during Pontiac's Rebellion, fought at Bunker Hill as a major general, and commanded at the Battle of Long Island. Exonerated of a later charge of insubordination, he remained in the service through 1779. He is the titular hero of a play by N.H. Bannister and often figures in literature about the Revolution.

Putnam's Monthly Magazine (1853–1910), founded by the New York publishing firm, with C.F. Briggs as editor and G.W. Curtis and Parke Godwin as associates. It was distinctively American, in contrast with *Harper's,* and its contributors included Longfellow, Lowell, Thoreau, Melville, Cooper, Bryant, Bayard Taylor, C.D. Warner, J.P. Kennedy, C.E. Norton, and R.H. Stoddard. Suspended in 1857, it was revived (1868–70) as *Putnam's Magazine,* with Briggs, Stedman, and Godwin as editors. Frank Stockton, Howells, Burroughs, and J.J. Piatt were contributors. A third *Putnam's* (1906–10), later merging with the *Atlantic Monthly,* printed works by Don Marquis, Neihardt, Henry James, H.W. Boynton, and Gelett Burgess.

PYLE, ERNIE (ERNEST TAYLOR PYLE) (1900–1945), journalist and war correspondent in North Africa, Europe, and the Pacific, whose syndicated articles formed the basis of *Ernie Pyle in England* (1941), *Here Is Your War* (1943), *Brave Men* (1944), and *Last Chapter* (1946). His familiar writing about American soldiers in World War II was the most popular produced during the war, and the author's death from a Japanese machine-gun bullet on Iwo Jima made him a national hero.

PYLE, HOWARD (1853–1911), illustrator, writer, and painter, established a great reputation in the last decades of the 19th century for his washes, colored drawings, and line drawings of American colonial life, buccaneers, and medieval legendry. His books for children, with his own illustrations, include *The Merry Adventures of Robin Hood* (1883), *Men of Iron* (1892), and *Howard Pyle's Book of Pirates* (1921).

PYNCHON, THOMAS (1937–   ), novelist, born on Long Island, N.Y., after service in the navy, graduation from Cornell (1958), work as a technical writer for Boeing Aircraft in Seattle, and a year in Mexico, published his first novel, *V.,* ♦ in 1963. A richly complex work, philosophically influenced by *The Education of Henry Adams* and Wittgenstein, it deals with two major figures in its plot. One is Benny Profane, a constant failure, who drifts through life in such enterprises as hunting alligators in New York's sewers and is associated with his friends, the Whole Sick Crew. Another major figure, the cultivated Herbert Stencil, is more purposeful as he searches the world for V., the mysterious female spy and anarchist, who is by turns Venus, Virgin, and Void. Pynchon's second novel, *The Crying of Lot 49* ♦ (1966), is a shorter fable but marked by the same characteristics. Pynchon's plots are mystery stories combined with science fiction, but the novels' larger metaphors present in baroque fashion motifs not only of quest but of entropy, showing a closed world losing energy as time decays toward timelessness, and order disintegrates into alienation or chaos. Filled with endless esoteric references (including the parodying of other authors' styles) that range from high culture to trivial events, and marked by humor of wild comedy, the mock-heroic, and satire, the novels present the reader a huge array of clues but no clear direction in their purposeful ambiguity. In his second novel the main figure is Oedipa Maas, a California woman whose legacy from a friend requires her to discover the true nature of her inheritance by following clues to a cabalistic social system known to many dispossessed Americans but hidden from people who live within conventional society. Pynchon's very long third novel, *Gravity's Rainbow* ♦ (1973, National Book Award), set in the closing years of World War II, is a story of plots and counterplots involving a Nazi Lieutenant Weissmann (once V.'s lover, for Pynchon's novels have echoes), disguised as Captain Blicero, and the American sleuth, Lieutenant Tyrone Slothrop, while V-2 rockets fall on London. Like all Pynchon's works, the mood moves from black humor to lyricism, and the dream-like fantasy is marked by labyrinthine interconnections until the reader is uncertain about what is "real" and what is imagined. More than a decade passed before Pynchon published another book, *Slow Learner* (1984), collecting five previously published stories, thus making even more distant and more remote his new novel, *Vineland* (1990). It is set during 1984, though with much reminiscence of the 1960s, in a so-called Vineyard County of northern California and involves situations that are both exotic and strangely humorous. It concentrates on an uneasy family, particularly its young member, Prairie, daughter of an unusual man, Zoyd Wheeler, and her mother, Frenesi Gates, who has long since left to pursue her own romance with Brook Zond, a federal prosecutor who leads her into FBI officialdom as she undergoes many changes. Along with William Gaddis among the most experimental of contemporary American writers, Pynchon incorporates myriad influences and draws widely on science, from physics to information theory.

Q

QBVII, novel by Leon Uris.♦

Quadroon, *The,* novel by Mayne Reid,♦ published in 1856 and dramatized by the author. It formed the basis of the play *The Octoroon* (1859), by Dion Boucicault.

Quakers, the religious body properly called the Society of Friends. They originally called themselves Children of Truth, Children of Light, or Friends of Truth, and received their sobriquet either because of association with highly emotional states manifested physically or because their leader once commanded a judge to "tremble at the word of the Lord." The Society of Friends arose in England under the guidance of George Fox (1624–91), who after 1647 preached a simple personal religion, as opposed to formal worship and ceremonial. Their fundamental doctrines do not differ greatly from those of other Christian bodies, but they avoid rigid creeds, making their belief less a system than an attitude of mind. They believe that the same spirit that gave forth the Scriptures still guides men to a right understanding of them, and therefore they refuse set forms of worship and have no trained leaders. Because they declined to support the Established Church, resisted the taking of oaths, and were pacifistic, they were continually persecuted in England until the Toleration Act (1689). In America, whence they came in the 1650s, they were likewise persecuted by the Puritans because of their opposition to theocracy. They flourished nevertheless, and in 1681 the colony of Pennsylvania was granted to their leader, William Penn. They became widely known for their humanitarianism, both in their relations with the Indians and in their opposition to slavery of blacks. This attitude may be seen in the writings of John Woolman, while such Quakers as Whittier and Lucretia Mott were prominent among 19th-century Abolitionists. Although for conscience' sake most Quakers refused to participate in the Revolutionary War, some of them, called Free Quakers, took up arms. In 1827 Elias Hicks pressed the doctrine of the "inward light" to its extreme, and split the Society of Friends into two parts, the Hicksites and the orthodox group. Another schism occurred (1845), with the Wilburites following John Wilbur in returning to what they considered the original principles of the movement. Various groups, holding to common fundamental beliefs, had over 130,000 members in 1990.

QUEEN, ELLERY, pseudonym of Frederic Dannay (1905–82) and Manfred Lee (1905–71), under which they wrote many detective novels, beginning with *The Roman Hat Mystery* (1929). They also collaborated on an anthology of detective stories, *A Challenge to the Reader* (1938), and editorship of *Ellery Queen's Mystery Magazine* (1941–).

Queen Anne's War, see *French and Indian Wars.*

Queequeg, character in *Moby-Dick.*♦

Quick or the Dead?, *The,* novelette by Amélie Rives.♦

QUIN, DAN, pseudonym of Alfred Henry Lewis.♦

QUINCE, PETER, pseudonym of Isaac Story.♦

QUINCY, JOSIAH (1744–75), member of a prominent Boston family, graduated from Harvard (B.A., 1759; M.A., 1763), practiced law, and became an ardent supporter of the patriots. Although he wrote anonymous articles against Parliament, he joined John Adams in defending in court the British soldiers whose attack had resulted in the Boston Massacre. After a trip to Charleston in a vain attempt to recover from tuberculosis, he wrote an important patriot tract, *Observations on . . . the Boston Port-Bill* (1774), and in the same year was sent to England to plead the cause of the colonies, but died on the way home. What he accomplished in England has never been learned.

QUINCY, JOSIAH (1772–1864), son of the elder Josiah Quincy, graduated from Harvard (1790), was a Federalist congressman (1805–12), opposing Jefferson and Madison, and attacked the admission of the state of Louisiana and the War of 1812. Continuing this attitude in state politics, he became mayor of Boston (1823–28), and distinguished himself as a practical reformer. Harvard elected him president (1829–45) to obtain a business-like administration, but his Unitarianism greatly offended conservative interests. To illustrate the liberal traditions of the university, he wrote *The History of Harvard University* (2 vols., 1840), which became a standard work. Although his relations with the students were marked by quarrels and misunderstandings, he established the law school and observatory, extended the library, obtained a good faculty, and increased the endowment and student body. After retiring he turned to writing, and his works include a history of the Boston Athenaeum (1851), a history of Boston (1852), and one of J.Q. Adams (1858), as well as a work on agriculture. He wrote a memoir of his father (1825).

EDMUND QUINCY (1808–77), his son, renounced his background as a member of Boston's hegemony to become an ardent Abolitionist and an editor of *The Liberator*. His writings include *Wensley, a Story Without a Moral* (1854), depicting colonial society; a biography of his father (1867); and *The Haunted Adjutant* (1885), a collection of short stories.

QUINN, JOHN (1870–1924), New York lawyer, early became a major collector of books and manuscripts, concentrating on the modern authors of Ireland, the land from which his father had emigrated. A friend of Yeats, he purchased many of his papers, the manuscript of Joyce's *Ulysses,* the manuscripts of Conrad's novels, and many of Pound's and Eliot's manuscripts, includ-

ing the original version of *The Waste Land*. Most of these he sold (1923) to have funds for purchasing modern French paintings. A biography of Quinn by B.L. Reid, *The Man from New York* (1968), was awarded a Pulitzer Prize.

Quint, PETER, character in *The Turn of the Screw*. ◆

Quinto Sol Movement, named for the group of Chicano writers who published with Quinto Sol Publications (1967–1977), established in Berkeley to publish Mexican-American writing. The concept of Atzlan, the supposed ancient home of the Aztecs somewhere in the American Southwest, was adopted by many of the writers as a way of fostering pride in both their Indian and Mexican heritages. Quinto Sol introduced the work of Hinojosa-Smith ◆ and Rudofo Anaya ◆.

QUOD, JOHN, pseudonym of J.T. Irving. ◆

Quodlibet, satire by J.P. Kennedy. ◆

R

Rabbit, Run, novel by John Updike, ♦ published in 1960. The first in a series of four, it was considerably revised in text for the edition of 1964 and again for publication in 1970. The novel presents 26-year-old Harry Angstrom, whose nickname, Rabbit, comes from his glorious days as a highschool basketball champion in the small town of Brewer, Pa. Now, frustrated by the responsibilities of marriage to Janice (pregnant and an alcoholic) and fatherhood to three-year-old Nelson, and by an inconsequential job demonstrating the MagiPeel kitchen implement, he decides to run away. His former athletic coach, Tothero, bucks him up and introduces him to an appealing young woman, Ruth, who becomes pregnant by him. With tragic irony, his legitimate child is born but soon accidentally drowns when his drunken wife is bathing her.

Rabbit, Redux (1971) depicts the Angstrom household just ten years later, long after Harry's return to a marriage that is still a shambles. He gets no stability from his father-in-law's successful place in the town's middle-class society as owner of an automobile sales agency. On the contrary, a suave Greek salesman for Springer Motors, Charlie Stavros, temporarily woos Janice away from Rabbit. Caught up in the social turmoil of the 1960s, he befriends two radicals, a young man and woman, and the latter is accidentally killed by neighbors who are infuriated by the young people's way of life.

Rabbit Is Rich (1981) treats the Angstroms still another decade later. Rabbit and Janice have now inherited a half interest in his late father-in-law's business and, having found a kind of place in society, he is a member of the local country club. He is resigned to good relations with Stavros, and he sees Ruth to determine if a chance acquaintance is their daughter. Rabbit finds that the girl is not his daughter, but he does become involved in paternal problems with his son Nelson, now in college, who has gotten his girl friend pregnant.

Rabbit at Rest (1990), necessarily the last in the series, finds Janice and Rabbit still warring, son Nelson now running the car dealership while doing drugs, and Rabbit much overweight. He has a brief affair with Nelson's wife and then dies of a massive heart attack sustained during a playground basketball game.

RABE, DAVID [WILLIAM] (1940–), Iowaborn dramatist, after army service in Vietnam and teaching at Villanova University began his career as playwright with *The Basic Training of Pavlo*

Hummel (1971) and *Sticks and Bones* (1971), both published in 1973, both treating the effect of the Vietnam War on people, the latter presenting a blinded soldier returning to his commonplace family and ironically being the only one capable of seeing. *The Orphan* (1973), also with a Vietnam background, relates the mythology of the *Oresteia* to modern cruelty. *In the Boom Boom Room* (produced 1973, published 1975) presents the sleazy life of a tawdry woman. *Streamers* (produced 1976, published 1977) is a violent depiction of homosexuality and murders in an army camp. *Goose and Tomtom* (1982) is a two-act comedy about fights between jewel thieves. *Hurlyburly* (1984) is a grim comedy drawing upon Rabe's experiences while writing screenplays in Hollywood. *Those the River Keeps* (1994) has two hoodlums meeting and remembering fearful pasts. The title comes from the criminal underworld belief that a corpse slit open will remain beneath the surface. A Novel, *Recital of the Dog* (1993) is bitterly comic.

Radical Club, THE, informal association of New England ministers and laymen, who desired to abolish vestiges of Christian supernaturalism and to embody in a free religion the spiritual intuitions of humanity at large. The Club met informally at the Boston home of J.T. Sargent and included virtually all the advanced Unitarian and Transcendentalist thinkers. It flourished in 1867–80, and similar societies existed elsewhere. *The Radical* (1865–72), an outgrowth of the Club, was the chief organ of the heterodox religious and social thinkers of New England at this time. Contributors included Moncure Conway, the elder James, T.W. Higginson, W. Phillips, J.F. Clarke, Alcott, and E.R. Sill.

RAFINESQUE, CONSTANTINE SAMUEL (1783–1840), European naturalist, first visited the U.S. in 1802 for a three-year stay that included work in a countinghouse, study of the Osage language, and the collection of botanical specimens. He returned in 1815 to remain for the rest of his life, serving as professor of botany, natural history, and modern languages (1818–26) at Transylvania University, Kentucky. During these latter years his publications included *A History of Kentucky* (1824) and *A Life of Travels and Researchers in North America and South Europe* (1836), along with works on banking, botany, the Bible, ichthyology, Indian culture and language, and many other topics, as well as original verse, so that a modern bibliography lists 939 items, ranging from books to circulars, that came from his pen. Among these is a translation of the *Walam Olum*♦ in his *The American Nations* (1836), a work on Indian tribes.

Ragtime, novel by E.L. Doctorow. ♦

Rahel to Varnhagen, blank-verse dramatic monologue by E.A. Robinson, ♦ published in *The Three Taverns* (1920).

The poem represents an episode in the courtship (1814) of the German historical figures Varnhagen von Ense, diplomat and biographer, and Rahel Robert, 14 years his senior but a woman of charm and intellect. Shrewdly and wittily, Rahel derides her youthful lover's presumption in seeking to win "these aged hands." She tells of earlier affairs, shows him old love letters, and chides his folly, but to no avail (as perhaps she has expected), for he smiles at her arguments and seems to have foreseen each of them. Finally she concedes his victory: "You know so dismal much As that about me? . . . Well, I believe you do."

RAHV, PHILIP (1908–73), Ukrainian-born literary critic, came to the U.S. in 1922 and within a decade became an important figure in its culture as co-founder and editor of *Partisan Review.* ♦ His essays are collected in *Image and Idea* (1949), including the seminal "Paleface and Redskin" on the dichotomy between experience and consciousness in American writers; *The Myth and the Powerhouse* (1965); and *Literature and the Sixth Sense* (1969). *Essays on Literature and Politics* (1978) is a posthumous collection. Beginning in 1957 he was a member of the Brandeis faculty.

RAIMOND, C.E., pseudonym of Elizabeth Robins. ♦

Raise High the Roof-Beam, Carpenters, stories by J.D. Salinger. ♦

RÂLE (or RASLES), SÉBASTIEN (1657?–1724), French Jesuit missionary, came to New France (1689) and established a mission among the Abnaki Indians in the disputed territory of Maine (1696). There he influenced the Indians to oppose the English, who later executed him. His *Dictionary of the Abnaki Language* was published in 1833.

RALPH, JAMES (c.1705–62), probably born in America, accompanied Franklin to London (1724), where he remained to establish himself as a poet, historian, journalist, and dramatist. His ballad opera *The Fashionable Lady* (1730) was the first play by an American to be produced in London. Although he was associated with Garrick in political journalism, Fielding in theatrical journalism, and Franklin in the writing of *An Histori-*

cal Review of the Constitution and Government of Pennsylvania (1759), Ralph was primarily a hack writer. He figures in Franklin's *Autobiography.*

Ramona, novel by Helen Hunt Jackson, ♦ published in 1884.

On the southern California ranch of Señora Moreno, a haughty Spaniard who refuses to yield to the onrushing tide of American conquest, live her son Felipe and Ramona Ortegna, a half-Indian and half-Scotch girl who does not realize that she has been adopted. To this ranch comes Alessandro, a full-blooded Indian, who falls in love with Ramona and has his love reciprocated until Señora Moreno, enraged at the union between her adopted daughter and an Indian, attempts to sever the romance. Alessandro returns to his native village, which he finds has been destroyed by the Americans, who have also killed his father in seizing the Indian land. He returns to the Spanish ranch, and Ramona elopes with him to San Diego. They are driven from place to place by the avaricious hordes of Americans, until Alessandro loses his reason and is killed by an American whose horse he had temporarily taken. Ramona and her child are found by Felipe, who brings them back to the old Mexican estate, now his property since Señora Moreno's death. After a temporarily peaceful period, Felipe is forced to sell the ranch to the powerful Americans, and he and his foster sister are married and remove to Mexico.

RAMSAY, DAVID (1749–1815), South Carolina physician, historian, and political figure, is most famous for his *History of the Revolution of South Carolina* (2 vols., 1785) and the complementary *History of South Carolina from Its First Settlement in 1670, to . . . 1808* (2 vols., 1809). The first part of the work is known to be partly plagiarized from the *Annual Register,* while the second occasionally borrows from the work of Alexander Hewat. ♦ Ramsay's posthumously published works are *Universal History Americanized* (12 vols., 1819), the last four volumes dealing with America, and *History of the United States* (3 vols., 1816–17), completed by Samuel Stanhope Smith.

RAND, AYN (1905–82), Russian-born novelist, graduated from the University of Leningrad, came to the U.S. (1926), where she was naturalized. Her first writing was a mystery play, *The Night of January 16th* (1935), but later works shows her deep concern with the theme of extreme individualism. Her first novel, *We, the Living* (1936), depicts young Russian individualists trapped and destroyed by totalitarian dictatorship. *Anthem* (England, 1938; U.S., 1946) is a short novel about a heroic dissenter in a future monolithic and collectivized state. *The Fountainhead*♦ (1943) is a long biographical novel praising the independence of an architect ostensibly modeled on Frank Lloyd Wright. *Atlas Shrugged* (1957) treats the value of a superior concept of individualism related to people who plan a new society based on the oath "I will never live for the sake of another man, nor ask any other man to live for mine." *For the New Intellectual* (1961) collects the philosophic passages of these four novels to present her theory of Objectivism, which is antiromantic and antialtruistic in its fervent appeal to a code of "rational self-interest." *The Romantic Manifesto* (1969) is her "philosophy of literature."

RANDALL, JAMES RYDER (1839–1908), native of Baltimore, teacher in Louisiana, and author of "Maryland, My Maryland" (1861), Civil War lyric sung to a modified tune of "Tannenbaum, O Tannenbaum." His complete *Poems* was published in 1910.

RANSOM, JOHN CROWE (1888–1974), Tennessee poet, was educated in his native state and as a Rhodes Scholar at Oxford (1913). He was a member of the English department of Vanderbilt University (1914–37) and early became a leader of the Agrarians♦ and an editor of *The Fugitive*♦ In 1937 he joined the faculty of Kenyon College, where he remained until retiring in 1958. He founded and edited the *Kenyon Review,*♦ placing stress on the New Criticism more than on the regionalism that he formerly emphasized. His first verse, *Poems About God* (1919), although not sufficiently valued by him for selection in later volumes, was already marked by the irony that is more accomplished in *Chills and Fever* (1924). *Grace After Meat* (1924) is an English selection from these two books, which was followed by *Two Gentlemen in Bonds* (1927). His balanced judgment of opposites and his portraits of people in his elegies are distinguished by a witty and oblique style. His *Selected Poems* (1945) was issued in revised, enlarged editions (1963, 1969). His criticism appears in *God Without Thunder: An Unorthodox Defense of Orthodoxy* (1930), an attack on science as destructive of the old mystery of God, a theme to which he returned in *The World's Body* (1938), on the failure of science to achieve the body that is in poetry; and he gathered later essays in *Beating the Bushes* (1972). He contributed to the Agrarian anthology *I'll Take My Stand*♦ (1930), and later analyzed contemporaries and called for an ontological critic in *The New Criticism* (1941).

Ranson's Folly, title story in a collection of novelettes by Richard Harding Davis,♦ published in 1902. It was dramatized by the author in 1904.

Rappaccini's Daughter, allegorical tale by Hawthorne,♦ published in 1844 and reprinted in *Mosses from an Old Manse* (1846).

Giovanni Guasconti comes to study at the University of Padua and lodges next door to the house of Giacomo Rappaccini, a doctor. In the latter's

garden he sees and falls in love with Rappaccini's daughter Beatrice, whose beauty strangely resembles that of her father's poisonous flowers. Pietro Baglioni, a friendly professor, warns Giovanni that Rappaccini's love of science has led him beyond moral or humane considerations, and that the girl's nature seems a product of his sinister art, but the young man is undeterred. Under the scientific regard of her father, the affection of the two grows deeper, and Giovanni himself becomes tainted by the poisonous breath of the garden. Then he gives Beatrice a potion that Baglioni has supplied him as an antidote to all poisons. She drinks it, but "as poison had been life, so the powerful antidote was death; and thus the poor victim of man's ingenuity and of thwarted nature . . . perished there, at the feet of her father and Giovanni."

Rappists, German religious communist sect, founded by George Rapp (1757–1847), who led his followers to settle in American communities. The most prominent of these were the Harmony Society♦ and New Harmony.♦

RASCOE, [ARTHUR] BURTON (1892–1957), critic, editor, and columnist, whose books include *Theodore Dreiser* (1925), *A Bookman's Daybook* (1929), *Titans of Literature* (1932), *Prometheans* (1933), and *Belle Starr* (1941), a biography of a Southwest "Bandit Queen." *The Smart Set Anthology* (1934) collects material from the magazine. *Before I Forget* (1937) and *We Were Interrupted* (1947) are autobiographies.

RASLES, SÉBASTIEN, see *Râle.*

Rationale of Verse, *The,* essay by Poe,♦ published as "Notes on English Verse" in *The Pioneer* (1843), and in its final form under the present title in the *Southern Literary Messenger* (1848). It is the most complete expression of Poe's theories of poetic technique, although critics, indicating its inconsistencies, assert that he did not follow his own dicta.

Refuting the notion that prosody is concerned with the regular "alternation of long and short syllables," Poe establishes a distinction between "natural" and "unnatural" metrical units. "The *natural* long syllables are those encumbered . . . with [difficult] consonants. . . . *Accented* syllables are of course always long, but, where *un*encumbered with consonants, must be classed among the *unnaturally* long." He upholds a "principle of equality," according to which each verse foot must be pronounced in the same time as every other foot in the line, regardless of the number of its syllables. This applies only to single lines, although to be effective a stanza should contain lines arranged in strict pattern; and rhyme, alliteration, and the use of refrains should be governed by the same rule. Since duration is the standard by which this "equality" is to be judged, there should be no "blending" or substitution of one metrical foot for another. Contractions or elisions should be avoided, although additional unstressed syllables may be used if they can be pronounced rapidly. The "cæsura" (in this usage, a "variable foot" occurring at the end or middle of a line, and consisting of one long syllable) is discussed as being one of the most important of metrical feet. The essay concludes with a passage, especially referring to Longfellow's poems, which denies the possibility of the successful use of Greek hexameters in English, because of the "natural" pronunciation peculiar to English words.

RAUSCHENBUSCH, WALTER (1861–1918), Baptist minister of New York and professor of church history at Rochester Theological Seminary (1897–1918), was a leader of the Christian Socialist movement. His books include *Christianity and the Social Crisis* (1907), *Prayers of . . . Social Awakening* (1910), *Christianizing the Social Order* (1912), and *Theology for the Social Gospel* (1917).

Raven, The, poem by Poe,♦ the title piece of a volume (1845), was several times revised in later publications. To Poe's account of writing it, in "The Philosophy of Composition,"♦ must be added the influence upon the meter of Mrs. Browning's "Lady Geraldine's Courtship" and Chivers's "Isadore." The poem consists of 18 six-line stanzas, the first five lines of each being in trochaic octameter, and the sixth line trochaic tetrameter. The rhythm is varied by frequent syncopation, caused by effects of double rhyme and alliteration. The rhyme pattern is *abcbbb,* in which the *b* rhymes are based on the constant refrain, "Nevermore," a word that merged Poe's favorite theme of grief occasioned by the death of a beautiful woman (in this case "Lenore"), the distinctive theme of despair at the denial of personal immortality, and the sonorous sound of the *o* and *r* in the refrain itself.

A weary student is visited in his room, one stormy midnight, by a raven who can speak the single word, "Nevermore." Tortured by grief over the loss of his beloved, the student questions the bird concerning the possibility of meeting her in another world. He is driven to wilder demands by the repetition of the fatal word, until the raven becomes an irremovable symbol of his dark doubts and frustrated longing.

RAWLINGS, MARJORIE KINNAN (1896–1953), born in Washington, D.C., graduated from the University of Wisconsin (1918), became a journalist, and in 1928 "deliberately cut her civilized ties . . . and migrated to the firmly intrenched outpost of the vanishing frontier," the hummock country of Florida that forms the setting of her fiction. *Cross Creek* (1942) is a humorous account of her adoption of Florida as a home and a source of literary material. She published her first novelette, *Jacob's Ladder,* and stories of

the region's poor-white farmers, hunters, trappers, fishermen, and moonshiners in *When the Whippoorwill* (1940). She further depicted this region in her novels *South Moon Under* (1933), *Golden Apples* (1935), and *The Yearling* (1938, Pulitzer Prize), about a boy's love for his pet fawn, which his father is forced to kill when it ruins his meager crops. Her *Selected Letters* was published in 1982.

RAYMOND, HENRY JARVIS (1820–69), after a brief association with Horace Greeley, founded his own paper, *The New York Times* ♦ (1851), to oppose the intemperate and distorted journalism of the period. His sound, impartial policies soon won the paper great success. He was also editor of *Harper's Monthly* (1850–56), but had little time for active work on it after the first year. He was a member of Congress (1865–67) and was the author of *History of the Administration of President Lincoln* (1864), a campaign document, later expanded into *The Life and Public Services of Abraham Lincoln* (1865).

RAYNAL, GUILLAUME THOMAS FRANÇOIS (1713–96), French author, usually called Abbé Raynal because as a young man he received orders as a Jesuit. He is best known as the author of *L'Histoire philosophique et politique des établissements et du commerce des Européens dans les deux Indes* (Amsterdam, 4 vols., 1770), written with the assistance of such *philosophes* as Diderot. The work lacks unity and proportion and merely summarizes the ideas of others, but its indictment of royalty, attack on the tyranny of the Church, and praise of the English settlers in America made it democratic propaganda, read with enthusiasm by Chateaubriand, Jefferson, and Crèvecœur. The last's *Letters from an American Farmer* was dedicated to Raynal and often paralleled his work, whose revised and enlarged edition in French (1772–74) was translated into English (1776), extracts being frequently issued under other titles. Paine's *Letter to the Abbé Raynal* (1782) corrects errors in Raynal's *The Revolution of America* (1781).

READ, OPIE [PERCIVAL] (1852–1939), born in Tennessee, began his journalistic career in Kentucky, then moved to Arkansas, where he conducted the humorous weekly paper *The Arkansas Traveler* (1882–92). When his satirical sketches of backcountry people made him unpopular in the region, he moved with the journal to Chicago (1891). His popular humorous works, such as *A Kentucky Colonel* (1890), seem to be purely ephemeral best sellers. *I Remember* (1930) is his autobiography.

READ, THOMAS BUCHANAN (1822–72), Pennsylvania poetaster and minor painter, wrote more than ten volumes of verse, but is best remembered for "Sheridan's Ride," a short piece describing the breakneck journey of General

Philip Sheridan 20 miles from Winchester to rally his retreating army, which was also the subject of his best-known painting. The poem was published in *A Summer Story, Sheridan's Ride, and Other Poems* (1865). *The Wagoner of the Alleghanies* (1862) is a poem of the Revolutionary War. His *Poetical Works* were collected in 3 volumes (1866).

Reader's Digest, *The* (1922–   ), monthly magazine featuring condensations of articles reprinted from other periodicals. It had a circulation (1994) of 16,250,000 in the U.S. and of 31,000,000 in all of its 16 language editions, making it the widest circulated magazine in the U.S. and in the world. It also publishes a Braille edition, a school edition, and a phonograph transcription. About 60% of its articles are original works, generally farmed out to other magazines for first publication, the remaining being legitimate reprints. Until 1955 it did not carry advertising. It has always featured many filler items such as a department of picturesque speech, and maxims and epigrams. It also features condensations of books and human-interest material. The editorial content is conservative and geared to the average mind. It is optimistic in depicting the joys of living on a small income, the ways of overcoming misfortune, the wonders of science, and the easy means of learning about "difficult" subjects.

REALF, RICHARD (1834–78), English-born poet, began his career with the precocious collection *Guesses at the Beautiful* (1852). He came to the U.S. (1854), served as a newspaper correspondent in Kansas, and there met John Brown, whose Abolitionist plans he supported. After his service in the Civil War, and a stormy private life, friends sent him to San Francisco, where, broken in health, he soon committed suicide. *Poems by Richard Realf, Poet, Soldier, Workman* (1898), though admired by Bierce, is generally considered bombastically impassioned.

Realism, term applied to literary composition that aims at an interpretation of the actualities of any aspect of life, free from subjective prejudice, idealism, or romantic color. It is opposed to the concern with the unusual which forms the basis of romance, but it does not proceed, as does naturalism,♦ to the philosophy of determinism and a completely amoral attitude. Although the novel has generally been considered the form best suited to the artistic treatment of reality, realism is not limited to any one form. As an attitude of the writer toward his materials, it is relative, and no chronological point may be indicated as the beginning of realism, but the 19th century is considered to mark its origin as a literary movement. The example of science, the influence of rational philosophy, the use of documentation in historical study, as well as the reaction against attenuated romanticism, all had their effect in creating the dominance of realism at this time. Although influenced by English and foreign authors, to a great extent the American transition from romance to realism in fiction was indigenous, but it occurred gradually. Frontier literature, frequently realistic in its observation of detail, merged in the general stream of influence through the work of such authors as Clemens, while the all-inclusive zest for experience displayed in Whitman's descriptive poems is another primary source of modern realism. A realistic attitude toward their materials may be noted in the stories of Harriet Beecher Stowe, De Forest, and Rebecca H. Davis, but the first concerted movement was probably that excited by the interest in local color. ♦ Although such writers as Harte, Sarah Orne Jewett, Cable, and F.H. Smith were frequently romantic in stressing eccentric manners, they were realistic in attending to minute details, and to some extent in their treatment of character. The tendencies of these writers were carried further by such novelists as Joseph Kirkland, Edward Eggleston, Hamlin Garland, and E.W. Howe. Although far less concerned with homely setting or themes, Howells, Henry James, and later Edith Wharton were also realistic in their depiction of certain special social environments, extending realism into the comedy of manners and into psychological perception of character. Somewhat later novelists such as H.B. Fuller, Upton Sinclair, and Ernest Poole, although often sentimental, were concerned with exposing the social evils that thwarted the happiness of their characters, and thereby used realism for humanitarian protest of a sort that later became much more determined as used by writers of proletarian literature. Although there have been substantial shifts of sensibility in 20th-century American literature, as for example to a new concern with the novel as romance, realism has continued to be a major mode of expression.

Realms of Being, *The,* general title of a series of philosophical works by Santayana,♦ to which *Scepticism and Animal Faith* (1923) serves as an introduction, while *The Realm of Essence* (1927), *The Realm of Matter* (1930), *The Realm of Truth* (1937), and *The Realm of Spirit* (1940) form the body. In these books, Santayana modifies and supplements his philosophy as expressed in *The Life of Reason*♦ (1905–6).

Investigating being, of which Nature is only one aspect, the author considers that there can be no first principle of skepticism, since such a principle is already an assumption. Hence the skeptic ultimately arrives at the conclusion that "nothing given exists," and all data are intuitive, without any guarantee of their existence in nature. "The sceptic, then, as a consequence of carrying his scepticism to the greatest lengths, finds himself in the presence of more luminous and less equivocal objects than does the working and believing mind; only these objects are without meaning, they are only what they are obviously, all surface." Such objects Santayana calls essences. Material events, then, arouse intuitions, and the system men make of these signs of their environment constitutes their concept of the realm of matter. "This world of free expression, this drift of sensations, passions, and ideas, perpetually kindled and fading in the light of consciousness, I call the *Realm of Spirit.*" Behind this lies matter, which Santayana recognizes as the unknowable but ever-present basis of action. There are, then, four realms: matter, essence, spirit, and truth. The last is considered as "frozen history," the standard comprehensive description of existence, a segment of the realm of essence formed of approximately correct views referring to the same system of facts. Knowledge is faith in the unknowable, symbolized by essences. Logical analysis may lead to complete skepticism concerning the existence of anything, but animal faith continues and believes in a world whose material events have aroused intuitive essences as signs of the environment in which all animals live and suffer. Essences, in themselves significant and eternal, are logically, though not cosmologically, prior to that which they designate, so that the world remains unknowable only in its inmost intrinsic character, and comes to be comprehensible through these reports lying in the realm of essence.

Reason the Only Oracle of Man, deistic book attributed to Ethan Allen,♦ published in 1784. Later scholarship has contended that, though the work has been popularly known as "Ethan Allen's Bible," approximately four-fifths of it was written by the free-thinker Dr. Thomas Young (1732–77), to whose posthumously obtained manuscript Allen gave no credit.

Rebecca of Sunnybrook Farm, novel by Kate Douglas Wiggin,♦ published in 1903.

The heroine of this popular story for children is precocious, lovable Rebecca Randall, whose adventures are described from her early years as one of seven children on her widowed mother's farm, to her life in Riverboro with her Aunts Miranda and Jane and her friends, Emma Jane Perkins, the stage driver Mr. Cobb, and generous Adam Ladd, her "Mr. Aladdin."

Rebellion, War of the, see *Civil War.*

RECHY, JOHN [FRANCISCO] (1934–   ), born in Texas, served in the army in Germany, is a novelist of the underground life of sex and drugs, mainly of homosexuals, presented with candid directness in *City of Night* (1963), *Numbers* (1967), *This Day's Death* (1970), *The Vampires* (1971), *The Fourth Angel* (1973), *Rushes* (1979), *Bodies and Souls* (1983), and *Marilyn's Daughter* (1988), more bisexual in theme and treatment, and *The Miraculous Day of Amalia Gomez* (1992). *The Sexual Outlaw* (1978), set in Hollywood, is a documentary account of men engaged in promiscuous, anonymous sex in public places.

Reconstruction, name applied to the reorganization of state governments in the South after the Civil War, the constitutional processes of their readmission to the Union, and the social adjustments made necessary by altered economic conditions, especially the emancipation and enfranchisement of blacks. The name also refers to the period of social, military, and political history in which, after Lincoln's assassination, power passed from the conservative group in the Republican party, inclined toward leniency and the rapid reinstatement of the seceded states, to the radical Republicans, who favored military rule and the suppression of civil rights in the conquered states. Reconstruction is considered to have terminated with the presidential election of 1876, despite the doubtful victory of Hayes over the Democratic candidate Tilden. Histories of the Reconstruction include Paul Buck's *Road to Reunion* and Claude Bowers's *The Tragic Era,* while events and social conditions in the South during this period are depicted in many novels, e.g. De Forest's *Kate Beaumont* (1872), Albion Tourgée's *A Fool's Errand* (1879) and *Bricks Without Straw* (1880), G.W. Cable's *John March, Southerner* (1894), Thomas Nelson Page's *Red Rock* (1898), Joel Chandler Harris's *Gabriel Tolliver* (1902), and Thomas Dixon's *The Leopard's Spots* (1902), *The Clansman* (1905), and *The Traitor* (1907).

Red Badge of Courage, The: *An Episode of the American Civil War,* novel by Stephen Crane,♦ published in 1895. The original manuscript, containing an added 5000 words (about 10% of the entirety) deleted by the original publisher, was printed for the first time in 1982. This psychological study of a soldier's reactions to warfare was written before Crane had ever seen a battle. His knowledge was at least partly derived from a popular anthology, *Battles and Leaders of the Civil War.* The unnamed battle of the novel has been identified as that at Chancellorsville.

Henry Fleming, generally called simply "the youth" or "he," is an ordinary, inexperienced soldier, "an unknown quantity," torn between a "little panic-fear" and "visions of broken-bladed glory" as he faces his first battle. He begins with the state of mind of the raw recruit who is anxious to get into battle so that he may show his patriotism and prove himself a hero. He swaggers to keep up his spirits during the delay that precedes his suddenly being thrust into the slaughter. Then he is overcome by unthinking fear and runs from the field. He is ashamed when he joins the wounded, for he has not earned their "red badge of courage," and then he becomes enraged when he witnesses the horrid dance of death of his terribly maimed friend, Jim Conklin. Later, by chance, he gets a minor head wound in a confused struggle with one of the retreating infantrymen of his own army. The next day, when his pretense is accepted that the wound is the result of enemy gunfire, he suddenly begins to fight frantically, and then automatically seizes the regiment's colors in the charge that reestablishes its reputation. He moves through this sultry nightmare with unconscious heroism, and emerges steady, quiet, and truly courageous.

Red Pony, The, story by Steinbeck, reprinted in *The Long Valley.* ◆

Red Rover, The, romance by Cooper, ◆ published in 1827 and dramatized by S.H. Chapman (1828).

Lieutenant Henry Ark, on the track of the Red Rover, a notorious pirate, disguises himself as a common sailor ("Wilder") and enlists as second in command of the mysterious *Dolphin.* When the captain of the merchant ship *Caroline* is accidentally injured, Ark is sent to take his place. Both ships sail immediately from Newport, and the youthful commander's skillful seamanship disturbs the superstitious crew of the *Caroline,* who desert him. He is left with the two passengers, Gertrude Grayson and her governess, Mrs. Wyllys, to escape the sinking ship in a small boat, from which they are rescued by the *Dolphin.* Captain Heidegger (the Rover) is attracted to Mrs. Wyllys, and becomes friendly with Ark, confessing to him that he had been a seaman in the royal navy, but that his loyalty to the colonies had led him into a quarrel in which he killed an officer and escaped to become a pirate. Ark's former ship, the *Dart,* is now sighted, and, when the Rover goes aboard her, disguised as a naval officer, he learns Ark's true identity. Returning, he is persuaded to put the women and Ark aboard the *Dart.* A fierce battle ensues, in which the pirate is victorious. Ark is about to be hanged, when it is revealed that he is actually Paul de Lacey, the long-lost son of Mrs. Wyllys. At this, the Rover sets his prisoners free, sends them ashore, dismisses his crew, burns his ship, and disappears. After the close of the Revolutionary War, 20 years later, he is brought, dying, to the home of De Lacey, who has married Gertrude. He discloses that he is the brother of Mrs. Wyllys, and that after ending his piracies he reformed, led a virtuous life, and served honorably in the patriot cause.

Red Score, English title given to the Indian chronicle *Walam Olum.* ◆

Redburn: His First Voyage, novel by Melville, ◆ published in 1849 and based on his own experiences during his first voyage (1837).

Wellingborough Redburn, son of an impoverished middle-class New York family, ships as a "boy" on the *Highlander,* bound for Liverpool. Captain Riga treats him with ironic kindness until the ship sails, after which he withdraws to his solitary cabin, placing his mate in command. Clumsy and inexperienced, Redburn receives only contempt from the sailors. During six weeks in Liverpool, he explores the city, aided by his guidebook, and sees especially the lack of democracy and the vicious living conditions of the poor. He becomes friendly with Harry Bolton, a spendthrift young aristocrat, who takes him on a riotous trip to London, shocking the boy by his excesses and reckless actions. The return voyage, on which Harry is also a sailor, is full of tragic incidents, for the steerage passengers nearly starve, an epidemic of cholera kills many, and the crew is maltreated. In New York, Captain Riga refuses to pay Redburn and Harry, and the friends part, the boy going to his home and the Englishman signing for a whaling voyage, during which he is killed.

REDPATH, JAMES (1833–91), Scottish-born journalist and reformer, came to the U.S. (*c.*1850), was Kansas correspondent for the New York *Tribune,* and became a zealous Abolitionist, as revealed in *The Roving Editor; or, Talks with Slaves in the Southern States* (1859), *Hand-book to Kansas Territory* . . . (1859), *The Public Life of Captain John Brown* (1860), *Echoes of Harper's Ferry* (1860), and *A Guide to Hayti* (1860). The last was part of his campaign to establish Haiti as an asylum for blacks. In 1868 he founded the Boston Lyceum Bureau, which later bore his name, and he became the leading lecture promoter of his time. *Tales and Traditions of the Border* (1849) is an early work on Scotland in collaboration with his father, and *Talks About Ireland* (1881) is a collection of letters denouncing the English administration.

Redskins, The; or, Indian and Injin, novel by Cooper, ◆ published in 1846 as the third of the Littlepage Manuscripts, dealing with the Anti-Rent War. ◆

Much of the land in New York state is held by absentee landlords, in the manner of feudal estates, and during the 1840s there is a popular anti-rent uprising. Bands of agitators, armed and disguised as "Injins," intimidate wealthy families and raid their property. Hugh Littlepage and his uncle Roger visit their estate, Ravensnest, to investigate the activities of the redskins. Hugh becomes engaged to Mary Warren, daughter of the local rector, although Seneca Newcome, an unscrupulous lawyer, attempts to arrange a match between Hugh and his daughter Opportunity. Hugh and Roger have been disguised as German peddlers, but they reveal themselves to the family after they are recognized by the faithful old Indian Susquesus and the black servant Jaap. A band of anti-renters arrives in "Injin" disguise and is contrasted unfavorably with a group of Western Indians who come to confer with Susquesus. Hugh, aided by Mary and the real Indians, discovers and foils the arson plot of Newcome and the anti-renters. The sheriff disperses the raiders, and, when Ravensnest is finally made safe again, Hugh and Mary are married.

Ree Indians, see *Arikara Indians.*

REED, ISHMAEL [SCOTT] (1938–), Chattanooga-born black author, long resident in Berkeley, Calif. His experimental novels of preposterous plots marked by fantasy, sometimes surrealistic, sometimes caricatured and satiric, include *The Free-Lance Pallbearers* (1967), depicting violence and corruption in a fictive land and satirizing its mistreatment of blacks; *Yellow Back Radio Broke Down* (1969), presenting the fantastic adventures of a black cowboy; *Mumbo Jumbo* (1972), a freewheeling tale about black-white relations over the ages; *The Quality of Hurt* (1973), containing bitter autobiographical comments on whites; *The Last Days of Louisiana Red* (1974), a bizarre tale of black and whites set in Berkeley during the 1960s; *Flight to Canada* (1976), fusing 19th- and 20th-century characters and situations in a surrealistic presentation of American slavery; *Reckless Eyeballing* (1980), displaying both humor and horror; and *The Terrible Twos* (1982), a bitter, satirical fantasy of political and social corruption in the U.S. of today and the future, contained in *The Terrible Threes* (1989), marked by both terror and humor. *Japanese by Spring* (1993) satirizes factional struggles and questions of political correctness among the faculty and students of a fictional Oakland college. His poetry is collected in *Catechism of the Neo-American HooDoo Church* (1970), *Conjure* (1972), *Chattanooga* (1973), *Secretary to the Spirits* (1978), and *New and Collected Poems* (1988). *Writin' Is Fightin'* (1988) gathers editorials, book reviews, and essays. *Shrovetime in Old New Orleans* (1978) and *God Made Alaska for the Indians* (1982) are gatherings of essays. *Airing Dirty Laundry* (1994) collects previously published essays as well as new work, much of it confronting the media for misrepresentations of African-Americans.

REED, JOHN (1887–1920), born of wealthy parents in Portland, Ore., graduated from Harvard (1910), then traveled in Europe. Aided by Lincoln Steffens, he obtained employment with *The American Magazine,* but he submitted his most sincere work to *The Masses.* His report of the Paterson silk mills strike won him recognition, and in 1913 he was sent by the New York *World* to cover the Mexican revolt of Villa. During the same year he reported the miners' strike at Ludlow, Colo., for the *Metropolitan Magazine,* and wrote his impressions of Villa and others in *Insurgent Mexico* (1914). As a war correspondent for the *Metropolitan,* as well as for *The Masses* and *The Seven Arts,* he wrote the articles republished in *The War in Eastern Europe* (1916). Already sympathetic with the cause of the Russian Revolution, Reed became friendly with the Bolshevik leaders and, after reporting their coup (1917), returned to America to be active in the organization of the first Communist party of the U.S. Difficulties encountered in this enterprise sent him back to Russia, where he died and was accorded the honor of burial in the Kremlin. His eyewitness story of the Russian Revolution is contained in *Red Russia* (1919) and his most important work, *Ten Days That Shook the World*♦ (1919). The latter graphic account was officially approved by the Soviets, and Lenin wrote an introduction to a later edition. In 1985 Corliss Lamont gathered from early sources a volume of Reed's *Collected Poems.*

REED, SAMPSON (1800–1880), born in Massachusetts, graduated from Harvard (1818), and left its Divinity School after being converted to the beliefs of Swedenborg. With his brother he edited the *New Jerusalem Magazine,* founded a Swedenborgian magazine for children, and otherwise spread the doctrines of his church. His *Observations on the Growth of the Mind* (1826), an essay on Swedenborgian thought, greatly impressed Emerson, who was particularly interested by the doctrine of correspondence and the prophetic optimism of its teachings, and seems to have derived from it much of his knowledge of Swedenborgianism.

REEDY, WILLIAM MARION (1862–1920), Missouri journalist, in 1893 became editor of the St. Louis *Sunday Mirror,* a local society journal that he transformed into a weekly literary and critical magazine, and later published as *Reedy's Mirror* (1913–20). The *Mirror* was politically liberal, and championed the theories of Henry George, while artistically it was a little magazine, introducing such authors as Fannie Hurst, Zoë Akins, Sara Teasdale, and E.L. Masters, whose *Spoon River Anthology* it first published. Other authors whose reputations it helped establish include J.G. Fletcher, Julia Peterkin, and Babette Deutsch.

REESE, LIZETTE WOODWORTH (1856–1935), Baltimore poet and schoolteacher, whose poetry is distinguished for its concision, intense emotion, and simple personal interpretation of pastoral subjects. The direct and rather crisp quality of the lyrics in her early books, *A Branch of May* (1887), *A Handful of Lavender* (1891), and *A Quiet Road* (1896), marks a great advance over the Victorian sentimental treatment of nature, and she maintained her high standards in later collections: *A Wayside Lute* (1909), containing her best-known poem, "Tears," in which she prays for clear vision with which to "see aright How each hath back what once he stayed to weep"; *Spicewood* (1920); *Wild Cherry* (1923); *Little Henrietta* (1927), whose title poem is a narrative "memorial" to a small child; *White April* (1930); *Pastures* (1933); and *The Old House in the Country* (1936). *Selected Poems* was issued in 1926. *A Victorian Village* (1929) and *The York Road* (1931) are autobiographical narratives, and *Worleys* (1936) is a fictional fragment.

Reformed Church in America, founded in colonial times by Protestant settlers from the Netherlands, is Calvinistic in faith and presbyterian in government. Until the English conquest in 1664, it was the established church of New Netherland. In 1771 it became independent of the mother church. For a long time it was a strong denomination in New York and New Jersey, moving toward the Middle West in the mid-19th century. Among the educational institutions it has sponsored is Rutgers University.

Reformed Church in the United States, established in America in the early 18th century by German, Swiss, and French settlers, was known officially until 1869 as the German Reformed Church. Its origin stems from the works of Zwingli, Calvin, and Melanchthon, and the Heidelberg Catechism of 1563 is still its standard for Scriptural instruction. In 1793 it declared itself independent of the Classis of Amsterdam, and at later dates it has been allied with other reformed churches in America.

Regionalism, term applied to literature which emphasizes a special geographical setting and concentrates upon the history, manners, and folkways of the area as these help to shape the lives or behavior of the characters. It generally differs from local color♦ in that it lays less stress upon quaint oddities of dialect, mannerisms, and costume and more on basic philosophical or sociological distinctions which the writer often views as though he were a cultural anthropologist. One major form of regionalism flourished in the South, particularly among the Agrarians of the 1920s and '30s. Its adherents contended that their ideas were based on a creative, scientific approach to the cultural, geographic, and economic differences of particular sections of the U.S. This detached view necessitated scholarly antiquarianism in studying the relation of folklore to literature, and led away from realism toward a critical interpretation of historical backgrounds. Allen Tate, one of its proponents, declared, "Only a return to the provinces, to the small self-contained centres of life, will put the all-destroying abstraction America safely to rest." Tate collaborated with J.C. Ransom, Donald Davidson, and R.P. Warren in publishing *The Fugitive* (1922–25) and the symposia *I'll Take My Stand* (1930), *Culture in the South* (1934), and *Who Owns America?* (1936). These works assert that as people adapt their lives to the geography of a region and create an economic system that gradually becomes natural, this pattern in turn becomes aesthetic. Their program was intended to combat the Northern drive toward industrializing the South, which would have made for eclecticism and standardization; to champion an agrarian economy; and, as Davidson said, to "speak for the South as a living historic entity which is separate from America though bound to it."

REID, [THOMAS] MAYNE (1818–83), Irish-born novelist, came to the U.S. (1840), where he had a varied career as journalist, storekeeper, overseer of slaves, schoolmaster, captain in the Mexican War, actor, dramatist, Indian fighter, and frontier hunter. He returned to England (1850) and was in America again only from 1867 to 1870, but during his years in the U.S. he knew not only the East but also the South, the prairies, and the Western frontier. He wrote a long series of romances, whose exciting adventures endeared him to millions of boys, and whose descriptions of the Southern and Western U.S. made him a prominent foreign follower of Cooper in depicting pioneer customs and the life of the Indians. His bibliography includes more than 90 titles, nearly 70 of which are stories of romance and adventure, many of them concerned with the American scene. Among the most popular were *The Rifle Rangers* (1850), *The Scalp Hunters* (1851), and *The Boy Hunters* (1852). One of his plays, *The Quadroon*♦ (1856), was the basis of Boucicault's *The Octoroon.*

REID, WHITELAW (1837–1912), Cincinnati journalist, whose reporting of the Civil War and the South during Reconstruction is partially republished in *After the War* (1866). He became Greeley's assistant on the New York *Tribune,* and was editor after 1872. Besides various diplomatic assignments, he published several books on historical and political subjects.

Reivers, The, novel by Faulkner,♦ published in 1962 and awarded a Pulitzer Prize.

Told to his grandson as "A Reminiscence," Lucius Priest's monologue recalls his adventures in 1905 as an 11-year-old, when he, the gigantic but childish part-Indian Boon Hogganbeck, and a black family servant, Ned William McCaslin, become reivers (stealthy plunderers) of the automobile of his grandfather, the senior banker of Jefferson, Miss. Driving 80 miles to Memphis, they stay at Miss Reba's brothel, where Boon falls in love with one of the girls, Everbe Corinthia, whom he later weds, while Ned, believing the grandfather would prefer a racehorse, trades the car for a poor mount. After various machinations the horse is successfully jockeyed by Lucius in a race that wins back the car and delights his grandfather, only to lead to another race in which both horse and a $500 bet of the grandfather are lost, although the grandfather counts the experience worthwhile.

Remarkable Providences, essay by Increase Mather,♦ published in 1684 under the title *An Essay for the Recording of Illustrious Providences.* It is based on a manuscript of 1658, containing accounts of extraordinary interpositions of Providence in human affairs, gathered by Puritan ministers in England and Ireland. The manuscript found its way to Boston, where it was discovered by Mather, who added further instances of providential events, collected by New England ministers. To this compilation he added his own observations, comments, and speculations, as well as similar information culled from other books. Although lacking any critical inspection of testimony, the work was intended to be scientific proof of the presence of supernatural forces in the world.

Rembrandt to Rembrandt, blank-verse dramatic monologue by E.A. Robinson,♦ published in *Avon's Harvest* (1921).

The Dutch painter contemplates his self-portrait, three years after the death of his beloved wife Saskia, and reflects on his diminishing popularity and prestige. He wonders if the current opinion is true, that he is now "a fellow painting in the dark,—a loon who cannot see that he is dead." Perhaps Saskia was "appointed well to die," for his present poverty and obscurity would cause her grief and suffering, although his failure is due to his refusal to compromise with commercialism. He has wished only to be sincere, to paint the values in light and human nature that his discerning eye reports. He is overcome, however, with doubts of his work and of artistic "immortality," summing up his life to himself as "your particular consistency in your peculiar folly." He proposes nevertheless to continue, despite his realization that the goals he seeks are comprehensible only to himself and a hypothetical posterity.

REMINGTON, FREDERIC [SACKRIDER] (1861–1909), sculptor, illustrator, and painter, chose for his different media the subjects of soldiers, Indians, and cowboys, frequently in lively action. His bronze statuettes and frequently reproduced canvases are of more historical than artistic value. In addition to being a popular magazine illustrator, he was the author of several books displaying the same temper as his graphic art. These include *Pony Tracks* (1895), *Crooked Trails* (1898), and *The Way of an Indian* (1906). *My Dear Wister* (1972) collects his correspondence with Owen Wister.

Remus, see *Uncle Remus.*

Renascence, poem in octosyllabic couplets by Edna St. Vincent Millay,♦ published in 1912 and collected in *Renascence and Other Poems* (1917).

With an air of casual simplicity, the poet tells how "Infinity came down and settled over me . . . I saw and heard, and knew at last the How and Why of all things. . . . " For this omniscience she pays in "infinite remorse," feeling as her own all the sin, regret, and agony of mankind. "Close-sepulchred" thus, she cries to God for new birth, and, upon casting off her self-centered belief and discovering again "Thy radiant identity," is granted the return of her own life to enjoy the freshness and beauty of the world.

René, romance by Chateaubriand,♦ first published as an episode of *Le Génie du christianisme* (1802) and separately in a pirated edition at Leipzig in the same year. Intended, along with *Atala,*♦ as an episode in *Les Natchez,*♦ the story is a brief monologue delivered by the young Frenchman René to his adopted father, Chactas, chief of the Natchez Indians, and the French missionary Father Souël. It tells of his wanderings in quest of peace and how he found it in living with his sister Amélie until she entered a convent to restrain her unnaturally strong feeling for her brother and he accordingly emigrated to the American wilderness.

REPPLIER, AGNES (1858–1950), Philadelphia author, known for her gracefully witty and scholarly essays, collected in *Books and Men* (1888), *Points of View* (1891), *Essays in Miniature* (1892), *Essays in Idleness* (1893), *In the Dozy Hours* (1894), *The Fireside Sphinx* (1901), *Compromises* (1904), *Americans and Others* (1912), *Counter-Currents* (1916), *Under Dispute* (1924), *To Think of Tea!* (1932), *Eight Decades* (1937), and other volumes. Her biographical studies include *Père Marquette* (1929), *Mère Marie of the Ursulines* (1931), and *Junipero Serra* (1933). *In Pursuit of Laughter* (1936) is a historical study of types of humor. *In Our Convent Days (1905)* and *A Happy Half-Century* (1908) are autobiographical works.

Representative Men, seven essays by Emerson,♦ published in 1850. Probably suggested by Carlyle's *Heroes and Hero-Worship,* they were originally lectures delivered in Boston (1845–46), and in Manchester and London (1847).

The six representative men are Plato, the philosopher; Swedenborg, the mystic; Montaigne, the skeptic; Shakespeare, the poet; Napoleon, the man of the world; and Goethe, the writer. In the first lecture, "On the Uses of Great Men," Emerson contends that humanity, being pervaded by the spirit of Deity, is not made up of a number of individuals. A great man is one who represents more of this divine essence than his fellows, and thus enables mankind to appreciate its own possibilities.

Requiem for a Nun, novel by Faulkner,♦ partly in dramatic form, published in 1951 as a sequel to *Sanctuary* (1931).

Responsibilities of the Novelist, The, essay by Frank Norris♦ used as the title piece of the posthumously published collection of his literary criticism, issued in 1903.

Retrospect of Western Travel, sketches by Harriet Martineau.♦

Return of Peter Grimm, The, play by David Belasco,♦ based on an idea suggested by Cecil B.
DeMille, produced in 1911 and published in
1920.

Reverberator, The, novelette by Henry James.♦

REVERE, PAUL (1735–1818), Boston silversmith and engraver, early associated himself with
the Revolutionary cause by joining the Sons of
Liberty, taking a leading part in the Boston Tea
Party, and drawing satirical cartoons at the time
of the Stamp Act. He was the official courier of
the Massachusetts Committee of Correspondence, in which capacity he became famous for
his ride from Charlestown to Lexington on the
night of April 18, 1775, to announce the approach of British troops. Samuel Prescott and
William Dawes also acted as couriers the same
night, but Revere is remembered because he
alone is mentioned in Longfellow's poem "Paul
Revere's Ride."♦ He later designed and printed
the first Continental currency and the first official
seals of the colonies and of Massachusetts. His
subsequent military career was without distinction, and he returned to business. His own account of his celebrated ride is contained in a letter
to Jeremy Belknap, first printed in the *Proceedings*
of the Massachusetts Historical Society (Nov.
1878), which indicates that Longfellow's account
is fictitious in such incidents as Revere's waiting
for lantern signals. Esther Forbes's biography *Paul
Revere and the World He Lived In* (1942) won a
Pulitzer Prize for American history.

Reverend Griffith Davenport, The, play by James
A. Herne,♦ produced in 1899 but unpublished.
It was adopted from *An Unofficial Patriot,* a novel
by Helen H. Gardener.

REVERIE, REGINALD, pseudonym of Grenville Mellen.♦

Reveries of a Bachelor; or, A Book of the Heart,
essays by D.G. Mitchell,♦ published in 1850 under his pseudonym Ik Marvel. The first "Reverie" was originally published in the *Southern
Literary Messenger* (1849). There are three other
"Reveries," familiar essays presenting the sentimental musings of the Bachelor on the subjects of
marriage, love, and friendship, based on his
knowledge gained through experience and imagination.

Review of Reviews (1891–1937), monthly magazine established as a U.S. counterpart of the English magazine of the same name. The policy was
"to follow with intelligent interest movements of
contemporary history, and to understand something of the real character of men and women
who rank among the living forces of our time."
The contents included editorial comment on
current events, leading articles reprinted from

other periodicals, and reviews of new books and
magazines. The *Review of Reviews* worked for a
union among "English-speaking communities,"
and tended to be Anglophile until after World
War I, when it became primarily concerned with
American problems. In 1932 it absorbed *World's
Work,♦* but its original policy was continued by
Albert Shaw, who edited it from its founding
until competition from such news magazines as
Time caused it to merge with the *Literary Digest♦*
(1937), a combination which failed within the
year.

Reviewer, The (1921–25), little magazine published at Richmond, Va., edited by Emily Clark
and others, including Cabell, who alone edited
three issues (Oct.–Dec. 1921). Although intended to champion the cause of Southern literature, the magazine published contributions from
most of the leading American authors of the time.
Its Southern "discoveries" included Frances
Newman, Julia Peterkin, DuBose Heyward, and
Paul Green. During its last year, it was edited by
Green from North Carolina. The letters of Emily
Clark to Hergesheimer appear in *Ingénue Among
the Lions* (1965).

Revolutionary Romances, series of narratives
by Simms,♦ dealing with life in the South during
the Revolutionary War. They are *The Partisan;
Mellichampe; The Kinsmen,* revised as *The Scout;
Katharine Walton; The Sword and the Distaff,* revised as *Woodcraft; The Forayers;* and *Eutaw.* "Joscelyn: A Tale of the Revolution" is not usually
considered one of the series.

Revolutionary War, name applied to the War
of Independence (1775–83) fought by the British
colonies in the present U.S. against the mother
country. Underlying causes were social, economic, political, religious, and geographic, but signs
of the coming struggle were first marked by such
difficulties between governors and assemblies as
that involving Andros. Colonists were particularly stirred by the imperialist policies exhibited
in the Navigation Acts which attempted to com-
pel importation and exportation exclusively with
England, the Molasses Act, the Stamp Act, and
the Townshend acts. Opposition to these measures appeared in many published works, ranging
from the constitutional objections of John Dickinson's *Letters from a Farmer in Pennsylvania* (1768)
to the inflammatory writings of Samuel Adams. It
included also the more literary propaganda of
Benjamin Franklin and Francis Hopkinson, such
as, respectively, *Edict by the King of Prussia* (1773)
and *A Pretty Story* (1774); the satirical mock-epic
M'Fingal (1775–76) by John Trumbull; and the
political satires in dramatic form by Mercy Otis
Warren. Prior to the beginning of hostilities and
all through them, Freneau wrote so much on
public and personal issues of the times that he
earned the sobriquet "the poet of the American

Revolution." After the further cleavages following the Boston Massacre, the Boston Tea Party, the Boston Port bill, and the Quebec Act, the Continental Congresses were convened. When Governor Gage tried to seize ammunition and stores at Concord after the famous midnight ride of Paul Revere, memorialized and popularized by Longfellow almost a century later, he met armed resistance (April 19, 1775), later celebrated in Emerson's "Concord Hymn." Washington was made the commander of the Revolutionary Forces (June 1775), but the colonies were split between the predominantly middle-class and lower-class advocates of independence and the generally wealthy Loyalists, who found their spokesmen in the poets Jonathan Odell and Joseph Stansbury. The moderate nonpartisan view appears in Robert Munford's play *The Patriots.* The British suffered heavy losses in taking Bunker Hill, the subject of a verse play by Brackenridge, but they occupied Boston, where General Burgoyne wrote and produced his play *The Blockade.* A fictive incident of the time is treated in Hawthorne's "Howe's Masquerade." During this period Paine's *Common Sense* was a stirring call to liberty, but it was more than a year after the Battle of Lexington that the Declaration of Independence was signed. The first issue of *The Crisis* by Paine was published in a period of desperation after the rapid retreat of the patriots and the capture of New York by Howe, but five days after it was issued Washington recrossed the Delaware (Dec. 23, 1776) and captured Trenton and Princeton. The next year Washington suffered heavy losses, particularly at Brandywine, and retreated north of Philadelphia for a winter of extreme hardship, the subject of Maxwell Anderson's historical drama *Valley Forge.* In 1778 the Americans began to win victories, and while the French fleet aided on the coast, George Rogers Clark gained success in the west, a subject of later historical novels, including Churchill's *The Crossing.* Benedict Arnold's treason was discovered, and his collaborator André became a sentimentalized figure in a play by William Dunlap and in later drama and fiction. Battles in the South were treated later as the subject of the Revolutionary Romances of William Gilmore Simms. The chief naval maneuvers of the war consisted of the privateering activities of John Paul Jones, celebrated by Cooper in *The Pilot,* and the naval aid given to various land campaigns. The war concluded after the French fleet blockaded Cornwallis in Virginia, while Washington, assisted by Lafayette and Rochambeau, came south to force his surrender at Yorktown (Oct. 19, 1781).

REXROTH, KENNETH (1905–82), Indiana-born poet and critic, resident in San Francisco after 1927, where he was associated in different eras with radical social views, Objectivist poetry, and the Beat movement. His collections of poems include *In What Hour* (1940), *The Phoenix*

and the Tortoise (1944), *The Signature of All Things* (1949), *In Defence of the Earth* (1956), *Natural Numbers* (1963), *Shorter Poems* (1966), *Longer Poems* (1968), and *New Poems* (1974). He also wrote verse plays; *Beyond the Mountains* (1951), a verse travel journal; *The Dragon and the Unicorn* (1952); and many adaptations or translations from the French, Chinese, and Japanese. His essays have appeared in many volumes including *Bird in the Bush* (1959), *Assays* (1961), *The Alternative Society* (1971), *With Eye and Ear* (1971), and *The Elastic Retort* (1974). His orphaned youth and experiences to the age of 21 appear in *An Autobiographical Novel* (1966), and a brief treatment of later years appears in *Excerpts from a Life* (1981). His anti-Establishment beliefs are treated in a survey, *Communalism* (1975), and his dedication to great literature of the past is seen in his *Classics Revisited* (1969). A gathering of his essays was published posthumously in *World Outside the Window* (1987).

REYNOLDS, JEREMIAH N. (1799?–1858), reared in Ohio, came to public notice (1825) when he championed the theory of Captain J.C. Symmes, Jr., according to which the world is compounded of five concentric spheres, with a hollow core and polar openings so wide that a voyager "might pass from the outer side of the earth over the rim and down the inner side a great distance before becoming aware of the fact at all." After publishing a review of Symmes's theory, Reynolds made a voyage to South America and upon his return agitated for a polar expedition. His polar theory may have influenced Poe's "The Unparalleled Adventure of One Hans Pfaall" (*Southern Literary Messenger,* June 1835), and Poe employed part of Reynolds's address to Congress in *The Narrative of Arthur Gordon Pym◆* (1838). Reynolds's tale of Mocha Dick◆ was a source of *Moby-Dick.* After obtaining a grant of $300,000 for polar exploration, Reynolds became involved in difficulties, and the expedition, which produced important Antarctic research, was conducted without him.

REYNOLDS, JOHN (1788–1865), born in Pennsylvania, was reared in frontier Tennessee and Illinois, and became a lawyer and jurist in the latter state. He was elected governor (1830), and served in the state legislature and in Congress as a proslavery Democrat. His *Pioneer History of Illinois* (1852) is considered a valuable source. *The Life and Adventures of John Kelly* (1853) is a semi-autobiographical romance that contains some of his scientific lectures. In addition to other works, he wrote an autobiography, *My Own Times* (1855).

REZNIKOFF, CHARLES (1894–1976), poet of the Objectivist◆ school, so little known during his lifetime in New York that he published many of his works himself. Marked by a deep dedication to a Jewish tradition and by his talent for imagistic lyrics, they include *Inscriptions* (1959) and *By the Waters of Manhattan* (1962). *Testimony: The United States 1885–1915* (1965) is the initial part (to 1890) of a projected four-volume recitative narrating diverse aspects of U.S. history. *Holocaust* (1975) prints poems based on testimony at the Nuremberg trials. *By the Well of Living and Seeing* (1974) is a selection of poems since 1918 made by Seamus Cooney (1933–), an Irish-born professor of English in the U.S. who is also editing Reznikoff's complete poems. *Family Chronicle* (1969) is a prose account of New York City ghetto life.

Rhett Butler, character in *Gone with the Wind.* ◆

RHODES, EUGENE MANLOVE (1869–1934), Nebraska-born author, lived as a boy and into his late thirties mostly in New Mexico, where he was both cowboy and writer, and, after a long residence in New York (1906–26), returned late in life to New Mexico and California. He wrote a great many stories for *The Saturday Evening Post* and other popular journals, sometimes revising and expanding these, so that his novel *Bransford in Arcadia* (1914), variously retitled in reprints, was an outgrowth of "The Little Eohippus," and *West Is West* (1917) fused several stories. The others of his ten novels, mainly about ranch and range life in the Southwest, are *Good Men and True* (1910), *The Desire of the Moth* (1916), *Stepsons of Light* (1921), *Copper Streak Trail* (1922), *Once in the Saddle* (1927), *The Trusty Knaves* (1933), *Beyond the Desert* (1934), and *The Proud Sheriff* (1935). The works were not only widely read but were praised for their interpretations of cowboy life and their descriptions of its scene. His subject was primarily the romance of the cattle business during the late 19th century, but his faithful depiction of the contemporary background and characters and the quality of his prose keep his work from the sentimentality and cheap melodrama of the usual tales of cowboy adventure.

RHODES, JAMES FORD (1848–1927), historian principally famous for his *History of the United States from the Compromise of 1850* (7 vols., 1893–1906), which covered the years 1850–77 as a clash between civilizations based on opposed abstract ideas. Other works are *History of the Civil War* (1917, Pulitzer Prize) and *History of the United States from Hayes to McKinley* (1919). Prior to his work as a historian he had been in the iron and steel business with his brother-in-law Mark Hanna.

Rhodes Scholarships, founded by Cecil John Rhodes (1853–1902), British statesmen and South African empire builder. He left the bulk of his £6,000,000 fortune to provide scholarships to Oxford University for men students from the British colonies, the U.S., and Germany. The first candidates were selected in 1903 and, like subsequent winners, were judged on the basis of previous college records, including scholarship, character, and leadership in athletics and other activities. The scholarships for German students were cancelled during World War I and discontinued permanently during World War II. U.S. and British scholarships were temporarily suspended during the two wars. The U.S. receives 32 scholarships, restricted to men until women were included in 1976. Among the American literary figures who have received Rhodes Scholarships are Christopher Morley, J.C. Ransom, R.P. Warren, Paul Engle, and R.P.T. Coffin.

Rhodora, The: On Being Asked, Whence Is the Flower?, poem in iambic pentameter couplets by Emerson, ◆ written in 1834 and first published in *The Western Messenger* (1839). It is collected in *Poems* (1847). Apropos of the beautiful New England flower, the poet condemns the questioning of the divine creative power: " . . . if eyes were made for seeing. Then Beauty is its own excuse for being."

Rhymes To Be Traded for Bread, poems by Vachel Lindsay. ◆

RIBAUT (or RIBAULT), JEAN (*c.*1520–65), French Huguenot navigator and colonizer, with Laudonnière ◆ founded a colony at the present Port Royal, S.C., and claimed the territory of Florida for France (1562). He published an account of his expedition as *The Whole and True Discoverye of Terra Florida* (1563). In 1565 he returned to reinforce the colony, but in a Spanish attack he and most of the colonists were massacred. A modern account is contained in Parkman's *Pioneers of France in the New World.*

RIBMAN, RONALD [BURT] (1932–), born in New York City, educated at the University of Pittsburgh through a Ph.D., but after a year of teaching moved to the stage with his first play, *Harry, Noon and Night* (1965, published 1967), which also appeared in a publication of 1978, along with: *Journey of the Fifth Horse* (1966), based on a Turgenev story; *The Final War of Olly Winter* (1967), written for television; and other plays including *Cold Storage* (1977), which ran for 180 performances on Broadway. Later works include three 1987 productions: *The Cannibal Masque, A Serpent's Egg,* and *Sweet Table at the Richelieu,* all serious plays of different eras but each marked by an oppressor and an oppressed.

RICE, ALICE [CALDWELL] HEGAN (1870–1942), Kentucky-born author of stories for children, whose best-known work is *Mrs. Wiggs of the Cabbage Patch* ◆ (1901), *The Inky Way* (1940) and *Happiness Road* (1942) are autobiographical works.

CALE YOUNG RICE (1872–1943), her husband, wrote verse, dramas, and an autobiography. *Bridging the Years* (1939).

RICE, ANNE (1941–   ), novelist born in New Orleans and educated in various colleges in California including Berkeley. Rice began to develop a cult following with her "Vampire Chronicles" series, of which the first, *Interview with the Vampire* (1976), is best known. The point of view is that of the vampire, not the victim, a reversal that speaks to the reader's own darkest shadow self. Others in the series are *The Vampire Lestat* (1985) and *The Queen of the Damned* (1988). She writes of the supernatural also in her other popular books, among them: *The Mummy: Or Ramses the Damned* (1989), in which a 3000-year-old mummy is awakened by an Egyptologist and brought to London, and *The Witching Hour* (1990), about one of three generations of witches in New Orleans, a saga continued in *Lasher* (1993) and *Taltos* (1994). Under the pseudonym A.N. Roquelaure she has published a series of sexually vivid and somewhat sadistic renderings of the Sleeping Beauty story: *The Claiming of Sleeping Beauty* (1983), *Beauty's Punishment* (1984), and *Beauty's Release: The Continued Erotic Adventures of Sleeping Beauty* (1985). She has also published under the name Anne Rampling.

RICE, ELMER (ELMER REIZENSTEIN) (1892–1967), New York dramatist, producer, and novelist, graduated from the New York Law School (1912), but soon abandoned this profession for writing. His first play, *On Trial* (1914), was a murder mystery employing the technique of the motion-picture "cutback" to present scenes that are described by the trial witnesses. His works for the Morningside Players, a little-theater group, were published in *Morningside Plays* (1917). In 1923 he obtained his second success with *The Adding Machine,*♦ a satirical, Expressionistic fantasy. His interest in the social aspects of life is further exhibited in the realistic play *Street Scene*♦ (1929, Pulitzer Prize); *We, the People* (1933); *Judgment Day* (1934), dealing with the ideologies involved in the trials for the burning of the Reichstag building; *Between Two Worlds* (1934); *American Landscape* (1938); *Two on an Island* (1940); *Flight to the West* (1941); and *A New Life* (1943). His other plays, mainly farces and melodramas, include *Wake Up, Jonathan* (1921), with Hatcher Hughes; *Cock Robin* (1928), with Philip Barry; *Close Harmony* (1929), with Dorothy Parker; *The Subway* (1929); *See Naples and Die* (1929); *The Left Bank* (1931); *Counsellor-at-Law* (1931); *Black Sheep* (1932); *and Dream Girl* (1945). His novels include *A Voyage to Purilia* (1930); *Imperial City* (1937), on New York; and *The Show Must Go On* (1949). *The Living Theatre* (1959) collects essays, originally lectures, on the theater as a social institution. *Minority Report* (1963) is an autobiography from his beginnings as a lawyer through his theat-

rical career, which included regional directorship of the New York Federal Theatre Project and helping to found the Playwright's Producing Company and to direct some of its plays.

RICH, ADRIENNE [CECILE] (1929–   ), Baltimore-born poet, whose first volume, *A Change of World* (1951), was published in the Yale Series of Younger Poets the year she graduated from Radcliffe. Succeeding collections were *The Diamond Cutters* (1955), *Snapshots of a Daughter-in-Law* (1963), *Necessities of Life* (1966), *Selected Poems* (1967), *Leaflets* (1969), *The Will To Change* (1971), *Diving into the Wreck* (1973), *Poems Selected and New* (1975), *The Dream of a Common Language* (1978), *A Wild Patience Has Taken Me This Far* (1981), *The Fact of a Doorframe* (1984), *Your Native Land, Your Life* (1986), and *Time's Power* (1989), further poems all displaying her commitment to radical politics and to women's causes. *Of Woman Born* (1976) is a study of motherhood as a social institution. *Blood, Bread, and Poetry* (1987), in the foreword to which she identifies herself as a radical feminist and lesbian, collects her prose since 1979. In 1986 she became a professor at Stanford. *What Is Found There: Notebooks on Poetry and Politics* (1993) remarks upon the work of mainly young, mainly female poets, but also elevates Muriel Rukeyser♦ to the rank of Emily Dickinson.

RICH, OBADIAH (1783–1850), Massachusetts bibliographer, as consul to Valencia (1816–29) and in the Balearic Islands (1834–45) gathered book and manuscript collections, furnishing the stock for his London bookstore (founded *c.*1829). His catalogues helped direct the scholarship of Irving, Prescott, Ticknor, and George Bancroft.

RICH, RICHARD (*fl.*1609–10), English soldier, sailed for Virginia on the *Sea Adventure,* when it accompanied Somers's fleet (June 1609). He witnessed the severe storm that drove the ship on the rocks off St. George's Island in the Bermudas, and participated in the near-abandonment of the Virginia colony (June 1610). He arrived in England (Sept. 1610) with Gates, and published his *Newes from Virginia,* a ballad based on these experiences. The work contains information regarding the settlement in Virginia and was probably influential in the sailing of two further fleets the following year. It may have suggested scenes in Shakespeare's *The Tempest.*

Richard Carvel, novel by Winston Churchill,♦ published in 1899. It owes obvious debts to Thackeray and S. Weir Mitchell. Descendants of the hero appear in *The Crisis.*♦

Richard Cory, poem by Robinson.♦

Richard Hurdis; *or, The Avenger of Blood,* romance by Simms,♦ published in 1838 as one of his series of Border Romances. Like its sequel, *Border Beagles*, ♦ it is based on the activities of the bandit Murrell. ♦

Richard Hurdis, an impetuous youth, leaves home after a quarrel with his villainous half-brother John over the affections of Mary Easterly. Accompanied by a friend, he rides into Alabama, where he becomes acquainted with the operations of a mysterious outlaw clan, led by the bandit Foster. After his companion is killed, Richard poses as a gambler, worms his way into Foster's confidence, and learns the organization of the gang. With this information he is able to lead an attack that results in the band's overthrow. Although Foster escapes, John, who has been forced to join the outlaws, is killed. Richard returns home and marries Mary.

RICHARDS, LAURA ELIZABETH (1850–1943), daughter of Samuel Gridley Howe and Julia Ward Howe. With her sister, Maud Howe Elliott, she wrote *Julia Ward Howe* (1915, Pulitzer Prize). She also wrote a life of her father (1935), a short life of Edwin Arlington Robinson (1936), and the autobiographical *Stepping Westward* (1931). Most of her other books, numbering about 80 in all, were for children, including *Captain January* (1890) and *When I Was Your Age* (1893).

RICHARDSON, JACK [CARTER] (1935–), New York City-born dramatist, graduate of Columbia, whose plays include *The Prodigal* (1960), a version of the Orestes-Agamemnon tale as a tragi-comic conflict between idealism and society's demands; *Gallows Humor* (1961), a two-part play contrasting a condemned man's acceptance of his execution and the hangman's loathing of his life; *Lorenzo* (1963), set in renaissance Italy; *Xmas in Las Vegas* (1965); and *As Happy as Kings* (1968). *The Prison Life of Harris Fillmore* (1963) is a novel about a banker who prefers jail to freedom. *Memoir of a Gambler* (1980) is a memoir of the author's addiction to gaming.

RICHARDSON, WILLIS (1899–1977), lived in Washington, D.C., and had many of his plays presented by Howard University. *The Chipp Woman's Fortune* (1917) was, however, produced on Broadway (1923). Most of his plays were one-acters and many dealt with historical events, like *The Flight of the Natives* (1927).

Richelieu: *A Domestic Tragedy,* play by J.H. Payne, ♦ adapted from a French drama by A. Duval, produced in London and the U.S. (1826), in the former as *The French Libertine*. It was revived (1850) as *Remorse*.

Richmond Enquirer (1804–77), semi-weekly newspaper edited (1804–45) by Thomas Ritchie, absorbed the Jeffersonian *Richmond Examiner* and was later Jacksonian in its political view.

RICHTER, CONRAD [MICHAEL] (1890–1968), Pennsylvania-born author, later long resident in New Mexico before returning to his native state. His novels include the trilogy *The Trees* (1940), about a rough, 18th-century pioneering family in Ohio; *The Fields* (1946), concerning the family and the region during the Civil War era; and *The Town* (1950, Pulitzer Prize), on the later family, its pioneer spirit urbanized, torn between idealism and realism. His other novels include *The Sea of Grass* (1937), about an Eastern woman's life in the Southwest; *Tacey Cromwell* (1942), about a prostitute in early 20th-century Arizona; *The Free Man* (1943), concerning the social rise of a German in colonial Philadelphia; *Always Young and Fair* (1947), about the destructiveness of an unhappy woman living in a Pennsylvania town; *The Light in the Forest* (1953), about a white boy captured by Delaware Indians, rescued, and then nostalgic for their way of life; *The Lady* (1957), set in New Mexico in the 1880s; *The Waters of Kronos* (1960), a novella of mysticism in which a man in old age returns as a stranger to his Pennsylvania hometown to see himself as a youth; *A Simple Honorable Man* (1962), treating the noble character of the father of the hero of *The Waters of Kronos,* a Lutheran minister who aids the poor miners of Pennsylvania; and *The Grandfathers* (1964), an easy, comic tale of western Maryland mountain people and the ways of their community. *Early Americana* (1936) collects stories of the Southwest, and *The Rawhide Knot* (1978) collects stories of marriages on the frontier. *The Mountain on the Desert* (1955) considers regionalism and writing in a mystical vein, and general views from his private notebooks appear in *Writing To Survive* (1988). His daughter Harvena edited *Private Notebooks* (1988).

Rickaree Indians, see *Arikara Indians*.

RICKETSON, DANIEL (1813–98), Massachusetts poet whose work includes *The Factory Bell and Other Poems* (1873), revealing his sympathy with working people. He was a friend of the Transcendentalists and was intimate with Thoreau.

RIDGE, JOHN ROLLIN (1827–67), born in Georgia, son of a prominent Cherokee Indian and a white woman, after a turbulent youth went to the California gold mines (1850) and drifted into journalism. His works, signed Yellow Bird, a translation of his Cherokee name, include *The Life and Adventures of Joaquin Murieta, the Celebrated California Bandit* (1854), a colored, fictionalized treatment that created a local Robin Hood legend, and romantic *Poems* (1868), collected after his death in California. *A Trumpet of Our Own* (1981) assembles from newspapers and magazines his essays on Indians.

RIDGE, LOLA (1871–1941), Irish-born poet, after living in Australia came to the U.S. (1907).

Her first book, *The Ghetto and Other Poems* (1918), influenced by Imagism, depicts New York life. After *Sun-Up* (1920) and *Red Flag* (1927), she wrote *Firehead* (1929), inspired by the Sacco-Vanzetti case, a psychological tale of the Crucifixion as seen by John, Peter, Mary, and Mary Magdalene. *Dance of Fire* (1935) shows further technical development in the use of symbolism and deals with her consistent theme of the martyrdom of the downtrodden.

RIDING, Laura (Laura Reichenthal) (1901–91), born in New York City, once associated with the group that published *The Fugitive,*◆ was long expatriated in Mallorca and England before returning to the U.S. (1959) to live in Florida. Her early writings include *Contemporaries and Snobs* (1928) and other critical works, as well as *A Survey of Modernist Poetry* (1927), one of several collaborations with Robert Graves. Her fiction includes *A Trojan Ending* (1937), about the Trojan War; *Lives of Wives* (1939), considering Cyrus, Aristotle, Caesar, and other pre-Christian figures as husbands; and *Progress of Stories* (1935), a series of 17 stories, progressively "of Lives . . . of Ideas . . . and Nearly True," and an essay on storytelling. An enlarged edition appeared in 1982. Her early poetry is gathered in *Collected Poems* (1938). After a long silence she published *Selected Poems* (England, 1970; U.S., 1973) and *The Telling* (1975), a philosophic essay. *First Awakenings: The Early Poems of Laura Riding* (1993) prints hitherto unpublished poems, written between 1920 and 1925. *The Word "Woman" and Other Related Writings* (1993) collects essays, some previously unpublished. She was married (1941–69) to Schuyler B. Jackson and sometimes published as Laura (Riding) Jackson.

RIESENBERG, Felix (1879–1939), engineer and sailor, whose voyages in both sailing craft and steamships furnished material for his books, including *Under Sail* (1915), *The Men on Deck* (1918), *Vignettes of the Sea* (1926), *Shipmates* (1928), *Clipper Ships* (1932), *Log of the Sea* (1933), *Cape Horn* (1939), and *The Pacific Ocean* (1940). His novels about life at sea include *East Side, West Side* (1927), *Red Horses* (1928), and *Mother Sea* (1933).

RIGDON, Sidney (1793–1876), Mormon leader, whose rewriting of a religious novel is sometimes said to have been the basis of the *Book of Mormon* (1830). After he and Joseph Smith had become involved in a financial scheme in Ohio, they fled to Missouri (1838), where they barely escaped execution for armed clashes in favor of Mormonism. At the Mormon settlement at Nauvoo, Ill., Smith and Rigdon split, partly because Rigdon did not accept the doctrine of polygamy; when Brigham Young succeeded Smith, Rigdon was excommunicated (1844) and at Pittsburgh founded (1845) his own Church of Christ.

RIGGS, Lynn (1899–1954), Oklahoma poet and dramatist, known for his plays on the people and folk themes of the southern Plains region. The most noted of these are *Roadside* (1930), a romantic comedy; *Green Grow the Lilacs*◆ (1931), a folk play set in the Indian Territory in 1900 and intended to dramatize the spirit of Western folk songs; *Russet Mantle* (1936), a comedy concerned with the problems of youth in a transitional culture; and *The Cherokee Night* (1936), a tragedy dealing with the degradation of the Cherokee Indians following the U.S. occupation of Oklahoma. Other plays include *Big Lake* (1927), *Sump'n Like Wings* (1928), *A Lantern To See By* (1928), and *The Cream in the Well* (1941). He also published a book of poetry, *The Iron Dish* (1930).

Right of Way, The, novel by Gilbert Parker.◆

Rights of Man, The, political tract by Thomas Paine,◆ published at London (2 parts, 1791–92). A defense of the French Revolution against the attacks of Burke, it resulted in a British law against seditious publications and in Paine's flight to France to escape prosecution.

The argument is based on the principle that sovereignty inheres in the will of the present majority, as a continuous compact reaffirmed by each generation. Men left the state of nature because moral virtue was insufficient to rule them, and the end of government is the freedom and security of the individual. In civil communities, civil rights rest on the natural rights inherited from the original condition of mankind. These natural rights include the maximum of freedom of action and thought that is compatible with the natural rights of others. Civil authority should interfere with the natural freedom of individuals only in so far as is required to ensure and protect the security and happiness of the majority of the people.

RIIS, Jacob August (1849–1914), Danish-born reformer, journalist, and author, came to New York City (1870), where his own experiences in the slums and his observations as a police reporter on New York papers led him to declare war on tenement conditions, child labor, and other abuses of lower-class urban life. His lone fight was aided later by Theodore Roosevelt, who, as head of the city police board, as New York governor, and as U.S. President, gave him great support. Among Riis's books describing his work were *How the Other Half Lives* (1890), *The Children of the Poor* (1892), *Out of Mulberry Street* (1898), and *The Battle with the Slum* (1902). *The Making of an American* (1901) is an autobiography.

RILEY, James Whitcomb (1849–1916), Indiana poet, tried his hand at such diverse occupations as acting with a patent medicine show and house painting, until his connection with a local newspaper led him into a career of journalism and the writing of verse. His popularity dates from his period on the *Indianapolis Journal* (1877–85), to which he contributed a series of genial poems in rustic dialect, ostensibly written by "Benj. F. Johnson, of Boone." The series, which included "When the Frost Is on the Punkin," was published in *The Old Swimmin'-Hole and 'Leven More Poems*♦ (1883). This was the first of a number of books marked by the frequent use of Hoosier dialect, a simple sentimentality, a quaint whimsical kindliness, and cheerful philosophy, blended with a frequently obtrusive pathos. The most popular of the poems were "Little Orphant Annie," "The Old Man and Jim," "Knee-Deep in June," and "The Raggedy Man," while the most successful of his books were *Afterwhiles* (1887), *Pipes o'Pan at Zekesbury* (1888), *Rhymes of Childhood* (1890), and *Poems Here at Home* (1893). He was also popular as a reader of his own poems, and frequently appeared with "Bill" Nye, whose broad humor he complemented with his appealing sentimentality. Meredith Nicholson's *The Poet* is a fictional biography of Riley.

RILEY, [ISAAC] WOODBRIDGE (1869–1933), professor of philosophy at Vassar (1908–33), was a leader in the study of American philosophic thought. His books include *American Philosophy* (1907) and *American Thought from Puritanism to Pragmatism* (1915, enlarged 1923).

RIMMER, WILLIAM (1816–79), English-born sculptor and painter, was brought to the U.S. (c.1824), and became noted as a sculptor through his interest in direct carving and sculptural form, his knowledge of anatomy gained as a physician, and his attempt to escape the formal neoclassical modeling of his time. He lectured at the Lowell Institute, Cooper Institute, and Boston Museum, and wrote *Elements of Design* (1864) and *Art Anatomy* (1877).

RINEHART, MARY ROBERTS (1876–1958), born in Pittsburgh, established herself as a leading author of mystery stories with her first books, *The Circular Staircase* (1908) and *The Man in Lower Ten* (1909). The former was dramatized with Avery Hopwood as *The Bat* (1920). She continued to write popular stories of horror and crime detection, as well as several plays and a series of humorous novels whose heroine is the eccentric old maid "Tish." *My Story* (1931, revised 1948) is her autobiography.

Rip Van Winkle, tale by Irving,♦ published in *The Sketch Book*♦ (1819–20). Joseph Jefferson is famous for his acting of the title role in a dramatic version, which he made with Boucicault in 1865.

Rip, an indolent, good-natured Dutch-American, lives with his shrewish wife in a village on the Hudson during the years before the Revolution. One day, while hunting in the Catskills with his dog Wolf, he meets a dwarf-like stranger dressed in the ancient Dutch fashion. He helps him to carry a keg, and with him joins a party silently engaged in a game of ninepins. After drinking of the liquor they furnish, he falls into a sleep which lasts 20 years, during which the Revolutionary War takes place. He awakes as an old man, returns to his altered village, is greeted by his old dog, who dies of the excitement, and finds that his wife has long been dead. Rip and his associates are almost forgotten, but he goes to live with his daughter, now grown and the mother of a family, and soon wins new friends by his generosity and cheerfulness.

RIPLEY, GEORGE (1802–80), Massachusetts religious thinker, writer, and reformer, graduated from Harvard (1823) and its Divinity School (1826), after which he began his 15-year ministry of a Boston Unitarian church. He exhibited his literary and philosophical interest in the German transcendental thinkers in his editorship of the *Christian Register,* a Unitarian paper which he made so liberal that he was attacked by Andrews Norton for a "leaning toward infidelity." He made a more direct contribution to American knowledge of idealistic philosophy in *Specimens of Foreign Standard Literature* (14 vols., 1838–42), edited with F.H. Hedge, which included contributions from Margaret Fuller, W.H. Channing, J.S. Dwight, and J.F. Clarke. This work had a considerable effect on the Transcendentalists, since it contained the documents on which their philosophy was partly based. Ripley's *Discourses on the Philosophy of Religion* (1836) precipitated another attack by Norton, which he answered in *Letters on the Latest Form of Infidelity* (1840). In 1841 he retired from the ministry. He put his Transcendentalist theories into practice by helping to found *The Dial* and to organize Brook Farm. As president of this community, he guided it through the period of Fourierism, and he helped to found the North American Phalanx on Fourierist principles. At Brook Farm he edited *The Harbinger*♦ (1845–49), and after the colony's failure he continued it in New York with Parke Godwin. Ripley created the first daily book reviews in the U.S. for the New York *Tribune* (1849–80). During these years he also continued his interest in reform, edited such works as *A Handbook of Literature on the Fine Arts* (1852) with Bayard Taylor and *New American Cyclopaedia* (16 vols., 1858–63) with C.A. Dana, and made trips to Europe (1866, 1869–70), where he met with many authors and philosophers whose views he had championed.

RIPLEY, ROBERT L[EROY] (1893–1949), California-born New York cartoonist, radio speaker, and writer. The first collected volume of his syndicated series "Believe It or Not!" appeared in 1928.

Rise of American Civilization, *The,* history by Charles A. Beard♦ and Mary R. Beard.♦

Rise of Silas Lapham, THE, novel by Howells, ♦ published in 1885.

Colonel Silas Lapham, a typical self-made businessman, has risen from a Vermont farm to wealth and prominence as a paint manufacturer. He establishes his family in Boston, where he begins to build a mansion, and urges his wife, Persis, and their daughters, Penelope and Irene, to enter Brahmin society, for which their wealth would seem to qualify them. Tom Corey and Penelope, the older and more intelligent sister, are in love, but he belongs to the social group to which the Laphams cannot attain, and there is a misunderstanding when Irene, immature and impulsive, believes that Tom returns her love for him. Penelope refuses his proposal, and, at the Coreys' dinner party, which Penelope does not attend, Silas gets drunk and reveals himself as a brash and sturdy *nouveau riche*. He has meanwhile been speculating unsuccessfully and faces bankruptcy. His only hope is the sale of a milling property to an English syndicate, and his former partner, Rogers, presses him to this action, although both know that this will result in disaster to the syndicate. When Lapham's fair play and integrity cause him to refuse the opportunity, he is ruined and returns to Vermont. Although he has fallen in the social scale, he has risen morally. Tom and Penelope are married and go to Mexico to escape the unhappy background of social distinctions between their families.

Rise of the Dutch Republic, *The,* history by J.L. Motley. ♦

RIVES, AMÉLIE (1863–1945), Virginia-born novelist, poet, and playwright, lived for some time in England, where she fell under the influence of the attenuated impressionism of the *fin de siècle* authors, as is revealed in her novelette *The Quick or the Dead?* (1888), a psychological study of a woman torn between love for her dead husband and for the living cousin who strongly resembles him. Among her other works are *A Brother to Dragons* (1888), a collection of tales; *Barbara Dering* (1892), a sequel to *The Quick or the Dead?;* *Herod and Mariamne* (1888), *Athelwold* (1893), and *Augustine the Man* (1906), blank-verse tragedies; *Seléné* (1905), a dramatic poem; and *Love-in-a-Mist* (1927), a comedy written with Gilbert Emery. She also wrote the romantic novels *Virginia of Virginia* (1888), *The Witness of the Sun* (1889), *According to St. John* (1891), *The Golden Rose* (1908), *Pan's Mountain* (1910), *Hidden House* (1912), *World's End* (1914), *The Ghost Garden* (1918), and *Firedamp* (1930). In 1896 she married the Russian Prince Troubetzkoy.

Rivington's New-York Gazetteer (1773–83), New York City Tory newspaper, founded by James Rivington (1724–1802). It was issued under the protection of the British army, being suspended from 1775 to 1777, revived as *Rivington's*

New-York Loyal Gazette and later *Royal Gazette,* and continued until the withdrawal of the army. Jonathan Odell was a contributor.

Road Not Taken, *The,* poem in iambic tetrameter by Robert Frost, ♦ published in *Mountain Interval* (1916).

The poet tells how the course of his life was determined when he came upon two roads that diverged in a wood. Forced to choose, he "took the one less traveled by, And that has made all the difference."

Road to Xanadu, *The,* critical study of Coleridge's "Kubla Khan" by John Livingston Lowes. ♦

Roan Stallion, allegorical narrative in free verse, by Jeffers, ♦ published in *Roan Stallion, Tamar, and Other Poems* (1925).

California, a young half-breed woman, is married to Johnny, a farmer of the California mountains. Although she is devoted to her daughter Christine, she loathes her sordid life with her brutal and obscene husband, and longs for a passionate emotional experience, which even her Catholic faith fails to give her. Then her husband brings home a beautiful roan stallion, who arouses in California's primitive mind a feeling of love and adoration, partly sexual, partly religious. After a wild ride in the night, which she imagines to be a sexual encounter, she returns to the drunkenly amorous Johnny, from whose advances she escapes in disgust. She runs to the corral, where he follows, and California helps the stallion to kill her husband, by shooting a dog who interferes. After Johnny has been trampled to death, she is "moved by some obscure human fidelity" to shoot the stallion, and then turns to her daughter "the mask of a woman who has killed God."

Roanoke Island, off the coast of North Carolina, south of the town of Kitty Hawk, was first settled in 1584, when Raleigh dispatched Sir Richard Grenville to plant a colony there. In 1585 Drake visited the colony, found it in bad straits, and took all the settlers back to England. A few days after his departure, Grenville arrived with a relief ship, and, finding the settlement deserted, left a party of 15 men for recolonization. Among them was Thomas Hariot. ♦ In 1587 Raleigh sent another colony of 117 people under John White, who found that the previous 15 colonists had disappeared. White returned (1591) to the colonists he had left, but found that they too had vanished without any trace, except the single word "Croatan," mysteriously carved on a tree. Among those who had disappeared was White's granddaughter, Virginia Dare (1587–?), the first white child of English parents born in America. Some evidence has been advanced for the traditional belief that the colonists lived and intermar-

ried among the Croatan Indians on a nearby island, leaving half-breed descendants who moved
to the southern part of the state. Among the literature concerned with Roanoke is Paul Green's
The Lost Colony (1937), a historical pageant produced annually on the island. The most famous
event of its later history is the Battle of Roanoke
Island (Feb. 8, 1862), in which Union troops and
vessels under the command of Burnside captured
this strategic Confederate position.

Rob of the Bowl: A Legend of St. Inigoes, romance
by J.P. Kennedy,♦ published in 1838. This story
of colonial Maryland in 1681, realistically treated
although the subject is melodramatic, is concerned with the attempt by Protestant factions to
overthrow the Catholic Lord Baltimore.

ROBB, JOHN S. (*fl.* 1847). St. Louis journeyman
printer, whose typical Southwestern frontier
humor and extravagant tales about Mike Fink
were collected from various periodicals in *Streaks
of Squatter Life, and Far-West Scenes* (1847). He
was also the author of *Kaam; or, Daylight . . . A
Tale of the Rocky Mountains* (1847).

ROBBINS, HAROLD (1916–   ), had early careers in the food industry and with a motion-
picture studio before becoming a successful novelist, beginning with *Never Love a Stranger* (1948),
the first of a long line of works marked by much
glamour and sex, now totaling over two dozen
and none selling fewer than 600,000 copies. His
best-known book, *The Carpetbaggers* (1961), is an
action novel about malefactions in industry.

ROBBINS, TOM (1936–   ), North Carolina-
born author of bizarre fiction very popular in
paperback. *Another Roadside Attraction* (1971) is set
at the hot dog stand north of Seattle (the author's
home area) owned by John and Amanda Ziller,
whose friend Plucky Purcell chances on the
mummified body of Christ, which he delivers to
them as an adornment for their place of business.
His next novel, *Even Cowgirls Get the Blues*
(1976), almost equally fantastic, is a picaresque
tale of a hitchhiking girl with vastly oversized
thumbs who ends up at a wild health ranch for
cowgirls. *Still Life with Woodpecker* (1980) deals
with the daughter of a foreign king exiled in
Seattle who has a love affair with a rebellious
young American who believes in remaking the
world with dynamite and drugs and from whom
she learns how to decipher cabalistic messages, of
which the most meaningful is found in the pictures and text of a pack of Camel cigarettes. Robbins's eccentric themes, somewhat in the vein of
Vonnegut, Brautigan, and Pynchon, are treated
in a style marked by whimsical similes and wild
wisecracks. His fourth novel, *Jitterbug Perfume*
(1984), is in the vein of the earlier ones as marked
in one passage: "It is better to be small, colorful,
sexy, careless, and peaceful, like the flowers, than

large, conservative, repressed, fearful, and agres-
sive, like the thunder lizards." It was followed by
Skinny Legs and All (1990), about exotic experi-
ences of a newly married couple in New York
City, and the erotic, comic *Half Asleep in Frog
Pajamas* (1994).

ROBERTS, SIR CHARLES GEORGE DOUGLAS
(1860–1943), Canadian poet, novelist, editor,
and university professor, after the popular success
of his history of Canada (1897) and other writings
moved to New York to devote himself to literature. He published several volumes of poetry, but
was best known for his historical fiction for children and adults, including *The Raid from Beausé-
jour* (1894), *A Sister to Evangeline* (1898), *Barbara
Ladd* (1902), *The Watchers of the Trails* (1904), *Red
Fox* (1905), and *Haunters of the Silences* (1907).

ROBERTS, ELIZABETH MADOX (1881–1941),
born in the Kentucky farming region, which she
described in her fiction, graduated from the University of Chicago (1921). Her first publications
were volumes of verse, *In the Great Steep's Garden*
(1915) and *Under the Tree* (1922, enlarged 1930),
and her later poetry is collected in *Song in the
Meadow* (1940), containing lyrics and verse legends. *The Time of Man*♦ (1926), her first novel,
set in the Kentucky countryside, deals with poor
whites possessed by the restless pioneer urge. *My
Heart and My Flesh*♦ (1927), another novel with a
pastoral background, is the tragic story of a woman driven to the verge of madness. The author's
scrupulous and effective re-creation of folk customs and speech distinguishes her further fiction,
which includes *Jingling in the Wind* (1928), a satirical fantasy whose chief character is a rainmaker
on his way to a professional convention; *The
Great Meadow*♦ (1930), a historical novel, depicting the beauty and terror of pioneer life in Kentucky; *A Buried Treasure* (1931), a humorous narrative about a farmer and his wife who discover a
pot of gold; *The Haunted Mirror* (1932), short stories of Kentucky mountain folk; *He Sent Forth a
Raven* (1935), a novel concerned with the relation of farmers to the soil they till; *Black Is My
Truelove's Hair* (1938), the story of a village girl
and the two love affairs that shape her life; and
Not by Strange Gods (1941), stories mainly about
Kentucky women.

ROBERTS, KENNETH [LEWIS] (1885–1957),
Maine novelist, graduated from Cornell (1908),
became a journalist, and later achieved recognition as a vivid and accurate historical novelist. His
fiction includes *Arundel* (1930), the story of Benedict Arnold's expedition against Quebec; *The
Lively Lady* (1931), dealing with the War of 1812;
Rabble in Arms (1933) and *Captain Caution* (1934),
sequels to *Arundel; Northwest Passage* (1937), the
story of Robert Rogers, the campaigns of his
Rangers against the Indians, and his later attempts
to find a Northwest Passage; *Oliver Wiswell*

(1940), a tale of the American Revolution as seen by a colonial Loyalist soldier and historian; *Lydia Bailey* (1947), a picaresque romance about a young Maine lawyer's pursuit of a girl through Toussaint's uprising in Haiti, the Tripolitan War, and political machinations of the Federal era; and *Boon Island* (1956), based on the shipwreck of 18th-century Britons off Maine's coast. He also wrote *For Authors Only* (1935), essays showing his salty humor; *Trending into Maine* (1938, revised 1944), including writings of others on his native state; *March to Quebec* (1938), compiling source materials of *Arundel; I Wanted To Write* (1949), on literary problems; several books on his belief in dowsing, including *Seventh Sense* (1953) and *Water Unlimited* (1957); and *The Battle of Cowpens* (1958), a history of a Revolutionary War engagement.

Robert's Rules of Order, manual of parliamentary procedure (1876, revised 1915, 1943), by General Henry Martyn Robert (1837–1923), a military engineer.

ROBERTSON, MORGAN ANDREW (1861–1915), popular author of romantic sea stories, which include *Spun-Yarn* (1898), *Where Angels Fear To Tread* (1899), and *Land-Ho!* (1905).

ROBERTSON, WILLIAM (1721–93), Scottish historian, educator, and Church of Scotland leader, whose masterpiece, *The History of the Reign of the Emperor Charles the Fifth* (1769), was republished (1857) with an appendix by W.H. Prescott, an enthusiastic follower of Robertson's concepts of historical writing. An outgrowth of Robertson's interest in the New World, awakened by his research for this work, was his *History of America* (2 vols., 1777), interrupted by the outbreak of the Revolutionary War. Although criticized for its omissions and inaccuracies, this vivid and moving narrative was very popular in its time.

Robin Day, *The Adventures of,* novel by R.M. Bird. ♦

ROBINS, ELIZABETH (1865–1952), American actress, famous for her creation of Ibsen roles in London during the 1890s, wrote such works as *The Magnetic North* (1904), a novel set in the Klondike, which she visited during the gold rush; *A Dark Lantern* (1905); *Votes for Women* (1906), a play, and *The Convert* (1907), a novel, both setting forth ideas of woman suffrage; and *Come and Find Me* (1908), a novel set in Alaska and California. She wrote of her stage experiences in *Ibsen and the Actress* (1928), and in 1932 published *Theatre and Friendship,* a volume of letters written to her by Henry James, which she edited with an autobiographical commentary. Some of her books were published under the pseudonym C.E. Raimond.

ROBINSON, CHARLES (1818–94), Massachusetts antislavery leader, emigrated to California (1849), where he established a newspaper and became a member of the legislature, opposing California's entrance into the Union as a slave state. He continued his adherence to the Free-Soil program as a leader of the Emigrant Aid Society in Kansas (1854), where he became territorial governor (1856), as well as first governor of the state (1861) after it was admitted to the Union. His books include *Kansas: Its Interior and Exterior Life* (1856) and *The Kansas Conflict* (1892), histories of the struggle for free soil.

ROBINSON, EDWIN ARLINGTON (1869–1935), was reared in Gardiner, Me., the prototype of his Tilbury Town, and after studying at Harvard (1891–93) was employed in New York City. His first volume of poems, *The Torrent and the Night Before* (1896), was privately printed. In these early poems, strongly influenced by his reading of Hardy, he presents the first of his spare, incisive portraits of the people of his Tilbury Town, ♦ marked by a dry New England manner that proved cryptic to his few readers. One reviewer stated that "The world is not beautiful to him, but a prison house," to which Robinson later replied: "The world is not a 'prison-house,' but a kind of spiritual kindergarten where bewildered infants are trying to spell God with the wrong blocks." Some of the poems of this book were reprinted, with additions, in *The Children of the Night* (1897), containing the "Credo" in which the poet recognizes that there is "not a glimmer" for one who "welcomes when he fears, the black and awful chaos of the night"; but states that he feels "the coming glory of the Light" through an intuition of a spiritual guidance that transcends the life of the senses. Many of the other poems are psychological portraits, similar in form to those of Browning, including such character studies as those of the wealthy and wise Richard Cory, who committed suicide for lack of a positive reason for being; Cliff Klingenhagen, with his mysterious ironic philosophy of life; the spiteful miser Aaron Stark; Luke Havergal, the bereaved lover; and romantic old John Evereldown.

The Children of the Night impressed Theodore Roosevelt, and, upon the publication of *Captain Craig* ♦ (1902), the President helped Robinson escape from work as inspector of subway construction to a clerkship in the New York Custom House (1905–10). Included in *Captain Craig* are such character studies as "Isaac and Archibald" ♦ and "The Book of Annandale," ♦ while *The Town Down the River* (1910) contains "Miniver Cheevy," ♦ "How Annandale Went Out," and other portraits. After this date, Robinson was able to give his entire time to poetry, much of which he wrote during his annual summer residence at the MacDowell Colony in New Hampshire. His next works were plays: *Van Zorn* (1914), a "comedy" whose titular figure, mysteriously able to learn the secrets of others, aids in solving their personal problems; and *The Porcupine* (1915), a tragedy founded on a similar psychological situation.

"The Man Against the Sky"♦ is the title piece of a collection of poems (1916) setting forth the author's philosophy of life with striking symbolic power. Other poems in the volume include "Flammonde,"♦ "Cassandra,"♦ and the Shakespearean study "Ben Johnson Entertains a Man from Stratford."♦ With *Merlin*♦ (1917) he began the Arthurian trilogy completed by *Lancelot*♦ (1920) and *Tristram*♦ (1927, Pulitzer Prize), in which he studied the characters as individuals who act according to their particular passions, independently of supernatural powers. *The Three Taverns* (1920) contains poems further illustrating this attitude, such as "Rahel to Varnhagen"♦ and "Rembrandt to Rembrandt,"♦ and further Tilbury portraits such as "Mr. Flood's Party," describing the pathetically humorous old town drunkard. *Avon's Harvest*♦ (1921) traces the consequences of an obsessive hatred and fear on a sensitive mind, and a volume of *Collected Poems* of this year won a Pulitzer Prize.

Robinson's steady production of verse continued with *Roman Bartholow*♦ (1923), a dramatic narrative presenting a subtle psychological analysis of a sick soul; *The Man Who Died Twice*♦ (1924, Pulitzer Prize), telling the tragic story of a man's dissipation of his artistic genius; ""Dionysus in Doubt,"♦ the title poem in a collection (1925), and "Demos and Dionysus,"♦ criticizing the standardization and materialism of equalitarian society, which the poet found inimical to "romance and love and art" and to the development in a transcendental fashion of the individual "self and soul"; *Cavender's House*♦ (1929), a blank-verse dialogue between Cavender and the ghost of the wife he murdered for a supposed infidelity; *The Glory of the Nightingales* (1930), a verse narrative concerned with the rivalry between two friends for the love of a woman, and their later reconciliation; *Matthias at the Door*♦ (1931), a narrative in which the chief figure, through bitter disillusion, loses his egocentric complacency and learns to understand others; *Nicodemus* (1932), adding ten poems to the body of his work, including four on Biblical themes; *Talifer*♦ (1933), a narrative of modern life, which shows the poet in a novel mood of optimistic cheer; *Amaranth* (1934), a somber narrative concerned with a group of frustrated artists; and *King Jasper*♦ (1935), a poetic narrative that constitutes a final statement of Robinson's sense of the tragedy of human life in a chaotic world, and of his unfaltering mystic faith in a "glimmer" of light beyond. He collected his *Sonnets, 1889–1927* (1928), and a selection from his letters was published in 1940.

As an heir of the New England traditions of Puritanism and Transcendentalism, with their emphasis upon the individual, Robinson has been termed a sober Transcendentalist who dealt primarily with the ethical conflicts within the individual and measured the value of the isolated person by his truth to himself. With the reserve typical of the New Englander, he most frequently employed the objective form of dramatic monologue, and, with the traditionalism inherent in his background, confined his experimentation to the use of common speech rhythms, rather than to the creation of new stanzaic forms. His quality of mind is organically expressed by his style, which itself quietly fuses tradition with originality, and romance with realism.

ROBINSON, HARRIET JANE HANSON (1825–1911), Massachusetts mill worker and woman suffrage leader, contributed to the *Lowell Offering,*♦ and, in addition to her political activities, wrote histories of women's life in factories, and such suffrage dramas as *Captain Mary Miller* (1887) and *The New Pandora* (1889).

ROBINSON, ROWLAND EVANS (1833–1900), Vermont author, began in 1877 to write sketches on rural sports and the simple life he knew as a farmer. His first book, *Forest and Stream Fables* (1886), was followed by such collections as *In New England Fields and Woods* (1896), *Hunting Without a Gun and Other Papers* (1905), and *Silver Fields and Other Sketches of a Farmer-Sportsman* (1921). His appreciation of the scenery of his native state, understanding of the Vermont farmers and English-speaking French Canadians, and sensitive ear for their dialects made him an important writer in the local-color tradition. These qualities and his typical Down East humor and homely philosophy are best exhibited in his collections of fiction, including *Uncle Lisha's Shop: Life in a Corner of Yankeeland* (1887); *Sam Lovel's Camps: Uncle Lisha's Friends Under Bark and Canvas* (1889); *Danvis Folks* (1894); *Uncle Lisha's Outing* (1897); *A Hero of Ticonderoga* (1898); *A Danvis Pioneer* (1900), a story of the Green Mountain Boys; and *Out of Bondage and Other Stories* (1905). He also wrote *Vermont: A Study of Independence* (1892). The "Centennial Edition" of his works (7 vols., 1933–36) contains many formerly uncollected sketches and stories.

ROBINSON, SOLON (1803–80), born in Connecticut, emigrated to northern Indiana (1834), where he became a leader in politics, journalism, and trade, and wrote about the frontier society. He was instrumental in the establishment of the Department of Agriculture (1862), and his books, written in New York and Florida, present a vivid picture of rural and pioneer life. They include *The Will: A Tale of the Lake of the Red Cedars and Shabbona* (1841), *Hot Corn: Life Scenes in New York Illustrated* (1854), and *Me-Won-I-Toc, A Tale of Frontier Life and Indian Character* (1867).

Rock Me to Sleep, see *Akers, Elizabeth.*

Rocked in the Cradle of the Deep, poem by Emma Willard.♦

Rocky Mountain Review (1938–59), quarterly regional magazine founded as *Intermountain Review* (1937), was issued from Utah until 1946, when, under the title *Western Review* and still under the editorship of Ray B. West, it moved to Lawrence, Kan., and again (1949) to the State University of Iowa. It became less regional and more generally literary and critical as time went on. Contributors included Kenneth Burke, R.V. Cassill, Walter Van Tilburg Clark, Evan Connell, George P. Elliott, Vardis Fisher, Wallace Stegner, Harvey Swados, and William Carlos Williams.

Roderick Hudson, novel by Henry James,♦ published in 1876. The character Christina also appears in *The Princess Casamassima.* ♦

Rowland Mallet, a wealthy connoisseur, struck by the genius of the amateur sculptor Roderick Hudson, takes the youth abroad to develop his art. Among their friends in Rome are Gloriani, a brilliant French sculptor; Sam Singleton, a modest American painter; Augusta Blanchard, an undistinguished American art student; and shrewd, benevolent old Madame Grandoni. Gloriani predicts that Roderick will "fizzle out," but this does not disturb the confident youth, who studies enthusiastically and produces several fine statues in the intervals between "sterile moods." He depends much on the stimulation of others and is considerably altered after meeting Christina Light, fascinating daughter of an expatriated American widow. He loses interest in sculpture, and Rowland summons from New England Roderick's mother and his fiancée, Mary Garland, who has also attracted Rowland. Roderick's fine bust of his mother is his last important work, for Christina, bowing to her mother's ambitious urging, marries the rich Prince Casamassima. The youth cannot overcome his infatuation, and after a time goes with his friends to Switzerland, where they meet Christina and her husband. With a sudden return of ardor, Roderick attempts to follow her, and for this purpose even attempts to borrow from Mary, at which Rowland angrily condemns him as an ungrateful egotist. Roderick walks off into the mountains, where he is caught in a thunderstorm. When his body is discovered, it is uncertain whether he fell or jumped from a cliff.

RODMAN, SELDEN (1909–   ), born in New York City, after graduation from Yale, where he was co-editor of the *Harkness Hoot* (1930–31), an iconoclastic literary journal, became a co-founder and editor (1932–43) of *Common Sense,* a liberal review. For a time he was co-director of Le Centre d'Art of Haiti, sponsoring primitive painting in this land, of which he wrote in *Renaissance in Haiti* (1948) and *Haiti: The Black Republic* (1954). Other works include *Lawrence: The Last Crusade* (1937), a long narrative poem on T.E. Lawrence: *The Airmen* (1941), another narrative poem, this one celebrating man in flight from Icarus to men in the 20th century; *The Revolutionists* (1942), a three-act verse play on the slave revolt in Haiti in 1791; *The Amazing Year: A Diary in Verse* (1947), treating public and personal affairs of 1945–46; *Portrait of the Artist as an American* (1951), an unorthodox biography of Ben Shahn; *Mexican Journal* (1958), record of a visit; *The Insiders* (1960), a personal view of contemporary painting; several guidebooks to Mexico, Central America, Brazil, and *Haiti* (1984); *Tongues of Fallen Angels* (1974), the author's conversations with Ginsberg, Mailer, and other writers of both Americas; and *Where Art Is Joy* (1988), on Haitian art.

ROE, E[DWARD] P[AYSON] (1838–88), born in New York, educated at Williams College and Auburn Theological Seminary, was a Presbyterian minister until the Chicago fire (1871) attracted him as an appropriate setting for a story of spiritual conversion. The resulting novel, *Barriers Burned Away*♦ (1872), became immensely popular, and after the success of a novel with a similar formula, *Opening a Chestnut Burr* (1874), he resigned from the ministry to become a professional author. These two works were his most popular and set the pattern for their successors, depending on a topical event, characters and incidents selected from personal observation or newspaper reports, an enthusiasm for rural life, and a plot of a search for a wife or a fortune, all overlaid with sentimental piety. Among his later novels are *Near to Nature's Heart* (1876), *A Knight of the Nineteenth Century* (1877), *Without a Home* (1881), *He Fell in Love with His Wife* (1886), and *The Earth Trembled* (1887).

ROETHKE, THEODORE (1908–63), born in Michigan, graduated from its state university and after further study at Harvard began a career of teaching English at various universities, from 1947 at the University of Washington. His career as a poet began with *Open House* (1941), brief, intense lyrics already marked by the plant imagery of growth and decay that so pervades all his poetry. *The Lost Son* (1948) lyrically presents psychic and physical biographical experiences of the maturing boy and man. *Praise to the End!* (1951) continues in a more mystic, visionary strain, showing an affinity to Yeats. *The Waking* (1953, Pulitzer Prize) and *Words for the Wind* (1958, Bollingen Prize) collect early and late work, showing great variety and great sensitivity. *I Am! Says the Lamb* (1961) is light verse but in the vein of Blake, and *The Far Field* (1964) is a posthumous gathering, whose final section was printed in a limited education as *Sequence, Sometimes Metaphysical* (1964). *On the Poet and His Craft* (1965) contains essays and lectures, and his *Selected Letters* appeared in 1968. *Straw for the Fire* (1972) comes from his notebooks.

Roger Malvin's Burial, story by Hawthorne,♦ published in *The Token* (1832) and in *Mosses from an Old Manse* (1846).

Two wounded survivors of a foray against Indians, led by John Lovewell, make their escape through the Maine woods. Roger Malvin, an old man mortally injured, urges his young companion, Reuben Bourne, to desert him and seek safety. Reuben protests, but is finally persuaded and promises to send help. He makes his way home, but cannot bring himself to tell Dorcas Malvin of the circumstances in which he left her father. He claims to have buried him in the forest, is hailed as a hero, and soon marries Dorcas. Their life is not happy, for his conscience disturbs him, and when their son Cyrus is 15, they leave the settlement to seek a new home in the wilderness. One evening Reuben accidentally shoots his son while hunting, and is horrified to discover the boy's body at the same spot where he left Malvin, years before. Dorcas discovers her son's death, and falls unconscious. The upper branch of an oak, where Reuben hung a bloody handkerchief as a signal, has withered and now crumbles and drops, while Reuben prays, feeling that at last his crime is expiated and the curse lifted.

Rogerenes, see *Rogers, John.*

ROGERS, BRUCE (1870–1957), Indiana-born book designer, was associated with the Riverside Press at Cambridge (1900–1912), where he became distinguished for his work in relating the style of each volume to its subject matter. He was later associated with C.P. Rollins and W.E. Rudge, and gradually changed his style from a clear, simple craftsmanship to a whimsical but skillful use of type ornament.

ROGERS, JOHN (1648–1721), Connecticut religious leader, originally a Baptist, founded the Rogerene sect opposed to formal clergy, prayers, and church meetings, and any connection between church and state. Although he had many followers, his liberal religious ideas constantly brought him into conflict with state and ecclesiastical authorities. The most important of his defenses of his beliefs was *The Book of the Revelation of Jesus Christ* (1720).

ROGERS, ROBERT (1731–95), born in Massachusetts, distinguished himself in the last of the French and Indian Wars, commanding some 600 Rangers who used the independent guerrilla technique of Indian warfare. After the British victory Rogers was sent to Detroit to receive the surrender of western French posts, as recorded in his *Journal* (1933). He later defended Detroit against the attack of Pontiac, but his illicit trading with the Indians disgraced him, and he went to England, where he published his *Journals* (1765), *A Concise Account of North America* (1765), and his play *Ponteach*♦ (1766). Appointed to command a Michigan fort, he commissioned the exploration of Jonathan Carver, but again found himself in difficulties when he administered the territory for his own profit and was suspected of treasonable relations with the French. After another period in England (1769–75), he returned to America, where he was apparently unable to decide if British or American service was of more value to himself, and was accordingly imprisoned as a spy by Washington. Escaping to the British, he took to the field unsuccessfully, and was then set to recruiting, in which he reverted to his former dishonest practices. In 1780 he returned to England, where he remained the rest of his life. He figures in most of the fiction and history concerning Pontiac,♦ as well as in Kenneth Roberts's *Northwest Passage.*

ROGERS, WILL[IAM] (1879–1935), was born near Claremore, Okla., of a family that was part Indian. After brief schooling he went to the Argentine and then to Africa, where he broke horses for the English during the Boer War and joined a Wild West show that took him to Australia and back to the U.S. His steer-roping act was soon altered to one of lariat tricks performed during a humorous monologue on current events. In 1913 he joined the Ziegfeld Follies, in which he remained an outstanding attraction, although after 1919 he also became a motion-picture actor. Both in his roping act and in his widely syndicated newspaper column, he was a homespun philosopher in the tradition of Petroleum V. Nasby, Artemus Ward, and Mr. Dooley, and although under the guise of ignorance he declared "All I know is just what I read in the papers," he was a pungent commentator on society and politics. He was at his best in aphorisms restricted to a newspaper paragraph, and his books, including *The Cowboy Philosopher on Prohibition* (1919), *The Illiterate Digest* (1924), and *Letters of a Self-Made Diplomat to His President* (1927), are considered less important. He died in an airplane crash in Alaska.

Rogêt, MARIE, character in *The Mystery of Marie Rogêt.*♦

ROLFE, JOHN (1585–1622), English-born colonist, came to Virginia (1609), where he was a leading cultivator of tobacco, and instrumental in making it Virginia's staple commodity. He fell in love with Pocahontas,♦ daughter of a leading Indian chief, and his marriage to her (1614) ensured peace with the Indians for several years. While on a voyage to England his wife died (1617), and he returned to become a colonial official. In 1622 the Indians destroyed his home, and he seems to have died at their hands. He wrote a description of Virginia for the king, first printed in the *Southern Literary Messenger* (June 1839), and is a figure in J.E. Cooke's novel *My Lady Pokahontas*♦ (1885) and other fiction about his wife.

Rolling Stones, stories by W.S. Porter.♦

ROLLINS, Carl Purington (1880–1960), Massachusetts printer, associated with the Yale University Press as typographic adviser, and distinguished for his simple design and period typography.

Rollo books, series of juvenile novels by Jacob Abbott.♦

RÖLVAAG, O[le] E[dvart] (1876–1931), born in Norway, came to the U.S. in 1896, and attended St. Olaf College, Minnesota, at which he became a professor of Norwegian (1907–31). His *Letters from America* (1912), like all his works, was written in his native language. This book purported to be a collection of correspondence from a young Norwegian in America to his family at home, and was a semi-autobiographical account of the gradual adjustment of an immigrant to the U.S. Rölvaag's greatest works were *Giants in the Earth*♦ (1927), *Peder Victorious*♦ (1929), and *Their Fathers' God*♦ (1931), a trilogy of epic power, realistically depicting the life of the Norwegian immigrants on the northwestern frontier of the U.S., and the psychological effect of the stern pioneer life upon the people whose titanic labors are a constant struggle against the impersonal forces of nature. His other novels include *Pure Gold* (1930) and *The Boat of Longing* (1933), the latter, written before his great trilogy, foreshadowing it both in its combination of realism and mysticism and in its theme of a young Norwegian's emigration to the U.S.

Roman Bartholow, blank-verse narrative by E.A. Robinson,♦ published in 1923.

Bartholow, a wealthy, middle-aged aristocrat, has gone through a long period of despair, from which his marriage to the beautiful Gabrielle does not rescue him. The instrument of his surprising deliverance is his friend Penn-Raven, an unconventional private evangelist and bland rhetorician, who calls himself frankly a "blackguard," but somehow maintains a profound spiritual wisdom and influence over others. The joyous, grateful Bartholow, inspired with hope, wishes Penn-Raven to live on his bounty, and cannot understand his friend's desire to leave him. The truth is that Penn-Raven has been paying court, though without success, to Gabrielle. She refuses his advances, not out of love for Bartholow, but because, without the capacity to understand his problems, she has lost during the years of their loveless marriage all contact with humanity. When Bartholow discovers her in Penn-Raven's embrace, he attacks his friend, who saves himself from being strangled by a shrewd spiritual discussion, half truthful, half hypocritical. Gabrielle drowns herself, and Bartholow forces Penn-Raven to leave, giving himself up to grief for a time, then going abroad for consolation and to share the "Power," which he still retains.

Roman Catholic Church in America had its beginnings in the legendary connection between the Norse discoveries of the New World and the medieval church in Greenland. Its modern history began with the colonization by Spain and France. Permanent dioceses were established in Santo Domingo, Haiti, and Puerto Rico (1511), and the see of Cuba ruled the mainland churches (1522–45). The first parish within the boundaries of the present U.S. was established at St. Augustine, Fla. (1565). During the ensuing centuries, much missionary work was done by the Capuchins, Jesuits,♦ and Franciscans. In the American territories outside the present U.S., colonization and proselyting have resulted in the dominance of the Catholic faith. In the English colonies, Catholicism was generally attacked, except in Maryland, which was founded by the Catholic Calvert family, and in Rhode Island and Pennsylvania, where there was religious toleration. John Carroll became the first Catholic bishop in the U.S. (1789), when there were approximately 30,000 Catholics in the country. The increase to the millions in the 19th century, owing in large part to immigration from first Ireland and Germany and later from Italy and Eastern Europe, occasioned sharp antagonism in this Protestant-founded country. Although localized, this feeling resulted in politico-religious movements like the Know-Nothings. The change from a priest-centered to member-centered service, in English, resulting from decisions of Vatican II in the 1960s, led to further growth, and by 1993 the number of American Roman Catholics was 59,220,723, or 23% of the population.

Roman Spring of Mrs. Stone, The, novelette by Tennessee Williams.♦

Romance, generic name applied to prose fiction that is conceived in terms of the fanciful and idealistic, rather than in terms of observation and faithful description of fact. In his preface to *The House of the Seven Gables,* Hawthorne states that a novel "is presumed to aim at a very minute fidelity, not merely to the possible, but to the probable and ordinary course of man's experience." A romance, on the other hand, while it must keep to "the truth of the human heart—has fairly a right to present that truth under circumstances . . . of the writer's own choosing or creation . . . he may so manage his atmospherical medium as to bring out or mellow the lights and deepen and enrich the shadows of the picture."

Romance, play by Edward Sheldon,♦ produced in 1913 and published in 1914.

ROMANS, Bernard (*c.*1720–*c.*1784), born in the Netherlands, was sent by the British government as a surveyor to America (*c.*1757), where he worked in Georgia and Florida, receiving an additional appointment as the king's botanist in the province of Florida. During the Revolution he served in the Continental army, in both Canada and the southern colonies. In addition to making maps of America and writing historical and nautical books, he wrote *A Concise Natural History of East and West Florida* (1775).

Romantic Comedians, The, novel by Ellen Glasgow,♦ published in 1926.

Judge Gamaliel Bland Honeywell of Queenborough (Richmond, Va.), although he is 65 and had been married for 36 years to his wife Cordelia, a year after her death is unable to recall her face, and finds his thoughts straying to other women. Before his marriage he had been engaged to Amanda Lightfoot, who is still unmarried although she is 58, and their friends now expect him to marry her. The Judge determines to avoid her "tedious fidelity," and, although he disapproves of the life of his libidinous sister, Mrs. Edmonia Bredalbane, he falls in love with and marries Annabel Upchurch, a young cousin of Cordelia. Annabel has just been jilted by Angus Blount, and frankly marries the Judge for his wealth, feeling that she can never love again. After their honeymoon she is immediately unfaithful, falls in love with Dabney Birdsong, and elopes with him to New York. The Judge follows, and attempts vainly to win her back. Upon his return he is consoled by Bella, Annabel's mother, who hopes he will now marry Amanda. He becomes seriously ill, waxes disconsolate, and believes himself beyond happiness. But when it is spring again, he notices the attractiveness of his young nurse, and he thinks dreamily, "Spring is here, and I am feeling almost as young as I felt last year."

Romanticism, term that is associated with imagination and boundlessness, and in critical usage is contrasted with classicism, which is commonly associated with reason and restriction. A romantic attitude may be detected in literature of any period, but as a historical movement it arose in the 18th and 19th centuries in reaction to more rational literary, philosophic, artistic, religious, and economic standards. Since it gathered force gradually in its various manifestations, it does not lend itself to the limitations of a concise summary. The most profound and comprehensive ideal of romanticism is the vision of a greater personal freedom for the individual. Its origins may be traced to the economic rise of the middle class, struggling to free itself from feudal and monarchial restrictions; to the individualism of the Renaissance; to the Reformation, which was based on the belief in an immediate relationship between man and God; to scientific deism, which emphasized the deity's benevolence; to the psychology of Locke, Hartley, and others, who contended that minds are formed by environmental conditions, thus seeming to indicate that all men are created equal and may be im-

proved by environmental changes; to the optimistic humanitarianism of Shaftesbury; and to the writings of Rousseau, who contended that man is naturally good, institutions alone having made him wicked. In American literature, such general influences were strengthened by the great English and French romantic authors, the "storm and stress" writers of Germany, and the idealistic philosophy of Kant. To these were added many indigenous forces: a realized political democracy; the individualism, buoyancy, and optimism of the frontier; the idealism latent in Calvinism, as expressed by Jonathan Edwards and others; intimacy with the wilderness; a predominantly agrarian background; and recognition of the heroism of early Americans.

The romantic movement in America, as elsewhere, left its impression not only on the arts, but also in the more practical spheres of action, as in revolutionary activities for political freedom and individual rights; humanitarian reform (Abolitionism and feminism); liberal religious movements (Unitarianism and Universalism); labor reform (Knights of Labor); and economic experiments in communal living (Brook Farm and New Harmony). The most clearly defined romantic literary movement in the U.S. was Transcendentalism,♦ centered at Concord (*c.*1836–60). Characteristics of the romantic movement exemplified in American literature are sentimentalism (*Charlotte Temple, The Sketch Book*); primitivism and the cult of the "noble savage" (*Hiawatha*); political liberalism (Jefferson, Paine, Barlow); the celebration of natural beauty and the simple life (Cooper, Emerson, Thoreau); introspection (Poe, Thoreau); idealization of the common man, uncorrupted by civilization (Whittier, Cooper); interest in the picturesque past (Irving, Hawthorne); interest in remote places (Melville, Bayard Taylor); medievalism (Longfellow); antiquarianism leading to the revival of the popular ballad (Longfellow, Whittier); the Gothic romance (Brown); concern with a crepuscular world of mystery (Poe, Chivers); individualism (Emerson, Thoreau, Whitman); technical innovation (Whitman's prosody); humanitarianism (*The Biglow Papers, Uncle Tom's Cabin*); morbid melancholy (Poe); native legendry (*Evangeline*); and the historical romance (Simms, Cooper).

These characteristics also appear in other arts. The interests that created the Gothic romance♦ also created the Gothic Revival,♦ an architectural movement based on medieval styles, whose design carried the eye above the actual form and conjured up imaginative associations. In painting, romanticism effected the change from the severe portraiture of the 18th century to the work of the Hudson River school,♦ which emphasized the charm and grandeur of the American landscape. American music, which had no important exponents until late in the 19th century, echoed contemporary European romanticism in the compositions of such men as MacDowell and Chadwick.

After the original impulse of the movement declined, its forces continued as fashions down to the turn of the century. Although the local-color movement♦ fostered the rise of realism, it also perpetuated the romanticist's interest in strange places and unusual customs. Sentimentalism appeared in the stories of Bret Harte, and exoticism in those of Cable and Hearn. Even such predominantly realistic authors as Clemens veered from vivid depiction of contemporary scenes to historical romancing and idyllic representations of youth. Lesser novelists like Lew Wallace and F.M. Crawford purveyed romantic ideas to the masses. Aldrich, Boker, Taylor, Stoddard, Stedman, and Gilder tended to imitate earlier romantic poets, and, lacking originality, so relied on attenuated romantic conventions that they came to represent the last stand for the genteel elements in the movement. While the genteel tradition found many revolutionary opponents in the advocates of realism♦ and naturalism,♦ both tradition and iconoclasm were products of the romantic movement. New forces were coupled with the old, as for instance when romanticism felt the impact of Freudian psychology, as seen in works by innumerable American authors from the 1920s on.

ROOSEVELT, [ANNA] ELEANOR (1884–1962), wife of Franklin D. Roosevelt, was a social welfare worker, lecturer, writer of a newspaper column, "My Day," and of books, including *It's Up to the Women* (1933); *This Troubled World* (1938); *The Moral Basis of Democracy* (1940); *If You Ask Me* (1946), answering readers' questions; *India and the Awakening East* (1953); and *This Is My Story* (1937), *This I Remember* (1949), and *On My Own* (1958), autobiographies. She was a U.S. representative to the General Assembly of the United Nations (1945–53, 1961–62).

ROOSEVELT, FRANKLIN DELANO (1882–1945), 32nd President of the U.S. (1933–45), was born at Hyde Park, N.Y., a fifth cousin of Theodore Roosevelt. Educated in Europe, at Groton, Harvard (1904), and Columbia law school (1907), he practiced law in New York City and became an independent Democratic state senator (1910). A progressive, he was influential in Wilson's election, was assistant secretary of the navy (1913–21) under Josephus Daniels, and a proponent of a large navy and naval reserve, serving in Europe in World War I as a naval administrator. He was nominated for the vice-presidency (1920), and after the defeat of his party returned to law practice, although stricken with infantile paralysis, from which he slowly recovered. In 1929 he succeeded Alfred E. Smith as governor of New York, holding this office until 1932, when he won the presidency by a large majority. His administrative program to correct economic and social abuses was widely criticized for its program of taxation and expenditures, re-

valuation of the dollar, employment of a "brain trust," ostensible opposition to great fortunes and corporate power, and tendency to experimentation in government, but its popularity was proved by the majority by which he was re-elected in 1936. For this "New Deal" administration Congress granted him greater powers than those given in peacetime to any of his predecessors. In 1940 he was again elected, the first President to serve a third term. This and the fourth term (just begun before his death) were devoted in large part to fighting World War II and to planning the peace that was to follow. His country estate, Hyde Park, where he is buried, was deeded to the U.S. with a library to house his documents, manuscripts, and effects and became a national monument (1946). His *Public Papers and Addresses* are collected in 13 volumes (1938–50) and his *Personal Letters* in 4 volumes (1947–50), and his books include *Whither Bound?* (1926), *The Happy Warrior: Alfred E. Smith* (1928), *Government—Not Politics* (1932), and *Looking Forward* (1933).

ROOSEVELT, THEODORE (1858–1919), 26th President of the U.S. (1901–9), born in New York City of a distinguished family, graduated from Harvard (1880). After writing a history of *The Naval Operations of the War Between Great Britain and the United States—1812–1815* (1882), he entered politics, serving in the state legislature (1882–84), where he led the Republican "insurgents" against Blaine. He retired to his ranch in Dakota Territory after Blaine's nomination, wrote books on his life in the West and biographies of Thomas Hart Benton (1886) and Gouverneur Morris (1888), and began *The Winning of the West,* before returning to politics in an unsuccessful campaign for the mayoralty of New York (1886). President Harrison appointed him to the Civil Service Commission (1889–95), after which he headed the New York City Police Board (1895–97), working against corrupt politics and collaborating with Jacob Riis in an attack on slum conditions. He was assistant secretary of the navy (1896–98), retiring to help organize the Rough Riders, in whose Spanish-American War exploits he became the popular hero. His newly won reputation brought him the governorship of New York (1898–1900), but his reforms alienated conservatives, who "shelved" him in the vice-presidency (1900), only to have him become President (1901) upon McKinley's assassination. During his two terms he championed the rights of "the little man," made a war against "malefactors of great wealth" in his regulation of trusts, and supported such reforms as the Meat Inspection Act and the Pure Food and Drugs Act. Although Congress claimed he had usurped its powers, he worked for the conservation of natural resources, and in this and in other matters his technique brought opposition on the grounds that he was attempting to dominate a government based on the theory of checks and balances.

His foreign policy was marked by jingoism, exhibited in the aid advanced to Panama in its revolution against Colombia, in order that the U.S. might begin the Panama Canal, and a "big stick" policy giving the U.S. a sort of police power in Latin American affairs. Other matters of foreign policy were a retention of the "Open Door" in China, mediation to end the Russo-Japanese War (1905), and the instigation of the Algeciras Conference to settle colonial problems of European powers. He virtually dictated the nomination of Taft (1908), but was alienated by his successor's conservative policies, and in 1912 formed the "Bull Moose" or Progressive Republican party, which nominated him for a third presidential term, but the split gave the election to Wilson.

In addition to his early books, he used authorship to promote his beliefs and tell of his adventures in and out of politics. *The Winning of the West*♦ (4 vols., 1889–96) is considered his most significant work, and others include *American Ideals and Other Essays* (1897); *The Rough Riders* (1899); *The Strenuous Life* (1900), concerned with personal conflicts resulting from his philosophy of life; *African Game Trails* (1910), an account of his hunting expeditions; *African and European Addresses* (1910), a discussion of colonial problems; *The New Nationalism* (1910), a statement of beliefs embodied in his Bull Moose party; *History as Literature, and Other Essays* (1913), on the theory of history illustrated in *The Winning of the West; Theodore Roosevelt: An Autobiography* (1913); *Through the Brazilian Wilderness* (1914), an account of an exploration; and *America and the World War* (1915), *Fear God and Take Your Own Part* (1916), and *The Great Adventure* (1918), views on World War I.

ROOT, GEORGE FREDERICK (1820–95), musician and music publisher, whose compositions with facile rhymes or martial or sentimental subjects were in great favor during the Civil War. The best known are "The Battle Cry of Freedom," "Tramp, Tramp, Tramp, the Boys Are Marching," and "Just Before the Battle, Mother."

ROOT, JOHN WELLBORN (1850–91), Chicago architect, was influenced by the honesty of structure of Richardson, and in turn influenced the work of Louis Sullivan. He was a pioneer in the construction of steel-frame office buildings, as in the 15-story Monadnock Building (Chicago), a straight vertical design with an unornamented façade. His firm planned the Columbian Exposition at Chicago (1893). He was a brother-in-law of Harriet Monroe, who wrote his biography (1896).

Rootabaga Stories, book for children by Sandburg. ♦

Roots, account by Alex Haley♦ of the successful search for his antecedents, imported to America in slavery from Gambia. Published in 1976, it won a Pulitzer Prize and when dramatized for television inspired a very large audience to an interest in black history and in genealogy.

ROSE, AQUILA (*c.*1695–1723), English-born poet and typographer, arrived in Philadelphia some time before 1717 and obtained a place in the printing office of Andrew Bradford, to which Franklin succeeded upon Rose's death. He was the subject of a poem by Samuel Keimer. His son Joseph Rose, with Franklin, to whom he was then apprenticed, collected his *Poems on Several Occasions* (1740), in which his work is that of a cultured amateur in the neoclassic tradition.

Rose of Dutcher's Coolly, novel by Hamlin Garland,♦ published in 1895.

Rose Tattoo, The, play by Tennessee Williams. ♦

ROSENBACH, A[BRAHAM] S[IMON] W[OLF] (1876–1952), Philadelphia dealer in rare books and manuscripts, and prominent collector, whose writings include *The Unpublishable Memoirs* (1917), a satire on bibliomania; *Books and Bidders* (1927); *A Book Hunter's Holiday* (1936); and bibliographical works. He was formally called Dr. Rosenbach because he had a Ph.D. The University of Pennsylvania, where he taught English for a time, remembers him with its Rosenbach Fellowship in Bibliography, whose lectures are published.

ROSENFELD, MORRIS (1862–1923), born in Russian Poland, came to the U.S. (1886), where he eked out an existence in New York City sweatshops. His Yiddish poems, plaintively singing the woes of the workers or satirizing social injustices, attracted the attention of Leo Wiener of Harvard, who translated his work as *Songs from the Ghetto* (1898). This, and later works on similar subjects and on the problems of his fellow Jews, brought Rosenfeld wide notice. His verses are among the earliest Yiddish literature in America.

ROSENFELD, PAUL (1890–1946), New York critic of music and literature, whose works include *Musical Portraits* (1920); *Musical Chronicle* (1923); *Port of New York* (1924), essays on 14 contemporary artists and authors; *Men Seen* (1925), criticisms of modern authors; *The Boy in the Sun* (1928), a novel; *By Way of Art* (1928), essays; *An Hour with American Music* (1929); and *Discoveries of a Music Critic* (1936). He was an editor of *The American Caravan.*

ROSIER, JAMES (*c.*1575–1635), English explorer, author of *A True Relation of the Most Prosperous Voyage Made This Present Yeere 1605 by Captaine George Waymouth* (London, 1605), which contains the first account of exploration in Maine. It was reprinted in part by Purchas.

ROSS, ALEXANDER (1783–1856), Scottish-born fur trader in Canada and the Columbia River country whose writings of historical importance include *Adventures of the First Settlers on the Oregon or Columbia River* (1849), *The Fur Hunters of the Far West* (1855), and *The Red River Settlement* (1856).

ROSS, LEONARD Q., pseudonym of Leo Rosten. ◆

ROSTEN, LEO [CALVIN] (1908–), political scientist, teacher, and humorist, born in Poland, was brought to the U.S. as an infant, and later educated at the University of Chicago (A.B., 1930; Ph.D., 1937). He is the author of *The Washington Correspondents* (1937), a study of the function, techniques, and personnel of the capital's journalists, and of *Hollywood: The Movie Colony, The Movie Makers* (1941), a similar sociological study of the film center. Under his pseudonym Leonard Q. Ross he has written popular fiction: *The Education of H*Y*M*A*N K*A*P*L*A*N** (1937), humorous sketches of a New York evening school for adults and its immigrant students' unorthodox approach to the English language, and *The Return of H*Y*M*A*N K*A*P*L*A*N* (1959) and *O K*A*P*L*A*N! My K*A*P*L*A*N!* (1976), sequels. Under his own name he has published *Captain Newman, M.D.* (1961), a witty but serious novel about an army psychiatrist; *The Many Worlds of L*E*O R*O*S*T*E*N* (1964), a collection of 30 years of writing; *A Most Private Intrigue* (1967), a spy story; *The Joys of Yiddish* (1968); *The 3:10 to Anywhere* (1976), reminiscences of travel; *Passions and Prejudices* (1978), essays; *Silky* (1978) and *King Silky* (1981), detective novels involving much Yiddish; and, as successor to earlier lexicons, *The Joys of Yinglish* (1989).

ROTH, HENRY (1906?–), novelist. Brought to New York City from Austria when he was 18 months old, Roth grew up on the Lower East Side, in poverty but withal enjoying a sense of community he was never to find later. At City College he published a sketch called "Impressions of a Plumber" in the college paper. It brought him to the attention of Eda Lou Walton of the English Department faculty. Roth began living with Walton in 1928, and the works of O'Neill, Eliot, and especially Joyce provided him narrative techniques to deal with the material of his childhood. The result was a major and to-be-influential work, *Call It Sleep* ◆ (1934). Published in the depth of the Great Depression, the novel got some good reviews but was attacked by the influential left as lacking "social realism" and "proletarian awareness." It went almost immediately out of print, until the critics Leslie Fiedler and Alfred Kazin called attention to it in the late

'50s, prompting the publication of a paperback edition in 1964 that was heralded by Irving Howe in a front-page *New York Times Book Review* piece. *Call It Sleep* was at last fully recognized and became a popular success—over a million copies sold, many translations, a place in some college courses. It is generally conceded to be the best of all U.S. Jewish ghetto novels. But for more than 50 years Roth never wrote another. In 1987 he published a slight second book of short writings, *Shifting Landscapes,* some of the pieces from his youth. Leonard Michaels, a professor at Berkeley, reported in 1993 that Roth had completed five books of a multi-volume autobiographical novel with the overall title *Mercy of a Rude Stream;* the first volume, *A Star Shines Over Mount Morris Park,* was published in 1994.

ROTH, PHILIP (1933–), New Jersey-born author, after graduation from Bucknell and an M.A. from the University of Chicago taught English there and creative writing at Iowa and Princeton. His first book, for which he won a National Book Award, was *Goodbye, Columbus* (1959), whose title novella and five short stories present witty, ironic, and perceptive depictions of Jewish life in the U.S. in a flip, personal style. *Letting Go* (1962), his first novel, employs something of the same vein less successfully in treating the lives of young Jewish intellectuals at the University of Chicago, in New York, and elsewhere. His succeeding fiction is *When She Was Good* (1967), a removal from his basic subject and territory in treating a Midwestern Protestant housewife who is destructively dedicated to reforming first her father, then her husband; *Portnoy's Complaint* ◆ (1969), a wildly comic depiction of his middle-class New York Jewish world in the portrait of Alexander Portnoy, whose possessive mother makes him so guiltily insecure that he can seek relief only in elaborate masturbation and sex with forbidden Gentile girls; *Our Gang* (1971), a broad satire of President Trick E. Dixon; *The Breast* (1972), a novella about a male professor of literature who suffers a Kafka-like transformation into a gigantic breast; *The Great American Novel* (1973), at once a burlesque and an allegory, its telling of the downfall of a great baseball team serving as a satirical parallel to contemporary American political and social events; *My Life as a Man* (1974), depicting the personal and literary frustrations of an author, partly through two of his short stories; and *The Professor of Desire* (1977), a novel about the romances of the Jewish professor who was the subject of *The Breast. The Ghost Writer* (1979) is a brief but intricate tale about a young writer who, when accused of travestying his fellow Jews, seeks counsel from a respected older Jewish author and finds this distinguished figure ambiguously involved with a girl whom the young writer fantasizes to be Anne Frank. *Zuckerman Unbound* (1981) is a sequel about the young writer years later as a major

American author and his poignant personal life; *The Anatomy Lesson* (1983) is a third portrayal of Zuckerman, aged 40 and having lost "his health, his hair, and his subject"; and *Zuckerman Bound* (1985) prints the trilogy and an epilogue, "The Prague Orgy," briefly treating Zuckerman's concern with the work of a recently deceased Jewish writer from Prague. Zuckerman, psychosomatically sick, caught in a writer's block, and castigated by an academic critic as the writer of trivial, scurrilous, and anti-Semitic fiction, yearns for a new career as a doctor. *The Counterlife* (1986) is another novel about Nathan Zuckerman bound up with problems varying from physical sexual issues to those related to a visit to Israel. *The Facts* (1988) continues the Zuckerman saga in a book that is a letter to his character in which the author dwells upon his own real life with some invention. A more exotic conception of real life occurs in Roth's next novel, *Deception* (1990), setting forth a conversation about love between an American novelist named Philip and some women. *Operation Shylock: A Confession* (1993) is a novel in which a novelist called Philip Roth, suffering from a breakdown, learns that an impostor using his name in Israel is advocating "Diasporism"—that Jews should quit Israel to avoid an Arab Holocaust and should again settle in their true home, Europe. *Reading Myself* (1975) collects interviews, essays, and articles. *Patrimony* (1991) is a memoir about his father's life and death.

Roughing It, autobiographical narrative by Clemens,♦ published in 1872 under his pseudonym Mark Twain. He records a journey from St. Louis across the plains to Nevada, a visit to the Mormons, and life and adventures in Virginia City, San Francisco, and the Sandwich Islands. The book is based on Clemens's own experiences during the 1860s, but facts are left far behind in his creation of a picture of the frontier spirit and its lusty humor. The entire work is unified by the character of the author and the ways in which his experiences changed him into a representative of the Far West, but seemingly little attempt is made to integrate the tall tales, vivid descriptions, narratives of adventure, and character sketches, except in so far as all of them constitute a vigorous, many-sided portrait of the Western frontier.

Round Table, *The* (1863–69), New York weekly journal of opinion, had an informal staff of contributors, rather than a regular corps of editors. Its chief interest was in literary criticism, which it insisted must be from the American point of view. Among the contributors were R.H. Stoddard, Aldrich, Stedman, William Winter, and M.D. Conway. Publication was suspended (1864–65), and when a new group came into control (1866), the magazine lost its vigorously critical attitude.

ROUQUETTE, Adrien Emmanuel (1813–87), born in New Orleans of a French father and a Creole mother, as a youth often ran away from his parents' summer home to live with the nearby Choctaw Indians, and returned to them even after he was sent to France to complete his education. His love of the primitive and of nature and his poetic feelings found expression in two volumes of verse, *Les Savanes* (1841) and *Wild Flowers: Sacred Poetry* (1848), and in a mystical prose work, *La Thebaïde en Amérique, ou Apologie de la vie solitaire et contemplative* (1852), the last two appearing after he had finally found direction in becoming a priest. His antislavery views, expressed through his sermons, made his life in New Orleans intolerable and so he once again went to the Choctaw, now as a priest. His later works include *L'Antoniade, ou La Solitude avec Dieu* (1860), mystical poetry; *La Nouvelle Atala* (1879), a romance inspired by Chateaubriand; and, under the pseudonym E. Junius, *Critical Dialogue Between Aboo and Caboo* (1880), a violent denunciation of Cable's depiction of Creoles in *The Grandissimes.*

ROUQUETTE, François Dominique (1810–90), brother of Adrien Rouquette, also had an affection for the life of the Choctaw and a feeling for poetry, expressed in *Meschacébéennes* (1839), a volume of verse praised by Victor Hugo, and *Fleurs d'Amérique* (1856); and he also made an English translation of Bossu's *Nouveaux Voyages* as *The Arkansas* (1850).

ROURKE, Constance [Mayfield] (1885–1941), graduated from Vassar (1907), where she taught (1910–15), and began her interpretations of the American scene, particularly its "vagaries, . . . from the belief that these have woven together a tradition which is various, subtle, sinewy, scant at times but not poor." These fused historical, biographical, and critical studies include *Trumpets of Jubilee* (1927), dealing with such figures as the Beechers and P.T. Barnum; *Troupers of the Gold Coast* (1928), dealing with Lotta Crabtree, Lola Montez, Adah Menken, and other actresses of the California frontier; *American Humor: A Study of the National Character* (1931); *Davy Crockett* (1934); and *Audubon* (1936). *Roots of American Culture, and Other Essays* (1942) is a posthumous collection.

Rousseau and Romanticism, critical work by Irving Babbitt.♦

Rover Boys, series of books for boys by Edward Stratemeyer.♦

ROVERE, Richard [Halworth] (1915–79), after graduation from Columbia began his journalistic career, which included service as associate editor of the *New Masses* (1938–39), assistant editor of *The Nation* (1940–43), editor of

Common Sense (1943–44), and staff writer of *The New Yorker* (1944–79). His books are *Howe and Hummel: Their True and Scandalous History* (1947), about two 19th-century shyster lawyers of New York; *The General and the President* (1951), written with A.M. Schlesinger, Jr., about the conflict between MacArthur and Truman; *Affairs of State: The Eisenhower Years* (1956), collecting some of his "Washington Letter" columns from *The New Yorker; Senator Joe McCarthy* (1959), a portrait of a demagogue; *The American Establishment* (1962), essays on a wide variety of people and subjects of the times; *The Goldwater Caper* (1965), about the Republican candidate for president in 1964; *Waist Deep in the Big Muddy* (1968), an analysis of contemporary U.S. foreign policy and domestic effects; and *Arrivals and Departures* (1976), essays as memoirs.

ROWLANDSON, Mary [White] (*c*.1635– *c*.1678), daughter of John White, an early settler and wealthy proprietor of Lancaster, Mass., in 1656 married Joseph Rowlandson, a Congregational minister. During King Philip's War, when the Narragansett attacked Lancaster (Feb. 10, 1676), she was abducted by the Indians, who held her for 11 weeks and five days, until she was ransomed. Her account of this captivity was published in Cambridge (1682) as *The Sovereignty & Goodness of God, Together with the Faithfulness of His Promises Displayed; Being a Narrative of the Captivity and Restauration of Mrs. Mary Rowlandson.* This was the second edition; the first edition, which has not been found, was apparently published earlier in the same year. The book is one of the most popular examples of 17th-century American prose and has been reprinted and reedited approximately 30 times. In pure, idiomatic, sinewy English, Mrs. Rowlandson shows the dangers in which the settlers lived, their contempt for the Indians, their devout dependence upon the Bible for support, and their actual treatment during such enforced captivities.

ROWSON, Susanna [Haswell] (*c*.1762– 1824), English-born author, accompanied her father, a naval lieutenant, to his station in Massachusetts. The family returned to England in 1777, where she published the novels *Victoria* (1786) and *Mary; or, The Test of Honour* (1789); *The Inquisitor; or, Invisible Rambler* (1788), modeled on Sterne's *Sentimental Journey; Poems on Various Subjects* (1788); and *A Trip to Parnassus* (1788), versified criticism on the theater. She first won fame with the novel *Charlotte Temple*♦ (1791), a sentimental didactic romance, which was extremely popular in the U.S., where it is mainly set. This was followed by *Mentoria: or, The Young Lady's Friend* (1791), didactic tales and essays on education, and *Rebecca; or, The Fille de Chambre* (1794), a semi-autobiographical work. After her husband's failure in business, the Rowsons turned to

acting careers, and came to the U.S. in 1793, where she appeared on the stage, and wrote a topical comic opera, *Slaves in Algiers* (1794); *The Volunteers* (1795), a musical farce; *The Female Patriot* (1795), adapted from Massinger's *The Bondsman;* and *Americans in England* (1796), a social comedy revised as *The Columbian Daughter* (1800). Her excessive sympathy with American patriotism caused Cobbett to criticize her betrayal of England in *A Kick for a Bite* (1795), and she in turn called him "a kind of loathsome reptile" in the preface to her *Trials of the Human Heart* (1795), a melodramatic romance set in London. She abandoned the stage in 1797 to conduct a girls' boarding school near Boston, and, in addition to writing texts and didactic works for students, edited a literary magazine there and wrote *Reuben and Rachel; or, Tales of Old Times* (1798), a historical novel tracing the lives of some descendants of Columbus; *Miscellaneous Poems* (1804); *Sarah; or, The Exemplary Wife* (1813), a semi-autobiographical novel; and the posthumously published *Charlotte's Daughter; or, The Three Orphans* (1828), a sequel to *Charlotte Temple,* usually known as *Lucy Temple.*

Roxy, novel by Edward Eggleston,♦ published in 1878.

Royal American Magazine, The (Jan. 1774–Mar. 1775), Boston monthly, a "Universal Repository of Instruction and Amusement." Under the editorship of Isaiah Thomas♦ until July 1774, it was violently patriotic. This fervor abated somewhat under the editorship of Joseph Greenleaf, who nevertheless published political burlesques and Paul Revere's political cartoons.

Royal Family, The, play by George S. Kaufman♦ and Edna Ferber.♦

ROYALL, Anne Newport (1769–1854), born in Maryland, after the loss of property inherited from her wealthy Virginian husband (1824) supported herself by traveling through the U.S. and writing accounts of her shrewd observations. Among the ten books of this nature, describing the society of virtually every important settlement in the U.S., are *Sketches of History, Life, and Manners in the United States* (1826), *The Black Book . . .* (3 vols., 1828–29), and *Letters from Alabama* (1830). She also published two newspapers, *Paul Pry* (1831–36) and *The Huntress* (1836–54), in which she vigorously set forth her own ideas on contemporary matters of government and religion, and bitterly attacked what she considered to be corrupt. She published a novel, *The Tennessean* (1827), a romantic tale of adventures in Boston and New Orleans.

ROYCE, Josiah (1855–1916), born in California, graduated from the state university (1875), was an advanced student in Germany and at Johns Hopkins, and became an instructor of English at his alma mater (1878–82). Although the remainder of his life was spent as a professor of philosophy at Harvard, his deep feeling for his native background is exhibited in *California . . . A Study of American Character* (1886) and his only novel, *The Feud of Oakfield Creek* (1887), treating the same conflict that is central to Frank Norris's *The Octopus*. Brought to Harvard by William James, he at first believed himself in complete accord with James's philosophy, but, though they remained friendly, they soon split on philosophic ideas. James's *Will To Believe* referred to specific human minds, whereas Royce considered consciousness to be a universal principle; James was a pluralist, believing God only one of many, Royce was a monist, affirming the essential, necessary oneness of things. *The Religious Aspect of Philosophy* (1885) first postulates a goodness at the heart of things that "satisfies the highest moral needs," and then proceeds to prove that there is an absolute or universal knower affirming judgments and experiencing objects transcending man's limitations. *The Conception of God* (1897) sustains the autonomy of the individual in face of this absolute, by contending that the absolute Will is distributed among human beings for independent use. His lectures at the University of Aberdeen were published as *The World and the Individual* (2 vols., 1900–1901), which first analyzes other philosophies and argues for an idealism in which reality is the possession solely of an all-enveloping mind, and then applies this to practical matters on the same basis developed in *The Conception of God*. He accounts for sin in the individual by contending that the highest value of the world lies in a moral conflict and victory, and that what is sinful in the finite view is in the higher view accepted as giving the necessary resistance to the moral will. After 1900 Royce became more interested in technical logic and the application of his philosophy to specific contemporary moral issues. *The Philosophy of Loyalty* (1908) contends that individual salvation lies in loyalty to a cause, supplemented by "loyalty to loyalty," and these ideas are further propounded in *The Problem of Christianity* (2 vols., 1913), lectures delivered at Oxford. His emphasis on the problem of loyalty and belief that knowledge is a social affair, resulting from a community of interpretation, was applied to the moral issues of World War I in *The Hope of the Great Community* (1916). Among his many other works, the most popular was *The Spirit of Modern Philosophy* (1892), which brilliantly examines the whole field, with particular attention to such German idealists as Fichte, to whom his beliefs were indebted.

ROYLE, EDWIN MILTON (1862–1942), author of melodramas, romantic plays, and farces, was best known for his romantic Indian play *The Squaw Man* (1905).

Rudder Grange, humorous novel by Frank Stockton,♦ published in 1879. Its popularity led to several sequels, including *The Rudder Grangers Abroad* (1891) and *Pomona's Travels* (1894).

RUDGE, WILLIAM EDWIN (1876–1931), New York printer and publisher, distinguished as a typographer and designer of beautiful books, was influential in translating the ideals of the private press into commercial bookmaking. Occasional collaborators included Goudy, Bruce Rogers, Frederic Warde, and Dwiggins.

Rugg, PETER, see *Austin, William.*

Ruggles of Red Gap, novel by H.L. Wilson.♦

RUKEYSER, MURIEL (1913–80), New York poet, whose poems in *Theory of Flight* (1935), *U.S. 1* (1938), *A Turning Wind* (1939), *Wake Island* (1942), *Beast in View* (1944), *The Green Wave* (1948), *Orpheus* (1949), *Body of Waking* (1958), *Waterlily Fire* (1962), *The Speed of Darkness* (1968), *Breaking Open* (1973), *The Gates* (1976), and *Collected Poems* (1979) are marked by elliptical, metaphysical style and intense feeling concerned with the solution of individual problems through social justice, also seen in her long poem, *The Soul and Body of John Brown* (1940). Her other books include *Willard Gibbs: American Genius* (1942), a prose study; *One Life* (1957), an interpretation of Wendell Willkie in prose and verse; *The Life of Poetry* (1949); translations of the *Selected Poems of Octavio Paz* (1963); *The Orgy* (1965), evoking the rites of Ireland's Puck Fair; and *The Traces of Thomas Hariot* (1971), a study of the English scientist and his influence.

Rules by Which a Great Empire May Be Reduced to a Small One, satirical essay by Franklin,♦ published in the *Public Advertiser* (London, Sept. 1773).

In this popular hoax, Franklin ironically assumes that the minister to whom his rules are addressed wishes to reduce the extensive dominions that he must govern. The rules that he offers as solutions of this problem contain actual grievances of the American colonies against the mother country, e.g. don't send wise or good governors, don't hesitate to impose heavy taxes, don't fail to perplex colonial commerce with infinite regulations, don't notice petitions, don't treat the colonists except as though they were about to revolt. He blandly affirms that close adherence to such rules will assuredly have the desired result of losing the colonies.

RUMFORD, COUNT, see *Thompson, Benjamin.*

RUNYON, [ALFRED] DAMON (1884–1946), journalist and sports columnist, also known for his short stories of the underworld, professional athletes, Broadway hangers-on, and other American types, distinguished for their use and invention of slang. These were collected in such volumes as *Guys and Dolls* (1932), which inspired the musical comedy of the same title (1950) by Abe Burrows and others, *Take It Easy* (1938), *My Wife Ethel* (1940), *Runyon à la Carte* (1944), *In Our Town* (1946), and *Short Takes* (1946). With Howard Lindsay he wrote the farce *A Slight Case of Murder* (1935).

RUSH, REBECCA (*fl.*1812), Philadelphia novelist, whose *Kelroy* (1812), a novel of manners in her native city, shows an advance from the didacticism, sentimentality, and affected elegance of earlier American women authors.

RUSS, JOANNA (1937–   ), born in New York City, educated at Cornell and Yale, a career academic, is a committed feminist who writes experimental works exploring gay issues, ethics, politics. Most of her work is science fiction. It includes *Picnic in Paradise* (1968); *And Chaos Died* (1970); *The Female Man* (1975), probably her most critically noticed work; *The Adventures of Alyx* (1983); *Extraordinary People* (1984); and the polemic *How To Suppress Women's Writing* (1983).

RUSSELL, IRWIN (1853–79), Mississippi poet, known for his works in black dialect. His accuracy of language and understanding of character were recognized by Joel Chandler Harris, who compiled Russell's single volume of verse as *Poems by Irwin Russell* (1888), in 1917 enlarged and reissued as *Christmas-Night in the Quarters*.

RUSSELL, OSBORNE (1814–*c.*1865), frontiersman, associated with James Bridger, later became a California and Oregon pioneer. His *Journal of a Trapper, or Nine Years in the Rocky Mountains, 1834–43* (1914) is considered an important account of frontier life.

Russell's Bookstore Group, informal literary association, met in Charleston during the 1850s at

the shop of John Russell. Among the members were Timrod, Simms, Hayne, W.J. Grayson, and S.H. Dickson. An outcome of these informal gatherings was the founding of *Russell's Magazine* (1857–60), a monthly magazine edited by Hayne, frankly modeled on the Scottish *Blackwood's,* and sectional in point of view.

Russet Mantle, play by Lynn Riggs,♦ produced and published in 1936.

RUXTON, GEORGE [AUGUSTUS] FREDERICK (1820–48), English adventurer, after education at Sandhurst, service in the Carlist civil war in Spain, and British army experience in Canada joined some mountain men of the American Far West for a time and thereby gained a knowledge of their behavior and speech that marks his novel *Life in the Far West*♦ (1848). Other experiences during his brief but exciting life provided the subject of his *Adventures in Mexico and the Rocky Mountains* (1847).

RYAN, ABRAM JOSEPH (1838–86), Maryland-born poet and Catholic priest, whose mystical lyrics upholding the Confederacy won him the name of "the Tom Moore of Dixie." Such popular Southern poems as the melancholy "Gather the Sacred Dust," "The Conquered Banner," and "The Lost Cause" were collected in *Father Ryan's Poems* (1879). *A Crown for Our Queen* (1882) is a book of devotions.

RYNNING, OLE (1809–38), leader of Norwegian colonists, came to Illinois (1837), where before his untimely death he wrote the book published in Norway (1838) and later translated as *A True Account of America for the Information and Help of Peasant and Commoner.* This work, comprehensively surveying American climate, soil, government, language, religious toleration, and opportunities for immigration, was known among Norwegian peasants as the "America Book," and was instrumental in encouraging the great Norwegian migration.

S

Saadi, poem by Emerson, ♦ first published in *The Dial* (1842) and collected in *Poems* (1847). It presents Saadi as the ideal poet dwelling apart from men's distractions, comforted by the Muse enjoining him to be serene. By loving the commonplace in Nature, he finds absolute beauty.

SABINE, LORENZO (1803–77), New England historian, best known for his work *The American Loyalists . . .* (1847), revised as *Biographical Sketches of the Loyalists of the American Revolution* (2 vols., 1864).

Sabin's Dictionary, name generally given to *A Dictionary of Books Relating to America, from Its Discovery to the Present Time,* also titled on the flyleaf, *Bibliotheca Americana,* an outstanding bibliographical work on Americana. It was begun by the English-born rare-book dealer of New York City, Joseph Sabin (1821–81), in 1856; its first volume was dated 1868, and the last of his making (fourteenth) was published in 1884. It lists alphabetically by author every book and pamphlet, in any language, related to America and provides bibliographical data and some sense of the work. The *Dictionary* through volume 20 was continued (1885–92) by Wilberforce Eames♦ and concluded with volume 29 (1936) by a staff under the administration of R.W.G. Vail. A three-volume *Author-Title Index* compiled by John E. Molnar appeared in 1974. In 1974 Lawrence S. Thompson began publishing *The New Sabin,* a reexamination of the listed works in a revised edition with the addition of others derived from other bibliographies. The tenth and final volume appeared in 1986.

Sac Indians, see *Sauk Indians.*

SACAGAWEA (*c.*1787–1812?), Shoshone squaw, was married (*c.*1800) to the French-Canadian trader Toussaint Charbonneau, with whom she accompanied the Lewis and Clark expedition, proving valuable as interpreter, peacemaker with the Shoshone, and guide over the Great Divide. Under her own name, which is variously spelled, or the nickname "The Bird Woman," she is frequently mentioned by early travelers, with praise for her character and services. She also appears in fiction, as in Emerson Hough's *The Magnificent Adventure.*

Sacco-Vanzetti case originated in the robbery (April 15, 1920) of a Massachusetts shoe com-

pany's payroll by two men who killed the paymaster and his guard. Nicola Sacco (1891–1927) and Bartolomeo Vanzetti (1888–1927) were charged with the crime, when it was discovered that they carried firearms and laid claim to the car that police identified with the crime. In their trial at Dedham, Mass. (May–July 1921), both had witnesses to prove that they were not at the scene of the crime, but these statements were discredited by state witnesses. Much of the evidence against them was later refuted, but prejudice was strong in their disfavor because they had been draft dodgers, anarchists, and labor agitators. In 1927 Governor Fuller of Massachusetts appointed an advisory investigating committee, consisting of President Lowell of Harvard, President Stratton of the Massachusetts Institute of Technology, and Judge Robert Grant. Although a condemned criminal, Madeiros, exonerated Sacco and Vanzetti, and admitted he had been a member of a gang of robbers responsible for the shoe-company killings, death sentences were upheld by the committee, and in 1927 Sacco and Vanzetti were executed. G. Louis Joughin and Edmund M. Morgan in *The Legacy of Sacco and Vanzetti* (1948) find 144 poems treating the case, including works by Witter Bynner, Malcolm Cowley, Countee Cullen, Edna St. Vincent Millay, and Lola Ridge; six plays, including *Winterset* by Maxwell Anderson, *Gods of the Lightning* by Anderson and Harold Hickerson, and *The Male Animal* by Thurber and Elliott Nugent, which uses a letter by Vanzetti as an important issue; and eight novels, including Upton Sinclair's *Boston,* Nathan Asch's *Pay Day,* De Voto's *We Accept with Pleasure,* Ruth McKenney's *Jake Home,* and, less directly, Dos Passos's *The Big Money* and Farrell's *Bernard Clare.* A section of C.E.S. Wood's *Heavenly Discourse* deals with the case, as does Katherine Anne Porter's *The Never-Ending Wrong. The Letters of Sacco and Vanzetti* was published in 1928.

SACKLER, HOWARD (1929–82), New York-born dramatist, director, and film writer, whose first major play, *The Great White Hope* (1967, published 1968), about Jack Johnson, the first black heavy-weight boxing champion of the world, won a Pulitzer Prize. Earlier he had staged *Mr. Welk and Jersey Jim* (1960); *Skippy,* also titled *The Yellow Loves* (1966); and *The Nine O'Clock Mail* (1965), a quartet of one-act plays about disparate people's unhappy, searching lives, produced together and printed as *A Few Enquiries* (1970). *Uriel Acosta* (1954) and *The Pastime of*

Monsieur Robert (1966) are other early plays. *Want My Shepherd* (1954) prints his poems.

Sacred Fount, The, novelette by Henry James,♦ published in 1901.

The narrator, whose temperament and interests resemble those of the author, is a guest at an English weekend party, where his excessively refined curiosity becomes absorbed in studying Guy and Grace Brissenden, the husband not yet 30, and the wife in her middle forties, who after a few years of marriage seem to have exchanged physical and mental ages. He derives from their case a "law" that, in such uneven matches, the older partner always draws energy, youth, and wit from the "sacred fount" of the other's personality, which becomes correspondingly depleted. Then he attempts to apply his law to another guest, Gilbert Long, who seems to have exchanged his character of a stupid though handsome young man for that of a witty and understanding man of the world. The narrator's prying mind seeks to discover the mistress who must have given Long this new power. Rejecting the bright, superficial Lady John, he settles on Mrs. May Server, an attractive woman who is obviously attempting to conceal a profound emotional disturbance and weakness. He even believes that he observes a realignment of the couples, resulting from the mutual weakness and defeat of Brissenden and Mrs. Server, and the common vigor and strength of will of Long and "poor Briss's" wife. His whole structure of hypothesis is overthrown, however, when Mrs. Brissenden says he is "crazy" and repudiates his hinted accusations as "houses of cards," though it is never certain whether his rout is caused by lies on her part or by his own unduly fanciful conjectures.

Sacred Wood, The, essays by T.S. Eliot.♦

Sag Harbor, play by James A. Herne,♦ a revision of his *Hearts of Oak* (1879), written with Belasco, was produced in 1899.

St. Clare, family name of characters in *Uncle Tom's Cabin.*♦

St. Elmo, novel by Augusta Jane Evans,♦ published in 1867.

SAINT-GAUDENS, Augustus (1848–1907), Irish-born American sculptor, whose style shows the changing direction of American sculpture, in its fusion of exalted realism with more animated poses, and its broken picturesque surfaces, as opposed to the cold, formal ideal of Italian neoclassicism, practiced by such members of the previous generation as Hiram Powers and Horatio Greenough. The general high standard of his work had an important influence on monument sculpture in the U.S. The dignified and simple *Lincoln* (1887) in Chicago, with its moderate im-

pressionistic treatment of surface; the grave, thoughtful *Adams Memorial* (1891) in Rock Creek Cemetery in Washington, D.C., a monument to the wife of his friend Henry Adams, which Adams called "The Peace of God"; the *Shaw Memorial* (opposite the State House, Boston) in high relief; and his many splendid bas-reliefs, which include the bronze tablet of Stevenson in Edinburgh, are outstanding among Saint-Gaudens's noble, sedate sculptures. He is the prototype of Mr. Wharton in Adams's novel *Esther.*♦ His *Reminiscences* (2 vols., 1913) was edited by his son, Homer Saint-Gaudens.

ST. JOHN, J. Hector, pseudonym of Crèvecœur.♦

Saint Katy the Virgin, story by Steinbeck.♦ reprinted in *The Long Valley.*♦

St. Nicholas (1873–1940), monthly magazine for children, was long distinguished for the high quality of its fiction, and its realization that a children's magazine should not "be a milk-and-water variety of the periodical for adults," or a place for "sermonizing" or "wearisome spinning out of facts." In addition to Mary Mapes Dodge, the editor (1873–1905), contributors included Rebecca Harding Davis, D.G. Mitchell, Trowbridge, Louisa May Alcott, Frank Stockton, Frances Hodgson Burnett, C.E. Carryl, Edward Eggleston, Mayne Reid, T.N. Page, Clemens, Howard Pyle, Stevenson, Henty, Kipling, Cable, Howells, Burroughs, Harte, A.B. Paine, Palmer Cox, and Gelett Burgess. At the turn of the century, when the regular contributions seemed to be less significant, the magazine established a department of contributions from its juvenile readers. Among the authors who thus received their first publication were E.B. White, Edna St. Vincent Millay, Faulkner, the Benéts, Robert Benchley, Elinor Wylie, Edmund Wilson, and Babette Deutsch. After 1930 it changed owners and policies several times, finally becoming in 1939 a picture magazine for very young children.

Saint-Simonism (or Saint-Simonianism), socialistic system based on the economic, religious, and social ideas of Claude-Henri de Rouvroy, Comte de Saint-Simon (1760–1825). It aims to create an industrial society scientifically administered by experts (scientists, technicians, property owners, and financiers) for the benefit of the "poorest and most numerous classes." It abolishes inheritance, socializes the means of production, and bases distribution on the merits of the individual recipients. The system exerted considerable influence on movements toward a scientifically planned economy even though the distortion of certain aspects of Saint-Simon's *New Christianity* (1825) by his disciples resulted in the discrediting and disbanding of the new sect they had organized. Michel Chevalier♦ was among the Saint-Simonians who visited the U.S. Although no communities were founded in the U.S., Orestes Brownson was a notable convert who expounded these social and religious doctrines, especially in his *Boston Quarterly Review.*

Salem witchcraft trials occurred at Salem, Mass., the result of a belief in witchcraft assignable not to Puritanism, but to the temper of the times as evidenced also in England and on the Continent. Before 1688 four persons had been hanged for witchcraft near Boston, but the principal outbreak of persecution took place in 1692, when an epidemic disease resembling epilepsy spread through Danvers (part of Salem). Discouraged by the inability of physicians to control this disease, and encouraged by sermons from such clergymen as Cotton Mather,♦ the belief was soon widespread that evil spirits in the form of witches were able to afflict the people at large. Increase Mather is frequently held responsible for fomenting the trials, although his *Cases of Conscience Concerning Evil Spirits* (1693) showed a rational attitude in disapproving "spectral evidence." During the prevalence of the delusion, in the spring and summer of 1692, 19 persons were hanged; one, Giles Corey, was pressed to death; 55 were frightened or tortured into confessions of guilt; 150 were imprisoned; and more than 200 were named as deserving arrest. Learned and distinguished men promoted the delusion by acquiescing in the proceedings of the court instituted by the governor, Sir William Phips. When the governor's wife, some near relatives of Cotton Mather, and the sons of ex-Governor Bradstreet became objects of suspicion, the spell began to break. Many of the accusers published solemn recantations, and Samuel Sewall was among those who did public penance, he for his part as a member of the Special Court of Oyer and Terminer.

A Brief and True Narrative of Witchcraft at Salem Village (1692) was written by Deodat Lawson; Cotton Mather's affirmations are to be found in *The Wonders of the Invisible World*♦ (1693) and *A Brand Pluck'd Out of the Burning* (1693), to which Robert Calef♦ replied in *More Wonders of the Invisible World* (1700). Mather in turn replied in *Some Few Remarks Upon a Scandalous Book . . . by One Robert Calef* (1701). A 20th-century edition of the *Narratives of the Witchcraft Cases* (1914) was edited by G.L. Burr. Novels about Salem's witchcraft cases include John Neal's *Rachel Dyer,* Paulding's *The Puritan and His Daughter,* De Forest's "Witching Times," and Esther Forbes's *A Mirror for Witches;* poems include Longfellow's *New England Tragedies;* and plays include J.N. Barker's *Superstition,* Cornelius Mathews's *Witchcraft,* Mary W. Freeman's *Giles Corey, Yeoman,* and Arthur Miller's *The Crucible.*

SALINGER, J[EROME] D[AVID] (1919–   ), New York-born writer, resident in New Hamp-

shire, began to publish stories in the early 1940s; and after service as an infantry sergeant in Europe during World War II he wrote more stories, but has not chosen to collect them from *Collier's, The Saturday Evening Post, Story,* and other journals. His first book was *The Catcher in the Rye*♦ (1951), about an unhappy teenage boy, Holden Caulfield, who runs away from his boarding school as part of his disgust with "phoniness," and who because of his feelings and the idiom in which he communicated them, particularly for a generation of high-school and college students, a symbol of purity and sensitivity. In *Nine Stories* (1953), printing stories written beginning in 1948, including "A Perfect Day for Bananafish," Salinger introduced his chronicle of an eccentric, warm-hearted family named Glass, continued in his next books of stories. *Franny and Zooey* (1961) presents two members of the Glass family, sister and brother, in two long stories. Franny, a college senior, visits her boyfriend on a football weekend which is made desperately unhappy because she is dissatisfied with him, herself, and life. Zooey, her older brother, a television actor, tries to ease her feelings after this weekend, and his sensitive aid is first described by their still older brother, Buddy, whom the author calls his "alter ego." *Raise High the Roof-Beam, Carpenters and Seymour: An Introduction* (1963), a single volume, reprints stories from *The New Yorker* (1955, 1959), in which Buddy Glass tells, first, of his return to New York during the war to attend his brother Seymour's wedding and of Seymour's jilting of the bride and then of their later elopement; and, second, after Seymour's suicide, of Buddy's own brooding, to the point of breakdown, upon Seymour's virtues, human and literary. In the early 1960s Salinger retired to his rural home, withdrew from the literary scene, and has not published since "Hapworth 16, 1924," a story about Seymour aged seven, in *The New Yorker* (June 19, 1965).

Salmagundi, quarterly little magazine, founded in 1965, since 1969 sponsored by Skidmore College. Concentrating on the humanities and social sciences, it is essentially a literary journal with one issue a year devoted to a single subject, e.g. "Contemporary Poetry in America," "Saul Bellow."

Salmagundi; or, the Whim-Whams and Opinions of Launcelot Langstaff, Esq. and Others, satirical essays and poems, published in 20 periodical pamphlets (Jan. 24, 1807–Jan. 25, 1808), by Washington♦ and William Irving♦ and J.K. Paulding,♦ who used such pseudonyms as Anthony Evergreen, Jeremy Cockloft the Younger, Will Wizard, and Pindar Cockloft, Esq. The work was collected in book form (1808).

Modeled on the *Spectator,* these whimsical pieces travesty contemporary New York's tastes, society, and politics, showing the authors' aristocratic Federalism. The "letters" of the visiting

Mustapha-Rub-a-Dub Keli Khan to Asem Haachem satirically describe "mobocratic" and "logocratic" Jeffersonian democracy, while other essays and poems deal in a humorous, pseudolearned style with such various topics as fashions in women's clothing, the vulgarity of *parvenus,* theatrical and musical criticism, style in literature, and caricatures of celebrities. A second series of *Salmagundi* papers was written by Paulding alone (May 1819–Sept. 1820).

SALTUS, EDGAR [EVERTSON] (1855–1921), born in New York City, after studying at Yale and abroad and receiving an LL.B. from Columbia began his literary career with a biography of Balzac (1884); volumes of translations from French fiction; *The Philosophy of Disenchantment* (1885), popularizing the pessimism of Schopenhauer and Hartmann; and *The Anatomy of Negation* (1886), a history of antitheistic philosophies. This philosophic attitude and the resulting lack of faith in anything but an esoteric hedonism, devoid of social or moral considerations, was elaborated in his fiction dealing with New York society. *Mr. Incoul's Misadventure* (1887) was the first of a long series of novels whose melodramatic plots were clothed in an epigrammatic style, a lush use of bizarre language, and an extravagant adaptation of *fin de siècle* romanticism, as expressed in his dictum: "In fiction as in history it is the shudder that tells." Among the later novels are *The Truth About Tristrem Varick* (1888); *The Pace That Kills* (1889); *Madame Sapphira* (1893); *Enthralled* (1894); *The Pomps of Satan* (1904); *The Perfume of Eros* (1905); *Vanity Square* (1906); *The Monster* (1912), which he made into an unproduced play, *The Gates of Life;* and *The Paliser Case* (1919). He also published two volumes of short stories, *A Transient Guest and Other Episodes* (1889) and *Purple and Fine Women* (1903), and his attitude of mind and manner of presentation were further illustrated in treatments of such exotic subjects as apocryphal Bible history, in *Mary Magdalen* (1891); the history of the Roman emperors, in *Imperial Purple* (1892); eroticism, in *Historia Amoris* (1906); the history of religions, in *The Lords of the Ghostland* (1907); the history of the Romanoffs, in *The Orgy* (1920); and similar subjects in a collection of essays, *Love and Lore* (1890). His cynicism, exotic eroticism, and rebellion against conventional standards caused Saltus to be attacked by many critics, and championed by such writers as Van Vechten and Huneker, in whose novel *Painted Veils* he is a minor character. His last works show a change from the dependence upon an aesthetic doctrine of art for art's sake to a belief in theosophy, in which he was largely influenced by the views of his third wife, Marie Saltus, who wrote a biography (1925) and edited his posthumous works.

Salut au Monde, poem by Whitman,♦ published as "Poem and Salutation" in *Leaves of Grass* (1856) and given its present title in 1867.

In the form of a colloquy, the poem opens with the demand, "O take my hand, Walt Whitman!" and the question, "What widens within you, Walt Whitman?" This is answered by long catalogues of what the poet sees and hears throughout the world, and the statement.

> My spirit has passed in compassion and determination around the whole earth; I have look'd for equals and lovers, and found them ready for me in all lands; I think some divine rapport has equalized me with them.

Sam Slick, character in *The Clockmaker,*♦ *The Attaché,*♦ and other sketches by T.C. Haliburton♦ and also in other writings by S.A. Hammett.♦

Sam Spade, detective in novels by Dashiell Hammett.♦

SAMPSON, DEBORAH (1760–1827), born in Massachusetts, after a rather peripatetic youth as an orphan disguised herself as a man and served in the Continental army for more than two years. Not until after the war did she reveal herself to be a woman, but in 1784 she married and settled down to a normal quiet life. *The Female Review; or, Life of Deborah Sampson* (1797) is an anonymous biography, obviously bordering on fiction.

San Francisco, situated on one of the world's largest bays, on the central California coast, had a population in 1990 of approximately 750,000. The bay may have been sighted by Drake (1579), but the discoverer of the city's site is usually considered to be Portola, whose expedition arrived in 1770. Anza founded the mission and presidio (1776), which, under the administration of Serra, was the beginning of the pueblo Yerba Buena, the present San Francisco. The region became Mexican territory (1821), but a local insurrection, the Bear Flag War (1846), resulted in the establishment of a temporary republic, and a month later California was taken by the U.S. The gold rush of the forty-niners caused San Francisco's mushroom growth into a busy, lawless frontier town, whose most notorious area was the Barbary Coast. The city's port flourished, with trade and immigration from the Orient, around Cape Horn, and across Panama. Overland communication with the East was established in 1860 by the pony express, and in 1869 by railroad, so that, until the rise of Los Angeles, San Francisco was the key city of the business and culture of the Far West. The discovery of the Comstock Lode♦ created a second boom period, but later the city settled into a more conservative way of life, which has caused it to be characterized as the most Eastern of the Western cities.

On April 18, 1906, occurred the San Francisco earthquake, followed by a disastrous four-day fire that could not be controlled, because the water mains were destroyed. The events resulted in the loss of some 500 lives, the demolition of a large part of the city's central business district and residential sections, and a loss of property estimated at between $500,000,000 and $1,000,000,000. The city emerged from the disaster with a better plan and more permanent buildings, but still retains its romantic cosmopolitan character, marked by its large Chinatown and Italian district. It is connected with the East Bay cities of Oakland and Berkeley by an eight-mile suspension bridge, and with suburban and rural Marin County by a bridge across the Golden Gate, the mouth of the harbor. Two famous expositions have been held in San Francisco, one celebrating the completion of the Panama Canal (1915), and another the building of the two bay bridges (1939–40). The University of California♦ is located in Berkeley, and on the peninsula south of the city is Stanford University.♦

The period of Mexican occupation is described in R.H. Dana's *Two Years Before the Mast,* and the city's literary flowering occurred during the post-gold-rush period (*c.*1850–70), when its authors included Bret Harte, Clemens, Joaquin Miller, Bierce, C.W. Stoddard, Alonzo Delano, G.H. Derby, Prentice Mulford, Ina Coolbrith, H.H. Bancroft, E.R. Sill, John Muir, Clarence King, and Henry George, many of whom contributed to the *Overland Monthly♦* and *The Golden Era.♦* Among the most prominent of the many visitors to write about the area was Robert Louis Stevenson. Later writers more permanently associated with the city and its environs included Frank Norris, Jack London, Gertrude Atherton, Edwin Markham, George Sterling, and the bohemian group Les Jeunes, led by Gelett Burgess, which published *The Lark.* Writers who later lived to the south respectively in Carmel♦ and the Salinas Valley included Jeffers and Steinbeck. Authors associated with the city and its environs include Oscar Lewis, Evan Connell, Herbert Gold, Alice Adams, and Ella Leffland, and Saroyan lived there for a time. In the mid- to late 1950s the Beat movement♦ was so centered there that it was also called the San Francisco Renaissance. Its authors included Kenneth Rexroth, as an elder figure, and Allen Ginsberg, Lawrence Ferlinghetti, Gary Snyder, Gregory Corso, Philip Whalen, and Michael McClure. Also related were Richard Brautigan, James Broughton, Robert Creeley, Robert Duncan, and John Wieners. At Big Sur, south of Carmel, Henry Miller lived, and to the town's north, in Santa Cruz, William Everson settled after a period, as Brother Antoninus, in the East Bay. Authors on nearby university faculties have included Kay Boyle and Wright Morris at San Francisco State University; Yvor Winters, Wallace Stegner, Albert Guerard, and Al Young at Stanford; and Josephine Miles, Ishmael Reed, Mark Schorer, and George R. Stewart at the University of California, Berkeley.

SANBORN, Franklin Benjamin (1831–1917), born in New Hampshire, graduated from Harvard (1855), and settled in Concord as a schoolteacher, where his pupils included the children of Emerson, Hawthorne, and the elder Henry James. He became an Abolitionist leader, and was arrested for refusing to testify concerning his aid to John Brown. He was associated with the *Springfield Republican* (1856–1914), and was also active in humanitarian work as the head of state charities. His acquaintance with the Transcendentalists resulted in the publication of many books, which include *Henry D. Thoreau* (1882); *A. Bronson Alcott: His Life and Philosophy* (2 vols., 1893), written with W.T. Harris, who also contributed to his *Genius and Character of Emerson* (1885); *The Personality of Thoreau* (1901); *Hawthorne and His Friends* (1908); and *Recollections of Seventy Years* (2 vols., 1909).

SANCHEZ, Sonia (1934–   ), African-American poet born in Birmingham, educated at Hunter College, New York City. Identifying solely with other African-Americans and writing in urban speech rhythms and dialect, her titles explain her themes: *Homecoming* (1964), *We a BaddDDD People* (1970), *It's a New Day: Poems for Young Brothas and Sistuhs* (1971), *Ima Talken bout the Nation of Islam* (1972), *A Blues Book for Blue Black Magical Women* (1973), *I've Been a Woman: New and Selected Poems* (1978), *Homegirls and Handgrenades* (1984), and *Under a Soprano Sky* (1987). In 1971 she edited *Three Hundred and Sixty Degrees of Blackness Comin' at You.* She has been a full professor at the University of Pennsylvania since 1979.

Sanctuary, novel by Faulkner,♦ published in 1931. The original text, in which Horace Benbow is the central character, was published in 1981. *Requiem for a Nun* (1951) is a sequel.

Temple Drake, an 18-year-old Mississippi college girl, goes to a petting party with a drunken escort, Gowan Stevens (see *Gavin Stevens*), who wrecks his car on a lonely road. They walk to a nearby house, which is a bootleggers' hideout, inhabited by a number of vicious criminals of whom the chief is the killer Popeye, emasculated and of subnormal intellect as the result of a childhood accident. Temple's cowardly escort escapes after a severe beating, but the girl, whose virginity makes her the object of several attacks, is finally raped by Popeye, who incidentally murders one of his men. He then places her in the Memphis brothel of Miss Reba, who is at first pleased to have the custom of this influential man, then horrified by his degenerate conduct. Goodwin, one of the bootleggers, is arrested for the murder that Popeye committed and is defended by a member of the distinguished Benbow family♦ of Jefferson, Horace Benbow, a lawyer who wishes to redeem his conventional career by serving justice in this unpopular case. He learns of Popeye's guilt and of the plight of Temple, whom he persuades to testify. The girl's mind is already unbalanced, and her testimony only increases the un-reasoning vindictiveness of the jurors, who convict Goodwin. The latter is brutally lynched; Benbow manages to escape with his life; Temple is taken by her broken father to live in Paris; and Popeye, who has escaped to Alabama, is apprehended and hanged for another murder, which he did not commit.

Sandbox, The, play by Edward Albee. ♦

SANDBURG, CARL [AUGUST] (1878–1967), born in Galesburg, Ill., of a Swedish immigrant family, after irregular schooling, and a youth spent as an itinerant laborer throughout the Middle West, went to Puerto Rico as a soldier in the Spanish-American War. On his return he worked his way through Lombard College in Galesburg, and after leaving (1902) became an advertising writer, journalist, and organizer for the Social Democratic party in Wisconsin. He was secretary to the socialist mayor of Milwaukee (1910–12).

His earliest poems were privately printed in a small pamphlet (1904), but he was unknown as a poet until 1914, when *Poetry* published a number of his short pieces, including "Chicago," ♦ whose fearless colloquialism and vigorous free verse stimulated a critical controversy and established him as the leading figure in the Chicago group of authors that was then beginning to flourish. *Chicago Poems* (1916), besides its title piece, contained such vivid impressionistic poems as "Fog," "Grass," and "Nocturne in a Deserted Brickyard," and verses defining the poet's liberal social position, such as "I Am the People, the Mob," and "To a Contemporary Bunk Shooter." These simple, powerful utterances depicted the crude, vital American that the author knew at first hand, and that Whitman had taught him to recognize as symbolic of a free, untrammeled, democratic promised life.

His sensitive appreciation of the beauty of ordinary people and commonplace things, in which he accepted the rude and savage ("Galoots") as well as the delicate and lovely ("Smoke Rose Gold"), was expressed with a firmer touch and greater power in the succeeding collections, *Cornhuskers* (1918; special Pulitzer award, 1919), *Smoke and Steel* (1920), *Slabs of the Sunburnt West* (1922), and *Good Morning, America* (1928). These volumes included such characteristic poems as "Cool Tombs," ♦ "Smoke and Steel," "Broken-Face Gargoyles," ♦ "Prairie," ♦ "Good Morning, America," ♦ "Prayers of Steel," ♦ "Four Preludes on Playthings of the Wind," "Clean Curtains," and "Losers," all of which display a combination of precise realism, born of personal experience, with playful fantasy and love of color. *The People, Yes* ♦ (1936) is a panoramic depiction in verse of America and the American spirit as expressed in folklore and folk history, which sums up Sandburg's profound social sympathies and his faith in

the future of the working classes. His *Complete Poems* (1950) was awarded a Pulitzer Prize. *Harvest Poems, 1910–1960* (1960), *Wind Song* (1960), *Honey and Salt* (1963), and *Complete Poems* (1970) collect late poems.

Throughout his work there is a constant, and frequently successful, attempt to capture the distinctive flavor of the American idiom and way of thought, particularly of his native Middle West. This interest led also to his compilation of ballads and folk songs in *The American Songbag* (1927), and strongly influenced his original books for children, *Rootabaga Stories* (1922), *Rootabaga Pigeons* (1923), and *Potato Face* (1930). Besides his poetry and journalism, he devoted much time and careful research to his monumental biography of Lincoln, *Abraham Lincoln: The Prairie Years* (2 vols., 1926) and *Abraham Lincoln: The War Years* (4 vols., 1939, Pulitzer Prize), both abridged by the author in one volume (1954), and from which he selected a "profile" of the Civil War years titled *Storm Over the Land* (1942). His other prose includes *The Chicago Race Riots* (1919); *Steichen the Photographer* (1929), whose subject was the author's brother-in-law; *Mary Lincoln, Wife and Widow* (1932), written with Paul M. Angle; *Home Front Memo* (1943), a collection of wartime writings in verse and prose; *Remembrance Rock* (1948), a large, loose, poetic novel tracing an American family from its 17th-century English origins to World War II as it develops the theme of the American Dream; and *Always the Young Strangers* (1953), a memoir about his youth, from which he excerpted for children a section titled *Prairie-Town Boy* (1955). His *Letters* was published in 1968.

SANDEMAN, ROBERT (1718–71), Scottish-born leader of the religious sect of Sandemanians, which protested against the established Church of Scotland, believed that church and state should be separate, and contended that "the bare Work of Jesus Christ without a Deed or Thought on the Part of Man is sufficient to present the chief of Sinners spotless before God." Sandeman emigrated to New England in 1764, where he published *Some Thoughts on Christianity* (1764), and established his sect, despite the opposition of Congregational ministers.

SANDERSON, JOHN (1783–1844), Pennsylvania writer and teacher, contributor to the anti-Federalist *Aurora,* was best known for his witty *Sketches of Paris: In Familiar Letters to His Friends* (1838), written during a visit abroad.

SANDOZ, MARI (1896–1966), Nebraska author, whose books include *Old Jules* (1935), a biography of her Swiss emigrant father, recounting his heroic efforts to wrest a living from his frontier farm; *Slogum House* (1937), a historical novel of late 19th-century Nebraska; *Capital City* (1939) and *The Tom-Walker* (1947), novels about descendants of Midwestern pioneers and the corruption of their civic and moral responsibility; *Crazy Horse* (1942), a life of the Sioux chief; *The Buffalo Hunters* (1954), a historical study; *Son of the Gamblin' Man* (1960), a novel about the young Robert Henri in frontier Nebraska before he became a famous painter; *Love Song to the Plains* (1961), recording history and personal feelings; *These Were the Sioux* (1961); *The Beaver Men* (1964), a history of the American fur trade; and *The Battle of the Little Big Horn* (1978). *The Christmas of Phonograph Records* (1966) is a memoir.

SANDS, ROBERT C[HARLES] (1799–1832), New York author and journalist, with Bryant edited *The New York Review and Athenæum Magazine*♦ (1825–26), and independently edited the *Commercial Advertiser* (1827–32). For *The Talisman,* an annual, he wrote essays and poetry. As a figure in the New York literary and social life of the time, he earned a great reputation, although he published only a few separate works, such as a *Life and Correspondence of John Paul Jones* (1830). His humorous works and other writings were collected in 1834. One of his most popular poems was *Yamoyden*♦ (1820), written with J.W. Eastburn.

SANDYS, GEORGE (1578–1644), English-born colonist in Virginia (1621–25), treasurer of the London Company, and member of its council. While in Virginia he made a verse translation of the last ten books of the *Metamorphoses* to accompany his previous translation of five books, and the whole was published as *Ovid's Metamorphosis Englished by G.S.* (1626). This was the first translation of a classic made in America, and it contains many references to America. The remainder of his works, written when he resided in England, include poetic paraphrases of the Psalms of David, the hymns of the Old and New Testaments, and the Song of Solomon.

SANGER, MARGARET [HIGGINS] (1883–1966), New York leader of the movement for birth control, author of such books as *Happiness in Marriage* (1927). *My Fight for Birth Control* (1931) and *Margaret Sanger* (1938) are autobiographical works.

SANKEY, IRA DAVID, see *Moody, D.L.*

Santa Fe Trail, caravan route from Independence, Mo., to Santa Fe, N.M., which from the time of William Becknell, its "founder" in 1821–22, until late in the century served as an important trade route, and caused the growth of such communities as Taos.♦ Josiah Gregg♦ and Lewis H. Garrard♦ wrote works on its early history, and Harvey Fergusson's trilogy *Followers of the Sun* (1921–29) is concerned with life along the trail from Spanish times to the present.

Santa-Fé Trail, The *(A Humoresque),* poem by Vachel Lindsay,♦ published in *The Congo and Other Poems* (1914). With frequent onomatopoetic effects, the poet presents the vision of a cavalcade of automobiles on the Kansas highway, in which "the United States goes by!," and alternates the cacophonous noise of the horns with the distant but persistent song of a bird "amid a hedge of thorns."

SANTAYANA, GEORGE (1863–1952), born in Spain, was christened Jorge Ruiz de Santayana y Borrais, but always used the English form of his name after he was brought to the U.S. (1872). Reared in Boston, he graduated from Harvard (1886), and after study in Germany and England received his Ph.D. from Harvard (1889). From that year until 1912 he was professor of philosophy at that university. After 1914 he made his home in Europe, first in France and England, and thereafter in Italy.

He is known as both a philosopher and a man of letters, having begun his literary career with *Sonnets and Other Verses* (1894); *The Sense of Beauty*♦ (1896), a treatise on aesthetics; *Lucifer: A Theological Tragedy* (1899, revised 1924), a play in verse; *Interpretations of Poetry and Religion* (1900); and another book of poems, *A Hermit of Carmel* (1901). He collected his *Poems* in 1923, but after the turn of the century the body of his work was philosophical, having literary significance because of his rich style, whose cadence, reminiscent of Pater, is illumined by lucid, pithy statements of philosophical problems. His outstanding early work is *The Life of Reason*♦ (5 vols., 1905–6), a study of reason in common sense, society, religion, art, and science, in which he finds matter to be the only reality, and the source of the myths, institutions, and definitions that men use to describe or express that reality. With *Scepticism and Animal Faith* (1923), he introduced a new philosophy to modify and supplement this concept. This books serves as a prologue to the series entitled *The Realms of Being,*♦ including *The Realm of Essence* (1927), *The Realm of Matter* (1930), *The Realm of Truth* (1937), and *The Realm of Spirit* (1940). In these works he found knowledge to be faith in the unknowable, symbolized by essences. He contended that, though logical analysis may lead to complete skepticism concerning the existence of anything, animal faith continues to believe in a world whose material events have aroused intuitive essences, which are signs of the environment in which all animals live and suffer. Santayana's other works include *Three Philosophical Poets* (1910), studies of Lucretius, Dante, and Goethe; *Winds of Doctrine* (1913); *Egotism in German Philosophy* (1916, revised 1940), attacking the romantic willfulness of the Germans; *Soliloquies in England*♦ (1922), a subtle interpretation of the Anglo-Saxon character; *Dialogues in Limbo*♦ (1925), a series of Platonic dialogues; *Platonism and the Spiritual Life* (1927); and *Some Turns of Thought in Modern Philosophy* (1933).

His works dealing specifically with the American character are *Philosophical Opinion in America* (1918); *Character and Opinion in the United States*◆ (1920), concerned with the conflict of materialism and idealism in American life; and *The Genteel Tradition at Bay*◆ (1931), analyzing the adulteration and formalization of Calvinism and Transcendentalism. *The Last Puritan*◆ (1935) is a novel set in America during the period of the waning strength of Calvinism, in which the contrasting characters, one a Puritan, the other a hedonist, represent "potentialities which from my earliest youth I felt in myself . . ."; through such concrete externalizations Santayana gave fictional form to his argumentative philosophy.

The Idea of Christ in the Gospels (1946) is an interpretation of the Gospels and an investigation of the philosophic validity of the idea of God in man. His memoirs, *Persons and Places,* were published as *The Backgrounds of My Life* (1944), *The Middle Span* (1945), and *My Host the World* (1953). *Obiter Scripta* (1936) contains essays, lectures, and reviews; his *Works* was published in 14 volumes (1936–37), and some of his letters were collected in 1955.

Sapphira and the Slave Girl, novel by Willa Cather,◆ published in 1940.

Recalling a story current during her Virginia childhood, the author describes events that occurred in the neighborhood in 1856. The pious miller, Henry Colbert, is unusually kind to a beautiful mulatto slave, Nancy Till, illegitimate daughter of a white artist and a black servant. His invalid wife, Sapphira, groundlessly jealous, persecutes the girl in various subtle ways, finally inviting a philandering nephew for a visit and encouraging him to seduce Nancy. The girl resists, placing herself under the protection of the Colberts' widowed daughter, Rachel Blake, who secretly helps her to escape to Canada by way of the Underground Railroad. Sapphira, already estranged from her generous, humanitarian daughter by her own pride and gentility, suspects the source of the plot and refuses to recognize Mrs. Blake until the death of a beloved grandchild causes a formal reconciliation. Twenty-five years later Nancy returns to visit her mother and Mrs. Blake, and impresses them by the poise she has acquired through her experiences as a housekeeper for a wealthy Canadian family.

SARETT, LEW (1888–1954), born in Chicago, spent a great part of his life in the Rocky Mountains and northern Canada, the background of his ruggedly pantheistic poems interpreting Indian and frontier life. He also taught English at the University of Illinois (1912–20) and Northwestern (1921–54). His books are *Many Many Moons* (1920), *The Box of God* (1922), *Slow Smoke* (1925), *Wings Against the Moon* (1931), *Collected Poems* (1941), and a posthumous collection, *Covenant with Earth* (1956).

SARGENT, EPES (1813–80), Boston author and journalist, was a member of the editorial staffs of various Boston papers, and, while resident in New York (1839–47), helped edit the *New-York Mirror* and other publications. He was well known in his time for miscellaneous writings, which ranged from *American Adventure by Land and Sea* (1841) to some of the Peter Parley◆ books, and anthologies for schools and the general public. His best works include the romantic tragedies *The Bride of Genoa* (1837); *Velasco* (1837), set in 11th-century Spain and dealing with the Cid; and *The Priestess* (1854); the satirical comedy *Change Makes Change* (1845); *Songs of the Sea with Other Poems* (1847), sonnets describing a voyage to Cuba, remembered for the song "A Life on the Ocean Wave"; *The Woman Who Dared* (1870), a long verse narrative; and the romantic novels *Fleetwood; or, The Stain of Birth* (1845) and *Peculiar; A Tale of the Great Transition* (1864). In later years Sargent devoted most of his writing to proof of spiritualism, in such books as *The Proof Palpable of Immortality* (1875) and *The Scientific Basis of Spiritualism* (1880).

SARGENT, LUCIUS MANLIUS (1786–1867), Boston author and antiquary, attended Harvard, where he published (1807) an invidious pamphlet on its living conditions. He then studied law but, being of independent means, turned to the writing of original Latin verse, translations of Virgil, articles on antiquarian matters for the *Boston Transcript,* and a vigorous series of temperance tracts, collected as *The Temperance Tales* (6 vols., 1863–64). His humanitarianism permitted him to attack the British coolie trade but his close alliance with the Boston hegemony made it impossible for him to stomach antislavery, which he blasted in *The Ballad of the Abolition Blunderbuss* (1861), leveled against Emerson and other liberals.

SARGENT, WINTHROP (1825–70), historian whose works include *The History of an Expedition against Fort Du Quesne . . .* (1855), a scholarly account of Braddock's campaign; and *Life and Career of Major John André* (1861), a highly eulogistic study. He also edited *The Loyal Verses of Joseph Stansbury and Doctor Jonathan Odell, Relating to the American Revolution* (1860).

SAROYAN, WILLIAM (1908–81), California author, whose short stories are marked by an impressionistic, rhapsodic manner, and a sentimental exaltation of characters ranging from Armenian-American workers like himself to middle-class businessmen, all somehow optimistically associated with the glory of an American dream. His impetuous and undiscriminating love for all sorts of people and situations, his very common fictionalizing of personal experience, and his ability to use what he calls the "jump-in-the-river-and-start-to-swim-immediately" type of writing allowed him to produce a steady flow of short fiction, published in *The Daring Young Man on the Flying Trapeze* (1934); *Inhale and Exhale* (1936); *Three Times Three* (1936); *Little Children* (1937); *A Native American* (1938); *The Trouble with Tigers* (1938); *Love, Here Is My Hat* (1938); *Peace, It's Wonderful* (1939); *My Name Is Aram* (1940), about the exuberant experiences of some Armenian children in California; *Fables* (1941); *Dear Baby* (1944); *The Whole Voyald* (1956); and *I Used To Believe I Had Forever, Now I'm Not So Sure* (1967), composed of stories, essays, and poems.

His novels include *The Human Comedy* (1943), set in California and mainly about children; *The Adventures of Wesley Jackson* (1946), a loosely knit, whimsical account of a Saroyanesque army private's war experiences, incorporated in *The Twin Adventures* (1950) with "The Adventures of William Saroyan," an "hour-to-hour chronicle of a writer at work on the writing of a novel"; *Rock Wagram* (1951); *Mama, I Love You* (1956), about a nine-year-old girl's fantastic theatrical life with her mother; *Papa, You're Crazy* (1957); *Boys and Girls Together* (1963), a novella about a young writer and his wife; and *One Day in the Afternoon of the World* (1964), a bittersweet picture of an aging author.

His many plays are also written in his own characteristic loose style and set forth views like those of his fiction. *My Heart's in the Highlands* (1939) is an amorphous short play illustrating the idea that worldly success means nothing and that only aspiration counts. *The Time of Your Life* (1939), awarded a Pulitzer Prize that Saroyan refused, is a full-length play about people at a San Francisco waterfront bar, whose basic virtue is revealed when a wealthy drunk gives them money to pursue their hopes and dreams. Other plays include *Love's Old Sweet Song* (1941), a farce comedy; *The Beautiful People* (1941), with a theme like that of *The Time of Your Life*, and included with *Sweeney in the Trees* and *Across the Board on Tomorrow Morning* in *Three Plays* (1941); *Razzle-Dazzle* (1942), short plays; *Get Away Old Man* (1944), about a young writer in Hollywood; *Jim Dandy, Fat Man in a Famine* (1947), symbolizing Saroyan's conception of brotherly love; *Don't Go Away Mad* (1949); and *The Cave Dwellers* (1958), a fantasy set in New York.

The Bicycle Rider in Beverly Hills (1952) is an autobiographical work, and he wrote more in this vein and less fiction as he grew older, but his recollections are also very creative. They include *Here Comes, There Goes, You Know Who* (1962); *Not Dying* (1963); *Short Drive, Sweet Chariot* (1966), musings and a conversation while driving across the U.S.; *Days of Life and Death and Escape to the Moon* (1970); *Places Where I've Done Time* (1972); *Sons Come and Go, Mothers Hang In Forever* (1976); *Chance Meetings* (1978); and *Obituaries* (1979), digressive recollections of deceased celebrities with reflections on death and life.

Sartain's Union Magazine, see *Union Magazine.*

SARTON, [ELEANOR] May (1912–   ), born in Belgium, brought to Massachusetts at age four when her father became a professor at Harvard; she, like her parents, became a U.S. citizen. Her first book, *Encounter in April* (1937), collected lyrics; later volumes of poetry include *Inner Landscape* (1939), *The Lion and the Rose* (1948), *The Land of Silence* (1953), *In Time Like Air* (1957), *Cloud, Stone, Sun, Vine* (1961), *A Private Mythology* (1965), *Collected Poems* (1974), *Halfway to Silence* (1980), *Letters from Maine* (1984), and *The Silence Now: New and Uncollected Earlier Poems* (1988), in ideas, expression, and language generally effective even though cast in rather established forms. She has been equally definite in writing fiction, her novels beginning early with *The Single Hound* (1938), about a young English poet solaced by an elderly Belgian woman and by her poetry; *The Bridge of Years* (1946), dealing with Belgian life between the world wars; *Shadow of a Man* (1950); *A Shower of Summer Days* (1952); *Faithful Are the Wounds* (1955), about the life and suicide of a distinguished Harvard professor, dedicated to literature and to social and political movements on the left; *The Birth of a Grandfather* (1957), about an old New England family; *The Small Room* (1961), set at a New England women's college; *Mrs. Stevens Hears the Mermaids Singing* (1965), about the nature of artistic creativity; *Crucial Conversations* (1975), depicting the breakup of a marriage through conversations of related persons; *As We Are Now* (1973), presenting the diary of a retired schoolteacher coping with life in an old people's home; *A Reckoning* (1978), depicting the recollections of a woman dying of cancer; *Anger* (1982), about an unhappy marriage; *The Magnificent Spinster* (1985), concerned essentially with the ideas and ways of women; and her 20th novel, *The Education of Harriet Hatfield* (1989). She has taught at Harvard and Wellesley, has written a play, *The Underground River* (1947), and in *I Knew a Phoenix* (1959) has created what she subtitles "sketches for an autobiography," continued in *A Plant Dreaming Deep* (1968) and *A World of Light* (1976). *Journal of a Solitude* (1973) records reflections during one year, as do *Recovering* (1980) and *At Seventy* (1984), and *After the Stroke* (1988). *Endgame, a Journal of the Seventy-ninth Year* (1992) is "the journal of a woman who now knows she will never get well." *Encore, a Journal of the Eightieth Year* (1993) is another installment of the diary/journal, now spoken into a machine. She declares it "the last journal."

Sartoris, novel by Faulkner, ♦ published in 1929 with editorial cuts. *Flags in the Dust* (1973) is the full text.

Bayard Sartoris comes home to Jefferson, Miss., from combat as an aviator in World War I, in which his twin brother John, also a flyer, has been killed. His grandfather, old Bayard, head of the Sartoris banking interests, and Miss Jenny, old Bayard's aunt, and others, including prewar associates and black tenants, frame young Bayard's attempted reentry into normal life, along with a complex family background of feudal tradition, stubborn pride, and a certain "glamorous fatality" bound up in the family names themselves. The names recall old Bayard's father, John, the founder of the Sartoris house in Mississippi, and his brother, another Bayard, killed in the Civil War, as well as young John, who all exist as active presences and influences, "palpable ghosts." Desolated by his twin's death, and the deaths of his wife Caroline and their infant son, Bayard rides, drives, drinks, and hunts with cold recklessness, alone in the "bleak and barren world" of his despair, deliberately courting death. He marries Narcissa, of the prominent Benbow family,♦ to whom Byron Snopes, a bookkeeper at the bank, has been sending anonymous letters of crazed lust, and whose brother Horace, like Bayard, has returned from the war obsessed with a poetic image of "the meaning of peace." But neither Narcissa's love nor their expected child, nor even his guilt over old Bayard's death from heart failure during a wild auto ride, can alter his despair. He leaves home, wanders in South America and the U.S., and is killed testing a new kind of aircraft he seems to know is unsafe. On the day he dies his son is born and named Benbow Sartoris, Narcissa's gesture away from the Sartoris nomenclature, the "dusk" of names "peopled with ghosts of glamorous and old disastrous things."

Sartoris family, characters in Faulkner's fiction, figuring most importantly in *Sartoris*♦ and *The Unvanquished.*♦ The founder of the Jefferson, Yoknapatawpha County, family, Colonel John, arrives soon after the town's establishment and becomes the commander of its first regiment in the Civil War. First married to Rosa Millard's daughter, by whom he has all his children, he later weds Drusilla Hawk, who rode with his regiment after her fiancé was killed. A man of violence, Colonel John kills two men for trying to permit black people to vote and goads his partner Ben Redmond (or Redlaw) until he is shot by him. His widowed sister Virginia (Aunt Jenny) bears this death with resignation, as she had the death in war of her other brother, Bayard. Colonel John's son Bayard (later called "old Bayard") as a boy worships his father, whose violence he emulates by killing Grumbly, a Southern renegade who had murdered Bayard's grandmother Rosa. Later he cools temperamentally and leaves his father's death unavenged, and in course of time he becomes the old aristocrat trying to withstand change and the coming of the Snopeses. His son John has twins, Bayard (young Bayard) and John, who both join the RAF in World War I, John dying in combat and Bayard returning home, feeling morbidly guilty over his brother's death and the deaths of his wife Caroline and their infant son. Bayard marries Narcissa Benbow, becomes increasingly restless, causes

old Bayard's death of heart failure in a wild auto ride, and, cut off from associations, abandons Narcissa and is killed testing an aircraft he suspects to be a deathtrap. On the day he dies his son is born and named by his mother Benbow Sartoris as if to break the spell of violence associated with Sartoris names. Benbow appears as a ten-year-old in *Sanctuary,* is one of the county's best shots at 17 in *The Mansion,* and is an officer in World War II in *Knight's Gambit.*

SASSACUS, see *Pequot Indians.*

Satanstoe, novel by Cooper,♦ published in 1845 as the first of the Littlepage Manuscripts.♦

Cornelius ("Corny") Littlepage is reared as an 18th-century country gentleman on the family estate Satanstoe, in Westchester County, New York, guided by his grandfather, Captain Hugh Littlepage, and Mr. Worden, an English parson. With his friends, Dirck Follock, descendant of a Dutch family, and Jason Newcome, the shrewd Yankee schoolmaster, he visits New York City, whose aspect and ways are described, with views of the theater and the black festival of "Pinkster." Corny falls in love with Dirck's cousin, Anneke Mordaunt, a belle whose other suitors include Dirck and Major Bulstrode. The fathers of Dirck and Corny send the young men with Jason and Mr. Worden to Albany to survey large grants of land where they plan to settle tenant farmers. The Mordaunts are there for like reasons, and all are befriended by Guert Ten Eyck, a young "buck" of the town, who loves Anneke's companion, Mary Wallace. Bulstrode is also present as the troops prepare for battles in the French and Indian War. Guert and Corny go to Mooseridge, the Littlepage lands, where their work is interrupted by the war. Susquesus, an Onondaga scout, guides them to the troops at Ticonderoga. After the British defeat there, they go to Ravensnest, the Mordaunt estate, where they fight off an Indian attack in which Guert is mortally wounded. At the end Anneke and Corny wed.

Saturday Club, THE, dinner club founded at Boston for informal literary discussion (1855). The organization was foreshadowed by the Symposia of Emerson and Alcott (c.1836–44), but credit for bringing the group together is given to Horatio Woodman, a lawyer and publishing agent. At first there were really two clubs, both nameless. The one was purely social; the other, sometimes later called the Magazine Club or the Atlantic Club, was concerned with promoting a literary journal. After the founding of the *Atlantic Monthly* (1857), this group held banquets for the contributors. By 1857 the Saturday Club was named, and its membership included Emerson, Lowell, Longfellow, Dana, Holmes, Prescott, Whittier, C.E. Norton, Parkman, Howells, Henry James, and other notable figures in New England literature. A history down to 1920 was written by E.W. Emerson and M.A. DeW. Howe (2 vols., 1918, 1927).

Saturday Evening Post, *The* (1821–1969, 1971–), Philadelphia weekly, whose first issue appeared August 18, 1821, although beginning in 1897 the cover page has carried the statement that it was founded by Franklin in 1728. Its only connection with Franklin is that it was originally issued from an office at one time occupied by his *Pennsylvania Gazette,* one of whose later publishers founded the *Post.* Its original purpose was to furnish light Sunday reading for Philadelphians, and its contributors included Cooper, Poe, N.P. Willis, and Harriet Beecher Stowe. Its modern period did not come until it was purchased by Cyrus H.K. Curtis (1897). It was edited by George Horace Lorimer♦ from 1899 to 1936. He increased its circulation from 1800 to 3,000,000 copies weekly by making it a popular magazine for the average American, and publishing stories with mass appeal. He also emphasized advertising, to which about 60 percent of the *c.*125 pages were devoted. A *Treasury* of selections appeared in 1954. Changing managements tinkered with design, editorial policy, and frequency of issue to offset loss of advertising revenue in the 1960s, but in 1969 the *Post* succumbed. It was revived as a quarterly in 1971, and is now published six times a year.

Saturday Press (1858–66), New York weekly miscellany edited by Henry Clapp, drew its literary contributions mainly from such other frequenters of Pfaff's Cellar as Aldrich, Fitz-James O'Brien, Whitman, Ada Clare, and William Winter. The paper suspended publication in 1860, but in 1865 was revived with the announcement: "This paper was stopped in 1860 for want of means. It is now started again for the same reason." One of its last issues (Nov. 18, 1865) contained Clemens's "Celebrated Jumping Frog" and work by Josh Billings.

Saturday Review, *The* (1924–82), journal, until 1952 subtitled "of Literature," emphasized book reviews and literary comment but also dealt with drama, recorded music, motion pictures, photography, travel, education, and science. Editors have been Canby (1924–36), De Voto (1936–38), George Stevens (1938–40), and Norman Cousins (1940–71, 1973–79).

Sauk (or SAC) **Indians,** Algonquian tribe related to the Fox Indians of the Great Lakes region, inhabited the Rock River country of Illinois, and the adjacent region in Wisconsin, Iowa, and Missouri. They were united with the Fox after 1730, aided the British in the War of 1812, and in 1832 participated in the Black Hawk War. They figure in historical studies of these battles, Jonathan Carver's *Travels,* W.J. Snelling's *Tales of the Northwest,* and fiction by August Derleth.

SAUNDERS, RICHARD, pseudonym of Franklin. ♦

SAVAGE, PHILIP HENRY (1868–99), Boston poet, whose *First Poems and Fragments* (1895) and *Poems* (1898), although slight in quantity, have been considered important for their simple and clear lyric quality.

SAVAGE, THOMAS (1608–82), Massachusetts settler who became a founder of Rhode Island because he held the Antinomian views of his mother-in-law, Anne Hutchinson. He later held public and military posts in Massachusetts. His son of the same name (1640–1705) served as a major under Phips, as reported in his *Account of the Late Action . . . Against the French at Canada* (London, 1691).

SAVAGE, THOMAS (1915–), novelist. Born in Utah, Savage grew up in Montana, where some of his most powerful and characteristic works have their setting. *The Power of the Dog* (1967) deals with a complicated Montana ranching family and involves family jealousy, suppressed homosexuality, and a grotesque killing. Among his other novels, two of the most powerful are *I Heard My Sister Speak My Name* (1977), about the sibling problems of a family in Seattle, and *The Corner of Rife and Pacific* (1988), again set on a Montana ranch, which has as the central character a matriarch, "The Sheep Queen," shrewd, loving, super-competent, rich at last but then sustaining a terrible loss. Savage has earned wide and consistent critical acclaim but little popular—or academic—acceptance. Yet these novels are as strong as those of any other American novelist of the 20th century.

Sawyer, TOM, see *Tom Sawyer.*

SAXE, JOHN GODFREY (1816–87), born in Vermont, after graduating from Middlebury College was prominent in the law and politics of his native state, though he considered his other activities less important than his literary career. In addition to editing a weekly paper, the *Burlington Sentinel* (1850–56), he had a local reputation as a wit and after-dinner poet. His contributions to *The Knickerbocker Magazine* and other literary journals widened the scope of his fame in the vein of light verse, less deft and polished than that of his master Holmes, though for a time equally popular. His many volumes of familiar and comic verse include *Progress: A Satirical Poem* (1846), *Humorous and Satirical Poems* (1850), *Clever Stories of Many Nations Rendered in Rhyme* (1865), and *Leisure-Day Rhymes* (1875). After 1860 his home was in New York state, where he consistently spent the social seasons at Saratoga Springs until personal tragedies made him a recluse.

Saybrook Platform, declaration of principles of a synod of Congregationalists, drawn up at Saybrook, Conn., in 1708. It reaffirmed the Savoy Confession of Faith, adopted in England (1691) by Congregationalists and Presbyterians, but differed from the Cambridge Platform (1648) in stressing the establishment of associations, and of consociations or tribunals with final and appellate jurisdiction. It thus turned from the earlier independency of Congregationalism to the centralized administration of Presbyterianism. It continued in force until 1784.

Scarecrow, The, play by Percy MacKaye,♦ published in 1908. It was produced by the Harvard Dramatic Club (1909) and in a professional performance (1910). It is based on Hawthorne's story "Feathertop" in *Mosses from an Old Manse.*

Scarlet Letter, The, romance by Hawthorne,♦ published in 1850. Based on a theme that appears in "Endicott and the Red Cross," this somber romance of conscience and the tragic consequences of concealed guilt is set in Puritan Boston during the mid-17th century. An introductory essay describes the author's experiences as an official of the Salem Custom House and his supposed discovery of a scarlet cloth letter and documents relating the story of Hester.

An aged English scholar sends his young wife, Hester Prynne, to establish their home in Boston. When he arrives two years later, he finds Hester in the pillory with her illegitimate child in her arms. She refuses to name her lover and is sentenced to wear a scarlet A, signifying Adulteress, as a token of her sin. The husband conceals his identity, assumes the name Roger Chillingworth, and in the guise of a doctor seeks to discover her paramour. Hester, a woman of strong independent nature, in her ostracism becomes sympathetic with other unfortunates, and her works of mercy gradually win her the respect of her neighbors. Chillingworth meanwhile discovers that the Rev. Arthur Dimmesdale, a revered, seemingly saintly young minister, is the father of Hester's beautiful, mischievous child, Pearl. Dimmesdale has struggled for years with his burden of hidden guilt, but, though he does secret penance, pride prevents him from confessing publicly, and he continues to be tortured by his conscience. Chillingworth's life is ruined by his preoccupation with his cruel search, and he becomes a morally degraded monomaniac. Hester wishes her lover to flee with her to Europe, but he refuses the plan as a temptation from the Evil One, and makes a public confession on the pillory in which Hester had once been placed. He dies there in her arms, a man broken by his concealed guilt, but Hester lives on, triumphant over her sin because she openly confessed it, to devote herself to ensuring a happy life in Europe for Pearl and helping others in misfortune.

Scarlet Sister Mary, novel by Julia Peterkin,♦ published in 1928, awarded a Pulitzer Prize, and dramatized in 1930.

In a settlement of blacks who speak Gullah♦ on a South Carolina cotton plantation, the orphan "Sister" Mary is reared by her pious, kindly, superstitious aunt, Maum Hannah. Mary, slender and spirited, at 15 marries July Pinesett, a young buck of the settlement, although Maum Hannah wanted her to marry his twin, June, the steadier and more considerate of the two. Their child, Unex ("Unexpected"), is born a few months after their marriage, and July is soon unfaithful. When he deserts Mary, she is desperately unhappy for a long time, until she becomes June's mistress, bearing him a daughter, Seraphine. During the next 15 years, she becomes vigorous and independent. Her nine children have as many different fathers, and, though she is cast out of the church and incurs the active enmity of the other plantation women, she thrives on rivalry and adversity. Her proud self-reliance begins to waver, however, when Unex leaves to seek work in the North, and a younger son, Keepsie, loses a leg in an accident. She nevertheless retains her gaiety and unconcern, and, when July suddenly reappears, she refuses to live with him. She accepts Seraphine's illegitimate daughter as her own, and finally Unex comes home, sick with fever and bringing his motherless child. He soon dies, and this loss of her one "heart-child" breaks Mary's self-confidence. She seeks divine forgiveness in a night of wild prayer, which ends in a vision of her sins as a series of bloody lashes on the body of Jesus, washed white again by her penitence. Admitted into the church, she vows a life of sinless devotion but secretly declines to give up the love charm she has always carried: "'E's all I got now to keep me young."

SCHAEFER, Jack (1907–), born and raised in Cleveland, graduated from Oberlin and did graduate study in English at Columbia before going into journalism. His first novel was *Shane* (1949), a story narrated by Bob Starrett, who was a boy at the time of action when the man Shane wanders into the frontier ranch that in time gets him involved in a great fight of homesteaders against cattlemen. The novel had a huge success in some 70 editions and 31 languages by 1975 and with a very popular film written by A.B. Guthrie. Later fiction included *The Canyon* (1953), a novel about the Cheyenne; *The Big Range* (1953) and *The Kean Land* (1959), stories; *Monte Walsh* (1963), a novel about life on a huge cattle settlement; and *Mavericks* (1967), a short novel.

SCHLESINGER, Arthur [Meier], Jr. (1917–), son of Arthur Meier Schlesinger (1888–1965) and like his father a professor of history at Harvard (1946–61) and at CUNY since 1966. He is the author of *Orestes A. Brownson* (1939) and *The Age of Jackson* (1945, Pulitzer Prize), in which the struggle of Jacksonian Democracy is shown to be not against Hamiltonian conservatism but against the traditional antistatism of the Jeffersonians. His *Age of Roosevelt* includes *The Crisis of the Old Order* (1957), *The Coming of the New Deal* (1959), and *The Politics of Upheaval* (1960). *The Politics of Hope* (1962) contains essays. He served as a special assistant to President Kennedy, about whose administration he wrote *A Thousand Days* (1965, Pulitzer Prize, National Book Award). *The Bitter Heritage* (1967) treats the effects of American involvement in Vietnam, and *The Crisis of Confidence* (1969) gathers essays on the U.S. in the 1960s. *The Imperial Presidency* (1973) traces the growth of presidential power. *Robert F. Kennedy and His Times* (1978, National Book Award) treats another member of the family to which he has maintained close ties. The more recent *The Cycles of American History* (1986) brings previously issued essays together. He expresses concern for the future of the Republic if "politically correct" educational agendas prosper in *The Disuniting of America: Reflections on a Multicultural Society* (1992).

SCHMITT, GLADYS (1909–72), Pennsylvania author, long on the faculty of Carnegie-Mellon University, was the author of 11 novels, including *The Gates of Aulis* (1942), about a German family in America and their concern for the social good; *Alexandra* (1947); *Confessors of the Name* (1952); *The Persistent Image* (1955); and *A Small Fire* (1957). *David the King* (1946) and *Rembrandt* (1961) are historical novels. *Electra* (1964) is a novel based on the Greek theme. *The Godforgotten* (1974) is an allegorical novel about an isolated 11th-century Benedictine community.

SCHOOLCRAFT, HENRY ROWE (1793–1864), ethnologist and geologist, accompanied the expedition of Lewis Cass to northern Michigan and Lake Superior (1820), and wrote *Narrative Journal of Travels through the Northwestern Regions of the United States . . .* (1821). A journey to the sources of the Mississippi (1832) is described in *Narrative of an Expedition through the Upper Mississippi . . .* (1834). As Indian agent at Sault Ste. Marie and Superintendent of Indian Affairs, he made researches into the natural history and ethnology of the North American Indians, upon which he based his voluminous studies, including *Algic Researches* (1839), treating all tribes of his so-called Algic (Allegheny to Atlantic) region; *One-óta, or Characteristics of the Red Race of America* (1844–45); and *Historical and Statistical Information Respecting the History, Condition, and Prospects of the Indian Tribes of the United States* (6 vols., 1851–57). Longfellow depended upon these works in writing *Hiawatha,* as did many other writers on Indian life.

SCHORER, MARK (1908–77), born in Wisconsin, received his A.B. and Ph.D. from the University of Wisconsin, and while still a graduate student published his first novel, *A House Too Old* (1935), set in his native state. His career then continued to include achievements in both scholarship and fiction. He was a professor of English at the University of California, Berkeley (1945–73). His later novels are *The Hermit Place* (1941) and *The Wars of Love* (1954), and his sensitive stories, many first printed in *The New Yorker,* appear in *The State of Mind* (1947). His major scholarly works are *William Blake: The Politics of Vision* (1946) and *Sinclair Lewis: An American Life* (1961), a monumental biography. His essays are collected as *The World We Imagine* (1968). *Pieces of Life* (1977) contains autobiographical sketches and short stories.

SCHULBERG, BUDD [WILSON] (1914–   ), New York-born novelist, reared in Hollywood, which he satirized in *What Makes Sammy Run?* (1941), about a dynamic but vicious opportunist. His other novels are *The Harder They Fall* (1947), about crookedness in prizefighting; *The Disenchanted* (1950), about the last year of an author modeled on F. Scott Fitzgerald, and partly set at Dartmouth, from which Schulberg was graduated in 1936; *Sanctuary V* (1969), about the president of a Latin American nation seeking sanctuary from revolutionaries; and *Everything That Moves* (1980), about a labor union leader's entanglement with gangsters. *Waterfront* (1955) is a fictive version of his film scenario *On the Waterfront. Some Faces in the Crowd* (1950) collects stories as does *Love, Action, Laughter* (1990). He collaborated on a musical version of *What Makes Sammy Run?* (1964) and dramatized *The Disenchanted* (1958). His nonfiction includes *The Four Seasons of Success* (1972), about changing opinions of the achievements of six U.S. novelists of which a revised and updated version appeared as *Writers in America* in 1983, and *Lover and Still Champion: Muhammad Ali* (1972). Schulberg established a writers' workshop for underprivileged blacks in Watts, Calif., and edited their work as *From the Ashes* (1967). *Moving Pictures: Memories of a Hollywood Prince* (1981) is autobiographical.

SCHURZ, CARL (1829–1906), born in Germany, participated in the unsuccessful revolutionary movement (1848–49), and emigrated to the U.S. (1852), where he became prominent in the Republican party and was active in antislavery work. His other services in behalf of Lincoln brought him an appointment as minister to Spain (1861–62), from which he resigned to become a brigadier general. Although his division was accused of cowardice at Gettysburg, a court of inquiry found the charges unwarranted and commended him for his actions. After the war he was Washington correspondent of the New York *Tribune,* and edited a Detroit paper and a German daily published in St. Louis. He left journalism to become a senator from Missouri (1869–75), in which capacity he opposed political corruption and jingoism. Hayes appointed him secretary of the interior (1877–81), in which office he was noted for his iinstallation of a merit promotion system, humanitarian treatment of the Indians, and interest in the conservation of natural resources. With E.L. Godkin and Horace White, he became editor of the New York *Evening Post,*♦ which they made famous for its liberal independence. After differing on editorial policies, he resigned to write for *Harper's Weekly* (1892–98), which he left when he refused to support the policy favoring war with Spain. His later years were devoted to writing and speaking on domestic and foreign matters. In addition to his *Life of Henry Clay* (1887) he left for publication *Reminiscences* (3 vols., 1907–8) and *Speeches, Correspondence, and Political Papers* (6 vols., 1913).

SCHUYLER, GEORGE S. (1895–1977), born in Rhode Island, became a journalist and then an author with *Black No More* (1931), which displayed his conservativism, a point of view more personally set forth in his autobiography, *Black and Conservative* (1966).

SCHUYLER, JAMES [MARCUS] (1923–91) Chicago-born author associated with the New York school of poets, including Ashbery, Kenneth Koch, and Frank O'Hara♦ was on the staff of the Museum of Modern Art. His first poems, *Salute* (1960), part of a series to which the other members of the school also contributed, showed their close relation to painting by being issued with prints that are not intended to be illustrative but are just as important as the texts. Later poems, generally underplayed and quietly observant of particulars, pastoral and urban, appear in *May 24th or So* (1966), *Freely Espousing* (1969), *The Crystal Lithium* (1972), *Hymn to Life* (1974), *The Morning of the Poet* (1980, Pulitzer Prize), *A Few Days* (1985), and *Selected Poems* (1988). He also wrote experimental plays and collected prose and poetry in *The Home Book* (1977). *Alfred and Guinevere* (1958) is a short novel about the summer holiday of a boy and his sister; *A Nest of Ninnies* (1969) is a novel written with Ashbery that comically travesties the lives of suburbanites; and *What's for Dinner?* (1979) is an amusing but serious novel about middle-class suburbanites, some "normal," others institutionalized as mentally troubled.

SCHWARTZ, DELMORE (1913–66), Brooklyn-born poet, critic, and teacher, graduated from New York University (1935), and was an editor of *Partisan Review* (1943–55). His books include *In Dreams Begin Responsibilities* (1938), poems; a translation of Rimbaud's *A Season in Hell* (1939); *Shenandoah* (1941), a verse play; *Genesis* (1943), a tale in prose and poetry about the identity of an American Jew; *Vaudeville for a Princess* (1950), poems; *Summer Knowledge* (1959, Bollingen Prize), collecting the poems in his first volume, selecting some from other early books, and adding new works; and collections of stories, *The World Is a Wedding* (1948) and *Successful Love*

(1961). His *Last and Lost Poems* was published in 1979 and a previously unpublished group of rather light prose sketches appeared as *The Ego Is Always at the Wheel,* issued in 1986. His correspondence with his publisher, *Delmore Schwartz and James Laughlin: Selected Letters,* appeared in 1993. He was the model for Von Humboldt Fleisher in Saul Bellow's *Humboldt's Gift.* ♦

Science and Health with Key to the Scriptures, authorized textbook of Christian Science, ♦ published by Mary Baker Eddy in 1875. In 1886 Mrs. Eddy employed the Rev. James Henry Wiggin, a former Unitarian minister and then an editor of the University Press at Cambridge, Mass., to rewrite large portions of the book. She continued to make slight changes from time to time, and at the time of her death more than 400,000 copies had been sold.

Science fiction, stories of fantasy dealing with the unknown in scientifically conceivable terms of reference. They use imaginary inventions and discoveries; settings that include the earth's interior, other planets, and the atom; and time in the remote future, the prehistoric past, and a new dimension. They sometimes resemble Utopian fiction, but their direct ancestors include Mary Shelley's *Frankenstein* and works by Poe, Verne, Fitz-James O'Brien, and H.G. Wells. Although Utopias and satires occasionally use some of the materials or techniques of science fiction and although Mark Twain's *A Connecticut Yankee in King Arthur's Court* used a favorite theme of traveling through time, the emphasis is not on pseudo-science and the creation of a sense of wonder. The vogue for science fiction became particularly evident around the turn into the 20th century, perhaps because people felt they were moving into a new era and because they were much impressed by the many recent inventions. The genre was given further impetus by the founding of *Amazing Stories* (1926) by Hugo Gernsback (1884–1967), an émigré from Luxembourg, who is commemorated by annual (since 1953) Hugo awards, and by the founding (1937) of another magazine, *Astounding,* by John W. Campbell, the "discoverer" of Asimov and Heinlein. The awe-inspiring scientific inventions of World War II and the subsequent era of manned travel into outer space made science fiction both more interesting and more acceptable to many readers. Postwar science fiction placed more emphasis on accuracy and less on weird adventures and also became more concerned with socio-political ideas; it also moved out of magazine publication to the greater solidity of books, both paperback and hardbound. Prominent science fiction writers of this century include Isaac Asimov, Ray Bradbury, Edgar Rice Burroughs, August Derleth, R.A. Heinlein, Frank Herbert, Stephen King, Ursula Le Guin, H.P. Lovecraft, Theodore Sturgeon, and A.E. van Vogt.

SCOLLARD, CLINTON (1860–1932), professor of English at Hamilton College (1888–96, 1911–12), whose long poetic career was marked by several different trends, including versions of precise classical French forms, songs of the open road, mystical pantheistic poems, lyrical romantic treatments of foreign lands in which he traveled, and poems inspired by World War I. A selection of his poems was published as *The Singing Heart* (1934). He also collaborated with his wife Jessie B. Rittenhouse (1869–1948), and his friend Frank D. Sherman, as well as writing essays, travel sketches, and prose romances.

Scopes trial, see *Fundamentalism.*

SCOTT, EVELYN (1893–1963), born in Tennessee, reared in New Orleans, and at the age of 20, in revolt against contemporary U.S. standards, became an expatriate in Brazil, which she describes in her autobiographical narrative *Escapade* (1923). Returning to the U.S., she published her first work, *Precipitations* (1920), a book of poetry; and a play, *Love* (1920). Her first two novels, *The Narrow House* (1921) and *Narcissus* (1922), attack middle-class morality and aims. Other fiction of this period include *The Golden Door* (1925), a novel; *Migrations: An Arabesque in Histories* (1927); and *Ideals* (1927), a collection of lighter short stories. *The Wave* (1929), her first popular novel, deals with the Civil War. After another volume of poetry, *The Winter Alone* (1930), and *Blue Rum* (1930), an adventure story set in Portugal and published under the pseudonym E. Souza, she returned to serious fiction in *A Calendar of Sin* (1931), chronicling the life of five generations of one family; *Eva Gay* (1933), studies of a woman and her lovers; *Breathe Upon These Slain* (1934), reconstructing the lives of people whom the narrator knows only through their photographs and the furniture that she finds in her rented house; *Bread and a Sword* (1937), the story of the struggles of an author for life in the modern economic order; and *The Shadow of the Hawk* (1941), about a boy who grows up knowing his father had been executed for a murder he did not commit. *Background in Tennessee* (1937) is an autobiographical account of the author's youth.

SCOTT, JOB (1751–93), Quaker preacher, traveled throughout the U.S., England, and Ireland, and was noted as a mystic. After his death, the orthodox church disavowed him, but the liberal group under Elias Hicks considered him a prophet and published his *Works* (1831).

SCOTT, WINFIELD TOWNLEY (1910–68), born in Massachusetts, after graduation from Brown University (1931) was on the staff of *The Providence Journal* (1931–51), meanwhile making a reputation for poetry that often deals with people and values of his native New England region, published in *Elegy for Robinson* (1936), *Wind the*

Clock (1941), *Mr. Whittier* (1948), and *Collected Poems* (1962), among other volumes. His literary notebooks were posthumously gathered as "*A Dirty Hand*" (1969).

Scottsboro case, *cause célèbre* concerning nine black men charged with the rape of two white girls on a freight train in Alabama. The first trial in Scottsboro, Ala. (1931), resulted in death sentences for eight of the men, and after liberals and radicals came to their aid, charging that the verdict was the result of racial prejudice, the decision was appealed to the U.S. Supreme Court, which declared (1932) that the defendants' right to counsel had been infringed. Despite the recantation of one of the girls, one of the men was again sentenced to death, and the case once more came before the Supreme Court, which in 1935 decided that there must be a retrial, since the constitutional rights of the defendants had been violated by the illegal exclusion of blacks from jury service. Four of the defendants were subsequently convicted, receiving sentences equivalent to life imprisonment, and the court, although refusing a retrial for them, dropped the rape charges against the five other defendants. The case has frequently figured in literature, and has been the subject of the plays *Scottsboro Limited* (1932), by Langston Hughes, and *They Shall Not Die* (1934), by John Wexley.

Scout, The; or, The Black Riders of the Congaree, romance by Simms,♦ published as *The Kinsmen* (1841) and reissued under the present title (1854). It is one of his Revolutionary Romances.

Scribner's Magazine (1887–1939), literary monthly, founded by the younger Charles Scribner (1854–1930), after his father sold *Scribner's Monthly*. It immediately won distinction as a dignified literary journal for educated readers. Contributors included Stevenson, Henry and William James, Harte, Kipling, Cable, Edith Wharton, Meredith, Stephen Crane, and Huneker, and among the illustrators were Stanford White, Howard Pyle, A.B. Frost, and Frederic Remington. Through the years the magazine maintained its high standards, ever open to new authors, and was the first important magazine to publish the fiction of Hemingway and Wolfe. During its later period, one of its regular departments was Phelps's book reviews, "As I Like It." Loss of circulation resulted in its purchase by a new editor (1936), who attempted to popularize it by meeting a lower level of public taste. When this failed, the magazine suspended publication (1939). It was purchased the same year by *The Commentator,* renamed *Scribner's Commentator,* and reissued with a propagandistic and political policy.

Scribner's Monthly (1870–81), literary journal founded by the elder Charles Scribner (1821–71), with J.G. Holland as editor. It was notable for its many departments; for its serials, including the editor's *Sevenoaks,* Hale's *Philip Nolan's Friends,* Stockton's *Rudder Grange,* Harte's *Gabriel Conroy,* Eggleston's *Roxy,* and Cable's *The Grandissimes;* for its short stories by such authors as Julian Hawthorne, Constance F. Woolson, and Helen Hunt Jackson; for its essays by C.D. Warner, Burroughs, Muir, Stedman, and W.C. Brownell; and for its poems by R.H. Stoddard, Emma Lazarus, Hayne, Lanier, Irwin Russell, and Joaquin Miller. The magazine was also distinguished for its engravings and typography. Its policies were continued after 1881 in *The Century Illustrated Monthly Magazine.* ◆

SCUDDER, HORACE ELISHA (1838–1902), Boston editor and author, was associated with the publishing firm that became Houghton, Mifflin (1864–1902), and served as editor of the *Atlantic Monthly* (1890–98). In addition to novels and books for children, he wrote biographies of Noah Webster (1882), Bayard Taylor (1884), and Lowell (1901).

Sea Lions, *The,* novel by Cooper. ◆

Sea of Cortez, *The,* travel account and philosophic narrative by Steinbeck ◆ and E.F. Ricketts.

Sea-Wolf, *The,* novel by Jack London, ◆ published in 1904.

Humphrey Van Weyden, a dilettante literary critic, is picked up by the sealing schooner *Ghost,* when the ferry boat on which he is traveling across San Francisco Bay collides with a tramp steamer. The captain of the *Ghost,* Wolf Larsen, is a man of tremendous physical power who is utterly ruthless. When the *Ghost,* on the sealing grounds off Japan, saves some refugees from an ocean disaster, a struggle commences between the hyper-civilized, moral Van Weyden and the primitive, individualistic Larsen over the poet Maude Brewster. Miss Brewster and Van Weyden escape to a deserted island to which the *Ghost,* dismasted and near sinking, is later driven. Larsen, deserted by his crew, is aboard, but, blinded by cerebral cancer, is doomed to slow paralysis. Van Weyden and Miss Brewster manage to rehabilitate the vessel and sail back to civilization, but Larsen dies, indomitably pagan.

SEABURY, SAMUEL (1729–96), born in Connecticut, graduated from Yale (1748) and the University of Edinburgh (1753), completed his medical study there, and became an Anglican minister in his native colony. Prior to the outbreak of the Revolution, he became an author of Loyalist pamphlets. Under the pseudonym "A Westchester Farmer," he published *Free Thoughts on the Proceedings of the Continental Congress* (Nov. 16, 1774), which attempted to arouse the opposition of the agricultural class to the proposals of the Congress. Twelve days later he issued *The Congress Canvassed,* further attacking Congress

and pleading for allegiance to the king. Answered by Hamilton in *A Full Vindication of the Measures of Congress,* Seabury published *A View of the Controversy Between Great Britain and Her Colonies* (Dec. 24, 1774), in which he proposed colonial home-rule under the authority of Parliament, preferring modification to independence. To this Hamilton replied with *The Farmer Refuted.* Seabury continued to press his view in *An Alarm to the Legislature of the Province of New York* (Jan. 17, 1775). The keen style of Seabury's pamphlets made them powerful weapons against the Revolutionary cause. He was seized by a mob (1775), imprisoned, and upon release so persecuted that at length he entered the British lines. After serving as a chaplain with the British troops, he was made a bishop, and in 1789 became presiding bishop of the Episcopal Church in the U.S., holding this office until his death. His *Discourses on Several Subjects* was published (3 vols., 1791–98).

SEALSFIELD, CHARLES, alias of Karl Postl (1793–1864), Moravian-born monk, who escaped from his monastery to become an author in Switzerland. During his various journeys to the U.S. (1824–25), 1826, 1827–32, 1837, 1850, 1853–58), he was upon occasion a merchant and a journalist. He was most famous for his depictions of frontier life in the Southwest and for his humanitarian championing of the Indians. Among his translated works are *The Americans as They Are* (1828), *The United States as They Are* (1828), *Tokeah; or, The White Rose* (1828), *The Cabin Book; or, Sketches of Life in Texas* (1844), and *Frontier Life* (1856).

SEAMAN, ELIZABETH COCHRANE (1867–1922), journalist under the pseudonym Nelly Bly, adopted from a song by Stephen Foster, specialized in sensational exposures of abuses in domestic employment, divorce, politics, and prison conditions. While working for the New York *World,* she had herself committed to Blackwell's Island by feigning insanity, and recorded the horrible conditions there in *Ten Days in a Mad House* (1887). Sponsored by the *World,* she made a tour of the world in 72 days, 6 hours, and 11 minutes (1889), which brought her international notice and furnished material for *Nelly Bly's Book: Around the World in Seventy-Two Days* (1890).

Seaside and the Fireside, *The,* poems by Longfellow, ◆ published in 1849. Among them are "The Building of the Ship," ◆ "The Builders," "King Witlaf's Drinking-Horn," and "Pegasus in Pound."

SEATTLE, CHIEF (1786–1866), chief of the Suquamish and Dewamish tribes of the Pacific Northwest. He converted to Christianity in the 1830s. He signed the Treaty of Port Elliott in 1855, guaranteeing his people a reservation in what became the state of Washington. A text of his speech at the signing, generally agreed to be corrupt with white journalistic emendations for effect, survives. It is in any case a haunting elegy. By then, Chief Seattle believed that he had embraced the wrong god: "Our people are ebbing away like a . . . tide that will never return. The white man's God can not love our people or He would protect them."

SECCOMB, JOHN (1708–92), while a student at Harvard wrote "Father Abbey's Will" (1731), a humorous verse on the college janitor, which was extremely popular in New England, and was reprinted in London (1732). Its sequel, "A Letter of Courtship," is supposedly addressed to Father Abbey's widow by the janitor of Yale. Seccomb was later a Congregational clergyman in his native Massachusetts, and, as an orthodox Calvinist, was prominent in the Great Awakening.

Secession, see *Confederacy* and *Civil War*.

Secession (1922–24), little magazine edited by Gorham B. Munson, Kenneth Burke, and Matthew Josephson. It was issued from various European cities and New York.

Second Adventists, see *Millerites*.

Secret Life of Walter Mitty, The, short story by James Thurber,♦ published in *The New Yorker* (1939) and collected in *My World—and Welcome to It* (1942).

Henpecked Walter Mitty daydreams as he drives his wife downtown, attends to errands she requires, and waits while she has her hair done, envisioning himself as the beloved commander who gets his men through the worst storm in 20 years of navy flying; as the brilliant surgeon who saves the life of a millionaire banker; as the world's greatest pistol shot testifying in a murder case and refusing to be bullied by a nasty district attorney; as the British bombardier preparing to attack a German ammunition dump on a dangerous solo flight; and then, as his wife momentarily leaves him waiting outside a drugstore, he snaps away his cigarette, disdains a blindfold, and faces "the firing squad; erect and motionless, proud and disdainful, Walter Mitty the Undefeated, inscrutable to the last."

Secret Service, play by William Gillette.♦

SEDGWICK, ANNE DOUGLAS (1873–1935), born in New Jersey, taken to England at the age of nine, lived the rest of her life abroad, where in 1908 she married the English author Basil de Sélincourt. Her novels, which follow in the school of Henry James, are concerned with problems of social relationship and the contrasts of American with English and continental standards. The more important of her early novels include *The Rescue* (1902) and *A Fountain Sealed* (1907), both dealing with the hatred between a mother and

daughter, the former set in Paris and the latter in Boston. *Amabel Channice* (1908) is the story of a woman who idolizes her husband, Sir Hugh Channice, because he has forgiven her infidelity and reared her illegitimate child as his own, until her illusions are destroyed by the revelation of his real character by his mistress. *Franklin Winslow Kane* (1910) contrasts an American and an English couple. *Tante*♦ (1911) is a psychological study of a genius. *The Encounter* (1914), another study of genius, concerns an aging German philosopher and his jealous insistence upon adoration. *The Third Window* (1920) deals with the attempt of a woman to prevent by supernatural means the remarriage of the widow of the man whom she had idolized. *Adrienne Toner*♦ (1922) is a character study of an American girl and her power over the English among whom she lives. *The Little French Girl*♦ (1924) presents a contrast of French and English standards of life. *The Old Countess* (1927), a tragic story again contrasting French and English characters, was followed by *Dark Hester* (1929), dealing with hatred between a mother-in-law and daughter-in-law and their love for the same man. *Philippa* (1930) is the story of a selfish man whose wife sacrifices her life to him and their equally selfish daughter. Her collections of short stories were published as *The Nest* (1913) and *Christmas Roses* (1920), the latter published in England as *Autumn Crocuses* (1920). Her letters were edited by her husband (1936).

SEDGWICK, CATHARINE MARIA (1789–1867), Massachusetts author of fiction depicting the simple domestic virtues of the American home, which she considered the safeguard of the Republic. *A New-England Tale* (1822) and *Redwood* (1824) are conventional romantic novels, illustrating their author's moral belief, and valuable for their realistic depiction of social customs in early 19th-century New England. *Hope Leslie; or, Early Times in the Massachusetts* (1827) tells of the romantic adventures which befall colonial settlers, through Indian captivities and massacres. *Clarence; or, A Tale of Our Own Times* (1830), set in and around New York City, contrasts the lives of a sensible and an adventurous girl, and *The Linwoods; or, "Sixty Years Since" in America* (1835) presents the social life of New York City during the last two years of the Revolution. *Married or Single?* (1857), her last novel, was again a story of society and a contrast of different types of women, with the ostensible purpose of showing the valuable activities in which an unmarried woman might engage. She also wrote many moral tracts, sometimes in the form of fiction, for children as well as adults. Besides contributing widely to periodicals, she was active in the Unitarian Church and as a feminist, although remaining apart from radical reform movements.

SEDGWICK, SUSAN [RIDLEY] (1789?–1867), sister-in-law of C.M. Sedgwick, was the author of *The Young Emigrants* (1836), a juvenile tale about a New York family's emigration to Ohio in the late 18th century. This was distinguished as an early example of nonreligious fiction for children. Her other books include *Allen Prescott; or, The Fortunes of a New England Boy* (1834) and *Alida; or, Town and Country* (1844).

SEEGER, ALAN (1888–1916), New York-born poet, graduated from Harvard (1910), went to Paris (1913), and at the beginning of World War I enlisted in the French Foreign Legion. He was killed at Belloy-en-Santerre, in the Battle of the Somme. "I Have a Rendezvous with Death" (*North American Review*, Oct. 1916) is the most famous of his war poems, which were collected in *Poems* (1916). His *Letters and Diary* was published in 1917.

SELBY, HUBERT (1928–), Brooklyn-born novelist whose fiction, set in his native area, is *Last Exit to Brooklyn* (1964), a vivid view of corruption and violence in contemporary urban life; *The Room* (1971), depicting the sadistic and sexual fantasies of a jailed prisoner; *The Demon* (1976), presenting a young businessman's "dark consciousness" and sexual impulses; and *Requiem for a Dream* (1978), about heroin addicts and others frustrated in their dreams. *Song of the Silent Snow* (1986) collects short stories.

SELDES, GILBERT [VIVIAN] (1893–1970), graduated from Harvard (1914), was a war correspondent in Europe, and returned to become a journalist, drama critic, and editor of *The Dial* (1920–23). His books include *The United States and the War* (1917); *The Seven Lively Arts* (1924), a critical examination of such arts as the comic strip, motion pictures, vaudeville, and popular songs; *The Stammering Century* (1928), an informal survey of 19th-century America; *The Wings of the Eagle* (1929), a novel; *The Movies and the Talkies* (1929); *Lysistrata* (1930), an adaptation of Aristophanes' comedy; *The Future of Drinking* (1930), a study of the effects of the 18th Amendment on drinking manners; *Against Revolution* (1932); *The Years of the Locust* (1932), a survey of the U.S. during the Depression; *Mainland* (1936), an analysis of contemporary America; *The Movies Come from America* (1937); and *The Great Audience* (1950), on movie, radio, and television publics. He also wrote detective stories under the name Foster Johns.

Self, social comedy by Sidney Bateman,♦ produced and published in 1856. It satirizes New York society in the vein of Anna Mowatt's *Fashion,* which obviously inspired it, and is concerned with the financial difficulties of the fashionable Apex family and its salvation by the commonsense banker John Unit.

Self-Reliance, essay by Emerson,♦ published in *Essays, First Series* (1841).

"Trust thyself," a central doctrine in the author's ethical thought, is the theme developed here. "Envy is ignorance . . . imitation is suicide"; a man "must take himself for better, for worse, as his portion." "Society everywhere is in conspiracy against the manhood of every one of its members. . . . Whoso would be a man must be a nonconformist." The two terrors that discourage originality and creative living are fear of public opinion and undue reverence for one's own consistency. The great figures of history have not cared for the opinions of their contemporaries; "to be great is to be misunderstood"; and if a man honestly expresses his nature he will be largely consistent. Deference to authority, to institutions, or to tradition is disobedience to the inner law that each of us must follow in order to do justice to himself and to society. We must speak the truth, and truth, revealed intuitively, cannot be achieved except through the development and expression of one's individual nature. "Nothing is at last sacred but the integrity of your own mind."

Sellers, COLONEL BERIAH, character in *The Gilded Age.*♦ In the dramatization he was called Colonel Mulberry Sellers, and under the latter name reappears in *The American Claimant.*♦

SELLERS, ISAIAH, see *Mark Twain.*

Selling of Joseph, The, antislavery tract by Samuel Sewall,♦ published in 1700 in the form of a lawyer's brief fortified by Scriptural text. In this pamphlet occurs the sentence often cited by later Abolitionists: "There is no proportion between twenty pieces of silver and liberty."

Seminole Indians, Florida tribe composed mainly of refugees from the Creeks,♦ with a large element of black ex-slaves. Still under Spanish rule, they were hostile to the U.S. in the War of 1812. In the first Seminole War (1817–18) they were subdued by Andrew Jackson, after which Spain ceded Florida to the U.S. The attempt to remove the tribe beyond the Mississippi provoked a second Seminole War (1835–42), which, at a cost of 1500 American lives and $20,000,000, resulted in the removal of most of the Seminoles and the death of their leader Osceola. The present Seminoles live in Oklahoma and southern Florida. Kirk Munroe's *The Flamingo Feather* (1887) is a romance about the tribe in the 16th century.

SENDAK, MAURICE [BERNARD] (1928–), Brooklyn-born illustrator and author, known for his playfully grotesque stories and drawings for children. His fantasies, comic but touched with eerie imagination, feature impish menacing creatures of strange scale, some dwarf-like, some depicting babies or small animals of gigantic size. His prolific publications include *The Sign on*

Rosie's Door (1960), which led to a television show and a musical play; *Where the Wild Things Ar* (1963, Caldecott Medal), *In the Night Kitchen* (1970), and *OUtside Over There* (1981), a trilogy; *Zlateh the Goat* (1966); *Higglety Pigglety Pop, or There Must Be More to Life* (1967); *Caldecott & Co., Notes on Books and Pictures* (1988); and *We Are All in the Dumps with Jack and Guy* (1993), about the homeless. He was the illustrator for *Dear Mili* (1988), a newly discovered Wilhelm Grimm tale.

Seneca Indians, tribe of the Iroquois Confederacy.♦ They were allied with Pontiac, aided the British during the Revolution, and largely supported the American side in the War of 1812. They now live mainly on several reservations in New York state. They are celebrated in poems by William H.C. Hosmer,♦ and Edmund Wilson's *Apologies to the Iroquois* (1960) tells of the modern status of the tribes in the Confederacy.

Sense of Beauty, *The,* study of aesthetics by Santayana,♦ published in 1896 and based on lectures delivered at Harvard (1892–95). Intending to "put together the scattered commonplaces of criticism into a system, under the inspiration of a naturalistic psychology," the author organizes his discussion in four parts; "The Nature of Beauty"; "The Materials of Beauty"; "Form"; and "Expression." He argues that "as truth is . . . the co-operation of perceptions, so beauty is the co-operation of pleasures. . . . [Beauty] is pleasure objectified." He further asserts that pleasures are primarily rooted in sensation, and that the materials with which the aesthetic function is associated are based on sensuous and ideal experiences of pleasure, when these are given expression through form. "Beauty," he concludes, "seems to be the clearest manifestation of perfection, and the best evidence of its possibility. . . . Beauty is a pledge of the possible conformity between the soul and nature, and consequently a ground of faith in the supremacy of the good."

Separatist Society of Zoar, see *Zoar.*

Separatists, name applied to those who split from the Established Church of England in the 17th century, organizing independent congregations. They had much in common with the Puritan party within the State Church, but went beyond them in desiring not merely a purification in ceremonial but also complete independence. Frequently they had no stated ministry, emphasizing only the bare letter of Scripture, believing in voluntary church membership, and a relatively democratic organization within the local church. The Pilgrims♦ were Separatists, but most of the other New England settlers, such as those of the Massachusetts Bay Colony, were Puritans. In America the two groups tended to merge, but

extreme Separatists, such as Roger Williams and Anne Hutchinson, were persecuted. Certain ministers, such as Thomas Hooker and John Wise, opposed the dominant oligarchy of New England ministers on essentially Separatist principles.

Septimius Felton; *or, The Elixir of Life,* unfinished romance by Hawthorne,♦ posthumously published in 1872.

During the Revolutionary War, Septimius Felton, a scholar who seeks a method of attaining earthly immortality, kills a British officer who has insulted his fiancée, Rose Garfield. On the hill top where he has buried the officer, he meets Sybil Dacy, a strange, unearthly creature, who is looking for a flower she expects to grow from the grave, and they become close friends. Before he died, the officer gave Septimius an old manuscript, containing the formula for an elixir of life, requiring the juice of the flower Sybil seeks. A Dr. Portsoaken, her uncle, visits Septimius and reveals that the scholar may be the heir to a British estate. Robert Hagburn, an American soldier and friend of Septimius, becomes engaged to Rose, after it is discovered that she is the scholar's half-sister. At the wedding of Robert and Rose, Sybil discloses to Septimius, who is about to drink the potion he has finally concocted, that the officer he killed was her lover, and that she has intended to seek revenge, but now loves Septimius. She drinks part of the potion, throws away the rest, and dies. Septimius disappears, and is believed to have gone to claim his English estate.

SEQUOYAH (*c.*1770–1843), half-breed Cherokee, also known as George Guess, who created a syllabary for his people's language by formulating a set of 85 characters. This principle has since been used for other Indian languages. He printed parts of the Bible and a newspaper, *The Cherokee Phoenix* (1828*ff.*), in his adaptation of ordinary type and numerals.

Servant to Servants, *A,* blank-verse dramatic monologue by Robert Frost,♦ published in *North of Boston* (1914).

A lonely, overworked New England farm wife talks with a visiting naturalist, and through her eager conversation reveals the tragic story of her life. Reared in a loveless family, in which her mother's life had been embittered by the necessity of caring for an obscenely mad brother-in-law, she herself had been influenced for a time by the inherited strain of insanity, and welcomed the opportunity to marry Len, the unfeeling husband who neglects her for his many business enterprises. Though she craves personal freedom, love, and the touch of beauty, she is burdened by innumerable menial tasks, including the feeding of the brutal farmhands, whose "servant" she has become.

SETON, ANYA (1916–90), daughter of Ernest Thompson Seton; her popular fiction includes the historical romances *My Theodosia* (1941), about Aaron Burr's daughter; *Katherine* (1954), about John of Gaunt's wife; and *The Winthrop Woman* (1958), set in Massachusetts Bay Colony. *Dragonwyck* (1944) and *The Turquoise* (1946) are romantic novels set in 19th-century America. Later novels are *Devil Water* (1962), set in England and Virginia of the 18th century; *Avalon* (1965), which deals with King Arthur's era and his descendants; *Green Darkness* (1973), on occult situations; and *Smouldering Fires* (1975).

SETON, ERNEST [EVAN] THOMPSON (1860–1946), English-born author, artist, and naturalist, was reared in Canada, where he won a reputation for his books on wildlife. These include *Wild Animals I Have Known* (1898), *The Biography of a Grizzly* (1900), *Lives of the Hunted* (1901), and *Biography of an Arctic Fox* (1937). *Trail of an Artist-Naturalist* (1940) is his autobiography. His name was originally Ernest Seton Thompson.

Seven Arts, The (Nov. 1916–Oct. 1917), monthly little magazine intended to foster native talents and points of view and encourage freer expression than could be countenanced in the more conservative quality magazines. Its editors included James Oppenheim, Waldo Frank, and Van Wyck Brooks, and among its contributors were Anderson, Amy Lowell, Frost, John Reed, Dos Passos, R.S. Bourne, Vachel Lindsay, Dreiser, Spingarn, W.H. Wright, and Mencken. The magazine's pacifism caused its subsidy to be withdrawn, and its financial failure.

Seven Cities of Cibola, see *Zuñi Indians.*

Sevenoaks, novel by J.G. Holland, ♦ published in 1875.

Seventh-Day Adventists, see *Millerites.*

Seventh-Day Baptists, see *Dunkers.*

Seventh of March Speech, name generally given to the speech by Daniel Webster, ♦ "For the Union and Constitution," delivered in the Senate, March 7, 1850. This reply to Calhoun's "Fourth of March Speech"—which had attacked Clay's Compromise bill—championed the cause of the Union and advocated that Abolitionists yield some of their principles to maintain the Union in harmony. Whittier's "Ichabod" ♦ is a typical expression of the reaction of the Abolitionists, who considered that Webster had betrayed them and was now a "lost leader."

SEWALL, JONATHAN MITCHELL (1748–1808), Massachusetts lawyer and ardent Federalist, was a grand-nephew of Samuel Sewall. His occasional

poetry reflects his patriotism and political beliefs, and includes a *Versification of President Washington's Excellent Farewell-Address* (1798) and a *Eulogy on the Late General Washington* (1800). He published his *Miscellaneous Poems* in 1801.

SEWALL, SAMUEL (1652–1730), born in England of a family that had previously resided in the colonies, was brought at the age of nine to Boston, with which his later life is identified. After graduation from Harvard (1671), he was for a long time a tutor at the college, but in 1679 began his long political career, including such early offices as manager of the colony's printing press, deputy to the general court, and member of the Council (1684–86). While in England on business (1688–89), he aided Increase Mather in appealing to William III to recover the abrogated Massachusetts charter. Upon his return he resumed his position on the Council, and was a councilor of the new charter (1691–1725).

In 1692 he was appointed by Governor Phips as a special commissioner in the Salem witchcraft trials, in which he later regretted having participated, and in 1697, on a fast day set aside for repentance concerning errors in the trials, he was the only judge publicly to recant by standing in the Old South Church while the clergyman read his confession of error and guilt. After holding several judicial posts, he became chief justice of the superior court of judicature (1718–28), and despite his lack of legal training was considered a good and rather liberal jurist.

His various pamphlets give evidence of the many different matters in which he was interested. *The Revolution in New England Justified* (1691), written with Edward Rawson, is a loquacious but logical justification of the New Englanders who deposed Andros and resumed charter government in 1689. *Phænomena quædam apocalyptica . . .*♦ (1697) is a prediction that New England will be the eventual seat of the New Jerusalem. *The Selling of Joseph*♦ (1700) is an early antislavery appeal, and other works include *Proposals Touching the Accomplishment of Prophecies* (1713) and *A Memorial Relating to the Kennebeck Indians* (1721), an early argument for humane treatment of the Indians. "Talitha Cumi" ♦ is an essay, not published until 1873, which argues against those who deny the resurrection of women.

Both as man and as author, Sewall is now best remembered for the *Diary,* which was published by the Massachusetts Historical Society (3 vols., 1878–82), and which covers the period from 1674 to 1729, with a gap between 1677 and 1685, in an intimate and minute manner. Because he not only relates in detail the homely activities of Boston but also gives an honest revelation of his own character, he has been compared with his British contemporary, Samuel Pepys. He reveals, evidently unconsciously, the twilight of the Puritan tradition and the rise of the New England

Yankee period, which transition he himself represented in his religious orthodoxy, tempered by an emphasis upon mercantilism in his capacity as a merchant. His practical Yankee bent made him less concerned with abstract ideas and more with daily happenings. The abstract thought in Cotton Mather's *Diary* thus receives a complementary balance for the student of the period in the journal of Sewall, which recounts such incidents as his unsuccessful wooing of Madam Winthrop with gifts of gingerbread, sermons, and a shilling and a half worth of sugar almonds, and their disputes over the marriage settlement and whether he should wear a wig and keep a coach. *The Letters of Samuel Lee and Samuel Sewall Relating to New England and the Indians* were published in the Colonial Society of Massachusetts Collections (XIV, 1913). Whittier describes Sewall in "The Prophecy of Samuel Sewall."

Sewanee Review (1892–   ), literary quarterly published by the University of the South, Sewanee, Tenn.; founded by William Peterfield Trent (1862–1932) while he was a professor of English there (1888–1900). It is now the oldest critical and literary quarterly in the U.S. and, though academic in outlook, is not a university organ. Its contributors are mainly Southerners, and it devotes much attention to the reinterpretation of the role of the South in U.S. culture. Beginning with Allen Tate's editorship (1944–46) it has laid more emphasis on modern literature. Andrew Lytle was the editor (1961–73).

SEXTON, ANNE (1928–74), poet who lived in her native Massachusetts and traced her ancestry to *Mayflower* Pilgrims, but whose writing is concerned not with heritage or religion but very frankly with her firsthand experience. Her first book, *To Bedlam and Part Way Back* (1960), was the outcome of a nervous breakdown. The poems in *All My Pretty Ones* (1962) are equally revealing. The same characteristics are evident also in the lyrics of *Live or Die* (1966, Pulitzer Prize) and *Love Poems* (1969). Her dark, bitter views of life are evident in *Transformations* (1971), retellings of the Grimms' fairy tales; *The Book of Folly* (1972), poems and prose parables; and *The Death Notebooks* (1974), which were followed by the poems in *The Awful Rowing Toward God* (1975), published after her suicide. *45 Mercy Street* (1976), *Words for Dr. Y* (1978), and *The Complete Poems* (1981) are posthumous collections of poems. A *Self-Portrait in Letters* appeared in 1977. In 1985 was published *No Evil Star,* a collection of essays, interviews, and other prose.

SHAARA, MICHAEL [JOSEPH, JR.] (1929–88), New Jersey-born author, after graduation from Rutgers and service as a paratrooper was a professor of English at Florida State University (1961–73). His novels are *The Broken Place* (1968), about a soldier who is a boxer, and *The*

Killer Angels (1974, Pulitzer Prize), which presents the Battle of Gettysburg as seen by both Northern and Southern officers.

Shadows on the Rock, novel by Willa Cather,◆ published in 1931.

Life in early 17th-century Quebec is depicted on this "rock" in the St. Lawrence, between visits by ships from France. Against a background of such figures as the Intendant, Frontenac, the rival bishops—generous, self-sacrificing old Bishop Laval and extravagant, haughty young Monseigneur de Saint-Vallier—and Mother Juschereau and her nuns are placed the stories of humble citizens. Euclide Auclair, "the philosopher apothecary," has followed Frontenac from France, and after his wife's death lives with his daughter Cécile, cherishing memories of Europe. Cécile and her father befriend Jacques, son of a sailor and a woman of the town, 'Toinette Gaux. Among their friends are Bishop Laval; Noël Pommier, the cobbler; Father Hector Saint Cyr, the missionary; Antoine Frichette, the trapper; and Pierre Charron, *coureur de bois* and fur trader, a romantic figure driven to his lonely occupation by a love affair with a girl who chose to become a religious recluse. The apothecary is despondent at the death of Frontenac, and when Charron comes to cheer his friend, he discovers that he loves Cécile. They marry, and Jacques becomes a sailor, while Auclair, no longer caring to return to France, spends his last years on "the rock."

SHAHN, BEN (1898–1969), Russian-born artist, brought to the U.S. in 1906, and reared in Brooklyn, whose life and settings he sometimes recalled in paintings. His works, showing his sense that art should be "first, and above all things, a product of the spirit," often treat public issues with a keen sense of social justice, as in his 23 gouache paintings of the Sacco-Vanzetti case and 15 of the Tom Mooney case. His forceful drawing, clear color contrasts, and monumental simplicity of structure are dominant in his easel paintings too. He also illustrated books, often using a straightforward calligraphy; like folk lettering. His Norton lectures at Harvard appeared as *The Shape of Content* (1957), and he also wrote *Love and Joy About Letters* (1963). Selden Rodman wrote an unusual biography, *Portrait of the Artist as an American* (1951).

Shakers, see *Lee, Ann.*

Shane, novel by Jack Schaefer◆ with screenplay by A.B. Guthrie.

SHANGE, NTOZAKE (1948–   ), New Jersey-born author, graduated from Barnard (1970), in 1971 changed her original name, Paulette Williams, which she called a slave name because the first one derived from a man and the second from an irrelevant Anglo-Saxon culture, to a Zulu combination meaning "she who comes with her own things" and "she who walks like a lion." Her first successful work was *for colored girls who have considered suicide/when the rainbow is enuf* (1977), which she called a choreo-poem, a stage production loosely combining poetry, dance, and music in evoking experiences of black women. Such dramas that followed included *three pieces* (1981), three verse plays about black people, and *from okra to greens: a different kinda love story* (1983). She also followed with novels, *Sassafras, Cypress, Indigo* (1982), about the experiences and ideas of three young black girls; *Betsey Brown* (1985), revealing the experiences of three generations of women in one family during a period of early school desegregation; and *Liliane: Resurrection of a Daughter* (1994), about the last days of legal segregation in Mississippi. She has also written several books of poetry, including *Natural Disasters and Other Festive Occasions* (1977), *a daughter's geography* (1983), and *Ridin' the Moon in Texas* (1987).

SHAPIRO, KARL [JAY] (1913–   ), Baltimore-born author whose first volume of *Poems* (1935) was followed by *Person, Place and Thing* and *The Place of Love,* both issued in 1942. He came to major prominence with *V-Letter and Other Poems* (1944, Pulitzer Prize), written while he was a soldier in the South Pacific. Later volumes of his pungent poetry include *Essay on Rime* (1945), a critique in verse of modern poetry; *Trial of a Poet* (1947); *Poems 1940–1953* (1953); *Poems of a Jew* (1958), on coming to terms with his heritage; *Selected Poems* (1968); and *Adult Bookstore* (1976). He has written a novel, *Edsel* (1971), about an aging poet-professor at a Midwestern state university, and literary studies, including *Beyond Criticism* (1953), essays on poetry; *In Defense of Ignorance* (1960), polemical lectures and essays praising Whitman and D.H. Lawrence and attacking highly intellectual writers; *Prose Keys to Modern Poetry* (1962); *The Bourgeois Poet* (1964), a poetic treatment of the poet's relation to other men and of men to society; *To Abolish Children* (1968), essays and fiction; and *The Poetry Wreck* (1975), essays. He edited *Poetry* (1950–55) and *Prairie Schooner* (1956–66) and has taught at the University of Nebraska (1956–66) and the University of California, Davis (1968–86). A projected three-volume autobiography appeared as *Poet* (1988) and *Reports of My Death* (1990).

SHAW, HENRY WHEELER (1818–85), Massachusetts-born humorist, better known under his pseudonym Josh Billings. Until the age of 45, when he began his literary career by writing for small newspapers, he attempted a variety of occupations, including Western exploration, farming, commanding a riverboat, selling real estate, and auctioneering. His writings soon attracted the at-

tention of C.F. Browne, who arranged for the publication of his first book, *Josh Billings, His Sayings* (1865). Thereafter he became a popular crackerbox philosopher, employing the devices popular among the literary comedians of the time: ridiculous spellings, deformed grammar, monstrous logic, puns, malapropisms, incongruous juxtapositions of idea, and anticlimax. Both in his lectures and in his books, he showed his gift for aphorism rather than sustained storytelling or characterization. From 1869 to 1880 he issued annual *Allminax,* and his other works include *Josh Billings on Ice, and Other Things* (1868), *Everybody's Friend* (1874), *Josh Billings' Trump Kards* (1877), *Old Probability: Perhaps Rain—Perhaps Not* (1879), and *Josh Billings Struggling with Things* (1881).

SHAW, IRWIN (1913–84), Brooklyn-born writer whose works are marked by dramatic intensity and social awareness. His plays include *Bury the Dead♦* (1936); *Siege* (1937); *The Gentle People* (1939); *Retreat to Pleasure* (1940); *Sons and Soldiers* (1944), about a woman dreaming of the life of her unborn son; *The Assassin* (1944), set in World War II; and *Children from Their Games* (1963), a comedy. His novels are *The Young Lions* (1948), tracing the fortunes of two American soldiers, one a Jew, the other a Gentile, and of the Nazi who kills the first and is killed by the second; *The Troubled Air* (1951), about radio actors harried by flimsy charges of Communist sympathies; *Lucy Crown* (1956), about a middle-aged woman's romance; *Two Weeks in Another Town* (1960); *Voices of a Summer Day* (1965), a middle-aged man's bittersweet memories; *Rich Man, Poor Man* (1970), the stories of two brothers and their sister set against the world scene from the 1940s to 1970; *Evening in Byzantium* (1973), portraying an aging Hollywood producer; *Nightwork* (1975), a lively depiction of a sophisticated international confidence man; *Beggarman, Thief* (1977), a melodramatic sequel to *Rich Man, Poor Man; The Top of the Hill* (1979), about a successful businessman trying to find himself; *Bread Upon the Waters* (1981); and *Acceptable Losses* (1982). *Sailor Off the Bremen* (1939), *Welcome to the City* (1941), *Act of Faith* (1946), *Mixed Faith* (1950), *Tip on a Dead Jockey* (1957), *Love on a Dark Street* (1965), *God Was Here But He Left Early* (1973), and *Five Decades* (1978) collect stories. *In the Company of Dolphins* (1964) describes a cruise Shaw made in the Mediterranean, and *Paris! Paris!* (1977) contains essays.

Shawnee Indians, Algonquian tribe related to the Sauk, Fox, and Kickapoo, migrated from the Cumberland and Savannah rivers to Pennsylvania and Ohio, in the 17th century. Their principal opposition to the whites occurred in the rebellion led by Tecumseh. ♦ They now live in Oklahoma. The Shawnee figure in R.M. Bird's *Nick of the Woods* and other works concerned with Tecumseh, and an 18th-century white boy reared by Shawnees in New York colony is the hero of a trilogy by Hervey Allen, *The City in the Dawn.*

Shays's Rebellion (1786–87), insurrection of Massachusetts farmers, led by Daniel Shays (1747–1825), a Revolutionary War captain, to stop the foreclosure of mortgages and to prevent the farmers' imprisonment for debts arising from high land taxes after the Revolution. Bellamy's novel *The Duke of Stockbridge* (1900) deals with this subject.

She Would Be a Soldier, or, The Plains of Chippewa, play by Mordecai M. Noah,♦ produced and published in 1819.

SHEEAN, [JAMES] VINCENT (1899–1975), born in Illinois, attended the University of Chicago, and became a European correspondent for the *Chicago Tribune* (1922–25), and later for news syndicates, reporting the Fascist march on Rome, the wars on the Rif tribes, and other events of the postwar decade. In *Personal History* (1935) he records the development of his mind through these experiences. *Between the Thunder and the Sun* (1943) and *This House Against This House* (1946) contain further personal history. His other books include the novels *The Anatomy of Virtue* (1927), *Gog and Magog* (1930), *The Tide* (1933), *Sanfelice* (1936), *A Day of Battle* (1938), *Bird of the Wilderness* (1941), *A Certain Rich Man* (1947), and *Beware of Caesar* (1965). His biographies include *Lead, Kindly Light* (1949), about Gandhi; *The Indigo Bunting* (1951), a memoir of Edna St. Vincent Millay: *Oscar Hammerstein I* (1956); *Orpheus at Eighty* (1958), a life of Verdi; *Nehru: The Years of Power* (1959); *Dorothy and Red* (1963), a memoir of the married life of his friends Dorothy Thompson and Sinclair Lewis; and *Faisal: The King and His Kingdom* (1975).

SHEED, WILFRID [JOHN JOSEPH] (1930–), English-born, Oxford-educated author, came to the U.S. (1947), has long been a resident of New York City. His humorous satirical novels include *A Middle Class Education* (1961), about a student at Oxford who comes on a scholarship to the U.S.; *The Hack* (1963), presenting a writer of inspirational verse and fiction for American Catholic journals; *Square's Progress* (1965), depicting an easygoing middle-class American who becomes a hippie; *Office Politics* (1966); *The Blacking Factory and Pennsylvania Gothic* (1968), a short novel and a long story; *Max Jamison* (1970), characterizing a journalistic drama critic; *People Will Always Be Kind* (1973), about an Irish-American's rise in politics; and *Transatlantic Blues* (1978), tracing an American at Oxford who goes on to become a television personality. Other writings include *The Morning After* (1971) and *The Good Word and Other Words* (1979), forerunners of *Essays in Disguise* (1990), essays; *Three Mobs: Labor, Church and Ma-*

fia (1975); and *Muhammad Ali* (1976) and *Clare Boothe Luce* (1982), biographies. *Frank and Maisie* (1985) is a memoir of his parents.

SHEEHAN, NEIL (1936–), Massachusetts-born and Harvard graduate, became a reporter for *The New York Times* and author of books that include *A Bright Shining Lie: John Paul Vann and America in Vietnam* (1988), awarded a Pulitzer Prize for general nonfiction. He is married to Susan Sheehan.

SHEEHAN, SUSAN (1937–), born in Vienna, brought to the U.S. in 1941; after graduation from Wellesley College became a freelance writer, publishing much of her work in *The New Yorker.* After her first book, *Ten Vietnamese* (1967), her fourth work, *Is There No Place on Earth for Me?* (1982) was awarded a Pulitzer Prize for general nonfiction.

Shelburne Essays, on literary, philosophical, and religious subjects, by Paul Elmer More,♦ were published in 11 volumes (1904–21), and *The New Shelburne Essays* (3 vols., 1928–36). All show the views of the New Humanism,♦ classical learning, and an elevated style, but the subjects range from Oriental revelations to modern European and U.S. books.

SHELDON, CHARLES M[ONROE] (1857–1946), born in New York, attended Brown University and Andover Theological Seminary, and became pastor of the Central Congregational Church of Topeka, Kan., which he left in 1919 to edit *The Christian Herald.* His novel *In His Steps* (1896), a story of a minister following the example of Jesus, was an extraordinary success, being translated into 23 languages and selling millions of copies. His other books include *Richard Bruce* (1892), *His Brother's Keeper; or, Christian Stewardship* (1895), *The Heart of the World* (1905), *Charles M. Sheldon: His Life Story* (1925), *Let's Talk It Over* (1929), and *He Is Here* (1931).

SHELDON, EDWARD [BREWSTER] (1886–1946), born in Chicago, graduated from Harvard (1907), where he studied under G.P. Baker. His first play, *Salvation Nell* (1908), is the story of a reformed saloon girl. After two dramas on American politics, *The Nigger*♦ (1909) and *The Boss*♦ (1911), he wrote *The Princess Zim-Zim* (1911), a romantic play laid in Coney Island. His other plays include *Egypt* (1912), melodrama; *The High Road* (1912), a study of a woman who rises from farm life to make her husband a presidential candidate; *Romance*♦ (1913), concerned with an old man's memories of a love affair; *The Song of Songs* (1914), an adaptation with an American setting of a novel by Sudermann; *The Garden of Paradise* (1914), a poetic fantasy based on Andersen's "The Little Mermaid"; *Bewitched* (1924), a romantic play, written with Sidney Howard; *Lulu Belle*

(1926), a study of a black prostitute, written with his nephew, Charles MacArthur; and *Jenny* (1929) and *Dishonored Lady* (1930), written with Margaret Ayer Barnes. *Ned and Jack* is a play (1981) about Sheldon and John Barrymore, written by Sheldon Rosen.

Sheltered Life, The, novel by Ellen Glasgow, ♦ published in 1932.

In Queensborough (Richmond), Virginia, Jenny Blair Archbald is reared by her widowed mother, her spinster Aunt Etta, and her grandfather, General David Archbald. Members of the decaying aristocratic class, they attempt to preserve the social traditions of the 19th century, but live in a section giving way to industrial encroachments. Their neighbors are George Birdsong and his wife Eva, a famous belle of the 1890s, extravagantly in love with her handsome but weak husband, who tries without success to be faithful. Jenny Blair, innocent and self-contained, is influenced by her grandfather's devotion to Eva, the miseries of her frustrated aunt, and the atmosphere of genteel decadence. As she reaches adolescence, she continues to "hate boys," especially Mrs. Birdsong's ward, John Welch, a radical-thinking youth. She prefers older men, such as her grandfather and George, and during an emotional crisis, when Eva, whom she adores, is critically ill, she falls in love with George. He laughs at her feeling, and at her 18 years, but begins to respond in spite of himself. He insists that he will do "nothing to hurt her," and they are separated during the summer vacation, from which the Birdsongs return ill, weary, and verging on nervous collapse. Jenny Blair, overcome with adolescent love, cannot keep away from George, and Eva surprises them in each other's arms. The girl flees into the garden, whence she is recalled by John Welch's frantic announcement of an "accident": George has killed his wife and committed suicide.

SHELTON, FREDERICK WILLIAM (1815–81), Episcopal clergyman of New York, was also an author. *The Trollopiad; or, Travelling Gentlemen in America* (1837) is a verse satire on Mrs. Trollope, Captain Basil Hall, and other English critics of American life. *Up the River* (1853) is a series of letters on the New York countryside, while *Peeps from a Belfry; or, The Parish Sketch Book* (1855) is a description of a winter in Vermont. Both show his indebtedness to Irving, as do many of his magazine tales and essays. *Salander and the Dragon, a Romance of The Hartz Prison* (1850) is an allegory in the vein of *Pilgrim's Progress,* and *The Rector of St. Bardolph's* (1853) is a story of a country parson.

Shenandoah, play by Bronson Howard, ♦ produced in 1888, revived in 1889 with success, and published in 1897.

Kerchival West, with his sister Madeline, visits his former West Point classmate Robert Elling-ham and his sister Gertrude in their Virginia home. Their two love affairs are interrupted when, at the outbreak of the Civil War, Kerchival becomes a colonel in the Union army and Robert attains the same rank in the Confederate army. When they next meet, Robert has become a prisoner, Gertrude has been captured as a spy and brought before Kerchival, and Madeline has come to comfort Gertrude. Kerchival is wounded by Gertrude's accomplice, Captain Thornton, who to save himself tells the Union commander, General Haverhill, that Kerchival has been Mrs. Haverhill's lover. This is believed because Kerchival possesses Mrs. Haverhill's locket, but he accounts for this when he proves that he obtained it from the young soldier, Frank Bedloe, who turns out to be the disguised son of Haverhill. Robert is exchanged for Bedloe, Bedloe is killed, Kerchival recovers to help resist a Confederate attack, and with the end of the war the two couples are reunited.

SHEPARD, BENJAMIN HENRY, see *Grierson, Francis.*

SHEPARD, ODELL (1884–1967), born in Illinois, graduated from the University of Chicago, after receiving his Ph.D. from Harvard became a professor of English at Trinity College (1917–46). His books include essays, criticism, and poetry, but he is best known for *Pedlar's Progress: The Life of Bronson Alcott* (1937, Pulitzer Prize) and two historical novels written with his son Willard Odell Shepard, *Holdfast Gaines* (1946) and *Jenkins' Ear* (1951).

SHEPARD, SAM (SAMUEL SHEPARD ROGERS, JR.) (1943–   ), Illinois-born playwright, reared and resident in California. His first works were short plays, beginning with *Cowboys* and *The Rock Garden* (1964), presented off-Broadway. *La Turista* (1967) was his first long play. Other productions followed rapidly from Shepard's prolific writing, which, with substantial selectivity, includes *The Tooth of Crime* (1972), a fantasy about rock-and-roll pop singers that is a commentary on contemporary American social values, and *Curse of the Starving Class* (1978), depicting a lower-middle-class family symbolic of social chaos in the U.S. *Buried Child* (1978, Pulitzer Prize) deals with an even more macabre disintegrating family in Illinois. In general the dramas of Shepherd are marked by an improvisational feeling because of their great variety in moving from the surreal to the realistic in treating people and situations ranging from the mythic to the abstract. Many of these early plays and more of the 1960s and 1970s were put into print in *Seven Plays* (1981), *Fool for Love* (1984), and *The Unseen Hand* (1986). More recent significant plays include the frequently staged, extremely popular *True West* (1980), depicting family feuding begun by a Los Angeles mother and her estranged husband, the father from the not-too-distant desert, that involves two sons, one, a film writer, who is close to their mother, and the other as empty as the desert itself; *Fool for Love* (1983), depicting the psychological unravelling of a man who, believing his wife sexually unfair to him, indulges in a vicious assault on her; and *A Lie of the Mind* (1985) about the adventures and fragmentation leading to the fury of a deserted woman against the men with whom she has been involved, and *Simpatico* (1994), Shepard's homage to the film-noir genre, set in a world of professional horse-racing; the complicated plot involves blackmail and false identities. Among screenplays Shepard wrote was that of Antonioni's *Zabriskie Point* (1965). He has written short stories, poems, and monologues, published in *Hawk Moon* (1972). Letters with Joseph Chaikin, a major actor in his plays, were published in 1989.

SHEPARD, THOMAS (1605–49), educated at Cambridge, became a preacher in England until banned for his puritanism, when he went to New England (1635). There he became pastor of the church at Cambridge and was one of the leaders in New England religious and intellectual life. He was instrumental in the founding of Harvard, was one of the leaders of the synod (1637) that condemned Anne Hutchinson and the Antinomians, was prominent in the conversion of the Indians, and helped draft the Cambridge Platform. He was a tireless worker, and in his preaching and writing was an outstanding though typical representative of the New England Calvinists. His most popular work, *The Sincere Convert* (1641), was frequently reprinted, and was translated into the Indian language by John Eliot (1689). In it he preaches a gospel of love and infinite compassion, indicating that anyone might be saved if he would open his heart to God. His other works include *The Clear Sun-shine of the Gospel Breaking Forth upon the Indians* (1648); *Theses Sabbaticae* (1649), rules for New England religious life; *The Parable of the Ten Virgins Opened and Applied* (1660); *Three Valuable Pieces* (1747), a posthumous collection containing a diary; and *The Autobiography of Thomas Shepard* (1832). His *Works* was published in three volumes (1853).

Sheriffs of Bristol, see *Letter to the Sheriffs of Bristol.*

SHERMAN, FRANK DEMPSTER (1860–1916), professor of architecture and graphics at Columbia (1887–1916), who was known for his charming, witty, occasional verse, published in such books as *Lyrics for a Lute* (1890), *Little-Folk Lyrics* (1892), and *Lyrics of Joy* (1904). He frequently wrote under the pseudonym Felix Carmen. With J.K. Bangs he wrote *New Waggings of Old Tales* (1888). Clinton Scollard, with whom he had collaborated in *A Southern Flight* (1905), edited his collected *Poems* (1917).

SHERMAN, STUART P[RATT] (1881–1926), after graduation from Williams College (1903)

continued his studies at Harvard, where he fell under the influence of the New Humanism♦ of Irving Babbitt, as may be observed in his works such as *Matthew Arnold: How To Know Him* (1917) and *On Contemporary Literature* (1917). His moderate conservatism, defense of the American Puritan tradition, and almost chauvinistic patriotism led him into many literary quarrels with such critics as H.L. Mencken. His change to a more liberal point of view may be traced through *Americans* (1922), *The Genius of America* (1923), *Points of View* (1924), and *Critical Woodcuts* (1926). He was a professor of English at the University of Illinois (1907–24), and edited the literary supplement of the New York *Herald-Tribune* (1924–26). He was an editor of *The Cambridge History of American Literature.* Jacob Zeitlin and Homer Woodbridge edited his *Life and Letters* (2 vols., 1929).

SHERMAN, WILLIAM TECUMSEH (1820–91), after graduation from West Point served in the Mexican War, and was superintendent of a military academy that later became Louisiana State University when the Civil War erupted. He refused high rank in the Confederacy. Under Grant♦ he distinguished himself at Shiloh and was soon promoted to major general. In a speech of 1880 he said, "There is many a boy here today who looks on war as all glory, but boys, it is just all hell." His march from Atlanta to the sea is celebrated in the powerful song "Marching Through Georgia" (1865). His *Memoirs* (2 vols., 1875), full, crisp, and strong, were published as a single volume (1990) in the Library of America♦ series, using the revised text of the 1886 edition. Sherman figures in Winston Churchill's *The Crisis,* Mary Johnston's *Cease Firing,* and John Brick's *Jubilee,* and his men figure as devilish forces in Margaret Mitchell's *Gone with the Wind.* ♦

SHERWOOD, ROBERT [EMMET] (1896–1955), New York dramatist, after graduation from Harvard (1918) and service in World War I became a drama critic and later an editor of *Life* and *Scribner's Magazine.* His first play was *The Road to Rome* (1927), a comedy concerning Hannibal's march on Rome and his decision to turn from his goal, which served as a plea against war. This was followed by *The Love Nest♦* (1927), dramatizing a story by Ring Lardner, and *The Queen's Husband* (1928), a comedy about a timid king who assumes power during the absence of his queen. *Waterloo Bridge* (1930), set in London during World War I, is concerned with a chorus girl turned prostitute, who, in order to preserve the chivalric ideals of a doughboy, refuses to give herself to him. After a melodrama, *This Is New York* (1930), Sherwood returned to comedy with *Reunion in Vienna* (1931), presenting a nostalgic assembly of the exiled Hapsburgs, at which is revived the love of Prince Maximilian

Rudolph and his former mistress, Elena. Sherwood next spent several years in Hollywood and England, writing for motion pictures, but in 1935 produced *The Petrified Forest,*♦ a melodramatic play concerned with frustrated lives during a period of social transition, and the following year won a Pulitzer Prize for *Idiot's Delight,*♦ a dramatic setting of a plea for world peace. After *Tovarich* (1936), a comedy adapted from the French, he was awarded a Pulitzer Prize again, this time for *Abe Lincoln in Illinois*♦ (1938), concerned with Lincoln's early years and his preparation for his lifework. *There Shall Be No Night* (1940, Pulitzer Prize) deals with the Russian attack on Finland, and its consequences in altering the attitude of a liberal Finnish scientist. He also wrote *The Virtuous Knight* (1931), a novel about the Third Crusade, and *Roosevelt and Hopkins* (1948, Pulitzer Prize), "an intimate biography," deriving in part from his association with the president as a speech writer. His life to 1939 is described in John Mason Brown's *The Worlds of Robert E. Sherwood* (1965).

SHILLABER, BENJAMIN PENHALLOW (1814–90), Boston author and printer, in 1847 created the character of Mrs. Partington for a newspaper on which he was employed. This character, a small-town Yankee Mrs. Malaprop, who discourses amiably and ignorantly about gardening, pets, Calvinism, and current events, and is ever baffled by her mischievous nephew, Ike, became popular in such books as *Life and Sayings of Mrs. Partington* (1854), *Mrs. Partington's Knitting Work* (1859), *Partingtonian Patchwork* (1873), and *Mrs. Partington's Grab Bag* (1893). Shillaber founded a humorous weekly, *The Carpet-Bag*♦ (1851–53), which was important in developing the new school of American humor and for printing the first work of Clemens. Critics have discovered that Clemens was indebted to Mrs. Partington for his character Aunt Polly. In turn Shillaber was accused of having taken the character from Sydney Smith.♦ Although he denied this, he admitted that the name came from the Englishman's allusion to Dame Partington, whose attempt to brush away the Atlantic Ocean had been compared in a speech (1831) with the opposition of the House of Lords to the progress of reform.

Ship of Fools, novel by Katherine Anne Porter.♦

Shirer, WILLIAM L[AWRENCE] (1904–93), Illinois-born journalist, war correspondent, and commentator on radio, best known for his firsthand studies of Germany, *Berlin Diary* (1941), *End of a Berlin Diary* (1947), *The Rise and Fall of the Third Reich* (1960), *The Rise and Fall of Adolf Hitler* (1961), and *The Collapse of the Third Republic* (1969). *20th Century Journey* (1976) is a memoir to 1930. He wrote a second volume of memoirs, *Nightmare Years* (1984), and a final one, *20th Century Journey: A Native's Return 1945–1988* (1990).

He also wrote novels: *The Traitor* (1950), *Stranger Come Home* (1954), and *The Consul's Wife* (1956).

Shock of Recognition, The, anthology with critical commentary by Edmund Wilson,♦ subtitled "The Development of Literature in the United States Recorded by the Men Who Made It," and collecting articles about American authors by their literary contemporaries from 1845 to the publication date of 1943.

SHOLOM ALEICHEM, pen name of Solomon Rabinowitz (1859–1916), meaning "Peace be with you" in Hebrew. Ukrainian-born, a popular and influential journalist, and a leading figure of Yiddish literature for his stories and plays. Sholom Aleichem left Russia because of pogroms. He lived in New York City (Oct. 1906–June 1907), contributing some of his bittersweet tales of Jewish village life to Lower East Side journals and having two of his plays produced there. However, he did not have financial success so he returned to Europe for a reading tour. Experience in the U.S. contributed to his long series of stories, including *The Adventures of Mottel, the Cantor's Son* (1953), about a boy sometimes called a Jewish Tom Sawyer, just as their author was said to be a Yiddish Mark Twain. When World War I broke out in Europe, Sholom Aleichem returned to New York for the last two years of his life, during which he worked on his incomplete autobiographical fiction. This includes, in posthumous English translation, *The Old Country* (1946), *Tevye's Daughters* (1949), and *The Great Fair* (1955). He was buried in Brooklyn. The success, popular and critical, of Jewish writers in the U.S. during the 1950s and later brought attention to Sholom Aleichem, particularly when the musical play *Fiddler on the Roof* (1964), based on some of his sketches, had 3242 performances in the U.S., making it in its time the longest-running musical production on Broadway. An autobiography of his youthful years was published as *From the Fair* (1985).

Shore Acres, play by James A. Herne,♦ produced in 1893 as a revision of his play *The Hawthornes* (1889). It is primarily a character study of the homespun philosopher "Uncle Nat" Berry, who circumvents the plans of his younger brother, Martin, to sell the old homestead in Maine and prohibit the marriage of their niece, Helen, to Dr. Sam Warren. Martin objects to the doctor because of his "free-thinkin' ideas." Although containing a melodramatic scene of the elopement of Helen, the play is distinguished for its quiet realism.

SHORT, BOB, pseudonym of A.B. Longstreet.♦

Short Happy Life of Francis Macomber, The, short story by Ernest Hemingway,♦ published in

Cosmopolitan (Sept. 1936) and collected in *The Fifth Column and the First Forty-Nine Stories* (1938).

An American couple on a safari in Kenya, the Macombers have long given the impression of a glamorous and comparatively happy marriage, although the basis for their union is that "Margot was too beautiful for Macomber to divorce her and Macomber had too much money for Margot ever to leave him." The marriage comes to a new straining point when in cowardice he runs from a wounded lion that he has shot badly, and she, in disgust, gives herself that night to the professional hunter and guide, the sturdy Englishman Robert Wilson. The next day, in a surge of excitement, Macomber discovers self-confidence and happiness as he shoots three wild buffalo, but Margot is suddenly made insecure as she sees him at last a man who will dominate their marriage. Forced to go into the hiding place of one of the animals he has only wounded to administer the *coup de grâce,* Macomber seems about to be gored by the buffalo when from the car Mrs. Macomber shoots at the beast and kills her husband instead, after which Wilson says wryly, "Of course it's an accident. I know that."

"Short Sixes": Stories To Be Read While the Candle Burns, 13 tales by H.C. Bunner,♦ published in 1891.

Shoshone Indians, primitive Northwestern tribe, sometimes erroneously called Snake Indians, which gave its name to a great linguistic family of various cultures, scattered through Montana, Wyoming, New Mexico, Texas, Oregon, and California. The Shoshonean tribes include the Comanche, Ute, Paiute, Hopi, Bannock, and Mission Indians. The Shoshone figure in books by Joaquin Miller, the Mission Indians in Helen Hunt Jackson's *Ramona* and Mary Austin's *Isidro,* and the Paiute in Mrs. Austin's *The Land of Little Rain.*

Showboats, floating theaters that give performances at waterfront towns. Such companies of strolling players were known early in the American occupation of the Mississippi basin, and performed on canalboats, flatboats, and keelboats. Later troupes, with more elegant accommodations on Ohio and Mississippi River steamboats, continued to present melodramas and variety shows, and there were also floating circuses and minstrel shows. The Chapman family, well known during the 1830s, were among the outstanding showboat actors. The main period of the showboats was during the 19th century, but they continue to exist, and an antiquarian interest has recently led to their revival and that of their early productions. The literature concerned with this form of theater includes Edna Ferber's novel *Show Boat* (1926), adapted as a musical play by Jerome Kern and Oscar Hammerstein II; David

Graham Phillips's novel *Susan Lenox*♦ (1917); and John Barth's novel *The Floating Opera* (1956).

Show-Off, The, comedy by George Kelly. ♦

SHUTE, HENRY AUGUSTUS (1856–1943), author of *The Real Diary of a Real Boy* (1902) and other humorous narratives largely concerned with the psychology and exploits of the "real" boys Plupy, Beany, and Pewt.

SIDNEY, EDWARD WILLIAM, pseudonym of N.B. Tucker. ♦

SIDNEY, MARGARET, pseudonym of Harriet Lothrop. ♦

Siege of London, The, novelette by Henry James,♦ the title story of a volume published in 1883.

Nancy Headway, several times married and divorced and now a wealthy widow, leaves the Western U.S. to exert her fascination in Europe, the constant goal of her vulgar ambition. Notorious throughout the West, she is snubbed in New York, and her dearest hope is to annoy her detractors by a social success in Paris and London. She attracts Sir Arthur Demesne, a weak, cautious, but romantically inclined English Tory, who follows her about without being able to decide to marry her. She meets a former Western acquaintance, Mr. Littlemore, who introduces her to his friend Waterville, an undersecretary of the U.S. ministry in London. Through these two she tries to establish contacts in British society, and finally, though she arouses the enmity of Sir Arthur's careful mother, she becomes popular because of her naïveté and fresh humor. Lady Demesne appeals to Littlemore and Waterville to disclose their knowledge of Mrs. Headway's past, but, though she wrests from Littlemore the admission that Nancy is "not respectable," the young woman triumphs, marrying her baronet and continuing to be a novel and slightly scandalous social celebrity.

SIGOURNEY, LYDIA HUNTLEY (1791–1865), Connecticut poetaster whose sentimental and pious verses were enormously popular, winning her the title "the Mrs. Hemans of America." Her lugubrious preoccupation with death caused her to look at every sick child as a potential angel, and she so consistently wrote melancholy verses on the decease of any prominent person that an elegy from her pen seemed as natural a sequence to death as interment. She wrote some 60 books, ranging from *Moral Pieces in Prose and Verse* (1815) to an autobiography, *Letters of Life* (1866). In addition to editing religious and juvenile publications, she was also a pioneer in the cause of higher education for women.

SILKO, LESLIE MARMON (1948–   ), reared with her Plains Indian family in New Mexico, the place she wrote about in her first book, *Laguna Woman* (1974), a collection of poems. She then wrote her first novel, *Ceremony* (1977), dealing with a Native American who seeks to recover heritage and old lore. *Storyteller* (1981) collects her versions of folktales and legends, as well as her poems and photographs; her novel *Almanac of the Dead* (1991) again celebrates Native American values, especially reverence for ancestral land. It presents the contemporary Western United States as an ecological as well as spiritual disaster area.

SILL, EDWARD ROWLAND (1841–87), born in Connecticut, graduated from Yale (1861) and attempted to fortify his frail health by following Dana's example in making a sea voyage around the Horn to California. During the ensuing years he held various odd jobs, read law, and studied medicine, returning east to study at the Harvard Divinity School and try his hand at New York journalism. In 1868 he published *The Hermitage and Other Poems,* the only volume of his verse issued publicly during his lifetime. After teaching school in Ohio and California, he became a professor of English at the University of California (1874–82), where he showed that, though not a great scholar, he was a man of wide culture, brilliant insight, and high spiritual quality. His last years were spent in Ohio, where he contributed essays and poems to magazines under the pseudonym Andrew Hedbrooke, and in 1883 privately issued *The Venus of Milo and Other Poems.* His collected *Poems* (1902) are marked by a classic finish and a stoic idealistic spirit in face of the problems of religious skepticism which racked his mind. His collected *Prose* (1900) contains charming treatments of slight literary subjects.

Silver Cord, The, play by Sidney Howard, ♦ produced in 1926 and published in 1927.

Mrs. Phelps, the widowed mother of David and Robert, has a pathological love for her sons that passes the maternal and causes her to employ every possible means to hold their love and destroy any attachment they may have for others. Her constant threatening and wheedling lead the younger son, Robert, to remain faithful to her, even though it means the breaking of his engagement with Hester, who in her desperation attempts suicide. David is nearly captured, but his stronger will, bolstered by that of his wife, Christina, permits him to escape from the silver cord of a mother fixation after Christina has finally made clear the nature of his mother's influence.

Silverado Squatters, The, autobiographical narrative by Stevenson, ♦ published in 1883. Written after the author's return to Europe (1882), it describes his trip, with his bride and his stepson Sam (Lloyd Osbourne), from San Francisco through the Napa Valley to Calistoga, and their sojourn

(June–July 1880) in a shanty at the deserted mining town of Silverado, on Mt. St. Helena in central California. The book is notable for its character sketches of the Hansons, who were the Stevensons' only neighbors at Silverado; Mr. Kelmar, the shrewd, good-natured Jewish merchant who directed them there; and other people of the countryside; as well as for realistic descriptions of the picturesque scene of their mountain idyll.

SILVERMAN, KENNETH (1936–   ), born in New York City, received his B.A. through Ph.D. from Columbia, became a professor of English at New York University in 1964. His books include *Timothy Dwight* (1969), *A Cultural History of the American Revolution* (1976), and *The Life and Times of Cotton Mather* (1984), awarded a Pulitzer Prize for biography. In 1992 he published *Edgar A. Poe: Mournful and Never-Ending Remembrance.*

SIMIC, CHARLES (1938–   ), poet. Born in what was Yugoslavia of Serbian parents, he settled with his family in Chicago in 1954 and began writing poetry in English while in high school. After education at the University of Chicago as well as at New York University, and service in the army, Simic published his first collection of poems, *What the Grass Says* (1967). *Selected Poems 1963–1983* was published in 1985. He has been the recipient of a Guggenheim and a MacArthur award. Later poems appear in *Unending Blues* (1986), *The Book of Gods and Devils* (1990), and *Hotel Insomnia* (1993). *The World Doesn't End* (1989), prose poems, won a Pulitzer Prize. Simic's poems are short, mixing realism with surrealism, and sometimes myth.

SIMMS, WILLIAM GILMORE (1806–70), Charleston author, began his literary career by writing romantic verse in the vein of Byron, who strongly influenced the local literary standards that Simms earnestly tried to meet. He began to write novels during a brief visit to the North, but his first work, *Martin Faber♦* (1833), a psychological study of a criminal, was not indicative of his talents, for he made his reputation with romances of the frontier and South Carolina history. *Guy Rivers♦* (1834), which he called the first of his "regular novels," deals with the life of Georgia desperadoes. *The Yemassee♦* (1835) is a story of Indian warfare in his own state, and *The Partisan♦* (1835), also set there, is a romance of the Revolution. Thus, within two years, Simms had begun writing on the three different subjects for which he is noted.

In the vein of *Guy Rivers* followed the series known as the Border Romances, concerned with colonial and 19th-century life in the South, which includes *Richard Hurdis♦* (1838), *Border Beagles♦* (1840), *Beauchampe♦* (1842), *Helen Halsey; or, The Swamp State of Conelachita* (1845), *Charlemont* (1856), and, in magazine form only,

"Voltmeier; or, The Mountain Men" (1869) and "The Club of the Panther: A Mountain Legend" (1869). Generally included with the Border Romances are *The Yemassee* and his other depictions of Indians, *The Wigwam and the Cabin*♦ (1845–46) and *The Cassique of Kiawah* (1859), a novel.

The Partisan was the first of a series known as the Revolutionary Romances, dealing with life in the South during the Revolution and centering on the activities of Marion, Greene, and other generals. Among these books are *Mellichampe*♦ (1836); *The Kinsmen* (1841), revised as *The Scout* (1854); *Katharine Walton*♦ (1851); *The Sword and the Distaff* (1853), revised as *Woodcraft* (1854); *The Forayers*♦ (1855); and *Eutaw*♦ (1856). "Joscelyn: A Tale of the Revolution" (1867) is not usually considered one of the series.

Two of the Border Romances, *Beauchampe* and *Charlemont,* form a sequence dealing with the Kentucky Tragedy,♦ and show Simms tending toward the psychological interest of his first novel. He also made unsuccessful attempts to deal with Spanish backgrounds in *Pelayo* (1838) and its sequel, *Count Julian* (1845). *The Damsel of Darien* (1839) is concerned with Balboa, and *Vasconselos* (1853) deals with Mexican history.

Simms, who was tremendously proud of South Carolina, and particularly of genteel, conservative Charleston, was, as the son of a poor storekeeper, snubbed by the social oligarchy, and yet remained loyal to the local taboos. The more he was slighted, the more he defended the society. Writing romances was an insufficient means of expressing his local patriotism, and he tried also to make himself a typical South Carolina litterateur by editing such magazines as *The Southern Quarterly Review* (1856–57) and *The Southern and Western Monthly Magazine* (1845), writing a *History* (1840) and a *Geography* (1843) of the state, and biographies of Francis Marion (1844), John Smith (1846), the Chevalier Bayard (1847), and Nathaniel Greene (1849), as well as delivering orations and writing essays, which began with the academic championing of slavery and in time became bitter denunciations of Northern attacks.

His blind adoration of local economic, political, and social standards is considered to have damaged the innate realism of his novels. The leading characters are generally more aristocratic than vital, and it is only in the secondary figures, the low-life characters, among whom is included his Falstaffian creation, Captain Porgy, that he presents fully rounded figures. Because of his two great topics, the frontier and the Revolution, he is invariably called a Southern Cooper, and he does resemble the New York novelist in his themes, fluent romantic style, use of stock figures, and melodramatic plots. Though he fails to attain the poetic quality of Cooper's depictions of nature, he seldom betrays such obvious faults as those of the Northerner. If he did not create a character comparable to Natty Bumppo, or a series comparable to the Leather-Stocking Tales,

he was in general a more accurate delineator of life. Simms's *Letters* were collected in 5 volumes (1952–56), and a scholarly edition of his works, projected for 15 volumes, began publication in 1969. He appears as a character in DuBose Heyward's *Peter Ashley* (1932).

Simon Legree, villain in *Uncle Tom's Cabin.*♦

Simon Suggs, Some Adventures of, tales by Johnson J. Hooper.♦

Simple, name given to the titular character, properly Jesse B. Semple, in several works by Langston Hughes.♦ A black resident of Harlem, Simple is a seemingly naïve or stupid man but actually smart in the vein of the shrewd cracker-barrel homespun figure. The satirical sketches in which he surveys contemporary issues were published in newspapers and are collected in *Simple Speaks His Mind* (1950), *Simple Takes a Wife* (1953), *Simple Stakes a Claim* (1957), *The Best of Simple* (1961), and *Simple's Uncle Sam* (1965). *Simply Heavenly* (1963) is a musical play by Hughes adapting some of these stories.

Simple Cobler of Aggawam, The, satirical work by Nathaniel Ward,♦ published under the pseudonym Theodore de la Guard (London, 1647), Theodore being the Greek equivalent of the Hebrew Nathaniel, and de la Guard a free French rendering of Ward. Aggawam was the original name of Ipswich, Mass., and the sobriquet "simple cobler" is explained in the subtitle: "Willing to help 'mend his Native Country, lamentably tattered, both in the upper-Leather and sole, with all the honest stitches he can take." The book is a partisan denunciation of undue tolerance in England and New England of the strife between Parliament and Charles I and of the frivolity of women and foppish fashions of men. In the style of a belated euphuist, Ward grumbles sincerely but wittily concerning all his particular dislikes. His manner recalls the Elizabethan pamphleteers, such as Nashe, Harvey, and Greene.

SIMPSON, Louis [Aston Marantz] (1923–   ), born in Jamaica, received his B.S. from Columbia (1948) after service in an airborne division in World War II. He received his Ph.D. from Columbia and has taught at the University of California, Berkeley (1959–67), and the State University of New York, Stony Brook (1967–   ). His poetry, marked by vivid imagination and fine craftsmanship, has been published in *The Arrivistes* (1949); *Good News of Death* (1955); *A Dream of Governors* (1959), including the long narrative poem "The Runner," set in the invasion of Europe in World War II; *At the End of the Open Road* (1963, Pulitzer Prize), including the long poem "The Marriage of Pocahontas," developing history into myth; *Selected Poems* (1965);

Adventures of the Letter I (1971); *Searching for the Ox* (1976); *Caviare at the Funeral* (1980); *People Live Here* (1983), selected poems since 1949; *The Best Hour of the Night* (1984); and *Collected Poems* (1988), selections from ten preceding volumes. He has also written a novel, *Riverside Drive* (1962), about a young man from Jamaica, his experiences in New York and the army, and his private life; an autobiography, *North of Jamaica* (1972); and critical works; *James Hogg* (1962); *Three on a Tower* (1975), about Pound, Eliot, and W.C. Williams; *A Revolution in Taste* (1979), about Dylan Thomas, Allen Ginsberg, Sylvia Plath, and Robert Lowell, poets who "created art out of the confusion of their lives"; *A Company of Poets* (1981), essays, reviews, talks, and autobiography, all materials evident again in *The Character of the Poet* (1986) and *Selected Prose* (1989).

Sincere Convert, The, see *Shepard, Thomas.*

SINCLAIR, UPTON [BEALL][(1878]–1968), born in Baltimore of a prominent but impoverished family, began writing dime novels at the age of 15 in order to pay his way through the College of the City of New York. While doing graduate work at Columbia, he wrote six novels, among them *Springtime and Harvest* (1901), retitled *King Midas* (1901); *Prince Hagen* (1903), a fantasy about U.S. high finance and politics; *The Journal of Arthur Stirling* (1903), about an insufficiently appreciated young poet; and *Manassas* (1904), set in the Civil War. The tone of these early works was suggested by Sinclair himself, who said that Jesus, Hamlet, and Shelley shaped his thought, and that he was disillusioned when the world did not meet him with the love and trust with which he approached it. After participating in an investigation of the Chicago stockyards, he wrote *The Jungle♦* (1906), in which he first indicated his conversion to socialism. His earnings were later invested in his cooperative colony, The Helicon Home Colony♦ at Englewood, N.J., and, after his removal to California (1915), in four unsuccessful campaigns for public office. In 1934 he united large sections of the unemployed and progressive elements in an EPIC (End Poverty in California) league, which captured the Democratic party machinery, nearly won him the governorship, and aided a follower to become Democratic governor in 1938.

Sinclair was a prolific writer, having published from 1901 to 1940 more than 100 works, ranging from pamphlets, social studies, boys' books, and studies in health, religion, and telepathy to novels, short stories, and plays. The most important of these include *The Metropolis* (1908), describing the morals of a society created by great fortunes; *King Coal♦* (1917); *The Profits of Religion* (1918), contending that organized religion is a capitalist tool in teaching the poor that God has allotted them their positions; *Jimmie Higgins* (1919), a pac-

ifist novel; *The Brass Check♦* (1919); *100%, the Story of a Patriot* (1920); *They Call Me Carpenter* (1922), a rich man's dream of a meeting with Christ; *The Goose-Step* (1923), a study of higher education in the U.S.; *The Goslings* (1924), about American schools; *Oil!♦* (1927); *Boston♦* (1928); *Mountain City* (1930), about a man dedicated to becoming a tycoon; *The Wet Parade* (1931), a fictive plea for prohibition of liquor; *American Outpost* (1932), an autobiography; *Upton Sinclair Presents William Fox* (1933), a study of finance in motion pictures; and *The Flivver King* (1937), a study of the automobile industry.

World's End (1940) is the first of a series of novels in which Lanny Budd, illegitimate son of a munitions manufacturer and a famous beauty, travels throughout the world, meets famous people, and is a figure in international intrigues and political maneuvers. That novel covers the years 1913–19; *Between Two Worlds* (1941) proceeds from the Versailles Treaty to the stock market crash of 1929; *Dragon's Teeth* (1942, Pulitzer Prize) covers 1930–34; *Wide Is the Gate* (1943) is concerned with anti-Nazi activities from the French Popular Front through part of the Spanish Civil War; *Presidential Agent* (1944) has Lanny become confidential agent of President Roosevelt, and carries the narrative to Munich in 1938; *Dragon Harvest* (1945) continues to the fall of Paris; *A World To Win* (1946) and *Presidential Mission* (1947) deal with events on the Continent, in North Africa, and the Orient, from 1940 to 1943; *One Clear Call* (1948) deals with the war to the time of Roosevelt's fourth term; *O Shepherd, Speak!* (1949) describes the war's end and Lanny's peace plans. *The Return of Lanny Budd* (1953), a sequel to the series of ten novels, warns against the dangers of Soviet Russia's policies.

Even in his eightieth year Sinclair published a novel, *It Happened to Didymus* (1958), about the modern reincarnation of an apostle. In *My Lifetime in Letters* (1960) he sampled the voluminous correspondence he received over the years, and he added to his memoirs with an *Autobiography* (1962). Sinclair's pseudonyms included Clarke Fitch, Frederick Garrison, and Arthur Stirling.

SINGER, ISAAC BASHEVIS (1904–91), Polish-born author of Yiddish fiction, descendant of rabbis, like his elder brother, Israel Joshua Singer,♦ turned from a rabbinical background to a career as a writer. In 1935 he followed his brother to New York City, where he became a journalist, writing in Yiddish for the *Jewish Daily Forward,* in which he has also published most of his fiction. His work deals mostly with the exotic heritage of Polish Jews, their traditional faith and folkways, their daily village life, their mysticism, their colorful personal relationships, their religious fanaticism, and their sexuality. His first major work, *Satan in Goray* (Yiddish, 1935; English, 1955) treats the aftermath of a 17th-century polish pogrom, when the remaining Jews turned to a messianic sect with mystic and erotic beliefs. The first of his books to appear in English (and all dates following refer to first publications in English) was *The Family Moskat* (1950), realistically presenting the degeneration of a Jewish family in Warsaw from the turn of the 20th century to World War II. This was followed by *The Magician of Lublin* (1960) and *The Slave* (1962), portrayals of diverse aspects of Jewish character in Poland. *The Manor* (1967) and *The Estate* (1969), its sequel, chronicle the lives of Polish Jews during the latter half of the 19th century. *Enemies* (1970) is his first novel set in the U.S., about a Polish Jew who, out of gratitude, marries the girl who helped him escape the Nazis after he believes his wife is dead, takes a mistress whom he bigamously weds when she becomes pregnant, and then discovers that his first wife has also escaped from Poland to New York. In *Shosha* (1978) Singer returned to treat the ghetto life of Poland before World War II. *The Penitent* (1983) is a lesser and a less compassionate novel. His last novel, *Scum* (1991), is also set in the prewar Polish-Jewish community of the *shtetl*. Two posthumously published novels, *The Certificate* (1992) and *Meshugah* (1994), were first published serially in the *Jewish Daily Forward.*

His stories are generally even more esteemed than his longer fiction, portraying more pungently the lives of curious characters in their ghetto settings in situations marked by fantasy and humor. His collections include *Gimpel the Fool* (1957), whose title tale was translated by Saul Bellow, about an innocent man gulled by his shrewish wife and all the world; *The Spinoza of Market Street* (1961); *Short Friday* (1964); *Zlateh the Goat* (1966); *The Séance* (1968); *A Friend of Kafka* (1970); *A Crown of Feathers* (1973); and *Passions* (1978). *Collected Stories* (1982) contains 47 of these tales. Later he wrote *The Death of Methuselah* (1985), inspired by Jewish folklore and legend.

Singer has also written books for children, including *When Shlemiel Went to Warsaw* (1968), folk tales, and *A Day of Pleasure* (1970), reminiscences of his own childhood. His memoirs include *In My Father's Court* (1966), an adult version of *A Day of Pleasure; A Little Boy in Search of God* (1976); *A Young Man in Search of Love* (1978); *Lost in America* (1981); and *Love and Exile* (1984). In 1978 he was awarded a Nobel Prize.

SINGER, ISRAEL JOSHUA (1893–1944), Polish-born Yiddish novelist, after a literary career in his homeland came to the U.S. (1934), sponsored by his American publisher, Abraham Cahan.♦ The next year he was followed by his brother Isaac Bashevis Singer.♦ In the U.S. he wrote *The Brothers Ashkenazi* (1936), a saga of Polish Jews; *In die Berg* (1942), a novel set in the U.S.; and *The Family Carnovsky* (1943), dealing with the wanderings in Europe of a Jewish family.

Single Hound, The, 146 brief poems by Emily Dickinson,♦ posthumously edited and published by her niece, Martha Dickinson Bianchi (1914). The selection consists largely of verses sent with flowers or messages to "Sister Sue," Emily's sister-in-law and next-door neighbor, Susan Gilbert Dickinson. Besides several poems expressing her warm feelings of friendship for her sister-in-law, there is a lyric on the death of Elizabeth Barrett Browning. The title of the volume is derived from the first poem:

> Adventure most unto itself
> The Soul condemned to be;
> Attended by a Single Hound—
> Its own Identity.

Many of the verses are metaphysical or religious meditations, concerned with ecstatic personal concepts of the Deity and natural phenomena. Others combine fantasy with a transcendental attitude toward Biblical subjects, birds, flowers, the seasons, and the constellations, all in her delicate, elliptical, metaphoric manner.

Single Tax, see *Progress and Poverty.*

SINGMASTER, ELSIE (1879–1958), author of novels about her Pennsylvania Dutch background, including *Katy Gaumer* (1914), *Basil Everman* (1920), *Keller's Anna Ruth* (1926), *A High Wind Rising* (1942), and the fictionalized biography *I Speak for Thaddeus Stevens* (1947).

Sinners in the Hands of an Angry God, sermon by Jonathan Edwards,♦ delivered in 1741 at Enfield, Mass., and published the same year. This fervid, imprecatory sermon was his most famous single contribution to the exposition of God's vindictive justice and man's natural corruption, and its vivid presentation had a strong effect in connection with the Great Awakening.

Sioux (or DAKOTA) **Indians,** confederation of tribes that occupied territory in the present states of Wisconsin, Minnesota, and the Dakotas, and smaller sections in Virginia and the Carolinas. The Siouan linguistic family was the most numerous among the Plains Indians, and included the Assiniboin, Mandan, Hidatsa, Crow, Omaha, Osage, and other tribes. The Sioux proper were friendly with the English, aiding them in the Revolution and the War of 1812. After several unsuccessful treaties, they rose under Little Crow (1862) and massacred more than 800 Minnesota settlers. In a subsequent revolt, when prospectors overran their Dakota reservation, the Sioux were led by such chiefs as Sitting Bull♦ and Crazy Horse♦ against Custer,♦ whose forces they annihilated. They were quelled in 1891. In Cooper's *The Prairie,* the Sioux figure as the "Ishmaelites of the American deserts," and they appear in Neihardt's *Song of the Indian Wars,* Garland's *The Captain of the Gray Horse Troop,* and Longfellow's *The Song of Hiawatha.* Nonfictional descriptions are to be found in Parkman's *The Oregon Trail,* W.J. Snelling's *Tales of the Northwest,* and Mari Sandoz's *Crazy Horse* and *These Were the Sioux.* Charles A. Eastman's works are concerned with the Sioux.

SIRINGO, CHARLES A. (1855–1928), Texas-born cowboy best known for his lusty, realistic autobiography *A Texas Cowboy, or Fifteen Years on the Hurricane Deck of a Spanish Pony* (1885), supplanted by *A Lone Star Cowboy* (1919). His work for the Pinkerton detective agency on cases ranging from cattle rustling to the Homestead strike led to his writing *A Cowboy Detective* (1912), and when the agency had it suppressed he issued *Two Evil Isms: Pinkertonism and Anarchism* (1915). Material from his previous books was reorganized as *Riata and Spurs* (1927).

Sister Carrie, novel by Dreiser.♦ The first edition was printed in 1900 but is said to have been withheld from circulation by the publisher because of its supposed immorality. It was reissued in 1907.

Carrie Meeber, penniless and "full of the illusions of ignorance and youth," leaves her rural home to seek work in Chicago, and becomes acquainted with Charles Drouet, a salesman who impresses her by his worldliness and affluence. In Chicago she lives with her sister and brother-in-law, and works for a time at jobs that pay little and oppress her imaginative spirit. After a period of unemployment and loneliness, she allows Drouet to establish her as his mistress, and finds temporary happiness with him. She becomes aware of his inferiority, however, and during his absences falls under the influence of his friend George Hurstwood, middle-aged, married, and comparatively intelligent and cultured, who is the manager of a celebrated bar. They finally elope, first to Montreal and then to New York, where he opens a saloon, and they live together for more than three years. Carrie grows in intellectual and emotional stature, while Hurstwood, away from the atmosphere of success on which his life has been based, steadily declines. When they are impoverished, their relations become strained, until Carrie goes on the stage and begins to support Hurstwood, rising from the chorus to minor acting parts. At last she deserts him, feeling that he is too great a burden, since he has not tried to obtain work except for a brief time as a strikebreaker during a trolley strike. Carrie becomes a star of musical comedies, but in spite of her success she is lonely and dissatisfied. Without her knowledge, Hurstwood sinks lower and lower, and after becoming a beggar, commits suicide.

SITTING BULL (1834?–90), Sioux chief who was on the warpath almost continually after 1866. When a punitive expedition was sent against his tribes, Sitting Bull was instrumental in annihilating the forces of Custer at the battle of Little Big Horn in Montana Territory (June 25, 1876). He later went to Canada, but came back on offer of pardon in 1881. He was a main attraction in both the U.S. and England with Buffalo Bill's Wild West Show in 1885. He was killed near Fort Yates, N.D., while trying to escape arrest. He appears as a central figure in Garland's *Book of the American Indian* (1923), and in Neihardt's *Song of the Indian Wars* (1925).

Six Nations, see *Iroquois Indians.*

1601, Conversation, As It Was by the Social Fireside, in the Time of the Tudors, sketch written by Clemens,♦ under his pseudonym Mark Twain, in 1876 and purporting to transcribe a ribald conversation of Queen Elizabeth, Raleigh, Bacon, Shakespeare, and others on the subjects of flatulency and sexual relations. First privately printed in 1880, the work has often been reprinted.

Sketch Book, The, familiar essays and tales by Irving,♦ written under the pseudonym Geoffrey Crayon, Gent., published serially in the U.S. (1819–20) and in book form in England (1820). Its genial humor and graceful style made it successful both in the U.S. and abroad, where American authors were not yet recognized. Most of the sketches concern his observations as an American visitor in England (e.g. "Westminster Abbey," "The Christmas Dinner," "Stratford-on-Avon," "John Bull," and "The Stage-Coach"), but six chapters deal with American scenes. Of these "Rip Van Winkle"♦ and "The Legend of Sleepy Hollow"♦ are adaptations of German folk tales to the New York backgrounds of Diedrich Knickerbocker; "English Writers of America" opposes the criticisms of the U.S. by British tourists; "Traits of Indian Character" is a romantic defense of the American tribes; "Philip of Pokanoket" is an account of King Philip; and "The Angler" is a whimsical self-exposure of the author as preferring to read Izaak Walton rather than pursue the art of angling in person.

Sketch Club, see *Bread and Cheese Club* and *Century Association.*

Skin of Our Teeth, The, comedy by Thornton Wilder,♦ produced and published in 1942, winning a Pulitzer Prize. The unconventional use of theatrical devices, such as asides and interruptions, increases the audience's feeling of participation.

George Antrobus, his wife, and his son and daughter represent humanity—the parents are Adam and Eve, and their son Henry is Cain—engaged in the struggle to survive. Their home in Excelsior, N.J., is threatened first by a creeping wall of ice, and later by a long war. Each time they barely escape annihilation, but George, inventor of the alphabet and the wheel, maintains the continuity of learning and culture. Lily

Sabina, their maid, the eternal Lilith, nearly succeeds in winning George away from his wife on the Atlantic City boardwalk during a convention of which George is elected president. Constructive attitudes prevail after the war, in which Henry is the enemy. Having reassembled his family, George feels the "most important thing of all: The desire to begin again to start building," and seeks his books to guide him in his struggle.

SKINNER, CONSTANCE LINDSAY (1879–1939), Canadian-born author, whose novels about the life of the Far North include *Builder of Men* (Germany, 1913), "*Good-Morning, Rosamond*" (1917, dramatized the same year), *The Search Relentless* (1925), and *Red Willows* (1929). For the Yale Chronicles of America she wrote *Pioneers of the Old Southwest* (1919) and *Adventurer of Oregon* (1920), and her other works include *Songs of the Coast Dwellers* (1930) and *Beaver, Kings and Cabins* (1933), a history of the American fur trade. In addition to writing children's books, she was the first editor of the Rivers of America series, an interpretation of American history in terms of its rivers.

SKINNER, CORNELIA OTIS (1901–79), long noted for her monologues and solo performances of such plays as *The Wives of Henry VIII* and her adaptation of Margaret Ayer Barnes's *Edna His Wife* (1937). She also wrote humorous autobiographical books, including *Tiny Garments* (1932) and *Soap Behind the Ears* (1941). With Emily Kimbrough she wrote *Our Hearts Were Young and Gay* (1942), about youthful adventures in Paris. *Family Circle* (1948) is autobiographical.

Skipper Ireson's Ride, ballad by Whittier♦ written in 1828, revised and published in the *Atlantic Monthly* (1857) and reprinted in *Home Ballads* (1860). It tells of the vengeance of women in the village of Marblehead, Mass., on "Old Floyd Ireson," because he deserted the wreck of a ship in Chaleur Bay, leaving rival local fishermen to drown. Whittier later learned that Ireson was innocent.

Slaughterhouse-Five; or The Children's Crusade. A Duty-Dance with Death, novel by Vonnegut,♦ published in 1969.

In telegraphic style and brief impressionistic scenes out of chronological sequence the work tells of the life and death of Billy Pilgrim, once an optometrist in Ilium, N.Y., later a "spastic in time" because he has been chosen by the inhabitants of Tralfamadore, a planet millions of light-years away, to inhabit their zoo. As a result he is freed from time and place, living in present, past, and future, now on earth, now in a distant galaxy. In the U.S. he comes to be considered crazy by everybody except a few eccentrics like the philanthropist Eliot Rosewater (of Vonnegut's novel

God Bless You, Mr. Rosewater) and the misanthropic science-fiction writer Kilgore Trout (also a figure in Vonnegut's other writings). In Germany, where he is held as a prisoner of war during World War II, he sees how mad most of humanity is. Forced to work in an underground slaughterhouse in Dresden, he becomes a witness of the terrible firebombing of the city that kills 135,000 people, the greatest single killing of human beings and a dreadful example of the tragic absurdity of mankind.

Slaves in Algiers, or a *Struggle for Freedom,* first and only surviving comic opera by Susanna Rowson,♦ produced and published in 1794. It is concerned with the barbarities practiced by Tripolitan pirates upon American citizens, prior to the Tripolitan War.

Sleepy Hollow, see *Sunnyside* and *Legend of Sleepy Hollow.*

SLOCUM, JOSHUA (1844–c.1910), Nova Scotia-born mariner who from 1895 to 1898 became the first man to achieve the feat described in his *Sailing Alone Around the World* (1900). Written in elegantly spare style, Slocum's account of his rebuilding *Spray* from the keel up in a Massachusetts meadow and sailing her on his epic voyage has been called "The *Walden* of the Sea." Other adventures of this naturalized American, told in his salty style, were collected in *The Voyages of Joshua Slocum* (1959). On a voyage to the Caribbean, he was lost at sea in the 37-foot boat he had once sailed around the world.

Slouching Towards Bethlehem, collection of essays by Joan Didion,♦ published in 1968. The title derives from a poem by Yeats that includes the line "Things fall apart; the center cannot hold." The pieces, reprinted from journals, fall into three groups: "Life Styles in the Golden Land," on California; ""Personals," about herself; and "Seven Places of the Mind," about places significant in her experiences.

Small Boy and Others, A, autobiographical narrative by Henry James,♦ published in 1913. Originally intending "to place together some particulars of the early life of William James and present him in his setting," the author found, he says, that "To knock at the door of the past was . . . to see it open to me quite wide—to see the world within begin to 'compose' . . . round the primary figure, see it people itself vividly and insistently." This account, consequently, is a richly detailed narrative, vivacious and revealing, of the boyhood experiences of the celebrated brothers, their family circle, and the cosmopolitan background that formed their minds, from the period of James's earliest recollections to the year 1859. The narrative is continued in *Notes of a Son and Brother*♦ (1914).

SMALLEY, GEORGE WASHBURN (1833–1916), journalist famous for his firsthand reports to the New York *Tribune* of the Civil War, the Austro-Prussian War, and the Franco-Prussian War. He was connected with the London *Times* (1895–1905), where he did much to further the cause of Anglo-American amity. His books include *London Letters* (1891), *Studies of Men* (1895), and *Anglo-American Memories* (2 vols., 1911, 1912).

Smart Set, The (1890–1930), monthly magazine founded by William D'Alton Mann as a journal for New York society, by whose members it was primarily written. Under the editorship of Arthur Grissom and C.H. Towne, it grew beyond its original plan to become a witty literary journal of material not compatible with the standards of larger magazines, and included among its contributions the first short story by O. Henry. In 1900 it was purchased by John A. Thayer, who attracted to it such authors as Gertrude Atherton, Richard Le Gallienne, Cabell, Mencken, and Nathan. Under the editorship of Willard Huntington Wright (1913–14), its primary purpose was "to provide lively entertainment for minds that are not primitive." Although the circulation was far greater than that of the average little magazine, its gaiety, vitality, and aesthetic credo were akin to the traits of this type of publication. Wright attracted new and stimulating American authors, and was also the first American editor to publish periodical contributions by such authors as George Moore, D.H. Lawrence, Joyce, D'Annunzio, and Ford Madox Ford. In 1914 Mencken and Nathan assumed joint editorship, and, although their policy was somewhat less stirring during the World War, after 1918 they continued Wright's vigorous policy, beginning such satirical departments as that of "Americana," which baited what they called the "booboisie." They also published the early writings of such authors as Eugene O'Neill, F. Scott Fitzgerald, J.W. Krutch, Waldo Frank, Lewis Mumford, Thomas Beer, and Julia Peterkin. When the magazine was purchased by Hearst (1924), new editors and a more conventional policy were introduced. Burton Rascoe and Groff Conklin edited *The Smart Set Anthology* (1934).

SMET, PIERRE JEAN DE (1801–73), Jesuit missionary. Father Smet came to the U.S. from Belgium in 1821 and after training in Maryland and Missouri, was ordained at the latter place in 1827. He was missionary to various tribes from 1838 on and was known among them as "Blackrobe." He wrote accounts of his ministry and mission-foundings in *Letters and Sketches, with a Narrative of a Year's Residence Among the Indian Tribes of the Rocky Mountains* (1843), *Oregon Missions and Travels over the Rocky Mountains* (1847), and *New Indian Sketches* (1863).

SMITH, BETTY [WEHNER] (1904–72), writer, whose novels about her native New York City are *A Tree Grows in Brooklyn* (1943), *Tomorrow Will Be Better* (1948), and *Maggie-Now* (1958), treating the lives of girls growing up in slums. *Joy in the Morning* (1964) is a novel about a very young couple beginning marriage. With George Abbott she made a musical drama (1951) of her first book.

SMITH, CHARD POWERS (1894–1977), New York-born author, who lived in New England, whose poetry includes *Along the Wind* (1925), *The Quest of Pan* (1930), *Hamilton: A Poetic Drama* (1930), and *Prelude to Man* (1935), an epic on evolution. *Artillery of Time* (1939) and *Ladies' Day* (1941) are novels depicting degradation in the U.S. during the second part of the 19th century. *Turn of the Dial* (1943) treats the corruption of radio advertising. *The Housatonic* (1946) is part of the Rivers of America series, and *Where the Light Falls* (1965) is a study of Edwin Arlington Robinson.

SMITH, CHARLES HENRY (1826–1903), Southern humorist known by his pseudonym Bill Arp, practiced law, and, loyal to the Confederacy, "joined the army and succeeded in killing about as many of them as they of me." His humorous writing was begun during the first year of the war, when he contributed to a newspaper of his native Georgia letters addressed to "Mr. Abe Linkhorn," signed "Bill Arp," which satirized the North by sympathizing with the Yankees in a deliberately inept manner. This device, used by D.R. Locke for the North, won Smith great popularity, causing him to devote most of the remainder of his life to writing. Although he retained the character of Bill Arp, he transformed him into a shrewd, cracker-barrel philosopher, and by 1866 dropped the device of comic misspelling to depend upon direct satire and homespun philosophy in his comments on woman suffrage, income tax, Reconstruction, rights for blacks, etc. Upon occasion he employed the dialect of the Georgia "cracker" and the Negro, in which he is supposed to have influenced Joel Chandler Harris. His works include *Bill Arp, So-Called* (1866), *Bill Arp's Letters* (1868), *Bill Arp's Peace Papers* (1873), *Bill Arp's Scrap Book* (1884), and *Bill Arp: From the Uncivil War to Date* (1903).

SMITH, DAVE [DAVID JEDDIE] (1942–), poet born in Portsmouth, Va., and educated at the University of Virginia. He served four years in the Air Force and then began an academic-based literary career. He founded a poetry magazine, *Back Door*, in 1969. His early collections of poems, *Mean Rufus Throw Down* (1973), *The Fisherman's Whore* (1974), and *Drunks* (1975), are all close to bedrock elemental experiences. *Goshawk, Antelope* (1970) placed Smith in the first line of

American poets. *Dream Flights* and *Onliness,* both 1981, reveal other talents, the latter being a novelistic allegory. *In the House of the Judge* (1983) explores connections between personal and formal history, as does *The Roundhouse Voices: Selected and New Poems* (1985). *Cuba Night* (1989) displays stylistic experimentation.

SMITH, ELIHU HUBBARD (1771–98), after graduation from Yale (1786) and medical education became a practicing physician in Connecticut, where he was a minor member of the Connecticut Wits,♦ contributing to *The Echo*♦ (1791–1805). Another literary project was the editing of *American Poems* (1793), the earliest anthology of American poetry, primarily devoted to the Wits. In 1794 he moved to New York, where he became prominent as a physician and as a member of literary society. He formed the Friendly Club, wrote a ballad opera, *Edwin and Angelina* (1796), and composed prefaces for *Alcuin* and *André,* by his friends Brown and Dunlap. Contracting yellow fever from a patient, he died at the age of 27.

SMITH, ELIZABETH OAKES (1806–93), wife of Seba Smith, was a popular novelist and contributor to literary magazines. Her novels include *The Western Captive* (1842), *Black Hollow* (1864), *Bald Eagle* (1867), and *The Sagamore of Saco* (1868), romantic tales of the frontier; *The Salamander: A Legend for Christmas* (1848), a story of the supernatural; *Bertha and Lily* (1854), a pious sentimental treatment of social, moral, and religious problems; and *The Newsboy* (1854), a sentimental story of life in the slums. Some of her works appeared under the pseudonym Ernest Helfenstein. *Woman and Her Needs* (1851) advocates woman suffrage. Her *Autobiography* was published in 1924.

SMITH, FRANCIS HOPKINSON (1838–1915), great-grandson of Francis Hopkinson, was born in Baltimore and became an engineer, with painting as an avocation. At the age of 50 he turned to literature, and his first books, *Well-Worn Roads of Spain, Holland, and Italy* (1887) and *A White Umbrella in Mexico* (1889), are charming travel sketches illustrated by his own drawings. He became widely known following the publication of *Colonel Carter of Cartersville*♦ (1891), a novelette in the local-color manner, portraying a Southern gentleman down on his luck. *Colonel Carter's Christmas* (1903) is a sequel. Smith's other fiction includes *A Day at Laguerre's and Other Days* (1892), stories set in places as widely varied as the Bronx and Constantinople; *Tom Grogan* (1896), a novel about an Irishwoman who fights unions and politicians to run her business as a contracting stevedore; *The Fortunes of Oliver Horn* (1902), a semi-autobiographical story of the life of a young painter in Baltimore and New York; *The Tides of Barnegat* (1906), a story of moral con-

trasts in a New Jersey family; and *Kennedy Square* (1911), concerned with social codes of the Old South. He also published books of charcoal sketches, such as *In Thackeray's London* (1913) and *In Dickens's London* (1914).

SMITH, JAMES (*c.*1737–*c.*1814), Pennsylvania frontiersman and Indian fighter whose *An Account of Remarkable Occurrences in the Life and Travels of Col. James Smith* (1799) is considered a primary source concerning pioneer life in the Ohio Valley. *A Treatise on the Mode and Manner of Indian War* (1812) is mainly drawn from his earlier work.

SMITH, JEDEDIAH STRONG (1798–1831), New York-born fur trader and explorer in the Far West, was a member of Ashley's expedition up the Missouri (1823) and led the party that established the South Pass route to the Green River Valley. Bridger, while employed by Smith, was the first white man to reach the Great Salt Lake. In 1826–27 Smith led a small exploring party from the Salt Lake, by way of the Colorado River and Santa Fe Trail, to southern California, and back across the Sierra Nevada. This was the first American crossing of the Sierra and the central overland route. He also led the first overland expedition from California to the Oregon country (1828). He was killed by Indians while guiding a party on the Santa Fe Trail. His knowledge was employed in maps and sketches by others, but his own journal was almost completely destroyed by a fire. H.C. Dale's *The Ashley-Smith Explorations* (1918) described his early career, and he is the central figure of Neihardt's novel *The Splendid Wayfaring* (1920).

SMITH, JOHN (1580–1631), English explorer and adventurer, left home at the age of about 16 to begin life as a soldier of fortune, in the Low Countries and elsewhere on the Continent. In 1602 he served with the Austrian forces against the Turks, on the Hungarian and Transylvanian border. The only sources of information for his life during these years are Smith's *The True Travels* and a lost Italian source mentioned by Purchas, so that his veracity has frequently been questioned. He claims to have distinguished himself in battles, and to have been granted a coat of arms (which has been authenticated), to have been enslaved and taken to Constantinople, and to have been presented as a gift to Tragabigzanda, the Turkish pasha's wife, who, falling in love with him, won him safety by sending him to her brother, the ruler of a country vaguely east of the Black Sea. Enslaved there, he escaped and passed through many exciting adventures before returning to England (*c.*1604).

Although only 26 when the Virginia Company received its patent, he energetically participated in the promotion and organization of the enterprise, and set sail with the early colonists, who disembarked at Jamestown (1607). Sealed orders, opened upon arrival in Virginia, gave him a post in the council, although he was not at first allowed to serve because of charges of mutiny on the voyage. He was active in exploration and in procuring food from the hostile Indians for the famished colony. On one of his expeditions, he was supposedly captured and condemned to death by the chief Powhatan, and dramatically rescued by the intercession of Pocahontas. ◆ This story, which Smith told in varying versions in different books, has sometimes been considered apocryphal. He returned to the colony (Jan. 1608) to find himself again faced with death, this time at the hands of his rivals on the council, who condemned him for having lost two of his men. He was rescued again, in dramatic fashion, when Christopher Newport arrived from England with supplies and settlers, on the eve of his execution. Restored to his place on the council, he continued his explorations, this time to Chesapeake Bay and the Potomac and Rappahannock rivers.

Despite continued friction among the councilors he was selected president because of his resourcefulness, bravery, and ability to deal with the Indians. During the winter of 1608–9, the colony again being faced by starvation, Smith divided it into three parts to search for food. During the summer, more colonists came, and with them letters from England criticizing his administration and treatment of the Indians, occasioning a demand by his enemies that he give up his office. In the midst of wrangling about authority, he was dangerously burned by a gunpowder explosion, and forced to leave for England (Oct. 1609), where the charges were dropped, though he was refused further employment by the Virginia Company.

Still interested in exploration, he was next employed by some London merchants to explore the region that he named New England, and to find gold mines and kill whales for them. Because he brought back fish and furs instead of fulfilling their fantastic desires, for which he showed contempt, he received only the empty title of Admiral of New England, and had to seek elsewhere for support of his plans for exploration and colonization. Under the patronage of Gorges, he made two unsuccessful attempts to reach New England, once being captured by pirates. He next tried to interest the Puritans in his guiding them to New England, but they loftily replied that, though his books and maps were valuable to them, he himself was not a desirable person.

He then settled in London to continue his writings on his own life and in furtherance of colonization in the New World. His books are *A True Relation of such occurrences and accidents of noate as hath hapned in Virginia since the first planting of that Collony* (1608), a pamphlet giving the earliest firsthand account of the settlement, but not mentioning his rescue by Pocahontas; *A Map of Vir-*

ginia with a Description of the Country (1612), continuing the account of his governorship; *A Description of New England: or the Observations and Discoveries of Captain John Smith . . .* (1616), a narrative of his later ventures in New England and unsuccessful voyages while in the employ of Gorges; *New Englands Trials* (1620), a pamphlet that has been called "essentially a plea for employment," and which was enlarged (1622) to give an account of the successes of the Pilgrims; *The Generall Historie of Virginia, New England, and the Summer Isles* (1624), a lengthy and more magniloquent reworking of his earlier writings, containing an extended account of the Pocahontas story; *An Accidence, or The Pathway to Experience Necessary for all Young Seamen* (1626), a pamphlet that was recast, probably by another hand, as *A Sea Grammar* (1627) and *The Seaman's Grammar* (1692); *The True Travels, Adventures, and Observations of Captaine John Smith in Europe, Asia, Africa, and America, from . . . 1593 to 1629 . . .* (1630), the autobiography that furnishes information about his early life; and *Advertisements for the Unexperienced Planters of New England, or Anywhere; or, The Pathway to Erect a Plantation* (1631), which, in the manner of a wise scholar counseling a young pupil, addresses advice to Winthrop and his Massachusetts settlers, and contains Smith's pathetic autobiographical poem "The Sea-Mark."

He often figures in historical fiction, including works by John Davis and John Esten Cooke, and as part of the romance and myth about Pocahontas. In *The Sot-Weed Factor*◆ John Barth concocts a bawdy secret journal ostensibly kept by John Smith. Among Smith's biographers is William Gilmore Simms.

SMITH, JOSEPH (1805–44), founder of the Church of Jesus Christ of Latter-Day Saints, commonly called Mormon, ◆ was born in Vermont and raised in Palmyra, N.Y., an area of ephemeral revivalist sects. He had virtually no formal education, but at the age of 14 he seems to have undergone the first of a series of visions that culminated in 1823 with the appearance of an angel, Moroni, and the discovery of a book written on golden plates. After the angel delivered them to Smith (1827), he moved to Pennsylvania and, with the aid of a magic device called Urim and Thummim, translated and published them as the *Book of Mormon* (1830). He founded his church in New York state that year and, aided by Sidney Rigdon, ◆ gained many followers. The leaders and their flock moved to Ohio and then Missouri (1831), but friction drove them to Nauvoo, Ill. (1839). There Smith ruled so autocratically that Rigdon and others seceded, also in part because of Smith's revelation (1843) sanctioning polygamy. He destroyed the press of a paper that opposed him, and while jailed for this act, a mob broke in and killed him and his brother Hyrum. This martyrdom stabilized the church, which, under the leadership of Brigham Young, moved to Utah (1847).

JOSEPH SMITH (1832–1914), his son, having failed to become president in 1852, founded the Reorganized Church of Jesus Christ of Latter-day Saints, which disavowed polygamy. Under his leadership this church grew to c.70,000 members. By 1990 it numbered more than 200,000 members.

SMITH, LILLIAN [EUGENIA] (1897–1966), Florida-born social worker in Georgia, whose treatment of Southern problems in novels appears in the love story of a mulatto girl in *Strange Fruit*♦ (1944), which she dramatized (1945), and *One Hour* (1960), about the response of a Southern town to the hysterical accusation of immorality that a young girl makes against an older man. Her nonfiction includes *Killers of the Dream* (1949, revised 1961); *The Journey* (1954); *Now Is the Time* (1955), on the need to implement the Supreme Court decision against school segregation; and *Our Faces, Our Words* (1964), another work on civil rights. *Memory of a Large Christmas* (1962) is a reminiscence.

SMITH, [LLOYD] LOGAN PEARSALL (1865–1946), New Jersey-born essayist reared in Philadelphia, educated at Haverford, Harvard, and Oxford, resided in England and on the Continent after 1888. His books of aphorisms and essays include *Trivia* (1902), *More Trivia* (1921), *Afterthoughts* (1931), the collection *All Trivia* (1933, revised 1945), and *Reperusals and Re-collections* (1936). He also published *The Youth of Parnassus* (1895), short stories; two slight collections of poetry, *Sonnets* (1908) and *Songs and Sonnets* (1909); various pamphlets on English vocabulary; *On Reading Shakespeare* (1933); a biography of Sir Henry Wotton (1907); and editions of authors as various as Donne and Santayana. *Milton and His Modern Critics* (1941) is a defense of Milton and an attack on T.S. Eliot and Ezra Pound. His autobiography, *Unforgotten Years* (1938), describes his Quaker boyhood, his acquaintance with Whitman, his activities as a bibliophile, and his experiences as an expatriate.

SMITH, MARGARET BAYARD (1778–1844), Washington society leader, author of the novels *A Winter in Washington* (1824) and *What Is Gentility?* (1828). Her best-known work, *The First Forty Years of Washington Society* (1906), is a posthumous collection of sprightly letters.

SMITH, RICHARD PENN (1799–1854), Philadelphia playwright, grandson of provost William Smith, was significant for introducing romantic tragedy in the U.S. and using foreign sources. Of his plays on American historical themes, *William Penn; or, The Elm Tree* (1829) and *The Triumph at Plattsburg*♦ (1830) were original, while *The Eighth of January*♦ (1829), although indebted to a

French melodrama, dramatized political feeling at the time of Jackson's election as President by celebrating his victory at the Battle of New Orleans. Most of his other plays were adaptations of foreign works; among those suggested by French models are *The Disowned* (1829), a melodrama; *The Sentinels; or, The Two Sergeants* (1829); *Is She a Brigand?* (1833), a farce comedy of mistaken identities; *The Daughter* (1836); and *The Actress of Padua*♦ (1836), based on a tragedy by Victor Hugo. *The Deformed*♦ (1830), a verse drama, a revision of his own play *The Divorce* (1825), owes a debt to both Dekker's *The Honest Whore* and Dunlap's *The Italian Father;* while *Caius Marius* (staged 1831, published 1968) is an original blank-verse romantic tragedy, produced by Forrest. He dramatized two novels by Cooper, *The Water Witch* (1830) and *The Bravo* (1837). His fiction includes *The Forsaken* (1831), a novel of the Revolution; *The Actress of Padua and Other Tales* (1836), containing a revision in narrative form of his play; and *Col. Crockett's Exploits and Adventures in Texas* (1836), which is generally considered to be Smith's work, although purporting to be by the frontiersman.

SMITH, SAMUEL (1720–76), Quaker public official of New Jersey, author of *The History of the Colony of Nova-Caesaria, or New Jersey . . . to the Year 1721* (1765), a patriotic but even-tempered study which, though it begins its general account with Columbus, places primary emphasis on the 17th century.

SMITH, SAMUEL FRANCIS (1808–95), Boston Baptist clergyman, who while a student at Andover Theological Seminary wrote the patriotic hymn "America"♦ (1831). His verses were collected in *Poems of Home and Country* (1895), and he was also the author of a book on mythology, travel sketches, and other prose.

SMITH, SAMUEL STANHOPE (1750–1819), Presbyterian clergyman and president of the College of New Jersey (1795–1819), distinguished not only for improving the standards of the institution, particularly in scientific training, but also for his pragmatic philosophy, which followed the school of John Witherspoon. His books include *Lectures on the Evidences of the Christian Religion* (1809) and *Lectures . . . on the Subjects of Moral and Political Philosophy* (2 vols., 1812). He also wrote a sequel to David Ramsay's *History of the United States* (1816–17).

SMITH, SEBA (1792–1868), born in Maine, graduated from Bowdoin (1818), founded the daily *Portland Courier* (1829), and achieved fame when he began to publish in his newspaper (1830) a series of letters from "Major Jack Downing," a Down East Yankee, whose comic rustic speech and homespun sagacity made him an outstanding character in the development of American humor. Although Smith created the character as a Yankee peddler, he soon had him turn his attention to local politics, and then, as the letters began to be printed in other newspapers and Downing began to capture the popular imagination, he made him into a confidant of Andrew Jackson, so that he might shrewdly satirize Jacksonian Democracy and matters of contemporary politics.

This use of his character and Smith's freedom from party politics made him the inaugurator of the American tradition of commenting on current events with great shrewdness cloaked under a guise of simplicity, and gave to the country a line of homespun political philosophers that has included Hosea Biglow, Mr. Dooley, and Will Rogers. In his own day, Smith found so many imitators, some of whom used Downing's own name, that Downing said he knew himself only by a scar on his left arm. The pirated edition of *Letters Written During the President's Tour, "Down East," by Myself, Major Jack Downing, of Downingville* (1833), which contained letters by Smith as well as by Charles A. Davis♦ and other imitators, caused Smith to print his own letters in *The Life and Writings of Major Jack Downing of Downingville* (1833), to which, however, he added some letters by "Uncle Josh Downing," written by J.L. Motley. The numerous imitations of the Downing letters also called forth many cartoons of the character, who was the prototype of Uncle Sam as a symbol of the U.S.

Smith continued to write for newspapers and collected his contributions in *John Smith's Letters with "Picters" To Match* (1839); *May-Day in New York* (1845), republished as *Jack Downing's Letters* (1845); *'Way Down East, or Portraitures of Yankee Life* (1854), a collection of local-color tales; and *My Thirty Years Out of the Senate* (1859), whose title was a satire of T.H. Benton's *Thirty Years' View of the American Government*. Smith also edited various magazines and wrote books which ranged from *Powhatan* (1841), a metrical romance, to *New Elements of Geometry* (1850). His wife was Elizabeth Oakes Smith.

SMITH, SOL[OMON FRANKLIN] (1801–69), editor, actor, theatrical manager, and lawyer of the old Southwest, whose books, *Sol Smith's Theatrical Apprenticeship* (1845) and *Theatrical Journey-Work* (1854), are important for their tall tales, which reveal the customs and characters of the region.

SMITH, SYDNEY (1771–1845), English clergyman and author, famous as a critic for the *Edinburgh Review* and creator of many *bons mots,* one of which made him notorious in America because he asked in a review of Seybert's *Annals of the United States* (*Edinburgh Review,* Jan. 1820): "In the four quarters of the globe, who reads an American book? or goes to an American play? or looks at an American picture or statue?" In a

speech (1831) Smith compared the opposition of the House of Lords to the progress of reform with the attempt of Dame Partington to brush away the Atlantic Ocean, and this suggested to B.P. Shillaber♦ his humorous character Mrs. Partington.

SMITH, THORNE (1892–1934), humorist whose first book, *Biltmore Oswald: The Diary of a Hapless Recruit* (1918), based on his experiences in the navy during World War I, was enormously popular at the time. With *Topper* (1926) he established the vein of ribald fantasy for which he is best known. This novel deals with two capricious ghosts, whose ectoplasmic reappearances and whimsically insane actions disturb the staid life of the inhibited banker Cosmo Topper. Later books in this manner include *Did She Fall?* (1930), *The Night Life of the Gods* (1931), *Turnabout* (1931), *The Bishop's Jaegers* (1932), *Topper Takes a Trip* (1932), and *Skin and Bones* (1933).

SMITH, WILLIAM (1727–1803), Scottish-born educator and Episcopal minister, came to America (1751), and, after outlining his theories of education in *A General Idea of the College of Mirania* (1753), was made provost of the College of Philadelphia (1755–79). He was prominent in politics as a supporter of the Crown and the Penn family, opposing the Quakers and such liberals as Franklin, and his opposition to the assembly occasioned a temporary imprisonment. To further his conservative beliefs, he edited *The American Magazine and Monthly Chronicle♦* (1752–58), and at the approach of the Revolution attacked Paine's *Common Sense* in a series of weekly letters to *The Pennsylvania Gazette,♦* written under the pseudonym Cato. These were answered by Paine in the *Pennsylvania Packet.* Although Smith opposed the Stamp Act as contrary to the rights of Englishmen, he was equally set against the independence of the colonies. His *Sermon on the Present Situation of American Affairs* (1775) created a sensation, and was considered by many to be a Loyalist document. The Assembly voided the charter of his college (1779), contending that the administration was hostile to the state government and opposed to equal privileges for all religious denominations. Smith then went to Maryland to found Washington College, of which he was president until the Pennsylvania college charter was restored (1789). He was again provost, until the college became the University of Pennsylvania (1791).

SMITH, WILLIAM (1728–93), born in New York, graduated from Yale (1745), became a lawyer, and with William Livingston prepared the first digest of New York statutes (1752) and *A Review of the Military Operations in North America . . . 1753–1756* (1757). He is best known for *The History of the Province of New York* (1757), which chronicles events to 1732, with primary emphasis on the 18th century. He was inclined to the Loyalist side, went to England (1783), and was later Chief Justice of Canada (1786–93).

SMITH, WILLIAM JAY (1918–   ), Louisiana-born poet whose education came from Washington University, St. Louis, a Rhodes Scholarship, and graduate study in Florence and whose later affiliations include service in the navy, membership in the Vermont House of Representatives, and teaching at Williams and at Hollins College. He is married to the poet Barbara Howes.♦ His poetry is as various as his career, as may be seen in *Poems* (1947); *Celebration at Dark* (1950), lyrics of diverse styles and moods; *The Tin Can* (1966), long poems and translations of Voznesensky; *Mr. Smith* (1968), light and nonsense verse for children; *Poems from Italy* (1972), translations; *Venice in the Fog* (1975); *The Telephone* (1978), a verse adaptation of a Russian children's story; and *The Traveler's Tree* (1980), new and selected poems. *The Spectra Hoax* (1961), dealing in part with the parodies of Witter Bynner♦ and A.D. Ficke, and *The Streaks of the Tulip* (1972) are critical works. *Army Brat* (1980) is a memoir of his youth.

SMITH, WINCHELL (1871–1933), actor, playwright, and director, whose most famous accomplishment as a producer was the introduction of the plays of Shaw to the U.S. (1904ff.). His own most successful play, written with Frank Bacon, was *Lightnin'* (1918), a character study of the ingratiating, inebriated liar "Lightnin' Bill Jones." This sentimental comedy had one of the longest continuous runs in American dramatic history. Smith's other plays include a dramatization of *Brewster's Millions*♦ (1906); *Turn to the Right* (1916), a farce; and *The Vinegar Tree* (1930), a comedy.

Smoke and Steel, free-verse poem by Sandburg,♦ the title piece of a volume published in 1920.

Smoke Bellew, novel by Jack London,♦ published in 1912.

Christopher Bellew, a San Francisco dilettante journalist, goes to the Klondike with his uncle, and there meets Joy Gastell, a spirited girl who scorns him as a tenderfoot. In his search for gold and his attempt to prove his worth to Joy, he undergoes a series of adventures that include riding a canoe across a dangerous rapids; discovering a lake; running races for claims, once losing in a friendly rivalry with Joy's father; rescuing starving natives; captivity by Indians; and rescue by the chief's daughter, who dies as she guides him back to Joy.

Snake Indians, name loosely applied to the Shoshone and related tribes. It is now used by scholars to refer to certain Oregon tribes. Beginning with the *Journals* of Lewis and Clark, the Snake Indians often figure in accounts of overland crossings.

SNELLING, WILLIAM JOSEPH (1804–48), Boston author and journalist, as a young man lived for a time among the Dakota Indians near the present St. Paul, Minn., thus gathering information for his charming and accurate *Tales of the Northwest; or, Sketches of Indian Life and Character* (1830). In his own day he was better known for *Truth: A New Year's Gift for Scribblers* (1831), a verse satire on contemporary poets. Attacks by literary and political figures who disliked his satire drove him to drink, for which he was sent to the House of Correction in Boston. He wrote of this in *The Rat-Trap; or, Cogitations of a Convict in the House of Correction* (1837). In the last year of his life, he edited the *Boston Herald,* continuing his zealous work for reforms.

SNIDER, DENTON JAQUES (1841–1925), teacher in St. Louis schools, was a follower of W.T. Harris♦ and the St. Louis school of Idealism, in propounding the philosophy of Hegel. His books include *Psychology and the Psychosis* (1890) and *The St. Louis Movement in Philosophy . . . with Chapters of Autobiography* (1920); as well as many other scholarly works, travel accounts, and poems.

SNODGRASS, W[ILLIAM] D[EWITT] (1926–   ), born in Pennsylvania, educated at the University of Iowa (B.A., 1949), where he also did graduate work, has taught English and speech at Syracuse and the University of Delaware (1979–   ). He is known for the fine craftsmanship and deep feeling of his first collection of poems, *Heart's Needle* (1959, Pulitzer Prize), whose title work about a father's love for a daughter he can see only infrequently, is perhaps autobiographical but has universality in its theme of separation. Later works, also marked by formal technique and personal revelation, include *After Experience* (1968), incorporating translations of Rilke; *Gallows Songs of Christian Morgenstern* (1967); *The Führer Bunker* (1977), poems on the end of the Third Reich in the voices of major Nazis; *Selected Poems 1957–1987* (1987); and *Remains* (1985), seven poems originally printed in another limited edition in 1970. *Six Troubadour Songs* (1977) prints translations. *Each in His Season* (1994) is a book of new poems organized in four parts, using both free and formal verse and ranging widely in subjects and themes: for example, "In Memory of Lost Brain Cells" and "The Ballad of Jesse Helms," the latter a rancorous satire in 16 stanzas. "The Drunken Minstrel Rags His Bluegrass Lute" parodies Stevens's "Man with a Blue Guitar." *In Radical Pursuit* (1975) collects essays and lectures on poetry.

Snopes family, characters in Faulkner's fiction, figuring most prominently in the trilogy, *The Hamlet,*♦ *The Town,*♦ and *The Mansion,*♦ but appearing also in *The Unvanquished, Sartoris,* and *As I Lay Dying.* Their origins obscure, they are "just Snopeses, like colonies of rats or termites are just rats and termites." They emerge from the Yoknapatawpha country, entrench themselves in Frenchman's Bend and later in the county seat, Jefferson, and finally replace, largely in the person of Flem Snopes, the old order as represented by the Sartoris◆ and Compson◆ families. Abner (Ab) Snopes, who settles as a sharecropper on Will Varner's land in Frenchman's Bend in the 1890s, a bitter man with a reputation for sharp horse trading and barn burning, is the most successful family member of his generation. His son Flem continues his father's rapacity and corruption, surpassing his cousins: Mink, who is imprisoned for murder; Ike, an idiot who falls in love with a cow; Wesley, tarred and feathered for his relations with a young girl; I.O., a bigamist; Launcelot (Lump), who sells tickets to view Ike's perverted relations with the cow; and Eckrum (Eck), atypically honest, but who blows himself to bits in an explosion. Flem is also more successful in his rapacious progress toward power and seeming respectability than is the next generation, which includes Wesley's son Byron, who absconds with a little money from a bank, marries an Apache squaw, and "mails" their four children back to Flem; I.O.'s sons, including Montgomery Ward, who makes money from pornographic pictures and bootlegging, the twins Bilbo and Vardaman, and Clarence, a venal state senator; and Eckrum's sons, Admiral Dewey and Wallstreet Panic, the latter as honest and therefore as unlike a Snopes as his father. Although Flem succeeds beyond any other Snopes, becoming president of the Sartoris bank, the owner of the De Spain mansion, and the possessor of wealth, it is Linda, his wife's daughter by another man, a Snopes in name only, who brings him down to death. In revenge for his treatment of her, which included obtaining her inheritance and driving her mother, Eula Varner Snopes, to suicide, Linda persuades Gavin Stevens to obtain a pardon for Mink. Suffering from the hardships of 38 years in prison, attributing his long sentence to Flem's initial failure to help him, and knowing that it was extended by a plot which Flem engineered, Mink comes to Flem's home and shoots him dead.

SNOW, [CHARLES] WILBERT (1884–1977), Maine poet, after graduation from Bowdoin (1907) studied at Columbia, and later taught at several colleges. His simple and direct poems of life in his native state have been published in *Maine Coast* (1923), *The Inner Harbor* (1926), *Down East* (1932), *Before the Wind* (1938), *Maine Tides* (1940), *Sonnets to Steve* (1957), and *Collected Poems* (1963). *Codline's Child* (1974) is an autobiography, mainly about poetry.

Snow-Bound: *A Winter Idyl*, poem by Whittier,◆ published in 1866. It is mainly in iambic tetrameter couplets, although the verse is sometimes varied by alternating rhymes.

The poet recalls the years of his boyhood, when a sudden snowstorm would transform his Quaker father's Massachusetts farm and its usual routine into an enchanted white realm of adventure. The family gathered during the evening before the fireplace, where his father told of his early experiences in the Canadian woods and the New England farms and fisheries, and his mother read from Quaker religious books, or described family adventures during Indian raids. An uncle, "innocent of books," offered tales of hunting and fishing, and an aunt shared memories of her girlhood, while other participants in the quiet festivities were the poet's brother and sisters, the merry schoolmaster, and a guest, the religious enthusiast Harriet Livermore. Later, after all retired, they lay awake listening to the unaccustomed sounds of the storm. In the morning, the snow-blanketed world outside appeared quiet and strange, but soon there was a bustle of visits and domestic activity, although the little community might remain isolated for weeks. After the poet has given these minute Flemish pictures of his own childhood, he realizes that the "Angel of the backward look" must clasp the book of the past, and recognizes that he must attend to the duties of later years. Yet haply, as life slopes down to death, he may pause in some lull of life, realize "the grateful sense of sweetness near," stretch forth the hands of memory "and, pausing, take with forehead bare the benediction of the air."

Snow-Image, *The, and Other Twice-Told Tales,* 17 short stories by Hawthorne,◆ published in 1851. The volume includes historical sketches, tales of the supernatural, and such allegorical stories as "Ethan Brand,"◆ "My Kinsman, Major Molyneux,"◆ and "The Great Stone Face."◆

"The Snow-Image: A Childish Miracle" is an allegory in which Peony and Violet Lindsey, gay, fanciful children, build an image of snow, encouraged by their mother, who tells them it will be their snow-sister and playfellow. In their enthusiasm they are hardly surprised when the image comes to life as a beautiful child in a flimsy white dress, who plays with them in the garden. When the children's father, a matter-of-fact merchant, comes home, he disregards their remonstrances and takes the snow-child into the house, intending to clothe her, feed her, and take her to her own home. But the child vanishes, and only a pool of water remains before the stove. The author concludes that "should some phenomenon of nature or providence transcend" the system of men of Lindsey's stamp, "they will not recognize it, even if it come to pass under their very noses. What has been established as an element of good to one being may prove absolute mischief to another."

Snow White, novel by Donald Barthelme.◆

Snowden's Ladies' Companion, see *Ladies' Companion.*

Snows of Kilimanjaro, The, story by Heming-way,♦ published in *Esquire* (Aug. 1936) and col-lected in *The Fifth Column and the First Forty-Nine Stories* (1938).

Dying with "a great tiredness and anger" of blood poisoning from his gangrenous leg, the novelist Harry lies in camp on his African safari, accompanied by his wife and native attendants, waiting for a rescue plane that he knows will arrive too late, and remembers experiences that were to have served as subjects of stories when he knew enough to write them well. But he realizes too that he has destroyed his talent by sloth, by enjoyments such as the marriage with his rich wife could bring, and that he hates himself as he vents his cruelty on her. As he knows he will die that night, he tries to write, but vividly he feels and sees and smells death as he drops off, dream-ing that the plane has come and taken him not to a hospital but to the very top of Kilimanjaro, said to be the highest mountain in Africa, where, ac-cording to the story's epigraph, close to the sum-mit that is called the House of God "there is the dried and frozen carcass of a leopard. No one has explained what the leopard was seeking at that altitude."

SNYDER, Gary [Sherman] (1930–   ), San Francisco-born poet, reared on a Washington farm and in Portland, after graduation from Reed College, work in the Forest Service, and study of Oriental languages at the University of Califor-nia, Berkeley, participated in the local poetic re-naissance that featured the Beat movement.♦ He was later a tanker seaman and lived in Japan to take formal Zen training until he settled on a northern California farm. He has said, "I hold the most archaic values . . . the fertility of the soul, the magic of animals, the power-vision in soli-tude, . . . the common work of the tribe" in his sacramental view of man's relation to the uni-verse. His poems appear in *Riprap* (1959), based on his experiences in the woods and at sea; *Myths and Texts* (1960), a series unified by the themes of the failure of Western culture and the contrasting values of Buddhism and American Indian primi-tivism (enlarged in 1965 with "Cold Mountain Poems," translations from the Chinese); *Six Sec-tions from Mountains and Rivers Without End* (1965, expanded 1970), part of an ongoing long work treating journeys, literal and metaphoric; *A Range of Poems* (1966), a selection of previous publica-tions with additions; *The Back Country* (1968), on early experiences in the Far West, Japan, and In-dia and his return to the U.S.; *Regarding Wave* (1970), poems both philosophic in his dedication to Buddhism and personal in telling of his love for his Japanese wife; *Manzanita* (1972), a limited edition forming part of *Turtle Island* (1974, Pu-litzer Prize), poetry and prose setting forth his views of humanity, nature, and religion; and *Left Out in the Rain* (1986), containing brief poems often in quite conventional forms written since

1947. *No Nature, New and Selected Poems* (1992) is a sampling of his life's work. *Earth House Hold* (1969) collects essays and journal jottings on po-etry, primitivism, communal life, and ecology, and *The Old Ways* (1977) is a small, lesser collec-tion of essays. Snyder figures as Japhy Ryder in Kerouac's *The Dharma Bums.* Since 1985 he has taught at the University of California, Davis.

Society and Solitude, essays by Emerson,♦ based on lectures delivered as early as 1858, revised and published in 1870. The subjects are "Society and Solitude," "Civilization," "Art," "Eloquence," "Domestic Life," "Farming," "Works and Days," "Books," "Clubs," "Courage," "Success," and "Old Age."

The title piece is concerned with the individu-al's problem of social conduct. For those who have originality and a sense of personal integrity, the necessity for solitude is deeply felt and "or-ganic." Constant social friction is wearing and difficult, and one naturally seeks to be alone. "But this banishment to the rocks and echoes . . . is so against nature, such a half-view, that it must be corrected by a common sense and experi-ence." A man can live significantly only through contact with his fellows; sympathy and coopera-tion]make possible the advancement of common causes; "the benefits of affection are immense"; and, moreover, "society cannot do without culti-vated men." On the other hand, "the people are to be taken in very small doses." Overmuch company is degrading, since "men cannot afford to live together on their merits, and they adjust themselves by their demerits." The remedy is to strike a balance between social and solitary ways of living, "and a sound mind will derive its prin-ciples from insight, with ever a purer ascent to the sufficient and absolute right, and will accept society as the natural element in which they are to be applied."

Society for the Propagation of the Gospel in Foreign Parts, London organization of Puritans (1649–61, reorganized 1662), best known for its distribution to the Massachuset Indians of John Eliot's tracts, and for the work of Thomas and Experience Mayhew. An Anglican organization of the same name was founded in 1701 to foster the Church of England in the American colonies through missionary work and the distribution of tracts. It quit missionary work in the U.S. in 1785.

Society in America, see *Martineau, Harriet.*

Society, Manners, and Politics in the United States, English translation (1839) of the French work (1834) by Michel Chevalier (1806–79), a young Saint-Simonian commissioned by the states-man Thiers to inspect U.S. public works. His book, the result of a two-year observation of the social, political, and economic machinery of the

U.S., is an acute and impersonal survey of U.S. democracy, industrial conditions, Jacksonian politics, preoccupation with business, influence of the frontier, ending with a speculation on the country's future.

Society of Friends, see *Quakers.*

Society of Gentlemen, see *American Magazine and Monthly Chronicle.*

Soldiers of Fortune, novel by R.H. Davis, ♦ published in 1897 and dramatized in 1902 with the aid of Augustus Thomas.

Soldiers' Pay, novel by Faulkner, ♦ published in 1926.

Lieutenant Donald Mahon, an American in the British air force during World War I, is discharged from the hospital where he has been treated for a critical head wound, and makes his way home to Georgia. The wound leaves a horrible scar, and causes loss of memory and later blindness. On the train from New York he is aided by Joe Gilligan, an awkward, friendly, footloose ex-soldier, and Margaret Powers, an attractive young widow whose husband was killed in the war. Margaret, strangely attracted to the dying, subhuman Donald, decides to go home with him, as does Gilligan, who is in love with her. Their reception in the Georgia town reveals the character of the fickle people: Donald's father, an Episcopal minister whose optimism and idealism prevent his recognition of his son's tragedy, until the accumulation of ugly facts destroys his faith; Donald's pathetic, homely cousin, Emmy, whom he had loved; his fiancée, Cecily Saunders, a selfish girl now in love with another man but afraid of her conventional parents and public opinion; and George Farr, Cecily's lover, who considers nothing but his own desire. Sentiment in town soon turns against Donald because of his fearful appearance and his suspected liaison with Margaret, who remains to nurse him. As months pass, Cecily elopes with George, and Gilligan good-naturedly stays on, despite Margaret's rejection of his proposals and her eventual marriage to Donald. The suffering aviator finally dies, and Margaret leaves, once more refusing Gilligan, who remains for a time with the elder Mahon. The latter is a changed man as the result of his ordeal: "Who knows; perhaps when we die we may not be required to go anywhere nor do anything at all. That would be heaven."

Soliloquies in England, and Later Soliloquies, brief, familiar essays by Santayana, ♦ published in 1922. The author spent the years of World War I in England, and though events "extorted" "desperate verses" from him, three of which are included in this book, he devoted himself while at Oxford and Cambridge to composing these autobiographical and philosophical meditations, whose subjects are as widely varied as "The English Church," "Death-Bed Manners," "Seafaring," "Dons," "Apology for Snobs," and "On My Friendly Critics." The English background is everywhere implicit in his attitude, and, he states, "What I love in Greece and in England is contentment in finitude, fair outward ways, manly perfection and simplicity." The second half of the book contains postwar essays written mainly on the Continent, dealing more generally with ethical, political and esthetic problems, but preserving the author's familiar manner, firm wit, and sonorous, richly textured prose.

SONDHEIM, STEPHEN [JOSHUA] (1930–), grew up in Pennsylvania a neighbor of Oscar Hammerstein II, who gave him serious early encouragement and criticism in lyricizing. Not long after graduation from Williams College (1950) he began his career as a significant lyricist and composer for the musical theater. He wrote the lyrics for Bernstein's *West Side Story* (1957). Works with both words and music by Sondheim include *A Funny Thing Happened on the Way to the Forum* (1962); *Company* (1970); *Follies* (1971); *A Little Night Music* (1973); *Sweeney Todd* (1979); *Sunday in the Park with George* (1984), with James Lapine, which won a Pulitzer Prize for drama; *Into the Woods* (1987); and *Passion* (1994).

Son of Royal Langbrith, The, novel by Howells, ♦ published in 1904.

Dr. Anther courts Mrs. Royal Langbrith, widow of a New England paper manufacturer who had the reputation of a social benefactor, although he was actually a scoundrel. James Langbrith is violently opposed to the match between his mother and the doctor, and Dr. Anther is only dissuaded from revealing the dead man's true character by the hope that the son will withdraw his objections to the marriage. Further to ensure that end, the doctor uses his medical skill to help cure the father of Hope Hawken, the girl loved by James. Paradoxically, Hope, who had been cool to James because his father had exploited her father, is then reconciled to him in gratitude for Dr. Anther's aid, and Hope marries the son of Royal Langbrith. As a further irony, Dr. Anther dies before he can marry Mrs. Langbrith.

Son of the Middle Border, A, autobiographical narrative by Hamlin Garland, ♦ published serially in *Collier's* (1914) and in book form in 1917.

Beginning with the western emigration of the Garland and McClintock families in the years following the Civil War, the author tells the story of his family background and his own youthful adventures among the pioneer farmers of South Dakota, his trip to Boston, and the period in which he struggled to establish himself as an author. The narrative, brought in this book to his thirty-third year, is continued in a later series: *A Daughter of the Middle Border* (1921), *Trail-Makers* of the *Middle Border* (1926), and *Back-Trailers from the Middle Border* (1928).

Son of the Wolf, *The,* nine short stories by Jack London,♦ published in 1900. These tales of white men in the Klondike and Yukon have their tone set in the title story, in which the daughter of an Indian chief is captured by her white lover, Scruff Mackenzie, despite the racial antipathy of her native suitors.

Song of Hiawatha, *The,* see *Hiawatha, The Song of.*

Song of Marion's Men, *The,* ballad by Bryant,♦ published in 1831. It celebrates the Revolutionary exploits of the frontier troops led by Francis Marion.

Song of Myself, poem by Whitman,♦ the untitled introduction to the first edition of *Leaves of Grass* (1855), later called "A Poem of Walt Whitman, An American" and "Walt Whitman," and given its present title in 1881.

Declaring "I celebrate myself . . . Walt Whitman, a kosmos," the poet sets forth two principal beliefs: the first, a theory of universality ("of every hue and caste am I, of every rank and religion"), is illustrated by lengthy catalogues of people and things; the second is that all things are equal in value ("I am the poet of the Body and . . . of the Soul . . . not the poet of goodness only, . . . of wickedness also. . . . I believe a leaf of grass is no less than the journey-work of the stars."). This equalitarian doctrine is based both on the theory of evolution and on a pantheistic belief; at one time Whitman is a mystic, and at another he proclaims, "Hurrah for positive science!," while yet admitting that facts serve only to give entrance to "an area of my dwelling." This inconsistency, however, he confesses and accepts: "Do I contradict myself? Very well then, I contradict myself; (I am large, I contain multitudes.)" and at the end he reiterates his mystical pantheism ("I bequeath myself to the dirt, to grow from the grass I love, If you want me again look for me under your boot-soles . . .").

Song of the Broad-Axe, poem by Whitman,♦ published in *Leaves of Grass* (1856) as "Broad-Axe Poem," and given its present title in 1867.

The "weapon, shapely, naked, wan," is traced from the extraction of the rough ore from the earth to its shaping for the utilitarian purposes to which it has been put in different periods of history. The use of the axe by American pioneers, firemen, shipbuilders, carpenters, and butchers is contrasted with its use in foreign countries at earlier periods by sacrificial priests, warriors, and executioners. Thus it becomes symbolic of the freedom of democracy, contrasted with the restrictions of autocratic rule.

Song of the Chattahoochee, *The,* poem by Lanier,♦ published in 1883 and reprinted in *Poems*

(1884). Mainly in iambics, with a variation of meters to produce musical sounds, the poem is an onomatopoetic expression of the river's flow "to be mixed with the main," obeying "the voices of Duty" to turn the mills and water the fields during its course.

Song of the Indian Wars, *The,* narrative poem in heroic couplets by J.G. Neihardt,♦ published in 1925. Set in the decade following the Civil War, it "deals with the last great fight for the bison pastures of the Plains between the westering white men and the prairie tribes," and forms the third part of the author's "Epic Cycle of the West."

Song of the Lark, *The,* novel by Willa Cather,♦ published in 1915.

Thea Kronborg, daughter of a Swedish minister in Colorado, during her growth to adolescence develops an obsessive interest in music. Her ability on the piano is encouraged by her eccentric German music teacher, Professor Wunsch, and by Dr. Howard Archie, a kindly, educated physician whose unfortunate marriage taints his life. Set apart from the townspeople by her talents and ardent nature, she prefers such friends as "Spanish Johnny" Tellamantez and the railroad worker Ray Kennedy, who falls in love with her but dies in a train wreck, leaving her his insurance. With this sum she goes to Chicago, at 17, to study with the pianist Andor Harsanyi, who finds in her the same innate taste and artistic integrity that mark his own character. When he discovers that she is earning her way by singing in a church choir, he listens to her voice, and finds it has great possibilities. He sends her to study voice with Madison Bowers, whose chill, selfish attitude repels her, but through him she meets the wealthy young brewer Fred Ottenburg, who introduces her to such socially prominent friends and art patrons as the Nathanmeyers. After she becomes ill and discouraged, despite her progress, Ottenburg invites her to his father's Arizona ranch. They fall in love, and travel together in Mexico, but separate because Fred, already married, is unable to obtain a divorce. Dr. Archie advances her the money necessary for study in Europe, and after ten years she becomes a great Wagnerian soprano of the Metropolitan Opera. Although she later marries Ottenburg after his wife's death, her life is expressed and bound up in her career, in which she finds not happiness but the fulfillment of the driving artistic impulse that has always ruled her.

Songs for the Nursery; *or, Mother Goose's Melodies,* nursery rhymes said to have been first printed at Boston (1719) by Thomas Fleet, from verses known by his mother-in-law, Mrs. Elizabeth Goose or Vergoose. This claim, advanced in 1860 and apparently unfounded, is denied by later bibliographers, who generally agree that the collection was first published at London (1760), from English and French sources including Perrault's *Contes de ma mère l'oye* (1697).

Songs from Vagabondia, poems by Bliss Carman♦ and Richard Hovey.♦

Songs of Labor, group of six poems and a dedication by Whittier,♦ forming the title section of a volume published in 1850. The poems, in various meters, celebrate the dignity and delights of labor for "The Shoemakers," "The Fishermen," "The Lumbermen," "The Ship-Builders," "The Drovers," and "The Huskers."

Songs of the Sierras, poems by Joaquin Miller.♦

SONTAG, SUSAN (1933–), best known for her essays collected in *Against Interpretation* (1966), arguing that the proper response to creative works is sensory or emotive, not intellectual; *Trip to Hanoi* (1968), about her view of North Vietnam during the U.S. war against it; *Styles of Radical Will* (1969), on different ways of changing consciousness, as through drugs, for aesthetic purposes; *On Photography* (1977), about the social and cultural roles of photography; *Illness as Metaphor* (1978), concerning psychological relations to physical ailments; *Under the Sign of Saturn* (1980); and *AIDS and Its Metaphors* (1988). She has also written novels, *The Benefactor* (1963) and *Death Kit* (1967), and stories, *I, etcetera* (1978). In 1992 appeared *The Volcano Lover, a Romance*. It is set in Naples and based on historical persons: Emma Hamilton, Sir William Hamilton, and Lord Nelson. She published a closet drama, *Alice in Bed, a Play* (1993), in which she fuses Alice James,♦ the troubled sister of William and Henry, with Lewis Carroll's Alice. There is a mad tea party scene which includes among others the ghosts of Emily Dickinson♦ and Margaret Fuller.♦

Sophie's Choice, novel by William Styron,♦ published in 1979.

Narrated by the author's autobiographical persona, Stingo, a young would-be novelist from Tidewater Virginia, it tells of his experiences in New York City, where he was first a publisher's reader, then a resident of the Bronx, able to be jobless and to concentrate on the creation of his first novel thanks to a small legacy of money deriving directly from the sale, generations before, of a family slave. In his boardinghouse Stingo becomes the devoted friend of Nathan Landau, a slightly older, brilliant but drug-deranged manic-depressive Jewish intellectual, and his beloved Sophie Zawistowska, an émigré Polish Catholic beauty, with whom he has a tortured relationship marked by frenzied sex. The account of her frightful experiences during World War II as told to Stingo make him recognize "a sinister zone of likeness between Poland

and the American South," thus creating another dimension for the novel and its narrator. Her father, a professor of law, and her husband had been killed by the Nazis, and she and her children had been imprisoned in the concentration death camp of Auschwitz. From it she had escaped, first by becoming the secretary of its commandant, Rudolf Höss, then by appealing to him by diverse means, including a pamphlet written years before by her anti-Semitic father. Although thus saved from death, she suffers her own perdition in the years of life left to her.

SORENSEN, VIRGINIA (1912–), Utah-born novelist, many of whose works, including *A Little Lower Than the Angels* (1942), *On This Star* (1946), *The Evening and the Morning* (1949), *Many Heavens* (1954), and *Kingdom Come* (1960), deal sympathetically and knowingly with Mormon life. *The Man with the Key* (1974) is a novel with a different subject: a love affair between an older white woman and a black handy man. She has also written books for children and *Where Nothing Is Long Ago* (1963), recollections of her childhood as a Mormon.

SORRENTINO, GILBERT (1929–), Brooklyn-born poet and experimental novelist. His first novel, *The Sky Changes* (1966), is a parody telling of an unhappily married couple driving across the U.S. on a "second honeymoon" that ends when she leaves him. It was followed by *Steelwork* (1970), depicting Brooklyn from the 1930s through World War II; *Imaginary Qualities of Actual Things* (1971), like its predecessor a work of fiction without plot, but a bitter satire on New York literati; *Mulligan Stew* (1979), a comic novel about a novelist; *Flawless Play Restored* (1975), a segment in the form of a drama from the novel *Aberration of Starlight* (1980), a quasi-autobiographical story of life in a New Jersey boardinghouse, seen from four points of view; *Crystal Vision* (1981), an early but previously unpublished comic novel; and a trilogy of novels, *Odd Number* (1985), *Rose Theatre* (1987), and *Misterioso* (1989). *The Darkness Surrounds Us* (1960), *Black and White* (1964), *The Perfect Fiction* (1968), *Corrosive Sublimate* (1971), and *The Orangery* (1978) collect poems that belong to the school of Pound, Williams, and Creeley. *Splendide-Hotel* (1973) is a novella-like essay about the role of the poet. His *Selected Poems* appeared in 1981. His essays and reviews are collected in *Something Said* (1984). He edited the little magazine *Neon* (1956–60), featuring Beat authors. He became a faculty member at Stanford in 1982.

Sot-Weed Factor, The, Hudibrastic satirical poem by Ebenezer Cook,♦ published at London (1708). It is ostensibly the record of an Englishman's visit to Maryland, although it is now considered to be by an American. The subtitle amply indicates the contents: "A Voyage to Maryland,

A Satyr. In which Is Described, The Laws, Government, Courts, and Constitutions of the Country; and also the Buildings, Feasts, Frolics, Entertainments and Drunken Humours of the Inhabitants of that Part of America. In Burlesque Verse." *Sot-Weed Redivivus: or The Planter's Looking-Glass . . . by E.C., Gent.* (1730) has been attributed to the same author.

Sot-Weed Factor, The, novel by John Barth♦; published in 1960 and in a revised version in 1966.

In a lusty picaresque tale that satirizes conventional historical fiction, the novel creates a fictive biography of the real Ebenezer Cook,♦ endowing him with a twin sister, Anna. After failing in his studies at Cambridge, though abetted by a tutor, Henry Burlingame, Ebenezer is ordered by his father to manage the family tobacco plantation in Maryland. There he spends most of his time writing poetry and protecting his virginity, both of which are under constant assault. Finally he achieves fame as a writer while simultaneously losing his poetic inspiration and his virginity.

SOTO, GARY (1952–   ), Californian who is an important representative of his Chicano heritage as a faculty instructor of English and Chicano Studies at the University of California, Berkeley (1980–   ), and as an active poet, whose works include *The Elements of San Joaquin* (1977), *Black Hair* (1985), and *Who Will Know Us?* (1990), as well as *Lesser Evils* (1988), relevant prose essays; *A Summer Life* (1990), about his growing up; and *Baseball in April* (1990), stories for young Chicanos.

Souls of Black Folk, The, collection of essays and sketches by W.E.B. DuBois, published in 1903. The 15 pieces in the book include sociological studies of sharecroppers and small farmers, sensitive interpretation of music related to black religious services, a historical study of the Freedmen's Bureau, and a searching consideration of Booker T. Washington, praising some of his activities but going beyond him in calling for higher education for blacks and for more militant action.

Sound and the Fury, The, novel by Faulkner,♦ published in 1929. The story is told in four parts, through the stream of consciousness of three characters (the sons of the Compson family,♦ Benjy, Quentin, and Jason), and finally in an objective account.

The Compson family, formerly genteel Southern patricians, now lead a degenerate, perverted life on their shrunken plantation near Jefferson, Miss. The disintegration of the family, which clings to outworn aristocratic conventions, is counterpointed by the strength of the black servants, who include old Dilsey and her son Luster. The latter tends the idiot Benjy Compson, who is

33 and incapable of speech or any but the simplest actions. Through his broken thoughts, which revert to his childhood at every chance stimulation of his acute senses, is disclosed the tragedy of his drunken father; his proud, sniveling, hypochondriac mother; his weak-minded Uncle Maury; his sister Candace (Caddy), whom he adores because she is kind to him; his mean, dishonest brother Jason; and his sensitive brother Quentin, a promising student at Harvard, who goes mad, obsessed by love of Caddy, and, shamed by her seduction, commits suicide. When Caddy is forced to marry and leave home, Benjy is desolate, but he plays like a child with her illegitimate daughter, until she grows up, gives evidence of her mother's nymphomaniac strain, runs away with a tent-show performer, and steals a sum of money from Jason.

South, THE, region including the present states of Maryland, Virginia, North Carolina, South Carolina, Georgia, Kentucky, Tennessee, Louisiana, Mississippi, Alabama, Missouri, Arkansas, Florida, West Virginia, eastern Texas, and formerly Delaware. The area was explored and colonized by the French and Spanish during the 16th century, among their leaders being Narváez, Ponce de León, Cabeza de Vaca, De Soto, Ribault, Laudonnière, Jolliet, Marquette, and La Salle. The first settlement was made at St. Augustine, Fla. (1565), and Franciscan and Jesuit missionaries were prominent in the early colonization, although the settlers also included Huguenots. Roanoke♦ and Jamestown♦ were the first English settlements, the latter being founded by the Virginia Company.♦ Except for the books of Sandys and John Smith, the English writing of this period was mainly promotional or descriptive, e.g. the works of Whitaker, Pory, Alsop, Hammond, Strachey, Hariot, and the authors of the Burwell Papers.

From the beginning, the South was characteristically agrarian, and the second wave of colonists, including wealthy Cavaliers who came during the interregnum, stimulated the growth of the aristocratic plantation system, in which the staple crops of tobacco, rice, and later cotton were worked under the institution of slavery. There was little popular education, and, even after the founding of William and Mary (1693), education was mostly restricted to the upper classes. Southern culture thus tended to follow the aristocratic Cavalier tradition. The dominant Episcopal Church crushed dissent in most of the colonies, although Catholicism flourished in Maryland under the Calverts, Oglethorpe's Georgia was nonsectarian, and in the 18th century Virginia became comparatively tolerant. As a result of various restraining forces, art and literature in the early South were of little consequence. Most of the writing was historical, as in the works of Beverley, Lawson, Blair, Stith, and Hugh Jones, although there were also the satires of Tailfer and Ebenezer Cook, and the charming journals of Byrd. Southern patriot leaders in the Revolutionary struggle included Patrick Henry, Washington, Jefferson, the Lees, Madison, the Randolphs, Francis Marion, George Mason, and Pickens, and many battles in the later phases of the war took place in the South. These men continued as leaders of the new republic; of the first five presidents, four were Southerners, while Washington, D.C., became the capital of the U.S.

During the 19th century, however, the economic system of the South, based on slave labor, separated the region from the North, which became increasingly industrial, and, with the frontier West, assumed greater political and financial power. Such differences as had appeared in the Federal Constitutional Convention led to the Southern emphasis on states' rights, especially after the Louisiana Purchase (1803), which brought within the U.S. the whole region of the Mississippi River. ♦ The widening schism was marked by such crises as the Missouri Compromise (1820), Calhoun's opposition to the Northern "Tariff of Abominations," the conflict over the Mexican War and its spoils, the Compromise of 1850, the struggles in Kansas and Nebraska, and the Dred Scott case. The survival of Spanish and French traditions, especially among the Creoles and Cajuns of Louisiana, made for distinctions, as did the tendency of the Border States to share the interests of the North. Southern aristocrats tended toward statesmanship rather than literature.

The agrarian emphasis may be seen in Jefferson and John Taylor of Caroline, the feudal gentility in J.P. Kennedy and the laudatory biographies by Marshall, Wirt, and Weems. The English Augustan tradition appears in the Tuesday Club of Annapolis, the Delphian Club of Baltimore, and the Russell's Bookstore Group♦ in Charleston, influenced both by neoclassical views and by the romanticism of Scott, as is evident in the writings of Legaré, Simms, and others. The fiction of N.B. Tucker was based on Calhoun's philosophy; William J. Grayson was an apologist for slavery; W.A. Caruthers and J.E. Cooke were slight historical romancers; Lamar shows the influence of Byron; and Poe and Chivers represent Southern romanticism carried into the realm of metaphysical mysticism. Regional periodicals included the *Southern Literary Messenger, De Bow's Review,* and *The Southern Quarterly Review.* The sectional feeling expressed through these and other media reached its peak in the Civil War,♦ when the South seceded from the Union, to form the temporary political association of the Confederacy.♦ During this time the enslaved blacks♦ of the region, kept from education, rarely had an opportunity to express themselves in the written word, although it was occasionally achieved, often by freed persons, like Benjamin Banneker, Martin Delany, and David Walker.

With secession came increased chauvinistic literature from white authors. Among the poets of the war and its sequel were Hayne, Timrod, J.R. Randall, Father Ryan, Lanier, J.R. Thompson, and Margaret Preston.

During the period of Reconstruction,♦ the former social and economic framework was overturned by the abolition of slavery and the new status of blacks. Something of the Southern situation in this period was depicted by the Northerner Albion Tourgée. The local-color movement included such Southern authors as Joel Chandler Harris, Richard M. Johnston, George W. Cable, Kate Chopin, Mary Murfree, John Fox, Lafcadio Hearn, and John T. Moore.

In the 20th century the literature of the South has become not only distinguished but very diverse, yet it has often laid stress on regionalism.♦ The most outstanding fiction, like Faulkner's Yoknapatawpha saga, has used precisely delineated local settings and situations to create a microcosm for the treatment of universal issues. Some fiction has emphasized romance, the past, and fantasy, as in different ways the novels of Margaret Mitchell, Hervey Allen, and Cabell have. Some fiction has concerned itself with the problems of a new industrialism, like the novels of Olive Dargan and T.S. Stribling. Some of the novels and plays have concentrated on the ways of life and the folklore of blacks, as have the works of Roark Bradford, Paul Green, DuBose Heyward, and Julia Peterkin. At long last black writers have been able to treat their own heritage in significant works of literature, although in many instances the authors have been from the South but have not remained residents of the region. Black writers who have depicted the South or its impact on their lives and their culture are very various and include William Attaway, Arna Bontemps, Sterling Brown, C.W. Chesnutt, William Demby, W.E.B. DuBois, P.L. Dunbar, Ernest Gaines, Alex Haley, Chester Himes, Langston Hughes, Zora Neale Hurston, Ishmael Reed, Albery Whitman, and Richard Wright. But the 20th-century South is too large, its writers are too many, too individual, and too important to be grouped according to subject, school, or heritage.

South Atlantic Quarterly (1902–), founded at Trinity College (since 1924, Duke University) at Durham, N.C., by John S. Bassett, a professor of history, primarily as a sober but generally liberal medium for discussion of Southern history, economics, education, and culture in a broad perspective. The policy continued after Bassett's editorship ended (1905), as may be seen in W.B. Hamilton's history and anthology, *Fifty Years of the South Atlantic Quarterly* (1952). A few special issues (e.g. on 18th-century literature, the Renaissance, and Soviet foreign policy) have served as *festschrifts* for university professors. It has recently grown livelier in text and appearance.

Southern and Western Monthly Magazine and Review, The (1845), Charleston periodical edited by Simms, whose policy combined the serious tone of a literary review with the attractive qualities of a popular magazine. Simms was the principal contributor, and others included E.A. Duyckinck and T.H. Chivers. The magazine was absorbed by the *Southern Literary Messenger.*

Southern Literary Journal and Monthly Magazine (1835–38), Charleston periodical that championed the cause of slavery and recorded the progress of Southern culture. Its most distinguished contributor was Simms, whose leading article was "American Criticism and Critics."

Southern Literary Messenger (1834–64, 1939–44), magazine founded at Richmond by Thomas W. White, whose first nine numbers were edited by James E. Heath. Poe's first contribution was "Berenice" (March 1835), and in December of that year he became the editor, at a salary of $15 per week. He published 83 reviews, 6 poems, 4 essays, and 3 stories, and increased the magazine's subscription list from 500 to more than 3500. His "tomahawk" method of criticism made the *Messenger* famous, and led to literary feuds with such authors as those of the Knickerbocker Group.♦ His persistent drinking led to his loss of the editorship (Jan. 1837). White then became editor, with aid from others, until his death (1843), after which Benjamin B. Minor became publisher and editor. Although Poe wrote two unimportant articles, and other former contributors continued, the magazine declined in literary significance, and gave great attention to military and naval affairs. Under J.R. Thompson (1847–60), G.W. Bagby (1860–64), and Frank H. Alfriend (1864), it dwindled to death. *The Contributors and Contributions to the Southern Literary Messenger* was published in 1936, and the magazine was revived (1939–44).

Southern Quarterly Review, The (1842–57), proslavery journal mainly issued from Charleston, which opposed British aggression and advocated states' rights and free trade. It was not as important as *The Southern Review* but included notable contributions. D.K. Whitaker was founder and first editor (1842–47); others included Simms (1849–55).

Southern Review, The (1828–32), quarterly literary magazine, published from Charleston as an expression of the culture of the South. Hugh S. Legaré was an editor and contributor.

Another quarterly of the same name (1867–79), published in Baltimore, had a similar purpose.

A third quarterly *Southern Review* (1935–42, 1965–   ) was published at Baton Rouge, La. Although issued by the Louisiana State University Press, it was not a university organ, but was primarily a regional review. Its editors included R.P. Warren, and it printed contributions from J.P. Bishop, Kenneth Burke, Herbert Agar, Katherine Anne Porter, J.C. Ransom, and Allen Tate. It was revived with similar policies under new editors in 1965, including Lewis Simpson. Later contributors were Walker Percy and Ernest Gaines.

Southwest, as distinguished from the Old Southwest♦ of the early 19th-century frontier, is the region including the border states of Arizona, New Mexico, and western Texas. Although the region is generally composed of deserts and mountains, its arable land has been increased by irrigation. The Santa Fe Trail♦ was an important trade route during the 19th century, leading to the growth of such communities as Santa Fe and Taos,♦ the home of Kit Carson and other scouts, some of whom had been famous in the region as mountain men. As the native land of the Navajo,♦ Apache,♦ Hopi,♦ and Zuñi Indians,♦ and the refuge of such frontier types as the cowboy, the prospector, and the two-gun sheriff, the Southwest is a favorite setting for the popular romantic fiction of such authors as Zane Grey and Harold Bell Wright, and the more substantial novels of Andy Adams and Eugene Manlove Rhodes. Cowboy folk ballads and tales have been collected by Lomax, Sandburg, J. Frank Dobie, and others, and the literature of the Southwest includes works about the Indians by Adolf Bandelier, Oliver La Farge, Mary Austin, and Edwin Corle, as well as by Indians, notably Scott Momaday; Stanley Vestal's books about Kit Carson; local-color stories of Arizona mining towns and cattle ranches by Stephen Crane, A.H. Lewis, Conrad Richter, and others; Willa Cather's *Death Comes for the Archbishop,* concerned with Catholic missionaries in New Mexico; and the writings of authors associated with the Taos and Santa Fe artist colonies, including Mabel Dodge Luhan, D.H. Lawrence, Harvey Fergusson, Paul Horgan, Witter Bynner, and Maxwell Anderson.

SOUTHWORTH, E[MMA] D[OROTHY] E[LIZA] N[EVITTE] (1819–99), popular feminine novelist of the domestic-sentimental school, lived most of her life in Washington, D.C. Her *Retribution* (1849) was followed by some 60 similar romances with melodramatic plots, originally written as magazine serials, and usually set in the South. Among the most popular works were *The Curse of Clifton* (1852), *The Missing Bride* (1855), *The Hidden Hand* (1859), *The Fatal Marriage* (1869), *The Maiden Widow* (1870), and *Self-Raised* (1876).

SOWER (SAUER), CHRISTOPHER (1693–1758), German-born printer, whose Pennsylvania press issued a Bible in German (1743), the second Bible to be printed in America, since it was preceded only by the Indian translation of John Eliot.

Spanish-American War, fought (April–Aug. 1898) between Spain and the U.S., following years of antagonism over the growing struggle for the independence of Cuba. The U.S. supported Cuban liberals because of the island's strategic position, American financial interests in Cuban agriculture and industry, and sympathy for the oppressed people. These motives and the feeling of "manifest destiny" led to U.S. intervention, after the sinking of the *Maine* and the publication of a letter from the Spanish minister at Washington, which insulted President McKinley. Feeling was aroused by provocative articles in the yellow press, and in rapid order Manila was captured by Commodore Dewey, General Shafter and his troops invaded Cuba, and the Spanish fleet was destroyed at Santiago by a U.S. fleet under Sampson and Schley. The Rough Riders, under Leonard Wood and Theodore Roosevelt, figured in the highly publicized capture of San Juan Hill. By the Treaty of Paris (Dec. 10), Spain relinquished her power in Cuba, gave Puerto Rico and Guam to the U.S. as indemnity, and sold the Philippines to the U.S. for $20,000,000. The U.S. was now first considered a world power, and important revisions of foreign policy resulted, including involvement in the Far East.

Among authors who fought in the war were Sherwood Anderson, George Cabot Lodge, and Carl Sandburg. Writings about it included the dispatches of Stephen Crane, published in New York newspapers and *McClure's;* of Richard Harding Davis, collected in *Cuba in War Time;* and of Frank Norris, printed in *Century Magazine* and *Atlantic Monthly* and in his pamphlet *The Surrender of Santiago.* In addition, Crane wrote *The Open Boat*◆ (1898), whose title story and "Flanagan and His Short Filibustering Adventure" deal with incidents related to but preceding the war, and *Wounds in the Rain* (1900), which collects sketches. William Graham Sumner was a leader in opposing imperialism and war, while Elbert Hubbard celebrated its heroism in his inspirational essay "A Message to Garcia"◆ (1899). Richard Hovey also showed chauvinistic enthusiasm in his poems "Unmanifest Destiny" and "The Word of the Lord from Havana." Shrewd, wry comments appeared in Finley Peter Dunne's *Mr. Dooley in Peace and War* (1898). Novels celebrating the excitements of the war include Kirk Munroe's *Forward March* (1899), Hergesheimer's *The Bright Shawl* (1922), and Herman Hagedorn's *The Rough Riders* (1927), about Theodore Roosevelt.

SPARKS, JARED (1789–1866), born in Connecticut, after graduation from Harvard (1815) became a tutor at the college (1817–19), a Unitarian minister at Baltimore (1819–23), and editor of *The North American Review* (1817–18, 1824–30). Returning to Harvard to become the first professor of history in any American university (1839–49), he was elected president (1849–

53), in which capacity he failed to further the historical program he had so promisingly begun. In his writings he broke the ground for the modern study of American history, and as editor of *The Library of American Biography* contributed lives of John Ledyard (1828) and of Gouverneur Morris (3 vols., 1832). Although his editorship did much to make known previously unprinted manuscripts, he was not a scientific historian, and frequently bowdlerized in order to present his subjects as gentlemen and heroes, in such works as *The Writings of George Washington,* containing a biography in volume I (12 vols., 1834–37), *The Diplomatic Correspondence of the American Revolution* (12 vols., 1829–30), and *The Works of Benjamin Franklin* (10 vols., 1836–40).

***Sparrowgrass Papers,** The,* collection of humorous articles by Frederick S. Cozzens.◆

Spartacus to the Gladiators, see *Kellogg, Elijah.*

Specimen Days and Collect, autobiographical narrative by Whitman,◆ published in 1882. It incorporates *Memoranda During the War* (1875).

The first part contains the author's reminiscences of his early life and the fascinating panorama of New York. This is followed by journal jottings and memoranda of the Civil War, both on the front and in Washington hospitals. The last part of the book deals with his observations of nature and his own sensations, and incorporates travel sketches of his excursions to the West, Canada, and Boston, with literary criticism of the authors he met and others who interested him, such as Carlyle.

Spectra, satirical parody of the technique and diction of modern poetry, was published in 1916. Written by Witter Bynner,◆ under the pseudonym Emanuel Morgan, and A.D. Ficke,◆ under the pseudonym Anne Knish, the hoax was for a time considered a serious contribution to contemporary verse experiments.

SPENCER, ELIZABETH (1921–   ), Mississippi-born novelist, resident for some time in Italy. Since 1958 she and her husband have lived in Canada. Her first novels, *Fire in the Morning* (1948), *This Crooked Way* (1952), and *The Voice at the Back Door* (1956), are set in her native state and in various ways contrast established and new modes of life in the Old South. Her next novels, *The Light in the Piazza* (1960) and *Knights and Dragons* (1965), both set in Italy, are very brief works sensitively dealing with Americans in Italy. Like her earlier fiction they are distinguished by fine craftsmanship and intense plots that reveal the essential natures of the characters. *The Snare* (1972) is a longer, more complex novel set in the underworld of New Orleans, while the recently hurricane-wrecked region of the Mississippi Gulf Coast in *The Salt Line* (1984) is symbolic of its resident characters' lives. Stories are collected in *Ship Island* (1968), *The Stories of Elizabeth Spencer* (1981), and *Jack of Diamonds* (1988), while *Marilee* (1981) groups three stories about the maturing of a girl in the deep South.

SPEYER, Leonora (1872–1956), New York poet whose lyrics in *A Canopic Jar* (1921) promised the command of form and intense personal idiom that were fulfilled in *Fiddler's Farewell* (1926, Pulitzer Prize), especially noted for its wit and understanding of feminine character. The poems in *Naked Heel* (1931) have been criticized as emotionally "thin" and excessively formal. *Slow Wall* (1939) appeared in an enlarged edition in 1946.

Sphinx, The, poem by Emerson,♦ first published in *The Dial* (1841) and collected in his *Poems* (1847).

In 17 stanzas of two quatrains with irregular two- and three-stress lines, it tells of a poet meeting the Sphinx and solving the riddle of the all-inclusive divine spirit: "Who telleth one of my meanings, Is master of all I am." Emerson paraphrased the poem in his notebook (1859): "The perception of identity unites all things and explains one by another. . . . But if the mind live only in particulars . . . then the world addresses to this mind a question it cannot answer."

SPICER, Jack (1925–65), California poet whose works, locally issued, include *After Lorca* (1957), translations, original poems, and letters addressed to the Spanish poet killed in Spain's civil war when Spicer was still a child; *Billy the Kid* (1959), a paean to the Western hero; *The Heads of the Town Up to the Aether* (1962), short poems with commentaries, including a section of "Homage to [Robert] Creeley," and "A Fake Novel About the Life of Arthur Rimbaud"; *Language* (1965), showing the poet's concern with linguistics; and *Book of Magazine Verse* (1966), poems ostensibly suited to various journals. All are gathered in *The Collected Books* (1975).

SPILLANE, Mickey [Frank Morrison] (1918–), author of tough detective stories, emphasizing sadism more than mystery. His enormously popular books include *I, The Jury* (1947), *My Gun Is Quick* (1950), *The Big Kill* (1951), and many others published during the 1960s. He returned to writing and publication with *Tomorrow I Die* (1984) and *The Killing Man* (1989).

SPINGARN, J[oel] E[lias] (1875–1939), professor of comparative literature at Columbia (1899–1911) and literary critic, whose works include *A History of Literary Criticism in the Renaissance* (1899), *The New Criticism* (1911), *Creative Criticism* (1917), and volumes of verse including *The New Hesperides* (1911) and *Poems* (1924). *A Spingarn Enchiridion* (1929) is his reply to P.E.

More's contention that he taught that criticism is "only impression." He also edited many works, and in 1914 established the award of the Spingarn Medal, granted annually to an outstanding black.

Spirit of the Age, The (Feb. 1849–Apr. 1850), New York weekly journal, edited by W.H. Channing with the purpose of seeking "the Peaceful Transformation of human society from isolated to associated interests." The many reforms it advocated included antislavery, abolition of the death penalty, universal education, pacifism, and temperance. Contributors included C.A. Dana, Parke Godwin, the elder Henry James, J.S. Dwight, Albert Brisbane, and Ripley, and there were also translations from foreign socialist writers.

Spirit of the Times (1831–61), New York journal founded by W.T. Porter.♦ This racy "Chronicle of the Turf, Agriculture, Field Sports, Literature, and the Stage" at one time probably had a circulation over 40,000, and was the medium for many "original contributions" from subscribers in every section of the country, but particularly in the Old Southwest. These contributions were distinctly masculine tales based on oral humor of the frontier. Some of the Sut Lovingood sketches were first published here, and other contributions included T.B. Thorpe's "The Big Bear of Arkansas" and work by J.J. Hooper, W.T. Thompson, Sol Smith, and J.M. Field. Porter left his journal to found *Porter's Spirit of the Times* (1856–61?) with George Wilkes (1819–85). Wilkes next founded his own *Spirit of the Times* (1859–1902).

Spiritual, religious folk song of blacks, perhaps stemming from the camp-meeting songs and spirituals of the white evangelistic sects, and characterized by melancholy, pathos, and naïve faith. It frequently consists of stanzas in which a single line is repeated several times with a line of refrain which unites the whole. The songs are essentially folk creations, often the result of mass extemporizing, lending themselves to many variations. Among the more famous are "Golden Slippers," "Roll, Jordan, Roll," and "Swing Low, Sweet Chariot."

Splendid Idle Forties, The, collection of stories by Gertrude Atherton,♦ published in 1902, is a revised and enlarged version of a collection issued as *Before the Gringo Came* (1894).

Subtitled "Stories of Old California," the 13 very romantic tales depict aspects of life in California under Mexican rule and directly after the American conquest, presenting the former era as an idyllic pastoral time.

SPOFFORD, Harriet [Elizabeth] Prescott (1835–1921), New England author best known for her numerous romantic short stories. Her reputation began when the *Atlantic Monthly* published "In a Cellar" (Feb. 1859), a tale of adventure characterized by its glowing descriptive passages. Her first novel, *Sir Rohan's Ghost* (1860), in the tradition of Poe and the Gothic romance, is the story of a man who tries to kill his mistress and is later plagued by her daughter, with whom he falls in love. *Azarian: An Episode* (1864) is a poetic tale concerning Constant Azarian, an artistic Bostonian who is too self-centered to appreciate the devotion of idealistic Ruth Yetton. *The Amber Gods and Other Stories* (1863) was the first of Mrs. Spofford's many collections of romantic tales, which include *New-England Legends* (1871), *A Scarlet Poppy and Other Stories* (1894), *Hester Stanley's Friends* (1898), *Old Madame and Other Tragedies* (1900), and *The Elder's People* (1920). After her marriage (1865) she lived much of the time in Washington, D.C., and her interest in the local color of this city is shown in *Old Washington* (1906). She wrote other novels and published many volumes of poetry, including *In Titian's Garden* (1903). Some of her many literary friendships in New England are recalled in *A Little Book of Friends* (1916).

Spoils of Poynton, The, novel by Henry James,♦ published in 1897.

Old Mrs. Gereth and young Fleda Vetch, while visiting the English country place of the vulgar Brigstocks, find a bond of sympathy in their dislike of their hosts' bad taste. Mrs. Gereth, who has been seeking a desirable wife for her undistinguished son Owen, invites Fleda to visit her at her house at Poynton, in which she takes great pride. There she has assembled a magnificent collection of furniture and objects of art, and Fleda is moved to tears by its splendor. In that setting Fleda falls in love with Owen, but he has decided to marry Mona Brigstock, whom he brings to visit Poynton, his property under his father's will. The antipathy of Mona and Mrs. Gereth flares up at once, and Owen, realizing that his mother must vacate the house, asks Fleda's aid in persuading her to leave. Mrs. Gereth takes revenge by removing her greatest treasures from Poynton, and Mona threatens to break with Owen unless they are returned. He has meanwhile fallen in love with Fleda, who urges his mother to send the "spoils" back to Poynton. When Owen comes to Fleda's shabby home and asks her to marry him, she tells him that he must first break with Mona. The next news received by Mrs. Gereth and Fleda is that of his sudden marriage to Mona. After a time Fleda receives a letter from Owen, asking her to take from the house whatever object she values most. On arriving at Poynton, she finds the place in ruins as the result of an accidental fire. Its treasures, which have twisted so many lives, have been entirely destroyed.

Spontaneous Me, poem by Whitman,♦ published in *Leaves of Grass* (1856) as "Bunch Poem," in-

cluded in "Children of Adam" (1860), and given its present title in 1867. It illustrates the author's pantheism and his amorous hyper-sensitivity by a catalogue of vital experiences—"the real poems, (what we call poems being merely pictures)."

Spoon River Anthology, free-verse poems of Edgar Lee Masters,♦ first printed serially in *Reedy's Mirror* in 1914, and published in book form in 1915. Basing his form on that of the Greek *Anthology,* the author presents a series of realistic, candid epitaphs, in which some 250 people buried in the cemetery of a small town of the Middle West reveal the essence of their secret lives. Many of the portraits are interrelated, so that 19 family histories are presented in the form of individual confessions, showing the typical frustrated ideals, petty intrigues, monotonous lives, and occasional exalted experiences of these representative characters. *The New Spoon River* (1924) is a less successful employment of the same concept. *Spoon River* (1963) by Charles Aidman is a play based on the work.

Among the best known of the epitaphs are those of "Anne Rutledge," presenting Lincoln's youthful love as the inspiration of his later humanity and charity, "Wedded to him, not through union, But through separation," and the source of "vibrations of deathless music"; "Petit, The Poet," expressing the futility of the career of the town's poetaster, who ignored the real life of the place, devoting himself to "little iambics, While Homer and Whitman roared in the pines!"; "Lucinda Matlock," the epitaph of a vigorous old woman, who died at 96 because she "had lived enough, that is all," and who looks with scorn on the "anger, discontent, and drooping hopes" of a "degenerate" generation, having learned that "It takes life to love Life"; "Benjamin Pantier" and "Mrs. Benjamin Pantier," showing the two sides of a domestic tragedy; "The Village Atheist," telling of the tubercular "infidel" who found that "Immortality is an achievement; And only those who strive mightily Shall possess it"; and "Fiddler Jones," the epitaph of a farmer who spent his life making music for others, ending with "forty acres . . . a broken fiddle . . . And not a single regret."

SPOTSWOOD, ALEXANDER (1676–1740), colonial governor of Virginia (1710–22), was at first popular because of the favorable concessions he acquired from the Indians, his introduction of the writ of habeas corpus, and his improvement of trade conditions. He was removed from office (1722) because of difficulties over ecclesiastical patronage. His *Official Letters* (2 vols., 1882–85) is a valuable source for students of the economic and social problems of 18th-century Virginia, and his career is the basis of W.A. Caruthers's novel *The Knights of the Horseshoe* (1845).

SPRAGUE, CHARLES (1791–1875), Boston poet, whose work ranges from the influence of Collins and Gray, in his "Shakespeare Ode," through the sentimentalized vein of the graveyard school in "The Funeral" and a simple statement of deism in "The Winged Worshippers" to the homely sincerity of "The Brothers." He collected his *Writings* (1841).

Springfield Republican, The (1824–   ), Massachusetts newspaper, founded as a weekly by Samuel Bowles. It became a daily under the direction of his son, the younger Samuel Bowles♦ (1844ff.). Although it originally supported the Whigs, it became politically independent as the result of opposition to slavery and the Mexican War, and has consistently maintained an independent policy. Despite its national importance, the *Republican* has always been considered a New England product, and has given much space to such contributors as J.G. Holland, who reflected local views. During the Civil War it supported Lincoln, but it later attacked the corruption of Grant's administration. The Bowles family in 1926 bought the city's three other newspapers, maintaining them independently with different policies, the *Republican* becoming a Sunday journal only. Upon the death of Sherman Bowles (1952) ownership passed to a trust fund for employees created by the family.

Spy, The: A Tale of the Neutral Ground, romance by Cooper,♦ published in 1821, and dramatized by C.P. Clinch (1822).

Harvey Birch, supposed to be a Loyalist spy but secretly in the intelligence service of General Washington, operates in the "neutral ground" of his native Westchester County, New York, and aids his neighbors, Henry Wharton, a Loyalist who pretends to be neutral, his daughters Sarah and Frances, and a son, Captain Henry Wharton of the British army. In 1780, Washington, in his accustomed disguise as Mr. Harper, is sheltered at the Wharton home, where he is impressed by the rebel sympathies of Frances. To repay the family's hospitality, Birch warns Captain Henry of his impending capture, but the young man, refusing to leave, is taken by a rebel force under Captain Jack Lawton. Frances appeals to her fiancé, the patriot Major Peyton Dunwoodie, but meanwhile Captain Henry escapes during a battle, only to be recaptured with Colonel Wellemere, Sarah's British admirer. Birch is almost captured by Lawton, who mistakes him for a spy, but in their struggle he spares Lawton's life, a good deed repaid by Lawton when Birch is later turned over to him by the "Skinners," a band of marauding patriots. The wedding of Wellemere and Sarah is interrupted by Birch, who reveals that Wellemere is already married, and the Englishman escapes during a raid by the marauders, who destroy the Wharton home. Captain Henry is sentenced to be executed as a spy, but Birch helps him escape, and Frances, seeking them, goes to Birch's mountain retreat, where she finds "Mr.

Harper" and persuades him to end the pursuit of her brother. Birch takes Captain Henry to a British ship, Frances and Dunwoodie are married, Lawton is killed in battle, and Birch, ending his service to Washington, refuses rewards, preferring to remain an itinerant peddler.

Squaw Man, The, play by E.M. Royle,♦ produced in 1905 and revived in England as *The White Man* (1908). It was adapted by Brian Hooker and W.H. Post as the libretto of the musical play *White Eagle* (1927).

SQUIBOB, pseudonym of G.H. Derby.♦

SQUIER, EPHRAIM GEORGE (1821–88), New York archaeologist whose writings include *Ancient Monuments of the Mississippi Valley* (1848) and *Aboriginal Monuments of the State of New York* (1851). His other books, *Nicaragua* (1852), *The States of Central America* (1858), and *Peru* (1877), are based on knowledge gathered during diplomatic missions to Central and South America.

STACTON, DAVID [DEREK] (1923–68), San Francisco-born novelist, after graduating from the University of California (1956) lived abroad. He was a prolific novelist, focusing on historical themes and figures, and his fiction, sometimes so-called triplets of three related works, is frequently macabre and ironic, basically psychological, and cast in an epigrammatic style. His novels first published in England include *Dolores* (1954); *A Ride on a Tiger* (1954); *A Fox Inside* (1955); *The Self-Enchanted* (1956); *Remember Me* (1957), about Ludwig II of Bavaria; *On a Balcony* (1958), about Nefertiti of Egypt; *Segaki* (1958), about a Zen master of feudal Japan, which with the preceding two forms a trilogy; *The Invincible Question; A Signal Victory* (1960), about a Spanish sailor who becomes a leader of the Mayans; *A Dancer in Darkness* (1960), about the Duchess of Malfi; *Tom Fool* (1962), on Wendell Willkie; and *Old Acquaintance* (1962). His works first published in America are *The Judges of the Secret Court* (1961), about John Wilkes Booth; *Sir William* (1963), about Lady Emma Hamilton, her husband, and Nelson; and *People of the Book* (1965), set during the Thirty Years' War. *The Bonapartes* (1966) is a historical study.

STAFFORD, JEAN (1915–79), California-born novelist reared in Colorado, after graduation from the University of Colorado and further study there and in Germany began the writing of fiction noted for sensitive interpretations of adult isolation and the problems of adolescence. *Boston Adventure* (1944) presents the character of a foreign girl working as secretary to a wealthy Boston spinster; her second novel, *The Mountain Lion* (1947), depicts the unhappy youth of a brother and sister and their escape on a Colorado ranch. Later novels include *The Catherine Wheel* (1952) and *A Winter's Tale* (1954). *Children Are Bored on Sunday* (1953) and *Bad Characters* (1964) collect stories, definitively assembled in *Collected Stories* (1969, Pulitzer Prize). Her only work of nonfiction was *A Mother in History* (1966), about Lee Harvey Oswald's mother. She was married to Robert Lowell (1940–48) and A.J. Leibling (1959–63).

STAFFORD, WILLIAM [EDGAR] (1914–   ), Kansas-born poet and professor at Lewis and Clark College (Portland, Ore.) (1948–80). His poems, mostly short lyrics, have been published in *West of Your City* (1960); *Traveling Through the Dark* (1962, National Book Award); *The Rescued Year* (1966), recalling his rural youth; *Allegiances* (1970); *Someday, Maybe* (1973); *Stories That Could Be True: New and Collected Poems* (1977); *The Quiet of the Land* (1982); *A Glass Face in the Rain* (1982); and *An Oregon Message* (1987). *Segues* (1984) prints correspondence written in poetry with Marvin Bell, each man the author of 22 poems. Stafford's critical writing appears in a work on Brother Antoninus◆ (1967) and *Friends to This Ground* (1968). *Writing the Australian Crawl* (1978) collects articles and interviews on his poetry and that of others. *Down in My Heart* (1947) remembers experiences as a conscientious objector during World War II. *The Darkness Around Us Is Deep* (1994) is a selection of Stafford's work edited and chosen by Robert Bly.

STALLINGS, LAURENCE (1894–1968), born in Georgia, had a brief journalistic career, served in World War I, in which he was seriously wounded, and returned to become a critic on the New York *World.* His war experiences furnished the background for his novel *Plumes* (1924) and for the play *What Price Glory?*◆ (1924), written with Maxwell Anderson. With Anderson he also wrote *First Flight* (1925), concerned with an episode in the youth of Andrew Jackson, and *The Buccaneer* (1925), dealing with the pirate Morgan. These were published as *Three American Plays* (1926). Stallings next wrote the books and lyrics for two operettas, *Deep River* (1926), set in 19th-century New Orleans, and *Rainbow* (1928), set in the Far West. He also dramatized *A Farewell to Arms* (1930), wrote many motion-picture scenarios, edited *The First World War* (1933), a collection of photographs and commentary, and wrote *The Doughboys, the Story of the A.E.F.* (1963).

STANDISH, BURT L., pseudonym of W.G. Patten.◆

STANDISH, MYLES (or MILES) (*c.*1584–1656), born in England, served in the Low Countries as a mercenary soldier, and was engaged by the Pilgrims to sail with them on the *Mayflower* (1620) as a military leader. His measures of defense and diplomatic ability in handling his soldiers soon made him more than an employee, and he may

have become a member of their church. Among his important actions were the building of the first port; the dispersal of the settlement of Thomas Morton, by whom, in the *New English Canaan,* he was called "Captain Shrimp, a quondam drummer"; the negotiation for loans and property rights from English merchants and the Council for New England; the administration of the treasury; and the founding with John Alden of the town of Duxbury. There is no historical basis for Longfellow's "The Courtship of Miles Standish,"◆ for Standish was twice married. He also figures in Jane G. Austin's *Standish of Standish* and Motley's *Merry Mount.*

STANLEY, SIR HENRY MORTON (1841–1904), English-born explorer, came to the U.S. (1859), where he adopted the name of his employer, and dropped his original name, John Rowlands. After serving in the Confederate army and U.S. navy, he became a reporter for the New York *Herald,* and his most exciting of many dramatic assignments was the search in central Africa (1871) for the lost Scottish missionary and explorer David Livingstone, whom he finally discovered and greeted with the famous sentence, "Dr. Livingstone, I presume?" Then and on later trips he continued the explorations of Livingstone, and for some time worked to establish the Congo Free State. Although an American citizen (1862–95), he resumed his English citizenship and was knighted (1899). His writings include *How I Found Livingstone* (1872), *Through the Dark Continent* (1878), and *In Darkest Africa* (1890).

STANSBURY, JOSEPH (1742–1809), English-born Loyalist poet, came to Philadelphia (1767), where during the Revolution he was in high favor with the British as an urbane and witty satirist of the patriots. Although he opposed the Revolution he did not, like the other major Loyalist poet Jonathan Odell, become virulent or descend to invective, but chose instead with gay humor to show the foibles and inconsistencies of the patriots. His opposition took a more serious turn when he acted as a go-between in the treasonable negotiations of Benedict Arnold and André. Although he tolerantly tried to forget differences of opinion after the war, destroyed his earlier political verse, and wrote some conciliatory lines, the erstwhile rebels temporarily imprisoned him, causing him to flee to Nova Scotia. Not until 1793 was he able to return in safety to the U.S. His poetry was first collected in *The Loyal Verses of Joseph Stansbury and Jonathan Odell* (1860). Caroline Kirkland was his granddaughter.

STANTON, ELIZABETH CADY (1815–1902), began her long career for woman's rights at the convention dedicated to this subject in her hometown of Seneca Falls, N.Y., in 1848. Soon thereafter she became the lifelong collaborator with Susan B. Anthony♦ in working for woman suffrage, as well as for temperance laws and the abolition of slavery. While the plain Miss Anthony was a talented organizer, the warm, attractive Mrs. Stanton was more effective as a public speaker and a vigorous journalist. The differences in abilities and temperaments often caused disagreements, but they worked together in many ways to promote the women's cause, publishing the journal *Revolution* (1868–69) and compiling and editing the three volumes of the monumental *History of Woman Suffrage* (1881–86). Mrs. Stanton alone created *The Woman's Bible* (2 vols., 1895, 1898), interpreting from her point of view all references to women in the Bible. She was president of the National Woman Suffrage Association (1869–90) and a successor organization for two years and a promulgator of the International Council of Women, the latter in part an outgrowth of frequent long visits late in life to be with her daughter Harriet Stanton Blatch,♦ married to an Englishman. Her last major work was her autobiography, *Eighty Years and More* (1898).

STANTON, FRANK LEBBY (1857–1927), Georgia poet, popular for his simple, optimistic, patriotic lyrics. These were published in such volumes as *Comes One with a Song* (1898) and *Songs from Dixie Land* (1900). His newspaper column in the *Atlanta Constitution* was republished in part in *Frank L. Stanton's Just from Georgia* (1927).

"Star-Spangled Banner, THE," song by Francis Scott Key,♦ became the U.S. national anthem by act of Congress (1931), although it had long been popularly considered the anthem and had been officially used by the army and navy since the Spanish-American War. Key, on a legal mission, was detained by the British and forced to view the bombardment of Fort McHenry, near Baltimore, during the night of September 13–14, 1814. The sight of the flag still flying inspired his verses, set to the music of "Anacreon in Heaven" by the Englishman John Stafford Smith (1750–1836), the anthem of the Anacreontic Societies, clubs of musical amateurs. Key's song was published as "Defence of Fort M'Henry" in *Baltimore Patriot* (Sept. 20, 1814), perhaps preceded by a broadside. It was collected in Key's *Poems* (1857).

Star-Splitter, *The*, blank-verse narrative by Robert Frost,♦ published in *New Hampshire* (1923). Brad McLaughlin's "life-long curiosity About our place among the infinities" culminates in his burning his house down for the insurance, to buy a telescope. He earns a living as a railroad ticket agent and uses his leisure "for star-gazing" through his glass, "the Star-splitter." Brad and his friend, the poet, often spend their nights in this activity, but though it provides material for "some of the best things we ever said," they remain in ignorance of the real nature of the universe: "We've looked and looked, but after all where are we?"

STARBUCK, GEORGE [EDWIN] (1931–), Ohio-born poet, has been on the faculty of the University of Iowa and of Boston University, whose works include *Bone Thoughts* (1960), *White Paper* (1966), *Elegy in a Country Church Yard* (1975), and *Desperate Measures* (1977).

Stars and Stripes, *The* (1918–19), official newspaper of the American Expeditionary Force, printed in France, included among its editorial staff F.P. Adams, John T. Winterich, and Alexander Woollcott. It was continued as an independent paper in the U.S. (1919–26). Woollcott collected his tales of the AEF from it in *The Command Is Forward* (1919), and Winterich's informal history of the paper *Squads Write!* (1931) includes some of its prose, verse, and cartoons.

A paper of the same name was founded in 1942 as the newspaper of the U.S. armed forces during World War II. It was issued in most of the theaters in which U.S. troops were stationed, and continued after the war, in smaller size, to serve occupation forces. The largest editions were those for the European theater, published in Paris, Rome, and other cities (1942–45).

Starting from Paumanok, poem by Whitman first published in *Leaves of Grass* in 1860 as "Proto-Leaf," revised and given its present title in 1867, and further revised in 1881. Beginning with reference to his birth on Paumanok, the Indian name of Long Island, in 19 sections the poem treats such major themes as the subject matter with which the author will deal in all his writing, the New World and the United States, comradeship, love, individualism, equality, liberty, and the soul.

STEARNS, HAROLD [EDMUND] (1891–1943), in *America and the Young Intellectual* (1921) stated the credo of the postwar generation, which he said "*does* dislike, almost to the point of hatred and certainly to the point of contempt, the type of people who dominate in our present civilization. . . ." A definitive statement of this attitude appeared in the symposium he edited, *Civilization in the United States: An Inquiry by Thirty Americans* (1922). With his return from expatriation in France and growing awareness of social action in place of escape, described in *The Street I Know* (1935), he prepared a new manifesto, *America: A Re-Appraisal* (1937), again a symposium by leading critics.

STEARNS, OLIVER (1807–85), after graduation from Harvard (1826) and Harvard Divinity School became a Unitarian clergyman. His ideas are expressed in such works as *The Gospel as Applied to the Fugitive Slave Law* (1851). With J.F. Clarke and F.H. Hedge he was in the vanguard of the progressive Unitarian thinkers and is said to be the first American theologian to champion the theory of evolution as a cosmic law. He was a professor at Harvard Divinity School (1863–78).

STEDMAN, EDMUND CLARENCE (1833–1908), was both a poet and a successful Wall Street broker, as may be seen in his most famous work, "Pan in Wall Street," a poem published in *The Blameless Prince* (1869). Also an essayist and critic, he was a noted literary figure in his time, although later critics have considered his several volumes of verse, collected in *Poetical Works* (1873), to be rather frigid reflections of the genteel tradition, or echoes of Tennyson and other contemporary poets. His work as a critic was of higher rank, particularly in his notable edition of Poe with G.E. Woodberry, and in *The Poets of America* (2 vols., 1885). This work, along with *A Library of American Literature* (11 vols., 1888–90), edited with Ellen M. Hutchinson, and *An American Anthology* (1900), did much to establish both a finer appreciation of and a greater interest in American literature.

STEEGMULLER, FRANCIS (1906–94), author of literary and biographical studies, including *Flaubert and Madame Bovary* (1939), *Maupassant: A Lion in the Path* (1949), *The Two Lives of James Jackson Jarves* (1951), *Apollinaire, Poet Among the Painters* (1963), and *Cocteau* (1970); lesser critical studies under the pseudonym Byron Steel; crime novels under the pseudonym David Keith; and light fiction, including *The Christening Party* (1961), *Stories and True Stories* (1972), and *Silence at Salerno* (1978). *French Follies and Other Follies* (1946) collects sketches from *The New Yorker* on the author's experiences in France and the U.S. *Stories and True Stories* (1972) collects articles and fiction. He also translated and edited many important works. His wife was Shirley Hazzard.

STEEL, DANIELLE (1947–   ), New York-born, longtime San Francisco resident who moved beyond journalism and public relations to the writing of much very popular fiction. Her best-sellers continue from *Going Home* (1973) to annual publications like *Daddy* (1989), about an "ideal" husband deserted by his wife, and *Wings* (1994), about a female aviator. All featuring contemporary settings, her novels are said to have sold up to 13,000,000 paperbacks in a two-year period. Many are adapted for television or films.

STEELE, WILBUR DANIEL (1886–1970), born in North Carolina and reared in Denver, is best known as a short-story writer whose plots are frequently set in New England and South Carolina, his later homes. His stories are collected in *Land's End* (1918), *The Shame Dance* (1923), *Urkey Island* (1926), *Tower of Sand* (1929), and other volumes. His novels include *Storm* (1914), *Isles of the Blest* (1924), *Taboo* (1925), *Sound of Rowlocks* (1938), and *That Girl from Memphis* (1945). *Diamond Wedding* (1950), *Their Town*

(1952), and *The Way to the Gold* (1955) are set in the Far West. *The Terrible Woman* (1925) is a collection of one-act plays, and in collaboration with his wife, Norma Mitchell Steele, he wrote *Post Road* (1934) and *Penny,* full-length plays. With Anthony Brown he dramatized one of his stories as *How Beautiful with Shoes*♦ (1935).

STEENDAM, JACOB (*c.*1616–*c.*1672), Dutch-born poet, came to New Netherland (*c.*1650) as a merchant and trader. To attract colonists to America, he published poems whose English translations bear the title *Complaint of New Amsterdam in New Netherland* (1659), a petition for aid from Holland; *Praise of New Netherland* (1661); and "Spurring Verses" (1662), prefixed to a pamphlet on a plan for colonization on the Delaware River. He seems to have returned to Holland (*c.*1662), and his later life was spent in the East Indies. His poems were reprinted in a biography (1861) by H.C. Murphy, who also published them in *Anthology of New Netherland* (1865).

STEFÁNSSON, VILHJÁLMUR (1879–1962), Canadian-born anthropologist, archaeologist, and Arctic explorer, long resident in the U.S., whose books include *My Life with the Eskimo* (1913), *The Friendly Arctic* (1921, revised 1943), *The Northward Course of Empire* (1922), *The Adventure of Wrangel Island* (1925), *The Standardization of Error* (1927), *Adventures in Error* (1936), *Unsolved Mysteries of the Arctic* (1938), *Iceland: The First American Republic* (1939), *Ultima Thule* (1940), *Greenland* (1942), and *Not by Bread Alone* (1946).

STEFFENS, [JOSEPH] LINCOLN (1866–1936), born in San Francisco, graduated from the University of California (1889), studied abroad, and entered New York journalism (1892). He is best known for his leadership of the muckraking movement.♦ As managing editor of *McClure's Magazine* (1902–6) and associate editor of *American Magazine* and *Everybody's* (1906–11), he was a contributor to the journalistic exposé of business and government corruption. His articles were collected in *The Shame of the Cities* (1904), *The Struggle for Self-Government* (1906), and *Upbuilders* (1909). His *Autobiography* (1931) tells the story of his gradual evolution of a theory of government and his transition from sensational reporting to the belief in a fundamental relation between the various forms of corruption he had discovered. It also contains an account of modern liberal and radical movements, with which he was affiliated during much of his life. *Lincoln Steffens Speaking* (1936) is a posthumous collection of articles written during his later years, and his *Letters* were collected in 1938.

STEGNER, WALLACE [EARLE] (1909–93), Iowa-born author, graduated from the University of Utah and in 1945 began his remaining academic career at Stanford as professor of English and head of its creative writing program. His own literary career is marked by many novels: *Remembering Laughter* (1937), set in Iowa; *On a Darkling Plain* (1940), about a Canadian veteran seeking solitude on the prairie; *Fire and Ice* (1941), about a college student temporarily joining the Communist party; *The Big Rock Candy Mountain* (1943), about a Far Westerner who moves his family from one home to another in a futile search for fortune; *Second Growth* (1947), contrasting the lives of visitors and villagers in New Hampshire; *The Preacher and the Slave* (1950), about Joe Hill of the I.W.W.; *A Shooting Star* (1961), presenting ways of life among established, wealthy northern Californians; *All the Little Live Things* (1967), contrasting ways of life of a cultivated older man and a young hippie; *Angle of Repose* (1971), a fictional rendering of the life of Mary Hallock Foote that won a Pulitzer Prize and was adapted as an opera by Oakley Hall and Andrew Imbrie (1976); *The Spectator Bird* (1976, National Book Award), in which the older man of *All the Little Live Things* recalls a romantic interlude of his youth; *Recapitulation* (1979), presenting a retired U.S. ambassador's unsettling return to Utah, where he was reared; and *Crossing to Safety* (1987), about two young men serving as beginning college instructors and how one gets ahead conventionally and the other does not. *The Women on the Wall* (1950), *The City of the Living* (1956), and *Collected Stories* (1990) present his short fiction. His nonfiction includes *Mormon Country* (1942), presenting the local scene and its folkways; *One Nation* (1945), depicting U.S. minorities; *Beyond the Hundredth Meridian* (1954), about John Wesley Powell's explorations of the western U.S.; *This Is Dinosaur* (1955), a conservationist plea for a Utah and Colorado national monument; *Wolf Willow* (1962), a warmly understanding personal and public history and recollection of the "last plains frontier" where Montana and Saskatchewan meet, the area where the author's youth was spent; *The Gathering of Zion* (1964), about the Mormon trek and trail to Utah; *The Sound of Mountain Water* (1969), diverse considerations of the West; *The Uneasy Chair* (1974), a life of Bernard De Voto, whose *Letters* (1975) Stegner edited; and *One Way To Spell Man* (1982), essays. *Collected Stories* (1990) were mostly written 30 years earlier before Stegner abandoned that form. *Where the Bluebird Sings to the Lemonade Springs, Living and Writing in the West* (1992) contains 16 more recent essays on subjects ranging from family memories to environmental challenges.

STEIN, GERTRUDE (1874–1946), born in Pennsylvania, was educated abroad, at California schools, and graduated from Radcliffe (1897). She was stimulated at college by William James, and her psychological experiments led her to study the anatomy of the brain at Johns Hopkins.

Tiring of scientific work, she went abroad (1902), where she lived until her death, her *salon* in France attracting prominent writers as well as painters, particularly Matisse, Picasso, and Juan Gris, whose works she collected. Her early fiction, including *Three Lives* (1909), stories of two servant girls and an unhappy black woman; *The Making of Americans*♦ (1925); and *A Long Gay Book* (1932), shows a breakdown of traditional plot structure and discursive writing, and dependence upon intuitive means of expressing the actual present.

Her later writings include *Tender Buttons* (1914), poetry without conventional logic or grammar, intended to express the qualities of objects; *Geography and Plays* (1922); *Composition as Explanation* (1926), lectures given at Oxford and Cambridge; *Lucy Church Amiably* (1930), a novel; *How To Write* (1931), a book of examples; *The Autobiography of Alice B. Toklas* (1933), her own autobiography, composed as though by her secretary and friend Alice B. Toklas♦; *Four Saints in Three Acts* (1934), an opera with music by Virgil Thomson; *Portraits and Prayers* (1934); *Narration* (1935), four critical lectures delivered at the University of Chicago; *The Geographical History of America* (1936), a formless work illustrating her literary theories; *Everybody's Autobiography* (1937), an account of her American lecture tour; *Picasso* (1938); *The World Is Round* (1939), a book for children; *Paris France* (1940), a sympathetic study of the French way of life; *Ida* (1941), a "novel"; *Wars I Have Seen* (1945) and *Yes Is For a Very Young Man*♦ (1946), about life in France during World War II, respectively in a personal account and a play; and *Brewsie and Willie* (1946), about lives of American soldiers in France during World War II.

Her *Lectures in America* (1935) explains her philosophy of composition, which is partly indebted to the aesthetic theories of William James and Bergson's concept of time. She contends that it is the "business of art" to live in "the complete actual present," and in describing her technique she compares it with that of the cinema. No two frames of a motion picture are exactly alike, yet the sequence presents to the eye a flowing continuity. Similarly, Miss Stein, by the use of partly repetitive statements, each making a limited advance in the theme, presents an uninterrupted series of instantaneous visions, so that one grasps a living moment in precise, ordered forms. This "moment to moment emphasis in what is happening" appears particularly in her early "portraits," and in *Three Lives* and *The Making of Americans*. Another of her concerns was "to tell what each one is without telling stories . . . so that the essence of what happened would be . . . the essence of the portraits." She was also interested in "the relation between color and sound."

In order to convey her concept of movement in the motion-picture manner, she set up a rhythmic pattern and placed her emphasis upon the verb. Nouns being names, she felt that "things once they are named the name does not go on doing anything to them and so why write in nouns." She felt that most punctuation is "an unnecessary name of something." "It is evident that when you ask a question you ask a question . . . and so why add to it the question mark." Other punctuation also interfered with the need for capturing motion: "If writing should go on what had colons and semicolons to do with it." In her poetry she holds a different theory about language; for, though naming, or noun-using, does not carry prose forward, "you can love a name and if you love a name then saying that name any number of times only makes you love it more . . ." and poetry is "really loving the name of anything." Thus, for her, poetry is a method of dealing "with everything that was not movement in space."

Her practice of these theories influenced other authors. Sherwood Anderson felt that she reviv-ified language and was stimulated by her method of repetition with minute variations, as was Hemingway, both in the rhythms of his prose and in his way of conveying emotions as immedi-ate experience. Yale, which inherited her manu-scripts, in 1951 began printing all unpublished works, initially edited by Van Vechten.

STEIN, Leo (1872–1947), brother of Gertrude Stein, like her was long an expatriate in Europe, where he too was an early collector of unrecog-nized contemporary artists; but their tastes and temperaments differed and they became es-tranged. His aesthetic judgments are to be found in *Appreciations* (1947) and his letters, papers, and journals, many showing his concern with psy-choanalysis, were edited as *Journey into the Self* (1950).

STEINBECK, John [Ernst] (1902–68), Cali-fornia novelist, attended Stanford University (1919–20, 1922–23, 1924–25), and worked at odd jobs, beginning his literary career with *Cup of Gold* (1929), a romantic novel based on the career of Sir Henry Morgan, the buccaneer. This was followed by *The Pastures of Heaven* (1932), a col-lection of short stories portraying the people of a farm community in a California valley. His second novel, *To a God Unknown* (1933), tells of a California farmer whose pagan religion of fertility becomes a mystical obsession, and after a season of drought leads to his suicide as a sacrifice on the sylvan altar at which he has worshiped.

Tortilla Flat♦ (1935) won Steinbeck popular attention for the first time, with its sympathet-ically humorous depiction of the lives of Mon-terey *paisanos*. *In Dubious Battle*♦ (1936), the sto-ry of a strike of migratory fruit pickers, was the first of his novels concerned with the conditions of this class, which continued to hold his interest. In *Of Mice and Men*♦ (1937), the story of two itinerant farmhands represents the tragedy of a

class that yearns for a home, of which it is perpet-ually deprived. After dramatizing this work with great success (1937), Steinbeck published a vol-ume of short stories, *The Long Valley*♦ (1938), containing the previously published *Saint Katy the Virgin* (1936) and *The Red Pony* (1937), published separately with additional material in 1945. His concern with the problems of the landless farm laborer received greatest emphasis in *The Grapes of Wrath*♦ (1939, Pulitzer Prize), a saga of a refu-gee family from the Dust Bowl, its migration to California, and the struggle to find work under an almost feudal system of agricultural exploita-tion.

In the 1940s Steinbeck wrote very various works. They include *The Forgotten Village* (1941), the script of a film depicting Mexican village life; *Sea of Cortez* (1941), written with his friend Ed-ward F. Ricketts, a marine biologist, presenting a journal of their travels and marine research in the Gulf of California and containing Steinbeck's re-flections on life; and *The Pearl* (1948), a short parable about a Mexican fisherman who finds a great pearl that brings evil to his family. This decade was also one of war writings: *Bombs Away: The Story of a Bomber Team* (1942); his dispatches of 1943 gathered in *Once There Was a War* (1958); and *A Russian Journal* (1948). Out of the same background came *The Moon Is Down* (1942), a novelette he dramatized (1942), about Norwegian resistance to the German occupation.

He returned to the setting and mood of *Tortilla Flat* in *Cannery Row*♦ (1945), a whimsical tale of idlers in Monterey and their relations with a sym-pathetic biologist. These people and this place appear again in *Sweet Thursday* (1954). *The Way-ward Bus* (1947) is a novel presenting a microcosm of frustrations in contemporary America through the stresses on a group of people stranded on a bus in rural California. *Burning Bright* (1950) in novelette form is a symbolic morality play about a man whose sterility forces him to accept anoth-er's child as his own. *East of Eden*♦ (1952), his first major novel after *The Grapes of Wrath,* is a long family saga from the Civil War to World War I, partly set in the Salinas Valley, using the theme of Cain and Abel in a story both symbolic and realistic of man's struggle between good and evil. After a brief and minor novel, *The Short Reign of Pippin IV* (1957), a lighthearted comedy about a 20th-century French king, Steinbeck re-turned to full-bodied and serious fiction with *The Winter of Our Discontent* (1961), treating the moral collapse of a descendant of an old New England family, a man of high integrity, under the pres-sures of the mid-20th century.

Steinbeck's fiction combines realism and ro-mance, but not always harmoniously. His settings are often rural areas, where people live most hap-pily when close to nature, but where malevolent forces, such as drought or labor and market con-ditions or human greed, destroy this vital rela-tionship. In dealing with the consequent problems Steinbeck's approach is sometimes lyric and mystical, sometimes realistic and sociological. Although he suffered a long period of adverse criticism, particularly in the United States, he remained popular and esteemed in Europe, and in the year when he published his account of a tour of 40 states, accompanied by his poodle, as *Travels with Charley in Search of America* (1962), he became the seventh American-born author to win a Nobel Prize.

His posthumously published works include *The Acts of King Arthur and His Noble Knights* (1976), a retelling of the tales. Correspondence appears in *Journals of a Novel: The East of Eden Letters* (1969), *Steinbeck: A Life in Letters* (1975), and *Letters to Elizabeth* (1978).

STEINBERG, SAUL (1914–   ), Rumanian-born artist, was educated as an architect in Italy. He came to the U.S. in 1942 and was naturalized in 1943. Here he has made a reputation as an artist and graphic satirist, noted for his precise line, his use of rubber stamps as bases of some designs, and his wordless comment on people, architecture, contraptions, and institutions, and a variety of other aspects of modern life, all treated with wit to expose their basic pomposity, fantastic nature, and grotesque appearance. His work frequently appears in *The New Yorker* and has been collected in books that include *All in Line* (1945), *The Art of Living* (1949), *The Passport* (1954), *The Labyrinth* (1960), *The Catalogue* (1962), *Confessions* (1965), and *The Inspector* (1973).

STEINEM, GLORIA (1934–   ), editor, writer, feminist spokesperson. Born in Ohio, Steinem graduated from Smith College and undertook further studies in India. She began to write on feminist issues for *Esquire, Vogue,* and *Cosmopolitan,* and in 1972 was co-founder of *Ms.* magazine and was its editor until 1987. *Outrageous Acts and Everyday Rebellions* (1983) collects 20 years of her feminist pieces. *Marilyn: Norma Jean* (1986) is a counter-biography to Norman Mailer's on the same subject. Steinem also wrote *Revolution from Within: A Book of Self-Esteem* (1992). *Moving Beyond Words* (1994) prints six essays, three of them new and three previously published in shorter form.

Stella Dallas, novel by Olive Higgins Prouty. ♦

STEPHENS, ANN SOPHIA (1810–86), in addition to contributions to leading literary magazines and an editorial position on *Graham's Magazine,* wrote some 25 books, chiefly fictionized treatments of English and American history. *Alice Copley: A Tale of Queen Mary's Time* (1844) and *The Diamond Necklace, and Other Tales* (1846) are typical of her flamboyant depictions of old England's nobility; and *The Rejected Wife* (1863) is representative of her handling of American history. *Fashion and Famine* (1854) is a melodramatic

story of the contrasts of New York life. *Malaeska: The Indian Wife of the White Hunter* (1860), probably her most famous book, sold some 300,000 copies and was the first dime novel, a genre to which she contributed other stories. *High Life in New York* (1843), written under the pseudonym Jonathan Slick, is Down East humor.

STEPHENS, JOHN LLOYD (1805–52), New Jersey-born author, left his legal practice in 1834 to begin the travels that resulted in his lively, colorful *Incidents of Travel in Egypt, Arabia Petraea, and the Holy Land* (2 vols., 1837) and *Incidents of Travel in Greece, Turkey, Russia, and Poland* (2 vols., 1838). President Van Buren sent him on a vague, confidential mission to Central America, out of which came his enthusiastic accounts of the physical remains of ancient civilizations in the jungles, illustrated by his fellow voyager, Frederick Catherwood, an English artist with some knowledge of archaeology. These were published as *Incidents of Travel in Central America, Chiapas and Yucatán* (2 vols., 1841) and the supplementary *Incidents of Travel in Yucatán* (2 vols., 1843).

STERLING, GEORGE (1869–1926), born in New York, was educated under Father Tabb in Maryland, went to California, and was thereafter identified with the state as a noted author and bohemian. He fell under the influence of Bierce, "the Great Cham" of literature on the West Coast, and consistently submitted his poetry to his master for criticism. Although later he recognized the significance of modern poets, as evidenced in his *Robinson Jeffers, the Man and the Artist* (1926), his own verse harked back to what he had been taught by Bierce, and, with its emphasis upon exotic romanticism and rhythmical regularity, looked backward rather than forward and failed to appeal to Eastern critics. He was best known for his sonnets, influenced by Keats, his simple musical lyrics, and his lush, grandiose longer poems. His most important books, whose titles reveal his characteristic attitude, include *The Testimony of the Suns* (1903), *A Wine of Wizardry* (1909), and *The House of Orchids* (1911). Among his later books are *Thirty-Five Sonnets* (1917) and *Selected Poems* (1923). He committed suicide in 1926. He is said to be the prototype of Brissenden in London's *Martin Eden.*

STERLING, JAMES (1701?–63), Irish-born poet and dramatist, emigrated to Maryland (1737) as an Anglican clergyman, and expressed colonial ideals in a series of conventional verses. He also wrote *An Epistle to the Hon. Arthur Dobbs* (1752), on the idea that Britain's future lay in America, and *Zeal Against the Enemies of Our Country Pathetically Recommended* (1755), against French interests in America.

STERN, RICHARD G[USTAVE] (1928–   ), born in New York City, a professor of English at the University of Chicago, whose novels include *Golk* (1960), a satire on television production; *Europe; or Up and Down with Baggish and Schreiber* (1961), about U.S. civil service men in postwar Germany; *In Any Case* (1963), treating a father's fight to clear his dead son of a charge of treason while being essentially treasonable to him; *Stitch* (1965), depicting an aged, expatriate American sculptor modeled on Ezra Pound; *Other Men's Daughters* (1973), the story of a middle-aged Harvard professor who falls in love with a young student; *Natural Shocks* (1978), treating a journalist who has to cope with the subject of death; and *A Father's Words* (1986), the effects, largely unhappy, that a post-middle-age man has upon relations with his family. Stories are collected in *Teeth, Dying and Other Matters* (1964), *1968: A Short Novel* (1970), *Packages* (1980), and *Noble Rot* (1989). Essays appear in *The Books in Fred Hampton's Apartment* (1973). *The Invention of the Real* (1982) collects essays, poems, and short prose pieces, as does *The Position of the Body* (1986).

STEVENS, ABEL (1815–97), Methodist clergyman, known for works on his church, which include *The History of the Religious Movement of the Eighteenth Century, Called Methodism* (3 vols., 1858–61) and *History of the Methodist Episcopal Church in the United States* (4 vols., 1864–67).

STEVENS, BENJAMIN FRANKLIN (1833–1902) and HENRY STEVENS (1819–86) were born in Vermont but emigrated to England, respectively in the 1860s and 1840s, where their interests as bibliophiles and antiquarians led them into the rare-book business, for a time together, later separately. The younger created a 180-volume manuscript index to the manuscripts in foreign archives relating to America between 1773 and 1783; the elder reprinted rare items from his collections and wrote *Recollections of Mr. James Lenox* (1886), telling of his part in creating the great Lenox Library (see *Lenox, James*).

Stevens, GAVIN, character in Faulkner's Yoknapatawpha saga, first appears as a Harvard graduate and young district attorney in *Light in August*. As Uncle Gavin, a county attorney in *Intruder in the Dust,*♦ he is persuaded by his nephew Chick Mallison to defend Lucas Beauchamp against the murder charge of which he is innocent. Gavin solves various crimes in *Knight's Gambit,* and in *Requiem for a Nun* he defends Nancy Mannigoe and takes Temple Drake to confess to the governor. In *The Town* he fights the rising power of the Snopeses while falling in love with Eula Varner Snopes, who tries to have him wed her daughter Linda. In *The Mansion* he continues his idealistic and "meddlesome" ways but he marries Melisandre Backus Harris, a widow.

GOWAN STEVENS, Gavin's nephew, in *Sanctuary* is the man whose drunken actions lead to Temple Drake being seized by bootleggers. In *Requiem for a Nun* he has atoned by marrying Temple. In *The Town* Gowan is called Gavin's cousin and is the source of much of the novel's lore.

STEVENS, HENRY, see *Stevens, Benjamin F.*

STEVENS, JAMES [FLOYD] (1892–1971), born in Iowa, after serving in World War I lived for a time in the Northwest, which furnished the background for his semi-autobiographical novels, *Brawnyman* (1926) and *Mattock* (1927). The tall tales of the lumbermen provided material for *Paul Bunyan* (1925) and *The Saginaw Paul Bunyan* (1932). *Homer in the Sagebrush* (1928) is a collection of Western short stories.

STEVENS, WALLACE (1879–1955), Pennsylvania-born poet, educated at Harvard (1897–1900) and at New York University Law School, made his business career as an executive of an insurance firm in Hartford, Conn. The few early poems he chose to save appear among later work in *Harmonium*♦ (1923), published when he was almost 44, but most of his poetry was written after he was 50, although its gaiety, vitality, and exotic imagination give no sense that it is the work of a man of such age and with a full-time business. His earliest poems have the finish, the elegant wit, the bizarre images, the lush figures, and the recondite diction that characterize all his work.

His poems range from descriptive and dramatic lyrics to meditative and discursive discourse, but all show a deep engagement in experience and in art. His musical verse, rich in tropic imagery but precise and intense in statement, is marked by concern with means of knowledge, with the contrast between reality and appearance, and the emphasis upon imagination as giving an aesthetic insight and order to life. These ideas are treated in "Sunday Morning,"♦ "Thirteen Ways of Looking At a Blackbird,"♦ "The Emperor of Ice Cream,"♦ and "Anecdote of the Jar,"♦ among other poems in *Harmonium*. *The Man with the Blue Guitar*♦ (1937) and *Notes Toward a Supreme Fiction*♦ (1942) are longer works that develop the ideas and techniques of the early poems at greater length.

Other collections of poems include an altered, enlarged edition of *Harmonium* (1931), *Ideas of Order* (1935), *Owl's Clover* (1936), *Parts of a World* (1942), *Transport to Summer* (1947), *The Auroras of Autumn* (1950), and *Collected Poems* (1954). *Opus Posthumous* (1957) collects plays, essays, some poems, including the full version of *Owl's Clover*, and epigrams. *The Palm at the End of the Mind* (1971) prints a selection of poems and the play "Bowl, Cat and Broomstick," complete in a book for the first time. Throughout this substantial body of work Stevens's philosophic views remain constant, as does the belief that

The poem is the cry of its occasion
Part of the res itself and not about it.

The Necessary Angel (1951) collects seven essays "on Reality and the Imagination." A collection of Stevens's *Letters* (1966) was selected and edited by his daughter Holly Stevens.

STEVENSON, ROBERT LOUIS (1850–94), Scottish novelist, essayist, poet, and traveler, in 1880 married an American, Fanny Van de Grift Osbourne, whom he had followed from Europe to California. Among the literary results of his sojourn in the U.S. are *The Silverado Squatters*♦ (1883), *The Amateur Emigrant*♦ (1894), *Across the Plains*♦ (1894), and a lost, unpublished "experiment in sensation," "Arizona Breckonridge; or, A Vendetta of the West," of which he finished only three parts. In 1887–88 he returned to the U.S., living for several months at Saranac Lake, writing essays for *Scribner's Magazine* and, with his stepson Lloyd Osbourne,♦ a farcical story, *The Wrong Box* (1888). In 1888, financed by the publisher S.S. McClure, he went to Samoa and the South Seas, where his writing included a vindication of Father Damien♦; and, with Osbourne, *The Wrecker* (1892), partly set in San Francisco, in which Pinkerton is modeled on McClure, and *The Ebb-Tide* (1894), set in the South Seas.

STEWART, DONALD OGDEN (1894–1980), humorist whose books include *A Parody Outline of History* (1921), *Aunt Polly's Story of Mankind* (1923), *Mr. and Mrs. Haddock Abroad* (1924), *The Crazy Fool* (1925), and *Father William* (1929). He also wrote for motion pictures and acted in his own play *Rebound* (1930). *By a Stroke of Luck!* (1975) is an autobiography.

STEWART, GEORGE R[IPPEY] (1895–1980), Pennsylvania-born educator and author, graduated from Princeton (1917), was a professor of English at the University of California, Berkeley (1923–62). His nonfiction includes *Bret Harte* (1931); *Ordeal by Hunger* (1936), about the Donner Party; *John Phoenix, Esquire* (1937), a life of George H. Derby; *Take Your Bible in One Hand* (1939), a life of W.H. Thomes; *Names on the Land* (1945, extended 1957), a historical account of place-naming in the U.S.; *Pickett's Charge* (1959), a vivid history of the final attack at Gettysburg; *The California Trail* (1962), a study of the main overland route to California in the 1840s and '50s; *Committee of Vigilance* (1964), about an episode in early San Francisco history; *Good Lives* (1967), studies of diverse people who had fulfilled lives; *Not So Rich as You Think* (1968), about man's despoiling of his environment, related to Stewart's long-time concern with ecology; and two compendia, *American Place-Names* (1970) and *American Given Names* (1979). Stewart's novels are *East of the Giants* (1938), set in pre-gold-rush California; *Doctor's Oral* (1939), about a Ph.D. examination; *Storm*

(1941), whose main "character" is a low-pressure area that occasions dramatic events as it bursts over California and sweeps the continent; *Fire* (1948), a similar treatment of a forest fire; *Earth Abides* (1949), about life after a disaster has killed all but a few people; *Sheep Rock* (1951), the ages-long history of a Nevada site; and *The Years of the City* (1955), the life cycle of a Greek city.

STICKNEY, [JOSEPH] TRUMBULL (1874–1904), New England poet, was known during his lifetime only as a classical student, despite the publication of his *Dramatic Verses* (1902). When his *Poems* was published by William Vaughn Moody and others (1905), it was discovered that he was a representative poet of his period.

STILES, EZRA (1727–95), grandson of Edward Taylor, graduated from Yale (1746) and became a tutor at the college (1749–55). During two of these years he practiced law at New Haven, after which for 22 years he was a pastor of Congregational churches in Rhode Island and New Hampshire, returning to Yale to become its president (1778–95). He was one of the most learned Americans of his time, and his ruling passion was to be a universal scholar. He was engaged in activities that ranged from the promulgation of silk manufacture in New England to helping found Brown University, and his boundless intellectual pleasure in the acquisition of knowledge is evidenced in the posthumously published *Literary Diary* (3 vols., 1901), *Extracts from the Itineraries and Other Miscellanies* (1916), and *Letters and Papers* (1933), although he wrote little for publication during his lifetime. Except for a few Latin orations and some sermons, he produced only *An Account of the Settlement of Bristol, Rhode Island* (1785) and *A History of Three of the Judges of King Charles I* (1794), a study of the regicides Whalley, Dixwell, and Goffe, who had fled to New England. *The Life of Ezra Stiles* (1798) was written by his son-in-law, Abiel Holmes.

Stillwater Tragedy, novel by Thomas Bailey Aldrich,♦ published in 1880.

STIRLING, ARTHUR, pseudonym of Upton Sinclair.♦

Stirling, PETER, see *Honorable Peter Stirling.*

STITH, WILLIAM (1707–55), born in Virginia, was educated at William and Mary and at Oxford, and wrote *The History of the First Discovery and Settlement of Virginia* (1747), based on careful study of the writings of John Smith and Robert Beverley and the records of the London Company. This is the earliest important secondary account of the colony to 1624, and shows Stith's sympathies to lie with the Company and against James I. He was chaplain to the House of Burgesses, and published several sermons, besides serving as president of William and Mary (1752–55).

STOBO, ROBERT (1727–c.1772), Scottish-born soldier, migrated to Virginia and served in the French and Indian Wars under Amherst and Wolfe. There is no record of him after 1770, but his *Memoirs* was published in 1800. He figures in Sir Gilbert Parker's novel *The Seats of the Mighty* and is considered the prototype of Lismahago in *The Expedition of Humphry Clinker,* written by his friend Smollett.

STOCKTON, FRANK R. (FRANCIS RICHARD STOCKTON) (1834–1902), Philadelphia novelist and short-story writer, was first known as an author of children's stories, some of which were contributed to *St. Nicholas,* ◆ of which he was an editor (1873–81). His juvenile stories are collected in *Ting-a-Ling* (1870), *The Floating Prince and Other Fairy Tales* (1881), and *The Bee Man of Orn and Other Fanciful Tales* (1887). After the publication of his whimsically fantastic novel *Rudder Grange* (1879), he began to write for adults, although continuing the same use of absurd situations that had made his juvenile tales popular. His chief books, after *Rudder Grange,* were the volume of short stories (1884) whose title piece was the sensationally popular "The Lady or the Tiger?" ◆ and the amusing novel *The Casting Away of Mrs. Lecks and Mrs. Aleshine* ◆ (1886), and its sequel *The Dusantes* (1888). The public also clamored for sequels to his first novel, which he furnished in *The Rudder Grangers Abroad* (1891) and *Pomona's Travels* (1894). His lively fancy continued to create many other tales and novels, but in later life took a somewhat different direction in such works as *The Great War Syndicate* (1889), *The Great Stone of Sardis* (1898), and *A Vizier of the Two Horned Alexander* (1899), which are sometimes humorously, sometimes seriously, concerned with pseudo-scientific matters. The comic *Buccaneers and Pirates of Our Coast* (1898) indicates another interest, continued in *Kate Bonnet* (1902), a satirical novel of 17th-century piracy, ridiculing conventional romances on the subject. During the last three years of his life, Stockton lived in West Virginia, which he had already known and described in his novels *The Late Mrs. Null* (1886) and *Ardis Claverden* (1890). A collected edition of his fiction was published (23 vols., 1899–1904).

STODDARD, CHARLES WARREN (1843–1909), California author, whose *Poems* (1867), edited by Bret Harte, preceded his wide travels that furnished material for his more famous works. Before 1873 he made two trips to Hawaii and one to Tahiti, resulting in the sketches *South-Sea Idyls* (1873; English edition, *Summer Cruising in the South Seas,* 1874), which range from delicately tinted description to the lush prose which caused him to be compared with Pierre Loti. His

voyage to Egypt and the Holy Land (1876–77) formed the basis for his narratives *Mashallah!* (1880) and *A Cruise Under the Crescent* (1898). He returned to live in Hawaii (1881–84), where he wrote *The Lepers of Molokai* (1885), first calling public attention to Father Damien ◆ and probably prompting his friend Stevenson ◆ to write his famous defense of the missionary. Other books resulting from this residence were *Hawaiian Life* (1894) and *The Island of Tranquil Delights* (1904). While in Hawaii he also wrote *A Troubled Heart* (1885), the story of his conversion to Catholicism. Upon his return he was a professor of English at the University of Notre Dame (1885–86) and at the Catholic University of America (1889–1902). His last years were spent in California, where, among other books, he wrote *In the Footsteps of the Padres* (1902). A posthumous collection of his *Poems* was made by Ina Coolbrith (1917), and *Diary of a Visit to Molokai in 1884* was published in 1933.

STODDARD, RICHARD HENRY (1825–1903), born in Massachusetts, was reared in squalid surroundings there and in New York City, and educated himself while working as an iron molder. He published a volume of romantic *Poems* (1852), and through Hawthorne's aid obtained a position as inspector of customs in New York (1853–70). After occupying other political posts, he became the literary editor of the New York *Mail and Express* (1880–1903), having during the previous 20 years written reviews for the New York *World.* His poetry, published in such volumes as *Songs of Summer* (1857), *Abraham Lincoln: An Horatian Ode* (1865), *Poems* (1880), and *The Lion's Cub, and Other Poems* (1890), was greatly admired in his day, but has come to be considered artificial, sentimental, and lacking in force, despite his gifts of melody and imagery. After 1870 Stoddard and his wife held a salon that was considered a center of New York literary life, and included not only such prominent contemporaries as Bayard Taylor and E.C. Stedman, but lesser-known figures like Melville, whom he befriended. During the last quarter of the century, Stoddard was a literary arbiter of the U.S., through both his newspaper criticisms and his editorial work, which included an edition of Poe (1894), with a complacent memoir attacking the character of this acquaintance of his youth. His autobiography, *Recollections Personal and Literary,* was published in 1903.

ELIZABETH DREW [BARSTOW] STODDARD (1823–1902), his wife, in addition to their collaborations, wrote *The Morgesons* (1862), *Two Men* (1865), and *Temple House* (1867), realistic novels set in her native Massachusetts. Although praised by Hawthorne, these were considered too grim for the average reader because of their truthful use of local color, anticipating Sarah Orne Jewett and Mary W. Freeman. Her *Poems* (1895) display poor technique, but have an intense, sometimes morbid, quality of personal revelation.

STODDARD, SOLOMON (1643–1729), Congregational clergyman, graduated from Harvard (1662), served as the college librarian (1667–74), was for a time a chaplain in Barbados (1667–69), and became pastor at Northampton (1672–1729). One of the most influential men in Massachusetts, he was concerned not only with theology but also with governmental policy and public morals. He was an early champion of the Half-Way Covenant, and introduced in his church the practice called Stoddardianism, which required merely a profession of faith and repentance, and not a relation of a personal experience of grace, as the prerequisite for the communion and other privileges of full church membership. He defended this policy against the attacks of Increase Mather in *The Doctrine of Instituted Churches* (1700), *The Inexcusableness of Neglecting the Worship of God, Under a Pretense of Being in an Unconverted Condition* (1708), and *An Appeal to the Learned* (1709). In these pamphlets he also advocated a national church and the vesting of greater power in the clergy. In *An Answer to Some Cases of Conscience Respecting the Country* (1722), he attacked contemporary foibles, immorality, wigs, lavish dress, and undue bibulousness. His belief that ministers should frighten congregations with threats of damnation is expounded in *The Efficacy of the Fear of Hell To Restrain Men from Sin* (1713) and *A Guide to Christ* (1714). His grandson, Jonathan Edwards, who followed him at Northampton, did not believe in Stoddardianism.

STODDARD, WILLIAM OSBORN (1835–1925), served for some time as a secretary to Lincoln, of whom he wrote a biography (1884) and whose *Table Talk* he collected (1894). In addition to a book concerning his life, *Inside the White House in War Times* (1890), and *The Lives of the Presidents* (10 vols., 1886–89), he wrote some 70 books for boys, of which the best known is *Little Smoke: A Tale of the Sioux* (1891).

STONE, BARTON WARREN (1772–1844), frontier evangelist who seceded from the Presbyterian church (1804). He and his associates called themselves simply "Christians," and acknowledged no creed but the Bible. In 1832 they united with the Disciples of Christ of Alexander Campbell. ◆ In addition to theological treatises, Stone wrote an autobiography (1847).

STONE, GRACE ZARING (1896–?), popular novelist whose books include *The Heaven and Earth of Doña Elena* (1929), the story of a Spanish nun; *The Bitter Tea of General Yen* (1930), the story of a New England girl involved in a Chinese uprising; *The Almond Tree* (1931); *The Cold Journey* (1934); *The Grotto* (1951); *Althea* (1962); and *Dear Deadly Cara* (1968). Under the name

Ethel Vance she wrote *Escape* (1939), *Reprisal* (1942), *Winter Meeting* (1946), and *The Secret Thread* (1948).

STONE, IRVING (1903–89), California author of widely popular fictionized biographies that include *Lust for Life* (1934), on van Gogh; *Sailor on Horseback* (1938), on Jack London; *Immortal Wife* (1944), on Jessie Benton Frémont; *Adversary in the House* (1947), on Debs; *The President's Lady* (1951), on Rachel Jackson; *Love Is Eternal* (1954), on Mary Todd Lincoln; *The Agony and the Ecstasy* (1961), on Michelangelo; *Passions of the Mind* (1971), on Freud; *The Greek Treasure* (1975), on Schliemann; *The Origin* (1980), on Darwin; and *Depths of Glory* (1985), on Pissarro.

STONE, JOHN AUGUSTUS (1800–1834), Massachusetts actor and playwright, best known for his romantic tragedy *Metamora, or the Last of the Wampanoags*◆ (1829), written for Edwin Forrest. He acted in his own plays, *Tancred: King of Sicily* (1831) and *The Demoniac; or, The Prophet's Bride* (1831), and revised Paulding's *The Lion of the West*◆ (1831). Another play for Forrest, *The Ancient Briton* (1833), concerned Boadicea. Stone committed suicide in Philadelphia, where Forrest erected a monument to him.

STONE, LUCY (1818–93), after graduation from Oberlin (1847) began her life work in her native Massachusetts, New Jersey, and elsewhere, for the causes of woman suffrage and antislavery. Although she was married (1855), she retained her maiden name as a matter of principle. She founded the *Woman's Journal* (1870), which for nearly half a century was the official publication of the National American Woman Suffrage Association, which split (1869) from the organization led by Elizabeth Cady Stanton and Susan B. Anthony, in part because they opposed passage of the 15th Amendment since it did not extend suffrage to women.

STONE, ROBERT [ANTHONY] (1937–), Brooklyn-born novelist, after service in the navy (1955–58) studied a year at New York University and another at Stanford before beginning to write. His works are *A Hall of Mirrors* (1967), a dark, intense story set in New Orleans during Mardi Gras, which is seen as a shocking nightmare; *Dog Soldiers* (1974, National Book Award), another view of a corrupt world, this one of drug dealing from Vietnam to California; *A Flag for Sunrise* (1982), a dramatic tale with political and philosophic views of a Latin American country undergoing revolution in the post-Vietnam era; *Children of Light* (1986), about a love affair between a screenwriter and a film actress; and *Outerbridge Reach* (1992), about a boat salesman failing in a marriage and in a round-the-world race in which he cheats, then commits suicide.

STONE, SAMUEL (1602–63), English nonconformist, emigrated to America (1633) with

Thomas Hooker, where he selected the site of Hartford, Conn., and removed there from Cambridge with members of his congregation (1636). He was a leader of the New England synods, and after Hooker's death (1647) became sole minister of the Hartford Church. During the latter part of his life, he entered into a violent controversy on matters of church polity, seemingly occasioned by personal friction with the ruling elder. His view, verging on Presbyterianism, was called by Cotton Mather "a speaking *Aristocracy* in the Face of a silent *Democracy*." His only book was *A Congregational Church Is a Catholike Visible Church* (1652).

STONE, WILLIAM LEETE (1792–1844), New York journalist and author, whose *Tales and Sketches* (2 vols., 1834) and *The Mysterious Bridal and Other Tales* (3 vols., 1835) depict the colonial life of Connecticut and other parts of New England. His interest in Indian life led him to write *Life of Joseph Brant* (1838), *Life and Times of Red-Jacket* (1841), *The Poetry and History of Wyoming* (1841), *Uncas and Miantonomoh* (1842), and *Border Wars of the American Revolution* (1843). Among his works on topical subjects was an exposé of Maria Monk (1836). As editor of the *Commercial Advertiser,* he was successfully sued for slanderous criticism of Cooper's *History of the Navy* and *Home as Found,* and he was the subject of a satire by Laughton Osborne.

WILLIAM LEETE STONE, JR. (1835–1908), his son, continued his father's career of journalist and completed his *Life and Times of Sir William Johnson* (1865). He was the author of several books on the Revolution and of a *History of New York City* (1868).

STONG, PHIL[IP DUFFIELD] (1899–1957), Iowa author, journalist, and Hollywood scenarist, wrote many novels of rural life in Iowa, including *State Fair* (1932), a tale of the Frake family and their week at the fair; *Stranger's Return* (1933), telling of a New York girl's visit to her grandfather's Iowa farm; *Village Tale* (1934); *The Farmer in the Dell* (1935), concerned with a retired farmer and his success in Hollywood motion pictures; *Week-End* (1935); *Career* (1936), telling of a crime wave in an Iowa town; *Buckskin Breeches* (1937), a story of pioneer life in the 1830s and 1840s; *The Long Lane* (1939); *Ivanhoe Keeler* (1939); *Miss Edeson* (1941); *Iron Mountain* (1942); *One Destiny* (1942); *Jessamy John* (1947), about John Law; *Forty Pounds of Gold* (1951); and *Blizzard* (1955). *Adventures of "Horse" Barnsby* (1956) is a flip satire in picaresque form of romances about the gold rush, and *Gold in Them Hills* (1957) is an informal history of the rush of 1849 to California. He also wrote humorous fantasies and books for boys, including *Honk: The Moose* (1935) and *No-Sitch: The Hound* (1936). He supplied the text for *County Fair* (1938), a book of photographs, and in *Horses and Americans* (1939) described the role played by the horse in the development of the U.S. *Hawkeyes* (1940) is a "biography of the state of Iowa," and *If School Keeps* (1940) is an account of the author's education and schoolteaching.

Stopping by Woods on a Snowy Evening, lyric poem in iambic tetrameter quatrains by Robert Frost, ♦ published in *New Hampshire* (1923). The poet stops his horse in the winter twilight to observe the beauty of the forest scene, and then is moved to continue his journey:

> The woods are lovely, dark and deep.
> But I have promises to keep,
> And miles to go before I sleep. . . .

Story (1931–53), monthly magazine founded at Vienna by Whit Burnett and his wife Martha Foley. It was devoted to short stories, often by unknown writers, which large commercial journals would refuse "because of tabooed subject matter or treatment." Printed for a time in Mallorca, it moved to New York (1933), became a bimonthly (1938) with book reviews and critical statements on the short story, and became a semiannual in book form (1951). *The Story of Story Magazine* (1980) is a posthumous, unfinished memoir by Martha Foley.

STORY, ISAAC (1774–1803), Massachusetts author whose *A Parnassian Shop, Opened in the Pindaric Stile; by Peter Quince, Esq.* (1801), a verse satire against Democrats, was modeled after the English "Peter Pindar." *Liberty* (1795) and *All the World's a Stage* (1796) were conventional 18th-century poems, and his essays "From the Desk of Beri Hesdin," contributed to the *Farmer's Weekly Museum,* imitated the "Lay Preacher" essays of the editor Joseph Dennie.

STORY, JOSEPH (1779–1845), Massachusetts jurist, was active in state politics and was a Democratic Republican congressman (1808–9) before he was appointed to the U.S. Supreme Court (1811). He held this position for the rest of his life, made many important decisions on admiralty and prize law, and virtually established American patent law. After 1829 he held a professorship of law at Harvard, where he was distinguished both as a teacher and as a pioneer in modern law-school training. In addition to other writings, his series of *Commentaries* (1832–45) is particularly important for *On the Constitution* (1833) and *Equity Jurisprudence* (2 vols., 1836).

STORY, WILLIAM WETMORE (1819–95), son of Joseph Story, graduated from Harvard (1838) and followed a legal career varied by his avocations of sculpture and literature, indicated in his *Poems* (1847). From 1847 he devoted his time to sculpture and spent most of his life in Rome, where he was influenced by sentimental neo-classicism. His *Cleopatra* and *Medea,* the former described at length in Hawthorne's *The Marble*

Faun, are representative of his choice of subjects, to which he gave plastic expression in a smooth, cool, but rather lifeless form. His books on Italy include *Roba di Roma* (1862), *Vallombrosa* (1881), *Fiammetta: A Summer Idyl* (1886), and *Excursions in Art and Letters* (1891). *Graffiti d'Italia* (1868), a book of poems, shows the influence of his friend Browning. He edited the *Life and Letters* (2 vols., 1851) and *Miscellaneous Writings* (1852) of his father. Henry James wrote *William Wetmore Story and His Friends* (2 vols., 1903).

Story of a Bad Boy, The, semi-autobiographical novel by Aldrich,♦ published in 1869 but dated 1870.

Tom Bailey's adventures begin with his sea voyage from New Orleans to Rivermouth (Portsmouth, N.H.), in the course of which he meets an old tar, "Sailor Ben." In Rivermouth he lives with his Grandfather Nutter, his maiden grand-aunt Miss Abigail, and the trusted Irish maid, Kitty Collins. Sent to grammar school, he enjoys a typical boy's life, and among his adventures with his gang, the Rivermouth Centipedes, are the presentation of plays, the burning of a stagecoach, snow fights, the thrashing of the town bully, and the firing of a collection of old cannon. Later, when he again meets Sailor Ben and brings him home to visit, it is discovered that the seaman is the long-lost husband of Kitty Collins. The story closes with the death of Tom's father, and the boy's going to seek a position in a countinghouse.

Story of a Country Town, The, novel by E.W. Howe,♦ published in 1883.

Story Teller's Story, A, autobiographical narrative by Sherwood Anderson,♦ published in 1924.

STOUGHTON, WILLIAM (1631–1701), probably born in England, graduated from Harvard (1650), studied at Oxford, and after losing his fellowship because of nonconformist ideas returned to Massachusetts (1662) to hold various political posts. He was on the council of Andros, but turned against the governor, and was later lieutenant-governor under Phips. After the latter's departure (1694), Stoughton was acting governor, except for one year, until his death. He presided at the Salem witchcraft trials and was largely responsible for their severe results. His views of a "Covenant-state" appear in the sermon *New Englands True Interest* (1670).

STOUT, REX [TODHUNTER] (1886–1975), novelist and publicist whose fiction includes such studies of contemporary character as *How Like a God* (1929), *Seed on the Wind* (1930), and *Forest Fire* (1933). He is best known for detective novels about Nero Wolfe, gourmet and connoisseur, who solves crimes without leaving his desk, including *The League of Frightened Men* (1935), *The*

Hand in the Glove (1937), *Too Many Cooks* (1938), *Some Buried Caesar* (1939), *Not Quite Dead Enough* (1944), *Murder by the Book* (1951), *If Death Ever Slept* (1957), *Death of a Doxy* (1966), *A Family Affair* (1975), and others, for they appeared at the rate of one or two a year.

Stover at Yale, novel by Owen Johnson.♦

STOWE, CALVIN ELLIS (1802–86), born in Massachusetts, graduated from Bowdoin (1824), studied at Andover Theological Seminary, and became professor of Greek at Dartmouth (1831–33) and of Biblical literature at Lane Theological Seminary, Cincinnati (1833–50). He was appointed commissioner for investigating European public schools, and his *Report on Elementary Instruction in Europe* (1837) had a great effect on American pedagogy. He was later professor of religion at Bowdoin (1850–52) and of sacred literature at Andover (1852–64). His books include *Introduction to the Criticism and Interpretation of the Bible* (1835) and *Origin and History of the Books of the Bible* (1867). He was married to Harriet Beecher Stowe.

STOWE, HARRIET [ELIZABETH] BEECHER (1811–96), daughter of Lyman Beecher, was reared in Connecticut under the Calvinist tutelage of her father. Her youth was one of morbid introspection, tempered partly by the liberal beliefs of her uncle, Samuel Foote, and the reading of such romantic fiction as that of Scott, which influenced her own later work. In 1832 she moved with her family to Cincinnati, where she taught at a girls' school, and began to write sketches of New England life. In 1836 she married C.E. Stowe, who was then a professor in her father's theological seminary. She observed the life of slaves during a visit to Kentucky, was influenced by the antislavery sentiment prevailing at her father's school, and stored impressions that she used later in fiction.

Upon moving to Maine (1850), she was stirred more than ever by antislavery discussion and availed herself of leisure time to write *Uncle Tom's Cabin*♦ (1852), which brought her nationwide prominence. Although she was not an Abolitionist, her supporters were, and to defend herself from attacks on the accuracy of her book she wrote *A Key to Uncle Tom's Cabin* (1853), a compilation of facts drawn from laws, court records, newspapers, and private letters. At the height of her fame, she made a trip to England (1853), where she was enthusiastically received, and of which she wrote in *Sunny Memories of Foreign Lands* (1854). To further the antislavery cause, she wrote her second novel, *Dred: A Tale of the Great Dismal Swamp*♦ (1856), which showed the demoralizing influence of slavery upon the whites.

After another trip abroad, during which she was honored by Queen Victoria, Mrs. Stowe returned to begin the writing of a series of books set in New England and having fiction rather than propaganda for their purpose. *The Minister's Wooing*♦ (1859) was a romance partly based on her sister's life, and contained an attack on the injustices of Calvinism, a religion that she eventually deserted. *The Pearl of Orr's Island*♦ (1862) was another novel using New England local color, as was also *Oldtown Folks*♦ (1869). In 1869 she again went abroad and met Lady Byron, from whom she obtained the information she published in *Lady Byron Vindicated* (1870). Her charge that Byron had had incestuous relations with his sister caused her to be accused of scandal mongering, and turned a great part of the English public against her.

She returned to New England themes in *Sam Lawson's Oldtown Fireside Stories* (1872), and in *Poganuc People* (1878) she wrote a novel closely based on her own childhood. *Agnes of Sorrento* (1862) is a historical novel set in Italy; *Pink and White Tyranny* (1871), a social satire; and *My Wife and I* (1871), a fictional essay defending woman's right to a career, which had as its sequel *We and Our Neighbors* (1875). Her *Religious Poems* was published in 1867, and some of her many lesser works were issued under the pseudonym Christopher Crowfield. After the Civil War, Mrs. Stowe lived mainly in Florida, and she described her quiet life there in *Palmetto-Leaves* (1873).

STRACHEY, WILLIAM (*fl.*1606–18), first secretary of the Virginia colony, after a literary career in England and a position as secretary of the ambassador to Constantinople (1606) accompanied Gates and Somers on the Virginia expedition of the *Sea Adventure,* which was wrecked in the Bermudas (July 1609), reaching Virginia the following May. During the year that he remained in the colony, he wrote a letter describing the wreck, which was first printed by Purchas (1625). The manuscript describing the storm may have influenced Shakespeare in writing *The Tempest.* Strachey's other works include *For the Colony of Virginea Britannia: Lawes Divine, Morall, and Martiall* (1612), the first legal codification for Virginia, and *The Historie of Travaile into Virginia Britannia . . . ,* inscribed to Bacon in 1618, but first published by the Hakluyt Society (1849).

STRAND, MARK (1934–   ), Canadian-born poet, educated in the U.S., has taught at various universities. His poems of alienation, treating darkness and doubleness in man, are minimalist in style and affected by surrealism. His lyrics appear in *Sleeping with One Eye Open* (1964), *Reasons for Moving* (1968), *Darker* (1970), *The Story of Our Lives* (1973), *Another Republic* (1976), *The Monument* (1978), *The Late Hour* (1978), *Selected Poems* (1980), and *The Planet of Lost Things* (1981). *Dark Harbor* (1992) contains a narrative poem in 45 sections, as well as reissues of his first two books,

plus a book of aphorisms. He has also written stories collected in *Mr. and Mrs. Baby* (1985).

Strange Fruit, novel by Lillian Smith,♦ published in 1944.

Nonnie Anderson, an educated mulatto girl, and Tracy Deen, son of a white doctor, grow up in a Georgia town, where their love affair must remain clandestine despite the girl's desire to devote her life to Tracy, and his sincere affection. Tracy is torn between class tradition and his suppressed wish to marry her. Her brother Ed, arriving from Washington for a vacation, tries to persuade Nonnie to go north, and her sister Bess, wife of a Pullman porter, also urges this, until Nonnie, pregnant, refuses an abortion and insists that the only happiness she wants is to bear Tracy's child. Tracy, meanwhile, is unable to resist his dominating mother's appeal that he marry their neighbor, Dorothy Pusey. He gives money to Henry, a black servant, to marry Nonnie and legitimize their child. When Henry drunkenly boasts of this, he is overheard by Ed, who intercepts Tracy after a rendezvous with Nonnie and kills him. Sam Perry, a black doctor, helps Ed escape north, but Henry is suspected. Although friendly white men attempt to protect him in the town jail, Henry is removed by a lynching party, who burn him to death. Nonnie returns to her work as nursemaid, her life blasted by events whose nature she does not try to understand. Sam, who hopes to marry her, and Bess, who from the first has accurately judged the weight of oppression over them, also return to their tasks, groping for meaning in the tragic plight of Southern whites and blacks.

Strange Interlude, drama in two parts and nine acts by O'Neill,♦ produced and published in 1928 and awarded a Pulitzer Prize. Its stream-of-consciousness technique uses asides to reveal the inner thoughts of the characters, often in ironic contrast with their speech.

Stranger in a Strange Land, novel by Robert A. Heinlein.♦

STRATEMEYER, EDWARD (1863–1930), author of several series of fiction for boys and girls, often under a variety of pen names. His most popular series includes 20 volumes of the Rover Boys (1899–1916) under the pseudonym Arthur M. Winfield, tales of preparatory school and college life, continued with ten volumes (1917–26) on the original boys' sons, and 40 volumes of works about the inventive Tom Swift (1910ff.). Other popular series include those about the peripatetic Motor Boys (1906ff.) and those for girls concerning the Bobbsey Twins, written under the name Laura Lee Hope. The Stratemeyer Syndicate (established 1914) produced books that Stratemeyer himself outlined and edited. All told, he is supposed to have written at least 150 full-length, hardbound novels.

HARRIET STRATEMEYER ADAMS (1894–1982), his daughter, continued all his series after her father's death, and expanded considerably on her father's three volumes about Nancy Drew, a girl detective whose exploits were described in works attributed to Carolyn Keene. Mrs. Adams was the major author of the Hardy Boys series, begun in 1927 by the Syndicate.

STRATTON-PORTER, GENE[VA] (1863–1924), Indiana author of books for girls, including sentimental novels and nature studies illustrated by her own drawings. Her most popular are *Freckles* (1904), about an Indiana waif who believes himself to be an orphan but is eventually reclaimed by his wealthy father; *A Girl of the Limberlost* (1909), the story of the companion of Freckles, Eleanora, who hunts the swamps for moths, which she sells to get money for an education; and *The Harvester* (1911), about a naturalist who resembles Thoreau. The author was known in private life as Mrs. Porter but signed her books by hyphenating her maiden and married names.

Straw, The, play by Eugene O'Neill. ♦

Stream of consciousness, a development of realism, ♦ influenced by modern psychological knowledge, is a method of the contemporary novel used to depict the mental and emotional reactions of characters to external events, rather than the events themselves. As opposed to the usages of conventional plot structure, description, and characterization, the action is presented in terms of images and attitudes within the mind of one or more figures, often to get at the psychic nature of the characters at a level distinct from that of their expression of ordered, verbalized thought. The term was coined by William James in *The Principles of Psychology* (1890) for psychologists but has long been applied to literature along with Edouard Dujardin's term, "interior monologue." Poe, especially in such a story as "The Tell-Tale Heart," and Melville and Henry James are considered to be among the American predecessors of the technique, even if Poe and James did not specifically practice it. Dujardin's *Les Lauriers sont coupés* (1887) and Joyce's *Ulysses* (1922) are considered the real forerunners and influences. After the impact of Joyce's work, the technique became pervasive and American novelists who have used it include Conrad Aiken, Sherwood Anderson, Dos Passos, James T. Farrell, Faulkner, Hemingway, Robert Penn Warren, Eudora Welty, W.C. Williams, and Thomas Wolfe. In *Strange Interlude,* O'Neill transferred this approach to the theater by the use of soliloquies and asides.

STREET, ALFRED BILLINGS (1811–81), New York lawyer and librarian, whose books of poetry, greatly admired in their time, include *The Burning of Schenectady* (1842) and *Frontenac* (1849). His descriptions of nature were especially appreciated.

Street Scene, play by Elmer Rice, ♦ produced and published in 1929 and awarded a Pulitzer Prize. A musical version was written with Kurt Weill and Langston Hughes in 1947 and titled *Street Scenes.*

Against the background of life in a New York tenement are presented the lives of the Kaplan and Maurrant families: Samuel Kaplan, a Jewish youth, falls in love with Rose Maurrant, an Irish girl, whose browbeaten mother, Anna, has taken as her lover the milk driver Steve Sankey. Her father, Frank, in a drunken rage kills Anna and Sankey. Rose, meanwhile, having refused a prosperous married man who wants to take her "away from all this," tells Sam that though she loves him she can never belong to anyone, for she must care for her brother and save him from an environment that leaves no life unblighted.

Streetcar Named Desire, A, play by Tennessee Williams, ♦ produced and published in 1947 and awarded a Pulitzer Prize.

Blanche DuBois, visiting the New Orleans home of her sister Stella and brother-in-law Stanley Kowalski, is horrified by the contrast between their squalid surroundings and her idealization of life at Belle Reve, the family estate now lost through bankruptcy. She reacts against Stanley's crude humor and animal maleness, while he resents her affected refinement and intrusion on his sensual privacy with his wife. At Stanley's poker party, Blanche meets Mitch and, sensing that he is lonely like herself and "superior to the others," she begins to think of marriage to him as a refuge from the past, which she has already sought in liquor and self-delusions about her age, beauty, and former admirers. Blanche contends that Stella's marriage and unborn child are products of lust, as aimless as the "street-car named Desire" shuttling through the narrow streets, and urges her not to "hang back with the brutes." In retaliation Stanley tells Mitch that Blanche lost her schoolteaching job because of an affair with a student and that she has become a nymphomaniac in quest of love to compensate for the loss of her homosexual husband by suicide. Mitch accordingly makes the kind of advances that he now thinks suitable, and although Blanche refuses him hysterically she is violently raped by Stanley in angry lust. Upon her return from the hospital with her baby, Stella is told the story by Blanche, but believing it an example of her fantasies, she has her committed to a mental institution. Blanche leaves with the doctor, saying, "Whoever you are—I have always depended on the kindness of strangers."

STREETER, EDWARD (1891–1976), author of *Dere Mable: Love Letters of a Rookie* (1918), *"Same*

Old Bill, eh Mable!" (1919), and *As You Were, Bill!* (1920), popular humorous treatments of the U.S. soldier in World War I. Later humorous books include *Father of the Bride* (1949) and *Chairman of the Bored* (1961).

Strenuous Life, The, essays by Theodore Roosevelt. ◆

STRONG, JOSIAH (1847–1916), born in Illinois, after graduation from Western Reserve University (1869) became a Congregational minister preaching the "social gospel" outlined in his book *Our Country* (1885), which called for a humanitarian purification of capitalism and a spreading of Christianity and this liberalized Anglo-Saxon civilization throughout the world. His other books include *The Twentieth Century City* (1898), *Religious Movements for Social Betterment* (1900), and *The Next Great Awakening* (1902).

STRUBBERG, FRIEDRICH ARMAND (1806–89), German author, lived in the U.S. (1826–29), and again as a Texas colonist (c.1839–54). His frontier life afforded material for many novels depicting German colonization in the Southwest, the lives of slaves, the Mexican War, the life of the Indians, and frontier conditions. None of his works was translated into English, but he attained great fame abroad as a counterpart of Cooper and an accurate portrayer of American life. He wrote under the pseudonym Armand.

STUART, CHARLES (1783–1865), born in Jamaica, served in the British East India Company and emigrated to the U.S., where he became converted to antislavery. His tract *The West India Question: Immediate Emancipation Safe and Practical* (1832), became the great text of abolitionists both in Great Britain and in America and was followed by many similar pamphlets. His most famous American disciple was Theodore Weld.

STUART, JESSE [HILTON] (1907–   ), Kentucky author of regional literature. His works on his native state include poems: *Man with a Bull-Tongue Plow* (1934), 700 sonnets; *Album of Destiny* (1944); *Kentucky Is My Land* (1952); and *Hold April* (1962); and collections of stories, including *Head o' W-Hollow* (1936), *Men of the Mountains* (1941), *Tales from the Plum Grove Hills* (1946), *Plowshare in Heaven* (1958), and *Save Every Lamb* (1964). His novels, also set in Kentucky, include *Trees of Heaven* (1940), about a farm couple and their son's love for the daughter of poor-white squatters; *Mongrel Mettle* (1944), a satirical story of a dog; *Taps for Private Tussie* (1943), about a mountain family's partly humorous adventures in spending insurance money paid after the supposed death of a son in the army; *Foretaste of Glory* (1946); and *Hie to the Hunters* (1950). *Beyond Dark Hills* (1938); *The Thread That Runs So True*

(1949); and *Year of My Rebirth* (1956), about his recovery from a heart attack, are autobiographies. Other personal works include *God's Oddling* (1960), tales about his father and his own youth; *To Teach, To Love* (1970), reminiscences of his teachers and his teaching; *The Seasons* (1976), a poetic autobiography; and *If I Were Seventeen Again* (1980). *Lost Sandstones and Lonely Skies* (1979) collects essays.

STUART, ROBERT (1785–1848), Scottish-born fur trader, was one of the party that went from New York by sea to found Astoria ◆ (1811). His return overland (1811–12) in a hazardous expedition is described at length in Irving's *Astoria,* and Stuart's own journal was first printed in P.A. Rollins's *The Discovery of the Oregon Trail* (1935).

STUART, RUTH [MCENERY] (1849–1917), Louisiana author of local-color stories, which depict the characters of the South in postbellum times. Her sentimentality, optimism, and ability at dialect won her a wide popularity. Her collections include *A Golden Wedding and Other Tales* (1893); *In Simpkinsville: Character Tales* (1897), treating backcountry hill people of Arkansas; *Napoleon Jackson: The Gentleman of the Plush Rocker* (1902), about black people; and *Aunt Amity's Silver Wedding, and Other Stories* (1909). *Sonny* (1896) is a long story, told in monologues, about the poor whites of Arkansas.

Stubb, character in *Moby-Dick.* ◆

Studs Lonigan, hero of a fictional trilogy by James T. Farrell, ◆ which includes *Young Lonigan,* ◆ *The Young Manhood of Studs Lonigan,* ◆ and *Judgment Day.* ◆

STURGEON, THEODORE [HAMILTON] (1918–85), novelist of fantasy and science fiction, ◆ noted particularly for tales that are psychodramas exploring loneliness, alienation, and shared consciousness, as in his most widely read novel, *More Than Human* (1953), which achieved cult status. His many collections of stories include *A Touch of Strange* (1958), *Sturgeon in Orbit* (1964), *Sturgeon Is Alive and Well* (1971), *Visions and Venturers* (1978), and *The Stars Are the Styx* (1979).

STURGIS, HOWARD OVERING (1855–1920), born in London of wealthy Massachusetts parents, lived most of his life abroad, where he was an intimate of such literary celebrities as Henry James, Edith Wharton, and his "quasi-cousin" Santayana. He wrote several novels with English settings, the best known being *Belchamber* (1904), the story of a tender young marquis in opposition to his own class and bent upon creating a universal brotherhood.

STYRON, WILLIAM [CLARK] (1925–   ), born in Newport News, Va., served in the marine corps before his graduation from Duke (1947). His first novel, which won great critical praise, was *Lie Down in Darkness*♦ (1951), revealing the tragic life and suicide of a girl whose rich Virginia family was unable to provide her or themselves love, understanding, and security. *The Long March* (1953) is a short novel about a forced training march of marines that results in the deaths of eight men. *Set This House on Fire* (1960) presents the hectic, finally violent, lives of some drifting, decadent American expatriates in Italy, exploring the mysteries of their complex relations. Styron's next novel, *The Confessions of Nat Turner*♦ (1967), won him his greatest critical acclaim (including a Pulitzer Prize) while stirring strong protests, mainly from black critics, of the way in which he conceived the protagonist and his followers in the fictive first-person rendering of the historical Nat Turner, leader of a slave rebellion in Virginia during 1831. Thirteen years passed before Styron published another novel, *Sophie's Choice*♦ (1979), which had comparably great sales and critical approval and denunciation, as he this time dealt with another subject alien to his background: experiences in a Nazi concentration death camp. *In the Clap Shack* (1972) is a comic play set in a venereal disease ward of the World War II navy. *This Quiet Dust* (1982) collects essays, reviews, and reminiscences. *Darkness Visible: A Memoir of Madness* (1990) is a narrative of Styron's struggle to understand and overcome clinical depression. Three long stories are collected in *A Tidewater Morning: Three Tales from Youth* (1993).

Such Counsels You Gave to Me, free-verse narrative by Jeffers,♦ the title poem of a volume published in 1937. It is based on the old Scottish ballad "Edward, Edward."

Howard Howren, eager for knowledge and success, has worked his way through high school and a year of college, unaided by his brutal, stupid father. Ill and overworked, he fears a nervous collapse, and returns to the family farm on the California coast, carrying a phial of poison with which to kill himself if his demand for financial aid is refused. His neurotic mother suspects his purpose, and, after his father laughs at his request, she persuades her son that it is better to live, even though he must work on the farm. At the same time she reveals her hatred and fear of her husband, of whose death she says she has been dreaming. A few months later, during an emotional crisis, Howard poisons his father. His mother then reveals her incestuous passion for him, and he realizes that his ambition and inner conflict have arisen from an unnatural love for her. He refuses to possess her, however, and she becomes insane. He acknowledges to himself that his crime developed inevitably from "divided desire and the split will," but decides that, rather than "escape easily" by suicide, he must undergo the ordeal of trial and execution. "There are cer-

tain duties," he tells himself, "Even for . . . what did you say? . . . modern man."

SUCKOW, RUTH (1892–1960), Iowa author, whose first novel, *Country People* (1924), is a strongly realistic study of three generations in a German-American family, the Kaetterhenrys, from their settlement in Iowa (1850) to their contemporary wealth and consequent loss of their original culture. *The Odyssey of a Nice Girl* (1925) tells of a young Iowa girl's struggle against the repressions of her family and the surrounding culture, and her eventual escape through marriage. Her subsequent fiction on the life of the region includes *Iowa Interiors* (1926), a collection of short stories published in England as *People and Houses* (1927); *The Bonney Family* (1928), a novel about a minister's household in the mean, unimaginative surroundings of a small Iowa town; *Cora* (1929), relating the Americanization of a German immigrant girl and her family; *The Kramer Girls* (1930), a novel; *Children and Older People* (1931), short stories; *The Folks* (1934), about the good but dull middle-class Fergusons; *New Hope* (1942), about a small-town minister; and *The John Wood Case* (1959), about the effects on others of an embezzlement by a respected citizen. *Carry-Over* (1936) collects *Country People, The Bonney Family,* and stories. *Some Others and Myself* (1952) includes stories and memoirs.

SUKENICK, RONALD (1932–), Brooklyn-born author, educated at Cornell and Brandeis, directed the creative writing program at the University of Colorado. His books include *Up* (1968), a satirical novel compounded of autobiography and fantasy in telling of a young man's maturing and his attempts to write a first novel; *Out* (1973), a novel about disaffected young New Yorkers of the 1960s trying to find a better life in southern California; *98.6* (1975), about life on an isolated Far Western commune; and *Blown Away* (1986), a curious tale related to Hollywood. *The Death of the Novel* (1969) and *The Endless Short Story* (1986) collect his stories, also radically innovative in style and structure. Other works include a study of Wallace Stevens (1967), *Down and In* (1987), a personal view of Manhattan bars, and *In Form* (1985), essays on the nature of fiction, prose, and, with Stevens, poetry.

SULLIVAN, FRANK (FRANCIS JOHN SULLIVAN) (1892–1976), humorist associated with the Algonquin Round Table♦ and longtime staff member of *The New Yorker,* to which he contributed a series of gently satirical interviews with Mr. Arbuthnot, an expert user of clichés, and an annual Christmas poem extending greetings to a great variety of people whose names formed the rhymes. Collections of his writings appear in a number of his volumes, including *Life and Times of Martha Hepplethwaite* (1926), *In One Ear* (1933), *The Night the Old Nostalgia Burned*

Down (1953), *A Moose in the Hoose* (1959), and *Frank Sullivan Through the Looking Glass* (1970).

SULLIVAN, MARK (1874–1952), journalist who is best known for *Our Times: The United States, 1900–1925* (6 vols., 1926–35), a survey of the American scene, divided into eras studied both in their large events and in the more informal matters that helped mold contemporary opinion. His autobiography, *The Education of an American* (1938), deals with his youth in Pennsylvania, schooling at Harvard, muckraking journalism with such magazines as *McClure's* and *Collier's*, and militant liberalism in behalf of the early Progressive party, and carries the account of his life to his mid-forties, after which he became a conservative Republican.

SUMMERFIELD, CHARLES, pseudonym of Alfred W. Arrington. ♦

SUMNER, CHARLES (1811–74), Boston lawyer, was elected on the Free-Soil ticket to the U.S. Senate (1851), where he became the spearhead of New England liberal opposition to the South. His vehement oratory in opposition to the Fugitive Slave Law and the Kansas-Nebraska bill reached its height in the speech "The Crime Against Kansas" (May 19–20, 1856), invidiously attacking Senator Butler of South Carolina and other Southerners. Two days later he was physically assaulted in the Senate by Representative Preston S. Brooks, a relative of Butler. This brutal beating made Sumner a martyr, and, though he was forced by ill-health to be absent from the Senate for three and a half years, he continued to hold his position, and was reelected. Upon his return he was the leading representative of the Republican party, which he had helped to found, and was not only among the first to suggest emancipation, but also urged equal civil rights for blacks, although he opposed Lincoln by contending that the seceded states had no rights under the Constitution. Under Johnson this difference on Reconstruction policy grew to such an extent that he was a leader of the radical Republicans, and took a prominent part in the impeachment proceedings. He also opposed Grant, particularly on his desire to annex Santo Domingo. His courageous crusading and the lofty eloquence of his speeches are preserved in his *Works* (15 vols., 1870–83). Longfellow wrote a memorial tribute, "Charles Sumner," in 1874, and Thomas Wentworth Higginson recalls him in *Contemporaries* (1884).

SUMNER, WILLIAM GRAHAM (1840–1910), professor of political and social science at Yale (1872–1909), is famous for both his economic and his sociological treatises. In economics he championed free trade, and is usually considered an advocate of laissez-faire, although his opposition to governmental control and labor organization was founded on the theory that they were likely to be unintelligent experimentation instead of scientific and unsentimental correction. In sociology, he believed that the science of society must be based on the study of the full interrelations of all institutions, from their most primitive to their most complex forms. He found that custom was the basis of all institutions, and in his book *Folkways* (1907) made a careful study of this underlying factor, showing the anthropological and sociological evolution of social institutions. His books on economics include *What Social Classes Owe to Each Other* (1883) and *Protectionism* (1885). His unfinished *Science in Society* (4 vols., 1927) was completed by A.G. Keller, who edited other works under the titles *War and Other Essays* (1911), *Earth Hunger and Other Essays* (1913), and *The Forgotten Man and Other Essays* (1919).

Sun Also Rises, The, novel by Hemingway, ♦ published in 1926. The title is derived from a pessimistic passage in Ecclesiastes, expressing a cynical disillusion in keeping with the postwar attitude. The English title of the work is *Fiesta*.

Lady Brett Ashley, "as charming when she is drunk as when she is sober," is traveling on the Continent, waiting for a divorce in order to marry Michael Campbell. Among her other satellites are Jake Barnes, an American newspaper correspondent; his friend Bill Gorton; Robert Cohn, an American Jewish novelist; and an eccentric Greek count. Cohn is weary of his mistress, Frances Clyne, and falls in love with Brett, although neither she nor his other acquaintances feel any real affection for him. The group leave Paris for an excursion in Spain, where they visit the fiesta at Pamplona. They are enthusiastic fans of the bullfights, finding in the ritualistic spectacle a mysterious beauty of precision. Brett and Jake are in love, but unhappily, because a wartime injury has emasculated him. She falls in love with a young bullfighter, Pedro Romero, with whom she elopes; and Cohn departs, expressing his anger by beating Jake, Michael, and Romero. When Romero wants to marry her, Brett decides to return to Michael, who is one of her own kind. She tells Jake, "we could have had such a damned good time together," and he concludes, "Yes. Isn't it pretty to think so?"

Sunday Morning, poem by Wallace Stevens, ♦ written in 1915 and published in *Harmonium* ♦ in 1923.

In eight 15-line stanzas of blank verse is presented, in the manner of a dialogue, a consideration of the end of life in two senses: its purpose and its conclusion. The issues are raised by an elegant, emancipated modern woman on her tropical patio rather than in church as she meditates upon secular and religious conceptions of reality, death, and the pleasures and beauties of this world as against those of heaven.

Sunnyside, country estate of Irving♦ on the Hudson River near Tarrytown, N.Y. He lived there (1836–42, 1846–59), receiving the visits of other men of letters and writing such works as *Astoria, The Crayon Miscellany, Wolfert's Roost,* and *The Life of George Washington.* The region about Sunnyside is described by Irving in many places, notably in "Sleepy Hollow" (in *Wolfert's Roost*) and "The Legend of Sleepy Hollow."

Sunthin' in the Pastoral Line, dialect verse by Lowell, in *The Biglow Papers.*♦

Superstition, blank-verse tragedy by J.N. Barker,♦ produced in 1824 and published in 1826.

Survey of the Summe of Church Discipline, A, treatise by Thomas Hooker.♦

Susan Lenox: *Her Fall and Rise,* novel by D.G. Phillips,♦ written in 1908 and posthumously published (2 vols., 1917).

Susan, the illegitimate daughter of a woman who died at her birth, is reared in a small Ohio town by an aunt and uncle, who force her to marry a loutish farmer, Jeb Ferguson. Running away from him, she is helped by a young newspaperman, Roderick Spenser, then gets a job as an entertainer on a showboat run by a man named Burlingham. When the boat is wrecked they are without money and he becomes sick. To pay for Burlingham's hospitalization Susan becomes a prostitute, and when he dies she becomes the mistress of a law student but refuses his proposal of marriage so as not to hurt his career. Upon meeting Spenser again, now an aspiring dramatist, she gives him money but also leaves him, having recognized that she is bad for him. She drifts into prostitution again, working for a gangster, Freddie Palmer, but meets a successful playwright, Brent, who helps her to become an actress and assists Spenser to get his play produced. Freddie out of jealousy murders Brent, and Susan is left lonely despite success starring in Brent's plays.

Sut Lovingood. *Yarns Spun by a "Nat'ral Born Durn'd Fool,"* 24 sketches by G.W. Harris,♦ contributed to the *Spirit of the Times* and Tennessee newspapers, collected in 1867. Previously uncollected sketches appear in *The Lovingood Papers* (2 vols., 1962–63).

Sut is a lanky, uncouth Tennessee mountaineer, who loves two things—corn whiskey and a joke. Hence come his humorous adventures in breaking up a black funeral, a wedding party, and a quilting, and being blown up by Seidlitz powders. His vivid, earthy dialect and tall tales come close to the true oral humor of the Southwestern frontier, and he foreshadows *Huckleberry Finn,* whose adventures have been called parlor versions of Sut's crude pranks.

Sutpen, THOMAS, and his family, white and black, are characters in the Yoknapatawpha saga of Faulkner and the subject of *Absalom, Absalom!*♦ They are also mentioned in other novels as one of the region's old families. In *The Unvanquished* Thomas Sutpen is described as second-in-command to John Sartoris but elected by the Jefferson regiment to succeed him and therefore to have the title of Colonel.

SUTTER, JOHN AUGUSTUS (JOHANN AUGUST SUTTER) (1803–80), Swiss adventurer and colonist, settled in California (1839) as proprietor of the wealthy New Helvetia Colony, protected by Sutter's Fort (Sacramento). When gold was discovered on the site of his sawmill, on the south fork of the American River at Coloma, by his partner James W. Marshall (Jan. 22, 1848) the influx of miners ruined his property, and as a result he died in poverty. His *Diary,* first published in the San Francisco *Argonaut* (1878), was republished in 1932, and his *New Helvetia Diary* (Sept. 1845–May 1848) was published in 1939.

SWADOS, HARVEY (1920–72), born in Buffalo, educated at the University of Michigan, was author of the novels *Out Went the Candle* (1955), a study of modern America, treating an opportunistic self-made businessman who alienates his children by trying to mold them; *False Coin* (1959), dealing with the problem of the artist trying to preserve integrity in a commercial society; *The Will* (1963), about three very different brothers trying to get their own ways as they struggle over an inheritance; *Standing Fast* (1970), recounting the experiences of a small group of dedicated Marxists; and *Celebration* (1975), depicting the relationship of a 90-year-old progressive educator and his radical grandson. *On the Line* (1957) collects stories about men on an auto assembly line; and other stories appear in *Nights in the Gardens of Brooklyn* (1961) and *A Story for Teddy* (1965). *A Radical's America* (1962) collects essays surveying America from a socialist point of view.

Swallow Barn; or, *A Sojourn in the Old Dominion,* 49 interrelated sketches by J.P. Kennedy,♦ published in 1832 and revised in 1851. In an Addisonian style, and undoubtedly under the influence of Irving, the work is a sketchbook of country life in Virginia during the first quarter of the 19th century. The slender thread of story, concerned with a friendly litigation between neighbors, which terminates in a love affair, has as a background a charming picture of Virginian life and local types, including the old Southern gentleman, the eccentric, oracular country lawyer, and the lovely young Southern girl.

Swamp Fox, sobriquet of Francis Marion.♦

"Swanee River," see *Old Folks at Home.*

Swedenborgianism, religious system incorporated in the Church of the New Jerusalem, based on the beliefs of the Swedish theologian Emmanuel Swedenborg (1688–1772). He contended that the inner meaning of the Bible is made clear through understanding that each natural object is the expression of a spiritual cause. He taught that there is one God, and that the Trinity is a division of essences, not of persons. The Father is the divine essence of love, the Son the divine Wisdom or Word to accomplish the redemption of mankind, and the Holy Spirit the divine proceeding by which life and love flow forth in act. The death and resurrection of Jesus symbolize the fate of man, who, if he has worked with the spirit of Jesus in love and obedience, will put aside his material body to pass from this probationary world to assume a spiritual body, becoming subject to a process of infinite perfectibility. The Church of the New Jerusalem held its first meeting in London (1788), although its teachings were known previously and had reached America in 1785. The formal organization was begun in America (1792), and has been strongest in Boston, Philadelphia, and Baltimore. One of its leaders was Sampson Reed, whose writings influenced Emerson, and the philosophy of Transcendentalism is indebted to Swedenborgianism for its prophetic optimism and doctrine of correspondence. The elder Henry James was also strongly impressed by these doctrines.

Sweeney, symbolic character in the poetry of T.S. Eliot,♦ representing the vulgar but vital force of life, particularly in modern man. He is introduced in "Mr. Eliot's Sunday Morning Service" (1918) as a contrast to the febrile presbyters. In "Sweeney Among the Nightingales" (1918) this ape-like man is ironically contrasted to Agamemnon, and in "Sweeney Erect" (1919) the sordid figure is further juxtaposed with great persons and ideas of cultural history. He appears incidentally in *The Waste Land* (1922) as a symbol of lust. *Sweeney Agonistes* (originally published in parts, 1926–27; combined, 1932) presents a different concept of Sweeney, who had formerly been associated with the slain Agamemnon, but who in this play becomes analogous to the slayer Orestes.

Sweet Alice, see *Ben Bolt.*

Sweet Singer of Michigan, THE, sobriquet of Julia A. Moore.♦

SWENSON, MAY (1927–89), born and reared in Utah of Swedish parents who were Mormons. Her poems, oracular, imagistic, and marked by experimentalism in technique and typography of shaped forms, appear in *Another Animal* (1954), *A Cage of Spines* (1958), *To Mix with Time* (1963), *Half Sun Half Sleep* (1967), *Iconographs* (1970), and *New and Selected Things Taking Place* (1979). *Poems To Solve* (1966) and *More Poems To Solve* (1971) are riddles for children. *Windows and Stones* (1972) is a translation of a Swedish poet. She was a co-winner of the Bollingen Prize♦ (1979–80). *In Other Words* (1987) was the last of her works published in her lifetime. *The Love Poems of May Swenson* (1992) contains 13 previously unpublished poems.

Swift, TOM, hero of books for boys by Edward Stratemeyer.♦

SWINTON, WILLIAM (1833–92), born in Scotland, was taken to Canada in 1843 and later removed to the U.S., where he joined the staff of *The New York Times.* His experiences as a correspondent furnished the background for his several books on the Civil War, which include *Campaigns of the Army of the Potomac* (1866) and *The Twelve Decisive Battles of the War* (1867). He was professor of English at the University of California (1869–74).

Symphony, The, poem by Lanier,♦ published in 1875 and collected in his *Poems* (1884). Employing a rich, complex versification to give an onomatopoetic expression to the different instruments in an orchestra, Lanier personifies each of them to discuss social questions of the time, particularly the inhumanities of trade and industrialism, and to set forth a philosophy of aesthetics, ending "Music is Love in search of a word."

Symposium Club, see *Transcendental Club.*

T

TABB, JOHN B[ANISTER] (1845–1909), Virginia-born poet, served as a Confederate blockade runner in the Civil War, and taught school in Baltimore. He was converted to Catholicism, and after ordination as a priest taught at St. Charles's College, near Baltimore (1884–1909), where George Sterling was one of his students. Tabb began early to write poetry but first attained fame when he published his *Poems* (1894). Later books included *Lyrics* (1897), *Later Lyrics* (1902), and *The Rosary in Rhyme* (1904). His brief, classically modeled poems, generally in the form of quatrains or musical lyrics, are marked by religious intensity and a cryptic, epigrammatic manner. His occasional humor, based on conceits, has caused his poetry to be compared both to that of his contemporary, Emily Dickinson, and to the work of the 17th-century English metaphysical poets.

Tablets, essays by Bronson Alcott,♦ published in 1868. The book is divided into two parts, the first "Practical," containing discussions on "The Garden," "Books," "Counsels," "Friendship," and other subjects in a manner somewhat reminiscent of Montaigne; the second "Speculative," dealing with "Instrumentalities," "Mind," "Genesis," and "Metamorphoses," in a more transcendental vein. The philosophic ideas in both sections are interspersed by original poems, which supplement the prose and frequently carry it beyond the logical development onto a more spiritual plane.

TAGGARD, GENEVIEVE (1894–1948), born in Washington, reared in Hawaii, graduated from the University of California (1919), and began her career as a poet with the publication of *For Eager Lovers* (1922) and *Hawaiian Hilltop* (1923). *Words for the Chisel* (1926) shows a greater maturity and a more metaphysical style, and *Travelling Standing Still* (1928) is a selection from these earlier volumes. Her only prose work, *The Life and Mind of Emily Dickinson* (1930), was followed by further poetry, including *Remembering Vaughan in New England* (1933), *Not Mine To Finish* (1934), *Calling Western Union* (1936), *Collected Poems* (1938), *Long View* (1942), and *Slow Music* (1946). Her literary interests are indicated by her anthologies *May Days* (1925), a selection of verse from *The Masses* and *The Liberator;* and *Circumference* (1929), a collection of metaphysical verse from Donne to E.E. Cummings. She taught English at Mount Holyoke (1929–31) and Sarah Lawrence (1935–48).

TAILFER, PATRICK (*fl.* 1741), an original settler of Georgia, quarreled with Governor Oglethorpe♦ and fled to Charleston, where he published *A True and Historical Narrative of the Colony of Georgia* (1741). This work, in which he was assisted by Hugh Anderson, David Douglas, and other Georgia settlers, is a carefully documented history of early Georgia, though its primary purpose is to satirize Oglethorpe's administration, which in a politely cold style is characterized as despotic and corrupt.

Tales of a Traveller, 32 stories and sketches by Irving,♦ published in 1824. The volume, resembling its predecessors *The Sketch Book* and *Bracebridge Hall,* was the product of notes and anecdotes gathered mainly during a tour of Germany (1822–23). The first three sections deal with European backgrounds: "Strange Stories by a Nervous Gentleman," "Buckthorne and His Friends," and "The Italian Banditti'; while the fourth section, "The Money-Diggers," contains five tales "found among the papers of the late Diedrich Knickerbocker," set in New York, and dealing with buried-treasure legends about Captain Kidd and other pirates.

Tales of a Wayside Inn, series of narrative poems by Longfellow,♦ published in three parts (1863, 1872, and 1874) and collected in 1886. The concept of a succession of tales by a group of congenial acquaintances was obviously derived from Chaucer, Boccaccio, and other authors. The setting is at a real inn near Boston, and the characters are based on Longfellow's friends. The musician is Ole Bull♦; the Spanish Jew, Israel Edrehi; the poet, T.W. Parsons♦; the theologian, Professor Daniel Treadwell; the student, Henry Ware Wales, a young Harvard scholar; the Sicilian, Luigi Monti; and the landlord, Lyman Howe, actual keeper of the inn at Sudbury. Of the 21 stories, only three deal directly with American themes:

Part First opens with the description of the inn and the members of the group. The first tale, "Paul Revere's Ride,"♦ is told by the landlord; the poet's tale, "The Birds of Killingworth," concerns Connecticut farmers who killed the small birds that destroyed their crops, and the way in which the birds were avenged by a plague of caterpillars who made the lands a desert; the theologian's tale is a love story set in rural Pennsylvania among Quakers.

Tales of Soldiers and Civilians, 19 stories by Ambrose Bierce,♦ published in 1891 and retitled *In the Midst of Life* (1892, revised 1898).

These grim, vivid stories, reminiscent of Poe's tales of horror, are marked by an ingenious use of the surprise ending and a realistic study of tense emotional states. Among the tales of soldiers, dealing with Civil War scenes, are "A Horseman in the Sky," telling of a soldier in the Union army, who, stationed as a picket near his Southern mountain home, encounters his father, a Confederate cavalry officer, and is forced to shoot, plunging him over a steep cliff to his death; "An Occurrence at Owl Creek Bridge," which is concerned with the illusory thoughts of a Southern planter who is being hanged by Union soldiers, depicting his mind in the interval between the tightening of the rope and the breaking of his neck, during which he imagines that he has escaped; and "Chickamauga," a lurid account of a deaf-mute child amid the horrors of a bloody battle that destroys his home and family. The tales of civilians also deal with sensational effects of mystery and terror, as in "The Middle Toe of the Right Foot," the story of the ghostly return of a wife to terrify the husband who murdered her, causing his death in a duel.

Tales of the Grotesque and Arabesque, first collection of stories by Poe,♦ published in two volumes in December 1839, dated 1840. The title was suggested by an essay of Sir Walter Scott, and the collection included 25 stories, among them "MS. Found in a Bottle,"♦ "The Assignation,"♦ "Berenice,"♦ "Morella," "Ligeia,"♦ "The Fall of the House of Usher,"♦ "William Wilson,"♦ and "The Unparalleled Adventure of One Hans Pfaall."♦

TALIAFERRO, HARDEN E. (1818–75), Baptist minister and editor in North Carolina and Alabama, known for his volume of *Fisher's River (North Carolina) Scenes and Characters* (1859), describing the Old Southwest frontier on which he grew up, in the manner of Longstreet's *Georgia Scenes.* A second series of sketches, contributed under the pseudonym Skitt to the *Southern Literary Messenger* between 1860 and 1863, was issued in book form as *Carolina Humor* (1938).

Talifer, blank-verse narrative by E.A. Robinson,♦ published in 1933.

Samuel Talifer, a middle-aged businessman, who has been engaged to the attractive but rather immature Althea, is now about to marry Karen, a woman of exotic beauty and complex intellect, with whom he claims to have "found Peace." This assertion amuses his wise and witty friend Dr. Quick, who sees that, while Althea genuinely loves and admires Talifer, Karen is motivated chiefly by a jealous hatred of Althea, and is interested in the theft of his affections rather than the man himself. Althea is meanwhile heartbroken, and the solitary Quick, who in his own way loves both women, can comfort her only by advising patience. Talifer and Karen are married, but immediately suffer from their extreme incompatibility. Karen, scholarly and remote, despises her undiscerning husband, who finds her impossibly refined and unsympathetic. The natural course of events, with Quick as catalyst, precipitates a crisis, during which Talifer secretly promises Althea that he will return to her, and Karen, because of a hysterical, ungrounded fear of murder by her husband, flees to the doctor's home. Quick sends her to his estate in Wales, to which he follows, while Talifer obtains a divorce and marries Althea. Two years later, the genial physician returns to find the Talifers happy at the birth of a son, and tells them that Karen has now devoted herself to study at Oxford.

Talisman, The (1827–30), New York gift book, published the works of Bryant, Verplanck, and R.C. Sands, all under the pseudonym Francis Herbert.

Talitha Cumi, essay by Samuel Sewall,♦ attacking theologians who denied the resurrection of women. It is subtitled "An Invitation to Women to look after their Inheritance in the Heavenly Mansions," and with characteristic wit the author says, "If we should wait till all the ancients are agreed in their opinions, neither men nor women would ever get to heaven." It was first printed in the *Proceedings* of the Massachusetts Historical Society (1873). The title in Aramaic means "maiden arise," and is from Mark 5:41.

Tall tale, term applied to the type of frontier anecdote characterized by exaggeration or violent understatement, with realistic details of character or local customs that work toward a cumulative effect of the grotesque, romantic, or humorous. Tall tales depend for their humor partly upon the incongruity between the realism in which the scene and narrator are portrayed and the fantastically comic world of the enclosed narrative. Frontier storytellers created the oral tradition of the tall tale, and folk legends and myths were developed through this medium, especially about such heroes as Paul Bunyan,♦ Mike Fink,♦ and Davy Crockett.♦ Later, the anecdotes began to be printed, and the tall tale became a distinct literary genre, which delightfully pictures the social life of the frontier. These mock oral tales were frequently published in almanacs and in such newspapers as the *Spirit of the Times,*♦ and were of a length dictated by the necessities of such publication. They were not only the creation of the frontier journalist, but the occasional amusement of lawyers, merchants, doctors, soldiers, actors, travelers, and gamblers, who turned amateur writer. Among the most famous literary examples are Longstreet's *Georgia Scenes,* Hooper's *Simon Suggs,* Thompson's *Major Jones,* Harris's *Sut Lovingood,* Baldwin's *Flush Times of Alabama and Mississippi,* Thorpe's "Big Bear of Arkansas," and many passages in the works of Clemens.

Talley's Folly, play by Lanford Wilson. ♦

Tamar and Other Poems, collection by Jeffers, ♦ published in 1924. The volume contains "The Tower Beyond Tragedy," ♦ "Night," ♦ "Shine, Perishing Republic," and "The Coast Range Christ." The title piece is a free-verse narrative, suggested by a passage in II Samuel 13.

An incestuous strain in the Cauldwell family, farmers on the California coast, begins with the passion of David and his sister Helen. Helen dies, but a generation later David's son and daughter by his wife, Lee and Tamar, break the same moral law, and Tamar becomes pregnant. She has desired "a love sterile and sacred as the stars," and now, terrified, attempts to conceal her sin by taking Will Andrews, a former suitor, as her lover. David's sister Stella becomes a psychic medium for the restless spirit of the dead Helen, impelling Tamar to further crime, for Tamar is jealous of Lee, who is about to leave for France to serve in the World War, and stirs her father to lust. In a paroxysm of contempt and desire, she brings Lee, Will, and David together in her bedroom, and by a fabric of lies sets them to fighting. During this violent encounter, an idiot aunt, Jinny, sets fire to the house, which is destroyed with all its occupants. This dramatic tale, of "passions turned inward, incestuous desires, and a fighting against ghosts," embodies the poet's allegorical warning to humanity against its growing introversion of values. Ending with desolation after a holocaust, it serves to demonstrate his vision of a culminating disaster, to be desired rather than feared, which threatens mankind because of its foolish and perverse attempt at self-deification.

Tamerlane and Other Poems, first collection by Poe, ♦ anonymously published in Boston (1827). The title piece is a narrative poem, revised in later editions, which shows the strong influence of Byron and purports to be the dying confession of the Asiatic conqueror to a strange friar, mainly concerned with memories of a passionate love.

TAN, AMY (1952–   ), born in Oakland, educated at San Jose State and at Berkeley, achieved wide critical and popular success with her first novel, *The Joy Luck Club* (1989), concerning the generation gap between the protagonist June, and three older Chinese women, members of the social group Joy Luck Club, which June's mother co-founded. The real theme is the difficulty of love and communication between mothers and daughters. Her next, *The Kitchen-God's Wife* (1991), also about a mother and daughter and the struggle to communicate well between old and new cultures and generations, was again both a critical and popular success.

Tanglewood Tales, see *Wonder-Book.*

Tante, novel by Anne Sedgwick, ♦ published in 1911.

Madame Okraska, a great concert pianist, insists upon adoration from her young protégée, Karen Woodruff, who blindly admires her as her "Tante." While the pianist is absent on an American tour, Karen marries Gregory Jardine, a conventional Englishman, but their happy life together ends when the hatred of the older woman for Jardine causes Karen to leave him. Madame Okraska's latest lover, Drew, wearies of her and falls in love with Karen, at which the older woman in a fury turns upon her. Karen realizes the true character of her tyrannical mentor and returns to Jardine.

Taos, village in New Mexico, north of Santa Fe, was a leading commercial center of the Santa Fe Trail ♦ and the home of such scouts as Kit Carson. It is now known for its Taos Indian pueblo, the finest example of Indian architecture in the Southwest, probably built in the 17th century, and for its artist colony. Maxwell Anderson's play *Night Over Taos* deals with the downfall of Mexican rule there in 1847, and Kit Carson's home is described in Willa Cather's *Death Comes for the Archbishop.* Harvey Fergusson's *Footloose McGarnigal* (1930) is concerned with the artist colony, of which such members as Mabel Dodge Luhan also wrote. D.H. Lawrence was a resident (1922, 1924).

Tar, *A Midwest Childhood,* autobiographical novel by Sherwood Anderson. ♦

TARBELL, IDA M[INERVA] (1857–1944), Pennsylvania author, editor, and lecturer, first became known as a leader of the muckraking movement for her articles in *McClure's Magazine.* From some of these was gathered her sensational exposé *The History of the Standard Oil Company* (2 vols., 1904). For the same magazine she had earlier written a *Life of Abraham Lincoln* (2 vols., 1900). She is the author of other books on Lincoln, *The Nationalizing of Business, 1878–1898* (1936), and an autobiography, *All in the Day's Work* (1939).

TARKINGTON, [NEWTON] BOOTH (1869–1946), Indiana novelist, first won popularity with his *Monsieur Beaucaire* (1900), the adventures in 18th-century England of the Duke of Orleans, who, disguised as a barber, has an affair with Lady Mary Carlisle from which he emerges a hero and she a cheat. Tarkington had already published *The Gentleman from Indiana* (1899), concerned with the crusade of a country editor against political corruption, and he now wrote a series of novels of life in the Middle West, of which two won Pulitzer Prizes: *The Magnificent Ambersons* ♦ (1918), the chronicle of three generations of a leading Indiana family and their decline during a period of transition, and *Alice Adams*♦ (1921), a study of a commonplace girl whose illusions are destroyed when a love affair with a man above her in social rank is ended by his acquaintance with her mediocre family. *Growth* (1927) is the title given to his trilogy of Midwestern city life: *The Turmoil* (1915), *The Magnificent Ambersons,* and *The Midlander* (1923); and other novels of the region include *The Conquest of Canaan* (1905), the story of an Indiana town; *The Plutocrat* (1927), a study of a self-made businessman traveling abroad; *The Heritage of Hatcher Ide* (1941), about the Depression years in a Midwestern city; *Kate Fennigate* (1943), the humorous story of a "managing" woman; and *The Image of Josephine* (1945), a story of a modern girl. Tarkington is also noted for his books about boys and adolescents, of which the most famous are *Penrod*♦ (1914), its sequels *Penrod and Sam* (1916) and *Penrod Jashber* (1929), and *Seventeen* (1916), about "Silly Billy" Baxter's puppy-love romance. His many plays include dramatizations of *Monsieur Beaucaire* (1901) and *Clarence* (1919) and several comedies with Harry Leon Wilson and Julian Street. He also wrote short stories, essays, and *The World Does Move* (1928), a book of reminiscences.

Tarzan, hero of juvenile adventure stories by Edgar Rice Burroughs.♦

TATE, [JOHN ORLEY] ALLEN (1899–1979), Tennessee author, began his career as an editor of *The Fugitive*♦ (1922) and also showed interest in regionalism through his contributions to the symposia *I'll Take My Stand*♦ (1930), *The Critique of Humanism* (1930), and *Who Owns America?* (1936), and in his interpretive biographies of Stonewall Jackson (1928) and Jefferson Davis (1929). He is best known for his poems, published in *Mr. Pope and Other Poems* (1928), *Three Poems* (1930), *Poems, 1928–1931* (1932), *The Mediterranean and Other Poems* (1936), *Selected Poems* (1937), *Winter Sea* (1944), *Poems, 1922–1947* (1948), *The Swimmers* (1971), and *Collected Poems* (1977).

His metaphysical poetry is distinguished by a neoclassical polish and satire, achieving sharp contrasts through use of archaisms verging on the baroque. He described his technique as "gradually circling round the subject, threatening it and filling it with suspense, and finally accomplishing its demise without ever quite using the ultimate violence upon it."

His criticism has been published as *Reactionary Essays on Poetry and Ideas* (1936); *Reason in Madness* (1941); *On the Limits of Poetry* (1948), including essays from the preceding volumes; *The Hovering Fly* (1949), literary essays; *The Forlorn Demon* (1953), "didactic and critical essays"; *Collected Essays* (1959); *Essays of Four Decades* (1969); and *Memoirs and Opinions* (1975). *The Fathers* (1938) is a novel set in pre-Civil War Virginia.

His anthologies include *American Harvest* (1942), edited with John Peale Bishop, a collec-

tion of creative writing, 1920–40; and, with his former wife (1924–59), Caroline Gordon, he wrote the text *The House of Fiction* (1950). Tate edited the *Sewanee Review* (1944–46) and taught at the University of Minnesota (1951–68). His correspondence with Donald Davidson was published in 1974, that with John Peale Bishop in 1981, and that with Andrew Lytle in 1987.

TATE, JAMES [VINCENT] (1943–), poet born in Kansas City, a member of the English department at the University of Massachusetts (1967–), came to prominence aged only 23 when his *The Lost Pilot* (1967) won the award of the Yale Series of Younger Poets. Praised by Robert Lowell for his "low-keyed, offhand style," counterpointing "feelings of estrangement, anger, and self-abasing humor," and noted too for his wit, later lyrics have been collected in *The Oblivion Ha-Ha* (1970), *Absences* (1972), *Hints to Pilgrims* (1971, revised 1982), *Viper Jazz* (1976), *Riven Doggeries* (1979), *Constant Defender* (1983), *Reckoner* (1986), *Selected Poems* (1992, Pulitzer Prize), *Worshipful Company of Fletchers* (1994, National Book Award), and other publications.

Taxation No Tyranny, tract by Dr. Samuel Johnson.♦

TAYLOR, [JAMES] BAYARD (1825–78), born in Pennsylvania of a Quaker family, early showed a poetic gift and desire to escape from his quiet surroundings. After the publication of his romantic verse, *Ximena* (1844), he went to England and the Continent, writing letters for the *New-York Tribune* and collecting material for *Views A-foot* (1846). The *Tribune,* delighted by his charming exoticism, made him manager of its literary section and sent him to California during the gold rush. After a year, he returned to publish *Eldorado* (2 vols., 1850), which augmented his popularity as an adventurous hero.

The following year, he departed for travels in Egypt, Abyssinia, Turkey, India, and China, and joined the Pacific squadron of Commodore Perry. Upon his return to New York (1853), he published in quick succession *A Journey to Central Africa* (1854), *The Lands of the Saracen* (1855), and *A Visit to India, China, and Japan, in the Year 1853* (1855), and was in steady demand as a lyceum lecturer. His prose accounts were supplemented by *Rhymes of Travel, Ballads and Poems* (1849), *A Book of Romances, Lyrics, and Songs* (1852), *Poems of the Orient* (1855), and other verse. Although he preferred to live as a conventional great man of letters, habit, public demand, and need of funds sent him off again in 1856 for two more years of romantic voyages, whose results were embodied in *Northern Travel* (1858), *Travels in Greece and Russia* (1859), and *At Home and Abroad* (1860).

After his return he was engaged in journalism during the Civil War and a good deal of hackwork, which was interrupted by a year (1862) as secretary of legation in St. Petersburg. From 1863 to 1870 he wrote novels, in which for the first time he considered his native country. *Hannah Thurston* (1863), a conventional love story set in upstate New York, is peppered by shots at the small-town mind and social reformers. *John Godfrey's Fortunes* (1864) is a realistic story of contemporary New York literary life. *The Story of Kennett* (1866) is a character study set in his native town of Kennett Square during the 18th century. *Joseph and His Friend* (1870) is another study of rural life in Pennsylvania, and *Beauty and the Beast and Tales of Home* (1872) is a collection of short stories that range from romantic depictions of Russia and realistic studies of Quaker life to satires on 19th-century reform. His poetry shows the same versatility, ranging from *Lars: A Pastoral of Norway* (1873) and *Home Pastorals, Ballads and Lyrics* (1875) to *The Echo Club and Other Literary Diversions* (1876), containing parodies of Whitman and other contemporary poets. Taylor's last years were devoted to a translation of Goethe's *Faust,* in the original meters (2 vols., 1870–71), which brought him a nonresident professorship of German at Cornell (1870–77) and the ministry to Germany (1878). This has come to be considered his most lasting work, even though the poetry itself rarely rises above the mediocrity that stamps all Taylor's sonorous but shallow verse, and which won him the somewhat hollow title of "laureate of the Gilded Age."

TAYLOR, EDWARD (*c.*1644–1729), English-born poet, emigrated to Boston (1668) and after graduation from Harvard (1671) became the pastor and physician of the Massachusetts frontier town Westfield, where he remained until his death. Not until 1937, when some of his poems were first published from manuscript, was he discovered to be an author of importance. His work as a Puritan sacred poet has been hailed as the finest 17th-century American verse. He is in the direct line of the English devotional metaphysical poets, such as Herbert, Crashaw, and Quarles, and his writings, though considered less important than those of his masters, are matched by none of his colonial contemporaries. His grandson, Ezra Stiles, in accordance with the request that none of his "poetical works" should be published, kept them in manuscript. Not until 1939 was the volume *Poetical Works,* edited by Thomas H. Johnson, published from the papers at Yale, followed by a more comprehensive edition of *Poems* in 1960. Fourteen related sermons, delivered 1701–3, and preparatory meditations in verse were first edited as *Christographia* (1962). Diverse *Unpublished Writings* were collected in three volumes (1981).

TAYLOR, EDWARD THOMPSON (1793–1871), as an orphan of seven began his life at sea, which lasted ten years. Ashore at Boston, he experienced an old-fashioned conversion in a Methodist chapel. Although he was not formally schooled, his fervor and unusual natural gifts brought him a ministry in the Methodist Episcopal Church. In 1829 the Seamen's Bethel was established at Boston to further the moral and religious welfare of sailors, and "Father Taylor," as he was affectionately known, was chosen to be its minister. His manner, which was like a sea captain's rather than a preacher's, and his sermons, which were full of imagery and language of the sea, are reproduced in the sermon of Father Mapple in *Moby-Dick.* His popularity may be judged by Dana's remark in *Two Years Before the Mast* that the first inquiry of the far-off California sailors was for Father Taylor. He is mentioned in Harriet Martineau's *Retrospect of Western Travel,* Dicken's *American Notes,* and Emerson's *Journals,* and is the subject of an article by Whitman.

TAYLOR, GRAHAM (1851–1938), began his career as a religious and social thinker as a pastor of the Dutch Reformed Church, became a professor at the Chicago Theological Seminary, and founded the Chicago Commons Social Settlement (1894). His writings include *Religion and Social Action* (1913), setting forth his belief that men can be truly devout only if they negate their individuality and recognize themselves to be members of society; *Pioneering on Social Frontiers* (1930), an autobiography; and *Chicago Commons Through Forty Years* (1936).

TAYLOR, HENRY [SPLAWN] (1942–), poet born in Virginia and educated at its state university, has long been a professor at the University of Washington (1971–). His first book of poetry, *The Horse Show at Midnight* (1966), has been followed by others, leading to *The Flying Change* (1985), marked by interest in the natural scene of his native state, awarded a Pulitzer Prize for poetry.

TAYLOR, JOHN (1753–1824), called "John Taylor of Caroline," was born in Virginia, and educated privately and at William and Mary (1770). After practicing law and serving in the Revolutionary army, he was elected to the Virginia House of Delegates (1779–81, 1783–85, 1796–1800). He served as U.S. senator (1792–94), joining Patrick Henry and George Mason in opposing ratification of the Constitution, on the ground that it failed to provide adequate individual and states' rights. Taylor was considered the theorist of Jeffersonian democracy, and fear of aristocracy and commercial autocracy permeates all his writings, in which he looks upon politics from the point of view of an economist believing in local government and states' rights. *An Inquiry into the Principles and Policy of the Government of the United States* (1814) is an attack on the Hamiltonian fiscal system and on John Adams's theory of a natural aristocracy. In *Construction Construed and Constitutions Vindicated* (1820), a reply to Marshall's decisions, he contended the Supreme

Court had no jurisdiction over appeals from state courts. *Tyranny Unmasked* (1822) attacked high protective tariffs to aid American industry. His attitude toward constitutional government is expressed in *New Views of the Constitution* (1823); and *Arator* (1831), 61 "agricultural essays, practical and political," sets forth his belief in an agrarian order.

TAYLOR, PETER [HILLSMAN] (1917–94), born in Tennessee. His stories, which sensitively depict characters and situations of contemporary middle-class life in the South, appear in *A Long Fourth* (1948), *The Widows of Thornton* (1954), *Happy Families Are All Alike* (1959), *Miss Leonora When Last Seen* (1963), *Collected Stories* (1969), *In the Miro District* (1977), and *The Old Forest* (1985). His novels are *A Woman of Means* (1950), *A Summons to Memphis* (1986, Pulitzer Prize), and *In the Tennessee Country* (1994). *Tennessee Day in St. Louis* (1956), *A Stand in the Mountains* (1968), and *Presences* (1973) are plays. *The Oracle of Stoneleigh Court* (1993), containing a novella, ten stories, and three one-act plays, is rife with ghosts and other supernatural phenomena.

TAYLOR, ROBERT LEWIS (1912–   ), Illinois-born novelist and journalist, wrote profiles for *The New Yorker* (1939–48) collected in *Doctor, Lawyer, Merchant, Chief* (1948) and *The Running Pianist* (1950). He also wrote *W.C. Fields, His Follies and Fortunes* (1949), *Winston Churchill* (1952), and *Vessel of Wrath* (1966), a life of Carry Nation. His fiction includes the satirical novels *Adrift in a Boneyard* (1947), *Professor Fodorski* (1950), and *The Bright Sands* (1954). *The Travels of Jamie McPheeters* (1958, Pulitzer Prize) is a rollicking picaresque tale of a teenage boy and his father en route from Louisville to California in 1849 and of life in the gold rush. *A Journey to Matecumbe* (1961) is another picaresque tale, about a boy and his uncle fleeing the Ku Klux Klan during Reconstruction; *Two Roads to Guadalupé* (1964) is still another lusty adventure story, about a teenage boy and his older brother in the Mexican War; *A Roaring in the Wind* (1978) is about an expelled Harvard student of the mid-19th century who tells of his adventures in a lusty Montana town; and *Niagara* (1980) is a rambunctious tale of life in the upstate New York resort town.

Tea and Sympathy, play by Robert W. Anderson.♦

TEACH, EDWARD, see *Blackbeard.*

TEALE, EDWIN WAY (1899–1980), Illinois-born journalist and author of numerous books on nature and ecology, whose works include *Grassroots Jungles* (1937), *Near Horizons: The Story of an Insect Garden* (1942), *Dune Boy: The Early Years of a Naturalist* (1943), *Journey into Summer* (1960), *Wandering Through Winter* (1965, Pulitzer Prize), and *A Naturalist Buys an Old Farm* (1974).

TEASDALE, SARA (1884–1933), lyric poet born in Missouri, made her home in New York, and became known for her unaffected quatrains, which, almost bare of imagery and sparing in metaphor, attempt the articulation of a mood, rather than the quest of universals. Her works include *Sonnets to Duse and Other Poems* (1907), *Helen of Troy* (1911), *Rivers to the Sea* (1915), *Love Songs* (1917, special Pulitzer award), *Flame and Shadow* (1920), *Dark of the Moon* (1926), *Strange Victory* (1933), and *Collected Poems* (1937).

TECUMSEH (1768?–1813), Shawnee Indian chief, who established a confederacy of tribes, and was led into a war (1811) with the U.S. when the government refused to recognize his principle that all Indian lands were a common possession that could not be ceded by or purchased from individual tribes. During his absence, Tenskwatawa (1768?–1834?), the "Shawnee Prophet," who is considered to have been Tecumseh's twin brother, was maneuvered by W.H. Harrison into the disastrous battle of Tippecanoe♦ (1811), and the war came to an end. During the War of 1812, Tecumseh was made a brigadier general by the British, and was killed in battle. In 1836 Dr. William Emmons published "a national drama" called *Tecumseh,* a subject he had previously employed in his epic *The Fredoniad; or Independence Preserved* (4 vols., 1827), a poetic history of the War of 1812. The Indian chief also figures in James Strange French's *Elkswatawa; or, The Prophet of the West* (1836), Edward S. Ellis's *The Forest Spy* (1861), and other melodramatic novels, as well as being the subject of a romantic biography (1841) by Benjamin Drake.

Telling the Bees, poem by Whittier,♦ in an approximation of ballad meter, published in 1858 and collected in *Home Ballads* (1860). A young man passes the farm of his beloved, where he sees the hired girl observing the old New England custom of dressing the hives in mourning and informing the bees of a death. He thinks his Mary's grandfather has died, but is stunned to hear the chore girl tell the bees "Mistress Mary is dead and gone!"

Tell-Tale Heart, The, story by Poe,♦ published in *The Pioneer* (1843). It has been considered the most influential of Poe's stories in the later development of stream-of-consciousness fiction.

A victim of a nervous disease is overcome by homicidal mania and murders an innocent old man in whose home he lives. He confuses the ticking of the old man's watch with an excited heartbeat, and although he dismembers the body he neglects to remove the watch when he buries the pieces beneath the floor. The old man's dying shriek has been overheard, and three police officers come to investigate. They discover nothing, and the murderer claims that the old man is absent in the country, but when they remain to question him he hears a loud rhythmic sound that he believes to be the beating of the buried heart. This so distracts his diseased mind that he suspects the officers know the truth and are merely trying his patience, and in an insane fit he confesses his crime.

Temple, family name of characters in the Leather-Stocking Tales♦ and other novels of Cooper.

Temple, CHARLOTTE, see *Charlotte Temple.*

Temple Drake, character in Faulkner's *Sanctuary*♦ and its sequel, *Requiem for a Nun.*

Ten Days That Shook the World, history by John Reed,♦ published in 1919. A dramatization by Robert E. Lee was produced in 1973.

A reportorial, firsthand, and sympathetic account of the November Revolution in Russia (1917), when, as the author puts it, "the Bolsheviki, at the head of the workers and soldiers, seized the state power of Russia and placed it in the hands of the Soviets." After prefatory explanation of political groups and other organizations, and of the background of the uprising, the work tells with graphic detail of the fall of the provisional government, the revolution and counterrevolution, the solidifying of power, and the resultant congress.

Ten Nights in a Barroom and What I Saw There, melodramatic story by T.S. Arthur,♦ published in 1854. It became a favorite text for temperance lecturers, and was popular in the dramatic version by William W. Pratt (1858). A temperance song by Henry Clay Work, "Come Home, Father," which begins:

> Father, dear father, come home with me now,
> The clock in the belfry strikes one

was introduced into the play about 1864.

A traveler, who visits the town of Cedarville from time to time during a period of ten years, notes the changing fortunes of the citizens, and places the responsibility on the evil influences of Simon Slade's saloon, the "Sickle and Sheaf." The landlord rises to affluence but then gradually sinks into poverty and degradation, and among the gruesome events that are described are Slade's accidental murder of little Mary, the daughter of Joe Morgan the drunkard, who comes to fetch her father home from the saloon and is hit by a glass which is thrown at him in a brawl; the disastrous gambling experiences of Willy Hammond with the cheating Harvey Green, who murders him; the insanity of Mrs. Slade, resulting from her son's rowdyism; and finally the son's murder of his father. Following this last outrage, the townspeople hold a mass meeting, decree a prohibition on the sale of liquor, destroy the saloon's stock, and disperse with new hope for the town's future.

Tender Is the Night, novel by F. Scott Fitzgerald,♦ published in 1934. Early versions date back to 1925, and the one first published began with Rosemary's arrival in the Diver circle; but in the last two years of his life Fitzgerald reorganized the story into chronological order in a version first issued, with Malcolm Cowley's commentary, in 1948.

Dick Diver, a young American psychiatrist completing his training in Zurich at the end of World War I, becomes interested in the case of Nicole Warren, a beautiful American girl with acute schizophrenia resulting from an incestuous relation with her father. As she recovers, she falls in love with Dick and comes to rely on him for stability and identity in what is for her a new and uncertain world. He returns her love, but also allows himself to acknowledge, if not to accept, a suggestion from her wealthy family, represented by her sister Baby, that he remain with her in order to care for her. Thus, in their marriage, the psychiatrist is involved, and to a degree confused, with the lover and the companion, and "her problem was one they had together for good now." Dick ceases "temporarily" to practice, though continuing to work on a new book. They have two children, and settle into a life of leisure on the Riviera with a circle of friends including Abe North, an alcoholic composer, and Tommy Barban, a French soldier of fortune in love with Nicole. Dick's effortless charm, which lets people feel at ease, makes him an ideal host, but although he is loved and admired, he is spending emotional resources which are not being replenished. Rosemary Hoyt, a naïve American movie actress who joins the group, falls in love with Dick and, attending a party at the Divers' villa, sees their life as magnificent, tasteful, and free, but she is "unaware of its complexity and lack of innocence." Out of touch with his work, his marriage and his very love for Nicole increasingly defined in terms of her illness, Dick becomes infatuated with Rosemary. He begins to drink more; his easy confidence begins to wear thin; and though in moments of crisis and relapse Nicole appeals to him, both her confidence in him and her dependence on him are gradually undermined. The same "transference" that partially drew her to him at the outset now draws his psychological strength toward her. Abe, long recognized by Dick as a hopeless case, fails in an effort to go back to America and to work, and is beaten to death in a Paris bar. Dick himself is involved in a brawl in Rome, and Baby, who extricates him, thus gains a "moral superiority" as well as a financial one over him. He is without illusions, having "managed to keep alive the low painful fire of intelligence," but he has lost himself through the intricacies of his relation to Nicole and his habitual desire to please her. Tommy, who loves Nicole but does not try to understand her, becomes her lover, and after they confront Dick for a divorce, he returns to America to sink into final obscurity.

Tennessee's Partner, tale by Bret Harte,♦ published in the *Overland Monthly* (1869) and in *The Luck of Roaring Camp and Other Sketches* (1870).

Tennessee, "known to be a gambler . . . suspected to be a thief," works a mining claim at Sandy Bar, Cal., with his unnamed "Partner." Although Tennessee once eloped with his Partner's wife, returning after she deserted him too, the Partner remains his affectionate friend. One day Tennessee is captured as a highway robber, and during an impromptu trial his Partner innocently offers his entire "stake" in return for Tennessee's life. This strengthens the determination of the "court" to punish the thief, and he is hanged from a nearby tree. Tennessee's Partner arrives with a donkey cart to claim the body of "the diseased," and the crowd joins him in a rude but tender funeral ceremony. After this loss, the Partner declines in health. When he dies the following spring, he imagines that he sees his friend coming to welcome him.

TENNEY, TABITHA [GILMAN] (1762–1837), New Hampshire novelist, resided in Washington, D.C. (1800–1807), during her husband's terms in Congress and wrote there her only novel, *Female Quixotism♦* (1801). This satire is in itself somewhat crude, but it is important for its understanding of the absurdities of contemporary feminine fiction.

TENSAS, MADISON, M.D., pseudonym of Dr. Henry Clay Lewis (1825–50), whose *Odd Leaves from the Life of a Louisiana Swamp Doctor* (1850) is a humorous work of the Old Southwestern frontier based on experiences in Kentucky and Louisiana.

TENSKWATAWA, see *Tecumseh.*

Tenth Muse, The, see *Bradstreet, Anne.*

TERHUNE, ALBERT PAYSON (1872–1942), son of the novelist Mary Virginia Terhune, with whom he collaborated on *Dr. Dale: A Story Without a Moral* (1900), became known for his fiction about collies, which includes *Lad: A Dog* (1919), *Bruce* (1920), and *Lad of Sunnybank* (1928). Other works include two autobiographical books, *Now That I'm Fifty* (1924) and *To the Best of My Memory* (1930).

TERHUNE, MARY VIRGINIA (1830–1922), popular romantic novelist, whose 26 novels, mostly concerned with the South before or during the Civil War, marked by a strongly moral manner, include *Alone* (1854), *Sunnybank* (1866), and *A Gallant Fight* (1888). She wrote under the pseudonym Marion Harland, and was also well known for her travel books, biographical studies, and works on household management. Albert Payson Terhune was her son.

TERKEL, STUDS [LOUIS] (1912–), Chicago radio and television interviewer, whose books are *Giants of Jazz* (1957), brief biographies of 12 musicians; *Division Street: America* (1966), transcriptions of his conversations with 70 very diverse persons of the Chicago area presenting a cross section of people and their concerns; *Hard Times* (1970), comparable conversations to create "an Oral History of the Great Depression"; *Working* (1974), further interviews; *Talking to Myself* (1977), "a memoir of my times"; *American Dreams: Lost and Found* (1980), interviews with plain people, which tell their autobiographies; and *The Good War* (1984), using the same techniques to document World War II, awarded a Pulitzer Prize for a general nonfiction work. He also wrote a play, *Amazing Grace* (1959).

Testament of Man, THE, cycle of 12 novels by Vardis Fisher.♦

TEUFFEL, BARONESS VON, see *Howard, Blanche.*

THACHER, JAMES (1754–1844), Massachusetts physician, served as a surgeon in the Continental army, and published an account of his experiences in *A Military Journal During the American Revolutionary War* (1823), which, like his *American Medical Biography* (1828), is a valuable source.

THACKERAY, WILLIAM MAKEPEACE (1811–63), English novelist, twice visited the U.S. (Nov. 1852–April 1853; Oct. 1855–April 1856), delivering lectures on English literature and history. Prior to his first trip he had published *Henry Esmond,♦* the conclusion of which deals with colonial Virginia. Its sequel, *The Virginians,♦* was the result of research begun during the second visit, when he outlined the idea to Cooke and received suggestions from J.P. Kennedy.

Thanatopsis, blank-verse poem by Bryant,♦ written when he was 16 years old, after reading Blair's *Grave,* Cowper's *Task,* and various poems by Southey and Henry Kirke White. The early version of "Thanatopsis," whose Greek title means "view of death," was published in *The North American Review* (1817). It lacked the first 17 lines and the last 15 of the present work, which was first collected in the author's *Poems* (1821). These passages materially altered the philosophic significance of the poem, in which Nature, rather than the author's "better genius," now discusses death. Nature speaks a varied language to man, the poet observes; when "thoughts of the last bitter hour" come, it teaches that earth claims all it has nourished. Man must therefore learn to conduct his life in such a way that he need have no fear when his summons comes to join the "innumerable caravan."

THANET, OCTAVE, see *French, Alice.*

THATCHER, BENJAMIN BUSSEY (1809–40), Boston antislavery leader, opposed the policies of

Garrison and urged African repatriation. In addition to his *Memoir of Phillis Wheatley* (1834), he wrote other books on blacks, and was also known for his *Indian Biography* (1832) and *Indian Traits* (1833).

THAXTER, CELIA [LAIGHTON] (1835–94), was the daughter of a lighthouse keeper on the Isles of Shoals, off the New Hampshire coast, where she spent most of her life. Her depiction of the various moods of the sea form the subject matter of her *Poems* (1872), *Drift-Weed* (1879), *Idyls and Pastorals* (1886), and other volumes. Her prose sketches devoted to the same subjects appear in *Among the Isles of Shoals* (1873) and *An Island Garden* (1894). She was as well known for her personality as for her poetry, and visitors at the hotel conducted by her family included Thoreau, Lowell, Whittier, and other authors and artists.

THAYER, ALEXANDER WHEELOCK (1817–97), born in Massachusetts, graduated from Harvard (1843), and became famous as a music critic for the New York *Tribune* and other papers. He was U.S. consul at Trieste (1864–82). His most famous work is his *Life of Beethoven* (3 vols., 1866–79).

THAYER, CAROLINE, see *Warren, Caroline.*

THAYER, WILLIAM ROSCOE (1859–1923), Boston author and editor whose works include *The Life and Letters of John Hay* (1915), *Theodore Roosevelt: An Intimate Biography* (1919), and several important works on Italian history.

Theatre Arts (1916–64), journal dealing with all the arts of the theater in the U.S. and abroad, for a long time sympathetic to experimentation. Begun as a quarterly, it became a monthly (1924), had slight changes of title, and upon occasion (1945–63) was more conservative in outlook.

Theatre Guild, THE, was founded by former members of the Washington Square Players♦ (1918). Originally a little-theater group, it specialized in the production of contemporary work, producing most of Shaw's plays after *Heartbreak House* (1920), and O'Neill's plays after *Marco Millions* (1928). It also revived such plays as Jonson's *Volpone.* Shrewdness in play selection, skill in production, and ability in financial management permitted the Guild to build its own million-dollar theater (1925) and thus take itself outside the scope of the movement into conventional commercial production. The theater was sold in 1944. Over the years the Guild mounted fewer and fewer plays of its own, turning into a subscription and tour-booking agency in association with the American Theatre Society. The Group Theatre♦ was an outgrowth (1931–41) of the Guild.

Their Fathers' God, novel by Rölvaag,♦ published in Norway (1931) and in translation in the U.S. the same year. It is the concluding volume of a trilogy which includes *Giants in the Earth*♦ and *Peder Victorious.*

Their Wedding Journey, novel by Howells,♦ published in 1871. *A Hazard of New Fortunes*♦ (1890), *An Open-Eyed Conspiracy* (1897), and *Their Silver Wedding Journey* (1899) are also concerned with the Marches.

This simple, episodic story deals with the honeymoon trip of Basil and Isabel March from Boston to Niagara, Montreal, and other scenic points. There is no stirring incident and the book depends upon its evocation of a charming mood, the description of types met in transit, and the places visited.

Theory of the Leisure Class, The, economic treatise by Thorstein Veblen,♦ published in 1899. The book enjoyed a popular vogue and profoundly influenced economic thought, but provoked controversial replies, of which the most sensational was Mencken's "Professor Veblen" in *Prejudices* (1919).

This description of habits and customs in modern life as "atavistic cultural survivals" contends that the institution of the Leisure Class arose during a predatory stage of barbarism, in conjunction with the institution of ownership. This was foreshadowed during the initial stage of peaceful savagery, when there began to be distinctions between the status of men and women. Woman's work, creation by the manipulation of inanimate materials, symbolized the instinct of workmanship and the beginning of industry. Man's work came to symbolize the advent of nonindustrial employments by acts of exploit, "the conversion to his own ends of energies previously directed to some other by another agent." Employment of other classes for wages is the modern form of exploit of that class, which emerges from the predatory stage as a social group living without recourse to industrial employment. The Leisure Class in the modern environment consists of those who enjoy freedom from irksome and undignified labor and who through successful acts of aggression are bent upon establishing their honorific distinction by conspicuous leisure and notable accumulations of wealth. Entrance to this class is by pecuniary fitness, which is exhibited by conspicuously wasteful consumption, setting standards according to canons of taste determined by wealth. This class, by force of mutual interest and instinct, and by precept and proscriptive example, not only perpetuates the existing maladjustment of institutions, but even favors a reversion to a somewhat more archaic scheme of life.

There Shall Be No Night, play by Robert Sherwood.♦

There Was a Child Went Forth, poem by Whitman,♦ published without title in *Leaves of Grass*

(1855), as "Poem of the Child That Went Forth, and Always Goes Forth, Forever and Forever" (1860), and under its present title in 1871.

This short poem states in simple terms Whitman's concept of man's identification with nature and the persons who surround him, and declares that those objects and people that he looked upon "became part of that child who went forth every day and who now goes, and will always go forth, every day."

THEROUX, PAUL [EDWARD] (1941–), Massachusetts-born author, resident abroad (1963–72) as a teacher of English in Italy, Malawi, Uganda, and Singapore, began his prolific literary career with *Waldo* (1966), a comic, surreal novel about eccentric individuals encountered by the title character as he travels after leaving a school for delinquent boys. Later novels include *Fong and the Indians* (1968), a satiric view of preposterous residents of a new east African country: natives, Chinese, and Americans; *Girls at Play* (1969), depicting in crueler fashion Afro-Indian, American, and English women schoolteachers in Kenya; *Jungle Lovers* (1971), set in Malawi and presenting a New England insurance salesman married to a native; *Saint Jack* (1973), treating people of diverse nations and natures drifting through life in Singapore; *The Black House* (1974), about an anthropologist returning from Africa to his native England and finding it stranger than the land he has been studying; *The Family Arsenal* (1976), dealing with professional terrorists in the seamy underworld of London; *Picture Palace* (1977), a fictive biography of a famous, aging woman photographer; and *The Mosquito Coast* (1982), about a Yankee engineer who seeks a new life in Honduras; *O-Zone* (1986), about New Yorkers adventuring in the Ozarks; and *My Secret History* (1989), a first-person novel about the sexual adventures and misadventures of a professional traveler and writer. In *Chicago Loop* (1991), an ordinary married businessman answers a lonely hearts ad, then kills the woman senselessly, afterwards sinking into a half-life. Stories are collected in *Sinning with Annie* (1972), *World's End* (1980), and *The London Embassy* (1982), while two novellas are combined in *Half Moon Street* (1984). Direct accounts of his own travels by train through Asia are in *The Great Railway Bazaar* (1975) and *Riding the Iron Rooster* (1988); through the Americas in *The Old Patagonian Express* (1979); and by other means and to other places in *Sailing Through China* (1984) and *Sunrise with Seamonsters* (1985). *The Kingdom by the Sea* (1983) tells of travels around the English coastline. *The Happy Isles of Oceania: Paddling the Pacific* (1992) chronicles his experiences in Polynesia packing and unpacking his collapsible sailing kayak. This trip also takes in what he calls "Meganesia"—New Zealand and Australia. Theroux is a travel writer in the 19th-century British tradition, experiencing native living and giving us commentary and meditations. He has also written a book about the West

Indian novelist V.S. Naipaul and, by contrast, several tales for children.

They Knew What They Wanted, play by Sidney Howard,♦ produced in 1924 and published in 1925, when it won a Pulitzer Prize.

They Stooped to Folly: *A Comedy of Morals,* novel by Ellen Glasgow,♦ published in 1929.

Virginius Littlepage, a lawyer in Queenborough (Richmond, Va.), at 57 believes that life has disappointed his hopes. His wife Victoria has long been his moral support, but he finds little satisfaction now in family life and feels more affection for Milly Burden, his secretary. During the World War, Milly had a child by Martin Welding; concealing the fact from him to spare him anxiety, but he never returned to her. Mary Victoria, Littlepage's daughter, returns from European war work and philanthropy, after an absence of five years, bringing Martin, now her husband, whom she "rescued" from illness and despair in France. She is a domineering, rigidly moral young woman, who administers the lives of all about her, and Martin feels "smothered" by excessive managing. Virginius drifts with comical caution into an affair with the amiable widow Amy Dalrymple, but when Victoria dies he feels lonely and lost. Martin deserts Mary Victoria, tries to persuade Milly to elope with him, but she refuses, deciding he desires only loneliness, and he leaves alone for Europe. Milly at last feels free of her bond to Martin, and Mary Victoria, after a brief period of frantic grief, turns to her duties to her unborn child and her father, sustained by her moral sense and essential egotism.

Thirteen Ways of Looking at a Blackbird, poem by Wallace Stevens,♦ composed in 1917 and published in *Harmonium*♦ (1923).

The work comprises 13 brief but suggestive imagistic statements, in each of which a blackbird is the point of reference. Although the blackbird is central to the context of each verse, the bird does not possess a constant symbolic meaning. It is considered in more general philosophic terms that relate the 13 views to issues concerning reality and the imagination, but these are not presented in an orderly or sequential relationship.

This Side of Paradise, novel by F. Scott Fitzgerald,♦ published in 1920.

Amory Blaine, after a pampered childhood with his wealthy, affected mother, Beatrice, attends preparatory school, where his indolence and aristocratic pose set him apart, until after an unhappy year he is accepted as a brilliant though eccentric athlete and leader. Although he is never religious, he has an affectionate father-and-son relation with his mother's friend Monsignor Darcy, a hedonist converted to Catholicism. He goes to Princeton, and there becomes a "literary bird," writing for the *Princetonian,* joining the Triangle Club, and discovering the English *fin de siècle* poets. Among his companions are Alec Connage, an unoriginal youth, and Tom D'Invilliers, whose radicalism and poetry they try to reform. Amory has a romance with a childhood friend, Isabelle; is involved in a student revolt led by Burne Holiday, an earnest radical who becomes a pacifist during the World War; nearly falls in love with his widowed cousin Clara, a beautiful "St. Cecilia" who has "never been in love"; and goes to France as a lieutenant. On his return he finds Beatrice dead and his wealth diminished, and he becomes an advertising writer. He has a passionate affair with Alec's debutante sister Rosaline—his one unselfish emotional experience—but she marries another man because she believes she cannot be happy without wealth. Amory drowns his disillusion in drink, but on a visit to Maryland meets Eleanor, a vivid, nervous personality even more egocentric than himself. They love for a few "bitter-sweet" weeks, and Amory continues his search for inner peace. He is penniless, and seeks employment. After Darcy's death, Amory realizes that his own unselfishness is the "the most living part" of himself, and considers his total experience at 24: "'I know myself,' he cried, 'but that is all.'"

THOMAS, AUGUSTUS (1857–1934), popular dramatist, whose more than 60 plays cover a wide range of subject matter and treatment, but whose most significant work had as its purpose the depiction of American background, as in *Alabama* (1891), *In Mizzoura* (1893), *The Capitol* (1895), *Arizona* (1899), and *The Copperhead* (1918), or the presentation of a character whose desire for individual liberty is obstructed by immediate surroundings or fate. Plays developing this theme include *The Witching Hour* (1907) and *The Harvest Moon* (1909), about hypnotism and psychological domination; and *As a Man Thinks* (1911), a problem play partly concerned with mental healing. Thomas also adapted Frances Hodgson Burnett's *Editha's Burglar*, first as a one-act and then as a four-act play, *The Burglar* (1889); and F.H. Smith's *Colonel Carter of Cartersville* (1892). With R.H. Davis he dramatized *Soldiers of Fortune* (1902).

THOMAS, EDITH MATILDA (1854–1925), Ohio-born poet whose works include *Lyrics and Sonnets* (1887), *The Inverted Torch* (1890), *In Sunshine Land* (1895), and *The Flower from the Ashes* (1915), distinguished by a classical craftsmanship and called "more Greek than American."

THOMAS, FREDERICK WILLIAM (1806–66), novelist whose various residences, in Rhode Island, Maryland, the Middle West, Kentucky, and Washington, D.C., and activities in such undertakings as journalism, legal practice, teaching, and the ministry gave him the backgrounds for his fiction. This realistic knowledge marks his novels, which include *Clinton Bradshaw; or, The Ad-*

ventures of a Lawyer (1835), *East and West* (1836), *Howard Pinckney* (1840), and *An Autobiography of William Russell* (1852), as well as his essays *Sketches of Character, and Tales Founded on Fact* (1849), and his long poem *The Emigrant* (1833). In addition to his own writing, he is remembered as a friend of Poe.

THOMAS, ISAIAH (1749–1831), printer, editor, and publisher of Worcester, Mass., whose publications included the *Massachusetts Spy*♦ and *The Royal American Magazine.*♦ He was the leading publisher of his day, the quality of his work causing Franklin to call him "the Baskerville of America," and the quantity of his printing, which included numerous chapbooks, causing him to establish branches in other New England towns. He issued *A Specimen* of his types (1785), which gives important evidence concerning early American printing. His *History of Printing in America* (2 vols., 1810) is the most significant early work on the subject. He founded the American Antiquarian Society (1812).

THOMAS, NORMAN [MATTOON] (1884–1968), born in Ohio, graduated from Princeton (1905) and was a Presbyterian minister in New York City until his Socialist interest caused him to turn to other activities. He was an editor of *The Nation* (1921–22), and a writer, speaker, and editor on social reform and pacifism. His unsuccessful Socialist candidacies for public office include those for governor of New York (1924), mayor of New York City (1925, 1929), U.S. representative (1930), and President (1928–44). Among his writings are *The Conscientious Objector in America* (1923), revised as *Is Conscience a Crime?* (1927); *The Challenge of War* (1925); *What Is Industrial Democracy?* (1927); *Socialism of Our Time* (1929); *The Choice Before Us* (1934); *Socialism on the Defensive* (1938); *Keep America Out of War* (1939), with Bertram D. Wolfe; *We Have a Future* (1941); *What Is Our Destiny?* (1944); *A Socialist's Faith* (1951); *The Test of Freedom* (1954); *The Prerequisites for Peace* (1959); and *The Great Dissenters* (1961).

THOMES, WILLIAM HENRY (1824–95), born in Maine, as a young boy was inspired by R.H. Dana's *Two Years Before the Mast* to ship to California (1842), where he engaged in the hide trade, as recounted in *On Land and Sea* (1883). Of his adventurous life in California until 1846 he left an account in the semi-fictional *Lewey and I* (1884). He went to Boston via England, and, attracted by the gold rush, he returned to San Francisco in 1849. Lack of success there and in the Philippines, China, and the gold mines of Victoria led him to return to Boston (1855). Five years later he founded a successful publishing firm, for which he wrote melodramatic works resembling the quality of the dime novel. These include *The Gold Hunters' Adventures; or, Life in*

Australia (1864), *The Bushrangers* (1866), *The Whaleman's Adventures* (1872), *A Slaver's Adventures* (1872), and *The Ocean Rovers* (1896). *Recollections of Old Times in California* (1974) is a brief memoir.

THOMPSON, BENJAMIN (1753–1814), Massachusetts-born mathematician and scientist, during the Revolution served as a Loyalist soldier and in the Colonial Office of England. After being knighted for his services, he joined the army of the Elector of Bavaria (1783), who made him head of the war department (1788) and a count of the Holy Roman Empire (1791). His title, Count Rumford, is derived from the name of the home of his wife, from whom he had been separated. He returned to England (1795) to continue his experiments on gunpowder, heat transmission, and moisture absorption, and published his *Essays, Political, Economical, and Philosophical* (4 vols., 1796–1802). In Munich (1796–98) he served on the council of regency, reorganized the Bavarian army, and headed the police. During another brief period in London, he attended to the organization of the Royal Institution (1800), based on his *Proposals for Forming . . . a Public Institution . . . for the Application of Science to the Common Purposes of Life* (1799). After 1802 he lived in France, where he married Madame Lavoisier, widow of the chemist. He contributed to English, American, and European scientific institutes, and continued his experiments, some of which were described in reports published in *Philosophical Papers* (1802).

THOMPSON, DANIEL PIERCE (1795–1868), Vermont author and lawyer, whose political career led him into literature when he published *The Adventures of Timothy Peacock, Esquire* (1835), a satire on Masonry in his state. This was followed by another novel, *May Martin; or, The Money Diggers* (1835), which dealt with local traditions. As a natural antiquarian and born storyteller, obviously influenced by Scott and Cooper, Thompson came into his own as an author with *The Green Mountain Boys*◆ (1839), a historical romance dealing with Ethan Allen and the New Hampshire land grants. *Locke Amsden; or, The Schoolmaster* (1847) presents a faithful picture of Vermont frontier life, and embodies the author's theories on education. *The Rangers; or, The Tory's Daughter* (1851) is a novel of the Revolution in Vermont. His other works, more lurid and less significant, include *Lucy Hosmer; or, The Guardian and the Ghost* (1848); *Gaut Gurley; or, The Trappers of Umbabog* (1857), a tale of border smuggling; *The Doomed Chief* (1860), an Indian story; and collections of short stories, including *The Shaker Lovers, and Other Tales* (1848) and *Centeola and Other Tales* (1864). In addition to his novels of the region, Thompson wrote *History of Vermont, and the Northern Campaign of 1777* (1851) and *History of the Town of Montpelier* (1860).

THOMPSON, DENMAN (1833–1911), Pennsylvania-born itinerant actor and dramatist, developed his play *Joshua Whitcomb* (1877) into *The Old Homestead* (1886), a homely rural drama of Yankee life whose chief claim to notice is its popularity for more than 20 years.

THOMPSON, DOROTHY (1894–1961), journalist known as a foreign correspondent and as a columnist for the New York *Herald Tribune* (1936–41) and for other newspapers. Her syndicated column "On the Record" dealt with foreign and domestic political affairs from the point of view of a rather liberal conservative. Her books include *The New Russia* (1928), which won notoriety because she accused Dreiser of plagiarizing it; *"I Saw Hitler!"* (1932), which contended that Hitler would never achieve national power; *Dorothy Thompson's Political Guide* (1938); and *Let the Record Speak* (1939), a compilation from her columns. She was married to Sinclair Lewis (1928–42), and their marriage was described both in Mark Schorer's biography of Lewis (1961) and in Vincent Sheean's *Dorothy and Red* (1963).

THOMPSON, ERNEST SETON, see *Seton, Ernest.*

THOMPSON, JOHN REUBEN (1823–73), Virginia author, owned and edited the *Southern Literary Messenger* (1847–60). He supported the Confederacy, both during a residence in England (1864–66) and in the U.S., by literary contributions that included the poem "Lee to the Rear." His *Poems* on Southern life and conditions were issued in 1920, and his lecture on his friend Poe was first published as *The Genius and Character of Edgar Allan Poe* (1929).

THOMPSON, [JAMES] MAURICE (1844–1901), Indiana author, whose first book, *Hoosier Mosaics* (1875), a forceful series of dialect sketches, was followed by several nature books, collections of poems that included *Songs of Fair Weather* (1883) and *Poems* (1892), and the romantic regional novels for which he is best known. His first novels, which include *A Tallahassee Girl* (1881) and *At Love's Extremes* (1885), are sentimental depictions of the South, where he was reared. *His Second Campaign* (1883) contrasts characters from the South and the West, and looked forward to his development of the romantic historical novel, a form in which he achieved greatest success with *Alice of Old Vincennes*◆ (1900), a story of the Northwest Territory and George Rogers Clark.

THOMPSON, MORTIMER NEAL, see *Thomson.*

THOMPSON, VANCE [CHARLES] (1863–1925), founder and editor of the urbane biweekly little magazine *M'lle New York* (1895–98), was an author of romantic novels, plays, verse, and essays, and was noted for his impressionistic literary criticism in such books as *French Portraits* (1900) and *Strindberg and His Plays* (1921).

THOMPSON, WILLIAM TAPPAN (1812–82), Ohio-born humorist of the Old Southwest, after 1835 lived mainly in Georgia, where for a time he was associated as a newspaper editor with A.B. Longstreet, his model in his humorous depictions of the Georgia cracker. ◆ His dialect short stories, which capture the quality of the oral storyteller, realistically portray the life of Georgia in the way Seba Smith's letters treat the Down East background. These tales are collected in *Major Jones's Courtship* (1843, enlarged 1844); *Chronicles of Pineville* (1845), republished as *Scenes in Georgia* (1858?); and *Major Jones's Sketches of Travel* (1848). In addition to his editorial work on various newspapers, Thompson wrote *Rancy Cottem's Courtship* (1879) and *John's Alive . . . and Other Sketches* (1883).

THOMPSON, ZADOCK (1796–1856), Vermont historian and naturalist, whose *History of Vermont, Natural, Civil and Statistical* (1842) is considered a primary source book for the region.

THOMSON (or THOMPSON), MORTIMER NEAL (1831–75), New York author, one of the earliest of American professional humorists, wrote under the pseudonym Q.K. Philander Doesticks, P.B. His contributions to such papers as the *Spirit of the Times,* which he called "roving unsubstantial inkbrats," were collected in *Doesticks, What He Says* ◆ (1855), sketches of American persons, places, and events, "dressed up in a lingual garb so quaint, eccentric, fantastic, or extravagant, that each lender will be sadly puzzled to recognize his own." *Plu-ri-bus-tah, A Song That's By No Author* (1856), a long parody of *Hiawatha,* was important for its satire on feminism, Barnum, the Kansas civil war, the Know-Nothing movement, spiritualism, free love, and the almighty dollar. Thomson next parodied W.A. Butler's *Nothing To Wear* in *Nothing To Say: A Slight Slap at Mobocratic Snobbery, Which Has "Nothing To Do" with "Nothing To Wear"* (1857). His articles for the *New-York Tribune* on criminal life were collected as *The History and Records of the Elephant Club* (1856), and those on fortune-telling frauds as *The Witches, Prophets, and Planet Readers of New York* (1859).

THOREAU, HENRY DAVID (1817–62), born in Concord of a family whose French, Scottish, Quaker, and Puritan stock helps to account for his temper of mind. Just as his heritage was mixed, so his philosophy of life combined diverse strains, and he called himself "a mystic, a transcendentalist, and a natural philosopher to boot." At heart, he was predominantly individualistic, and his great interest was "to observe what transpires, not in the street, but in the mind and heart of me!" Although his reading carried him far afield, he could truthfully say "I have travelled a good deal in Concord." In addition to his natural education in the woods near Concord, and the ordinary preparatory schooling, he graduated from Harvard (1837), where he was primarily influenced by E.T. Channing's teaching of composition, and the knowledge of Greek and the metaphysical poets that he derived from Jones Very. His temporary residence in the home of Orestes Brownson, from whom he learned German, was also influential. Above all he fell under the sway of Emerson, and it has been frequently said that he was the answer to Emerson's plea for an "American Scholar."

After graduation he taught school in his native town, for a time in collaboration with his brother John, following the principles of Bronson Alcott. With his brother he also made a trip on the Concord and Merrimack rivers (1839), of which he wrote during his residence at Walden in *A Week on the Concord and Merrimack Rivers* ◆ (1849). After closing his school, he lived with Emerson (1841–43), serving him as a general handyman, although their relation was also one of master and disciple. At this time he became an intimate of the members of the Transcendental Club ◆ and a contributor to *The Dial* and other magazines. During 1843 he was a tutor in the Staten Island home of William Emerson, where he made the acquaintance of Horace Greeley, Lucretia Mott, and the elder Henry James.

After his return to Concord, Thoreau built himself a hut at nearby Walden Pond, where he lived from July 4, 1845, to September 6, 1847, a period of which he wrote in his most famous book, *Walden* ◆ (1854). While other Transcendentalists sought a retreat at Brook Farm, Thoreau, ever an individualist, having no use for cooperative plans, found his solution at Walden. He wanted to get back to the naked simplicity of life, where he might "subdue and cultivate a few cubic feet of flesh," chew the cud of his thoughts, and get to the very core of the universe, by living deep and sucking out all the "marrow of life." His desire was "so to love wisdom as to live according to its dictates, a life of simplicity, independence, magnanimity, and trust . . . to solve some of the problems of life, not only theoretically, but practically." He wanted neither to be interfered with nor to interfere with others, and he declared, "I would not have anyone adopt my mode of living, each should find out his own way, not his neighbor's or his parents'."

His residence at the Pond was interrupted by a day's imprisonment for refusal to pay a poll tax to a government that supported the Mexican War, a war he considered merely a land-grabbing scheme of the Southern slaveholders. This action was in accord with his belief in passive resistance, a means of protest he explained in his essay "Civil Disobedience" ◆ (1849). It was a means of accentuating his belief, expressed in *Walden,* that each man should save himself and all would be saved.

He not only believed with Jefferson that that government is best which governs least, but he also contended that "they are the lovers of law and order who observe the law when the government breaks it." His belief in the individual and in a moral law superior to statutes and constitutions was also expressed in "Life Without Principle"♦ (1863).

After his return to Concord, he lived for a year in Emerson's home while the essayist was abroad, and during this period formed his close friendship with the younger W.E. Channing, who in writing the first biography of Thoreau aptly called him "the poet-naturalist." His observations of nature were distinguished not merely by his scientific knowledge, which was occasionally erroneous, but by his all-inclusive love of life, expressed now in an earthy manner with a Yankee twang, now with a sweet, pure English, having, as Lowell said, "an antique purity like wine grown colorless with age." Though he enjoyed the scientific view of nature, he was also a Transcendentalist,♦ defining his attitude when he said he wanted more the wideness of heaven than the limit of the microscope. His statement that he liked "better the surliness with which the wood chopper speaks of his woods, handling them as indifferently as his axe, than the mealy-mouthed enthusiasm of the lover of nature" shows him as an observer who wanted his answers concerning nature not only in facts but in terms of faith.

He made several brief trips (1849–53), which supplied the material for his posthumously published books *Excursions*♦ (1863), *The Maine Woods*♦ (1864), *Cape Cod*♦ (1865), and *A Yankee in Canada*♦ (1866). Meanwhile he continued his outwardly parochial life in Concord, where he wrote his journals, containing some two million words, the basis of all his books. During these years he became increasingly involved in the antislavery movement and delivered such speeches as "Slavery in Massachusetts" (1854). He was profoundly stirred by his meeting with John Brown at Emerson's home (1857) and praised Brown's actions at Harpers Ferry, for here was a man who was carrying out the principles that he himself championed. He eulogized him in three lectures, "A Plea for Captain John Brown" (1859), "The Last Days of John Brown" (1860), and "After the Death of John Brown" (1860).

During his last years, Thoreau made further trips to Cape Cod and Maine, and to New York City, where he met Whitman, but he was a victim of tuberculosis, which gradually weakened him and finally caused his death. He worked indefatigably, in spite of this handicap, on a long, unpublished ethnological study of the Indians and continued to make scientific observations and to carry on his own way of life both privately and as a lyceum lecturer. An invalid, he made an attempt to recapture health by journeying to the Great Lakes and the Mississippi (1861), but returned home, knowing that he was shortly to die,

to engage in a last attempt to edit his journals for publication. He published two books and a few articles and speeches during his lifetime, but it was not until after his death that selections from his journals were edited by his friend Harrison G.O. Blake♦ as *Early Spring in Massachusetts* (1881), *Summer* (1884), *Winter* (1888), and *Autumn* (1892). The complete *Journal* was issued (14 vols.) in 1906 and the text of a lost journal (1840–41) was edited by Perry Miller as *Consciousness in Concord* (1958). Other miscellaneous work was published in his collected *Writings* (20 vols., 1906), and Emerson's edition of the *Letters* (1865) was enlarged (1894) and further amplified and edited as *Correspondence* (1958). His *Poems of Nature* appeared in 1895 and Carl Bode edited the *Collected Poems* in 1943. A scholarly edition of his *Writings,* which will supersede that of 1906, began publication in 1971. In 1993 appeared *Faith in a Seed: "The Dispersion of Seeds" and Other Late Natural History Writings,* edited by Bradley Dean, proto-chapters from the journals, not shaped by Thoreau for publication, but pioneering notes on processes of plant succession and dispersal in the Concord environs.

THORNTON, WILLIAM (1759–1828), born in the West Indies, came from London to the U.S. (1793), where he was selected by Washington as the architect of the Capitol, whose construction he supervised with the assistance of James Hoban and others. He was the author of books on subjects as varied as the origin of steamboats, the education of the deaf, the abolition of slavery, and a plan for uniting North and South America by a Panama Canal.

THORPE, ROSE HARTWICK (1850–1939), author of "Curfew Must Not Ring Tonight," a popular ballad contributed to a Detroit newspaper in 1867. It deals with the son of an English lord of the manor, who is arrested as a spy, condemned to death, and saved by his sweetheart, who clings to the clapper of the bell that is supposed to toll curfew, the time of his execution.

THORPE, T[HOMAS] B[ANGS] (1815–78), humorist of the Old Southwest, was born in Massachusetts, but lived in Louisiana (1833–53) during the years in which he wrote tales of the frontier. The best of these is "The Big Bear of Arkansas,"♦ first printed in the *Spirit of the Times,* and from this and other magazines he collected his sketches in *The Mysteries of the Backwoods* (1846) and *The Hive of the Bee Hunter* (1854). Colonel *Thorpe's Scenes in Arkansaw* (1858) is an anthology whose title comes from one of his stories. His service in the Mexican War resulted in *Our Army on the Rio Grande* (1846), *Our Army at Monterey* (1847), and *The Taylor Anecdote Book* (1848). He was later an editor of the *Spirit of the Times,* and served in the Civil War. His other books include *The Master's House* (1854) and *A Voice to America*

(1855). He was also known for his vivid landscape paintings and portraits.

Three Black Pennys, The, novel in three parts by Hergesheimer,♦ published in 1917.

Three Lives, stories by Gertrude Stein,♦ published in 1909.

These unconventional character portraits, the author's first published fiction, exhibit her typical experimental attitude toward style and subject matter, and her attempt to reach an intuitive expression of consciousness and emotions. "The Good Anna" tells of Anna Federner, a sober, faithful housekeeper "of solid lower middle-class south German stock," who comes to the American city of Bridgepoint, and works successively for Miss Mary Wadsmith, "a large, fair, helpless woman," whose nephew and niece she helps to raise; Dr. Shonjen, a friendly physician; and Miss Mathilda, who goes to Europe and leaves Anna her house. She takes in boarders, but loses money by her simple generosity, and dies as a result of overwork. "The Gentle Lena" is concerned with a German girl who works as a maid in Bridgepoint, is married by her aunt to a stupid German tailor, apathetically endures her miserable life, and dies at the birth of her fourth child. The long story, "Melanctha," tells of the "subtle, intelligent, attractive, half white girl" Melanctha Herbert, who grows up in a Southern town, unloved by her brutal black father and weak mulatto mother. She has an unhappy love affair with the mulatto Dr. Jeff Campbell, who never returns her passionate affection. After she breaks with Jeff, she is engaged to a black gambler, Jem Richards, but, after he deserts her, she contracts consumption and dies.

Three Soldiers, novel by John Dos Passos,♦ published in 1921.

The effect of the World War upon the characters of ordinary doughboys is shown in the lives of three privates: Dan Fuselli, an Italian-American who is a fatuously cheerful conformist, and only desires to secure an advance in rank; Chrisfield, a homesick Indiana farm boy who does become a corporal, but who consistently hates the horrors and regimentation of wartime and vents his feelings in violent outbursts; and his friend John Andrews, a hypersensitive, introverted Harvard graduate, whose ambition is to be a musician. He too hates the war, but, unable to find an outlet for his emotions, he is sullenly resigned until he achieves an escape through temporary service in Paris, where he studies music. Arrested for lack of a pass to the countryside, where he takes his French girl on an outing, Andrews is sent to a labor battalion. From it he escapes, meeting other deserters, including Chrisfield, who in the confusion of a battle had thrown a grenade and killed his hated sergeant. For a time Andrews hides successfully and begins to com-

pose a symphonic work. When he is discovered, he faces the prospect of a firing squad with calm defiance and leaves his manuscript to be scattered by the wind.

Threnody, elegiac poem by Emerson,♦ published in *Poems* (1847). Arranged in alternately rhymed couplets of irregular four-stress lines, the work is a lyric expression of the poet's sorrow at the death of his five-year-old son Waldo. Following a passage of deep grief and lamentation, he concludes by finding consolation in the Platonic theory of an eternal changeless divinity into which all transitory appearances are finally resolved:

> House and tenant go to ground,
> Lost in God, in Godhead found.

Through the Eye of the Needle, epistolary novel by Howells,♦ published in 1907 as a sequel to *A Traveler from Altruria.* ♦

THURBER, JAMES [GROVER] (1894–1961), Ohio-born humorous writer and artist, in 1927 began his lifelong association with *The New Yorker,* in which most of his work first appeared. Of the journal and its editor, Harold Ross, he wrote a personal history, *The Years with Ross* (1959). His essays, sketches, fables, stories, parables, and reminiscences, illustrated by his distinctive and fluid drawings, include *Is Sex Necessary?* (1929), written with E.B. White, satirizing pseudo-scientific sex manuals; *The Owl in the Attic and Other Perplexities* (1931); *The Seal in the Bedroom & Other Predicaments* (1932); *My Life and Hard Times* (1933), amusing recollections; *The Middle-Aged Man on the Flying Trapeze* (1935); *Let Your Mind Alone!* (1937), satirizing inspirational books and popularizations of psychology; *The Last Flower* (1939), an ironic parable of modern war; *Fables for Our Time, and Famous Poems Illustrated*♦ (1940); *My World—and Welcome to It* (1942), essays, sketches, and stories, including the well-known tale "The Secret Life of Walter Mitty"♦; *Thurber's Men, Women, and Dogs* (1943), drawings; *The Thurber Carnival* (1945); *The Beast in Me and Other Animals* (1948); *Thurber Country* (1953); *Further Fables for Our Time* (1956); *Alarms and Diversions* (1957); *Lanterns & Lances* (1961), essays that are final examples of light and shafts cast by the author; and *Credos and Curios* (1962), a posthumous collection of stories and sketches. *Many Moons* (1943), *The Great Quillow* (1944), *The White Deer* (1945), *The 13 Clocks* (1950), and *The Wonderful O* (1957) are fantasies for children. With Elliott Nugent he wrote *The Male Animal* (1940), a comedy dealing with the rivalry between an English professor and an ex-football player for the love of the professor's wife.

Thurber's humorous prose and drawings are never raucous, for, as he said, "the little wheels of their invention are set in motion by the damp hand of melancholy," in keeping with his view that "humor is a kind of emotional chaos told about calmly and quietly in retrospect." His fantastic people and animals move with sad persistence through incredible upsets, and are all misshapen and repressed, products of a malignant fate which they stoically survive or combat. Across the puzzling scene that is surveyed by resigned dogs move predatory women at war with docile men who, caught by life's conventions, quietly dream of escape and deeds of derring-do.

Thurso's Landing, free-verse narrative by Jeffers, ♦ the title poem of a volume published in 1932.

This tale of suffering, violence, and desperate courage on a California coast farm is principally concerned with stubborn, powerful Reave Thurso, his wife Helen, and his brother Mark, who has been crippled in the World War and loves and sympathizes with his lonely sister-in-law, as her unfeeling husband cannot. Grim old Mrs. Thurso hates Helen, realizing the younger woman's passionate, sensual nature and her dissatisfaction with the limited life of the Landing, but is powerless to prevent Reave from bringing her home again after she elopes with his friend Rick Armstrong. When Reave takes a girl servant as his mistress, Helen is wildly jealous, but he is soon crippled and made impotent when a cable snaps while he is felling trees. A struggle of wills ensues between husband and wife, he clinging grimly to his useless life, and she wishing him dead but admiring his immense courage. Mark goes mad because of his lust for Helen and visions of his father's ghost, and hangs himself, after which Helen kills Reave and commits suicide. Old Mrs. Thurso, who says of Helen that she "had a wasteful gallant spirit," calls herself "the last And worst of four: and at last the unhappiest: but that's nothing."

THWAITES, REUBEN GOLD (1853–1913), historian, editor, and librarian, whose most important works are editions of *Early Western Travels, 1748–1846* (32 vols., 1904–7), and *The Jesuit Relations* (73 vols., 1896–1901), carefully edited reprints of source materials on the West. Besides editing *Original Journals of the Lewis and Clark Expedition* (8 vols., 1904–5), he was a prolific author of works on the West and on French colonization in America.

TICKNOR, GEORGE (1791–1871), born in Boston and graduated from Dartmouth (1807), became an important literary historian and scholar of his time. His education came from contacts with leading Americans and Europeans during his grand tour of the Atlantic states (1814–15) and his *Wanderjahre* abroad with Edward Everett (1815–19). Study at Göttingen and extensive travel through the Latin countries further prepared him for his position as first Abiel Smith Professor of the French and Spanish Languages and Literatures and Professor of Belles Lettres at Harvard (1819–35). In addition to improving instruction in modern languages, Ticknor affected

the rising generation of American poets by stimulating interest in romantic lore. After another visit to Europe (1835–38), he began his *History of Spanish Literature* (3 vols., 1849; final revision, 1872), which illustrated his acute scholarship in a pioneer field. He wrote a biography of Prescott (1864), and his *Life, Letters, and Journals* was published in two volumes (1876). He was a cousin of W.D. Ticknor and an uncle of Charles W. Eliot.

TICKNOR, WILLIAM DAVIS (1810–64), Boston publisher, in 1832 founded the firm known after 1854 as Ticknor and Fields, which published the works of his friends Longfellow, Holmes, Lowell, Emerson, Thoreau, Hawthorne, and many of their distinguished contemporaries. The firm published the *Atlantic Monthly* (1859ff.) and *The North American Review* (1854–64), and owned the Old Corner Bookstore. ♦

Tides of Barnegat, The, novel by F. Hopkinson Smith, ♦ published in 1906.

TIERNAN, MARY SPEAR (1836–91), Baltimore novelist long resident in Virginia, whose pre-Civil War life she described in many novels, including *Homoselle* (1881) and *Suzette* (1885).

TIETJENS, EUNICE (1884–1944), Chicago poet, best known for her *Profiles from China* (1917), free-verse sketches of the country in which she lived for two years. *Profiles from Home* (1925), on American life, is less distinguished. *Leaves in Windy Weather* (1929) is a miscellaneous collection of her poems, and *Poetry of the Orient* (1928) is an anthology containing her translations. *The World at My Shoulder* (1938) is an autobiography.

Tilbury Town, fictitious setting of many poems by Edwin Arlington Robinson, ♦ a place of conventional and materialistic values, presumably modeled on his hometown, Gardiner, Me. In it dwell such characters as Miniver Cheevy, ♦ Flammonde, ♦ Annandale, ♦ Richard Cory, John Evereldown, Mr. Flood, and Luke Havergal, whose characterizations and soliloquies reveal their conflicts with the prevailing town mores. Sixty-three of the poems were gathered as *Tilbury Town* (1953) by Lawrance Thompson.

TILLICH, PAUL [JOHANNES OSKAR] (1886–1965), German-born theologian, a member of the United Church of Christ, came to the U.S. (1933), was naturalized (1940), and served as a professor at Union Theological Seminary (1933–55), Harvard (1955–62), and the University of Chicago (1962–65). He was a leader in dialectical theology, and his works, which relate philosophic and existential religious views, include *The Religious Situation* (1932), *The Interpretation of History* (1936), *The Protestant Era* (1948), *Systematic Theology* (3 vols., 1951, 1957, 1963), *The Courage To Be* (1952), *Love, Power, and Justice* (1954), *Biblical Re-*

ligion and the Search for Ultimate Reality (1955), *Dynamics of Faith* (1956), *Theology of Culture* (1959), and *The Eternal Now* (1963).

TILTON, THEODORE (1835–1907), New York City author and journalist, noted for his editorship of the *Independent*♦ (1856–71), a Congregationalist journal that attracted wide attention for its championing of such reform movements as antislavery and woman suffrage. Tilton was also extremely popular as a lyceum lecturer, until he brought suit against Henry Ward Beecher for adultery with his wife (1874). The scandal caused a division of public opinion, reflected in the hung jury, but so completely ruined Tilton's reputation that he went abroad (1883), where he spent the remainder of his life. His publications include a sensational romance, *Tempest-Tossed* (1874); some musical ballads, *Swabian Stories* (1882); and *Sonnets to the Memory of Frederick Douglass* (1895).

Time (1923–   ), New York weekly "newsmagazine" founded by Briton Hadden and Henry Robinson Luce to present a concise and comprehensive summary of current news related to its larger background, grouped in various general and specialized departments that are changed or augmented from time to time. Each issue includes one long article treating the subject that is featured on its pictorial cover, and annually, with fanfare, the year's first issue presents a cover and long story on the "Man of the Year." The journal maintains correspondents throughout the world and has a staff of research workers, in addition to subscribing to news services and depending upon other periodicals. It is written in an impersonal though lively style that was at one time marked by a rather flip manner and a prose noted for concentrated language and arch use of neologisms, but it has outgrown most of these mannerisms. Mostly staff-written, it does contain some signed reviews and feature articles. *Time* absorbed *The Literary Digest* (1938) and has long had international circulation with special European, Latin American, Canadian, and Asian and South Pacific editions. The parent company, Time, Inc., owns *Fortune,* a magazine of business; *Life,* a magazine of news and features presented through pictures; *Sports Illustrated,* a weekly sports magazine; and *People,* a journal of brief pictorial and textual concern with personalities. Men of letters who have served on the staff of *Time* include James Agee, Louis Kronenberger, and Theodore White. In 1989 the firm of Time, Inc. was merged with Warner Communications Inc. to become the largest media and entertainment conglomerate in the world.

Time of Man, *The,* novel by Elizabeth M. Roberts.♦ published in 1926.

During her childhood, Ellen Chesser wanders with her parents through Kentucky, Tennessee, and Georgia, while her restless father seeks work as a farmhand or sharecropper. She grows up barefooted and ill-fed, working in the fields and feeling an intimate relation with things of earth. When the family finally settles in one place, Ellen falls in love with Jasper Kent, a fellow worker. Although he leaves temporarily, to escape punishment for accidentally burning a barn, he returns to marry her. Ellen bears children, they try sharecropping, and then Jasper returns to his former employer, Joe Phillips. Jasper and Ellen quarrel over his interest in Hester Shuck and Joe's in Ellen, but they are reconciled by the birth and early death of their fifth child. They become more prosperous, and hope to buy the farm they are working, but a neighbor's barn burns, and rumors of the old accusation against Jasper lead a group of rioters to drive them away. Once more Ellen packs her belongings in a wagon, headed, as she tells her children, "somewheres. . . ."

Time of Your Life, *The,* play by William Saroyan.♦

Timoleon, poems by Melville,♦ privately printed in 1891. Besides the title piece, the volume contains some 40 other light poems inspired by the author's travels in Greece and Italy (1857), as well as the unique and contrasting "After the Pleasure Party," which is concerned with "the sexual feud that clogs the aspiring life" and a bitter arraignment of the fate that makes "selfhood" seem "incomplete" and yet seldom allows the mating of "matching halves."

Timothy Titcomb, pseudonym of J.G. Holland.♦

TIMROD, HENRY (1828–67), born in Charleston, was educated at Franklin College (the present University of Georgia), and was a member of the Russell's Bookstore Group.♦ During his brief life he published only one volume of *Poems* (1860), delicate treatments of nature showing his training in the classics. During the Civil War, the tuberculosis from which he later died made him unfit for military service, and he unsuccessfully attempted to eke out a living by editing a Columbia newspaper and writing poetry. These sad last years he summed up when he wrote to his friend Hayne, "You ask me to tell you my story for the last year. . . . I can embody it all in a few words: beggary, starvation, death, bitter grief, utter want of hope!" Nevertheless, his trials stirred him to write his greatest poetry, which, no longer showing the dependence of his earlier work, included such poems as "Ethnogenesis,"♦ "The Cotton Boll,"♦ and "Ode"♦ on the graves of the Confederate dead, whose passionate emotion is the more effective because of the cool, severe utterance. After his death, his friend Hayne collected his *Poems* (1873), with a sympathetic introduction. Later publications include *Katie* (1884), a long love lyric addressed to his wife, and *Com-*

plete Poems (1899). He is called "the laureate of the Confederacy."

Tin Pan Alley, name applied to the New York City district engaged in the composing and publishing of popular dance music and ballads, and more generally to the industry as a whole. The distinctive name and the conception of such an industry is credited to the songwriter and publisher Charles K. Harris (1865–1930), author of "After the Ball Is Over" (1892). Tin Pan Alley had its inception in the 14th Street area of New York, gradually moving uptown with the theater and amusement district, and later, because of its combination with the motion-picture industry and radio, became a general term applied to all its ramifications, whether in Hollywood or New York. Famous Tin Pan Alley composers include George M. Cohan, Irving Berlin, W.C. Handy, Jerome Kern, George Gershwin, Rudolph Friml, and Sigmund Romberg. The commercialism and superficiality of Tin Pan Alley have been frequently satirized, as in *Beggar on Horseback* by Marc Connelly and George S. Kaufman, and *June Moon* by Kaufman and Ring Lardner.

Titan, The, novel by Dreiser, ♦ published in 1914 as a sequel to *The Financier* ♦ and based on the career of C.T. Yerkes, a flamboyant financier of Philadelphia, Chicago, and London.

Frank Cowperwood, having married his mistress Aileen Butler, establishes a home in Chicago. Their history becomes known, and they fail to make their desired entry into society, but Cowperwood's business affairs prosper. After successful speculations in the grain exchange and in stocks, he effects a great merger of the growing city's public utilities, and acquires a tremendous fortune, as well as political power and prestige, through his streetcar business, his gift of an observatory to a university, and his fine collection of paintings acquired during trips to Europe. Meanwhile he is dissatisfied with Aileen and pursues other women, arousing her bitter resentment. Once she physically attacks a current mistress, but even this cannot restore her control of him, and she becomes increasingly coarse and dissipated, taking several lovers herself. When he establishes a palatial residence in New York City, Cowperwood discovers his "ideal" in Berenice Fleming, the beautiful, sensitive, and innocent daughter of a former brothel keeper. Although he is twice her age, he succeeds in winning the girl's love, and she accompanies him to Europe after he is finally ousted by his Chicago competitors.

To a Waterfowl, lyric poem by Bryant, ♦ written in 1815, published in 1818, and collected in *Poems* (1821). Called by Matthew Arnold "the most perfect brief poem in the language," it is arranged in alternately rhymed quatrains, and expresses the poet's grateful vision, at the close of a day of self-doubt and despair, of a solitary bird on

the horizon, and his sense of the protective guidance of everything in nature by a divine Power, who "In the long way that I must tread alone, Will lead my steps aright."

To Build a Fire, short story by Jack London, ♦ first published in *The Century* (Aug. 1908) and collected in *Lost Face* (1910).

A *chechaquo,* as newcomers to the Arctic are called, travels on a little-used route off the main Yukon trail one sunless winter day of "tremendous cold" at 75 degrees below zero. His every action has to be careful, but nevertheless he accidentally steps into a spring hidden under the snow and so immediately has to dry his boots and feet. The fire he builds is put out by snow that falls from a bough, and his hands and feet begin to freeze. With the heels of his frozen hands he awkwardly grasps and lights his matches but burns himself and the fire fails to catch the twigs and grasses painfully scraped together. To save himself he decides to kill his husky dog and to bury his hands in the warm body until the numbness might go out of them, but he cannot hold his knife, and the frightened dog evades him. In desperation he runs to restore circulation, but he flounders, lies down, and drowses off to death.

To Earthward, lyric poem in three- and two-stress iambic meter, by Robert Frost, ♦ published in *New Hampshire* (1923). The poet contrasts the sweet joys of youthful experience ("The petal of the rose It was that stung") with the bitter passions of maturity ("Now no joy but lacks salt That is not dashed with pain And weariness and fault . . .").

To Have and Have Not, novel by Hemingway, ♦ published in 1937.

Harry Morgan, a tough "conch," as natives of Key West, Fla., call themselves, has devoted his life to the single-minded effort to keep himself, his wife, and his children on the upper fringe of the "have-nots." He hires out his powerboat to wealthy men for fishing trips, but, when the Depression destroys this source of income and a rich tourist welshes on payment for lost fishing tackle, he is obliged to turn to illegal activities. He contracts to smuggle Chinese from Cuba into the U.S., but, taking their money, murders their leader and abandons the others. While smuggling illegal liquor, he is captured in a gun battle by federal officers, loses an arm, and has his boat confiscated. In a last desperate attempt to obtain money, he aids in the escape of four bank robbers, although realizing that unless he kills them, they will kill him. This he does, but they wound him fatally. Picked up by the Coast Guard and accused of being a member of the gang, he stammers, "'A man . . . ain't got no hasn't got any can't really isn't any way out. . . . One man alone ain't got . . . no chance.' He shut his eyes. It had taken him a long time to get it out and it had taken him all his life to learn it."

To Have and To Hold, novel by Mary Johnston,♦ published in 1900.

To Helen, title of two lyric poems by Poe.♦

To One in Paradise, poem by Poe.♦

To Science, sonnet by Poe,♦ published as a prologue to "Al Aaraaf"♦ in *Al Aaraaf, Tamerlane, and Minor Poems* (1829). The poet apostrophizes Science as one whose peering eyes alter all things, as a destroyer of beauty, preying upon the heart of its lover, and as a "Vulture, whose wings are dull realities." Poe developed the theme of the conflict of scientific thought and poetic feeling in his prose, but later, as in *Eureka,* considered that the beauty of poetry depended on its representing a scientific concept of an ordered universe.

To the Finland Station, work by Edmund Wilson,♦ published in 1940 and subtitled "A Study in the Writing and Acting of History."

The study treats European ideas of socialism and revolution from their intellectual rise with Michelet through the activities of Saint-Simon, Fourier, and Robert Owen to anarchistic deviation by Bakunin, their dwindling in Renan, Taine, and Anatole France, then to the heights of theory in Marx and Engels, and finally to the actions and ideas of Trotsky and Lenin, who both wrote and made history. They are all treated in terms of character studies as well as elements of intellectual history.

To the Fringed Gentian, poem by Bryant,♦ published in *Poems* (1832). In iambic tetrameter quatrains, it depicts the blossom, "colored with heaven's own blue," which blooms late in autumn after other flowers are gone, and expresses the poet's wish that, as death approaches, "Hope, blossoming within my heart, May look to heaven as I depart."

Tobacco Road, novel by Erskine Caldwell,♦ published in 1932. The sensational dramatization by Jack Kirkland (1933) had a continuous run of 3182 Broadway performances.

In the squalid, cotton-raising backcountry of contemporary Georgia live the sharecropper Jeeter Lester and his miserable, starving family, which includes his sick wife Ada, his neglected mother, his 16-year-old son Dude, and his repulsive, hare-lipped daughter Ellie May. Nearby lives the railroad worker Lov Benson, who has recently married Jeeter's 12-year-old daughter Pearl. Lov comes to ask Jeeter's aid in forcing the unwilling Pearl to sleep with him, and, while Lov's attention is diverted by the sex-hungry Ellie May, Jeeter steals the turnips that Lov has been carrying. The Lesters devour Lov's turnips, being joined by ugly Sister Bessie Rice, a widowed preacher who then leads them in penitential prayer. It is six years since Jeeter has been able

to plant cotton, because he has neither money nor credit to buy seed and fertilizer. A "born" farmer, he stubbornly persists on his sterile acres, refusing to seek work in town as most of his 15 children have already done. Sister Bessie, who wants a husband to help her preach and "for other purposes," induces Dude to marry her by buying a new automobile. Subsequent events include futile attempts by Jeeter to obtain credit, further sexual diversions by the entire group, and the rapid ruin of the new auto, owing to Dude's ignorance and reckless driving, which also result in the accidental deaths of Jeeter's mother and a black farmer. Pearl runs away to find work and escape her husband's attempt to rape her, and Ellie May goes to live with Lov. Jeeter and Ada are left alone one night. The house catches fire and burns to the ground, ending their oppressed and degraded lives.

TOCQUEVILLE, ALEXIS, Comte de (1805–59), French liberal politician and writer, at the request of his government came to the U.S. (May 1831–Feb. 1832), to report on the penitentiary system and its possible application in France. His general observations of American society during this period resulted in *De la démocratie en Amérique* (2 vols., 1835; 2 supplementary vols., 1840; first American edition, 1838). The work deals with the social conditions in the U.S. and the governmental and administrative systems. The advantages and disadvantages of democracies are treated according to their influences on American intellect, feelings, manners, and politics. Generally impartial, the study has taken its place as the earliest important analysis of its subject. In his survey of American literature, Tocqueville finds a retardation attributable to the disrepute in which art and letters were held by early settlers, as well as to lack of leisure and easily accessible English writings. Since there was a large, heterogeneous potential reading public, he expected that a literature would be created that would be free from conventional rules, vehement and bold, lacking in profundity, of great variety, quickly read, easily understood, and obsessed with a magnificent image of patriotic exaltation. He thought that equalitarianism would give poets an instinctive distaste for the ancient, make the use of demigods or heroes impossible, and leave as the only subject man himself, his passions, doubts, propensities, and wretchedness, standing in the presence of nature and God.

TODD, MABEL LOOMIS (1856–1932), Massachusetts author, wife of David Peck Todd, professor of astronomy at Amherst, came to know Emily Dickinson because she had a long and intense love affair with Emily's older brother, Austin. She edited two series of Emily's *Poems* (1890–91) with T.W. Higginson and then she alone edited a third series (1896) and the *Letters of Emily Dickinson* (2 vols., 1894). Her own books include popular works on science, a novel, and *A Cycle of Sonnets* (1896).

Together, novel by Robert Herrick,♦ published in 1908.

Togo, HASHIMURA, character in humorous books by Wallace Irwin.♦

Token, *The* (1827–42), Boston gift book, published by S.G. Goodrich. It was the first medium to give Hawthorne's work wide circulation, and the *Twice-Told Tales* were mostly reprinted from *The Token.* Among other prose contributors were Timothy Flint, Lydia Child, Edward Everett, Longfellow, James Hall, Sarah J. Hale, and Harriet Beecher Stowe. The level of its poetry is indicated by the prominent representation of Goodrich and Lydia Huntley Sigourney, although Holmes, Longfellow, and Lowell contributed occasionally. N.P. Willis edited the 1829 issue.

TOKLAS, ALICE B[ABETTE] (1877–1967), San Francisco-born friend, constant companion, and secretary of Gertrude Stein♦ from 1907 on. Gertrude Stein made her the ostensible author of *The Autobiography of Alice B. Toklas* (1933), which she declared was written "as simply as Defoe did the autobiography of Robinson Crusoe," although it was her own life story. Miss Toklas finally spoke out herself in a brief memoir, *What Is Remembered* (1963), and she also wrote *The Alice B. Toklas Cook Book* (1954), recipes and reminiscences; and *Aromas and Flavors of Past and Present* (1958), a French cookbook. *Staying On Alone* (1973) collects letters written after Gertrude Stein's death.

Tol'able David, story by Hergesheimer,♦ published in *The Happy End* (1919).

TOLSON, MELVIN B[EAUNORUS] (1898–1966), Missouri-born black poet, after graduation from Lincoln University (Pennsylvania) taught at Langston University (Missouri), of whose town he was also the mayor. His works appear as *Rendezvous with America* (1944); *Libretto for the Republic of Liberia* (1953), written for the nation's centennial; and *Harlem Gallery; Book 1, The Curator* (1965), the beginning of a projected, uncompleted epic on blacks in America. He also wrote plays, *Black No More* (1952) and *The Fire in the Flint* (1952), adaptations of others' narratives; and *Black Boy* (1963). Two posthumous collections of his writings were published, poetry in *A Gallery of Harlem Portraits* (1979) and newspaper articles in *Caviar and Cabbage* (1982).

Tom Sawyer, Detective, story by Clemens,♦ published in 1896 under his pseudonym Mark Twain.

As a final sequel to previous adventures, Huck Finn tells of the remarkable way in which Tom Sawyer solves an intricate mystery involving a diamond robbery and a false accusation of murder made against his Uncle Silas, as well as a case of mistaken identity between a real and a supposed corpse.

Tom Sawyer, *The Adventures of,* novel by Clemens,♦ published in 1876 under his pseudonym Mark Twain. Its classic sequel, *Huckleberry Finn,*♦ was followed by the relatively unimportant *Tom Sawyer Abroad*♦ and *Tom Sawyer, Detective.*♦

In the drowsy Mississippi River town of St. Petersburg, Mo., Tom Sawyer, imaginative and mischievous, and his priggish brother Sid live with their simple, kind-hearted Aunt Polly. Sid "peaches" on Tom for playing hooky, and Tom is punished by being made to whitewash a fence, but ingeniously leads his friends to do this job for him by pretending it is a privilege. When his sweetheart, Becky Thatcher, is angered because Tom reveals that he has previously been in love, he forsakes a temporary effort at virtue, plays hooky, and decides to become a pirate or a Robin Hood. With his boon companion, Huck Finn, a good-natured, irresponsible river rat, Tom goes to a graveyard at midnight to swing a dead cat, an act advised by Huck as a cure for warts. They watch Injun Joe, a half-breed criminal, stab the town doctor to death and place the knife in the hands of drunken Muff Potter. After being further scolded by Aunt Polly, and further spurned by Becky, Tom, with Huck and Joe Harper, another good friend, hides on nearby Jackson's Island. Their friends believe them drowned, but their funeral service is interrupted by the discovery of the "corpses," who are listening from the church gallery. Tom returns to school, is reconciled with Becky and his aunt, and becomes a hero at the trial of Muff Potter, when he reveals Injun Joe's guilt. Tom and Becky attend a school picnic, and are lost for several days in a cave, where Tom spies Injun Joe. Later the half-breed is found dead, and his treasure is divided between Tom and Huck, after which the latter is adopted by the Widow Douglas. His only consolation, since he has surrendered his state of unwashed happiness, lies in Tom's promise to admit him to his robber gang on the strength of his social standing.

Tom Sawyer Abroad, short novel by Clemens,♦ published in 1894 under his pseudonym Mark Twain.

As a sequel to "all them adventures" in the book bearing his name, Huck Finn tells of further exploits with Tom Sawyer and Jim, the former slave, in a story that concerns a balloon voyage to the Sahara and Near East, involving a mid-Atlantic storm, encounters with Bedouins and wild lions, and a final takeoff for the return home from Mt. Sinai. Tom's romancing and knowledge, Huck's common sense, and Jim's superstitions are revealed by various incidents.

Tom Swift, hero of a series of books for boys by Edward Stratemeyer.♦

Tomorrow and Tomorrow, play by Philip Barry,♦ produced and published in 1931.

TOMPSON, BENJAMIN (1642–1714), born in Quincy, Mass., graduated from Harvard (1662) and became a physician and a teacher at the Boston Latin School and the Roxbury Latin School. He is known today as the first native-born colonial poet. *New Englands Crisis. Or a Brief Narrative, of New-Englands Lamentable Estate at Present . . .* (1676) is a satirical depiction in heroic couplets of what he considered to be the degeneracy of the period of King Philip's War. Most of this was reprinted in *New-Englands Tears for Her Present Miseries* (1676). Lesser verse was contributed to the *Magnalia* of Cotton Mather, and the *Narrative* of King Philip's War by William Hubbard.

Tony Beaver, see *Beaver, Tony.*

TOOLE, JOHN KENNEDY (1937–69), born in New Orleans, educated at Tulane and at Columbia University (M.A.), served in the army and taught at colleges, but, depressed at his inability to find a publisher for his novel, *A Confederacy of Dunces,* committed suicide. His mother urged it on Walker Percy, who convinced a university press to print it (1980). It was soon recognized as a great comic and satirical view of the contemporary U.S., set in the raffish French Quarter of New Orleans. It won a Pulitzer Prize.

TOOMER, JEAN (1894–1967), black author, born in Washington, D.C., after graduation from New York University (1918) wrote *Cane*♦ (1923), a miscellany of stories, verses, and a drama concerned with the emotional life of black people. His other books are *Essentials* (1931), aphorisms, and *Portage Potential* (1932). *The Wayward and the Seeking* (1980) is a selection from his writings, and his *Collected Poems* was issued in 1988.

Topper, novel by Thorne Smith.♦

Topsy, character in *Uncle Tom's Cabin.*♦

TORRENCE, [FREDERIC] RIDGELY (1875–1950), New York poet, dramatist, and journalist, whose first volume of poetry, *The House of a Hundred Lights* (1900), a whimsical, sentimental mixture of *fin de siècle* ideas, was very unlike his more mature poetry in *Hesperides* (1925), an expression of his dignified, moving transcendental faith. With further lyrics, *Hesperides* was extended in two volumes titled simply *Poems* (1941, 1952). His plays include *El Dorado* (1903), a tragedy; *Abelard and Héloïse* (1907), a poetic drama; and *Granny Maumee, The Rider of Dreams,* and *Simon*

the Cyrenian (1917), plays about blacks. He also wrote *The Story of John Hope* (1948), a biography of the black educator, and edited the *Selected Letters* (1940) of his friend Edwin Arlington Robinson.

TORREY, BRADFORD (1843–1912), Massachusetts-born essayist on ornithology and life in the outdoors of various parts of the U.S., including *Birds in the Bush* (1885), *A Rambler's Lease* (1889), *The Foot-Path Way* (1892), *A Florida Sketch-Book* (1894), *Spring Notes from Tennessee* (1896), *Footing It in Franconia* (1901), and *Field-Days in California* (1913). He was an admirer of Thoreau, about whom he wrote in *Friends on the Shelf* (1906), and whose *Journal* he edited, for the first time, in 14 volumes in 1906.

Tortesa, the Usurer, blank-verse romantic drama by N.P. Willis,♦ produced and published in 1839.

Tortilla Flat, novel by Steinbeck,♦ published in 1935 and dramatized by Jack Kirkland in 1937.

In the uphill district above Monterey, Cal., live *paisanos,* colored like "a well-browned meerschaum pipe" and combining "Spanish, Indian, Mexican and assorted Caucasian bloods," a feckless, innocently amoral group of men and women. Among them is Danny, the chance owner of two houses, one of which he rents to his friend Pilon for $15, which is never paid, and to their drinking companion Pablo. The three of them pilfer from their neighbors, drink gallons of wine from the saloon of the formidable Torrelli, and pursue amours with such gallant ladies as Sweets Ramirez, Tia Ignacio, Mrs. Morales, and the incredibly promiscuous Cornelia Ruiz. The circle of "Danny's friends" also includes Big Joe Portagee, Jesus Maria Corcoran, and the half-witted Pirate, always accompanied by five dogs. This "Round Table" of friends, whose primitive love of pleasure is balanced by a superstitious love of the Church, comes to an end when an unusually uproarious party leads to Danny's death and the burning of his house.

TOTHEROH, DAN (1895–1976), California dramatist, whose first play, *Wild Birds,* was produced at the state university (1922) before its New York production (1925). It is a tragic love story of an orphan girl and a reform-school boy, whose attempt to escape from the farm where they work leads to his being beaten to death and her suicide. His other plays include *One-Act Plays for Everyone* (1931); *Distant Drums* (1932), a play of the pioneer West; *Moor Born* (1934), a play about the Brontës; *Mother Lode* (1934), concerned with early San Francisco; and *Searching for the Sun* (1936). He also wrote and produced outdoor pageants, and directed the Greek Theatre at the University of California, Berkeley. His novels include *Wild Orchard* (1927), *Men Call Me Fool* (1929), and *Deep Valley* (1942).

Touchett, RALPH, character in *The Portrait of a Lady.* ◆

Tour on the Prairies, A, autobiographical narrative by Irving, ◆ published as the first volume of *The Crayon Miscellany* (1835). The narrative describes the author's adventures in the Indian territories of the Midwestern frontier, during a journey (Oct.–Nov. 1832) in which he was accompanied by Charles J. Latrobe, a British traveler; Count de Pourtalès, a Swiss youth; Henry L. Ellsworth, a government commissioner; and "a little swarthy, meagre, wiry French creole, named Antoine, but familiarly dubbed Tonish: a kind of Gil Blas of the frontier." From Fort Gibson, in the present Oklahoma, Irving and his companions traveled westward, living among the frontiersmen and in camps and buffalo-hunting grounds of the Pawnee, Osage, and Creek tribes. Irving was particularly interested in gathering examples of folklore, and the *Tour* recounts such legends as that of the Pacing Mustang. ◆ The descriptions of Western life are presented in Irving's characteristically softened and romanticized manner, and when compared with Ellsworth's manuscript account show many omissions and alterations of fact.

TOURGÉE, ALBION W[INEGAR] (1838–1905), born in Ohio, was for two years a student at the University of Rochester, but left to become a Union officer in the Civil War, in which he was seriously wounded. In 1865 he moved his family to North Carolina, where he practiced law and entered politics as a carpetbagger. His venomous political stand and obviously biased attitude as a judge made him unpopular with his fellow citizens, but he became wealthy through corrupt administration of the courts. He founded and edited journals primarily devoted to a radical Reconstruction policy, and wrote several novels setting forth his political beliefs and depicting the South during Reconstruction. After 1878 he made his home in New York, and his only political affiliation was an appointment as consul at Bordeaux (1897). His fiction, which is romantic in plot but realistic in its presentation of the contemporary scene, includes *'Toinette* (1874), republished as *A Royal Gentleman* (1881), a story of the antebellum and Civil War South; *Figs and Thistles* (1879), set in Ohio and the South during the Civil War, and said to be a fictional account of the political career of Garfield, though others claim it to be semi-autobiographical; *A Fool's Errand* ◆ (1879), a story of Reconstruction, definitely based on the author's own life and considered his best work; *Bricks Without Straw* ◆ (1880), concerned with blacks and whites in North Carolina during the turbulent postwar period; *John Eax and Mamelon* (1882) and *Hot Plowshares* (1883), also dealing with this period; and *Pactolus*

Prime (1890), set in Washington and telling of a black who brings up his own light-complexioned child as a white. He published and edited *The Continent* (1882–84), a weekly literary magazine that serialized his own work and was flavored by his strong Republican attitude, defense of the blacks, and antipathy to the Ku Klux Klan.

Tower Beyond Tragedy, The, free-verse drama by Jeffers, ◆ published in *Tamar and Other Poems* (1924).

In this original treatment of the Electra theme, Jeffers represents the homecoming of Agamemnon to Mycenæ; his murder by his queen Clytemnestra and her lover Ægisthus; the entry of Agamemnon's spirit into the body of the captive Trojan princess, Cassandra, to prophesy the retribution at the hands of Orestes; and the escape of the child Orestes with his sister Electra. When Orestes reaches manhood, he and Electra, determined to accomplish their filial obligation, return to Mycenæ, where Clytemnestra and Ægisthus have established their rule. With the assistance of Cassandra, who has served as the queen's slave, they arouse the palace, and Orestes kills both his mother and her consort. The people choose their returned prince to be king, but the horror of matricide drives him temporarily insane, and he spends a night in the hills. The following morning he reappears, announcing to Electra his return to sanity, despite a dream vision in which he possessed her, "entered the fountain," as he had, in a different sense, by killing his mother. Electra tries to persuade him to remain as ruler, even offering, with some eagerness, to accept him as her lover. The youth declines, asserting that his crime and the consequent derangement have left him with a new wisdom, which impels him to lead a wandering life away from the city. Lying on the hillside at night, he came to realize that men have gone mad by a sort of racial introversion. He himself has discovered peace by a pantheistic identification of himself with all nature. He has attained "the pure flame and the white," having "fallen in love outward." With this phrase, the key to the author's philosophic pantheism, Orestes dismisses Electra's plea, and departs to pass his life in exile from humanity, having

> . . . climbed the tower beyond time,
>   consciously,
> and cast humanity, entered the earlier fountain.

Town, The, novel by William Faulkner, ◆ published in 1957, the second of a trilogy including *The Hamlet* ◆ and *The Mansion.* ◆

Having come from Frenchman's Bend to Jefferson, Yoknapatawpha County, Mississippi, with his wife Eula Varner Snopes and Linda, her daughter by a former lover, Flem Snopes gradually entrenches himself in the town's economic life, moving through a succession of jobs up to a vice-presidency of the Sartoris bank. In his wake come his cousins and their offspring like "rats or termites" to infest the town: Byron, a bank clerk and embezzler; I.O., a bigamist; Montgomery Ward, a pornographic photographer, who is a son of I.O.; and Eck, atypically honest, who is blown to bits in an explosion. Accompanying them are their offspring, including I.O.'s twins, Bilbo and Vardaman, and his oldest son, Clarence, and Eck's boy, Wallstreet Panic Snopes. Himself impotent and his marriage but a means of furthering his ambition and greed, Flem feigns ignorance of Eula's affair with Manfred de Spain, the mayor and bank president, biding his time until his knowledge can be turned to most advantage. The worldly De Spain's rival for Eula is Gavin Stevens, an idealistic yet naïve attorney who with his friend, the shrewd trader V.K. Ratcliff, is the Snopeses' chief opponent. Taunted by De Spain, Gavin challenges and is bloodied by the mayor at the Cotillion Ball, defending "chastity and virtue in women . . . whether they exist or not." Flem, who has been given a sinecure by De Spain as superintendent of the town power plant, makes a rare error in his pursuit of profit when he steals some brass, leading Gavin to file suit, as much against De Spain as Flem. Eula offers herself to Gavin to drop the charge, but Gavin cannot reconcile her unashamed sensual pragmatism with his ideal view of her and sends her away. He turns his attention to Linda, trying to raise her above the Snopes level through books he gives her and his plans for a college education for her, but Flem refuses to send her away to school. Doubting that he is really her father, Linda rebels, although he cynically wins back her confidence so as to secure for himself her future inheritance of Will Varner's bank stock. With this achieved, Flem finally exposes Eula's long liaison with De Spain, who is forced to sell his stock to him and hand over the bank presidency. Eula, now aware of Flem's deception and the threat to Linda's future, commits suicide after asking Gavin to marry Linda, although he agrees only to help her. Gavin gets Linda away by sending her to New York to enjoy new surroundings, De Spain leaves Jefferson, and Flem moves into the De Spain mansion, having rid himself of other Snopeses who threaten his "respectability."

Town and Country, see *Home Journal.*

Town Down the River, *The,* poems by E.A. Robinson. ◆

TOWNSEND, Edward Waterman (1855–1942), author of stories about a tough young man from the Bowery, ◆ first printed in a New York newspaper and later collected with additions in *Chimmie Fadden, Major Max, and Other Stories* (1895) and *Chimmie Fadden Explains* (1895).

TOWNSEND, George Alfred (1841–1914), Delaware-born journalist, became known for his vivid Civil War dispatches, collected in *Campaigns of a Non-Combatant* (1866). After the war he became one of the first syndicated correspondents, writing for some one hundred newspapers under the pseudonym Gath. Although he wrote many books based upon his journalism, biographies of Garibaldi (1867) and Lincoln (1867), *Poems* (1870), plays, and historical romances, he is best remembered for his *Tales of the Chesapeake* (1880), a collection of local-color stories, and *The Entailed Hat* (1884), a novel about the kidnapping of free blacks before the Civil War.

TOWNSEND, Mary Ashley [Van Voorhis] (1832–1901), New York novelist, whose residence in New Orleans provided the background for her melodramatic novel *The Brother Clerks* (1857), and *The Captain's Story* (1874), a poem concerning a supposedly white man who discovers his mother to have been a mulatto. She also wrote *Down the Bayou and Other Poems* (1882). Some of her early writings were published under the name Xariffa or Mary Ashley.

Track of the Cat, *The,* novel by Walter Van Tilburg Clark, ◆ published in 1949.

Tragic Muse, *The,* novel by Henry James, ◆ published in 1890.

To Paris from London comes widowed Lady Agnes Dormer, who wishes to "settle" the lives of her children: Nick, whom she desires to turn from painting to politics; Grace, a conventional girl for whom she seeks a successful marriage; and young Biddy (Bridget), who shares Nick's artistic interests, and whom she also wishes to be married. Among their acquaintances are the aesthete Gabriel Nash, who encourages Nick to paint; Peter Sherringham, a cousin in the diplomatic service, whose avocation is theatergoing; Miriam Rooth, a bold, talented girl, whose genteelly poor mother fosters her ambition to be an actress and uses Peter to obtain an introduction to the great Mme Carré, who trains the girl; and Julia Dallow, Peter's widowed sister, who loves Nick and employs her fortune to back him in a parliamentary election, which causes the family's return to England. To please his mother, Nick proposes to Julia after his election, and for a time concentrates on his political career. He drifts back to painting, however, and one day, when Miriam is posing for a portrait, Julia pays him a visit, after which she breaks their engagement. Nick resigns his seat in Parliament and devotes himself to portraiture. Although Biddy is obviously in love with Peter, the latter has become infatuated with Miriam, who develops into a fine and famous London actress. She refuses Peter, marries her leading man, Basil Dashwood, and causes Peter to pass through a period of despair, from which he emerges to fall in love with Biddy, whom he marries and takes to America. Nick has achieved a modest success as a portraitist, and the unhappy

Julia, who has abandoned her political ambitions, invites him to paint her. It seems, to the immense relief of Lady Agnes, that the two may yet marry.

Trail of the Lonesome Pine, The, novel by John Fox,♦ published in 1908 and dramatized by Eugene Walter (1912).

John Hale, a young engineer, comes to the lawless Kentucky mountain region, to develop a coal mine on the property of "Devil" Judd Tolliver, leader of his family in the feud against the Falin clan. Hale's attempts to keep order arouse the hatred of both families, and the Tollivers are particularly bitter when Judd's daughter June falls in love with Hale, although her cousin Dave looks upon her as his future wife. Hale sends June east for an education, and upon her return she testifies against her own family in the trial of a Tolliver for killing a policeman. After the deaths of Judd and Dave, she marries Hale.

TRAIN, ARTHUR [CHENEY] (1875–1945), born in Massachusetts, became prominent both as a New York lawyer and public official and as an author of fiction. He is particularly noted for his stories with a legal background and concerned with Mr. Tutt, an aging lawyer whose ingenuous manner conceals a shrewd wit and brilliant knowledge of his profession. The many tales in which he figures have been collected in such volumes as *Tutt and Mr. Tutt* (1920), *The Adventures of Ephraim Tutt* (1930), *Mr. Tutt's Case Book* (1936), and *Mr. Tutt Finds a Way* (1945). *Yankee Lawyer: The Autobiography of Ephraim Tutt* (1943) contains the story of his fictional career. *Puritan's Progress* (1931) is an account of the puritan tradition in America. *My Day in Court* (1939) is an autobiography; *From the District Attorney's Office* (1939) explains the administration of criminal justice; and *Tassels on Her Boots* (1940) is a novel of the days of Boss Tweed. Train was president of the National Institute of Arts and Letters (1941–45).

Tramp Abroad, A, travel narrative by Clemens,♦ published in 1880 under his pseudonym Mark Twain. It is a record of his European tour (1878) with Joseph H. Twichell,♦ whom he calls "Harris," and describes their adventures in Germany, Italy, and Switzerland, chiefly during a walking trip through the Black Forest and the Alps. Besides the serious, journalistic account of European natural beauties, society, folklore, and history, including enthusiastic descriptions of Alpine scenery that do not fail to praise comparable regions of the U.S., there are passages ranging from crude farce to tall tales and typical satire. Thus a retelling of Whymper's conquest of the Matterhorn is complemented by the author's "ascent of Mont Blanc by telescope," and a description of ravens in the Black Forest prompts him to recount "Baker's Blue-Jay Yarn," concerned with the sense of humor of California jays. Characteristic

humor also appears in Clemens's inept drawings, purportedly the work of an art student, and the satirical passages on subjects alien to the average American, such as "the awful German language," Wagnerian opera, and "The Great French Duel."

Transcendental Club, name applied by outsiders to the New England intellectuals who met occasionally and informally, during the seven or eight years following 1836, at Emerson's home in Concord and elsewhere, to discuss philosophy, theology, and literature. The members called themselves the Symposium, or the Hedge Club, the latter name being due to the fact that meetings were frequently called when Dr. F.H. Hedge made a trip from his Bangor home to Boston. The assemblage, which assumed the nature of an open forum, included Emerson, Alcott, J.F. Clarke, the younger W.E. Channing, Parker, Margaret Fuller, Ripley, Brownson, Elizabeth Peabody, Thoreau, Hawthorne, Jones Very, C.P. Cranch, Charles Follen, W.H. Channing, Convers Francis, and others. The Brook Farm enterprise was only remotely connected with the Club, whereas *The Dial*♦ was more intimately associated with the group, who led the movement called Transcendentalism.♦

Transcendentalism, a philosophic and literary movement that flourished in New England, particularly at Concord (*c.*1836–60), as a reaction against 18th-century rationalism, the skeptical philosophy of Locke, and the confining religious orthodoxy of New England Calvinism. This romantic, idealistic, mystical, and individualistic belief was more a cast of thought than a systematic philosophy. It was eclectic in nature and had many sources. Its qualities may be discerned in Jonathan Edwards's belief in "a Divine and Supernatural Light, immediately imparted to the soul by the spirit of God," and the idealism of Channing, whose Unitarianism was a religious predecessor of this belief in an indwelling God and intuitive thought. It was also a manifestation of the general humanitarian trend of 19th-century thought. The name, as well as many of the ideas, was derived from Kant's *Critique of Practical Reason* (1788), in which he declares: "I call all knowledge *transcendental* which is concerned, not with objects, but with our mode of knowing objects so far as this is possible *a priori.*" From other German philosophers, such as Jacobi, Fichte, Schleiermacher, Schelling, and Herder, it received impulses toward mysticism and toward practical action as an expression of the will. Through Goethe, Richter, Novalis, and other literary figures, the philosophy was more easily communicated to American authors, and, at second remove, the doctrines of German transcendentalism were reflected in the poetry and criticism of such English authors as Coleridge, Carlyle, and Wordsworth. In addition, the New England Transcendentalist belief was shaped by the ideas of Plato, Plotinus, and such English neo-Platonists as Cudworth and More, as well as by certain aspects of the teachings of Confucius, the Mohammedan Sufis, the writers of the Upanishads and the *Bhagavad-Gita,* the Buddhists, the eclectic idealist Victor Cousin, the Hebrew and Greek scriptural authors, Thomas à Kempis, Pascal, and Swedenborg.

Although the very spirit of Transcendentalism permitted contradiction, and its eclectic sources made for diverse concepts, in its larger outlines the belief had as its fundamental base a monism holding to the unity of the world and God and the immanence of God in the world. Because of this indwelling of divinity, everything in the world is a microcosm containing within itself all the laws and meaning of existence. Likewise, the soul of each individual is identical with the soul of the world, and latently contains all that the world contains. Man may fulfill his divine potentialities either through a rapt mystical state, in which the divine is infused into the human, or through coming into contact with the truth, beauty, and goodness embodied in nature and originating in the Over-Soul. Thus occurs the doctrine of correspondence between the tangible world and the human mind, and the identity of moral and physical laws. Through belief in the divine authority of the soul's intuitions and impulses, based on this identification of the individual soul with God, there developed the doctrine of self-reliance and individualism, the disregard of external authority, tradition, and logical demonstration, and the absolute optimism of the movement.

These primary beliefs varied greatly as they were interpreted in the writings of different authors, although the most important literary expression of transcendental thought is considered to lie in Thoreau's *Walden*♦ and in such works of Emerson as *Nature,*♦ *The American Scholar,*♦ the Divinity School Address,♦ "The Over-Soul,"♦ "Self-Reliance,"♦ and "Compensation."♦ Other members of the informal Transcendental Club♦ whose prose and poetry express similar ideas, included Alcott, Margaret Fuller, the younger W.E. Channing, Ripley, Jones Very, C.P. Cranch, J.F. Clarke, Theodore Parker, Brownson, Elizabeth Peabody, and W.H. Channing. Since there was no formal association, many writers of the time, such as Hawthorne and Julia Ward Howe, were on the fringe of the steadfast believers, and in one way or another the beliefs affected many not usually associated with the movement, including Lowell, Longfellow, Bryant, Whittier, Melville, and Whitman. So far as the movement had a central voice, *The Dial*♦ (1840–44) may be considered its organ, and, although it necessarily remained on an idealistic plane, it was instrumental in the formation of such social experiments as Brook Farm♦ and Fruitlands.♦

Transformation, see *Marble Faun.*

transition (1927–38), monthly little magazine founded in Paris as "an international magazine for creative experiment." Its editors, Eugene Jolas and Elliot Paul, believed that the literary imagination of the time was too photographic and that the study of the irrational was an *a priori* condition for giving the imagination a new dimension. They therefore explored "a nightworld hitherto neglected" and tried to liberate conventional language, using new words and new grammar to evoke such states of mind as dream, hallucination, and half-sleep. Joyce's "Work in Progress" (*Finnegans Wake*), which attempted, according to the editor, "to give a time-and-space-less panorama of the nocturnal world," was one of their leading documents. Other contributors included Gertrude Stein, Hemingway, Hart Crane, and W.C. Williams, and the magazine published translations of foreign authors. In the summer of 1928 it became a quarterly, and it was temporarily discontinued (1930–32) when "it threatened to become a mercantile success."

Traveler from Altruria, A, novel by Howells,♦ published in 1894. *Through the Eye of the Needle*♦ is a sequel.

Mr. Homos, a visitor from the Utopian republic Altruria, founded on principles of altruism, comes to spend his vacation at a fashionable American summer resort. In a series of discussions with Mr. Twelvemough, a fashionable novelist, and other wealthy Americans, he applies his naïve Christian socialism to modern society. Mrs. Makely, a fashionable bourgeois intellectual, arranges for Homos to lecture on Altrurian conditions, and, though his point of view is antithetical to that of most of the hotel guests, he is loudly cheered by the impoverished farmers of the neighborhood. The local minister looks upon Altruria as heaven on earth, a manufacturer's faith in the profit system is shaken, Professor Lumen, avoiding principles, damns the republic as a rehash of famous Utopias, and Mrs. Makely is entirely unmoved by the results of her stimulating evening. The economy of Altruria, as outlined by Homos, requires all citizens to work three hours a day at manual tasks, in return for food and other goods from government sources. In this thoroughly equalitarian state, property is communally owned, most modern machinery is outlawed, family life is subordinated to civic life, and fashions in everything from dress to architecture are under the supervision of aesthetic commissioners.

TRAVEN, B., pseudonym of a mysterious author whose full name is believed to be Berick Traven Torsvan. He is said to have been born in Chicago in 1890 of Swedish parents, but it has also been said that he was a German named Ret Marut or used that name during residence in Germany. He seems to have been active in the I.W.W. in the U.S., to have been in Germany during World War I, and to have lived in Mexico from the 1920s or '30s to his death in 1969. His novels include *The Death Ship* (Germany, 1926; U.S., 1934), about a New Orleans sailor stranded in Antwerp, shunted around Europe, and finally hired on a ship which the owners plan to sink for insurance money; *The Treasure of the Sierra Madre* (Germany, 1927; U.S., 1935), analyzing the psychology of greed in telling of three Americans searching for a lost gold mine in Mexican mountains; *The Bridge and the Jungle* (Germany, 1929; U.S., 1938), in which an explorer in a Central American jungle becomes involved in the drowning of a boy; and *The Rebellion of the Hanged* (Germany, 1936; U.S., 1952), treating the exploitation of Indian lumber camp workers in Mexico during the 1910 revolt against Diaz. This novel was one of a series of six in *The Caoba Cycle,* the latest of which to be translated is *Trozas* (1994). Other novels were published in Germany and England, and shorter fiction is collected in the U.S. as *Stories by the Man Nobody Knows* (1961) and *The Night Visitor* (1973).

Tree Grows in Brooklyn, A, novel by Betty Smith. ♦

TRENT, William Peterfield, see *Sewanee Review.*

TRILLIN, Calvin (1935–), Kansas City-born journalist, after graduation from Yale was a reporter for *Time* and then a staff writer for *The New Yorker.* His nonfictional works include *An Education in Georgia* (1964), about the first blacks to be admitted to a public university in Georgia; *U.S. Journal* (1971), vignettes of life in varied parts of the nation; *American Fried* (1974), on good food in the U.S.; *Alice, Let's Eat* (1978) and *Third Helpings* (1983), further adventures of a happy eater; and *Uncivil Liberties* (1982), witty essays, a form continued in *With All Disrespect* (1985) and *If You Can't Say Something Nice* (1987). *Killings* (1984) deals with sudden deaths, mainly murders. *Travels with Alice* (1989) tells of his wide-ranging trips, often abroad, with his wife. *Remembering Denny* (1993) probes the suicide of a classmate at Yale from whom great things were expected. His fiction includes *Barnett Frummer Is an Unbloomed Flower* (1969), humorous stories; *Runestruck* (1977), a funny tale of a New England town thought to be a Viking landing place; and *Floater* (1980), a comic treatment of work on a weekly news magazine.

TRILLING, Diana (1905–), essayist on literary, social, and political subjects, whose books include *Claremont Essays* (1964), *We Must March My Darlings* (1977), *Reviewing the Forties* (1978), and *Mrs. Harris* (1981), a study of an elegant lady condemned for murdering her lover.

TRILLING, Lionel (1905–75), professor of English at Columbia, also affiliated with the Ken-

yon School of English, *The Kenyon Review,* and the *Partisan Review.* He wrote the studies *Matthew Arnold* (1939) and *E.M. Forster* (1943), and his other critical writings include *The Liberal Imagination* ♦ (1950) and *The Opposing Self* ♦ (1955), essays; *Freud and the Crisis of Our Culture* (1956), lectures; *A Gathering of Fugitives* (1956), brief essays; *The Life and Work of Sigmund Freud* (1962); *Beyond Culture* (1965), essays; *Sincerity and Authenticity* (1972); and *Mind in the Modern World* (1973). *The Middle of the Journey* ♦ (1947) is a novel of the moral and political climate of the 1930s and '40s. Posthumous publications include his *Collected Works* (12 vols., 1978–80) and *Speaking of Literature and Society* (1980), previously uncollected critical writings. Diana Trilling was his wife.

Tripolitan War, or Barbary Wars, naval expeditions against the Barbary states (Morocco, Algiers, Tripoli, and Tunis), which for more than two centuries had preyed on the commerce of Christian nations and captured Christians as slaves. Forbearance was customarily obtained by paying annual tribute, but Jefferson opposed this practice, sending successful expeditions against the pirates (1801–5), led by Preble and Decatur. While the U.S. was engaged in the War of 1812, the Barbary states renewed their ship raiding, and Algiers declared war (1815). Decatur and others were responsible for the conclusion of the war by an American victory. The campaigns furnished the theme of Susanna Rowson's *Slaves in Algiers,* Payne's *Fall of Algiers,* Tyler's *The Algerine Captive,* and other contemporary literature. Later fictional treatments include Kenneth Roberts's *Lydia Bailey* and H.L. Davis's *Harp of a Thousand Strings.*

Tri-Quarterly, little magazine founded (1958) as a publication of Northwestern University but since 1964 addressed to a general public, although still under the university's auspices. In special issues or substantial sections of regular issues it deals in depth with a particular subject, such as contemporary American fiction or a modern literary movement or a single U.S. or foreign author.

Tristram, blank-verse dramatic narrative by E.A. Robinson, ♦ published in 1927 and awarded a Pulitzer Prize. It belongs with *Lancelot* ♦ and *Merlin* ♦ in the author's Arthurian trilogy.

    Prince Tristram of Lyonesse, wounded in combat in Ireland, is nursed to health by Princess Isolt. He tells his uncle, King Mark of Cornwall, of Isolt's beauty, and Mark sends him to bring her to be his queen. During the return voyage, Tristram falls in love with Isolt, but feels honor bound to carry out his mission. He contemplates suicide and refuses to attend the marriage feast. Three messengers are sent to persuade him: Gouvernail, his friend and counselor; Queen Morgan, who attempts to renew her former hold on him; and Brangwaine, Isolt's attendant. All fail, and Isolt herself comes. Their farewell embrace is spied by his treacherous cousin Andred, whom Tristram wounds. For this act Mark exiles Tristram, and Gouvernail follows him, rescuing Tristram when a fever overcomes him. While he is recuperating, Morgan tries to make him love her. He goes with Gouvernail to Brittany, where another Isolt—Isolt of the White Hands—daughter of King Howel, counters his indifference with her passionate love, and he marries her. Later he becomes a knight of Arthur's Round Table, and, when Mark is imprisoned for opposing the papal government, Tristram and Isolt of Ireland spend a blissful time together in Joyous Gard. Mark is released and takes his queen back to Cornwall. She is dying, and Mark, resigned and generous, allows Tristram to attend her. The final embrace of the lovers is interrupted by Andred, who brings about the death of Tristram and Isolt in each other's arms.

Triumph at Plattsburg, The, play by R.P. Smith,♦ produced in 1830 and first published in Quinn's *Representative American Plays* (1917). The play deals with the defeat of the British fleet at Plattsburg Bay in the War of 1812, the escape of Major McCrea from the British, and the actions of his daughter Elinor, married to Captain Stanley of the British army.

Triumph of Infidelity, poem by Timothy Dwight,♦ published anonymously in 1788. Written in heroic couplets, this satire lacks the light touch of Dwight's master, Pope, and is characterized by abusiveness that has led it to be compared with "good old-fashioned pulpit-thumping." He violently defends Calvinist orthodoxy and defies Voltaire, Hume, Priestley, and their "infidel" followers.

Triumph of the Egg, The, collection by Sherwood Anderson,♦ published in 1921, is subtitled "A Book of Impressions from American Life in Tales and Poems."

Triumphs of Love, The, or *Happy Reconciliation,* play by John Murdock, produced and printed in 1795. It deals with the Quakers, the Whiskey Rebellion, and other matters of contemporary interest. It is chiefly remembered for Sambo, the first black to be portrayed on the American stage.

Trivia, volume of aphorisms and essays written by Logan Pearsall Smith. ♦

TROLLOPE, FRANCES (1780–1863), English author, resided in the U.S. (1827–30), during which time her husband operated a fancy-goods bazaar in Cincinnati. The business failed, but Mrs. Trollope's book *Domestic Manners of the Americans* (1832) attained notoriety. Although she admitted that the material status of Americans

was superior to that of Europeans, she remarked on the tendency of democracy to lower the level of intellectual attainment, attacked slavery, was offended by revivals, disliked the affected delicacy of American women, and criticized the general boastfulness and sharp practices in business. The work caused a sensation and prompted many replies both in magazines and in books. Mrs. Trollope wrote other travel books and novels, of which four deal with America: *The Refugee in America* (1832); *Jonathan Jefferson Whitlaw* (1836), attacking black slavery; *The Barnabys in America* (1843); and *The Old World and the New* (1849). Her sons, the novelist Anthony Trollope (1815–82) and Thomas Adolphus Trollope (1810–92), both wrote studies of American institutions. The several trips that Anthony made to America resulted in *North America* (1862) and some letters in the Liverpool *Weekly Mercury* (1875), of which one was reprinted as *A Letter from Anthony Trollope Describing a Visit to California* (1946).

Tropic of Cancer, novel in the form of a personal narrative by Henry Miller,♦ first published in Paris in 1934 but censored in the U.S., where it was not printed until 1961.

In a first-person monologue that is heavily anecdotal and quasi-philosophic, it tells of the life of an expatriate American author in Paris during the 1920s and '30s. By turns angry and humorous, it presents very frankly the doings of an impoverished artist, including his sexual experiences, which are good when animated by love and when not are viewed as being as vulgar as the ultimate obscenity of inertia.

Tropic of Capricorn, novel in the form of a personal narrative by Henry Miller,♦ first published in Paris in 1939 but because of censorship not printed in the U.S. until 1962.

In a form like that of *Tropic of Cancer*♦ the autobiographical account describes the writer's boyhood in Brooklyn, his quest to discover himself by sexual experiences and by other means, and his fury at the faults he finds in many of the values and ways of life in the U.S.

TROUBETZKOY, PRINCESS, see *Rives, Amélie.*

TROWBRIDGE, J[OHN] T[OWNSEND] (1827–1916), New York-born author, lived in Boston after 1848, and there wrote some 40 novels for boys, which had much to do with raising juvenile literature from didacticism to a higher plane. The best known of his books are the antislavery novels *Cudjo's Cave*♦ (1864), written for children, and *Neighbor Jackwood*♦ (1857). *Coupon Bonds* (1866), which the author dramatized in 1876, is a story of a rural New England family whose sole interest is money. His poems, collected in 1903, include several long narratives and some light verse, such as "Darius Green and His Flying Machine." His autobiography is *My Own Story* (1903).

True Relation, *A, of . . . occurrences . . . in Virginia*, see Smith, John.

TRUMBO, DALTON (1905–76), Colorado-born film writer and novelist. His masterpiece is *Johnny Got His Gun* (1939), a powerful telling, from inside the sufferer's mind, of the struggle to break through and reach out of a World War I soldier who has lost both arms, both legs, had his whole face scooped out by a shell, and is deaf. So he is a medical curiosity, imprisoned with his brain, until one doctor detects the movements of his head as signals in Morse code. Trumbo was jailed for contempt of Congress in the early fifties after refusing to testify before the House Committee on Un-American Activities. He was blacklisted by Hollywood, went to Mexico, and wrote scripts under various names, and under his own, when the ban was lifted, *Exodus* (1960) and *Spartacus* (1960). *Additional Dialogue* (1970) is a collection of letters.

TRUMBULL, BENJAMIN (1735–1820), Connecticut Congregational clergyman, wrote *A Complete History of Connecticut* (1797, revised 1818), which was an accurate but heavy work. Only one volume of his projected *General History of the United States* was published (1810), although *A Compendium of the Indian Wars in New England* was edited and published (1924).

TRUMBULL, JOHN (1750–1831), member of the Connecticut Wits,♦ graduated from Yale (1767), where with Timothy Dwight and David Humphreys he attempted to liberalize the course of studies and create an interest in modern literature. His valedictory oration, *An Essay on the Uses and Advantages of the Fine Arts*, attacks subservience to neoclassical rules, but its concluding verses, "Prospect of the Future Glory of America," are perfect examples of neoclassical versification. After receiving his master's degree (1770), and while tutoring at the college, he wrote *The Progress of Dulness*♦ (1772–73), a satire on college education, as well as a series of Addisonian essays printed in *The Boston Chronicle* (1769–70) and graceful verse. Removing to Boston (1773), he studied law in the office of John Adams, and was stimulated by him to interest himself in the patriotic movement and write his bombastic poem *An Elegy on the Times* (1774). While practicing law at New Haven and Hartford (1774–1825), he was drawn into the poetic circle of the Wits and into politics. Although he aligned himself on the side of the revolutionaries, he was cautious and moderate, as indicated in his literary contributions to the cause. He was a thinker rather than a man of action. At the instigation of "some leading members of the first Congress," he wrote the mock epic *M'Fingal*♦ (1782), satirizing the stupidity of

the British. Later, he joined the conservative Federalists, cooperating with them in *The Anarchiad,*♦ satirizing democratic liberalism. Although he remained active in legal matters, he outlived his literary vitality, and did no more than contribute to these collections during the last half-century of his life. He was a first cousin of Jonathan Trumbull.

TRUMBULL, JONATHAN (1710–85), chief justice of the Connecticut supreme court (1766–69) and governor of the colony and later the state (1769–84), was the only colonial governor to champion the Revolutionary cause. He was an adviser of Washington and has been considered the original of the name "Brother Jonathan."♦ He was the father of John Trumbull (1756–1843), a painter of grand, historical canvases and portraits.

TRUTH, SOJOURNER [ISABELLA VAN WAGENER] (c. 1797–1883), orator, advocate for women's rights. A New York-born former slave who spoke Dutch first, then learned English, she grew up on a Dutch estate in Ulster County and was sold several times, sometimes to English-speakers who beat her for being slow in the language. She had two of her children sold away from her and when she was 30 she bolted from a hard master, and following her own revelations from God, renamed herself and embarked on her mission, as commanded, to "sojourn" in the land and spread His truth. In Northampton, Mass., she came under the influence of abolitionists and sharpened her message. She chose a white amanuensis to write her narrative—it is unclear whether she was illiterate—but her own voice comes through in *Narrative of Sojourner Truth; A Bondswoman of Olden Time, with a History of Her Labors and Correspondence Drawn from Her "Book of Life."* It appeared in the *Anti-Slavery Bugle* issue of June 1851 and features her "three hearts"—millennialism, abolitionism, and women's rights. Sojourner's attestation of God giving her Truth for her name appeared in Harriet Beecher Stowe's piece "The Libyan Sibyl."

TUCHMAN, BARBARA W[ERTHEIM] (1912–89), New York-born journalist and historian, author under her maiden name of *The Lost British Policy* (1938); *Bible and Sword* (1956); and *The Zimmerman Telegram* (1958), about the German foreign minister's cable in World War I proposing that Mexico attack the U.S. and regain Southwestern territory. Under her married name she wrote *The Guns of August* (1962, Pulitzer Prize), on the battles during the first month of World War I; *The Proud Tower* (1965), on the 24 years preceding that month; *Stilwell and the American Experience in China, 1911–45* (1972, Pulitzer Prize); *Notes from China* (1972); *A Distant Mirror* (1978), on Europe in the 14th century; *The March of Folly* (1984), treating political inanity throughout history; and *The First Salute* (1988), treating the first foreign official recognition of the United States by the Dutch, and focusing on the maritime side of the Revolutionary War. *Practicing History* (1981) collects essays.

TUCKER, GEORGE (1775–1861), born in Bermuda, reared in Virginia, was a member of Congress (1819–25), where his views attracted Jefferson, who appointed him professor at the University of Virginia (1825–45). He had already written a volume of essays, *Letters from Virginia* (1816), satirizing the decadent gentility of the Old Dominion, and two novels, *The Valley of Shenandoah* (1824) and *A Voyage to the Moon* (1827), the latter being a Swiftian satire of human follies, but during his later years his literary reputation was based on his histories and writings on political economy. His *Progress of the United States . . .* (1843; appendix, 1855) shows the influence of Malthus, and his *History of the United States* (4 vols., 1856–57) is a conservative Virginian's championing of the theory of states' rights. His *Life of Thomas Jefferson* (2 vols., 1837), although laudatory, is considered the most satisfactory and impartial of the early biographies. His works on political economy, *The Law of Wages, Profits, and Rent Investigated* (1837), *The Theory of Money and Banks Investigated* (1839), and *Political Economy for the People* (1859), follow the theories of Adam Smith.

TUCKER, NATHANIEL BEVERLEY (1784–1851), son of St. George Tucker, was a professor of law at William and Mary and author of several works on political economy and law, which show him to be a highly reactionary Virginia aristocrat. He is best known for his novels: *George Balcombe* (1836), a realistic picture of contemporary Virginia and Missouri; and *The Partisan Leader*♦ (1836), a romance telling of events supposed to take place in 1849, which was intended to sway the election of 1836 against Van Buren, but whose political philosophy made it more than a campaign document and caused it to be reissued as propaganda during the Civil War. He is sometimes known as Beverley Tucker, and used the pseudonym Edward William Sidney.

TUCKER, ST. GEORGE (1752–1827), Virginia jurist, in addition to his legal writings was the author of *Liberty, a Poem on the Independence of America* (1788); *Dissertation on Slavery* (1796), suggesting a plan for gradual emancipation; and *The Probationary Odes of Jonathan Pindar* (1796), a volume of political satires. He was the stepfather of John Randolph.

TUCKERMAN, FREDERICK GODDARD (1821–73), member of a distinguished Massachusetts family and cousin of Henry Theodore Tuckerman, was himself generally little known during his lifetime because, after graduation from Har-

vard and a short period of legal practice, he lived as a recluse and issued only one volume of *Poems* (1860), for which he is now highly regarded. This privately printed collection was reissued in 1864 and 1869, and *Complete Poems* (1965) was edited from manuscripts. The modern discovery of Tuckerman was effected by Witter Bynner, who republished the best of his *Poems,* together with three hitherto unpublished sonnet sequences, as *Sonnets* (1931). In a highly eulogistic introduction Bynner calls these works among "the noblest in the language" for their expression of grief, their imagery, and their radical use of a conventional form. Yvor Winters contends that "in the description of natural detail . . . he surpasses the British romantics except, perhaps, for an occasional line or short passage in Wordsworth." Winters lays particular stress on a late poem, "The Cricket" (first published in an imperfect text, 1950), an ode sensitively evoking the insect and treating the theme of differences and relations between the human and natural worlds.

TUCKERMAN, HENRY THEODORE (1813–71), Boston-born author, after 1845 lived in New York, where he wrote serenely sympathetic books of criticism, such as *Thoughts on the Poets* (1846), *Characteristics of Literature* (1849, 1851); leisurely essays, *The Optimist* (1850) and *The Criterion* (1866); sketches in the vein of Irving, *Leaves from the Diary of a Dreamer* (1853); biographies, including one of J.P. Kennedy (1871); a scholarly work on travel in the U.S., *America and Her Commentators* (1864); a volume of sentimental *Poems* (1851); and romantic travel books.

TUDOR, WILLIAM (1779–1830), Boston merchant, was a founder of the Anthology Club,♦ and contributed to its magazine and to *The North American Review,* of which he was the first editor. His *Miscellanies* (1821) range from the "Secret Causes of the American and French Revolutions" to the satires on scholarly papers in "On Cranberry Sauce" and "A Dissertation Upon Things in General." His other books are *Letters on the Eastern States* (1820), social criticism; *The Life of James Otis of Massachusetts* (1823); and a novel, *Gebel Teir* (1829).

Tuesday Club of Annapolis (1745–56), founded by Dr. Alexander Hamilton and Jonas Green, editor of *The Maryland Gazette.* It was a typical colonial coffeehouse gathering of literary figures and other intellectuals. Hamilton's records of the meetings were written under the pseudonym Loquacious Scribble, Esq.

Tuesday Club of Philadelphia (1800–?), founded by Joseph Dennie and the group that supported his *Port Folio.* ♦ Its sympathies were Federalist, aristocratic, and intensely pro-English. Among the members were Joseph Hopkinson and Nicholas Biddle. Little is known of the club after 1804.

TULLEY, JOHN (*c.*1639–1701), born in England, lived most of his life in Connecticut, where from 1687 until his death he issued annual almanacs, significant as the first continuous series in this form. The edition of 1687 is said to have begun the tradition of the humorous almanac in America.

TULLY, RICHARD WALTON (1877–1945), California playwright whose works include *Rose of the Rancho* (1906), written with Belasco; *The Bird of Paradise* (1912), a play about an American's love for a Hawaiian girl, adapted by H.E. Rogers and Rudolf Friml as an operetta (1930); *Omar the Tentmaker* (1914); and *The Flame* (1916), contrasting American businessmen in Mexico with the native people.

TURELL, JANE [COLMAN] (1708–35), daughter of Benjamin Colman, and wife of another Congregational minister, Ebenezer Turell (1702–78), was the author of pious poems, published in *Reliquiae Turellae* (1735), reprinted as *Memoirs . . .* (1741). The latter also includes her verses on Waller and Richard Blackmore, and all are more significant as examples of contemporary taste than as poetry.

Turn of the Screw, The, story by Henry James, ♦ published in 1898. The ambiguities of the tale have led to a large body of interpretations, particularly Freudian and anti-Freudian analyses, of which the best known is Edmund Wilson's in *The Triple Thinkers,* itself twice revised. The story was dramatized by William Archibald as *The Innocents* (1950) and Benjamin Britten created an operatic version under the original title in 1954.

This mysterious tale of ghastly apparitions is recounted from the diary of a neurotic spinster who in her youth was a governess on a lonely British estate. Her unusually beautiful and precocious pupils, the children Miles and Flora, are subjected, she believes, respectively to the evil influence of two ghosts: Peter Quint, once a valet on the estate, and Miss Jessel, their former governess. The frustrated new governess, infatuated by the children and particularly by the boy, pits her will against that of the ghosts, for these specters, she believes, morally dominate the children and have an evil relationship with them. She justifies her belief by winning the housekeeper to her cause, although this kindly, simple woman never sees the apparitions. Fearing to report the untoward events to her employer, the children's uncle, for whom she entertains an unrealized and thwarted passion, the governess attempts to exorcise the malicious influences by directly challenging Flora, whose resultant fear is so great she cannot again face the governess. A similarly impassioned attack on Miles results in his death in the arms of the governess, who thought she was saving his life from a demon.

TURNER, FREDERICK JACKSON (1861–1932), born in Wisconsin, taught history at the state university (1889–1910) and at Harvard (1910–24), and was later associated in his research with the Huntington Library. Before the American Historical Association (Chicago, July 1893), he read a paper on "The Significance of the Frontier in American History" (printed 1894), which inaugurated a new interpretation of the West. He wrote little, and when he published *The Frontier in American History* (1920) there were only a dozen short essays that he cared to reprint along with his original paper on the frontier. *The Significance of Sections in American History* (1932) was a posthumous recipient of a Pulitzer Prize. In the *Rise of the New West, 1819–1829* (1906), a volume in A.B. Hart's cooperative work *The American Nation,* he disclosed the sectional unities of the period 1819–29. At his death he left incomplete a continuation of this work, published as *The United States, 1830–1850: The Nation and Its Sections* (1935). (For a brief survey of his theory, see *Frontier.*)

TURNER, NAT, see *Confessions of Nat Turner* and *Dred.*

Tuscarora Indians, tribe related to the Iroquois, which was driven by white settlers from its original home in North Carolina to take refuge with the Iroquois Confederacy, which then became the Six Nations. Because they remained friendly with the Americans in the Revolution, they were attacked and dispersed by the British. The Tuscarora chief Wyandotté is the central figure in Cooper's novel of that name, and Edmund Wilson's *Apologies to the Iroquois* (1960) tells of the 20th-century situation of the tribes in the Confederacy.

Tutt, MR., character in the short stories of Arthur Train. ♦

TWAIN, MARK, see *Mark Twain.*

'Twas the Night Before Christmas, poem by C.C. Moore. ♦

Twentieth Century Magazine (1909–13), Boston monthly journal, prominent in the muckraking movement. Its contributors included Hamlin Garland and Edwin Markham.

Twice a Year (1938–48), semi-annual "journal of literature, the arts and civil liberties," concerned with a synthesis of aesthetic and social expression. It published translations of such authors as Proust, Kafka, and Lorca, and its contributors included Muriel Rukeyser, Henry Miller, Stieglitz, Saroyan, and Kenneth Patchen.

Twice-Told Tales, 39 stories by Hawthorne, ♦ printed in *The Token,* collected (1837) and enlarged (1842). Among the tales, many of them marked by the author's interest in the supernatural, are sketches of New England history, like

"The Grey Champion,"♦ "Endicott and the Red Cross,"♦ "The Maypole of Merrymount,"♦ and the four "Legends of the Province House," which include "Howe's Masquerade"♦ and "Lady Eleanor's Mantle"♦; stories of incident, like "Mr. Higginbotham's Catastrophe"♦; and moral allegories, like "The Minister's Black Veil,"♦ "Dr. Heidegger's Experiment,"♦ and "The Ambitious Guest."♦

TWICHELL, JOSEPH HOPKINS (1838–1918), Congregational clergyman of Hartford, Conn., was a member of the circle which included Harriet Beecher Stowe, C.D. Warner, and Clemens. He suggested that Clemens write *Life on the Mississippi,* and accompanied him on the European tour described in *A Tramp Abroad,* in which Twichell figures as "Harris." His own writings include a biography of John Winthrop (1891), whose letters he edited.

Two Look at Two, blank-verse poem by Robert Frost,♦ published in *New Hampshire* (1923).

A pair of lovers climb a wooded mountain, and at the approach of night prepare to turn back but are halted on seeing a doe staring at them across a fence. The spell broken when she calmly walks off, they are about to go on again, but are stopped a second time by the appearance in the same place of "an antlered buck of lusty nostril" who "viewed them quizzically with jerks of head." After a moment he too disappears, but the lovers stand spellbound,

> As if the earth in one unlooked-for favor
> Had made them certain earth returned their
> love.

Two Magics, The, tales of the supernatural by Henry James.♦

Two Rivulets, discursive work by Whitman,♦ the second volume of a collected edition (1876) whose first volume was *Leaves of Grass.* The title suggests not only the blending of prose and verse, but also the combination of thoughts on American politics and literature with realistic and imaginative speculations on death and immortality. *Two Rivulets* incorporates *Democratic Vistas*♦ (1871) and *Memoranda During the War* (1875) as prose, and its poetry includes the previous pamphlets *As a Strong Bird on Pinions Free* (1872) and *Passage to India*♦ (1871), a group of "Centennial Songs," and other fugitive writings.

Two Years Before the Mast, personal narrative of life at sea by R.H. Dana, Jr.,♦ published anonymously in 1840. It is written in the form of an extended diary, based on a journal that the author kept during his voyage, for the purpose of presenting "the life of a common sailor at sea as it really is,—the light and the dark together." A concluding chapter furnishes a general statement of conditions prevailing on merchant ships at the time, and suggests measures to diminish the hardships of the sailors' daily lives.

The narrative begins with Dana's abrupt change from the life of a Harvard undergraduate to that of an ordinary seaman, sailing on the brig *Pilgrim* (Aug. 14, 1834) for a voyage from Boston around Cape Horn to California. In a clear-sighted, hard-headed, and self-controlled manner, he describes the 150-day voyage, with all its petty details and routine, as well as the sailors' off-hour occupations and conversation. One of the most dramatic events is the flogging of two of his shipmates, and his vow "to redress the grievances and sufferings of that class of beings with whom my lot had so long been cast." During his residence on the California coast (Jan. 13, 1835–May 8, 1836), he describes with similar detailed realism his life on shore, curing hides and gathering them at such ports as Santa Barbara, San Diego, Monterey, and San Francisco. There are also character portraits of such persons as Hope, a Kanaka "noble savage" who blindly adored Dana; his young shipmate, self-educated Tom Harris; the older high-tempered sailor, John the Swede; and the cruel Captain Thompson, who could gladly knock a sailor down with a handspike. Although designed to be purely objective, the narrative also reveals the author as torn between antagonistic points of view, and during the return trip on the ship *Alert* (May 8–Sept. 20, 1836) and the stormy rounding of Cape Horn, he tells of his intense desire to return to his original milieu and his eventual discovery that when the hardships and the realities of the voyage were finished, it assumed the character of a symbol of liberation, so that "the emotions which I had so long anticipated feeling I did not find, and in their place was a state of very nearly entire apathy." To later editions was added the chapter "Twenty-Four Years After," describing Dana's nostalgic return to California in 1859.

TYLER, ANNE (1941–   ), novelist born in Minneapolis, educated at Duke University (B.A., 1961), lives in Baltimore, the scene of some of her fiction, which also is often set in small Southern towns. Her first novels—*If Morning Ever Comes* (1965), *The Tin Can Tree* (1966), and *A Slipping Down Life* (1970)—published before she was 30, deal with families and the separations they suffer through deaths and through the unhappy isolation of one member from another. These themes are also presented in later novels: *The Clock Winder* (1973); *Celestial Navigation* (1975); *Searching for Caleb* (1976); *Earthly Possessions* (1977); *Morgan's Passing* (1980); *Dinner at the Homesick Restaurant* (1982), telling of the long, often unhappy life of a deserted wife who is a possessive and domineering mother; *The Accidental Tourist* (1985), about a sad travel writer, from which a film was made; *Breathing Lessons* (1988), concerning moving away from and back to family roots, honored by a Pulitzer Prize; and *Saint Maybe* (1992) exploring religious preoccupations with faith and deliverance.

TYLER, ROYALL (1757–1826), born in Boston, after graduation from Harvard (1776) practiced law and helped to suppress Shays's Rebellion. While on a visit to New York City, he saw a production of *The School for Scandal,* and within three weeks wrote *The Contrast*♦ (1787), a social comedy contrasting homespun American dignity with the alien foppery of the British, the second play and the first comedy to be written by an American. Within a month of its production, he followed it with a two-act comic opera, *May Day in Town; or, New York in an Uproar,* which has not survived and is known only to have been a satire on contemporary manners, concerned with the confusion caused by spring housecleaning and moving. Another comedy, *The Georgia Spec; or, Land in the Moon* (1797), is also lost, but is known to have ridiculed the Yazoo frauds. In addition, Tyler wrote four unproduced and unpublished plays: *The Island of Barrataria,* a farce based on *Don Quixote;* and *The Origin of the Feast of Purim, Joseph and His Brethren,* and *The Judgment of Solomon,* blank-verse Biblical dramas. Having moved from Boston to Vermont (1790) to continue his legal career, eventually becoming chief justice of the state supreme court (1807–13) and professor of jurisprudence at the University of Vermont (1811–14), he entered into a close friendship with Joseph Dennie. Using the pseudonym Spondee, while Dennie employed that of Colon, he collaborated in writing satirical verse and light essays, frequently showing a Federalist bias, which they contributed to the *Farmer's Weekly Museum* and other journals. In addition to a long poem, *The Chestnut Tree,* written in 1824 and first published in 1931, which depicts contemporary rural life but prophesies the rise of industrialism, Tyler is known for his picaresque novel *The Algerine Captive*♦ (1797) and his *Yankey in London* (1809), a series of letters supposedly written by an American resident in England. Previously uncollected *Verse* and *Prose* appeared respectively in 1968 and 1972.

Typee, fictional narrative by Melville,♦ published in 1846. It is based on the author's experiences when he deserted the whaler *Acushnet* (1842).

Tom and Toby desert their whaling ship because the poor food, hard work, and tyranny of the captain have become unbearable. They take refuge with the peaceful Typee savages on a Marquesas island. When Tom falls sick, Toby seeks aid and through misadventure is shipped aboard a vessel bound for the U.S. Left alone with the Typees, Tom makes sharp observation of the social, religious, and moral standards of the natives. Tom enjoys the idyllic life with Fayaway, a native belle, and is aroused from his pleasant captivity of three months only when the tribe insists he be tattooed and when he fears the cannibals may turn from eating Happars to eating white men. He finally escapes on an Australian trading vessel. A second edition (1846) containing some deletions and revisions prints a sequel telling the story of Toby's safe return.

U

U.S.A., trilogy by Dos Passos,♦ which includes the novels *The 42nd Parallel,♦ 1919,♦* and *The Big Money.♦*

UHRY, ALFRED (1937–), out of his childhood in Atlanta, Ga., and after graduation from Brown University, moved into the world of theater and drama. He wrote or collaborated on several productions as lyricist and librettist. His play *Driving Miss Daisy* (1987), about the relationship between an elderly Southern woman and her black chauffeur, was awarded a Pulitzer Prize in 1988.

Ulalume, poem by Poe,♦ published in the *American Whig Review* (Dec. 1847). This lyrical poem, called by Poe a ballad, expresses the writer's grief over the death of his beloved "Ulalume," and in its first magazine publication had ten stanzas ranging from the nine lines of the first stanza to the 13 of the penultimate, which in later publications became the final stanza. The meter is anapestic trimeter. It tells of the lover's unwitting return to the tomb where he had buried his Ulalume:

> It was hard by the dim lake of Auber
> In the misty mid region of Weir—
> It was down by the dank tarn of Auber,
> In the ghoul-haunted woodland of Weir.

ULLOA, ANTONIO DE (1716–95), Spanish naval officer, scientist, and government official, was governor of Louisiana (1766–68). He is best known for his books translated as *A Voyage to South America* (1758), *Secret Information Concerning America* (1826), and *Secret Expedition to Peru . . .* (1851), the last written with Jorge Juan y Santacilia.

Ulster County Gazette (1798–1822), New York Federalist newspaper, widely known for the issue (Jan. 4, 1800) that contained an account of Washington's funeral and the congressional proceedings upon his death. No original copy of this issue is known, but there have been 21 spurious reprints, often sold at high prices as rare antiques.

UNCAS (fl.1600–1683), chief of the Mohegan Indians,♦ sided with the British in the Pequot War (1637), figures as the titular character in *The Last of the Mohicans,♦* and also appears in Cooper's *Wept of Wish-ton-Wish.* However, he has only his name in common with Cooper's hero. The historical Uncas was tolerated by the English

colonists of Massachusetts and Connecticut because he made war on Miantonomo, the Indian protector of Roger Williams, who was anathema to their religious hegemony, but was later considered an "underminer of praying to God" because he attacked Massasoit, the friend of the Massachusetts colony. He is the subject of a biography by W.L. Stone (1842).

Uncle Lisha's Shop, stories by R.E. Robinson.♦

"Uncle Ned," minstrel-show song by Stephen Foster.♦

Uncle Remus: *His Songs and His Sayings,* verses and tales based on black folklore, by Joel Chandler Harris,♦ published in periodicals and collected in 1881.

Whimsical, lovable old Uncle Remus, once a slave, is now a trusted family servant who entertains the young son of his employers with traditional fables of his race. Included in the collection are the famous "Tar-Baby" stories and others in which the chief figures are animals endowed with human qualities, such as Brer Rabbit, Brer Fox, and Brer Wolf. The dialect is authentic and the author gathered his materials at first hand among Southern blacks. He published many other Uncle Remus collections.

Uncle Sam, nickname for the people or government of the U.S. The first recorded use occurs in the *Troy Post* (Sept. 7, 1813), where it is said to be derived from the letters U.S. on government wagons. Thereafter it appeared frequently in upstate New York newspapers, and seems to have been derisively used by those who opposed the War of 1812. Other theories concerning its origin may be found, but the one above seems the most acceptable. The first appearance of the name in book form was in *The Adventures of Uncle Sam* (1816) by "Frederick Augustus Fidfaddy, Esq." The first foreigner to use the term was the Englishman William Faux, who employed it frequently in his *Memorable Days in America* (1823). By 1860 the term had passed into the dictionary without any opprobrious connotation. The costume of Uncle Sam derives from that of Jack Downing,♦ whom he replaced as the national symbol in cartoons. The clown Dan Rice performed in such a costume.

Uncle Tom's Cabin, *or, Life Among the Lowly,* novel by Harriet Beecher Stowe,♦ published serially in the *National Era* (1851–52) and in book form in 1852. During its first year after publication, more than 300,000 copies were sold, and it became the most popular American novel, having a powerful antislavery influence. Attacks upon its truth caused Mrs. Stowe to publish *A Key to Uncle Tom's Cabin* (1853), defending the accuracy of its facts. The story was frequently translated and republished and was successfully dramatized by George Aiken♦ (1852), without Mrs. Stowe's consent.

Uncle Tom is a noble, high-minded, devoutly Christian black slave in the kindly Shelby family. The Shelbys, in financial difficulties, are about to sell their slaves, and the mulatto girl Eliza and her child escape across the frozen Ohio River, but Tom remains because he does not wish to embarrass his master. Separated from his wife and children, he is sold to a slave trader, and young George Shelby promises some day to redeem him. On the voyage down the Mississippi, Tom saves the life of little Eva, the daughter of St. Clare, who in gratitude purchases him as a servant for his New Orleans home. Tom is happy for two years with the easygoing St. Clare, the angelic little Eva, and her mischievous companion, the black child Topsy, who, when questioned about her family, says: "Never was born, never had no father, nor mother, nor nothin' . . . I 'spect I growed." Eva's delicate constitution fails, and she soon dies. St. Clare is accidentally killed, and Tom is sold at auction to Simon Legree, a brutal, drunken, degenerate planter. The slave's courage and religious fortitude impress his criminal master, who becomes desperately fear-ridden. Cassie and Emmaline, two female slaves, take advantage of his state of mind and pretend to escape. When Tom refuses to reveal their hiding place, Legree is furious, and has him flogged to death. George Shelby arrives as Tom is dying, and vows to devote himself to the cause of abolition.

Uncle Tom's Children, stories by Richard Wright. ♦

UNDERHILL, JOHN (c. 1597–1672), Massachusetts military leader in the war against the Pequot Indians, of which he published an account in *Newes from America* (1638). Because he was an Antinomian he was banished and excommunicated, but later he was allowed to return and helped the English to gain control of New Amsterdam. He is the subject of a poem by Whittier.

UNDERWOOD, FRANCIS HENRY (1825–94), Massachusetts author and lawyer, was one of the founders of the *Atlantic Monthly,* which he helped to edit (1857–59). His novels include *Quabbin: The Story of a Small Town* (1893).

Union Colony, see *Meeker, N.C.*

Union Magazine, The (1847–52), New York monthly, edited for the first year by Caroline

Stansbury Kirkland, who contributed Western stories, and obtained reviews, essays, sketches, and sentimental, moral, and didactic tales from Simms, C.F. Hoffman, Lydia Huntley Sigourney, T.S. Arthur, and Park Benjamin. Poe contributed "An Enigma" and "To Helen." The magazine was purchased by John Sartain (1848), who added his name to the title. Contributors under his editorship included Longfellow, Lowell, N.P. Willis, Boker, Stoddard, T.D. English, Griswold, J.G. Saxe, and T.B. Read. At this time Poe contributed "The Bells" and "The Poetic Principle," and Thoreau contributed the first part of *The Maine Woods.*

Unitarianism, religious doctrine of the single personality of God, as contrasted with the Trinitarian concept. The name does not fully indicate the significance of the Unitarian movement, which lies in its liberal rationalism and its opposition to the doctrines of inherited guilt, loss of free will, eternal punishment, and vicarious atonement. Modern Unitarianism traces its origin to the Reformation, and its history in England and America began in the 17th and 18th centuries. More a cast of thought than a systematic theology, the movement in America was at first a reaction against the confining orthodoxy of New England Calvinism, and was to a large extent the result of liberal scientific thought. It was first evidenced in the rationalistic teachings of such divines as Jonathan Mayhew. ♦ Independently, the Anglicans of King's Chapel, Boston, adopted a liturgy eliminating the doctrine of the Trinity (1785) and so became America's first Unitarian church. Congregational churches in Salem were influenced by English Unitarians, of whom the most prominent, Joseph Priestley, emigrated to organize Unitarian churches in the U.S. (1794). Henry Ware was instrumental in promulgating Unitarian ideas as the first nonorthodox professor of divinity at Harvard (1805–40) and as founder of the college's Divinity School (1819). William Ellery Channing, whose sermon at the ordination of Jared Sparks (1819) indicated a clear break with orthodox Calvinism, was looked upon as the great apostle of Unitarianism. The thought at this time was an attempt to combine rationalism with a modified supernaturalism, and was devoted to practical Christianity and humanitarianism. From about 1835, it was strongly influenced by German idealistic philosophy in both its mystical and its rationalistic aspects, and Theodore Parker, George Ripley, and J.F. Clarke were its great exponents. As a stimulating force in the intellectual life of New England, it did much to prepare the way for Transcendentalism, whose leaders included former Unitarian ministers. Since 1885 Unitarianism has been increasingly rational, employing independent judgment, common sense, and the scientific method. The Church in 1993 had some 180,000 members, including followers of Universalism. ♦

United Brethren, see *Moravian Church.*

United Colonies of New England, see *New England Confederation.*

United Society of Believers, see *Lee, Ann.*

United States Gazette, see *Gazette of the United States.*

United States Literary Gazette (1824–26), Boston semi-monthly periodical of literary news and criticism. Edited by Theophilus Parsons (1797–1882), a Harvard law professor, it contained writing by Bryant, R.H. Dana, Sr., Longfellow, and J.G. Percival. In 1826 it merged with *The New York Review and Athenaeum Magazine,*◆ and for one year, under the editorship of Charles Folsom and Bryant, appeared as the *United States Review and Literary Gazette.*

United States Magazine, The (Jan.–Dec. 1779), Philadelphia monthly periodical, edited by H.H. Brackenridge. Contributions included a satire on James Rivington by John Witherspoon, Freneau's parody of Psalm 137, and other witty and sometimes scurrilous works.
  Another *United States Magazine* (1854–58) was edited at New York by Seba Smith.

United States Magazine and Democratic Review (1837–49), monthly literary and political journal founded at Washington. Among its contributors were Whittier ("Songs of Labor"), Hawthorne ("Legends of the Province House"), Poe ("Marginalia"), Whitman (short stories), Bryant, Paulding, Simms, C.P. Cranch, and Epes Sargent. It was moved to New York (1841) and the following year absorbed Brownson's *Boston Quarterly Review,* becoming further devoted to politics and serving as the mouthpiece of exuberant nationalism. In an article (1845), John L. O'Sullivan, the founder and editor, coined the jingoistic phrase "manifest destiny." The magazine merged with the *United States Review* (1846) and thereafter declined.

Universal Asylum, see *Columbian Magazine.*

Universal Instructor, see *Keimer, Samuel.*

Universalism, religious belief in universal salvation or the eternal progress of all souls. Since its followers consider that truth and righteousness are the controlling powers of the universe, good inevitably triumphs over evil and all mankind is brought into harmony with God. This belief has existed in one form or another since the earliest days of the Christian church, but as an organized Protestant denomination it is primarily centered in the U.S., where it owes its origin to John Murray,◆ an English minister who came to this country in 1770. The Church had 73,194 members in 1954, but in 1961 it gave up independent identity by merging with the Unitarians, their combined membership (1981) being some 170,000 members. Early forerunners of Universalism include Samuel Gorton,◆ the younger Henry Vane,◆ Charles Chauncey,◆ and Jonathan Mayhew,◆ and later important members included Adin Ballou◆ and Hosea Ballou.◆

Unleavened Bread, novel by Robert Grant,◆ published in 1900 and dramatized by Grant and Leo Ditrichstein (1901).

Unparalleled Adventure of One Hans Pfaall, The, story by Poe,◆ published in the *Southern Literary Messenger* (June 1835) and collected in *Tales of the Grotesque and Arabesque* (1840).
  Five years after the disappearance of Hans Pfaall from Rotterdam a balloon of odd shape and structure came over the city and from it a strange little person dropped a letter describing in pseudoscientific detail Pfaall's own balloon ascension to the moon on a 19-day voyage that began on April 1 of an unnamed year. In a concluding Note the author declares the "sketchy trifle" is a hoax and links it to the Moon Hoax◆ of Richard A. Locke.

Unpopular Review, The (1914–21), quarterly journal which analyzed contemporary social, economic, philosophic, and aesthetic problems from an avowedly conservative point of view. Its contributors included P.E. More, D.S. Jordan, Brander Matthews, Dorothy Canfield Fisher, Mary Austin, and Amy Lowell. The name was changed to *The Unpartisan Review* (1919).

UNTERMEYER, JEAN STARR (1886–1970), a poet known for *Steep Ascent* (1927) and other volumes, marked by a simple austerity that has been termed "classically Hebraic." Her poems are collected in *Love and Need* (1940). *Private Collection* (1965) is an autobiography. She was married to Louis Untermeyer.

UNTERMEYER, LOUIS (1885–1977), New York poet, most of whose writings may be classified in four categories: his original poetry, distinguished by a luxurious romantic quality, such as *Roast Leviathan* (1923) and *Burning Bush* (1928), brought together in *Long Feud: Selected Poems* (1962); paraphrases of Horace as various poets would have rendered his subjects, and similar witty imitations of modern poets, in *Collected Parodies* (1926); translations, such as those which form the first volume of his biography *Heinrich Heine: Paradox and Poet* (1937); and critical anthologies, such as *Modern American Poetry* (1919, frequently revised). However, he also wrote works in other veins, including *Moses* (1928), a free handling in prose of the Biblical narrative; *The Donkey of God* (1932), a children's travel book about Italy; *Play in Poetry* (1938), a critical study; *The Wonderful Adventures of Paul Bunyan* (1945), a verse version of the tall tales; and *Lives of the Poets* (1960), treating writers from the author of *Beowulf* to Dylan Thomas. *From Another World* (1939) and *Bygones* (1965) are autobiographies. *The Letters of Robert Frost to Louis Untermeyer* was published in 1963.

Unvanquished, The, novel by Faulkner,♦ published in 1938. The first six of the seven chapters were originally published as short stories, all but one in *The Saturday Evening Post.*

Young Bayard Sartoris♦ from his teens to his young manhood tells about his own experiences as well as the exploits of his father, Colonel John Sartoris, and other members of his clan during the Civil War and the resultant era of the collapse of the old Southern order.

Up from Slavery, autobiography of Booker T. Washington,♦ published in 1901. Developed from a series of articles in *The Outlook,* it tells of his childhood in slavery on a Virginia plantation, of his struggle for education, his schooling at Hampton Institute, and his presidency of Tuskegee Institute in Alabama. The work concludes with an account of travels, speeches, meetings with leaders including Theodore Roosevelt in the White House, and testimonials to his beliefs and accomplishments. The work has a didactic tone as it sets forth the author's views on the social separation of the races, his faith in education, largely vocational for blacks, and his belief in honesty, industry, frugality, and self-discipline.

UPDIKE, DANIEL BERKELEY (1860–1941), Massachusetts printer, whose Merrymount Press was founded in 1893. Although he began by introducing the heavily ornamented style of William Morris, all of his later work is distinguished by a simple use of type without embellishment, depending for effect upon harmonious proportion. His writings include *Printing Types: Their History, Forms, and Use* (2 vols., 1922) and *In the Day's Work* (1924), essays on typography.

UPDIKE, JOHN [HOYER] (1932–   ), Pennsylvania-born novelist and poet, after graduation from Harvard (1954) worked for *The New Yorker* (1955–57), before publishing his first novel, *The Poorhouse Fair* (1959), a short work about the revolt of a poorhouse's aged inhabitants against a sociologically oriented director, a seeming parable about individuals' antipathy to the welfare state. *Rabbit, Run*♦ (1960), a full-length novel, treats an unstable, immature young man who, still hankering for the glamour and applause of his days as a high-school athlete, deserts his wife and child. *Rabbit Redux*♦ (1971) is a sequel whose protagonist, age 36, is now seen with his life having crumbled around him. In a later sequel, *Rabbit Is Rich*♦ (1981, Pulitzer Prize), the major character is middle-aged and well-to-do. *Rabbit*

at Rest (1990) is the final novel about ex-basketball player Harry Rabbit Angstrom, his lively complaints, and his end. *The Centaur*♦ (1963) combines realism with mythology in presenting three days important in the lives of a teenager and his father, a high-school science teacher, who, like other characters, are also presented as figures of Greek mythology, respectively Prometheus and Chiron, the centaur who was a teacher of heroes. *Of the Farm* (1965) presents tensions between a man's mother and his second wife. Updike's fiction had all been set in or near his hometown in Pennsylvania, but his next novel, *Couples*♦ (1968), like many succeeding works, takes place in Tarbox, which is similar to Ipswich, Mass., to which he moved in 1957. It depicts the town's stylish set of young marrieds in their almost religious observance of modern morality with its easygoing sexual pairings. *Bech: A Book*♦ (1970) takes a new subject in portraying a successful Jewish novelist in a quest for approbation; *Bech Is Back* (1982) is a sequel. *A Month of Sundays* (1975) portrays a clergyman's sexual adventures during a month's enforced stay in a rest home. *Marry Me* (1976) tells of two couples' affairs when they exchange mates. *The Coup* (1979) is a semi-comic view of the head of state of a barren African nation. *The Witches of Eastwick* (1984) concerns three mischievous suburban divorcees, their sexual adventures with Satan, and the curse they put on Eastwick, Rhode Island. *Roger's Version* (1986) is about Professor Roger Lambert, whose life is disrupted by an intense student with whom his wife has an affair. *S* (1988) treats worthless 42-year-old Sarah Worth of New England, who joins a fallacious pseudo-Hindu religious colony in Arizona from which she disputatiously writes to her husband, other family, and associates. *Buchanan Dying* (1974) is a play about the onetime President. Updike returns to this subject in *Memories of the Ford Administration* (1992), a novel wherein the narrator, a professor of history at "a third-rate college," has spent years on his unfinished biography of Buchanan, large portions of which we read, alternating with chapters in the professor's love life reminiscent of *Couples*. *Brazil* (1994) is a novel of love and criminality whose main characters, Isabel and Tristão, take their tone, as Updike notes in an afterword, from Joseph Bédier's "Romance of Tristan and Iseult." Stories are collected in many volumes, including *The Same Door* (1959), *Pigeon Feathers* (1962), *The Music School* (1966), *Museums and Women* (1972), *Too Far To Go* (1979), *Problems* (1979), *Trust Me* (1987), and *The After Life: And Other Stories* (1994), variations on the theme of middle age. Updike is a brilliant stylist in his fiction, but he has also written many poems, generally light, collected in *The Carpentered Hen and Other Tame Creatures* (1958), *Telephone Poles* (1963), *Midpoint* (1969), *Seventy Poems* (1972), *Tossing and Turning* (1977), *Facing Nature* (1985), and *Collected Poems* (1993). *Picking Up*

Pieces (1975), *Hugging the Shore* (1983), and *Odd Jobs* (1991) contain book reviews, interviews, and essays, while *Just Looking* (1989) focuses exclusively on essays on art. *Self-Consciousness* (1989) is a memoir, in part of youth, but also a comment on his belief in a personal God and recollections of his acceptance of the U.S. warfare in Vietnam during the 1960s.

UPHAM, CHARLES WENTWORTH (1802–75), Unitarian minister at Salem, Mass., known for his investigations *Salem Witchcraft* (1867) and *Salem Witchcraft and Cotton Mather* (1869). A brother-in-law of Oliver Wendell Holmes, he is said to be the prototype of Judge Pyncheon in *The House of the Seven Gables*.

Upstream, see *Lewisohn, Ludwig.*

URIS, LEON (1924–   ), Baltimore-born author of very popular novels that include *Battle Cry* (1953), about the U.S. Marines in World War II, with whom he served as a private (1942–46); *The Angry Hills* (1955), treating the Palestine Brigade's service in Greece; *Exodus* (1958), the tale of the creation of Israel; *Mila 18* (1961), about the revolt of the Warsaw ghetto against the Nazis; *Armageddon* (1964), set in Berlin after World War II; *Topaz* (1967), a romantic story of Soviet espionage in France; *QBVII,* about the trial of an American novelist in Queen's Bench 7 for libeling a Polish surgeon by contending he performed experimental sterilizations of Jews in a concentration camp; *Trinity* (1976), concerning conflicts in Northern Ireland from 1840 to 1916 among Catholics, Protestants, and British gentry; *The Haj* (1984), treating modern Palestinians in relation to other Arabs and Israel; and *Mitla Pass* (1988), about an American novelist and screenwriter coming to Israel during the 1956 Sinai War and falling in love. *Ireland: A Terrible Beauty* (1975) is a work on contemporary Ireland, and *Jerusalem: Song of Songs* (1981) is a history of Israel, both books with photos by Leon's wife Jill.

Ushant, autobiography of Conrad Aiken. ♦

Usher, RODERICK, character in "The Fall of the House of Usher." ♦

V

V., novel by Thomas Pynchon,♦ published in 1963.

Benny Profane, a schlemiel as sailor and human being, recently discharged from the U.S.S. *Scaffold,* after wandering around the East Coast of the U.S. looking for a way of life, joins Zeitzuss's Alligator Patrol, a quasi-military organization whose business is to hunt through the sewers of New York City for the blind, albino alligators that roam there, having been flushed down toilets when they grew too large to be children's pets. Also traveling through this underground world but in a purposeful way is Herbert Stencil, trying to trace the secret of a 19th-century manuscript dealing with one V., a mysterious woman involved in anarchic plots and international spying. By turns she is associated with Victoria Wren, an expatriate British aristocrat and "self-proclaimed citizen of the world," with Vera Meroving, a German woman possessed of an artificial eye in which is implanted a clock, and with other esoteric figures to be conceived variously as Venus, Virgin, and Void. The quest for V. involves Stencil in investigations of remote and exotic regions and curious historical lore as well as encounters with many odd characters, including Benny Profane, whose path he crosses more than once. The ceaseless pursuit of his mysterious woman takes Stencil, as it took his father before him, through a maze of complex puzzles whose relationships are both labyrinthine and phantasmagoric.

Vagabondia, *Songs from,* poems by Richard Hovey♦ and Bliss Carman.♦

Valentine, *Alias Jimmy,* see Porter, W.S.

VALENTINE, DAVID THOMAS (1801–69), New York antiquarian whose yearly *Manual of the Corporation of the City of New York* (1841–67), a conglomeration of historical and contemporary material, furnishes a primary source for the city's history.

VALENTINE, JEAN (1934–   ), born in Chicago and educated at Radcliffe, had her first collection of verse published in the Yale Younger Poets Series: *Dream Barker and Other Poems* (1965). The title poem is a vivid and haunting dream wherein the narrator and "a Virgilian Nigger Jim" go in his flat-bottomed boat to a joyous "seafood barker's cave," but the speaker at last wakes "Bone dry, old, in a dry land, Jim, my Jim." Poems from *Pilgrims* (1969), *Ordinary*

Things (1974), and *The Messenger* (1979) are reprinted in *Deep Blue, New and Selected Poems* (1989).

VALLENTINE, BENJAMIN BENNATON (1843–1926), English-born journalist, came to New York in 1871, where he was one of the founders of *Puck.* He wrote a series of satirical articles for this journal supposedly by a British fop, titled "The Fitznoodle Papers" and "Fitznoodle in America." He was also the author of plays and a comic opera, *Fadette* (1892).

Valley of Decision, *The,* historical novel by Edith Wharton,♦ published in 1902.

Odo Valsecca, a young Italian nobleman, preserves from his neglected childhood among the family servants an interest in the lower classes, which brings him into accord with the liberal tendencies of the 18th century. In spite of his attitude, when he becomes heir presumptive to the duchy of Pianura (Lombardy), he is befriended by the minister of state Trescorre, the duchess's lover, who represents the conservative aristocratic and clerical classes. Odo continues to sympathize, however, with the intellectual group led by the philosopher Orazio Vivaldi, whose daughter Fulvia he loves. When Vivaldi is exiled because of his political beliefs, Odo rescues Fulvia from the convent in which she is imprisoned and takes her to Switzerland. From there he is recalled by his cousin's death to become Duke of Pianura, but he intends to help his people to gain political liberty. Trescorre arranges a marriage between Odo and the widowed duchess, and when Fulvia returns to encourage his liberal program and become his mistress, she is killed by a shot intended for him. He passes through an illness and spiritual crisis, from which he emerges with his popular sympathies dissipated. He withdraws the constitution he has offered the people, and, when the influence of the French Revolution reaches Pianura, he is unable to agree with the advanced liberals who openly revolt under their leader Gamba. Odo is forced into exile, embittered and defeated.

Valley of the Moon, *The,* novel by Jack London,♦ published in 1913.

Saxon Brown, a young girl who works in a laundry at Oakland, Cal., falls in love with Billy Roberts, a teamster and ex-prizefighter, who is also attempting to maintain himself in the industrial society of the town. Not long after their marriage, the teamsters' union goes on strike, and Billy, an ardent advocate of the strike, becomes poverty-stricken. Saxon's baby is born dead when she witnesses a horrible fight between police and strikers, in which Billy's best friend is killed. Brutalized by his ensuing economic struggle, Billy is jailed for assault. Upon his release, he and Saxon leave the town and the unsuccessful strike, determining to find a homestead. At Carmel they are befriended by various bohemians, on whose advice they go to the "Valley of the Moon," in Sonoma County, where they find peace and economic stability, and await the birth of another child.

VANCOUVER, George (1758?–98), English naval explorer who came to the Northwest coast of America in 1792 via Australia and the Hawaiian Islands. The record of his extended explorations during the next three years was published in his *Voyage of Discovery to the North Pacific Ocean, and Round the World* (3 vols., 1798).

Vandemark's Folly, by Herbert Quick,♦ published in 1922, is the first volume of a trilogy including *The Hawkeye* (1923) and *The Invisible Woman* (1924).

VAN DINE, S.S., see *Wright, W.H.*

VAN DOREN, Carl [Clinton] (1885–1950), professor at Columbia (1911–34), and literary editor of *The Nation* (1919–22) and *The Century* (1922–25), whose critical works include *The American Novel* (1921, revised 1940), *Contemporary American Novelists, 1900–1920* (1922), *James Branch Cabell* (1925), *Swift* (1930), *Sinclair Lewis* (1933), and managing editorship of the *Cambridge History of American Literature* (4 vols., 1917–20). Studies of American history include *Benjamin Franklin* (1938, Pulitzer Prize), a biography; *Secret History of the American Revolution* (1941); *Mutiny in January* (1943), about an incident in the Continental army in 1780–81; *The Great Rehearsal* (1948), about "the making and ratifying of the Constitution"; and *Jane Mecom* (1950), a life of Franklin's sister. *Three Worlds* (1936) is his autobiography. Mark Van Doren was his brother.

VAN DOREN, Mark [Albert] (1894–1972), brother of Carl Van Doren, was also a professor of English at Columbia (1920–59) and literary editor of *The Nation* (1924–28). He wrote critical studies of Thoreau (1916), Dryden (1920), Shakespeare (1939), and Hawthorne (1949). Major criticism is collected in *Private Reader* (1942), *The Happy Critic* (1961), and other volumes; and he published his views in *Liberal Education* (1942) and studied ten great poems in *The Noble Voice* (1946). His novels include *The Transients* (1935) and *Windless Cabins* (1940), the latter a study of a youth haunted by fear after inadvertently killing an evil man. *Nobody Say a Word* (1953) and *Home*

with Hazel (1957) are among the sources of *Collected Stories* (1962). His poetry includes *Spring Thunder* (1924), bucolic verse; *Jonathan Gentry* (1931), a narrative; *Collected Poems* (1939, Pulitzer Prize); *The Mayfield Deer* (1941), retelling a frontier legend; *Our Lady Peace* (1942) and *The Seven Sleepers* (1944), war poems; *The Country New Year* (1946), lyrics on rural life; *New Poems* (1948); *Morning Worship* (1960); *Collected and New Poems* (1963); and *Good Morning* (1973). *The Last Days of Lincoln* (1959) is a play. He wrote an *Autobiography* (1958), and his wife Dorothy wrote *The Professor and I* (1958).

Vandover and the Brute, novel by Frank Norris,♦ written in 1894–95 and posthumously published from an unfinished manuscript in 1914.

VAN DRUTEN, John [William] (1901–57), English-born playwright and novelist, came to the U.S. in 1925 with his first play, *Young Woodley,* after it had been banned from production in England. He later rewrote the play as a novel (1929) with the same title. He became a U.S. citizen in 1944. His later plays include *The Voice of the Turtle* (1943), a bittersweet romantic comedy; *I Remember Mama* (1944), based on autobiographical sketches of San Francisco life by Kathryn Forbes; *Bell, Book, and Candle* (1950), a light comedy about modern witchcraft; and *I Am a Camera* (1951; published, 1952), based on Christopher Isherwood's sketches of Berlin life, *Goodbye to Berlin.*

VAN DUYN, Mona (1921–   ), Poet Laureate of the U.S., 1992–93. Van Duyn was born and educated in Iowa. She was a lecturer at Washington University, St. Louis (1950–67). Van Duyn constructs her poems in strict forms, with subjects ranging from romantic love to the grittily diurnal. Her volumes are *Valentines to the Wide World* (1959), *To See, To Take* (1970), *Merciful Disguises* (1973), *Letters from a Father* (1982), *Near Changes* (1990), and *Firefall* (1993). *If It Be Not I: Collected Poems 1959–1982* (1992) prints all of her earlier work.

VAN DYKE, Henry (1852–1933), Presbyterian minister, later a professor at Princeton (1900–1923), was the author of a great many books, extremely popular in their time, which include essays on outdoor life, such as *Little Rivers* (1895) and *Fisherman's Luck* (1899); moralistic essays, first delivered as sermons, such as *The Story of the Other Wise Man* (1896) and *The First Christmas Tree* (1897); collections of short stories and romances, including *The Ruling Passion* (1901), *The Blue Flower* (1902), and *The Unknown Quantity* (1912); volumes of travel sketches; melodious but facile poems; and volumes of literary criticism, distinguished for their graceful style but representative of the Victorian standards of taste. He served as minister to the Netherlands (1913–17), but resigned because he could not reconcile service in a neutral country with his ardent desire to arouse public opinion against Germany.

VAN DYKE, JOHN C[HARLES] (1856–1932), born in New Jersey, reared in Minnesota, and traveled west into lands of which he wrote in *The Desert* (1901), popular in many succeeding editions and a major creator of very favorable appreciation of a different landscape form and color. He also traveled elsewhere in the U.S. and abroad, becoming a scholar of fine art which he taught at Rutgers and other major institutions, and wrote books like *Rembrandt and His School* (1923).

Vanity Fair (1859–63), New York humorous weekly, concerned with national, social, and political affairs, had no policy other than to bring its sophisticated wit to bear upon matters of contemporary interest. It was edited by C.G. Leland (1860–61) and C.F. Browne (1862). Its contributors included Aldrich, Stoddard, Howells, Saxe, Fitz-James O'Brien, George Arnold, and Winter. Among its features were the burlesques of Arnold, the fantastic interviews of Artemus Ward, and its cartoons.

Another *Vanity Fair* (1868–1936) was issued in New York with various subtitles. Its purpose was "a weekly show of political, social, literary, and financial wares." It was edited for a time by Frank Harris. In 1913 it was purchased by Condé Nast, and until it was absorbed by *Vogue* (1936), a women's fashion magazine, it was edited as a sophisticated review of contemporary literature, art, and society. It was revived in 1983.

VAN LOON, HENDRIK WILLEM (1882–1944), born in Holland, came to the U.S. as a young man and graduated from Cornell (1905). He served as a foreign correspondent and attended the University of Munich (Ph.D., 1911). *A Short History of Discovery* (1918) was the first of the books that won him a reputation as a popularizer of encyclopedic subjects. His surveys, marked by a genially familiar style that is reflected in his own sketchy illustrations, include *Ancient Man* (1920); *The Story of Mankind* (1921); *The Story of the Bible* (1923); *Tolerance* (1925), a history of the rise of religious tolerance; *America* (1927); *Man, the Miracle Maker* (1928); *Van Loon's Geography* (1932); *Ships & How They Sailed the Seven Seas* (1935); *The Arts* (1937); and *The Story of the Pacific* (1940). His other works include *Life and Times of Pieter Stuyvesant* (1928); *R. v. R.* (1930), a fictional biography of Rembrandt; *Thomas Jefferson* (1943), an intimate biography; and *Van Loon's Lives* (1942) and *Report to St. Peter* (1947), autobiographies.

VAN TWILLER, WOUTER (1580?–1656?), Dutch governor of New Netherland (1633–37). Although ably attending to the commercial interests of the colony, he was considered incompetent and was constantly quarreling with the English of Massachusetts and Connecticut colonies. He is satirized as Walter the Doubter in Irving's *History of New York*.

VAN VECHTEN, CARL (1880–1964), born in Iowa, graduated from the University of Chicago (1903), and became assistant music critic for *The New York Times* and dramatic critic for the New York *Press*. His critical articles are collected in several books, and the leading contents of these are preserved in two later selections, *Red* (1925) and *Excavations* (1926). At the age of 40 he declared that his intellectual arteries had hardened for criticism, and, turning to fiction, he wrote *Peter Whiffle* (1922), a witty, pseudo-biographical novel revealing the author's refined dilettante temperament. With continued urbanity, Gallic sophistication, watered aesthetics, and an agile pen, Van Vechten described the manners and mannerisms of his era's decadent elegance in several other novels: *The Blind Bow-Boy* (1923) and *Firecrackers* (1925), dealing with the sophisticated artistic set of New York; *Spider Boy* (1928), a satirical extravaganza on Hollywood; and *Parties* (1930), dealing with a group of sophisticated New York idlers. *The Tattooed Countess* (1924) is a novel set in the Iowa of the author's youth, and *Nigger Heaven*♦ (1926) is a sympathetic, realistic treatment of Harlem life, which did much to stimulate the interest of sophisticates in black culture. *The Tiger in the House* (1920) deals with cats. After *Sacred and Profane Memories* (1932) he forsook writing for photography. He was editor of Gertrude Stein's posthumously published books.

Varieties of Religious Experience, The, psychological study by William James,♦ published in 1902, originally delivered in two courses of lectures at the University of Edinburgh (1901–2).

This "description of man's religious constitution" is written from the point of view of a psychologist, and based on the principle that "all states of mind are neurally conditioned" and that "their significance must be tested not by their origin but by the value of their fruits." Asserting that institutional religion is "an external art" of "ritual acts," the author limits his study to personal religion, in which "the inner dispositions of man himself . . . form the center of interest, his conscience, his deserts, his helplessness, his incompleteness." He offers an "arbitrary" definition of religion: "the feelings, acts, and experiences of individual men in their solitude, so far as they apprehend themselves to stand in relation to whatever they may consider the divine." Pointing out that it is thus a "way of accepting the universe," and is of great value "from the biological point of view," he proceeds to the consideration, profusely documented by individual case histories, of such phenomena as "the religion of healthy-mindedness," "the sick soul," "the divided self, and the process of its unification," conversion, and saintliness. The study concludes with a discussion of values in the religious life, mysticism, and religious philosophy, as well as a definition of the author's own position as a refined "piecemeal supernaturalism" and philosophic pluralism.

Variety (1905–   ), New York theatrical trade journal, founded and edited by Sime Silverman (1873–1933). It is distinguished not only for its impartial reporting of theatrical events, but also for a cynical humor expressed in its own faithful usage of the racy argot of Broadway. An example of this cryptic headline style may be noticed in an article which, discussing the unpopularity with rural audiences of pictures burlesquing their own lives, was headed: "Stix Nix Hix Pix." For many years the tabloid has dealt also with films, radio, television, and music.

Varner, WILL, character in Faulkner's *The Hamlet,* ♦ *The Town,* ♦ and *The Mansion,* ♦ who has economic control of Frenchman's Bend. He arranges for his pregnant daughter Eula to marry Flem Snopes, son of his tenant, Ab Snopes, for which he gives the old Frenchman's Place as dowry. Although angered at being bested by the Snopes clan on deals, he is later forced into making his son-in-law the president of the bank once run by Major de Spain. ♦ Another of Will's 16 children by his first marriage is Jody, involved in many of his adventures. In *As I Lay Dying* Will and Jody are neighbors of the Bundrens, and they are mentioned in *Light in August, Intruder in the Dust,* and *Knight's Gambit.*

VASSA, GUSTAVAS, see *Equiano, Olaudah.*

VEBLEN, THORSTEIN [BUNDE] (1857–1929), born of Norwegian immigrant parents in Wisconsin, studied at Carleton College, Johns Hopkins, and Yale (Ph.D., 1884), and taught at the University of Chicago (1892). In 1899 he published *The Theory of the Leisure Class,* ♦ a merciless attack on the commercial values of the monied class, which was received with hostility by the academic world, but at once secured the author a solid place as an economist and writer. *The Theory of Business Enterprise* (1904) is a more direct analysis of business and the price system. Veblen taught at Stanford University (1906–9), the University of Missouri (1911–18), and The New School for Social Research. *The Instinct of Workmanship* (1914) established his leadership of the institutional school of economics, and contended that the instinct of workmanship, deeply ingrained in man since his days of savagery, has been thwarted throughout history by predatory and pecuniary institutions. *The Vested Interests and the State of the Industrial Arts* (1919) began a change in thought from subtle statement and intellectual detachment to more direct attacks on the dominant financial order, which is definitely stated in *The*

Engineers and the Price System (1921), a sketch of the technique of revolution through organization of a soviet of engineers and technicians, who could assume leadership of the productive activities of the nation. Although his last book, *Absentee Ownership and Business Enterprise in Recent Times* (1923), summarizes his ideas, it shows that in his last years he had lost his trenchant power of attack. Veblen's works were crucial in weakening the hold of neoclassical theory and in introducing a more realistic outlook through the institutional school, which is recognized as an American contribution to the science of economics. Veblen was in part responsible for a trend toward social control, and, although the implications of his criticisms of capitalism were revolutionary, his intellectual attitude and methods were liberal.

VEDDER, ELIHU (1836–1923), painter known for his mystical subjects treated in a symbolic manner and his book illustrations, of which those made for the *Rubáiyát* (1884) are in the sensuous vein of Art Nouveau. He was long expatriated, as described in his rambling, whimsical memoir, *The Digressions of V* (1910). Subsequent books are *Miscellaneous Moods in Verse* (1914) and *Doubt and Other Things* (1922).

Vein of Iron, novel by Ellen Glasgow, ♦ published in 1935.

Ada Fincastle is reared in Shut-In Valley, in the Virginia mountains, where her ancestors have been ministers and leaders since colonial days. Her father, John, repudiated by his congregation for his unorthodox ideas, has become a schoolteacher, and Ada is accustomed to the pinch of poverty. The Fincastles nevertheless retain the respect of the community through the activities of John's proud old mother, his devoted wife Mary Evelyn, who works herself to an early death, his homely, pious sister Meggie, and the black servant Aunt Abigail Geddy. Willful, inquisitive, and passionate, Ada is jealous of Janet Rowan, a petulant beauty who marries her father's brilliant student, Ralph McBride. Ralph gives up the law to sell automobiles, and, tormented by his loveless marriage, grows morose and longs for escape. Six years afterward, Janet seeks a divorce to marry a wealthy lover, and Ralph enlists to fight in World War I. Before he leaves, he and Ada become lovers. To spare him in his already neurotic condition, she does not disclose her pregnancy; ostracized by the village, after her grandmother's death she moves the household to Queenborough (Richmond), where the boy Rannie is born. When Ralph returns they are married, and he becomes prosperous until an automobile accident temporarily paralyzes him. Employed only occasionally, he grows bitter and cynical, and Ada returns to work. Her gentle old father rapidly declines, having completed his great idealistic metaphysical treatise, which is neglected except by a few foreign scholars. During the Depression of the 1930s, the family is sustained only by the "vein of iron" in Ada's character. After her father's death, his insurance enables the other members of the family to buy back the ancestral home, to which they return, determined to make a new life.

VENABLE, WILLIAM HENRY (1836–1920), Cincinnati high-school teacher, author of *Beginnings of Literary Culture in the Ohio Valley* (1891), an important early study, and *Buckeye Boyhood* (1911), about his youth as a pioneer in the Midwest.

Venner, ELSIE, see *Elsie Venner.*

VÉRENDRYE, PIERRE, see *La Vérendrye.*

Veritism, see *Garland, Hamlin.*

VERPLANCK, GULIAN CROMMELIN (1786–1870), New York lawyer, journalist, politician, and author, who carried on a pamphlet war for almost ten years with DeWitt Clinton, whom he satirized in such erudite and invidious publications as *A Fable for Statesmen and Politicians* (1815) and *The State Triumvirate* (1819). He served in Congress (1825–33), and upon returning to literary life published a scholarly edition of Shakespeare's plays (3 vols., 1847) and helped edit *The Talisman.*♦ He delivered many lectures and wrote essays, collected in *Discourses and Addresses on Subjects of American History, Arts, and Literature* (1833).

Vers libre, see *Free verse.*

VERY, JONES (1813–80), born in Salem, Mass., graduated from Harvard (1836) and was a tutor of Greek while studying at the Divinity School. During this period he turned from his previous mild Unitarianism under the influence of a spiritual exaltation in which he had poetic visions of the Holy Ghost. He claimed that his religious sonnets were communicated to him in these visions. Although Emerson appreciated his poetry and prose and arranged for him to speak at Concord, the Harvard faculty questioned his sanity, and he allowed himself to be committed to an asylum for the insane. He continued to write, however, and some of his verse was published in *The Western Messenger,* through the influence of J.F. Clarke, who in answer to critics declared that, instead of monomania, Very had "monosania." Emerson, who also thought him "profoundly sane," helped in the selection of his *Essays and Poems* (1839), Very's only book published during his lifetime. He was a friend of the Transcendentalists, but his poems show that he was a mystic, whose belief in the absolute surrender of the will to God made his theological and spiritual affiliations closer to those of the early Puritans and Quakers. His poems of religious experience rightly caused him to be compared

with George Herbert and other 17th-century metaphysical poets. His essays in literary criticism, such as "Epic Poetry," "Hamlet," and "Shakespeare," also reveal his mystic approach. After a brief time (1838) in the asylum, Very, without a degree in divinity, held temporary pastorates in Maine and Massachusetts, but, being too shy to preach well, retired to live as a recluse under the care of his sister Lydia. He wrote little during his remaining 40 years. Two posthumous editions of his works were published, *Poems* (1883) and *Poems and Essays* (1886), "a complete" edition containing some 600 poems, edited by J.F. Clarke.

VERY, LYDIA LOUISE ANN (1823–1901), sister of Jones Very, also wrote verse, published in *Poems* (1856), which, however, shows none of her brother's transcendental mysticism in interpreting nature, although nature was her primary subject. Most of her life was devoted to caring for him, but after his death she returned to writing and published *Poems and Prose Writings* (1890), reprinting her earlier work together with sketches of Salem scenery. Later works included *Sayings and Doings Among the Insects and Flowers* (1897), simple stories of nature; *The Better Path* (1898), *A Strange Disclosure* (1898), and *A Strange Recluse* (1899), romantic novels; and *An Old-Fashioned Garden, and Walks and Musings Therein* (1900), a volume of charmingly simple anecdotes about her life.

VESPUCCI, AMERIGO (1454–1512), born in Florence, early entered the commercial house of the Medici, and after 1492 resided in Spain as their agent. According to his own account, he obtained a commission to fit out 12 ships for the king of Spain (1495) and set sail from Cadiz (May 10, 1497), reaching the mainland of the American continent (June 16, 1497) eight days before John Cabot. These statements are not convincing and the consensus of scholarly opinion is that he never made this voyage. He made a "second" voyage across the Atlantic (1499), entered the service of Dom Manuel of Portugal (1501), and made a "third" voyage to America via Cape Verde (1502); also in the service of Portugal, he made his last voyage (1503), intending to reach Malacca, whose location he completely misjudged. He landed at Bahia in the present Brazil, returning to Lisbon (1504). All knowledge concerning these voyages rests on Vespucci's doubtful accounts. He received Spanish letters of naturalization (1505), and the following year was appointed chief pilot of Spain, a post he held until his death. In 1503 he wrote to Lorenzo di Medici from Lisbon, describing the alleged Portuguese voyage of 1501–2, and the supposed 1499 voyage. This document is lost, but a Latin translation was printed variously as *Mundus Novus* and *Epistola Albericii de Novo Mundo.* His letter written from Portugal (1504) to Pier Soderini, Gonfalonier of the Republic of Florence, still exists in the original printing in Italian. From this a French version was made, and from this in turn a Latin translation was published (1507). The last was used in Waldseemuller's *Cosmographiæ Introductio* (1507), which contains the first use of the name America. ♦ An English translation of his letters was published in 1894.

VESTAL, STANLEY, see *Campbell, W.S.*

VICTOR, FRANCES FULLER (1826–1902), began her literary career with *Poems of Sentiment and Imagination* (1851), written with her sister Metta Victoria Victor. The two married brothers, but Frances moved from New York to California and Oregon. She wrote local-color stories and poems of the West and the volumes on Oregon in the *History of the Pacific States* issued by H.H. Bancroft, ♦ as well as contributing to other parts of his work on the Northwest and writing a section of his *History of California* (7 vols., 1886–90). *The River of the West* (1870), based on the reminiscences of the old mountain man and pioneer Joseph L. Meek, combines history with fiction.

VICTOR, METTA VICTORIA (1831–86), was married to Orville James Victor (1827–1910), a publisher of dime novels for whom she wrote works including the antislavery *Maum Guinea and Her Plantation Children* (1862).

VIDAL, GORE (1925–   ), after army service in World War II published his first novel, *Williwaw* (1946), about the reactions of passengers on a freighter caught in an Aleutian storm. Later novels include *In a Yellow Wood* (1947), characterizing a nonconforming army veteran; *The City and the Pillar* (1948, revised 1965), a sympathetic portrait of a young man isolated from most people because he is a homosexual; *The Season of Comfort* (1949), about a boy's conflict with his mother; *A Search for the King* (1950), about a troubadour's affection for his king, Richard the Lion-Hearted; *Dark Green, Bright Red* (1950), about a U.S. army officer in a Latin-American revolution; *The Judgment of Paris* (1952, revised 1965), a modern version of the Trojan tale applied to an American who finds himself during European travel; *Messiah* (1954, revised 1965), on a modern Madison Avenue messiah; *Julian* (1964), about the 4th-century Roman emperor who renounced Christianity; *Washington, D.C.* (1967), treating politics in the F.D.R. and Truman years; *Myra Breckinridge* (1968), a satire about the lurid adventures of a transsexual, and *Myron* (1974), a sequel, set in Hollywood; *Two Sisters* (1970), counterpointing the 4th-century Roman empire and modern life; *Burr* (1973), a favorable fictive view of Aaron Burr; *1876* (1976), a story of American society a century earlier; *Kalki* (1978), a satire on feminism in the post-Vietnam War world; *Creation* (1981), set in the 5th-century world of Darius, Xerxes,

and Confucius; *Duluth* (1983), set in the late 20th-century U.S.; *Lincoln* (1984), another historical novel; and *Hollywood* (1990), subtitled "A Novel of America in the 1920s." *Live from Golgotha* (1992) is the New Testament according to Vidal; in it a 20th-century television executive treats with the apostle Paul to film the Crucifixion via new technology. Among his television plays, *Visit to a Small Planet* (1956) was rewritten for a Broadway production (1957). This satire drawing upon science fiction was followed by another legitimate drama, *The Best Man* (1960), on politics. *A Thirsty Evil* (1956) collects stories. *Rocking the Boat* (1962); *Reflections on a Sinking Ship* (1969), incorporating two essays explaining his revision of earlier works on the grounds that "what's worth keeping should be made as good as possible"; *Homage to Daniel Shays* (1973); *Matters of Fact and of Fiction* (1977); *The Second American Revolution* (1982); *At Home* (1988); and *United States, Essays 1952–1992* (1993) collect essays. *Screening History* (1992) is drawn from the William E. Massey Sr. lectures given at Harvard; these essays are memories, with reflections, often biting, on American politics from F.D.R. to Bush; the author also reflects upon the hold that movies acquired and still retain on the American sense of history.

VIERECK, GEORGE SYLVESTER (1884–1962), born in Germany, came to the U.S. (1895) and later became a citizen. His writings include *A Game at Love and Other Plays* (1906); *Nineveh* (1907), *Songs of Armageddon* (1916), and other poems collected in *My Flesh and Blood; A Lyric Autobiography, with Indiscreet Annotations* (1931); *The House of Vampire* (1907), a novel, as is *My First Two Thousand Years* (1928), "the autobiography of the Wandering Jew," written with Paul Eldridge. He championed the Germans in World War I in *The Fatherland*, a journal renamed the *American Monthly*, and was imprisoned in World War II for failure to register as a foreign agent. Peter Viereck is his son.

VIERECK, PETER (1916–   ), professor of history at Mount Holyoke College (1948–   ), author of *Metapolitics—From the Romantics to Hitler* (1941), *Conservatism Revisited—The Revolt Against Revolt—1815–1949* (1949), *Shame and Glory of the Intellectuals* (1953), *Dream and Responsibility: The Tension Between Poetry and Society* (1953), *The Unadjusted Man: A New Hero for Americans* (1956), *Conservatism from John Adams to Churchill* (1956), *Metapolitics, the Roots of the Nazi Mind* (1961), and *Conservatism Revisited* and *The New Conservatism—What Went Wrong?* (two works combined and revised 1962). His lyric poems include *Terror and Decorum* (1948, Pulitzer Prize), *Strike Through the Mask!* (1950), *The First Morning* (1952), *The Persimmon Tree* (1956), and *New and Selected Poems* (1967). *The Tree Witch* (1961) is a verse drama. His father was George S. Viereck, who he possibly has in mind in *Archer in the Marrow* (1987), a poetic dialogue between father and son on the history of poetry and its variety of forms.

Vigilantes, members of secret volunteer organizations for the summary suppression of lawless conditions, where formal means of law enforcement are lacking, or where they are considered to be inadequate. Such vigilance committees consistently flourished on the frontier, and were particularly prominent in California during the gold-rush era, and in other parts of the West as the result of cattle and horse thefts. The committees frequently resorted to lynch law. Even during periods of settled order, vigilance committees have been formed because of racial conflict, crime waves, labor disorders, and radical activities. Literary treatments include Bret Harte's "The Outcasts of Poker Flat," Norris's *The Octopus,* Steinbeck's *In Dubious Battle,* and Van Tilburg Clark's *The Ox-Bow Incident.*

Village Blacksmith, The, eight-stanza poem in ballad measure by Longfellow,♦ published in *Ballads and Other Poems* (1841). The smith is described at work, with the children stopping on the way from school to watch his flaming forge and roaring bellows, his mighty arms and hands, and his brow "wet with honest sweat." At church, his daughter's voice in the choir reminds him of "her mother's voice, Singing in Paradise!" In the last stanza, the poet makes of him a symbol of the proper conduct of life. The poem was suggested by a smithy under a spreading chestnut tree, near the poet's house in Cambridge.

VILLAGRÁ, GASPAR PÉREZ DE (*c.*1555–*c.*1620), Spanish explorer and officer on the expedition of Juan de Oñate,♦ of which he wrote an epic poem (1610), translated as *History of New Mexico* (1933).

VILLARD, HENRY (1835–1900), Bavarian-born journalist and financier, emigrated to the U.S. (1853) and studied law in Illinois, where in 1858 began his friendship with Lincoln. *Lincoln on the Eve of '61* (1941) is a collection of his newspaper dispatches between Lincoln's election and his inauguration. He participated in the Pike's Peak gold rush (1859) and wrote a guidebook, *The Past and Present of the Pike's Peak Gold Regions* (1860). His later career was mainly concerned with railroad building and finance in the Northwest, where besides controlling Oregon and California railways he was president of the Northern Pacific (1881–84). Villard helped found the Edison General Electric Company (1889) and bought the New York *Evening Post* (1881). He married the daughter of W.L. Garrison.

VILLARD, OSWALD GARRISON (1872–1949), son of Henry Villard, born in Germany, was educated at Harvard and began his journalistic career

in Philadelphia (1896). He was an editorial writer for the New York *Evening Post* (1897–1918), of which he was owner and president after his father's death. Villard purchased *The Nation♦* (1908), which, during his editorship until 1933, was established as a leading journal of liberal opinion. His books include *John Brown, 1800–1859—A Biography Fifty Years After* (1910), *Some Newspapers and Newspaper Men* (1923), an autobiography entitled *Fighting Years* (1939), and *The Disappearing Daily* (1944), the development of the U.S. press brought up to date from his 1923 volume.

VINAL, HAROLD (1891–1965), Maine poet, descendant of a family long established there, best known for his rather sweet poetry about his region, published in *White April* (1922), *Hurricane* (1936), *The Compass Eye* (1944), and other volumes. He also published a magazine of poetry, *Voices* (1921ff.). He was the subject of a satirical poem by E.E. Cummings, "Poem, or Beauty Hurts Mr. Vinal."

Vindication of the Government of New-England Churches, A, by John Wise,♦ published in 1717, is a forceful exposition of the principles of ecclesiastical polity of New England Congregationalism, based on the theory that the best government of the church derives from the best government of the state, which Wise believed to be founded on the idea of human equality. His discussion of the rights of man presents him as one of the forerunners of Jeffersonian ideas. Because of the democratic theme, which transcends the specific issues, the book was republished in 1772 and widely read prior to the Revolution and again in 1860 before the Civil War.

Virginia, novel by Ellen Glasgow,♦ published in 1913.

Virginia Dinwiddie, reared during the 1880s in the state for which she is named and in keeping with its ideals of gentility and propriety, subordinates herself to her husband, Oliver Treadwell, a poor, aspiring, and egocentric playwright, and their three children. Finally he becomes a successful dramatist with plays produced in New York, but by this time Virginia is middle-aged, worn, and limited in interests to her domestic obligations, so he deserts her for Margaret Oldcastle, the star of his plays. Virginia is left without a purpose in life except the devotion to her son Harry, who loves her, for she has little in common with her independent, feminist, and aggressive daughters.

Virginia City, see *Comstock Lode.*

Virginia Comedians, The; or, Old Days in the Old Dominion, romance by J.E. Cooke,♦ published anonymously in 1854. *Henry St. John, Gentleman♦* is a sequel.

Virginia Company, joint-stock corporation chartered by James I (1606) to settle colonies in America. There were two branches. That which had jurisdiction over the southern colonies, from 34° to 41° north latitude, was known as the Virginia Company of London, since its headquarters were in that city. That which was to manage the northern colonies, from 45° to 38° south latitude, was called the Virginia Company of Plymouth, and its office was in Plymouth, Devonshire. In 1607 the London Company sent an expedition under Christopher Newport, which settled Jamestown. ♦ The Plymouth Company failing to establish a settlement, the London Company obtained a new charter (1609) when Sir Thomas Gates was made absolute governor in Virginia. De la Warr arrived in 1610, when the colony was on the verge of dissolution, and served as governor until 1618. In 1612, a third charter made the Company self-governing, and in 1619 the first legislative assembly convened. James I annulled the charter (1624) and the colony became a royal province, directly administered under the king's authority. John Smith ♦ was long the actual, if not the titular, head of the colony. Among the important sources of the colony's early history are Smith's *A True Relation,* Beverley's *History of Virginia,* Stith's *History of . . . Virginia,* and the Company's records edited by S.M. Kingsbury (1906).

Virginia Gazette (1736–66, 1766–73), first newspaper in Virginia, founded at Williamsburg by William Parks, who was its editor until his death (1750). The paper was under the influence of the governor, but in addition to its news it is significant for its essays, many of which are concerned with London life in the spirit of the Queen Anne writers but are considered to have originated in Virginia. After Parks's death, it changed hands several times, and in 1766 another paper of the same name was founded, since the original *Gazette* was entirely under the influence of the governor. The second *Gazette* lasted until 1773.

Virginia Quarterly Review, The (1925–   ), journal of liberal opinion on social and economic affairs, which also publishes fiction, poetry, and literary criticism. Although issued at the University of Virginia, the review is neither an academic organ nor sectional in point of view. In addition to foreign authors, its contributors have included Allen Tate, Robert Frost, Sherwood Anderson, Thomas Wolfe, Conrad Aiken, T.S. Eliot, C.A. Beard, E.A. Robinson, Elizabeth Madox Roberts, John Berryman, and Julian Green.

Virginian, The: A Horseman of the Plains, romantic novel by Owen Wister, ♦ published in 1902 as a companion piece to his *Lin McLean* (1898).

This tale of the cowpunchers of the Wyoming cattle country during the exciting 1870s and '80s is chiefly concerned with the adventures of a handsome, heroic figure known only as "the Virginian," his chivalry and daring, and his successful wooing of Molly Wood, a pretty schoolteacher from Vermont. The celebrated phrase, "When you call me that, *smile!,*" is one of the many colloquial expressions with which the book is peppered.

Virginians, The; A Tale of the Last Century, romance by Thackeray, ♦ published in England (2 vols., 1858–59), in the U.S. in 1859. Thackeray conceived the idea and began his research during a visit to the U.S. (1855–56) and received information and suggestions from J.P. Kennedy, who accompanied him on a tour of Virginia. The work is a sequel to *Henry Esmond.*

Rachel Warrington, widowed daughter of Henry Esmond, affectionately dominates her twin sons, Harry and George, whom she rears at Castlewood, the Virginia estate inherited from her father. George accompanies Washington, then a young officer and friend of his mother, on the expedition of Braddock, and in the rout of the British force is believed to have been killed. Harry goes to England as heir to the estate, where he meets the English Castlewoods. They cultivate him because of his wealth and he is led into a life of extravagance and dissipation by Baroness Bernstein, once his father's fiancée Beatrix, but now twice widowed and an unscrupulous social leader. Imprisoned for gambling debts, he is released on the arrival of George, who had only been injured and captured by the French. Harry serves in Canada under Wolfe, while George turns London playwright. Their tyrannical mother spurns both, Harry for marrying Hetty Mountain, her housekeeper's daughter, George for marrying Theo Lambert, a penniless English girl. During the Revolution George, who has inherited the title and property of the English Warringtons, joins the Loyalists, and Harry becomes a patriot leader. Later reconciled, Harry becomes master of the family's Virginia property, George of the English estate.

Vision of Columbus, The, see *Columbiad.*

Vision of Sir Launfal, The, verse parable by Lowell, ♦ published in 1848. The work is in two parts, each with a prelude, and the basic meter is iambic tetrameter. The plot is derived from legends of the Holy Grail in Malory, and perhaps influenced by Tennyson.

Visit from St. Nicholas, A, poem by C.C. Moore. ♦

VIZENOR, GERALD (1934–   ), poet and novelist born in Minneapolis of Ojibway and French ancestry, later an enrolled member of the Chippewa. His rather formal verse is printed in *Raising the Moon* (1964), *Two Wings the Butterfly* (1967), and *Matushima Haiku* (1984). His novels are *Darkness in St. Louis Bearheart* (1978) and *Trickster of*

Liberty (1988), both ironic depictions of contemporary Native American lives. *Cross Bloods* (1990) collects essays.

VIZETELLY, FRANK HORACE (1864–1938), English-born lexicographer and editor, came to the U.S. (1891), and is best known for his editorship of Funk and Wagnalls's *New Standard Dictionary* and various reference books, and as a contributor to the *Literary Digest.* He wrote some 20 books pertaining to the English language and other philological subjects, and was a popular authority in sanctioning American colloquialisms.

Voices of the Night, first collection of poems by Longfellow,♦ published in 1839. It contains such famous works as "Hymn to the Night,"♦ "A Psalm of Life,"♦ and "The Beleaguered City."

VOLLMER, LULA (18??–1955), North Carolina dramatist, whose plays, concerned with the character of the people of her native mountains, include *Sun-Up*♦ (1923); *The Shame Woman* (1923), the story of a woman who willingly meets the death sentence in order to kill the man who had once been her lover and later her daughter's paramour; *The Dunce Boy* (1925), dealing with a mother's love for her half-wit son; and *Trigger* (1927), the story of a girl struggling against the stultifying standards of her native mountain people.

Voluntaries, poem by Emerson,♦ published in the *Atlantic Monthly* (1863) to commemorate the death in battle of Colonel Robert G. Shaw, leader of a regiment of black soldiers in the Civil War. It was collected in *May-Day* (1867). In five stanzas of alternately rhymed, irregular four-stress lines, it celebrates the heroism of those who sacrifice their lives in the cause of freedom:

> So nigh is grandeur to our dust,
> So near is God to man.
> When duty whispers low, *Thou must,*
> The youth replies, *I can.*

VON HOLST, HERMANN, see *Holst.*

VONNEGUT, KURT, JR. (1922–), born in Indianapolis, studied biochemistry at Cornell before being drafted into the infantry in World War II. Captured by the Germans, he was working in the underground meat locker of a slaughterhouse in Dresden when that city was annihilated by U.S. and British bombs. He emerged to find "135,000 Hansels and Gretels had been baked like gingerbread men." After the war Vonnegut studied anthropology at the University of Chicago and worked in public relations for General Electric. His first novel, *Player Piano* (1952), satirizes the tyrannies of automation observed at G.E. and his second, *The Sirens of Titan* (1959), uses the mode of science fiction. *Mother Night* (1961) pre-

sents an American spy in Germany during World War II who transmits secret messages via open pro-Nazi, anti-Semitic radio talks; its moral, Vonnegut declared, was that "We are what we pretend to be." *Cat's Cradle*♦ (1963), like his other novels, uses science fiction concepts for quietly satirical consideration of mankind and its need for sympathy and compassion, proposing that we live by "foma," lies that make for human happiness. *God Bless You, Mr. Rosewater*♦ (1965), in a similar vein, is also marked by freedom of form and by fanciful black humor in presenting the duplicity and absurdity of modern life, and its lack of generosity and gentleness. *Slaughterhouse-Five; or The Children's Crusade*♦ (1969), inspired by his Dresden experience, also uses the vein of surrealism and science fiction, and is marked by the dark comedy, philosophic meditation, and brief, impressionistic scenes of the sort that characterized *Cat's Cradle. Breakfast of Champions; or, Goodbye Blue Monday!* (1973) is a lesser, though popular, novel that in chronicling the fantastic adventures of several Americans makes nihilistic comment upon contemporary society. *Slapstick; or, Lonesome No More!* (1976), also a slighter novel, as a broad comedy treats the problem of loneliness. *Jailbird* (1979) is a more straightforward novel portraying the fanciful life of a fictitious participant in the Watergate conspiracy as it satirizes American politics. *Deadeye Dick* (1982) deals with the accidental explosion of a neutron bomb in Ohio. *Galapagos* (1985) deals with a confusion of past, future, and present related to various human views. *Bluebeard* (1987), Vonnegut's 13th novel, employs a minor character from *Breakfast of Champions* to treat major themes prominent in the preceding fiction. *Hocus Pocus* (1990) is a narrative by a Vietnam veteran, set in 2001. *Welcome to the Monkey House* (1968) collects stories and essays, and *Wampeters, Foma and Granfalloons* (1974) is a volume of essays, reviews, and speeches, whose title employs words used in *Cat's Cradle. Palm Sunday* (1981) is a similar collection. *Happy Birthday, Wanda June* (1970) is a play that satirically presents the afterlife (on earth and in heaven) of two American military heroes who dropped the atomic bomb on Nagasaki, and *Between Time and Timbuktu* (1973) is a television script drawing upon *Cat's Cradle* and *The Sirens of Titan.*

VON TEUFFEL, BARONESS, see *Howard, Blanche.*

VORSE, MARY [MARVIN] HEATON (1874–1966), lived in Provincetown from 1907 to her death, as described in *Time and the Town* (1942), and was a sponsor of the Provincetown Players. She was known for her proletarian novels, including *The Prestons* (1918), *Passaic* (1926), *Second Cabin* (1928), and *Strike!* (1930), the last about Gastonia.♦ *Footnote to Folly* (1935) is an autobiography.

W

Waifs and Strays, stories by W.S. Porter. ♦

Waiting for Lefty, short play by Clifford Odets, ♦ produced by the Group Theatre in 1935 and published the same year.

Members of the taxicab drivers' union meet to decide whether or not to strike, and while they await the arrival of the popular committeeman Lefty Costello, they are addressed by the capitalist agent Harry Fatt, who attempts to discourage the plan. Six blackout scenes show the causes of the strike in terms of injustice, corrupt practices, and personal tragedy: "Joe and Edna" and "The Young Hack and His Girl" depict estrangement and frustration resulting from economic difficulties; "Lab Assistant Episode" and "Interne Episode" show demoralized capitalistic ethics; "The Young Actor" demonstrates the unequal conflict between art and commercialism; and "Labor Spy Episode" presents the perjured evidence of a bribed witness. The labor leader Agate Keller confutes the spy's testimony, and, when a messenger arrives to report the murder of Lefty, arouses the men's fighting spirit and leads them in declaring the strike.

WAGONER, DAVID [RUSSELL] (1926–), born in Ohio, a professor at the University of Washington since 1954, is best known as a poet of quiet and accomplished lyric power, often writing of the Northwestern scene. His poems are collected in *Dry Sun, Dry Wind* (1953), *A Place to Stand* (1958), *The Nesting Ground* (1963), *Staying Alive* (1966), *New and Selected Poems* (1969), *Working Against Time* (1970), *Riverbed* (1972), *Sleeping in the Woods* (1974), *Collected Poems* (1976), *In Broken Country* (1979), *Landfall* (1981), *First Light* (1983), and *Through the Forest* (1987). He has also written numerous novels, some serious fables set in the present day, others lighthearted tales of amusing adventures in the 19th-century U.S. They are *The Man in the Middle* (1954), *Money Money Money* (1955), *Rock* (1958), *The Escape Artist* (1965), *Baby, Come On Inside* (1968), *Where Is My Wandering Boy Tonight?* (1970), *The Road to Many a Wonder* (1974), *Tracker* (1975), *Whole Hog* (1976), and *The Hanging Garden* (1980). He has written a volume of poems derived from the legendry of Northwest Indians, *Who Shall Be the Sun?* (1978), and edited as *Straw for the Fire* (1972) the notebooks of Theodore Roethke, who was a great influence upon him.

WAKOSKI, DIANE (1937–), California-born poet who began to publish books soon after graduation from the University of California, Berkeley (1960). Her very personal, intense poems appear in *Coins and Coffins* (1961), *Discrepancies and Apparitions* (1966), *The George Washington Poems* (1967), *Inside the Blood Factory* (1968), *Motorcycle Betrayal Poems* (1971), *Virtuoso Literature for Two and Four Hands* (1976), *Waiting for the King of Spain* (1977), *The Man Who Shook Hands* (1978), *Cap of Darkness* (1980), *The Magician's Feastletters* (1982), *The Rings of Saturn* (1986), and *Emerald Ice* (1988), a selection from the 15 books published since 1962. Much of the poetry is concerned with difficult personal experience from an unhappy childhood to unpleasant relations with men. For some time she has taught at or been a writer in residence at several institutions, particularly Michigan State University. Somewhat related is her book on contemporary poetry, *Toward a New Poetry* (1980).

Walam Olum, tribal chronicle of the Leni-Lenape, or Delaware Indians, divided into five books of 183 short verses that relate the story of the tribe from creation through its migration to North America and to its meeting with white men. The title is translated as Red Score, or "painted record," for the work was written in the form of pictographs on sticks. The originals have been lost, but a manuscript copy was made by Constantine Rafinesque ♦ in 1833 to accompany his translation of "the songs annexed thereto in the original language" that he also collected. This text he published in his book *The American Nations* (1836) and later translations were made by E.G. Squier ♦ and Daniel G. Brinton. ♦ Not only is the work important to anthropologists but the songs have been acclaimed as a great Indian epic poem.

Walden, or *Life in the Woods,* narrative by Thoreau, ♦ published in 1854. Between the end of March 1845 and July 4, when he began occupation, the author constructed a cabin on the shore of Walden Pond, near Concord. There he lived alone until September 1847, supplying his needs by his own labor and developing and testing his transcendental philosophy of individualism, self-reliance, and material economy for the sake of spiritual wealth. He sought to reduce his physical needs to a minimum, in order to free himself for study, thought, and observation of nature and himself; therefore his cabin was a simple room and he wore the cheapest essential clothing and restricted his diet to what he found growing wild and the beans and vegetables he himself raised. When not engaged in domestic and agricultural labors, or in fishing, swimming, and rowing, Thoreau devoted himself enthusiastically to careful observation and recording of the flora and fauna of the locality, to writing his voluminous journals, and to reading ancient and modern poetry and philosophy. His thought about this experience was developed in the journals over a period of years, and the result is *Walden,* a series of 18 essays describing Thoreau's idealistic creed as affected by and expressed in his life at the Pond. The chapter on "Economy" asserts that the only standard of value is in vital experience, and that the complexities of civilization stand in the way of significant living. To escape the demands of society and to realize the best powers of mind and body, Thoreau decides for an ascetic withdrawal from organized society, since in his desire "to live deep and suck out all the marrow of life," he found that the essential necessity was to "simplify, simplify." Among the matters described in subsequent chapters are the practical operation of this economy; Thoreau's intimacy with such different neighbors as the moles in his cellar, an educated Canadian woodcutter, and the pickerel in Walden Pond; his temporary imprisonment for refusing to pay a poll tax because he would not support a state that returned fugitive slaves to the South; the music of the wind in the telegraph wires, and the distant railroad whistle; the varied seasonal aspects of the woods; and the joys of outdoor labor and solitary study. From this many-sided discussion, expressed in an agile, compact, lucid, and often poetic style, emerges Thoreau's philosophy of individualism brought almost to the point of anarchy, and his idealistic exaltation of arts and ideas balanced by a vital appreciation of the life of the senses.

WALKER, ALICE [MALSENIOR] (1944–), Georgia-born author of fiction and poetry about African Americans. Her novels include *The Third Life of Grange Copeland* (1970), depicting violence among three generations of men in a black sharecropping family; *Meridian* (1976), about a black woman torn between the revolutionary civil rights movement of the 1960s in the North and her affection for the unsophisticated blacks of the South; *The Color Purple* (1982), treating two devoted sisters, black women, one of whom goes to live in Africa; and *The Temple of My Familiar* (1989), involving three marriages over a long period of time and place, ranging from pre-colonial Africa, post-slavery North Carolina, and modern San Francisco. Her poems include *Once* (1968), dealing with both the civil rights movement and her experiences of living in Africa; *Revolutionary Petunias* (1973), autobiographical works about a Georgia childhood, black militancy in the North, and love poems; *"Good Night, Willie Lee, I'll See You in the Morning"* (1979); and *Horses Make a Landscape Look More Beautiful* (1984). Her short

stories about black women are collected in *In Love and Trouble* (1973) and *You Can't Keep a Good Woman Down* (1981). She has also written a biography of Langston Hughes for children (1974), edited an anthology of the writings of Zora Neale Hurston (1979), and collected articles, reviews, journal entries, and other prose in *In Search of Our Mother's Gardens* (1984) and *Living By the Word* (1988).

WALKER, DAVID (1785?–1830), free-born black of North Carolina, who settled in Boston and there published a pamphlet, *Walker's Appeal* (1829), calling on his fellow blacks to unite and act against slavery.

WALKER, MARGARET ABIGAIL (1915–), born in Birmingham and educated at Northwestern University and the University of Iowa (M.A., 1940; Ph.D., 1965). Walker was the youngest African-American woman to win a prestigious national award for literature with *For My People* (1942), which received the Yale Younger Poets Series Award. It is a book of ballads, sonnets, and free verse, tales of folk heroes and heroines, and it established her reputation as well as being a commercial success. Her reputation as a poet rests also on *Prophets for a New Day* (1970), informed by religious faith, in which Martin Luther King, Medgar Evers, and others are tandemed with Bible characters. Finally, Walker's reputation also is anchored on a book that was 30 years in the writing–the historical novel *Jubilee* (1965), about a slave family during and after the Civil War. The book was originally inspired by bedtime stories of "the slave time" told her by her maternal grandmother about Walker's great-grandmother, but richly based on historical research. It was a prototype of the novel giving African-American history from an African-American viewpoint.

Wall Street, narrow thoroughfare of New York City, situated in lower Manhattan, received its name from a stockade erected there by Stuyvesant. It has long been the greatest financial district of the U.S., and by extension the name implies international corporate finance. During the 19th century, it was the center of operations for such celebrated financiers as Vanderbilt, Drew, and Morgan. There has been a great deal of literature making use of Wall Street as setting or subject. Its appearance in fiction includes several novels by Richard B. Kimball, Brander Matthews's *His Father's Son,* Joaquin Miller's melodramatic *The Destruction of Gotham,* and a trilogy by Charles Dudley Warner. Other literature about Wall Street includes Bronson Howard's satirical play *The Henrietta;* E.C. Stedman's whimsical poem "Pan in Wall Street," in which Pan visits the "bulls" and "bears" of the street, but is removed by a blue-coated policeman; and more recently *The Big Money* and other novels by Dos Passos, the novels *The Embezzler* by Louis Auchincloss and

The Bonfire of the Vanities by Tom Wolfe, as well as nonfictional studies, including *The Robber Barons* by Matthew Josephson.

WALLACE, HORACE BINNEY (1817–52), Philadelphia lawyer and author, best known for his posthumous collections of essays, *Art, Scenery, and Philosophy in Europe* (1855) and *Literary Criticisms and Other Papers* (1856), which show him to have been an early follower of the positivist philosophy of Comte.

WALLACE, LEW[IS] (1827–1905), Indiana author, whose career included military service in the Mexican War and the Civil War, in which he rose to the rank of major general and redeemed a failure at Shiloh by defending Washington from capture by a Confederate force under Jubal Early. After a residence in Mexico, where he interested himself in the attempt of Juárez to gain power, he returned to his native state to practice law and complete his novel *The Fair God*♦ (1873), a story of the Spanish conquest of Mexico. The success of this romance caused him to write *Ben-Hur*♦ (1880), a romantic depiction of the late Roman empire and the rise of Christianity, which is said to have sold 2,000,000 copies, besides being translated into many foreign languages. He followed this with a narrative, *The Boyhood of Christ* (1888). After having served as territorial governor of New Mexico (1878–81), he became minister to Turkey (1881–85), and his interest in that country inspired him to write *The Prince of India* (1893), a turgid novel based on the story of the Wandering Jew. His other works include *The Wooing of Malkatoon* (1898), a long poem which incorporates his earlier tragedy, *Commodus* (1877); and *Lew Wallace: An Autobiography* (1906), completed by his wife Susan Arnold Wallace (1830–1907), an author in her own right.

WALLACE, WILLIAM ROSS (1819–81), born in Kentucky, moved in 1841 to New York, where he became a lawyer and poet. His works include *Alban the Pirate* (1848), a long verse romance; *Meditations in America, and Other Poems* (1851), ardently patriotic in describing American scenery; and *The Liberty Bell* (1862), militant poems upholding the Union, which were set to music. Although he himself has been forgotten, his poem "The Hand That Rocks the Cradle" has been a popular anthology piece. He was an intimate friend of Poe, whom he is said to have resembled in both appearance and temperament, and whom he defended against the attacks of John Neal.

WALLANT, EDWARD LEWIS (1926–62), author and graphic artist whose novels *The Human Season* (1960), *The Pawnbroker* (1961), *The Tenants of Moonbloom* (1963), and *The Children at the Gate* (1964) present Jewish characters, lonely and anguished, but with a warm sense of humanity.

Walpole Literary Club (*c.*1795–1800), New Hampshire social and literary coterie led by Joseph Dennie. Its members contributed to his paper, the *Farmer's Weekly Museum.*♦ Among them were Royall Tyler and T.G. Fessenden.

WALSH, ROBERT (1784–1859), Federalist journalist who edited *The American Register* (1809–10) and other journals, was a professor at the University of Pennsylvania (1828–33), wrote *An Appeal from the Judgments of Great Britain Respecting the United States of America* (1819), defending this nation from the views of English writers and visitors, and collected his various papers in *Didactics: Social, Literary, and Political* (2 vols., 1836), the occasion of Poe's eulogy of him as a thinker, scholar, and writer.

WALTER, EUGENE (1874–1941), born in Cleveland, was the author of 16 plays during his heyday (1902–21), which included *Paid in Full* (1908), *The Easiest Way* (1909), and *Fine Feathers* (1911), successful melodramas that were considered steps in the direction of realistic drama. He dramatized John Fox's *The Trail of the Lonesome Pine* (1911) and *The Little Shepherd of Kingdom Come* (1916), and analyzed his technique in *How to Write a Play* (1925).

WALTER, THOMAS (1696–1725), Congregational minister of Massachusetts, author of *The Grounds and Rules of Musick Explained; or, an Introduction to the Art of Singing by Note* (1721); a book of poems, *The Sweet Psalmist of Israel* (1722); and an attack on radical theological views, *A Choice Dialogue Between John Faustus, a Conjuror, and Jack Tory, His Friend* (1720), for which material was gathered by his uncle, Cotton Mather.

Wampanoag Indians, Algonquian tribe of Massachusetts, the first to be encountered by the Pilgrims. Under Massasoit♦ they were friendly with the whites, but his son King Philip♦ precipitated a war (1675) that ended disastrously, the Indians being nearly exterminated. They figure in J.A. Stone's *Metamora* and in the many accounts of King Philip.

Wapshot Chronicle, The, novel by John Cheever,♦ published in 1957.

The quaint, rather run-down old fishing town of St. Botolphs, Mass., is the home of the eccentric Wapshot family. Its senior members are the cousins Leander and Honora. In his old age Leander operates a decrepit ferryboat to a nearby island tourist park (until his second wife, Sarah, renovates it as "The Only Floating Gift Shoppe in New England"), and keeps a laconic journal with reminiscences about his raffish life, until one day he swims out from shore, never to return. The diminutive Honora, possessed of a leonine face, feuds with Leander, whose house and boat she owns, but is fond of his sons, Moses and

Coverly. In time both young men leave home to seek their fortunes. Moses, in picaresque style, gets a fine post in a secret government agency until ousted as a security risk because of his liaison with a woman of erratic behavior. He then obtains an executive position in New York City and becomes the second husband of Melissa, the ward of his quirky relative, the misanthropic Justina Wapshot Molesworth Scaddon. Coverly follows a simpler path as the husband of Betsy, an initially pleasant young woman from Georgia, but their marriage also appears unpromising as she is left friendless during their life on a Midwestern military base where he has found a job.

The Wapshot Scandal, a sequel, published in 1964, continues the family saga after the deaths of Leander and Sarah. Honora, who has grown more eccentric over the years, throws all her mail unopened into the fireplace and so has never paid income taxes. When approached by a government agent, she flees to Italy but is relieved to be extradited home. In time she drinks and starves herself to death. Meanwhile Coverly and Betsy continue in their unhappy marriage, while Moses and Melissa drift into even greater instability and inconstancy. Melissa takes a young grocery boy as lover and in a fantastic sequence of events they go to live together in Italy. Moses finds what comfort he can in alcohol and copulation with the widow Willston of St. Botolphs for, like his brother, he has drifted back to their ancestral hometown.

War Between the States, see *Civil War.*

War Is Kind, poems by Stephen Crane. ♦

War of 1812, fought between the U.S. and Great Britain (1812–15). During the Napoleonic Wars, American shipping flourished to such an extent that it harmed both French and English commerce and led the British to impress British sailors on board American ships, and the Americans retaliated with embargo and nonintercourse acts. Meanwhile Clay, Calhoun, and other "war hawks" in Congress felt that the British were unfairly preventing American expansion in the West by such means as inciting Indians to hostilities along the frontier, and they desired war to conquer Canada and west Florida. War was declared June 18, 1812, and the land forces were soon forced to surrender to the British. At sea the Americans were more successful; the *Constitution* defeated the *Guerrière,* and the *United States,* commanded by Decatur, defeated the *Macedonian,* although the *Chesapeake* under James Lawrence was defeated by the *Shannon.* Perry's victory on Lake Erie (Sept. 1813) and the recapture of Detroit were in 1814 offset by fears that England, temporarily free from the Napoleonic Wars, would crush the Americans, and at the Hartford Convention Federalist New Englanders, who

dubbed this "Mr. Madison's War," talked of secession. Meanwhile Republicans in the North were uninterested in seizing Florida and the Southern Republicans were unenthusiastic about the attempts to capture Canada. The British blockaded the Atlantic coast, captured Washington (1814), and burned the White House and Capitol, but were stopped before Baltimore (see *"Star-Spangled Banner"*); the invasion from Canada was halted at Plattsburg. The indecisive victories on both sides and English fear of European war led to peace negotiations ending in the Treaty of Ghent (Dec. 24, 1814). Not a single aim of the war was attained, and the American commissioners did not even feel strong enough to demand the abandonment of impressment or to ask for more than the surrender of territory gained by Great Britain during the war. Jackson's victory at New Orleans (Jan. 8, 1815) occurred before he was notified of the treaty, and this last American success did much to restore national confidence.

Contemporary novels about the war include James K. Paulding's *Diverting History of John Bull and Brother Jonathan* (1812), an attack on British tyranny, and Samuel Woodworth's *The Champions of Freedom* (1816), an extravagant moral romance. The chauvinistic drama of a later day included Mordecai Noah's *She Would Be a Soldier*♦ (1819), Richard Penn Smith's *The Eighth of January*♦ (1829) and *The Triumph of Plattsburg*♦ (1830), and William Emmons's *Tecumseh* (1836), a reworking of his poetic history *The Fredoniad; or Independence Preserved* (4 vols., 1827). The most famous work to come out of the war was "The Star-Spangled Banner" and the most famous later work was Holmes's "Old Ironsides"♦ (1830), celebrating the *Constitution.* Later historical fiction includes Irving Bacheller's *D'ri and I* (1901), about the Canadian frontier and the Battle of Lake Erie; Edward L. Bynner's *Zachary Phipps* (1892), about Aaron Burr's machinations; Edward Everett Hale's *Man Without a Country* (1863), incidentally treating a naval battle; John T. Moore's *Hearts of Hickory* (1926), on Andrew Jackson; and Kenneth Roberts's *Lively Lady* (1931), about the war in the North.

War of Independence, see *Revolutionary War.*

War of the Rebellion, see *Civil War.*

WARD, Artemus, pseudonym of C.F. Browne. ♦

WARD, Elizabeth Stuart Phelps (1844–1911), Massachusetts author, daughter of Elizabeth Stuart Phelps, ♦ continued her mother's interest in religious fiction by writing her fervently emotional novel *The Gates Ajar*♦ (1868), which is less a novel than a series of conversations by fictional characters concerning the beauties of Heaven. The immense popularity of this work, which seems to have brought solace to innumerable women, was continued in other fictional discussions of the future life: *Beyond the Gates* (1883), recounting the dream of a woman who thinks she dies and goes to Heaven; *The Gates Between* (1887), telling the afterlife adventures of an agnostic doctor; and *Within the Gates* (1901), a reworking of the latter novel. *Hedged In* (1870), a novel having as its theme the hypocrisy of society in its treatment of women who transgress against conventional moral standards, was followed by other pleas for social justice for women. These are *The Silent Partner* (1871), a story of New England mill girls; *The Story of Avis* (1877), concerned with a woman's attempt to have a career as a painter; and *Dr. Zay* (1882), an account of a woman physician. *The Madonna of the Tubs* (1886) and *Jack, the Fisherman* (1887) are novelettes, more realistic in their presentation of the lives of Gloucester fishermen. *A Singular Life* (1894) parallels the life of Christ in that of a young New England minister whose sincerity causes him to be rejected by the orthodox church. In addition to other lesser novels and collections of short stories whose themes are like those of her longer works, she wrote spiritual poetry and the autobiographical *Chapters from a Life* (1896), and collaborated with her husband Herbert Dickinson Ward (1861–1932) on several biblical romances.

WARD, LESTER FRANK (1841–1913), sociologist who, in addition to writing many works on the natural sciences, developed a theory that the human mind, when honestly and scientifically instructed, can take an active rather than a passive part in planning the process of human evolution, thus proceeding beyond the bounds of the ordinary evolutionary hypothesis. These ideas are developed in such books as *Dynamic Sociology* (1883), *The Psychic Factors of Civilization* (1893), and *Pure Sociology* (1903). His *Glimpses of the Cosmos* (6 vols., 1913–18) reprints many of his works in their biographical context, developing what he called his "mental autobiography."

WARD, NATHANIEL (c.1578–1652), Englishborn Congregational clergyman, emigrated to Massachusetts (1634), where he served as minister (1634–36) at Aggawam (now Ipswich). Upon retiring from the ministry, he formulated the colony's first code of laws, "The Body of Liberties" (1641), which is considered fundamental in American constitutional history. His best-known work, *The Simple Cobler of Aggawam*♦ (1647), is a crotchety and amusing satirical blast against religious toleration and other matters of annoyance to him. Ward also wrote commendatory verse prefixed to the poems of Anne Bradstreet, and published some poetry in his own book. He returned to England as a clergyman (1647) and several later political and ecclesiastical tracts have been attributed to him.

WARD, NED [EDWARD] (1667–1731), English poet, satirist, and tavern keeper, probably did not come to America as he alleged in *A Trip to New England. With a Character of the Country and People, both English and Indians* (London, 1699), but got his material from secondary sources and his imagination. This lively account briefly discusses blue laws, witchcraft, and racy aspects of the life of the Puritans, characterized as "*Saints* without *Religion, Traders* without *Honesty, Christians* without *Charity* . . . *Neighbours* without *Amity, Faithless Friends, Implacable Enemies,* and *Rich Men* without *Money.*"

WARD, SAMUEL (1814 84), brother of Julia Ward Howe, after graduation from Columbia (1831) tried the family banking business, emigrated to California, of which he wrote journalistic accounts collected in *Sam Ward in California* (1949), enjoyed Washington social life as "King of the Lobby" for financial interests in the capital, and presumably wrote "The Diary of a Public Man" (1879) about Lincoln before his presidency, as well as his only signed volume, *Lyrical Recreations* (1865). As a kindly, witty bon vivant he was well known in England and on the Continent and became the inspiration for the character Horace Bellingham in *Dr. Claudius* (1883) by his nephew, F. Marion Crawford.

WARE, HENRY (1764–1845), Massachusetts clergyman of the liberal branch of the Congregational Church, was instrumental in the establishment of Unitarianism in the U.S., being the first nonorthodox professor of divinity at Harvard (1805–40) and a founder of the college's Divinity School (1819). He wrote several controversial works, including *Letters Addressed to Trinitarians and Calvinists* (1820). His son Henry Ware (1794–1843) was also a Unitarian clergyman.

WILLIAM WARE (1797–1852), another son, was a Unitarian clergyman and author of a popular trilogy on the social and political struggles between the early Christians and the dominant hierarchies of their time. The three epistolary novels are *Zenobia,* first called *Letters . . . from Palmyra* (1837); *Aurelian,* first called *Probus* (1838); and *Julian* (1841). He is also the author of *Lectures on . . . Washington Allston* (1852).

Ware, THERON, see *Damnation of Theron Ware.*

WARNER, CHARLES DUDLEY (1829–1900), was born in Massachusetts, reared in western New York, and graduated from Hamilton College (1851). After publishing his commencement oration as *The Book of Eloquence* (1851), he went to Missouri as a railroad surveyor, then to the University of Pennsylvania (LL.B., 1858), and practiced law in Chicago (1858–60). Determining upon a literary and journalistic career, he made his home in Hartford, Conn., and after 1861 was editor of the *Courant,* although frequently occupied in other matters. His first mature book, *My Summer in a Garden* (1870), a series of essays about his farm, possessed the quiet humor and mellow grace of Irving, which also characterized his later essays, ranging from recollections of his childhood to literary criticism, and including *Backlog Studies* (1873), *Baddeck* (1874), *Being a Boy* (1878), *On Horseback* (1888), *As We Were Saying* (1891), *The Relation of Literature to Life* (1896), and *Fashions in Literature* (1902). His travel sketches, concerning his five trips to Europe and other journeys, are marked by similar qualities and include *Saunterings* (1872), *My Winter on the Nile* (1876), *In the Levant* (1877), *In the Wilderness* (1878), *A Roundabout Journey* (1883), and *Our Italy* (1891). Warner's biographies include *Captain John Smith* (1881) and, as editor of the American Men of Letters Series, ♦ *Washington Irving* (1881).

His first novel, written with his friend Clemens, was *The Gilded Age*♦ (1873). The original idea has been attributed to Warner, and the character Philip Sterling is considered partly autobiographical, but the book's realism is more attributable to Clemens. Possibly prompted by this investigation of the shoddy Reconstruction era of big finance, Warner forsook the easy, rather shallow character of his essays to write his trilogy on the creation, immoral use, and dissipation of a great fortune. *A Little Journey in the World* (1889) depicts the ruin of the character of Margaret Debree through her reconciliation with the ruthless methods employed by her husband, Rodney Henderson, in accumulating his great fortune. *The Golden House* (1894) is centered on Henderson's second wife, Carmen, whose morality in her affair with Jack Delancy is shown to be on the same plane as that of her husband, who financially ruins the young aristocrat. *That Fortune* (1899) concerns the marriage of Carmen, after her husband's death, to Mavick, a wily politician who loses her fortune and thus destroys the sole distinction she enjoyed. The regeneration of values is suggested by the marriage of her daughter to Philip Burnett, an honest but socially undistinguished young lawyer, who becomes a journalist.

WARNER, SUSAN BOGERT (1819–85), New York author of juvenile novels, distinguished by sentimental piety, who wrote under the pseudonym Elizabeth Wetherell. *The Wide, Wide World* (3 vols., 1850) recounts the moral development of a young orphan, as does *Queechy* (1852), another popular work.

ANNA BARTLETT WARNER (1827–1915), her sister, collaborated with her on several works, and independently wrote similar novels, including *Dollars and Cents* (1852), under the pseudonym of Amy Lothrop, and *My Brother's Keeper* (1855).

WARNER, WILLIAM WHITESIDES (1920–), Princeton graduate, executive of the Smithsonian Institution, and author of *Beautiful Swimmers: Watermen, Crabs and the Chesapeake Bay* (1976, Pulitzer Prize) and *Distant Water: The Fate of the North Atlantic Fisherman* (1983).

WARREN, CAROLINE MATILDA (1787?–1844), New England schoolteacher and author of *The Gamesters: or, Ruins of Innocence* (1805), a typical sentimental didactic novel of the period. She is sometimes known by her married name of Thayer, and wrote an American history for children and some religious tracts.

WARREN, MERCY OTIS (1728–1814), sister of James Otis, wife of James Warren (1726–1808), president of the Provincial Congress of Massachusetts, was herself at the center of Revolutionary politics and a frequent correspondent with the leaders. Her political satires in dramatic form, *The Adulateur*♦ (1773) and *The Group*♦ (1775), attack Governor Hutchinson and other Loyalists. Probably neither play was performed, and both are conversations rather than dramas. Her *History of the Rise, Progress, and Termination of the American Revolution* (3 vols., 1805) is a lively and astute work, important as a contemporary record. *The Blockheads* (1776), a prose farce in answer to Burgoyne's *The Blockade*♦ (1775), has been attributed to her, probably erroneously. *The Motley Assembly* (1779), also attributed to her, is a farce ridiculing types of Boston society who opposed the Revolution as incompatible with their aristocratic notions. Her *Poems Dramatic and Miscellaneous* (1790) contains two verse tragedies, "The Sack of Rome" and "The Ladies of Castile."

WARREN, ROBERT PENN (1905–89), born in Kentucky, by heritage had deep associations with the issues and traditions of the South, early indicated by his affiliation with the regionalist group that published *The Fugitive*♦ while he was a student at Vanderbilt University (B.A., 1925). After receiving an M.A. at the University of California (1927) and further study at Yale and as a Rhodes Scholar at Oxford, Warren, while establishing himself as an author, began an academic career that included posts as a professor at Louisiana State University (1934–42), Minnesota (1942–50), and Yale (1950–73). The range and variety of his talents as well as a continuing concern with his regional background are evident in his early works: *John Brown: The Making of a Martyr* (1929), a biographical study; *Thirty-Six Poems* (1935); and *Night Rider* (1939), a novel treating moral issues relating to the fight between tobacco growers and manufacturers in Kentucky at the opening of the 20th century. At this time he was also a founder and editor of *The Southern Review* (1935–42).

His second novel was *At Heaven's Gate* (1943), depicting an unscrupulous financier who, though he controls his Southern state, loses his daughter, who commits suicide; followed by *All the King's*

Men ♦ (1946, Pulitzer Prize), treating a corrupt Southern governor like Huey Long but having a moral significance extending far beyond its topical subject; *World Enough and Time* (1950), a version of the notorious Kentucky Tragedy; *Band of Angels* ♦ (1955), a lush, full-bodied Civil War story about a Kentucky plantation owner's daughter sold into slavery whose fight becomes an inquiry into the nature of freedom and the quest for individual identity; *The Cave* (1959), a labyrinthine study of the way in which diverse people, affected by the plight of a young Tennessee hillbilly immured in a cave, reveal in thought and action their basic natures; *Wilderness* (1961), the portrait of a Bavarian Jew who comes to the U.S. to fight for freedom with the Union army; *Flood* (1964), presenting people in a small western Tennessee town that is to be obliterated by the building of a dam and who are thereby forced to face their essential natures; *Meet Me in the Green Glen* (1971), about the tragic romance of a young Italian-American and a middle-aged farm wife of western Tennessee; and *A Place To Come To* (1977), the reminiscences of a 60-year-old classics scholar from his youth in Alabama. *The Circus in the Attic* (1947) collects stories.

Warren's poetry, first marked by metaphysical influences but later simpler, more regional, and more narrative in character, is published in *Eleven Poems on the Same Theme* (1942); *Selected Poems, 1923–1943* (1944); *Brother to Dragons* (1953, revised 1979), a "tale in verse and voices" of the lurid early-19th-century Kentucky frontier murder of a black by nephews of Jefferson, and also an inquiry into the nature of evil and the quest of the individual for order; *Promises* (1957, Pulitzer Prize); *You, Emperors, and Others* (1960); *Incarnations* (1968); *Audubon: A Vision* (1969); *Or Else-Poem* (1975); *Now and Then* (1978); *Being Here* (1980); *Rumor Verified* (1981); and *Chief Joseph of the Nez Percé* (1983). His *New and Selected Poems* since 1923 was published in 1985. Two brief nonfictional works are *Segregation: The Inner Conflict in the South* (1956) and *The Legacy of the Civil War* (1961), on the ways the war shaped American society and sensibilities. *Who Speaks for the Negro?* (1965) treats problems of integration, in large part through interviews with black leaders. A volume of *New and Selected Essays* (1989) gathers 13 literary studies dating back to the 1940s.

Warren's literary essays associate him with the New Criticism, ♦ as do several works, written with Cleanth Brooks, that served as influential college texts, including *Understanding Poetry* (1938) and *Understanding Fiction* (1943). His other critical writings include *Homage to Theodore Dreiser* (1971), *John Greenleaf Whittier* (1971), and *Democracy and Poetry* (1975). He was the nation's first Poet Laureate (1986–87). He was married to Eleanor Clark. ♦

WASHINGTON, BOOKER T[ALIAFERRO] (1856–1915), son of a black slave and a white man, was born into slavery on a Virginia plantation. Freed, he taught himself to read from Webster's "Blue-back spelling book," adopted his inspirational surname, and walked most of the 500 miles to attend Hampton Institute (Virginia) for vocational training. Ten years later, aged 25, he was selected to head Tuskegee Institute (Alabama), a normal school for blacks. He developed it beyond a school for industrial training into a college with nearly 200 faculty members offering instruction in professions as well as in trades. His leadership in education as well as his talents as a public speaker made him the outstanding black man of his time and a spokesman for his people, although many persons considered his approval of the separation of the races, lack of emphasis on political rights, and stress on industrial training were inhibiting to the progress of his people. His books include *Up from Slavery* ♦ (1901), an autobiography; *The Future of the American Negro* (1899); *Working with the Hands* (1904); and *The Story of the Negro* (1909). His *Papers* (1972–) are being published in a 13-volume set.

WASHINGTON, GEORGE (1732–99), 1st President of the U.S. (1789–97), was born on the family estate in Westmoreland County, Virginia. His education was elementary, and after his father's death (1743) he was guided mainly by his half-brother Lawrence, who obtained him a position as surveyor. His first military experience (1753) was in the Ohio country against the French and Indians, and is recorded in his report *The Journal of Major George Washington* (1754). His next service was to build Fort Necessity at Great Meadows, near the present site of Pittsburgh, where he defeated the French of Fort Duquesne (May 1754), but was soon forced to retreat and arrange a peace. He then accompanied Braddock in his unsuccessful attack (1755) on Fort Duquesne.

On his return, Washington was engaged for two years as commander of the Virginia forces in repelling attacks on the colony's western frontier. In 1759 he married Mrs. Martha Dandridge Custis (1732–1802), and settled down on the Mount Vernon estate inherited from his brother, to lead the life of a country gentleman, though also serving in the House of Burgesses. The conflict with Great Britain drew him into larger colonial politics, and he was a member of both Continental Congresses, upon the outbreak of the Revolutionary War being chosen commander in chief of the Continental army (June 1775).

After assuming command of a raw, loosely organized army at Cambridge (July 1775), he began his first campaign, which ended with the capture of Dorchester Heights and the British evacuation of Boston (March 1776). He then attempted the untenable defense of New York, in which he was forced to retreat, although he soon recrossed the Delaware (Christmas, 1776) into New Jersey and took Trenton and Princeton in a counterattack. The next months were consumed by attempts to build a larger and better disciplined army, but ended with the defeat by Howe at Brandywine (Sept. 1777), and the loss of Philadelphia to the British. The failure to destroy Howe's army at Germantown (Oct. 1777) caused him to retreat to Valley Forge for the hard winter, which was made even more difficult by the Conway Cabal. ♦ His army nevertheless emerged stronger and better drilled after the arduous winter, and at the Battle of Monmouth (June 1778) showed itself the equal of the British. The assistance of the French troops and a strong southern campaign aided his final victory over Cornwallis at Yorktown (Oct. 1781).

The war dragged to an end, and after indignantly refusing the suggestion of some of his soldiers that he be crowned king, Washington retired to Mount Vernon, only to return to public affairs as president of the Federal Constitutional Convention (1787). He was elected President of the new government, and drew his cabinet from all factions. He mainly supported the national or federalistic policies of Hamilton, basing financial stability on manufacturing and commerce, and when Jefferson resigned from the cabinet because of this and the failure to aid France in the war against Great Britain, the two-party system came into being, Jefferson leading the Democratic Republicans and Hamilton the Federalists.

Washington's second administration was definitely Federalist, and there was much opposition to his so-called aristocratic tendencies, to Jay's Treaty, and to the tax that led to the Whiskey Rebellion (1794). Nevertheless, he had brought the country power, credit, and prestige, had through the exploits of Anthony Wayne temporarily ended severe Indian troubles, opened the Mississippi to navigation through treaties with Spain and Great Britain, and settled financial difficulties through the policies of Hamilton.

His writings are important historically, but lack the literary merit of similar contemporary documents. Of these the foremost is the *Farewell Address*♦ (1796), a monument of American policy, probably written with the aid of Hamilton and Madison. His *Writings* have been collected in 39 volumes (1931–44) and his *Diaries, 1748–1799* in 4 volumes (1925), but the first collection of *Letters and Papers* (12 vols., 1837) by Jared Sparks was bowdlerized to make Washington a gentlemanly hero. His apotheosis began immediately upon his death, with the famous phrase "First in war, first in peace, first in the hearts of his countrymen" spoken by "Light-Horse Harry" Lee in his memorial resolution delivered before Congress (Dec. 27, 1799). The glorification was further exaggerated in the biography by Parson Mason Locke Weems, ♦ which first came out about 1800 and was expanded in 1806 to introduce the cherry-tree story. The best of the early biographies are those by John Marshall (5 vols., 1804–7), Jared Sparks (1839), and Washington Irving (5 vols., 1855–59). An outstanding scholarly

biography is Douglas Southall Freeman's (6 vols., 1948–54).

Even during his life Washington passed beyond the bounds of biography to become a heroic character in literature. The verse that eulogized him includes Trumbull's *M'Fingal* (1782), Joel Barlow's *The Vision of Columbus* (1787), John Blair Linn's elegy *The Death of Washington* (1800), and Richard Alsop's *A Poem: Sacred to the Memory of George Washington* (1800). In drama he appears as a character in Dunlap's *André* (1798), G.W.P. Custis's *The Indian Prophecy* (1828), and other works. More frequently he was made a personage in fiction; some of the earlier works include Jeremy Belknap's *The Foresters* (1792), Samuel Woodworth's *The Champions of Freedom* (1816), Cooper's *The Spy* (1821), John Neal's *Seventy-Six* (1823), James McHenry's *The Wilderness* (1823), Catharine M. Sedgwick's *The Linwoods* (1835), J.H. Ingraham's *Burton* (1838), Jeremiah Clemens's *The Rivals* (1860), John Esten Cooke's *Fairfax* (1868), and S. Weir Mitchell's *Hugh Wynne* (1897). Not only has Washington appeared in foreign fiction, notably Thackeray's *The Virginians* (1858–59), but he has continued to be treated in 20th-century American novels, including Gertrude Atherton's *The Conqueror* (1902), Hergesheimer's *Balisand* (1924), Kenneth Roberts's *Oliver Wiswell* (1940), and Howard Fast's *The Unvanquished* (1942), as well as in such modern American plays as Maxwell Anderson's *Valley Forge* (1934) and Sidney Kingsley's *The Patriots* (1942).

Washington Square, novel by Henry James, ♦ published in 1881.

As Catherine Sloper grows up in her father's New York house in Washington Square, she realizes that he has been embittered by the early loss of his wife and son, and that her own plainness and lack of wit further disappoint him. At 20, Catherine's one advantage is her prospect of inheriting a fortune, and this attracts a suitor, Morris Townsend. The girl is overjoyed, but Dr. Sloper investigates Townsend's status and finds him penniless. When Catherine dutifully tells her father that she has accepted Townsend's proposal, the doctor refuses his consent, stating that if she marries she will forfeit her inheritance. She is deeply hurt, and after her father forbids Townsend's visits she continues to meet him secretly, finally promising to marry him when he is ready, for she does not realize that what he is waiting for is a change in Dr. Sloper's attitude. Exasperated at his daughter's obstinacy, the doctor takes her to Europe for a year, but this only strengthens her feeling for Townsend. At length, however, she realizes the reason for his interest, and, assuming a stolid calm, informs her father that she has broken the engagement. She refuses to see Townsend again, although later she declines her father's dying request that she vow never to marry Townsend, and he consequently reduces his bequest to her. After a time, Townsend proposes again, abetted by Catherine's aunt, Mrs. Penniman, who had encouraged his suit before, but the disillusioned girl refuses him. She feels that emotion and affection are now past in her life, and remains with the integrity of her sentiment and her position as "maiden-aunt to the younger portion of society."

Washington Square Players, THE, New York City little theater, founded in 1915, initially to encourage native talents and American themes. Its members included Zoë Akins, Zona Gale, and Philip Moeller as playwrights, Katharine Cornell as an actress, and Robert Edmond Jones as a stage designer. U.S. entry into World War I helped to end the enterprise in 1918, and the following year many of its participants founded the Theatre Guild.

WASSERSTEIN, WENDY (1950–), born in Brooklyn, after graduate work at Yale early got into writing and publication for the stage and television with *Any Woman Can't* (1973) and, among other productions, *Uncommon Women and Others* (1975), begun as a one-act text and developed into a full-length text for New York and very numerous productions nationwide. It was followed by *Isn't It Romantic* in versions of 1979 and 1983. Her growing production and reputation were increased with *The Heidi Chronicles* (1988), awarded a Pulitzer Prize. It is another inquiry into the nature and activities of women, with comic treatment as part of a serious overall theme. *Bachelor Girls* (1990) treats similar themes. *The Sisters Rosensweig* (1992) is another "serious comedy," about a reunion in London of three American Jewish sisters.

Waste Land, The, poem on the theme of the sterility and chaos of the contemporary world by T.S. Eliot,♦ published in 1922. This most widely known expression of the despair of the postwar era has as a structural framework the symbolism of certain fertility myths that reputedly formed the pagan origins of the Christian Grail legend.

The Waste Land itself is a desolate and sterile country ruled by an impotent king, and the poem is divided into five parts: "The Burial of the Dead," representing the rebirth of the land after the barren winter; "The Game of Chess," a contrast between the splendor of the past and the squalor of modern life; "The Fire Sermon," vignettes of the sordidness of modern life; "Death by Water," the vision of a drowned Phoenician sailor who at least dies by water, not thirst; and "What the Thunder Said," representing the decay of modern Europe through symbols of the Grail legend. The poem concludes with quotations from the Upanishads, its last word, three times repeated, being "Shantih," meaning "the peace which passeth understanding." In the 433 lines of the poem are included quotations from,

allusions to, or imitations of some 35 different writers, as well as several popular songs and passages in six foreign languages, including Sanskrit. The original poem was far longer than the published text, which was severely pruned and edited by Ezra Pound, to whom the work is dedicated. The original version with Pound's annotations was published in 1971.

Water Witch, The, romance by Cooper,♦ published in 1830. Several dramatic versions, including one by R.P. Smith, were produced in 1830 and 1831.

Set in the region of New York City at the close of the 17th century, the story is concerned with the admirable small brigantine *Water Witch* and its pirate captain, known as "The Skimmer of the Seas," whose romantic abduction of a beautiful heiress, Alinda de Barberie, begins the action. Pursued by the English sloop of war, the *Coquette,* whose commander, Captain Ludlow, is Alinda's suitor, the *Water Witch* manages to escape, though remaining in Long Island Sound, until the *Coquette* is engaged in battle by two French ships. The Skimmer of the Seas cannot desert his fellow countrymen in time of danger, and joins forces with Ludlow, helping to destroy the enemy craft. Ludlow is doubly grateful when his fiancée is restored to him, and offers his protection to the patriotic pirate, but The Skimmer of the Seas embarks for new adventures in his own favorite, the *Water Witch.*

WATERS, FRANK (1902–), born in Colorado, began his literary career with *Wild Earth's Nobility* (1935), about a young man's career in the area's mining development to 1902; *Below Grass Roots* (1937), a sequel in the man's personal life and his search for gold; *Dust Within the Rock* (1940), the third novel to complete a trilogy; *People of the Valley* (1941), about people of the Southwest cultures; *The Man Who Killed the Deer* (1942), a tale of Pueblo Indians and of a young man fighting their and his own rituals; *The Yogi of Cockroach Court* (1947), about life in a Mexican border town; *Pike's Peak: A Family Saga* (1971); and *Flight from Fiesta* (1986), a tale of friction and friendship between a Pueblo Indian and a young Anglo tourist. He wrote as many works of nonfiction as novels, including one on *The Colorado* (1946), a studious *Book of the Hopi* (1964), a study of *Mexico Mystique* (1975), and a book of essays both autobiographical and mystical in *Mountain Dialogues* (1982).

Watson, MISS, character in *Huckleberry Finn.*♦

WATTERSON, HENRY (1840–1921), editor of the Louisville *Courier-Journal♦* (1868–1918). He was considered a typical Southerner and was called "Marse Henry," the title also of his autobiography (1919). A collection of his *Editorials* was published in 1923.

WATTS, Alan (1915–73), English-born leader of the Zen Buddhist movement in U.S., where he lived after 1938 and where he was naturalized in 1943. For a time an Episcopal minister and university chaplain and teacher, he became more widely known as a lecturer on Oriental philosophy, an experimenter with mind-altering drugs, described in *The Joyous Cosmology* (1962), and associate of the Beat movement.♦ His books include *The Spirit of Zen* (1936), *Behold the Spirit* (1947), *The Way of Zen* (1957), *Beat Zen, Square Zen and Zen* (1967), *Beyond Theology* (1973), and *In My Own Way* (1973), an autobiography.

WATTS, Mary S[tanbery] (1868–1958), Ohio novelist whose works include *Nathan Burke* (1910), a story of an Ohio backwoods boy in the Mexican War; *Van Cleve* (1913), dealing with the Middle West during the period of the Spanish-American War; *The Rise of Jennie Cushing* (1914), dealing with the career of a slum girl and her humanitarian work; *From Father to Son* (1919), a story showing the changing standards of the 20th century by the refusal of a boy to accept the fortune of a profiteering grandfather; *The Boardman Family* (1918); *The House of Rimmon* (1922); *Luther Nichols* (1923); and *The Fabric of the Loom* (1924).

Way Down East, sentimental melodrama by Lottie Blair Parker, produced in 1898, which was for many years one of the most popular vehicles of stock companies.

Way to Wealth, The, see *Poor Richard's Almanack.*

Wayside Inn, located near the village of Sudbury, about 20 miles from Cambridge, Mass., is also known as the Red-Horse Inn (founded 1686). It was originally the country house of an English family named Howe, who later kept it as a public place. It is famous as the scene of *Tales of a Wayside Inn.*♦ In 1923 Henry Ford made it a Longfellow shrine and colonial museum; it was partially burned (1955) and has been restored.

We Are Coming, Father Abraham, Three Hundred Thousand More, poem by James Sloan Gibbons (1810–92), a Quaker Abolitionist. Prompted by Lincoln's call for 300,000 new troops in 1862, the poem appeared in the New York *Evening Post* (July 1862). Set to music by Luther O. Emerson, Stephen Foster, and others, it became a favorite song of Union partisans.

Weary Blues, The, first collection of poetry by Langston Hughes.♦

WEAVER, John V[an] A[lstyn] (1893–1938), North Carolina-born author, whose poems, using American slang to depict shopgirls, salesmen, and other urban types in a toughly sen-

timental style, appear in *In American* (1921), *Finders* (1923), *More "In American"* (1925), *Trial Balance* (1931), and other books. He also wrote novels and scenarios, and of his plays the best known, written with George Abbott, is *Love 'Em and Leave 'Em* (1926).

Web and the Rock, The, novel by Thomas Wolfe,♦ posthumously published in 1939. *You Can't Go Home Again*♦ is a sequel. Both are clearly autobiographical.

George Webber, born in 1900 in Libya Hill, a small city in the state of Old Catawba (North Carolina), grows up torn between the Southern values of his mother's family and the more dynamic ways of his father, who came from Pennsylvania and who deserted his family when George was a boy. When his father dies, George receives a small inheritance that allows him to attend a local Baptist college, where his friends include Jim Randolph, a football star, and Gerald Alsop, an intellectual aesthete. In time all seek a larger life in New York City, but Jim goes on to South America, looking for the excitement and adulation he had known in college, and Alsop grows more and more precious and reactionary. George has an affair with Esther Jack, an older, married woman, a sophisticated member of theatrical and literary society. Although she helps him by trying to get his lengthy novel published, their relations are tempestuous and he storms off to Europe. There he is torn between the desires of his Mind and his Body, as he puts it, as well as between the inspiration of foreign lands and recollections of youth, and the recognition that "you can't go home again."

WEBB, Charles Henry (1834–1905), New York-born humorist, after writing for *Harper's Weekly* and *The New York Times* went to California (1863–66), where he founded *The Californian,* a journal which his friends Harte and Twain contributed. His works include *Liffith Lank* (1866) and *St. Twel'mo* (1866), respectively parodies of Reade's *Griffith Gaunt* and of Augusta Jane Evans's *St. Elmo; John Paul's Book* (1874), humorous sketches; and *Parodies: Prose and Verse* (1876).

WEBB, Walter Prescott (1888–1963), Texas-born scholar and educator, professor at the University of Texas from 1918 to his death. His studies of the frontier include *The Great Plains* (1931), *The Texas Rangers* (1935), *Divided We Stand: The Crisis of a Frontierless Democracy* (1937), and *The Great Frontier* (1952).

WEBBER, Charles Wilkins (1819–56), Kentucky-born adventurer, served as a Texas Ranger, was briefly a prominent New York journalist, tried frontier exploration, and died in battle serving in Walker's filibustering campaign in Nicaragua. His lurid Wild West tales include *Old*

Hicks, the Guide (1848), *The Gold Mines of the Gila* (1849), and *Tales of the Southern Border* (1852). His close friendship with Audubon may have inspired his books of natural history, *The Hunter-Naturalist* (1851) and *Wild Scenes and Song Birds* (1854).

WEBSTER, DANIEL (1782–1852), born in New Hampshire, graduated from Dartmouth (1801), and was admitted to the bar (1805). He was a Federalist congressman (1813–17, 1823–27), championing the New England shipping and mercantile interests, and meanwhile gaining a great reputation as a Boston lawyer and orator. As senator (1827–41) he became a leading Whig opponent of Calhoun's theory of states' rights and Jackson's war on the Bank of the United States, which was one of Webster's principal clients. Although he was considered for the Whig presidential candidacy, he never attained this ambition. He served as secretary of state (1841–43) in the cabinets of Harrison and Tyler, but after terminating the Webster-Ashburton Treaty negotiations (1842), which settled the Maine-Canada boundary dispute with Great Britain, he followed the other Whigs in resigning from the cabinet because Tyler showed himself to be a believer in states' rights and an opponent of the main principles of the party.

Webster returned to the Senate (1845–50), where he championed the protective tariff views of New England's vested interests, for he had been ruined financially in the panic of 1837 and was virtually a hired retainer of the conservative Massachusetts businessmen. Although he continued his moderate stand against slavery, he adhered to the constitutional rights of the slaveholders, since he realized that Southern Whigs must be propitiated if the wealthy Northerners were to obtain revision of the tariff toward further protection. He was consequently reviled as a traitor by the antislavery Northerners when he championed the Compromise of 1850 in his conciliatory "Seventh of March Speech"♦ on "The Constitution and the Union." Whittier attacked Webster in his poem "Ichabod,"♦ and Emerson declared that "all the drops of his blood have eyes that look downward" and he was a fallen star in the regard of all liberal thinkers. However, Whittier came to regret the severe castigation and wrote an apology, "The Lost Occasion" (1880), and others did likewise at a late date. Webster's last office was that of secretary of state in Fillmore's cabinet (1850–52), where he continued to work for Clay's compromise measures.

Among his famous legal arguments were the Dartmouth College case (1816–19) and the Rhode Island case, concerned with Dorr's Rebellion. His reputation as an orator was based on such legal cases, his many public addresses, such as those at Bunker Hill (1825, 1843) and a *Discourse in Commemoration of Jefferson and Adams* (1826), the speeches in the Senate and House of Representatives, and other addresses, all characterized by an eloquent Ciceronian rhetoric. His *Writings and Speeches* were collected in 18 volumes (1903).

His imposing appearance and impressive speech have made him into a folk figure, as in Stephen Vincent Benét's *The Devil and Daniel Webster♦* (1939), and he has also appeared in novels, notably Honoré Willsie Morrow's *Black Daniel* (1931).

WEBSTER, JEAN (1876–1916), New York author of juvenile novels, whose best-known works are *Daddy-Long-Legs* (1912), a sentimental, humorous story of orphanage life, and the Patty series about a young college girl. The prototype of the heroine of both the novel and the series is said to have been her friend Adelaide Crapsey, whose *Verse* she edited (1915).

WEBSTER, NOAH (1758–1843), Connecticut lexicographer and philologist, after graduation from Yale (1778) began his career with the publication of *A Grammatical Institute of the English Language* (1783–85). The first part of this work became his famous *Spelling Book,* which was designed to meet American needs and long played a fundamental part in American education by its aid in standardizing spellings that differed from the English. It was so widely used that by 1890 this work, with its various revisions, had sold more than 60,000,000 copies. His attempts to obtain a copyright for his book led Webster into politics as a zealous Federalist, for his need to obtain the proper legislation in 13 states caused him to champion a strong central government that could control matters of this sort. His ideas on a federal union were set forth in *Sketches of American Policy* (1785). Between periods of school-teaching and legal practice, he edited the Federalist journals *American Minerva♦* (1793–1803) and *Herald* (1794–1803). He also wrote graceful essays, works on economics, science, and medicine, edited the *Journal* of John Winthrop (1790), and, prompted by Franklin, wrote *Dissertations on the English Language* (1789), with radical views on reformed spelling, although his other orthographical works were on the whole traditional. His *Compendious Dictionary of the English Language* (1806) was a forerunner of his scholarly work, *An American Dictionary of the English Language* (2 vols., 1828). At the time of its publication, there raged a "War of the Dictionaries" with the rival lexicographer Joseph Worcester,♦ but Webster's work, adding some 5000 words not before included in English dictionaries, making use of Americanisms, and basing its definitions on the usage of American as well as English writers, soon became the recognized authority. In 1840 Webster revised his work to include 70,000 words instead of the original 38,000, and it has remained a recognized American authority in the many revisions made since his death.

WECHSBERG, JOSEPH (1907–1983), Czecho-slovakian-born journalist and novelist, came to the U.S. in 1938 and was naturalized in 1944. His writings include *Looking for a Bluebird* (1945) and *Sweet and Sour* (1948), witty sketches, many first published in *The New Yorker,* of his life as a musician in Europe and his travels; *Homecoming* (1946), describing his return as a U.S. soldier to his old home of Prague; *The Continental Touch* (1948) and *The Self-Betrayed* (1955), novels; *Avalanche!* (1958), an account of a disastrous Austrian landslide; and *Blue Trout and Black Truffles* (1953), on fine cuisine, one of his subjects, along with music, wine, and travel, in *The Best Things of Life* (1964). Some of these enthusiasms led to books on opera (1972) and violin (1972), and lives of Dame Nellie Melba (1961), the waltz-composing Strausses (1973), Verdi (1974), and Schubert (1978). He has also written recollections and familiar histories of East Germany (1964), Prague (1971), and Leningrad (1977). *The First Time Around* (1970) is a memoir.

Week on the Concord and Merrimack Rivers, A, autobiographical narrative by Thoreau, ♦ published in 1849. It was written, mainly during the period described in *Walden,* from earlier journal entries, poems, and essays. The narrative describes seven days in a small boat during a trip (Aug. 31–Sept. 13, 1839), which the author made with his brother John to the White Mountains in New Hampshire. From the description of the homemade dory, which was "painted green below, with a border of blue, with reference to the two elements in which it was to spend its existence," to the account of New Hampshire people, the book maintains a certain air of romantic adventure, but the travel narrative is subordinated to learned digressions into history, religion, and philosophy; poetry; discussions of literary classics; and such Emersonian essays as the one on friendship. Some of the passages have been frequently quoted, for Thoreau's style was already fully developed, and was said by Lowell to have "an antique purity." During the author's lifetime, the book was not popular. Later editors, like H.S. Canby, have given it a more compact form by eliminating "indoor additions."

Weekly Rehearsal, The (1731–35), Boston newspaper, was founded by Jeremy Gridley, who filled half the paper with his Addisonian essays. It was taken over by his printer, Thomas Fleet (1733), who impartially opened its columns to any political views. Fleet renamed the paper the *Boston Evening Post* ♦ (1735).

WEEMS, MASON LOCKE (1759–1825), Episcopal clergyman, temporarily at Pohick Church, Mount Vernon parish, where Washington is supposed to have been one of his parishioners. For more than 30 years he was also an author and peddler of chapbooks, and a book agent, mainly for Mathew Carey, contending that the selling of "good books" was a field for God's work. Among his short biographies the best known is *The Life and Memorable Actions of George Washington* (c.1800), which first gives the story of the cherry-tree episode in the so-called Fifth Edition of 1806 and is responsible for much of the Washington myth. He also wrote lives of Francis Marion (1809), Franklin (1815), and Penn (1822), and moral tracts, ranging from *Hymen's Recruiting Sergeant* (c.1799), a plea for brotherly love, to *God's Revenge Against Adultery* (1815).

WEIDMAN, JEROME (1913–), New York author, known for his frank, unpleasant portraits of Jewish characters, whose novels include *I Can Get It For You Wholesale* (1937) and its sequel, *What's in It for Me?* (1938), about an unscrupulous New Yorker's dress-manufacturing business; *I'll Never Go There Any More* (1941); *Too Early To Tell* (1946), satirizing a wartime government agency; *The Price Is Right* (1949), about a ruthless businessman; *Your Daughter Iris* (1955), an epistolary tale of a young woman from the Bronx living in England; *The Enemy Camp* (1958), about a Jew's ambivalent attitudes toward Christian society; *Before You Go* (1960), about the fictitious private life of a man whose public life resembles that of Roosevelt's adviser Harry Hopkins; *The Sound of Bow Bells* (1962), about a Jewish novelist striving for fame by any means; *Word of Mouth* (1964), about a New York lawyer and the theater world; *Other People's Money* (1968) and *The Center of the Action* (1969), about the business rise of New Yorkers; *Fourth Street East* (1971), a fictive memoir of youth on the Lower East Side, also the setting of *Last Respects* (1971); *Tiffany Street* (1974); *The Temple* (1975); *A Family Fortune* (1978), concerning the rise and fall of a Jewish racketeer; and *Counselors-at-Law* (1980), a mystery novel involving chicanery of lawyers. Weidman's plays include *Fiorello!* (1960, Pulitzer Prize), a collaboration with George Abbott ♦; *Tenderloin* (1961); a dramatization of *I Can Get It for You Wholesale* (1962); *Ivory Tower* (1969); and *Asterisk* (1969). *The Horse That Could Whistle "Dixie"* (1939), *The Captain's Tiger* (1947), and *The Death of Dickie Draper* (1965) collect stories. *Letter of Credit* (1940) describes a world tour. *Back Talk* (1963) collects magazine sketches. *Praying for Rain* (1986) is a work of autobiography.

WEISS, JOHN (1818–79), Unitarian minister of Massachusetts, and prominent reformer, upon returning from Heidelberg helped to introduce idealistic German literature to New England with his translations of Schiller (1845) and other authors. His other works include *Life and Correspondence of Theodore Parker* (2 vols., 1863), *American Religion* (1871), and *Wit, Humor, and Shakespeare: Twelve Essays* (1876).

WELCH, JAMES (1940–), born in Montana to a Blackfoot father and a Gros Ventre mother, was schooled on a reservation and at the University of Montana. He has been a firefighter, educational counselor, and served on the Montana State Board of Pardons. His first book was *Riding the Earthboy 40: Poems* (1971). *Winter in the Blood* (1974) is a novel of a young man struggling for insight amid the hardships of reservation life. *The Death of Jim Loney* (1979) treats the differences between white and Native American moral codes. *Fools Crow* (1986) deals with the Blackfeet in the 1870s. A more contemporary novel is *The Indian Lawyer* (1990).

WELD, THEODORE DWIGHT (1803–95), Massachusetts reformer, was a disciple of Charles Stuart♦ and himself the earliest and most influential of American Abolitionists. His speeches and campaigning in New York, Ohio, the Southern states, and elsewhere were largely responsible for consolidating antislavery feeling and for converting such later leaders as J.G. Birney, E.M. Stanton, Lyman Beecher, and the Grimké sisters. Harriet Beecher Stowe attributed the inspiration for *Uncle Tom's Cabin* to the tract *American Slavery as It Is* (1839), compiled by him and his wife Angelina Grimké.♦ Among his own few published works is *The Bible Against Slavery* (1837). His belief in anonymity kept him from publishing his numerous speeches.

WELD (or WELDE), THOMAS (1595–1661), English Congregational minister, resided in Massachusetts (1632–41), where he took a leading part in combating the teachings of Anne Hutchinson, and with John Eliot and Richard Mather wrote the *Bay Psalm Book*♦ (1640). In 1641, with Hugh Peter, he returned to England to represent the colony, and never returned to America. With Peter he edited and in part wrote *New Englands First Fruits*♦ (1643), but his failure to stop Roger Williams from acquiring a grant of land and his inefficient handling of funds caused his dismissal from the post of representing the Massachusetts Bay Colony in England. He then turned his attention to English religious and political affairs. His interest in New England continued, as may be seen in his *An Answer to W.R. . . .* (1644), attacking William Rathband's criticisms of New England's "Godly and Orthodoxicall Churches"; *A Short Story of the Rise, Reign, and Ruine of the Antinomians . . .* (1644), compiled from Winthrop's account of the Hutchinson episode; and *A Brief Narration of the Practices of the Churches in New-England* (1645).

WELLS, HELENA (*fl.*1799–1800), writer of didactic sentimental novels, is described on the title page of her novel *The Stepmother* (1799) as a resident "of Charleston, South Carolina," and seems to have been a Loyalist who later served as a governess in London. Her other novel is *Constantia Neville; or, The West Indian* (1800).

WELTY, EUDORA (1909–), Mississippi author, whose books include *A Curtain of Green* (1941),

The Wide Net (1943), *The Golden Apples* (1949), *The Bride of the Innisfallen* (1955), and *Moon Lake* (1980), stories set mainly in her region and depicting characters, often grotesque, who fail to know themselves or their neighbors; and *The Shoe Bird* (1964), tales for children. Her longer works include *The Robber Bridegroom* (1942), a novelette combining fairy tale and ballad form, telling of the wooing of Rosamond, the daughter of a Mississippi planter, by a bandit chief; *Delta Wedding* (1946), a novel subtly revealing the sensibilities of a modern plantation family; *The Ponder Heart* (1954), a comic fantasy of small-town Mississippi life, dramatized (1957) by Jerome Chodorov and Joseph Fields; *Losing Battles* (1970), depicting a family of Mississippians trying to preserve their way of life in the 1930s; and *The Optimist's Daughter* (1972, Pulitzer Prize), treating conflicts between the daughter and the second wife of a New Orleans judge. *One Time, One Place* (1971) collects snapshots of Mississippi taken just after the author returned home following graduation from the University of Wisconsin (1929), while *Photographs* (1990) collects pictures illustrating Welty's life and works, with much emphasis on the South during the Depression. *The Eye of the Story* (1978), essays and reviews, was followed by a volume of *Collected Stories* (1980). *The Robber Bridegroom* was made into a musical (1975) by Alfred Uhry and Robert Waldman.

WENDELL, BARRETT (1855–1921), professor of English at Harvard (1880–1917), was known both for his teaching and scholarship and as an early instructor in American literature. His works include a biography of Cotton Mather (1891), a critical study, *William Shakspere* (1894), *A Literary History of America* (1900), and *The Temper of the Seventeenth Century in English Literature* (1904).

Wept of Wish-ton-Wish, The, romance by Cooper,♦ published in 1829. In England it was titled *The Borderers* (1829) and *The Heathcotes* (1854). An anonymous dramatization was produced (1834) and published (1856).

In 1666 in the Connecticut settlement of Wish-ton-Wish the old colonist Mark Heathcote is threatened by Indian attacks, but he is aided by the advice and warnings of the mysterious stranger Submission (the regicide Goffe) and a captive Indian lad who is especially befriended by Heathcote's daughter-in-law, Ruth. The boy disappears during an attack, taking with him her small daughter, also named Ruth. The main part of the story deals with King Philip's War, ten years later. The Heathcote settlement is attacked by Indians under Metacomet (King Philip) and Conanchet (Canonchet), the latter being the former boy captive, now grown and a chief of the Narragansett. His wife, Narra-mattah, is the kidnapped Ruth, and when the Heathcotes are captured, she and Conanchet save them from execution. A few days later, Conanchet's intervention in behalf of Submission and the Heathcotes results in his capture and execution in Philip's camp, following a chase by his old enemies, the Pequot and Mohegan, under their chief, Uncas. Narra-mattah dies beside the body of her husband, and her mother dies soon afterward, "the wept of Wish-ton-Wish."

WERNER, M[ORRIS] R[OBERT] (1897–1981), journalist and author, known for his debunking studies of famous American persons and institutions: *Barnum* (1923), *Brigham Young* (1925), *Tammany Hall* (1928), *Bryan* (1929), *Little Napoleons and Dummy Directors* (1933), *Privileged Characters* (1935), about postwar graft; *It Happened in New York* (1957), sensational events of the city in the 19th century; and *Teapot Dome* (1959). *"Orderly!"* (1930) deals with his World War I experiences.

WESCOTT, GLENWAY (1901–87), Wisconsin author, known for his writings about his native region, although he had lived mainly abroad. After publishing *The Bitterns* (1920), poems, he wrote *The Apple of the Eye* (1924), a novel of the frontier West about a boy torn between the crabbed orthodoxy of his aunt, a typical pioneer woman, and the pagan acceptance of the beauty of life taught him by a friend. After *Natives of Rock* (1925), a volume of poems, and *Like a Lover* (1926), short stories, he wrote his best-known work, *The Grandmothers* (1927), published in England as *A Family Portrait*. This is the story of a pioneer Midwestern family told through the imagination of a youth, Alwyn Tower, who, having escaped to Europe from his uncongenial background, nostalgically turns the pages of a photograph album and from the faces of his ancestors reconstructs their sad, frustrated lives. *Good-Bye, Wisconsin* (1928) is a collection of short stories presenting the same dour interpretation of the Midwest. *The Pilgrim Hawk* (1940), his first work of fiction in ten years, is set in a Paris suburb during the 1920s and concerns three couples, linked by three different kinds of love. *Images of Truth* (1962) is a collection of essays about literary friends, subtitled "Remembrances and Criticism." *The Best of All Possible Worlds* (1975) contains letters and reminiscences from 1914 to 1937.

WEST, JESSAMYN (1907–84), Indiana-born author, graduate of Whittier College, had long residence in California. Her first work, *The Friendly Persuasion* (1945), gives a sense of her heritage through its tender, fictive sketches of mid-19th-century Quaker life in Indiana. Her next work, *The Witch Diggers* (1951), also set in her native state, is a symbolic novel about life on a poor farm in the 1890s and of the experiences of the superintendent's family and some inmates who dig for Truth. Other fiction includes *Cress Delahanty* (1953), charming sketches of the life of an adolescent California girl on a ranch and in town.

South of the Angels (1960) is a large and panoramic novel about settlers on a vast real-estate development near Los Angeles at the opening of the 20th century; *A Matter of Time* (1966) is a semi-autobiographical tale of a woman attending to her "young-middle-aged" sister dying of cancer; *Leafy Rivers* (1967), set on the 19th-century Ohio frontier, is a story of a young woman growing to maturity during the early years of her marriage; *Except for Me and Thee* (1969) is in spirit and subject a companion piece to *The Friendly Persuasion;* *The Massacre at Fall Creek* (1975), also set on the Indiana frontier, is a depiction of the trial of whites who murdered Indians; and *The Life I Really Lived* (1979) is about the complex loving relations and affairs of a Midwestern woman transplanted to California. Stories are collected in *Love, Death, and the Ladies' Drill Team* (1959) and *Crimson Ramblers of the World, Farewell* (1970). *Love Is Not What You Think* (1959) is an essay; *To See the Dream* (1957) treats her experiences with the filming of her first book; and *A Mirror for the Sky* (1948) is a libretto for an opera about Audubon. Autobiographies are *Hide and Seek* (1973), from childhood to young womanhood; and *The Woman Said Yes* (1976), about her own sickness, tuberculosis, and the sickness and suicide of her sister that she had fictionalized in *A Matter of Time. The Secret Look* (1974) collects poems. *Double Discovery* (1980) prints her European travel diary of 1929.

WEST, NATHANAEL (1903–40), pseudonym of Nathan Wallenstein Weinstein, New York author who, after graduation from Brown University (1924) and two years in Paris, returned to his native city to begin writing his bitter, macabre fiction, which attracted little notice in his time but great recognition from critics after his death. His first works were *The Dream Life of Balso Snell* (1931), a scatological fantasy dwelling on human corruption; *Miss Lonelyhearts*♦ (1933), a sad and bitter satire of a newspaperman enmeshed in the lives of the writers to his lovelorn column; and *A Cool Million* (1934), a fantastic travesty and savage attack on the Horatio Alger theme. Script writing in Hollywood gave West a sense of that community and business that led to his most significant novel, *The Day of the Locust*♦ (1939), a grotesque depiction in surrealist style of the sham of the city and the pathological misfits who inhabit it. West, who was S.J. Perelman's brother-in-law, was married to Eileen McKenney, the heroine of Ruth McKenney's *My Sister Eileen*.

WEST, THOMAS, see *De La Warr*.

West Point, site on the western bank of the Hudson River, 45 miles north of New York City, of the U.S. Military Academy (founded 1802). The number of the present corps of cadets is more than 4000. During the Revolution, Washington's headquarters were at West Point (1779); and the following year, when Benedict Arnold was in command there, he plotted to deliver it to André. In addition to most of the distinguished officers of the U.S. Army, students at West Point have included Poe, G.H. Derby, and Whistler.

West-Running Brook, poems by Robert Frost. ♦

Westchester Farmer, pseudonym of Samuel Seabury. ♦

WESTCOTT, EDWARD NOYES (1846–98), after a successful career as a banker in Syracuse, N.Y., wrote the posthumously published *David Harum, A Story of American Life* ♦ (1898), a popular novel built around the character of a shrewd, humorous country banker in upstate New York. A short story was posthumously published with his letters in *The Teller* (1901).

Western American Literature (1966–), quarterly journal of The Western Literature Association, published at Utah State University, prints scholarly studies, bibliographies, and reviews of all phases of the literature of the American West.

Western Messenger, *The* (1835–41), monthly religious and literary magazine, edited from Cincinnati and Louisville by W.H. Channing, assisted by J.F. Clarke (1836–39). Some attempt was made to interpret the West to the East, but the literary contributions were mainly Transcendentalist and Unitarian discussions or interpretations of German and Oriental literature, in which, as in other particulars, the *Messenger* preceded *The Dial.* ♦ Emerson contributed "Goodbye," "The Rhodora," "Each and All," and "The Humble-Bee," while Keats's "Ode to Apollo" and a part of his journal were contributed by his brother George. Other contributors included Margaret Fuller, Jones Very, Parker, C.P. Cranch, Elizabeth Peabody, and Parkman.

Westover Manuscripts, journals of William Byrd, ♦ which remained unpublished from 1728 to 1841. They contain his *History of the Dividing Line,* ♦ *Journey to the Land of Eden,* ♦ and *Progress to the Mines,* ♦ records of his frontier expeditions. The name refers to the author's estate, Westover, on the James River in Virginia.

WETHERELL, ELIZABETH, pseudonym of Susan B. Warner. ♦

WETZEL (or WEITZEL), LEWIS (1764–1808?), Indian fighter and border scout, famous as a frontier figure in West Virginia and Ohio. As a youth he was captured by Indians, and as a result became their confirmed and barbarous opponent. He figures as Timothy Weasel in Paulding's *The Dutchman's Fireside.*

WEXLEY, JOHN (1907–85), New York dramatist, whose plays include *The Last Mile* (1930),

dealing with the last days of a condemned prisoner; *Steel* (1931); *They Shall Not Die* (1934), concerned with the Scottsboro case ♦; and *Running Dogs* (1938), dealing with the struggle between Chinese conservatives and Communists prior to the Japanese invasion. *The Judgment of Julius and Ethel Rosenberg* (1955) is a work of nonfiction.

Whale, *The,* see *Moby-Dick.*

WHALEN, PHILIP (1923–), Oregon-born poet, associated with the Beat movement, ♦ later resident for some time in Japan. His avant-garde poetry, some of which has its layout and typography designed to reinforce the text, has appeared in *Self-Portrait from Another Direction* (1959), *Memoirs of an Inter-Glacial Age* (1960), *Like I Say* (1960), *Monday in the Evening* (1964), *Every Day* (1965), *Highgrade* (1966), *On Bear's Head* (1969), *The Kindness of Strangers* (1976), *Enough Said* (1980), and *Heavy Breathing* (1983). He has also written two novels: *You Didn't Even Try* (1966) and *Imaginary Speech for a Brazen Head* (1972). Interviews with him were issued as *Off the Wall* (1978).

WHALLEY, EDWARD, see *Goffe, William.*

Wharf Theatre, see *Provincetown Players.*

WHARTON, EDITH [NEWBOLD JONES] (1862–1937), member of a distinguished New York family, was privately educated in the U.S. and abroad. Her short stories, *The Greater Inclination* (1899), were followed by *The Touchstone* (1900), published in England as *A Gift from the Grave* (1900), which showed the influence of Henry James both in its form as a novelette and in its occupation with ethical values. It is concerned with a man torn between his desire to obtain money to marry the woman he loves and his reluctance to sell the love letters written to him by a celebrated woman. *The Valley of Decision* ♦ (1902), her first long novel, is notable for its depiction of an 18th-century Italian aristocrat of liberal sympathies. After another novelette, *Sanctuary* (1903), she wrote *The House of Mirth* ♦ (1905), the story of a New York girl whose attempts to make a brilliant marriage lead to ostracism because she breaks conventional standards. As in Henry James, her study of the effects of false values here rises above the level of the novel of manners to become tragedy.

In 1907 Mrs. Wharton moved to France, which she made the scene of her novelette *Madame de Treymes* (1907), contrasting French and American concepts of honor. Her next novel, *The Fruit of the Tree* (1907), set with a background of a great American woolen mill, is concerned with the inner conflict of a business executive between the demands of his work and those of the two women he loves. *Ethan Frome* ♦ (1911), a sharply etched novelette concerning simple New England people, is considered her greatest tragic story, and shows a marked departure from the ironic contemplation of aristocratic mores and highly complex characters. Yet, as in *The House of Mirth,* the central problem is that of the barriers imposed by local conventions upon an individual whose happiness depends on rising above them. From the fine simplicity of this work the author returned to complex treatments of moral and social conflicts in *The Reef* (1912) and *The Custom of the Country* (1913), stories of Americans in France. The latter is an international novel of manners, contrasting the background of an American social climber with the standards of her third husband, a French patrician. *Summer* (1917) again employs the direct realism of *Ethan Frome,* in the study of a New England girl who returns to live with a degenerate group of outlaws in order to escape the mean life of the village to which she has been taken.

During World War I, Mrs. Wharton not only gave her energy to relief work, as described in *Fighting France, from Dunkerque to Belfort* (1915), but also made the events of the time the subject of her fiction in *The Marne* (1918) and *A Son at the Front* (1923). *The Age of Innocence*♦ (1920, Pulitzer Prize), considered her most skillfully constructed work, shows the obvious influence of James in the unified view of the action as revealed through the consciousness of one character, and in the ironic handling of Victorian social standards in New York high society. After an international novel of manners, *The Glimpses of the Moon* (1922), the author returned to the American scene in *Old New York* (1924), four novelettes, *False Dawn, The Old Maid,*♦ *The Spark,* and *New Year's Day,* depicting the decades from the 1840s through the 1870s. Her next three novels deal with the relations of parents and children; they are *The Mother's Recompense*♦ (1925), *Twilight Sleep* (1927), and *The Children* (1928). *Hudson River Bracketed* (1929) is a contrast of the culture of the Middle West with that of settled New York society, and its sequel, *The Gods Arrive* (1932), carries the contrast of morals and social conventions to England and the Continent.

Although she wrote two volumes of poetry, *Artemis to Actæon* (1909) and *Twelve Poems* (1926), Mrs. Wharton's main form outside the novel was the short story. Her stories are collected in *Crucial Instances* (1901); *The Descent of Man* (1904); *The Hermit and the Wild Woman* (1908); *Tales of Men and Ghosts* (1910), cerebral ghost stories in the James manner, in which the ghosts are projections of men's mental obsessions; *Xingu and Other Stories*♦ (1916), which in brief form uses her major themes—the brittle standards of high society, the supernatural, the background of the World War, the historical study, the stunted middle-class lives in 19th-century New York; *Here and Beyond* (1926); *Certain People* (1930); *Human Nature* (1933); *The World Over* (1936); and *Ghosts* (1937).

The Writing of Fiction (1925) shows her artistic

credo to be that of James, who felt, she says, "every great novel must first of all be based on a profound sense of moral values, and then constructed with a classical unity and economy of means." She insists that the author must "bear in mind at each step that his business is not to ask what the situation would be likely to make of his characters, but what his characters, being what they are, would make of the situation. . . ." In addition to travel books, such as *Italian Backgrounds* (1905), *A Motor-Flight Through France* (1908), and *In Morocco* (1920), she wrote an autobiography, *A Backward Glance* (1934). She left an unfinished novel, *The Buccaneers* (1938), concerned with the attempt of socially unsuccessful American girls to enter English society.

WHARTON, WILLIAM (1925–), Philadelphia-born novelist of "magic realism," seen especially in *Birdy* (1979), concerning a man who studies birds in order to become one, and in the powerful novel *Dad,* (1981), wherein the title character escapes what appears to be a stable marriage by summoning up a fantasy wife and family on the Jersey shore. *A Midnight Clear* (1982) concerns soldiers in the World War II Battle of the Bulge in the Ardennes. *Scumbler* (1984) follows an American painter in Paris, and *Pride* (1985) is set in the Great Depression.

What Is Man?, essay by Clemens♦ based on his paper, "What is Happiness?," delivered before the Monday Evening Club of Hartford (Feb. 1883), rewritten (1898), privately published without the author's name (1906), and posthumously collected in *What Is Man? and Other Essays* (1917).

In this Platonic dialogue between a Young Man and a disillusioned Old Man, the mouthpiece of the author's pessimistic view of mankind, the Old Man considers human beings to be merely mechanisms, lacking free will, motivated selfishly by a need for self-approval, and completely the products of their environment. In an "Admonition to the Human Race," he pleads for the raising of ideals of conduct to a point where the individual's satisfaction will coincide with the best interests of the community.

What Maisie Knew, novel by Henry James,♦ published in 1897.

Beale and Ida Farange, an idle, spendthrift English couple, are divorced when their daughter Maisie is six. Each sues for custody of the unwanted child, and the court arranges that she shall live with them alternately for six-month periods. This serves their purpose of spite, and they earnestly indoctrinate Maisie with hateful notions of each other. First she stays with Beale, and then with her mother and a governess, attractive Miss Overmore. The governess is apparently strongly attached to her pupil, but quarrels with Ida, who discharges her in favor of Mrs. Wix, an untidy, incompetent old woman whose sentimentality and motherliness win Maisie's confidence. The child, precociously acute, has become aware of her position and knows the wisdom of silence, which is misunderstood as a symptom of stupidity. At Beale's again, she finds Miss Overmore as governess, but the young woman now neglects Maisie to busy herself in the affairs of Beale. Mrs. Wix announces the engagement of Ida to Sir Claude, with whom she says Maisie is to stay, but Miss Overmore retorts by telling of her own marriage to Beale. Maisie is now an encumbrance, and when Ida tires of Sir Claude and has a succession of lovers, he in turn falls in love with "Mrs. Beale." Mrs. Wix appeals to him to leave the "bad women" and devote himself to Maisie. The appeal is futile, though Sir Claude goes to France with Maisie, after she refuses to accompany Beale to America with his latest consort. Mrs. Wix joins them in France, informing Sir Claude that "Mrs. Beale" is now free, which causes him to hurry back to England. When he returns, he asks Maisie to give up Mrs. Wix, whom "Mrs. Beale" hates, and come to live with them. The child replies that she will give up Mrs. Wix if he will give up "Mrs. Beale." He loves Maisie, but cannot do this, and Maisie and Mrs. Wix return to England, their income assured by Sir Claude. Still a "little girl," Maisie is far beyond her years in "what she knows," for in her strange situation, aided by her sharp vision and the constant moralizing of Mrs. Wix, she has come to understand "everything."

What Makes Sammy Run?, novel by Budd Schulberg. ♦

What Price Glory?, play by Maxwell Anderson ♦ and Laurence Stallings, ♦ produced in 1924 and published in 1926.

WHEATLEY, PHILLIS (1753?–84), as a black child from Africa was purchased into slavery by a Boston merchant, John Wheatley, who with his wife treated the girl almost as a daughter and encouraged her education and poetic talent. In 1773 they even sent her to England, accompanied by their son, and there, as previously in the colonies, her deportment, intelligence, and poetry were appreciated. Her *Poems on Various Subjects, Religious and Moral* was published in London (1773) with a foreword by various distinguished Massachusetts men testifying that she indeed had the powers to write the poems signed by her, although Jefferson elsewhere declared her verse was beneath the dignity of criticism. It was conventional in the neoclassical mode of the time and concentrated on the matters cited in the book's subtitle.

WHEATON, HENRY (1785–1848), born in Rhode Island, studied law in the U.S. and abroad, and became a leading New York lawyer

and an editor of a Jeffersonian newspaper. While chargé d'affaires to Denmark (1827–35), he wrote *History of the Northmen* (1831), defending the pre-Columbian discovery of America. Holding a similar post in Berlin (1835–46), he published *Elements of International Law* (1836) and *History of the Law of Nations . . .* (1845), complementary volumes that caused him to be ranked as the outstanding American expounder and historian of international law. The former work was later edited in a notable edition by R.H. Dana, Jr.

WHEELER, EDWARD L., see *Deadwood Dick.*

WHEELOCK, ELEAZAR (1711–79), Congregational clergyman of Connecticut, became the first president of Dartmouth College (1769–79) when the institution was founded both as a classical seminary and to continue his former school for Indians (founded 1754 in Lebanon, N.H.). His *Plain and Faithful Narrative of the . . . Indian Charity-School at Lebanon* was published in 1763, with additions following until 1775.

WHEELOCK, JOHN HALL (1886–1978), New York poet, while at Harvard wrote, with Van Wyck Brooks, *Verses by Two Undergraduates* (1905). His next works, *The Human Fantasy* (1911) and *The Belovéd Adventure* (1912), are exuberant, athletic lyrics indicating the influence of Whitman and Henley. His later verse, in *Love and Liberation* (1913), *Dust and Light* (1919), *The Black Panther* (1922), *The Bright Doom* (1927), and other volumes, shows a change to philosophic poetry, tinged by ethereal mysticism, though still possessed of the same rhetorical qualities. A collection, *Poems, 1911–1936* (1936), was followed by *Poems Old and New* (1956). Later works include *The Gardener* (1961, Bollingen Prize), *Dear Men and Women* (1966), *By Daylight and In Dream* (1970), *In Love and Song* (1971), and *This Blessed Earth* (1978). His prose includes *Alan Seeger* (1918) and *What Is Poetry?* (1963). He edited the letters of Maxwell Perkins (1950).

WHEELWRIGHT, JOHN (c.1592–1679), Congregational clergyman, emigrated to New England (1636), where in the ensuing Antinomian controversy he supported the views of his sister-in-law Anne Hutchinson. ♦ He was therefore banished (1637), and became a pastor of churches outside the Massachusetts jurisdiction. His *Mercurius Americanus* (1645) was a reply to the history of the Antinomians written by Thomas Weld. ♦ He was later allowed to return to the colony and held a pastorate.

When Knighthood Was in Flower, novel by Charles Major. ♦

When Lilacs Last in the Dooryard Bloom'd, elegy on the death of Lincoln by Whitman, ♦ first published in *Sequel to Drum-Taps* (1865–66) and incorporated in *Leaves of Grass* (1867).

The poet, lamenting the death of his hero, brings a sprig of lilac for the "coffin that slowly passes . . ." and perfumes "the grave of him I love" with "the breath of my chant" and "sea-winds, blown from east and west." Held by the lilac and the drooping star in the west, representative of Lincoln the man, the poet cannot answer the "song of the bleeding throat" of the "shy and hidden" thrush until he finds consolation in the thought of immortality announced in the carol of death sung by the gray-brown bird. Hearing it "joyously sing the dead, . . . Laved in the flood of thy bliss, O death," the poet sees a vision of the late war, whose dead are at rest, and whose living alone suffer. Finally the song of the thrush arouses an echo in the poet's soul, and

> Lilac and star and bird twined with the chant of my soul,
> There in the fragrant pines and the cedars dusk and dim.

When the Frost Is on the Punkin, poem by James Whitcomb Riley. ♦

Where the Blue Begins, fantasy by Christopher Morley, ♦ published in 1922.

Whilomville Stories, 13 tales by Stephen Crane, ♦ published in 1900. Except for "The Knife," concerned with the humorous tribulations of two black men in the town of Whilomville, when both try to steal the same watermelon, the stories deal with typical childhood incidents among boys and girls of this small New York town.

"The Angel Child" tells of an ingenious birthday entertainment invented by little Cora Trescott, who treats her friends to haircuts at the shop of an unperceptive barber, to the alarm and sorrow of their parents. "Lynx-Hunting" details the adventures of three small boys with a rifle, who seek a lynx, aim at a chipmunk, and hit a farmer's cow. "The Lover and the Telltale" is concerned with the tragedy of Jimmie Trescott, who attacks his school-fellows because they have derided him for writing a love letter to his cousin Cora, and is kept after school by his teacher. "The Trial, Execution, and Burial of Homer Phelps" tells of the imaginative play of a group of boys, and the misfortunes of their unwilling victim. "A Little Pilgrimage" deals with the disastrous error of Jimmie Trescott, who leaves his Sunday school because it has been announced there will be no Christmas tree this year, only to join another that follows the same policy. "'Showin' Off'" is a humorous account of the rivalry between two youngsters for the favors of a vain little girl in a red hood.

WHIPPLE, EDWIN PERCY (1819–86), Massachusetts author and lyceum lecturer, who in his day was ranked with Poe and Lowell as an authoritative American critic. He is now best re-membered for his rather generous estimates of early American writers in *American Literature and Other Papers* (1887) and *Recollections of Eminent Men* (1887). More discriminating appraisals of foreign literature are included in *Essays and Reviews* (2 vols., 1848–49), *Lectures on Subjects Connected with Literature and Life* (1850), and *Literature of the Age of Elizabeth* (1869), collected from his addresses, lectures, and articles first published in *The North American Review* and other periodicals. *Charles Dickens, The Man and His Work* (2 vols., 1912) was posthumously published.

WHISTLER, JAMES ABBOT MCNEILL (1834–1903), born in Lowell, Mass., was reared in Russia, England, and the U.S., and attended West Point, from which he was dismissed (1854) because of failure in chemistry. "Had silicon been a gas, I would have been a major-general" was one of his later *bons mots*. In 1855 he went abroad for the remainder of his life, first to Paris, then to London in the 1860s, where he became noted for his paintings called nocturnes, harmonies, and symphonies, which rejected the illusion of the third dimension and replaced contrasting colors with tones of gray. He was also distinguished for his etchings, but it was his canvases that particularly enraged the academicians, because his art for art's sake ran counter to their vivid storytelling, as well as the Pre-Raphaelites, who emphasized meticulous detail. His *Nocturne in Black and Gold: The Falling Rocket* (exhibited, 1877) led Ruskin, the leading English art critic, to denounce him for "flinging a pot of paint in the public's face." Whistler brought suit (he was awarded a farthing but bankrupted by expenses of the trial) and with acidulous, epigrammatic humor wrote *Whistler v. Ruskin: Art and Art Critics* (1878). With a statement of his aesthetic creed, *Mr. Whistler's "Ten O'Clock"* (1888), he reprinted the earlier text and developed his views in *The Gentle Art of Making Enemies* (1890). Further statements of his views appear in *Eden versus Whistler. The Baronet and the Butterfly. A Valentine with a Verdict* (1899), an account of another lawsuit, this one pertaining to his portrait of Lady Eden. His friends Joseph and Elizabeth Pennell ♦ wrote his official *Life* (1908) and edited his *Journal* (1921).

WHITAKER, ALEXANDER (1585–1617?), Anglican clergyman, emigrated to Virginia (1611), where he resided as a minister. He is best remembered for his instruction and conversion of Pocahontas, and for his book *Good News from Virginia* (1613), a sermon which, in urging greater support from the mother country, gives a clear picture of the character and climate of the region and the native tribes.

WHITCHER, FRANCES MIRIAM (1814–52), New York author of a popular series of humorous sketches in colloquial dialect. These sketches of Yankee characters contain the first American female comic figures to be portrayed at length, and with good-natured satire depicted typical feminine foibles of the time. After publication in *Godey's Lady's Book* and other magazines, they were collected in *The Widow Bedott Papers* (1856) and *Widow Spriggins, Mary Elmer, and Other Sketches* (1867). In 1879 Petroleum V. Nasby dramatized the Widow Bedott sketches, preserving much of the original dialogue.

WHITE, ANDREW DICKSON (1832–1918), born in New York, graduated from Yale (1853), studied abroad, and became a professor of history at the University of Michigan (1857–63). As a founder of Cornell and its first president (1867–85) he made it a coeducational, nonsectarian university to "battle mercantile morality and temper military passion," emphasizing the natural sciences, agriculture, and engineering. His books include the rationalistic *History of the Warfare of Science with Theology in Christendom* (2 vols., 1896), *Seven Great Statesmen in the Warfare of Humanity with Unreason* (1910), and an *Autobiography* (2 vols., 1905).

WHITE, EDWARD LUCAS (1866–1934), Maryland author, graduate of Johns Hopkins, and classics teacher in his state's schools. His romantic novels include *El Supremo* (1916), set in 19th-century Paraguay, and *Andivius Hedulio* (1921), set in the later Roman empire.

WHITE, E[LWYN] B[ROOKS] (1899–1985), humorist and witty critical commentator on contemporary culture, was born in Mt. Vernon, N.Y., and educated at Cornell (A.B., 1921). After newspaper work he became a contributing editor of *The New Yorker,* primarily responsible for "The Talk of the Town" column, from which some of his books were drawn. From 1938 to 1943 he wrote the "One Man's Meat" department for *Harper's.* His books include *The Lady Is Cold* (1929) and *The Fox of Peapack* (1938), poems; *Alice Through the Cellophane* (1933), witty criticism of modern trends; *Every Day Is Saturday* (1934), collecting *New Yorker* editorial essays; *Quo Vadimus? or, The Case for the Bicycle* (1939), stories and sketches about complexities of urban and suburban life; *One Man's Meat* (1942, enlarged 1944), essays on conflicts in life and his solution of rural family living; *The Wild Flag* (1946), reprinting *New Yorker* editorials on world government; *Here Is New York* (1949), an impression of the city; *The Second Tree from the Corner* (1954), essays and poems; and *The Points of My Compass* (1962), further essays. *Stuart Little* (1945), a fantasy about a mouse in a human family, and *Charlotte's Web* (1952), about a girl's pets, a pig and a spider, are children's books also appreciated by adults. With Thurber he wrote the satire *Is Sex Necessary?* (1929), and with his wife Katharine he edited *A Subtreasury of American Humor* (1941). A

brilliant stylist himself, he revised *The Elements of Style* (1959), a manual by William Strunk, Jr. White's *Letters* were published in 1976, and selected *Poems and Sketches* were collected in 1981.

WHITE, JOHN (1575–1648), English Puritan clergyman, did not emigrate to the American colonies but helped found both the Dorchester Company♦ (1623) and the Massachusetts Bay Company♦ (1629). His tract *The Planters Plea* (1630) shows the economic and social value of emigration and furnishes a pleasant account of the colony's early history.

WHITE, JOHN (*fl.*1585–93), Virginia colonist, noted for his watercolors of the flora and fauna of America, and of the native Indians, published to illustrate the *Briefe and True Report of . . . Virginia* by Thomas Hariot♦ (1590). A John White, considered to be the same man, was Raleigh's governor of the Roanoke colony (1587) and Hakluyt published his account of a voyage to Virginia (1590).

WHITE, RICHARD GRANT (1821–85), New York critic, self-appointed arbiter of literature, music, and art for the city. Despite his emphasis on social distinctions and his occasional scholastic errors, he was a graceful man of letters somewhat akin to his friend C.E. Norton and obviously of Brahmin stock. In addition to his many contributions to periodicals, he was the author of *Handbook of Christian Art* (1853); *The New Gospel of Peace* (1863–66), a satire on the Copperheads♦; *Words and Their Uses* (1870); *Studies in Shakespeare* (1885); and an edition of Shakespeare republished as the *Riverside* text. His son was Stanford White (1853–1906), a distinguished architect.

WHITE, STEWART EDWARD (1873–1946), Michigan author, long resident in California, whose early experiences among rivermen, miners, and lumberjacks furnished the setting and subjects for his novels of rugged outdoor life, including *The Claim Jumpers* (1901), *The Blazed Trail* (1902), and *The Rules of the Game* (1910). His *Story of California* (1927) is a trilogy composed of three historical romances: *Gold* (1913), *The Gray Dawn* (1915), and *The Rose Dawn* (1920). Later novels include *The Long Rifle* (1932), *Ranchero* (1933), *Folded Hills* (1934), and *Stampede* (1942), set in California, and *Wild Geese Calling* (1940), about pioneer farmers in Alaska. *Anchors to Windward* (1943) and *Speaking for Myself* (1943) express his beliefs.

WHITE, THEODORE H[AROLD] (1915–86), after graduation from Harvard (1938) became chief of the China Bureau of *Time* (1939–45) and from his observations came *Thunder Out of China* (1946), written with Annalee Jacoby. Work as a European correspondent led to *Fire in the Ashes* (1953), a study of the postwar Continent. *The*

Mountain Road (1958) and The View from the Fortieth Floor (1960) are novels, respectively about World War II in China and a large New York news magazine. White was closely associated with President Kennedy and wrote The Making of the President 1960 (1961, Pulitzer Prize), a public and private view of the campaign that put Kennedy in the White House. Similar studies of "American politics in action" are made in identically titled books (1965, 1969, 1973) about succeeding presidential elections. Breach of Faith (1975) is about the downfall of Nixon, and Caesar at the Rubicon (1968) is a play about Caesar's seizure of power. In Search of History (1978) is a memoir.

WHITE, WILLIAM ALLEN (1868–1944), born in Kansas, purchased the Emporia Gazette (1895) and became a famous independent editor following publication of his editorial "What's the Matter with Kansas?" (Aug. 15, 1896), a conservative attack on the Populists, indirectly aiding McKinley's election. White was prominent in the Bull Moose party and became a leader of the Republican party. His Gazette editorials are collected in The Editor and His People (1924) and Forty Years on Main Street (1937). His many books expressing his social and political views include The Real Issue and Other Stories (1896); The Court of Boyville (1899); Stratagems and Spoils (1901); In Our Town (1906); A Certain Rich Man (1909), a novel about a corrupt small-town Kansas banker in the post-Civil War era whose conscience finally leads him to decency in finance and politics; The Old Order Changeth (1910); God's Puppets (1916); In the Heart of a Fool (1918); Masks in a Pageant (1928), A Puritan in Babylon: The Story of Calvin Coolidge (1938); and The Changing West (1939). His Autobiography (1946, Pulitzer Prize) and Selected Letters (1947) were published posthumously.

White Album, The, collection of essays by Joan Didion,♦ published in 1979. Opening with a partly autobiographical section that also provides background on persons and situations about which she wrote in the 1960s, it continues with a section of vignettes on California life, followed by one on women, and another on places the author has visited, concluding with "On the Morning After the Sixties." The title derives from an album of recordings by the Beatles; the title of one song, "Helter Skelter," was written in blood by the murderers in the La Bianca-Tate massacre, a subject symbolically cited in the book.

White Buildings, first collection of poems by Hart Crane.♦

White Fang, novel by Jack London,♦ published in 1906 as a complement to The Call of the Wild.♦

White Fang, offspring of an Indian wolf-dog and a wolf, is sold by his Indian owner to Beauty Smith, a white man who torments him to make him even more savage, in order that he may win in professional dogfights. He is rescued by a mining engineer, Weedon Scott, who subdues his ferocity by kindness. His master takes White Fang from his home in the Yukon to California, where the process of domestication is completed. There he is severely wounded while saving the Scott home from an attack by an escaped convict.

White-Jacket; or, The World in a Man-of-War, semi-autobiographical novel by Melville,♦ based on his service on the man-of-war United States (Aug. 1843–Oct. 1844), published in 1850.

The narrator, a young seaman nearing the end of a three-year cruise on the U.S. frigate Neversink, is nicknamed "White-Jacket" after he buys a white pea jacket in Callao, Peru. On the voyage around Cape Horn and up the Atlantic coast, it protects him in rough weather, distinguishes him among the crew, and nearly causes his death when it wraps about his head in a storm, so that he falls from a yardarm into the sea. There are few other catastrophes, for the interest of the tale derives not from plot but from character and observed detail. The most striking characters include Jack Chase, "our noble first captain of the top," handsome, cultured, "incomparable" young officer who wins the love and admiration of White-Jacket and all the crew; Captain Claret, "a large, portly man, a Harry the Eighth afloat, bluff and hearty"; Mr. Pert, the youthful midshipman; and Surgeon Cuticle, whose indifference to suffering and human values is shown in his unnecessary amputation of the leg of a seaman, which results in the patient's death. During the long voyage from Peru to Virginia, these officers and the diverse crew are depicted in their daily activities, including scenes of ferocious punishment for minor misdeeds, and other malpractices; and the author discusses other evils inherent in the autocratic system, the inhumane regimentation, and the degrading effects of the prevailing living conditions, partly counteracted by the exuberant joys of sea life.

White Steed of the Prairies, see Pacing Mustang.

White Wings, dramatic fantasy by Philip Barry,♦ produced in 1926 and published in 1927. An opera based on the play was written by Douglas Moore in 1935.

WHITEFIELD, GEORGE (1714–70), English evangelist, while at Oxford (1735) came under the influence of John and Charles Wesley, the founders of Methodism.♦ His histrionic ability, zeal, and belief in himself as a divinely inspired teacher made him the leader of the Methodists after the departure of the Wesleys for Georgia, and he drew large audiences throughout England. After a short stay in Georgia (May–Sept. 1738), he returned to preach in England at outdoor meetings, since the Church of England was now closed to him. He returned to America (1739) and was instrumental in promoting the Great Awakening. ♦ Although he made many enemies and was suspended from his ecclesiastical office for his irregular doctrine and actions, he nevertheless attracted such diverse adherents as the Tennents and Jonathan Edwards, and even won the financial support of Franklin. In England (1741–44) Whitefield continued his inflexible but emotional way, even breaking with the Wesleys and becoming a leader of the Calvinistic Methodists, although on his next trip to America (1744–48) many Congregationalists turned against him, the fervor of the Great Awakening having waned. He made later visits to America (1751, 1754–55, 1763–64, 1769–70), continuing to be famous for his dynamic preaching, since the manner more than the matter attracted his large audiences, and his many sermons, pamphlets, and letters, though widely read, were less effective. A selection of his *Works* was published (6 vols., 1771–72).

WHITEHEAD, ALFRED NORTH (1861–1947), English philosopher and mathematician, was a leading author and educator in his native country, and a professor of philosophy at Harvard (1924–36). He developed a philosophy of "organism," based on modern scientific knowledge but essentially idealistic, conceiving a universal, impersonal deity as the source of all existence, and religious experience as the unifying and supremely rational path to knowledge. Objects in nature are then viewed as organically interrelated and engaged in a constant process of evolutionary change which is divinely ordered. Written in occasionally highly technical language, his principal works include *Principia Mathematica* (3 vols., 1910–13), written with Bertrand Russell; *The Organisation of Thought* (1916); *Enquiry Concerning . . . Natural Knowledge* (1919); *The Concept of Nature* (1920); *The Principle of Relativity* (1922); *Science and the Modern World* (1925); *Religion in the Making* (1926); *Symbolism: Its Meaning and Effect* (1927); *The Aims of Education* (1929); *Process and Reality* (1929); *The Function of Reason* (1929); *Adventures of Ideas* (1933); *Nature and Life* (1934); and *Modes of Thought* (1938), the last being a summary introduction to his philosophy. *Essays in Science and Philosophy* (1947) includes autobiographical material.

WHITLOCK, BRAND (1869–1934), Ohio journalist and lawyer, after serving as a liberal reform mayor of Toledo (1905–13) was appointed minister (later ambassador) to Belgium (1913–22). During the war he distinguished himself as a humanitarian worker, both in behalf of such individuals as Edith Cavell and in relief administra-

tion. His liberal interests are shown in novels that belong to the nascent period of realism, mainly set in the town of Macochee, whose original was his home, Urbana, Ohio. These include *The 13th District* (1902), an objective depiction of the corruption of American politics and the inevitable moral disintegration of those concerned in it; *Her Infinite Variety* (1904), a light account of the embroilments of suffragettes in politics; *The Happy Average* (1904), a semi-autobiographical novel; *The Turn of the Balance* (1907), a realistic story of the relation of criminals to modern society, and a humanitarian plea for social and prison reform; *J. Hardin & Son* (1923), a character study of the contrasts between two generations; *Uprooted* (1926) and *Transplanted* (1927), novels contrasting American and continental standards; and *Big Matt* (1928), a character study of a typical machine politician. In addition to his autobiography, *Forty Years of It* (1910), Whitlock wrote *Belgium: A Personal Narrative* (1919), books on contemporary politics, and biographies.

WHITMAN, ALBERY ALLSON (1851–1901), black poet and clergyman, whose poems *Not a Man and Yet a Man* (1877), *The Rape of Florida* (1884), reprinted as *Twasinta's Seminoles* (1885), and *An Idyl of the South* (1901) are narratives dealing with blacks and Indians.

WHITMAN, MARCUS (1802–47), Oregon pioneer, born in New York, was sent by the American Board of Commissioners for Foreign Missions (Presbyterian) as a physician and missionary to the Indians of the Pacific Northwest (1835), and settled near the site of the present Walla Walla, Wash. (1836). Conflicts with other denominations led him to make an arduous seven months' horseback trip east (1842–43) to strengthen his missionary position, and not, as is often claimed, to "save Oregon" for the U.S. He returned (1843) with a great company of emigrants, whose actions and introduction of an epidemic turned the Indians against Whitman and caused an uprising in which he and his wife were murdered. This tragedy and the Indian war that ensued may have hastened the passage of the Oregon Territory law. Whitman wrote many pamphlets and newspaper articles pointing out the resources of the Territory. He and his wife are the subjects of Honoré Morrow's novel *We Must March* (1925).

WHITMAN, SARAH HELEN [POWER] (1803–78), Rhode Island poet, after the death of her husband became engaged to Poe (*c.*1848). Several of her poems concern him and more bear the obvious influence of his style. Some of her verse is collected in *Hours of Life* (1853), and a complete edition appeared posthumously (1879). She defended Poe against Griswold and others in *Edgar Poe and His Critics* (1860). The second of Poe's poems entitled "To Helen" was addressed to her, and his *Last Letters* to her were published in 1909.

WHITMAN, WALT[ER] (1819–92), was born on Long Island, of English, Dutch, and Welsh stock. His family lived in Brooklyn (*c.*1823–33), where Walt was educated, and he later served as printer's devil, journeyman compositor, and itinerant schoolteacher, besides editing the *Long Islander* (1838–39). Meanwhile he was reading the Bible, Shakespeare, Ossian, Scott, Homer, and something of the Greek and Hindu poets, the Nibelungenlied, and Dante, all of which, either in rhythm or thought, influenced his later writing. He entered politics as a Democrat, and after 1841 was actively associated with at least ten newspapers and magazines in New York and Brooklyn. Such poems as he published were conventional and mediocre, and to the *Democratic Review* (1841–45) he contributed many thin, sentimental, melancholy stories. These early writings were gathered in *The Uncollected Poetry and Prose of Walt Whitman* (2 vols., 1921) and *The Half-Breed and Other Stories* (1927). At this time he also wrote a temperance tract, *Franklin Evans; or, The Inebriate: A Tale of the Times* (1842). He became editor of *The Brooklyn Eagle*♦ (1846), a Democratic party paper in which he denounced the "mad fanaticism" of the Abolitionists, but so obviously favored the Free-Soil party that he was discharged (1848). His writings for this paper have been collected as *The Gathering of the Forces* (2 vols., 1920).

In February 1848 he went to New Orleans with his brother Jeff, who with George was the most intimate with him among his nine brothers and sisters. He was an editor of the New Orleans *Crescent* for three months, during which many biographers have contended he had a love affair with an octoroon, which was the chief force in altering his character. Such assertions are primarily based on interpretations of "Once I Pass'd Through a Populous City,"♦ which is probably more literary than biographical. Whitman's later statement to J.A. Symonds and others that he was the father of illegitimate children is probably one of the legends with which he liked to endow himself.

Returning to Brooklyn, he came by way of St. Louis, Chicago, and upstate New York, for the first time seeing something of the frontier that so strongly affected his philosophy, as in such poems as "Pioneers! O Pioneers!"♦ and "The Song of the Broad Axe."♦ He edited various papers, including the Brooklyn *Times,* from which his contributions have been collected in *I Sit and Look Out* (1932). Meanwhile, as before, he was acquainted with the varying aspects of the metropolis, listening to the oratory of the time, becoming intimate with omnibus drivers and ferryboat pilots, joining the crowds at bathing beaches, and hearing Shakespeare and Italian opera, all of which had an effect on the themes and manner of his poetry. Although he had earlier affected the mien of a dandy, he now dressed as a "rough," and his actions and ideas were leading toward the climax of 1855. Just as it has been supposed that he underwent a transformation in New Orleans, it is thought that he passed through some mystical experience at this time. It is probably more realistic to suppose that *Leaves of Grass* grew out of a slow and conscious effort to employ his experiences and his own maturity. Although he consistently celebrated himself as an average man, he was probably feeling his unique qualities more definitely than ever. Divided between faith in democratic equality and belief in the individual rebel against society's restrictions, he combined the figure of the average man and the superman in his conception of himself. He certainly differed in the hypersensitivity that made him as zealous in pursuing emotional freedom through love as he had been in pursuing social freedom through democracy. He differed also in his frequent, forceful declarations of his democratic love for man, and he has been considered a homosexual.

Such abnormal sensitivity and extreme sensuousness appear to be primary forces in his poetry. Other influences included Goethe's autobiography, which showed him a man surveying the universe in terms of himself; Hegel's philosophy, which supplied the idea of a cosmic consciousness evolving through conflict and contradiction toward a definite objective; and Carlyle's *Heroes and Hero Worship,* which suggested that a superior individual is a power above man-made laws. Above all literary influences was that of the Transcendentalists, particularly Emerson, from whom he learned that the individual was not merely an eccentric but an impersonal seer at one with Nature, perceiving what is permanent in flux and revealing its development. He was affected by the typical interest of his period in science, although he considered it cold and intellectual as compared with faith in a divine purpose. He was also concerned with such pseudosciences as phrenology, adopting its specialized terms for his poetry, though his unique use of words comes from sources as widely separated as George Sand and the American Indian.

The first 12 poems written under these many influences were collected, with a critical preface, as *Leaves of Grass*♦ (1855). Although Whitman uncritically accepted many divergent philosophies and seems at first to have been unconscious of any unifying purpose in *Leaves,* he eventually worked out the belief that it was to show how man might achieve for himself the greatest possible freedom within the limits of natural law, for the mind and body through democracy, for the heart through love, and for the soul through religion. Although his ideas of prosody were also refined later, he already illustrated his belief in a simple style devoid of the ordinary usages of rhyme, meter, or ornament, and distinguished by a natural organic growth, with each part in proportion with the whole. He himself compared his poetry with the "liquid, billowy waves," and some of its most distinctive features are the use of repetition, parallelism, rhetorical mannerisms, and the employment of the phrase instead of the foot as a unit of rhythm, to create forms later called free verse.

Except for his own anonymous and enthusiastic reviews, *Leaves* received comparatively little attention, though Emerson wrote a letter of high praise. Whitman published an enlarged second edition (1856), and during the following years, continuing his writing, became prominent among the bohemian frequenters of Pfaff's Cellar.♦ The 1860 edition of *Leaves of Grass* for the first time found a regular publisher, and was greatly enlarged, containing two new sections, "Children of Adam"♦ and "Calamus."♦

The poet was not intimately affected by the Civil War until late in 1862, when he went to Virginia to see his wounded brother George, and then to Washington to become an unofficial nurse to Northern and Southern soldiers in the army hospitals. He left a record of this period in his prose *Memoranda During the War* (1875), reprinted in *Specimen Days and Collect*♦ (1882), and in the poems published in *Drum-Taps*♦ (1865) and *Sequel to Drum-Taps* (1865–66), containing his dirges for Lincoln, "When Lilacs Last in the Dooryard Bloom'd"♦ and "O Captain! My Captain!"♦ Nominally a Republican at this time, he became a clerk in the Indian Bureau of the Department of the Interior, but was shortly dismissed by the Secretary, on the ground that *Leaves of Grass* was an immoral book. Whitman was defended by his friends, William O'Connor, who wrote *The Good Gray Poet* (1866), and John Burroughs, who with Whitman's assistance published *Notes on Walt Whitman as Poet and Person* (1867). During these years, Whitman issued two new editions of *Leaves of Grass* (1867, 1871); *Democratic Vistas*♦ (1871), a prose work; and *Passage to India*♦ (1871), embodying the concept of the regeneration of the human race through uniting the spiritual wisdom of the East with the materialism of the West.

His Washington residence ended (1873) when he suffered a paralytic stroke, possibly induced by an infection during his hospital work. From this time his writing shows a change of thought. His realistic style becomes one of indirection and suggestion, his materialistic pantheism a more spiritualized idealism, his political views change from individualism to nationalism, and even internationalism, and in general he is less interested in freedom than in regulation. During his last 19 years he lived at Camden, N.J., continuing to revise *Leaves of Grass* and to publish new editions. *Two Rivulets*♦ (1876) incorporated *Democratic Vistas* and some new poems. His newspaper poems were collected as *November Boughs* (1888), incorporated in the *Leaves* (1889), and contain the preface "A Backward Glance o'er Travel'd Roads."♦ *Good-Bye, My Fancy* (1891) is a final collection of poems and prose.

Although not previously neglected, he was particularly in the public eye during the 1870s, when such English writers as William Rossetti, Swinburne, Symonds, Anne Gilchrist, and Stevenson contended that Americans did not fully appreciate him. He also had a circle of immediate disciples, including the Canadian physician Richard M. Bucke,♦ whose official biography (1883) was partly written by Whitman, and Horace Traubel, an enthusiastic young Boswell who preserved every scrap of the poet's conversation in his book *With Walt Whitman in Camden* (3 vols., 1906–14; 3 vols., 1953, 1963, 1982).

During the final years, the poet mellowed, and was content to live quietly at Camden, except for a brief trip to Colorado (1879) for his health, to Canada (1880) to visit Dr. Bucke, and to Boston (1881), where he visited Emerson, for whom he still felt a strong sympathy, although he had long since set himself up as an original genius owing no debt to his onetime master. His executors published a standard edition of his *Complete Writings* (10 vols., 1902), but a scholarly edition of *The Collected Writings of Walt Whitman,* begun in 1961 and projected for 18 volumes, is more complete, including correspondence and all minor writing.

WHITTEMORE, [Edward] Reed [II] (1919–), after graduation from Yale (1941) and service in the air force during World War II began his academic career as a professor of English at Carleton College in Minnesota (1947–67) and his literary career as a poet whose lyrics, often witty and light, appear in *Heroes and Heroines* (1946); *An American Takes a Walk* (1956); *The Self-Made Man* (1959); *The Boy from Iowa: Poems and Essays* (1962); *The Fascination of the Abomination* (1963), a collection of poems, stories, and essays; *Poems, New and Selected* (1967); *From Zero to the Absolute* (1967); *50 Poems 50* (1970); and *The Mother's Breast and the Father's House* (1974). *William Carlos Williams* (1975) is a critical biography, and *The Poet as Journalist* (1976) collects essays and reviews from *The New Republic.* He has written two books on biography with examples from Plutarch to Leon Edel in *Pure Lives* (1988) and *Whole Lives* (1989). He was co-editor of the little magazine *Furioso* (1939–53) and a professor at the University of Maryland (1968–81).

WHITTIER, John Greenleaf (1807–92), Massachusetts poet, born of Quaker stock, had little formal education but found his most important intellectual influences in his religion and in the books he read as a boy, especially Burns, whose poetry led him to see the romance underlying the everyday rural life of New England. His earliest poems were published in Garrison's newspaper, and similar country journals, and through the aid of Garrison he was given an editorial position on a Boston paper (1829), soon followed by similar work on country newspapers. His first book, *Legends of New-England in Prose* *and Verse* (1831), shows his interest in local historical themes, as does his pamphlet *Moll Pitcher* (1832), on Molly Pitcher, and *Mogg Megone* (1836), a narrative of Indian life in colonial times.

Through the influence of Garrison and his own Quaker conscience, Whittier was now deflected from his original purpose of interpreting the American background to ally his writing with activities in the cause of social justice. As he says, he "left the Muses' haunt to turn the crank of an opinion mill" (*c.*1833–59), becoming an ardent Abolitionist. He was elected to the Massachusetts legislature (1835), spoke at antislavery meetings, edited *The Pennsylvania Freeman* (1838–40) of Benjamin Lundy,♦ and wrote tracts and the verse collected in *Poems Written During the Progress of the Abolition Question* (1838). Disliking the methods of Garrison, Whittier became a founder of the Liberty party, for which he also edited newspapers. He published *Lays of My Home and Other Poems* (1843), and his antislavery verse was collected in *Voices of Freedom* (1846), which included "Massachusetts to Virginia."♦

As an editor of the *National Era* (1847–60), he contributed to this paper most of the poems and articles which he wrote, and though he continued his antislavery work he had not forgotten his earlier interests, as may be seen in *Leaves from Margaret Smith's Journal in the Province of Massachusetts Bay, 1678–79* (1849). This, his only long work of fiction, is based on records of the period of the Salem witchcraft trials, and is a semi-fictional romance uncovering the mind of Puritan New England in the manner of Hawthorne, steering a middle course between vilification and praise. Other prose works collected from this paper were *Old Portraits and Modern Sketches* (1850) and *Literary Recreations and Miscellanies* (1854). That his humanitarian interests were still predominant may be seen in "Proem" in his first collected *Poems* (1849), in which he says that though he cannot equal "the old melodious lays" of Spenser and Sidney, he can atone for his artistic limitations by "a hate of tyranny intense" and a sympathy for his "brother's pain and sorrow." This creed can be seen in his *Songs of Labor*♦ (1850).

Whittier continued also to write on antislavery matters during the eventful years prior to and during the Civil War, on subjects ranging from the Kansas-Nebraska bill and Webster's defection in "Ichabod"♦ to the 13th Amendment in "Laus Deo!"♦ (1865). Meanwhile his reputation as a pure poet of the countryside was increased with *The Chapel of the Hermits* (1853); *The Panorama and Other Poems* (1856), containing "Maud Muller"♦ and "The Barefoot Boy"♦; and *Home Ballads, Poems and Lyrics* (1860), containing "Skipper Ireson's Ride"♦ and "Telling the Bees."♦ Another volume of verse, dealing with contemporary matters, was published as *In War Time and Other Poems* (1864), which included "Barbara Frietchie."♦

After the Civil War, Whittier returned to his poetic interest in the New England scene to write his winter idyll *Snow-Bound*♦ (1866), which is considered his greatest work. This was followed by *The Tent on the Beach* (1867), a cycle of verse narratives in the manner of Longfellow's *Tales of a Wayside Inn,* but also containing his poem "The Eternal Goodness," which praises the "pitying love" of God and sets forth the poet's "fixed trust" in "His goodness and His love." Other volumes of this period, showing his recaptured interest in rural life and colonial history, include *Among the Hills* (1869), *Miriam and Other Poems* (1871), *Hazel-Blossoms* (1875), *The Vision of Echard* (1878), *St. Gregory's Guest* (1886), and *At Sundown* (1890). Many of his poems have been set to music as hymns. In addition, he edited or contributed introductions to many other people's works, of which the best known is his sympathetic edition of Woolman's *Journal* (1871). Whittier's *Letters* was published in three volumes (1975).

Whittier's work, which falls roughly into three periods, has been variously estimated at different times. The poems written up to 1833, in which he is a romantic follower of Burns, are youthful works that he himself attempted to suppress. The poems from 1833 to 1859 present him as a militant Quaker, with liberal political and humanitarian beliefs, and have been most appreciated in recent years. The poems from 1859 to his death show him both as a poet of nature and of homely incidents, rising to his loftiest in *Snow-Bound,* and as a thinker assured of a comprehensive religious faith that led him to become devoted to religious tolerance, humanism, and democratic justice. Whittier has consistently been praised for his ballads and such long narratives as *Snow-Bound.* Many of his poems suffer from either sentimentality or lack of technical ability, and even his best works are not altogether free from faults. Much of his poetry, which is still widely read for its simple sentiment or moral beauty, is marred by flaccidity, diffuseness, undue affection for preaching, and lack of discipline. He properly estimated one of his technical faults by saying he wrote "good Yankee rhymes, but out of New England they would be cashiered." Both his virtues and his vices probably derive from the fact that he was a man of conscience rather than of intellect, and lacked the power to discriminate between his poems of force and spontaneity and his inferior verse.

Who's Afraid of Virginia Woolf?, play by Edward Albee,♦ produced in 1962.

Martha, the middle-aged daughter of the president of a small New England college, and her husband George, an unsuccessful professor in its History Department, entertain a new faculty member, Nick, and his wife Honey in an evening of drunken antagonism, much of it devoted to Martha's game "Humiliate the Host." George and Martha's elliptical references to their 21-year-old son and other revelations lead Nick to confide that he married Honey only because she said she was pregnant. As the evening goes on, Honey gets sick, George wanders off, and Nick tries to sleep with Martha but is impotent. Through all the wild affairs it becomes clear that the older couple invented the story that they have a child and the younger couple's marriage is also sterile because Honey fears childbirth. The entire night is an intense exposure of sadism and masochism, aggression and fearfulness, expressed in an orgy of emotions.

Who's Who in America, biographical dictionary of notable living men and women of the U.S., revised and reissued biennially. It was founded in 1900 by A.N. Marquis.

WIDDEMER, MARGARET (1884–1978), Pennsylvania poet whose first book, *The Factories with Other Lyrics* (1915), contains poems passionately championing the rights of oppressed workers. *Old Road to Paradise* (1918, special Pulitzer award) contains softer and more sentimental verse, as does *Ballads and Lyrics* (1925). *The Singing Wood* (1926) is a verse play, and *A Tree with a Bird in It* (1923) is a volume of satirical verse. *The Dark Cavalier* (1958) collects her poems. Miss Widdemer's works also include many novels, on both contemporary issues and historical subjects, and short stories. Her memoirs appear as *Golden Friends I Had* (1964).

WIDEMAN, JOHN EDGAR (1941–), born in Washington, D.C., grew up in the Homewood black ghetto of Pittsburgh, a place from which he draws much of his material. A basketball star recruited by the University of Pennsylvania, he did well at the sport, but aware he could not make the NBA, he accepted a Rhodes Scholarship and earned a degree in 18th-century English literature. He was successful with his first novel, *A Glance Away* (1967), about a day in the life of a drug addict. The novels that followed, *Hurry Home* (1970), *The Lynchers* (1973), *Hiding Place* (1981), and *Sent for You Yesterday* (1983), the last selected for the 1984 PEN/Faulkner Award, all describe experiences of black urban life. *Damballah* (1981) collects short stories. *Brothers and Keepers* (1984) is a memoir. Since 1975 Wideman has been a professor of English at the University of Wyoming.

Widow Bedott, pseudonym of Frances Whitcher.♦

Widow Douglas, character in *Tom Sawyer*♦ and *Huckleberry Finn.*♦

Widow's Son, The; or, Which Is the Traitor?, domestic tragedy by Samuel Woodworth,♦ produced and published in 1825.

William Darby, falsely accused of being a Tory during the Revolutionary War, revenges himself on the patriots by actual treachery as a British spy. His mother, Margaret, chagrined by her son's treason, offers her services to Washington as a spy. Although her work is so successful as to undo that of her son, who is executed by the British, she is content with the knowledge that she has worked for the good of her country and saved him from dishonorable execution by his own countrymen.

Wieland; or, The Transformation, epistolary Gothic romance by C.B. Brown, ♦ published in 1798.

The elder Wieland, a German mystic, emigrates to Pennsylvania, erects a mysterious temple on his estate, and dies there one night by spontaneous combustion. His wife dies soon afterward, and their children, Clara and the younger Wieland, depend for friendship on Catharine Pleyel. Wieland marries Catharine, and Clara falls in love with Henry Pleyel, who is engaged to a woman in Germany. Into their happy circle enters a mysterious vagabond, Carwin (see *Memoirs of Carwin*), and at the same time comes the first of a series of warnings from unearthly voices. Henry falls in love with Clara after one of these disembodied voices announces the death of his German fiancée. When circumstances force him to believe that Clara and Carwin have had an affair, Pleyel deserts her, discovers his former fiancée to be alive, and marries her. Wieland, inheriting his father's fanaticism, is driven mad by the voices, and murders his wife and children. Carwin then confesses to Clara that a "mischievous daemon" led him to test the family courage, producing the mysterious voices by ventriloquism. Wieland, escaping from an asylum, is about to murder his sister when Carwin for the last time uses ventriloquism to command Wieland to desist. The unhappy madman commits suicide, Carwin departs to a remote district of Pennsylvania, and Clara marries Pleyel after the death of his first wife.

WIENERS, JOHN (1934–), Boston-born poet, attended Black Mountain College, where he was influenced by Olson and Robert Duncan, and of which he wrote *A Memory* (1969). In San Francisco (1957–60) during the period of the Beat movement,♦ he came to prominence with his locally issued *The Hotel Wentley Poems* (1958), eight poems related to experiences of that year, presenting with deep emotion a world of outcasts, particularly dope addicts and homosexuals. In addition to many broadsides and leaflets, he has published *Nerves* (1970) and *Selected Poems* (1971), the latter revised and reissued in 1987. His plays, including *Jive Shoelaces and Anklesox* (1967), have been produced in little theaters.

WIGGIN, KATE DOUGLAS (1856–1923), born in Philadelphia, studied under Emma Marwedel, and moved to San Francisco to conduct one of the first kindergartens in the U.S. (1878–84). She wrote novels for adults, and an autobiography, *My Garden of Memory* (1923), but is best known as a successful author of children's books. The most famous of these are *The Birds' Christmas Carol* (1887), telling of the life and death of an ethereal child, Carol Bird; *Rebecca of Sunnybrook Farm* ♦ (1903), about a lovable, precocious little girl; and *Mother Carey's Chickens* (1911), dramatized with Rachel Crothers (1917), the story of a kindly widow and her many children.

WIGGLESWORTH, MICHAEL (1631–1705), brought from England as a child (1638), graduated from Harvard (1651) and during most of his life served as minister of the Congregational church at Malden, Mass. After 1663 he also practiced medicine. He is remembered for his long theological poem in ballad meter *The Day of Doom* ♦ (1662). His other poetical works, also theological treatises in rhyme, include "A Short Discourse on Eternity," "Vanity of Vanities," and "A Postscript unto the Reader," all annexed to this book. Other versified theology of a similarly edifying nature includes *Meat Out of the Eater* (1670) and "God's Controversy with New-England," inspired by the drought of 1662, and first published by the Massachusetts Historical Society (1873).

EDWARD WIGGLESWORTH (c.1693–1765), his son, graduated from Harvard (1710) and became a Congregational minister and professor of divinity at Harvard (1722–65). He was noted as a pamphleteer and stout defender of orthodoxy against the evangelicalism of George Whitefield.

Wigwam and Cabin, 13 stories by Simms, ♦ published in 1845–46. They deal with the backwoods, the Revolution, Indian lore, and the supernatural.

WILBARGER, JOHN WESLEY (*fl.*1839–89), Texas pioneer whose *Indian Depredations in Texas* (1889) is an important source concerning the early settlement of the region by Americans, based on stories told by surviving pioneers.

WILBUR, RICHARD [PURDY] (1921–), after graduation from Amherst (1942) and an M.A. from Harvard (1947) began his teaching career at Harvard (1950–54), continued as a professor at Wesleyan (1955–), and commenced his career as a poet with the mature and polished lyrics of *The Beautiful Changes* (1947). His cultivated and formal poetry, although influenced by the French Symbolists, Marianne Moore, and Wallace Stevens, among others, is highly original in the classic, urbane, often witty, and always intellectual works collected in *Ceremony* (1950), *A Bestiary* (1955), *Things of This World* (1956), *Poems* (1957, Pulitzer Prize), *Advice to a Prophet* (1961), *Walking to Sleep* (1969), *The Mind-Reader* (1976), *Seven Poems* (1981), and *New and Collected Poems* (1988),

awarded another Pulitzer Prize. *Responses* (1976) collects essays on poetry and other literary subjects. He translated Molière's *Misanthrope* (1955), *Tartuffe* (1963), and *The Learned Ladies* (1978) into English verse, and collaborated with Lillian Hellman on the comic opera *Candide* (1957), based on Voltaire's work, for which he also wrote the lyrics. He turned to French tragedy in a verse translation of Racine's *Andromache* (1982). He has also published *The Whale and Other Uncollected Translations* (1983) and written *Opposites* (1973) and other poems for children. In 1987 Wilbur was named Poet Laureate of the U.S. for the year.

WILCOX, CARLOS (1794–1827), born in New Hampshire, lived in Connecticut, where he was a Congregational pastor during the two years prior to his early death. His *Remains* (1828), which reprints his sermons and the long didactic poem "The Age of Benevolence," in the school of Young and Cowper, has received attention from scholars for its distinguished nature poetry.

WILCOX, ELLA WHEELER (1850–1919), Wisconsin poetaster, whose first book, *Drops of Water* (1872), a collection of temperance verse, was followed by nearly 40 volumes of romantic, unctuous verse in the "Oh God, the pain" school, distinguished by a sentimental approach to spiritualistic, metaphysical, and pseudo-erotic subjects. Her popular reputation was ensured when *Poems of Passion* (1883) was rejected for "immorality." Her platitudes also found expression in many short stories, sketches, and novels. *The Story of a Literary Career* (1905) and *The Worlds and I* (1918) are autobiographical works. Her most famous lines are from her poem "Solitude":

> Laugh, and the world laughs with you;
>   weep, and you weep alone.

Wild Honey Suckle, The, poem by Freneau, ♦ published in his *Poems* (1786). In six-line tetrameter stanzas, this brief work, considered one of the author's finest nature poems, celebrates the beauty of the frail forest flower.

WILDE, RICHARD HENRY (1789–1847), Irish-born poet, lawyer, and at various times congressman from Georgia (1815–35). Part of his projected epic on the Seminole War, "The Lament of the Captive," was published without his knowledge (1819), and stirred a tempest of speculation, being variously claimed as the work of another or as a translation from Alcaeus. Anthony Barclay, English consul at Savannah, circulated a translation into Greek, which he later published in an *Authentic Account of Wilde's Alleged Plagiarism* (1871). The poem was enthusiastically praised, and set to music by Lanier and others as "My Life Is Like the Summer Rose." In Italy (1835–40) he wrote romantic *Conjectures . . . Concerning . . . Tasso* (2 vols., 1842). While in New Orleans (1843–47) he was a professor of constitutional law and wrote *Hesperia* (1867), a long poem in Tom Moore's vein. His lyric poems are uncollected.

WILDER, Laura Ingalls (1867–1957), author of popular children's books about life in her native frontier Wisconsin, including *Little House in the Big Woods* (1932) and *Little House on the Prairie* (1935).

WILDER, Thornton [Niven] (1897–1975), born in Wisconsin, was reared in China and the U.S., and after graduation from Yale (1920) became a teacher at the Lawrenceville School (1921–28) and a professor of English at the University of Chicago (1930–36). His first book, *The Cabala* (1926), is a gracefully written and deftly ironic novel, concerning the sophisticated but decaying Italian nobility of the post-World War I period. After producing *The Trumpet Shall Sound* (1926) at a little theater, he suddenly achieved wide popularity with *The Bridge of San Luis Rey*♦ (1927, Pulitzer Prize), a delicately ironic study of the way Providence has directed disparate lives to one end. His next novels are *The Woman of Andros* (1930), an urbane treatment of human relations and ethical values in its story of a Greek concubine, based on Terence's Latin comedy *Andrea; Heaven's My Destination* (1935), an amused, ironic portrait of an evangelically religious American salesman; and *The Ides of March* (1948), divergent views of Caesar's last months seen through letters and documents.

Having published collections of one-act plays, *The Angel That Troubled the Waters* (1928) and *The Long Christmas Dinner* (1931), and made adaptations, Wilder came to his full development as a playwright with *Our Town*♦ (1938, Pulitzer Prize), depicting the qualities of small-town New England life. Later plays include *The Merchant of Yonkers* (1938), a comedy revised as *The Matchmaker* (1954), and by others made into the musical comedy *Hello, Dolly!* (1963); *The Skin of Our Teeth*♦ (1942, Pulitzer Prize), said to have been inspired by Joyce's *Finnegans Wake; A Life in the Sun* (London, 1955), based on Euripides' *Alcestis* and produced in dramatic (1960) and operatic (1962) versions as *The Alcestiad* in German and finally published in its English text in the U.S. in 1977; and *Plays for Bleecker Street* (1962), three unpublished one-act plays, part of a projected 14-play cycle on the Seven Ages of Man and the Seven Deadly Sins.

Wilder returned to the novel with *The Eighth Day* (1967, National Book Award), a chronicle of two early 20th-century Midwestern families and their involvement in a murder case raising serious questions about human nature; and *Theophilus North* (1973), portraying the good deeds of the title character, a tutor in Newport, R.I., during the 1920s, whose various saintly actions are presented in closely related short stories, by turns comic, sentimental, serious, and optimistic. Wil-

der's essays were posthumously collected as *American Characteristics* (1979). He was the first person to be awarded a National Medal for Literature (1965).

Wilderness Road, pioneer route, known also as Boone's Trace, blazed by Daniel Boone (1775) from eastern Virginia through the Cumberland Gap to Kentucky, and used by many frontier settlers in the first great westward migration. The region forms the setting of Churchill's *The Crossing* and E.M. Roberts's *The Great Meadow.*

WILKINS, Mary E., see *Freeman, Mary Wilkins.*

Will To Believe, *The, and Other Essays in Popular Philosophy,* ten essays by William James♦ collected with a preface in 1896. The ideas of the title piece are amplified in such essays as "Is Life Worth Living?," "The Sentiment of Rationality," "Reflex Action and Theism," and "The Dilemma of Determinism," while other essays treat other ethical and moral problems.

"The Will To Believe" begins by defining "hypothesis" and "option," and stating the basic principles that "As a rule we disbelieve all facts and theories for which we have no use" and that "Our nonintellectual nature does influence our convictions." The author summarizes his thesis: "Our passional nature not only lawfully may, but must, decide an option between propositions, whenever it is a genuine option that cannot by its nature be decided on intellectual grounds. . . ." He shows the distinction between an empiricist and an absolutist belief in truth, and defines his own position as empirical, but points out that "The greatest empiricists among us are only empiricists on reflection: when left to their instincts, they dogmatize like infallible popes." Pyrrhonistic skepticism would condemn this absolutism of instinct, but James argues for its acceptance. "In our dealings with objective nature we . . . are recorders, not makers, of the truth . . . ," but in regard to the solution of moral questions "faith in a fact can help create the fact." Therefore, even in the absence of factual evidence, we have the right to accept idealistic beliefs which lead to action for desirable ends. This is not an argument for an indiscriminate embracing of faiths, and "the freedom to believe can only cover living options which the intellect of the individual cannot by itself resolve." Finally, the author applies his thesis to the question of religious belief, foreshadowing his attitude in *The Varieties of Religious Experience,*♦ and concludes: "Indeed we *may* wait if we will [for evidential confirmation] . . . but if we do so, we do so at our peril as much as if we believed. In either case we *act,* taking our life in our hands. . . ."

WILLARD, Emma [Hart] (1787–1870), pioneer in women's education, at Middlebury, Vt.

(1814), opened her Female Seminary to teach such subjects as mathematics, philosophy, history, and the sciences, which had been previously closed to women. Her *Address . . . Proposing a Plan for Improving Female Education* (1819), sent to Governor Clinton of New York, attracted attention that led to her founding another seminary in Troy (1821), which offered the equivalent of a college education for women, 16 years before Mount Holyoke, the first women's college, was founded. In addition to works on female education and texts for her school, she published a volume of mediocre verse, *The Fulfillment of a Promise* (1831), still remembered for "Rocked in the Cradle of the Deep," which became extremely popular in its musical setting by the English composer Joseph P. Knight.

WILLARD, FRANCES E[LIZABETH] (1839–98), born in New York, was first known for her teaching and other work in behalf of women's education in Illinois, serving as president of the Evanston College for Ladies (1871–74). She became a leader of the temperance movement, and from 1879 was president of the Women's Christian Temperance Union. She was one of the organizers of the Prohibition party. Her books include *Woman and Temperance* (1883) and *Glimpses of Fifty Years* (1889).

WILLARD, JOSIAH FLINT (1869–1907), nephew of Frances E. Willard, tired of settled life as an Illinois college student and took to the road as a vagrant, although other experiences included study of political science at the University of Berlin, life in literary London as a friend of Arthur Symons, laboring on Tolstoy's Russian estate, and work for a railroad that needed advice on eliminating tramps. From these experiences came his books written under the pseudonym Josiah Flynt: *Tramping with Tramps* (1899); *Notes of an Itinerant Policeman* (1900); *The World of Graft* (1901); a novel, *The Little Brother: A Story of Tramp Life* (1902); and an autobiography, *My Life* (1908).

WILLARD, SAMUEL (1640–1707), Congregational clergyman, graduated from Harvard (1659), preached in western Massachusetts, and became pastor of the Old South Church (1678–1707), where he established himself as an influence second only to Increase Mather. His many sermons, precisely expounding orthodox theology, condemning those of different faiths, and questioning the court judgment in the Salem witchcraft trials, were collected in *Compleat Body of Divinity* (1726), the largest volume ever published by a colonial press. His orthodoxy and sound scholarship led to his being made vice-president of Harvard (1700–1707), of which he was nominally president for six years while Increase Mather was at odds with the colonial government. An elegy on Willard was written by Benjamin Colman.

William Wilson, story by Poe,♦ published in 1839 and collected in *Tales of the Grotesque and Arabesque* (1840). The description of school life in England is partly autobiographical.

The central figure is a willful, passionate youth, who at Dr. Bransby's boarding school leads all his companions except one, a boy of his own age and appearance who bears the same name of William Wilson. This double maintains an easy superiority, which frightens Wilson, and haunts him by constant patronage and protection, noticed only by Wilson himself, whose sense of persecution increases until he flees from the school. He goes to Eton and Oxford, and then travels about Europe, following a career of extravagant indulgence, and becoming degenerate and vicious. At critical times his double invariably appears to warn him or destroy his power over others. Finally at Rome, when the double appears to prevent his planned seduction of the Duchess Di Broglio, Wilson is infuriated, engages the other in a sword fight, and murders him. As the double lies dying, he tells Wilson: "You have conquered . . . Yet henceforward art thou also dead. . . . In me didst thou exist—and, in my death, see by this image, which is thine own, how utterly thou hast murdered thyself."

WILLIAMS, BEN AMES (1889–1953), born in Mississippi, graduated from Dartmouth (1910) and became a journalist in Boston until he published his first novel, *All the Brothers Were Valiant* (1919). Of his many popular novels, several are detective stories such as *The Silver Forest* (1926), *The Dreadful Night* (1928), and *Money Musk* (1932). *Evered* (1921), *Audacity* (1924), and *Immortal Longings* (1927) are concerned with Maine life; *Black Pawl* (1922), *Touchstone* (1930), *Honeyflow* (1932), *Leave Her to Heaven* (1944), and *It's a Free Country* (1945) are character studies; *Splendor* (1927) deals with newspapermen; *Great Oaks* (1930), *Come Spring* (1940), and *Time of Peace* (1942) are panoramas of American life; *House Divided* (1947) is a long novel about the Civil War; and *The Unconquered* (1953) deals with interracial strife in post-Civil War New Orleans. *Thrifty Stock* (1923) and other books collect his popular stories. He edited (1949) the *Diary* of life during the Confederacy by Mary Boykin Chesnut.♦

WILLIAMS, JOHN (1664–1729), after graduation from Harvard (1683) became pastor of the Congregational church at Deerfield in western Massachusetts, where during the French and Indian Wars he and his entire family were captured by Indians. His account of his two-year captivity and his resistance to Jesuit attempts to convert him, written with Cotton Mather, was published as *The Redeemed Captive, Returning to Zion* (1707).

WILLIAMS, JOHN (1761–1818), better known by his pseudonym Anthony Pasquin, after a career as a scurrilous satirist and critic in England found it necessary to emigrate to America (c.1797), where he continued his vitriolic writings on literary and political matters in various newspapers. His best-known American work, the *Hamiltoniad* (1804?), is a vicious verse satire of the Federalists. His language was so outrageous that it drove Macaulay to call him a "polecat" and "malignant and filthy baboon."

WILLIAMS, JOHN A[LFRED] (1925–), Mississippi-born author, reared in Syracuse, N.Y., from whose university he graduated after naval service in World War II. His novels include *The Angry Ones* (1960), a bitter book about Greenwich Village and the world of black musicians; *Night Song* (1961); *Sissie* (1963), presenting the sad life of an old black woman; *The Man Who Cried I Am* (1967), the autobiographical recollections of a dying black author in the U.S. and Europe; *Sons of Darkness, Sons of Light* (1969), depicting racial conflict in New York City; *Captain Blackman* (1972), about a black soldier wounded in the Vietnam War and the similarity of his experiences to those of blacks in earlier wars; *Mothersill and the Foxes* (1975), depicting a black man's experiences with love and sex; *The Junior Bachelor Society* (1976), about nine middle-aged black men who grew up together and meet again after long separation; *! Click Song* (1982), treating the difficulties a black man has in trying to become a successful novelist; *The Berhama Account* (1985), treating events on a Caribbean island; and *Jacob's Ladder* (1987), concerning a black U.S. military attaché trapped in a West African nation. Williams's other writings include poems; a biography of Martin Luther King, Jr., *The King God Didn't Save* (1970); a biography of Richard Wright, *The Most Native of Sons* (1970); and *This Is My Country Too* (1965), about his experiences as a black man traveling in the U.S.

WILLIAMS, ROGER (c.1603–83), born in London, early became the protégé of the great lawyer Sir Edward Coke, and was educated at Cambridge and destined for the law. After receiving his B.A. (1627), he determined to become a minister, and by 1629 had taken orders in the Anglican Church. He became increasingly influenced by the Puritans, though he soon went beyond their beliefs. Arriving in Massachusetts (1631), he refused a call from a Boston church because it was not Separatist and after a brief period at the more liberal Plymouth he went to Salem as a minister, holding democratic views of church government even beyond those of Separatists. ♦

He became anathema to the Massachusetts theocracy because of his "leveler" principles, ♦ based on the ideals of the New Testament and representing the incarnation of Protestant individualism, as well as for his political views, which caused him to attack the royal charter as an imperialistic expropriation of Indian rights. His extremely democratic church at Salem so disturbed

the hegemony that the General Court banished him (1635), and, "sorely tossed for one fourteen weeks, in a bitter winter season, not knowing what bread or bed did mean," he made his way to Rhode Island to found its earliest settlement at Providence (1636). Carrying out his democratic principles, he entered upon his apostolic labors among the Indians, living with them "in their filthy smoky holes . . . to gain their tongue," which efforts resulted in *A Key into the Language of America* (1643).

Meanwhile he became a Baptist for a few months (1639), then a Seeker, believing in the fundamentals of Christianity but in no creed, and espousing a mysticism that held to an indwelling God of love. His colony of those who had followed him from Salem was based on the compact theory which held that government is a man-made institution resting on the consent and equality of its subjects: church and state were separate, family heads had a voice in government, and all shared equally in a land association.

Opposition from the encircling New England Confederation and antagonisms among his own individualistic settlers posed problems that led him to go to England (1643), where through the aid of his friend Sir Henry Vane he got a charter for the "Providence Plantations" ♦ (1644). While abroad he became an intimate of Milton and Cromwell, taking part in the Revolution. To current arguments on church government he added *Queries of Highest Consideration* (1644), addressed to both houses of Parliament as objection to the establishment of a national church. He also composed an answer to a letter written six years before by John Cotton, which had justified Williams's banishment, and published the reply as *Mr. Cotton's Letter Lately Printed, Examined and Answered* (1644). This statement of his side of the controversy, with the representation of his own view that "persecutors of men's bodies seldom or never do these men's souls good," was followed by a more famous controversy with Cotton. Challenging the views of the Massachusetts hierarchy, and pleading for a complete religious and political liberty, he published his most celebrated work, *The Bloudy Tenent of Persecution* ♦ (1644).

Returning to his colony in the autumn of the same year, he found that William Coddington had usurped leadership, and opposed both Williams's democracy and his desire to unite the various Rhode Island settlements. After a temporary settlement, Williams again went to England (1651), where he succeeded in overthrowing his rival. While there, he wrote *The Bloudy Tenent Yet More Bloudy . . .* (1652) in reply to Cotton's *The Bloudy Tenent Washed and Made White in the Bloud of the Lamb* (1647). Williams returned to become president of his colony (1654) and obtained a new charter (1663). Illustrating his belief in complete toleration, he admitted both Jews and Quakers, but nevertheless soon found himself involved in a dispute with the latter group.

With great vituperation he attacked the followers of the English Quaker, Fox (1672), and published *George Fox Digg'd out of his Burrowes* (1676). Although this and other controversies embittered his last years, as did the necessity to take part with the other colonies in King Philip's War (1675–76) against the Indians, whom he had so long befriended, he continued to the end of his life to be a democratic leader, in both religious and temporal affairs. In addition to lesser writings such as *Christenings Make Not Christians* (1645) and *The Hireling Ministry None of Christs* (1652), various fugitive materials have been gathered in *Letters and Papers of Roger Williams* (1924).

WILLIAMS, TENNESSEE (THOMAS LANIER WILLIAMS) (1911–83), born in Mississippi and reared there and in St. Louis, began his career as a dramatist with *American Blues* (1939, published 1948), one-act plays, and *Battle of Angels* (1940, published 1945), revised as *Orpheus Descending* (1957). He first achieved success with *The Glass Menagerie*♦ (1944), a play of sentiment and pathos about a frustrated mother, who is a victim of fantasies, and her withdrawn daughter. It not only is his most tender story but also is rather autobiographical.

After publishing a collection of 11 one-act plays, *27 Wagons Full of Cotton* (1946), he adapted, with Donald Windham, a D.H. Lawrence story as *You Touched Me!* (1947), and then wrote his next important play, *A Streetcar Named Desire*♦ (1947), set in a New Orleans slum and bringing into violent contrast a neurotic woman's dreamworld and the animalistic realism of her brother-in-law. *Summer and Smoke* (1948), another study of sexual maladjustment, revised as *The Eccentricities of a Nightingale* (1964), was followed by a comedy of sex, *The Rose Tattoo* (1950), set in a Gulf Coast town and treating a perfervid Sicilian woman's eager quest for love. In *I Rise in Flame, Cried the Phoenix* (1951) he further revealed the influence of D.H. Lawrence, about whose death the play revolves. This was followed by his fantasy play *Camino Real* (1953) and *Cat on a Hot Tin Roof*♦ (1955, Pulitzer Prize), depicting bitter, abnormal family tensions in a struggle for control of a plantation.

These plays reveal the darkest side of life in Gothic situations and settings, but Williams's characters live by experiencing a full emotional involvement in life rather than shrinking from or denying it, despite the terrible violence they encounter. In his depiction of horror he went on to create other treatments of evil in *Suddenly Last Summer* (1958), produced with *Something Unspoken* (1958) as *Garden District,* and telling of the egocentric, sadistic, homosexual son of a doting mother who is killed and eaten by cannibal natives on a savage island; *Sweet Bird of Youth* (1959), about an aging movie star whose kept young man is castrated by the father of the girl he deserted; *Triple Play* (1959); *Period of Adjustment*

(1960), a "serious comedy"; and *The Night of the Iguana* (1962), adapted from an earlier short story, presenting diverse characters in a mean Mexican hotel who, like its chained iguana, are balked and imprisoned.

Later plays include *Slapstick Tragedy* (1965), composed of two short works, *The Mutilated* and *The Gnaidige Fräulein; Kingdom of Earth* (1968), acted in abbreviated form as *The Seven Descents of Myrtle,* presenting relations among a dying transvestite, his sluttish bride, and his brother; *In the Bar of a Tokyo Hotel* (1969), a bitter characterization of a painter; *Small Craft Warnings* (1972), portraying a group of "castoffs" gathered at a California coastside bar; and *Outcry* (1973), a slightly altered version of *The Two-Character Play* (1969), presenting two actors, a brother and sister, deserted by their company and trying to sort out the relations between life and art.

Nondramatic works include *The Roman Spring of Mrs. Stone* (1950), a novelette about an aging actress and her sordid last affair with a gigolo; *One Arm* (1948, revised 1954), *Hard Candy* (1954), and *Eight Mortal Ladies Possessed* (1974), stories; *The Knightly Quest* (1966), a Gothic science fiction novella and four stories; *Moise and the World of Reason* (1975), a novel about a homosexual writer recalling his childhood and his search for love; *In the Winter of Cities* (1956) and *Androgyne, Mon Amour* (1977), collections of poems; and *Memoirs* (1975), reminiscences and discussion of the creation of his plays. Williams's letters to Donald Windham were published by the recipient in 1977. *Baby Doll* (1956) is a film script Williams created from two of his one-act plays.

WILLIAMS, WILLIAM CARLOS (1883–1963), born in Rutherford, N.J., his lifelong home, where he practiced medicine as a pediatrician. While studying at the University of Pennsylvania Medical School he became a friend of Pound and of H.D. and shared their subscription to the tenets of Imagism,♦ as is evident in his first books, *Poems* (1909) and *The Tempers* (1913), and, to some extent, in all the writing of his long career. However, the limited nature of Imagism was extended in *Al Que Quiere!* (1917), the prose poems of *Kora in Hell* (1920), *Sour Grapes* (1921), and *Spring and All* (1922) to Expressionism,♦ characterized by a clean stripping of poetry to essentials, by a holding of emotion at arm's length, and by vivid observations, restricted almost entirely to sensory experience. Williams declared that his poetry belonged to the school of Objectivism,♦ whose publications, like his *Collected Poems, 1921–1931* (1934), were issued from the short-lived Objectivist Press. In its defense, Williams said: "Imagism . . . though it had been useful in ridding the field of verbiage, had no formal necessity implicit in it" and so "it had dribbled off into so-called 'free verse' . . . but, we argued, the poem . . . is an object . . . that in itself formally presents its case and its meaning by the very form it assumes . . . this was what we wished to imply by Objectivism."

In this vein his poetry was continued in *An Early Martyr* (1935), *Adam & Eve & The City* (1936), *The Complete Collected Poems . . . 1906–1938* (1938), *The Broken Span* (1941), *The Wedge* (1944), *The Desert Music* (1954), *Journey to Love* (1955), and *Pictures from Brueghel* (1963, Pulitzer Prize). Marked by vernacular American speech and direct observation, his poetry has the character, he declared, that one finds "as a physician works upon a patient, upon the thing before him, in the particular to discover the universal." *Paterson*♦ (5 vols., 1946–58) is a long, structureless poem, including much quoted prose, relating to the history, formal and informal, the surroundings, and the appearance of a New Jersey city and about one human figure, partly autobiographical, partly mythic.

His prose includes *The Great American Novel* (1923), impressionistic essays; *In the American Grain*♦ (1925), more impressionistic essays, on discoverers of the New World from Eric the Red to Lincoln, bodying forth American values; and *Selected Essays* (1954). He wrote plays collected in *Many Loves* (1961); stories collected in *The Knife of the Times* (1932), *Life Along the Passaic River* (1938), *Make Light of It* (1950), and *The Farmers' Daughters* (1961); and four novels: *A Voyage to Pagany* (1928), autobiographical fiction about a small-town American doctor in Europe; and a trilogy, *White Mule* (1937), about immigrants adjusting to the U.S.; *In the Money* (1940), continuing the chronicle of a middle-class family and its young children; and *The Build-Up* (1952), carrying the story along in its New Jersey setting from 1900 to World War I. He published an *Autobiography* (1951), *Selected Letters* (1957), and *Yes, Mrs. Williams* (1960), a memoir of his mother. This material was increased by his correspondence with James Laughlin, his publisher, in 1989.

WILLIAMSON, MICHAEL, see *Maharidge, Dale.*

WILLINGHAM, CALDER [BAYNARD, JR.] (1922–95), Georgia-born novelist whose works include *End as a Man* (1947), a satirical view of a Southern military academy like the one the author attended; *Geraldine Bradshaw* (1950) and *Reach to the Stars* (1951), both views of life as seen by hotel bellboys; *Natural Child* (1952); *To Eat a Peach* (1955); *Eternal Fire* (1963); *Providence Island* (1969); *Rambling Rose* (1972); and *The Big Nickel* (1975). He adapted his first novel as a play (1953), and he wrote several successful film scenarios. *The Gates of Hell* (1951) collects stories.

WILLIS, N[ATHANIEL] P[ARKER] (1806–67), born in Maine and reared in Boston, while at Yale published blank-verse paraphrases of Biblical themes, for which he was hailed as a leading U.S. poet. His collection of verse *Sketches* was published the year of his graduation (1827). After a brief employment by S.G. Goodrich, he founded the *American Monthly Magazine*♦ (1829–31), a literary journal in which he published some of his best stories and sketches, later frequently reprinted. Although the magazine lasted only two years, and Willis was less than 25, he was established as the most worldly and fluent of American editors. His representation of himself as an aesthete led Holmes to say "He was something between a remembrance of Count D'Orsay and an anticipation of Oscar Wilde." After publishing two more books of poems, Willis became associated with G.P. Morris as a sort of foreign correspondent on social affairs for the *New-York Mirror.*♦ He traveled on the Continent, in England, and through Turkey and Asia Minor (1832–36), writing letters about his acquaintanceships, which were collected in *Pencillings by the Way* (3 vols., London, 1835; Philadelphia, 1836; complete edition, New York, 1844) and *Loiterings of Travel* (3 vols., 1840). In England, where he was popular but irritated some of the stouter minds, he published *Melanie and Other Poems* (1835), and a series of sketches under the pseudonym Philip Slingsby, collected in *Inklings of Adventure* (1836). Returning to the U.S., he wrote such romantic tragedies as *Bianca Visconti*♦ (1837) and *Tortesa the Usurer*♦ (1839), as well as helping to edit the *Mirror* and writing American sketches for it, which were collected in *A l'Abri: or, The Tent Pitch'd* (1839) and *American Scenery* (2 vols., 1840). As a coeditor of the *Mirror* he engaged his friend Poe to be literary critic. Meanwhile he published society verse and *Dashes at Life with a Free Pencil* (1845), short stories whose surprise endings foreshadow those of O. Henry. In addition to magazine contributions and collections of letters concerning two trips to Europe and one to the West Indies, Willis published his only novel, *Paul Fane* (1857), the story of a young painter adored by women as a celebrity but disdained as a social inferior. He reissued his earlier books under new titles, collected short stories in such volumes as *Life, Here and There* (1850), engaged in further editorial work, and was noted as a host at his celebrated country residence on the Hudson.

WILLIS, SARA PAYSON (1811–72), sister of N.P. Willis, was a popular author under the pseudonym Fanny Fern. Her first book, *Fern Leaves from Fanny's Portfolio* (1853), became popular for its sharp, playful sketches. This was followed by several similar works, continuing her style of feminine wit plus bloodcurdling melodrama and touchingly tender tales. Her brother's reputation as a rake so infuriated her that she wrote *Ruth Hall* (1855), a scurrilous fictional satire. For many years she was a columnist for the *New York Ledger*. She married James Parton in 1856.

WILSON, ALEXANDER (1766–1813), Scottish-born ornithologist, emigrated to the U.S. (1794) and was urged by William Bartram to begin the scientific investigation which culminated in *American Ornithology* (9 vols., 1808–14), dealing with the eastern part of the U.S. north of Florida. The work is considered both accurate and brilliant, and, preceding Audubon by some 20 years, was the pioneer study in its field. His nature poems, published in *The Foresters* (1805) and *Poems: Chiefly in the Scottish Dialect . . .* (1816), are less important.

WILSON, AUGUST (1945–), born and raised in Pittsburgh by a poor family, although he said, "My generation of blacks knew very little about the past of our parents." He dropped out of school at 16 and, in addition to working at menial jobs, wrote poems and plays. His plays included *Ma Rainey's Black Bottom* (1984), in which a blues singer and others suffer racist treatment. It was followed by *Fences* (1985)—like its predecessor published a year after production—about the troubles of two generations of black athletes, and *Joe Turner's Come and Gone* (1986), concerning an ex-convict's troubles. *Fences* was awarded a Pulitzer Prize, as was his later play, *The Piano Lesson,* first produced in 1987, dealing with a dispute between a brother and sister over a handsome piano they have inherited: he wants to sell it and buy some land on which his family lived as slaves and she wants to retain it as an elegant souvenir of those ancestors.

WILSON, EDMUND (1895–1972), born in New Jersey, graduated from Princeton (1916), after service abroad during World War I began the writing career that made him a leading man of letters in various genres, best known as a literary critic. He long held several journalistic posts, including managing editor of *Vanity Fair* (1920–21), associate editor of *The New Republic* (1926–31), and book reviewer for *The New Yorker* (1944–48), but he always kept himself independent of organizations in pursuing his own varied interests that led to his many diverse books.

His works of nonfiction begin with *Axel's Castle*◆ (1931), a study of Symbolist literature, and during the succeeding 16 years include *The American Jitters: A Year of the Slump* (1932) and *Travels in Two Democracies* (1936), social reporting from a Marxist point of view, the latter concerning Russia and the U.S., combined in *The American Earthquake* (1958); *The Triple Thinkers* (1938, revised and enlarged 1948) and *The Wound and the Bow* (1941), essays on literature ranging from analyses of particular authors—Hemingway, James, Edith Wharton—to Freudian literary theory and the relationship of Marxism and historical interpretation to literature; *To The Finland Station*◆ (1940), tracing European revolutionary traditions from Michelet to Lenin to Trotsky; *The Boys in the Back Room* (1941), notes on modern California authors; *The Shock of Recognition* (1943), an anthology of American writers' critical views of one another, from the mid-19th century on; and *Europe Without Baedeker* (1947, revised 1966), travel sketches. From his journal publications during these years he collected *Classics and Commercials* (1950), articles and reviews about the 1940s; *The Shores of Light* (1952), a comparable anthology of his writings of the 1920s and 1930s; and *The Bit Between My Teeth* (1965), a similar literary chronicle of the 1950s and '60s. During the 1950s and 1960s he published *The Scrolls from the Dead Sea* (1955), revised and extended on new findings as *The Dead Sea Scrolls, 1947–1969* (1969); *Red, Black, Blond and Olive* (1956), studies in four civilizations: Zuñi, Haitian, Russian, and Israeli; *A Piece of My Mind* (1956), "reflections at sixty" in the form of essays on diverse and important topics; *Apologies to the Iroquois* (1960), on the history and present status of the Indian Confederacy; *Patriotic Gore*◆ (1962), substantial "studies in the literature of the American Civil War"; *The Cold War and the Income Tax* (1963), on his difficulties with, and objections to, federal taxation; and *O Canada* (1965), on Canadian culture. In the last year of his life and following his death there appeared *A Window on Russia* (1972), essays on Russian literature and language; *The Devils and Canon Barham* (1973), literary essays; and *The Twenties* (1975), from his notebooks of the time, a compilation completed by Leon Edel.

Wilson published his verse in *The Undertaker's Garland* (1922), a collaboration with John Peale Bishop; *Poets, Farewell!* (1929); *Note-Books of Night* (1942), which, like the others, contains some prose; and *Night Thoughts* (1961), collecting from the two previous books. Wilson's fiction is printed in *I Thought of Daisy* (1929, revised 1967), a novel about bohemian literary New York, and *Memoirs of Hecate County* (1946), stories about the lives of wealthy New York suburban intelligentsia. His plays are *Discordant Encounters* (1926), dialogues and short dramas; *This Room and This Gin and These Sandwiches* (1937), three "experimental" plays; *The Little Blue Light* (1950); *Five Plays* (1954), adding one work to the two previous books; and *The Duke of Palermo* (1969).

A Prelude (1967) draws on journals (1908–19) to portray his early life; *Upstate* (1971) contains recollections (1950–70) of his life in the family house of northern New York, where he summered. Correspondence is gathered in *Letters on Literature and Politics* (1977) and *The Nabokov-Wilson Letters* (1979). *The Sixties: The Last Journal, 1960–1972* (1993) ends the day before his death.

WILSON, HARRIET (1808–c.1870), wrote the first novel by an African-American published in the U.S.: *Our Nig: Sketches from the Life of a Free Black, in a Two-Story White House, North, Showing That Slavery's Shadows Fall Even There* (1859). Frado, a mulatto abandoned by her white mother, suffers continual abuse in the family she is hired to—a family who espouse abolitionism. Thus Northern economic racism is exposed, for Frado is in effect "commodified."

WILSON, HARRY LEON (1867–1939), was an editor of the humorous weekly *Puck* (1896–1902), after which he began writing fiction. His novels include *The Spenders* (1902), contrasting a pioneer of the Far West and his grandchildren, effete Easterners; *The Lions of the Lord* (1903), on the great Mormon trek to Utah under Brigham Young; *Bunker Bean* (1913), about a timorous man who suddenly asserts himself; *Ruggles of Red Gap* (1915), the story of a British valet employed in a Far Western cattle town; and *Merton of the Movies* (1922), about a movie-struck clerk who achieves success because he unconsciously burlesques serious roles. *Merton* was dramatized (1922) by Marc Connelly and George S. Kaufman, and Wilson collaborated with Tarkington in writing *The Man from Home* (1907) and other plays. After 1912 Wilson, who was born in Illinois, lived in Carmel, California.

WILSON, JAMES (1742–98), Scottish-born jurist and political figure, emigrated to America (1765) and early entered the Revolutionary movement. His *Considerations on the Nature and Extent of the Legislative Authority of the British Parliament* (1774) contended that Parliament had no authority over the colonies, since they were separate states connected only by a common sovereign. Wilson was a delegate to the Continental Congress, a signer of the Declaration of Independence, and a member of the Federal Constitutional Convention, where he worked for a strong national government. He later became conservative and framed a reactionary constitution for Pennsylvania. He was a justice of the U.S. Supreme Court (1789–98) and a professor of law at the College of Philadelphia. His *Works* was published in three volumes (1804).

WILSON, JOHN (*c.*1591–1667), English-born Congregational minister, emigrated to Boston (1630), where he was also known as a versifier. His longest published work, *A Song or, Story, for the Lasting Remembrance of Divers Famous Works* (1626), reissued as *A Song of Deliverance* (1680), in rough ballad meter, was written to teach children how nobly God had shaped English history under Protestant rule. "Memoria Wilsoniana" (1685), a biography by Cotton Mather, was republished in Mather's *Magnalia*.

WILSON, LANFORD (1937–), Missouri-born playwright, reared by his mother in the Ozarks and then in the Midwest until, as a teenager, he went to southern California to be with his long-divorced father. Wilson's dramatic career began at Caffe Cino, a small off-off-Broadway coffeehouse in Greenwich Village. His one-act plays produced there include *So Long at the Fair* (1963);

Home Free (1964), about the incestuous love of a brother and sister; and *The Madness of Lady Bright* (1964), presenting a pathetic, aging, flamboyant homosexual. These were followed by a move to off-Broadway with the full-length plays *Balm in Gilead* (1964), a view of life in an all-night New York diner; and *The Rimers of Eldritch* (1965), depicting blighted lives in a Midwestern ghost town. *This Is the Rill Speaking* (1965) is a happier nostalgic view of life in an Ozarks village. Wilson's plays moved to Broadway and other major producing centers with *The Gingham Dog* (1968), treating the breakup of the marriage of a liberal white architect and his young black wife; *Lemon Sky* (1970), about a young boy leaving his divorced mother to live in California with his father and finding that no better as he is falsely accused of homosexuality; and *Serenading Louie* (1970), presenting the deteriorating lives of two couples, which had seemed so bright in college days. Wilson joined the Circle Repertory Company (founded 1969), a small off-Broadway team of actors, playwrights, and designers, for which he wrote one-act plays and longer works. *The Hot l Baltimore* (1973), set in a derelict hotel whose sign has even lost a letter, is peopled in its last days by pathetic outcasts who still live on wistful hopes. *The Mound Builders* (1975) contrasts views of the earth, and thus metaphorically of life, by archaeologists digging an ancient Indian site in the Midwest and the realtor who hopes to develop it. *5th of July* (1978) views the disintegration of radicals and flower children of the 1960s as they live into a new decade. The parents of some of these characters are presented in *Talley's Folly* (1979, Pulitzer Prize), treating the romance of an unlikely couple, a shy Missouri village girl and an older, Jewish accountant from a big city. *A Tale Told* (1981) is a third view of the Talley family, set in 1944 at the same time as the preceding play's depiction of the romance between Matt Friedman and Sally Talley. *Angels Fall* (1982) brings together at an isolated mission in New Mexico a disparate group of people stranded because of an accident at a nearby uranium mine. They are a jolly priest, an insecure New England college professor of art history and his wife, the widow of a local painter and her lover, a professional tennis player, and an educated Indian of the region, and all reveal themselves through their plotless relationships. Wilson has also written an adaptation for the screen (1970) of Tennessee Williams's story "One Arm"; a television play, *The Migrants* (1974), with him; and the libretto for an operatic version (1971) of his *Summer and Smoke*.

Windy McPherson's Son, novel by Sherwood Anderson. ♦

Winesburg, Ohio, 23 stories by Sherwood Anderson, ♦ published in 1919. The preface, "The Book of the Grotesque," explains the author's unifying conception of his characters: "It was the truths that made the people grotesques. . . . The moment one of the people took one of the truths to himself, called it his truth, and tried to live his life by it, he became a grotesque and the truth he embraced became a falsehood." In a simple and intense style these psychological portraits of the sensitive and imaginative of Winesburg's population are seen through the eyes of a young reporter, George Willard.

"Hands" is the story of Wing Biddlebaum, who has an innocent passion for caressing living things and is driven from the town because of this misunderstood eccentricity. "Queer" tells of Elmer Cowley, who has grown up on a farm, and is lonely and frustrated in Winesburg, until, obsessed by the idea that he is considered "queer," he runs away to begin life anew. "Godliness" is a long tale concerned with Jesse Bentley, who prays for a David to help him despoil his Philistine neighbors of their farms and is himself nearly slain by a stone from the sling of the young David, his grandson. "The Strength of God" tells of the religious Rev. Curtis Hartman, who is obsessed with sexual desire until his "cure" after an intense inner struggle, in which he believes that "God has manifested himself to me in the body of a woman."

Wing-and-Wing, romance by Cooper,♦ published in 1842.

On the island of Elba, at the height of the Napoleonic empire, lives Ghita Caraccioli, granddaughter of the Neapolitan admiral and beloved of the French privateer Raoul Yverne. Raoul's ship is the *Wing-and-Wing,* a lugger carrying British colors but actually preying on British shipping. The romantic privateer visits Ghita, who refuses to marry him unless he becomes a Catholic and gives up his occupation. He is nearly trapped by the arrival of an English frigate, the *Proserpine,* but with the aid of his lieutenant, Ithuel Bolt, a Yankee soldier of fortune, he manages to reach his ship. The *Proserpine* pursues the *Wing-and-Wing* for several exciting days, but by his daring and superior seamanship the privateer escapes. The notorious execution of Admiral Caraccioli by order of Lord Nelson takes place at Naples, and Ghita, present for a last interview with her grandfather, is joined by Raoul in disguise. Attempting to take her and her uncle to their home, Raoul and Ithuel are apprehended. Ithuel is released on the condition that he serve again in the British navy, but Raoul is sentenced to death. A delay is granted, for the unjust Caraccioli execution has had an unfortunate effect on the people, and Ithuel and Ghita help Raoul to escape. They regain the *Wing-and-Wing,* but the ship is soon wrecked on a dangerous reef. The British attack, and Raoul is fatally wounded, but Ithuel helps Ghita to escape.

Wingless Victory, *The,* play by Maxwell Anderson. ♦

Wings of the Dove, *The,* novel by Henry James, ♦ published in 1902. The novel formed the basis for an opera of this title (1961) by Douglas Moore.

Kate Croy, daughter of an impoverished English social adventurer, is in love with Merton Densher, a London journalist, and they become secretly engaged, although she will not marry him while he is without wealth. While Densher is in America on business, Kate's shrewd, worldly aunt Mrs. Lowder has as guests the Americans Mrs. Stringham and her wealthy protégée, Milly Theale. The latter, an unselfish, poetically lovely girl suffering from a mysterious illness, confides in Kate, who in turn tells everything of herself except her affair with Densher, who has previously been acquainted with Milly, deeply attracting her by his charm and honesty. Sir Luke Strett, a celebrated surgeon, reveals to Mrs. Stringham that Milly's only possibility of postponing her approaching death is to be as happy and cheerful as possible. Kate, learning of this, devises a scheme that she thinks will solve the problems of all. Densher returns to London, and Kate encourages Milly's interest in him, believing that her marriage to the journalist will contribute to her happiness, while, following the girl's imminent death, Densher will inherit her fortune and be able to marry Kate. She simply tells him to be kind to Milly, and, carried away by his love and faith in her ability to manage affairs, he obeys. Milly, who thinks that Densher has been rejected by Kate, is ecstatically happy for a time. In the autumn they all meet at Venice, where Milly arouses the resentment of Lord Mark, a British fortune-seeker, by refusing his proposal of marriage. Kate exposes her entire scheme to her lover, who weakly consents to go through with it if she will give herself to him at once. She fulfills her part of the bargain and returns to London. Lord Mark, who knows the relations of Kate and Densher, vents his spite by divulging the plot to Milly, and the dying girl, deprived of hope, quickly declines. Mrs. Stringham asks Densher to save Milly by telling her he is not engaged to Kate, but this he will not do. He returns to London, and after Milly's death receives a large legacy. He offers to marry Kate if she will consent to destroy the check, and she replies that she will if he can swear that he is "not in love with her memory." He cannot, for, as Kate realizes, they are now separated by the barriers of Densher's conscience and their tragic memories.

Winner Take Nothing, 14 stories by Hemingway, ♦ published in 1933.

"The Light of the World," set in a small town in the Middle West, has for its chief character a fat, blonde prostitute, who recalls nostalgically the prizefighter who furnished the one rudimentary romantic episode of her life. "A Clean, Well-Lighted Place" ♦ portrays the desolate lives of a waiter and a customer of a Spanish café. "The Sea

Change" tells of the tragic separation of a young couple, when the girl drifts into a homosexual relation with another woman. "A Way You'll Never Be" describes the hysterical reaction of a young American officer in the Italian army, when he is relieved from active duty and thus has time to become aware of the significance of the war. "Homage to Switzerland" contains three vignettes of fatuous middle-class American tourists in Europe. "A Natural History of the Dead" is a bitter satire on the results of modern warfare. "The Gambler, the Nun, and the Radio" is concerned with two hospital patients, a Mexican gambler and an author, and the way in which the writer cynically plays upon the phrase "the opium of the people."

Winning of Barbara Worth, The, novel by Harold Bell Wright.♦

Winning of the West, The, historical study by Theodore Roosevelt,♦ published in four volumes (1889–96). It deals with the settlement of the Northwest Territory following the Revolutionary War, and specifically with the events leading up to the Ordinance of 1787, which established the conditions of expansion and the development of political and social institutions in the U.S. beyond the Ohio. The work used original sources and influenced later histories in reconsidering the significance of this period, but is generally considered to follow Parkman in its romantic portrayal of heroic events and emphasis on literary qualities rather than scholarship.

WINSLOW, EDWARD (1595–1655), English-born Puritan, came to America on the *Mayflower. Mourt's Relation♦* (1622), concerning this voyage and the earliest days of the Plymouth Colony, is considered to be based on his journal and that of William Bradford. When Winslow returned to England (1623–24) as agent of the Colony, he published *Good News from New England* (1624), a continuation of his previous narrative to September 1623. The graphic account ends with a warning "to discourage such as with too great lightness undertake" the business of colonization. On his return, he took a leading part in the Colony's affairs, serving three times as governor (1633, 1636, 1644), and was continuously assistant until 1647. On a journey to England (1634) he was briefly imprisoned for his religious beliefs. He went to England again (1646) to remain after the triumph of Cromwell, and published *Hypocrisie Unmasked* (1646), a spirited defense of the colony, attacking Samuel Gorton. *New Englands Salamander Discovered by an Irreligious and Scornfull Pamphlet* (1647), a reply to Major John Child's *New-Englands Jonas Cast Up at London* (1647), answers this criticism, which was unfavorable to the Puritan regime and specifically to Winslow. The latter was sent by Cromwell on a mission to the West Indies, where he died of a fever.

JOSIAH WINSLOW (*c.*1629–80), his son, was also prominent in the government of the Plymouth Colony, serving as assistant governor (1657–73) and governor (1673–80), as Plymouth commissioner in the New England Confederation, and as a commander of forces in King Philip's War. His elegy on Bradford was published in Morton's *New Englands Memoriall.*

WINSLOW, THYRA SAMTER (1893–1961), popular writer of short stories, whose tales, mainly based on her knowledge of small-town life in her native Arkansas and elsewhere, or on the romance of the theater she discovered as a New York dramatic critic, are collected in *Picture Frames* (1923), *Show Business* (1926), *People Round the Corner* (1927), *Blueberry Pie* (1932), *My Own, My Native Land* (1935), and *The Sex Without Sentiment* (1954).

WINSOR, JUSTIN (1831–97), librarian of Harvard University (1877–97), whose historical work included the editorship of the cooperative *Narrative and Critical History of America* (8 vols., 1884–89), in which his own scholarly notes and bibliographical essays were interspersed with the text. He advanced the scientific study of American history by making available new materials.

WINTER, WILLIAM (1836–1917), was a writer in his native Massachusetts, a bohemian journalist in the group at Pfaff's Cellar, and became dramatic critic of the *New-York Tribune* (1865–1909). Although during the first 25 years he was respected as the Great Cham of the New York theater, he was later considered a relic of the Victorian era because of his romanticism, sentimentalism, insistence upon morality, and hatred of the rising realism. In addition to his daily columns, in part reprinted in *The Wallet of Time* (1913), he wrote such theatrical reminiscences as *Other Days* (1908) and *Old Friends* (1909), and biographies of such theatrical figures as Joseph Jefferson, Henry Irving, Edwin Booth, Ada Rehan, Richard Mansfield, and Belasco. *Shakespeare on the Stage* (2 vols., 1911, 1915) is a valuable work of theatrical scholarship, dealing with interpretations of Shakespearean roles by leading actors. He was the author of a great many occasional poems and of funeral verse on the deaths of important actors, which, because of his longevity, were so frequent that he came to be known as "Weeping Willie." His *Poems* were collected in 1909.

WINTERICH, JOHN T[RACY] (1891–1970), journalist and author of books for bibliophiles and students of literary history, which include *A Primer of Book Collecting* (1927); *Collector's Choice* (1928); *Books and the Man* (1929); *An American Friend of Dickens* (1933); *Early American Books and Printing* (1935); *Twenty-Three Books* (1938); and *Three Lantern Slides* (1949), on the U.S. book trade, 1876, 1901, and 1926. *Another Day, Another Dollar* (1947) contains reminiscences.

WINTERS, [ARTHUR] YVOR (1900–1968), born in Chicago, was a member of the Department of English, Stanford University, from 1928. There he edited *The Gyroscope* (1929–31), and was the Western editor of *Hound and Horn* (1932–34). His poetry, published in *The Immobile Wind* (1921), *The Magpie's Shadow* (1922), and *The Bare Hills* (1927)—all collected in *The Early Poems* (1966)—*The Proof* (1930), *The Journey* (1931), *Before Disaster* (1934), *Poems* (1940), and *The Giant Weapon* (1943), is marked by those qualities he asks for as a critic: classical order, dignity, restraint, and moral judgment. His *Collected Poems* (1952) was revised and enlarged (1960) and at that time was awarded a Bollingen Prize. His critical works are *Primitivism and Decadence* (1937), showing the obscurity of modern American poetry as the result of romanticism qualified by certain aspects of American history, *Maule's Curse* (1938), on obscurantism in 19th-century American authors, and *The Anatomy of Nonsense* (1943), on 20th-century poets and critics—all three books collected in *In Defense of Reason* (1947); *Edwin Arlington Robinson* (1946); *The Function of Criticism: Problems and Exercises* (1957); *Forms of Discovery* (1967); and *Uncollected Essays* (1973). He was married to Janet Lewis.

Winterset, verse play by Maxwell Anderson,♦ produced and published in 1935. Its theme was suggested by the Sacco-Vanzetti case.♦

Thirteen years before the time of the play, Romagna, an Italian radical, was "framed" on a murder charge and executed. His wife died, and their son Mio, wandering through the country as a tramp, becomes passionately certain of his father's innocence. He comes to a New York tenement district, where in a mean dwelling under a bridge he locates Garth Esdras, a reformed gangster who has come home in an attempt to escape the domination of Trock, the gangster leader who actually committed the murder of which Romagna was convicted. Mio meets Garth's sister Miriamne, and they fall in love, finding an intimate bond in their mutual loneliness and terror. Then, in the Esdras cellar apartment, he discovers Garth with Judge Gaunt, who participated in the Romagna "frame-up," and whose sense of guilt has driven him mad. The judge is being nursed by Garth's father, a kindly and wise old rabbi. When Garth and Gaunt deny Mio's accusations, he begins to doubt his father's innocence, until Trock is shocked into confession by the reappearance of his gunman, Shadow, whom he thought he had murdered. Police take the insane Gaunt into custody, but after Miriamne prevents Mio from accusing Trock, the gangster and his men surround the tenement when the officers leave. Trock shoots Mio and as he dies Miriamne assures him that she will carry his message to the world, but she too is killed.

WINTHROP, JOHN (1588–1649), a member of an English upper-class family, attended Cambridge and took his position in the English social scheme as lord of the manor at Groton and as an important lawyer. His Puritan sympathies worked against his success, however, and he determined to join the Massachusetts Bay Company. Selected as governor, he sailed on the *Arbella* (1630), after collaborating with the other leaders in writing *The Humble Request of . . . the Company Late Gone for New England* (1630), affirming their belief in Puritanism, and disclaiming any intention of separating from the Established Church. While at sea Winthrop wrote "A Modell of Christian Charity," pointing out what the colony should be and the manner of the colonists' necessary cooperation. For nine of his remaining 19 years he was governor, and during the other ten deputy-governor.

Since the charter of the company had been transferred to New England, and was not, as in other colonies, held by an English corporation, this Puritan commonwealth had in it the seeds of democracy. Winthrop and the other upper-class leaders, however, had their own ideas on how a democracy should operate, and they attempted to create a sort of benevolent despotism, despite the opposition of the freemen, the original stockholders who held the franchise. Because of John Cotton, the company became increasingly an aristocratic theocracy. Quarrels with the freemen were frequent, and their leader, Sir Henry Vane, was governor until he sided with Anne Hutchinson,♦ after which Winthrop resumed power. His manuscript war with Vane has been printed, and his contribution to the controversy was compiled at the time by Thomas Weld.♦ In 1642 occurred the *cause célèbre* of Goody Sherman, whose stray sow had been impounded by wealthy Robert Keayne. The aristocratic Court of Assistance vetoed the action of the larger and more democratic General Court, which sided with the poor woman, and thus definitively established its power and created a precedent for American legislatures. Winthrop indicated his views at the time, proclaiming, "If we should change from a mixt aristocratie to a mere Democratie, first we should have no warrant in scripture for it: there is no such government in Israel . . . a Democratie is, amongst most civil nations, accounted the meanest and worst forms of government." He founded the New England Confederation♦ (1643), but exceeded his authority when, without referring to his colonists or the Confederation, he took sides in a local French dispute in Acadia. Such actions as this, and his writing of a discourse on "Arbitrary Government" (1644), so inflamed the people that he was impeached, although he escaped conviction by delivering a speech on liberty, thus satisfying the colonists to such an extent that they elected him governor annually until his death.

His most famous piece of writing is his *Journal,*

of which the first two parts were published in 1790, and the complete work as *The History of New England* (2 vols., 1825–26). This important source book, begun on the *Arbella* voyage and continued intermittently until his death, is composed of brief jottings. It records not only the great events but also the minute happenings, for as a Puritan he conceived of formal history as specific and concrete anecdotes, all equally important, since all occur through the will of God. The *Winthrop Papers,* a scholarly edition of his *Journal,* was published by the Massachusetts Historical Society (5 vols., 1929–47). Winthrop figures frequently in literature, as in Hawthorne's *The Scarlet Letter,* "Howe's Masquerade," and "Endicott and the Red Cross."

JOHN WINTHROP (1606–76), his son, was educated in England and Ireland, served in the British navy, traveled widely on the Continent, and emigrated to join his father in Boston (1631). During a trip to England (1634), he was appointed by Lord Say and Sele and Lord Brooke to be governor of the plantation that they founded in Connecticut. Although he returned to the colonies (1635), he barely visited Connecticut but continued to make his home in Massachusetts. After another trip to England (1641–43), he settled in Connecticut, built an iron works, and, although holding posts in both colonies, became definitely associated with the new one on resuming the post of governor (1657). From 1659 until his death, he was annually elected governor, and in 1663 won his colony so liberal a charter that it became virtually an independent state. In his time he was known for his scientific investigations, and he was the first colonial to be elected a Fellow of the Royal Society.

JOHN WINTHROP (1638–1707), his son, commonly known as Fitz-John Winthrop, was prominent as a soldier in Cromwell's parliamentary army and as a commander of colonial troops. He was governor of Connecticut (1698–1707).

WINTHROP, THEODORE (1828–61), Connecticut novelist, graduated from Yale (1848) and traveled extensively in Europe, on horseback across the U.S. to California and Oregon, to Panama, and through the Maine woods. Although for a time in the steamship business and a lawyer, he devoted most of his time to travel and writing. His books were posthumously published after he was killed in the Civil War. His novels include *Cecil Dreeme* (1861), the story of a New York girl who escapes an undesirable marriage by masquerading as a man among the artists of the Washington Square district; *John Brent*♦ (1862), an early novel of Western life; and *Edwin Brothertoft* (1862), a romance of the Revolution in New York. All of these are marked by melodramatic plots and a breathless narrative style. *The Canoe and the Saddle* (1863) contains vivid sketches of his journey to the Northwest, with an addendum on his trip to Panama to survey a canal

route, and *Life in the Open Air* (1863) is a similar work.

WINWAR, FRANCES (1900–), born in Sicily, brought to the U.S. (1907), later naturalized, she adopted as a pseudonym the Anglicization of her Italian name, Vinciguerra, and under it has written romantic novels, including *Gallows Hill* (1937), about the Salem witchcraft trials, and popular, colorful biographies, including *Poor Splendid Wings* (1933), about the Pre-Raphaelites; *The Romantic Rebels* (1935), about Byron, Shelley, and Keats; *Oscar Wilde and the Yellow Nineties* (1940); *American Giant: Walt Whitman and His Times* (1941); *The Haunted Palace* (1959), about Poe; and *Jean-Jacques Rousseau; Conscience of an Era* (1961).

WIRT, WILLIAM (1772–1834), Virginia lawyer and U.S. attorney general under Monroe and Adams (1817–29), was the presidential candidate of the Anti-Masonic party (1832). His first book, the popular *Letters of the British Spy*♦ (1803), was followed by other essays sketching Southern customs and manners, *The Rainbow* (1804) and *The Old Bachelor* (1812), the latter written with friends. All were published anonymously. Wirt's *Life* of Patrick Henry (1817) re-created many of his speeches from notes and tradition. J.P. Kennedy wrote his *Memoirs* (2 vols., 1849).

WISE, HENRY AUGUSTUS (1819–69), naval officer, whose writings include *Los Gringos; or, An Inside View of Mexico and California . . .* (1849), *Tales for the Marines* (1855), and several melodramatic novels published under the pseudonym Harry Gringo.

WISE, JOHN (1652–1725), born at Roxbury, Mass., was minister of the Second Church of Ipswich (1680–1725), except for a brief period (1687) when Governor Andros deprived him of his ministry and jailed him for leading his townsmen in refusing to pay taxes that violated their charter rights. His pamphlets *The Churches Quarrel Espoused*♦ (1710) and *A Vindication of the Government of New-England Churches*♦ (1717) opposed the attempts of the Mathers to establish a centralized association for regulating the churches. Their underlying ideas of democracy caused the pamphlets to be reissued and widely read before the revolution and the Civil War. *A Word of Comfort to a Melancholy Country* (1721) is a plea for paper money.

Wise Blood, novel by Flannery O'Connor,♦ published in 1952.

A 22-year-old soldier, Hazel Motes, upon being released from the army because of a wound, makes his way to his home state of Tennessee. There he founds a Church Without Christ, not only in revolt against his grandfather, a preacher, but in opposition to Asa Hawkes, a religious charlatan who pretends to be blind. Hazel's follower, Hoover Shoates, who calls himself Onnie Jay Holy, comes to champion a rival prophet of the Church Without Christ. After killing the false prophet by running him down with an auto, Hazel blinds himself, stops preaching, tortures himself, sickens, and dies.

WISLIZENUS, FREDERICK ADOLPH (1810–89), German-born physician and adventurer, came to the U.S. (1835) and made a trip to the Far West, recorded in a book (1840) translated as *A Journey to the Rocky Mountains in the Year 1839* (1912). He joined a trading caravan on a trip from St. Louis to Chihuahua, Mexico (1846), and described the journey in *Memoir of a Tour to Northern Mexico* (1848).

WISTER, OWEN (1860–1938), member of a distinguished Pennsylvania family and a grandson of Fanny Kemble, graduated from Harvard (1882), and found the subject matter for a literary career when ill health caused his doctor to advise him to follow the example of his classmate Theodore Roosevelt and go West. Out of summer trips to Wyoming ranches came the material for *Red Men and White* (1896), stories of the Western cattle country; *Lin McLean* (1898), another collection but more unified; *The Jimmyjohn Boss* (1900), a final collection of stories; and the extremely popular novel *The Virginian*♦ (1902), about Wyoming cowpunchers during the 1870s and '80s, which established many of the patterns of fiction about the West and created a native mythology. His journals of his Western years, 1885–95, were published as *Owen Wister Out West* (1958), but he himself turned to other regions and subjects for the rest of his literary career. Later works include *Philosophy 4* (1903), a tale about Harvard undergraduate life; *Lady Baltimore* (1906), a romantic novel of life in Charleston; a biography of Grant (1900); *The Seven Ages of Washington* (1907); and *Roosevelt, the Story of a Friendship, 1880–1919* (1930). His collected works (11 vols., 1928) also include poems, nature studies, other stories of the West, further fiction, and humorous writings. *My Dear Wister* (1972) collects his correspondence with Frederic Remington.

Witchcraft, see *Salem witchcraft trials.*

Witchcraft; or, The Martyrs of Salem, blank-verse tragedy by Cornelius Mathews,♦ produced in 1846 and published in 1852.
  Ambla Bodish, a 17th-century Massachusetts woman accused of witchcraft, is unsuccessfully defended by her son Gideon. Susanna Peache, who loves Gideon, testifies against Ambla, believing that she has used witchcraft to alienate his affections. Despairing of recovering Gideon's love, Susanna commits suicide, and he is killed by Jarvis Dane, another lover of the girl.

With the Procession, novel by H.B. Fuller,♦ published in 1895.

WITHERSPOON, JOHN (1723–94), Scottish-born Presbyterian minister, came to America to accept the presidency of the College of New Jersey (1768). He healed the breach between the New Side and the Old Side, revitalized his church in the Middle colonies, and as a philosopher denounced the theories of Berkeley and championed empirical common sense. He encouraged advanced methods of instruction, and enlarged the curriculum, but because of the suspension of exercises during the Revolution, the institution suffered during his administration, and he turned his interest to political affairs. A member of the Continental Congress, he signed both the Declaration of Independence and the Articles of Confederation. His hand can be traced in several keen political publications of the period, to which he contributed anonymously. His most memorable sermon, "The Dominion of Providence Over the Passions of Men," preached at Princeton (May 17, 1776), is a calm statement of his advocacy of independence. His best secular writing is the *Essay on Money* (1786), opposing paper currency. He is better remembered for his coinage of the word "Americanism" in "The Druid," a denunciation of the American language published in the *Pennsylvania Journal* (1781). His writings were collected (4 vols., 1800–1801).

Wizard of Oz, character in children's books by L. Frank Baum. ♦

Wobblies, see *I.W.W.*

WOIWODE, LARRY [ALFRED] (1941–), North Dakota-born author whose novels, set in the Midwest, are *What I'm Going To Do, I Think* (1969), a bittersweet tale of a young couple's romance and their return to the site of their honeymoon two years later; *Beyond the Bedroom Wall: A Family Album* (1975), a portrayal of several generations of a North Dakota family; *Poppa John* (1981), about an aging television character actor who preaches religious platitudes; and *Born Brothers* (1988), a sequel to *Beyond the Bedroom Wall,* tracing two boys from childhood to young adult achievement. *Even Tide* (1977) collects poems; *The Neumiller Stories* (1989) gathers short stories.

WOLCOTT, ROGER (1679–1767), after serving in the French and Indian Wars became prominent in the politics of his native Connecticut and served as its governor (1751–54). His *Poetical Meditations* (1725) contains "A Brief Account of the Agency of the Honourable John Winthrop" (in obtaining the Connecticut charter), a rugged attempt at an epic which is an interesting link between earlier New England elegies and the American epics of the Connecticut Wits.

Wolcott's prose pamphlets were concerned with religious controversies.

WOLFE, THOMAS [CLAYTON] (1900–1938), was born and reared in Asheville, N.C. (the "Altamont, Old Catawba" of his fiction). His father, a powerful stonecutter from the North, is the prototype of Oliver Gant, and his mother, a member of a typical puritanical mountain family, is the original of the mother of Eugene Gant, whose drab life and eventual escape parallels the author's own youth. The lifelong influence of his mother is shown in his *Letters to His Mother* (1943).

After graduation from the University of North Carolina (1920), where he wrote and acted for the Carolina Playmakers,♦ he studied playwriting at Harvard and received an M.A. (1922). His work included the writing of three plays, one of which, *The Iron of Melancholy,* was published in 1983. Another of his early plays, *Mannerhouse,* was published posthumously in 1948 and reissued in a more accurate text in 1985. He returned from a period abroad to teach English at New York University (1924–30) but after the publication of *Look Homeward, Angel♦* (1929) devoted his full time to writing. This strongly autobiographical novel, displaying originality and intensity as well as debts to Dreiser, Lewis, Joyce, and other contemporary novelists, was continued in a sequel, *Of Time and the River♦* (1935), incorporating a short novel, "A Portrait of Bascom Hawke," previously printed in *Scribner's* in 1932.

A posthumous novel, *The Web and the Rock♦* (1939), has as its central character George Webber, apparently the Eugene Gant of the previous books. Despite the author's claim that "It is the most objective novel that I have written," the first half of the book closely parallels the material of *Look Homeward, Angel,* and the second part serves as a sequel to *Of Time and the River.* The title indicates symbolically the problem of his first book: the web of experience, environment, and ancestry, in which the hero is snared; and his attempt to escape by finding the rock, which is the original strength and beauty of vision of his father. He concludes that "you can't go home again," that you must go forward, you can't return to a dead past. The sequel, *You Can't Go Home Again♦* (1940), deals with George's life after his return to the U.S.: his continued unsatisfactory romance; his success in writing novels reminiscent of Wolfe's own; his kindly relation and later dissatisfaction with an internationally famous but disillusioned novelist and with his editor, who fatalistically accepts the sickness of civilization; his unsuccessful attempt to return to the roots of his hometown, whose morality has become shoddy during the prosperous decade of the '20s; and his horrid discovery of the destruction of the Germany he had once loved. It is the story of a man who recognizes that a corrupt society destroys each individual in it, but nevertheless believes that "the true fulfillment of our spirit, of our people, of our mighty and immortal land is yet to come."

In addition to his lengthy fiction, Wolfe published short stories, *From Death to Morning* (1935), and a critical examination of his own work, *The Story of a Novel* (1936). Volumes that appeared after his death include *The Hills Beyond* (1941), an unfinished novel and some short stories, the latter separately issued as *The Lost Boy* (1965); two plays, *Gentlemen of the Press* (1942) and *Mannerhouse* (1948); *A Western Journal . . . of the Great Parks Trip . . . 1938* (1951); a collection of *Letters* (1956); *Letters . . . to His Mother* (1968); and his *Notebooks* (2 vols., 1970). "Poetical Passages" from his novels have been collected in *The Face of a Nation* (1939) and *A Stone, a Leaf, a Door* (1945), the latter arranged as verse.

Throughout his fiction there is a self-fascination and self-torment that endow his writing now with a lofty romantic quality, now with the prosaic quality of literal reporting of the hero's life. His intensity results in both a powerful emotional evocation and a sprawling unrestrained formlessness. His prose is sometimes highly lyrical, but there are many passages characterized by swollen, frenzied rhetoric. His books cling always to the story of his life; however, he rises above egocentricity in his mystical, patriotic belief that there is something great in America that haunts and kindles the imaginations of its young men.

Since his death various letters of his have been collected and published, e.g. two volumes in 1983 to two different women.

WOLFE, TOM (THOMAS KENNERLY WOLFE, JR.) (1931–), Virginia-born journalist, known for his treatment of contemporary American culture from its popular heroes to its alternative lifestyles, a jet-set sociology written in a baroque pop style. His collections of articles include *The Kandy-Kolored Tangerine-Flake Streamline Baby* (1965), *The Pump House Gang* (1968), and *Radical Chic and Mau-Mauing the Flak Catchers* (1970). Other books include *The Electric Kool-Aid Acid Test* (1968), partly about Ken Kesey♦ and his Merry Pranksters; *The New Journalism* (1973); *The Painted Word* (1975), commentary on the current art world's pretensions; *Mauve Gloves and Madmen* (1976), stories, essays, and sketches; *The Right Stuff* (1979), about U.S. astronauts, "gods for a day"; and *From Bauhaus to Our House* (1981), a satirical view of contemporary U.S. architecture. *In Our Time* (1980) collects his drawings, and *The Purple Decades* (1982) collects 20 essays from previous books. *The Bonfire of the Vanities♦* (1987), his first novel, presents a successful young New York financial trader in trouble.

Wolfert's Roost and Miscellanies, 19 stories and sketches by Irving,♦ published under various pseudonyms in *The Knickerbocker Magazine* and collected in 1855. The volume contains tales based on Spanish legends, stories of colonial America, familiar essays on "National Nomenclature" and "Criticism," and a sketch of the region of the author's home ("Sleepy Hollow"). The title "chronicle" deals with New York in the time of Peter Stuyvesant.

WOLFF, GEOFFREY ANSELL (1937–), came to critical attention with a brilliant memoir of his con-man father, *The Duke of Deception* (1979). When his parents divorced, Geoffrey chose to live with his father, while his younger brother Tobias went with their mother, and Geoffrey did not communicate with either of them until his senior year at Princeton. His account of growing up with a deadbeat, indulgent, conscienceless father whom he loved but finally had to abandon has the same holding honesty as Conroy's *Stop-Time.* Wolff's novels include *Bad Debts* (1969) and *Providence* (1986). *The Final Club* (1990) is a memoir of Princeton from an insider/outsider's view. *A Day at the Beach* (1992) is biographical sketches of his own wife and sons.

WOLFF, TOBIAS (1945–), younger brother of Geoffrey, lived with his mother, who had "gone to deep cover" in Connecticut, Florida, Utah, and Washington, with frequent interruptions of Tobias's formal education. After Army service in Vietnam, Wolff took a degree at Oxford, and after a job on the *Washington Post,* then further study at Stanford, became writer in residence at Syracuse University. His story collections include *In the Garden of North American Martyrs* (1981) and *Back in the World* (1985). A novella, *The Barracks Thief* (1985), won the PEN/Faulkner Award. *This Boy's Life* (1989) is a harrowing memoir of growing up in his stepfather's house.

Wolfville, 24 stories by A.H. Lewis,♦ published in 1897 under the pseudonym Dan Quin.

Woman in the Nineteenth Century, feminist study by Margaret Fuller.♦

Woman of Andros, *The,* novel by Thornton Wilder.♦

Woman's Home Companion (1873–1957), founded as the semi-monthly *Home Companion* at Cleveland, Ohio, became the *Ladies' Home Companion* (1886), and in 1897 became a monthly under the title *Woman's Home Companion,* later moving to New York City. Besides its departments of household interest, and such lengthy serials as Dorothy Canfield's *The Deepening Stream,* it mainly featured popular fiction by women authors, among them Willa Cather, Zona Gale, and Edna Ferber. Gertrude B. Lane was the editor from 1911 to 1940.

Women at Point Sur, *The,* free-verse narrative by Jeffers,♦ published in 1927. A "Prelude" reveals the author's personal philosophy, which in this narrative, as in "Tamar"♦ and "Roan Stallion,"♦ reasserts the need "to uncenter the human mind from itself." It also constitutes a "warning" against abuses or irrelevant applications of such an idea.

Dr. Barclay, a preacher in a California coast town, after learning of the death of his son in the World War, announces to his congregation that "Christianity is false," and that he is leaving them to create a new religion based on energy and violence. He goes to a farm near Point Lobos, where he elaborates his mystical faith, preaching to the trees and stones of the desolate mountainside, and "breaking from the mold" of his former gentleness and continence. Convinced that

> All the relations of the world have changed in a moment.
> If there was anything forbidden you may do it,

he sleeps with the Indian serving-woman Maruca, and then, having achieved "deliverance," goes mad with an indiscriminate lust that causes him to rape his daughter April and infects all the residents of the Morhaus farm, including the daughter Natalia, who murders her child to rectify the "sin" of bearing it; Randal, Natalia's husband, and Faith Heriot, her lesbian lover, whom Randal has previously possessed; and even crippled old Morhaus. The insane liberation of evil impulses that Barclay's nihilism has effected ends with April's suicide and her father's escape to starve to death in the hills, where he thinks "on the nothing Outside the stars, the other shore of me, there's peace."

Women's Liberation, see *Feminism.*

Wonder-Book, *A,* tales for children adapted from Greek myths by Hawthorne,♦ published in 1852. *Tanglewood Tales* (1853) is a similar collection.

Wonder-Working Providence of Sions Saviour in New England, *The,* chronicle of 17th-century New England by Edward Johnson,♦ first published anonymously at London (1653, dated 1654) with the title *A History of New-England.* This vigorous history, covering the period from 1628 to 1652, takes an epic view of the founding of the colony as a spiritual crusade by settlers who are all soldiers of Christ in a war against unbelievers and the wilderness. The rhapsodic quality of the work precludes it from being an accepted authority, but preserves the spirit of 17th-century thought. The prose, which is interspersed with many stalwart verse tributes to contemporary men and events, is ornate and verbose, and yet has a typical Elizabethan zest in its ecstatic view of New England as a land whose settlement is assisted by God working wonders for those who cooperate with Him.

Wonderful One-Hoss Shay, see *Deacon's Masterpiece.*

Wonders of the Invisible World, The, by Cotton Mather,♦ published in 1693 as a narrative of some of the Salem witchcraft trials. It contains theological observations on the operations of devils, and was answered by Robert Calef♦ in *More Wonders of the Invisible World* (1700).

WOOD, CHARLES ERSKINE SCOTT (1852–1944), born in Pennsylvania, after an army career in the West became an Oregon lawyer (1884–1919) and published his first poetry in *A Masque of Love* (1904), followed by *The Poet in the Desert* (1915), a dialogue between Truth and a Poet, protesting against social injustice and championing humanitarian ideals. Later poetry appears in *Maia* (1918), a sonnet sequence, and *Poems from the Ranges* (1929). Colonel Wood, who long lived in California, is best known for *Heavenly Discourse* (1927), a series of 40 dialogues written during World War I for *The Masses,* although only a few were published before the magazine was suppressed. Satirizing the folly and inhumanity of the war, as well as other manifestations of meanness, irreligion, economic inequality, sentimental art, Puritanism, political abuses, and persecution, these ironically humorous conversations take place in Heaven among God, Satan, Jesus, and such angels or temporary visitors as Rabelais, Voltaire, Paine, Clemens, Jefferson, Carry Nation, Bryan, Billy Sunday, Ingersoll, Joan of Arc, Anthony Comstock, and Charles Evans Hughes. A 41st dialogue on Sacco and Vanzetti♦ was added in 1928. A second collection, *Earthly Discourse,* was published in 1937.

WOOD, SARAH SAYWARD BARRELL KEATING (1759–1855), Maine author of Gothic romances, whose *Julia and the Illuminated Baron* (1800) is a wildly melodramatic tale of the subversive, atheistic activities of the French society of the Illuminati, as conducted by a miscreant baron. *Dorval; or, The Speculator* (1801) is again a fantastic story, dealing with a villain, Dorval, and his machinations in the Yazoo fraud. Her last two novels, like her first, are set in Europe and show the same absurd plot structure. They are *Amelia; or, The Influence of Virtue* (1802), concerned with the travails of a cloyingly perfect heroine; and *Ferdinand and Elmira: A Russian Story* (1804). *Tales of the Night* (1827) contains two long stories, set in Maine, which, though still showing a romantic and moralistic turn of mind, are slightly more realistic.

WOOD, WILLIAM (*fl.*1629–35), English colonist in Massachusetts (1629–33). He is the author of *New Englands Prospect♦* (1634), an important early description of the country. In the book he speaks of his intention to return, but nothing is known of his later life.

WOODBERRY, GEORGE EDWARD (1855–1930), Massachusetts critic, poet, and professor, first won notice for his life of Poe (1885, enlarged 1909), a subject for which he had little sympathy but which he treated with scholarly impartiality. In 1890 he published his first book of poetry, *The North Shore Watch,* and collected his magazine articles as *Studies in Letters and Life,* a critique of literature in relation to the experiences that produce it. As professor of comparative literature at Columbia (1891–1904), he was known for his stimulating instruction and personal guidance of students. During this period he published further volumes of poetry; two collections of essays, *Heart of Man* (1899) and *Makers of Literature* (1900), which show him to be in accord with the movement later known as the New Humanism♦; a biography of Hawthorne (1902), considered his best biographical work; and *America in Literature* (1903), a literary history illustrating his antipathy to realism in its failure to consider such authors as Whitman and Clemens. After resigning from Columbia, he made his home in Massachusetts, but led a life of academic and literary vagabondage, teaching for brief periods at colleges in the East and West, and spending much time abroad. His works of this later period include collections of his lectures, such as *The Torch* (1905) and *The Appreciation of Literature* (1907); a biography of Emerson (1907); a book of travels, *North Africa and the Desert* (1914); *Ideal Passion* (1917), a sonnet sequence that expresses his idealistic philosophy of beauty; and *The Roamer* (1920), a long narrative poem reflecting his personal creed and spiritual autobiography. His scholarship is demonstrated in his editions of the works of Shelley (1892) and, with E.C. Stedman, of the works of Poe (10 vols., 1894–95).

WOODHULL, VICTORIA [CLAFLIN] (1838–1927), born in Ohio, during her early years figured with her mother and her sister Tennessee Celeste Claflin (1846–1923) in spiritualistic and mesmeric exhibitions. In 1868 the sisters went to New York City, where the elder Cornelius Vanderbilt set them up as "lady brokers" in Wall Street. With the aid of Stephen P. Andrews, they inaugurated *Woodhull and Claflin's Weekly* (1870–76), a journal advocating socialism, woman suffrage, free love, birth control, and vegetarianism. It published the scandalous Beecher-Tilton story that occasioned the trial of Henry Ward Beecher, and in the same year (1872) printed the first English translation of the *Communist Manifesto.* Victoria was nominated for President by the Equal Rights party (1872), with Frederick Douglass for Vice-President. The sisters moved to England (1877), where each got married. Together they wrote *The Human Body as the Temple of God* (1890). Victoria's principal works were *Origin, Tendencies, and Principles of Government* (1871), *Stirpiculture* (1888), and *Humanitarian Money* (1892).

Woodman, Spare That Tree!, poem by G.P. Morris.♦

Wood-Pile, *The,* blank-verse poem by Robert Frost,♦ published in *North of Boston* (1914).

The poet suggests a cosmic symbol in his discovery of a weathered, long-abandoned cord of maple, "cut and split and piled," held from being scattered by a growing tree on one side and on the other "a stake and prop, these latter about to fall." This wasted labor can be the work only of "someone who lived in turning to fresh tasks," and could leave his creation "To warm the frozen swamp as best it could With the slow smokeless burning of decay."

WOODWARD, C[OMER] VANN (1908–), premier historian of the American South, divided his career between Johns Hopkins (1946–61) and Yale (1961–77), where he was Sterling Professor of History. Woodward has concentrated on the American South since the Civil War. He established his reputation with *Tom Watson: Agrarian Rebel* (1938), and after an interval of service in World War II, *Origins of the New South: 1877–1913* (1951), which had the then revisionist view that internal Southern conflicts rather than Northern carpetbaggers were at root of the long poverty of the region. Among his many titles are *The Strange Career of Jim Crow* (1955) and *Thinking Back: The Perils of Writing History* (1986). He is General Editor of the *Oxford History of the United States* (11 vols., 1982–), and he edited *Mary Chesnut's Civil War* (1981), which won a Pulitzer Prize. With Elisabeth Muhlenfeld he edited *The Private Mary Chesnut: The Unpublished Civil War Diaries* (1984).

WOODWARD, W[ILLIAM] E. (1874–1950), born in South Carolina, author of the novels *Bunk* (1923), *Lottery* (1924), *Bread and Circuses* (1925), and *Evelyn Prentice* (1933), in addition to popular debunking books for which he was known. His biographies include *George Washington: The Image and the Man* (1926), *Meet General Grant* (1928), and *Tom Paine: America's Godfather* (1945). *A New American History* (1936) is a breezy narrative; *The Way Our People Lived* (1944) selects representative episodes; *Years of Madness* (1951) deals with the Civil War. *The Gift of Life* (1947) is his autobiography.

WOODWORTH, SAMUEL (1785–1842), Massachusetts-born author, after 1809 was a journalist in New York, edited the *New-York Mirror* and other papers, and wrote plays and poems. He is remembered today for "The Old Oaken Bucket," first titled "The Bucket," collected in his *Melodies, Duets, Songs, and Ballads* (1826), and set to music by Frederick Smith. The same volume contains his "The Hunters of Kentucky," a ballad written to celebrate the riflemen who under Jackson repulsed the British at New Orleans in 1815. His plays include *LaFayette* (1824), a melodrama; *The Forest Rose*♦ (1825), a comedy known for its Yankee character, Jonathan Ploughboy;

and *The Widow's Son* (1825), a domestic tragedy of the Revolutionary period. His sole novel, *The Champions of Freedom* (2 vols., 1816), is a fantastic moral romance with the War of 1812 as background to a plot involving the spirit of George Washington as a "Mysterious Chief" who guides the destinies of Decatur, Harrison, Jackson, and other heroes of the time.

WOOLLCOTT, ALEXANDER [HUMPHREYS] (1887–1943), New York dramatic and literary critic, and whimsical, gossipy essayist. His books, written in a fancifully embroidered style, include *Mrs. Fiske* (1917), *Shouts and Murmurs* (1922), *Mr. Dickens Goes to the Play* (1923), *Enchanted Aisles* (1924), *The Story of Irving Berlin* (1925), *Going to Pieces* (1928), *While Rome Burns* (1934), and *Long, Long Ago* (1943). His other activities included radio, stage, and screen performances, the compilation of anthologies, and collaboration with George S. Kaufman on the melodrama *The Dark Tower* (1933). *The Man Who Came to Dinner* (1939), a play by Moss Hart and Kaufman, is based on the character of Woollcott, who appeared in the leading role. His *Letters* (1944) were edited by Beatrice Kaufman and Joseph Hennessey, and his biography was written by Samuel Hopkins Adams (1945).

WOOLMAN, JOHN (1720–72), New Jersey-born Quaker, had little formal education, and was a tailor's apprentice, baker, and shopkeeper until age 26, when he felt the presence of God in his heart commanding him to preach the gospel. As a preacher and leader of his faith, he began the long series of journeys which, with intermittent schoolteaching, occupied the rest of his life. His ardent humanitarianism aroused his interest in the problems of black slavery and the distribution of wealth. His two essays entitled *Some Considerations on the Keeping of Negroes* (1754, 1762) are among the earliest American antislavery works, and his other pamphlets include *Considerations on Pure Wisdom and Human Policy* (1758), on labor, education, and "the right use of the Lord's outward gifts"; *Considerations on the True Harmony of Mankind* (1770); *A Plea for the Poor* (written 1763), first published (1793) under the title "A Word of Remembrance and Caution to the Rich"; and *An Epistle* (1772), setting forth his religious belief in a farewell to friends before his departure for England, where he died. Woolman was consistently interested in social problems, but, when in opposition to the prevailing ideas of this world, governed himself by a principle of "passive obedience," obeying the letter of the law but not its spirit, for though he "studied to be quiet" and live according to his own views, he reasonably accepted that which was required of him. Although having frequently to bow to external authority, in personal matters he did what he wished, giving up dyed clothes because he knew dyes were harmful to workers and giving up sugar because of conditions among plantation slaves. He is best known for his lengthy *Journal* (1774), a classic document of the inner life characterized by a crystal-pure style, of which Whittier in his edition of 1871 said "it has a sweetness as of violets." Others have paid similar tributes, Channing finding it "beyond comparison the sweetest and purest autobiography in the language," and Charles Lamb exhorting his readers to "get the writings of John Woolman by heart."

WOOLSON, CONSTANCE FENIMORE (1840–94), New Hampshire-born grandniece of Cooper, spent her youth mainly in Ohio, of which she wrote in her early local-color stories and novels. *Castle Nowhere* (1875) collects stories dealing chiefly with the primitive French inhabitants near the Great Lakes. Later, as in the title story of *Rodman the Keeper: Southern Sketches* (1880), she wrote of the contrasts between the prewar South and its life during Reconstruction, which she studied at first hand during her residence in the Carolinas and Florida (1873–79). *The Front Yard* (1895) and *Dorothy* (1896) are collections of tales presenting character studies of Americans in Italy, where the author lived after 1879. Her five novels, written while she was abroad, use American settings. *Anne* (1882) deals with a simple Mackinac Island girl, thrown into the social life of New York; *For the Major* (1883), set in North Carolina, is a study of a woman's self-sacrifice for her husband to preserve his cherished illusions of the Old South; *East Angels* (1886) is a study of moral contrasts with a lush Florida background; *Jupiter Lights* (1889) is a story of the conflict between sisters-in-law representative of the Southern and Northern characters. Her last novel, *Horace Chase* (1894), is about a self-made man and his wife, who looks down upon him until she discovers his true character.

WORCESTER, JOSEPH EMERSON (1784–1865), New England lexicographer, graduated from Yale (1811) and for five years taught at Salem, Mass., where, while writing his early textbooks, he had Hawthorne as one of his students. After moving to Cambridge (1819) he began his long series of dictionaries, first editing Dr. Johnson's, then Webster's, and finally compiling his own *Comprehensive Pronouncing and Explanatory Dictionary of the English Language* (1830). This led Webster to charge his rival with plagiarism, and precipitated the long "War of Dictionaries," intermittently intensified when each philologist followed the other in publishing new editions, and causing such by-products as Worcester's pamphlet *A Gross Literary Fraud Exposed* (1835), an invidious denial of his dependence upon Webster. Worcester was an uncompromising advocate of philological orthodoxy and English examples, zealously and consistently combating Webster's attempts at national independence. He frowned upon the imported Bostonian broad *a*,

and suggested a "compromise vowel," since, as another critic said, "our *grass* really lies between the *grahs* of a British lawn, and the *grass* of the boundless prairies." His conservatism in pronunciation and purism in spelling were accepted at Harvard and the University of Virginia, but elsewhere Webster prevailed, although Holmes was speaking for the best New England writers when he declared in favor of "Mr. Worcester's Dictionary, on which as is well known, the literary men of this metropolis are by special statutes allowed to be sworn in place of the Bible." Worcester's last great revision appeared as *A Dictionary of the English Language* (1860), but, with the 1864 revision of Webster by a company of scholars, the Webster supremacy was definitely established.

WORCESTER, NOAH (1758–1837), nephew of Joseph E. Worcester, was a New Hampshire clergyman and editor. His *Bible News . . .* (1810) and *Respectful Address . . .* (1811) are essentially Unitarian and led him to desert the Congregational Church to become the editor of *The Christian Disciple* (1813). From Unitarianism he developed an interest in pacifism, becoming the secretary of the Massachusetts Peace Society (1815–28), editor of *The Friend of Peace* (1819–28), and, under the pseudonym Philo Pacificus, author of *A Solemn Review of the Custom of War* (1814) and other popular pacifist works.

Worcester Magazine, see *Massachusetts Spy.*

WORK, HENRY CLAY, see *Ten Nights in a Barroom.*

World According to Garp, *The,* novel by John Irving,♦ published in 1978.

Jenny Fields, a dedicated New England heiress, drops out of Wellesley College to nurse warshattered soldiers in a Boston hospital during World War II. There she quixotically decides to have a child and therefore gives herself to a dying, brain-damaged airplane gunner who can only shout the meaningless exclamation, "Garp." Therefore she calls their child T.S. (for Technical Sergeant) Garp. In time he goes to a New England preparatory school, where she serves as a nurse and writes the book *A Sexual Suspect,* a statement on women's sensibilities and rights. Garp too becomes an author, matures to marry a bookish woman, Helen, and fathers two children, Duncan and Walt, while his mother becomes a leader of the women's rights movement. In an auto accident, while Garp is driving, Walt is killed, Duncan loses an eye, and Helen is severely injured. With his remaining family Garp then goes to live in a home for battered women run by his mother, which houses a cult of Ellen Jamesians, named for a folk hero, an 11-year-old girl who was raped. There he writes a novel, *The World According to Bensenhaver,* a tale of ghastly happenings and some compassionate people. Violent tragedy occurs in real life too as Jenny is killed by a demented man and Garp is later shot down by a woman who mistakenly believes he raped her sister. Although mother and son are murdered, their ideas, respectively about women and about people of sensitivity, continue to affect followers.

World War I, major conflict involving most of the nations of the world (1914–18), and sometimes called the Great War. It was an outgrowth of European territorial problems and nationalism, but the U.S. was finally brought to take an active part (April 6, 1917), the immediate cause being the unrestricted German submarine warfare upon Atlantic shipping. On the side of the British, French, Belgian, and other Allied forces, opposing Germany and the Central Powers, the American Expeditionary Force from October 23, 1917, until the Armistice (Nov. 11, 1918) participated in many battles on the western front, including such critical engagements as the battles of Cantigny, Château-Thierry, Belleau Wood, Saint-Mihiel, the Marne, and the Argonne offensive. The U.S. Senate refused to ratify the Treaty of Versailles, and a separate treaty of peace was signed by the U.S. and Germany at Berlin (Aug. 25, 1921).

The many works of American literature that deal with the war and its aftermath include Anderson and Stallings's *What Price Glory?*, E.E. Cummings's *The Enormous Room*, Dos Passos's *Three Soldiers*, Faulkner's *Soldiers' Pay* and *A Fable*, and Hemingway's *A Farewell to Arms.*

World War II broke into active combat with Germany's attack on Poland (Sept. 1939). During 1939–41 the U.S. was split by views ranging from intervention to isolationism. Meanwhile Japan, seeking expansion in a so-called Greater East Asia co-prosperity sphere, pursued undeclared war in China and seized the opportunity of French defeat to establish troops in southeast Asia and enter the Rome-Berlin "axis." On December 7, 1941, Japanese aircraft bombed Pearl Harbor, crippling the U.S. Pacific fleet, after which Germany and Italy followed Japan in declaring war on the U.S. After great losses in the Orient and the Pacific, including the Philippines, the U.S. and Allied forces began an offensive over island "stepping stones" to the Philippines (Oct. 1944) and to Iwo Jima and Okinawa, within bombing distance of the enemy's home islands. During this time the Russians had turned back besieging Germans at Stalingrad (Nov. 1942) and the U.S. air forces had joined Allied raids on strategic European military and industrial installations, systematically reducing Germany's ability to wage war. In November 1942, Anglo-American forces landed in Algeria and Morocco and, in a campaign climaxed by a fierce struggle for Tunisia, drove the enemy from North Africa (May 1943). During 1943 the tide of Axis success was turned by the maturing of the vast industrial power of the U.S., the stubborn military might of the U.S.S.R., the tenacity of a Britain fighting for survival, and underground resistance in occupied countries. General Dwight D. Eisenhower, who had commanded Allied troops in the African campaign, led the invasions of Sicily (July 1943) and Italy (Sept. 1943), and became supreme commander of the Allied forces that invaded the Normandy peninsula on "D-Day" (June 6, 1944). Germany finally capitulated on "V-E Day" (May 8, 1945). Faced by the might of the Allied nations and appalled by the atomic bombs' devastation of Hiroshima (Aug. 6) and Nagasaki (Aug. 8), the Japanese surrendered on "V-J Day" (Aug. 14, 1945). The wartime cooperation of the Allied nations was formalized into the United Nations.

Besides reportage, including the works of Ernie Pyle and William L. White, American writings concerned with the war include Maxwell Anderson's *The Eve of St. Mark,* Harry Brown's *A Walk in the Sun,* Cozzens's *Guard of Honor;* Joseph Heller's *Catch-22;* Hersey's *A Bell for Adano, Hiroshima,* and *The Wall;* James Jones's *From Here to Eternity, The Thin Red Line,* and *Whistle;* Mailer's *The Naked and the Dead;* Arthur Miller's *Incident at Vichy;* Shapiro's *V-Letter;* Shaw's *The Young Lions;* Stein's *Brewsie and Willie* and *Wars I Have Seen;* Vonnegut's *Slaughterhouse-Five;* and Wouk's *The Caine Mutiny, The Winds of War,* and *War and Remembrance.*

World's Work (1900–1932), monthly magazine, founded and edited by W.H. Page until 1913. It concentrated on the American way of life and the U.S. position in the "newly organized world . . . trying to convey the cheerful spirit of men who do things." An independent British counterpart, with which it cooperated, was founded in 1902. The original policy, but a less optimistic attitude during the Depression, continued until the magazine was absorbed by the *Review of Reviews.* ◆

WOUK, HERMAN (1915–), New York City author, after graduation from Columbia and navy service in World War II published *Aurora Dawn* (1947), a mannered satire on the advertising business; *The City Boy* (1948), sympathetically and humorously describing a New York boy's life in the 1920s; *The Caine Mutiny*◆ (1951, Pulitzer Prize), about cruelties and cowardice on a minesweeper in the Pacific war, adapted by him as the play *The Caine Mutiny Court-Martial* (1954); *Marjorie Morningstar* (1955), about a Jewish girl's quest for romance and a stage career until she settles down as a New Jersey matron; *Youngblood Hawke* (1962), about a young Kentucky author (perhaps partly suggested by Thomas Wolfe), who is commercially successful but destroyed as artist and person in New York; and *Don't Stop the Carnival* (1965), a comic novel about a resort in the Caribbean. *The Winds of War* (1971) and *War and Remembrance* (1978) are two lengthy novels comprising a saga of World War II in its vast scope, often concentrating on Pacific operations but also vividly depicting the Holocaust. *Inside, Outside* (1985) deals with the life of an Orthodox Jew from the days of his Czarist Russian-era family to his own lively days as a young American in Nixon's era. *The Hope* (1993) chronicles the first 20 years of the state of Israel, a saga continued in *The Glory* (1994). The novels of the 1970s and later are not only morally serious and documented by thorough research but also popular presentations of fictive characters mingling with great historic figures and situations. *The Traitor* (1949) and *Nature's Way* (1957) are plays. *The "Lomokome" Papers* (1968) is a brief and minor work of science fiction, written in 1949. *This Is My God* (1959) is about Judaism.

Wounds in the Rain, collection of stories and sketches by Stephen Crane.◆

Wreck of the Hesperus, *The,* literary ballad by Longfellow,◆ published in *Ballads and Other Poems* (1841).

Based on the actual wreck of the *Hesperus,* in which one body was found lashed to a piece of wreckage, the poem tells of the ill-fated voyage of the schooner, whose skipper refuses to head for port despite an approaching hurricane. When the gale descends, he wraps his little daughter in a seaman's coat, lashes her to the mast, and remains at the helm until he is overcome by the cold. The ship is shattered upon the reef of Norman's Woe near Gloucester, and at dawn a fisherman finds the child's body near the shore, still lashed to the mast.

WRIGHT, AUSTIN TAPPAN (1883–1931), New Hampshire-born, Harvard-educated professor of law at the University of California, Berkeley, and the University of Pennsylvania, author of a posthumously published, very lengthy Utopian novel, *Islandia* (1942). It completely documents an imaginary insular nation (with full data on its weather, peerage, etc.) that is based on an agricultural economy and a transcendental sort of philosophy.

WRIGHT, CHAUNCEY (1830–75), Massachusetts mathematician and philosopher, wrote for *The Mathematical Monthly, The North American Review,* and *The Nation.* His paper on the law of the arrangement of leaves (1873) was reissued as a pamphlet by Darwin. He lectured at Harvard (1870) and was appointed instructor in mathematical physics there (1874). His *Philosophical Discussions* (1877) were collected by C.E. Norton, and his *Letters* (1878) give a clue to his brilliant conversation.

WRIGHT, FRANCES (1795–1852), Scottish-born free-thinker and author, who spent two years in the U.S. (1818–20), where she produced her play *Altorf* (1819), about the Swiss fight for independence, and toured the country as reported in her enthusiastic *Views of Society and Manners in America* (1821). While abroad she wrote *A Few Days in Athens* (1822), fiction about a young disciple of Epicurus, which Whitman later called his "daily food." Returning to the U.S. (1824), she accompanied Lafayette on his triumphal tour and through him met Jefferson and Madison. Encouraged by them, she founded the Nashoba Community (1825–28) in Tennessee as part of her plan for gradual emancipation of blacks. Influenced by Robert Dale Owen,◆ she joined him in editing *The New-Harmony Gazette* (1828–29), meanwhile giving public talks on women's rights, free education, birth control, equitable distribution of wealth, and errors of organized religion. These and later talks, given after an absence abroad (1830–35), were published as *Course of Popular Lectures* (2 vols., 1829, 1836).

WRIGHT, FRANK LLOYD (1869–1959), Wisconsin-born architect, began work as an assistant to Louis Sullivan (1887–94). He developed a Prairie style having low horizontal lines to harmonize with the Midwestern landscape, large windows, open terraces, and interiors treated as unified flowing space. His cantilever construction and poured and reinforced concrete also illustrate his creed that form should follow function. After 1910 he replaced his simple surfaces by external ornamentation, as in Tokyo's Imperial Hotel (1916–22), also known for the floating cantilever construction, which enabled it to withstand the earthquake of 1923. During the 1920s, he stressed patterned blocks of precast concrete, reinforced at the joints, which produced an austere effect, as in the Millard house (1921). Later he became more occupied with homes and office buildings that achieve their effect mainly through the disposition of masses and the frank emphasis upon modern materials rather than decoration. His books include *Modern Architecture* (1931), *An Autobiography* (1932, revised 1943), *Frank Lloyd Wright on Architecture* (1941), *When Democracy Builds* (1945), revised as *The Living City* (1958), and *The Natural House* (1954). He was the inspiration for the hero of Ayn Rand's novel *The Fountainhead* and of Meyer Levin's novel *The Architect.*

WRIGHT, HAROLD BELL (1872–1944), popular novelist whose works include *The Shepherd of the Hills* (1907), *The Calling of Dan Matthews* (1909), and *When a Man's a Man* (1916). His stories, set in the great open spaces of the Southwest, are concerned with love and adventure, and emphasize an incredibly wholesome morality and the superiority of the rugged natural man. His books had a tremendous sale; *The Winning of Barbara Worth* (1911) sold 1,500,000 copies in 25 years.

WRIGHT, JAMES [ARLINGTON] (1927–80), Ohio-born poet, graduated from Kenyon College, received a Ph.D. from the University of Washington, and from 1966 on taught at Hunter College. His first book, *The Green Wall* (1957), in the Yale Series of Younger Poets, was followed by *Saint Judas* (1959), *The Lion's Tail and Eyes* (1962), *The Branch Will Not Break* (1963), *Shall We Gather at the River?* (1968), *Collected Poems* (1971, Pulitzer Prize), *Two Citizens* (1973), *Moments of the Italian Summer* (1976), *To a Blossoming Pear Tree* (1977), and *This Journey* (1982), whose poems are heavily imaged and often formal. His complete collected poems were incorporated in *Above the River* (1990).

WRIGHT, RICHARD [NATHANIEL] (1908–60), self-educated black author, born near Natchez, Miss., and reared in Memphis. After many menial jobs there and in Chicago, to which he migrated at age 19, he had to go on relief during the Depression. During the 1930s he joined the Communist party but left it in the 1940s, as recorded in the anthology *The God That Failed* (1950). His *Uncle Tom's Children* (1938, enlarged 1940), a collection of four long stories, received the Story prize for the best book submitted by anyone associated with the Federal Writers' Project. ♦ The stories tell of race prejudice in the South and contain graphic descriptions of lynchings. With the publication in 1940 of *Native Son,* ♦ Wright was considered not only the leading black author of the U.S. but also a major force in the naturalistic tradition in his story of the tragedy of a black boy reared in the Chicago slums. The novel was successfully dramatized (1941) by Wright and Paul Green, and in 1950 the author made a film of it in Argentina, with himself in the lead role. After his major novel, Wright participated in the creation of *12 Million Black Voices* (1941), a text and photo folk history of American blacks, and wrote *Black Boy* ♦ (1945), an autobiography of his childhood and youth. After World War II he became an expatriate in Paris and while there wrote *The Outsider* ♦ (1953), a sensational novel of a black man's life in Chicago and New York City and his fatal involvement with the Communist party, and *The Long Dream* (1958), a novel about a black boy in Mississippi and his father's corrupt business dealings with both blacks and whites. Other books include *Black Power* (1954), his reactions to "a land of pathos," Africa's Gold Coast; *The Color Curtain* (1956), reporting the Bandung Conference of Asian and African nations; and *Pagan Spain* (1957), his bitter personal observations of Spain. Posthumously issued works include *Eight Men* (1961), stories; *Lawd Today* (1963), a novel written prior to *Native Son* and dealing in great detail with one unhappy day—February 12, 1936—in the life of a black postal clerk in Chicago; and *American Hunger* (1977), an autobiographical account written as a sequel to *Black Boy.*

WRIGHT, WILLARD HUNTINGTON (1888–1939), born in Virginia, was educated in California and at Harvard and became an editor of *The Smart Set* ♦ (1913–14), distinguishing himself as a sophisticated student of esoteric subjects. His writings, during this period in New York and a residence in Europe, included *Europe After 8:15* (1913), in collaboration with H.L. Mencken and G.J. Nathan, co-editors of *The Smart Set; What Nietzsche Taught* (1914); *Modern Painting* (1915); and *The Future of Painting* (1923). In 1925 he suffered a serious illness, and, being unable to undertake more formidable work, began writing detective novels. The principal character of his popular series in this genre is the master sleuth Philo Vance, whose urbanity and scholarship were obviously modeled on the author's. *The Benson Murder Case* (1926) was followed by many other Philo Vance stories, all written under the pseudonym S.S. Van Dine.

WRIGHT, WILLIAM, see *De Quille, Dan.*

WROTH, L[AWRENCE] C[OUNSELMAN] (1884–1970), librarian of the John Carter Brown Library (1923–57) and research professor of American history at Brown University, was the author of several bibliographical and historical works, including *Parson Weems* (1911), *The Colonial Printer* (1931), and *An American Bookshelf, 1755* (1934).

WURDEMANN, AUDREY (1911–60), born in Seattle, graduated from the University of Washington and moved to New York (1932). Her poems are collected in *The House of Silk* (1927), *Bright Ambush* (1934, Pulitzer Prize), *The Seven Sins* (1935), *Splendour in the Grass* (1936), and a sonnet sequence, *Testament of Love* (1938). She was the wife of Joseph Auslander, ♦ with whom she collaborated on a novel and a volume of poems.

Wyandot Indians, see *Huron Indians.*

Wyandotté, romance by Cooper. ♦

WYETH, NATHANIEL JARVIS (1802–56), Boston merchant, attempted to build a fur-trading and salmon-shipping business in Oregon, but his overland expeditions (1832–33, 1834–36) were unsuccessful. His *Correspondence and Journals* was published in 1899, and contemporary records by companions, John B. Wyeth and John Kirk Townsend, were issued respectively as *Oregon, or, A Short History of a Long Journey* (1833) and *Narrative of a Journey . . . to the Columbia River* (1839). Wyeth figures prominently in Irving's *Adventures of Captain Bonneville.*

WYLIE, ELINOR [HOYT] (1885–1928), born in New Jersey, published her first collection of poems in England, the anonymous, privately issued *Incidental Numbers* (1912). Her brilliant though brief literary career began with the publication of *Nets To Catch the Wind* (1921), highly polished verse influenced by the metaphysical poets, whose emotion has been described as "a passion frozen at its source." This was followed by a similar collection, *Black Armour* (1923). Her four novels are distinguished by a very mannered craftmanship and a juxtaposition of artificial formality and fantasy like that of her verse. *Jennifer Lorn* (1923), subtitled "A Sedate Extravaganza," deals with 18th-century aristocrats in England and colonial India. *The Venetian Glass Nephew* (1925) has the same delicate color and fragility, which caused Cabell to characterize the author as a "Dresden china shepherdess." *The Orphan Angel* (1926), which appeared in England as *Mortal Image* (1927), is an imaginative story of Shelley, who, instead of being drowned, is picked up by a Yankee ship and brought to America, where his character is contrasted with the pioneer environment. *Mr. Hodge & Mr. Hazard* (1928) is a more realistic tale of English life during the 1830s, after the departure of such romantic figures as Byron and Shelley, whose spirits hover over the prosaic period. *One Person* (1928), a passionately intense sonnet sequence, was republished in *Angels and Earthly Creatures* (1929). *Trivial Breath* (1928) is a final selection of the poems after *Black Armour* which she wished to preserve. Her *Collected Poems* (1932) and *Collected Prose* (1933) were edited by her husband William Rose Benét, and *Last Poems* appeared in 1943.

Wynne, HUGH, see *Hugh Wynne*.

X–Y

Xingu, and Other Stories, eight tales by Edith Wharton,♦ published in 1916.

"Xingu" is a witty account of the Hillbridge Lunch Club, a gathering of "indomitable huntresses of erudition"—hypocrites and snobs, with the single exception of a newcomer, Mrs. Roby—who entertain a famous woman author. Her indifference to the "topics" advanced for discussion ends only when Mrs. Roby refers familiarly to "Xingu," an esoteric subject that she and the other members then pretend to know thoroughly. The ladies of the Lunch Club discover the Xingu to be a Brazilian river, and, crestfallen and indignant, expel Mrs. Roby. "Coming Home," a story of the World War, is concerned with a young Frenchwoman who gives herself to a German officer to save her fiancé's home and family from destruction. The fiancé takes revenge by murdering the German, now a wounded prisoner, who is entrusted to his care. "Autres Temps . . ." is a poignant tale of a woman's personal tragedy, contrasting the attitudes toward divorce of two generations of New York society. "Kerfol" and "The Triumph of Night" are subtle delineations of ghosts, mystery, and terror. "Bunner Sisters," a novelette, tells of the lives of two commonplace spinsters who operate a small shop near Stuyvesant Square, in 19th-century New York City.

Yale Series of Younger Poets, volumes issued annually since 1919 by Yale University Press to print the work of promising American poets under 40 who have not previously published a book of poetry. Stephen Vincent Benét, MacLeish, Auden, and Dudley Fitts have been judges of manuscripts submitted for this literary award and editors of the published books. Winners have included Hervey Allen (1921), Oscar Williams (1922), Paul Engle (1932), James Agee (1934), Muriel Rukeyser (1935), Ted Olson (1937), William Meredith (1946), Eve Merriam (1948), Adrienne Rich (1952), W.S. Merwin (1953), Daniel Hoffman (1955), John Ashbery (1956), James Wright (1957), John Hollander (1958), William Dickey (1959), Alan Dugan (1961), Jean Valentine (1965), Peter Davidson (1964), James Tate (1966), and Robert Hass (1972).

Yamasee Indians, war-like tribe in South Carolina and Georgia during colonial times. After 1715 reduced to a small number, they took refuge mainly in Florida. They are often referred to by Southern authors, notably in Simms's *The Yemassee,*♦ which deals with their attempt to massacre the English of South Carolina, when incited by the Spanish of Florida (1715).

Yamoyden, poem in six cantos on the wars of King Philip,♦ written by J.W. Eastburn♦ and R.C. Sands,♦ published in 1820. It is based upon a cursory knowledge of Hubbard's *Narrative of the Indian Wars* and similar studies, but the Puritans are depicted as wholly wrong, the Indians as wholly right. The work was extremely popular and inaugurated a new literary subject.

Yank (1942–45), weekly magazine written by and published for enlisted men of the army. The most widely circulated service periodical during World War II, its most popular features were cartoons, such as "The Sad Sack" by George Baker, pinup pictures of girls, letters from soldiers, and editorial comment on issues of importance to men in the ranks.

Yankee, term of unknown origin, applied during the 18th century to New Englanders. One hypothetical origin is an attempt by the Indians to pronounce either *English* or *Anglais.* This seems unlikely, since the word was first applied to the Dutch in the 17th century and may have been derived from *Janke,* diminutive of the common Dutch name *Jan,* or from *Jankees,* a blend of *Jan* and *Cornelis.* At some time in the 18th century the name began to be applied to the English colonists rather than the Dutch. The song "Yankee Doodle"♦ did much to establish the name, which was adopted by the Americans after it had been contemptuously applied by the British in the Revolution. During the Civil War it was invidiously applied to Northerners, usually as "damn Yankee." During World War I it had mainly a kindly, facetious connotation, and long before that it was applied to Americans generally, although it is more properly restricted to the typical New England native and associated with the Down East♦ character. The Yankee has long been a stock comic figure, and some of the notable characters of this type are Royall Tyler's Jonathan in *The Contrast,* Seba Smith's Major Jack Downing, T.C. Haliburton's Sam Slick, and Lowell's Hosea Biglow. Irving's Ichabod Crane, although he has some of the usual characteristics, lacks the conventional acuteness. The figure is usually marked by shrewd, homespun wit, caution, ability in trading, and taciturnity. When he speaks, it is frequently to ask a dry but astute question, or to make a striking understatement in his famous nasal twang. Later examples of the type include the title characters of Mark Twain's *Connecticut Yankee in King Arthur's Court* and E.N. Westcott's *David Harum*.

"Yankee Doodle," popular song of the patriot troops during the Revolutionary War, the origin of whose title, words, and tune is unknown. It has often been attributed to a Dr. Shuckburg, a British army surgeon, who supposedly wrote the words in derision of the motley American army. The earliest manuscript version is dated 1775, and the earliest known printing was in a Scottish collection *c.*1778. In Tyler's *The Contrast*♦ (1787), Jonathan says he knows only 190 of its verses, although "our Tabitha at home can sing it all."

Yankee in Canada, A, travel narrative by Thoreau, ♦ partly published in *Putnam's Monthly Magazine* (1853), and issued posthumously in a volume with his "Anti-Slavery and Reform Papers" (1866). Derived from his journal notes during a week's trip (Sept. 25–Oct. 3, 1850) from his home in Concord to Montreal and Quebec, the narrative presents homely impressions of the farmers and townspeople, and the intimate details of travel and scenery, with digressions of literary criticism and comments on fortresses, Roman Catholicism, the railroad, and comparative manners in Canada and New England.

Yankey in England, The, comedy by David Humphreys, ♦ produced by amateurs in 1814 and published in 1815. The play is set in a London hotel, where American Whig and Tory officers meet a French nobleman and an adventuress. Their actions furnish a background for Doolittle and Newman, the Yankees, who straighten out their complicated affairs. The last two are significant as showing the Yankee tradition of paradoxical simplicity and cunning, in contrast to the refinement of the other characters.

Yardbird Reader, literary annual founded (1972) by Ishmael Reed♦ in Berkeley, Cal., as an anthology of writings by contemporary Afro-American authors. In 1978 it was renamed *Y'Bird Magazine.* Editorship has been circulated among several authors, some representative of other minorities, on whose writings special issues have concentrated.

Yazoo frauds, Georgia land speculation (1795), in which four companies bribed the state legislature, in order to obtain grants for large areas of land to which the state itself had doubtful claims. This territory lay in the present Alabama and Mississippi, some near the Yazoo River. The sale was revoked the following year. *The Georgia Spec; or, Land in the Moon* (1797), a lost play by Royall Tyler, ridiculed the scheme, and Sarah Wood's *Dorval; or, The Speculator* (1801) is also concerned with the episode.

Yearling, The, novel by Marjorie K. Rawlings.♦

Yellow Bird, pseudonym of John R. Ridge.♦

Yellow Jack, play by Sidney Howard, ♦ produced and published in 1934.

Yellow Jacket, The, drama by George C. Hazelton and J. Harry Benrimo, produced in 1912. This play, on a Chinese theme concerned with the life of a boy and his attempt to win his rightful claim to the throne from his half-brother, was successful not only for its subject matter but because of its novelty in employing the technique of native Chinese drama, preserving such conventions as the property man and the chorus.

Yellow press, term applied to unscrupulously sensational newspapers. In 1894 the New York *World* printed the first colored comic strip, "Hogan's Alley," by R.F. Outcault, whose "bad boy" hero, the Yellow Kid, attracted subscribers by the cartoon and the novelty of color printing. Hearst's New York *Journal* employed Outcault (1896ff.), and from the sensational controversy between the two papers, both of which printed Yellow Kid serials, the term originated.

Yemassee, The, romance by Simms,♦ published in 1835 as one of his Border Romances. It deals with the warfare of the Yamasee♦ in colonial South Carolina.

YERBY, FRANK [GARVIN] (1916–91), Georgia-born African-American author, after receiving an M.A. from Fisk (1938) taught briefly at Southern universities but concentrated on the writing of historical romances after the great success of his *The Foxes of Harrow* (1946), set in the pre-Civil War South. He continued to write such popular fiction, some in part concerned with black people. His novels include *A Woman Called Fancy* (1951); *The Garfield Honor* (1961); *An Odor of Sanctity* (1965); *Goat Song: A Novel of Ancient Greece* (1967); *Judas, My Brother* (1968); *A Darkness at Ingraham's Crest* (1979); *Western: A Saga of the Great Plains* (1982); *Devilseed* (1984), dealing with a prostitute in gold rush San Francisco who becomes rich and proper; and his 32nd novel, *McKenzie's Hundred* (1985), concerning a questing woman in Virginia on the eve of the Civil War. From 1959 Yerby was an expatriate living in Spain.

Yes Is for a Very Young Man, play by Gertrude Stein♦ (produced 1946, published 1947), about life and loyalties in World War II France under German occupation, drawing upon her *Wars I Have Seen.* It was titled *In Savoy* in England.

YEZIERSKA, ANZIA (1885–1970), Russian-Jewish immigrant, among the most noted Jewish-American writers in the period 1920–32, during which time this former schoolteacher and housewife published two short story collections and four novels about the struggles of Jewish immigrants on New York's Lower East Side. Yezierska's first collection, *Hungry Hearts* (1920), contained her most famous story, "Fat of the Land," which not only gives a feminist view of the often futile fight against poverty but also explores the difficult choice of Jewish women between a quest for self-determination or a submission to Old World patriarchy. Her best novel, *Bread Givers* (1925), had a similar theme of self-liberation. Sara Smolinsky rebels hard against her tyrant father, an unsuccessful teacher of Hebrew, then works through night school and college to become a schoolteacher. Still not fulfilled, Sara marries the principal of her school, who then gets her to invite her father, now widowed, to live with them—a conclusion that pleased neither feminists nor the Jewish critics, who deplored her portrayals of Jewish men and her quest for freedom at the expense of family and community life. *Salome of the Tenements* had appeared in 1922. Samuel Goldwyn bought *Hungry Hearts* and *Salome* for the screen, and brought Yezierska to Hollywood to collaborate on the screenplays and to promote her among the gossip columnists. The publicity made her famous. She published *All I Could Never Be* (1932), an autobiographical novel, but then dropped from notice, although her autobiography, *Red Ribbon on a White Horse,* was published in 1950 with an introduction by W.H. Auden.

Yoknapatawpha County, fictional setting in northern Mississippi for the saga of 14 novels and many stories by William Faulkner.♦ Based on Lafayette County and its capital, Oxford, Faulkner's mythical land, whose capital is called Jefferson, has an area of 2400 square miles and a population of 6298 whites and 9313 blacks, according to the map that its creator printed in the 1951 edition of *Absalom, Absalom!* The name of the county is presumably of Chickasaw derivation, for these Indians, such as Ikkemotubbe,♦ are presented as the original possessors of the land. In order of their publication, the novels set in whole or in part in this land are *Sartoris, The Sound and the Fury, As I Lay Dying, Sanctuary, Light in August, Absalom, Absalom!, The Unvanquished, The Hamlet, Intruder in the Dust, Knight's Gambit, Requiem for a Nun, The Town, The Mansion,* and *The Reivers,* and the stories set there include "The Bear" and other tales in *Go Down, Moses.* The characters involved in the life of this land include the Benbow, Compson, De Spain, McCaslin, Sartoris, Snopes, Stevens, Sutpen, and Varner families. (See also *individual entries for titles and characters.*)

You Can't Go Home Again, novel by Thomas Wolfe,♦ published in 1940. It is a sequel to *The Web and the Rock.*♦

George Webber, aged 29, returns to New York City from his emotional residence in Germany to resume his love affair with Esther Jack, the older, married, wealthy society woman who is an acclaimed stage designer. George also returns to an earlier life when he revisits his hometown of Libya Hill in the Southern state of Old Catawba to attend the funeral of his Aunt Joyner, who reared him after his father deserted the family and his mother died. But he sees how much his childhood world has changed as the townspeople are intent on making money during boom times to such an extent that even a leading citizen like Judge Rumford Bland takes usurious advantage of black people to become rich but morally bankrupt. Returning to New York George falls prey to social lion hunters when his novel is published as a great success. Disaffected by both worlds, he becomes a recluse in Brooklyn, trying unsuccessfully to write a second novel, then flees to London and to Germany. But everywhere George is disillusioned, by contemporary values in the U.S., by the sterility and frustration of its most famous author, and by the evil he discerns in the rise of Nazism. Even upon his return to New York George can find no surcease and breaks with Fox Edwards, the brilliant editor who had helped to shape his novel, accusing him of fatalistically accepting the world as it is, while George declares that although "I believe that we are lost here in America, . . . I believe we shall be found."

You Can't Take It with You, comedy by Moss Hart♦ and George S. Kaufman,♦ produced in 1936 and published in 1937, when it was awarded a Pulitzer Prize.

You Know Me Al, stories by Ring Lardner.♦

Youma, novel by Lafcadio Hearn,♦ published in 1890. It is based on an actual occurrence in the Martinique slave rebellion of 1848.

YOUNG, AL[BERT JAMES] (1939–), Mississippi-born novelist and poet, long resident in California, a graduate of the University of California, Berkeley (1969), and a teacher of creative writing at Stanford. His first, brief novel, *Snakes* (1970), is the story of a black jazz musician; *Who Is Angelina?* (1975) depicts a young black woman in quest of herself; *Sitting Pretty* (1976) is the autobiographical recollection of a black man, told in the vernacular and ostensibly into a tape recorder; *Ask Me Now* (1980) presents an overage black professional basketball player in retirement; and *Seduction by Light* (1988) is about a black woman from Mississippi living uneasily in Hollywood. Young's poems, also drawing on the experiences and attitudes of his race, and obviously influenced by Whitman, appear in *Dancing* (1969), *The Song Turning Back into Itself* (1971), *Geography of the Near Past* (1976), and *The Blues Don't Change* (1982). He has written two books of memoirs related to his concern with music: *Kinds of Blue*

(1984) and *Things Ain't What They Used To Be*
(1987). He was also a major contributor to *Mingus / Mingus* (1989), devoted to a major figure of
jazz who had died ten years earlier.

YOUNG, ALEXANDER (1800–1854), Massachusetts antiquarian and Unitarian minister,
noted for his critical reprinting of source material
in *Chronicles of the Pilgrim Fathers . . . from 1602 to
1625* (1841) and *Chronicles of the First Planters of the
Colony of Massachusetts Bay from 1623 to 1636*
(1846).

YOUNG, ART[HUR] (1866–1943), cartoonist
noted for his striking satirical drawings for liberal
and radical publications. His pacifistic cartoons
during World War I led to a trial for sedition. His
books include *Hell Up to Date* (1893) and *Art
Young's Inferno* (1934), showing Hell as the abode
of reactionaries; and two autobiographical works,
On My Way (1928) and *Art Young: His Life and
Times* (1939).

YOUNG, BRIGHAM (1801–77), born in Vermont near the birthplace of Joseph Smith, of a
poor, semi-literate frontier family, was baptized
as a Mormon♦ (1832). He became a leading missionary in both the U.S. and England, and upon
the assassination of Smith (1844) had himself
elected president of the church. He led the mass
migration from Illinois to the valley of Great Salt
Lake in the present Utah (1846–47). Developing
the agriculture there, he made the colony a
strong theocratic state and ruled it dictatorially.
He had little effect on the theological beliefs, but
proved himself a successful social and economic
administrator of the church. Young was constantly embroiled with the U.S. government, but
when his colony was made into a territory he
became its first civil governor (1850–58) and
controlled his successors. Although he was harsh
with both Mormons who disagreed with him and
all outsiders, he acted with pure realism as a utilitarian whose one aim was to preserve his church.
He was extremely moral, although his concept of
morality included polygamy, and he is said to
have had at various times between 19 and 27
wives, many of them holding that position in
name only for doctrinal purposes. Young's sermons appear in his *Journal of Discourses* (26 vols.,
1854–86). He appears in the accounts of many
travelers to the Far West, including the works of
foreigners, such as Sir Richard Burton's *City of
the Saints,* and such different American views as
Samuel Bowles's *Across the Continent* and Mark
Twain's *Roughing It.* Studies include M.R.
Werner's *Brigham Young,* Ray B. West's *Kingdom
of the Saints,* and Wallace Stegner's *The Gathering
of Zion.* He appears as a character in the novels
The Lions of the Lord by Harry Leon Wilson and
Children of God by Vardis Fisher.

YOUNG, STARK (1881–1963), graduated from
the University of Mississippi (1901) and taught

English literature there, at the University of
Texas, and at Amherst, until 1921. Meanwhile he
published *The Blind Man at the Window* (1906),
poems; *Guenevere* (1906), a verse play; one-act
prose plays; and *The Flower in Drama* (1923), essays on the theater. Later works include *The Three
Fountains* (1924), Italian sketches; *The Colonnade*
(1924) and *The Saint* (1925), plays; *Glamour*
(1925) and *The Theater* (1927), essays on drama
and the stage; the novels *Heaven Trees* (1926), *The
Torches Flare* (1928), *River House* (1929), and *So
Red the Rose* (1934), set in Mississippi during the
Civil War; *The Street of the Islands* (1930) and
Feliciana (1935), stories; and a translation of
Chekhov's *The Sea Gull* (1939). Drama criticism
for *The New Republic* is collected in *Immortal
Shadows* (1948). *The Pavilion* (1951) contains rem-
iniscences.

YOUNG, THOMAS, see *Allen, Ethan.*

Young Goodman Brown, allegorical tale by Hawthorne, ♦ published in *The New England Magazine*
(1835) and in *Mosses from an Old Manse* (1846).

Goodman Brown, a Puritan of early Salem,
leaves his young wife Faith, who pleads with him
not to go, to attend a witches' sabbath in the
woods. Among the congregation are many
prominent people of the village and church. At
the climax of the ceremonies, he and a young
woman are about to be confirmed into the
group, but he finds she is Faith, and cries to her to
"look up to heaven, and resist the wicked one."
Immediately he is alone in the forest, and all the
fearful, flaming spectacle has disappeared. He returns to his home, but lives a dismal, gloomy life,
doomed to skeptical doubt of all about him, and
never able to believe in goodness or piety.

Young Lonigan: *A Boyhood in Chicago Streets,*
novel by James T. Farrell, ♦ published in 1932.
This naturalistic study of the mind of a 15-year-
old boy, utilizing a stream-of-consciousness technique, is the first part of the Studs Lonigan trilogy, which includes *The Young Manhood of Studs
Lonigan* ♦ and *Judgment Day.* ♦

The son of a lower-class Catholic family, William Lonigan, nicknamed Studs, is depicted in
the common experiences of a boyhood on the
South Side of Chicago. He smokes secretly, plays
baseball and basketball, experiments with sex,
fights, swims, enjoys his first familiarity with the
older toughs he admires, and participates in Jew-
baiting, shoplifting, and other activities of the
youthful gang. Lucy Scanlan, a girl of his own
age, provides his first romantic affair; he has a
comradely friendship with the tomboy Helen
Shires; and shares with other boys the attentions
of Iris, a 14-year-old exponent of "free love."
Other characters include Studs's father and mother; his sister Frances; the priest, Father Gilhooley;
Leon, a middle-aged homosexual; Davey Cohen,
who deserts the gang when Iris refuses him be-

cause he is a Jew; and such intimates of Studs as "Weary" Reilley, Paulie Haggerty, and Kenny Killarney. The boy is shown throughout to have healthy impulses and attitudes, but these are perverted by his environment and partially repressed in order that he may display the hard, unsentimental exterior prevalent among his fellows.

Young Manhood of Studs Lonigan, The, novel by James T. Farrell,♦ published in 1934. The second part of his Studs Lonigan trilogy, it follows *Young Lonigan*♦ and precedes *Judgment Day.*♦

Continuing his naturalistic study of the experiences of a Chicago youth, the author follows young Lonigan from the end of his schooling, during World War I, to a New Year's Eve celebration of a decade later. Studs tries to join the army but fails because of his youth; attempts a holdup; goes to work with his father as a house painter; helps his gang to torture a black child during race riots; plays football in a rough game that ends in a gang fight; frequently becomes drunk; learns to dance; joins the YMCA but gives it up because the "joint looks phony"; has various experiences with girls, including his early sweetheart Lucy, who rejects him after he contracts a venereal disease from a "pickup"; is impressed by the dedication ceremonies of a new church and is nearly persuaded by his mother to undertake a mission; but reverts to hard drinking and narrowly escapes incrimination in his friend Weary's rape of a pickup during a New Year's Eve party. Brief alternating chapters show the universality of the main narrative, by presenting the similar experiences of Studs's younger brother Martin and of a black boy; the love affair of

Phil Rolfe, a Jew who accepts Catholicism because he wishes to marry Loretta Lonigan; the dreary lives of Studs's parents; the communistic ideas of the waiter Christy; Davey Cohen's degradation and beggary; and the views of Danny O'Neill, a university student and gas-station attendant, who seems to express the author's own commentary on these events.

Young Mrs. Winthrop, play by Bronson Howard,♦ produced in 1882 and published in 1899.

Youth's Companion, The (1827–1929), Boston weekly magazine, of which Nathaniel Willis was a founder, provided an amusing and instructive children's periodical unconnected with Sunday schools. Early contributors included the editor's son N.P. Willis, Felicia Hemans, and Lydia Huntley Sigourney. In 1857 it was purchased by Daniel Sharp Ford, who raised the circulation from 4000 to 500,000 before his death (1899), and began to print material for adult reading. The authors included Harriet Beecher Stowe, Gladstone, Tennyson, Whittier, Sarah Orne Jewett, Hardy, Kipling, T.H. Huxley, C.E. Craddock, James Bryce, Louisa May Alcott, and Rebecca Harding Davis. Before the turn of the century, the list of contributors included Howells, J.T. Trowbridge, Stevenson, Theodore Roosevelt, Jules Verne, Cleveland, Jack London, Aldrich, Garland, and Woodrow Wilson. In 1929 the magazine was merged with *The American Boy,* suspended in 1941. An anthology of selections was issued in 1954.

Yukon, see *Klondike gold rush.*

Z

ZATURENSKA, MARYA (1902–82), Russian-born poet, educated at the University of Wisconsin, whose verse is collected in *Cold Morning Sky* (1937, Pulitzer Prize), *The Listening Landscape* (1941), *The Golden Mirror* (1944), *Selected Poems* (1954), *Terraces of Light* (1960), *Collected Poems* (1965), and *The Hidden Waterfall* (1974). She also wrote *Christina Rossetti* (1949), a biography, and, with her husband, Horace Gregory, *A History of American Poetry, 1900–1940* (1946).

ZENGER, JOHN PETER (1697–1746), German-born printer and journalist in New York, served as an apprentice to William Bradford, and established the *New-York Weekly Journal*♦ (1733) to oppose Bradford's *New York Gazette* and assail the administration of the provincial governor. His polemical articles and rhymes caused him to be arrested and tried for criminal libel (1735). Despite the opposition of the judge, the jury found him not guilty, and his acquittal has been considered instrumental in establishing American freedom of the press. He published a verbatim account of the trial as *A Brief Narrative of the Case and Tryal of John Peter Zenger* (1736), and continued to edit the *Journal* until his death.

Zenobia, character in *The Blithedale Romance.*♦

ZINDEL, PAUL (1936–), New York-born dramatist whose *The Effect of Gamma Rays on Man-in-the-Moon Marigolds* (first produced 1964, published 1970), about the relationship of a teenage girl and her unhappy mother and sister, won a Pulitzer Prize (1971). Later plays include *And Miss Rearden Drinks a Little* (1967, produced 1971), *Let Me Hear You Whisper* (1974), and *Ladies at the Alamo* (1975). He has also written fiction and plays for children and teenagers.

ZINZENDORF, NICOLAUS, see *Moravian Church.*

Zoar, community established in Tuscarawas County, Ohio (1819), by a society of German Separatists, incorporated as the Separatist Society of Zoar (1832). Their spiritual and temporal head, Joseph Bäumeler, later spelled his name Bimeler, and the people were commonly called Bimelers. Marriage was at first prohibited, but this rule was set aside (*c.*1828). The community prospered and in 1874 had 300 members and more than a million dollars. Because of internal dissension it was dissolved (1898).

Zoo Story, The, play by Edward Albee.♦

Zooey Glass, character in *Franny and Zooey,* stories by J.D. Salinger.♦

ZUGSMITH, LEANE (1903–69), Kentucky-born proletarian author, whose novels include *All Victories Are Alike* (1929), the story of a newspaper columnist's loss of ideals; *Goodbye and Tomorrow* (1931), about a romantic spinster who seeks happiness by patronizing artists; *Never Enough* (1932), a panorama of American life during the 1920s; *The Reckoning* (1934), the story of a New York slum boy; *A Time To Remember* (1936), concerned with labor troubles and unionization in a New York department store; and *The Summer Soldier* (1938), about 20th-century injustices to blacks. *Home Is Where You Hang Your Childhood* (1937) and *Hard Times with Easy Payments* (1941) are collections of short stories.

ZUKOFSKY, LOUIS (1904–78), born of Russian immigrant parents on New York's Lower East Side, has come to be recognized as a major poet although his work was not commercially printed in a book until he was in his fifties. His lyric poems, spare, precise, and powerful, were first gathered from little magazines and booklets when he was in his sixties into *All the Collected Short Poems, 1923–1958* (1965) and *All the Collected Short Poems, 1956–1964* (1966). His works are marked by organic form, sharp observation, and verbal association with the object with which the poem began, and he was considered a leader of the Objectivist♦ school. In 1927 he started his great poem *"A,"* presenting in diverse forms his experience of art and life, of personal and public events, that began in *"A" 1–12* (1959) and *"A" 13–21* (1969) and was finally completed with the publication in 832 pages of *"A"* (1979). His poetic theories and other critical concepts are found in *Le Style Apollinaire* (Paris, 1934), *A Test of Poetry* (1948), *Prepositions* (1967), and *The Gas Age* (1969). His aesthetic views are also to be found in *Bottom: On Shakespeare* (2 vols., 1963), whose second part contains his wife Celia's musical setting for *Pericles.* With her he translated Catullus (1969), and to the poetic personal statements that comprise his *Autobiography* (1970) she contributed musical settings for his lyrics. He also published works of fiction: *It Was* (1961), revised as *Ferdinand* (1968), and *Little; for Careenagers* (1970), a comic tale of a prodigy violinist from his birth to age 12. These and other works were gathered in

Collected Fiction (1990). Zukofsky was a professor of English at various institutions, notably Polytechnic Institute, Brooklyn, and the University of Connecticut.

Zuñi Indians, agricultural tribe of western New Mexico, was visited by early Spanish explorers of the region. Incited by glowing accounts of the wealth of their seven pueblos, Coronado led an expedition against them in 1540, only to find that the "Seven Cities of Cibola" were ordinary Indian villages. The tribe is now concentrated in a single town, Zuñi, noted for its preservation of aboriginal pueblo customs and religion. F.H. Cushing, ♦ who lived among the Zuñi, published several volumes dealing with their life, and Edmund Wilson wrote of them in *Red, Black, Blond and Olive.*

Zury, the Meanest Man in Spring County, novel by Joseph Kirkland, ♦ published in 1887. A sequel, *The McVeys,* was published in 1888.

CHRONOLOGICAL INDEX

This is a year-by-year outline in parallel sequence of the social and literary history sumarized in *The Oxford Companion to American Literature*. While only the most significant events and writings are mentioned, the selection has not always been in accordance with conventional standards. The literary index attempts to include not only the leading authors, books, and periodicals, but also those less distinguished writers and works whose qualities make them noteworthy as representative of their time. In the social-historical index, each event and personality in some way constitutes a milestone in the progress of the American nation and its culture.

Since they are intended merely for reference to the discussions and summaries in the text, titles are not given in full. Plays and playwrights are included in the literary outline, the former under the date of first production. Only a few actors, painters, and other artists are included, and they are arbitrarily placed in the index of social history. In general terms, the index provides a means of ready comparison of the political, economic, religious, scientific, and aesthetic background of a given period with the chief literary events and personalities which it produced.

LITERARY HISTORY	SOCIAL HISTORY
	1577 Drake takes possession of New Albion
1578 Nathaniel Ward (*c.*1578–1652); Sandys (1578–1644)	
1580 John Smith (1580–1631)	
1584 John Cotton (1584–1652)	**1584** Roanoke founded
	Myles Standish (*c.*1584–1656)
1586 Thomas Hooker (1586–1647)	
	1587 Virginia Dare (1587—?)
1588 Hariot, *Briefe and True Report*	
John Winthrop (1588–1649)	
1589 Hakluyt, *The Principal Navigations*	
1590 William Bradford (1590–1657);	
Thomas Morton (1590?–1647)	
1595 Edward Winslow (1595–1655)	
1596 Richard Mather (1596–1669)	
1603 Roger William (*c.*1603–83)	
1604 John Eliot (1604–90)	
1605 Thomas Shepard (1605–49)	
	1606 Virginia and Plymouth Companies chartered
	1607 Jamestown founded
1608 Smith, *A True Relation*	**1608** Pocahontas "saves" Smith
1609 Gray, *Good Speed to Virginia*	**1609** Hudson discovers Hudson River, claims New Netherland
1610 Rich, *Newes from Virginia*	
1612 Smith, *A Map of Virginia*	
Anne Bradstreet (*c.*1612–72)	
1613 *Purchas His Pilgrimage;* Whitaker, *Good News from Virginia*	**1613** Sir Henry Vane (1613–62)
	1614 John Smith explores New England
1616 Smith, *A Description of New-England*	
Steendam (*c.*1616–*c.*1672)	
	1619 Black slavery introduced in Virginia
	1620 Council for New England
	Voyage of *Mayflower*
	Plymouth founded
	1621 New Amsterdam founded
1622 *Mourt's Relation*	
	1623 Dorchester Company of Adventurers
1624 Smith, *Generall Historie;* Winslow, *Good News from New England*	**1624** Virginia becomes royal colony
1625 Morrell, *Nova Anglia;* Purchas, *Hakluytus Posthumus*	**1625** Merry Mount settled
1626 Sandys, *Ovid*	**1626** Minuit director of New Netherland (1626–31); purchase of Manhattan

	1627 Suppression of Merry Mount
	1629 Massachusetts Bay Company chartered (Endecott governor, 1629–30)
1630 Smith, *The True Travels;* Cotton, *God's Promise to His Plantation;* Bradford, *History of Plimmoth Plantation* (1630–51); Winthrop, *Journals* (1630–49)	**1630** Voyage of *Arbella* Massachusetts Bay Colony
1631 Wigglesworth (1631–1705)	
	1633 Van Twiller, director of New Netherland (1633–37)
1634 Wood, *New Englands Prospect*	
	1635 Boston Latin School
	1636 Roger Williams at Providence Harvard College founded
1637 Morton, *New English Canaan*	**1637** Pequot War
	1638 Anne Hutchinson banished New Sweden founded
1639 Daye's press founded; first American almanac Increase Mather (1639–1723)	**1639** *Oath of a Free-man*
1640 *Bay Psalm Book*	**1640** Population of colonies, *c.*27,950
	1641 *Body of Liberties*
1642 Shepard, *The Sincere Convert*	**1642** Sir William Berkeley governor of Virginia (1642–52, 1660–77)
1643 *New Englands First Fruits;* Williams, *A Key into the Language*	**1643** New England Confederation (1643–84)
1644 Williams, *Bloudy Tenent of Persecution* Cotton, *Keys of the Kingdom of Heaven* Edward Taylor (*c.*1644–1729)	**1644** William Penn (1644–1718)
	1645 Roxbury Latin School
1646 Cotton, *Milk for Babes*	
1647 Ward, *Simple Cobler;* Cotton, *The Bloudy Tenent Washed*	**1647** Stuyvesant director of New Netherland (1647–64)
1648 Hooker, *Summe of Church Discipline*	**1648** Cambridge Platform
1649 *Platform of Church-Discipline*	**1649** Society for the Propagation of the Gospel in Foreign Parts
1650 Bradstreet, *The Tenth Muse*	**1650** Population, 51,700
	1651 First Navigation Act
1652 Samuel Sewall (1652–1730)	
1653 Johnson, *Wonder-Working Providence*	
	1655 Dutch take New Sweden
1656 Hammond, *Leah and Rachel*	
	1660 Population, 84,800 Second Navigation Act
1661 Eliot's translation of New Testament into Algonquin	
1662 Wigglesworth, *Day of Doom*	**1662** Half-Way Convenant
1663 Davenport, *Discourse about Civil Government* Cotton Mather (1663–1728)	
	1664 English seize New Amsterdam (now New York)
1665 *Ye Beare and Ye Club*	
1666 Pain, *Daily Meditations*	
1669 Wigglesworth, *Meat Out of the Eater;* Eliot, *The Indian Primer*	
	1670 Population, 114,500 Hudson's Bay Company chartered Charleston founded
	1671 Sir Henry Morgan captures Panama
	1672 Frontenac governor of New France (1672–82, 1689–98)
	1673 Jolliet and Marquette explore upper Mississippi
1674 Sewall's diary (1674–1729) William Byrd (1674–1744)	**1675** King Philip's War (1675–76)
1676 Thompson, *New Englands Crisis*	**1676** Bacon's Rebellion
1677 Mather, *A Relation of the Troubles*	
1678 Bradstreet, *Poems*	**1678** Duluth claims upper Missippi for France
	1680 Population, 155,600

LITERARY HISTORY	SOCIAL HISTORY
1682 Rowlandson, *Captivity and Restauration*	**1682** Penn settles Pennsylvania; La Salle explores Louisiana Philadelphia founded
1683 *New England Primer* (1683?) **1684** Mather, *Remarkable Providences*	**1684** Massachusetts charter revoked **1686** Andros governor of consolidated northern colonies
1687 Tulley's almanacs (1687–1701)	
1689 Mather, *Memorable Providences* **1690** *Publick Occurrences*	**1688** Smibert (1688–1751) **1689** Andros overthrown; Leisler's revolt **1690** Population, 213,500 King William's War (1690–97) **1692** Salem witchcraft trials Massachusetts under new charter; Phips governor (1692–95)
1693 Mather, *Wonders of the Invisible World;* Mather, *Cases of Conscience Concerning Evil Spirits* **1700** Sewall, *The Selling of Joseph;* Calef, *More Wonders of the Invisible World*	**1693** College of William and Mary founded **1700** Population, 275,000 **1701** Captain Kidd hanged Detroit founded; Yale College founded
1702 Mather, *Magnalia Christi Americana* **1703** Jonathan Edwards (1703–58) **1704** Sarah Knight's diary (1704–5); *Boston News Letter* (1704–76) **1705** Beverley, *History of Virginia* **1706** Benjamin Franklin (1706–90) **1708** Cook, *Sot-Weed Factor* **1710** Mather, *Bonifacius* ("Essays To Do Good") Wise, *The Churches Quarrel Espoused*	**1702** Queen Anne's War (1702–13) **1708** Saybrook Platform **1710** Population, 375,500 **1713** Treaty of Utrecht
1714 *Androboros* **1717** Wise, *Vindication of the Government of New England Churches*	**1717** Mississippi Bubble (1717–20) **1718** New Orleans founded Israel Putnam (1718–90)
1719 *Songs for the Nursery* *Boston Gazette* (1719–41) **1720** John Woolman (1720–72) **1721** Mather, *The Christian Philosopher* *New England Courant* (1721–26) Hell-Fire Club (1721–24) **1722** Franklin, "Dogood Papers" **1724** Mather, *Parentator* **1725** Ames almanacs (1725–75)	**1720** Population, 474,400 **1722** Samuel Adams (1722–1803) **1725** Lovewell's Fight James Otis (1725–83)
1726 Mather, *Manuductio ad Ministerium* **1727** Colden, *History of the Five Indian Nations* Junto Club founded Ezra Stiles (1727–95) **1728** *Pennsylvania Gazette* (1728–1815); Byrd runs dividing line **1729** Franklin, "Busy-Body Papers" Samuel Seabury (1729–96)	 **1729** Berkeley comes to America Baltimore founded **1730** Population, 654,950 **1731** Robert Rogers (1731?–95)
1732 John Dickinson (1732–1808) **1733** Franklin, *Poor Richard's Almanack* (1733–58); Byrd, *Journey to the Land of Eden*	**1732** Ephrata Community Washington (1732–99); R.H. Lee (1732–94) **1733** Oglethorpe settles Georgia Molasses Act Richmond founded **1734** Great Awakening (*c.*1734ff.) Daniel Boone (1734–1820); Robert Morris (1734–1806)
1735 Crèvecœur (1735–1813)	**1735** Zenger trial John Adams (1735–1826); Paul Revere (1735–1818) **1736** Patrick Henry (1736–99)

LITERARY HISTORY	SOCIAL HISTORY
1737 Paine (1737–1809); Hopkinson (1737–91); Jonathan Odell (1737–1818)	
	1738 Whitefield's first visit to America (1738–39) Copley (1738?–1815); Benjamin West (1738–1820)
1740 Tailfer, *Narrative of the Colony of Georgia*	**1740** Population, 889,000 Faneuil Hall erected
1741 Edwards, *Sinners in the Hands of an Angry God* Bradford, *The American Magazine;* Franklin, *The General Magazine*	**1741** C.W. Peale (1741–1827)
1743 Sower's German Bible American Philosophical Society founded	**1743** Jefferson (1743–1826)
	1745 King George's War (1745–48); capture of Louisburg Anthony Wayne (1745–96); John Jay (1745–1829); Benjamin Rush (1745–1813)
1746 Shirley, *Siege of Louisburg*	**1746** College of New Jersey founded (now Princeton University) C.C. Pinckney (1746–1825)
1747 Stith, *Settlement of Virginia*	**1747** John Paul Jones (1747–92)
1748 Brackenridge (1748–1816)	**1748** Treaty of Aix-la-Chapelle
1749 First dramatic company in America at Philadelphia (later moved to New York)	**1749** First Ohio Company chartered
1750 John Trumbull (1750–1831)	**1750** Population, 1,207,000
	1751 Philadelphia Academy founded (now University of Pennsylvania) Madison (1751–1836)
1752 Freneau (1752–1832); Timothy Dwight (1752–1817)	**1752** George Rogers Clark (1752–1818); Gouverneur Morris (1752–1816)
	1753 Edmund Randolph (1753–1813); Benjamin Thompson (1753–1814)
1754 Edwards, *Freedom of Will* Barlow (1754–1812)	**1754** Albany Congress French and Indian War (1754–60); Braddock commander in chief of British forces (1754–55) King's College founded (now Columbia University)
	1755 Acadians deported John Marshall (1755–1835); Gilbert Stuart (1755–1828)
1756 Woolman's *Journal* (1756–72)	**1756** John Trumbull (1756–1843); Aaron Burr (1756–1836); "Light-Horse Harry" Lee (1756–1818)
1757 *The American Magazine and Monthly Chronicle* (1757–58) Royall Tyler (1757–1826)	**1757** Hamilton (1757–1804); Charles Pinckney (1757–1824)
1758 Franklin, "The Way to Wealth"; Maylem, *Conquest of Louisburg;* Prince, *Psalms, Hymns, and Spiritual Songs* Noah Webster (1758–1843)	**1758** Mary Jemison captured Pittsburgh founded Monroe (1758–1831)
	1760 Population, 1,610,000
	1761 Gallatin (1761–1849)
1762 Susanna Rowson (*c.*1762–1824)	**1762** Pontiac's Conspiracy (1762–65) Louisiana secretly transferred by France to Spain St. Louis founded
	1763 Gage commander in chief of British forces (1763–75) Treaty of Paris Mason-Dixon survey (1763–67) Astor (1763–1848); Charles Bulfinch (1763–1844); James Kent (1763–1847)
1764 Otis, *Rights of British Colonies;* Hutchinson, *History of Massachusetts Bay*	**1764** Sugar Act; Colonial Currency Act Brown University founded
1765 Godfrey, *Prince of Parthia;* Samuel Adams, *Resolutions*	**1765** Stamp Act; Patrick Henry's resolutions; Stamp Act Congress, *Declaration of Rights;* Quartering Act; Regulators (1765–71) Robert Fulton (1765–1815)

LITERARY HISTORY	SOCIAL HISTORY
1766 Rogers, *Ponteach* William Dunlap (1766–1839)	**1766** Stamp Act repealed; Westmoreland Association Queen's College founded (now Rutgers University) **1767** Townshend acts; Nonimportation agreements Monticello erected Andrew Jackson (1767–1845); John Quincy Adams (1767–1848); Black Hawk (1767–1838)
1768 Dickinson, *Letters from a Farmer in Pennsylvania*	**1768** Troops sent to Boston **1769** Portolá's expedition to California (1769ff.); Serra's first mission Dartmouth College founded DeWitt Clinton (1769–1828)
1770 *Massachusetts Spy* (1770–1904)	**1770** Population 2,205,000 Boston Massacre Watauga Association
1771 Franklin begins autobiography C.B. Brown (1771–1810) **1772** Freneau and Brackenridge, *Rising Glory of America;* Trumbull, *Progress of Dulness* (1772–73)	**1772** First Committees of Correspondence
1773 Wheatley, *Poems;* Warren, *The Adulateur;* Franklin, "Edict of the King of Prussia" and "Rules by Which a Great Empire May Be Reduced to a Small One" *Rivington's New-York Gazetteer* (1773–83)	**1773** Boston Tea Party Boone settles in Kentucky John Randolph (1773–1833); W.H. Harrison (1773–1841)
1774 Hopkinson, *A Pretty Story;* Duché, *Caspipina's Letters*	**1774** First Continental Congress; Burke's speech on taxation; Dunmore's War; second Quartering Act Shakers in America Meriwether Lewis (1774–1809)
1775 Burgoyne, *The Blockade;* Burke, *On Conciliation;* Warren, *The Group;* Freneau, "A Political Litany"; Trumbull, *M'Fingal* (1775–82)	**1775** Second Continental Congress Revolutionary War (1775–83); battles of Lexington and Concord; Arnold and Allen capture Ticonderoga and Crown Point; unsuccessful campaign against Canada; Washington commander in chief of Continental army; Siege of Boston; Battle of Bunker Hill
1776 Paine, *Common Sense;* Brackenridge, *Battle of Bunkers-Hill;* Leacock, *Fall of British Tyranny;* Freneau, "The Beauties of Santa Cruz"; Munford, *The Patriots* Paine, *The American Crisis* (1776–83)	**1776** Declaration of Independence; Virginia Bill of Rights; Boston Port bill; separation from England; Nathan Hale executed; Battles of Trenton and Long Island San Francisco mission and presidio founded Phi Beta Kappa founded
1777 Hopkinson, *A Political Catechism;* Burke, *Letter to the Sheriffs of Bristol*	**1777** Stars and Stripes adopted as national flag Battles of Princeton, Brandywine, Germantown, and Saratoga; Valley Forge (1777–78); Conway Cabal Henry Clay (1777–1852); R.B. Taney (1777–1864)
1778 Hopkinson, "The Battle of the Kegs" J.K. Paulding (1778–1860)	**1778** Alliance with France Wyoming Valley massacre; Battle of Monmouth Articles of Confederation
1779 Freneau, "The House of Night" *United States Magazine* Francis Scott Key (1779–1843)	**1779** *Bonhomme Richard* vs. *Serapis;* Vincennes captured; Battle of Stony Point University of Pennsylvania founded Decatur (1779–1820); Joseph Story (1779–1845)
	1780 Population, 2,781,000 Benedict Arnold's treason discovered, André captured; battles of Camden and King's Mountain; Rochambeau arrives with French troops David Porter (1780–1843)
1781 Freneau, *The British Prison Ship*	**1781** Battle of Eutaw Springs; Cornwallis surrenders at Yorktown James Lawrence (1781–1813)

LITERARY HISTORY	SOCIAL HISTORY
1782 Crèvecœur, *Letters from an American Farmer;* Aitken Bible (first complete English Bible printed in America)	**1782** Lewis Cass (1782–1866); Calhoun (1782–1850); Van Buren (1782–1862); Webster (1782–1852); T.H. Benton (1782–1858)
1783 Webster, *Spelling Book* Irving (1783–1859)	**1783** Treaty of Paris
1784 Allen, *Reason the Only Oracle of Man* *Massachusetts Centinel* (1784–1840) Joseph Worcester (1784–1865)	**1784** Zachary Taylor (1784–1850)
1785 Dwight, *Conquest of Canaan;* Webster, *Sketches of American Policy* Friendly Club of Hartford (c. 1785–1807)	**1785** Audubon (1785–1851); O.H. Perry (1785–1819)
1786 Freneau, *Poems; The Anarchiad* (1786–87) *Columbian Magazine* (1786–92)	**1786** Annapolis Convention Shays's Rebellion (1786–87) Ohio Company of Associates; Tammany Society Nicholas Biddle (1786–1844); Crockett (1786–1836); W.L. Marcy (1786–1857); Winfield Scott (1786–1866)
1787 Jefferson, *Notes on Virginia;* Barlow, *The Vision of Columbus;* Tyler, *The Contrast;* Adams, *Defence of the Constitutions; The Federalist* (1787–88)	**1787** Federal Constitutional Convention Ordinance of 1787 Emma Willard (1787–1870)
1788 Freneau, *Miscellaneous Works*	**1788** Constitution ratified First settlement by Ohio Company
1789 Dunlap, *The Father;* Webster, *Dissertations on the English Language;* Brown, *The Power of Sympathy* *Gazette of the United States* (1789–1847) Cooper (1789–1851)	**1789** Washington's administration (1789–97) First Congress University of North Carolina founded
1790 Webster, *Essays* Halleck (1790–1867)	**1790** Population according to first national census, 3,929,214 John Tyler (1790–1862)
1791 Hamilton, *Report on Manufactures;* Adams, *Discourses of Davila;* Bartram, *Travels;* Paine, *Rights of Man* (1791–92); *The Echo* (1791–1805) J.H. Payne (1791–1852)	**1791** Bill of Rights Bank of the U.S. Vermont admitted as 14th state Williams College founded Peter Cooper (1791–1883); James Buchanan (1791–1868)
1792 Barlow, *Advice to the Privileged Orders;* Hopkinson, *Essays;* Odiorne, *Progress of Refinement;* Brackenridge, *Modern Chivalry* (1792–1815) Seba Smith (1792–1868)	**1792** White House cornerstone laid Thaddeus Stevens (1792–1868); Francis M. Drexel (1792–1863)
1793 *The Hapless Orphan* *Farmer's Almanack* (1793–) John Neal (1793–1876)	**1793** Genêt mission Fugitive Slave Law Capitol cornerstone laid Cotton gin Houston (1793–1863)
1794 Dwight, *Greenfield Hill;* Rowson, *Charlotte Temple* and *Slaves in Algiers;* Paine, *The Age of Reason* (1794–95) Bryant (1794–1878)	**1794** Whiskey Rebellion Jay's Treaty; Neutrality Act Bowdoin College founded Edward Everett (1794–1865); Matthew Perry (1794–1858); Vanderbilt (1794–1877)
1795 Freneau, *Poems* J.R. Drake (1795–1820); J.P. Kennedy (1795–1870); J.G. Percival (1795–1856)	**1795** Yazoo frauds Pinckney's Treaty Boston State House erected First American circus Polk (1795–1849)
1796 Washington, "Farewell Address"; Barlow, *Hasty Pudding;* first of Dennie's "Lay Preacher" essays T.C. Haliburton (1796–1865); W.H. Prescott (1796–1859)	**1796** Greek Revival introduced in U.S. Horace Mann (1796–1859)
1797 Foster, *The Coquette;* Burk, *Bunker Hill;* Tyler, *The Algerine Captive;* Dwight, *The Triumph of Infidelity* *Porcupine's Gazette* (1797–99)	**1797** John Adams's administration (1797–1801) XYZ Affair (1797–98) Daniel Drew (1797–1879)

LITERARY HISTORY	SOCIAL HISTORY
1798 Brown, *Wieland;* Dunlap, *André;* "Hail Columbia"	**1798** Alien and Sedition acts; Kentucky and Virginia Resolutions Jedediah Smith (1798–1831)
1799 Brown, *Edgar Huntly* and *Ormond* and *Arthur Mervyn; The Political Greenhouse* Bronson Alcott (1799–1889); R.P. Smith (1799–1854)	
1800 Weems, *Life of Washington* (1800?); Wood, *Julia and the Illuminated Baron* Library of Congress founded; Tuesday Club of Philadelphia (1800–?); *National Intelligencer* (1800–1870) George Bancroft (1800–1891)	**1800** Population, 5,308,483 Washington, D.C., becomes capital Gothic Revival introduced in U.S. John Brown (1800–1859); Caleb Cushing (1800–1879); Fillmore (1800–1874)
1801 Brown, *Clara Howard* and *Jane Talbot;* Chateaubriand, *Atala;* Tenney, *Female Quixotism* New York *Evening Post* (1801–); *The Port Folio* (1801–27)	**1801** Jefferson's administration (1801–9) Barbary Wars (1801–5) W.H. Seward (1801–72); Brigham Young (1801–77)
	1802 U.S. Military Academy founded Dorothea Dix (1802–87)
1803 Wirt, *Letters of the British Spy;* Fessenden, *Terrible Tractoration* Emerson (1803–82)	**1803** Louisiana Purchase *Marbury* vs. *Madison*
1804 Marshall, *Life of Washington* Anthology Club (*c.*1804–11) Hawthorne (1804–64)	**1804** Lewis and Clark expedition (1804–6) Burr-Hamilton duel Harmony Society founded Franklin Pierce (1804–69)
1805 Boston Athenaeum (1805–)	**1805** Garrison (1805–79); Joseph Smith (1805–44)
1806 Webster, *Compendious Dictionary* R.M. Bird (1806–54); W.G. Simms (1806–70); N.P. Willis (1806–67)	**1806** Nonimportation Act Edwin Forrest (1806–72); J.A. Roebling (1806–69)
1807 Barlow, *The Columbiad;* Irving and Paulding, *Salmagundi* (1807–8) Longfellow (1807–82); Whittier (1807–92)	**1807** Embargo Act Burr tried for treason *Clermont's* first voyage Agassiz (1807–73); R.E. Lee (1807–70)
	1808 Importation of slaves prohibited Salmon P. Chase (1808–73); Jefferson Davis (1808–89); Andrew Johnson (1808–75)
1809 Irving, *History of New York;* Campbell, *Gertrude of Wyoming* Holmes (1809–94); Poe (1809–49)	**1809** Madison's administration (1809–17) Repeal of Embargo Act; Nonintercourse Act Lincoln (1809–65); Kit Carson (1809–68); Albert Brisbane (1809–90)
1810 Ingersoll, *Inchiquin;* Thomas, *History of Printing in America* Margaret Fuller (1810–50); Theodore Parker (1810–60)	**1810** Population, 7,239,881 P.T. Barnum (1810–91)
1811 Mitchell, *The Asylum* Greeley (1811–72); Henry James, Sr. (1811–82); Harriet Beecher Stowe (1811–96)	**1811** Steamboats on the Mississippi Battle of Tippecanoe G.C. Bingham (1811–79); Charles Sumner (1811–74)
1812 Barker, *Marmion;* Paulding, *John Bull and Brother Jonathan;* Melish, *Travels in the United States* American Antiquarian Society (1812–)	**1812** War of 1812 (1812–15); *Constitution* vs. *Guerrière* "Gerrymander" A.H. Stephens (1812–83)
1813 Taylor, *Arator* *Boston Daily Advertiser* (1813–1929) Jones Very (1813–80)	**1813** Battle of Lake Erie Frémont (1813–90); Stephen Douglas (1813–61); H.W. Beecher (1813–87)
1814 Key, "Star-Spangled Banner"; Humphreys, *Yankey in England; History of the Expedition of Captains Lewis and Clark*	**1814** Hartford Convention (1814–15) British invade Washington; Battle of Lake Champlain; Creek Indians defeated; Treaty of Ghent W.L. Yancey (1814–63); Stanton (1814–69); Tilden (1814—86)
1815 Freneau, *Poems* *North American Review* (1815–1939) R.H. Dana, Jr. (1815–82)	**1815** Battle of New Orleans Tripolitan War

LITERARY HISTORY	SOCIAL HISTORY
1816 Drake, "The Culprit Fay"; Woodworth, *Champions of Freedom*	**1816** Second Bank of the U.S.
The Portico (1816–18)	Regular transatlantic shipping inaugurated
Parke Godwin (1816–1904)	
1817 Bryant, "Thanatopsis"; Barker, *How to Try a Lover;* Neal, *Keep Cool*	**1817** Monroe's administration (1817–25)
	First Seminole War (1817–18)
Thoreau (1817–62)	University of Michigan founded
1818 Payne, *Brutus;* Bryant, "To a Waterfowl"	**1818** Northern boundary (to Rocky Mountains) fixed at 49th parallel
	Lucy Stone (1818–93)
1819 Drake and Halleck, "Croaker Papers"; Noah, *She Would Be A Soldier;* Channing, *Baltimore Sermon;* Irving, *The Sketch Book* (1819–20)	**1819** Transatlantic voyage of the *Savannah*
	Purchase of Florida
	Dartmouth College case
Lowell (1819–91); Melville (1819–91); Whitman (1819–92)	University of Virginia founded
1820 Cooper, *Precaution;* Eastburn and Sands, *Yamoyden;* Sydney Smith, "Who reads an American book?"	**1820** Population, 9,638,453
	Missouri Compromise
	First American missionaries in Hawaii
Boucicault (1820–90)	Susan B. Anthony (1820–1906); Sherman (1820–91)
1821 Cooper, *The Spy;* Bryant, *Poems;* Percival, *Poems;* Wright, *Views of Society and Manners in America;* Dwight, *Travels* (1821–22)	**1821** Santa Fe Trail
	James Longstreet (1821–1904); Mary Baker Eddy (1821–1910); Jay Cooke (1821–1905); C.P. Huntington (1821–1900); Clara Barton (1821–1912)
The Saturday Evening Post (1821–1969); *Genius of Universal Emancipation* (1821–39)	
1822 Irving, *Bracebridge Hall;* Neal, *Logan;* Halleck, "Alnwick Castle"; Trumbull, *Works*	**1822** Grant (1822–85); Hayes (1822–93)
Bread and Cheese Club (*c.*1822–27)	
E.E. Hale (1822–1909)	
1823 Cooper, *The Pioneers* and *The Pilot;* Paulding, *Koningsmarke;* Neal, *Seventy-Six;* Moore, "A Visit from St. Nicholas"	**1823** Monroe Doctrine
New-York Mirror (1823–60)	
G. H. Boker (1823–90)	
1824 Irving, *Tales of a Traveller;* Payne, *Charles the Second;* Barker, *Superstition;* Neal, "American Writers" (1824–25)	**1824** National Republican party (1824–32)
	Tour of Lafayette
Springfield Republican (1824–)	"Stonewall" Jackson (1824–63)
G.W. Curtis (1824–92)	
1825 Halleck, "Marco Bozzaris"; Webster, Bunker Hill oration; Bryant, "A Forest Hymn"; Woodworth, *The Widow's Son*	**1825** John Quincy Adams's administration (1825–29)
	Erie Canal opened
	Nashoba Community (1825–28); New Harmony (1825–28)
Atlantic Souvenir (1925–32)	Rutgers College founded
R.H. Stoddard (1825–1903); Bayard Taylor (1825–78)	
1826 Cooper, *Last of the Mohicans;* Woodworth, *Ballads;* Payne, *Richelieu;* Kent, *Commentaries;* Flint, *Recollections of the Last Ten Years*	**1826** First lyceum
	McClelland (1826–85)
Graham's Magazine (1826–58)	
De Forest (1826–1906); Stephen Foster (1826–64)	
1827 Poe, *Tamerlane and Other Poems;* Cooper, *The Prairie;* Sedgwick, *Hope Leslie;* Tucker, *A Voyage to the Moon;* Simms, *Poems*	
The Token (1827–42); *Youth's Companion* (1817–1929)	
1828 Hawthorne, *Fanshawe;* Webster, *American Dictionary of the English Language;* Cooper, *Red Rover;* Irving, *Columbus;* Sealsfield, *Americans as They Are;* Calhoun, "South Carolina Exposition"	**1828** Tariff of Abominations
	American Peace Society
1829 Poe, *Al Aaraaf, Tamerlane, and Other Poems;* Irving, *Conquest of Granada;* Stone, *Metamora;* Smith, *Eighth of January;* Cooper, *Wept of Wish-ton-Wish;* Knapp, *Lectures on American Literature;* Kettell, *Specimens of American Poetry*	**1829** Andrew Jackson's administration (1829–37)
	Tom Thumb, first steam locomotive in U.S.
	Workingmen's party
S. Weir Mitchell (1829–1914); C.D. Warner (1829–1900)	Roscoe Conkling (1829–88); Carl Schurz (1829–1906)

LITERARY HISTORY	SOCIAL HISTORY

1830 Holmes, "Old Ironsides"; Paulding, *Lion of the West; Book of Mormon;* Smith, *Triumph at Plattsburg;* Worcester, *Dictionary;* Seba Smith begins "Jack Downing" letters; Hale, "Mary Had a Little Lamb"
Godey's Lady's Book (1830–98); Boston *Daily Evening Transcript* (1830–1941)
J.E. Cooke (1830–86); Emily Dickinson (1830–86); P.H. Hayne (1830–86)

1830 Population, 12,866,020
Mormon church
Blaine (1830–93)

1831 Poe, *Poems;* Bird, *The Gladiator;* Whittier, *Legends of New England;* Smith, "America"; Paulding, *Dutchman's Fireside*
Liberator (1831–65); *Spirit of the Times* (1831–58)
Rebecca H. Davis (1831–1910)

1831 Southampton Insurrection
New England Anti-Slavery Society
New York University founded
Garfield (1831–81); Sheridan (1831–88)

1832 Bryant, *Poems;* Kennedy, *Swallow Barn;* Mason, *The Choir;* Bird, *Oralloossa;* Irving, *The Alhambra;* Trollope, *Domestic Manners of the Americans;* Hawthorne, "Roger Malvin's Burial"; Dunlap, *History of the American Theatre;* Story, *Commentaries* (1832–45)
Louisa May Alcott (1832–88); H.H. Bancroft (1832–1918)

1832 Ordinance of Nullification; beginning of U.S. Bank controversy

1833 Longfellow, *Outre-Mer;* Simms, *Martin Faber;* Neal, *The Down-Easters;* Poe, "MS. Found in a Bottle"
Knickerbocker Magazine (1833–65); New York *Sun* (1833–1966); *Parley's Magazine* (1833–41)

1833 American Anti-Slavery Society
Haverford College founded; Oberlin College founded
Chicago incorporated
Benjamin Harrison (1833–1901); R.G. Ingersoll (1833–99); J.E.B. Stuart (1833–64)

1834 *Life of David Crockett;* Simms, *Guy Rivers;* Abbott, first of the Rollo books; Bancroft, *History of the United States* (1834–76)
Southern Literary Messenger (1834–64)
Frank Stockton (1834–1902); Horatio Alger (1834–99)

1834 McCormick reaper
Whistler (1834–1903); Langley (1834–1906); James Fisk (1834–72)

1835 Longstreet, *Georgia Scenes;* Simms, *The Yemassee* and *The Partisan;* Hawthorne, "Young Goodman Brown"; Sparks, *Life of Washington;* Irving, *Tour on the Prairies;* Drake, *The Culprit Fay;* Poe, "Berenice" and "Morella"; Bird, *The Hawks of Hawk-Hollow;* Kennedy, *Horse-Shoe Robinson*
Crockett alamanacs (1835–56); New York *Herald* (1835–1966); *Western Messenger* (1835–41)
Clemens (1835–1910)

1835 Locofocos (*c.*1835–40)
Second Seminole War (1835–42)
Adah Menken (1835–68); Carnegie (1835–1919), John La Farge (1835–1910)

1836 Emerson, *Nature;* Haliburton, *The Clockmaker;* Hildreth, *The Slave;* Holmes, *Poems;* Tucker, *Partisan Leader;* McGuffey, *Eclectic Readers* (1836–57)
Transcendental Club (1836–*c.*1844)
Aldrich (1836–1907); Bret Harte (1836–1902)

1836 Lone Star Republic (1836–45); Battle of the Alamo
Whig party
Colt revolver
Mt. Holyoke Seminary (first women's college)
Jay Gould (1836–92); Winslow Homer (1836–1910)

1837 Hawthorne, *Twice-Told Tales;* Emerson, *The American Scholar;* Carey, *Principles of Political Economy;* Willis, *Bianca Visconti;* Bird, *Nick of the Woods;* Prescott, *Ferdinand and Isabella;* Cooper, *Gleanings in Europe* (1837–38)
Baltimore *Sun* (1837–   ); *New Orleans Picayune* (1837–   ); *United States Magazine and Democratic Review* (1837–49); *Burton's Gentleman's Magazine* (1837–40)
Burroughs (1837–1921); Howells (1837–1920); Edward Eggleston (1837–1902)

1837 Van Buren's administration (1837–41)
Caroline Affair
Financial panic
Cleveland (1837–1908); Mark Hanna (1837–1904); J.P. Morgan (1837–1913)

1838	Emerson, "Divinity School Address"; Cooper, *American Democrat;* Kennedy, *Rob of the Bowl;* Whittier, *Ballads and Anti-Slavery Poems;* Martineau, *Retrospect of Western Travel;* Neal, *Charcoal Sketches;* Tocqueville, *Democracy in America;* Poe, "Silence" and "Ligeia" and *Narrative of A. Gordon Pym* Henry Adams (1838–1918); John Hay (1838–1905); Muir (1838–1914); F.H. Smith (1838–1915); Tourgée (1838–1905)	**1838**	Underground Railroad established J.J. Hill (1838–1916); H.H. Richardson (1838–86)
1839	Longfellow, *Hyperion* and *Voices of the Night;* Very, *Essays and Poems;* Willis, *Tortesa;* Marryat, *Diary in America;* Kirkland, *A New Home;* Poe, *Tales of the Grotesque and Arabesque;* Thompson, *The Green Mountain Boys* Liberty Bell (1839–58) Henry George (1839–97)	**1839**	Aroostook War Rockfeller (1839–1937)
1840	Dana, *Two Years Before the Mast;* Cooper, *The Pathfinder;* Alcott, "Orphic Sayings"; Simms, *Border Beagles;* Hoffman, *Greyslaer* *The Dial* (1840–44)	**1840**	Population, 17,069,453 Chardon Street Convention (1840–41) Thomas Nast (1840–1902)
1841	Emerson, *Essays, First Series;* Cooper, *The Deerslayer;* Lowell, *A Year's Life;* Thorpe, "Big Bear of Arkansas"; Catlin, *North American Indians;* Poe, "Murders in the Rue Morgue"; Longfellow, *Ballads and Other Poems* *New-York Tribune* (1841–1966) Joaquin Miller (1841?–1913)	**1841**	Harrison's administration (1841); Tyler's administration (1841–45) Dorr's Rebellion Brook Farm (1841–47)
1842	Hawthorne, *Twice-Told Tales* (enlarged); Simms, *Beauchampe;* Dickens, *American Notes;* Whittier, "Massachusetts to Virginia"; Cooper, *Wing-and-Wing;* Poe, "Eleonora" and "Masque of the Red Death"; Griswold, *Poets and Poetry of America* Lanier (1842–81); William James (1842–1910); Bronson Howard (1842–1908); Bierce (1842–1914?)	**1842**	Amana Community; Fruitlands (1842–43); Hopedale (1842–56) Webster-Ashburton Treaty Barnum's American Museum
1843	Prescott, *Conquest of Mexico;* Webster, second Bunker Hill oration; Pierpont, *Anti-Slavery Poems;* Thompson, *Major Jones's Courtship;* Poe, "The Gold Bug" and "The Black Cat" Henry James, Jr. (1843–1916)	**1843**	North American Phalanx (1843–54) Barnburners (1843–48) McKinley (1843–1901)
1844	Emerson, *Essays, Second Series;* Cooper, *Afloat and Ashore;* Whittier, *Voices of Freedom;* Smith, *The Drunkard;* Dickens, *Martin Chuzzlewit* *Littell's Living Age* (1844–1941); *Brownson's Quarterly Review* (1844–75) G.W. Cable (1844–1925)	**1844**	"Fifty-four forty or fight" Hunkers (1844–52) Vulcanizing process patented; Morse demonstrates telegraph Bethel Community (1844–80) Eakins (1844–1916); Comstock (1844–1915)
1845	Poe, *The Raven and Other Poems* and "The Literati"; Mowatt, *Fashion; Life of Frederick Douglass;* Fuller, *Woman in the Nineteenth Century;* Judd, *Margaret;* Cooper, *Satanstoe;* Hooper, *Simon Suggs* *Broadway Journal* (1845–46); *Harbinger* (1845–49)	**1845**	Polk's administration (1845–49) Texas annexed U.S. Naval Academy founded Elihu Root (1845–1937)
1846	Melville, *Typee;* Hawthorne, *Mosses from an Old Manse;* Holmes, *Poems;* Emerson, *Poems;* Mathews, *Witchcraft;* Poe, "Cask of Amontillado" and "The Philosophy of Composition" *DeBow's Review* (1846–80)	**1846**	Mexican War (1846–48); Oregon acquired; Bear Flag War; Wilmot Proviso Hoe rotary press; Morton's use of ether as anaesthetic; Howe sewing machine Donner Party Smithsonian Institution Carry Nation (1846–1911); Elbert Gary (1846–1927); W.F. Cody (1846–1917)
1847	Longfellow, *Evangeline;* Melville, *Omoo;* Field, *The Drama in Pokerville;* Prescott, *Conquest of Peru;* Paulding, *The Bucktails;* Griswold, *Prose Writers of America* *Union Magazine* (1847–52)	**1847**	Free soil party (1847–54) Mormons in Utah Edison (1847–1931); Jesse James (1847–82); C.F. McKim (1847–1909); Alexander G. Bell (1847–1922)

LITERARY HISTORY	SOCIAL HISTORY

1848 Lowell, *Biglow Papers* and *Fable for Critics* and *Vision of Sir Launfal;* Poe, *Eureka;* Foster, *Songs of the Sable Harmonists*
The Independent (1848–1928)
H.H. Boyesen (1848–95); J.C. Harris (1848–1908)

1848 Gold discovered in California
Treaty of Guadalupe Hidalgo
Oneida Community (1848–79)
College of the City of New York founded; University of Wisconsin founded
Seneca Falls woman suffrage meeting
Saint-Gaudens (1848–1907); Harriman (1848–1909)

1849 Parkman, *Oregon Trail;* Melville, *Mardi* and *Redburn;* Longfellow, *Kavanagh;* Thoreau, *Week on the Concord and Merrimack* and "Civil Disobedience"; Whittier, *Margaret Smith's Journal;* Southworth, *Retribution;* Paulding, *The Puritan and His Daughter;* Poe, "Annabel Lee" and "The Bells" and "Eldorado"; Griswold, *Female Poets of America*
Sarah Orne Jewett (1849–1909); J.L. Allen (1849–1925); J.W. Riley (1849–1916)

1849 Taylor's administration (1849–50)
California gold rush
Astor Place riot
Burbank (1849–1926)

1850 Hawthorne, *The Scarlet Letter;* Taylor, *Eldorado;* Mitchell, *Reveries of a Bachelor;* Melville, *White-Jacket;* Garrard, *Wah-tó-yah;* Emerson, *Representative Men;* Whittier, "Ichabod," *Songs of Labor;* Calhoun, "Fourth of March" speech; Webster, "Seventh of March" speech
Bellamy (1850–98); Eugene Field (1850–1902); Hearn (1850–1904)

1850 Fillmore's administration (1850–53)
Population, 23,191,876
Clayton-Bulwer Treaty; Fugitive Slave Law; Compromise of 1850
Currier and Ives partnership established
Jenny Lind's tour (1850–52)
Gompers (1850–1924); H.C. Lodge (1850–1924); Seth Low (1850–1916)

1851 Melville, *Moby-Dick;* Parkman, *Conspiracy of Pontiac;* Simms, *Katharine Walton;* Hawthorne, *The Snow-Image* and *The House of the Seven Gables;* Mitchell, *Dream Life;* Foster, "Old Folks at Home"; Morgan, *League of the Ho-dé-no-sau-nee;* Schoolcraft, *Indian Tribes* (1851–57)
Kate Chopin (1851–1904)

1851 "Go West, young man"
Maine becomes first state with long-term "dry" law
Northwestern University founded

1852 Stowe, *Uncle Tom's Cabin* (the novel and the Aiken dramatization); Hawthorne, *The Blithedale Romance;* Melville, *Pierre*
San Francisco *Golden Era* (1852–93)
Mary Wilkins Freeman (1852–1930)

1853 Baldwin, *Flush Times;* Curtis, *Potiphar Papers,* Simms, *The Sword and the Distaff*
Putnam's Monthly Magazine (1853–1910)
E.W. Howe (1853–1937); T.N. Page (1853–1922)

1853 Pierce's administration (1853–57)
Gadsden Purchase; Perry's voyage to Japan
Kane's Arctic expedition (1853–55)
Rail connection, New York to Chicago
Antioch College founded

1854 Thoreau, *Walden;* Arthur, *Ten Nights in a Barroom;* Cooke, *Leather Stocking and Silk* and *The Virginia Comedians;* Melville, "The Encantadas"; Grayson, *The Hireling and the Slave;* Shillaber, *Mrs. Partington;* Thorpe, *Hive of the Bee Hunter;* Cummins, *The Lamplighter*
F.M. Crawford (1854–1909)

1854 Trade treaty with Japan; Ostend Manifesto
Kansas-Nebraska Act; Emigrant Aid Company

1855 Whitman, *Leaves of Grass;* Longfellow, *Hiawatha;* Melville, "Benito Cereno"; Simms, *The Forayers;* Bartlett, *Familiar Quotations;* Boker, *Francesca da Rimini;* Bulfinch, *Age of Fable;* Thomson, *Doesticks;* Parton, *Horace Greeley;* Duyckinck, *Cyclopaedia of American Literature;* Irving, *Life of Washington* (1855–59)
Saturday Club of Boston (1855–); *New York Ledger* (1855–1903)
Belasco (1855?–1931); Bunner (1855–96); Royce (1855–1916); Saltus (1855?–1921); Woodberry (1855–1930)

1855 Mellon (1855–1937); Debs (1855–1926); La Follette (1855–1925); W.H. Page (1855–1918)

LITERARY HISTORY | SOCIAL HISTORY

1856 Stowe, *Dred;* Motley, *Rise of the Dutch Republic;* Simms, *Eutaw;* Emerson, *English Traits;* Curtis, *Prue and I;* Reid, *The Quadroon;* Bateman, *Self;* Thomson, *Pluri-bus-tah;* Whitcher, *Widow Bedott Papers; Sabin's Dictionary* (1856–1936)
Copyright law
Lizette Reese (1856–1935)

1856 Know-Nothing movement; national organization of Republican party
Wilson (1856–1924); Brandeis (1856–1941); J.S. Sargent (1856–1925); L.H. Sullivan (1856–1924)

1857 Bunce, *Love in '76;* Butler, "Nothing To Wear"; Helper, *Impending Crisis of the South;* Boucicault, *The Poor of New York;* Trowbridge, *Neighbor Jackwood*
Atlantic Monthly (1857–); *Harper's Weekly* (1857–1916); *Russell's Magazine* (1857–60)
Gertrude Atherton (1857–1948); Margaret Deland (1857–1945); H.B. Fuller (1857–1929); Veblen (1857–1929)

1857 Buchanan's administration (1857–61)
Dred Scott decision
Financial panic
First Otis elevator
Clarence Darrow (1857–1938); Pennell (1857–1926); Taft (1857–1930)

1858 Longfellow, *Courtship of Miles Standish;* Holmes, *Autocrat of the Breakfast-Table;* O'Brien, "The Diamond Lens"; Taylor, *Our American Authors* (1858–71)
C.W. Chesnutt (1858–1932); Agnes Repplier (1858–1950)

1858 Lincoln-Douglas debates
First transatlantic cable
Theodore Roosevelt (1858–1919); E.M. House (1858–1938)

1859 Stowe, *The Minister's Wooing;* Boucicault, *The Octoroon;* Simms, *The Cassique of Kiawah;* "Dixie"; Thackeray, *The Virginians*
Vanity Fair (1859–63)
John Dewey (1859–1952)

1859 Brown's raid on Harpers Ferry
First commercial production of petroleum
Cooper Union founded

1860 Hawthorne, *The Marble Faun;* Holmes, *Professor at the Breakfast-Table;* Timrod, *Poems;* Emerson, *Conduct of Life;* Boucicault, *The Colleen Bawn;* Whittier, *Home Ballads;* Tuckerman, *Poems;* Stephens, *Malaeska* (first dime novel)
Huneker (1860–1921); Garland (1860–1940)

1860 Population, 31,443,321
Tweed Ring (*c.*1860–71)
Pony Express (1860–61)
Crittenden Resolutions; South Carolina secedes
Bryan (1860–1925; Pershing (1860–1948)

1861 Holmes, *Elsie Venner;* Timrod, "Ethnogenesis"; Longfellow, "Paul Revere's Ride"

1861 Lincoln's administration (1861–65)
Secession of Mississippi, Florida, Alabama, Georgia, Louisiana, Texas, Virginia, Tennessee, Arkansas, and North Carolina; Jefferson Davis president of Confederate States of America; attack on Fort Sumter begins Civil War; first Battle of Bull Run; Trent Affair
Gatling machine gun
Vassar College founded
Alfred North Whitehead (1861–1947)

1862 Browne, *Artemus Ward;* Howe, "Battle Hymn of the Republic"; Davis, *Margaret Howth;* Winthrop, *John Brent;* Stowe, *The Pearl of Orr's Island;* Newell, *The Orpheus C. Kerr Papers* (1862–71)
Edith Wharton (1862–1937); W.S. Porter (1862–1910)

1862 Lee in command of Confederate army; *Monitor* vs. *Merrimac;* Peninsular campaign; battles of Shiloh, Antietam, second Bull Run; Siege of Vicksburg (1862–63)
Homestead Act
Union and Central Pacific railways chartered
C.E. Hughes (1862–1948)

1863 Longfellow, *Tales of a Wayside Inn;* Lincoln, "Gettysburg Address"; Thoreau, *Excursions;* Hawthorne, *Our Old Home;* Hale, "The Man Without a Country"
Santayana (1863–1952); John Fox, Jr. (1863–1919)

1863 Battles of Chancellorsville, Gettysburg, and Chattanooga
Emancipation Proclamation
National Banking Act
Henry Ford (1863–1947); W.R. Hearst (1863–1951)

1864 Boker, *Poems of the War;* Trowbridge, *Cudjo's Cave;* Halpine, *Private Miles O'Reilly;* Locke, *The Nasby Papers*
Richard H. Davis (1864–1916); Richard Hovey (1864–1900); P.E. More (1864–1937)

1864 Maximilian's regime in Mexico (1864–67)
Grant in command of Union army; Sherman's march to the sea; *Alabama* vs. *Kearsarge;* battle of Wilderness, Spotsylvania, and Mobile Bay
First Pullman car
Stieglitz (1864–1946)

LITERARY HISTORY	SOCIAL HISTORY
1865 Whitman, *Drum-Taps;* Clemens, "The Celebrated Jumping Frog"; Thoreau, *Cape Cod;* Parkman, *Pioneers of France in the New World;* Boucicault and Jefferson, *Rip Van Winkle;* Dodge, *Hans Brinker;* Shaw, *Josh Billings* *The Nation* (1865–) Irving Babbitt (1865–1933); P.L. Ford (1865–1902)	**1865** Johnson's administration (1865–69) Lee's surrender at Appomattox ends war Lincoln assassinated 13th Amendment outlaws slavery Molly Maguires (1865–67); first Ku Klux Klan organization Cornell University founded Harding (1865–1923); Steinmetz (1865–1923)
1866 Whittier, *Snow-Bound;* Howells, *Venetian Life;* Emerson, "Terminus"; Smith, *Bill Arp;* Cooke, *Surry of Eagle's Nest* New York *World* (1866–1931); *Galaxy* (1866–78) George Ade (1866–1944); Steffens (1866–1936)	**1866** Civil Rights bill Grand Army of the Republic Second Atlantic cable
1867 Harte, *Condensed Novels;* Harris, *Sut Lovingood Yarns;* De Forest, *Miss Ravenel's Conversion;* Longfellow, translation of the *Divine Comedy;* Parkman, *The Jesuits in North America;* Timrod, "Ode"; Daly, *Under the Gaslight;* Evans, *St. Elmo;* Burroughs, *Notes on Walt Whitman;* Whittier, *The Tent on the Beach;* Lowell, *Biglow Papers* (second series); Emerson, *May-Day and Other Poems* *Journal of Speculative Philosophy* (1867–93); Radical Club (1867–80); *Oliver Optic's Magazine* (1867–75) D.G. Phillips (1867–1911)	**1867** National Ku Klux Klan Reconstruction Act; purchase of Alaska Granger movement Howard University founded J.P. Morgan, Jr. (1867–1943)
1868 Harte, "The Luck of Roaring Camp"; Ward, *The Gates Ajar;* Holmes, *The Guardian Angel;* Alcott, *Tablets;* Louisa May Alcott, *Little Women* (1868–69) *Hearth and Home* (1868–75); *Lippincott's Magazine* (1868–1916); *Overland Monthly* (1868–1933); *Vanity Fair* (1868–1936) Mary Austin (1868–1934); W.E.B. DuBois (1868–1963); Robert Herrick (1868–1938); W.A. White (1868–1944); Masters (1868–1950)	**1868** 14th Amendment: rights of citizenship Johnson impeached; acquitted
1869 Clemens, *Innocents Abroad;* Stowe, *Oldtown Folks;* Harte, "Tennessee's Partner" and "Outcasts of Poker Flat"; Parkman, *La Salle;* Aldrich, *Story of a Bad Boy;* Lowell, "The Cathedral" *Appleton's Journal* (1869–81) Herbert Croly (1869–1930); Stephen Leacock (1869–1944); W.V. Moody (1869–1910); E.A. Robinson (1869–1935); George Sterling (1869–1926); Tarkington (1869–1946)	**1869** Grant's administration (1869–77) 15th Amendment: right to vote Knights of Labor; Prohibition party Union Pacific railroad completed "Black Friday" C.W. Eliot president of Harvard (1869–1909) Brady's *National Photographic Collection of War Views* Frank Lloyd Wright (1869–1959)
1870 Harte, "Plain Language from Truthful James"; Emerson, *Society and Solitude;* Howard, *Saratoga;* Bryant, translation of the *Iliad* *Scribner's Monthly* (1870–81) Frank Norris (1870–1902); Ray S. Baker (1870–1946)	**1870** Population, 38,818,449 Standard Oil Company founded Moody and Sankey begin revivalist campaign Cardozo (1870–1938)
1871 James, "A Passionate Pilgrim"; Burroughs, *Wake-Robin;* Harte, *East and West Poems;* Hay, *Pike County Ballads;* Eggleston, *Hoosier Schoolmaster;* Lowell, *My Study Windows;* Miller, *Songs of the Sierras;* Johnston, *Dukesborough Tales;* Howells, *Their Wedding Journey;* Whitman, *Democratic Vistas* and *Passage to India;* Bryant, translation of the *Odyssey* (1871–72); Furness, *New Variorum Shakespeare* (1871–1913) Winston Churchill (1871–1947); Stephen Crane (1871–1900); Dreiser (1871–1945)	**1871** Tweed Ring overthrown Treaty of Washington Chicago fire Smith College founded Barnum opens circus

LITERARY HISTORY	SOCIAL HISTORY
1872 Clemens, *Roughing It;* Hayne, *Legends and Lyrics;* Stanley, *How I Found Livingstone;* King, *Mountaineering in the Sierra Nevada;* Murdoch and Mayo, *Davy Crockett;* Roe, *Barriers Burned Away;* Holmes, *Poet at the Breakfast Table* *Congressional Record* (1872–) P.L. Dunbar (1872–1906)	**1872** Crédit Mobilier scandal (1872–73) Muybridge's pictures of movement Coolidge (1872–1933)
1873 Howells, *A Chance Acquaintance;* Clemens and Warner, *The Gilded Age;* Aldrich, "Marjorie Daw"; Wallace, *The Fair God;* Timrod, *The Cotton Boll* *Delineator* (1873–1937); *St. Nicholas* (1873–1940); *Woman's Home Companion* (1873–1957) Anne D. Sedgwick (1873–1935); Willa Cather (1873–1947)	**1873** Financial panic Slaughterhouse cases Nevada silver rush Alfred E. Smith (1873–1944)
1874 Eggleston, *The Circuit Rider;* Fiske, *Outlines of Cosmic Philosophy* Ellen Glasgow (1874–1945); Charles Beard (1874–1948); Owen Davis (1874–1956); Clarence Day (1874–1935); Zona Gale (1874–1938); Amy Lowell (1874–1925); Gertrude Stein (1874–1946); Frost (1874–1963)	**1874** Women's Christian Temperance Union Massachusetts legalizes ten-hour work day for women Hoover (1874–1964)
1875 Eddy, *Science and Health;* Howells, *A Foregone Conclusion;* Holland, *Sevenoaks* *Chicago Daily News* (1875–1978) Lambs Club (1875–)	**1875** Greenback party Brigham Young University founded Arbor Day
1876 Clemens, *Tom Sawyer;* James, *Roderick Hudson;* Whitman, *Leaves of Grass* (Centennial Edition); Moore, *Sweet Singer of Michigan;* Julian Hawthorne, *Garth;* Melville, *Clarel* *Frank Leslie's Popular Monthly* (1876–1906) Sherwood Anderson (1876–1941); Jack London (1876–1916); Rölvaag (1876–1931)	**1876** Bell telephone; barbed wire Battle of Little Big Horn Centennial Exposition Johns Hopkins opened University of Texas founded Socialist-Labor party Disputed election of Tilden and Hayes
1877 Jewett, *Deephaven;* James, *The American;* Lanier, *Poems;* Morgan, *Ancient Society;* Burroughs, *Birds and Poets;* Parkman, *Count Frontenac* *Puck* (1877–1918) William Beebe (1877–1962)	**1877** Hayes's administration (1877–81) End of Reconstruction Chief Joseph's revolt Railroad and coal strikes Edison's phonograph
1878 James, *Daisy Miller* and *The Europeans;* Eggleston, *Roxy;* Green, *Leavenworth Case;* Lanier, "The Marshes of Glynn"; Tyler, *American Literature, 1607–1765* Upton Sinclair (1878–1968; Sandburg (1878–1967); Don Marquis (1878–1937)	**1878** "Solid South" Bland-Allison silver act Arc light Isadora Duncan (1878–1927)
1879 George, *Progress and Poverty;* Cable, *Old Creole Days;* Tourgée, *A Fool's Errand;* Burroughs, *Locusts and Wild Honey;* Herne and Belasco, *Hearts of Oak;* Stockton, *Rudder Grange;* Howells, *Lady of the Aroostook* Cabell (1879–1955); Vachel Lindsay (1879–1931); Dorothy Canfield Fisher (1879–1958); Wallace Stevens (1879–1955	**1879** Edison's incandescent lamp First Madison Square Garden Chicago Art Institute founded
1880 Adams, *Democracy;* Cable, *The Grandissimes;* Wallace, *Ben-Hur;* Aldrich, *Stillwater Tragedy;* Tourgée, *Bricks Without Straw;* Clemens, *A Tramp Abroad;* MacKaye, *Hazel Kirke* *The Dial* (1880–1929) Sholem Asch (1880–1957); Hergesheimer (1880–1954); Mencken (1880–1956); Julia Peterkin (1880–1961); Ernest Poole (1880–1950); Van Vechten (1880–1964); Channing Pollock (1880–1946)	**1880** Population, 50,155,783 Bryn Mawr College founded
1881 James, *Washington Square* and *The Portrait of a Lady;* Harris, *Uncle Remus;* Lothrop, *Five Little Peppers* *Century* (1881–1930); *Judge* (1881–1939) William McFee (1881–1966); Neihardt (1881–1973); Stribling (1881–1965)	**1881** Garfield's administration (1881); Arthur's administration (1881–85) Greely's Arctic expedition (1881–83) Standard Oil incorporated American Federation of Labor Tuskegee Institute founded

1882 Clemens, *Prince and the Pauper;* Crawford, *Mr. Isaacs;* Stockton, "The Lady or the Tiger?"; Howard, *Young Mrs. Winthrop;* Whitman, *Specimen Days and Collect;* Howells, *A Modern Instance*
Susan Glaspell (1882–1948); G.J. Nathan (1882–1958)

1883 Clemens, *Life on the Mississippi;* Howe, *Story of a Country Town;* James, *Siege of London;* Stevenson, *Silverado Squatters;* Riley, *Old Swimmin'-Hole;* Peck, *Peck's Bad Boy;* Rives, *Quick or the Dead?;* Grant, *An Average Man;* Wilcox, *Poems of Passion;* Eggleston, *Hoosier Schoolboy*
Ladies' Home Journal (1883–   ); *Life* (1883–1936)
Max Eastman (1883–1969)

1884 Clemens, *Huckleberry Finn;* Murfree, *In the Tennessee Mountains;* Parkman, *Montcalm and Wolfe;* Harris, *Mingo;* Jackson, *Ramona;* Jewett, *A Country Doctor;* Lowell, "On Democracy"; Hay, *Bread-Winners*
Damon Runyon (1884–1946); Sara Teasdale (1884–1933)

1885 Howells, *Rise of Silas Lapham;* Janvier, *Color Studies;* Keenan, *Money-Makers;* Royce, *Religious Aspect of Philosophy;* Grant, *Personal Memoirs* (1885–86)
DuBose Heyward (1885–1940); Lardner (1885–1933); Sinclair Lewis (1885–1951); Ezra Pound (1885–1972); Elinor Wylie (1885–1928)

1886 James, *The Bostonians* and *The Princess Casamassima;* Jewett, *A White Heron;* Burnett, *Little Lord Fauntleroy;* Grady, "The New South"; Howells, *Indian Summer;* Carnegie, *Triumphant Democracy;* Thompson, *The Old Homestead*
Cosmopolitan (1886–   ); *Forum* (1886–1950)
Van Wyck Brooks (1886–1963); Elizabeth M. Roberts (1886–1941)

1887 Page, *In Ole Virginia;* Howard, *The Henrietta;* Kirkland, *Zury;* French, *Knitters in the Sun;* Freeman, *A Humble Romance;* Wiggin, *Birds' Christmas Carol;* Crawford, *Saracinesca;* Frederic, *Seth's Brother's Wife;* Robinson, *Uncle Lisha's Shop*
Scribner's Magazine (1887–1939)
Floyd Dell (1887–1969); Edna Ferber (1887–1968); Jeffers (1887–1962); John Reed (1887–1920)

1888 Whitman, *November Boughs;* Bellamy, *Looking Backward;* Howard, *Shenandoah;* Lowell, *Political Essays;* Bryce, *American Commonwealth;* James, *Aspern Papers;* Conwell, *Acres of Diamonds;* Whitman, *Complete Poems and Prose* (1888–89); Stedman, *Library of American Literature* (1888–90)
Collier's (1888–1957); American Folk-Lore Society (1888–   )
T.S. Eliot (1888–1965); O'Neill (1888–1953); Maxwell Anderson (1888–1959)

1882 Immigration of Chinese labor suspended
Knights of Columbus
W.H. Vanderbilt: "The public be damned"
Jesse James shot to death
F.D. Roosevelt (1882–1945); Frankfurter (1882–1965)

1883 Civil Service Reform Act
Brooklyn Bridge completed
New steel navy begun
Maxim machine gun
Pulitzer buys the New York *World*
Metropolitan Opera founded

1884 National Bureau of Labor
"Mugwumps"
"Rum, Romanism, and Rebellion"
Norman Thomas (1884–1969)
Truman (1884–1972)

1885 Cleveland's first administration (1885–89)
Statue of Liberty; Washington Monument dedicated
Stanford University founded

1886 Haymarket Riot
Mergenthaler linotype first used
Presidential succession law
Statue of Liberty dedicated
Last major war with Indians ends with Geronimo's capture
Sears Roebuck founded
Coca-Cola put on sale

1887 Interstate Commerce Act
First electric streetcar
First U.S. social register

1888 Department of Labor
National Geographic founded
Irving Berlin (1888–1989)

766

LITERARY HISTORY	SOCIAL HISTORY

1889 Howells, *Annie Kilburn;* Field, *A Little Book of Western Verse;* Clemens, *A Connecticut Yankee;* Carnegie, *Gospel of Wealth;* Hearn, *Chita;* Smith, *A White Umbrella in Mexico;* Adams, *History of the United States* (1889–91); Roosevelt, *Winning of the West* (1889–96)
Munsey's (1889–1929)
Conrad Aiken (1889–1973); Hervey Allen (1889–1949); Waldo Frank (1889–1967); George S. Kaufman (1889–1961)

1889 Harrison's administration (1889–93)
Australian ballot system adopted in ten states
Department of Agriculture
Barnard College founded
Oklahoma opened for settlement
Johnstown flood
First Pan-American Congress
Samoan treaty

1890 Dickinson, *Poems;* William James, *Principles of Psychology;* Riis, *How the Other Half Lives;* Mahan, *Influence of Sea Power;* Nicolay and Hay, *Abraham Lincoln;* Howells, *A Hazard of New Fortunes;* Hearn, *Youma;* James, *The Tragic Muse;* Woodberry, *Poems*
Literary Digest (1890–1938); *Smart Set* (1890–1930)
Marc Connelly (1890–1980); Christopher Morley (1890–1957); Katherine Anne Porter (1890–1980); Conrad Richter (1890–1968)

1890 Population, 62,947,714
Sherman Anti-Trust and Silver Purchase acts
Nelly Bly completes 72-day tour of the world
Daughters of the American Revolution organized
New Madison Square Garden
Dwight D. Eisenhower (1890–1969)

1891 Bierce, *Tales of Soldiers and Civilians;* Garland, *Main-Travelled Roads;* Howells, *Criticism and Fiction;* Freeman, *A New England Nun;* Smith, *Colonel Carter of Cartersville;* Dickinson, *Poems: Second Series;* Fiske, *The American Revolution;* Cooke, *Huckleberries Gathered from New England Hills;* Allen, *Flute and Violin;* Hoyt, *A Trip to Chinatown;* Norton, translation of *Divine Comedy* (1891–92)
First international copyright law
Review of Reviews (1891–1937)
Sidney Howard (1891–1939); Henry Miller (1891–1980)

1891 Forest Reserve Act (beginning of conservation movement)
Populist party
Basketball game invented
Thomas's Chicago Orchestra (1891–1905)

1892 Herne, *Shore Acres;* Page, *The Old South*
Sewanee Review (1892–1973)
Pearl Buck (1892–1973); MacLeish (1892–1982); Edna St. Vincent Millay (1892–1950); Elmer Rice (1892–1967); R.P.T. Coffin (1892–1955)

1892 Coeur d'Alene and Homestead strikes
Ellis Island becomes immigrant station
Lizzie Borden case
Ward McCallister: "The Four Hundred"
University of Chicago founded
Wendell Willkie (1892–1944)

1893 Fuller, *The Cliff-Dwellers;* Crane, *Maggie;* Turner, "Significance of the Frontier"
McClure's Magazine (1893–1929); *Outlook* (1893–1915)
Dorothy Parker (1893–1967); S.N. Behrman (1893–1973)

1893 Cleveland's second administration (1893–97)
Gold Panic
Chicago World Fair
Anti-Saloon League
Treaty of annexation of Hawaii signed, then withdrawn
Huey Long (1893–1935)

1894 Carman and Hovey, *Songs from Vagabondia;* Muir, *Mountains of California;* Clemens, *Pudd'nhead Wilson;* Santayana, *Sonnets;* Warner, *Golden House;* Allen, *Kentucky Cardinal;* Chopin, *Bayou Folk;* Tabb, *Poems;* Ford, *Honorable Peter Stirling;* Howells, *A Traveler from Altruria*
Chap Book (1894–98)
E.E. Cummings (1894–1962); Paul Green (1894–1981); Robert Nathan (1894–1985); James Thurber (1894–1961)

1894 Coxey's army; Pullman, coal, and American Railway Union strikes
U.S. recognizes Republic of Hawaii
First U.S. open golf tournament

1895 Crane, *Red Badge of Courage* and *Black Riders;* Gillette, *Secret Service;* Mitchell, *Amos Judd;* Garland, *Rose of Dutcher's Coolly;* Fuller, *With the Procession;* Bates, "America the Beautiful"
Bookman (1895–1933); *White's Emporia Gazette* (1895–   ); *Collier's Weekly* (1895–1957)
Vardis Fisher (1895–1968); Edmund Wilson (1895–1972)

1895 Cuban rebellion; Venezuela affair
Income Tax Law declared unconstitutional
New York Public Library

1896 Clemens, *Joan of Arc;* Dickinson, *Poems: Third Series;* Jewett, *Country of the Pointed Firs;* Robinson, *Torrent and the Night Before;* Van Dyke, *Story of the Other Wise Man;* Santayana, *The Sense of Beauty;* Bangs, *Houseboat on the Styx;* Frederic, *Damnation of Theron Ware;* Parker, *Seats of the Mighty;* Patten, first of the "Frank Merriwell" books; Sheldon, *In His Steps*
Philip Barry (1896–1949); Bromfield (1896–1956); Dos Passos (1896–1970); Fitzgerald (1896–1940); Sherwood (1896–1955)

1896 Klondike gold rush (1896ff.)
Bryan's "Cross of Gold" speech
Rural free delivery
Edison introduces motion pictures in U.S.
Princeton University given present name

1897 James, *What Maisie Knew* and *The Spoils of Poynton;* Allen, *The Choir Invisible;* Mitchell, *Hugh Wynne;* Kipling, *Captains Courageous;* Davis, *Soldiers of Fortune;* Freeman, *Jerome;* Lewis, *Wolfville;* Robinson, *Children of the Night;* Tyler, *Literary History of the American Revolution;* William James, *The Will to Believe*
Survey Graphic (1897–1944)
Faulkner (1897–1962); Thornton Wilder (1897–1975); Lillian Smith (1897–1967)

1897 McKinley's administration (1897–1901)
Sousa, "The Stars and Stripes Forever"
Library of Congress building

1898 Dunne, *Mr. Dooley in Peace and War;* Rosenfeld, *Songs from the Ghetto;* Crane, *The Open Boat;* Johnston, *Prisoners of Hope;* Westcott, *David Harum;* Major, *When Knighthood Was in Flower;* Mitchell, *Adventures of François;* James, "Turn of the Screw"
Stephen Benét (1898–1943); Hemingway (1898–1961)

1898 Spanish-American War; *Maine* incident; Battle of Manila Bay; Treaty of Paris
Annexation of Hawaii
Uniform Bankruptcy law
George Gershwin (1898–1937)

1899 Crane, *The Monster* and *War Is Kind;* Gillette, *Sherlock Holmes;* Ade, *Fables in Slang;* Markham, "The Man with the Hoe"; Hubbard, *Message to Garcia;* Norris, *McTeague;* Churchill, *Richard Carvel;* Veblen, *Theory of the Leisure Class;* Ford, *Janice Meredith;* James, *The Awkward Age;* Chesnutt, *The Conjure Woman;* Tarkington, *Gentleman from Indiana*
Everybody's (1899–1928); *Pearson's* (1899–1925); *American Boy* (1899–1941)
Hart Crane (1899–1932); Vincent Sheean (1899–1975); E.B. White (1899–1985)

1899 Philippine insurrection (1899–1902)
First Hague conference
"Open Door" policy in China
United Mine Workers organized
Carnegie Steel Company created

1900 London, *Son of the Wolf;* Roosevelt, *The Strenuous Life;* Crane, *Whilomville Stories;* Grant, *Unleavened Bread;* Dreiser, *Sister Carrie;* Belasco and Long, *Madame Butterfly;* Bacheller, *Eben Holden;* Thompson, *Alice of Old Vincennes;* Johnston, *To Have and To Hold;* Tarkington, *Monsieur Beaucaire;* Stedman, *An American Anthology;* Howells, *Literary Friends and Acquaintances;* Wendell, *Literary History of America;* Baum, *Wonderful Wizard of Oz;* Royce, *The World and the Individual* (1900–1901); Socum, *Sailing Alone Around the World*
Thomas Wolfe (1900–1938); V.F. Calverton (1900–1940)

1900 Population, 75,994,575
Galveston tornado
Socialist party
College Entrance Aptitude Tests
Carnegie Institute of Technology
First U.S. national automobile show
Aaron Copland (1900–1991); Helen Hayes (1900–1992)

1901 Norris, *The Octopus;* Moody, *Poems;* Fitch, *The Climbers;* Churchill, *The Crisis;* McCutcheon, *Graustark;* Rice, *Mrs. Wiggs of the Cabbage Patch;* Riis, *Making of an American;* James, *Sacred Fount;* Washington, *Up from Slavery;* Muir, *Our National Parks*
Granville Hicks (1901–82); Glenway Wescott (1901–87)

1901 Theodore Roosevelt's administration (1901–9)
Hay-Pauncefote Treaty (Panama Canal)
Northern Pacific panic
First transatlantic radio
Consolidation of U.S. Steel Corporation and of Union, Central, and Southern Pacific railroads

1902 Robinson, *Captain Craig;* William James, *Varieties of Religious Experience;* Riis, *The Battle with the Slum;* Wilson, *History of the American People;* Wister, *The Virginian;* James, *Wings of the Dove;* Fitch, *Girl with the Green Eyes;* Wharton, *Valley of Decision;* Glasgow, *The Battle Ground;* White, *The Blazed Trail;* Davis, *Ranson's Folly*
South Atlantic Quarterly (1902–   )
Langston Hughes (1902–67); Steinbeck (1902–67); Ogden Nash (1902–71)

1903 London, *Call of the Wild;* Norris, *The Pit;* Adams, *Log of a Cowboy;* Austin, *Land of Little Rain;* DuBois, *Souls of Black Folk;* James, *The Ambassadors;* Wiggin, *Rebecca of Sunnybrook Farm;* Trent, *History of American Literature;* Woodberry, *America in Literature;* Sterling, *Testimony of the Suns;* Fox, *Little Shepherd of Kingdom Come*
Kay Boyle (1903–94); Erskine Caldwell (1903–85); James Gould Cozzens (1903–78); Countee Cullen (1903–46); Nathanael West (1903–40)

1904 James, *The Golden Bowl;* London, *The Sea-Wolf;* Cabell, *The Eagle's Shadow;* Tarbell, *History of the Standard Oil Company;* Porter, *Cabbages and Kings;* Stratton-Porter, *Freckles;* Steffens, *Shame of the Cities;* Belasco, *Girl of the Golden West;* Galsgow, *Deliverance;* Churchill, *The Crossing;* Howells, *Son of Royal Langbrith;* More, *Shelburne Essays* (1904–35); Adams, *Mont-Saint-Michel and Chartres*
American Academy of Arts and Letters (1904–   )
James T. Farrell (1904–79); Louis Zukofsky (1904–78)

1905 De Leon, *Socialist Reconstruction of Society;* London, *War of the Classes;* Dixon, *The Clansman;* Austin, *Isidro;* Wharton, *House of Mirth;* Royle, *Squaw Man;* Santayana, *Life of Reason* (1905–6)
Variety (1905–   )
Harvard's 47 Workshop
R.P. Warren (1905–89)

1906 Austin, *The Flock;* Porter, *The Four Million;* Sinclair, *The Jungle;* Mitchell, *The New York Idea;* Churchill, *Coniston;* Deland, *Awakening of Helena Ritchie;* Traubel, *With Walt Whitman in Camden* (1906–82)
Clifford Odets (1906–63)

1907 *Education of Henry Adams;* Sumner, *Folkways;* James, *The American Scene;* William James, *Pragmatism;* Porter, *Trimmed Lamp;* Fitch, *The Truth;* Thomas, *Witching Hour;* Wharton, *Madame de Treymes;*
Jesse Stuart (1907–   )

1908 Herrick, *Together* and *Master of the Inn;* Royce, *Philosophy of Loyalty;* Fox, *Trial of the Lonesome Pine;* Gale, *Friendship Village;* MacKaye, *The Scarecrow;* London, *The Iron Heel*
Paul Engle (1908–91); Theodore Roethke (1908–63); Saroyan (1908–81); Richard Wright (1908–60)

1902 Reclamation Act; Isthmian Canal Act
Anthracite coal strike
Maryland enacts first state workmen's compensation law; Oregon adopts first state initiative and referendum laws

1903 Department of Commerce and Labor
Wisconsin enacts first state direct primary law
Postal scandal
Pacific cable from San Francisco to Manila
Revolt of Panama from Colombia; independence of Panama recognized by U.S.
Wright brothers' airplane
Rhodes Scholarships

1904 Pacific cable completed; Panama Canal begun
Northern Securities case
Chicago meat packers strike

1905 Insurance companies investigated
Rotary clubs; I.W.W.

1906 San Francisco earthquake and fire
Pure Food and Drug Act; Meat Inspection Act
Helicon Home Colony (1906–7)

1907 Second Hague Conference
Georgia and Alabama adopt prohibition
First Ziegfeld Follies
De Forest's vacuum tube

1908 "Gentlemen's agreement" with Japan restricts immigration
Lyndon B. Johnson (1908–73)

1909 Stein, *Three Lives;* Croly, *The Promise of American Life;* White, *A Certain Rich Man;* Crothers, *A Man's World;* Porter, *Roads of Destiny;* Stratton-Porter, *Girl of the Limberlost;* London, *Martin Eden;* Moody, *Great Divide* and *Faith Healer;* Pound, *Personae;* Sheldon, *The Nigger* James Agee (1909–55); Wallace Stegner (1909–93); Eudora Welty (1909–)	**1909** Taft's administration (1909–13) Peary's last North Pole expedition Rise of "Progressive" movement "Dollar diplomacy" Model T Ford marks first mass production of automobiles
1910 Robinson, *Town Down the River;* Myers, *History of the Great American Fortunes;* Peabody, *The Piper;* Lomax, *Cowboy Songs;* Addams, *Twenty Years at Hull-House; Harvard Classics;* Huneker, *Promenades of an Impressionist* Peter De Vries (1910–93)	**1910** Population, 91,972,266 First long-distance flight, from Albany to New York City NAACP founded Boy Scouts of America founded
1911 Dreiser, *Jennie Gerhardt;* Wharton, *Ethan Frome;* Belasco, *Return of Peter Grimm;* Spingarn, *The New Criticism;* Sheldon, *The Boss;* Wright, *Winning of Barbara Worth;* Harrison, *Queed;* Bierce, *Devil's Dictionary;* Johnston, *Long Roll;* Sedgwick, *Tante* *Masses,* later *New Masses* (1911–53)	**1911** La Follette forms National Republic Progressive League Standard Oil and American Tobacco trusts dissolved First flight across U.S. (68 landings during 49 days)
1912 Johnson, *Autobiography of an Ex-Colored Man;* Dreiser, *The Financier;* Antin, *Promised Land;* Grey, *Riders of the Purple Sage;* Millay, "Renascence"; London, *Smoke Bellew;* Lowell, *Dome of Many-Coloured Glass* *Poetry: A Magazine of Verse* (1912–) John Cheever (1912–82); William Everson (1912–94)	**1912** Progressive party (1912–46) Massachusetts establishes first minimum wage for women and children Stokowski leader of Philadelphia Orchestra (1912–36)
1913 Cather, *O Pioneers!;* Frost, *A Boy's Will;* Wilson, *The New Freedom;* Sheldon, *Romance;* Glasgow, *Virginia;* Beard, *Economic Interpretation of the Constitution;* London, *Valley of the Moon;* Lindsay, *General William Booth Enters into Heaven;* Churchill, *Inside of the Cup;* Eastman, *Enjoyment of Poetry;* Herrick, *One Woman's Life;* James, *A Small Boy and Others;* Macy, *Spirit of American Literature* *Reedy's Mirror* (1913–20) Karl Shapiro (1913–)	**1913** Wilson's administration (1913–21) 16th and 17th Amendments: Federal Reserve Bank Act; Parcel Post system; Department of Labor Armory Show of modern art Ludlow strike (1913–14) Richard Nixon (1913–94)
1914 Dickinson, *Single Hound;* Frost, *North of Boston;* Lowell, *Sword Blades and Poppy Seed;* Tarkington, *Penrod;* Oppenheim, *Songs for the New Age;* Brandeis, *Other People's Money;* Lindsay, *The Congo;* Herrick, *Clark's Field;* Giovannitti, *Arrows in the Gale* *New Republic* (1914–); *Little Review* (1914–29) Ralph Ellison (1914–94); Howard Fast (1914–); John Hersey (1914–93); Irwin Shaw (1914–84); Tennessee Williams (1914–83); John Berryman (1914–72)	**1914** Panama Canal opened Financial crisis Federal Trade Commission; Clayton Anti-Trust Act U.S. fleet in Vera Cruz; protest against British interference with American shipping Kiwanis clubs
1915 Widdemer, *Factories;* Brooks, *America's Coming-of-Age; Some Imagist Poets;* Masters, *Spoon River Anthology;* Teasdale, *Rivers to the Sea;* Dreiser, *The "Genius";* Poole, *The Harbor;* Neihardt, *Song of Hugh Glass;* Cather, *Song of the Lark;* Pattee, *History of American Literature Since 1870* Provincetown and Washington Square Players Saul Bellow (1915–); Alfred Kazin (1915–)	**1915** *Lusitania* sunk; Ford's "Peace Ship" Wilson: "Too proud to fight" 1,000,000th Ford auto Widener Library opened at Harvard Revival of Ku Klux Klan

LITERARY HISTORY	SOCIAL HISTORY

1916 Frost, *Mountain Interval;* Sandburg, *Chicago Poems;* Clemens, *Mysterious Stranger;* Tarkington, *Seventeen;* Robinson, *Man Against the Sky;* McFee, *Casuals of the Sea;* Lowell, *Men, Women and Ghosts;* O'Neill, *Bound East for Cardiff;* Dewey, *Democracy and Education;* Wharton, *Xingu;* Bynner and Ficke, *Spectra;* Glasgow, *Life and Gabriella;* Lardner, *You Know Me Al*
Seven Arts (1916–17); *Theatre Arts Magazine* (1916–64)
Walker Percy (1916–90)

1916 American punitive expedition in Mexico
U.S. Shipping Board; Federal Farm Loan Bank Act; 17th Amendment: election of senators by popular vote
San Francisco Preparedness Day bombing

1917 Eliot, *Prufrock;* Garland, *Son of the Middle Border;* Teasdale, *Love Songs;* Robinson, *Merlin;* Moeller, *Madame Sand;* Morley, *Parnassus on Wheels;* Cabell, *Cream of the Jest;* Williams, *Why Marry?;* Lindsay, *Chinese Nightingale;* Austin, *The Ford;* Hergesheimer, *Three Black Pennys;* Phillips, *Susan Lenox;* Poole, *His Family;* Smith, *Trivia;* Cambridge *History of American Literature* (1917–20)
Pulitzer Prizes (1917–   )
The Dial (1917–29)
Gwendolyn Brooks (1917–   ); Carson McCullers (1917–67); Robert Lowell (1917–77)

1917 Germans renew unrestricted submarine warfare; U.S. enters World War I; draft; AEF in France; Espionage Act; War Industries Board; food production and control bills; government control of railroads
Prohibition amendment submitted to states
Lansing-Ishii Agreement
Rosenwald Fund
Lions clubs
John F. Kennedy (1917–63)

1918 Sandburg, *Cornhuskers;* Gale, *Birth;* Wharton, *The Marne;* Tarkington, *Magnificent Ambersons;* O'Neill, *Moon of the Caribbees;* Beebe, *Jungle Peace;* Ridge, *The Ghetto;* Smith and Bacon, *Lightnin';* Streeter, *Dere Mable!;* Cather, *My Ántonia; I.W.W. Songs;* Perry, *American Spirit in Literature*
Theatre Guild (1918–   ); Carolina Playmakers (1918–   )

1918 Battles of Belleau Wood and Château-Thierry; Argonne and St. Mihiel offensives; second Battle of the Marne
"Fourteen points"; armistice; Wilson at peace conference

1919 Anderson, *Winesburg, Ohio;* Mencken, *The American Language;* Veblen, *Higher Learning in America;* Moeller, *Molière and Sophie;* Reed, *Ten Days That Shook the World;* Frank, *Our America;* Untermeyer, *Modern American Poetry;* Cabell, *Jurgen and Beyond Life;* Hergesheimer, *Linda Condon;* O'Brien, *White Shadows in the South Seas;* Mencken, *Prejudices* (1919–27)

1919 Treaty of Versailles (not signed by U.S.)
18th Amendment: prohibition of liquor; Volstead Act
Steel strike; National Industrial Conference
American Legion; Communist Party

1920 Eliot, *Poems;* Lewis, *Main Street;* Sandburg, *Smoke and Steel;* Huneker, *Painted Veils;* Wharton, *Age of Innocence;* Robinson, *Lancelot;* Brooks, *Ordeal of Mark Twain;* Gale, *Miss Lulu Bett;* O'Neill, *Emperor Jones* and *Beyond the Horizon;* Anderson, *Poor White;* Dell, *Moon-Calf;* Sinclair, *The Brass Check;* Millay, *A Few Figs from Thistles;* Fitzgerald, *This Side of Paradise;* Yezierska, *Hungry Hearts*
Frontier (1920–39)

1920 Population, 105,710,620
19th Amendment: woman suffrage
Transcontinental airmail; first commercial radio broadcasting
Transportation, Merchant Marine, and Water-Power acts
Socialists poll 919,799 votes in presidential election

1921 Dos Passos, *Three Soldiers;* O'Neill, *Anna Christie;* Robinson, *Collected Poems;* Tarkington, *Alice Adams;* Davis, *The Detour;* McFee, *Harbours of Memory;* Marquis, *The Old Soak;* Anderson, *Triumph of the Egg;* Adams, *Founding of New England;* Hecht, *Erik Dorn;* Donn-Byrne, *Messer Marco Polo;* Cabell, *Figures of Earth;* Wylie, *Nets To Catch the Wind;* Kaufman and Connelly, *Dulcy;* C. Van Doren, *The American Novel*
Richard Wilbur (1921–   )

1921 Harding's administration (1921–23)
Industrial depression (nearly 6,000,000 unemployed)
Emergency Tariff Act; immigration quotas
First Sacco-Vanzetti trial
Separate peace with Germany; Washington Armament Limitation Conference

1922 Eliot, *The Waste Land;* Lewis, *Babbitt;* Cummings, *The Enormous Room;* Santayana, *Soliloquies in England;* Van Vechten, *Peter Whiffle;* Quick, *Vandemark's Folly;* Cather, *One of Ours; Civilization in the United States;* Sedgwick, *Adrienne Toner;* Colton, *Rain;* O'Neill, *The Hairy Ape;* Lowell, *Critical Fable;* Hough, *Covered Wagon;* Pound, *American Songs and Ballads* *Secession* (1922–24); *The Fugitive* (1922–25); *Reader's Digest* (1922–) Kurt Vonnegut (1922–)	**1922** Coal and railway strikes Fordney-McCumber tariff, higher than any before Nine-Power Treaty concerning China First one-day coast-to-coast flight
1923 Millay, *Harp-Weaver;* Cather, *A Lost Lady;* Davis, *Icebound;* Leonard, *Two Lives;* Sinclair, *Goose Step;* Bradford, *Damaged Souls;* Wylie, *Black Armour* and *Jennifer Lorn;* Frost, *New Hampshire;* Atherton, *Black Oxen;* Rice, *Adding Machine;* Stevens, *Harmonium;* D.H. Lawrence, *Studies in Classic American Literature;* Quinn, *History of American Drama* (1923–27); Santayana, *Realms of Being* (1923–40) *Time* (1923–) Norman Mailer (1923–); James Purdy (1923–)	**1923** Coolidge's administration (1923–29) Minimum wage law held unconstitutional Teapot Dome scandal (1923–24)
1924 Jeffers, *Tamar;* Lardner, *How To Write Short Stories;* Seldes, *Seven Lively Arts;* Anderson, *Story Teller's Story;* Dickinson, *Complete Poems;* Clemens, *Autobiography;* O'Neill, *All God's Chillun* and *Desire Under the Elms;* Anderson and Stallings, *What Price Glory?;* Kaufman and Connelly, *Beggar on Horseback;* Howard, *They Knew What They Wanted;* Melville, *Billy Budd;* Bromfield, *Green Bay Tree;* Hemingway, *In Our Time;* Wharton, "Old New York"; Sedgwick, *Little French Girl* James Baldwin (1924–87)	**1924** Industrial depression Soldiers' bonus passed over veto; new immigration quotas, with exclusion of Japanese; child labor amendment submitted Second Progressive party London reparations conference ("Dawes Plan")
1925 Dos Passos, *Manhattan Transfer;* Anderson, *Dark Laughter;* Dreiser, *An American Tragedy;* Lewis, *Arrowsmith;* Cather, *Professor's House;* Heyward, *Porgy;* Kelly, *Craig's Wife;* Glasgow, *Barren Ground;* H.D., *Collected Poems;* Boyd, *Drums;* Fitzgerald, *The Great Gatsby;* Jeffers, *Roan Stallion;* Neihardt, *Song of the Indian Wars;* Loos, *Gentlemen Prefer Blondes;* Green, *In Abraham's Bosom;* Pound, *Cantos* (1925–70) *American Speech* (1925–); *New Yorker* (1925–) Guggenheim Fellowships (1925–) Truman Capote (1925–84); William Styron (1925–); Gore Vidal (1925–)	**1925** Scopes trial Trinity College becomes Duke University U.S. initiates air freight service Standard Oil Co. adopts eight-hour day
1926 Hemingway, *The Sun Also Rises;* Sandburg, *Abraham Lincoln: The Prairie Years;* O'Neill, *The Great God Brown;* Hughes, *The Weary Blues;* Van Vechten, *Nigger Heaven;* Parker, *Enough Rope;* Stribling, *Teeftallow;* Roberts, *Time of Man;* Cabell, *Silver Stallion;* Howard, *Silver Cord;* Beer, *Mauve Decade;* De Kruif, *Microbe Hunters;* Sullivan, *Our Times* (1926–35); Faulkner, *Soldiers' Pay* Book-of-the-Month Club founded Allen Ginsberg (1926–)	**1926** Transatlantic wireless telephone Byrd flies over North Pole Army Air Corps created

LITERARY HISTORY	SOCIAL HISTORY

1927 Robinson, *Tristram;* Sinclair, *Oil!;* Cather, *Death Comes for the Archbishop;* Peterkin, *Black April;* Aiken, *Blue Voyage;* Rourke, *Trumpets of Jubilee;* Marquis, *archy and mehitabel;* Wescott, *The Grandmothers;* Rölvaag, *Giants in the Earth;* Sandburg, *American Songbag;* Parrington, *Main Currents in American Thought* (vols. I, II); Beard, *Rise of American Civilization;* Wilder, *Bridge of San Luis Rey;* Hemingway, *Men Without Women;* O'Neill, *Marco Millions*
Hound and Horn (1927–34); *American Caravan* (1927–36); *transition* (1927–38)
Literary Guild founded
John Ashbery (1927–   )

1927 Lindbergh flight, New York to Paris
Transatlantic telephone
Sacco and Vanzetti executed
U.S. Marines in Nicaragua (1927–33)

1928 O'Neill, *Strange Interlude;* MacLeish, *Hamlet of A. MacLeish;* Benét, *John Brown's Body;* Sandburg, *Good Morning, America;* Sinclair, *Boston;* Peterkin, *Scarlet Sister Mary;* Frost, *West-Running Brook;* Bradford, *Ol' Man Adam an' His Chillun;* Foerster, *American Criticism;* Whipple, *Spokesmen; Dictionary of American Biography* (1928–36)
American Literature (1928–   )
Edward Albee (1928–   )

1928 Pan-American Conference; Kellogg Pact to outlaw war
First Byrd explorations of Antarctica from Little America
Talking pictures; first Mickey Mouse cartoon

1929 Hemingway, *Farewell to Arms;* Krutch, *Modern Temper;* Wolfe, *Look Homeward, Angel;* Faulkner, *Sound and the Fury;* Frank, *Re-Discovery of America;* Aiken, *Selected Poems;* Lewis, *Dodsworth;* Rölvaag, *Peder Victorious;* Rice, *Street Scene;* La Farge, *Laughing Boy;* Lynd, *Middletown;* Lippmann, *Preface to Morals;* Glasgow, *They Stooped to Folly*
John Hollander (1929–   )

1929 Hoover's administration (1929–33)
Stock market collapse begins Depression; Gastonia strike; Agricultural Marketing Act
Byrd flies over South Pole
Museum of Modern Art founded
Martin Luther King, Jr. (1929–68)

1930 Eliot, *Ash-Wednesday;* Crane, *The Bridge;* Faulkner, *As I Lay Dying;* MacLeish, *New Found Land; I'll Take My Stand; Humanism and America;* Connelly, *Green Pastures;* Gold, *Jews Without Mercy;* Barry, *Hotel Universe;* Glaspell, *Alison's House;* Dos Passos, *42nd Parallel;* Roberts, *Great Meadow;* Gregory, *Chelsea Rooming House;* Porter, *Flowering Judas;* Roberts, *Arundel;* Mott, *History of American Magazines* (1930–38); *Encyclopaedia of the Social Sciences* (1930–35)
Lewis receives Nobel Prize
Fortune (1930—   );
John Barth (1930—   ) Gary Snyder (1930–   )

1930 Population, 122,775,046
London Naval Treaty; Smoot-Hawley high tariff
Institute for Advanced Study (Princeton)
First supermarket

1931 O'Neill, *Mourning Becomes Electra;* Steffens, *Autobiography;* Cather, *Shadows on the Rock;* Wilson, *Axel's Castle;* Stribling, *The Forge;* Aiken, *Preludes for Memnon;* Allen, *Only Yesterday;* Buck, *Good Earth;* Rölvaag, *Their Fathers' God;* Kaufman and Ryskind, *Of Thee I Sing;* Faulkner, *Sanctuary;* Riggs, *Green Grow the Lilacs;* Canby, *Classic Americans*
Story (1931–53)
Group Theatre (1931–41)
Tom Wolfe (1931–   )

1931 Debt and reparations moratorium; Norris Anti-Injunction Act
Ford's 20-millionth automobile
First Scottsboro trial

LITERARY HISTORY	SOCIAL HISTORY

1932 Caldwell, *Tobacco Road;* Farrell, *Young Lonigan;* Galsgow, *Sheltered Life;* Austin, *Earth Horizon;* Calverton, *Liberation of American Literature;* MacLeish, *Conquistador;* De Voto, *Mark Twain's America;* Dos Passos, *1919;* Fisher, *In Tragic Life;* Anderson, *Night Over Taos;* Nordhoff and Hall, *Mutiny on the Bounty;* Jeffers, *Thurso's Landing;* Faulkner, *Light in August;* Stong, *State Fair*
Common Sense (1932–46)
John Updike (1932–   ); Robert Coover (1932–   )

1933 Stein, *Autobiography of Alice B. Toklas;* Caldwell, *God's Little Acre;* Allen, *Anthony Adverse;* O'Neill, *Ah, Wilderness!;* Hicks, *Great Tradition;* MacLeish, *Frescoes;* Hemingway, *Winner Take Nothing;* Howard, *Alien Corn;* Kingsley, *Men in White;* Nathan, *One More Spring;* Robinson, *Talifer;* Kirkland and Caldwell, *Tobacco Road* (1933–41)
Philip Roth (1933–   ); John Gardner (1933–82)

1934 Saroyan, *Daring Young Man on the Flying Trapeze;* Adamic, *Native's Return;* Fitzgerald, *Tender Is the Night;* Cantwell, *Land of Plenty;* Hellman, *Children's Hour;* Sherwood, *Petrified Forest;* Farrell, *Young Manhood of Studs Lonigan;* Suckow, *The Folks;* Anderson, *Valley Forge;* Millay, *Wine from These Grapes;* Young, *So Red the Rose;* Lomax, *American Ballads and Folk Songs;* Stuart, *Man with a Bull-Tongue Plow;* Miller, *Tropic of Cancer*
Partisan Review (1934–   )
Joan Didion (1934–   ); N. Scott Momaday (1934–   )

1935 Lewis, *It Can't Happen Here;* MacLeish, *Panic;* Wolfe, *Of Time and the River;* Sheean, *Personal History;* Steinbeck, *Tortilla Flat;* Freeman, *R.E. Lee;* Perry, *William James;* Day, *Life with Father;* Glasgow, *Vein of Iron;* Anderson, *Winterset;* Odets, *Waiting for Lefty* and *Awake and Sing;* Kingsley, *Dead End*
Federal Writers' Project (1935–39); American Writers Congress
Southern Review (1935–42)
Richard Brautigan (1935–84); Ken Kesey (1935–   )

1936 Brooks, *Flowering of New England;* Dos Passos, *The Big Money;* Santayana, *The Last Puritan;* Faulkner, *Absalom, Absalom!;* Frost, *A Further Range;* MacLeish, *Public Speech;* Sandburg, *The People, Yes;* Mitchell, *Gone with the Wind;* Steinbeck, *In Dubious Battle;* Jeffers, *Solstice;* Eliot, *Collected Poems;* Sherwood, *Idiot's Delight;* Shaw, *Bury the Dead*
O'Neill receives Nobel Prize
Federal Theatre Project (1936–39)
New Life (1936–   ); *New Directions* (1936–   )
Tom Robbins (1936–   )

1932 Reconstruction Finance Corporation
War veterans' bonus march on Washington
St. Lawrence Waterway Treaty signed
Charles A. Lindbergh, Jr., kidnap-murder

1933 Franklin Roosevelt's administration (1933–45)
Bank "holidays"; National Industrial Recovery Act; Civilian Conservation Corps; Tennessee Valley power project; Home Owners' Loan Act; Agricultural Adjustment and Farm Credit acts; Banking and Gold Reserve acts; Emergency Relief Act
U.S. recognizes U.S.S.R.
20th and 21st Amendments
Einstein and other German émigrés come to U.S.

1934 Reciprocal trade treaties
Securities Exchange Act; National Housing Act; Tyding-McDuffie Independence Act grants autonomy to Philippines in 1946
Federal Communications Commission
Upton Sinclair's EPIC campaign in California

1935 Works Progress Administration ("work relief"); Social Security Act; Agricultural Adjustment Act; National Labor Relations Act; Public Utility Holding Company Act
Congress of Industrial Organizations founded
Regular trans-Pacific air service
Alcoholics Anonymous founded in Akron, Ohio

1936 Rural electrification act; AAA declared unconstitutional; Merchant Marine Act; Soil Conservation and Domestic Allotment Act; Roosevelt reelected, winning electoral votes of all but two states
CIO expelled from AFL
Inter-American Peace Conference

LITERARY HISTORY	SOCIAL HISTORY
1937 Hemingway, *To Have and Have Not;* Roberts, *Northwest Passage;* MacLeish, *The Fall of the City;* Marquand, *The Late George Apley;* Zaturenska, *Cold Morning Sky;* Blitzstein, *The Cradle Will Rock;* Millay, *Conversation at Midnight;* Steinbeck, *Of Mice and Men* and *The Red Pony;* Paul, *Life and Death of a Spanish Town;* Anderson, *High Tor;* Jeffers, *Such Counsels You Gave to Me* Thomas Pynchon (1937–)	**1937** CIO "sit-down" strikes in glass and automobile industries Roosevelt asks for reorganization of federal judiciary; Supreme Court validates National Labor Relations Act "Quarantine aggressors" speech of Roosevelt; third Neutrality Act Business recession; migrant labor problem increased by drought Bonneville dam project; U.S. Housing Authority
1938 Sherwood, *Abe Lincoln in Illinois;* Wilder, *Our Town;* C. Van Doren, *Benjamin Franklin;* Rawlings, *The Yearling;* Hemingway, *The Fifth Column;* Peattie, *Prairie Grove;* Dictionary of American English (1938–44) Pearl Buck receives Nobel Prize *Rocky Mountain Review* (1938–59); *Twice a Year* (1938–48) Joyce Carol Oates (1938–)	**1938** Naval bill larger than any previous peacetime bill Wages and Hours Law Mexico expropriates foreign oil holdings Howard Hughes flies around world in 91 hours
1939 Steinbeck, *The Grapes of Wrath;* Edward Taylor, *Poetical Works;* Nathanael West, *The Day of the Locust;* Beard, *America in Midpassage;* Dos Passos, *Adventures of a Young Man;* Frost, *Collected Poems;* Marquand, *Wickford Point;* Parker, *Here Lies;* Sandburg, *Abraham Lincoln: The War Years;* Saroyan, *The Time of Your Life;* Thurber, *The Last Flower;* M. Van Doren, *Collected Poems;* Wolfe, *The Web and the Rock;* Benét, *The Devil and Daniel Webster;* Crouse and Lindsay, *Life with Father* *Kenyon Review* (1939–)	**1939** Regular trans-Atlantic air service King George and Queen Elizabeth tour U.S. and Canada Neutrality Act amended, repealing arms embargo Hatch Act forbids political activity by government employees Tom Mooney pardoned
1940 *Dictionary of American History;* Brooks, *New England Indian Summer;* Lindbergh, *The Wave of the Future;* MacLeish, *The Irresponsibles;* Wright, *Native Son;* McCullers, *The Heart Is a Lonely Hunter;* Clark, *The Ox-Bow Incident;* Wolfe, *You Can't Go Home Again;* Sinclair, *World's End;* Hemingway, *For Whom the Bell Tolls;* Saroyan, *My Name is Aram;* Sherwood, *There Shall Be No Night;* Cather, *Sapphira and the Slave Girl;* Roberts, *Oliver Wiswell;* Wescott, *The Pilgrim Hawk* *PM* (1940–48)	**1940** Population, 131,669,275 Limited national emergency declared; first peacetime conscription; National Guard, naval and marine reserves called to active duty; bases acquired in British possessions; "two-ocean" navy; joint defense with Canada; aid to Great Britain "short of war"; transfer of warships to Britain Refugee children from Europe admitted to U.S. as "visitors"; aliens required to register; Communist party ends affiliation with Communist International
1941 Fast, *The Last Frontier;* Adamic, *Two-Way Passage;* Marquand, *H.M. Pulham, Esq.;* Benét, *The Dust Which is God;* Sinclair, *Between Two Worlds;* Glasgow, *In This Our Life;* Saroyan, *The Beautiful People;* Hellman, *Watch on the Rhine;* Fitzgerald, *The Last Tycoon;* Millay, *Collected Sonnets;* Wilson, *The Wound and the Bow*	**1941** Roosevelt inaugurated for third term "Lend-lease" bill to aid anti-Axis powers; Greenland bases acquired to maintain "present status"; unlimited national emergency declared; Axis ships seized; Nazi consulates closed; U.S. becomes "arsenal of democracy"; Iceland occupied; Atlantic Charter; U.S. enters "shooting war" in Atlantic; Roosevelt's "Four Freedoms" speech Japanese attack Pearl Harbor; U.S. at war with Japan, Germany, Italy, and Axis satellites; Japanese capture Guam and Wake, and invade Philippines Hoover Library on War, Revolution, and Peace opened at Stanford; National Gallery of Art opened

LITERARY HISTORY	SOCIAL HISTORY
1942 Anderson, *Eve of St. Mark;* Berlin, *This Is the Army;* Faulkner, *Go Down, Moses;* Freeman, *Lee's Lieutenants;* Paul, *Last Time I Saw Paris;* Sinclair, *Dragon's Teeth;* Wilder, *Skin of Our Teeth;* E.B. White, *One Man's Meat;* W.L. White, *They Were Expendable* Yank (1942–45)	**1942** U.S. and Philippine forces surrender after battles of Bataan and Corregidor; General MacArthur commands forces in southwest Pacific; Doolittle fliers bomb Tokyo; naval battles of Coral Sea, Midway, Santa Cruz, Solomons; battle of Guadalcanal; U.S. air forces begin European bombing raids; American and British troops land in North Africa War Manpower Commission, Office of War Information, War Production Board, Office of Civilian Defense, War Labor Board formed; price control and rationing Twenty-six signatories to "Declaration by United Nations"
1943 Benét, *Western Star;* De Voto, *Year of Decision;* Dos Passos, *Number One;* Fast, *Citizen Tom Paine;* Rodgers and Hammerstein, *Oklahoma!;* Santayana, *Persons and Places;* Smith, *A Tree Grows in Brooklyn;* Thurber, *Men, Women, and Dogs;* Willkie, *One World;* T.S. Eliot, *Four Quartets* James Tate (1943–)	**1943** General Eisenhower leads forces in driving Germans from North Africa, invading Sicily and Italy, and is made supreme Allied commander in Europe; Japanese offensive power destroyed in southwest Pacific and Aleutians; Italian armistice; Roosevelt and Churchill meet at Casablanca, decide on "unconditional surrender" of Axis as war aim; Roosevelt, Churchill, Stalin meet at Teheran United Nations Relief and Rehabilitation Administration organized
1944 Hersey, *A Bell for Adano;* Brown, *A Walk in the Sun;* Chase, *Harvey;* Jackson, *The Lost Weekend;* Pyle, *Brave Men;* Shapiro, *V-Letter;* Smith, *Strange Fruit;* Bellow, *Dangling Man*	**1944** U.S. forces return to Philippines, begin air bombardment of Japan; D-Day invasion of western Europe, battles from Normandy beachhead to German frontiers; "round-the-clock" bombing of German military and industrial installations Servicemen's Readjustment Act (G.I. Bill of Rights) Dumbarton Oaks conference plans United Nations organization; Bretton Woods conference plans World Bank and International Monetary Fund
1945 Frost, *Masque of Reason;* Crouse and Lindsay, *State of the Union;* Mauldin, *Up Front;* Mencken, *The American Language; Supplement I;* Schlesinger, *The Age of Jackson;* Shapiro, *Essay on Rime;* Stein, *Wars I Have Seen;* Stewart, *Names on the Land;* Williams, *The Glass Menagerie;* Wright, *Black Boy* Commentary (1945–)	**1945** Roosevelt inaugurated for fourth term; "Big Three" confer at Yalta Truman's administration (1945–53) Invaded Germany capitulates on V-E Day; battles of Iwo Jima and Okinawa; atomic bombs dropped on Hiroshima and Nagasaki; Japan surrenders on V-J Day United Nations charter written at San Francisco Rationing, wartime controls relaxed or abandoned
1946 Dreiser, *The Bulwark;* Fast, *The American;* Hersey, *Hiroshima;* Williams, *Paterson;* McCullers, *The Member of the Wedding;* W.A. White, *Autobiography;* R.P. Warren, *All the King's Men;* Welty, *Delta Wedding;* Stein, *Brewsie and Willie;* Jeffers, *Medea;* Lowell, *Lord Weary's Castle;* Vidal, *Williwaw*	**1946** First meetings of United Nations; Paris Conference plans peace treaty with Axis satellite nations Lewis and United Mine Workers return to AFL; price controls relaxed; coal, railroad, maritime, and other major strikes Atomic bomb tests in Pacific; United Nations commission considers international control of atomic energy
1947 Canby, *American Memoir;* De Voto, *Across the Wide Missouri;* Frost, *Masque of Mercy;* James, *Notebooks;* Lewis, *Kingsblood Royal;* Nevins, *Ordeal of the Union;* Steinbeck, *The Wayward Bus;* Michener, *Tales of the South Pacific;* Williams, *A Streetcar Named Desire* Ann Beattie (1947–)	**1947** Truman Doctrine aiding foreign nations "to maintain independence"; Marshall Plan offering cooperation for economic reconstruction; Western Hemisphere Mutual Defense Treaty; Armed Forces under a secretary of defense; Air Forces co-equal with Army and Navy; U.S. Trusteeship of 625 Pacific isles; Taft-Hartley Labor Relations Act

LITERARY HISTORY	SOCIAL HISTORY

1948 Faulkner, *Intruder in the Dust;* Mailer, *The Naked and the Dead;* Cozzens, *Guard of Honor; Literary History of the United States;* Pound, *Pisan Cantos;* Capote, *Other Voices, Other Rooms;* Auden, *Age of Anxiety;* Sandburg, *Remembrance Rock*
T.S. Eliot receives Nobel Prize

1948 Truman elected to full term; first peacetime selective service act; Berlin blockade and airlift; many investigations by House Committee on Un-American Activities; Organization of American States created

1949 Clark, *Track of the Cat;* Miller, *Death of a Salesman;* Buechner, *A Long Day's Dying;* Bowles, *The Sheltering Sky*

1949 American Communist party leaders convicted of conspiracy
U.S. nuclear monopoly ended as U.S.S.R. explodes atom bomb
North Atlantic Defense Pact signed

1950 Eliot, *The Cocktail Party;* Hemingway, *Across the River and into the Trees;* Schulberg, *The Disenchanted*
Faulkner receives Nobel Prize
National Book Awards (1950–   )

1950 Population, 150,597,361
Peace treaty with Japan; South Korea invaded by forces from north, including Chinese "volunteers"; U.N. sends troops and support to South Korea; U.S. proclaims state of national emergency

1951 Carson, *The Sea Around Us;* Faulkner, *Requiem for a Nun;* Jones, *From Here to Eternity;* McCullers, *Ballad of the Sad Café;* Moore, *Collected Poems;* Salinger, *Catcher in the Rye;* Saroyan, *Rock Wagram;* Styron, *Lie Down in Darkness;* Wouk, *The Caine Mutiny*

1951 22nd Amendment: President limited to two terms; Puerto Rico becomes a commonwealth; Truman relieves MacArthur of Far East command; Japanese Peace Treaty signed

1952 Hemingway, *The Old Man and the Sea;* De Voto, *Course of Empire;* MacLeish, *Collected Poems;* Steinbeck, *East of Eden*

1952 Eisenhower elected President; strong wave of anti-communism; investigations into "un-American" activities; increasing sweep to "loyalty" oaths

1953 Eliot, *The Confidential Clerk;* Warren, *Brother to Dragons;* Roethke, *The Waking;* Bellow, *Adventures of Augie March;* Wright, *The Outsider*

1953 Truce in Korea; U.S. pledges atomic aid to NATO forces; Eisenhower creates Health, Education, and Welfare cabinet post

1954 Welty, *The Ponder Heart;* Hecht, *A Child of the Century;* Steinbeck, *Sweet Thursday;* Faulkner, *A Fable;* Glasgow, *The Woman Within;* Jeffers, *Hungerfield;* Wallace Stevens, *Collected Poems*
Hemingway receives Nobel Prize

1954 Supreme Court rules racial segregation in schools unconstitutional; McCarthy censured by Senate
St. Lawrence Seaway construction begins
Southeast Asia Treaty Organization

1955 Anderson, *The Bad Seed;* Bishop, *North & South;* Inge, *Bus Stop;* Mailer, *Deer Park;* Miller, *A View from the Bridge;* O'Hara, *Ten North Frederick;* Williams, *Cat on a Hot Tin Roof*

1955 AFL and CIO merge
Salk antipolio vaccine developed
Supreme Court orders reasonable speed in implementation of 1954 decision on racial desegregation in schools

1956 Algren, *A Walk on the Wild Side;* Berryman, *Homage to Mistress Bradstreet;* Ginsberg, *Howl;* Kennedy, *Profiles in Courage;* O'Connor, *The Last Hurrah;* O'Neill, *Long Day's Journey into Night;* Thurber, *Fables for Our Time*

1956 Eisenhower reelected

1957 Agee, *A Death in the Family;* Cheever, *Wapshot Chronicle;* Cozzens, *By Love Possessed;* Faulkner, *The Town;* Kerouac, *On the Road;* Malamud, *The Assistant;* Wilbur, *Poems*

1957 International Geophysical Year begins
Eisenhower sends National Guard to Little Rock, Ark., in school integration crisis
Truman Library dedicated

1958 Eliot, *The Elder Statesman;* MacLeish, *J.B.;* Nabokov, *Lolita;* Roethke, *Words for the Wind;* Williams, *Suddenly Last Summer*

1958 Alaska admitted as 49th state
U.S. launches earth satellite
U.S. inaugurates jet airline service

1959 Bellow, *Henderson the Rain King;* Hansberry, *A Raisin in the Sun;* Lowell, *Life Studies;* Pound, *Thrones;* Roth, *Goodbye, Columbus;* Snodgrass, *Heart's Needle;* Warren, *The Cave*

1959 Hawaii admitted as 50th state
St. Lawrence Seaway opened
Antarctica designated scientific preserve by international treaty

1960 Faulkner, *The Mansion;* Jarrell, *The Woman at the Washington Zoo;* Morris, *Ceremony in Lone Tree;* Styron, *Set This House on Fire;* Updike, *Rabbit, Run*

1960 Kennedy elected President
Population, 170,323,175; New York, 7,781,984; Chicago, 3,550,404; Los Angeles, 2,479,015
U.S. and Japan sign treaty of mutual security and cooperation

1961 Baldwin, *Nobody Knows My Name;* Dugan, *Poems;* Heinlein, *Stranger in a Strange Land;* Heller, *Catch-22;* McCullers, *Clock Without Hands;* Salinger, *Franny and Zooey;* Steinbeck, *The Winter of Our Discontent*

1961 Peace Corps created
U.S. severs relations with Cuba; Cuba invasion fails
First U.S. manned suborbital space flight

LITERARY HISTORY	SOCIAL HISTORY
1962 Albee, *Who's Afraid of Virginia Woolf?*; Auden, *The Dyer's Hand*; Faulkner, *The Reivers*; Nabokov, *Pale Fire*; Porter, *Ship of Fools*; Saroyan, *Here Comes, There Goes, You Know Who*; Williams, *The Night of the Iguana*; Wilson, *Patriotic Gore* Steinbeck receives Nobel Prize	**1962** Two Americans and two Russians orbit the earth Soviet arming of Cuba causes crisis Telstar, first private communications satellite
1963 Jeffers, *The Beginning and the End*; McCarthy, *The Group*; Malamud, *Idiots First*; Pynchon, *V.*; Updike, *The Centaur*; Williams, *Pictures from Brueghel* *New York Review of Books* (1963–)	**1963** Kennedy assassinated (Nov. 22); Johnson becomes President California most populous state Widespread civil rights demonstrations "Big Three" sign limited nuclear test ban
1964 Bellow, *Herzog*; Berryman, *77 Dream Songs*; Hemingway, *A Moveable Feast*; Vidal, *Julian*; Warren, *Flood*	**1964** Antipoverty and civil rights legislation; Johnson elected President Martin Luther King, Jr., receives Nobel Peace Prize
1965 Albee, *Tiny Alice*; Ammons, *Tape for the Turn of the Year*; Haley, *The Autobiography of Malcolm X*; Mailer, *American Dream* Wilder receives first National Medal for Literature	**1965** Military support of South Vietnam Intervention in Dominican Republic revolt 25th Amendment: presidential succession stipulated
1966 Alfred, *Hogan's Goat*; Barth, *Giles Goat-Boy*; Capote, *In Cold Blood*; Malamud, *The Fixer*; Merrill, *Nights and Days*; Pynchon, *The Crying of Lot 49*	**1966** Medicare established U.S. planes begin bombing North Vietnam; antiwar protests Racial riot in Watts, Cal.
1967 Brautigan, *Trout Fishing in America*; Podhoretz, *Making It*; Styron, *The Confessions of Nat Turner*; Wilder, *The Eighth Day*	**1967** Vietnam War intensified; 475,000 U.S. troops in South Vietnam; protests against war increased Racial disturbances in U.S. cities
1968 Didion, *Slouching Towards Bethlehem*; Mailer, *The Armies of the Night*; Miller, *The Price*; Updike, *Couples*; Vidal, *Myra Breckenridge*	**1968** *Pueblo* seized by North Korea, crew later released Martin Luther King, Jr., assassinated American astronauts orbit moon Nixon elected President
1969 Bishop, *Complete Poems*; Hellman, *An Unfinished Woman*; Howard, *Untitled Subjects*; Momaday, *House Made of Dawn*; Roth, *Portnoy's Complaint*	**1969** Large-scale anti-Vietnam-War demonstrations Peace talks with Vietnam begun Limited military withdrawal from Vietnam Astronauts Neil A. Armstrong and Colonel Edwin E. Aldrin, Jr., are first men to walk on the moon
1970 Dickey, *Deliverance*; Didion, *Play It as It Lays*; Hemingway, *Islands in the Stream*; Pound, *Cantos* (collected); Wolfe, *Radical Chic and Mau-Mauing the Flak Catchers*	**1970** Population, 203,235,298; New York, 7,895,563; Chicago, 3,369,357; Los Angeles, 2,811,801 Four Kent State University students protesting Vietnam War shot to death by National Guardsmen Independent U.S. Postal Service created
1971 Ammons, *Collected Poems*; DeVries, *Into Your Tent I'll Creep*; Doctorow, *The Book of Daniel*; Gaines, *The Autobiography of Miss Jane Pitman*; Malamud, *Tenants*; Stegner, *Angle of Repose*; Wilson, *Upstate*	**1971** 26th Amendment lowers voting age to 18 New national railway system, Amtrak, inaugurated
1972 Barth, *Chimera*; Oates, *Marriages and Infidelities*; Purdy, *I Am Elijah Thrush*; Reed, *Mumbo-Jumbo*; Welty, *Optimist's Daughter*; T. Williams, *Small Craft Warnings*	**1972** President Nixon visits China U.S. troops leave Vietnam Democratic National Committee headquarters in Watergate building (Washington, D.C.) broken into by people associated with Republican party's committee to reelect Nixon Nixon reelected
1973 Ginsberg, *The Fall of America*; Hellman, *Pentimento*; Lowell, *The Dolphin*; Pynchon, *Gravity's Rainbow*; Vidal, *Burr*; Vonnegut, *Breakfast of Champions*; Wilder, *Theophilus North*	**1973** Vietnam War ended Military draft ended Watergate and allied scandals involve Nixon administration; several chief administrators resign Vice-President Agnew sentenced to probation and fine for evading taxes on undercover payments Agnew resigns

LITERARY HISTORY	SOCIAL HISTORY
1974 Connell, *The Connoisseur;* Everson, *Man-Fate;* Lurie, *The War Between the Tates;* Olson, *Yonnondio;* Synder, *Turtle Island*	**1974** Nixon impeachment hearings begun Watergate scandals spread Nixon resigns Ford succeeds to presidency, grants unconditional pardon to Nixon
1975 Albee, *Seascape;* Ashbery, *Self-Portrait in a Convex Mirror;* Bellow, *Humboldt's Gift;* Doctorow, *Ragtime;* Sexton, *The Awful Rowing Toward God*	**1975** U.S. merchant ship *Mayaguez* seized by Cambodia; 38 of the 39 crewmen freed by U.S. marines are killed in rescue
1976 D.L. Coburn, *The Gin Game;* Everson, *River-Root;* Gass, *On Being Blue;* Haley, *Roots;* Hellman, *Scoundrel Time;* Isherwood, *Christopher and His Kind;* Stegner, *The Spectator Bird* Saul Bellow awarded Nobel Prize	**1976** U.S. celebrates Bicentennial Viking II lands on Mars Carter elected President
1977 Coover, *The Public Burning;* Dunne, *True Confessions;* Percy, *Lancelot;* Perelman, *Eastward Ha!*	**1977** Most Vietnam War draft evaders pardoned by Carter First National Women's Conference drafts women's rights program
1978 Cowley, *And I Worked at the Writer's Trade;* Gardner, *On Moral Fiction;* Irving, *The World According to Garp;* Kazin, *New York Jew;* Tuchman, *A Distant Mirror;* Warren, *Now and Then;* Wouk, *The Winds of War* I. B. Singer awarded Nobel Prize	**1978** Panama Canal turned over to Panama Mass suicide of over 900 persons in People's Temple cult, Jonestown, Guyana Carter promotes peace treaty between Israel and Egypt
1979 Barth, *Letters;* Didion, *The White Album;* Justice, *Selected Poems;* Mailer, *The Executioner's Song;* Roth, *The Ghost Writer;* Styron, *Sophie's Choice;* Zukofsky, *A*	**1979** American citizens taken hostage by Iran Last Watergate convict (former Attorney General Mitchell) released U.S. and China establish formal diplomatic relations Large antinuclear demonstration in Washington, D.C.
1980 Ferlinghetti and Peters, *Literary San Francisco;* Gold, *He/She;* Kinnell, *Mortal Acts, Mortal Words;* Morris, *Plains Song;* Oates, *Bellefleur;* Percy, *The Second Coming;* Robbins, *Still Life with Woodpecker* Milosz awarded Nobel Prize	**1980** Population, 224,599,260; New York, 7,035,348; Chicago, 3,005,072; Los Angeles, 2,952,511 Miami race riots Reagan elected President
1981 Ashbery, *Shadow Train;* Hemingway, *Letters;* Roth, *Zuckerman Unbound;* Vidal, *Creation;* Tuchman, *Practicing History;* Updike, *Rabbit Is Rich*	**1981** American hostages released by Iran Severe federal budget cuts Reagan assassination attempt
1982 Bellow, *The Dean's December;* Dunne, *Dutch Shea, Jr.;* Stegner, *One Way To Spell Man;* *The Library of America* begun	**1982** Increased concern with Central American civil strife Economic recession 12,000,000 unemployed (10.8 % of work force)
1983 Mailer, *Ancient Evenings;* Rodriguez, *Hunger of Memory;* Shepard, *Fool for Love;* Walker, *The Color Purple*	**1983** U.S. involved in civil wars in Central America Soviets shoot down Korean airliner Terrorist blows up U.S. Marine barracks at Beirut, killing 183
1984 Erdrich, *Love Medicine;* LeRoi Jones, *Autobiography;* Mamet, *Glengarry Glen Ross;* M. Oliver, *American Primitive*	**1984** Reagan re-elected Jesse Jackson becomes first African American to make a serious bid for major party presidential nomination
1985 Baldwin, *Evidence of Things Not Seen;* Carolyn Kizer, *Yin;* S. Olds, *The Dead and the Living;* Studs Terkel, *The Good War*	**1985** Giant corporate merger frenzy Number of people classified poor declines by 2 million Gorbachev becomes leader of USSR Deficit in national budget exceeds $200 billion
1986 DeLillo, *White Noise;* McMurtry, *Lonesome Dove;* Tyler, *The Accidental Tourist;* Welch, *Fool's Crow*	**1986** Space Shuttle *Challenger* explodes "Star Wars" national defense program started U.S. bombs Libya
1987 Rita Dove, *Thomas and Beulah;* B. Lopez, *Arctic Dreams;* A. Wilson, *Fences;* Wolfe, *Bonfire of the Vanities*	**1987** Dow-Jones plunges 508 points in one day 50,000 cases of AIDS reported in U.S. Iran-contra affair: arms for hostages Reagan and Gorbachev sign missile treaty

LITERARY HISTORY	SOCIAL HISTORY
1988 Boyle, *World's End;* Hongo, *The River of Heaven;* Toni Morrison, *Beloved;* Uhry, *Driving Miss Daisy*	**1988** Bush elected President Unemployment at 5.2% U.S. Navy missile downs Iranian airliner, killing 290
1989 Donald Hall, *The One Day;* Tyler, *Breathing Lessons;* Wasserstein, *The Heidi Chronicles*	**1989** Student demonstrations crushed in China Supreme Court partly restrains abortions 200,000 infected with HIV virus *Exxon Valdez* oil spill in Alaska U.S. overthrows Noriega in Panama
1990 Doctorow, *Billy Bathgate;* Simic, *The World Doesn't End;* Updike, *Rabbit at Rest;* A. Wilson, *The Piano Lesson*	**1990** Population, 248,709,873: New York City, 7,322,564; Los Angeles, 3,485,398; Chicago, 2,783,726 War against Iran Eastern Europe released from control of USSR
1991 Banks, *The Sweet Hereafter;* Roth, *Patrimony;* Tan, *The Kitchen God's Wife;* Van Duyn, *Near Changes*	**1991** Collapse of communism in Eastern Europe and in USSR Soviet Union ceases existence, Cold War ends Pan-Am out of business, TWA bankrupt
1992 Brodkey, *The Runaway Soul;* DeLillo, *MAO II;* P. Levine, *What Work Is;* Mamet, *Oleanna;* Paglia, *Sex, Art, and American Culture*	**1992** Severe recession Clinton elected President 52 killed in L.A. riot after acquittal of 4 white police officers in beating of black motorist Rodney King
1993 Boyle, *The Road to Wellville;* R. Butler, *A Good Scent from a Strange Mountain;* Updike, *Collected Poems* Toni Morrison awarded Nobel Prize.	**1993** Congressional struggle to control $4 trillion national debt National Health Plan fails to pass Debate over open acceptance of gays in military; "don't ask, don't tell"
1994 Albee, *Three Tall Women;* Gaddis, *A Frolic of His Own;* Bishop, *One Art: Letters*	**1994** Republican landslide, largest since Reconstruction Era, captures both houses of Congress Struggle to control huge national debt continues Mexico near financial collapse Dollar drops sharply against Yen and Mark O. J. Simpson "Trial of the Century" rivets country's attention Baseball players strike in August; World Series cancelled.